Mediterranean Europe

on a shoestring

Tom Brosnahan	**Frances Linzee Gordon**
Colin Clement	**Jon Murray**
Steve Fallon	**John Noble**
Helen Gillman	**Jeanne Oliver**
Paul Hellander	**Corinne Simcock**
Charlotte Hindle	**Dorinda Talbot**
John King	**David Willett**
	Julia Wilkinson

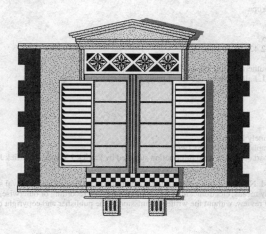

Mediterranean Europe

3rd edition

Published by
Lonely Planet Publications
Head Office: PO Box 617, Hawthorn, Vic 3122, Australia
Branches: 155 Filbert St, Suite 251, Oakland, CA 94607, USA
               10 Barley Mow Passage, Chiswick, London W4 4PH, UK
               71 bis rue du Cardinal Lemoine, 75005 Paris, France

Printed by
Colorcraft Ltd, Hong Kong

Photographs by

Vicki Beale (VB)	Sonia Berto (SB)	Tom Brosnahan (TB)	Bethune Carmichael (BC)
Geert Cole (GC)	John Gillman (JG)	David Hall (DH)	Rosemary Hall (RH)
Damien Simonis (DS)	David Willett (DW)		

Cover photograph by Nikos Desyllas, International Photographic Library

First Published
January 1993

This Edition
January 1997

Although the authors and publisher have tried to make the information as accurate as possible, they accept no responsibility for any loss, injury or inconvenience sustained by any person using this book.

National Library of Australia Cataloguing in Publication Data

Mediterranean Europe

   3rd ed.
   Includes index.
   ISBN 0 86442 428 0

   1. Europe, Southern - Guidebooks. 2. Mediterranean Region -
   Guidebooks. I. Fallon, Steve. (Series : Lonely Planet on a shoestring)

   914

Tom Brosnahan

Tom wrote the Turkey chapter. He was born in Pennsylvania, went to college in Boston, then set out on the road. He first went to Turkey as a US Peace Corps volunteer, teaching English and learning to speak Turkish. He studied Ottoman Turkish history and language for eight years, but abandoned the writing of his PhD dissertation in order to write guidebooks. Tom is also the author of Lonely Planet's guides to *Turkey*, *Istanbul*, *Guatemala, Belize & Yucatán: La Ruta Maya*, and of the *Turkish phrasebook*, as well as coauthor of *Mexico*, *Central America on a shoestring* and other Lonely Planet guides. His e-mail address is tbros@infoexchange.com.

Colin Clement

Colin updated the Morocco chapter. He was born and raised in Edinburgh, Scotland, and after graduating from university with a degree in philosophy, politics and economics, set off wandering around the world working as a teacher, tour guide, bus driver, barman, construction worker, etc. Since 1990 he has lived in Alexandria, Egypt, making a living as a freelance writer and translator. Colin likes green hills and good wine, and often wonders why he doesn't base himself in France or Italy.

Steve Fallon

Steve worked on the introductory chapters and updated the Slovenia chapter. Born in Boston, Massachusetts, Steve graduated from Georgetown University in 1975 with a Bachelor of Science in modern languages. The following year he taught English at the University of Silesia near Katowice, Poland. After he had worked for several years for a Gannett newspaper and obtained a master's degree in journalism, his fascination with the 'new' Asia took him to Hong Kong, where he lived and worked for 13 years for a variety of publications and was editor of *Business Traveller* magazine. In 1987, he put journalism on hold when he opened Wanderlust Books, Asia's only travel bookshop. Steve lived in Budapest for 2½ years from where he wrote LP's guides to *Hungary* and *Slovenia* before moving to London in 1994.

Helen Gillman

Helen wrote the Italy chapter and updated the Malta chapter. She worked as a journalist and editor in Melbourne, Australia, for 12 years, including three years as the editorial manager of 10 suburban newspapers. Trying to manage journalists is not easy, so Helen decided to 'retire' in 1990 and went to live in Italy. She continues to work on a freelance basis as an editor and writer and has coauthored and updated Lonely Planet's *Italy*. She lives in Rome with her husband, Stefano Cavedoni, and their three-year-old daughter, Virginia.

Paul Hellander

Paul updated the chapters on Albania, Macedonia and Yugoslavia. A freelance writer, translator and coordinator of an Internet-based translation agency, Paul lives in Adelaide, South Australia. Originally from the UK, he came to Australia, via Greece and a number of other countries, where he taught Modern Greek for 14 years to trainee interpreters and translators before belatedly turning to writing. Paul's other Lonely Planet publications are a *Greek phrasebook* and the 2nd edition of *Greece* on which he worked as updater and coauthor. Paul's ambition is to travel by train from Thurso to Saigon and write a book about it. When not translating, researching or writing, Paul can be found in cyberspace at sals@adelaide.dialix.oz.au.

Charlotte Hindle

Charlotte updated the Cyprus chapter. Born in Caerphilly, Wales, she studied art history at Leicester University. She au-paired in France, worked in a Swiss ski resort and sold theatre tickets in London before travelling to Australia. In 1988 she joined Lonely Planet and worked at the head office in Melbourne for 3½ years. In 1991 she returned to London to set up and run Lonely Planet's London office.

Frances Linzee Gordon

Frances updated the France chapter with Dorinda Talbot. She grew up in Scotland but later went to London University, where she read Latin. Overcome by her usefulness to society, she decided modern languages might be more the thing, and lived in Spain, Germany and Belgium for a number of years. After returning to London, she worked for a travel publisher and read French and European Studies with the University of Lille at the French Institute. She now works – even more usefully – as a freelance travel writer and photographer. She lives in London with her zebra finch, George.

John Noble

John updated the Spain and Andorra chapters. He comes from the Ribble valley in northern England. After studies at Cambridge University, a spell in mainstream journalism carried him to London's Fleet Street. Increasing interruptions for foreign travel eventually led to him updating Lonely Planet's *Sri Lanka – travel survival kit*, since when he has been mixed up in numerous Lonely Planet titles, from *Mexico* and *Indonesia* to *Russia, Ukraine & Belarus* and *Central Asia* – supported on many expeditions by his wife and coauthor, Susan Forsyth, and, in recent years, their children Isabella and Jack.

Jeanne Oliver

Jeanne updated the Croatia chapter. She was born in New Jersey but soon moved to New York City where she got a job at the *Village Voice* newspaper and then a law degree. Her legal practice was interrupted by ever more frequent trips – to Central and South America, Europe and the Middle East. Finally travel won and she set off on a trip around the world that took her through Africa and South-East Asia before winding up in Paris, where she worked as a tour director on bus tours. Now she makes a living as a freelance travel writer.

Corinne Simcock

Corinne updated the Greece chapter with David Willett. Born in London, she spent the first 10 years of her career as a sound engineer in the music industry. In 1988, sick of spending 18 hours a day in a basement listening to people who couldn't play, she chucked it all in to become a journalist, writing for national newspapers and magazines about everything from travel and crime to business and personal finance. She has travelled through more than 30 countries and her passion in life is deserts.

Dorinda Talbot

Dorinda updated the France chapter with Frances Linzee Gordon. Born in Melbourne, she began travelling at the age of 18 months – to visit her grandparents in Blighty – and has since taken in a fair slice of the world, including Papua New Guinea, South-East Asia, the USA, Britain and Europe. Dorinda studied journalism at Deakin University in Geelong before working as a reporter in Alice Springs and subeditor in Melbourne and London. Still based in London, she now works as a freelance journalist and travel writer. Dorinda also helped to update LP's *Canada* guide.

Julia Wilkinson & John King

Julia and John updated the Portugal chapter. Julia first set off on her own at the age of four, when she grabbed a backpack and headed down the road in a moment of furious independence. Some 20 years later, en route to Australia, she discovered Asia. With Hong Kong as her base, she has worked as a freelance travel writer and photographer for the past 15 years, writing about the remoter parts of Asia for publications worldwide. The contributor to guidebooks on Thailand and Hong Kong, she is also coauthor, with John, of LP's *Portugal* guide.

John grew up in the USA, destined for the academic life, but in a rash moment in 1984 he took off for China, teaching English and travelling for a year. In Tibet he met Julia and in Hong Kong they laid plans for future 'joint ventures'. Since then John has squeezed out a living as a travel writer. John is also author of LP's *Karakoram Highway*, and coauthor of *Portugal, Czech & Slovak Republics, Prague, Pakistan, Russia, Ukraine & Belarus* and *Central Asia*.

Julia and John now split their time at 'home' between south-west England and Hong Kong. Life and work have been considerably altered by the arrival of their son Kit, who complicated and enlivened the Portugal research on his first trip out of Hong Kong.

David Willett
David updated the Greece and Tunisia chapters. David is a freelance journalist based near Bellingen on the north coast of New South Wales, Australia. He grew up in Hampshire, England, and wound up in Australia after stints on newspapers in Iran (1975-78) and Bahrain. He spent two years as a subeditor on the Melbourne *Sun* newspaper before trading a steady job for a warmer climate. Between jobs, David has travelled extensively in Europe, the Middle East and Asia. He has previously worked on LP's guides to *Greece*, *North Africa*, *Indonesia* and *Australia*.

From the Authors

Tom Brosnahan Thanks to Pat Yale, coauthor of Lonely Planet's *Turkey*; Leyla Özhan of the Turkish tourism office in New York City; Mustafa Siyahhan of the Turkish tourism office in Washington, DC; Cansen Beklerîz of the tourism office in İstanbul's Sirkeci station; Ersan Atsür of Orion-Tour in İstanbul; Çelik Gülersoy of the Turkish Touring & Automobile Association; Süha Ersöz of the Esbelli Evi in Ürgüp; Ann Nevens of the Hotel Empress Zoe in İstanbul; and, as always, the Turkish people (especially the cooks!) who made my research trips so enjoyable.

Colin Clement Many thanks to the people of Morocco, to Magda Aboulfadl, to Les Celliers de Meknès, and to my mum, Margaret.

Steve Fallon *Najlepša hvala* for assistance and kindness to Tatjana Radovič and Janja Romih of the Ljubljana Promotion Centre; Janko Štebej and Alenka Brežnik of Kompas Holidays, Ljubljana; Jure Golob of Markom, Ljubljana; Jana Hojnik at the Park Hotel, Ljubljana; Marjana Gruber at Hotel Fiesa, Piran; and Norman Knapp of Slovenija Pursuits in Royston, Hertfordshire. As always, special thanks to Michael Rothschild for keeping the fires burning (home and otherwise) over the past 20 years.

Helen Gillman Special thanks to my sister Nicole and to Stefano for their invaluable assistance. Thanks also to the various tourism offices in Italy for their help, in particular to Aldo Cianci (Naples EPT), Cecilia and Giovanni (Pisa APT's station branch), Mimmo Ziino (AAST delle Isole Eolie), Signora Albani (Syracuse AAT), Giuseppe (Agrigento AAST), Dottoressa Benci (Siena APT) and Pierluigi and Fulvia (Enjoy Rome). Thanks to Mr Louis Azzopardi and Marika Doublet at the Malta National Tourism Organisation for their invaluable assistance.

Paul Hellander The task of updating this book would have been very difficult without the assistance of the following people and organisations: Ljupčo Naumovski and Makedonijaturist in Macedonia; Miroslav Savić, Professor Olga Mišeska-Tomić and Predrag Maksimović in Yugoslavia; Dr Xhani and Hinemoa Xhori, Ilir Zenku and Valentin Priffti in Albania; Radek Adameć; Kevin Bell; Tim Smith; Geoff Sarbutt; Angela Hassane; John Fuller; Greg Umbach; Pavlinka Georgiev; Bujar Sulemani; my many Internet contacts on ALBANIAN; and especially Carmen and Dan Clay of San Francisco for Neil Young, Tom Petty and peanut butter and for proving that campervanning round Albania can be done. Last but not least, my thanks to my wife, Stella, who gives me her blessing to undertake these assignments. As always, my work is done with Byron and Marcus in mind. May they one day take after their peripatetic father.

Charlotte Hindle Charlotte would like to thank her father, Tom Hindle, for accompanying her to southern Cyprus, and Simon, who helped to research North Cyprus. She would also like to thank Andreas Christodoulides from the Cyprus Tourism Organisation in London.

Frances Linzee Gordon Thanks for the endless patience shown at tourist boards across France, and particularly to Vanina Plotard

(Lyon), Sophie Leloup (Normandy), Méanie Sylvester (Calvi), Sandra Oliel (French Alps). Thanks also to M Lavêcque for a wonderful day touring his chateau; to Xavier, to Stéphane and his beautiful island of Corsica, and to M Jacques Tartarin of Crédit Agricole for miracle-working at a dark hour. Finally to all those little, old men across France who helped me always so gallantly back onto the right route. I dedicate my infinitesimal contribution to this book to my father.

John Noble Special thanks to Mark Armstrong, Susan Forsyth and Damien Simonis for their generous help on the Spain chapter, and Albert Padrol and Josep Maria Romero for their hospitality and insights into Catalonia and Andorra.

Jeanne Oliver Special thanks to Mirjana Žilić of the Croatian National Tourism Office – her warmth and enthusiasm are the best advertisement for Croatia. Thanks also to Vesna Jovićić of Pula for her help and valuable insights. Other tourism workers and government officials whose patient assistance made my trip a pleasure include Vladimir Bakić of Dubrovnik, Josip Karabaić and Nedo Pinezić of Krk, Alyoša Milat and Stanka of Korčula, and Bruno Petruz of Rovinj.

Corinne Simcock Thanks to Adrienne Costanzo at LP for bothering to take my details to Australia, and to Mike Elder from Ourios Travel in Iraklio and Anna from Dakoutros Travel on Santorini for their spectacular assistance. Among the other friends who helped with fact-finding missions, thanks to Josette and Dimitri at Pension Andreas and Jean from Le Bistrot on Rhodes; George at Olga's Pension in Rethymno; Rooms for Rent George in Hania; and Vasso and Manolis at Pension Vasso on Samos.

Dorinda Talbot Thanks to Mark Baker, Virginie Patheron, Corinne Gripekoven and Dawn Chapman for their boundless hospitality and support. Also special thanks to Lydia Megert, Claudia Rohrbach, tourist office staff in Paris and across France, fellow travellers and all the staff at the LP Paris office.

Julia Wilkinson & John King Thanks to Robert Strauss and Deanna Swaney for laying the groundwork for the Portugal chapter, upon which we have depended heavily. Again we are indebted to Pilar Pereira of the London ICEP office for significant logistical support and information gathering. For extraordinary help, both with research and with our two-year-old 'research assistant', we are indebted to Amélia Paulo (Sintra Turismo) and her daughter Andraia Paulo. Staff at the municipal tourist offices in Tavira, Évora, Sintra and Coimbra, and at the ICEP offices in Porto and Lisbon, provided assistance well beyond the call of duty. Finally, *obrigado* to Barry Girling for his house and the soft landing it gave us on arrival.

David Willett In Greece, my thanks go to Tolis and Steve (Athens) and to George and Magda (Corfu) for their help and hospitality. In Tunisia, thanks to Kamel, Anis and Larbi Grar, Chokri ben Nessir and Henda Salhi.

This Book
Many people have helped to bring about this 3rd edition. In past editions we also had the benefit of the following writers on whose sound foundations this edition was laid: Mark Armstrong, Mark Balla, Adrienne Costanzo, Geoff Crowther, Rob van Driesum, Richard Everist, Hugh Finlay, Rosemary Hall, Daniel Robinson, Damien Simonis, David Stanley (whose *Eastern Europe on a shoestring* provided the chapters on Albania and all of former Yugoslavia), Robert Strauss, Gary Walsh, Tony Wheeler and Pat Yale. Mark Honan, as always, researched the Getting Around chapter.

This edition was updated by Tom Brosnahan, Steve Fallon, Helen Gillman, Frances Linzee Gordon, John King, John Noble, Corinne Simcock, Dorinda Talbot, Julia Wilkinson and David Willett. Mark Honan researched the Getting Around chapter.

Mediterranean Europe is part of the LP Europe shoestring series, which includes *Western Europe*, *Eastern Europe*, *Central Europe* and *Scandinavian & Baltic Europe*. Lonely Planet also publishes phrasebooks for these regions.

From the Publisher

The editing of this book was coordinated by Brigitte Barta. The cartography was coordinated by Jane Hart and Michelle Stamp. All three coordinators were ably assisted by a cast of thousands, in particular: Rob van Driesum, Adrienne Costanzo, Jane Fitzpatrick, Mary Neighbour, Suzi Petkovski, Paul Harding, Steve Womersley, Liz Filleul, Diana Saad, Anne Mulvaney, Rachel Black, Lyndell Taylor, Anthony Phelan, Dorothy Natsikas, Michael Signal, Tony Fankhauser, Nick Tapp, Cathy Oliver, Chris Wyness and Tom Smallman. Thanks to Claude Calleja for help with the Maltese language guide; to Paul Hellander for the e-mail advice; to Vicky Wayland (LP UK), Sacha Pearson (LP US) and Rob van Driesum (LP Aus) for comments on the introductory chapters; to Paul Clifton for the colour and back cover maps, and to David Kemp and Simon Bracken for the cover. Special thanks to Dan Levin for technical wizardry.

Thanks

Many thanks to the travellers who used the last edition and wrote to us with helpful hints, useful advice and interesting anecdotes:

Jonathan Bryan, Helene Budinski, Sid Cara, Richard Carnell, Christopher Clarke, M Cresp, Fiona Dent, Veronica Egron, Sara Elison, Diane Fahey, Mrs M Foster, Dave Fuller, Andy Ganner, Jenny Garcia, Anne Geange, Joel Goldsmith, Gorrit Goslinga, Rene Granacher, Maria Heritage, NG Hetterley, Kate Hill, Timothy Hill, C Jackson, Chris James, Peter James, J Jarman, Arthur Jones, AJ Julicher, Dr Christoph Lenssen, Peter Lyon, Jodi McMillan, Heico Neumeyer, Sara Newhall, Pasco Panconcelli, Paula Park, Renee Petry, Scott Reardon, Karen Sackler Novick, Robert Saltzstein, Julien Scaife, Pushparcy Shetty, Peter Thayer, Sharda Ugra, Dorothea Vafiadis, P Walsh.

Warning & Request

Things change – prices go up, schedules change, good places go bad and bad places go bankrupt – nothing stays the same. So, if you find things better or worse, recently opened or long since closed, please tell us and help make the next edition even more accurate and useful.

We value all of the feedback we receive from travellers. Julie Young coordinates a small team who read and acknowledge every letter, postcard and e-mail, and ensure that every morsel of information finds its way to the appropriate authors, editors and publishers.

Everyone who writes to us will find their name in the next edition of the appropriate guide and will also receive a free subscription to our quarterly newsletter, *Planet Talk*. The very best contributions will be rewarded with a free Lonely Planet guide.

Excerpts from your correspondence may appear in updates (which we add to the end pages of reprints); new editions of this guide; in our newsletter, *Planet Talk*; or in the Postcards section of our Web site – so please let us know if you don't want your letter published or your name acknowledged.

Contents

Map Legend

BOUNDARIES

— International Boundary
— Regional Boundary
— Suburban Boundary

ROUTES

Freeway
Highway
Major Road
Unsealed Road or Track
City Road
City Street
Railway
Underground Railway
Tram
Walking Track
Walking Tour
Ferry Route
Cable Car or Chairlift

SYMBOLS

✪ CAPITAL	National Capital		
◉ Capital	Regional Capital		
◯ CITY	Major City		
● City	City		
● Town	Town		
● Village	Village		

Place to Stay, Place to Eat
Cafe, Pub or Bar
Post Office, Telephone
Tourist Information, Bank
Transport, Parking
Museum, Youth Hostel
Caravan Park, Camping Ground
Church, Cathedral
Mosque, Synagogue
Buddhist Temple, Hindu Temple
Hospital, Police Station

AREA FEATURES

Parks
Built-Up Area
Pedestrian Mall
Market
Christian Cemetery
Non-Christian Cemetery
Beach or Desert
Mountain Range

HYDROGRAPHIC FEATURES

Coastline
River, Creek
Intermittent River or Creek
Rapids, Waterfalls
Lake, Intermittent Lake
Canal
Swamp

Embassy, Petrol Station
Airport, Airfield
Swimming Pool, Gardens
Shopping Centre, Zoo
Winery or Vineyard, Trail Head
One Way Street, Route Number
Stately Home, Monument
Castle, Tomb
Cave, Hut or Chalet
Mountain or Hill, Lookout
Lighthouse, Shipwreck
Pass, Spring
Beach, Ski Field
Archaeological Site or Ruins
Ancient or City Wall
Cliff or Escarpment, Tunnel
Railway Station, Metro Station

Note: not all symbols displayed above appear in this book

Introduction

Mediterranean Europe evokes images of beautiful beaches, the brilliant blue of the Mediterranean Sea, spectacular landscapes dotted with olive and citrus groves, outdoor cafés, wonderful food, friendly local people, exuberant festivals and a relaxed way of life. It *is* all this – and even more.

This book offers an insight into the many different countries of the region, its peoples and its cultures, and provides practical information to help you get the most out of your time and money. It covers the area from Portugal and Morocco in the west to Cyprus and Turkey in the east. Although Portugal is not on the Mediterranean, and Morocco, Tunisia and most of Turkey are not part of Europe, these countries have been included because of their proximity and accessibility as well as their historical ties to the region.

Given the exceptional diversity of the countries and cultures in Mediterranean Europe, the choice of things to see and do is almost limitless. Some of Europe's earliest and most powerful civilisations flourished around the Mediterranean, and traces of them remain in the many archaeological sites and in the monuments, architecture, art, writings and music they created. There are countless churches, galleries and museums with works of art ranging from the Renaissance masters to 20th-century innovators. The region features architectural masterpieces as diverse as the Parthenon in Athens, Chartres' cathedral in France, the Hagia Sofia in İstanbul, St Peter's Basilica in Rome, the Alhambra in Granada and Gaudí's extraordinary creations in Barcelona.

When museums and churches begin to overwhelm you, turn to the many more active pursuits Mediterranean Europe has to offer. There is skiing or trekking in the Alps, Apennines, Pyrenees and Atlas mountains; island-hopping in Greece; or you can simply laze on a beach anywhere along the coast. The food of the Mediterranean region is one of its principal delights, not to mention the wine of Burgundy, Tuscany and elsewhere. There are even places where you can escape from other travellers, as relatively few tourists have made their way to Albania or to many parts of eastern Turkey and southern Italy.

Mediterranean Europe includes much practical information on how to get there and how to get around once you've arrived, whether it's by road, rail or ferry. There are extensive details on what to see, when to see it and how much it all costs. The thousands of recommendations about places to stay range from *domatia* (rooms to rent) in Greece to cheap hotels in the medinas (old towns) of Morocco. Restaurant recommendations include outdoor cafés in France, trattorias in Italy and *gostilne* in Slovenia. If shopping appeals, the Mediterranean area offers outlets ranging from chic boutiques in Paris and İstanbul's Grand Bazar to flea markets.

It's 3000 km from the Strait of Gibraltar to the Turkish coast – a huge region with a huge number of attractions waiting to be enjoyed. To experience them, all you have to do is go.

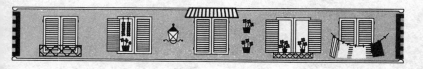

A	B	C
D	E	F
G	H	I

A: Spain (DS)   B: Italy (JG)   C: Greece (RH)
D: Tunisia (DW)   E: France (GC)   F: Italy (JG)
G: Morocco (DS)   H: Spain (DS)   I: Portugal (BC)

SWEDEN

BALTIC SEA

16°E
24°E
32°E
LATVIA
40°E
54°N
Moscow

LITHUANIA
Smolensk
RUSSIA

Kaliningrad
Kaunas
Vitsebsk

RUSSIA
Vilnius

Gdańsk
Brest

oznań
Vistula
Warsaw
Minsk

P O L A N D
BELARUS

Wrocław
Kiev

Ostrava
Kraków
Lviv
Zhytomyr

rno
Košice
U K R A I N E
Dnipro

SLOVAKIA

Bratislava
CARPATHIAN MTNS
MOLDOVA

enna
Győr
Cluj-Napoca
Kishinev

HUNGARY
Budapest
Timişoara
Braşov
Odessa

Pécs
Novi Sad
R O M A N I A
Crimea

Zagreb
CROATIA
Danube
Sevastopol

BOSNIA-HERCEGOVINA
Belgrade
Craiova
Bucharest
Constanţa
BLACK SEA

lit
Sarajevo
YUGOSLAVIA
BULGARIA
Varna

ubrovnik
Podgorica
Priština
Sofia
Plovdiv
Burgas

Shkodra
Skopje
Sinop

Tirana
MACEDONIA
İstanbul
Zonguldak
Samsun

Bari
Durrës
Ohrid
Thessaloniki
Xanthi
Bursa
Ankara

Taranto
ALBANIA
Çanakkale
Kızıl Irmak
Sivas

Golfo di Taranto
Vlora
Ioannina
Larisa
T U R K E Y
Kayseri

Corfu
GREECE
Lesvos
İzmir
Konya
Tuz Gölü
Adana

Ionian Islands
Evia
Aegean Sea
Kuşadası
Antalya
Mersin

Patras
Athens
Piraeus
Cyclades Islands
Bodrum
Alanya

Peloponnese
Kaş
Latakia

Kalamata
Sea of Crete
Rhodes
Lefkosia (Nicosia)

Hania
Iraklio
Dodecanese Islands
CYPRUS
Aleppo

Crete
Lemessos
SYRIA

MEDITERRANEAN SEA
LEBANON
Beirut
Damascus
IRAQ

ISRAEL

Benghazi
Tel Aviv-Jaffa
Amman

Gulf of Sidra
Jerusalem
JORDAN

Alexandria
Port Said

Cairo
EGYPT
SAUDI ARABIA

MEDITERRANEAN EUROPE
0   250   500 km

S A H A R A
Nile
RED SEA
24°E
32°E
26°E

EASTERN TURKEY

40°E
GEORGIA
Tbilisi

BLACK SEA
Batumi
AZERBAIJAN

42°N
Kars
ARMENIA
Yerevan

Trabzon
Mt Ararat 5123m
Doğubeyazıt

Giresun
Erzurum
IRAN

Sivas
Van
Van Gölü

Kızıl Irmak
T U R K E Y
Euphrates

38°N
Diyarbakır
Tigris

Gaziantep
IRAQ
Mosul

Aleppo
SYRIA

EASTERN TURKEY
Same Scale as Main Map

Continued on Eastern Turkey Inset
RUSSIA
Krasnodar

Sea of Azov
GEORGIA
Sukhumi

46°N
42°N
Batumi

BLACK SEA
Trabzon

Erzurum

38°N
Sivas
Diyarbakır

Gaziantep
Euphrates

Aleppo

34°N

30°N

A	B
C	D	E
F	G	H

A: Morocco (DS)
D: Italy (SB)
G: Morocco (DS)

B: Morocco (DS)
E: Greece (DH)
H: Turkey (TB)

C: Greece (VB)
F: Turkey (TB)

Facts for the Visitor

There are those who say that Mediterranean Europe is so well developed that you don't have to plan a thing before your trip since anything can be arranged on the spot. As any experienced traveller knows, the problems you worried about at home often turn out to be irrelevant or sort themselves out once you're on the move.

This is fine if you've decided to blow the massive inheritance sitting in your bank account, but if your financial status is somewhat more modest, a bit of prior knowledge and careful planning can make your budget stretch further than you thought it would. You'll also want to make sure that the things you plan to see and do will be possible at the particular time of year you'll be travelling.

PLANNING
When to Go
Any time can be the best time to visit Mediterranean Europe, depending on what you want to do. Summer lasts roughly from June to September, and offers the most pleasant climate for outdoor pursuits in the northern half of Europe. Along the Mediterranean coast, on the Iberian Peninsula and in southern Italy and Greece, where the summers tend to be hotter, you can extend that period by one or even two months either way, when temperatures may also be more agreeable.

Unfortunately, you won't be the only tourist during summer – everyone in France and Italy, for instance, goes on holiday in August. Prices can be high, accommodation fully booked, and the sights packed. You'll find much better deals – and far fewer crowds – in the shoulder seasons either side of summer; in April and May, for instance, flowers are in bloom and the weather can be surprisingly mild, and indian summers are common in September and October.

On the other hand, if you're keen on winter sports, resorts in the Alps and the Pyrenees begin operating in November or early December and move into full swing after the New Year, closing down again when the snows begin to melt in March or April.

The Climate & When to Go sections in the individual country chapters explain what to expect and when to expect it, and the Climate Charts appendix in the back of the book will help you compare the weather in different destinations. The temperate maritime climate along the Atlantic seaboard is relatively wet all year, with moderate extremes in temperature; the Mediterranean coast is hotter and drier, with most rainfall during the mild winter; and the continental climate in eastern France and the Alps has greater extremes between summer and winter.

What Kind of Trip?
Travelling Companions Travelling alone is not a problem in most parts of Mediterranean Europe; the region is well developed and relatively safe.

If you decide to travel with others, keep in mind that travel can put relationships to the test like few other experiences can. Many a long-term friendship has collapsed under the strain of constant negotiations about where to stay and eat, what to see and where to go next. But many friendships also become closer than ever before. You won't find out until you try, but make sure you agree on itineraries and routines beforehand and try to remain flexible about everything – even in the heat of an August afternoon in Rome.

If travel is a good way of testing established friendships, it's also a great way of making new ones. Hostels and camping grounds are good places to meet fellow travellers, so even if you're travelling alone, you need never be lonely.

The Getting Around chapter has information on organised tours.

Move or Stay? 'If this is Tuesday, it must be Barcelona.' Though often ridiculed, the mad dash that crams six countries into a month does have its merits. If you've never visited Europe before, you won't know which areas you'll like, and a quick 'scouting tour' will give an overview of the options. A rail pass that offers

17

unlimited travel within a set period of time is the best way to do this.

But if you know where you want to go, or find a place you like, the best advice is to stay put for a while, discover some lesser known sights, make a few local friends and settle in. It's also cheaper in the long run.

Maps

Good maps are easy to come by once you're in Europe, but you might want to buy a few beforehand. The maps in this book will help you get an idea of where you want to go and will be a useful first reference when you arrive in a city. Proper road maps are essential if you're driving or cycling.

You can't go wrong with Michelin maps and, because of their soft covers, they fold up easily so you can stick them in your bag or pocket. Some people prefer the meticulously produced Freytag & Berndt, Kümmerly & Frey or Hallwag maps.

The British AA maps are also good – as a rule, maps published by European automobile associations are excellent, and they're sometimes free if membership of your local association gives you reciprocal rights. Tourist offices are often another good source of (usually free) maps.

Online Services

The following web sites offer useful general information about Europe, its cities, transport systems, currencies etc.

Lonely Planet
  http://www.lonelyplanet.com. Lonely Planet's own web site is packed with information on Mediterranean Europe and other destinations, and is extensively hot-linked to other useful sites.
Tourist Offices
  http://www.mbnet.mb.ca/lucas/travel. Lists tourist offices at home and around the world.
Rail Information
  http://www.raileurope.com. Train fares and schedules for the most popular routes in Europe, including information on rail and youth passes.
Airline Information
  http://www.travelocity.com. Which airlines fly where, when and for how much.
Currency Converters
  http://bin.gnn.com/cgi-bin/gnn/currency & http://pacific.commerce.ubc.ca/xr. Exchange rates for hundreds of currencies worldwide.

US State Department Travel Advisories
  http://www.stolaf.edu/network/travel-advisories. html. May have some useful tips for countries where safety could be an issue.

See the E-mail section under Post & Communications for some general advice on gaining access to the Internet while on the move in Europe.

What to Bring

Taking along as little as possible is the best policy. It's very easy to find almost anything you need in Mediterranean Europe, and since you'll probably buy things as you go, it's better to start with too little rather than too much.

A backpack is still the most popular method of carrying gear as it is convenient, especially for walking. On the down side, a backpack doesn't offer too much protection for your valuables, the straps tend to get caught on things and some airlines may refuse to accept responsibility if the pack is damaged or tampered with.

Travelpacks, a combination backpack and shoulder bag, are also very popular. The backpack straps zip away inside the pack when they are not needed so you almost have the best of both worlds. Some packs have sophisticated shoulder-strap adjustment systems and can be used comfortably even on long hikes. Backpacks and travelpacks are always much easier to carry than a bag and they can be made reasonably theft-proof with small padlocks. Another alternative is a large, soft zip-bag with a wide shoulder strap so it can be carried with relative ease if necessary.

As for clothing, the climate will have a bearing on what you bring along. Remember that insulation works on the principle of trapped air, so several layers of thin clothing are warmer than a single thick one (and will be easier to dry, too). You'll also be better prepared if the weather suddenly turns warm on you. Just be ready for rain at any time of year. Bearing in mind that you can buy virtually anything on the spot, a packing list could include:

- underwear, socks and swimming gear
- a pair of jeans and a pair of shorts or a skirt
- a few T-shirts
- a warm sweater (jumper)

- a solid pair of walking shoes
- sandals or thongs for showers
- a coat or jacket
- a raincoat, waterproof jacket or umbrella
- a medical kit and sewing kit
- a padlock
- a Swiss Army knife
- soap and towel
- toothpaste, toothbrush and other toiletries
- an elastic clothes line and a few clothes pins

A padlock is useful for locking your bag to a luggage rack in a bus or train; it may also be needed to secure your hostel locker. A Swiss Army knife comes in handy for all sorts of things. *Any* pocket knife is fine but make sure it includes such essentials as a bottle opener and strong corkscrew! Soap, toothpaste and toilet paper are readily obtainable almost anywhere, but you'll need your own supply of paper in many public toilets and those at camping grounds. In some countries, it's a good idea to have some small change handy when using public toilets as you may be charged a small fee. Tampons are available in all but the most remote places, but are hard to find in Turkey. Condoms are widely available in the region; you can find them in Morocco, but the quality there is dubious.

A tent and sleeping bag are vital if you want to save money by camping. Even if you're not camping, a sleeping bag is still very useful. Get one that can be used as a quilt. A sleeping sheet with pillow cover (case) is necessary if you plan to stay in hostels – you may have to hire or purchase one if you don't bring your own. In any case, a sheet that fits into your sleeping bag is easier to wash than the bag itself. Make one yourself out of old sheets (include a built-in pillow cover), or buy one from your hostel association.

Other optional items include a compass, a torch (flashlight), an alarm clock, an adapter plug for electrical appliances (such as a cup or coil immersion water heater to save on expensive tea and coffee), a universal sink plug (a film canister sometimes works), sunglasses, premoistened towelettes or a large cotton handkerchief that you can soak in fountains and use to cool off while touring cities in the hot summer months. During city sightseeing, a small daypack deters snatch thieves better

than a shoulder bag (see Theft in the Dangers & Annoyances section in this chapter).

Finally, consider using plastic carry bags or rubbish bags inside your backpack to keep things separate but also dry if the pack gets soaked. Airlines do lose luggage from time to time, but you have a much better chance of it not being yours if it is tagged with your name and address *inside* the bag as well as outside; outside tags can always fall off or be removed.

Appearances & Conduct

Most Mediterranean countries attach a great deal of importance to appearances, so your clothes may well have some bearing on how you're treated, especially in Spain, Portugal, Italy and Greece.

By all means dress casually, but keep your clothes clean and ensure sufficient body cover (trousers or knee-length dress) if your sightseeing includes churches, monasteries, mosques and synagogues. Wearing shorts away from the beach is not very common among men in Mediterranean Europe. Also keep in mind that in most Muslim countries, such as Morocco, Western women *or* men in shorts or sleeveless shirts are virtually in their underwear in the eyes of the more conservative locals. Some nightclubs and fancy restaurants refuse entry to anyone wearing jeans, a tracksuit or sneakers (trainers); men might consider packing a tie as well, just in case.

Europeans have 'been there, done that' with hair length. Nevertheless, the 'long hair equals despicable hippy' syndrome still survives in some places (in Morocco, for instance), especially if it's dirty or unkempt hair. Dreadlocks, for example, don't go down very well there.

Most border guards and immigration officials are too professional to judge people entirely by their appearance, but first impressions do count and you'll find life easier if you are well presented when dealing with officialdom.

On the beach, nude bathing is usually limited to restricted areas, but topless bathing is common in many parts of Mediterranean Europe. Nevertheless, women should be wary of sunbathing topless in more conservative countries or untouristed areas. If nobody else seems to be doing it, you shouldn't do it either.

You'll soon notice that Europeans often shake hands and kiss when they greet one another. If you can't handle the kissing, that's fine, but get used to shaking hands with virtually everyone you meet as it's an important ritual. It's also customary to greet the proprietor when entering a shop, café or quiet bar, and to say goodbye when you leave.

The Top 10

There is so much to see in Mediterranean Europe, that compiling a top 10 is almost impossible. However, we asked the authors involved in this book to list their personal highlights. The results are as follows:

1. Paris
2. Rome
3. The Alps
4. Florence
5. Epiros in north-west Greece
6. Venice
7. Istanbul
8. Morocco's High Atlas Mountains
9. Tuscany
10. Lake Bled in Slovenia

Other nominations included Greek island-hopping, Barcelona, Umbria, Provence, the Pyrenees, Corsica, Andalucía and Seville.

The Bottom 10

The writers were also asked to list the 10 worst 'attractions' of the region:

1. Spain's Costa del Sol
2. The Greek island of Kos
3. Albufeira on Portugal's Algarve
4. EuroDisney in France
5. Palma de Mallorca
6. France's northern coast
7. Milan
8. The Monte Carlo casino
9. Agios Nikolaos on Crete
10. Bullfights in Spain

VISAS & DOCUMENTS
Passport

Your most important travel document is your passport, which should remain valid until well after you return home. If it's just about to expire, renew it before you go. This may not be easy to do overseas, and some countries insist on your passport remaining valid for a specified period (usually three to six months after you visit). Even if they don't insist on this, you can expect questions from immigration officials if it's due to expire in a matter of days.

Applying for or renewing a passport can take anything from an hour to several months, so don't leave it till the last minute. Bureaucracy usually grinds faster if you do everything in person rather than relying on the mail or agents, but check first what you need to take with you: photos of a certain size, birth certificate, population register extract, signed statements, exact payment in cash etc.

Australian citizens can apply at a post office or the passport office in their state capital; Britons can pick up application forms from major post offices, and the passport is issued by the regional passport office; Canadians can apply at regional passport offices; New Zealanders can apply at any district office of the Department of Internal Affairs; US citizens must apply in person (but may usually renew by mail) at a US Passport Agency office or at some courthouses and post offices.

Once you start travelling, carry your passport at all times and guard it carefully. The nationals of some countries in Mediterranean Europe are required by law to carry personal identification, and the same applies to foreigners. See the following Photocopies entry for advice about carrying copies of your passport and other important documents.

Camping grounds and hotels sometimes insist that you hand over your passport for the duration of your stay, which is very inconvenient, but a driving licence or Camping Card International usually solves the problem.

Citizens of many European countries don't always need a valid passport to travel within the region; a national identity card may be sufficient. A citizen of the European Union (EU) travelling to another EU country will generally face the least problems. But if you want to exercise any of these options, check with your travel agent or the embassies of the countries you plan to visit.

Visas

A visa is a stamp in your passport or a separate piece of paper permitting you to enter the country in question and stay for a specified period of time. Often you can get the visa at the border or at the airport on arrival, but not always – check first with the embassies or consulates of the countries you plan to visit – and seldom on trains. Most readers of this book, however, will have very little to do with

Visa Requirements
Country of Origin

	Aust	Can	Ire	Isr	NZ	Sing	UK	USA
Albania	–	–	–	✶	–	✓	–	–
Andorra	–	–	–	–	–	–	–	–
Croatia	Visas, if required, issued at border.							
Cyprus	–	–	–	✓	–	–	–	–
France	✓	–	–	–	–	–	–	–
Greece	–	–	–	–	–	✦	–	–
Italy	–	–	–	–	–	–	–	–
Macedonia	✶	✶	–	✓	✓	✓	–	✶
Malta	–	–	–	✓	–	–	–	–
Morocco	–	–	–	✓	–	✓	–	–
Portugal	–	✶	–	✓	–	✓	–	✶
Slovenia	–	–	–	–	–	–	–	–
Spain	✓	–	–	–	–	–	–	–
Tunisia	✓	–	–	✓	✓	✓	–	–
Turkey	–	–	✶	–	–	–	✶	–
Yugoslavia	✓	✓	✓	✓	✓	✓	✓	✓

✓ tourist visa required   ✦ no visa required for stays of up to 14 days

✶ 60-day maximum stay without visa   ✶ visa issued at point of entry

visas. With a valid passport they'll be able to visit most of the countries around the Mediterranean for up to three (sometimes even six) months, provided they have some sort of onward or return ticket and/or 'sufficient means of support' (ie money).

In line with the Schengen Agreement there are no passport controls at the borders between Germany, France, Spain, Portugal and the Benelux countries and an identity card should be sufficient, but it's always safest to carry your passport. The other EU members are not yet full members of Schengen and still maintain (low-key) border controls over traffic from other EU countries. Border procedures between EU and non-EU countries can still be fairly thorough. For those who do require visas, it's important to remember that these will have an expiry date and you'll be refused entry after that period has elapsed.

In the past, South Africans have had little joy travelling on their passports but this is changing – though not as fast as one would hope. Australians still need a so-called Schengen Visa to visit France or Spain – it may not be checked when entering these countries overland, but major problems can arise if it is requested during your stay or on departure and you can't produce it.

Visa requirements can change, and you should always check with the individual embassies or a reputable travel agent before travelling. It's generally easier to get your visas as you go along, rather than arranging them all beforehand. Carry spare passport photos (you may need one to four every time you apply for a visa). The accompanying table lists visa requirements for some nationalities.

Photocopies
The hassles created by losing your passport can be reduced considerably if you have a record of its number and issue date, or even better, photocopies of the relevant data pages. A photocopy of your birth certificate can also be useful.

Also keep a record of the serial numbers of your travellers' cheques (cross them off as you cash them) and photocopies of your credit cards, airline ticket and other travel documents. Keep all this emergency material separate from your passport, cheques and cash, and leave extra copies with someone you can rely on back home. Add some emergency money, say US$50 in cash, to this separate stash as well. If you do lose your passport, notify the police immediately (make sure you get a statement), and contact your nearest consulate.

Travel Insurance

You should seriously consider taking out travel insurance. This not only covers you for medical expenses and luggage theft or loss but also for cancellation or delays in your travel arrangements. (You could fall seriously ill two days before departure, for example.) Cover depends on the insurance and your type of airline ticket, so ask both your insurer and your ticket-issuing agency to explain where you stand. Ticket loss is also covered by travel insurance.

Buy travel insurance as early as possible. If you buy it the week before you fly, you may find, for instance, that you're not covered for delays to your flight caused by strikes or other industrial actions that may have started or been threatened before you took out the insurance.

Paying for your airline ticket with a credit card often provides limited travel accident insurance, and you may be able to reclaim the payment if the operator doesn't deliver. In the UK, for instance, institutions issuing credit cards are required by law to reimburse consumers if a company goes into liquidation and the amount in contention is more than UK£100. Ask your credit-card company what it's prepared to cover.

International Driving Permit

If you don't hold a European driving licence and plan to drive in the region, obtain an International Driving Permit (IDP) from your local automobile association before you leave – you'll need a passport photo and a valid licence. They are usually inexpensive and valid for one year only. Although American, Canadian and Australian driving licences are usually accepted throughout Mediterranean Europe, an IDP helps Europeans make sense of your unfamiliar local licence (make sure you take that with you, too) and can make life much simpler, especially when hiring cars and motorcycles.

While you're at it, if you're a member, ask your automobile association for a Letter of Introduction (Lettre de Recommandation). This entitles you to services offered by sister organisations in Europe, which are usually free of charge (touring maps and information, help

with breakdowns, technical and legal advice and so on).

Camping Card International

Your local automobile association also issues the Camping Card International, which is basically a camping ground ID. Cards are also available from your local camping federation, and sometimes on the spot at camping grounds. They incorporate third-party insurance for damage you may cause, and many camping grounds offer a small discount if you sign in with one.

Hostelling Card

A hostelling card is useful, if not always mandatory, for those staying at hostels. Many – perhaps even most – hostels in Mediterranean Europe don't require that you be a hostelling association member, but they sometimes charge less if you have a card. Many hostels will issue one on the spot or after a few stays, though this might cost a bit more than getting it in your home country. See Hostels in the Accommodation section later.

Student & Youth Cards

The most useful of these is the International Student Identity Card (ISIC), a plastic ID-style card with your photograph, which provides discounts on many forms of transport (including flights and local public transport), cheap or free admission to museums and sights, and cheap meals in some student restaurants.

There is a worldwide industry in fake student cards, and many places now stipulate a maximum age for student discounts or, more simply, they've substituted a 'youth discount' for a 'student discount'. If you're aged under 26 but not a student, you can apply for a GO25 card issued by the Federation of International Youth Travel Organisations (FIYTO) or the Euro<26 card, which goes under different names in various countries (eg Under 26 in England and Wales, Carte Jeunes in France). Both the GO25 and the Euro<26 cards give much the same discounts and benefits as an ISIC.

All these cards are issued by student unions, hostelling organisations and youth-oriented travel agencies. The cards don't automatically entitle you to discounts, and some companies and institutions refuse to recognise them altogether, but you won't find out until you flash the card.

Senior Cards
Museums and other sights, public swimming pools and spas and transport companies may also offer discounts to retired people, old-age pensioners or those over 60 (slightly younger for women). Make sure you bring proof of age; that suave *signore* in Italy or that polite Parisian *madame* is not going to believe you're a day over 39.

For a small fee, European nationals aged over 60 can get a Rail Europe Senior Card as an add-on to their national rail senior pass. For more information see Cheap Tickets under Train in the Getting Around chapter.

International Health Certificate
You'll need this yellow booklet only if you're coming to the region from certain parts of Asia, Africa and South America where outbreaks of yellow fever have been reported. See Immunisations in the Health section for more information on jabs.

CUSTOMS
Throughout most of Mediterranean Europe, the usual allowances on tobacco (eg 200 cigarettes), alcohol (two litres of wine, one of spirits) and perfume (50 grams) apply to duty-free goods purchased at the airport or on ferries. When travelling within the borders of the EU, do not confuse these with *duty-paid* items bought at normal shops and supermarkets in one EU country and brought into another, where certain goods (eg alcohol and tobacco) might be more expensive or the selection limited. Then the allowances are more than generous: 800 cigarettes, 90 litres of wine, 10 litres of spirits and unlimited quantities of perfume.

Customs inspections among EU countries have now all but ceased. At most border crossings and airports elsewhere they are pretty cursory but don't be lulled into a false sense of security. When you least expect it...

MONEY
Costs
The secret to budget travel in Mediterranean Europe is cheap accommodation. Europe has a highly developed network of camping grounds and hostels, some of them quite luxurious, and they're great places to meet people.

Other money-saving strategies include preparing your own meals and avoiding alcohol; using a student card (see the previous Visas & Documents section) and buying any of the various rail and public transport passes (see the Getting Around chapter). Also remember that the more time you spend in any one place, the lower your daily expenses are likely to be as you get to know your way around.

Including transport, but not private motorised transport, your daily expenses could work out to around US$30 to US$40 a day if you're operating on a rock-bottom budget. This means camping or staying in hostels, eating economically and using a transport pass. In Greece, Portugal and Spain, you could probably get the daily cost down below that.

Travelling on a moderate budget, you should be able to manage on about US$40 to US$50 in the cheaper countries and US$60 to US$80 a day elsewhere in the region. This would allow you to stay at cheap hotels, guesthouses or B&Bs. You could afford meals in economical restaurants and even a few beers! Again Greece and Portugal would be somewhat cheaper, while France and Italy would be pricier.

Price Levels
A general warning about all those prices that we list throughout this book: they're likely to change, usually moving upward, but if last season was particularly slow they may remain the same or even come down. Nevertheless, relative price levels should stay fairly constant – if hotel A costs twice as much as hotel B, it's likely to stay that way.

Cash
Nothing beats cash for convenience...or risk. If you lose it, it's gone forever and very few travel insurers will come to your rescue. Those that will, limit the amount to about US$300.

It's still a good idea, though, to bring some local currency in cash, if only to tide you over until you get to an exchange facility or find an automatic teller machine (ATM), both of which have become common in Mediterranean Europe in recent years. The equivalent of, say, US$50 should usually be enough. Some extra cash in an easily exchanged currency (eg US dollars or Deutschmarks) is also a good idea. Remember that banks will always accept paper money but very rarely coins in foreign currencies, so you might want to spend (or donate) your local coins before you cross a border.

Travellers' Cheques

The main idea of carrying travellers' cheques rather than cash is the protection that they offer from theft, though they are losing their popularity as more travellers – including those on tight budgets – deposit their money in their bank at home and withdraw it from ATMs as they go along.

American Express, Visa and Thomas Cook cheques are widely accepted and have efficient replacement policies. If you're going to remote places, it's worth sticking to American Express since small local banks may not always accept other brands.

Keeping a record of the cheque numbers and those you have used is vital when it comes to replacing lost travellers' cheques. You should keep this separate from the cheques themselves. Cheques are available in various currencies; choose the currency you're likely to need most – French francs, say, if you're going to spend most of your time and money in France – or one you can easily 'think' in.

When you change cheques, don't just look at the exchange rate; ask about fees and commissions as well. These may be a per-cheque service fee, a flat transaction fee, or a percentage of the total amount irrespective of the number of cheques. Some banks charge fees to cash cheques and not cash; others do the reverse. But in most European countries these days, the exchange rate for travellers' cheques is slightly better than the exchange rate for cash.

Plastic Cards & ATMs

If you're not familiar with the options, ask your bank to explain the workings and relative merits of credit, credit/debit, debit, charge and cash cards.

A major advantage of credit cards is that they allow you to pay for expensive items (eg airline tickets) without your having to carry great wads of cash around. They may also allow you to withdraw cash at selected banks or from the many ATMs that are now linked up internationally in many European countries.

However, if an ATM in Europe swallows a card that was issued outside Europe, it could be a major headache. Check that your credit card is hooked up to overseas ATM networks; ask your bank to do this and request a 'personal identification number' (PIN).

Cash cards, which you use at home to withdraw money directly from your bank account or savings account, are widely linked up internationally. Ask your bank at home for advice.

Credit and credit/debit cards like Visa and MasterCard are widely accepted. MasterCard (also known as Access in the UK) is linked to Europe's extensive Eurocard system, and Visa (sometimes called Carte Bleue) is particularly strong in France and Spain. However these cards often have a credit limit that is too low to cover major expenses like long-term car rental or airline tickets and can be difficult to replace if lost abroad.

Charge cards like American Express and Diners Club have offices that will replace a lost card within 24 hours in most major cities. However, charge cards are not widely accepted off the beaten track.

The best advice is not to put all your eggs in one basket. If you want to rely heavily on bits of plastic, go for two different cards – an American Express or Diners Club card, for instance, along with a Visa or MasterCard. Better still is a combination of credit or cash card and travellers' cheques so you have something to fall back on if an ATM swallows your card or the banks in the area are closed.

A word of warning: fraudulent shopkeepers in the region have been known to quickly make several charge-slip imprints with your credit card when you're not looking, and then simply copy your signature from the one that you authorise. Try not to let your card out of sight, and always check your statements upon your return.

International Transfers

Transferring money from your home bank will be easier if you've authorised someone back home to access your account. Also, a transfer to a tiny bank branch in a remote village in Corsica is obviously going to be more difficult than to the bank's head office in Paris. If you have the option, find a large bank and ask for the international division.

Money sent by telegraphic transfer (which

typically costs from US$40) should reach you within a week; by mail, allow at least two weeks.

You can also transfer money by American Express or Thomas Cook; the former charges US$40 for amounts up to US$300 and US$70 for amounts over US$500. Western Union money transfers can be collected at associated banks throughout Europe.

Guaranteed Cheques

Guaranteed personal cheques are another way of carrying money or obtaining cash. The most popular of these is the Eurocheque. To get Eurocheques, you need a European bank account and a cheque-cashing card; depending on the bank, it takes at least two weeks to apply for the cheques. Some countries have similar systems operating nationally, such as the 'postgiro' system in the Netherlands.

Currency Exchange

In general, US dollars, Deutschmarks, pounds sterling, and French and Swiss francs are the most easily exchanged, followed by Italian lire and Dutch guilders. You lose out through commissions and customer exchange rates every time you change money, so if you only plan to visit Portugal, for example, you may be better off buying escudos before you leave home if you can find a bank able to provide them.

The importation and exportation of certain currencies (eg Moroccan dirham, Tunisian dinar and Cypriot pounds) is restricted or banned entirely so get rid of any local currency before you leave the country. Try not to have too many leftover Portuguese escudos or Maltese lire, and definitely get rid of any Yugoslav dinar as it is impossible to change them back into hard currency. Some banks and bureaux de change just over the border will exchange Croatian kuna and Slovenian tolar, but don't count on it.

Most airports, central train stations, some fancy hotels and many border posts have banking facilities outside working hours, sometimes open on a 24-hour basis. Post offices in Europe often perform banking tasks, tend to have longer opening hours, and outnumber banks in remote places. Be aware, though, that while they always exchange cash, they might not be prepared to change travellers' cheques.

The best exchange rates are usually at banks. Bureaux de change usually (but not always) offer worse rates or charge higher commissions. Hotels are almost always the worst places to change money. American Express and Thomas Cook offices usually do not charge commissions for changing their own cheques but they may offer a less favourable exchange rate than banks.

By the year 2000, the EU should have a single currency called the euro. Until then francs, marks, pesetas, pounds and so on remain in place.

Tipping

In many European countries it's common (and the law in France) for a service charge to be added to restaurant bills, in which case no tipping is necessary. In others, simply rounding up the bill is sufficient. See the individual country chapters for details.

Taxes & Refunds

A kind of sales tax called value-added tax (VAT) applies to most goods and services throughout Europe. In most countries visitors can claim back the VAT on purchases that are being taken out of the country. Those residing in one EU country are not entitled to a refund on VAT paid on goods bought in another EU country. The procedure for making the claim is fairly straightforward though it may vary somewhat from country to country and there are minimum-purchase amounts imposed. When making your purchase ask the shop attendant for a VAT refund voucher filled in with the correct amount and the date. This can either be refunded directly at international airports on departure or stamped at ferry ports or border crossings and mailed back for a refund.

POST & COMMUNICATIONS
Post

From major European centres, air mail typically takes about five days to North America and a week to Australasian destinations. Postage costs do vary from country to country, and so does post office efficiency – the Italian post office is notoriously unreliable and Lonely Planet manuscripts sent special delivery air mail have taken up to two months to reach Australia. The postal systems in Greece and Tunisia are also less than reliable.

You can collect mail from poste restante sections at major post offices. Ask people writing to you to print your name clearly and underline your surname. When collecting mail, your passport may be required for identification and you may have to pay a small fee. If an expected letter is not awaiting you, ask the clerk to check under your first name: letters commonly get misfiled. Post offices usually hold mail for about a month, but sometimes less. Unless the sender specifies otherwise, mail will always be sent to the city's main post office.

You can also have mail (but not parcels) sent to you at American Express offices so long as you have an American Express card or are carrying Amex travellers' cheques. When you buy American Express cheques, ask for their booklet listing all its office addresses worldwide.

Telephone

You can ring abroad from almost any phone box in Europe. Public telephones accepting stored-value phonecards, available from post offices, telephone centres, newsstands or retail outlets, are almost the norm in Europe now; in some countries, coin-operated phones are increasingly difficult to find. The card solves the problem of finding the correct coins for calls (or lots of correct coins for international calls), but it can be annoying having to buy a 100FF phonecard when you just want to make a 2FF call.

A new product called the Country Card is available in some areas. With one of these cards (available from post offices or telephone centres), you get a 15% to 20% discount on calls to certain countries, making it even cheaper to use than one of the standard phonecards. Ask at the post office if these things are available in the country you're visiting.

Without a phonecard or Country Card, you can ring from a booth inside a post office or telephone centre and settle your bill at the counter. Reverse-charge (collect) calls are often possible, but not always – for a start, you'll have to be able to communicate with the local operator, who might not always speak English. From many countries, however, you can dial direct to your home operator, which solves the problem. See the Telephones appendix at the back of this book for information on international dialling, local phones, costs and country codes.

Fax & Telegraph

You can send faxes and telegrams from most main post offices in Mediterranean Europe.

E-mail

Maintaining your Internet connectivity while you are on the road in Europe can be done with a little planning. All European countries are now connected to the Internet and finding access is becoming easier. You have a few options. You can take your laptop PC and modem and dial your home country service provider, or take out a local account in the region you will be visiting most (there are kits to help you cope with local telephone plugs). For more information take a look at Lonely Planet's site at http://www.lonelyplanet.com.

Internet cafés, where you can buy online time and have a coffee are springing up all over Europe. Check http://www.cyberiacafe.net/cyberia/guide/ccafe.htm for the latest list. Failing that, make friends with local students and ask if you can sneak time on a university, or even private, machine. Before leaving home, contact your service provider to see if they can offer any specific advice about the countries you intend to visit.

NEWSPAPERS & MAGAZINES

In larger towns and cities you'll be able to get the excellent *International Herald Tribune* on the day of publication as well as the colourful but superficial *USA Today*. The *Guardian*, *Financial Times* and some other UK papers are often available but usually a day or so late. The lightweight weekly newspaper *The European* can be found everywhere as can the news magazines *Time*, *Newsweek* and *The Economist*.

RADIO & TV

The BBC World Service can be found on medium wave at 648 kHz, on short wave at 6195, 9410, 12095 and 15575 kHz, and on long wave at 198 kHz; the appropriate frequency depends on where you are and the time of day. The Voice of America (VOA) can usually be found on short wave at 15205 kHz. There are also numerous English-language broadcasts (and BBC World Service and VOA repeats) on local AM and FM radio stations. Monte Carlo based Riviera Radio, for example, broadcasts 24 hours a day on 106.3 MHz FM in Monaco and 106.5 and 98.8 MHz FM along the rest of the Côte d'Azur.

Cable and satellite TV have spread across Europe with much more gusto than radio. Sky TV can be found in many hotels throughout Mediterranean Europe, as can CNN and other networks. You can also pick up many cross-border TV stations, including UK stations close to the English Channel in France.

VIDEO SYSTEMS

If you want to record or buy video tapes to play back home, you won't get a picture if the image registration systems are different. Europe generally uses PAL (though France uses SECAM), which is incompatible with the North American and Japanese NTSC system. Australia uses PAL.

PHOTOGRAPHY

Mediterranean Europe is extremely photogenic, but the weather and where you'll be travelling will dictate what film to take or buy locally. In places like northern France where the sky can often be overcast, photographers should bring high-speed film (200 or 400 ASA), but for most of the sunny Mediterranean, slower film is the answer.

Film and camera equipment are available everywhere in the region, but obviously shops in the larger towns and cities will have a wider selection. Avoid buying film at tourist sites in Europe – eg at the kiosks below the Leaning Tower of Pisa or at the entrance to the Acropolis. It may have been stored badly or have reached its sell-by date. It will certainly be more expensive.

ELECTRICITY

Voltage & Cycle

Most of Europe runs on 220V, 50 Hz AC. The exceptions are the UK and Malta, which have 240V, and Spain and Andorra, which usually have 220V but sometimes still the old 125V depending on the network (some houses can have both). Some old buildings and hotels in Italy might also have 125V. All EU countries were supposed to have been standardised at 230V by now, but like everything else in the EU, this is taking a bit longer than anticipated.

Check the voltage and cycle (usually 50 Hz) used in your home country. Most appliances that are set up for 220V will handle 240V without modifications (and vice versa); the same goes for 110 and 125V combinations. It's always preferable to adjust your appliance to the exact voltage if you can (some modern battery chargers and radios will do this automatically). Just don't mix 110/125V with 220/240V without a transformer (which will be built into an adjustable appliance).

Several countries outside Europe (such as the USA and Canada) use 60 Hz AC, which will affect the speed of electric motors even after the voltage has been adjusted to European values, so CD and tape players (where motor speed is all-important) will be useless. But things like electric razors, hair dryers, irons and radios will be fine.

Plugs & Sockets

Cyprus and Malta use a design with three flat pins – two for current and one for earth (ground). The rest of Mediterranean Europe uses the 'europlug' with two round pins. Many europlugs and some sockets don't have provision for earth, since most local home appliances are double-insulated; when provided, earth usually consists of two contact points along the edge, although Italy and Greece use a third round pin. In Greece the standard two-pin plug still fits the sockets.

If your plugs are of a different design, you'll need an adapter. Get one before you leave, since the adapters available in Europe usually go the other way. If you find yourself without one, however, a specialist electrical-supply shop should be able to help.

HEALTH

Your main health risks in Mediterranean Europe are likely to be sunburn, dehydration, foot blisters, insect bites and upset stomachs from eating and drinking too much. You might experience mild gut problems if you're not used to copious amounts of olive oil, but you'll get used to it.

If you plan to visit North Africa or the more remote parts of Turkey, health risks increase and you'll want to consult your doctor beforehand, especially if you're going to be roughing it. Discuss your plans with your physician or local travellers' health agency, and ask about protection against hepatitis, typhoid, malaria, rabies and giardiasis.

If you are reasonably fit, the only things to organise before departure are a visit to your dentist, and travel insurance with good medical cover (see the following section). You should also make sure that your normal childhood vaccines (against diphtheria, tetanus and polio) are up to date.

Predeparture Planning

Health Insurance A travel insurance policy to cover theft, loss, personal liability and medical problems is highly recommended; check with your travel agent. The international student travel policies handled by STA Travel and other student travel organisations are usually good value. Some policies offer lower and higher medical-expense options. Check the small print: many policies specifically exclude 'dangerous activities' such as scuba diving, motorcycling, skiing, mountaineering and even trekking.

A policy that pays doctors or hospitals directly may be preferable to one where you pay on the spot and claim later. If you have to claim later, make sure you keep all documentation. Some policies ask you to call back (reverse charges) to a centre in your home country where an immediate assessment of your problem is made.

Check if the policy covers ambulances or helicopter rescue and an emergency flight home. If you have to stretch out you will need two seats and somebody has to pay for them!

Citizens of EU countries are covered for emergency medical treatment throughout the EU on presentation of an E111 form. Enquire about this at your national health service or travel agent well in advance; post offices in some countries also have these forms. Australian Medicare covers emergency treatment in Italy, Malta and the UK as well as in the Netherlands, Sweden and Finland. You may still have to pay on the spot, but you'll be able to reclaim these expenses at home. However, travel insurance is still advisable because of the flexibility it offers as to where and how you're treated, as well as covering ambulance and repatriation expenses.

Medical Kit It's wise to carry a small, straight-forward medical kit. The kit should include:

- aspirin or paracetamol (acetominophen in the US) – for pain or fever
- antihistamine (such as Benadryl) – useful as a decongestant for colds, allergies, to ease the itch from insect bites or stings or to help prevent motion sickness
- kaolin preparation (eg Pepto-Bismol), Imodium or Lomotil – for possible stomach upsets; anti-diarrhoea medication should not be given to children under the age of 12
- antiseptic, such as povidone-iodine (eg Betadine), which comes as a solution, ointment, powder and impregnated swabs – for cuts and grazes
- calamine lotion or Stingose spray – to ease irrita-tion from insect bites or stings
- bandages and Band-aids – for minor injuries
- scissors, tweezers and a thermometer (note that mercury thermometers are prohibited by airlines)
- insect repellent, sunblock cream, lip balm and perhaps water-purification tablets

When buying medicines over the counter in southern Europe, North Africa and Turkey, check the expiry date and make sure that correct storage conditions have been followed.

Health Preparations If you wear glasses, take a spare pair as well as your prescription. Losing your glasses can be a problem, though you can usually get new spectacles made up quickly, cheaply and competently in Mediterranean Europe.

If you require a particular medication, take an adequate supply; the same applies for oral contraceptives. Take the prescription or, better still, part of the packaging showing the generic rather than the brand name, as it will be easier to obtain replacements.

It's wise to have a legible prescription to show that you legally use the medication – it's surprising how often over-the-counter drugs from one place are illegal without a prescrip-tion or even banned in another. Keep the medication in its original container. If you're carrying a syringe for some reason, make sure you have a note from your doctor to explain why you're doing so.

A Medic Alert tag is worth having if your medical condition is not always easily recognisable (heart trouble, diabetes, asthma, allergic reactions to antibiotics etc).

Immunisations For Europe, jabs are not necessary, but they may be an entry requirement if you're coming from an infected area – an inoculation against yellow fever is the most likely requirement. If you're going to Europe with stopovers in Africa, Asia or Latin America, check with your travel agent or with the embassies of the countries you plan to visit.

There are, however, a few routine vaccinations that are recommended whether you're travelling or not, and this Health section assumes that you've had them: polio (usually administered during childhood), tetanus and diphtheria (usually administered together during childhood, with a booster shot every 10 years), and sometimes measles. See your physician or nearest health agency about these. You'll also need a malaria prophylactic and protection against hepatitis and typhoid if you plan to travel in some parts of North Africa and Turkey. You might also consider a rabies (pre-exposure) vaccination.

All vaccinations should be recorded on an International Health Certificate, which is available from your physician or government health department. Don't wait till the last minute to have your vaccinations, as some of them require an initial shot followed by a booster, while other vaccinations should not be given together. It is recommended that you seek medical advice at least six weeks prior to travel.

Basic Rules
Care in what you eat and drink is the most important health rule in North Africa and the more remote parts of Turkey and southern Europe; stomach upsets are the most likely travel health problem here but most of these upsets will be relatively minor.

Water Tap water is almost always safe to drink in Europe, but be wary of water taken directly from rivers or lakes unless you can be sure that there are no people or cattle upstream. Run-off from fertilised fields is also a concern. Tap water is usually *not* safe to drink in North Africa or Turkey, so stick to bottled water and avoid ice cubes, fresh salads and even fruit juice, as water may have been added to it. In these areas, use purified water rather than tap water to brush your teeth.

Dairy products are fine throughout Europe, but should be treated with suspicion in North Africa and Turkey because milk is often unpasteurised. Boiled milk is fine if it is kept hygienically, and yoghurt is always good.

If you're going to spend some time in North Africa or Turkey, or are planning extended hikes where you have to rely on water from rivers or streams, you'll need to know about water purification.

The simplest way of purifying water is to boil it thoroughly. Technically this means boiling for 10 minutes. Remember that at high altitudes water boils at a lower temperature, so germs are less likely to be killed.

Simple filtering will not remove all dangerous organisms, so if you cannot boil water, treat it chemically. Chlorine tablets (Puritabs, Steritabs or other brand names) will kill many but not all pathogens. Iodine is very effective for purifying water and is available in tablet form, such as Potable Aqua, but follow the directions carefully and remember that too much iodine can be harmful.

Food Salads and fruit should be safe throughout Europe, but elsewhere they should be washed with purified water or peeled where possible. Ice cream is usually OK, but beware of street vendors in North Africa and Turkey, and of any ice cream that has melted and been refrozen.

Take great care with fish or shellfish (for instance, cooked mussels that haven't opened properly can be dangerous), and avoid undercooked meat. In general, places that are packed with either travellers or locals (or both) should be fine. Always be wary of an empty budget restaurant.

Mushroom-picking is a favourite pastime in Europe (especially as autumn approaches), but make sure that you don't eat any mushrooms that haven't been positively identified as safe. Many cities and towns set up inspection tables at markets or at entrances to national parks to separate the good from the deadly.

Nutrition If you don't vary your diet, are travelling hard and fast and therefore missing meals, or simply lose your appetite, you can soon start to lose weight and place your health at risk – just as you would at home.

If you rely on fast food, you'll get plenty of fats and carbohydrates but little else of value. Remember that overcooked food loses much of its nutritional value. If your diet isn't well balanced, it's a good idea to take vitamin and iron pills (women lose a lot of iron through menstruation). Fruit and vegetables are good sources of vitamins.

In warm climates make sure you drink enough – don't rely on feeling thirsty to indicate when you should drink. Very dark yellow or strong-smelling urine (or not needing to urinate) is a danger sign. Carry a water bottle on long trips. Excessive sweating can lead to loss of salt and therefore to muscle cramping and dehydration. Salt tablets are not a good idea as a preventative, but in places where salt is not used much, adding salt to food can help.

Medical Problems & Treatment

Local pharmacies or neighbourhood medical centres are helpful if you have a small medical problem and can explain what the problem is. Hospital casualty wards will assist if the problem is more serious, and they'll tell you if it's not. Major hospitals and emergency numbers are mentioned in the various country chapters of this book. Tourist offices and hotels can put you on to a doctor or dentist, and your embassy or consulate will probably know one who speaks your language.

Sunburn In southern Europe and North Africa (and anywhere on water, sand, ice or snow) you can get sunburned surprisingly quickly, even through cloud. Use a sunscreen and take extra care to cover areas that don't normally see sun, eg your feet. A hat provides added protection, and it may be a good idea to use a sunblock cream for your nose and lips. Calamine lotion is good for relieving mild sunburn.

Remember that too much sunlight can

damage your eyes, whether it's direct or reflected (glare). If your plans include being near water, sand, ice or snow, then good sunglasses are doubly important. Make sure they're treated to absorb ultraviolet radiation – if not, they'll do more harm than good as they dilate your pupils and make it easier for ultraviolet light to damage the retina.

Prickly Heat Prickly heat is an itchy rash caused by excessive perspiration trapped under the skin. It usually strikes people who have just arrived in a hot climate and whose pores have not yet opened sufficiently to cope with greater sweating. Keeping cool, bathing often, using a mild talcum powder or even resorting to air-conditioning may help until you acclimatise.

Heat Exhaustion Dehydration or salt deficiency can cause heat exhaustion. Take time to acclimatise to high temperatures and make sure you get sufficient (nonalcoholic) liquids. Salt deficiency is characterised by fatigue, lethargy, headaches, giddiness and muscle cramps, and in this case salt tablets may help. Vomiting or diarrhoea can also deplete your liquid and salt levels.

Anhydrotic heat exhaustion, caused by an inability to sweat, is quite rare. Unlike the other forms of heat exhaustion it is likely to strike people who have been in a hot climate for some time, rather than recent arrivals.

Heatstroke This serious, sometimes fatal, condition occurs if the body's heat-regulating mechanism breaks down and the body temperature rises to dangerous levels. Long, continuous periods of exposure to high temperatures can leave you vulnerable to heatstroke. You should try to avoid excessive

---

Vital Signs
The normal body temperature for an adult human being is 98.6°F or 37°C; more than 2°C (4°F) higher than that is a high fever. A normal adult pulse rate is 60 to 100 per minute (children 80 to 100, babies 100 to 140). You should know how to take a temperature and a pulse rate. As a general rule, the pulse increases about 20 beats per minute for each °C (2°F) rise in body temperature.

The respiration rate is also an indicator of illness. Count the number of breaths per minute: between 12 and 20 is normal for adults and older children (up to 30 for younger children, 40 for babies). People with a high fever or serious respiratory illness (like pneumonia) breathe more quickly than normal. More than 40 shallow breaths a minute could indicate pneumonia. ■

alcohol and strenuous activity when you first arrive in a hot climate.

Feeling unwell, not sweating very much or at all and a high body temperature (39°C to 41°C) are the symptoms. When sweating has ceased, the skin becomes flushed and red. Severe, throbbing headaches and lack of coordination will also occur, and the sufferer may become confused or aggressive. Eventually the victim will become delirious or convulse. Hospitalisation is essential, but meanwhile get victims out of the sun, remove their clothing, cover them with a wet sheet or towel and fan them continually.

Fungal Infections Hot-weather fungal infections are most likely to occur on the scalp, between the toes or fingers (athlete's foot), in the groin (jock itch or crotch rot) and on the body (ringworm). You get ringworm (a fungal infection, not a worm) from infected animals or by walking on damp areas, like shower floors.

To prevent fungal infections, wear loose, comfortable clothes, avoid artificial fibres, wash frequently and dry carefully. Always wear plastic sandals or thongs in showers that you suspect might be less than hygienic. If you do get an infection, wash the infected area daily with a disinfectant or medicated soap and water, and rinse and dry well. Apply an antifungal powder like the widely available Tinaderm. Try to expose the infected area to air or sunlight as much as possible, wash all towels and underwear in hot water and change them often.

Hypothermia Too much cold is just as dangerous as too much heat, especially if it leads to hypothermia. Cold combined with wind and moisture (ie soaking rain) is particularly risky. If you are trekking at high altitudes or in a cool, wet environment, be prepared.

Hypothermia occurs when the body loses heat faster than it can produce it, and the core temperature of the body falls. It is surprisingly easy to progress from being very cold to being dangerously cold through a combination of wind, wet clothing, fatigue and hunger, even if the air temperature is above freezing. It is best to dress in layers – silk, wool and some of the new artificial fibres are all good insulating

materials. A hat is important, as a lot of heat is lost through the head. A strong, waterproof outer layer is essential, as keeping dry is vital. Carry basic supplies, including food that contains simple sugars to generate heat quickly, and lots of fluid to drink.

Symptoms of hypothermia are exhaustion, numb skin (particularly toes and fingers), shivering, slurred speech, irrational or violent behaviour, lethargy, stumbling, dizzy spells, muscle cramps and violent bursts of energy. Irrationality may take the form of sufferers claiming that they are warm and trying to take off their clothes.

To treat hypothermia, first get the person out of the wind and/or rain, remove their clothing if it's wet and replace it with dry, warm clothing. Give them hot, nonalcoholic liquids and some high-kilojoule (high-calorie), easily digestible food. Do not rub victims' skin; instead allow them to slowly warm themselves. This should be enough for the early stages of hypothermia. The early recognition and treatment of mild hypothermia is the only way to prevent severe hypothermia, which is a critical condition.

Altitude Sickness Acute mountain sickness (AMS) occurs at high altitude and can be fatal. There is no hard-and-fast rule as to how high is too high: AMS can strike at altitudes of 3000 metres, although 3500 to 4500 metres is the usual range. Very few treks or ski runs in the Alps and Pyrenees reach heights of 3000 metres or more so it's not a major concern, though Jebel Toubkal in Morocco's High Atlas Mountains is over 4000 metres high.

Breathlessness, a dry, irritative cough (which may progress to the of production pink, frothy sputum), severe headache, lack of coordination and balance, confusion, irrational behaviour, vomiting and drowsiness are all signs to heed; if the symptoms persist or become worse, the only treatment is to descend – even 500 metres can help.

Motion Sickness Eating lightly before and during a trip will reduce the chances of motion sickness. If you are prone to motion sickness, try to find a place that minimises disturbance – near the wing on aircraft, close to midships on boats, near the centre on buses. Fresh air and looking at a steady reference point such as the horizon usually help, whereas cigarette smoke and reading don't. The commercially made motion-sickness preparations, which can cause drowsiness, have to be taken before the trip commences; when you're feeling sick it's too late. Ginger (available in capsule form) and peppermint (including mint-flavoured sweets) are natural preventatives.

Jet Lag Jet lag is experienced when a person travels by air across more than three time zones (each time zone usually represents a one-hour time difference). It occurs because many of the functions of the human body (such as temperature, pulse rate and the emptying of the bladder and bowels) are regulated by internal 24-hour cycles called circadian rhythms. When we travel long distances rapidly, our bodies take time to adjust to the 'new time' of our destination, and we may experience fatigue, disorientation, insomnia, anxiety, impaired concentration and loss of appetite. These effects will usually be gone within three days of arrival, but there are ways of minimising the impact of jet lag:

- Rest for a couple of days prior to departure; try to avoid late nights, too many bon voyage parties, and last-minute dashes for travellers' cheques, visas etc.
- Try to select flight schedules that minimise sleep deprivation; arriving late in the day means you can go to sleep soon after you arrive. For very long flights, try to organise a stopover.
- Avoid excessive eating (which bloats the stomach) and alcohol (which causes dehydration) during the flight. Instead, drink plenty of noncarbonated, nonalcoholic drinks such as fruit juice or mineral water.
- Avoid smoking, as this reduces the amount of oxygen in the aircraft cabin even further and causes greater fatigue.
- Make yourself comfortable by wearing loose-fitting clothes and perhaps bringing an eye mask and ear plugs to help you sleep.

Diarrhoea A change of water, food or climate can all cause the runs, but diarrhoea caused by contaminated food or water is more serious. Despite all your precautions, you may still have a bout of mild travellers' diarrhoea, but a few rushed toilet trips with no other symptoms is not indicative of a serious problem.

Moderate diarrhoea, involving half a dozen

loose movements in a day, is more of a nuisance. Dehydration is the main danger with diarrhoea, particularly for children, so fluid replenishment is the very important. Weak black tea with a little sugar, soda water, or soft drinks allowed to go flat and diluted 50% with water are all good.

With any diarrhoea more severe than this, go straight to the casualty ward of the nearest hospital.

Viral Gastroenteritis This is caused not by bacteria but, as the name suggests, by a virus. It is characterised by stomach cramps, diarrhoea, and sometimes by vomiting and a slight fever. All you can do is rest and drink lots of fluids.

Giardiasis The parasite causing this intestinal disorder is present in contaminated water. The symptoms are stomach cramps, nausea, a bloated stomach, watery, foul-smelling diarrhoea and frequent gas. Giardiasis can appear several weeks after you have been exposed to the parasite. The symptoms may disappear for a few days and then return. Tinidazole, known as Fasigyn, or metronidazole (Flagyl) are the recommended drugs for treatment. Either can be used in a single treatment dose. Other antibiotics are of no use.

Hepatitis Hepatitis A is a very common problem among travellers to areas with poor sanitation. Protection is through the Havrix vaccine, or the antibody gamma globulin, which does not last long. The disease is spread by contaminated food or water. The symptoms are fever, chills and fatigue, followed by vomiting, dark urine and jaundiced skin. Seek medical advice; in general, there's not much you can do apart from rest, drink lots of fluids, eat lightly and avoid fatty foods. Avoid alcohol for at least six months after the illness as hepatitis attacks the liver.

Hepatitis B is spread through contact with infected blood, blood products or bodily fluids – for example, through sexual contact, unsterilised needles and blood transfusions. Other risk situations include tattooing and body piercing. The symptoms are much the same as hepatitis A. Hepatitis B can lead to irreparable liver damage, even liver cancer.

There is no treatment (except resting, drinking lots of fluids and eating lightly), but an effective prophylactic vaccine is readily available in most countries.

Rabies Though rare in Europe, rabies is found in many countries, including Morocco, Tunisia and Turkey. It is caused by a bite or scratch from an infected animal; dogs are a noted carrier, but cats, foxes and bats can also be affected. Any bite, scratch or even lick from a warm-blooded furry animal should be cleaned immediately and thoroughly. Scrub with soap and running water, and then clean scratches or cuts with an alcohol solution. If there is any possibility that the animal is infected, particularly if it froths at the mouth and behaves strangely, medical help should be sought immediately. Even if it is not rabid, all bites should be treated seriously as they can become infected or can result in tetanus.

A rabies vaccination is available and should be considered if you are in a high-risk category – eg if you intend to explore caves (bat bites can be dangerous), work with animals, or travel so far off the beaten track that medical help is more than two days away.

Tuberculosis TB is most likely to be of concern if you are going to be travelling in North Africa and Turkey. It is not a serious risk to healthy travellers, but children are more susceptible than adults and vaccination is a sensible precaution for children under 12 travelling in endemic areas. TB is commonly spread by coughing or by eating or drinking unpasteurised dairy products from infected cows. Milk that has been boiled is safe to drink; the souring of milk to make yoghurt or cheese also kills the bacilli.

Sexually Transmitted Diseases Sexual contact with an infected partner spreads what are now commonly called STDs.

Abstinence – admittedly an unrealistic expectation – is the only 100% effective preventative, but the proper use of condoms can be almost as effective. Gonorrhoea and syphilis are the most common of these diseases: in men the symptoms are sores, blisters or rashes around the genitals, discharges, or pain when urinating. Symptoms may be less marked or not observed at all in women. Symptoms of syphilis eventually disappear completely, but the disease continues and can cause severe problems in later years. The treatment of gonorrhoea and syphilis is with antibiotics. STD clinics are widespread in Europe. Don't be shy about visiting them if you think you may have contracted something; they are there to help and have seen it all before.

There are numerous other STDs. Effective treatment is available for most but as yet there is no cure for herpes or HIV/AIDS. The latter has become a considerable problem in Europe. HIV, the human immunodeficiency virus, may develop into AIDS (acquired immune deficiency syndrome). Apart from abstinence, the most effective preventative is always to practise safe sex using condoms. It is impossible to detect the HIV-positive status of an otherwise healthy-looking person without a blood test.

HIV/AIDS can also be spread through infected blood transfusions or by dirty needles – vaccinations, acupuncture, tattooing and body piercing can be potentially as dangerous as intravenous drug use if the equipment is not sterile.

Bites & Stings Bee and wasp stings are usually painful rather than dangerous. Calamine lotion will give relief; ice packs will reduce the pain and swelling. There are some spiders with dangerous bites (though rare in Europe) but antivenenes are usually available. Scorpion stings are notoriously painful, but the small scorpions occasionally found in southern Europe are not considered fatal. Scorpions often shelter in shoes or clothing – always give your shoes a good shake-out before putting them on in the morning, especially when camping.

There are various fish and other sea creatures that can sting or bite or that are dangerous to eat. Seek local advice to avoid problems.

Stings from most jellyfish are merely painful. Seek local advice before swimming in the sea to avoid contact with these creatures. Dousing the affected area in vinegar will deactivate any stingers which have not 'fired'. Calamine lotion, antihistamines and analgesics may reduce the reaction and relieve the pain.

Mosquitoes can be a nuisance in southern

Europe, but most people get used to mosquito bites after a few days as their bodies adjust and the itching and swelling become less severe. An antihistamine cream may help to alleviate the symptoms. For some people, a daily dose of vitamin B will keep mosquitoes at bay.

The only countries where they present a real problem are Morocco and Turkey, as they may spread malaria. In Morocco, the risk of catching malaria is minimal between October and May and only slight during the rest of the year, unless you travel within the more remote southern provinces. The risk of contact is always much higher in rural areas and during the wet season.

In Turkey, the areas to watch out for are Çukurova, the muggy agricultural region north of Adana (from March to November), and south-east Anatolia (from mid-May to mid-October). If you are going to travel in endemic areas, it is important to take malarial prophylactics. Make sure you follow the course through to the end.

Avoid bites by covering bare skin and using an insect repellent. Insect screens on windows and mosquito nets on beds offer protection. Mosquito coils give mixed results but the electrical 'vapour' repellents are very good.

Bedbugs are not uncommon in cheap hotels in North Africa and Turkey. They are found particularly in dirty mattresses and bedding. If you find spots of blood on bedclothes or on the wall around the bed, find another hotel. Calamine lotion may help to soothe the itching.

All lice cause itching and discomfort. They make themselves at home in your hair (head lice), your clothing (body lice) or in your pubic hair (crabs). You catch lice through direct contact with infected people or by sharing combs, clothing and the like. Powder or shampoo treatment will kill the lice, and infected clothing should then be washed in very hot water.

Snakes tend to keep a very low profile, but to minimise your chances of being bitten always wear boots, socks and long trousers when walking through undergrowth or rocky areas where snakes may be present. Tramp heavily and they'll usually slither away before you come near. Don't put your hands into holes and crevices, and be careful when collecting firewood (dead wood also attracts scorpions). Snake bites do not cause instantaneous

death and antivenenes are usually available. Keep the victim calm and still, wrap the bitten limb tightly, as you would for a sprained ankle, and attach a splint to immobilise it. Then seek medical help, if possible with the dead snake for identification. Don't attempt to catch the snake if there is even a remote possibility of it biting again. Tourniquets and sucking out the poison are now completely discredited.

Women's Health

Poor diet, lowered resistance through the use of antibiotics for stomach upsets, and even contraceptive pills, can lead to vaginal infections when you're travelling in hot climates. Maintaining good personal hygiene, and wearing skirts or loose-fitting trousers and cotton underwear will help to prevent infections.

Yeast infections (thrush), characterised by a rash, itch and discharge, can be treated with a vinegar or lemon-juice douche or with yoghurt. Nystatin suppositories are the usual medical prescription. Trichomonas is a more serious infection; symptoms are a discharge and a burning sensation when urinating, and if a vinegar-water douche is not effective, medical attention should be sought. Metronidazole (Flagyl) is the prescribed drug. In both cases, male sexual partners must also be treated.

Some women experience an irregular menstrual cycle when travelling because of the upset in routine. Don't forget to take time zones into account if you're on the pill. Ask your physician about these matters.

WOMEN TRAVELLERS

For women travellers, common sense is the best guide to dealing with possibly dangerous situations like hitchhiking, walking alone at night etc.

Women are more likely to experience problems in rural Spain, southern Italy, Morocco, Turkey and Tunisia. Slightly conservative dress can help to avoid attention, and dark sunglasses help to avoid unwanted eye contact. Marriage is highly respected in the region, and a wedding ring (on the left ring finger) sometimes helps, along with talk about 'my husband'.

In Muslim countries, a Western woman without a male companion will have a trying time coping with constant attention from males. The average Muslim woman is still bound to very strict codes of behaviour and dress, so it's not surprising that her Western sister is seen as being freer of moral or sexual constraints. Although head cover is not compulsory in these countries, it's a good idea to wear a headscarf if you're visiting mosques and so on. Hitching alone in these areas is definitely asking for trouble.

The *Handbook for Women Travellers* (Judy Piatkus Publishers, London) by M & G Moss is recommended.

GAY & LESBIAN TRAVELLERS

This book lists contact addresses and gay and lesbian venues in the individual country chapters, but your national organisation should be able to give you much more information. The *Spartacus Guide for Gay Men* (Bruno Gmünder, Berlin) is a good international directory of gay entertainment venues and includes all the countries in this book. It's best used in conjunction with listings in local papers. For lesbians, *Places for Women* (Ferrari Publications) is the best international guide.

DISABLED TRAVELLERS

If you have a physical disability, get in touch with your national support organisation (preferably the 'travel officer' if there is one) and ask about the countries you plan to visit. They often have complete libraries devoted to travel, and they can put you in touch with travel agents who specialise in tours for the disabled.

The British-based Royal Association for Disability & Rehabilitation (RADAR) publishes a useful guide entitled *Holidays & Travel Abroad: A Guide for Disabled People* (UK£5), which gives a good overview of facilities available to disabled travellers in Europe (in even-numbered years) and further afield (published in odd-numbered years). Contact RADAR (☎ 0171-250 3222) at 12 City Forum, 250 City Rd, London EC1V 8AF.

SENIOR TRAVELLERS

Senior citizens are entitled to many discounts in Europe on things like public transport, museum admission fees etc, provided they show proof of their age. In some cases they might need a special pass. The minimum qualifying age is generally 60 or 65 for men and slightly younger for women. European residents over 60 are also eligible for the Rail Europe Senior Card – see Train in the Getting Around chapter for details.

In your home country, a lower age may already entitle you to all sorts of interesting travel packages and discounts (on car hire, for instance) through organisations and travel agents that cater for senior travellers. Start hunting at your local senior citizens' advice bureau.

TRAVEL WITH CHILDREN

Successful travel with young children requires planning and effort. Don't try to overdo things; even for adults, packing too much into the time available can cause problems. And make sure the activities include the kids as well – balance that day at the Louvre with a day at Euro-Disney. Include children in the planning of the trip; if they've helped to work out where you will be going, they will be much more interested when they get there. Lonely Planet's *Travel with Children* by Maureen Wheeler is a good source of information.

In Europe most car-rental firms have children's safety seats for hire at a nominal cost but it is essential that you book them in advance. The same goes for highchairs and cots (cribs); they're standard in many restaurants and hotels but numbers are limited. The choice of baby food, infant formulas, soy and cow's milk, disposable nappies (diapers) and the like is as great in the supermarkets of southern Europe as it is back home but you may have trouble finding certain items in North Africa and Albania.

DANGERS & ANNOYANCES

On the whole, you should experience few problems in Mediterranean Europe, so long as you exercise common sense. Whatever you do, don't leave friends and relatives back home worrying about how to get in touch with you in case of emergency. Work out a list of places where they can contact you. Better still, phone home now and then.

Theft

Theft is definitely a problem in Europe, and it's not just other travellers you have to be wary of. The most important things to guard are your passport, papers, tickets and money – in that order. It's always best to carry these next to your skin or in a sturdy leather pouch on your belt. Train station lockers or luggage storage counters are useful places to store your bags (but *never* valuables) while you get your bearings in a new town. Be very suspicious about people who offer to help you operate your locker. Carry your own padlock for hostel lockers.

You can further lessen the risks by being careful of snatch thieves. Cameras or shoulder bags are great for these people, who sometimes operate from motorcycles or scooters and expertly slash the strap before you have a chance to react. A small daypack is better, but watch your rear. Be very careful at cafés and bars; loop the strap around your leg while seated.

Pickpockets are most active in dense crowds, especially in busy train stations and on public transport during peak hours. A common ploy is for one person to distract you while another zips through your pockets. Beware of gangs of kids (particularly in Morocco, Italy and France), waving newspapers and demanding attention. In the blink of an eye, a wallet or camera can go missing.

Be careful even in hotels: don't leave valuables lying around in your room. Parked cars are prime targets for petty criminals in most cities, especially cars with foreign number plates and/or rental-agency stickers. Remove the stickers (or cover them with local football club stickers or something similar), leave a local newspaper on the seat and generally try to make it look like a local car. Don't ever leave valuables in the car, and remove all luggage overnight, even if it's in a parking garage. In some places even freeway service centres have become unsafe territory – in the time it takes to drink a cup of coffee or use the toilet your car can be broken into and cleared out.

Another ploy is for muggers to pull up alongside your car and point to the wheel; when you get out to have a look, you become one more robbery statistic. While driving in cities, beware of snatch thieves when you pull up at the lights – keep doors locked and windows rolled up high. In case of theft or loss, always report the incident to the police and ask for a statement. Otherwise your travel insurance won't pay up.

Drugs

Always treat drugs with a great deal of caution. There is a fair bit of dope available in Mediterranean Europe, sometimes quite openly, but that doesn't mean it's legal. Even a little harmless hashish can cause a great deal of trouble.

Don't bother bringing drugs home with you either. With 'suspect' stamps in your passport (eg Morocco), energetic customs officials could well decide to take a closer look.

ACTIVITIES

Europe offers countless opportunities to indulge in more active pursuits than sightseeing. The varied geography and climate supports the full range of outdoor pursuits: windsurfing, skiing, fishing, trekking, cycling and mountaineering – you name it, Europe will have several great places to do it. For more local information, see the individual country chapters.

Windsurfing & Surfing

After swimming and fishing, windsurfing could well be the most popular of the many water sports on offer in Europe. It's easy to rent sailboards in many tourist centres, and courses are usually available for beginners.

Believe it or not, you can also go surfing in Europe. While the calm Mediterranean is not the best place for the sport, there can be excellent surf (and an accompanying surfer scene) along the Atlantic coast of France and Portugal, and along the north and south-west coasts of Spain. The Atlantic seaboard of Morocco, too, has some excellent waves and deserted beaches.

Skiing

In winter, Europeans flock to the hundreds of resorts in the Alps and Pyrenees for downhill skiing, though cross-country has also become very popular.

Skiing is quite expensive due to the costs of ski lifts, accommodation and the inevitable après-ski drinking sessions. Equipment hire (or even purchase), on the other hand, can be relatively cheap if you follow the tips in this book, and the hassle of bringing your own skis may not be worth it. As a rule, a skiing holiday in Europe will work out twice as expensive as a summer holiday of the same length. Cross-country skiing costs less than downhill since you don't rely as much on ski lifts.

The skiing season generally lasts from early December to late March, though at higher altitudes it may extend an extra month either way. Snow conditions can vary greatly from one year to the next and from region to region, but January and February tend to be the best (and busiest) months. During the ski season, the English-language *International Herald Tribune* newspaper publishes a daily report on snow conditions at every major ski resort in Europe.

Ski resorts in the French Alps offer great skiing and facilities but are also among the most expensive in Europe. Prices in the French Pyrenees and Italian Alps and Apennines are slightly cheaper (with up-market exceptions like Cortina d'Ampezzo), and can work out to be relatively cheap with the right package. Cheaper still are the Julian Alps in Slovenia, across the border from Austria and Italy, which are luring skiers away from the flashier resorts.

Possibly the cheapest skiing in Europe can be found in the Pyrenees in Spain and Andorra, and in the Sierra Nevada mountain range in the south of Spain. Greece also boasts a growing ski industry and skiing there is good value. See the individual country chapters for more information.

Hiking

Keen hikers can spend a lifetime exploring Europe's many exciting trails. Probably the most spectacular are in the Alps and Italian Dolomites, which are crisscrossed with well-marked trails during the summer months; food and accommodation are available along the way. The equally sensational Pyrenees are less developed, which can add to the experience as you often rely on remote mountain villages for rest and sustenance. Hiking areas that are less well known but nothing short of stunning can be found in Corsica, Sardinia and Crete, while the High Atlas mountains in Morocco offer a mind-blowing experience through tumble-down Berber villages in untamed country.

The Ramblers' Association (☎ 0171-582 6878) is a London charity that promotes long-distance walking in the UK and can help with maps and information. The British-based Ramblers Holidays (☎ 01707-331133) offers hiking-oriented trips in Europe and elsewhere.

Lonely Planet also publishes trekking guides to Spain, Greece and Turkey.

Every country in Europe has national parks and other interesting areas that may qualify as a trekker's paradise, depending on your preferences. Guided treks are often available for those who aren't sure about their physical abilities or who simply don't know what to look for. Read the Hiking information in the individual country chapters in this book and take your pick.

Cycling

Along with hiking, cycling is the best way to really get close to the scenery and the people, while keeping yourself fit in the process. It's also a good way to get around many cities and towns.

Much of Europe is ideally suited to cycling. In the north-west, the flat terrain ensures that bicycles are a popular form of everyday transport, though rampant headwinds often spoil the fun. In the rest of the continent, hills and mountains can make for heavy going, but this is offset by the dense concentration of things to see. Cycling is a great way to explore many of the Mediterranean islands, though the heat can get to you after a while (make sure you drink enough fluids).

Popular cycling areas include the coastal areas of Sardinia (around Alghero) and Apulia, and the hills of Tuscany and Umbria in Italy, anywhere in the Alps (for those fit enough), and the south of France. The French in particular take their cycling very seriously, and the annual Tour de France marathon is followed closely by much of the population.

If you are arriving from outside Europe, you can often bring your own bicycle along on the plane. Alternatively, this book lists many places where you can hire one (make sure it has plenty of gears if you plan anything serious), though they might take a dim view of rentals lasting more than a week.

See the Getting Around chapter for more information on bicycle touring, and the individual country chapters for rental agencies and tips on places to go to.

Boating

Europe's many lakes, rivers and diverse coastlines offer a variety of boating options unmatched anywhere in the world. You can kayak down rapids in Slovenia, charter a yacht in the Aegean, row on a peaceful alpine lake, rent a sailing boat on the Côte d'Azur, cruise the canals of France – the possibilities are endless. The country chapters have more details.

COURSES

If your interests are more cerebral, you can enrol in courses in Europe on anything from language to alternative medicine. Language courses are often available to foreigners through universities or private schools, and are justifiably popular since the best way to learn a language is in the country where it's spoken. But you can also take courses in art, literature, architecture, drama, music, cooking, alternative energy, photography and organic farming, among other subjects.

The individual country chapters in this book give pointers on where to start looking. In general, the best sources of information are the cultural institutes maintained by many European countries around the world; failing that, try their national tourist offices or embassies. Student exchange organisations, student travel agencies, and organisations like the YMCA/YWCA and Hostelling International (HI) can also put you on the right track. Ask about special holiday packages that include a course.

WORK

European countries aren't keen on handing out jobs to foreigners with unemployment so high in many areas. Officially, an EU citizen is allowed to work in any other EU country, but the paperwork isn't always straightforward for longer term employment. Other country/nationality combinations require special work permits that can be almost impossible to arrange, especially for temporary work. That doesn't prevent enterprising travellers from topping up their funds occasionally by working in the hotel or restaurant trades or teaching a little English, and they don't always have to do this illegally either.

The UK, for example, issues special 'working holidaymaker' visas to Commonwealth citizens aged between 17 and 27. In France you can get a visa for work as an au pair if you are going to follow a recognised course of study (eg a French-language course) and complete all the paperwork before leaving your country. Your national student exchange organisation may be able to arrange temporary work permits to several countries through special programmes. For more details on working as a foreigner, see Work in the Facts for the Visitor sections of the individual country chapters.

If you have a parent or grandparent who was born in an EU country, you may have certain rights you never knew about. Get in touch with that country's embassy and ask about dual citizenship and work permits – if you go for citizenship, also ask about any obligations, such as military service and residency. Ireland is particularly easy-going about granting citizenship to people with an Irish parent or grandparent, and with an Irish passport, the EU is your oyster. You should be aware that your home country may not recognise dual citizenship.

If you do find a temporary job, the pay may be less than that offered to local people. The one big exception is teaching English, but these jobs are hard to come by – at least officially. Other typical tourist jobs (picking grapes in France, washing dishes in Alpine resorts) often come with board and lodging, and the pay is little more than pocket money, but you'll have a good time partying with other travellers.

Work Your Way around the World by Susan Griffith provides good, practical advice on a wide range of issues. The same publisher, Vacation Work, has many other useful titles, including *The Au Pair and Nanny's Guide to Working Abroad* by Susan Griffith & Sharon Legg.

If you play an instrument or have other artistic talents, you could try working the streets. As every Peruvian pipe player (and his fifth cousin) knows, busking is fairly common in major Mediterranean European cities, especially in France, Spain and Italy. Beware though: many countries require municipal permits that can be hard to obtain. Talk to other buskers first.

Selling goods on the street is generally frowned upon and can be tantamount to vagrancy apart from at flea markets. It's also a hard way to make money if you're not selling something special. Most countries require permits for this sort of thing. It's fairly common, though officially illegal, in Spain.

ACCOMMODATION

The cheapest places to stay in Europe are camping grounds, followed by hostels and accommodation in student dormitories. Cheap hotels, guesthouses, pensions, private rooms and B&Bs often present good value. If you're with a group, self-catering flats and cottages are worth considering, especially if you plan to stay somewhere for a while.

See the Facts for the Visitor sections in the country chapters for an overview of the local accommodation options. During peak holiday periods, accommodation can be hard to find, and unless you're camping, it's advisable to book ahead. Even camping grounds can fill up, especially in or around big cities.

Reservations & Bookings

If you arrive in a country by air, there is often an airport hotel-booking desk, although it rarely covers the lower strata of hotels. Tourist offices often have extensive accommodation lists, and the more helpful ones will go out of their way to find you something suitable. In most countries the fee for this service is very low and if accommodation is tight, it can save you a lot of running around. This is also an easy way to get around any language problems. Agencies offering private rooms can be good value. Staying with a local family doesn't always mean that you'll lack privacy, but you'll probably have less freedom than in a hotel.

Sometimes people will come up to you on the street offering a private room or a hostel bed. This can be good or bad, there's no hard-and-fast rule – just make sure it's not way out in a dingy suburb somewhere, and that you negotiate a clear price. As always, be careful when someone offers to carry your luggage: they might carry it away altogether.

Camping

Camping is immensely popular in Mediterranean Europe (especially among German and Dutch tourists) and provides the cheapest accommodation. There's usually a charge per tent or site, per person and per vehicle. National tourist offices should have booklets or brochures listing camping grounds all over their country. See the earlier Visas & Documents section for information on the Camping Card International.

In large cities, most camping grounds will be some distance from the centre. For this reason, camping is most popular with people who have their own transport. If you're on foot, the money you save by camping can quickly be outweighed by the money you spend on commuting to/from the town centre. You may also need a tent, sleeping bag and cooking equipment, though not always: many camping grounds rent out bungalows or cottages accommodating from two to eight people.

Camping other than at designated camping grounds is difficult because the population density makes it hard to find a suitable spot to pitch a tent away from prying eyes. It is also illegal without permission from the local authorities (the police or local council office) or from the owner of the land (don't be shy about asking – you may be pleasantly surprised by the response).

In some countries, free camping is illegal on all but private land, and in Greece it's illegal everywhere. This doesn't prevent hikers from occasionally pitching their tent for the night, and they'll usually get away with it if they keep a low profile (don't make a lot of noise, build a fire or leave rubbish). At worst, they'll be woken up by the police and asked to move on. Beware of camping freelance near camping grounds. In Tunisia, you can sleep on the beach in the north, but it is not acceptable to do so in the resort areas of Cap Bon Peninsula or Sousse.

Hostels

Hostels offer the cheapest roof over your head in Europe, and you don't have to be a youngster (though some French hostels have age limits) to use them. Most hostels are part of the national YHA (Youth Hostel Association), which is affiliated with what was formerly called the IYHF (International Youth Hostel Federation) and has now been renamed Hostelling International (HI) in order to attract a wider clientele and move away from the emphasis on 'youth'. The situation remains slightly confused at the moment, however. Some countries, such as the USA and Canada, immediately adopted the new name, but many European countries may take a few years to change their logos. In practice it makes no difference: IYHF and HI are the same thing and the domestic YHA almost always belongs to the parent group.

Technically you're supposed to be a YHA or HI member to use affiliated hostels, but you can often stay by paying an extra charge and this will usually be set against future membership. Stay enough nights as a nonmember and you're automatically a member.

To join the HI, ask at any hostel or contact your local or national hostelling office. The offices for English-speaking countries appear below. Otherwise, check the individual country chapters for addresses.

Australia
Australian Youth Hostels Association, Level 3, 10 Mallett St, Camperdown, NSW 2050 (☎ 02-9565 1699)

Canada
Hostelling International Canada, 1600 James Naismith Drive, Suite 608, Gloucester, Ontario K1B 5N4 (☎ 613-237 7884)

England & Wales
Youth Hostels Association, Trevelyan House, 8 St Stephen's Hill, St Albans, Herts AL1 2DY (☎ 01727-855215)

Ireland
An Óige, 61 Mountjoy St, Dublin 7 (☎ 01-830 4555)

New Zealand
Youth Hostels Association of New Zealand, PO Box 436, 173 Gloucester St, Christchurch 1 (☎ 03-379 9970)

Northern Ireland
Youth Hostel Association of Northern Ireland (YHANI), 22-32 Donegall Rd, Belfast BT12 5JN (☎ 01232-324733)

Scotland
Scottish Youth Hostels Association, 7 Glebe Crescent, Stirling FK8 2JA (☎ 01786-451181)

South Africa
Hostel Association of South Africa, 101 Boston House, 46 Strand St, Cape Town 8001 (☎ 021-419 1853)

USA
Hostelling International/American Youth Hostels, 733 15th St NW, Suite 840, Washington, DC, 20005 (☎ 202-783 6161)

At a hostel, you get a bed for the night, plus use of communal facilities, which often include a kitchen where you can prepare your own meals. You are usually required to have a sleeping sheet – simply using your sleeping bag is not permitted. If you don't have your own approved sleeping sheet, you can usually hire or buy one.

Hostels vary widely in character, but the growing number of travellers and the increased competition from other forms of accommodation (particularly private 'backpacker hostels') have prompted many hostels to improve their facilities and cut back on rules and regulations. Increasingly, hostels are open all day, curfews are gradually disappearing and 'wardens' with a sergeant-major mentality are an endangered species. In some places you'll even find hostels with single and double rooms. Everywhere the trend has been towards smaller dormitories with just four to six beds.

There are many hostel guides with listings available, including HI's *Europe* guide. Many hostels accept reservations by phone or fax but usually not during peak periods; for a small fee they'll often book you a place at the next one you're headed to. You can also book hostels through national hostel offices. Popular hostels can be heavily booked in summer and limits may even be placed on how many nights you can stay.

Student Accommodation

Some university towns rent out student accommodation during holiday periods. This is very popular in France (see the France chapter for details). Accommodation will sometimes be in single rooms (more commonly in doubles or triples) and may have cooking facilities. Enquire at the college or university, at student information services or at local tourist offices.

B&Bs, Guesthouses & Hotels

There's a huge range of accommodation above the hostel level. In some countries private accommodation similar to the B&Bs in the UK may go under the name of pension, guesthouse, *chambre d'hôte*, *domatia* and so on. Although the majority of B&Bs are simple affairs, there are more expensive ones where you will find attached bathrooms and other luxuries.

Above this level are hotels, which at the bottom of the bracket may be no more expensive than B&Bs or guesthouses, while at the other extreme extend to luxury five-star properties with price tags to match. Although categorisation depends on the country, the hotels recommended in this book will generally range from no stars to one or two stars. You'll often find inexpensive hotels clustered around the bus and train station areas – always good places to start hunting.

Check your hotel room and the bathroom

before you agree to take it, and make sure you know what it's going to cost – discounts are often available for groups or for longer stays. Ask about breakfast: sometimes it's included but other times it may be obligatory and you'll have to pay extra for it. If the sheets don't look clean, ask to have them changed right away. Check where the fire exits are.

If you think a hotel room is too expensive, ask if there's anything cheaper. (Often, hotel owners may have tried to steer you into more expensive rooms.) In southern Europe in particular, hotel owners may be open to a little bargaining if times are slack. In France it is now common practice for business hotels (usually rated higher than two stars) to slash their rates by up to 40% on Friday and Saturday nights when business is dead. Save your big hotel splurge for the weekend here.

FOOD

Few regions in the world offer such a variety of cuisines in such a small area. Dishes are completely different from one country (and even region) to the next, and sampling the local food can be one of the most enjoyable aspects of travel. The Facts for the Visitor sections in the individual country chapters contain details of local cuisine, and there are many places to eat recommended in the chapters themselves.

Restaurant prices vary enormously. The cheapest places for a decent meal are often the self-service restaurants in department stores. University restaurants are dirt cheap, but the food tends to be bland and it's not always clear whether you'll be allowed in if you're not a local student. Kiosks often sell cheap snacks that can be as much a part of the national cuisine as the fancy dishes.

Self-catering – buying your ingredients at a shop or market and preparing them yourself – can be a cheap and wholesome way of eating. Even if you don't cook, a picnic lunch with a fresh stick of bread, some local cheese and salami and a tomato or two, washed down with a bottle of local wine, can be one of the recurring highlights of your trip. It also makes a nice change from restaurant food.

Most campers will probably end up preparing at least some of their meals, and hostels and student accommodation often have cooking facilities. Camping Gaz replacement canisters are widely available.

If you have dietary restrictions – you're a vegetarian or you keep kosher, for example – tourist organisations may be able to provide lists of suitable restaurants. Some vegetarian and kosher restaurants are listed in this book.

In general vegetarians needn't worry about going hungry in Mediterranean Europe; except in Morocco, many restaurants have one or two vegetarian dishes, and southern European menus in particular tend to contain many vegetable dishes and salads. Some restaurants will prepare special dishes on request (approach them about this in advance).

Getting There & Away

Step one is to get to Europe and, in these days of severe competition among airlines, there are plenty of opportunities to find cheap tickets to a variety of 'gateway' cities.

Forget shipping, unless by 'shipping' you mean the many ferry services between Europe and North Africa. Only a handful of ships still carry passengers across the Atlantic; they don't sail often and are expensive even compared with full-fare air tickets. The days of ocean liners as modes of transport are well and truly over, but if you're still keen, refer to the Sea section at the end of this chapter for more details.

Some travellers still arrive or leave overland – the options being Africa, the Middle East and Asia, and what used to be the Soviet Union. The Trans-Siberian and associated railways offer an exciting approach to Europe that needn't be expensive. See the Land section later in this chapter for more information.

AIR

Remember always to reconfirm your onward (if you break your journey for more than 72 hours) or return bookings by the specified time – at least three days before departure on international flights. Otherwise there's a real risk that you'll turn up at the airport only to find that you've missed your flight because it was rescheduled, or that you've been reclassified as a 'no show' and been 'bumped' (see the Air Travel Glossary).

Buying Tickets

Your plane ticket will probably be the single most expensive item in your travel budget, and it's worth taking some time to research the current state of the market. Start early: some of the cheapest tickets have to be bought well in advance, and some popular flights sell out early. Have a talk to recent travellers, look at the ads in newspapers and magazines, and watch for special offers.

Cheap tickets are available in two distinct categories: official and unofficial. Official ones have a variety of names, including advance purchase tickets, advance purchase excursion (Apex) fares, super-Apex and simply budget fares.

Unofficial tickets are simply discounted tickets that the airlines release through selected travel agents (usually not sold by the airline offices themselves). Airlines can, however, supply information on routes and timetables and make bookings; their low-season, student and senior citizens' fares can be competitive. Also, normal full-fare airline tickets sometimes include one or more side trips in Europe free of charge, which can make them good value.

Return (round-trip) tickets usually work out cheaper than two one-way fares – often *much* cheaper. Be aware that immigration officials often ask for return or onward tickets, and that if you can't show either, you'll have to provide proof of 'sufficient means of support', which means you have to show a lot of money or, in some cases, valid credit cards.

Round-the-world (RTW) tickets are often real bargains, and can work out to be no more expensive or even cheaper than an ordinary return ticket. The official airline RTW tickets are usually put together by a combination of two or more airlines, and permit you to fly anywhere you want on their route systems so long as you don't backtrack. Other restrictions are that you (usually) must book the first sector in advance and cancellation penalties then apply. There may be restrictions on how many stops (or miles) you are permitted, and usually the tickets are valid for 90 days up to a year. Prices start at about UK£1000/US$1500, depending on the season and length of validity. An alternative type of RTW ticket is one put together by a travel agent using a combination of discounted tickets. These 'tailor-made' RTW tickets can be much cheaper than the official ones but usually carry a lot more restrictions.

Generally, you can find discounted tickets at prices as low as, or lower than, advance purchase or budget tickets. Phone around the travel agencies for bargains. You may discover that those impossibly cheap flights are 'fully booked, but we have another one that costs a

Air Travel Glossary

Apex Tickets Apex ('advance purchase excursion') fares are usually between 30 and 40% cheaper than full economy ones, but there are restrictions. You must purchase the ticket at least 21 days (sometimes more) in advance, be away for a minimum period (normally 14 days) and return within a maximum period (90 or 180 days). Stopovers are not allowed, and if you have to change your travel dates or routing, there will be extra charges. These tickets are not fully refundable; if you cancel your trip, the refund is often considerably less than what you paid for the ticket. Take out travel insurance to cover yourself in case you have to call off your trip unexpectedly (eg due to illness).

Baggage Allowance This will be written on your ticket; you are usually allowed one item weighing 20 kg to go in the hold, plus one item of hand luggage. Many airlines flying transatlantic routes allow for two pieces of luggage with relatively generous limits on their dimensions and weight.

Bucket Shops At certain times of the year and/or on certain routes, many airlines fly with empty seats. This isn't profitable (or good PR) and it's often more cost-effective for them to fly full, even if that means having to sell a certain number of drastically discounted tickets. They do this by off-loading them onto bucket shops (or consolidators), travel agents who specialise in such discounted fares. The agents, in turn, sell them to the public at reduced prices. These tickets are often the cheapest you'll find, but you usually can't purchase them directly from the airlines, restrictions abound and long-haul journeys can be extremely time-consuming, with several stops along the way. Availability varies widely, so you'll not only have to be flexible in your travel plans, you'll also have to be quick off the mark as soon as an advertisement appears in the press.

Bucket-shop agents advertise in newspapers and magazines, and there's a lot of competition – especially in places like Amsterdam, London and Hong Kong, three places that are crawling with them. It's always a good idea to telephone first to ascertain availability before rushing to some out-of-the-way shop. Naturally, they'll advertise the cheapest available tickets, but by the time you get there, these may be sold out (or were nonexistent in the first place) and you may be looking at something slightly more expensive.

Bumping Just because you have a confirmed seat doesn't mean you're going to get on the plane (see Overbooking).

Cancellation Penalties If you have to cancel or change an Apex or other discounted ticket, there may be heavy penalties involved; travel insurance can sometimes be taken out against these penalties. Some airlines now impose penalties on regular tickets as well, particularly against 'no show' passengers.

Check In Airlines ask you to check in a certain time ahead of the flight departure (usually two hours on international flights but longer on particularly security-conscious ones like El Al, the Israeli carrier). If you fail to check in on time and the flight is overbooked, the airline can cancel your reservation and give your seat to somebody else.

Confirmation Having a ticket written out with the flight and date on it doesn't mean you have a seat until the agent has confirmed with the airline that your status is 'OK' and has written or stamped that on your ticket. Prior to this confirmation, your status is 'on request'.

Courier Fares Businesses often send their urgent documents or freight through courier companies. These companies hire people to accompany the package through customs and, in return, offer cheap tickets that used to be phenomenal bargains but nowadays are just like decent discounted fares. In effect, what the courier companies do is ship their goods as your luggage on regular commercial flights; you are usually only allowed carry-on. This is a legitimate operation – all freight is completely legal. There are two drawbacks, however: the short turnaround time of the ticket (usually not longer than a month) and the limitation on your baggage allowance.

Discounted Tickets There are two types of discounted fares: officially discounted (such as Apex) ones and unofficially discounted tickets (see Bucket Shops). The latter can save you more than money – you may be able to pay Apex prices without the associated advance-purchase and other requirements. The lowest prices often impose drawbacks, such as flying with unpopular airlines, inconvenient schedules, or unpleasant routings and connections.

Economy Class Economy-class tickets are usually not the cheapest way to go, but they do give you maximum flexibility and they are valid for 12 months. If you don't use them, most are fully refundable, as are unused sectors of a multiple ticket.

Full Fares Airlines traditionally offer first-class (coded F), business-class (coded J) and economy-class (coded Y) tickets. These days there are so many promotional and discounted fares available that the only passengers paying full fare are on expense accounts or at the gate and in a hurry.

Lost Tickets If you lose your ticket, an airline will usually treat it like a travellers' cheque and, after inquiries, issue you with a replacement. Legally, however, an airline is entitled to treat it like cash, so a loss could be permanent. Consider them as valuables.

MCO A 'miscellaneous charges order' is a voucher for a given amount, usually issued by an airline as a refund or against a lost ticket. It can be used to pay for a flight with any IATA (International Air Transport Association) airline. MCOs, which are more flexible than a regular ticket, may satisfy the irritating onward ticket requirement, but some countries are now reluctant to accept them.

No Shows No shows are passengers who fail to turn up for their flight for whatever reason. Full-fare no shows are sometimes entitled to travel on a later flight. The rest are penalised (see Cancellation Penalties), but it all depends on the circumstances and availability of space.

Open-Jaw Tickets These are return tickets that allow you to fly to one place but return from another, and travel between the two 'jaws' by any means of transport at your own expense. If available, this can save you backtracking to your arrival point.
Overbooking Airlines hate to fly with empty seats, and since every flight has some passengers who fail to show up, they often book more passengers than there are seats available. Usually the excess passengers balance those who fail to show up, but occasionally somebody gets bumped – usually the last passenger(s) to check in.

Promotional Fares These are officially discounted fares, such as Apex ones, which are available from travel agents or direct from the airline.

Reconfirmation If you break your journey, you must contact the airline at least 72 hours prior to departure of the ongoing flight to 'reconfirm' that you intend to fly. If you don't do this, the airline is entitled to delete your name from the passenger list.
Restrictions Discounted tickets often have various constraints placed on them, such as advance purchase, limitations on the minimum and maximum period you must be away, restrictions on breaking the journey or changing the booking or routing etc.

Standby This is a discounted ticket where you only fly if there is a seat free at the last moment. Standby fares are usually only available directly at the airport, but may sometimes also be handled by an airline's city office. To give yourself the best possible chance of getting on the flight you want, get there early and have your name placed on the waiting list immediately. It's first come, first served.
Student Discounts Some airlines offer student-card holders 15% to 25% off certain fares. The same often applies to anyone under the age of 26. These discounts are generally only available on normal economy-class fares; you wouldn't get one, for instance, on an Apex or an RTW ticket, since these are already discounted. Take a calculator and do the sums; discounted tickets – both the official and bucket-shop ones – are often better value than student fares.

Tickets Out An entry requirement for many countries is that you have an onward (ie out of the country) ticket. If you're not sure of your travel plans, the easiest solution is to buy the cheapest onward ticket to a neighbouring country or a ticket from a reliable airline that can be refunded later if you do not use it.
Transferred Tickets Airline tickets cannot be transferred from one person to another. Travellers sometimes try to sell the return half of their ticket, but officials can ask you to prove that you are the person named on the ticket. This may not be checked on domestic flights, but on international flights, tickets are usually compared with passports. Remember that if you are flying on a transferred ticket and something goes wrong with the flight (hijack, crash), there will be no record of your presence on board.
Travel Periods Some officially discounted fares – Apex fares in particular – vary with the seasons. There is often a low (off-peak) season and a high (peak) season. Sometimes there's an intermediate (or shoulder) season as well. At peak times, when everyone wants to fly, both officially and unofficially discounted fares will be higher and discounted tickets may not be available. Usually the fare depends on your outward flight – if you depart in the high season and return in the low season, you still pay the high-season fare. ■

bit more'. Or that the flight is on an airline notorious for its poor safety standards and leaves you in the world's least favourite airport in mid-journey for 14 hours – where you're confined to the transit lounge because you don't have a visa. Or the agent claims to have the last two seats available for that country for the whole of August, which will be held for you for a maximum of two hours as long as you come in and pay cash. Don't panic – keep ringing around.

If you are travelling from the USA or South-East Asia, or you are trying to exit Europe from the UK, you will probably find that the cheapest flights are being advertised by obscure agencies whose names probably haven't even reached the telephone directory. Many such firms are honest and solvent, but there are a few rogues who will take your money and disappear – only to reopen elsewhere a month or two later under a new name.

If you feel suspicious about a firm, don't give them all the money at once – leave a deposit of 20% or so and pay the balance when you get the ticket. If they insist on cash in advance, go somewhere else or be prepared to take a very big risk. And once you have the ticket, ring the airline to confirm that you are booked onto the flight.

You may decide to pay more than the rock-bottom fare by opting for the safety of a better known travel agent. Firms such as STA Travel, which has offices worldwide, Council Travel in the USA and elsewhere or Travel CUTS in Canada offer good prices to most destinations, and won't disappear overnight leaving you clutching a receipt for a nonexistent ticket.

Use the fares quoted in this book as a guide only. They are approximate and based on the rates advertised by travel agents at the time of research. Most are likely to have changed by the time you read this.

Travellers with Special Needs

If you have special needs of any sort – you're vegetarian or require a special diet (salt-free, kosher etc), you're travelling in a wheelchair, taking the baby, terrified of flying, whatever – let the airline people know as soon as possible so that they can make the necessary arrangements. Remind them when you reconfirm your booking (at least 72 hours before departure) and again when you check in at the airport. It may also be worth ringing around the airlines before you make your booking to find out how they can handle your particular needs.

Children aged under two travel for 10% of the full fare (or free on some airlines) as long as they don't occupy a seat. They don't get a baggage allowance in this case. 'Skycots', baby food and nappies (diapers) should be provided by the airline if requested in advance. Children aged between two and 12 can usually occupy a seat for half to two-thirds of the full fare. They do get the standard baggage allowance.

The USA

The North Atlantic is the world's busiest long-haul air corridor, and the flight options are bewildering. The *New York Times*, *LA Times*, *Chicago Tribune*, *San Francisco Chronicle* and the *Boston Globe* all publish weekly travel sections in which you'll find any number of travel agents' ads. Council Travel and STA Travel have offices in major cities nationwide. You should be able to fly New York-London return for around US$370 in the low season, or US$600 in the high season. Tack on another US$80 or so from the West Coast. Flights to Paris from New York start from US$425 or US$525, depending on the season.

One-way fares can work out to about half of this on a stand-by basis. Airhitch (☎ 212-864 2000) specialises in this sort of thing and can get you to Europe one way for US$169/$269/$229 from the East/West Coast/elsewhere in the USA.

An interesting alternative to the boring New York-London flight is offered by Icelandair (☎ 800-223 5500), which has competitive year-round fares to Luxembourg with a stop-over in Iceland's capital, Reykjavík – a great way of spending a few days in an unusual country that is otherwise hard to get to.

Another option is a courier flight, where you accompany a parcel or freight to be picked up at the other end. A New York-London return courier flight can be had for about US$300/$400 or even less in the low/high season.

You can also fly one way. The drawbacks are that your stay in Europe may be limited to one or two weeks on a return ticket, your luggage is usually restricted to hand baggage (the parcel or freight you carry comes out of your luggage allowance) and you may have to be a resident and apply for an interview before they'll take you on.

Find out more about courier flights from Discount Travel International in New York (☎ 212-362 3636) and Orbit Travel in Los Angeles (☎ 213-466 7248). Call two or three months in advance and at the start of the calendar month when rosters are being written.

The *Travel Unlimited* newsletter, PO Box 1058, Allston, Massachusetts 02134, publishes details of the cheapest airfares and courier possibilities for destinations all over the world from the USA and other countries including the UK. The newsletter is a treasure trove of information. A single monthly issue costs US$5 and a year's subscription US$25 (US$35 abroad).

Canada

Travel CUTS has offices in all major Canadian cities. Scan the budget travel agents' ads in the *Toronto Globe & Mail*, *Toronto Star* and *Vancouver Province*.

See the previous USA section for general information on courier flights. For flights originating in Canada, contact FB on Board Courier Services (☎ 905-612 8095 in Toronto, ☎ 604-278 1266 in Vancouver). A courier return flight to London will start at about C$350 from Toronto or Montreal, C$570 from Vancouver, depending on the season. Airhitch (see the USA section) has stand-by fares to/from Toronto, Montreal and Vancouver.

Australia

STA Travel and Flight Centres International are major dealers in cheap airfares. Check the travel agents' ads in the Yellow Pages and ring around.

The Saturday travel sections of the *Sydney Morning Herald* and Melbourne's *The Age* newspapers have many ads offering cheap fares to Europe, but don't be surprised if they happen to be 'sold out' when you contact the agents: they're usually low-season fares on obscure airlines with conditions attached. With Australia's large and well-organised ethnic populations, it pays to check special deals in the ethnic press – Olympic Airways sometimes has good deals to Athens, for example.

Discounted return fares on mainstream airlines through a reputable agent like STA Travel cost between A$1500 (low season) and A$2500 (high season). Flights to/from Perth are a couple of hundred dollars cheaper.

New Zealand

As in Australia, STA Travel and Flight Centres International are popular travel agencies. Not surprisingly, the cheapest fares to Europe are routed through the USA, and a RTW ticket can be cheaper than an advance purchase return ticket.

Africa

Nairobi is probably the best place in Africa to buy tickets to Europe, thanks to the strong competition between its many bucket shops. Several West African countries such as Burkina Faso and The Gambia offer cheap charter flights to France, and charter fares from Morocco can be incredibly cheap if you're lucky enough to find a seat.

From South Africa, Air Namibia has particularly cheap return youth fares to London from as low as R2819. The big carriers' return fares range from R2900 to R3815. These fares are expected to rise shortly following the devaluation of the rand. Students' Travel (☎ 011-716 3945) in Johannesburg and the Africa Travel Centre (☎ 021-235 555) in Cape Town are worth trying for cheap tickets.

Asia

Hong Kong is still the discount plane-ticket capital of Asia, and its bucket shops offer some great bargains. But be careful: not all are reliable. Ask the advice of other travellers before buying tickets. Many of the cheapest fares from South-East Asia to Europe are offered by Eastern European carriers (eg LOT or Aeroflot), though Gulf Air often has some good deals. STA Travel has branches in Hong Kong, Tokyo, Singapore, Bangkok and Kuala Lumpur.

To/from India, the cheapest flights tend to be with Eastern European carriers or certain Middle Eastern airlines like Syrian Arab Airlines. Bombay is India's air transport hub, with many transit options to/from South-East Asia, but tickets are slightly cheaper in Delhi.

The UK

London is Europe's major centre for discounted fares. The following are some of the best agencies to contact:

Trailfinders
   198 Kensington High St, London W8 (☎ 0171-938
   3232); tube: High St Kensington
STA Travel
   86 Old Brompton Rd, London SW7 3LQ (☎ 0171-
   581 4132); tube: South Kensington
Campus Travel
   52 Grosvenor Gardens, London SW1W OAG
   (☎ 0171-730 8832); tube: Victoria
Council Travel
   28A Poland St, London W1V 3DB (☎ 0171-287
   3337); tube: Oxford Circus

The weekly listings magazine *Time Out* and the weekend newspapers like the *Daily Telegraph* and the *Evening Standard* carry ads for cheap fares. Also look out for the free magazines and newspapers widely available in London, especially *TNT* and *Southern Cross*. You can often pick them up outside main railway and tube stations.

Make sure the agent is a member of some sort of traveller-protection scheme, such as that offered by the ABTA (Association of British Travel Agents). If you have bought your ticket from an ABTA-registered agent who then goes out of business, ABTA will guarantee a refund or an alternative. Unregistered bucket shops are riskier but usually cheaper.

From Continental Europe
Though London is the travel discount capital of Europe, there are several other cities in the region where you'll find a wide range of good deals, particularly Athens and Amsterdam.

Many travel agents in Europe have ties with STA Travel, whose tickets can often be altered free of charge the first time round. Outlets in major transport hubs include: CTS Voyages (☎ 01 43 25 00 76), 20 Rue des Carmes, 75005 Paris; SRID Reisen (☎ 069-70 30 35), Bockenheimer Landstrasse 133, 60325 Frankfurt; and International Student & Youth Travel Service (☎ 01-322 1267), Nikis 11, 10557 Athens.

LAND
Train
Morocco and most of Turkey lie outside Europe, but the rail systems of both countries are still covered by Inter-Rail (though only the 26+ version is valid in Turkey). The price of a cheap return train ticket from London to Morocco compares favourably with equivalent bus fares.

To/from Asia, a train can work out at about the same price as flying, depending on how much time and money you spend along the way, and it can be a lot more fun. There are three routes to/from Moscow across Siberia: the Trans-Siberian to/from Vladivostok, and the Trans-Mongolian and Trans-Manchurian, both to/from Beijing. There's a fourth route south from Moscow and across Kazakstan, following part of the old Silk Road to Beijing. Prices vary enormously, depending on where you buy the ticket and what is included – the prices quoted here are a rough indication only.

The Trans-Siberian takes just under seven days from Moscow via Khabarovsk to Vladivostok, from where there is a boat to Niigata in Japan from May to October. Otherwise you can fly to Niigata as well as to Seattle, Washington, and Anchorage, Alaska, in the USA. The complete journey from Moscow to Niigata costs from about US$600 per person for a 2nd-class sleeper in a four-berth cabin.

The Trans-Mongolian passes through Mongolia to Beijing and takes about 5½ days. A 2nd-class sleeper in a four-berth compartment would cost around US$265 if purchased in Moscow or Beijing. If you want to stop off along the way or spend some time in Moscow, you'll need 'visa support' – a letter from a travel agent confirming that they're making the travel/accommodation bookings you require in Russia or Mongolia. Locally based companies that do all-inclusive packages (with visa support) include the Travellers Guest House (☎ 095-971 4059; fax 280 9786) in Moscow; and Monkey Business (☎ 2723 1376; fax 2723 6653) in Hong Kong, with an information centre in Beijing. There are a number of other budget operators.

The Trans-Manchurian passes through Manchuria to Beijing and takes 6½ days, costing about US$225.

A trans-Central Asia route runs from Moscow to Almaty in Kazakstan, crosses the border on the new line to Ürümqi (northwestern China), and follows part of the old Silk Road to Beijing. At present you can't buy through tickets. Moscow to Ürümqi in 2nd class costs about US$160 and takes five or more days, depending on connections.

There are countless travel options between

Moscow and the rest of Europe. Most people will opt for the train, usually to/from Berlin, Helsinki, Munich, Budapest or Vienna, where they can make connections to Mediterranean Europe. The *Trans-Siberian Handbook* (Trailblazer) by Bryn Thomas is a comprehensive guide to the route, and Lonely Planet's *Russia, Ukraine & Belarus* has a separate chapter on trans-Siberian travel.

Overland Trails

Asia In the early 1980s, the overland trail to/from Asia lost much of its popularity as the Islamic regime in Iran made life difficult for most independent travellers, and the war in Afghanistan closed that country off to all but the foolhardy. Now that Iran seems to be rediscovering the merits of tourism, the Asia route has begun to pick up again, though unsettled conditions in Afghanistan, southern Pakistan and north-west India could prevent the trickle of travellers from turning into a flood for the time being.

A new overland route through the former Soviet Union could become important over the next decade. At this stage the options are more or less confined to the Trans-Siberian/Trans-Mongolian railway lines to/from Moscow (see the previous Train section), but other modes of transport are likely to become available beyond the Urals as the newly independent states open up to travellers.

Africa Apart from the complicated Middle East route, going to/from Africa involves a Mediterranean ferry crossing (see the Boat section in the Getting Around chapter). Due to political problems in Africa (eg war between Morocco and the Polisario in the west, civil wars in Algeria and Sudan), the most feasible Africa overland routes of the past have all but shut down.

Travelling by private transport beyond Europe requires plenty of paperwork and other preparations. A detailed description is beyond the scope of this book, but the following Getting Around chapter tells you what's required within Europe.

SEA
Ferry

Several different ferry companies compete on all the main ferry routes. The resulting service is comprehensive but complicated. The same ferry company can have a host of different prices for the same route, depending upon the time of day or year, the validity of the ticket, or the length of your vehicle. Vehicle tickets include the driver and often up to five passengers free of charge. It is worth planning (and booking) ahead where possible as there may be special reductions on off-peak crossings and advance purchase tickets. On English Channel routes, apart from one-day or short-term excursion returns, there is little advantage in buying a return ticket as against two singles.

Stena Line is the largest ferry company in the world and serves British, Irish and Scandinavian routes (but from England to/from Norway it's Color Line). P&O European Ferries and Brittany Ferries sail direct between England and northern Spain, taking 24 to 35 hours. The shortest cross-Channel routes (Dover to Calais, and Folkestone to Boulogne) are also the busiest, though there is now great competition from the Channel Tunnel.

Rail-pass holders are entitled to discounts or free travel on some lines (see the earlier Train section), and most ferry companies give discounts to disabled drivers. Food on ferries is often expensive (and lousy), so it is worth bringing your own when possible. It is also worth knowing that if you take your vehicle on board, you are usually denied access to it during the voyage.

Passenger Ships & Freighters

Regular, long-distance passenger ships disappeared with the advent of cheap air travel and were replaced by a small number of luxury cruise ships. Cunard's *Queen Elizabeth 2* sails between New York and Southampton 20 times a year; the trip takes six nights each way and costs around UK£1500 for the return trip, though there are also one-way and 'fly one-way' deals. Your travel agent will have more details. The standard reference for passenger ships is the *OAG Cruise & Ferry Guide* published by the UK-based Reed Travel Group (☎ 01582-600111), Church St, Dunstable, Bedfordshire LU5 4HB.

A more adventurous (though not necessarily cheaper) alternative is as a paying passenger on a freighter. Freighters are far more numerous than cruise ships, and there are many more routes from which to choose. With a bit of homework, you'll be able to sail between Europe and just about anywhere else in the world, with stopovers at exotic ports that you may never have heard of. The previously mentioned *OAG Cruise & Ferry Guide* is the most comprehensive source of information though *Travel by Cruise Ship* (Cadogan, London) is also a good source.

Passenger freighters typically carry six to 12 passengers (more than 12 would require a doctor on board) and, though less luxurious than dedicated cruise ships, give you a real taste of life at sea. Schedules tend to be flexible and costs vary, but seem to hover around US$100 a day; vehicles can often be included for an additional fee.

LEAVING MEDITERRANEAN EUROPE

A few countries charge you a small fee for the privilege of leaving from their airports. Some also charge port fees when departing by ship. Such fees are usually included in the price of your ticket, but it pays to check this when purchasing it. If not, you'll have to have the fee ready when leaving. Details of departure taxes

are given at the end of the Getting There & Away section in the individual country chapters.

WARNING

This chapter is particularly vulnerable to change – prices for international travel are volatile, routes are introduced and cancelled, schedules change, special deals come and go, and rules and visa requirements are amended. Airlines seem to take a perverse pleasure in making price structures and regulations as complicated as possible; you should check directly with the airline or travel agent to make sure you understand how a fare (and ticket you may buy) works. In addition, the travel industry is highly competitive and there are many schemes and bonuses. The upshot of this is that you should get opinions, quotes and advice from as many airlines and travel agents as possible before you part with your hard-earned cash. The details given in this chapter should be regarded as pointers and are not a substitute for careful, up-to-date research.

Getting Around

AIR

From 1997, as part of the EU's 'open skies' policy, national airlines will no longer have to include a domestic airport in their routings and can fly directly from one EU city to another. Pundits forecast increased competition and lower prices, but additional take-off slots at oversubscribed airports are hard to come by. Look out for the new breed of small airlines, such as the UK-based EasyJet, which sell budget tickets directly to the customer.

Refer to the Air Glossary in the previous Getting There & Away chapter for information on types of air tickets. London is a good centre for picking up cheap, restricted-validity tickets through bucket shops. Amsterdam and Athens are other good places for bucket-shop tickets. For more information, see the individual country chapters.

For longer journeys, you can sometimes find airfares that beat or at least equal surface-travel alternatives in terms of cost, depending on the season. A discounted return airfare from London to Madrid, for example, is available through discount travel agents for UK£139 throughout most of the year but it rises to UK£195 in the height of summer and certain other peak periods. Comparable fares from London to Rome would be UK£183 and UK£234. A two-month return by rail and ferry from London to Madrid is UK£195 (from UK£201 by Eurostar to Paris and rail to Madrid) and London to Rome UK£177 (from UK£190 by Eurostar to Paris and rail to Rome). Depending on the season, there are cheap charter flights from London, Paris and Madrid to Morocco and Tunisia.

Air travel is best viewed as a means to get you to the starting point of your itinerary rather than as your main means of travel since it lacks the flexibility of ground transport. Also, if you start taking flights for relatively short hops it gets extremely expensive, particularly as special deals are not as common on domestic flights as they are on international ones.

So-called open-jaw returns, by which you can travel into one city and exit from another, are worth considering, though they sometimes work out more expensive than simple returns. In the UK, Trailfinders (☎ 0171-938 3232) and STA Travel (☎ 0171-581 4132) can give you tailor-made versions of these tickets. Your chosen cities don't necessarily have to be in the same country. Lufthansa has Young Europe Special (YES) flights, which allow travel around Europe by air at UK£59 or UK£69 per flight (minimum four flights, maximum 10). The UK is the starting point, and the offer is open to students under 31 years of age and anybody under 26. Alitalia's Europa Pass is a similar deal.

If you are travelling alone, courier flights are a possibility. You get cheap passage in return for accompanying a package or documents through customs and delivering it to a representative at the destination airport. EU integration and electronic communications means there's increasingly less call for couriers, but you might find something. British Airways, for example, offers courier flights through the Travel Shop (☎ 0181-564 7009). Sample courier return fares from London are UK£80 to Barcelona and the same to Lisbon.

Getting between airports and city centres is rarely a problem in Europe thanks to ever improving underground networks and good bus services.

BUS
International Buses

International bus travel tends to take second place to going by train. The bus has the edge in terms of cost, sometimes quite substantially, but is generally slower and less comfortable.

UK-based Eurolines (☎ 0990-143219 or ☎ 01582-404511), 52 Grosvenor Gardens, London SW1W 0AU, is the main international bus company. European representatives include Eurolines Nederland (☎ 020-627 5151), Rokin 10, 1012 KR Amsterdam; Eurolines Peninsular (☎ 93-490 4000), Estació d'Autobuses de Sants, Calle Viriato, Barcelona; Eurolines France (☎ 01 49 72 51 51), Gare Routière Internationale, 28 Ave du Général de Gaulle, Porte de Bagnolet, 75020 Paris; Deutsche Touring (☎ 089-545 8700),

Amulfstrasse 3, Im Stamberger, 80335 Munich; and Eurolines Italy (☎ 06-44 23 39 28), Ciconvallazione Nonentana 574, Lato Stazione Tiburtina, Rome. These companies may also be able to advise you on other bus companies and deals.

Eurolines has 10 circular Explorer routes, always starting and ending in London. The popular London-Amsterdam-Paris route costs UK£71 (no youth reductions). Eurolines now also offers passes, but they're neither as extensive nor as flexible as rail passes. They cover 18 European cities as far apart as London, Barcelona, Rome, Budapest and Copenhagen, and cost UK£229 for 30 days (UK£199 for students and senior citizens) or UK£279 for 60 days (UK£249). The passes are cheaper in the off season.

On ordinary return trips, youth (under 26) fares are about 10% less than the adult full fare, eg a London-Madrid return ticket costs UK£154 for adults or UK£139 for those under 26. The adult/youth fares to Rome from London are UK£137/£127. Explorer or return tickets are valid for six months. One of Eurolines' three daily London-Paris buses goes on Le Shuttle via the Channel Tunnel.

Eurobus started up in 1995. In addition to hop-on, hop-off buses equipped with WC and video, the company offers services such as on-board guides and mail-forwarding. Buses complete a figure-of-eight loop of Europe every two days, taking in Amsterdam, Brussels, Paris, Zürich, Prague, Vienna, Budapest and major cities in Germany and Italy; there's also a Spanish link reaching as far as Valencia and Madrid and one into Italy to Florence and Rome.

You can only get on/off at the specified stops on the loop, but you can complete as many loops as you like. Reservations are advised, though only the first sector *must* be booked. Unlimited travel costs are US$360/ $460 for two/three months for students and those under 26; US$499/$599 for those 26 years of age and over. Tickets are available in many countries worldwide (eg from STA Travel in the UK), though you need to make your own way to a city on the loop to start off.

The Moroccan national bus line, CTM (Compagnie des Transports Marocains), operates buses to/from France, Belgium and northern Italy to most of the largest Moroccan towns. Eurolines has a London-Tangier service via Paris for UK£133.

See the individual country chapters for more information about long-distance buses.

National Buses

Domestic buses provide a viable alternative to the rail network in most countries. Again, compared to trains they are usually slightly cheaper and, with the exception of Spain, Portugal and Greece, somewhat slower.

Buses tend to be best for shorter hops such as getting around cities and reaching remote villages. They are often the only option in mountainous regions where rail tracks don't exist. Advance reservations are rarely necessary. On many city buses you usually buy your ticket in advance from a kiosk or machine and cancel it on boarding.

See the individual country chapters and city sections for more details on local buses.

TRAIN

Trains are a popular way of getting around: they are comfortable, frequent and generally on time. In some countries, such as Italy, Spain and Portugal, fares are heavily subsidised; in others, European rail passes make travel more affordable. Supplements and reservation costs are not covered by passes, and pass-holders must always carry their passport for identification purposes.

If you plan to travel extensively by train, it might be worth getting a copy of the *Thomas Cook European Timetable*, which gives a complete listing of train schedules and indicates where supplements apply and where reservations are necessary. It is updated monthly and is available from Thomas Cook outlets in the UK and Australia and in the USA from Forsyth Travel Library (☎ 800-367 7984), 9154 West 57th St, PO Box 2975, Shawnee Mission, Kansas 66201-1375. If you are planning to do a lot of train travel in one or a handful of countries – Spain and Portugal, say – it might be worthwhile getting hold of the national timetables published by the state railroads.

In Mediterranean Europe, Paris and Milan are important hubs for international rail connections; see the relevant city sections for details and budget ticket agents.

Note that European trains sometimes split en route in order to service two destinations, so

Channel Tunnel
The Channel Tunnel, which opened in November 1994, links England and France by rail. At 50 km it's the longest undersea tunnel in the world and a remarkable engineering feat.

There are two ways of using the tunnel: the Eurostar passenger train and Le Shuttle for cars, motorcycles, buses and freight vehicles and their passengers.

Eurostar
The Eurostar train link enables passengers to take a direct train from London's Waterloo train station to Paris' Gare du Nord (three hours) or Brussels Midi/Zuid (3¼ hours). These times will come down once high-speed rail has been laid on the British side, but that's not expected until 2002.

From about 6.30 am to 8 pm there's a train every one or two hours in each direction between London and Paris, and London and Brussels. There are easy onward connections from London to Scotland and Wales, and from Brussels to Germany and the Netherlands. Tickets are widely available – from some 3000 travel agencies and at major train stations – and include a seat reservation on a particular train. For information and credit-card bookings, call ☎ 0345-881 881 in the UK or ☎ 01233-617 575 from abroad. Passengers can transport bicycles on Eurostar.

Le Shuttle
Le Shuttle, the vehicle-carrying service, runs only between the two tunnel terminals, Folkestone and Calais (actually just west of Calais at Coquelles). The crossing takes 35 minutes, but actual travel time with loading and unloading is closer to an hour. Shuttle trains run 24 hours a day, departing every 15 minutes in each direction at peak times and at least every 1¼ hours during the quietest periods of the night.

Shuttles are designed to carry up to 180 cars (or 120 cars and 12 coaches). Bicycles, motorcycles, cars, camper vans, caravans and trailers can all be carried, though the maximum vehicle length is 6.5 metres. Ferries normally have a limit of five passengers per car, but with Le Shuttle you can transport up to eight, if you can cram them all in (hitchers, take note!). Facilities are minimal and travellers stay in or with their vehicle.

Prices vary according to the time of year, and may also fluctuate as the tunnel and the ferry companies compete for market share. You can pre-pay or pay on arrival (by cash or credit card at a toll booth), but you can't reserve a place on a particular shuttle. For further information or credit-card bookings, call the customer service centre on ☎ 0990-353 535. Passport and immigration controls for the UK and France are passed before boarding Le Shuttle. ■

even if you know you're on the right train, make sure you're in the correct carriage as well.

Express Trains
Fast trains or ones that make few stops are identified by the symbols EC (Eurocity) or IC (intercity). The French TGV and Spanish AVE are even faster. Supplements can apply on fast trains, and it is a good idea (sometimes obligatory) to make seat reservations at peak times and on certain lines.

Overnight Trains
Overnight trains will usually offer a choice of couchette or sleeper if you don't fancy sleeping in your seat with somebody else's head on your shoulder. Again, reservations are advisable as sleeping options are allocated on a first-come, first-served basis. Couchettes have four bunks per compartment in 1st class and six in 2nd class. They are comfortable enough, if lacking a bit in privacy. A bunk costs around US$25 for most international trains, irrespective of the length of the journey.

Sleepers are the most comfortable option, offering beds for one or two passengers in 1st class, and two or three passengers in 2nd class. Charges vary depending upon the journey, but they are significantly more expensive than couchettes. Most long-distance trains have a dining or buffet (café) car or an attendant who wheels a snack trolley through carriages. Prices tend to be steep.

Security
Stories occasionally surface about train passengers being gassed or drugged and then robbed, though bag-snatching is more of a worry. Sensible security measures include not

letting your bags out of your sight (especially when stopping at stations), chaining them to the luggage rack, and locking compartment doors overnight.

Rail Passes

Shop around, as pass prices can vary between different outlets. Once purchased, take care of your pass, as it cannot be replaced or refunded if lost or stolen. European passes get reductions on Eurostar through the Channel Tunnel and on certain ferries.

Eurail These passes can only be bought by residents of non-European countries and are supposed to be purchased before arriving in Europe. However, Eurail passes can be purchased within Europe, so long as your passport proves you've been there for less than six months, but the outlets where you can do this are limited and the passes will be more expensive than getting them outside Europe. The Rail Shop (☎ 0990-300003), 179 Piccadilly, London W1V 0BA, is one such outlet. If you've lived in Europe for more than six months, you are eligible for an Inter-Rail pass, which is a better buy.

Eurail passes are valid for unlimited travel on national railways and some private lines in Austria, Belgium, Denmark, Finland, France (and Monaco), Germany, Greece, Hungary, Ireland, Italy, Luxembourg, the Netherlands, Norway, Portugal, Spain, Sweden and Switzerland (including Liechtenstein). The UK is not covered.

Eurail is also valid on certain ferries between Italy and Greece, for example. Reductions are given on some other ferry routes and on steamer services in various countries.

Eurail passes offer reasonable value to people aged under 26. A Youthpass is valid for unlimited 2nd-class travel for 15 days (US$418), one month (US$598) or two months (US$798). The Youth Flexipass, also for 2nd class, is valid for freely chosen days within a two-month period: 10 days for US$438 or 15 days for US$588. Overnight journeys commencing after 7 pm count as the following day's travel. The traveller must fill out in ink the relevant box in the calendar before starting a day's travel; not validating the pass in this way incurs a fine of US$50. Tampering with

the pass (eg using an erasable pen and later rubbing out earlier days) costs the perpetrator the full fare plus US$100.

For those over 26, a Flexipass (available in 1st class only) costs US$616 or US$812 for 10 or 15 freely chosen days in two months. The standard Eurail pass has five versions, costing from US$522 for 15 days unlimited travel up to US$1468 for three months. Two or more people travelling together (minimum three people between April and September) can get good discounts on a Saverpass, which works like the standard Eurail pass. Eurail passes for children are also available.

Europass Also for non-Europeans, the Europass gives between five and 15 freely chosen days of unlimited travel within a two-month period. Youth (under 26) and adult (solo, or two sharing) versions are available, and purchasing requirements and sales outlets are as for Eurail passes. They are a little cheaper than Eurail passes as they cover fewer countries. You can choose to travel in three to five countries: France, Italy, Spain, Germany and Switzerland. For a small additional charge each or all of Greece (including ferries from Italy), Portugal, Austria, Belgium (including Luxembourg and the Netherlands) can be added on. But beware: the countries you choose must be adjacent.

Inter-Rail Inter-Rail passes are available to European residents of six months standing (passport identification is required). Terms and conditions vary slightly from country to country, but in the country of origin there is only a discount of around 50% on normal fares.

Travellers over 26 can get the Inter-Rail 26-plus ticket, valid for unlimited rail travel in Austria, Bulgaria, Croatia, Czech Republic, Denmark, Finland, Germany, Greece, Hungary, Luxembourg, Netherlands, Norway, Poland, Romania, Ireland, Slovakia, Slovenia, Sweden, Turkey and Yugoslavia. The pass also gives free travel on some ferries from the Italian port of Brindisi to Patras in Greece, as well as discounts of 30% to 50% on various other ferry routes (more than covered by Eurail) and certain river and lake services. A 15-day pass costs UK£215 and one month costs UK£275.

The Inter-Rail pass for those under 26 is split into zones. Zone A is Ireland; B is Sweden, Norway and Finland; C is Denmark, Germany, Switzerland and Austria; D is the Czech Republic, Slovakia, Poland, Hungary, Bulgaria, Romania and Croatia; E is France, Belgium, Netherlands and Luxembourg; F is Spain, Portugal and Morocco; and G is Italy, Greece, Turkey and Slovenia. The price for any one zone is UK£185 for 15 days. Multizone passes are better value and are valid for one month: a pass for two zones is UK£220, for three zones it's UK£245, and for all zones it's UK£275.

Euro Domino There is a Euro Domino pass (called a Freedom pass in the UK) for each of the countries covered in the zonal Inter-Rail pass, except for Croatia and Romania. Adults (travelling in 1st or 2nd class) and those under 26 can choose from three, five, or 10 days validity within one month. Examples of adult/youth prices for 10 days in 2nd class are UK£239/£179 for Italy and UK£239/£189 for Spain.

National Rail Passes If you intend to travel extensively within one country, check which national rail passes are available. These can sometimes save you a lot of money; details can be found in the Getting Around sections in the individual country chapters. You need to plan ahead if you intend to take this option, as some passes can only be purchased prior to arrival in the country concerned.

Cheap Tickets
European rail passes are only worth buying if you plan to do a reasonable amount of inter-country travelling within a short space of time. Some people tend to overdo it and spend every night they can on the train, ending up too tired to enjoy sightseeing the next day.

When weighing up options, consider the cost of other cheap ticket deals. Travellers aged under 26 can pick up BIJ (Billet International de Jeunesse) tickets which can cut fares by up to about 30%. Unfortunately, you can't always bank on a substantial reduction. London to Madrid one way/return is UK£93/£186 instead of UK£124/£195, London to Rome one way/return is UK£92/£173 instead of UK£111/

£177. Various agents issue BIJ tickets in Europe, eg Campus Travel (☎ 0171-730 8832), 52 Grosvenor Gardens, London SW1 0AG, which also sells Eurotrain tickets for people aged under 26. Eurotrain options include circular Explorer tickets, allowing a different route for the return trip: London to Madrid, for instance, takes in Barcelona, Paris and numerous other cities. The fare for this 'Spanish Explorer' ticket is UK£195 and it's valid for two months. British Rail International (☎ 0171-834 2345) and Wasteels (☎ 0171-834 7066), both in London's Victoria train station, sell BIJ tickets and other rail deals.

For a small fee, European residents aged over 60 can get a Rail Europe Senior Card as an add-on to their national rail senior pass. It entitles the holder to reduced European fares. The percentage saving varies according to the route.

TAXI
Taxis in Europe are metered and rates are high. There might also be supplements (depending on the country) for things like luggage, the time of day, the location from which you were picked up, and extra passengers. Good bus, rail and underground railway networks make taxis all but unnecessary for most travellers, but if you need one in a hurry taxi ranks can usually be found near train stations or outside big hotels. Lower fares make taxis more viable in some countries, such as Spain, Greece and Portugal.

CAR & MOTORCYCLE
Travelling with your own vehicle is the best way to get to remote places and it gives you the most flexibility. Unfortunately, the independence you enjoy does tend to isolate you from the local people. Also, cars are usually inconvenient in city centres, where it is generally worth ditching your vehicle and relying on public transport. Various car-carrying trains can help you avoid long, tiring drives.

A useful general reference on motoring in Europe is Eric Bredesen's *Moto Europa* (Seren Publishing). It's updated annually and contains information on rental, purchase, documents, tax and road rules. It can be ordered from US and Canadian bookshops (US$24.95) or directly from Seren Publishing (☎ 800-EUROPA-8 or ☎ 319-583 1068 from abroad) at PO Box 1212, Dubuque, Iowa 52004 (add US$3 for shipping).

Paperwork & Preparations

Proof of ownership of a private vehicle should always be carried (the vehicle registration document for British-registered cars) when touring Europe. An EU driving licence is acceptable for driving throughout Europe. However, old-style green UK licences are no good for Spain and should be backed up by an Italian translation in Italy and a German translation in Austria. If you have any other type of licence it is advisable or necessary to obtain an International Driving Permit (IDP) from your motoring organisation (see Visas & Documents in the Facts for the Visitor chapter earlier). An IDP is recommended for Turkey even if you have a European licence.

Third-party motor insurance is a minimum requirement in Europe. Most UK motor insurance policies automatically provide this for EU countries and some others. Get your insurer to issue a Green Card (which may cost extra), which is internationally recognised proof of insurance, and check that it lists all the countries you intend to visit. You'll need this in the event of an accident outside the country where the vehicle is insured. Also ask your insurer for a European Accident Statement form, which can simplify things if the worst comes to the worst. Never sign statements you can't read or understand – insist on a translation and sign that only if it's acceptable.

If you want to insure a vehicle you've just purchased (see the Purchase & Leasing section) and have a good insurance record, you might be eligible for considerable discounts if you can show a letter to this effect from your insurance company back home.

Taking out a European motoring assistance policy is a good investment, such as the AA's Five Star Service or the RAC's Eurocover Motoring Assistance. Expect to pay about UK£46 for 14 days cover with a small discount for association members. Both of these include a bail bond for Spain, which is also recommended. Ask your motoring organisation for details about free and reciprocal services offered by affiliated organisations around Europe.

Every vehicle travelling across an international border should display a sticker showing its country of registration (see the International Country Abbreviations appendix). A warning triangle, to be used in the event of breakdown, is compulsory almost everywhere; in Spain you need two of them. Recommended accessories include a first-aid kit (compulsory in Slovenia, Croatia, Yugoslavia, Greece and Austria), a spare bulb kit, and a fire extinguisher (compulsory in Greece and Turkey). For more information contact the RAC (☎ 0800-550055) or the AA (☎ 0900-500600) in the UK.

Road Rules

With the exception of Malta and Cyprus, driving is on the right in Mediterranean Europe. Vehicles brought over from the UK or Ireland, where driving is on the left, should have their headlights adjusted to avoid blinding oncoming traffic at night (a simple solution on older headlight lenses is to cover up the triangular section of the lens with tape). Priority is usually given to traffic approaching from the right in countries that drive on the right-hand side. The RAC publishes an annual *European Motoring Guide*, which gives an excellent summary of regulations in each country, including parking rules. Motoring organisations in other countries have similar publications.

Take care with speed limits, as they vary from country to country. You may be surprised at the apparent disregard for traffic regulations in some places (particularly in Italy and Greece), but as a visitor it is always best to be cautious. Many driving infringements are subject to an on-the-spot fine in most European countries now. Always ask for a receipt.

European drink-driving laws are particularly strict. The blood-alcohol concentration (BAC) limit when driving is between 0.05% and 0.08%. See the introductory Getting Around sections in the country chapters for more details on traffic laws.

Roads

Conditions and types of roads vary across Europe, but it is possible to make some generalisations. The fastest routes are four or six-lane dual carriageways/highways (ie two or three lanes either side) called *autoroutes*, *autostrade* etc. These tend to skirt cities and plough through the countryside in straight lines, often avoiding the most scenic bits. Some of these roads incur tolls, which are often quite hefty (eg in Italy and France), but there will always be an alternative route you can take. Motorways and other primary routes are generally in good condition.

Road surfaces on minor routes are not so reliable in some countries (eg Morocco, Portugal and Greece) although normally they will be more than adequate. These roads are narrower and progress is generally much slower. To compensate, you can expect much better scenery and plenty of interesting villages along the way.

Rental
The big international firms – Hertz, Avis, Budget Car, Eurodollar, and Europe's largest rental agency, Europcar – will give you reliable service and a good standard of vehicle. Usually you will have the option of returning the car to a different outlet at the end of the rental period.

Unfortunately, if you walk into an office and ask for a car on the spot, you will pay more, even allowing for special weekend deals. If you want to rent a car and haven't prebooked, look for national or local firms, which can often undercut the big companies by up to 40%. Nevertheless, you need to be wary of dodgy deals where they take your money and point you towards some clapped-out wreck, or where the rental agreement is bad news if you have an accident or the car is stolen – a cause for concern if you can't even read what you sign.

Prebooked and prepaid rates are always cheaper, and there are fly-drive combinations and other programmes that are worth looking into. Holiday Autos (☎ 909-949 1737), 1425 W Foothill Blvd, Upland, California 91786, has good rates for Europe, for which you need to prebook; it has offices in the UK (☎ 0990-300400) and many European countries.

No matter where you rent, make sure you understand what is included in the price (unlimited or paid km, tax, injury insurance, collision damage waiver etc) and what your liabilities are. Always take the collision damage waiver, though you can probably skip the injury insurance if you and your passengers have decent travel insurance.

The minimum rental age is usually 21 or even 23, and you'll probably need a credit card.

Note that prices at airport rental offices are usually higher than at branches in the city centre.

Motorcycle and moped rental is common in Italy, Spain, Greece and the south of France, but it is all too common to see inexperienced riders leap on bikes and very quickly fall off them again.

Purchase & Leasing
The purchase of vehicles in some European countries is illegal for nonresidents of that country. The UK is probably the best place to buy: second-hand prices are good and, whether buying privately or from a dealer, the absence of language difficulties will help you to establish exactly what you are getting and what guarantees you can expect in the event of a breakdown.

Bear in mind, though, that you will be getting a car with the steering wheel on the right in the UK. If you want left-hand drive and can afford to buy new, prices are reasonable in the Netherlands and Greece (without tax), in France and Germany (with tax), and in Belgium and Luxembourg (regardless of tax). Paperwork can be tricky wherever you buy, and many countries have compulsory roadworthiness checks on older vehicles.

Leasing a vehicle has none of the hassles of purchasing and can work out considerably cheaper than hiring over longer periods. The Renault Eurodrive Scheme provides new cars for non-EU residents for a period of between 17 days and six months. Under this scheme, a Renault Clio 1.2 for 30 days, for example, would cost 4688FF, including insurance and roadside assistance. Peugeot's European Self-Drive programme is slightly more expensive.

Camper Van
A popular way to tour Europe is for three or four people to band together to buy or rent a camper van. London is the usual embarkation point. Look at the advertisements in London's free magazine *TNT* if you wish to form or join a group. *TNT* is also a good source for purchasing a van, as is the *Loot* newspaper and the Van Market in Market Rd, London N7 (near the Caledonian Rd tube station), where private vendors congregate on a daily basis. Some second-hand dealers offer a 'buy-back' scheme for when you return from the Continent, but

buying and reselling privately should be more advantageous if you have the time.

Camper vans usually feature a fixed high-top or elevating roof and two to five bunk beds. Apart from the essential camping gas cooker, professional conversions may include a sink, fridge and built-in cupboards. You will need to spend from at least UK£1500 (US$2325) for something reliable enough to get you around Europe for any length of time. An eternal favourite for budget travellers is the VW Kombi; they aren't made any more but the old ones seem to go on forever, and getting spare parts isn't a problem. Once on the road you should be able to keep budgets lower than backpackers using trains, but don't forget to set some money aside for emergency repairs.

The main advantage of going by camper van is flexibility: with transport, eating and sleeping requirements all taken care of in one unit, you are tied to nobody's timetable but your own.

A disadvantage of camper vans is that you are in a confined space for much of the time. (Four adults in a small van can soon get on each other's nerves, particularly if the group has been formed at short notice.) Another drawback is that they're not very manoeuvrable around town, and you'll often have to leave your gear unattended inside (many people bolt extra locks onto the van). They're also expensive to buy in spring and hard to sell in autumn. As an alternative, consider a car and tent.

Motorcycle Touring

Mediterranean Europe is made for motorcycle touring, with good-quality winding roads, stunning scenery, and an active motorcycling scene.

The wearing of helmets for both rider and passenger is compulsory everywhere in Europe. Portugal, Spain and all of former Yugoslavia as well as Austria, Belgium, France, Germany and Luxembourg also require that motorcyclists use headlights during the day.

On ferries, motorcyclists rarely have to book ahead as they can generally be squeezed in. Take note of local custom about parking motorcycles on pavements (sidewalks). Though this is illegal in some countries, the police usually turn a blind eye so long as the vehicle doesn't obstruct pedestrians.

Anyone considering a motorcycle tour from the UK might benefit from joining the International Motorcyclists Tour Club (UK£19 per annum plus UK£3 joining fee). It organises European (and worldwide) biking jaunts, and members regularly meet to swap information. Contact James Clegg (☎ 01489-664868), Membership Secretary, 238 Nettham Rd, Netherton, Huddersfield, HD4 7HL.

Fuel

Fuel prices can vary enormously from country to country, and may bear little relation to the general cost of living; eg Spain is cheaper than Portugal, and Gibraltar and Andorra are cheaper still. France and Italy have Europe's most expensive petrol.

Unleaded petrol is now widely available throughout Europe (except in Morocco) and is usually slightly cheaper than super (premium grade, the only 'leaded' choice in some countries). Diesel is usually significantly cheaper.

BICYCLE

A tour of Europe by bike may seem a daunting prospect, but one organisation in the UK that can help is the Cyclists' Touring Club (CTC; ☎ 01483-417 217), Cotterell House, 69 Meadrow, Godalming, Surrey GU7 3HS. It can supply information to members on cycling conditions in Europe as well as detailed routes, itineraries, maps and cheap specialised insurance. Membership costs UK£25 per annum (UK£12.50 for students and people under 18, or UK£16.50 for senior citizens).

Europe by Bike, by Karen & Terry Whitehall, a paperback available in the USA and selected outlets in the UK, is a little out of date but has good descriptions of 18 cycling tours of up to 19 days duration.

A primary consideration on a cycling tour is to travel light, but you should take a few tools and spare parts, including a puncture repair kit and an extra inner tube. Panniers are essential to balance your possessions on either side of the bike frame. A bike helmet is also a very good idea. Take a good lock and always use it when you leave your bike unattended.

Seasoned cyclists can average 80 km a day, but there's no point in overdoing it. The slower you travel, the more local people you are likely to meet. If you get tired of pedalling or simply want to skip a boring transport section, you can put your feet up on the train. On slower trains, bikes can usually be transported as luggage, subject to a small supplementary fee. Fast trains can rarely accommodate bikes: they need to be sent as registered luggage and may end up on a different train from the one you take. The Eurostar train, which links the UK with France and Belgium via the Channel Tunnel, charges UK£20 to send a bike as registered luggage on its routes.

The European Bike Express is a coach service where cyclists can travel with their bicycles. It runs in the summer from north-east England to France and Spain, with pick-up/drop-off points en route. The return fare is UK£149 (£139 for CTC members); phone ☎ 01642-251 440 in the UK for details.

For more information about cycling, see Activities in the Facts for the Visitor chapter and in the individual country chapters.

Rental

It is not as easy to hire bikes in Mediterranean Europe as it is elsewhere on the Continent, but where available they are hired out on an hourly, half-day, daily or weekly basis. It is sometimes possible to return the machine at a different outlet so you don't have to retrace your route. Many train stations have bike-rental counters, some of which are open 24 hours a day. See the country chapters for more details.

Purchase

For major cycling tours, it's best to have a bike you're familiar with, so consider bringing your own (see the following section) rather than buying on arrival. There are plenty of places to buy in Europe (shops sell new and second-hand bicycles or you can check local papers for private vendors), but you'll need a specialist bicycle shop for a machine capable of withstanding European touring. CTC can provide a leaflet on purchasing. European prices are quite high (certainly higher than in North America), but non-Europeans should be able to claim back VAT on the purchase.

Bringing Your Own

If you want to bring your own bicycle to Europe, you should be able to take it along with you on the plane relatively easily. You can either take it apart and pack everything in a bike bag or box, or simply wheel it to the check-in desk, where it should be treated as a piece of luggage. You may have to remove the pedals and turn the handlebars sideways so that it takes up less space in the aircraft's hold; check all this with the airline well in advance, preferably before you pay for your ticket. If your bicycle and other luggage exceed your weight allowance, ask about alternatives or you may suddenly find yourself being charged a fortune for excess baggage.

HITCHING

Hitching is never entirely safe in any country in the world, and we don't recommend it. Travellers who decide to hitch should understand that they are taking a small but potentially serious risk. People who do choose to hitch will be safer if they travel in pairs and let someone know where they plan to go.

Hitching can be the most rewarding and frustrating way of getting around. Rewarding, because you get to meet and interact with local people and are forced into unplanned detours that may yield unexpected highlights off the beaten track. Frustrating, because you may get stuck on the side of the road to nowhere with nowhere (or nowhere cheap) to stay.

That said, hitchers can end up making good time, but obviously your plans need to be flexible in case a trick of the light makes you appear invisible to passing motorists. A man and woman travelling together is probably the best combination. Two or more men must expect some delays; two women together will make good time and should be relatively safe. A woman hitching on her own is taking a big risk, particularly in parts of southern Europe, Turkey and North Africa.

Don't try to hitch from city centres: take public transport to suburban exit routes. Hitching is usually illegal on motorways (freeways) – stand on the slip roads, or approach drivers at petrol stations and truck stops. Look presentable and cheerful and make a cardboard sign indicating your intended destination in the local language. Never hitch where drivers can't stop in good time or without causing an obstruction. At dusk, give up and think about finding somewhere to stay. If your itinerary includes a ferry crossing (from mainland France to Corsica, for instance), it's worth trying to score a ride before the ferry rather than after, since vehicle tickets sometimes include a number of passengers free of charge. This also applies to Le Shuttle, the car and lorry train that connects France and the UK via the Channel Tunnel.

It is sometimes possible to arrange a lift in advance: scan student notice boards in colleges, or contact car-sharing agencies. Such agencies are particularly popular in France (Allostop Provoya, Auto-Partage).

BOAT
Mediterranean Ferries

There are many ferries across the Mediterranean between southern Europe and North Africa, including ones from Spain to Morocco, Italy to Tunisia and France to Algeria, Morocco and Tunisia. There are also ferries between Italy and Greece (eg Brindisi or Bari to Corfu, Igoumenitsa or Patras), and Greece and Israel. Ferries are often filled to capacity in summer, especially to/from Tunisia, so book well in advance if you're taking a vehicle across.

The Greek islands are connected to the mainland and each other by a spider's web of routings; the excellent *Thomas Cook Guide to Greek Island Hopping* gives comprehensive listings of ferry times and routes, as well as information on sightseeing. Ferries also link other islands in the Mediterranean with mainland ports: Corsica with Nice, Marseille and Toulon (France) and Genoa, La Spezia, Piombino and Livorno (Italy); Sicily and Sardinia with Genoa and Naples (among other Italian ports) as well as Tunis; and Malta with Sicily and Naples. See the relevant country chapters in this book for more details.

ORGANISED TOURS

Tailor-made tours abound; see your travel agent or look for the small ads in newspaper travel pages. Specialists in the UK include Ramblers Holidays (☎ 01707-331133) for walkers and Arctic Experience Discover the World (☎ 016977-48361) for wilderness and wildlife holidays.

Young revellers can party on Europe-wide bus tours. An outfit called Tracks offers budget coach/camping tours for under US$40 per day, plus food fund. It has a London office (☎ 0171-937 3028) and is represented in Australia and New Zealand by Adventure World; in North America, call ☎ 800-233 6046. Contiki (☎ 0181-290 6422) and Top Deck (☎ 0171-370 4555) offer camping or hotel-based bus tours, also for the 18 to 35 age group. The latter's 12-day Taste of Europe tour costs UK£299 plus food fund. Both have offices or representatives in North America, Australasia and South Africa.

For people aged over 50, Saga Holidays (☎ 0800-300500), Saga Building, Middelburg Square, Folkestone, Kent CT20 1AZ, offers holidays ranging from cheap coach tours to luxury cruises (and has cheap travel insurance). Saga also operates in the USA as Saga International Holidays (☎ 617-262 2262) 222 Berkeley St, Boston, Massachusetts 02116, and in Australia as Saga Holidays Australasia (☎ 02-9957 5660), Level One, 110 Pacific Highway, North Sydney, NSW 2060.

National tourist offices in most countries offer organised trips to points of interest. These may range from one-hour city tours to several-day circular excursions. They often work out more expensive than going it alone, but are sometimes worth it if you are pressed for time. A short city tour will give you a quick overview of the place and can be a good way to begin your visit.

Albania

Until recently a closed communist country, Albania caught world attention in late 1990 as the last domino to tumble in Eastern Europe's sudden series of democratic revolutions. Yet the recent changes date back to 1985 and the death of Enver Hoxha, Albania's Stalinist leader since 1944. The statues of Stalin and Hoxha toppled, and the non-communist opposition was elevated to power in March 1992, putting Albania at a crossroads. Its first years of attempted democracy have been troubled by economic chaos and controversy over the less-than-democratic May 1996 election.

Long considered fair prey by every imperialist power, Albania chose a curious form of isolation. Blood vendettas and illiteracy were replaced by what some claimed was the purest form of communism. Right up until December 1990, monuments, factories, boulevards and towns were dedicated to the memory of Joseph Stalin. Although Hoxha's iron-fisted rule did save Albania from annexation by Yugoslavia after WWII, it's unlikely that you'll find many in Albania with much good to say about him. On the contrary, most blame him for the country's present problems.

Politics aside, few European countries have the allure of the mysterious Republika e Shqipërisë. Albanians call their country the 'Land of the Eagle'. Albania is Europe's last unknown, with enchanting classical ruins at Apollonia, Butrint and Durrës, the charming 'museum towns' of Gjirokastra and Berat, vibrant cities like Tirana, Shkodra, Korça and Durrës, colourful folklore and majestic landscapes of mountains, forests, lakes and sea. You can see a great number of things in a pocket-sized area and the Albanians are extremely friendly and curious about their handful of visitors.

In the capital, Tirana, and the port of Durrës people are already quite used to seeing foreigners, but almost everywhere else you'll be an object of curiosity. Things have greatly improved since the collapse of the old system in 1992 – trains are back on the rails, increasing numbers of private buses are plying the roads, private rooms are becoming more readily available in the towns, fine restaurants have

opened up, travel agencies are in operation and all areas of the country are now accessible to travellers. As Albania opens up to the world for the first time, visitors have the chance to meet the people in a way that's almost impossible elsewhere in Europe.

Facts about the Country

HISTORY

In the 2nd millennium BC, the Illyrians, ancestors of today's Albanians, occupied the western Balkans. The Greeks arrived in the 7th century BC to establish self-governing colonies at Epidamnos (now Durrës), Apollonia and Butrint. They traded peacefully with the Illyrians, who formed tribal states in the 4th century BC. The south became part of Greek Epirus.

In the second half of the 3rd century BC, an expanding Illyrian kingdom based at Shkodra

ALBANIA

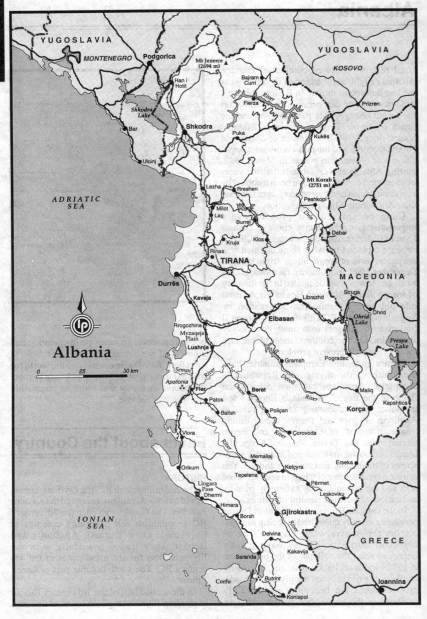

came into conflict with Rome, which sent a fleet of 200 vessels against Queen Teuta (who ruled over the Illyrian Ardian kingdom) in 228 BC. In 214 BC, after a second Roman naval expedition in 219 BC, Philip V of Macedonia came to the aid of his Illyrian allies. This led to a long war which resulted in the extension of Roman control over the entire Balkans by 167 BC.

Like the Greeks, the Illyrians preserved their own language and traditions despite centuries of Roman rule. Under the Romans, Illyria enjoyed peace and prosperity, though the large agricultural estates were worked by slave labour. The main trade route between Rome and Constantinople, the Via Egnatia, ran from Durrës to Thessaloniki. In 285 AD, a provincial reorganisation carried out by the Roman emperor Diocletian (an Illyrian himself) broke Illyria up into four provinces: Epirus Vetus (capital Ioannina), Epirus Nova (capital Durrës), Praevalitana (capital Shkodra) and Dardania (today the Kosovo region of Yugoslavia).

When the Roman Empire was divided in 395 AD, Illyria fell within the Eastern Roman Empire, later known as Byzantium. Invasions by migrating peoples – Visigoths, Huns, Ostrogoths and Slavs – continued through the 5th and 6th centuries and only in the south did the ethnic Illyrians survive. Prior to the Roman conquest, Illyria had stretched north to the Danube. In the 11th century, control of this region passed back and forth between the Byzantines, the Bulgarians and the Normans.

The feudal principality of Arbëria was established at Kruja in 1190. Other independent feudal states appeared in the 14th century and towns then developed. In 1344 Albania was annexed by Serbia, but after the defeat of Serbia by the Turks in 1389 the whole region was open to Ottoman attack. The Venetians occupied some coastal towns, and from 1443 to 1468 the national hero Skanderbeg (George Kastrioti) led Albanian resistance to the Turks from his castle at Kruja. Skanderbeg (Skënderbeg in Albanian) won all 25 battles he fought against the Turks, and even Sultan Mehmet-Fatih, conqueror of Constantinople, could not take Kruja.

Albania was not definitively incorporated into the Ottoman empire until 1479. It remained there until 1912, the most backward corner of Europe. In the 15th and 16th centuries thousands of Albanians fled to southern Italy to escape Turkish rule and over half of those who remained converted to Islam so as to become first-class citizens of the theocratic Ottoman empire. In the late 18th century, the Albanian nobles Karamahmut Pasha Bushatlli of Shkodra and Ali Pasha Tepelena of Ioannina (Janina) established semi-independent pashaliks (military districts), but Ottoman despotism was reimposed in the early 19th century.

In 1878 the Albanian League at Prizren (in present-day Kosovo, Yugoslavia) began a struggle for autonomy that was put down by the Turkish army in 1881. Uprisings between 1910 and 1912 culminated in a proclamation of independence and the formation of a provisional government led by Ismail Qemali at Vlora in 1912. These achievements were severely compromised by the London ambassador's conference, which handed Kosova, nearly half of Albania, over to Serbia in 1913. In 1914 the Great Powers (Britain, France, Germany, Italy, Austria-Hungary and Russia) imposed a German aristocrat named Wilhelm von Wied on Albania as head of state but an uprising soon forced his departure. With the outbreak of WWI, Albania was occupied by the armies of Greece, Serbia, France, Italy and Austria-Hungary in succession.

In 1920 the Congress of Lushnja denounced foreign intervention and moved the capital from Durrës to less vulnerable Tirana. Thousands of Albanian volunteers converged on Vlora and forced the occupying Italians to withdraw. In May 1924, Bishop Fan Noli established a fairly liberal government which was overthrown on Christmas Eve that year by Ahmet Zogu, who represented the landed aristocracy of the lowlands and the tribal chieftains of the highlands. Zogu ruled with Italian support, declaring himself King Zog I in 1928, but his close collaboration with Italy backfired in April 1939 when Mussolini ordered an invasion of Albania. Zog fled to Britain and used gold looted from the Albanian treasury to rent a floor at London's Ritz Hotel.

On 8 November 1941 the Albanian Communist Party was founded with Enver Hoxha (pronounced Hodja) as first secretary, a position he held until his death in April 1985. The communists led the resistance against the Italians and, after 1943, against the Germans. A provisional government was formed at Berat in October 1944, and by 29 November the Albanian Army of National Liberation had crushed the 'Balli Kombetar', a grouping of tribal quislings in the north, and pursued the last Nazi troops from the country. Albania was the only Eastern European country where the Soviet army was not involved in these operations. By tying down some 15 combined German-Italian divisions, Albania made an important contribution to the final outcome.

The Rise of Communism

After the fighting died down, the communists consolidated power. In January 1946 the People's Republic of Albania was proclaimed, with Enver Hoxha as president. In February a programme of socialist construction was adopted and all large economic enterprises were nationalised. By 1952 seven years of elementary education had become mandatory (this was raised to eight years in 1963) and literacy was increased from just 15% before WWII to 72% in 1995.

In October 1946 two British warships struck mines in the Corfu Channel, causing the loss of 44 lives. The British government blamed Albania and demanded £843,947 compensation. To back their claim they impounded 1574 kg of gold (now worth £10 million) which the fascists had stolen from Albania and which had passed into British hands at the end of WWII. Albania has never accepted responsibility for the incident, nor has it agreed to pay damages. The stubborn British are still holding Albania's gold, despite agreeing in principle in 1992 to return it, less reparations. It is now widely believed that Yugoslavia placed the mines. Good relations with Tito were always important to the British, whereas Albania was expendable.

In September 1948, Albania broke off relations with Yugoslavia, which had hoped to incorporate the country into the Yugoslav Federation. Instead, Albania allied itself with Stalin's USSR and put into effect a series of Soviet-style economic plans, the first a two-year plan, and then five-year plans beginning in 1951. After WWII there were British and US-backed landings in Albania by right-wing émigrés. One British attempt in 1949 was

thwarted when Stalin passed to Hoxha a warning he had received from double agent Kim Philby.

Albania collaborated closely with the USSR until 1960, when a heavy-handed Khrushchev demanded a submarine base at Vlora. With the Soviet alliance becoming a liability, Albania broke off diplomatic relations with the USSR in 1961 and reoriented itself towards the People's Republic of China.

From 1966 to 1967 Albania experienced a Chinese-style cultural revolution. Administrative workers were suddenly transferred to remote areas and younger cadres were placed in leading positions. The collectivisation of agriculture was completed and organised religion banned. Western literary works were withdrawn from circulation and a strong national culture firmly rooted in socialist ideals was carefully cultivated.

After the Soviet invasion of Czechoslovakia in 1968, Albania left the Warsaw Pact and embarked on a self-reliant defence policy. Today, some 750,000 igloo-shaped concrete bunkers and pillboxes with narrow gun slits are strung along all borders, both terrestrial and maritime, as well as the approaches to all towns. The highway from Durrës to Tirana is one bunker after another for 35 km. The amount of time and materials employed in creating these defences must have been tremendous and the bunkers still occupy much agricultural land today.

With the death of Mao Zedong in 1976 and the changes in China after 1978, Albania's unique relationship with China came to an end. In 1981 there was a power struggle within the Albanian Party of Labour (as the Communist Party had been called since November 1948) and former partisan hero and prime minister Mehmet Shehu 'committed suicide' after being accused of being a 'polyagent' (multiple spy).

Shehu had wanted to expand Albania's foreign contacts, an orientation which brought him into direct conflict with Hoxha. Until 1978 Albania had thrived on massive Yugoslav, Soviet and Chinese aid in succession, but building socialism alone, without foreign loans or credit, proved to be difficult. Because its exports didn't earn sufficient hard currency to pay for the import of essential equipment, the country fell far behind technologically.

Post-Hoxha

Hoxha died after a long illness in April 1985 and his longtime associate Ramiz Alia assumed leadership of the 147,000-member Party of Labour. Aware of the economic decay caused by Albania's isolation, Alia began a liberalisation programme in 1986 and broadened Albania's ties with foreign countries. Travellers arriving in Albania at this time no longer had their guidebooks confiscated and their beards and long hair clipped by border barbers, and short skirts were allowed.

By early 1990 the collapse of communism in most of Eastern Europe had created a sense of expectation in Albania and in June some 4500 Albanians took refuge in Western embassies in Tirana. After a brief confrontation with police and the Sigurimi (secret police) these people were allowed to board ships to Brindisi, Italy, where they were granted political asylum.

After student demonstrations in December 1990, the government agreed to allow opposition parties. The Democratic Party, led by heart surgeon Sali Berisha, was formed. Further demonstrations won new concessions, including the promise of free elections and independent trade unions. The government announced a reform programme and party hardliners were purged.

In early March 1991, as the election date approached, some 20,000 Albanians fled to Brindisi by ship, creating a crisis for the Italian government, which had begun to view them as economic refugees. Most were eventually allowed to stay. In the run-up to the 31 March 1991 elections, Alia won the support of the peasants by turning over state lands and granting them the right to sell their produce at markets. This manoeuvre netted the Party of Labour 169 seats in the 250-member People's Assembly, which promptly re-elected Alia president for a five-year term.

In mid-May a general strike forced the renamed Socialist Party (formerly the Party of Labour) to form a coalition with the opposition Democrats in preparation for fresh elections the following year. As central economic planning collapsed, factories ceased production and the food distribution network broke down. In August another 15,000 young male Albanians attempted to take refuge in Italy, but this time they were met by Italian riot police

and quickly deported. By late 1991 mass unemployment, rampant inflation and shortages of almost everything were throwing Albania into chaos and in December food riots began. Fearful of another refugee crisis, the European Community (now known as the European Union) stepped up economic aid and the Italian army established a large military base just south of Durrës, ostensibly to supervise EC food shipments.

The March 1992 elections ended 47 years of communist rule as the Democratic Party took 92 of the 140 seats in a revamped parliament. After the resignation of Ramiz Alia, parliament elected Sali Berisha president in April. In their campaign, the Democrats promised that their victory would attract foreign investors and gain Western immigration quotas for Albanian workers. When these failed to materialise the socialists bounced back to win the municipal elections of July 1992.

In September 1992 Ramiz Alia was placed under house arrest after he wrote articles critical of the Democratic government, and in January 1993 the 73-year-old widow of Enver Hoxha, Nexhmije Hoxha, was sentenced to nine years imprisonment for allegedly misappropriating government funds between 1985 and 1990. In August 1993 the leader of the Socialist Party, Fatos Nano, was also arrested on corruption charges. He was sentenced to 12 years imprisonment in April 1994. Persons once associated with the old regime are now being purged from the public service, their places taken by Democratic Party supporters (even though President Berisha and all the others are themselves former communists – hardly surprising, since everyone in the old Albania had to be communist to get anywhere). In November 1993 Amnesty International issued a report condemning increasing human rights violations by the police against political opponents of the government. Meanwhile King Zog's son, a resident of South Africa, is manoeuvring for a return to Albania as King Leka I – an unlikely event.

In mid-1992 Albania signed a military agreement with Turkey, and followed in December by joining the Islamic Conference Association. This reorientation towards the Islamic world stems from practical security considerations. Greek politicians have made territorial claims to southern Albania (which they call Northern Epiros) and the alliance with Turkey is seen as a balance. In mid-1993 relations with Greece hit a new low following the deportation from Albania of a hardline Greek bishop who had attempted to organise the Greek minority in Albania for political ends. In retaliation, Athens ordered the expulsion of 20,000 of the 150,000 Albanian immigrants in Greece.

President Berisha has denounced Serbian oppression of the large Albanian majority in Yugoslav Kosovo and has repeatedly called for the deployment of United Nations peacekeeping troops in that area, warning that Albanians would react as a nation if Yugoslavia provoked a massacre of Albanians in Kosovo.

Foreign investment in Albania has been steady and is made obvious by the number of new buildings and projects established by foreign concerns. Investment interest has been expressed from as far away as New Zealand and elections in May 1996, while ultimately boycotted by the socialist opposition following charges of intimidation and poll-rigging, returned the Democrats to power thus bolstering investor confidence in a country that needs strong investment to catch up with the rest of Europe.

GEOGRAPHY

Albania's strategic position between Greece, Macedonia, Yugoslavia and Italy has been important throughout its history. Vlora watches over the narrow Strait of Otranto, which links the Adriatic Sea to the Ionian Sea. For decades Albania has acted as a barrier separating Greece from the rest of Europe. The Greek island of Corfu is only a few km from Saranda in the Ionian Sea.

Over three-quarters of this 28,748-sq-km country (a bit smaller than Belgium) consists of mountains and hills. There are three zones: a coastal plain, a mountainous region and an interior plain. The coastal plain extends over 200 km from north to south and up to 50 km inland. The 2000-metre-high forested mountain spine that stretches along the entire length of Albania culminates at Mt Jezerce (2694 metres) in the north. Although Mt Jezerce is the highest mountain entirely within the country, Albania's highest peak is Mt Korab (2751 metres), on the border with Macedonia. The country is subject to destructive earthquakes,

such as the one in 1979 which left 100,000 people homeless.

The longest river is the Drin River (285 km), which drains Lake Ohrid. In the north the Drin flows into the Buna, Albania's only navigable river, which connects shallow Lake Shkodra to the sea. Albania shares three large tectonic lakes with Yugoslavia, Macedonia and Greece: Shkodra, Ohrid and Prespa respectively. Ohrid is the deepest lake in the Balkans (294 metres), while Lake Prespa, at 853 metres elevation, is one of the highest. The Ionian littoral, especially the 'Riviera of Flowers' from Vlora to Saranda, offers magnificent scenery. Forests cover 40% of the land, and the many olive trees, citrus plantations and vineyards give Albania a true Mediterranean air.

ECONOMY

Albania stuck to strict Stalinist central planning and wage and price controls longer than any other Eastern European country. Under communism two-thirds of the national income was directed towards consumption and social benefits, and the rest was used for capital investment. Industrial development was spread out, with factories in all regions. Unfortunately, much of the technology used is now thoroughly outdated and the goods produced are unable to compete on world markets. Between 1990 and 1992 industrial production fell 60%; huge investments, now gradually entering the economy, will be required to turn the situation around.

The communist quest for higher production was carried out with little or no consideration for the environment and today's industrial wastelands are scenes of utter desolation far beyond anything else in Europe. You'll see ponds covered with a slick of oil leaking from a nearby oil well and large buildings with every window broken and the walls collapsing. Many Albanians treat their country like a giant garbage dump, the aluminium cans, chocolate wrappers and other debris of capitalism joining the tens of thousands of broken concrete bunkers and dozens of derelict factories left behind by communism. It's hard to believe this country will ever be cleaned up.

Albania is rich in natural resources such as crude oil, natural gas, coal, copper, iron, nickel and timber and is the world's third-largest producer of chrome, accounting for about 10% o the world's supply. The Central Mountains yield minerals such as copper (in the north-east around Kukës), chromium (farther south near the Drin River), and iron nickel (closer to Lake Ohrid). There are textiles industries at Berat, Korça and Tirana. Oil was discovered in Albania in 1917 and the country was until recently supplying all its own petroleum requirements. Oil and gas from Fier also enabled the production of chemical fertilisers.

There are several huge hydroelectric dams on the Drin River in the north. Albania obtains 80% of its electricity from such dams and by 1970 electricity had reached every village in the country. From 1972 to 1990 Albania exported hydroelectricity to Yugoslavia and Greece. The dams were built with Chinese technical assistance.

Under communist central planning Albania grew all its own food on collective farms, with surpluses available for export. About 20% of these farms were state farms run directly by the government, and the rest were cooperatives. The main crops were corn, cotton, potatoes, sugar beet, tobacco, vegetables and wheat. Lowland areas were collectivised in the 1950s, mountain areas during the 1967 Cultural Revolution.

Following the breakdown of authority in 1991, peasants seized the cooperatives' lands, livestock and buildings and terminated deliveries to the state distribution network, leading to widespread food shortages. After a period of neglect in the agricultural sector, farmers have begun the long task of rebuilding the rural infrastructure. Land is once more heavily cultivated and farms are once again providing produce for the markets.

Considering the country's small size, self-sufficiency was a real challenge, yet before 1990 Albania was one of the few countries in the world with no foreign debt (in 1976 a provision was included in its constitution forbidding any overseas loans). By 1994, however, the government had accumulated an estimated US$920 million foreign debt and must seek new loans just to cover interest on the existing loans.

With the public sector bankrupt, the government has drastically increased taxation on the private sector. Enver Hoxha's Sigurimi has been replaced by the powerful tax-collecting Policia Financiare, who drive expensive Italian vehicles and are almost a law unto themselves.

After the breaks with the USSR and China, Albania's foreign trade had to be completely redirected. Until 1990 its main trading partners were Bulgaria, Czechoslovakia, Hungary, Italy and Yugoslavia, which purchased Albanian food products, asphalt, bitumen, chromium, crude oil and tobacco. Minerals, fuels and metals accounted for 47% of Albania's exports. Today Albania still trades with its Balkan neighbours and Italy, though new trading partners from further afield are appearing on the scene. A new east-west trading route is slowly taking shape from Turkey through Bulgaria, Macedonia and Albania to Italy. New highways and railways are on the drawing board and investments of US$2.5 billion are envisioned over the next 10 years.

POPULATION & PEOPLE

The Albanians are a hardy Mediterranean people, physically different from the more nordic Slavs. Although the Slavs and Greeks look down on the Albanians, the Albanians themselves have a sense of racial superiority based on their descent from the ancient Illyrians, who inhabited the region before the coming of the Romans. The country's name comes from the Albanoi, an ancient Illyrian tribe.

Approximately 3.5 million Albanians live in Albania and a further two million suffer Serbian oppression in Kosovo (regarded by Albanians as part of greater Albania), in Yugoslavia, another Balkan tinderbox waiting to explode. (Whilst in Albania you'll avoid offence by calling the region Kosova instead of Kosovo.) A further 400,000 are in western Macedonia. Harsh economic conditions in Albania have unleashed successive waves of emigration: to Serbia in the 15th century, to Greece and Italy in the 16th century, to the USA in the 19th and 20th centuries and to Greece, Italy and Switzerland today. The Arbereshi, longtime Albanian residents of 50 scattered villages in southern Italy, fled west in the 16th century to escape the Turks. As many as two million ethnic Albanians live in Turkey, emigrants from Serb-dominated Yugoslavia between 1912 and 1966.

Since 1990 some 300,000 Albanians – 10% of the population – have migrated to Western

Europe (especially Greece and Italy) to escape the economic hardships at home. Albania's largest source of income is now remittances from Albanian workers abroad, as witnessed by the large number of consumer goods now available on the market and the disproportionately high number of motor vehicles brought in (often under shady circumstances) from Western Europe.

Minorities inside Albania include Greeks (3% of the population) and Vlachs, Macedonians and Gypsies (comprising a further 2% of the population). Greek sources argue that Greeks are far more numerous than the official figure cited above, although such claims are often estimates based on factors such as the number of Greek Orthodox parishes in Albania before WWII and are thus inaccurate. The ethnic Greeks reside in southern Albania and they have often found themselves at the centre of political conflict. In 1975 the Albanian government implemented an assimilation programme to force Albanian Greeks to adopt 'acceptable' Albanian names and in late 1991 thousands fled from Albania to Greece. Greek nationalists have used the Greek minority as a pretext for territorial claims against Albania.

Albania is one of the most densely populated states of Europe, with 36% of the people living in urban areas (compared with only 15% before WWII). Under the communists birth control was forbidden (as part of the effort to make Albania self-sufficient by increasing the workforce); since WWII the population growth rate has been the highest in Europe (2.5% per annum). The population doubled between 1923 and 1960 and again between 1960 and 1990. Part of this growth can be ascribed to an increase in life expectancy from 38 years in 1938 to 73.8 years today. However, population growth dropped off to 1.16% by 1995, due in part to losses brought about by emigration.

Tirana, the capital, is the largest city, with 400,000 inhabitants, followed by Durrës, Shkodra, Elbasan, Vlora, Korça, Fier and Berat. The apartment buildings which house a high percentage of the population may look decrepit on the outside but inside they're quite attractive. If you travel around the country much you'll most likely be invited to visit one.

The Shkumbin River forms a boundary between the Gheg cultural region of the north and the Tosk region in the south. The people in these regions still vary in dialect, musical culture and traditional dress (the Ghegs are also said to have larger noses). The communists worked hard to level regional differences by building an industrial complex in the Durrës-Tirana-Elbasan triangle, well away from the old tribal centres of Shkodra and Korça.

ARTS

Literature

Prior to the adoption of a standardised orthography in 1909, very little literature was produced in Albania, though Albanians resident elsewhere in the Ottoman empire and in Italy did write works. Among these was the noted poet Naim Frashëri (1846-1900), who lived in Istanbul and wrote in Greek. About the time of independence (1912), a group of romantic patriotic writers at Shkodra wrote epics and historical novels.

Perhaps the most interesting writer of the interwar period was Fan Noli (1880-1965). Educated as a priest in the USA, Fan Noli returned there to head the Albanian Orthodox Church in America after the Democratic government of Albania, in which he served as premier, was overthrown in 1924. Although many of his books are based on religious subjects, the introductions he wrote to his own translations of Cervantes, Ibsen, Omar Khayyám and Shakespeare established him as Albania's foremost literary critic.

Fan Noli's contemporary, the poet Migjeni (1911-38), focused on social issues until his early death from tuberculosis. In his 1936 poem, *Vargjet e lira* (Free Verse), Migjeni seeks to dispel the magic of the old myths and awaken the reader to present injustices.

Albania's best known contemporary writer is Ismail Kadare, born in 1935, whose 15 novels have been translated into 40 languages. Unfortunately the English editions are sometimes disappointing as they are translated from the French version rather than the Albanian original. *The Castle* (1970) describes the 15th-century Turkish invasion of Albania, while *Chronicle in Stone* (1971) relates wartime experiences in Kadare's birthplace, Gjirokastra, as seen through the eyes of a boy. *Broken April* deals with the blood vendettas of the northern highlands before the 1939 Italian invasion. Among Kadare's other novels available in English are *The General of the Dead Army* (1963), *The Palace of Dreams* (1981) and *Doruntina* (1988). Although Kadare lived in Tirana throughout the Hoxha years and even wrote a book, *The Great Winter* (1972), extolling Hoxha's defiance of Moscow, he sought political asylum in Paris in October 1990. His latest book, *Printemps Albanais* (Fayard, Paris, 1990), tells why.

Cinema

A recent film worth checking out is *Lamerica*, a brilliant and stark look at Albanian postcommunist culture. Despite its title, it is about Albanians seeking to escape to Bari, Italy, in the immediate postcommunist era. The title is a symbol for ordinary Albanians seeking a better and more materially fulfilling life in the West. Woven loosely around a plot concerning a couple of Italian scam artists, the essence of the film is the unquenchable dignity of ordinary Albanians in the face of adversity.

Music

Polyphony, the blending of several independent vocal or instrumental parts, is a southern Albanian tradition that dates back to ancient Illyrian times. Peasant choirs perform in a variety of styles, and the songs, usually with epic-lyrical or historical themes, may be dramatic to the point of yodelling or slow and sober, with alternate male or female voices combining in harmonies of unexpected beauty. Instrumental polyphonic *kabas* are played by small Gypsy ensembles usually led by a clarinet. Improvisation gives way to dancing at colourful village weddings. One well-known group which often tours outside Albania is the Lela Family of Përmet.

An outstanding recording of traditional Albanian music is the compact disc *Albania, Vocal and Instrumental Polyphony* (LDX 274 897) in the series 'Le Chant du Monde' (Musée de l'Homme, Paris).

The folk music of the Albanian-speaking villages founded five centuries ago in southern Italy has been popularised by Italian singer Silvana Licursi. Although Licursi sings in the Albanian language, her music bears a strong Italian imprint.

CULTURE

Traditional dress is still common in rural areas, especially on Sunday and holidays. Men wear embroidered white shirts and knee trousers, the Ghegs with a white felt skullcap and the Tosks with a flat-topped white fezzes. Women's clothing is brighter than that of the men. Along with the standard white blouses with wide sleeves, women from Christian areas wear red vests, while Muslim women wear baggy pants tied at the ankles and coloured headscarves. Older Muslim women wear white scarves around the neck; white scarves may also be a sign of mourning.

RELIGION

From 1967 to 1990 Albania was the only officially atheist state in the world. Public religious services were banned and many churches were converted into theatres or cinemas. In mid-1990 this situation ended and in December of that year Nobel Prize-winner Mother Teresa of Calcutta, an ethnic Albanian from Macedonia, visited Albania and met President Alia. Traditionally, Albania has been 70% Sunni Muslim, 10% Roman Catholic (mostly in the north) and 20% Albanian Orthodox (mostly in the south). Albania is the only country in Europe with an Islamic majority. The spiritual vacuum left by the demise of communism is being filled by US evangelical imperialists. New churches and mosques are springing up all over the country as evidence of the revival of traditional spiritual customs.

LANGUAGE

Albanian (Shqipja) is an Indo-European dialect of ancient Illyrian, with many Latin, Slavonic and (modern) Greek words. The two main dialects of Albanian diverged over the past 1000 years. In 1909 a standardised form of the Gheg dialect of Elbasan was adopted as the official language, but since WWII a modified version of the Tosk dialect of southern Albania has been used. Outside the country, Albanians resident in former Yugoslavia speak Gheg, those in Greece speak Tosk, whereas in Italy they speak another dialect called Arberesh. With practice you can sometimes differentiate between the dialects by listening for the nasalised vowels of Gheg. The Congress of Orthography at Tirana in 1972 established a unified written language based on the two dialects which is now universally accepted.

Italian is the most useful foreign language to know in Albania, with English a strong second. Some of the older people will have learnt Italian in school before 1943; others have picked it up by watching Italian TV stations or through recent trips to Italy (as is the case with many of the young men).

Lonely Planet's *Mediterranean Europe Phrasebook* contains a helpful list of translated Albanian words and phrases. A complete 24-lesson Albanian language course with text and cassette tape is available for US$40 from Jack Shulman (☎ 718-633 0530), PO Box 912, Church Street Station, New York, NY 10008, USA.

Many Albanian place names have two forms because the definite article is a suffix. In this book we use the form most commonly used in English, but Tirana actually means *the* Tiranë. On signs at archaeological sites, *p.e.sonë* means BC, and *e sonë* means AD. Public toilets may be marked *burra* for men and *gra* for women or may simply show a man's or a woman's shoe or the figure of a man or woman. Albanians, like Bulgarians, shake their heads to say yes and nod to say no.

See the Language Guide at the back of the book for pronunciation guidelines and useful words and phrases.

Facts for the Visitor

PLANNING
Climate & When to Go

Albania has a warm Mediterranean climate. The summers are hot, clear and dry, and the winters, when 40% of the rain falls, are cool, cloudy and moist. In winter the high interior plateau can be very cold as continental air masses move in. Along the coast the climate is moderated by sea winds. Gjirokastra and Shkodra receive twice as much rain as Korça, with November, December and April being the wettest months. The sun shines longest from May to September and July is the warmest month, but even April and October are quite pleasant. The best month to visit is September, as it's still warm and fruit and vegetables are abundant. Winter is uncomfortable as most rooms are unheated and tap water is ice-cold.

Books & Maps

Previously, one of the best travel guidebooks to Albania was *Nagel's Encyclopedia-Guide Albania* (Nagel Publishers, 5-7, Rue de l'Orangerie, 1211 Geneva 7, Switzerland), published in English and German editions in 1990. It's seldom found in bookshops, however, so consider ordering a copy through the mail well ahead. Nagel's provides no practical hotel or restaurant information but it's good on historical background up to 1990.

The first noteworthy postcommunist (1994) travel guide to the country is the *Blue Guide Albania* by James Pettifer, now in its 2nd (1996) edition and available from A & C Black, Box 19, Huntingdon, Cambs PE19 3SF, England, UK.

High Albania by Edith Durham, first published in 1909 and recently reissued by Virago in the UK and Beacon Press in the USA, is an Englishwoman's account of the tribes of northern Albania based on seven years of travel in the area.

In *Albania, The Search for the Eagle's Song* (Brewin Books, Studley, Warwickshire, England, UK), June Emerson gives a picture of what it was like to visit Albania just before 1990. Untainted by hindsight, her book is an unwitting snapshot of a time that has vanished forever.

The Artful Albanian: The Memoirs of Enver Hoxha (Chatto & Windus, London, UK, 1986), edited by Jon Halliday, contains selected passages from the 3400 pages of Hoxha's six volumes of memoirs. Chapters like 'Decoding China' and 'Battling Khrushchev' give an insight into the mind of this controversial figure.

Anton Logoreci's political and factual narrative *Albanians* is a well-balanced and readable account of Albanian history up to 1987, while *Albania and the Albanians* by Derek Hall (Pinter Publishers, London, England, UK) is a comprehensive political history of Albania published in 1994.

Biografi by New Zealand writer Lloyd Jones is a fanciful but very readable tale set in immediate postcommunist Albania involving the search for Enver Hoxha's alleged double, Petar Shapallo.

Online Services

Useful World Wide Web sites to point your browser at are: http://www.ios.com/ulpiana/Albanian/index.html (the Albanian WWW Home Page) which has a link to the first WWW site established in Albania (http://www.tirana.al), set up by the United Nations Development Project. People interested in business might care to check out the Albanian Business Forum on the Web: http://members.aol.com/ElbaTirana/a1.htm.

What to Bring

Most essential items found in Western Europe are available in Tirana. If you are planning to spend some time in the country, bring with you all your personal toiletries and medications. A universal sink plug is about the most practical commodity you can take to Albania.

SUGGESTED ITINERARIES

Depending on the length of your stay, you might want to see and do the following things in Albania:

Two days
  Visit Gjirokastra, Saranda and Butrint.
One week
  Visit Gjirokastra, Fier/Apollonia, Berat, Durrës, Tirana and Pogradec or Korça.
Two weeks
  Visit Gjirokastra, Fier/Apollonia, Berat, Durrës, Tirana, Kruja, Lezha, Shkodra and Kukës.
One month
  Visit every place included in this chapter.

HIGHLIGHTS
Museums & Galleries

The Onufri Museum in Berat Citadel houses real masterpieces of medieval icon painting. The National Museum of History in Tirana and the historical museum in Kruja Citadel are excellent. Tirana also has a good archaeological museum.

Castles & Historic Towns

Albania's two 'museum towns', Berat and Gjirokastra, each have a remarkable citadel (kalaja). The Tepelena Citadel on the road to Gjirokastra is also magnificent. Earthquakes, such as the one in 1979, have damaged many of the country's other historic towns, although Skënderbeg's Kruja Citadel has been carefully restored. The Rozafa Fortress at Shkodra is perhaps Albania's most evocative castle.

TOURIST INFORMATION

There are no tourist information offices in Albania, but hotel receptionists will sometimes give you directions. The moribund state tourism authority Albturist may eventually be reincarnated in privatised form, but don't count on it just yet. You can buy city maps of Tirana, but in most other towns they're unobtainable. In addition, many streets lack signs and the buildings have no numbers! Some streets don't seem to have any name at all. Most of the towns are small enough for you to do without such things.

The Albania Society of Britain (☎ 0181-540 6824), 7 Nelson Road, London SW19 1HS, England, exists 'to promote contacts between Albania and Britain, to offer factual information concerning Albania and to foster cultural and social bonds between the two peoples'. The Society's quarterly journal Albanian Life carries a good range of interesting, readable articles, and membership (£8 in the UK, £12 overseas) includes a subscription.

In Australasia write to FG Clements, The Albania Society, PO Box 14074, Wellington, New Zealand.

In the USA, Jack Shulman (☎ 718-633 0530), PO Box 912, Church Street Station, New York, NY 10008, sells by mail order Albanian books, maps, videos, folk-music cassettes and English-Albanian language courses. Jack also carries English translations of Ismail Kadare's best novels.

In Germany you can contact the Deutsch-Albanische Freundschaftsgesellschaft (☎ & fax 040-511 1320), Bilser Strasse 9, D-22297 Hamburg, Germany, which publishes the quarterly magazine Albanische Hefte.

An excellent source of rare and out-of-print books on Albania is Eastern Books (☎ 0181-871 0880), 125a Astonville St, Southfields, London SW18 5AQ, England, UK. Write for their 24-page catalogue of books about Albania, or point your WWW browser at their URL: http://ourworld.compuserve.com/home pages/EasternBooks/albania.htm.

You can also e-mail them at 100753.1153@compuserve.com. Also try Oxus Books (☎ 0181-870 3854), 121 Astonville St, London SW18 5AQ, England, UK.

ALBANIA

VISAS & EMBASSIES

No visa is required from citizens of Australia, Bulgaria, Canada, Iceland, New Zealand, Norway, Switzerland, Turkey, the USA and EU countries. Travellers from other countries can obtain their Albanian visa at the border for a price equivalent to what an Albanian would pay for a tourist visa in those countries. Those who don't need a visa must still pay an 'entry tax' of US$5. Citizens of the USA do not have to pay the US$5 entry tax. Land border authorities may try to take anything up to US$20 from you. Insist on $5 and ask for a receipt.

Upon arrival you will fill in an arrival and departure card. Keep the departure card with your passport and present it when you leave.

Albanian Embassies Abroad

Albanian embassies are found in the following cities: Ankara, Athens, Beijing, Belgrade, Bonn, Brussels, Bucharest, Budapest, Cairo, Geneva, Havana, Istanbul, London, New York, Paris, Prague, Rome, Skopje, Sofia, Stockholm, Vienna, Warsaw and Washington.

Greece
  Karahristou 1, 115 21 Athens
  (☎ 01-723 4412; fax 01-723 1972)
France
  13 rue de la Pompe, Paris, France 75016
  (☎ 01 45 53 50 95)
UK
  38 Grosvenor Gardens, London SW1 0EB
  (☎ 0171-730 5709; fax 0171-730 5747)
USA
  1150 18th St, Washington, DC 20036
  (☎ 202-249 2059)
Yugoslavia
  Kneza Miloša 56, Belgrade (☎ 011-646 864)

Foreign Embassies in Albania

Bulgaria
  Rruga Skënderbeg; open Tuesday and Thursday noon to 1.30 pm only.
Hungary
  Rruga Skënderbeg (the street between Rruga Durrësit and Rruga Kavajes blocked off with a big iron gate); open Monday and Wednesday 9 to 11 am only.
Macedonia
  Rruga Skënderbeg, 2nd floor of the apartment building marked 'Ushqimore', near the Banka e Kursimeve kiosk.
UK
  Rruga Vaso Pasha (☎ 42 849); open weekdays 9 am to 12 pm.

USA
  Rruga Labinoti (☎ 32 875, 32 222); open weekdays 8 am to 4.30 pm.
Yugoslavia
  Rruga Durrësit, entry from the rear of the building; open weekdays 9 am to noon. This embassy is always crowded with Albanians, so get your visa elsewhere if possible.

MONEY

Albanian banknotes come in denominations of one, three, five, 10, 25, 50, 100, 500 and 1000 lekë. Coins have all but disappeared from circulation. Albania's huge, torn, dirty banknotes will strain your wallet, though the newer notes are a little easier to manage. In 1964 the currency was revalued 10 times and prices are often still quoted at the old rate. Thus if people tell you that a ticket costs 1000 lekë, they may really mean 100 lekë, so take care not to pay 10 times more! Conversely, a taxi driver who quotes a fare of 1000 lekë may actually mean 1000 new lekë, so watch out. This situation can be very confusing.

In mid-1996, US$1 got you about 104 lekë. Everything can be paid for with lek; prices are often quoted in dollars but you can pay in lek at the current rate. Although Albania is an inexpensive country for foreigners, for Albanians it's different as the average monthly wage is only 10,000 lekë, though this is changing quickly. For the most recent currency rates of the Albanian lek, point your Web browser at: gopher://gopher.undp.org:70/00/uncurr/exchrates.

The private Banka e Kursimeve is usually the most efficient when it comes to changing travellers' cheques and they keep longer hours than the National Bank. Some banks will change US dollar travellers' cheques into US dollars cash without commission. Travellers' cheques in small denominations may be used when paying bills at major hotels but cash is preferred everywhere. Credit cards are not accepted in Albania.

Every town has its free currency market which usually operates on the street in front of the main post office or state bank. Look for the men standing with pocket calculators in hand. Such transactions are not dangerous and it all takes place quite openly, but make sure you count their money twice before tendering yours. The rate will be about the same as at a bank. The advantages with changing money on the street are that you avoid the 1% commission, save time and don't have to worry about banking hours. Unlike the banks, private moneychangers never run out of currency notes.

Deutschmarks are preferred in Yugoslavia but in Albania US dollars are the favourite foreign currency; you should bring along a supply of dollars in small bills as they can be used to bargain for everything from hotel rooms to curios and taxi rides. The import and export of Albanian currency is prohibited, but there's no reason to do either. Conversion rates for major currencies in mid-1996 are listed below:

Exchange Rates

Australia	A$1	=	75 lekë
Canada	C$1	=	74 lekë
France	1FF	=	19.5 lekë
Germany	DM1	=	69 lekë
Japan	¥100	=	88 lekë
United Kingdom	UK£1	=	154 lekë
United States	US$1	=	104 lekë

Tipping

Albania is a tip-conscious society. You should leave a reasonable tip in restaurants. You're allowed to import a litre of alcohol duty-free and this will make an excellent gift for anyone who has been especially helpful. Don't bother bringing the permitted carton of duty-free cigarettes, however, as these are readily available from street vendors in Albania.

Discretion should be used in tipping in order to avoid spoiling Albania. Tourists who hand out chewing gum or pens to children on the street are encouraging them to be a serious nuisance.

POST & COMMUNICATIONS
Post
Sending Mail Postage is inexpensive and the service surprisingly reliable, but always use air mail. There are no public mailboxes in Albania; you must hand in your letters at a post office in person. Leaving letters at hotel reception for mailing is unwise. Mail your parcels from the main post office in Tirana to reduce the amount of handling.

If you buy any books in Albania, be aware that all material printed in Albania or in the

Albanian language is confiscated by Yugoslav border guards. Anyone leaving Albania via Montenegro or Kosovo should mail all Albanian publications home before leaving Tirana. Bring some padded envelopes or wrapping paper and string for the purpose. You shouldn't have any problems of this kind at the Macedonian or Greek borders.

Receiving Mail American Express cardholders can have their mail sent c/o American Express (World Travel), Rruga Durrësit 65, Tirana, Albania. Otherwise just use Poste Restante, Tirana, Albania. However, Albania is not a good country for receiving mail as letters to Albania are often opened by people looking for money.

Telephone
Long-distance telephone calls made from main post offices are cheap, costing about 100 lekë a minute to Western Europe. You may be pleasantly surprised by how fast your calls go through but come early or late as these offices are often crowded around mid-afternoon.

Getting through to Albania (country code ☎ 355) takes persistence, and only Tirana (area code ☎ 42), Durrës (☎ 52), Elbasan (☎ 545) and Korça (☎ 824) have direct dialling; elsewhere you must go through an operator.

Albania's international access code is ☎00.

Fax & E-mail
Faxing can be done fairly easily from Tirana. Albania is connected to the Internet, but access to casual visitors is limited at the moment. The Open Society Foundation of Albania (OSFA) may be able to answer your queries. Try contacting postmaster@osfa. tirana.al for the latest information.

NEWSPAPERS & MAGAZINES
Some 18 newspapers are published in Tirana, up from seven in 1989. Many are sponsored by political parties, such as Zëri i Popullit (The People's Voice), organ of the Socialist Party; RD (Democratic Renaissance), the Democratic Party's paper; Alternativa, the Social Democratic Party's paper; and Republika, the Republican Party's paper. Koha Jonë is the paper with the widest readership. The Gazeta Shqiptare is published in Albanian and Italian. Drita (Light), the weekly periodical of the

League of Writers & Artists, features poetry in Albanian. The daily *Albania* has a page in English.

RADIO & TV

There are many TV channels available in Albania including the state TV service TVSH and, among others, CNN, Euronews, Eurosport, several Italian channels and a couple of French ones to boot.

The BBC World Service can be picked up in and around Tirana on 103.9 FM.

PHOTOGRAPHY & VIDEO

Plenty of film is sold in Tirana, and there are several good one-hour developing and printing services. In the country it's considered rude to take pictures of people without asking permission, but this will almost never be refused. If you promise to send prints to local people, be sure to honour those promises. As a photographer you'll arouse a lot of friendly curiosity. Don't photograph military or government establishments. Bring your own video paraphernalia – batteries and tapes etc – even though these are now available in Tirana.

TIME

Albania is one hour ahead of GMT/UTC, the same as Yugoslavia, Macedonia and Italy, but one hour behind Greece. Albania goes on summer time at the end of March, when clocks are turned forward an hour. At the end of September, they're turned back an hour.

ELECTRICITY

The electric current is 220 V, 50 Hz, and plugs have two round pins.

WEIGHTS & MEASURES

Albania uses the metric system.

TOILETS

Public toilets in Albania are to be used in dire circumstances only! There are only three in the whole of Tirana. Use hotel or restaurant toilets whenever you can. The ones in the main hotels in Tirana are very clean and modern. Plan your 'rest' stops carefully when travelling in the country.

HEALTH

Health services are available to tourists for a small fee at state-run hospitals, but service and standards are not crash hot. You are better off taking out health insurance and using the private clinics where available.

WOMEN TRAVELLERS

While women are not likely to encounter any predictable dangers, it is recommended that you travel in pairs or with male companions, in order to avoid unwanted attention – particularly outside of Tirana. Bear in mind that Albania is a predominantly Muslim country. Dress should be conservative both for cultural and for personal reasons.

GAY & LESBIAN TRAVELLERS

Gay sex became legal in Albania early in 1995, however attitudes towards homosexuality are still highly conservative. The Gay Albania Society (Shoqata Gay Albania) is at PO Box 104, Tirana, Albania.

DISABLED TRAVELLERS

Getting around Tirana and Albania in general will be problematic for travellers in wheelchairs since few special facilities exist. There are toilets for disabled people in the Tirana International and the Europapark (Rogner) Hotel in Tirana.

DANGERS & ANNOYANCES

Beware of pickpockets on crowded city buses and don't flash money around! Walking around the towns is safe during the day, even in small streets and among desolate apartment blocks, but at night you must beware of falling into deep potholes in the unlit streets, and occasional gangs of youths. Be aware of theft generally but don't believe the horror stories you hear about Albania in Greece and elsewhere.

Take special care if accosted by gypsy women and children begging, as they target foreigners and are very pushy. If you give them money once, they'll stick to you like glue. When accosted, do not respond and avoid eye contact. Just keep walking and they will soon give up. Head for the nearest hotel if they haven't given up in five minutes. They will soon scarper.

Corrupt police may attempt to extort money

from you by claiming that something is wrong with your documentation, or on another pretext. Strongly resist paying them anything without an official receipt. If they threaten to take you to the police station, just go along for the experience and see things through to the end. Always have your passport with you.

Hepatitis B is prevalent in Albania. Get a vaccination before arriving and take care swimming near built-up areas and drinking tap water.

BUSINESS HOURS
Most shops open at 7 am and close for a siesta from noon to 4 pm. They open again until 7 pm and some also open on Sunday. In summer the main shops stay open one hour later but private shops keep whatever hours they like. State banks will change travellers' cheques from 7.30 to 11 am only.

Albanian museums don't follow any pattern as far as opening hours go. Museums in small towns may only open for a couple of hours a week. You may find them inexplicably closed during the posted hours or simply closed with no hours posted. Since state subsidies have been slashed, foreigners must pay 100 to 300 lekë admission to major museums.

PUBLIC HOLIDAYS & SPECIAL EVENTS
Public holidays in Albania include New Year's Day (1 January), Easter Monday (March/April), Labour Day (1 May), Independence & Liberation Day (28 November) and Christmas (25 December).

Ramadan and Bajram, variable Muslim holidays, are also celebrated.

ACCOMMODATION
Many of the large tourist hotels are still owned by the State Bureau for Tourism, Alburist, though many are being privatised. Most Alburist hotels are in pretty bad shape, so it's always a good idea to check your room before committing yourself. Alburist itself is barely hanging on in the changing tourist market, so don't depend on it for too much advice on places to stay.

Accommodation is undergoing a rapid transformation in Albania with the opening up of new custom-built private hotels, and the conversion of homes or villas into so-called private hotels. For budget travellers, these are without doubt the best way to go.

New custom-built hotels tend to have Western European prices, ie 5000 lekë per person per night and upwards, but these are modern, well-appointed establishments – a far cry from the state-run hotels of old – and they usually include breakfast.

In this book we have tended to provide advice on private accommodation and on state accommodation when that is the only option. You can very often find unofficial accommodation in private homes by asking around. You may even get a meal or two thrown in as well.

There are no camping grounds but free camping is possible in emergencies. For security, camp out of sight of the road and never go off and leave your tent unattended. Don't camp in the same area more than one night, unless you have permission to camp next to someone's house (even then you risk losing things). Expect to arouse considerable curiosity.

FOOD
Lunch is the main meal of the day though eating out in the evening is very common in Tirana. The quality of restaurants in the capital has improved greatly. In the country and other towns things are also getting much better, so you should have no problem getting a decent meal.

State-owned hotel restaurants are cheaper but the standards are low and they're also poor value. Everywhere beware of waiters who refuse to bring the menu, pad your bill with extras and 'forget' to bring your change. The many hamburger stands in the towns are a much better deal, but choose one that is patronised by a lot of people.

Albanian cuisine, like that of Serbia, has been strongly influenced by Turkey. Grilled meats like *shishqebap* (shish kebab), *romstek* (minced meat patties) and *qofte* (meat balls) are served all across the Balkans. Some local dishes include *çomlek* (meat and onion stew), *fërges* (a rich beef stew), *rosto me salcë kosi* (roast beef with sour cream) and *tavë kosi* (mutton with yoghurt). Lake Shkodra carp and Lake Ohrid trout are the most common fish dishes. Try the ice cream *(akullore)*, which is very popular everywhere.

ALBANIA

DRINKS

Albanians take their coffee both as *kafe turke* (Turkish coffee) and *kafe ekspres* (espresso). If you ask for *kafe surogato* you will get what is the closest to filter coffee. Any tourist or resident expatriate will tell you not to drink the water, but Albanians do so all the time with no consequences. It all depends on what your stomach is acclimatised to. Avoid unbottled, ungased drinks as they may be questionable.

Albanian white wine is better than the vinegary red. However the red *Shesi e Zi* from either Librazhd or Berat is an excellent drop. Most of the beer consumed in Albania is imported from Macedonia or Greece, but draught Austrian or Italian beer is available in the posher joints in Tirana. *Raki* (a clear brandy distilled from grapes) is taken as an apéritif. There's also *konjak* (cognac), *uzo* (a colourless aniseed-flavoured liqueur like Greek ouzo) and various fruit liqueurs. *Fërnet* is a medicinal apéritif containing herbal essences, made at Korça.

Public bars and cafés patronised mostly by local men are very sociable and if you enter one for a drink with an Albanian always try to pay. Nine times out of 10 your money will be refused and by having the opportunity to insist on paying your host will gain face in front of those present. The favourite Albanian drinking toast is *gëzuar!*

ENTERTAINMENT

Check the local theatre for performances. These are usually advertised on painted boards either in front of the theatre or on main streets. Ask someone to direct you to the venue if it's not clear. Soccer games take place at local stadiums on Saturday and Sunday afternoons. As a foreigner, you may need to ask someone to help you to obtain tickets.

THINGS TO BUY

Most of the hotels have tourist shops where you can buy Albanian handicrafts such as carpets, silk, ornaments (made from silver, copper and wood), embroidery, shoulder bags, handmade shoes, picture books, musical instruments, and records and cassettes of folk music.

Getting There & Away

AIR

Rinas Airport is 23 km north-west of Tirana. Taxis and a bus ply the route to Tirana.

Ada Air arrives from Bari; Adria Airways from Ljubljana; Albanian Airlines from Rome, Zürich, Munich and Vienna; Alitalia from Rome; Arbëria Airlines from New York; Hemus Air from Sofia; Malév Hungarian Airlines from Budapest; Olympic Airlines from Athens via Ioannina or Thessaloniki; and Swissair from Zürich.

These expensive flights are used mostly by business people or Albanians resident abroad and are of little interest to budget travellers, who can come more cheaply and easily by road. An exception is Malév Hungarian Airlines' service three times a week from Budapest to Tirana, which is good value at 26,700 lekë return and you avoid having to transit Yugoslavia.

Unfortunately, the Italian government requires its state airline flying between Italy and Albania to charge business class fares for one-way tickets, which makes Italy a poor gateway. For example, with Alitalia, Tirana-Bari is 31,800 lekë one way, Tirana-Rome 46,200 lekë one way. However, Alitalia does do weekend return specials to/from Rome for 33,990 lekë. In comparison to flying to Rome, it is cheaper to fly further on Albanian Airlines (☎ & fax 42 857), a joint venture with a Kuwaiti concern, which has flights to Zürich (twice weekly, 38,800 lekë one way), Munich (three times a week, 39,500 lekë one way) and Vienna (three times a week, 37,000 lekë one way). Return flights to/from Rome or Bologna with Albanian Airlines cost 29,600 lekë.

Before investing in any of the above fares, compare them with the price of a cheap flight to Athens or Thessaloniki, from where Albania is easily accessible by local bus with a change of bus at the border; you could also look at the cost of a charter flight to Corfu, from where you can take a ferry to Saranda in southern Albania.

LAND

Bus

The simplest way to get into Albania by bus is from Greece. Nine buses a day run from

Ioannina, Greece, to the Albanian border at Kakavija (one hour, 960 dr). You must arrive at the border before 11 am to connect with the regular Albanian bus on to Tirana (242 km). In the other direction, you are better off taking the early morning bus from Tirana to either Ioannina or Athens directly, in order to avoid transport delays at the border post.

Alternatively, it's fairly easy to cover the 93 km from Korça to Florina, Greece, via Kapshtica (see the Korça section in this chapter for details). Unscheduled local buses from Tirana to Kakavija and Korça to Kapshtica leave throughout the day. To/from Athens you're better off going via Kakavija, to/from Thessaloniki via Kapshtica.

If you're Macedonia-bound, take a bus to Pogradec on the south side of Lake Ohrid and cross on foot via Sveti Naum, as described in the Pogradec section in this chapter. Buses for destinations in Macedonia depart at 8 am daily from behind the Palace of Culture in Tirana. Tickets can be bought from Esterida Bus Services. A one-way ticket to Skopje costs 2070 lekë.

Buses for Sofia (505 km, US$26 – payable only in US dollars) depart on Tuesday and Wednesday at 10 am from Albtransport on Rruga Mina Peza in Tirana. Buses for Athens (732 km, 3640 lekë) leave every day at 6 am except Tuesday, and for Istanbul (1080 km, 4160 lekë) at noon on Friday only from the Axhensi bus office on a side street near the art gallery in Tirana.

Although Shkodra is linked to Podgorica, Yugoslavia, by freight train, there's no passenger service.

Car & Motorcycle

In the recent past, bringing a car to Albania was a risky business. Today there is no real reason why you should not travel by car through Albania. Travel is slow because of the poor condition of the roads and the arterial infrastructure cannot yet properly support the marked increase in vehicular traffic that Albania has recently experienced. Apart from an eight-km stretch of 'freeway' between Tirana and Durrës there has been no visible improvement in the roads since the days of communism. See the following Getting Around section for further information on local driving conditions.

It should be possible to transit the country from Hani i Hotit on the Montenegran border to the Kakavija border with Greece (or vice versa) in about eight or nine hours, though Tirana makes for a convenient overnight stop, should you decide to make the trip. The following highway border crossings are open to both motorists and persons on foot or bicycle.

Yugoslavia You can cross at Han i Hotit (between Podgorica and Shkodra) and at Morina (between Prizren and Kukës). For information about crossing at Morina, see the Kukës section in this chapter and Prizren in the Yugoslavia chapter. A new border crossing was due to open by September 1996 at Muriqan, between Shkodra and Ulcinj in Montenegro, but the access road on the Albanian side is pretty rough.

Macedonia Cross at Tushemisht (near Sveti Naum, 29 km south of Ohrid), Qafa e Thanës (between Struga and Pogradec) and Maqellare (between Debar and Peshkopi). See the Pogradec section of this chapter for information about crossing at Tushemisht.

Greece The border crossings are Kapshtica (between Florina and Korça) and Kakavija (between Ioannina and Gjirokastra). A new EU-funded border crossing between Sagiada and Konispol, south of Saranda, was due to open in mid-1996.

SEA

The Italian company Adriatica di Navigazione offers ferry services to Durrës from Bari (220 km, nine hours), Ancona (550 km, 20 hours) and Trieste (750 km, 25 hours) several times a week. The routes are served by 272-vehicle, 1088-passenger ships of the *Palladio* class. The food aboard ship is good.

Deck fares are 7000 lekë Bari-Durrës, 10,000 lekë Ancona-Durrës and 12,000 lekë Trieste-Durrës. Pullman (airline-style) seats cost 8000 lekë Bari-Durrës, 11,000 lekë Ancona-Durrës, and 13,500 lekë Trieste-Durrës. Cabins for the Trieste-Durrës trip vary in price from 15,500 lekë for a bed in a four-bed C-class cabin to 19,500 lekë for an A-class cabin.

These are high-season fares, applicable

eastbound from July to mid-August, west-bound from mid-August to mid-September. During other months it's about 25% cheaper. The cost of a return fare is double the one-way fare. Meals are not included and an Italian port tax of US$3 is charged on departures from Italy.

In Trieste ferry tickets are available from Agenzia Marittima 'Agemar' (☎ 40-363 737), Via Rossini 2, right on the old harbour five blocks from Trieste railway station. The booking office is closed from noon to 3 pm and on weekends. In Bari the agent is 'Agestea' (☎ 80-331 555), Via Liside 4. In Ancona it's Maritime Agency Srl (☎ 71-204 915), Via XXIX Settembre 2/0. In Albania tickets are sold at the harbour in Durrës.

Illyria Lines SA in Durrës (☎ & fax 052-23 723), in Vlora (☎ & fax 063-25 533) and in Brindisi (☎ 831-562 043; fax 831-562 005) runs two ferries between these three ports. Prices are 6900 lekë for a deck ticket or 8280 lekë for an aircraft-type seat.

The fastest ferry connection between Bari and Durrës is the 315-passenger catamaran *La Vikinga* (3½ hours, 11,500 lekë, students 8700 lekë). This high-speed vessel departs almost daily and travels at speeds of up to 90 km/h. The Bari agent is Morfimare (☎080-521 0022), Corso de Tullio 36/40.

The shortest and least expensive ferry trip to/from Italy is the Otranto-Vlora link (100 km, three times a week, 4500 lekë). Tickets are available from Biglietteria Linee Lauro (☎ 0836-806 061; fax 0836-806 062), at the port in Otranto, or Albania Travel & Tours (☎ 042-32 983) in Tirana.

The Transeuropa ferry between Koper, Slovenia, and Durrës runs three times a week (11,200 lekë deck, 14,200 lekë in a four-bed cabin, 17,200 lekë in a two-bed cabin and 22,200 lekë for a single). The ticket office is at the harbour in Durrës. In Koper contact Inter-agent (☎ 66-456 100).

Travellers from Corfu are advised to look for the ticket vendors (from any of the three ferry companies) who hang around the New Harbour before the ferries depart. The *Kamelia* departs Corfu at 10 am, the *Oleg Volvać* at 10.30 am and the *Harikla* at 3 pm.

ORGANISED TOURS

Several companies offer package tours to Albania which include transport, accommodation, meals, admission fees and guides, but not visa fees, airport taxes, or alcohol with the meals. Single hotel rooms also cost extra. As always, group travel involves a trade-off: having everything arranged for you against lack of control over the itinerary and the obligation to wait around for slower group members. Tours also tend to isolate you from the everyday life of Albania, though the trekking tours bring you more into contact with people and places.

The companies to contact are:

Regent Holidays, 15 John St, Bristol BS1 2HR, UK (☎ 0117-921 1711; fax 0117-925 4866)
ITS, 546-550 Royal Exchange, Old Bank Street, Manchester M2 7EN, UK (☎ 0161-839 111; fax 0161-839 000)
Kutrubes Travel, 328 Tremont St, Boston, MA 02116 USA (☎ 617-426 5668)
Scope Reizen, Spoorstraat 41, NL-5931 PS Tegelen, The Netherlands (☎ 077-735 533)
Skënderbeg-Reisen GmbH, Postfach 102204, D-44722 Bochum, Germany (☎ 0234-308 686)
Egnatia Tours, Piaristengasse 60, A-1082 Vienna, Austria (☎ 0222-406 97 32)
Hauser Exkursionen International, Marienstrasse 17, D-80331 München, Germany (☎ 089-235 006; fax 291 3714)
Intertrek BV Postbus 18760, NL-2502 ET Den Haag, Netherlands (☎ 070-363 6416)
Exodus, 9 Weir Rd London SW12 0LT, England, UK (☎ 0181-675 5550; fax 0181-673 0779)

Regent Holidays has a five-day bus tour of central Albania four times a year at £508, return flight from London included. ITS offers eight-day tours of 'Classical Albania' for £799, covering most of the major sights. Kutrubes Travel offers a 10-day bus tour of southern Albania every two weeks from May to October at US$2260, including return air fare from Boston. Northern Albania is offered once in July and again in August (US$2367).

Exodus offers 15-day hiking and discovery tours between May and September. Their free brochure is quite informative.

LEAVING ALBANIA

Airport departure tax is US$10, which is payable in lekë. Departure tax from Albanian ports is US$2. Private cars departing from Albania pay US$5 road tax per day for each day spent in the country.

Getting Around

BUS

Most Albanians travel around their country in private minibuses or state-owned buses. These run fairly frequently throughout the day between Tirana and Durrës (38 km) and other towns north and south. Buses to Tirana depart from towns all around Albania at the crack of dawn. Tickets are sold by a conductor on board, and for foreigners the fares are low. Although old, the buses are usually comfortable enough, as the number of passengers is controlled by police.

TRAIN

Before 1948, Albania had no railways, but the communists built up a limited north-south rail network based at the port of Durrës, with daily passenger trains leaving Tirana for Shkodra (98 km, 3½ hours), Fier (121 km, 4¼ hours), Ballsh (146 km, five hours), Vlora (155 km, 5½ hours) and Pogradec (189 km, seven hours). Seven trains a day make the 1½-hour, 36-km trip between Tirana and Durrës. In August 1986 a railway was completed from Shkodra to Podgorica, Yugoslavia, but this is for freight only.

Albanian railways use mostly old Italian rolling stock seconded as a form of aid. There's still only one type of train ticket, so you can sit in 1st or 2nd class for the same price. Train fares are about a third cheaper than bus fares, but both are very cheap by European standards.

Train travel is really only useful between Tirana and Durrës. All trains to southern Albania call at Durrës, a roundabout route that makes them much slower than bus. The bus to Shkodra in the north is also much faster. Still, travelling by train is an interesting way to see the country and meet the people. But be warned: many trains don't have toilets and the carriages can be very decrepit, with broken windows.

CAR & MOTORCYCLE

Albania still does not have an official road traffic code and most motorists have only learned to drive in the last few years. The road infrastructure is poor and the roads badly maintained, but the number of cars on the road is growing daily. Petrol stations are available in the cities, but are fewer and further between in the country. Very few people ride motorcycles as yet and the poor road conditions are a concern for motorcyclists planning to tour the country. You can hire a car, but if you are a timid driver, hiring a car and a driver is the best way to get around.

Hazards you should look out for are pedestrians who use the roads as an extension of the footpaths; animals being herded along country roads; gaping potholes; a lack of road warning and general road signs and occasionally reckless drivers. Security is an issue that needs addressing. Although there are now many cars in the country and cars are parked freely, you are advised to park your vehicle in a secure location, like in hotel grounds, or in a guarded parking lot. You might also want to store removables like hubcaps inside the car when parked. An immobiliser alarm is a good idea.

Police are everywhere and stop cars regularly, often on a whim. The police are generally pretty laid-back, but may try to separate you from a few dollars to supplement their meagre incomes. If you are stopped, smile a lot and politely refuse to be parted from your cash.

Modern petrol stations are opening up all over the country so fuel is no longer a problem, although unleaded fuel may only be available closer to Tirana, so fill up when you can.

BICYCLE

Cycling around Albania, while not unheard of, is still a novelty. A number of foreign cyclists, including solo riders, have written of interesting and hassle-free trips through the country, though some caution should still be exercised. If you are planning to cycle into the country, it is preferable to do so in groups of two or more for security – primarily for your belongings on the bike. Facilities outside of Tirana, while improving, are not very sophisticated yet. You will need to be as self-sufficient as possible. Car drivers may not show much respect for cyclists, so ride defensively. Potholed roads make it necessary to keep a sharp eye out so as to avoid damage to your bike. Mountain bikes are a better option than road bikes.

HITCHING

With buses so cheap, hitching will probably only be an emergency means of transport. You can afford to be selective about the rides you accept as everyone will take you if they possibly can. Truck drivers usually refuse payment from foreigners for lifts (even if Albanian passengers must pay). Never accept rides in cars containing three or more excited young men as they will drive wildly and do things which could get you into trouble.

You can get an indication of where a vehicle might be going from the letters on the licence plate: Berat (BR), Durrës (DR), Elbasan (EL), Fier (FR), Gjirokastra (GJ), Korça (KO), Kruja (KR), Lezha (LE), Pogradec (PG), Saranda (SR), Shkodra (SH), Tirana (TR), Vlora (VL).

LOCAL TRANSPORT

Shared minibuses run between cities. They usually cost about five times the bus fare but for foreigners they're still relatively cheap. Ask locals what they think the fare should be and then bargain for something approaching that.

City buses operate in Tirana, Durrës and Shkodra (pay the conductor). Watch your possessions on city buses as they're very crowded.

There are two types of taxis: the older private taxis, which are usually found around the market or at bus and train stations, and the shiny Mercedes tourist taxis parked outside the Rogner and Tirana International hotels (which quote fares in US dollars but also take lekë). Taxi fares are set at approximately 45 lekë per kilometre. Work out the price in your head before getting in and make sure you reach an agreement with the driver before setting off. Car rentals with or without a company driver are available in Tirana.

Don't trust truck drivers who enthusiastically offer to give you a lift somewhere the following day as their plans could change and all the morning buses may have left before you find out about it.

Tirana

Tirana (Tiranë) is a pleasant city of 400,000 (compared with 30,000 before WWII), almost exactly midway between Rome and Istanbul. Mt Dajti (1612 metres) rises to the east. Founded by a Turkish pasha (military governor) in 1614, Tirana developed into a craft centre with a lively bazar. In 1920 the city was made capital of Albania and the bulky Italianate government buildings went up in the 1930s. In the communist era, larger-than-life 'palaces of the people' blossomed around Skënderbeg Square and along Bulevardi Dëshmorët e Kombit (Martyrs of the Nation Blvd). You'll see Italian parks and a Turkish mosque, but the market area on the east side of Tirana is also worth exploring. The city is compact and can be visited on foot.

Information

Money The State Bank of Albania (Banka e Shtetit Shqiptar) on Skënderbeg Square (open weekdays from 8.30 am to noon) changes travellers' cheques for 1% commission.

A free currency market operates on the square directly in front of the State Bank. One of the men with a pocket calculator in hand will take you aside. A number of small kiosks here will also change your cash for a similar rate.

The Unioni Financiar Tiranë Exchange just south of the post office is a good place to send and receive money electronically and to cash your money as well.

Post & Communications The telephone centre is on Bulevardi Dëshmorët e Kombit, opposite Hotel Arbëria and a little towards Skënderbeg Square. It's open 21 hours a day and calls go straight through. This is also the cheapest place to send a fax. Tirana's telephone code is ☎ 042.

Travel Agencies The American Express representative is World Travel (☎ & fax 27 908), Rruga Durrësit 65. They can cash and supply travellers' cheques, provide air and ferry tickets and arrange private or group tours around Albania.

Albania Travel & Tours (☎ 32 983; fax 33 981), Rruga Durrësit 102, sells tickets for the ferry from Vlora to Otranto, Italy (three a week, 3500 lekë), perhaps the cheapest way across the Adriatic. Skanderbeg Travel, a few blocks north-west up the same street, is good about providing general information.

Newspapers & Magazines Foreign newspapers and magazines are sold at all major hotels and at many street kiosks.

Medical & Emergency Services Hospital services at the Policlinic will cost you a minimum fee of about 500 lekë, but if you have travel insurance you would probably be better off heading for the new and private Poliklinika at Luigji Monti on Rruga Kavajes.

Things to See & Do

Most visits to Tirana begin at **Skënderbeg Square**, a great open space in the heart of the city.

Beside the 15-storey Tirana International hotel (the tallest building in Albania), on the north side of the square, is the **National Museum of History** (1981), the largest and finest museum in Albania (open Tuesday to Saturday from 9 am to noon and 4 to 7 pm, Friday and Sunday 9 am to 1 pm, admission 200 lekë). A huge mosaic mural entitled *Albania* covers the façade of the museum building (the rooms describing the communist era are closed). Temporary exhibits are shown in the gallery on the side of the building facing the Tirana International Hotel (admission free).

To the east is another massive building, the **Palace of Culture**, which has a theatre, restaurant, cafés and art galleries. Construction of the palace began as a gift from the Soviet people in 1960 and was completed in 1966, after the 1961 Soviet-Albanian split. The entrance to the **National Library** is on the south side of the building. Opposite this is the cupola and minaret of the **Mosque of Ethem Bey** (1793), one of the most distinctive buildings in the city. Enter to see the beautifully painted dome. Tirana's **clock tower** (1830) stands beside the mosque.

On the west side of Skënderbeg Square is the State Bank of Albania, with the main post office behind it. The south side of the square is taken up by the massive ochre-coloured buildings of various government ministries. In the middle of the square is an equestrian statue (1968) of Skënderbeg himself looking straight up Bulevardi Dëshmorët e Kombit (formerly Bulevardi Stalin and before that, Bulevardi Zog I), north towards the train station.

A massive statue of Enver Hoxha stood on the high marble plinth between the National Museum of History and the State Bank but it was unceremoniously toppled after the return to democracy. A small fairground now occupies the central part of the square.

Behind Skënderbeg's statue extends Bulevardi Dëshmorët e Kombit, leading directly south to the three arches of **Tirana University** (1957). As you stroll down this tree-lined boulevard, you'll see Tirana's **art gallery** (closed Monday), a one-time stronghold of socialist realism, with a significant permanent collection that has been exhibited here since 1976.

Continue south on Bulevardi Dëshmorët e Kombit to the bridge over the Lana River. On the left just across the river are the sloping white-marble walls of the **former Enver Hoxha Museum** (1988), occasionally used as an exhibition centre but now likely to be turned into a disco (Enver would be spinning in his grave!). The museum closed down at the start of 1991 and the brilliant red star was removed from the pyramid-shaped building's tip. Just beyond, on the right, is the four-storey former **Central Committee building** (1955) of the Party of Labour, which now houses various ministries.

Follow Rruga Ismail Qemali, the street on the south side of the Central Committee building, a long block west to the **former residence of Enver Hoxha** (on the north-west corner of the intersection). Formerly it was forbidden to walk along these streets, since many other party leaders lived in the surrounding mansions. When the area was first opened to the general public in 1991, great crowds of Albanians flocked here to see the style in which their 'proletarian' leaders lived.

On the left, farther south on Bulevardi Dëshmorët e Kombit, is the ultramodern **Palace of Congresses** (1986), next to which is the **Archaeological Museum** (open Monday to Saturday 7 am to 3 pm). There are no captions but a tour in English is usually included in the 200 lekë admission price.

Some 1800 selected objects from prehistoric times to the Middle Ages are on display and it's interesting to note how the simple artefacts of the Palaeolithic and Neolithic periods give way to the weapons and jewellery of the Copper and Bronze ages, with evidence of social differentiation. Although Greek and

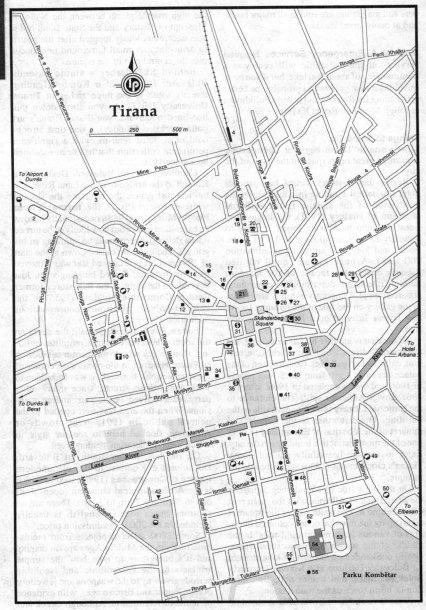

Tirana

0   250   500 m

PLACES TO STAY		3	Buses to Kruja	32	Main Post Office
12	Hotel California	4	Train Station	35	Unioni Financiar Tiranë
19	Hotel Arbëria	5	Yugoslav Embassy		Exchange
22	Hotel Tirana	6	Hungarian Embassy	36	Teatri i Kukallave
	International	7	Bulgarian Embassy	37	Teatri Kombetar
25	Hotel Miniri	8	Poliklinika At Luigji	38	Guarded Parking
33	Hotel Klodiana		Monti	39	Parliament
34	Europa International	9	Macedonian Embassy	40	Art Gallery
	Hotel	10	Orthodox Church	43	Dinamo Bus Station
41	Hotel Dajti	11	Cathedral of St Anthony	44	UK Embassy
48	Hotel Europapark	13	World Travel	45	Former Residence of
		14	Skanderbeg Travel		Enver Hoxha
PLACES TO EAT		15	Albtransport	46	Former Central
17	Piazza Restaurant	16	Albania Travel & Tours		Committee Building
24	Restorant Popullor	18	Philatelic Bureau	47	Former Enver Hoxha
27	Berlusconi Restaurant	20	Telephone Centre		Museum
29	Qendra Stefan	21	National Museum of	49	Italian Embassy
42	Ujvara Restaurant		History	50	US Embassy
55	Bar Artisti	23	Policlinic	51	Romanian Embassy
		26	Palace of Culture	52	Palace of Congresses
OTHER		28	Market	53	Qemal Stafa Stadium
1	Northern Bus Station	30	Mosque of Ethem Bey	54	Archaeological Museum
2	Asllan Rusi Stadium	31	State Bank of Albania	56	Tirana University

Roman relics are well represented, evidence of the parallel Illyrian culture is present throughout, illustrating that the ancestors of the present Albanians inhabited these lands since time immemorial.

Behind the museum is the **Qemal Stafa Stadium** (1946) where football matches are held every Saturday and Sunday afternoon, except during July and August. The boulevard terminates at the university, with the Faculty of Music on the right.

Beyond the university is **Parku Kombëtar** (National Park), a large park with an open-air theatre (Teatri Veror) and an artificial lake. There's a superb view across the lake to the olive-coloured hills. Cross the dam retaining the lake to **Tirana Zoo**. The excellent **botanical gardens** are just west of the zoo (ask directions). If you're keen, you can hire a rowing boat and paddle on the lake.

About five km south-east on Rruga Labinoti, which becomes the Elbasan Highway, is the **Martyrs' Cemetery** (Varrezat e Dëshmorëve), where some 900 partisans who died during WWII are buried. Large crowds once gathered here each year on 16 October, Enver Hoxha's birthday, since this is where he and other leading revolutionaries such as Gog Nushi, Qemal Stafa and Hysni Kapo were formerly interred. (In May 1992 Hoxha's lead

coffin was dug up and reburied in a common grave in a public cemetery on the other side of town.) The hilltop setting with a beautiful view over the city and mountains is subdued, and a great white figure of Mother Albania (1972) stands watch. Nearby, on the opposite side of the highway, is the **former palace of King Zog**, now a government guesthouse.

West of Tirana's centre on Rruga Kavajes is the Catholic **Cathedral of St Anthony**, which served as the Rinia Cinema from 1967 to 1990. Many foreign embassies are situated along Rruga Skënderbeg just beyond the cathedral. Since the rush of refugees into these in 1991, access for Albanians is restricted.

Organised Tours
World Travel on Rruga Durrësit 65, can arrange individual or group tours around Albania, depending on demand and requirements.

Places to Stay
Private Rooms Staying in private rented apartments or with local families is the best budget accommodation in Tirana. The formerly cheap (and often dire) state-owned hotels have either closed or been renovated, with accordingly higher prices. Newer private hotels are similarly high priced.

World Travel, Rruga Durrësit 65, arranges accommodation in private rooms or apartments for between 2000 and 3500 lekë per person. Albania Travel & Tours, Rruga Durrësit 102 (weekdays 8 am to 7 pm), has private rooms at around 1500 lekë per person. They can also organise private rooms or hotels in Gjirokastra, Korça, Vlora and Durrës.

Skanderbeg Travel (☎ & fax 23 946), Rruga Durrësit 5/11, a couple of blocks west of Albania Travel & Tours (weekdays 8.30 am to 1.30 pm and 4.30 to 7.30 pm), arranges private apartments with TV and fridge for between 3000 and 3500 lekë.

Hotels The newest and best hotel in Tirana is the *Hotel Europapark* (☎ 35 035; fax 35 050) at Blvd. Dëshmorët e Kombit 1, run by the Rogner group. Rooms are a pricey 15,000 lekë per night.

The high-rise *Tirana International* (☎ 34 185; fax 34 188) on Skënderbeg Square is now an Italian-run concern. Rooms cost 9025/12,350 lekë plus 24% tax for well-appointed singles/doubles. The room price includes breakfast. Full board supplement is 1800 lekë.

To the right of the Tirana International is the newer but smaller *Hotel Miniri* (☎ & fax 30 930) at Rruga e Dibres 3. Their single/double rooms with phone and TV are 6000/10,000 lekë.

A nice private hotel is the *Europa International Hotel* (☎ & fax 27 403), which has very modern single/double rooms for 6000/7000 lekë. Look for the sign on Rruga Myslym Shyri. Just off Rruga Durrësit, at Rruga Mihal Duri 2/7, is the nifty *Hotel California* (☎ 24 493). Nice rooms with mini-bar and TV cost 5500/6500 lekë for singles/doubles.

The aging and somewhat old-fashioned *Hotel Dajti* (☎ 33 327) on Bulevardi Dëshmorët e Kombit was erected in the 1930s by the Italians. The 90 rooms with bath are 3500/6500 lekë for singles/doubles.

The *Hotel Klodiana* (☎ 27 403) is just a few private rooms but is OK. A single/double goes for 3000/4000 lekë. It is just back from Rruga Myslym Shyri and shares the same phone number as the Europa International Hotel.

The 96 rooms at the state-run, six-storey *Hotel Arbëria* (☎ 60 813) on Bulevardi Dëshmorët e Kombit, to the north of Skënderbeg Square, cost 2500/3500 lekë for a single/double with bath. Check your room as some have broken windows and no running water, and the hotel is unheated in winter.

Places to Eat

There is no shortage of small restaurants and snack bars on and around Skënderbeg Square and Blvd Dëshmorët e Kombit, and small, stylish bars have mushroomed everywhere. Here are some places that you might not easily stumble across.

The *Piazza Restaurant* is a tastefully designed and well-appointed establishment just north of Skënderbeg Square. The food and service are excellent and prices, for what you get, are reasonable. The adjoining *Piano Bar* is a relaxing place to unwind with a predinner drink.

The *Berlusconi* bar and restaurant is a trendy Italian-influenced place hidden away just behind the Palace of Culture. Pasta and pizza are the main fare and prices are very reasonable.

The *Ujvara* restaurant on the south side of the river near the Dinamo bus station is another nice spot for an evening meal. Ignore the apparent squalor of the neighbourhood; the restaurant is top-notch. Restaurants at both the *Tirana International Hotel* and the *Hotel Europapark* are also very good. At the latter you will find some excellent Albanian food.

Check out the *Bar Artisti* cafeteria at the Institute of Art if you want to have a coffee and snack and mingle with the Tirana arty set. If you fancy a cuppa and a sandwich – or even a pizza – call into *Qendra Stefan*, a friendly, American-run place. It's near the fruit-and-vegetable market.

You can enjoy nice kebabs, salad and beer at the convenient and economical *Restorant Popullor*, close to Hotel Miniri on Rruga e Dibres.

Entertainment

As soon as you arrive, check the *Palace of Culture* on Skënderbeg Square for opera or ballet performances. Most events in Tirana are advertised on placards in front of this building. The ticket window opens at 5 pm and most performances begin at 7 pm.

The *Teatri i Kukallave*, beside the State Bank on Skënderbeg Square, presents puppet shows for children on Sunday at 10 and 11 am all year round. During the school year there are also morning shows on certain weekdays (ask when you get there).

Pop concerts and other musical events often take place in the *Qemal Stafa Stadium* next to the university. Look out for street banners bearing details of upcoming events.

If you really must, you can play bingo and poker machines in Tirana now. *Bingo* is next to the Theatri Kombetar while the poker machines are at *Admiral* at the southern end of Blvd Dëshmorët e Kombit.

The *London Bar* at Blvd Dëshmorët e Kombit 51 (near the Hotel Tirana International) is a mixed gay and straight bar.

Things to Buy

Tirana's public market, just north of the Sheshi Avni Rustemi roundabout several blocks east of the clock tower, is at its largest on Thursday and Sunday. A few shops here sell folkloric objects such as carved wooden trays, small boxes, wall hangings and bone necklaces.

The Philatelic Bureau (Filatelia), on Bulevardi Dëshmorët e Kombit, north-west of Hotel Tirana International, charges 40 times the face value of the stamps but they're still not too expensive by Western standards and there is a good selection.

Getting There & Away

Air For information about routes and fares of flights to/from Rinas Airport see the Getting There & Away section earlier in this chapter.

Many of the airline offices are on Rruga Durrësit, just off Skënderbeg Square. Here you'll find Ada Air, Adria Airways, Arbëria Airlines, Albanian Airlines, Hemus Air and Malév Hungarian Airlines. Alitalia has an office on Skënderbeg Square behind the National Museum of History and Swissair is at Hotel Europapark. To confirm an Olympic Airways flight, go to Albtransport on Rruga Mine Peza.

Bus Both private and state-owned buses operate between Tirana and most towns. There's no one central bus station in Tirana and pick-up venues may change, so check for the latest departure points. Service to/from Durrës (38 km, 40 lekë) is fairly frequent, leaving from the block adjacent to the train station.

Buses to Berat (122 km), Elbasan (54 km), Fier (113 km), Gjirokastra (232 km), Kakavija (263 km), Korça (179 km), Lushnja (83 km),

Pogradec (140 km), Saranda (289 km) and Vlora (147 km) leave from Dinamo bus station, on the west side of Dinamo Stadium. From about 6 am every day you can get buses to almost anywhere from here: they leave when full throughout the day. As late as 5 pm you'll still find some to Berat, Elbasan, Fier and perhaps further.

Buses to Kruja (32 km) leave from Rruga Mine Peza, at the beginning of the highway to Durrës.

North-bound buses to Lezha (69 km), Shkodra (116 km), Kukës (208 km) and other places leave from a station out on the Durrës highway just beyond the Asllan Rusi Stadium. Buses to Shkodra leave throughout the day but those to Kukës leave at 4 and 5 am only.

Information on all bus services out of Tirana can be obtained by calling ☎ 26 818.

Train The train station is at the north end of Bulevardi Dëshmorët e Kombit. Seven trains a day go to Durrës, a one-hour journey (36 km, 50 lekë). Trains also depart for Ballsh (146 km, four hours, daily), Elbasan (four hours, three daily), Pogradec (189 km, seven hours, twice daily), Shkodra (98 km, 3½ hours, twice daily), Fier (121 km, 4¼ hours, daily) and Vlora (155 km, 5½ hours, daily).

Getting Around

To/From the Airport The bus to the airport leaves from in front of the Albtransport office, Rruga Durrësit (23 km, 300 lekë; pay the driver). A tourist taxi from the airport to Tirana should cost between 2000 and 3000 lekë.

Car & Motorcycle There are two guarded parking lots, both charging 200 lekë a night. One is on Rruga Myslym Shyri, around the corner from Hotel Dajti, and the other is directly behind the Hotel Tirana International.

World Travel, Rruga Durrësit 65, rents cars at 4500 lekë daily without a driver, 6500 lekë daily with a driver/guide. As you may expect, they feel more comfortable with their own employee behind the wheel.

Taxi Local taxis park on the south side of the roundabout at the market. These are much cheaper for excursions out into the countryside than the Mercedes taxis parked at Hotel Tirana

International, but the drivers don't speak English so take along someone to bargain and act as interpreter.

AROUND TIRANA
Durrës

Unlike Tirana, Durrës (Durazzo in Italian) is an ancient city. In 627 BC the Greeks founded Epidamnos (Durrës) whose name the Romans changed to Dyrrhachium. It was the largest port on the eastern Adriatic and the start of the Via Egnatia (an extension of the Via Appia) to Constantinople. The famous Via Appia (Appian Way) to Rome began 150 km south-west of Durrës at Brindisi, Italy.

Durrës changed hands frequently before being taken by the Turks in 1501, under whom the port dwindled into insignificance. A slow revival began in the 17th century and from 1914 to 1920 Durrës was the capital of Albania. Landings here by Mussolini's troops on 7 April 1939 met fierce though brief resistance and those who fell are regarded as the first martyrs in the War of National Liberation.

Today, Roman ruins and Byzantine fortifications embellish this major industrial city and commercial port, which lies 38 km west of Tirana. Durrës is Albania's second-largest city, with 85,000 inhabitants. On a bay south-east of the city are long, sandy beaches where all the tourist hotels are concentrated. In 1991 the city saw desperate mobs attempting to escape by ship to Italy and there's now a heavy Italian military presence in the area. Car ferries from Italy dock on the east side of the port. The entry/exit point is even further east. Look for road signs to the ferry quay when departing.

Information The National Bank near the port (open weekdays from 8 to 11 am) changes travellers' cheques for a commission of 100 lekë per cheque, as does the Banka e Kursimeve up the street, half-way between the port and the large mosque (open Monday to Saturday from 9 am to 2 pm). Unofficial currency exchange is carried out on the street around the main post office in town.

The post office and phone centre are located one block west of the train and bus stations. Look for the big Telekom sign. The telephone code for Durrës is ☎ 052.

Things to See A good place to begin your visit to Durrës is the **Archaeological Museum** (open 9 am to 1 pm, closed Monday, 100 lekë admission), which faces the waterfront promenade near the port. Its two rooms are small but each object here is unique and there's a large sculpture garden outside. Behind the museum are the 6th-century Byzantine **city walls**, built

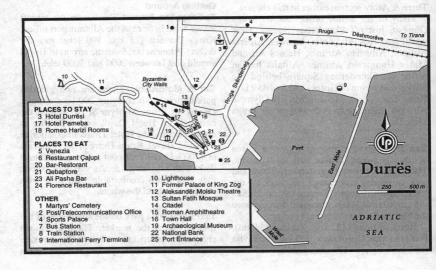

PLACES TO STAY
3 Hotel Durrësi
17 Hotel Pameba
18 Romeo Harizi Rooms

PLACES TO EAT
5 Venezia
6 Restaurant Çajupi
20 Bar-Restorant
21 Qebaptore
23 Ali Pasha Bar
24 Florence Restaurant

OTHER
1 Martyrs' Cemetery
2 Post/Telecommunications Office
4 Sports Palace
7 Bus Station
8 Train Station
9 International Ferry Terminal
10 Lighthouse
11 Former Palace of King Zog
12 Aleksandër Moisiu Theatre
13 Sultan Fatih Mosque
14 Citadel
15 Roman Amphitheatre
16 Town Hall
19 Archaeological Museum
22 National Bank
25 Port Entrance

Durrës

ADRIATIC SEA

Rruga Dëshmorëve — To Tirana

Byzantine City Walls

Rruga Skënderbeg

Port

East Mole

West Mole

0   250   500 m

after the Visigoth invasion of 481 and supplemented by round Venetian towers in the 14th century.

The town's impressive **Roman amphitheatre**, built between the 1st and 2nd centuries AD, is on the hillside just inside the walls. Much of the amphitheatre has now been excavated and you can see a small built-in 10th-century Byzantine church decorated with wall mosaics. Follow the road just inside the walls down towards the port and you'll find the **Sultan Fatih Mosque** (1502) and the **Moisiut Ekspozita e Kulturës Popullore**, with ethnographic displays housed in the former home of actor Alexander Moisiu (1879-1935). It's open in the morning only.

The former **palace of King Ahmet Zog** is on the hill top west of the amphitheatre. In front of the palace is a statue of Skënderbeg and huge radar disks set up by the Italian army. The next hill beyond bears a **lighthouse** which affords a splendid view of Albanian coastal defences, Durrës and the entire coast. The soldiers guarding the lighthouse will allow you to climb up for the view.

As you're exploring the centre of the city, stop to see the **Roman baths** directly behind Aleksandër Moisiu Theatre, on the central square. The large **mosque** on the square was erected with Egyptian aid in 1993, to replace one destroyed during the 1979 earthquake. At the western end of Rruga Dëshmorevë is the **Martyrs' Cemetery**, guarded by half a dozen decrepit bunkers.

Places to Stay Durrës offers cheap private rooms and a few hotels.

In Town There is not much choice these days in Durrës town. The best hotel is *Hotel Pameba* (☎ & fax 24 149), about 400 metres up the hill from the port entrance. Singles/doubles with a TV go for 5000/7000 lekë, including breakfast.

The Romeo Harizi family, left along the waterfront from the tower, a block beyond the Archaeological Museum, rents private rooms very cheaply. There's a sign outside in English.

You may be able to scrounge a room at the rather run-down four-storey *Hotel Durrësi*, next to the main post office in town. If you manage to get in, expect to pay about 1000 lekë but the amenities are pretty basic.

At the Beach The main tourist hotel is the *Adriatik* (☎ 23 612 or 23 001), on the long sandy beach five km south-east of Durrës. The 60 rooms in this appealing Stalin-era building are 4300/4600 lekë for a single/double, with bath and breakfast included. At five storeys it's the highest along the entire Albanian coast, a good indication of just how undeveloped tourism is here. The quality of the water lapping the Adriatik's beach is of dubious quality, so have a look before plunging in.

Near the Adriatik are the *Durrësi*, *Apollonia*, *Butrinti* and *Kruja* hotels, all in some kind of renovation or privatisation process. Prices, once the work is complete, can be expected to be higher than those of the Adriatik.

One traveller reported getting a room in a private *villa* near the beach just south-east of Hotel Adriatik for 1500 lekë, so it pays to look around.

Places to Eat There's a modern restaurant/bar called the *Florence* opposite the port entrance.

On Rruga Durrah, the main street, is a fairly modern and clean nameless kebab place. Look for the *Qebaptore* sign outside. Almost opposite is another nice restaurant simply called *Bar-Restorant*. Look out for the Löwenbräu sign. The *Hotel Pameba* also has a nice small restaurant.

Restorant Çajupi, west across the square from the train station, is a private restaurant which serves a bowl of rich beef soup. Just behind the Çajupi is the *Venezia*, with good coffee and ice cream. Unfortunately neither place has a menu so get the staff to write down the prices before ordering.

Entertainment Visit the *Aleksandër Moisiu Theatre* in the centre of Durrës and the *Sports Palace* on Rruga Dëshmorevë to see if anything is on.

There are any number of new bars and cafeterias opening up on and around the main street. There is a disco and even a poker machines joint. Try the pleasant outdoor *Ali Pasha* bar, very close to the port entrance, for a relaxing drink while you watch the street activity.

Getting There & Away Albania's 720-km

railway network centres on Durrës. There are seven trains a day to Tirana (36 km, 1½ hours, 50 lekë), two to Shkodra, one to Elbasan, two to Pogradec, one to Vlora and one to Ballsh. The station is beside the Tirana Highway, conveniently close to central Durrës. Tickets are sold at the 'Biletaria Trenit' office below the apartment building nearest the station or at a similar office below the next building. Buses to Tirana and elsewhere leave from in front of the train station and service is fairly frequent.

Ferry Agjencia Detare Shteterore per Adriatica at the entrance to the port sells tickets for the car ferries to Trieste, Ancona and Bari. Shpresa Transeuropa (☎ 22 423) in a kiosk nearby handles the ferries between Durrës and Koper, Slovenia, but schedules can be very flexible and the ferry may not leave on the day indicated.

The ticket office of the fast catamaran *La Vikinga* from Durrës to Bari is on Rruga Durrah, the street from the port to the mosque.

Some of the agencies require payment in Italian lira which you must purchase on the black market. If you have a valid ISIC student card always try for a student discount.

Ferries arrive in Durrës several times a week from Bari, Otranto, Ancona and Trieste in Italy and from Koper in Slovenia. If boarding a ferry at Durrës allow plenty of time, as it can be a long, complicated process, especially at night.

Getting Around There's a bus service on the main highway from the Adriatik Hotel into Durrës. For the return journey, look for the bus near the main post office in Durrës. Pay the conductor.

Northern Albania

A visit to northern Albania usually takes in only the coastal strip, but a journey into the interior is well worth while for the marvellous scenery. Between Puka and Kukës the road winds through 60 km of spectacular mountains.

Shkodra, the old Gheg capital near the lake of the same name, is a pleasant introduction to Albania for those arriving from Montenegro.

South of here is Lezha and Skënderbeg's tomb. Kruja is 6.5 km off the main road but is often visited for its crucial historical importance and striking location 608 metres up on the side of a mountain.

KRUJA
In the 12th century, Kruja was the capital of the Principality of Arberit, but this hill-top town attained its greatest fame between 1443 and 1468 when national hero George Kastrioti (1405-68), also known as Skënderbeg, made Kruja his seat.

At a young age, Kastrioti, son of an Albanian prince, was handed over as a hostage to the Turks, who converted him to Islam and gave him a military education at Edirne. There he became known as Iskënder (after Alexander the Great) and Sultan Murat II promoted him to the rank of bey (governor), thus the name Skënderbeg.

In 1443 the Turks suffered a defeat at the hands of the Hungarians at Niš, giving the nationally minded Skënderbeg the opportunity he had been waiting for to abandon Islam and the Ottoman army and rally his fellow Albanians against the Turks. Among the 13 Turkish invasions he subsequently repulsed was that led by Murat II himself in 1450. Pope Calixtus III named Skënderbeg 'captain general of the Holy See' and Venice formed an alliance with him. The Turks besieged Kruja four times. Though beaten back in 1450, 1466 and 1467, they took control of Kruja in 1478 (after Skënderbeg's death) and Albanian resistance was suppressed.

Things to See & Do
Set below towering mountains, the **citadel** that Skënderbeg defended still stands on an abrupt ridge above the modern town. In 1982 an excellent **historical museum** (open from 9 am to 1 pm and 3 to 6 pm, Thursday 9 am to 1 pm, closed Monday, admission 100 lekë) opened in the citadel. The saga of the Albanian struggle against the Ottoman empire is richly told with models, maps and statuary. The museum was designed by Pranvera Hoxha, Enver's daughter, who attempted to portray Hoxha and Skënderbeg as parallel champions of Albanian independence. Like Hoxha, Skënderbeg was something of a social reformer. He abolished

the blood vendetta (*gjakmarrje*) but the feuds began afresh soon after his death.

In an old house opposite the main citadel museum is an **ethnographical museum** (open from 9 am to 3 pm, Thursday 9 am to 1 pm and 3 to 6 pm, closed Wednesday).

Hidden in the lower part of the citadel are the Teqja e Dollmës or **Bektashi Tekke** (1773), place of worship of a mystical Islamic sect, and the 16th-century **Turkish baths** (*hammam*), which are just below the tekke.

Between the citadel and Hotel Skënderbeu is Kruja's 18th-century **Turkish bazar**, which was later destroyed but has now been fully restored and made into a workplace for local artisans and craftspeople.

It's possible to climb to the top of the mountain above Kruja in an hour or so and it's even possible to hike back to Tirana along a path that begins near the citadel entrance.

Places to Stay & Eat

The four-storey *Hotel Skënderbeu* (☎ 529) is next to the equestrian statue of Skënderbeg near the terminus of the buses from Tirana. The 33 rooms are 750/1000 lekë for a single/double without bath and 1250/2500 lekë with bath. A speciality of the hotel restaurant is a mixed plate with skallop (beef in sauce), kanellane (minced meat wrapped in pastry) and qofte (a long, minced-meat patty).

The *Pestiqe* restaurant in the main street of the artisans' quarter is very good value for money and does nice meals in comfortable traditional surroundings, with chairs covered in woollen rugs.

The *Karakteristik* restaurant, just up the hill from the museum in the citadel, is also very cosy, but a little more expensive.

Getting There & Away

It's possible to visit Kruja by local bus as a day trip from Tirana (32 km). If there's no bus direct to Kruja, get a bus to Fush-Kruja where you'll find many buses to Kruja. For example, the Laç bus stops at Fush-Kruja. In the afternoon it's much easier to get back to Tirana from Kruja than vice versa.

LEZHA

It was at Lezha (Alessio) in March 1444 that Skënderbeg succeeded in convincing the Albanian feudal lords to unite in a League of Lezha

to resist the Turks. Skënderbeg died of fever here in 1468 and today his tomb may be visited among the ruins of the Franciscan **Church of St Nicholas**. Reproductions of his helmet and sword grace the gravestone and along the walls are 25 shields bearing the names and dates of battles he fought against the Turks.

Near the tomb, beside the grey apartment blocks, is the **Ethnographical Museum**, and on the hill top above is the medieval **Lezha Citadel**. Much of old Lezha was destroyed by an earthquake on 15 April 1979.

Places to Stay & Eat

The only real option is the state-run but still cosy *Hotel Gjuetisë*, commonly known as the Hunting Lodge. It is some five km off the main road at Ishull i Lezhës, a lagoon popular for bird-watching. Double rooms here go for 5000 lekë including breakfast. There is also a nice restaurant. The only disadvantage is the surly, state-appointed staff who seem to treat guests as annoyances.

Getting There & Away

There's a bus from Tirana to Lezha.

SHKODRA

Shkodra (also Shkodër and, in Italian, Scutari), the traditional centre of the Gheg cultural region, is one of the oldest cities in Europe. In 500 BC an Illyrian fortress already guarded the strategic crossing just west of the city where the Buna and Drin rivers meet and all traffic moving up the coast from Greece to Montenegro must pass. These rivers drain two of the Balkans' largest lakes: Shkodra, just northwest of the city, and Ohrid, far up the Drin River, beyond several massive hydroelectric dams. The route inland to Kosovo also begins in Shkodra. North of Shkodra, line after line of cement bunkers point the way to the Han i Hotit border crossing into Montenegro (33 km). Tirana is 116 km south.

In the 3rd century BC, Queen Teuta's Illyrian kingdom was centred here. Despite wars with Rome in 228 and 219 BC, Shkodra was not taken by the Romans until 168 BC. Later the region passed to Byzantium before becoming the capital of the feudal realm of the Balshas in 1350. In 1396 the Venetians occupied Shkodra's Rozafa Fortress, which they held against Suleiman Pasha in 1473 but lost

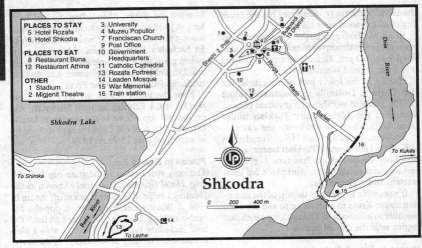

PLACES TO STAY
5 Hotel Rozafa
6 Hotel Shkodra

PLACES TO EAT
8 Restaurant Buna
12 Restaurant Athina

OTHER
1 Stadium
2 Migjenit Theatre
3 University
4 Muzeu Popullor
7 Franciscan Church
9 Post Office
10 Government Headquarters
11 Catholic Cathedral
13 Rozafa Fortress
14 Leaden Mosque
15 War Memorial
16 Train station

Shkodra Lake

Shkodra

0   200   400 m

To Shiroka

To Lezha

To Kukës

to Mehmet Pasha in 1479. The Turks lost 14,000 men in the first siege and 30,000 in the second.

As the Ottoman empire declined in the late 18th century, Shkodra became the centre of a semi-independent pashalik, which led to a blossoming of commerce and crafts. In 1913, Montenegro attempted to annex Shkodra (it succeeded in taking Ulcinj, but this was not recognised by the international community and the town changed hands often during WWI. Badly damaged by the 1979 earthquake, Shkodra was subsequently repaired and now, with a population of 81,000, is Albania's fourth-largest city.

Orientation & Information

From the Migjenit Theatre on the Five Heroes Roundabout, Rruga Marin Barleti (formerly Bulevardi Stalin) runs south-east past Hotel Rozafa and the post office. The post office faces north-east up Bulevardi 13 Dhjetori, a delightful old street lit by antique lamps in the evening and lined with harmonious buildings, many of which are now shops selling Albanian handicrafts. The train station is at the far south-east end of Rruga Marin Barleti, 1.5 km from the centre of town, whereas buses leave from around Migjenit Theatre.

Money Two adjacent banks on Bulevardi 13 Dhjetori change travellers' cheques for 1% commission (open weekdays 7 am to 1 pm). Otherwise look for moneychangers along the street between these banks and the post office.

Post & Communications The post office on Rruga Marin Barleti, across the square from the Rozafa Hotel, is open Monday to Saturday from 7 am to 2 pm, Sunday 8 am to noon. The telephone centre here operates around the clock.

The telephone code for Shkodra is ☎ 0224.

Things to See

Shkodra's skyline is dominated by the brand new and impressive **Sheik Zamil Abdullah Al-Zamil** mosque, completed in 1995. It stands next to the Muzeo Popullor on the corner of Rruga Marin Barleti and Bulevardi 13 Dhjetori. Its pastel façade and silver domes are very striking.

The **Muzeu Popullor**, in the eclectic palace (1860) of an English aristocrat opposite Hotel Rozafa, contains recent paintings and historic photos upstairs, and an excellent archaeological collection downstairs.

Shkodra was the most influential Catholic city of Albania, with a large cathedral and

Jesuit and Franciscan monasteries, seminaries and religious libraries. From 1967 to 1990 the **Franciscan Church** on Rruga Ndre Mjeda off Bulevardi 13 Dhjetori was used as an auditorium but now it's a church once again. Just inside is a photo exhibit of Shkodra priests who died in communist prisons. Note especially the photos of Catholic poet Gjergj Fishta (1871-1940), formerly buried here but whose bones were dug up and thrown in the Drin River during the Cultural Revolution. A few blocks south-east is the **Catholic cathedral** (1858), converted into a palace of sport by the communists and rededicated just in time for the papal visit in April 1993.

Rozafa Fortress Two km south-west of Shkodra, near the southern end of Lake Shkodra, is the Rozafa Fortress, founded by the Illyrians in antiquity and rebuilt much later by the Venetians and Turks. Upon entering the second enclosure you pass a ruined church (which was first converted into a mosque) and then reach a restored stone palace. From the highest point there's a marvellous view on all sides.

The fortress derived its name from a woman named Rozafa, who was allegedly walled into the ramparts as an offering to the gods so that the construction would stand. The story goes that Rozafa asked that two holes be left in the stonework so that she could continue to suckle her baby. Nursing women still come to the fortress to smear their breasts with milky water taken from a spring here.

Below the fortress is the many-domed **Leaden Mosque** (1774), the only Shkodra mosque to escape destruction in the 1967 Cultural Revolution. At **Shiroka**, seven km north of the Buna Bridge, there's a pleasant café beside Lake Shkodra.

Places to Stay
The *Hotel Shkodra*, Bulevardi 13 Dhjetori 14, has two sparse double rooms with shared bath at 100 lekë per person and three five-bed dormitories at 100 lekë per person. The old people who run this place in their old home are very friendly.

The city's main tourist hotel, where all tourists were required to stay until 1991, is the *Hotel Rozafa* (☎ 27 67), a nine-storey building

on the Five Heroes Roundabout. Rooms are 2000/4000 lekë for singles/doubles with bath, breakfast included.

The ramshackle *Hotel Kaduku* (☎ 22 16) can be hard to find but it's adequate and clean enough. It's right next to the Hotel Rozafa; look for the 'Dentist' sign. The owner charges 1500 lekë per person.

Places to Eat
Shkodra's best restaurant is the *Restaurant Athina*, a little way from the older part of town. The food is nominally Greek and is reasonably good value. The toilet has an electronic soap dispenser (!).

Restaurant Buna, close to the big mosque, is also very nice and a little more convenient to reach if you don't feel like walking.

Around sunset half the population of Shkodra go for a stroll along the lakeside promenade towards the Buna Bridge and there are several small restaurants where you can have fried fish, tomato salad and beer while observing the passing parade.

Getting There & Away
Buses to Tirana (frequent, 116 km, 110 lekë) and Durrës (infrequent, 124 km, 100 lekë) depart from near Migjenit Theatre, most reliably around 7 am and also at 1 pm.

Two direct daily trains from Shkodra to Tirana depart at 5 am and 1.15 pm (98 km, 3½ hours, 100 lekë). These trains don't pass Durrës. The train station is on the south-east side of town. Bus travel is more convenient, though perhaps less picturesque.

KUKËS
Kukës has perhaps the most beautiful location of any town in Albania, set high above Lake Fierza below the bald summit of Mt Gjalica (2486 metres). Old Kukës formerly stood at the junction of two important rivers, the White Drin from Kosovo and the Black Drin from Lake Ohrid, but beginning in 1962 the town was moved to its present location when it was decided that the 72-sq-km reservoir of the 'Light of the Party' hydroelectric dam would cover the old site. It's a pleasant place to get in tune with Albania if you've just arrived from Kosovo, and a good stop on your way around the country.

ALBANIA

Money
Cash changes hands among the trees at the market, not far from the bus stop.

Places to Stay & Eat
Cheapest is the *Hotel Gjalica*, an unmarked three-storey building on the nameless main street in the centre of town, opposite a place with the large yellow sign 'Fruta Perime'. A simple but adequate room with washbasin and lumpy, smelly bed will be 700 lekë per person.

For a room with private bath the price jumps to 2000 lekë per person at the four-storey *Hotel Drini* overlooking the lake on the same street as the post office.

One of Albania's finest hotels is the *Hotel Turizmi* (☎ 452), a five-storey cubist edifice on a peninsula jutting out into the lake, a five-minute walk from town. Rooms here are 3000 lekë per person – better value than the Drini.

All three hotels have restaurants but forget the wretched one at the Gjalica. The terrace at the Turizmi is great for a drink and their restaurant is the best in town. A few basic places near the market serve lunch.

Getting There & Away
Minibuses to Kukës from Tirana ✆ ave from the minibus stand near the guarded parking lot. The fare is 500 lekë per person and the trip takes 6½ hours with meal stops. Look for the KU license plates or ask.

Several buses to Tirana (208 km, 300 lekë) leave Kukës around 6 am. Getting to Shkodra (129 km, 200 lekë) is problematic; if you can't find a direct bus it's best to take the Tirana bus to Puka (60 km) and look for an onward bus from there.

Occasional buses run the 17 km from Kukës to the Yugoslav border at Morina. The Albanian and Yugoslav border posts are adjacent and once across it should be fairly easy to cover the remaining 18 km to Prizren by hitchhiking or taxi. Any Albanian books or newspapers will be confiscated by the Yugoslav border guards.

Southern Albania

The south of the country is rich in historical and natural beauty. Apollonia and Butrint are renowned classical ruins, while Berat and Gjirokastra are museum towns and strongholds of Tosk tradition. Korça is the cultural capital of the south, whereas Pogradec and Saranda, on Lake Ohrid and the Ionian Sea respectively, are undeveloped resort towns.

South-east of the vast, agricultural Myzaqeja plain, the land becomes extremely mountainous, with lovely valleys such as those of the Osum and Drino rivers, where Berat and Gjirokastra are situated. The 124 km of Ionian coast north from Saranda to Vlora are stunning, with 2000-metre mountains falling directly to the sea and not a hotel in sight.

The 115-km road from Tepelena to Korça is one of the most scenic in Albania. About 60 km from Tepelena it takes a sharp turn north at a small village and from here to Erseka there are many switchbacks. There are through buses from Korça to Gjirokastra and Saranda in the early morning. Because of the relatively light traffic this is one road that is in reasonable shape, though winter driving is not advised. You may be stopped by curious police on this section, probably more out of boredom than anything else. Bring your own food supplies since the towns along the way are not used to servicing travellers.

FIER & APOLLONIA
Fier is a large town by the Gjanica River at a junction of road and rail routes, 89 km south of Durrës. Albania's oil industry is centred at Fier, with a fertiliser plant, an oil refinery and a thermal power plant fuelled by natural gas. Fier has a pleasant riverside promenade.

Things to See
Visitors first reach Fier's imposing 13th-century Orthodox **Monastery of St Mary**. The icons in the church, the capitals in the narthex and the Byzantine murals in the adjacent refectory are outstanding. The monastery now houses an extremely rich **archaeological museum** (admission 100 lekë) with a large collection of ceramics and statuary from the ruins of Apollonia. Near the post office is a **historical museum** with well-presented exhibits covering the district's long history.

By far the most interesting sight in the vicinity is the ruins of ancient **Apollonia** (Pojan) 12 km west of Fier, set on a hill top surrounded by impressive bunkers. Apollonia was founded by Corinthian Greeks in 588 BC and quickly grew into an important city-state, minting its own currency. Under the Romans the city became a great cultural centre with a famous school of philosophy. Julius Caesar rewarded Apollonia with the title 'free city' for supporting him against Pompey the Great during a civil war in the 1st century BC and sent his nephew Octavius, the future Emperor Augustus, to complete his studies there. After a series of military disasters, the population moved south to present-day Vlora (the ancient Avlon), and by the 5th century only a small village with its own bishop remained at Apollonia.

Only a small part of ancient Apollonia has so far been uncovered. The first ruin to catch the eye is the roughly restored 2nd-century **bouleuterion**, or Hall of the Agonothetes. In front of it is the 2nd-century **odeon** (a small theatre). To the west of this is a long, 3rd-century BC **portico** with niches that once contained statues.

Apollonia's **defensive walls** are nearby. The lower portion of these massive walls, which are four km long and up to 6.5 metres high, date back to the 4th century BC.

Places to Stay & Eat

The six-storey *Hotel Fieri* (☎ 23 94), by the river, has 50 rooms, with prices ranging from 2000/2500 lekë to 5000/5500 lekë for singles/doubles, depending on the facilities provided. *Hotel Apollonia* (☎ 21 11), a somewhat run-down four-storey hotel across the street from the Fieri, has basic singles/doubles for 1600 lekë .

Hotel Fieri has a nice clean restaurant. The *Restorant Kosova* on the main square near Hotel Fieri is basic but OK. If you want a pizza or a hamburger, try the *Llapi*, also on the main square.

Getting There & Away

All buses between Tirana and Vlora or Gjirokastra pass this way and other buses run from Fier to Berat (42 km). There's also a daily train to/from Tirana (121 km, 4¼ hours).

Getting Around

There are village buses from Fier direct to Apollonia in the morning. You can also get there on the Seman bus but you'll have to walk

four km from the junction to the ruins. In Fier the Seman bus leaves from a place called Zogu i Zi near the Historical Museum, or from the train station.

VLORA

Vlora (Vlorë), the main port of southern Albania, sits on lovely Vlora Bay just across an 80-km strait from Otranto, Italy. Inexpensive ferries run between these towns three times a week, making Vlora a useful gateway to/from southern Italy. This is probably the only real reason to come here as Vlora's own attractions don't warrant a special trip.

Money

Moneychangers hang around the corner between Hotel Sazani and the post office. The Banka e Shtetit Shqiptar is a long block away, if you have travellers' cheques and are there on a weekday morning.

Things to See & Do

The **archaeological museum** is across the street from Hotel Sazani, and a house museum dedicated to the Laberia Patriotic Club (1908) is nearby.

In the park behind Hotel Sazani is a large stone **monument** commemorating the proclamation of an independent Albania at Vlora in 1912. A block south of this monument is the well-preserved **Murad Mosque** (1542). In 1480 and 1536 the Turks used Vlora as a base for unsuccessful invasions of Italy.

A **war cemetery** on the hillside directly opposite the 1912 monument overlooks the town and from the cemetery a road winds around to the Liria Café, on a hill top with a sweeping view of the entire vicinity – a good place for a drink at sunset. A stone stairway descends directly back to town from the café.

You can take a bus from the 1912 monument down Vlora's main street to the south end of the **city beach** every half-hour.

Places to Stay & Eat

Accommodation choices in Vlora are limited. The best option is the *Kompleksi Turistik VEFA* (☎ 063-24 179), on the beach about eight km south of Vlora. This modern complex provides motel-style rooms and has a nice restaurant and guarded parking. Prices are 3000 lekë per person including breakfast.

The very run-down three-storey *Hotel Sazani* (☎ 063-31 52), near the post office and market in the centre of town, will start off asking 1000 lekë per person for a basic room with shared bath, but try bargaining. The buffet at the Sazani serves reasonable meals (with beer).

Hotel Meeting on Rruga Jonaq Kilica, opposite the Halim Dhelo school, has been recommended by one traveller who was charged 1200 lekë for a double room without a bath.

There are a number of very pleasant restaurants in and around the central area near Hotel Sazani, as well as any number of beachside restaurants on the south side of town.

Getting There & Away
There are daily trains to Tirana (155 km, 5½ hours) and Durrës but buses are more frequent and convenient. Unfortunately, no bus runs the full length of the spectacular 124-km Riviera of Flowers – you can only get as far as Himara, from where you will need to take a taxi onwards. The early morning bus to Saranda takes a roundabout 190-km route through Fier, Tepelena and Gjirokastra.

If you're interested in taking the Linee Lauro ferry to Otranto, Italy (three times a week, 100 km, 4500 lekë), pick up tickets beforehand at Albania Travel & Tours in Tirana. The Otranto agent is listed in the introductory Getting There & Away section earlier this chapter. This is probably the cheapest way to cross the Adriatic.

SARANDA
Saranda (Sarandë) is an animated town on the Gulf of Saranda, between the mountains and the Ionian Sea, 61 km south-west of Gjirokastra. An early Christian monastery here dedicated to 40 saints (Santi Quaranta) gave Saranda its name. This southernmost harbour of Albania was once the ancient port of Onchesmos. Saranda's pebble beach is nothing special although the setting of the town is nice. Today, Saranda's main attractions are its sunny climate and the nearby ruins of Butrint. It is also a very convenient entry and exit point for travellers arriving in Albania via Corfu in Greece.

Orientation & Information
Saranda is spread out around a bay. Most tourist accommodation and eating places are on the south side of the bay. The main bus station is right in the centre of town, about 200 metres back from the waterfront. Taxis congregate on the main square in front of the town hall, which is 200 metres south of the bus station. The ferry terminal is at the north end of the bay.

Money There are two banks on the main street, but the simplest and best way to change money is to use the money changers behind the town hall on the main square.

Post & Communications The most efficient way to call home from Saranda is to use the informal cellular phone entrepreneurs who congregate around the little boat harbour. A quick and easy-to-make call to the US or Australia will cost you 250 lekë a minute. Calls are routed via Greece.

Things to See
Saranda's palm-fringed waterfront promenade is attractive and is gradually livening up, with new restaurants and bars opening every month. In the centre of town are some ancient ruins with a large mosaic covered with sand. Ask around town if you are interested in seeing the recently discovered **catacombs** of the Church of the 40 Saints. The **Blue Eye spring**, 15 km east of Saranda, to the left off the Gjirokastra road and before the ascent over the pass to the Drino valley, is definitely worth seeing. Its iridescent blue water gushes from the depths of the earth and feeds the Bistrica River. French divers have descended to a depth of 70 metres, but its actual depth is still unknown.

Places to Stay & Eat
The seven-storey, state-run *Hotel Butrinti* (☎ 417), overlooking the harbour just south of town, has single/double/triple rooms for 3000/4500/5000 lekë. Like most state-run hotels, the place is run-down and not all that appealing.

Just 100 metres north is the attractive but pricey *Kaoni Villa* (mobile phone ☎ 30 94 348 921). Single/double rates here are 4500/6000 lekë for spacious rooms with shared bathroom. Look for the big green gates. About 500 metres south of Hotel Butrinti is the attractively sited

Hotel Delfini, with rooms overlooking the water. Rates are 3500 lekë per room. The Delfini also has a very pleasant restaurant.

The *Halyl Hyseni* hotel (really just private rooms) on Rruga Adam Sheme has very comfortable single/doubles for 4000/4500 lekë, with private bathroom and TV. It is about 150 metres inland from the waterfront. The rooms suffer from some street noise. The rooms of *Panayot Qyro* (☎ 25 64) further up the same street are basic but clean and have a modern communal bathroom. Single/double/triple rates are 500/1000/1500 lekë. Look for the blue railings of the electricity sub-station. The rooms are right opposite.

The *Paradise Restaurant* close to Hotel Butrinti has excellent food and the service is top notch. The *Three Roses* restaurant in the middle of Saranda is another good place to eat. It is set back from the waterfront on the 2nd floor of a big building. Look for the prominent sign.

Getting There & Away

Buses to Saranda from both Tirana and Vlora follow an interior route via Gjirokastra; unfortunately, no buses connect Saranda with Himara, north along the coast. A taxi to Himara should cost about 3000 lekë one way or 4000 lekë return. From Himara there is a daily bus to Vlora. Several buses to Gjirokastra (62 km) and Tirana (289 km) leave Saranda in the morning.

Three daily passenger ferries cross between Corfu and Saranda. One of the ferries takes up to five cars. The *Harikla* leaves Saranda at 10 am; the *Oleg Volvaç* leaves at 1 pm; the car-carrying *Kamelia* leaves at 2 pm. The crossing takes 60 to 90 minutes. One-way fares cost 1600 lekë. Taking a car costs 4000 lekë.

BUTRINT

The ancient ruins of Butrint, 18 km south of Saranda, are surprisingly extensive and interesting. Virgil claimed that the Trojans founded Buthroton (Butrint), but no evidence of this has been found. Although the site had been inhabited long before, Greeks from Corfu settled on the hill in Butrint in the 6th century BC. Within a century Butrint had become a fortified trading city with an acropolis. The lower town began to develop in the 3rd century BC and many large stone buildings existed when the

Romans took over in 167 BC. Butrint's prosperity continued throughout the Roman period and the Byzantines made it an ecclesiastical centre. Then the city declined; it was almost abandoned when Italian archaeologists arrived in 1927 and began carting off any relics of value to Italy until WWII interrupted their work. In recent years the Italian government has returned some important Butrint sculptures to Albania. These are now in Tirana's National Museum of History.

There are two buses daily to Butrint, leaving Saranda at 6.30 am and noon.

Things to See

The site (open daily 7 am to 2 pm, 200 lekë) lies by a channel connecting salty Lake Butrint to the sea. A triangular **fortress** erected by warlord Ali Pasha Tepelena in the early 19th century watches over the ramshackle vehicular ferry that crosses the narrow channel.

In the forest below the acropolis is Butrint's 3rd-century BC **Greek theatre**, which was also in use during the Roman period. Nearby are the small **public baths**, which have geometrical mosaics. Deeper in the forest is a wall covered with crisp Greek inscriptions, and a 6th-century palaeo-Christian **baptistry** decorated with colourful mosaics of animals and birds. The mosaics are covered by protective sand. Beyond a 6th-century basilica stands a massive **Cyclopean wall** dating from the 4th century BC. Over one gate is a splendid relief of a lion killing a bull, symbolic of a protective force vanquishing assailants.

In a crenellated brick building on top of the acropolis is a **museum** (if it is open) full of statuary from the site. There are good views from the terrace.

GJIROKASTRA

This strikingly picturesque museum town, midway between Fier and Ioannina, is like an Albanian eagle perched on the mountainside with a mighty citadel for its head. The fortress surveys the Drino Valley above the three and four-storey tower houses clinging to the slopes. Both buildings and streets are made of the same white-and-black stone. For defence purposes during blood feuds, these unique stone-roofed houses *(kulla)* had no windows on the ground floor, which was used for storage, and the living quarters above were reached by an exterior stairway.

The town's Greek name, Argyrokastro, is said to refer to a Princess Argyro, who chose to throw herself from a tower rather than fall into the hands of enemies, though it's more likely to be derived from the Illyrian Argyres tribe which inhabited these parts.

Gjirokastra was well established by the 13th century, but the arrival of the Turks in 1417 brought on a decline. By the 17th century Gjirokastra was thriving again with a flourishing bazar where embroidery, felt, silk and the still-famous white cheese were traded. Ali Pasha Tepelena took the town in the early 19th century and strengthened the citadel. Today all new buildings must conform to a historical preservation plan.

Things to See

Above the **Bazar Mosque** (1757) in the centre of town is the **Mëmëdheu ABC Monument**, commemorating the renaissance of Albanian education around the turn of the century. The monument, which you may have to ask directions to find, affords an excellent view of the town.

Dominating the town is the 14th-century **citadel**, now a Museum of Armaments (8 am to noon and 4 to 7 pm, closed Monday and Tuesday, 200 lekë), with a collection of old cannons and guns and a two-seater US reconnaissance plane that made a forced landing near Berat in 1957. During the 1920s the fortress was converted into a prison and the Nazis made full use of it during their stay in 1943-44. Do not miss visiting the prison: the water torture cells are particularly grim.

A National Folk Festival used to be held every five years in the open-air theatre beside the citadel but the last one was in 1988 and now the festival rotates round various cities in the country.

Enver Hoxha was born in 1908 in the winter room of his family home, among the narrow cobbled streets of the Palorto quarter, up Rruga Bashkim Kokona beyond the Gjimnazi Asim Zeneli. The original house burned down in 1916, but the building was reconstructed in 1966 as a Museum of the National Liberation War and now houses the **Ethnographic Museum** (100 lekë).

The 17th-century **Turkish baths** are below the Çayupi Hotel in the lower town, near the polyclinic. The remnants of the **Mecate Mosque** are nearby. Gjirokastra has a lively Sunday market.

Places to Stay & Eat

The **Çayupi Hotel** is another run-down former state enterprise. It is located prominently on the main taxi square, just before the old town. Single/double rooms with bath go for 2500/3500 lekë.

Two cheaper hotels are nearby and they're always worth a try. The **Argjiro Hotel** is right next to the Çayupi. A very basic single/double room goes for 700/1400 lekë with shared, smelly toilets. Across the street is the **Hotel Sapoti** with similarly basic single/double rooms for 600/1200 lekë.

By far the most accommodating place to stay is the rooms of **Haxhi Kotoni**. Very cosy single/double rooms cost 2000/3000 lekë, including breakfast. The 'Bing Crosby' suite is a sight to behold. To reach the rooms, bear left by the mosque and after 50 metres take a sharp right turn downwards. You will find a sign on the wall on your left after about another 50 metres.

Eating places are thin on the ground in Gjirokastra. The **Argjiro Restaurant** next to the hotel of the same name is about as cheap and convenient as you will get. On the hill high above the town is the **Tourist Restaurant** with a great view but higher prices. Follow the road past the Kotoni rooms to walk to it in about 20 minutes.

Getting There & Away

Gjirokastra is on the main bus route from Tirana to Kakavija and Saranda. Most through buses stop on the main highway below Gjirokastra though some buses depart from the Çayupi Hotel below the citadel, including one to Tirana at 5 am.

BERAT

Although not as enchanting as Gjirokastra, Berat deserves its status as Albania's second most important museum town. Berat is sometimes called the 'city of a thousand windows' for the many openings in the white-plastered red-roofed houses on terraces overlooking the Osum River. Along a ridge high above the gorge is a 14th-century citadel that shelters small Orthodox churches. On the slope below this, all the way down to the river, is Mangalem, the old Muslim quarter. A seven-arched stone bridge (1780) leads to Gorica, the Christian quarter.

In the 3rd century BC an Illyrian fortress called Antipatria was built here on the site of an earlier settlement. The Byzantines strengthened the hill-top fortifications in the 5th and 6th centuries, as did the Bulgarians 400 years later. The Serbs, who occupied the citadel in 1345, renamed it Beligrad, or 'White City', which has become today's Berat. In 1450 the Ottoman Turks took Berat. The town revived in the 18th and 19th centuries as a Turkish crafts centre specialising in woodcarving. For a brief time in 1944, Berat was the capital of liberated Albania. Today, most of Albania's crude oil is extracted from wells just northwest of the city, but Berat itself is a textile town with a mill once known as Mao Zedong.

Things to See

On the square in front of Hotel Tomori is a white hall where the National Liberation Council met from 20 to 23 October 1944 and formed a Provisional government of Albania, with Enver Hoxha as prime minister. It is now a billiard hall. Beyond this is the **Leaden Mosque** (1555), named for the material covering its great dome. Under the communists it was turned into a museum of architecture, but it is now a mosque again.

Follow the busy street north towards the citadel and after a few blocks, behind the market building, you'll reach the **King's Mosque** (1512), formerly the Archaeological Museum. Inside is a fine wooden gallery for female worshippers and across the courtyard is the **Alveti Tekke** (1790), a smaller shrine where Islamic sects such as the Dervishes were once based.

By the nearby river is the Margarita Tutulani Palace of Culture, a theatre worth checking for events. Beyond this is the **Bachelor's Mosque** (1827), now a folk-art museum (open Tuesday and Thursday only). A shop downstairs sells cassettes of Albanian folk music.

Continue on towards the old stone bridge (1780) and you'll see the 14th-century **Church of St Michael** high up on the hillside, below the citadel. In Mangalem, behind the Bachelor's Mosque, is the **Muzeu i Luftes** (closed Monday),

which is worth seeing as much for its old Berati house as for its exhibits on the partisan struggle during WWII. Beyond the bank on the stone road leading up towards the citadel is the **Muzeu Etnografik** (open Wednesday and Friday only) in another fine old building.

After entering the **citadel** through its massive gate, continue straight ahead on the main street and you will see the sign to the **Muzeu Onufri** (open daily from 9 am to 3 pm, 200 lekë). This museum and the **Orthodox Cathedral of Our Lady** (1797) are both within the monastery walls. The wooden iconostasis (1850) and pulpit in the cathedral are splendid. The museum has a large collection of icons, including many by the famous mid-16th century artist after whom the museum is named. Onufri's paintings are more realistic, dramatic and colourful than those of his predecessors.

Other churches in the citadel include the 14th-century **Church of the Holy Trinity** (Shen Triadhes), on the west side near the walls. Its exterior is impressive but the frescos inside are badly damaged. The 16th-century **Church of the Evangelists** is most easily found by following the eastern citadel wall. At the south end of the citadel is a rustic **tavern** and battlements offering splendid views of Gorica and the modern city.

Places to Stay

The five-storey *Hotel Tomori* (☎ 062-32 462) is named after Mt Tomori (2416 metres), which towers above Berat to the east. The hotel is by the river on the east side of town. It has no lift but the balcony views of the riverside park compensate for the climb. The 56 rooms are 3000/5000 lekë for a single/double with bath and breakfast included. The hotel sign lacks the word 'Tomori'.

The *Hotel Gega* was being renovated but should have reopened by the time you read this. It's a couple of hundred metres east of the Leaden Mosque along the main street.

The basic *Hotel Dyrmo* has three rooms with a bath. They charge 500/1000 lekë for a single/double. It is just back from the west end of the main street. Ask at the restaurant if no-one is around.

Places to Eat

The *Iliri Restorant* alongside the river has good food and a nice upstairs balcony. The atmosphere, however, can get a little rowdy at times. The cosy little *Onufri Restorant*, very close to the Onufri Museum in the citadel, is very good value for money.

Getting There & Away

The bus station is next to the Leaden Mosque near Hotel Tomori. A bus from Tirana to Berat (122 km) takes three hours, a little long for a day trip. Buses to Fier (47 km) and Tirana are fairly frequent and some buses run from Berat direct to Gjirokastra (120 km). Minibus taxis also run from here to Fier, Tirana and Gjirokastra, and to places south of Berat.

ELBASAN

Elbasan is on the Shkumbin River, midway between Durrës and Pogradec and 54 km south-east of Tirana. It has been prominent since 1974, when the Chinese built the mammoth 'Steel of the Party' steel mill. It also has a cement factory and burgeoning pollution, though the old town retains a certain charm. With 83,000 inhabitants, Elbasan is Albania's third-largest city, having more than doubled in size since 1970.

The Romans founded Skampa (Elbasan) in the 1st century AD as a stopping point on the Via Egnatia. Stout stone walls with 26 towers were added in the 4th century to protect against invading barbarians. The Byzantines continued this trend, also making Skampa the seat of a bishopric. In 1466, Sultan Mohammed II rebuilt the walls as a check against Skënderbeg at Kruja and renamed the town El Basan ('The Fortress' in Turkish). Elbasan was an important trade and handicrafts centre throughout the Turkish period.

Elbasan can be visited as a day trip from Tirana and the drive across the mountains is spectacular. Look out for the Citadel of Petrela, which stands on a hill top above the Erzen River.

Things to See

The 17th-century **Turkish baths** are in the centre of town, beside Hotel Skampa. Directly across the park on the other side of the hotel is Sejdini House, a typical 19th-century Balkan building, now the **Ethnographical Museum**.

Opposite the hotel are the **city walls**, erected by the Turks and still relatively intact on the south and west sides. Go through the **Bazar Gate** near the clock tower and follow a road directly north past the 15th-century **King's Mosque** to **St Mary's Orthodox Church**, which has a fine stone arcade on each exterior side and a gilded pulpit and iconostasis inside. This church is usually locked to prevent theft but it's worth asking around for the person with the key (who will expect a tip). Visible from behind St Mary's is a large Catholic church (closed). On the west city wall is a museum dedicated to the partisan war.

Places to Stay & Eat

The eight-storey *Hotel Skampa* (☎ 22 40) has 112 rooms at 2150/3820 lekë for a single/double with bath. It also has an OK restaurant downstairs.

The *Restaurant Universi*, about 200 metres west of Hotel Skampa, is another eating option. It is clean and prices are low. Failing that there are any number of snack bars or hamburger stands along or opposite the city walls nearby.

Getting There & Away

All buses to/from Pogradec (86 km) pass through here but they arrive full. Getting a bus to Tirana is easier and there are also minibus taxis, departing from the parking lot next to the Skampa Hotel.

The train station is about five blocks from the Skampa Hotel. There are trains to Tirana and Durrës three times a day.

POGRADEC

Pogradec is a pleasant beach resort at the southern end of Lake Ohrid, 140 km south-east of Tirana. The 700-metre elevation gives the area a brisk, healthy climate and the scenery is beautiful. Pogradec is much less developed than the Macedonian lake towns of Ohrid and Struga. The nearby border crossing at Svet Naum makes Pogradec a natural gateway to/from Macedonia.

Places to Stay & Eat

The eight-storey *Guri i Kuq Hotel* (☎ 414) opposite the post office, is named after the 'red-stone' mountain on the west side of the lake where nickel and chrome ore are extracted. Rooms are 1250/2500 lekë for a single/double with bath.

A much cheaper place to stay is the old privately operated *Hotel Turizmi i Vjetar* o the beach about 200 yards west of the Guri i Kuq.

The private *Hotel Koço Llakmani* is essentially private rooms above a restaurant/bar of the same name. It is on the little square 100 metres west of the Guri i Kuq Hotel. Just round the corner is the *Greek Taverna* which has very little Greek about it but serves excellent Ohrid trout at a third the price you'd pay in Ohrid.

Facing the lakeshore a km east of the centre is the *Shtepia e Pushimit te Ushterakëve* (☎ 348), formerly a military officers' holiday resort. In early 1996 it was undergoing renovation, but it should be open as a hotel by the time you read this.

Getting There & Away
The train station, with two daily services to Tirana (189 km, seven hours) and Durrës, is near the mineral-processing factory, about four km from the Guri i Kuq Hotel. Buses run to Tirana (140 km), Korça (46 km) and other towns.

Macedonia It's fairly easy to hitch the six km east from Pogradec to the Tushemisht border post with Macedonia. Halfway is Drilon, a well-known tourist picnic spot, then the lakeside road goes through Tushemisht village and along the hillside to the border crossing. On the Macedonian side is the monastery of Sveti Naum, where there is a bus to Ohrid (29 km), and a boat service in summer.

Tushemisht is a much better crossing for pedestrians and private cars than the Qafa e Thanës border crossing on the west side of the lake, which is used mostly by trucks and other commercial vehicles.

KORÇA
The main city of the south-eastern interior, Korça sits on a 869-metre-high plateau west of Florina, Greece, 39 km south of Lake Ohrid. Under the Turks, Korça was a major trading post and carpet-making town – it's still Albania's biggest carpet and rug-producing centre. Although it is in the heart of a rich agricultural area, Korça saw hard times in the late 19th and early 20th centuries and became a centre of emigration. Albanians abroad often regard Korça as home and quite a few still come back to retire here. Moneychangers work the street just west of Hotel Iliria.

Things to See
The **Muzeu Historik** is in the old two-storey building on Bulevardi Themistokli Gërmenji behind Hotel Iliria. Further up the boulevard on the left is the **Muzeu i Arsimit Kombëtar**, or Education Museum (open Tuesday, Thursday and Sunday only), housed in the first school to teach in the Albanian language (in 1887). Nearby at the top of the boulevard is the **statue of the National Warrior** (1932) by Odhise Paskali.

Delve into the small streets behind this statue and veer left to find the former **Muzeu i Artet Mesjetar Shqiptar** (Museum of Albanian Medieval Art), once the most important of Korça's museums, with several icons by Onufri. In a striking reversal of roles, Orthodox Albanians have recently taken over the modern museum building and turned it into a church to replace their original place of worship, which was destroyed by the communists.

Much of the old city centre was gouged out by urban renewal after devastating earthquakes in 1931 and 1960 which toppled the minarets and flattened the churches. Some of the colour of old Korça still remains in the Oriental-style **bazar area** west of Hotel Iliria. Walk the crumbling cobbled streets lined with quaint old shops and swing south to the **Mirahorit Mosque** (1485), one of the oldest in Albania.

Places to Stay & Eat
The eight-storey *Hotel Iliria* (☎ 0824-31 68) costs 1600/2600 lekë for a single/double without bath, 3000/4800 lekë with bath. Breakfast is included.

Among Korça's hotels catering mostly to Albanians is the friendly *Hotel Pallas*, on Bulevardi Themistokli Gërmenji just up from Hotel Iliria. On the opposite side of the same building is the *Hotel Gramosi* (it has no sign, so just ask). The prices asked of foreigners at these places varies, but for Albanians it's considerably cheaper.

Rozetta Qirjako and her husband Niko are a friendly couple and will take people in for about 1000 lekë per person. Their address is Rruga Dhori Lako L1, No 8. Niko is also a mechanic.

The **Alfa Restaurant** close to the above hotels is a good place to eat, otherwise Hotel Iliria has a restaurant. **Dolce Vita** on Bulevardi Republike offers fine Italian food and a surreal ambience. It's open until 11 pm.

Getting There & Away

There are buses to/from Tirana (179 km) via Elbasan. Korça is a gateway to Albania for anyone arriving from Florina, Greece, via the Kapshtica border crossing 28 km east. Buses to Kapshtica leave when full throughout the day from near Skënderbeg Stadium at the east end of Bulevardi Republike. From Kapshtica it's 65 km to Florina, a major Greek city with good connections to/from Thessaloniki.

Andorra

The princedom of Andorra, covering just 468 sq km, is nestled between France and Spain in the midst of the Pyrenees. Though it *is* tiny, this political anomaly is at the heart of some of the most dramatic scenery in Europe.

Once a real backwater, Andorra has developed since the 1950s as a skiing centre and duty-free shopping haven, bringing not only wealth and foreign workers but also some unsightly development around the capital, Andorra la Vella. Until 1993, the country was a 'co-princedom' with its sovereignty invested in two 'princes': the Catholic bishop of the Spanish town of La Seu d'Urgell and the French president (who inherited the job from France's pre-Revolutionary kings). This arrangement dated back some seven centuries. Now Andorra has a constitution which puts full control in the hands of its people. The elected parliament, the Consell General (General Council), has 28 members, four from each parish. Andorra is not a member of the European Union (EU).

Andorrans form only about a quarter of Andorra's total population (65,000) and are outnumbered by Spaniards. The official language is Catalan, which is related to both Spanish and French. Most people speak a couple of these languages, sometimes all three.

Facts for the Visitor

VISAS & EMBASSIES
You do not need a visa to visit Andorra, but you must carry your passport or national identity card. Andorra does not have any diplomatic missions abroad, but Spain and France have embassies in Andorra la Vella.

MONEY
Andorra, which has no currency of its own, uses both the French franc and the Spanish peseta. Except in Pas de la Casa on the French border, prices are usually given in pesetas. It's best to use pesetas: the exchange rate for francs in shops and restaurants is seldom in your favour. See the France and Spain chapters for exchange rates.

1FF = 24.50 ptas
100 ptas = 4.08FF

Andorra's very low tax regime has made it a famous duty-free bazar for electronic goods, cameras, alcohol, etc. Today prices for these things no longer justify a special trip, but if you're prepared to shop around, you can find some cameras or electronic goods about 20% or 30% cheaper than in France or Spain. There are limits on what you can take out of Andorra duty-free – tourist offices have details.

POST & COMMUNICATIONS
Post
Andorra has no postal system of its own; France and Spain each operate separate systems with their own Andorran stamps.

ANDORRA

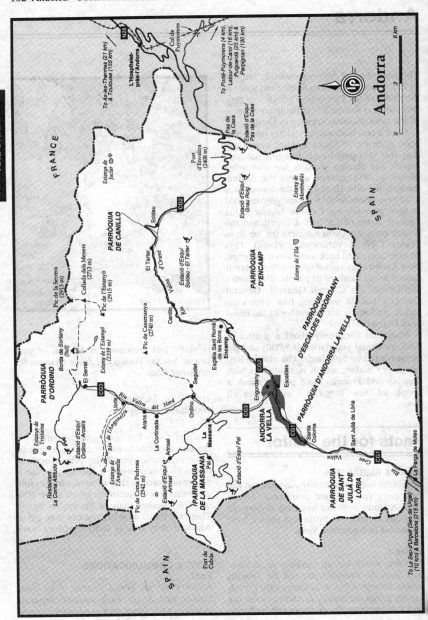

Andorra

Andorran stamps of both types are valid only for mail posted in Andorra and are needed only for international mail – letters within the country are free and do not need stamps. Regular French and Spanish stamps cannot be used in Andorra.

Postal rates are the same as those of the issuing country, with the French tariffs slightly cheaper. You are better off routing all international mail (except letters to Spain) through the French postal system. Poste restante mail to Andorra la Vella goes to the French post office there.

Telephone

Andorra's country code is ☎ 376. To call Andorra from any other country, dial the international access code, then ☎ 376, then the six-digit local number. To call other countries from Andorra, dial ☎ 00, then the country code, area code and local number.

Public telephones take pesetas (francs in Pas de la Casa) or an Andorran *teletarja*, which works like telephone cards in most European countries. Teletarges (plural) worth 500 and 900 ptas are sold at post offices, tourist offices and some shops. Andorra does *not* have reverse-charge (collect) calling facilities.

TIME & ELECTRICITY

Andorra is one hour ahead of GMT/UTC in winter and two hours ahead from the last Sunday in March to the last Sunday in September. Electric current is either 220V or 125V, both at 50 Hz.

HEALTH & EMERGENCY

Medical care has to be paid for. For emergency medical help, call ☎ 116; for an ambulance ☎ 118; for the police ☎ 110.

BUSINESS HOURS

Shops in Andorra la Vella are open daily from 9.30 am to 1 pm and 3.30 to 8 pm, except (in most cases) Sunday afternoon.

ACTIVITIES

Above the main valleys where most people live is plenty of high, attractive, lake-dotted mountain country, good for skiing in winter and walking in summer. Some peaks remain snow-capped until July or even later. Tourist offices give out a useful English-language booklet,

Sport Activities, describing numerous walking and mountain-bike routes. In summer, mountain bikes can be rented at several places for around 2500 ptas a day.

Hiking

There are some beautiful hiking areas in the north and north-west of Andorra (see the Parròquia d'Ordino section for more information). Several long-distance walking routes, including the Spanish GR11 and the mainly French Haute Randonnée Pyrenéenne, which both traverse the Pyrenees from the Mediterranean to the Atlantic, cross the country. The best season for hiking is June to September, when temperatures climb well into the 20s in the day, though they drop to around 10°C at night. June can be wet.

A 1:25,000-scale *mapa topogràfic* of the country costs 1200 ptas in bookshops and tourist offices. Maps at 1:10,000 (10 cm = 1 km) are also available. Hikers can sleep for free in more than two dozen *refugi* (mountain huts).

Skiing

Andorra has the best inexpensive skiing and snowboarding in the Pyrenees. The season lasts from December to April (snow cover permitting). For information on the five downhill ski areas (*estacós d'esquí*), ask at one of the capital's tourist offices or contact Ski Andorra (☎ 864389). The largest and best resorts are Soldeu-El Tarter and Pas de la Casa/Grau Roig, but the others – Ordino-Arcalís, Arinsal and Pal – are a bit cheaper. Ski passes cost 2500 to 3700 ptas a day, depending on the location and season; ski-gear rental is around 1500 ptas a day.

ACCOMMODATION

There are no youth hostels, but plenty of camping grounds, hotels and cheaper *pensiós, residèncias*, etc. Prices in many places are the same year-round, though some go up in August and/or at Christmas, Easter and the height of the ski season.

The 26 mountain refuges have bunks and fireplaces, and all except one are free. Nearly all have drinking water. Tourist offices have more info, and maps indicating their locations.

ANDORRA

Getting There & Away

The only way into Andorra is by road. If you're coming from France, you won't soon forget Port d'Envalira (2408 metres), the highest pass in the Pyrenees. The municipal tourist office in Andorra la Vella has bus timetables and knows ticket office hours.

From France, by public transport you need to approach by train and then get a bus for the final leg. The nearest station is L'Hospitalet-près-l'Andorre, two hours from Toulouse by four daily trains (102 FF). The two daily buses between L'Hospitalet and Plaça Guillemó in Andorra la Vella (1½ to 2¼ hours, 925 ptas) connect with trains.

From Barcelona, Alsina Graells runs five buses daily to and from Andorra la Vella's Estació d'Autobusos on Carrer Bonaventura Riberaygua (four hours, 2500 ptas). Other services to/from the Estació d'Autobusos include: Tarragona daily (four hours, 1260 ptas); Zaragoza and Madrid Estación Sur (8½ hours, 4300 ptas), three per week; Burgos, Valladolid and Tuy, two per week. There are up to eight buses daily between La Seu d'Urgell and Plaça Guillemó in Andorra la Vella (30 minutes, 315 ptas).

The nearest Spanish train station to Andorra is Puigcerdà. The first two trains from Barcelona's Estació Sants (6.15 and 9.18 am) get you to Puigcerdà in time to reach Andorra la Vella (with a change of bus at La Seu d'Urgell) the same day – a trip of about 6½ hours in total for about 2000 ptas.

Getting Around

BUS

Cooperativa Interurbana (☎ 820412) runs eight bus lines along the three main highways from Andorra la Vella. Autobus Parroquial de La Massana i d'Ordino operates a few services from La Massana. The municipal tourist office in Andorra la Vella has timetables. Destinations from Andorra la Vella include Ordino (125 ptas), daily every 20 or 30 minutes from 7.30 am to 8.30 pm; Arinsal (175 ptas) three times daily; Soldeu (325 ptas) hourly from 9

am to 8 pm; Pas de la Casa (560 ptas) at 9 am. Buses to all these places leave from the Plaça Príncep Benlloch stop in Andorra la Vella.

CAR & MOTORCYCLE

With all the twists and turns, it's almost impossible to reach the inter-hamlet speed limit of 90 km/h. The biggest problems are Andorra la Vella's traffic jams and the ever-vigilant parking officers. If you don't buy a coupon (available from machines everywhere) and place it on the dashboard, you will be fined for sure.

Petrol in Andorra is about 15% cheaper than in Spain and 25% cheaper than in France.

Andorra la Vella

Andorra la Vella (Vella is pronounced 'VEY-yah'; population 22,000) is in the Riu Valira valley at an elevation of just over 1000 metres. The town is given over almost entirely to retailing of electronic and luxury goods. With its mountains, constant din of jack-hammers and 'mall' architecture, travellers familiar with Asia may be reminded of Hong Kong. The only differences seem to be the snow-capped peaks and lack of noodle shops!

Orientation

Andorra la Vella is strung out along the main drag, called Avinguda Meritxell in the east and Avinguda Príncep Benlloch in the west. The tiny historic quarter (Barri Antic) lies south-west of Plaça Príncep Benlloch. The town merges with the once-separate villages of Escaldes and Engordany to the east and Santa Coloma to the south-west.

Information

Tourist Offices The helpful municipal tourist office (Oficina d'Informació i Turisme; ☎ 827117), on Plaça de la Rotonda, has maps, all sorts of brochures, stamps and telephone cards. It's open daily from 9 am to 1 pm and 3.30 to 8 pm (on Sunday to 7 pm). In July and August it foregoes the afternoon break.

The national tourist office (Sindicat d'Iniciativa Oficina de Turisme; ☎ 820214) is on Carrer Doctor Vilanova just down from

Plaça Rebés; it's open Monday to Saturday from 10 am (9 am from July to September) to 1 pm and 3 to 7 pm, and on Sunday mornings.

Money Banks are open weekdays from 9 am to 1 pm and 3 to 5 pm and on Saturday to noon. There are banks every 100 metres or so along Avinguda Meritxell and Avinguda Príncep Benlloch in the town centre, most with ATMs. American Express is represented by Viatges Relax (☎ 822044) at Carrer Roc dels Escolls 12. It doesn't change money but can replace American Express cards and travellers' cheques, and sell travellers' cheques against card-holders' personal cheques.

Post & Communications The main French post office (La Poste) is at Carrer Pere d'Urg 1. It is open Monday to Friday from 8.30 am to 2.30 pm (to 7 pm in July and August), Saturday from 9 am to noon. Payment is in French francs only.

The main Spanish post office (Correus i Telègrafs) is nearby at Carrer Joan Maragall 10. It's open Monday to Friday from 8.30 am to 2.30 pm, and Saturday from 9.30 am to 1 pm, and only accepts pesetas.

You can make international telephone calls from street pay phones.

Medical Services The main hospital is the modern Hospital Nostra Senyora de Meritxell (☎ 868000) at Avinguda Fiter i Rossell 1-13, about 1.5 km east of Plaça Guillemó.

Things to See & Do

Casa de la Vall Built in 1580 as a private home, Casa de la Vall (☎ 829129), on Carrer de la Vall in the Barri Antic, has been the seat of Andorra's parliament and its forerunners for almost three centuries. Downstairs is the Sala de la Justicia, the only courtroom in the whole country. Free guided tours (sometimes in English) are given about once an hour on weekdays from 9 am to 1 pm and 3 to 7 pm: you should book a week ahead to ensure a place, but individuals can sometimes join a group at the last minute.

Caldea Caldea (☎ 865777) in Escaldes is an enormous spa complex of pools, hot tubs and saunas fed by thermal springs, all enclosed in

what looks like a futuristic cathedral. Three-hour tickets (2000 ptas) are available from the tourist offices. Caldea is just east of Avinguda Fiter i Rossell, the continuation of Avinguda Doctor Mitjavila, a two-km walk from Plaça Guillemó.

Places to Stay

Camping About 1.5 km south-west of Plaça Guillemó on Avinguda de Salou, *Camping Valira* (☎ 822384) charges 500 ptas per person and the same for a tent and for a car. It's open all year, and has a heated covered swimming pool.

Hotels – Plaça Guillemó & Barri Antic At Carrer La Llacuna 21, just off Plaça Guillemó, *Residència Benazet* (☎ 820698) has large, serviceable rooms with washbasin and bidet at 1300 ptas per person. *Hotel Les Arcades* (☎ 821355) at Plaça Guillemó 5 has singles/doubles with shower and toilet from 2000/3000 to 3000/5400 ptas depending on the season.

In the Barri Antic, the nondescript rooms at *Pensió La Rosa* (☎ 821810) at Antic Carrer Major 18, not far from the Casa de la Vall, are 1700/3000 ptas. Quiet *Hostal Calones* (☎ 821312), Antic Carrer Major 8, has better rooms with big bathrooms for 2800/3700 ptas. *Habitacions Baró* (☎ 821484) at Carrer del Puial 21 – up the steps opposite Avinguda Príncep Benlloch 53 – has rooms for 1300/2600 ptas, or 1800/3600 ptas with bath.

Hotel Pyrénées (☎ 860006; fax 820265), at Avinguda Príncep Benlloch 20, has a tennis court, swimming pool, and all mod cons and is priced accordingly at 5300/8700 ptas including breakfast.

Hotels – further east At Avinguda Meritxell 44, *Hotel Costa* (☎ 821439) has basic but clean rooms for 1300/2600 ptas. Bathrooms are shared. *Hotel Residència Albert* (☎ 820156) at Avinguda Doctor Mitjavila 16 has rooms for 1500/3000 ptas, or doubles with shower for 3500 ptas.

Places to Eat

The *Hotel Les Arcades* restaurant, Plaça Guillemó 5, has a decent three-course Spanish set meal for 800 ptas. *El Timbaler del Bruch*

ANDORRA

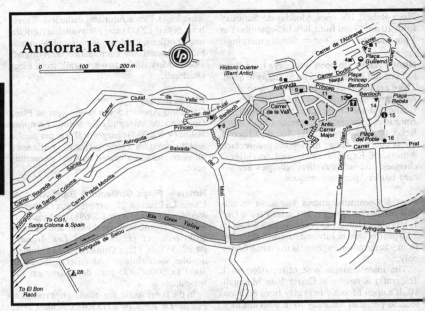

Andorra la Vella

0   100   200 m

Historic Quarter
(Barri Antic)

To CG1,
Santa Coloma & Spain

To El Bon
Racó

PLACES TO STAY
1 Residència Benazet
4 Hotel Les Arcades
6 Hotel Pyrénées
7 Habitacions Baró
9 Pensió La Rosa
11 Hostal Calones
19 Hotel Costa
22 Hotel Residència Albert
28 Camping Valira

PLACES TO EAT
2 El Timbaler del Bruch
5 Pizzeria Primavera

8 Tex-Mex Café
14 Pans & Company
21 Pizzeria La Mossegada
23 Pans & Company

OTHER
3 Plaça Guillemó Bus
   Stop
10 Casa de la Vall
12 Plaça Príncep Benlloch
   Bus Stop
13 Església de Sant
   Esteve
15 National Tourist Office

16 Public Lift to Plaça del
   Poble
17 Viatges Relax/Ameri-
   can Express
18 Pyrénées Department
   Store
20 Municipal Tourist Office
24 Spanish Post Office
25 French Post Office
26 Police Station
27 Estació d'Autobusos

on the same square does good, generous tor-
rades (open toasted sandwiches) from 375
ptas. *Pizzeria Primavera* nearby at Carrer
Doctor Nequi 4 has pizzas and pasta for 500 to
750 ptas, and a set meal for 900 ptas. It is closed
on Wednesday. *Pans & Company* at Plaça
Rebés 2 and Avinguda Meritxell 91 is good for
hot and cold baguettes with a range of fillings
(300 to 400 ptas).

Pizzeria La Mossegada, closed Wednesday,
overlooks the Riu Valira at Avinguda Doctor
Mitjavila 3. Pizzas cost between 750 and 875
ptas. Fancy Mexican in Andorra? The *Tex-
Mex Café* at Avinguda Príncep Benlloch 49
has tacos with chilli (850 ptas) and Mexican
spareribs (1200 ptas).

The best place for real Catalan cooking is
the up-market *El Bon Racó* (☎ 822085) at

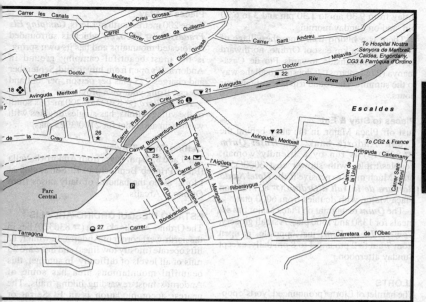

Avinguda de Salou 86 in Santa Coloma, about a km west of Camping Valira. Meat – especially xai (lamb) – roasted in an open hearth is the speciality (1200 ptas). The big supermarket on the 2nd floor of the Pyrénées department store at Avinguda Meritxell 21 is open Monday to Saturday from 9.30 am to 8 pm and on Sunday to 7 pm.

Getting There & Away

See the Getting There & Away and Getting Around sections at the start of this chapter for international and domestic transport options to/from Andorra la Vella.

Parròquia d'Ordino

The mountainous parish of Ordino, north of Andorra la Vella, is arguably the country's most beautiful region, with slate and fieldstone farmhouses, gushing streams and picturesque stone bridges. Virtually everything of interest is along the 35-km highway CG3.

ORDINO

Ordino (population 1000; 1300 metres) is much larger than other villages in the area, but remains peaceful and Andorran in character, with most buildings still in stone.

Orientation & Information

The tourist office (☎ 836963), on highway CG3, is open Monday to Saturday from 9 am to 1 pm and 3 to 7 pm, and on Sunday morning. There are several banks and two post offices.

Things to See & Do

The **Museu d'Areny i Plandolit** (☎ 836908), just off Plaça Major, is a 17th-century house of typically rugged Andorran design that once belonged to one of the princedom's most illustrious families. The library and dining room are particularly fine. Half-hour guided visits cost 200 ptas; it's open Tuesday to Saturday from 9.30 am to 1.30 pm and 3 to 6.30 pm, and on Sunday morning.

There is a **hiking trail** from the village of Segudet, half a km east of Ordino, northward up the mountainside towards Pic de Casamanya (2740 metres). It doesn't go all the way to the summit. The round trip takes about four hours.

Places to Stay & Eat
Just off Plaça Major, in the alley behind the Crèdit Andorrà bank, the *Hotel Quim* (☎ 835013) is run by a friendly woman; doubles/triples with shower cost 3000/3500 ptas. Much more expensive is the *Hotel Santa Bàrbara de la Vall d'Ordino* (☎ 837100) on Plaça Major, with doubles from 6000 ptas.

The *Quim* restaurant on Plaça Major has set meals for 1350 and 1500 ptas. A small grocery, *Comerç Fleca Font*, just opposite, is open from 7 am to 2 pm and 4 to 8 pm daily, except Sunday afternoon.

LLORTS
The hamlet of Llorts (pronounced 'yorts'; population 100; 1413 metres), six km north of Ordino, has traditional architecture set amid tobacco fields and near-pristine mountains. This is one of the most unadulterated spots in the whole country.

Things to See & Do
Llorts is a good area for **hiking** trails. One leads west from the village up the Riu de l'Angonella valley to a group of lakes, Estanys de l'Angonella, at about 2300 metres. Count on about three hours to get there.

From slightly north of the village of El Serrat (population 60; 1600 metres), which is three km up the valley from Llorts, a secondary road leads four km east to the Borda de Sorteny mountain shelter. From there, trails go on to Estany de l'Estanyó (2339 metres) and to peaks such as Pic de la Serrera (2913 metres) and Pic de l'Estanyó (2915 metres), Andorra's fourth and second highest.

The partly Romanesque **Església de Sant Martí** in La Cortinada, 2.5 km south of Llorts, has 12th-century frescos in remarkably good condition.

Places to Stay
Some 200 metres north of Llorts, *Camping Els Pradassos* (☎ 850022), which is surrounded by forested mountains and has its own spring, is the most beautiful camping ground in Andorra. It's open from July to mid-September and charges 275 ptas per person, per tent and per car. Bring your own provisions.

Hotel Vilaró (☎ 850225), 200 metres south of the village limits, has singles/doubles with washbasin and bidet for 2100/3925 ptas.

Getting There & Away
The 1 and 8.30 pm buses from Andorra la Vella (Plaça Príncep Benlloch) to El Serrat stop at Llorts, as do the handful of daily buses from Ordino to Arcalís.

ESTACIÓ D'ESQUÍ ORDINO-ARCALÍS
The Ordino-Arcalís ski area (☎ 836320) lies in the north-west corner of Andorra. In winter, 12 lifts operate (mostly tow lines) and there are 23 runs of all levels of difficulty. In summer, this beautiful mountainous area has some of Andorra's most rewarding hiking trails. The nearest accommodation is in El Serrat or Llorts.

Restaurant La Coma Altitude, at 2200 metres near the third car park, is a useful landmark. It is open from December to early May and, except on Monday, from the end of June to early September. The long Telecadira La Coma chairlift rises opposite.

Things to Do
The souvenir kiosk opposite the foot of Telecadira La Coma rents out mountain bikes for 3100 ptas a day between late June and mid-September (daily, except Monday in June and July, from 10 am to 6 pm). The trail behind Restaurant La Coma Altitude leads eastward across the hill then north over the ridge to a group of beautiful lakes, Estanys de Tristaina. You can also start walking from the top of Telecadira La Coma (2700 metres), which operates daily from late June to early September from 10 am to 6 pm.

Getting There & Away
There are a few buses (150 ptas) daily from Ordino, through Llorts and El Serrat.

Bosnia-Hercegovina

Bosnia-Hercegovina straddles the Dinaric Alps, which separate the Pannonian Plain from the Adriatic. Sandwiched between Croatia and Serbia, this mountainous country has been a meeting point of East and West for nearly two millennia. Here the realm of Orthodox Byzantium mingled with Catholic Rome, and the 15th-century swell of Turkish power settled among the Slavs. This unique history created one of the most fascinating cultures in Europe, with a heterogeneous population of Croats, Serbs and Slavic converts to Islam.

In the 20th century Bosnia-Hercegovina has had more than its share of strife. WWI began at Sarajevo when a Serb nationalist assassinated an Austrian aristocrat, and much of the bitter partisan fighting of WWII took place in this region. After the war it seemed Bosnia-Hercegovina's varied peoples had learned to live together, and this third-largest republic of Yugoslavia enjoyed 45 years of peace. All that ended in 1992 when Serb super-nationalists shattered the country's social harmony with the active assistance of the federal army and hard-line Serb officials in Belgrade.

In October 1991 Bosnia-Hercegovina declared its independence from former Yugoslavia but six months later the three-way war began. Although the war is officially over, and a trickle of tourists has begun to arrive, it will be some time before the country's tourism infrastructure is restored.

Facts about the Country

HISTORY

The ancient inhabitants of this region were Illyrians, followed by the Romans who settled around the mineral springs at Ilidža near Sarajevo. When the Roman Empire was divided in 395 AD, the Drina River, today the border between Bosnia-Hercegovina and Serbia, became the line which divided the Western Roman Empire from Byzantium.

The Slavs arrived in the 7th century and in 960 the area became independent of Serbia. From the mid-12th century, the Hungarians exercised some control. The first Turkish raids came in 1383 and by 1463 Bosnia was a Turkish province with Sarajevo as capital. Hercegovina is named after Herceg (Duke) Stjepan Vukčić, who ruled the southern portion of the present republic from his mountaintop castle at Blagaj near Mostar until the Turkish conquest in 1468.

During the 400-year Turkish period, Bosnia-Hercegovina was completely assimilated and became the boundary between the Islamic and Christian worlds. Wars with Venice and Austria were frequent. After the Turkish conquest, a Christian heretic sect, the Bogomils, converted to Islam, and the region still forms a Muslim enclave deep within Christian Europe. Forty per cent of the local Slavic population is Sunni Muslim.

As Ottoman rule weakened in the 16th and 17th centuries, the Turks strengthened their hold on Bosnia-Hercegovina as an advance bulwark of their empire. The national revival

Bosnia-Hercegovina

movements of the mid-19th century led to a reawakening among the South Slavs, and in 1875-76 there were uprisings against the Turks in Bosnia and Bulgaria. In 1878 Turkey suffered a crushing defeat by Russia in a war over Bulgaria and it was decided at the Congress of Berlin that Bosnia-Hercegovina would be occupied by Austria-Hungary. However, the population desired autonomy and had to be brought under Habsburg rule by force.

Resentment that one foreign occupation had been replaced by another became more intense in 1908 when Austria annexed Bosnia-Hercegovina outright. The assassination of the Habsburg heir Archduke Franz Ferdinand by a Bosnian Serb at Sarajevo on 28 June 1914 (the 525th anniversary of the Battle of Kosovo), led Austria to declare war on Serbia. When Russia supported Serbia, and Germany came to the aid of Austria, the world was soon at war.

Following WWI, Bosnia-Hercegovina was annexed to royalist Serbia, then in 1941 to fascist Croatia. During WWII this rugged area became a partisan stronghold. The foundations of postwar Yugoslavia were laid at Jajce in 1943, and after the war Bosnia-Hercegovina was granted republic status within Yugoslavia.

In the republic's first free elections in November 1990, the communists were easily defeated by nationalist Serbian and Croatian parties, representing their respective communities, and a predominantly Muslim party favouring a multi-ethnic Bosnia-Hercegovina.

The Croat and Muslim parties united against the Serb nationalists and independence from Yugoslavia was declared on 15 October 1991, breaking an unwritten rule of Bosnian politics that each of the three nationalities would have a veto on important issues. The Serb parliamentarians withdrew and set up a parliament of their own at Pale, 20 km east of Sarajevo. Bosnia-Hercegovina was recognised internationally and admitted to the UN. This over-hasty recognition caused talks between the parties to break down.

Although Bosnia-Hercegovina's Muslim president went out of his way to guarantee Serb rights, the Belgrade leadership incited Serbian extremists to defend Bosnian Serbs from 'genocide'.

The UN declared a ban on arms sales to ex-Yugoslavia, but this was only effective against the poorly armed Bosnian (mostly Muslim) government forces, as the Serbs had inherited almost the entire arms stock of the federal army and Croatia was able to import vast quantities of Warsaw Pact weapons via Hungary.

The War

Civil war broke out in April 1992, shortly after Serb snipers in the Sarajevo Holiday Inn opened fire on unarmed civilians demonstrating for peace in Sarajevo, killing over a dozen people. The first to die was a young student from Dubrovnik, Suada Dilberović, and the bridge on which she fell is now known as Suada Most.

Serbs began seizing territory with the support of some of the 50,000 ex-Yugoslavian federal troops in Bosnia-Hercegovina, as had been done in Croatia. Sarajevo came under siege by Serbian irregulars on 5 April 1992 and shelling by Serbian artillery began soon after.

The Serbs began a process of 'ethnic cleansing', brutally expelling the Muslim population from northern and eastern Bosnia to create a 300-km corridor between Serb ethnic areas in the west of Bosnia and Serbia proper. Villages were terrorised until their inhabitants fled for their lives. The terrorists entered the villages, looting and destroying homes to prevent anyone from returning. Elderly people who refused to leave were massacred.

In June 1992 the Croatian Community of Herceg-Bosna was set up at Mostar and in November heavy fighting erupted between Croats and Muslims after the presidents of Croatia and Yugoslavia cut a deal to partition Bosnia between themselves. The Croats' deadly mini-siege of the Muslim quarter of Mostar received far less publicity than the siege of Sarajevo.

In August 1992 the UN Security Council authorised the use of force to deliver humanitarian relief supplies and in September 6000 UN troops were sent to Bosnia-Hercegovina to protect aid shipments, joining the 1500 already deployed at Sarajevo airport. The impotence of these troops was dramatically displayed in January 1993 when the vice-premier of Bosnia-Hercegovina, Hakija Turajlić, was pulled out of a UN armoured personnel carrier at a Serb checkpoint and executed in front of French peacekeepers. Only in 1993 did the Security Council pass a motion allowing the peacekeepers to shoot back if fired upon.

By mid-1993, with Serb 'ethnic cleansing' almost complete, the UN proposed setting up 'safe areas' for Muslims around Bihać, Goražde, Sarajevo, Srebrenica, Tuzla and Žepa.

The Security Council finally endorsed the use of force to police the no-fly zone over Bosnia in March 1993 but the Serbs defied this without penalty. By August 1993 the Bosnian Serbs were so sure Western nations would not intervene that when NATO threatened air strikes unless the siege of Sarajevo was lifted, Bosnian Serb leader Radovan Karadžić warned that if a single bomb hit a Serb position it would mean all-out war, and NATO quickly backed down.

The elected Bosnian government repeatedly emphasised that it didn't want foreign ground troops to push back the Serb rebels, but only the right to purchase arms so they could do the job themselves.

But the Serbs were not the only worry facing the Muslim government and population. At a peace conference in January 1993, the EC negotiator Lord Owen and the UN representative Cyrus Vance proposed dividing Bosnia into 10 ethnically based autonomous provinces. The Bosnian government initially rejected the Vance-Owen Plan because it rewarded 'ethnic cleansing', while the Serbs said no because it frustrated their principal aim of a 'Greater Serbia'. Only the Croats accepted the deal, which they used as a pretext to consolidate their control of the areas assigned to them.

In May 1993 Croatian president Franjo Tudjman made a bid for a 'Greater Croatia' by making a separate deal with the Bosnian Serbs to carve up Bosnia between themselves. Tudjman secretly sent regular Croatian troops to Bosnia and began cooperating with the Serbs militarily. Tudjman's cynical scheme hit a snag when the Croat forces were pushed back by the numerically superior Bosnian government army and the carnage in Bosnia spread. In early 1994 some 5000 regular Croatian army troops were deployed in Bosnia-Hercegovina.

After a Serb mortar attack on a Sarajevo market in February 1994 left 68 dead and 200 injured, NATO issued an ultimatum to the Bosnian Serbs to either withdraw their guns from the hills around the city within 10 days or face air strikes. After stalling for a week, the Serbs quickly began withdrawing their guns when Russia offered to send peacekeeping troops to Sarajevo, thereby freezing the front lines and making the partition of the city permanent.

US fighters belatedly began enforcing the no-fly zone over Bosnia by shooting down four Serb aircraft in February 1994 (the first actual combat in NATO's 45-year history). Two months later, NATO aircraft carried out their first air strikes against Bosnian Serb ground positions after the Serbs advanced on the UN 'protected area' around Goražde. The NATO raids quickly ceased when a British plane was shot down.

Meanwhile, at talks held in Washington in March 1994, the United States pressured the Bosnian government to join the Bosnian Croats in a federation which might perhaps be linked to Croatia. Tudjman was presented with the choice of giving up his dream of a 'Greater Croatia' or facing UN economic sanctions.

Croatia was also becoming worried about Serb enclaves on its own soil and in May 1995 Croatia again went on the offensive. Ignoring UN peacekeepers the Croat army rapidly over-ran Croatian Serb positions and towns in western Slavonia, within Croatia. For the first time in the conflict it was Serb soldiers who were captured by the truckload and Serb civilians who clogged the roads as they fled from burning towns. The attack was so swift that the Bosnian Serb army was unable to respond before it was all over.

The Croats' decisive action took the situation to a critical point. Many of the parties and factions in the region were on the point of deciding that all-out war was a better choice than an uncertain stalemate, and the impotence of the UN had yet again been demonstrated.

A pan-Balkan war seemed closer than ever. Again, Bosnian Serb tanks and artillery attacked Sarajevo, again the peacekeepers requested NATO air strikes, and yet again they were vetoed by the UN. Bosnian Serb forces, reinforced by Serb forces from the neighboring Krajina region of Croatia, captured the region around Bihać. Finally, air strikes to protect Bosnian towns were authorised, but the Serbs captured 300 peacekeepers, chaining some to potential targets to keep the planes away.

The UN's continued presence in Bosnia was a day-to-day proposition. In July 1995, attacks by the Bosnian Serbs on so-called 'safe areas' and the fall of Srebrenica showed that the while the UN's new 'rapid reaction force' did react, it was not rapid, and as a force it was a farce. The Žepa enclave also fell and Goražde teetered. It did not seem so at the time, but this was the beginning of the end of Bosnian Serb military dominance.

The US senate voted to lift the arms embargo on Bosnia, and European leaders were calling loudly for strong action not just to defend the Bosnians (which had proved a miserable failure) but to defeat the Bosnian Serbs. (Admittedly, strong calls from world leaders had been common and ineffectual for years.) Croatia renewed its offensive, taking territory from the Bosnian Serbs in western Bosnia, and threatening the rebel Serb 'state' of Krajina. This relieved the beleaguered Muslim enclave of Bihać, and partly for that reason the Croatian advance was not opposed by the international community.

In August, the Croat army took Krajina, a region where Serbs had lived for centuries. There is speculation that the Serbian government had done a deal with Croatia, whereby Serbia would forsake Krajina if Croatia stayed out of eastern Slavonia.

US president Bill Clinton proposed a new peace plan, dividing Bosnia between the main adversaries. It was the right moment for such a plan, as the Bosnian Serbs were on the defensive but the Muslims and Croats had not yet reached the point where they prefered to keep fighting in the hope of winning more territory. Two weeks of NATO air strikes in September 1995 helped the Bosnian Serbs decide to talk peace.

The Dayton Accord

The peace conference in Dayton, Ohio, USA, began in November 1995 and the final agreement was signed in Paris in December.

The Dayton agreement stated that the country would retain its pre-war external boundaries, but would be composed of two parts or 'entities'. The Federation of Bosnia & Hercegovina (the Muslim and Croat portion) would administer 51% of the country, and the Serb Republic of Bosnia & Hercegovina 49%.

Sarajevo was reunified and Goražde was linked to the Federation by a land corridor. The Serbs retained Žepa and Srebrenica, former UN safe areas, but agreed to hand back eastern Slavonia to Croatia. The Posavina Corridor, a 60-km strip linking Serb territory in eastern and western Bosnia, was ceded to the Serbs. The town of Brčko, within the corridor, is presently Serb-held but its final fate will be decided by international arbitration.

A Human Rights Commission and a War Crimes Tribunal were established. The accord is supervised by a peace implementation force, (IFOR), under the command of NATO. The USA has provided IFOR with most of its muscle.

War Crimes

As early as 1992 there had been reports of massacres, mass rape, torture and concentration camps in Serb-held areas. In January 1993 US secretary of state Lawrence Eagleburger, a former US ambassador to Yugoslavia, named 10 Serb leaders who warranted war crimes prosecution, beginning with Serbian president Slobodan Milošević. In February 1993 the UN Security Council voted to set up a war crimes tribunal for ex-Yugoslavia and in May this was established at The Hague. In June 1994 the tribunal reported that in certain areas such as Prijedor in north-west Bosnia the Serb leader-

ship had planned acts of genocide as long as six months in advance. Atrocities were no doubt committed by all sides, but a CIA report concluded that the Serbs were responsible for 90% of 'ethnic cleansing' and its associated horrors.

IFOR has the authority to arrest indicted war criminals but it will not try to track them down. So far, more than 50 people have been indicted although few have been captured.

After Dayton

In early 1996 Bosnian, Serb and Croat forces withdrew to the agreed lines, and the international force took up positions between them. This has significantly eased the possibility of war breaking out again, in the short term at least. US troops are set to leave at the end of 1996 and it's anybody's guess what will happen then.

Bosnian Serb leader and indicted war criminal Radovan Karadžić stepped down from the presidency in July 1996, under pressure from the international community, which threatened to reintroduce sanctions against the Serbs if he did not quit public office. Removed from power, Karadžić continued to exercise influence through his loyal and hardline replacement, Biljana Plavšić.

Even if peace prevails, it seems likely that instead of being a united country, Bosnia-Hercegovina will split into more-or-less autonomous Muslim, Croat and Serb sections.

Meanwhile, more and more evidence of atrocities committed during the war is being found. Bitterness on both sides will poison relations for a long time to come. Repairing the infrastructure of the country (especially the battered Muslim parts) will take an estimated US$5 billion over three years, and there are nearly three million refugees to relocate.

GEOGRAPHY

Bosnia-Hercegovina is a mountainous country of 51,129 sq km on the west side of the Balkan Peninsula, almost cut off from the sea by Croatia. Most of the country's rivers flow north into the Sava; only the Neretva cuts south from Jablanica through the Dinaric chain to Ploče (formerly called Kardeljevo) on the Adriatic Sea. Bosnia-Hercegovina contains over 30 mountain peaks from 1700 to 2386 metres high.

GOVERNMENT

The Dayton accord stipulates that the central government will comprise a House of Peoples selected from the legislatures of the two entities and a House of Representatives directly elected by each entity. Two-thirds of each house will be from the Federation, one third from the Serb Republic. There will be a three-person Presidency, one elected by the Serb Republic, the others by the Federation, and a Council of Ministers, responsible for carrying out government policies and decisions.

The process of establishing this new system of government has begun, but as it ultimately depends on cooperation between the two entities, you wouldn't want to bet on a speedy implementation.

ECONOMY

Bosnia-Hercegovina was one of the poorest regions of Yugoslavia. War has cemented the poverty. At the end of 1995 unemployment was a catastrophic 80% and the average per capita annual income stood at US$500, a quarter of what it was before the war. The terrain makes agriculture difficult in many places, although the northern and central areas are heavily cultivated and support grain crops.

The split between urban and rural lifestyles is marked. During the war, when many rural people sought refuge in Sarajevo, urbanites complained that their cosmopolitan culture was threatened by their less wordly country cousins.

Various minerals are mined and hydroelectricity is a potentially important industry. With half the country forested, timber and timber products are important exports. The Bosnian maple is highly prized by violin makers.

POPULATION & PEOPLE

Before the war, Bosnia-Hercegovina's population stood at around five million. In 1991 the largest cities were Sarajevo (525,980), Banja Luka (195,139), Zenica (145,577), Tuzla (131,861) and Mostar (126,067).

The pre-war population was incredibly mixed, with Croats concentrated in northeastern Bosnia and western Hercegovina and many ethnic Serbs living in areas adjacent to Croatia in the north-west and west. 'Ethnic cleansing' has forced most of the Muslims out of areas separating Bosnian Serbs from Serbia proper. The Croats conducted their own campaign of ethnic cleansing around Mostar.

Serbs, Croats and Bosnian Muslims are all South Slavs of the same ethnic stock. Physically the three peoples are indistinguishable.

ARTS

Bosnia's best known writer is Ivo Andrić (1892-1975), winner of the 1961 Nobel Prize for Literature. His novels *Travnik Chronicle* and *Bridge over the Drina*, both written during WWII, are fictional histories which deal with the intermingling of Islamic and Orthodox societies in the small Bosnian towns of Travnik and Višegrad.

RELIGION

Religious conflict is one of the unavoidable facts about this devastated country. Despite wishful thinking about a renewal of tolerance and integration, the Serb Republic is almost entirely Christian and the Federation is almost entirely Muslim. Before the war, Bosnia-Hercegovina's five million people were 43% Muslim Slavs, 31% Orthodox Serbs and 17% Catholic Croats.

LANGUAGE

Dialects notwithstanding, the people of Bosnia-Hercegovina speak the same language, called Croatian if written in Latin letters, Serbian if in Cyrillic. See the Croatian & Serbian section of the Language Guide at the back of the book for pronunciation guidelines and useful words and phrases.

Facts for the Visitor

VISAS

The visa situation remains unclear. Because of the war-wrought chaos, Bosnia is said to be the only country in the world where no-one needs a visa to enter or leave. This will presumably change as the situation stabilises.

The constitution guarantees freedom of movement between the two entities for citizens of the country, and by implication this might be supposed to apply to visitors as well. However, it seems likely that the two entities will be at least antagonistic to each other, which probably means problems crossing between the two.

In the past, if you planned to visit the Serbian-controlled portions of Bosnia-Hercegovina from Yugoslavia, you needed a double-entry visa for Yugoslavia as you had to return the way you came. This was much less of a problem when entering from Croatia as Croatian visas were available at the border and the Croat officials are usually helpful to Westerners.

ONLINE SERVICES

If Vietnam was the first televised war, Bosnia was the first war to feature on the Internet. Many sites and news groups sprang up, some within the country (especially Sarajevo), some outside. Perhaps the most ambitious site (probably also the first real attempt to use the Internet to create a new form of media) is *Beserkistan* (http://www.linder.com/berserk/berserk.html). It has maps, good background and correspondents' reports, not to mention a logo for the war. It isn't exactly 'infotainment', but it isn't straight reporting either. Other sites worth a look are *Bosnia Homepage* (http://www.cco.caltech.edu/bosnia. htm) and *Bosnia*

Virtual Fieldtrip (http://geog.gmu.edu/gess/jwc/bosnia/bosnia.html).

A wire service from Sarajevo keeps you up to date with daily news, much of it not related to the war these days (http://www.axime. com/wm/sarajevo/onasa.html).

MONEY

You might be able to use the Croatian dinar (HRD) in the border areas of the Federation but Deutschmarks are best. With so many American troops around, US dollars would probably also be accepted. The Federation government has introduced Bosnia-Hercegovina dinars, at a rate of 100BHD to 1 DM.

POST & COMMUNICATIONS

To call Bosnia-Hercegovina, dial the international access code (different from each country), ☎ 387 (the country code for Bosnia-Hercegovina), the area code (without the initial zero) and the number. Area codes include ☎ 070 (Jajce), ☎ 071 (Sarajevo), ☎ 078 (Banja Luka) and ☎ 088 (Mostar).

DANGERS & ANNOYANCES

Any area which saw fighting during the war should be regarded as dangerous because of land mines. Do not drive off the shoulder of roads, do not poke around in damaged buildings or abandoned villages, and regard every centimetre of ground as suspicious unless you are absolutely certain that it is safe. You can't trust local knowledge because civilians generally left the area during the fighting and probably don't know where mines were laid.

Hijacking and looting of vehicles on highways is a potential danger, especially in the Posavina Corridor area. Always find out the local conditions before undertaking a journey, and if IFOR is still in operation see if you can tag along with a military convoy. Apart from bandits, the driving habits of locals pose a real threat on the highways.

During the chaos of war local 'mafias' sprang up in several towns, and armed robbery is a real possibility.

ACCOMMODATION

In the past you had a choice of hotels (rather expensive), private rooms and camping. There was a youth hostel on a hill near Sarajevo railway station. What is left today is uncertain.

BOSNIA

FOOD

Bosnia's Oriental background is savoured in its grilled meats, *bosanski lonac* (Bosnian stew of cabbage and meat), baklava (a Turkish sweet) and the ubiquitous *burek* (a layered cheese or meat pie).

Getting There & Away

AIR

Air Bosnia, a new and tiny airline part-owned by the Federation government, plans flights into Sarajevo from Croatia, Germany and Turkey.

Croatia Airlines planned to have flights to Sarajevo and Mostar from mid-1996.

LAND

In August 1996, Sarajevo celebrated as the first train to depart the city in over four years resumed its normal journey to the coast, following a spectacular route down the Neretva River past Mostar to the Adriatic at Ploče. (In April 1992 the line was blown up and many highway bridges were destroyed.)

Bus travel between Croatia and the Croat-Muslim Federation of Bosnia-Hercegovina is fairly easy. A daily bus travels between Sarajevo and Zagreb (417 km) and Sarajevo and Split. The Sarajevo-Dubrovnik bus makes three trips per week.

Two daily buses link Mostar and Dubrovnik, four daily buses travel between Međugorje and Zagreb, the same number shuttle between Međugorje and Split (156 km), and five daily buses connect Mostar with Split (179 km).

Various bus and train services operate between Serbia proper and the Bosnian Serb Republic. Ask at Belgrade bus station about direct buses to Bijeljina and Banja Luka. Always check the current situation before leaving either Serbia or the Serb Republic.

From the north it should be possible to cross the border near Županja (Croatia) and Orašje. The US Army has constructed a bridge across the Sava river here. If it is still closed to non-military traffic you can use the nearby vehicle ferry (free).

Around the Country

SARAJEVO

Sarajevo, near the geographical centre of former Yugoslavia, is the capital of the Republic of Bosnia-Hercegovina. Sarajevo's 73 mosques by the Miljacka River in hilly, broken countryside, once gave Sarajevo the strongest Turkish flavour of any city in the Balkans. Apart from being the seat of Islam in former Yugoslavia, this large city had an Orthodox metropolitan and a Catholic archbishop.

From the mid-15th century until 1878, Turkish governors ruled Bosnia from Sarajevo. The name comes from *saraj*, Turkish for 'palace'. When the Turks finally withdrew, half a century of Austro-Hungarian domination began, culminating in the assassination of Archduke Franz Ferdinand and his wife, Sophie, by Serbian nationalists.

Until the recent war, Sarajevo was the most Oriental city in Europe, retaining the essence of its rich history with its mosques, markets and local colour of Baščaršija, the picturesque old Turkish bazar. The riverfront remained largely unchanged since that fateful day in 1914 when history was irrevocably altered here. Seventy years later in 1984 Sarajevo again attracted world attention by hosting the 14th Winter Olympic Games.

For hundreds of years Sarajevo was a place where Muslims, Serbs, Croats, Turks, Jews and others could peacefully coexist. According to the 1991 census, the 525,980 inhabitants were 49.3% Muslim, 29.9% Serb, 6.6% Croat and 14.2% 'other'. However, the Sarajevan tradition of tolerance and the heritage of six centuries was pounded into rubble by Serbian artillery during the recent war, leaving over 10,500 people dead and 50,000 wounded.

During the three-year siege, a km-long tunnel under the airport linked Sarajevo to the outside world. Some electricity for the government made it through, supplies came in and troops were rostered. Refugees were moved out, but young men of military age were not allowed to leave. By night, the army rented the tunnel to black marketeers for about US$25,000 for eight hours.

Despite the barbarity which surrounded them, the citizens of Sarajevo attempted to retain some semblance of normality. It wasn't easy. Most people went to work but were not paid. At the notorious Snipers' Alley, a UN armoured vehicle sheltered pedestrians as they crossed the street. However, if they didn't stand behind the wheels, the snipers would try to hit their legs. Armoured jeeps full of press photographers also waited by the intersection. They didn't shelter civilians – they were waiting for the chance to take photos of a newly killed pedestrian.

The end of the war and the reunification of the city brought weary relief but not a return to the old days of tolerance and cohabitation. The Serbs moved out as their suburbs came under Bosnian control, despite assurances of protection. People burned their apartment buildings as they left. In some Serb suburbs elderly Muslims who had stayed on unscathed throughout the war were murdered by their departing neighbours. IFOR did little to stop the burning and killing because maintaining law and order was not part of its mandate.

The respected mayor of Sarajevo resigned after the ruling Muslim Party allotted only two of the 47 council seats to non-Muslims. He said, 'I think this is Sarajevo's suicide'.

Despite the continuing problems, Sarajevo is again a fairly normal city. The trams are running and many pleasant cafés are open. The tourist office and main travel agency have reopened and in mid-1996 the city welcomed its first postwar tourists, from Spain. Early visitors tended to be 'war groupies' – less interested in the city's historical and cultural sights than in places which gained horrible notoriety during the war.

Places to Stay

Before the war, Sarajevo boasted 100 accommodation venues. Only a few remain. The *Holiday Inn* charges DM300 per night – expensive, but there's not much else going. There's the possibility of staying in a private home. Arrange this through *Bosnia Tours*, near Snipers' Alley. Rooms cost a standard DM60 per night.

JAJCE

Jajce (pronounced 'yaitse') is a medieval walled city of cobbled streets and old houses in hilly country on the main highway from Sarajevo to Zagreb. Prior to the 15th-century Turkish conquest, Jajce was the seat of the Christian kings of Bosnia and for a short period in 1943 it was the capital of liberated Yugoslavia. Here in 1943 the 142 delegates to the second session of the Antifascist Council for the National Liberation of Yugoslavia (AVNOJ) proclaimed a constitution outlining the principles of a new federal Yugoslavia and Marshal Tito officially replaced King Peter II as Yugoslavia's legitimate leader.

In October 1992 Serbian separatists brutally expelled 35,000 Muslims from this historic city where they had previously been the largest ethnic group.

BANJA LUKA

This important crossroads on the Vrbas River in north-western Bosnia has the dubious distinction of being the military headquarters of the Serbian separatists. Banja Luka was never much of a tourist centre and in 1993 local Serbs made sure it never would be by blowing up all 16 of the city's mosques, complementing the damage previously done by WWII bombings and a 1969 earthquake.

MOSTAR

A medium-sized city among the vineyards between Dubrovnik and Sarajevo, Mostar is the main centre of Hercegovina. Founded by the Turks in the 15th century at a strategic river crossing, **Kujundžiluk**, the old quarter, once greeted thousands of daily visitors from the coastal resorts who came in search of instant Islamic culture.

In May 1993 Croat forces in the western part of the city began a 10-month siege of the Muslim quarter east of the Neretva River, which was treated to sporadic artillery fire by night, sniper fire by day. The Croats forcibly expelled thousands of Muslims from the west bank of the Neretva and slaughtered hundreds more, and all of the town's 16th and 17th-century mosques were destroyed. In November 1993 Mostar's famous **Turkish Bridge**, which had arched 20 metres above the green waters of the Neretva since 1566, was smashed by Croat artillery.

The current population is around 60,000 – half that of pre-war days, and the city remains divided by the war because of the Bosnian Croats' refusal to give up their statelet of

BOSNIA

'Herzeg-Bosna', in brazen defiance of the Dayton peace agreement. Months after the accord, Bosnian Croats appointed a government for the rebel state, with hardliner Pero Marković as prime minister.

However, rebuilding (on the Croat side at least) is proceeding rapidly. Mostar currently has a bad reputation for gangsters; foreigners working in the town prefer to live in nearby Medugorje.

MEDUGORJE

Medugorje is one of Europe's most remarkable sights. On 24 June 1981 six teenagers in this dirt-poor mountain village between Čitluk and Ljubuški, 23 km south-west of Mostar, saw a miraculous apparition of the Virgin Mary, and Medugorje's instant economic boom began. A decade later Medugorje was awash with tour buses, duty-free shops, souvenir stands, car-rental offices, travel agencies, furnished apartments, restaurants, traffic jams and shiny Mercedes taxis. 'Religious tourism' was developed as if this were a beach resort and shops sold postcards of Christ and the Virgin.

The civil war greatly reduced the number of package pilgrims, but it should be still possible to enter by bus from Split. Most of the tourist facilities are intact. Check at the Church of St James (1969) for the daily programme of masses, meetings, recitations, blessings and prayers. Major feasts include the anniversary of the first apparition (June 24), the Assumption of the Virgin (15 August) and the Nativity of the Virgin (8 September).

In the past, apparitions appeared on Monday and Friday on the side of Podbrdo, the Hill of Apparitions, and you had a good chance of seeing a miracle there. It's about an hour's walk to this rocky hill from St James. Ask if the visionaries still receive their daily messages from the Virgin and if audiences are possible with them. (The Catholic Church has not officially acknowledged the Medugorje apparitions, the first in Europe since those of Lourdes, France, in 1858 and Fatima, Portugal, in 1917.)

Croatia

Croatia (Hrvatska) extends in an arc from the Danube River in the east to Istria in the west and south along the Adriatic coast to Dubrovnik. Roman Catholic since the 9th century, and under Hungary since 1102, Croatia only united with Orthodox Serbia in 1918. Croatia's centuries-long resistance to Hungarian and Austrian domination was manifested in 1991 in its determined struggle for nationhood. Yet within Croatia, cultural differences remain between the Habsburg-influenced central European interior and the formerly Venetian Mediterranean coast.

Croatia's capital, Zagreb, is the country's cultural centre, while coastal towns such as Poreč, Rovinj, Pula, Mali Lošinj, Krk, Rab, Zadar, Šibenik, Trogir, Split, Hvar, Korčula and Dubrovnik all have well-preserved historic centres with lots to see.

Before 1991 the strikingly beautiful Mediterranean landscapes of this 56,538-sq-km country attracted nearly 10 million foreign visitors a year.

Traditionally, tourism has been focused along the Adriatic coast, with its unsurpassed combination of history, natural beauty, good climate, clear water and easy access. Seaside resorts are numerous, the swimming is good, and the atmosphere is relaxed – there are few rules about behaviour and few formalities. Since 1960 nudism has been promoted and Croatia is now *the* place to go in Europe to practise naturism.

When Yugoslavia split apart in 1991, no less than 80% of the country's tourist resorts ended up in Croatia. Istria and the lovely Adriatic islands were largely untouched by the fighting and remained peaceful and safe even during the dark days when Osijek, Vukovar and Dubrovnik were world headlines.

The publicity brought tourism almost to a standstill and although Istria and Krk are again popular, it will probably take years before the millions of annual visitors return to Dalmatia. The lack of tourists means that, south of Krk in particular, you'll have some beautiful places all to yourself.

Effects of War

In mid-1991 heavy fighting erupted between Serbs and Croats in areas of Croatia with a large Serbian population. Within a year a solid quarter of Croatian territory was under Serbian control. Most of the occupied land was recaptured by Croatia in the summer of 1995 except for the north-east portion known as eastern Slavonia. The USA-brokered Dayton Peace Accord brought peace and stability to Croatia's borders and provided for the peaceful transfer of eastern Slavonia to Croatian control within two years. This transitional area is still administered by the NATO military Implementation Force known as IFOR. The former frontline in this region had been heavily mined, making travel there inadvisable.

The rest of Croatia is completely safe to visit. Zagreb is calm again and the Adriatic resorts right down to Dubrovnik are as enchanting as ever, although you might encounter occasional inconveniences. Some hotels still house refugees and not all museums have reopened; many still have exhibits in

Croatia (Hrvatska)

storage. The splendid national parks at Plitvice, Paklenica and Krka are scrambling to put their facilities in order after years of occupation. Luxury may be in short supply, but there is an abundance of natural beauty.

If you want to see reminders of the brutal war, they are there for the viewing. Large swathes of formerly occupied territory from Knin in the south to Karlovac in the north are wastelands of blown-apart villages from which the inhabitants have fled. No matter where you go you can talk to people about the price of war. You'll learn about lowered living standards, disrupted lives, relatives in other areas killed or forced to flee their homes. Such insights

bring you closer to the human component behind the headlines, which is what real travel is all about.

Facts about the Country

HISTORY

In 229 BC the Romans began their conquest of the indigenous Illyrians, establishing a colony at Salona (near Split) in Dalmatia. Emperor Augustus extended the empire and created the provinces of Illyricum (Dalmatia and Bosnia) and Pannonia (Croatia). In 285 AD, Emperor

Diocletian decided to retire to his palace fortress in Split, today the greatest Roman ruin in Eastern Europe. When the empire was divided in 395, what is now Slovenia, Croatia and Bosnia-Hercegovina stayed with the Western Roman Empire, while present-day Serbia, Kosovo and Macedonia went to the Eastern Roman Empire, later known as the Byzantine Empire. Visigoth, Hun and Lombard invasions marked the fall of the Western Roman Empire in the 5th century.

Around the year 625, Slavic tribes migrated from present-day Poland. The Serbian tribe settled in the region that is now southwestern Serbia and extended their influence southward and westward. The Croatian tribe moved into what is now Croatia and occupied two former Roman provinces: Dalmatian Croatia along the Adriatic, and Pannonian Croatia to the north.

By the early part of the ninth century, both settlements had accepted Christianity but the northern Croats fell under Frankish domination while Dalmatian Croats came under the nominal control of the Byzantine Empire. The Dalmatian duke, Tomislav, united the two groups in 925 in a single kingdom which prospered for nearly 200 years.

Late in the 11th century, the throne fell vacant and a series of ensuing power struggles weakened central authority and split the kingdom. The northern Croats, unable to agree upon a ruler, united with Hungary in 1102 for protection against the Orthodox Byzantine Empire.

In 1242 a Tatar invasion devastated both Hungary and Croatia. In the 14th century the Turks began pushing into the Balkans, defeating the Serbs in 1389 and the Hungarians in 1526. Northern Croatia in 1527 turned to the Habsburgs of Austria for protection against the Turks and remained under their influence until 1918. To form a buffer against the Turks, in the 16th century the Austrians invited Serbs to settle the Vojna Krajina (military frontier) along the Bosnian border. The Serbs in the borderlands had an autonomous administration under Austrian control and these areas were not reincorporated into Croatia until 1881.

The Adriatic coast fell under Venetian influence as early as the 12th century although Hungary continued to struggle for control of the region. Some Dalmatian cities changed hands repeatedly until Venice imposed its rule on the Adriatic coast in the early 15th century and occupied it for nearly four centuries. Only the Republic of Ragusa (Dubrovnik) maintained its independence. The Adriatic coast was threatened, but never conquered, by the Turks, and, after the naval Battle of Lepanto in 1571, when Spanish and Venetian forces wiped out the Turkish fleet, this threat receded.

After Venice was shattered by Napoleonic France in 1797, the French occupied southern Croatia, entering Ragusa (Dubrovnik) in 1808. Napoleon's merger of Dalmatia, Istria and Slovenia into the 'Illyrian provinces' in 1809 stimulated the concept of South Slav ('Yugoslav') unity. After Napoleon's defeat at Waterloo in 1815, Austria-Hungary moved in to pick up the pieces along the coast.

A revival of Croatian cultural and political life began in 1835. In 1848 a liberal democratic revolution led by Josip Jelačić was suppressed, but serfdom was abolished. An 1868 reform transferred northern Croatia from Austria to Hungary, united the territory with Hungarian Slavonia and granted a degree of internal autonomy. Dalmatia remained under Austria. In the decade before the outbreak of WWI, some 50,000 Croats emigrated to the USA.

With the defeat of the Austro-Hungarian empire in WWI, Croatia became part of the Kingdom of Serbs, Croats & Slovenes (called Yugoslavia after 1929), which had a centralised government in Belgrade. This was strongly resisted by Croatian nationalists, who organised the Paris assassination of King Alexander I in 1934. Italy had been promised the Adriatic coast as an incentive to join the war against Austria-Hungary in 1915 and it held much of northern Dalmatia from 1918 to 1943.

After the German invasion of Yugoslavia in March 1941, a puppet government dominated by the fascist Ustaša movement was set up in Croatia and Bosnia-Hercegovina under Ante Pavelić (who fled to Argentina after the war). At first the Ustaša tried to expel all Serbs from Croatia to Serbia, but when the Germans stopped this because of the problems it was causing, the Ustaša launched an extermination campaign which surpassed even that of the Nazis in scale, brutally murdering some 350,000 ethnic Serbs, Jews and Gypsies. The Ustaša programme called for 'one-third of

CROATIA

Serbs killed, one-third expelled and one-third converted to Catholicism'.

Not all Croats supported these policies, however. Maršal Tito was himself of Croat-Slovene parentage and tens of thousands of Croats fought bravely with his partisans. Massacres of Croats conducted by Serbian Četniks in southern Croatia and Bosnia forced almost all antifascist Croats into the communist ranks, where they joined the numerous Serbs trying to defend themselves from the Ustaša. In all, about a million people died violently in a war which was fought mostly in Croatia and Bosnia-Hercegovina.

Recent History

Postwar Croatia was granted republic status within the Yugoslav Federation. During the 1960s Croatia and Slovenia moved far ahead of the southern republics economically, leading to demands for greater autonomy. The 'Croatian Spring' of 1971 caused a backlash and purge of reformers, and increasing economic inertia due to a cumbersome system of 'self-management' of state enterprises by employees. After Tito died in 1980 the paralysis spread to government; the federal presidency began rotating annually among the republics.

In 1989 severe repression of the Albanian majority in Serbia's Kosovo province sparked renewed fears of Serbian hegemony and heralded the end of the Yugoslav Federation. With political changes sweeping Eastern Europe, many Croats felt the time had come to end more than four decades of communist rule and attain complete autonomy into the bargain. In the free elections of April 1990 Franjo Tudjman's Croatian Democratic Union (Hrvatska Demokratska Zajednica) easily defeated the old Communist Party. On 22 December 1990 a new Croatian constitution was promulgated, changing the status of Serbs in Croatia from that of a 'constituent nation' to a national minority.

The constitution's failure to guarantee minority rights, and mass dismissals of Serbs from the public service, stimulated the 600,000-strong ethnic Serb community within Croatia to demand autonomy. In early 1991 Serb extremists within Croatia staged provocations designed to force federal military intervention. A May 1991 referendum (boy-cotted by the Serbs) produced a 93% vote in favour of independence, but when Croatia declared independence on 25 June 1991, the Serbian enclave of Krajina proclaimed its independence from Croatia.

Heavy fighting broke out in Krajina (the area around Knin north of Split), Baranja (the area north of the Drava River opposite Osijek) and Slavonia (the region west of the Danube). The 180,000-member, 2000-tank Yugoslav People's Army, dominated by Serbian communists, began to intervene on its own authority in support of Serbian irregulars under the pretext of halting ethnic violence. After European Community (EC) mediation, Croatia agreed to freeze its independence declaration for three months to avoid bloodshed.

In the three months following 25 June, a quarter of Croatia fell to Serbian militias and the federal army. In September the Croatian Government ordered a blockade of 32 federal military installations in the republic, lifting morale and gaining much-needed military equipment. In response, the Yugoslav navy blockaded the Adriatic coast and laid siege to the strategic town of Vukovar on the Danube.

In early October 1991 the federal army and Montenegrin militia moved against Dubrovnik to protest against the ongoing blockade of their garrisons in Croatia, and on 7 October the presidential palace in Zagreb was hit by rockets fired by Yugoslav air-force jets in an unsuccessful assassination attempt against President Tudjman. As outrage spread over the siege of historic Dubrovnik, the EC ordered punitive sanctions against Serbia and Montenegro. On 19 November heroic Vukovar finally fell when the army culminated a bloody three-month siege by concentrating 600 tanks and 30,000 soldiers there. During six months of fighting in Croatia 10,000 people died, hundreds of thousands fled and tens of thousands of homes were deliberately destroyed.

The EC's envoy, Lord Carrington, and other mediators cobbled together successive cease-fires which were soon broken. However, in early December the United Nations special envoy, Cyrus Vance, began more successful negotiations with Serbia over the deployment of a 14,000-member UN Protection Force (UNPROFOR) in the Serbian-held areas of Croatia. Beginning on 3 January 1992, a 15th cease-fire generally held. The federal army was allowed to withdraw from its bases inside Croatia without having to shamefully surrender its weapons and thus tensions diminished.

When the three-month moratorium on independence expired on 8 October 1991, Croatia declared full independence. To fulfil a condition for EC recognition, in December the Croatian parliament belatedly amended its constitution to protect minority and human rights. In January 1992 the EC, succumbing to strong pressure from Germany, recognised Croatia. This was followed three months later by US recognition and in May 1992 Croatia was admitted to the United Nations.

The UN peace plan in Krajina was supposed to have led to the disarming of local Serb paramilitary formations, the repatriation of refugees and the return of the region to Croatia. Instead it only froze the existing situation and offered no permanent solution.

In January 1993 the Croatian army suddenly launched an offensive in southern Krajina, pushing the Serbs back as much as 24 km in some areas and recapturing strategic points such as the site of the destroyed Maslenica bridge, Zemunik airport near Zadar and the Peručać hydroelectric dam in the hills between Split and Bosnia-Hercegovina. The Krajina Serbs vowed never to accept rule from Zagreb and in June 1993 they voted overwhelmingly to join the Bosnian Serbs (and eventually Greater Serbia).

The self-proclaimed 'Republic of Serbian Krajina' held elections in December 1993 which no international body recognised as legitimate or fair. Meanwhile continued ethnic cleansing' left only about 900 Croats in the Krajina out of an original population of 44,000. Although no further progress was made in implementing the Vance Peace Plan, the Krajina Serbs signed a comprehensive cease-fire on 29 March 1994 which substantially reduced the violence in the region and established demilitarised 'zones of separation' between the parties.

While the world's attention turned to the grim events unfolding in Bosnia-Hercegovina, the Croatian government quietly began procuring arms from abroad. On 1 May 1995, the Croatian army and police entered occupied western Slavonia, east of Zagreb, and seized control of the region within days. The Krajina

Serbs responded by shelling Zagreb in an attack that left seven people dead and 130 wounded. As the Croatian military consolidated its hold in western Slavonia, some 15,000 Serbs fled the region despite assurances from the Croatian government that they were safe from retribution.

Belgrade's silence throughout this campaign made it clear that the Krajina Serbs had lost the support of their Serbian sponsors, encouraging the Croats to forge ahead. At dawn on 4 August the military launched a massive assault on the rebel Serb capital of Knin, pummelling it with shells, mortars and bombs. Outnumbered by two to one, the Serb army fled towards northern Bosnia, along with 150,000 civilians whose roots in the Krajina stretched back centuries. The military operation ended in days, but was followed by months of terror. Widespread looting and burning of Serb villages, as well as attacks upon the few remaining elderly Serbs, seemed designed to ensure the permanence of this massive population shift.

The Dayton agreement signed at Paris in December 1995 recognised Croatia's traditional borders and provided for the return of eastern Slavonia. A sense of stability began to return to the country. Nevertheless, masses of refugees live in a kind of twilight zone, waiting to learn their fate. Although the Croatian government agreed in principle to the repatriation of displaced Serbs, in fact they have created insurmountable bureaucratic obstacles to block their return. Dealing with the human and economic wreckage of this war, including finding jobs for demobilised soldiers, housing for displaced Croats and repairing damaged infrastructure, has left the government with a dizzying array of problems. As in any particularly nasty divorce nothing remains but bills, bitterness and an uncertain future for the children.

GEOGRAPHY & ECOLOGY

Croatia is half the size of present-day Yugoslavia in area (56,538 sq km) and population. The republic swings around like a boomerang from the Pannonian plains of Slavonia between the Sava, Drava and Danube rivers, across hilly central Croatia to the Istrian Peninsula, then south through Dalmatia along the rugged Adriatic coast.

The narrow Croatian coastal belt at the foot of the Dinaric Alps is only about 600 km long as the crow flies, but it's so indented that the actual length is 1778 km. If the 4012 km of coastline around the offshore islands is added to the total, the length becomes 5790 km.

Most of the 'beaches' along this jagged coast consist of slabs of rock sprinkled with naturists – don't come expecting to find sand. Beach shoes are worth having along the rocky, urchin-infested shores. Officially there are no private beaches in Croatia, but you must pay to use 'managed' beaches. The waters are sparkling clean even around large towns.

Croatia's offshore islands are every bit as beautiful as those in Greece. There are 1185 islands and islets along the tectonically submerged Adriatic coastline, 66 of them inhabited. The largest are Cres, Krk, Lošinj, Pag and Rab in the north; Dugiotok in the middle; and Brač, Hvar, Korčula, Mljet and Vis in the south. Most are elongated from north-west to south-east and barren, with high mountains that drop right into the sea.

When the Yugoslav Federation collapsed, seven of its finest national parks ended up in Croatia. Brijuni near Pula is the most carefully cultivated park, with well-preserved Mediterranean holm oak forests. Mountainous Risnjak National Park near Delnice, east of Rijeka, is named after one of its inhabitants – the *ris* or lynx. Dense forests of beech trees and black pine in Paklenica National Park near Zadar are home for a number of endemic insects, reptiles and birds, as well as the endangered griffon vulture. The abundant plant and animal life, including bears, wolves and deer, in Plitvice National Park between Zagreb and Zadar has put it onto UNESCO's list of world natural heritage sites. Both Plitvice and Krka National Park near Šibenik feature a dramatic series of cascades. The 101 stark and rocky islands of the Kornati Archipelago and National Park make it the largest in the Mediterranean. The island of Mljet near Korčula also contains a national park.

ECONOMY

The former communist government of Yugoslavia emphasised heavy industry, especially in aluminium, chemicals, petroleum and shipbuilding. Today Croatia is the world's third-largest shipbuilder, with most of the output from the shipyards of Pula, Rijeka and Split intended for export. The chemical industry is concentrated at Krk, Rijeka, Split and Zagreb; machine-tool manufacture at Karlovac, Slavonski Brod and Zagreb; heavy electrical engineering at Zagreb; and textiles at Zagreb and in north-west Croatia.

Eighty per cent of Croatia's petroleum comes from local oil wells – in fact most of the wells of ex-Yugoslavia were in Croatia, north and east of Zagreb. Fortunately these wells were outside the area of the recent war, though the refinery at Sisak burned down after being hit by federal shells.

In the past a third of Croatia's national income came from tourism, but between 1991 and 1995 tourism fell dramatically. Dalmatia was the hardest hit while Istria and Krk have begun to climb back, with an influx of Germans, Austrians and some Italians. The collectivisation of agriculture just after WWII failed and private farmers with small plots continue to work most of the land. The interior plains produce fruit, vegetables and grains (especially corn and wheat), while olives and grapes are cultivated along the coast.

Since independence Croatia has had to completely reorient its trade after the loss of markets in the southern regions of former Yugoslavia. In 1994, Italy, Germany and Slovenia together accounted for well over half of Croatia's imports and exports. Due to the war, the average wage is less than US$350 a month, and a high percentage of the population is unemployed (17.1% in 1995), with the number due to increase sharply when troops are demobilised. The current policy of over valuing the kuna penalises exporters while making imports cheap, a situation that will be difficult to sustain in the long term.

Damage from four years of war is estimated at US$27 billion, which the government hopes to raise by borrowing from abroad and by economic growth. Another source of funds is the release of assets held by Belgrade. The return of resource-rich eastern Slavonia is also expected to give the economy a boost. The main priority is to revitalise tourism which before the war, was yielding an average US$ billion a year. Privatisation of state-owned companies is proceeding but not as rapidly as hoped.

POPULATION & PEOPLE

Of Croatia's population of nearly five million, 78% are Croats and 12% are Serbs. Small communities of Slavic Muslims, Hungarians, Slovenes, Italians, Czechs and Albanians complete the mosaic. Some 200,000 war refugees from Bosnia-Hercegovina exist in precarious conditions in Croatia.

Another million Croats live in the other states of ex-Yugoslavia, especially Bosnia-Hercegovina, northern Vojvodina and around the Bay of Kotor in Montenegro. Some 2.3 million ethnic Croats live abroad, including almost 1.5 million in the USA, 270,000 in Germany, 240,000 in Australia, 150,000 in Canada and 150,000 in Argentina. Pittsburgh and Buenos Aires have the largest Croatian communities outside Europe. The largest cities in Croatia are Zagreb (one million), Split (300,000), Rijeka (225,000), Osijek (175,000) and Zadar (150,000).

Sadly, ethnic discrimination has been institutionalised in the Law of Citizenship passed by the Croatian parliament in October 1991. It states that to become a citizen, non-Croats (including Serbs born in Croatia) must demonstrate a knowledge of the Croatian language and Latin alphabet, and show an acceptance of Croatian culture. Dual citizenship is abolished and children from mixed marriages must declare themselves Croats to become citizens able to own property and obtain a work permit. State employees who refuse to take an oath of loyalty to Croatia are fired from their jobs.

ARTS

The work of sculptor Ivan Meštrović (1883-1962) is seen in town squares all around Croatia. Besides creating public monuments, Meštrović designed imposing buildings such as the circular Croatian History Museum in Zagreb (presently closed). Both his sculpture and architecture display a powerful classical restraint that he learned from Rodin. Meštrović's studio in Zagreb and his retirement home at Split have been made into galleries of his work.

Literature

Croatian literary figures include 16th-century playwright Marin Držić and 20th-century novelist, playwright and poet Miroslav Krleža, whose works depict the concerns of a changing Yugoslavia. His most popular novels include *The Return of Philip Latinovicz* (1932) and *Banners* (1963-65), a multivolume saga about middle-class Croatian life at the turn of the century.

Music

Croatian folk music bears many influences. The *kolo*, a lively Slavic round dance in which men and women alternate in the circle, is accompanied by Gypsy-style violinists or players of the *tambura*, a three or five-string mandolin popular throughout Croatia. The measured guitar-playing and rhythmic accordions of Dalmatia have a gentle Italian air.

A recommended recording available locally on compact disc (DD-0030) is *Narodne Pjesme i Plesovi Sjeverne Hrvatske* (Northern Croatian Folk Songs & Dances) by the Croatian folkloric ensemble Lado. The 22 tracks on this album represent nine regions, with everything from haunting Balkan voices reminiscent of Bulgaria to lively Mediterranean dance rhythms.

CULTURE

Croats take pride in keeping up appearances. Despite a fragile economy money can usually be found to brighten up the town centre with a fresh coat of paint or to repair a historic building. Even as their own bank accounts diminish most people will cut out restaurants and movies in order to afford a shopping trip to Italy for some new clothes. The tidy streets and stylish clothes are rooted in the Croats' image of themselves as Western Europeans, not Yugoslavs, a word that makes Croats wince. Because of the intense propaganda surrounding the recent war, Croats are inclined to see themselves as wholly right and the other side as wholly wrong. Comments questioning this assumption are not appreciated.

RELIGION

Croats (78% of the total population) are overwhelmingly Roman Catholic, while virtually all Serbs belong to the Eastern Orthodox Church. In addition to various doctrinal differences, Orthodox Christians venerate icons, allow priests to marry and do not accept the authority of the Roman Catholic pope. Long suppressed under communism, Catholicism is

CROATIA

undergoing a strong resurgence in Croatia; churches are strongly attended every Sunday. Muslims make up 1.2% of the population and Protestants 0.4%, with a tiny Jewish population in Zagreb.

LANGUAGE

As a result of history, tourism and the number of returned 'guest workers' from Germany, German is the most commonly spoken second language in Croatia. Many people in Istria understand Italian, and throughout Slovenia and Croatia, English is popular among the young.

Croatian is a South Slavic language, as are Serbian, Slovene, Macedonian and Bulgarian. Prior to 1991 both Croatian and Serbian were considered dialects of a single language known as Serbo-Croatian. As a result of the civil war in former Yugoslavia, the local languages are being revised, so spellings and idioms may change.

The most obvious difference between Serbian and Croatian is that Serbian is written in Cyrillic script and Croatian in Roman script. There are also a number of variations in vocabulary.

Geographical terms worth knowing are *aleja* (walkway), *cesta* (road), *donji* (lower), *gora* (hill), *grad* (town), *jezero* (lake), *krajina* (frontier), *luka* (harbour), *malo* (little), *novo* (new), *obala* (bank, shore), *otok* (island), *planina* (mountain), *polje* (valley), *prolaz* (strait), *put* (path), *rijeka* (river), *selo* (village), *šetalište* (way), *stanica* (station, stop), *stari* (old), *šuma* (forest), *sveti* (saint), *toplice* (spa), *trg* (square), *ulica* (street), *veliko* (big), *vrata* (pass), *vrh* (peak) and *zaljev* (bay).

Two words everyone should know are *ima* (there is) and *nema* (there isn't). If you make just a small effort to learn a few words, you'll distinguish yourself from the packaged tourists and be greatly appreciated by the local people.

Lonely Planet's *Mediterranean Europe phrasebook* includes a useful chapter on the Serbian and Croatian languages, with translations of key words and phrases from each appearing side by side, providing a clear comparison of the languages. For a basic rundown on travellers' Croatian and Serbian, see the Language Guide at the end of this book.

Facts for the Visitor

PLANNING
Climate & When to Go

The climate varies from Mediterranean along the Adriatic coast to continental inland. The high coastal mountains help to shield the coast from cold northerly winds, making for an early spring and late autumn. In spring and early summer a sea breeze called the *maestral* keeps the temperature down along the coast. Winter winds include the cold *bura* from the north and humid *široko* from the south.

The sunny coastal areas experience hot, dry summers and mild, rainy winters, while the interior regions are cold in winter and warm in summer. Because of a warm current flowing north up the Adriatic coast, sea temperatures never fall below 10°C in winter, and in August they go as high as 26°C. You can swim in the sea from mid-June until late September. The resorts south of Split are the warmest.

May is a nice month to travel along the Adriatic coast, with good weather and few tourists. June and September are also good, but in July and August all Europe arrives and prices soar. September is perhaps the best month since it's not as hot as summer, though the sea remains warm, the crowds will have thinned out as children return to school, off-season accommodation rates will be in place and fruit such as figs and grapes will be abundant. In April and October it may be too cool for camping but the weather should still be fine along the coast, and private rooms will be plentiful and inexpensive.

Books & Maps

For a comprehensive account of the personalities and events surrounding the collapse of ex-Yugoslavia it would be hard to surpass *The Death of Yugoslavia* by Laura Silber & Allan Little, based on the 1995 BBC television series of the same name. A couple of years earlier another BBC correspondent, Misha Glenny, also wrote about his journey through the disintegrating country in *The Fall of Yugoslavia: The Third Balkan War*. Brian Hall's more personal travelogue, *The Impossible Country: A Journey through the Last Days of Yugoslavia*, is occasionally funny and often moving. Rebecca West's 1937 travel classic, *Black Lamb & Grey Falcon*, contains a long section on Croatia as part of her trip through Yugoslavia. Robert Kaplan's *Balkan Ghosts* touches on Croatia's part in the tangled web of Balkan history.

Kimmerley & Frey's map *Croatia & Slovenia* (1:500,000) is detailed and depicts the latest borders. Most tourist offices in the country have local maps, but make sure the street names are up to date.

Online Services

The Croatian Information Service maintains a web site (http://vukovar.unm.edu/wtc/wtc.html) that contains useful practical information and some interesting links. A good site for detailed regional maps is http://www.acs.supernet.net/maps/.

SUGGESTED ITINERARIES

Depending on the length of your stay, you might want to see and do the following things:

Two days
    Visit Zagreb.
One week
    Visit Zagreb, Split and Dubrovnik.
Two weeks
    Visit Zagreb and all of Dalmatia.
One month
    Visit all the areas covered in this chapter.

HIGHLIGHTS
Museums & Galleries

Art museums and galleries are easier for a foreign visitor to enjoy than historical museums, which are usually captioned in Croatian only. In Zagreb the Museum Mimara contains an outstanding collection of Spanish, Italian and Dutch paintings as well as an archaeological collection, exhibits of ancient art from the Far East and collections of glass, textiles, sculpture and furniture. The Strossmayer Gallery, also in Zagreb, is worthwhile for its exhibits of Italian, Flemish, French and Croatian paintings.

If the Meštrović Gallery reopens in Split it would be worth a detour to see. In Zagreb the Meštrović Studio is open by appointment only but gives a fascinating insight into the life and work of this remarkable sculptor.

Castles

The palace of the Roman emperor, Diocletian, in Split has been named a world heritage site by UNESCO. Despite a weathered facade, this sprawling imperial residence and fortress is considered the finest intact example of classical defence architecture in Europe.

Just outside Zagreb is an impressive circle of castles. To the north is Veliki Tabor, a fortified medieval castle, and Trakošćan, beside a long lake. Medvedgrad, west of Zagreb, was built by bishops in the 13th century. The square baroque castle of Lukavec lies in the picturesque Turopolje region south-east of Zagreb. The Varaždin Castle in northern Croatia has recently been restored and hosts an annual music festival. Trsat Castle in Rijeka offers a stunning view of the Kvarner Gulf.

Historic Towns

All along the Adriatic coast are white-stone towns with narrow, winding streets enclosed by defensive walls. Each town has its own flavour. Hilly Rovinj looks out over the sea, while the peninsula of Korčula town burrows into it. Zadar retains echoes of its original Roman street plan while Hvar and Trogir are traditional medieval towns. None can match the exquisite harmony of Dubrovnik, with its blend of elements of medieval and Renaissance architecture.

TOURIST OFFICES

Municipal tourist offices and any office marked 'Turist Biro' will have free brochures and good information on local events. These offices are found in Dubrovnik, Pula, Rijeka, Split and Zagreb. Most towns also have an office selling theatre and concert tickets.

Tourist information is also dispensed by commercial travel agencies such as Kompas, Atlas, Arenatourist, Dalmacijaturist, Generalturist, Croatia Express and Kvarner Express, which also arrange private rooms, sightseeing tours etc.

Keep in mind that these are profit-making businesses, so don't be put off if you're asked to pay for a town map etc. The agencies often sell local guidebooks which are excellent value if you'll be staying long in one place. Ask if they have the schedule for coastal ferries.

CROATIA

Croatian Tour Companies Abroad

The Croatian Ministry of Tourism has few offices abroad, but the tour companies listed here specialise in Croatia and will gladly mail you their brochures containing much information on the country:

Germany
    Kroatische Zentrale für Tourismus, Karlsluher Strasse 18, D-60329 Frankfurt (☎ 069-252 045)
Netherlands
    Phoenix Vakanties, Nieuwe Haven 133, 3116 AC Schiedam (☎ 010-426 2726)
UK
    Phoenix Holidays, 2 The Lanchesters, 162-164 Fulham Palace Rd, London W69ER (☎ 0181-563 0022)
USA
    Atlas Ambassador of Dubrovnik, 60 East 42nd St, New York, NY 10165 (☎ 212-697 6767)

VISAS & EMBASSIES

Visitors from Australia, Canada, New Zealand and the USA require a visa to enter Croatia but visas are issued free of charge at Croatian consulates. Although visas can be obtained at the border, some airlines have been known to refuse passengers without a visa. UK nationals don't require a visa. Visas are valid for a maximum of three months with extensions possible.

While in Croatia, you're supposed to have your passport with you at all times. If you stay at a hotel or camping ground, the staff may keep your passport at the desk and give you a stamped card that serves the same purpose.

Many camping grounds in Croatia are happy to hold your camping carnet instead of the passport – you can't cash travellers' cheques without a passport.

Croatian Embassies Abroad

Croatian embassies and consulates around the world include the following:

Australia
    6 Bulwarra Close, O'Malley, Canberra, ACT 2606 (☎ 062-86 6988)
    9-24 Albert Rd, South Melbourne, Victoria 3205 (☎ 03-9699 2633)
    379 Kent St, Level 4, Sydney, NSW 2000 (☎ 02-9299 8899)
    68 St George's Terrace, Perth, WA 6832 (☎ 09-321 6044)

Canada
    130 Albert St, Suite 1700, Ottawa, ON K1P 5G4 (☎ 613-230 7351)
    918 Dundas St E, Suite 302, Mississauga, ON L4Y 2B8 (☎ 905-277 9051)
New Zealand
    131 Lincoln Rd, Henderson, Box 83200, Edmonton, Auckland (☎ 09-836 5581)
UK
    21 Conway St, London W1P 5HL (☎ 0171-387 1144)
USA
    2343 Massachusetts Ave NW, Washington, DC 20008 (☎ 202-588 5899)

For the addresses of Croatian embassies in Bucharest, Budapest, Ljubljana, Prague and Sofia, turn to the sections of this book relating to those cities.

Foreign Embassies in Croatia

All the following addresses are in Zagreb unless otherwise noted:

Albania
    Vrhovec 231 (☎ 01-777 659)
Australia
    Mihanovićeva 1 (☎ 01-45 77 433)
Bosnia-Hercegovina
    Veslačka 2 (☎ 01-277 715)
Bulgaria
    Novi Goljak 25 (☎ 01-45 52 287)
Canada
    Mihanovićeva 1 (☎ 01-45 77 905)
Czech Republic
    Savska 41 (☎ 01-61 15 914)
Hungary
    Cvetno naselje 17b (☎ 01-61 10 430)
Poland
    Krležin Gvozd 3 (☎ 01-278 818)
Romania
    Becićeve stube 2 (☎ 01-432 226)
Slovakia
    Prilaz Gjure Deželića 10 (☎ 01-430 099)
Slovenia
    Savska 41 (☎ 01-535 122)
UK
    Vlaška 121 (☎ 01 -45 55 310)
    Obala hrvatskog narodnog preporoda 10, Split 21000 (☎ 021-341 464)
USA
    Andrije Hebranga 2 (☎ 01-45 55 500)

MONEY
Currency

In May 1994 the Croatian dinar was replaced by the kuna, which takes its name from the marten, a fox-like animal whose pelt served as a means of exchange in the Middle Ages. You're allowed to import or export Croatian banknotes up to a value of around US$350 but there's no reason to do either.

Exchange Rates

Since 1994 inflation has been brought under control and the kuna has held steady against the Deutschmark at about 3.66 kuna to 1DM. Exchange rates are as follows:

Australia	A$	=	4.1 kuna
Canada	C$1	=	3.8 kuna
France	1FF	=	1.03 kuna
Germany	DM1	=	3.6 kuna
Japan	¥100	=	4.83 kuna
United Kingdom	UK£1	=	8.3 kuna
United States	US$1	=	5.2 kuna

Changing Money

There are numerous places to change money, all offering similar rates; ask at any travel agency for the location of the nearest exchange. Banks and exchange offices keep long hours. Exchange offices deduct a commission of 1.5% to change cash or travellers' cheques but some banks do not. Kuna can be converted into hard currency only at a bank and if you submit a receipt of a previous transaction. Hungarian currency is difficult to change in Croatia.

Credit Cards

Visa credit cards are accepted for cash advances in Croatia only at Splitska Banka. (American Express, MasterCard and Diners Club cards are easier.) Cirrus cards can be used for cash advances only in Zagreb right now but that is changing.

Costs

The government deliberately overvalues the kuna to obtain cheap foreign currency. Hotel prices are set in Deutschmarks and thus are fairly constant, though you pay in Croatian kuna calculated at the daily official rate. Accommodation is more expensive than it should be for a country trying to lure world tourism; real budget accommodation is in short supply. Transport, concert and theatre tickets, and food are reasonably priced for Europe.

Average prices per person are US$10 to US$25 for a private room, US$4 to US$6 for a meal at a self-service restaurant and US$5 to US$8 for an average intercity bus fare. It's not that hard to do it on US$35 a day if you stay in hostels or private rooms and you'll pay less if you camp and self-cater, eating only things such as bread, cheese and canned fish or meat with yoghurt or wine (cooking facilities are seldom provided). A student card will get you half-price admission at some museums and galleries.

Your daily expenses will come way down if you can find a private room to use as a base for exploring nearby areas. Coastal towns which lend themselves to this include Rovinj, Mali Lošinj, Rab, Split, Korčula and Dubrovnik.

You'll get more of a feel for your surroundings if you spend four nights in a place, and using a town as a base allows you to make day trips without hassles over luggage or worrying about where you'll sleep. You will also escape the 30% to 50% surcharge on private rooms rented for under five nights.

If it still seems expensive, keep in mind that the average monthly income in Croatia is less than US$350, so it's much more difficult for the Croats. Most only manage to make ends meet because they still receive subsidised housing, health care and education, and many hold down two or three jobs. Relatives abroad send money home and country people grow much of their own food. Others have savings from the good years before 1991.

Tipping

If you're served fairly and well at a restaurant, you should round up the bill as you're paying. (Don't leave money on the table.) If a service charge has been added to the bill no tip is necessary. Bar bills and taxi fares can also be rounded up. Tour guides on day excursions expect to be tipped.

POST & COMMUNICATIONS
Post

Mail sent to Poste Restante, 10000 Zagreb, Croatia, is held at the post office next to Zagreb railway station. A good coastal address to use is c/o Poste Restante, Main Post Office, 21000 Split, Croatia.

If you have an American Express card, you can have your mail addressed to Atlas travel agency, Trg Nikole Zrinjskog 17, 10000 Zagreb, Croatia, or Atlas travel agency, Trg Brace Radić, 21000 Split, Croatia.

CROATIA

Telephone

To call Croatia from abroad, dial your international access code, ☎ 385 (the country code for Croatia), the area code (without the initial zero) and the local number.

To make a phone call from Croatia, go to the main post office – phone calls placed from hotel rooms are much more expensive. As there are no coins you'll need tokens or a telephone card to use public telephones.

Phonecards come in three values: A, B and C. These can be purchased at any post office and most tobacco shops and newspaper kiosks. A three-minute call from Croatia will be around US$5 to the UK and US$10 to the USA or Australia. The international access code is ☎ 99. Some other useful numbers are ☎ 92 for the police, ☎ 93 for the fire department, ☎ 94 for emergency medical assistance and ☎ 901 to place an operator-assisted call.

NEWSPAPERS & MAGAZINES

The most respected daily newspaper in Croatia is *Vjesnik* but the most daring is the satirical newsweekly *Feral Tribune*. Its investigative articles and sly graphics target increasingly unamused political parties, who have responded by attempting to tax the newspaper out of existence. German and Italian newspapers are widely available and a daily newspaper in Italian, *La Voce del Popolo*, is published in Rijeka. American, British and French newspapers and magazines can be hard to find outside of large cities.

RADIO & TV

The three national television stations in Croatia fill a lot of air time with foreign programming, usually American and always in the original language. For local news, residents of Zadar, Split, Vinkovci and Osijek turn to their regional stations. Croatian Radio broadcasts news in English four times a day (8 am, 10 am, 2 pm, 11 pm) on frequencies 88.9, 91.3 and 99.3.

TIME

Croatia is on Central European Time (GMT/UTC plus one hour). Daylight saving comes into effect at the end of March when clocks are turned forward an hour. At the end of September they're turned back an hour.

ELECTRICITY

Electricity is 220V, 50 Hz AC. Croatia uses the standard European round-pronged plugs.

WEIGHTS & MEASURES

The metric system is used. Like other continental Europeans, Croats indicate decimals with commas and thousands with points.

HEALTH

Everyone must pay to see a doctor at a public hospital *(bolnica)* or medical centre *(dom zdravcja)* but the charges are reasonable. Travel insurance would only pay off if you had a very serious accident and had to be hospitalised. Medical centres often have dentists on the staff, otherwise you can go to a private dental clinic *(zubna ordinacija)*.

WOMEN TRAVELLERS

Women face no special danger in Croatia although women on their own may be harassed and followed in large coastal cities. Some of the local bars and cafés seem like private men's clubs; a woman alone is likely to be greeted with sudden silence and cold stares. Topless sunbathing is considered acceptable; judging from the ubiquitous photos of topless women in tourist brochures it seems almost obligatory.

DANGERS & ANNOYANCES

Personal security and theft are not problems in Croatia. The police and military are well disciplined and it's highly unlikely you'll have any problems with them in any of the places covered in this chapter. The biggest nuisance is aggressive cigarette smoking.

BUSINESS HOURS

Banking hours are 7.30 am to 7 pm weekdays, 8 am to noon Saturday. Many shops open from 8 am to 7 pm weekdays, 8 am to 2 pm Saturday. Along the coast, life is more relaxed; shops and offices frequently close for an afternoon break. Croats are early risers and by 7 am there will be lots of people on the street and many places will already be open.

PUBLIC HOLIDAYS & SPECIAL EVENTS

The public holidays of Croatia are New Year's Day (1 January), Orthodox Christmas (6 and 7 January), Easter Monday (March/April), Labour Day (1 May), Statehood Day (30 May).

Croatian National Uprising Day (22 June), Feast of the Assumption (15 August), All Saints' Day (1 November) and Christmas (25 and 26 December). Statehood Day marks the anniversary of the declaration of independence in 1991 while National Uprising Day commemorates the outbreak of resistance in 1941.

In July and August there are summer festivals in Dubrovnik, Opatija, Split and Zagreb. The many traditional annual events held around Croatia are included under Special Events in the city and town sections.

ACTIVITIES
Yachting
The long, rugged islands off Croatia's mountainous coast all the way from Istria to Dubrovnik make this a yachting paradise. Fine, deep channels with abundant anchorage and steady winds attract yachties from around the world. Throughout the region there are quaint little ports where you can get provisions, and yachts can tie up right in the middle of everything. Information is available from the Adriatic Croatia International Club (☎ 051-271 288; fax 051-271 824), M Tita 221, 51410 Opatija, Croatia.

The only company that currently arranges charters along the Croatian coast is Adria Yacht Center (☎ 0222-533 0640; fax 0222-535 0501), Passauer Platz 6, 1010 Vienna, Austria. All charters are for a minimum of one week (Saturday evening to Saturday morning) and prices range from US$667 to US$5000 a week, depending on the type of yacht and the season. Add US$100 a day for the skipper. Of course, all food, drink and fuel are extra. Boats are available from April to September.

Kayaking
There are countless possibilities for anyone carrying a folding sea kayak, especially among the Elafiti Islands (take the daily ferry from Dubrovnik to Lopud) and the Kornati Islands (take the daily ferry from Zadar to Sali). See Organised Tours in the Getting Around section for information on sailing and kayaking tours.

Hiking
Risnjak National Park at Crni Lug, 12 km west of Delnice between Zagreb and Rijeka, is a good hiking area in summer. Buses run from Delnice to Crni Lug near the park entrance about three times a day, and there's a small park-operated hotel (☎ 051-836 133) at Crni Lug, with rooms at US$18 per person including breakfast. (For accommodation at Delnice turn to the Rijeka section.) Because of the likelihood of heavy snowfalls, hiking is only advisable from late spring to early autumn. It's a nine-km, 2½-hour climb from the park entrance at Bijela Vodica to Veliki Risnjak (1528 metres). At last report, park admission was US$1.50.

The steep gorges and beech forests of Paklenica National Park, 40 km north-east of Zadar, also offer excellent hiking. Starigrad, the main access town for the park, is well connected by hourly buses from Zadar. Hotels and private accommodation are available in Starigrad, as well as a camping ground, Paklenica (☎ 023-369 236), open May to September.

For a great view of the barren coastal mountains, climb Mt Ilija (961 metres) above Orebić, opposite Korčula.

Scuba Diving
The clear waters and varied underwater life would seem to encourage a flourishing dive industry in Croatia but in fact dive shops are just starting to pop up. Most offer certification courses at about US$320 and a dive with rented equipment for US$43. Night diving and wreck diving are also offered. Try Divecentre Hvar (☎ 021-761 026) at Hotel Jadran, 58465 Jelsa, Hvar, or Tauchschule (☎ 051-721 154), Barbat 710, 51280 Rab. In Medveja, outside Opatija, there's a dive centre at Hotel Castello (☎ 051-291 016).

COURSES
The Croatian Heritage Foundation (Hrvatska matica iseljenika), Trg Stjepana Radića 3, 10000 Zagreb (☎ 01-530 005; fax 01-539 111) runs a series of programmes on Croatian language and culture during July and August (exact dates become known the preceding February). Though designed for people of Croatian descent living abroad, everyone is welcome. On the island of Badija near Korčula two 10-day programmes explore Croatian folk dances and Croatian folk music. The cost is US$133 tuition plus US$18 daily board. Three 14-day 'Croaticum' programmes are offered at

Supetar on Brač Island (in association with the National University of Split), costing US$580 with tuition, full board and excursions to Split, Trogir and other places included.

The Faculty of Arts at the University of Zagreb (founded in 1669) organises a more intensive, academically oriented four-week course, (US$580 school fees plus US$190 registration). Room and board (sharing a twin room) at a student dormitory is US$21 a day. Students sit for an exam at the end of the course and those who pass receive a certificate of merit.

Contact the Croatian Heritage Foundation in Zagreb for application information or Professor Luka Budak (☎ 02-9805 7054), Croatian Studies Department, Macquarie University, Sydney, NSW 2109, Australia; Dr Vinko Grubišić (☎ 519-746 5243), Faculty of Arts, University of Waterloo, Waterloo, ON N2L 3G1, Canada, or Dr William March (☎ 913-864 4298), Department of Slavic Languages, University of Kansas, Lawrence, KS 66045, USA. Also ask about regular semester courses offered throughout the academic year.

These courses are an excellent way to learn about Croatian culture and meet a lot of interesting people, while providing a productive anchor for a Mediterranean holiday – highly recommended.

WORK

The Croatian Heritage Foundation also organises summer 'task forces' of young people from around the world who gather to assist in war reconstruction. Often these programmes have an ecological slant such as repairing the bridges in Plitvice National Park or saving the griffon vulture. For details, contact the Croatian Heritage Foundation or call Ms Slavka Jureta (☎ 03-9482 4388) in Australia or Ms Sylvia Hrkač (☎ 905-270 2672) in the USA. One American participant wrote, 'The experience I had and the friends I made changed my life'.

Suncokret (fax 01-222 715), Seferova 10, 10000 Zagreb, Croatia, accepts summer volunteers to do unpaid relief work among war refugees in Croatia. Preference is given to teachers, social workers, counsellors and applicants with prior experience working with refugees.

ACCOMMODATION

Along the coast, accommodation is priced according to three seasons, which vary from place to place. Generally April, May and October are the cheapest months, June and September are medium, but in July and August count on paying at least 50% more. Prices for rooms in the interior regions are often constant all year. Add US$1 to US$1.50 per person per night 'residence tax'.

Beware of the prices listed in official tourist brochures as these are often much lower than what is actually charged. Accommodation is generally cheaper in Dalmatia than in Kvarner or Istria.

This chapter provides the phone numbers of most accommodation facilities. Once you know your itinerary it pays to go to a post office, buy a telephone card and start calling around to check prices, availability etc. Most receptionists speak English.

Camping

Nearly 100 camping grounds are scattered along the Croatian coast. Most operate from mid-May to September only, although a few are open in April and October. In May and late September, call ahead to make sure that the camping ground is open before beginning the long trek out. Don't go by the opening and closing dates you read in travel brochures or this book, as these are only approximate. Even local tourist offices can be wrong.

Many camping grounds are expensive for backpackers because the prices are set in dollars or Deutschmarks per person, and include the charge per tent, caravan, car, electric hook-up etc. This is fine for people with mobile homes who occupy a large area but bad news for those with only a small tent. If you don't have a vehicle, you're better off at camping grounds which have a much smaller fee per person and charge extra per tent, car, caravan, electric hook-up etc.

Germans are the leading users of Croatian camping grounds. Unfortunately, many of these are gigantic 'autocamps' with restaurants, shops and row upon row of caravans. Nudist camping grounds (marked FKK) are among the best because their secluded locations ensure peace and quiet. Freelance camping is officially prohibited.

Hostels

The Croatian YHA (☎ 01-278 239), at Dež-manova 9, 10000 Zagreb, operates summer youth hostels in Dubrovnik, Šibenik and Zadar, and year-round hostels at Zagreb and Pula. Bed and breakfast at these is around US$8 for YHA members in the low season (May, June, September and October), and US$12 for members in July and August. Non-members pay an additional US$4 per person daily for a welcome card; six stamps on the card then entitles you to a membership. The Zagreb hostel has higher prices.

Private Rooms

The best accommodation in Croatia is private rooms in local homes, the equivalent of small private guesthouses in other countries. Such rooms can be arranged by travel agencies but they add a lot of taxes and commission to your bill, so you'll almost always do better dealing directly with proprietors you meet on the street or by knocking on the doors of houses with *sobe* or *zimmer* signs. This way you avoid the residence tax and four-night minimum stay, but you also forgo the agency's quality control. Hang around coastal bus stations and ferry terminals, luggage in hand, looking lost, and someone may find you.

If the price asked is too high, bargain. Be sure to clarify whether the price agreed upon is per person or for the room. Tell the proprietor in advance how long you plan to stay or they may try to add a surprise 'supplement' when you leave after a night or two. At the agencies, singles are expensive and scarce, but on the street, sobe prices are usually per person, which favours the single traveller. Showers are always included. It often works out cheaper if you pay in cash Deutschmarks rather than kuna. Although renting an unofficial room is common practice along the Adriatic coast, be discreet, as technically you're breaking the law by not registering with the police. Don't brag to travel agencies about the low rate you got, for example.

If you stay less than four nights, the agencies add a 20% to 30% surcharge. Travel agencies classify the rooms according to categories I, II or III. If you want the cheapest room, ask for category III. In the resort areas many category I rooms have cooking facilities, and private apartments are available.

Some rooms are excellent, but at others the landlord comes in every half-hour with only a brief knock on the door. Staying in a private room is a way of meeting a local family but unfortunately, private rooms are usually unavailable in interior towns, and very expensive in Zagreb.

Hotels

There are few cheap hotels in Croatia – prices generally begin around US$35 double, even in the off season. Still, if you're only staying one night and the private room agency is going to levy a 50% surcharge, you might consider getting a hotel room. In the off season when most rooms are empty you could try bargaining for a more realistic rate.

The staff at many of the state-run hotels have a couldn't-care-less attitude and just laugh at complaints. Maintenance isn't their concern and the level of service is often geared towards group tours, not the individual, who has to pay a lot more.

Since 1991 a number of resort hotels along the Adriatic coast have been filled with refugees from the fighting in interior areas. Although the refugees are gradually leaving, the hotels may need to remain closed for some time in order to renovate.

FOOD

A restaurant *(restauracija)* or pub may also be called a *gostionica* and a café a *kavana*. Self-service cafeterias are quick, easy and inexpensive, though the quality of the food varies. If the samples behind glass look cold or dried out, ask them to dish out a fresh plate for you. Better restaurants aren't that much more expensive if you choose carefully. In most of them the vegetables, salads and bread cost extra, and some deluxe restaurants add a 10% service charge (not mentioned on the menu). Fish dishes are often charged by weight, which makes it difficult to know how much a certain dish will cost. Ice-cream cones are priced by the scoop.

Restaurants in Croatia can be a hassle because they rarely post their menus outside, so to find out what they offer and the price range you have to walk in and ask to see the menu. Then if you don't like what you see, you must walk back out and appear rude. Always check the menu, however, and if the price of the drinks or something else isn't listed, ask, otherwise you'll automatically be charged the 'tourist price'.

Breakfast is difficult in Croatia as all you can get easily is coffee. For eggs, toast and jam you'll have to go somewhere expensive, otherwise you can buy some bread, cheese and milk at a supermarket and picnic somewhere. Throughout ex-Yugoslavia the breakfast of the people is *burek*, a greasy layered pie made with meat *(mesa)* or cheese *(sira)* and cut on a huge metal tray.

A load of fruit and vegetables from the local market can make a healthy, cheap picnic lunch. There are plenty of supermarkets in Croatia – cheese, bread, wine and milk are readily available and fairly cheap. The person behind the meat counter at supermarkets will make a big cheese or bologna sandwich for you upon request and you only pay the regular price of the ingredients.

Regional Dishes

Italian pizza and pasta are a good option in Istria and Dalmatia, costing about half of what you'd pay in Western Europe. The Adriatic coast excels in seafood, including scampi, *prstaci* (shellfish) and Dalmatian *brodet* (mixed fish stewed with rice), all cooked in olive oil and served with boiled vegetables or *tartufe* (mushrooms) in Istria. In the Croatian interior, watch for *manistra od bobića* (beans and fresh maize soup) or *štrukle* (cottage cheese rolls). A Zagreb speciality is *štrukli* (boiled cheesecake).

DRINKS

It's customary to have a small glass of brandy before a meal and to accompany the food with one of Croatia's fine wines. Ask for the local regional wine. Croatia is also famous for its plum brandies *(šljivovica)*, herbal brandies *(travarica)*, cognacs *(vinjak)* and liqueurs such as maraschino, a cherry liqueur made in Zadar, or herbal *pelinkovac*. Italian-style espresso coffee (infused by a machine) is popular in Croatia.

Zagreb's Ožujsko beer *(pivo)* is very good but Karlovačko beer from Karlovac is better. You'll want to practise saying the word *živjeli!* (cheers!).

ENTERTAINMENT

Culture was heavily subsidised by the communists, and admission to operas, operettas and concerts is still reasonable. The main theatres offering musical programmes are listed herein, so note the location and drop by some time during the day to see what's on and purchase tickets. In the interior cities, winter is the best time to enjoy the theatres and concert halls. The main season at the opera houses of Rijeka, Split and Zagreb runs from October to May. These close for holidays in summer and the cultural scene shifts to the many summer festivals. Ask municipal tourist offices about cultural events in their area.

Discos operate in summer in the coastal resorts and all year in the interior cities. If you're male, you'll find the local women aren't interested in meeting you; if you're female, you'll find the local men are *too* interested in meeting you, so it's always a good idea to go accompanied. It doesn't cost anything at all to participate in the early evening *korzo*, a casual promenade enjoyed by great crowds in the town centres.

The cheapest entertainment in Croatia is a movie at a *kino* (cinema). Admission fees are always low and the soundtracks are in the original language. The selection leans towards popular American blockbusters and the last film of the day is usually hard-core pornography. Check the time on your ticket carefully, as admission is not allowed once the film has started.

THINGS TO BUY

Among the traditional handicraft products of Croatia are fine lace from the Dalmatian islands, handmade embroidery, woodcarvings, woollen and leather items, carpets, filigree jewellery, ceramics, national costumes and tapestries.

Getting There & Away

AIR

Croatia Airlines (☎ 01-45 51 244), ulica Teslina 5, Zagreb, has flights from Zagreb to Amsterdam, Berlin, Brussels, Copenhagen, Dublin, Düsseldorf, Frankfurt, London,

Moscow, Mostar, Munich, Paris, Prague, Rome, Sarajevo, Skopje, Stuttgart, Tirana, Vienna and Zürich.

LAND
Bus

Hungary There are frequent connections between Zagreb and Nagykanizsa (145 km, twice daily, US$10) and Zagreb and Barcs (202 km, four daily, US$16), going onto Pécs. From Barcs there are frequent trains to Pécs (67 km) and then less-frequent buses to Szeged (188 km), where there are trains and buses to Subotica (47 km) in Vojvodina (Yugoslavia). Nagykanizsa is more convenient if you're travelling to/from Budapest. No buses are running from Croatia to Serbia at the moment although that is expected to change soon.

Germany The buses of the Deutsche Touring GmbH are cheaper than the train. Buses to Croatia depart from Berlin, Cologne, Dortmund, Frankfurt/Main, Mannheim, Munich, Nuremberg and Stuttgart. Baggage is DM3 extra per piece. Service is usually only once or twice a week, but buses operate all year. Information is available at bus stations in the cities just mentioned.

The Netherlands Budget Bus/Eurolines (☎ 020-627 5151), Rokin 10, Amsterdam, offers a weekly service all year to Zagreb (US$125 one way, US$203 return, 22 hours), Rijeka and Split (US$139 one way, US$215 return). Reductions are available for children under 13, but not for students or seniors. Eurolines (☎ 03-266 8662) operates a similar weekly service all year from Antwerp (Belgium) to Zagreb. On all of the Dutch and Belgian services you must change buses at Frankfurt, where you will be charged DM3 per piece for luggage. An advance reservation (US$3) is recommended.

Train

Italy Railway fares in Italy are relatively cheap, so if you can get across the Italian border from France or Switzerland, it won't cost an arm and a leg to take a train on to Trieste, where there are frequent bus connections to Croatia via Koper. Between Venice and Zagreb (US$28) there are the *Kras, Simplon*

and *Venezia* express trains via Trieste and Ljubljana (seven hours).

Germany Intercity 296/297 goes overnight nightly from Munich to Zagreb (613 km, nine hours, US$69) via Salzburg and Ljubljana. Reservations are required southbound but not northbound. The *Eurocity Mimara* between Leipzig and Zagreb, stopping at Munich, travels by day.

Austria The *Ljubljana* express from Vienna to Rijeka (615 km, eight hours), via Ljubljana, and the *Eurocity Croatia* from Vienna to Zagreb (472 km, 6½ hours, US$46) both travel via Maribor.

Hungary To go from Budapest to Zagreb (412 km, 6½ hours, US$28) you have a choice of five trains. A direct daily train links Zagreb to Pécs (267 km, four hours, US$18), leaving Pécs in the early morning and Zagreb in the afternoon. Since July 1991 no trains have linked Croatia directly with Serbia, but train service is due to be reinstated as soon as repair work is finished.

As well as the international express trains, there are unreserved local trains between Gyékényes (Hungary) and Koprivnica (15 km, 20 minutes, US$4) three times a day, with connections in Gyékényes to/from Nagykanizsa, Pécs and Kaposvár. Two unreserved trains a day travel between Varaždin and Nagykanizsa (72 km, 1½ hours, US$6).

Romania From Bucharest there are two daily trains to Zagreb (26 hours, US$112) or you can take the overnight train to Arad and a local train to Nadlac on the Hungarian border. Crossing the border on foot has been known to irritate border guards but it's easy enough to hitch. Catch a train from Nagylak, Hungary to Szeged (47 km, 1¼ hours) and then a bus to Pécs, from where there are frequent trains to Barcs and Zagreb.

Car & Motorcycle

The main highway entry/exit points between Croatia and Hungary are Goričan (between Nagykanizsa and Varaždin), Gola (23 km east of Koprivnica), Terezino Polje (opposite Barcs) and Donji Miholjac (seven km south of

Harkány). There are 29 crossing points to/from Slovenia, too many to list here. There are 23 border crossings into Bosnia-Hercegovina and seven into Yugoslavia. The main Zagreb to Belgrade highway has reopened and major destinations in Bosnia-Hercegovina such as Sarajevo, Mostar and Međugorje are accessible from Zagreb, Split and Dubrovnik.

SEA

International ferry services are just getting back on track after four years of disrupted service because of the war. Although there used to be direct services between Croatia and Italy, Greece and Albania, only Croatia and Italy are directly linked today. The Croatian Jadrolinija line, the Italian Adriatica Navigazione and the Croatian company Lošinjska Plovidba all serve the Adriatic coast. All year round there's an overnight, twice weekly Jadrolinija ferry between Ancona and Split (10 hours, US$44) and weekly service between Dubrovnik and Bari (eight hours, US$44), with additional service in summer. At about the same price, Adriatica Navigazione also connects Ancona and Split all year. Other Jadrolinija lines from Ancona stop at Zadar, Stari Grad on Hvar Island, and Vela Luka on Korčula Island. See the Getting There & Away sections in those destinations for further details.

Both Adriatica Navigazione and Lošinjska Plovidba connect Italy with the Istrian coast in summer. From May to September Adriatica Navigazione runs the *Marconi* between Trieste and Rovinj (eight hours, US$19) six times a week, stopping on certain days at Poreč, the Brijuni Islands and Mali Lošinj. Lošinjska Plovidba's *Marina* connects Venice with Zadar (14½ hours, US$48) twice a week from late June to September, stopping at Pula and Mali Lošinj. Departure tax from Italian ports is US$3.

Unless the ferry service to Greece and Albania resumes, there is no choice but to connect via Ancona or Bari. Both the Jadrolinija line to Bari and the Adriatica Navigazione line to Ancona connect well to other Adriatica Navigazione ferries to Durrës. From Ancona and Bari it is also possible to catch the Anek Lines boats to Igoumenitsa, Patrasso and Corfu.

LEAVING CROATIA

The airport departure tax is US$8. There is no port tax if you are leaving the country by boat.

Getting Around

AIR

Croatia Airlines has daily flights from Zagreb to Dubrovnik (US$100), Pula (US$71) and Split (US$93). Its twice-weekly flight to Skopje is very expensive at US$202 one way.

BUS

Bus services in Croatia are excellent. Fast express buses go everywhere, often many times a day, and they'll stop to pick up passengers at designated stops anywhere along their route. Buses charge about US$0.50 for each kilometre of travel. Luggage stowed in the baggage compartment under the bus is extra, costing around US$1 apiece, including insurance. If your bag is small you could carry it onto the bus, although the seats are often placed close together, making this impossible on crowded buses.

At large stations, bus tickets must be purchased at the office, not from drivers; try to book ahead to be sure of a seat. Lists of departures over the various windows at the bus stations tell you which one has tickets for your bus. Tickets for buses that arrive from somewhere else are usually purchased from the conductor. On Croatian bus schedules, *vozi svaki dan* means every day, *ne vozi nedjeljom ni praznikom* means not Sundays and public holidays.

Some buses travel overnight, saving you having to pay for a room. Don't expect to get much sleep, however, as the inside lights will be on and music will be blasting the whole night. Take care not to be left behind at meal or rest stops and beware of buses leaving 10 minutes early.

TRAIN

Train travel is about 15% cheaper than bus travel and often more comfortable, if slower. Baggage is free. Local trains usually have only unreserved 2nd-class seats but they're rarely crowded. Reservations may be required on express trains. 'Executive' trains have only 1st-class seats and are 40% more expensive than local trains. No couchettes are available on any domestic services. Most train stations have left-luggage offices charging US$1 apiece (passport required).

Daily train service from Zagreb to Zadar (11 hours, US$14) and Split (10 hours, US$13) has been restored, both trains stopping at Knin. Other trains include Zagreb to Osijek (288 km, five hours), Koprivnica (92 km, 1½ hours, local), Varaždin (110 km, three hours, local), Ljubljana (160 km, three hours, local) and Rijeka (243 km, five hours, local). There are also trains from Rijeka to Ljubljana (155 km, 2½ hours, local) and Pula to Ljubljana (258 km, five hours, local).

On posted timetables in Croatia the word for arrivals is *dolazak*, and for departures it's *odlazak* or *polazak*. Other terms you may encounter include *poslovni* (executive train), *brzi* or *ubrazni* (fast train), *putnički* (local train), *rezerviranje mjesta obvezatno* (compulsory seat reservation), *presjedanje* (change of trains), *ne vozi nedjeljom i blagdanom* (no service Sundays and holidays) and *svakodnevno* (daily).

CAR & MOTORCYCLE

Motorists require vehicle registration papers and the green insurance card to enter Croatia. Two-way amateur radios built into cars are no problem but must be reported at the border.

Petrol is either leaded super, unleaded (*bezolovni*), or diesel. You have to pay tolls on the motorways around Zagreb, to use the Učka tunnel between Rijeka and Istria, and for the bridge to Krk Island.

Along the coast, the spectacular Adriatic highway from Italy to Albania hugs the steep slopes of the coastal range, with abrupt drops to the sea and a curve a minute. You can drive as far south as Vitaljina, 56 km south-east of Dubrovnik.

The bridge at Maslenica on the main highway east of Zadar was destroyed by the federal army in November 1991, then held by Serb separatists for over a year before being recaptured by the Croatian army during their surprise January 1993 offensive. A pontoon bridge has been erected to replace the destroyed bridge but traffic is often heavy.

Motorists can turn to the Hrvatski Auto-klub (HAK) or Croatian Auto Club for help or advice. Addresses of local HAK offices are provided throughout this chapter and the nationwide HAK road assistance (*vučna služba*) number is ☎ 987.

Road Rules

Unless otherwise posted, the speed limits for cars and motorcycles are 60 km/h in built-up areas, 90 km/h on main highways and 130 km/h on motorways. Police systematically fine motorists exceeding these limits. On any of Croatia's winding two-lane highways, it's illegal to pass long military convoys or a whole line of cars caught behind a slow-moving truck. Drive defensively, as local motorists lack discipline.

Rental

The large car-rental chains represented in Croatia are Avis, Budget, Europcar and Hertz, with Europcar (offices in Opatija, Split and Zagreb) generally the cheapest and Hertz the most expensive. Avis, Budget and Hertz have offices at Zagreb and Split airports. Throughout Croatia, Avis is allied with Autotehna, while Hertz is often represented by Kompas. Independent local companies are often less expensive than the international chains, but Avis, Budget, Europcar and Hertz have the big advantage of offering one-way rentals which allow you to drop the car off at any of their stations in Croatia free of charge.

The cheapest cars include the Renault 5, Peugeot 106, Fiat Panda and Fiat Uno. Prices begin around US$20 a day plus US$0.25 per km (100 km minimum), or US$350 a week with unlimited km. Shop around as deals vary widely and 'special' discounts and weekend rates are often available. Third-party public liability insurance is included by law, but make sure your quoted price includes full collision insurance, called collision damage waiver (CDW). Otherwise your responsibility for damage done to the vehicle is usually determined as a percentage of the car's value. Full CDW is usually US$8 a day extra (compulsory for those aged under 25), theft insurance is US$8 a day, and personal accident insurance is another US$5 a day. Add 10% to 20% local tax to all charges. You may be able to get a reduced tax rate by paying in foreign currency or in cash – ask about this.

CROATIA

Age limits vary from company to company. Budget will rent to 18-year-olds who have had their licence for at least a year, but at Hertz, Avis and Europcar you have to be 21. If you're paying by cash the amount of the cash deposit is usually based upon the type of car and the length of the rental.

Sometimes you can get a lower car-rental rate by booking the car from abroad. Tour companies in Western Europe often have fly-drive packages which include a flight to Croatia and a car (two-person minimum).

HITCHING

The hitchhiking in Croatia is lousy. There are lots of little cars but they're usually full and the local motorists are not noted for their courtesy. Tourists never stop. Unfortunately, the image many Croats have of this activity is based on violent movies like *Hitchhiker*.

BOAT
Jadrolinija Ferries

All year round big, white and blue international Jadrolinija car ferries operate along the Rijeka-Dubrovnik coastal route, with service almost daily during summer. The most scenic section is Split to Dubrovnik, which all of the Jadrolinija ferries cover during the day. Rijeka to Split (13 hours) is usually an overnight trip in either direction.

Ferries are a lot more comfortable than buses, though considerably more expensive. From Rijeka to Dubrovnik deck fare is US$28 but at least 10% cheaper October to May. With a through ticket, you can stop at any port for up to a week, provided you notify the purser beforehand and have your ticket validated. This is much cheaper than buying individual sector tickets. Cabins should be booked a week ahead, but deck space is usually available on all sailings.

Deck passage on Jadrolinija is just that: reclining seats (*poltrone*) are about US$6 extra and four-berth cabins (if available) begin at US$44 per person (US$60 Rijeka to Dubrovnik). Cabins can be arranged at the reservation counter aboard ship, but advance bookings are recommended if you want to be sure of a place. Deck space is fine for passages during daylight hours and when you can stretch out a sleeping bag on the upper deck in good weather, but if

it's rainy you could end up sitting in the smoky cafeteria which stays open all night. During the crowded midsummer season, deck class can be unpleasant in wet weather.

Meals in the restaurants aboard Jadrolinija ships are about US$11 for a set menu. All the cafeteria offers is ham-and-cheese sandwiches for US$3. Coffee is cheap in the cafeteria but wine and spirits tend to be expensive. Breakfast in the restaurant is about US$5. It's best to bring some food and drink with you.

Other Ferries

There are weekly ferries all year between Pula and Zadar (US$9.30) via Mali Lošinj and also between Mali Lošinj and Zadar (US$8). The latter service runs daily in summer.

Other local ferries connect the bigger offshore islands with each other and with the mainland. The most important routes are Valbiska on Krk Island to Merag on Cres Island (nine daily all year), Baška on Krk Island to Lopar on Rab Island (three or four daily from June to September), Jablanac to Mišnjak on Rab Island (nine daily all year), Zadar to Preko on Ugljan Island (eight daily all year), Split to Supetar on Brač Island (six daily all year), Split to Stari Grad on Hvar Island (two or three daily all year), Drvenik to Sućuraj on Hvar Island (four daily all year), Split to Vela Luka on Korčula Island via Hvar (daily all year), Orebić to Korčula Island (eight daily all year) and Dubrovnik to Sobra on Mljet Island (weekdays all year).

Taking a bicycle on these services incurs an extra charge. Some of the ferries operate only a couple of times a day, and once the vehicular capacity is reached, remaining motorists must wait for the next service. In summer the lines of waiting cars can be long, so it's important to arrive early. Foot passengers and cyclists should have no problem getting on.

Throughout Croatia, when asking about ferry times beware of ticket agents who give incomplete or misleading information about departures. Study the posted Croatian timetable carefully, *then* ask your questions.

Travel agencies such as Atlas run fast hydrofoils up and down the coast, especially between Rijeka and Split, with Rab and Hvar also served (Rijeka-Split is five hours, US$40). These services normally operate only once a week during summer and are advertised on placards outside the agencies.

ORGANISED TOURS

Atlas travel agency sometimes offers 'adventure' tours which feature bird-watching, canoeing, caving, cycling, diving, fishing, hiking, riding, sailing, sea kayaking and whitewater rafting in both Croatia and Slovenia. The eight-day tours, if they are offered, begin at US$496 all-inclusive and you join the group in Croatia. These tours allow you to combine the advantages of group and individual travel. Travel agents in North America book through Atlas Ambassador of Dubrovnik (☎ 212-697 6767), 60 East 42nd St, New York, NY 10165. An interesting alternative for sailing enthusiasts is Katarina Line (☎ 051-272 110), Hotel Admiral 51410 Opatija, which offers weeklong cruises from Rijeka to Krk, Rab, Pag, Mali Lošinj and Cres. Prices start at US$280 (US$333 with the Kornati Islands) and include half-board.

Zagreb

Zagreb, an attractive city of over a million inhabitants, has been the capital of Croatia since 1557. Spread up from the Sava River, Zagreb sits on the southern slopes of Medvednica, the Zagreb uplands. Medieval Zagreb developed from the 11th to the 13th centuries in the twin towns of Kaptol and Gradec. Kaptol grew around St Stephen's Cathedral and Gradec centred on St Mark's Church. Clerics established themselves in Kaptol as early as 1094, whereas Gradec was the craftspeople's quarter.

Much of medieval Zagreb remains today, although the stately 19th-century city between the old town and the train station is the present commercial centre. There are many fine parks, galleries and museums in both the upper and lower towns. Zagreb is Croatia's main centre for primitive or naive art.

For a time it appeared that Zagreb would escape the havoc surrounding the break-up of Yugoslavia but its tranquillity was shaken by the rocket attacks of May 1995 which left seven people dead. Now that peace has returned, affluent-looking consumers throng Ilica, and the clientele of the elegant cafés around Trg Jelačića is as sophisticated as ever. The people are well dressed and smiling, but many of Zagreb's museums are still closed (some for 'reinterpretation'), with the exhibits removed for safekeeping. Finding a place to stay at a reasonable price remains the biggest problem for a traveller in this calm and graceful city.

Orientation

As you come out of the train station, you'll see a series of parks and pavilions directly in front of you and the twin neo-Gothic towers of the cathedral in the distance. Trg Jelačića, beyond the north end of the parks, is the main city square. The bus station is one km east of the train station. Tram Nos 2, 3 and 6 run from the bus station to the train station, with No 6 continuing to Trg Jelačića.

Left-luggage offices in both the bus and train stations are open 24 hours a day. The price posted at the left-luggage office in the bus station is *per hour* and it works out to US$3 a day, so be careful. At the train station you pay a fixed price of about US$1.50 per day.

Information

The tourist office (☎ 272 530), Trg Jelačića 11, is open weekdays from 8 am to 8 pm, weekends from 9 am to 6 pm.

The Croatian Auto Club (HAK) has two travel offices in Zagreb: a smaller office (☎ 431 142) at Draškovićeva ulica 46 and a main information centre (☎ 415 800) six blocks east at Derenčinova 20.

Plitvice National Park maintains an information office (☎ 442 448) at Trg Tomislava 19. It also has information on other national parks around Croatia.

Money Exchange offices at the bus and train stations change money at the bank rate with 1.5% commission. Both the exchange office in the train station (open 7 am to 7.30 pm) and in the bus station (open 6 am to 8 pm) accept travellers' cheques.

Post & Communications Any poste-restante mail is held (for one month) in the post office on the east side of the train station. Zagreb is a good

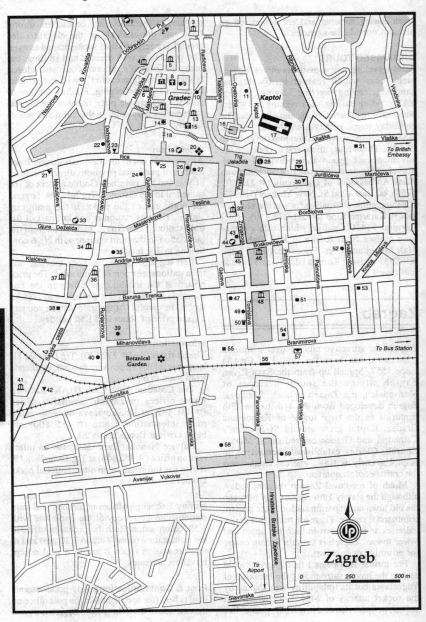

Put

2 ▼

3

Dobravkin

Radićeva

Filipvić

4 ●

5

Mesnička

Matoševa

7 ■

8

■ ●9

6 ●

10 ●

Gradec

Tkalčićeva

Opatovina

11 ●

Kaptol

Kaptol

Vončinina

Vlaška

12 ■

13

14 ●

□18

16

15 ■

17

Vlaška

G. Kovačića

Nazorova

Dežmanova

22 ●

23 ▼

Ilica

19 ◑

20 ✳

Trg
Jelačića

i 28

● 31

To British
Embassy

29 ▼

21 ▼

Medulićeva

24 ●

Gundulićeva

▼25

26 ●

● 27

Preradovićeva

Jurišićeva

30 ▼

Martićeva

Teslina

33 ◐

Gjure Deželića

Masarykova

Frankopanska

32 ■

43 ●

44 ◑

Zrinjevac

Đorđićeva

Boškovićeva

52 ●

Draškovićeva

Kneza Mislava

34 ■

● 35

Andrije Hebranga

45 ■

46 ■

Gajeva

Petrinjska

Palmotićeva

Klaićeva

37 ■

36 ▽

△

Baruna Trenka

47 ●

48 ■

● 51

■ 53

38 ■

Runjaninova

39 ●

49 ●

50 ■

Tomislava

54 ▽

Mihanovićeva

Savska cesta

40 ●

**Botanical
Garden** ✳

● 55

Branimirova

57 ▼

56

To Bus Station

41 ■

▼42

Koturaška

Miramarska

Paromlinska

Trnjanska cesta

● 58

● 59

Avenijar Vukovar

Hvatske

Bratske Zajednice

To
Airport

Slavonska

Zagreb

0   250   500 m

PLACES TO STAY		6	Historical Museum of	33	Embassy of Slovakia
31	Hotel Jadran		Croatia	34	Arts & Crafts Museum
38	Inter-Continental Hotel	7	Banski Dvori Palace	35	Croatian National
51	Omladinski Hotel	8	St Mark's Church		Theatre
	(Youth Hostel) &	9	Sabor (Parliament)	36	Ethnographic Museum
	Hotel Astoria	10	Stone Gate	37	Museum Mimara
53	Sheraton	11	Komedija Theatre	39	National Library
54	Central Hotel	12	Gallery of Naive Art	40	Dom Zdravlja Centar
55	Hotel Esplanade	13	Muzejski Prostor	41	Technical Museum
		14	Lotršćak Tower	43	Atlas Travel Agency
PLACES TO EAT		15	St Catherine's Church	44	US Embassy
2	Restauracija Dubravkin	16	Dolac Market	45	Gallery of Modern Art
	put	17	St Stephen's Cathedral	46	Strossmayer Gallery
21	Medulić Restaurant	18	Funicular Railway	47	Puppet Theatre
23	Pizzeria Delfino	19	British Council	48	Exhibition Pavilion
25	Restaurant Split	20	Nama Department	49	Plitvice National Park
30	Slavija Restaurant		Store		Office
42	Studentski Centar	22	Croatian YHA/Dali	50	Pivnica Tomaslav
			Travel	52	Croatian Auto Club
OTHER		24	Academy of Music		(HAK)
1	Polish Embassy	26	Trg Petra Preradovića	56	Train Station
3	City Museum	27	Blagasija Oktogon	57	Post Office
4	Natural History	28	Tourist Office	58	City Hall
	Museum	29	Post Office/Telephone	59	Vatroslav Lisinski
5	Meštrović Studio		Centre		Concert Hall
		32	Archaeological Museum		

place to pick up mail, as the poste-restante office here is open around the clock (except Sunday morning). Have your letters addressed to Poste Restante, 10000 Zagreb, Croatia.

This same post office is also the best place to make long-distance telephone calls. Public telephones in Zagreb use phonecards. Zagreb's telephone code is ☎ 01.

Travel Agencies Dali Travel, Dežmanova 9, the travel branch of the Croatian YHA, can provide information on HI hostels throughout Croatia and make advance bookings. It also sells ISIC student cards (US$6). It's open weekdays from 8 am to 4 pm.

The American Express representative is Atlas (☎ 427 623), Trg Zrinjskoga 17, Zagreb 10000. It will hold clients' mail.

Bookshops Antikvarijat, next to Atlas travel agency, has a wide selection of paperbacks in English as well as several excellent (though expensive) maps.

Laundry Predom, across the street from HAK on Draškovića 31, is open Saturday mornings and weekdays from 7 am to 7 pm. Jeans and

shirts cost US$1 each to wash and press. Underwear and socks are washed for US$0.25 each.

Medical & Emergency Services If you need to see a doctor, your best bet is the ultramodern Dom Zdravlja Centar (☎ 273 555), Runjaninova 4 near the Botanical Garden. It's open daily from 7 am to 10 pm and at last report the consultation fee was US$6.

The police station for foreigners is at Petrinjska 30.

Things to See

Kaptol Zagreb's colourful **Dolac vegetable market** is just up the steps from Trg Jelačića and continues north along Opatovina. It functions daily, with especially large gatherings on Friday and Saturday. The twin neo-Gothic spires of **St Stephen's Cathedral** (1899), now renamed The Cathedral of the Assumption of the Blessed Virgin Mary, are nearby. Elements from the medieval cathedral on this site, destroyed by an earthquake in 1880, can be seen inside, including 13th-century frescos, Renaissance pews, marble altars and a baroque pulpit. The baroque **Archiepiscopal Palace** surrounds the cathedral, as do 16th-century

CROATIA

fortifications constructed when Zagreb was threatened by the Turks.

Gradec From ulica Radićeva 5 off Trg Jelačića a pedestrian walkway, stube Ivana Zakmardija, leads to the **Lotršćak Tower** and a funicular railway (1888), which connects the lower and upper towns. The tower may be climbed for a sweeping 360-degree view of the city (closed Sunday). To the right is the baroque **St Catherine's Church**, with Jezuitski trg beyond. The **Muzejski prostor**, Jezuitski trg 4 (free admission on Monday), is Zagreb's premier exhibition hall where superb art shows are staged. Further north and to the right is the 13th-century **Stone Gate**, with a miraculous painting of the Virgin which escaped the devastating fire of 1731.

The colourful painted-tile roof of the Gothic **St Mark's Church** on Markov trg marks the centre of Gradec. Inside are works by Ivan Meštrović, Croatia's most famous modern sculptor, but the church is only open irregularly. On the east side of St Mark's is the **Sabor** (1908), Croatia's National Assembly.

To the west of St Mark's is the 18th-century **Banski Dvori Palace**, the presidential palace with guards at the door in red ceremonial uniform.

At Mletačka 8 nearby is the former **Meštrović Studio**, now a museum which can be visited by appointment only from 8 am to 3 pm. Other museums in this area include the **Historical Museum of Croatia**, Matoševa 9, the **Gallery of Naive Art**, Ćirilometodska 3 (temporarily closed), and the **Natural History Museum**, Demetrova 1 (closed Monday). More interesting is the recently renovated **City Museum**, Opatićka 20, with a scale model of old Gradec. Summaries in English and German are in each room of the museum, which is housed in the former Convent of St Claire (1650).

The Lower Town Zagreb really is a city of museums. There are four on the parks between the train station and Trg Jelačića. The yellow **exhibition pavilion** (1897) across the park from the station presents changing contemporary art exhibitions. The second building north, also in the park, houses the **Strossmayer Gallery** of the Academy of Arts & Sciences,

with old master paintings. It's closed on Monday, but you can enter the interior courtyard anyway to see the Baška Slab (1102) from the island of Krk, one of the oldest inscriptions in the Croatian language.

The **Gallery of Modern Art** (closed Monday), adjacent at Andrije Hebranga 1, has a large collection of rather uninspiring paintings. The nearby **Archaeological Museum** (closed Saturday), at Trg Nikole Zrinjskog 19, displays prehistoric to medieval artefacts, as well as Egyptian mummies. Behind the museum is a garden of Roman sculpture. (At last report both these museums were closed.)

West of the Centre The **Museum Mimara**, (open Tuesday to Sunday from 10 am to 8 pm, Monday 2 to 8 pm, US$4, free on Monday) at Rooseveltov trg 5, is one of the finest art galleries in Europe. Housed in a neo-Renaissance former school building (1883), this diverse collection shows the loving hand of Ante Topić Mimara, a private collector who donated over 3750 priceless objects to his native Zagreb, even though he spent much of his life in Salzburg, Austria. The Spanish, Italian and Dutch paintings are the highlight, but there are also large sections of glassware, sculpture and Oriental art. (At present only the paintings may be seen.)

Nearby on Trg Maršala Tita is the neobaroque **Croatian National Theatre** (1895), with Ivan Meštrović's sculpture *Fountain of Life* (1905) standing in front. The **Ethnographic Museum** (closed Monday), at Trg Mažuranića 14, has a large collection of Croatian folk costumes with English explanations. South is the Art-Nouveau **National Library** (1907). The **Botanical Garden** on ulica Mihanovićeva (closed Monday, free admission) is attractive for the plants and landscaping as well as its restful corners.

North of the Centre A 20-minute ride north on bus No 106 from the cathedral takes you to **Mirogoj**, one of the most beautiful cemeteries in Europe. One wag commented that the people here are better housed in death than they ever were in life. The English-style landscaping is enclosed by a long 19th-century neo-Renaissance arcade.

Organised Tours
Within Zagreb, Adriatours (☎ 45 52 868), Zrinjevac 14, organises walking tours for US$8 per person. Minibus tours (US$15) leave every Wednesday morning from the Hotel Esplanade and the InterContinental. Generalturist (☎ 45 50 888), Praška 5, runs day trips outside Zagreb, visiting castles and manors in the surrounding hills.

Special Events
In odd years in April there's the Zagreb Biennial of Contemporary Music, since 1961 Croatia's most important music event. Zagreb also hosts a festival of animated films every other year in June. Croatia's largest international fairs are the Zagreb spring (mid-April) and autumn (mid-September) grand trade fairs. In July and August the Zagreb Summer Festival presents a cycle of concerts and theatre performances on open stages in the upper town.

Places to Stay
Camping There's a camping area beside the Pod starim hrastovima Restaurant at Sesvete, east of Zagreb. Take tram No 4, 7, 11 or 12 to Dubrava, then bus No 212 to Sesvete and get out at Varaždinska cesta. From the bus stop it's only an eight-minute walk north along the highway to the signposted camping ground. You may arrive to find the camping ground completely abandoned, in which case there'd probably be no problem pitching a tent for one night. Check with the tourist office and try to get information before heading out there.

Hostels Budget accommodation is in short supply in Zagreb. An early arrival is recommended, since private room-finding agencies are an attractive alternative and refuse telephone bookings.

The noisy 215-bed *Omladinski Hotel* (actually a youth hostel) at Petrinjska 77 near the train station (☎ 434 964) is open all year and costs US$35 for a double without bath, US$47 with bath, plus US$1.30 per person tax (no singles). Some of the six-bed dormitories here (at US$12.50 per person) are occupied by war refugees but many rooms remain available. The 10% YHA discount is only available to persons under 27 sleeping in the dormitory.

You must check out by 9 am and you can't occupy the room until 2 pm.

The *Studenthotel Cvjetno Naselje* (☎ 534 524 or ☎45 93 560), off Slavonska avenija in the south of the city, charges US$34/53 for a single/double plus US$1.30 tax, breakfast included. The rooms are good, each with private bath, and the staff are friendly. It's expensive because the 'higher ups' have decided foreigners can afford to pay a lot more than Croats. There's no student discount, although showing your ISIC and pleading poverty occasionally works. There's a self-service student restaurant here where a filling meal with a Coke will cost US$5. The Cvjetno Naselje is available to visitors only from mid-July to the end of September – the rest of the year it's a student dormitory. Take tram No 4, 5, 14, 16 or 17 south-west on Savska cesta to 'Vjesnik'. Opposite the stop is a tall building marked 'Vjesnik'. The student complex is just behind it. (Anyone needing a Hungarian visa should note that the Hungarian Embassy is only a few hundred metres from the hostel.)

In July and August make straight for the *Studentski dom Stjepan Radić*, Jarunska ulica 3, off Horvaćanska ulica in the south of the city near the Sava River (tram No 5 or 17). Rooms in this huge student complex cost US$20/26 for a single/double.

Private Rooms Staza Agency (☎ 213 082), Heinzelova 3, off Kvaternikov trg in the east of the city (tram Nos 4, 7, 11 or 12), has private rooms for US$26/44 a single/double. If you only stay one or two nights the price increases to US$31/52. Prices are high because almost half the money goes in taxes. Another half goes to the agency and your host pockets only a quarter of the money you pay!

Staza's sign gives its office hours as 9 am to 6 pm weekdays, 9 am to 1 pm Saturday, but the reliable English-speaking manager, Nadica Kratko, lives on the premises and says visitors can ring her doorbell anytime and she'll give them a room if she has one. Telephone reservations are not accepted. Nadica's standards are high and it's unlikely you'll have any complaints about your room.

Private rooms are also available from the Diprom Agency (☎ 523 617), Trnsko 25a, in Novi Zagreb south of the Sava River (tram

CROATIA

No 7, 14 or 16 to Trnsko). Prices are US$22/ 40 for a single/double with a 30% surcharge if you stay only one night. Apartments are US$48 a double and a US$1.30 per person per day tax is additional. Ninety per cent of their rooms are in high-rise apartment blocks in Novi Zagreb although they do have a few rooms in the city centre at the same price. The office is in a school building and is only open weekdays from 8 am to 4 pm, Saturday 8 am to noon.

Two buildings away from Di-prom is the Turističko Društvo Novi Zagreb (☎ 521 523 or 770 117), Trnsko 15e, which has private rooms in apartment buildings in this area at US$36/48 a single/double, plus the US$1.30 tax, with a 30% surcharge for one-night stays, 20% extra for two or three nights. The office is theoretically open weekdays 8 am to 6 pm, Saturday 9 am to 1 pm.

If you're new to Croatia, don't be put off by these high prices. Along the coast, especially from Rab south, private rooms cost less than half as much.

Hotels There aren't any cheap hotels in Zagreb. Most of the older hotels have been renovated and the prices raised to B category. To make matters worse, United Nations personnel with fat expense allowances have flooded into Zagreb, exacerbating an already dismal accommodation situation. Even at the rip-off rates quoted here the snooty hotel clerks act as if they're doing you a favour giving you a room at all!

If you can't arrange a morning arrival and afternoon departure to avoid spending the night in Zagreb, be prepared to bite the bullet and pay a lot more for a place to sleep than you would elsewhere in Croatia. The only easy escape is to book an overnight bus to Split or Dubrovnik.

The 110-room *Central Hotel* (☎ 425 777), Branimirova 3 opposite the train station, is US$50/76 a single/double with bath and breakfast.

The six-storey *Hotel Astoria* (☎ 430 444), Petrinjska 71 near the Omladinski Hotel, has 130 rooms at US$64/109 with private bath and breakfast.

The six-storey *Hotel Jadran* (☎ 414 600), Vlaška 50 near the city centre, charges US$57/84 with shower and breakfast.

If you're willing to spend that much consider a splurge at the five-star *Hotel Esplanade* (☎ 435 666) next to the train station (US$186/ 240 plus tax with bath and a buffet breakfast). This six-storey, 215-room hotel erected in 1924 is very elegant and there's a casino on the premises.

Places to Eat

Restaurants & Fast Food One of the most elegant places in town is undoubtedly the *Paviljon* in the yellow exhibition pavilion across the park from the train station. Main courses with an Italian accent start at US$10. The fresh fish and local wines at *Split*, Ilica 19, also make a delicious treat. For regional dishes and lots of local colour, dine in one of the outdoor restaurants along ulica Tkalčićeva, up from Trg Jelačića, on summer evenings.

Pizzeria Delfino, at Dežmanova 2 on the corner of Ilica, moves its tables out onto the street in summer and dispenses pizza at reasonable prices. The *Slavija Restaurant*, Jurišićeva 18 in the city centre, has a pleasant decor and serves tasty spaghetti for US$6. *Medulić*, Medulićeva 2 at Ilica, serves vegetarian food in the back dining room and the menu is in English.

Palačinke, on Ilica across from Tomićeva, is a lively fast-food joint where you can grab a quick salad or sandwich.

Cafés & Bars The *Rock Forum Café*, Gajeva ulica 13, occupies the rear sculpture garden of the Archaeological Museum (open in summer only) and across the street is the *Hard Rock Café*, full of 1950s and 1960s memorabilia. Farther back in the passageway from Hard Rock is the *Art Café Thalia* which really tries to live up to its name. A couple of other cafés, art galleries and music shops share this lively complex at the corner of Teslina and Gajeva streets. If you're in Zagreb between October and May check out the *BP Club* in the complex basement where there's jazz nightly.

In the evening the cafés along Tkalčićeva, north off Trg Jelačića, buzz with activity as crowds spill out onto the street, drinks in hand. Farther up on Kozarska ulica the city's young people cluster shoulder to shoulder. Trg Petra Preradovića, Zagreb's flower-market square, is also interesting. Zagreb's most pretentious cafés are *Gradska Kavana* on Trg Jelačića and *Kazališna Kavana* on Trg Maršala Tita opposite the Croatian National Theatre.

Café Centar, Jurišićeva ulica 24, has great cakes and ice cream. The *Pivnica Tomislav*, Trg Tomislava 18, facing the park in front of the train station, is a good local bar with inexpensive draught beer.

Entertainment

Zagreb is a happening city. Its theatres and concert halls present a great variety of programmes throughout the year. Many (but not all) are listed in the monthly brochure *Zagreb Events & Performances*, which is usually available from the tourist office.

It's worth making the rounds of the theatres in person to check the calendars. Tickets are usually available, even for the best shows. A small office marked 'Kazalište Komedija' (look for the posters) in the Blagasija Oktogon, a passage connecting Trg Petra Preradovića to Ilica near Trg Jelačića, also sells theatre tickets.

Theatre The neobaroque *Croatian National Theatre*, at Trg Maršala Tita 15, was established in 1895. It stages opera and ballet performances and the box office is open weekdays from 10 am to 7.30 pm, Saturday 10 am to 1 pm as well as for a half-hour before performances. You have a choice of orchestra (parket), lodge (lože) or balcony (balkon) seats.

The *Komedija Theatre*, Kaptol 9 near the cathedral, stages operettas and musicals.

The ticket office of the *Vatroslav Lisinski Concert Hall*, just south of the train station, is open weekdays from 9 am to 8 pm, Saturday 9 am to 2 pm.

Concerts also take place at the *Academy of Music*, Gundulićeva 6a, off Ilica.

There are performances at the *Puppet Theatre*, ulica Baruna Trenka 3, Saturday at 5 pm and Sunday at 10 am.

Discos Zagreb's most popular disco is *Sokol club*, across the street from the Ethnographic Museum (open Wednesday to Sunday 10 pm to 4 am, entry US$8). Live concerts are presented every Wednesday. Women are admitted free on Friday for a Chippendales-style male strip show.

Cinemas A notice board in the passage at Ilica 10 displays what's showing at all the cinemas of Zagreb (with addresses and times).

Spectator Sport

Basketball is popular in Zagreb, and from October to April games take place at the Cibona Centar, Savska cesta 30 opposite the Technical Museum, usually on Saturday at 7.30 pm. Tickets are available at the door.

Soccer games are held on Sunday afternoon at the Maksimir Stadium, Maksimirska 128 on the east side of Zagreb (tram No 4, 7, 11 or 12 to Bukovačka). If you arrive too early for the game, Zagreb's zoo is just across the street.

Things to Buy

Ilica is Zagreb's main shopping street. Get in touch with Croatian consumerism at the Nama department store on Ilica near Trg Jelačića. Some souvenirs are also sold here.

Folk-music compact discs are available from Fonoteca at Nama, Ilica 6, and Orfej, ulica Mirka Bogovića 1 (a block apart). The tourist office has a small assortment of appealing handicraft items, such as Croatian dolls, wall hangings, wooden objects and pottery.

The shops and grocery stores in the passage under the tracks beside the train station have long opening hours.

Getting There & Away

Bus Zagreb's big, modern bus station has a large, enclosed waiting room where you can stretch out while waiting for your bus (but there's no heating in winter). Buy most international tickets at window Nos 13 and 14, and change money (including travellers' cheques) at A Tours. The left-luggage office is always open (take care – they charge *per hour*).

Buses depart from Zagreb for most of Croatia, Slovenia and places beyond. Buy an advance ticket at the station if you're travelling far.

The following domestic buses depart from Zagreb: Bled (200 km, four daily), Dubrovnik (713 km, five daily, US$25), Koper (253 km, five daily), Krk (229 km, three daily), Ljubljana (135 km, five daily), Piran (273 km, daily), Plitvice (140 km, 19 daily), Poreč (264 km, five daily), Pula (283 km, 12 daily), Rab (211 km, daily), Rijeka (173 km, 21 daily), Rovinj (278 km, eight daily), Split (478 km, 19

CROATIA

daily), Varaždin (77 km, 27 daily), Mali Lošinj (298 km, daily) and Zadar (320 km, 14 daily). No buses operate to Serbia.

Daily bus service to Sarajevo (417 km, US$57) has resumed and there are four daily buses to Međugorje (420 km, US$25), including one overnight.

To Hungary, there's Zagreb-Nagykanizsa (145 km, twice daily, US$10) or four daily Zagreb-Barcs buses (202 km, US$16). Nagykanizsa is preferable if you're bound for Budapest or Balaton Lake, Barcs for Pécs or Yugoslavia.

Other international buses worth knowing about are Zagreb to Vienna (371 km, twice daily at 6 am and 9.30 pm, US$35), Munich (576 km, twice daily at 7 and 8 pm, US$50), Berlin (three times a week, DM159, payment in Deutschmarks only), Amsterdam (Sunday at 4 pm, US$124) and Istanbul (weekly, US$90). Luggage is DM3 per piece.

Train The *Maestral* express train departs from Zagreb for Budapest (412 km, seven hours, US$28) every morning. The *Adriatica* runs overnight. A ticket from Zagreb to Nagykanizsa, the first main junction inside Hungary, is US$10. Alternatively, take a train to Koprivnica or Varaždin and one of the two or three local trains into Hungary from there. A useful daily train runs between Zagreb and Pécs, Hungary (267 km, five hours, US$18), leaving Zagreb in the afternoon.

Zagreb is on both the Munich-Ljubljana and Vienna-Maribor main lines. There are trains twice a day between Munich and Zagreb (613 km, eight hours, US$69) via Salzburg. Five trains a day arrive from Venice (seven hours, US$28).

Five trains a day run from Zagreb to Osijek (288 km, 4½ hours), 20 to Koprivnica (92 km, two hours), 11 to Varaždin (110 km, three hours, US$4), six to Ljubljana (160 km, 2¼ hours), four to Rijeka (243 km, five hours) and two to Pula (418 km, 5½ hours). Both daily trains to Zadar (11 hours, US$14) and Split (10 hours, US$13) stop at Knin. Reservations are required on some trains, so check. Beware of overcharging in the 1st-class ticket office (check the price beforehand at information).

In mid-1991 all rail, road and air routes between Zagreb and Belgrade were cut, and to travel between the two cities it was necessary to do a loop through Hungary. The Zagreb to Belgrade highway (390 km) has reopened but the cities are not yet connected by train because of heavy damage from the war. This situation is due to change so check for the latest information upon arrival.

Getting Around

Public transport is based on an efficient but overcrowded network of trams, although the city centre is compact enough to make them unnecessary. Tram Nos 3 and 8 don't run on weekends. Buy tickets (US$0.70) at newspaper kiosks. You can use your ticket for transfers within 90 minutes but only in one direction.

A *dnevna karta* (day ticket) valid on all public transport until 4 am the next morning is available for US$2 at most Vjesnik or Tisak news outlets.

To/From the Airport The Eurokont bus to Pleso Airport, 17 km south-east of Zagreb, leaves from the bus station every hour on the half-hour from 4.30 am to 7.30 pm and later if there are flights (US$3).

Taxi Zagreb's taxis all have meters which begin at a whopping US$3 and then ring up US$1.10 a km. On Sunday and nights from 10 pm to 5 am there's a 20% surcharge. Waiting time is US$8 an hour. The baggage surcharge is US$0.25 for more than one bag.

Car Europcar (☎ 271 469), Varšavska 13, often has the lowest rates (from US$27 a day plus US$0.27 a km or US$442 a week with unlimited km). Other companies are Budget Rent-a-Car (☎ 45 62 221) in the Hotel Sheraton, Avis Autotehna (☎ 172 133) at the InterContinental Hotel and Hertz (☎ 442 423), Kršnjavoga 13 near the InterContinental Hotel.

VARAŽDIN

Varaždin, between Zagreb and Balaton Lake, may be a useful transit point on the way to/from Hungary. It's a rather pleasant little town with a few baroque churches and a medieval castle which now contains the municipal museum. You can see it all in a couple of hours.

Turistička Agencija in the train station (ope

weekdays and Saturday 8.30 am to 8.30 pm) changes travellers' cheques and sells international train tickets. *Pansion Maltar*, Prešernova 1, diagonally opposite the expensive Hotel Turist between the train and bus stations, has single/double rooms for US$27/53.

Train service from Zagreb to Varaždin (110 km) is every couple of hours and there are two unreserved local trains a day between Varaždin and Nagykanizsa, Hungary (72 km, US$6). The left-luggage office at the train station is open 24 hours a day.

Varaždin's bus and train stations are on opposite sides of town and not linked by public transport. There are 27 buses a day to Zagreb, six to Maribor, one to Rijeka, two to Ljubljana, two to Nagykanizsa (US$4.50) and daily services to Stuttgart, Munich and Vienna.

PLITVICE

Plitvice Lakes National Park lies midway between Zagreb and Zadar. The 19½ hectares of wooded hills enclose 16 turquoise lakes which are linked by a series of waterfalls and cascades. The mineral-rich waters carve new paths through the rock, depositing tufa in continually changing formations. Wooden footbridges follow the lakes and streams over, under and across the rumbling water for an exhilaratingly damp 18 km. Swimming is allowed in several lakes. Park admission is US$10 (US$5 for students) but is valid for the entire stay.

The civil war in ex-Yugoslavia actually began in Plitvice on 31 March 1991 when rebel Serbs took control of the park headquarters. The murder of a Croatian police officer, Josip Jović, that Easter Sunday was the first casualty of this ruthless war. When the Croatian army finally retook the park in August 1995 they found the natural beauty intact but the hotels completely gutted.

Places to Stay

The only functioning hotel at the time of writing was the *Hotel Bellevue* (☎ 053-774 015), which has single/double rooms at US$37/60 with a reduction of 20% for stays longer than three nights. The camping ground at *Kolana* outside the park is currently closed for renovation as are the hotels *Jezero* and *Plitvice*. Private accommodation is not yet available since the towns and villages on the

edge of the park were thoroughly trashed during the conflict. Check at the Hotel Bellevue or the Plitvice National Park office in Zagreb for the latest information on accommodation.

Getting There & Away

Buses run hourly from Zagreb to Plitvice (140km, three hours, US$6) and then continue on to Zadar or Split. If you want to see the aftermath of war the road from Zagreb to Plitvice provides a vivid picture. It is possible to visit Plitvice for the day on the way to or from the coast but be aware that buses will not pick up passengers at Plitvice if they are full. Luggage can be left at the tourist information centre (open daily 8 am to 6.30 pm) at the first entrance to the park.

Istria

Istria (Istra to Croatians), the heart-shaped 3600-sq-km peninsula just south of Trieste, Italy, is named after the Illyrian Histri tribe conquered by the Romans in 177 BC.

In the 20th century Istria has been a political basketball. Italy took Istria from Austria-Hungary in 1919, then had to give it to Yugoslavia in 1947. A large Italian minority lives in Istria and Italian is widely spoken. Tito wanted Trieste (Trst) as part of Yugoslavia too, but in 1954 the Anglo-American occupiers returned the city to Italy so that it wouldn't fall into the hands of the 'communists'. Today the Koper-Piran strip belongs to Slovenia, the rest to Croatia.

The 430-km Istrian Riviera basks in the Mediterranean landscapes and climate for which the Adriatic coast is famous. The long summer season from May to October attracts large crowds. Mercifully, Istria was spared the fighting that occurred elsewhere in former Yugoslavia, and it's a peaceful place to visit. Industry and heavy shipping are concentrated along the north side of Istria around Koper and Izola, and Umag is a scattered, characterless resort you could easily skip. Novigrad is nicer, but the farther south you go in Istria the quieter it gets, with cleaner water, fewer visitors and cars and less industry. See Piran quickly, then move south to Rovinj, a perfect base from which to explore Poreč and Pula.

Getting There & Away

Bus Koper and Rijeka are the main entry/exit points, with buses to most towns on Istria's west coast every couple of hours. Train service in Istria is limited, so plan on getting around by bus.

Boat From May to September the Italian shipping company Adriatica Navigazione operates the fast motor vessel *Marconi* between Trieste and Istria every day but Tuesday, departing from Trieste at 8 am and returning from Istria in the afternoon. The *Marconi* visits Rovinj (three hours, US$19) every trip, but calls on Poreč (US$17) only on Monday and Wednesday from mid-July to September. All voyages go on to the Brijuni islands (US$24) and call on Mali Lošinj (US$42) as well, weekends from mid-July to September. An embarkation/disembarkation tax of US$3 is charged at some ports. In Trieste, tickets are available from Agemar (☎ 040-363 737), Piazza Duca degli Abruzzi 1a.

Also in summer you can take Lošinjska Plovidba's boat, *Marina*, from Venice to Zadar, stopping at Pula and Mali Lošinj. The agency Traspedi (☎ 041-521 0631), Dorsoduro 1826 in Venice, has information. In Istria, travel agencies such as Kvarner Express should know the departure times although tickets may only be available on board. Both boats depart from the landings marked 'Customs Wharf' on the maps in this book; schedules are sometimes posted there. It's an exciting way to go.

POREČ

Poreč (Italian: Parenzo), the Roman Parentium, sits on a low, narrow peninsula about halfway down the west coast of Istria. The ancient Dekumanus with its polished stones is still the main street of town. Even after the fall of Rome, Poreč remained important as a centre of early Christianity, with a bishop and a famous basilica. Although it's now the largest tourist resort in Istria, the vestiges of earlier times and its small-town atmosphere make it well worth a stop. There are many places to swim in the clear water off the rocks north of the old town.

Orientation

The bus station (with a left-luggage office open from 6 am to 8 pm except Sunday when it closes at 5 pm) is directly opposite the small-boat harbour just outside the old town.

Information

The tourist office (☎ 451 293) is at Zagrebačka 11. Atlas travel agency, at Eufrazijeva 63, represents American Express.

The Auto-Klub Poreč (☎ 431 503) is in the large white building next to the Citroën garage, visible across the field north of the market.

Post & Communications The telephone centre in the main post office, Trg Slobode 14, is open Monday to Saturday from 7 am to 9 pm, Sunday 9 am to noon. The telephone code for Poreč is ☎ 052.

Things to See

The many historic sites in the old town include the ruins of two **Roman temples**, between Trg Marafor and the west end of the peninsula. Archaeology and history are featured in the four-floor **Regional Museum** (open daily all year round), in an old baroque palace at Dekumanus 9 (captions in German and Italian).

The main reason to visit Poreč, however, is to see the 6th-century **Euphrasian basilica**, which features wonderfully preserved Byzantine gold mosaics. The capitals, sculpture and architecture are remarkable survivors of that distant period. Entry to the church is free, and for a small fee you may visit the 4th-century mosaic floor of the adjacent Early Christian basilica.

From May to mid-October there are passenger boats (US$2 return) every half-hour 24 hours a day to **Sveti Nikola**, the small island opposite Poreč harbour, departing from the new wharf on Obala Maršala Tita.

Special Events

Annual events include the Folk Festival (June) the Inter Folk Fest (August), the Annual Ar Exhibition (all summer until late August) and the Musical Summer (May to September). Ask about these at the tourist office.

Places to Stay

Accommodation in Poreč is tight and the camping grounds are far from the town centre

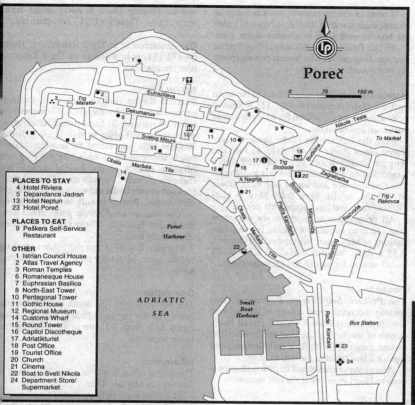

Poreč

PLACES TO STAY
4 Hotel Riviera
5 Depandance Jadran
13 Hotel Neptun
23 Hotel Poreč

PLACES TO EAT
9 Peškera Self-Service
  Restaurant

OTHER
1 Istrian Council House
2 Atlas Travel Agency
3 Roman Temples
6 Romanesque House
7 Euphrasian Basilica
8 North-East Tower
10 Pentagonal Tower
11 Gothic House
12 Regional Museum
14 Customs Wharf
15 Round Tower
16 Capitol Discotheque
17 Adriatikturist
18 Post Office
19 Tourist Office
20 Church
21 Cinema
22 Boat to Sveti Nikola
24 Department Store/
  Supermarket

o you might want to stop off only for the day
n your way south or north.

Camping There are two camping grounds at
Zelena Laguna, six km south of Poreč. Both
Autocamp Zelena Laguna (☎ 451 696) and
Autocamp Bijela Uvala (☎ 451 083) are open
rom mid-April to September and charge
round US$3.50 per person, US$2 per tent.
There are buses to Zelena Laguna from Poreč
us station every couple of hours, or catch the
ourly boat from the small-boat harbour in
ont of Hotel Poreč (summer only). The boat
nding at the Parentium Hotel is nearly two
m from Autocamp Zelena Laguna, however,

and even further from Bijela Uvala. Ask if the
boat will go on to Hotel Delfin, which is closer.

Private Rooms Adriatikturist (☎ 452 458),
Trg Slobode 3 (and a second Adriatikturist
office near the market), rents private rooms for
US$14/21 for a single/double with a shared
bath in July and August. Rooms are about 40%
cheaper in the off season. Kompas (☎ 32 339),
Kvarner Express near Hotel Neptun, and Atlas
travel agency at Eufrazijeva 63 also have
private rooms for the same price. Make sure to
arrive early in the day outside the main May to
September tourist season as many agencies
close around noon.

If none of the agencies in town has private rooms, walk south on Rade Končara and watch for houses with sobe or zimmer signs. Near Caffe Bar Janko this way is Sun Tourist Service, Butorac 18, which rents private rooms all year round.

Hotels The only year-round hotel in the town centre is *Hotel Neptun* (☎ 451 711). Rooms in peak season cost US$40/66 for a single/double with bath and breakfast.

Near the bus station is the modern, five-storey *Hotel Poreč* (☎ 451 811). In July and August rooms here cost US$40/69 for a single/double with bath, breakfast and dinner. The *Depandance Jadran* (☎ 451 422), Obala M Tita 24, is also open from May to mid-October only and has comparable prices.

All prices assume a four-night minimum stay and drop about 50% during the shoulder seasons of May, June, September and October. Add a daily 'residence tax' of US$1.30/$1 on/off season for all official accommodation.

Places to Eat
The *Peškera Self-Service Restaurant*, just outside the north-west corner of the old city wall (open daily from 9 am to 8 pm all year), is one of the best of its kind in Croatia. The posted menu is in English and German, and there's a free toilet at the entrance.

A large supermarket and department store is next to Hotel Poreč near the bus station.

Entertainment
Poreč's top disco is *Capitol Discotheque*, downstairs at V Nazor 9.

Getting There & Away
The nearest train station is at Pazin, 30 km east (five buses daily from Poreč). Buses run twice a day to Portorož (54 km), Trieste (89 km) and Ljubljana (176 km); five times a day to Rovinj (38 km); five times a day to Zagreb (264 km) and Rijeka (80 km); and 11 times a day to Pula (56 km). Between Poreč and Rovinj the bus runs along the Lim Channel, a drowned valley. To see it, sit on the right-hand side southbound, or the left-hand side northbound.

For information on the fast motor vessel *Marconi* that shuttles between Trieste and Poreč ask the port captain at Obala M Tita 17

and see Getting There & Away in the Istri introduction. There's a US$3 departure tax.

Car Autotehna is at Trg J Rakovca 1; Hert (☎ 432 113) is in a corner of Trg J Rakovc near the market.

ROVINJ
Relaxed Rovinj (Italian: Rovigno), its hig peninsula topped by the great 57-metre-hig tower of massive St Euphemia Cathedral, i perhaps the best place to visit in all of Istria Wooded hills punctuated by low-rise luxur hotels surround the town, while the 13 gree offshore islands of the Rovinj archipelag make for pleasant, varied views. The cobbled inclined streets in the old town are charming picturesque. Rovinj is still an active fishin port, so you see local people going about thei day-to-day business. There's a large Italia community here.

Friendly Rovinj is just the place to rest u before your island-hopping journey furthe south.

Orientation
The bus station is just south-east of the ol town. The left-luggage office at the bus statio opens daily from 5.15 am to 9 pm (ask at th ticket window).

Information
The tourist office is at Obala Pina Budicina 1 just off Trg Maršala Tita.

Motorists can turn to the Auto Moto Društv (HAK) next to the large parking lot on Obal Palih Boraca.

Phone calls can be made from the post offic behind the bus station. The telephone code fo Rovinj is ☎ 052.

Things to See
The **Cathedral of St Euphemia** (1736), whic completely dominates the town from its hil top location, is the largest baroque building i Istria, reflecting the period during the 18 century when Rovinj was the most populou town in Istria, an important fishing centre an the bulwark of the Venetian fleet.

Inside the cathedral, don't miss the tomb St Euphemia (martyred in 304 AD) behind th right-hand altar. The saint's remains wer brought here from Constantinople in 800. O

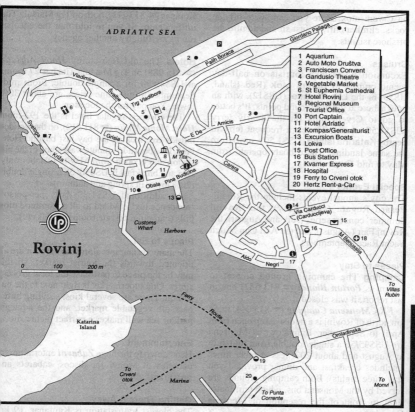

Rovinj

ADRIATIC SEA

1 Aquarium
2 Auto Moto Društva
3 Franciscan Convent
4 Gandusio Theatre
5 Vegetable Market
6 St Euphemia Cathedral
7 Hotel Rovinj
8 Regional Museum
9 Tourist Office
10 Port Captain
11 Hotel Adriatic
12 Kompas/Generalturist
13 Excursion Boats
14 Lokva
15 Post Office
16 Bus Station
17 Kvarner Express
18 Hospital
19 Ferry to Crveni otok
20 Hertz Rent-a-Car

0   100   200 m

the anniversary of her martyrdom (16 September) devotees congregate here. A copper statue of St Euphemia tops the cathedral's mighty tower.

Take a wander along the winding narrow backstreets below the cathedral, such as ulica Grisia, where local artists sell their work. Rovinj has developed into an important art centre, and each year in mid-August Rovinj's painters stage a big open-air art show in the town.

The **Regional Museum** on Trg Maršala Tita (closed Sunday and Monday) contains an unexciting collection of paintings and a few Etruscan artefacts found in Istria. These might

attract some interest if the captions were in something other than Croatian and Italian. The **Franciscan convent**, up the hill at E de Amicis 36, also has a small museum.

Better than either of these is the **Rovinj Aquarium** (established in 1891), at Obala Giordano Paliaga 5 (open daily, US$1.50, closed mid-October to April). It exhibits a good collection of local marine life, from poisonous scorpion fish to colourful anemones.

When you've seen enough of the town, follow the waterfront south past the Park Hotel to **Punta Corrente Forest Park**, which was afforested way back in 1890 by Baron Hütterodt, an Austrian admiral who kept a villa on Crveni otok. Here you can swim off the rocks, climb a cliff, or just sit and admire the offshore islands.

Cruises

Excursion boats take tourists on half-day scenic cruises to **Crveni otok** (Red Island, US$3) or the **Lim Channel** (US$12), with an hour ashore at the turnaround points. It's better to go to Crveni otok on the hourly ferry (US$1.50 return). There's a frequent ferry to nearby **Katarina Island** (US$1.50 return) from the same landing. These boats operate from May to mid-October only.

Special Events

The city's annual events include the Rovinj-Pesaro Regata (early May), the 'Rovinj Summer' concert series (July and August), the Rovinj Fair (August), and the ACI Cup Match Yacht Race (September).

Places to Stay

Camping The camping ground closest to Rovinj is *Porton Biondi* (☎ 813 557) but, at last report, it was closed.

FKK Monsena Camping (☎ 813 044) three km north of Rovinj is a nudist camp open from April to September. Bungalows at Monsena are US$35/56 a single/ double from mid-July to August and about 20% less at other times (includes breakfast and dinner provided you stay three nights). Both camping grounds are served by the Monsena bus, which terminates right in front of the reception of Monsena Camping.

Five km south-east of Rovinj is *Polari Camping* (☎ 813 441), open from May to mid-October. Get there on the Villas Rubin bus. All of these camping grounds charge about US$3.50 per person, plus US$4 per tent.

Private Rooms Many offices in Rovinj offer private rooms beginning at US$10 per person double occupancy with a 30% surcharge for a stay of less than four nights. Pula and Poreč are within easy commuting distance from Rovinj, so having to stay four nights may not be such a problem. Try Lokva (☎ 813 365), ulica Via Carducci 4, or Marco Polo (☎ 816 955), both opposite the bus station; Kvarner Express (☎ 811 155) on the harbour near the bus station; or Generalturist (☎ 811 402) and

Kompas (☎ 813 211), both on Trg Maršala Tita in the centre. If you're told that the cheape rooms are full, try another agency.

Hotels The old four-storey *Hotel Adriatic* (☎ 815 088) on Trg Maršala Tita has 27 room at US$40/80 for a single/double. From mid September to mid-June prices are about 30% lower. You pay for the location.

The cheapest regular hotel is the 192-room *Hotel Monte Mulin* (☎ 811 512), on the wooded hillside overlooking the bay just beyond Hote Park. It's about a 15-minute walk south of the bus station and is open from May to October only Bed and breakfast is US$30/ 58 a single/doubl (20% lower in spring and autumn).

An additional US$1.30 daily per-person 'residence tax' is added to all accommodation bills (camping, private rooms, hotels etc).

Places to Eat

The many restaurants along the harbour are a oriented towards the tourist market, so thi may be the place to patronise the local grocer stores. One supermarket is right next to the bu station. There are several kiosks selling bure near the vegetable market, and the adjacer park or sea wall makes a perfect picnic site.

Entertainment

Head down to the huge *Zabavni* entertainmer complex at Monvi for discos, cabarets an restaurants.

Getting There & Away

The closest train station is Kanfanar, 19 k away on the Pula-Divača line.

There's a bus from Rovinj to Pula (34 km every hour or so, eight a day to Poreč (38 km six a day to Rijeka (84 km), eight a day Zagreb (278 km), two a day to Koper (81 km Split (509 km) and Ljubljana (190 km), an one a day to Dubrovnik (744 km).

From May to September the fast moto vessel *Marconi* glides between Rovinj an Trieste six times a week (three hours, US$19 Eurostar Travel on the harbour may hav tickets (which must be paid in Italian lire otherwise try asking the port captain on th opposite side of the same building.

Getting Around

Local buses run every two hours from the bu

station north to Monsena and south to Villas Rubin.

PULA

Pula (the ancient Polensium) is a large regional centre with some industry, a big naval base and a busy commercial harbour. The old town with its museums and well-preserved Roman ruins is certainly worth a visit and nearby are rocky wooded peninsulas overlooking the clear Adriatic waters, which explains the many resort hotels and camping grounds.

Orientation

The bus station (with a left-luggage office open daily from 5 am to 10 pm except for two half-hour breaks) is on ulica Mate Balote in the centre of town. One block south is Giardini, the central hub, while the harbour is just north of the bus station. The train station is near the water about one km north of town (with a left-luggage service from 9 am to 4 pm, closed Sunday).

The town planners of Pula are in the process of renaming many streets in order to banish reminders of the ex-Yugoslavia. There are also plans afoot to move the bus station away from the town centre.

Information

The Tourist Association of Pula, at ulica Istarska 13 (weekdays 9 am to 1 pm and 5 to 8 pm), will have the latest city map. The American Express representative is Atlas travel agency (☎ 214 172), Petra Drapšina 1, Pula 2000. It will hold clients' mail.

Post & Communications Long-distance telephone calls may be placed at the main post office at Dante Trg 4 (open till 8 pm daily). The telephone code for Pula is ☎ 052.

Travel Agencies Jadroagent (☎ 41 878), Obala 14, and the adjacent Kvarner Express office sell ferry tickets.

Via Tours on ulica Mate Balote next to the bus station sells express bus tickets to Zagreb (283 km, US$17) and Trieste (US$14) and train tickets to Munich and Vienna.

Things to See

Pula's most imposing sight is the 1st-century

Roman amphitheatre overlooking the harbour north-east of the old town. At US$2.50 admission the visit is expensive, but you can see plenty for free from outside. Around the end of July a Croatian film festival is held in the amphitheatre, with an Italian film festival held a week later.

The **Archaeological Museum** (open daily in summer, closed weekends in winter, admission US$2, students US$1) is on the hill opposite the bus station. Even if you don't get into the museum be sure to visit the large sculpture garden around it, and the **Roman Theatre** behind. The garden is entered through 2nd-century twin gates.

Along the street facing the bus station are **Roman walls** which mark the east boundary of old Pula. Follow these walls south and continue down Giardini to the **Triumphal Arch of Sergius** (27 BC). The street beyond the arch winds right around old Pula, changing names several times as it goes. Follow it to Forum (the former Trg Republike), where you'll find the ancient **Temple of Augustus** and the **old town hall** (1296). Above this square is the **Franciscan church** (1314), with a museum in the cloister (entry from around the other side) containing paintings, medieval frescos and a Roman mosaic.

The **Museum of History** (open daily) is in the 17th-century Venetian citadel on a high hill in the centre of the old town. The meagre exhibits deal mostly with the maritime history of Pula but the views of Pula from the citadel walls are good.

Places to Stay

Camping The closest camping ground to Pula is *Autocamp Stoja* (☎ 24 144; open mid-April to mid-October), three km south-west of the centre (take bus No 1 to the terminus at Stoja). There's lots of space on the shady promontory, with swimming possible off the rocks. The two restaurants at the camping ground are good. There are more camping grounds at Medulin and Premantura, coastal resorts south-east of Pula.

Hostels The *Ljetovalište Ferijalnog Saveza Youth Hostel* (☎ 34 595), Zaljev Valsaline 4, is three km south of central Pula in a great location overlooking a clean pebble beach.

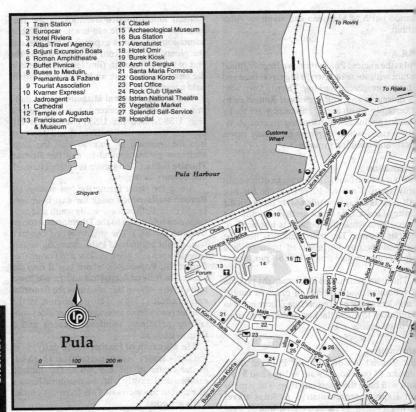

1	Train Station	
2	Europcar	
3	Hotel Riviera	
4	Atlas Travel Agency	
5	Brijuni Excursion Boats	
6	Roman Amphitheatre	
7	Buffet Pivnica	
8	Buses to Medulin, Premantura & Fažana	
9	Tourist Association	
10	Kvarner Express/ Jadroagent	
11	Cathedral	
12	Temple of Augustus	
13	Franciscan Church & Museum	
14	Citadel	
15	Archaeological Museum	
16	Bus Station	
17	Arenaturist	
18	Hotel Omir	
19	Burek Kiosk	
20	Arch of Sergius	
21	Santa Maria Formosa	
22	Gostiona Korzo	
23	Post Office	
24	Rock Club Uljanik	
25	Istrian National Theatre	
26	Vegetable Market	
27	Splendid Self-Service	
28	Hospital	

Pula

0   100   200 m

Take the No 2 Verudela bus to the 'Piramida' stop and walk back to the first street, turn left and look for the sign. Bed and breakfast is US$10 per person, and camping is allowed (US$4). The hostel is now heated and open all year. You can sit and sip cold beer on the terrace, where a rock band plays on some summer evenings. Ask also about Disco Piramida nearby. If the youth hostel is full and you have a tent, it's only a 10-minute walk to *Autocamp Ribarska Koliba* (☎ 22 966), open from May to October.

Private Rooms Arenaturist (☎ 34 355), Giardini 4 a block south of the bus station, and

Via Tours on ulica Mate Balote right next the bus station, have private rooms all ye round for US$8 per person, with an addition 50% surcharge for one night stays and 25% surcharge if you stay less than four night Brijuni Turist Biro (☎ 216 601), ulica Istarsk 3 beside the bus station, has rooms at simil. rates.

Hotels The cheapest hotel is the 112-room *Pension Ribarska Koliba* (☎ 22 966) near th camping ground of the same name, toward Verudela about three km south of Pula (No Verudela bus). Singles/doubles with share bath are US$23/39 in July and August (30)

wer in the off season) but the place is often
ull with groups. The pension has a nice terrace
verlooking a bay full of small boats. It's open
rom April to mid-October only.

For a little luxury, try the elegant, old *Hotel
Riviera* (☎ 211 166), Splitska ulica 1 overlook-
ng the harbour. Erected in 1908, it offers
omfortable, B-category rooms for US$29/49
single/double with shared bath, US$36/59
vith private bath, breakfast included. From
›ctober to May prices are about 25% lower.
'ompare the price of a room with half and full
›oard when you check in.

Hotel Omir (☎ 22 019), Serdo Dobrića 6
ust off Zagrebačka ulica near Giardini, is a
·rivate hotel with 11 rooms for US$47/73/100/
14 single/double/triple/quad with bath and
›reakfast. If you're willing to pay that, you're
etter off at the Riviera.

laces to Eat

›r grilled meats and local dishes such as
›oulash, smoked ham and squid risotto, try
ostiona Korzo, ulica Prvog maja 34 (closed
unday). Despite the plain exterior, it's a little
·xpensive but manageable if you order care-
·lly.

Splendid Self-Service, Narodni trg 5 oppo-
·te the vegetable market (open daily from 9.30
n to 9 pm), is easy since you see what you're
·tting and pay at the end of the line.

Pula's most prestigious café is *Kavana
orum*, at Forum.

There are a couple of good burek and ham-
urger kiosks on the corner of Zagrebačka and
·akima Rakovca, open from 7 to 1 am.

The people at the cheese counter in *Vesna*,
·xt to Kino Istra on Giardini, prepare healthy
·ndwiches while you wait. They're open
fonday to Saturday from 6.30 am to 8 pm.

ntertainment

›sters around Pula advertise live perfor-
ances. *Rock Club Uljanik*, Jurja Dobrile 2,
great whenever something's on. You can
unce there.

Buffet Pivnica, in the back courtyard at
·arska 34 near the Roman amphitheatre (open
uily from 8 am to 4 pm), is one of the least
·pensive places in Pula to get a draught beer,
·ass of wine or espresso coffee, and all prices
·e clearly listed. No food is available but
·ere's a convenient free toilet.

Two cinemas on Giardini are the *Istra* at No
13 and *Giardini* at No 2. Quality art films are
shown at the *Istrian National Theatre* a couple
of times a week.

Getting There & Away

Bus The 18 daily buses to Rijeka (110 km,
1½ hours) are sometimes crowded, especially
the eight which continue on to Zagreb, so
reserve a seat a day in advance if you can.
Going from Pula to Rijeka, be sure to sit on the
right-hand side of the bus for a stunning view
of the Gulf of Kvarner.

Other buses from Pula include 20 a day to
Rovinj (42 km), 12 to Poreč (56 km), eight to
Zagreb (292 km), three to Zadar (333 km), two
each to Postojna (161 km), Trieste (124 km)
and Split (514 km) and one each to Portorož
(90 km), Koper (104 km), Ljubljana (211 km)
and Dubrovnik (749 km).

Train Ever since Pula was the main port of the
Austro-Hungarian empire, the railway line in
Istria has run north towards Italy and Austria
instead of east into Croatia. Now that a new
international border has been drawn across the
line it's even more irrelevant and most local
trains terminate at Buzet near the Slovenian
border. However, two go on to Divača (140 km)
near Trieste, where you connect for Ljubljana.

One early morning train and one afternoon
train run through to Zagreb (418 km) via
Ljubljana but both services involve two sets of
border controls and a new Croatian visa, so the
only real reason to use the train would be to go
to Ljubljana (258 km, four daily, US$11 local,
US$14 express).

Boat From late June to September the fast boat
Marina runs from Venice to Pula (six hours,
US$29) twice a week and from Pula to Zadar
(7½ hours, US$19) four times a week, stopping
at Mali Lošinj (three hours, US$16). The ferry to
Mali Lošinj (US$8 one way) and Zadar
(US$9.30 one way) runs once a week all year.
Ask at Jadroagent or Kvarner Express on the
harbour.

Getting Around

Only two city buses are of use to visitors, and
both stop at Giardini. Bus No 1 runs to the
camping ground at Stoja, while bus No 2 to

Verudela passes the youth hostel and Pension Ribarska Koliba. Frequency varies from every 15 minutes to every 30 minutes, with service from 5 am to 11.30 pm daily. Tickets for both these rides are sold at newsstands for US$1.50.

BRIJUNI

The Brijuni (Italian: Brioni) island group consists of two main pine-covered islands and 12 islets off the coast of Istria just north-west of Pula. Each year from 1949 until his death in 1980, Maršal Tito spent six months at his summer residences on Brijuni in a style any Western capitalist would admire. Tito received 90 heads of state here, and at a meeting on Veli Brijun (the main island) in 1956 Tito, Nasser and Nehru laid the foundations of the non-aligned movement.

Tito had three palaces on Veli Brijun: Vila Jadranka, Bijela Vila and Vila Brionka. The famous 1956 Brijuni Declaration was signed in Bijela Vila, Tito's 'White House'. Tourists are driven past these three, but Tito's private retreat on the tiny islet of Vanga cannot be visited. In 1984 Brijuni was proclaimed a national park. Some 680 species of plants grow on the islands, including many exotic subtropical species planted at Tito's request.

As you arrive, after a half-hour boat ride from Fažana on the mainland, you'll see Tito's two private yachts still tied up in the harbour, and, near the landing, four luxury hotels where his guests once stayed. The four-hour tour of Veli Brijun begins with a visit to **St German Church**, now a gallery of copies of medieval frescos in Istrian churches. The **'Tito on Brijuni'** exhibit in another building includes large photos of Tito with film stars such as Gina Lollobrigida, Sophia Loren, Elizabeth Taylor and Richard Burton, all of whom visited Tito here.

Then you're driven around the island in a small train, past the palaces and through a **safari park**. The fenced area was Tito's private hunting ground, and the exotic animals there were given to Tito by world leaders. Deer wander wild across the island. You pass the ruins of a 1st-century **Roman villa** without stopping, then have a walk around an unexciting zoo. Towards the end of the tour you're herded quickly through the excellent **ethnographical museum** which has Croatian folk costumes.

Getting There & Away

You may only visit Brijuni National Park with a group. Instead of booking an excursion with one of the travel agencies in Pula, Rovinj, or Poreč, you can take a public bus from Pula to Fažana (eight km), then sign up for a tour (US$20) at the Brijuni Tourist Service office near the wharf. You must arrive at Fažana before noon to be sure of getting over that day.

Also check along the Pula waterfront for excursion boats to Brijuni. The five-hour boat trips from Pula to Brijuni may not actually visit the islands but only sail around them. Still, it makes a nice day out.

Gulf of Kvarner

The Gulf of Kvarner (Italian: Quarnero) stretches 100 km south from Rijeka, between the Istrian Peninsula on the west and the Croatian littoral on the east. The many elongated islands are the peaks of a submerged branch of the Dinaric Alps, the range which follows the coast south all the way to Albania. Krk, Cres and Pag are among the largest islands in Croatia.

Rijeka, a bustling commercial port and communications hub at the north end of the gulf, is well connected to Italy and Austria by road and rail. The railway built from Budapest to Rijeka in 1845 gave Hungary its first direct outlet to the sea. Big crowds frequent nearby Opatija, a one-time bathing resort of the Habsburg elite and Krk Island, now linked to the mainland by bridge. Historic Rab, the jewel of the Gulf of Kvarner, is much harder to reach; with some difficulty it can be used as a stepping stone on the way south.

RIJEKA

Rijeka (Italian: Fiume), 126 km south of Ljubljana, is the sort of place you try to avoid but sometimes can't since it's a bus, train and ferry hub for most coastal routes. Although the city does have a few saving graces, such as the pedestrian mall, Korzo, and a colourful market, it seems to have lost its soul under a hail of WWII bombs. The belching industry, cars, shipyards, refineries, cranes and container ships jammed into the narrow coastal

CROATIA

PLACES TO STAY
9 Hotel Bonavia

PLACES TO EAT
17 Express Restaurant

OTHER
1 National Revolution Museum
2 Maritime Museum
3 Courthouse
4 Church of St Guido
5 Turistički Savez
6 Jadroagent
7 St Jerome Church
8 Generalturist
10 Club Palach
11 Auto-Klub Rijeka
12 Kino Fenice
13 Capuchin Church
14 Bus Station
15 Kvarner Express
16 Jadrolinija Office
18 Jadrolinija Ferry Wharf
19 Post Office
20 City Tower
21 Serbian Orthodox Church
22 Market

Rijeka

0   50   100 m

Rijeka Harbour

CROATIA

trip aren't beautiful. This largest of all Croatian ports does have a sort of crude energy, however, and if you like punishment Rijeka will give it to you.

Orientation

The bus station is on Trg Žabica below the Capuchin Church in the centre of town. If the left-luggage office in the bus station (open daily 5.30 am to 10.30 pm) is full, there's a larger *garderoba* (cloakroom) in the train station (open 24 hours), a seven-minute walk west on ulica Krešimirova. The Jadrolinija ferry wharf (no left-luggage) is just a few minutes east of the bus station.

Korzo runs east through the city centre towards the fast-moving Rječina River, once the border of Italy and Yugoslavia (the Italian and Croatian names of the city, Fiume and Rijeka, both mean river). Until 1918 Rijeka was the main port of Hungary. When Italy took Rijeka from Austria-Hungary in 1919, neighbouring Sušak was developed as a port by Yugoslavia. The cities merged when the whole area came under Yugoslav control after WWII.

Information

Try Kvarner Express, Trg Jadranski near the bus station, or the Turistički Savez Općine Rijeka (☎ 213 145) at Užarska 2.

The Auto-Klub Rijeka (☎ 212 442), Dolac 11, assists motorists.

Money You can change money at Croatia Express on platform No 1 at the train station Monday to Saturday from 7 am to 9 pm, Sunday 8 am to 9 pm.

There's an exchange counter in the main post office, opposite the old city tower on Korzo.

Post & Communications The telephone centre in the main post office on Korzo is open from 7 am to 9 pm daily.

Rijeka's telephone code is ☎ 051.

Travel Agencies The American Express representative is Atlas travel agency (☎ 271 032) across the street from Hotel Kvarner in nearby Opatija.

Jadroagent (☎ 211 276; fax 335 172), at Trg Ivana Koblera 2, is an excellent source of information on all ferry sailings from Croatia.

Things to See
The **Modern Art Gallery** (closed Sunday and Monday) is at Dolac 1, upstairs in the scientific library across from Hotel Bonavia. The **Maritime Museum** and the **National Revolution Museum** (both closed Sunday and Monday) are adjacent at Žrtava fašizma 18, above the city centre. Worth a visit if you have time is the 13th-century **Trsat Castle** (closed Monday), on a high ridge overlooking Rijeka and the canyon of the Rječina River.

Places to Stay – Rijeka
Camping The closest camping ground is listed in the following Opatija section.

Private Rooms Kvarner Express (☎ 213 613), Trg Jadranski 3, and Autotrans Turist Biro, Riva 20 just around the corner from the bus station (open Monday to Saturday from 7.30 am to 3 pm), have private rooms for US$13/18 a single/double, with a 30% surcharge if you stay less than three nights. Singles are seldom available and frequently all rooms are full.

Hotels The A-category *Hotel Bonavia* (☎ 333 744) is central and has single/double rooms with bath for US$54/67. The C-category *Hotel*

Neboder (☎ 217 355) and the B-category *Hotel Kontinental* (☎ 216 477) are a block apart in an uninspiring neighbourhood northeast of the town centre. Single/double rooms with bath cost US$27/44 at Neboder and US$44/53 at Kontinental. For those prices you might as well pay more and stay in Opatija.

Places to Stay – Delnice
Another alternative to staying in Rijeka is to go on to Delnice, 44 km east on the main road to Zagreb. The wooded countryside around Delnice is pleasant and Risnjak National Park is just 13 km north-west, but the immediate reason for coming is *Hotel Risnjak* (☎ 051-812 261), next to Delnice bus station and only about 200 metres from the train station. The 20 rooms with shower are US$16/27 for a single/double with breakfast and there's a large restaurant on the premises. It's seldom full. Most international trains from Rijeka stop at Delnice.

Places to Eat
Restoran Index, at ulica Krešimirova 18 between the bus and train stations, has a good self-service section (samoposluzi). *Express 14* Riva near the Jadrolinija office, is another self-service open every day 7 am to 9 pm.

Entertainment
Performances at the *Ivan Zajc National Theatre* (1885) are mostly drama in Croatian though opera and ballet are sometimes offered. The ticket office is open weekdays.

Club Palach, in the back alley accessible through a small passageway next to the Riječka Banka on Trg Jadranski, opens at 8 pm daily. It's a good, noncommercial place to drink and dance. The best chance of seeing a worthwhile film is at *Kino Fenice*, Dolac 13.

Getting There & Away
Bus There are 12 buses a day between Rijeka and Krk (56 km, 1½ hours, US$4), using the huge Krk Bridge. Buses to Krk are overcrowded and a seat reservation in no way guarantees you a seat. Don't worry – the bus from Rijeka to Krk empties fairly fast so you won't be standing for long.

Other buses depart from Rijeka for Baška also on Krk island (76 km, six daily, US$6) Dubrovnik (639 km, two daily), Koper (8 km), Ljubljana (128 km, once a day, US$9), Mali Lošinj (122 km, four daily), Poreč (91 km, five daily), Pula (110 km, 14 daily,), Rab (115 km, two daily, US$11), Rovinj (105 km, four daily), Split (404 km, nine daily), Trieste (70 km, four daily), Zadar (228 km, 12 daily) and Zagreb (173 km, 3½ hours, 16 daily).

Several international 'touring buses' leave from Rijeka bus station, all of them around 5.30 pm. There are buses five times a week to Zürich (801 km), and daily buses to Frankfurt, Munich (571 km) and Stuttgart (786 km). The bus to Amsterdam (US$130) is every Sunday. Luggage is DM3 per piece on all international services (Deutschmarks in cash required).

Train Overnight trains leave Rijeka daily for Budapest (595 km, 11 hours, US$42), Munich, Salzburg (US$44) and Zagreb. Four trains a day run to Zagreb (243 km, five hours, US$15). Several of the seven daily services to Ljubljana (155 km, three hours, US$7) require a change of trains at the Slovenian border and again at Pivka or Postojna. The *poslovni* (executive) trains have only 1st-class seats and reservations are compulsory.

Car ATR Rent a Car (☎ 337 544), Riva 20 near the bus station, has rental cars from US$100 a day with unlimited km. On a weekly basis it's US$400 with unlimited km. These prices are all-inclusive and they'll often give you a 10% discount in the off season. Also try Europcar Hertz (☎ 339 900), Zagrebačka 21.

Boat Jadrolinija (☎ 211 444), Riva 16, has tickets for the large coastal ferries between Rijeka and Dubrovnik that run all year. Southbound ferries depart from Rijeka at 6 am daily.

Fares are US$10 to Rab (three hours), US$21 to Split (13 hours) US$23 to Hvar (16 hours), US$25 to Korčula (18 hours) and US$28 to Dubrovnik (22 hours). Fares are lightly lower in winter. Berths to Split are US$44 for one bed in a four-bed cabin, US$56 per person in a double or US$66 in a single. With a through ticket from Rijeka to Dubrovnik, you can have the purser validate your ticket for free stopovers. The ferry occasionally doesn't call at Rab if there's 'fog' (ie not enough passengers to drop off or pick up).

Since the Jadrolinija ferries travel between Rijeka and Split at night, you don't get to see a lot so it's probably better to go from Rijeka to Split by bus and enjoy excellent views of the Adriatic coast. In contrast, the ferry trip from Split to Dubrovnik is highly recommended.

OPATIJA

Opatija, just a few km due west of Rijeka, was *the* fashionable seaside resort of the Austro-Hungarian empire until WWI. Many grand old hotels remain from this time, and the elegant waterfront promenade affords a fine view of the Gulf of Kvarner. The busy highway runs right along the coast and you get a passing glance of Opatija (the name means 'abbey') from the Pula bus. West of Opatija rises Mt Učka (1396 metres), the highest point on the Istrian Peninsula.

Information

The tourist office is at Maršala Tita 183.

The main post office, at Eugena Kumičića 2 behind the market *(tržnica)*, opens Monday to Saturday from 8 am to 7 pm, Sunday 9 am to noon. The telephone code for Opatija is ☎ 051.

Places to Stay

Preluk Autokamp (☎ 621 913), beside the busy highway between Rijeka and Opatija, is unreliably open from May to September. City bus No 32 stops near the camping ground.

For private rooms, try the following places along Maršala Tita: Kvarner Express at No 188, Generalturist at No 178 and Kompas at No 170. All have rooms for US$10 per person plus a 50% surcharge for single-room occupancy.

The cheapest hotel is the old three-storey *Hotel Continental* (☎ 271 511), Maršala Tita 169, but it is currently occupied by war refugees. The elegant *Hotel Paris* has single/double rooms with private bath and breakfast for US$38/63.

Getting There & Away

Bus No 32 stops in front of the train station in Rijeka (11 km, US$1.50) and runs right along the Opatija Riviera west from Rijeka to Lovran every 20 minutes until late in the evening. There's no left-luggage facility at Opatija bus station, which is on Trg Vladimira Gortana in the town centre, but Autotrans Agency at the station will usually watch luggage.

CROATIA

KRK ISLAND

Croatia's largest island, 409-sq-km Krk (Italian: Veglia) is barren and rocky with little vegetation. In 1980 Krk was joined to the mainland by the massive Krk Bridge, the largest concrete arch bridge in the world with a span of 390 metres. Since then, Krk has suffered from too-rapid development – Rijeka airport and some industry at the north end of Krk, and big tourist hotels in the middle and far south. Still, the main town (also called Krk) is rather picturesque and Baška has an impressive setting. You can easily stop at Krk town for a few hours of sightseeing, then catch a bus to Baška and Krk's longest beach.

Krk Town

From the 12th to the 15th centuries, Krk town and the surrounding region remained semi-independent under the Frankopan Dukes of Krk, an indigenous Croatian dynasty, at a time when much of the Adriatic was controlled by Venice. This history explains the various medieval sights in Krk town, the ducal seat.

Orientation & Information The bus from Baška and Rijeka stops by the harbour, a few minutes walk from the old town of Krk. There's no left-luggage facility at Krk bus station. Krk's telephone code is ☎ 051.

Things to See The 14th-century **Frankopan Castle** and lovely 12th-century Romanesque **cathedral** are in the lower town near the harbour. In the upper part of Krk town are three old monastic churches. The narrow streets of Krk are worth exploring.

Places to Stay There is a range of accommodation options in and around Krk, but many places only open for the summer.

Camping There are three camping grounds. The closest is *Autocamp Ježevac* (☎ 221 081) on the coast, 10 minutes walk south-west of Krk town. The rocky soil makes it nearly impossible to use tent pegs, but there are lots of stones to anchor your lines. There's good shade and places to swim.
  Camping Bor (☎ 221 581) is on a hill inland from Ježevac. *Camp Politin FKK*

(☎ 221 351) is a naturist camp south-east of Krk just beyond the large resort hotels.

Hostel From mid-June to September youth hostel accommodation is available at the *Ljetovalište Ferialnog Saveza* (☎ 854 037) at Punat, between Krk town and Baška. All the buses to Baška stop here.

Private Rooms Kvarner Express on the harbour at Krk has private rooms for US$19 a double plus a 30% surcharge for stays of less than four nights. Similar rooms can be booked from a tourist agency at the bus station and another at Adriatours in the old town.

Getting There & Away About 14 buses a day travel between Rijeka and Krk town (56 km, 1½ hours), of which six continue on to Baška (20 km, one hour). One of the Rijeka buses is to/from Zagreb (229 km). To go from Krk to the island of Mali Lošinj, change buses at Malinska for the Lošinj-bound bus that comes from Rijeka but check the times carefully as the connection only works once or twice a day.

Baška

Baška, at the south end of Krk Island, is a popular resort with a two-km-long pebbly beach set below a high ridge. The swimming and scenery are better at Baška than at Krk and the old town has a lot of charm. This is a good base for hiking; the Chapel of Sveti Ivan on the hillside above Baška offers splendid views.

Orientation & Information The bus from Krk stops at the edge of the old town, between the beach and the harbour.
  The tourist office (☎ 856 971) is at Zvoni mirova 114 just up the street from the bus stop.

Places to Stay The places to try for private room bookings are the tourist office; Amplu Agency, next to the Riječka Banka adjacent to the tourist office; Kvarner Express; and Kompas, both at the Hotel Corinthia nearby.

Camping There are two camping options a Baška. *Camping Zablaće* (☎ 856 909), open from May to September, is on the beach visible south-west of the bus stop (look for the row

CROATIA

of caravans). In heavy rain you risk getting flooded here.

A better bet is **FKK Camp Bunculuka** (☎ 856 806), open from May to September. A naturist camping ground over the hill east of the harbour (a 15-minute walk), it's quiet, shady and conveniently close to town.

Private Rooms The people renting private rooms at Baška don't like you to sleep alone and single rooms are almost impossible to find, either at the agencies or by knocking on doors with *sobe* signs. Most people will also refuse to rent you a room for one night and just tell you to go to a hotel. They have enough German and Austrian tourists screaming for rooms that they can afford to be choosy, especially in July and August.

All the room-finding agencies (see Places to Stay, above) charge exactly the same prices for private rooms and most have only expensive 1st-category rooms with a few 2nd-category and no 3rd-category. Expect to pay at least US$28 a double (plus 20% if you stay less than four nights). The tourist tax of US$1.30 per person per day is extra.

Hotels Small, basic rooms without private bath are available at hotels **Velebit** and **Baška** right on the main beach for US$18/29 a single/double, including breakfast (25% higher in midsummer, open June to mid-September). Bookings must be made at the reception of the nearby **Hotel Corinthia** (☎ 856 824), where you'll have breakfast. You must insist on these rooms, as the Corinthia staff will try to steer you into much more expensive rooms in the main hotel.

Getting There & Away The ferry from Baška to Lopar on Rab Island operates three or four times a day from June to mid-September US$6). The rest of the year you could be forced to backtrack to Rijeka to get further south. To reach the Lopar ferry, follow the street closest to the water through the old town, heading south-east for less than a km.

RAB ISLAND

Rab (Italian: Arbe) Island, near the centre of the Kvarner island group, is one of the most enticing in the Adriatic. The north-east side is barren and rocky, whereas the south-west is green with pine forests. High mountains protect Rab's interior from cold north and east winds.

Rab Town

Medieval Rab town is built on a narrow peninsula which encloses a sheltered harbour. The old stone buildings climb from the harbour to a cliff overlooking the sea. For hundreds of years Rab was an outpost of Venice until the Austrians took over in the 19th century.

Even today you'll hear as much German as Croatian spoken on Rab and you'll find that transport, accommodation and food – virtually everything connected with a visit – is expensive. Even so, Rab is a convenient stepping stone between Krk and Zadar and one of the prettiest little towns on the Adriatic.

Orientation The bus station is at the rear of a new commercial centre opposite Merkur department store, a five-minute walk from the old town. Despite a sign at the bus station advertising a *garderoba* (left-luggage office), it's not operational because the station is only open limited hours. The large Jadrolinija ferries tie up near the Riva Hotel in the old town.

Information The tourist office is on Arba Municipium opposite the post office in the old town. Rab's post office is open Monday to Saturday from 7 am to 8 pm.

Rab's telephone code is ☎ 051.

Things to See Four tall church towers rise above the red-roofed mass of houses on Rab's high peninsula. If you follow Rade Končara north from the **Monastery of St Anthony** (1175), you soon reach the Romanesque **cathedral**, alongside a pleasant terrace with a view overlooking the sea. Farther along, beyond a tall **Romanesque tower** and another convent, is a second terrace and **St Justine Church**, now a small museum of religious art. Just past the next chapel, look for a small gate giving access to a park with the foundations of Rab's oldest church and the fourth tower (which you can climb).

Rade Končara ends at the north city wall, which affords a splendid view of the town,

CROATIA

harbour, sea and hill. The scene is especially beautiful just after sunset. North of the wall is the extensive **city park** with many shady walkways.

Special Events Annual events to ask about include the Rab Fair (25 to 27 July) and the Rab Music Evenings (June to September).

Places to Stay Everything from camping to expensive hotels can be found in and around Rab town.

Camping To sleep cheap, carry your tent south along the waterfront about 25 minutes to *Autocamp Padova* (☎ 724 355) at Banjol (US$3 per person, US$1.50 per tent). There's a wooded ridge by the camping ground where you can pitch a tent away from the noise and caravans. The beach is just below.

Private Rooms Several agencies rent private rooms, including Turist biro Palit (open April to October only) and Turist biro Kristofor, both on the corner near the bus station. If they are closed, try the Turist Biro on Arba Municipium and Arba Kompas next door. The official tariff is US$15/24 a single/double 1st category (private bath) in July and August (US$13/19 in June and September, US$11/16 the rest of the year), or US$10/14 a single/double in 3rd category in July and August (cheaper during other months). For stays of less than three nights there's a 30% surcharge. Some agencies forgo the single supplement, taxes and surcharges when things are slow.

You could be approached by women at the bus station offering private rooms.

Hotels The *Hotel International* (☎ 711 266), on Obala kralja Petra Krešimira IV facing the harbour, has rooms at US$27/40 a single/double with bath and breakfast in June and September, 30% more in midsummer. It's a pleasant place to stay if you don't mind the price.

Add US$1.30 per person per night 'tourist tax' to all accommodation rates.

Places to Eat One of the few restaurants in Rab which posts a menu outside is *Alibaba* on ulica Ivana Lole Ribara in the old town. It's not cheap but it does have a good selection of seafood; according to the locals it's the best place in town.

The buffet at Merkur department store near the bus station posts drink prices and serves grilled meat dishes in the dining room. There's a good supermarket in the basement at Merkur for picnic supplies.

Getting There & Away All the local travel agencies have bus and ferry schedules posted in their offices.

Bus The most reliable way to come or go is on one of the two daily buses between Rab and Rijeka (115 km, US$10). In the tourist season there's also a direct bus from Zagreb to Rab (211 km, five hours, US$18). These services can fill up, so book ahead if possible.

There's no direct bus from Rab to Zadar. You must take the Rijeka or Zagreb bus up to the main highway at Jablanac (US$3.50) and wait there. This is fairly easy as connecting buses to Zadar run down the main coastal highway all day. Going from Zadar to Rab by bus is much more difficult as you probably won't find a bus from Jablanac to Rab and may have to walk or hitchhike.

Boat The ferry from Baška on Krk Island to Lopar at the north end of Rab operates three or four times a day from June to mid-September only (US$6).

Unless you're on a through bus to/from Rijeka or Zagreb, the more frequent year-round ferry from Jablanac on the mainland to Mišnjak on Rab Island is problematic. Jablanac is four km off the main Rijeka-Split highway (downhill all the way) and there are no local buses from Mišnjak into Rab town (11 km), only the through buses from Rijeka or Zagreb.

The large Jadrolinija coastal ferries between Rijeka and Dubrovnik are supposed to call at Rab a few times a week and this would certainly be the easiest, if not the cheapest or most convenient, way to come, *except* that northbound they arrive in the middle of the night and they don't stop at all in bad weather.

In summer tourist boats make day excursions to Lošinj Island once or twice a week (US$17 return).

Lopar

The bus from Lopar to Rab town stops in front of Pizzeria Aloha opposite the small-boat harbour about 300 metres ahead of the Lopar ferry landing. The stop is unmarked, so ask. There's a bus every hour or two to Rab town (12 km). Several houses around here have *sobe* signs. Camping San Marino is about three km south of the Lopar ferry landing, across the peninsula.

Dalmatia

Dalmatia (Dalmacija) occupies the central 375 km of Croatia's Adriatic coast, from the Gulf of Kvarner in the north to the Bay of Kotor in the south, offshore islands included. The rugged Dinaric Alps form a 1500-metre-high barrier separating Dalmatia from Bosnia, with only two breaks: the Krka River canyon at Knin and the Neretva Valley at Mostar, both of which have railways.

After the last Ice Age, part of the coastal mountains were flooded, creating the same sort of long, high islands seen in the Gulf of Kvarner. The deep, protected passages that lie between these islands are a paradise for sailors and cruisers.

Historical relics abound in towns like Zadar, Trogir, Split, Hvar, Korčula and Dubrovnik, framed by a striking natural beauty of barren slopes, green valleys and clear water. The ferry trip from Split to Dubrovnik is one of the classic journeys of Eastern Europe. The vineyards of Dalmatia supply half of Croatia's wine. A warm current flowing north up the coast keeps the climate mild – dry in summer, damp in winter. Dalmatia is noticeably warmer than Istria or the Gulf of Kvarner and it's possible to swim in the sea right up until the end of September. This is the Mediterranean at its best.

Unfortunately Dalmatia suffered badly in the civil war that tore apart ex-Yugoslavia. Zadar and Dubrovnik were especially hard hit by shelling in late 1991 and early 1992. Šibenik and Split also came under fire. Although the physical damage has largely been repaired and the region is now completely safe to visit, the virtual collapse of a once-thriving tourist industry has left the population demoralised. Some hotels are still filled with refugees, excursions attract too few visitors to operate regularly and many museums remain closed for lack of money. Still, the warm welcome extended to tourists can more than compensate for a few hassles. The people you meet are usually quite willing to talk about their experiences in 1991-92 and the first-hand knowledge you'll gain will add a new dimension to your trip. To attract business, prices here are much lower than they are further north and at least one hotel in each town is reserved for visitors. The Jadrolinija ferries continue to ply the lovely coastal route from Rijeka to Dubrovnik. Zadar, Trogir, Split, Hvar, Korčula and Dubrovnik are all easily accessible by bus or boat. As peace slowly settles over Dalmatia, the tourist industry will inevitably crank up but for now you'll have the old stone towns and sparkling coastline all to yourself.

History

The Illyrians settled here around 1000 BC, followed in the 4th century BC by the Greeks, who established colonies at Korčula, Hvar and Solin. When Greek and Illyrian interests collided, the Romans intervened and after 74 years of wars they succeeded in subjugating the province of Dalmatia in 155 BC. Major Roman ruins are still seen in Zadar, Solin and Split. After the Western Roman Empire fell in the 5th century AD, the region became a battleground for barbarians, Byzantines and many other conquerors. The present inhabitants are descended from Slavic tribes which arrived in the 6th century.

Medieval Dalmatia was ruled at different times by Venice and Croatia. Venice purchased Dalmatia from the Hungaro-Croatian king in 1409 and held it until Napoleon captured Venice itself in 1797. Most of the coastal towns still bear a deep Italian imprint, quite a contrast to the Turkish influence just a few dozen km inland. Through diplomatic deals Dalmatia was eventually handed to Austria, which held it until 1918.

In 1915 Britain and France promised northern Dalmatia to Italy if Italy would enter WWI on their side. After postwar wrangles, it was finally agreed that Italy could have Istria, Cres, Lošinj, Zadar and Lastovo while Yugoslavia got the rest. In 1941 Mussolini annexed the

CROATIA

whole of Dalmatia to Italy but in 1947 everything was formally given back to Yugoslavia, including the territory Italy got from Austria in 1920.

ZADAR

Zadar (the ancient Zara), the main city of northern Dalmatia, occupies a long peninsula which separates the harbour on the east from the Zadar Channel on the west. The city of Iader was laid out by the Romans, who left behind considerable ruins. Later the area fell under the Byzantine Empire, which explains the Orthodox churches with their central domes. In 1409 Venice took Zadar from Croatia and held it for four centuries. Dalmatia was part of the Austro-Hungarian empire during most of the 19th century, with Italy exercising control from 1918 to 1943. Badly damaged by Anglo-American bombing raids in 1943-44, much of the city had to be rebuilt. Luckily, the original street plan was respected and an effort made to harmonise the new with what remained of old Zadar.

In November 1991, Zadar seemed to be reliving history as Yugoslav rockets ploughed into the old city, damaging the cathedral. For the next three months the city's inhabitants had to sleep on cots in their basements without running water, electricity or heating, unable to go out of their homes for fear of being hit. Ask any of the older people how much weight they lost during this dark time. This experience has embittered many residents and you may encounter some suspicion until people know who you are. Despite being shelled indiscriminately from Serb positions in the surrounding countryside, Zadar sustained remarkably little damage, although some buildings are still pockmarked with bullet holes. The Serb gunners were pushed back by the Croatian army during its January 1993 offensive and the city has been safe to visit ever since.

Although the scars of both wars are visible, Zadar's narrow, traffic-free stone streets are again full of life and the tree-lined promenade along Obala kralja Petra Krešimira IV is perfect for a lazy stroll or a picnic. Zadar can be a fascinating place in which to wander. Tremendous 16th-century fortifications still shield the city on the landward side, and high walls run along the harbour. Even though the museums and monuments are in poor repair

and usually closed, Zadar is surprising for its variety of sights. It's also famous for its maraschino cherry liqueur.

Orientation

The train and bus stations are adjacent, a 15-minute walk south-east of the harbour and old town. The left-luggage office in the train station is closed (and there never was one in the bus station).

From the train and bus stations, Zrinsko-Frankopanska ulica leads north-west past the main post office to the harbour. Buses marked 'Poluotok' run from the bus station to the harbour. Narodni trg is the heart of Zadar.

Information

Croatia Express is on Široka ulica. The American Express representative is Atlas travel agency (☎ 314 339), Branimirova Obala 12, across the footbridge over the harbour just north-east of Narodni trg.

Telephone calls can be made from the main post office at Zrinsko-Frankopanska ulica 8 (open from 7 am to 8 pm daily).

Zadar's telephone code is ☎023.

Things to See

The main things to see are near the circular St Donatus Church, a 9th-century Byzantine structure built over the Roman forum. In summer, ask about musical evenings here (Renaissance and early baroque music). The outstanding Museum of Church Art (currently closed) in the Benedictine Monastery opposite offers a substantial display of reliquaries and religious paintings. The obscure lighting deliberately recreates the environment in which the objects were originally kept.

The 13th-century Romanesque Cathedral of St Anastasia nearby never really recovered from WWII destruction; the Franciscan Monastery a few blocks away is more cheerful. The large Romanesque cross in the treasury behind the sacristy is worth seeing.

Other museums include the Archaeological Museum (closed Monday) across from St Donatus, and the Ethnological Museum in the Town Watchtower (1562) on Narodni trg. The latter should reopen as soon as renovations on the Watchtower are completed. More interesting is the National Museum on Poljana Pape Aleksandra III just inside the Sea Gate. This

Harbour

Zadar

0   50   100 m

Liburnska obala

Bedemi zadarskin pobuna

Istarska obala

Luke Jelíca

Petranovíća

Božídara

Bersa

Natka

Nodila

Aleksandra III

Brne Krnarulíća

Bedemi zadarskin pobuna

Obala kralja Petra Krešimira IV

Zeleni trg

Široka

Nikole Matafara

Benje

S Kožíča

ulica

Borelli

Excursion Boat Wharf

Narodni trg

E. Kotromanić

Spire Brusine

Varoška

Pavlinovíća

Obala kralja Petra Krešimira IV

Rudera

Smiljaníća

Boškovíća

Zadar Channel

Zvonimira

Fošá

PLACES TO EAT
13 Samoposluzivanje Self-
    Service
25 Dalmacija Restaurant

OTHER
1   Ancona Ferry
2   Jadrolinija
3   Rowing Boat Ride
4   Arsenal
5   Croatia Airlines
6   Jadroagent
7   Franciscan Monastery
8   Serbian Church
9   Cathedral
10 Post Office (not GPO)
11 St Krsevan
12 National Museum
14 St Donatus Church
15 Archaeological Museum
16 Museum of Church Art
17 Kompas
18 St Petar Stari
19 Vegetable Market
20 National Theatre
21 Central Kavana
22 Town Watchtower
23 Liburnija Tourist
    Office
24 Kvarner Express
26 St Simun
27 Turistička Zajednica
28 Art Gallery
29 Medieval Tower
30 Town Gate
31 Ruins

CROATIA

excellent historical museum features scale models of Zadar from different periods and old paintings and engravings of many coastal cities. The same admission ticket will get you into the local **art gallery**. Unfortunately, the captions in all of Zadar's museums are in Croatian only and most museums are closed in winter.

Organised Tours

Any of the many travel agencies around town can supply information on the daily tourist cruises to the beautiful Kornati Islands (US$40, including lunch and a swim in the sea or a salt lake). As this is about the only way to see these 101 barren, uninhabited islands, islets and cliffs it's worthwhile if you can spare the cash, but the trips are cancelled during bad weather and throughout winter. Check with Kvarner Express on Kraljice Elizabete Kotromanić, Kompas on Široka and Croatia Express across the street. The Kornati boats leave from the wharf near Hotel Zagreb. Also ask about excursions to the national parks of Plitvice and Krka.

Special Events

Major annual events include the town fair (July and August), the Dalmatian Song Festival (July and August), the Musical Evenings in St Donatus Church (August) and the Choral Festival (October).

Places to Stay

In no event should you arrive in Zadar without pre-arranged accommodation. Facilities not closed for renovation or lack of guests are filled with refugees and closed to tourists. You may have better luck heading out to nearby Borik a few km north-west; there are buses from the main bus station every half hour.

Camping *Zaton* (☎ 64 444) is 16 km northwest of Zadar on a sandy beach and should be open May to September. There are 12 buses daily. Nearer to Zadar is *Autocamp Borik* (☎ 23 677), only steps away from Borik beach.

Hostels Also near the beach at Borik is the *Borik Youth Hostel* (☎ 443 145), Obala Kneza Trpimira 76, open from May to September. Out of 330 beds only 35 are available to tourists,

the rest are for refugees. An advance reservation is strongly recommended.

Private Rooms Private rooms exist but can be hard to find mainly because no one has bothered to reinstate a system to put the people who have rooms together with the people who want them. Call in advance. Try Kompas (☎ 433 380) on Široka or Kvarner Express (☎ 24 864) at Kraljice Elizabete Kotromanić or Marlin Tours (☎ 23 599), around the corner from Atlas. Liburnija tourist office next to Kvarner Express might have rooms. In a pinch, Turistička Zajednica (☎ 25 948), the local tourist authority at Smiljanića 1, may be able to help. Expect to pay about US$20 for a double in July/August.

Hotels The only hotel presently open in Zadar is the *Hotel Kolovare* (☎ 433 022), ulica Bože Peričića, 200 metres from the bus station. About half the hotel is occupied by refugees, EU monitors and UN peacekeepers; the rest is open to tourists all year. Single/double rooms are US$50/76 in the high season, 10% less in spring and autumn. There is a swimming pool, a pleasant private beach and the food is good if you decide to take half-board. In Borik, the B-category *Novi Park* (☎ 22 177) and *Hotel Borik* (☎ 332 151) have rooms that are about 25% cheaper.

Places to Eat

Dalmacija, at the end of Kraljice Elizabete Kotromanić, is a good place for pizza, spaghetti, fish and local specialities. At the south-east end of the harbour, on the corner of Obala Kralja Tomislava, is *Restaurant Basket*. The *Samoposluzivanje*, a self-service restaurant in the passage at Nikole Matafara 9, has hot dishes starting at US$3 (open from 7 am to 9 pm daily).

Central Kavana on Široka is a spacious café and hang-out with live music on weekends. For drinks you can also try *Bife Agava*, ulica Jurja Barakovića 6, a block towards the harbour from Narodni trg. In the summer the many cafés along Varoška place their tables on the street; it's great for people-watching. There's a large supermarket on Široka ulica where you can buy picnic supplies.

Entertainment

The National Theatre box office on Široka ulica has tickets to cultural programmes advertised on posters outside.

Getting There & Away

Bus & Train There is a daily morning train to Zagreb (11 hours, US$12) that changes at Knin. The bus to Zagreb (320 km) is quicker. There are also buses to Rijeka (228 km), Split (158 km), Mostar (301 km) and Dubrovnik (393 km, four daily, US$16).

Croatia Express travel agency (see Information section for the address) sells bus tickets to many German cities, including Munich (US$64), Frankfurt (US$100), Cologne (US$117) and Berlin (US$126).

Boat From late June to September the fast boat *Marina* runs from Venice to Zadar (14½ hours, US$48) twice a week and from Pula to Zadar (7½ hours, US$19) four times a week, stopping at Mali Lošinj. There are weekly local ferries all year between Mali Lošinj and Zadar (six hours, US$8) and between Pula and Zadar (eight hours, US$9.30), stopping at Mali Lošinj. The Jadrolinija coastal ferry from Rijeka to Dubrovnik calls at Zadar four times a week (US$21 from Rijeka, US$23 from Dubrovnik).

From June to September Jadrolinija also runs a car ferry three times a week (four in August) from Zadar to Ancona, Italy (six hours, US$40). The rest of the year the service is weekly. The same ferry runs to Šibenik once a week.

On Monday and Saturday there's a ferry to Zaglav on Dugi otok (US$6), a good day trip on other days there's no connection to return to Zadar).

For information on the *Marina*, contact Jadroagent (☎ 23 210) on ulica Natka Nodila just inside the city walls. Jadrolinija (☎ 24 843), Liburnska obala 7 on the harbour, has tickets for all local ferries.

TROGIR

Trogir (formerly Trau), a lovely medieval town on the coast just 20 km west of Split, is well worth a stop if you're coming down from Zadar. A day trip to Trogir from Split can easily be combined with a visit to the Roman ruins of Salona (see the section on Salona later in this chapter).

The old town of Trogir occupies a tiny island in the narrow channel between Čiovo Island and the mainland, just off the coastal highway. Many sights are seen on a 15-minute walk around this island. The nearest beach is four km west at the Medena Hotel.

Orientation

The heart of the old town is a few minutes walk from the bus station. After crossing the small bridge near the station, go through the North Gate. Trogir's finest sights are around Narodni trg, slightly left and ahead.

There's no left-luggage office in Trogir bus station, so you'll end up toting your bags around town if you only visit on a stopover.

Information

The tourist office (☎ 881 554) opposite the cathedral sells a map of the area. The telephone code for Trogir is ☎ 021.

Things to See

The glory of the three-naved Venetian **Cathedral of St Lovro** on Narodni trg is the Romanesque portal of Adam & Eve (1240) by Master Radovan, which you can admire for free any time. Enter the building through an obscure back door to see the perfect Renaissance Chapel of St Ivan, and the choir, pulpit, ciborium and treasury. You can even climb the cathedral tower for a delightful view. Also on Narodni trg is the **town hall**, with an excellent Gothic staircase and Renaissance loggia.

Places to Stay

Camping On Čiovo Island, *Camping Rožac* is connected to Trogir by a bridge. It's a half-hour walk from Trogir bus station, or you can take the Okrug bus. *Medena Camping* (☎ 894 141) is just off the highway to Zadar about four km west of Trogir. Check with the Turist Biro to make sure they're open before trekking out.

Private Rooms The Turist Biro opposite the cathedral has private rooms for US$11/18 a single/double.

Getting There & Away

Southbound buses from Zadar (130 km) will drop you off in Trogir. Getting buses north can

CROATIA

be more difficult, as they often arrive full from Split.

City bus No 37 runs between Trogir and Split (28 km) every 20 minutes throughout the day with a stop at Split airport en route. In Split bus No 37 leaves from the local bus station. If you're making a day trip to Trogir also buy your ticket back to Split, as the ticket window at Trogir bus station is often closed. Drivers also sell tickets if you're stuck.

SPLIT

Split (Italian: Spalato), the largest Croatian city on the Adriatic coast, is the heart of Dalmatia. The old town is built around the harbour, on the south side of a high peninsula sheltered from the open sea by many islands. Ferries to these islands are constantly coming and going. The entire west end of the peninsula is a vast wooded mountain park, while industry, shipyards, limestone quarries and the ugly commercial/military port are mercifully far enough away on the north side of the peninsula. High coastal mountains set against the blue Adriatic provide a striking frame to the scene.

Split achieved fame when the Roman emperor Diocletian (245-313 AD), noted for his persecution of early Christians, had his retirement palace built here from 295 to 305. After his death the great stone palace continued to be used as a retreat by Roman rulers. When the nearby colony of Salona was abandoned in the 7th century, many of the Romanised inhabitants fled to Split and barricaded themselves behind the high palace walls, where their descendants live to this day.

First Byzantium and then Croatia controlled the area, but from the 12th to the 14th centuries medieval Split enjoyed a large measure of autonomy which favoured its development. The western part of the old town around Narodni trg, which dates from this time, became the focus of municipal life, while the area within the palace walls proper continued as the ecclesiastical centre.

In 1420 the Venetians conquered Split, which led to a slow decline. During the 17th century, strong walls were built around the city as a defence against the Turks. In 1797 the Austrians arrived; they remained until 1918, with only a brief interruption during the Napoleonic wars.

Since 1945, Split has grown into a major industrial city with large apartment-block housing areas. Much of old Split remains, however, and this combined with its exuberant nature makes it one of the most fascinating cities in Europe. It's also the perfect base for excursions to many nearby attractions, so settle in for a few days.

Be prepared, however, to find the doors of many museums securely locked. During the war many exhibits were removed for safe-keeping and haven't yet been returned although you'll see few other signs of the war.

Orientation

The bus, train and ferry terminals are adjacent on the east side of the harbour, a short walk from the old town. The *garderoba* (left-luggage) kiosk at the bus station is open from 6 am to 8 pm. The left-luggage office at the train station is about 50 metres north of the station at Domagoja 6 and is open from 5 am to 11 pm. Obala hrvatskog narodnog preporoda, the waterfront promenade, is your best central reference point in Split.

Information

The tourist office is at Obala hrvatskog narodnog preporoda 12.

Post & Communications Poste-restante mail can be collected at window No 7 at the main post office, Kralja Tomislava 9. The post office is open weekdays from 7 am to 8 pm, and Saturday from 7 am to 2 pm. The telephone centre here is open daily from 7 am to 9 pm. On Sunday and in the early evening there's always a line of people waiting to place calls, so it's better to go in the morning.

Split's telephone code is ☎ 021.

Travel Agency The American Express representative, Atlas travel agency (☎ 43 055), is at Trg Braće Radića, Split 21000.

Bookshops The so-called International Book Shop, Obala hrvatskog narodnog preporoda 20, sells foreign newspapers (but few books).

Things to See

There's much more to see than can be mentioned here, so pick up a local guidebook if you're staying longer than a day or two. The

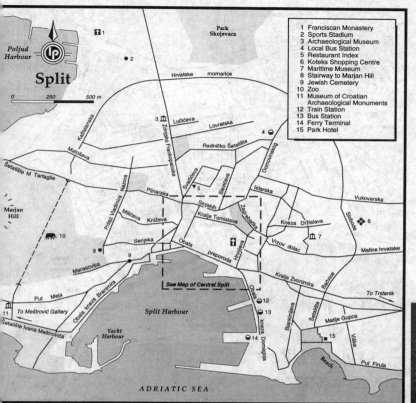

Split

```
1   Franciscan Monastery
2   Sports Stadium
3   Archaeological Museum
4   Local Bus Station
5   Restaurant Index
6   Koteks Shopping Centre
7   Maritime Museum
8   Stairway to Marjan Hill
9   Jewish Cemetery
10  Zoo
11  Museum of Croatian
    Archaeological Monuments
12  Train Station
13  Bus Station
14  Ferry Terminal
15  Park Hotel
```

ld town is a vast open-air museum made all
ne more interesting by the everyday life still
oing on throughout.

Diocletian's Palace facing the harbour is
ne of the most imposing Roman ruins in
xistence. It was built as a strong rectangular
ortress with walls 215 by 180 metres long
nd reinforced by towers. The imperial resi-
ence, temples and mausoleum were south of
ne main street connecting the east and west
ates.

Enter through the central ground floor of the
alace at Obala hrvatskog narodnog preporoda
2. On the left you'll see the excavated base-
nent halls, which are empty but impressive.

Continue through the passage to the **Peristyle**,
a picturesque colonnaded square, with the neo-
Romanesque cathedral tower rising above. The
vestibule, an open dome above the ground-
floor passageway at the south end of the
Peristyle, is overpowering. A lane off the Peristyle opposite the cathedral leads to the
Temple of Jupiter, now a baptistry.

On the east side of the Peristyle is the **cathedral**, originally Diocletian's mausoleum.
The only reminder of Diocletian in the cathedral is a sculpture of his head in a circular stone
wreath below the dome directly above the
baroque white-marble altar. The Romanesque
wooden doors (1214) and stone pulpit are

CROATIA

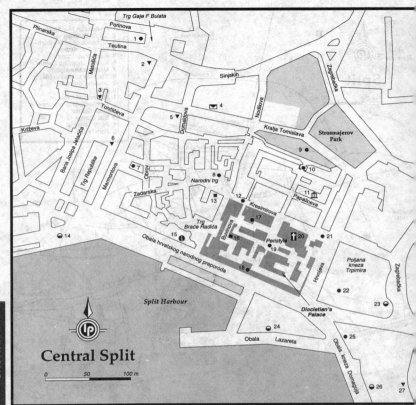

Plinarska
Porinova
Trg Gaje F Bulata
1
Teutina
Matošića
2
3
Tončićeva
Domaldova
Sinjskih
4
5
Nodilova
Zagrebačka
Kralja Tomislava
Strosmajerov Park
9
10
Križeva
Bana Josipa Jelačića
Trg Republike
Marmontova
6
Obrov
7
Zadarska
Narodni trg
8
11
Papaličeva
12
13
Kresimirova
17
Buvinova
Trg Braće Radića
15
16
Obala hrvatskog narodnog preporoda
Peristyle
19
20
21
14
18
Split Harbour
22
23
Poljana kneza Trpimira
Zagrebačka
Diocletian's Palace
24
Obala   Lazareta
25
Obala kneza Domagoja
26
27

Central Split

0   50   100 m

worth noting. You may climb the tower for a small fee.

The west palace gate opens onto medieval Narodni trg, dominated by the 15th-century Venetian Gothic **old town hall**. Trg Braće Radića, between Narodni trg and the harbour, contains the surviving north tower of the 15th-century Venetian garrison castle, which once extended to the water's edge. The east palace gate leads into the market area.

In the Middle Ages the nobility and rich merchants built residences within the old palace walls, one of which, the Papalic Palace, at Papaličeva (also known as Žarkova) ulica 5, is now the town museum. Go through the north palace gate to see the powerful **statue** (1929) by Ivan Meštrović of 10th-century Slavic religious leader Gregorius of Nin, who fought for the right to say mass in Croatian.

Museums & Galleries Split's least known yet most interesting museum is the **maritime museum** (open 9 am to noon, closed Monday, free entry) in Gripe Fortress (1657), on a hilltop east of the old town. The large collection of wartime maps, photos, artefacts and scale models is fascinating, but unfortunately all the captions are in Croatian only. This museum has not yet reopened following the war.

PLACES TO STAY
13 Central Hotel
16 Prenoćište Slavija

PLACES TO EAT
2 Bastion Self-Service Restaurant
3 Galija
5 Burek Bar
6 Ero Lunch Counter
27 Pizzeria Bakra

OTHER
1 Croatian National Theatre
4 Main Post Office
7 Fish Market
8 Old Town Hall
9 Statue of Gregorius of Nin
10 North Palace Gate
11 Town Museum
12 West Palace Gate
14 Salona Bus Stop
15 Turistički biro
17 Temple of Jupiter
18 Basement Halls of Palace
19 Vestibule
20 Cathedral
21 East Palace Gate
22 Vegetable Market
23 Bus No 17 to Camping Ground
24 Airport Bus Stop
25 Adria Airlines
26 Bus & Train Stations

Also worth the walk is the **archaeological museum**, Zrinjsko-Frankopanska 25, north of own (open mornings only, closed Monday). The best of this valuable collection, first assembled in 1820, is in the garden outside. The items in the showcases inside the museum building would be a lot more interesting if the captions were in something other than Croatian. This museum also has not yet reopened.

The **town museum** on Papaliceva, east of Narodni trg (open Tuesday to Friday from 10 am to 5 pm, weekends 10 am to noon, closed Monday), has a well-displayed collection of artefacts, paintings, furniture and clothes from Split. Captions are in Croatian.

Other Split museums are west of the old own. The impressive-looking **Museum of Croatian Archaeological Monuments**, on Šetalište Ivana Meštrovića (closed Monday), disappoints on the inside. Its lack of captions in any languages other than Croatian makes it hardly worth seeing. Some of the exhibits appear o be replicas, but it doesn't really matter since

you don't know what you're looking at anyway!

A welcome contrast is the **Meštrović Gallery**, Šetalište Ivana Meštrovića 46 (presently closed). When the gallery reopens you'll see a comprehensive, well-arranged collection of works by Ivan Meštrović, Croatia's premier modern sculptor, who built the gallery as a personal residence in 1931-39. Although Meštrović intended to retire here, he emigrated to the USA soon after WWII. Bus No 12 passes the gate infrequently. There are beaches on the south side of the peninsula below the gallery.

From the Meštrović Gallery it's possible to hike straight up **Marjan Hill**. Go up ulica Tonča Petrasova Marovića on the west side of the gallery and continue straight up the stairway to Put Meja ulica. Turn left and walk west to Put Meja 76. The trail begins on the west side of this building. Marjan Hill offers trails through the forest, lookouts, old chapels and the local zoo.

Special Events
The Split Summer Festival from mid-July to mid-August features opera, drama, ballet and concerts on open-air stages. There's also the Feast of St Dujo (7 May) and the four-day Festival of Popular Music around the end of June. From June to September a variety of evening entertainment is presented in the old town.

Places to Stay
Camping The nearest camp site is at Trstenik, five km east of the centre near the beach (bus No 17 from the east side of the market). *Autocamp Trstenik* (☎ 521 971), just beyond the last stop of bus No 17, on a cliff overlooking the sea, is shady with many pine trees and stairs leading down to the beach, but lately it has been filled with refugees.

Private Rooms Although women used to offer a good deal on *zimmer* at the bus station, lately the lack of business has discouraged them from appearing. Your only choice may be to head for the Turistički biro, Obala hrvatskog narodnog preporoda 12. Prices begin at US$18/30 for a single/double including 'residence tax', less 30% if you stay three nights or more. Singles are seldom available. Many travellers find private rooms in the area around the Koteks shopping centre.

Hotels The current hotel situation in Split is bleak. Most hotels are housing refugees; those that are available to guests extract top dollar. The ageing *Central Hotel* (☎ 48 242) used to offer the cheapest rooms but is now filled with refugees. The 32-room *Prenoćište Slavija* (☎ 47 053), Buvinova 3, has a few rooms available for US$46 which is as cheap as you'll find. The B-category *Park Hotel* (☎ 021-515 411), Šetalište Bačvice 15, has plenty of rooms if you want to pay US$83/100 for a single/double. This attractive 58-room resort hotel is a 10-minute walk from the old town, but close to the bus and train stations and the beach.

Places to Eat
Pizza, lasagne and draught beer are offered at both the up-market *Galija* on Tončićeva (daily until 11 pm), and *Pizzeria Bakra*, Radovanova 2, off ulica Sv Petra Starog just down from the vegetable market. If you want a slice of suburban Croatian life with your pizza, head to *Pizzeria Koteks* in the Koteks shopping centre, a huge white complex 10 minutes' walk east of the old town beyond the Maritime Museum. It is the largest of its kind in Dalmatia and includes a supermarket, department store, boutiques, restaurants, bars, banks, post office, two bowling alleys, sports centre etc.

The cheapest place in town is *Restaurant Index*, a self-service student eatery at Svačićeva 8. Vegetarians should avoid this place. Better fare for only a little more is available at the *Bastion Self-Service*, Marmontova 9 (open daily). It's clean and inexpensive.

The *Burek Bar*, Domaldova 13, just down from the main post office, serves a good breakfast or lunch of burek and yoghurt for about a dollar. There are tables where you can sit.

Entertainment
In summer you'll probably find the best evening entertainment in the small streets of the old town, or along the waterfront promenade. During winter, opera and ballet are presented at the *Croatian National Theatre*, Trg Gaje Bulata. The best seats are about US$10 and tickets for the same night are usually available. Erected in 1891, the theatre

was fully restored in 1979 in the original style; it's worth attending a performance for the architecture alone. At intermission, head upstairs to see the foyer.

Split's best known disco is *Metropole* in the Koteks Shopping Centre.

Getting There & Away
Air Croatia Airlines operates one-hour flights to/from Zagreb about four times a day (US$93).

Bus Advance bus tickets with seat reservations are recommended. There are through buses from the main bus station beside the harbour to Zadar (158 km, 25 daily), Zagreb (478 km, 26 daily), Rijeka (404 km, 11 daily), Ljubljana (532 km, one daily), Pula (514 km, two daily) and Rovinj (509 km, daily). To Bosnia-Hercegovina there are four daily buses from Split to Međugorje (156 km), five to Mostar (179 km) and one to Sarajevo (271 km). Croatia Express next to the bus station has a convenient overnight bus to Zagreb (US$14).

Bus No 37 to Solin, Split airport and Trogir leaves from a local bus station on Domovinskog, one km north-east of the city centre (see the map).

Lenhard Tours next to the bus station has buses to Amsterdam (weekly, US$140) and many German cities, including Munich (912 km, daily, US$69). Agencija Touring at the bus station also has many buses to Germany.

Dubrovnik The 10 daily buses between Split and Dubrovnik (235 km) pass through the small resort town of Neum which belongs to Bosnia-Hercegovina; expect a border check. Signs of war (ethnic cleansing to be exact) are clearly visible here in the form of the burned and looted homes of Muslim 'departed residents', although the large tourist hotels are untouched.

Train Service between Split and Zagreb (daily, nine hours, US$14) has been restored. Two trains operate daily between Split and Šibenik (74 km).

Boat Jadrolinija (☎ 355 673), in the large ferry terminal opposite the bus station, handles services to Hvar (US$10), operating three or four

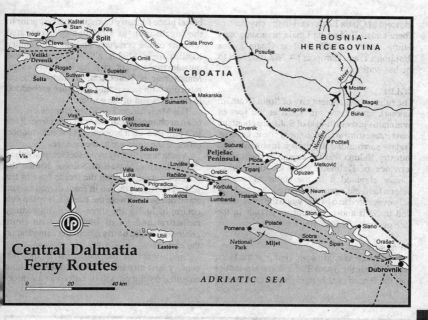

Central Dalmatia Ferry Routes

0   20   40 km

ADRIATIC SEA

times a week all year round. The most useful local ferry is the daily service between Split and Ubli on the island of Lastovo, which calls at Hvar (US$7) and Vela Luka on Korčula Island (US$8) daily. This ferry departs from Vela Luka in the morning and Split in the afternoon (the latter does not return to Split the same day).

The Jadrolinija coastal ferries usually leave Split at 8 am southbound and 7 pm northbound, but service is not always daily, so check the schedule at a travel agency beforehand. With a through ticket (US$21) from Split to Dubrovnik, you can get free stops at Hvar and Korčula.

All year round there's an overnight Jadrolinija ferry between Ancona and Split (10 hours, US$44) at least twice a week and up to five times a week in summer. Adriatica Navigazione also has a year-round service between Ancona and Split (US$38 off season, US$44 July and August). Most trips are overnight but once a week Adriatica makes a day run. For information on international ferries to Italy check with Jadroagent

in the ferry terminal (open daily from 8 am to 1.30 pm and 5 to 8 pm).

Getting Around

To/From the Airport The bus to Split airport (US$4.50) leaves from Obala Lazareta 3, a five-minute walk from the train station. This bus departs 90 minutes before flight times. You can also get there on bus No 37, as described in Getting There & Away (two-zone ticket).

Bus Line up for city bus tickets at one of the very few kiosks around town which sell them, as newsstands don't have these tickets. For Trogir, buy a zone 3 ticket; Split airport is zone 2; Solin and Trstenik are zone 1. Validate the ticket once aboard. Bus tickets with an arrow at each end are good for two trips – you cancel one end at a time. You can also pay the driver, but that costs almost double.

Car Compare prices at Cobra Rent-a-Car (☎ 356 865) and ST Rent-a-Car (☎ 46 473), adjacent at Obala Lazareta 3 in the city centre. There's also Budget on Obala hrvatskog narodnog, Hertz (☎ 585 840) at Obala kneza Branimira 1, and Europcar (☎ 362 700) next to the bus station.

SOLIN

The ruins of the ancient city of Solin (Roman: Salona), among the vineyards at the foot of mountains just north-east of Split, are about the most interesting archaeological site in Croatia. Today surrounded by noisy highways and industry, Salona was the capital of the Roman province of Dalmatia from the time Julius Caesar elevated it to the status of colony. Salona held out against the barbarians and was only evacuated in 614 AD when the inhabitants fled to Split and neighbouring islands in the face of Avar and Slav attacks.

Things to See

A good place to begin your visit is at the large car park near the Snack Bar Salona. **Manastirine**, the fenced area behind the car park, was a burial place for early Christian martyrs prior to the legalisation of Christianity. Excavated remains of the cemetery and the 5th-century basilica are highlights, although this area was outside the ancient city itself. Overlooking Manastirine is **Tusculum**, an archaeological museum with interesting sculpture embedded in the walls and in the garden.

The Manastirine/Tusculum complex is part of an **archaeological reserve** open from 8 am to 3 pm. Pick up a brochure in the information office at the entrance to the reserve.

A path bordered by cypresses leads south to the northern **city wall** of Salona. Notice the covered aqueduct along the inside base of the wall. The ruins you see in front of you as you stand on the wall were the Early-Christian cult centre, including the three-aisled 5th-century **cathedral** and small **baptistry** with inner columns. **Public baths** adjoin the cathedral on the east.

South-west of the cathedral is the 1st-century east city gate, **Porta Caesarea**, later engulfed by the growth of Salona in all direc-

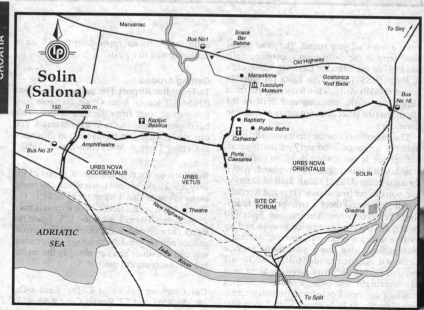

tions. Grooves in the stone road left by ancient chariots can still be seen at this gate.

Walk west along the city wall 500 metres to **Kapljuc Basilica** on the right, another martyrs' burial place. At the west end of Salona is the huge 2nd-century **amphitheatre**, destroyed in the 17th century by the Venetians to prevent it from being used as a refuge by Turkish raiders.

Getting There & Away
The ruins are easily accessible on Split city bus No 1 direct to Snack Bar Salona (look for the yellow bus shelter on the left) every half-hour from opposite Trg Republike. Bus No 16 will also take you to Solin, but you have to get out where the Sinj Highway and city wall meet and then walk west along the old highway one km to the snack bar.

From the amphitheatre at Solin it's easy to continue on to Trogir by catching a westbound bus No 37 from the nearby stop on the adjacent new highway (buy a three-zone ticket in Split if you plan to do this). If, on the other hand, you want to return to Split, use the underpass to cross the highway and catch an eastbound bus No 37 (one-zone ticket).

HVAR ISLAND
Called the 'Croatian Madeira', Hvar is said to receive more sunshine than anywhere else in the country, a total of 2724 hours each year. Yet the island is luxuriantly green, with brilliant patches of lavender, rosemary and heather. It also has a health centre for the treatment of allergies.

Hvar Town
Hvar town cherishes its reputation as one of the most exclusive, chic resorts on the Dalmatian coast, and prices for meals and accommodation reflect the fashionable crowd. Medieval Hvar lies between protective pine-covered slopes and the azure Adriatic, its Gothic palaces hidden among narrow backstreets below the 13th-century city walls. The traffic-free marble avenues of Hvar have an air of Venice, and it was under Venetian rule that Hvar grew rich exporting wine, figs and fish.

Orientation & Information The big Jadrolinija ferries drop you off right in the centre of old Hvar. The barge from Split calls at Stari Grad, 20 km east.

Atlas travel agency, facing the harbour, represents American Express. Public telephones are in the post office (open Monday to Saturday from 7 am to 8 pm) on the waterfront. The telephone code for Hvar is ☎ 021.

The attendant at the public toilets beside the market adjoining the bus station holds luggage for US$1 apiece, but the toilets are only open during market hours, so check the closing time carefully.

Things to See The full flavour of medieval Hvar is best savoured on the backstreets of the old town. At each end of Hvar is a monastery with a prominent tower. The **Dominican monastery** at the head of the bay was destroyed by Turks in the 16th century, and the local **archaeological museum** is now housed among the ruins. If the museum is closed (as it usually is), you'll still get a good view of the ruins from the road just above, which leads up to a stone cross on a hill top offering a picture-postcard view of Hvar.

At the south-east end of Hvar is the 15th-century Renaissance **Franciscan monastery**, with a fine collection of Venetian paintings in the church and adjacent museum, including *The Last Supper* by Matteo Ingoli.

Smack in the middle of Hvar is the imposing Gothic **arsenal**, its great arch visible from afar. The local commune's war galley was once kept here. Upstairs off the arsenal terrace is Hvar's prize, the first **municipal theatre** in Europe (1612), rebuilt in the 19th century. Try to get into the theatre (not the sex-and-violence Kino Madeira downstairs!) to appreciate its delightful human proportions.

On the hill top high above Hvar town is a **Venetian fortress** (1551), well worth the climb for the sweeping panoramic views. Inside is a tiny collection of ancient amphoras recovered from the seabed. The fort was built to defend Hvar from the Turks, who sacked the town in 1539 and 1571.

Beaches are scarce at Hvar, so everyone ends up taking a launch to the **naturist islands** of Jerolim and Stipanska, just offshore. Stipanska is much larger than Jerolim.

Places to Stay Four km north of Hvar town is *Camping Vira* (☎ 741 112). *Mengola Travel* (☎ 742 099) is presently the only agency

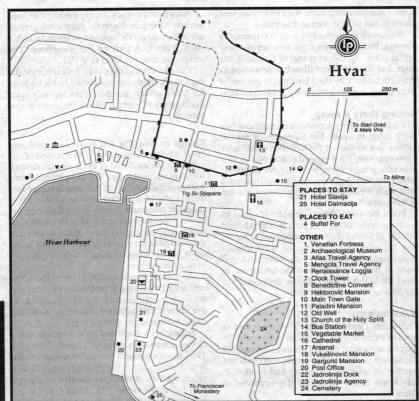

Hvar

0   125   250 m

PLACES TO STAY
21 Hotel Slavija
25 Hotel Dalmacija

PLACES TO EAT
4 Buffet For

OTHER
1 Venetian Fortress
2 Archaeological Museum
3 Atlas Travel Agency
5 Mengola Travel Agency
6 Renaissance Loggia
7 Clock Tower
8 Benedictine Convent
9 Hektorović Mansion
10 Main Town Gate
11 Paladini Mansion
12 Old Well
13 Church of the Holy Spirit
14 Bus Station
15 Vegetable Market
16 Cathedral
17 Arsenal
18 Vukašinović Mansion
19 Gargurić Mansion
20 Post Office
22 Jadrolinija Dock
23 Jadrolinija Agency
24 Cemetery

finding private accommodation and they only have 1st-category rooms. Expect to pay US$19/25 for a single/double in the high season, 20% less in May, June, September and October. You can bargain for a lower rate with proprietors who approach you at the ferry landing. In midsummer everything fills up, so try coming in spring or autumn.

The cheapest hotel is the *Dalmacija* (☎ 741 120), overlooking a quiet cove with single/ double rooms at US$36/57 in July and August but much less the rest of the year.

Places to Eat The restaurant at *Hotel Palace*, next to the clock tower, offers an appetiser,

main course and dessert, all Dalmatian specialities, for only US$8. The pizzerias of Hvar offer the most predictable inexpensive eating. *Buffet For* facing the harbour has good prices for drinks.

The grocery store on Trg Sv Stjepana is your best alternative to a restaurant, and there's a nice park in front of the harbour just made for picnics. A filling breakfast of bread, cheese and yoghurt will cost less than a coffee at the various cafés. The store sells out of bread by noon, however, so shop early.

Entertainment Hvar has a very lively nightlife when the tourist season is in full swing. In the evening the town comes alive, with crowds of locals and tourists promenading along the waterfront and up the huge town square as music drifts across the water from the outdoor cafés. On summer evenings a live band plays on the terrace of the *Hotel Slavija*, just as you would expect to see in Venice. From 10 pm to 4 am at this magical time of year the fortress above Hvar functions as a disco.

Getting There & Away The Jadrolinija ferries between Rijeka and Dubrovnik call at Hvar three or four times a week all year – by far the nicest if not the cheapest way to come. Northbound they leave around 4 pm, southbound at 10 am. The Jadrolinija agency (☎ 741 132) beside the landing sells ferry tickets (US$10 to Split, US$23 to Rijeka, US$12 to Dubrovnik).

The local ferry that runs daily between Vela Luka on Korčula Island and Split calls at Hvar northbound in the morning, southbound in the afternoon, five times a week. This ferry is much cheaper: US$7 Hvar-Split, US$5 Hvar-Vela Luka.

. It's possible to visit Hvar on a day trip from Split by catching the morning Jadrolinija ferry to Hvar town, a bus to Stari Grad, then the last ferry from Stari Grad directly back to Split.

Stari Grad

Stari Grad (Old Town), 20 km away on the island's north coast, is rather picturesque, though somewhat of a disappointment after Hvar. Stari Grad is on the site of an ancient beacon which once stood at the east end of the long inlet which bisects western Hvar. (Hvar gets its name from *pharos*, Greek for lighthouse.)

Stari Grad was the capital of the island until 1331 when the Venetians shifted the administration to Hvar. This explains the extensive medieval quarter you still see at Stari Grad. The palace of the Croat poet Petar Hektorović (1487-1572) is worth a visit to see the fish pond and garden.

Places to Stay Just off the harbour right in the centre of Stari Grad is *Kamp Jurjevac* (open from June to early September). There's no sign, so ask for directions.

Private-room proprietors are less likely to meet the buses and ferries here than in Hvar

town and at last report there was no agency renting such rooms, so you'll just have to ask around.

Getting There & Away Besides the local ferries that run from Split to Stari Grad (US$7) three times a day, Jadro-linija's weekly car ferry from Vela Luka stops at Stari Grad on Sunday evening before going on to Ancona, Italy (US$44 to Ancona). The ferry landing at Stari Grad is about two km from town along a pleasant path by the pine-fringed bay. Buses meet ferries at Stari Grad.

There are three buses a day from Stari Grad to Hvar town (US$2 plus US$1 per piece of baggage).

KORČULA ISLAND

Korčula is the largest island in an archipelago of 48 islets. Rich in vineyards and olive trees, the original Greek settlers called the island Korkyra Melaina (Black Korčula) because of its dense woods and plant life. The southern coast is dotted with quiet coves and small beaches linked to the interior by winding, scenic roads. Korčulans are proud of their musical tradition; some of Croatia's most popular singers come from Korčula.

Korčula Town

The town of Korčula (Italian: Curzola), at the north-east tip of the island, hugs a small, hilly peninsula jutting into the Adriatic Sea. With its round defensive towers and compact cluster of red-roofed houses, Korčula is a typical medieval Dalmatian town. In contrast to Turkish cities like Mostar and Sarajevo, Korčula was controlled by Venice from the 14th to the 18th century. Venetian rule left its mark, especially on Cathedral Square. It's a peaceful little place (population 4000), with grey stone houses nestling between the deep-green hills and gun-metal-blue sea. There are rustling palms all around.

Korčula is noticeably cheaper than Hvar and there's lots to see and do, so it's worth planning a relaxed four-night stay to avoid the 30% surcharge on private rooms. Day trips are possible to Lumbarda and Vela Luka, to Orebić on the Pelješac Peninsula, and to the islands of Badija and Mljet.

CROATIA

Orientation The big Jadrolinija car ferry drops you off below the walls of the old town of Korčula. The passenger launch from Orebić is also convenient, terminating at the old harbour, but the barge from Orebić goes to Bon Repos in Dominče, several km south-east of the centre. There's no left-luggage office at the bus station.

Information The Turist Biro is near the old town. Atlas travel agency is the local American Express representative.

The post office (with public telephones) is rather hidden next to the stairs up to the old town. Korčula's telephone code is ☎ 020.

Things to See Other than following the circuit of the former town walls or walking along the shore, sightseeing in Korčula centres on Cathedral Square. The Gothic **Cathedral of St Mark** features two paintings by Tintoretto (*Three Saints* on the altar and *Annunciation* to one side).

The **treasury** in the 14th-century Abbey Palace next to the cathedral is worth a look, and even better is the **town museum** in the 15th-century Gabriellis Palace opposite. The exhibits of Greek pottery, Roman ceramics and home furnishings have explanations in English. It's said that Marco Polo was born in Korčula in 1254; for a small fee, you can climb the tower of the house that is supposed to have been his. There's also an **icon museum** in the old town. It isn't much of a museum, but visitors are let into the beautiful old **Church of All Saints** as a bonus.

In the high summer season ask about shuttle boats from Korčula to **Badija Island**, which features a 15th-century Franciscan monastery (now a D-category hotel) and a naturist beach.

Organised Tours Marco Polo Tours (☎ 715 400) offers tours to Mljet Island and guided tours of Korčula Island (both for US$20), as well as hiking tours. They also rent small motorboats for US$35.

Places to Stay Korčula offers quite a range of accommodation, though prices are high in July and August.

Camping The *Autocamp Kalac* (☎ 711 182) is behind Hotel Bon Repos, not far from the Orebić car ferry terminal. There are no bungalows, but the beach is close by.

Private Rooms The Turist Biro (☎ 711 067) and Marko Polo Tours (facing the East Harbour) arrange private rooms in town, charging US$13/18/25 for a single/double/triple, except in July and August, when prices increase by 50%. They can also arrange accommodation in the small villages lining the coast. Some of the private operators who meet the boats ask exorbitant rates for private rooms. If their price is more than you're accustomed to paying, check the agencies (which may, however, charge a 30% supplement if you stay fewer than three nights).

There are numerous sobe and zimmer signs around town, so you could try knocking on doors. The houses on the road along the waterfront north-west of the old town are a good bet.

Hotels The B-category *Hotel Korčula* (☎ 711 078), facing Pelješac Channel on the edge of the old town, is about US$43/53 for a single/double with breakfast (30% higher in July and August). The 22 rooms are often full. *Hotel Bon Repos* (☎ 711 102) overlooks a small beach and offers singles/doubles at US$33/40. The Lumbarda bus will drop you off at the hotel.

Places to Eat Just around the corner from Marco Polo's house, *Adio Mare* has a charming maritime decor and a variety of fresh fish. Restaurant Grill Planjak, between the supermarket and the Jadrolinija office in town, is good for chicken and steaks, national specialities like ražnjici, čevapčići and pljeskavici and huge mugs of draught beer. You can also get morning coffee here.

The terrace at *Hotel Korčula* is a nice place for a coffee.

Entertainment From May to September there's moreška sword dancing by the old town gate every Thursday evening at 8.30 pm. Tickets cost US$7 and can be purchased from the Turist Biro. *Cinema Liburna* is in the building marked 'kino' behind the Liburna Restaurant near the bus station.

Getting There & Away Getting to Korčula is easy since there's a daily bus service from Dubrovnik to Korčula (113 km, US$6). Four times a week there's a Zagreb-Korčula bus (US$24).

Six daily buses link Korčula town to Vela Luka at the west end of the island (48 km, 1½ hours, US$2.50). Buses to Lumbarda run about hourly (seven km, US$1.50). No bus runs to Lumbarda on Sunday and service to Vela Luka is sharply reduced on weekends.

Boat Getting to Korčula is easy since all the Jadrolinija ferries between Split and Dubrovnik tie up at the landing next to the old town. If it's too windy in the east harbour, this ferry moors at the west harbour in front of Hotel Korčula. If you didn't plan a stop, one glimpse of Korčula from the ferry will make you regret it. Car-ferry tickets may be bought at the Jadrolinija office (☎ 715 410) or the Turist Biro (same prices). Departures from Korčula are usually around noon in both directions.

Between Orebić and Korčula, instead of the barge-type car ferry which lands at Bon Repos a couple of km from town, look for the passenger launch (four times a day year-round, 15 minutes, US$1 one way) which will drop you off at the Hotel Korčula right below the old town's towers. This is best if you're looking for a private room, but if you want to camp or stay at the hotel be sure to take the auto barge to Bon Repos in Dominče.

Lumbarda
Just 15 minutes from Korčula town by bus, Lumbarda is a picturesque small settlement near the south-east end of Korčula Island. A good ocean beach (Plaza Pržina) is on the other side of the vineyards beyond the supermarket. 'Grk' is the name given by the Greek settlers to the dry white wine originating in the vineyards around Lumbarda.

Staff at the *Hotel Lumbarda* (☎ 712 602) reception arrange private rooms and there are a couple of camping grounds just up the road beside the hotel.

Vela Luka
Vela Luka, at the west end of Korčula, is the centre of the island's fishing industry because of its large sheltered harbour. Tiny, wooded

Ošjak Island in the bay just off Vela Luka is a national park. There isn't a lot to see at Vela Luka and no real beaches, so if you're arriving by ferry from Split or Hvar you might jump right on the waiting bus to Korčula town and look for a room there. Vela Luka does have the advantage of being less touristy than Korčula.

Places to Stay Six km north-west of Vela Luka (no bus service) is *Camping Mindel* (☎ 812 494). The Turist Biro (☎ 82 042), open in summer only, arranges private rooms. It is beside the Jadran Hotel on the waterfront 100 metres from the ferry landing.

If the Turist Biro is closed your next best bet is the *Pansion u Domaćinstva Barčot* (☎ 812 014), directly behind the Jadran Hotel. This attractive 24-room guesthouse is open all year and prices are just a little above what you'd pay for private rooms. Some rooms on the 3rd floor have balconies.

Getting There & Away Ferries from Split land at the west end of the harbour, and buses to Korčula town meet all arrivals. There's at least one boat a day from Vela Luka to Split (US$8), calling at Hvar five times a week throughout the year. It leaves Vela Luka very early in the morning, so you might want to spend the night if you'll be catching it, although a bus from Korčula does connect. Once a week from June to September Jadro-linija runs a car ferry between Vela Luka and Ancona, Italy (US$44), stopping at Stari Grad and Vis. It leaves Vela Luka at 4 pm Sunday and arrives in Ancona Monday at 8 am.

OREBIĆ
Orebić, on the south coast of the Pelješac Peninsula between Korčula and Ploče, offers better beaches than those found at Korčula, 2.5 km across the water. The easy access by ferry from Korčula makes it the perfect place to go for the day, and a good alternative place to stay. All bus passengers to/from Dubrovnik or Zagreb transit the town.

Things to See & Do
There's a good beach east of the port, two km along a peaceful waterfront road. A trail leads up from Hotel Bellevue to an old **Franciscan monastery** on a ridge high above the sea. The

CROATIA

monastery is worth seeing and the view makes the climb worthwhile.

A more daring climb is to the top of **Mt Ilija** (961 metres), the bare grey massif that hangs above Orebić. The three-hour hike through thick vegetation begins on ulica Kralja Tomislava beside the cathedral near the port and is marked with red-and-white circles or red arrows.

A second, more difficult route up Mt Ilija departs from the Franciscan monastery. The last half-hour is very steep and the final bit is a scramble over the rocks. The trail is safe and well marked, but avoid getting lost near the top as there's no rescue service. Your reward is a sweeping view of the entire coast.

Places to Stay

The helpful Turistički ured Orebić (☎ 713 014), next to the post office near the ferry landings (open April to September), rents private rooms and can provide a town map. If the office is closed just walk around looking for 'sobe' signs – you'll soon find something.

Autokamp Hauptstrand (☎ 713 399) is a pleasant 15-minute walk east along the shore from the port. It overlooks an excellent long beach. There are several other camping grounds near Orebić, but in the off-season check first at the tourist office to make sure they're open.

If you arrive late in the afternoon on the bus from Dubrovnik it's probably better to spend the night in Orebić and take the morning ferry over to Korčula. In fact, Orebić would be well worth a couple of nights if you're a hiker or beach lover.

Getting There & Away

In Orebić the two ferry terminals and the bus station are all adjacent. One bus leaves Orebić for Dubrovnik (113 km, US$6) in the morning and returns in the afternoon. See Korčula for additional bus and ferry information.

MLJET ISLAND

Created in 1960, **Mljet National Park** occupies the western third of the green island of Mljet (Italian: Meleda), between Korčula and Dubrovnik. The park centres around two salt-water lakes surrounded by pine-clad slopes. Most people visit on day trips from Korčula but it's possible to come by regular ferry and spend

a few days. If you do, you'll have Mljet almost to yourself!

Orientation

Tour boats from Korčula arrive at Pomena wharf at Mljet's west end, where a good map of the island is posted.

Things to See & Do

From Pomena it's a 15-minute walk to a jetty on **Veliko jezero**, the larger of the two lakes. Here the groups board a boat to a small lake islet where lunch is served at a 12th-century **Benedictine monastery**, now a hotel.

Those who don't want to spend the rest of the afternoon swimming and sunbathing on the monastery island can catch an early boat back to the main island, and spend a couple of hours walking along the lakeshore before catching the late-afternoon boat back to Korčula. There's a small landing opposite the monastery where the boat operator drops off passengers upon request. It's not possible to walk right around the larger lake as there's no bridge over the channel connecting the lakes to the sea.

Mljet is good for cycling; the hotels rent bicycles.

Organised Tours

Atlas travel agency (☎ 711 060) in Korčula offers a day trip to Mljet Island twice a week from May to mid-October. The tour lasts from 8.30 am to 6 pm, and is US$33 per person including the US$6 park entry fee. The boat trip from Korčula to Pomena takes two hours. Lunch isn't included in the tour price and meals at the hotels on Mljet are very expensive, so it's best to bring a picnic lunch.

Places to Stay

You can either find a private room in Sobra, about 14 km east of Pomena on the north side of Mljet, or take the local bus that meets the ferry and go on to Pomena. Just east of Pomena is *Autokamp Sikjerica*.

Getting There & Away

A regular ferry (daily except Sunday, US$7) leaves from Dubrovnik at 2 pm and goes to Sobra. The big Jadrolinija coastal ferries also stop at Mljet twice a week in summer and once a week the rest of the year.

Dubrovnik

Founded 1300 years ago by refugees from Epidaurus in Greece, medieval Dubrovnik (Ragusa until 1918) was the most important independent city-state on the Adriatic after Venice. Until the Napoleonic invasion of 1806, it remained an independent republic of merchants and sailors.

Like Venice, Dubrovnik's fortunes now depend upon its tourist industry. Stari Grad, the perfectly preserved old town, is unique for its marble-paved squares, steep cobbled streets, tall houses, convents, churches, palaces, fountains and museums, all cut from the same light-coloured stone. The intact city walls keep motorists at bay, and the southerly position between Split and Albania makes for an agreeable climate and lush vegetation.

For those who watched the shelling of Dubrovnik on TV in late 1991, here's a bit of good news: the city is still there, as beautiful as ever, though many of the old stone buildings are now pocked with bullet holes – reminders of the naval bombardments, artillery attacks and incendiary bombing during the eight-month siege by the federal army from October 1991 to May 1992. The cable car up 412-metre Srd Mountain was destroyed. This brutal assault on a city classed a world heritage treasure by UNESCO marked a low point in the conflict.

Fortunately, most of the damage to Dubrovnik has been repaired. UNESCO supervision ensured that the buildings and monuments have been restored with traditional techniques using the same stone quarried from nearby Korčula. Some buildings are still damaged but you don't see it as the shutters will be down and the windows closed. The palaces, churches and museums have reopened, hotels are shedding their refugee guests and everyone wants to know when the tourists are coming back. The total abandonment of the city by tourists has left its residents feeling isolated and apprehensive about their future. Yet for a visitor there is no better time to discover this highlight of Eastern Europe. The streets are refreshingly free of crowds, fine museums can be explored in peace and the magical interplay of light and stone enchant as never before. Don't miss it.

Orientation

The Jadrolinija ferry terminal and the bus station are a few hundred metres apart at Gruž, several km north-west of the old town. The camping ground and most of the luxury tourist hotels are on the Lapad Peninsula, west of the bus station.

Information

The tourist office is on Placa, opposite the Franciscan monastery in the old town. The American Express representative is Atlas travel agency (☎ 442 222), Brsalje 17 outside Pile gate next to the old town. There's another Atlas office across from Fort Revelin at Frana Supila 2.

Post & Communications The main post office is at Ante Starčevića 2, a block up from Pile Gate (Monday to Saturday 7 am to 8 pm, Sunday 8 am to 2 pm). Place international telephone calls here. There's another post office/telephone centre at Lapad near Hotel Kompas.

The telephone code for Dubrovnik is ☎ 020.

Left-Luggage Left-luggage at the bus station is open from 4.30 am to 9 pm. The bus service into town is fairly frequent.

Things to See

You'll probably begin your visit at the city bus stop outside **Pile Gate**. As you enter the city, Placa, Dubrovnik's wonderful pedestrian promenade, extends before you all the way to the clock tower at the other end of town. Just inside Pile Gate is the huge **Onofrio Fountain** (1438) and the **Franciscan monastery**, with the third-oldest functioning pharmacy in Europe by the cloister (operating since 1391).

In front of the clock tower at the east end of Placa, you'll find the **Orlando Column** (1419) – a favourite meeting place. On opposite sides of Orlando are the 16th-century **Sponza Palace** (now the State Archives) and **St Blaise's Church**, a lovely Italian baroque building.

At the end of the broad street beside St Blaise is the baroque **cathedral** and, between the two churches, the Gothic **Rector's Palace** (1441), now a museum with furnished rooms, baroque paintings and historical exhibits. The elected rector was not permitted to leave the

CROATIA

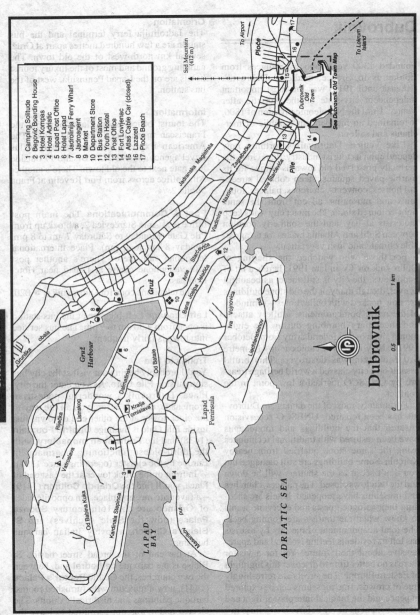

KEY

1 Camping Solitude
2 Begovic Boarding House
3 Hotel Kompas
4 Hotel Adriatic
5 Lapad Post Office
6 Hotel Lapad
7 Jadrolinija Ferry Wharf
8 Jadroagent
9 Market
10 Department Store
11 Bus Station
12 Youth Hostel
13 Post Office
14 Fort Lovrijenac
15 Atlas Cable Car (closed)
16 Lazareti
17 Ploče Beach

CROATIA

Dubrovnik

building during his one-month term without the permission of the senate. The narrow street opposite this palace opens onto Gundulićeva Poljana, a bustling morning market. Up the stairway at the south end of the square is the imposing **Jesuit monastery** (1725).

Return to the cathedral and take the narrow street in front to the **aquarium** in Fort St John. Through an obscure entrance off the city walls, above the aquarium, is the **Maritime Museum**. If you're 'museumed out' you can safely give these two a miss.

By this time you'll be ready for a leisurely walk around the **city walls** themselves. Built between the 13th and 16th centuries and still intact today, these powerful walls are the finest in the world and Dubrovnik's main claim to fame. They enclose the entire city in a curtain of stone over two km long and up to 25 metres high, with two round towers, 14 square towers, two corner fortifications and a large fortress. The views over the town and sea are great, so make this walk the high point of your visit.

Whichever way you go, you'll notice the large **Dominican monastery** in the north-east corner of the city. Of all Dubrovnik's religious museums, the one in the Dominican Monastery is the largest and most worth paying to enter.

Dubrovnik has many other sights, such as the unmarked **synagogue** at ulica Žudioska 5 near the clock tower (open 10 am to noon on Friday, 5 to 7 pm on Tuesday). The uppermost streets of the old town below the north and south walls are pleasant to wander along.

Beaches The closest beach to the old city is just beyond the 17th-century **Lazareti** (former quarantine station) outside Ploče Gate. There are also 'managed' hotel beaches on the **Lapad Peninsula**, but you could be charged admission unless they think you're a guest.

A far better option is to take the ferry which shuttles six times a day from the small-boat harbour (May to October, US$2 return) to **Lokrum Island**, a national park with a rocky nudist (FKK) beach, a botanical garden and the ruins of a medieval Benedictine monastery.

A day trip can be made from Dubrovnik to the resort town of **Cavtat** just south-east. Bus No 10 runs often to Cavtat from Dubrovnik's bus station. Like Dubrovnik, Cavtat was founded by Greeks from Epidaurus and there

are several churches, museums and historic monuments as well as beaches. Don't miss the memorial chapel to the Račič family by Ivan Meštrović.

Special Events
The Dubrovnik Summer Festival from mid-July to mid-August is a major cultural event with over 100 performances at different venues in the old city.

The Feast of St Blaise (3 February) and carnival (February) are also celebrated.

Places to Stay
Camping Open from May to mid-October, *Camping Solitude* (☎ 448 166) is on the Lapad Peninsula (walk or catch bus No 6).

Hostels The *YHA hostel*, up Vinka Sagrestana from Bana Josipa Jelačića 17, is newly opened and refurbished. A bed in a room for four with breakfast is US$8. Lunch and dinner can also be arranged.

Private Rooms The easiest way to find a place to stay is to accept the offer of a sobe from one of the women who might approach you at the ferry terminal. Their prices are lower than those charged by the room-finding agencies and they are open to bargaining (from around US$10 per person). With tourism down, landladies no longer bothered waiting at the bus station for the few arriving passengers. This will undoubtedly change.

Dalmacijaturist opposite the port at Gruž arranges private rooms for about US$14/20 a single/double. They may levy a 30% surcharge if you stay less than three nights. Also charging these prices are Atlas travel agency and Kompas, at Brsalje 10. The tourist office on Placa opposite the Franciscan monastery is another place to try.

Hotels Dubrovnik's hotels are much more expensive than private rooms. Less expensive hotels such as *Hotel Stadion* (☎ 411 449), right behind the bus station (same building), and *Hotel Gruž*, Pionirska 4, directly above the Jadrolinija ferry landing, are presently occupied by refugees and closed, although this could change.

The bullet-scarred five-storey *Hotel Petka*

CROATIA

CROATIA

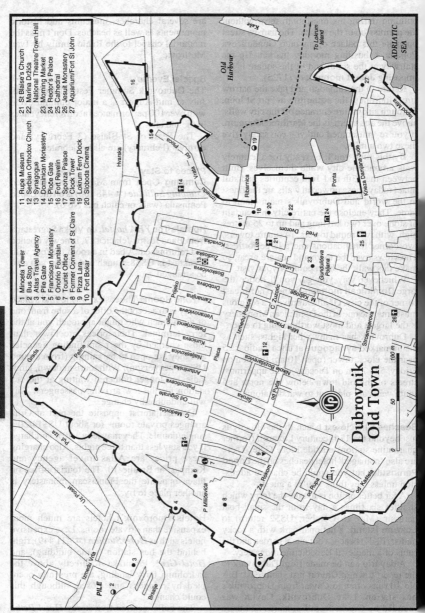

1 Minceta Tower
2 Bus Stop
3 Atlas Travel Agency
4 Pile Gate
5 Franciscan Monastery
6 Onofrio Fountain
7 Tourist Office
8 Former Convent of St Claire
9 Pizzeria Lara
10 Fort Bokar

11 Rupe Museum
12 Serbian Orthodox Church
13 Synagogue
14 Dominican Monastery
15 Ploče Gate
16 Fort Revelin
17 Sponza Palace
18 Clock Tower
19 Lokrum Ferry Dock
20 Sloboda Cinema

21 St Blaise's Church
22 Marina Držića
23 National Theatre/Town Hall
24 Morning Market
25 Rector's Palace
26 Jesuit Monastery
27 Aquarium/Fort St John

Dubrovnik Old Town

(☎ 24 933), Obala Stjepana Radića 38, opposite the Jadrolinija ferry landing, has 104 rooms at US$19/37 a single/double with bath and breakfast. It's reliably open all year round.

A much nicer B-category place is *Hotel Lapad* (☎ 432 922) on Lapadska obala, an old hotel full of character facing the small-boat harbour. Rooms are US$33/53 for a single/double. They have a swimming pool.

The *Begović Boarding House* (☎ 28 563), Primorska 17, a couple of blocks up from Lapad post office (bus No 6), has three rooms with shared bath at US$13 per person and three small apartments for US$33. There's a nice terrace out the back with a good view. Call ahead as they do fill up at peak periods. They'll gladly pick you up at the port or bus station.

Places to Eat

You can get a decent meal at one of the expensive seafood or Italian restaurants along ulica Prijeko, a narrow street parallel to Placa. The restaurants at the west end of the street are slightly cheaper.

Konoba Primorka, Nikole Tesle 8 just west of the department store in Gruž, has a good selection of seafood and national dishes at medium prices. In summer you dine below the trees on a lamp-lit terrace.

A slice of pizza or some burek costs only US$2 at *Pizza Lara* south of Placa, but the cheapest way to fill up in Dubrovnik is to buy the makings of a picnic at a local supermarket, such as the one in the department store near the bus station.

Entertainment

Sun City Disco, Dubrovnik's most popular disco, is next to the bus station. The modern *Sloboda Cinema* is at the foot of the clock tower.

Ask at the tourist office about concerts and folk dancing.

Getting There & Away

Air Daily flights to/from Zagreb are operated by Croatia Airlines. The fare is about US$100 one way.

Bus Daily buses from Dubrovnik include one to Pula (749 km), three to Rijeka (639 km),

nine to Zadar (393 km), 11 to Split (235 km), five to Zagreb (713 km) and one to Orebić (113 km, US$6) and Korčula. With the resumption of service to Mostar (143 km, twice daily) and Sarajevo (278 km, three times a week) travellers from Dubrovnik no longer need to backtrack. In a busy summer season and on weekends, buses out of Dubrovnik can be crowded, so book a ticket well before the scheduled departure time.

Boat The Jadrolinija coastal ferry north to Hvar (US$12), Split (US$15), Zadar (US$23) and Rijeka (US$28) is far more comfortable than the bus, if somewhat more expensive. Still, it's well worth the extra money. The ferry leaves around 10 am several times a week all year round. A local ferry leaves Dubrovnik for Sobra on Mljet Island (2½ hours, US$7) at 2 pm daily except Sunday throughout the year.

Information on domestic ferries is available from Jadrolinija (☎ 23 068), at Obala S Radića 40.

From June to September there's a Jadrolinija car ferry from Dubrovnik to Bari, Italy (nine hours, US$44 one way) twice a week but only once a week the rest of the year. Tickets for international ferries are sold by Jadroagent, Obala S Radića 32 at the port.

Getting Around

To/From the Airport Čilipi international airport is 24 km south-east of Dubrovnik. Adria Airways and Croatia Airlines airport buses (US$3) leave from in front of Atlas travel agency, Brsalje 17, just outside Pile Gate, 1½ hours before flight times.

Bus Pay your fare in exact change on city buses as you board – have small coins ready.

Car Gulliver Rent-a-Car (☎ 411 088), Obala Stjepana Radića 31, rents cars for US$15 a day plus US$0.20 a km or US$60 with unlimited km. Hertz (☎ 23 779), at Hotel Kompas in Lapad, is more expensive and, unlike Gulliver, you must be at least 21 years old. The biggest advantage of Hertz is that you can drop the car off at any Hertz office around Croatia and Slovenia.

CROATIA

Cyprus

Cyprus, the Mediterranean's third-largest island, is the legendary birthplace of Aphrodite. Close to Greece, Turkey, Jordan, Israel and Egypt, it is a useful stepping stone for those travelling between East and West.

Cyprus presents an infinite variety of natural and architectural delights. Two high mountain ranges tower above a fertile plain. Landscapes are dotted with ancient Greek and Roman ruins, Orthodox monasteries and crusader castles.

The lifestyle on the island is easy-going, the crime rate is low and the sun shines a lot. All of this makes Cyprus sound like a paradise, and perhaps it would be, were it not for the Turkish invasion of 1974 and subsequent partition of the island. Despite this, its people are friendly, relaxed and hospitable.

Facts about the Country

HISTORY

Cyprus' position in the eastern Mediterranean has meant that since ancient times it has been an important trading post, hence its history has been fraught with battles and conquests.

Cyprus has been inhabited since the Neolithic period and colonised by the Mycenaeans, Phoenicians, Egyptians, Assyrians and Persians. The latter were defeated by Alexander the Great. In 295 BC, Ptolemy I, king of Egypt, won control. The Ptolemy dynasty ruled until Cyprus was annexed to Rome in 58 BC.

As part of the Roman Empire, Cyprus enjoyed relative peace and prosperity, but by the mid-7th century AD it was torn between two warring empires, the Byzantine and the Islamic, and over the next three centuries it changed hands at least 11 times.

In 1191 Richard the Lionheart (king of England from 1189 to 1199) conquered the island during the Third Crusade, but when the Cypriots rebelled he sold the island to the Knights Templar, a military religious order. They then sold it to Guy de Lusignan, the deposed king of Jerusalem. The Lusignan dynasty ruled from 1192 to 1489. This was a period of prosperity but also oppression of Cypriot culture and Orthodoxy.

By the late 14th century the dynasty was in decline and in 1489 the Venetians moved in. They strengthened the island's fortifications, but in 1570 the Turks attacked, killing some 2000 people, and 300 years of Ottoman rule began.

In 1878 the Turks ceded administration of Cyprus to Britain. They did this out of fear of Russia's expansionist policy, as Britain had promised to help Turkey in the event of a Russian attack.

In 1925 Cyprus became a Crown colony of the UK. By now Cypriots were deeply frustrated by their lack of self-determination, and the first stirrings of *enosis* (union with Greece) were felt. This led to intercommunal riots between Greeks and Turks. The Turkish population (18%) opposed enosis, believing it would lead to greater oppression than they felt they were already subjected to. By the late

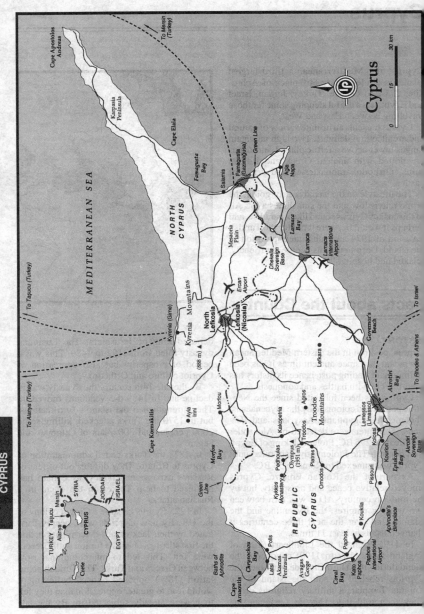

CYPRUS

1940s the Cypriot Orthodox Church had come
out openly in support of enosis, and in 1951 a
plebiscite showed that 96% of Greek Cypriots
were also in its favour.

During the next couple of years little
changed. In 1954 Britain prepared a new con-
titution for Cyprus which was accepted by the
Turkish population but opposed by extremists
in the National Organisation of Cypriot
Freedom Fighters (EOKA). They wanted
enosis and began guerilla activities against the
British administration, resulting in much suf-
ering and many deaths.

In August 1960 the UK granted independence to Cyprus with Archbishop Makarios as
president and a Turk, Fasal Kükük, as vice
president.

In December 1963 Makarios proposed some
amendments which would have given the
Greeks greater control of the government. The
Turkish government rejected these and threat-
ned military intervention but refrained due to
international pressure. Intercommunal vio-
ence increased significantly and in 1964 the
United Nations sent in a peacekeeping force.

In 1967 a military junta seized power in
Greece and the demands for enosis ceased –
obody wanted union with such a repressive
egime. However, on 15 July 1974 Greece
mounted a coup d'état and overthrew Maka-
ios. When he escaped an assasination attempt
and fled the country, Greece put ex-guerilla
eader Nicos Samson in power. The Turks
eacted by invading the island, and the Greek
unta realised they'd made a huge mistake.
Greece removed Samson and their offensive
ollapsed. The Turkish troops continued to
dvance until they occupied the northern third
f the island, forcing some 180,000 Greek
Cypriots to flee their homes for the safety of
outhern Cyprus. Neither the UK nor the USA
ntervened.

Cyprus has remained a divided island.
Unsuccessful peace talks, mostly under the
uspices of the UN, have been held sporadi-
ally and there was real hope that a solution
might have been found during the 12-month
eriod from March 1993 but, again, the initia-
ve came to nothing. More recently Richard
Holbrooke, the US diplomat who did much to
nd the war in Bosnia, said that he plans to
make 1996 'the year of the big push' in Cyprus.
However, in August 1996 Greek-Cypriots

clashed with Turks in the worst violence since
the Turkish invasion in 1974, making any
chance of a settlement unlikely.

GEOGRAPHY & ECOLOGY

The land area of Cyprus is 9251 sq km. There
are two mountain ranges: the Kyrenia Mountains in North Cyprus and the Troodos Massif
in the centre of the Republic. Between them is
the Mesaoria Plain.

Much of southern Cyprus' coastline has
been spoilt by tourism, so most of the island's
impressive range of flora and fauna (especially
birds) is found in the well-managed areas of
the Troodos Mountains and the Akamas Peninsula, near Polis. Being far less touristed, a
diverse range of wildlife is found all over North
Cyprus, particularly on the relatively unex-
plored Karpasia Peninsula.

GOVERNMENT & POLITICS

In 1960 Cyprus was declared an independent
sovereign republic with a presidential system
of government. In November 1983, however,
Rauf Denktash declared the northern part of
Cyprus an independent republic (Turkish
Republic of Northern Cyprus) with himself as
president. Only Turkey recognises this self-
styled nation.

Southern Cyprus is governed by a coalition
between the right-wing Democratic Rally
Party (DYSY) and the centre-right Democratic
Party with DYSY's Glafkos Clerides as president.

Northern Cyprus is governed by a coalition
of the Democrat Party and the Republican
Turkish Party under the presidential leadership
of Rauf Denktash.

ECONOMY

Partition had a devastating effect on Cyprus'
economy. The Republic (southern Cyprus),
which has its own currency, has made a steady
recovery and tourism is now its biggest source
of income. In North Cyprus the Turkish lira is
used, tying the area's economy to Turkey's
high inflation; agriculture and a developing
tourist industry provide most of the income.

POPULATION & PEOPLE

Since partition the vast majority of Greek Cypriots live in the Republic, while Turkish
Cypriots and Turkish colonists live in the

north. Cyprus' total population is 885,800, with 163,000 living in the north.

ARTS
Artistic reminders of Cyprus' history include ancient Greek temples, Roman mosaics and 15th-century church frescos. Building on a rich and varied tradition, the visual arts are very much alive today. Many villages specialise in one art form or another, whether it be pottery, silver and copperware, basket-weaving, tapestry work, or the famous Cyprus lace from Lefkara.

CULTURE
Cypriots are very proud of their cultural heritage which stretches back more than 9000 years. However, life in Cyprus today is influenced more by recent historical events than ancient ones.

Since the island's split, the Turks have succeeded in imbuing North Cyprus with an all-pervasive Turkishness. They have even changed the Greek place names to Turkish ones and embraced the life and culture of Turkey.

There is a feeling that the Republic is striving to find its own cultural identity. A recent example of this is the Republic's decision to rename some of the island's place names, making them more Cypriot than English.

RELIGION
Most Greek Cypriots belong to the Greek Orthodox Church and most Turkish Cypriots are Sunni Muslims.

LANGUAGE
Most Cypriots in the Republic speak English and many road signs are in Greek and English. In North Cyprus this is not the case outside the touristy areas and you'll have to brush up on your Turkish. In both areas, the spelling of place and street names varies enormously.

Since the middle of 1995 the Republic has converted all place names into Latin characters according to the official system of transliteration of the Greek alphabet. As a result, Nicosia has become Lefkosia, Limassol is now Lemessos, Famagusta is Ammochostos, and Kyrenia is now Keryneia. Throughout this chapter the new names for places in southern Cyprus are used because the old ones are being phased out on all tourist maps and road signs. The new Greek names for Famagusta and Kyrenia in North Cyprus have not been used.

See the Turkish and Greek language guides at the back of the book for pronunciation guidelines and useful words and phrases.

Facts for the Visitor

PLANNING
Climate & When to Go
Cyprus has a typically Mediterranean climate. April/May and September/October are the most pleasant times to visit.

Books & Maps
Bitter Lemons by Lawrence Durrell and *Journey into Cyprus* by Colin Thubron are both worth reading. The free CTO maps are adequate for most purposes.

Online Services
There is a very nice Internet site about North Cyprus at http://www.brad.ac.uk/yysentur/ncyprus/doc2.html, and information on the Republic can be found at http://www.wam.umd.edu/cyprus/tourist.html and http://www.webm.com/homepage.html.

SUGGESTED ITINERARIES
Republic of Cyprus
Depending on the length of your stay, you might want to see and do the following things:

One week
  Allow two days for Lefkosia, two days for Paphos and the rest for exploring the Troodos Massif.
Two weeks
  As above but make a day trip into North Cyprus, add Polis and the Akamas Peninsula (beaches and walks) and spend one day in Larnaca.

North Cyprus
One week
  Allow one day for North Lefkosia, one day for Famagusta, half a day for Salamis, and spend the rest staying in Kyrenia and visiting the castles in the Kyrenia Mountains.
Two weeks
  As above but have a Turkish bath in North Lefkosia and spend some time exploring the near-deserted Karpasia Peninsula and its archaeological sites.

HIGHLIGHTS

Republic of Cyprus

Nine of the frescoed Byzantine churches in the Troodos Massif are on UNESCO's World Heritage List and they really are special. The Tombs of the Kings, dating back to the 4th century, are a lot more fun than the Paphos Mosaics, and only half as crowded.

North Cyprus

With the castle at one end, Kyrenia's waterfront must be one of the most beautiful and least spoilt in the Mediterranean. Some people are a bit disappointed by the archaeological site at Salamis but the number of well-preserved upright columns in the gymnasium is incredible.

TOURIST OFFICES

The Cyprus Tourism Organisation (CTO) has offices in major towns in the Republic, as well as in most European countries, the USA and Japan. Their leaflets and maps are excellent.

In North Cyprus there are tourist offices in North Lefkosia, Famagusta and Kyrenia which have a few free country and town maps but not many good brochures. There are also tourist offices in the UK and Turkey, otherwise enquiries are handled by Turkish tourist offices.

VISAS & EMBASSIES

In both the Republic and North Cyprus, nationals of the USA, Australia, Canada, Japan, New Zealand, Singapore and EU countries can stay for up to three months without a visa.

If you have a North Cyprus stamp in your passport you can still visit the Republic, but it will be deleted by customs on entry. A North Cyprus stamp will not prevent you from visiting Greece either. Despite this, it is advisable to get immigration to stamp a piece of paper rather than your passport when entering North Cyprus.

Cypriot Diplomatic Missions Abroad

The Republic of Cyprus has diplomatic representation in the following countries:

Australia
   30 Beale Crescent, Deakon, ACT 2600 (☎ 06-281 0832)
Canada
   all enquiries should be addressed to the US office
Germany
   Kronprinzenstrasse 58, D-53173 Bonn (☎ 228-363 336)

UK
   93 Park St, London W1Y 4ET (☎ 0171-499 8272)
USA
   2211 R St North West, Washington, DC, 20008 (☎ 202-462 5772)

The Turkish Republic of Northern Cyprus has offices in:

Canada
   328 Highway 7 East, Suite 308, Richmond Hill, Ontario (☎ 416-771 8556)
Germany
   Auf Dem Platz 3, 53577 Neustadt Wied-Neschen (☎ 02683-32748)
Japan
   4, F1 6th Arai Blog 1-5-4, Kabuki-Chad, Shinjuku-ku, Tokyo 160 (☎ 03-3205 1313)
UK
   28 Cockspur St, London SW1Y 5BN (☎ 0171-839 4577)
USA
   821 United Nations Plaza, 6th floor, New York, NY 10017 (☎ 212-687 2350)

Diplomatic Missions in Cyprus

Countries with diplomatic representation in the Republic of Cyprus include:

Australia
   Gonia Leoforos Stassinou & Annis Komninis St, 2nd Floor, Lefkosia (☎ 02-473001)
Canada
   Office 403, 15 Themistokli Dervi St, Lefkosia (☎ 02-451630)
Germany
   10 Nikitara St, Lefkosia (☎ 02-444362)
UK
   Alexandrou Palli St, Lefkosia (☎ 02-473131)
USA
   Gonia Metochiou & Ploutarchou Sts, Egkomi, Lefkosia (☎ 02-476100)

Countries with diplomatic representation in North Cyprus include:

UK
   23 Mehmet Akif Sokak, North Lefkosia (☎ 228 3861)
USA
   20 Güner Türkmen Caddesi, North Lefkosia (☎ 227 2443)

CUSTOMS

Items which can be imported duty-free into Cyprus are 250 grams of tobacco or the equivalent in cigarettes, 0.75 litres of wine, one litre of spirits, and 300 ml of perfume.

MONEY
Currency
The unit of currency in the Republic is the Cyprus pound (CY£), which is divided into 100 cents. There is no limit on the amount of Cyprus pounds you can bring into the country, but foreign currency equivalent to US$1000 has to be declared. You can leave Cyprus with either CY£100 or the amount with which you entered. The unit of currency in North Cyprus is the Turkish lira (TL) and there are no official restrictions.

Banks throughout Cyprus will exchange all major currencies in either cash or travellers' cheques. Most shops, hotels etc in North Cyprus accept CY£ and other hard currencies.

In the Republic you can get a cash advance on a Visa card at most banks. In North Cyprus cash advances are given on Visa cards at the Yapi Vekredi banks in North Lefkosia, Kyrenia and Famagusta. You can no longer get any cash with an American Express card in either part of the island.

Exchange Rates
Exchange rates for the Cyprus pound are as follows:

Australia	A$1	=	CY£0.36
France	1FF	=	CY£0.09
Germany	1DM	=	CY£0.31
Japan	¥100	=	CY£0.43
New Zealand	NZ$1	=	CY£0.32
United Kingdom	UK£1	=	CY£0.72
United States	US$1	=	CY£0.46

Exchange rates for the Turkish lira are not worth giving as high inflation will make them quickly out of date. As a result, all prices quoted in the North Cyprus section are in UK pounds.

Costs
Cyprus is a cheaper place to visit than most European countries and in North Cyprus costs are slightly lower. Living frugally, you could just get by on CY£10 a day and you could live quite adequately on CY£26.

POST & COMMUNICATIONS
In the Republic, postal rates for cards and letters are between 21 and 41 cents. There are poste-restante services in Lefkosia, Larnaca, Paphos and Lemessos.

In North Cyprus, postal rates are between UK£0.05 and UK£0.08. There are poste-restante services in North Lefkosia, Kyrenia and Famagusta. All mail must be addressed to Mersin 10, Turkey, *not* North Cyprus.

You can make direct overseas calls from any phone boxes either with coins or telephone cards. The Republic's international country code is ☎ 357. You can send a telegram from the Republic's telephone company (CYTA) but faxes are handled by the post office.

To call North Cyprus from abroad you need to dial ☎ 90 (Turkey), then the country code ☎ 392, and then the area code and the number. Area codes also have to be used when calling locally (codes have been incorporated into all phone numbers in the North Cyprus section).

To make a call from a phone box you need either a telephone card or tokens (*jetonlar*) obtained from any Turkish Telecom administration office or from street stalls. You can make overseas calls from all public and private phones, and sending a fax is easy from the Turkish Telecom administration office in North Lefkosia.

NEWSPAPERS & MAGAZINES
The Republic's English-language papers are the *Cyprus Mail* and the *Cyprus Weekly*. The North Cyprus English-language newspapers are the *Turkish Daily News* and *Cyprus Today*.

RADIO & TV
CyBC (Cyprus Broadcasting Corporation) has programmes and news bulletins in English on Radio 2, and BFBS (British Forces Broadcasting Services) has two channels broadcasting in English. The BBC World Service is also easy to pick up.

On CyBC TV there is news in English at pm on Channel 2. Satellite dishes are very common, so in many hotels you can also watch CNN, BBC, SKY or NBC.

TIME
Cyprus is two hours ahead of GMT/UTC. Clocks go forward one hour on the last weekend in March and back one hour on the last weekend in September.

ELECTRICITY

The electric current is 240V, 50 Hz. Plugs are large with three square pins as in the UK.

WEIGHTS & MEASURES

Cyprus uses the metric system.

LAUNDRY

There are laundrettes and dry-cleaners in all main towns, and most hotels have a laundry service.

TOILETS

In the Republic there are public toilets in the main towns and at tourist sites; they are invariably clean and Western-style. In North Cyprus there are fewer public facilities and often toilets, even in restaurants, can be dirty and of the squat variety.

HEALTH

Tap water is safe to drink everywhere. The greatest health risk comes from the sun, so take care against sunstroke, heat exhaustion and dehydration.

Foreigners do not receive free health care in the Republic but they do in North Cyprus.

WOMEN TRAVELLERS

Women travellers will encounter little sexual harassment, although it is worth steering clear of any red-light areas and some of the cheaper hotels because they may be brothels.

GAY & LESBIAN TRAVELLERS

Due to pressure from the Gay Liberation Movement (PO Box 1947, Lefkosia; ☎ 02-43346) and the EU, homosexual conduct between consenting adults in private is no longer illegal in the Republic.

In North Cyprus homosexuality is still legal.

DISABLED TRAVELLERS

Any CTO can send you a fact sheet called *What the Disabled Visitor Needs to Know about Cyprus* which lists some useful organisations. At the Republic's airports there are truck-lifts for arriving or departing disabled travellers. Some of the hotels have facilities for the disabled, but at sites or museums little help is given. In North Cyprus there are few facilities for the disabled visitor.

SENIOR TRAVELLERS

Older visitors will find travelling around both the Republic and North Cyprus fairly easy. In general, no concessions exist for tourists; the exception is the Cyprus Folk Art Museum in Lefkosia where there is a lower admission fee for those over 60.

DANGERS & ANNOYANCES

For locals and tourists alike, Cyprus is a safe place to travel and there is very little street crime or vandalism.

BUSINESS HOURS

In the Republic, banks are open Monday to Friday from 8.15 am to 12.30 pm and some large banks offer a tourist service in the afternoon. In North Cyprus they are open from 8 am to noon.

In summer, shops are open Monday to Saturday from 8 am to 1 pm and 4 to 7 pm, closing at 1 pm on Wednesday and Saturday. In winter the afternoon hours are from 2.30 to 5.30 pm.

PUBLIC HOLIDAYS & SPECIAL EVENTS

Holidays in the Republic are the same as in Greece, with the addition of Greek Cypriot Day (1 April) and Cyprus Independence Day (1 October). Easter is the most important religious festival and just about everything stops. Fifty days before this is carnival time. A useful publication is the *Diary of Events* which you can get from any CTO.

North Cyprus observes Muslim holidays, including Ramadan, but this is not very strictly adhered to. In addition they have Turkish Cypriot Resistance Day (1 August) and the Proclamation of the Turkish Republic of Northern Cyprus (15 November).

WORK

In the Republic, work permits can only be obtained through a prospective employer applying on your behalf. The best place to look for jobs is in the *Cyprus Weekly*. During the tourist season you can sometimes pick up bar or café work in return for accommodation and food but rarely do you get paid (if you don't have a permit).

ACCOMMODATION

There are six licensed camping grounds in the Republic. They are all equipped with hot showers, a minimarket and a snack bar, and they charge around CY£1.50 a day for a tent space and CY£1 per person per day. In the North there are two camping grounds.

There are six HI hostels in the Republic; these are slightly cheaper if you are a member. The Cyprus Youth Hostel Association (☎ 442027) is at PO Box 1328, Lefkosia. There are no HI hostels in North Cyprus.

Hotels in the Republic are classified from one to five stars and prices for a double room range from CY£20 to CY£100. Guesthouses cost anything from CY£8 to CY£20. Accommodation costs are negotiable in winter. In North Cyprus these prices are slightly lower.

In southern Cyprus you can sometimes stay overnight at the monasteries for free, but a donation is expected.

FOOD & DRINKS

Cypriot food is a combination of Greek and Turkish cuisine, much of it meat, salad and fruit-based. The barbecue is a very popular way of cooking meat and fish, and a *meze* is a traditional meal consisting of around 20 different small dishes.

Cypriot wine, made in the villages of the Troodos, is excellent and Greek/Turkish coffee and Nescafé are widely available.

ENTERTAINMENT

Restaurants sometimes have live music and there are cinemas and discos in most major towns and tourist areas.

THINGS TO BUY

Good buys include wines and spirits made in Cyprus, most leather items and the crafts mentioned in the Arts section of this chapter. The government-run Cyprus Handicraft Service sells high-quality goods; the shops are marked on the CTO's free town maps.

Getting There & Away

AIR

The Republic's airports are at Larnaca and Paphos. There are scheduled and charter flights from most European cities and the Middle East (around UK£240 return from London), with discounts for students, but they are heavily booked in the high season. From Cyprus there are daily flights to Greece (CY£95) and the UK (CY£176), and frequent services to Israel (CY£130), Egypt (CY£105) and Jordan (CY£87), again with student discounts.

Ercan airport in North Cyprus is not recognised by international airline authorities so you can't get there direct. Turkish airlines touch down in Turkey and then continue on to North Cyprus (around UK£260 from London) and other airlines can fly you to Turkey, where you'll have to change planes.

SEA

The Republic's passenger ferry port is in Lemessos. In summer there are regular boats to Greece (CY£44), Rhodes (CY£41), and Israel (CY£37). To get to the Greek islands from Lemessos you need to change in Athens and the only boats now going to Egypt are cruise ships which don't take one-way passengers. The prices quoted are deck-only and student discounts are available. Any travel agent in Lemessos can sell you tickets.

From North Cyprus there are three routes to mainland Turkey. They are Famagusta to Mersin (UK£17.50), Kyrenia to Taşucu (UK£14) and, during peak season, to Alanya.

LEAVING CYPRUS

The departure tax of CY£11 when leaving by sea, and CY£7 when leaving by air, is usually added on to your ticket.

Getting Around

You can usually make a day trip into North Cyprus from the Republic (see Lefkosia Getting There & Away section). It is impossible to travel in the opposite direction.

BUS

Urban and long-distance buses run Monday to Saturday and are operated by a host of private companies. There are no services on Sunday. Buses between major towns are frequent and efficient, charging around CY£1.50 for most journeys.

SERVICE TAXI

Service taxis, which take up to eight people, are owned by a number of private firms and you'll usually find at least one of them operating on a Sunday. You can get to most places in the Republic by service taxi but often not direct. The fares are fixed but still competitive with bus travel. Either go to the taxi office or telephone them and the driver will pick you up at your hotel. In North Cyprus there are only service taxis between Kyrenia and North Lefkosia. There are also normal (more expensive) taxis everywhere.

CAR & MOTORCYCLE

Cars and 4WD vehicles are widely available for hire and cost between CY£18 and CY£50 a day. You can also rent motorbikes (CY£9) or mopeds (CY£5) in some towns. Driving is on the left and international road signs are used. Car parking is cheap. Super and low-lead petrol cost 37 cents a litre, regular costs 35 cents and diesel just 11 cents.

The Cyprus Automobile Association (☎ 313233) is at 12 Chr. Mylona St, Lefkosia.

BICYCLE

Bicycles can be hired in most areas but particularly in the Troodos where mountain biking is very popular. Rates start from around CY£3 a day.

HITCHING

Hitching is easy and the locals are very hospitable.

The Republic of Cyprus

In the Republic, which comprises 63% of the island, you'll find a real mix of Greek, Eastern and Western cultures. The UK's legacy lives on in the island's two sovereign military bases at Akrotiri, near Lemessos, and Dhekelia, near Larnaca.

LEFKOSIA

Lefkosia (formerly Nicosia), the capital, is cut in two by the Green Line which divides the Republic from North Cyprus. As a sign at one of the UN-patrolled barriers states, it is 'the last divided Capital', and a visit is essential to appreciate the island's plight. Being inland, it attracts far less visitors and so the life you see here is much more genuine than in the touristy coastal towns.

Orientation

The old town is inside the 16th-century Venetian wall and is the most interesting area for visitors; the new town sprawls without. The wall is so reduced in height and dissected by wide thoroughfares that sometimes it is hardly visible. The city centre is Plateia Eleftherias on the south-western edge of the wall. The Green Line runs through the old city. The UN crossover point (Ledra Palace Hotel checkpoint) is at the far west and Famagusta Gate is to the east. At the base of the wall there are car parks and the municipal gardens.

Information

Tourist Office The CTO (☎ 444264) is in Laiki Yitonia (see map inset), a fairly touristy, restored area of the old town. It is open Monday to Friday from 8.30 am to 4 pm and on Saturday from 8.30 am to 2 pm.

Money The Popular Bank on Plateia Eleftherias opens from 3.15 to 4.45 pm in addition to normal banking hours. American Express is represented by AL Mantovani & Sons Ltd (☎ 443777) in the new town at 2D Agapinoros, off Leoforos Archiepiskopou Makariou III.

Post & Communications The main post office is on Leoforos Konstantinou Palaiologou. Opening hours are Monday to Friday from 7.30 am to 1.30 pm and 3 to 6 pm (closed Wednesday afternoon). On Saturday it is open from 9 to 11 am. The telecommunications office (CYTA) is on Leoforos Aigyptou and opens from 7.30 am to 7 pm daily.

The telephone code for Lefkosia is ☎ 02.

Laundry There is a laundrette at 121z Prodromou St, in the new town. Express Dry-cleaners at 49 Ippokratous St, in the old town, also does service washes.

Emergency The police station (☎ 305000) is on the corner of Leoforos Archiepiskopou Makariou III and Leoforos Santaroza. The

CYPRUS

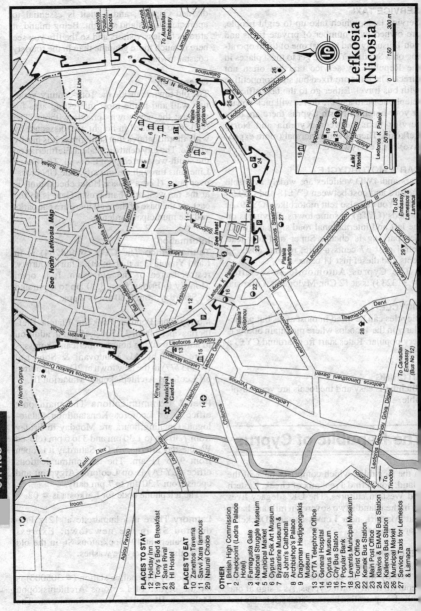

Lefkosia (Nicosia)

See North Lefkosia Map

See Inset

Green Line

To North Cyprus

To Troodos

To US Embassy, Lemesos & Larnaca

To Canadian Embassy (Bus No 12)

Municipal Gardens

PLACES TO STAY
12 Holiday Inn
19 Tony's Bed & Breakfast
21 Sans Rival
28 HI Hostel

PLACES TO EAT
10 Zanettos Taverna
11 Savvi Xara Iampous
29 Natural Choice

OTHER
1 British High Commission
2 Checkpoint (Ledra Palace Hotel)
3 Famagusta Gate
4 National Struggle Museum
5 Municipal Market
6 Cyprus Folk Art Museum
7 Byzantine Museum & St John's Cathedral
8 Archbishop's Palace
9 Dragoman Hadjigeorgakis Museum
13 CYTA Telephone Office
14 General Hospital
15 Cyprus Museum
16 City Bus Station
17 Popular Bank
18 Leventis Municipal Museum
20 Tourist Office
22 Kemek Bus Station
23 Main Post Office
24 Klavios & EMAN Bus Station
25 Kallenos Bus Station
26 Municipal Market
27 Service Taxis for Lemesos & Larnaca

mergency number for the police is ☎ 199. Lefkosia's general hospital (☎ 451111) is on Leoforos Nechrou.

Things to See

Walking Tours Every Monday and Thursday at 10 am there are free walking tours of the old city which depart from the CTO; the two routes are in the CTO's *Walking Tours* brochure. Otherwise, the following walk will take you along some of the main streets of the old city and past many of its museums.

From Plateia Eleftherias go along Lidras St and turn right onto Ippokratous St. At No 17 is the **Leventis Municipal Museum**, which traces the city's development from prehistoric times to the present day. It's open Tuesday to Sunday from 10 am to 4.30 pm and is free.

Continue to the end of Ippokratous St, turn left onto Thrakis St and then veer right and left into Trikoupi St. Soon you'll see the Omeriyeh Mosque on your right, after which you turn right onto Patriarchou Grigoriou St. On the right along this street is the 18th-century house of **Dragoman Hadjigeorgakis**, which is now a museum. Opening times are Monday to Friday from 8 am to 2 pm and Saturday from 9 am to 1 pm; entrance is 50 cents.

The next turning left leads to Plateia Archiepiskopou Kyprianou, dominated by the **Archbishop's Palace** and a colossal statue of Makarios III. Here you'll find the **Byzantine Museum**, with a superb collection of icons. It's open Monday to Friday from 9 am to 4.30 pm and on Saturday from 9 am to 1 pm; admission is CY£1. In its grounds is **St John's Cathedral**, which was built in 1662 and has the most wonderful frescos dating from 1736 inside. It's open Monday to Saturday from 9 am to noon and 2 to 4 pm (closed Saturday afternoon); admission is free. Next door is the newly renovated **Cyprus Folk Art Museum**, open Monday to Friday from 9 am to 5 pm and at weekends from 10 am to 1 pm; admission is CY£1. The **National Struggle Museum**, next door, is currently closed and being renovated.

Continue north along Agiou Ioannou St and turn right onto Thiseos St, which leads to Leoforos N Foka. Turn left here and you will see the imposing **Famagusta Gate** ahead. This was once the main entrance to the city and is now a cultural centre. The most direct way

back to Laiki Yitonia is to walk along Leoforos N Foka, following the signposts to the CTO.

Cyprus Museum Near the CYTA office, this museum has an extraordinary collection of 2000 7th-century BC terracotta figurines found at the sanctuary of Ayia Irini, as well as the original Leda & the Swan mosaic found at Aphrodite's sanctuary near Kouklia. It is open Monday to Saturday from 9 am to 5 pm and on Sunday from 10 am to 1 pm; admission is CY£1.50.

Places to Stay

The HI *hostel* (☎ 444808) is in a quiet part of the new town at 5 Hadjidakis St, about six blocks from Plateia Eleftherias. Follow the signs from Tefkrou St, off Themistokli Dervi St. The hostel charges CY£3.50 a night and is very pleasant.

A good B&B is the newly refurbished *Tony's Bed & Breakfast* (☎ 466752) at 13 Solonos St, where rooms either with or without private bathroom cost from CY£11 to CY£16 for singles, CY£17 to CY£22 for doubles and CY£27/32 for triples/quadruples. Tony also has cheaper rooms in a nearby villa for self-catering stays of a week or more. Less clean and sometimes noisy is *Sans Rival* (☎ 474383) at 7c Solonos St, where rooms cost from CY£13 to CY£15 for singles and from CY£12 to CY£14 for doubles.

Most of the more expensive hotels are found in the new town, but inside the city walls at 70 Rigainis St is the *Holiday Inn* (☎ 475131) where standard singles/doubles cost CY£39/53 without breakfast.

Places to Eat

Zanettos Taverna at 65 Trikoupi St is where the locals eat and it's a real winner with huge mezedes for CY£4 and bottles of village wine for CY£2. Also worth checking out is *Savvi Xara Iampous* (name in Greek) at 65 Solonos St.

Not far from the HI hostel at 11 Chytron St is *Natural Choice*, a health-food shop and restaurant. At the moment it is not open in the evening but from Monday to Saturday you can get a delicious lunchtime salad buffet for CY£4.20.

In the old city the *municipal market* is on Diogenous St, and in the new town there's one on the corner of Leoforos Evgenias Kai Antoniou Theodotou and Digeni Akrita St. Both are open Monday to Saturday from 6 am to 1 pm; except Wednesday and Saturday, they are also open from 4 to 6 pm.

Getting There & Away

To North Cyprus Depending on diplomatic relations you are usually allowed into North Cyprus for one day, but check at the CTO first. The border crossing is at the Ledra Palace Hotel and you are allowed through for the day from 8 am to 1 pm, returning at 5 pm. From the Greek side you simply walk to the Turkish checkpoint, pay CY£1 for an entry permit, and that's it. Private cars can be taken over the border but not hired ones.

Air Lefkosia's international airport is in the UN buffer zone and is no longer a passenger airport.

Bus There are lots of private companies operating out of Lefkosia. Kemek, at 3 Omirou St (just round the corner from its former office at 34 Leonidou St), has five buses a day to Lemessos (CY£1.25; fewer on Saturday), one bus to Paphos (CY£2.50) and one to Platres (CY£2). Kallenos operates from the car park north of Leoforos Salaminos and has five or six buses a day to Larnaca (CY£1.10). Klarios goes to Troodos (CY£1.50) and EMAN goes to Agia Napa (CY£2); both operate out of the Constanza car park.

Service Taxi Nearest to Laiki Yitonia are A Makris (☎ 466201) and Kypros (☎ 464811) at 11 and 9 Leoforos Stasinou respectively; both operate taxis to Larnaca (CY£1.95) and Lemessos (CY£2.60).

Getting Around

The city bus station is at Plateia Solomou (west of Eleftherias) and Nicosia Buses operates numerous routes to and from the city and suburbs.

You can hire cars from A Petsas & Sons (☎ 462650), 24 Leoforos Kostaki Pantelidi, in front of the bus station. To hire motorcycles go to Geofil Ltd at 18 Thermopilon St, north-east of the main post office. There are no bicycles for rent in or around the old city.

LARNACA

Larnaca is a coastal resort built over the once important ancient city of Kition. It has a city beach, an old Turkish area and a fort. North of the fort, touristy cafés line the seafront but the other side is less spoilt and much quieter. The CTO (☎ 654322) is on Plateia Vasileos Pavlou two blocks west of the Sun Hall Hotel. It is open Monday to Friday from 8.15 am to 2.30 pm and on Monday and Thursday from 3 to 6.15 pm. On Saturday it is open from 8.15 am to 1.30 pm. There is also a CTO at the airport.

Larnaca's telephone code is ☎ 04.

Things to See

The site of ancient **Kition** is about 1.5 km outside Larnaca. It dates back to the 13th century BC but was completely rebuilt by the Phoenicians in the 9th century BC. The Cyclopean city walls are impressive, otherwise it is not that thrilling. En route is the **District Archaeological Museum** where artefacts found at Kition are on display. Both Kition and the museum are open Monday to Friday from 7.30 am to 2.30 pm and entry is 75 cents at both; they are signposted from the centre of town.

On Agiou Lazarou, the ornately decorated Byzantine church of **St Lazaros** and its museum are worth a visit, as is the city **fort**.

Places to Stay & Eat

The nearest camping ground is *Forest Beach Camping* (☎ 644514), eight km along the beach road towards Agia Napa, but it's a bit run-down; to get there take the tourist bus from the north side of the Sun Hall Hotel.

The HI *hostel* (☎ 621188), 27 N Rossou St, is just east of St Lazaros church and charges CY£3.50 a night. Also near St Lazaros church is the one-star *Hotel Pavion* (☎ 656688) where B&B is CY£11/16/22/28 for singles/doubles/triples/quadruples. The rooms have private bathrooms and the staff are very friendly.

At the other end of town, near the CTO on Stasinou St, is *1900 Art Café*. It is an art gallery, a bookshop and also a restaurant with an ever-changing menu of home-cooked Cypriot dishes for CY£3.50. Also good is *Militzis Restaurant* on the waterfront south of the fort.

The *municipal market* is at the northern end of N Rossou St.

Getting There & Away

Bus The bus stop for Lefkosia (CY£1.10), Lemessos (CY£1.20) and Agia Napa (CY£1) is opposite the Yin Yang Chinese Restaurant on the waterfront. On Sunday there is only a service to Agia Napa.

Service Taxi Acropolis (☎ 655555), opposite the police station on Leoforos Archiepiskopou Makariou III, and A Makris (☎ 652929), on the north side of the Sun Hall Hotel, operate service taxis to Lefkosia (CY£1.95) and Lemessos (CY£2.25).

Getting Around

To/From the Airport Bus No 19 from St Lazaros church goes near the airport, which is six km away. The first bus is at 6.20 am and the last at 7 pm in summer or 5.45 pm in winter. A private taxi costs CY£3; there are no service taxis on this route.

Bus A Makris runs buses every 20 minutes from the north side of the Sun Hall Hotel to the tourist hotel area, eight km along the coast towards Agia Napa (CY£1.60 return).

Car & Motorcycle Thames (☎ 656333), next door to A Makris, rents cars and there are also car-rental booths at the airport. You can hire motorcycles or mopeds from Theodoros (☎ 655186) at 41 Leoforos Archiepiskopou Makariou III.

Bicycle Bicycles can be hired at Anemayia. To get there, turn west along Leoforos Grigori Afxentiou from the police station and it is 100 metres on the left past the second traffic lights.

AGIA NAPA

On the coast 35 km east of Larnaca is Agia Napa, Cyprus' main package-tourist resort. It is expensive, crowded and ugly. If you do go there, however, the HI *hostel* (☎ 723433) is at 23 Dionysios Solomos St, near the main square. See Larnaca's Getting There & Away section for transport details.

The telephone code for Agia Napa is ☎ 03.

LEMESSOS

Lemessos (formerly Limassol) is Cyprus' second-largest city and the main passenger and cargo port. Bland hotels and public gardens line the waterfront; behind these and to the west is the more attractive old town with crumbling houses, a mosque, old-fashioned artisans' shops and a castle. Behind the old section sprawls the new town. The CTO (☎ 362756) is at 15 Spyros Araouzou St on the waterfront near the old harbour. It's open Monday to Friday from 8.15 am to 2.30 pm, on Monday and Thursday from 3 to 6.15 pm, and on Saturday from 8.15 am to 1.30 pm.

The telephone code for Lemessos is ☎ 05.

Things to See

The main attraction is the **castle** where Richard the Lionheart married Berengaria of Navarre in 1191. Occupied and refashioned by Lusignans, crusaders, Venetians and Turks, it has been well restored and its many rooms and passageways now house the **Medieval Museum**. It is open Monday to Friday from 7.30 am to 5 pm and Saturday from 9 am to 5 pm. Entry costs CY£1.

Lemessos has a number of other museums and sights, but of greater interest are **Kolossi Castle**, 14 km east of town on the road to Paphos, and the ancient, extensive site of **Kourion**, another five km away.

Places to Stay & Eat

The nearest camping ground is *Governor's Beach Camping* (☎ 632300 or 632878), 20 km east of town.

If you're on a tight budget, the cheapest hotels are clustered in the old town, on the eastern side of the castle. A good one with large, clean rooms is the *Luxor Guest House* (☎ 362265), 101 Agiou Andreou St, where single/doubles cost CY£5/8.

Another option is the *Continental Hotel* (☎ 362530) at 137 Spyrou Araouzou St, on the waterfront, which has very pleasant singles/doubles with private bathroom for CY£15/25 including breakfast.

The locals eat at *Mikph Mapia* at 3 Ankara St to the left of the castle, where the 24-dish meze costs CY£4. Another good place to eat is the unlikely *Richard & Berengaria* café, just by the castle.

Getting There & Away

Bus Kemek has frequent daily services to Lefkosia (CY£1.25) and Paphos (CY£1.25)

CYPRUS

from its station on the corner of Enoeos and Eirinis Sts, north of the castle. From here there is also a weekday bus at noon to Agros (CY£1) in the Troodos Mountains. Kallenos goes to Larnaca (CY£1.10) from the bus stop outside the CTO. From Monday to Saturday, Kyriakos/Karydas service taxis has a minibus to Platres (CY£1.50) at 11.30 am from its office (see below).

Service Taxi Close to the CTO at 65 Spyros Araouzou St, Acropolis Taxis (☎ 366766) has taxis every half-hour to Lefkosia (CY£2.60), Larnaca (CY£2.25) and Paphos (CY£2.05). Kyriakos/Karydas (☎ 364114), at 21 Thessalonikis St, travels the same routes.

Ferry You can buy ferry tickets from any travel agency or direct from Amathus Navigation Co Ltd, on the waterfront between the CTO and the old harbour. The port is five km south-west of town. See the Getting There & Away section at the start of this chapter for more information.

Getting Around
The city bus station is on A Themistokleous St, close to the municipal market. Bus No 1 goes to the port, Bus No 16-17 goes to Kolossi, and bus No 30 goes north-east along the seafront. Frequent buses also run from Lemessos Castle to Kourion and its beach. From April to October there's a Governor's Beach bus which leaves from the Continental Hotel every day at 9.50 am, returning at 4.30 pm.

Lipsos Rent-a-Car (☎ 365295) is at 6 Richard & Berengaria St (opposite the castle). The Oceanic Supermarket at 232 Oktovriou 28 St rents mopeds and bicycles.

TROODOS MASSIF
The mountains of the Troodos region are unforgettable with their secluded Byzantine monasteries, 15th-century frescoed churches, small wine-making villages and numerous walking trails. In summer the area offers some respite from the heat and in winter there's enough snow to ski. The CTO (☎ 421316) in the square at Platres is open Monday to Friday from 9 am to 3.30 pm and Saturday from 9 am to 2.30 pm.

Things to See & Do
The **Kykkos Monastery**, 20 km west of Pedhoulas village, is the best known but also the most touristy of the monasteries. Although it dates from the 12th century, it has been completely renovated and all the mosaics, frescos and stonework are new. It also has a museum containing priceless religious icons and relics.

In Pedhoulas village there is the small **Church of Archangelos**, a World Heritage-listed church, with frescos dating from 1474. The key to the church is at the house with the light green door, to the right of the church as you face the entrance.

Omodos village is in the wine-growing region, almost directly south of Pedhoulas, and home-made wine is available for sale and tastings. You can also visit **Socrates' Traditional House**, a 500-year-old village house with a wine cellar and distillery dating from this time. Also in Omodos is the old **Stavros Monastery** which makes quite a contrast to the larger, more renowned ones.

The walking in this area is superb and well marked; ask at the CTO for details.

Places to Stay & Eat
Even though there are hotels or rooms in almost all the villages, there aren't enough so in July and August it is wise to book. Outside these months, you can negotiate on prices.

The only reason to stay in Troodos itself, more a touristy hill station than a village, is for the walks. Two km north, in a pine forest, there is a *camping ground* (☎ 421624) which is open from May to October. The Troodos Hostel (☎ 422400) is open from April to October and charges CY£5 for the first night and CY£4 thereafter. Rather more luxurious is the three-star *Troodos Hotel* (☎ 421635) where singles/doubles cost CY£29/38 for B&B.

A good base for this area is Platres. The *Pafsilypon Hotel* (☎ 421738) is a lovely old place. Singles/doubles/triples with shared bathroom cost CY£8.50/17/22 with breakfast. The friendly *Kallithea Hotel* (☎ 421746) is smarter and B&B costs CY£13 for a room with a private bathroom. The owner also has cheaper accommodation across the road. There are signposts to these hotels and many more in the village.

The best restaurant in Platres is the good-value *Kalidonia*. Just outside Platres on the road to Troodos is the *Psilo Dendro* lunchtime restaurant and trout farm, where fresh trout costs CY£4.20.

Getting There & Away

See the Lemessos and Lefkosia Getting There & Away sections for details of buses to the Troodos region.

Buses from Platres to Lemessos (CY£1.50) leave at around 6.30 am every day except Sunday. One bus leaves Platres at 5.30 am for Lefkosia and another leaves Troodos village for Lefkosia at 6.30 am. Service taxis also leave from the main square in Platres for Lemessos (CY£1.50) at 7 am, Monday to Saturday, with more regular trips in August.

PAPHOS

Once the capital of Cyprus, Paphos has always been historically and mythologically important. Today it consists of Kato (lower) Paphos on the coast, where you'll find most of the places of interest, and Paphos, which is one km inland. Kato Paphos is a horrendous monument to package tourism which spoils most of the old harbour and port area. Paphos itself is much more pleasant, with a more authentic life of its own.

The tourist office (☎ 232841) is at 3 Gladstonos St, just down from Paphos' main square. It opens Monday to Friday from 8.15 am to 2.30 pm and from 3 to 6.15 pm. Sometimes it is closed on Wednesday and Friday afternoons. On Saturday it is open from 8.15 am to 1.30 pm. In July and August it often closes at 3.45 pm. (There is another tourist office at the airport.)

The telephone code for Paphos is ☎ 06.

Things to See

There is a lot to see in Paphos but most renowned are the **Paphos Mosaics** which are well-preserved (if a bit dusty) mosaic floors from the villas of 3rd-century Roman nobles. They mostly depict mythological themes with an emphasis on the exploits of Dionysos. At present they are displayed in three main indoor areas but as the site is developing there should be more to see soon. It is open every day from am to 7 pm in summer, closing at 4.30 pm in winter, and admission is CY£1.50. On the way

to the mosaics you pass a **Byzantine castle** and an **odeon**.

About two km north of Kato Paphos, on the coastal road to Polis, are the **Tombs of the Kings** which date from the 4th century BC. These underground tombs are fascinating to explore and are open from 7.30 am to 7 pm; entry is 75 cents.

Places to Stay & Eat

The nearest camping ground is *Zenon Gardens* (☎ 242277), five km south of Kato Paphos. It is very close to the beach and you camp in the shade of trees.

The HI *hostel* (☎ 232588) is quite a way north of Paphos at 37 Leoforos Eleftheriou Venizelou. To get there, walk up Leoforos Evagora Pallikaridi and it is off on the right. The hostel is very cosy and quiet and a bed costs CY£3.50.

At the top of Gladstonos St is Leoforos Archiepiskopou Makariou III where, at No 99, the *Trianon Guest House* (☎ 232193) has basic rooms, some with private facilities and all sharing a communal kitchen, for between CY£4 and CY£8 per person. More up-market but good value is the *Agapinor Hotel* (☎ 233926) at 26 Nikodimou Mylona St where B&B costs CY£13/26 for singles/doubles with private facilities.

Two recommended restaurants in Paphos are the *Trianon Restaurant*, opposite the Trianon Hotel, and *Demetris Tavern*, 12 Petraki Miltiadous St, near the food market.

Getting There & Away

Bus The Amaroza bus company has buses to Polis and Lemessos. Their office is at 79 Leoforos Evagora Pallikaridi, north of Paphos' main square; there are around 11 buses a day to Polis (95 cents) and one to Lemessos at 2 pm. Alepa Ltd (☎ 231755) has buses to Lemessos (CY£1.50) and Lefkosia (CY£3) daily. If you book in advance they'll pick you up from your hotel; otherwise they depart from the urban bus station and also stop outside the food market.

Service Taxi Karydas/Kyriakos (☎ 232424) at 9 Leoforos Evagora Pallikaridi and A Makris (☎ 246802) at 2 Grammou St, opposite the police station, have service taxis to Lemessos (CY£2.05) every half-hour.

Getting Around

There are no buses or service taxis to/from the airport and a normal taxi costs CY£6.

The urban bus station is at Karavella Parking, behind the Amaroza bus company office. Bus No 1 goes to Geroskipou Tourist Beach, nine km north of Paphos; Bus No 11 goes to Kato Paphos; and bus No 10 goes to Coral Bay.

D Antoniades Ltd (☎ 233301), 111-113 Leoforos Evagora Pallikaridi, rents out mountain bikes, motorcycles and mopeds.

POLIS

Near deserted beaches and the wild, remote hiking region of the Akamas Peninsula is the small town of Polis. Not half as spoilt by tourism as Cyprus' other coastal towns, Polis is a charming and serene base from which to explore Chrysochou Bay and the surrounding area. There are plenty of mountain-bike, motorcycle and car-rental companies in town.

The telephone code for Polis is ☎ 06.

Things to See & Do

The **Akamas Peninsula** is one of the last wild and unspoilt places on the island's coast. The landscape is a patchwork of barren rock and lush vegetation, with a wide variety of flora and fauna, including some rare species. A network of paths crisscross the peninsula, making it an ideal place for walkers.

At the start of these trails are the famous and much-visited **Baths of Aphrodite**, 10 km west of Polis. According to legend the goddess used to bathe there to renew her virginity after amorous encounters with her many lovers.

Places to Stay & Eat

About one km north of Polis towards the sea and surrounded by gum trees, is the *Camping Site* (☎ 321526); there are signs to it from the town centre. Many of the houses have rooms to rent for around CY£7 and there are plenty of apartments for hire. Otherwise, a good hotel is the *Akamas* (☎ 322507), on the main street, where smallish rooms (mostly with wonderful views) cost CY£5 a night. The hotel has a good restaurant too.

The most popular eatery in town is the *Arsinoe Fish Tavern* where you can get a delicious fish meze for CY£5 and other fresh fish dishes.

Getting There & Away

The New Amaroza/ALEPA bus company office is on Kyproleontos St, beside the Old Town Restaurant. They run 11 buses a day to Paphos (95 cents) and also have services to Latsi (35 cents) and the Baths of Aphrodite (50 cents).

North Cyprus

The Turkish Republic of Northern Cyprus occupies 37% of the island. Almost completely unspoilt by tourism, it has some of the island's best beaches, as well as some of its most awe-inspiring monasteries, archaeological sites and castles.

In this section, Greek place names are used with the Turkish in brackets.

NORTH LEFKOSIA (LEFKOŞA)

North Lefkosia, the capital of North Cyprus, is a quiet city with some good examples of Gothic and Ottoman architecture. Although it can sometimes seem populated only by soldiers, if you wander the backstreets of the old town you'll find lots of its inhabitants toiling away in small workshops, making or mending a whole variety of everyday articles.

Orientation

The city centre is Atatürk Square in the old city. Girne Caddesi is the main thoroughfare and runs north from Atatürk Square to the very well-preserved Girne Gate. To the east of the square is the Selimiye quarter, where you'll find most places of interest.

Information

There isn't a proper tourist office but you can get information from the Ministry of Tourism (☎ 2283666) which is the last building on Selçuklu Caddesi. As this is some way from the old town, your best bet is to use the free town map stocked at most travel agents.

The main post office is on Sarayonu Sokak just west of Atatürk Square. The telecommunications office is on Kizilay Sokak, out of the old town and west of the telecom tower; it is open seven days a week from 8 am to midnight. In an emergency, ring ☎ 112 for the hospital.

☎ 155 for the police or ☎ 199 for the fire station.

North Lefkosia's telephone code is ☎ 22.

Things to See & Do

The **Turkish Museum** at the northern end of Girne Caddesi is housed in a 17th-century Islamic monastery which was used by dervishes (Muslim ascetics) in the 19th century and now has a display of dervish memorabilia. Extending from the museum is a long, thin mausoleum lined with the tombs of 16 sheikhs. The museum is open Monday to Friday from 8 am to 5 pm.

The old quarter east of Atatürk Square is dominated by the **Selimiye Mosque**, which was originally a cathedral built between 1209 and 1326. Next to it is the **Bedesten**, a building comprising two churches, which was used in the Ottoman period as a covered bazar.

The **Büyük Hamam**, by the Antalya Pansiyon, is a world-famous Turkish bath and is used by both locals and tourists. A steam bath costs UK£2.50 and a massage (there are only male masseurs) costs UK£7.

Places to Stay & Eat

Most of the budget hotels around the Selimiye Mosque area have dormitory-style rooms where a bed costs around UK£3. These are

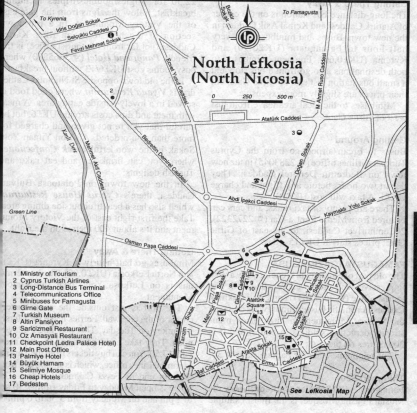

North Lefkosia (North Nicosia)

To Kyrenia
To Famagusta

Idris Doğan Sokak
Selçuklu Caddesi
Fevzi Mehmet Sokak
Eqvit Yusuf Caddesi
Kanil Deri
Mehmet Akif Caddesi
Bedrettin Demirel Caddesi
Atatürk Caddesi
Dogan Sokak
M Ahmet Ruso Caddesi
Bozkir Sokak
Abdi İpekci Caddesi
Kaymaklı Yolu Sokak
Green Line
Osman Paşa Caddesi
Mahmut Paşa Sokak
Girne Caddesi
Tanzim Sokak
Tekçamı Sokak
Kılızade Sokak
Atatürk Square
Arasta Sokak
Ermu Caddesi
Bat Caddesi

See Lefkosia Map

0   250   500 m

1 Ministry of Tourism
2 Cyprus Turkish Airlines
3 Long-Distance Bus Terminal
4 Telecommunications Office
5 Minibuses for Famagusta
6 Girne Gate
7 Turkish Museum
8 Altin Pansiyon
9 Saricizmeli Restaurant
10 Oz Amasyali Restaurant
11 Checkpoint (Ledra Palace Hotel)
12 Main Post Office
13 Palmiye Hotel
14 Büyük Hamam
15 Selimiye Mosque
16 Cheap Hotels
17 Bedesten

CYPRUS

pretty dire places except for the **Kalkan Pansiyon** (☎ 2278130), which is clean and just in front of the mosque, and the **Palmiye Hotel** (☎ 2287733) on Mecidiye Sokak. Also good is the **Altin Pansiyon** (☎ 2285049), 63 Girne Caddesi, where doubles/triples cost UK£7/10.

On the opposite side of the road are two friendly restaurants, **Saricizmeli** and **Oz Amasyali**, which are open all day. A substantial plate of mixed fare in either will cost around UK£2.50

In Arasta Sokak, opposite the Bedesten, is a shop which makes delicious halva on the premises. Beside the Bedesten is the **Belediyepazari**, a large covered market selling fresh produce as well as clothes and knick-knacks.

Getting There & Away

The long-distance bus station is on the corner of Atatürk Caddesi and Kemal Asik Caddesi in the new town. Buses and minibuses go every half-hour to Famagusta (UK£0.90) and Kyrenia (UK£0.60). Frequent minibuses to both destinations also go from a bus stop and a small bus station just east of Girne Gate, but their prices are slightly more expensive.

Minibuses to the local area leave from just west of Girne Gate.

Getting Around

Buses to Ercan airport go from the Cyprus Turkish Airlines office (☎ 2283045) in the new town on Bedrettin Demirel Caddesi. They depart two hours before any flight and charge UK£1. A taxi will cost UK£10.

There are plenty of taxi ranks, and cars can be hired from Memo Rent-a-Car (☎ 2272322), 2 Cumhuriyet Caddesi, to the east of Girne Gate; prices start at UK£15 a day.

FAMAGUSTA (GAZIMAĞUSA)

The old part of Famagusta is enclosed by a very impressive, well-preserved Venetian wall. The tourist office (☎ 3662864) is on Fevzi Cakmak Caddesi. From the bus terminus, walk past the Victory Monument (a huge black monstrosity depicting soldiers in battle) and it is 300 metres on the right.

The telephone code for Famagusta is ☎ 36.

Things to See

Famagusta's **St Nicholas Cathedral**, now the Mustafa Pasha Mosque, is the finest example of Gothic architecture in Cyprus. Rather incongruously, a small minaret perches on top of one of its ruined towers.

Othello's Castle, part of the city walls and battlements, was built by the Lusignans in the 13th century. According to legend it was here that Christophore Moro (governor of Cyprus from 1506 to 1508) killed his wife, Desdemona, in a fit of jealous rage. It is said that Shakespeare based his tragedy *Othello* on the legend. There are good views from the ramparts. It's open every day from 10 am to 5 pm; admission is UK£1.20.

Places to Stay & Eat

Inside the city walls is the **Altun Tabaya Hotel** (☎ 3665363), 7 Kizilkule Yolu, where rooms with a private bathroom cost UK£12.50/17.50/ 22.50 for singles/doubles/triples including breakfast; follow the signs from the gate east of the Victory Monument. In a run-down section of the new town on Ilker Karter Caddesi (not far from the tourist office) is the friendly **Panorama Hotel** (☎ 3665880) where cosy rooms cost UK£6/13 without breakfast.

In the old town opposite St Nicholas Cathedral is **Viyana Restaurant** where good food is served in a lovely outside eating area. A meal with meat and dips costs around UK£6, but be careful that you're not given and charged for more than you ordered. Also on Yiman Yolu Sokak is the wonderful **Petek Confectioner** where you can drink tea and eat cake and Turkish delights.

In the new town, on Polatpasa Bulvari Caddesi, there's **Cyprus House Restaurant** which also has a beautiful outside dining area. Take the first right east of the Victory Monument and it's about 400 metres on the right.

Getting There & Away

Minibuses go half-hourly to Kyrenia (UK£1 and North Lefkosia (UK£0.90). The bus terminus is on Lefkoşa Yolu, near the Victory Monument.

The port is just outside the south-eastern corner of the city wall. Ferries leave for Mersin in Turkey on Tuesday, Thursday and Friday at noon. They take eight hours and the trip cost UK£17.50. You can buy tickets from the Turkish Maritime Lines office, which is signposted from the port end of Fevzi Cakmak Caddesi. The office is open Monday to Friday from 7.30 am to 2 pm and on Monday from 3.30 to 6 pm.

SALAMIS

Nine km north of Famagusta is the huge site of Cyprus' most important pre-Christian city. Among many other remains, there is a fully restored Roman amphitheatre, a gymnasium still surrounded by the majority of its marble columns with adjacent baths, and some interesting mosaics. The site is open daily from 7.30 am to 6.30 pm in summer and entry costs UK£1.20. There is a bar/restaurant (with very clean Western-style toilets) in the car park by the ticket office. Allow a day here as there is also a long sandy beach next to the site. There are no buses to Salamis and a taxi will cost UK£5 (one way) from Famagusta.

KYRENIA (GIRNE)

Kyrenia is a very attractive town built around a horseshoe-shaped harbour dominated on one side by an impressive Byzantine castle. The tourist office (☎ 8152145) is at the opposite end of the harbour to the castle. The waterfront is lined with lovely outdoor cafés and restaurants where it is delightful to sit and watch the boats.

The telephone code for Kyrenia is ☎ 81.

Things to See

The star attraction of the castle is the **Ship-wreck Museum**, which houses the world's oldest shipwreck and its cargo. The ship is believed to have sunk in a storm near Kyrenia around 3000 BC. The castle was built by the Byzantines as a defence against marauding Arabs. Both the castle and the museum are open from 8 am to 5 pm every day; admission is UK£1.20.

Places to Stay & Eat

Hürriyet Caddesi runs west from the town hall and at No 6 you'll find the *Bingöl Guest House* (☎ 8152749) where B&B costs UK£10/20/30 for a single/double/triple. Further down is the *New Bristol Hotel* (☎ 8156570) where en suite rooms cost UK£7.50/15. Just opposite is the *Ercan Motel* (☎ 815 1200) where B&B with private facilities costs UK£12.50/17.50 for a single/double. There are also some cheaper options along Ecevit Caddesi, on the main road to North Lefkosia, and behind Hürriyet Caddesi towards the harbour.

Little Arif's Restaurant, on the same side of the road as the New Bristol Hotel, is very good value; turn right into a cul-de-sac opposite the Onder taxi office. On the harbour is the *Set Fish Restaurant* where a wonderful fish meal with cost UK£8.

Getting There & Away

The long-distance bus station is on Ecevit Caddesi at the southern end of the new town. Minibuses to Famagusta (UK£1) and shared taxis to North Lefkosia (UK£0.70) depart from the roundabout in front of the town hall.

There are express boats between Kyrenia and Taşucu in Turkey every day at 11 am and from Monday to Friday there's also a ferry at 2 pm. Tickets cost UK£14 one way and the trip takes four to six hours. From Tuesday to Thursday during peak season there's an express boat to Alanya in Turkey at 6.30 pm. This sometimes runs on a Friday. You can get tickets either from the passenger lounge at the port or from Fergün Shipping Co Ltd at the roundabout in front of the town hall.

CYPRUS

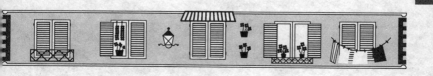

France

France's most salient characteristic is its exceptional diversity. The largest country in Western Europe, France stretches from the rolling hills of the north to the seemingly endless beaches of the south; from the wild coastline of Brittany to the icy crags of the Alps, with cliff-lined canyons, dense forest and vineyards in between. France's towns and cities also hold many charms. Whether strolling along grand boulevards, sitting at a café terrace or picnicking in the beautiful public parks, it's easy to sense the famous *joie de vivre* of the country. Outstanding museums and galleries are also a nationwide phenomenon. This chapter will help you decide where to go and what to see.

Over the centuries, France has received more immigrants than any other country in Europe. From the ancient Celtic Gauls and Romans to the more recent arrivals from France's former colonies in Indochina and Africa, these peoples have introduced new elements of culture, cuisine and art, all of which have contributed to create France's unique and diverse civilisation.

At one time, France was on the western edge of Europe. Today, as Europe moves towards unification of one sort or another, it is at the crossroads: between England and Italy, Belgium and Spain, North Africa and Scandinavia. Of course, this is exactly how the French have always regarded their country – at the very centre of things.

Facts about the Country

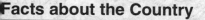

HISTORY
Prehistory
Human presence in France is known to date from the middle Palaeolithic period, about 90,000 to 40,000 years ago. Around 25,000 BC the Stone Age Cro-Magnon people appeared on the scene and left their mark in the form of cave paintings and engravings. The most visible evidence of France's Neolithic age are the menhirs and dolmens dating from 4000 to 2500 BC. With the dawning of the Bronze Age,

and the demand for copper and tin for bronze, trade began to develop between France and the rest of Europe around 2000 BC.

Ancient & Medieval History
The Celtic Gauls moved into what is now France between 1500 and 500 BC. By about 600 BC, they had established trading links with the Greeks, whose colonies on the Mediterranean coast included Massilia (Marseille). After several centuries of conflict between Rome and the Gauls, Julius Caesar's legions took control of the territory around 52 BC, when a revolt led by the Gallic chief Vercingétorix was crushed. Christianity was introduced to Roman Gaul early in the 2nd century AD.

France remained under Roman rule until the 5th century, when the Franks (thus 'France') and other Germanic groups overran the country. These peoples adopted important parts of Gallo-Roman civilisation – including Christianity – and their eventual assimilation resulted in a fusion of Germanic, Roman and Celtic cultures.

France

GREAT BRITAIN

LONDON
Channel Tunnel
Ramsgate
Dover
Folkstone
Zeebrugge
Ostende
Antwerp

Southampton
Portsmouth
Weymouth
Poole
Newhaven
BELGIUM
Calais
Dunkirk
BRUSSELS

Plymouth
Boulogne
Lille
PICARDY & LE NORD
Arras
Saint Quentin

English Channel (La Manche)
Dieppe
Somme River
Amiens
Beauvais

To Rosslare & Cork
Cherbourg
Le Havre
Rouen
Reir
Chak sur-Me

To Rosslare & Cork
Guernsey
Sark
Jersey
D-Day Beaches
Ouistreham
Bayeux
Seine River
PARIS
Marne River
CHAMPAGN

To Cork
Channel Islands (GB)
Caen
NORMANDY
Évreux
Versailles
EURO Disney

Roscoff
Saint Malo
Dinard
Mont-Saint-Michel
Pontorson
Alençon
Chartres
Melun
Seine River
Troyes

Brest
BRITTANY
MASSIF ARMORICAIN
Rennes
Le Mans
Orléans
BURGUNDY
Auxerre
FRANCHE-COMTE

Point du Raz
Quimper
Concarneau
Lorient
Carnac
Angers
Tours
Amboise
Blois
Loire River
Bourges
Cher River
Nevers

ATLANTIC OCEAN
Saint Nazaire
Nantes
LOIRE VALLEY
Indre River
Allier River

POITOU & AQUITAINE
Poitiers
Vienne River
Creuse River

Île de Ré
La Rochelle
Île d'Oléron

Limoges
Puy de Dôme (1465 m)
Clermont-Ferrand

LIMOUSIN
Angoulême
PÉRIGORD (DORDOGNE)
Périgueux
Vézère River
Brive
Dordogne River
Montignac
MASSIF

Gironde Estuary

Bordeaux
Saint Émilion
Sarlat-la-Canéda
Lot River
CENTRAL

Arcachon
Garonne River
Cahors
QUERCY

BAY OF BISCAY
Agen
Tarn River
Albi
LANGUEDOC
Nîme

Biarritz
St Jean de Luz
Bayonne
Toulouse
Castres
Montpellier
Béziers

Bilbao
San Sebastián
BASQUE COUNTRY
Pau
Garonne River
Narbonne
Sète

St Jean Pied de Port
Lourdes
Tarbes
Carcassonne
Golfe de Lion

SPAIN
Pamplona
Cauterets
THE PYRENEES
Foix
ROUSSILLON
Perpignan
Mo

ANDORRA
ANDORRA LA VELLA

0   75   150 km

FRANCE

Two Frankish dynasties, the Merovingians and the Carolingians, ruled from the 5th to the 10th century. The Frankish tradition by which the king was succeeded by all of his sons led to power struggles and the eventual disintegration of the kingdom into a collection of small, feudal states. In 732, Charles Martel defeated the Moors at Poitiers, thus ensuring that France would not follow Spain and come under Muslim rule.

Charles Martel's grandson, Charlemagne, significantly extended the power and boundaries of the kingdom and was crowned Holy Roman Emperor (Emperor of the West) in 800. But during the 9th century, the Scandinavian Vikings (also known as the Normans, ie Northmen) began raiding France's western coast. They eventually settled in the lower Seine Valley and formed the Duchy of Normandy in the early 10th century.

The Capetian dynasty was founded in 987, when the nobles elected Hugh Capet as their king. At the time, the king's domains were quite modest, consisting mostly of small pieces of land around Paris and Orléans.

Under William the Conqueror, Duke of Normandy, Norman forces occupied England in 1066, making Normandy – and later, Plantagenet-ruled England – a formidable rival of the kingdom of France. A further third of France came under the control of the English Crown in 1154, when Eleanor of Aquitaine married Henry of Anjou (later King Henry II of England). The subsequent battle between France and England for control of Aquitaine and the vast English territories in France lasted for three centuries.

The struggle between the Capetians and the English king Edward III (a member of the Plantagenet family) over the powerful French throne set off the Hundred Years' War, which was fought on and off from 1337 to 1453. The Black Death ravaged the country in 1348, killing about a third of the population, but the plague only briefly interrupted the fighting.

In 1415, French forces were defeated at Agincourt; in 1420, the English took control of Paris, and two years later King Henry IV of England became king of France. Just when it seemed that the Plantagenets had pulled off a dynastic union of England and France, a 17-year-old peasant girl known to history as Jeanne d'Arc (Joan of Arc) surfaced in 1429 and rallied the French troops at Orléans. She was captured, convicted of heresy by a court of French ecclesiastics and burned at the stake two years later, but her efforts helped to turn the war in favour of the French. With the exception of Calais, the English were expelled from French territory in 1453.

The Renaissance

The ideals and aesthetics of the Italian Renaissance arrived in France towards the end of the 15th century, introduced in part by the French aristocracy returning from military campaigns in Italy. The influence was most evident during the reign of François I, and the chateaux of Fontainebleau, near Paris, and Chenonceau in the Loire are good examples of Renaissance architectural style.

The Reformation

By the 1530s the position of the Protestant Reformation sweeping Europe had been strengthened in France by the ideas of the Frenchman John Calvin, an exile in Geneva. The Edict of January (1562), which afforded the Protestants certain rights, was violently opposed by ultra-Catholic nobles, whose fidelity to their religion was mixed with a desire to strengthen their power base in the provinces.

The Wars of Religion (1562-98) involved three groups: the Huguenots (French Protestants); the Catholic League, led by the House of Guise; and the Catholic monarchy. The fighting severely weakened the position of the king and brought the French state close to disintegration. The most outrageous massacre took place in Paris in 1572, when some 3000 Huguenots who had come to Paris to celebrate the wedding of Henry of Navarre were slaughtered in the Saint Bartholomew's Day Massacre (24 August).

Henry of Navarre, a Huguenot who had embraced Catholicism, eventually became King Henry IV. In 1598, he promulgated the Edict of Nantes, which guaranteed the Huguenots freedom of conscience and many civil and political rights. It was revoked by Louis XIV less than 100 years later.

Louis XIV & the Ancien Régime

Le Roi Soleil (the Sun King) ascended the throne in 1643 at the age of five and ruled until 1715. Throughout his long reign, he sought to extend the power of the French monarchy – bolstered by claims of divine right – both at home and abroad. He involved France in a long series of costly wars that gained it territory but nearly bankrupted the treasury. Louis XIV was not known for his parsimony domestically either, and poured huge sums of money into building his extravagant palace at Versailles.

His successor, Louis XV (ruled 1715-74), was followed by the incompetent – and later universally despised – Louis XVI. As the 18th century progressed, new economic and social circumstances rendered the old order *(ancien régime)* dangerously at odds with the needs of the country. The regime was further weakened by the anti-Establishment and anticlerical ideas of the Enlightenment, whose leading lights included Voltaire, Rousseau and Montesquieu. But entrenched vested interests, a cumbersome power structure and royal lassitude delayed reform until it was too late.

The Seven Years' War (1756-63), fought by France and Austria against Britain and Prussia, was one of a series of ruinous wars pursued by Louis XV, culminating in the loss of France's flourishing colonies in Canada, the West Indies and India to the English. It was in part to avenge these losses that Louis XVI sided with the colonists in the American War of Independence. But the Seven Years' War cost a fortune and, even more disastrous for the monarchy, it helped to disseminate in France the radical democratic ideas which the American Revolution had thrust onto the world stage.

The French Revolution

By the late 1780s, Louis XVI and his queen, Marie-Antoinette, had managed to alienate virtually every segment of society – from enlightened groups to conservatives. When the king tried to neutralise the power of the more reform-minded delegates at a meeting of the Estates General in 1789, the urban masses took to the streets and, on 14 July, a Parisian mob stormed the Bastille prison – the ultimate symbol of the despotism of the ancien régime.

At first, the Revolution was in the hands of relative moderates. France was declared a constitutional monarchy and various reforms were made, including the adoption of the Declaration of the Rights of Man. But as the masses armed themselves against the external threat to the Revolution posed by Austria, Prussia and the many exiled French nobles, patriotism and nationalism melded with revolutionary fervour, thereby popularising and radicalising the Revolution. It was not long before the moderate, republican Girondists (Girondins in French) lost power to the radical Jacobins, led by Robespierre, Danton and Marat who established the First Republic in 1792, after Louis XVI proved unreliable as a constitutional monarch. In January 1793, Louis was guillotined in what is now Place de la Concorde in Paris. In March, the Jacobins set up the notorious Committee of Public Safety. This body had virtually dictatorial control over the country during the Reign of Terror (September 1793 to July 1794), which saw religious freedoms revoked and churches desecrated.

By autumn, the Reign of Terror was in full swing, and by the middle of 1794 some 17,000 people in every part of the country had been beheaded. In the end, the Revolution turned on its own, and many of its leaders, including Robespierre, followed their victims to the guillotine.

Napoleon

In the resulting chaos, the leaders of the French military began disregarding instructions from the increasingly corrupt and tyrannical Directory (the executive power in Paris), pursuing instead their own ambitions on the battlefield. One dashing young general by the name of Napoleon Bonaparte was particularly successful in the Italian campaign of the war against Austria, and his victories soon turned him into an independent political force. In 1799, when it appeared that the Jacobins were again on the ascendancy in the legislature, Napoleon overthrew the discredited Directory and assumed power himself.

At first, Napoleon took the title of First Consul. In 1802, a referendum declared him 'consul for life' and his birthday became a national holiday. By 1804, when he had himself crowned Emperor of the French by Pope Pius VII at Notre Dame Cathedral in Paris, the scope and nature of Napoleon's ambitions were obvious to all. But to consolidate and legitimise his authority, Napoleon needed more victories on the battlefield. So began a seemingly endless series of wars in which France came to control most of Europe.

But in 1812, in an attempt to do away with his last major rival on the continent, Tsar Alexander I, Napoleon invaded Russia. Although his Grande Armée (Grand Army) captured Moscow, it was wiped out shortly after by the brutal Russian winter. Prussia and Napoleon's other enemies quickly recovered from their earlier defeats, and less than two years after the fiasco in Russia, the Allied armies entered Paris. Napoleon abdicated and left France for his tiny Mediterranean island-kingdom of Elba.

At the Congress of Vienna (1814-15), the Allies restored the House of Bourbon to the French throne, installing Louis XVI's brother as Louis XVIII (Louis XVII, Louis XVI's son, had died in exile in 1795). But in March 1815, Napoleon escaped from Elba, landed in southern France and gathered a large army as he marched northward towards Paris. His 'Hundred Days' back in power ended when his forces were defeated by the English at Waterloo in Belgium. Napoleon was exiled to the remote South Atlantic island of Saint Helena, where he died in 1821.

Although reactionary in some ways – slavery was re-established in the colonies, for instance – Napoleon instituted a number of important reforms, including a reorganisation of the judicial system and the promulgation of a new legal code, the Code Civil (or Napoleonic Code), which forms the basis of the French legal system (and many others in Europe) to this day. More importantly, he preserved the essence of the changes wrought by the Revolution. Napoleon is therefore remembered by the French as a great hero.

The 19th Century

The 19th century was a chaotic one for France. Louis XVIII's reign (1815-24) was dominated by the struggle between extreme monarchists, who wanted a return to the ancien régime, and those who saw the changes wrought by the Revolution as irreversible. Charles X (ruled 1824-30) handled the struggle between reactionaries and liberals with great ineptitude and was overthrown in the July Revolution of 1830. Louis-Philippe (ruled 1830-48), an ostensibly constitutional monarch of upper bourgeois sympathies and tastes, was then chosen by parliament to head what became known as the July Monarchy.

Louis-Philippe was in turn overthrown in the February Revolution of 1848, in whose wake the Second Republic was established. In presidential elections held that year, Napoleon's undistinguished nephew Louis-Napoleon Bonaparte was overwhelmingly elected. A legislative deadlock led Louis-Napoleon to lead a coup d'état in 1851, after which he was proclaimed Napoleon III, Emperor of the French.

The second empire lasted from 1852 until 1870. During this period, France enjoyed significant economic growth. But as his uncle had done, Napoleon III embroiled France in a number of conflicts, including the disastrous Crimean War (1853-56). It was the Prussians, however, who ended the second empire. In 1870, the Prussian prime minister Bismarck goaded Napoleon III into declaring war on Prussia. Within months the thoroughly unprepared French army had been defeated and the emperor taken prisoner.

When news of the debacle reached the French capital, the Parisian masses took to the streets and demanded that a republic be declared. The Third Republic began as a provisional government of national defence – the Prussians were, at the time, advancing on Paris. But in the Assemblée Nationale (National Assembly) elections of February 1871 (required by the armistice which had been signed after a four-month siege of Paris by the Prussians), the republicans, who had called on the nation to continue resistance, lost to the monarchists, who had campaigned on a peace platform.

As expected, the monarchist-controlled National Assembly ratified the Treaty of Frankfurt (1871). However, when ordinary Parisians heard of its harsh terms – a five billion franc war indemnity and surrender of the provinces of Alsace and Lorraine – they revolted against the government. The Communards, as the supporters of the Paris Commune were known, took over the city but were slowly pushed back in bloody fighting in which several thousand rebels were killed. A further 20,000 or so Communards, mostly from the working class, were summarily executed.

The greatest moral and political crisis of the Third Republic was the infamous Dreyfus Affair, which began in 1894 when a Jewish army officer named Captain Alfred Dreyfus

was framed as a German spy, court-martialled and sentenced to life imprisonment. Despite bitter opposition from the army command, right-wing politicians and many Catholic groups, the case was eventually reopened and Dreyfus vindicated. The affair greatly discredited both the army and the Church. The result was more rigorous civilian control of the military and, in 1905, the legal separation of church and state.

WWI

Central to France's entry into WWI was the desire to regain Alsace and Lorraine, lost to Germany in 1871. This was achieved but at immense human cost: of the eight million French men who were called to arms, 1.3 million were killed and almost one million crippled. The war was officially ended by the Treaty of Versailles in 1919, whose severe terms (Germany was to pay US$33 billion in reparations) were heavily influenced by the uncompromising French prime minister Georges Clemenceau.

WWII

During the 1930s the French, like the British, did their best to appease Hitler, but two days after the 1939 German invasion of Poland, the two countries reluctantly declared war on Germany. By June of the following year, France had capitulated. The British expeditionary force sent to help the French barely managed to avoid capture by retreating to Dunkirk and crossing the English Channel in small boats. The hugely expensive Maginot Line, a supposedly impregnable wall of fortifications along the Franco-German border, had proved useless: the German armoured divisions had simply outflanked it by going through Belgium.

The Germans divided France into a zone under direct German occupation (in the north and along the west coast) and a puppet state based in the spa town of Vichy, which was led by the ageing WWI hero, General Philippe Pétain. Both Pétain's collaborationist government (whose leaders and supporters assumed that the Nazis were Europe's new masters and had to be accommodated) and French police forces in German-occupied areas were very helpful to the Nazis in rounding up French

Jews and other targeted groups for deportation to concentration camps.

After the capitulation, General Charles de Gaulle, France's undersecretary of war, fled to London and set up a French government-in-exile. He also established the Forces Françaises Libres (Free French Forces), a military force dedicated to continuing the fight against Germany. The underground movement known as the Résistance, which included no more than perhaps 5% of the population (the other 95% either collaborated or did nothing), engaged in such activities as railway sabotage, collecting intelligence for the Allies, helping Allied airmen who had been shot down, and publishing anti-German leaflets.

The liberation of France began with the US, British and Canadian landings in Normandy on D-Day (6 June 1944). On 15 August, Allied forces also landed in southern France. After a brief insurrection by the Résistance, Paris was liberated on 25 August by an Allied force spearheaded somewhat superficially by Free French units.

The Fourth Republic

De Gaulle soon returned to Paris and set up a provisional government, but in January 1946 he resigned as its president, miscalculating that such a move would create a popular outcry for his return. A few months later, a new constitution was approved by referendum. The Fourth Republic was a period of unstable coalition cabinets that followed one another with bewildering speed (on average one every six months). It was characterised by slow economic recovery helped by massive US aid (the Marshall Plan), an unsuccessful war to reassert French colonial control of Indochina and an uprising by Arab nationalists in Algeria, whose population included over one million French settlers.

The Fifth Republic

The Fourth Republic came to an end in 1958, when extreme right-wingers, furious at what they saw as defeatism in dealing with the uprising in Algeria, began conspiring to overthrow the government. De Gaulle was brought back to power to prevent a military coup and even civil war. He soon drafted a new constitution that gave considerable powers to the president at the expense of the National Assembly.

The Fifth Republic (which continues to this day) was rocked in 1961 by an attempted coup staged in Algiers by a group of right-wing military officers. When it failed, the Organisation de l'Armée Secrète (OAS; a group of French settlers and sympathisers opposed to Algerian independence) turned to terrorism, trying several times to assassinate De Gaulle. In 1962, de Gaulle negotiated an end to the war in Algeria. Some 750,000 *pieds noirs* ('black feet' – as Algerian-born French people are known in France) flooded into France. In the meantime, almost all of the other French colonies and protectorates in Africa had demanded and achieved independence. Shrewdly, the French government began a programme of economic and military aid to its former colonies in order to bolster France's waning international importance.

The crisis of May 1968 took the government, and much of the country, by total surprise. A seemingly insignificant incident, in which police broke up yet another protest by university students, sparked a violent reaction on the streets of Paris: students occupied the Sorbonne, barricades were erected in the Latin Quarter and unrest spread to other universities. Workers then joined in the protests. About nine million people participated in a general strike, virtually paralysing the country. But just when the country seemed on the brink of revolution, de Gaulle defused the crisis by successfully appealing to people's fear of anarchy. With stability restored, the government made a number of important changes, including a reform of the higher education system.

In 1969, de Gaulle was succeeded as president by the Gaullist leader Georges Pompidou, who was in turn succeeded by Valéry Giscard d'Estaing in 1974. François Mitterrand, a Socialist, was elected president in 1981 and re-elected for a second seven-year term in 1988. In the 1986 parliamentary elections, the right-wing opposition led by Jacques Chirac received a majority in the National Assembly. For the next two years, Mitterrand was forced to work with a prime minister and cabinet from the opposition, an unprecedented arrangement which became known as *cohabitation*.

Cohabitation was again the order of the day after the 1993 parliamentary elections, in

FRANCE

which a centre-right coalition took 480 of 577 seats in the National Assembly and Édouard Balladur of Chirac's party was named prime minister.

The closely contested presidential election of May 1995 resulted in Chirac winning the mandate with 52% of the vote, and naming Alain Juppé as prime minister. More surprising was the considerable success of the extreme-right Front National (FN) led by Jean-Marie Le Pen. In the presidential elections, this party took 15% of votes in the first round, and in the municipal elections of June that year won some 1249 seats, notably in southern France.

Chirac has earned credit for decisive words and actions in matters relating to the EU and the war in former Yugoslavia. His decision however to resume nuclear testing on the Polynesian island of Moruroa was met with outrage both in France and abroad. On the home front, Chirac's moves to restrict welfare payments led to the largest protests and strikes since 1968. In January 1996, François Mitterrand died.

GEOGRAPHY & ECOLOGY

France covers an area of 551,000 sq km and is the largest country in Europe after Russia and Ukraine. It is shaped like a hexagon bordered by either mountains or water except for the relatively flat, north-east frontier which abuts Germany, Luxembourg and Belgium.

France has a rich variety of flora and fauna, including some 113 species of mammals (more than any other country in Europe). Unfortunately, intensive agriculture, the draining of wetlands, the encroachment of industry and the expansion of the tourism infrastructure are amongst the problems threatening some species. The proportion of protected land is relatively low in France, but animal reintroduction programmes, such as storks bred in Alsace, have met with some success. France is home to nearly two million hunters. The 1979 Directive de Bruxelles, introduced to protect wild birds and their habitats, was signed by the French government but has yet to become part of French law.

France's nuclear energy industry continues to thrive and about three-quarters of the country's electricity is produced in this way. Since 1960, France has also maintained an independent arsenal of nuclear weapons. In 1992, the French government finally agreed to suspend nuclear testing on the Polynesian island of Moruroa and a nearby atoll, and this decision was reaffirmed in 1994. In 1995, however, Jacques Chirac decided to conduct one last round of tests before supporting a worldwide test ban treaty. The tests were concluded in January 1996, but France has yet to commit itself to the test ban.

GOVERNMENT & POLITICS

Despite a long tradition of highly centralised government, the country remains linguistically and culturally heterogeneous, and in some areas there's less than complete acceptance of control by Paris. There are even groups in the Basque Country, Brittany and Corsica demanding complete independence from France.

France has had 11 constitutions since 1789. The present one, which was instituted by de Gaulle in 1958, established what is known as the Fifth Republic (see the previous History section). It gives considerable power to the president of the republic.

The 577 members of the National Assembly are directly elected in single-member constituencies for five-year terms. The 321 members of the rather powerless Sénat, who serve for nine years, are indirectly elected. The president of France is elected directly for a seven-year term. The voting age is 18 and women were given the franchise in 1944.

Executive power is shared by the president and the Council of Ministers, whose members, including the prime minister, are appointed by the president but are responsible to parliament. The president, who resides in the Palais de l'Élysée in Paris, makes all major policy decisions.

France is one of the five permanent members of the UN Security Council. It withdrew from NATO's joint military command in 1966.

Local Administration

Before the Revolution, the country consisted of about two dozen regions. Their names are still widely used, but for administrative purposes the country has been divided into units called *départements* since 1790. At present there are 96 departments in metropolitan

France and another five overseas. The government in Paris is represented in each department by a *préfet* (prefect). A department's main town, where the departmental government and the prefect are based, is known as a *préfecture*.

ECONOMY

The recession hit France especially hard in the early 1990s. Unemployment, which has plagued the country for years, has risen to near crisis proportions with over 3.3 million workers (12.2% of the workforce) jobless in the first half of 1995. The situation among young people is so bleak that since 1994 the government has been offering bonuses and tax exemptions to employers for hiring anyone under 25 years of age who has never held a steady job.

The government has long played a significant interventionist *(dirigiste)* role in managing and running the French economy, which during the 1950s was one of the most tariff-protected and government-subsidised in Europe. Under direct government control is the world-famous Renault car works and most of the major banks. Although privatisation has been embraced in some sectors and will probably accelerate under Chirac, the lack of competition in other areas can mean poor service.

Union activity is strongest in the public sector where strike action is often a daily occurrence. But only about 15% of the French workforce is unionised – amongst the lowest rates in the EU – despite the fact that France is one of the most industrialised nations in the world, with around 40% of the workforce employed in the industrial sector. France is also the largest agricultural producer and exporter in the EU. Nearly one in 10 workers is engaged in agricultural production, which helps to account for the attention given by the government to French farmers during their periodic protests against cheaper imports.

POPULATION & PEOPLE

France has a population of 58 million, more than 20% of whom live in the Paris greater metropolitan area. The number of French people living in rural and mountain areas has been declining since the 1950s. For much of the last two centuries, France has had a considerably lower rate of population growth than its neighbours.

On the other hand, during the last 150 years France has received more immigrants than any other European country (4.3 million between 1850 and 1945), including significant numbers of political refugees. During the late 1950s and early 1960s, as the French colonial empire collapsed, more than one million French settlers returned to metropolitan France from Algeria, Morocco, Tunisia and Indochina.

In recent years, there has been a racist backlash against France's nonwhite immigrant communities, especially Muslims from North Africa. The extreme-right FN party has fanned these racist sentiments in a bid to win more votes. In 1993, the French government tightened its immigration laws, making it harder for immigrants to get French citizenship.

ARTS
Architecture

A religious revival in the 11th century led to the construction of a large number of Romanesque churches, so called because their architects adopted many elements (eg vaulting) from Gallo-Roman buildings still standing at the time. Romanesque buildings typically have round arches, heavy walls that let in very little light and a lack of ornamentation bordering on the austere.

The Gothic style originated in the mid-12th century in northern France, whose great wealth enabled it to attract the finest architects, engineers and artisans. Gothic structures are characterised by ribbed vaults, pointed arches and stained-glass windows, with the emphasis on space, verticality and light. The invention of the flying buttress (a structural support which conducts the thrust of the building down through a series of arches to the ground) meant that greater height and width were now possible. This new technology subsequently spread to the rest of Europe. By the 15th century, decorative extravagance led to the Flamboyant Gothic style, so named because its wavy stone carving was said to resemble flames.

Painting

An extraordinary flowering of artistic talent took place in France during the late 19th and early 20th centuries. The impressionists, who

FRANCE

dealt with colour as a property of light (rather than of objects) and endeavoured to capture the ever-changing aspects of reflected light, included Édouard Manet, Claude Monet, Edgar Degas, Camille Pissarro and Pierre-Auguste Renoir. They were followed by a diverse but equally creative group of artists known as the postimpressionists, among whose ranks were Paul Cézanne, Paul Gauguin and Georges Seurat. A little later, the Fauves (literally, 'wild beasts'), the most famous of whom was Henri Matisse, became known for their radical use of vibrant colour. In the years before WWI Pablo Picasso, who was living in Paris, and Georges Braque pioneered cubism, a school of art which concentrated on the analysis of form through abstract and geometric representation.

Music

When French music comes to mind, most people hear accordions and *chansonniers* (cabaret singers) like Édith Piaf. But they're only part of a much larger and more complex picture. At many points in history France has been at the centre of musical culture in Europe.

In the 17th and 18th centuries, French baroque music greatly influenced European musical output. Composers such as François Couperin (1668 -1733), noted for his harpsicord studies, and Jean Phillipe Rameau (1683-1764), a key figure in the development of modern harmony, were two major contributors. The opulence of the baroque era is reflected also in the art and architecture of the time.

France's two greatest classical composers of the 19th century were the Romantic Hector Berlioz, the founder of modern orchestration, and César Franck. Berlioz's operas and symphonies and Franck's organ compositions sparked a musical renaissance in France that would produce such greats as Gabriel Fauré and the impressionists Claude Debase and Maurice Ravel.

Jazz hit Paris in the 1920s and has remained popular ever since. France's contribution to the world of jazz includes the violinist Stéfane Grappelli and, in the 1950s, Claude Luter and his Dixieland Band.

Popular music has come a long way since the *yéyé* (imitative rock) of the 1960s sung by Johnny Halliday – though you might not think

so listening to middle-of-the-roaders Vanessa Paradis and Patrick Bruel. Watch out for rappers MC Solaar, Reg'lyss and I Am from Marseille. Evergreen balladeers/folk singers include Francis Cabrel and Julien Clerc. Some people like the new age space music of Jean-Michel Jarre; others say his name fits his sound.

France's claim to fame over the past decade has been *sono mondial* (world music) – from Algerian *raï* (Cheb Khaled, Zahouania) and Senegalese *mbalax* (Youssou N'Dour) to West Indian *zouk* (Kassav, Zouk Machine). La Mano Negra and Négresses Vertes are two bands that combine many of these styles – often with outstanding results.

Literature

To get a feel for France and its literature of the 19th century, you might pick up a translation of any novel by Victor Hugo *(Les Misérables* or *The Hunchback of Notre Dame)*, Stendahl *(The Red and the Black)*, Honoré de Balzac *(Old Goriot)*, Émile Zola *(Germinal)* or Gustave Flaubert *(A Sentimental Education)*.

After WWII, existentialism, a significant literary movement, emerged. Based upon the philosophy that people are self-creating beings, it placed total moral responsibility upon individuals to give meaning to their existence. The most prominent figures of the movement – Jean-Paul Sartre *(Being & Nothingness)*, Simone de Beauvoir, and Albert Camus *(The Plague)* – stressed the importance of the writer's political commitment. De Beauvoir, author of the ground-breaking study *The Second Sex*, has had a profound influence on feminist thinking.

In the late 1950s, some younger novelists began to experiment with the novel in an attempt to show different aspects of reality. Critics began to speak of the *nouveau roman* (new novel), referring to the works of Alain Robbe-Grillet, Nathalie Sarraute, Michel Butor and Claude Simon among others. Although these writers did not form a school, they all rejected the traditional novel with its conventions of plot, linear narrative and identifiable characters. Other authors who enjoy a wide following are: Marguerite Duras, Françoise Sagan, Patrick Modiano, Pascal Quignard and Denis Tillinac.

Cinema

Film has always been taken very seriously as an art form in France, and as such has attracted artists, intellectuals and theorists. Some of the most innovative and influential film-makers of the 1920s and 1930s were Jean Vigo, Marcel Pagnol and Jean Renoir.

After WWII, a new generation of directors burst onto the scene with experimental films that abandoned such constraints as temporal continuity and traditional narrative. Known as the *nouvelle vague* (new wave), this genre includes many disparate directors such as Jean-Luc Godard, François Truffaut, Claude Chabrol, Alain Resnais, Agnès Varda and Eric Rohmer, whose main tenet was that a film should be the conception of the film-maker – not the product of a studio or a producer.

Despite the onslaught of American films in Europe, France is still producing commercially viable (albeit subsidised) films. Contemporary directors of note include Bertrand Blier *(Trop belle pour toi)*, Jean-Jacques Beineix *(Betty Blue)* and Jacques Rivette *(Jeanne la Pucelle)*. The French film industry's main annual event is the Cannes Film Festival held in May, when the coveted Palme d'Or is awarded to French and foreign films.

CULTURE

Some visitors to France conclude that it would be a lovely country if it weren't for the French. As in other countries, however, the more tourists a particular town or neighbourhood attracts, the less patience the locals tend to have for them. The following tips might prove useful when interacting with the French:

Never address a waiter or bartender as *garçon* (boy); *s'il vous plaît* is the way it's done nowadays. Avoid discussing money, keep off the manicured French lawns *(Pelouse Interdite)*, and resist handling produce in markets; trust the shopkeeper to choose for you.

Perhaps the easiest way to improve the quality of your relations with the French is always to address people as *Monsieur/Madame/Mademoiselle*. Monsieur means 'sir' and can be used with any male person who isn't a child. Madame is used where 'Mrs' would apply in English; Mademoiselle is equivalent to 'Miss' and is used when addressing unmarried women. When in doubt, use 'Madame'.

Finally, when you go out for the evening, it's a good idea to follow the local custom of being relatively well dressed, particularly in a restaurant. If invited to someone's home or a party, always bring some sort of gift, such as good wine.

RELIGION

Some 80% of French people say they are Catholic, but although most have been baptised very few attend church – especially among the middle classes. The French Catholic church is generally progressive and ecumenically minded.

Protestants, who were severely persecuted during much of the 16th and 17th centuries, now number about one million. They are concentrated in Alsace, the Jura, the south-eastern part of the Massif Central and along the Atlantic coast.

France now has at least four million Muslims, making Islam the second-largest religion in the country. The vast majority are immigrants (or their offspring) who came from North Africa during the 1950s and 1960s.

There has been a Jewish community in France almost continuously since the Roman period. About 75,000 Jews resident in France were killed during the Holocaust. The country's Jewish community now numbers some 600,000.

LANGUAGE

Around 122 million people worldwide speak French as their first language; it is an official language in Belgium, Switzerland, Luxembourg, Canada and over two dozen other countries, most of them former French colonies in Africa. It is also spoken in the Val d'Aosta region of north-western Italy. Various forms of creole are used in Haiti, French Guiana and parts of Louisiana. France has a special government ministry (Ministère de la Francophonie) to deal with the country's relations with the French-speaking world.

The French tend to take it for granted that all human beings should speak French; it was the international language of culture and diplomacy until WWI. Your best bet is always to approach people politely in French, even if the only words you know are *'Pardon, Monsieur/Madame/Mademoiselle, parlez-vous anglais?'* ('Excuse me Sir/Madam/Miss, do you speak English?').

See the Language Guide at the back of the book for pronunciation guidelines and useful words and phrases.

Facts for the Visitor

PLANNING
Climate & When to Go

Weather-wise, France is at its best in spring, though winter-like relapses are not unknown in April and the beach resorts only begin to pick up in mid-May. Autumn is pleasant, too, but later on (late October) it gets a bit cool for sunbathing. Winter is great for snow sports in the Alps and Pyrenees, but Christmas, New Year and the February/March school holidays create surges in domestic and foreign tourism that can make it very difficult to find accommodation. On the other hand, Paris always has all sorts of cultural activities during its rather wet winter.

In summer, the weather is warm and even hot, especially in the south, which is one reason why the beaches, resorts and camping grounds are packed to the gills. Also, millions of French people take their annual month-long holiday (congé) in August. Resort hotel rooms and camp sites are in extremely short supply, while in the half-deserted cities – only partly refilled by the zillions of foreign tourists – many shops, restaurants, cinemas, cultural institutions and even hotels simply shut down. If at all possible, avoid travelling in France during August.

Books

There are many excellent histories of France in English. Among the best is Fernand Braudel's two-volume The Identity of France (History & Environment and People & Production). Citizens, a very readable work by Simon Schama, looks at the first few years of the French Revolution. France Today by John Ardagh provides excellent insights into the way French society has evolved since WWII.

Paul Rambali's French Blues is a series of uncompromising yet sympathetic snapshots of modern France, while Paris Notebooks by veteran journalist Mavis Gallant reviews the years 1968 to 1985. Patrick Howarth's When the Riviera Was Ours traces the lives of expatriates who frequented the Mediterranean coast during the two centuries up to WWII. A Year in Provence by Peter Mayle is an irresistible account of country life in southern France. Toujours Provence is its witty sequel.

France has long attracted expatriate writers from the UK, North America and Australasia, many of whom spent at least part of their stay writing in the country. A Moveable Feast by Ernest Hemingway portrays Bohemian life in 1920s Paris. Henry Miller also wrote some pretty dramatic stuff set in the French capital of the 1930s, including Tropic of Cancer and Tropic of Capricorn. Gertrude Stein's The Autobiography of Alice B Toklas is an entertaining account of Paris' literary and artistic circles from WWI to the mid-1930s, featuring such figures as Picasso, Matisse and Apollinaire.

Travel Guides Lonely Planet's France – a travel survival kit by Steve Fallon & Daniel Robinson is a comprehensive guide to France and includes chapters on Andorra and Monaco.

Michelin's hardcover Guide Rouge (red guide) to France, published annually, has more than 1200 pages of maps and practical travel information (hotels, restaurants, garages for car repairs, etc) for every corner of the country, but it's best known for rating France's greatest restaurants with one, two or three stars. Michelin's green guides, covering France in 24 regional volumes (10 of which are available in English), are full of generally interesting historical information, though the prose can hardly be called lively. The green guide to all of France, with brief entries on the most touristed sights, is also available in English.

Maps

For driving, the best road map is Michelin's Motoring Atlas France, which covers the whole country in 1:200,000 scale (1 cm = 2 km). If you'll only be in one or several regions of France, you might prefer to use Michelin's yellow-jacketed 1:200,000 scale sheet maps.

Éditions Didier & Richard's series of 1:50,000 scale trail maps are adequate for most hiking and cycling excursions. The Institut Géographique National (IGN) publishes maps of France in both 1:50,000 and 1:25,000 scale. Topoguides are little booklets for hikers that include trail maps and information (in French) on trail conditions, flora, fauna, villages en route etc.

Abbreviations commonly used on city maps include: *R* for *rue* (street); *Boul* or *Bd* for boulevard; *Av* for avenue; *Q* for *quai* (quay); *C* or *Cr* for *cours* (avenue); *Pl* for *place* (square); *Pte* for *porte* (gate); *Imp* for *impasse* (dead-end street); and *St* and *Ste* for saint (masculine and feminine, respectively). The street numbers 14bis (14 twice) or 92ter (92 thrice) are the equivalent of 14A or 92B.

What to Bring

English-language books, including used ones, cost about 50% more in France than in the UK (double North American prices), so voracious readers might want to bring along a supply. A pocketknife (penknife) and eating utensils are invaluable for picnicking. Bikini tops are not used much in France; you might leave them at home! And, of course, bring as much money as you can afford – France can be an expensive (and a very tempting) place to visit.

SUGGESTED ITINERARIES

Depending on the length of your stay, you might want to consider the following options:

Two days
    Paris – the most beautiful city in the world.
One week
    Paris plus a nearby area, such as the Loire Valley, Champagne, Alsace or Normandy.
Two weeks
    As above, plus one area in the west or south, such as Brittany, the Alps or Provence.
One month
    As above, but spending more time in each place and visiting more of the west or south – Brittany, say, or the Côte d'Azur.
Two months
    In summer, hiking in the Pyrenees or Alps; hanging out at one of the beach areas on the English Channel, Atlantic coast or the Mediterranean; spending some time in more remote areas (eg the Basque Country or Corsica).

HIGHLIGHTS
Beaches

The Côte d'Azur – the French Riviera – has some of the best known beaches in the world, but you'll also find lovely beaches further west

on the Mediterranean coast as well as on Corsica, along the Atlantic coast (eg at Biarritz) and even along the English Channel (eg Dinard).

Museums

Every city and town in France has at least one museum, but a good number of the country's most exceptional ones are in Paris. In addition to the rather overwhelming Louvre, Parisian museums not to be missed include the Musée d'Orsay (late 19th and early 20th-century art), the Pompidou Centre (modern and contemporary art), the Musée Rodin, and the Musée National du Moyen Age (Museum of the Middle Ages) at the Hôtel de Cluny. Other cities known for their museums include Nice, Bordeaux, Strasbourg and Lyon.

Chateaux

The royal palace at Versailles is the largest and most grandiose of the hundreds of chateaux located all over the country. Many of the most impressive ones, including Chambord, Cheverny, Chenonceau and Azay-le-Rideau, are in the Loire Valley around Blois and Tours.

Cathedrals

The cathedrals at Chartres, Strasbourg and Rouen are among the most beautiful in France.

TOURIST OFFICES
Local Tourist Offices

Virtually every French city, town and one-chateau village has some sort of tourist office. See Information under each town or city for details.

Tourist Offices Abroad

French Government Tourist Offices are located in the following countries and can provide brochures and tourist information.

Australia
    BNP Building, 12 Castlereagh St, Sydney, NSW 2000 (☎ 02-9231 5244; fax 02-9221 8682)
Canada
    30 Saint Patrick St, suite 700, Toronto, Ontario M5T 3A3 (☎ 416-593 4723; fax 416-979 7587)
UK
    178 Piccadilly, London W1V OAL (☎ 0891-244 123; fax 0171-493 6594)
USA
    444 Madison Ave, New York, NY 10020-2452 (☎ 212-838-7800; fax 212-838-7855)

FRANCE

VISAS & EMBASSIES

Citizens of the USA, Canada, most European countries and a handful of other nations can enter France for up to three months without a visa. Australians, however, must have visas to visit France, even as tourists. The usual length of a tourist visa is three months.

If you plan to stay in France for over three months to study or work, apply to the French consulate nearest where you live for the appropriate sort of long-stay visa. If you're not an EU citizen, it is extremely difficult to get a work visa; one of the few exceptions is the provision that people with student visas can apply for permission to work part-time. For any sort of long-stay visa, begin the paperwork several months before you leave home. By law, everyone in France, including tourists, must carry identification with them. For visitors, this means a passport. A national identity card is sufficient for EU citizens.

Visa Extensions

Tourist visas *cannot* be extended. If you qualify for an automatic three-month stay upon arrival, you'll get another three months if you exit and then re-enter France. The fewer French entry stamps you have in your passport, the easier this is likely to be.

French Embassies Abroad

Australia
  6 Perth Ave, Yarralumla, ACT 2600 (☎ 06-270 5111)
Canada
  42 Sussex Drive, Ottawa, Ontario K1M 2 C9 (☎ 613-789 1795)
Germany
  Kappellenweg 1A, 5300 Bonn 2 (☎ 228-35 18 32)
Italy
  consulate: Via Giulia 251, 00186 Rome (☎ 06-68 80 64 37)
New Zealand
  Robert Jones House, 1-3 Willeston St (PO Box 1695), Wellington (☎ 04-472 0200)
Spain
  consulate: Calle Marques de la Enseñada 10, 28004 Madrid (☎ 91-319 7188)
UK
  consulate: 6A Cromwell Place, London SW7 (☎ 0171-838 2051; 0891-887733 for general information on visa requirements)
USA
  4101 Reservoir Rd, NW Washington, DC, 20007-2185 (☎ 202-944 6195)

Foreign Embassies in Paris

Australia
  4 Rue Jean Rey, 15e; metro Bir Hakeim (☎ 01 40 59 33 00)
Canada
  35 Ave Montaigne, 8e; metro Alma Marceau or Franklin D Roosevelt (☎ 01 44 43 29 00)
New Zealand
  7ter Rue Léonard de Vinci, 16e; metro Victor Hugo (☎ 01 45 00 24 11)
Spain
  consulate: 165 Blvd Malesherbes, 17e; metro Wagram (01 47 66 03 32)
UK
  Embassy: 35 Rue du Faubourg Saint Honoré, 8e; metro Concorde (☎ 01 42 66 91 42)
  consulate: 16 Rue d'Anjou, 8e; metro Concorde (☎ 01 42 66 38 10)
USA
  2 Ave Gabriel, 8e; metro Concorde (☎ 01 43 12 22 22)

MONEY

Generally you'll get a better exchange rate for travellers' cheques than for cash. The most useful travellers' cheques are those issued by American Express in US dollars or French francs, which can be exchanged at many post offices.

Do not bring travellers' cheques in Australian dollars as they are hard to change, especially outside Paris. US$100 dollar bills are also difficult to change because there are so many counterfeits around; many Banque de France branches refuse them.

Visa (Carte Bleue in France) is more widely accepted than MasterCard (Eurocard). Visa card-holders with a 'PIN' number can get cash advances from banks and automatic teller machines nationwide – even in remote Corsican towns. American Express cards are not very useful except to get cash at American Express offices in big cities or to pay for things in up-market shops and restaurants. To have money sent from abroad, have it wired to either Citicorp's Paris office (see Money in the Paris section) or to a specific branch of a French or foreign bank. You can also have money easily sent via American Express.

Currency

One French franc (FF) equals 100 centimes. French coins come in denominations of five, 10 and 20 centimes and half, one, two, five, 10 and 20FF (the last two are two-tone). Banknotes are issued in denominations of 20, 50,

00, 200 and 500FF. The higher the denomination, the larger the bill. It can be difficult to get change for a 500FF bill.

Exchange Rates

Australia	A$1	=	3.93FF
Canada	C$1	=	3.66FF
Germany	DM1	=	3.39FF
Japan	¥100	=	4.64FF
New Zealand	NZ$1	=	3.50FF
Spain	100 ptas	=	3.99FF
United Kingdom	UK£1	=	7.81FF
United States	US$1	=	5.02FF

Banque de France, France's central bank, offers the best exchange rates, especially for travellers' cheques, and it does not charge any commission (except 1% for travellers' cheques in French francs). There are Banque de France bureaus in the prefectures of each department.

Many post offices make exchange transactions at a very good rate. They accept banknotes in a variety of currencies as well as American Express travellers' cheques, but *only* if the cheques are in US dollars or French francs.

In large cities, *bureaux de change* (currency exchange offices) are faster, easier, have longer opening hours and often give better rates than the banks, but are not beyond milking clueless tourists. As always, your best bet is to compare the rates offered by various banks, which charge at least 20 to 30FF per transaction, and exchange bureaus, which are not allowed to charge commission.

If your American Express travellers' cheques or credit card are lost or stolen, call ☎ 08 00 90 86 00, American Express' 24-hour toll-free number in France. For lost or stolen Visa cards, call ☎ 01 42 77 11 90.

Costs

If you stay in hostels (or, if there are two or more of you, the cheapest hotels) and buy provisions from grocery stores rather than eating at restaurants, it is possible to tour France on as little as US$35 a day per person (US$45 in Paris). Eating out, lots of travel or treating yourself to France's many little luxuries can increase this figure dramatically. A student card can significantly reduce the price of getting into museums and other sights,

cinemas etc. Always check to see if you qualify for the *tarif réduit* (reduced price), as the rules vary tremendously.

Tipping

It is not necessary to leave a tip *(pourboire)* in restaurants, hotels etc; under French law, the bill must already include a 15% service charge. Some people leave a few francs on the table for the waiter, but this is not expected (especially for drinks). At truly posh restaurants, however, a more generous gratuity will be anticipated. For a taxi ride, the usual tip is about 2 or 3FF no matter what the fare.

Consumer Taxes

France's VAT (value-added tax, ie sales tax) is known in French as TVA *(taxe sur la valeur ajoutée)*. The TVA is 20.6% on the purchase price of most goods (and for noncommercial vehicle rental). Prices that include TVA are often marked TTC *(toutes taxes comprises)*, which means 'all taxes included'.

It is possible (though rather complicated) to get a reimbursement for TVA if you meet several conditions: 1) You are not an EU national and are over 15 years of age; 2) you have stayed in France less than six months; 3) you are buying more than 2000FF worth of goods at a single shop (not including foodstuffs); and 4) the establishment offers duty-free sales *(vente en détaxe)*.

To claim a TVA, you fill out the proper export sales invoice *(bordereau de vente)* at the time you make your purchase. This is then stamped at your port of exit, thereby proving that you have taken the goods out of the country. The shop then reimburses you – by mail or bank transfer within 30 days – for the TVA you've paid.

POST & COMMUNICATIONS
Post
Postal Rates Postal services in France are fast, reliable and expensive. Postcards and letters up to 20g cost 3FF within the EU, 4.40FF to the USA and Canada and 5.20FF to Australasia. Aerograms cost 5.10FF to all destinations. All overseas packages are now sent by air only, which is very expensive.

Receiving Mail All mail to France *must* include the area's five-digit postcode, which begins with the two-digit number of the department. In Paris, all postcodes begin with 750 and end with the arrondissement number, eg 75004 for the 4th arrondissement, 75013 for the 13th. The local postcode appears in each destination in this book under Information or Post.

Since poste restante mail is held alphabetically by family name, it is important that you follow the French practice of having your last name written in capital letters. Poste restante mail not sent to a particular branch post office ends up at the town's main post office *(recette principale)*. In Paris, this means it goes to the central post office (☎ 01 40 28 20 00) at 48-52 Rue du Louvre (1er; metro Sentier or Les Halles). See Post in the Paris section for details. There is a 2.80FF charge for every poste restante claimed.

It is also possible to receive mail care of American Express offices, although if you do not have an American Express card or travellers' cheques there is a 5FF charge each time you check to see if you have received any mail.

Telephone

Once saddled with one of the worst telephone systems in Western Europe, over the last two decades France has leapfrogged into the era of high-tech telecommunications. Today, you can dial direct to almost anywhere in the world from any phone in France. The Minitel system, which gives online access to computer data bases, allows you to look up phone numbers throughout France and to make air, rail and concert reservations as well as access a wide range of data bases and services. Minitel is available in most major post offices.

Public Telephones Most public phones in France now require phonecards *(télécartes)*, which are sold at post offices, tobacconists' shops *(tabacs)*, Paris metro ticket counters and supermarket check-out counters. Cards with 50/120 units cost 40.60/97.50FF. Each unit is good for one three-minute local call. Rates for calls abroad vary according to the time of day, so you will need to ask the French operator (see International Dialling below). To make a call with a phonecard, pick up the receiver, insert

the card and dial when the LCD screen reads 'Numérotez'.

All telephone cabins can take incoming calls, so if you want someone to call you back, give them the new 10-digit number (see Domestic Dialling below) written after the words *'ici le'* on the information sheet next to the phone.

Domestic Dialling In October 1996, the old system of dialling ☎ 16 to the provinces and ☎ 1 to Paris was abolished. France is now divided into five telephone zones and all telephone numbers, no matter what number you are calling or where you are calling from, are 10-digit rather than eight-digit.

Paris and Île de France numbers now begin with ☎ 01. The other codes are: ☎ 02 for areas in the north-west; ☎ 03 for the north-east; ☎ 04 for the south-east; and ☎ 05 for the south-west

Toll-free numbers *(numéros verts)* now begin with ☎ 0800 instead of ☎ 05. Two-digit emergency numbers have not changed. For directory assistance *(service des renseignements)*, dial ☎ 12.

International Dialling To call France from abroad, first dial the international access code then ☎ 33 (France's country code), but omit the 0 at the beginning of the new 10-digit number (see Domestic Dialling above).

Direct-dial calls to almost anywhere in the world can be placed using a phonecard. Just dial ☎ 00, wait for the second tone, and then add the country code, area code and local number. If the country code is not on the information sheet posted in phone cabins, consult a phone book or dial ☎ 12 (directory assistance).

To make a reverse-charge call *(en PCV)* or person-to-person *(avec préavis)* from France to other countries, dial ☎ 00 (the international operator), wait for the second tone and then dial ☎ 33 plus the country code of the place you're calling. If you're using a public phone you must insert a phonecard (or, in the case of coin telephones, deposit 1FF) first.

For directory enquiries outside France, dial ☎ 00, and when the second tone sounds, dial ☎ 33, then ☎ 12, and finally the country code. For information on home-country direct calls, see the Telephones Appendix in the back of this book.

Fax & Telegram
Virtually all French post offices can send and receive domestic and international faxes (*télécopies* or *téléfaxes*), telexes and telegrams. It costs around 20FF to send a one-page fax within France, 45FF to the USA and 60FF to Australia.

NEWSPAPERS & MAGAZINES
The excellent *International Herald Tribune*, published six times a week and distributed around the globe, is edited in Paris. It is sold at many news kiosks throughout France for 10FF. Other English-language papers you can find include two British papers with European editions, the *Guardian* and the *Financial Times*; *The European*; and the colourful *USA Today*. *Newsweek*, *Time* and the *Economist* are also widely available.

RADIO & TV
The BBC World Service can be picked up on 195 kHz AM and 6195 kHz, 9410 kHz, 9760 kHz and 12095 kHz short wave. In northern France, BBC for Europe is on 648 kHz AM. Up-market hotels often offer cable TV access to CNN, BBC TV and other networks. Canal+ (pronounced 'ka-NAHL pluce'), a French subscription TV station available in many mid-range hotels, sometimes screens non-dubbed English movies.

PHOTOGRAPHY & VIDEO
Be prepared to have your camera and film forced through the ostensibly film-safe x-ray machines at airports and when entering sensitive public buildings such as any Palais de Justice (Law Courts) or Banque de France branch. The most you can do is ask that they hand-check your film, if not your whole camera.

Unlike the rest of Western Europe and Australia, which use PAL (phase alternation line), French TV broadcasts are in SECAM (*système électronique couleur avec mémoire*). North America and Japan use a third incompatible system, NTSC (National Television Systems Committee). French videotapes cannot be played on video cassette recorders or TVs that are not equipped with SECAM.

TIME
France is one hour ahead of GMT/UTC in winter and two hours ahead in summer. The 24-hour clock is widely used in France – even informally. Thus 14.30 (or 14h30) is 2.30 pm, 00.15 (00h15) is 12.15 am and so on.

ELECTRICITY
The electric current in France is 220V, 50 Hz. Plugs have two round pins.

WEIGHTS & MEASURES
France uses the metric system, which was invented by the French Academy of Sciences and adopted by the French government in 1795. For a chart of metric equivalents, see the inside back cover of this guide.

LAUNDRY
To find a self-service laundrette (*laverie libre service*), ask at the front desk of your hotel or hostel. Be prepared to pay about 22FF per load and around 2FF for six minutes of drying and a cup of washing powder (*lessive*). Bring lots of coins; few laundrettes have change machines.

TOILETS
Public toilets, signposted as *toilettes* or *wc*, are few and far between, though small towns often have them near the town hall (*mairie*). In Paris, you're more likely to come upon one of the tan, self-disinfecting toilet pods. Get your change ready: many public toilets cost 2FF or even 2.50FF. In the absence of public amenities, you can try ducking into a fast-food outlet or department store. Except in the most tourist-filled areas, café owners are usually amenable to your using their toilets provided you ask politely (and with just a hint of urgency).

HEALTH
Public Health System
France has an extensive public health care system. Anyone who is sick can receive treatment in the emergency room (*service des urgences*) of any public hospital. Such treatment costs much less in France than in many other countries, especially the USA. Hospitals usually ask that foreigners settle their account right after receiving treatment.

Condoms
Many pharmacies have 24-hour automatic condom (*préservatif*) dispensers near the door.

Some brasseries and discothèques also have condom-vending machines.

WOMEN TRAVELLERS

In general, women need not walk around in fear of passers-by – women are rarely physically attacked on the street. However, you are more likely to be left alone if you have about you a purposeful air that implies that you know exactly where you're going – even if you haven't a clue!

If you are subject to catcalls or are hassled in any way while walking down the street, the best strategy is usually to carry on and ignore the macho lowlife who is disrupting your holiday. Making a cutting retort is ineffective in English and risky in French if your slang isn't extremely proficient.

France's national rape crisis hotline, which is run by a women's organisation called Viols Femmes Informations, can be reached toll-free by dialling ☎ 0800 05 95 95. It is staffed by volunteers Monday to Friday from 10 am to 6 pm.

GAY & LESBIAN TRAVELLERS

Most of France's major gay organisations are based in Paris. Centre Gai et Lesbien (CGL; ☎ 01 43 57 21 47), 3 Rue Keller (11e; metro Ledru Rollin) 500 metres east of Place de la Bastille, serves as a headquarters for lots of organisations that hold a variety of meetings and activities each week. The bar, library etc are open Monday to Saturday from 2 to 8 pm; the Sunday activities (2 to 7 pm) are mainly for people who are HIV positive.

Archives Lesbiennes (☎ 01 43 56 11 49) holds meetings on the ground floor of the Maison des Femmes (☎ 01 43 48 24 91) at 8 Cité Prost (11e; metro Charonne) every Friday from 7 to 10 pm. Écoute Gaie runs a hotline (☎ 01 44 93 01 02) for gays and lesbians that's staffed on weekdays from 6 to 10 pm.

Gay male-oriented publications include *Illico*, published at the beginning of each month, with articles (in French) and lots of ads for places that cater to gays, and the monthly *Double Face*, which has fewer articles and more information on nightlife. For lesbians, the monthly national magazine *Lesbia* gives a rundown of what's happening around the country.

DISABLED TRAVELLERS

France is not particularly well equipped for disabled people *(handicapés)*: kerb ramps are few and far between, older public facilities and bottom-end hotels often lack lifts, and the Paris metro, most of it built decades ago, is hopeless. But physically disabled people who would like to travel in France can overcome these problems. For instance, most hotels with two or more stars are equipped with lifts, and Michelin's *Guide Rouge* indicates hotels with lifts and facilities for disabled people.

Hostels in Paris that cater to disabled travellers include the Foyer International d'Accueil de Paris Jean Monnet and the Centre International de Séjour de Paris Kellermann (see Hostels & Foyers under Places to Stay in the Paris section).

The Comité National Français de Liaison pour la Réadaptation des Handicapés (☎ 01 53 80 66 66), at 236 Rue de Tolbiac (13e; metro Glacière) in Paris, can provide information or accommodation, sports and leisure pursuits, transport and access to tourist sites throughout France. The Association des Paralysés de France (☎ 01 40 78 69 00), at 17 Blvd Auguste Blanqui (13e; metro Porte d'Italie), may be able to help with specific enquiries and can supply the addresses of branches across France.

SENIOR TRAVELLERS

People aged over 60 are eligible for a reduction of up to 50% on 1st and 2nd-class train travel with a Carte Vermeil Plein Temps. It cost 270FF and is valid in 21 European countries for one year (see Train in the Getting Around section). Entry to most museums and monuments in France is half price for people over 60 – always check the tariff rules to see if you are eligible for a reduction. Senior citizens are usually offered a reduction on cinema tickets during the week. Some hostels, particularly in Paris, only offer accommodation to 'young' people; again, check the rules if you're thinking of hostelling.

DANGERS & ANNOYANCES

The biggest crime problem for tourists in France is theft – especially of and from cars. Never, *ever* leave anything in a parked motor vehicle or you'll learn the hard way. Pickpockets are a problem, and women are a common target because of their handbags. Be especially careful at airports and on crowded public transport in cities.

France's laws regarding even small quantities of drugs are very strict. Thanks to the Napoleonic Code, the police have the right to search anyone they want at any time, whether or not there is probable cause, and they have been known to stop and search charter buses coming from Amsterdam.

If stopped by the police for any reason, your best course of action is to be polite and to remain calm. It is a very bad idea to be overly assertive, and being rude or disrespectful is asking for serious trouble. Emergency telephone numbers in use all over France include:

Ambulance (SAMU)	☎ 15
Fire Brigade	☎ 18
Police	☎ 17

The rise in support for the extreme right-wing National Front in recent years reflects the growing racial intolerance in France, particularly against Muslim North Africans and, to a lesser extent, blacks from sub-Saharan Africa and France's former territories in the Caribbean. In many parts of France, especially in the south (eg Provence and the Côte d'Azur), entertainment places such as bars and discos are, for all intents and purposes, segregated: owners and their ferocious-looking bouncers make it quite clear who is 'invited' to use their public facilities and who is not.

BUSINESS HOURS

Most museums are closed on either Monday or Tuesday and on public holidays (jours fériés), though during the summer some stay open seven days a week. Most small businesses are open from 9 or 10 am to 6.30 or 7 pm daily except Sunday and perhaps Monday, with a break between noon and 2 pm or 1 and 3 pm. In the south, midday closures are more like siestas and may continue until 3.30 or even 4 pm.

Many food shops are open daily except Sunday afternoon and Monday. As a result, Sunday morning may be your last chance to stock up on provisions until Tuesday. Most restaurants are open only for lunch (noon to 2 or 3 pm) and dinner (6.30 to about 10 or 11 pm); outside Paris, very few serve meals throughout

the day. All are closed at least one full day per week and sometimes a lunchtime as well. In August, lots of establishments simply close so that their owners and employees alike can take their annual month-long holiday. With most museums and other sights closed at midday and lunch menus cheaper than dinner ones, it pays to take your main meal at lunch and picnic at night.

Banque de France branches throughout France are open Monday to Friday from around 8.45 am to 12.15 pm and 1.30 to 3.30 pm. The opening hours of other banks vary. The main post office in towns and cities, and all branches in Paris, are open weekdays from 8 am to 6.30 or 7 pm and on Saturday to noon. Branches outside Paris are generally open from 8.30 am to noon and 1.30 or 2 to 5.30 or 6.30 pm weekdays and on Saturday morning.

PUBLIC HOLIDAYS & SPECIAL EVENTS

National public holidays in France include New Year's Day, Easter Sunday & Monday, May Day (1 May), 1945 Victory Day (8 May), Ascension Thursday (40th day after Easter), Pentecost Sunday and Whit Monday (seventh Sunday and Monday after Easter), Bastille Day (14 July), Assumption Day (15 August), All Saints' Day (1 November), 1918 Armistice Day (11 November) and Christmas Day.

Most French cities have at least one major cultural festival each year. For details about what's on and when (dates change from year to year), contact the main tourist office in Paris or a French Government Tourist Office abroad.

ACTIVITIES

Skiing
The French Alps have some of the finest skiing in Europe. Smaller, low-altitude stations are much cheaper than their classier, high-altitude cousins. There are quite a few low-altitude ski stations in the Pyrenees.

Surfing
The best surfing in France (and some of the best in all of Europe) is on the Atlantic coast around Biarritz.

Hiking
France has thousands of km of hiking trails in every region of the country and through every kind of terrain. These include *sentiers de*

FRANCE

grande randonnée, long-distance hiking paths whose alphanumeric names begin with the letters GR and are sometimes hundreds of km long (as in Corsica).

Canoeing

The Fédération Française de Canoë-Kayak (☎ 01 45 11 08 50) at 87 Quai de la Marne, 94340 Joinville-le-Pont, can supply information on canoeing and kayaking clubs around the country. The sports are very popular in the Périgord (Dordogne) area. See Getting Around for information about houseboats and canal boats.

COURSES

For details on language and cooking courses, see Courses in the Paris section. For water sports courses see Courses in Bayonne.

Information on studying in France is available from French consulates and French Government Tourist Offices abroad. In Paris, the Centre Régional des Œuvres Universitaires et Scolaires (CROUS; ☎ 01 40 51 37 10), 39 Ave Georges Bernanos (5e; metro Port Royal), provides information on matters of interest to students.

WORK

Getting a *carte de séjour* (temporary residence permit), which in most cases lets you work in France, is almost automatic for EU citizens; contact the Préfecture de Police in Paris or, in the provinces, the *mairie* (town hall) or nearest prefecture. For anyone else, it is almost impossible, though the government does seem to tolerate undocumented workers helping out with some agricultural work, especially the apple and grape harvests in autumn. It's hard work and you are usually put up in barracks, but it's paid.

Working as an au pair – a kind of mother's helper – is very common in France, especially in Paris. Single young people – particularly women – receive board, lodging and a bit of money (500FF per week is the going rate) in exchange for taking care of the kids and doing light housework. Knowing at least a bit of French may be a prerequisite. Even US and other non-EU citizens can become au pairs, but they must be studying something (eg a recognised language course) and have to apply

for an au pair's visa three months *before* leaving home.

For information on au pair placement contact a French consulate or the Paris touri[st] office. Most private agencies charge the au pai[r] 600 to 800FF and collect an additional fee fro[m] the family. Some agencies check the famil[y] and the living conditions they are offering[;] others are less thorough. In any case, be asser[t]ive in dealing with the agency to make sure yo[u] get what you want.

ACCOMMODATION

More and more cities and towns in France ar[e] instituting a *taxe de séjour*, which is a tax o[n] each night you stay in a hotel and sometime[s] even hostels or camping grounds. In Paris, th[e] tax ranges from 1 to 7FF per person per nig[ht] but is usually included in the quoted price.

Camping

France has thousands of seasonal and yea[r-] round camping grounds, many of which ar[e] situated near streams, rivers, lakes or th[e] ocean. Facilities and amenities, which ar[e] reflected in the number of stars the site ha[s] been awarded, determine the price. At the les[s] fancy places, two people with a small te[nt] should expect to pay 25 to 55FF a nigh[t.] Another option in some rural areas is far[m] camping *(camping à la ferme)*. Tourist office[s] will have details.

Camping grounds near cities and tow[ns] covered in this guide are detailed under Place[s] to Stay for each city or town. For informatio[n] on other camping grounds, enquire at a touri[st] office or consult the *Guide Officiel Camping[-] Caravaning* or Michelin's *Camping/Caravan[-] ing France*. Both are updated annually.

Campers who arrive at a camping groun[d] without a vehicle can usually get a spot, eve[n] late in the day, but not in July and especiall[y] not in August, when most are packed wi[th] families on their annual holiday.

If you'll be doing overnight backpackin[g,] remember that in national and regional park[s] camping is permitted only in proper campin[g] grounds. Camping elsewhere, eg in a road o[r] trailside meadow *(camping sauvage)*, is tole[r-] ated to varying degrees (but not at all i[n] Corsica); you probably won't have any prob[-] lems with the police if you're not on priva[te] land, have only a small tent, are discreet, sta[y] only one night and are at least 1500 metres from a camping ground.

Refuges & Gîtes d'Étape

Refuges (mountain huts or shelters) are basic dorm rooms operated by national park authorities, the Club Alpin Français and other private organisations along trails in uninhabited mountainous areas frequented by hikers and mountain climbers. They are marked on hiking and climbing maps. Some are open all year, others only during the warm months.

In general, refuges are equipped with mattresses and blankets but not sheets, which you have to bring yourself. Charges average 50 to 70FF per night per person. Meals, prepared by the *gardien* (attendant), are sometimes available. Most refuges are equipped with a telephone, so it's a good idea to call ahead and make a reservation. For details on refuges, contact a tourist office near where you'll be hiking.

Gîtes d'étape, which are usually better equipped and more comfortable than refuges (some even have showers), are found in less remote areas, often in villages. They also cost around 50 to 70FF per person. *Les Gîtes d'Étape* published annually by Fivedit covers the whole of France and should be available in bookshops or at newsstands.

Hostels

In the provinces, hostels *(auberges de jeunesse)* generally charge from 45FF (for out-of-the-way places with basic facilities) to 70FF for a bunk in a single-sex dorm room. A few of the more comfortable places that aren't officially auberges de jeunesse charge from 70 to 90FF, usually including breakfast. In Paris, expect to pay 95 to 120FF a night, including breakfast. In the cities, especially Paris, you will also find *foyers*, student dorms used by travellers in summer. Information on hostels and foyers is available from tourist offices. Most of France's hostels belong to one of three Paris-based organisations:

Fédération Unie des Auberges de Jeunesse (FUAJ)
    27 Rue Pajol, 18e; metro La Chapelle (☎ 01 44 89 87 27; fax 01 44 89 87 10). FUAJ has 190 hostels in France and is the only group affiliated with Hostelling International (HI).

Ligue Française pour les Auberges de la Jeunesse (LFAJ)
    38 Blvd Raspail, 7e; metro Sèvres Babylone (☎ 01 45 48 69 84; fax 01 45 44 57 47)
Union des Centres de Rencontres Internationales de France (UCRIF)
    27 Rue de Turbigo, 2e; metro Étienne Marcel (☎ 01 40 26 57 64; fax 01 40 26 58 20)

Cheap Hotels

Staying in an inexpensive hotel often costs less than a hostel when two or more people share a room. Unless otherwise indicated, prices quoted in this chapter refer to rooms in unrated or one-star hotels equipped with a washbasin (and usually a bidet, too) but without a toilet or shower. Most doubles, which generally cost the same or only marginally more than singles, have only one bed. Doubles with two beds usually cost a little more. Taking a shower *(douche)* in the hall bathroom can be free or cost between 10 and 25FF.

Reservations If you'll be arriving after noon (or after 10 am during peak tourism periods), it is a good idea to call ahead and make reservations; it will save you a lot of time and hassle in the long run. For advance reservations, most hotels require that you send them a deposit by post. But if you call on the day you'll be coming and sound credible, many hotels will hold a room for you until a set hour (rarely later than 6 or 7 pm). At small hotels, reception is usually closed on Sunday morning or afternoon. Local tourist offices will also make reservations for you, usually for a small fee.

FOOD

A fully fledged traditional French dinner – usually begun about 8.30 pm – has quite a few distinct courses: an apéritif or cocktail; a first course *(entrée)*; the main course *(plat principal)*; salad *(salade)*; cheese *(fromage)*; dessert *(dessert)*; fruit *(fruit)*; coffee *(café)*; and a *digestif*.

France has lots of restaurants where several hundred francs gets you excellent French cuisine, but inexpensive French restaurants are in short supply. Fortunately, delicious and surprisingly cheap ethnic cuisine is available from the many restaurants specialising in dishes from France's former colonies in Africa, Indochina, India, the Caribbean and the South Pacific. One of the most delicious of the North African dishes is *couscous*, steamed semolina eaten with vegetables and some sort of meat: lamb shish kebab, *merguez* (North African sausage), *mechoui* (lamb on the bone) or chicken.

Restaurants & Brasseries

There are two principal differences between restaurants and brasseries: restaurants usually specialise in a particular cuisine while brasseries – which look very much like cafés – serve quicker meals of more standard fare (eg steak and chips/French fries, omelettes etc). Restaurants are usually open only for lunch and dinner; brasseries, on the other hand, serve meals (or at least something solid) throughout the day.

Most restaurants offer at least one fixed-price, multicourse meal known in French as a *menu*, *menu à prix fixe* or *menu du jour*. In general, menus cost much less than ordering each dish separately (*à la carte*), but some may be only available at lunch. When you order the menu, you usually get to choose a first course, a main meat or fish dish and a cheese or dessert course. A *formule* usually allows you to choose two of the three courses. Drinks (*boissons*) cost extra unless the menu says *boisson comprise* (drink included), which usually means a quarter litre of wine.

Cafés

Sitting in a café to read, write or talk with friends is an integral part of everyday life in France. People use cafés as a way to keep in touch with their neighbourhood and friends, and to generally participate in the social life of their town or city.

A café located on a grand boulevard (such as Blvd du Montparnasse or the Champs Élysées in Paris) will charge considerably more than a place that fronts a side street. Once inside, progressively more expensive tariffs apply at the counter (*comptoir*), in the café itself (*salle*) and outside on the *terrasse*. The price of drinks goes up at night, usually after 8 pm, but the price of a cup of coffee (or anything else) earns you the right to sit for as long as you like.

Self-Catering

France is justly renowned for its extraordinary chefs and restaurants, but one of the country's premier culinary delights – especially for vegetarians, who will find France's restaurants obsessed with meat and seafood – is to stock up on fresh breads, cheeses, fruit, vegetables, prepared dishes etc and have a picnic. Although prices are likely to be much higher than you're used to, you will find that the food is of excellent quality.

While supermarkets (*supermarchés*) and slightly more expensive grocery shops (*épiceries*) are more and more popular with working people in cities, many people still buy their food from small neighbourhood shops, each with its own speciality. The whole setup is geared towards people buying fresh food each day, so it's completely acceptable to purchase very small quantities – a few slices (*tranches*) of sliced meat or a few hundred grams of salad.

Fresh *baguettes* and other breads are baked and sold at a *boulangerie*. They may also sell sandwiches, quiches and small (very ordinary) pizzas. Mouthwatering pastries are available from a *pâtisserie*. For chocolate and sweets look for a *confiserie*. (These three shops are often combined.) For a selection of superb cheeses, such as *chèvre* (goat's-milk cheese) and a half-round of perfectly ripe Camembert go to a *fromagerie* (also called a *crémerie*). Fruit and vegetables are sold by a *marchand de legumes et de fruits*. Wine is sold by a *marchand de vin*.

A general butcher is a *boucherie*, but for specialised poultry you have to go to a *marchand de volaille*, and a *boucherie chevaline* will sell you horsemeat, still popular in France all these years after the war. Fish is available from a *poissonnerie*. A *charcuterie* is a delicatessen offering pricey but delicious sliced meats, seafood salads, pâtés and ready-to-eat main dishes. Most supermarkets have a charcuterie counter. The word *traiteur* (caterer) means the establishment sells ready-to-eat takeaway dishes.

In most towns and cities, most foods are available one or more days a week at open-air markets (*marchés découverts*) or their covered equivalents (*marchés couverts* or *halles*).

DRINKS
Nonalcoholic Drinks

There is no medical reason to buy expensive bottled water; the tap water in France is perfectly safe. Make sure you ask for *une carafe d'eau* (a jug of water) or *de l'eau du robinet* (tap water) or you may get costly mineral water *(eau de source)*.

A small cup of espresso is called *un café, un café noir* or *un express*. You can also ask for a large *(grand)* version. *Un café crème* is espresso with steamed cream. *Un café au lait* is espresso served in a large cup with lots of steamed milk. Decaffeinated coffee is *un café décaféiné* or simply *un déca*.

Other hot drinks that are popular include: tea *(thé)*, but if you want milk you ask for *'un peu de lait frais'*; herbal tea *(tisane)*; and usually excellent hot chocolate *(chocolat chaud)*.

Alcohol

The French almost always take their meals with wine – red *(rouge)*, white *(blanc)* or rosé, chosen to complement what's being eaten. The least expensive wines cost less per litre than soft drinks. Wines that meet stringent regulations governing where, how and under what conditions the grapes are grown, fermented and bottled, bear the abbreviation AOC *(Appellation d'Origine Contrôlée,* which means 'mark of controlled place of origin'). The cheapest wines have no AOC certification and are known as *vins ordinaires* or *vins de table* (table wines). They sell for as little as 5FF a litre in wine-producing areas and closer to 10 or 12FF a litre in supermarkets, but spending an extra 5 or 10FF per bottle can make all the difference.

Alcoholic drinks other than wine include apéritifs, such as *kir* (dry white wine sweetened with *cassis* – blackcurrant liqueur), *kir royale* (champagne with cassis), and *pastis* (anise-flavoured alcohol drunk with ice and water); and *digestifs* such as brandy or Calvados (apple brandy). Beer is usually either from Alsace or imported. A *demi* (about 250 ml) is cheaper on draught *(à la pression)* than from a bottle.

ENTERTAINMENT

If you don't fancy seeing your favourite actors lip-synching in French, look in the film listings and on the theatre marquee for the letters 'VO' *(version originale)* or 'VOST' *(version originale sous-titrée)*, which mean the film retains its original foreign soundtrack but has been given French subtitles. If there's no VO or if you see 'VF' *(version française)*, the film has been dubbed.

THINGS TO BUY

France is renowned for its luxury goods, including *haute couture* fashion, expensive accessories (eg Hermès scarves), perfume and such alcoholic beverages as champagne and brandy. Purchases of over 2000FF by people who live outside the EU are eligible for a rebate of the value added tax (TVA) on most goods. See Consumer Taxes under Money earlier in this section.

Getting There & Away

AIR

Air France and scores of other airlines link Paris with every part of the globe. Other French cities with direct international air links include Nice, Lyon and Marseille. For details on agencies selling discount international tickets in Paris, see Travel Agencies in the Paris section. For information on Paris' two international airports, Orly and Roissy-Charles de Gaulle, see Getting There & Away in the Paris section. Information on how to get from the airports into Paris (and vice versa) is given under Getting Around in the Paris section.

Britain

Return flights between Paris' Charles de Gaulle airport and London start at 611FF (British Midland) to Heathrow and 618FF (British Airways and Air UK) to Gatwick and Stanstead. You must stay over a Saturday night. In Paris contact Nouvelles Frontières (☎ 01 46 34 55 30) at 66 Blvd Saint Michel (6e; metro Luxembourg). SOS Charters (☎ 01 49 59 09 09; recorded message) has information on round-trip packages. On Minitel, key in 3615 SOS Charters.

Elsewhere in Europe

One-way discount charter fares available for flights from Paris start at 580FF to Rome; 920FF to Athens; 730FF to Dublin; 940FF to Istanbul; and 710FF to Madrid. Contact a travel agent or call SOS Charters for more information.

FRANCE

LAND
Britain

The highly civilised Eurostar – the passenger train service through the Channel Tunnel – began operating between Paris' Gare du Nord and London's Waterloo Station in late 1994. The journey takes about three hours (20 minutes through the tunnel) and will be shortened when Britain completes its portion of high-speed track at the end of the decade. The full one-way/return fare between Paris and London is 645/1290FF, but if you travel during the week and spend more than three nights away you can get a return fare for as little as 490FF.

Le Shuttle, which also began operating in 1994, whisks buses and cars (and their passengers) on single and double-deck wagons from near Folkstone to Coquelles just west of Calais in 35 minutes. Actual travel time from *auto-route* (the A26 to/from Paris) to motorway (the M20 to/from London) is closer to an hour, though. One-way fares start at 590FF. Shuttles run round the clock, and no bookings are required.

The Eurostar and Le Shuttle office in Paris (☎ 01 44 51 06 02) is in the Maison de la Grande Bretagne at 19 Rue des Mathurins (9e; metro Havre Caumartin), north-west of Place de l'Opéra. Information is also available on Minitel 3615 SNCF/Le Shuttle.

Elsewhere in Europe

Bus For bus services between France and other parts of Europe, see Getting There & Away in the Paris section.

Train Paris, France's main rail hub, is linked with every part of Europe. Depending on where you're coming from, you may have to transit through Paris to get to the provinces. For details on Paris' six train stations, each of which handles traffic to/from different parts of France and Europe, see Train under Getting There & Away in the Paris section.

BIJ (Billet International Jeunes) tickets, which are available to people under 26, cost about 20% or 25% less than regular tickets on international 2nd-class train travel started during off-peak periods. See Discounts under Train in the following Getting Around section for details. BIJ tickets are not sold at train station ticket windows; you have to go to an office of Transalpino, Frantour Tourisme or Voyages Wasteels. There's usually one in the vicinity of a major train station.

SEA
Britain & the Channel Islands

The hovercraft *(aéroglisseur)* takes 30 minutes to cross the Channel. Hoverspeed (☎ 01 40 25 22 00 in France, 01304-24 0241 in Dover) runs both giant catamarans (SeaCats) and hovercraft from Calais to Dover (Douvres), Boulogne to Dover and Boulogne to Folkstone. Passage costs from 200FF one way, up to 400FF for a five-day return. A small car with four passengers costs at least 525FF return on a SeaCat. Bus-boat combos from Victoria Coach Station in London to 165 Ave de Clichy (17e; RER C Porte de Clichy) take about eight hours and start at 270FF one way. Train-boat combos are sold at train stations. Hoverspeed's Paris office is at 165 Ave de Clichy (17e; RER C Porte de Clichy).

Sealink (☎ 01 44 94 40 40 in Paris, 03 21 34 55 00 in Calais and 01304-20 4204 in Dover), in Paris' Maison de la Grande Bretagne at 19 Rue des Mathurins (9e; metro Havre Caumartin), runs car ferries from Calais to Dover (1½ hours). One-way fares for passengers and cyclists start at 180FF. Cars cost from 400 to 1180FF one way.

Stena Line (☎ 01 53 43 40 00), 38 Ave de l'Opéra (2e; metro Opéra), operates car ferries (from 180FF one way, four hours) and catamarans (from 220FF, two hours) from Dieppe to Newhaven; and ferries from Cherbourg to Southampton (180 to 390FF one way, six/eight hours during the day/night).

P&O European Ferries (☎ 01 44 51 00 51 in Paris, 01304-22 3000 in Dover), in the same building as Sealink in Paris, runs car ferries from Calais to Dover (1¼ hours), Le Havre to Portsmouth (5¾ hours) and Cherbourg to Portsmouth (3¾ hours). If you're going to far northern France, you might consider the company's Dover-Ostende (Belgium) route.

For information on ferries from Saint Malo to Weymouth, Poole, Portsmouth, Jersey, Guernsey (Guernesey) and Sark (Sercq), see Ferry under Getting There & Away in the Saint Malo (Brittany) section.

Ireland

Irish Ferries (☎ 01 42 66 90 90) links Le Havre

and Cherbourg with Cork and Rosslare. The trip takes about 20 hours. There are only two or three ferries a week from October to March but daily runs the rest of the year. Passengers pay from 530FF one way, depending on when they travel, and students get a small discount. The cheapest couchette is an extra 38FF. Irish Ferries' Paris office is at 32 Rue du 4 Septembre (2e; metro Opéra). Eurail passes are valid on some of these ferry services.

Italy

For information on ferry services between Italy and Corsica, see Getting There & Away in the Corsica section. You can purchase tickets from many French travel agents.

North Africa

The Société Nationale Maritime Corse Méditerranée (SNCM) and its Algerian counterpart, Algérie Ferries, operate ferry services from Marseille to the Algerian ports of Algiers (Alger), Annaba, Bejaia, Skikda and Oran. Passage to the first four cities (from 950FF one way) takes 18 to 24 hours – and slightly more to Oran (from 1050FF one way). SNCM also has services from Marseille to Tunis in Tunisia (from 915FF) and Porto Torres in Sardinia. For details, see Ferry under Getting There & Away in the Marseille section.

The Compagnie Marocaine de Navigation (☎ 04 91 56 32 00 in Marseille) runs ferries from Sète (near Montpellier) to the Moroccan cities of Tangier (Tanger) and Nador. The trip takes about 36 hours.

Getting Around

AIR

Air France Europe (Air Inter until the end of 1996; ☎ 01 45 46 90 00 in Paris) handles domestic passenger flights. Flying within France is quite expensive, but people under 25 (and students under 27) can get discounts of 50% and more on certain Air Inter flights. The most heavily discounted flights may be cheaper than long-distance rail travel. Details are available from travel agents.

BUS

Because the French train network is state-owned and the government prefers to operate a monopoly, the country has only a limited intercity bus service. Buses are widely used, however, for short-distance intra-departmental routes, especially in rural areas with relatively few train lines (eg Brittany and Normandy).

Costs

In some areas (eg along the Côte d'Azur), you may have the choice of going by either bus or train. For longer trips, buses tend to be much slower but slightly cheaper than trains. On short runs they are slower and usually more expensive.

TRAIN

France's excellent rail network, operated by the Société Nationale des Chemins de Fer (SNCF), reaches almost every part of the country. Places not served by train are linked with major railheads by SNCF buses. France's most important train lines fan out from Paris like the spokes of a wheel, making rail travel between certain provincial towns and cities infrequent and rather slow. In some cases, you have to transit through Paris, which may require transferring from one of Paris' six train stations to another (see Train under Getting There & Away in the Paris section for details).

The pride and joy of the SNCF is the world-famous TGV *(train à grande vitesse)*, which means 'high-speed train'. There are three TGV lines: the TGV Sud-Est, which links Paris' Gare de Lyon with Lyon, Valence and – via non-TGV tracks – the south-east; the TGV Atlantique, which runs from Paris' Gare Montparnasse to the Loire Valley, Bordeaux and the south-west; and the TGV Nord Europe, which goes from Paris' Gare du Nord to Calais and London. Although it usually travels at 300 km/h, the TGV Atlantique has, in test runs, reached over 515 km/h, the world speed record for trains. Going by TGV costs the same as travelling on regular trains except that you must pay a reservation fee (see Costs & Reservations below) of 18 to 99FF, depending on when you travel.

Most larger SNCF stations have a left-luggage office *(consigne manuelle)* which charges 30FF per bag (35FF for a bicycle) for 24 hours.

FRANCE

Information

Most train stations have both ticket windows *(guichets)* and an information and reservation office or desk. SNCF now has a nationwide telephone number (☎ 08 36 35 35 35 in French, ☎ 08 36 35 35 39 in English) for all rail enquiries and reservations.

Formalities

Before boarding the train on each leg of your journey, you must validate your ticket *and* your reservation card by time-stamping them in one of the *composteurs*, postbox-like orange machines that are located somewhere between the ticket windows and the tracks. Eurail passes and France Railpasses *must* be time-stamped before you begin your first journey to initiate the period of validity.

Costs & Reservations

Train fares consist of two parts: the cost of passage, which is calculated according to the number of km you'll be travelling, and a reservation fee. The reservation fee is optional unless you travel by TGV or want a couchette or special reclining seat. In addition, on especially popular trains (eg on holiday weekends) you may have to make advance reservations in order to get a seat. Eurail-pass holders should bear in mind that they must pay any applicable reservation fees. Since some overnight trains are equipped only with couchettes – eg most of the overnight trains on the Paris-Nice run – there's no way Eurail-pass holders can avoid the reservation fee except by taking a day train with a supply of unreserved seats.

Discounts

For the purpose of granting discounts, SNCF now divides train travel into two periods: blue *(bleue)*, when the largest discounts are available, and white *(blanche)*, when there are far fewer bargains. To be eligible for the discount, your journey must begin during a period of the appropriate colour. For a chart of blue and white periods, ask for a *Calendrier Voyageurs* at any SNCF information counter.

Discounts for Non-EU Citizens The France Vacances Pass (called the France Railpass in North America) allows unlimited travel by rail in France for three to nine days over the course of a month. The pass can be purchased in France (from Gare du Nord, Gare de Lyon, Gare Saint Lazare and the two airports in Paris and the main train stations in Nice and Marseille only) but will be more expensive than buying it before you leave home. A three-day pass bought in France costs 1169FF. In the USA, the three-day 2nd-class version costs US$145; each additional day is US$30. The pass is available through travel agents anywhere outside Europe and from a limited number of places within Europe. In North America, Rail Europe (☎ 800-438 7245) has all the information.

Discounts Available in France The Carrissimo card, valid for travel within France *only*, grants the holder (who must be 12 to 25 years old) and up to four travelling companions (who must also be aged 12 to 25) a 50% discount for journeys begun during blue periods and a 20% discount for travel begun during white periods. A Carrissimo card costs 190FF for four trips or 295FF for eight trips and is available from SNCF information offices.

For travel within France, students aged 12 to 25 can purchase BSE (Billet Scolaire et Étudiants) tickets, which cost 20% to 25% less than regular one-way or return fares. Like BIJ tickets (see Train in the Getting There & Away section), they cannot be purchased from SNCF – you have to go to a Wasteels, Transalpino or Frantour Tourisme office.

No matter what age you are, the Billet Séjour excursion fare gives you a 25% reduction for round-trip travel within France if you meet three conditions: the total length of your trip is at least 1000 km; you'll be spending at least part of a Sunday at your destination; and you begin travel in both directions during blue periods. It is available at ticket counters or the station's information and reservation office. With a Carte Couple – which is available free to any two people who are living together and can prove it – one of the two people who appear on the card pays full fare and the other gets 50% off on travel undertaken together provided it's begun during blue periods.

People aged 60 or over can get a Carte Vermeil Plein Temps, which entitles the bearer to a 50% reduction for 1st or 2nd-class travel begun during blue periods and 20% during white periods. It costs 270FF, is valid for one year in 21 European countries and is available from the information offices of major European train stations. A four-journey version valid for France only, the Carte Vermeil Quatre Temps, costs 135FF.

The Carte Kiwi is useful for people travelling with a child under 16. With the Carte Kiwi 4 x 4 (285FF), the child (who is the cardholder) and up to four companions of any age or relation get 50% off four trips for a year. The Carte Kiwi Tutti (444FF) allows unlimited travel under the same conditions for a year.

Anyone can take advantage of *les prix Joker* (Joker prices). Buy your ticket eight days in advance and you'll get a 30% discount. More than a month before earns you 60% off. But discounts are not available on all lines.

TAXI

France's cities and larger towns all have 24-hour taxi service. French taxis are always equipped with meters; prices range from 3.23FF per km in Paris to as high as 10FF in Corsica. Tariffs are quite a bit higher after 7 pm and on Sunday and public holidays. There are often surcharges (5FF or so) for each piece of heavy luggage or if you are picked up or dropped off at a train station or airport. Passengers always sit in the back seat.

CAR & MOTORCYCLE

There's nothing like exploring the back roads of the Loire Valley or the Alps on your own, free of train and bus schedules. Unfortunately, travelling around France by car or motorcycle is expensive: petrol is costly and tolls can reach hundreds of francs a day if you're going cross-country in a hurry. Three or four people travelling together, however, may find that renting a car is cheaper than taking the train. Throughout France, you must use a meter to park. Buy a ticket from the machine you'll see on every block and display it *inside* the car on the dashboard.

Road Rules

To drive in France, you must carry a passport or EU national identity card, a valid driver's licence, proof of insurance and car-ownership papers.

Unless otherwise posted, speed limits are 130 km/h (110 km/h in the rain) on the *autoroutes* (dual carriageways/expressways whose alphanumeric names begin with A); 110/90 km/h on the *routes nationales* (highways whose names begin with N); and 90 km/h on the *routes départementales* (rural highways whose names start with D). The moment you pass a sign indicating that you've entered the boundaries of a town, village or hamlet, the speed limit automatically drops to 50 km/h (or less as posted) and stays there until you pass an identical sign with a red bar across it.

The maximum permissible blood-alcohol level in France is 0.07%.

Expenses

Petrol prices in France can vary by half a franc or more per litre depending on the station – it pays to shop around. Regular leaded petrol (*essence*) with an octane rating of 97, usually sold as *super*, costs about 5.90FF a litre. Unleaded (*sans plomb*) petrol with an octane rating of 98 costs around 5.80FF a litre. Diesel fuel (*gasoil* or *gazole*) is about 4.20FF a litre. Fuel is most expensive at the rest stops along the autoroutes.

Tolls are another major expense: expect to pay around 40FF per 100 km.

Rental

Renting a car in France is expensive, especially if you do it through one of the international car-hire companies. In the Getting Around sections for many cities, the Car & Motorcycle entry supplies details on the cheapest places to rent cars.

If you get into a minor accident, fill out a Constat Aimable d'Accident Automobile (joint car accident report) – there should be one in the glove compartment – with the other driver. You both sign and each of you gets a copy. If you were not at fault, make sure all the facts reflecting this are included on the form which, unless your French is really fluent, should be filled out with the assistance of someone who can translate all the French automobile terms.

Purchase-Repurchase Plans

If you'll be needing a car in France for a minimum of 23 days and a maximum of 180, it is *much* cheaper to 'purchase' one from the manufacturer and then 'sell' it back than it is to rent one. In reality, you only pay for the number of days you use the vehicle, but the

FRANCE

purchase-repurchase *(achat-rachat)* aspect of the paperwork, none of which is your responsibility, lets you save France's whopping 20.6% VAT on noncommercial car rentals.

Both Renault and Citroën have excellent-value purchase-repurchase plans – contact the dealer in your country. It can be up to 35% cheaper arranging your purchase-repurchase car abroad, where various discounts are available, than in France. You usually have to book and pay about a month before you pick up the car.

Useful Organisations

For further information on driving in France contact the Automobile Club de France (☎ 01 43 12 43 12; fax 01 43 12 43 43) at 8 Place de la Concorde (8e; metro Concorde) or its Paris affiliate, the Automobile Club de l'Île de France (☎ 01 40 55 43 00; fax 01 43 80 90 51) at 14 Ave de la Grande Armée (17e; metro Argentine).

BICYCLE

Most large towns have at least one cycling shop that hires out bikes by the hour, day or week. You can still get low-tech one and three-speeds or 10-speeds *(vélos à 10 vitesses)*, but in some areas such antiquated contrivances are going the way of the penny-farthing. A growing number of shops only have mountain bikes *(vélos tout-terrain* or VTTs), which generally cost 70 to 120FF a day. Most places, especially those renting expensive mountain bikes, require a substantial deposit (though a passport will often suffice).

HITCHING

Hitching in France is more difficult than almost anywhere else in Europe. (See the Hitching section in the introductory Getting Around chapter for general information.) Getting out of big cities like Paris, Lyon and Marseille or travelling around the Côte d'Azur by thumb is well nigh impossible. Remote rural areas are your best bet, but few cars are likely to be going further than the next large town. Women should not hitch alone.

It is an excellent idea to hold up a sign with your destination followed by the letters *s.v.p.* (for *s'il vous plaît* – 'please'). Some people have reported good luck hitching with truck drivers from truck stops. It is illegal to hitch on autoroutes and other major expressways, but you can stand near the entrance ramps.

In Paris, Allostop-Provoya (☎ 01 53 20 42 42; metro Cadet) at 8 Rue Rochambeau (9e) can put you in touch with a driver who is going your way. If you are not a member (250FF for up to eight journeys over two years), there is a per-trip fee of between 30FF (for distances under 200 km) and 70FF (for distances over 500 km). In addition, you have to pay the driver 0.20FF per km for expenses.

BOAT

Travelling through some of France's 7500 km of navigable waterways on a houseboat or canal boat is a unique and relaxing way to see the country. For a brochure listing boat-rental companies around France, contact the Paris-based Syndicat National des Loueurs de Bateaux de Plaisance (☎ 01 44 37 04 00) at Port de Javel Haut (15e; metro Javel).

ORGANISED TOURS

Though independent travel is usually far more rewarding then being led from coach to sight and back to coach, some areas in France are difficult to visit on your own unless you have wheels. Tour options are mentioned under Organised Tours in sections where they are relevant (eg Loire Valley, the D-Day Beaches in Normandy, the Vézère Valley in Périgord). A number of Paris-based companies have tours of various lengths into the hinterland (Champagne, Burgundy, the Loire Valley, Normandy) including Cityrama Gray Line (☎ 01 44 55 61 00; metro Palais Royal) at 4 Place des Pyramides (1er). The tourist office in Paris has a complete list.

Paris

By now, Paris (population 2.15 million; metropolitan area 10.6 million) has almost exhausted the superlatives that can reasonably be applied to a city. Notre Dame and the Eiffel Tower – at sunrise, at sunset, at night – have been described ad nauseam as have the Seine and the subtle (and not-so-subtle) differences between the Left and Right banks. But what writers have been unable to capture is the grandness and even the magic of strolling along the city's broad avenues – a legacy of the 19th century – which lead from impressive public buildings and exceptional museums to parks, gardens and esplanades. Paris is enchanting at any time, in every season. You too may find yourself humming that old Cole Porter favourite as you walk the streets: 'I love Paris in the springtime, I love Paris in the fall...'

Orientation

In central Paris (which the French call Intra-Muros – 'within the walls'), the Rive Droite (Right Bank) is north of the Seine, while the Rive Gauche (Left Bank) is south of the river. For administrative purposes, Paris is divided into 20 *arrondissements* (districts), which spiral out clockwise from the centre of the city. Paris addresses always include the arrondissement number. In this section, these numbers are listed in parentheses immediately after the street address, using the usual French notation. For example, *1er* stands for *premier* (1st), *4e* for *quatrième* (4th) and 19e for *dix-neuvième* (19th). When an address includes the full five-digit postal code, the last two digits indicate the arrondissement: 75001 for the 1st, 75014 for the 14th etc.

As there is nearly always a metro station within 500 metres, you can whiz around under the traffic and pop up wherever you choose. To help you find your way, we've included the station nearest each hotel, museum etc, immediately after the telephone or arrondissement number.

Maps The best map of Paris is Michelin's 1:10,000 scale *Paris Plan*. It comes both in booklet *(Paris Plan 11)* and sheet form *(Paris Plan 10)* and is available in bookshops, stationery stores and kiosks around the city.

Information

Tourist Offices Paris' main tourist office (☎ 01 49 52 53 54; fax 01 49 52 53 00; metro Charles de Gaulle-Étoile) is 100 metres east of the Arc de Triomphe at 127 Ave des Champs Élysées (8e). It is open every day of the year except 1 May from 9 am to 8 pm. This is the best source of information on the city's museums, concerts, expositions, theatre performances and the like. Information on other parts of France is also available. For a small fee and a deposit, the office can find you a place to stay in Paris for that night or in the provinces up to eight days in advance.

There are tourist office annexes open Monday to Saturday from 8 am to 8 pm (9 pm in summer) in all of Paris' train stations except Gare Saint Lazare. From May to September, the tourist office annexe (☎ 01 45 51 22 15) at the Eiffel Tower (7e) is open from 11 am to 6 pm.

Both international airports have Aéroports de Paris (ADP) tourist information desks. The one at Orly is in the Orly-Sud terminal on the ground floor opposite Gate H; it is open daily from 6 am to 11.45 pm. At Roissy-Charles de Gaulle, there's a tourist information bureau (☎ 01 48 62 27 29) on the arrival level of Aérogare 1 and one in each of the three terminals of Aérogare 2.

For recorded information on cultural and other events taking place in Paris, call ☎ 01 49 52 53 56 (English) or ☎ 01 49 52 53 55 (French) any time. Many French regions and departments such as Périgord, Pyrénées and Hautes-Alpes have tourist outlets (Maisons du Tourisme) in Paris. Ask at the main tourist office for a list.

Money All of Paris' six major train stations have exchange bureaus open seven days a week until at least 8 pm (7 pm at Gare Montparnasse), but the rates are not very good. The exchange offices at Orly (Orly-Sud terminal) and Roissy-Charles de Gaulle (both Aérogares) are open until 10 or 11 pm. Unless you want to get about 10% less than a fair rate, avoid the big exchange-bureau chains like Chequepoint and ExactChange.

Banque de France By far the best rate in town is offered by Banque de France, France's central bank, whose headquarters (☎ 01 42 92 22 27; metro Palais Royal-Musée du Louvre) is three blocks north of the Louvre at 31 Rue Croix des Petits Champs (1er). The exchange service is open Monday to Friday from 9.30 am to 12.30 pm and 1.30 to 4 pm. The Banque de France branch (☎ 01 44 61 15 30; metro Bastille) at 5 Place de la Bastille (4e), which is opposite the new Opéra-Bastille, is open weekdays from 9 am to noon and 1.30 to 3.30 pm.

To Grande Arche de la Défense
(Tête Défense)

Rue V. Hugo

Boulevard

51

Rue A. France

50

La Défense

River

Seine

Blvd

Bineau

49

Pont de Neuilly

Avenue Charles de Gaulle

Les Sablons

48

Cimetière
Montma...

17^e

Avenue de Wagram

Rue d'Amsterdam

Blvd Pereire

Parc de
Monceau

Gare St
Lazare

Route du M. Gandhi

47

See Central Paris map

Boulevard — Haussmann

Avenue Foch

Arc de Triomphe

8^e

46

Avenue des Champs Elysées

To Camping du Bois
de Boulogne

45

Lac
Inférieur

Blvd Périphérique

Avenue Victor Hugo

Avenue Kléber

Avenue d'Iéna

Place
de la
Concorde

Bois de
Boulogne

44

7^e

Eiffel Tower

Hôtel des
Invalides

To Camping du Bois
de Boulogne (1 km)

43

16^e

LEFT BA

42

Seine River

Blvd. Montparn

41

To Autoroute A13,
Versailles (12 km),
Chartres (via N10, 80 km),
Rouen (128 km),
Bayeux (257 km) &
Normandy

Avenue de Versailles

Quai André Citroën

Rue de la Convention

15^e

Lecourbe

Gare Montparnasse

40

Avenue Félix Faure

Rue de Vaugirard

31

Cimetière
Montparn

Avenue Édouard Vaillant

Avenue P. Grenier

39 38

Rue

Rue des Morillons

37

14^e

Avenue du Maine

Pla
Den
Roche

Blvd

36

Lefebvre

Rue d'Alésia

35 34

Blvd Brune

Périphérique

33

32

Paris

To Charles de Gaulle Airport (21 km), Autoroute A1, Calais (289 km), Brussels & Antwerp

Blvd Ney

phérique

Blvd Ornano

18e

Rue de la Chapelle

Ave de Flandre

Canal de l'Ourcq

Parc de la Villette

19e

Avenue Jean Jaurès

0   0.5   1 km

arrondissement boundaries

Sacré Cœur Basilica

Blvd Barbès

de Clichy

Gare du Nord

9e

Rue La Fayette

Gare de l'Est

Parc des Buttes Chaumont

Belleville

éra-Garnier

2e

Blvd de Magenta

10e

Rue de

Blvd Sébastopol

Place de la République

See Marais & Île St Louis map

Blvd Jules Ferry

11e

Blvd de Ménilmontant

Cimetière du Père Lachaise

To Autoroutes A1 & A3

GHT BANK

1er

3e

Rue de Rivoli

re

4e

Notre Dame

Rue de la Roquette

Rue de

Rue de Lappe

Rue Voltaire

Blvd de Charonne

To Château de Vincennes (1.5 km) & Jardin Tropical (4.4 km)

6e

Blvd St Michel

Rue St Jacques

5e

Panthéon

Place de la Bastille

Rue du Faubourg St Antoine

ain

See the Latin Quarter & Île de la Cité map

Seine River

Diderot

Gare de Lyon

Avenue Daumesnil

Place de la Nation

Cours de Vincennes

12e

To Château de Vincennes (1.6 km); Park Floral (2.4 km) & Jardin Tropical (4 km)

Gare d'Austerlitz

Blvd St Marcel

Blvd de l'Hôpital

vd Arago

Blvd Saint Jacques

28

Place d'Italie

Blvd Vincent Auriol

Quai de Bercy

Quai de la Gare

Zoo

29

Glacière

13e

Avenue d'Italie

Boulevard Poniatowski

Bois de Vincennes

Rue de Tolbiac

To Orly Airport, Autoroutes A6, A10 & A11, Chartres, Brittany, Blois, Tours, Bordeaux, Dijon, Lyon, Alps, Marseille & Nice

Blvd Masséna

urdan

Blvd Kellermann

26

24

To Reims (136 km), Strasbourg (482 km), Alsace, Lorraine, Luxembourg & Stuttgart

Autoroute A4

27

25

PLACES TO STAY		6	Porte de Pantin	32	Porte d'Orléans
14	Hôtel Sainte Marguerite	7	Porte du Pré St Gervais	33	Porte de Châtillon
15	Maison Internationale	8	Porte des Lilas	34	Porte de Vanves
	des Jeunes	9	Gare Routière	35	Porte Brancion
19	CISP Ravel		Internationale	36	Porte de la Plaine
26	CISP Kellermann		(International Bus	37	Lost Property Office
28	Maison des Clubs		Terminal)	38	Porte de Sèvres
	UNESCO	10	Porte de Bagnolet	39	Paris Heliport
29	FIAP Jean Monnet	12	Le Balajo Discothèque	40	Porte de St Cloud
		16	Porte de Montreuil	41	Porte Molitor
PLACES TO EAT		17	Porte de Vincennes	42	Porte d'Auteuil
11	Ethnic Restaurants	18	Porte de St Mandé	43	Porte de Passy
13	Hamilton's Fish & Chips	20	Musée des Arts	44	Porte de la Muette
31	La Cagouille		d'Afrique et	45	Paris Cycles
	Restaurant		d'Océanie	46	Porte Dauphine
		21	Porte Dorée	47	Paris Cycles
OTHER		22	Porte de Charenton	48	Porte Maillot
1	Porte de Saint Ouen	23	Porte de Bercy	49	Porte de Champerret
2	Porte de Clignancourt	24	Porte d'Ivry	50	Porte d'Asnières
3	Porte de la Chapelle	25	Porte d'Italie	51	Porte de Clichy
4	Porte d'Aubervilliers	27	Porte de Gentilly		
5	Porte de la Villette	30	Catacombs		

American Express Paris' landmark American Express office (☎ 01 47 77 77 07; metro Auber or Opéra) at 11 Rue Scribe (9e) faces the west side of Opéra-Garnier. Exchange services, cash advances, refunds and poste restante are available Monday to Saturday from 9 am to 6.30 pm (5.30 pm on Saturday). Since you can get slightly better exchange rates elsewhere and the office is usually jammed, try to avoid it.

Citibank Money wired from abroad by or to Citibank usually arrives at its head office (☎ 01 49 06 10 10; metro Grande Arche de la Défense) in the suburb of La Défense, which is west of the Arc de Triomphe. The address is 19 Le Parvis, and it is open Monday to Friday from 10 am to 5.30 pm.

Notre Dame (4e & 5e) Le Change de Paris (☎ 01 43 54 76 55; metro Saint Michel) at 2 Place Saint Michel (6e) has some of the best rates in all of Paris. It is open daily from 10 am to 7 pm. There is another exchange bureau (☎ 01 46 34 70 46; metro Saint Michel) with good rates one block south of Place Saint Michel at 1 Rue Hautefeuille (6e). This place is open daily from 9 am (11 am on Sunday) to 8 pm (11 pm from May to October).

Panthéon (5e) The Banque Nationale de Paris (☎ 01 43 29 45 50; metro Luxembourg) at 7 Rue Soufflot exchanges foreign currency Monday to Friday from 9 am to noon and 1 to 5 pm.

Champs Élysées (8e) Thanks to fierce competition, the Champs Élysées is an excellent place to change money. The bureau de change (☎ 01 42 25 38 14; metro Franklin D Roosevelt) at 25 Ave des Champs Élysées is open every day of the year from 9 am to 8 pm.

Montmartre (18e) There's a bureau de change (☎ 01 42 52 67 19; metro Abbesses) at 6 Rue Yvonne Le Tac, two blocks east of Place des Abbesses. It is open Monday to Saturday from 10 am (10.30 am on Saturday) to 6.30 pm.

Post & Communications Paris' main post office (☎ 01 40 28 20 00; metro Sentier or Les Halles) at 48-52 Rue du Louvre (1er) offers all the usual services every day round the clock. Foreign exchange is only available on weekdays from 8 am to 7 pm and Saturday from 8 am to noon. All poste restante mail not specifically addressed to a particular branch post office ends up here.

At the post office (☎ 01 44 13 66 00; metro

George V) at 71 Ave des Champs Élysées (8e), you can place telephone calls with phonecards, pick up poste restante mail and send letters, telegrams and faxes Monday to Saturday from 8 am to 10 pm and on Sunday and public holidays from 10 am to noon and 2 to 8 pm. See Orientation for an explanation of Paris postcodes.

Travel Agencies Nouvelles Frontières (☎ 01 46 34 55 30; metro Luxembourg) at 66 Blvd Saint Michel (6e) specialises in discount long-distance airfares and is open Monday to Saturday from 9 am to 7 pm. Another agent, Selectour Voyages (☎ 01 43 29 64 00; metro Saint Michel) at 29 Rue de la Huchette (5e), is open weekdays from 9 am to 7 pm and on Saturday from 10 am to 6.30 pm. Council Travel (☎ 01 44 55 55 65; metro Pyramides) has its main Paris office at 22 Rue des Pyramides (1er). It is open Monday to Friday from 9.30 am to 6.30 pm and on Saturday from 10 am to 5.30 pm.

Bookshops Paris' famous English-language bookshop Shakespeare & Company (☎ 01 43 26 96 50; metro Saint Michel) is at 37 Rue de la Bûcherie (5e), which is across the Seine from Notre Dame Cathedral. The shop has an unpredictable collection of new and used books in English, but even the second-hand stuff doesn't come cheap. There's a library/reading room on the 1st floor. Shakespeare & Company is generally open daily from noon to midnight.

The largest English-language bookshop in the city, WH Smith (☎ 01 44 77 88 99; metro Concorde) at 248 Rue de Rivoli (1er), is a block east of Place de la Concorde. It's open Monday to Saturday from 9.30 am to 7 pm and on Sunday from 1 to 6 pm. At 29 Rue de la Parcheminerie (5e), the mellow, Canadian-run Abbey Bookshop (☎ 01 46 33 16 24; metro Cluny-La Sorbonne) has an eclectic, though somewhat limited, selection of titles. It's open daily from 10 am to 7 pm (10 pm Wednesday to Saturday in the summer).

Lonely Planet books and other travel guides are available from Ulysse (☎ 01 43 25 17 35; metro Pont Marie) at 26 Ave St Louis en L'Île (4e); from FNAC Librairie Internationale (☎ 01 44 41 31 50; metro Cluny-La Sorbonne)

at 71 Blvd Saint Germain (5e); and from L'Astrolabe Rive Gauche (☎ 01 46 33 80 06; metro Cluny-La Sorbonne) at 14 Rue Serpente (6e).

Cultural & Religious Centres The British Council (☎ 01 49 55 73 00; metro Invalides) at 9-11 Rue de Constantine (7e) has a lending library (230FF a year for membership) and a free reference library. The bulletin board outside the entrance has information on the many cultural activities sponsored by the council.

The newly restored Canadian Cultural Centre (☎ 01 44 43 21 31; metro Invalides) at 5 Rue de Constantine has an art gallery, a reference library and an extensive multimedia section which, among other things, offers access to the Internet. The centre is open Monday to Friday from 9 am to 7 pm.

The American Church (☎ 01 47 05 07 99; metro Invalides) at 65 Quai d'Orsay (7e) is a place of worship and something of a community centre for English speakers, and its announcement board is an excellent source of information on all sorts of subjects, including job openings and apartments for rent. Reception is staffed daily from 9 am to 10 pm (7.30 pm on Sunday).

Laundry The laundrettes *(laveries)* mentioned here are near many of the hotels and hostels listed under Places to Stay. Near the BVJ hostels, the Laverie Libre Service (metro: Louvre Rivoli) at 7 Rue Jean-Jacques Rousseau (1er) is open daily from 7.30 am to 10 pm. In the Marais, the Laverie Libre Service (metro: Saint Paul) at 25 Rue des Rosiers (3e) is open daily from 7.30 am to 10 pm.

Thanks to the Latin Quarter's student population, laundrettes are plentiful in this part of Paris. Three blocks south-west of the Panthéon, the laundrette (metro: Luxembourg) at 216 Rue Saint Jacques (5e), near the Hôtel de Médicis, is open from 7 am to 10.30 pm. Just south of the Arènes de Lutèce, the Lav-omatique (metro: Monge) at 63 Rue Monge (5e) is open daily from 6.30 am to 10 pm.

Near Gare de l'Est, the Lav' Club (metro: Gare de l'Est) at 55 Blvd de Magenta (10e) stays open daily until 10 pm. In Montmartre, the Laverie Libre Service (metro: Blanche) at

4 Rue Burq (18e) is open daily from 7.30 am to 10 pm.

Lost & Found Paris' Bureau des Objets Trouvés (Lost & Found Office; ☎ 01 45 31 14 80), run by the Préfecture de Police, is at 36 Rue des Morillons (15e; metro Convention). The only lost objects that do not make their way here are those found in SNCF train stations. Since telephone enquiries are impossible, you have to go in person and fill out forms to see if what you've lost has been located. The office is open weekdays from 8.30 am to 5 pm (8 pm on Tuesday and Thursday).

Medical Services Paris has about 50 Assistance Publique hospitals. An easy one to find is the Hôtel Dieu hospital (☎ 01 42 34 82 34; metro Cité), on the northern side of Place du Parvis Notre Dame (4e), the square in front of the cathedral. The emergency room (*service des urgences*) is open 24 hours a day.

Dangers & Annoyances For its size, Paris is a safe city, but you should always use common sense; for instance, avoid the large Bois de Boulogne and Bois de Vincennes forested parks after nightfall. Although it's fine to use the metro until it stops running at about 12.45 am, some stations may be best avoided late at night, especially if alone. These include Châtelet (1er) and its many seemingly endless tunnels to the Les Halles and Châtelet-Les Halles stops; Château Rouge in Montmartre (18e); Gare du Nord (10e); Strasbourg-Saint Denis (2e & 10e); Réaumur-Sébastopol (2e); and Montparnasse-Bienvenüe (6e and 15e).

Museum Hours & Discounts Paris has more than 100 museums of all sizes and types; a comprehensive list is available from the tourist office for 10FF. Government-run museums (*musées nationaux*) in Paris and the Île de France (eg the Louvre, the Musée Picasso) are open daily except Tuesday. The only exceptions are the Musée d'Orsay, Musée Rodin and Versailles, which are closed Monday. Entry to most of the national museums is free for people 17 or younger and half-price for those aged 18 to 25 or over 60. Paris' municipal museums (Musées de la Ville de Paris; ☎ 01 42 76 65 68)

are open daily except Monday and are free on Sunday.

The Carte Musées et Monuments (☎ 01 44 78 45 81) museum pass gets you into some 75 museums and monuments in Paris and the surrounding region without having to queue for a ticket. The card costs 70/140/200FF for one/three/five consecutive days and is on sale at the museums and monuments it covers, at some metro ticket windows and at the tourist office.

Things to See – Left Bank

Île de la Cité (1er & 4e) Paris was founded sometime during the 3rd century BC, when members of a tribe known as the Parisii set up a few huts on Île de la Cité. By the Middle Ages, the city had grown to encompass both banks of the Seine, but Île de la Cité remained the centre of royal and ecclesiastical power.

Notre Dame Paris' cathedral (☎ 01 42 34 56 10; metro Cité or Saint Michel) is one of the most magnificent achievements of Gothic architecture. Its construction was begun in 1163 and completed around 1345. Exceptional features include the three spectacular rose windows, especially the one over the west facade, and the window on the north side of the transept, which has remained virtually unchanged since the 13th century. One of the best views of Notre Dame is from the lovely little park behind the cathedral, where you can see the mass of ornate flying buttresses that encircle the chancel and hold up its walls and roof. (While there, have a look at the haunting **Mémorial des Martyrs de la Déportation** in memory of the more than 200,000 people deported by the Nazis and French fascists during WWII.)

Notre Dame is open daily from 8 am to 7 pm (but is closed on Saturday from 12.30 to 2 pm). There is no entrance fee. Free concerts are held every Sunday at 5.30 pm. The **Trésor** (Treasury) at the back of the cathedral, which contains precious liturgical objects, is open Monday to Saturday from 9.30 to 11.45 am and 12.30 to 5.30 pm (2 to 5.30 pm on Saturday); admission is 15FF (10FF for students). The top of the west façade, from where you can view many of the cathedral's most ferocious-looking gargoyles and a good deal of Paris, can be reached via 387 steps. It is open daily from 9.30 am to 6.30 pm during summer; until 5 pm in winter. The entrance is at the base of the north tower. Entry is 28FF (18FF reduced rate).

The **Crypte Archéologique** (☎ 01 43 29 83 51) under the square in front of the cathedral displays Gallo-Roman and later remains found on the site. Entrance costs 28FF (18FF reduced rate).

Sainte Chapelle The gem-like upper chapel of Sainte Chapelle (☎ 01 43 54 30 09; metro Cité), illuminated by a veritable curtain of 13th-century stained glass, is inside the **Palais de Justice** (Law Courts) at 4 Blvd du Palais (1er). Consecrated in 1248, Sainte Chapelle was built in only 33 months to house a crown of thorns (supposedly worn by the crucified Christ) and other relics purchased by King Louis IX (later Saint Louis) earlier in the 13th century. From October to March, it is open daily from 10 am to 5 pm; the rest of the year, from 9.30 am to 6.30 pm. Tickets cost 32FF (21FF reduced rate). A ticket valid for both Sainte Chapelle and the nearby Conciergerie costs 45FF. The high-security visitors' entrance to the Palais de Justice is opposite 7 Blvd du Palais (1er).

Conciergerie The Conciergerie (☎ 01 43 54 30 06; metro Cité) was a luxurious royal palace when it was built in the 14th century – the **Salle des Gens d'Armes** (Cavalrymen's Room) is the oldest medieval hall in Europe – but was later transformed into a prison and continued as such until 1914. During the Reign of Terror (1793-94), the Conciergerie was used to incarcerate 'enemies' of the Revolution before they were brought before the tribunal, which met next door in what is now the Palais de Justice. Among the almost 2800 prisoners held here before being bundled off to the guillotine were Queen Marie-Antoinette and the Revolutionary radicals Danton and Robespierre. The Conciergerie is open daily from 10 am to 5 pm (9.30 am to 6.30 pm from April to September). Guided visits in French leave every half-hour. The entrance is at 1 Quai de l'Horloge (1er) and tickets cost 28FF (18FF reduced rate).

Ile Saint Louis (4e) Île Saint Louis, the smaller of Paris' two islands, is just east of Île de la Cité. The 17th-century houses of grey stone and the small-town shops that line the streets and quays impart an almost provincial feel, making this quarter a great place for a quiet stroll. If circumnavigating the island makes you hungry, you might want to join the line in front of Berthillon at 31 Rue Saint Louis en l'Île (4e; metro Pont Marie), which is reputed to have Paris' best ice cream. On foot, the shortest route between Notre Dame and the Marais passes through Île Saint Louis.

Latin Quarter (5e & 6e) This area is known as the Quartier Latin because, up till the Revolution, all communication between students and their professors took place here in Latin. The 5e has become increasingly touristy but still has a large population of students and academics affiliated with the University of Paris and other institutions. Shop-lined **Blvd Saint Michel**, known as the 'Boul Mich', runs along the border of the 5e and the 6e.

Panthéon (5e) The Latin Quarter landmark now known as the Panthéon (☎ 01 43 54 34 51; metro Luxembourg or Cardinal Lemoine), which is at the eastern end of Rue Soufflot, was commissioned as an abbey church in the mid-18th century. In 1791, the Constituent Assembly converted it into a mausoleum for the 'great men of the era of French liberty'. Permanent residents include Victor Hugo, Émile Zola, Voltaire and Jean-Jacques Rousseau. The Panthéon's ornate marble interior is gloomy in the extreme, but you get a great view of the city from around the colonnaded dome (261 steps). From October to March, the Panthéon is open daily from 10 am to 5.30 pm (9.30 am to 6.30 pm the rest of the year when there are guided visits). Entrance costs 32FF (21FF reduced rate).

Sorbonne (5e) Paris' most famous university was founded in 1253 as a college for 16 poor theology students. After serving for centuries as France's major theological centre, it was closed in 1792 by the Revolutionary government but reopened under Napoleon. Today, the Sorbonne's main campus complex (bounded by Rue Victor Cousin, Rue Saint Jacques, Rue des Écoles and Rue Cujas) and other buildings nearby house several of the 13 autonomous

Central Paris

FRANCE

arrondissement boundaries

1 km

0.5

0

RIGHT BANK

LEFT BANK

Palais du Louvre

Jardin des Tuileries

Place de la Concorde

Place Vendôme

Place de la Madeleine

Place de l'Opéra

Place d'Italie

Place de la République

Place d'Iéna

Place Charles de Gaulle

Jardin du Luxembourg

Jardin des Plantes

Champ de Mars

Champ de Mars (Tour Eiffel)

Notre Dame

Île de la Cité

Île St Louis

Châtelet Les Halles

Panthéon

Esplanade des Invalides

Pont Neuf

Pont d'Iéna

Seine River

Trocadéro

See Marais & Île St Louis Map

See the Latin Quarter & Île de la Cité Map

To Gare du Nord (600 m)

To Montmartre (1 km)

To La Défense Skyscraper District (3.7 km)

To Place Denfert Rochereau (650 m)

Blvd Jules Ferry

Blvd de Magenta

Blvd de Strasbourg

Blvd de Sébastopol

Blvd Montmartre

Blvd des Capucines

Blvd des Italiens

Blvd Haussmann

Blvd Malesherbes

Blvd Raspail

Blvd du Montparnasse

Blvd des Invalides

Blvd St Germain

Blvd St Michel

Blvd Saint Germain

Blvd de Grenelle

Blvd de Vaugirard

Blvd Garibaldi

Blvd de Beauséjour

Rue de Rivoli

Rue du Louvre

Rue Montmartre

Rue St Honoré

Rue Réaumur

Rue de Turbigo

Rue Beaubourg

Rue Monge

Rue des Écoles

Rue Saint Jacques

Rue de Rennes

Rue de Vaugirard

Rue d'Assas

Rue de Sèvres

Rue de Babylone

Rue Vaneau

Rue de Varenne

Rue St Placide

Rue de la Croix des Petits Champs

Rue Croix des Petits Champs

Rue de Richelieu

Ave de l'Opéra

Ave des Champs Élysées

Ave F D Roosevelt

Ave George V

Ave Marceau

Ave d'Iéna

Ave Victor Hugo

Avenue Kléber

Avenue Foch

Ave de la Grande Armée

Ave de Friedland

Ave Georges V

Ave W Churchill

Ave Bosquet

Ave Rapp

Ave de la Motte Picquet

Ave Duquesne

Ave de Suffren

Ave de Breteuil

Ave de Tourville

Ave Latour Maubourg

Quai d'Orsay

Quai de l'Université

Quai Saint Bernard

Quai Saint Hilaire

Rue de Buffon

Rue Geoffroy St Hilaire

Rue Lafayette

Rue La Boétie

Faubourg St Honoré

Rue Montmartre

Blvd Denis

President Wilson

Rue du Commerce

Rue Cambronne

Rue Mademoiselle

Rue des Entrepreneurs

1er 2e 3e 4e 5e 6e 7e 8e 9e 10e 11e 12e 13e 15e 16e 17e

	PLACES TO STAY			
28	Auberge de Jeunesse Jules Ferry	8	Au Printemps (Department Store)	36	Bateaux Mouches (Boat Tours)
31	Centre International BVJ Paris-Louvre & Laundrette	9	Galeries Lafayette (Department Store)	37	Cinémathèque
		10	Galeries Lafayette	38	Palais de Chaillot
50	Three Ducks Hostel & Bicycle Tours/Rental	11	Eurostar & Ferry Offices	39	Jardins du Trocadéro
		12	American Express	40	American Church
51	Aloha Hostel	13	Opéra-Garnier	41	Aérogare des Invalides (Buses to Orly)
		16	Canadian Embassy	42	Palais Bourbon (National Assembly Building)
	PLACES TO EAT	17	Grand Palais		
14	Chartier Restaurant	18	Musée du Petit Palais		
15	Le Drouot Restaurant	19	US Embassy	43	British Council
33	Léon de Bruxelles & Batifol	20	WH Smith Bookshop	44	Musée d'Orsay
		21	Food Shops	45	Eiffel Tower
56	Le Caméléon Restaurant	22	Council Travel	46	Hôtel des Invalides
		23	Musée de l'Orangerie	47	Église du Dôme
57	CROUS Restaurant Universitaire (6e)	24	Banque de France	48	Musée Rodin
		25	Main Post Office	49	École Militaire
58	CROUS Restaurant Universitaire Bullier	26	Rue Saint Denis Sex District	52	FNAC Store & Ticket Outlet
		27	Cinémathèque	53	Montparnasse Tower
	OTHER	29	Louvre Museum	54	Gare Montparnasse
1	Gare Saint Lazare	30	Change du Louvre (Currency Exchange)	55	Cimetière du Montparnasse
2	Gare de l'Est			59	Institut du Monde Arabe
3	Arc de Triomphe	32	Église Saint Eustache	60	Paris Mosque & Hammam
4	Main Tourist Office	34	Forum des Halles (Shopping Mall & Park)	61	Museum of Natural History
5	Post Office			
6	Bureau de Change			62	Gare d'Austerlitz
7	La Madeleine Church	35	Musée Guimet		

universities created when the University of Paris was reorganised in 1968. **Place de la Sorbonne** links Blvd Saint Michel with **Église de la Sorbonne**, the university's domed 17th-century church.

Jardin du Luxembourg (6e) When the weather is warm, Parisians flock to the Luxembourg Gardens (metro: Luxembourg) in their thousands to sit and read, write, relax, talk and sunbathe while their children sail little boats in the fountains. The gardens' main entrance is across the street from 65 Blvd Saint Michel. The **Palais du Luxembourg**, fronting Rue de Vaugirard at the northern end of the Jardin du Luxembourg, was built for Maria de' Medici (Marie de Médicis in French), queen of France from 1600 to 1610. It now houses the Sénat, the upper house of the French parliament.

Musée du Moyen Age (5e) The Museum of the Middle Ages (☎ 01 43 25 62 00; metro Cluny-La Sorbonne) houses one of France's finest collections of medieval art. Its prized

possession is a series of six late 15th-century tapestries from the southern Netherlands known as *La Dame à la Licorne* (the Lady & the Unicorn). The museum is housed in two structures: the frigidarium (cold room) and other remains of Gallo-Roman baths from around the year 200 AD, and the late 15th-century residence of the abbots of Cluny. The museum's entrance is at 6 Place Paul Painlevé, and is open from 9.15 am to 5.45 pm daily except Tuesday. Entry is 27FF (18FF reduced rate). On Sunday, everyone pays 18FF.

Paris Mosque (5e) Paris' central mosque (☎ 01 45 35 97 33; metro Monge) at Place du Puits de l'Ermite was built between 1922 and 1926 in an ornate Moorish style. There are tours from 10 am to noon and 2 to 6 pm daily except Friday. The mosque complex includes a small souk (marketplace), a salon de thé, an excellent couscous restaurant and a public bath *(hammam)*. The hammam (☎ 01 43 31 18 14) is open from 10 am to 9 pm on Monday, Wednesday, Thursday, Friday and Saturday for women and from 2 to 9 pm on Tuesday and 10 am to 9 pm on Sunday for men. It costs 85FF. The entrance is at 39 Rue Geoffroy Saint Hilaire.

The mosque is opposite the western end of the **Jardin des Plantes** (Botanical Gardens), which includes a small **zoo** (☎ 01 40 79 37 94) as well as the recently renovated **Muséum d'Histoire Naturelle** (☎ 01 40 79 30 00; metro Monge). It is open weekdays except Tuesday from 10 am to 6 pm (until 10 pm on Thursday). Entrance is 40FF (30FF reduced rate).

Institut du Monde Arabe (5e) Established by 20 Arab countries to showcase Arab and Islamic culture and to promote cultural contacts, this institute (☎ 01 40 51 38 38; metro Jussieu) at 1 Rue des Fossés Saint Bernard occupies one of the most graceful and highly praised modern buildings in Paris. The 7th-floor **museum** (buy your tickets on the ground floor) of 9th to 19th-century Muslim art and artisanship is open daily except Monday from 10 am to 6 pm and costs 25FF (20FF reduced rate).

Catacombs (14e) In 1785, it was decided that the hygiene problems posed by Paris' overflowing cemeteries could be solved by exhuming the bones and storing them in the tunnels of three disused quarries. One such ossuary is the Catacombes (☎ 01 43 22 47 63; metro Denfert Rochereau), in which the bones and skulls of millions of Parisians from centuries past are neatly stacked along the walls. During WWII, these tunnels were used by the Résistance as headquarters. The route through the Catacombs begins from the small green building at 1 Place Denfert Rochereau. The site is open Tuesday to Friday from 2 to 4 pm and on weekends from 9 to 11 am and 2 to 4 pm. Tickets cost 27FF (15FF reduced rate).

Musée d'Orsay (7e) The Musée d'Orsay (☎ 01 40 49 48 14; metro Musée d'Orsay), along the Seine at 1 Rue de Bellechasse, exhibits paintings, sculptures, *objets d'art* and other works of art produced between 1848 and 1914, including the fruits of the impressionist, post-impressionist and Art-Nouveau movements. It thus fills the chronological gap between the Louvre and the Musée d'Art Moderne at the Centre Pompidou. The Musée d'Orsay is spectacularly housed in a former train station built in 1900 and re-inaugurated in its present form in 1986. It is open daily, except Monday, from 10 am (9 am on Sunday) to 6 pm (9.45 pm on Thursday). Entrance costs 35FF (24FF reduced rate).

Musée Rodin (7e) The Musée Auguste Rodin (☎ 01 44 18 61 10; metro Varenne) at 77 Rue Varenne is one of the most pleasant museums in Paris. Rodin's extraordinarily vital bronze and marble sculptures (look for *The Kiss*, *Cathedral* and, of course, *The Thinker*) are on display both inside the 18th-century Hôtel Biron and in the delightful garden out the back. The Musée Rodin is open from 9.30 am to 5.45 pm (4.45 pm during winter) daily except Monday. Entrance costs 27FF (18FF reduced rate). On Sunday, everyone gets in for 18FF.

Invalides (7e) The **Hôtel des Invalides** (metro Invalides for the Esplanade, metro Varenne or Latour Maubourg for the main building) was built in the 1670s by Louis XIV to provide housing for 4000 disabled veterans *(invalides)*. On 14 July 1789, the Paris mob forced its way into the building and, after fierce fighting, took 28,000 rifles before heading for the Bastille prison.

The **Église du Dôme**, whose dome sparkles again after a 1989 regilding, was built between 1677 and 1735 and is considered one of the finest religious edifices erected under Louis XIV. The church was initially a mausoleum for military leaders in 1800, and in 1861 received the remains of Napoleon, encased in six concentric coffins.

The buildings on either side of the **Cour d'Honneur** (Main Courtyard) house the **Musée de l'Armée** (☎ 01 44 42 37 72), a huge military museum. The Musée de l'Armée and the light and airy **Tombeau de Napoléon 1er** (Napoleon's Tomb) are open daily from 10 am to 5 pm (6 pm in summer). Entrance costs 34FF (24FF reduced rate).

Eiffel Tower (7e) The Tour Eiffel (☎ 01 44 11 23 11; metro Champ de Mars-Tour Eiffel) faced massive opposition from Paris' artistic and literary elite when it was built for the 1889 Exposition Universelle (World's Fair), held to commemorate the Revolution. It was almost torn down in 1909 but was spared for practical reasons – it proved an ideal platform for new-fangled transmitting antennae. The Eiffel Tower is 318 metres high, including the television antenna at the very tip. This figure can vary by as much as 15 cm as the tower's 7000 tonnes of steel, held together by 2.5 million rivets, expand in warm weather and contract when it's cold.

You can choose to visit any of the three levels open to the public. The lift (west and north pillars) costs 20FF for the 1st platform (57 metres above ground), 40FF for the 2nd (115 metres) and 56FF for the 3rd (276 metres). Walking up the stairs (south pillar) to the 1st or 2nd platforms costs 12FF. The tower is open every day from 9.30 am to 11 pm (9 am to midnight in summer). You can walk up from 9 am to 6.30 pm (11 pm or midnight from early July to mid-September).

Champ de Mars (7e) The Champ de Mars, the grassy park around the Eiffel Tower, was originally a parade ground for the **École Militaire** (France's military academy), the huge, 18th-century building at the south-eastern end of the lawns.

Things to See – Right Bank
Jardins du Trocadéro (16e) The Jardins du Trocadéro (metro: Trocadéro), whose fountain and nearby statue garden are grandly illuminated at night, are across the Pont d'Iéna from the Eiffel Tower. The colonnaded Paris and Passy wings of the **Palais de Chaillot**, built in 1937, house a number of museums, including the Musée de la Marine (☎ 01 45 53 31 70), the Musée du Cinéma (☎ 01 45 53 21 86) and the Musée des Monuments Français (☎ 01 44 05 39 10), all of which are closed on Tuesday. The view from the terrace between the two wings is one of the most impressive in Paris.

Musée Guimet (16e) The Guimet museum (☎ 01 47 23 61 65; metro Iéna) at 6 Place d'Iéna, about midway between the Eiffel Tower and the Arc de Triomphe, displays a fabulous collection of antiquities and works of art from throughout Asia. Large sections of the museum, however, will be closed for renova-

tion until 1999. It is open daily except Tuesday from 9.45 am to 6 pm. Entrance costs 27FF (18FF reduced rate and on Sunday for all).

Louvre (1er) The Louvre Museum (☎ 01 40 20 53 17, 01 40 20 51 51; metro Palais Royal-Musée du Louvre), constructed around 1200 as a fortress and rebuilt in the mid-16th century as a royal palace, became a public museum in 1793. The paintings, sculptures and artefacts on display have been assembled by French governments over the past five centuries and include works of art and artisanship from all over Europe as well as important collections of Assyrian, Egyptian, Etruscan, Greek, Coptic, Roman and Islamic art. The Louvre's most famous work is undoubtedly Leonardo da Vinci's *Mona Lisa*. Since it takes several serious visits to get anything more than the briefest glimpse of the offerings, your best bet – after seeking out a few things you really want to see (eg masterpieces such as the Winged Victory of Samothrace and Venus de Milo) – is to choose a period or section of the museum and pretend the rest is somewhere across town.

The Louvre's entrance is covered by a glass pyramid designed by American architect IM Pei. Commissioned by François Mitterrand and completed in 1990, the design generated bitter opposition but is now generally acknowledged as a brilliant success.

The Louvre is open daily except Tuesday from 9 am to 6 pm (until 9.45 pm on Monday and Wednesday). Ticket sales end 30 minutes before closing time. The entry fee is 45FF (26FF reduced rate), but on Sunday and every day after 3 pm everyone pays just 26FF. Entry is free for all on the first Sunday of every month.

Free brochures with rudimentary maps of the museum are available at the information desk in Hall Napoléon, where you can also get details on guided tours. Cassette tours in six languages can be rented for 28FF on the mezzanine level. Detailed explanations in a variety of languages, printed on heavy plastic-coated pages, are stored on racks in each display room.

Place Vendôme (1er) The arcaded buildings around Place Vendôme (metro: Tuileries) and the square itself were designed in the 17th century to display a giant statue of Louis XIV that was later destroyed during the Revolution. The present 44-metre column in the middle of Place Vendôme consists of a stone core wrapped in a spiral of bronze made from 1250 cannons captured by Napoleon at the Battle of Austerlitz (1805). The shops around the square are among the most fashionable – and expensive – in Paris.

Musée de l'Orangerie (1er) The Musée de l'Orangerie (☎ 01 42 97 48 16; metro Concorde), which is in the south-east corner of Place de la Concorde, displays important impressionist works, including a series of Monet's spectacular *Nymphéas* (Water Lilies) and paintings by Cézanne, Matisse, Modigliani, Picasso and Renoir. It is open daily except Tuesday from 9.45 am to 5 pm. The entry fee is 27FF (18FF reduced rate and on Sunday for all).

Place de la Concorde (8e) This vast, cobbled square, set between the Jardin des Tuileries and the eastern end of the Champs Élysées, was laid out between 1755 and 1775. Louis XVI was guillotined here in 1793 – as were another 1343 people over the next two years including his wife, Marie-Antoinette, and Robespierre. The 3300-year-old Egyptian **obelisk** in the middle of the square was given to France in 1829 by the ruler of Egypt, Mohammed Ali.

La Madeleine (8e) The church of Saint Mary Magdalene (☎ 01 44 51 69 00; metro Madeleine) is 350 metres north of Place de la Concorde along Rue Royale. Built in the style of a Greek temple, it was consecrated in 1842 after almost a century of design changes and construction delays. The front porch affords a superb view of the square and, across the river, the 18th-century **Palais Bourbon**, whose façade dates from the early 19th century. It is now the home of the National Assembly.

Fauchon (☎ 01 47 42 60 11; metro Madeleine) at 26 Place de la Madeleine, Paris' most famous gourmet food shop, is open daily except Sunday from 9.40 am to 7 pm.

Champs Élysées (8e) The two-km-long Ave des Champs Élysées links Place de la Concorde with the Arc de Triomphe. Once popular with the aristocracy as a stage on which t[o] parade their wealth, it has, in recent decade[s] been partly taken over by fast-food restaurant[s] and overpriced cafés. The nicest bit is the par[k] with the Petit Palais and the Grand Palai[s] between Place de la Concorde and Rond Poin[t] des Champs Élysées.

Musée du Petit Palais (8e) The Petit Palai[s] (☎ 01 42 65 12 73; metro Champs Élysée[s] Clemenceau), built for the 1900 Expositio[n] Universelle, is on Ave Winston Churchill[,] which runs between Ave des Champs Élysée[s] and the Seine. Its museum specialises in medi[-] eval and Renaissance porcelain, clocks[,] tapestries, drawings and 19th-century Frenc[h] painting and sculpture. It is open from 10 a[m] to 5.40 pm daily except Monday. The entry fe[e] is 27FF (14.50FF reduced tariff). Temporar[y] exhibitions usually cost 35FF extra (25FF i[f] you qualify for the reduction).

The **Grand Palais** (☎ 01 44 13 17 17[)] which is across Ave Winston Churchill fro[m] the Petit Palais on Square Jean Perrin, was als[o] built for the 1900 World's Fair. It is now use[d] for temporary exhibitions.

Arc de Triomphe (8e) The Arc de Triomph[e] (☎ 01 43 80 31 31; metro Charles de Gaull[e] Étoile), Paris' second most famous landmar[k] is a couple of km north-west of Place de [la] Concorde in the middle of Place Charles d[e] Gaulle. Also called Place de l'Étoile, this is th[e] world's largest traffic roundabout and th[e] meeting point of 12 avenues. The Arc d[e] Triomphe was commissioned in 1806 b[y] Napoleon to commemorate his imperial victo[-] ries but remained unfinished when he starte[d] losing battles and then entire wars. It wa[s] finally completed in the 1830s. An Unknow[n] Soldier from WWI is buried under the arch, hi[s] fate and that of countless others like him com[-] memorated by a memorial flame that is lit wit[h] ceremony each evening.

The platform atop the arch (lift up, step[s] down) is open from 9.30 am to 6 pm (10 pm o[n] Friday) daily except on public holidays. Winte[r] hours are 10 am to 5.30 pm. It costs 31F[F] (20FF reduced rate), and there's a sma[ll] **museum** with a short videotape. The only saf[e] way to get to the base of the arch is via th[e] underground passageways from its perimeter; trying to cross the traffic on foot is suicidal.

From the Arc de Triomphe, the **Voie Triomphale** (Triumphal Way) stretches another 4.5 km north-west along Ave de la Grande Armée and beyond to the new skyscraper district of **La Défense**. Its best known landmark, the **Grande Arche** (Grand Arch), is a hollow cube (112 metres to a side) completed in 1989.

Centre Georges Pompidou (4e) This centre (☎ 01 44 78 12 33; metro Rambuteau or Châtelet-Les Halles), also known as the Centre Beaubourg, is dedicated to displaying and promoting modern and contemporary art. Thanks in part to its outstanding temporary exhibitions, it is by far the most frequented sight in Paris and the tens of thousands of daily visitors have forced a major renovation of the building. **Place Igor Stravinsky** and its crazy fountains south of the centre and the large square to the west attract street artists, mimes, musicians, jugglers and 'artisans' who will write your name on a grain of rice.

The design of the Centre Pompidou has not ceased drawing wide-eyed gazes and critical comment since it was built between 1972 and 1977. In order to keep the exhibition halls as spacious and uncluttered as possible, the architects put the building's 'insides' on the outside.

The Centre Pompidou consists of six floors and several sections. The **Musée National d'Art Moderne**, which displays the national collection of modern and contemporary art on the 4th floor, is open daily except Tuesday from noon (10 am on weekends and public holidays) to 10 pm. Entrance costs 35FF (24FF reduced rate), but everyone gets in for free on Sunday from 10 am to 2 pm. The free **Bibliothèque Publique d'Information**, with the same opening hours, is a huge, nonlending library equipped with the latest high-tech information retrieval systems. The entrance is on the 2nd floor.

If you'll be visiting several parts of the complex in the same day, the one-day pass Forfait Journalier, which costs 70FF (45FF if you're 13 to 25), is a good deal, especially if you take a guided tour. Tours in English, which last 1½ hours, leave at 2.30 and 3.30 pm daily except Tuesday from the main information desk (*accueil général*).

Les Halles (1er) Paris' central food market, Les Halles, occupied this site from the 12th century until 1969, when it was moved out to the suburb of Rungis. A huge underground shopping mall (Forum des Halles) was built in its place and has proved highly popular with Parisian shoppers. Just north of the grassy area on top of Les Halles is one of Paris' most attractive churches, the mostly 16th-century **Église Saint Eustache**, noted for its wonderful pipe organ.

Hôtel de Ville (4e) Paris' city hall (☎ 01 42 76 40 40; metro Hôtel de Ville) at Place de l'Hôtel de Ville was burned down during the Paris Commune of 1871 and rebuilt in the neo-Renaissance style between 1874 and 1882. There are guided tours in French every Monday at 10.30 am, and the small **museum** has imaginative exhibits on Paris. The visitors' entrance is at 29 Rue de Rivoli.

Marais Area (4e) The Marais, the part of the 4e east of the Centre Pompidou and north of Île Saint Louis, was a marsh *(marais)* until the 13th century, when it was converted to agricultural use. During the 17th century this was the most fashionable part of the city, and the nobility erected luxurious but discreet mansions known as *hôtels particuliers*. When the aristocracy moved to trendier pastures, the Marais was taken over by ordinary Parisians. By the time renovation was begun in the 1960s, the Marais had become a poor but lively Jewish neighbourhood centred around **Rue des Rosiers**. In the 1980s the area underwent serious gentrification and is today one of the trendiest neighbourhoods to live and shop in. It is also something of a gay quarter.

Place des Vosges (4e) In 1605, King Henri IV decided to turn the Marais into Paris' most fashionable district. The result of this initiative, completed in 1612, was the Place Royale – now Place des Vosges (metro: Chemin Vert) – a square ensemble of 36 symmetrical houses with ground-floor arcades, steep slate roofs and large dormer windows north of Rue Saint Antoine. Duels were once fought in the elegant park in the middle. Today, the arcades around Place des Vosges are occupied by up-market art galleries, antique shops and salons de thé.

The **Maison de Victor Hugo** (☎ 01 42 72 10 16), where the author lived from 1832 to 1848, is open daily except Monday from 10 am to 5.40 pm. The entry fee is 17.50FF (9FF reduced rate).

Musée Picasso (3e) The Picasso Museum (☎ 01 42 71 25 21; metro Saint Sébastien-Froissart), housed in the mid-17th century Hôtel Salé, is a few hundred metres north-east of the Marais at 5 Rue de Thorigny. Paintings, sculptures, ceramic works, engravings and drawings donated to the French government by the heirs of Pablo Picasso (1881-1973) to avoid huge inheritance taxes are on display, as is Picasso's personal art collection (Braque, Cézanne, Matisse, Rousseau etc). The museum is open daily except Tuesday from 9.30 am to 6 pm (5.30 pm in the winter). The entry fee is 27FF (18FF reduced rate).

Bastille (4e, 11e & 12e) The Bastille is the most famous nonexistent monument in Paris; the notorious prison was demolished shortly after the mob stormed it on 14 July 1789 and freed all seven prisoners. Today, the site where it stood is known as Place de la Bastille; the 52-metre **Colonne de Juillet** in the centre was erected in 1830. The new (and rather drab) **Opéra-Bastille** (☎ 01 40 01 19 71; metro Bastille) at 2-6 Place de la Bastille (12e) is another grandiose project initiated by President François Mitterrand.

Opéra-Garnier (9e) Paris' better known opera house (☎ 01 40 01 25 14; metro Opéra) at Place de l'Opéra was designed in 1860 by Charles Garnier to display the splendour of Napoleon III's France and is one of the most impressive monuments erected during the second empire. The extravagant **entrance hall**, with its grand staircase, is decorated with multicoloured marble and a gigantic chandelier. The **ceiling** of the auditorium was painted by Marc Chagall in 1964. Opéra-Garnier is open to visitors from 10 am to 5 pm daily except Sunday. Entrance is 30FF (18FF reduced rate). Opéra-Garnier is used for concerts and ballets; opera performances now take place at Opéra-Bastille.

Montmartre (18e) During the 19th century – and especially after 1871, when the Commu-nard uprising began here – Montmartre's Bohemian lifestyle attracted artists and writers, whose presence turned the area into Paris' most vibrant centre of artistic and literary creativity. In English-speaking countries, Montmartre's mystique of unconventionality has been magnified by the notoriety of the **Moulin Rouge** (☎ 01 46 06 00 19; metro Blanche) at 82 Blvd de Clichy, a nightclub founded in 1889 and known for its twice-nightly *revue* (at 10 pm and midnight) of nearly naked chorus girls. Today it is an area of mimes, buskers, tacky souvenir shops and commercial artists.

Basilique du Sacré Cœur Perched at the very top of Butte de Montmartre, the Basilica of the Sacred Heart (metro: Lamarck Caulaincourt) was built to fulfil a vow taken by many Parisian Catholics after the disastrous Franco-Prussian War of 1870-71. On warm evenings, groups of young people gather on the steps below the church to contemplate the view, play guitar and sing. Although the basilica's domes are a well-loved part of the Parisian skyline, the architecture of the rest of the building, which is typical of the style of the late 19th century, is not very graceful.

The basilica is open daily from 6.45 am to 11 pm. The entrance to the **dome** and the **crypt**, which costs 15FF (8FF for students), is on the west side of the basilica. Both are open daily from 9 am to 6 pm; they say you can see for 30 km on a clear day from the dome. The recently rebuilt funicular up the hill's southern slope costs one metro/bus ticket each way. It runs from 6 am to 12.45 am.

The **Musée d'Art Naïf** (Museum of Naive Art) in Halle Saint Pierre (☎ 01 42 58 72 89; metro Anvers), south-west of the basilica at 2 Rue Ronsard, is worth a visit (40FF; 30FF for students).

Place du Tertre Just west of **Église Saint Pierre**, the only building left from the great abbey of Montmartre, Place du Tertre is filled with cafés, restaurants, portrait artists and tourists and is always animated. But the real attractions of the area, apart from the view, are the quiet, twisting streets and shaded parks. Look for the two **windmills** west on Rue Lepic and the last **vineyard** extant in Paris on the corner of Rue des Saules and Rue Saint Vincent.

Pigalle (9e & 18e) Pigalle, only a few blocks south-west of the tranquil, residential areas of Montmartre, is one of Paris' major sex districts. Although the area along Blvd de Clichy between the Pigalle and Blanche metro stops is lined with sex shops and striptease parlours, the area has plenty of legitimate nightspots too, including La Locomotive discothèque (see Entertainment later in the Paris section) and several all-night cafés.

Cimetière du Père Lachaise (20e) Père Lachaise Cemetery (☎ 01 43 70 70 33; metro Père Lachaise), final resting place of such notables as Chopin, Proust, Oscar Wilde, Édith Piaf and Sarah Bernhardt, may be the most visited cemetery in the world. The best known tomb (and the one most visitors come to see) is that of 1960s rock star Jim Morrison, lead singer for the Doors, who died in 1971. It is in Division 6. Maps indicating the graves' locations are posted around the cemetery.

The cemetery is open daily from 8.30 am to 6 pm (7.30 am to 6 pm from mid-March to early November). On Sundays and public holidays, it opens at 9.30 am. The cemetery has five entrances; the main one is opposite 23 Blvd de Ménilmontant. Admission is free.

Bois de Vincennes (12e) This large English-style park, the 9.29-sq-km Bois de Vincennes, is in the far south-eastern corner of the city. Highlights include the **Parc Floral** (Floral Garden; metro Château de Vincennes) on Route de la Pyramide; the Parc Zoologique de Paris (Paris Zoo; ☎ 01 44 75 20 10) at 53 Ave de Saint Maurice (metro: Porte Dorée); and, at the park's eastern edge, the **Jardin Tropical** Tropical Garden; RER stop Nogent-sur-Marne) on Ave de la Belle Gabrielle.

Château de Vincennes (12e) The Château de Vincennes (☎ 01 43 28 15 48; metro Château de Vincennes), at the northern edge of the Bois de Vincennes, is a bona fide 14th-century royal chateau complete with massive fortifications and a moat. You can walk around the grounds for free, but to see the Gothic **Chapelle Royale**, built between the 14th and 16th cen-

turies, and the 14th-century **donjon** (keep), with its small historical museum, you must take a guided tour (26FF; 17FF reduced rate). Daily opening hours are from 10 am to 5 pm (6 pm in summer). The main entrance, which is opposite 18 Ave de Paris in the inner suburb of Vincennes, is right next to the Château de Vincennes metro stop.

Musée des Arts d'Afrique et d'Océanie (12e) This museum (☎ 01 44 74 84 80; metro Porte Dorée) at 293 Ave Daumesnil specialises in art from Africa and the South Pacific. It is open weekdays except Tuesday from 10 am to noon and 1.30 to 5.30 pm (12.30 to 6 pm on weekends). The entry fee is 27FF (18FF reduced rate).

Bois de Boulogne (16e) The 8.65-sq-km Bois de Boulogne, located on the western edge of the city, is endowed with meandering trails, gardens, forested areas, cycling paths and *belle époque*-style cafés. Rowing boats can be rented at the **Lac Inférieur** (metro: Ave Henri Martin), the largest of the park's lakes.

Paris Cycles (☎ 01 47 47 76 50) rents city and mountain bicycles at two locations: on Route du Mahatma Gandhi (metro: Les Sablons), opposite the Porte des Sablons entrance to the Jardin d'Acclimatation amusement park; and near the Pavillon Royal (metro: Ave Foch) at the northern end of the Lac Inférieur. Charges are 30FF an hour or 80FF a day. From mid-April to mid-October, bicycles are available daily from 10 am to sundown. During the rest of the year, you can rent them on Wednesday, Saturday and Sunday only.

Courses

Language Courses The Alliance Française (☎ 01 45 44 38 28; metro Saint Placide) at 101 Blvd Raspail (6e) has month-long French courses beginning the first week of each month. The registration office is open Monday to Friday from 9 am to 6 pm. French courses with the same schedule offered by the Accord Language School (☎ 01 42 36 24 95; metro Rambuteau or Les Halles) at 72 Rue Rambuteau (1er) get high marks from students. A one-month course (10 hours a week) costs 1900FF.

Cooking Courses Several cooking schools offer courses of various lengths including the famed École Ritz Escoffier (☎ 01 42 60 38 30; metro Concorde) at 38 Rue Cambon (1er) and École Le Cordon Bleu (☎ 01 48 56 06 06; metro Vaugirard) at 8 Rue Léon Delhomme (15e). A one-day hands-on course at the latter is 1250FF and from 4590FF for a week.

Organised Tours
Bus The cheapest way to see Paris on wheels between mid-April and late September is to hop aboard RATP's Balabus (☎ 01 43 46 14 14) which follows a 50-minute route from the Gare de Lyon to the Grande Arche de la Défense and back, passing many of the city's most famous sights. Buses leave every 10 to 20 minutes from 12.30 to 8 pm; the fare is one to three bus/metro tickets, depending on how far you go. ParisBus (☎ 01 42 30 55 50) offers a longer (2¼ hours) tour with English and French commentary year-round on red double-decker buses. There are nine stops (including the Eiffel Tower and Notre Dame) and you can get on and off as you wish. Tickets, available on the bus, are 125FF (half-price for children under 12).

Bicycle Mountain Bike Trip (☎ 01 48 42 57 87; metro Commerce), based in the Three Ducks Hostel at 6 Place Étienne Pernet (15e, metro Commerce), runs popular six-hour mountain bike tours of Paris in English for 135FF. Phone to reserve a place between 8 am and 9 pm the day before. Here you can also rent a mountain bike for 90FF a day.

Boat In summer, the Batobus river shuttle (☎ 01 44 11 33 44) stops at half a dozen places along the Seine, including Notre Dame and the Musée d'Orsay. The boats come by every 35 minutes and cost 12FF per journey or 60FF for the whole day. The Bateaux Mouches company (☎ 01 40 76 99 99; metro Alma Marceau), which is based on the north bank of the Seine just east of Pont de l'Alma (8e), runs the biggest tour boats on the Seine. The cost for a one-hour cruise with commentary is 40FF (no student discount). Vedettes du Pont Neuf (☎ 01 46 33 98 38; metro Pont Neuf), whose home port is on the western tip of Île de la Cité (1er) near the newly cleaned Pont Neuf, oper-

ates one-hour boat circuits day and night fo 45FF.

Places to Stay
Accommodation Services Accueil de Jeunes en France (AJF) can always fin anyone accommodation in a hostel, hotel o private home, even in summer. It works lik this: you come in on the day you need a plac to stay and pay AJF for the accommodatior plus a 10FF fee, and they give you a vouche to take to the establishment. The earlier in th day you come the better, as the convenient anc cheap places always go first. Prices start a 120FF per person. AJF's main office (☎ 01 4 77 87 80; metro Rambuteau) is at 119 Ru Saint Martin (4e), just west of the Centr Pompidou's main entrance. It is open Monda to Saturday from 10 am to 6.45 pm. Be pre pared for long queues during the summer. Th AJF annexe (☎ 01 42 85 86 19; metro Gare d Nord) at the Gare du Nord train station (10e is open daily from June to mid-September.

The main Paris tourist office (☎ 01 49 52 5 54) can also find you accommodation in Pari for the evening of the day you visit its offic There is an 8FF charge for a spot at a hoste and a 20FF charge for reservations at a one-sta hotel. For information on the tourist office an its annexes, see Tourist Offices under Informa tion at the start of the Paris section.

Camping The only camping ground actuall within the Paris city limits, *Camping du Boi de Boulogne* (☎ 01 45 24 30 00) on Allée d Bord de l'Eau (16e), is along the Seine at th far western edge of the Bois de Boulogne. I summer, two people with a tent pay aroun 65FF or 80FF with a car. From April to Sep tember, privately operated shuttle buses fron the Porte Maillot metro stop (16e & 17e) ru daily from 8.30 am to 1 pm and 5 pm t sometime between 11 pm and 1 am. Durin July and August, the shuttles run every hal hour from 8.30 am to 1 am. Throughout th year, you can take either bus No 244 from Port Maillot or bus No 144 from the Pont de Neuill metro stop from 6 am to about 9 pm.

Hostels & Foyers Many hostels allow guest to stay for only three nights, especially i summer. Places that have age limits (eg up t

30) tend not to enforce them very rigorously. Only official hostels require that guests present Hostelling International cards. Curfews at Paris hostels tend to be 1 or 2 am though some are earlier. Few hostels accept reservations by telephone; those that do are noted in the text.

Louvre Area (1er) The *Centre International BVJ Paris-Louvre* (☎ 01 42 36 88 18; metro Louvre-Rivoli) at 20 Rue Jean-Jacques Rousseau is only a few blocks north-east of the Louvre. Beds in single-sex rooms cost 120FF, including breakfast. There is a second BVJ hostel, the *Centre International BVJ Paris-Les Halles* (☎ 01 40 26 92 45), around the corner at 5 Rue du Pélican.

Marais (4e) The Maison Internationale de la Jeunesse et des Étudiants, better known as MIJE, runs three hostels (☎ 01 42 74 23 45 for all) in attractively renovated 17th and 18th-century residences in the Marais. A bed in a single-sex dorm with shower costs 120FF, including breakfast. The nicest of the three, *MIJE Fourcy* is at 6 Rue de Fourcy (metro: Saint Paul), 100 metres south of Rue de Rivoli. *MIJE Fauconnier* is two blocks away at 11 Rue du Fauconnier (metro: Pont Marie). *MIJE Maubisson* is at 12 Rue des Barres (metro: Hôtel de Ville). Individuals can make reservations for all three hostels, up to seven days in advance, by calling in at MIJE Fourcy.

Panthéon Area (5e) The clean and friendly *Y&H Hostel* (☎ 01 45 35 09 53; metro Monge) is at 80 Rue Mouffetard, a hopping, happening street known for its restaurants and pubs. A bed in a cramped room with a sink costs 97FF plus 5FF for sheets. Reservations can be made only if you leave a deposit for the first night. Reception is open from 8 to 11 am and 5 pm to 2 am.

11e Arrondissement The *Auberge de Jeunesse Jules Ferry* (☎ 01 43 57 55 60; metro République) is at 8 Blvd Jules Ferry. This hostel is a bit institutional but the atmosphere is fairly relaxed and – an added bonus – it doesn't accept large groups. A bed costs 110FF, including breakfast.

The friendly *Hôtel Sainte Marguerite* (☎ 01 47 00 62 00; metro Ledru Rollin) at 10 Rue Trousseau, 700 metres east of Place de la Bastille, is run like an HI hostel and attracts a young, international crowd. Beds in rooms for two, three or four people cost 91FF per person, including breakfast.

The *Maison Internationale des Jeunes* (☎ 01 43 71 99 21; metro Faidherbe Chaligny) at 4 Rue Titon is about a km east of Place de la Bastille. A bed in a spartan dorm room for two, three, five or eight people costs 110FF, including breakfast. If you don't have your own sheets, there's a 15FF rental charge. Telephone reservations are accepted only for the day you call.

12e Arrondissement The *Centre International de Séjour de Paris (CISP) Ravel* (☎ 01 44 75 60 00; metro Porte de Vincennes) is on the south-eastern edge of the city at 4-6 Ave Maurice Ravel. A bed in a 12-person dormitory is 105FF. Rooms for two to five people cost 118FF per person, and singles are 135FF. All prices include breakfast (provided you stay more than one night) and student card-holders get a 10% discount. Reservations are accepted from individuals no more than 24 hours in advance.

13e & 14e Arrondissements The *Foyer International d'Accueil de Paris (FIAP) Jean Monnet* (☎ 01 45 89 89 15; metro Glacière) is at 30 Rue Cabanis (14e), a few blocks south-east of Place Denfert Rochereau. A bed costs 126/151FF (including breakfast) in modern rooms for eight/four people. Singles/doubles cost 260/170FF per person. Rooms specially outfitted for disabled people (handicapés) are available.

The *Centre International de Séjour de Paris (CISP) Kellermann* (☎ 01 44 16 37 38; metro Porte d'Italie) is at 17 Blvd Kellermann (13e). A bed in an attractive dorm for eight costs 109FF, and staying in a double or quad will cost 134FF per person. Singles are 151FF (181FF with toilet and shower). All prices include sheets and breakfast. This place also has facilities for disabled people on the 1st floor. Telephone reservations are accepted if you call the same day you arrive.

The rather institutional *Maison des Clubs UNESCO* (☎ 01 43 36 00 63; metro Glacière) is at 43 Rue de la Glacière (13e), midway

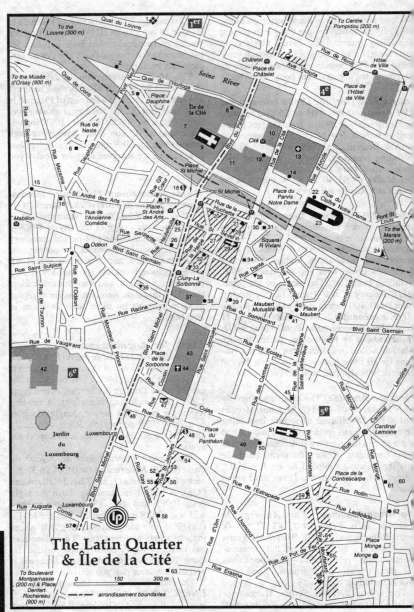

The Latin Quarter
& Île de la Cité

0   150   300 m

- · - · - · - arrondissement boundaries

To Boulevard
Montparnasse
(200 m) & Place
Denfert
Rochereau
(900 m)

FRANCE

PLACES TO STAY		OTHER		29	Église Saint Séverin
5	Hôtel Henri IV	1	Samaritaine	30	Shakespeare & Co
6	Hôtel de Nesle		(Department Store)		Bookshop
16	Hôtel Petit Trianon	2	Vedettes du Pont Neuf	32	Abbey Bookshop
19	Hôtel Saint Michel		(Boat Tours)	37	Musée du Moyen Age
31	Hôtel Esmerelda	3	Noctambus (All-Night		(Thermes de Cluny)
34	Hôtel du Centre, Le		Bus) Stops	38	Musée du Moyen Age
	Cloître Pub & Polly	4	Hôtel de Ville (City Hall)		Entrance
	Maggoo Pub	7	Palais de Justice &	39	Eurolines Bus Office
52	Hôtel de Médicis		Conciergerie	40	Food Shops
58	Hôtel Gay Lussac	8	Conciergerie Entrance	41	Fromagerie (Cheese
61	Hôtel des Arènes	9	Sainte Chapelle		Shop)
63	Grand Hôtel du Progrès	10	Flower Market	42	Palais du Luxembourg
66	Y & H Hostel	11	Préfecture de Police		(French Senate
		12	Préfecture Entrance		Building)
PLACES TO EAT		13	Hôtel Dieu (Hospital)	43	Sorbonne (University
27	Restaurants ('Bacteria	14	Hospital Entrance		of Paris)
	Alley')	15	Food Shops	44	Église de la Sorbonne
28	L'Année du Dragon	17	Carrefour de l'Odéon	45	Le Violon Dingue Pub
	Chinese Restaurant	18	Le Change de Paris	47	Post Office
33	McDonald's	19		48	Banque Nationale de
35	Au Coin des Gourmets	20	Selectour Voyages		Paris
	Indochinese		(Travel Agent)	49	Panthéon
	Restaurant	21	Caveau de la Huchette	50	Panthéon Entrance
36	Pâtisserie Viennoise		Jazz Club	51	Église Saint Étienne du
46	McDonald's	22	Notre Dame Tower		Mont
54	Tashi Delek Tibetan		Entrance	53	Food Shops
	Restaurant	23	Notre Dame Cathedral	55	Laundrette
56	Aleka Restaurant	24	WWII Deportation	57	Nouvelles Frontières
59	La Rose de Mouffetard		Memorial		(Travel Agency)
64	Restaurants	25	Bureau de Change	60	Arènes de Lutèce
65	Crêpe Stand	26	L'Astrolabe Rive	62	Laundrette
			Gauche Travel		
			Bookshop		

etween Place Denfert Rochereau and Place l'Italie. A bed in a large, unsurprising room for three or four people is 120FF; singles/doubles ost 160/140FF per person.

5e Arrondissement The friendly, helpful *Three Ducks Hostel* (☎ 01 48 42 04 05; metro Commerce), a favourite with young backpackers, is at 6 Place Étienne Pernet. A bunk bed osts 97FF, and if you don't have your own heets, there is a one-time charge of 15FF. elephone reservations are accepted. For nformation on their mountain bike tours, see Bicycle under Organised Tours earlier in this ection. The *Aloha Hostel* (☎ 01 42 73 03 03; netro Volontaires), run by the same people, is t 1 Rue Borromée about a km west of Gare Montparnasse. Beds cost 107FF and sheets, if ou don't have your own, cost 15FF.

lotels A rash of renovations, redecorations nd other improvements has turned many of

Paris' best budget hotels into quaint and spotless two-star places where the sheets are changed daily and the minibar is full. But there are still bargains to be had.

Marais (4e) One of the best deals in town is the friendly *Hôtel Rivoli* (☎ 01 42 72 08 41; metro Hôtel de Ville) at 44 Rue de Rivoli. Room rates range from 110FF (for singles without shower) to 230FF (for doubles with bath and toilet). The front door is locked at 2 am. The *Grand Hôtel du Loiret* (☎ 01 48 87 77 00; metro Hôtel de Ville) is two buildings away at 8 Rue des Mauvais Garçons. Singles/doubles start at 140/160FF. Rooms with shower and toilet start at 250FF.

The *Hôtel Moderne* (☎ 01 48 87 97 05; metro Saint Paul) at 3 Rue Caron has basic singles/doubles for 130/160FF, 190FF with shower and 220FF with shower and toilet. The *Hôtel Pratic* (☎ 01 48 87 80 47; metro Saint Paul) is just around the corner at 9 Rue

FRANCE

d'Ormesson. Singles/doubles cost 150/230FF with washbasin; double rooms cost 275FF with shower, 340FF with bath and toilet.

One of the most attractive medium-priced hotels in the area is the *Hôtel de Nice* (☎ 01 42 78 55 29; fax 01 42 78 36 07; metro Hôtel de Ville), a comfortable oasis at 42bis Rue de Rivoli. Doubles/triples/quads with shower and toilet are 400/500/600FF and many of the rooms have balconies. The completely over-hauled *Grand Hôtel Mahler* (☎ 01 42 72 60 92; fax 01 42 72 25 37; metro Saint Paul) is at 5 Rue Mahler. Singles/doubles with everything start at 470/570FF (add 100FF in summer).

Notre Dame Area (5e) The run-down *Hôtel du Centre* (☎ 01 43 26 13 07; metro Saint Michel) at 5 Rue Saint Jacques has very basic singles/doubles starting at 100/150FF. Doubles with shower cost from 180FF. Hall showers are 20FF. Reservations are not accepted, but reception is open 24 hours a day.

Because of its location at 4 Rue Saint Julien le Pauvre directly across the Seine from Notre Dame, the *Hôtel Esmerelda* (☎ 01 43 54 19 20; metro Saint Michel) is everybody's favourite. Its three simple singles (160FF) are almost always booked up months in advance – other singles/doubles (with shower and toilet) start at 320FF.

Panthéon Area (5e) The *Hôtel de Médicis* (☎ 01 43 54 14 66; metro Luxembourg) at 214 Rue Saint Jacques is exactly what a dilapidated Latin Quarter dive for impoverished travellers should be like. Very basic singles start at 75FF, but the cheapest rooms are usually occupied. Basic doubles/triples are 150/240FF and hall showers are 10FF.

A much better deal is the *Grand Hôtel du Progrès* (☎ 01 43 54 53 18; metro Luxembourg) at 50 Rue Gay Lussac. Singles with washbasin start at 150FF and there are larger rooms with fine views of the Panthéon for 240FF. Hall showers are free. There are also large old-fashioned singles/doubles with shower and toilet for 310/330FF. A cut above, the *Hôtel Gay Lussac* (☎ 01 43 54 23 96; metro Luxembourg) at No 29 on the same street has small singles/doubles with washbasin for 200/260FF; doubles/quads with shower and toilet are 360/500FF.

A quiet, up-market hotel with views from the back of a 2nd-century Roman amphitheatre (Arènes de Lutèce) is the *Hôtel des Arènes* (☎ 01 43 25 09 26; fax 01 43 25 79 56; metro Monge) at 51 Rue Monge. Singles/doubles triples with shower and toilet are 595/662 900FF.

Saint Germain des Prés (6e) The wonderfully eccentric *Hôtel de Nesle* (☎ 01 43 54 6 41; metro Odéon or Mabillon) at 7 Rue d Nesle, with its frescoed rooms and cool garden out the back, is a favourite with students an young people from all over the world. Single cost 195FF, and a bed in a double is 220FF Doubles with shower and toilet are 350FF. The only way to get a place here is to book in perso in the morning. The nearby *Hôtel Peti Trianon* (☎ 01 43 54 94 64; metro Odéon) a 2 Rue de l'Ancienne Comédie also attracts lot of young travellers. Singles start at 170FF Doubles with shower are 320FF.

The well-positioned *Hôtel Henri IV* (☎ 0 43 54 44 53; metro Pont Neuf) is at 25 Plac Dauphine (1er), a quiet square at the wester end of Île de la Cité near Pont Neuf. Perfectl adequate singles without toilet or shower ar 140FF, doubles are 195 to 270FF, and hal showers are 15FF. This place is usually booke up months in advance.

The *Hôtel Saint Michel* (☎ 01 43 26 98 7(metro Saint Michel) is a block west of Plac Saint Michel and a block south of the Seine a 17 Rue Gît le Cœur. Singles/doubles ar 215/240FF, with shower 310/335FF. All price include breakfast.

Montmartre (18e) The metro station Abbesse is convenient for all the following hotels. Th *Idéal Hôtel* (☎ 01 46 06 63 63) at 3 Rue de Trois Frères has simple but acceptabl singles/doubles starting at 125/170FF. A ha shower is 20FF; rooms with showers ar 250FF. The *Hôtel Bonséjour* (☎ 01 42 54 2 53), a block north of Rue des Abbesses at 1 Rue Burq, has basic but pleasant singles fror 110 to 130FF and doubles for 170FF; shower are 10FF.

The *Hôtel Audran* (☎ 01 42 58 79 59) is o the other side of Rue des Abbesses at 7 Ru Audran. Singles/doubles start at 100/140F with showers costing 10FF. A cut above is th renovated *Hôtel des Arts* (☎ 01 46 06 30 52; fax 01 46 06 10 83) at 5 Rue Tholozé. This two-star place has singles/doubles with shower and toilet starting at 340/460FF.

Places to Eat

Restaurants Except for those in touristy areas (Notre Dame, Louvre, Champs Élysées), most of the city's thousands of restaurants are pretty good value for money – at least by Parisian standards. Intense competition tends to rid the city quickly of places with bad food or prices that are out of line. Still, you can be unlucky. Study the posted menus carefully and check to see how busy the place is before entering.

Forum des Halles One of a chain of seven restaurants, *Léon de Bruxelles* (☎ 01 42 36 18 50; metro Les Halles) at 120 Rue Rambuteau (1er) is dedicated to only one thing: moules et frites (mussels and chips/French fries). Meal-size bowls of the bivalves start at 60FF. This place is open nonstop from 11.45 am to midnight (1 am on Friday and Saturday nights). A favourite with young Parisian branchés (trendies), *Batifol* ☎ 01 42 36 85 50; metro Les Halles or Étienne Marcel) at 14 Rue Mondétour (1er) excels at making pot au feu (beef and vegetables cooked in a clay pot) for 60FF. It's open daily from noon to midnight.

Opéra Area (2e & 9e) On the 1st floor at 103 Rue de Richelieu (2e), 500 metres east of Opéra-Garnier, is *Le Drouot* (☎ 01 42 96 68 23; metro Richelieu Drouot), whose décor and ambience haven't changed much since the late 1930s. A three-course traditional French meal with wine costs only 80FF. Le Drouot is open daily for lunch and dinner. *Chartier* (☎ 01 47 70 86 29; metro Rue Montmartre) at 7 Rue du Faubourg Montmartre (9e), under the same management, is famous for its ornate, late 19th-century dining room. Prices, fare and hours are similar to those at Le Drouot, but it closes a little earlier (9.30 pm).

Marais (4e) The heart of the old Jewish neighbourhood, Rue des Rosiers (metro: Saint Paul), has quite a few kosher (cacher) and kosher-style restaurants but most of them are European-orientated. If you're after kosher

couscous and kebabs, check out the restaurants along Blvd de Belleville (11e and 20e; metro Belleville or Couronnes).

Société Rosiers Alimentation (☎ 01 48 87 63 60), at 34 Rue des Rosiers, is one of several places along Rue des Rosiers selling Israeli takeaway food and Middle Eastern snacks such as shwarma and felafel. Paris' best known Jewish restaurant, founded in 1920, is *Restaurant Jo Goldenberg* (☎ 01 48 87 20 16) at 7 Rue des Rosiers. The food (main dishes about 70FF) is Jewish but not kosher. Jo Goldenberg is open from 8.30 am until about midnight daily except on Yom Kippur.

Le P'tit Gavroche (☎ 01 48 87 74 26; metro Hôtel de Ville), at 15 Rue Sainte Croix de la Bretonnerie, is a favourite with crowds of raucous working-class regulars. It is open daily except Sunday for lunch and dinner to midnight. The menu, available until about 10 pm or whenever the food runs out, costs around 48FF.

For vegetarian food, a good bet is *Aquarius* (☎ 01 48 87 48 71; metro Rambuteau) at 54 Rue Sainte Croix de la Bretonnerie, which has a calming, airy atmosphere. It is open Monday to Saturday from noon to 10 pm but the plat du jour is available only at lunch and dinner times. There's a two-course menu for 56FF.

Bastille (4e, 11e & 12e) Lots of ethnic restaurants line Rue de la Roquette and Rue de Lappe (11e), which intersects Rue de la Roquette 200 metres north-east of Place de la Bastille. Among the pizza joints and Chinese, North African and Japanese places, you'll find Paris' only fish and chips shop, *Hamilton's* (☎ 01 48 06 77 92; metro Bastille or Ledru Rollin) at 51 Rue de Lappe, which gets good reviews from homesick English expats. It is open Monday to Friday from noon to 2.30 pm and 6 pm to midnight and on Saturday from 1 pm to 1 am.

Notre Dame Area (4e, 5e & 6e) The Greek, North African and Middle Eastern restaurants in the area bounded by Rue Saint Jacques, Blvd Saint Germain, Blvd Saint Michel and the Seine attract mainly foreign tourists, who are unaware that some people refer to Rue de la Huchette and its nearby streets as 'bacteria alley' because of the high incidence of food

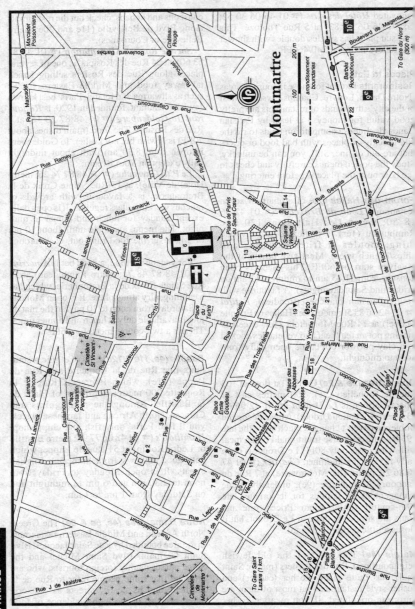

Montmartre

0   100   200 m

— arrondissement boundaries

PLACES TO STAY

7 Hôtel des Arts
8 Hôtel Bonséjour
11 Hôtel Audran
21 Idéal Hôtel

PLACES TO EAT

10 Le Mono African Restaurant
19 Refuge des Fondus Restaurant
22 Le Delta Brasserie

OTHER

1 Vineyard
2 Moulin de la Galette (Windmill)
3 Moulin Radet (Windmill)
4 Église Saint Pierre
5 Crypt & Dome Entrance
6 Sacré Cœur Basilica
9 Laundrette
12 Food Shops
13 Funicular Railway
14 Museum of Naive Art
15 La Locomotive Discothèque
16 Moulin Rouge Nightclub
17 Pigalle Sex & Entertainment District
18 Post Office
20 Bureau de Change

oisoning at restaurants there. But the
akeaway kebab and shwarma sandwiches
20FF) aren't bad.

L'Année du Dragon (☎ 01 46 34 23 46;
metro Saint Michel) at 10 Rue Saint Séverin
5e), which serves Chinese and Vietnamese
ood, has menus for as little as 36FF. It is open
laily for lunch and dinner. Sandwich shops sell
aguette halves with various fillings for around
8FF, and there's always *McDonald's* (metro:
Cluny-La Sorbonne) on the corner of Blvd
aint Germain and Rue de la Harpe (5e) open
o midnight.

East of Rue Saint Jacques, *Au Coin des
Gourmets* (☎ 01 43 26 12 92; metro Maubert
Mutualité) at 5 Rue Dante (5e) serves decent
ndochinese food. It is open for lunch and
inner every day but Tuesday. The lunch menu
s 68FF; main dishes are 40 to 55FF. For a
elightful selection of scrumptious central
uropean pastries and tourtes (quiche-like
ies), drop by *Pâtisserie Viennoise* (☎ 01 43
6 60 48; metro Cluny-La Sorbonne or Saint
Michel) at 8 Rue de l'École de Médicine (6e),
hich is on the other side of Blvd Saint Michel
om the Musée du Moyen Age. It is open

weekdays from 9 am to 7.15 pm but is closed
from mid-July to the end of August.

Panthéon (5e) The area around Rue Mouffetard is filled with dozens of places to eat and is
especially popular with students. Some of the
best discount crêpes in Paris are sold from a
little stall across the street from 68 Rue
Mouffetard between 11 am and 2 am. They
start at 11FF. *La Rose de Mouffetard* (☎ 01 43
26 66 43; metro Monge) at 6 Rue Mouffetard
serves some of the cheapest sit-down food in
town, including generous portions of tasty
couscous starting at only 25FF. This place is
open daily from 11 am to midnight.

For Tibetan food, a good choice is the
friendly *Tashi Delek* (☎ 01 43 26 55 55;
metro Luxembourg) – that's 'bon jour' in
Tibetan – at 4 Rue des Fossés Saint Jacques.
Tashi Delek is open for lunch and dinner
from Monday night to Saturday. Lunch/
dinner menus start at 40/105FF. If someone
else is treating, try *Aleka* (☎ 01 44 07 02 75)
at 187 Rue Saint Jacques for some of the
freshest Greek-style hors d'oeuvres (from
25FF) and grilled salmon and tuna (79FF) in
Paris. Aleka is open weekdays for lunch and
every night to 2 am for dinner.

Montparnasse (6e & 14e) Two somewhat
pricey places but real 'finds' in this area are *Le
Caméléon* (☎ 01 43 20 63 43; metro Vavin) at
6 Rue de Chevreuse (6e), which has never-to-
be-forgotten lobster ravioli on its menu, and *La
Cagouille* (☎ 01 43 22 09 01; metro Gaîté) at
10-12 Place Brancusi (14e), which faces 23
Rue de l'Ouest. Fish and shellfish are the
latter's speciality. Bookings at both are essential.

Montmartre (9e & 18e) There are dozens of
cafés and restaurants around Place du Tertre
but they tend to be touristy and overpriced. An
old Montmartre favourite is *Refuge des
Fondus* (☎ 01 42 55 22 65) at 17 Rue des Trois
Frères (18e), whose speciality is fondues. For
87FF, you get wine and a good quantity of
either cheese fondue Savoyarde or meat
fondue Bourguignonne (minimum of two). It's
open daily from 7 pm to 2 am and is very
popular, so book. *Le Mono* (☎ 01 46 06 99 20)
at 40 Rue Véron (18e) serves West African

dishes (Togolese to be exact) priced from 25 to 70FF. It's open every night except Wednesday. Get off at metro station Abbesses for the above restaurants.

Le Delta Brasserie (☎ 01 42 85 74 15; metro Barbès Rochechouart) at 17 Blvd Rochechouart (9e) caters to shoppers perusing the clothing and fabric stalls in the area and has plats du jour for 55FF.

University Restaurants The Centre Régional des Œuvres Universitaires et Scolaires, or CROUS (☎ 01 40 51 37 10), runs 15 student cafeterias (restaurants universitaires) in the city. Tickets (on sale at meal times) cost 21.10FF for students and 26.40FF for others. Some of the restaurants also have à la carte brasseries. In general, CROUS restaurants have rather confusing opening times that change according to rotational agreements among the restaurants and school holiday schedules (eg most are closed on weekends and during July and August).

Restaurant Universitaire Bullier (metro: Port Royal) is on the 2nd floor of the Centre Jean Sarrailh at 39 Rue Bernanos (5e). Lunch and dinner are served Monday to Friday and, during some months, on weekends as well. The ticket window, which is up one flight of stairs, is open from 11.30 am to 2 pm and 6.15 to 8 pm. One of the nicest CROUS restaurants in town is on the 7th floor of the Faculté de Droit et des Sciences Économiques (Faculty of Law & Economics; metro Vavin), which is south of the Jardin du Luxembourg at 92 Rue d'Assas (6e). It's open weekdays from 11.30 am to 3 pm. The ticket window is on the 6th floor.

Self-Catering Buying your own food is one of the best ways to keep down the cost of visiting Paris. Supermarkets are always cheaper than small grocery shops.

Food Markets The freshest and best-quality fruits, vegetables, cheeses and meats at the lowest prices in town are on offer at Paris' neighbourhood food markets. The city's dozen or so covered markets are open from 8 am to sometime between 12.30 and 1.30 pm and from 3.30 or 4 to 7.30 pm daily except Sunday afternoon and Monday. The open-air markets – about 60 scattered around town – are set up two or three mornings a week in squares and streets like Rue Mouffetard (5e) and Rue Daguerre (14e) and are open from 7 am to 1 pm.

Notre Dame Area (4e & 5e) On Île Saint Louis, there are boulangeries, fromageries and fruit and vegetable shops on Rue Saint Louis en l'Île and Rue des Deux Ponts (4e; metro Pont Marie). There is a cluster of food shops in the vicinity of Place Maubert (5e; metro Maubert-Mutualité), which is 300 metres south of Notre Dame, and on Rue Lagrange. On Tuesday, Thursday and Saturday from 7 am to 1 pm, Place Maubert is transformed into an outdoor produce market. There's an excellent fromagerie (metro: Maubert-Mutualité) at 47 Blvd Saint Germain (5e).

Saint Germain des Prés (6e) The largest cluster of food shops in the neighbourhood is one block north of Blvd Saint Germain around the intersection of Rue de Buci and Rue de Seine. There are also food shops along Rue Dauphine and the two streets that link it with Blvd Saint Germain, Rue de l'Ancienne Comédie and Rue de Buci.

Panthéon Area (5e) There are several food shops (metro: Luxembourg) along Rue Saint Jacques between Nos 172 and 218 (the area just south of Rue Soufflot).

Marais (4e) Fresh breads and Jewish-style central European pastries are available at the two *Finkelsztajn* bakeries (metro: Saint Paul) at 27 Rue des Rosiers and 24 Rue des Écouffes. There are quite a few food shops on Rue de Rivoli and Rue Saint Antoine around the Saint Paul metro stop.

Louvre Area (1er) You'll find a number of food shops one block north of where the western part of the Louvre meets the eastern end of Jardin des Tuileries.

Montmartre (18e) Most of the food shops in this area are along Rue des Abbesses, which about 500 metres south-west of Sacré Cœur and Rue Lepic.

Entertainment

Information in French on cultural events, music concerts, theatre performances, films, museum exhibitions, festivals, circuses etc is listed in two publications that come out each Wednesday: *Pariscope* (3FF), which includes an eight-page English section, and *L'Officiel des Spectacles* (2FF). They are available at most news kiosks.

Tickets Reservations and ticketing for all sorts of cultural events are handled by the ticket outlets in the FNAC stores at 136 Rue de Rennes (6e; ☎ 01 49 54 30 00; metro Saint Placide) and at the 3rd underground level of the Forum des Halles shopping mall (☎ 01 40 41 40 00; metro Châtelet-Les Halles) at 1-7 Rue Pierre Lescot (1er).

Cinemas The fashionable cinemas on Blvd du Montparnasse (6e & 14e; metro Montparnasse Bienvenüe) show both dubbed (VF) and original (VO) feature films. There's another cluster of cinemas at Carrefour de l'Odéon (6e; metro Odéon) and lots more movie theatres along the Ave des Champs Élysées (8e; metro George V) and Blvd Saint Germain (6e; metro Saint Germain des Prés).

The *Cinémathèque Française* (☎ 01 47 04 24 24) almost always leaves its foreign offerings non-dubbed. Several screenings take place almost every day at two locations: in the far eastern tip of the Palais de Chaillot on Ave Albert de Mun (16e; metro Trocadéro or Iéna) and at 18 Rue du Faubourg du Temple (11e; metro République). Tickets cost 30FF.

Parisian movie-going is rather pricey. Expect to pay around 45FF for a ticket. Students and people under 18 and over 60 usually get discounts of about 25% except on weekend nights. On Monday and/or Wednesday most cinemas give everyone discounts.

Pubs At 19 Rue Saint Jacques (5e), *Le Cloître* (☎ 01 43 25 19 92; metro Saint Michel) is an unpretentious, relaxed place with mellow background music which seems to please the young Parisians who congregate there. It is open daily from 3 pm to 2 am. Informal, friendly *Polly Maggoo* (☎ 01 46 33 33 64; metro Saint Michel), up the street at 11 Rue Saint Jacques, was founded in 1967 and still plays music from that era. It is open daily from 3 pm to the wee hours.

Another favourite with Anglo-Saxons is a rather loud American-style bar named *Le Violon Dingue* (☎ 01 43 25 79 93; metro Maubert-Mutualité), which is at 46 Rue de la Montagne Sainte Geneviève (5e). It is open daily from 7.30 pm to 2 am; live bands start at 10 pm on Thursday, Friday and Saturday. *Café Oz* (☎ 01 43 54 30 48; metro Luxembourg), at 18 Rue Saint Jacques, is a casual, friendly Australian pub with Fosters on tap. It is open daily from 11 am to 1.30 am.

Discothèques The discothèques – not really 'discos' as we know them but any place where there's music and dancing – favoured by the Parisian 'in' crowd change frequently, and many are officially private, which means that the gorilla-like bouncers can refuse entry to whomever they don't like the look of. Single men, for example, may not be admitted simply because they're alone and male. Women, on the other hand, get in free on some nights. Expect to pay at least 50FF on weekdays and 100FF on weekends.

Le Balajo (☎ 01 47 00 07 87; metro Bastille), a mainstay of the Parisian dance-hall scene since the time of Édith Piaf, is at 9 Rue de Lappe (11e), two blocks north-east of Place de la Bastille. It offers accordion music on Friday, Saturday and Sunday afternoons from 3 to 7 pm and dancing on Thursday, Friday and Saturday nights from 11.30 pm to 5 am. On Saturday and Sunday admission costs 40/50FF. At night admission is 100FF and includes one drink.

La Locomotive (☎ 01 42 57 37 37; metro Blanche) at 90 Blvd de Clichy (18e), which is in Pigalle next to the Moulin Rouge nightclub, occupies three floors, each offering a different ambience and kind of music. It is open from 11 pm until 6 am nightly except Monday. Entrance costs 65FF on weekdays and 100FF on Friday and Saturday nights, including one drink.

Jazz For the latest on jazz happenings in town, check the listings (see the beginning of this section). *Caveau de la Huchette* (☎ 01 43 26 65 05; metro Saint Michel) at 5 Rue de la Huchette (5e) is an old favourite with live jazz.

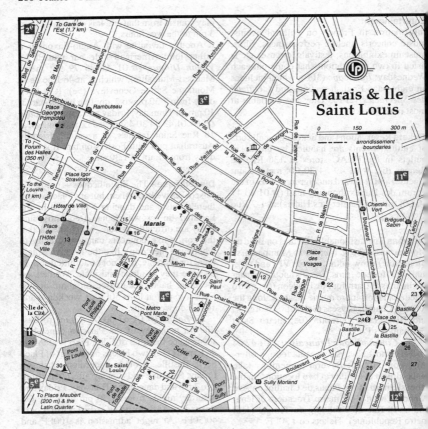

Marais & Île Saint Louis

0   150   300 m

arrondissement boundaries

PLACES TO STAY		9	Restaurant Jo Goldenberg	22	Victor Hugo's House

PLACES TO STAY
- 10 Grand Hôtel Mahler
- 11 Hôtel Pratic
- 12 Hôtel Moderne
- 14 Hôtel Rivoli
- 15 Grand Hôtel du Loiret
- 16 Hôtel de Nice
- 17 MIJE Maubisson
- 19 MIJE Fourcy
- 20 MIJE Fauconnier

PLACES TO EAT
- 3 Aquarius Vegetarian Restaurant
- 4 Le P'tit Gavroche Restaurant
- 8 Restaurants

- 9 Restaurant Jo Goldenberg
- 23 Ethnic Restaurants
- 31 Berthillon Ice Cream

OTHER
- 1 Accueil des Jeunes en France (AJF)
- 2 Centre Pompidou
- 5 Musée Picasso
- 6 Finkelsztajn Bakery
- 7 Laundrette
- 13 Hôtel de Ville (City Hall)
- 18 Memorial to the Unknown Jewish Martyr
- 21 Food Shops

- 22 Victor Hugo's House
- 24 Banque de France
- 25 Colonne de Juillet
- 26 Entrance to Opéra-Bastille
- 27 Opéra-Bastille
- 28 Port de Plaisance de Paris Arsenal
- 29 Notre Dame
- 30 WWII Deportation Memorial
- 32 Food Shops
- 33 Ulysse Bookshop

FRANCE

is open every night from 9.30 pm to 2.30 am
Sunday to Thursday nights), 3.30 am (Friday
ight) or 4 am (Saturday and holiday nights).
rom Sunday to Thursday, entry costs 60FF
55FF for students) and 70FF on Friday and
aturday.

oncerts & Opera Paris has all sorts of
rchestra, organ and chamber music concerts.
ome are even free, such as the organ concerts
eld at Notre Dame every Sunday at 5.30 pm.
péra-Bastille (☎ 01 44 73 13 99; metro Bas-
lle) at 2-6 Place de la Bastille (12e) has been
aris' main opera house since its opening in
989. The old – some would say real – opera
ouse, *Opéra-Garnier* (☎ 01 44 73 13 99;
etro Opéra) at Place de l'Opéra (9e) now
tages concerts and ballets. The cheapest
egular tickets, which get you a seat with an
bstructed view high above the stage, cost as
ttle as 20 to 30FF. Subject to availability,
eople under 25 and over 65 may be able to
urchase decent seats 15 minutes before the
urtain rises for the 100FF tarif spécial.

hings to Buy
ashion For fashionable clothing and acces-
ories, some of the fanciest shops in Paris are
ong Ave Montaigne (8e), Rue Saint Honoré
er & 8e), Place Vendôme (1er) and Rue du
aubourg Saint Honoré (8e). Rue Bonaparte
e) offers a good choice of mid-range bou-
ques.

epartment Stores Right behind Opéra-
arnier are two of Paris' largest department
ores. Au Printemps (☎ 01 42 82 50 00; metro
avre Caumartin) is at 64 Blvd Haussmann
e) and Galeries Lafayette (☎ 01 42 82 36 40;
etro Auber ou Chaussée), at 40 Blvd
aussmann (9e), is housed in two adjacent
uildings linked by a pedestrian bridge. The
ird of Paris' 'big three', Samaritaine (☎ 01
)41 20 20; metro Pont Neuf), consists of four
uildings between Pont Neuf and Rue de
ivoli. There is an amazing 360° view of the
ty from the 10th-floor terrace of Building 2
19 Rue de la Monnaie. Take the lift to the
h floor and walk up the narrow staircase. All
ree stores are open Monday to Saturday from
30 am to 7 pm (10 pm on Thursday).

Getting There & Away

Air Paris has two major international airports.
Aéroport d'Orly is 14 km south of central
Paris. For flight and other information, call
☎ 01 49 75 15 15. Aéroport Charles de Gaulle
(☎ 01 48 62 22 80), also known as Roissy-
Charles de Gaulle because it is in the Paris
suburb of Roissy, is 23 km north-east of central
Paris. Telephone numbers for information at
Paris' airline offices are:

Airline Office	Telephone
Air France	☎ 01 44 08 22 22
Air Inte	☎ 01 45 46 90 00
American Airline	☎ 01 42 89 05 22
British Airways	☎ 01 47 78 14 14
Continental Airline	☎ 01 42 99 09 09
Delta Air Lines	☎ 01 47 68 92 92
Northwest Airlines	☎ 01 42 66 90 00
Qantas Airways	☎ 01 44 55 52 00
Singapore Airlines	☎ 01 45 53 90 90
Thai Airways	☎ 01 44 20 70 80
Tower Air	☎ 01 44 51 56 56
TWA	☎ 01 49 19 20 00
United Airlines	☎ 01 48 97 82 82

Bus Eurolines runs buses from Paris to cities
all over Europe. The company's terminal, Gare
Routière Internationale (☎ 01 49 72 51 51;
metro Gallieni), is at Porte de Bagnolet (20e)
on the eastern edge of Paris. Its ticket office in
town (☎ 01 43 54 11 99; metro Cluny-La Sorbonne) at 55 Rue Saint Jacques (5e) is open
Tuesday to Friday from 9.30 am to 1 pm and
2.30 to 7 pm and on Monday and Saturday to
6 pm.

Cities served include Amsterdam (250FF
one way, eight hours), London (290FF, nine
hours), Madrid (590FF, 17 hours) and Rome
(590FF, 26 hours). People under 26 and over
60 get a discount of about 10%. Because the
French government prefers to avoid competition with the state-owned rail system and
regulated domestic airlines, there is no domestic, intercity bus service to or from Paris.

Train Paris has six major train stations (*gares*),
each handling traffic to different parts of
France and Europe. For information in English
call ☎ 08 36 35 35 39; the switchboards are
staffed from 7 am to 10 pm. All the stations
have exchange bureaus, and there is a tourist
office annexe at each one except Gare Saint
Lazare. The metro station attached to each

train station bears the same name as the gare. Paris' major train stations are:

Gare d'Austerlitz (13e) Quai d'Austerlitz (metro: Gare d'Austerlitz) – trains to the Loire Valley, Spain and Portugal and non-TGV trains to south-western France (Bordeaux, the Basque Country)

Gare de l'Est (10e) Place du 11 Novembre 1918 (metro: Gare de l'Est) – trains to parts of France east of Paris (Champagne, Alsace, Lorraine), Luxembourg, parts of Switzerland (Basel, Lucerne, Zürich), southern Germany (Frankfurt, Munich) and Austria

Gare de Lyon (12e) Place Louis Armand (metro: Gare de Lyon) – regular and TGV Sud-Est trains to points south-east of Paris, including Dijon, Lyon, Provence, Côte d'Azur, Alps, parts of Switzerland, Italy and Greece

Gare Montparnasse (15e) Blvd de Vaugirard (metro: Montparnasse Bienvenüe) – trains to Brittany and places on the way (Chartres, Angers, Nantes); and the TGV Atlantique, which serves Tours, Bordeaux and other places in south-western France

Gare du Nord (10e) Rue de Dunkerque (metro: Gare du Nord) – trains to northern France (Lille, Calais), the UK via the Channel Tunnel (TGV Nord), Belgium, Netherlands, northern Germany, Scandinavia, Moscow etc

Gare Saint Lazare (8e) Rue Saint Lazare (metro: Saint Lazare) – trains to Normandy and, via the Channel ports, ferries to England. The SNCF information office (☎ 01 53 42 00 00), which is 50 metres behind *voie* 2 (track 2), can also help tourists with matters not concerning train travel.

Getting Around

RATP, Paris' public transit system, is one of the most efficient in the world and one of the biggest urban transport bargains (see Metro/Bus Tickets). Free metro/RER/bus maps are available at the ticket windows of most stations and at tourist offices. For information on metros and RER commuter trains and buses, call ☎ 08 36 68 77 14 between 6 am and 9 pm.

To/From Orly Airport Orly Rail is the quickest way to get to the Left Bank and the 16e. Take the free shuttle bus to the Pont de Rungis-Aéroport d'Orly RER (commuter rail) station, which is on the C2 line, and get on a train (30FF) heading into the city. Another fast way into town is to hop on the Orlyval shuttle train (52FF); it stops near Orly-Sud's Porte F and links Orly with the Antony RER station, which is on line B4. Orlybus (30FF or six bus/metro tickets), takes you to the Denfert-Rochereau metro station (14e).

Air France buses charge 40FF to take you to Ave du Maine at the Gare Montparnasse (15e) or the Aérogare des Invalides, which is next to Esplanade des Invalides (7e). RATP bus No 183 (four tickets) goes to Porte de Choisy (13e) but is very slow. All the services between Orly airport and Paris run every 15 minutes or so (less frequently late at night) from early in the morning (sometime between 5.30 and 6.30 am) to 11 or 11.30 pm.

Taking a taxi from Orly airport can work out cheaper per person if there are four people to share it.

To/From Charles de Gaulle (CDG) Airport The fastest way to get to/from the city is by Roissy Rail. Free shuttle buses take you from the airport terminals to the Roissy-Charles de Gaulle RER (commuter rail) station. You can buy tickets to CDG (45FF) at RER stations. If you get on at an ordinary metro station you can buy a ticket when you change to the RER or pay at the other end or on the train (with a fine if you get caught).

Air France buses will take you to Porte Maillot (16e & 17e; metro Porte Maillot) or the corner of Ave Carnot near the Arc de Triomphe (17e) for 55FF. Its buses to Blvd de Vaugirard at the Gare Montparnasse (15e) cost 65FF. Roissybus (RATP bus No 352) goes to the American Express office (9e) near Place de l'Opéra and costs 35FF. RATP bus No 350 goes to Gare du Nord (10e) and Gare de l'Est (10e). Until 9.15 pm (heading into the city) and 8.2? am (towards the airport), RATP bus No 35? goes to Ave du Trône (11e & 12e), on the eastern side of Place de la Nation. Both RATP buses require six tickets.

Unless otherwise indicated, the buses and trains from CDG to Paris run from sometime between 5 and 6.30 am until 11 or 11.30 pm.

Bus Paris' extensive bus network tends to get overlooked by visitors, in part because the metro is so quick, efficient and easy to use. Bus routes are indicated on the free RATP maps No 1, *Petit Plan de Paris*, and No 3, *Grand Plan Île de France*.

Short trips cost one bus/metro/RER ticket (see Underground/Bus Tickets below), while longer rides require two. Travellers without tickets can purchase them from the driver

Whatever kind of ticket *(coupon)* you have, you must cancel it in the little machine next to the driver. The fines are hefty if you're caught without a ticket or without a cancelled ticket. If you have a Carte Orange, Formule 1 or Paris Visite pass (see the following Metro & RER section), just flash it at the driver – do not cancel your ticket.

After the metro shuts down at around 12.45 am, the Noctambus network, whose symbol is a black owl silhouetted against a yellow moon, links the Châtelet-Hôtel de Ville area (4e) with lots of places on the Right Bank (lines A to H) and a few on the Left Bank (lines J and R). Noctambuses begin their runs from the even-numbered side of Ave Victoria (4e), which is between the Hôtel de Ville and Place du Châtelet, every hour on the half-hour from 1.30 to 5.30 am. A ride requires three tickets (four tickets if your journey involves a transfer).

Metro & RER Paris' underground rail network consists of two separate but linked systems: the Métropolitain, known as the metro, which has 13 lines and over 300 stations, many marked by Hector Guimard's famous noodle-like Art-Nouveau entrances with the red 'eyes', and the suburban commuter rail network, the RER which, along with certain SNCF lines, is divided into eight concentric zones. The term 'metro' is used in this chapter to refer to the Métropolitain and any part of the RER system within Paris. The whole system has been designed so that no point in Paris is more than 500 metres from a metro stop; in fact, some places in the city centre are within a few hundred metres of up to three stations.

You may be able to reduce the number of transfers you'll have to make by going to a station a bit further on from your destination. For metro stations to avoid late at night, see Dangers & Annoyances earlier in the Paris section.

How it Works Each metro train is known by the name of its terminus; trains on the same line have different names depending on which direction they are travelling in. On lines that split into several branches and thus have more than one end-of-the-line station, the final destination of each train is indicated on the front, sides and interior of the train cars. In the sta-

tions, white-on-blue *sortie* signs indicate exits and black-on-orange *correspondance* signs show how to get to connecting trains. The last metro train sets out on its final run at 12.30 am. Plan ahead so as not to miss your connection. The metro starts up again at 5.30 am.

Metro/Bus Tickets The same green 2nd-class tickets are valid on the metro, the bus and, for travel within the Paris city limits, the RER's 2nd-class carriages. They cost 7.50FF if bought separately and 44FF for a booklet *(carnet)* of 10. For children aged four to nine a carnet costs 22FF. One ticket lets you travel between any two metro stations, including stations outside of the Paris city limits, no matter how many transfers are required. You can also use it on the RER commuter rail system for travel within Paris (within zone 1).

For travel on the RER to destinations outside the city, purchase a special ticket *before* you board the train or you won't be able to get out of the station and could be fined. Always keep your ticket until you reach your destination and exit the station; if you're caught without a ticket, or with an invalid one, you'll be fined. A weekly and monthly bus/metro/RER pass, known as the Carte Orange, is available for travel in two to eight urban and suburban zones; you must present a photograph of yourself to buy one. The weekly ticket *(coupon hebdomadaire)*, which costs 67FF for travel in zones 1 and 2 (covering all of Paris proper plus a few RER stops in the inner suburbs), is valid from Monday to Sunday. The validity of the monthly *(mensuel)* ticket (230FF for zones 1 and 2) begins on the first day of each calendar month. You *must* write your name on the Carte Orange and the number of your Carte Orange on your weekly/monthly ticket.

Formule 1 and Paris Visite passes, designed to facilitate bus, metro and RER travel for tourists, are on sale in many metro stations, the train stations and international airports. The Formule 1 card (and its *coupon*) allows unlimited travel for one day in two to four zones. The version valid for zones 1 and 2 costs 30FF. The four-zone version (60FF) lets you go all the way out to Versailles and both airports (but not on Orlyval). Paris Visite passes are valid for three consecutive days of travel in three to five zones. The 1 to 3-zone version costs 105/165FF (three/five days). Obviously a Paris Visite pass is much dearer than a weekly two-zone Carte Orange ticket.

Taxi Paris' 15,000 taxis have a reputation for paying little heed to riders' convenience. Another common complaint is that it can be difficult to find a taxi late at night (after 11 pm) or in the rain. The flag fall is 12FF; within the city, it costs 3.23FF per km between 7 am and 7 pm Monday to Saturday. On nights, Sunday and holidays, it's 5.10FF per km. Animals, a fourth passenger and heavy luggage cost extra. Tips are not obligatory, but no matter what the fare is, usual tips range from 2FF to a maximum of 5FF.

The easiest way to find a taxi is to walk to the nearest taxi stand (*tête de station*), of which there are 500 scattered around the city and marked on any of the Michelin 1:10,000 maps. Radio-dispatched taxis include Taxis Bleus (☎ 01 49 36 10 10), G7 Taxis (☎ 01 47 39 47 39), Alpha Taxis (☎ 01 45 85 85 85), Taxis-Radio Étoile (☎ 01 42 70 41 41) and Artaxi (☎ 01 42 41 50 50). If you order a taxi by phone, the meter is switched on as soon as the driver gets word of your call – wherever that may be (but usually not too far away).

Car & Motorcycle Driving in Paris is nerve-racking but not impossible. Most side streets are one way (*sens unique*) and, without a good map, trying to get around town by car will make you feel like a rat in a maze. In general, the best way to get across the city is via one of the major boulevards, except during rush hour. If you're caught in rush hour, all you can do is find a parking space and take the metro. You must feed Paris meters every two hours. The fastest way to get all the way across Paris is usually the Blvd Périphérique, the ring road (beltway) around the city.

Rent A Car (☎ 01 43 45 15 15), has offices at 79 Rue de Bercy (12e; metro Bercy) and 84 Ave de Versailles (16e; metro Mirabeau), and has Fiat Pandas with unlimited km for 298FF a day, including insurance. The weekly rate is 1398FF. The Rue de Bercy office is open Monday to Thursday from 8 am to 6.30 pm, Friday from 8 am to 7 pm and on Saturday from 9 am to 6 pm. Avis (☎ 01 46 10 60 60) has offices at all six train stations, both airports and several other locations in the Paris area. Europcar (☎ 01 30 43 82 82) has bureaus at both airports and almost 20 other locations. Hertz (☎ 01 47 88 51 51) also has offices at the airports and at many other places around Paris.

For information on purchase/repurchase plans, see the Getting Around section at the start of this chapter.

Bicycle With its heavy traffic and impatient drivers Paris has never been a cyclist's paradise. But things are improving. In early 1996 the city unveiled a plan to establish a 50-km network of bicycle lanes across Paris. By early 1997, there will be lanes stretching from Porte de Pantin in the north to Porte de Vanves in the south, and east to west from the Bois de Vincennes to the Bois de Boulogne. Centrally, the lanes run along Rue de Rivoli and the Blvd Saint Germain. The tourist office should have detailed maps.

Maison du Velo (☎ 01 42 81 24 72), at Rue Fénélan (10e; metro Gare du Nord), has bicycles available for 150FF per day, 260FF per weekend and 575FF per week.

Cyclic (☎ 01 43 25 63 67), at 19 Rue Mange (5e; metro Cardinal Lemoine), rents bikes by the hour (20FF), day (100FF) and week (300FF).

See the sections on Bois de Boulogne (under Things to See) and Bicycle (under Organised Tours) for more information.

Around Paris

The region surrounding Paris is known as the Île de France (Island of France) because of its position between four rivers: the Aube, Marne, Oise and Seine. It was from this relatively small area that, starting around 1100 AD, the kingdom of France began to expand. Today, the region's proximity to Paris and a number of remarkable sights make it an especially popular day-trip destination for people staying in Paris.

EURODISNEY

It took US$4 billion to turn beet fields 32 km east of Paris into the much heralded

EuroDisney theme park (☎ 01 64 74 30 00), which opened in April 1992 amid much moaning from France's intellectuals. Though far from turning a profit, the park is pulling in European crowds by the hundreds of thousands.

From June to September EuroDisney is open daily from 9 am to 8 pm (11 pm on Saturday and Sunday), the rest of the year it's open daily from 10 am to 6 pm (8 pm on Sunday). All-day entry costs 195FF for everyone over age 12 (150FF for children aged three to 11). Three-day passes are 505/390FF.

To get there, take RER line A4 to the terminus (Marne-la-Vallée Chessy), but check the destination boards to ensure your train goes all the way to the end. Trains, which take 35 minutes from the Nation stop on Place de la Nation (12e), run every 10 or 15 minutes or so. Sometimes, usually during the off-peak season, RER/EuroDisney offer cheap promotional fares. There are also shuttle buses from Orly and Roissy-Charles de Gaulle airports (80FF one way).

VERSAILLES

Site of France's grandest and most famous chateau, Versailles (population 92,000) served as the country's political capital and the seat of the royal court from 1682 until 1789, when revolutionary mobs massacred the palace guard and dragged Louis XVI and Marie-Antoinette off to Paris, where they were later guillotined. After the Franco-Prussian War of 1870-71, the victorious Prussians proclaimed the establishment of the German empire from the chateau's Galerie des Glaces (Hall of Mirrors). In 1919 the Treaty of Versailles was signed in the same room, officially ending WWI and imposing harsh conditions on a defeated Germany, Austria and Hungary.

Because Versailles is on most travellers' 'must-see' lists, the chateau can be jammed with tourists, especially on weekends, in summer and most especially on summer Sundays. The best way to avoid the lines is to arrive early in the morning.

Information
The tourist office (☎ 01 39 50 36 22) is at 7 rue des Réservoirs, just north of the chateau. From November to April, it is open Monday to Saturday from 9 am to 12.30 pm and 2 to 6.15

pm (on Saturday to 5 pm). During the rest of the year, it is open daily from 9 am to 7 pm.

Château de Versailles
The enormous Château de Versailles (☎ 01 30 84 74 00) was built in the mid-17th century during the reign of Louis XIV (the Sun King). Among the advantages of Versailles was its distance from the political intrigues of Paris; out here, it was much easier for the king to contain and keep an eye on his scheming nobles. The plan worked brilliantly, all the more so because court life turned the nobles into sycophantic courtiers who expended most of their energy vying for royal favour à la Les Liaisons Dangereuses.

The chateau essentially consists of four parts: the main palace building, which is a classical structure with innumerable wings, sumptuous bedchambers and grand halls; the vast 17th-century gardens, laid out in the formal French style; and two out-palaces, the late 17th-century Grand Trianon and the mid-18th century Petit Trianon.

Opening Hours & Tickets The main building is open daily except Monday and public holidays from 9 am to 5.30 pm (6.30 pm from May to September). Entrance to the **Grands Appartements** (State Apartments), which include the 73-metre-long **Galerie des Glaces** (Hall of Mirrors) and the **Appartement de la Reine** (Queen's Suite), costs 45FF (35FF reduced rate). Everyone pays 35FF on Sunday. Tickets are on sale at Entrée A (Entrance A), which is off to the right from the equestrian statue of Louis XIV as you approach the building. You won't be able to visit other parts of the main palace unless you take one of the guided tours (see Guided Tours below). Entrée H has facilities for the disabled, including a lift.

The **Grand Trianon**, which costs 25FF (15FF reduced rate), is open daily except Monday. From October to April, opening hours are 10 am to 12.30 pm and 2 to 5.30 pm (10 am to 5.30 pm on weekends). During the rest of the year, hours are 10 am to 6.30 pm. The **Petit Trianon**, open the same hours as the Grand Trianon, costs 15FF (10FF reduced rate).

The gardens are open every day of the week from 7 am to nightfall. Entry is free except on Sundays from May to early October when the baroque fountains 'perform'. The **Grandes Eaux** show takes place from 3.30 to 5 pm and costs 25FF.

At the time of writing, Versailles was in the process of being privatised; you may want to call the chateau or tourist office to check whether hours and prices have changed drastically.

Guided Tours Eight different guided tours are available in English. A one-hour tour costs 25FF in addition to the regular entry fee. To buy tickets and make advance reservations (☎ 01 30 84 76 18), go to entrées C or D. Cassette-guided tours in six different languages are also available at entrées A and C for 25FF.

Other Attractions

The city of Versailles is filled with beautiful buildings from the 17th and 18th centuries. The tourist office has a brochure of historic walks (*promenades historiques*) pinpointing more than two dozen of these structures. They include: the **Jeu de Paume** (check the opening hours with the tourist office) on Rue du Jeu de Paume, where the representatives of the Third Estate constituted themselves as a National Assembly in June 1789; the **Musée Lambinet** (☎ 01 39 50 30 32) at 54 Blvd de la Reine (open Tuesday to Sunday from 2 to 6 pm); and the mid-18th century **Cathédrale Saint Louis** at Place Saint Louis, renowned for its enormous pipe organ.

Getting There & Away

Bus Bus No 171 takes you from the Pont de Sèvres metro stop in Paris all the way to Place d'Armes, right in front of the chateau.

Train Versailles, 23 km south-west of central Paris, has three train stations: Versailles-Rive Gauche, Versailles-Chantiers and Versailles-Rive Droite. Each is served by one of the three rail services that link Versailles with Paris.

RER line C5 takes you from Paris' Gare d'Austerlitz and various other RER stations on the Left Bank (including Saint Michel and Champ de Mars-Tour Eiffel) to Versailles-Rive Gauche, which is 700 metres south-east of the chateau on Ave Général de Gaulle. Check the electronic destination lists on the platform to make sure you take a train that goes all the way there.

SNCF trains go from Paris' Gare Montparnasse to Versailles-Chantiers, which is 1.3 km south-east of the chateau just off Ave de Sceaux. SNCF trains also run from Paris' Gare Saint Lazare to Versailles-Rive Droite, 1.2 km north-east of the chateau. Many of the trains from Gare Montparnasse to Versailles continue on to Chartres. Eurail-pass holders can travel free on the SNCF trains but not on those operated by the RER.

CHARTRES

The indescribably beautiful 13th-century cathedral of Chartres (population 43,000) rises abruptly from the corn fields 88 km south-west of Paris. Crowned by two soaring spires – one Gothic, the other Romanesque – it dominates the attractive medieval town clustered around its base. The present cathedral has been attracting pilgrims for eight centuries, but the city has been a site of pilgrimage for over two millennia: the Gallic Druids may have had a sanctuary here, and the Romans apparently built a temple dedicated to the Dea Mater (mother goddess).

Orientation

The medieval sections of Chartres are situated along the Eure River and the hillside to the west. The cathedral, which is visible from almost everywhere, is about 500 metres east of the train station.

Information

Tourist Office The tourist office (☎ 02 37 21 50 00) is one block south-west of the cathedral's main entrance at Place de la Cathédrale. It is open Monday to Friday from 9.30 am to 6, 6.30 or 6.45 pm, depending on the season. Saturday hours are 9.30 am to 5 pm (6 pm from March to October). From May to September, the office is also open on Sunday from 10.30 am to 12.30 pm and 2.30 to 5.30 pm; during the rest of the year it is open on Sunday morning only. Hotel reservations cost 10FF (plus a 50FF deposit).

Money & Post Banks are usually open Tuesday to Saturday, including the Banque de France (☎ 02 37 91 59 03) at 32 Rue du Docteur Maunoury about a km south of the

-ain station. The main post office is at Place
es Épars. Chartres' postcode is 28000.

hings to See & Do

:athédrale Notre Dame Chartres' cathedral
☎ 02 37 21 56 33) was built in the first quarter
f the 13th century and, unlike so many of its
:ontemporaries, it has not been significantly
nodified since then. Built to replace an earlier
tructure devastated by fire in 1194, the con-
truction of this early Gothic masterpiece took
nly 25 years, which is why the cathedral has
 high degree of architectural unity. It was
lmost torn down during the Reign of Terror
nd managed to survive WWII bombing raids
nscathed.

The cathedral is open daily from 7 am to 7
m (7.30 pm from April to September). From
pril to November (and sometimes in winter),
nglishman Malcolm Miller gives fascinating
ours (30FF) of what he calls 'this book of
tained glass and sculpture' at noon and 2.45
m every day except Sunday.

The 105-metre Clocher Vieux (old bell
)wer), the tallest Romanesque steeple still
:anding, is to the right as you face the Roman-
sque Portail Royal (the main entrance). The
:locher Neuf (new bell tower) has a Gothic
)ire dating from 1513 and can be visited daily,
xcept Sunday morning, from 9.30 or 10 to
1.30 am and 2 to 4 or 4.30 pm (October to
larch) or 5.30 pm (April to September). The
e is 14FF (10FF reduced rate).

Inside, the cathedral's most exceptional
:ature is its extraordinary stained-glass
indows, most of which are 13th-century orig-
als and are slowly being cleaned at great
xpense. The three exceptional windows over
e main entrance date from around 1150. The
range labyrinth on the nave floor in dark and
ght stone was used by medieval pilgrims while
aying. The trésor (treasury) displays a piece
f cloth given to the cathedral in 876 said to have
en worn by the Virgin Mary. It is open every
ternoon from Tuesday to Saturday and in the
orning as well from April to October.

The early 11th-century Romanesque crypt,
e largest in France, can be visited by a half-
)ur guided tour in French for 11FF. Tours
:part from the cathedral's gift shop, La
rypte, which is outside the south entrance at
3 Rue du Cloître Notre Dame, every day at 11
n, 2.15, 3.30 and 4.30 pm. From mid-June to

mid-September there's an additional tour at
5.15 pm.

Centre International du Vitrail The International Centre of Stained Glass Art (☎ 02 37 21
65 72), partly housed in a 13th-century underground storehouse north of the cathedral at 5
Rue du Cardinal Pie, has exhibits on stained-
glass production, restoration, history and
symbolism; it's not a bad idea to stop by here
before visiting the cathedral if you read French.
The centre is open Monday to Friday from 9.30
am to 12.30 pm and 1.30 to 6 pm and on
weekends and holidays from 10 am to 12.30
pm and 2.30 to 6 pm. The entry fee is 15FF
(12FF reduced rate).

Musée des Beaux-Arts The fine arts museum
(☎ 02 37 36 41 39), which is behind (north of)
the cathedral at 29 Cloître Notre Dame, is housed
in the 17th- and 18th-century Palais Épiscopal
(Bishop's Palace). Its collections include paintings from the 16th to 19th centuries, wooden
sculptures from the Middle Ages, a number of
17th- and 18th-century harpsichords and some
tapestries. The museum is open daily, except
Tuesday, from 10 am to noon and 2 to 5 pm (10
am to 6 pm from April to October). Entrance is
10FF (5FF reduced rate).

Old City During the Middle Ages, the city of
Chartres grew and developed along the banks
of the Eure River. Among the many buildings
remaining from that period are private residences, stone bridges, tanneries, wash houses
and a number of churches. Streets with buildings of interest include Rue de la Tannerie,
which runs along the Eure, and Rue des
Écuyers, which is midway between the cathedral and the river. Église Saint Pierre at Place
Saint Pierre has a massive bell tower dating
from around 1000 and some fine (and often
overlooked) medieval stained-glass windows.

Walking Tour Self-guided cassette-tape tours
of the old city can be rented at the tourist office
for 35/40FF for one or two people (plus 100FF
deposit).

Places to Stay
Camping About 2.5 km south-east of the train
station on Rue de Launay is *Les Bords de*

FRANCE

l'Eure camping ground (☎ 02 37 28 79 43), which is open from April to early September. Two adults with a tent and car pay 47FF. To get there from the train station take bus No 8 to the Vignes stop.

Hostel The pleasant and calm *Auberge de Jeunesse* (☎ 02 37 34 27 64) at 23 Ave Neigre is about 1.5 km east of the train station via the ring road (Blvd Charles Péguy and Blvd Jean Jaurès). By bus, take line No 3 from the train station and get off at the Rouliers stop. Reception is open daily from 8 to 10 am and from 3 to 10 pm (11 pm in summer). A bed costs 65FF, including breakfast. The hostel may be closed between December and January.

Hotels The cheapest hotel in town is the *Hôtel Le Goût Royal* (☎ 02 37 36 57 45) at 17 Rue Nicole, which is 200 metres south-west of the train station. Very basic doubles with communal showers and toilets cost 120FF. The *Hôtel de l'Ouest* (☎ 02 37 21 43 27), a two-star place opposite the train station at 3 Place Pierre Sémard, has clean, carpeted doubles/triples for 120/170FF (with washbasin and bidet), 140/240FF (with shower) and 210/260FF (with shower and toilet).

A lovely two-star choice is *Hôtel de la Poste* (☎ 02 37 21 04 27; fax 02 37 36 42 17), north-west of Place des Épars at 3 Rue du Général Koening, with singles/doubles from 215FF with shower (265/290FF with shower and toilet). Triples/quads with shower cost 360/430FF.

Places to Eat

Café Serpente (☎ 02 37 21 68 81), a brasserie and salon de thé across from the south porch of the cathedral at 2 Rue du Cloître Notre Dame, has main dishes for 72 to 98FF and large salads for 40 to 68FF. It is open daily from 10 am to 1 pm. *Le Petit Bistro* (☎ 02 37 21 09 23), three blocks south of the cathedral at 12 Place Billard, is a casual wine bar/bistro with generous charcuterie (42FF) and cheese platters (25FF). It is open daily from 9 am to 10 pm. The *Monoprix* supermarket at 21 Rue Noël Ballay north-east of Place des Épars is open daily from 9 am to 7.30 pm.

Getting There & Around

Train The train station (☎ 08 36 35 35 39) is at Place Pierre Sémard. The trip from Paris' Gare Montparnasse (69FF one way) takes 50 to 70 minutes. The last train back to Paris leaves Chartres just after 9 pm on weekdays and an hour or so later on weekends. There is also direct rail service to/from Nantes, Quimper, Rennes and Versailles.

Taxi For a taxi in Chartres, call ☎ 02 37 36 00 00.

Alsace

Alsace, the easternmost part of northern France, is nestled between the Vosges Mountains and, about 30 km to the east, the Rhine River, marking the Franco-German border. The area owes its unique language, architecture, cuisine and atmosphere to both sides of this river.

Most of Alsace became part of France in 1648, although Strasbourg, the region's largest city, retained its independence until 1681. But more than two centuries of French rule did little to dampen 19th and early 20th-century German enthusiasm for a foothold on the west bank of the southern Rhine, and Alsace was twice annexed by Germany: from the Franco-Prussian War (1871) until the end of WWI and again between 1939 and 1944.

Language

The Alsatian language, a Germanic dialect similar to that spoken in nearby parts of Germany and Switzerland, is still used by many Alsatians, especially older people in rural areas. Alsatian is known for its singsong intonations, which also characterise the way some Alsatians speak French.

STRASBOURG

The cosmopolitan city of Strasbourg (population 256,000), just a couple of km west of the Rhine, is Alsace's great metropolis and intellectual and cultural capital. Towering above the restaurants, pubs and *bars à musique* of the lively old city is the cathedral, a medieval marvel in pink sandstone near which is clustered one of the finest ensembles of museums in France. Strasbourg's distinctive architecture, including the centuries-old half-timbered houses, and its exemplary orderliness impart an unmistakably Alsatian ambience.

When it was founded in 1949, the Council of Europe (Conseil de l'Europe) decided to base itself in Strasbourg. The organisation's huge headquarters, the Palais de l'Europe, is used for one week each month (except in summer) by the European Parliament, the legislative branch of the EU.

Orientation
The train station is 350 metres west of the old city, which is an island delimited by the Ill River to the south and the Fossé du Faux Rempart to the north. The main public square in the old city is Place Kléber, which is 400 metres north-west of the cathedral. The quaint Petite France area is in the old city's south-west corner.

Information
Tourist Office The main tourist office (☎ 03 88 52 28 28) at 17 Place de la Cathédrale is open from 9 am to 6 pm, and from May to September daily from 8.30 am to 7 pm.

There's a tourist office annexe (☎ 03 88 32 51 49) in the underground complex beneath the Place de la Gare in front of the train station. It's open weekdays from 9 am to 12.30 pm and 1.45 to 6 pm. From April to June it's also open on the weekend, and from June to September hours are 8.30 am to 7 pm daily. This is a good place to pick up bus tickets. The office also sells the Strasbourg Pass (50FF, valid for three days) which includes free/reduced admission to museums.

Money The Banque de France is at 9 Place Broglie. The Banque CIAL bureau in the train station is open weekdays from 9 am to 1 pm and 2 to 7.30 pm and weekends from 9 am to 8 pm. The commission is 15FF on weekdays and 26FF on weekends. There's a 24-hour exchange machine outside the Sogenal bank at Place Gutenberg; American Express (☎ 03 88 75 78 75) at 31 Place Kléber is open weekdays from 8.45 am to noon and 1.30 to 6 pm.

Post The main post office (☎ 03 88 52 31 00), opposite 8 Ave de la Marseillaise, is open

weekdays from 8 am to 7 pm and on Saturday till noon. The branch post office to the left of the train station keeps the same hours. Both offer currency exchange. The postcode of central Strasbourg is 67000.

Things to See & Do
Walking Tour Strasbourg is a great place for an aimless stroll. The bustling **Vieille Ville** is filled with pedestrian malls, up-market shopping streets and lively public squares. There are river views from the quays and paths along the Ill River and the Fossé du Faux Rempart, and in **La Petite France**, half-timbered houses line the narrow streets and canals. The city's parks – **Parc de l'Orangerie** and **Place de la République** particularly – provide a welcome respite from the traffic and bustle. Guided tours of the town (38FF) are organised by the tourist office every Saturday from April to December and from Tuesday to Saturday in July and August.

Cathédrale Strasbourg's impossibly lacy Gothic cathedral was begun in 1176 after an earlier cathedral had burnt down. The west façade was completed in 1284, but the spire (its southern companion was never built) was not in place until 1439. Following the Reformation and a long period of bitter struggle, the cathedral came under Protestant control and was not returned to the Catholic Church until 1681. Many of the statues decorating the cathedral are copies – the originals can be seen in the Musée de l'Œuvre Notre-Dame (see the Museums section).

The cathedral is open from 7 to 11.30 am and 12.40 to 7 pm daily except during masses. The 30-metre-high Gothic and Renaissance contraption just inside the south entrance is the **horloge astronomique**, a 16th-century clock (the mechanism dates from 1842) that strikes every day at precisely 12.30 pm. There is a 5FF charge to see the carved wooden figures do their thing.

The 66-metre-high platform above the façade (from which the tower and its spire soar another 76 metres) can be visited daily – if you don't mind the 330 steps to the top. It's open from 9 am (8.30 am in July and August) to 4.30 pm (November to February), 5.30 pm (March and October), 6.30 pm (April to June and September) or 7 pm

PLACES TO STAY
2   CIARUS (Hostel)
19 Hôtel de Bruxelles
21 Hôtel Le Colmar
24 Hôtel Weber
36 Hôtel Michelet
43 Hôtel de la Cruche d'Or
44 Hôtel Patricia
49 Hôtel de l'Ill

PLACES TO EAT
18 Restaurant Le Cappadoce
22 Pâtisserie
32 Au Crocodile
33 Aldo Pizzeria
42 Winstub Zuem Strissel
45 Au Pont Saint Martin Restaurant
51 Le Bouchon & Festival Bar
    Américain
52 La Michaudière
54 Adan Vegetarian Restaurant

OTHER
1   Synagogue de la Paix
3   Law Courts
4   Palais du Rhin
5   Préfecture
6   Bibliothèque Nationale et
    Universitaire
7   US Consulate
8   Église Saint Paul
9   Main Post Office
10 Théâtro National
11 Banque de France
12 Église Saint Pierre-le-Jeune
    (Prostestant)
13 Post Office Branch
14 Train Station
15 Tourist Office Annexe
16 Europcar Car Rental
17 Voyages Wasteels (Travel
    Agency)
20 Budget Car Rental
23 Coop Supermarket
25 L'Académie de la Bière

26 Église Saint Pierre-le-Vieux (Catholic)
27 Cinéma Club
28 Cinéma Star
29 Printemps (Department Store)
30 American Express
31 Nouvelles Galeries-Magmod
    (Department Store)
34 Main Tourist Office
35 24-Hour Exchange Machine
    (Sogenal Bank)
37 Cathédrale Notre Dame
38 Bar des Aviateurs
39 Château des Rohan, Musée
    Archéologique, Musée des Arts
    Décoratifs & Musée des Beaux-Arts
40 Musée d'Art Moderne & Post Office
    Branch
41 Musée de l'Œuvre Notre-Dame
46 Église Saint Thomas
47 Musée Alsacien
48 Bierstub Le Trou
50 Café des Anges (Live Music Bar)
53 Bus Station

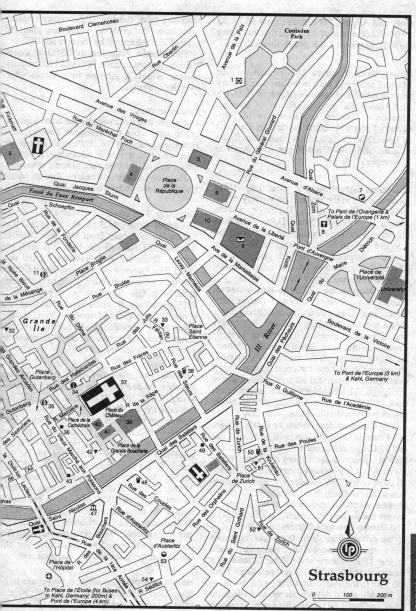

Boulevard Clemenceau
Rue Oberlin
Avenue de la Paix
Contades Park
1
Avenue des Vosges
Rue du Maréchal Foch
Rue du Général Gourard
3
5
Quai Jacques Sturm
4
Place de la République
6
Avenue d'Alsace
7
Quai du Zorn
To Parc de l'Orangerie & Palais de l'Europe (1 km)
8
Fossé du Faux Rempart
Quai
Rue de la Fonderie
Schoepflin
10
Avenue de la Liberté
Quai
Lezay - Marnésia
9
Ave de la Marseillaise
Koch
Pont d'Auvergne
Quai du Maire
Dietrich
11
Place Broglie
Rue Brûlée
Place de l'Université
University
32
Grande Île
Rue des Juifs
33
Rue du Faisan
Place Saint Etienne
Ill River
Boulevard de la Victoire
Rue des Dômes
Rue des Frères
Rue des Sœurs
38
Quai des Pêcheurs
To Pont de l'Europe (3 km) & Kehl, Germany
Place Gutenberg
Rue des Hallebardes
37
Rue St Guillaume
Rue de l'Académie
Gutenberg
34
35
R Mercière
36
R de la Râpe
Place du Château
39
Quai des Bateliers
Rue des Bateliers
Rue de Zurich
Rue de la Krutenau
Rue des Poules
Place de la Cathédrale
40
41
42
Place de la Grande Boucherie
49
50
51
43
48
Rue des Couples
Rue d'Austerlitz
47
Rue des Orphelins
Place de Zurich
52
Rue de Zurich
Rue du Saint Gothard
Quai Saint Nicolas
Rue des Bouchers
Place d'Austerlitz
53
Place de l'Hôpital
54
R Sédillot
To Place de l'Étoile (for Buses to Kehl, Germany; 200m) & Pont de l'Europe (4 km)

Strasbourg

0   100   200 m

FRANCE

(July and August). The entrance (☎ 03 88 32 59 00) is at the base of the tower that was never built. Tickets cost 13FF (10FF for students).

Église Saint Thomas This church on Rue Mártin Luther was built in the late 12th century and turned into a Lutheran church in 1529. It's best known for the mausoleum of Marshal Maurice of Saxony, a masterpiece of 18th-century French sculpture erected on the order of Louis XV. The church is open from 10 am to noon and 2 to 5 pm (6 pm from April to November).

Museums Strasbourg's most important museums are in the immediate vicinity of the cathedral. All are closed on Tuesday except the Musée de l'Œuvre Notre-Dame which is closed on Monday. Hours are 10 am to noon and 1.30 to 6 pm (10 am to 5 pm on Sunday). Each museum charges 15FF (8FF for students under 25, free for those under 18). For information on all these museums, call ☎ 03 88 52 50 00.

The **Musée de l'Œuvre Notre-Dame**, housed in a group of 14th and 15th-century buildings at 3 Place du Château, is Strasbourg's single most outstanding museum. It displays one of France's finest collections of Romanesque, Gothic and Renaissance sculpture, including many of the cathedral's original statues, brought here for preservation. Don't overlook the beautiful and celebrated statue *Synagoga*. The booklet for sale at the ticket desk (28FF) provides a useful though rather pricey introduction to items on display.

The **Château des Rohan** or Palais Rohan, at 2 Place du Château, was built between 1732 and 1742 as a residence for the city's princely bishops. It now houses three museums; entry for each is 15FF though a combined ticket for all three costs 30FF (students 16FF). Information sheets in English are available. The large **Musée Archéologique** in the basement covers the period from prehistory to 800 AD. The **Musée des Arts Décoratifs**, which takes up the ground floor, includes clocks, ceramics and a series of episcopal state rooms decorated in the 18th-century style. The **Musée des Beaux-Arts**, which displays paintings from the 14th to the 19th century, is on the 1st floor. The **Musée d'Art Moderne**, at 5 Place du Château (2nd floor), specialises in painting and sculpture from the late 19th-century impressionists to the present. There are plans to enlarge and relocate it by the end of 1997.

The **Musée Alsacien** at 23 Quai Saint Nicolas, housed in three 16th and 17th-century houses, affords a glimpse into Alsatian life over the centuries.

Places to Stay

During the one week each month from September to June when the European Parliament is in session, many of the city's hotel rooms are reserved up to a year in advance. The tourist office will tell you the parliament's schedule.

Place de la Gare and nearby Rue du Maire Kuss are lined with two and three-star hotels.

Camping The municipal *Camping de la Montagne Verte* (☎ 03 88 30 25 46) at 2 Rue Robert Forrer is open from March to October. It costs 23FF for a tent and car and 18FF per person. There are also facilities for the disabled. The *Auberge de Jeunesse René Cassin* (see the next section) has a place to pitch tents at the back. The charge, including breakfast, is 41FF per person. Bus Nos 3 and 23 link the city centre (Rue du Vieux Marché aux Vins) and the train station (Rue Sainte Marguerite) with the camping ground and the auberge. Get off at the Auberge de la Jeunesse stop.

Hostels The modern *Centre International d'Accueil et de Rencontre Unioniste de Strasbourg* (CIARUS; ☎ 03 88 32 12 12), a 200-bed Protestant-run hostel at 7 Rue Finkmatt, is about a km north-east of the train station. Per person tariffs, including breakfast, range from 86FF in a room with eight beds to 177FF in a single. CIARUS also has facilities for the disabled. To get there from the train station, take bus No 10 and get off at the Place de Pierre stop.

The 286-bed *Auberge de Jeunesse René Cassin* (☎ 03 88 30 26 46) is two km south-west of the train station at 9 Rue de l'Auberge de Jeunesse. A bed costs 68FF (in a room for four to six people), 97FF (in a double) or 147FF (in a single), including breakfast. See the earlier Camping section for bus transport.

Hotels Strasbourg's cheapest hotels are to be found near the train station but the old city also offers several good options.

Train Station Area The *Hôtel Le Colmar* (☎ 03 88 32 16 89) at 1 Rue du Maire Kuss (1st floor) is a bit sterile, but it's convenient and clean. Singles/doubles start at 130/150FF, or 190/200FF with shower. Hall showers are 15FF. The *Hôtel Weber* (☎ 03 88 32 36 47) at 22 Blvd de Nancy is on the grim side, but it's cheap, and convenient if you arrive by train. Singles or doubles cost 110 to 150FF and 205/240FF with shower. Triples or quads with shower and toilet are 290FF. Hall showers are 12FF.

The two-star *Hôtel de Bruxelles* (☎ 03 88 32 45 31) at 13 Rue Kuhn has clean and fairly large singles/doubles from 145FF, or 215/250FF with shower, toilet and TV; triples/quads are 280/350FF.

Old City The small, family-run *Hôtel Michelet* (☎ 03 88 32 47 38) is at 48 Rue du Vieux Marché aux Poissons. Singles/doubles cost 125/135FF, or 170/200FF with shower and 190/220FF with shower and toilet. An extra bed costs 30FF. Breakfast in your room costs 15FF. The *Hôtel Patricia* (☎ 03 88 32 14 60) at 1a Rue du Puits, a few blocks further west, has very ordinary singles/doubles for 135/160FF and doubles with shower and toilet for 210FF. Hall showers at both these hotels are 12FF.

The pleasant two-star *Hôtel de l'Ill* (☎ 03 88 36 20 01), across the river from the cathedral at 8 Rue des Bateliers, has comfortable singles/doubles for 190/230FF with shower, and more spacious rooms with TV for 275/298FF. Hall showers are free. Breakfast is 29 to 38FF.

More expensive is the two-star *Hôtel de la Cruche d'Or* (☎ 03 88 32 11 23) at 6 Rue des Tonneliers, south-west of the cathedral. Singles/doubles cost 160/280FF with shower, toilet and TV. Breakfast is 35FF.

Places to Eat

Local specialities can be sampled at two uniquely Alsatian kinds of eating establishments. Winstub ('VEEN-shtub') serve both wine and typically hearty Alsatian fare such as choucroute (sauerkraut) and baeckeoffe (pork, beef and lamb marinated in wine for one to two days before being cooked with vegetables in a baeckeoffe, or baker's oven). Some places serve baeckeoffe only on certain days (eg Friday).

Bierstubs ('BEER-shtub') primarily serve beer – the selection may include dozens, scores, even hundreds! Although they do have food (such as tarte flambée, a pastry base with cream, onion and bacon), they don't usually serve multicourse meals (see also Entertainment).

Restaurants In La Petite France, *Au Pont Saint Martin* (☎ 03 88 32 45 13) at 15 Rue des Moulins specialises in Alsatian dishes, including choucroute (68FF) and baeckeoffe (86FF). Vegetarians can order the fricassée de champignons (46FF). The restaurant is open daily except Sunday afternoon and Monday.

The hugely popular *Aldo Pizzeria* (☎ 03 88 36 00 49) at 3 Rue du Faisan has design-it-yourself pizzas for 44FF, huge salads for 42FF and pasta dishes from 44FF. It's open daily. *Le Bouchon* (☎ 03 88 37 32 40) at 6 Rue Sainte Catherine offers Lyonnais specialities at reasonable prices. A chanteuse (singer) performs most evenings. It's open Monday to Saturday from 7 pm to 4 am; meals are served until 2 am.

The area of La Krutenau, south-east of the centre, has quite a few up-market restaurants, including *La Michaudière* (☎ 03 88 24 28 12) at 52 Rue de Zurich; it's closed on Sunday and Monday evening.

Near the train station, *Restaurant Le Cappadoce* (☎ 03 88 32 88 95) at 15 Rue Kuhn serves excellent, freshly prepared Turkish food in an informal dining room. Main dishes are 35 to 85FF, salads 15 to 25FF. It's open Monday to Saturday till 1 am.

For all-out indulgence, head for the three-Michelin-star *Au Crocodile* (☎ 03 88 32 13 02) at 10 Rue de l'Outre, east of Place Kléber. On offer are dishes such as truffle-flavoured pig's trotters and ears, and foie gras set in Gewürztraminer jelly. The four-course menus start at a mere 295/395FF for lunch/dinner. Au Crocodile is closed on Sunday and Monday and during the last three weeks of July.

Winstubs The *Winstub Zuem Strissel* (☎ 03 88 32 14 73), close to the the cathedral at 5 Place de la Grande Boucherie, has a typical winstub ambience – wooden floors, benches and panelling and colourful stained-glass windows. A quarter-litre of wine costs 17 to 27FF and menus start at 60FF. Strissel is open Tuesday to Saturday from 10 am to 11 pm.

Self-Catering There is an excellent selection of picnic food at the *Suma* supermarket. It's on the 3rd floor of the Nouvelles Galeries-Magmod store at 34 Rue du 22 Novembre, just off Place Kléber, and is open every day except Sunday.

Entertainment

Live Music The mellow *Café des Anges* (☎ 03 88 37 12 67) at 5 Rue Sainte Catherine is a music bar that puts on live jazz or blues concerts almost every night at around 9 pm. Tickets cost around 50FF (40FF for students), though entry to the bœufs (jam sessions) on Monday is free. Beers are 9FF (17FF after 10 pm). The café is open Monday to Saturday from 5 pm until late and on Saturday from 3 pm to 1 am or later.

Bars The *Festival Bar Américain* (☎ 03 88 36 31 28), a fashionable American-style bar at 4 Rue Sainte Catherine, is open daily from 8 pm to 4 am (from 9 pm during October to March). The lively *Bar des Aviateurs* (☎ 03 88 36 52 69) at 12 Rue des Sœurs, whose poster-covered walls and long wooden counter impart a 1940s sort of atmosphere, is open from 6 pm to 4 am (closed Sunday evening).

Bierstubs Housed in a vaulted brick cellar at 5 Rue des Couples, *Le Trou* (☎ 03 88 36 91 04) serves over 100 kinds of beer and is open daily from 8 pm to 4 am. Prices for a demi (33 ml) on tap start at 15FF. At *L'Académie de la Bière* (☎ 03 88 32 61 08), 17 Rue Adolphe Seyboth, you can sit at rough-hewn wooden tables and sip one of 80 beers (from 12FF). It's open from 8 pm (7.30 pm Wednesday and Friday, 10 am on Saturday, 11 am Sunday) to 4 am.

Brewery Tours Free guided tours of the city's brasseries are conducted on weekday mornings and afternoons – ask at the tourist office for details.

Getting There & Away

Bus Strasbourg's municipal bus No 21 goes from Place de l'Étoile (take a tram from the train station) to Kehl across the Rhine in Germany.

Train For information on trains call (☎ 08 36 35 35 39). At the train station, there is always at least one ticket counter open every day from 6 am to midnight. Strasbourg is well connected by rail with Basel (Bâle; 100FF), Colmar (56FF, 30 minutes, a dozen a day), Munich (368FF) and Paris (263FF, four to 4½ hours, at least 10 a day). There are also trains to Amsterdam (463FF), Chamonix (332FF) and Nice (460FF). Certain trains at the weekend to/from Paris require payment of a 30FF supplement.

BIJ discounted tickets are available for those under 26 from Wasteels (☎ 03 88 32 40 82) at 13 Place de la Gare, which is open Monday to Saturday from 9 am to 7 pm (6 pm on Saturday).

Car Near the train station, Budget (☎ 03 88 52 87 52) at 14 Rue Déserte rents small cars at 395FF a day with 300 km included, and 525FF (with 700 km) for a two-day weekend. The office is open Monday to Saturday from 8 am to noon and 2 to 7 pm. Cheaper cars can be found at Europcar (☎ 03 88 22 18 00) at 16 Place de la Gare. Prices are 375FF a day (200 km) and 398/459FF for a two/three-day weekend with 400/600 km. Opening hours are Monday to Saturday from 8 am to noon and 2 to 7 pm (3 pm on Saturday).

Free parking can be found along Quai du Woerthel in La Petite France.

Getting Around

Bus and tram tickets (7FF) or a Multipass (29/56FF) good for five/10 trips are available from the tourist office and the CTS office in the train station. Tourpasses (22FF) are valid for 24 hours of travel from the moment you time-stamp them. Buses from Strasbourg's city centre run until about 11.30 pm.

Strasbourg's new 12.6-km-long tram line stops at various places in the city centre, including the train station, Place de l'Homme de Fer, Place Kléber and Place de l'Étoile.

Tickets can be bought from the machines at each stop.

There are taxi ranks at the train station and Place de la République. To order a cab, call ☎ 03 88 36 13 13.

COLMAR

Colmar (population 64,000), an easy day trip from Strasbourg, is famous for the typically Alsatian architecture of its older neighbourhoods and the unparalleled *Issenheim Altarpiece* in the Musée d'Unterlinden.

Orientation

Ave de la République stretches from one block in front of the train station to the Musée d'Unterlinden; the streets of the old city are to the south-east. Petite Venise, a neighbourhood of old, half-timbered buildings, runs along the Lauch River at the southern edge of the old city.

Information

Tourist Office The efficient tourist office (☎ 03 89 20 68 92) is opposite the museum at 4 Rue d'Unterlinden. It's open Monday to Saturday from 9 am to 6 pm (7 pm in July and August), and Sunday from 10 am to 2 pm.

Money & Post The Banque de France is at 46 Ave de la République. The main post office (☎ 03 89 41 19 19) at 36 Ave de la République also has exchange services. Colmar's postcode is 68000.

Things to See

Musée d'Unterlinden This museum (☎ 03 89 20 15 50) houses the famous *Issenheim Altarpiece (Retable d'Issenheim)*, acclaimed as one of the most dramatic and moving works of art ever created. The gilded wooden figures of this reredos (ornamental screen) were carved by Nicolas of Hagenau in the late 15th century; the wooden wings – which originally closed over each other to form a three-layered panel painting – are the work of Matthias Grünewald, and were painted between 1512 and 1516. The museum's other displays include an Alsatian wine cellar, 15th and 16th-century armour and weapons, pewterware and Strasbourg faïence.

From November to March, the museum is open from 9 am to noon and 2 to 5 pm (closed Tuesday); from April to October, it's open daily from 9 am to 6 pm. Tickets cost 30FF (20FF for students under 30).

Musée Bartholdi This museum (☎ 03 89 41 90 60) at 30 Rue des Marchands – once the home of Frédéric Auguste Bartholdi (1834-1904), creator of the *Statue of Liberty* – displays some of the sculptor's work and personal memorabilia. The museum is open from 10 am to noon and 2 to 6 pm (closed Tuesday and in January and February). Entry is 20FF (10FF for students).

Église des Dominicains This desanctified church at Place des Dominicains is known for its 14th and 15th-century stained glass and the celebrated triptych, *La Vierge au Buisson de Roses* (The Virgin & the Rosebush), painted by Martin Schongauer in 1473. It's open from 10 am to 6 pm daily from mid-March to November only. Entry is 8FF (5FF for students under 30).

Old City The medieval streets of the old city, including **Rue des Marchands** and much of **Petite Venise**, are lined with half-timbered buildings. **Maison Pfister**, opposite 36 Rue des Marchands, was built in 1537 and is remarkable for its exterior decoration (frescos, medallions and a carved wooden balcony). The **Maison des Têtes** at 19 Rue des Têtes is known for its façade covered with all manner of carved stone heads and faces; it was built in 1609.

Places to Stay

Camping The *Camping de l'Ill* (☎ 03 89 41 15 94) is four km from the train station in Horbourg-Wihr. It's open from February to November, but tent camping is only possible from May to mid-September. It costs 16FF for a tent and car plus 14FF per person. Take bus No 1 from the train station.

Hostels The *Maison des Jeunes et de la Culture* (MJC; ☎ 03 89 41 26 87) is five minutes walk south of the train station at 17 Rue Camille Schlumberger. A bed costs 40FF, and curfew is at 11 pm. The *Auberge de Jeunesse Mittelharth* (☎ 03 89 80 57 39) at 2 Rue Pasteur is just over two km north of the station. You can take bus No 4 from here or from the Unterlinden stop and get off at the Pont Rouge stop. Reception is open before 10 am or after 5 pm. A bed costs 64FF and singles are 89FF, including breakfast. Curfew is at midnight.

Hotels The one-star *Hôtel La Chaumière* (☎ 03 89 41 08 99) at 74 Ave de la République is Colmar's cheapest hotel with simple rooms for 150FF. Singles/doubles with shower, toilet and TV are 220/240FF. The two-star *Hôtel Rhin et Danube* (☎ 03 89 41 31 44) at 26 Ave de la République has old-fashioned and rather dark doubles for 250FF or 320FF with shower. A triple/quad with bath is 390/400FF.

The *Hôtel Primo* (☎ 03 89 24 22 24) at 5 Rue des Ancêtres is two blocks from the Musée d'Unterlinden. The rooms, which are accessible by lift, are modern in a tacky sort of way and cost 139/199FF or 219/279FF with shower. All rooms have TV and hall showers are free.

Places to Eat
Reasonably priced restaurants are not Colmar's forte, but one good bet is *La Maison Rouge* (☎ 03 89 23 53 22) at 9 Rue des Écoles, which specialises in Alsatian cuisine, including ham on the bone cooked on a spit (57FF). The four-course menu costs 78FF. The restaurant is open daily except Sunday evening and Wednesday. The inexpensive *Flunch cafeteria* (☎ 03 89 23 56 56) at 8 Ave de la République is open daily from 11 am to 9.30 pm.

There is a *Monoprix* supermarket (closed Sunday) across the square from the Musée d'Unterlinden. *Fromagerie Saint Nicolas* at 18 Rue Saint Nicolas sells fine, traditionally made cheeses. It's closed all day Sunday and Monday morning.

Getting There & Around
The train trip to/from Strasbourg takes about 30 minutes and costs 56FF each way.

All nine of Colmar's bus lines – which operate Monday to Saturday until 7.30 or 8 pm – serve the Unterlinden (Point Central) stop next to the tourist office and the Musée d'Unterlinden. To get to the museum from the train station, take bus No 1, 2, 3, 4 or 5. On Sunday, lines A and B operate about once an hour between 1 and 6.30 or 7 pm.

ROUTE DU VIN
The Route du Vin winds its way some 120 km south of Strasbourg to Thann, south of Colmar. This area is famous not only for its excellent Alsatian wines but also for its picturesque villages of half-timbered houses set amid vine-covered hills and overlooked by hilltop castles. The tourist office in Colmar has brochures on the wine route and information about tours.

Riquewihr and Ribeauvillé are perhaps the most attractive villages – and the most visited. Less touristy places include Mittelbergheim, Eguisheim and Turkheim, all of which can be seen on a day trip from Colmar. If you have your own transport, you might visit the imposing chateau of Haut-Koenigsbourg, rebuilt early this century by Emperor William II. The wine route is also where you're most likely to see some of Alsace's few remaining storks.

Normandy

The one-time duchy of Normandy (Normandie) derives its name from the Norsemen (or Vikings) who took control of the area in the early 10th century.

Often compared with the countryside of southern England, Normandy is the land of the *bocage*, farmland subdivided by hedges and trees. Set among this lush, pastoral landscape are Normandy's cities and towns. Rouen, the region's capital, is especially rich in medieval architecture, including a spectacular cathedral. Bayeux is home to the 11th-century Bayeux Tapestry and is only about 12 km from the D-Day landing beaches. In Normandy's southwestern corner is one of France's greatest attractions: the island abbey of Mont-St-Michel. Because of its proximity to Paris, the Normandy coastline is lined with beach resorts, including the fashionable twin towns of Deauville and Trouville. Rural Normandy is famed for its cheeses and other dairy products, apples and cider brandy (Calvados).

Ferries link southern England with four ports in Normandy: Dieppe, Le Havre,

Cherbourg and Ouistreham, north-east of Caen.

Getting Around

Given rural Normandy's beauty and its limited public transport, renting a car will add more to your visit here than almost anywhere else in France.

ROUEN

The city of Rouen (population 105,000), for centuries the furthest point downriver where you could cross the Seine by bridge, is known for its many spires and church towers. The old city is graced with over 800 half-timbered houses, a renowned Gothic cathedral and a number of excellent museums. The city can be visited on an overnight or even a day trip from Paris.

Orientation

The train station (Gare Rouen-Rive Droite) is at the northern end of Rue Jeanne d'Arc, the major thoroughfare running south to the Seine. The old city is centred around Rue du Gros Horloge between the Place du Vieux Marché and the cathedral.

Information

Tourist Office The tourist office (☎ 02 32 08 32 40) is in an early 16th-century building at 25 Place de la Cathédrale. It's open Monday to Saturday from 9 am to 6.30 pm and Sunday from 10 am to 1 pm. From May to September, opening hours are Monday to Saturday from 9 am to 7 pm and on Sunday and holidays from 9.30 am to noon and 2.30 to 6 pm. In summer, guided tours of the city (30FF) depart from the tourist office daily at 10 am and 3 pm. The Carte des Musées de Rouen (60FF) is also available here and allows entry to five of the city's museums.

Money & Post The Banque de France is at 32 Rue Jean Lecanuet. Albuquerque Bureau de Change near the cathedral at 9 Rue des Bonnetiers offers good rates. It is open from 10 am to 7 pm daily except Sunday.

Rouen's main post office (☎ 02 35 08 73 73), which also has exchange services, is at 45bis Rue Jeanne d'Arc. Rouen's postcode is 76000.

Things to See

Old City Rouen's old city suffered enormous damage during WWII but has since been painstakingly restored. The main street, **Rue du Gros Horloge**, runs from the cathedral to **Place du Vieux Marché**, where 19-year-old Joan of Arc was burned at the stake for heresy in 1431. The striking **Église Jeanne d'Arc** marking the site was completed in 1979; you'll learn more about her life from its stained-glass windows than at the tacky **Musée Jeanne d'Arc** across the square at No 33.

The pedestrians-only Rue du Gros Horloge is spanned by an early 16th-century gatehouse holding aloft the **Gros Horloge**, a large medieval clock with only one hand. The late 14th-century belfry above it was under renovation at the time of going to press and could not be visited.

The incredibly ornate **Palais de Justice** (law courts) was left a shell at the end of WWII, but has since been restored to its early 16th-century Gothic glory. The courtyard, entered through a gate on Rue aux Juifs, is well worth a look for its spires, gargoyles and statuary. Under the courtyard is the **Monument Juif**, a stone building used by Rouen's Jewish community in the early 12th century.

Cathédrale Notre Dame Rouen's cathedral, which was the subject of a series of paintings by the impressionist painter Claude Monet, is considered a masterpiece of French Gothic architecture. Built between 1201 and 1514, it suffered extensive damage during the war and has been undergoing restoration and cleaning for decades. The Romanesque **crypt** was part of a cathedral completed in 1062 and destroyed by fire in 1200. There are several guided visits (15FF) a day to the crypt, ambulatory (containing Richard the Lion-Heart's tomb) and **Chapel of the Virgin** between July and August but only on weekends the rest of the year. The cathedral is open Monday to Saturday from 8 am to 7 pm (6 pm on Sunday).

Museums The **Musée Le Secq des Tournelles** (☎ 02 35 71 28 40) is dedicated to the blacksmith's craft and displays some 12,000 locks, keys, scissors, tongs and other wrought-iron utensils made between the 3rd and 19th centuries. Located on Rue Jacques Villon

Place Bernard Tissot
Place Beauvoisine
Rue du Champ des Oiseaux
Rue Bouquet
Rue de la Rochefoucauld
R du Donjon
Blvd de l'Yser
Boulevard de l'Yser
Place Cauchoise
Boulevard de la Marne
Rue du Moulinet
Rue Jeanne d'Arc
Rue du Faucon
Rue du Cordier
Rue de Joyeuse
Rue du Bailliage
Rue Louis Ricard
Rue Jean Lecanuet
Rue des Bons Enfants
Rue de Fontenelle
Square Verdrel
Place du Vieux Marché
Rue de Crosne
Boulevard des Belges
Rue de Bihorel
Rue des Bas
Rue J Villon
Place du Général de Gaulle
Rue du Vieux Palais
Place Maréchal Fuch
Rue du Tambour
Ganterie
Rue de l'Hôpital
Rue de Harcourt
Rue du Vieux Palais
Rue aux Juifs
OLD CITY
Rue des Carmes
Rue St-Eloi
Rue du Général Giraud
Rue du Gros Horloge
Rue Saint Nicolas
Rue des Faulx
Rue Eau de Robec
Rue des Charrettes
Rue du Petit Salut
Place de la Cathédrale
Rue d'Amiens
Rue Jeanne d'Arc
Rue aux Ours
Rue Saint-Romain
Rue Armand Carrel
Quai du Havre
Rue Saint Étienne des Tonneliers
Rue Général
Rue de la Tour de Beurre
Leclerc
Rue de la République
Rue Victor Hugo
Rue Martainville
To N15 & Camping Municipal (Déville-lès-Rouen) (4.5 km)
Rue de la Calende
Rue des Bonnetiers
Rue Alsace-Lorraine
Place Saint Marc
Quai de la Bourse
Rue Grand-Pont
Rue des Augustins
Quai Pierre Corneille
Quai Cavalier de la Salle
Pont Jeanne d'Arc
Seine River
Quai Jean Moulin
Quai de Paris
Rue Corneille
Pont
To Auberge de Jeunesse (500 m)
Cours Clemenceau
Ave de Bretagne
Place Carnot
Quai d'Elbeuf
Rue La Fayette
To A13, Le Havre, Caen & Paris
Rouen
0   100   200 m

FRANCE

PLACES TO STAY		OTHER		22	Palais de Justice
3	Hôtel Normandya	1	Gare Rouen-Rive		Courtyard &
5	Hôtel Sphinx		Droite (Train Station)		Monument Juif
6	Hostellerie du Vieux	2	La Tour Jeanne d'Arc	26	Banks
	Logis	4	Laundrette	27	Gros Horloge (Medi-
7	Hôtel du Square	8	Musée de la Céramique		eval Clock)
14	Hôtel Saint Ouen	9	Banque de France	28	Rouen Cycles
15	Hôtel des Flandres	10	Musée des Beaux-Arts	29	Bus Station
23	Hôtel Le Palais	11	Musée Le Secq des	30	Métrobus (Local Bus
36	Hôtel de la Cathédrale		Tournelles		Information)
		12	Hôtel de Ville	31	Théâtre des Arts
PLACES TO EAT		13	Église Saint Ouen	33	Tourist Office
17	Pascaline	16	Main Post Office	34	Cathédrale Notre Dame
24	Chez Pépé	18	Covered Food Market	35	Albuquerque Bureau
25	La Galetteria	19	Église Jeanne d'Arc		de Change
32	Natural	20	Musée Jeanne d'Arc	37	Église Saint Maclou
39	Kim Ngoc	21	Palais de Justice	38	Aître Saint Maclou
40	Chez Zaza			41	Prefecture

(opposite 27 Rue Jean Lecanuet), it is open from 10 am to 1 pm and 2 to 6 pm daily except Tuesday. The entry fee is 13FF (9FF for students).

The **Musée de la Céramique** (☎ 02 35 07 31 74), whose speciality is 16th to 19th-century Rouen ceramics, is north of Square Verdrel up some stairs at 1 Rue du Faucon. Opening hours and ticket prices are the same as at the Musée Le Secq des Tournelles. The recently renovated **Musée des Beaux-Arts** (☎ 02 35 71 28 40) facing the square at 26bis Rue Jean Lecanuet features some major paintings from the 16th to 20th centuries, including some of Monet's cathedral series. The museum is open from 10 am to 6 pm and entry is 20FF (13FF for students).

Aître Saint Maclou Behind the Gothic **Église Saint Maclou** at 186 Rue Martainville is the *aître*, or ossuary, a rare surviving example of a medieval burial ground for plague victims. The curious ensemble of 16th-century buildings that surround the courtyard is decorated with macabre carvings of skulls, crossbones, grave-diggers' tools and hourglasses. It's open every day from 8 am to 6 pm, and entry is free.

La Tour Jeanne d'Arc This tower (☎ 02 35 98 16 21) in Rue du Donjon south of the train station is the only one left of the eight that once ringed the chateau built by Philippe Auguste in the early 13th century. Joan of Arc was imprisoned here before her execution. The

tower and its two exhibition rooms are open from 10 am to noon and 2 to 5.30 pm daily except Tuesday. Entrance is 10FF (free for students).

Places to Stay

Camping The *Camping Municipal* (☎ 02 35 74 07 59) in the suburb of Déville-lès-Rouen is five km north-west of the train station on Rue Jules Ferry. From the Théâtre des Arts on Rue Jeanne d'Arc or the nearby bus station, take bus No 2 and get off at the mairie (town hall) of Déville-lès-Rouen. Two people with a tent are charged 51FF, or 58FF with a car. It is open from March to December.

Hostel Rouen's *Auberge de Jeunesse* (☎ 02 35 72 06 45) is at 118 Blvd de l'Europe, three km south of the train station. The new metro runs there: take the train in the direction of Hôtel de Ville and get off at the Europe station. A bed in a dorm costs 56FF, including breakfast, shower and sheets (100FF deposit required).

Hotels – north of the centre The spotless and friendly *Hôtel Normandya* (☎ 02 35 71 46 15), at 32 Rue du Cordier, is on a quiet street 300 metres south-east of the train station. Singles (some with shower) are 90 to 140FF, doubles are 10FF more; an additional bed costs 40FF and a hall shower is 15FF. The quiet *Hôtel du Square* (☎ 02 35 71 56 07) at 9 Rue du Moulinet, a few hundred metres south of the station,

FRANCE

has singles/doubles without shower for 110 to 130FF, and with shower for 150 to 180FF. There are no hall showers.

The *Hôtel Sphinx* (☎ 02 35 71 35 86) at 130 Rue Beauvoisine is a cosy, friendly place with some timbered rooms. Doubles range from 90 to 100FF; an additional bed is 60FF. Showers cost 10FF.

The very French *Hostellerie du Vieux Logis* (☎ 02 35 71 55 30) at 5 Rue de Joyeuse, almost a km to the east of the train station, has a relaxed and pleasantly frayed atmosphere with a lovely little garden out the back. Singles/doubles start at 120FF, two-bed triples cost 150FF. Showers are free.

Hotels – city centre The attractive *Hôtel Saint Ouen* (☎ 02 35 71 46 44) is opposite the garden of Église Saint Ouen at 43 Rue des Faulx. Simple singles/doubles cost from 115/125FF and 130/140FF with shower. Hall showers are 16FF. The *Hôtel des Flandres* (☎ 02 35 71 56 88) at 5 Rue des Bons Enfants has doubles for 120/145FF without/with shower. The *Hôtel Le Palais* (☎ 02 35 71 41 40), between the Palais de Justice and the Gros Horloge at 12 Rue du Tambour, has singles and doubles without/with shower for 130/150FF.

If you're feeling flush, the *Hôtel de la Cathédrale* (☎ 02 35 71 57 95) sits in the shadow of Rouen's cathedral in a 17th-century house at 12 Rue Saint Romain. Rooms are from 300 to 415FF. Ask for a room looking onto the courtyard.

Places to Eat
Near Place du Vieux Marché *La Galetteria* (☎ 02 35 88 98 98), opposite 17 Rue du Vieux Palais, has savoury-filled galettes and crêpes for 12 to 43FF. It is open daily except Saturday at midday and Sunday.

Chez Pépé (☎ 02 35 07 44 94) at 19 Rue du Vieux Palais is a pizzeria open from noon to 2 pm and 7 to 11.30 pm daily except Monday at lunchtime and Sunday. *Natural* (☎ 02 35 98 15 74), near the tourist office at 3 Rue du Petit Salut, is a lunchtime vegetarian café with good salads and health-food menus for 39 and 61FF.

Near Église Saint Maclou, *Chez Zaza* (☎ 02 35 71 33 57) at 85 Rue Martainville specialises in couscous (from 45FF) and is open daily. *Kim Ngoc* (☎ 02 35 98 76 33), nearby at No 168, is

one of Rouen's many Vietnamese restaurants with menus for 65 and 80FF. It is open every day but Monday.

For a splurge, the old-time bistro *Pascaline* (☎ 02 35 89 67 44) at 5 Rue de la Poterne has two/three-course menus for 77/97FF. It's open until 11.30 pm every day.

Dairy products, fish and fresh produce are on sale from 7 am to 12.30 pm daily except Monday at the covered market at Place du Vieux Marché.

Getting There & Away
Bus Buses to Dieppe and Le Havre are slower and more expensive than the train. The bus station (☎ 02 35 52 92 29) is on 25 Rue des Charrettes near the Théâtre des Arts.

Train There are 24 trains a day to and from Paris' Gare Saint Lazare (70 minutes). The last leaves at about 9 pm for Paris and 10 pm for Rouen. The information office at Rouen's train station (☎ 08 36 35 35 39) is open Monday to Saturday from 7.15 am to 7 pm.

Getting Around
Bus & Metro TCAR operates Rouen's local bus network as well as its metro line. The metro links the train station with the Théâtre des Arts before crossing the Seine into the southern suburbs, and runs between 5.30 am and 11 pm daily. Bus tickets cost 7.50FF, a carnet of 10 is 56FF, and the Carte Découverte, good for one/two/three days unlimited travel, costs 20/30/40FF. They can be purchased at the Métrobus counters in the train station, in front of the Théâtre des Arts and in the Place du Général de Gaulle near the Hôtel de Ville.

Bicycle Rouen Cycles (☎ 02 35 71 34 30) at 45 Rue Saint Éloi rents mountain bikes and 10-speeds for 120FF a day (320FF a week). The shop is open Tuesday to Saturday from 9 am to noon and 2 to 7.30 pm.

BAYEUX
Bayeux (population 15,000) is celebrated for two trans-Channel invasions: the conquest of England by the Normans under William the Conqueror in 1066 (an event chronicled in the Bayeux Tapestry) and the Allied D-Day landings of 6 June 1944, which launched the

liberation of Nazi-occupied France. Bayeux was the first town in France to be freed.

Bayeux is an attractive – though fairly touristy – town with several excellent museums. It also serves as a base for visits to the D-Day beaches (see that section for details).

Orientation & Information

The cathedral, the major landmark in the centre of Bayeux and visible throughout the town, is one km north-west of the train station. The tourist office (☎ 02 31 92 16 26) is at Pont Saint Jean just off the northern end of Rue Larcher. It is open Monday to Saturday from 9 am to noon and 2 to 6 pm. During July and August, it opens on Sunday from 10 am to 12.30 pm and 3 to 6.30 pm.

Money & Post Banks are open Tuesday to Saturday from 8.30 am to noon and from about 2 to 5 pm. There is a Société Générale at 26 Rue Saint Malo and a Caisse d'Épargne at No 59 of the same street. The main post office (☎ 02 31 92 01 00), at 29 Rue Larcher opposite the Hôtel de Ville, also has exchange operations. Bayeux's postcode is 14400.

Things to See

A multipass ticket *(billet jumelé)* valid for all four museums listed here, and available at each, costs 65FF (30FF for students).

Bayeux Tapestry The world-famous Bayeux Tapestry – actually a 70-metre-long strip of coarse linen decorated with woollen embroidery – was commissioned by Odo, bishop of Bayeux and half-brother to William the Conqueror (Guillaume le Conquérant), sometime between the Norman invasion of England in 1066 and 1082, when Odo was disgraced for raising troops without William's consent. The tapestry, which was probably made in England for the consecration of the cathedral in Bayeux in 1077, recounts the dramatic story of the Norman invasion and the events that led up to it – from the Norman perspective. The story is told in 58 panels presented like a modern comic strip, with action-packed scenes following each other in quick succession. The events are accompanied by a written commentary in dog Latin. The scenes themselves are filled with depictions of 11th-century Norman and Saxon dress, food, cooking, weapons and tools. Halley's Comet, which passed through our part of the solar system in 1066, also makes an appearance.

The tapestry is housed in the **Musée de la Tapisserie de Bayeux** (☎ 02 31 92 05 48), on Rue de Nesmond. It is open daily from 9.30 am (8 am in July and August) to 12.30 pm and 2 to 6 or 6.30 pm. From May to mid-September, the museum is open all day until 7 pm. Entry is 35FF (14FF for students). There is an excellent taped commentary available (5FF) and a 14-minute video (screened in English eight times a day).

Cathédrale Notre Dame Most of Bayeux's spectacular cathedral, an exceptional example of Norman-Gothic architecture, dates from the 13th century, though the crypt, the arches of the nave and the lower portions of the towers on either side of the main entrance, are Romanesque from the late 11th century. Look out for the 15th-century frescos of angels playing musical instruments in the south transept. The cathedral is open daily from 9 am (8 am in July and August) to 12.30 pm and 2 to 6.30 or 7 pm.

Musée Diocésain d'Art Religieux The Diocesan Museum of Religious Art (☎ 02 31 92 14 21), full of liturgical objects and clerical garb, is just south of the cathedral at 6 Rue Lambert Leforestier. It is open daily from 10 am to 12.30 pm and 2 to 6 pm (7 pm from July to September). The 15FF entry fee (6FF for students), also gets you in to the **Conservatoire de la Dentelle** (☎ 02 31 92 73 80) in the same building. It's dedicated to the preservation of traditional Norman lace-making techniques.

Musée Baron Gérard This pleasant museum (☎ 02 31 92 14 21), next to the cathedral at Place de la Liberté, specialises in local porcelain, lace and 15th to 19th-century European paintings. Out front there is a huge plane tree known as the Arbre de la Liberté which, like many such 'Freedom Trees', was planted in the years after the French Revolution (1797). It is one of only nine left in all of France. The museum is open daily from 10 am to noon and from 2 to 6 pm (9 am to 7 pm from June to mid-September). The entry fee is 20FF (10FF for students).

FRANCE

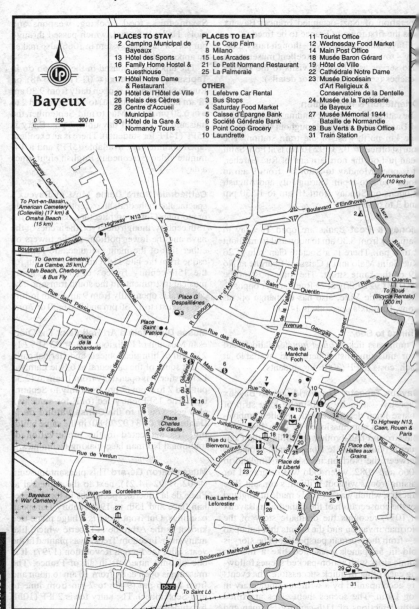

PLACES TO STAY
- 2 Camping Municipal de Bayeaux
- 13 Hôtel des Sports
- 16 Family Home Hostel & Guesthouse
- 17 Hôtel Notre Dame & Restaurant
- 20 Hôtel de l'Hôtel de Ville
- 26 Relais des Cèdres
- 28 Centre d'Accueil Municipal
- 30 Hôtel de la Gare & Normandy Tours

PLACES TO EAT
- 7 Le Coup Faim
- 8 Milano
- 15 Les Arcades
- 21 Le Petit Normand Restaurant
- 25 La Palmeraie

OTHER
- 1 Lefebvre Car Rental
- 3 Bus Stops
- 4 Saturday Food Market
- 5 Caisse d'Épargne Bank
- 6 Société Générale Bank
- 9 Point Coop Grocery
- 10 Laundrette
- 11 Tourist Office
- 12 Wednesday Food Market
- 14 Main Post Office
- 18 Musée Baron Gérard
- 19 Hôtel de Ville
- 22 Cathédrale Notre Dame
- 23 Musée Diocésain d'Art Religieux & Conservatoire de la Dentelle
- 24 Musée de la Tapisserie de Bayeux
- 27 Musée Mémorial 1944 Bataille de Normandie
- 29 Bus Verts & Bybus Office
- 31 Train Station

Bayeux

0   150   300 m

Musée Mémorial 1944 Bataille de Normandie
Bayeux's huge war museum (☎ 02 31 92 93 41) on Blvd Fabien Ware displays a rather haphazard collection of photos, uniforms, weapons, newspaper clippings and life-like scenes associated with D-Day and the Battle of Normandy. It is open daily from 10 am to 12.30 pm and from 2 to 6 pm (9.30 am to 6.30 pm from May to mid-September). Entry costs 30FF (12FF for students). There's an excellent 30-minute film compiled from archive news-reels which is screened in English three to five times a day.

The **Bayeux War Cemetery**, a British cemetery on Blvd Fabien Ware a few hundred metres west of the museum, is the largest of the 18 Commonwealth military cemeteries in Normandy. It contains the tombs of 4868 soldiers from 11 countries, including the graves of 466 Germans. Many of the headstones are inscribed with poignant epitaphs.

Places to Stay
Camping The *Camping Municipal de Bayeux* (☎ 02 31 92 08 43) is two km north of the town centre, just south of Blvd d'Eindhoven. It's open from mid-March to mid-November. A tent site costs from 7.40FF and adults pay 13.60FF each.

Bus Nos 5 and 6 from the train station will take you there.

Hostels The *Family Home* hostel and guesthouse (☎ 02 31 92 15 22) in three old buildings at 39 Rue du Général de Dais is an excellent place to meet other travellers. A bed in a dorm room costs 100FF (90FF if you've got a HI card), including breakfast. Singles with showers are 160FF. Multicourse French dinners, prepared by the indefatigable Mme Lefebvre, cost 65FF, including wine. Vegetarian dishes are available on request or you can cook for yourself.

The efficient *Centre d'Accueil Municipal* hostel (☎ 02 31 92 08 19) is housed in a large, modern building at 21 Rue des Marettes, one km south-west of the cathedral. Sterile but comfortable singles are good value at 89FF, including breakfast. A HI card is not necessary.

Hotels The old but well-maintained *Hôtel de la Gare* (☎ 02 31 92 10 70) at 26 Place de la Gare opposite the train station has singles/doubles from 85/100FF. Two-bed triples/quads are 160FF and showers are free.

The *Hôtel de l'Hôtel de Ville* (☎ 02 31 92 30 08), in the centre of town at 31 Rue Larcher, has large, quiet singles/doubles for 150FF. An extra bed is 50FF, and showers are free. Telephone reservations are not accepted. A few hundred metres north at 19 Rue Saint Martin, the *Hôtel des Sports* (☎ 02 31 92 28 53) has decent singles/doubles (most with shower or free use of those along the hall) starting at 160/200FF.

The *Relais des Cèdres* (☎ 02 31 21 98 07), somewhat fussily done out in 'French country' style, is in an old mansion at 1 Blvd Sadi Carnot. Doubles cost 150 to 220FF, or 270FF with shower. Hall showers are free.

If you can afford something more up-market, you might try *Hôtel Notre Dame* (☎ 02 31 92 87 24) at 44 Rue des Cuisiniers, a two-star (though not officially) place opposite the western façade of the cathedral. Doubles are 240 to 250FF with shower or bath, but they have half a dozen cheaper rooms for 150FF. Hall showers cost 20FF.

Places to Eat
Le Petit Normand (☎ 02 31 22 88 66) at 35 Rue Larcher specialises in traditional Norman food prepared with apple cider, and is popular with English tourists. Simple fixed-price menus start at 58FF. The restaurant is open every day except Sunday evening (daily in July and August). *Les Arcades* (☎ 02 31 92 72 79), at 10 Rue Laitière close to Hôtel des Sports, is popular with the locals and has excellent four-course menus from 68FF. It's open every day and serves dinner until 11 pm.

For couscous (from 55FF), try *La Palmeraie* (☎ 02 31 92 72 08) near the Bayeux Tapestry Museum at 62-64 Rue de Nesmond. It's open for lunch and dinner every day except Monday and midday on Saturday. *Milano* (☎ 02 31 92 15 10) at 18 Rue Saint Martin serves very good pizza. It's open every day except Sunday and daily from June to October.

The food at the *Hôtel Notre Dame* restaurant (☎ 02 31 92 87 24) is Norman at its best; count on 55FF for a lunch menu and 88FF per person at dinner. It is open every day except Sunday midday and Monday (daily from June to August).

FRANCE

There are lots of takeaway places and food shops along or near Rue Saint Martin and Rue Saint Jean, including *Le Coup Faim* at 42 Rue Saint Martin and the *Point Coop* grocery at 25 Rue du Maréchal Foch, open Tuesday to Saturday from 8.30 am to 12.15 pm and 2.30 to 7.15 pm and on Sunday from 9 am to noon. There are open-air markets in Rue Saint Jean on Wednesday morning and in Place Saint Patrice on Saturday morning.

Getting There & Away

The train station (☎ 02 31 92 80 50) is open daily from about 6 am to 9.30 or 10 pm. Trains serve Paris' Gare Saint Lazare (via Caen), Cherbourg, Rennes and points beyond.

Getting Around

The local bus line, Bybus, schedules buses to meet train arrivals. Bus Nos 1 and 3 go to the centre and end up at Place Saint Patrice. See the D-Day Beaches section for information on car rental and transport to places in the vicinity of Bayeux.

Taxis can be ordered 24 hours a day by calling ☎ 02 31 92 92 40.

D-DAY BEACHES

The D-Day landings, codenamed 'Operation Overlord', were the largest military operation in history. Early on the morning of 6 June 1944, swarms of landing craft – part of a flotilla of almost 7000 boats – hit the beaches, and tens of thousands of soldiers from the USA, UK, Canada and elsewhere began pouring onto French soil. Most of the 135,000 Allied troops stormed ashore along 80 km of beach north of Bayeux codenamed (from west to east) Utah and Omaha (in the American sector) and Gold, Juno and Sword (in the British and Canadian ones). The landings on D-Day – Jour J in French – were followed by the start of the 76-day battle of Normandy that would lead to the liberation of Europe from Nazi occupation.

Things to See

Arromanches In order to unload the vast quantities of cargo necessary for the invasion, the Allies established two prefabricated ports codenamed **Mulberry Harbour**. The remains of one of them, Port Winston, can still be seen at Arromanches, a seaside town 10 km northeast of Bayeux. The harbour consisted of 146

massive cement caissons towed over from England and sunk to form a semicircular breakwater in which floating bridge spans were moored. In the three months after D-Day, 2½ million men, four million tonnes of equipment and 500,000 vehicles were unloaded there. At low tide you can walk out to many of the caissons. The best view of Port Winston is from the hill east of town topped with a statue of the Virgin Mary.

The well-regarded **Musée du Débarquement** (Landing Museum; ☎ 02 31 22 34 31) explains the logistics and importance of Port Winston and makes a good first stop before visiting the beaches. It is open daily from 9.30 am (10 am on Sunday) to 5 pm (until 6 pm in April). From May to September, it's open from 9 am to 7 pm. The museum is closed for most of January. Entrance is 32FF (17FF for students). The last guided tour (in French, with a written text in English) leaves 45 minutes before closing time. Forget about the diorama/slide show, but don't miss the film showing archival news footage. Both are screened in English, last about 10 minutes and run throughout the day.

Omaha Beach The most brutal fighting of 6 June was fought 20 km west of Arromanches along Omaha Beach, which had to be abandoned in storms two weeks later. A memorial marks the site of the first US military cemetery on French soil, where soldiers killed right on the beach were first buried. Today, Omaha Beach is lined with holiday cottages and is popular with swimmers and sunbathers. Little evidence of the war remains except the bunkers and munitions sites of a German fortified point to the west (look for the tall obelisk on the hill).

American Military Cemetery The remains of the Americans who lost their lives during the Battle of Normandy were either sent back to the USA or buried in the American Military Cemetery (☎ 02 31 51 62 00) at Colleville-sur-Mer above Omaha Beach. The cemetery contains the graves of 9386 American soldiers and a memorial to 1557 others whose bodies were never found. The huge, immaculately tended expanse of white crosses and Stars of David, set on a hill overlooking Omaha Beach, testifies to the extent of the killing which took

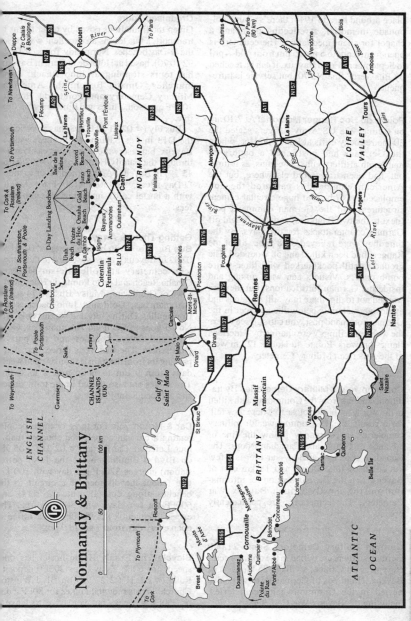

Normandy & Brittany

place around here in 1944; there's a large colonnade memorial, a reflecting pond and a chapel for silent meditation. The cemetery is open from 8 am to 5 pm (6 pm from mid-April to September). From Bayeux, it can be reached by Bus Verts' line No 70, but service is infrequent.

Pointe du Hoc Ranger Memorial At 7.10 am on 6 June, 225 US Army Rangers scaled the 30-metre rocky cliffs at Pointe du Hoc, where the Germans had positioned a battery of mammoth artillery guns. The guns, as it turns out, had been transferred elsewhere, but the American commandos captured the gun emplacements (the two huge circular cement structures) and the German command post (next to the two flagpoles) and then fought off German counterattacks for two days. By the time they were relieved on 8 June, 81 of the Rangers had been killed and 58 wounded. The ground is still pockmarked with three-metre bomb craters. Visitors can walk among and inside the German fortifications, but they are warned not to dig: there may still be mines and explosive materials below the surface. In the German command post, you can still see where the wooden ceilings were charred by American flame-throwers. Pointe du Hoc is 12 km west of the American Military Cemetery.

Commonwealth Military Cemeteries By tradition, soldiers from the Commonwealth killed in the war were buried close to where they fell. As a result, the 18 Commonwealth military cemeteries in Normandy follow the line of advance of British and Canadian troops. The Canadian cemetery at Bény-sur-Mer is a few km south of Juno Beach and 18 km east of Bayeux. See the Bayeux section for information on the mostly British Bayeux War Cemetery. The cemeteries are permanently open.

German Military Cemetery Some 21,000 German soldiers are buried in the military cemetery near La Cambe, a village 25 km west of Bayeux. Hundreds of German dead were also buried in the Commonwealth cemeteries, including the Bayeux War Cemetery.

Organised Tours

Given the limitations posed by other forms of transport, a bus tour is an excellent way to see the D-Day beaches. Normandy Tours (☎ 02 31 92 10 70), based at Hôtel de la Gare in Bayeux has tours stopping at Juno Beach, Arromanches, Omaha Beach, the American Military Cemetery and Pointe du Hoc fo 100FF a person. Times and itineraries are flexible.

Bus Fly (☎ 02 31 22 00 08) has an office on the D13 in Les Sablons (Vaucelles) west o Bayeux, but reservations are most easily made through the Family Home hostel (☎ 02 31 92 15 22) in Bayeux. An afternoon tour to majo D-Day sites costs 150FF (130FF for student with a hostel card), including museum entr fees.

Getting There & Away

Bus Bus No 70 run by Bus Verts (☎ 02 31 9. 02 92 in Bayeux), goes westward to the American cemetery at Colleville-sur-Mer an Omaha Beach and on to Pointe du Hoc and th town of Grandcamp-Maisy. Bus No 74 serve Arromanches, Gold and Juno beaches an Courseulles. During July and August only, Bu No 75 goes to Caen via Arromanches, Gold Juno and Sword beaches and the port o Ouistreham. The Bus Verts office, across th parking lot from the train station, is open week days from 9 am to noon and 2 to 6 pm Timetables are also posted in the train statio and at Place Saint Patrice.

Car & Motorcycle For three or more people renting a car can actually be cheaper than tour. Lefebvre Car Rental (☎ 02 31 92 05 96 on Blvd d'Eindhoven (at the Esso petro station) charges 320FF per day with 100 kr free (about the distance of a circuit to th beaches along coastal route No 514) an 600FF for two days with 300 km free. Th excess (deductible) is 2000FF. The office i open every day from 7 am to 9 pm.

Bicycle The Family Home hostel has one speeds for 60FF a day (plus 200FF deposit Roué (☎ 02 31 92 27 75) on Blvd Winsto Churchill rents mountain bikes for 80FF a da or 350FF a week, but you have to leave

MONT-SAINT-MICHEL

It is difficult not to be impressed with your first sighting of Mont-Saint-Michel. Covering the summit is the massive abbey, a soaring ensemble of buildings in a hotchpotch of architectural styles. Topping the abbey – 80 metres above the sea – is a slender spire, at the tip of which is a gilded copper statue of Michael the Archangel slaying a dragon. Around the base are the ancient ramparts and a jumble of buildings that house the 120 people who still live there.

Mont-Saint-Michel's fame derives equally from the bay's extraordinary tides. Depending on the orbits of the moon and, to a lesser extent, of the sun, the difference in the level of the sea between low tide and high tides can reach 12 metres. At low tide, the Mont looks out onto bare sand stretching many km off into the distance. At high tide – only about six hours later – this huge expanse of tideland will be under water (though the Mont and its causeway are completely surrounded by the sea only during the highest of tides, which occur at seasonal equinoxes).

History

According to Celtic mythology, Mont-Saint-Michel was one of the sea tombs to which the souls of the dead were conveyed. In 708 AD, Saint Michel appeared to Aubert, Bishop of Avranches, and told him to build a devotional chapel at the top of the Mont. In 966, Richard I, Duke of Normandy, transferred Mont-Saint-Michel to the Benedictines, who turned it into an important centre of learning. The monastery was at its most influential in the 12th and 13th centuries, and pilgrims journeyed from miles around to honour the cult of St Michel. In the 13th century, the Mont became something of an ecclesiastical fortress, with a military garrison at the disposal of the abbot and the king.

In the early 15th century, during the Hundred Years' War, the English blockaded and besieged Mont-Saint-Michel three times. But the fortified abbey withstood these assaults; it was the only place in all of western and northern France not to fall into English hands. After the French Revolution, Mont-Saint-Michel was turned into a prison. In 1966 the abbey was symbolically returned to the Benedictines as part of the celebrations marking its millennium.

Orientation

There is only one opening in the ramparts, Porte de l'Avancée, immediately to the west as you walk down the causeway. The single street (Grande Rue), for pedestrians only, is lined with restaurants, a few hotels, souvenir shops and entrances to some rather tacky exhibits in the crypts below. **Pontorson**, the nearest town, is nine km south and the base for most travellers. Route D976 from Mont-Saint-Michel runs right into Pontorson's main thoroughfare, Rue du Couësnon.

Information

Tourist Office The tourist office (☎ 02 33 60 14 30) is up the stairs to the left as you enter Porte de l'Avancée. It is open every day except Sunday from 9 am to noon and 2 to 5.45 pm (6.30 pm from Easter to September). In July and August hours are from 9 am to 7 pm daily. If you are interested in what the tide will be doing during your visit, look for the *horaire des marées* posted outside. In July and August – when up to 9000 people a day visit – children under eight can be left at the day nursery *(garderie)* near the abbey church.

The friendly staff at Pontorson's tourist office (☎ 02 33 60 20 65) in the Place de l'Église (just west of the Place de l'Hôtel de Ville) are on duty from 9.30 am to 12.30 pm and from 2.30 to 5 pm (to 7.30 pm from mid-June to mid-September).

Money & Post There are several places to change money in Mont-Saint-Michel, but the best rate is at the CIC bank at 98 Rue du Couësnon in Pontorson. It's open Tuesday to Friday from 8.30 am to 12.15 pm and 1.45 to 5.45 pm (4.50 pm on Saturday).

The Pontorson post office (☎ 02 33 60 01 66) is on the east side of the Place de l'Hôtel de Ville.

Things to See & Do

Walking Tour When the tide is out, you can walk all the way around Mont-Saint-Michel, a distance of about one km. Straying too far from the Mont is extremely inadvisable: you might get stuck in quicksand – from which Norman soldiers are depicted being rescued in one

FRANCE

scene of the Bayeux Tapestry. For information on guided tours, call the Maison de la Baie (☎ 02 33 70 86 46).

Abbaye du Mont-Saint-Michel The Mont's major attraction is the renowned abbey (☎ 02 33 89 80 00), at the top of the Grande Rue, up the stairway. It's open daily from 9.30 am to 4.30 pm. From mid-May to September, it's open from 9 am to 5.30 pm, and there are also night-time visits of the abbey (60FF) every evening except Sunday (May to August from 10 pm to 1 am, and September from 9 pm to midnight). Visitors explore at their own pace the illuminated and music-filled rooms.

During the day, it's worth taking the guided tour included in the ticket price (36FF or 23FF for students under 25). One-hour tours in English depart three to eight times a day.

In the 11th century, the Romanesque **Église Abbatiale** (Abbey Church) was built on the rocky tip of the mountain cone over its 10th-century predecessor, now the underground chapel of **Notre Dame de Sous Terre**. When the Romanesque choir collapsed in 1421, a Flamboyant Gothic choir replaced it in the 15th century, held up from below by crypts with vast supporting columns. The church is famous for this mixture of architectural styles.

In the early 13th century, **La Merveille** (literally, the 'wonder' or 'marvel') monastery was built on three levels and added to the church's north side. Considered a Gothic masterpiece, it was completed in only 16 years. The famous **cloître** (cloister) is an ambulatory surrounded by a double row of delicately carved arches resting on slender marble pillars, and is a good example of the Anglo-Norman style. The early 13th-century **réfectoire** (dining hall) is illuminated by a wall of recessed windows, a remarkable arrangement given that the sheer drop-off precluded the use of flying buttresses. The High Gothic **salle des hôtes** (guest hall), which dates from 1213, has two giant fireplaces.

Places to Stay

Camping The *Camping du Mont-Saint-Michel* (☎ 02 33 60 09 33) is on the road to Pontorson (D976), two km from the Mont. It's open from mid-February to mid-November and charges 15FF per person, 11FF for a tent

and 13FF for a car. Bungalows with showe and toilet are also available for 210 to 230FF for two people. There are several othe camping grounds a couple of km furthe towards Pontorson.

Hostel *Centre Duguesclin* (☎ 02 33 60 18 65 in Pontorson operates as a hostel from Easte to mid-September. A bed in a three-bunk roon costs 43FF a night, but you must bring you own sheets. There are kitchen facilities on the ground floor. The hostel is closed from noon t 5 pm, but there is no curfew. The hostel is abou one km west of the train station on Rue d Général Patton, which runs parallel to th Couësnon River north of Rue du Couësnon The hostel is on the left side in an old three storey stone building opposite No 26.

Hotels Mont-Saint-Michel has about 15 hotel but almost all are at least two-star and expen sive. Don't forget that you'll have to drag you luggage up here too, as vehicles must be left i the parking lot below. *La Mère Poulard* (☎ 0 33 60 14 01), the first hotel on the left as yo walk up the Grande Rue, has twins with showe from 250FF.

Your best bet is to stay in Pontorson. Acros Place de la Gare from the train station, ther are a couple of cheap hotels. The *Hôtel d l'Arrivée* (☎ 02 33 60 01 57) at 14 Rue d Docteur Tizon has doubles for 87/150F without/with shower. Triples/quads ar 160/200FF and from 200FF with shower. Hal showers are 15FF. The *Hôtel Le Rénové* (☎ 0 33 60 00 21), nearby at 2 Rue de Rennes, ha doubles for 140/180FF without/with shower Triples or quads cost 250FF.

The *Hôtel La Tour de Brette* (☎ 02 33 6 10 69) at 8 Rue du Couësnon is an exceller deal. Its singles and doubles – all with showe and TV – are 165FF to 220FF. The touris office can arrange private accommodation c farm stays from 150 to 200FF per double including breakfast.

Places to Eat
The tourist restaurants around the base of th Mont have lovely views but they aren't bar gains; menus start at about 90FF.

In Pontorson, *La Squadra* (☎ 02 33 68 3 17) at 102 Rue Couësnon has decent pizz from 37FF), salads and pasta and is open daily. For crêpes and savoury galettes (15FF), try *La Crêperie du Couësnon* (☎ 02 33 60 16 67) at 21 Rue du Couësnon. *La Tour de Brette* (☎ 02 33 60 10 69), across from the river at 8 Rue du Couësnon, has very good menus from 57FF.

The supermarket nearest the Mont is next to the Camping du Mont-Saint-Michel on the D976. It's open daily except Sunday from 9 am to 1 pm and 2.30 to 7 pm from mid-February to October and from 7.30 am to 10 pm in July and August.

Getting There & Away

Bus Bus No 15 run by STN (☎ 02 33 58 03 07 in Avranches) goes from Pontorson train station to Mont-Saint-Michel. There are nine buses a day in July and August (six on weekends and holidays) and three or four during the rest of the year. Most of the buses connect with trains to/from Paris, Rennes and Caen.

For information on bus transport to/from Saint Malo, 43 km to the west, see Getting There & Away in the Saint Malo section. The Pontorson office of Courriers Bretons buses ☎ 02 33 60 11 43; ☎ 02 99 56 79 09 in Saint Malo) is 50 metres west of the train station at 2 Rue du Docteur Tizon. It is open weekdays from 9.30 to 11.30 am and 5.45 to 7 pm.

Train There are trains to the Pontorson train station (☎ 02 33 60 00 35) from Caen (via Folligny) and Rennes (via Dol). From Paris, take the train to Caen (from Gare Saint Lazare), Rennes (from Gare Montparnasse) or direct to Pontorson via Folligny (Gare Montparnasse).

Bicycle Bikes can be rented at the train station 55FF per day plus 1000FF deposit) and from E Videloup (☎ 02 33 60 11 40) at 1bis Rue du Couësnon, which charges 35FF/70FF per day for one-speeds/mountain bikes. E Videloup is open from 8.30 am to 12.30 pm and 2 to 7 pm from Monday afternoon to Saturday.

Brittany

Brittany (Bretagne in French, Breizh in Breton), the westernmost region of France, is famous for its rugged countryside and wild coastline. The area is also known for its many colourful religious celebrations *(pardons)*. Traditional costumes, including extraordinarily tall headdresses of lace worn by the women, can still be seen at some of these and other local festivals, including night-time dance meets called *fest-noz*.

Breton customs are most in evidence in Cornouaille, the area at the south-western tip of the Breton peninsula, whose largest city is Quimper. Saint Malo is a popular tourist destination and seaside resort on Brittany's north coast.

Breton Identity

The people of Brittany, driven from their homes in what is now Great Britain by the Anglo-Saxon invasions, migrated across the English Channel in the 5th and 6th centuries, bringing with them their Celtic language and traditions. For centuries a rich and powerful duchy, Brittany became part of France in 1532. To this day, many Bretons have not abandoned the hope that their region will one day regain its independence or at least a greater degree of autonomy.

Language

The indigenous language of Brittany is Breton, a Celtic language related to Welsh and, more distantly, to Irish and Scottish Gaelic. Breton – which, to the untrained ear, sounds like Gaelic with a French accent – can sometimes still be heard in western Brittany and especially in Cornouaille, where perhaps a third of the population understands it. However, only a tiny fraction of the people speak Breton at home.

Getting Around

Brittany's lack of convenient, intercity public transport and the appeal of exploring out-of-the-way destinations make renting a car or motorcycle worth considering. Brittany – especially Cornouaille – is an excellent area for cycling, and bike-rental places are never hard to find.

QUIMPER

Situated at the confluence *(kemper* in Breton) of two rivers, the Odet and the Steïr, Quimper (which is pronounced 'cam-PAIR'; population 62,000) has managed to preserve its Breton architecture and atmosphere and is considered by many to be the cultural and artistic capital of Brittany. Some even refer to the city as the 'soul of Brittany'.

The Festival de Cornouaille, a showcase for traditional Breton music, costumes and culture, is held here every year between the third and fourth Sundays in July.

Orientation

The old city, largely pedestrianised, is to the west and north-west of the cathedral. The train and bus stations are just under a km east of the old city. Mont Frugy overlooks the city centre from the south bank of the Odet River.

Information

Tourist Office The tourist office (☎ 02 98 53 04 05) at Place de la Résistance is open Monday to Saturday from 9 am to noon and 1.30 to 6 or 7 pm. In July and August, the hours are from 8.30 am to 8 pm. From May to mid-September, the office is also open on Sunday from 9.30 am to 12.30 pm.

Money & Post The Banque de France is 150 metres from the train station at 29 Ave de la Gare, and is open Tuesday to Saturday from 8.45 am to noon and 1.30 to 3.30 pm. Crédit Agricole at 10 Rue René Madec is open Monday to Saturday and keeps similar hours but closes at 5.30 pm (4 pm on Monday and Saturday). The main post office (☎ 02 98 64 28 28) is at 37 Blvd Amiral de Kerguélen. Quimper's postcode is 29000.

Things to See

Walking Tour Strolling the quays that flank both banks of the Odet River is a fine way to get a feel for the city. The old city is known for its centuries-old houses, which are especially in evidence on **Rue Kéréon** and around **Place au Beurre**. To climb 72-metre-high **Mont Frugy**, which offers great views of the city, follow the switchback path **Promenade du Mont Frugy** next to the tourist office.

Cathédrale Saint Corentin Built between 1239 and 1515 (with spires added in the 1850s), Quimper's cathedral incorporates many Breton elements, including – on the west façade between the spires – an equestrian

statue of King Gradlon, the city's mythical 5th-century founder. The early 15th-century nave is out of line with the choir, built two centuries earlier. The cathedral's patron saint is Saint Corentin, the city's first bishop who according to legend, ate half a fish each morning and threw the rest back in the river. The next day the miraculous fish would reappear whole and offer itself once again to the saint. The loaf of bread you'll see in the south transept in front of a relic of Blessed Jean Discalcéat (1279-1349) was left by one of the faithful asking for a blessing. The really poor – not you – are entitled to it. Mass in Breton is said on the first Sunday of every month. In July and August, there are guided tours of the cathedral every day at 3 pm; in May and June tours are every other day at 2 pm.

Museums The **Musée Départemental Breton** (☎ 02 98 95 21 60), next to the cathedral in the former bishop's palace on Place Saint Corentin, houses exhibits on the history, furniture, costumes, crafts and archaeology of the area. It opens from 9 am to noon and 2 to 5 pm daily except Sunday morning and Monday. From June to September it's open daily from 9 am to 6 pm. Entry is 20FF (10FF for students) but rises to 25/12FF in summer. The **Musée des Beaux-Arts** (☎ 02 98 95 45 20), in the Hôtel de Ville at 40 Place Saint Corentin, has a wide collection of European paintings from the 16th to early 20th centuries. It is open from 10 am to noon and 2 to 6 pm every day except Tuesday, and in July and August daily from 10 am to 7 pm. The entry fee is 25FF (15FF for students).

Faïencerie Tour

Faïenceries HB Henriot (☎ 02 98 90 09 36) has been turning out the famous Quimper (or Kemper) porcelain since 1690. It has tours of the factory, which is on Rue Haute south-west of the cathedral, on weekdays from 9 to 11.15 am and 1.30 to 4 pm on weekdays (3 pm on Friday). The cost is 15FF (12FF for students).

Places to Stay

It is extremely difficult to find accommodation in Quimper during the Festival de Cornouaille. The tourist office can make bookings for you for 2FF in Quimper, and 10FF elsewhere in

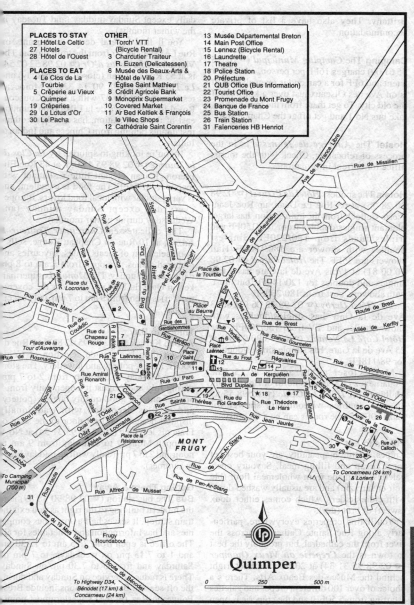

PLACES TO STAY
2 Hôtel Le Celtic
27 Hotels
28 Hôtel de l'Ouest

PLACES TO EAT
4 Le Clos de La Tourbie
5 Crêperie au Vieux Quimper
19 Crêperies
29 Le Lotus d'Or
30 Le Pacha

OTHER
1 Torch' VTT (Bicycle Rental)
3 Charcutier Traiteur R. Euzen (Delicatessen)
6 Musée des Beaux-Arts & Hôtel de Ville
7 Église Saint Mathieu
8 Crédit Agricole Bank
9 Monoprix Supermarket
10 Covered Market
11 Ar Bed Keltiek & François le Villec Shops
12 Cathédrale Saint Corentin

13 Musée Départemental Breton
14 Main Post Office
15 Lennez (Bicycle Rental)
16 Laundrette
17 Theatre
18 Police Station
20 Préfecture
21 QUB Office (Bus Information)
22 Tourist Office
23 Promenade du Mont Frugy
24 Banque de France
25 Bus Station
26 Train Station
31 Faïenceries HB Henriot

Quimper

0   250   500 m

FRANCE

Brittany. They also have a list of private accommodation.

Camping The *Camping Municipal* (☎ 02 98 55 61 09) charges 16FF per person, 3.50FF for a tent and 6FF for a car, and is open all year. It is on Ave des Oiseaux just over a km west of the old city. To get there from the train station, take bus No 1 and get off at the Chaptal stop.

Hostel The *Auberge de Jeunesse* is in the process of relocating. Check with the tourist office for current information.

Hotels The spotless *Hôtel de l'Ouest* (☎ 02 98 90 28 35) at 63 Rue Le Déan, up Rue Jean-Pierre Calloch from the train station, has large, pleasant singles/doubles from 100/150FF and triples/quads from 180/220FF. Singles/doubles with shower are 180/190FF. Hall showers are 15FF. The *Hôtel Pascal* (☎ 02 98 90 00 81) at 17bis Ave de la Gare has a few singles and doubles for 120/140FF, but most, with showers, cost from 180/200FF.

The *Hôtel Derby* (☎ 02 98 52 06 91) at 13 Ave de la Gare has singles/doubles with shower, toilet and TV from 150/200FF. The *Hôtel Café Le Nantaïs* (☎ 02 98 90 07 84) at 23 Ave de la Gare, has simple singles/doubles for 98/118FF.

Much closer to the action at 13 Rue Douarnenez (100 metres north of Église Saint Mathieu), the *Hôtel Le Celtic* (☎ 02 98 55 59 35) has doubles without/with shower for 120/160FF. Some rooms can be a bit noisy.

Places to Eat

Crêpes, a Breton speciality, are your best bet for a cheap and filling meal. Savoury ones, galettes, are made from wholemeal flour (blé noir or sarrazin) and are usually washed down with cidre (cider), which comes either doux (sweet) or brut (dry).

You'll find crêperies everywhere, particularly along Rue Sainte Catherine, across the river from the cathedral, but probably the best in town is the *Crêperie au Vieux Quimper* (☎ 02 98 95 31 34) at 20 Rue Verdelet, right behind the Musée des Beaux Arts. There's a choice of over 100 different crêpes and galettes (starting from 5.50FF) and the crêperie is open

daily except Sunday midday (and Tuesday in the winter months).

You'll find several decent restaurants on Rue Le Déan not far from the train station. The Vietnamese *Le Lotus d'Or* (☎ 02 98 53 02 54) is at 53 Rue Le Déan (closed Wednesday) and *Le Pacha* (☎ 02 98 90 14 32), a Moroccan restaurant, is at No 37 with a killer Couscous Royal for 99FF. Ave de la Libération, running east of the train station, has a strip of ethnic restaurants ranging from Chinese and Indian to Italian.

If you're looking to splurge, try *Le Clos de la Tourbie* (☎ 02 98 95 45 03), at 43 Rue Elie Fréron. It's an elegant little restaurant with menus from 74FF. The food is excellent, and is very popular with local food lovers. It's open every day except Sunday midday (and Wednesday during winter months).

The delicatessen *Charcutier Traiteur F Euzen*, at 10 Rue du Chapeau Rouge, sells a good selection of meats, patés, savouries and prepared dishes. It's open from 8 am to 8 pm daily except Sunday. The *Monoprix* supermarket on Quai du Port au Vin (near the covered market) is open from 9 am to 7 pm daily except Sunday.

Things to Buy

Ar Bed Keltiek (☎ 02 98 95 42 82) at 2 Rue du Roi Gradlon has a wide selection of Celtic books, music, pottery and jewellery. The store is open Monday to Saturday from 2 to 7 pm; during July and August it's open daily from ? am to 7 pm. For good-quality faïence (pottery and textiles decorated with traditionally inspired designs, go next door to the shop o François le Villec (☎ 02 98 95 31 54) at No 4 It's open Monday to Saturday from 9 am to noon and 2 to 7 pm (daily with no midday break in summer).

Getting There & Away

Bus The bus station (☎ 02 98 90 88 89) is in the modern building to the right as you exit the train station. It serves half a dozen bus companies and has information and timetables for all The office is open from 7.15 am to 12.30 pm and 1 to 7.15 pm on weekdays, to 7 pm on Saturday and from 5 to 7.30 pm on Sunday There is reduced service on Sunday and during the off season. Bus destinations include Brest Pointe du Raz (France's westernmost point)

...oscoff (from where there are ferries to Plymouth, England), Concarneau and Quimperlé. For information on SNCF buses to Douarnenez, Camaret-sur-Mer, Concarneau and Quiberon, enquire at the train station.

Train The train station (☎ 08 36 35 35 39) is east of the city centre on Ave de la Gare. The information counters are open daily from 8.30 am to 6.30 pm (8 am to 7 pm in July and August). A one-way ticket on the TGV to Paris' Gare Montparnasse costs 357FF (4½ hours). You can also reach Saint Malo by train via Rennes. The station has luggage lockers (30FF).

Getting Around
Bus QUB (☎ 02 98 95 26 27), which runs the local buses, is opposite the tourist office at 2 Quai de l'Odet. It's open weekdays from 8 am to 12.15 pm and 1.30 to 6.30 pm and on Saturday from 9 am to noon and 2 to 6 pm. Tickets are 6FF each or 45FF for a carnet of 10. Buses stop running around 7 pm and do not operate on Sunday. To reach the old city from the stations, take any bus from No 1 to No 7.

Taxi Radio taxis can be reached on ☎ 02 98 90 21 21.

Bicycle Possible cycling destinations from Quimper include Bénodet, Concarneau and even Pointe du Raz in Cornouaille. Torch' VTT (☎ 02 98 53 84 41) at 58 Rue de la Providence rents mountain bikes for 90/50FF a day/half day (70/45FF from October to April). The shop, which is open from 9.30 am to 7 pm daily except Sunday, is a good source of information on cycling routes. Bikes are a little bit cheaper at Lennez (☎ 02 98 90 14 81) just west of the train station at 13 Rue Aristide Briand. Lennez also rent *cyclos* and scooters for 150FF and 200FF a day.

CONCARNEAU
Concarneau (Konk-Kerne in Breton; population 19,000), 24 km south-east of Quimper, is France's third most important trawler port. Much of the tuna brought ashore here is caught in the Indian Ocean and off the coast of Africa; you'll see handbills announcing the size of the incoming fleet's catch all around town. Con-

carneau is slightly scruffy and at the same time a bit touristy, but it's refreshingly unpretentious and is near several decent beaches.

Orientation & Information
Concarneau curls around the busy fishing port, the Port de Pêche, with the two main quays running north-south along the harbour. The tourist office (☎ 02 98 97 01 44) is on Quai d'Aiguillon, 150 metres north of the main (west) gate to the Ville Close. It is open Monday to Saturday from 9 am to noon and from 2 to 6 pm. From mid-May to June, it keeps Sunday hours from 9 am to 12.30 pm, and in July and August, it's open daily from 9 am to 8 pm.

Money & Post The Société Générale at 10 Rue du Général Morvan, half a block west of the tourist office, is open weekdays from 8.10 am to noon and from 1.35 to 5.10 pm. Caisse d'Épargne on Rue Charles Linement, which runs parallel two streets south, keeps similar hours but is open on Saturday (until 4 pm) and closed Monday. The main post office, which has an exchange service, is at 14 Quai Carnot. Concarneau's postcode is 29900.

Things to See & Do
The **Ville Close** (walled city), built on a small island measuring 350 metres by 100 metres and fortified between the 14th and 17th centuries, is reached from Place Jean Jaurès by a footbridge. As you enter, note the sundial warning us all that 'Time passes like a shadow'. Ville Close is packed with shops and restaurants, and there are nice views of the town, the port and the bay from the **ramparts**, which are open throughout the year for strolling. From mid-June to mid-September, however, there is a charge of 5FF, and opening times are from 10 am to 7.30 pm daily. The ticket office is up the stairs to the left just inside the main gate.

The **Musée de la Pêche** (☎ 02 98 97 10 20), on Rue Vauban just beyond the gate, has four aquariums and interesting exhibits on everything you could possibly want to know about fish and the fishing industry over the centuries. It's open daily from 9.30 am to 12.30 pm and 2 to 6 pm (9.30 am to 7 pm from mid-June to

FRANCE

mid-September). The entry fee is 30/20FF for adults/under 18s.

The **Château de Keriolet** (02 98 97 36 50) about three km north of town is an extravagant neo-Gothic building with a colourful history. Five rooms are open to the public from June to September from 10.30 am to 6.30 pm. Entry is 25FF and includes a guided tour lasting an hour. To get there, take the bus to Beuzec-Conq which departs about every 10 minutes from the bus terminal at Place Jean Jaurès.

Plage des Sables Blancs (White Sands Beach) is 1.5 km north-west of the tourist office on Baie de la Forêt; **Plage du Cabellou** is several km south of town. Both beaches can be reached by taking bus No 2.

From April to September, three companies offer excursions to **Îles Glénan**, nine little islands about 20 km south of Concarneau with sailing and scuba-diving schools, an 18th-century fort, a bird sanctuary and a few houses. Fares are around 100FF. See Vedettes Glenn (☎ 02 98 97 10 31) at 17 Ave du Docteur Nicolas or call Vedettes de L'Odet (☎ 02 98 57 00 58) or Vedette Taxi (☎ 02 98 97 25 25).

Places to Stay

Camping Concarneau's half a dozen camping grounds include *Camping du Moulin d'Aurore* (☎ 02 98 50 53 08), 600 metres south-east of the Ville Close at 49 Rue de Trégunc. It's open from April to September and costs 18.50FF per person and 16.50FF for a tent and car. To get there take bus No 1 or 2 (to stop: Le Rouz) or the little ferry from Ville Close to Place Duquesne and walk south along Rue Mauduit Duplessis.

Hostel The *Auberge de Jeunesse* (☎ 02 98 97 03 47) is right on the water at Quai de la Croix, next to the Marinarium. To get there from the tourist office, walk south to the end of Quai Peneroff and turn right. A bed is 45FF, breakfast is 18FF. Reception is open from 9 am to noon and 6 to 8 pm.

Hotels The cheapest hotel in town is the *Hôtel Renaissance* (☎ 02 98 97 04 23) at the northern end of town at 56 Ave de la Gare. Rooms start at 130/185FF without/with shower. Opposite the tourist office, *Hôtel Le Jockey* (☎ 02 98 97 31 52) at Ave Pierre Guéguin has singles/

doubles with shower from 230FF. Just south a 9 Place Jean Jaurès, the *Hôtel Les Voyageurs* (☎ 02 98 97 08 06) has doubles without/with shower for 165/190FF. Hall showers are free.

If you can afford a bit more, *Hôtel des Halles* (☎ 02 98 97 11 41) around the corner from Hotel Les Voyageurs on Place de l'Hôtel de Ville charges from 260FF for a double with shower and TV. *Hôtel Modern* (☎ 02 98 97 03 36) is north of the port at 5 Rue du Lin, a quiet back street. It has singles/doubles with shower from 260FF (190FF without) and use of a private garage (40FF).

Places to Eat

Designed like the interior of an old fishing boat, *L'Écume* (☎ 02 98 97 33 27) at 3 Place Saint Guénolé in the Ville Close has excellent wholemeal crêpes and draught cider served in pewter cups. Back on the mainland, *Le Men Fall* (☎ 02 98 50 80 80), down narrow Rue Fresnel from Quai de la Croix, has good pizzas and pasta and is open daily to 11 pm except Monday and Sunday at midday. *Le Chalut* (☎ 02 98 97 02 12) at 20 Quai Carnot has a 50FF menu which is popular with local people

The covered market on Place Jean Jaurès is open to 1 pm daily except Sunday. There's a large *Super U* supermarket on Quai Carnot next to the post office.

Getting There & Away

The bus station is in the parking lot next to the tourist office. Caoudal (☎ 02 98 56 96 72) runs nine buses a day (three on Sunday) between Quimper and Quimperlé (via Concarneau and Pont Aven). The trip from Quimper to Concarneau costs 23FF and takes 30 minutes.

Getting Around

Bus Concarneau's three bus lines run by Busco operate between 7.20 am and 6.30 pm daily except Sunday. All of them stop at the bus terminal next to the tourist office and tickets are 5FF (44FF for a 10-ticket carnet). For information, consult the Busco office (☎ 02 98 60 53 76) in the covered market on Ave de Docteur Nicolas. It's open from 9.30 am to noon and from 2 to 5 pm on weekdays.

Taxi For taxis in Concarneau call ☎ 02 98 97 24 18.

Boat A small passenger ferry links the Ville Close and Place Duquesne on Concarneau's eastern shore year-round. From mid-June to August, sailings are between 7 am and 8.30 pm. Off season, they start an hour later, take a lunch break and finish at 6.20 pm (7.20 pm at the weekend). One way is 3FF (20FF for 10 tickets).

SAINT MALO

The Channel port of Saint Malo (population 48,000) is one of the most popular tourist destinations in Brittany – and with good reason. Situated at the mouth of the Rance River, it is famed for its walled city and nearby beaches. The Saint Malo area has some of the highest tidal variations in the world – depending on the lunar and solar cycles, the high-water mark is often 13 metres or more above the low-water mark.

Saint Malo is an excellent base from which to explore the Côte d'Émeraude, the northern 'Emerald Coast' of Brittany between Pointe du Grouin and Le Val André. Mont-Saint-Michel (see Normandy, earlier) can be visited easily as a day trip from Saint Malo.

Saint Malo reached the height of its importance during the 17th and 18th centuries, when it was one of France's most active ports for both merchant ships and privateers, whose favourite targets were, of course, the English.

Orientation

Saint Malo consists of the resort towns of Saint Servan, Saint Malo, Paramé and Rothéneuf. The old city, signposted as Intra-Muros ('within the walls') and also known as the Ville Close, is connected to Paramé by the Sillon Isthmus. Esplanade Saint Vincent, where the tourist office and bus station are located, is a giant parking lot just outside Porte Saint Vincent, one of the old city gates. The train station is 1.2 km east of Esplanade Saint Vincent.

Information

Tourist Office Saint Malo's tourist office (☎ 02 99 56 64 48) is just outside the old city on Esplanade Saint Vincent. It's open Monday to Saturday from 9 am to noon and 2 to 6.30 pm. From April to September, it's also open on Sunday from 10 am to noon and 2 to 5.30 pm. In July and August, it's open Monday to Satur-

day from 8.30 am to 8 pm and on Sunday from 10 am to 6.30 pm.

Money There are half a dozen banks near the train station, along Blvd de la République and at Place de Rocabey. All are open on weekdays and keep about the same hours: 8.30 am to noon and 1.30 to 4.30 pm. In the old city, the Banque de France is at 7 Rue d'Asfeld.

Post The main post office (☎ 02 99 20 51 78) is near Place de Rocabey at 1 Blvd de la Tour d'Auvergne. Currency exchange services are available. In the old city, there's a branch at 4 Place des Frères Lamennais. Saint Malo's postcode is 35400.

Things to See & Do

Old City During the fighting of August 1944, which drove the Germans from Saint Malo, 80% of the old city was destroyed. After the war, the principal historical monuments were faithfully reconstructed but the rest of the area was rebuilt in the style of the 17th and 18th centuries. **Cathédrale Saint Vincent**, begun in the 11th century, is noted for its medieval stained-glass windows. The striking modern altar in bronze reveals a Celtic influence.

The **ramparts**, built over the course of many centuries, survived the war and are largely original. They afford superb views in all directions: the freight port, the interior of the old city and the English Channel. There is free access to the **ramparts walk** at Porte de Dinan, the Grande Porte, Porte Saint Vincent and elsewhere. The remains of the 17th-century **Fort National**, for many years a prison, are just beyond the northern stretch.

The **Musée de la Ville** (☎ 02 99 40 71 57), in the Château de Saint Malo at Porte Saint Vincent, deals with the history of the city and the Pays Malouin (the area around Saint Malo). It is open daily from 10 am to noon and 2 to 6 pm (closed on Monday in winter). Entry is 25FF (12.50FF for students).

The **aquarium** (☎ 02 99 40 91 86), with over 100 tanks, is built into the walls of the old city, next to Place Vauban. It's open daily from 9.30 am to noon and 2.30 to 6 pm (to 11 pm with no midday break from July to mid-August). Entry is 30FF (22FF for students). (A giant new aquarium, **Le Grand Aquarium**

FRANCE

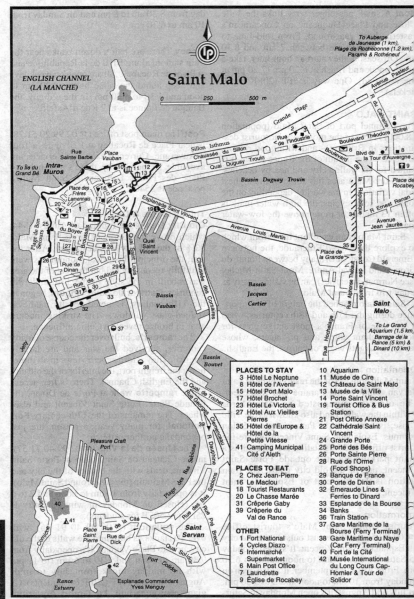

Saint Malo

ENGLISH CHANNEL
(LA MANCHE)

Intra-Muros

To Auberge
de Jeunesse (1 km),
Plage de Rochebonne (1.2 km),
Paramé & Rothéneuf

English Channel / La Manche, Grande Plage, Sillon Isthmus, Chaussée du Sillon, Quai Duguay Trouin, Bassin Duguay Trouin, Esplanade Saint Vincent, Avenue Louis Martin, Quai Saint Vincent, Chaussée des Corsaires, Bassin Jacques Cartier, Bassin Vauban, Bassin Bouvet, Pleasure Craft Port, Saint Servan, Rance Estuary, Port Solidor

To Île du Grand Bé
To le Grand Aquarium (1.5 km), Barrage de la Rance (5 km) & Dinard (10 km)

Place Vauban, Rue Sainte Barbe, Place des Frères Lamennais, Rue du Boyer, Rue Broussais, Rue de Dinan, Rue de Toulouse, Rue Saint Louis, Plage de Bon Secours, Jetty

Boulevard Théodore Botrel, Blvd de la Tour d'Auvergne, Place de Rocabey, Avenue Jean Jaurès, Avenue Pasteur, R du Calvaire, R Ernest Renan, Boulevard de la République, Rue Athone Théore, Boulevard des Talards, Place de la Grande, Rue Hochange, Saint Malo

Quai de Trichet, Rue Georges Clemenceau, R Dauphine, Rue des Bas Sablons, Plage des Bas Sablons, Rue des Bas, Rue Pré Bricet, Rue de la Cité, Place Saint Pierre, Rue du Dick, Corniche d'Aleth, Quai Solidor, Esplanade Commandant Yves Menguy

0 250 500 m

PLACES TO STAY
3 Hôtel Le Neptune
8 Hôtel de l'Avenir
15 Hôtel Port Malo
17 Hôtel Brochet
23 Hôtel Le Victoria
27 Hôtel Aux Vieilles Pierres
35 Hôtel de l'Europe & Hôtel de la Petite Vitesse
41 Camping Municipal Cité d'Aleth

PLACES TO EAT
2 Chez Jean-Pierre
16 Le Maclou
18 Tourist Restaurants
20 Le Chasse Marée
31 Crêperie Gaby
39 Crêperie du Val de Rance

OTHER
1 Fort National
4 Cycles Diazo
5 Intermarché Supermarket
6 Main Post Office
7 Laundrette
9 Église de Rocabey
10 Aquarium
11 Musée de Cire
12 Château de Saint Malo
13 Musée de la Ville
14 Porte Saint Vincent
19 Tourist Office & Bus Station
21 Post Office Annexe
22 Cathédrale Saint Vincent
24 Grande Porte
25 Porte des Bés
26 Porte Sainte Pierre
28 Rue de l'Orme (Food Shops)
29 Banque de France
30 Porte de Dinan
32 Émeraude Lines & Ferries to Dinard
33 Esplanade de la Bourse
34 Banks
36 Train Station
37 Gare Maritime de la Bourse (Ferry Terminal)
38 Gare Maritime du Naye (Car Ferry Terminal)
40 Fort de la Cité
42 Musée International du Long Cours Cap-Hornier & Tour de Solidor

02 99 21 19 02) is scheduled to open in June
)96 on Ave Général Patton, about a km to the
uth of St Malo's centre. It will spread over
)00 sq metres, with exotic fish, turtles, croc-
liles and sharks displayed in 40 aquariums
ncluding a circular one offering a 360-degree
anoramic view). Entry is expected to cost
)FF (students, 44FF). Bus No 5 from the
ilway station should run past there, but check
ith the tourist office first.

e du Grand Bé You can reach the Île du
rand Bé, where the 18th-century writer Cha-
aubriand is buried, on foot at low tide via the
orte des Bés and the nearby old city gates. Be
arned: when the tide comes in (and it comes
fast), the causeway remains impassable for
out six hours.

aint Servan Saint Servan's fortress, **Fort de
Cité**, was built in the mid-18th century and
rved as a German base during WWII. The
erman pillboxes of thick steel flanking the
rtress walls were heavily scarred by Allied
ells in August 1944. The interior of the fort
now used by camper vans.

The **Musée International du Long Cours
ap-Hornier** (☎ 02 99 40 71 58), housed in the
4th-century **Tour de Solidor** on Esplanade
lenguy, displays nautical instruments, ship
odels and other exhibits relating to the sailors
ho sailed around Cape Horn between the
rly 17th and early 20th centuries. There is a
eat view from the top of the tower. The
useum is open from 10 am to noon and 2 to
pm daily (closed Monday from October to
pril). Tickets cost 25FF (12.50FF for stu-
nts).

eaches Just outside the old city walls to the
est is **Plage de Bon Secours**. Saint Servan's
age des Bas Sablons is popular with older
inbathers. The **Grande Plage**, which
retches north-eastward from the Sillon
thmus, is spiked with tree trunks that act as
eakers. **Plage de Rochebonne** is a km or so
the north-east.

laces to Stay
amping The **Camping Municipal Cité
'Aleth** (☎ 02 99 81 60 91) is at the northern
p of Saint Servan next to Fort de la Cité. It's

open all year and charges 18.50FF per person
and 26FF for a tent and car. In summer, take
bus No 1. During the rest of the year, your best
bet is to take bus No 6 and walk.

Hostel The *Auberge de Jeunesse* (☎ 02 99 40
29 80) is at 37 Ave du Père Umbricht in
Paramé, a bit under two km north-east of the
train station. A bed in a four or six-person room
costs from 64 to 67FF, doubles are from 74 to
81FF per person, and singles with shower and
toilet are 108FF, all including breakfast. From
the train station, take bus No 5.

Hotels It can be difficult finding a hotel room
in Saint Malo during July and August. Among
the cheaper places, the noisy and charmless
hotels near the train station are the first to fill
up. If you're looking for a bargain, the hotels
around Place de Rocabey are probably your
best bet, though there are also a few good deals
in the old city.

Place de Rocabey The small *Hôtel de
l'Avenir* (☎ 02 99 56 13 33) at 31 Blvd de la
Tour d'Auvergne has singles and doubles for
120FF (150FF with shower). Hall showers cost
15FF. Close to the Grande Plage, *Hôtel Le
Neptune* (☎ 02 99 56 82 15) is an older, family-
run place at 21 Rue de l'Industrie. Adequate
doubles with free hall showers cost from
120FF. Doubles with shower and toilet cost
170FF.

Train Station Area The *Hôtel de l'Europe*
(☎ 02 99 56 13 42) is at 44 Blvd de la
République, across the roundabout from the
train station. Modern, nondescript doubles
start at 140FF (175FF from mid-April to
August). Shower-equipped rooms without/
with toilet are 170/180FF (220/250FF from
mid-April to August). There are no hall
showers. Like other places in this area, it's
somewhat noisy. The *Hôtel de la Petite Vitesse*
(☎ 02 99 56 01 93), next door at No 42, has
good-sized but noisy doubles from 160FF
(180FF with shower) and two-bed quads from
270FF. Hall showers are 20FF.

Old City The friendly, family-run *Hôtel Aux
Vieilles Pierres* (☎ 02 99 56 46 80) is in a quiet
part of the old city at 4 Rue des Lauriers.

Singles/doubles start at 135FF (160FF with shower); hall showers are free. The *Hôtel Le Victoria* (☎ 02 99 56 34 01) is more in the thick of things at 4 Rue des Orbettes. It has doubles from 150FF (185FF with shower). Hall showers are free.

The *Hôtel Port Malo* (☎ 02 99 20 52 99), 150 metres from Porte Saint Vincent at 15 Rue Sainte Barbe, has singles/doubles with shower and toilet for 180/240FF (200/260FF from May to September). The *Hôtel Brochet* (☎ 02 99 56 30 00), due south at 1 Rue Corne de Cerf, has singles/doubles (accessible by lift) with shower and TV for 180/200FF (230/290FF in summer).

Places to Eat

The old city has lots of tourist restaurants, crêperies and pizzerias in the area between Porte Saint Vincent, the cathedral and the Grande Porte, but if you're after better food, and better value, avoid this area completely.

The *Auberge Aux Vieilles Pierres* (☎ 02 99 56 46 80), below the Hotel in 4 Rue des Lauriers, has excellent menus from 85FF. The building was one of the very few in Saint Malo to survive the war. It is open daily (except Monday midday) until 11 pm. Popular with the locals is *Le Chasse Marée* (☎ 02 99 40 85 10) at 4 Rue du Grout Saint-Georges, off Place des Frères Lamennais. Menus start at 87FF, and it's open daily (except Monday in winter). For crêpes and galettes, try *Crêperie Gaby* at 2 Rue de Dinan, which has become a bit of an institution; the indefatigable Mme Gaby has been turning out her delicious crêpes for over 30 years. Crêpes start at 8.50FF, galettes at 7.50FF.

Chez Jean-Pierre (☎ 02 99 40 40 48), popular for pizza and pasta (from 44FF), has an enviable location across from the Grande Plage at 60 Chaussée du Sillon. It's open daily.

For takeaway sandwiches available until 1 am daily, head for *Le Maclou* (☎ 02 99 56 50 41) at 22 Rue Sainte Barbe. Near Plage des Bas Sablons in Saint Servan, *Crêperie du Val de Rance* (☎ 02 99 81 64 68) at 11 Rue Dauphine serves Breton-style crêpes and galettes all day. Order a bottle of Val de Rance cider and drink it, as they do here, from a teacup.

In the old city, you'll find a number of food shops along Rue de l'Orme, including the excellent cheese shop *Bordier* at No 9 (closed Sunday and Monday), a fruit and vegetable shop (closed Sunday) at No 8 and two boulangeries. A large *Intermarché* supermarket is two blocks from Place de Rocabey on Blvd Théodore Botrel.

Getting There & Away

Bus The bus station, from which several bus companies operate, is at Esplanade Saint Vincent, next door to the tourist office. Many of the buses departing from here also stop at the train station.

Les Courriers Bretons (☎ 02 99 56 79 09) has regular services to destinations such as Cancale (20.50FF), Fougères (48FF, Monday to Saturday only) and Mont-Saint-Michel (50FF, one hour). The daily bus to Mont-Saint-Michel leaves at 11.10 am and returns around 6.30 pm. During July and August, there are five return trips a day. The Courriers Bretons office is open Monday to Friday from 8.30 am to 12.15 pm and 2.15 to 6 pm and Saturday morning (all day in summer).

Tourisme Verney (☎ 02 99 40 82 67), with identical opening hours, has buses to Cancale (19.50FF), Dinan (33FF), Dinard (18.50FF) and Rennes (54FF).

Voyages Pansart (☎ 02 99 40 85 96), whose office is open Monday to Saturday (daily in July and August), offers various excursions. All-day tours to Mont-Saint-Michel (110FF, 99FF for students) operate daily from June to mid-September and three times a week in April and May.

Train The train station (☎ 02 99 40 70 20) is one km east of the old city along Ave Louis Martin. The information counters are open daily from 9 am to 12.30 pm and 2 to 7 pm. There is direct service to Paris' Gare Montparnasse (248FF, 4½ hours) in summer only. During the rest of the year, you have to change trains at Rennes. There are also services to Dinan (44FF) and Quimper (210FF).

Ferry Ferries link Saint Malo with the Channel Islands, Weymouth, Portsmouth and Poole in England and Cork in Ireland. There are two ferry terminals: hydrofoils, catamarans and the like depart from Gare Maritime de la Bourse; car ferries leave from the Gare Maritime de la Naye. Both terminals are south of the walled city. Shuttles to Dinard (see the Dinard section for details) depart from just outside the old city's Porte de Dinan.

From Gare Maritime de la Bourse, Condor (☎ 02 99 20 03 00) has hydrofoil services to Jersey (275FF one-day excursion) and Guernsey (315FF) from mid-April to October and up to mid-September to Sark and Alderney (560FF three-day excursion). Condor's service to Weymouth (579FF one way, seven hours) operates daily from late April to October.

Émeraude Lines (☎ 02 99 40 48 40) has ferries to Jersey, Guernsey and Sark. Service is most regular between late March and mid-November. Car ferries to Jersey run all year long, except in January.

Between mid-March and mid-December, Brittany Ferries (☎ 02 99 40 64 41) has boats to Portsmouth once or twice a day (except Sunday during some months) leaving from the Gare Maritime du Naye. One-way fares are 210 to 240FF and 910 to 1210FF for a car. In winter, ferries sail twice a week. There are also services to Poole (four times weekly) from late May to September, and to Portsmouth, Plymouth and Cork.

Getting Around
Bus Saint Malo Bus has seven lines, but line No 1 runs only in summer. Tickets cost 7FF and can be used as transfers for one hour after they're time-stamped; a carnet of 10 costs 59FF and a one-day pass, 20FF. In summer, Saint Malo Bus tickets are also valid on Courriers Bretons buses for travel within Saint Malo. Buses run until about 7.15 pm, but in summer certain lines keep running until about midnight. The company's information office at Esplanade Saint Vincent (☎ 02 99 56 06 06) is open from 8.30 to noon and 2 to 6.15 or 6.30 pm daily except Saturday afternoon and Sunday (daily except Sunday in summer).

Esplanade Saint Vincent, where the tourist office and bus station are, is linked with the train station by bus Nos 1, 2, 3 and 4.

Taxi Taxis can be ordered on ☎ 02 99 81 30 30.

Bicycle Cycles Diazo (☎ 02 99 40 31 63) at 47 Quai Duguay Trouin is open Monday to Friday from 9 am to noon and 2 to 6 pm. Three-speeds cost 50FF and mountain bikes are 80FF a day.

DINARD
While Saint Malo's old city and beaches are oriented towards middle-class families, Dinard (population 10,000) attracts a well-heeled clientele – especially from the UK – who have been coming here since the town first became popular with the English upper classes in the mid-19th century. Indeed, Dinard has the feel of a turn-of-the-century English beach resort, especially in summer, with its candy-cane bathing tents, beachside carnival rides and spiked-roof *belle époque* mansions perched above the waters.

Staying in Dinard can be a bit hard on the budget, but since the town is just across the Rance Estuary from Saint Malo, a day trip by bus or boat is an easy option.

Orientation
Plage de l'Écluse (also called Grande Plage), down the hill from the tourist office, runs along the northern edge of town between Pointe du Moulinet and Pointe de la Malouine. To get there from the Embarcadère (the pier where boats from Saint Malo dock), climb the stairs and walk 200 metres along Rue Georges Clemenceau. Place de Newquay (formerly Place de la Gare) is one km south-west of the tourist office.

Information
The tourist office (☎ 02 99 46 94 12) is in a round, colonnaded building at 2 Blvd Féart. It is open Monday to Saturday from 9 am to noon and 2 to 6 pm (from 9.30 am to 7.30 pm with no midday break in July and August and including Sunday).

There are a number of banks on Rue Levavasseur east of Blvd Féart and a Caisse d'Épargne at Place Rochaid close to the post office, open weekdays from 8.45 am to 12.15 pm and 1.45 to 5.30 pm (4 pm on Saturday). The main post office (☎ 02 99 16 34 00) is just south of Ave Édouard VII at Place Rochaid. Dinard's postcode is 35800.

Things to See & Do
Musée du Site Balnéaire The town's only real museum (☎ 02 99 46 81 05), at 12 Rue des Français Libres, focuses on the history of the area and, in particular, Dinard's development as a seaside resort. The Villa Eugénie was built in 1868 for the wife of Napoleon III who – alas

FRANCE

– never got to stay here. It's open April to October from 10 am to noon and 2 to 6 pm (on Saturday and Sunday, only in the afternoon) and costs 16FF (10FF for students).

Walks Beautiful seaside trails extend along the coast in both directions from Dinard. The tourist office sells a topoguide (5FF) with maps and information in French on five coastal trails entitled *Sentiers du Littoral du Canton du Dinard*.

Dinard's famous **Promenade du Clair de Lune** (Moonlight Promenade) runs along the Baie du Prieuré, which is south-west of the Embarcadère at the Place du Général de Gaulle. Perhaps the town's most attractive walk is the one which links the Promenade du Clair de Lune with **Plage de l'Écluse** via the rocky coast of **Pointe du Moulinet**, from where Saint Malo's old city can be seen across the water. This trail continues westward along the coast, passing **Plage de Saint Énogat** en route to Saint Briac, some 14 km away. Bikes are not allowed. There's a sound-and-light show on the Promenade du Clair de Lune from mid-June to mid-September.

If you are in the mood for a bit of a hike, you can take the bus or ferry over from Saint Malo and walk the 12 km back via the Barrage de la Rance (see below).

Swimming Wide, sandy **Plage de l'Écluse** is surrounded by fashionable hotels, a casino and changing cubicles. Next to the beach is the **Piscine Olympique** (☎ 02 99 46 22 77), an Olympic-sized swimming pool filled with heated sea water. It's open mornings, afternoons or evenings (except in December) depending on the day and costs 12FF/10FF for adults/students on weekdays and 24FF/15FF on weekends, holidays and during July and August. **Plage du Prieuré**, one km to the south along Blvd Féart, isn't as smart but it's less crowded. **Plage de Saint Énogat** is a km west of Plage de l'Écluse on the other side of Pointe de la Malouine.

Windsurfing The Wishbone Club (☎ 02 99 88 15 20) next to the swimming pool on the Plage de l'Écluse offers windsurfing instruction for 150FF per hour and rents boards. Depending on the make, they're 80 and 100FF an hour

(190 and 240FF for half a day). Wishbone operates every day from 9 am to 7 pm from March to October, and on weekends only during the rest of the year.

Barrage de la Rance If you're driving or walking along the D168 between Saint Malo and Dinard, you'll pass over the Rance Tidal Power Station (☎ 02 99 16 37 00), a hydroelectric dam across the estuary of the Rance River that uses Saint Malo's extraordinarily high tides to generate 3% of the electricity consumed in Brittany. The 750-metre-long dam, built between 1961 and 1966, has 24 generators that are turned at high tide by sea water flowing into the estuary and at low tide by water draining into the sea. Near the lock on the Dinard side is a small, subterranean visitors' centre open daily from 8.30 am to ? pm. It has a film in English on how the power station works.

Places to Stay

Hostel The *Auberge de Jeunesse Ker Charles* (☎ 02 99 46 40 02) at 8 Blvd l'Hôtelier (about 600 metres west of the tourist office) is open all year. A bed costs 80FF including breakfast; evening meals are 40FF.

Hotels A number of relatively inexpensive hotels can be found around Place de Newquay. The friendly *Hôtel de la Gare* (☎ 02 99 46 1? 84) at 28 Rue de la Corbinais has doubles without shower for 120 to 170FF. The reception is inside the ground-floor restaurant. The newly refurbished *Hôtel L'Étoile de Mer* (☎ 02 99 46 11 19) at 52 Rue de la Gare has singles/doubles with shower from 150/190FF.

The *Hôtel du Parc* (☎ 02 99 46 11 39), a bit closer to the centre of town at 20 Ave Édouard VII, has rooms starting at 145FF for one or two people. Doubles with shower and toilet are 270FF.

If you can afford a little more, *Hôtel du Prieuré* (☎ 02 99 46 13 74) is a lovely little place overlooking the beach and the town at Place du Général de Gaulle. Singles/doubles with shower are 260/270FF.

Places to Eat

There are a plenty of places around the tourist office that sell crêpes and the like. *L'Épicurien* at the Hôtel de la Gare (☎ 02 99 46 10 84) is a family-style restaurant with a good-value lunch menu for 45FF which includes a choice from the salad bar.

Le Grill de la Croisette (☎ 02 99 16 00 01), a few steps west of the tourist office at 2 Place de la Republique, specialises in meat grilled over an open fire and has a good three-course meal available for 59FF. The restaurant is open until around midnight daily except Tuesday.

The *Shopi* supermarket north of the Place de Newquay at 45 Rue Gardiner is open from 8.30 am to 12.30 pm and 2.30 to 7.30 pm Monday to Saturday and on Sunday morning.

Getting There & Around

Bus TIV buses (☎ 02 99 40 83 33, 02 99 82 26 26 in Saint Malo) leave Esplanade Saint Vincent in Saint Malo and pick up passengers at the train station before continuing on via the Barrage de la Rance to Dinard. The buses run almost once an hour until about 6 pm (to Saint Malo) and 7 pm (to Dinard).

Taxi You can order a taxi on ☎ 02 99 46 88 80.

Boat From April to September, the Bus de Mer ferry run by Émeraude Lines links Saint Malo with Dinard. The trip costs 20/30FF one way/return and takes 10 minutes. In Saint Malo, the dock (☎ 02 99 40 48 40) is just outside the Porte de Dinan; the Dinard dock (☎ 02 96 46 10 45) is at 27 Ave George V. There are eight to 17 trips a day from 9.30 am to around 6 pm, and until 11 pm in July and August.

Loire Valley

From the 15th to 18th centuries, the Loire Valley (Vallée de la Loire) was the playground of kings, princes, dukes and nobles who expended family fortunes and the wealth of the nation to turn it into a vast neighbourhood of lavish chateaux. Today, the region is a favourite destination of tourists seeking architectural testimony to the glories of the Middle Ages and the Renaissance.

The earliest chateaux in the Loire Valley were medieval fortresses (*châteaux forts*),

some constructed hastily in the 9th century as a defence against the marauding Vikings. These structures were built on high ground and, from the 11th century, when stone came into wide use, were often outfitted with fortified keeps, massive walls topped with battlements, loopholes (arrow slits) and moats spanned by drawbridges.

As the threat of invasion diminished – and the cannon (in use by the mid-15th century) rendered castles almost useless for defence – the architecture of new chateaux (and the new wings added to older ones) began to reflect a different set of priorities, including aesthetics and comfort. Under the influence of the Italian Renaissance, with its many innovations introduced to France at the end of the 15th century, the defensive structures so prominent in the early chateaux metamorphosed into whimsical, decorative features such as can be seen at Azay-le-Rideau, Chambord and Chenonceau. Instead of being built on isolated hilltops, the Renaissance chateaux were placed near a body of water or in a valley and proportioned to harmonise with their surroundings. Most chateaux from the 17th and 18th centuries are grand country houses built in the neoclassical style and set amid formal gardens.

BLOIS

The medieval town of Blois (population 50,000), whose name is pronounced 'blwah', was a major centre of court intrigue between the 15th and 17th centuries, and during the 16th century served as something of a second capital of France. A number of dramatic events, involving some of the most important kings and other personages of French history (Louis XII, François I and Henri III among them), took place inside the city's outstanding attraction, the Château de Blois. The old city, seriously damaged by German attacks in 1940, retains its steep, twisting medieval streets. Several of the most rewarding chateaux in the Loire Valley, including Chambord and Cheverny, are within a 20-km radius of the city.

Orientation

Blois, lying on the north bank of the Loire River, is quite a compact town and almost everything is within walking distance of the train station. The old city is both south and east of the Château de Blois, which towers over Place Victor Hugo.

Information

Tourist Office The local tourist office (☎ 02 54 74 06 49) at 3 Ave Jean Laigret is housed in an early 16th-century pavilion which used to stand in the middle of the chateau's gardens. From October to April, it's open Monday to Saturday from 9 am to noon and 2 to 6 pm, and on Sunday from 10.30 am to 12.30 pm and 2 to 5 pm. From May to September it's open daily from 9 am to 7 pm.

Money & Post The Banque de France (☎ 02 54 55 44 00), one block east of the train station at 4 Ave Jean Laigret, is open Tuesday to Saturday from 8.45 am to 12.15 pm and 1.45 to 3.45 pm. Crédit Agricole (☎ 02 54 74 30 68) at 6 Place Louis XII is open Tuesday to Saturday from 8.45 am to 5.30 pm (4.30 pm on Saturday) but charges a 40FF commission for changing money. The post office (☎ 02 54 78 08 01), which also has a currency exchange service, is north of Place Victor Hugo at 2 Rue Gallois. The postcode for Blois is 41000.

Things to See

Château de Blois This chateau (☎ 02 54 74 16 06) is not the most impressive in the Loire Valley, but it has a compellingly bloody history and an extraordinary mixture of architectural styles. The chateau's four distinct sections are: early Gothic (13th century), Flamboyant Gothic (the reign of Louis XII around 1500), early Renaissance (from the reign of François I, about 1520) and classical (towards the end of the reign of Louis XIII, around 1630). In the Louis XII section, look out for the porcupines (his symbol) carved into the stonework. The Italianate François I wing, which includes the famous **spiral staircase**, is decorated with repetitions of François I's insignia, a capital 'F' and the salamander.

The chateau also houses a small **archaeological museum** (closed until 1998 for refurbishment) and the **Musée des Beaux-Arts**. The chateau is open daily from 9 am to noon and 2 to 5 pm from October to mid-March. During the rest of the year, opening hours are from 9 am to 6 pm (until 7.30 pm during July and August). The entry fee is 33FF (17FF if you are under 25 or over 60). There is a sound-and-light show at the chateau during some evenings in May and every night from June to September. Prices are 60FF. For show times, check with the tourist office.

The entry ticket for the chateau also gets you into the museums of religious art and natural history in the 15th-century **Les Jacobins** convent across from 15 Rue Anne de Bretagne. Both are open every day from 2 to pm except Sunday and Monday.

A new museum, the **Maison de la Magie** (House of Magic; ☎ 02 54 55 26 26) is due to open towards the end of 1997 across the square from the chateau at 1 Place du Château. It will exhibit a collection of clocks and other objects invented by the 19th-century scientist/magician Robert Houdin (after whom the great Houdini named himself), and will stage magic shows in the theatre.

Old City Much of the area has been turned into a pedestrian mall and there are informative explanatory signs (in brown) tacked up around the old city in English. The tourist office has a good brochure suggesting walking tour (itinéraires), and guided tours (in French) leave every day from the chateau at 6 pm in July and August, and on Saturdays at 3 pm during May, June, September and October. Prices are 42FF (26FF for students).

Cathédrale Saint Louis is named after Louis XIV, who assisted in rebuilding it after a devastating hurricane in 1678. The crypt dates from the 10th century. There's a great view of both banks of the Loire River from the **Terrasse de l'Évêché** (terrace of the bishop's palace), directly behind the cathedral. The 15th-century **Maison des Acrobates** at Place Saint Louis, with its carved faces of acrobats, is one of the few medieval houses in Blois not destroyed during WWII.

Places to Stay

Camping The *Camping Municipal de la Boire* (☎ 02 54 74 22 78), open from March to November, is 2.5 km east of the train station on the south bank of the Loire. It is on Blvd René Gentil near the heliport and Pont Charles de Gaulle, a highway bridge over the river. Two people with a tent are charged 34FF, 40FF with a car. There's no bus service from town.

PLACES TO STAY
4 Hôtel Saint Jacques
5 Hôtel Le Savoie
11 Hôtel du Bellay
12 Hôtel L'Étoile d'Or
13 Hôtel Le Lys

PLACES TO EAT
21 La Salamandre
22 La Mesa
28 Au Bouchon Lyonnais
30 Restaurant Le Maïdi
31 Banquettes Rouges

OTHER
1 Bus Station
2 Taxi Booth
3 Train Station
6 Banque de France
7 Avis Car Rental
8 Tourist Office
9 Église Saint Vincent
10 Post Office
14 Palais de Justice
15 Bus Stops
16 Préfecture Building
17 Palais de la Culture et de Congrès
18 Maison des Acrobates
19 Cathédrale Saint Louis
20 Hôtel de Ville
23 Laundrette
24 Sports Motos Cycles
25 Maison de la Magie
26 Point Bus Office
27 Château de Blois
29 Crédit Agricole
32 Église Saint Nicolas
33 Les Jacobins

Blois

0   100   200 m

Loire River

To Héliport,
Camping Municipal de
la Boire (2 km) &
D951 & Chambord

To Beauregard (6 km) &
Cheverny (16 km)

To Autoroute A10, Tours (64 km)
& Paris (180 km)

To Basilique Notre
Dame de la Trinité
(700 m)

To Centre Hospitalier (1.5 km),
ADA Car Rental (1.2 km) & D149

To Cloître Saint Saturnin (300m)

To Cloître Saint Saturnin (20 km) & Amboise (34 km)

To N152, Auberge de
Jeunesse (Les Grouëts; 4 km)
& Tours (60 km)

Old City

Quartier
Saint
Nicolas

FRANCE

Hostel The *Auberge de Jeunesse* (☎ 02 54 78 27 21), open during the same period as the camp site, is 4.5 km south-west of the train station at 18 Rue de l'Hôtel Pasquier in the village of Les Grouëts. Call before heading out there as it's often full. Beds in a dorm are 40FF and breakfast (optional) is 18FF. The hostel is closed from 10 am to 6 pm. To get there, take bus No 4, which runs until 7 or 7.30 pm, from Place de Valin-de-la-Vaissière.

Hotels Near the train station, your best bet is the friendly *Hôtel Saint Jacques* (☎ 02 54 78 04 15) at 7 Rue Ducoux. Basic doubles start at 125FF; with shower, toilet and TV they're 176FF. Just opposite at No 6-8, the family-run *Hôtel Le Savoie* (☎ 02 54 74 32 21) has well-kept singles/doubles with shower, toilet and TV for 210/230FF.

A couple of hundred metres north-west of the old city, the *Hôtel du Bellay* (☎ 02 54 78 23 62) at 12 Rue des Minimes has doubles for 135FF; hall showers are free. Doubles with shower are 160FF, or 185FF with shower, toilet and cable TV. The hotel is closed during February. Nearby, the *Hôtel L'Étoile d'Or* (☎ 02 54 78 46 93) at 7 Rue du Bourg Neuf has doubles from 120FF (240FF with shower and toilet). Hall showers cost 12FF. Another good medium-priced deal in this area is the *Hôtel Le Lys* (☎ 02 54 74 66 08) at 3 Rue des Cordeliers, where singles/doubles with shower are 200FF.

Places to Eat
Le Maïdi (☎ 02 54 74 38 58), a North African restaurant in the old city at 42 Rue Saint Lubin, serves excellent couscous from 55FF, and menus from 65FF. It's open till 10 or 11 pm daily except Thursday. *La Mesa* (☎ 02 54 78 70 70) is a pleasant place at 11 Rue Vauvert, up tiny Rue du Grenier à Sel from 44 Rue Foulerie. It serves good pizzas (from 35FF) and salads, and you can eat al fresco in the courtyard.

For something a bit more up-market, try the local favourite *Au Bouchon Lyonnais* (☎ 02 54 74 12 87) at 25 Rue des Violettes (above Rue Saint Lubin). Menus are 110 and 165FF. The restaurant is open daily except Monday. Another good bet is *Banquettes Rouges* (☎ 02 54 78 74 92), an old-fashioned bistro at 16 Rues des Trois Marchands with a menu at 120FF. By

far the best value in town is the restaurant *La Salamandre* (☎ 02 54 74 09 18) at 34 Rue Foulerie. Good four-course menus including an aperitif are 72 and 98FF. It is open every day except Saturday and Sunday midday.

In the old city, there's a food market along Rue Anne de Bretagne, off Place Louis XII, on Tuesday, Thursday and Saturday until 1 pm.

Getting There & Away
The train station (☎ 08 36 35 35 39) is at the western end of Ave Jean Laigret on Place de la Gare. The information office is open from 9 am to 6.30 pm daily except Sunday. Service between Blois and Paris' Gare d'Austerlitz takes about 1½ hours by direct train (119FF) but less than an hour via Orléans. Tours (50FF) is 30 minutes away and Bordeaux (228FF) is four hours by direct train (less if you change to a TGV at Saint Pierre des Corps near Tours).

Getting Around
Bus Buses within Blois proper – run by TUB – operate from Monday to Saturday until 7.30 pm (to 11 pm on Saturday). On Sundays, service is greatly reduced. All lines except TUB No 4 stop at the train station. Tickets cost 5.80FF or 39.50FF for a carnet of 10. For information, consult the Point Bus office (☎ 02 54 78 15 66) at 2 Place Victor Hugo beneath the chateau (closed Sunday).

Taxi Taxis (☎ 02 54 78 07 65) can be hired for trips into the Loire Valley (see Getting There & Away in the Blois Area Chateaux section).

Car & Bicycle See Getting There & Away in the Blois Area Chateaux section for rental information.

BLOIS AREA CHATEAUX
The Blois area is endowed with some of the finest chateaux in the Loire Valley, including the spectacular Château de Chambord, the magnificently furnished Château de Cheverny, the beautifully situated Château de Chaumont (also accessible from Tours) and the modest but more personal Beauregard. The town of Amboise (see the Tours Area Chateaux section) can also be reached from Blois. Don't try to visit too many though; you'll soon find yourself 'chateau-saturated'.

Organised Tours

Without your own wheels, the best way to see more than one chateau in one day is with an organised tour. The regional TLC bus company (same office as Point Bus; ☎ 02 54 78 15 66) in Blois offers two Circuits Châteaux itineraries (prices do not include admission fees): Chambord and Cheverny (65FF return, 50FF for students) and Chaumont and Chenonceau (110/90FF for students). Both operate daily from mid-June to mid-September and on weekends between late May and mid-June.

Getting There & Away

Bus TLC runs limited bus services to destinations in the vicinity of Blois. All times quoted here are approximate and should be verified with the company first. Buses depart from Place Victor Hugo (in front of the Point Bus office) and from the bus station to the left of the train station as you exit.

Taxi If there are a few of you, you might consider visiting one or several chateaux by taxi (☎ 02 54 78 07 65 in Blois), which can be boarded at the taxi booth just outside the train station. Sample fares on weekdays/Sundays are: Chaumont 250/350FF; Cheverny 240/340FF; Chambord 260/365. For 950/1340FF you can (somehow) manage Chaumont, Cheverny, Chambord, Amboise and Chenonceau in one day.

Car Avis (☎ 02 54 74 48 15) at 6 Rue Jean Moulin is open Monday to Saturday from 8 am to noon and 2 to 7 pm.

Bicycle The countryside around Blois, with its quiet country back roads, is perfect for cycling. Unfortunately, Chambord, Cheverny and Chaumont are each about 20 km from Blois. An excursion to all, which are 20 km apart, is a 60-km proposition – quite a bit for one day if you're not in shape. A 1:200,000 scale Michelin road map or a 1:50,000 scale IGN is indispensable to find your way around the rural back roads.

Sports Motos Cycles (☎ 02 54 78 02 64) at 6 Rue Henry Drussy rents 10-speeds at 35FF a day. It is open Tuesday to Saturday from 9 am to noon and 2 to 6.30 pm.

Château de Chambord

The Château de Chambord (☎ 02 54 20 40 18), begun in 1519 by François I (1515-47), is the largest and most visited chateau in the Loire Valley. Its Renaissance architecture and decoration, grafted onto a feudal ground plan, may have been inspired by Leonardo da Vinci who, at the invitation of the king, lived in Amboise (45 km south-west of here) from 1516 until his death three years later.

Chambord is the creation of François I, whose emblems – a royal monogram of the letter F and a salamander of a particularly fierce disposition – adorn many parts of the building. Though forced by liquidity problems to leave his two sons unransomed in Spain and to help himself to both the treasuries of his churches and his subjects' silver, the king kept 1800 workers and artisans at work on Chambord for 15 years. At one point he even demanded that the Loire River be rerouted so that it would pass by Chambord; eventually, a smaller river, the Cosson, was diverted instead (you can still see a bridge spanning dry land on the road from Blois). Molière first staged two of his most famous plays at Chambord to audiences that included Louis XIV.

The chateau's famed **double-helix staircase**, attributed by some to Leonardo, consists of two spiral staircases that wind around the same central axis but never meet. The rich ornamentation is in the style of the early French Renaissance. Of the chateau's 440 rooms, only about 10 are open to the public. Watch out for the **tapestries** in the lovely chapel, the **Count de Chambord bedroom** (a late 19th-century pretender to the throne) and the fine collection of **Dresden tiles** on the 1st floor.

The royal court used to assemble on the Italianate **rooftop terrace** to watch military exercises, tournaments and the hounds and hunters returning from a day of stalking deer. As you stand on the terrace (once described as resembling an overcrowded chessboard), you will see all around you the towers, cupolas, domes, chimneys, dormers and slate roofs with geometric shapes that create the chateau's imposing skyline.

Tickets to the chateau are on sale daily from 9.30 am to 5.15 pm (October to March), to 6.15 pm (April to June and in September) and to 7.15 pm (July and August). The entry fee is

36FF (22FF for those under 24). A brochure in English (3FF) is available, but there are good (multilingual) explanatory signs posted in the major rooms. There are also tours of the chateau in English; these last about an hour and the price is included in the entry fee. During July and August, a nursery is available for children over two years. A sound-and-light show (50FF or 40FF for students) takes place nightly at 10.30 pm between mid-June and mid-September and on weekends from mid-April to mid-June and mid-September to mid-October.

The Centre d'Information Touristique (☎ 02 54 20 34 86) is at Place Saint Michel, the parking lot surrounded by tourist shops. It's open from mid-March to September daily from 10 am to 6 pm.

Getting There & Away Chambord is 16 km east of Blois and 18 km north-east of Cheverny. During the school year, TLC line No 2 averages three daily return trips from Blois to Chambord (18.40FF one way). The first bus out to Chambord leaves Blois at 12.10 pm Monday to Saturday and at 1.45 pm on Sundays. The last bus back to Blois leaves Chambord at 6.45 pm every day except Friday (6.03 pm) and Sunday (5.15 pm). There is very limited service in July and August.

Getting Around Bicycles are available from the Centre d'Information Touristique for 25FF an hour, 40FF for two hours and 80FF a day.

Château de Cheverny

The Château de Cheverny (☎ 02 54 79 96 29), the most magnificently furnished of the Loire Valley chateaux and still privately owned, was completed in 1634. After entering the building through its finely-proportioned neoclassical façade, visitors are treated to some 17 sumptuous rooms outfitted with the finest of period appointments: canopied beds, tapestries (note the *Abduction of Helen* in the **Salle d'Armes**, the former armoury), paintings, mantelpieces, parquet floors, painted ceilings and walls covered with embossed Córdoba leather. The pamphlet provided is extremely useful. Don't miss the three dozen panels illustrating the story of *Don Quixote* in the 1st-floor dining room.

On exiting the chateau, you can visit the **Salle des Trophées** – exhibiting the antlers of almost 2000 stags – and the kennels where a pack of some 80 hounds are still kept.

Cheverny is open daily from 9.15 or 9.30 am to noon and 2.15 to 5 pm (November to February), to 5.30 pm (October and March), to 6 pm (the last half of September) or 6.30 pm (April and May). From June to mid-September, the chateau stays open every day from 9.15 am to 6.45 pm. The entry fee is 32FF (21FF for students).

Getting There & Away Cheverny is 15 km south-east of Blois. TLC bus No 4 from Blois to Romorantin stops at Cheverny. Buses leave Blois Monday to Saturday at 6.50 am and 12.20 pm, Sundays at 11.10 am. Heading back to Blois, the last buses depart before 7 pm from Monday to Saturday (6.30 pm during July and August) and at 8.25 pm on Sunday and holidays.

By car from Blois, follow route D765 south to Cour-Cheverny. From Chambord, take the D112 south to Bracieux and then head west on route D102.

Château de Beauregard

Beauregard (☎ 02 54 70 46 64), the closest chateau to Blois, is relatively modest in size and a bit scruffy on the outside, which somehow adds to its charm. Built in the early 16th century as a hunting lodge for François I and enlarged 100 years later, it is set in the middle of a large park which is now being converted (with EU assistance) to what will be one of the largest gardens (70 hectares) in Europe. The count and countess who own the place still live in one wing, which is why only five rooms are open to the public.

Beauregard's most famous feature is the **Galerie des Portraits** on the 1st floor, featuring 327 portraits of 'who was who' in France from the 14th to 17th centuries. The floor is very unusual also, covered with 17th-century Dutch tiles.

From April to September, Beauregard is open daily from 9.30 am to noon and 2 to 6.30 pm; there is no closure at midday during July and August. During the rest of the year (except from mid-January to mid-February, when it's closed), the chateau is open from 9.30 am to noon and 2 to 5 pm daily except Wednesday. Entry is 35FF (25FF for students under 25 and people over 60).

Getting There & Away

The Château de Beauregard, only six km south of Blois, makes a good destination for a short bike ride. There is road access to the chateau from both the D765 (the Blois-Cheverny road) and the D956 (turn left at the village of Cellettes).

TLC bus No 5 heading towards the town of Saint Aignan stops at the village of Cellettes, one km south-west of the chateau, on Wednesday, Friday and Saturday. The first leaves at noon. Unfortunately, there is no afternoon bus back except the one operated by Transports Boutet (☎ 02 54 34 43 95), which passes through Cellettes at about 6.30 pm from Monday to Saturday and at about 6 pm on Sunday (except during August).

Château de Chaumont

The Château de Chaumont (☎ 02 54 20 98 03), set on a bluff overlooking the Loire, looks as much like a feudal castle as any chateau in the area. Built in the late 15th century, it served as a 'booby prize' for Diane de Poitier when her lover, Henry II, died in 1559, and hosted Benjamin Franklin several times when he served as ambassador to France after the American Revolution. The luxurious **stables** (*écuries*) are Chaumont's most famous feature, but the **Salle du Conseil** (Council Chamber) on the 1st floor with its majolica-tile floor and tapestries and **Catherine de' Medici's bedroom** overlooking the chapel are remarkable.

Tickets are on sale daily from 10 am to 4.30 pm (9.30 am to 6 pm from mid-March to mid-October); the chateau stays open for half an hour after sales end. The entry fee is 28FF (18FF for people under 24). The park around the chateau, with its many cedar trees, is open daily from 9 am to 5 pm (7 pm from April to September).

Wine Tasting

There are many wine cellars in the area offering tastings; consult the tourist office (☎ 02 54 20 91 73) just below the chateau on Rue du Maréchal Leclerc as times vary. From around Easter to September, for example, there is free tasting in the small build-

ing 50 metres up Rue du Village Neuf from the beginning of the path up to the chateau.

Getting There & Away

The Château de Chaumont is 21 km south-west of Blois and 15 km north-east of Amboise in the village of Chaumont-sur-Loire. The path leading up to the park and the chateau begins at the intersection of Rue du Village Neuf and Rue Maréchal Leclerc (route D751). By rail, you can take a local train on the Orléans-Tours line and get off at Onzain (16FF), which is a two-km walk across the river from the chateau.

TOURS

While Blois remains essentially medieval in layout and small-townish in atmosphere, Tours (population 136,000) has the cosmopolitan and bourgeois air of a real French provincial city. Tours was devastated by German bombardment and an accompanying fire in June 1940; much of it has been rebuilt since WWII. It is said that the French spoken in Tours is the purest in all of France.

Orientation

Tours' focal point is Place Jean Jaurès, where the city's major thoroughfares (Rue Nationale, Blvd Heurteloup, Ave de Grammont and Blvd Béranger) join up. The train station is 300 metres to the east along Blvd Heurteloup. The old city, centred around Place Plumereau, is about 400 metres west of Rue Nationale.

Information

Tourist Office The tourist office (☎ 02 47 70 37 37) is at 78-82 Rue Bernard Palissy opposite the new Centre International de Congrès (International Convention Centre). From June to September, the office is open Monday to Saturday from 8.30 am to 7 pm and on Sunday from 10 am to 12.30 pm and 3 to 6 pm. The rest of the year it opens daily from 9 am to 12.30 pm and 1.30 to 6 pm and on Sunday from 10 am to 1 pm.

Money & Post Most banks in Tours are closed on Monday. The Crédit Agricole (☎ 02 47 20 84 85), just east of the train station at 10 Rue Édouard Vaillant, is open Tuesday to Saturday from 9 am to 12.30 pm and 1.30 to 5.15 pm (4.15 pm on Friday). Banque de France, at 2

Rue Chanoineau, has similar opening hours but closes at 3.30 pm.

The main post office (☎ 02 47 60 34 20) is 200 metres west of Place Jean Jaurès on 1 Blvd Béranger. It also offers currency exchange. Tours' postcode is 37000.

Things to See

Walking Tour Tours is a great city for strolling. Areas worth exploring include the **old city** around Place Plumereau, which is surrounded by half-timbered houses, **Rue du Grand Marché** and **Rue Colbert**. Also of interest is the neighbourhood around the Musée des Beaux-Arts, which includes **Cathédrale Saint Gatien**, built between 1220 and 1547 and renowned for its spectacular 13th and 15th-century stained glass. It is open from 8.30 am to noon and 2 to 7.30 pm (8 pm in July and August). Tours of the cathedral's Renaissance **cloître** (cloister) can be visited with a guide (14FF) daily except Sunday morning from 10 am to noon and 2 to 5 pm (9 am to noon and 2 to 6 pm from April to September).

Museums The tourist office offers a 'Carte multi-visite' for 50FF allowing entry to seven museums in Tours.

The **Musée Archéologique de Touraine** (☎ 02 47 66 22 32) is at 25 Rue du Commerce in the Hôtel Gouïn, a splendid Renaissance residence built around 1510 for a wealthy merchant. Its Italian-style façade, all that was left after the 1940 conflagration, is worth seeing even if the eclectic assemblage of pottery, scientific instruments, art etc inside doesn't interest you. The museum is open from 10 am to 12.30 pm and 2 to 5.30 or 6.30 pm; in July and August, it's open until 7 pm. Entry is 18FF (15FF for students).

The **Musée du Compagnonnage** (☎ 02 47 61 07 93) overlooking the courtyard of **Église Saint Julien** at 8 Rue Nationale, is a celebration of the skill of the French artisan; exhibits include examples of woodcarving, metalwork and even cake-icing. It's open every day except Tuesday from 9 am to noon and 2 to 5 or 6 pm, and from 9 am to 6.30 pm (mid-June to mid-September). Tickets cost 21FF (12FF for students). The **Musée des Vins de Touraine** (Museum of Touraine Wines; ☎ 02 47 61 07 93), a few metres away at No 16, is in the 13th-century wine cellars of Église Saint Julien. Hours are the same as those of the Musée du Campagnonnage, and so is the level of interest: neither are must-sees. Entry costs 12FF (6FF for students).

The **Musée des Beaux-Arts** (☎ 02 47 05 68 73) at 18 Place François Sicard has a good collection of works from the 14th to 20th centuries but is especially proud of two 15th-century altar paintings by the Italian painter Andrea Mantegna, brought from Italy by Napoleon. The museum is open every day except Tuesday from 9 am to 12.45 pm and 2 to 6 pm. Entry costs 30FF (15FF for students).

Places to Stay

Camping The *Camping Édouard Péron* (☎ 02 47 54 11 11) at Place Édouard Péron about 2.5 km north-east of the train station on the north bank of the Loire, is open from June to mid-September. To get there, take bus No 7 towards Sainte Radegonde Ermitage. The per-person charge is 14FF and a tent site is 10 to 18FF.

Hostels At 16 Rue Bernard Palissy, 400 metres north of the train station, *Le Foyer* (☎ 02 47 60 51 51) has singles/doubles for 80/160FF. Reception is open weekdays from 9 am to 7 pm (to 2.30 pm on Saturday).

The *Auberge de Jeunesse* (☎ 02 47 25 14 45) is five km south of the train station in Parc de Grand Mont. A bed with/without breakfast costs 63/45FF a night, and sheets/sleeping bags are an extra 17FF. Rooms are locked from 10 am to 5 pm. To get there, take bus No 1 or 6 from Place Jean Jaurès (Auberge de Jeunesse stop). Between about 9.30 pm and midnight take the Bleu de Nuit line N1 (southbound) and get off at the Monge stop.

Hotels Most of the cheapest hotels – those close to the train station – are pretty basic. The ones near the river are slightly more expensive but are also good value.

Train Station Area The cheapest hotel in town is the *Tours Hôtel* (☎ 02 47 05 59 35), directly to the east of the train station at 10 Rue Édouard Vaillant. Basic singles/doubles start at 70/75FF, and a two-bed quad is 120FF. Showers cost 10FF. On the other side of the station, the

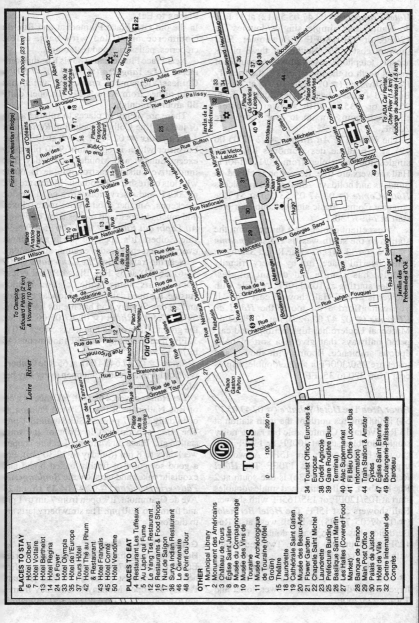

Tours

Scale: 0   100   200 m

PLACES TO STAY
6   Hôtel Colbert
7   Hôtel Voltaire
13 Hôtel Berthelot
14 Hôtel Regina
24 Le Foyer
33 Hôtel Olympia
35 Hôtel de l'Europe
37 Tours Hôtel
42 Hôtel Thé au Rhum & Restaurant
43 Hôtel Français
45 Hôtel Comté
50 Hôtel Vendôme

PLACES TO EAT
4   Restaurant Les Tuffeaux
5   Au Lapin qui Fume
12 Le Yang Tse Restaurant
16 Restaurants & Food Shops
17 Nuit de Saigon
36 Surya Indian Restaurant
46 Le Centenaire
48 Le Point du Jour

OTHER
1   Municipal Library
2   Monument des Américains
3   Château de Tours
8   Église Saint Julien
9   Musée du Compagnonnage
10 Musée des Vins de Touraine
11 Musée Archéologique de Touraine (Hôtel Goüin)
15 Théâtre
18 Laundrette
19 Cathédrale Saint Gatien
20 Musée des Beaux-Arts
21 Flower Garden
22 Chapelle Saint Michel
23 Préfecture Building
25 Basilique Saint Martin
26 Église Saint Martin
27 Les Halles (Covered Food Market)
28 Banque de France
29 Main Post Office
30 Palais de Justice
31 Hôtel de Ville
32 Centre International de Congrès
34 Tourist Office, Eurolines & Europcar
38 Crédit Agricole
39 Gare Routière (Bus Terminal)
40 Atac Supermarket
41 Fil Bleu Office (Local Bus Information)
44 Train Station & Amster Cycles
47 Église Saint Étienne
49 Boulangerie-Pâtisserie Dardeau

Loire River

Pont Wilson

Pont de Fil (Pedestrian Bridge)

To Amboise (23 km)

To Camping Édouard Péron (2 km) & Vouvray (10 km)

To ADA Car Rental, Cher River (1.5 km) & Auberge de Jeunesse (4.5 km)

Hôtel Français (☎ 02 47 05 59 12) at 11 Rue de Nantes has simple singles/doubles for 120FF, or 150/180FF with shower. Hall showers cost 10FF. Neither of these places accepts telephone reservations. A couple of metres north of the tourist office, the friendly *Hôtel Olympia* (☎ 02 47 05 10 17) at 74 Rue Bernard Palissy has singles/doubles from 95FF, or 135FF with shower. Shower-equipped rooms for up to four people are 200FF.

The *Hôtel Thé Au Rhum* (☎ 02 47 05 06 99) at 4-6 Place des Aumônes has clean singles/doubles/triples from 90/110/140FF. Hall showers are free. Reception is closed on Sundays and holidays. Another good choice is *Hôtel Comté* (☎ 02 47 05 53 16) at 51 Rue Auguste Comte. Basic singles/doubles/triples start at 74/97/130FF.

An excellent choice a bit further from the station to the south-west is *Hôtel Vendôme* (☎ 02 47 64 33 54) at 24 Rue Roger Salengro. This cheerful place, run by a very friendly couple, has simple but decent singles/doubles starting at 105/110FF. A triple with shower is 210FF. Hall showers cost 15FF. If you can afford a bit more, the *Hôtel de l'Europe* (☎ 02 47 05 42 07) at 12 Place du Maréchal Leclerc has high ceilings and carpeted hallways that give it a sort of belle époque ambience. Rooms with shower and toilet are 250/300FF a single/double; triples cost from 320 to 350FF.

River Area The *Hôtel Voltaire* (☎ 02 47 05 77 51) is 900 metres north of the train station at 13 Rue Voltaire. Comfortable but rather noisy singles/doubles start at 100FF, or 130FF with shower. Hall showers are 15FF. A two-bed triple with shower costs 170FF. The *Hôtel Regina* (☎ 02 47 05 25 36) is due south at 2 Rue Pimbert. Well-maintained singles/doubles start at 105/120FF, or 135/165FF with shower. Hall showers cost 15FF. The *Hôtel Berthelot* (☎ 02 47 05 71 95), a block west at 8 Rue Berthelot, has clean, basic doubles for 105/125FF without/with shower. Two-bed triples with shower cost 175FF.

A cut above in this area is the *Hôtel Colbert* (☎ 02 47 66 61 56) at 78 Rue Colbert, with large singles/doubles with shower, toilet and TV for 225/260FF.

Places to Eat

In the old city, Place Plumereau and Rue du Commerce are filled with bars, cafés, crêperies, pâtisseries and restaurants.

Near Place Plumereau at 83bis Rue du Commerce is *Le Yang Tse* (☎ 02 47 61 47 59), a Chinese/Vietnamese restaurant which has main dishes from 30 to 35FF. It's open daily till around midnight.

There are plenty of places to splurge along or just off Rue Colbert, including *Restaurant Les Tuffeaux* (☎ 02 47 47 19 89) at 19-21 Rue Lavoisier which is open until 9.30 pm daily except Sunday and Monday at midday. The innovative cuisine gastronomique is made with lots of fresh local products. Menus are 110 to 200FF, and reservations are a good idea on weekends. Another good place – more relaxed and much cheaper with menus from 65FF – is *Au Lapin qui Fume* (☎ 02 47 66 95 49) at 90 Rue Colbert. It's open for lunch and dinner every day except Tuesday evening and Sunday.

Near the train station, *Le Centenaire* (☎ 02 47 61 86 93) at 39 Rue Blaise Pascal prides itself on its home-made, classic French cuisine. It's open daily except Monday evening and all day Sunday, and has menus for 52 and 59FF. *Thé Au Rhum* (☎ 02 47 05 06 99), on the ground floor of the hotel, has crêpes (10 to 35FF), meat dishes (30 to 45FF) and menus (45 to 70FF).

Surya (☎ 02 47 64 34 04), at 65 Rue Colbert, is a North Indian restaurant open every day but Monday lunch.

Les Halles covered market, 500 metres west of Rue Nationale at Place Gaston Pailhou, is open daily until 7 pm and Sunday until 1 pm. The *Atac* supermarket in front of the train station at 5 Place du Maréchal Leclerc is open weekdays to 8 pm (Sunday to 12.30 pm). For a good selection of freshly baked bread and exquisite cakes and tarts, try the *Boulangerie-Pâtisserie Dardeau* (☎ 02 47 64 35 18) on 29 Ave de Grammont. It's open from 7 am to 1 pm and from 4 to 7.30 pm. The strawberry tarts are to die for.

Getting There & Away

Bus The long-haul international carrier Eurolines (☎ 02 47 66 45 56) has a ticket office next to the tourist office at 76 Rue Bernard Palissy. It's open Monday to Saturday from 9 am to noon and 1.30 to 6.30 pm. La Compagnie d'Autocars de Touraine (CAT; ☎ 02 47 37 81 81) handles services within the department of Indre-et-Loire. Schedules are posted at the bus terminal, which is in front of the train station at Place du Maréchal Leclerc. The information office is open from 7 am to 12.15 pm and 2 to 6.30 pm Monday to Friday and on Saturday from 8 am to 12.15 pm and 2 to 5.30 pm. See each Getting There & Away section under Tours Area Chateaux for details.

Train The train station (☎ 08 36 35 35 39) is off Blvd Heurteloup at Place du Maréchal Leclerc. The information office is open Monday to Saturday from 8.30 am to 6.30 pm. Paris' Gare Montparnasse is about an hour away by TGV (196 to 251FF). There is also service to Paris' Gare d'Austerlitz, Bordeaux (218FF, 2½ hours) and Nantes (134FF, two hours). Some of the chateaux around Tours can be reached by train or SNCF bus, both of which accept Eurail passes. See the Getting There & Away section under Tours Area Chateaux for details.

Car Europcar (☎ 02 47 64 47 76), next to the tourist office at 76 Blvd Bernard Palissy, is open from 8 am to noon and 2 to 6.30 pm Monday to Saturday.

Getting Around

Bus Fil Bleu is the bus network serving Tours and its suburbs. Almost all lines stop near Place Jean Jaurès. Three Bleu de Nuit lines operate about every hour from around 9.15 pm to just after midnight. Tickets (6.50FF) are valid for one hour after being time-stamped; a carnet of five/10 tickets is 29/56FF. A day pass costs 23FF.

Fil Bleu has an information office (☎ 02 47 56 70 70) in the Jean Jaurès centre, at 5bis Rue de la Dolve, 50 metres west of Place Jean Jaurès. It's open daily except Sunday from 7.30 am to 7 pm (9 am to 6.30 pm on Saturday).

Taxi Call Taxi Radio (☎ 02 47 20 30 40) to order a cab 24 hours a day.

Bicycle See the Getting There & Away section under Tours Area Chateaux for information on renting a bike.

TOURS AREA CHATEAUX

Tours makes a good base for visits to some of the Loire chateaux, including Chenonceau (which you can also visit on a tour from Blois), Azay-le-Rideau, Amboise (also accessible from Blois) and Chaumont (listed under Blois Area Châteaux). If you have a Eurail pass, more chateaux can be reached from Tours than from any other railhead in the region.

Organised Tours

Three companies offer English-language tours of the chateaux. Reservations can be made at the Tours tourist office or you can phone the company directly. Prices quoted here do not include entrance fees – a major expense if you go alone – but you will benefit from group prices on arrival with a tour.

Touraine Évasion (☎ 02 47 60 30 00), which uses minibuses, charges from 75 to 170FF for half-day and from 215 to 245FF for full-day tours. Half-day tours with Acco-Dispo (☎ 02 47 57 67 13) are from 100 to 130FF, and from 180 to 200FF for full days. Services Touristiques de Touraine (☎ 02 47 58 32 06), based at the train station, has bus tours from 158 to 176FF for a half-day and 245 to 260FF for a full day.

Getting There & Away

Bus CAT (☎ 02 47 37 81 81) runs a limited bus service to the area around Tours every day except Sunday. If you work fast, you can see two chateaux – Chenonceau and Amboise – by public transport on the same day. Take the bus from Quai 7 at the bus station in Tours to Chenonceaux (the town has an 'x' at the end) at 10 am, arriving at 11.14 am, and have a quick look at the chateau. The bus to Amboise leaves at 12.40 pm and returns to Tours at 5.25 pm. The total price is 65.90FF.

All times quoted are approximate, so verify them before making plans.

Train Some of the chateaux (including Azay-le-Rideau, Chenonceau and Chaumont) can be reached from Tours by train or SNCF bus. In summer, certain trains allow you to take a bicycle along free of charge, which makes it possible to cycle either there or back. For up-to-date schedules, ask for the brochure *Les Châteaux de la Loire en Train* at the Tours train station.

Bicycle From May to September, Amster Cycles (☎ 02 47 61 22 23) has a rental point inside the train station. For an 18-speed/tandem the price is 65/140FF per day (cheaper for longer periods). They can also lend you maps.

Château de Chenonceau

With its stylised (rather than defensive) moat, drawbridge, towers and turrets straddling the Cher River, 16th-century Chenonceau (☎ 02 47 23 90 07) is everything you imagine a fairy-tale castle to be. The chateau's interior, however, filled with period furniture, tourists, paintings, tourists, tapestries and more tourists, is of only moderate interest.

One of the series of remarkable women who created Chenonceau, Diane de Poitiers, mistress of King Henri II, planted the garden to the left (east) as you approach the chateau down the avenue of plane trees. After Henri's death in 1559, she was forced to give up her beloved Chenonceau by the vengeful Catherine de' Medici, Henri's wife. Catherine then applied her own formidable energies to the chateau and, among other works, laid out the garden to the west. (Diane's is prettier.)

The 60-metre-long **Galerie**, spanning the Cher River, was built by Catherine de' Medici and was converted into a hospital during WWI. Between 1940 and 1942, the demarcation line between Vichy-ruled France and the German-occupied zone ran down the middle of the Cher. For many people trying to escape to Vichy, this room served as a crossing point. Two other must-see rooms are Catherine's lovely little **library** on the ground floor with the oldest original ceiling (1521) in the castle and the **bedroom** where Louise de Lorraine lived her final days after the assassination of her husband, Henri III, in 1589. Macabre illustrations of bones, skulls, shovels and tear-drops adorn the walls.

Chenonceau is open all year from 9 am to 4.30 pm from mid-November to January, until 5 to 6.30 pm for the rest of the year (check with the tourist office for exact times). From mid-March to mid-September it's open until 7 pm. The entry fee is 40FF (25FF for students). You'll be given an easy-to-follow tour brochure in English as you enter.

Getting There & Away The Château de Chenonceau is 34 km east of Tours, 10 km south-east of Amboise and 40 km south-west of Blois. A couple of trains a day go from Tours to the town of Chenonceaux (33FF one way), 500 metres from the chateau. There are two CAT buses a day from Monday to Saturday, one departing at 10 am, the other at 2.15 pm; both take about an hour. The one-way/return fare is 36.60/65.90FF.

Château d'Azay-le-Rideau

Azay-le-Rideau (☎ 02 47 45 42 04), built on an island in the Indre River and surrounded by a quiet pool and lovely park, is one of the most harmonious and elegant of the Loire chateaux. It is adorned with stylised fortifications and turrets intended both as decoration and to indicate the owners' rank. But only seven rooms are open to the public, and their contents are disappointing (apart from a few 16th-century Flemish tapestries). The self-guiding brochure is a bit sketchy.

The chateau can be visited daily from October to March from 9 am to noon and 2 to 5.30 pm. From April to June and in September it's open from 9.30 am to 6 pm. During July and August, the hours are from 9 am to 7 pm. Tickets cost 32FF (21FF under 25). There's a sound-and-light show nightly from May to September at 10 or 10.30 pm (60FF).

Getting There & Away Azay-le-Rideau is 26 km south-west of Tours. SNCF has a year-round service two or three times a day from Tours to Azay (the station is 2.5 km from the chateau) by either train or bus for 27FF one way. The train is faster, but the bus goes direct to the chateau. The last train/bus back to Tours leaves Azay at about 6 pm (just after 8 pm on Sunday).

Amboise

The picturesque hillside town of Amboise (population 11,400), an easy day trip from Tours, is known for its chateau which reached the pinnacle of its importance around the turn of the 16th century.

Tourist Office The tourist office (Accueil d'Amboise; ☎ 02 47 57 09 28), along the river opposite 7 Quai Général de Gaulle, is open

Monday to Saturday from 9 am to 12.30 pm and from 2 or 3 pm to 6 or 6.30 pm, depending on the season. Between mid-June and mid-September there's no midday break and the office stays open to 8.30 pm. It also keeps Sunday hours from 10 am to noon and 4 to 7 pm. 'Passport tickets' which allow entry to Amboise's five museums are available for 80FF.

Château d'Amboise The rocky outcrop overlooking the town has been fortified since Gallo-Roman times, but the Château d'Amboise (☎ 02 47 57 00 98), which now lies atop it, began to take form in the 11th and 12th centuries. King Charles VIII, who grew up here, began work to enlarge it in 1492 after a visit to Italy, the artistic creativity and luxurious lifestyle of which had deeply impressed him. François I lived here during the first few years of his reign, a wild period marked by balls, masquerade parties and tournaments.

The chateau's ramparts and open gallery afford a panoramic view of the town, the Loire Valley and – on a clear day – Tours. The most notable features of the chateau are the **Tour des Chevaliers**, with a vaulted spiral ramp once used to ride horses in and out of the castle, and the Flamboyant Gothic **Chapelle Saint Hubert**, with a curious spire decorated with antlers. The remains of Leonardo da Vinci 1452-1519), who lived in Amboise for the last three years of his life, are supposedly under the chapel's northern transept. Exit the chateau via the souvenir shop: the side door leads to the 15th-century **Tour Hurtault**, whose interior consists of a circular ramp decorated with sculptured faces, animals and angels.

The entrance to the chateau is on Rue François Ier, a block east of Quai Général de Gaulle. It's open daily from 9 am to noon and to 5 or 6.30 pm, depending on the season. During July and August, the hours are 9 am to 7.30 pm without a break. The entry fee is 34FF (24FF for students under 26). Tours are in French only, but you are given a fact sheet in the language of your choice.

e Clos Lucé Leonardo da Vinci came to Amboise at the invitation of François I in 1516. Until his death at the age of 67 three years later, Leonardo lived and worked in Le Clos Lucé

(☎ 02 47 57 62 88), a 15th-century brick manor house 500 metres south-east of the chateau on Rue Victor Hugo. The building now contains restored rooms and scale models of some 40 of Leonardo's inventions – including a proto-automobile, armoured tank, parachute and hydraulic turbine. It's a fascinating place with a lovely garden, watchtower and recorded Renaissance music – infinitely more evocative of the age than the chateau. Le Clos Lucé is open daily from 9 am to 7 pm (closed in January). The entry fee is 37FF (28FF for students). Rue Victor Hugo to Clos Lucé passes several troglodyte dwellings – caves in the limestone hillside in which local people still live (with all the mod cons and a mortgage, of course).

Wine Tasting If you are driving, you can't see for all the *caves* (wine cellars) and wine-tasting places on route No 751, which runs parallel to the Loire (south side) from Chaumont. Closer to town the Caveau de Dégustation (wine-tasting cellar run by local growers; ☎ 02 47 57 23 69), in the base of the south side of the chateau, is open from April to September daily from 10 am to 7 pm.

Getting There & Away Amboise is 23 km east of Tours and 35 km west of Blois. Several trains a day between those two cities stop right across the river from Amboise (27FF one way from Tours). The last train back to Tours departs around 8.30 pm. From Tours, you can also take the CAT bus from Quai No 7 (23.50/42.30FF one way/return).

South-Western France

The south-western part of France includes a number of diverse regions, ranging from the Bordeaux wine-growing area near the beach-lined Atlantic seaboard to the Basque Country and the Pyrenees mountains in the south. There is convenient rail transport from this region to Paris, Spain and the Côte d'Azur.

LA ROCHELLE

La Rochelle (population 78,000) is a lively city midway down France's Atlantic coast and is

FRANCE

popular with middle-class French families and students on holiday. A university opened there in 1995, further boosting the student population. The nearby Île de Ré is surrounded by tens of km of fine-sand beaches. The quais of La Rochelle are lined with pleasant cafés and bars.

La Rochelle was one of France's most important seaports between the 14th and 17th centuries, and it was here that Protestantism first took root in France, incurring the wrath of Catholic authorities during the Wars of Religion in the latter half of the 16th century. In 1628 this Huguenot stronghold surrendered to Louis XIII's forces after all but 5000 of its 28,000 residents had starved to death during a 15-month siege orchestrated by Cardinal Richelieu, the principal minister to Louis XIII. There was a German submarine base here during WWII; Allied attacks on it devastated La Rochelle.

Orientation

The old city is at the northern end of Quai Valin, which runs more or less north-south along the Vieux Port (old port). Quai Valin is linked to the train station – 500 metres south-east – by Ave du Général de Gaulle. To get to Place du Marché, with a covered market and lots of restaurants, walk 250 metres north along Rue des Merciers from the old city's Hôtel de Ville. Rue du Palais, with its arcades and 18th-century merchants' homes, is the main shopping street.

Information

The tourist office (☎ 05 46 41 14 68) is in Le Gabut, the area due west of where Quai Valin and Ave du Général de Gaulle meet. It is open Monday to Saturday from 9 am to 12.30 pm and 2 to 6 pm. From June to September, opening hours are Monday to Saturday from 9 am to 7 pm (8 pm in July and August) and Sunday from 11 am to 5 pm.

The Banque de France is at 22 Rue Réaumur. The main post office (☎ 05 46 30 41 35) is to the north-east on Place de l'Hôtel de Ville. La Rochelle's postcode is 17000.

Things to See & Do

Old City To protect the harbour at night and defend it in times of war, a chain used to be stretched between the two 14th-century stone towers at the harbour entrance. Visitors can climb to the top of the 36-metre **Tour Saint Nicolas** (☎ 05 46 41 74 13) daily except Tuesday between 9.30 am and 12.30 pm and from 2 to 6.30 pm for 22FF (10FF for students). It's open every day to 7 pm in July and August with no midday break. **Tour de la Chaîne** (☎ 05 46 50 52 36), which houses a rather corny exhibition called 'La Rochelle in the Middle Ages', costs 20FF (12FF for students). West along the old city wall is **Tour de la Lanterne** (☎ 05 46 41 56 04), which was used for a long time as a prison. It now houses a museum with essentially the same hours and entry fees as the other two towers. The English-language graffiti you'll see on the wall was written by English privateers held here during the 18th century.

Parts of the **Tour de la Grosse Horloge** (☎ 05 46 51 51 51), the imposing clock tower on Quai Duperré, were built in the 13th century but most of it dates from the 18th century. From July to mid-September, the archaeological museum (15FF) inside is open from 10 am to 7 pm. There's an excellent view of the city from the roof.

The **Hôtel de Ville** (☎ 05 46 41 14 68) at Place de l'Hôtel de Ville in the old city was begun in the late 15th century and still houses the municipal government. Guided tours of the interior (16FF, 10FF for students) take place on Saturday and Sunday at 3 pm and daily from June to September.

Île de Ré & Beaches The Île de Ré, a 30-km long island whose eastern tip is nine km west of La Rochelle's centre, is reached by a three km toll bridge. In summer, the island's many beaches are a favourite destination for families with young children. The island is accessible from Quai Valin and the train station by Autoplus bus No 1, which goes to Sablanceaux (the narrow bit of the island nearest La Rochelle). The entire island is served by Rébus (☎ 05 46 09 20 15 in Saint Martin de Ré) from Place de Verdun and the train station. Eight buses a day go to both Saint Martin de Ré (23FF one way) and La Flotte (17FF). If you decide to drive, be prepared for the 110FF bridge toll from June to September (60FF at other times).

Another excellent beach about 10 km south of La Rochelle is **Châtelaillon**. It is accessible by Autoplus bus No 16.

Places to Stay

During July and August, most places in La Rochelle are full by noon and prices are higher than during the rest of the year.

Camping In summer, many camping grounds open up in the La Rochelle area, especially on the Île de Ré. The closest is *Camping du Soleil* (☎ 05 46 44 42 53) on Ave des Minimes in Les Minimes, a beachside suburb of La Rochelle about 1.5 km south of the city centre. It's open from mid-May to mid-September and is often full. Two people with a tent are charged about 45FF. From Quai Valin or the train station, take bus No 10.

Hostel The *Auberge de Jeunesse* (☎ 05 46 44 43 11) is half a km south of Camping du Soleil on Ave des Minimes. Beds are 72FF and singles/doubles are from 107FF including breakfast. There's a bus service (No 10; get off at the Lycée Hôtelier stop) until about 7.15 pm.

Hotels The *Hôtel Henri IV* (☎ 05 46 41 25 19), near the Vieux Port at 31 Rue des Gentilshommes, has doubles from 150FF but for 50FF more you get a room with shower, toilet and TV. Just south, the *Hôtel de Bordeaux* (☎ 05 46 41 31 22) at 43-45 Rue Saint Nicolas has pleasant singles/doubles for 145FF (185FF from May to September). For something a little more up-market, try *Hôtel de l'Arrivée et des Voyageurs* (☎ 05 46 41 40 18), some 50 metres south at 5 Rue de la Fabrique. Its comfortable doubles/quads with shower, toilet and TV are 275/440FF (cheaper off season). Breakfast is 30FF.

A number of cheap hotels can be found in the vicinity of Place du Marché, 250 metres north of the old city. The renovated *Hôtel Printania* (☎ 05 46 41 22 86) at 9 Rue du Brave Rondeau has singles/doubles from 150FF and triples/quads with shower for 195FF. Hall showers cost 10FF. Breakfast is 28FF. The *Hôtel de la Paix* (☎ 05 46 41 33 44), housed in an 18th-century building at 14 Rue Gargoulleau, has a few doubles for 150FF (170FF with shower, 180FF with shower and toilet). There are also triples and quads with shower for 230 to 310FF. Hall showers are free.

One of the nicest hotels in La Rochelle and convenient to the Place du Marché is the *Hôtel* *François 1er* (☎ 05 46 41 28 46) at tranquil 13-15 Rue Bazoges. It has doubles with all the mod cons for 278 to 475FF (cheaper in winter). Several French kings stayed in this building in the 15th and 16th centuries.

Places to Eat

There's always room at the *Brasserie Spaten* (☎ 05 46 41 42 88), a large seafood place at 15 Quai Valin with a 79FF menu. It's open daily from noon to midnight. A pizzeria in the immediate area can be recommended: the friendly *Papageno* (☎ 05 46 41 05 34) at 46 Rue Saint Nicolas. Homesick Yanks may want to try *Molly's Lone Star* (☎ 05 46 41 57 05) at 16 Rue de la Chaîne with buffalo wings, chilli, real cheeseburgers and brownies. It's open seven days a week from noon to 1 am.

Two areas chock-a-block with restaurants are the streets around the Place du Marché and Rue Saint Jean du Pérot, which is west of the Vieux Port. Choose the former for ethnic eateries – Moroccan, Chinese, Vietnamese – and food shops. On Rue Saint Jean du Pérot, three French restaurants worthy of a splurge are *La Marmite* (☎ 05 46 41 17 03) at No 14 with seafood menus from 185FF (closed Wednesday); the more reasonably priced *L'Assiette Saint Jean* (☎ 05 46 41 75 75) at No 18 with a 95FF seafood menu; and *Bistro l'Entr'acte* (☎ 05 46 50 62 60) at No 22 with an astonishing three-course meal for 145FF (closed Sunday).

Coop, a small grocery store near the Hôtel de Bordeaux on Rue Sardinerie, is open daily from 9 am to 1 pm and from 4 to 9 pm. For the sweetest North African pastries this side of the Mediterranean, try *El Souk* at 3 Rue de la Ferté which is open to 7.30 pm Tuesday to Saturday. It also has an excellent choice of olives and nuts.

Getting There & Away

Bus Océcars (☎ 05 46 00 21 01) and Citram (☎ 05 46 99 01 36 in Rochefort), which handle destinations in the department of Charente-Maritime, have buses which stop at Place de Verdun.

Train La Rochelle's train station (☎ 08 36 35 35 39) is at the southern end of Ave du Général de Gaulle. The information office is open

Monday to Saturday from 9 am to 6.45 pm. Destinations served by direct trains include: Bordeaux (131FF, two hours); Nantes (123FF, two hours); Marseille (404FF, nine hours); and Toulouse (243FF, 4½ hours). From Paris (320FF), you can take a TGV from Gare Montparnasse (three hours) or a non-TGV from Gare d'Austerlitz (five hours), which usually requires a change at Poitiers.

Getting Around
Bus Local buses run by Autoplus (☎ 05 46 34 02 22) all stop at the central station (*gare centrale*) on Place de Verdun. Most of the 10 lines run until sometime between 7.15 and 8 pm. A single ticket is 8FF; one-day and three-day passes are available for 24FF (including bicycle hire) and 58FF. The information office at the bus station is open Monday to Friday from 9 am to noon and 2 to 6 pm and on Saturday morning.

Car A small fleet of bright yellow electric cars and scooters are available for rent from the Autoplus bus company at Place de Verdun. The cars are good for 50 km and cost 100FF per day; scooters need to be recharged after 35 km and cost 70/40FF per day/half-day. Both require a 2500FF deposit.

Bicycle The Autoplus bus company runs an unusual bicycle rental called Les Vélos Autoplus opposite 11 Quai Valin from May to September. An adult's or child's yellow bike (lock included) is free for the first two hours; after that the charge is 6FF per hour and 60FF overnight (the one-day bus pass also covers bicycle rental). The bike depot is open every day from 9 am to 12.30 pm and 1.30 to 7 pm. The tourist office has a good biking map brochure called *Guide des Itinéraires Cyclables*.

Boat Autoplus' Bus de Mer links the Vieux Port with the beach at Les Minimes. From April to September boats leave from the pier just north of Tour de la Chaîne every hour from 10 am to 8 pm (10FF one way). In July and August departures are increased to two per hour to 11.30 pm. During the rest of the year Bus de Mer runs only at weekends.

BORDEAUX
Bordeaux (population 260,000) is known for its neoclassical architecture, wide avenues, colossal statues and well-tended public squares and parks. The city's ethnic diversity (there are three universities here with 60,000 students, many from developing countries), excellent museums and untouristed atmosphere make it much more than just a convenient stop between Paris and Spain.

Bordeaux was founded by the Romans in the 3rd century BC. From 1154 to 1453, it prospered under the rule of the English, whose fondness for the region's red wines (known as claret across the Channel) gave impetus to the local wine industry. The marketing and export of Bordeaux wine remains the single most important economic activity.

Orientation
Cours de la Marne stretches from the train station to Place de la Victoire, which is linked to Place de la Comédie by the pedestrians-only Rue Sainte Catherine. The city centre lies between Place Gambetta and the Garonne River. Cours de l'Intendance is the city's main shopping street. Rue de la Porte Dijeaux is also a pedestrian mall.

Information
Tourist Office The very efficient main tourist office (☎ 05 56 00 66 00) at 12 Cours du 30 Juillet is open daily from 9 am to 6 pm (to 8 pm from June to September). Its free maps and brochures are first-class, and there are daily city and 'theme' tours on foot from 40FF (30FF for students). The tourist office annexe at the train station (☎ 05 56 91 64 70) is open daily from 9 am (10 am on off-season Sundays) to 7 pm, and there is an airport branch (☎ 05 56 34 50 50).

For information about the Gironde department, contact the Maison du Tourisme de la Gironde (☎ 05 56 52 61 40) at 21 Cours de l'Intendance Monday to Saturday from 9 am to 7 pm.

Foreign Consulates Bordeaux has some 40 consulates, including the UK's at 353 Blvd du Président Wilson (☎ 05 56 42 34 13). The US consulate, however, has recently closed.

Money & Post Banque de France is around the corner from the tourist office at 13 Rue Esprit les Lois. American Express (☎ 05 56 52 40 52) t 14 Cours de l'Intendance is open Monday to Friday from 8.45 am to noon and 1.30 to 6 pm. The rate at the Thomas Cook bureau (☎ 05 56 1 58 80) in the train station is lower than that of the banks, but its services are available Monday to Saturday from 9 am to 6.50 pm and on Sunday from 10 am to 5.50 pm. It's open daily until 9 pm in summer.

The main post office (☎ 05 56 48 87 48) is west of the city centre at 52 Rue Georges Bonnac. Central Bordeaux's postcode is 3000.

Laundry The laundrette at 6 Rue de l'ondaudège, near Place de Tourny, is open even days a week from 7 am to 8.30 pm. At O Rue La Faurie de Monbadon, near the Hôtel Balzac, there's a laundrette open daily from 7 am to 9 pm. The laundrette on Rue La Boetie, round the corner from the Hôtel Boulan, is lso open daily from 7 am to 9 pm.

Things to See
The most prominent feature of the **Esplanade es Quinconces**, laid out in 1820, is a tower- ng fountain-monument to the Girondists, a roup of moderate, bourgeois legislative dep- ties during the French Revolution, 22 of whom were executed in 1793 for alleged unter-revolutionary activities. The **Jardin ublic**, an 18th-century 'English park', is long Cours de Verdun. It includes Bordeaux's **otanical garden** and **Musée d'Histoire aturelle** (Natural History Museum).

The much-praised, neoclassical **Grand héâtre** at Place de la Comédie was built in ne 1770s. Lovely **Place de la Bourse**, anked by the old Hôtel de la Douane (customs ouse) and the Bourse du Commerce (stock xchange), was built between 1731 and 1755. he riverside area nearby is run-down and irly lifeless.

Porte Dijeaux, which dates from 1748 and one of the few city gates still standing, leads **Place Gambetta**, a beautiful garden by a ond. Today it is an island of calm in the midst f the urban hustle and bustle, but during the eign of Terror, a guillotine was used here to ver the heads of 300 people.

Cathédrale Saint André in the Place Pey- erland was where the future King Louis VII married Eleanor of Aquitaine in 1137. The cathedral's 15th-century belfry, **Tour Pey- Berland**, stands behind the choir, whose chapels are nestled among the flying but- tresses. The cathedral is open Monday to Saturday from 8 am to noon and 2 to 7 pm (on Sunday from 8 am to noon and 3 to 6 pm).

Bordeaux' Moorish **synagogue** (☎ 05 56 91 79 39), inaugurated in 1882, is just west of Rue Sainte Catherine on Rue du Grand Rabbin Joseph Cohen. During WWII, the interior was ripped apart by the Nazis, who turned the complex into a prison. Visits are possible Monday to Thursday from 3 to 5 pm from the rabbi's office at 213 Rue Sainte Catherine.

Museums Most museums in Bordeaux charge adults 18FF (9FF for students), but almost all are free on Wednesday. The outstanding **Musée d'Aquitaine** (☎ 05 56 01 51 00) at 20 Cours Pasteur illustrates the history and eth- nography of the Bordeaux area from prehistory to the 19th century and the exhibits are excep- tionally well designed. The museum is open daily except Monday from 10 am to 6 pm.

At 20 Cours d'Albert, the **Musée des Beaux-Arts** (☎ 05 56 10 16 93) occupies two wings of the 18th-century Hôtel de Ville, between which is an attractive public garden called Jardin de la Mairie. The museum houses a large collection of paintings, including 17th- century Flemish, Dutch and Italian works and a major painting by Delacroix. It's open from 10 am to 5 or 6 pm daily except Tuesday.

At 39 Rue Bouffard, the **Musée des Arts Décoratifs** (☎ 05 56 00 72 50) specialises in porcelain, silverware, glassware, furniture and so on. It is open daily except Tuesday from 2 to 6 pm. Temporary exhibits stay open from 10 am to 6 pm.

The excellent **Musée d'Art Contemporain** (☎ 05 56 44 16 35) at 7 Rue Ferrère hosts temporary exhibits by contemporary artists on three floors. It is open from noon to 7 pm (to 10 pm on Wednesday) daily except Monday. Entry is 30FF (20FF for students), but is free if you arrive between noon and 2 pm. The museum is housed in the Entrepôts Lainé, built in 1824 as a warehouse for the exotic products of France's colonies: coffee, cocoa, peanuts, vanilla etc.

FRANCE

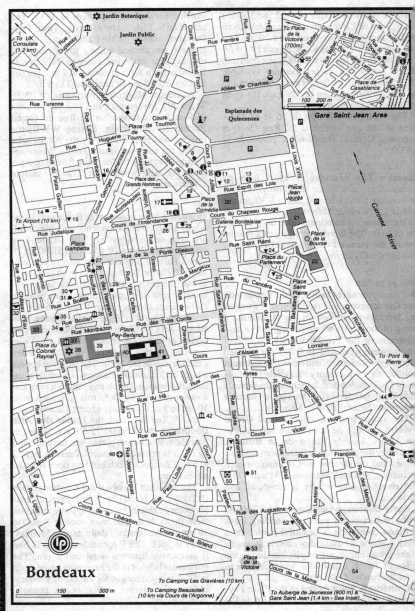

✿ Jardin Botanique

Rue Duplessy

To UK
Consulate
(1.2 km)

Rue de Fondaudège

Rue Turenne

Rue Lalande de Montbadon

Rue du Palais Gallien

To Airport (10 km)

Rue Judaïque

Place
Gambetta

Rue du Château d'Eau

Rue Saint Sernin

Rue de Belfort

Rue Mouneyra

Rue L'Isler

Cours de la Libération

✦ Bordeaux

0   150   300 m

To Camping Les Gravières (10 km)
To Camping Beausoleil
(10 km via Cours de l'Argonne)

Jardin Public ✿

Rue Foy

Cours du Maréchal Foch

Cours de Verdun

Rue Ferrère

Cours Georges Clémenceau

Huguerie

Place
de
Tournon

Rue JJ Rousseau

Cours de Tournon

Allées de Tournon

Rue Montesquieu

Place des
Grands Hommes

Cours de l'Intendance

Rue de la Porte Dijeaux

Rue de Grassi

Rue Vital Carles

R des Remparts

Rue Boudet

Rue La Boëtie

Rue Boulan

Rue Montbazon

Place
Pey-Berland

Cours du Maréchal Joffre

Rue du Hâ

Rue de Cursol

Rue Jean Burguet

Cours Pasteur

Cours Paul Louis Landes

Cours Aristide Briand

Allées de Chartres

Esplanade des
Quinconces

Quai Louis XVIII

Cours du 30 Juillet

Rue Esprit des Lois

Place
Jean
Jaurès

Place
de la
Comédie

Cours du Chapeau Rouge

Galerie Bordelaise

Rue Saint Rémi

Place
de la
Bourse

Place du
Parlement

Rue Margaux

Rue Sainte Catherine

Rue du Cancéra

Rue du Pas Saint Georges

Place
Saint
Pierre

Rue des Bahutiers

Quai Richelieu

Garonne River

To Pont de
Pierre

Rue des Trois Conils

Chevereus

Cours
d'Alsace

Ayres

Rue
des

Rue Sainte Catherine

Rue Saint Georges

Rue Saint James

Lorraine

Rue
Bouquière

Rue du Mirail

Victor
Hugo

Rue des Faures

Rue des Menuts

Rue Saint François

Rue Leyteire

Rue Bergeret

Rue Sainte Catherine

Cours Victor

Rue des Augustins

R Gratelot

Place du
Colonel
Raynal

Cours d'Albret

Place
de la
Victoire

Cours de la Marne

To Auberge de Jeunesse (800 m) &
Gare Saint Jean (1.4 km - See Inset)

To Place
de la
Victoire
(700m)

Cours de la Marne

Cours Barbey

Rue Malbec

Rue Eugène Leroy

Rue Vincennes

Rue des Douves

Rue Tauzia

Place
de
Casablanca

Rue Furado

Rue Charles Domercq

Place de la Victoire

0   100   200 m

Gare Saint Jean Area

PLACES TO STAY		OTHER		33	Galerie de Beaux-Arts
5	Hôtel Touring & Hôtel Studio	1	Musée d'Histoire Naturelle	35	Bradley's Bookshop
6	Hôtel de Sèze	2	Musée d'Art Contemporain	36	Musée des Arts Décoratifs
14	Hôtel Le Provence			37	Musée des Beaux-Arts
16	Hôtel Balzac & Laundrette	3	CITRAM Bus Station	38	Jardin de la Mairie
		4	Laundrette	39	Hôtel de Ville
19	Hôtel Blayais	7	Monument des Girondins	40	Cathédrale Saint André
28	Hôtel Bristol			41	Tour Pey-Berland
29	Hôtel de Lyon	8	Bordeaux Magnum (Wine Shop)	42	Musée d'Aquitaine
34	Hôtel Boulan			43	Porte de la Grosse Cloche
49	Maison des Etudiantes	9	Banks & Cash Machines		
55	Auberge de Jeunesse			44	Porte des Salinières
56	Hôtel Les Deux Mondes & Hôtel La Terasse	10	Maison du Vin de Bordeaux	45	Église Saint Michel
				46	Tour Saint Michel
		11	Tourist Office	48	Hôpital Saint André
		13	Banque de France	50	Synagogue
PLACES TO EAT		17	Église Notre Dame	51	Champion Supermarket
12	Les Quatre Sœurs Bistro	18	Maison du Tourisme de la Gironde	53	Porte d'Aquitaine
				54	Marché des Capucins (Wholesale Food Market)
15	Le Mechoui	20	Grand Théâtre		
23	La Galluchat	21	Bourse du Commerce		
24	Chez Edouard	22	Hôtel de la Douane (Customs)	57	Thomas Cook
26	Pizza Païe			58	SNCF Information Office
30	Cân Tho Restaurant	25	American Express		
47	The Blarney Stone	27	Porte Dijeaux (Gate)	59	Bus Stops
52	La Dakaroise	31	Laundrette	60	Train Station (Gare Saint Jean)
		32	Main Post Office		

Places to Stay

Camping *Camping Beausoleil* (☎ 05 56 89 17 16; open all year) charges 59FF for two people with their own tent (84FF with a car). It is about 10 km south-west of the city centre at 371 Cours du Général de Gaulle (route N10) in Gradignan. To get there, take bus G from Place de la Victoire towards Gradignan Beausoleil and get off at the terminus.

Camping Les Gravières (☎ 05 56 87 00 36; open all year) charges 28FF for a tent and 19FF per person; there's no extra charge for a car. It's 10 km south-east of central Bordeaux at Place de Courréjean in Villenave d'Ornon. Take bus B from Place de la Victoire towards Courréjean and get off at the terminus.

Hostels The *Maison des Étudiantes* (☎ 05 56 96 48 30) at 50 Rue Ligier, a dormitory during the academic year, offers accommodation from July to September. A bed costs 55FF with a student card (75FF without), including sheets and use of the showers and kitchen. To get there from the train station, take bus No 7 or 8 to the Course du Travail stop and walk 400 metres west on Cours de la Libération.

The charmless *Auberge de Jeunesse* (☎ 05 56 91 59 51) at 22 Cours Barbey is 650 metres west of the train station. A spot in a utilitarian, eight-bed room is only 40FF but the 1st floor (women's section) and the 2nd floor (men's section) are reached by separate staircases! There's an 11 pm curfew, but have a word with the manager in advance if you'll be staying out late. The hostel accepts telephone reservations and reception is open daily from 8 to 9.30 am and 6 to 11 pm.

Hotels Hotels in the area around the train station are convenient for rail passengers, but the neighbourhood is rather seedy. In terms of both price and value, you're much better off staying around the tourist office, Place de Tourny or Place Gambetta.

Tourist Office Area The old-fashioned *Hôtel Blayais* (☎ 05 56 48 17 87), east of the baroque Église Notre Dame at 17 Rue Mautrec, has fairly large singles/doubles for 110FF (with washbasin and bidet) and 150FF (with shower). Hall showers are free.

FRANCE

Place de Tourny The best inexpensive choice here is the two-star *Hôtel Touring* (☎ 05 56 81 56 73) at 16 Rue Huguerie, which has gigantic, spotless singles/doubles for 120/140FF (with washbasin and bidet), 180/200FF (with shower and TV) and 200/220FF (with shower, toilet and TV). The *Hôtel Studio* (☎ 05 56 48 00 14), nearby at No 26, has basic singles from 98FF, doubles from 120FF and triples from 180FF. All have shower, toilet and TV with cable.

The best choice in a higher price range in this area is *Hôtel de Sèze* (☎ 05 56 52 65 54) at 7 Rue de Sèze with comfortable singles/ doubles from 250/380FF. South-west of Place de Tourny the *Hôtel Le Provence* (☎ 05 56 52 00 05), at 2 Rue Castéja, has basic singles/ doubles from 110/130FF.

Place Gambetta There are several excellent deals in the area between Place Gambetta and the Musée des Beaux-Arts. The quiet *Hôtel Boulan* (☎ 05 56 52 23 62) at 28 Rue Boulan has pleasant singles/doubles with high ceilings for 100/110FF (120/130FF with shower). Hall showers cost 15FF.

The friendly *Hôtel de Lyon* (☎ 05 56 81 34 38, at 31 Rue des Remparts has singles/doubles with shower, toilet and TV for 120/135FF. Try not to get one of the cramped rooms on the 3rd floor though.

The excellent *Hôtel Bristol* (☎ 05 56 81 85 01) at 2 Rue Bouffard has pleasant singles/ doubles with four-metre-high ceilings, a bathroom, toilet and TV for 210/300FF.

Train Station Area The popular *Hôtel La Terrasse* (☎ 05 56 91 42 87) at 20 Rue Saint Vincent de Paul has clean singles/doubles from 70/120FF. Doubles with shower cost 150FF. Hall showers are 20FF. The *Hôtel Les Deux Mondes* (☎ 05 56 91 63 09), nearby at No 10, is a decent place with lots of foreign guests during the summer. Rates are 110/165FF for singles/doubles with shower.

Places to Eat

The plats du jour at *Les Quatre Sœurs* (☎ 05 56 48 16 00), a bistro next to the tourist office at 6 Cours de 30 Juillet, are tasty and reliable. A two-course menu is 65FF. *Pizza Paï* (☎ 05 56 81 35 80) at 26 Cours de l'Intendance has that most un-French of things: an all-you-can-

eat salad bar (40FF). Generous pizza men start at 50FF. It's open every day from 11 a to 10 pm. Looking out onto the attracti square and fountain at Place du Parlemen *Chez Edourd* (☎ 05 56 81 48 87) has trad tional French lunch menus from 58FF. Nearb at 29 Rue du Parlement St Pierre, *Le Galluch* (☎ 05 56 44 86 67) has excellent lunch men from 45FF. It's open every day except Tuesd for lunch and dinner.

Bordeaux is a multicultural city and its re taurants reflect that. Around Place de l Victoire, *La Dakaroise* (☎ 05 56 92 77 32) 9 Rue Gratiolet specialises in West Afric dishes like yassa poisson (fish cooked wi lime) and maffé (beef in a peanut sauce) fro around 65FF. It's open daily from 7 to 11.. pm. A few minutes walk to the north-west 144 Cours Victor Hugo is the *Blarney Stor* (☎ 05 56 31 87 20), an Irish bar and restaura with pub food from 25FF. It's open Monday Saturday from 11.30 am to 2 am and on Sund from 6.30 pm to 2 am. There's live music Monday evenings.

Rue du Palais Gallien is loaded wi Chinese, Vietnamese and North African re taurants. *Le Mechoui* (☎ 05 56 44 58 81) at N 20 has decent couscous from 65FF. The *Cá Tho* (☎ 05 56 81 40 38), south of Pla Gambetta at 16 Rue Villeneuve, has goo Chinese and Vietnamese dishes from 30FF. I open seven days a week.

If price is no object, eat at *La Chantere* (☎ 05 56 81 75 43), one of the best restauran in Bordeaux with menus starting at 95F (65FF at lunch). It's at 3 Rue Martign (heading east, Rue Martignac is left off Cou de l'Intendance, just after Place de la Comédi and is open for lunch and dinner every d except Monday night and all day Sunday.

The modern, mirrored *Marché des Gran Hommes* at Place des Grands Hommes, 10 metres north of Cours de l'Intendance, h stalls in the basement selling fruit, vegetable cheese, bread, pastry and sandwiches. It's op Monday to Saturday from 7 am to 7.30 p *Champion* supermarket at 190 Rue Sain Catherine is open from 8.30 am to 8 pm dai except Sunday.

Things to Buy

Bordeaux wine in all price ranges is on sale three speciality shops near the main touri

office: Vinothèque de Bordeaux at 8 Cours du
30 Juillet, L'Intendant at 2 Allées de Tourny
and Bordeaux Magnum at 3 Rue Gobineau.

Getting There & Away

Bus Buses to places all over the Gironde and
nearby departments leave from the CITRAM
bus station (☎ 05 56 43 68 43) at the western
end of Allée de Chartres, north-east of Place de
Tourny. The information office is open
Monday to Friday from 9 am to noon and 2 to
5 pm (5 pm on Friday). Destinations include
Soulac (on the coast near the mouth of the
Gironde River) and Cap Ferret (south-west of
Bordeaux near the Bassin d'Arcachon, a bay
on the coast west of Bordeaux). There's also
year-round service to the medieval vineyard
town of Saint Émilion. See the Bordeaux Vineyard Visits section for fares and frequencies.

Train Bordeaux's train station, Gare Saint Jean
(☎ 08 36 35 35 39), is about three km south-
east of the city centre at the end of Cours de la
Marne. It is one of France's major rail transit
points – there are trains from here to almost
everywhere. The station's information office is
open Monday to Saturday from 9 am to 7 pm.
If you take the TGV Atlantique, Bordeaux is
only about three hours from Paris' Gare
Montparnasse (non-TGV trains use the Gare
d'Austerlitz).

Getting Around

Bus Single tickets on Bordeaux's urban bus
network, CGFTE (☎ 05 57 57 88 88), cost
7.50FF (52FF for 10) and are valid for one hour
after being time-stamped. Bus information
bureaus (*espaces rouges*) on Place Gambetta
and at the southern end of the train station
(open every day to 7.30 pm) have user-friendly
route maps. Carte Bordeaux Découverte
allows unlimited bus travel for one day (22FF)
or three days (52FF).

Bus Nos 7 and 8 link the train station with
the city centre. Place de la Comédie is the
correct stop for the tourist office; the Place
Gambetta stop is also good for Place de
Tourny.

Taxi To order a cab in central Bordeaux, ring
☎ 05 56 48 03 25 or ☎ 05 56 91 47 05.

BORDEAUX VINEYARD VISITS

The Bordeaux wine-producing region is subdivided into 53 production areas *(appellations)*,
whose climate and soil impart distinctive characteristics upon the wine produced there.
These are grouped into six families *(familles)*.
The majority of the region's diverse wines
(reds, rosés, sweet and dry whites, sparkling
wines) have earned the right to include the
abbreviation AOC on their labels, indicating
that the contents have been grown, fermented
and aged according to strict regulations. The
region's production averages 660 million
bottles of wine a year.

The areas to the east, north-east and south-
east of Bordeaux have many thousands of
chateaux, which indicates properties where
grapes are raised, fermented and matured, and
some of the names may be familiar: Graves,
Sauternes, Pommarol, Saint Émilion. The
smaller chateaux often accept walk-in visitors
year-round except in August, but many of the
larger and better known ones (eg Château
Mouton-Rothschild) accept visitors only by
appointment. Each vineyard has different rules
about tasting – at some it's free, others make
you pay, and others do not serve wine at all. As
you drive around, look for signs that say
dégustation (wine tasting), *en vente directe*
(direct sales) or *vin à emporter* (wine to take
away/to go).

Information

Opposite Bordeaux's main tourist office at 3
Cours du 30 Juillet, the Maison du Vin de
Bordeaux (☎ 05 56 00 22 66) has lots of information on visiting vineyards. First decide
which growing area you would like to visit (use
the maison's colour-coded map of *appellations)*; the staff will give you the address of the
local *maison du vin* (a sort of tourist office for
wine-growing areas), which has details on
which chateaux are open and when.

The Maison du Vin de Bordeaux is open
weekdays from 8.30 am to 5.30 or 6 pm. From
mid-June to mid-October it is also open on
Saturday from 9 am to 12.30 pm and 1.30 to 7
pm. There is free wine tasting here at 10.30 and
11.30 am and at 2.30 and 4.30 pm.

Organised Tours

Bus tours organised by the tourist office to
various chateaux in the Bordeaux area are a

FRANCE

solution to transport difficulties. Afternoon excursions, which take place throughout the year on Wednesday and Saturday (daily from mid-June to mid-September) and last from 1.30 to 6.30 pm, cost 150FF (130FF for students). Commentary is in French and English.

Saint Émilion

One easily accessible wine-producing area to visit on your own is Saint Émilion, a medieval gem of a village 42 km east of Bordeaux and famous for its full-bodied, deeply coloured reds. The local tourist office (☎ 05 57 24 72 03) is open daily at Place du Clocher. From Bordeaux, Saint Émilion is accessible by train with at least one return trip every day (8 or 9 am, returning at 6.30 pm, 42FF one way). CITRAM buses go there and back about five times a day (there may be a transfer at Libourne). The one-way fare is 37FF. If you're driving take route D89 east to D670.

Virtually every shop in Saint Émilion sells wine (which you can also sample) but stick with the professionals. Maison du Vin (☎ 05 57 55 50 55) around the corner from the tourist office on Place Pierre Meyrat has an enormous selection and one-hour introductory wine-tasting courses (100FF) in summer. The English proprietor at Maison des Vins du Libournais (☎ 05 57 24 65 60) on Rue Guadet, with a more eclectic selection, is particularly knowledgeable and helpful.

If you get hungry in Saint Émilion, *L'Envers du Décor* (☎ 05 57 74 48 31) next to the tourist office on Rue Clocher has excellent plats du jour for around 65FF and vintage wine by the glass from 20 to 35FF. For something more romantic, try the excellent *Le Tertre* (☎ 05 57 74 46 33) on Rue du Tertre de La Tente. Macaroons – soft cookies made from almond flour, egg whites and sugar – are a speciality of Saint Émilion. Fabrique de Macarons Matthieu Mouliérac just up from Le Tertre has the best.

BAYONNE

Bayonne (population 41,000) is the most important city in the French part of the Basque Country (Euzkadi in Basque, Pays Basque in French), a region straddling the French-Spanish border with its own unique language, culture, history and identity. Unlike the up-market beach resort of Biarritz a short bus ride away, Bayonne retains much of its Basque ness: the riverside buildings with their green red and white shutters are typical of the region and you'll hear almost as much Euskara (Basque language) as French. Most of the graf fiti you'll see around town – like *Amnistia!* in bold letters on the massive Château Neuf – i the work of nationalist groups seeking an inde pendent Basque state.

Bayonne's most important festival is the annual Fête de Bayonne, which begins on the first Wednesday in August. The festiva includes a 'running of the bulls' like the one in Pamplona except that here they have cow rather than bulls and usually it's the people dressed in white with red scarves around thei necks – who chase the cows rather than th other way around. The festival also include Basque music, bullfighting, a float parade and rugby matches (a favourite sport in south-wes France).

Orientation

The Adour and Nive rivers split Bayonne int three parts: Saint Esprit, the area north of th Adour, where the train station is located; Gran Bayonne, the oldest part of the city, on the wes bank of the Nive; and very Basque Peti Bayonne to the east. The suburban area o Anglet is sandwiched between Bayonne an the beach resort of Biarritz, eight km to th west.

Information

Tourist Office The tourist office (☎ 05 59 4 01 46) is on Place des Basques just north-wes of Grand Bayonne. It's open Monday to Frida from 9 am to 6.30 pm and on Saturday from 1 am to 6 pm. In July and August, it's open dail from 9 am to 7 pm and from 10 am to 1 pm o Sunday. Its brochure *Programme des Fêtes e Pays Basque* is useful for cultural and sportin events. The freebie *Découverte et Activités e Pays Basque* is indispensable for organisin hiking, biking, climbing, diving etc.

The tourist office for the Basque Country the Agence de Tourisme du Pays Basque (☎ 0 59 46 46 64), is a km north of Place de Basques at 1 Rue Donzac.

Money & Post Banks in Bayonne are ope from Monday to Friday; those in Anglet ope

Tuesday to Saturday. The Banque de France is at 18 Rue Albert 1er, and there are more banks in Grand Bayonne near the Hôtel de Ville, along Rue Thiers and on Rue du 49ème Régiment d'Infanterie behind the post office.

The post office (☎ 05 59 59 32 00), which has exchange operations, is at 11 Rue Jules Labat. Bayonne's postcode is 64100.

Things to See & Do

Cathédrale Sainte Marie This Gothic cathedral is on Rue de la Monnaie at the southern end of the Rue du Port Neuf pedestrian mall in the heart of the oldest part of town. Construction of the cathedral was begun in the 13th century, when Bayonne was ruled by the English, and completed after the area came under French control in 1451. These political changes are reflected in the ornamentation on the vaulted ceiling of the nave, which includes both the English arms, three leopards, and that most French of emblems, the *fleur-de-lis*. Some of the stained glass dates from the Renaissance but many of the statues that once graced the church's very crumbly exterior were smashed during the Revolution.

Sainte Marie is open daily from 7 am to 12.30 pm and 2.30 to 7.30 pm. The **cloître**, the beautiful 13th-century cloister south of the cathedral on Place Louis Pasteur, is open every day except Saturday from 9.30 am to 12.30 pm and 2 to 5 pm (to 6 pm from April to October). Entry is 14FF (10FF reduced).

Musée Bonnat This museum (☎ 05 59 59 08 52) at 5 Rue Jacques Laffitte in Petit Bayonne has a diverse collection of works, including a whole room of paintings by Peter Paul Rubens (1577-1640). It is open from 10 am to noon and 2.30 to 6.30 pm (8.30 pm on Friday) daily except Tuesday. From mid-September to mid-June, opening hours on Friday are 3 to 8.30 pm only. The entry fee is 20FF (10FF for students).

Izarra Tasting Izarra, a local liqueur supposedly distilled from '100 flowers of the Pyrenees', is produced at the **Distillerie de la Côte Basque** (☎ 05 59 55 07 48) at 9 Quai Amiral Bergeret in Saint Esprit. Half-hour free tours of the plant and the little museum with a tasting at the end take place on weekdays from 9 to 11.30 am and 2 to 4.30 pm (to 6 pm from mid-July to August).

Sports Courses

The Auberge de Jeunesse d'Anglet (see Places to Stay) offers very popular one-week courses *(stages)* in surfing, body-boarding *(morey boogie)*, scuba diving and horse riding throughout the year. The courses, which are in French (though the instructors usually speak a little English), last from Sunday evening to Saturday afternoon and cost between 2150 and 2800FF, including accommodation, meals and equipment.

Places to Stay

Accommodation is most difficult to find from mid-July to mid-August, especially during the five-day Fête de Bayonne in August.

Camping There are several camping grounds in Anglet. The one-star *Camping du Fontaine Laborde* (☎ 05 59 03 48 16), open June to September, is on Allée Fontaine Laborde not far from the hostel. It often fills up in July and August. To get there, follow the instructions for taking the bus to the auberge de jeunesse (see Hostel below) but get off at Fontaine Laborde two stops later. You can also take bus No 2 from Bayonne's train station and get off at Place Leclerc.

You might also try *Camping de Parme* (☎ 05 59 23 03 00), open all year, which is on Route l'Aviation in Anglet. It costs 29FF to pitch a tent and 29FF per adult. Take bus line No 6 and ask for Camping de Parme.

Hostel The *auberge de jeunesse* (☎ 05 59 63 86 49) nearest Bayonne is at 19 Route des Vignes in Anglet. It is open all year and charges 69FF for a bed, including breakfast. To get there from the Bayonne train station, take bus No 4 heading for Biarritz and get off at the Auberge de Jeunesse stop. From the Biarritz train station, it's bus No 2 (direction Bayonne) to the Hôtel de Ville stop where you change to bus No 4.

Hotels There are a number of hotels right around the train station in Saint Esprit. The *Hôtel Paris Madrid* (☎ 05 59 55 13 98) is to the left (east) as you exit the station. The cheapest singles cost 90FF. Big, pleasant singles and

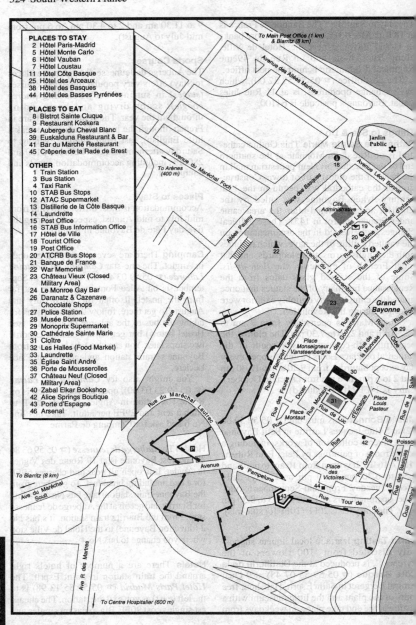

PLACES TO STAY
2 Hôtel Paris-Madrid
5 Hôtel Monte Carlo
6 Hôtel Vauban
7 Hôtel Loustau
11 Hôtel Côte Basque
25 Hôtel des Arceaux
38 Hôtel des Basques
44 Hôtel des Basses Pyrénées

PLACES TO EAT
8 Bistrot Sainte Cluque
9 Restaurant Koskera
34 Auberge du Cheval Blanc
39 Euskalduna Restaurant & Bar
41 Bar du Marché Restaurant
45 Crêperie de la Rade de Brest

OTHER
1 Train Station
3 Bus Station
4 Taxi Rank
10 STAB Bus Stops
12 ATAC Supermarket
13 Distillerie de la Côte Basque
14 Laundrette
15 Post Office
16 STAB Bus Information Office
17 Hôtel de Ville
18 Tourist Office
19 Post Office
20 ATCRB Bus Stops
21 Banque de France
22 War Memorial
23 Château Vieux (Closed Military Area)
24 Le Monroe Gay Bar
26 Daranatz & Cazenave Chocolate Shops
27 Police Station
28 Musée Bonnart
29 Monoprix Supermarket
30 Cathédrale Sainte Marie
31 Cloître
32 Les Halles (Food Market)
33 Laundrette
35 Église Saint André
36 Porte de Mousserolles
37 Château Neuf (Closed Military Area)
40 Zabal Elkar Bookshop
41 Alice Springs Boutique
43 Porte d'Espagne
46 Arsenal

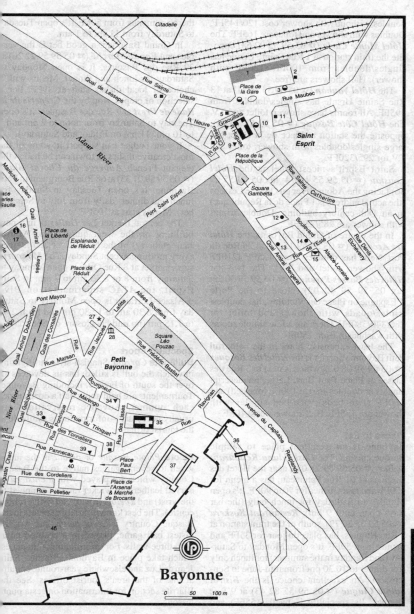

Citadelle

Quai de Lesseps

Rue Sainte

6

Ursule

Place de
la Gare

1

2

3

Rue Maubec

Adour River

R Neuve

5

Graouillats

R Hugues

4

11

10

Saint
Esprit

9

7 8

Rue Sainte Catherine

Place de la
République

Pont Saint Esprit

Square
Gambetta

12

Boulevard

14

13

Rue de l'Esté

15

Alsace-Lorraine

Rue Denis

Etcheverry

Quai Amiral Bergeret

Maréchal Leclerc

Place
Charles
de Gaulle

Quai Amiral Lesseps

16

17

Place
de la Liberté

Esplanade
de Réduit

Place de
Réduit

Pont Mayou

Nive River

Quai des Corsaires

Quai Amiral Dubourdieu

Allées Boufflers

Rue Lafitte

27

28

Rue Jacques

Square
Léo
Pouzac

Rue Frédéric Bastiat

Petit
Bayonne

Rue Marsan

Bourgneuf

Rue Marengo

34

Quai Galuperie

33

Rue Pontrique

Rue du Trinquet

Rue des Lisses

35

Rue

Ravignan

Avenue du Capitaine Resplandy

36

Rue des Tonneliers

Rue Pannecau

39

38

40

Place
Paul
Bert

Rue des Cordeliers

Place de
l'Arsenal
& Marché
de Brocante

37

Rue Pelletier

46

Bayonne

0   50   100 m

doubles without/with shower cost 120/145FF. Doubles with shower and toilet are 165FF. The **Hôtel Monte Carlo** (☎ 05 59 55 02 68) opposite the train station at 1 Rue Sainte Ursule has singles/doubles from 100FF (120FF with shower). Hall showers are free.

The **Hôtel Vauban** (☎ 05 59 55 11 31) at 13 Rue Sainte Ursule has singles/doubles from 195FF. All rooms have shower, toilet and TV. The **Hôtel Côte Basque** (☎ 05 59 55 10 21), opposite the station at Place de la Gare, has large singles/doubles with shower, toilet and TV for 295/320FF.

Saint Esprit's nicest hotel is the **Hôtel Loustau** (☎ 05 59 55 16 74; fax 05 59 55 69 36) facing the Adour River on Quai de Lesseps (the actual address is 1 Place de la République) in an 18th-century building. Doubles/triples with shower are 285/350FF.

In the centre of Grand Bayonne, the **Hôtel des Arceaux** (☎ 05 59 59 15 53) at 26 Rue du Port Neuf has doubles from 125FF (210FF with shower, toilet and TV). The two-star **Hôtel des Basses Pyrénées** (☎ 05 59 59 00 29; fax 05 59 59 42 02), close to the Porte d'Espagne on Place des Victoires, has doubles/ triples/quads with shower and toilet for 280/340/380FF. There are a few simple rooms with washbasin from 150FF.

The least expensive hotel in the colourful Petit Bayonne quarter is the **Hôtel des Basques** (☎ 05 59 59 08 02), which is next to 3 Rue des Lisses at Place Paul Bert. Large, nondescript singles or doubles start at 100FF (one bed) and 150FF (two beds); one-bed singles with shower are 135FF. Hall showers cost 10FF.

Places to Eat

Bayonne is an excellent place to sample Basque cuisine. The **Euskalduna Restaurant & Bar** (☎ 05 59 59 28 02), near the Hôtel des Basques at 61 Rue Pannecau, has a menu for 100FF and main dishes for 70 to 90FF. It's open Monday to Saturday for lunch only (the bar stays open until 9 pm). **Restaurant Koskera** (☎ 05 55 59 20 79), south of the train station at 3 Rue Hugues, has plats du jour for 35FF and menus from 59FF. It's open Monday to Saturday (and Sunday in the summer) for lunch only (for dinner to 10.30 pm from mid-June to September). An excellent choice is the **Bistrot Sainte Cluque** (☎ 05 59 55 82 43) at 9 Rue Hugues. Its speciality is paella (55FF) and

there are menus from 50FF. It's open Tuesda to Saturday from 11 am to 1 am.

In Grand Bayonne, a good bet is the ver pleasant **Bar du Marché** (☎ 05 59 59 22 26) i 39 Rue des Basques. It is open Monday t Saturday for lunch and dinner. Menus with choice of local dishes start at 39FF. For a selection of crêpes, stop by the **Crêperie de l Rade de Brest** at 7 Rue des Basques. It's ope Tuesday to Saturday from noon to 2 pm and to 10 pm (11 pm on Friday and Saturday).

If your budget can support it, some of th most creative dishes in town can be had at th elegant French **Auberge du Cheval Blan** (☎ 05 59 59 01 33) at 68 Rue Bourgneuf in Pet Bayonne. It's open Tuesday to Sunday fe lunch and dinner (daily from July to Septem ber). Menus start at 105FF.

The central market **Les Halles** is in a ne building on the west quay (Quai Amira Jauréguiberry) of the Nive River and is ope every morning except Sunday. The **Monopri** supermarket at 8 Rue Orbe is open Monday t Saturday from 8 or 8.30 am to 7 pm. In Sai Esprit, the **ATAC** supermarket on Blv d'Alsace-Lorraine is open Monday to Satu day from 8.30 am to 12.30 pm and from 2.4 to 7.15 pm (no midday closure on Saturday).

Spectator Sport

Bullfights *Corrida*, Spanish-style bullfightin in which the bull is killed, has its devotees a over the south of France, including Bayonne Tournaments are held about half a dozen time each summer. Advance reservations ar usually necessary – information is available a the tourist office.

Pelote *Pelote Basque* or *pelota* is the nam given to several games native to the Basqu Country which are played with a *chistera* (curved leather and wicker racquet strapped t the wrist) and a *pelote* (a hard ball with a rubbe centre). The best known variety of pelota in th Basque Country is *cesta punta*, the world' fastest ball game, played in a covered cou with three walls. For information on matches which take place in Bayonne, Biarritz, Sain Jean de Luz and elsewhere year-round, enquire at one of the area's tourist offices. See th Biarritz section for information on cesta punt lessons.

Things to Buy

Bayonne is famous throughout France for its ham and chocolate. Buy the former at Au Jambon de Bayonne Brouchican (☎ 05 59 59 27 18) at 20 Quai Augustin Chao in Petit Bayonne; the latter at the very traditional chocolaterie Cazenave (☎ 05 59 59 03 16) at 19 Rue Port Neuf.

Zabal Elkar (☎ 05 59 25 43 90) at 52 Rue Pannecau has a large selection of cassettes and CDs of Basque music. It also carries lots of books on Basque history and culture and hiking in the Basque Country as well as maps. The shop is open from 9.15 am to 12.30 pm and 2.30 to 7.30 pm daily except Monday morning and all day Sunday.

Homesick Aussies should check out Alice Springs (☎ 05 59 59 13 72), a boutique australienne at 25 Rue Poissonnerie open weekdays from 10 am to 7 pm.

Getting There & Away

Bus The tiny bus station (☎ 05 59 55 17 59) is in front of the train station at Place de la Gare. The information office is open weekdays from 8.45 am to 12.15 pm and 2 to 5.30 pm. RDTL serves destinations in Les Landes, the department to the north, including Dax, Léon and Vieux Boucau. To get to the beaches along the coast north of Bayonne such as Mimizan and Moliets, take the bus heading for Vieux Boucau (37FF, 1¼ hours).

Buses run by ATCRB (☎ 05 59 26 06 99 in Saint Jean de Luz) serve Saint Jean de Luz (20FF), Hendaye (40.50FF) and San Sebastián (Spain). They leave from the bus stop at 9 Rue du 49ème Régiment d'Infanterie.

Train The train station (☎ 08 36 35 35 39) is in Saint Esprit at Place de la Gare. The information office is open Monday to Saturday from 9 am to noon and 2 to 6.30 pm (daily from 9 am to 7.30 pm in July and August). TGVs to/from Paris (406FF) take 4½ hours and go to Gare Montparnasse. Other Paris-bound trains take about eight hours and stop at Gare d'Austerlitz. There are also trains to Bordeaux (141FF, two hours), Lourdes (102FF), Pau (79FF, one hour), Saint Jean de Luz (24FF) and Saint Jean Pied de Port (45FF).

For travel to Spain, change trains at Irún. Night trains to the Italian border town of Ventimiglia go via Lourdes, Marseille and the Côte d'Azur.

Getting Around

Bus The bus network serving the BAB metropolitan area – Bayonne, Anglet and Biarritz – is called STAB. Single tickets cost 7FF (31/62FF for a carnet of five/10) and remain valid for an hour after they are time-stamped.

In Bayonne, STAB has an information office (☎ 05 59 59 04 61) in the Hôtel de Ville. It is open Monday to Saturday from 8 am to noon and 1.30 to 6 pm. Line No 1 links Bayonne's train station with the centre of Biarritz (Hôtel de Ville stop). Line No 2 starts at Bayonne's train station and passes through the centre of Biarritz before continuing on to the Biarritz-La Négresse train station. Bus No 4 links the train station in Bayonne and the centre of Biarritz via the Anglet coast and its beaches. No 9 is a scenic – if slow – way to get from Bayonne to Biarritz.

Taxi To order a taxi, call ☎ 05 59 59 48 48. There's a large rank in front of the train station.

BIARRITZ

The classy coastal town of Biarritz (population 30,000 but four times that in summer), which is eight km west of Bayonne, got its start as a resort in the mid-19th century when Emperor Napoleon III and his Spanish-born wife, Eugénie, began coming here. In later decades, Biarritz became popular with wealthy Britons and was visited by Queen Victoria and King Edward VII, both of whom have streets named in their honour. These days, Biarritz is known for its fine beaches and some of the best surfing in Europe.

Biarritz can be a real budget-buster. Consider making it a day trip from Bayonne or the HI hostel in Anglet.

Information

Tourist Office The tourist office (☎ 05 59 24 20 24) is one block east of Ave Édouard VII at 1 Square d'Ixelles. It's open daily from 9 am to 6.45 pm. From June to September it's open from 8 am to 8 pm when there is also an annexe at the train station open from 8.30 am to 7.30 pm.

Money & Post Change Plus (☎ 05 59 24 82 47) at 9 Rue Mazagram, west off Place Bellevue, offers pretty good rates and is open Monday to Friday from 9.30 am to 12.30 pm and 2 to 7 pm. From June to September it's open Monday to Saturday from 8 am to 8 pm and on Sunday from 10 am to 1 pm and 4 to 7 pm.

The main post office is between Place Clemenceau and Ave Jaulerry on Rue de la Poste. Biarritz' postcode is 64200.

Things to See & Do

The **Grande Plage**, lined in season with striped bathing tents, stretches from the Casino Bellevue to the grand old Hôtel du Palais, built in the mid-19th century as a villa for Napoleon III and Empress Eugénie. North of the Hôtel du Palais is **Plage Miramar**, bounded on the north by **Pointe Saint Martin** and the **Phare de Biarritz** (lighthouse), erected in 1834. There are four km of beaches north of Pointe Saint Martin in Anglet.

Heading southward from the Grande Plage, you can walk along the coast past the old fishing port and around the mauve cliffs of **Rocher de la Vierge**, a stone island topped with a white statue of the Virgin Mary and reached by a footbridge. There's a small beach just south of Rocher de la Vierge at the **Port Vieux**. The long **Plage de la Côte des Basques** begins a few hundred metres further down the coast.

The **Musée de la Mer** (☎ 05 59 24 02 59), Biarritz' sea museum, is on the esplanade near the Rocher de la Vierge footbridge. It has a 24-tank aquarium, exhibits on commercial fishing, and seal and shark pools. The museum is open daily from 9.30 am to 12.30 pm and 2 to 6 pm (to 7 pm with no midday closure from July to September and to midnight from mid-July to mid-August). Entry is 45FF (40FF reduced rate).

Introductory one-hour **cesta punta lessons** (100FF per person) are available at the Biarritz Athletic Club (☎ 05 59 23 91 09) in the Parc des Sports d'Aguilera south of the town centre.

Places to Stay

Most hotels raise their rates substantially in summer, sometimes by almost 100%.

The friendly *Hôtel Berthouet* (☎ 05 59 24 63 36), near the market at 29 Rue Gambetta,

has clean singles/doubles with hardwood floors and outdated furniture for 90/130FF with washbasin and 150/210FF with shower. Hall showers are 20FF. The *Hôtel La Marine* (☎ 05 59 24 34 09) at 1 Rue des Goélands, off Rue Mazagram west from Place Bellevue, is a popular place with young travellers. Singles/doubles with shower are 130/150FF. Doubles with shower and toilet are 180FF.

One of the most attractive – and quiet – hotels in Biarritz is the *Hôtel Etche-Gorria* (☎ 05 59 24 00 74) at 21 Ave du Maréchal Foch. Situated in an old villa with a terrace and charming garden, it has doubles with washbasin and bidet from 200FF and with shower and toilet from 280FF.

Places to Eat

An excellent place for lunch is the central *O Frango* (☎ 05 59 24 20 12) at 11 Ave du Maréchal Foch with Portuguese and Spanish specialities starting at 45FF. Try the morue (salt cod) in garlic and olive oil or the tortilla española. Around the corner at 6 Rue Jean Bart *Le Dahu* (☎ 05 59 22 01 02) serves traditional French cuisine daily except Monday in a rustic setting. Menus start at 85FF.

Pizzeria Les Princes (☎ 05 59 24 21 78) at 13 Rue Gambetta has pizzas for 45 to 55FF and pasta from 45FF. It's open for lunch and dinner (to 11.30 pm) daily except Wednesday and at lunch on Thursday. *Bar Jean* (☎ 05 59 24 80 38), right by the market at 5 Rue des Halles, serves super fresh tapas from 5FF.

Les Halles, the large food market south along Rue Gambetta, is open seven days a week from 5 am to 1.30 pm.

Getting There & Away

Bus For information on STAB buses to/from Bayonne and Anglet, see Getting Around in the Bayonne section. The STAB information office in Biarritz (☎ 05 59 24 26 53) is across Square d'Ixelles from the tourist office. It's open Monday to Saturday from 8 am to noon and 1 to 6 pm.

Train The Biarritz-La Négresse train station (☎ 08 36 35 35 39) is three km south of the centre at the southern end of Ave du Président John F Kennedy (the continuation of Ave du Maréchal Foch). SNCF has a downtown office

☎ 05 59 24 00 94) at 1 Rue Étienne Ardoin at the corner of Ave du Maréchal Foch. It is open Monday to Friday from 9 am to noon and 2 to pm.

Getting Around

Taxi To summon a taxi, call ☎ 05 59 23 18 18 or 05 59 63 17 17.

Motorcycle & Bicycle Two-wheeled conveyances of all sorts can be rented from Sobilo (☎ 05 59 24 94 47) at 24 Rue Peyroloubilh, which is south of Place Clemenceau where Rue Gambetta becomes Ave Beaurivage. Mountain bikes cost 70FF a day; scooters/motorcycles are 240/360FF.

AROUND BIARRITZ

Saint Jean de Luz

The seaside town of Saint Jean de Luz (Donibane Lohitzun in Basque; population 13,000), 23 km south-west of Bayonne and 15 km from Biarritz, is an attractive beach resort with a colourful history of whaling and piracy. It's still an active fishing port and is celebrated for its fine Basque linen.

The richly decorated (and almost windowless) **Église Saint Jean Baptiste**, a mid-17th century church built in the traditional Basque style on Rue Gambetta, was the scene in 1660 of the marriage of King Louis XIV to the Spanish princess Marie-Thérèse, only an infant at the time. Don't miss the exceptional 17th-century **altar screen** with gilded wooden statues.

The tourist office (☎ 05 59 26 03 16) is south of the Église Saint Jean Baptiste on Place du Maréchal Foch and is open Monday to Sunday from 9 am to 12.30 pm and 2 (3 pm on Sunday) to 7 pm (to 8 pm without interruption in July and August).

If you want to spend the night (Saint Jean de Luz is an easy day trip from Bayonne or Biarritz), one of the nicest – if not cheapest – places is the two-star *Hôtel Ohartzia* (☎ 05 59 26 00 06), a few steps from the ocean at 28 Rue Garat. Doubles with shower and TV start at 280FF (higher in summer).

For a meal, *Tarterie-Saladerie Muscade* (☎ 05 59 26 96 73) nearby at 20 Rue Garat specialises in savoury tartes (30 to 45FF) and mixed salads (38 to 75FF). The speciality at *La Vieille Auberge* (☎ 05 59 26 19 61) at 22 Rue

Tourasse, the street running parallel to the west, is ttoro (Basque fish soup). Menus start at 75FF.

Frequent trains and buses link Saint Jean de Luz with Bayonne and Biarritz (see Getting There & Away and Getting Around in the Bayonne section). Buses leave from Place du Maréchal Foch. The train station is 200 metres south.

Saint Jean Pied de Port

The walled Pyrenean town of Saint Jean Pied de Port (Donibane Garazi in Basque; population 1800), 54 km south-east of Bayonne, was once the last stop in France for pilgrims on their way south to the Spanish city of Santiago de Compostela, the most important Christian pilgrimage site after Jerusalem and Rome in the Middle Ages. Today the town, which is in a hilly rural area, retains much of its Basque character. The views from the 17th-century **Citadelle** are picture-postcard perfect.

The tourist office (☎ 05 59 37 03 57), at 14 Place Charles de Gaulle just north of the Nive River, has a set of five maps for hiking in the area. The office is open Monday to Saturday from 9 am to noon and 2 to 7 pm (to 6 pm on Saturday). It opens on Sunday from mid-June to mid-September.

The cheapest place to stay in town is the *Hôtel des Remparts* (☎ 05 59 37 13 79) south of the Nive at 16 Place Fouquet. Singles/ doubles with shower are 180/205FF. For more comfort, head north from the tourist office to the *Hôtel Itzalpea* (☎ 05 59 37 03 66) at 5 Place du Trinquet which has doubles with shower and toilet from 220FF. It also has a restaurant with hearty regional cuisine and menus from around 65FF. For a real splurge, try the *Restaurant des Pyrénées* (☎ 05 59 37 01 01), which boasts two Michelin stars. Menus are from 220 to 500FF.

Half the reason for coming to Saint Jean Pied de Port is the scenic train trip (three to six a day) from Bayonne, which takes about an hour. The cost from Bayonne is 45FF one way.

LOURDES

Lourdes (population 16,300) was just a sleepy market town on the edge of the snowcapped Pyrenees in 1858 when Bernadette Soubirous, a 14-year-old peasant girl, saw the Virgin Mary in a series of 18 visions that took place in a

FRANCE

grotto near the town. The girl's account was eventually investigated by the Vatican, which confirmed them as bona fide apparitions. Bernadette, who lived out her short life as a nun and died in 1879, was canonised as Saint Bernadette in 1933.

These events set Lourdes on the path to becoming one of the world's most important pilgrimage sites. Some five million pilgrims from all over the world converge on Lourdes annually, including many sick people seeking cures. But accompanying the fervent, almost medieval piety of the pilgrims is an astounding display of commercial exuberance that can seem unspeakably tacky. Wall thermometers, snowballs and plastic statues of the Virgin are easy to mock; just remember that people have spent their life savings to come here and for many of the Catholic faithful Lourdes is as sacred a place as Mecca, the Ganges, or the Wailing Wall in Jerusalem.

Orientation

Lourdes' two main east-west streets are Rue de la Grotte and, 300 metres north, Blvd de la Grotte. Both lead to the Sanctuaires Notre Dame de Lourdes, but Blvd de la Grotte takes you to the main entrance at Pont Saint Michel. The principal north-south thoroughfare, known as Chaussée Maransin when it passes over Blvd de la Grotte, connects Ave de la Gare and the train station with Place Peyramale.

Information

Tourist Office The new horseshoe-shaped glass-and-steel tourist office (☎ 05 62 42 77 40) at Place Peyramale is open Monday to Saturday from 9 am to noon and 2 to 6 pm (7 pm from Easter to mid-October when it's also open on Sunday). From May to September, there is no midday closure. The office sells a pass called Visa Passeport Touristique (139FF; 69.50FF for children under 12) allowing entry to seven museums in Lourdes.

Money & Post The Caisse d'Épargne at 17 Place du Marcadal is open weekdays from 8.45 am to noon and from 1.15 to 5 pm. There are several other banks nearby. The main post office (☎ 05 62 42 72 00), east of the tourist office at 1 Rue de Langelle, has a foreign exchange service. Lourdes' postcode is 65100.

Things to See

The huge religious complex that has grown around the cave where Bernadette saw the Virgin, **Sanctuaires Notre Dame de Lourdes**, is west of the city centre across the small Gave de Pau River. The grounds can be entered 24 hours a day via the Entrée des Lacets, which is on Place Monseigneur Laurence at the end of Rue de La Grotte. The Pont Saint Michel entrance is open from 5 am to midnight.

The more noteworthy sites in the complex include the **Grotte de Massabielle**, where Bernadette had her visions and which today hung with the crutches of cured cripples, the nearby **pools** in which 400,000 people seeking to be healed immerse themselves each year and the **Basilique du Rosaire** (Basilica of the Rosary), which was built at the end of the 19th century in an overwrought pseudo-Byzantine style. Proper dress is required within the complex (don't wear short shorts, skirts or sleeveless shirts) and smoking is prohibited.

From the Sunday before Easter to at least mid-October, there are solemn **torch-lit processions** nightly at 8.45 pm from the Grotte de Massabielle. The **Procession Eucaristique** (Blessed Sacrament Procession), in which groups of pilgrims carrying banners march along the esplanade, takes place daily during the same period at 4.30 pm.

Other attractions in Lourdes include the **Musée Grévin** wax museum (☎ 05 62 94 3 74) at 87 Rue de la Grotte, where you can see life-size dioramas of important events in the lives of both Jesus Christ and Bernadette Soubirous, and the **Musée de Lourdes** (☎ 05 62 94 28 00), with similar exhibits a few steps south in the Parking de l'Égalité. The museums are open from 9 to 11.40 am and 1.30 to 6.30 pm (from 8.30 to 10 pm in July and August). Admission to the Musée Grévin is 33FF (17FF reduced rate), and 30FF (15FF reduced rate) to the Musée de Lourdes.

Sites directly related to the life of Saint Bernadette include: her birthplace, the **Moulin de Boly** (Boly Mill), down the alley next to 5 Blvd de la Grotte (12 Rue Bernadette Soubirous); the **Cachot**, the former prison where the impoverished Soubirous family was forced to move in 1857, at 15 Rue des Petits Fossés; and **Bernadette's school** in the Centre Hospitalier Général west of the train station on Chaussée

Maransin. Visits to all three are free and self-guided.

Between April and mid-October, the same two films about Saint Bernadette play at the **Cinéma Pax** (☎ 05 62 94 52 01), which is down the small street opposite 64 Rue de la Grotte. The eyrie-like medieval **Château Fort**, with the majority of its present buildings dating from the 17th or 18th centuries, houses the **Musée Pyrénéen** (☎ 05 62 94 02 04). The entrances to the chateau (opposite 42 Rue du Fort and off Rue du Bourg) are open daily except Tuesday from mid-October to March) from 9 am to noon and 2 to 6 pm. Entry is 26FF.

Places to Stay

Lourdes has over 350 hotels, more than any city in France except Paris; even in winter, when many places close, it is no problem finding a relatively cheap room.

Camping The camping ground nearest the centre of town is **Camping de la Poste** (☎ 05 2 94 40 35) at 26 Rue de Langelle, a few locks east of the main post office. It's open from late April to mid-October and charges 2FF for two people plus a tent. It also has doubles/quads with washbasin and bidet for 20/160FF in a nearby building.

Hotels The family-run **Hôtel de l'Annon-iation** (☎ 05 62 94 22 78) at 23 Blvd de la Grotte has ordinary singles/doubles/quads with shower and toilet from 160/170/330FF. It's open from April to the end of October. The tidy **Hôtel Saint Sylve** (☎ 05 62 94 63 48) to the south at 9 Rue de la Fontaine has large singles/doubles with washbasin for 70/120FF. With shower, they're 90/140FF and with shower and toilet 100/150FF. Half-board, which includes room, breakfast and dinner, costs 120FF per person. The Saint Sylve is open all year.

A much more stylish place (and priced accordingly) is the fin de siècle **Hôtel de la Grotte** (☎ 05 62 94 58 87; fax 05 62 94 20 50) at 66 Rue de la Grotte, with balconies and a pretty garden. Singles/doubles with all the mod cons start at 320/340FF (higher in summer).

Places to Eat

Most hotels offer pilgrims half or full-board plans; some even require guests to stay on those terms. It usually works out cheaper than eating elsewhere, but the food is seldom very inspiring. Restaurants close early in this pious town; even **McDonald's** at 7 Place du Marcadal is slammed shut at 10 pm.

The friendly **Restaurant Les Tilleuls** (☎ 05 62 94 01 63) at 75 Rue de la Grotte has one of the cheapest menus around – 55FF for four courses. The **Restaurant Croix du Périgord** (☎ 05 62 94 26 65) at 13-15 Rue Basse just west of the tourist office serves up steak frites and a salad at lunch for only 38FF. **Restaurant La Rose des Sables** (☎ 05 62 42 06 82) across from the tourist office at 8 Rue des Quatre Frères Soulas specialises in couscous (from 66FF) and is open for lunch and dinner every day except Tuesday.

Les Halles, the covered market on Place du Champ Commun south of the tourist office, is open Monday to Saturday from 7 am to 2 pm. There's a **Prisunic** supermarket across the road on Rue Laffitte open Monday to Saturday from 8.30 am to 7.30 pm.

Getting There & Away

Bus The bus station (☎ 05 62 94 31 15), down Rue Anselme Lacadé from the covered market, has TER services to regional towns and cities including Pau (34.50FF, 1¼ hours). SNCF buses to the Pyrenean towns of Cauterets (36FF, one hour) and Luz Saint Sauveur (36FF, 1¼ hours) leave from the train station parking lot.

Train The train station (☎ 08 36 35 35 39) is one km east of the Sanctuaires on Ave de la Gare. Trains connect Lourdes with many cities including Bayonne (107FF, two hours), Bordeaux (169FF, 2½ hours) and Marseille (304FF, six hours). To Paris (395FF) there are three non-TGV trains to Gare d'Austerlitz and several TGVs to Gare Montparnasse. Local buses link the train station with the Grotte de Massabielle from April to mid-October.

AROUND LOURDES

The resort town of **Cauterets** (population 1200), 30 km south of Lourdes and accessible from there by SNCF bus, makes an excellent base for exploring the Parc National des

Pyrénées, which stretches for about 100 km along the Franco-Spanish border.

Cauterets (935 metres) is in a valley surrounded by mountains of up to 2800 metres, which offer some of the best skiing in the Pyrenees (at **Circuit du Lys** and **Pont d'Espagne**). The École de Ski Français (☎ 05 62 92 58 16) at Place Georges Clemenceau gives group and individual lessons. Other activities include taking the waters in the **Thermes César** (☎ 05 62 92 51 60) at 3 Place de la Victoire or hiking in the park. For information and maps, contact the Maison du Parc National des Pyrénées (☎ 05 62 92 52 56) at Place de la Gare.

The helpful tourist office (☎ 05 62 92 50 27) at Place du Maréchal Foch can book hotel rooms, but the cheapest places in town are the *Hôtel du Béarn* (☎ 05 62 92 53 54), around the corner at 4 Ave du Général Leclerc, and the friendly *Hôtel Le Grum* (☎ 05 62 92 53 01) at 4 Rue de l'Église. Both have simple rooms from 95FF; doubles with shower and toilet are around 190FF.

Périgord (Dordogne)

Although the name Périgord dates from pre-Roman times, the region is better known in English-speaking countries as the Dordogne, referring both to the department that covers most of the area and one of Périgord's seven rivers.

Périgord was one of the cradles of human civilisation. A number of local caves, including the world-famous Lascaux, are adorned with extraordinary prehistoric paintings, and there have been major finds here of the remains of Neanderthal and Cro-Magnon people. Périgord is also justly renowned for its cuisine, which makes ample use of those very French products, black *truffes* (truffles – subterranean fungi with a very distinct aroma and taste) and *foie gras*, the fatty liver of force-fed geese served on its own or used in preparing the finest *pâté*.

PÉRIGUEUX
Built over 2000 years ago around a curve in the gentle Isle River, Périgueux (population 36,000) rests these days on its two laurels: it proximity to the prehistoric sites of the Vézèr Valley to the south-east and its status as th capital of one of France's true gourmet regions

Orientation
The town is composed of three sections. Th main one is the medieval and Renaissance ol city (Puy Saint Front), which was built on a hil and whose pedestrians-only streets swee down from Blvd Michel Montaigne to the Isl River. To the south-west is the older Gallo Roman quarter (La Cité), whose centre is ruined 2nd-century amphitheatre. The trai station area and its cheap hotels are about on km north-west of the old city.

Information
The tourist office (☎ 05 53 53 10 63) is at 2 Place Francheville next to the 15th-centur Tour Mataguerre. It's open Monday to Satu day from 9 am to noon and 2 to 6 pm; fro mid-June to mid-September, the hours are am to 7 pm, and 10 am to 5 pm on Sunday For regional information, contact the Comit Départementale du Tourisme de la Dordogn (☎ 05 53 35 50 24) at 25 Rue du Présider Wilson. It's open Monday to Friday fro 9.30 am to noon and 2 to 5.30 pm and o Saturday from 9.30 am to noon (to 2 pm i summer).

The Banque de France is on Place Frankli Roosevelt. Other banks line Blvd Montaign The main post office (☎ 05 53 53 60 82) is 15 metres south-east at Rue du 4 Septembre Périgueux's postcode is 24000.

Things to See & Do
The most appealing part of Périgueux is th **Puy Saint Front** quarter around the cathedra which has a marked circuit you can follow wit a walking map provided by the tourist offic When viewed at sunset, the five-dom **Cathédrale Saint Front** looks like somethin transported from Istanbul. Originally Roman esque, the massive church (the largest i south-western France) was almost totall rebuilt in a mock-Byzantine style in the mi 19th century. The interior (open from 8 am 12.30 pm and 2.30 to 7.30 pm) is devoid o distinctive characteristics while the 12th century cloister displays an odd mixture o styles.

The **Musée du Périgord** (☎ 05 53 53 16 42), north of the cathedral at 22 Cours Tourny, is France's second-most important prehistoric museum after the one at Les Eyzies de Tayac (see that section). It is open daily except Tuesday from 10 am to noon and 2 to 5 pm (6 pm in summer). Admission for adults/students is 12/6FF and free for those under 18.

The regional tourist office organises hiking, bicycling, horse riding and canoe excursions from April to October. Two days on the Vézère River costs 520FF per person, including equipment, board and tent accommodation. A weekend of guided mountain biking in the Dordogne Valley costs 750FF.

Organised Tours
Taxi Flanchec (☎ 05 53 53 70 47) offers regional circuits, including a trip to Les Eyzies de Tayac and Lascaux II (see Montignac in the Vézère Valley section) from 240FF. There must be a minimum of three people, and bookings will need to be made by telephone two days in advance.

Places to Stay
Camping The *Barnabé Plage* camp site (☎ 05 53 53 41 45) is about 2.5 km east of the train station along the Isle River. Open all year, it charges 15FF per adult and 14.50/9.50FF for a tent/car. To get there take bus No D from Place Michel Montaigne to the Rue des Bains stop.

Hostel The small *Foyer Des Jeunes Travailleurs* (☎ 05 53 53 52 05) south of the Puy Saint Front quarter is open all year and charges 65FF a night, including breakfast. Reception is open weekdays from 4 to 8 pm and weekends from noon to 1 pm and 7 to 8 pm. Bus No G from Place Montaigne goes to the nearby Lakanal stop.

Hotels One of the cheapest places near the train station is the *Hôtel des Voyageurs* (☎ 05 53 53 17 44) at 26 Rue Denis Papin, with basic singles/doubles for 74/80FF (hall showers are free) and 100FF for a double with shower. The *Hôtel du Midi et Terminus* (☎ 05 53 53 41 06), on the same street at No 18-20, is a huge, amiable place with basic singles from 125FF and doubles with shower from 155FF. Quads with two beds plus shower go for 185FF.

Near the old city, *Le Lion d'Or* (☎ 05 53 53 49 03) at 17 Cours Fenelon is on a busy road and locks the front door at 11 pm, but the large singles/doubles start at only 140FF (160FF with shower). A much more pleasant option is the two-star *Hôtel de l'Univers* (☎ 05 53 53 34 79) at 18 Cours Michel Montaigne. It has three small attic doubles without shower (hall showers are free) for 150FF and rooms with shower from 250FF.

Places to Eat
A few places, such as the homely *Vieux Pavé* (☎ 05 53 08 53 97) at 4 Rue de la Sagesse, have three-course formule rapide menus (quick-order meals) from 68FF. Inexpensive salads and vegetarian snacks can be found at *Le Tonic* (☎ 05 53 53 51 94), a café in a health club/gym at 4 Rue Gambetta. *Le Grange* (☎ 05 53 53 74 88) on Place Saint Silain is a popular pizzeria with tables set out in a pleasant, shady square. Daily specials start at 36FF. *Sorrentino* (☎ 05 53 53 20 45) at 1 Rue Chanzy near the amphitheatre is another pizzeria and pasta place.

The *Monoprix* on Place Bugeaud has a huge grocery section upstairs and is open Monday to Saturday from 8.30 am to 8 pm.

Getting There & Away
Bus The bus station (☎ 05 53 08 91 06) is on Place Francheville south-west of the city tourist office. CFTA runs three buses a day to Bergerac (42.20FF) and Sarlat (43.20FF), and there's a bus to Montignac weekdays at 6 pm (31.50FF, one hour).

Train Périgueux's train station (☎ 08 36 35 35 39) is on Rue Denis Papin, about one km north-west of the city tourist office. It's connected to Place Montaigne by bus Nos A and C. There are connections from here to Bordeaux (97FF, 1¼ hours), Limoges (78FF, one hour) and Toulouse (170FF, four hours). Short-haul destinations include Bergerac (74FF, 1½ hours), Sarlat (73FF, 1½ hours) and Les Eyzies de Tayac (39FF, 40 minutes).

Getting Around
Péribus' main hub is Place Montaigne; for information go to the Péribus kiosk (☎ 05 53 53 30 37) there. Single tickets are 7FF; a 10-ticket carnet costs 45FF.

FRANCE

VÉZÈRE VALLEY

Périgord's most important prehistoric caves are in the Vézère Valley south-east of Périgueux. Stretching from Le Bugue, near where the Vézère and Dordogne rivers meet, north to Montignac, the valley's centre is the village of Les Eyzies de Tayac, 45 km from Périgueux. Another 22 km south-east is Sarlat-la-Canéda, a lovely Renaissance town and the most pleasant base from which to explore the valley with a car. Montignac is the town closest to the Lascaux II cave. Those not under their own steam might consider a day tour (see Organised Tours in the Périgueux and Sarlat sections). Bus and train connections are very limited in the valley.

Les Eyzies de Tayac

As one of the world's major prehistoric centres, this tiny village (population 800) at the confluence of the Vézère and Beune rivers attracts a great many tourists. Most come to see some of the oldest art works in the world at the **Musée National de la Préhistoire** (☎ 05 53 06 97 03) or visit the **Musée de l'Abri Pataud** (☎ 05 53 06 92 46), an impressive Cro-Magnon rock shelter towering above the town. From mid-November to March, the museum is open daily except Tuesday from 9.30 am to noon and 2 to 5 pm (6 pm the rest of the year with no midday closure in July and August). Entry is 20FF (13FF for students and free for those under 18). The rock shelter is open daily except Monday and all of January from 10 am to noon and 2 to 5.30 pm (10 am to 7 pm in July and August). Entry is 25FF (12FF for students).

Two caves, **Grotte de Font de Gaume** and **Grotte des Combarelles**, are one and three km respectively north-east of Les Eyzies de Tayac on Route D47 (Route de Sarlat). Combarelles has thousands of animal engravings dating back some 15,000 years, but the narrow passages of Font de Gaume (with Lascaux and, in Spain, Altamira, one of only three Palaeolithic polychrome caves in the world) are covered with lifelike paintings of bison, reindeer, woolly rhinoceros and wolves in red, brown, white and black. Each cave costs 32/21FF for adults/students and both are open from 9 or 10 am to noon and 2 to 5 or 6 pm (Combarelles closes on Wednesday, Font de Gaume on Tuesday). Because the number of visitors allowed in each day is limited, you must book ahead on site or by phone (☎ 05 53 06 90 80).

Les Eyzies de Tayac's tourist office (☎ 0 53 06 97 05) is in the centre of the village a Place de la Mairie and is open weekdays (an weekends from April to October) from 9 am t noon and from 2 to 6 pm. The *Restaura Chateaubriant* (☎ 05 53 06 91 74), a few step to the north along the village's single road, i a good place to sample local specialities lik cou d'oie farci (stuffed goose neck) or confi de canard (duck joints cooked very slowly i their own fat). There's an excellent-valu lunch menu for 60FF. Train service to/from Périgueux and Sarlat exists but is infrequent.

Montignac

Montignac (population 2900), picturesquel situated on the Vézère River, is near Lascau Cave and the facsimile Lascaux II. The touris office (☎ 05 53 51 82 60) is on Place Bertra de Born and can help with bicycle rentals.

Lascaux Cave About 2.5 km south o Montignac off route D704 is the Lascaux Cave discovered by four teenage boys in 1940 an sometimes called 'the Sistine Chapel of prehis toric art'. The cave was closed to visitors i 1960 when it was discovered that carbo dioxide and condensation from human breat were creating green fungus and even tiny sta lactites on the 17,000-year-old paintings Today the cave is kept at a constant 12°C (98% humidity), and visitors are allowed in at a rat of five a day, three times a week. The waitin list for visitors is more than two years long.

But everyone can visit **Lascaux II** (☎ 05 5. 51 95 03), a very exact paint and cement replic. of the most important section of the original The reproductions of the bison, horses an reindeer are so clear and alive that the painting in the real caves may be disappointing! Onl 2300 people can enter Lascaux II daily. Tour take 40 people and in the high season leave every 10 or 15 minutes.

Lascaux II is open Tuesday to Sunda (closed January) from 10 am to noon and 2 t 5.30 pm. In July and August, when tickets *mus* be purchased from the Montignac touris office, Lascaux II is open daily from 9.30 an to 7 pm. There are guided visits in Englis every hour.

Tickets, which cost 50FF (no discounts), also allow entry into **Le Thot** (☎ 05 53 50 70 44), a prehistoric theme park with a museum, mock-ups of Palaeolithic huts and living examples of some of the animals as seen in the cave paintings. It's all very *Flintstones*. Le Thot is just off lovely route D706 about four km south of Lascaux II and has the same opening hours.

Sarlat-la-Canéda

Despite centuries of war and conflagration, this beautiful Renaissance town (population 10,650) north of the Dordogne River has managed to retain most of its 16th and 17th-century limestone buildings.

Orientation & Information Modern Sarlat stretches for 2.5 km from the town hospital in the north to the train station in the south. The main drag linking the two is known as Rue de la République where it slices the heart-shaped old town almost in half. Three lovely squares – Place du Marché aux Oies, Place de la Liberté and Place du Peyrou – are in the restored eastern half.

The tourist office (☎ 05 53 59 27 67) is in the beautiful Hôtel de Maleville on Place de la Liberté. It's open Monday to Saturday from 9 am to noon and 2 to 6 pm. From June to September, it's also open on Sunday from 10 am to noon and 2 to 6 pm.

Things to See & Do The **Cathédrale Saint Sacerdos** on Place du Peyrou was originally part of a 9th-century Benedictine abbey but has been extended and rebuilt in a mixture of styles over the centuries. To the east is the **Jardin des Pénitents**, Sarlat's medieval cemetery, and the beehive-shaped **Lanterne des Morts** (Light of the Dead), a 12th-century tower dedicated to Saint Bernard. There's a colourful **Saturday market** on Place de la Liberté chock-full with truffles, mushrooms, geese and parts thereof.

Organised Tours HEP! Excursions (☎ 05 53 28 10 04) runs various tours to regional destinations, including the southern Vézère Valley 180FF, excluding entry to sights).

Places to Stay The closest camping ground to Sarlat is the expensive *Les Périères* (☎ 05 53 59 05 84), about 800 metres to the north-east

along route D47 towards Sainte Nathalène. It charges 104FF for two people including tent and is open from April to September. From the train station take the minibus to the La Bouquerie stop.

Hostel Sarlat's *Auberge de Jeunesse* (☎ 05 53 59 47 59) at 77 Ave de Selves is open from mid-March to late November. Charges are 40FF a night or 25FF for those who want to pitch their tent in the tiny backyard. It's just over two km from the train station, but the minibus stops close by at Le Cimetière on Rue du 26 Juin 1944.

Hotels One of the cheapest places in this relatively expensive town is the *Hôtel de la Mairie* (☎ 05 53 59 05 71) near the tourist office at 13 Place de la Liberté. Pleasant singles/doubles start at 170FF. Hall showers are free. The renovated *Hôtel les Récollets* (☎ 05 53 59 00 49), west of Rue de la République at 4 Rue Jean-Jacques Rousseau, has attractive rooms with washbasin and bidet for 190FF, with toilet and shower for 240FF.

Rooms with shower, toilet and TV at the large, chateau-like *Hôtel La Couleuvrine* (☎ 05 53 59 27 80; fax 05 53 31 26 83) start at 200FF though there is one small room for 160FF.

Places to Eat Two reasonably priced places facing each other on steep, narrow Côte de Toulouse west of Rue de la République are the *Pizzeria Romane* (☎ 05 53 59 23 88) at No 3 with pasta and pizza (from 35FF) and *La Petite Taverne* (☎ 05 53 28 35 52), opposite at No 2, with a 60FF Périgord menu.

For more salubrious surrounds, head for the *Auberge de Mirandol* (☎ 05 53 29 53 89) in a lovely Renaissance house at 7 Rue des Conseils just north of the Place du Marché aux Oies. An excellent-value menu costs 85FF.

Getting There & Away CFTA buses to Périgueux via Montignac (22.50FF, 25 minutes) leave from Place de la Petite Rigaudie north of the old town. The CFTA information office (☎ 05 53 59 01 48) is at 31 Rue de Cahors halfway between the old town and the train station.

Sarlat's tiny train station (☎ 08 36 35 35 39) is just over a km south of town at the end of

FRANCE

Ave de la Gare. Trains go to Périgueux (73FF, 1½ hours), Les Eyzies de Tayac (50FF, 40 minutes), Bordeaux (two via Saint Émilion: 117FF, 2½ hours) and Toulouse via Souillac (120FF, three hours).

Getting Around Sarlat's two bus routes (Nos A and B), serviced by minibus, run the length of the modern town and point north and south. To reach the old town from the train station, take bus No B and get off at the Jules Ferry stop.

Peugeot Cycles (☎ 05 53 28 51 87), north of the train station at 36 Ave Thiers, rents bicycles for 50FF a day and organises excursions in the countryside.

Burgundy & the Rhône Region

The Duchy of Burgundy (Bourgogne), situated on the great trade route between the Mediterranean and northern Europe, was wealthier and more powerful than the kingdom of France during the 14th and 15th centuries. These days, the region and its capital, Dijon, are known for their superb wines, great gastronomy and a rich architectural heritage.

By far the most important urban centre in the Rhône region, which lies south of Burgundy, is Lyon, France's second-largest city in area. Lyon's centuries of commercial and industrial prosperity, made possible by the mighty Rhône River and its tributary the Saône, have created an appealing city with superb museums, an attractive centre, shopping to rival that of Paris and a flourishing cultural life.

DIJON

Dijon (population 150,000), the prosperous capital of the dukes of Burgundy for almost 500 years, is one of France's most appealing provincial cities, its centre graced by elegant residences built during the Middle Ages and the Renaissance. Despite its long history, Dijon has a distinctly youthful air, in part because of the major university situated there. The city is a good starting point for visits to the nearby

vineyards of the Côte d'Or, arguably the greatest wine-growing region in the world.

Orientation
Dijon's main thoroughfare runs eastward from the train station to Église Saint Michel. Ave Maréchal Foch links the train station with the tourist office. Rue de la Liberté, the principal shopping street, runs between Porte Guillaume (a triumphal arch erected in 1788) and the Palais des Ducs. The social centre of Dijon is Place François Rude, a popular hang-out in good weather.

Information
Tourist Office The tourist office (☎ 03 80 43 42 12), 300 metres east of the train station at Place Darcy, is open daily from mid-October to April from 9 am to 1 pm and 2 to 7 pm. During the rest of the year, hours are 9 am to 9 pm. The tourist office annexe (☎ 03 80 44 11 44) at 34 Rue des Forges, opposite the north side of the Palais des Ducs, is open from 9 am to noon and 1 to 6 pm.

Money & Post The Banque de France is at 2 Place de la Banque (just north of the covered market). There are quite a few banks along Rue de la Liberté. The main post office (☎ 03 80 50 62 14) is at Place Grangier. Exchange services are available. Dijon's postcode is 21000.

Things to See
The classical appearance of the **Palais des Ducs et des États de Bourgogne** (Palace of the Dukes & States-General of Burgundy) is the result of 17th and 18th-century remodelling. The mid-15th century **Tour Philippe le Bon**, in the palace's central building, offers a great view of the city. Between April and mid November the tower is open daily from 9 am to noon and 1.45 to 5.30 pm. For the rest of the year, it's open on weekends only from 9 to 11 am and 1.30 to 3.30 pm, and on Wednesday from 1.30 to 3.30 pm. Across the courtyard are the vaulted **Cuisines Ducales** (Ducal Kitchens) built in 1445, a fine example of Gothic civic architecture. The front of the palace looks out onto the semicircular **Place de la Libération**, a gracious, arcaded public square laid out in 1686.

Some of the finest of Dijon's many medieval and Renaissance hôtels particuliers are along

Rue Verrerie and Rue des Forges, Dijon's main street until the 18th century. The splendid Flamboyant Gothic courtyard of the **Hôtel Chambellan** (1490) at 34 Rue des Forges, now home to a branch of the tourist office, is worth at least a peek. There's some remarkable vaulting at the top of the spiral staircase. **Rue de la Chouette**, where there are more old residences, runs along the north side of Église Notre Dame. It is named after the small stone owl *(chouette)* carved into the corner of one of the church's chapels, which people stroke for good luck and happiness.

Churches The Burgundian-Gothic **Cathédrale Saint Bénigne**, built in the late 13th century over what may be the tomb of St Benignus (who by tradition is believed to have brought Christianity to Burgundy in the 2nd century), is open daily from 8.45 am to 7 pm. Many of the great figures of Burgundy's history are buried here. The multicoloured tile roof is typically Burgundian.

The **Église Saint Michel**, begun in 1499, is a flamboyant Gothic church with an impressive Renaissance façade added in 1661. The unusual **Église Notre Dame** was built in the Burgundian-Gothic style during the first half of the 13th century. The three tiers of the extraordinary façade are decorated with dozens of false gargoyles (they aren't there to throw rainwater clear of the building). The **Horloge à Jacquemart** (mechanical clock) on the right tower dates from the late 14th century.

Museums The Carte d'Accès aux Musées is a combo ticket that gets you into seven major museums. It costs 20FF (10FF for students and people over 60). The Clé de la Ville-Dijon is similar but is valid for three days and includes a guided visit of the town. You can purchase both at museum ticket counters or at the tourist office. All museums are closed on Tuesday except the Musée Magnin, which is closed on Monday.

The **Musée des Beaux-Arts** (☎ 03 80 74 52 70), one of the most renowned fine arts museums in the provinces, is in the east wing of the Palais des Ducs. It's worth a visit just for the magnificent **Salle des Gardes** (Room of the Guards), rebuilt after a fire in 1502, which houses the extraordinary 15th-century Flamboyant Gothic sepulchres of two of the first Valois dukes of Burgundy. The museum is open from 10 am to 6 pm. Entry is 18FF (9FF for students and free for those under 18 and for everyone on Sunday).

Next to the cathedral at 5 Rue du Docteur Maret is the **Musée Archéologique** (☎ 03 80 30 88 54), containing a number of very rare Celtic and Gallo-Roman artefacts. It's open from 9 am to noon and 2 to 6 pm. From June to September hours are 9.30 am to 6 pm. Entry costs 12FF (6FF for students and free for teachers with ID and everyone on Sundays).

The **Musée Magnin** (☎ 03 80 67 11 10) is just off Place de la Libération at 4 Rue des Bons Enfants. This pleasant, mid-17th century residence contains a collection of 2000 assorted works of art assembled by Jeanne Magnin and her brother Maurice around the turn of the century. It's open from 10 am to noon and 2 to 6 pm (closed Monday). From June to September, it does not close at midday. Admission is 15FF (10FF for students, and free for art, art history and archaeology students and teachers with ID).

Places to Stay
Camping The *Camping du Lac* (☎ 03 80 43 54 72) at 3 Blvd Chanoine Kir is 1.2 km west of the train station, behind the psychiatric hospital. It's open from April to mid-November and charges 14/12/8FF per person/tent/car. From the train station, take bus No 12 and get off at the Hôpital des Chartreux stop.

Hostels The *Centre de Rencontres Internationales et de Séjour de Dijon* (CRISD; ☎ 03 80 71 32 12), Dijon's large, institutional hostel, is 2.5 km north-east of the town centre at 1 Blvd Champollion. A bed in a dorm costs 64FF, a single room 150FF, including breakfast. The hostel is closed from 10 am to 5 pm, but if you stay for a few days and pay in advance you can still get in during these hours. There's no curfew but you will need a hostelling card or an international student card. There are facilities for the disabled. To get to CRISD, take bus No 5 (towards Épirey) from Place Grangier. From 8.30 pm to midnight, Line A buses run hourly from the station or the centre.

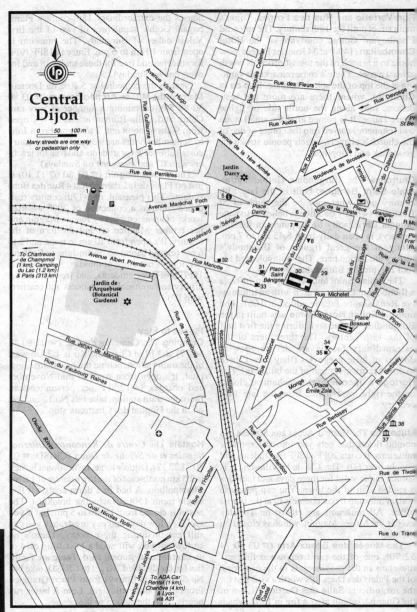

Central Dijon

0   50   100 m

Many streets are one way
or pedestrian only

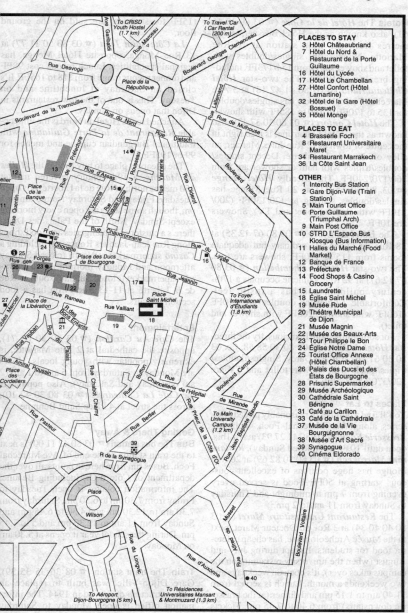

PLACES TO STAY
3   Hôtel Châteaubriand
7   Hôtel du Nord &
    Restaurant de la Porte
    Guillaume
16 Hôtel du Lycée
17 Hôtel Le Chambellan
27 Hôtel Confort (Hôtel
    Lamartine)
32 Hôtel de la Gare (Hôtel
    Bossuet)
35 Hôtel Monge

PLACES TO EAT
4   Brasserie Foch
8   Restaurant Universitaire
    Maret
34 Restaurant Marrakech
36 La Côte Saint Jean

OTHER
1   Intercity Bus Station
2   Gare Dijon-Ville (Train
    Station)
5   Main Tourist Office
6   Porte Guillaume
    (Triumphal Arch)
9   Main Post Office
10 STRD L'Espace Bus
    Kiosque (Bus Information)
11 Halles du Marché (Food
    Market)
12 Banque de France
13 Préfecture
14 Food Shops & Casino
    Grocery
15 Laundrette
18 Église Saint Michel
19 Musée Rude
20 Théâtre Municipal
    de Dijon
21 Musée Magnin
22 Musée des Beaux-Arts
23 Tour Philippe le Bon
24 Église Notre Dame
25 Tourist Office Annexe
    (Hôtel Chambellan)
26 Palais des Ducs et des
    États de Bourgogne
28 Prisunic Supermarket
29 Musée Archéologique
30 Cathédrale Saint
    Bénigne
31 Café au Carillon
33 Café de la Cathédrale
37 Musée de la Vie
    Bourguignonne
38 Musée d'Art Sacré
39 Synagogue
40 Cinéma Eldorado

Hotels The *Hôtel de la Gare* (☎ 03 80 30 46 61), also known as the Hôtel Bossuet, is 300 metres from the train station at 16 Rue Mariotte. Nondescript singles/doubles with toilet and shower start from 154/173FF, including breakfast (19FF). The two-star *Hôtel Châteaubriand* (☎ 03 80 41 42 18) at 3 Ave Maréchal Foch (1st floor) has singles/doubles for 135 to 170FF or 140 to 185FF with shower.

The *Hôtel Confort* (☎ 03 80 30 37 47), also known as the Hôtel Lamartine, is also right in the centre of town at 12 Rue Jules Mercier, an alley off Rue de la Liberté. Decent singles/doubles/triples with bath or shower are from 160/170/240FF. The friendly *Hôtel Monge* (☎ 03 80 30 55 41) at 20 Rue Monge has singles/doubles starting at 120/130FF (200/210FF with shower, toilet and TV). Showers are 10FF.

The *Hôtel du Lycée* (☎ 03 80 67 12 35) at 28 Rue du Lycée has ordinary but adequate rooms from 115 to 170FF; showers are free. The two-star *Hôtel Le Chambellan* (☎ 03 80 67 12 67) at 92 Rue Vannerie occupies a 17th-century building and has a rustic feel. Comfortable singles or doubles are 110FF (160FF with shower, 200FF with shower and toilet).

For something more luxurious, try the three-star *Hôtel du Nord* (☎ 03 80 30 58 58; fax 03 80 30 61 26) at Place Darcy. Singles/doubles/triples/quads with shower, toilet and TV are 320/370/455/470FF.

Places to Eat
You'll find a number of reasonably priced brasseries along Ave Maréchal Foch, including *Brasserie Foch* (☎ 03 80 41 27 93) at No 1bis, open until 10.30 pm (closed Sunday). *Restaurant Marrakech* (☎ 03 80 30 82 69) at 20 Rue Monge has huge portions of excellent couscous starting at 50FF. Food is served every evening from 7 pm to midnight and Thursday to Sunday from 11 am to 2 pm.

The *Restaurant Universitaire Maret* (☎ 03 80 40 40 34) at 3 Rue du Docteur Maret, next to the Musée Archéologique, has cheap cafeteria food for students. Except during July and August (when the university restaurant on the campus takes over), it's open on weekdays and two weekends a month. Lunch is served from 11.40 am to 1.15 pm and dinner (at the brasserie downstairs) from 6.40 to 7.45 pm. Tickets (15FF for students) are sold on the ground floor.

La Côte Saint Jean (☎ 03 80 50 11 77) at 13 Rue Monge, opposite Hôtel Monge, has regional specialities. Lunch menus cost 98FF and dinner menus range from 118 to 165FF. It's closed on Saturday at lunchtime and on Tuesday. This is one of the few restaurants in Dijon that opens on Sunday.

Attached to the Hotel du Nord is the impeccable *Restaurant de la Porte Guillaume* with traditional Burgundian cuisine and menus for 99 or 195FF.

The cheapest place to buy food is the *Halles du Marché*, a 19th-century covered market 150 metres north of Rue de la Liberté. It is open Tuesday, Friday and Saturday from 6 am to 1 pm, though some stalls are open every morning except Sunday. North of the Palais des Ducs, there's a cluster of boulangeries and food shops along Rue Jean-Jacques Rousseau, including a *Casino* supermarket at No 16 (closed Sunday afternoon and Monday morning). The *Prisunic* supermarket (closed Sunday) south of Rue de la Liberté at 11-13 Rue Piron has a food section upstairs.

Entertainment
The *Café Au Carillon* (☎ 03 80 30 63 71), opposite the cathedral at 2 Rue Mariotte, is extremely popular with young locals. Hours are Monday to Saturday from 6 am to 1 am (2 am on Friday and Saturday). Also popular is the *Café La Cathédrale* (☎ 03 80 30 42 10), across the street at 4 Place Saint Bénigne.

Getting There & Away
Bus The bus station (☎ 03 80 42 11 00) is next to the train station at the end of Ave Maréchal Foch. Buses run from here to points all over the department of Côte d'Or, including Beaune. The information counter is open Tuesday to Friday from 7.30 am to 6.30 pm, Saturday from 7.30 am to 12.30 pm and 4.30 to 6.45 pm and Sunday from 11 am to 12.30 pm and 5 to 7.45 pm. During the school year it opens at 5.30 am on Monday.

Train The train station (☎ 08 36 35 35 39), Gare Dijon-Ville, was built to replace an earlier structure destroyed in 1944. The information office is open Monday to Saturday from 9 am to 7 pm (6 pm on Saturday). At least one ticket counter is always open every day from 7 am to 10 pm. Going to/from Paris' Gare de Lyon by TGV (215 to 274FF) takes about 1¾ hours. Prices vary according to the day of travel; Friday and Saturday are generally the most expensive. There are non-TGV trains to Lyon (132 to 145FF, two hours) and Nice (from 372FF, eight hours).

Getting Around

Dijon's extensive urban bus network is run by STRD (☎ 03 80 30 60 90). Single trips cost 5.20FF; various bus passes are available, including a day ticket (15.14FF) and a 12-trip ticket (40FF). Eight different bus lines stop along Rue de la Liberté and six more stop at Place Grangier. Most STRD buses run Monday to Saturday from 6 am to 8 pm, and on Sunday from 1 to 8 pm. Six lines (A, B, C D, E and F) run from 8 pm to 12.15 am. STRD's L'Espace Bus Kiosque (information office) in the middle of Place Grangier is open Monday to Friday from 7.15 am to 7.15 pm, and Saturday from 8.30 am to 12.15 pm and 2.15 to 7.15 pm.

VINEYARDS AROUND DIJON

Burgundy's finest vineyards come from the vine-covered Côte d'Or, the eastern slopes of the limestone, flint and clay escarpment running for about 60 km south of Dijon. The northern section is known as the Côte de Nuits and the southern section as the Côte de Beaune. The tourist offices in Dijon, Beaune and nearby towns can provide details on wine cellars (caves) that offer tours and wine tasting (dégustation).

For detailed information on the region's wines, vineyards, wine cellars and merchants, get a copy of the booklet *Guide des Caves* (25FF), available at the tourist office in Beaune. The tourist office can also book you onto an organised tour of vineyards in a minibus. The trips last two hours, include a guide, and some wine tasting. There are three Safari Tours a day, and prices start at 170FF per person.

North of Beaune are the picturesque wine-making villages of Nuits Saint Georges, Vosne-Romanée, Clos de Vougeot and Gevrey-Chambertin, which are known for their fine reds and offer excellent wine-tasting opportu-

nities. You can also visit the **Clos de Vougeot chateau**, which was founded by Cistercian monks in the 12th century and owned by them until the Revolution. The chateau (☎ 03 80 62 89 09) is open daily from 9 to 11.30 am and 2 to 5.30 pm (from 9 am to 6.30 pm with no midday break from April to September). Entrance is 16FF (students 8FF) and includes a 45-minute guided tour (departing every half-hour in summer) but no tasting.

Gevrey-Chambertin chateau, where the staunchly monarchist and octogenarian Madame Masson gives you a charming tour (in English) of her home and cellar, is also worth visiting. Entry costs 20FF and includes one tasting.

Beaune

The attractive town of Beaune (population 22,000), a major wine-making centre about 40 km south of Dijon, makes an excellent day trip. Its most famous historical site is the Hôtel-Dieu, France's most opulent medieval charity hospital. The tourist office (☎ 03 80 26 21 30) is at Rue de l'Hôtel-Dieu, opposite the entrance to the Hôtel-Dieu.

The **Hôtel-Dieu**, founded in 1443 by Nicolas Rolin, is built in Flemish-Burgundian Gothic style and features a distinctive multicoloured tile roof. Of particular interest are the hospice's **Hall of the Poor** and the **Apothecary**, with a vast array of china and glass jars full of herbal potions. Don't miss the extraordinary polyptych of *The Last Judgment*, a medieval masterpiece by Roger van der Weyden. You'll find it in the darkened room off the hall. The Hôtel-Dieu is open from late March to late November from 9 am to 6.30 pm; the rest of the year, hours are 9 to 11.30 am and 2 to 5.30 pm. Entry is 29FF (22FF for students). Make sure you pick up the informative brochure (in English) at the ticket counter.

For wine tasting in Beaune, you can visit the **Marché aux Vins** at Rue Nicolas Rolin, where you can sample 15 wines for 50FF. It is closed from mid-December to 26 January. **Patriarche Père et Fils** at 7 Rue du Collège has the largest wine cellars in Burgundy, containing several million bottles. You can taste 13 wines for 40FF. It is open daily from 9 to 11.30 am and 2 to 5.30 pm.

FRANCE

Places to Eat As one of France's prime gastronomic centres, Beaune is a great place to indulge your taste buds. The town has an abundant selection of restaurants, including the *Restaurant Bernard Morillon* (☎ 03 80 24 12 06) at 31 Rue Maufoux, with one Michelin star and with menus from 180FF. *Les Jardins du Rempart* (☎ 03 80 24 79 41) at 10 Rue de l'Hôtel-Dieu offers impeccable food and service; menus range from 130 (170 at weekends) to 280FF. The restaurant is closed on Sunday evening and Monday. Another good (and more informal) choice is *La Grilladine* (☎ 03 80 22 22 36), just up the road from Bernard Morillon at 17 Rue Maufoux. Menus cost from 72 to 199FF.

The city also has a fantastic collection of food shops – if you want to prepare a gourmet picnic, this is the place to do it. The boulangerie-pâtisserie *Aux 3 Épis*, at 31 Rue d'Alsace, and the boucherie *J Rossignol* close by at 19 Rue Faubourg Madeleine have a great selection of edibles.

Getting There & Away You can get from Dijon to Beaune by train (36.80FF, about 30 minutes) or bus (36.40FF, one hour). Trains also stop at various villages along the way, including Gevrey-Chambertin, Vougeot and Nuits Saint Georges but services are limited in winter. Transco bus No 44 is a good bet if you want to stop along the way as there are vineyards at virtually every stop. Service is greatly reduced on Sunday.

LYON

The grand city of Lyon, with a population of 423,000, is part of a prosperous urban area of 1.26 million people, making it the second-largest conurbation in France. Founded by the Romans over 2000 years ago, it has spent the last 500 years as a commercial, industrial and banking powerhouse. Lyon is endowed with outstanding museums, a dynamic cultural life, an important university, up-market shops, lively pedestrian malls and excellent cuisine – it is, after all, one of France's gastronomic capitals, even for people on a budget.

Lyon, founded in 43 BC as the Roman military colony of Lugdunum, served as the capital of the Roman territories known as the Three Gauls under Augustus. The 16th century marked the beginning of the city's extraordinary prosperity. Banks were established, great commercial fairs were held, and trade flourished. Printing arrived before the end of the 15th century; within 50 years Lyon was home to several hundred printers. The city became Europe's silk-weaving capital in the mid-1700s. The famous *traboules*, a network of covered passageways in Croix Rousse and Vieux Lyon, originally built to facilitate the transport of silk during inclement weather, proved very useful to the Résistance during WWII. In 1944, the retreating Germans blew up all but one of the city's two dozen bridges.

Orientation

Lyon's city centre is on the Presqu'île, a long, thin peninsula bounded by the Rhône and Saône rivers. The elevated area north of Place des Terreaux is known as Croix Rousse. Place Bellecour is one km south of Place des Terreaux and one km north of Place Carnot, which is next to one of Lyon's train stations, Gare de Perrache. The city's other train station, Gare de la Part-Dieu, is two km east of the Presqu'île in a huge, modern commercial district known as La Part-Dieu. Vieux Lyon (the old city) is on the west bank of the Saône River between the city centre and Fourvière hill.

Information

Tourist Offices The main tourist office (☎ 04 78 42 25 75) is in the south-east corner of Place Bellecour. It is open Monday to Friday from 9 am to 6 pm and Saturday until 5 pm. From mid-June to mid-September, hours are 9 am to 7 pm (6 pm on Saturday). The same building houses an SNCF information and reservations desk, open Monday to Saturday from 9 am to 6 pm (5 pm on Saturday).

The tourist office annexe at Gare de Perrache (in the pedestrian flyover that links the train station with the upper level of the Centre d'Échange) is open Monday to Friday from 9 am to 6 pm and to 5 pm on Saturday; in summer, weekday hours are 9 am to 6 pm and to 7 pm on Saturday.

In Vieux Lyon, the tourist office annexe (☎ 04 78 42 25 75) on Ave Adolphe Max, right next to the lower funicular station, is open Monday to Friday from 9 am to 6 pm, on Saturday until 5 pm, and on Sunday from 10 am to 5 pm. Summer hours are 10.30 am to 7.30

pm Monday to Saturday and 10 am to 6 pm on Sunday.

Money The Banque de France is at 14 Rue de la République on Place de la Bourse. There is a Caisse d'Épargne de Lyon (open Tuesday to Friday and on Saturday mornings) at 2 Place Ampère, and there are other banks on Rue Victor Hugo just north of Place Ampère. Near Place des Terreaux, there are a number of banks on Rue de la République and Rue du Bât d'Argent.

American Express (☎ 04 78 37 40 69), near Place de la République at 6 Rue Childebert, is open weekdays from 9 am to noon and 2 to 6 pm and, from May to September, on Saturday morning also. At Gare de la Part-Dieu, Thomas Cook (☎ 04 72 33 48 55) is open daily from October to April from 8 am (10.30 am on Sunday) to 7 pm. During the rest of the year it's open daily from 8 am to 8 pm. The Thomas Cook office (☎ 04 78 38 38 84) at Gare de Perrache keeps roughly the same hours, but shuts at midday from 12.15 to 1.25 pm.

Post The main post office (☎ 04 72 40 60 50) at 10 Place Antonin Poncet has foreign currency services. The branch office at 3 Rue du Président Édouard Herriot, near Place des Terreaux, can also change money. There is another office at 8 Place Ampère.

Lyon's postcodes consist of the digits 6900 followed by the number of the arrondissement (one to nine).

Bookshops The Eton English Bookshop (☎ 04 78 92 92 36) at 1 Rue du Plat has lots of new paperbacks as well as some Lonely Planet titles. Students get a 5% discount.

Things to See
The tourist office has details of guided tours of Lyon on foot, by boat and by bus. You can also buy a Clé de la Ville ticket for 90FF which includes an audio-guided tour, and entrance to the six principal museums.

Vieux Lyon The old city, whose narrow streets are lined with over 300 meticulously restored medieval and Renaissance houses, lies at the base of Fourvière hill. The area underwent urban renewal two decades ago and has since become a trendy place in which to live and socialise. Many of the most interesting old buildings are along Rue du Bœuf, Rue Juiverie, Rue des Trois Maries and Rue Saint Jean. Traboules that can be explored include those at 68 Rue Saint Jean and 1 Rue du Bœuf; a comprehensive list is available at the tourist office.

Begun in the late 12th century, the mainly Romanesque **Cathédrale Saint Jean** has a Flamboyant Gothic façade and portals decorated with stone medallions from the early 14th century. Don't miss the 14th-century astronomical clock in the north transept. The cathedral can be visited daily from 8 am to noon and 2 to 7.30 pm (5 pm on weekends and holidays).

The **Musée Gadagne** (☎ 04 78 42 03 61) at 12 Rue de Gadagne (or Place du Petit Collège) has two sections: the Musée de la Marionette, featuring puppets of all sorts, including *guignol* (a French 'Punch-and-Judy'), created by the museum's founder, Laurent Mourguet (1769-1844), which has become one of the city's symbols; and the Musée Historique, which illustrates the history of Lyon. Both are open daily except Tuesday from 10.45 am to 6 pm (8.30 pm on Friday). The entry fee is 20FF (10FF for students). Puppet performances are held, amongst other places, at the Guignol de Lyon Theatre (☎ 04 78 28 92 57) at 2 Rue Louis Carrand north of Place du Change.

Fourvière Two millenniums ago, the Romans built the city of Lugdunum on the slopes of Fourvière. Today, the hill – topped by the Tour Métallique, a sort of stunted Eiffel Tower erected in 1893 and now used as a TV transmitter – offers spectacular views of Lyon and its two rivers.

Several paths lead up the slope, but the easiest way to get to the top is to take the funicular railway (metro: Vieux Lyon) from Place Édouard Commette in Vieux Lyon. The Fourvière line, with an upper terminus right behind the basilica, operates daily until 6 pm. You can use a bus/metro ticket or you can purchase a special return ticket for 12FF, which is valid all day for one trip up and one trip down.

The exceptional **Musée Gallo-Romain** (☎ 04 78 25 94 68) at 17 Rue Cléberg is well

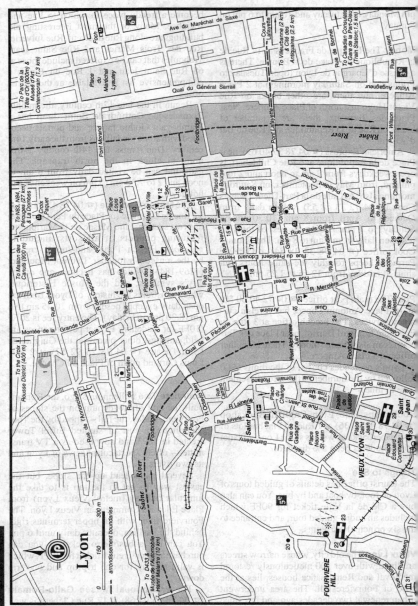

FRANCE

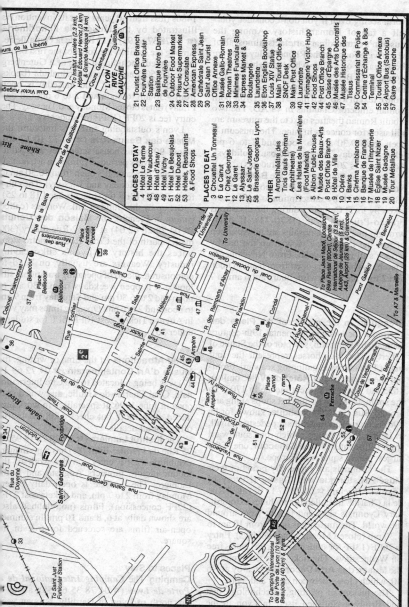

PLACES TO STAY

4 Hôtel Le Terme
43 Hôtel Vaubecour
48 Hôtel d'Ainay
49 Hôtel Vichy
51 Hôtel Le Beaujolais
52 Hôtel Dubost
53 Hôtels, Restaurants & Food Shops

PLACES TO EAT

3 Chouettel Un Tonneau
6 Le Canut
11 Chez Georges
12 Le Garet
13 Alyssaar
25 Le Saint Joseph
58 Brasserie Georges Lyon

OTHER

1 Amphithéâtre des Trois Gauls (Roman Amphitheatre)
2 Les Halles de la Martinière (Food Market)
5 Albion Public House
7 Musée des Beaux-Arts
8 Post Office Branch
9 Hôtel de Ville
10 Opéra
14 Banks
15 Cinéma Ambiance
16 Banque de France
17 Musée de l'Imprimerie
18 Église Saint Nizier
19 Musée Gadagne
20 Tour Métallique
21 Tourist Office Branch
22 Fourvière Funicular Station
23 Basilique Notre Dame de Fourvière
24 Outdoor Food Market
26 Prisunic Supermarket
27 UK Consulate
28 American Express
29 Cathédrale Saint Jean
30 Saint Jean Tourist Office Annexe
31 Musée Gallo-Romain
32 Roman Theatres
33 Minimes Funicular Stop
34 Express Market & Boulangerie
35 Laundrette
36 Eton English Bookshop
37 Louis XIV Statue
38 Main Tourist Office & SNCF Desk
39 Main Post Office
40 Laundrette
41 Fromagerie Victor Hugo
42 Food Shops
44 Post Office Branch
45 Caisse d'Epargne
46 Musée des Arts Décoratifs
47 Musée Historique des Tissus
50 Commissariat de Police
54 Centre d'Échange & Bus Terminal
55 Tourist Office Annexe
56 Airport Bus (Satobus)
57 Gare de Perrache

worth seeing even if you don't consider yourself a fan of Roman history. Among the museum's extraordinary artefacts, almost all of which were found in the Rhône Valley area, are the remains of a four-wheeled vehicle from around 700 BC, several sumptuous mosaics and lots of Latin inscriptions, including the bronze text of a speech made by the Lyon-born Roman emperor Claudius in 48 AD. The two rebuilt Roman theatres next to the museum are still used for concerts in June. The museum is open from 9.30 am to noon and 2 to 6 pm (closed Monday, Tuesday and bank holidays). Admission is 20FF (10FF for students).

Like Sacré Cœur in Paris, the **Basilique de Notre Dame de Fourvière**, completed in 1896, was built by subscription to fulfil a vow taken by local Catholics during the disastrous Franco-Prussian War (1870-71). If overwrought marble and mosaics are not your cup of tea, the panoramic view from the nearby terrace still merits a visit. From November to March, the basilica is open from 6 am to noon and 2 to 6 pm; otherwise, hours are 6 am to 7 pm.

Presqu'île In the middle of the **Place des Terreaux** there is a monumental 19th-century fountain by Bartholdi, sculptor of the Statue of Liberty. The four horses represent the four major French rivers galloping seaward. Fronting the square is the **Hôtel de Ville**, built in 1655 but given its present façade in 1702. To the south, there are up-market shops along and around **Rue de la République**, known for its 19th-century buildings; it's a pedestrian mall, as is Rue Victor Hugo, which runs southward from 17th-century **Place Bellecour**, one of the largest public squares in Europe.

The Lyonnais are especially proud of their **Musée Historique des Tissus** (History of Textiles Museum; ☎ 04 78 37 15 05) at 34 Rue de la Charité. Its collection includes extraordinary Lyonnais silks and fabrics from around the world. The museum is open from 10 am to 5.30 pm (closed Monday and holidays). Entry is 26FF (13FF for students under 25), but is free on Wednesdays. The ticket also gets you into the **Musée des Arts Décoratifs**, nearby at No 30, which closes between noon and 2 pm.

The history of printing, a technology that had firmly established itself in Lyon in the 1480s (less than 40 years after its invention) i illustrated by the **Musée de l'Imprimerie** (☎ 04 78 37 65 98) at 13 Rue de la Poulaillerie. Among the exhibits are some of the first book ever printed, including a page of a Gutenberg Bible (1450s) and several incunabula (book printed before 1500). The museum is ope from 9.30 am to noon and 2 to 6 pm (all da Friday) but is closed Monday and Tuesday. Th entry fee is 20FF (10FF for students).

Lyon's outstanding fine arts museum, th **Musée des Beaux-Arts** (☎ 04 72 10 17 40) whose 90 rooms house sculptures and paint ings from every period of European art, is at 20 Place des Terreaux. It's open from 10.30 am t 6 pm (closed Monday and Tuesday). The entr fee is 20FF (10FF for students aged 18 to 25)

Set up by the Guild of Silk Workers (calle *canuts* in French), the **Maison des Canut** (☎ 04 78 28 62 04) at 10-12 Rue d'Ivry (30 metres north of the Croix Rousse metro stop traces the history of Lyon's silk-weavin industry. Weavers are usually on hand t demonstrate the art of operating traditional sil looms. It is open weekdays from 8.30 am t noon and 2 to 6.30 pm and Saturday from 9 a to noon and 2 to 6 pm. Opening times may var in August. Tickets cost 10FF (5FF for student under 26).

Other Attractions At the time of writing, th **Musée d'Art Contemporain** (☎ 04 72 69 1 17) was being relocated to the Cité Internatio nale, Quai Charles-de-Gaulle, and was due t open in June 1996. It specialises in work pro duced after 1960, but check with the touri office for all details.

The **Institut Lumière** (☎ 04 78 78 18 95) a 25 Rue du Premier-Film (8e) has a permanen exhibition (25FF entry) on the work of th motion-picture pioneers Auguste and Lou Lumière. The institute is open daily excep Monday from 2 to 7 pm, and tickets cost 27F (22FF concession). Films (non-dubbed also are shown daily at 6, 8 and 10 pm. In summe open-air films are screened for free in th square.

Places to Stay
Camping The *Camping International de Porte de Lyon* (☎ 04 78 35 64 55), about 1 km north of Lyon in Dardilly, is open yea

round. This attractive and well-equipped camping ground (with facilities for the disabled) charges 32FF to park and pitch a tent and 17FF per person. It closes at 9 pm in winter and midnight in summer. Bus No 19 (towards Écully-Dardilly) from the Hôtel de Ville metro station stops right in front of it. To get there by car, take the A6 towards Paris.

Hostels The *Auberge de Jeunesse* (☎ 04 78 76 39 23) is about five km south-east of Gare de Perrache at 51 Rue Roger Salengro in Vénissieux. Beds cost 48FF, breakfast 18FF and sheets 16FF. Reception is open from 7.30 am to noon and from 5 pm to 12.30 am; curfew is also at 12.30 am. To get there from the Presqu'île, take bus No 35 from Place Bellecour (Georges Lévy stop); from Gare de Perrache take bus No 53 (États-Unis-Viviani top), and from Gare de la Part-Dieu take bus No 36 (Viviani-Joliot-Curie stop).

The *Centre International de Séjour* (☎ 04 78 01 23 45, 04 78 76 14 22) is about four km south-east of Gare de Perrache at 46 Rue du Commandant Pégoud, behind 101 Blvd des États-Unis. Guests staying more than one night must buy a membership card, which costs 4FF and is valid for a year. Weekday rates range from 83FF (for a bed in a quad with shower and breakfast) to 130FF (for a single with sheets and breakfast). Weekend rates are 8/123FF. From the train stations, take the same buses as for the Auberge de Jeunesse.

Hotels The neighbourhood around Place Carnot, just north of Gare de Perrache, is a bit on the seedy side, but the hotels here are convenient if you're travelling by train. The cheapest place in town is the very basic and unwelcoming *Hôtel Le Beaujolais* (☎ 04 78 7 39 15) at 22 Rue d'Enghien. Singles/doubles cost between 130 and 142FF; rooms with shower cost 161/162FF. Hall showers are 7FF. The two-star *Hôtel Dubost* (☎ 04 78 42 0 46) is at 19 Place Carnot, to the left as you come out of the train station. There are two singles for 215FF. Singles/doubles/triples with shower, toilet and TV are from 245/257/340FF.

In the area north of the train station, the old-fashioned *Hôtel Vaubecour* (☎ 04 78 37 4 91) at 28 Rue Vaubecour has singles from 05 to 120FF and doubles from 140 to 200FF.

Hall showers cost 15FF. The friendly, family-run *Hôtel d'Ainay* (☎ 04 78 42 43 42) at 14 Rue des Remparts d'Ainay (2nd floor), just off Place Ampère, has simply furnished singles/doubles for 155/165FF or 198/208FF with shower, and 215/225FF with shower, toilet and TV. Quads with shower are 416FF. Hall showers are 15FF and breakfast is 24FF.

One of the most affordable places in town is the family-run *Hôtel Vichy* (☎ 04 78 37 42 58) at 60bis Rue de la Charité (1st floor). Basic rooms range from 103 to 138FF or 148 to 175FF with shower. Hall showers are 20FF. The *Hôtel Le Terme* (☎ 04 78 28 30 45) at 7 Rue Sainte Catherine (1er) is in a lively area a few blocks north-west of the Hôtel de Ville. It has simply furnished singles or doubles from 150FF and more comfortable rooms for around 220FF.

Places to Eat

There are two *bouchons* – small, friendly, unpretentious restaurants that serve traditional Lyonnais cuisine – near Place des Terreaux. One is *Chez Georges* (☎ 04 78 28 30 46) at 8 Rue du Garet. The other is the cosy *Le Garet* (☎ 04 78 28 16 94) at 7 Rue du Garet, which is popular with locals. Both are open Monday to Friday. *Alyssaar* (☎ 04 78 29 57 66), a Syrian restaurant specialising in dishes from Aleppo (49 to 68FF), is at 29 Rue du Bât d'Argent. It's open Monday to Saturday until midnight.

Chouette! Un Tonneau! (☎ 04 78 27 42 42) at 17 Rue d'Algérie serves decent French food daily until midnight. *Le Canut* (☎ 04 78 28 19 59; closed Sunday) at 4 Place des Terreaux is a small, friendly place offering good Lyonnais cuisine as well as more innovative dishes. Dinner menus range from 68 to 127FF. Restaurants abound on the pedestrianised Rue Mercière (2e). A good choice is *Le Saint Joseph* (☎ 04 78 37 37 25) at No 46, which is open daily. There are also lots of places to eat, including several hamburger joints, along the Rue Victor Hugo pedestrian mall.

For a splurge, you might try *Brasserie Georges Lyon* (☎ 04 72 56 54 54) at 30 Cours de Verdun Perrache by the train station. It has been serving food in its vast Art Deco dining room since 1836 and has become a bit of an institution. Good-value menus are from 82FF (71FF for lunch).

The Presqu'île has lots of food shops along

FRANCE

Rue Vaubecour, including several boulangeries. *Fromagerie Victor Hugo* is a particularly good cheese shop at 26 Rue Sainte Hélène. The *Prisunic* (with an upstairs supermarket section) at 31 Rue de la République is open Monday to Saturday from 8.30 am to 7.30 pm.

In the old city, there are a number of food shops on Rue du Doyenné, including a Tunisian boulangerie and an *Express Market* grocery, both at No 11. The outdoor food market along the Saône River (Quai Saint Antoine and Quai des Célestins) on the Presqu'île is open from 7 am to 12.30 pm (closed Monday).

Entertainment
Ask at the tourist office for the free bimonthly publication *Lyon Spectacles Evènements*. It gives the latest on Lyon's lively cultural life, which includes theatre, opera, dance, classical music, jazz, variety shows, sporting events and films.

The *Albion Public House* (☎ 04 78 28 33 00) at 12 Rue Sainte Catherine is one of the city's most popular hang-outs at night. Live music, such as blues, jazz and R&B, is played on weekends after 9.30 pm. It is open Monday to Saturday from 5 pm to 2 am (3 am on Friday and Saturday) and Sunday from 6 pm to 1 am.

Getting There & Away
Air Aéroport Lyon-Satolas (☎ 04 72 22 72 21) is 25 km east of the city.

Bus Intercity buses (of which there are relatively few) depart from the bus terminal under the Centre d'Échange (the building next to Gare de Perrache). Timetables and other information are available from the information office of Lyon's mass transit authority, TCL (☎ 04 78 71 70 00) for intercity bus information), which is on the lower level of the Centre d'Échange. Tickets for travel on buses run by private companies are sold by the driver.

Train Lyon has two train stations: Gare de Perrache and Gare de la Part-Dieu. There are lots of exceptions, but in general trains which begin or end their runs in Lyon use Perrache, whereas trains passing through the city stop at Part-Dieu. As you would expect, trains to/from Paris (292 to 390FF) use the capital's Gare de

Lyon. Some trains, including all the Lyon-Paris TGVs, stop at both stations. For travel between the stations, you can go by metro (change at Charpennes), but if there happens to be an SNCF train going from one station to the other, you can take it without buying an additional ticket. Fares from Lyon include Marseille (20□ to 221FF), Nice (293 to 313FF) and Bordeaux (323 to 343FF). Prices vary according to the day on which you travel, and are more expensive on weekends.

The complex that includes Gare de Perrache (☎ 08 36 35 35 39) consists of two main buildings: the Centre d'Échange, the inside of which serves as a bus terminal and metro station; and southward over the pedestrian bridge, the SNCF station itself. In the latter, the information office on the lower level is open Monday to Saturday from 9 am to 6.30 pm.

Gare de la Part-Dieu (same phone number as Perrache) is two km east of Place de la République. The information office (same opening hours as Perrache) is to the right as you go out from the Sortie Vivier-Merle exit.

Getting Around
To/From the Airport The Navette (shuttle) buses to Aéroport Lyon-Satolas run daily from 5 am to 9 pm departing every 20 minutes. They cost 47FF and take about 40 minutes from Gare de Perrache (near the taxi stand), and 3□ minutes from Gare de la Part-Dieu. From the airport, there are buses to the city between □ am and 11 pm.

Bus & Metro The metro's four lines (A, B, □ and D) start operating at 5 am; the last train begin their final run at about midnight. Tickets, which cost 7.80FF if bought individually, are valid for one-way travel on buses, trolleybuses, the funicular and the metro for an hour after time-stamping. A carnet of 10 tickets is 66.50FF (55FF for students under 26). On the metro, tickets have to be validated before you enter the platform.

Shuttle buses (Navette Presqu'île) run between Saint Paul, Place des Terreaux, Place Bellecour, Gare de Perrache and Cours Charlemagne; tickets valid only for these buses cost 6FF each (55FF for a carnet of 10).

TCL (☎ 04 78 71 70 00) has information offices on the lower level of the Centre l'Échange; at 43 Rue de la République; underground at Place Bellecour at the entrance to line A; at Vieux Lyon next to the entrance to he line D metro; and at 19 Blvd Marius Vivier-Merle (near Gare de la Part-Dieu).

Taxi Taxi Lyonnais (☎ 04 78 26 81 81) operates 24 hours a day.

Bicycle Except in winter, mountain bikes can be rented for 100/350FF a day/week from Locasport (☎ 04 78 61 11 01), which is at 62 Rue Colombier, a block east of Place Jean Macé (east of Gare de Perrache). The shop is open Tuesday to Saturday from 9 am to noon and 2 to 7 pm.

The French Alps

The French Alps, where fertile valleys meet soaring peaks topped with craggy, snowbound summits, are without doubt one of the most awe-inspiring mountainscapes in the world. In summer, visitors can take advantage of hundreds of km of magnificent hiking trails and engage in all sorts of warm-weather sporting activities. In winter, the area's profusion of fine ski resorts attracts enthusiasts from around the world.

If you're going to ski, expect to pay at least 250FF a day (including equipment hire, lifts and transport) at low-altitude stations, which usually operate from December to March. The larger, high-altitude stations cost 350 to 450FF a day. The cheapest time to go skiing is in January, between the school holiday periods. Tourist offices have up-to-the-minute information on ski conditions, hotel availability and prices.

GRENOBLE

Grenoble (population 155,000) is the undisputed intellectual and economic capital of the French Alps. Set in a broad valley surrounded by the Alps on all sides, this spotlessly clean city has a Swiss feel to it.

Orientation

The old city is centred around Place Grenette, with its many cafés, and Place Notre Dame.

Both are about a km east of the train and bus stations.

Information

Tourist Offices The Maison du Tourisme at 14 Rue de la République houses the tourist office (☎ 04 76 42 41 41), an SNCF train information counter and a desk for information on the local bus network (TAG). The tourist office is open Monday to Saturday from 9 am to 12.30 pm and 1.30 to 6 pm (7 pm in summer) and Sunday from 10 am to noon. The TAG and SNCF counters are open Monday to Friday from 8.30 am to 6.30 pm and on Saturday from 9 am to 6 pm. The Maison du Tourisme is served by both tram lines.

Money & Post There are several banks along Blvd Édouard Rey, including the Lyonnaise de Banque at No 11 and the Banque de France on the corner of Blvd Édouard Rey and Ave Félix Viallet (open weekdays from 8.45 am to 12.15 pm and 1.30 to 3.30 pm). There's also a 24-hour exchange machine outside the tourist office that accepts foreign banknotes and credit cards. The branch post office next door to the tourist office is open on weekdays from 8 am to 6.30 pm (6 pm on Monday) and Saturday to noon. Grenoble's postcode is 38000.

Things to See

Built in the 16th century (and expanded in the 19th) to control the approaches to the city, **Fort de la Bastille** sits on the north side of the Isère River, 263 metres above the old city. The fort affords superb views of Grenoble and the surrounding mountain ranges, including Mont Blanc on clear days. A sign near the disused Mont Jalla chair lift (300 metres beyond the arch next to the toilets) indicates the hiking trails that pass by here. To reach the fort you can take the *téléphérique* (cable car) de Grenoble Bastille (☎ 04 76 44 33 65) from Quai Stéphane Jay, which costs 21/33FF one way/return (12/17FF for students).

Housed in a 17th-century convent, the **Musée Dauphinois** (☎ 04 76 85 19 00) at 30 Rue Maurice Gignoux (at the foot of the hill on which Fort de la Bastille sits) has displays on the history of the old Dauphiné region. It's open from 9 am to noon and 2 to 6 pm (closed

FRANCE

French Alps & Jura

0   20   40 km

uesday). Tickets cost 15FF (10FF for students nd people over 60).

Grenoble's fine arts museum, the **Musée de ;renoble** (☎ 04 76 63 44 44) at 5 Place de ,avalette, is known for its fine collection of ainting and sculpture, including a well-egarded modern section that features pieces y Matisse, Picasso and Chagall. The museum ; open daily except Tuesday from 11 am to 7 m (10 pm on Wednesday). Admission costs 5FF (15FF for students).

The **Musée de la Résistance et de la)éportation** (☎ 04 76 42 38 53) at 14 Rue lébert examines the region's role in the résistance, and the deportation of Jews from ;renoble to Nazi concentration camps. It's open aily except Tuesday from 9 am till noon and 2) 6 pm. Tickets cost 20FF (15FF for students).

At the time of writing, both **Cathédrale lotre Dame** and the adjoining **Bishop's 'alace** on Place Notre Dame were getting omplete face-lifts. They will contain three ew museums towards the end of 1996. Check /ith the tourist office for current details.

\ctivities

;kiing Downhill skiing *(ski de piste)* and ross-country skiing *(ski de fond)* are possible t a number of inexpensive, low-altitude ski tations which are day trips from Grenoble. "hese include Col de Porte and Le Sappey ›oth north of the city) and Saint Nizier du Moucherotte, Lans-en-Vercors, Villard-de-.ans and Méaudre (west of the city).

Summer skiing, which is relatively expen-ive, is possible during June and July (and even nto August) at several high-altitude ski sta-ons east of Grenoble. These include the Alpe 'Huez (tourist office ☎ 04 76 80 35 41), which ffers skiing (during July) on glaciers at eleva-ons of 2530 to 3350 metres, and Les Deux ,lpes (see Around Grenoble).

liking A number of beautiful trails can be icked up in Grenoble or nearby (eg from Fort e la Bastille). The northern part of the Parc laturel Régional du Vercors (☎ 04 76 95 15 99)r the administrative headquarters) is just rest of town.

The place in Grenoble to go for hiking infor-nation is CIMES and La Maison de la .andonnée (☎ 04 76 42 45 90) at 7 Rue Vol-taire. They have a large selection of hiking maps (57 to 79FF), topoguides, day-hike guides and information on places where you can stay overnight (gîtes d'étape and refuges) when hiking. They can also suggest itineraries. The office is open Monday to Saturday from 9 am to noon and 2 to 6 pm.

Places to Stay

Camping The *Camping Les Trois Pucelles* (☎ 04 76 96 45 73; open all year) is at 58 Rue des Allobroges, one block west of the Drac River, in Grenoble's western suburb of Seyssins. To get there from the train station, take the tram towards Fontaine and get off at the Maisonnat stop. Then take bus No 51 to Mas des Îles and walk east on Rue du Dauphiné. A place to camp and park costs 25/ 50FF for one/two people.

Hostel The *Auberge de Jeunesse* (☎ 04 76 09 33 52) is at 10 Ave du Grésivaudan in Échirolles, 5.5 km south of the train station. To get there from Cours Jean Jaurès, take bus No 8 (direction Pont de Claix, which runs until about 9 pm) and get off at the Quinzaine stop – look for the Casino supermarket. Reception is open from 7.30 am to 11 pm. Charges are 67FF per person, including breakfast, but you must have a hostelling card.

Hotels Near the train station, the *Hôtel Alizé* (☎ 04 76 43 12 91) at 1 Place de la Gare has ultramodern and somewhat sterile singles/ doubles from 120/200FF.

Quite a few cheap hotels are within a few blocks of Place Condorcet, a bit under a km south-east of the train station. The *Hôtel des Doges* (☎ 04 76 46 13 19) at 29 Cours Jean Jaurès has singles/doubles from 100/120FF. Rooms with shower or bath, toilet and TV are 160/170FF. Hall showers are 15FF.

The *Hôtel Victoria* (☎ 04 76 46 06 36), a quiet, well-maintained place at 17 Rue Thiers, has comfortable singles/doubles with shower for 165FF. All rooms have TV. The *Hôtel Beau Soleil* (☎ 04 76 46 29 40) at 9 Rue des Bons Enfants has simple singles/doubles from 130/ 140FF, and from 155/170FF with shower and TV. There is a 16FF charge for showers.

Hôtel du Moucherotte (☎ 04 76 54 61 40) at 1 Rue Auguste Gaché has huge, well-kept

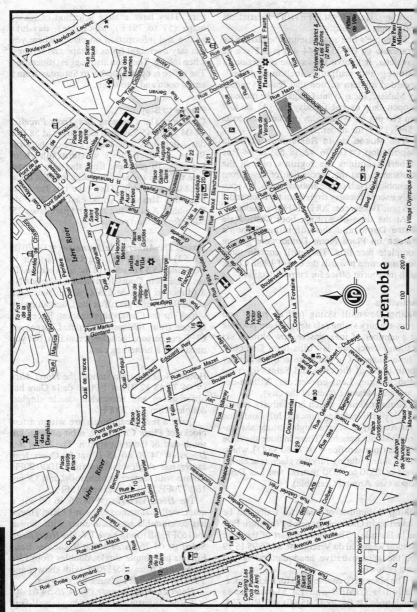

Grenoble

PLACES TO STAY		27	Lotus d'Or		16	Lyonnaise de Banque
4	Foyer de l'Étudiante				17	Église Saint Louis
	(Summer Hostel)	**OTHER**			18	Prisunic Supermarket
14	Hôtel Alizé	1	Musée Dauphinois		19	Post Office
23	Hôtel du Moucherotte	2	Musée de Grenoble		20	Tourist Office, TAG
28	Hôtel de la Poste	3	Police Headquaters			Bureau &
29	Hôtel des Doges	5	Cathédrale Notre			SNCF Counter
30	Hôtel Victoria		Dame &		21	Laundrette
31	Hôtel Beau Soleil		Bishop's Palace		22	Les Halles Sainte
		9	Téléphérique to Fort de			Claire
PLACES TO EAT			la Bastille			Market
6	Le Tonneau de Diogène	11	Bus Station		25	CIMES & Maison de la
7	Le Tunis Restaurant	12	Train Station			Randonnée
8	Namastay Indian	13	Post Office &		26	Musée de la Résistance
	Restaurant		Gare Europole Tram		32	Main Post Office
10	University Restaurant		Station			
24	La Panse Restaurant	15	Banque de France			

ooms and a central location. Singles/doubles
vithout shower are from 130/168FF, and hall
howers cost 25FF. Singles/doubles/triples/
uads with showers start at 140/194/218/
56FF.

The pleasant and friendly *Hôtel de la Poste*
☎ 04 76 46 67 25) at 25 Rue de la Poste has
ingles from 100 to 120FF, doubles and triples
or 160 to 190FF and quads for 200FF. Showers
re free. Overall, this is an excellent deal.

laces to Eat
or reasonable French food at good prices, try
e Tonneau de Diogène (☎ 04 76 42 38 40) at
Place Notre Dame, which attracts a young,
vely crowd. It's open daily from 8.30 am to 1
m. The 38FF three-course 'student' menu
unchtime only) is excellent value. *La Panse*
☎ 04 76 54 09 54) at 7 Rue de la Paix offers
aditional French cuisine at lunch and dinner
very day but is closed Sunday. The 71FF
unch menu is especially good value; dinner
enus are 98 and 148FF.

The popular *Lotus d'Or* (☎ 04 76 51 20 10)
6 Rue Vicat offers Vietnamese specialities
have there or take away; the plat du jour
osts 30FF. It's open from 10 am to 7 pm
losed on Sunday). You can get vegetarian and
on-vegetarian main dishes for 39 to 59FF at
e *Namastay Indian Restaurant* (☎ 04 76 54
89) at 2 Rue Renauldon. It's open from
Ionday evening to Saturday for lunch and
nner. *Le Tunis Restaurant* (☎ 04 76 42 47
) at 5 Rue Chenoise, open daily for lunch and
nner, has good Tunisian couscous from 38FF.

Les Halles Sainte Claire food market, near
the tourist office, is open daily except Tuesday
from 6.45 am to 12.30 pm. The *Prisunic*
(closed Sunday) at 22 Rue Lafayette, a block
west of the tourist office, has a supermarket in
the basement.

Getting There & Away
Bus The bus station (Gare Routière) is next to
the train station at Place de la Gare. VFD (☎ 04
76 47 77 77), which is open daily from 6.45 am
to 7 pm, has services to Geneva (140FF), Nice
(287FF), Annecy (90FF), Chamonix (149FF),
and many places in the Isère region, including
a number of ski stations. Unicar (☎ 04 76 87
90 31) handles tickets to Aéroport Lyon-
Satolas (the international airport for Lyon and
the Alps, 130FF), Marseille (145FF), Gap
(53FF), Valence (49FF) etc. Unicar is open
Monday to Saturday from 6.30 am to 7 pm and
Sunday from 7 am to 7 pm.

Train The train station (☎ 04 76 47 50 50) is
served by both tram lines (get off at the Gare
Europole stop). The information office is open
daily from 8.30 am to 7 pm and at least one
ticket counter will remain open from 5.15 am
to 11 pm. By TGV, the trip to Paris' Gare de
Lyon (from 342 to 430FF) takes about 3½
hours. There is also service to Lyon (93FF),
Nice (285FF) and Chamonix (160FF).

Getting Around
Bus & Tram The buses and trams (line Nos A
and B) take the same tickets (7.50FF, or 51FF

FRANCE

for a carnet of 10), which are sold by bus (but not tram) drivers and by ticket machines at tram stops. They are valid for same-direction transfers within one hour of time-stamping. Most buses stop running sometime between 6.30 and 9 pm, while the trams run until 11.30 pm or midnight. TAG (☎ 04 76 20 66 66), the local bus company, has an information desk inside the tourist office building and an office to the left as you exit the train station (open Monday to Friday from 7.15 am to 6.30 pm).

Taxi Radio taxis can be ordered by calling ☎ 04 76 54 42 54.

AROUND GRENOBLE
Les Deux Alpes
Les Deux Alpes (1650 metres) is the largest summer skiing area in Europe (mid-June to early September) and is also a popular winter resort. There are 196 km of marked ski runs and 64 ski lifts.

Information The tourist office (☎ 04 76 79 22 00) in the Maison des Deux Alpes on Place des Deux Alpes is open from 8 am to 7 pm daily, except in spring, when it's open from 8.30 am to 12.30 pm and 2 to 6.30 pm. There's a reservation centre here (☎ 04 76 79 75 10) which can help with accommodation.

In winter, equipment hire (skis, stocks/poles and boots) costs from about 60/300FF per day/seven days. Ski passes, available at the tourist office, start at 78FF for a one-day beginners' blue pass. The all-lifts red pass costs 170/965FF per day/seven days. In summer, a full/half-day ski pass costs 200/150FF. For ski lessons, contact the École de ski Français (☎ 04 76 79 21 21) which charges from 120FF for a 2½-hour group lesson.

Places to Stay The *Auberge de Jeunesse Les Brûleurs de Loups* (☎ 04 76 79 22 80) in the heart of the ski station at Ave de Muzelle is open from mid-June to early September and from late October to April. Dorm beds cost 66FF, including breakfast; sheets are 21FF. Reception is closed between 2 and 5 pm. The hostel sells ski passes, runs both winter and summer skiing courses (with a 10% discount for students) and organises various activities in summer.

Le Bel Alpe (☎ 04 76 80 52 11) at Place de Venosc, opposite the tourist office, has simpl singles/doubles for 150/240FF (160/250FF i summer). Singles/doubles with shower, toile and TV cost from 200/270FF (230/300FF i summer). The hotel is closed in May.

Getting There & Away Les Deux Alpes is 7 km south-east of Grenoble. VFD (☎ 04 76 4 77 77) runs buses from Grenoble (99FF, 1¾ hours) and Briançon.

CHAMONIX
The town of Chamonix (population 10,000 1037 metres) sits in a valley surrounded by th most spectacular scenery in the French Alp The area is almost Himalayan in its awesome ness: deeply crevassed glaciers many km lon ooze down the valley in the gullies between th icy spikes and needles around Mont Blan which soars 3.8 vertical km above the valle floor. In late spring and summer, the glacie and high-altitude snow serve as a glistenin white backdrop for meadows and hillsides ric in flowering plants, bushes and trees.

There are some 330 km of hiking trails i the Chamonix area. In winter, Chamonix an its environs offer superb skiing, with dozens ski lifts and over 200 km of downhill an cross-country ski runs.

Orientation
The mountain range to the east of the Cham onix Valley, the Aiguilles de Chamoni includes the mind-boggling mass of Mon Blanc (4807 metres), the highest mountain the Alps. The almost glacierless Aiguille Rouges range – its highest peak is Le Bréve (2525 metres) – runs along the western side the valley.

Information
Tourist Office The tourist office (☎ 04 50 00 24) at Place du Triangle de l'Amitié (opp site Place de l'Église) is open daily from 8 8.30 am to 12.30 pm and 2 to 7 pm. In July an August, it is open from 8.30 am to 7.30 pr Useful brochures on ski-lift hours and cos refuges, camping grounds and parapen schools are available. In winter it sells a ran of ski passes, including two-day/seven-da passes, valid for bus transport and all the s lifts in the valley (except Lognan-Les Gran

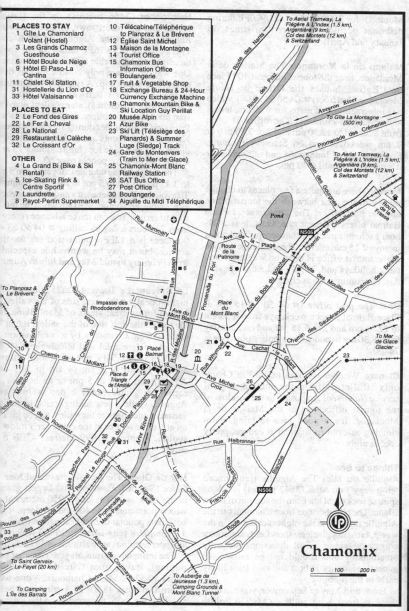

PLACES TO STAY
1 Gîte Le Chamoniard Volant (Hostel)
3 Les Grands Charmoz Guesthouse
6 Hôtel Boule de Neige
9 Hôtel El Paso-La Cantina
11 Chalet Ski Station
31 Hostellerie du Lion d'Or
33 Hôtel Valaisanne

PLACES TO EAT
2 Le Fond des Gires
22 Le Fer à Cheval
28 Le National
29 Restaurant Le Calèche
32 Le Croissant d'Or

OTHER
4 Le Grand Bi (Bike & Ski Rental)
5 Ice-Skating Rink & Centre Sportif
7 Laundrette
8 Payot-Pertin Supermarket

10 Télécabine/Téléphérique to Planpraz & Le Brévent
12 Église Saint Michel
13 Maison de la Montagne
14 Tourist Office
15 Chamonix Bus Information Office
16 Boulangerie
17 Fruit & Vegetable Shop
18 Exchange Bureau & 24-Hour Currency Exchange Machine
19 Chamonix Mountain Bike & Ski Location Guy Perillat
20 Musée Alpin
21 Azur Bike
23 Ski Lift (Télésiège des Planards) & Summer Luge (Sledge) Track
24 Gare du Montenvers (Train to Mer de Glace)
25 Chamonix-Mont Blanc Railway Station
26 SAT Bus Office
27 Post Office
30 Boulangerie
34 Aiguille du Midi Téléphérique

Chamonix

0   100   200 m

FRANCE

Montets), for 350/1050FF (325/920FF during discount periods – before Christmas, in January and April).

Maison de la Montagne The Maison de la Montagne, near the tourist office at 109 Place de l'Église, houses the Office de Haute Montagne (2nd floor; ☎ 04 50 53 22 08), which has information and maps for walkers, hikers and mountain climbers. The office is open from 8.30 am to 12.30 pm and 2 or 2.30 to 6 or 7 pm weekdays and on Saturday morning. From the end of June to the end of September it's open daily until 6.30 pm.

Money There are quite a few places to change money in the area between the tourist office and the post office. The Change at 21 Place Balmat offers a decent rate. Outside is a 24-hour exchange machine that accepts banknotes in any of 15 currencies. The exchange service at the tourist office is open on weekends and bank holidays and, in July and August, every day. No commission is charged.

Post The post office (☎ 04 50 53 15 90) at Place Balmat is open weekdays from 8.30 am to 12.15 pm and 2 to 6.15 pm and on Saturday from 8.30 am to noon. Chamonix's postcode is 74400.

Climate Weather changes rapidly in Chamonix. Bulletins from the meteorological service (la météo) are posted in the window of the tourist office and at the Maison de la Montagne. It's a good idea to bring warm clothing as even in summer it can get pretty cool at night.

Things to See
Aiguille du Midi The Aiguille (pronounced 'eh-gwee') du Midi (3842 metres) is a lone spire of rock eight km from the summit of Mont Blanc. The téléphérique from Chamonix to the Aiguille du Midi is the highest cable car in the world, crossing glaciers, snowfields and rocky crags; the views in all directions are truly breathtaking and should not be missed. In general, visibility is best and rain least likely early in the morning.

From mid-May to September, you can continue on from the Aiguille du Midi to **Pointe**

Helbronner (3466 metres) on the Italia border and the resort town of **Courmayeu** Return tickets to the Aiguille du Midi co 174FF; it's an extra 76FF return for the spe tacular transglacial ride to Pointe Helbronne One-way prices are only 20 to 25% less tha those for a return trip. A ride from Chamoni to the cable car's halfway point, Plan d l'Aiguille (2308 metres), an excellent place start hikes during summer, costs 55FF one wa Prices are 10FF higher during July and Augus No student discounts are available but a 50 discount is available for children under 13 an a 20% discount for people over 60.

The téléphérique operates all year from 8 a to 3.45 pm (6 am to 5 pm in July and August To avoid the long queues, try and arrive as ear as possible, and before 9.30 am when the bus start to arrive. You can make advance reserv tions 24 hours a day by calling ☎ 04 50 53 4 00; there is a 12FF commission fee for th service, but it may be worthwhile especial from February to mid-May and July to Augus

Le Brévent Le Brévent (2525 metres), t highest peak on the west side of the valley, known for its great views of Mont Blanc an the rest of the east side of the valley. It can reached from Chamonix by a combination télécabine (gondola) and téléphérique (☎ 50 53 13 18) for 54FF one way (76FF returr Service begins at 9 am (8 am in July an August) and stops at 5 pm or an hour or earlier in winter (until 6 pm in July an August). Quite a few hiking trails, includi various routes back to the valley, can be pick up at Le Brévent or at the cable car's midw station, Planpraz (1999 metres; 43FF o way).

Mer de Glace The heavily crevassed Mer Glace (Sea of Ice), the second-largest glaci in the Alps, is 14 km long, 1950 metres at widest point and up to 400 metres deep. It h become a major tourist destination thanks a crémaillère (cog-wheel rail line) which h an upper terminus at an altitude of 1913 metr

The train, which runs all year (weather p mitting), leaves from Gare du Montenv (☎ 04 50 53 12 54) in Chamonix. A one-wa return trip costs 48/65FF. A combined tick valid for the train, the gondola to the ice ca

Grotte de la Mer de Glace; 13FF return) and
ntry to the cave (14FF) costs 86FF. There are
often long queues for the train during July and
August. The ride takes 20 minutes each way.

The Mer de Glace can also be reached on
oot from Plan de l'Aiguille (take the Grand
Balcon Nord – see Activities below) and
Chamonix. The uphill trail, which takes about
wo or 2½ hours, begins near the summer bob
leigh track. Traversing the glacier, with its
nany crevasses, is dangerous without a guide
nd proper equipment.

Musée Alpin This museum (☎ 04 50 53 25 93)
t 89 Ave Michel Croz in Chamonix displays
rtefacts, lithographs and photos illustrating
he history of mountain climbing and other
Alpine sports. From June to September, it's
pen daily from 2 to 7 pm; between Christmas
nd Easter, hours are 3 to 7 pm. It's closed the
est of the year. The entry fee is 15FF (8FF for
nose under 16).

Activities

Hiking In late spring and summer (mid-June to
October), the Chamonix area has some of the
most spectacular hiking trails anywhere in the
Alps. In June and July there is enough light to
ike until at least 9 pm.

The *Carte des Sentiers de Montagne en Été*
summer mountain trails map; 25FF) is ade-
uate for straightforward day hikes. It includes
ots of trails and the locations of refuges. The
est map of the area is the 1:25,000 scale IGN
map (No 3630OT) entitled *Chamonix-Massif
u Mont Blanc* (54FF).

The fairly flat **Grand Balcon Sud** trail
long the Aiguilles Rouges (western) side of
e valley, which remains at about 2000
etres, offers great views of Mont Blanc and
e glaciers along the eastern side of the valley.
 you prefer to avoid a km of hard uphill
alking, take either the Planpraz lift (43FF one
ay) or La Flégère lift (40FF one way).

From Plan de l'Aiguille (55FF one way), the
idway point on the Aiguille du Midi cable
ar, the **Grand Balcon Nord** takes you to the
Ier de Glace, from where you can hike down
 Chamonix. There are a number of other trails
om Plan de l'Aiguille.

There are also trails to **Lac Blanc** (2350
etres), a turquoise lake surrounded by moun-

tains, from either the top of Les Praz-L'Index
cable car (55FF one way) or La Flégère (40FF
one way), the line's midway transfer point.

Cycling Many of the trails around the valley
are perfect for mountain biking (although the
well-known Petit Balcon Sud is no longer open
to cyclists during July and August). See
Getting Around in this section for information
on bike rentals.

Skiing The Chamonix area has 160 km of
marked ski runs, 42 km of cross-country trails
and 64 ski lifts of all sorts. These include
téléskis (tow lines), *télésièges* (chair lifts),
télécabines and téléphériques.

Many sports shops around Chamonix rent
skiing equipment. Count on paying around
39/220FF a day/week for regular skis or boots.
Ski Location Guy Perillat (☎ 04 50 53 54 76)
at 138 Rue des Moulins is open daily and also
rents out snowboards (99/148FF a day
without/with boots or 590/690FF a week).
Cross-country skis are available from Le
Grand Bi (☎ 04 50 53 14 16) at 240 Ave du
Bois du Bouchet.

Parapente Parapente is the sport of floating
down from somewhere high – the top of a cable
car line, for instance – suspended from a wing-
shaped, steerable parachute that allows you to
catch updraughts and fly around for quite a
while. An initiation flight *(baptême de l'air)*
with an instructor costs 500FF. A five-day
beginners' course *(stage d'initiation)* costs
around 3000FF. For information, contact the
tourist office.

Places to Stay
Camping Open from May to September, *L'Île
des Barrats* (☎ 04 50 53 51 44) is near the base
of the Aiguille du Midi cable car. The three-star
Camping Les Deux Glaciers (☎ 04 50 53 15
84) on the Route des Tissières in Les Bossons,
three km south of Chamonix, is open all year
except from mid-November to mid-December.
Two people with a car and tent pay 64FF. To
get there, take the train to Les Bossons or
Chamonix Bus to the Tremplin-le-Mont stop.
There are a number of camping grounds a
couple of km south of Chamonix in the village
of Les Pélerins (near the turn-off to the Mont

Blanc Tunnel to Italy), including *Camping Les Arolles* (☎ 04 50 53 14 30; open from late June to September) at 281 Chemin du Cry.

Refuges Most mountain refuges, which have dorm beds from 35 to 150FF a night, are accessible to hikers, though a few can be reached only by climbers. They are generally open from mid-June to mid-September. Half-board (demi-pension) costs from 145 to 290FF.

The easier-to-reach refuges include one at Plan de l'Aiguille (☎ 04 50 53 55 60) at 2308 metres, the intermediate stop on the Aiguille du Midi cable car, and another at La Flégère (☎ 04 50 53 06 13) at 877 metres, the midway station on the Les Praz-L'Index cable car. It is advisable to call ahead to reserve a place, especially in July and August. For information on other refuges, contact the Maison de la Montagne (☎ 04 50 53 22 08).

Hostels The *Chalet Ski Station* (☎ 04 50 53 20 25) is a gîte d'étape at 6 Route des Moussoux in Chamonix (next to the Planpraz/Le Brévent télécabine station). Beds cost 60FF a night, there's a 15FF charge for sheets, and showers are 5FF. Guests receive a discount on the Brévent cable car. This place is closed from 10 May to 20 June and from 20 September to 20 December. The semi-rustic *Gîte Le Chamoniard Volant* (☎ 04 50 53 14 09) is on the north-eastern outskirts of town at 45 Route de la Frasse. A bunk in a cramped, functional room of four, six or eight beds costs 65FF; sheets are 20FF, and an evening meal is available for 65FF. Showers and use of the kitchen are free. Reception is open from 10 am to 10 pm. The nearest bus stop is La Frasse.

The *Auberge de Jeunesse* (☎ 04 50 53 14 52) is a couple of km south-west of Chamonix at 127 Montée Jacques Balmat in Les Pélerins. By bus, take the Chamonix-Les Houches line and get off at the Pélerins École stop. Beds in rooms of four or six cost 74FF; doubles are 89/94FF per person without/with shower. The HI hostel is closed from October to November.

Hotels At 468 Chemin des Cristalliers next to the railway tracks, *Les Grands Charmoz Guesthouse* (☎ 04 50 53 45 57) is run by a friendly, easy-going American couple. Doubles cost 184FF, including use of the

shower and sheets (but not towels); dorm bee are 72FF. Guests also have use of the kitche This place is closed in November and som times also in October. *Hôtel El Paso-L Cantina* (☎ 04 50 53 64 20) at 37 Impasse de Rhododendrons has comfortable rooms fro 182/224FF in the low/high season, and fro 252/284FF with shower and toilet. Quads a 340/428FF in the low/high season. Som rooms can be a bit noisy as there's a lively b downstairs.

The *Hôtel Valaisanne* (☎ 04 50 53 17 98) a small, family-owned place at 454 A Ravanel Le Rouge, about a km south of th centre of town. Doubles cost 160FF (256F with bath and toilet). At the *Hostellerie Lion d'Or* (☎ 04 50 53 15 09) at 255 Rue Docteur Paccard, singles/doubles start 175/220FF; showers are free.

Places to Eat
Le Fer à Cheval restaurant (☎ 04 50 53 13 2 at 118 Rue Whymper is reputed to have the be fondue Savoyarde (cheese fondue) in tow Prices range from 71 to 120FF. During summ and the skiing seasons, it's a good idea reserve a day in advance. This place is clos on Tuesday during the off season and for th month of June.

Le Fonds des Gires (☎ 04 50 55 85 76), self-service restaurant on the north side town at 350 Route du Bois du Bouchet, is favourite with people staying at the nearl gîtes. It's open for lunch all year (exce January) every day and for dinner until 9 p in July and August.

Countless restaurants offering pizza, fond etc can be found in the centre of town. One these is *Le National* (☎ 04 50 53 02 23) on Rue du Docteur Paccard, a friendly place offe ing huge portions of local specialities. Disl go for 89 and 145FF. *La Cantina*, the Tex-Me restaurant attached to Hôtel El Paso-l Cantina, has copious main dishes from 55 110FF.

The *Payot-Pertin* supermarket at 117 R Joseph Vallot is open Monday to Saturday a Sunday morning.

Getting There & Away
Bus Chamonix's bus station is next to the tra station. SAT Autocar (☎ 04 50 53 01 15) h buses to Annecy (89FF), Courmayeur in Ita

OFF, 40 minutes), Geneva (188FF, two ours), Grenoble (152FF) and Turin (140FF, ree hours).

rain The narrow-gauge train line from Saint ervais-Le Fayet (20 km west of Chamonix) Martigny, Switzerland (42 km north of hamonix), stops at 11 towns in the Chamonix alley. There are nine to 12 return trips a day. ou have to change trains at Châtelard or allorcine on the Swiss border. Le Fayet serves a railhead for long-haul trains to destinations l over France.

Chamonix-Mont Blanc train station (☎ 04 0 53 00 44) is in the middle of Chamonix. The formation office is open Monday to Saturday om 9 am to noon and 2 to 6.30 pm. From June September and December to April, it's open n Sunday as well. Major destinations include aris' Gare de Lyon (400 to 480FF, six to seven ours, five trains a day plus one night train), yon (179FF, four to 4½ hours, four trains a ay) and Geneva (95FF, two to 2½ hours via aint Gervais).

etting Around

us Bus transport in the valley is handled by hamonix Bus, whose stops are marked by ack-on-yellow roadside signs. From mid- ecember to early April, there are 21 lines to l the ski lifts in the area; from April to early lay there are 12 lines; and during the rest of e year, there are only two, both of which ave from Place de l'Église and pass by the hamonix Sud stop. Chamonix Bus summer les do not run after about 7 pm (6 or 6.30 pm June and September).

The Chamonix Bus information office ☎ 04 50 53 05 55) at Place de l'Église (oppo- te the tourist office) is open daily in winter om 8 am to 7 pm. The rest of the year, hours e 8 am to noon and 2 to 6.30 pm (7.45 am to pm from June to August).

axi There is a taxi stand (☎ 04 50 53 13 94) tside the train station.

icycle Chamonix Mountain Bike (☎ 04 50 54 76) at 138 Rue des Moulins, run by an ssie and an Englishman, is open daily from am to 7 pm. Their hire charges are 50FF for o hours and 95FF a day. Azur Bike (☎ 04 50

53 50 14) at 79 Rue Whymper rents bikes for 140FF a day. It's open daily from 9 am to 7 pm during the biking season. Between April and October, Le Grand Bi (☎ 04 50 53 14 16) at 240 Ave du Bois du Bouchet has 10-speeds for 70FF a day and mountain bikes for 100FF. It is open Monday to Saturday from 9 am to noon and 2 to 7 pm.

ANNECY

Annecy (population 51,000; 448 metres), sit- uated at the northern tip of the incredibly blue Lac d'Annecy, is the perfect place to spend a relaxing holiday. Visitors in a sedentary mood can sit along the lake and feed the swans or mosey around the geranium-lined canals of the old city. Museums and other sights are limited, but for the athletically inclined, the town is an excellent base for water sports, hiking and biking. In winter, there is bus transport to low-altitude ski sta- tions nearby.

Orientation

The train and bus stations are 500 metres north- west of the old city, which is centred around the canalised Thiou River. The modern town centre is between the main post office and the Centre Bonlieu complex, home to the tourist office. The lake town of Annecy-le-Vieux is just east of Annecy.

A 1:25,000 scale map of the Lac d'Annecy area is on sale at the tourist office for 55FF.

Information

The tourist office (☎ 04 50 45 00 33), at 1 Rue Jean Jaurès in the Centre Bonlieu north of Place de la Libérations, is open Monday to Saturday from 9 am to noon and 1.45 to 6.30 pm and on Sunday from 3 to 6 pm. In July and August it does not close at midday and opens on Sunday from 9 am to noon and 1.45 to 6.30 pm.

There are several banks in the vicinity of the main post office. The Banque de Savoie opposite the tourist office at 2 Rue du Pâquier is open Monday to Friday from 9 am to 12.25 pm and 1.30 to 5.30 pm. There is a 24-hour currency exchange machine outside the Crédit Lyonnais in the Centre Bonlieu. In the old city, the Change at 20 Rue Perrière is generally open Tuesday to Saturday (daily from June to September). It's closed in January and February.

FRANCE

FRANCE

Annecy

To Plage de l'Impérial (700m),
Plage d'Annecy-le-Vieux &
Camping Grounds in
Annecy-le-Vieux (1.2 km)

Lake Annecy

Ile des Cygnes

0   50   100 m

To Camping Municipal Le
Belvédère (800m), Auberge
de Jeunesse (500m) &
Forêt du Crêt du Maure

To Base Nautique des Marquisats
(300m), Plage des Marquisats
(500m) & Sévrier (5 km)

To Hôtel
Plaisance

To Basilique
de la Visitation

PLACES TO STAY
1 Hôtel Les Terrasses
12 Central Hôtel
23 Hôtel de Savoie
27 Auberge du Lyonnais
29 Hôtel du Château

PLACES TO EAT
17 Pomme de Pain
24 Le Ramoneur Savoyard
32 Salle des Gardes
34 Le Pichet

OTHER
2 Bus Station & Voyages
   Crolard Office
3 Train Station
4 Lyonnaise de Banque
5 Centre Bonlieu
6 Tourist Office &
   SIBRA Office
7 24-Hour Currency
   Exchange Machine
8 Boat Rental
9 Banque de Savoie
10 Banque Populaire
11 Savoisienne de Crédit
13 Main Post Office
14 Boulangerie -
   Pâtisserie Royale
15 Église Notre Dame
   de Liesse
16 Prisunic Supermarket
18 Église Saint Maurice
19 Hôtel de Ville
20 Boat Rental
21 Boat Rental
22 Église Saint François
25 Food Shop
26 Cathédrale Saint Pierre
28 Morning Food Market
30 Château d'Annecy
31 Musée d'Histoire d'Annecy
33 Boulangerie
35 Pedal Boat Rental
36 Police Station
37 Hospital
38 Stade Nautique des
   Marquisats
39 Sports Évasion (Bicycle
   & Ski Rental)

The main post office (☎ 04 50 33 67 00) is at Rue des Glières. Foreign exchange services e available. Annecy's postcode is 74000.

Things to See & Do

Walking Tour Just walking around, taking in the water, flowers, grass and quaint buildings, the essence of a visit to Annecy.

Just east of the old city, behind the Hôtel de Ville, are the flowery **Jardins de l'Europe**, shaded by giant redwoods from California. There's a pleasant stroll from the Jardins de Europe along Quai de Bayreuth and Quai de la Tournette to the Base Nautique des Marquisats and beyond. Another fine promenade begins at the **Champ de Mars**, across the Canal du Vassé from the redwoods, and goes eastward around the lake towards **Annecy-le-Vieux**.

Old City The Vieille Ville, an area of narrow streets on either side of the Canal du Thiou, retains much of its 17th-century appearance despite recent 'quaintification'. On the island in the middle, the Palais de l'Isle (a former prison) houses the **Musée d'Histoire d'Annecy et de la Haute-Savoie** (☎ 04 50 33 87 31), which is open daily except Tuesday from 10 am to noon and 2 to 6 pm (daily from July to September). Entry costs 20FF (5FF for students).

Château d'Annecy The **Musée d'Annecy** (☎ 04 50 33 87 31), housed in the 13th to 16th-century chateau overlooking the town, puts on innovative temporary exhibitions and has a permanent collection of local craftwork and miscellaneous objects relating to the region's natural history. It keeps the same hours as Musée d'Histoire d'Annecy et de la Haute-Savoie. Entry is 30FF (10FF for students). The climb up to the chateau is worth it just for the view.

Activities

Beaches A km east of the Champ de Mars there is a free beach, **Plage d'Annecy-le-Vieux**. Slightly closer to town, next to the casino, is the **Plage de l'Impérial** (open from May to September), which costs 21FF (14FF for those under 13 or over 60) and is equipped with changing rooms, sporting facilities and

other amenities. Perhaps Annecy's most pleasant stretch of lawn-lined swimming beach is the free **Plage des Marquisats**, one km south of the old city along Rue des Marquisats.

Hiking The Forêt du Crêt du Maure, the forested area south of the old city, has lots of trails. There are nicer hiking areas, though, in and around two nature reserves: **Bout du Lac** (20 km from Annecy at the southern tip of the lake) and **Roc de Chère** (10 km from town on the east coast of the lake). Both can be reached by Voyages Crolard buses (see Getting There & Away).

Cycling There is a bike path along the western side of the lake. It starts 1.5 km south of Annecy (off Rue des Marquisats) and goes all the way to the lakeside town of Duingt, about 14 km to the south.

Bicycles can be rented from Sports Évasion (☎ 04 50 51 21 81) at 30 Rue des Marquisats, which is open Monday to Saturday from 9 am to noon and 2 to 7 pm (9 am to 7 pm in July and August). Mountain bikes cost 90/70FF a day/half-day.

Boating From late March to late October, pedal boats (60/70FF an hour for two/four people) and small boats with outboard motors can be hired (210FF an hour for four or five people, 250FF for up to seven) along the shore near the Jardins de l'Europe and the Champ de Mars. Boats are available daily (unless it's raining) from 9 am until sometime between 6 pm (in March) and 9 pm (in July and August). Various clubs at the Base Nautique des Marquisats, 800 metres south of the old city, rent kayaks, canoes, sailboats, sailboards, rowing hulls and diving equipment.

Swimming Pools The Stade Nautique des Marquisats (☎ 04 50 45 39 18) at 29 Rue des Marquisats has four swimming pools (including one for children) and acres of lawn. The complex is open from May to early September. Entry is 19FF.

The covered pool (☎ 04 50 57 56 02) at 90 Chemin des Fins, on the corner of Blvd du Fier, is open year-round except from 29 June to 29 August. The entry fee is 19FF (15FF for those under 18). The pool is served by bus Nos 2 and

3. There is an ice-skating rink *(patinoire)* in the same complex, open until mid-June. Entry and skate rental is 32FF (28FF for students).

Parapente Col de la Forclaz, the huge ridge overlooking Lac d'Annecy from the east, is a perfect spot from which to descend by parapente (see the Chamonix section for an explanation of this sport). For details on parapente and hang-gliding *(delta-plane)* schools, contact the tourist office in Annecy.

Winter Sports Not much snow falls in Annecy itself, but there's cross-country and downhill skiing at **Le Semnoz** (☎ 04 50 01 25 98 for information), about 15 km from town, and at **La Clusaz** (☎ 04 50 32 65 00) and **Le Grand Bornand** (☎ 04 50 02 78 00), both of which are 32 km east of Annecy. Count on paying 120 to 140FF a day for lift tickets. All three can be reached by Voyages Crolard buses.

In Annecy, skis can be rented from Sports Évasion (see Cycling earlier), which is also open on Sunday during the skiing season.

Places to Stay
Camping The *Camping Municipal Le Belvédère* (☎ 04 50 45 48 30) is 2.5 km south of the train station in the Forêt du Crêt du Maure. To get there, turn off Rue des Marquisats onto Ave de Trésum, take the first left and follow Blvd de la Corniche. From mid-June to early September you can take bus No 91 (Ligne des Vacances) from the train station. Charges are 23FF for a tent site and 25FF per person.

There are several other camping grounds near the lake in Annecy-le-Vieux. *Le Pré d'Avril* (☎ 04 50 23 64 46; open from Easter to 20 September) at 56 Rue du Pré d'Avril, charges 25FF for a place to camp and park and 20FF per person (70FF for two people with a tent and car in summer).

Hostels The *Auberge de Jeunesse* (☎ 04 50 45 33 19) is on Route du Semnoz, close to the camping ground. From mid-June to early September, bus No 91 goes there. Beds cost 67FF with a hostelling card, 86FF without, including breakfast. Sheets are an extra 17FF. You can check in between 8 am and noon and from 2 to 10 pm.

Hotels The *Hôtel Plaisance* (☎ 04 50 57 42) at 17 Rue de Narvik has simple but brig singles/doubles from 120/135FF and triples f 235FF. Rooms with shower are 180FF. Ha showers are 11FF and breakfast is 25FF. Fre parking is available. The pleasant *Hôtel L Terrasses* (☎ 04 50 57 08 98) at 15 Rue Lou Chaumontet, 300 metres north of the tra station, has singles/doubles from 120/150F (170/200FF in the high season). Rooms wi shower and toilet are 160/190FF (210/240FF From June to September, guests must pay hal board (255/440FF for singles/doubles witho shower, 295/480FF with). It is closed December and January.

One of the cheapest places close to the o city is the *Central Hôtel* (☎ 04 50 45 05 37) 6bis Rue Royale (enter through the courtyarc Basic rooms start at 200FF and go up to 220F with bath and toilet. Triples/quads are arou 210/230FF. In the heart of the old city, t **Auberge du Lyonnais** (☎ 04 50 51 26 10) at Rue de la République (on the corner of Qu de l'Évêché) occupies an idyllic setting ju next to the canal. Comfortable singles/doubl are from 160/200FF, from 170/200FF wi shower and toilet. All rooms have TV. Th place does not take reservations and has on a few rooms, so come by before 9 am.

Places to Eat
In the old city, there are a number of chea hole-in-the-wall sandwich shops along Ru Perrière and Rue de l'Isle, including a coup of good crêperies. Further north, *Pomme Pain* at 2 Rue Joseph Blanc has decent san wiches for 16 to 26FF. It is open daily from am to 7 pm (8 pm or later in summer).

The popular *Le Ramoneur Savoyard* (☎ 0 50 51 99 99) at 7 Rue de Grenette has reason ably priced regional dishes, with menus fro 69 to 175FF. It's open daily for lunch an dinner. *Le Pichet* (☎ 04 50 45 32 41) at 13 Ru Perrière has three-course menus from 61 110FF. The rather touristy *Salle des Garde* (☎ 04 50 51 52 00) at Quai des Vieilles Prison facing the old prison, has Savoyard special ties, such as fondue and tartiflette (a fillin concoction of oven-baked potatoes, reblocho cheese, and other ingredients such as onion and bacon). Menus start at 89FF (55FF fo lunch). It is closed on Monday and Tuesday midday during the low season.

In the old city, there is a food market along ue Sainte Claire on Sunday, Tuesday and riday from 6 am to 12.30 pm. Fancy vegetales, fruit, cheese and wine (at fancy prices) e on sale at the food shop *Mme de Warens* at Rue Jean-Jacques Rousseau.

etting There & Away

us The bus station, Gare Routière Sud, is on ue de l'Industrie next to the train station. oyages Crolard's office (☎ 04 50 45 08 12) ere is open Monday to Saturday from 6.15 am ▸ 12.10 pm and 1.30 to 7.30 pm. The company as regular services to Roc de Chère on the astern shore of Lac d'Annecy and Bout du ac at the far southern tip, as well as to places ast of Annecy, including La Clusaz and Le rand Bornand ski stations and the towns of lbertville and Chamonix. Autocars Frossard ☎ 04 50 45 73 90), open from 7.45 am to 12.30 m and 1.45 to 7 pm (closed Sunday and holiays), sells tickets to Geneva, Grenoble, Nice and lsewhere.

Autocars Francony (☎ 04 50 45 02 43) has uses to Chamonix. The office at the bus ation is open weekdays from 7.15 to 11 am nd 2.15 to 6.15 pm.

rain The train station (☎ 08 36 35 35 39) is a nodernistic structure at Place de la Gare. The nformation office, which is on the lower level, ; open daily from 8.35 am (9 am on Sunday) ▸ 7.15 pm. There is also at least one ticket ffice open from 4.45 am to 11.45 pm. There re frequent trains, not all of them direct, to aris' Gare de Lyon (335 to 423FF, 3¾ hours), lice (347FF via Lyon, 328FF via Grenoble, ight to nine hours, faster with a change of ain), Lyon (110FF, two hours), Chamonix 102FF, 2½ to three hours) and Aix-les-Bains 37FF, 30 to 45 minutes).

etting Around

us The local bus company SIBRA (☎ 04 50 1 72 72) has an information bureau (☎ 04 50 1 70 33) across the covered courtyard from he tourist office. It's open Monday to Saturday om 8.45 am to 7 pm. Tickets cost 7FF each r 37.50FF for a carnet of eight. Students and nose aged five to 20 pay 27FF for a carnet of 0. Annecy's buses run Monday to Saturday om 6 am to 8 pm. On Sundays, 20-seat

minibuses (identified by letters rather than numbers) provide limited service. Ligne des Vacances bus No 91 runs only from mid-June to early September.

Taxi Taxis based at the bus station can be ordered by calling ☎ 04 50 45 05 67.

Provence

Provence stretches along both sides of the Rhône River from just north of the town of Orange down to the Mediterranean and along France's southern coast from the Camargue salt marshes in the west to Marseille and beyond in the east. The spectacular Gorges d'Ardèche, created by the often torrential Ardèche River, are west of the Rhône, and to the east are the region's famous upland areas: 1909-metre Mt Ventoux, the Vaucluse Plateau, the Lubéron Range and the chain of hills known as the Alpilles. East of Marseille is the Côte d'Azur and its hinterland, which, though part of Provence, is treated as a separate region in this guide.

Provence was settled by the Ligurians, the Celts and the Greeks, but it was after its conquest by Julius Caesar in the mid-1st century BC that the region really began to flourish. Many exceptionally well-preserved amphitheatres, aqueducts (particularly Pont du Gard) and other buildings from the Roman period can still be seen in Arles, Nîmes and Orange. During the 14th century, the Catholic Church, then led by a series of French-born popes, moved its headquarters from feud-ridden Rome to Avignon, thus beginning the most resplendent period in that city's history.

Language

A thousand years ago, *oïl* and *oc* were the words for 'yes' in the Romance languages of what is now northern and southern France respectively. As Paris-based influence and control spread, so did the Langue d'Oïl, and thus the Langue d'Oc (the language of Provence) was gradually supplanted. The Provençal language is not spoken much these days, but it has left the world a rich literary legacy – the Langue d'Oc was used by the medieval troubadours,

FRANCE

whose melodies and poems were motivated by the ideal of courtly love.

Climate

Provence's weather is bright and sunny for much of the year, and the extraordinary light has attracted a number of painters, including Van Gogh, Cézanne and Picasso. The cold, dry winds of the mistral, which gain surprising fury as they careen down the Rhône Valley, can turn a fine spring day into a bone-chilling wintry one with little warning.

MARSEILLE

The cosmopolitan and much maligned port of Marseille, France's second-largest city with a population of 800,000 and third-most populous urban area (population 1.23 million), is not in the least bit prettified or quaintified for the benefit of tourists. Its urban geography and atmosphere are a function of the diversity of its inhabitants, the majority of whom are immigrants (or their descendants) from the Mediterranean basin, West Africa and Indochina. Although Marseille is notorious for organised crime and racial tensions (the extreme right polls about 17% here), the city has more to reward the visitor who likes exploring on foot than almost any other city in France.

Orientation

The city's main street, La Canebière, stretches eastward from the Vieux Port. The train station is north of La Canebière at the top of Blvd d'Athènes. The city centre is around Rue Paradis, which becomes more fashionable as you move south.

Information

Tourist Office The tourist office (☎ 04 91 13 89 00), next to the Vieux Port at 4 La Canebière, is open Monday to Saturday from 9 am to 7.15 pm and on Sunday from 10 am to 5 pm. From June to September, opening hours are 8.30 am to 8 pm daily. The tourist office annexe (☎ 04 91 50 59 18) at the train station (on the right as you exit the station's main doors) is open weekdays from 10 am to 1 pm and 1.30 to 6 pm (9 am to 7 pm from June to September).

Foreign Consulates There is a UK consulate (☎ 04 91 53 43 32) at 24 Ave du Prado (near Place Castellane and the Castellane metro stop). The US consulate (☎ 04 91 54 92 00) is across from the préfecture building at 12 Blvd Paul Peytral.

Money The Banque de France is at Place Estrangin Pastré, a block west of the préfecture. There are a number of banks on La Canebière near the tourist office. Change de la Bourse at 3 Place du Général de Gaulle will exchange dozens of currencies.

American Express (☎ 04 91 13 71 26) at 39 La Canebière is open weekdays from 8 am to 6 pm and on Saturday from 8.30 am to noon and 2 to 4.30 pm. The Comptoir de Change Méditerranéen at the train station will exchange foreign currencies daily.

Post The main post office (☎ 04 91 15 47 00) is at 1 Place de l'Hôtel des Postes. Exchange services are available. The postcode for Marseille consists of the digits 130 plus the arrondissement number (01 to 16). The areas covered by the Marseille map in this book are in 13001 except the area south of Rue Grignan, which is in 13006, and the area south of the Vieux Port, which is 13007.

Laundry The Laverie des Allées at 17 Allée Léon Gambetta is close to many of the hotels mentioned under Places to Stay and is open seven days a week from 9 am to 8 pm.

Dangers & Annoyances Despite its fearsome reputation for underground crime, Marseille is probably no more dangerous than other French cities. As elsewhere, street crime such as bag snatching and pickpocketing is best avoided by keeping your wits about you and your valuables hard to get at. Guard your luggage very carefully, especially at the train station, and *never* leave anything inside a parked vehicle. One Lonely Planet researcher did just that and lost all his clothes!

At night, it is best to avoid the Belsunce area, the poor, immigrant neighbourhood south-west of the train station bounded by La Canebière, Cours Belsunce/Rue d'Aix, Rue Bernard du Bois and Blvd d'Athènes.

Things to See & Do

Walking Tour Marseille grew up around the

Vieux Port, where Greeks from Asia Minor established a settlement around 600 BC. The quarter north of Quai du Port (around the Hôtel de Ville) was blown up by the Germans in 1943 and rebuilt after the war. The lively **Place Thiars** pedestrian zone, with its many late-night restaurants and cafés, is south of the Quai de Rive Neuve. To get from one side of the harbour entrance to the other, you can walk through the Saint Laurent Tunnel, which surfaces in front of the cathedral (near Fort Saint Jean) and, on the south side, just east of Fort Saint Nicolas. Also worth a stroll is the more fashionable **6e arrondissement**, especially the area between La Canebière and the préfecture building, and the Rue Saint Ferréol pedestrian mall.

Corniche Président John F Kennedy runs along the coast from 200 metres west of the **Jardin du Pharo**, a park with good harbour views, to the Plages Gaston Defferre, 4.5 km to the south. Along its entire length, the corniche is served by bus No 83, which goes to the Quai des Belges (the old port) and the Rond-Point du Prado metro stop.

If you like great panoramic views or overwrought mid-19th century architecture, consider a walk up to the **Basilique Notre Dame de la Garde**, which is one km south of the Vieux Port on a hilltop (154 metres) – the highest point in the city. The basilica and the crypt are open from 7.30 am to 5.30 pm (7 am to 7.30 pm in summer). Bus No 60 will get you back to the Vieux Port.

Museums Except where noted, the museums listed here are open daily from 10 am to 5 pm (11 am to 6 pm from June to September). All of them admit students and teachers for half the regular price.

The **Centre de la Vieille Charité** (☎ 04 91 56 28 38), which used to be a charity centre and is housed in a hospice built between 1671 and 1745, has superb permanent exhibits on ancient Egypt and Greece and all sorts of temporary exhibitions. It is in the mostly North African Panier quarter (north of the Vieux Port) at 2 Rue de la Charité. Adult entry fees are 10FF for the Museum of Mediterranean Archaeology, 10FF for the Museum of African Art and 20FF for special exhibitions.

The **Musée du Vieux Marseille** (☎ 04 91 55 10 19), behind the Hôtel de Ville in a 16th-century mansion at 2 Rue de la Prison, displays antique household items from Provence, playing cards (for which Marseille has been known since the 17th century) and the equipment to make them, and photos of the city under German occupation – among other things. Admission costs 10FF (5FF for students). The museum was closed for restoration at the time of writing, but was due to reopen in late 1996.

The **Musée Cantini** (☎ 04 91 54 77 75), off Rue Paradis at 19 Rue Grignan, has changing exhibitions of modern and contemporary art. From October to May the museum is open from 10 am to 5 pm (11 am to 6 pm from June to September); it's closed on Monday. Entry is 15FF.

Roman history buffs might want to visit the **Musée d'Histoire de Marseille** (☎ 04 91 90 42 22) on the ground floor of the Centre Bourse shopping mall (just north of La Canebière). Its exhibits include the freeze-dried remains of a merchant ship that plied the waters of the Mediterranean in the late 2nd century AD. It is open Monday to Saturday from noon to 7 pm. Entry is 10FF. The remains of Roman buildings, uncovered by accident during construction of the shopping mall, can be seen nearby in the **Jardin des Vestiges**, which lies between the Centre Bourse and Rue Henri Barbusse and can be entered via the museum.

Château d'If Château d'If (☎ 04 91 59 02 30), the 16th-century island fortress-turned-prison made infamous by Alexandre Dumas' *The Count of Monte Cristo*, can be visited daily from 9 am until 7 pm (or whenever the last boat of the day departs). The entry fee is 22FF for all. Boats (45FF return, 20 minutes each way) leave from near the GACM office (☎ 04 91 55 50 09) on Quai des Belges (old port) and go on to the nearby **Îles du Frioul** (45FF return, or 70FF for both the chateau and islands).

Beaches The city's most attractive beach, the **Plages Gaston Defferre** (commonly known as the Plage du Prado), is four km south of the city centre. To get there, take bus No 19, 72 or 83 from the Rond-Point du Prado metro stop or bus No 83 from the Quai des Belges. You

FRANCE

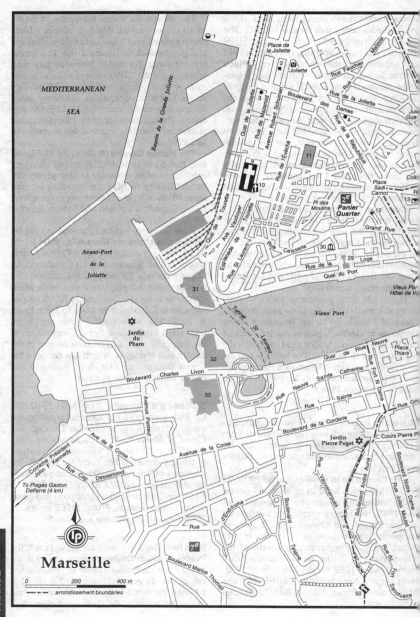

MEDITERRANEAN

SEA

Bassin de la Grande Joliette

Avant-Port
de la
Joliette

Jardin
du
Pharo

Boulevard Charles Livon

Avenue d'Endoume

Avenue Pasteur

Corniche Président John F Kennedy

Rue Cap Dessemond

Ave de la Corse

To Plages Gaston
Deflerre (4 km)

Rue

Boulevard Marius Thomas

7e

Marseille

0   200   400 m

- - - - - arrondissement boundaries

Place de
la Joliette

Joliette

Rue Fauchier

Rue de la Joliette

Boulevard des Dames

Quai de la Joliette

Rue de Mazenod

Avenue Robert Schuman

Rue de la République

Rue de l'Évêché

Rue St Laurent

Esplanade de la Tourette

Ave Vaudoyer

Quai de la Tourette

Place
Sadi
Carnot

2e

Panier
Quarter

Pl des
Moulins

Grand' Rue

Rue Caisserie

Rue de la Loge

Quai du Port

Vieux Port
Hôtel de Va

Vieux Port

Quai de Rive Neuve

Rue Fort N Dame

Place
Thiars

Rue Neuve Sainte Catherine

Rue Neuve Sainte

Boulevard de la Corderie

Jardin
Pierre Puget

Cours Pierre P

Avenue de la Corse

Rue Vauvenargues

Boulevard André Aune

Boulevard Notre Dame

Rue Jules Moulet

Boulevard Telline

Boulevard d'Endoume

Boulevard

Rue du Fort

Sanctuaire

Jules
Gue

Colb

13

12

9

10

1

11

3

2

4

30

29   Loge

31

32

33

50

FRANCE

PLACES TO STAY
2 Hôtel Breton
17 Hôtel de Bourgogne
18 Hôtel Gambetta
19 Hôtel Ozea & Hôtel Pied-à-Terre
21 Hôtel de Nice
22 Hôtel Sphinx
23 Cheap Hotels
49 Hôtel Béarn

PLACES TO EAT
12 Auberge 'In' Vegetarian Restaurant
25 Takeaway Restaurants
37 La Caucase & Le Resto Provençal
38 Ethnic Restaurants
40 Restaurant Antillais Madiana
41 Le Quinze

OTHER
1 Passenger Ferry Terminal
3 SNCM Ferries Office
4 Algérie Ferries
5 Bus Station
6 Taxi Stand
7 Post Office
8 Gare Saint Charles
9 Nouvelle Cathédrale
10 Ancienne Cathédrale de la Major
11 Centre de la Vielle Charité
13 Main Post Office
14 Jardin des Vestiges (Roman Ruins)
15 Musée d'Histoire de Marseille
16 Laundrette
20 New Can-Can Disco
24 Marché des Capucins (Food Market)
26 American Express
27 Espace Infos RTM (Bus & Metro Information)
28 Nouvelles Galeries Supermarket
29 Hôtel de Ville
30 Musée du Vieux Marseille
31 Fort Saint Jean
32 Bas Fort Saint Nicolas
33 Fort d'Entrecasteaux & Fort Saint Nicolas
34 Tourist Office
35 Opera
36 Change de la Bourse
39 La Maison Hantée
42 Musée Cantini
43 Law Courts
44 Préfecture de Police
45 Préfecture
46 US Consulate
47 Banque de France
48 Fruit & Vegetable Morning Market
50 Basilique Notre Dame de la Garde

368 France - Provence

can walk there along the Corniche Président John F Kennedy. For more information about beaches and the great range of water activities, ask for the *Marseille by the Sea* brochure at the tourist office.

Places to Stay

Camping All of Marseille's municipal camping grounds are presently closed. Contact the tourist office to find out if any have reopened. Travellers with tents can camp at the Auberge de Jeunesse de Bonneveine.

Hostels The *Auberge de Jeunesse de Bonneveine* (☎ 04 91 73 21 81) is at 47 Ave Joseph Vidal, about 4.5 km south of the Vieux Port. To get there, take bus No 44 from the Rond-Point du Prado metro stop and get off at Place Louis Bonnefon. A bed in a room for six is 66FF (72FF in summer), including breakfast. Sheets cost 16FF. Valuables should be kept in the 24-hour lockers, which cost 25FF.

There's another hostel, the *Auberge de Jeunesse de Bois Luzy* (☎ 04 91 49 06 18), 4.5 km east of the city centre at 76 Ave de Bois Luzy (in the Montolivet neighbourhood). To get there, take bus No 6 from near the Canebière-Réformés metro stop to the Marius-Richard stop. Beds are 43FF and breakfast is 18FF. The hostel is closed between 10 am and 5 pm.

Hotels Marseille has some of France's cheapest hotels; you can still find rooms for 50FF a night but most are filthy dives in unsafe areas which rent out rooms by the hour. All of the places listed by name in this section are reputable and relatively clean.

Ferry Terminal Area The *Hôtel Breton* (☎ 04 91 90 00 81), a stone's throw away from the ferry terminal at 52 Rue Mazenod, has clean, well-kept singles/doubles with shower, telephone and TV for 110/170FF.

Train Station Area The *Hôtel de Bourgogne* (☎ 04 91 62 19 49) at 31 Allées Léon Gambetta has singles/doubles from 80/140FF and triples for 180FF; showers are 10FF. Singles/doubles with shower are 150/160FF. If requested, they can add an extra bed. The *Hôtel Gambetta* (☎ 04 91 62 07 88), nearby at No 49, has

singles without shower for 95FF and singles/ doubles with shower from 130/160FF. Doubles with shower and toilet start at 215FF. Hall showers are 15FF.

There are several other one and two-star hotels nearby and a cluster of small, extremely cheap hotels of less-than-pristine reputation along Rue des Petites Maries.

South of La Canebière The *Hôtel Ozea* (☎ 04 91 47 91 84) is at 12 Rue Barbaroux, across Square Léon Blum from the eastern end of Allées Léon Gambetta. This place, which welcomes new guests 24 hours a day (if you arrive late at night just ring the bell), has clean, old-fashioned doubles without/with shower for 120/150FF. There are no hall showers. Nearby, the *Hôtel Pied-à-Terre* (☎ 04 91 92 00 95) at No 18 has singles/doubles without/with shower for 120/150FF.

There are lots of rock-bottom hotels along Rue Sénac de Meilhan and around Place du Lycée and a number of one-star hotels along Rue des Feuillants. The *Hôtel Sphinx* (☎ 04 91 48 70 59), at 16 Rue Sénac, has simple but well-kept singles/doubles from 68/116FF or 120/160FF with shower. Triples with shower are 200FF. Hall showers are 17FF. Another possibility is the *Hôtel de Nice* (☎ 04 91 48 73 07) on the same street at No 11. Doubles without/with rather dismal showers are 100/ 120FF; hall showers cost 20FF. Guests can register 24 hours a day.

Préfecture Area The *Hôtel Béarn* (☎ 04 91 37 75 83), at 63 Rue Sylvabelle, has comfortable singles/doubles with shower for 120FF and singles/doubles with shower, toilet and TV for 170FF.

Places to Eat

There are lots of cheap takeaway places selling pizza and Middle Eastern sandwiches of various sorts on Rue des Feuillants, which intersects La Canebière just east of Cours Saint Louis. Cours Belsunce is lined with inexpensive food kiosks.

Restaurants along and near the pedestrianised Cours Julien, a few blocks south of La Canebière, offer an incredible variety of cuisines: Antillean, Pakistani, Thai, Lebanese, Tunisian, Italian and more. *La Caucase* (☎ 04

'91 48 36 30) at No 62 specialises in Armenian dishes. It's open for dinner seven nights a week from about 6 pm and has menus for 85 and 145FF. If you'd rather have something French, try *Le Resto Provençal* (☎ 04 91 48 85 12) at No 64. There are pleasant outdoor tables and a good-value three-course lunch menu for 100FF. It's closed Sunday and Monday.

Le Quinze (☎ 04 91 92 00 52), at 15 Rue des Trois Rois, a small street running parallel to Cours Julien, offers Provençal menus from 89FF. Nearby, the West Indian restaurant *Antillais Madiana* (☎ 04 91 94 25 55) on Rue des Trois Mages has menus from 65FF.

Countless sandwich shops, cafés and restaurants line the pedestrian streets around Place Thiars, which is on the south side of the Vieux Port. Though many offer bouillabaisse, the rich fish stew for which Marseille is famous, it is difficult to find the real thing. Recommended for the real thing, however, is *La Maronaise* (☎ 04 91 73 25 21) at 'Les Gourdes' on Route de la Maronaise west of the city, on the way to Plages Gaston Defferre. Avoid the touristy restaurants on the Quai de Rive Neuve.

The *Auberge 'In'* (☎ 04 91 90 51 59) is a vegetarian restaurant a few hundred metres north of the Vieux Port at 25 Rue du Chevalier Roze. Giant salads cost 45 to 50FF. Meals are served at lunch and dinner daily except on Sunday. The attached food shop and salon de thé are open from 8 am to 11 pm.

There is an up-market supermarket, open Monday to Saturday, in the Nouvelles Galeries department store a block north of La Canebière in the Centre Bourse shopping mall complex. The most convenient entrance is at 28 Rue de Bir Hakeim. At the *Marché des Capucins*, one block south of La Canebière on Rue Longue des Capucins, you can buy fruit and vegetables Monday to Saturday from 7 am to 7 pm.

Getting There & Away

Air The Aéroport de Marseille-Provence (☎ 04 42 14 14 14) is 28 km north-west of the city.

Bus The bus station (☎ 04 91 08 16 40) at Place Victor Hugo, 150 metres to the right as you exit the train station, offers service to Aix-en-Provence, Arles, Avignon, Cannes, Carpentras, Nice (direct and via the coast), Nice airport, Orange and Salon. The buses, which are slower than the train, cost more or less the same unless you're a student under 26 (30% discount). The information counter and the left-luggage office are open Monday to Saturday from 7.45 am to 6.30 pm and on Sunday from 9 am to noon and 2 to 6 pm. Tickets are sold on the bus.

Train Marseille's passenger train station, Gare Saint Charles (☎ 08 36 35 35 39), is served by both metro lines. Trains from here go everywhere, including Paris' Gare de Lyon (409FF, five to eight hours), Bordeaux (339FF, five to six hours), Toulouse (232FF, three to four hours) and Nice (143FF, 1½ to two hours). The information office, one floor under the platforms, is open Monday to Saturday from 9 am to 8 pm. There's an SNCF office (☎ 04 91 54 42 61) at 17 Rue Grignon, off Rue St Ferréol a couple of blocks north of the préfecture. It's open weekdays from 9 am to 5 pm.

Ferry The Société Nationale Maritime Corse-Méditerranée (SNCM; ☎ 04 91 56 30 10) at 61 Blvd des Dames offers ferry service from the gare maritime (at the foot of Blvd des Dames) to Corsica (Corse), Sardinia (Sardaigne), Tunisia and Algeria. Discounts of up to 30%, some limited to the off season (October to April) or applicable only if you're a student or under 25 (or both), are available. The SNCM office is open weekdays from 8 am to 6 pm and on Saturday from 8.30 am to noon and 2 to 6 pm.

Getting Around

To/From the Airport TRPA buses from Gare Saint Charles go to the Marseille-Provence airport every 20 minutes from 5.30 am to 9.50 pm. From the airport, they go to the train station from 6.20 am to 10.20 pm. The trip takes about 25 minutes and costs 42FF.

Bus & Underground Marseille has two easy-to-follow metro lines (look for the white-on-brown signs bearing an angular letter 'M') and an extensive bus network.

Numbered buses run until 9 pm; lines identified with letters, known as the *autobus de nuit*, run from 9 pm to 12.30 am. Tickets (8FF) are valid for travel on both the bus and the metro for 70 minutes after they have been

FRANCE

time-stamped. When you buy a carnet of six tickets (available in metro stations for 42FF) you get two coupons *(talons* or *souches)* with the same serial number as your tickets; to use a ticket as a transfer you must show one of the coupons.

For more information, visit the Espace Infos RTM (☎ 04 91 91 92 10) at 6-8 Rue des Fabres, which is open weekdays from 8.30 am to 6 pm.

Taxi Marseille Taxi (☎ 04 91 02 20 20) and Allô Taxis (☎ 04 91 49 59 99) will dispatch taxis 24 hours a day.

AIX-EN-PROVENCE

One of the most appealing cities in Provence, Aix (population 159,000) is very lively, perhaps because of the high number of students, which make up over 20% of the population. One of the city's most prominent citizens was the postimpressionist painter Cézanne. Aix's main festival is the Festival International d'Art Lyrique, which is held in July. The city is also renowned for its *calissons*, almond-paste confectionery made with candied melon.

The mostly pedestrianised old city is a great place to explore, with its maze of tiny streets full of ethnic restaurants, specialist food shops and tempting designer shops. Apart from this, there are lots of mossy fountains, elegant 17th and 18th-century hôtels particuliers and popular outdoor cafés which give the city a relaxed, friendly atmosphere.

Aix also has several interesting museums, the finest of which is the **Musée Granet** (☎ 04 42 38 14 70) at Place Saint Jean de Malte. The collection includes Italian, Dutch and French paintings from the 16th to 19th centuries as well as some of Cézanne's lesser known paintings. Admission is 18FF (10FF for students). The **Musée des Tapisseries** (☎ 04 42 23 09 91), in the former bishop's palace at 28 Place des Martyrs de la Résistance, is worth visiting for its tapestries and sumptuous costumes. Entry is 15FF (9FF for students); during special exhibitions the fee goes up to 18FF (10FF concession). Both museums are closed on Tuesday.

Atelier Paul Cézanne (☎ 04 42 21 06 53), at 9 Ave Paul Cézanne, was the painter's last studio and has been left as it was when he died in 1906. It's open daily except Tuesday and entry is 16FF (10FF for students).

The tourist office (☎ 04 42 16 11 61) is on Place Général de Gaulle. Numerous cafés, brasseries and restaurants can be found in the heart of the city on Place des Cardeurs and Place de l'Hôtel de Ville. One of these is the *Brasserie de la Mairie* which has good, inexpensive salads. *Les Tournesols* (☎ 04 42 27 93 78) at 1 Rue Cardinale, close to Rue d'Italie, offers delectable, seasonal food at very reasonable prices. A colourful morning fruit and vegetable market is held on Place Richelme.

Frequent trains run between Marseille and Aix (32FF, 30 minutes).

AVIGNON

Avignon (population 100,000) acquired its ramparts and its reputation as a city of art and culture during the 14th century, when Pope Clement V and his court, fleeing political turmoil in Rome, established themselves here. From 1309 to 1377 huge sums of money were invested in building and decorating the popes' palace and other important church edifices. Even after the pontifical court returned to Rome amid bitter charges that Avignon had become a den of criminals and brothel-goers, Avignon, which remained under Vatican rule until the Revolution, continued to serve as an important cultural centre.

Today, Avignon maintains its tradition as a patron of the arts, most notably through its annual performing arts festival. The city's other attractions include a bustling (if slightly touristy) walled town and a number of interesting museums, including several across the Rhône in Villeneuve-lès-Avignon. Avignon is a good base for day trips to other parts of Provence.

The world-famous Festival d'Avignon, held every year during the last three weeks of July, attracts many hundreds of performers (actors, dancers, musicians etc) who put on some 300 performances of all sorts each day.

Orientation

The walled city's main avenue runs northward from the train station to Place de l'Horloge; it's called Cours Jean Jaurès south of the tourist office and Rue de la République north of it. Place de l'Horloge is 200 metres south of Place du Palais, which is next to the Palais des Papes.

The island that runs down the middle of the Rhône between Avignon and Villeneuve-lès-Avignon is known as Île de la Barthelasse.

Information

Tourist Office The tourist office (☎ 04 90 82 65 11) is 300 metres north of the train station at 41 Cours Jean Jaurès. The free guide *Avignon en Poche* has all the information you're likely to need while in Avignon. The office is open Monday to Saturday from 9 am to 1 pm and 2 to 6 pm (5 pm on Saturday). During the festival, hours are 10 am to 7 pm (5 pm on weekends and holidays). From October to March the tourist office annexe at the Pont Saint Bénézet (Pont d'Avignon) is open from 9 am to 1 pm and 2 to 5 pm (closed Monday); from April to September it's open daily from 9 am to 6.30 pm.

Money & Post There's a Banque de France at the northern end of Place de l'Horloge. The main post office (☎ 04 90 86 78 00) is on Cours Président Kennedy, which is through Porte de la République from the train station. It has currency exchange services. Avignon's postcode is 84000.

Laundry Laverie La Fontaine at 64 Place des Corps Saint, just around the corner from Rue Agricol Perdiguier, is open Monday to Saturday from 7 am to 8 pm.

Things to See

Avignon's most interesting areas are within the walled city *(intra-muros)*. The ramparts were restored during the 19th century but the original moats were not re-excavated, leaving the crenellated fortifications looking rather less imposing than they once probably did.

Palais des Papes Avignon's leading tourist attraction is the fortified Palace of the Popes (☎ 04 90 27 50 73/4) at Place du Palais, built during the 14th century. Six centuries ago, the seemingly endless halls, chapels, corridors and staircases were sumptuously decorated with tapestries, paintings etc but these days, except for a few damaged frescos, they are nearly empty. As a result, the palace is of interest more as a result of the dramatic events that took place here than for the inherent beauty of its stone halls.

The palace is open daily from 9 am to 12.45 pm and 2 to 6 pm. From April to October, hours are 9 am to 7 or 8 pm. When the palace closes at midday, morning ticket sales end at noon; in the evening, the ticket window closes 45 to 60 minutes before the palace does. Entry to the palace's interior is 34FF (26FF for students and people over 60). One-hour guided tours (43FF, or 38FF concession) are available in English from April to November *only*, usually at 10 am and 3.30 pm (10 am and 3 pm in July and August). Special exhibitions, especially during summer, may raise the entry fee by 10FF or so.

Around Place du Palais At the far northern end of Place du Palais, the **Musée du Petit Palais** (☎ 04 90 86 44 58) houses an outstanding collection of 13th to 16th-century Italian religious paintings. It's open from 9.30 am to noon and 2 to 6 pm (closed Tuesday); from July to August hours are 10 am to 6 pm. Tickets cost 20FF (10FF concession) but entry is free on Sunday from October to March. Just up the hill is **Rocher des Doms**, a delightful bluff-top park that offers great views of the Rhône, Pont Saint Bénézet, Villeneuve-lès-Avignon, the Alpilles, and so on.

Pont Saint Bénézet (☎ 04 90 85 60 16) was built in the 12th century to link Avignon with Villeneuve-lès-Avignon. The 900-metre-long structure was repaired and rebuilt several times, but four of its 22 spans were washed away once and for all in the mid-1600s. Yes, this is the Pont d'Avignon mentioned in the French nursery rhyme. If you want to stand *on* the bridge, you can do so – for 15FF (7FF concession) Tuesday to Sunday from 9 am to 1 pm and 2 to 5 pm (from April to September, daily from 9 am to 6.30 pm).

Synagogue The synagogue (☎ 04 90 85 21 24), at 2 Place Jérusalem, was established on this site in 1221. A 13th-century oven used to bake unleavened bread for Passover is still in place, but the rest of the present dome-topped, neoclassical structure dates from the 19th century. You can visit the synagogue Monday to Friday from 10 am to noon and 3 to 5 pm.

Avignon

To Lyon

To Orange & Lyon

Route de Lyon

Imp Mourre

Boulevard Limbert

Rhône River

Montfavet

de

Avenue

Pierre

To Airport, Aix-en-Provence & Marseille

Saimod

Boulevard du Quai Saint Lazare

Rue des Infirmières

Rue Carreterie

Rue Louis Pasteur

Place des Carmes

Rue Guillaume Puy

Rue Thiers

Rue Saint Christophe

Rue des Teinturiers

Boulevard Saint Michel

To Centre Hospitalier (2.5 km)

To Airport, Aix-en-Provence & Arles

To Hôpital (2.5 km)

Rue Palapharnerie

Rue Campane

Rue Paul Sain

Rue Philonarde

Rue des Lices

Rue de la Ligne

R Bertrand

Rue Banasterie

Place Pie

Rue Bonneterie

Rue du Roi René

Place des Corps Saints

Rue St Michel

Rue Agricol Perdiguier

Rocher des Doms

Rue Carnot

Place (Jérusalem)

Rue des

Rue Henri Fabre

Avenue Monclar

Boulevard du Rhône

Place du Palais

Place de la Balance

R. de la Balance

Place du Palais

Place de l'Horloge

Rue Joseph Vernet

Rue de la République

Rue St Agricol

Rue Bouquerie

Square Agricol Perdiguier

Cours Jean Jaurès

Place Campana

Rue des Grottes

Rue de la Grande Fusterie

Place Crillon

Rue St Didier

Rue Vernet

Cours Président Kennedy

Boulevard Saint Roch

Pont Saint Bénézet

Pont Saint Bénézet

Boulevard de l'Oulle

Rue du Rempart de l'Oulle

Rue Victor Hugo

Rue Annanelle

Rue Saint Charles

Rue Joseph

Boulevard Raspail

Allées des Oulles

Boulevard Saint Dominique

Rue Velouterie

Ave Eisenhower

Rue Paul Merindol

Île de la Barthelasse

Rhône River

Pont Édouard Daladier

To Saint Bénézet (300m)

To Villeneuve-lès-Avignon (500m), Municipal Camping Bagatelle Hostel (1.2 km) & Fort Saint André (2.1 km)

Chemin des Berges

To Hameau Champfleuri (250m)

Pont de l'Europe

FRANCE

0   150   300 m

Museums Housed in an 18th century mansion, and only partially reopened after extensive renovation, the **Musée Calvet** (☎ 04 90 86 33 84) at 65 Rue Joseph Vernet has a collection of Egyptian, Greek and Roman artefacts as well as paintings from the 16th to 20th centuries. Admission is free. The **Musée Lapidaire** (☎ 04 90 85 75 38) at 27 Rue de la République houses the city's archaeological collection. It's open from 10 am to noon and 2 to 6 pm (closed Tuesday). Entry is 10FF (free for students).

At 17 Rue Victor Hugo, the **Musée Louis Vouland** (☎ 04 90 86 03 79) exhibits a fine collection of faïence (ceramics) and some superb pieces of 18th-century French furniture. It's open Tuesday to Saturday from 2 to 6 pm (also 10 am to noon from June to September). Entry costs 20FF (10FF for students and people over 65).

Villeneuve-lès-Avignon Avignon's picturesque sister city also has a few interesting sights. The **Chartreuse du Val de Bénédiction** (☎ 04 90 15 24 24) at 60 Rue de la République, a Carthusian charterhouse founded in the 14th century, is open daily from 9.30 am to 5.30 pm (9 am to 6.30 pm from April to September), but the ticket office closes half an hour earlier. Entry is 27FF (18FF for those

under 25 or over 60). You can also buy a 50FF combined ticket which allows you to visit all of the town's major sights.

The **Musée Pierre de Luxembourg** (☎ 04 90 27 49 66) on Rue de la République near Place Jean Jaurès has a fine collection of religious paintings, many of them from the 15th to the 17th centuries. The museum is open from 10 am to noon and 2 to 5.30 pm (closed Tuesday); from April to September hours are 10 am to 12.30 pm and 3 to 7 pm. Admission is 20FF (12FF concession).

The **Tour Philippe le Bel** (☎ 04 90 27 49 68), a defensive tower built in the 14th century at what was then the western end of Pont Saint Bénézet, has great views of Avignon's walled city, the river and the surrounding countryside. Another place to visit for a wonderfully Provençal panorama is the 14th-century **Fort Saint André**, which is open daily from 10 am to noon and 2 to 5 pm (October to March) and 9.30 am to 12.30 pm and 2 to 7 pm (April to June and September). In July and August it's open from 9 am to 7 pm. Entry is 21FF (14FF for students and those over 60).

From Avignon, Villeneuve can be reached by bus No 10, which you can catch in front of the main post office. Unless you want to take the grand tour of the Avignon suburb of Les

FRANCE

Angles, take a bus marked 'Villeneuve puis (then) Les Angles' (rather than 'Les Angles puis Villeneuve').

Places to Stay

Camping The attractive, shaded *Camping Bagatelle* (☎ 04 90 85 78 45; open all year) is on Île de la Barthelasse, slightly north of Pont Édouard Daladier. Charges are 20FF per adult, 8.50FF to pitch a tent and 8.50FF to park a car. To get there take bus No 10 from the main post office and get off at La Barthelasse stop.

Hostels The 210-bed *Auberge Bagatelle* (☎ 04 90 86 30 39) and its many amenities are part of a large, park-like area on Île de la Barthelasse that includes Camping Bagatelle. A bed costs 58FF; doubles with twin beds cost 137FF. Rooms are locked from 1 to 5 pm, but there's no curfew. See the previous Camping section for bus directions.

The friendly *Avignon Squash Club* (☎ 04 90 85 27 78) at 32 Blvd Limbert also serves as a hostel. A bunk in a converted squash court costs only 54FF (74FF in summer). Breakfast is 16FF; sheets cost 16FF also. Travellers can check in Monday to Saturday from 10 am to 10 pm; from May to October reception is open daily from 9 to 11 am and 5 to 11 pm (10 to 11 am and 6 to 7 pm on Sunday). The hostel is closed in winter. There is a bus from the main post office (get off at the Thiers stop).

Hotels During the festival, it is nearly impossible to find accommodation in Avignon unless you've booked months in advance.

Walled City The very proper *Hôtel du Parc* (☎ 04 90 82 71 55) at 18 Rue Agricol Perdiguier, only 300 metres from the train station, has singles without/with shower for 120/145FF and doubles without/with shower for 140/155FF. Rooms with shower and toilet are 190FF and a quad with shower is 245FF. Hall showers are 10FF. Across the street at No 17 is the *Hôtel Splendid* (☎ 04 90 86 14 46). Small well-kept rooms – most have showers – start at 140FF (160FF in summer). Doubles with all the amenities cost from 160FF (200FF in summer). Prices are cheaper if you stay a week or more. The friendly *Hôtel Innova* (☎ 04 90 82 54 10) at 100 Rue Joseph Vernet has doubles

without/with run-down showers for 130/160FF; doubles with shower and toilet cost 200 to 250FF. Hall showers are free.

The *Hôtel Mignon* (☎ 04 90 82 17 30; fax 04 90 85 78 46), three blocks west of Place de l'Horloge at 12 Rue Joseph Vernet, has beautifully decorated rooms with shower for 185 to 210FF and doubles/triples with shower, toilet and TV for 250/300FF. To get there by bus, take No 10 from in front of the main post office and get off at the Porte de l'Oulle.

Outside the Walls The family-run *Hôtel Monclar* (☎ 04 90 86 20 14) is across the tracks from the train station at 13 Ave Monclar. Eminently serviceable singles/doubles cost 100/160FF, 184FF with shower and 215FF with shower and toilet. Triples/quads with shower and toilet are 245/265FF. Parking is available at 20FF a day. The pleasant *Hôtel Saint Roch* (☎ 04 90 82 18 63) at 9 Rue Paul Mérindol has large, airy singles or doubles with bath, toilet and TV for 200 to 250FF and triples/quads for 280/375FF. Several rooms look out onto the lovely garden at the back. Prices in winter are about 10% cheaper. Breakfast is 30FF.

Places to Eat

The *Brasserie Le Palais* (☎ 04 90 82 53 42) at 36 Cours Jean Jaurès has lunch menus starting at 56FF and dinner menus for 76 and 92FF. Meals are served every day of the year from 11.30 am to 3 pm and 6.45 pm to midnight; during the festival, hours are 11.30 am to 1 am. There are several cheap places along Rue de la République, including the excellent sandwich shop *Sur Le Pouce* at No 26.

Restaurant Song-Long (☎ 04 90 86 35 00) at 1 Rue Carnot (next to Place Carnot) offers a wide variety of Vietnamese dishes, including vegetarian soups, salads, first courses and main dishes. Menus start at 45FF (lunch) and 55 or 78FF (dinner to 11 pm). There are quite a few restaurants on Rue Galante (a small street running south off Rue Rouge, near Place de l'Horloge), including Chinese and Vietnamese places and a very popular tapas bar.

If you're in the mood to splurge on French cuisine, you might try *Le Petit Bedon* (☎ 04 90 82 33 98) at 70 Rue Joseph Vernet, whose specialities include frogs' legs and escargots.

Menus (there's no à la carte service) cost 100FF (lunch only) and 150FF. The restaurant is closed on Sunday. The attractive *Café des Artistes* (☎ 04 90 82 63 16), at 21 Place Crillon by the Porte de l'Oulle, serves very good French fare at reasonable prices. Excellent lunch menus start at 55FF. It's open Monday to Saturday (daily during the festival) from noon to 2 pm and 8 to 11 pm.

On the other side of town, a good choice is *Woolloomooloo* (☎ 04 90 85 28 44) at 16bis Rue des Teinturiers. This informal, lively restaurant is open Tuesday to Saturday from noon to 2 pm and 7.30 pm to 1 am. Lunchtime menus are 48 to 58FF and vegetarian and Antillean dishes are on offer.

Near Place de l'Horloge, there's a *Casino* grocery at 22 Rue Saint Agricol (closed on Sunday). Avignon's fanciest food shops are along Rue Joseph Vernet and Rue Saint Agricol.

Entertainment

The Australian-run *Koala Bar* (☎ 04 90 86 80 87), a popular hang-out for English speakers, is at 2 Place des Corps Saints. A small beer on tap costs from 10FF, but the price drops to 6FF during happy hour (9 to 10 pm on Wednesday, Friday and Saturday).

The only movie theatre in town with non-dubbed movies is *Cinéma Utopia* (☎ 04 90 82 65 36) at 4 Rue Escaliers Ste Anne, just north of the Palais des Papes (there's also one screen in the centre of town at 5 Rue Figuière). The cinema also functions as a mini-cultural centre and jazz club. Tickets cost 30FF (24FF each if you buy a carnet of 10).

The *Opéra d'Avignon* (☎ 04 90 82 42 42) at Place de l'Horloge stages operas, operettas, theatre, symphonic concerts, chamber music and ballet from October to June. Performance prices in the fourth gallery/orchestra range from 30/120FF to 120/360FF, depending on what's playing. The ticket office is open Monday to Saturday from 11 am to 6 pm except during August.

Getting There & Away

Bus The bus station (☎ 04 90 82 07 35) is down the ramp to the right as you exit the train station. The information windows are open Monday to Friday from 8 am to noon and 2 to 6 pm (5 pm on Friday). Tickets are sold on the

buses, which are run by 19 different companies.

Places you can get to by bus include Aix-en-Provence (11 a day), Arles (four direct a day), Carpentras (about 15 a day), Nice (one a day), Nîmes (five a day), Orange (17 a day) and Marseille (five a day). Service on Sundays and during winter is less frequent. A schedule is posted in the waiting room.

Train The train station (☎ 08 36 35 35 39) is across Blvd Saint Roch from Porte de la République. The information office is open from 9 am to 6.15 pm (closed on Sunday and holidays). There are frequent trains to Arles (33FF, 25 minutes, 18 a day), Nice (180FF, four hours), Nîmes (44FF, 30 minutes, 16 a day) and Paris (400FF).

Car & Motorcycle Europcar Interent (☎ 04 90 14 40 80), at 2a Ave Monclar, rents cars for 415FF a day (with 200 free km) and 775FF for the weekend (with 600 free km), including tax and insurance. It's open Monday to Saturday.

Getting Around

TCRA municipal buses operate from 7 am to about 7.40 pm. On Sunday, buses are less frequent and most lines run only between 8 am and 6 pm. TCRA has offices in the walled city at Porte de la République (☎ 04 90 82 68 19) and at Place Pie (☎ 04 90 85 44 93; closed on Sunday). Tickets cost 6.50FF.

AROUND AVIGNON

The Provençal cities of Arles and Nîmes, famed for their well-preserved Roman antiquities, are only a short train or bus ride from Avignon. See Getting There & Away under Avignon for transport details.

Arles

Arles (population 52,000), set on the northern edge of the Camargue alluvial plain, began its ascent to prosperity and political importance in 49 BC when Caesar (to whom the city had given its support) captured and despoiled Marseille, which had backed the Roman general Pompey. It soon became a major trading centre, the sort of place that, by the late 1st century, needed a 20,000-seat amphitheatre and a 12,000-seat theatre. Now known as the

FRANCE

Arènes and the **Théâtre Antique** respectively, the two structures are still used to stage bullfights and cultural events.

Arles is also known for its **Cathédrale Saint Trophime** and **Cloître Saint Trophime**; significant parts of both date from the 12th century and are in the Romanesque style. It is probably best known as the place where Van Gogh painted some of his most famous works, including *The Sunflowers*. The tourist office (☎ 04 90 18 41 20) is on Esplanade des Lices.

Nîmes

The city of Nîmes (population 130,000) has some of the best preserved Roman structures in all of Europe. The **Arènes** (amphitheatre), which, unlike its counterpart at Arles, retains its upper storey, dates from around 100 AD and could once seat 24,000 spectators. Entry is 30FF (22FF for students). The rectangular **Maison Carrée**, a Greek-style temple measuring 26 by 15 metres, dates from the late 1st century BC and is largely intact.

The most important festival in Nîmes is La Feria at the end of March, with bullfights and concerts in the Arènes and parades and music in the streets. The helpful tourist office (☎ 04 66 67 29 11) is at 6 Rue Auguste. There is an annexe (☎ 04 66 84 18 13) at the train station.

Pont du Gard

Built by the Roman general Agrippa around 19 BC, the mighty Pont du Gard is not to be missed. This aqueduct, which spans the Gard River, is 275 metres long and 49 metres high. Apart from admiring the Romans' handiwork from a distance, you can also walk inside the aqueduct, where the water once flowed. There are buses to the Pont du Gard from Avignon, but there are more services from Nîmes.

Côte d'Azur

The Côte d'Azur, also known as the French Riviera, stretches along France's Mediterranean coast from Toulon to Menton and the Italian border. Many of the towns along the coast – Saint Tropez, Cannes, Antibes, Nice, Monaco – have become world-famous thanks to the recreational activities of the rich, idle and tanned. The reality is rather less glamorous, but the Côte d'Azur still has a great deal to attract visitors: sun, 40 km of beaches, all sorts of cultural activities and, sometimes, even a bit of glitter.

Unless you'll be camping or hostelling, your best bet is to stay in Nice, which has a generous supply of cheap hotels, and take day trips to other places in the area. The Côte d'Azur includes many seafront and hillside towns, such as Toulon, Saint Tropez, the Massif de l'Esterel, Grasse (renowned for its perfume production), Vence, Saint Paul de Vence and Roquebrune-Cap Martin. Make sure you don't miss Villefranche-sur-Mer and Èze; though close to Nice they offer a completely different view of the Riviera.

Trains run between Ventimiglia (just across the border in Italy) and Saint Raphaël – via Menton, Monaco, Nice, Antibes, Cannes and the many smaller towns – from early morning until late at night. See Getting There & Away in the Nice section for details.

Radio

The English-language Riviera Radio, based in Monte Carlo, can be heard on 106.3 MHz FM (in Monaco) and 106.5 MHz FM (along the rest of the Côte d'Azur). It broadcasts BBC World Service news every hour.

Dangers & Annoyances

Theft from backpacks, pockets, cars and even laundrettes is a serious problem along the Côte d'Azur. To avoid unpleasantness, keep a sharp eye on your bags, especially at train and bus stations, and use the lockers at train and bus stations if you'll be sleeping outside (say, on the beach). Again, *never* leave anything in a parked vehicle.

Getting Around

The Côte d'Azur is notorious for its traffic jams, so if you'll be driving along the coast, especially in summer, be prepared for slow going. Around Saint Tropez, for instance, it can sometimes take hours to move just a few km, which is why some of the truly wealthy have taken to reaching their seaside properties by helicopter.

NICE

Known as the capital of the Riviera, the fashionable yet relaxed city of Nice (population

To Sisteron (9 km),
Gap (57 km) &
Grenoble (140 km)

Digne-les-
Bains

ALPES-MARITIMES

N204 **ITALY**
To Genoa

To Avignon (65 km),
Lyon (280 km)
& Paris (740 km)

Castellane

N202

Sainte
Agnès

Gorbio

Sospel

San
Remo

Lac de
St-Croix

N85

Vence
Saint Paul de Vence

Èze

Menton
Roquebrune-Cap-Martin

Ventimiglia

MONTE CARLO
MONACO

A51

Grasse

Cagnes-sur-Mer

Biot

Nice

Saint Jean-Cap Ferrat

Villefranche

A7

Mandelieu-La Napoule

Cannes

Antibes
Juan-les-Pins
Cap d'Antibes

A8

Îles de Lérins

Draguignan

VAR

Les Arcs

Massif de
l'Esterel

Théoule-sur-Mer

Aix-en-Provence

N7

Fréjus

Saint Raphaël

To
Corsica

A8

N560

Saint Maxime

Marseille

N8

N97

Massif des Maures

Saint Tropez

Cap Camarat

A57

N98

D559

Côte d'Azur

Cassis

A50

Toulon

Bormes-les-
Mimosas

Corniche des Maures

La Ciotat

Bandol

Hyères

Le Lavandou

0   15   30 km

Porquerolles

Port
Cros

Île du Levant

To Tunisia
& Algeria

To Corsica
& Algeria

To Corsica
& Sardinia

Île de Porquerolles

Îles d'Hyères

Île de Port Cros

**MEDITERRANEAN
SEA**

346,000) makes a great base from which to explore the entire Côte d'Azur. The city, which did not become part of France until 1860, has plenty of relatively cheap accommodation and is only a short train or bus ride away from the rest of the Riviera. Nice's beach may be nothing to write home about, but the city is blessed with a fine collection of museums.

Orientation

Ave Jean Médecin runs from near the train station to Place Masséna. The Promenade des Anglais follows the curved beachfront from the city centre all the way to the airport, six km to the west. Vieux Nice is the area delineated by the Quai des États-Unis, Blvd Jean Jaurès and the 92-metre hill known as Le Château. The neighbourhood of Cimiez, home to several very good museums, is north of the town centre.

Information

Tourist Office From July to September, the main tourist office (☎ 04 93 87 07 07) at the train station is open daily from 8 am to 8 pm (until 7 pm the rest of the year). The tourist office annexe (☎ 04 93 87 60 60) at 5 Promenade des Anglais is open Monday to Saturday from 8 am to 6 pm.

Money There's a Banque de France at 14 Ave Félix Faure. There are numerous places where you can change money along Ave Jean Médecin near Place Masséna. The Banque Populaire de la Côte d'Azur at 17 Ave Jean Médecin has a 24-hour currency exchange machine. The Office Provençal Change at 17 Ave Thiers (to the right as you exit the train station) offers less-than-optimal rates but is open every day of the year from 7 am to midnight.

American Express (☎ 04 93 16 53 53) at 11 Promenade des Anglais is open Monday to Saturday from 9 am to 8 pm and on Sunday from 10 am to 6 pm.

Post The main post office (☎ 04 93 82 65 00), which will exchange foreign currency, is at 23 Ave Thiers, one block to the right as you exit the train station. There are branch post offices at 4 Ave Georges Clemenceau, on the corner of Rue de Russie, and in the old city at 2 Rue Louis Gassin. Nice's postcode is 06000 north of Ave Jean Jaurès (including the train station area) and 06300 south and south-east of there (including the old city).

Travel Agencies Council Travel (☎ 04 93 82 23 33) is one block from the train station at

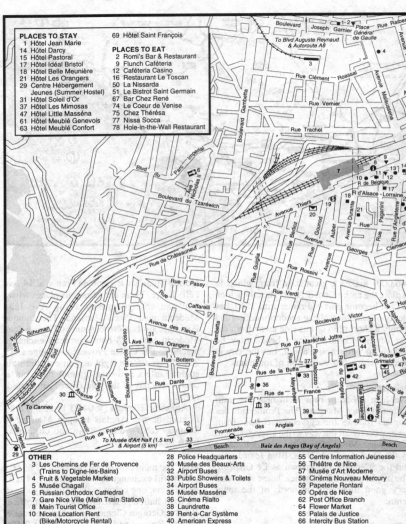

PLACES TO STAY
1   Hôtel Jean Marie
14 Hôtel Darcy
15 Hôtel Pastoral
17 Hôtel Idéal Bristol
18 Hôtel Belle Meunière
21 Hôtel Les Orangers
29 Centre Hébergement
    Jeunes (Summer Hostel)
31 Hôtel Soleil d'Or
37 Hôtel Les Mimosas
47 Hôtel Little Masséna
61 Hôtel Meublé Genevois
63 Hôtel Meublé Confort

69 Hôtel Saint François

PLACES TO EAT
2   Romi's Bar & Restaurant
9   Flunch Cafétéria
12 Caféteria Casino
16 Restaurant Le Toscan
50 La Nissarda
51 Le Bistrot Saint Germain
67 Bar Chez René
74 Le Coeur de Venise
75 Chez Thérésa
77 Nissa Socca
78 Hole-in-the-Wall Restaurant

OTHER
3   Les Chemins de Fer de Provence
    (Trains to Digne-les-Bains)
4   Fruit & Vegetable Market
5   Musée Chagall
6   Russian Orthodox Cathedral
7   Gare Nice Ville (Main Train Station)
8   Main Tourist Office
10 Nicea Location Rent
    (Bike/Motorcycle Rental)
11 USIT Voyages
13 Council Travel
16 Office Provençal Change
    (Currency Exchange)
20 Main Post Office
22 Laundrette
23 La Baraka Grocery
24 Église Notre Dame
25 The Cat's Whiskers (English Books)
26 Prisunic Supermarket
27 Nice Étoile Shopping Mall & FNAC Store

28 Police Headquarters
30 Musée des Beaux-Arts
32 Airport Buses
33 Public Showers & Toilets
34 Airport Buses
35 Musée Masséna
36 Cinéma Rialto
38 Laundrette
39 Rent-a-Car Système
40 American Express
41 Tourist Office Annexe
42 English-American Library
43 Anglican Church
44 US Consulate
45 Post Office Branch
46 Cycles Arnaud (Bike Rental)
48 UK Consulate
49 24-Hour Currency Exchange Machine
52 Banque de France
53 Sun Bus (Local Bus Information)
54 Station Centrale (Local Bus Terminus)

55 Centre Information Jeunesse
56 Théâtre de Nice
57 Musée d'Art Moderne
58 Cinéma Nouveau Mercury
59 Papeterie Rontani
60 Opéra de Nice
62 Post Office Branch
64 Flower Market
65 Palais de Justice
66 Intercity Bus Station
68 Food Shops (along Rue Pairolière)
70 William's Pub
71 Banque Populaire de la Côte d'Azur
72 Jonathan's Live Music Pub
73 Cathédrale Sainte Réparate
76 Église Saint Jacques le Majeur
79 Fruit & Vegetable Market
80 Buses to City Centre
81 Musée Terra Amata
82 Tour Bellanda & Lift
83 Ferry Terminal & SNCM Office

FRANCE

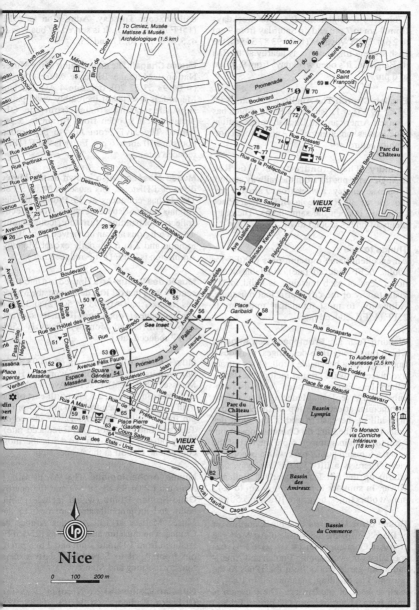

To Cimiez, Musée
Matisse & Musée
Archéologique (1.5 km)

0   100 m

Promenade

Boulevard

Jean

Pailon

66

67

68

Place
Saint
François

69   70

71

72

Rue de la Boucherie

Rue de la Côte

73

74   75

78   77

76

Rue Rossetti

Rue de la Préfecture

79

Cours Saleya

Parc du
Château

Allée Professeur Benoît

VIEUX
NICE

See Inset

To Cimiez

Tunnel

George V

Ménard

5

Blvd de Cimiez

Blvd de Cimiez

Avenue

Raimbaldi

Rue Assalit

Rue de départte

Rue Pertinax

Rue de Paris

Rue Lamartine

Rue Miron

Notre
Dame

Desambrois

Maréchal

Foch

25

Avenue

Biscarra

26

27

Rue

Dubouchage

Boulevard

Rue Delille

Rue Tondut de l'Escarène

Boulevard Carabacel

28

Avenue Jean Médecin

Boulevard

Rue Pastorelli

50

Rue Gubernatis

55

Avenue Saint Jean Baptiste

du

Pailon

57

56

Place
Garibaldi

58

Ave Gallieni

Esplanade Kennedy

Avenue de la République

Rue Barla

Rue Cassini

Rue Bonaparte

Rue Auguste Gal

Rue Arson

Rue de l'Hôtel des Postes

Rue
Blacas

Rue
Alberti

Giofredo

R Chauvain

51

49

52

Passage Émile
Négrin

Place
Masséna

té

Place
magenta

Verdun

din
pert
er

53

Avenue Félix Faure

Espace
Masséna

Square
Général
Leclerc

54

Promenade

Jean

Boulevard

Rue Rossetti

Rue de la
Préfecture

65

Rue A Mari

59   61

62

63

60

64

Place Pierre
Gautier

Cours Saleya

Quai des États - Unis

VIEUX
NICE

Parc du
Château

Jaurès

80

To Auberge de
Jeunesse (2.5 km)

Rue Foderé

Place Île de Beauté

Bassin
Lympia

Boulevard

81

Carnot

To Monaco
via Corniche
Inférieure
(18 km)

82

Bassin
des
Amiraux

Bassin
du
Commerce

83

Quai Rauba Capeu

Nice

0   100   200 m

37bis Rue d'Angleterre. It's open weekdays from 9 am to 7 pm and on Saturday from 9 am to 2 pm. USIT Voyages (☎ 04 93 87 34 96), the Irish student travel outfit, is nearby at 10 Rue de Belgique. It's open weekdays from 9.30 am to 6 pm.

English Church The Anglican Church (☎ 04 93 87 19 83) at 11 Rue de la Buffa, which has a mixed American and English congregation, functions as something of an Anglophone community centre.

Laundry The laundrette at 16 Rue d'Angleterre, not far from the railway station, is open seven days a week from 7 am to 9 pm; the one at 39 Rue de la Buffa, near Place Grimaldi, is open the same hours. There are plenty of others around town.

Things to See
An excellent-value museum pass (120FF for adults, 60FF reduced rate), available at the ticket desk of each museum, is valid for 15 visits to any of the city's principal museums. Admission to most municipal museums is 25FF (15FF reduced rate).

Walking Tour The **Promenade des Anglais**, which runs along Baie des Anges, provides a fine stage for a beachside stroll. Other attractive places to walk around include the Jardin Albert 1er, Espace Masséna (with its fountains) and Ave Jean Médecin (Nice's main commercial street). On top of the 92-metre-high hill at the eastern end of the Quai des États-Unis is the **Parc du Château** (open from 8 am to 7 pm in summer, 6 pm the rest of the year), a forested public park with a panoramic view. There is a lift (3.50FF one way, 5FF return) up the hill from under the Bellanda Tower. In summer it runs from 9 am to 6.45 pm. At other times, hours are 10 am to 5.50 pm.

Musée d'Art Moderne One block north-west of Place Garibaldi, the Musée d'Art Moderne et d'Art Contemporain (☎ 04 93 62 61 62) specialises in eye-popping French and American avant-garde works from the 1960s to the present. The building, inaugurated in 1990, is itself a work of modern art. The museum is open from 11 am to 6 pm (10 pm on Friday)

daily except Tuesday. Admission is 25FF (15FF for students). It is served by bus Nos 3, 4, 5, 7, 9, 10, 16, 17 and 25.

Musée Chagall The main exhibit of the Musée National Message Biblique Marc Chagall (☎ 04 93 53 87 20), opposite 4 Ave Docteur Ménard, is a series of incredibly vivid paintings illustrating stories from the Old Testament. It is open from 10 am to 5 pm (closed Tuesday). From July to September hours are 10 am to 6 pm. Entry is 28FF (18FF reduced rate).

Musée Masséna Also known as the Musée d'Art et d'Histoire, this museum (☎ 04 93 88 11 34) has entrances at 35 Promenade des Anglais and 65 Rue de France. The eclectic collection of paintings, furniture, icons, ceramics and religious art can be viewed from 10 am to noon and 2 to 6 pm daily except Monday. Admission is 25FF (15FF reduced rate).

Musée des Beaux-Arts Housed in a late 19th-century villa just off Rue de France, the Musée des Beaux-Arts (☎ 04 93 44 50 72) at 33 Ave des Baumettes is open from 10 am to noon and 2 to 6 pm (closed Monday). Entry is 25FF (15FF reduced rate).

Musée Matisse This museum (☎ 04 93 81 08 08), with its fine collection of works by Henri Matisse (1869-1954), is at 164 Ave des Arènes de Cimiez in Cimiez, 2.5 km north-east of the train station. It's open from 10 am to 5 pm (6 pm from April to September). It's closed on Tuesday. Entry is 25FF (15FF reduced rate). Many buses go there but No 15 is the most convenient. Get off at the Arènes stop.

Musée Archéologique The Archaeology Museum (☎ 04 93 81 59 57) and the nearby **Gallo-Roman Ruins** (which include public baths and an amphitheatre) are next to the Musée Matisse at 160 Ave des Arènes de Cimiez. The museum and the ruins (25/15FF) are open from 10 am to 1 pm and 2 to 5 pm (6 pm from April to September) daily except Sunday morning and Monday.

Russian Cathedral St Nicolas' Russian Orthodox Cathedral (☎ 04 93 96 88 02) crowned by six onion-shaped domes, was built between 1903 and 1912 in the style of the early 17th century. Step inside and you'll be transported to Imperial Russia, a world of Cyrillic script and gilded icons. The cathedral, opposite 17 Blvd Tzaréwitch, is open from 9 or 9.30 am to noon and 2.30 to 5 pm (5.30 pm in spring and autumn, and 6 pm in summer). The entry fee is 12FF (10FF for students). Shorts or short skirts and sleeveless shirts are forbidden.

Activities

Nice's **beach** is covered with smooth little rocks. Between mid-April and mid-October, the sections of beach open to the public without charge alternate with private beaches (60 to 70FF a day) offering all sorts of amenities (mattresses, showers, changing rooms, parasols, a reduced chance of theft etc). Along the beach you can hire catamaran paddle boats, sailboards and jet skis (300FF for 30 minutes), and go parasailing (200FF for 10 minutes) and water-skiing (100 to 130FF for 10 minutes). There are indoor showers (12FF) and toilets (2FF) open to the public opposite 50 Promenade des Anglais.

Places to Stay

In summer, lots of young people sleep on the beach. Theoretically this is illegal, but the Nice police usually look the other way.

Hostels The *Auberge de Jeunesse* (☎ 04 93 89 23 64) is five km east of the train station on Route Forestière du Mont Alban. Beds cost 64FF, including breakfast, and sheets are 15FF. There is a midnight curfew (1 am in summer). It's often full so call ahead. Take bus No 14 from the Station Centrale (the local bus terminal) on Square Général Leclerc, which is linked to the train station by bus Nos 15 and 17.

The *Relais International de la Jeunesse* (☎ 04 93 81 27 63; open all year) at 26 Ave Scuderi is four km north of the city centre in the wealthy neighbourhood of Cimiez. Take bus No 15 to get out there and get off at the Scuderi stop; it's a five-minute walk along Ave Scuderi. A dorm bed costs 70FF (including breakfast and showers) for the first night and 60FF for subsequent nights. The maximum stay in summer is three nights, but you can stay longer if you take half-board, which costs 120FF. This place is closed between 10 am and 5 pm and there is an 11 pm curfew. You can't make reservations, so call ahead to find out if there's room.

From mid-June to 10 September the *Centre Hébergement Jeunes* (☎ 04 93 86 28 75) serves as a hostel. It's at 31 Rue Louis de Coppet, half a block from 173 Rue de France. A bed in a six-bed room costs only 50FF. There is a midnight curfew. Bags must be stored in the luggage room during the day, which costs 10FF a day.

Hotels There are quite a few cheap hotels near the train station and lots of places in a slightly higher price bracket along Rue d'Angleterre, Rue d'Alsace-Lorraine, Rue de Suisse, Rue de Russie and Rue Durante, also near the station. There are plenty more to the east of the station, clustered around Rue Assalit and Rue Pertinax. In summer the inexpensive places fill up by late morning – come by or call ahead by 10 am.

Train Station Area The *Hôtel Belle Meunière* (☎ 04 93 88 66 15) at 21 Ave Durante, a clean, friendly place that attracts lots of young people, is an excellent bet. Dorm beds are 75 to 80FF. Large doubles/triples with high ceilings, some with century-old décor, or kitchenettes, start at 160/240FF (265/321FF with shower and toilet). All prices include breakfast. There's room to park out the front. This place is closed in December and January. Down the block at No 10bis, the *Hôtel Les Orangers* (☎ 04 93 87 51 41) has renovated but plain rooms with shower, hotplate and fridge. It costs 80FF for a dorm bed and from 90FF for a single. Doubles are 180 to 200FF and triples/quads are 270/340FF.

The *Hôtel Darcy* (☎ 04 93 88 67 06) at 28 Rue d'Angleterre has singles/doubles for 130/160FF (165/190FF with shower and toilet), breakfast included. From May to September, prices are increased by 10 to 30FF. The friendly *Hôtel Idéal Bristol* (☎ 04 93 88 60 72) at 22 Rue Paganini has cheaply furnished doubles, some with fridge, from 145FF (180FF with shower and toilet). Rooms with shower and toilet for four/five people are 340/425FF. There's no charge for showers and there's a rooftop terrace.

FRANCE

The *Hôtel Pastoral* (☎ 04 93 85 17 22) is just off Ave Jean Médecin at 27 Rue Assalit. Large, simple singles/doubles with fridge start at 105/120FF; showers cost 10FF. Doubles with shower and toilet are 170FF. Reception is open daily from 8 am to 3 pm and 6 to 10 pm.

Vieux Nice The *Hôtel Saint François* (☎ 04 93 85 88 69) at 3 Rue Saint François has small singles with small windows from 85FF, doubles with one/two beds for 127/164FF and triples from 216FF. Showers cost 15FF.

The *Hôtel Meublé Genevois* (☎ 04 93 85 00 58), in an unmarked building at 11 Rue Alexandre Mari (3rd floor), has 1950s-style singles/doubles with kitchenette from 120FF (with washbasin and bidet) and 180FF (with shower and toilet). Large studios with shower and toilet cost from 200FF for two people. Reception is open from 9.30 to 11 am and 3 to 6 pm. The *Hôtel Meublé Confort* (☎ 04 93 85 00 58), which is run by the same people and has similar prices, is down the block in an unmarked building at No 17 (4th floor). Both are near the Station Centrale – to get there take bus No 15 (or any of several other lines) from the train station.

Elsewhere in Town The *Hôtel Little Masséna* (☎ 04 93 87 72 34) is right in the centre of things at 22 Rue Masséna. Reception, which stays open until 7 pm, is on the 5th floor and, yes, there's a lift. Small studios for one or two people with hotplate, fridge and TV range from 130 to 220FF; showers are free. The relaxed, family-style *Hôtel Les Mimosas* (☎ 04 93 88 05 59) is at 26 Rue de la Buffa (2nd floor), a block north of the Musée Masséna. Depending on the season, good-sized, utilitarian rooms cost 100 to 130FF for one person and 120 to 180FF for two. Showers are free. You can check in here 24 hours a day.

The quiet *Hôtel Soleil d'Or* (☎ 04 93 96 55 94) is 1.3 km south-west of the train station at 16 Ave des Orangers. Simple singles with high ceilings cost 100FF, doubles start at 150FF, and an extra bed costs 50FF. Doubles with shower and toilet are 210FF. Hall showers cost 10FF.

The *Hôtel Jean Marie* (☎ 04 93 84 87 23) is 600 metres north of the train station at 15-17 Rue André Theuriet. The less-than-convenient location means that there may be rooms here

when other places are full. Dim but serviceable rooms (doubles only) start at 120/145FF without/with shower. There are no hall showers, but you can take a shower (11FF) in the annexe. Buses from Ave Jean Médecin include Nos 1, 2 and 22. Also in the northern part of town, *Madame Gregori Maurin* (☎ 04 93 52 84 15) has four rooms in a large house at 2 Rue Gare du Sud. A room for two costs 150FF including breakfast, lunch or dinner. Heading west from Place Général de Gaulle, Rue Gare du Sud is the first street on the left.

Places to Eat

Cheap places near the train station include the *Flunch Cafétéria* (☎ 04 93 88 41 35), which is to the left as you exit the station building and is open daily from 11 am to 9.30 pm (10 pm in summer) and, across the street at 7 Ave Thiers, the *Cafétéria Casino* (☎ 04 93 82 44 44) which is open from 8 am to 10 pm.

In the same vicinity, *Restaurant Le Toscan* (☎ 04 93 88 40 54; closed Sunday), a family-run Italian place at 1 Rue de Belgique, offers large portions of home-made ravioli. The menus (from 62FF) let you choose from a wide selection of dishes. There are lots of Vietnamese and Chinese restaurants on Rue Paganini, Rue d'Italie and Rue d'Alsace-Lorraine.

North of the railway station, *Romi's Bar & Restaurant* (☎ 04 93 51 83 71) at 7 Place Général de Gaulle offers a variety of wonderfully fresh plats du jour from 50FF. It's open for lunch and dinner daily except Tuesday. A huge traditional vegetable, fruit, flower and fish market is held nearby, along Ave Malaussena, every morning except Monday.

La Nissarda (☎ 04 93 85 26 29; closed Sunday) at 17 Rue Gubernatis has specialities of both Nice and Normandy. The menus are reasonably priced at 60, 78, 98 and 138FF. This place serves dinner to 9 pm. Nearby, *Le Bistrot Saint Germain* (☎ 04 93 13 45 12; closed Sunday) at 9 Rue Chauvain brings a touch of Paris to Nice, its walls decorated with photos of famous Parisian scenes. It offers fresh, seasonal food at affordable prices: you can choose from three plats du jour (59FF) or the menu (129FF).

In the old city, a perennial favourite with locals is *Nissa Socca* (☎ 04 93 80 18 35) at 5 Rue Sainte Reparate. Niçois specialities include socca, whose main ingredients are chickpea flour and olive oil. Pasta dishes are 36 to 40FF. Nissa Socca is closed all day Sunday, at midday on Monday, and all of January. Nearby streets, such as Rue de l'Abbaye, are lined with restaurants. For socca (10FF), Niçois-style sandwiches (12 to 17FF), pizza (6 to 10FF per piece) and other takeaway dishes, try *Bar Chez René* at 2 Rue Miralheti.

The *Prisunic* supermarket opposite 33 Ave Jean Médecin is open Monday to Saturday. A few blocks south-east of the train station, *La Baraka* grocery at 10 Rue de Suisse is open daily from 5 pm to 2 am. In Vieux Nice, there are a number of food shops along Rue Pairolière.

Entertainment

William's Pub-Biererie (☎ 04 93 85 84 66), opposite the intercity bus station at 4 Rue Centrale, has live rock music every night starting at around 10 pm (9 pm on Sunday). The pub itself is open Monday to Saturday from 9 pm to 6 am. There's pool, darts and chess in the basement. *Jonathan's Live Music Restaurant* (☎ 04 93 62 57 62), another bar à musique at 1 Rue de la Loge, near Rue Centrale, has live music (country, boogie-woogie, Irish folk etc) every night except Monday. *Hole-in-the-Wall Restaurant* (☎ 04 93 80 40 16) at 3 Rue de l'Abbaye offers both food and live music. Open from 8 pm to 1 am nightly except Monday, it has main dishes for 35 to 79FF and the famous salade niçoise for 38FF. Bottled beer is 22 to 40FF.

Getting There & Away

Air Nice's airport, Aéroport International Nice-Côte d'Azur (☎ 04 93 21 30 30), is six km west of the centre of town.

Bus Lines operated by some two dozen bus companies stop at the bus station, which is opposite 10 Blvd Jean Jaurès. The information counter (☎ 04 93 85 61 81) is open Monday to Saturday from 8 am to 6.30 pm. There is slow but frequent service every day until about 7.30 pm to Cannes (30FF one way, 1½ hours), Antibes (24.50FF one way, 1¼ hours), Monaco (18FF return, 45 minutes), Menton (24FF return, 1¼ hours) and Grasse (36FF one way, 1¼ hours).

Train The train station's information office (☎ 08 36 35 35 39) is open Monday to Saturday from 8 to 6.30 pm and Sunday from 8 to 11.30 am and 2 to 5.30 pm. There is fast, frequent service (up to 40 trains a day in each direction) to points all along the coast, including Monaco (18FF, 20 minutes), Antibes (21FF, 24 minutes) and Cannes (30FF, 35 minutes). From June to September there are trains every 20 minutes between 5 am and 11 or 11.30 pm. The rest of the year trains run at least once an hour except between 2 and 4 pm and after 8.30 pm. One of the two overnight trains to Paris (Gare de Lyon) is a sleeper (564FF). Second-class tickets cost 214FF to Rome and 362FF to Barcelona.

Ferry The fastest and least expensive ferries from mainland France to Corsica depart from Nice (see Getting There & Away in the Corsica section). The SNCM office (☎ 04 93 13 66 99) at the ferry port on Quai du Commerce is open from 8 am to noon and 2 to 5.45 pm daily except Saturday afternoon and Sunday. From mid-June to September, weekday hours are 6 am to 8 pm and Saturday hours are 6 am to noon. SNCM tickets can be purchased at many travel agencies. To get to the ferry port from Ave Jean Médecin, take bus No 1 or 2 and get off at the Port stop.

Getting Around

To/From the Airport From the bus station or the Promenade des Anglais, take the bus with the aeroplane logo (22FF). Buses run daily every 20 minutes (30 minutes on Sunday) from 5.50 am to 8.15 pm. From the train station or Rue de France, take bus No 23 (8FF). From the airport, buses run from 6.05 am to 10.45 pm (11.45 pm on Friday).

Bus Tickets cost 8FF for a single ride or 68FF for a carnet of 10. Bus No 12 links the train station with the beach. To go from the train station to Vieux Nice and the bus station, take bus No 15 or 17. Bus information and one, five and seven-day passes are available from the Centre d'Information (☎ 04 93 16 52 10) at 10 Ave Félix Faure (next to the Station Centrale, the main terminal for municipal buses).

Taxi Call ☎ 04 93 80 70 70 to order a taxi.

Car & Motorcycle Rent-a-Car Système (☎ 04 93 87 87 37) at 25 Promenade des Anglais rents Fiat Pandas for 298FF a day, including insurance and unlimited km. The excess is 1000FF. For 199FF a day, the excess is an outrageous 8000FF. The office is open Monday to Saturday from 8.30 am to 12.30 pm and 2 to 7 pm and Sunday from 9 am to noon.

Mopeds (from 150FF), scooters (from 325FF) and motorcycles can be rented from Nicea Location Rent (☎ 04 93 82 42 71) at 9 Ave Thiers, which is open Monday to Saturday from 9 am to 6 pm.

Bicycle Bicycles (120FF a day) can be rented from Nicea Location Rent (see Car & Motorcycle above). Cycles Arnaud (☎ 04 93 87 88 55) at 4 Place Grimaldi have mountain bikes for 100FF a day or 180FF for the weekend. It's open Monday to Friday from 9 am to noon and 2 to 7 pm.

ANTIBES

Across the Baie des Anges from Nice, Antibes has beautiful, sandy beaches, 16th-century ramparts that run along the sea, an attractive pleasure-boat harbour (Port Vauban) and an old city with narrow, winding streets and flower-bedecked houses. The tourist office (☎ 04 92 90 53 00) is at 11 Place de Gaulle.

The Château Grimaldi, set on a spectacular site overlooking the sea, now serves as the **Musée Picasso** (☎ 04 93 34 91 91). This outstanding museum at Place Mariejol is open from 10 am to noon and 2 to 6 pm (3 to 7 pm from July to September). It's closed on Tuesday and in November; entry is 20FF (10FF for students).

For accommodation, there is a *Relais International de la Jeunesse* (☎ 04 93 61 34 40; open all year) at 60 Blvd de la Garoupe at Cap d'Antibes. Dorm beds are 70FF a night. *La Belle Époque* (☎ 04 93 34 53 00) at 10 Ave du 24 Août, close to the bus station, has well-kept singles/doubles with shower for 173/196FF (223/246FF, including breakfast, from May to September). Doubles with shower and toilet are 236FF (286FF in the high season). From July to August you have to take half-board: 303/406FF for singles/doubles. For more luxurious accommodation try the *Relais du Postillon* (☎ 04 93 34 20 77) at 8 Rue Cham-

pionnet, across the park from the post office, or the *Auberge Provençale* (☎ 04 93 34 13 24) at 61 Place Nationale.

In the old city, Rue James Close has the greatest concentration of restaurants and food shops, but these establishments are fairly touristy. Further away, at 3 Rue Frédéric Isnard, near the town hall, the friendly *Le Brulot* (☎ 04 93 34 17 76) has lunch menus for 58FF. There are more restaurants nearby and on Place Nationale. A food market is held on Tuesday to Saturday mornings (daily from June to August) on Place Masséna, next to the Hôtel de Ville.

The bus station (☎ 04 93 34 37 60) is at Place Guynemer, just off Rue de la République. The train station is on Ave Robert Soleau; call ☎ 08 36 35 35 39 for information. There are frequent trains from Nice and Cannes.

CANNES

The harbour, the bay, Le Suquet hill, the beachside promenade, the beaches and the people sunning themselves provide more than enough natural beauty to make at least a day trip to Cannes (population 68,000) worth the effort. It's also fun watching the rich drop their money with such fashionable nonchalance.

Cannes is famous for its many festivals and cultural activities, the most renowned of which is the International Film Festival, which runs for two weeks in mid-May. People come to Cannes all year long, but the tourist season runs from May to October. During the off season, however, local people are more inclined to be friendly, prices are lower and there are no crowds to contend with.

Orientation

Rue Jean Jaurès, which runs in front of the train station, is four or five blocks north of the huge Palais des Festivals et des Congrès, to the west of which is the old port. Place Bernard Cornut Gentille (formerly Place de l'Hôtel de Ville) where the bus station is located, is on the north-western corner of the Vieux Port. Cannes' most famous promenade, the magnificent, hotel-lined Blvd de la Croisette, begins at the Palais des Festivals and continues eastward around the Baie de Cannes to Pointe de la Croisette.

Cannes

PLACES TO STAY

1. Pension Les Glycines
8. Hôtel de Bourgogne
10. Hôtel Atlantis
18. Hôtel National
19. Hôtel Chanteclair

PLACES TO EAT

9. Au Bec Fin
17. Restaurant Le Croco
20. Restaurants
21. Aux Bons Enfants

OTHER

2. Morning Food Market
3. Location Deux Roues (Bicycle & Scooter Rental)
4. Laundrette
5. Bus Station (to Grasse, Vallauris & Valbonne)
6. Tourist Office Annexe
7. Train Station
11. Office Provençal Change
12. Monoprix Supermarket
14. Champion Supermarket
15. Zanzi Bar
16. Food Shops
18. Marché Forville
22. Cristal Bar
23. Bus Station (To Nice)
24. Musée de la Castre
25. Cannes Info Jeunesse
26. CMC Ticket Office (Ferries to the Îles de Lérins)
27. Cannes English Bookshop
28. Post Office
29. American Express
30. Main Tourist Office
31. Palais des Festivals et des Congrès
32. Banque de France
33. Plages de la Croisette (Private Beaches)

To Auberge de Jeunesse (350 m)

To La Chalit Hostel (350 m)

To Pointe de la Croisette (2 km); Carlton Inter-Continental & Hôtel Martinez

To Free Public Beaches (Plages du Midi & Plages de la Bocca), Cannes-La Bocca & Caravaning Bellevue (Camping Ground) (5.5 km)

To Îles de Lérins

Baie de Cannes

Vieux Port

Public Beach

Jetée Albert Édouard

Esplanade George Pompidou

Boulevard de la Croisette

Square Brougham

Square J Hibert

Quai Saint Pierre

Le Suquet

Place Général de Gaulle

Place du 18 Juin

Place Gambetta

Place Bernard Cornut Gentille

Place Maréchal Joffre

Blvd de la République

Boulevard d'Alsace

Boulevard Jean Hibert

Blvd du Midi

Quai du Port

Rue d'Antibes
Rue Teisseire
Rue d'Antibes
Rue Chabaud
Rue des Frères
Rue Maceé
Rue H Vagliano
Rue Hoche
Rue Jean Jaurès
Rue des
Serbès
Rue Notre Dame
Rue du 24 Août
Rue des Belges
Rue Maréchal Foch
Rue Buttura
Rue Buttura
Rue d'Antibes
Rue Vénizélos
Rue Meynadier
Rue Faure
Rue Louis Blanc
Rue Félix Faure
Avenue de Grasse
Avenue du Nord
Avenue de Grasse
Avenue Buachaga Boualem
Avenue des Suisses
Avenue Louis Blanc
Rue Louis Pastour
Rue Louis
Rue G Guynemer
Rue Georges
Rue des Suisses
Rue du Suquet
Rue du Dr Sazagnac
Rue St Antoine
Rue de la Castre
Rue du Pré
Rue Clemenceau
Rue Maréchal Galliéni
Rue des Constantins en Constantins
Bivouac Napoléon
Pantiero
Rue Commandant André
Rue des États-Unis
Rue du Commandant André
Rue Perissol

Cannes

0   75   150 m

Information

Tourist Office The main tourist office (☎ 04 93 39 24 53) is on the ground floor of the Palais des Festivals. It's open Monday to Saturday from 9 am to 6.30 pm and, during festivals and conventions, on Sunday as well. In July and August, the office is open daily to 8 pm. The tourist office annexe (☎ 04 93 99 19 77) at the train station is open from 9 am to 1 pm and 2 to 6 pm. In July and August, it opens half an hour earlier and closes half an hour later. To get there, go left as you exit the terminal building and then walk up the stairs next to Frantour Tourisme.

Money & Post There are banks along Rue d'Antibes (two blocks towards the beach from Rue Jean Jaurès) and on Rue Buttura (across Blvd de la Croisette from the main tourist office). American Express (☎ 04 93 99 05 45) at 8 Rue des Belges, two blocks north-east of the Palais des Festivals, is open Monday to Friday from 9 am to 6 pm and on Saturday from 9 am to 1 pm.

There's a post office (☎ 04 93 39 14 11) at 22 Rue Bivouac Napoléon, two blocks inland from the Palais des Festivals, that exchanges foreign currency. Cannes' postcode is 06400.

Things to See & Do

Walking Tour Not surprisingly, the best places to walk are not far from the water. Some of the largest yachts you've ever seen are likely to be sitting in the **Vieux Port**, which was once a fishing port but is now given over to pleasure craft. The streets around the old port are particularly pleasant on a summer's night after dark, when the many cafés and restaurants – overflowing with well-heeled patrons – light up the whole area with coloured neon.

The hill just west of the old port, **Le Suquet**, affords magnificent views of Cannes, especially in the late afternoon and on clear nights. Musée de la Castre (see the following entry) is at the summit. The pine and palm-shaded walkway along **Blvd de la Croisette** is probably the classiest promenade on the whole Riviera.

Musée de la Castre This museum (☎ 04 93 38 55 26), housed in a chateau atop Le Suquet, has a diverse collection of Mediterranean and Middle Eastern antiquities as well as objects of ethnographic interest from all over the world. The museum, which costs 10FF (free for students), is open from 10 am to noon and 2 to 5 pm (closed Tuesday). From April to June and in September, afternoon hours are 2 to 6 pm; during July and August, they're 3 to 7 pm.

Beaches Each of the fancy hotels that line Blvd de la Croisette has its own private section of the beach. Unfortunately, this arrangement leaves only a small strip of sand near the Palais des Festivals for the bathing pleasure of the masses. Free public beaches, the **Plages du Midi** and **Plages de la Bocca**, stretch for several km westward from the old port along Blvd Jean Hibert and Blvd du Midi.

Islands The eucalyptus and pine-covered **Île Sainte Marguerite**, where the Man in the Iron Mask (made famous in the novel by Alexandre Dumas) was held captive during the late 17th century, lies just over a km from the mainland. The island, which measures 3.2 by 0.95 km, is crisscrossed and circumnavigated by many trails and paths. The smaller **Île Saint Honorat** was once the site of a renowned and powerful monastery founded in the 5th century.

The Compagnie Maritime Cannoise (☎ 04 93 38 66 33) and the Compagnie Esterel Chanteclair (☎ 04 93 39 11 82) run ferries to Île Saint Honorat (50FF return, 20 minutes) and Île Sainte Marguerite (45FF return, 20 minutes). Both islands (known as the Îles de Lérins) can be visited for 70FF. The ticket office, at the old port across Jetée Albert Édouard from the Palais des Festivals, is open daily from 7.30 am to 12.15 pm and 2 to 4.15 pm. From early May to August, it's open from 8.30 am to 6 pm and later for special outings.

Places to Stay

Hotel prices in Cannes fluctuate wildly according to seasonal demand. Tariffs can be up to 50% higher in July and August – when you'll be lucky to find a room at any price – than in winter. During the film festival, all the hotels are booked up to a year in advance.

Hostels Cannes' *Auberge de Jeunesse* (☎ 04 93 99 26 79), in a small villa at 35 Ave de Vallauris about 400 metres north-east of the

rain station, has beds in dorm rooms for four
o six people for about 80FF, though you must
ave an HI card (available for 75/104FF for
hose under/over 26). Sheets cost 10FF. Each
of the three floors has a kitchen, and there's a
aundry room. Reception is open from 8 am to
0.30 pm daily; curfew is at midnight (1 am at
veekends). The hostel is open all year.

An alternative to the official hostel is a very
leasant private one called *Le Chalit* (☎ 04 93
9 22 11) at 27 Ave du Maréchal Galliéni about
ive minutes walk north-west of the station. It
harges 80FF for a bed in rooms for four to
ight people. Sheets are 15FF extra. There are
wo kitchens. Le Chalit is open year-round and
here is no curfew, but you must leave a deposit
o get a key.

Iotels Cannes should have more places like
he *Hôtel Chanteclair* (☎ 04 93 39 68 88) at
2 Rue Forville. This well-maintained and
riendly hotel, a favourite with backpackers,
as singles/doubles from 140/180FF (mid-
October to mid-April) and rooms with shower
nd toilet for 260FF (during the film festival
nd from mid-July to mid-August). Triples/
uads with shower are 240/280FF (300/400FF
n the high season). Hall showers are free. The
Hôtel National (☎ 04 93 39 91 92) at 8 Rue
Maréchal Joffre has doubles starting at 160FF
190FF in the high season). Rooms with
hower are 190FF (250FF high season) or
20FF (300FF) with shower and toilet.

The large *Hôtel Atlantis* (☎ 04 93 39 18 72)
s half a block south of the train station at 4 Rue
u 24 Août. Despite its two-star rating, it has
ingles/doubles with washbasin, bidet and TV
rom only 145/160FF in the low season.
Rooms with shower cost 200/230FF or 230/
50FF with shower and toilet. Prices are hiked
p by about 50FF during the festival and in July
nd August. The *Hôtel de Bourgogne* (☎ 04
3 38 36 73) at 13 Rue du 24 Août has singles/
oubles for 160/180FF in the off season and
70/220FF in summer. Showers are free.
ingles or doubles with shower, toilet and TV
re 200FF (220 to 250FF in summer).

Places to Eat
There are a few small, cheap restaurants
round the Marché Forville (a block north of
Place Bernard Cornut Gentille) and many little

(but not necessarily cheap) restaurants along
Rue Saint Antoine, which runs north-west
from Place Bernard Cornut Gentille.

Near the train station, *Au Bec Fin* (☎ 04 93
38 35 86) at 12 Rue du 24 Août is often filled
with regulars. You can choose from two excellent plats du jour for 50 to 55FF. This place is
open for lunch and dinner, but is closed on
Saturday evening and Sunday. Another good
choice is the popular *Aux Bons Enfants* at 80
Rue Meynadier. It offers regional dishes in a
convivial atmosphere; menus are 59FF (lunch
only) and 90FF. It's open for lunch and dinner
on weekdays and for lunch on Saturday (in
June and July it's also open on Saturday
evening). There are several other small restaurants at this end of Rue Meynadier.

One of the cheapest restaurants in Cannes is
Restaurant Le Croco (☎ 04 93 68 60 55), on
Rue Louis Blanc, just south of Ave des Anciens
Combatants. Pizzas, grilled meat and fish and
shish kebabs are the main items on the menu.
Plats du jour start at 40FF and menus are 59FF
(lunch) and 89FF.

There's a *Monoprix* supermarket (closed
Sunday) on the corner of Rue Buttura and Rue
Vénizélos, half a block towards the beach from
the train station. A morning food market is held
on Place Gambetta from Tuesday to Sunday
(daily in summer). There are quite a few food
shops along Rue Meynadier, a pedestrian mall
two blocks inland from the old port. One block
north of Place Bernard Cornut Gentille along
Rue du Docteur Gazagnaire is the *Marché
Forville*, a fruit and vegetable market that's
open every Tuesday to Saturday morning
(daily in summer).

Getting There & Away
Bus Buses to Nice (30FF one way, 1½ hours),
Nice's airport (70FF one way, 45 minutes),
Antibes (12.50FF, 25 minutes) and other destinations, most of them operated by Rapides
Côte d'Azur, leave from Place Bernard Cornut
Gentille. Buses to Nice's airport leave every
hour on the hour from 8 am to 7 pm; the last
bus is at 9.15 pm. The bus information office
(☎ 04 93 39 11 39) is open Monday to Saturday
from 8 am to noon and 2 to 6 pm and Sunday
to 2 pm.

Buses to Grasse (line No 600), Vallauris,
Valbonne and elsewhere depart from the bus
station, which is to the left as you exit the train

FRANCE

station. The information counter (☎ 04 93 39 31 37) is open from 9 am to noon and 2 to 6.30 pm (closed Wednesday, Sunday and holidays).

Train The train station (☎ 08 36 35 35 39) is five blocks inland from the Palais des Festivals on Rue Jean Jaurès. The information office (on the 1st floor over the left-luggage office) is open Monday to Saturday from 8.30 am to 6 pm. Opening hours are 8.30 am to 7 pm from mid-July to mid-September. Trains to Antibes cost 13FF and take 10 minutes; to Fréjus-Saint Raphaël, the fare is 32FF (30 minutes).

Getting Around
Bus Bus Azur serves Cannes and destinations up to 11 km from town. Its office (☎ 04 93 39 18 71) at Place Bernard Cornut Gentille, in the same building as Rapides Côte d'Azur, is open Monday to Saturday from 7 am to 7 pm. Tickets cost 7FF and a carnet of 10 is 49FF.

Taxi Call ☎ 04 92 99 27 27 to order a taxi.

MENTON
Menton (population 30,000), reputed to be the warmest spot on the Côte d'Azur, is next to the Italian frontier. Set in the Baie du Garavan and the Baie du Soleil, it is encircled by mountains which protect it from the mistral. It's very pleasant to wander around the narrow, winding streets of the old city and up to the cemetery, from where there are scenic views of the bay and surrounding hills.

Menton is renowned for its production of lemons and holds a two-week Fête du Citron that begins every year sometime between mid-February and early March. During the Fête Médiévale de la Saint Jean (held on the third weekend in June) people don medieval garb for a historic parade complete with troubadours. Menton is a good base from which to explore the nearby historic villages of Sospel, Gorbio and Sainte Agnès, as well as the Parc National du Mercantour.

Orientation
The Promenade du Soleil runs more or less east-west along the beach; the railway tracks run more or less east-west about 400 metres inland. Ave Boyer and Ave de Verdun (on either side of the wide centre strip) run perpendicular

to both. The Vieille Ville is on and around the hill at the eastern end of the Promenade du Soleil. The port is east of the old city. Ave Édouard VII links the train station with the beach. Ave Boyer, where the tourist office is, is 200 metres west of the station along Ave de la Gare.

Information
The helpful tourist office (☎ 04 93 57 57 00) is in the Palais de l'Europe at 8 Ave Boyer. It's open Monday to Saturday from 8.30 am to 6 pm and, during winter festivals, on Sunday from 10 am to 12.30 pm. From mid-June to mid-September it's open from 8.30 am to 7.30 pm every day except Sunday, when hours are 8.30 am to 12.30 pm. There are lots of banks on Ave Carnot and Ave Félix Faure.

Things to See & Do
The **beach** along the Promenade du Soleil is public and, like Nice's, is carpeted with smooth pebbles. The better, private beaches lie east of the old city in the pleasure port area, the main one being **Plage des Sablettes**.

Église Saint Michel, the grandest baroque church in this part of France, sits perched in the centre of the **Vieille Ville**, with its many narrow and winding passageways. The church is open from 10 am to noon and 3 to 6 pm except Saturday mornings. The ornate interior is Italian in inspiration. Further up the hill is the cypress-shaded **Cimetière du Vieux Château**, which is open from 7 am to 6 pm (8 pm from May to September). Graves of English, Irish, North Americans, New Zealanders and other foreigners who died here during the 19th century can be seen in the cemetery's south-west corner (along the road called Montée du Souvenir). The view is worth the climb.

The **Musée Jean Cocteau** (☎ 04 93 57 7 30) is near the old city on Quai de Monléon and features the artist's drawings, tapestries and ceramics. It is open from 10 am to noon and 2 to 6 pm (closed Tuesday); afternoon hours are 3 to 7 pm from mid-June to mid-September. Entry is free. More of Cocteau's distinctive work can be seen in the Hôtel de Ville's Salle des Mariages (☎ 04 93 57 87 87) at Place Ardoïno, which is still used for wedding ceremonies. It is open Monday to Friday from 8.30 am to 12.30 pm and 1.30 to 5 pm. Entry is 5FF.

Places to Stay

Camping The *Camping Saint Michel* (☎ 04 93 35 81 23; open from April to 30 September), just off Route des Ciappes de Castellar, is best reached by walking eastward from the bus and train stations along Chemin des Terres Chaudes, which runs along the north side of the train tracks (turn left at the end). Tariffs are 16FF per person, 16FF for a small tent and 17FF for a car.

Camping Fleur de Mai (☎ 04 93 57 22 36; open from Easter to mid-October) at 67 Val de Gorbio is two km west of the train station. Two people with a car and a small tent pay 90FF. The simplest way to get there is to walk westward on the street one block inland from the Promenade du Soleil, and then turn right onto Ave Florette, which becomes Route de Gorbio. Both camping grounds have a two-star rating.

Hostel The *Auberge de Jeunesse* (☎ 04 93 35 93 14) on Plateau Saint Michel (the hill north-east of the train station) is next to Camping Saint Michel. Bed and breakfast is 64FF and sheets are 12FF. Daytime closure is from 10 am to 5 pm, and there is a midnight curfew. The hostel is closed in December and January. Between 7 am and 7 pm (8 pm in summer), you can get to the hostel from the train station by a privately run minibus that operates something like a shared taxi. From the bus station it only runs twice in the morning and twice in the afternoon. You can also take bus No 6 – get off at the Saint Michel stop.

Hotels Opposite the train station at Place de la Gare, *Hôtel Le Terminus* (☎ 04 93 35 77 00) has a few basic singles or doubles for 150FF; rooms with shower and toilet are 210FF. Showers are free. Reception is closed after noon on Saturday and after 5 pm on Sunday. The hotel may be closed for one week in mid-November. The friendly *Hôtel de Belgique* (☎ 04 93 35 72 66) at 1 Ave de la Gare has singles/doubles from 140/187FF or doubles with shower and toilet for 260FF. All rooms have TV. The *Hôtel Le Parisien* (☎ 04 93 35 54 08) at 27 Ave Cernuschi is just west of the train station and only 100 metres from the beach. Singles/doubles start at 160/200FF or 220/250FF with shower and toilet; all rooms have TV and air-con. Parking is free.

Places to Eat

Au Pistou (☎ 04 93 57 45 89) at 2 Rue du Fossan, behind the Nouvelles Galeries department store, has local specialities. The *Marché Municipal*, also known as Les Halles, is in the old city on Quai de Monléon. Food of all sorts is on sale daily from 5 am to 1 pm. Just across the border in Vintimille (Ventimiglia) is a huge market selling everything from food to imitation designer clothes every Friday until 5 pm.

Getting There & Away

Bus The bus station (☎ 04 93 35 93 60) is next to 12 Promenade Maréchal Leclerc, the northern continuation of Ave Boyer. The information office is open Monday to Friday from 9 am to noon and 2 to 6 pm and from 8 am to noon on Saturday.

Train The information desk at the train station, which is at Place de la Gare, is open daily. The ticket offices offer the same services daily from 5 am to 7.30 pm. Call ☎ 08 36 35 35 39 for more information.

Monaco

The Principality of Monaco, which has been under the rule of the Grimaldi family for most of the period since 1297, is a sovereign state whose territory, surrounded by France, covers only 1.95 sq km. It has been ruled since 1949 by Prince Rainier III (born in 1923), whose sweeping constitutional powers make him far more than a figurehead. The citizens of Monaco (Monégasques), of whom there are only 5070 (out of a total population of 30,000), pay no taxes. The official language is French, although efforts are being made to revive the country's traditional dialect. The official religion is Catholicism. There are no border formalities upon entering Monaco and a visit here makes a perfect day trip from Nice.

Orientation

Monaco consists of four principal areas: Monaco Ville, a 60-metre-high outcrop of rock 800 metres long (also known as the old city or the Rocher de Monaco), south of the Port of Monaco; Monte Carlo, famed for its casino and

FRANCE

Monaco

0   100   200 m

N7

To Menton

To Menton

To Lavotto, Cinéma
d'Eté & Monte
Carlo Sporting Club

Place
des
Moulins

Route de la Moyenne Corniche

Boulevard de Verdun

Boulevard de la Turbie

Avenue du Carnier

Avenue Maréchal Foch

Avenue de la République

Avenue de Grande Bretagne

Boulevard des Moulins

Boulevard du Larvotto

Avenue Princesse Grace

Avenue de France

Blvd de France

Blvd du Général
Leclerc

Escalier
du Riviéra

Blvd de la République

Avenue
Madone

Avenue de
la Madone

Avenue des Spélugues

Rue Princesse Charlotte

Rue Ste Céc

Beausoleil

FRANCE

To Nice

Boulevard Princesse Charlotte

Avenue
Henri
Dunant

Avenue
Princesse Alice

Square
Beaumarchais

Place du
Casino

Monte Carlo

Boulevard
Louis II

Avenue de la
Costa

Avenue

Avenue de Monte Carlo

Avenue de la Villaine

Avenue de

Ave Paul Doumer

Ave Paul Doumer

Rue Pasteur

Boulevard de Suisse

Avenue de la

Avenue d'Ostende

Avenue du Président JF Kennedy

Quai des Etats-Unis

**MEDITERRANEAN
SEA**

Place
Saint Dévote

Rue Grimaldi

Boulevard Albert 1er

Quai Albert 1er

Quai Albert 1er

Quai Albert 1er

*Port
de
Monaco*

Rue Suffren Reymond

Rue Princesse
Antoinette

Rainier III

Boulevard

**La
Condamine**

Quai Antoine 1er

Avenue de la Porte Neuve

Avenue de la Quarantaine

Ave des Jardins

Route de la Moyenne Corniche

Avenue Hector Otto

Avenue Hector Otto

Jardin
Exotique

Boulevard de Belgique

Avenue Crovetto Frères

Ave Hector Otto

Rue Plati

Rue Plati

Rue Plati

Boulevard Rainier III

Boulevard Charles III

Ave Prince

Rue de la
Turbie

R Princesse Caroline

R de Millo

Place
d'Armes

Place
du
Palais

**Monaco
Ville**

Avenue Saint Martin

Rue des Remparts

Avenue des Pins

Place de la
Visitation

Rue Pierre

Rue Comte
Félix Gastaldi

*Port
de
Fontvieille*

Avenue du
Hélitoire
Albert

Avenue des Papalins

Quai des
Sanbarbani

Fontvieille

To Cap d'Ail,
France (200 m)
& Nice (16 km)

2
3
4
5
6
7
8
9
10
11
12
13
14
15
16
17
18
19
20
21
22
23
24
25
26
27
28
29
30
31
32
33
34

FRANCE

PLACES TO STAY		4	Public Lift Entrance	22	Public Lift to Parking
6	Hôtel Cosmopolite (Beausoleil)	5	Public Lift		Pêcheurs
29	Hôtel Cosmopolite (La Condamine) & Hôtel de France	7	Laundrette	23	Musée Océanographique
		8	American Express	24	Cathedral
		9	Codec Top Supermaket	25	Musée des Souvenirs Napoléoniens
30	Youth Hostel	11	Tourist Office		
		12	Casino of Monte Carlo	26	Palais du Prince
PLACES TO EAT		14	Main Post Office	27	Rampe Major (Path to Palais du Prince)
10	Le Bistroquet	15	CAM Office (Local Bus Company)		
13	Café de Paris			28	Food Market
19	Stars 'n' Bars	16	Public Lift Entrance	31	Train Station
		17	Public Lift Entrance	32	Post Office
OTHER		18	Monaco Market Super- market	33	Musée d'Anthropologie Préhistorique
1	Plages du Larvotto				
2	Public Lift Entrance	20	Fort Antoine	34	Public Lift
3	Musée National	21	Post Office		

its Grand Prix motor race in late May, north of the port; La Condamine, the flat area around the port; and Fontvieille, an industrial area south-west of Monaco Ville and the port of Fontvieille. The French town of Beausoleil is just north of Monte Carlo.

Information

Tourist Office The Office National de Tourisme (☎ 04 92 16 61 16) is at 2a Blvd des Moulins, across the public gardens from the casino. It is open Monday to Saturday from 9 am to 7 pm, and Sunday from 10 am to noon. From mid-June to mid-September, several tourist office kiosks are set up around the principality, including one at the train station, next to the Jardin Exotique and on the Quai des États-Unis, which runs along the north side of the port.

Money The currency of Monaco is the French franc. Both French and Monégasque coins are in circulation, but the latter are not widely accepted outside the principality.

In Monte Carlo, you'll find lots of banks in the vicinity of the casino (along Ave Princesse Alice, for instance). In La Condamine, try Blvd Albert 1er. American Express (☎ 04 93 25 74 45), near the tourist office at 35 Blvd Princesse Charlotte, is open weekdays from 9 am to noon and 2 to 6 pm, and on Saturday to noon.

Post & Communications Monégasque stamps, one of the principality's few symbols of independence, are valid only within Monaco. Postal rates are the same as in France. The main post office (☎ 04 93 25 11 11) is in Monte Carlo at 1 Ave Henri Dunant (inside the Palais de la Scala). It does not exchange foreign currency. Other post offices are at Place de la Mairie in Monaco Ville, near the Musée Océanographique, and near the train station (look for the sign of the Hôtel Terminus). Monaco's postcode is 98000.

Monaco's public telephones accept either Monégasque or French phonecards. The country telephone code for Monaco is ☎ 377.

Things to See & Do

Palais du Prince The changing of the guard takes place outside the Palais du Prince de Monaco (☎ 04 93 25 18 31) every day at precisely 11.55 am. From June to September about 15 rooms in the palace are open to the public every day from 9.30 am to 6.30 pm (10 am to 5 pm in October). Entry is 30FF (15FF for children and students). Guided visits (35 minutes) in English leave every 15 or 20 minutes.

Musée des Souvenirs Napoléoniens In the south wing of the Palais du Prince, this museum (☎ 04 93 25 18 31) displays some of Napoleon's personal effects (handkerchiefs, a sock etc) and a fascinating collection of princely bric-a-brac (medals, coins, swords, uniforms). The museum is open daily except Monday and is closed in November. Tickets, which costs 20FF (10FF for children), are sold from 10.30 am to 12.30 pm and 2 to 5 pm. From

June to September they're on sale from 9.30 am to 6.30 pm.

Musée Océanographique If you're going to go to one aquarium on your whole trip, the world-renowned Oceanographic Museum (☎ 04 93 15 36 00), with its 90 sea-water aquariums, should be it. This is also one of the few aquariums in the world to have living coral. Upstairs are all sorts of exhibits on ocean exploration. The museum, which is on Ave Saint Martin in Monaco Ville, is open daily from 9 or 9.30 am to 7 pm (8 pm from June to August); from November to February hours are 10 am to 6 pm. The entry fee – brace yourself – is 60FF (30FF for students).

Walk around the Rock The touristy streets and alleys facing the palace are surrounded by beautiful, shaded gardens offering great views of the entire principality (as well as a good bit of France and some of Italy).

Jardin Exotique The steep slopes of the wonderful Jardin Exotique (☎ 04 93 30 33 65), which is at one end of the No 2 bus line, are home to some 7000 varieties of cacti and succulents from all over the world. The spectacular view is worth at least half the admission fee of 36FF (18FF for students), which also gets you into the **Musée d'Anthropologie Préhistorique** and includes a half-hour guided visit to the **Grottes de l'Observatoire**, caves located 279 steps down the hillside. The garden is open daily from 9 am to 6 or 7 pm depending on the season.

Casino The drama of watching people risk their money in Monte Carlo's incredibly ornate casino (☎ 04 92 16 21 21), built between 1878 and 1910, makes visiting the gaming rooms almost worth the stiff entry fees: 50FF for the Salon Ordinaire (which has French roulette and trente-quarante) and 100FF for the Salons Privés (baccarat, blackjack, craps, American roulette etc). You must be at least 21 to enter. Shorts are forbidden in the Salon Ordinaire; men must wear a tie and jacket after 9 pm in the Salons Privés. Income from gambling accounts for 4.95% of Monaco's total state revenues.

Places to Stay

There are no cheap places to stay in Monaco, and less expensive accommodation is scarce and often full. Over 75% of Monaco's hotel rooms are classified as 'four-star deluxe'.

Hostels The *Centre de la Jeunesse Princesse Stéphanie* (☎ 04 93 50 83 20), Monaco's HI hostel, is at 24 Ave Prince Pierre, 120 metres up the hill from the train station. You must be aged between 16 and 31 to stay here. The cost is 70FF per person, including breakfast and sheets. Stays are usually limited to one night during summer. Beds are given out each morning on a first-come-first-served basis; numbered tickets are distributed from 7.30 or 8 am. Registration begins at 10.30 am but rooms only become free after 11.30 am.

The *Relais International de la Jeunesse* (☎ 04 93 78 18 58) on the waterfront at Ave R Grammaglia in Cap d'Ail is another good option, as it is very close to the train station, which is the stop just before Monaco. This place, which is open from April to October, is run by the same people as the Relais International in Nice. See Places to Stay in the Nice section for information on prices, curfew and daytime closure.

Hotels The *Hôtel Cosmopolite* (☎ 04 93 30 16 95) at 4 Rue de la Turbie in La Condamine still has some of the cheapest rooms in the principality. Basic singles/doubles cost 186/200FF or 272/310FF with shower.

The other, unrelated *Hôtel Cosmopolite* (☎ 04 93 78 36 00), at 19 Blvd du Général Leclerc in Beausoleil and up the hill from the casino, offers better value if you want all the amenities. Very comfortable singles/doubles with shower, toilet and TV cost 250/280FF. The all-you-can-eat breakfast buffet is 30FF. The even-numbered side of the street is in Monaco and is called Blvd de France. The nearest bus stop is Crémaillère, served by bus Nos 2 and 4. The *Hôtel de France* (☎ 04 93 30 24 64) at 6 Rue de la Turbie has similar singles/doubles/triples with shower, toilet and TV for 295/360/450FF.

Places to Eat

There are a few cheap restaurants in La Condamine along Rue de la Turbie. Lots of touristy

estaurants of more or less the same quality can
be found in the streets leading off from Place
du Palais.

Le Bistroquet (☎ 04 93 50 65 03) at 11
Galerie Charles III on Ave des Spélugues in
Monte Carlo is fairly up-market but has good-
value plats du jour for 55FF. It's open from
noon to 6 am (7 am on weekends) and is closed
on Wednesday during the off season. A local
favourite is *Tea for Two* (☎ 04 93 50 10 10) at
1 Blvd Albert Ier in La Condamine. The *Café
de Paris* (☎ 04 92 16 23 00) at Place du Casino
is a great place to sit but a beer and a sandwich
will cost you around 72FF!

The *Codec Top* supermarket opposite 33
Blvd Princesse Charlotte, a block from the
main tourist office, is open daily except
Sunday. It has an in-house bakery. In La Condamine, there's a covered food market every
morning in the new building at Place d'Armes.

Getting There & Away

Bus There is no single bus station in Monaco;
intercity buses leave from various points
round the city.

Train The train station, which is part of the
French national railway network, is on Ave
Prince Pierre. See Getting There & Away in the
Nice section for more information. The
station's information office is open daily from
9.15 am to noon and 2.30 to 4.20 pm; in
summer it closes at 6 pm. You can exchange
foreign currency here, but the rates are not very
good.

Getting Around

Bus Monaco's urban bus system has six lines.
You're most likely to use line No 2, which links
Monaco Ville with Monte Carlo and then loops
back to the Jardin Exotique. Rides cost 8.50FF
and eight-ride magnetic cards are on sale from
bus drivers for 30FF. The bus system operates
daily until 8.45 or 9 pm; bus maps are available
at the tourist office. CAM, the bus company
(☎ 04 93 50 62 41 for information), has offices
at 3 Ave Président John F Kennedy, on the
north side of the port.

Taxi Taxis can be ordered by calling ☎ 04 93
50 01 01 or 04 93 50 56 28.

Lift Twelve large public lifts *(ascenceurs
publics)* operate up and down the hillside. Most
of them operate from 6 am to 10 pm.

Corsica

Corsica (Corse in French) is the most mountainous and geographically diverse of all the
islands of the Mediterranean. Though measuring only 8720 sq km, in many ways Corsica
resembles a miniature continent, with 1000 km
of coastline, soaring granite mountains that
stay snowcapped until July, a huge national
park (the Parc Naturel Régional de Corse),
flatland marshes (along the east coast), an
uninhabited desert (the Désert des Agriates) in
the north-west and a 'continental divide'
running down the middle of the island. Much
of the island is covered with the typically
Corsican form of vegetation called *maquis*,
with its low, dense shrubs providing many of
the spices used in Corsican cooking. During
WWII, the French Résistance became known
as Le Maquis because the movement was so
active in Corsica.

Corsica was ruled by Genoa from the 13th
century until the Corsicans *(u populu corsu)*,
led by the extraordinary Pasquale (Pascal in
French) Paoli, declared the island independent
in 1755. But its independence was short-lived.
France took over Corsica in 1769 and has ruled
it ever since – except for a period in 1794-96,
when it was under English domination, and
during the German and Italian occupation of
1940-43.

Despite having spent only 14 years as a
self-governed country, the people of Corsica
(who now number about a quarter of a million)
have retained a fiercely independent streak.
Though few support the Front de Libération
National de la Corse (FLNC) and other violent
separatist organisations, whose initials and
slogans are spray-painted on walls and road
signs all over the island, they remain very
proud of their language, culture and traditions.

The symbol of a black head wearing a ban-
danna that you see everywhere in Corsica is the
Tête de Maure (Moor's Head), the island's
emblem, which dates back to the time of the
Crusades. The Corsicans, like the Irish, have a

FRANCE

LIGURIAN
SEA

To Mainland France
(170 km)

To Marseille, Toulon & Nice

To Marseille & Nice

To Genoa

To Marseille, Toulon & Nice

To Genoa, La Spezia, Livorno & Piombino

NOTE: Some
ferry services
are infrequent
and/or seasonal

Barcaggio

Centuri-Port

Macinaggio

Pino

Cap
Corse

Nonza

Marine de
Pietracorbara

Erbalunga

Golfe de
Saint Florent

Désert des
Agriates

Saint Florent

Bastia

Étang de
Biguglia

D80

L'Île
Rousse

D81

HAUTE-
CORSE

N193

Algajola

Balagne Region

N197

Aéroport de
Bastia-Poretta

Plage de la Marana

Plage de Pineto

Calvi

Aéroport Calvi-
Sainte Catherine

Coastal
boat
services

Calenzana

Golo River

Ponte Leccia

Réserve de
Scandola

Galéria

Girolata

Haut
Asco

Parc Naturel
Régional
de la Corse

Monte
Cinto
(2706 m)

Castagniccia Region

Monte
San Petrone
(1767 m)

Morlani-Plage

Vergio
Ski Station

Gorges du Tavignano

Corte

Parc Naturel
Régional
de la Corse

N198

To Italy
(80 km)

Golfe de
Porto

Porto

Ota

Évisa

D84

Gorges de la Restonica

Les Calanche

Capo Rosso

Plana

Gorges de
Spelunca

Forêt
d'Altone

Monte
Rotondo
(2622 m)

Tavignano River

Plage
d'Arone

D81

Cargèse

D70

Vivario

N200

Aléria

Golfe de
Pero

D69

Ghisoni

D344

Golfe de
Sagone

N193

Bastelica

Ghisonaccia

TYRRHENIAN
SEA

D81

Aéroport d'Ajaccio-
Campo dell'Oro

Ajaccio

Taravo River

Zicavo

Monte Incudine
(2136m)

Solenzara

Pointe de
la Parata

Îles
Sanguinaires

Golfe de
Ajaccio

Porticcio

La Crociata

D69

Parc Naturel
Régional
de la Corse

Conca

To Genoa

N196

Quenza

To Marseille, Toulon & Nice

Filitosa

To Marseille & Toulon

To Marseille

Golfe de
Valinco

Propriano

CORSE-
DU-SUD

To Porto Torres

Sartène

Porto-
Vecchio

To Livorno

Golfe de
Porto-Vecchio

MEDITERRANEAN
SEA

N196

Cauria

Aéroport
de Figari

N198

To Porto Torres

Bonifacio

To Santa Teresa & Sardinia (12 km)

Strait of Bonifacio

LP

Corsica
(Corse)

0   10   20 km

long tradition of emigration. Many of the settlers in France's colonies were Corsican émigrés, and many young people still leave the island in search of better opportunities.

Language
The Corsican language (Corsu), which has been almost exclusively oral until recently, is more closely related to Italian than French. It constitutes an important component of Corsican identity and there is a movement afoot to ensure its survival (notably at the university of Corte). Street signs are now often bilingual or exclusively in Corsican.

Climate & When to Go
The best time of year to visit Corsica is in May and June. Outside these months, there are fewer visitors but a reduced tourist infrastructure (many hotels etc operate only seasonally). Avoid July and August when the island is overrun with mainly Italian and German holiday-makers.

Dangers & Annoyances
When Corsica makes the newspapers around the world, it's usually because separatist militants have engaged in some act of violence, such as bombing a public building, robbing a bank or blowing up a vacant holiday villa. But such attacks, which in 1994 included over 400 bombings and some 40 murders, are *not* targeted at tourists and there is no reason for visitors to fear for their safety.

Activities
Corsica's superb hiking trails include three *mare à mare* (sea-to-sea) trails that cross the island from east to west. The legendary GR20, also known as Li Monti (literally, 'between the mountains'), stretches over 160 km from Conca (20 km north of Porto-Vecchio) to Calenzana (10 km south-east of Calvi), and is passable from mid-June to October.

Some 600 km of trails are covered in the invaluable *Walks in Corsica*, published by Robertson McCarta, London. The book is currently out of print in Corsica itself, but you can get it in the UK for £9.95. If you read French, the Parc Naturel Régional de la Corse (☎ 04 95 21 56 54), based in Ajaccio, has useful fact sheets and a couple of guide books including

A Travers la Montagne Corse for 89FF. These are all available by mail order.

Accommodation
Camping Almost all of Corsica's many camping grounds close during the colder half of the year and some are open only from June to September. Charges are quite a bit higher than on the mainland – a rate of 28FF per person (minus tent) is usual. Camping outside recognised camping areas *(camping sauvage)* is strictly prohibited, partly because of the risk of fires.

Gîtes If you're staying put for a while and there are several of you, *gîtes ruraux* (country cottages) can be a good deal, ranging from 1000 to 3000FF a week from October to May but increasing considerably from June to September. Some are also rented out for weekends, and by the night in a bed and breakfast arrangement (from 200FF for a double room). In Ajaccio, contact Relais des Gîtes Ruraux (☎ 04 95 51 72 82; fax 04 95 51 72 89) at 1 Rue Général Fiorella, which provides information on available cottages.

Hotels Corsica's bottom-end hotel rooms are much more expensive than mainland counterparts and virtually nothing is available for less than 180FF. Many hotels in all price ranges raise their tariffs considerably in July and August (in some cases by over 200%!). But unless you make reservations months in advance (or arrive early in the morning and get lucky) you probably won't have the opportunity to pay them anyway. On the other hand, wintertime visitors will find that outside of Bastia and Ajaccio, most hotels shut down completely between November and Easter.

Getting There & Away
Visitors pay an arrival *and* departure tax of 30FF; this will probably have been calculated into your ferry or airfare.

Air Corsica's four main airports are at Ajaccio, Bastia, Calvi and Figari (near Bonifacio). Flights from Nice cost 464FF, but people under 25 or over 60 may qualify for a fare of 330FF. The regular one-way fare from Paris starts at 954FF, but charters and certain discounted (and very restricted) fares cost about 675FF one way, which is much cheaper than going by train and ferry.

Ferry During the summer – especially from mid-July to early September, reservations for vehicles and couchettes (berths) must be made well in advance (several months for the most popular routes).

To/From France Car and passenger ferry services between the French mainland (Nice, Marseille and Toulon) and Corsica (Ajaccio, Bastia, Calvi, L'Î Rousse, Propriano and Porto-Vecchio) are handled by the Société National Maritime Corse-Méditerranée, or SNCM (☎ 04 91 56 30 10 in Marseille).

For a one-way passage, individuals pay 304 to 340FF to/from Nice and 292 to 308FF to/from either Marseille or Toulon. Daytime crossings take from about three to 8½ hours, depending on where you get on and off. For overnight trips (departing at 8 pm and arriving at 7.30 or 8 am), the cheapest couchette costs an additional 80FF; the charge per person in a very comfortable cabin is 174FF. For people under 25, the basic passenger fare is from 177 to 249FF one way on all sailings to/from Nice. There are currently no youth fares available to/from Marseille and Toulon.

To/From Italy Corsica Ferries (☎ 04 95 32 95 95 in Bastia) has year-round car ferry services between Bastia and Genoa, La Spezia and Livorno (four to six hours or overnight). From mid-May to mid-September, the company also runs ferries between Genoa and Calvi. Depending on which route you take and when you travel, individuals pay 150 to 190FF. Bringing a car over costs from an additional 235 to 650FF (depending on the season).

From late March to October, Mobylines (☎ 04 95 31 46 29 in Bastia) also links Bastia with Genoa and Livorno. Between early July and early September, their car ferries also sail to/from Piombino. Depending on when you travel, the one-way passenger fare between Genoa and Bastia is 180 to 220FF. The smallest car costs 236 to 650FF.

SNCM has very infrequent sailings between Propriano or Ajaccio and Porto-Torres, in Sardinia, between April and September (147FF per person). For information on ferries from Sardinia to Bonifacio, see Getting There & Away in the Bonifacio section.

Getting Around

Bus Bus transport around the island is slow, infrequent (one to four runs a day), relatively expensive (105FF from Ajaccio to Bastia) and handled by an enormously complicated network of independent companies. Outside July and August, only a handful of intercity buses operate on Sunday and public holidays. Student discounts are available on some routes.

Train Chemins de Fer de la Corse, Corsica's metre-gauge, single-track train system has more in common with the Kalka-Simla line through the Himalayan foothills of northern India than it does with the TGV. The two and four-car trains make their way unhurriedly through the stunning mountain scenery, stopping at tiny rural stations and, when necessary, for sheep and cows. The two-line network links Ajaccio, Corte, Bastia, Ponte Leccia and Calvi on 232 km of track and is definitely the most interesting (and comfortable) way to tour the island.

Corsica's train system does *not* accept Eurail passes or give any discounts except to holders of Inter-Rail passes, who get 50% off. Tariffs are 118FF to go from Ajaccio to Bastia, 63FF to Corte and 89FF to travel from Bastia to Calvi. Transporting a bicycle is 63FF. Leaving luggage and bikes at the stations ticket offices costs a flat 19FF.

Car There's no doubt that a car is the most convenient way to get around Corsica. It's also the most stressful. Many of the roads are spectacular but narrow and serpentine (particularly D81 between Calvi and Porto and N196 from Ajaccio to Bonifacio). Count on averaging 50 km/h. A good road map is indispensable. Car rental agencies in Corsica are listed under Getting There & Away in the Ajaccio and Bastia sections.

AJACCIO

The port city of Ajaccio (Aiacciu in Corsican, population 58,000), birthplace of Napoleon Bonaparte in 1769, is a great place to begin visit to Corsica. This pastel-shaded, Mediterranean town is a fine place for strolling, but spending some time here can also be educational: Ajaccio's several museums and many statues dedicated to Bonaparte (who, local people will neglect to mention, never came back to visit after becoming emperor) speak volumes, not about Napoleon himself, but about how the people of his native town prefer to think of him.

Orientation
Ajaccio's main street is Cours Napoléon, which stretches from Place du Général de Gaulle northward to the train station and beyond. The old city is south of Place Foch.

Information
Tourist Office The tourist office (☎ 04 95 21 40 87) at 1 Place Foch is open Monday to Friday from 8.30 am to 6 pm and on Saturday from 9 am to noon. Between mid-June and mid-September, it is open daily from 8.30 am to 8 pm. At the airport, the information desk (☎ 04 95 21 03 64) is open daily from 6 am to 10.30 pm.

Money & Post The Banque de France is at 8 Rue Sergent Casalonga. The main post office (☎ 04 95 21 13 60), which has an exchange service, is at 5 Cours Napoléon. Ajaccio's postcode is 20000.

Hiking Information The Maison d'Information (☎ 04 95 51 79 10) at 2 Rue Sergent Casalonga has lots of information on the Parc Naturel Régional de Corse and the island's many hiking trails. It's open Monday to Friday from 9 am to noon and 2 to 6 pm.

Things to See & Do
Museums The house where Napoleon was born and raised, the **Maison Bonaparte** (☎ 04 95 21 43 89) on Rue Saint Charles in the old city, was sacked by Corsican nationalists in 1793 but rebuilt (with a grant from the government in Paris) later in the decade. It is open from 9 am (10 am from October to April) to noon and 2 to 6 pm (5 pm from October to April) daily except Sunday afternoon and Monday morning. The entry fee of 17FF (11FF for those 18 to 25 and over 60) includes a guided tour in French.

The sombre **Salon Napoléonien** (☎ 04 95 21 90 15), which exhibits memorabilia of the emperor on the 1st floor of the Hôtel de Ville at Place Foch, is open Monday to Friday from 9 am to noon and 2 to 6 pm. The fee is 5FF but visitors must be properly dressed. The **Musée A Bandera** (☎ 04 95 51 07 34) at 1 Rue Général Lévie deals with Corsican military history and costs 20FF (10FF for students) to visit. It's open Monday to Friday from 9 am to noon and from 2 to 6 pm.

The **Musée Fesch** (☎ 04 95 21 48 17) at 50 Rue du Cardinal Fesch has a fine collection of Italian primitive-art paintings (14th to 19th centuries) and yet another collection of Napoleonia in the basement. It is open from 9.30 am to 12.15 pm and 2.15 to 6 pm (3 to 7 pm from May to September) daily except Sunday and Monday. During July and August it's also open on Friday night from 9 pm to midnight. Entry costs 25FF (15FF for students aged 18 to 25 and people over 60). There is a separate fee of 10FF (5FF for students) to get into the Renaissance **Chapelle Impériale**, the Bonaparte family sepulchre built in 1857.

Cathédrale Ajaccio's Venetian Renaissance cathedral is in the **old city** on the corner of Rue Forcioli Conti and Rue Saint Charles. Built in the late 1500s, it contains Napoleon's marble baptismal font, which is to the right of the entrance, and the painting *Vierge au Sacré Cœur* (Virgin of the Sacred Heart) by Eugène Delacroix (1798-1863), which is to the left.

Pointe de la Parata This wild, black granite promontory is 12 km west of the city on Route des Sanguinaires (route D111). It's famed for its sunsets, which can be watched from the base of a crenellated, early 17th-century Genoan watchtower. Bus No 5 links Ajaccio with the Pointe.

The **Îles Sanguinaires**, a group of small islands visible offshore, can be visited on two to three-hour boat excursions between April and November which cost 100FF (120FF during July and August). Boats leave from the quayside opposite Place Foch.

Beaches Ajaccio's beaches are nothing special. Plage de Ricanto, popularly known as

PLACES TO STAY
4 Hôtel Kallysté
15 Hôtel Fesch
22 Hôtel Le Colomba

PLACES TO EAT
10 Da Mamma
28 U Scalone
29 Crêperie U San Carlu

OTHER
1 Train Station
2 Loca Corse
    (Bike Rental)
3 Vehicle Entrance to
    Ferry Port
5 Monoprix Supermarket
6 Musée Fesch &
    Chapelle Impériale
7 Terminal Routier (Bus
    Terminal)
8 Terminal Maritime
    (Ferry Terminal)

9 SNCM Ticketing Office
11 Main Post Office
12 Banque de France
13 Maison d'Information
    (Regional Park Office)
14 Marché Municipal
16 Préfecture
17 Relais de Gîtes Ruraux
    Office
18 Musée A Bandera
19 Assemblée Régionale
    de la Corse
20 Laundrette
21 Timy Supermarket
23 TCA Boutique (Local Bus
    Information)
24 Hôtel de Ville & Salon
    Napoléonien (Museum)
25 Tourist Office
26 Boats to Îles Sanguinaires
27 Taxi Rank
30 Cathédrale
31 Maison Bonaparte (Museum)

To Camping Les Mimosas (1.7 km),
Tahiti Plage (5 km), Airport (8 km),
Porticcio (17 km) & Porto (via D81)

Boulevard Dominique Paoli

Cours Napoléon

Rue du Docteur Pellegrino

Ave Colonel Colonna d'Ornano

Avenue Jean Léive

Square
Pierre
Griffi

Avenue Beverini Vico

Ave Pascal Paoli

Rue Frediani

Sampiero

Golfe
d'Ajaccio

Boulevard

Rue du Cardinal Fesch

Cours Napoléon

Rue du Roi Jérôme

Quai l'Herminier

Avenue de l'Impératrice Eugénie

Rue Sergent Casalonga

Rue Général Campi

Passage Ginchetta

Square Campinchi

To Sentier du
Bois des
Anglais (trail)

Rue Général Lévie

Rue Général Fiorella

Rue des Halles

Rue E Conti

To Place
d'Austerlitz
(450 m)

Rue Maréchal Ornano

Ajaccio

0   100   200 m

Cours Grandval

Avenue de Paris

Rue du Maréchal

Place Foch

To Place
des
Sanguinaires (D111),
Beaches & Pointe
de la Parata (12 km)

R P Mérimée

Boulevard Pascal

Plage Saint François

Rossini

Place du
Général
de Gaulle

Ave Eugène Macchini

Rue Charles
Rue du Roi de Rome
Rue Bonaparte
Rue Napoléon

Old
City

Rue St Charles

Casanova

Rue Forcioli Conti

Danielle

Boulevard

Vieux Port

Jetée de la
Citadelle

Citadelle
(Military Area)

FRANCE

Tahiti Plage, is about five km east of town on the way to the airport and can be reached on bus No 1. The more attractive and smaller, segmented beaches between Ajaccio and Pointe de la Parata (Ariane, Neptune, Palm Beach and Marinella) are served by bus No 5.

Places to Stay

Camping The *Camping Les Mimosas* (☎ 04 95 20 99 85; open April to October) is about three km north of the centre on Route d'Alata. To get there, take bus No 4 to the roundabout at the western end of Cours Jean Nicoli and walk up Route d'Alata for about one km. A tent site and a place to park cost 11FF each; adults pay 28FF each.

Hotels The best deal in town is the central *Hôtel Le Colomba* (☎ 04 95 21 12 66) on the 3rd floor at 8 Ave de Paris opposite Place du Général de Gaulle. It's run by a feisty Italian woman who offers clean, pleasant doubles without/with shower for 180/250FF and triples for 250FF. The friendly *Hôtel Kallysté* (☎ 04 95 51 34 45) at 51 Cours Napoléon has serviceable singles/doubles with shower and air-con off a large central stairway for 200/235FF (15 to 25% more from May to mid-November). Studios with kitchenettes for one/two people range from 235/260FF to 280/335FF, depending on the season.

The two-star *Hôtel Fesch* (☎ 04 95 21 50 52; fax 04 95 21 83 36) at 7 Rue du Cardinal Fesch has singles/doubles with satellite TV for 280/305FF (350/395FF from June to September). An extra bed costs 100FF (150FF during summer).

Places to Eat

U Scalone (☎ 04 95 21 50 05) at 2 Rue Roi de Rome caters to a well-heeled crowd (mains are 50 to 150FF) but it's a relaxing, comfortable place for a splurge.

The restaurant *Da Mamma* (☎ 04 95 21 39 44) is a charming, tucked-away place reached through a little tunnel off Rue du Cardinal Fesch. It has a small, outdoor terrace and serves menus from 60 to 145FF. For a taste of the local cuisine, the four-course menu Corse at 135FF is good value. It's open daily except Sunday and Monday lunchtime.

Crêperie U San Carlu (☎ 04 95 21 30 21)

at 16 Rue Saint Charles has crêpes of all descriptions for 15 to 50FF. It's open April to September from 11 am to 9.30 or 10 pm.

There's a big *Timy* supermarket opposite 4 Cours Grandval which is open Monday to Saturday from 9 am to 12.30 pm and 3.15 to 7.30 pm. The *Monoprix* supermarket opposite 40 Cours Napoléon is open Monday to Saturday from 8.30 am to 7.15 pm.

Getting There & Away

Air Aéroport d'Ajaccio-Campo dell'Oro is eight km east of the city along Cours Napoléon and its continuation. Bus No 1 links Place du Général de Gaulle and Cours Napoléon with the airport (20FF).

Bus The Terminal Routier (Ajaccio's bus terminal) is on Quai l'Herminier next to (and connected with) the Terminal Maritime (ferry terminal). About a dozen companies have daily services (except on Sunday and public holidays) to Bastia (105FF), Bonifacio (115FF), Calvi via Ponte Leccia (120FF), Corte (60FF), Porto (65FF), Sartène (70FF), Propriano and many other destinations.

The bus station's information booth (☎ 04 95 21 28 01), which can provide schedules for all routes, is open Monday to Saturday from 7 am to 6.30 or 7 pm. Eurocorse (☎ 04 95 21 06 30), which handles many of the long-distance lines, keeps its kiosk open Monday to Saturday from 7 to 11.30 am and from 2 to 6.30 pm (no break in July and August).

Train Trains to Corte, Bastia, Calvi and intermediate destinations are boarded at the train station (☎ 04 95 23 11 03) on Square Pierre Griffi. See Train under Getting Around at the start of the Corsica section for more information.

Car & Motorcycle About a dozen car-rental companies have bureaus at the airport, but the least expensive is Aloha (☎ 04 95 20 52 00). For a Fiat Panda, the charge is 975FF for three days, including insurance and unlimited km.

Loca Corse (☎ 04 95 20 71 20) at 10 Ave Beverini Vico rents 50/80 cc scooters for 200/250FF a day and 125 cc motorbikes for 350FF. It's open April to September from 9 am to noon and 2 to 6.30 pm.

Ferry The Terminal Maritime is on Quai l'Herminier next to the bus station. SNCM's ticketing office (☎ 04 95 29 66 99), across the street at 3 Quai l'Herminier, is open Monday to Friday from 8 to 11.45 am and 2 to 6 pm and on Saturday morning. For evening ferries, the SNCM bureau in the ferry terminal opens two or three hours before the scheduled departure time.

Getting Around
Bus Local bus maps and timetables can be picked up at the TCA Boutique (☎ 04 95 51 43 23) at 2 Ave de Paris from 8 am to noon and 3 to 6 pm Monday to Saturday. Local bus tickets cost 7.50FF (58FF for a carnet of 10).

Taxi There's a taxi rank on the east side of Place du Général de Gaulle or you can order one from Radio Taxis (☎ 04 95 51 15 67).

Bicycle Mountain bikes are available for 80/440FF a day/week from Loca Corse (see Car & Motorcycle earlier).

BASTIA
Bustling Bastia (population 38,000), Corsica's most important business and commercial centre, has rather an Italian feel to it. It was the seat of the Genoese governors of Corsica from the 15th century, when the *bastiglia* (fortress) from which the city derives its name was built. Though it's a pleasant enough place, there's not all that much to see or do here, and most travellers simply pass through. Bastia does, however, make a good base for exploring **Cap Corse**, the wild, 40-km-long peninsula to the north.

Orientation
The focal point of the town centre is 300-metre-long Place Saint Nicolas. Bastia's main thoroughfares are the east-west Ave Maréchal Sébastiani, which links the ferry terminal with the train station, and the north-south Blvd Paoli, a fashionable shopping street one block west of Place Saint Nicolas.

Information
The tourist office (☎ 04 95 31 00 89) at the northern edge of Place Saint Nicolas is open daily from 8 am to 6 pm (from 7 am to 10 pm during July and August when there's also tourist information available in the ferry terminal building). It has information on companies offering day trips to Cap Corse.

Banque de France is at 2bis Cours Henri Pierangeli, half a block south of Place Saint Nicolas. The main post office is on the even-numbered side of Ave Maréchal Sébastiani, a block west of Place Saint Nicolas. Exchange services are available. Bastia's postcode is 20200.

Things to See & Do
Place Saint Nicolas, a palm and plane tree-lined esplanade as long as three football pitches, was laid out in the late 19th century. The narrow streets and alleyways of **Terra Vecchia**, which is centred around Place de l'Hôtel de Ville, lie just south. The **Oratoire de l'Immaculée Conception**, opposite 3 Rue Napoléon, was decorated in rich baroque style in the early 18th century.

The picturesque, horseshoe-shaped **Vieux Port** is between Terra Vecchia and the **Citadelle**; you can reach the latter by climbing the stairs through the **Jardin Romieu**, the hillside park on the south side of the port. Inside the Citadelle, built by the Genoese in the 15th and 16th centuries, stands the mustard-coloured **Palais des Gouverneurs** (Governors' Palace). It houses a rather dull anthropology museum, but the views from the gardens behind the submarine conning tower (which served active and heroic duty during WWII) are worth the climb. **Église Sainte Marie**, whose entrance is on Rue de l'Evêché, was rebuilt in 1604 on the site of a much earlier church. Much more interesting is the **Église Saint Croix** down the alley to the right (south) of Sainte Marie. It's older (1543), the gilded coffered ceiling is Renaissance and the chapel to the right of the main altar contains a miraculous black statue of the crucified Christ found by two fishermen in the early 15th century.

Bastia's best beach is **Plage de la Marana**, about 12 km south at the southern edge of the Étang de Biguglia lagoon, a favourite nesting area for waterfowl. In summer it can be reached by bus No 8 from Rue du Nouveau Port.

Places to Stay
Camping In Miomo, about five km north of

Bastia, you'll find *Camping Casanova* (☎ 04 95 33 91 42), which is open from early May to October and charges 12FF for a tent and 22FF per person. To get there, take the bus towards Erbalunga from the terminal on Rue du Nouveau Port.

Hotels One of the most convenient hotels in Bastia is the *Hôtel de l'Univers* (☎ 04 95 31 03 38) at 3 Ave Maréchal Sébastiani. Singles/doubles/triples cost 130/170/200FF with washbasin and bidet and 200/300/350FF with shower and toilet. The hotel sometimes closes during the winter months, so check first. The one-star *Hôtel Le Riviera* (☎ 04 95 31 07 16) is 100 metres north of Place Saint Nicolas at 1 bis Rue du Nouveau Port. Fairly large singles/doubles with washbasin and bidet cost 150/180FF. Singles/doubles with shower, toilet and TV are 200/250FF (250/300FF during July and August).

If your budget can handle it, the very central, up-market *Hôtel Napoléon* (☎ 04 95 31 60 30; fax 04 95 31 77 83) at 43 Blvd Paoli is good value between October and May with fully equipped doubles at 290FF. Unfortunately the price jumps to 450FF in summer.

Places to Eat
There are plenty of restaurants around the Vieux Port, especially on the north side. Try *A Scaletta* (☎ 04 95 32 28 70) at 4 Rue Saint Jean and ask for a table on the tiny balcony overlooking the port. Scaletta's excellent-value menus include omelette with white brocciu cheese and mint (75FF) and fresh stuffed sardines (85FF). About 200 metres west in a square near the start of Rue Laurent Casanova, the *Chiangmai* (☎ 04 95 32 73 61) has reasonable, Vietnam-influenced Thai food.

The *Timy* supermarket at 2 Rue Campanelle (one block north of Ave Maréchal Sébastiani) is open Monday to Saturday from 8.30 am to 12.30 pm and 3.30 to 7.30 pm. The mammoth *Hyper Toga* supermarket north of the town centre on Rue de l'Impératrice Eugénie is open Monday to Saturday from 9 am to 8 pm.

Getting There & Away
Air France's fifth-busiest airport, Aéroport de Bastia-Poretta (☎ 04 95 54 54 54), is 20 km south of the town. Municipal buses to the airport (42FF) depart from the roundabout in front of the préfecture building (opposite the train station) about an hour before each flight's departure (nine to 10 times a day). A timetable is available at the tourist office.

Bus Rapides Bleus, whose buses serve Porto-Vecchio and Bonifacio (110FF), has a ticket office (☎ 04 95 31 03 79) at 1 Ave Maréchal Sébastiani from where the buses depart. Twice-daily buses run by Eurocorse (☎ 04 95 31 03 79) to Corte (55FF) and Ajaccio (105FF) also leave from here. The bus to Calvi (80FF), run by Autocars Beaux Voyages (☎ 04 95 65 15 02), leaves from the stop a short way up the block. Short-haul buses serving the Bastia area stop at the terminal along Rue du Nouveau Port, which is opposite the north-west corner of Place Saint Nicolas.

Train The train station (☎ 04 95 32 60 06) is across the roundabout at the northern end of Ave Maréchal Sébastiani. See Getting Around at the start of the Corsica section for information on the train system. Fares from Bastia are 118FF to Ajaccio, 89FF to Calvi and 55FF to Corte.

Car The cheapest place in Bastia to rent a car is ADA (☎ 04 95 31 48 95) next to the Renault office at 35 Rue César Campinchi, the street two blocks west of Place Saint Nicolas. It is open Monday to Saturday from 8 am to noon and 2 to 7 pm. Small cars (eg the Peugeot 106) cost 560FF for a weekend and 1790FF for a week, including unlimited km and insurance.

Ferry The ferry terminal is at the quayside end of Ave Maréchal Sébastiani. SNCM's office (☎ 04 95 54 66 88) is across the roundabout; it handles ferries to mainland France and is open from 8 to 11.30 am and 2 to 5.30 pm daily except Sunday, and Saturday afternoon in the winter, unless a boat has just arrived or departed. The SNCM counter in the ferry terminal itself is open two hours before each sailing (three hours on Sunday).

If you're headed for Italy, Mobylines' office (☎ 04 95 31 46 29) is 200 metres north of Place Saint Nicolas at 4 Rue du Commandant Luce de Casabianca. It is open Monday to Saturday from 8.30 am to noon and 2 to 6 pm. There is also a bureau (☎ 04 95 31 46 29) in the ferry terminal which is open daily from 9 to 11.30 am and 2 to 5.30 pm. Corsica Ferries' office (☎ 04 95 32 95 95) is 250 metres north of the ferry terminal at 5 Rue Chanoine Leschi next to the Mobil petrol station. It's open daily except Sunday from 8.30 am to noon and from 2 to 6 pm, and on Saturday from 8.30 am to noon. See Ferry under Getting There & Away at the start of the Corsica section for more information.

CALVI

Calvi (population 5000), where Nelson lost his eye, serves both as a military town and rather down-market holiday resort. The citadel, garrisoned by a crack regiment of the French Foreign Legion, sits atop a promontory at the western end of a beautiful half-moon shaped bay.

Orientation

The Citadelle – also known as the Haute Ville (upper town) – is north-east of the port. Blvd Wilson, the major thoroughfare in the Basse Ville (lower town), is set up the hill from Quai Landry and the marina.

Information

The tourist office (☎ 04 95 65 16 67) is on the marina just behind the train station. It's open Monday to Saturday from 9 am to noon and 2 to 6 pm (from mid-June to mid-September, it's open every day from 8.30 am to 7.30 pm). Guided visits of Calvi are available in English between mid-April and October for 45FF.

The Crédit Lyonnais opposite 10 Blvd Wilson is open weekdays from 8.20 am to 12.20 pm and from 1.50 to 4.40 pm. The main post office (☎ 04 95 65 00 40) is about 100 metres to the south on the same street. Calvi's postcode is 20260.

Things to See & Do

The **Citadelle**, set atop an 80-metre-high granite promontory and enclosed by ramparts built by the Genoese, affords great views of the surrounding area. **Église Saint Jean Baptiste** was built in the 13th century and rebuilt in 1570; inside is yet another miraculous ebony icon of Christ. West of the church, a marble plaque marks the site of the house where,

according to local tradition, Christopher Columbus was born. The imposing **palace of the Genoan governors**, built in the 13th century and enlarged in the mid-16th century, is above the entrance to the citadel. Now known as Caserne Sampiero, it serves as a barracks and mess hall for officers of the French Foreign Legion.

Beaches Calvi's four-km-long beach begins just east of the marina and stretches around the Golfe de Calvi. There are a number of other nice beaches, including one at **Algajola**, west of town. The port and resort town of L'Île Rousse (Red Island) east of Calvi is also endowed with a long, sandy beach with some of the cleanest water in the Mediterranean.

Between late April and October, many of the beaches between Calvi and L'Île can be reached by shuttle train (see Getting There & Away for details).

Places to Stay

Camping & Studios The *Camping Les Castors* (☎ 04 95 65 13 30), open from April to mid-October, is 800 metres south-east of the centre of town on Route de Pietra Maggiore. Campers pay 29FF per adult, 15FF for a camp site and 10FF for parking. Small studios for two people with shower, toilet and kitchenette cost 1040FF a week in the low season and between 2150 and 2450FF in summer.

Hostel The friendly, 133-bed *BVJ Corsotel* hostel (☎ 04 95 65 14 15), open from late March to October, is on Ave de la République, 70 metres to the left as you exit the train station. Beds in rooms for two to eight people cost 120FF per person, including breakfast, and 175/230FF for half/full board. No reservations are accepted from guests staying less than a week. A hostel card is not necessary.

Hotels The *Hôtel du Centre* (☎ 04 95 65 02 01), in an airy old building at 14 Rue Alsace-Lorraine (parallel to and one block down the hill from Blvd Wilson), is open from early June to mid-October. Basic doubles without/with shower are 180/200FF and rise to 250/280FF in the middle of summer. *Hôtel Le Belvédère* (☎ 04 95 65 01 25) at Place Christophe Colomb is open all year. Small, cheaply appointed doubles/triples/quads with shower and toilet start at 180/200/250FF (300/400/450FF during the summer).

The three-star *Grand Hôtel* (☎ 04 95 65 09 74; fax 04 95 65 25 18) at 3 Blvd Wilson charges 328FF for a double with shower and 358FF with shower and toilet (380 and 550FF in July and August).

Places to Eat

Calvi's attractive marina is lined with restaurants and cafés, and there are several budget places on Rue Clemenceau, which runs parallel to Blvd Wilson. One of the cheapest, *Astalla Crêperie-Snack* (☎ 04 95 65 06 29) at No 11, has crêpes and omelettes. *Au Poussin Bleu* (☎ 04 95 65 01 58) at 8 Blvd Wilson is good for sandwiches in the 17 to 22FF range.

The pleasant open-air restaurant at the *Grand Hôtel* (☎ 04 95 65 09 74) has pizza, pasta and one of the better three-course menus in town for a reasonable 80FF. Try the mixed deep-fried seafood.

There are a couple of supermarkets south of the town centre on Ave Christophe Colomb: *Timy* (next to the Mobil petrol station) and the massive *Super U*.

Getting There & Away

Air Aéroport Calvi-Sainte Catherine is seven km south-east of Calvi. There is no bus service from Calvi to the airport; taxis (☎ 04 95 65 03 10) cost between 70 and 90FF (depending on the time of day) to the centre of town.

Bus From Monday to Saturday, Autocars Beaux Voyages (☎ 04 95 65 15 02) runs a daily bus to Bastia (80FF) which leaves from Place de la Porteuse d'Eau opposite the post office. During summer, one bus a day goes to Calenzana (30FF) and another to Porto (100FF) from Place du Monument every day but Sunday.

Train Calvi's train station is between the marina and Ave de la République. Fares to Ajaccio are 137FF, Corte 75FF and Bastia 89FF.

From mid-April to mid-October, one-car shuttle trains *(navettes)* of Tramways de la Balagne make 19 stops between Calvi and L'Île Rousse. The line is divided into three

sectors, and it costs one ticket (9FF or 44FF for a carnet of six) for each sector you travel in. Getting to and from L'Île Rousse takes all six tickets. The navettes run on Sundays and holidays only in summer.

Ferry SNCM ferries (☎ 04 95 65 20 09) sail to Calvi from Nice, Marseille and Toulon, but during winter they can be very infrequent. Between mid-May and mid-September, Corsica Ferries links Calvi with Genoa. See Ferry under Getting There & Away at the start of the Corsica section for more information.

PORTO

The pleasant seaside town of Porto, nestled among huge outcrops of red granite and renowned for its sunsets, is an excellent base for exploring some of Corsica's natural wonders. **Les Calanche** (Les Calanques de Piana in French), a truly spectacular mountain landscape of red-and-orange granite forms resembling humans, animals, fortresses etc, towers above the azure waters of the Mediterranean slightly south of Porto along route D81. The **Gorges de Spelunca**, Corsica's most famous river gorges, stretch almost from the town of Ota, five km east of Porto, to the town of Evisa, 22 km away.

Orientation & Information

The marina is about 1.5 km down the hill from Porto's pharmacy – the local landmark – and the nearby Timy supermarket, both of which are on the D81. The area, known as Vaïta, is spread out along the road linking the D81 to the marina. The Porto River just south of the marina is linked by an arched pedestrian bridge to a fragrant eucalyptus grove and a small, pebble beach.

The tourist office (☎ 04 95 26 10 55) is built into the wall that separates the marina's upper and lower parking lots and is open from 9.30 am to noon and 2 to 6 pm Monday to Saturday (no break in July and August). Just around the corner is a Parc Naturel Régional de Corse office, open in summer only. Porto's postcode is 20150.

Things to See & Do

A short trail leads to the 16th-century **Genoese tower** on the outcrop above the town. It is open from April to September between 11 am and 7 pm (10FF).

From April to mid-October, the Compagnie des Promenades en Mer (☎ 04 95 26 15 16), whose bureau is across the parking lot from the tourist office, has two **boat excursions** a day (170FF) to Girolata (passing by the Scandola Nature Reserve), and occasionally to Les Calanche in the evenings. There are also glass-bottom boat excursions during July and August for 180FF. Keep a look out for dolphins following the boat as you leave and return to the port. Patrick & Toussaint (☎ 04 95 26 12 31), close to the bridge leading to the pebble beach, rents **motorboats** for up to seven people between April and October. Prices start at 400/600FF for a half/full day, not including petrol.

Places to Stay
Camping The *Camping Sole e Vista* (☎ 04 95 26 15 71), open from April to early November, is behind the Timy supermarket near the pharmacy. Charges are 10FF each for a tent and for a parking place and 30FF per person.

Hostels There are two hostels in the nearby village of Ota. *Gîte d'Étape Chez Félix* (☎ 04 95 26 12 92) and *Gîte d'Étape des Chasseurs* (☎ 04 95 26 11 37) are both open all year and charge 60/50FF respectively for a bed in a dormitory room. Chez Félix has doubles and triples for 200FF and a room for five for 320FF.

Hotels There are plenty of hotels in Vaïta and at the marina. One of the best deals, with great views of the marina, is the *Hôtel Le Golfe* (☎ 04 95 26 13 33), which charges 220FF for shower-equipped doubles with toilet (add 10FF in summer). *Hôtel Monte Rosso* (☎ 04 95 26 11 50) nearby has doubles with shower and toilet for 240FF (300FF in July and August). If you're not staying, at least have a cup of coffee at its lovely terrace café.

Places to Eat
Most of Porto's hotels double as restaurants. For a splurge and some seafood try the restaurant *Le Soleil Couchant* (☎ 04 95 26 10 12) on the marina. It has good-value menus from 85FF, pizzas from 38FF, and is open from April to mid-October. The grocery *Super Viva* near

the Porto River, just before the bridge to the beach, is open from April to September.

Getting There & Away
Between July and mid-September, two buses a day run daily (except on Sunday) between Porto and Ajaccio (65FF) operated by SAIB (☎ 04 95 26 13 70 in Porto; ☎ 04 95 22 41 99 in Ajaccio). From mid-May to mid-October, one bus a day goes to/from Calvi (100FF). Several buses a day link the village of Ota to both Ajaccio and Porto.

CORTE
When Pasquale Paoli led Corsica to independence in 1755, one of his first acts was to make Corte (Corti in Corsican; population 6000), a fortified town at the geographical centre of the island, the country's capital. To this day, the town remains a potent symbol of Corsican independence. In 1765, Paoli founded a national university there, but it was closed when his short-lived republic was taken over by France in 1769. The Università di Corsica Pasquale Paoli was reopened in 1981 and now has about 3000 students, making Corte the island's liveliest and least touristy town.

Information
The tourist office (☎ 04 95 46 24 20) is at the far end of the long building on your right as you pass through the Citadelle's main gate; look for the entrance with a '1' above it. It is open Monday to Friday from 9 am to noon and 1.30 to 5 pm. In summer, the office moves to the building on the left as you walk through the citadel gate.

There are several banks and automatic tellers on Cours Paoli, the main street which runs north-south through the town. The main post office is just off the northern end on Ave du Baron Mariani. Corte's postcode is 20250.

Things to See & Do
The **Citadelle**, built in the early 15th century and largely reconstructed during the 18th and 19th centuries, is perched on top of a hill, with the steep and twisted alleyways and streets of the **Ville Haute** and the Tavignanu and Restonica river valleys below. The Citadelle's **Belvédère** can be visited any time; the 15th-century **Nid d'Aigle** (eagle's nest) lookout 100

metres above is open from May to October (10FF).

The Citadelle houses the **Font Régional d'Art Contemporain** (☎ 04 95 46 22 18), which puts on temporary exhibitions of contemporary art. An ambitious anthropological museum, the **Musée de la Corse**, is being built with EU funding and is scheduled to open in June 1997.

The **Palazzu Naziunale** (National Palace; ☎ 04 95 61 02 62), down the hill from the Citadelle on Place Gaffori, was the governmental seat of the short-lived Corsican republic. It contains temporary exhibitions.

Università di Corsica Pasquale Paoli, Corsica's only university, is east of the town centre on Ave Jean Nicoli, on the way to the train station.

The **Gorges de la Restonica**, a deep valley cut through the mountains by the Restonica River, is a favourite with hikers. The river passes Corte, but some of the choicer trails begin about 16 km south-west of town at the Bergeries Grotelle sheepfolds. The trails are indicated on the free town map available at the tourist office.

Places to Stay

Camping The *Camping Alivetu* (☎ 04 95 46 11 09; open from Easter to mid-October), is in Faubourg Saint Antoine just south of Pont Restonica, the second bridge on Allée du Neuf Septembre crossing the Restonica River. It costs 13FF per tent and per car and 28FF per person.

Hostel The quiet and very rural *Gîte d'Étape U Tavignanu* (☎ 04 95 46 16 85), which is open all year, charges 60FF per person (or 160FF with half-board). To get there from Pont Tavignanu (the first bridge on Allée du Neuf Septembre over the Tavignanu River), walk westward along Chemin de Baliri and follow the signs (almost a km).

Hotels The 135-room *Hôtel HR* (☎ 04 95 45 11 11), housed in a complex of converted apartment blocks at 6 Allée du Neuf Septembre, is 300 metres to the left (south-west) as you exit the train station. Utilitarian singles/doubles/triples with a washbasin and bidet cost 135/145/170FF; doubles with shower and toilet are

195FF. Prices are slightly higher from August to mid-September.

The *Hôtel de la Poste* (☎ 04 95 46 01 37) is a few blocks north of the centre of town at 2 Place du Duc de Padoue. Simply furnished doubles with tiny shower cost 165 to 190FF, depending on how big it is and whether you want a window. They're 230FF with shower and toilet. The friendly *Hôtel Colonna* (☎ 04 95 46 01 09), in the centre just north of the main square (Place Paoli), has 18 rooms at 3 Ave Xavier Luciani and in an annexe opposite at No 4. Decent, renovated doubles are 180 to 250FF, and triples are 300FF.

Places to Eat

Le Bip's (☎ 04 95 46 06 26), down the steps and behind 14 Cours Paoli, is a cellar restaurant specialising in Corsican cuisine. The daily menu costs 75FF and is good value. Le Bip's is closed on Saturday, except in summer. *U Muntagnone* (☎ 04 95 61 09 77) has a pleasant terrace on 3 Place Paoli and is popular with the locals for its good-value fare. Pizzas start at 32FF, menus at 59FF and there's a special student deal for 54FF. It's open every day from mid-January to mid-November. The *Hôtel HR* (see above) also does student menus (49FF with a student card) at its brasserie. *Les Delices du Palais* pâtisserie diagonally opposite Le Bip's on Cours Paoli has a great selection of pastries.

Supermarkets in Corte include the *Eurospar* next to the Hôtel Colonna on Ave Xavier Luciani and the much larger *Casino*, a few steps west of the Hôtel HR. Both are open Monday to Saturday from 8.30 am to noon and 3 to 7 or 7.30 pm. Eurospar is also open on Sunday morning.

Getting There & Away

Corte is on Eurocorse's twice-daily (except Sunday) service in each direction between Bastia (50FF) and Ajaccio (60FF). The stop is in front of the Hôtel Colonna (3 Ave Xavier Luciani).

The train station (☎ 04 95 46 00 97) is about a km south-east of the town centre along Ave Jean Nicoli. Trains link Corte with Ajaccio (63FF, two hours), Bastia (55FF, 1½ hours) and Calvi (75FF, almost three hours).

SARTÈNE

The town of Sartène (Sartè in Corsican; population 3500), whose unofficial slogan is 'the most Corsican of Corsica's towns', is a delightful place to spend a morning or afternoon. Local people chatting in Corsican gather in **Place de la Libération**, the town's main square, where you'll find **Église Sainte Marie** – which contains a huge and very heavy wooden cross carried by a penitent every year on the eve of Good Friday – and the **Hôtel de Ville**, once the Genoan governor's palace. The **Musée de la Préhistoire Corse** (☎ 04 95 77 01 09) is up the hill. It's open Monday to Friday from 10 am to noon and 2 to 4 or 5 pm depending on the season. The tourist office (☎ 04 95 77 15 40) at 6 Rue Médecin-Capitaine Louis Bénédetti is open from 9 am to noon and, in summer, after lunch to 5 or 6 pm.

Places to Stay & Eat

The only hotel actually in Sartène is the two-star *Hôtel Les Roches* (☎ 04 95 77 07 61), just off the northern end of Ave Jean Jaurès. Singles/doubles/triples are 220/250/340FF, rising to 250/295/405FF from April to September.

A popular restaurant in Sartène is *La Chaumière* (☎ 04 95 77 07 13) at 39 Rue Médecin-Capitaine Louis Bénédetti, a couple of hundred metres south of the tourist office. Its evening menu is 90FF.

Getting There & Away

Given Sartène's dearth of reasonably priced hotels, your best bet is to stop off here on your way from Ajaccio to Bonifacio or to make it a day trip from the capital. Buses operated by Eurocorse between Ajaccio (70FF) and Bonifacio (55FF, two a day Monday to Saturday) stop at the Ollandini travel agency (☎ 04 95 77 18 41) on Cours Gabriel Péri.

BONIFACIO

The famed **Citadelle** of Bonifacio (Bunifaziu in Corsican; population 2700) and its medieval streets sit 70 metres above the translucent, turquoise waters of the Mediterranean, atop a long, narrow and eminently defensible promontory sometimes called 'Corsica's Gibraltar'. On all sides, limestone cliffs sculpted by the wind and the waves – topped in places with precariously perched apartment houses – drop almost vertically to the sea. The north side of the promontory looks out on 1.6-km-long Bonifacio Sound, at the eastern end of which is Bonifacio's **marina**. The southern ramparts of the citadel afford views of the coast of Sardinia, 12 km away.

Bonifacio was long associated with the Republic of Genoa. The local language – unintelligible to the rest of Corsicans – is a Genoan dialect and many of the traditions (including cooking methods) are Genoa-based.

Information

The tourist office (☎ 04 95 73 11 88) is in the old town at Place de l'Europe – go in through the ground-floor entrance on the eastern side of the Hôtel de Ville. It's open Monday to Friday from 8.30 am to 12.30 pm and 1.30 to 5.15 pm. From mid-June to mid-September, the hours are 9 am to 1 pm and 3 to 7 pm Monday to Saturday. There's also an annexe at the marina in summer.

In the port area, there's a Société Générale at 7 Rue Saint Erasme and a bureau de change with longer hours just opposite. The main post office (☎ 04 95 73 01 55) is in the old town, up the hill south of the tourist office, in Place Correga. Bonifacio's postcode is 20169.

Things to See

Walking around the old town and looking down the dramatic cliffs to the sea is a delight; the best views are to be had from **Place du Marché** and from the walk west towards and around the cemetery. Don't miss **Porte de Gênes**, which is reached by a tiny 16th-century drawbridge, or the Romanesque **Église Sainte Marie Majeure**, the oldest building in Bonifacio. **Rue des Deux Empereurs** (Street of the Two Emperors) is so-called because both Charles V and Napoleon himself slept there; look for the plaques at Nos 4 and 7. The **Foreign Legion Monument** east of the tourist office was brought back from Algeria in 1963 when that country won its independence.

Places to Stay

The olive-shaded *Camping Araguina* (☎ 04 95 73 02 96), open from mid-March to October, is 400 metres north of the marina on Ave Sylvère Bohn. Two people with a tent are charged 65FF (71FF during July and August) and 11FF to park.

Your best bet for budget hotel accommodation is the *Hôtel des Étrangers* (☎ 04 95 73 01 09), on Ave Sylvère Bohn 100 metres up the hill from the camping ground. It's open from April to October. Plain doubles with shower and toilet cost 180FF; from June to September, prices are 40 to 90FF higher.

In the citadel, the two-star *Hôtel Le Royal* (☎ 04 95 73 00 51) at 8 Rue Fred Scamaroni has doubles for 290FF (from 450 to 600FF from July to September).

Places to Eat

U Castille (☎ 04 95 73 04 99) on Rue Simon Varsi is a charming, family-run place converted from an old mill. Decent pizzas cost from 30FF, menus from 95FF. *Les Terrasses d'Aragon* (☎ 04 95 73 51 07) is just up the road at Place de la Poste. It has pizzas/menus from 39/70FF. It's a great place also for a cup of coffee (6FF); the terrace has good views over the cliffs. There's a supermarket at 15 Rue Oloria which is open from 8 am to noon and 3 to 6.30 pm.

For a real treat, visit *Boulangerie-Pâtisserie Faby* at 4 Rue Saint Jean Baptiste. It specialises in Corsican-Genoan treats like fougazi – big, flat biscuits flavoured with anis – and lemon canistrelli. It's open daily from 7.30 am to 12.30 pm and 3.30 to 7 pm (no midday closure from June to October).

Getting There & Away

Bus From Monday to Saturday, Rapides Bleus (☎ 04 95 70 10 36 in Porto-Vecchio) has up to two buses a day to Porto-Vecchio and daily buses to Bastia (110FF). Eurocorse (☎ 04 95 21 06 30 in Ajaccio; ☎ 04 95 70 13 83 in Porto-Vecchio) runs buses the 137 km to Ajaccio (115FF) via Sartène twice a day. All buses leave from the parking lot across the street from the eastern end of the marina.

Ferry Saremar (☎ 04 95 73 00 96) offers year-round car ferry service every day from Bonifacio's ferry port to Santa Teresa in Sardinia. One-way pedestrian passage costs 48 to 60FF depending on the season plus the 30FF departure tax (see Getting There & Away at the start of the Corsica section). If you want to get a vehicle across (from 124 to 234FF), make sure you have reservations at least a week in advance. Fares charged by their competition, Moby Lines (☎ 04 95 73 00 29), which has more frequent sailings, are a couple of francs more. The tax is the same.

Greece

The first travel guide to Greece was written
800 years ago by the Greek geographer and
historian Pausanias, so the tourism industry
isn't exactly in its infancy. In the 19th century,
wealthy young European aristocrats made it
part of their Grand Tour; in this century it has
become a mecca for sun and sea worshippers.

The country's enduring attraction is its
archaeological sites; those who travel through
Greece journey not only through the landscape
but also through time, witnessing the legacy of
Europe's greatest ages – the Mycenaean,
Minoan, classical, Hellenistic and Byzantine.

You cannot wander far in Greece without
stumbling across a broken column, a crumbling bastion or a tiny Byzantine church, each
perhaps neglected and forgotten but still retaining an aura of former glory.

Greece is much more than beaches and
ancient monuments. Its culture is a unique blend
of East and West, inherited from the long period
of Ottoman rule and apparent in its food, music
and traditions. The mountainous countryside is
a walker's paradise crisscrossed by age-old
donkey tracks leading to stunning vistas.

The magnetism of Greece is also due to less
tangible attributes – the dazzling clarity of the
light, the floral aromas which permeate the air,
the spirit of *place* – for there is hardly a grove,
mountain or stream which is not sacred to a
deity, and the ghosts of the past still linger.

And then again, many visitors come to
Greece simply to get away from it all and relax
in one of Europe's friendliest and safest countries.

Facts about the Country

HISTORY
Greece's strategic position at the crossroads of
Europe and Asia has resulted in a long and
turbulent history.

During the Bronze Age, which lasted from
3000 to 1200 BC in Greece, the advanced
Cycladic, Minoan and Mycenaean civilisations flourished. The Mycenaeans were
eventually swept aside by the Dorians in the
12th century BC. The next 400 years are often
referred to as the 'age of darkness' (1200-800
BC), which sounds a bit unfair for a period that
saw the arrival of the Iron Age and emergence
of geometric pottery. Homer's *Odyssey* and
Iliad were composed at this time.

By 800 BC, when Homer's works were first
written down, Greece was undergoing a cultural and military revival with the evolution of
the city-states, the most powerful of which
were Athens and Sparta. Greater Greece –
Magna Graecia – was created, with south Italy
as an important component. The unified
Greeks repelled the Persians twice, at Marathon (490 BC) and Salamis (480 BC). The
period which followed was an unparalleled
time of growth and prosperity, resulting in
what is called the classical (or golden) age.

The Golden Age
In this period, the Parthenon was commissioned by Pericles, Sophocles wrote *Oedipus*

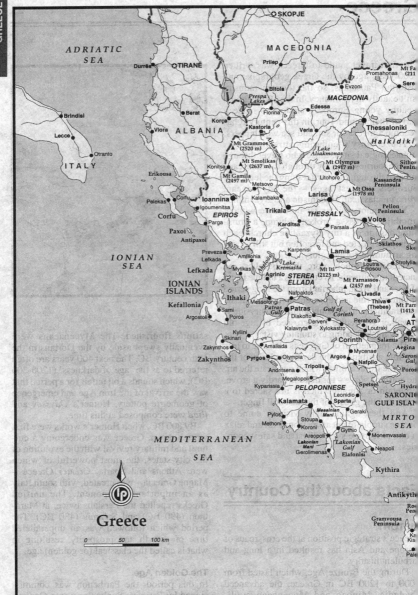

ADRIATIC
SEA

MACEDONIA

SKOPJE

Prilep

Durrës   TIRANË

Bitola   Evzoni

Promahonas   Mt Fa
(211

Sere

Prespa
Lakes

MACEDONIA

Brindisi

Berat

Vlora

ALBANIA

Korça

Florina

Edessa

Veria

Kastoria

Thessaloniki

Halkidiki

Lecce

Otranto

ITALY

Erikousa

Mt Grammos
(2520 m)

Mt Smolikas
(2637 m)

Konitsa

Mt Gamila
(2497 m)

Metsovo

Lake
Aliakmonas

Mt Olympus
(2917 m)

Litohoro

Kassandra
Peninsula

Sithon

Pelekas

Corfu

Ioannina

Igoumenitsa

Kalambaka

Larisa

Mt Ossa
(1978 m)

Corfu

EPIROS

Trikala

THESSALY

Pelion
Peninsula

Volos

Alonn

Paxoi

Parga

Karditsa

Farsala

Antipaxoi

Preveza

Arta

Skiathos

Ske

IONIAN
SEA

Lefkada

Amfilohia

Karpenisi

Lamia

Loutra
Edipsou

Strofylia

Lefkada

Mytikas

Lake
Kremasta

Mt Iti
(2125 m)

IONIAN
ISLANDS

Agrinio

STEREA
ELLADA

Mt Parnassos
(2457 m)

Nafpaktos

Livadia

Thiva
(Thebes)

Mt Parr
(1413

Ithaki

Messolongi

Kefallonia

Sami

Patras
Gulf

Patras

Diakofto

Gulf of
Corinth

Perahora

ATT

Argostoli

Poros

Derveni

Xylokastro

Loutraki

Kyllini

Kalavryta

Corinth

Salamis

Pira

Skinari

Mycenae

Aegina

Zakynthos

Amaliada

Olympia

Pyrgos

Argos

Nafplio

Saron
Gul

Zakynthos

Andritsena

Tripolis

Poros

Megalopoli

PELOPONNESE

Spetses

Hydra

Kyparissia

Leonidio

Sparta

SARONI
GULF ISLAN

Kalamata

Messinian
Mani

Geraki

MIRTO
SEA

Pylos

Koroni

Gythio

MEDITERRANEAN
SEA

Methoni

Stoupa

Areopoli

Lakonian
Mani

Lakonian
Gulf

Monemvassia

Gerolimenas

Elafonisi

Neapoli

Kythira

Antikyth

Ro
Pen

Greece

0   50   100 km

Gramvousa
Peninsula

Ka
Kis

Pale

the King, and Socrates taught young Athenians to think. At the same time, the Spartans were creating a military state. The golden age ended with the Peloponnesian War (431-404 BC) in which the militaristic Spartans defeated the Athenians. So embroiled were they in this war that they failed to notice the expansion of Macedonia to the north under King Philip II, who easily conquered the war-weary city-states.

Philip's ambitions were surpassed by those of his son Alexander the Great, who marched triumphantly into Asia Minor, Egypt, Persia and what are now parts of Afghanistan and India. In 323 BC he met an untimely death at the age of 33, ostensibly from food poisoning. (Today's Greeks prefer to attribute his death to the more 'exotic' disease of syphilis.) After his death, his generals divided his empire between themselves.

Roman Rule & the Byzantine Empire

Roman incursions into Greece began in 205 BC, and by 146 BC Greece and Macedonia had become Roman provinces. In 330 AD Emperor Constantine chose Byzantium as the new capital of the Roman Empire and renamed the city Constantinople. After the subdivision of the Roman Empire into Eastern and Western empires in 395 AD, Greece became part of the Eastern Roman Empire, leading to the illustrious Byzantine age.

In the centuries that followed, Venetians, Franks, Normans, Slavs, Persians, Arabs and, finally, Turks took their turns to chip away at the Byzantine Empire.

The Ottoman Empire & Independence

The end came in 1453 when Constantinople fell to the Turks. Most of Greece soon became part of the Ottoman Empire. Crete was not captured until 1670, leaving Corfu the only island never occupied by the Turks. By the 19th century the Ottoman Empire had become the 'sick man of Europe'. The Greeks, seeing nationalism sweep Europe, fought the War of Independence (1821-32). The Great Powers – Britain, France and Russia – intervened in 1827, in which year Ioannis Kapodistrias was elected the first Greek president.

In 1831 Kapodistrias was assassinated and in the ensuing anarchy the European powers stepped in again and declared that Greece should become a monarchy. In January 1833

Otho of Bavaria was installed as king. Hi ambition, called the Great Idea, was to unite al the lands of the Greek people to the Gree motherland. In 1862 he was peacefully ouste and the Greeks chose George I, a Danis prince, as king.

In WWI, Prime Minister Venizelos allie Greece with France and Britain. King Constan tine (George's son), who was married to th Kaiser's sister Sophia, disputed this and left th country.

Smyrna & WWII

After the war, Venizelos resurrected the Grea Idea and, underestimating the new-foun power of Turkey under the leadership o Atatürk, sent forces to occupy Smyrna (th present-day Turkish port of İzmir) which ha a large Greek population. The army wa repulsed and many Greeks were slaughtere This led to the brutal population exchang between the two countries in 1923, the aim c which was to eliminate the main reason behin Greece's territorial claims.

In 1930 George II, Constantine's son, wa reinstated as king and he appointed the dictatc General Metaxas as prime minister. Metaxas grandiose ambition was to take the best fror Greece's ancient and Byzantine past to creat a Third Greek Civilisation, though what h actually created was more a Greek version c the Third Reich. His chief claim to fame is h celebrated *okhi* (no) to Mussolini's request t allow Italian troops to traverse Greece in 194(Despite Allied help, Greece fell to Germany i 1941, after which followed carnage and mas starvation. Resistance movements sprang up eventually polarising into royalist and commu nist factions. A bloody civil war resulte lasting until 1949 and leaving the country i chaos.

The Colonels

Continuing political instability led to th colonels' coup d'état in 1967. King Constar tine (son of King Paul, who succeeded Georg II) staged an unsuccessful counter coup, the fled the country. The colonels' junta distir guished itself by inflicting appalling brutalit repression and political incompetence upc the people. In 1974 they attempted to assass nate Cyprus' leader, Archbishop Makario When Makarios escaped, the junta replace im with the extremist Nikos Samson, a convicted murderer. The Turks, who comprised 10% of the population, were alarmed at having Samson as leader. Consequently, mainland Turkey sent in troops and occupied North Cyprus, the continued occupation of which is one of the most contentious issues in Greek politics today. The junta, by now in a shambles, had little choice but to hand back power to civilians. In November 1974 a plebiscite voted 69% against restoration of the monarchy, and Greece became a republic. An election brought the right-wing New Democracy (ND) party into power.

The Socialist 1980s

In 1981 Greece entered the EC (European Community, now the EU). Andreas Papandreou's Panhellenic Socialist Movement (PASOK) won the next election, giving Greece its first socialist government. PASOK promised removal of US air bases and withdrawal from NATO, which Greece had joined in 1951.

Six years into government these promises remained unfulfilled, unemployment was high and reforms in education and welfare had been limited. Women's issues had fared better however – the dowry system was abolished, abortion legalised, and civil marriage and divorce were implemented. The crunch for the government came in 1988 when Papandreou's affair with air stewardess Dimitra Liana (whom he subsequently married) was widely publicised and PASOK became embroiled in a financial scandal involving the Bank of Crete.

In July 1989 an unprecedented conservative and communist coalition took over to implement a *katharsis* (campaign of purification) to investigate the scandals. It ruled that Papandreou and four ministers should stand trial for embezzlement, telephone tapping and illegal grain sales. It then stepped down in October 1990, stating that katharsis was completed.

The 1990s

The tough economic reforms that Prime Minister Konstantinos Mitsotakis was forced to introduce to counter a spiralling foreign debt soon made his government deeply unpopular. By late 1992, allegations began to emerge about the same sort government corruption and dirty tricks that had brought Papandreou

unstuck. Mitsotakis himself was accused of having a secret horde of Minoan art. He was forced to call an election in October 1993 after his foreign minister, Antonis Samaras, quit ND to found the Political Spring party.

Greeks again turned to PASOK and the ageing, ailing Papandreou, who had eventually been cleared of all the charges levelled in 1990. He marked his last brief period in power with a conspicuous display of the cronyism that had become his trademark. He appointed his wife as chief of staff, his son Giorgos as deputy foreign minister and his personal physician as minister of health.

He had little option but to continue with the same austerity program begun by Mitsotakis, quickly making his government equally unpopular.

Papandreou was finally forced to hand over the reins in January 1996 after a lengthy spell in hospital. His resignation marked the end of an era. After a tense two-round ballot, party reformist Costas Simitis narrowly defeated Papandreou loyalist Akis Tsochadzopoulos for the PASOK leadership. Simitis, an experienced economist and lawyer, came to power committed to further economic reform in preparation for involvement in the new Europe.

Foreign Policy

Greece's foreign policy is dominated by its extremely sensitive relationship with Turkey, its giant Muslim neighbour to the east. The two uneasy NATO allies have repeatedly come close to blows, most recently after Turkish journalists symbolically replaced the Greek flag on the tiny rocky outcrop of Imia (Kardak to the Turks) in February 1996. Both sides poured warships into the area before being persuaded to calm down.

The break-up of former Yugoslavia and the end of the Stalinist era in Albania have given Greece two new issues to worry about. The attempt by the former Yugoslav republic of Macedonia to become independent Macedonia prompted an emotional outburst from Greece, which argued that the name 'was, is, and always will be' Greek. Greece was able to persuade its EU partners to recognise Macedonia only if it changed its name. That's how the independent acronym of FYROM (Former Yugoslav Republic of Macedonia) came into being.

GREECE

Greece is also at odds with Albania over that country's treatment of its significant Greek-speaking minority.

GEOGRAPHY & ECOLOGY

Greece consists of the southern tip of the Balkan peninsula and about 2000 islands, only 166 of which are inhabited. The land mass is 131,900 sq km and Greek territorial waters cover a further 400,000 sq km.

Most of the country is mountainous. The Pindos Mountains in Epiros are the southern extension of the Dinaric Alps, which run the length of former Yugoslavia. The range continues down through central Greece and the Peloponnese, and re-emerges in the mountains of Crete. Less than a quarter of the country is suitable for agriculture.

The variety of flora is unrivalled in Europe. The wild flowers are spectacular. They continue to thrive because much of the land is too poor for agriculture and has escaped the ravages of modern fertilisers. The best places to see the amazing variety are the mountains of Crete and the southern Peloponnese.

You won't encounter many animals in the wild, mainly due to the macho male habit of blasting to bits anything that moves. The brown bear, Europe's largest mammal, survives in very small numbers in the Pindos Mountains, as does the grey wolf. Lake Mikri Prespa in Macedonia has the richest colony of fish-eating birds in Europe, while the Dadia Forest Reserve in Thrace numbers such majestic birds as the golden eagle and the giant black vulture among its residents.

Looking at the harsh, rocky landscapes of the 20th century, it's hard to believe that in ancient times Greece was a fertile land with extensive forests. The change represents an ecological disaster on a massive scale. The main culprit has been the olive tree. In ancient times, native forest was cleared on a massive scale to make way for a tree whose fruit produced an oil that could be used for everything from lighting to lubrication. Much of the land cleared was hill country that proved unsuitable for the olives. Without the surface roots of the native trees to bind it, the topsoil quickly disappeared. The ubiquitous goat has been another major contributor to ecological devastation.

The news from the Aegean Sea is both good and bad. According to EU findings, it is Europe's least polluted sea – apart from area immediately surrounding major cities. Like the rest of the Mediterranean, it has been over fished.

GOVERNMENT & POLITICS

Since 1975, democratic Greece has been a parliamentary republic with a president a head of state. The president and parliament which has 300 deputies, have joint legislative power. Prime Minister Simitis heads a 41 member cabinet.

Administratively, Greece is divided into regions and island groups. The mainland regions are the Peloponnese, Central Greece (officially called Sterea Ellada), Epiros, Thessaly, Macedonia and Thrace. The island group are the Sporades, North-Eastern Aegean Saronic Gulf, Cyclades, Dodecanese, and the Ionian, which is the only group not in the Aegean. The large islands of Evia and Crete do not belong to any group. For administrative purposes each region and group is divided into prefectures *(nomoi)*.

ECONOMY

Traditionally, Greece has been an agricultural country, but the importance of agriculture in the economy is declining. Greece has the second-lowest income per capita in the EU (Portugal's is lowest). Tourism is by far the biggest industry; shipping comes next.

Greece's politicians face a tough battle to meet conditions set down by the EU for the country's proposed entry into Europe's financially integrated elite. Austerity measure forced on previous governments went down like lead balloons, but still tougher measure are required if conditions are to be met. The inflation rate has been brought below 10% for the first time in donkeys' years, but efforts to get the economy moving have been hit hard by the loss of the main overland trade route through the Balkans to Europe. The economy grew by only 1.5% in 1994, well behind the rest of Europe.

POPULATION & PEOPLE

The 1991 census recorded a population of 10,264,146, an increase of 5.4% on the 1981 figure. Women outnumber men by more than 200,000. Greece is now a largely urban society with 68% of people living in cities. By far the argest is Athens, with more than 3.1 million in he greater Athens area – which includes 'iraeus (169,000). Other major cities and their opulations are Thessaloniki (740,000), Patras 172,800), Iraklio (127,600), Larisa (113,400) nd Volos (106,100). Less than 15% of people ive on the islands. The most populous are Crete (537,000), Evia (209,100) and Corfu 105,000).

It is doubtful that any Greek alive today is lirectly descended from an ancient Greek. Contemporary Greeks are a mixture of all of he invaders who have occupied the country ince ancient times. There are a number of listinct ethnic minorities – about 300,000 thnic Turks in Thrace; about 100,000 Britons 60,000 live in Athens); about 5000 Jews; Vlach and Sarakatsani shepherds in Epiros; Gypsies; and lately, a growing number of Albanians – many in Greece illegally.

ARTS

The arts have been integral to Greek life since ancient times. In summer, Greek dramas are taged in the ancient theatres where they were riginally performed.

The visual arts follow the mainstream of modern European art, and traditional folk arts uch as embroidery, weaving and tapestry continue.

The bouzouki is the most popular musical nstrument, but each region has its own speciality of instruments and sounds. *Rembetika* music, with its themes of poverty and suffering, was banned by the junta, but is now njoying a revival.

Architecture in the classical, Hellenistic and Roman periods was based on three column rders – simple, clear Doric; slender Ionic, opped with a scroll; and the more ornate Corinthian, surmounted by a flowery burst of laboration.

The blind bard Homer composed the narrave poems the *Odyssey* and the *Iliad*. These are ales of the Trojan war and the return to Greece f Odysseus, King of Ithaki, linking together ne legends sung by bards during the dark age. Plato was the most devoted pupil of Socrates, vriting down every dialogue he could recall etween Socrates, other philosophers and the outh of Athens. His most widely read work is ne *Republic*, which argued that the perfect

State could only be created with philosopher-rulers at the helm.

The Alexandrian, Constantine Cavafy (1863-1933), revolutionised Greek poetry by introducing a personal, conversational style. He is considered the TS Eliot of Greek literary verse. Nikos Kazantzakis, author of *Zorba the Greek* and numerous other novels, plays and poems, is the most famous of 20th-century Greek novelists.

CULTURE

Greece is steeped in traditional customs. Name days (celebrated instead of birthdays), weddings and funerals all have great significance. On someone's name day there is an open house and refreshments are served to well-wishers who stop by with gifts. Weddings are highly festive, with dancing, feasting and drinking sometimes continuing for days.

If you want to bare all, other than on a designated nude beach, remember that Greece is a traditional country, so take care not to offend the locals.

RELIGION

About 97% of Greeks nominally belong to the Greek Orthodox Church. The rest of the population is split between the Roman Catholic, Protestant, Evangelist, Jewish and Muslim faiths. While older Greeks and people in rural areas tend to be deeply religious, most young people are decidedly more interested in the secular.

LANGUAGE

Greeks are naturally delighted if you can speak a little of their language. But many Greeks have lived abroad, usually in Australia or the USA, so even in remote villages there are invariably one or two people who can speak English. If you arrive in such a place and make your presence known, the local linguist will soon be produced.

Greek is the oldest European language, with a 4000-year-old oral tradition and a 3000-year-old written tradition. Its evolution over the four millennia has been characterised by its strength during the golden age of Athens; its spread and use as a lingua franca by Alexander the Great and his successors as far east as India during the Hellenistic period (330 BC to 100 AD); its adaptation instead of Aramaic as the language of the new religion, Christianity; its status as the official language of the Eastern Roman Empire; and its eventual proclamation as the language of the Byzantine Empire (380-1453 AD).

Greek maintained its status and prestige during the Renaissance and was employed as the linguistic perspective for all contemporary sciences and terminologies during the period of the Enlightenment. The Modern Greek (MG) language is a southern Greek dialect now used by most Greek speakers in Greece and abroad. Modern Greek combines ancient vocabulary with Greek regional dialects – namely, Cretan, Cypriot and Macedonian.

See the Language Guide at the back of this book for pronunciation guidelines and useful words and phrases.

Transliteration

Travellers in Greece will frequently encounter confusing, seemingly illogical English transliterations of Greek words. Transliteration is a knotty problem – there are six ways of rendering the vowel sound 'ee' in Greek, and two ways of rendering the 'o' sound and the 'e' sound. This book has merely attempted to be consistent within itself, not to solve this long-standing difficulty.

As a general rule, the Greek letter gamma (γ) appears as a 'g' rather than a 'y'; thus *agios*, not *ayios*. The letter delta (δ) appears as 'd' rather than 'dh', so *domatia*, not dhomatia. The letter phi (φ) can be either 'f' or 'ph'. Here, we have used the general rule that classical names are spelt with a 'ph' and modern names with an 'f' – Phaestos (not Festos), but Folegandros, not Pholegandros. Please bear with us if signs in Greek don't agree with our spelling. It's that sort of language.

Facts for the Visitor

PLANNING
Climate & When to Go

The climate is typically Mediterranean with mild, wet winters followed by hot, dry summers. Spring and autumn are the best times to visit. Winter is pretty much a dead loss, unless you're coming to Greece to take advantage of the cheap skiing. Most of the tourist infrastructure goes into hibernation between late November and early April, particularly on the islands. Hotels and restaurants close up and buses and ferries operate on drastically reduced schedules.

The cobwebs are dusted off in time for Easter, and conditions are perfect until the end of June. Everything is open, public transport operates normally, but the crowds have yet to arrive. From July until mid-September, it's on for young and old as northern Europe heads for the Mediterranean en masse. If you want to party, this is the time to go. The flip side is that everywhere is packed out, and rooms can be hard to find.

The pace slows down again by mid-September, and conditions are ideal once more until the end of October.

Book & Maps

The 2nd edition of Lonely Planet's *Greece - travel survival kit* has been comprehensively updated, with particular emphasis on some of the less visited areas of central and northern Greece. Lonely Planet's *Trekking in Greece* is recommended for anyone considering any serious walking. Both books are strong on maps.

There are numerous books to choose from if you want to get a feel for the country. *Zorba the Greek* by Nikos Kazantzakis may seem an obvious choice, but read it and you'll understand why it's the most popular of all Greek novels translated into English. *A Traveller History of Greece* by Timothy Boatswain & Colin Nicholson covers Greek history from Neolithic times to the present day.

Mythology was such an intrinsic part of life in ancient Greece that some knowledge of will enhance your visit to the country. *The Greek Myths* by Robert Graves is very thorough, if a bit academic. Homer's *Odyssey* translated by EV Rien, is arguably the best translation of this epic.

The Colossus of Maroussi by Henry Miller is a gripping book. With senses heightened Miller relates his travels in Greece at the outbreak of WWII with feverish enthusiasm. *Hellas* and *Eleni*, both by Nicholas Gage, are portraits of contemporary Greece that will further whet your appetite for the country.

Detailed, although somewhat outdated ordnance survey maps are available from the

Athens Statistical Service (☎ 01-325 9302), Lykourgou 14; take your passport. Stanfords, 12 Long Acre, London WC2E 9LP, also stocks them. Freytag & Berndt produces 15 maps of Greece which are widely available and cost about US$10 each.

What to Bring

In summer, bring light cotton clothing, a sun hat and sunglasses; bring sunscreen too, as it's expensive in Greece. In spring and autumn, you will need light jumpers (sweaters) and thicker ones for the evenings.

In winter, thick jumpers and a raincoat are essential. You will need to wear sturdy walking shoes for trekking in the country, and comfortable shoes are a better idea than sandals for walking around ancient sites. An alarm clock for catching early-morning ferries, a torch (flashlight) for exploring caves, and a small backpack for day trips will also be useful.

SUGGESTED ITINERARIES

Depending on the length of your stay, you might want to see and do the following things:

Two days
    Spend both days in Athens seeing its museums and ancient sites.
One week
    Spend two days in Athens, four days in either Epiros or the Peloponnese, or four days visiting the Cycladic islands.
Two weeks
    Spend two days in Athens, three days each in Epiros and the Peloponnese and four days on the Cycladic islands, allowing two days travelling time.
One month
    Spend two days in Athens, four days in Epiros, a week in the Peloponnese, six days on the Dodecanese and North-Eastern Aegean islands and four days each in Crete and the Cyclades.

HIGHLIGHTS

Islands

Many islands are overrun with tourists in summer. For tranquillity, try lesser-known islands such as Kassos, Sikinos, Anafi, Koufonisi, Donoussa, Shinoussa, Iraklia and Kastellorizo. (See the sections on the Cyclades and the Dodecanese islands for more information.) If you enjoy mountain walks, then Naxos, Crete, Samothraki and Samos are all very rewarding. If you prefer the beach, try Paros.

Museums & Archaeological Sites

There are three museums which should not be missed. The National Archaeological Museum in Athens houses Heinrich Schliemann's finds from Mycenae and, temporarily, the Minoan frescos from Akrotiri on Santorini (Thira). The Thessaloniki Museum contains exquisite treasures from the graves of the Macedonian royal family, and the Iraklio Museum houses a vast collection from the Minoan sites of Crete.

Greece has more ancient sites than any other country in Europe. It's worth seeking out some of the lesser lights where you won't have to contend with the crowds that pour through famous sites like the Acropolis, Delphi, Knossos and Olympia.

The Sanctuary of the Great Gods on Samothraki is one of Greece's most evocative sites, and it's off the package-tourist circuit because there's no airport and there are no boats from Piraeus.

Museums and sites are free on Sunday, except for tour groups. They are free all the time for card-carrying students and teachers from EU countries. An International Student Identification Card (ISIC) gets non-EU students a 50% discount.

Historic Towns

Two of Greece's most spectacular medieval cities are in the Peloponnese. The ghostly Byzantine city of Mystras, west of Sparta, clambers up the slopes of Mt Taygetos, its winding paths and stairways leading to deserted palaces and churches. In contrast, Byzantine Monemvassia is still inhabited, but equally dramatic and full of atmosphere.

There are some stunning towns on the islands. Rhodes is the finest surviving example of a fortified medieval town, while Naxos' hora (main village) is a maze of narrow, stepped alleyways of whitewashed Venetian houses, their tiny gardens ablaze with flowers. Pyrgi, on Chios, is visually the most unusual village in Greece – the exterior walls of the houses are all decorated with striking black-and-white geometrical patterns.

TOURIST OFFICES

The Greek National Tourist Organisation (GNTO) is known as EOT in Greece. There is either an EOT office or a local tourist office in almost every town of consequence and on many islands. Most do no more than give out brochures and maps. Popular destinations have tourist police, who can often help in finding accommodation.

Local Tourist Offices

The EOT head office (☎ 01-322 3111) is at Amerikis 2, Athens 10564. This office does not deal directly with the general public. Some of the main tourist offices are:

Athens
    Syntagma/Karageorgi Servias 2 (in the National Bank) (☎ 01-322 2545)
Patras
    Iroön Polytehniou 110 (☎ 061-420 303/304)
Piraeus
    EOT Building, Zea Marina (☎ 01-413 5716)
Thessaloniki
    Plateia Aristotelous 8 (☎ 031-271 888)

Tourist Offices Abroad

Australia
    51 Pitt St, Sydney, NSW 2000 (☎ 02-9241 1663)
Canada
    1300 Bay St, Toronto, Ontario MSR 3K8 (☎ 416-968 2220); 1233 Rue de la Montagne, Suite 101, Montreal, Quebec H3G 1Z2 (☎ 514-871 1535)
France
    3 Ave de l'Opéra, Paris 75001 (☎ 01 42 60 65 75)
Germany
    Neue Mainzerstrasse 22, 6000 Frankfurt (☎ 69-237 735); Pacellistrasse 2, W 8000 Munich 2 (☎ 89-222 035); Abteistrasse 33, 2000 Hamburg 13 (☎ 40-454 498); Wittenplatz 3A,10789 Berlin 30 (☎ 30-217 6262)
Italy
    Via L Bissolati 78-80, Rome 00187 (☎ 06-474 4249); Piazza Diaz 1, 20123 Milan (☎ 02-860 470)
Japan
    Fukuda Building West, 5F 2-11-3 Akasaka, Minato-ku, Tokyo 107 (☎ 03-350 55 911)
UK
    4 Conduit St, London W1R ODJ (☎ 0171-499 9758)
USA
    Olympic Tower, 645 5th Ave, New York, NY 10022 (☎ 212-421 5777); Suite 160, 168 North Michigan Ave, Chicago, Illinois 60601 (☎ 312-782 1091); Suite 2198, 611 West 6th St, Los Angeles, California 92668 (☎ 213-626 6696)

VISAS & EMBASSIES

Nationals of Australia, Canada, EU countries, Israel, New Zealand and the USA are allowed to stay in Greece for up to three months without a visa. For longer stays, apply at a consulate abroad or at least 20 days in advance to the Aliens Bureau (☎ 01-770 5711), Leoforos

Alexandros 173, Athens. Elsewhere in Greece apply to the local police authority. Singapore nationals can stay in Greece for 14 days without a visa.

In the past, Greece has refused entry to people whose passport indicates that they have visited Turkish-occupied North Cyprus, though there are reports that this is less of a problem now. To be on the safe side, however, ask the North Cyprus immigration officials to stamp a piece of paper rather than your passport. If you enter North Cyprus from the Greek Republic of Cyprus, no exit stamp is put in your passport.

Greek Embassies Abroad

Greece has diplomatic representation in the following countries:

Australia
    9 Turrana St, Yarralumla, Canberra, ACT 260 (☎ 062-73 3011)
Canada
    76-80 Maclaren St, Ottawa, Ontario K2P 0K (☎ 613-238 6271)
France
    17 Rue Auguste Vacquerie, 75116 Paris (☎ 01 47 23 72 28)
Germany
    Koblenzer Str 103, 5300 Bonn 2 (☎ 228-83010)
Italy
    Via S Mercadante 36, Rome 00198 (☎ 06-854 9630)
Japan
    16-30 Nishi Azabu, 3-chome, Minato-ku, Tokyo 1 (☎ 03-340 0871/0872)
New Zealand
    5-7 Willeston St, Wellington (☎ 04-473 7775)
South Africa
    Reserve Bank Building, St George's Rd, Cape Tow (☎ 21-24 8161)
Turkey
    Ziya-ul-Rahman Caddesi 9-11, Gazi Osman Pa 06700, Ankara (☎ 312-446 5496)
UK
    1A Holland Park, London W11 3TP (☎ 0171-229 3850)
USA
    2221 Massachusetts Ave NW, Washington, D 20008 (☎ 202-667 3169)

Foreign Embassies in Greece

The following countries have diplomatic representation in Greece:

Australia
  Dimitriou Soutsou 37, Athens 11521
  (☎ 01-644 7303)
Canada
  Genadiou 4, Athens 11521 (☎ 01-725 4011)
France
  Leoforos Vasilissis Sofias 7, Athens 10671
  (☎ 01-361 1663)
Germany
  Dimitriou 3 & Karaoli, 10675 Kolonaki
  (☎ 01-728 5111)
Italy
  Sekeri 2, Athens 10674 (☎ 01-361 7260)
Japan
  Athens Tower, Leoforos Messogion 2-4, Athens
  11527 (☎ 01-775 8101)
New Zealand (honorary consulate)
  Semitelou 9, Athens 11528 (☎ 01-771 0112)
South Africa
  Kifissias 60, Maroussi, Athens 15125
  (☎ 01-689 5330)
Turkey
  Vasilissis Georgiou B 8, Athens 10674
  (☎ 01-724 5915)
UK
  Ploutarhou 1, Athens 10675 (☎ 01-723 6211)
USA
  Leoforos Vasilissis Sofias 91, Athens 11521
  (☎ 01-721 2951)

CUSTOMS

Duty-free allowances in Greece are the same as for other EU countries. Import regulations for medicines are strict; if you are taking medication, make sure you get a statement from your doctor before you leave home. It is illegal, for example, to take codeine into Greece. The export of antiques is prohibited. You can bring as much foreign currency as you like, but if you want to leave with more than US$1000 in foreign banknotes the money must be declared on entry. It is illegal to bring in more than 100,000 dr, and to leave with more than 20,000 dr.

MONEY

Banks will exchange all major currencies, in either cash or travellers' cheques and also eurocheques. All post offices have exchange facilities and charge less commission than banks. Most travel agencies also change money, but check the commission charged.

All major credit cards are accepted, but only in larger establishments. If you run out of money, you can get a cash advance on a Visa card at the Greek Commercial Bank and on Access/MasterCard/Eurocard at the National

Bank, or you can find a major bank and ask them to cable your home bank for money (see Money in the Facts for the Visitor chapter at the start of this book).

American Express card-holders can draw cash from Credit Bank automatic teller machines.

Currency

The Greek unit of currency is the drachma (dr). Coins come in denominations of one, two, five, 10, 20, 50 and 100 dr. Banknotes come in 50, 100, 500, 1000, 5000 and 10,000 dr denominations.

Exchange Rates

Australia	A$1	=	185.13 dr
Canada	C$1	=	172.11 dr
France	1FF	=	47.07 dr
Germany	DM1	=	159.60 dr
Italy	L1000	=	154.98 dr
Japan	¥100	=	218.41 dr
New Zealand	NZ$1	=	164.75 dr
United Kingdom	UK£1	=	367.82 dr
United States	US$1	=	236.13 dr

Costs

Greece is no longer dirt cheap. A rock-bottom daily budget would be about 4000 dr, which would mean staying in hostels, self-catering and seldom taking buses or ferries. Allow at least 9000 dr per day if you want your own room and plan to eat out regularly, as well as travelling and seeing the sites. If you want a real holiday – comfortable rooms and restaurants all the way – reckon on close to 15,000 dr per day.

Tipping & Bargaining

In restaurants the service charge is included on the bill, but it is the custom to leave a small tip – just round off the bill. There are plenty of opportunities to practise your bargaining skills. If you want to dive in the deep end, try haggling with the taxi drivers at Athens airport after a long flight! Accommodation is nearly always negotiable outside peak season, especially if you are staying more than one night. Souvenir shops are another place where substantial savings can be made. Prices in other shops are normally clearly marked and non-negotiable.

Consumer Taxes

The value-added tax (VAT) varies from 15 to 18%. A tax-rebate scheme applies at a restricted number of shops and stores; look for a Tax Free sign in the window. You must fill in a form at the shop and present it with the receipt at the airport on departure. A cheque will (hopefully) be sent to your home address.

POST & COMMUNICATIONS
Post

Postal rates for cards and small air-mail letters (up to 20g) are 120 dr to EU destinations, and 150 dr elsewhere. The service is slow but reliable – five to eight days within Europe and about 10 days to the USA, Australia and New Zealand.

Post offices are usually open from 7.30 am to 2 pm. In major cities they stay open until 8 pm and also open from 7.30 am to 2 pm on Saturday. Do not wrap up a parcel until it has been inspected at the post office.

Mail can be sent poste restante to any main post office and is held for up to one month. Your surname should be underlined and you will need to show your passport when you collect your mail. Parcels are not delivered in Greece – they must be collected from a post office.

Telephone

The phone system is modern and efficient. All public phone boxes use phonecards, sold at OTE telephone offices and *periptera* (kiosks). Three cards are available: 100 units (1300 dr), 500 units (6000 dr) and 1000 units (11,500 dr). A local call costs one unit. The 'i' at the top left hand of the dialling panel on public phones brings up the operating instructions in English. Some periptera have metered phones. On the islands, you can often use the phones at travel agents, but they add a hefty surcharge.

Direct-dial long-distance and international calls can also be made from public phones. Many countries participate in the Home Country Direct scheme, which allows you to access an operator in your home country for reverse-charge calls.

If you're calling Greece from abroad, the country code is ☎ 30. If you're making an international call from Greece, the international access code is ☎ 00.

Fax & Telex

Telegrams can be sent from any OTE office. Larger offices have telex facilities. Main city post offices have fax facilities.

NEWSPAPERS & MAGAZINES

The most widely read Greek newspapers are *Ethnos*, *Ta Nea* and *Apoyevmatini*, all of which are dailies.

Newspapers printed in English include the daily *Athens News* (250 dr) and the weekly *Greek Times* (300 dr). *The Athenian* (600 dr) is a quality monthly magazine with articles on politics and the arts. Foreign newspapers are widely available, although only between April and October in smaller resort areas. The papers reach Athens (Syntagma) at 1 pm on the day of publication on weekdays and 7 pm at weekends. They are not available until the following day in other areas.

RADIO & TV

There are plenty of radio stations to choose from, especially in Athens, but not many broadcast in English. Athens International FM broadcasts the BBC World Service live 24 hours a day, interspersed with occasional Greek programs. If you have a short-wave radio, the best frequencies for the World Service are 618, 941 and 1507 MHz.

The nine TV channels offer nine times as much rubbish as one channel. You'll find the occasional American action drama in English (with Greek subtitles). News junkies can get their fix with CNN and Euronews.

PHOTOGRAPHY

Major brands of film are widely available, but quite expensive outside major towns. In Athens, a 36-exposure role of Kodak Gold ASA 100 costs about 1500 dr. You'll pay at least 500 dr more on the islands.

Never photograph military installations or anything else with a sign forbidding pictures. Greeks usually love having their photos taken but ask first. Because of the brilliant sunlight in summer, it's a good idea to use a polarising lens filter.

TIME

Greece is two hours ahead of GMT/UTC, and three hours ahead on daylight-saving time which begins at 12.01 am on the last Sunday in March, when clocks are put forward one hour. Clocks are put back an hour at 12.01 am on the last Sunday in September.

Out of daylight-saving time, at noon in Greece it is also noon in İstanbul, 10 am in London, 11 am in Rome, 2 am in San Francisco, 5 am in New York and Toronto, 8 pm in Sydney and 10 pm in Auckland. These times do not make allowance for daylight saving in the other countries.

ELECTRICITY
The electric current is 220V, 50 Hz, and plugs have two round pins. All hotel rooms have power points, and most camping grounds have power.

WEIGHTS & MEASURES
Greece uses the metric system. Liquids are sold by weight rather than volume – 950g of wine, for example, is equivalent to 1000 ml. Like other Continental Europeans, Greeks indicate decimals with commas and thousands with points.

LAUNDRY
Large towns and some islands have laundrettes. They charge 2000 to 2500 dr to wash and dry a load, whether you do it yourself or leave it to them. Hotels can normally provide you with a wash tub.

TOILETS
You'll find public toilets at all major bus and train stations, but they are seldom very pleasant. You will need to supply your own paper. In town, a café is the best bet, but the owner won't be impressed if you don't buy something.

A warning: Greek plumbing cannot handle toilet paper; always put it in the bin provided.

HEALTH
Tap water is generally safe to drink in Greece. The biggest health risk comes from the sun, so take care against sunburn, heat exhaustion and dehydration. Mosquitoes can be troublesome but coils and repellents are widely available.

Watch out for sea urchins around rocky beaches; if you get some of their needles embedded in your skin, olive oil will help to loosen them. Beware also of jellyfish; although the Mediterranean species are not lethal, their sting can be painful. Greece's only poisonous

snake is the adder, but they are rare. They like to sunbathe on dry-stone walls, so it's worth having a look before climbing one.

Greece's notorious sheepdogs are almost always all bark and no bite, but if you are going to trek in remote areas, you should consider having rabies injections. There is at least one doctor on every island in Greece and larger islands have hospitals or major medical clinics. Pharmacies are widespread – in cities, at least one is rostered to be open 24 hours. All pharmacies have a list of all-night pharmacies on their doors. Remember that codeine is banned in Greece, and ensure that you carry a statement from your doctor if you have prescribed drugs with you.

The number to ring throughout Greece for advice on first aid is ☎ 166. (See the Health section in the Facts for the Visitor chapter at the start of this book for more details on travel health.)

WOMEN TRAVELLERS
Many foreign women travel alone in Greece. Hassles occur, but they tend to be a nuisance rather than threatening. Women travelling alone in rural areas are usually treated with respect. In rural areas it's a good idea to dress conservatively, although it is perfectly OK to wear shorts, short skirts etc in touristy places. If you are pestered, ignore the guy and you'll find that the hint is usually taken.

GAY & LESBIAN TRAVELLERS
Greece is a popular destination amongst gay and lesbian travellers and Mykonos and Lesvos are still the most popular islands. The address of the Greek Gay Liberation Organisation is PO Box 2777, Athens 10022. The monthly magazine To Kraximo has information about the local scene.

DISABLED TRAVELLERS
If mobility is a problem, the hard fact is that most hotels, museums and ancient sites are not wheelchair accessible. Lavinia Tours (☎ 031-23 2828), Egnatia 101 (PO Box 11106), Thessaloniki 54110, has information for disabled people coming to Greece.

SENIOR TRAVELLERS
Elderly people are shown great respect in Greece. There are some good deals available

for EU nationals. For starters, those over 60 qualify for a 50% discount on train travel plus five free journeys per year. Take your ID card or passport to a Greek Railways (OSE) office and you will be given a Senior Card. The five free journeys may not be taken 10 days before or after Christmas or Easter, or between 1 July and 30 September. Pensioners also get a discount at museums and ancient sites.

DANGERS & ANNOYANCES

Greece has the lowest crime rate in Europe, and crimes are most likely to be committed by other travellers. Drug laws are strict. There's a minimum seven-year sentence for possession of even a small quantity of dope.

BUSINESS HOURS

Banks are open Monday to Thursday from 8.30 am to 2.30 pm, and Friday from 8.30 am to 2 pm. Some city banks also open from 3.30 to 6.30 pm and on Saturday morning. Shops open from 8 am to 1.30 pm and 5.30 to 8.30 pm on Tuesday, Thursday and Friday, and from 8 am to 2.30 pm on Monday, Wednesday and Saturday, but these times are not always strictly adhered to. Periptera (kiosks) are open from early morning to midnight. All banks and shops, and most museums and archaeological sites, close during holidays.

PUBLIC HOLIDAYS & SPECIAL EVENTS

Public holidays are as follows: New Year's Day (1 January); Epiphany (6 January); Lent (first Sunday in March); Greek Independence Day (25 March); Good Friday; Easter Sunday; Spring Festival (1 May); Assumption Day (5 August); Okhi Day (28 October) – Metaxas' refusal to allow Mussolini's troops to cross Greece in WWII – is commemorated with military parades throughout the country; Christmas Day (25 December); and St Stephen's Day (26 December).

Easter is Greece's most important festival, with candle-lit processions, feasting and firework displays. The Orthodox Easter is 50 days after the first Sunday in Lent.

Numerous regional festivals take place throughout the year. If you're in the right place at the right time, you'll certainly be invited to join the revelry.

A number of cultural festivals are also held during the summer months. The most important is the Athens Festival, when plays, operas, ballet and classical music concerts are staged at the Theatre of Herodes Atticus. The festival is held in conjunction with the Epidaurus Festival, which features ancient Greek dramas at the theatre at Epidaurus. Ioannina, Patras and Thessaloniki also host cultural festivals.

ACTIVITIES
Windsurfing

Sailboards are widely available for hire at about 2000 dr an hour. The top spots for windsurfing are Hrysi Akti on Paros, and Vasiliki on Lefkada – reputedly one of the best places in the world to learn.

Skiing

Greece offers some of the cheapest skiing in Europe. There are 16 resorts dotted around the mainland, most of them in the north. They have all the basic facilities and are a pleasant alternative to the glitzy resorts of northern Europe. What's more, there are no package tours. More information is available from the Hellenic Ski Federation (☎ 01-524 0057), PO Box 8037, Omonia, Athens 10010, or from the EOT.

The largest resort is at Mt Parnassos, near Delphi. There are daily excursions to Mt Parnassos from Athens, organised by the ski department (☎ 01-324 1915) at Klaoudatos, a department store on Athinas. The return fare of 5000 dr includes a lift pass, and an extra 2500 dr gets you all the gear.

Hiking

The mountainous terrain is perfect for trekkers who want to get away from the crowds. Lonely Planet's *Trekking in Greece* is an in-depth guide to Greece's mountain trails. The popular routes are well marked and well maintained, including the E4 and E6 trans-European treks which both end in Greece. The Hellenic Federation of Mountaineering Clubs (also known as EOS; ☎ 01-323 4555), Karageorgi Servias 7, Athens, has information on conditions.

If you want someone to do the organising for you, Trekking Hellas, Filellinon 7, Athens 10557 (☎ 01-325 0853; fax 01-323 4548) offers a range of treks and other adventure activities throughout the country.

COURSES

If you are serious about learning Greek, an

intensive course at the start of your stay is a good way to go about it. Most of the courses are in Athens. The Athens Centre (☎ 01-701 2268; fax 01-701 8603), Archimidous 48, and the YWCA (XEN in Greek) (☎ 01-362 4291; fax 01-362 2400), Amerikis 11, both have good reputations.

There are also courses on the islands in summer. The Athens Centre moves to Spetses in June and July, while the Hellenic Culture Centre (☎ & fax 01-647 7465 or 0275-61 482) runs courses on the island of Ikaria from June to October.

More information about courses is available from EOT offices and Greek embassies.

WORK

The unemployment rate is one of the highest in Europe, so Greeks aren't exactly falling over themselves to give jobs to foreigners.

Your best chance of finding work is to do the rounds of the tourist hotels and bars at the beginning of the season. The few jobs available are hotly contested, despite the menial work and dreadful pay. EU nationals don't need a work permit, but everyone else does.

If you are an EU national, an employment agency worth contacting is Working Holidays, Pioneer Tours, Nikis 11, Athens (☎ 01-322 4321). It offers hotel and bar jobs, au pair work, fruit picking, etc.

ACCOMMODATION

There is a range of accommodation in Greece to suit every taste and pocket. All places to stay are subject to strict price controls set by the tourist police. By law, a notice must be displayed in every room, which states the category of the room and the price for each season. If you think you've been ripped off, contact the tourist police.

Many places – especially in rural areas and on the islands – are closed from the end of October until mid-April.

Camping

Greece has almost 350 camping grounds. Prices vary according to facilities, but reckon on about 1000 dr per person and about 750 dr for a small tent. Most sites are open only from April to October. Freelance camping is officially forbidden, but often tolerated in remoter areas.

Hostels

You'll find youth hostels in most major towns and on half a dozen islands. The only place affiliated to Hostelling International (HI) is the superb Athens International Youth Hostel (☎ 01-523 4170). Most hostels are run by the Greek Youth Hostel Organisation (☎ 01-751 9530), Damareos 75, 11633 Athens. There are affiliated hostels in Athens (two), Litohoro (Mt Olympus), Mycenae, Olympia, Patras and Thessaloniki on the mainland; and on the islands of Corfu, Crete, Ios, Naxos, Santorini (Thira) and Tinos. There are six on Crete – at Iraklio, Malia, Myrthios, Plakias, Rethymno and Sitia.

Other hostels belong to the Greek Youth Hostels Association (☎ 01-323 4107), Dragatsaniou 4, 105 59 Athens. It has hostels in Delphi and Nafplio on the mainland, and on the islands of Corfu, Crete (Hersonisos) and Santorini.

Whatever their affiliation, the hostels are mostly very casual places. Their rates vary from 1000 to 1500 dr.

Athens has a number of private hostels catering to budget travellers. Standards vary enormously – from clean, friendly places to veritable fleapits. Most charge from 1500 to 2000 dr for dorm beds.

There are YWCA hostels (XEN in Greek) for women only in Athens and Thessaloniki.

Domatia

Domatia are the Greek equivalent of the British bed and breakfast, minus the breakfast. Once upon a time, domatia consisted of little more than spare rooms that families would rent out in summer to supplement their income. Nowadays many domatia are purpose-built appendages to the family house. Rates start at about 3500/6000 dr for singles/doubles, rising to 5000/8000 dr.

Hotels

Hotels are classified as deluxe, A, B, C, D or E class. The ratings seldom seem to have much bearing on the price, but expect to pay 4000/8000 dr for singles/doubles in D and E class, and about 8000/12,000 dr in a decent C-class place. Some places are classified as pensions and rated differently. Both are allowed to levy a 10% surcharge for stays of less than three nights, but they seldom do. It normally works the other way, and you can bargain if you're staying more than one night. Prices are about 40% cheaper between October and May.

Apartments

Self-contained family apartments are available in some hotels and domatia. There are also a number of purpose-built apartments, particularly on the islands, which are available for either long or short-term rental.

Traditional Settlements

Traditional settlements are old buildings of architectural merit that have been renovated and turned into tourist accommodation. They are terrific places to stay if you can afford 10,000 to 15,000 dr for a double. The EOT has information on the settlements.

Houses & Flats

For long-term rental accommodation in Athens, check the advertisements in the English-language newspapers. (See also Places to Stay in the Athens section.) In rural areas, ask around in tavernas.

Refuges

Greece has 55 mountain refuges, which are listed in the booklet *Greece Mountain Refuges & Ski Centres*, available free of charge at EOT and EOS offices.

FOOD

If Greek food conjures up an uninspiring vision of lukewarm moussaka collapsing into a plate of olive oil, take heart – there's a lot more on offer.

Snacks

Greece has a great range of fast-food options for the inveterate snacker. Foremost among them are the *gyros* and the *souvlaki*. The gyros is a giant skewer laden with slabs of seasoned meat that grills slowly as it rotates, the meat being steadily trimmed from the outside. Souvlaki are small, individual kebabs. Both are served wrapped in pitta bread with salad and lashings of tzatziki (a yoghurt, cucumber and garlic dip). Other snacks are pretzel rings, *spanakopitta* (spinach and cheese pie) and *tyropitta* (cheese pie). Dried fruits and nuts are also very popular.

Starters

Greece is famous for its appetisers, known as *mezedes*, (literally, 'tastes'). Standards include tzatziki, *melitzanosalata* (aubergine dip), taramasalata (fish-roe dip), dolmades (stuffed vine leaves), *fasolia* (beans) and *oktapodi* (octopus). A selection of three or four represents a good meal and can be a good option for vegetarians. Most dishes cost between 400 dr and 800 dr.

Main Dishes

You'll find moussaka (layers of aubergine and mince, topped with cheese sauce and baked) on every menu, alongside a number of other taverna staples. They include *moschari* (oven-baked veal and potatoes), *keftedes* (meatballs), *stifado* (meat stew), *pastitsio* (macaroni with mince meat and béchamel sauce, baked) and *yemista* (either tomatoes or green peppers stuffed with mince meat and rice). Most main courses cost between 1000 dr and 1500 dr.

The most popular fish are *barbouni* (red mullet) and *ksifias* (swordfish), but they don't come cheap. Prices start at about 2000 dr for a serve. *Kalamaria* (fried squid) are readily available and cheap at about 1000 dr for a decent serve.

Fortunately for vegetarians, salad is a mainstay of the Greek diet. The most popular is *horiatiki salata*, normally listed on English menus as Greek or country salad. It's a mixed salad of cucumbers, peppers, onions, olives, tomatoes and feta (white sheep or goat cheese).

Desserts

Turkish in origin, most Greek desserts are variations on pastry soaked in honey. Popular ones include baklava (thin layers of pastry filled with honey and nuts) and kadaifi (shredded wheat soaked in honey). Delicious thick yoghurt *(yiaourti)* and rice pudding *(rizogalo)* are also available.

Restaurants

There are several varieties of restaurants. An *estiatoria* is a straightforward restaurant with a printed menu. A taverna is often cheaper and more typically Greek, and you'll probably be invited to peer into the pots. A *psistaria* specialises in charcoal-grilled dishes. *Ouzeria* (ouzo bars) often have such a good range of mezedes that they can be regarded as eating places.

Kafeneia

Kafeneia are the smoke-filled cafés where men gather to drink coffee, play backgammon and cards and engage in heated political discussion. They are a bastion of male chauvinism that Greek women have yet to break down. Female tourists tend to avoid them too, but those who venture in invariably find they are treated courteously.

Self-Catering

Buying and preparing your own food is easy in Greece as there are well-stocked grocery stores and fruit and vegetable shops everywhere. In addition, villages and each area of a town hold a once or twice-weekly *laiki agora* (street market) where goods are sold. These markets are great fun to stroll around, whether or not you are cooking for yourself.

DRINKS

Nonalcoholic Drinks

The tap water is safe to drink, but many people prefer bottled mineral water. It's cheap and available everywhere, as are soft drinks and packaged juices.

Greeks are great coffee drinkers. Greek coffee (known as Turkish coffee until the words became unspeakable after the 1974 invasion of Cyprus) comes three main ways. Greeks like it thick and sweet *(glyko)*. If you prefer less sugar, ask for *metrio*; *sketo* means without sugar. Instant coffee is known as Nescafé, which is what it usually is. If you want milk with your coffee, ask for *Nescafé me ghala*.

Alcohol

Greece is traditionally a wine-drinking society. If you're spending a bit of time in the country, it's worth acquiring a taste for retsina (resinated wine). The best (and worst) flows straight from the barrel in the main production areas of Attica and central Greece. Tavernas charge about 700 dr for a litre. Retsina is available by the bottle everywhere. Greece also produces a large range of non-resinated wines from traditional grape varieties.

Amstel is the cheapest of several northern European beers produced locally under

licence. Expect to pay about 180 dr in a supermarket, or 350 dr in a restaurant. The most popular aperitif is the aniseed-flavoured ouzo.

ENTERTAINMENT

The busy nightlife is a major attraction for many travellers. Nowhere is the pace more frenetic than on the islands in high season; Ios and Paros are famous for their raging discos and bars. Discos abound in all resort areas. If you enjoy theatre and classical music, Athens and Thessaloniki are the places to be.

Greeks are great movie-goers. You'll find cinemas everywhere. They show films in the original language (usually English) with Greek subtitles.

SPECTATOR SPORT

Greek men are football mad, both as spectators and participants. If you happen to be eating in a taverna on a night when a big match is being televised, expect indifferent service. Basketball is another boom sport.

THINGS TO BUY

Greece produces a vast array of handicrafts, including woollen rugs, ceramics, leather work, hand-woven woollen shoulder bags, embroidery, copperware and carved-wood products. Beware of tacky imitations in tourist areas.

Getting There & Away

AIR

There are no less than 16 international airports, but most of them handle only summer charter flights to the islands. Athens handles the vast majority of international flights, including all intercontinental flights. Athens has regular scheduled flights to all the European capitals, and Thessaloniki is also well served. Most flights are with the national carrier, Olympic Airways, or the flag carrier of the country concerned.

Europe

Flying is the fastest, easiest and cheapest way of getting to Greece from northern Europe. What's more, the scheduled flights are very competitvely priced these days so it's hardly worth hunting around for charter cheapies.

For example, Olympic Airways, British Airways and Virgin Atlantic all offer 30-day return tickets from London for under UK£220 (midweek departures) in high season, and Olympic and British Airways both offer returns to Thessaloniki for about UK£210.

Charter flights from London to Athens are readily available for UK£99/189 one way/return in high season, dropping to UK£70/129 in low season. Fares are about UK£109/209 to most island destinations in high season. Similar deals are available from charter operators throughout Europe.

There is one important condition for charter-flight travellers (only) to bear in mind. If you travel to Greece on a return ticket, you will invalidate the return portion if you visit Turkey. If you turn up at the airport for your return flight with a Turkish stamp in your passport, you will be forced to buy another ticket.

Athens is a good place to buy cheap air tickets. Examples of one-way fares include London (25,000 dr), Paris (40,000 dr) and Amsterdam (48,000 dr).

North America

Delta Airlines, Olympic and Trans-World Airlines all have daily flights from New York to Athens. Apex return fares range from US$900 to US$1400. Olympic also has a weekly flight from Boston (same fares), and two flights a week from Toronto via Montreal. Apex fares start at C$1098. You'll get better deals from the discount operators.

Australia

Olympic flies to Athens twice a week from Sydney via Melbourne. Fares range from A$1730 to A$2199.

LAND
Northern Europe

Overland travel between northern Europe and Greece is virtually a thing of the past. Buses and trains can't compete with cheap airfares, and the turmoil in former Yugoslavia has cut the shortest overland route. All bus and train services now go via Italy and take the ferries over to Greece.

Bus Olympic Bus operates the only year-round service between London and Athens, travelling via Brussels, Frankfurt, Munich, Innsbruck, Venice and Brindisi. Buses leave London (☎ 0171-837 9141) on Friday, and Athens (☎ 01-324 4633) on Tuesday. Fares drop as low as UK£50 one way at times. Eurolines operates between London and Athens only during August and September.

Train Unless you have a Eurail pass, travelling to Greece by train is prohibitively expensive. Greece is part of the Eurail network, and passes are valid on ferries operated by Adriatica di Navigazione and Hellenic Mediterranean Lines from Brindisi to Corfu, Igoumenitsa and Patras.

Neighbouring Countries

Bus The Hellenic Railways Organisation (OSE) has two buses a day from Athens to İstanbul (22 hours; 16,600 dr), leaving at 8 am and 7 pm. It also has daily services to Tirana (Albania) and Sofia (Bulgaria). All depart from the Peloponnese train station in Athens.

Train There are daily trains between Athens and İstanbul for 13,250 dr, but the service is incredibly slow, crowded and uncomfortable. Stick to the buses. There is also a daily train from Athens to Sofia (18 hours, 9000 dr).

Car & Motorcycle The crossing points into Turkey are at Kipi and Kastanies; the crossings into the Former Yugoslav Republic of Macedonia (FYROM) are at Evzoni and Niki; and the Bulgarian crossing is at Promahonas. All are open 24 hours a day. The crossing points to Albania are at Kakavia and Krystallopigi.

Hitching If you want to hitchhike to Turkey, look for a through-ride from Alexandroupolis because you cannot hitchhike across the border. If you're heading for Bulgaria, try to get a lift from Thessaloniki through to Sofia, as lifts are difficult to find after Servia.

SEA
Italy

The most popular crossing is from Brindisi to Patras (18 hours), via Corfu (nine hours) and Igoumenitsa (10 hours). There are numerous services. Deck-class fares start at about 7000 dr one way in low season, 10,000 dr in high season. Eurail pass-holders can travel free with both Adriatica di Navigazione and Hellenic Mediterranean. You still need to make a reservation and pay port taxes – L8000 in Italy, and 1500 dr in Greece.

There are also ferries to Patras from Ancona, Bari, Trieste and Venice, stopping at either Corfu or Igoumenitsa on the way. In summer there are also ferries from Bari and Brindisi to Kefallonia, from Otranto and Ortona to Igoumenitsa and from Ancona to Iraklio on Crete.

Turkey

There are five regular ferry services between the Greek islands and Turkey: Lesvos-Ayvalık, Chios-Çeşme, Samos-Kuşadası, Kos-Bodrum and Rhodes-Marmaris. All are daily services in summer, dropping to weekly in winter. Tickets must be bought a day in advance and you will be asked to hand over your passport. It will be returned on the boat.

Cyprus & Israel

Salamis Lines operates a weekly, year-round service from Piraeus to Lemessos (formerly Limassol) on Cyprus and the Israeli port of Haifa, stopping at Rhodes on the way. Deck-class fares from Haifa are US$105 to Rhodes and US$110 to Piraeus. The fares from Lemessos are US$70 to Rhodes and US$75 to Piraeus. There are two other services in summer, both travelling via Iraklio on Crete.

LEAVING GREECE

An airport tax of 6000 dr for international flights is included in airfares. The tax is to help pay for Athens' new airport. Port taxes are 1500 dr to Italy and 4000 dr to Turkey.

Getting Around

AIR

Most domestic flights are operated by Olympic Airways and its offshoot, Olympic Aviation. They offer a busy schedule in summer with flights from Athens to 22 islands and a range of mainland cities. Sample fares include

Athens-Iraklio for 20,500 dr, Athens-Rhodes for 23,100 dr and Athens-Thessaloniki for 20,700. There are also flights from Thessaloniki to the islands. It is advisable to book at least two weeks in advance, especially in summer. Services to the islands are fairly skeletal in winter. Air Greece provides competition on a few major routes, such as Athens-Iraklio (18,100 dr).

All the above fares include the 3100-dr tax on domestic flights, paid when you buy your ticket.

BUS

Buses are the most popular form of public transport. They are comfortable, they run on time and there are frequent services on all the major routes. Almost every town on the mainland (except in Thrace) has at least one bus a day to Athens. Local companies can get you to all but the remotest villages. Reckon on paying about 1000 dr per hour of journey time. Sample fares from Athens include 7300 dr to Thessaloniki (7½ hours) and 3200 dr to Patras (three hours). Tickets should be bought at least an hour in advance in summer to ensure a seat.

Major islands also have comprehensive local bus networks. In fact, every island with a road has a service of some sort, but they tend to operate at the whim of the driver.

TRAIN

Trains are generally looked on as a poor alternative to bus travel. The main problem is that there are only two main lines: to Thessaloniki and Alexandroupolis in the north and to the Peloponnese in the south. In addition there are a number of branch lines, such as Pyrgos-Olympia and the spectacular Diakofto-Kalavryta mountain railway.

If there are trains going in your direction, they are a good way to travel. Be aware though that there are two distinct levels of service: the painfully slow, dilapidated trains that stop at all stations and the faster, modern intercity trains.

The slow trains represent the cheapest form of transport. It may take five hours to crawl from Athens to Patras, but the 2nd-class fare is only 1580 dr. Intercity trains do the trip in just over three hours for 2580 dr – still cheaper than the bus.

Inter-Rail and Eurail passes are valid in Greece, but you still need to make a reservation. In summer, make reservations at least two days in advance.

CAR & MOTORCYCLE

Car is a great way to explore areas that are off the beaten track. Bear in mind that roads in remote regions are often poorly maintained. You'll need a good road map.

EU nationals need only their normal licence; others need an International Driving Permit. You can bring a vehicle into Greece for four months without a carnet – only a Green Card (international third-party insurance) is required.

Average prices for fuel are 210 dr per litre for super, 195 dr for unleaded and 140 dr for diesel.

Most islands are served by car ferries, but they are expensive. Sample fares for small cars from Piraeus include 15,200 dr to Crete and 18,600 dr to Rhodes. If you are going to take your car island-hopping, do some research first – cars are useless on some of the smaller islands.

Road Rules

Greek motorists are famous for ignoring the road rules, which is probably why the country has the highest road fatality rate in Europe. No casual observer would ever guess that it was compulsory to wear seat belts in the front seats of vehicles, nor that it was compulsory to wear a crash helmet on motorcycles of more than 50 cc – always insist on a helmet when renting a motorcycle.

The speed limit for cars is 120 km/h on toll roads, 90 km/h outside built-up areas and 50 km/h in built-up areas. For motorcycles, the speed limit outside built-up areas is 70 km/h. Speeding fines start at 30,000 dr. Drink-driving laws are strict – a blood alcohol content of 0.05% incurs a penalty and over 0.08% is a criminal offence.

All cars are required to have a first-aid kit, a fire extinguisher and triangular warning sign (in case of a breakdown).

Rental

Car hire is expensive, especially from the multinational hire companies. Their high-season weekly rates with unlimited mileage start at about 105,000 dr for the smallest

models, dropping to 85,000 dr in winter – and that's without tax and extras. You can generally do much better with local companies. Their advertised rates are 25% lower and they're often willing to bargain.

Mopeds, however, are cheap and available everywhere. Most places charge about 3000 dr per day.

Automobile Association

The Greek automobile club, ELPA, offers reciprocal services to members of other national motoring associations. If your vehicle breaks down, dial ☎ 104.

BICYCLE

People do cycle in Greece, but you'll need strong leg muscles to tackle the mountainous terrain. You can hire bicycles, but they are not nearly as widely available as cars and motorcycles. Prices range from about 1000 to 3000 dr. Bicycles are carried free on most ferries.

HITCHING

The further you are from a city, the easier hitching becomes. Getting out of major cities can be hard work, and Athens is notoriously difficult. In remote areas, people may stop to offer a lift even if you aren't hitching.

BOAT
Ferry

Every island has a ferry service of some sort. They come in all shapes and sizes, from the state-of-the-art 'superferries' that run on the major routes to the ageing open ferries that operate local services to outlying islands.

The hub of the vast ferry network is Piraeus, the main port of Athens. It has ferries to the Cyclades, Crete, the Dodecanese, the Saronic Gulf islands and the North-Eastern Aegean islands. Patras is the main port for ferries to the Ionian islands, while Volos and Agios Konstantinos are the ports for the Sporades.

Some of the smaller islands are virtually inaccessible in winter, when schedules are cut back to a minimum. Services start to pick up in April and are running at full steam from June to September.

Fares are fixed by the government. The small differences in price you may find between ticket agencies are the result of some agencies sacrificing part of their designated

Greece – Getting Around 429

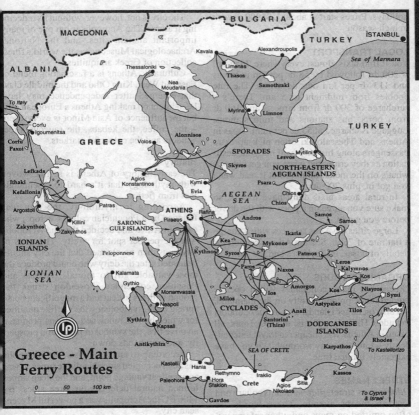

Greece - Main Ferry Routes

0   50   100 km

commission to qualify as a 'discount service'. The discount seldom amounts to more than 50 dr. Tickets can be bought at the last minute from quayside tables set up next to the boats. Prices are the same, contrary to what you will be told by agencies. Unless you specify otherwise, you will automatically be sold deck class, which is the cheapest fare. Sample fares from Piraeus include 3550 dr to Mykonos and 4280 dr to Santorini (Thira).

Hydrofoil

Hydrofoils operate competing services on some of the most popular routes. They cost about twice as much as the ferries, but get you there in half the time.

Yacht

It's hardly a budget option, but *the* way to see the islands is by yacht. There are numerous places to hire boats, both with and without crew. If you want to go it alone, two crew members must have sailing certificates. Prices start at about US$1200 per week for a four-person boat. A skipper will cost an extra US$700 per week.

Individuals can sign up with one of the companies that offer fully catered yachting holidays. Prices start at about US$900 a week in high season.

LOCAL TRANSPORT
You'll find taxis almost everywhere. Flag fall is 200 dr, followed by 58 dr per km in towns and 113 dr per km outside towns. The rate doubles from midnight to 5 am. There's a surcharge of 300 dr from airports and 160 dr from ports, bus stations and train stations. Luggage is charged at 55 dr per item. Taxis in Athens and Thessaloniki often pick up extra passengers along the way (yell out your destination as they cruise by; when you get out, pay what's on the meter, minus what it read when you got in, plus 200 dr).

In rural areas taxis don't have meters, so make sure you agree on a price with the driver before you get in.

Large cities have bus services which charge a flat rate of 75 dr. See the Athens section for details of buses, trolleybuses and the metro.

ORGANISED TOURS
Greece has many companies which operate guided tours, predominantly on the mainland, but also on larger islands. The major operators include CHAT, Key Tours and GO Tours, all based in Athens. It is cheaper to travel independently – tours are only worthwhile if you have extremely limited time.

STREET NAMES
Odos means street, *plateia* means square and *leoforos* means avenue. These words are often omitted on maps and other references, so we have done the same throughout this chapter, except when to do so would cause confusion.

Athens Αθήνα

Ancient Athens ranks alongside Rome and Jerusalem for its glorious past and its influence on Western civilisation, but the modern city is a place few people fall in love with.

However inspiring the Acropolis might be, most visitors have trouble coming to terms with the surrounding urban sprawl, the appalling traffic congestion and the pollution.

The city is not, however, without its redeeming features. The Acropolis is but one of many important ancient sites, and the National Archaeological Museum has the world's finest collection of Greek antiquities.

Culturally, Athens is a fascinating blend of East and West. King Otho and the middle class that emerged after Independence may have been intent on making Athens a European city, but the influence of Asia Minor is everywhere – the coffee, the kebabs, the raucous street vendors and the colourful markets.

History
The early history of Athens is so interwoven with mythology that it's hard to disentangle fact from fiction.

According to mythology, the city was founded by a Phoenician called Cecrops, who came to Attica and decided that the Acropolis was the perfect spot for a city. The gods of Olympus then proclaimed that the city should be named after the deity who could produce the most valuable gift to mortals. Athena and Poseidon contended. Poseidon struck the ground with his trident and a magnificent horse sprang forth, symbolising the warlike qualities for which he was renowned. Athena produced an olive tree, the symbol of peace and prosperity, and won hands down.

According to archaeologists, the Acropolis has been occupied since Neolithic times. It was an excellent vantage point, and the steep slopes formed natural defences on three sides. By 1400 BC the Acropolis was a powerful Mycenaean city.

Its power peaked during the so-called golden age of Athens in the 5th century BC, following the defeat of the Persians at the Battle of Salamis. It fell into decline after its defeat by Sparta in the long-running Peloponnesian War, but rallied again in Roman times when it became a seat of learning. The Roman emperors, particularly Hadrian, graced Athens with many grand buildings.

After the Roman Empire split into east and west, power shifted to Byzantium and the city fell into obscurity. By the end of Ottoman rule, Athens was little more than a dilapidated village (the area now known as Plaka).

Then, in 1834, Athens became the capital of independent Greece. The newly crowned King Otho, freshly arrived from Bavaria, began rebuilding the city along neoclassical lines, featuring large squares and tree-lined boulevards with imposing public buildings. The city grew steadily and enjoyed a brief heyday as the 'Paris of the Mediterranean' in the late 19th and early 20th centuries.

This came to an abrupt end with the forced population exchange between Greece and Turkey that followed the Treaty of Lausanne in 1923. The huge influx of refugees from Asia Minor virtually doubled the population overnight, forcing the hasty erection of the first of the concrete apartment blocks that dominate the city today. The belated advent of Greece's industrial age in the 1950s brought another wave of migration, this time of rural folk looking for jobs. This trend continues.

Orientation

Although Athens is a huge, sprawling city, nearly everything of interest to travellers is located within a small area bounded by Omonia Square (Plateia Omonias) to the north, Monastiraki Square (Plateia Monastirakiou) to the west, Syntagma Square (Plateia Syntagmatos) to the east and the Plaka district to the south. The city's two major landmarks, the Acropolis and Lykavittos Hill, can be seen from just about everywhere in this area.

Syntagma is the heart of modern Athens; it's flanked by luxury hotels, banks and expensive coffee shops and dominated by the old royal palace – home of the Greek parliament since 1935.

Omonia is decidedly sleazy these days. It's more of a transport hub than a square. The major streets of central Athens all meet here. Panepistimiou (El Venizelou) and Stadiou run parallel south-east to Syntagma, while Athinas leads south from Omonia to the market district of Monastiraki. Monastiraki is in turn linked to Syntagma by Ermou – home to some of the city's smartest shops – and Mitropoleos.

Mitropoleos skirts the northern edge of Plaka, the delightful old Turkish quarter which was virtually all that existed when Athens was declared the capital of independent Greece. Its labyrinthine streets are nestled on the northeastern slope of the Acropolis, and most of the city's ancient sites are close by. It may be touristy, but it's the most attractive and interesting part of Athens and the majority of visitors make it their base.

Streets are clearly signposted in Greek and English. If you do get lost, it's very easy to find help. A glance at a map is often enough to draw an offer of assistance. Anyone you ask will be able to direct you to Syntagma (say SYN-tagma).

Information

Tourist Offices EOT's head office (☎ 322 3111) at Amerikis 2 does not deal with enquiries from the general public. The organisation's public face is a small information window (☎ 322 2545) in the National Bank of Greece building on Syntagma. It's worth asking for their free map of Athens, which has most of the places of interest clearly marked and also shows the trolleybus routes. There's also a notice board with transport information, including ferry departures from Piraeus. This window is open Monday to Friday from 8 am to 6 pm and Saturday from 9 am to 2 pm.

The EOT office (☎ 979 9500) at the East airport terminal is open Monday to Friday from 9 am to 7 pm and Saturday from 10 am to 5 pm.

The tourist police (☎ 902 5992) are open 24 hours a day at Dimitrakopoulou 77, Veïkou. Take trolleybus No 1, 5 or 9 from Syntagma. They also have a 24-hour information service (☎ 171).

Money Most of the major banks have branches around Syntagma, open Monday to Thursday from 8 am to 2 pm and Friday from 8 am to 1.30 pm. The National Bank of Greece and the Credit Bank, on opposite sides of Stadiou at Syntagma, both have 24-hour automatic exchange machines.

American Express (☎ 324 4975), Ermou 2, Syntagma, is open Monday to Friday from 8.30 am to 4 pm, and Saturday from 8.30 am to 1.30 pm. Thomas Cook (☎ 322 0155) has an office at Karageorgi Servias 4, open Monday to Friday from 8.30 am to 8 pm, Saturday from 9 am to 6.30 pm and Sunday from 10 am to 2.30 pm.

In Plaka, Acropole Foreign Exchange, Kydathineon 23, is open from 9 am to midnight every day. The banks at both the East and West airport terminals are open 24 hours a day, although you may have trouble tracking down the staff late at night.

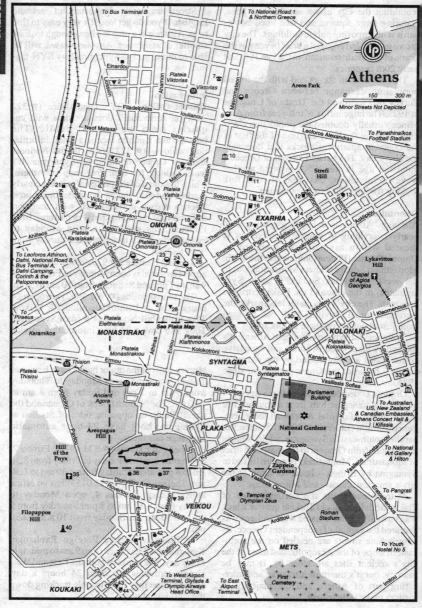

Athens

0   150   300 m

Minor Streets Not Depicted

To Bus Terminal B

To National Road 1 & Northern Greece

Einardou

Lofsson

Plateia Viktorias

Plateia Ahamon

Viktorias

7

Areos Park

8

9

Mavromateon

Filadelfias

Ioulianou

To Panathinaikos Football Stadium

Leoforos Alexandras

Neof Metaxa

Ipirou

Deligianni

Kerameon

3

4

Deligianni

5

Acharninon

Marni

28 Oktovriou – Patision

10

Tositsa

11

Strefi Hill

Solomou

15

16

12

13

21

Victor Hugo

19

20

Karolou

Veranzerou

18

OMONIA

EXARHIA

14

17

Lykavittos Hill

Ahilleos

Plateia Karaiskaki

Lehidiou

Agiou Konstantinou

Plateia Omonias

Omonia

Themistokleous

Emmanuel Benaki

Zoodohou Pigis

Harilaou Trikoupi

Mavromihali

Ippokratous

Akadimias

Solonos

Asklipiou

Chapel of Agios Georgios

Kleomenous

To Leoforos Athinon, Dafni, National Road 8, Bus Terminal A, Dafni Camping, Corinth & the Peloponnese

22

Plateia Vathis

23

24

25

Pireos

Panepistimiou (E Venizelou)

29

Stadiou

30

Amerikis

Voukourestiou

Lykavitou

KOLONAKI

Plateia Kolonakiou

To Piraeus

Keramikos

27

28

Plateia Eleftherias

See Plaka Map

MONASTIRAKI

Plateia Monastirakiou

Athinas

Eolou

Plateia Klafthmonos

Kolokotroni

SYNTAGMA

Kanaris

Ploutarhou

Kanari

31

32

33

Vasilissis Sofias

34

Plateia Thisiou

Thision

Ermou

Monastiraki

Ermou

Mitropoleos

Nikis

Filellinon

Plateia Syntagmatos

Parliament Building

Koumbari

To Australian, US, New Zealand & Canadian Embassies, Athens Concert Hall & Kifissia

Ancient Agora

Apostolou Pavlou

Areopagus Hill

PLAKA

Kydathineon

Amalias

National Gardens

Zappeio

To National Art Gallery & Hilton

Vasileos Konstantinou

Hill of the Pnyx

Acropolis

36

37

Dionysiou Areopagitou

Zappeio Gardens

Vasilissis Olgas

38

To Pangrati

35

Rovertou Galli

39

Misseon

Erehthiou

Hatzihristou

VEIKOU

Lembesi

Syngrou

Temple of Olympian Zeus

Vasileos Georgiou

Ardittou

Roman Stadium

Eratosthenous

Filopappos Hill

40

41

42

43

44

Veikou

Dimitrakopoulou

Drakou

Falirou

Kallirois

Voutadon

Zaharitsa

To West Airport Terminal, Glyfada & Olympic Airways Head Office

To East Airport Terminal

MEANS

METS

First Cemetery

Imitou

KOUKAKI

To Youth Hostel No 5

Post & Communications The main post office is at Eolou 100, Omonia (postcode 10200), which is where mail addressed to poste restante will be sent unless specified otherwise. If you're staying in Plaka, it's best to get mail sent to the Syntagma post office (postcode 10300). Both are open Monday to Friday from 7.30 am to 8 pm, Saturday from 7.30 am to 2 pm, and Sunday from 9 am to 1.30 pm. Parcels over two kg going abroad must be posted from the parcels office at Stadiou 4 (in the arcade). They should not be wrapped until they've been inspected.

The OTE telephone office at 28 Oktovriou-Patission 85 is open 24 hours a day, as is the office at Stadiou 15. The Omonia office, Athinas 50, is open from 7 am to 10 pm every day.

Athens' telephone code is ☎ 01.

If you need to send an e-mail, you could try the Saita (http://www.istos.net.gr/saita) cybercafé at Papathimiou 3.

Travel Agencies Most of the travel agencies are around Syntagma and Omonia, but only those around Syntagma deal in discount air fares. There are lots of them south of the square on Filellinon, Nikis and Voulis.

The International Student & Youth Travel Service (☎ 01-323 3767), 2nd floor, Nikis 11, is the city's official youth and student travel service. Apart from selling tickets, they also issue student cards.

Bookshops Athens has three good English-language bookshops: Pantelides Books at Amerikis 11, Eleftheroudakis at Nikis 4, and Compendium Bookshop at Nikis 28. Compendium also has a second-hand books section.

Cultural Centres The British Council (☎ 363 3215), Plateia Kolonaki 17, and the Hellenic American Union (☎ 362 9886), Massalias 22, hold frequent concerts, film shows, exhibitions etc. Both have libraries.

Laundry Plaka has a convenient laundry at Angelou Geronta 10, just off Kydathineon near the outdoor restaurants.

Medical & Emergency Services For emergency medical treatment, ring the tourist police (☎ 171) and they'll tell you where the nearest hospital is. Don't wait for an ambulance – get a taxi. Hospitals give free emergency treatment to tourists. For hospitals with outpatient departments on duty, ring ☎ 106. For first-aid advice, ring ☎ 166. You can get free dental treatment at the Evangelismos Hospital, Ipsilandou 45.

Dangers & Annoyances Although Athens is one of Europe's safest cities, a warning to solo male travellers about the following practice: a male traveller enters a bar, or is enticed there by a friendly local, and buys a drink; the owner then offers him a second drink. Girls appear, more drinks are provided and the visitor relaxes as he realises that the girls are not prostitutes, just friendly Greeks. The crunch comes when the traveller is eventually presented with an exorbitant bill. Beware of this scam, especially around Syntagma.

Things to See
Walking Tour The following walk starts and finishes at Syntagma Square and takes in most of Plaka's best-known sites. Without detours, it will take about 45 minutes. The route is marked with a dotted line on the Plaka map.

From Syntagma, walk along Mitropoleos and take the first turning left onto Nikis. Continue along here to the junction with Kydathineon, Plaka's main thoroughfare, and turn right. Opposite the church is the **Museum of Greek Folk Art**, which houses an excellent collection of embroidery, weaving and jewellery. It is open Tuesday to Sunday from 10 am to 2 pm; admission is 400 dr. After passing the square with the outdoor tavernas, take the second turning left onto Adrianou. A right turn at end of Adrianou leads to the small square with the **Choregic Monument of Lysicrates**, erected in 334 BC to commemorate victory in a choral festival.

Turn left and then right onto Epimenidou; at the top, turn right onto Thrasilou, which skirts the Acropolis. Where the road forks, veer left into the district of **Anafiotika**. Here the little white cubic houses resemble those of the Cyclades, and olive-oil cans brimming with flowers bedeck the walls of their tiny gardens. The houses were built by the people of Anafi, who were used as cheap labour in the rebuilding of Athens after Independence.

The path winds between the houses and comes to some steps on the right, at the bottom of which is a curving pathway leading downhill to Pratiniou. Turn left onto Pratiniou and veer right after 50 metres onto Tholou. The yellow-ochre Venetian building with brown shutters at No 5 is the old university, now the **Museum of the University**. It is open Monday and Wednesday from 2.30 to 7 pm, and Tues-

day, Thursday and Friday from 9.30 am to 2.30 pm. Admission is free.

At the end of Tholou, turn left onto Panos. At the top of the steps on the left is a restored 19th-century mansion which is now the **Paul & Alexandra Kanellopoulos Museum** – closed for repairs at the time of writing. Retracing your steps, go down Panos to the ruins of the **Roman Agora**, then turn left onto Polygnotou and walk to the crossroads. Opposite, Polygnotou continues to the **Ancient Agora**. At the crossroads, turn right and then left onto Poikilis, then immediately right onto Areos. On the right are the remains of the **Library of Hadrian** and next to it is the **Museum of Traditional Greek Ceramics**, open every day, except Tuesday, from 10 am to 2 pm. Admission is 500 dr. The museum is housed in the **Mosque of Tzistarakis**, built in 1759. After Independence it lost its minaret and was used as a prison.

Ahead is Monastiraki Square, named after the small church. To the left is the metro station and the **flea market**. Monastiraki is Athens at its noisiest, most colourful and chaotic; it's teeming with street vendors.

Turn right just beyond the mosque onto Pandrossou, a relic of the old Turkish bazar. At No 89 is Stavros Melissinos, the 'poet sandalmaker' of Athens who names the Beatles, Rudolph Nureyev and Jackie Onassis among his customers. Fame and fortune have not gone to his head – he still makes the best sandals in Athens, costing from 2400 dr per pair.

Pandrossou leads to Plateia Mitropoleos and the **Athens Cathedral**. The cathedral was constructed from the masonry of over 50 razed churches and from the designs of several architects. Next to it stands the much smaller, and far more appealing, old **Church of Agios Eleftherios**. Turn left after the cathedral, and then right onto Mitropoleos and back to Syntagma.

Acropolis Most of the buildings now gracing the Acropolis were commissioned by Pericles during the golden age of Athens in the 5th century BC. The site had been cleared for him by the Persians, who destroyed an earlier temple complex on the eve of the Battle of Salamis.

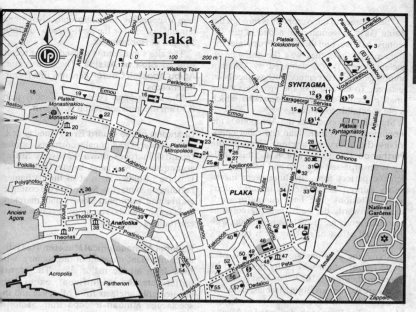

Plaka

0   100   200 m

Walking Tour

SYNTAGMA

Plateia
Kolokotroni

Plateia
Syntagmatos

PLAKA

National
Gardens

Ancient
Agora

Acropolis

Parthenon

Zappeio

PLACES TO STAY		49	The Cellar	24	Church of Agios
9	Hotel Grande Bretagne	52	Byzantino		Eleftherios
17	Hotel Tempi	53	Plaka Psistaria	25	National Welfare
27	John's Place	54	Ouzeri Kouklis		Organisation
40	Hotel Nefeli	55	Taverna Damigos	28	Syntagma Post Office
41	Acropolis House			29	Parliament
	Pension	**OTHER**		31	Bus 040 to Piraeus
42	Kouros Hotel	1	Pantiledes Books	32	International Student &
43	George's Guesthouse	2	OTE		Youth Travel Service
44	Festos Youth &	5	Parcel Post Office	33	Buses to Cape Sounion
	Student Guest	6	Festival Box Office	34	Compendium Books
	House	10	Credit Bank	35	Tower of the Winds
50	Student & Travellers'	11	EOT & National Bank	36	Roman Agora
	Inn		of Greece	37	Kanellopoulos Museum
		12	Thomas Cook	38	Museum of the
PLACES TO EAT		13	Buses to Airport		University
3	Apotsos Ouzeri	14	American Express	45	Trolley Stop for Plaka
4	Zonar's	15	Eleftheroudakis Books	46	Church of
7	Brazil Coffee Shop	16	Church of Kapnikarea		Metamorphosis
8	Wendy's	18	Flea Market	47	Museum of Greek Folk
19	Savas & Thanasis	20	Museum of Traditional		Art
26	Peristeria Taverna		Greek Ceramics	51	Acropole Foreign
30	Neon Café	21	Library of Hadrian		Exchange
39	Eden Vegetarian	22	Centre of Hellenic	56	Plateia Plakas
	Restaurant		Tradition	57	Laundrette
48	Taverna Saita	23	Athens Cathedral		

The entrance to the Acropolis is through the **Beule Gate**, a Roman arch added in the 3rd century AD. Beyond this is the **Propylaia**, the monumental gate that was the entrance in ancient times. It was damaged by Venetian bombing in the 17th century, but has since been restored. To the south of the Propylaia is the small, graceful **Temple of Athena Nike**, which is not accessible to visitors.

Standing supreme over the Acropolis is the monument which more than any other epitomises the glory of ancient Greece: the **Parthenon**. Completed in 438 BC, this building is unsurpassed in grace and harmony. To achieve perfect form, its lines were ingeniously curved to counteract unharmonious optical illusions. The base curves upwards slightly towards the ends, and the columns become slightly narrower towards the top, with the overall effect of making them both look straight.

Above the columns are the remains of a Doric frieze, which was partly destroyed by Venetian shelling in 1687. The best surviving pieces are the famous Elgin Marbles, carted off by Lord Elgin in 1801 and now in the British Museum. The Parthenon, dedicated to Athena, contained an 11-metre-tall gold and ivory statue of the goddess completed in 438 BC by Phidias of Athens; only the statue's foundations exist today).

To the north is the **Erechtheion** with its much-photographed Caryatids, the six maidens who support its southern portico. These are plaster casts – the originals (except for the one taken by Lord Elgin) are in the site's museum. The Erechtheion was dedicated to Athena and Poseidon and supposedly built on the spot where they competed for possession of ancient Athens. The Acropolis Museum has sculptures from the temples.

The site is open Monday to Friday from 8 am to 5.45 pm, and weekends and public holidays from 8.30 am to 2.45 pm. The museum is open on Monday from 11 am to 4 pm, Tuesday to Friday from 8 am to 6.30 pm, and weekends from 8.30 am to 2.30 pm. The combined admission fee is 2000 dr.

Ancient Agora The Agora was the marketplace of ancient Athens and the focal point of civic and social life. Socrates spent much time here expounding his philosophy. Not much remains except for the well-preserved **Doric Temple of Hephaestus**.

The site's museum is housed in the reconstructed **Stoa of Attalos**. The 11th-century **Agiou Apostoli Church** contains fine Byzantine frescos.

The site is open Tuesday to Sunday from 8.30 am to 3 pm; admission is 1200 dr.

Changing of the Guard Every Sunday at 11 am a platoon of traditionally costumed *evzones* (guards) marches down Vasilissis Sofias accompanied by a band, to the Tomb of the Unknown Soldier in front of the parliament building on Syntagma. Some find the costume (skirts and pom-pom shoes) and marching style comic, but the ceremony is colourful and entertaining.

National Archaeological Museum This is the most important museum in the country, with finds from all the major sites. The crowd pullers are the magnificent, exquisitely detailed gold artefacts from Mycenae and the spectacular **Minoan frescos** from Santorini (Thira), which are here until a suitable museum is built on the island. Allow a whole day to see the vast collection. The museum is at 2 Oktovriou-Patission 44, open Monday from 1 am to 7 pm, Tuesday to Friday from 8 am to 7 pm, and on weekends and public holidays from 8.30 am to 3 pm. It closes at 5 pm instead of 7 pm in winter. Admission is 2000 dr.

Benaki Museum This museum, on the corner of Vasilissis Sofias and Koumbari, houses the collection of Antoine Benaki, the son of a Alexandrian cotton magnate named Emmanuel Benaki. The collection includes ancient sculpture, Persian, Byzantine and Coptic objects, Chinese ceramics, icons, two El Greco paintings and a superb collection of traditional costumes. The museum was closed for repair at the time of writing.

Goulandris Museum of Cycladic & Ancient Greek Art This private museum is custom built to display a fabulous collection of Cycladic art, with an emphasis on the Early Bronze Age. Particularly impressive are the beautiful marble figurines. These simple elegant forms, mostly of naked women with arms folded under their breasts, inspired 20th-century artists such as Brancusi, Epstein, Modigliani and Picasso.

It's at Neofytou Douka 4 and is open Monday, Tuesday, Thursday and Friday from 10 am to 4 pm, and Saturday from 10 am to 3 pm. Admission is 400 dr.

Lykavittos Hill Pine-covered Lykavittos is the highest of the eight hills dotted around Athens. From the summit there are all-embracing views of the city, the Attic basin and the islands of Salamis and Aegina – pollution permitting.

The southern side of the hill is occupied by the posh residential suburb of Kolonaki. The main path to the summit starts at the top of Loukianou, or you can take the funicular railway from the top of Ploutarhou (400 dr).

National Gardens Formerly named the Royal Gardens, these offer a welcome shady retreat from the summer sun, with subtropical trees, peacocks, water fowl, ornamental ponds and a botanical museum.

Courses
The Athens Centre (☎ 701 2268; fax 701 2603), Archimidous 48, has a very good reputation. Its courses cover five levels of proficiency from beginners' to advanced. There are five immersion courses a year for beginners. The YWCA (XEN in Greek) (☎ 362 4291; fax 362 2400), Amerikis 11, has six-week beginners' courses starting in February, May, and October.

Other places in Athens offering courses are the Hellenic American Union (☎ 362 9886), Massalias 22, and the Hellenic Language School, Zalongou 4 (☎ 362 8161; fax 363 9951).

Organised Tours
Key Tours (☎ 923 3166), Kallirois 4; CHAT Tours (☎ 322 3137), Stadiou 4; and GO Tours (☎ 322 5951), Voulis 31-33, are the main operators. You'll see their brochures everywhere, offering identical tours and prices. They include a half-day bus tour (7700 dr), which does no more than point out the major sights.

Special Events
The Athens Festival is the city's most important cultural event, running from mid-June to the end of September, with plays, ballet and classical-music concerts. Performances are held in the Theatre of Herodes Atticus and begin at 9 pm. Information and tickets are available from the Festival Box Office, Stadiou 4.

If this all sounds too staid, the fringe International Jazz Festival runs concurrently. Venues include the theatre on Lykavittos Hill. Both festivals have discounts for students.

Places to Stay
Camping *Dafni Camping* (☎ 581 1562/ 1563) is a good shady site next to Dafni's famous Byzantine monastery, about 10 km from the city centre on the road to Corinth. Take bus No 880 or 860 from Panepistimiou. There are several camping grounds on the coast road to Cape Sounion.

Hostels There are a few places around town making a pitch for the hostelling market by tagging 'youth hostel' onto their name. There are some dreadful dumps among them.

The only youth hostel worth bothering with is the excellent HI-affiliated *Athens International Youth Hostel* (☎ 523 4170), Victor Hugo 16. Location is the only drawback, otherwise the place is almost too good to be true. The spotless rooms, each with bathroom, sleep two to four people. Rates are 2000 dr per person for HI members, 2500 dr for others.

The *YWCA* (XEN; ☎ 362 4291), Amerikis 11, is an option for women only. It has singles/doubles with shared bathroom for 3500/6000 dr, or 4500/6500 dr with private bathroom. There are laundry facilities and a snack bar. Annual membership is 600 dr.

Hotels Athens is a noisy city and Athenians keep late hours, so an effort has been made to select hotels in quiet areas. Plaka is the most popular place to stay, and it has a good choice of accommodation right across the price spectrum. Rooms fill up quickly in July and August, so it's wise to make a reservation. Some budget hotels let you sleep on the roof in summer. Checkout time in hotels is noon unless otherwise stated.

Plaka The **Student & Travellers' Inn** (☎ 324 4808), right in the heart of Plaka at Kyda thineon 16, is hard to look past. It's a friendly, well-run place with beautiful polished floors and spotless rooms. It has beds in four-person dorms for 2000 dr, while singles/doubles/triples are 4500/6000/7500 dr with shared bathroom. English breakfast is served in the vine-covered courtyard out the back for 1050 dr.

The huge timber spiral staircase at **George's Guesthouse** (☎ 322 6474) speaks of grander times at Nikis 46, but it's a friendly place with dorms for 2000 dr and doubles/triples for 5000/6000 dr with shared bathroom.

The **Festos Youth & Student Guest House** (☎ 323 2455), Filellinon 18, has been a popular place with travellers for a long time despite its noisy situation on one of the busiest streets in Athens. Dorm beds are 2000 dr, but they pack eight into a room. It charges 2500 dr per person in private rooms with shared bathroom.

The rooms at **John's Place** (☎ 322 9719), Patroou 5, are very basic but clean. Singles/doubles with shared bathroom are 4000/6000 dr. Patroou is on the left heading down Mitropoleos from Syntagma.

Slightly more expensive but much better value is the friendly **Hotel Tempi** (☎ 321 3175), near Monastiraki Square on the pedestrian precinct part of Eolou. The rooms at the front have balconies overlooking a little square with a church and a flower market. Rates are 4000/7000 dr with shared bathroom, or 8000 dr for doubles with private bathroom.

Plaka also has some good mid-range accommodation. The **Acropolis House Pension** (☎ 322 2344), Kodrou 6-8, is a beautifully preserved 19th-century house. Singles/doubles with shared bathroom are 7500/9000 dr, or 9100/10,900 dr with private bathroom. All rooms have central heating. Kodrou is the southern (pedestrian) extension of Voulis, leading onto Kydathineon.

Just around the corner from the Acropolis House is the **Hotel Nefeli** (☎ 322 8044/8045), Iperidou 16, a modern place with singles/doubles for 11,000/12,000 dr, including breakfast.

Veïkou & Koukaki There are a few good places to stay in this pleasant residential area just south of the Acropolis. The **Marble House** **Pension** (☎ 923 4058), Zini 35A, Koukaki, is a quiet, friendly place tucked away in a small cul-de-sac. Rates for the immaculate singles/doubles are 5800/8900 dr with shared bathroom or 6800/9900 dr with private bathroom. Special weekly and monthly rates are available in winter.

The comfortable **Art Gallery Pension** (☎ 923 8376/1933), Erehtheiou 5, Veïkou, is a fine family-run place with singles/doubles for 13,000/15,000 dr with balcony and private bathroom.

Both these places are just a short ride from Syntagma on trolleybus No 1, 5, 9 or 18. Coming from Syntagma, they travel along Veïkou. Get off at the Drakou stop for the Art Gallery Pension, and at Zini for the Marble House. The trolleybuses return to Syntagma along Dimitrakopoulou.

Omonia & Surrounds There are dozens of hotels around Omonia, but most of them are either bordellos masquerading as cheap hotels or uninspiring, overpriced C-class hotels. Only a couple of places are worth a mention.

The **Hostel Aphrodite** (☎ 881 0589), 1 minutes from the train stations, at Einardou 12 is well set up for budget travellers. It is very clean, with dazzling, white walls and good sized rooms, many with balconies. It has dorm beds for 1500 dr, singles/doubles/triples with shared bathroom for 4000/5000/6000 dr and few doubles with private bathroom for 6000 dr.

The **Hotel Mystras** (☎ 522 7737), just south of the stations at Kerameon 26, is also geared towards travellers. Singles/doubles/triples are 4000/5000/6000 dr with private bathroom.

The long-established **Museum Hotel** (☎ 380 5611), Bouboulinas 16, is behind the National Archaeological Museum. The rooms are comfortable and reasonably priced 5000/7000/8400 dr with private bathroom.

Long-Term Accommodation For long-term rentals, look in the classifieds of the English language newspapers and magazines. Another possibility is to look at the notice board outside Compendium Books, Nikis 28. One-bedroom furnished flats cost from 80,000 dr a month although less salubrious apartments can be found for 60,000 dr.

Places to Eat

Plaka For most people, Plaka is the place to be. It's hard to beat the atmosphere of dining out beneath the floodlit Acropolis.

You do, however, pay for the privilege – particularly at the outdoor restaurants around the square on Kydathineon. The best of this bunch is *Byzantino*, which prices its menu more realistically and is popular with Greek family groups. One of the best deals in the Plaka is the nearby *Plaka Psistaria*, Kydathineon 28, with a range of gyros and souvlakia to eat there or take away.

Ouzeri Kouklis, Tripodon 14, is an old-style ouzeri with an oak-beamed ceiling, marble tables and wicker chairs. It serves only mezedes, which are brought round on a large tray for you to take your pick. They include flaming sausages – ignited at your table – and cuttlefish for 800 dr, as well as the usual dips or 400 dr. The whole selection, enough for four hungry people, costs 6400 dr.

Vegetarian restaurants are thin on the ground in Athens. The *Eden Vegetarian Restaurant*, Lyssiou 12, is one of only three. The Eden has been around for years, substituting soya products for meat in tasty vegetarian versions of moussaka (1250 dr) and other Greek favourites.

With such an emphasis on outdoor eating in summer, it's no great surprise that the three cellar restaurants on Kydathineon are closed from mid-May until October. They are also three of Plaka's cheaper places, charging about 500 dr for a main dish washed down with half a litre of retsina. The best of them is the *Taverna Saita* at No 21 – near the Museum of Greek Folk Art. The others are *The Cellar* at No 10 and *Damigos* at No 41.

Peristeria Taverna, next to John's Place at Patroou 5, is a good, basic taverna that is open all year.

Monastiraki There are some excellent cheap places to eat around Monastiraki, particularly for gyros and souvlaki fans. *Thanasis* and *Savas*, opposite each other at the bottom end of Mitropoleos, are the places to go.

The best taverna food in this part of town is the *meat market*, on the right 400 metres along Athinas from Monastiraki Square. The place must resemble a vegetarian's vision of hell, but the food is great and the tavernas are

open 24 hours, except Sunday. They serve traditional meat dishes such as patsas (tripe soup), podarakia (pig-trotter soup) as well as regular dishes like stifado and meatballs. Soups start at 600 dr and main dishes at 1000 dr.

Opposite the meat market is the main *fruit & vegetable market*.

Syntagma The *Neon Café*, opposite the post office, has spaghetti or fettucine with a choice of sauces for 780 dr, moussaka for 1350 dr and roast beef for 1680 dr. It is probably the only eating place in Athens with a no-smoking area.

Apotsos Ouzeri, Panepistimiou 10 (in an arcade opposite Zonar's), is Athens' oldest ouzeri – it opened in 1900. It is a popular lunch-time venue for journalists and politicians. It has a huge choice of mezedes priced from 450 to 2500 dr.

Follow your nose to the *Brazil Coffee Shop* on Vorkourestiou for the best coffee in town.

Veïkou & Koukaki The *Gardenia Restaurant*, Zini 31 at the junction with Dimitrakopoulou, claims to be the cheapest taverna in Athens; it has moussaka for 650 dr and a litre of draught retsina for 450 dr. What's more, the food is good and the service is friendly.

Socrates Prison, Mitseon 20, is not named after the philosopher, but after the owner (also called Socrates) who reckons the restaurant is his prison. It's a stylish place with an imaginative range of mezedes from 450 dr and main dishes from 1250 dr.

Exarhia There are lots of ouzeria and tavernas to choose from in the lively suburb of Exarhia, just east of Omonia. Prices here are tailored to suit the pockets of the district's largely student clientele.

Emmanual Benaki, which leads from Panepistimiou to the base of Strefi Hill, is the place to look. The *Ouzeri Refenes*, at No 51, is a popular place that does a delicious pikilia (mixed plate) of mezedes for 1000 dr. The *Taverna Barbargiannis*, further up the hill on the corner of Emmanual Benaki and Dervenion, is another good place. It does a tasty bean soup for 650 dr as well as a selection of meat dishes for under 1200 dr.

It's quite a long hike to the area from Syntagma. An alternative is to catch bus No 230 from Amalias to Harilau Trikoupi and walk across.

Around the Train Stations Wherever you choose to eat in this area you will find the lack of tourist hype refreshing. The *O Makis Psistaria*, at Psaron 48 opposite the church, is a lively place serving hunks of freshly grilled pork or beef, plus chips, for 1200 dr.

Hidden away at Proussis 21 is one of Athens' real gems, the *Taverna Avli*. Although not a vegetarian restaurant, it has the best vegetarian food in town. It has a fabulous range of mezedes, including spicy Mykonos cheese salad, saganaki of smoked Macedonian cheese or mussels and deep-fried 'sausages' of aubergine and minced walnut. Expect to pay about 2500 dr per person.

Entertainment

Cinema Athenians are avid movie-goers and there are cinemas everywhere. The *Athens News*, *Greek Weekly Times* and *Athenscope* all have listings. Admission is about 1500 dr.

Discos & Bars Discos operate in central Athens only between October and April. In summer, the action moves to the coastal suburbs of Glyfada and Ellinikon.

The highest concentration of music bars is in Exarhia. The *Green Door Music Club*, Kalidromiou 52 at the junction with Emmanual Benaki, is one of the most popular. If you want to hear some good music and have a conversation at the same time, then try the *Passenger Club*, 1st floor, Mavromihali 168. The music is mellow (mostly jazz and R&B), with no hard rock or heavy metal. Cocktails are priced from 1200 dr, spirits are 1000 dr and beer 800 dr.

Popular gay bars include *Granazi Bar*, Lembesi 20, which is south of the Arch of Hadrian, and the *Alexander Club* at Anagnostopoulou 44, Kolonaki. Both attract a mixed clientele. *Iridis* is a lesbian bar on Apostolou Pavlou in the Thision district, west of the Agora.

Rock & Jazz Concerts The *Rodon Club* (☎ 524 7427) at Marni 24 hosts touring international rock bands, while local bands play at

the *AN Club* and *Ach Maria Club*, opposite each other on Solomou in Exarhia. Concerts are listed in the *Weekly Greek News*.

Greek Folk Dances The *Dora Stratou Dance Company* performs at its theatre on Filopappos Hill at 10.15 pm every night from mid-May to October, with additional performances at 8.15 pm on Wednesday. Tickets are 1500 dr. Filopappos Hill is west of the Acropolis, of Dionysiou Areopagitou. Bus No 230 from Syntagma will get you there.

Sound-and-Light Show Athens' endeavour at this spectacle is not one of the world's best. There are shows in English every night at 9 pm from the beginning of April until the end of October at the theatre on the Hill of the Pnyx (☎ 322 1459). Tickets are 1500 dr. The Hill of the Pnyx is opposite Filopappos Hill, and the show is timed so that you can cross straight to the folk dancing.

Rembetika Clubs Rembetika is the music of the working classes and has its roots in the sufferings of the refugees from Asia Minor in the 1920s. Songs are accompanied by bouzouki, guitar, violin and accordion. By the 1940s it had also become popular with the bourgeoisie. It was banned during the junta years, but has since experienced a resurgence, especially in Athens.

Rembetika Stoa Athanaton, Sofokleous 1 (in the meat market), is open in the afternoon from 3 to 6 pm as well as in the evenings. *Rembetiki Istoria*, Ippokratous 181, plays host to some top musicians. It's open Thursday to Sunday from 11 pm.

Spectator Sport

Soccer is the most popular sport in Greece. Six of the 18 teams in the Greek first division are from Athens: AEK, Apollon, Ethnikos, Olympiakos, Panathinaïkos and Panionios. The season lasts from September to mid-May. Matches are played on Wednesday and Sunday. Admission is 1200 dr. Fixtures and results are given in the *Weekly Greek News*.

Things to Buy

The National Welfare Organisation shop, on the corner of Apollonos and Ipatias, Plaka, is a good place to go shopping for handicrafts. It has top-quality goods and the money goes to a good cause – the organisation was formed to preserve and promote traditional Greek handicrafts. It has a wide range of knotted carpets, kilims, flokatis, needle-point rugs and embroidered cushion covers as well as a small selection of pottery, copper and wood-work.

The Centre of Hellenic Tradition, Pandros-sou 36, Plaka, has a display of traditional and modern handicrafts from each region of Greece. Most of the items are for sale.

Getting There & Away

Air Athens' dilapidated airport, Ellinikon, is nine km south of the city. There are two main terminals: West for all Olympic Airways flights, and East for all other flights. Occasion-ally, the old military terminal is dusted off for charter flights in peak season.

The Olympic Airways head office (☎ 926 9111) is at Syngrou 96. There was no office on Syntagma at the time of writing, following the closure of the branch at Othonos 6. A new office is due to open on Filellinon in 1997.

Bus Athens has two main intercity bus sta-tions. The EOT gives out comprehensive schedules for both with departure times, journey times and fares.

Terminal A is north-west of Omonia at Kifissou 100 and has departures to the Peloponnese, the Ionian islands and western Greece. To get there, take bus No 051 from the junction of Zinonos and Menandrou, near Omonia. Buses run every 15 minutes from 5 am to midnight.

Terminal B is north of Omonia off Liossion and has departures to central and northern Greece as well as to Evia. To get there, take bus No 024 from outside the main gate of the National Gardens on Amalias. EOT mislead-ingly gives the terminal's address as Liossion 260, which turns out to be a small workshop. Liossion 260 is where you should get off the bus. Turn right onto Gousiou and you'll see the terminal at the end of the road.

Buses for Attica leave from the Mavro-mateon terminal at the junction of Leoforos Alexandras and 28 Oktovriou-Patission.

Train Athens has two train stations, located about 200 metres apart on Deligianni, which is about a km north-west of Omonia. Trains to the Peloponnese leave from the Peloponnese station, while trains to the north leave from Larisis station – as do all the international trains.

Trolleybus No 1 stops 100 metres from Larisis station at the junction of Deligianni and Neofiliou Metaxa. Plaka residents can catch the trolleybus from the southern end of the National Gardens on Amalias. Peloponnese station is across the footbridge at the southern end of Larisis Station.

Services to the Peloponnese include 14 trains a day to Corinth (780 dr, or 1430 dr intercity). The Peloponnese line divides at Corinth, with nine trains heading along the north coast to Patras (1580/2580 dr), and five going south. Three of these go to Kalamata (2160 dr) via Tripolis, while two stop at Nafplio (1400 dr).

Services from Larisis station include nine trains a day to Thessaloniki (3500 dr), five of which are intercity services (7150 dr). The 7 am service from Athens is express right through to Alexandroupolis, arriving at 7 pm. There are also trains to Volos and Halkida, Evia.

Tickets can be bought at the stations or at the OSE offices at Filellinon 17, Sina 6 and Karolou 1.

Car & Motorcycle National Rd 1 is the main route north from Athens. It starts at Nea Kifis-sia. To get there from central Athens, take Vasilissis Sofias from Syntagma and follow the signs. National Rd 8, which begins beyond Dafni, is the road to the Peloponnese. Take Agiou Konstantinou from Omonia.

The northern reaches of Syngrou, just south of the Temple of Olympian Zeus, are packed solid with car-rental firms. Local companies offer much better deals than their international rivals. Motorcycles are available from Moto-rent (☎ 923 4939), Falirou 5 (parallel to and east of Syngrou), and from Papavassiliou Elef-therios (☎ 325 0677), Asomaton 6, Thision.

Hitching Athens is the most difficult place in Greece to hitchhike from. Your best bet is to ask the truck drivers at the Piraeus cargo wharves. Otherwise, for the Peloponnese, take a bus from Panepistimiou to Dafni, where National Rd 8 begins. For northern Greece, take the metro to Kifissia, then a bus to Nea Kifissia and walk to National Rd 1.

Ferry See the Piraeus section for information on ferries to/from the islands.

Getting Around

To/From the Airport There is a 24-hour express bus service (No 91) between central Athens and both the East and West terminals, also calling at the special charter terminal when in use.

The buses leave Stadiou, near Omonia, every half-hour from 6 am to 9 pm, every 40 minutes from 9 pm until 12.20 am, and then hourly through the night. They stop at Syntagma (outside the Macedonia-Thrace Bank) five minutes later. The trip takes from 30 minutes to an hour, depending on traffic. The fare is 160 dr (200 dr at night), and you pay the driver. There are also express buses between the airport and Plateia Karaïskaki in Piraeus.

A taxi from the airport to Syntagma should cost from 1200 to 2500 dr depending on the time of day.

Bus & Trolleybus You probably won't need to use the normal blue-and-white suburban buses. They run every 15 minutes from 5 am to midnight and charge a flat rate of 75 dr. Route numbers and destinations, but not the actual routes, are listed on the free EOT map.

The map does, however, mark the routes of the yellow trolleybuses, making them easy to use. They also run from 5 am to midnight and cost 75 dr.

There are special green buses that operate 24 hours a day to Piraeus. Bus No 040 leaves from the corner of Syntagma and Filellinon, and No 049 leaves from the Omonia end of Athinas. They run every 20 minutes from 6 am to midnight, and then hourly.

Tickets can be bought from ticket kiosks and periptera. Once on a bus, you must validate your ticket by putting it into a machine; the penalty for failing to do so is 1500 dr.

Metro Central Athens is dotted with construction sites for its new metro line, which is due to open in 1998. Until then, there is just one metro line running from Piraeus in the south to Kifissia in the north. The line is divided into three sections: Piraeus-Omonia, Omonia-Perissos and Perissos-Kifissia. The fares are 75 dr for travel within one or two sections, and 100 dr for three sections. Monastirakiou is the closest stop to Plaka.

Taxi Athenian taxis are yellow. Flag fall is 200 dr, with a 160 dr surcharge from ports, train and bus stations and 300 dr from airports. After that the day rate (tariff 1 on the meter) is 58 dr per km. Rates double between midnight and 5 am.

In theory, most trips around the city centre shouldn't cost more than about 400 dr on tariff 1, but Athenian taxi drivers are notorious for pulling every scam in the book. If a taxi driver refuses to use the meter, try another – and make sure it's set on the right tariff.

To hail taxis, stand on the edge of the street and shout your destination as they pass. They will stop if they are going your way even if the cab is already occupied. Take a note of the meter reading when you get in, and pay the difference when you get out – plus 200 dr flag fall.

Radio taxis are useful if you have to get somewhere on time. Operators include Athina (☎ 921 7942), Kosmos (☎ 493 3811), Parthenon (☎ 581 4711), Ermis (☎ 411 5200), Proodos (☎ 643 3400) and Enossi (☎ 644 3345).

Bicycle You'll rarely see anyone riding a bicycle in central Athens, and you'd need to have a death wish to attempt it.

Piraeus & Attica

PIRAEUS Πειραιάς

Piraeus has been the port of Athens since classical times. These days it's little more than an outer suburb of the space-hungry capital, linked by a mish-mash of factories, warehouses and apartment blocks. The streets are every bit as traffic-clogged as Athens, and behind the veneer of banks and shipping offices most of Piraeus is pretty seedy. The only reason to come here is to catch a ferry or hydrofoil.

Orientation & Information

Piraeus consists of a peninsula surrounded by harbours. The most important of them is the Great Harbour. All ferries leave from here, and it has excellent connections to Athens. There are dozens of shipping agents around the harbour, as well as banks and a post office. Zea Marina, on the other side of the peninsula, is the port for hydrofoils to the Saronic Gulf islands (except Aegina). North-east of here is the picturesque Mikrolimano (small harbour). There's a useless EOT office (☎ 413 5716) at Zea Marina.

The telephone code for Piraeus is ☎ 01.

Getting There & Away

Bus There are two 24-hour green bus services between central Athens and Piraeus. Bus No 049 runs from Omonia to the Great Harbour, and bus No 040 runs from Syntagma to the tip of the Piraeus peninsula. This is the service to catch for Zea Marina – get off at the Hotel Savoy on Vasileos Konstantinou. Leave plenty of time – the trip can take over an hour if the traffic is bad.

There are express buses to Athens airport from Plateia Karaïskaki between 5 am and 8.20 pm, and between 6 am and 9.25 pm in the other direction. The fare is 160 dr. Blue bus No 110

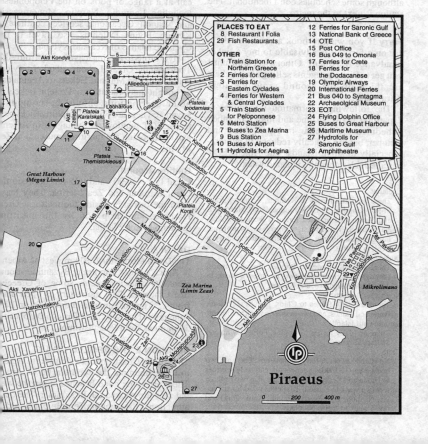

PLACES TO EAT
8 Restaurant I Folia
29 Fish Restaurants

OTHER
1 Train Station for Northern Greece
2 Ferries for Crete
3 Ferries for Eastern Cyclades
4 Ferries for Western & Central Cyclades
5 Train Station for Peloponnese
6 Metro Station
7 Buses to Zea Marina
9 Bus Station
10 Buses to Airport
11 Hydrofoils for Aegina
12 Ferries for Saronic Gulf
13 National Bank of Greece
14 OTE
15 Post Office
16 Bus 049 to Omonia
17 Ferries for Crete
18 Ferries for the Dodacanese
19 Olympic Airways
20 International Ferries
21 Bus 040 to Syntagma
22 Archaeolgical Museum
23 EOT
24 Flying Dolphin Office
25 Buses to Great Harbour
26 Maritime Museum
27 Hydrofoils for Saronic Gulf
28 Amphitheatre

Piraeus

runs from Plateia Karaïskaki to Glyfada and Voula every 15 minutes (75 dr). It stops outside the West terminal.

There are no intercity buses to or from Piraeus.

Metro The metro offers the fastest and most convenient link between the Great Harbour and Athens. The station is close to the ferries, at the northern end of Akti Kalimassioti. There are metro trains every 10 minutes from 5 am to midnight.

Train All services to the Peloponnese from Athens actually start and terminate at Piraeus, although some schedules don't mention it. The station is next to the metro.

Ferry If you want to book a cabin or take a car on a ferry, it is advisable to buy a ticket in advance in Athens. Otherwise, wait until you get to Piraeus; agents selling ferry tickets are thick on the ground around Plateia Karaïskaki.

The following information is a guide to departures between June and mid-September. Schedules are similar in April, May and October, but are radically reduced in winter – especially to small islands. The Athens EOT has a reliable schedule, updated weekly.

Cyclades
    There are daily ferries to Kythnos, Serifos, Sifnos, Milos, Kimolos, Syros, Mykonos, Paros, Naxos, Ios and Tinos; two or three ferries a week to Iraklia, Shinoussa, Koufonisi, Donoussa, Amorgos, Folegandros, Sikinos, and Anafi; and one ferry a week to Andros.
Dodecanese
    There are daily ferries to Rhodes, Kos, Kalymnos, Leros and Patmos; and two or three a week to Astypalea, Karpathos, and Kassos.
North-East Aegean
    There are daily ferries to Chios, Lesvos (Mytilini), Ikaria and Samos; and two or three a week to Limnos.
Saronic Gulf Islands
    There are daily ferries to Aegina, Poros, Hydra and Spetses all year.
Crete
    No island has better ferry connections. There are two boats a day to Iraklio year-round, and daily services to Hania and Rethymno. There are also two or three ferries a week to Kastelli-Kissamos (via Monemvassia, Neapoli, Gythio, Kythira and Antikythira) and one a week to Agios Nikolaos.

The departure points for the various ferry destinations are shown on the map of Piraeus. Note that there are two departure points for Crete. Check where to find your boat when you buy your ticket. All ferries display a clock face showing their departure time and have their ports of call written in English above their bows. See Boat in this chapter's Getting Around section and the Getting There & Away sections for each island for more information.

Hydrofoil Flying Dolphin hydrofoils operate a busy schedule around the Saronic Gulf between early April and the end of October. There are frequent services to the islands of Aegina, Poros, Hydra and Spetses. They also call at a range of ports on the Peloponnese including Leonidio, Nafplio, Monemvassia and Neapoli. Occasional services continue to Kythira. Flying Dolphins also travel to the Cycladic islands of Kea and Kythnos.

Hydrofoils to Aegina leave hourly from Akti Tzelepi at the Great Harbour; all other services leave from Zea Marina. Tickets to Aegina can be bought quayside at Akti Tzelepi; tickets to other destinations should be bought in advance. There are Flying Dolphin offices next to the EOT window on Syntagma in Athens and overlooking the maritime museum at Zea Marina.

Getting Around
Local bus Nos 904 and 905 run between the Great Harbour and Zea Marina. They leave from the bus stop beside the metro at Great Harbour, and drop you by the maritime museum at Zea Marina.

DAFNI Δαφνί
The **Dafni Monastery**, 10 km west of Athens, is Attica's most important Byzantine monument. Its church contains some of Greece's finest mosaics. The monastery is open daily from 8.30 am to 3 pm and entry is 800 dr. Blue Athens bus Nos 860 and 880 run to Dafni every 20 minutes from Panepistimiou.

SOUNION & THE APOLLO COAST
The Apollo Coast stretches south from Athens to Cape Sounion, the southern tip of Attica. There are some good beaches along the way but they are packed out in summer. The main attraction is the stunning **Temple of Poseidon**

at Cape Sounion, perched on a rocky headland that plunges 65 metres into the sea. The temple is open Monday to Saturday from 9 am to sunset, and from 10 am to sunset on Sunday. Sunset is the best time to be there. Admission is 800 dr.

Getting There & Away
Buses to Cape Sounion (two hours, 1050 dr) leave from the Mavromateon terminal in Athens. Services using the coast road leave hourly on the half-hour and stop on Filellinon 10 minutes later. Services travelling inland via Marcopoulo leave hourly on the hour.

The Peloponnese
Η Πελοπόννησος

The Peloponnese is the southern extremity of the rugged Balkan peninsula. Its strange geography, linked to the rest of Greece only by the narrow Isthmus of Corinth, has long prompted people to declare the Peloponnese to be more an island than part of the mainland. Its name – Peloponnisos in Greek – translates as Island of Pelops, the mythological father of the Mycenaean royal family. It technically became an island after the completion of the Corinth Canal across the isthmus in 1893, and it is now linked to the mainland only by road and rail bridges.

The Peloponnese is an area rich in history. The principal site is Olympia, birthplace of the Olympic Games, but there are many other sites worth seeking out. The ancient sites of Epidaurus, Corinth and Mycenae in the northeast are all within easy striking distance of the pretty Venetian town of Nafplio.

In the south are the magical old Byzantine towns of Monemvassia and Mystras. The rugged Mani peninsula is famous for its spectacular wild flowers in spring, as well as for the bizarre tower settlements that dot its landscape. The beaches south of Kalamata are some of the best in Greece.

NAFPLIO Ναύπλιο
Nafplio is a resort town with some fine Venetian buildings. The municipal tourist office is on 25 Martiou opposite the OTE office and is

open from 9 am to 1.30 pm and 4.30 to 9 pm daily. The bus station is on Syngrou, the street which separates the old town from the new.

Nafplio's telephone code is ☎ 0752.

Things to See
Folk Art Museum The museum has a fascinating display of traditional textile-producing techniques as well as beautiful costumes. The museum is in the old town at Ypsilandou 1. It's open Tuesday to Sunday from 9 am to 2.30 pm; admission is 300 dr.

Palamida Fortress There are terrific views of the old town and the surrounding coast from this ruined hill-top fortress. The climb is strenuous – there are almost 1000 steps – so start early and take water with you. The easy way out is to catch a taxi from town for about 1000 dr. The fortress is open daily from 8 am to 7 pm (5 pm in summer); admission is 800 dr.

Places to Stay & Eat
There are *camping grounds* galore along Tolo Beach, nine km east of town. The pleasant *youth hostel* (☎ 27 754) is in the new town at Argonafton 15. Beds cost 1000 dr and an HI card or student ID is required. It takes about 20 minutes to walk there from the bus station. Head east on 25 Martiou and fork left onto Asklipiou at the first traffic lights, then left again onto Argolis at the following traffic lights. Argonafton is the seventh street on the right.

Most of the domatia are in the old town in the streets between Staikopoulou and the Io Kale fortress. Also in this area is the D-class *Hotel Lito* (☎ 28 093), at the fortress end of Farmakopoulou. The *Hotel King Otto* (☎ 27 585), at the other end of Farmakopoulo, offers a similar deal.

The friendly *Hotel Acropol* (☎ 27 796), near the folk museum at Vasilissis Olgas 9, has clean singles/doubles with bathroom for 5700/8000 dr.

Zorbas and *Taverna Ta Fanaria* are two popular places opposite each other in the centre of the old town on Staikopoulou. Both have main courses priced from around 1000 dr.

Getting There & Away
There are hourly buses to Athens (2½ hours, 2250 dr), as well as services to Argos (for

Peloponnese connections), Mycenae, Epidaurus, Corinth and Tolo.

From May to September, there are hydrofoils to Piraeus every day except Sunday. Buy tickets from Iannopoulos Travel on Plateia Syntagmatos in the old town.

EPIDAURUS Επίδαυρος

The huge well-preserved **Theatre of Epidaurus** is the crowd-puller at this site, but don't miss the more peaceful **Sanctuary of Asclepius** nearby. Epidaurus was regarded as the birthplace of Asclepius, the god of healing, and the sanctuary was once a flourishing spa and healing centre. The setting alone would have been enough to cure many ailments.

The site is open every day from 8 am to 7 pm. Admission is 1000 dr, including the museum – closed on Monday afternoon.

You can enjoy the theatre's astounding acoustics first hand during the **Epidaurus Festival** from mid-June to mid-August.

The expensive *Xenia* is the only hotel in town.

Getting There & Away

There are two buses a day from Athens (2½ hours, 2100 dr), as well as three a day to Nafplio (40 minutes, 495 dr). During the festival, there are excursion buses from Nafplio and Athens.

ANCIENT CORINTH & ACROCORINTH

The sprawling ruins of ancient Corinth lie seven km south-west of the modern city. Corinth (Κόρινθος) was one of ancient Greece's wealthiest and most wanton cities. When Corinthians weren't clinching business deals, they were paying homage to Aphrodite in a temple dedicated to her, which meant they were having a rollicking time with the temple's sacred prostitutes. The only ancient Greek monument remaining here is the imposing **Temple of Apollo**; the others are Roman. Towering over the site is Acrocorinth, the ruins of an ancient citadel built on a massive outcrop of limestone.

Both sites are open daily from 8 am to 7 pm. Admission is 1200 dr for ancient Corinth and 500 dr for Acrocorinth.

Modern Corinth is an unprepossessing town which gives the impression that it has never quite recovered from the devastating earthquake of 1928. It is, however, a convenient base from which to visit ancient Corinth.

Corinth's telephone code is ☎ 0741.

Places to Stay & Eat

Buses to ancient Corinth go past *Corinth Beach Camping* (☎ 27 967), about three km west of town, and there are *domatia* near ancient Corinth.

There are a couple of reasonable cheap hotels in Corinth. The *Belle-Vue* (☎ 22 088) facing the harbour at Damaskinou 41, is an old place with clean singles/doubles with shared bathroom for 3500/4500 dr, and doubles with private bath for 6000 dr. The *Hotel Apollon* (☎ 22 587), near the train station at Pirinis 18 has singles/doubles with shower for 4000/5500 dr.

The *Kanita Restaurant*, near the Belle-Vue Hotel, serves generous helpings of traditional fare. Main meals are priced from 800 dr. As the name suggests, the *Restaurant To 24 Hour* never closes. It's on the waterfront south of the port.

Getting There & Away

Corinth has two bus stations. There are buses to Athens (1½ hours, 1350 dr) every 30 minutes from the bus station on Ermou, near the park in the city centre. It is also the departure point for hourly buses to ancient Corinth (20 minutes, 150 dr). Buses to other parts of the Peloponnese leave from the station at the junction of Ethnikis Antistaseos and Aratou.

There are 14 trains a day to Athens, five of them intercity services. There are also trains to Kalamata, Nafplio and Patras.

MYCENAE Μυκήνες

Mycenae was the most powerful influence in Greece for three centuries until about 1200 BC. The rise and fall of Mycenae is shrouded in myth, but the site was settled as early as the sixth millennium BC. Historians are divided as to whether the city's eventual destruction was due to outsiders or internal conflict between the various Mycenaean kingdoms. Described by Homer as 'rich in gold', Mycenae's entrance, the **Lion Gate**, is Europe's oldest monumental sculpture.

Excavations have uncovered the palace complex and royal tombs, shaft graves and extraordinary beehive-shaped tombs. The si haft graves known as the **First Royal Grave Circle** were uncovered by Heinrich Schliemann in 1873.

The gold treasures he found in these graves, including the so-called **Mask of Agamemnon**, are among the world's greatest archaeological finds. They are now in the National Archaeological Museum in Athens.

The site is open daily from 8 am to 7 pm; admission is 1500 dr.

Getting There & Away

There are buses to Argos and Nafplio.

SPARTA Σπάρτη

The bellicose Spartans sacrificed all the finer things in life to military expertise and left no monuments of any consequence. Ancient Sparta's forlorn ruins lie amidst olive groves at the northern end of town. Modern Sparta is a neat, unspectacular town, but a convenient base from which to visit Mystras.

Orientation & Information

Sparta is laid out on a grid system. The main street, Paleologou, runs north-south through the town. The EOT office (☎ 24 852) is in the town hall on the main square, Plateia Kentriki. It's open Monday to Saturday from 8 am to 2 pm.

Sparta's telephone code is ☎ 0731.

Places to Stay & Eat

Camping Mystra (☎ 22 724), on the Sparta-Mystras road, is open year-round. *Hotel Cecil* (☎ 24 980), at Paleologou 125, has cosy singles/doubles/triples for 4000/6500/8000 dr with shared bath. The *Hotel Maniatis* (☎ 22 565), Paleologou 72, has immaculate singles/doubles with air-con for 9000/11,500 dr.

The *Diethnes Restaurant*, Paleologou 105, does good traditional food and has garden seating in summer.

Getting There & Away

There are frequent buses to Mystras (30 minutes, 175 dr) from Lykourgou, two blocks west of the main square. The main bus terminal is on Vrasidou, off Paleologou. There are eight buses a day to Athens (4½ hours, 3300 dr), three a day to Monemvassia and two to Kalamata.

MYSTRAS Μυστράς

Mystras, seven km from Sparta, was once the shining light of the Byzantine world. Its ruins spill from a spur of Mt Taygetos, crowned by a mighty fortress built by the Franks in 1249. The streets of Mystras are lined with glorious palaces, monasteries and churches, most of them dating from the period between 1271 and 1460, when the town was the effective capital of the Byzantine Empire. The buildings, most of which have been restored, are among the finest examples of Byzantine architecture in Greece and contain many superb frescos.

On no account should you miss the **Church of Perivleptos**, whose walls are decorated with incredibly detailed paintings. Except for the **Pantanassa Convent**, which is occupied by nuns, the buildings are uninhabited.

The site is open every day from 8 am to 7 pm. Admission is 1000 dr, which includes entrance to the museum (closed Monday). You'll need a whole day to do this vast place justice. Take a taxi or hitch a ride to the upper Fortress Gate and work your way down. Take some water.

MONEMVASSIA Μονεμβασία

Monemvassia is no longer an undiscovered paradise, but mass tourism hasn't lessened the impact of one's first encounter with this extraordinary old town – nor the thrill of exploring it.

There's no EOT office but the staff at Malvasia Travel (☎ 61 752), near the bus station, are helpful.

Monemvassia's telephone code is ☎ 0732.

Things to See

Monemvassia occupies a great outcrop of rock that rises dramatically from the sea opposite the village of Gefyra. It was separated from the mainland by an earthquake in 375 AD and access is by a causeway from Gefyra. From the causeway, a road curves around the base of the rock for about a km until it comes to a narrow L-shaped tunnel in the massive fortifying wall. You emerge, blinking, in the **Byzantine town**, hitherto hidden from view.

The cobbled main street is flanked by stairways leading to a complex network of stone houses with tiny walled gardens and courtyards. Steps (signposted) lead to the ruins of the **fortress** built by the Venetians in the 16th century. The views are great, and there is the added bonus of being able to explore the Byzantine **Church of Agia Sophia**, perched precariously on the edge of the cliff.

Places to Stay & Eat

The nearest camping ground is *Camping Paradise* (☎ 61 123), 3.5 km to the north. There is no budget accommodation in Monemvassia, but there are domatia in Gefyra as well as cheap hotels.

The best place is the *Hotel Glyfada* (☎ 61 752), on the beach a short walk from town. It has spacious rooms with private bathroom for 5000/6500 dr. The basic *Hotel Akrogia* (☎ 61 360), opposite the National Bank of Greece, has singles/doubles with shower for 5000/7000 dr, while the *Hotel Aktaion* (☎ 61 234), by the causeway, charges 4000/8000 dr with bathroom.

If your budget permits, treat yourself to a night in one of the beautifully restored traditional settlements in Monemvassia. They include *Malvasia Guest Houses* (☎ 61 113), with singles/doubles for 7500/10,000 dr, and *Byzantino* (☎ 61 254), with doubles for 12,500 dr.

Taverna Nikolas is the place to go for a hearty meal in Gefyra, while *To Kanoni*, on the right of the main street in Monemvassia, has an imaginative menu.

Getting There & Away

Bus There are between two and four buses a day to Athens (six hours, 4900 dr), depending on the season. They travel via Sparta, Tripolis and Corinth. In summer, there is a daily bus to Gythio (1½ hours, 1400 dr).

Ferry In summer, ferries call at Monemvassia twice a week in each direction on the route between Piraeus and Kastelli-Kissamos on Crete, via Gythio, Kythira and Antikythira. Check the schedules at Malvasia Travel.

In July and August, there are at least two hydrofoils a day to Piraeus via the Saronic Gulf islands.

GYTHIO Γύθειο

Gythio, once the port of ancient Sparta, is an attractive fishing town at the head of the Lakonian Gulf. It is the gateway to the rugged Mani peninsula to the south.

The main attraction at Gythio is the picturesque islet of **Marathonisi**, linked to the mainland by a causeway. According to mythology, it is ancient Cranae, where Paris (a prince of Troy) and Helen (the wife of Menelaus of Sparta) consummated the love affair that sparked the Trojan War. An 18th-century tower on the islet has been turned into a **museum** of Mani history.

Gythio's telephone code is ☎ 0731.

Places to Stay & Eat

Gythio's *camping grounds* are dotted along the coast south of town.

There are numerous *domatia* on the waterfront near the main square. The *Saga Pension* (☎ 23 220), between the square and the causeway, has immaculate singles/doubles with bathroom for 5000/6000 dr.

The waterfront tavernas are tourist traps, so make for *Petakos Taverna* in the town's stadium at the northern end of town on the road to Skala. There's also a restaurant at the Saga Pension.

Getting There & Away

Bus There four buses a day to Athens (5½ hours, 3950 dr), and four a day to Kalamata. Two of these services go via the Mani, calling at Areopoli, Itilo, Kardamyli and Stoupa, and two go via Sparta. In summer, there is a daily bus to Monemvassia.

Services to the Inner Mani include three buses a day to the Diros Caves, two to Gerolimenas and one to Vathia – all via Areopoli. All buses heading south can drop you at the camping grounds.

Ferry In summer, there are two ferries a week to Kastelli-Kissamos on Crete via Kythira and Antikythira, and two a week to Piraeus via Monemvassia. For information and ferry tickets, contact Rozakis Travel Agency (☎ 2 207) opposite the port.

THE MANI

The Mani is divided into two regions, the Lakonian (inner) Mani in the south and Messinian (outer) Mani in the north-west below Kalamata.

Lakonian Mani

The Lakonian Mani is wild and remote, it

landscape dotted with the dramatic stone tower houses that are a trademark of the region. They were built as refuges from the clan wars of the 19th century. The best time to visit is in spring, when the barren countryside briefly bursts into life with a spectacular display of wild flowers.

The principal village of the region is **Areopoli**, about 30 km south-west of Gythio. There are a number of fine towers on the narrow, cobbled streets of the old town.

Just south of here are the magnificent **Diros Caves**, where a subterranean river flows. The caves are open 8 am to 6 pm from June to September and 8 am to 4.30 pm from October to May. Admission is 2300 dr and worth it.

Gerolimenas, 20 km further south, is a tranquil fishing village built around a sheltered bay. It's a short walk from Gerolimenas to the almost deserted villages of **Boulari** and **Kato Boulari**. **Vathia**, a village of towers built on a rocky peak, is 11 km south-east of Gero-limenas. Beyond Vathia, the coastline is a series of rocky outcrops sheltering pebbled beaches. At the hamlet of **Porto Kagia**, seven km south of Vathia, a path leads to the light-house at **Cape Matapan**, reckoned by some to be the mythical **Gate of Hades**.

Kotronas is the east coast's largest village, and further south are the villages of **Kokkala** and **Laggia**. The latter, 400 metres above sea level, has magnificent views.

The telephone code for Areopoli and the rest of the Lakonian Mani is ☎ 0733.

Places to Stay & Eat There are no official camp sites in the Lakonian Mani.

Areopoli The cheapest accommodation in Areopoli is at *Perros Bathrellos Rooms* (☎ 51 105) on Kapetan Matapan, the main street of the old town. Singles/doubles are 4000/5000 dr with shared bath.

Tsimova Rooms (☎ 51 301), signposted off Kapetan Matapan, offers beautiful doubles in a renovated tower house for 6000 dr. There's good food at the nameless *taverna* below Perros Bathrellos Rooms.

Gerolimenas & Vathia There are two hotels in Gerolimenas. The *Hotel Akrotenaritis* (☎ 54 254) has singles/doubles for 2500/4500 dr with shared bath, while the more luxurious

Hotel Akroyali (☎ 54 204) has rooms over-looking the beach for 4500/7000 dr with private bath. It also has an excellent restaurant. If you feel like a treat, check out the superb rooms at *Vathia Towers* (☎ 52 222). Doubles are 14,000 dr with breakfast. On the east coast there are domatia at Kotronas and Kokkala.

Getting There & Away There are direct buses to Gythio and Sparta from both Areopoli and Gerolimenas. Getting to Kalamata involves changing buses in Itilo, 11 km north of Areopoli.

Getting Around Areopoli is the focal point of the local bus network. There are three buses a day to Itilo, two a day to the Diros Caves and Gerolimenas, and one a day to Kotronas. There are occasional buses to Vathia.

Hitching in the Mani is fairly easy. An asphalt road skirts the coast, and minor roads lead to isolated churches and villages.

Messinian Mani
The Messinian Mani runs north along the coast from Itilo to Kalamata. The beaches here are some of the best in Greece, set against the dramatic backdrop of the Taygetos mountains.

Itilo, the medieval capital of all the Mani, is split by a ravine that is the traditional dividing line between inner and outer Mani.

The picturesque coastal village of **Karda-myli**, 37 km south of Kalamata, is the starting point for walks up the **Taygetos Gorge**. It takes about 2½ hours to walk to the deserted Monastery of the Saviour. Strong footwear is essential and take plenty of water.

The once small fishing village of **Stoupa**, 10 km south of Kardamyli, has become a popular package destination in summer.

The Messinian Mani's telephone code is ☎ 0721.

Places to Stay There are about half a dozen *camping grounds* along the coast between Kardamyli and Stoupa.

Kardamyli There are numerous domatia, but nowhere cheap. *Olivia Koumounakou* (☎ 73 326), opposite the post office, has immaculate doubles with private bathroom for 7500 dr. *Lela's Taverna & Rooms* (☎ 73 541) occupy a charming stone building overlooking the sea. It has stylish doubles with private bathroom for 10,000 dr.

Stoupa Accommodation is monopolised by package operators in summer. Groups of two or more can seek out Thanasis at his small office by the beach. The wacky *Thanasis* rents domatia in a variety of houses. Rates start at 7000 dr for two.

The *Ipocampus Taverna*, between the bus stop and the sea, has good seafood.

Getting There & Away Itilo, Kardamyli and Stoupa are all on the bus route between Kalamata and Gythio. There are two buses a day in each direction. There are also buses between Itilo and Areopoli, the only bus link between inner and outer Mani.

OLYMPIA Ολυμπία
The site of ancient Olympia lies just half a km beyond the modern town, surrounded by the green foothills of Mt Kronion. There is an

excellent tourist office on the main street, open from 8.30 am to 10 pm in summer and until 8.15 pm in winter. It will also change money.

Olympia's telephone code is ☎ 0624.

Things to See
In ancient times, Olympia was a sacred place of temples, priests' dwellings and public buildings, as well as being the venue for the quadrennial Olympic Games. The first Olympics were staged in 776 BC, reaching the peak of their prestige in the 6th century BC. The city-states were bound by a sacred truce to stop fighting for three months and compete.

The site is dominated by the immense ruined **Temple of Zeus**, to whom the games were dedicated. The site is open Monday to Friday from 8 am to 7 pm, and on weekends from 8.30 am to 3 pm. Admission is 1200 dr. There's also a **museum** north of the archaeological site. It keeps similar hours and admission is also 1200 dr. Allow a whole day to see both.

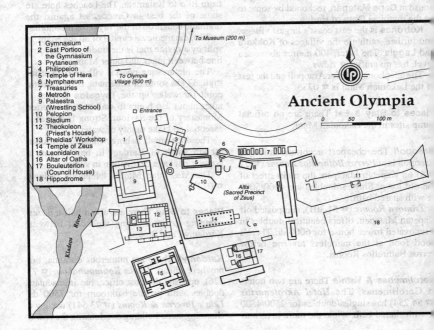

1 Gymnasium
2 East Portico of the Gymnasium
3 Prytaneum
4 Philippeion
5 Temple of Hera
6 Nymphaeum
7 Treasuries
8 Metroön
9 Palaestra (Wrestling School)
10 Pelopion
11 Stadium
12 Theokoleon (Priest's House)
13 Pheidias' Workshop
14 Temple of Zeus
15 Leonidaion
16 Altar of Oaths
17 Bouleuterion (Council House)
18 Hippodrome

Ancient Olympia

Places to Stay & Eat

Well signposted and only 250 metres from town is **Camping Diana** (☎ 22 314). It has excellent facilities and a pool.

The **youth hostel** (☎ 22 580), Kondili 18, has dorm beds for 1300 dr. No hostel card is required.

The **Pension Achilleys** (☎ 22 562), Stefanopoulou 4, has singles/doubles with shared bathroom for 3500/5000 dr, while the plant-festooned **Pension Poseidon** (☎ 22 567), at No 9, charges 4000/5000 dr for singles/doubles with shared shower. It also has an outside taverna serving tasty food in summer.

The **Taverna Praxitelous**, behind the tourist office, is a favourite with locals.

Getting There & Away

There four buses a day to Olympia from Athens 5½ hours, 5000 dr), but buses to Athens leave only from the town of Pyrgos, 24 km away. There are hourly buses from Olympia to Pyrgos (330 dr) and five trains a day. Regular buses and trains go from Pyrgos to Patras.

PATRAS Πάτρα

Patras is Greece's third-largest city and the principal port for ferries to Italy and the Ionian Islands. It's not particularly exciting and most travellers hang around only long enough for transport connections.

Orientation & Information

The city is easy to negotiate and is laid out on a grid stretching uphill from the port to the old *kastro* (castle). Most services of importance to travellers are to be found along the waterfront, known as Othonos Amalias in the middle of town and Iroön Politehniou to the north. All the various shipping offices are to be found along here. The train station is right in the middle of town on Othonos Amalias, and the bus station is close by. Customs and the EOT office (☎ 42 9303) are clustered together inside the port fence off Iroön Politehniou.

Money The National Bank of Greece on Plateia Trion Symahon has a 24-hour automatic exchange machine. American Express is represented by Albatros Travel at Othonos Amalias 48.

Post & Communications The post office, on the corner of Zaïmi and Mezonos, is open Monday to Friday from 7.30 am to 8 pm and Saturday from 7.30 am to 2 pm. There is also a mobile post office outside customs. The postcode is 26001.

The main OTE office, on the corner of Dimitriou Gounari and Kanakari, is open 24 hours. There are also OTE offices at customs and on Agiou Andreou at Plateia Trion Symahon.

Patras' telephone code is ☎ 061.

Medical & Emergency Services There is a first-aid centre (☎ 27 7386) on the corner of Karolou and Agiou Dionysiou.

The tourist police (☎ 22 0902), opposite the EOT at the port, are open 24 hours.

Things to See & Do

There are great views of Zakynthos and Kefallonia from the Venetian **kastro**, which is reached by the steps at the top of Agiou Nikolaou.

The **Achaïa Clauss Winery**, eight km south-east from Patras, has conducted tours offers free wine sampling between 7 am and 1 pm and 4 and 7 pm (10 am to 4.30 pm in the low season). Take bus No 7 from the corner of Kolokotroni and Kanakari.

Places to Stay & Eat

The nearest camping ground is **Kavouri Camping** (☎ 42 8066), three km east of town. Take bus No 1 from Agios Dionysios church.

The friendly **youth hostel** (☎ 42 7278) was still operating from Iroön Politehniou 68, 1.5 km along the same road, at the time of writing, but it's set to move to a restored neoclassical building at Tofalou 2. Dorm beds are 1500 dr and no card is required.

The best budget hotel is the **Pension Nicos** (☎ 27 6183), at Patreos 3 on the corner of Agiou Andreou. Its cheery singles/doubles cost 3000/4500 dr with shared bath, and doubles with private bath are 6000 dr. The **Hotel Metropolis** (☎ 27 7535), Plateia Trion Symahon, lingers on in faded grandeur; singles/doubles are 5500/9900 dr.

Nicolaros Taverna, Agiou Nikolaou 50, and the nameless **restaurant** at Michalakopoulou 3 both serve good traditional food.

PLACES TO STAY
6   Youth Hostel
17 Hotel Astir
22 Hotel Acropole
27 Hotel Metropolitan
28 Pension Nicos

PLACES TO EAT
14 Restaurant
30 Nicolaros Taverna

OTHER
1   Passport Control
2   Customs
3   EOT
4   Tourist Police
7   Buses to Lefkada
8   Boats to Ionian Islands
13 First-Aid Centre
18 Main Bus Station
18 Post Office
19 Archaeological Museum
20 Laundrette
22 Local Buses
23 Train Station
24 National Bank of Greece
25 Ferries to Italy
26 Albatros Travel
    (American Express)
29 English-Language Books
31 Supermarket
32 Church of Agios Nikolaos
33 Kastro
34 Ancient Odeion
35 Plateia Agios Georgiou
36 Galanopoulos House
37 OTE
38 Church of Agios Andreas

FERRY LINES
5   Hellenic
    Mediterranean Line
9   Adriatica
10 Superfast
11 Fragline
12 Minoan-Strintzis
16 ANEK

Patras

0   100   200 m

Gulf of
Patras

Getting There & Away

Bus Buses to Athens (three hours, 3200 dr) run every 30 minutes, with the last at 9.45 pm. There are also 10 buses a day to Pyrgos (for Olympia) and two a day to Kalamata.

Train There are nine trains a day to Athens. Four are slow trains (five hours, 1580 dr) and five are express intercity trains (3½ hours, 2580 dr). The last intercity train leaves at 6 pm. Trains also run south to Pyrgos and Kalamata.

Ferry There are daily ferries to Kefallonia (2½ hours, 2725 dr), Ithaki (3¾ hours, 2725 dr) and Corfu (10 hours, 4900 dr). Services to Italy are covered in the Getting There & Away section at the start of this chapter. Ticket agents line the waterfront.

DIAKOFTO-KALAVRYTA RAILWAY

This spectacular rack-and-pinion line climbs up the deep gorge of the Vouraikos River from the small coastal town of Diakofto to the mountain resort of **Kalavryta**, 22 km away. It is a thrilling journey, with dramatic scenery all the way. The trains leave Diakofto at 6, 9, 10.50 and 11.50 am, and 1.50 and 4.25 pm, returning at 7.10 and 10.10 am, 12.15, 1.10, 3.05 and 5.35 pm. Kalavryta is 45 minutes east of Patras by bus or train.

Kalavryta has some good hotels, but it can be hard to find a room at weekends and during the ski season. The *Hotel Paradissos* (☎ 22 803) on Kallimani has spotless singles/doubles with bathroom for 4000/7000 dr. To get there, cross the road from the train station and walk up Syngrou, then turn right onto Kallimani at the Hotel Maria. Kalavryta has five buses a day to Patras and two to Athens.

Central Greece

Central Greece has little going for it in terms of attractions – with the notable exception of Delphi and its surroundings.

DELPHI Δελφοί

Like so many of Greece's ancient sites, the setting at Delphi – overlooking the Gulf of Corinth from the slopes of Mt Parnassos – is stunning. The Delphic oracle is thought to have originated in Mycenaean times when the earth goddess Gaea was worshipped here.

By the 6th century BC, Delphi had become the Sanctuary of Apollo and thousands of pilgrims came to consult the oracle, who was always a peasant woman of 50 years or more. She sat at the mouth of a chasm which emitted fumes. These she inhaled, causing her to gasp, writhe and shudder in divine frenzy. The pilgrim, after sacrificing a sheep or goat, would deliver a question, and the priestess' incoherent mumblings were then translated by a priest. Wars were fought, voyages embarked upon, and business transactions undertaken on the strength of these prophecies.

Orientation & Information

The bus station, post office, OTE, National Bank of Greece and tourist office (☎ 82 900) are all on modern Delphi's main street, Vasileon Pavlou. The tourist office, at No 44, is open Monday to Saturday from 8 am to 2 pm. The ancient site is 1.5 km east of modern Delphi.

Delphi's telephone code is ☎ 0265.

Sanctuary of Apollo

The **Sacred Way** leads up from the entrance of the site to the **Temple of Apollo**. It was here that the oracle supposedly sat, although no chasm, let alone vapour, has been detected. The path continues to the theatre and stadium. Opposite this sanctuary is the **Sanctuary of Athena** (free admission) and the much photographed **tholos**, which is a columned rotunda of Pentelic marble. It was built in the 4th century BC and is the most striking of Delphi's monuments, but its purpose and to whom it was dedicated are unknown.

The site is open from Monday to Friday from 7.30 am to 7.15 pm, and on weekends and public holidays from 8.30 am to 2.45 pm. The museum is open similar hours, except on Monday when it's open only from noon until 6.15 pm. Entry to each is 1200 dr.

Places to Stay & Eat

The nearest camping ground to Delphi is *Apollon Camping* (☎ 82 750), 1.5 km west of modern Delphi.

The *youth hostel* (☎ 82 268), Apollonos 29, is one of Greece's best. It has dorm beds for

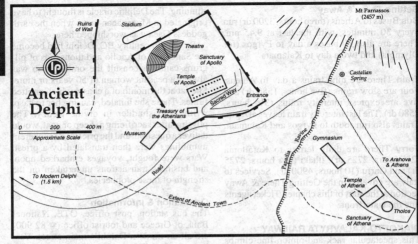

Ancient Delphi

Ruins of Wall

Stadium

Theatre

Sanctuary of Apollo

Temple of Apollo

Sacred Way

Entrance

Treasury of the Athenians

Museum

Road

To Modern Delphi (1.5 km)

Extent of Ancient Town

Papadia Ravine

Mt Parnassos (2457 m)

Castalian Spring

Gymnasium

To Arahova & Athens

Temple of Athena

Tholos

Sanctuary of Athena

0   200   400 m
Approximate Scale

1500 dr and doubles for 6000 dr. It's open from March to November.

There are hotels in Delphi to suit every budget. The *Hotel Athina* (☎ 82 239), on the corner of Vasileon Pavlou and Frederikis, has singles/doubles with shared bathroom for 4000/6000 dr, or 5200/7000 dr with private bathroom.

The food is good value at *Taverna Vakhos*, next to the youth hostel.

Getting There & Away
There are five buses a day to Delphi from Athens (three hours, 2600 dr).

Northern Greece

Northern Greece covers the regions of Epiros, Thessaly, Macedonia and Thrace. It includes some areas of outstanding natural beauty, such as the Zagoria region of north-western Epiros.

IGOUMENITSA Ηγουμενίτσα
Igoumenitsa, opposite the island of Corfu, is the main port of north-western Greece. Few people stay any longer than it takes to buy a ticket out. The bus station is on Kyprou. To get

there from the ferries, follow the waterfront (Ethnikis Antistasis) north for 500 metres and turn up El Venizelou. Kyprou is two blocks inland and the bus station is on the left.

Igoumenitsa's telephone code is ☎ 0665.

Places to Stay & Eat
If you get stuck for the night, the *Hotel Lux* (☎ 22 223) has singles/doubles for 2500/4800 dr with shared bathroom, or 4700/5400 dr with private bath. To get there, turn right onto Kyprou from El Venizelou and the hotel is on the left. The nearby *Hotel Egnatias* (☎ 23 648) has better singles/doubles with bathroom for 5500/10,000 dr.

To Astron Restaurant, El Venizelou 9, and *Restaurant Nikolas*, on the corner of 23 Fevrouariou and Gregoris Lambraki, both have main courses priced from 900 dr.

Getting There & Away
Bus Services include nine buses a day to Ioannina (two hours, 1600 dr), and three a day to Athens (8½ hours, 7350 dr).

Ferry In summer, there are daily ferries to the Italian ports of Brindisi and Bari, and occasional boats to Ortona and Otranto. Ticket agents are opposite the port.

There are ferries to Corfu (1½ hours, 850 dr) every hour between 5 am and 10 pm.

IOANNINA Ιωάννινα

Ioannina is the largest town in Epiros, sitting on the western shore of Lake Pamvotis. In Ottoman times, it was one of the most important towns in the country.

Orientation & Information

The main bus terminal is between Sini and Zossimadon. To reach the town centre, find the large pharmacy adjoining the terminal and take the road opposite. Turn right at the Hotel Egnatias, then left onto 28 Oktovriou, which meets Ioannina's main street at Plateia Dimokratias. The street is called Averof on the left and Dodonis on the right.

The helpful EOT office is 100 metres along Dodonis, set back on a small square at Napoleonda Zerva 2. It's open Monday to Friday from 7.30 am to 2.30 pm and from 5.30 to 8.30 pm, and on Saturday from 9 am to 2 pm. Robinsons Travel (☎ 29 402), 8 Merarhias Gramou 10, specialises in treks in the Zagoria region.

Ioannina's telephone code is ☎ 0651.

Things to See

The **old town** juts out into the lake on a small peninsula. Inside the impressive fortifications ies a maze of winding streets flanked by traditional Turkish houses.

The **Nisi** (island) is a serene spot in the middle of the lake, with four monasteries set among the trees. Ferries to the island leave from just north of the old town. They run half-hourly in summer and hourly in winter. The fare is 150 dr.

The **Perama Cave**, four km from Ioannina, has a mind-boggling array of stalactites and stalagmites. It's open from 8 am to 8 pm in summer and 8 am to 6.15 pm in winter; admission is 800 dr.

Places to Stay & Eat

On the lakeside two km north of town is *Camping Limnopoula* (☎ 25 265).

The cheapest hotel is the *Agapi Inn* (☎ 20 541), Tsirigoti 6, near the bus station. Basic doubles cost 4000 dr. Next door is the *Hotel Paris*, which has more comfortable singles/

doubles for 4000/6500 dr. There are domatia on the island.

There are several restaurants outside the entrance to the old town. *To Mantelo Psistaria* is recommended.

Getting There & Away

Air Ioannina has two flights a day to Athens (17,100 dr) and five a week to Thessaloniki (10,800 dr).

Bus Services include 12 buses a day to Athens (7½ hours, 6450 dr), nine to Igoumenitsa, five to Thessaloniki and three to Trikala via Kalambaka. The road from Ioannina to Kalambaka across the Pindos mountains is one of Greece's most spectacular drives.

ZAGORIA & VIKOS GORGE

The Zagoria (Ζαγώρια) region covers a large expanse of the Pindos mountains north of Ioannina. It's a wilderness of raging rivers, crashing waterfalls and deep gorges. Snow-capped mountains rise out of dense forests. The remote villages that dot the hillsides are famous for their impressive grey-slate architecture.

The fairytale village of **Monodendri** is the starting point for treks through the dramatic **Vikos Gorge**, with its awesome sheer limestone walls. It's a strenuous 7½-hour walk from Monodendri to the twin villages of **Megalo Papingo** and **Mikro Papingo**. The trek is very popular and the path is clearly marked. Ioannina's EOT office has information.

Other walks start from **Tsepelovo**, near Monodendri.

The telephone code for the Zagoria villages is ☎ 0653.

Places to Stay & Eat

There are some excellent places to stay, but none come cheap. The options in Monodendri include the lovely, traditional *Monodendri Pension & Restaurant* (☎ 61 233). Doubles are 8100 dr. *Alexis Gouris* (☎ 81 214) has a delightful pension in Tsepelovo with doubles for 7000 dr. Alexis also runs a shop and restaurant and can advise on treks.

Xenonas tou Kouli (☎ 41 138) is one of several options in Megalo Papingo. Rates start at 7000 dr for singles. The owners are official

EOS guides. The only rooms in Mikro Papingo are at *Xenonas O Dias* (☎ 41 257), a beautifully restored mansion with doubles for 9500 dr. It has an excellent restaurant specialising in charcoal grills.

Getting There & Away
Buses to the Zagoria leave from the main bus station in Ioannina. On weekdays, there are buses to Monodendri at 5.30 am and 4.15 pm and to Tsepelovo at 6 am and 3 pm. There are buses to the Papingo villages on Monday, Wednesday and Friday at 5.30 am and 2 pm, and on Sunday at 9 am.

TRIKALA Τρίκαλα
Trikala is a major transport hub, but otherwise has little of interest. Eight buses a day run between Trikala and Athens, (5½ hours, 4750 dr). There are also six buses a day to Thessaloniki, two to Ioannina and hourly buses to Kalambaka (for Meteora).

METEORA Μετέωρα
Meteora is an extraordinary place. The massive, sheer columns of rock that dot the landscape were created by wave action millions of years ago. Perched precariously atop these seemingly inaccessible outcrops are monasteries that date back to the late 14th century.

Meteora is just north of the town of Kalambaka, on the Ioannina-Trikala road. The rocks behind the town are spectacularly floodlit at night. **Kastraki**, two km from Kalambaka, is a charming village of red-tiled houses just west of the monasteries.

The telephone code for the area is ☎ 0432.

Things to See
There were once monasteries on each of the 24 pinnacles, but only five are still occupied. They are Metamorphosis (Grand Meteora, closed on Tuesday), Varlaam (closed Friday), Agios Stefanos (open daily), Agia Triada (open daily), Agios Nikolaos (open daily) and Roussanou (closed Wednesday). All keep similar hours – 9 am to 1 pm and 3 to 5 pm – except Agios Nikolaos, which opens from 9 am to 6 pm. Admission is 600 dr for Grand Meteora, 400 dr for the others.

Meteora is best explored on foot, following the old paths where they exist. Allow a whole

day to visit all of the monasteries and take food and water. Women must wear skirts that reach below their knees, men must wear long trousers, and arms must be covered.

Places to Stay & Eat
Kastraki is the best base for visiting Meteora. *Vrachos Camping* (☎ 22 293), on the edge of the village, is an excellent site. *Zozas Pallas* on the road to Kalambaka, has luxurious singles/doubles for 4000/8000 dr. The *Hotel France* (☎ 24 186), which is opposite Vrachos Camping, has rooms for 5000/7000 dr and a restaurant. The owner is a good source of information about walks.

In Kalambaka, *Koka Roka Rooms* (☎ 24 554), at the beginning of the path to Agia Triada, is popular travellers' place. Doubles with bath are 6000 dr; the taverna downstairs is good value.

Getting There & Away
Kalambaka is the hub of the transport network. There are frequent buses to Trikala and two

day to Ioannina. Local buses shuttle constantly between Kalambaka and Kastraki; five a day continue to Metamorphosis.

THESSALONIKI Θεσσαλονίκη

Thessaloniki, also known as Salonica, is Greece's second-largest city. It's a bustling, sophisticated place with good restaurants and a busy nightlife. It was once the second city of Byzantium, and there are some magnificent Byzantine churches, as well as a scattering of Roman ruins.

Orientation & Information

Thessaloniki is laid out on a grid system. The main thoroughfares – Tsimiski, Egnatia and Agiou Dimitriou – run parallel to Nikis, on the waterfront. Plateias Eleftherias and Aristotelous, both on Nikis, are the main squares. The city's most famous landmark is the White Tower (no longer white) at the eastern end of Nikis.

The train station is on Monastiriou, the westerly continuation of Egnatia beyond Plateia Dimokratias, and the airport is 16 km to the south-east. The old Turkish quarter is north of Athinas. The EOT office (☎ 271 888), at Plateia Aristotelous 8, is open Monday to Friday from 8 am to 8 pm, and Saturday from 8 am to 2 pm. USIT Travel (☎ 263 814), Ippodromiou 15, sells airline and ferry tickets.

Money The National Bank of Greece and the Commercial Bank have branches on Plateia Dimokratias. American Express (☎ 269 521) has an office at Tsimiski 19.

Post & Communications The main post office is at Tsimiski 45 and is open Monday to Friday from 7.30 am to 8 pm, Saturday from 7.30 am to 2 pm, and Sunday from 9 am to 1.30 pm. The OTE telephone office is at Karolou Dil 27 and is open 24 hours a day.

Thessaloniki's telephone code is ☎ 031.

Laundry Bianca Laundrette, on Antoniadou, charges 1200 dr to wash and dry a load. Antoniadou is just north of the Arch of Galerius, off Gournari.

Medical & Emergency Services There is a first-aid centre (☎ 530 530) at Nav Koundouriti

6. The tourist police (☎ 548 907), at Egnatia 10 (enter via Tandalidou), are open daily from 7.30 am to 11 pm from October to March, and 24 hours a day from April to September.

Things to See

The **archaeological museum**, at the eastern end of Tsimiski, houses a superb collection of treasures from the royal tombs of Philip II. It is open on Monday from 12.30 to 7 pm, Tuesday to Friday from 8 am to 7 pm (5 pm in winter) and on weekends from 8.30 am to 3 pm; admission is 1500 dr. The outstanding **Folkloric & Ethnological Museum of Macedonia**, at Vasilissis Olgas 68, includes traditional household utensils and northern Greek costumes. It's open every day, except Thursday, from 9.30 am to 4 pm; admission is 200 dr.

Places to Stay

The *youth hostel* (☎ 225 946), Alex Svolou 44, has dorm beds for 1800 dr. The doors are locked from 11 am to 7 pm, and there's an 11 pm curfew. An HI card is required and the hostel is closed from December to mid-May.

The best budget hotel in town is the friendly, family-run *Hotel Acropol* (☎ 531 670), on Tandalidou, a quiet side street off Egnatia. It has singles/doubles with shared bath for 5000/7500 dr. The *Hotel Atlantis* (☎ 540 131), Egnatia 14, has doubles with shared bathroom for 4500 dr. The rooms are tiny but clean.

The *Hotel Atlas* (☎ 510 038), Egnatia 40, has good doubles with bath for 8000 dr. The rooms at the front get a lot of traffic noise. Just around the corner from the Atlas is the quiet *Hotel Averof* (☎ 538 498) at Leontos Sofou 24. Pleasant singles/doubles with shared bath are 4500/7500 dr.

Rooms can be hard to find during the international trade fair in September.

Places to Eat

Adventurous eaters should head for *Patsas Ilias*, Egnatia 102, to sample the local speciality, tripe soup. Others may prefer the security of McDonald's, 50 metres away.

A place full of local colour is the lively *O Loutros Fish Taverna*, which occupies an old Turkish hammam near the flower market on Komninon. Excellent fish dishes start from 1000 dr. The place is always packed and there

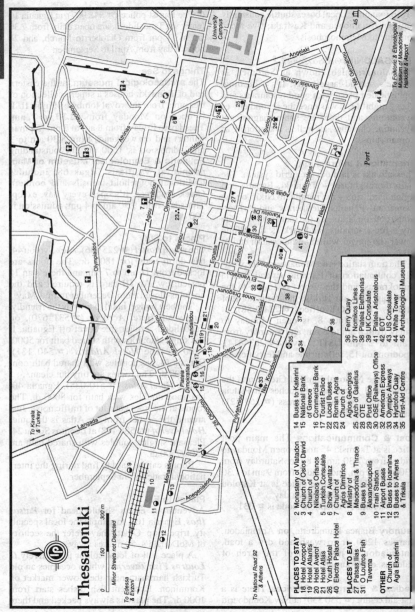

Thessaloniki

0   150   300 m

Minor Streets not Depicted

To Edessa
& Evzoni

To National Road 92
& Athens

To Kavala
& Turkey

To Folkloric & Ethnological
Museum of Macedonia,
Halkidiki & Airport

Port

University
Campus

PLACES TO STAY
18 Hotel Acropol
19 Hotel Atlantis
20 Hotel Averof
21 Hotel Atlas
26 Youth Hostel
40 Electra Palace Hotel

PLACES TO EAT
27 Patsas Ilias
31 O Loutros Fish
     Taverna

OTHER
1   Church of
     Agia Ekaterini
2   Monastery of Vlatadon
3   Church of Osios David
4   Church of
     Nikolaos Orfanos
5   Turkish Consulate
6   Show Avantaz
7   Church of
     Agios Dimitrios
8   Ministry of
     Macedonia & Thrace
9   Buses to
     Alexandroupolis
10 Train Station
11 Airport Buses
12 Buses to Ioannina
13 Buses to Athens
     & Trikala
14 Buses to Katerini
15 National Bank
     of Greece
16 Commercial Bank
17 Tourist Police
22 Local Buses
23 Roman Agora
24 Church of
     Agios Georgios
25 Arch of Galerius
28 OTE
29 Post Office
30 OSE (Railways) Office
32 American Express
33 Olympic Airways
34 Hydrofoil Quay
35 First-Aid Centre
36 Ferry Quay
37 Nomikos Lines
38 Plateia Eleftherias
39 UK Consulate
41 Plateia Aristotelous
42 EOT
43 US Consulate
44 White Tower
45 Archaeological Museum

are often spontaneous renderings of rembetika; it's closed at weekends.

Entertainment

Young people frequent the many bars along the waterfront before hitting the clubs. From October to May, the action is in town. You'll find live bouzouki and folk music every night at *Show Avantaz*, opposite the Turkish consulate at Agiou Dimitriou 156. It opens at 11 pm. *Traffic*, east of the university on Tritis Septemvriou, is a popular dance spot. In summer, the city discos close and others open up on the road to the airport.

Getting There & Away

Air The airport is 16 km to the south-east. There are six flights a day to Athens (19,200 dr) and daily flights to Limnos (12,800 dr). Other destinations include Ioannina, Lesvos, Iraklio and Rhodes. Olympic Airways (☎ 230 240) is at Nav Koundouriti 3. See the Getting There & Away section at the start of this chapter for information on international flights.

Bus There are several bus terminals, most of them near the train station. Buses for Athens, Igoumenitsa and Trikala leave from Monastiriou 65 & 67, and buses for Alexandroupolis leave from Plateia Galopourou. Buses for Pella, Florina, Kastoria and Volos leave from Anegeniseos 22, and buses to the Halkidiki peninsula from Karakassi 68 (off the map in the eastern part of town; it's marked on the free EOT map). To reach the Halkidiki terminal, take local bus No 10 to the Botsari stop, near Odos Markou Botsari. The OSE has two buses a day to Athens from the train station, as well as international services to İstanbul, Sofia (Bulgaria) and Korça (Albania).

Train There are eight trains a day to Athens and five to Alexandroupolis. All international trains from Athens stop at Thessaloniki. You can get more information from the OSE office at Aristotelous 18 or from the train station.

Ferry & Hydrofoil There's a Saturday ferry to Lesvos, Limnos and Chios throughout the year. In summer there are two ferries a week to Iraklio (Crete), stopping in the Sporades and the Cyclades on the way. Get your tickets from Nomikos Lines (☎ 524 544) by the port. In summer there are hydrofoils most days to Skiathos, Skopelos and Alonnisos. Tickets can be bought from Egnatias Tours (☎ 22 811), Kambouniou 9.

Getting Around

To/From the Airport There is no bus service from the Olympic Airways office. Take bus No 78 from the train station. A taxi from the airport costs about 1500 dr.

Bus There is a flat fare of 75 dr on city and suburban buses, paid either to a conductor at the rear door or to coin-operated machines on driver-only buses.

HALKIDIKI Χαλκιδική

Halkidiki is the three-pronged peninsula south-east of Thessaloniki. It's the main resort area of northern Greece, with superb sandy beaches right around its 500 km of coastline. **Kassandra**, the south-western prong of the peninsula, has surrendered irrevocably to mass tourism. **Sithonia**, the middle prong, is not as over the top and has some spectacular scenery.

Mt Athos

Halkidiki's third prong is occupied by the all-male Monastic Republic of Mt Athos (also called the Holy Mountain), where monasteries full of priceless treasures stand amid an impressive landscape of gorges, wooded mountains and precipitous rocks.

To acquire a four-day visitor's permit to Mt Athos you must be male and have a letter of recommendation from your embassy or consulate. You take it to either the Ministry of Foreign Affairs, Zalokosta 2, Athens, or the Ministry of Macedonia & Thrace, Plateia Diikitirio, Thessaloniki, between 10 am and 2 pm, Monday to Friday. Thessaloniki's UK consulate (☎ 278 006), which also represents Australian, Canadian and New Zealand citizens, is at El Venizelou 8, and the US consulate (☎ 266 121) is at Nikis 59. For more details, enquire at the EOT office. Armed with your permit, you can explore, on foot, the 20 monasteries and dependent religious communities of Mt Athos. You can stay only one night at each monastery.

MT OLYMPUS Ολυμπος Ορος

Mt Olympus is Greece's highest and mightiest mountain. The ancients chose it as the abode of their gods and assumed it to be the exact centre of the Earth. Olympus has eight peaks, the highest of which is Mytikas (2917 metres). The area is popular with trekkers, most of whom use the village of **Litohoro** as a base. Litohoro is five km inland from the Athens-Thessaloniki highway.

The telephone code is ☎ 0352. The EOS office (☎ 81 944) on Plateia Kentriki has information on the various treks and conditions.

The main route to the top takes two days, overnighting at one of the refuges on the mountain. Good protective clothing is essential, even in summer.

Places to Stay & Eat

Litohoro's *youth hostel* (☎ 82 176) charges 1300 for dorm beds and 500 dr for linen. The manager is a valuable source of information for serious trekkers and also hires out suitable clothing. Luggage can be stored here. The *Olympos Taverna* serves standard fare at reasonable prices.

There are four *refuges* on the mountain at altitudes ranging from 270 metres to 930 metres. They are all open from May to September.

Getting There & Away

There are eight buses a day to Litohoro from Thessaloniki and three from Athens (5½ hours, 6500 dr). There are frequent buses between Litohoro and the coastal village of Katerini.

ALEXANDROUPOLIS Αλεξανδρούπολη

Dusty Alexandroupolis doesn't have much going for it, but if you're going to Turkey or Samothraki, you may end up staying overnight here. There's a tourist office (☎ 24 998) in the town hall on Dimokratias.

Alexandroupolis' telephone code is ☎ 0551.

Places to Stay & Eat

The nearest camping ground, *Camping Alexandroupolis* (☎ 28 735), is on the beach two km west of town. Buses to Makri from Plateia Eleftherias, opposite the port, can drop you there. The *Hotel Lido* (☎ 28 808), one block north of the bus station at Paleologou 15, is a great budget option. Doubles are 2600 dr, or 5200 dr with private bathroom. The *Hotel*

Okeanis (☎ 28 830), almost opposite the Lido, has large, comfortable singles/doubles for 7000/9000 dr.

The *Neraida Restaurant*, on Kyprou, has a range of local specialities priced from 1400 dr. Kyprou starts opposite the pier where ferries leave for Samothraki.

Getting There & Away

There is at least one flight a day to Athens (17,100 dr) from the airport seven km west of town. There are five trains (3440 dr) and five buses (5100 dr) a day to Thessaloniki. There's also a daily train and a daily OSE bus to İstanbul, as well as daily buses to Plovdiv and Sofia in Bulgaria.

In summer there are at least two boats a day to Samothraki (two hours, 2200 dr), dropping to one in winter. There are also hydrofoils to Chios, via Lesvos and Limnos.

Saronic Gulf Islands
Νησιά του Σαρωνικού

The Saronic Gulf islands are the closest island group to Athens. Not surprisingly they are a very popular escape for residents of the congested capital. Accommodation can be hard to find between mid-June and September, and on weekends all year round.

The telephone code is ☎ 0298 for all the islands except Aegina (☎ 0297).

Getting There & Away

Ferries to all four islands, and hydrofoils to Aegina, leave from the Great Harbour in Piraeus. Hydrofoils to the other islands run from Zea Marina in Piraeus.

AEGINA Αίγινα

Aegina is the closest island to Athens and a popular destination for day-trippers. Many make for the lovely **Temple of Aphaia**, a well-preserved Doric temple 12 km east of Aegina town. It is open on weekdays from 8.15 am to 7 pm (5 pm in winter) and on weekends from 8.30 am to 3 pm. Admission is 800 dr. Buses from Aegina town to the small resort of **Agia Marina** can drop you at the site. Agia Marina has the best beach on the island, which isn't saying much.

Most travellers prefer to stay in Aegina town, where the *Hotel Plaza* (☎ 25 600) has singles/doubles overlooking the sea for 4000/7000 dr.

POROS Πόρος

Poros is a big hit with the Brits, but it's hard to work out why. The beaches are nothing to write home about and there are no sites of significance. The main attraction is pretty Poros town, draped over the Sferia peninsula. Sferia is linked to the rest of the island, known as Kalavria, by a narrow isthmus. Most of the package hotels are here. There are a few domatia in Poros town, signposted off the road to Kalavria.

The island lies little more than a stone's throw from the mainland, opposite the Peloponnesian village of Galatas.

HYDRA Ύδρα

Hydra is the island with the most style and is famous as the haunt of artists and jet-setters. Its gracious stone mansions are stacked up the rocky hillsides that surround the fine natural harbour. The main attraction is peace and quiet. There are no motorised vehicles on the island – apart from a garbage truck and a few construction vehicles.

Accommodation is expensive, but of a high standard. The friendly *Pension Theresia* (☎ 53 983) has quaint rooms around a leafy courtyard for 7000/9000 dr, negotiable on weekdays.

SPETSES Σπέτσες

Pine-covered Spetses is perhaps the most beautiful island in the group. It also has the best beaches, so it's packed with package tourists in summer. The **old harbour** in Spetses town is a delightful place to explore. The travel agents on the waterfront can organise accommodation.

Cyclades Κυκλάδες

The Cyclades, named after the rough circle they form around Delos, are quintessential Greek islands with brilliant white architecture, dazzling light and golden beaches.

Delos, historically the most important island of the group, is uninhabited. The inhabited islands of the archipelago are Mykonos, Syros, Tinos, Andros, Paros, Naxos, Ios, Santorini (Thira), Anafi, Amorgos, Sikinos, Folegandros and the tiny islands of Koufonisi, Shinoussa, Iraklia and Donoussa, which lie east of Naxos. The remaining six – Kea, Kythnos, Serifos, Sifnos, Kimolos and Milos – are referred to as the Western Cyclades.

Some of the Cyclades, like Mykonos, Paros and Santorini, have vigorously embraced the tourist industry, filling their coastlines with discos and bars, and their beaches with sun lounges, umbrellas and water-sports equipment for hire. But others, like Anafi, Sikinos and the tiny islands east of Naxos, are little more than clumps of rock, each with a village, a few secluded coves – and very few tourists.

To give even the briefest rundown on every island is impossible in a single chapter. The following gives information on a cross section of the islands, from those with packed beaches and a raucous nightlife, to those off the tourist circuit, where tranquillity and glimpses of a fast-dying, age-old way of life await the visitor.

History

The Cyclades enjoyed a flourishing Bronze Age civilisation (3000-1100 BC), more or less concurrent with the Minoan civilisation.

By the 5th century BC, the island of Delos had been taken over by Athens, which kept its treasury there.

Between the 4th and 7th centuries AD, the islands, like the rest of Greece, suffered a series of invasions and occupations. During the Middle Ages they were raided by pirates – hence the labyrinthine character of their towns, which was meant to confuse attackers. On some islands the whole population would move into the mountainous interior to escape the pirates, while on others they would brave it out on the coast. This is why on some islands the hora (main town) is on the coast and on others it is inland.

The Cyclades became part of independent Greece in 1827.

Orientation & Information

The islands lie in the central Aegean, southeast of Athens and north of Crete. In July, August and September the Cyclades are prone to the *meltemi*, a ferocious north-easterly wind which sends everything flying and disrupts ferry schedules. Paros, Ios, Milos, Serifos, Sifnos and Syros have either EOT or municipal tourist offices. On other islands, information is available from the tourist police, private travel agents and the regular police.

Getting There & Away

Air Mykonos and Santorini have international airports that receive charter flights from northern Europe. There are daily flights from Athens to Milos, Naxos, Paros, Mykonos and Santorini, and six flights a week between Mykonos and Santorini. Both islands have flights to Crete and Rhodes.

Boat The information on boat services supplied in this section is for April to October; in winter, services are severely curtailed. Most islands are served by daily boats from Piraeus.

A daily excursion boat travels between Mykonos, Paros, Naxos, Ios and Santorini. Hydrofoils and catamarans link Paros, Naxos, Syros, Tinos, Ios, Santorini and Crete in high season. Bear in mind, particularly if you're visiting a remote island, that ferries are prone to delays and cancellations. All the islands are served by car ferry. Hydrofoils do not carry cars.

Getting Around

Most islands have buses that link the port with villages on the island. On many islands *caïques* (fishing boats) connect the port with popular beaches.

Santorini, Paros, Naxos, Ios, Milos and Mykonos have car-rental firms. Most islands have motorcycle and moped-rental places, and some also have bicycles for rent.

Most islands are crisscrossed by donkey tracks, which are great to walk along.

NAXOS Νάξος

Naxos is the island where Theseus disloyally dumped Ariadne after she helped him to slay the Minotaur (half-bull, half-man) on the island of Crete. She gave him the thread that enabled him to find his way out of the Minotaur's labyrinth once he had killed the monster.

Naxos, the greenest and most beautiful island of the archipelago, is popular but big enough to allow you to escape the hordes.

Orientation & Information

Naxos town, on the west coast, is the island's capital and port. There is no EOT but there's an excellent unofficial tourist office (☎ 24 358) opposite the harbour, run by the inimitable Despina Kitini. Luggage storage is 300 dr, and the office is open daily from 8 am to midnight. The OTE is on the waterfront opposite the National Bank of Greece; for the post office, turn left beyond the OTE and then take the second right.

Naxos' telephone code is ☎ 0285.

Things to See

Naxos Town The winding alleyways of Naxos town, lined with immaculate whitewashed houses, clamber up to the crumbling 13th-century kastro walls. The well-stocked archaeological museum is here, housed in a former school where Nikos Kazantzakis was briefly a pupil. The museum is open Tuesday to Sunday from 8.30 am to 3 pm; admission is 500 dr.

Beaches After the town beach of Agios Georgios, sandy beaches – which become progressively less crowded – continue southwards as far as Pyrgaki Beach.

Apollonas On the north coast, Apollonas has a rocky beach and a pleasant sheltered bay. If you're curious about the *kouros* statues, you can see the largest one, 10.5 metres long, just outside of Apollonas, lying abandoned and unfinished in an ancient marble quarry. There are two more in the Melanes region.

It's worth taking the bus or driving from Naxos town to Apollonas for the scenery. The road winds its way through the Tragaea, gradually ascending through increasingly dramatic mountainscapes. After Apiranthos the road zigzags to Komiaki, the island's highest village. From here the descent begins to the lush valley of Apollonas.

Tragaea This gorgeous region is a vast Arcadian olive grove with Byzantine churches and

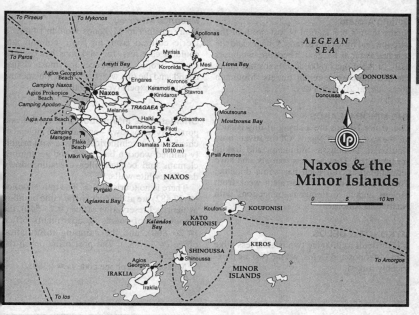

Naxos & the Minor Islands

tranquil villages. **Filoti**, the largest settlement, perches on the slopes of **Mt Zeus** (1004 metres). It takes three hours to climb the trail to the summit.

Filoti is also a good base from which to explore the region on foot. A dirt road leads from the village to the picturesque and isolated hamlets of **Damarionas** and **Damalas**. From Damalas it is a short walk to the village of **Halki**, from where another dirt road leads to the twin hamlets of **Khimaros** and **Tsikalario**.

Another village, **Apiranthos**, has many old houses of uncharacteristically bare stone, and some of the women who live here still weave on looms and wear traditional costumes.

Places to Stay & Eat

Naxos' three camping grounds are *Camping Naxos* (☎ 23 501), one km south of Agios Georgios Beach; *Camping Maragas* (☎ 24 552), Agia Anna Beach; and *Camping Apollon* (☎ 24 117), 700 metres from Agios Prokopios Beach. All are open from May to October.

Hotel Anixis (☎ 22 112) is one of Naxos

town's best budget hotels. Doubles/triples cost 8000/10,000 dr with private bath. Nearby, the unofficial *Dionyssos Hostel* (☎ 22 331) has dorm beds for 1500 dr and doubles/triples for 4000/6000 dr. No card is required. The easiest way to find these establishments is to follow the signs in the old town to the Hotel Panorama. *Pension Sofi* (☎ 25 582), 350 metres from the quay, has spotless doubles/triples for 10,000/12,000 dr.

O Tsitas Restaurant, in Naxos town, up the alleyway by Zas Travel Agency near the harbour, has tasty cheap food. *Maro's*, on the street bearing left after the roundabout 50 metres past the post office, has a wide range of dishes and is superb for breakfasts (omelettes from 400 dr). You will find bakeries, grocery shops and fruit and vegetable shops on Market St.

Getting There & Away

Naxos has daily ferries to Paros and Piraeus (3500 dr) and frequent ferries to the Minor Islands, other Cycladic ports, and to Samos and Chios. For the port police, call ☎ 22 300.

Getting Around

Naxos town's bus station is just north of the harbour, and buses run to most villages and the beaches as far as Pyrgaki. There are two buses daily to Apollonas (800 dr). Naxos has many car and motorcycle-rental outlets. Mountain bikes start at 2000 dr a day.

THE MINOR ISLANDS

The Minor Islands are a string of tiny islands off the east coast of Naxos. Of the seven, only Koufonisi, Donoussa, Shinoussa and Iraklia are inhabited. They see few tourists, and have few amenities, but each has some domatia. They are served by two ferries a week from Piraeus and have frequent connections with Naxos and Amorgos.

MYKONOS & DELOS

It is difficult to imagine two islands less alike than Mykonos and Delos, yet the two are inextricably linked.

Mykonos Μύκονος

Many visitors to Mykonos wouldn't know a Doric column from an Ionic column and couldn't care less, for Mykonos has become the St Tropez of Greece, the most visited island, and the one with the most sophisticated – and most expensive – nightlife.

Orientation & Information The capital and port is Mykonos town – an elaborate tableau of chic boutiques, chimerical houses with brightly painted wooden balconies, and geraniums, clematis and bougainvillea cascading down dazzling white walls.

There is no tourist office. The tourist police (☎ 22 482) are at the port, in the same building as the hotel reservation office (☎ 24 540), the association of rooms & apartments office (☎ 26 860), and the camping information office (☎ 22 852). The post office is on the waterfront.

Mykonos' telephone code is ☎ 0289.

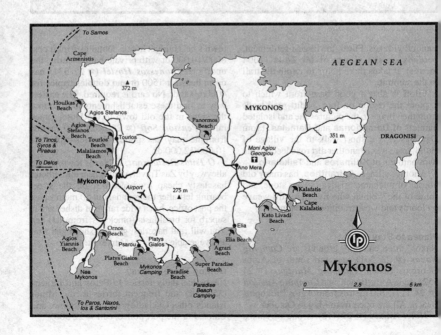

Mykonos

Things to See & Do The **archaeological museum** and **nautical museum** are mediocre, but the **folklore museum** (open Monday to Saturday from 5.30 to 8.30 pm; free entry) is well stocked with local memorabilia. Exhibits include reconstructions of traditional homes, and a somewhat macabre stuffed pelican, the erstwhile Petros, who was run over by a car in 1985. He was hastily supplanted by Petros II, who you will no doubt meet if you loiter around the fish market. The museum is near the Delos quay.

The most popular beaches are the mainly nude **Paradise** and **Super Paradise** (mainly gay), **Agrari** and **Elia**. The less crowded ones are **Panormos**, which is inaccessible by bus or caïque but can be walked to from the inland village of Ano Mera, and **Kato Livadi**, which you can walk to from Elia Beach.

Places to Stay Mykonos has two camping grounds: *Paradise Beach Camping* (☎ 22 937) and *Mykonos Camping* (☎ 24 578). Paradise charges 1500 dr per person and 850 dr per tent.

Rooms fill up quickly in summer, so it's prudent to succumb to the first domatia owner who accosts you.

The delightfully old-world *Apollon* (☎ 22 223) on the waterfront, run by two genteel elderly ladies, has doubles for 15,000 dr with private bath (closed in the low season), and *Angela's Rooms* (☎ 22 967), on Plateia Mavrogenous (usually called Taxi Square), has doubles with bath for 12,000 dr.

Places to Eat The *Sesame Kitchen*, near the nautical museum, serves mostly vegetarian dishes. *Niko's Taverna*, near the Delos quay, is popular, though prices are higher than at waterfront cafés.

Entertainment The *Scandinavian* bar, near Niko's Taverna, and the improbably named *Stavros Irish Pub*, near Taxi Square, have the cheapest drinks. For a more tasteful ambience, make for *Club Verandah* and *Montparnasse* bars in Little Venice, where classical music plays as the sun sets.

Getting There & Away Flights from Mykonos to Athens cost 17,300 dr, to Santorini 13,900

dr, and to both Rhodes and Crete 20,500 dr. The Olympic Airways office (☎ 22 490) is on Plateia Louka.

There are many ferries daily to Mykonos from Piraeus (6500 dr). Mykonos also has hydrofoil and excursion boats to the other major Cycladic islands.

Getting Around The north bus station is near the port, behind the OTE office. It serves Agios Stefanos, Elia, Kalafatis and Ano Mera. The south bus station serves Agios Yiannis, Psarou, Platys Gialos and the airport.

Super Paradise, Agrari and Elia beaches are served by caïque from Mykonos town, but easier access to these and Paradise Beach is by caïque from Platys Gialos.

There are at least six boats daily to Delos, in season, leaving between 8.45 am and 10.45 am. The round-trip is 1600 dr; entrance to the site is 1200 dr.

Most car, motorcycle and bicycle-rental firms are around the south bus station.

Delos Δήλος
Just south-east of Mykonos, the uninhabited island of Delos is the Cyclades' archaeological jewel. In ancient times, the island was both a religious site and the most important commercial port in the Aegean.

According to mythology, Delos was the birthplace of Apollo – the god of light, poetry, music, healing and prophecy. Delos flourished as a religious and commercial centre from the 3rd millennium BC, reaching its height in the 5th century BC, by which time its oracle was second only to Delphi's. It was sacked by Mithridates, king of the Black Sea region, in 88 BC and 20,000 people were killed.

The site of Delos is basically in three sections. To the north of the harbour is the **Sanctuary of Apollo**, containing temples dedicated to him, and the much photographed **Terrace of the Lions**. These proud beasts were carved in the 4th century BC from marble from Naxos, and their function was to guard the sacred area. The Venetians took a liking to them, and in the 17th century shipped one to Venice, where it can still be seen guarding the arsenal of the city. The **Sacred Lake** (dry since 1926) is where Leto supposedly gave birth to Apollo. The museum is east of this section.

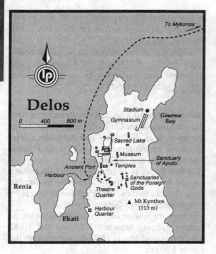

South of the harbour is the **Theatre Quarter**, where private houses were built around the **Theatre of Delos**. East of here, towards Mt Kynthos, are the **Sanctuaries of the Foreign Gods**, containing a shrine to the Samothracian Great Gods, the sanctuary of the Syrian Gods, and a sanctuary with temples to Serapis and Isis.

There are boats to Delos from Mykonos. No-one can stay overnight on Delos, and the boat schedule allows you only three hours there. Bring plenty of water and, if you want, some food, because the island's cafeteria is a rip-off.

IOS Ιος

More than any other Greek island, Ios epitomises the Greece of sun, sand, sex and souvlaki. Come here if you want to bake on a beach all day and drink all night. Young people hang out in the village, where the nightlife is. The older set tend to stay in the port.

Ios' telephone code is ☎ 0286.

Places to Stay & Eat

Ios Camping (☎ 91 329) is on the beach next to the port, but the camping grounds at Milopotas beach are preferable. They are *Milopotas Camping* (☎ 91 554), *Stars* (☎ 91 302) and, the best of all, *Far Out Camping* (☎ 91 468).

There is a wonderful view of the bay from *Francesco's* (☎ 91 223), in the village. A dorm bed is 2300 dr, and doubles/triples with private bath are 6000/8000 dr. It's a lively meeting place with a bar and terrace.

The Nest is an excellent eatery, with plenty of dishes at around 800 dr. It's opposite the village's only pharmacy. In season, *Zorba's Restaurant*, *Pithari Taverna* and *Pinocchio* are popular.

Getting There & Away

The island has daily connections with Piraeus (4700 dr) and there are frequent hydrofoils and excursion boats to the major Cycladic islands.

PAROS Πάρος

Physically, Paros is 16 km from Naxos, but metaphysically it hovers somewhere between Ios and Mykonos. It's popular with backpackers who crave style but can't afford Mykonos, yet still attracts some big spenders, as evidenced by its expensive jewellery shops (which are conspicuously absent on Ios). Like Mykonos, it's also popular with gay travellers. Paros is famous for its pure white marble – no less than the *Venus de Milo* herself was created from it.

Paros is an attractive island, although less

dramatically so than Naxos. Its softly con-
toured and terraced hills culminate in one
central mountain, Profitis Ilias. It has some of
the finest beaches in the Cyclades.

The small island of Antiparos (Αντίπαρος)
lies one km east of Paros. The two were originally joined, but were split by an earthquake
many millennia ago.

Orientation & Information

Paros' main town and port is Paroikia, on the
west coast. The municipal tourist office is by
the port. The OTE is on the south-west waterfront; turn right from the ferry pier. The post
office is also on the waterfront, but to the north
of the pier.

Paros' telephone code is ☎ 0284.

Things to See & Do

One of the most notable churches in Greece is
Paroikia's **Panagia Ekatontapyliani**, which
features a beautiful, highly ornate interior.

Petaloudes, 10 km from Paroikia, is better
known as the Valley of the Butterflies. In
summer, huge swarms of the creatures almost
conceal the copious foliage.

The charming village of **Naoussa**, filled with
white houses and labyrinthine alleyways, is still
a working fishing village, despite an enormous
growth in tourism over the last few years.

Paroikia's beaches are disappointing. Take a
caïque to a nearby beach or try Naoussa, which
has good beaches served by caïque. Most
popular are **Kolimvythres**, with bizarre rock
formations, **Monastiri**, a mainly nude beach, and
Santa Maria, which is good for windsurfing.

Paros' longest beach, **Hrysi Akti** (Golden
Beach) on the south coast, is reputedly brilliant
for windsurfing.

The picturesque villages of **Lefkes**, **Marmara**
and **Marpissa** are all worth a visit. The Moni
Agiou Antoniou (Monastery of St Anthony), on
a hill above Marpissa, offers breathtaking views.
From Lefkes, an ancient Byzantine path leads in
one hour of easy walking to the village of Pro-
dromos, from where it is a short walk to either
Marmara or Marpissa.

Antiparos This small island, less than two km
from Paros, has superb beaches, but is becoming too popular for its own good.

One of the chief attractions in Antiparos is
the cave, considered one of Europe's most
beautiful (open from 10 am to 4 pm daily in
summer only). Despite indiscriminate looting
of stalagmites and stalactites in times gone by,
it still has a profusion of them. Entry is 450 dr.

Places to Stay

Paros has five camping grounds. *Parasporas*
(☎ 22 268), *Koula Camping* (☎ 22 081) and
Krios (☎ 21 705) are near Paroikia, and
Naoussa Camping (☎ 51 595) and *Surfing
Beach* (☎ 51 013) are near Naoussa. Surfing
Beach is the largest and has the best facilities.

Antiparos has one camping ground, *Antiparos Camping* (☎ 61 221), on Agios Giannis
Theologos Beach.

Rooms Mike (☎ 22 856) is deservedly
popular with backpackers. Doubles/triples cost
7000/9000 dr, with a small kitchen and a roof
terrace. To get there, walk 50 metres left from the
pier and you'll find it next to the Memphis bar.
Around the corner, above Taverna Parikia, Mike
also has self-contained studios; doubles/triples
are 8000/10,000 dr. *Hotel Kypreou* (☎ 21 383)
has doubles/triples with private bath for
7000/10,000 dr; turn left from the pier and it's on
the first street to the right .

Places to Eat

No matter how late at night you arrive, *To
Proto*, 50 metres to the right from the pier, is
usually open; it serves bacon and eggs (500 dr),
home-made hamburgers (650 dr), gyros and
souvlaki (350 dr). *Ouzeri Albadross*, on the
south-west waterfront, is cosy and popular;
small/big mixed platters cost 900/1800 dr.

Getting There & Away

Flights from Athens cost 17,100 dr. Paros is a
major transport hub for ferries. Daily connections with Piraeus take seven hours and cost
3320 dr. There are frequent ferries to Naxos,
Ios, Santorini and Mykonos, and less frequent
ones to Astypalea, Kalymnos, Kos, Tilos, Symi
and Rhodes. There are hourly excursion boats
in season to Antiparos. You can contact the port
police on ☎ 21 240.

Getting Around

The bus station is 100 metres north of the
tourist office. There are frequent buses to Aliki,
Naoussa, Lefkes, Piso Livadi and Hrysi Akti.
For Petaloudes take the Aliki bus.

GREECE

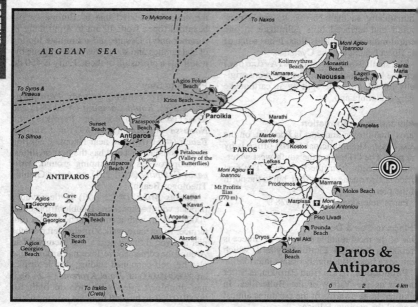

Paros & Antiparos

0   2   4 km

There are many car and motorcycle-rental places.

FOLEGANDROS & SIKINOS

Of these two sparsely populated islands, Sikinos (Σίκινος) is the less visited – you could be the only visitor during the low season. There are no hotels, but there are some domatia and pensions in the very pretty Hora. The island also has several good beaches.

Folegandros (Φολέγανδρος) has become too popular in recent years and is no longer an island where you can get away from it all. Even so, it is considerably quieter than the major islands in the Cyclades and has a dramatic landscape, with a hora perched precariously on top of a sheer cliff. *Livadi Camping* (☎ 0286-41 204) on Livadi Beach has good facilities. *Hotel Kastro Danassis* (☎ 0286-41 230) has doubles/triples at 12,000/16,000 dr.

Getting There & Away

There are three ferries a week between Sikinos (4650 dr), Folegandros (4030 dr) and Piraeus.

Two go via Kythnos, Serifos, Sifnos, Milos and Kimolos, and one goes via Syros, Paros, Naxos and Santorini.

SANTORINI (THIRA) Σαντορίνη (Θήρα)

Around 1450 BC, the volcanic heart of Santorini exploded and sank, leaving an extraordinary landscape. Today the startling sight of the malevolently steaming core almost encircled by sheer cliffs remains. It's possible that the catastrophe destroyed the Minoan civilisation, but neither this theory nor the claim that the island was part of the lost continent of Atlantis have been proven.

Since ancient times the Atlantis legend has fired the imaginations of writers, scientists and mystics, all of whom depict it as an advanced society destroyed by a volcanic eruption. Egyptian papyruses have been found which tell of a cataclysmic event which destroyed such a civilisation, but they place it further west than the Aegean. Solon, the 6th-century BC Athenian ruler, related that on his visit to Egypt he was told of a continent destroyed 9000 years before his birth. Believers say he merely made a mathematical error and that he meant 900 years, which would correspond with the Santorini eruption. Plato firmly believed in the existence of Atlantis and depicted it as a land of art, flowers and fruit, and the frescos from Akrotiri bear this out.

Orientation & Information

The capital, Fira, perches on top of the caldera on the west coast. The port of Athinios is 12 km away. There is no EOT or tourist police, but, the exceptionally helpful Dakoutros Travel Agency (☎ 22 958) gives advice, sells boat tickets, arranges accommodation and changes currency. It is open from 8 am to 9 pm every day. Facing north, turn right at the Commercial Bank on the main square (Plateia Theotokopoulou).

Santorini's telephone code is ☎ 0286.

Things to See & Do

Fira The commercialism of Fira has not reduced its all-pervasive dramatic aura. The **Megaron**

Gyzi Museum, behind the Catholic monastery, houses local memorabilia, including fascinating photographs of Fira before and immediately after the 1956 earthquake. It's open Monday to Saturday from 10.30 am to 1.30 pm and 5 to 8 pm, and on Sunday from 10.30 am to 4.30 pm. Admission is 400 dr. The **archaeological museum**, opposite the cable-car station, houses finds from ancient Akrotiri and ancient Thira. Opening times are Tuesday to Sunday from 8.30 am to 3 pm, and admission is 800 dr.

Ancient Sites Excavations in 1967 uncovered the remarkably well preserved Minoan settlement of **Akrotiri**. There are remains of two and three-storey buildings, and evidence of a sophisticated drainage system. The site is open Tuesday to Sunday from 8.30 am to 3 pm; admission is 1200 dr.

Less impressive than Akrotiri, the site of **ancient Thira** is still worth a visit for the stunning views. The **Moni Profiti Ilia**, built on the island's highest point, can be reached along a path from ancient Thira.

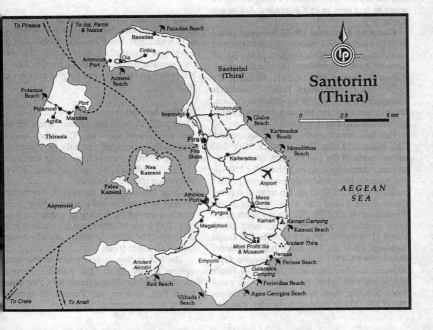

GREECE

Beaches Santorini's beaches are of black volcanic sand which becomes unbearably hot, making a beach mat essential. Kamari and Perissa get crowded, whereas those near Oia and Monolithos are quieter.

Other Attractions From Imerovigli, just north of Santorini, a 12-km coastal path leads to the picturesque village of **Oia**. On a clear day there are breathtaking views of Folegandros and Sikinos. Oia is built on a steep slope of the caldera, and many of its traditional white Cycladic houses nestle in niches hewn from the volcanic rock.

Of the surrounding islets, only **Thirasia** is inhabited. At Palia Kameni you can bathe in hot springs, and on Nea Kameni you can clamber around on volcanic lava.

Places to Stay
Non-ravers should avoid accommodation near the main square or on the road running east towards Camping Santorini. Beware of aggressive accommodation owners who meet boats and buses and claim that their rooms are in Fira when in fact they're in Karterados. Ask to see a map.

Camping Santorini (☎ 22 944) has many facilities including a restaurant and swimming pool. The cost is 1300 dr per person and 800 dr per tent. It's 400 metres east of the main square. *Kamari Camping* (☎ 31 453) is one km up the main road from Kamari Beach. *Galanakis Camping* (☎ 81 343), on the beach at Perissa, has a minimarket and bar, and charges 1300 dr per person and 800 dr per tent.

Fira has three hostels, all well signposted. The massive *Thira Hostel* (☎ 23 864), 200 metres north of the main square, has a variety of small dorms with up to 10 beds for 1500 dr per person, plus doubles/triples with private bath for 6000/7500 dr. At the time of writing there were plans for a swimming pool. *Kontohori* (☎ 22 722), 500 metres north of the main square, is a friendly place with cheap meals (500 to 900 dr) and satellite TV. Dorm beds are 1800 dr. The more basic *Kamares Hostel* (☎ 24 472) is near the Megaron Gyzi Museum and has dorm beds for 1600 dr. Fira's hotels are expensive, but a short walk away from the noise, *Rena Kavallari Rooms* charges 10,000/12,000 dr for doubles/triples, *Pension*

Horizon charges 11,000/13,000 and *Villa Gianna* – which has a pool – charges 14,000/ 16,800. All have private bath and balcony. To book, ring Dakoutros Travel (see Orientation and Information).

The same agent has a variety of properties in Oia on its books; most are in traditional houses with heart-stopping views. Prices for a double studio start at 18,000 dr; a house for four costs from 35,000 dr.

Places to Eat
Next to Thira Hostel, the *Bella Thira* looks expensive but isn't – some Italian and Greek dishes are less than 900 dr. *Restaurant Stamna*, towards the main square from Dakoutros, usually has specials for 800 or 900 dr.

There's a supermarket just north of the main square.

Getting There & Away
Air Flights cost 20,200 dr to Athens, 13,900 dr to Mykonos, 13,900 dr to Crete and 20,400 dr to Rhodes. The Olympic Airways office (☎ 22 493) is 200 metres south of the hospital.

Ferry The daily ferries to Piraeus cost 4650 dr and take 10 hours. There are frequent connections with Crete, Ios, Paros and Naxos. Ferries travel less frequently to/from Anafi, Sikinos, Folegandros, Sifnos, Serifos, Kimolos, Milos, Karpathos and Rhodes. For the port police, call ☎ 22 239.

Getting Around
There are daily boats from Athinios and the old port to Thirasia and Oia. The other islands surrounding Santorini can only be visited on excursions from Fira; volcano tours start from 1500 dr. A full-day Akrotiri tour costs 5500 dr and sunset tours are 3500 dr.

Large ferries use Athinios port, where they are met by buses. Small boats use Fira Scala, which is served by donkey or cable car from Fira (700 dr each); otherwise it's a clamber up 600 steps. The cable car runs every 15 minutes from 6.40 am to 9 pm.

The bus station is just south of the main square. Buses go to Oia, Kamari, Perissa, Akrotiri and Monolithos frequently. Port buses leave Fira, Kamari and Perissa 90 minutes before ferry departures.

Car & Motorcycle Fira has many car and motorcycle-rental firms.

ANAFI Ανάφη

Tiny Anafi, lying east of Santorini, is almost entirely overlooked by travellers – the island's amenities are limited and its ferry links with other islands are tenuous. It's a pristine island untainted by concessions to tourism. If you visit, be aware that the island has limited resources. The few tavernas will prevent you from starving but don't expect a wide choice. Take some food along and go easy with the water.

One or two boats a week from Piraeus (4930 dr) call in at Anafi via Paros, Naxos, Ios and Santorini.

Crete Κρήτη

Crete, Greece's largest island, has the dubious distinction of playing host to a quarter of all visitors to Greece. You can escape the hordes by visiting the undeveloped west coast, going into the rugged mountainous interior, or staying in one of the villages of the Lassithi Plateau which, when the tour buses depart, return to rural tranquillity.

Blessed with an auspicious climate and fertile soil, Crete is Greece's cornucopia, producing a wider variety of crops than anywhere else.

As well as water sports, Crete has many opportunities for trekking and climbing. It is also the best place in Greece for buying high-quality, inexpensive leather goods.

History

The island was the birthplace of Minoan culture, Europe's first advanced civilisation, which flourished from 2800 to 1450 BC. The palace of Knossos, discovered at the beginning of this century, gives clues to the advanced nature of Minoan culture. They were literate – their first script resembled Egyptian hieroglyphs, which progressed to a syllable-based script called Linear A (still undeciphered). In the ruins, archaeologists also found clay tablets with Linear B inscriptions, the form of writing used by the Mycenaeans, which suggests that Mycenaean invaders may have conquered the island, perhaps around 1500 BC.

Later, Crete passed from the warlike Dorians to the Romans, and then to the Genoese, who in turn sold it to the Venetians. Under the Venetians, Crete became a refuge for artists, writers and philosophers who fled Constantinople after it fell to the Turks. Their influence inspired the young Cretan painter Domenikos Theotokopoulos, who moved to Italy and won immortality as El Greco. The Turks finally conquered Crete in 1670. It became a British protectorate in 1898 after a series of insurrections and was united with independent Greece in 1913. There was fierce fighting during WWII when a German airborne invasion defeated Allied forces in the 10-day Battle of Crete. An active resistance movement drew heavy reprisals from the German occupiers.

Orientation & Information

Crete is divided into four prefectures: Hania, Rethymno, Iraklio and Lassithi. All of Crete's large towns are along the north coast, and it is in this area that the package tourist industry is concentrated.

Most of Crete's towns have tourist offices.

Getting There & Away

Air The international airport is at Iraklio, which is Crete's capital city. Hania and Sitia have domestic airports. There are several flights a day from Athens to Iraklio and Hania, and in summer there are two a week to Sitia. From Thessaloniki there are three flights a week to Iraklio and one a week to Hania. There are daily flights to Rhodes from Iraklio and several flights a week in high season to Mykonos and Santorini. In summer, Kassos and Karpathos are served by one flight a week from Sitia.

Ferry Kastelli-Kissamos, Rethymno, Hania, Iraklio, Agios Nikolaos and Sitia have ferry ports. Within Greece, direct ferries travel daily to Piraeus from Iraklio (5450 dr) and Hania (4990 dr), and three times a week from Rethymno (5500 dr), Agios Nikolaos and Sitia. From Monday to Saturday there are daily boats from Iraklio to Santorini.

Regular ferries from Iraklio serve the Cyclades. There are three ferries a week to

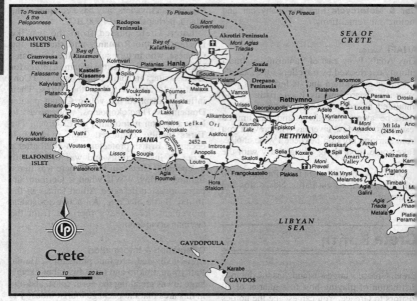

Crete

0   10   20 km

Rhodes (5500 dr) via Karpathos and in season at least two a week from Agios Nikolaos to Rhodes via Sitia, Kassos and Karpathos. Two or three boats a week run between Piraeus and Kastelli-Kissamos via Antikythira, Kythira and the Peloponnese.

In summer, two boats a week go from Iraklio to Cyprus via Rhodes and continue to Israel.

Hydrofoil In summer, four hydrofoils a week link Iraklio with Santorini, Ios, Naxos and Paros.

Getting Around
Frequent buses run between towns on the north coast, and less frequently to the south coast and mountain villages. Parts of the south coast are without roads, so boats are used to connect villages.

IRAKLIO Ηράκλειο
Iraklio, Crete's capital, lacks the charm of Rethymno or Hania, its old buildings having been swamped by modern apartment blocks,

yet it exudes a dynamism from its frenetically paced, neon-lit streets.

Orientation & Information
Iraklio's two main squares are Venizelou and Eleftherias. Dikeosynis and Dedalou run between them, and 25 Avgoustou is the main thoroughfare leading from the waterfront to Venizelou. The EOT (☎ 22 8225), which is open Monday to Friday from 8 am to 2 pm, and Olympic Airways offices (☎ 22 9191) are on Plateia Eleftherias. There is a laundrette and left-luggage storage at Handakos 18 (☎ 28 0858), open from 7.30 am to 9 pm. Lockers cost 400 dr per day.

Money Most of the city's banks are on 25 Avgoustou, but none open in the afternoon or on weekends. The American Express representative is at 25 Avgoustou 23.

Post & Communications The central post office is on Plateia Daskalogiani, and opening hours are Monday to Friday from 7.30 am to

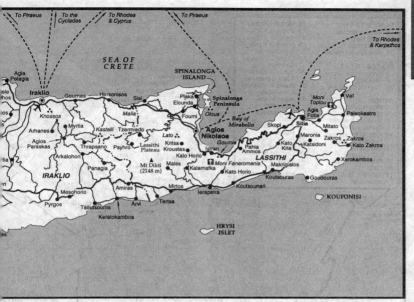

...m. The OTE telephone office is on the west ide of Plateia El Greco, and is open 24 hours.

Iraklio's telephone code is ☎ 081.

Medical & Emergency Services The Apollonia Hospital (☎ 22 9713) is on P Nikousiou. The Tourist police (☎ 28 3190) is at Dikeosynis 10. It's open from 7 am to 11 pm.

Things to See

Don't leave Iraklio until you've seen the **archaeological museum's** magnificent collection. Opening times are Tuesday to Sunday from 8 am to 6 pm and Monday from 12.30 to 6 pm. Admission is 1500 dr.

You can pay homage to the great writer Nikos Kazantzakis by visiting his grave. To get there, walk south on Evans and turn right onto Plastira.

Places to Stay

Beware of taxi drivers who tell you that the pension of your choice is dirty, dangerous or has a bad reputation. They're paid commissions by the big hotels.

Rent Rooms Hellas (☎ 28 0858), Handakos 24, has a lively atmosphere, with a roof garden and bar. Reception is on the roof. Singles/doubles/triples are 4500/5500/7000 dr, but they can fit up to six beds in some of the rooms for 2000 dr per extra person.

If you don't mind surly service, *Vergina Rooms* (☎ 24 2739), 32 Hortatson, is a turn-of-the-century house with a bit of character. Singles/doubles/triples are 4500/6500/8500 dr.

Hotel Rea (☎ 22 3638), 50 metres away at the junction of Handakos and Kalimeraki, has singles/doubles/triples for 5000/6400/8000 dr with private bath, 4500/5500/7000 dr without.

If you truly can't afford anything else, there is a *hostel* (☎ 28 6281) at Vyronos 5, off 25 Avgoustou. Dorms and roof beds are 1200 dr, but don't even think about the roof beds. There is a midnight curfew.

Places to Eat

The *Ippocampos Ouzeri*, on the waterfront just west of 25 Avgoustou, has a huge range of mezedes on offer from 400 dr. Go early to

PLACES TO STAY
4 Vergina Rooms
6 Hotel Rea
7 YHO Hostel
10 Rent Rooms Hellas

PLACES TO EAT
2 Ippocampos Ouzeri
9 Doukiani
26 Taverna Melandris

OTHER
1 Historical Museum of Crete
3 Venetian Fortress
5 Ourios Travel
8 American Express Representative
11 Laundrette/ Left Luggage
12 Planet Bookstore
13 OTE
14 National Bank of Greece
15 Morosini Fountain
16 Buses to Knossos
17 Venetian Loggia
18 Buses to Hania & Rethymno
19 Buses to Knossos & Airport
20 Buses to Eastern Crete (Station A)
21 Buses to Western Crete (Station B)
22 Agios Minos Cathedral
23 Tourist Police
24 EOT
25 Archaeological Museum
27 Post Office
28 Buses to Airport
29 Olympic Airways
30 Appolonia Hospital
31 Grave of Nikos Kazantzakis

Iraklio

0   250   500 m

get a table. It's closed between 3.30 pm and 7 pm.

Treat yourself to traditional Cretan cuisine – or even just a coffee – at the stylish *Doukiani* at Handakos 30. Mezedes start at 400 dr.

Half-way down the fish market on Karterou is *Taverna Malandris*, a lively restaurant popular with locals, serving main courses for between 900 and 1000 dr.

The bustling, colourful market is on Odos 1866.

Getting There & Away

For air and ferry information, see Getting There & Away at the start of the Crete section.

Iraklio has two main bus stations. Bus station A is 100 metres west of the new harbour and serves Agios Nikolaos, Ierapetra, Sitia, Malia and the Lassithi Plateau. Bus station B 50 metres beyond the Hania Gate, serves Phaestos, Matala, Anoghia and Fodele. The Hania/Rethymno terminal is opposite bus station A.

Ourios Travel (☎ 28 2977), in the hi-tech Candia Tower building at Monis Agarathou 20, is particularly helpful.

Getting Around

Bus No 1 goes to/from the airport every 1 minutes between 6 am and 1 am; it stops a

Plateia Eleftherias adjacent to the archaeological museum (120 dr). Local bus No 2 goes to Knossos every 15 minutes from bus station A and also stops on 25 Avgoustou.

Car and motorcycle-rental firms are mostly along 25 Avgoustou.

KNOSSOS Κνωσσός

The most famous of Crete's Minoan sites, Knossos, is eight km south-east of Iraklio. It inspired the myth of the Minotaur.

According to legend, King Minos of Knossos was given a bull to sacrifice to the god Poseidon, but he took such a liking to the bull that he decided to keep it. This enraged Poseidon, who punished the king by causing his wife Pasiphae to fall in love with the animal. The result of this bizarre union was the Minotaur – half-man and half-bull – who lived in a labyrinth beneath the king's palace, feeding on youths and maidens sent as tributes from Athens.

Theseus, an Athenian prince anxious to put an end to these tributes, posed as a sacrificial youth and planned to kill the monster. He fell in love with Ariadne, King Minos' daughter, who gave him a ball of wool to unwind, so that he could find his way out of the labyrinth. Theseus killed the monster and fled with Ariadne, only to later dump her on Naxos.

Classicists have speculated on the origins of the myth; one theory is that it may have been based on a Minoan religious ritual.

In 1900 the ruins of Knossos were uncovered by Arthur Evans, who spent a fortune reconstructing some of the buildings. The site consists of an immense palace, courtyards, public reception rooms, private apartments, baths, storage vaults and stairways. Although archaeologists tend to disparage Evans' reconstruction, the buildings do give the layperson a good idea of what a Minoan palace may have looked like.

Most visitors enter along the Corridor of the Procession Fresco. It is best then to leave the corridor and re-enter from the north, near the Royal Road which brought visitors in ancient times. Entering the Central Court, you will pass the relief Bull Fresco, which depicts a charging bull. The Throne Room is dominated by a simple, beautifully proportioned throne flanked by the Griffin Fresco. The room is thought to have been a shrine, and the throne the seat of a high priestess.

The grand staircase leads to the private apartments and the Hall of the Double Axes, from which a passage leads to the Queen's Megaron, where the exquisite Dolphin Fresco was found. Adjacent is the bathroom with a terracotta bathtub. Also just off the megaron is the water chamber, a masterpiece of archaic plumbing.

Very little is known of Minoan civilisation, which came to an abrupt end around 1450 BC, possibly destroyed by Santorini's volcanic eruption. The delightful frescos depict plants and animals, as well as people participating in sports, ceremonies and festivals, and generally enjoying life, in contrast to the battle scenes found in the art of classical Greece.

A whole day is needed to see the site, and a guidebook is immensely useful – one of the best is *The Palaces of Minoan Crete* by Gerald Cadogan (paperback), which is not always available on Crete. The site is open Monday to Friday from 8 am to 7 pm, and weekends and holidays from 8.30 am to 3 pm; entry is 1000 dr. Try to arrive early, unless you enjoy crowds.

PHAESTOS & OTHER MINOAN SITES

Phaestos (Φαιστός), Crete's second-most important Minoan site, is not as impressive as Knossos but worth a visit for its stunning views of the plain of Mesara. The palace was laid out on the same plan as Knossos, but excavations have not yielded a great many frescos. Opening times are the same as for Knossos and entry is 800 dr.

Crete's other important Minoan sites are **Malia**, 34 km to the east of Iraklio, where there is a palace complex and adjoining town, and **Zakros**, 40 km from Sitia. This was the smallest of the island's palatial complexes. The site is rather remote and overgrown, but the ruins are on a more human scale than at Knossos, Phaestos or Malia.

HANIA Χανιά

Hania, the old capital of Crete, has a harbour with crumbling, softly hued Venetian buildings. It oozes charm; unfortunately it also oozes package tourists.

Orientation & Information

Hania's bus station is on Kydonias, two blocks

GREECE

south-west of Plateia 1866, the town's main square. Halidon runs from here to the old harbour. The fortress separates the old harbour from the new.

The central post office is at Tzanakaki 3, open from 7.30 am to 8 pm on weekdays, and 7.30 am to 2 pm on Saturday. The OTE telephone office is next door and it operates from 6 am to 11 pm. The EOT office (☎ 92 624) is at Kriari 40, 20 metres from Plateia 1866. It is open Monday to Friday from 8 am to 3 pm. There is a laundrette next to the Fidias Pension on Sarpaki. Hania's port is at Souda, 10 km from town.

Hania's telephone code is ☎ 0821.

Things to See

The **archaeological museum** at Halidon 2 is housed in the former Venetian Church of Sa Francesco; the Turks converted it into mosque. Opening hours are Tuesday to Sunda from 8.30 am to 3 pm. Admission is 500 dr.

Places to Stay & Eat

The nearest camping ground is *Campin Hania* (☎ 31 138) which charges 1200 dr pe person and 800 dr per tent. Take a Kalamak bus from Plateia 1866.

If it's character you're after, try *Rooms fo Rent George* (☎ 88 715), Zambeliou 30, in 600-year-old house with antique furniture

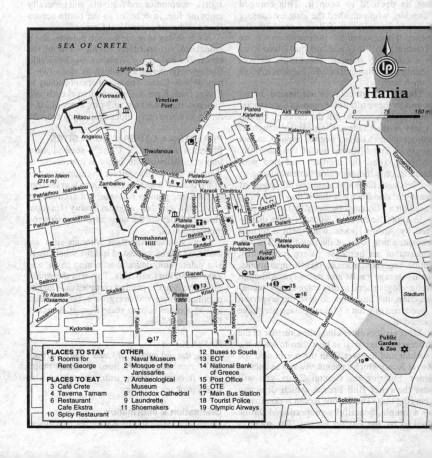

SEA OF CRETE

Lighthouse

Fortress

Venetian Port

Ritsou

Angelou

Hania

Plateia Katehari

Akti Enosis

Kalergon

0   75   150 m

Theofanous

Pension Ideon (215 m)

Zambeliou

Patriarhou Ioanikeiou

Patriarhou Gerasimou

Plateia Vanizelou

Karaoli Dimitriou

Plateia Afinagora

Promahonas Hill

Betola

Plateia Skridlof

Plateia Hortatson

Food Market

Plateia Markopoulou

Gianari

Selinou

To Kastelli-Kissamos

Skalidi

Plateia 1866

Kriari

Dimokratias

Stadium

Kydonias

El Venizelou

Public Garden & Zoo

Solomou

PLACES TO STAY	OTHER	
5 Rooms for Rent George	1 Naval Museum	12 Buses to Souda
	2 Mosque of the Janissaries	13 EOT
PLACES TO EAT	7 Archaeological Museum	14 National Bank of Greece
3 Café Crete	8 Orthodox Cathedral	15 Post Office
4 Taverna Tamam	9 Laundrette	16 OTE
6 Restaurant Cafe Ekstra	11 Shoemakers	17 Main Bus Station
10 Spicy Restaurant		18 Tourist Police
		19 Olympic Airways

ingles/doubles/triples are 3000/5000/6500 dr.
Turn left from Halidon onto Zambeliou one
block from the waterfront; the pension is on the
right.

There are many other pensions and domatia
in the old town near the old harbour. The area
round the new harbour is easier for parking
and has lots of accommodation bargains. The
opulent *Pension Ideon* (☎ 70 132) on Patri-
rhou Ioanikeiou has singles/doubles/triples
for 4000/6000/9000 dr.

Come early for a table at *Taverna Tamam*,
Zambeliou 51. Meatballs and souvlaki start at
200 dr. It is open only for dinner. *Restaurant
Cafe Ekstra*, at Zambeliou 8, serves Greek and
international dishes, with crêpes from 1200 dr.
Spicy Restaurant, Potie 19, is popular and
cheap. The central *food market* is a lively place
to go and eat; there are two inexpensive tavernas.

Entertainment

The authentic *Café Crete* at Kalergon 22 has
live Cretan music every evening.

Things to Buy

Good-quality, handmade leather goods are
available from the market on Skridlof, where
shoes cost from 9000 dr.

Getting There & Away

For air and ferry information, see Getting
There & Away at the start of the Crete section.
Olympic Airways (☎ 57 701) is at Tzanakaki
8.

There are frequent buses to Rethymno and
Kastelli-Kissamos, and less frequent ones to
Paleohora, Omalos, Hora Sfakion, Lakki and
Elafonisi. Buses for Souda (the port) leave
frequently from outside the food market.

THE WEST COAST

This is Crete's least developed coastline. At
Falassarna, 11 km west of Kastelli-Kissamos,
there's a magnificent sandy beach and a few
tavernas and domatia. The beach is five km
from Platanos, where you get off the bus.

South of Falassarna there are good sandy
beaches near the villages of Sfinario and
Kambos.

Further south you can wade out to more
beaches on Elafonisi islet. Travel agents in Hania
and Paleohora run excursions to the area.

SAMARIA GORGE Φαράγγι της Σαμαριάς

It's a wonder the rocks underfoot haven't worn
away completely as so many people trample
through the Samaria Gorge. But it is one of
Europe's most spectacular gorges, and worth
seeing. You can do it independently by taking
a bus to Omalos from Hania, returning by boat
to Hora Sfakion, and then returning by bus to
Hania. Or you can join one of the daily excursions from Hania.

The first public bus leaves at 6.15 am and
excursion buses also leave early so that people
get to the top of the gorge before the heat of the
day. You need good walking shoes and a hat,
as well as water and food. The gorge is 16 km
long and takes on average five or six hours to
walk. It is closed from autumn to spring
because of the danger of flash floods.

LEVKA ORI Λευκά Όρι

Crete's rugged White Mountains are south of
Hania. For information on climbing and trekking, contact the EOS (☎ 44 647), Tzanakaki
90, in Hania.

PALEOHORA & THE SOUTH-WEST COAST

Paleohora (Παλαιοχώρα) was discovered by
hippies back in the 1960s and from then on its
days as a tranquil fishing village were numbered. But it remains a relaxing resort favoured
by backpackers.

Further east, along Crete's south-west coast,
are the resorts of Sougia, Agia Roumeli, Loutro
and Hora Sfakion; of these, Loutro is the most
appealing and the least developed.

Paleohora's telephone code is ☎ 0823.

Places to Stay & Eat

One and a half km from town is *Camping
Paleohora* (☎ 41 120), which charges 800 dr per
person and 400 dr per tent. There are many domatia.

Rooms to Rent Anonymous (☎ 41 509) is a
great place for backpackers. It has clean rooms
set around a small courtyard; singles/doubles
are 3000/4000 dr and there is a communal kitchen.

Oriental Bay Rooms (☎ 41 076), at the northern end of the pebble beach, has comfortable
doubles/triples for 6500/8500 dr. The *Lissos
Hotel* (☎ 41 266), El Venizelou 12, opposite the
bus stop, has singles/doubles for 5000/5500 dr
with shared bath, and doubles/triples for
7200/8500 dr with private bath.

Getting There & Away

There is no road linking the coastal resorts, but they are connected by boats from Paleohora in summer. Twice weekly the boat goes to Gavdos Island. Coastal paths lead from Paleohora to Sougia and from Agia Roumeli to Loutro (make sure you take plenty of water, because you'll be walking in full sun). There are five or six buses a day from Paleohora to Hania.

GAVDOS ISLAND Νήσος Γαύδος

The small rocky island of Gavdos, off Crete's southern coast, has some good beaches, a few domatia and tavernas, and as yet, is little

visited. Freelance camping is tolerated all ov the island.

RETHYMNO Ρέθυμνο

Although similar to Hania in its Venetian an Turkish buildings (not to mention its packag tourists), Rethymno is smaller and has a di tinct character.

The EOT office (☎ 24 143) is on the beac side of El Venizelou and is open Monday t Friday from 8 am to 2.30 pm. The post offic is at Moatsou 21 and the OTE telephone offic is at Pavlou Kountouriotou 28. The latter open from 7 am to 10 pm. There is a laundret next to the hostel.

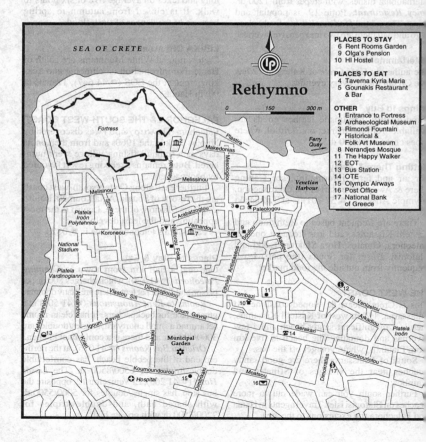

PLACES TO STAY
6 Rent Rooms Garden
9 Olga's Pension
10 HI Hostel

PLACES TO EAT
4 Taverna Kyria Maria
5 Gounakis Restaurant & Bar

OTHER
1 Entrance to Fortress
2 Archaeological Museum
3 Rimondi Fountain
7 Historical & Folk Art Museum
8 Nerandjes Mosque
11 The Happy Walker
12 EOT
13 Bus Station
14 OTE
15 Olympic Airways
16 Post Office
17 National Bank of Greece

SEA OF CRETE

Rethymno

0   150   300 m

Fortress

Venetian Harbour

Ferry Quay

ethymno's telephone code is ☎ 0831.

hings to See & Do
he imposing **Venetian fortress** is worth a
ander around, and the **archaeological mu-
eum** opposite the fortress entrance is well
ocked but disorganised. The fortress is open
aily from 9 am to 7 pm and the museum is
pen Tuesday to Sunday from 8.30 am to 3 pm.
.dmission to both is 500 dr. The **historical &
blk art museum** at Mesologiou 28 has a well-
resented display of Cretan crafts. Its opening
ours are Monday to Saturday from 9 am to 1
m; entry is 400 dr.

The Happy Walker (☎ 52 920), Tombazi 56,
as a programme of daily walks in the coun-
yside costing from 6000 dr per person.

laces to Stay
he nearest camping ground is *Elizabeth
'amping* (☎ 28 694) on Myssiria beach, three
m east of town.

The *youth hostel* (☎ 22 848), Tombazi 41,
 a friendly place with a bar; beds are 1000 dr
1 dorms or on the roof. There is no curfew and
 card is not required. *Olga's Pension* (☎ 29
51), in the heart of town at Souliou 57, is
pectacularly funky, with a wide choice of rooms
pread about in clusters off a network of terraces
ursting with greenery. Prices range from basic
ingles for 4000 dr up to triple rooms with private
ath for 9000 dr. *Rent Rooms Garden* (☎ 28
86), Nikiforou Foka 82, is an old Venetian
ouse with many original features and a delight-
il grape-arboured garden; doubles/triples are
000/10,000 dr with private bath.

Places to Eat
Taverna Kyria Maria, Diog Mesologiou 20,
ucked behind the Rimondi fountain, is a cosy
amily-run taverna.

Gounakis Restaurant & Bar, Koroneou 6,
as live Cretan music every evening and good,
easonably priced food.

Getting There & Away
There are frequent buses to Iraklio and Hania,
nd less frequent ones to Agia Galini, Arkadi
Monastery and Plakias.

For ferries, see Getting There & Away at the
tart of the Crete section.

AGIOS NIKOLAOS Αγιος Νικόλαος
The manifestations of package tourism gather
momentum as they advance eastwards, reaching their ghastly crescendo in Agios Nikolaos,
or Ag Nik in package-tourist jargon.

If you don't take the first bus out, you'll find
the municipal tourist office (☎ 22 357) next to
the bridge between the lake and the harbour;
follow the signs from the bus station and pick
up a map. The tourist police (☎ 26 900) are at
Kontogianni 34.

Ag Nik's telephone code is ☎ 0841.

Places to Stay & Eat
The nearest camping ground is *Gournia Moon
Camping* (☎ 0842-93 243), 19 km from Ag
Nik and almost opposite the Minoan site of
Gournia. Buses to Sitia can drop you off right
outside.

In town, the *Sunbeam* hotel (☎ 25 645),
Ethnikis Antistaseos 23, is outstanding and
certainly the best value for money. Immaculate
singles/doubles/triples are 4000/6000/7000 dr
with private bath, breakfast included. There is
also a bar. Walk up Paleologou and take the
fourth left after the lake.

For a balcony over the sea, try the spotless
Pension Mylos (☎ 23 783), at Sarolidi 24,
where doubles/triples cost 8500/10,500 dr with
private bath, or 6700/8700 dr without.

The ramshackle *Green House* (☎ 22 025),
Modatsou 15, is popular with backpackers;
singles/doubles are 3500/4500 dr. Walk up
Kapetan Tavla from the bus station and look
for the sign.

The waterfront tavernas are expensive –
head inland for better value. *Taverna Itanos*,
Kyprou 1, is a lively traditional restaurant. The
Taverna Pine Tree, next to the lake at Paleologou 18, specialises in charcoal-grilled food,
such as a plate of king prawns for 1800 dr.
Aouas Taverna, at Paleologou 44, has traditional décor and a lovely garden.

Things to See & Do
The **archaeological museum**, on Paleologou,
is open daily, except Monday, from 8.30 am to
3 pm. Admission is 500 dr. The **folk museum**
next to the tourist office is open daily, except
Saturday, from 9.30 am to 1 pm. Admission is
250 dr.

Getting There & Away

There are frequent buses from Agios Nikolaos to Iraklio, Malia, Ierapetra and Sitia, and two a day to Lassithi.

For boats, see Getting There & Away at the start of the Crete section. To contact the port police, call ☎ 22 312.

Getting Around

Car and motorcycle-rental firms are ubiquitous, but for bicycle rental try Ross Rentals (☎ 23 407), Koundourou 10, which has mountain bikes for 2000/10,500 dr per day/week.

LASSITHI PLATEAU Οροπέδιο Λασιθίου

Sadly, many of the windmills that gave Lassithi its picture-postcard fame have been replaced by electrically operated pumps, although if you're lucky you may still see some white sails unfurled. But windmills or not, the first view of this mountain-fringed plateau, laid out like an immense patchwork quilt, is breathtaking.

Things to See

The **Dikteon Cave**, on the side of Mt Dikti, is not as festooned with stalactites and stalagmites as some of Greece's other caves, but it's still worth a visit. Here, according to mythology, the Titan Rhea hid the newborn Zeus from Cronos, his offspring-gobbling father. It's open Monday to Saturday from 10.30 am to 5 pm; admission is 800 dr.

Places to Stay & Eat

Psychro is the best place to stay: it's near the cave and has the best views. The *Zeus Hotel* (☎ 0844-31 284) has singles/doubles for 5000/7500 dr. The taverna in the main square is good value.

Getting There & Away

From Psychro two or three buses a day go to Iraklio and Agios Nikolaos, and one goes to Malia.

SITIA Σητεία

Back on the north coast the tourist overkill dies down considerably by the time you reach Sitia. Skirting a commanding hotel-lined bay with a long sandy beach (more than can be said of Ag Nik), Sitia is an attractive town.

The post office is on Therissou, off I Venizelou; the OTE telephone office is o Kapetan Sifis, which runs inland from th central square. The tourist office can be cor tacted on ☎ 24 955.

Sitia's telephone code is ☎ 0843.

Places to Stay & Eat

There are no camp sites near Sitia, but it i possible to camp in the grounds of the *yout. hostel* at Therissou 4, on the road to Iraklio. Bed at the hostel are 1300 dr and double rooms ar 3000 dr.

The immaculate *Hotel Arhontiko* (☎ 2 172), Kondilaki 16, has singles/doubles/triple for 4000/5000/7000 dr. From the bus statior turn left onto the waterfront and 100 metre along you'll see a small harbour; turn left her and you'll see the sign.

To Kyma, on the waterfront, serves goo seafood and grills. There are many grocer shops on Thoyntaladou, one block south o Plateia Agonostos.

Getting There & Away

For air and ferry information, see Gettin; There & Away at the start of the Crete section There are at least five buses daily to Ierapetr and eight to Iraklio via Agios Nikolaos. I summer there are two or three buses daily t Vaï and Zakros.

AROUND SITIA

The reconstructed **Toplou Monastery**, 15 km from Sitia, houses some beautifully intricat icons and other fascinating relics.

Vaï Beach, famous for its palm tree forest gets pretty crowded, but it's a superb beach an well worth a visit.

For Toplou Monastery, get a Vaï bus from Sitia, get off at the fork for the monastery an walk the last three km.

Dodecanese Δωδεκάνησα

More verdant and mountainous than th Cyclades and with comparable beaches, th islands of the Dodecanese offer more tha natural beauty, for here more than anywher else you get a sense of Greece's proximity to

asia. Ancient temples, massive crusader forti-
ications, mosques and imposing Italian-built
eoclassical buildings stand juxtaposed, ves-
ges of a turbulent past. Even now, proximity
o Turkey makes the islands a contentious issue
whenever hostility between the two countries
ntensifies.

There are 16 inhabited islands in the group;
he most visited are Rhodes, Kos, Patmos and
ymi.

RHODES Ρόδος
According to mythology, the sun god Helios
hose Rhodes as his bride and bestowed light,
warmth and vegetation upon her. The blessing
seems to have paid off, for Rhodes produces
flowers in profusion and enjoys more sunny
days than most Greek islands.

The ancient sites of Lindos and Kamiros are
legacies of Rhodes' importance in antiquity.

In 1291 the Knights of St John, having fled
Jerusalem under siege, came to Rhodes and
established themselves as masters. In 1522
Süleyman I, sultan of the Ottoman Empire,
staged a massive attack on the island and took
Rhodes city. The island, along with the other
Dodecanese, then became part of the Ottoman
Empire.

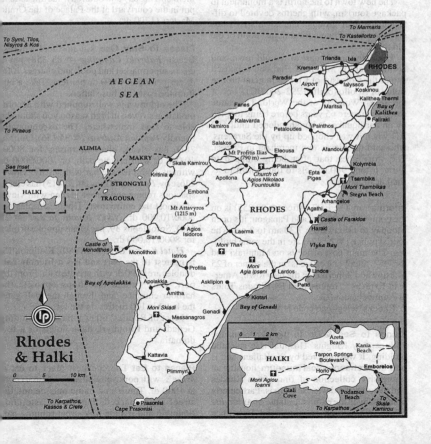

Rhodes & Halki

In 1912 it was the Italians' turn and in 1944 the Germans took over. The following year Rhodes was liberated by British and Greek commandos. In 1948, Rhodes, along with the other Dodecanese, became part of Greece.

Rhodes City

Rhodes' capital and port is Rhodes city, on the northern tip of the island. Almost everything of interest in the city lies within its walls. The main thoroughfares are Sokratous, Pythagora, Agiou Fanouriou and Ipodamou, with mazes of narrow streets between them. Many parts of the old town are prohibited to cars, but there are car parks around the periphery.

The new town to the north is a monument to package tourism, with ghettos devoted to different national groups. The town's two bus stations are on Plateia Rimini, just north of the old town.

The main port is east of the old town, and north of here is Mandraki Harbour, supposed site of the Colossus of Rhodes, a giant bronze statue of Apollo (built in 292-280 BC) – one of the Seven Wonders of the World. The statue stood for a mere 65 years before being toppled by an earthquake. It lay abandoned until 653 AD when it was chopped up by the Saracens, who sold the pieces to a merchant in Edessa. The story goes that after being shipped to Syria, it took 980 camels to transport it to its final destination.

Information The EOT office (☎ 23 255) is on the corner of Makariou and Papagou; it's open Monday to Friday from 7.30 am to 3 pm. The tourist police (☎ 27 423) are in the same building. The main post office is on Mandraki and the OTE telephone office is on the corner of 25 Martiou and Amerikis in the new town. American Express is represented by Rhodos Tours at Ammochostou 23.

Rhodes' telephone code is ☎ 0241.

Things to See & Do In the old town, the 15th-century Knights' Hospital is a splendid building. It was restored by the Italians and is now the **archaeological museum**, housing an impressive collection of finds from Rhodes and the other Dodecanese islands. Particularly noteworthy is the exquisite statue of *Aphrodite of Rhodes*, which so entranced Lawrence

Durrell that he named his book about the island, *Reflections on a Marine Venus*, after it. Opening times are Tuesday to Sunday from 8.30 am to 3 pm. Admission is 800 dr.

Odos Ippoton – the Avenue of the Knights – is lined with magnificent medieval buildings, the most imposing of which is the **Palace of the Grand Masters**, restored, but never used, as a holiday home for Mussolini. It is open Tuesday to Sunday from 8.30 am to 3 pm. Admission is 1200 dr.

The old town is reputedly the world's finest surviving example of medieval fortification. The 12-metre-thick walls are closed to the public, but you can take a **guided walk** along them on Tuesday and Saturday, starting at 2.45 pm in the courtyard at the Palace of the Grand Masters (1200 dr).

Places to Stay One km north of Faliraki Beach, *Faliraki Camping* (☎ 85 358) has a disco, supermarket and pool, and charges 1000 dr per person and 600 dr per tent. Take a bus from the east-side bus station.

The old town is well supplied with accommodation so even in high season you should be able to find somewhere. The exceptionally friendly *Pension Andreas* (☎ 34 156), Omirou 28D, has clean, pleasant rooms for 8000/10,000 dr with private bath, or 7000/9000 dr without, and a terrace bar with terrific views. Close by, *Pension Minos* (☎ 31 813) has clean, spacious rooms and a roof garden with views of almost the entire town. Doubles/triples are 8000/10,000 dr. *Niki's Rooms to Let* (☎ 25 115), Sofokleous 39, has clean doubles/triples for 8000/10,000 dr.

Hotel Kava d'Oro (☎ 36 980), Kistiniou 15, is nearest to the port and has a friendly bar; doubles are 9000 dr with private bath. From the port, walk behind the shops opposite the harbour entrance, and through the wall gate; the hotel is 100 metres on the left.

Most of Rhodes' other villages, including Genadi and Plimmyri, have hotels or a few domatia.

Places to Eat The cheapest place to eat is *Mike's*, with pork souvlaki and calamari both at 1000 dr. There's no name outside and the street isn't marked, but find Castellania Fountain and it's the tiny street running par-

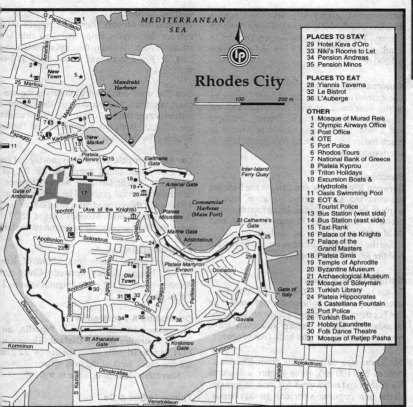

PLACES TO STAY
29 Hotel Kava d'Oro
33 Niki's Rooms to Let
34 Pension Andreas
35 Pension Minos

PLACES TO EAT
28 Yiannis Taverna
32 Le Bistrot
36 L'Auberge

OTHER
1 Mosque of Murad Reis
2 Olympic Airways Office
3 Post Office
4 OTE
5 Port Police
6 Rhodos Tours
7 National Bank of Greece
8 Plateia Kyprou
9 Triton Holidays
10 Excursion Boats & Hydrofoils
11 Oasis Swimming Pool
12 EOT & Tourist Police
13 Bus Station (west side)
14 Bus Station (east side)
15 Taxi Rank
16 Palace of the Knights
17 Palace of the Grand Masters
18 Plateia Simis
19 Temple of Aphrodite
20 Byzantine Museum
21 Archaeological Museum
22 Mosque of Süleyman
23 Turkish Library
24 Plateia Hippocrates & Castelliana Fountain
25 Port Police
26 Turkish Bath
27 Hobby Laundrette
30 Folk Dance Theatre
31 Mosque of Retjep Pasha

---

llel south of Sokratous. *Yiannis Taverna*, Apellou 41, is also very good value, but if you're sick of Greek food by now, *Le Bistrot*, Omirou 22-24, serves terrific French dishes, with main courses costing around 1500 dr. At the time of writing, the restaurant was planning to split into two, with Le Bistrot offering a variety of Créole appetisers and the French menu being served from *L'Auberge*, Praxitelous 19-21.

South of the old town, *To Steno*, Agion Anargiron 29, near the church, is popular with locals.

Self-caterers will find many food shops in the new market.

Entertainment The *sound-and-light show* at the Palace of the Knights, depicting the Turkish siege, is superior to most such efforts. Check the schedule with the EOT, but there is usually an English performance nightly except on Sunday. Admission is 1000 dr.

Homesick Aussies should make for the *Down Under Bar* at Orfanidi 37, north-west of the old town, where all the staff are Australian.

Lindos Λίνδος
The imposing **Acropolis of Lindos**, Rhodes' most important ancient city, shares a rocky outcrop with a **crusader castle**. Down below it there are labyrinths of winding streets with

whitewashed, elaborately decorated houses which are undeniably beautiful but extremely touristy. The site of Lindos is open Tuesday to Sunday from 8.30 am to 3 pm and admission is 1200 dr.

Kamiros Κάμειρος

The extensive ruins of this ancient Doric city on the west coast are well preserved, with the remains of houses, baths, a cemetery, a temple and a stoa. But the site should be visited as much for its lovely setting on a gentle hillside overlooking the sea.

Beaches

Between Rhodes city and Lindos the beaches are crowded. If you prefer isolation, venture south to the bay of Lardos. Even further south, between Genadi and Plimmyri, you'll find good stretches of deserted sandy beach.

On the west coast, beaches tend to be pebbly and the sea is often choppy.

Getting There & Away

Triton Holidays (☎ 21 690; fax 31 265), Plastira 9, is a particularly helpful travel agent. You can fax them for specialist advice on any of the islands and Turkey before you even leave home and they'll fax you back free of charge.

Air There are daily flights from Rhodes to Athens (23,100 dr), three flights a week to Karpathos and two a week to Crete. In summer there are regular services to Mykonos, Santorini, Kassos, Kastellorizo, Thessaloniki and Kos. The Olympic Airways office (☎ 24 555) is at Ierou Lohou 9.

Ferry There are daily ferries from Rhodes to Piraeus (7000 dr). Some go via Karpathos, Kassos, Crete and the Cyclades, others go via the Dodecanese north of Rhodes. There are two ferries a week to Kastellorizo and daily excursion boats to Symi. The EOT gives out a schedule.

There are regular boats from Rhodes to Marmaris (Turkey) between April and October; one-way tickets cost 16,000 dr by hydrofoil or 10,500 dr by ferry, including the 4000-dr port tax.

In summer there are regular ferries to Israel (from 27,000 dr) via Cyprus (19,000 dr).

Getting Around

To/From the Airport There are frequent buses to/from the airport from the west-side bus station (270 dr). A taxi to the airport costs about 2500 dr. For a radio taxi, phone ☎ 64 712 or ☎ 64 734.

Bus The west-side bus station serves the west coast, Embona and Koskinou; the east-side station serves the east coast and inland southern villages. Both bus stations are on Plateia Rimini. The EOT has a schedule.

Car & Motorcycle There is no shortage of car and motorcycle-rental firms, but the Bicycle Centre (☎ 28 315), Griva 39, is one of Greece's best bicycle-rental places. The daily rates are 800 dr for a three-speed bike and 1200 dr for a Scott mountain bike. Mopeds start at 2500 dr a day and there are discounts for longer rentals.

KARPATHOS Κάρπαθος

The picturesque, elongated island of Karpathos, lying midway between Crete and Rhodes, is one of the most singular islands in the Aegean.

Orientation & Information

The main port and capital is **Pigadia**, and there's a smaller port at **Diafani**. There's no EOT, but the friendly tourist police (☎ 22 218) are one block west of the post office.

Karpathos' telephone code is ☎ 0245.

Things to See & Do

Karpathos has glorious beaches, particularly at Apella and Kira Panagia. The northern village of **Olymbos** is like a living museum and is endlessly fascinating to ethnologists. Young women wear brightly coloured and embroidered skirts, waistcoats and headscarves and goatskin boots. The older women's apparel is more subdued but still distinctive. Interiors of houses are decorated with embroidered cloth and their façades with brightly painted moulded-plaster reliefs. The inhabitants speak a dialect which retains some Doric words, and the houses have wooden locks of the kind described by Homer. A two-hour uphill trail leads from Diafani to Olymbos.

Places to Stay & Eat

In Pigardia the delightfully kitsch *Carlo*

Rooms (☎ 22 477) has doubles and triples for 5000 dr. From the port take the left fork onto Karpathou, turn left two blocks along, turn right two blocks further on again, and turn left at the arts centre. It's 400 metres up the hill on the left. *Konaki Rooms* (☎ 22 908) is sparkling and has doubles/triples for 5000/6000 dr. It's just beyond the arts centre. Accommodation is also available at Diafani, Olymbos and several other villages.

The *Kali Kardia Restaurant* serves superb, fresh fish and inexpensive meat dishes. It's opposite the Hotel Atlantic in Pigadia.

Getting There & Away

Air Karpathos has an international airport that receives charter flights from northern Europe.

There are two flights a week to Athens (24,700 dr), four a week to Kassos (6000 dr), daily flights to Rhodes (12,100 dr), and one a week to Sitia on Crete (11,500 dr).

Ferry There are two ferries a week from Rhodes and from Piraeus (6340 dr) via the Cyclades and Crete. In bad weather, ferries do not stop at Diafani.

KASSOS Κάσσος

On the map, Kassos looks like a bit of Karpathos that has broken away; it's rocky and barren with a couple of sandy beaches, and it's a good choice if you yearn for isolation. Kassos has air connections with Sitia, Karpathos and Rhodes, and has the same ferry connections as Karpathos, but if the weather is bad, the ferries give it a miss.

Hotel Anagennisis (☎ 41 323) is highly recommended; singles/doubles cost 6600/10,750 dr with private bath.

Kassos' telephone code is ☎ 0245.

KOS Κως

Kos is renowned as the birthplace of Hippocrates, father of medicine. Kos town manifests the more ghastly aspects of mass tourism, and the beaches are horrendous, with wall-to-wall sun lounges and beach umbrellas.

Orientation & Information

Kos town, on the north-east coast, is the main town and the port. The municipal tourist office (☎ 26 583) is at Vasileos Georgiou 3, near the hydrofoil pier. It is open Monday to Friday from 8 am to 2.30 pm. The post office is at El Venizelou 16, one block from the OTE, on the corner of Vironos and Xanthou.

Kos' telephone code is ☎ 0242.

Things to See

Kos Town Before you beat a hasty retreat, check out the ruined **agora** and **odeion**, and also the 13th-century **fortress** and the **museum**, open Tuesday to Sunday from 8.30 am to 3 pm; admission to both the fortress and the museum is 800 dr.

Standing at the entrance to the castle is the **Hippocrates Plane Tree** beneath which, according to the EOT brochure, the great man taught – although plane trees don't usually live for more than 200 years.

Asclepion On a pine-clad hill, four km from Kos town, stand the extensive ruins of the renowned healing centre of Asclepion. The site is open Tuesday to Sunday from 8.30 am to 3 pm; admission is 800 dr.

Around the Island The villages in the **Asfendion** region of the Dikeos Mountains are reasonably tranquil. **Paradise** on the south-east coast is the most appealing beach, but don't expect to have it to yourself.

Places to Stay & Eat

Three km south-east of town is the friendly *Kos Camping* (☎ 23 275). In June, July and August their minibus meets most boats, including the 4 am ferry from Piraeus.

The *Dodekanissos Hotel* (☎ 28 460), Ipsilandou 9, has singles/doubles/triples with private bath for 5200/7700/9200 dr. From the port, with the castle wall to your left, turn right and then left at the sign for the centre. *Hotel Elena* (☎ 22 986), Megalou Alexandrou 5, has doubles with/without private bath for 6500/5500 dr. The street is off Akti Kondourioti in the middle of the waterfront.

Many of Kos' restaurants cater for the package-tourist trade, but one notable exception is the remarkably cheap and good *Olympiada Restaurant* behind the Olympic Airways office. It offers a good range of dishes from 850 dr.

The food market is on Plateia Eleftherias.

GREECE

Getting There & Away
Air Apart from European charter flights, there are daily flights from Kos to Athens (19,800 dr) and two a week to Rhodes (13,200 dr). The Olympic Airways office (☎ 28 330) is at Vasileos Pavlou 22, south of the agora.

Ferry There are frequent ferries from Rhodes which continue on to Piraeus (6330 dr) via Patmos, Leros and Kalymnos. There are less frequent connections to Nisyros, Tilos, Symi, Samos and Crete. Daily excursion boats also go to Nisyros, Kalymnos and Rhodes.

Ferries travel twice daily in summer to Bodrum in Turkey; fares are 10,500 dr one way or 13,000 dr return (including port tax).

Getting Around
Buses for Asclepion leave from opposite the town hall on the harbour; all other buses leave from behind the Olympic Airways office. Motorcycles, mopeds and bicycles are widely available for hire.

NISYROS & TILOS Νίσυρος & Τήλος
Volcanic Nisyros' caldera obligingly bubbles, hisses and spews – you must wear solid shoes as it gets very hot underfoot. Dramatic moonscapes combine with lush vegetation, and after the day-trippers from Kos depart, Nisyros reverts to its peaceful, unspoilt self.

Tilos is less visited than Nisyros and has gentle and enfolding hills offering many opportunities for walking, as well as some of the finest beaches in the Dodecanese.

PATMOS Πάτμος
Starkly scenic Patmos is where St John wrote his book of Revelations. It gets crowded in summer, but manages to remain remarkably tranquil.

Patmos' telephone code is ☎ 0247.

Orientation & Information
The tourist office (☎ 31 666), open Monday to Friday from 9 am to 1.30 pm and from 5 to 8 pm, is behind the post office at Skala, the port. The main town is the hill-top Hora.

Things to See & Do
The **Monastery of the Apocalypse**, on the site where St John wrote the Revelations, is between the port and the Hora. The attraction

here is the cave in which the saint lived and dictated his revelations. It's open on Monday, Wednesday, Friday and Saturday from 8 am to 1 pm, on Tuesday and Thursday from 8 am to 1 pm and 4 to 6 pm, and on Sunday from 10 am to noon and 4 to 6 pm. Admission is free.

The Hora's whitewashed houses huddle around the fortified **Monastery of St John**, which houses a vast collection of monastic treasures, including embroidered robes, ornate crosses and chalices, Byzantine jewellery and early manuscripts and icons. It's open the same hours as the Monastery of the Apocalypse. Admission to the monastery is free, but it's 1000 dr to see the treasury.

Patmos' indented coastline provides numerous secluded coves, mostly with pebble beaches.

Places to Stay & Eat
One of Greece's most pleasant camp sites is *Stefanos Flower Camping* (☎ 31 821). It's on the beach, two km north-east of Skala, and charges 1200 dr per person and 400 dr per tent.

Enthusiastic domatia owners will nearly knock you over as you disembark, and there are many rooms for rent in and around the harbour.

The *Pension Akteon* (☎ 31 187) has self-contained studios at 4000/8000/9600 dr for singles/doubles/triples. *Hotel Chris*, *Hotel Maria* and *Hotel Rex*, all close to the harbour and easy to find, are among the cheapest hotels.

O Pantelis Taverna, on the street a block back from the waterfront, and *Taverna Grigoris*, opposite the cafeteria/passenger transit building, are the two most popular eateries. The food market is well signposted from the waterfront.

Getting There & Away
Frequent ferries travel between Patmos and Piraeus (5340 dr), and to Rhodes (4640 dr) via Leros, Kalymnos and Kos. There are also frequent boats to Samos.

Getting Around
Skala, Hora, Grigos and Kambos are connected by buses which depart from beside the ferry port. In summer there are excursion boats from Skala to beaches and also to the island of Lipsi to the east of Patmos.

KASTELLORIZO Καστελλόριζο

Tiny Kastellorizo lies 116 km east of Rhodes, its nearest Greek neighbour, and only 2.5 km from the southern coast of Turkey. Its **Blue Grotto** is spectacular and comparable to its namesake in Capri. The name derives from the blue appearance of the water in the grotto, caused by refracted sunlight. Fishermen will take you to the cave in their boats, and also to some of the surrounding islets, all of which are uninhabited. The island's remoteness is drawing a steady trickle of visitors, but as yet it remains pristine. Three flights (10,600 dr) and two ferries a week operate between Rhodes and Kastellorizo. There are plenty of rooms for rent.

Kastellorizo's telephone code is ☎ 0241.

North-Eastern Aegean Islands

These islands are less visited than the Cyclades and the Dodecanese. There are seven major islands in this group: Chios, Ikaria, Lesvos, Limnos, Samos, Samothraki and Thasos.

Off-shore oil – albeit of a not very high quality – has been found around Thasos, leading to Turkey casting a covetous eye upon the whole group. The Turks claim that as this part of the Aegean lies off their coast, they should have a share of whatever it yields. But on the basis of the 1982 Law of the Sea the Aegean belongs to Greece. Turkey has not ratified this law and is pressing for negotiations. The dispute has necessitated a heavy military presence.

SAMOS Σάμος

Samos was an important centre of Hellenic culture and is reputedly the birthplace of the philosopher and mathematician Pythagoras. Lush and humid, its mountains are skirted by pine, sycamore and oak-forested hills, and its air is permeated with floral scents.

Orientation & Information

Vathy (Samos town) is the main town and port; the smaller port of Pythagorio is on the south-east coast. The municipal tourist office (☎ 28 530) is in Vathy, at 25 Martiou 4, and is open

from 8.30 am to 2.30 pm on weekdays. The post office is on Smyrnis, four blocks from the waterfront. The OTE telephone office is on Plateia Iroön, behind the municipal gardens, and is open from 7.30 am to 3 pm.

Samos' telephone code is ☎ 0273.

Things to See & Do

Very little is left of the **ancient city** of Samos, on which the town of Pythagorio now stands. The Sacred Way, once flanked by 2000 statues, has now metamorphosed into the airport's runway.

The extraordinary **Evpalinos Tunnel** is the site's most impressive surviving relic. It was built in the 6th century BC by Evpalinos who was the chief engineer of the tyrant Polycrates. The one-km-long tunnel was dug by political prisoners and used as an aqueduct to bring water from the springs of Mt Ampelos. Part of it can still be explored. It's two km north of Pythagorio and is open daily, except Monday, from 8.30 am to 3 pm. Entry is 800 dr.

Vathy's **archaeological museum** is outstanding, with an impressive collection of statues, votives and pottery. It is open daily, except Monday, from 8.30 am to 3 pm. Admission is 800 dr.

The villages of **Manolates** and **Vourliotes** on the slopes of Mt Ampelos are excellent walking territory, as there are many marked pathways in the region.

Quiet beaches can be found on the south-west coast in the Marathokampos area.

Places to Stay & Eat

Pythagorio, where you'll disembark if you've come from Patmos, is touristy and expensive.

Vathy – 20 minutes away by bus – is cheaper. The friendly *Pension Vasso* (☎ 23 258) is open all year round and has singles/doubles/triples for 3000/5000/6000 dr with private bath. To get there from the quay, turn right onto the waterfront, left into Stamatiadou and walk up the steps. The owners also have a charming three-bed country cottage for rent, right by the sea in the unspoilt village of Livadaki, on the north coast. It costs 8000/ 10,000/12,000 dr a day for two/four/six people.

Back in Vathy, *Pension Avli* (☎ 22 939), a former convent girls' school, has doubles for 6500 dr. It's on Kalomiri, close to the port, two blocks back from the waterfront. Nearby,

GREECE

Hotel Ionia (☎ 28 782) is cheap, with singles/doubles/triples for 2500/3500/4500 dr.

The popular *Taverna Gregory*, near the post office, is one of Greece's most authentic delights, serving good food at reasonable prices. On some nights three locals – the Tris Manolis – sing for their supper.

Getting There & Away

Air Samos has an international airport receiving European charter flights. There are also daily flights to Athens (16,100 dr).

Ferry There are ferries twice a week to Chios and Patmos, and also to Piraeus (4830 dr); some go via Paros and Naxos, others go via Mykonos. Avoid being hustled onto an excursion boat to Patmos. The normal ferry (2500 dr) is a quarter of the price.

There are daily boats to Kuşadası (for Ephesus) in Turkey, costing 11,000 dr one way and 14,000 dr return, including port tax. There are many travel agencies on the waterfront. For the port police, call ☎ 27 318.

Getting Around

To get to Vathy's bus station, turn left onto Lekadi, 250 metres south of Plateia Pythagora. Buses run to all the island's villages.

CHIOS Χίος

'Craggy Chios', as Homer described it, is less visited than Samos and almost as riotously fertile. Chios is famous for its mastic trees which produce a resin used in chewing gum and arrack, a liquor distilled from grain.

In 1822 an estimated 25,000 inhabitants on the island were massacred by the Turks.

Orientation & Information

The main town and port is Chios town, which is strident and unattractive; only the old Turkish quarter has any charm. It is, however, a good base from which to explore the island.

The municipal tourist office (☎ 44 389) is on Kanari, the main street running from the waterfront to Plateia Plastira in the town centre. The OTE telephone office is opposite the tourist office. The post office is on Rodokanaki, a block back from the waterfront.

Chios' telephone code is ☎ 0271.

Things to See

The **Philip Argenti Museum**, next to the cathedral in Chios town, contains exquisite embroideries and traditional costumes. It's open daily from 9 am to 1.30 pm except Sunday. Admission is 500 dr.

The **Nea Moni** (New Monastery), 14 km

west of Chios town, houses some of Greece's most important mosaics. They date from the 11th century and are among the finest examples of Byzantine art in Greece. It's open daily from 7 am to 1 pm and 4 to 6 pm; entry is 500 dr.

Pyrgi, 24 km from Chios town and the centre of the mastic-producing region, is one of Greece's most beautiful villages. The façades of its dwellings are decorated with intricate grey and white geometric patterns. **Emboreios**, six km south of Pyrgi, is an attractive, uncrowded black-pebble beach.

Places to Stay

Singles/doubles/triples with private bath and TV are available for 4000/6000/8000 dr at *Anesis Pension* (☎ 44 801). It is just off Aploaras, the main shopping street, parallel to the waterfront. *Hotel Filoxenia* (☎ 22 813), signposted from the waterfront, has simple singles/doubles for 4800/6500 dr.

Places to Eat

Right opposite the ferry disembarkation point in Neorion is *Ouzeri Theodosiou*, a popular old-style establishment. For the freshest possible fish, try *Iakovos Taverna* on the northern arm of the harbour by the fish terminal.

Getting There & Away

There are daily flights from Chios to Athens (14,600 dr) and twice-weekly flights to Thessaloniki (21,100 dr).

Ferries sail twice a week to Samos (2100 dr) and Piraeus (4800 dr) via Lesvos, and once a week to Thessaloniki via Lesvos and Limnos. There are also four boats a week to the small island of Psara, west of Chios, and in summer daily excursion boats to the even smaller island of Inousses. In summer daily boats travel to Çeşme in Turkey; tickets cost 11,000 dr one way and 14,000 dr return. You can contact the port police on ☎ 44 433.

Getting Around

The bus station is on Plateia Vournakio, just south of Plateia Plastira. Blue buses go to Frontados, Karyes and Karfas, all near Chios town. Green buses go to Emboreios, Pyrgi and Mesta.

LESVOS (MYTILINI) Λέσβος (Μυτιλήνη)

Lesvos, the third-largest island in the North-Eastern Aegean, has always been a centre of artistic and philosophical achievement and creativity. Sappho, one of the greatest poets of ancient Greece, lived here and today the island is visited by many lesbians paying homage to her. Lesvos was also the birthplace of the composer Terpander and the poet Arion – an influence on both Sophocles and Euripides – and boasted Aristotle and Epicurus among the teachers at its exceptional school of philosophy. It remains to this day a spawning ground for innovative ideas in the arts and politics.

Mytilini

Mytilini, the capital and port of Lesvos, is a large workaday town built around two harbours. All passenger ferries dock at the southern harbour. The tourist police (☎ 22 776) are at the entrance to the quay and the EOT (☎ 42 511) is at James Aristakou 6. The post office is on Vournazon, west of the southern harbour, and the OTE is in the same street.

Mytilini's telephone code is ☎ 0251.

Things to See Mytilini's imposing **castle** was built in early Byzantine times and renovated in the 14th century. It is open daily, except Monday, from 8.30 am to 2.50 pm. The **archaeological museum**, one block north of the quay, is open Tuesday to Sunday from 8.30 am to 3 pm. Admission to both is 500 dr. Don't miss the **Theophilos Museum**, which houses the works of the prolific primitive painter Theophilos; it's open Tuesday to Sunday from 9 am to 1 pm. Entry is 250 dr.

Places to Stay & Eat Domatia owners belong to a cooperative called *Sappho Self-Catering Rooms in Mytilini*. Most of these domatia are in little side streets off Ermou, near the northern harbour. The nearest to the quay is the *Panorea Pension* (☎ 42 650), Komninaki 21, where doubles/triples cost 6800/8500 dr. *Thalia Rooms* (☎ 24 640) has doubles/triples for 7000/8000 dr. *Salina's Garden Rooms* (☎ 42 073), Fokeas 7, has doubles for 7500 dr with private bath.

The *Albatross Ouzeri*, on the corner of Ermou and Adramytiou, is worth a visit just for the experience. It's packed with paraphernalia

GREECE

and looks more like a junk shop than an eating establishment. The *Restaurant Averof*, in the middle of the southern waterfront, is a no-nonsense traditional eatery serving hearty Greek staples. The small, friendly *Ta Stroggylia*, at Komninaki 9, has wine barrels and good food.

Around the Island

Northern Lesvos is best known for its exquisitely preserved traditional town of **Mithymna**. Its neighbouring beach resort of **Petra**, six km south, is affected by low-key package tourism, while the villages surrounding **Mt Lepetymnos** are authentic, picturesque and worth a day or two of exploration.

Western Lesvos is a popular destination for lesbians who come on a kind of pilgrimage in honour of the poet Sappho. The beach resort of **Skala Eresou** is built over ancient Eresos, where she was born in 628 BC.

Southern Lesvos is dominated by 968-metre **Mt Olympus** and the pine forests that decorate its flanks. **Plomari**, a large traditional coastal village, is popular with visitors, and the picturesque village of **Agiasos** is a favourite day-trip destination with some fairly genuine artisan workshops.

Getting There & Away

Air There are three flights a day from Lesvos to Athens (15,800 dr), one a day to Thessaloniki (19,600 dr) and Limnos (12,700 dr) and two a week to Chios (7100 dr). The Olympic Airways office (☎ 28 659) is at Kavetsou 44.

Ferry In summer there are daily boats to Piraeus (12 hours, 5300 dr), some via Chios. There are three a week to Kavala (5100 dr) via Limnos and two a week to Thessaloniki (7000 dr). Ferries to Turkey cost 16,000 dr. From May there are hydrofoils to Limnos, Chios, Samos, Patmos, Kavala and Alexandroupolis. You can contact the port police on ☎ 47 888.

Getting Around

There are two bus stations in Mytilini, both by the harbour. The one for long-distance buses is just beyond the south-western end of Pavlou Kountouriotou. For local villages go to the northernmost section. There are many car and motorcycle-rental firms.

SAMOTHRAKI Σαμοθράκη

Until a decade ago, Samothraki was Greece' best kept secret, visited only by archaeologist and a few adventurers. But inevitably this wild alluring island has been discovered by holiday makers. Most people stick to the resorts o Kamariotissa, Therma and Pahia Ammos leaving the rest of the island untouched.

Orientation & Information

Samothraki's port is Kamariotissa on the north-west coast. The main town, the Hor (also called Samothraki), is five km inland There is no EOT office or tourist police, but the regular police (☎ 41 203) are in the Hora, nea the kastro.

Samothraki's telephone code is ☎ 0551.

Things to See & Do

Sanctuary of the Great Gods This hushed ancient site at Paleopolis is shrouded i mystery. No-one knows quite what went o here, only that it was a place of initiation int the cult of the Kabeiroi, the gods of fertility They were believed to help seafarers, and to b initiated into their mysteries was seen as safeguard against misfortune and in particula against shipwreck. Its winding pathways lea through lush shrubbery to extensive ruins.

The famous Winged Victory of Samothrace which now has pride of place in the Louvre was taken from here in the last century. Th site's little museum is well laid out, and bot the site and the museum are open Tuesday t Sunday from 8.30 am to 3 pm. Admission t each is 500 dr.

Mt Fengari Legend tells that it was from th summit of Mt Fengari (1611 metres) tha Poseidon, god of the sea and of earthquake watched the progress of the Trojan War. difficult climb, Mt Fengari should only b tackled by experienced trekkers. Guides can b hired in Therma for about 12,000 dr.

Walks The island is a walker's paradise. Th glorious scenery combines the jagged rock of Mt Fengari's slopes with shady groves plane trees, bubbling waterfalls, gentle undu lating hills and meadows ablaze with wil flowers.

From the kastro ruin in the Hora, a dirt trac

leads to Paleopolis. It takes about an hour to get there.

Samothraki's only sandy beach, **Pahia Ammos**, a 700-metre-long stretch of sand sheltered by two rocky headlands, can be reached along a seven-km dirt track from Lakoma.

Places to Stay & Eat

There are several private camping grounds at Therma and free camp sites at Pahia Ammos. There are showers on the beach.

Samothraki's few hotels are expensive. The most pleasant place to stay is the Hora. Its Turkish-era houses are built in amphitheatre fashion on two adjacent mountain slopes and the town is totally authentic. There are no hotels, just rooms in private houses.

Cheap eateries line Kamariotissa's waterfront. The *psistaria* in Hora's main square serves large helpings of barbecued meat. The *nameless taverna* on the left of the nameless street which leads up to the kastro has delicious vegetable stews.

Getting There & Around

See Getting There & Away under Alexandroupolis in the Northern Greece section. There is one boat a week between Kavala and Samothraki. To contact the port police, call ☎ 41 305.

Buses run from Kamariotissa to the Hora, Lakoma, Profitis Ilias, Paleopolis and Therma. In summer, caïques sail between Kamariotissa and Pahia Ammos. There is a motorcycle-rental outlet opposite the harbour.

Sporades Σποράδες

The Sporades group comprises the lush, pine-forested islands of Skiathos, Skopelos and Alonnisos, south of the Halkidiki Peninsula, and far-flung Skyros, off Evia.

Getting There & Away

Air Skiathos receives lots of charter flights from northern Europe. In summer, there are up to three flights a day from Athens to Skiathos (15,300 dr) and daily flights to Skyros (13,900

dr). There's also the odd flight between the two (9100 dr).

Ferry Skiathos, Skopelos and Alonnisos have frequent ferry services to the mainland ports of Volos and Agios Konstantinos, as well as one or two a week to Kymi (Evia), via Skyros.

There's a bewildering array of hydrofoil services buzzing around the islands in summer. They include three services a week connecting Skyros and the other islands.

SKIATHOS Σκίαθος

Skiathos is tagged the Mykonos of the Sporades, which means it's crowded and expensive. If you decide to go, however, the tourist police (☎ 23 172) on Papadiamanti 8, the port's main street, will help you to find accommodation. Ferries dock at Skiathos town.

Skiathos' telephone code is ☎ 0427.

SKOPELOS Σκόπελος

Skopelos is less commercialised than Skiathos, but following hot on its trail. Skopelos town is an attractive place of white houses built on a hillside, with mazes of narrow streets and stairways leading up to the kastro. **Glossa**, the island's other town, lying inland in the north, is similarly appealing with fewer concessions to tourism. There is no tourist office or tourist police. The post office is signposted from the port, as is the OTE, although both are well hidden in the labyrinth of alleyways behind the waterfront.

Skopelos' telephone code is ☎ 0424.

Things to See

Four km from Skopelos town, **Staphylos** is a decent beach that gets very crowded; over a headland is **Velanio**, the island's designated nudist beach.

The two-km stretch of tiny pebbles at **Milia**, 10 km further on, is considered the island's best beach.

Places to Stay & Eat

The lovely traditional *Pension Lina* (☎ 22 637), with oak-beamed ceilings, brass bedsteads, and carpet throughout, has doubles/triples for 10,000/12,000 dr with private bath. The pension is on the waterfront, opposite the taxi stand. *Pension Sotos* (☎ 22 549), also on the waterfront 150 metres from the ferry pier, is another charming alternative. Spacious doubles/triples are 10,000/12,000 dr. There are many rooms to rent in private houses.

H Klimataria restaurant, opposite the ferry pier, has impressive food at reasonable prices.

Getting There & Away
There are frequent ferries to Volos (2820 dr) and Agios Konstantinos (3480 dr). These boats also call at Alonnisos and Skiathos. Many hydrofoil services to Skopelos also call at Loutraki, the port for Glossa.

Getting Around
There are frequent buses from Skopelos town to Glossa, stopping at the beaches on the way.

You can hire cars and motorcycles from Rent-a-Car Bike (☎ 22 986), which is at the southern end of the port, next to the Hotel Lena.

ALONNISOS Αλόννησος
Alonnisos is the least visited of these three islands. In 1963 the island suffered a major earthquake which devastated the inland Hora, and villagers were forced to move to the harbour town of Patitiri.

Alonnisos' telephone code is ☎ 0424.

Things to See & Do
One of the best beaches is **Kokkinokastro** (red castle), so named because the earth around here is red. Other good beaches line the coast. Alonnisos is an ideal island for walking. A winding path starting from just beyond Pension Galini in Patitiri leads within 40 minutes to the Hora. **Gialia Beach**, on the west coast, is a 20-minute walk from the Hora.

Places to Stay & Eat
Outstanding budget accommodation is offered by *Pension Galini* (☎ 65 573). It is well kept and beautifully furnished with lots of pine and has a flower-festooned terrace. Doubles/triples are 8000/9500 dr with private bath, breakfast included. Spacious, well-equipped apartments for five/six people are also available for 13,000/15,000 dr. The pension is on the left, 400 metres up Pelasgon, the main road leading up from the waterfront, to the left of the port. There are also many domatia in Patitiri.

On the waterfront, *To Dixty Taverna* has a larger selection of dishes than most.

Getting There & Away
There are frequent ferries to Volos (3180 dr) and Agios Konstantinos (3850 dr), via Skiathos and Skopelos.

Getting Around
In summer, caïques take passengers to the beaches of Milia, Hrysi Milia and Kokkinokastro.

Ionian Islands
Τα Επτάνησα

The Ionian islands stretch down the west coast of Greece from Corfu in the north to remote Kythira, off the southern tip of the Peloponnese.

Getting There & Away
Air There are lots of charter flights to Corfu from Northern Europe in summer, as well as a few flights to Kefallonia and Zakynthos. Olympic has daily flights from Athens to Corfu, Zakynthos and Kefallonia.

Ferry Most ferries between Italy and Patras call at Corfu. In summer, there are also direct services from Brindisi to Ithaki, Kefallonia, Paxoi and Zakynthos and from Bari to Kefallonia.

For inter-island ferries and ferries to the mainland, see the Getting There & Away sections under the respective islands.

CORFU Κέρκυρα
Corfu is the most important island in the group, with a population of more than 100,000. With its green hills and valleys of graceful cypress trees and olive groves, many visitors rate it Greece's most beautiful island.

Corfu Town
The old town of Corfu, wedged between two fortresses, occupies a peninsula on the island's east coast. The narrow alleyways of high shuttered tenements in mellow ochres and pinks are an immediate reminder of the town's long association with Venice.

Orientation & Information The town's old fortress (Palaio Frourio) stands on an eastern promontory, separated from the town by an

Corfu

To Brindisi,
Otranto, Bari,
Ortona &
Ancona (Italy)

Agios
Stefanos

Sidhari   Roda   Pelekito

Karoussades   Kassiopi

Agrilia   Perithia

                              Mt
                          ▲ Pantokrator
                    Strinila   (906 m)   ALBANIA

Makrades   Pyrgi
Krini   Lakones Ypos
Paleokastritsa   Kato Korlaklana
         Liapades   Dassia
         Danilia Village
                  Gouvia   PITHIA

Giannades
    Ropa Valley   Corfu
Ermones   (Kerkyra)
   Vatos   Kanoni
Myrtiotissa   Pelekas   Peninsula
    Glyfada   GREECE
                                 Perama
Sinarades   Gastouri

IONIAN   Agios   Agioi
SEA   Gordios   Deka   Benitses

                         Strongyli

Paramonas
   Skala   Agios
           Matheos
Prasouda
           Gardiki   Messongi
                              Boukari
                                 Petriti
           Panagia
           Messavrisi   To Igoumenitsa
                    Agios   Marathias   Lefkimmi
                    Giorgios   Vitalades
0   5   10 km   Kritika   Kavos
                         Paleohori   Spartera
                              Asprokavos   To Paxoi,
                                          Kefallonia
                                          & Patras

rea of parks and gardens known as the
pianada. The new fortress (Neo Frourio) lies
o the north-west. Ferries dock at the new port,
ust beyond the new fortress. The long-distance
us station in on Avrami, just inland from the
ort.

The EOT office (☎ 37 520) is on Rizospaston
Voulefton, between the OTE and the post office,
nd the tourist police (☎ 30 265) are at Plateia
Neou Frouriou 1. All the major Greek banks are
n town, including the National Bank on the
orner of Voulgareos and Theotoki. American
Express (☎ 30 661) is represented by Greek
kies Tours at Kapodistriou 20A.

Corfu's telephone code is ☎ 0661.

The Corfu General Hospital (☎ 45 811) is
on Polithroni Kostanda.

Things to See The **archaeological museum**,
Vraili 5, houses a collection of finds from
Mycenaean to classical times. The star attraction is the pediment from the Temple of
Artemis, decorated with gorgons. Opening
times are Tuesday to Saturday from 8.45 am to
3 pm and Sunday from 9.30 am to 2.30 pm;
admission is 800 dr.

The **Church of Agios Spiridon**, Corfu's
most famous church, has an elaborately decorated interior. Pride of place is given to the

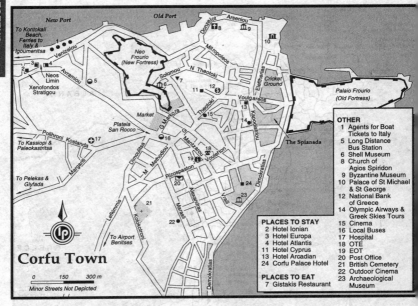

OTHER
1 Agents for Boat
  Tickets to Italy
5 Long Distance
  Bus Station
6 Shell Museum
8 Church of
  Agios Spiridon
9 Byzantine Museum
10 Palace of St Michael
  & St George
12 National Bank
  of Greece
14 Olympic Airways &
  Greek Skies Tours
15 Cinema
16 Local Buses
17 Hospital
18 OTE
19 EOT
20 Post Office
21 British Cemetery
22 Outdoor Cinema
23 Archaeological
  Museum

PLACES TO STAY
2 Hotel Ionian
3 Hotel Europa
4 Hotel Atlantis
11 Hotel Cyprus
13 Hotel Arcadian
24 Corfu Palace Hotel

PLACES TO EAT
7 Gistakis Restaurant

Corfu Town

0   150   300 m

Minor Streets Not Depicted

remains of St Spiridon, displayed in a silver casket; four times a year they are paraded around the town.

Places to Stay & Eat Five km north-west of town is *Camping Kontokali Beach* (☎ 91 202), the closest of the island's six camping grounds. Take bus No 7 from Plateia San Rocco. Next door is the co-managed *youth hostel* (☎ 91 292) where beds are 1200 dr per person.

There are no decent budget places in town. Most travellers wind up at the *Hotel Europa* (☎ 39 304), mainly because it's right next to the port. It charges 5500/6000 dr for reasonable singles/doubles. A better choice is the *Hotel Cyprus*, between the fortresses at Agiou Paterou 13. Doubles are 5500 dr.

Gistakis Restaurant, Solomou 20, serves excellent Corfiot regional food. Main dishes are priced from 900 dr.

Around the Island
There's hardly anywhere in Corfu that hasn't

made its play for the tourist dollar, but the north is totally over the top.

There's good snorkelling at **Paleokastritsa** the main resort on the west coast. The town i built round a series of pretty bays. Furthe south, the hill-top village of **Pelekas** is sup posedly the best place on Corfu to watch th sunset.

Many backpackers head straight for the *Pin Palace* (☎ 53 103/104), a huge complex of res taurants, bars and budget rooms that tumble down a hillside outside the village of **Agio Gordios**. It charges 4500 dr per day for be breakfast and dinner. The place is open fro April to November, and staff meet the boats.

There's a road from the village of **Strinila** t the top of **Mt Pantokrator** (906 metres) Corfu's highest mountain. You'll find a mon astery – and stupendous views over to th mountains of southern Albania.

Getting There & Away
Air Olympic Airways flies to Athens (19,10 dr) three times a day and to Thessalonik

(19,600 dr) twice a week. The Olympic Airways office (☎ 38 694) is at Kapodistriou 20.

Bus There are daily buses to Athens and Thessaloniki from the Avrami terminal in Corfu town. The fare of 8100 dr to Athens includes the ferry to Igoumenitsa. The trip takes 11 hours.

Ferry There are hourly ferries to Igoumenitsa (1½ hours, 850 dr) and a daily ferry to Paxoi. In summer, there are daily services to Patras (10 hours, 4900 dr) on the international ferries that call at Corfu on their way from Italy. (See Getting There & Away at the start of the Ionian Islands section.)

Getting Around

Buses for villages close to Corfu town leave from Plateia San Rocco. Services to other destinations leave from the bus terminal on Avrami. The EOT gives out a schedule.

ITHAKI Ιθάκη

Ithaki is the fabled home of Odysseus, the hero of Homer's *Odyssey*, who pined for his island during his journeys to far-flung lands. It's a quiet place with some isolated coves. From the main town of Vathy you can walk to the **Arethusa Fountain**, the fabled site of Odysseus' meeting with the swineherd Eumaeus on his return to Ithaki. Take water with you, as the fountain dries up in summer.

Ithaki has daily ferries to the mainland ports of Patras and Astrakos, as well as daily services to Kefallonia and Lefkada.

KEFALLONIA Κεφαλλονιά

Tourism remains relatively low-key on mountainous Kefallonia, the largest island of the Ionian group. Resort hotels are confined to the areas near the capital, the beaches in the southwest, Argostoli and the airport. Public transport is very limited, apart from regular services between Argostoli and the main port of Sami, 25 km away on the east coast. The **Melissani Cave**, signposted off the Argostoli road four km from Sami, is an underground lake lit by a small hole in the cave ceiling. The nearby **Drogarati Cave** has some impressive stalactites.

There are daily ferries from Sami to Patras (2½ hours, 2725 dr), as well as from Argostoli and the south-eastern port of Poros to Kyllini in the Peloponnese. There are also connections to Ithaki, Lefkada and Zakynthos.

ZAKYNTHOS Ζάκυνθος

Zakynthos, or Zante, is a beautiful island surrounded by great beaches – so it's hardly surprising that the place is completely overrun by package groups. Its capital and port, Zakynthos town, is an imposing old Venetian town that has been painstakingly reconstructed after being levelled by an earthquake in 1953.

Some of the best beaches are around **Laganas Bay** in the south, which is where endangered loggerhead turtles come ashore to lay their eggs in August – at the peak of the tourist invasion. Conservation groups are urging people to stay away.

There are regular ferries between Zakynthos and Kyllini in the Peloponnese.

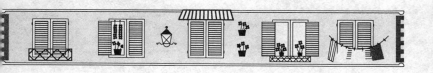

U9,600 daily twice a week. The Olympic Airways
office (☎ 38 694) is at Eleodoraton 20.

Bus There are daily buses to Athens and Thessaloniki from the Argostoli terminal on Co-op lane.
The fare of 8100 to Athens includes the ferry
to Igoumenitsa. The trip takes 11 hours.

Ferry There are nightly ferries to Igoumenitsa
(4½ hours, 850 dr) and a daily ferry service from
in summer; there are daily services to Patras
(4½ hours, 4300 dr) on the international ferries
that call at Corfu on their way from Italy. (See
Getting There & Away at the start of the Ionian
Islands section.)

Getting Around
Buses for villages close to Corfu town leave
from Plateia San Rocco. Services to other destinations leave from the bus terminal on
Avrami. The EOT gives out a schedule.

ITHAKI (Ithaca)
Ithaki is the fabled home of Odysseus, the hero
of Homer's Odyssey, who pined for his island
during his long years on far-flung lands. It's a
quiet place with some isolated coves. From the
main town of Vathy you can walk to the tiny village Perachori, the fabled site of Odysseus's
meeting with the swineherd Eumaeus on his
return to Ithaki. Take water with you as there's
often a dried-up summer.

Ithaki has daily ferries to the mainland ports
of Patras and Astakos, as well as daily services
to Kefallonia and Lefkada.

KEFALLONIA (Cephalonia)
Tourism remains relatively low-key in Kefallonia. Kefallonia, the largest island of the
Ionian group, lies on hopes and optimism on the
areas plan for the capital, the beaches in the south-
west, Argostoli and the airport. Public
transport is very limited, apart from regular
services between Argostoli and the main port
of Sami, 25 km away on the east coast. The
Melissani Cave, sign-posted off the Argostoli
road, four km from Sami, is an underground
lake fed by a small hole in the cave ceiling. The
nearby Drogarati Cave has some impressive
stalactites.

There are daily ferries from Sami to Patras
(2½ hours, 2295 dr) as well as from Argostoli
and the northern port of Fiskardo to Kyllini
on the Peloponnese. There are also connections
to Ithaki, Lefkada and Zakynthos.

ZAKYNTHOS (Zante)
Zakynthos, or Zante, is a beautiful island surrounded by great beaches – so it's hardly
surprising that the place is completely overrun
by package groups. Its capital and port,
Zakynthos town, is an immensely old Venetian
town that has been painstakingly reconstructed
after being levelled by an earthquake in 1953.
Some of the best beaches are around
Laganas Bay in the south, which is where
endangered loggerhead turtles come ashore to
lay their eggs in August – at the peak of the
tourist invasion. Conservation groups are
urging people to stay away.

There are regular ferries between Zakynthos
and Kyllini in the Peloponnese.

Italy

Since the days of the Grand Tour, travellers to Italy have speculated on the 'fatal spell' of the country. This special charm has been attributed to the women, the art, the history, even the air. What is it that makes Italy so seductive? The Italian writer, Luigi Barzini, had this to say on the question:

It made and still makes unwanted people feel wanted, unimportant people feel important and purposeless people believe that the real way to live intelligently is to have no earnest purpose in life.

This land of vibrant, expressive people has given the world pasta and pizza, da Vinci and Michelangelo, Dante and Machiavelli, Catholicism and a vast array of saints and martyrs, Verdi and Pavarotti, Fellini and Sophia Loren, not to mention the Mafia, a remarkable sense of style and *la dolce vita*. In Italy you can visit Roman ruins, study the art of the Renaissance, stay in tiny medieval hill towns, go mountaineering in the Alps and Apennines, feel romantic in Venice, participate in traditional festivals and see more beautiful churches than you imagined could exist in one country. Some people come simply to enjoy the food and wine.

Do your research before coming to Italy, but arrive with an open mind and you will find yourself agreeing with Henry James, who wrote on his arrival in Rome: 'At last, for the first time, I live'.

Facts about the Country

HISTORY

Italy's strategic position in the Mediterranean made it a target for colonisers and invaders over thousands of years. But it also gave the Romans an excellent base from which to expand their empire. Italy's history is thus a patchwork of powerful empires and foreign domination, its people have a diverse ethnic background, and, from the fall of the Roman Empire until the Risorgimento (the Italian unification movement) in 1860, the country was never a unified entity.

The traditional date for the founding of Rome by Romulus is 753 BC, but the country had been inhabited for thousands of years. Palaeolithic Neanderthals lived in Italy during the last Ice Age, more than 20,000 years ago, and by the start of the Bronze Age, around 2000 BC, the peninsula had been settled by several Italic tribes.

The Etruscans

From about 900 BC, or possibly earlier, the Etruscan civilisation developed until these mysterious people, whose origins are still controversial, dominated the area between the Arno and Tiber valleys.

After the foundation of Rome, Etruscan civilisation continued to flourish and Etruscan kings, known as the Tarquins, ruled Rome until 509 BC, when the Roman republic was established. By the end of the 3rd century BC the Romans had overwhelmed the last Etruscan city.

Italy
(Italia)

The Roman Republic

The new Roman republic, after recovering from the invasion of the Gauls in 390 BC, began its expansion into the south of Italy. The Greeks had colonised this area, which they called Magna Grecia, as early as the 8th century BC, and they had established cities such as Syracuse, which rivalled Athens in power.

By about 265 BC Rome had taken the south from Greece, and Sicily was held by Carthage. Rome claimed Sicily following the First Punic War against Hannibal in 241 BC, and although the Romans were defeated by Hannibal at Lake Trasimeno after his legendary crossing of the Alps, Rome defeated and destroyed Carthage in 202 BC. Within another few years they claimed Spain and Greece as colonies and had moved into North Africa.

Expansion & Empire

In the 1st century BC, under Julius Caesar, Rome conquered Gaul and moved into Egypt. After Caesar's assassination by his nephew, Brutus, on the Ides of March in 44 BC, a power struggle began between Mark Antony and Octavius, leading to the deaths of Antony and Cleopatra in Egypt in 31 BC and the establishment of the Roman Empire in 27 BC. Octavius, who had been adopted by Julius Caesar as his son and heir, took the title of Augustus Caesar and became the first emperor. During his rule Roman literature flourished, with great writers including Virgil, Horace and Livy. Augustus was succeeded by Tiberius, Caligula, Claudius and Nero.

The Eastern & Western Empires

By the end of the 3rd century, the empire had grown to such an extent that Emperor Diocletian divided it between east and west for administrative purposes. His reign was also noted for the persecution of Christians. His successor, Constantine, declared religious freedom for Christians and moved the seat of the empire to the eastern capital, Byzantium, which he renamed Constantinople. During the 4th century, Christianity was declared the official state religion and grew in power and influence; at the same time Rome was under constant threat of barbarian invasion.

By the early 5th century, German tribes had entered Rome, and in 476 the Western Roman Empire ended when the German warrior, Odoacer, deposed the emperor and declared himself ruler of Italy.

While the Eastern Roman Empire continued to exist and even retook part of the country for Byzantium in 553, this was the period of the Dark Ages during which Italy became a battleground of barbarians fighting for control. The south and Sicily were dominated by Muslim Arabs until the Normans invaded in 1036 and established a kingdom there.

With a view to re-establishing the Western Roman Empire, Pope Leo II crowned the Frankish king, Charlemagne, emperor in 800 AD. However, the empire again declined under Charlemagne's successors, culminating in the foundation of the Holy Roman Empire in 962 by the German king Otto I, who also declared himself emperor.

The City-States

The Middle Ages in Italy were marked by the development of powerful city-states in the north, while in the south the Normans were busily imposing a severe feudal system on their subjects. After the mid-12th century, when Frederick Barbarossa was crowned emperor, conflict between Pope Alexander III and the emperor reached the point where Italy again became a battleground as cities became either Guelph (supporters of the pope) or Ghibelline (supporters of the emperor). The factional struggles died gradually, but did not prevent a period of great economic, architectural and artistic development. This was the time of Dante, Petrarch and Boccaccio, Giotto, Cimabue and Pisano. The city-states flourished under the rule of powerful families and the papal states were established, even though the French had moved into the country and installed rival popes based in Avignon.

The Renaissance

It was not until the 15th century and the arrival of the Renaissance that Italy rediscovered its former glory. This period was marked by savage intercity wars, internal feuding and French invasions, but the Renaissance, which began in Florence, spread throughout the country, fostering genius of the likes of Brunelleschi, Donatello, Bramante, Botticelli, da Vinci, Masaccio, Lippi, Raphael and, of course, Michelangelo.

ITALY

By the early 16th century, the Reformation had arrived in Italy, and by 1559 much of the country was under Spanish rule. This lasted until 1713 when, following the War of Spanish Succession, control of Italy passed to the Austrians. The powerful states of the country's north, however, continued to grow in power. It was not until after the invasion by Napoleon in 1796 that a degree of unity was introduced into the country, for the first time since the fall of the Roman Empire. The Congress of Vienna in 1815, which restored power to the nobles and revived the old territorial divisions in Italy, created great discontent among the people and led directly to the Risorgimento, the movement to unite the country under one rule.

The Risorgimento

Under the leadership of Garibaldi, Cavour and Mazzini, the unification movement gained momentum until Garibaldi and his Expedition of One Thousand (also known as the Redshirts) took Sicily and Naples in 1860. The Kingdom of Italy was declared in 1861 and Vittorio Emanuele was proclaimed king. Venice was wrested from Austria in 1866 and Rome from the papacy in 1870. However, the new government had great difficulty achieving national unity. As Cavour noted before his death in 1861: 'To harmonise north and south is harder than fighting with Austria or struggling with Rome'.

Mussolini & WWII

In the years after WWI, Italy was in turmoil and in 1921 the Fascist Party, formed by Benito Mussolini in 1919, won 35 of the 135 seats in parliament. In October 1921, after a period of considerable unrest and strikes, the king asked Mussolini to form a government, and he became prime minister with only 7% representation in parliament.

The Fascists won the 1924 elections, following a campaign marked by violence and intimidation, and by the end of 1925 Mussolini had become head of state, expelled opposition parties from parliament, gained control of the press and trade unions and reduced the voting public by two-thirds. He formed the Rome-Berlin axis with Hitler in 1936 and Italy entered WWII as an ally of Germany in June 1941. After a series of military disasters and an invasion by the Allies in 1943, Mussolini surrendered Italy to the Allies and went into hiding. He was shot, along with his mistress, Clara Petacci, by partisans in April 1945.

The Italian Republic

In 1946, following a referendum, the constitutional monarchy was abolished and the republic established.

Italy was a founding member of the European Economic Community in 1957 and was seriously disrupted by terrorism in the 1970s following the appearance of the Red Brigades, who kidnapped and assassinated the Christian Democrat prime minister, Aldo Moro, in 1978.

In the decades following WWII, Italy's national government was consistently dominated by the centre-right Christian Democrats, usually in coalition with other parties (excluding the Communists). Italy enjoyed significant economic growth in the 1980s, but the 1990s heralded a new period of crisis for the country, both economically and politically. Against the backdrop of a severe economic crisis, the very foundations of Italian politics were shaken by a national bribery scandal.

The 1990s

The *tangentopoli* (translated as 'kickback cities') scandal broke in Milan in early 1992 when a functionary of the Socialist Party was arrested on charges of accepting bribes in exchange for public works contracts. Investigations eventually implicated thousands of politicians, public officials and businesspeople and left the main parties in tatters, effectively demolishing the centre of the Italian political spectrum.

National elections in March 1994 saw Italy move decisively to the right. A new right-wing coalition known as the Freedom Alliance, whose members include the Neo-Fascist National Alliance, and which is led by billionaire media magnate Silvio Berlusconi, won the elections. Berlusconi, who had entered politics only three months before the elections, was appointed prime minister, but his government fell after only nine months. The latest elections, held in April 1996, resulted in a centre-left coalition, led by economist Romano Prodi, winning the majority of votes. The win by the Olive Tree coalition represented a historic moment in Italian politics: for the first time since the establishment of the republic, the communists will participate in governing the country.

The 1990s have also seen Italy moving more decisively against the Sicilian Mafia, prompted by the 1992 assassinations of two prominent anti-Mafia judges. A major offensive in Sicily, plus the testimonies of several *pentiti* (repentant mafiosi-turned-informers), led to several important arrests – most notably of the Sicilian godfather, Salvatore 'Toto' Riina. The most recent breakthrough in the war against the Mafia came with the arrest in May 1996 of Giovanni Brusca, the man believed to have taken power after Riina's arrest. Brusca was implicated in the murder of anti-Mafia judge, Giovanni Falcone, as well as in the bombings in Florence, Milan and Rome in 1993, which damaged monuments and works of art and killed several people.

GEOGRAPHY & ECOLOGY

Italy's boot-shape makes it one of the most recognisable countries in the world. The country, incorporating the islands of Sicily and Sardinia, is bound by the Adriatic, Ligurian, Tyrrhenian and Ionian seas, which all form part of the Mediterranean Sea. About 75% of the Italian peninsula is mountainous, with the Alps dividing the country from France, Switzerland and Austria, and the Apennines forming a backbone which extends from the Alps into Sicily. There are three active volcanoes: Stromboli (in the Aeolian Islands), Vesuvius (near Naples) and Etna (Sicily). The countryside can be dramatically beautiful, but the long presence of humans on the peninsula has had a significant impact on the environment. Aesthetically the result is not always displeasing – much of the beauty of Tuscany, for instance, lies in the interaction of olive groves with vineyards, fallow fields and stands of cypress and pine.

However, this alteration of the environment, combined with the Italians' passion for hunting (*la caccia*), has led to many native animals and birds becoming extinct, rare or endangered. Under laws progressively introduced this century, many animals and birds are now protected.

There are numerous national parks in Italy. Among the most important are the Parco Nazionale del Gran Paradiso and the Parco Nazionale dello Stelvio, both in the Alps, and the Parco Nazionale d'Abruzzo.

Pollution caused by industrial and urban waste exists throughout Italy and many beaches are fouled to some extent, particularly on the Ligurian Coast, in the northern Adriatic (where there is an algae problem resulting from industrial pollution), and near major cities such as Rome and Naples. However, it is possible to find a clean beach, particularly in Sardinia. Air pollution is a problem in the industrialised north, as well as in major cities, where car emissions poison the atmosphere with carbon monoxide and lead. Litter-conscious visitors will be astounded by the Italians' habit of dumping rubbish when and where they like.

GOVERNMENT & POLITICS

For administrative purposes Italy is divided into 20 regions, which each have some degree of autonomy. The regions are then divided into provinces and municipalities.

The country is a parliamentary republic, headed by a president who appoints the prime minister. The parliament consists of a senate and chamber of deputies, both of which have equal legislative power. The seat of national government is in Rome. Italy's political situation is in a constant state of flux. Until reforms were introduced in 1994, members of parliament were elected by what was probably the purest system of proportional representation in the world. Two-thirds of both houses are now elected on the basis of who receives the most votes in their district, basically the same as the first-past-the-post system in the UK. The old system generally produced unstable coalition governments – Italy had 53 governments in the 48 years from the declaration of the republic to the introduction of the electoral reforms. But, even under the new system, there has been instability.

ECONOMY

Italy has the fifth-largest economy in the world, after enjoying spectacular growth in the 1980s. However, there has been much debate about the ability of the Italian economy to perform efficiently in the context of a unified Europe – a debate which has intensified following the country's severe economic crisis and political instability of the 1990s. Draconian measures were introduced by the

ITALY

Regions of Italy

FRANCE

GERMANY

AUSTRIA

HUNGARY

Lake Constance

LIECHTENSTEIN

SWITZERLAND

Bolzano

TRENTINO-ALTO ADIGE

Trento

FRIULI-VENEZIA GIULIA

SLOVENIA

Trieste

0   100   200 km

VALLE D'AOSTA

Aosta

LOMBARDY

Milan

VENETO

Venice

Turin

PIEDMONT

EMILIA-ROMAGNA

Bologna

CROATIA

BOSNIA-HERCEGOVINA

Genoa

LIGURIA

FRANCE

LIGURIAN SEA

Florence

TUSCANY

SAN MARINO

Ancona

ADRIATIC SEA

THE MARCHES

Perugia

UMBRIA

CORSICA

LAZIO

L'Aquila

ABRUZZO

Rome

MOLISE

Campobasso

Bari

CAMPANIA

Naples

APULIA

Potenza

BASILICATA

TYRRHENIAN SEA

SARDINIA

Cagliari

CALABRIA

Catanzaro

MEDITERRANEAN SEA

Palermo

IONIAN SEA

SICILY

MALTA

TUNISIA

YUGOSLAVIA

government to control public spending and reduce the massive public debt, including partial privatisation of the country's huge public sector.

There remains a significant economic gap between Italy's northern and southern regions, despite years of effort and the expenditure of trillions of lire. The fact remains that Italy's richest regions (Piedmont, Emilia-Romagna and Lombardy) are all northern, and its poorest (Calabria, Campania and Sicily) are all southern. One impact of this gap is that, generally, things don't work as well in the south as they do in the north – notably in hospitals, banks and public services such as the post office.

POPULATION & PEOPLE

The population of Italy is 57.8 million. The country has the lowest birthrate in Europe – a surprising fact considering the Italians' preoccupation with children and family. Foreigners may like to think of Italy as a land of passionate, animated people who gesticulate wildly when speaking, love to eat, drive like maniacs and don't like to work. However, it will take more than a holiday in Italy to understand its vigorous and remarkably diverse inhabitants. Overall the people remain fiercely protective of their regional customs, including their dialects and cuisine.

ARTS

Architecture, Painting & Sculpture

Italy has often been called a living art museum and certainly it is not always necessary to enter a gallery to appreciate the country's artistic wealth – it is all around you as you walk through Rome, or Florence, or Venice, or visit a tiny church in a tiny medieval hill town in Umbria. This visible evidence of the country's history is one of the most fascinating aspects of a visit to Italy. In Rome, for instance, the forum, the Colosseum and the Pantheon are juxtaposed with churches and palaces of the medieval, Renaissance and baroque periods. Near Rome, at Tarquinia, you can visit 2000-year-old Etruscan tombs to see the vibrant funerary artwork of this ancient civilisation.

In the south of Italy and in Sicily, where Greek colonisation preceded Roman domination, there are important Greek archaeological sites such as the temples at Paestum, south of Salerno, and at Agrigento in Sicily. Pompeii

and Herculaneum give an idea of how ancient Romans actually lived.

Byzantine mosaics adorn churches throughout Italy, most notably at Ravenna, in the Basilica of San Marco in Venice, and in Monreale cathedral near Palermo. There are also some interesting mosaics in churches in Rome. In Apulia, you can tour the magnificent Romanesque churches, a legacy of the Normans (the region's medieval rulers) and their successors, the Swabians.

The Renaissance The 15th and early 16th centuries in Italy saw one of the most remarkable explosions of artistic and literary achievement in recorded history – the Renaissance. Giotto di Bendone (1267-1337), known simply as Giotto, who revolutionised painting by introducing naturalism into his works, was one of the most important precursors of the Renaissance. Among his most noted works are the frescos of the Scrovegni Chapel in Padua.

Patronised mainly by the Medici family in Florence and the popes in Rome, painters, sculptors, architects and writers flourished and many artists of genius emerged. The High Renaissance (about 1490-1520) was dominated by three men – Leonardo da Vinci (1452-1519), Michelangelo Buonarrotti (1475-1564) and Raphael (1483-1520).

A tour of Renaissance artworks would alone fill an extended trip to Italy. In Florence there is Italy's best known art gallery, the Uffizi. Ten of its rooms trace the development of Florentine and Tuscan painting from the 13th to 16th centuries and works include Botticelli's *Birth of Venus* and *Primavera* (Spring) and Leonardo da Vinci's *Annunciation*. In the Accademia is Michelangelo's *David*, while the Bargello houses Donatello's bronze *David*. At the Vatican in Rome there is Michelangelo's ceiling and *Last Judgment* in the Sistine Chapel and Raphael's frescos in Pope Julius II's private apartment. In St Peter's Basilica is Michelangelo's *Pietà* and his *Moses* is in the church of San Pietro in Vincoli.

Baroque The baroque period (17th century) was characterised by sumptuous, often fantastic architecture and richly decorative painting and sculpture.

In Rome there are innumerable works by the great baroque sculptor and architect Gianlorenzo Bernini (1598-1680), including the central fountain in Piazza Navona. Rome's best loved baroque work is the Trevi Fountain. Cities which were literally transformed by baroque architecture include Lecce, Noto and Naples.

Later Styles Neoclassicism in Italy produced the sculptor, Canova (1757-1822). Of Italy's modern artists, Amadeo Modigliani (1884-1920) is perhaps the most famous. The early 20th century also produced an artistic movement known as the Futurists, who rejected the sentimental art of the past and were infatuated by new technology, including modern warfare. Fascism produced its own style of architecture in Italy, characterised by the work of Marcello Piacentini (1881-1960), which includes the *Stadio dei Marmi* at Rome's Olympic Stadium complex.

Music

Few modern Italian singers or musicians have made any impact outside Italy – one exception is Zucchero (Adelmo Fornaciari), who has become well known in the USA and UK as Sugar. Instead, it is in the realms of opera and instrumental music where Italian artists have always triumphed. Antonio Vivaldi (1675-1741) created the concerto in its present form. Verdi, Puccini, Bellini, Donizetti and Rossini, composers from the 19th and early 20th centuries, are all stars of the modern operatic era. Tenor Luciano Pavarotti (1935-) is today's luminary of Italian opera.

Literature

Before Dante wrote his *Divina Commedia* (Divine Comedy) and confirmed vernacular Italian as a serious medium for poetic expression, Latin was the language of writers. Among the greatest writers of ancient Rome were Cicero, Virgil, Ovid and Petronius.

A contemporary of Dante was Petrarch (Francesco Petrarca 1304-74). Giovanni Boccaccio (1313-75), author of the *Decameron*, is considered the first Italian novelist.

Machiavelli's *Il Principe* (The Prince), although a purely political work, has proved the most lasting of the Renaissance works.

Alessandro Manzoni (1785-1873) worked hard to establish a narrative language which was accessible to all Italians in his great historical novel *I Promessi Sposi* (The Betrothed).

The turbulence of political and social life in Italy in the 20th century has produced a wealth of literature. The often virulent poetry of ardent nationalist, Gabriele d'Annunzio, was perhaps not of the highest quality, but his voice was a prestige tool for Mussolini's Fascists.

Italy's richest contribution to modern literature has been in the novel and short story. Cesare Pavese and Carlo Levi both endured internal exile in southern Italy during Fascism. Levi based *Cristo si è Fermato a Eboli* (Christ Stopped at Eboli) on his experiences in exile in Basilicata. The works of Italo Calvino border on the fantastical, thinly veiling his preoccupation with human behaviour in society.

Natalia Ginzburg has produced prose, essays and theatre. Alberto Moravia was a prolific writer who concentrated on describing Rome and its people. The novels of Elsa Morante are characterised by a subtle psychological appraisal of her characters. Umberto Eco shot to fame with his first and best known work, *Il Nome della Rosa* (The Name of the Rose).

Theatre

At a time when French playwrights ruled the stage, the Venetian Carlo Goldoni (1707-1793) attempted to bring Italian theatre back into the limelight with the *commedia dell'arte*, the tradition of improvisational theatre based on a core of set characters including Pulcinella and Arlecchino. Luigi Pirandello (1867-1936) threw into question every preconception of what theatre should be with such classics as *Sei Personaggi in Cerca d'Autore* (Six Characters in Search of an Author). Pirandello won the Nobel Prize in 1934. Modern Italian theatre's most enduring contemporary representative is actor/director Dario Fo.

Cinema

Born in Turin in 1904, the Italian film industry originally made an impression with silent spectaculars. Its most glorious era began as WWII came to a close in Europe, when the Neo-Realists began making their films. One of the earliest examples of this new wave in cinema was Luchino Visconti's *Ossessione* (Obsession). From 1945 to 1947, Roberto Rossellini produced three Neo-Realist masterpieces, including *Roma Città Aperta* (Rome Open City), starring Anna Magnani. Vittorio de Sica produced another classic in 1948, *Ladri di Biciclette* (Bicycle Thieves).

Schooled with the masters of Neo-Realism, Federico Fellini in many senses took the creative baton from them and carried it into the following decades, with films such as *La Dolce Vita*, with Anita Ekberg and Marcello Mastroianni. The career of Michelangelo Antonioni reached a climax with *Blow-up* in 1967. Pier Paolo Pasolini's films included *Accattone* and *Decameron*.

Bernardo Bertolucci had his first international hit with *Last Tango in Paris*. He made the blockbuster *The Last Emperor* in 1987. Franco Zeffirelli's most recent film was *Jane Eyre*. Other notable directors include the Taviani brothers, Giuseppe Tornatore and Nanni Moretti.

Italy's first international film star was Rudolph Valentino. Among Italy's most successful actors since WWII are Marcello Mastroianni, Anna Magnani, Gina Lollobrigida and Sophia Loren.

CULTURE
Religious festivals and soccer are the two great passions of the average Italian, followed closely by eating and the traditional August holidays. The midday meal is a revered tradition which means that all shops, offices and most institutions close for three to four hours in the afternoon.

In August, particularly during the week round the Feast of the Assumption (August 15), known as *ferragosto*, a combination of summer heat and national holidays means that Italians evacuate the cities en masse and head for the hills and beaches. This means that almost *everything* closes down in the big cities during the peak tourist period.

Avoiding Offence
Women should note that light, skimpy clothing which might be acceptable in the north could attract unwanted attention in places such as Sicily and Sardinia. Churches enforce strict dress rules. Anyone wearing shorts (including men) will find it difficult to get into a church

anywhere in Italy. Remember that while churches are major tourist attractions in Italy, they are also places of worship, so try to avoid visiting during services.

RELIGION
Some 85% of Italians professed to be Catholic in a census taken in the early 1980s. The remaining 15% included about 500,000 evangelical Protestants; the rest professed to have no religion.

LANGUAGE
Although many Italians speak some English (as they study it in school), English is more widely understood in the north, particularly in major centres such as Milan, Florence and Venice, than in the south. Staff at most hotels, *pensioni* and restaurants usually speak a little English, but you will be better received if you at least attempt to communicate in Italian.

Italian is a Romance language which is related to French, Spanish, Portuguese and Romanian. The Romance languages belong to the Indo-European group of languages, which include English. Indeed, as English and Italian share common roots in Latin, you will recognise many Italian words.

Modern literary Italian began to be developed in the 13th and 14th centuries, predominantly through the works of Dante, Petrarch and Boccaccio, who wrote chiefly in the Florentine dialect. The language drew on its Latin heritage and the many dialects of Italy to develop into the standard Italian of today. Although many and varied dialects are spoken in everyday conversation, standard Italian is the national language of schools, media and literature, and is understood throughout the country.

There are 58 million speakers of Italian in Italy, half a million in Switzerland (where Italian is one of the four official languages) and 1.5 million speakers in France and former Yugoslavia. As a result of migration, Italian is also widely spoken in the USA, Argentina, Brazil and Australia.

Many older Italians still expect to be addressed by the third person formal, ie *Lei* instead of *tu*. Also, it is not polite to use the greeting *ciao* when addressing strangers, unless they use it first; use *buongiorno* and *arrivederci*.

See the Language Section at the back of the book for pronunciation guidelines and useful words and phrases.

Facts for the Visitor

PLANNING
Climate & When to Go
Italy lies in a temperate zone, but the climates of the north and south vary. Summers are uniformly hot, but are often extremely hot and dry in the south. Winters can be severely cold in the north – particularly in the Alps, but also in the Po Valley – whereas they are generally mild in the south and in Sicily and Sardinia. The best time to visit Italy is in the off season, particularly from April to June and September to October, when the weather is good, prices are lower and there are fewer tourists. During July and August (the high season) it is very hot, prices are inflated, the country swarms with tourists, and hotels by the sea and in the mountains are usually booked out. Many hotels and restaurants in seaside areas close down for the winter months.

Books & Maps
For a more comprehensive guide to Italy, pick up a copy of Lonely Planet's *Italy* guide.

For serious research on Italian history, culture and people, try the following books: *The Decline and Fall of the Roman Empire* by Edward Gibbons; *Concise History of Italy* by Vincent Cronin; *Painters of the Renaissance* by Bernard Berenson; and *The Penguin Book of the Renaissance* by J H Plumb.

For lighter reading, you will find many books written by travellers in Italy: *Venice* by James Morris; *Venice Observed* and *The Stones of Florence* by Mary McCarthy; and *A Traveller in Southern Italy* and *A Traveller in Italy* by H V Morton.

Companion Guides (Collins) are excellent and include *Rome* by Georgina Masson, *Venice* by Hugh Honour, *Tuscany* by Archibald Lyall and *Southern Italy* by Peter Gunn.

Luigi Barzini's classic *The Italians* is a must.

For maps of cities, you will generally find those provided by the tourist office adequate.

Excellent road and city maps are published by the Istituto Geografico de Agostini and are available in all major bookshops. If you are driving, invest in the De Agostini *Atlante Stradale Italiano* (L35,000).

What to Bring
A backpack is a definite advantage in Italy, but if you plan to use a suitcase and portable trolley be warned about the endless flights of stairs a train stations and in many of the smaller medieval towns, as well as the petty thieves who prey on tourists who have no hands free because they are carrying too much luggage. A small pack (with a lock) for use on day trips and for sight seeing is preferable to a handbag or shoulder bag particularly in the southern cities where motor cycle bandits are very active. A money belt i absolutely essential in Italy, particularly in the south and in Sicily, but also in the major cities where groups of dishevelled-looking women and children prey on tourists with bulging pockets. While travelling, it is best not to display any valuable jewellery, including rings and expensive watches.

In the more mountainous areas, the weather can change suddenly even in high summer, so remember to bring at least one item of warm clothing. Most importantly, bring a pair of hardy, comfortable, already worn-in walking shoes. In many cities, pavements are uneven and often made of cobblestones.

SUGGESTED ITINERARIES
Depending on the length of your stay, you might want to see and do the following things

Two days
    Visit Rome to see the Forum, the Colosseum, Peter's Basilica and the Vatican museums.
One week
    Visit Rome and Florence, with detours to Siena and San Gimignano.
Two weeks
    As above, plus Bologna, Verona, Ravenna and at lea three days in Venice.
One month
    As above, but go to Sicily and perhaps Sardinia for one week at least. Explore the north, includir Liguria, and the south, including Puglia.

HIGHLIGHTS
Museums & Galleries
The Vatican museums in Rome and the fabulous Uffizi Gallery in Florence are absolutely

not to be missed. The Bargello in Florence, with its excellent sculpture collection, is another must. In Venice visit the Peggy Guggenheim Gallery of Modern Art. The Museo Archeologico Nazionale in Naples houses finds from Pompeii, as well as the spectacular Farnese collection.

Historic Towns

There are so many fascinating and beautiful medieval towns in Italy that it seems a shame to confine your travels to the major cities. In Tuscany visit San Gimignano, Arezzo and Volterra, and in Umbria take a tour of the medieval hill towns, many still surrounded by their walls and crowned with ruined castles. The more interesting towns include Perugia, Assisi, Spoleto, Gubbio and Orvieto. In Liguria walk along the coast to visit the Cinque Terre, five tiny villages linked by a walking track on the Riviera di Levante. One of the most fascinating towns in Italy is Matera in Basilicata. Wandering through its famous *sassi* (stone houses) is an experience not easily forgotten.

Churches

A few highlights include the cathedrals in Florence, Milan, Siena and Orvieto (considered one of the most beautiful in Italy), and one at Monreale, near Palermo, for its beautiful mosaics. The Basilica di San Vitale in Ravenna is notable both for its mosaics and for the design of the church. The Romanesque cathedrals in Apulia are fascinating.

Beaches

Although the water is polluted, the beaches along the Riviera di Levante in Liguria are worth visiting. The beach resorts along the Amalfi Coast are particularly scenic, but again the water is not exactly clean. The cleanest beaches are in Sardinia and there are some lovely spots in Sicily.

Hotels & Restaurants

The following are hotels which are in characteristic locations. The Pensione Bellavista in Florence has two double rooms with views of the Duomo (cathedral) and the Palazzo Vecchio. Just outside Florence, near Fiesole, is Bencistà, a former villa with a terrace overlooking Florence. In Rome the Albergo

Abruzzi is in the same piazza as the Pantheon. In Naples, the best pizzas are at Trianon. In Florence, head for Mario's, a local institution.

General Sights

Italy itself is a virtual museum and in every part of the country you will come across monuments, works of art, views and special places which have the capacity to surprise even the most world-weary traveller. Here are a few of the more special ones: Michelangelo's *Pietà* in St Peter's Basilica, Rome; the Grand Canal in Venice; the Pala d'Oro (gold altarpiece) in the Basilica di San Marco (St Mark's Basilica) in Venice; the view of Tuscany from the top of the town hall tower in San Gimignano; the painted Etruscan tombs at Tarquinia; Giotto's frescos in the Cappella degli Scrovegni in Padua; the Valley of the Temples at Agrigento; and the floor mosaic in Otranto's cathedral.

TOURIST OFFICES

There are three main categories of tourist office in Italy: regional, provincial and local. Their names vary throughout the country, but they all offer basically the same services. Provincial offices are sometimes known as the Ente Provinciale per il Turismo (EPT) or, more commonly, the Azienda di Promozione Turistica (APT). The Azienda Autonoma di Soggiorno e Turismo (AAST) offices usually have information only on the town itself. In most of the very small towns and villages the local tourist office is called a Pro Loco.

The quality of services offered varies dramatically throughout the country and don't be surprised if you encounter lethargic or even hostile staff. You should be able to get a map, a *elenco degli alberghi* (a list of hotels), a *pianta della città* (map of the town) and information on the major sights. Staff speak English in larger towns, but in the more out-of-the-way places you may have to rely on sign language. Tourist offices are generally open from 8.30 am to 12.30 pm and 3 to 7 pm Monday to Friday and on Saturday morning. You can obtain some information on places throughout Italy at the EPT office in Rome, Via Parigi 11, 00185, and at the Rome office of the Italian State Tourist Office, Ente Nazionale Italiano per il Turismo (ENIT), Via Marghera 2.

ITALY

Italian Tourist Offices Abroad

Information about Italy can be obtained at Italian State Tourist Offices throughout the world, including:

Australia
   Alitalia, Orient Overseas Building, suite 202, 32 Bridge St, Sydney (☎ 02-9247 1308)
Canada
   1, Place Ville Marie, suite 1914, Montreal, Que H3B 3M9 (☎ 514-866 7667)
UK
   1 Princes St, London W1R 8AY (☎ 0171-408 1254)
USA
   630 Fifth Ave, suite 1565, New York, NY 10111 (☎ 212-245 4822)
   124000 Wilshire Blvd, suite 550, Los Angeles, CA 90025 (☎ 310-82 0098)
   401 North Michigan Ave, suite 3030, Chicago, IL 60611 (☎ 312-644 0990)

Sestante CIT, Italy's national travel agency, also has offices throughout the world (known as CIT outside Italy). It can provide extensive information on Italy, as well as book tours and accommodation. It can also make train bookings. Offices include:

Australia
   123 Clarence St, Sydney 2000 (☎ 02-9299 4754)
   suite 10, 6th floor, 422 Collins St, Melbourne 3000 (☎ 03-9670 1322)
Canada
   1450 City Councillors St, suite 750, Montreal, Que H3A 2E6 (☎ 514-954 8608)
   111 Avenue Rd, suite 808, Toronto, Ont M5R 3J8 (☎ 416-927 7712)
UK
   Marco Polo House, 3-5 Lansdown Rd, Croydon, Surrey CR9 1LL (☎ 0181-686 0677)
USA
   242 Madison Ave, suite 207, New York, NY 10173 (☎ 212-697 2497)
   6033 Century Blvd, suite 980, Los Angeles, CA 90045 (☎ 310-338 8615).

USEFUL ORGANISATIONS

The following organisations in Italy might prove useful:

Centro Turistico Studentesco e Giovanile (CTS)
   This agency has offices all over Italy and specialises in discounts for students and young people, but is also useful for travellers of any age looking for cheap flights and sightseeing discounts. It is linked with the International Student Travel Confederation. You can get a student card if you have documents proving that you are a student.

Touring Club Italiano (TCI)
   The head office (☎ 02-852 62 44) is at Corso Italia 10, Milan. It publishes useful trekking guides and maps (in Italian), and has offices throughout Italy.

VISAS & EMBASSIES

Residents of the USA, Australia, Canada and New Zealand do not need to apply for visas before arriving in Italy if they are entering the country as tourists only. While there is an official three-month limit on stays in the country border authorities no longer stamp the passports of visitors from Western nations. If you are entering the country for any reason other than tourism, you should insist on having your passport stamped. By law, visitors must go to a *questura* (police headquarters) if they plan to stay at the same address for more than one week, to receive a *permesso di soggiorno* – in effect, permission to remain in the country for a nominated period up to the three-month limit. Tourists who are staying in hotels are not required to do this. While it is extremely unlikely that tourists will encounter any problems without a permesso di soggiorno, authorities have the right to put you on the next plane, train or boat out of the country if they find you without one.

It is almost impossible to extend your visa within Italy and visitors of the nationalities just mentioned must theoretically leave the country after three months, even if this means simply crossing a border into France or Switzerland and then re-entering Italy to have their passport restamped.

Foreigners who want to study at a university in Italy must have a student visa. Australians and New Zealanders also require a visa to study at a language school. This can be obtained from the Italian embassy or consulate in your city, but you must have a letter of acceptance from the university or school you will be attending. This type of visa is renewable within Italy, but you will be required to continue studying and provide proof that you have enough money to support yourself during the period of study. It should be noted that the process to obtain a student visa can take some months.

While citizens of EU countries are able to travel and work freely in Italy, it is extremely difficult for other nationalities to obtain a visa to work in the country (see Work in this chapter).

Italian Embassies Abroad

Italian diplomatic missions abroad include:

Australia
Level 45, The Gateway, 1 Macquarie Place, Sydney (☎ 02-9392 7940)
509 St Kilda Rd, Melbourne (☎ 03-9867 5744)
Canada
136 Beverley St, Toronto (☎ 416-977 1566)
France
47 Rue de Varennes, 73343 Paris (☎ 01-44 30 47 00)
New Zealand
34 Grant Rd, Thorndon, Wellington (☎ 04-735 339)
UK
14 Three Kings Yard, London (☎ 0171-312 2200)
USA
690 Park Ave, New York (☎ 212-439 8600)
2590 Webster St, San Francisco (☎ 415-931 4924)

Foreign Embassies in Italy

The headquarters of most foreign embassies are in Rome, although there are generally British and US consulates in other major cities. The following addresses and phone numbers are for Rome (the telephone area code is ☎ 06):

Australia
Via Alessandria 215 (☎ 85 27 21)
Austria
Via Pergolesi 3 (☎ 855 82 41)
Consulate, Via Liegi 32 (☎ 855 29 66)
Canada
Via G B de Rossi 27 (☎ 44 59 81)
Consulate, Via Zara 30
France
Palazzo Farnese (☎ 68 60 11)
visas at Via Giulia 251
Germany
Via Po 25c (☎ 88 47 41)
Consulate, Via Francesco Siacci 2c.
Greece
Via Mercadante 36 (☎ 855 31 00)
Consulate, Via Stoppani 10 (☎ 807 08 49)
Japan
Via Sella 60 (☎ 48 79 91)
New Zealand
Via Zara 28 (☎ 440 29 28)
Spain
Largo Fontanella Borghese 19 (☎ 687 81 72)
Switzerland
Via Barnaba Oriani 61 (☎ 808 36 41)
Consulate, Largo Elvezia 15 (☎ 808 83 71)
UK
Via XX Settembre 80a (☎ 482 54 41)
USA
Via Vittorio Veneto 119a-121 (☎ 46 741)

For a complete list of all foreign embassies in Rome and other major cities throughout Italy,

look in the local telephone book under *Ambasciate* or *Consolati*, or ask for a list at the tourist office.

DOCUMENTS

A passport is the only important document you will need in Italy if you want to stay as a tourist for up to three months. It is necessary to produce your passport when you register in a hotel or *pensione*. You will find that many proprietors will want to keep your passport during your stay. This is not a legal requirement; they only need it long enough to take down the details. If you want to rent a car or motorcycle, you will need a valid EU driving licence, an International Driving Permit, or your driving permit from your own country. If you're driving your own car, you'll need an International Insurance Certificate, known as a *Carta Verde* (Green Card). Students should carry their student identity card, or obtain an International Student Identity Card (ISIC) before leaving home, in order to take advantage of student discounts while travelling.

CUSTOMS

People from outside Europe can import, without paying duty, two still cameras with 10 rolls of film, a movie or TV camera with 10 cartridges of film, a portable record player with 10 records or a tape recorder with 10 tapes, a CD player, a transistor radio, a pair of binoculars, up to 400 cigarettes, two bottles of wine and two bottles of liquor.

Visitors who are residents of a European country and enter from an EU country can import a maximum of 300 cigarettes, one bottle of wine and half a bottle of liquor. There is no limit on the amount of lire you can import.

MONEY

Anything to do with money and banks is likely to cause significant frustration and time-wasting in Italy. Banks are the most reliable (although not necessarily the fastest) places to exchange money or to obtain cash advances on your credit card, although some will charge up to L8000 commission on cheques. The dilemma here is that although it is best to exchange large sums at once to save on the commission, it is unwise throughout Italy to carry large amounts of cash. If you buy travellers' cheques in lire, generally there should be no commission charge when cashing them.

There are exchange offices at all major airports and train stations, but it is advisable to obtain a small amount of lire before arriving to avoid problems and queues at the airport and train stations.

Most of the major banks will give cash advances on Visa, but not all will honour MasterCard. The Banca Commerciale Italiana, one of Italy's major banks, *will* give cash advances on MasterCard, as will the Cassa di Risparmio and Credito Italiano. American Express and Thomas Cook have offices throughout the country, and for sheer convenience their travellers' cheques are a good option.

The fastest way to have money sent to you is by 'urgent telex' through the foreign office of a large Italian bank, or through major banks in your own country, to a nominated bank in Italy. It is important to have an exact record of all details associated with the money transfer, particularly the exact address of the Italian bank where the money has been sent. This will always be the head office of the bank in the town to which the money has been sent. Urgent telex transfers will take only a few days, while other means, such as by draft, can take weeks. You will be required to produce identification, usually a passport, in order to collect the money.

Major credit cards, including Visa, MasterCard and American Express, are accepted throughout Italy in shops, restaurants and larger hotels. However, many *trattorias*, *pizzerias*, most *pensioni* and one-star hotels do *not* accept credit cards. You will also find that while most stall holders at large flea markets accept credit cards, they will bargain only if you pay cash.

Currency

Italy's currency is the lira (plural: lire). The smallest note is L1000. Other denominations in notes are L2000, L5000, L10,000, L50,000 and L100,000. Coin denominations are L50, L100, L200 and L500. Remember that like other Continental Europeans, Italians indicate decimals with commas and thousands with points.

Exchange Rates

Australia	A$1	=	L1195
Canada	C$1	=	L1111
France	1FF	=	L304
Germany	DM1	=	L1030
Japan	¥100	=	L1409
New Zealand	NZ$1	=	L1063
United Kingdom	UK£1	=	L2373
United States	US$1	=	L1524

Costs

A *very* prudent traveller could get by o L60,000 per day, but only by staying in yout hostels, eating one meal a day (at the hostel buying a sandwich or pizza by the slice fc lunch and minimising the number of gallerie and museums visited, since the entrance fee most major museums is cripplingly expensiv at around L12,000. You save on transport cos by buying tourist or day tickets for city bus an underground services. When travelling b train, by avoiding the fast intercities you ca save on the *supplemento rapido*. Italy's rai ways also offer a few cut-price options fc students, young people and tourists for trav within a nominated period (see the Gettin Around section in this chapter for more infor mation). Museums and galleries usually giv discounts to students, but you will need a vali student card which you can obtain from CT offices if you have documents proving you a a student. A basic breakdown of costs durin an average day could be: accommodatio L20,000 to L30,000; breakfast (coffee ar croissant) L2000; lunch (sandwich an mineral water) L3000 to L5000; public tran port (bus or underground railway in a maj town) L5000-L6000; entry fee for one museu L12,000; dinner L15,000.

Tipping & Bargaining

You are not expected to tip on top of restaura service charges, but it is common practi among Italians to leave a small amount, arour 10%. In bars they will leave any small chang as a tip, often only L50 or L100.

Bargaining is common throughout Italy the various flea markets, but not normally shops. You can try bargaining for the price a room in a pensione, particularly if you pl to stay for more than a few days.

Consumer Taxes

Whenever you buy an item in Italy you will pay value-added tax, known as IVA. Tourists who are residents of countries outside the EU are able to claim back this tax if the item costs more than a certain amount (L400,000 at the time of writing). The goods must be for personal use, they must be carried with your luggage and you must keep the fiscal receipt. You have to fill in a form at the point of purchase, have the form checked and stamped by Italian customs and then return it by mail within 60 days to the vendor, who will then make the refund, either by cheque or to your credit card. At major airports and border points, there are places where you can get an immediate cash refund.

POST & COMMUNICATIONS

Italy's postal service is notoriously slow and unreliable. Don't expect to receive every letter sent to you, or that every letter you send will reach its destination.

Post

Rates The cost of sending a letter *via aerea* (air mail) depends on weight, but an average letter to Australia will cost L1400, L750 to the UK and around L1100 to the USA. It usually takes 10 days to two weeks for air mail to reach countries outside Europe and approximately one week to reach the UK.

Sending Mail Print the country of destination in block letters and underline it. If you want to mail something urgently, you can ask to send the article *espresso* (express). Registered mail is *raccomandato* and insured mail (for valuable items) is *assicurato*. If you want something to reach its destination quickly, use Express Mail Service (EMS), also known as CAI Post. A parcel weighing one kg will cost approximately L40,000 within Europe, L66,000 to the USA and Canada, and L95,000 to Australia and New Zealand. It will take four to eight days for a letter or parcel to reach Australia and two to four days to reach the USA. Ask at post offices for addresses of EMS outlets. The international courier DHL operates in Italy and offers a low-cost option for packages weighing up to 500 grams.

Francobolli (stamps) are available at authorised tobacconists, but any international

mail has to be weighed, so it is best to use the post office.

Fax & Telegraph Public fax services are available at large post offices, otherwise use one of the many private services. Telecom is introducing public fax telephones, although they are still few and far between. Telegrams can be sent from any post office.

Telephone

Rates, particularly for long-distance calls, are among the highest in Europe. Travellers from countries which offer direct dialling services paid for at home country rates (such as AT&T in the USA and Telecom in Australia) should take advantage of them. Local and long distance calls can be made from any public phone, or from a Telecom office in larger towns.

Local calls cost L200 for a few minutes. Most public phones accept only phonecards, however coin-operated phones accept L100, L200 and L500 coins. You can buy L5000, L10,000 and L15,000 phonecards at tobacconists and newsstands, or from vending machines at Telecom offices.

To call Italy from abroad, dial the international access code, ☎ 39 (the country code for Italy), the area code (dropping the initial zero) and the number. Important area codes include: ☎ 06 (Rome), ☎ 02 (Milan), ☎ 055 (Florence), ☎ 081 (Naples), ☎ 070 (Cagliari) and ☎ 091 (Palermo).

To make a reverse-charges (collect) call from a public telephone, dial ☎ 170. For calls to European countries, dial ☎ 15. All operators speak English. Otherwise, you can direct dial an operator in your own country and ask to make your collect call. Numbers for this service include: Australia (☎ 172 10 61), Canada (☎ 172 10 01), New Zealand (☎ 172 10 64), UK (☎ 172 10 44), and USA (through AT&T ☎ 172 10 11).

Receiving Mail

The Italian version of poste restante is fermo posta and is usually reliable. Tell friends and relatives to write your surname in block letters. It often happens that mail is filed under the first letter of your first name, instead of your surname, so ask staff to check under both letters.

512 Italy – Facts for the Visitor

E-mail
There are Internet cafés in Rome, where you can rent time on a PC and surf the Net or send messages to friends (see under Rome Entertainment).

NEWSPAPERS & MAGAZINES
The major English-language newspapers available in Italy are the *Herald Tribune*, an international newspaper available Monday to Saturday, and the *European* (available Friday). The major English newspapers, including the *Guardian*, *The Times* and the *Telegraph*, are sent from London, so outside major cities such as Rome, Milan and Venice, they are generally a few days old. *Time* magazine, *Newsweek* and the *Economist* are available weekly. The French newspaper *Le Monde* is also widely available.

RADIO & TV
At the time of writing, the Telemontecarlo (TMC) station broadcast CNN live from about 3 to 7.30 am. On channel 41, known as Autovox, the American PBS McNeill Lehrer News Hour was broadcast nightly at around 8 pm. Vatican Radio (526 on the AM dial or 93.3 and 105 on FM) broadcasts the news in English at 7 and 8.30 am, 6.15 and 9.50 pm. Pick up a pamphlet at the Vatican tourist office for more information.

PHOTOGRAPHY & VIDEO
A roll of normal Kodak film (36 exposures, 100 ASA) costs around L8000. It costs around L18,000 to have 36 exposures developed and L12,000 for 24 exposures. There are many outlets which provide cheap developing services, but beware of poor quality. A roll of 36 slides costs L10,000, and L7000 for processing. Tapes for video cameras are often available at film processing outlets, otherwise you can buy them at stores selling electrical goods.

TIME
Italy is one hour ahead of GMT/UTC, two hours ahead during summer. Daylight-saving time starts on the last Sunday in March, when clocks are put forward an hour. Clocks are put back an hour on the last Sunday in September. Remember to make allowances for daylight-saving time in your own country. Note that Italy operates on a 24-hour clock.

When it's noon in Rome, it's 11 pm in Auckland, 11 am in London, 6 am in New York, 3 am in San Francisco and 9 pm in Sydney. European cities such as Paris, Munich, Berlin, Vienna and Madrid are on the same time as Italy. Athens, Cairo and Tel Aviv are one hour ahead.

ELECTRICITY
The electric current in Italy is 220V, 50 Hz, but make a point of checking with your hotel management because in some areas, including parts of Rome, 125V is still used. Power points have two or three holes but do not have their own switches, while the plugs have two or three corresponding round pins.

WEIGHTS & MEASURES
Italy uses the metric system. Basic terms for weight include: *un etto* (100 grams) and *un chilo* (one kg). Note that Italians indicate decimals with commas and thousands with points.

LAUNDRY
The best place to wash your clothes is in your hotel room. Most laundries in Italy charge by the kg and do the laundry themselves, which makes it an expensive proposition. In some of the larger towns, particularly where there are universities, you can find laundries with coin-operated machines, but a load will still cost around L8000.

TOILETS
You'll find public toilets in locations such as train stations, service stations on the autostrade, and in department stores. Bars are obliged to have a toilet, but you might need to buy a coffee before they'll permit you to use it. Coin-operated, self-cleaning public toilets are being installed throughout the country, but they are still pretty rare.

HEALTH
Residents of EU countries, including the UK, are covered for emergency medical treatment in Italy on presentation of an E111 form (see the Facts for the Visitor chapter at the start of this book). Australia has a reciprocal arrangement with Italy whereby Australian citizens have access to free emergency medical services. Medicare publishes a brochure with the

details. The USA, New Zealand and Canada do not have reciprocal health care arrangements with Italy.

Travellers should seriously consider taking out a travel insurance policy which covers health care, in order to have greater flexibility in deciding where and how you are treated. The quality of public hospital care in Italy can vary dramatically. Basically, the further north you travel, the better the standard of care.

For emergency treatment, go straight to the *pronto soccorso* (casualty section) of a public hospital, where you can also get emergency dental treatment. Your own doctor and dentist may be able to give you some recommendations or referrals before you leave your country. Otherwise, embassies can usually be of assistance.

WOMEN TRAVELLERS

Italy is not a dangerous country for women, but women travelling alone will often find themselves plagued by unwanted attention from men. Most of the attention falls into the nuisance/harassment category and it is best to simply to ignore the catcalls, hisses and whistles. However, women on their own should use common sense. Avoid walking alone in dark and deserted streets and look for centrally located hotels which are within easy walking distance of places where you can eat at night.

Women travelling alone should be particularly careful in the south, Sicily, and Sardinia, especially in Naples, Palermo, Brindisi and Bari. Women should also avoid hitchhiking alone.

GAY & LESBIAN TRAVELLERS

Homosexuality is legal in Italy and generally well tolerated in major cities – although overt displays of affection might get a negative response in smaller towns and villages. National gay organisations include Arci Gay for men; ☎ 051-43 67 00) and ARCI Cordinamento Donne (for women; ☎ 06-325 09 1).

DISABLED TRAVELLERS

Italy has only recently started to become conscious of the particular needs of the disabled. The Italian travel agency CIT can advise on hotels which have special facilities. The UK-based Royal Association for Disability and

Rehabilitation (RADAR ☎ 0171-250 3222) publishes a useful guide called *Holidays & Travel Abroad; A Guide for Disabled People*.

TRAVEL WITH CHILDREN

Don't try to pack too much into the time available and make sure activities include the kids. Involve older kids in the planning of the trip and be sure to take time out to let the little ones play – keep an eye out for playgrounds. *Farmacie* (chemists) in Italy sell baby formula and sterilising solutions. Disposable nappies are widely available in supermarkets and chemists. Fresh cow's milk is found in bars bearing the *latteria* sign.

DANGERS & ANNOYANCES

Theft is the main problem for travellers in Italy. Thieves and pickpockets operate in most major cities, particularly in Rome, Florence and Milan. Watch out for groups of dishevelled-looking women and children. They generally work in groups of four or five and carry paper or cardboard which they use to distract your attention while they swarm around and rifle through your pockets and bag. Never underestimate their skill – they are lightning fast and very adept. The best way to avoid being robbed is to wear a money belt. Never carry a purse or wallet in your pockets and hold on tight to your bag. Pickpockets operate in crowded areas, such as markets and on buses. Motorcycle bandits are particularly active in Rome, Naples, Palermo and Syracuse. If you are using a shoulder bag, make sure that you wear the strap across your body and have the bag on the side away from the road.

Never leave valuables in a parked car – in fact, try not to leave anything in the car if you can help it. It is a good idea to park your car in a supervised car park if you are leaving it for any amount of time. Car theft is a major problem in Rome and Naples. Throughout Italy you can call police (☎ 113) or carabinieri (☎ 112) in an emergency.

BUSINESS HOURS

Business hours can vary from city to city, but generally shops and businesses are open Monday to Saturday from 8.30 am to 1 pm and from 5 to 7.30 pm. Banks are generally open Monday to Friday from 8.30 am to 1.30 pm and from 2.30 to 4.30 pm, but hours vary between banks and cities. Public offices are usually open Monday to Saturday from 8 am to 2 pm, although in major cities some open in the afternoon. Large post offices are open Monday to Saturday from 8 am to 6 or 7 pm. Most museums close on Monday, and restaurants and bars are required to close for one day each week. All food outlets close on Sundays and one weekday afternoon, which varies from town to town.

PUBLIC HOLIDAYS & SPECIAL EVENTS

National public holidays include: 6 January (Epiphany); Easter Monday; 25 April (Liberation Day); 1 May (Labour Day); 15 August (ferragosto, or the Feast of the Assumption); 1 November (All Saints' Day); 8 December (the Feast of the Immaculate Conception); 25 December (Christmas Day); and 26 December (the Feast of St Stephen).

Individual towns also have public holidays to celebrate the feasts of their patron saints. Some of these are the Feast of St Mark in Venice on 25 April; the Feast of St John the Baptist on 24 June in Florence, Genoa and Turin; the Feast of St Peter and St Paul in Rome on 29 June; the Feast of St Januarius in Naples on 19 September; and the Feast of St Ambrose in Milan on 7 December.

Annual events in Italy worth keeping in mind include:

Carnevale
  During the 10 days before Ash Wednesday, many towns stage carnivals. The one held in Venice is the best known, but there are also others, including at Viareggio in Liguria and Ivrea near Turin, where they hold the only carnival in the world which follows a script.
Holy Week (the week before Easter)
  There are important festivals during this week everywhere in Italy, in particular the colourful and sombre traditional festivals of Sicily. In Assisi the rituals of Holy Week attract thousands of pilgrims.
Scoppio del Carro (Explosion of the Cart)
  This colourful event held in Florence in Piazza del Duomo on Easter Sunday features the explosion of a cart full of fireworks and dates back to the Crusades. If all goes well, it is seen as a good omen for the city.
Corso dei Ceri
  One of the strangest festivals in Italy, this is held in Gubbio (Umbria) on 15 May, and features a race run by men carrying enormous wooden constructions called ceri, in honour of the town's patron saint, Sant'Ubaldo.

Il Palio
  On 2 July and on 16 August, Siena stages this extraordinary horse race in the town's main piazza.

ACTIVITIES

If the churches, museums, galleries and sightseeing are not sufficient to occupy your time in Italy, there are various options if you want to get off the main tourist routes or have specific interests.

Hiking

It is possible to go on organised treks in Italy but if you want to go it alone you will find that trails are well marked and there are plenty of refuges, especially in the Alps. The Dolomites in particular provide spectacular walking/trekking opportunities. There are also well-marked trails and refuges in the Alpi Apuane in Tuscany and in parts of the Appennines. In Sardinia the rugged landscape offers some spectacular hikes, particularly in the eastern mountain ranges, such as Gennargentu, and the gorges near Dorgali (see the Sardinia section for more details).

Skiing

The numerous excellent ski resorts in the Alps and the Apennines usually offer good conditions from December to April (see the Alps section).

Cycling

This is a good option if you can't afford a car but want to see the more isolated parts of the country. Classic cycling areas include Tuscany and Umbria. A bicycle would be particularly useful in Sardinia to explore the coast between Alghero and Bosa and the area around Dorgali (see the section on Sardinia).

In the south, try cycling along the coast of Apulia, starting from Lecce and continuing down the coast of Salento Province to the tip of the heel, and then up to Gallipoli.

COURSES

There are numerous private schools which offer Italian language courses, particularly in Rome, Florence and Siena (see under these cities for more details), but the cheapest option is to study at the University for Foreigners in Perugia. The average cost of a course in Florence is around L800,000 a month, whereas in

Perugia it costs L260,000 a month. Schools in Florence and Rome also offer courses in art, sculpture, architecture and cooking.

Italian cultural institutes and embassies in your country will provide information on schools and courses as well as enrolment forms. The university in Perugia and all private schools can arrange accommodation (see under Perugia for further information).

WORK

It is illegal for non-EU citizens to work in Italy without a work permit, but trying to obtain one is extremely difficult. EU citizens are allowed to work in Italy. After finding a job they must go to the questura with a letter promising employment and can then obtain a work permit and permesso di soggiorno for up to two years. For citizens of other countries it is not so simple. You must have a promise of a job which cannot be filled by an Italian or citizens of EU countries, and must apply for the visa in your country of nationality. A type of amnesty in early 1996, when the government gave illegal workers the opportunity to become legitimate, is expected to mean that it will become more difficult to find work which has in the past usually been done by people without permits, such as teaching English in language schools.

Traditionally, the main legal employment for foreigners is to teach English, but even with full qualifications an American, Australian, Canadian or New Zealander will find it difficult to secure a permanent position. Foreign visitors can still find 'black economy' work in bars and restaurants, or as babysitters and housekeepers. Most people get started by placing or responding to advertisements in local publications such as *Wanted in Rome*, or *Secondomano* in Milan. Another option is au pair work. A useful guide is *The Au Pair and Nanny's Guide to Working Abroad* by S Griffith & S Legg. Also see *Work Your Way Around the World* by Susan Griffith.

If you are looking to work legally in Italy for an extended period, you should seek information from the Italian embassy in your country.

ACCOMMODATION

Prices are intended as a guide only. There is generally a fair degree of fluctuation throughout the country, depending on the season.

Prices usually rise by 5% to 10% each year, although sometimes they remain fixed for years, or even drop.

Camping

Facilities throughout Italy are usually reasonable and vary from major complexes with swimming pools, tennis courts and restaurants, to simple camping grounds. Average prices are around L8000 per person and L10,000 or more for a site. Lists of camping grounds in and near major cities are usually available at tourist information offices.

The Touring Club Italiano (TIC) publishes an annual book on all camping sites in Italy, *Campeggi e Villaggi Turistici in Italia* (L22,000), and the Istituto Geografico de Agostini publishes the annual *Guida di Campeggi in Europa* (L20,000), available in major bookshops in Italy. Free camping is forbidden in many of the more beautiful parts of Italy, although the authorities pay less attention in the off season.

Hostels

Hostels in Italy are called *ostelli per la gioventù* and are run by the Associazione Italiana Alberghi per la Gioventù (AIG), which is affiliated with Hostelling International (HI). A HI membership card is not always required, but it is recommended that you have one. Membership cards can be purchased at major hostels, from student and youth travel centre (CTS) offices and from AIG offices throughout Italy. Pick up a list of all hostels in Italy, with details of prices, locations etc, from the AIG office (☎ 06-487 11 52) in Rome, Via Cavour 44.

Many Italian hostels are located in castles and old villas, most have bars and the cost per night often includes breakfast. Many also provide dinner, usually for around L12,000. Prices, including breakfast, range from L15,000 to L23,000. Closing times vary, but are usually from 9 am to 3 or 5 pm and curfews are around midnight. Men and women are often segregated, although some hostels have family accommodation.

Pensioni & Hotels

Establishments are required to notify local tourist boards of prices for the coming year and by law must then adhere to those prices (although they do have two legal opportunities each year to increase charges). If tourists believe they are being overcharged they can make a complaint to the local tourist office. The best advice is to confirm hotel charges before you put your bags down, since many proprietors employ various methods of bill padding. These include charges for showers (usually around L2000), a compulsory breakfast (up to L14,000 in the high season) and compulsory half or full board, although this can often be a good deal in some towns.

The cheapest way to stay in a hotel or pensione is to share a room with two or more people: the cost is usually no more than 15% of the cost of a double room for each additional person. Single rooms are uniformly expensive in Italy (from around L30,000) and quite a number of establishments do not even bother to cater for the single traveller.

There is often no difference between an establishment that calls itself a pensione and one that calls itself an *albergo* (hotel); in fact, some use both titles. *Locande* (similar to pensioni) and *alloggi*, sometimes also known as *affittacamere*, are generally cheaper, but not always. Tourist offices have booklets listing all pensioni and hotels, including prices, and lists of locande and affittacamere.

Rental Accommodation

Finding rental accommodation in the major cities can be difficult and time-consuming and you will often find the cost prohibitive, especially in Rome, Florence, Milan and Venice. For details on rental agencies, refer to the individual city chapters. If you are planning to study in an Italian city, the school or university will help you to find rental accommodation, or a room in the house of a family. In major resort areas, such as the Aeolian Islands and other parts of Sicily, and in the Alps, rental accommodation is reasonably priced and readily available. You can obtain information from local tourist offices, or from specialist travel agencies in your own country.

One organisation which publishes booklets on villas and houses in Tuscany, Umbria, Veneto, Sicily and Rome is Cuendet. Write to Signora N Cuendet, Località Il Cereto/Strove, 53035, Monteriggioni, Siena (☎ 0577-30 10 12; fax 0577-30 11 49) and ask for a catalogue

(US$15). Prices, however, are expensive. CI offices throughout the world also have lists of villas and apartments for rent in Italy.

Agriturismo

This is basically a farm holiday and is becoming increasingly popular in Italy. Traditionally the idea was that families rented out rooms in their farmhouses. However, the more common type of establishment these days is a restaurant/small hotel. All establishments are working farms and you will usually be able to sample the local produce. Recommended areas where you can try this type of holiday are Tuscany, Umbria and Trentino-Alto Adige. Information is available from local tourist offices.

For detailed information on all facilities in Italy contact Agriturist (☎ 06-6 85 21), Corso Vittorio Emanuele 89, 00186 Rome. It publishes a book listing establishments throughout Italy (L35,000), which is available at their office and in selected bookshops.

Religious Institutions

These institutions offer accommodation in most major cities. The standard is usually good, but prices are no longer low. You can expect to pay about the same as for a one-star hotel, if not more. Information about the various institutions is available at all tourist offices, or you can contact the archdiocese in your city.

Refuges

Before you go hiking in any part of Italy, obtain information about refuges from the local tourist offices. Some refuges have private rooms, but many offer dorm-style accommodation, particularly those which are more isolated. Average prices are L20,000 per person for B&B. A meal costs around the same as at a trattoria. The locations of refuges are marked on good hiking maps and most open only from July to September.

FOOD

Eating is one of life's great pleasures for Italians. Be adventurous and never be intimidated by eccentric waiters or indecipherable menus and you will find yourself agreeing with the locals, who believe that nowhere in the world is the food as good as in Italy and, more specifically, in their own town.

Cooking styles vary notably from region to region and significantly between the north and south. In the north the food is rich and often creamy, and the regional specialities of Emilia-Romagna, including *spaghetti bolognese* (known in Italy as *spaghetti al ragù*), *tortellini*, and *mortadella* are perhaps the best known throughout the world.

In Tuscany and Umbria the locals use a lot of olive oil and herbs, and regional specialities are noted for their simplicity, fine flavour and the use of fresh produce. As you go further south the food becomes hotter and spicier and the *dolci* (cakes and pastries) sweeter and richer. Don't miss the experience of eating a pizza in Naples and don't leave Sicily without trying their *dolce di mandorle* (almond pastries), or the rich and very sweet ricotta cake known as *cassata*.

Vegetarians will have no problems eating in Italy. Though there are very few restaurants devoted to them (and these few tend to be expensive and on the trendy side), vegetable dishes are a staple of the Italian diet. Most eating establishments serve a selection of *contorni* (vegetables prepared in a variety of ways), and the further south you go, the more excellent vegetable dishes you'll find.

Self-Catering

For a light lunch, or a snack, most bars serve *panini* (sandwiches), and there are numerous outlets where you can buy pizza by the slice. Another option is to go to one of the many *alimentari* (grocery stores) and ask them to make a panino with the filling of your choice. At a *pasticceria* you can buy pastries, cakes and biscuits.

If you have access to cooking facilities, you can buy fruit and vegetables at open markets (see the individual towns for information), and salami, cheese and wine at alimentari or *salumerie* (a cross between a grocery store and a delicatessen). Fresh bread is available at a *forno* or *panetteria*.

Restaurants

Eating establishments are divided into several categories. A *tavola calda* (literally hot table) usually offers cheap, pre-prepared meat, pasta and vegetable dishes in a self-service style. A *rosticceria* usually offers cooked meats, but also often has a larger selection of takeaway food. A pizzeria will of course serve pizza, but usually also a full menu. An *osteria* is likely to be either a wine bar offering a small selection of dishes, or a small trattoria. A trattoria is basically a cheaper version of a *ristorante* (restaurant). The problem is that many of the establishments that are in fact ristoranti call themselves trattorias and vice versa for reasons best known to themselves. It is best to check the menu, which is usually posted by the door, for prices.

Don't panic if you find yourself in a trattoria which has no printed menu, as they are often the ones which offer the best and most authentic food and have menus which change daily according to the availability of fresh produce. Just hope that the waiter will patiently explain the dishes and tell you how much they cost.

Most eating establishments charge a *coperto* (cover charge) of around L1000 to L3000, and a *servizio* (service charge) of 10 to 15%. Restaurants are usually open for lunch from 12.30 to 3 pm, but will rarely take orders after 2 pm. In the evening, opening hours vary from north to south. In the north they eat dinner earlier, usually from 7.30 pm, but in Sicily you will be hard-pressed to find a restaurant open before 8 pm. Note that very few restaurants stay open after 11.30 pm.

Italians rarely eat a sit-down breakfast. Their custom is to drink a cappuccino, usually *tiepido* (lukewarm), and eat a *brioche*, *cornetto*, or other type of pastry while standing at a bar. Lunch is the main meal of the day, and shops and businesses close for three to four hours each afternoon to accommodate the meal and the siesta which follows.

A full meal will consist of an antipasto, which can vary from *bruschetta*, a type of garlic bread with various toppings, to fried vegetables, or *prosciutto e melone* (ham wrapped around melon). Next comes the *primo piatto*, a pasta dish or risotto, followed by the *secondo piatto* of meat or fish. Italians often then eat an *insalata* (salad) or contorni and round off the meal with dolci and caffè, often at a bar on the way home or back to work.

Numerous restaurants offer tourist menus, at an average price of L18,000 to L24,000. Generally the food is of a reasonable standard, but choices will be limited and you can usually get away with paying less if you want only pasta, salad and wine.

After lunch and dinner, head for the nearest *gelateria* to round off the meal with some excellent Italian *gelati* (ice cream), followed by a *digestivo* (liqueur) at a bar.

Remember that as soon as you sit down in Italy, prices go up considerably. A cappuccino at the bar will cost around L1500, but if you sit down, you will pay anything from L2500 to L5000 or more, especially in touristy areas such as Piazza San Marco in Venice (L10,000) and the Spanish Steps in Rome.

DRINKS

Italian wine is justifiably world-famous. Few Italians can live without it, and even fewer abuse it, generally drinking wine only with meals. Going out for a drink is still considered unusual in Italy. Fortunately, wine is reasonably priced so you will rarely pay more than L10,000 for a bottle of drinkable wine and as little as L5000 will still buy OK quality. The styles of wine vary throughout the country, so make a point of sampling the local produce in your travels. Try the famous *chianti* in Tuscany, but also the *vernaccia* of San Gimignano, the *soave* in Verona and the *valpolicella* around Venice. Orvieto's wines are excellent, as are those from Trentino; in Rome try the local *frascati*.

Italians drink wine with lunch and dinner, but prefer to drink beer with pizza, which means that many pizzerias do not serve wine. Beer is known as *birra* and the cheapest local variety is *Peroni*, but a wide range of imported beers are also available, either in bars or at a *birrerria* or pub.

ENTERTAINMENT

Whatever your tastes, there should be some form of entertainment in Italy to keep you amused, from the national obsession, *il calcio* (soccer), to the opera, theatre, classical music concerts, rock concerts and traditional festivals. Major entertainment festivals are also held, such as the Festival of Two Worlds in June/July at Spoleto, Umbria Jazz in Perugia in July, and the Venice Biennale every odd-numbered year. Operas are performed in Verona and Rome throughout summer (for details see the Entertainment sections under both cities) and at various times of the year throughout the country, notably at the opera houses in Milan and Rome.

The main theatre season is during winter, and classical music concerts are generally performed throughout the year. Nightclubs, indoor bars and discotheques are more popular during winter and many close down for the summer months. For up-to-date information on entertainment in each city, buy the local newspaper. Tourist offices will also provide information on important events, festivals performances and concerts.

SPECTATOR SPORT

Soccer *(calcio)* is the national passion and there are stadiums in all the major towns. If you'd rather watch a game than visit a Roman ruin, check newspapers for details of who's playing where.

THINGS TO BUY

Italy is synonymous with elegant, fashionable and high-quality clothing. The problem is that most of the clothes are very expensive. However, if you can manage to be in the country during the summer sales in July and August and the winter sales in December and January, you can pick up incredible bargains.

Italy is renowned for the quality of its leather goods, so plan to stock up on bags, wallets, purses, belts and gloves. At markets such as Porta Portese in Rome and the San Lorenzo leather market in Florence you can find some remarkable bargains – but check carefully for quality.

Other items of interest are Venetian glass, and the great diversity of ceramics produced throughout Italy, notably on the Amalfi Coast at Deruta and Orvieto in Umbria, and in Sicily. The beautiful Florentine paper goods also make great gifts and are reasonably priced.

Getting There & Away

AIR

Although paying full fare to travel by plane in Europe is expensive, there are various discount options, including cut-price fares for students and people aged under 25 or 26 (depending on the airline). There are also stand-by fares which are usually around 60% of the full fare. Several airlines, including Alitalia, Qantas and

Air France, offer cut-rate fares on legs of international flights between European cities. These are usually the cheapest fares available, but the catch is that they are usually during the night or very early in the morning, and the days on which you can fly are severely restricted. Some examples of cheap one-way fares at the time of writing were: Rome-Paris L167,000 (L278,000 return); Rome-London L177,000 (L295,000 return); Rome-Amsterdam L250,000 (L340,000 return).

Another option is to travel on charter flights. There are several companies throughout Europe which operate these, and fares are usually cheaper than for normal scheduled flights. Italy Sky Shuttle (☎ 0181-748 1333), part of the Air Travel Group, 227 Shepherd's Bush Rd, London W6 7AS, specialises in charter flights, but also offers scheduled flights.

Look in the classified pages of the London Sunday newspapers for information on other cheap flights. Campus Travel (☎ 0171-730 3402), 52 Grosvenor Gardens, SW1W OAG, and STA Travel (☎ 0171-939 3232), 74 Old Brompton Rd, London SW7, both offer reasonably cheap fares. Within Italy, information on discount fares is available from CTS and Sestante CIT offices (see the earlier Useful Organisations section).

LAND
If you are travelling by bus, train or car to Italy, it will be necessary to cross various borders, so remember to check whether you require visas for those countries before leaving home.

Bus
Eurolines is the main international carrier in Europe, with representatives in Italy and throughout the continent. Its head office (☎ 0171-730 0202), is at 52 Grosvenor Gardens, Victoria, London SW1, and it has representatives in Italy and throughout Europe. The main bus company operating this service in Italy is Lazzi: in Florence (☎ 055-21 51 55), Piazza Adua; and Rome (☎ 06-884 08 40), Via Tagliamento 27b. Buses leave from Rome, Florence, Milan, Turin, Venice and Naples, as well as numerous other Italian towns, for major cities throughout Europe including London, Paris, Barcelona, Amsterdam, Vienna, Prague, Athens and Istanbul. A guide to the cost of one-way tickets is Rome-Paris L162,000;

Rome-London L217,000; and Rome-Barcelona L180,000.

Train
Eurocity (EC) trains run from major destinations throughout Europe direct to major Italian cities. On overnight hauls you can book a *cuccetta* (known outside Italy as a *couchette* or sleeping berth).

Travellers aged under 26 can take advantage of Billet International de Jeunesse tickets (BIJ, also known in Italy as BIGE), which can cut fares by up to 50%. They are sold at Transalpino offices at most train stations and at CTS and Sestante CIT offices in Italy, Europe and overseas. Examples of one-way fares include: Rome-Amsterdam L315,100 and Rome-London L280,700.

Examples of normal one-way 2nd-class fares are Rome-London L285,000; and Rome-Amsterdam L325,400. Throughout Europe and in Italy it is worth paying extra for a couchette on night trains. A couchette from Rome to Paris is an extra L24,500.

You can book tickets at train stations or at CTS, Sestante CIT and most other travel agency offices. Eurocity trains, like the internal intercity trains, carry a supplement (see Costs & Reservations in the Getting Around section).

Car & Motorcycle
Travelling with your own vehicle certainly gives you more flexibility. The drawbacks in Italy are that cars can be inconvenient in larger cities where you'll have to deal with heavy traffic, parking problems and the risk of car theft in some cities. Driving in Italy is expensive once you add up the cost of petrol and toll charges on the autostrade. Foreign tourists driving cars with non-Italian numberplates are entitled to a free breakdown service, including emergency tow-truck service. The service is provided by the Italian Automobile Club (ACI; see Car & Motorcycle in the Getting Around section).

You will need a valid driver's licence from your own country, or an International Driving Permit, as well as proof of ownership (if you are driving your own car) and a Green Card, an internationally recognised proof of insurance, which can be obtained from your insurer.

The main points of entry into Italy are the

Mont Blanc tunnel from France at Chamonix, which connects to the A5 for Turin and Milan; the Grand St Bernard tunnel from Switzerland, which also connects to the A5; and the Brenner Pass from Austria, which connects with the A22 to Bologna. Italy has an excellent autostrada system; the main north-south link is the Autostrada del Sole from Milan to Reggio di Calabria (A1 from Milan to Rome, A2 from Rome to Naples and A3 to Reggio di Calabria).

Hitching

Your best bet is to enquire at hostels throughout Europe, where you can often arrange a lift. Otherwise, follow the same advice as for within Italy and stand, with a sign stating your destination, near the entrance to an autostrada (it is illegal to hitch on the autostrade).

SEA

Ferries connect Italy to Greece, Tunisia, Turkey and Malta. There are also services to Corsica (from Livorno) and Albania (from Trieste, Bari and Ancona). See Getting There & Away under Brindisi (ferries to/from Greece), Ancona (to/from Greece, Albania and Turkey), Venice (to/from Croatia), and Sicily (to/from Malta and Tunisia).

The company Adriatica runs the Albania service, with ferries leaving Trieste and Ancona twice a week for Durrës and three times a week from Bari. You can pick up an Adriatica brochure at many travel agencies. In Bari, contact the agency Agestea (☎ 080-523 58 25) at the Stazione Marittima. In Trieste, contact the agency Agemar (☎ 040-36 32 22), Piazza Duca degli Abruzzi 1a.

LEAVING ITALY

There is a departure tax on international flights, which is built into the cost of your ticket.

Getting Around

AIR

Travelling by plane is expensive within Italy and it makes much better sense to use the efficient and considerably cheaper rail and bus services. The domestic airlines are Alitalia and Meridiana. The main airports are in Rome, Pisa, Milan, Naples, Catania and Cagliari, but there are other, smaller airports throughout Italy. Domestic flights can be booked directly with the airlines or through Sestante CIT, CTS and other travel agencies.

Alitalia offers a range of discounts for students, young people and families (40%), and weekend travel (50%). Another option is Apex fares, limited to certain flights and requiring a minimum two-night stay.

BUS

Bus travel within Italy is provided by numerous companies, and services vary from local routes linking small villages to major intercity connections. It is usually necessary to make reservations only for long trips, such as Rome to Palermo or Brindisi. Otherwise, just arrive early enough to claim a seat.

Buses can be a cheaper and faster way to get around if your destination is not on major rail lines, for instance from Umbria to Rome or Florence, and in the interior areas of Sicily and Sardinia. Some examples of prices for bus travel are Rome-Palermo L70,000; Rome-Siena L22,000; and Rome-Pompeii L25,000.

You can usually get bus timetables from local tourist offices and, if not, staff will be able to point you in the direction of the main bus companies. See Rome's Getting There & Away section for more details.

TRAIN

Travelling by train in Italy is simple, relatively cheap and generally efficient. The Ferrovie dello Stato (FS) is the partially privatised state train system and there are several private railway services throughout the country.

There are several types of trains: *regionale*, which usually stops at all stations and can be very slow; *interregionale*, which runs between the regions; *diretto*, which indicates that you do not need to change trains to reach the final destination; an *espresso*, which stops only at major stations; and an intercity (IC), or Eurocity (EC), which services only the major cities. There is also the new ETR 450, a fast train service between major cities, known as the *pendolino*, which has both 1st and 2nd class.

Costs & Reservations

To travel on the intercity, Eurocity and pendolino trains, you have to pay a *supplemento*, an additional charge determined by the distance you are travelling. For instance, on the intercity train between Florence and Bologna (about 100 km) you will pay a L4900 supplemento. Always check whether the train you are about to catch is an intercity or Eurocity, and pay the supplement before you get on the train, otherwise you will pay extra. It's obligatory to book a seat on the pendolino, since it doesn't carry standing-room passengers. The difference in second-class fares for the pendolino and intercity trains is around L8000 from Rome to Florence, and you arrive half an hour earlier.

There are left-luggage facilities at all major train stations and at other train stations, except for the smallest, throughout Italy. They are usually open seven days a week, 24 hours a day, but if not, they close for only a few hours after midnight.

Discounts

It is not worth buying a Eurail or Inter-Rail pass if you are going to travel only in Italy. The FS offers its own discount passes for travel within the country. These include the Cartaverde for those aged 26 years and under. It costs L40,000, is valid for one year, and entitles you to a 20% discount on all train travel. You can buy a biglietto chilometrico (kilometric ticket), which is valid for two months and allows you to cover 3000 km, with a maximum of 20 trips. It costs L186,000 (2nd class) and you must pay the rapido supplement if you catch an intercity train. Its main attraction is that it can be used by up to five people, either singly or together. Some examples of normal, 2nd-class train fares are: Rome-Florence L24,400 (plus L11,800 supplement); Rome-Naples L17,200 (plus L9700 supplement). A 2nd-class fare on the pendolino from Rome to Florence (less than a 1¾-hour journey) is L45,800.

CAR & MOTORCYCLE

Trains and buses are fine for travelling through most of Italy but, if you want to get off the beaten track, renting a car or motorcycle is a good idea, particularly in Sicily and Sardinia where some of the most interesting and beautiful places are difficult to reach by public transport. The Istituto Geografico de Agostini publishes detailed road maps for all of Italy. Its book entitled *Atlante Stradale Italiano* has road maps as well as town maps. You can also buy individual maps of the regions you plan to visit.

Automobile Club d'Italia (ACI) offers free roadside assistance to tourists driving cars with foreign numberplates (☎ 116). They will also tow your car for free to the nearest garage – you will be up for the cost of repairs.

Roads are generally good throughout the country and there is an excellent system of autostrade (freeways). The main north-south link is the Autostrada del Sole, which extends from Milan to Reggio di Calabria (called the A1 from Milan to Naples and the A3 from Naples to Reggio). The only problem with the autostrade is that they are toll roads. Connecting roads provide access to Italy's major cities from the autostrada system.

Road Rules

Italian traffic, particularly in the cities, can appear extremely chaotic, and people drive at high speed on the autostrade (never remain in the left-hand fast lane longer than is necessary to pass a car).

In Italy, as throughout Continental Europe, people drive on the right-hand side of the road and pass on the left. Unless otherwise indicated, you must give way to cars coming from the right. It is compulsory to wear seat belts if they are fitted to the car (front seat belts on all cars and back seat belts on cars produced after 26 April 1990). Most Italians ignore this requirement and generally wear seat belts only on the autostrade. If caught not wearing your seat belt, you will be required to pay a L50,000 on-the-spot fine.

You don't need a licence to ride a moped under 50 cc, but you should be aged 14 years or over, and a helmet is compulsory up to age 18; you can't carry passengers or ride on the autostrade. To ride a motorcycle or scooter up to 125 cc, you must be at least 16 years old and have a licence (a car licence will do). Helmets are compulsory. Over 125 cc, you need a motorcycle licence and, of course, a helmet.

The limit on blood-alcohol content is 0.08% and random breath tests have now been introduced.

In Rome and Naples you might have difficulty negotiating the extraordinarily chaotic traffic, but remain calm, keep your eyes on the car in front of you and you should be OK. Most roads are well signposted and once you arrive in a city or village, follow the *centro* signs to reach the centre of town. Be extremely careful where you park your car. In the major cities it will almost certainly be towed away and you will pay a heavy fine if you leave it near a sign reading 'Zona di Rimozione' (Removal Zone) and featuring a tow truck.

Some Italian cities, including Rome, Florence, Milan and Turin, have introduced restricted access to motorists (both private and rental cars) in their historical centres. The restrictions, however, do not apply to vehicles with foreign registrations, to allow tourists to reach their hotels. If you are stopped by a traffic police officer, you will need to name the hotel where you are staying and produce a pass (provided by the hotel) if required. Motorcyclists with large bikes may be stopped, but *motorini* (mopeds) and scooters (such as Vespas) are able to enter the zones without any problems.

Speed limits, unless otherwise indicated by local signs, are: on autostrade 130 km/h for cars of 1100 cc or more, 110 km/h for smaller cars and motorcycles under 350 cc; on all main, non-urban highways 100 km/h; on secondary non-urban highways 90km/h; in built-up areas 50 km/h.

Expenses

Petrol prices are high in Italy – around L1800 per litre. Autostrada tolls are also expensive: you will pay around L55,000 for the trip from Rome to Milan. Petrol is called *benzina*, unleaded petrol is *benzina senza piombo* and diesel is *gasolio*. If you are driving a car which uses liquid petroleum gas (LPG), you will need to buy a special guide to service stations which have *gasauto*, also known as GPL. By law these must be located in nonresidential areas and are usually in the country or on city outskirts. The guides are available at service stations selling GPL.

Rental

It is cheaper to organise a rental car before you leave your own country, for instance through some sort of fly/drive deal. Most major firms, including Hertz, Avis and Budget, will arrange this and you simply pick up the vehicle at a nominated point when in Italy. Foreign offices of Sestante CIT can also help to organise car or camper-van rental before you leave home.

You will need to be aged 21 years or over (23 years or over for some companies) to rent a car in Italy, and you will find the deal a lot easier to organise if you have a credit card. You'll find that most firms will accept your standard licence or an International Driving Permit.

At the time of writing, Hertz was offering a special weekend rate which compared well with rates offered by other firms. This was L190,000 for a small car from Friday 9 am to Monday 9 am. The cost for a week was L611,000. Other discounts are also offered to tourists. If you need a baby car seat, call one day ahead to ensure the company has one available. They cost an extra L50,000.

Rental motorcycles are usually mopeds and scooters such as Vespas (50 cc and 125 cc), but it is also possible to rent big touring motorcycles. The cost for a 50-cc Vespa is around L60,000 a day or L300,000 a week. An 800-cc BMW costs L120,000 a day and L800,000 a week. Note that most places require a sizable deposit, sometimes around L300,000, and that you could be responsible for reimbursing part of the value of the vehicle if it is stolen. Always check the fine print in the contract.

Rental agencies are listed under the major cities in this chapter. Most tourist offices have information about where to rent a car or motorcycle, or you can look in the *Yellow Pages* for each town.

Purchase

Car Basically, it is not possible for foreigners to buy a car in Italy, since the law requires that you must be a resident to own and register one. However, if you manage to find a way around this, the average cost of a cheap car is L1,500,000 to L2,500,000, ranging up to around L5,000,000 for a decent second-hand Fiat Uno. The best way to find a car is to look in the classified section of local newspapers in each town or city.

Motorcycle The same laws apply to owning and registering a motorcycle. The cost of a second-hand Vespa ranges from L500,000 to L1,000,000, and a motorino will cost from L200,000 to L1,000,000. Prices for more powerful bikes start at L1,500,000.

BICYCLE

Bikes are available for rent in most Italian towns – the cost ranges from L8000 to L15,000 a day and up to L50,000 a week (see the Getting Around section in each city). But if you are planning to do a lot of cycling, consider buying a bike in Italy; you can buy a decent second-hand bicycle for L200,000. See the Activities section earlier in this chapter for some suggestions on places to cycle. Bikes can travel in the baggage compartment of Italian trains (not on the pendolino, Eurocities or intercities).

HITCHING

It is illegal to hitchhike on Italy's autostrade, but quite acceptable to stand near the entrance to the toll booths. It is not often done in Italy, but Italians are friendly people and you will generally find a lift. Women travelling alone should be extremely cautious about hitchhiking, particularly in the south, Sicily and Sardinia. It is preferable to travel with a companion in these areas. In Rome, go to the Enjoy Rome office (☎ 06-445 1843) at Via Varese 39 for advice.

BOAT

Navi (large ferries) service the islands of Sicily and Sardinia, and *traghetti* (smaller ferries) and *aliscafi* (hydrofoils) service areas such as Elba, the Aeolian Islands, Capri and Ischia. The main embarkation points for Sicily and Sardinia are Genoa, Livorno, Civitavecchia and Naples. In Sicily the main points of arrival are Palermo and Messina, and in Sardinia they are Cagliari, Arbatax, Olbia and Porto Torres. Tirrenia Navigazione is the major company servicing the Mediterranean and it has offices throughout Italy. The FS also operates ferries to Sicily and Sardinia. Further information is provided in the Getting There & Away sections under both islands. Most long-distance services are overnight and all ferries carry vehicles (you can usually take a bicycle free of charge).

LOCAL TRANSPORT

All the major cities have good transport systems, including buses and, in Rome, Milan and Naples, underground railways. In Venice, however, your only options are to get around by boat or on foot. Efficient bus services also operate between neighbouring towns and villages. Tourist offices will provide information on urban public transport systems, including bus routes and maps of the underground railway systems.

Bus

Urban buses are usually frequent and reliable and operate on an honour system. You must buy a ticket beforehand and validate it in the machine on the bus. Tickets generally cost from L1500 to L1800, although most cities offer 24-hour tourist tickets for around L4000 to L6000.

The trend in the larger cities is towards integration of public transport services, which means the same ticket is used for buses, trams and the underground. Tickets are sold at authorised tobacconists, bars and newspaper stands and at ticket booths at bus terminals (for instance, outside Stazione Termini in Rome where most of the major buses stop).

Think twice before travelling without a ticket, as in most cities the army of inspectors has been increased along with fines. In Rome you will be fined L50,000 on the spot if caught without a validated ticket.

Underground

On the underground railways (called the *Metropolitana*) in Rome, Naples and Milan (where they are referred to as the MM), you must buy tickets and validate them before getting on the train.

Taxi

Try to avoid using taxis in Italy, as they are very expensive, and you can usually catch a bus instead. The shortest taxi ride in Rome will cost around L10,000, since the flag fall is L6400. Generally taxis will not stop if you hail them in the street. Instead head for the taxi ranks at train and bus stations or you can telephone for one (radio taxi phone numbers are listed throughout this chapter in the Getting Around sections of the major cities).

ORGANISED TOURS

It is less expensive and more enjoyable to do some research and see the sights independently, but if you are in a hurry or prefer guided tours, go to Sestante CIT or American Express offices. Both offer city and package tours (see under Organised Tours in the major cities for further information). Offices of CIT abroad (see Useful Organisations earlier) can provide information about and organise package tours to Italy.

Rome

'I now realise all the dreams of my youth', wrote Goethe on his arrival in Rome in the winter of 1786. Perhaps Rome today is more chaotic, but certainly no less romantic or fascinating. A phenomenal concentration of history, legend and monuments coexists with an equally phenomenal concentration of people busily going about everyday life. It is easy to pick the tourists because they are the only ones to turn their heads as the bus passes the Colosseum.

Rome had its origins in Etruscan, Latin and Sabine settlements on the Palatine, Esquiline, Quirinal and surrounding hills (archaeological evidence shows that the Palatine settlement was the earliest). It is, however, the legend of Romulus and Remus which has captured the popular imagination. They were the twin sons of Rhea Silvia and the Roman war god Mars, and were raised by a she-wolf after being abandoned on the banks of the Tiber (Tevere). The myth says Romulus killed his brother during a battle over who should govern, and then established the city on the Palatine (Palatino), one of the famous Seven Hills of Rome. Romulus, who established himself as the first king of Rome, disappeared one day, enveloped in a cloud which carried him back to the domain of the gods.

From the legend grew an empire which eventually controlled almost the entire world known to Europeans at the time, an achievement described by a historian of the day as being 'without parallel in human history'.

In Rome there is visible evidence of the two great empires of the Western world: the Roman Empire and the Christian Church. On the one hand there are the forum and the Colosseum, and on the other St Peter's and the Vatican. In between, in almost every piazza, lies history on so many levels that what you actually see is only the tip of the iceberg – a phenomenon exemplified by St Peter's Basilica, which stands on the site of an earlier basilica built by the Emperor Constantine over the necropolis where St Peter was buried.

Realistically, at least a week is probably a reasonable amount of time to explore Rome, but whatever time you devote to the city, put on your walking shoes, buy a good map and plan your time carefully – the city will eventually seem less chaotic and overwhelming than it first appears.

Orientation

Rome is a vast city, but the historical centre is relatively small. Most of the major sights are within walking distance of the central train station, Stazione Termini. It is, for instance, possible to walk from the Colosseum, through the Forum and the Palatine, up to the Spanish Steps and across to the Vatican in one day, though this is hardly recommended even for the most dedicated tourist. One of the great pleasures of Rome is to allow time for wandering through the many beautiful *piazzas* (squares), stopping now and again for a caffè and *paste* (pastries). All the major monuments are to the west of the station area, but make sure you use a map. Although it can be enjoyable to get lost in Rome, it can also be very frustrating and time-consuming.

It can be difficult to plan an itinerary if your time is limited. Some museums and galleries are now open all day, while others close around 1.30 pm – it is a good idea to check. Some of the major monuments which open in the afternoon include the Colosseum, St Peter's Basilica and the Roman Forum (the latter in summer only). Remember that many museums are closed on Monday.

Most new arrivals in Rome will end up at Stazione Termini. It is the terminus for all international and national trains; the main city bus terminus is in Piazza dei Cinquecento, directly in front of the station. Many intercity buses arrive and depart from the Piazzale Tiburtina, in front of the Stazione Tiburtina, accessible from Termini on the Metropolitana Linea B. Get off at Tiburtina.

The main airport is Leonardo da Vinci, at Fiumicino (about half an hour by train or an hour by car from the centre). For more information, see To/From the Airport under the Rome Getting Around section.

If you're arriving in Rome by car, invest in

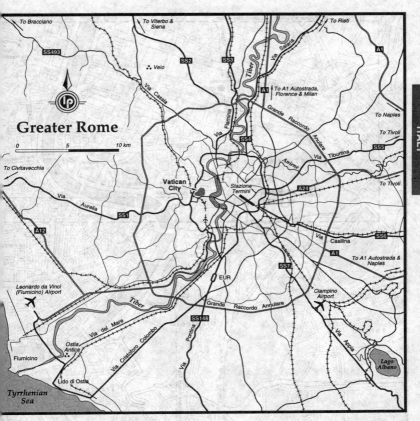

good road map of the city beforehand so as to have an idea of the various routes into the city centre: easy access routes from the Grande Raccordo Anulare (the ring road encircling the city, which is connected to the Autostrada del Sole) include Via Salaria from the north, Via Aurelia from the north-west and Via Cristoforo Colombo from the south. Normal traffic is not permitted into the city centre, but tourists are allowed to drive to their hotels.

The majority of cheap hotels and pensioni are concentrated around Stazione Termini, but if you are prepared to go the extra distance, it is more expensive but definitely more enjoyable to stay closer to the centre. The area

around the station, particularly to the south-west, is unpleasant, seedy and can be dangerous at night, especially for women, but it is the most popular area for budget travellers.

Invest L5000 in the street map and bus guide simply entitled *Roma*, with a red-and-blue cover, which is published by Editrice Lozzi in Rome; it is available at any newsstand in Stazione Termini. It lists all streets, with map references, as well as all bus routes.

Information

Tourist Offices There is a tourist information office (EPT) at Stazione Termini, open

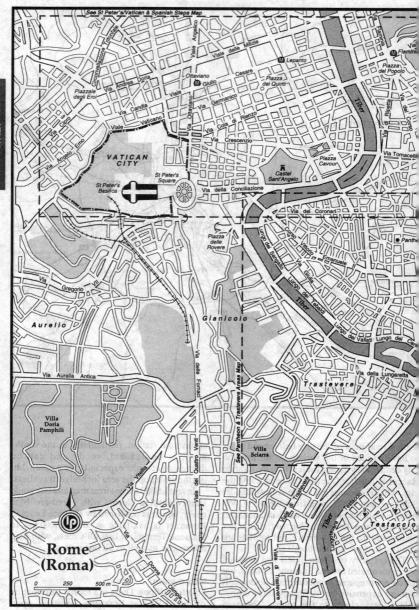

See St Peter's/Vatican & Spanish Steps Map

Circonvallazione Trionfale

Viale Angelico

Viale delle Milizie

Via Flaminia

Flaminio

Piazza del Popolo

Lepanto

Ottaviano

Giulio Cesare

Piazza dei Quiriti

Via Andrea Doria

Piazzale degli Eroi

Viale Vaticano

Via Candia

Via Ottaviano

Via Germanico

Via Cola di Rienzo

Via Crescenzio

Via Cipro

Via Angelo Emo

VATICAN CITY

St Peter's Square

St Peter's Basilica

Piazza Cavour

Castel Sant'Angelo

Via della Conciliazione

Via Tomacelli

Via dei Coronari

Piazza delle Rovere

Corso Vittorio Emanuele

Panth

Lungo del Sangallo

Via Giulia

Lungo dei Tebaldi

Lungo dei Vallati

Tiber

Lungo dei Cen

Gianicolo

Aurelio

Via Gregorio VII

Via della Lungaretta

Trastevere

Via Aurelia Antica

Via delle Fornaci

Villa Doria Pamphili

See Pantheon & Trastevere Areas Map

Villa Sciarra

Via del Quattro Venti

Via Vitellia

Viale del Trastevere

Tiber

Lungotevere Testaccio

Testaccio

Rome (Roma)

0   250   500 m

Viale di Trastevere

Via Donna Olimpia

Villa
Borghese

To Australian Embassy &
Consulate & Canadian
Embassy & Consulate

Villa
Torlonia

Corso
d'Italia

Piazza
Fiume

Via Nomentana

Viale Regina Margherita

Via Boncompagni

Via del Policlinico

Viale del Policlinico

Viale Regina Elena

See Stazione Termini Area Map

Via Castro Pretorio

Hospital

Viale dell'Università

della Trinità dei Monti

Spagna

Via Sistina

Via Barberini

Via IX Settembre

Piazza
Barberini

Via del Tritone

Trevi Fountain

Piazza
della
Repubblica

Piazza
Venezia

Repubblica

Stazione
Termini

Termini

Via Marsala

Via Pretoriano

Via dei
Reti

Via Nazionale

Basilica di
Santa Maria
Maggiore

Via Cavour

Via C. Alberto

Via Tiburtina

Via dei Sardi

Cavour

Via Merulana

Vittorio
Piazza V
Emanuele

Roman
Forum

Viale del Monte Oppio

Colosseo

Piazza
di Porta
Maggiore

Colosseum

Via Labicana

Manzoni

Viale Manzoni

Via Filippo

Palatine
Hill

Via S. Gregorio

Piazza
della
Navicella

Piazza
San Giovanni
in Laterano

Piazza di
Porta San
Giovanni

San Giovanni

Celian
Hill

Villa
Cellimontana

Via Appia Nuova

Via dei Cerchi

Circo
Massimo

Via Aventino

Via delle Terme di Caracalla

Re di Roma

ventino

Via Piramide

Viale delle Terme di Caracalla

Via Etruria

Piramide

To the Catacombs
of San Callisto &
the Appian Way

1	Alien
2	British Embassy & Consulate
3	Formula 1
4	Hotel Il Castello
5	Basilica di San Giovanni in Laterano
6	Baths of Caracalla
7	Il Canestro
8	Pizzeria Remo
9	Augustarello

Monday to Saturday from 9 am to 7 pm. It is opposite platform No 4.

The main EPT office (☎ 48 89 92 53) is at Via Parigi 11 and is open from 8.15 am to 7 pm Monday to Saturday. Walk north-west from Stazione Termini, through Piazza della Repubblica. Via Parigi runs to the right from the top of the piazza, about a five-minute walk from the station. It has information on hotels and museum opening hours and entrance fees. The office also has information on summer festivals and concert seasons. Staff can also provide information about provincial and intercity bus services, but you need to be specific about where and when you want to go (see the Getting Around section for further information).

It's likely that you'll get all the information and assistance you need at Enjoy Rome (☎ 445 18 43; fax 445 07 34), Via Varese 39 (a few minutes north-east of the station). This is a privately run tourist office which offers a free hotel reservation service. Staff can also organise alternative accommodation such as apartments. They have extensive up-to-date information about Rome. The owners speak English and are very keen to help. The office is open Monday to Friday from 8.30 am to 1 pm and 3.30 to 6 pm and Saturday from 8.30 am to 1 pm.

Money Banks are open Monday to Friday from 8.30 am to 1.30 pm and usually from 2.45 to 3.45 pm. You will find a bank and exchange offices at Stazione Termini. There is also an exchange office (Banco di Santo Spirito) at Fiumicino airport, to your right as you exit from the customs area.

Numerous other exchange offices are scattered throughout the city, including American Express in Piazza di Spagna and Thomas Cook in Piazza della Repubblica and several other locations.

Otherwise, go to any bank in the city centre. The Banca Commerciale Italiana, Piazza Venezia, is reliable for receiving money transfers and will give cash advances on both Visa and MasterCard. Credit cards can also be used in automatic teller machines (ATMs), known as *bancomats*, to obtain cash 24 hours a day throughout Italy. You'll need to get a PIN number from your bank.

Post & Communications The main post office is at Piazza San Silvestro 19, just off Via del Tritone, and is open Monday to Friday from 8.30 am to 8 pm and Saturday from 8.30 am to noon. Fermo posta (the Italian version of poste restante) is available here. You can send telegrams from the office next door (open 24 hours).

The Vatican post office, in Piazza San Pietro (St Peter's Square), is open Monday to Friday from 8.30 am to 7 pm and Saturday to 6 pm. The service is supposedly faster and more reliable, but there's no fermo posta. The postcode for central Rome is 00100, although for fermo posta at the main post office it is 00186.

There is a Telecom office at Stazione Termini, from where you can make international calls direct or through an operator. Another office is near the station, in Via San Martino della Battaglia opposite the Pensione Lachea. International calls can easily be made with a phonecard from any public telephone. Phonecards can be purchased at tobacconists and newspaper stands.

Rome's telephone code is ☎ 06.

At Explorer Café (☎ 32 41 17 57), Via dei Gracchi 83/85 (near the Vatican), you can pay by the hour (about L12,000) to use their computers to have access to an e-mail service, the WWW and CD-Rom and Multi Media libraries. Another Internet café is Music All (☎ 784 29 33), Via Manlio Torquato 21 (near the Metro stop in Largo Colli Albani).

A new Internet centre opened in Rome in mid-1996. Itaca Multimedia (☎ 686 14 64; fax 689 60 96) at Via della Fosse di Castello 8, allows you to access Internet services, and send and receive e-mail messages. The service costs L7000 for a half-hour, L100,000 for a 10-hour subscription, and L30,000 a month for a personal mail box.

Travel Agencies There is a Sestante CIT office (Italy's national tourist agency; ☎ 4 79 41) in Piazza della Repubblica, where you can make bookings for planes, trains, buses and ferries, and another in Stazione Termini near the exit to Via Marsala. The staff speak English and have information on fares for students and young people. They also arrange tours of Rome and the surrounding areas. CTS (the student tourist centre; ☎ 4 67 91), Via Genova 16, off

Via Nazionale, offers much the same services and will also make hotel reservations, but focuses on discount and student travel. There is a branch office at Termini. The staff at both offices speak English. American Express (☎ 6 76 41 for travel information; ☎ 7 22 82 for 24-hour client service for lost or stolen cards; ☎ 167-87 20 00 for lost or stolen travellers' cheques), Piazza di Spagna 38, has a travel service similar to CIT and CTS, as well as a hotel reservation service, and can arrange tours of the city and surrounding areas.

Bookshops The Corner Bookshop, at Via del Moro 48 in Trastevere, is very well stocked with English-language books (including Lonely Planet guides). It is run by a helpful and friendly Australian woman named Claire Hammond. The Anglo-American Bookshop, Via della Vite 102, off Piazza di Spagna, also has an excellent selection of literature, travel guides and reference books. The Lion Bookshop, Via del Babuino 181, also has a good range, as does the Economy Book and Video Center, Via Torino 136, off Via Nazionale.

Laundry There is a coin laundrette, Onda Blu, at Via Principe Amadeo 70b, near the train station.

Medical Services Emergency medical treatment is available in the Pronto Soccorso (casualty sections) at public hospitals including: Policlinico Umberto I (☎ 446 23 41), Via del Policlinico 255, near Stazione Termini; Policlinico A Gemelli (☎ 3 01 51), Largo A Gemelli 8. The Rome American Hospital (☎ 2 56 71), Via E Longoni 69, is a private hospital and you should use its services only if you have health insurance and have consulted your insurance company. Rome's paediatric hospital is Bambino Gesù (☎ 68 59 23 51) on the Janiculum (Gianicolo) Hill at Piazza Sant'Onofrio.

For an ambulance call ☎ 5510, and for first aid call ☎ 118.

There is a pharmacy in Stazione Termini, open daily from 7 am to 11 pm (closed in August). For information (in Italian) on all-night pharmacies in Rome, ring ☎ 1921. Otherwise, closed pharmacies should post a list in their windows of others open nearby.

Emergency The questura (police head-quarters; ☎ 4686) is at Via San Vitale 15. Its Foreigners' Bureau (Ufficio Stranieri; ☎ 46 86 29 87) is around the corner at Via Genova 2. It is open 24 hours a day and thefts can be reported here. For immediate police attendance call ☎ 112 or 113.

Dangers & Annoyances Thieves are very active in the areas in and around Stazione Termini, at major sights such as the Colosseum and Roman Forum, and in the city's most expensive shopping streets, such as Via Condotti. Pickpockets like to work on crowded buses, particularly No 64 from St Peter's to Termini and the No 27 from Termini to the Colosseum. For more comprehensive information on how to avoid being robbed see the Dangers and Annoyances section earlier in this chapter.

Things to See & Do

It would take years to explore every corner of Rome, months to begin to appreciate the incredible number of monuments and weeks for a thorough tour of the city. You can, however, cover most of the important monuments in five days, or three at a minimum.

Walking Tour A good, but rather long walk to help orient yourself in Rome is to start from Piazza della Repubblica and head north-west along Via Vittorio Emanuele Orlando, turning left into Via XX Settembre (which becomes Via del Quirinale) to reach the **Piazza del Quirinale**. Along the way you'll pass by two churches, Borromini's **San Carlo alle Quattro Fontane** at the intersection known as the Quattro Fontane, and Bernini's **Sant'Andrea al Quirinale**. Set on the Quirinal Hill, the Piazza del Quirinale affords an interesting view of Rome and St Peter's. Italy's president lives at the Palazzo del Quirinale. The palace and its gardens are opened to the public on the last Sunday of each month from 9 am to 1 pm. Admission is free. From Piazza del Quirinale walk back down Via del Quirinale and turn left into Via delle Quattro Fontane to get to **Piazza Barberini**. From here you can wander up **Via Veneto**, or take Via Sistina to the **Spanish Steps**.

From Piazza di Spagna take Via Condotti

and turn left on to Via del Corso, crossing over Via del Tritone. Then take the second left (Via delle Muratte) to see the **Trevi Fountain**. Return to Via del Corso and cross into the **Piazza Colonna**. Things get a bit complicated here, but use a good map, follow the tourist signs and you won't get lost. Walk through the piazza into the **Piazza di Montecitorio**, and continue straight ahead along Via degli Uffici del Vicario, where you can buy a gelato at Giolitti. Then turn left at Via della Maddalena to get to the **Pantheon**.

Take Via Giustiniani from the north-western corner of Piazza della Rotonda to get to **Piazza Navona**. Leave the piazza from Via Cuccagna, cross Corso Vittorio Emanuele II and take Via Cancelleria to reach the **Campo de' Fiori**. From here go down Via Gallo into the **Piazza Farnese** and then walk directly ahead out of the piazza on Via dei Farnesi into **Via Giulia**.

If you still have the energy, you have two choices. Either continue along Via Giulia and cross the Ponte Vittorio Emanuele II to get to **St Peter's Basilica** and the **Vatican**, or cross the **Ponte Sisto** at the southern end of Via Giulia and wander through the streets of **Trastevere**.

Piazza del Campidoglio Designed by Michelangelo in 1538, the piazza is on the Capitolino (Capitoline Hill), the most important of Rome's seven hills. The hill was the seat of the ancient Roman government and is now the seat of Rome's municipal government. Michelangelo also designed the façades of the three palaces which border the piazza. A bronze equestrian statue of Emperor Marcus Aurelius once stood in the centre of the piazza. It was removed for restoration and is now on display in the ground floor portico of the Palazzo del Museo Capitolino. A copy will eventually be placed in the piazza. In the two palaces flanking the piazza are the **Musei Capitolini**, which are well worth visiting. They are open Tuesday to Saturday 9 am to 7 pm and Sunday until 1.30 pm. Admission is L10,000.

Walk to the right of the Palazzo del Senato to see a panorama of the Roman Forum. Walk to the left of the same building to reach the ancient Roman **Carcere Mamertino**, where prisoners were put through a hole in the floor to starve to death. St Peter was believed to have

been imprisoned there. The **Chiesa di Santa Maria d'Aracoeli** is between the Campidoglio and the Monumento Vittorio Emanuele II at the highest point of the Capitoline Hill. Built on the site where legend says the Tiburtine Sybil told Augustus of the coming birth of Christ, it features frescos by Pinturicchio in the first chapel of the south aisle.

Piazza Venezia This piazza is overshadowed by a monument dedicated to Vittorio Emanuele II, which is often referred to by Italians as the *macchina da scrivere* (typewriter) – because it resembles one.

Built to commemorate Italian unification, the piazza incorporates the **Altare della Patria** and the tomb of the unknown soldier, as well as the **Museo del Risorgimento**. Also in the piazza is the 15th-century **Palazzo Venezia**, which was Mussolini's official residence.

Roman Forum & Palatine Hill The commercial, political and religious centre of ancient Rome, the forum stands in a valley between the Capitoline and Palatine (Palatino) hills. Originally marshland, the area was drained during the early Republican era and became a centre for political rallies, public ceremonies and senate meetings. Its importance declined along with the empire after the 4th century, and the temples, monuments and buildings constructed by successive emperors, consuls and senators over a period of 900 years fell into ruin, eventually to be used as pasture land.

The area was systematically excavated in the 18th and 19th centuries, and excavations are continuing. You can enter the forum from Via dei Fori Imperiali, which leads from Piazza Venezia to the Colosseum. The forum and Palatine are open in summer from 9 am to 6 pm (3 pm in winter), and on Sunday from 9 am to 1 pm year-round. Admission is L12,000 and covers entrance to both the forum and the Palatine Hill.

As you enter the forum, to your left is the **Tempio di Antonino e Faustina**, erected by the Senate in 141 AD and transformed into a church in the 8th century. To your right are the remains of the **Basilica Aemilia**, built in 179 BC and demolished during the Renaissance, when it was plundered for its precious marble. The Via Sacra, which traverses the forum from north-west to south-east, runs in front of the basilica. Towards the Campidoglio the **Curia**, once the meeting place of the Roman Senate and converted to a Christian church in the Middle Ages. The church was dismantled and the Curia restored in the 1930s. In front of the Curia is the **Lapis Niger**, a large piece of black marble which legend says covered the grave of Romulus. Under the Lapis Niger is the oldest known Latin inscription, dating to the 6th century BC.

The **Arco di Settimo Severo** was erected in 203 AD in honour of this emperor and his sons, and is considered one of Italy's major triumphal arches. A circular base stone beside the arch marks the *umbilicus urbis*, the symbolic centre of ancient Rome. To the south is the **Rostrum**, used in ancient times by public speakers and once decorated by the rams of captured ships.

South along the Via Sacra is the **Tempio di Saturno**, one of the most important temples in ancient Rome. Eight granite columns remain. The **Basilica Julia**, in front of the temple, was the seat of justice, and nearby is the Tempio di Giulio Cesare (Temple of Julius Caesar), which was erected by Augustus in 29 BC on the site where Caesar's body was burned and Mark Antony read his famous speech. Back towards the Palatine Hill is the **Tempio dei Castori**, built in 489 BC to mark the defeat of the Etruscan Tarquins and in honour of the Heavenly Twins, or Dioscuri. It is easily recognisable by its three remaining columns.

In the area south-east of the temple is the **Chiesa di Santa Maria Antiqua**, the oldest Christian church in the forum. It is closed to the public. Back on the Via Sacra is the **Case delle Vestali**, home of the virgins who tended the sacred flame in the adjoining **Tempio di Vesta**. If the flame went out, it was seen as a bad omen. The next major monument is the vast **Basilica di Costantino**. Its impressive design inspired Renaissance architects. The **Arco di Tito**, at the Colosseum end of the forum, was built in 81 AD in honour of the victories of the emperors Titus and Vespasian against Jerusalem.

From here climb the **Palatino**, where wealthy Romans built their homes and where legend says that Romulus founded the city. Archaeological evidence shows that the earliest settlements in the area were on the Palatine.

Like the forum, the buildings of the Palatine fell into ruin and in the Middle Ages the hill became the site of convents and churches. During the Renaissance, wealthy families established their gardens here. The Farnese gardens were built over the ruins of the Domus Tiberiana, which is now under excavation.

Worth a look are the impressive **Domus Augustana**, which was the private residence of the emperors, and the **Domus Flavia**, the residence of Domitian; the **Tempio della Magna Mater**, built in 204 BC to house a black stone connected with the Asiatic goddess, Cybele; and the **Casa di Livia**, thought to have been the house of the wife of Emperor Augustus, and decorated with frescos. Bring a picnic lunch.

Colosseum Originally known as the Flavian Amphitheatre, its construction was started by Emperor Vespasian in 72 AD in the grounds of Nero's Golden House, and completed by his son Titus. The massive structure could seat 80,000 and the bloody gladiator combat and wild beast shows, when thousands of wild animals were slashed to death, give some insight into Roman people of the day.

In the Middle Ages the Colosseum became a fortress and was later used as a quarry for travertine and marble for the Palazzo Venezia and other buildings. Restoration works have been underway since 1992. Opening hours are from 9 am to 7 pm in summer (3 pm in winter) and to 1 pm Wednesday, Sunday and public holidays. General entry is free, although there are plans to introduce an entry fee. It costs L8000 to go to the top levels.

Arch of Constantine On the west side of the Colosseum is the triumphal arch built to honour Constantine following his victory over his rival Maxentius at the battle of Milvian Bridge (near the present-day Zona Olimpica, north-west of the Villa Borghese) in 312 AD. Its decorative reliefs were taken from earlier structures. A major restoration was completed in 1987.

Circus Maximus There is not much to see here apart from the few ruins that remain of what was once a chariot racetrack big enough to hold more than 200,000 people.

Baths of Caracalla This huge complex, covering 10 hectares, could hold 1600 people and included shops, gardens, libraries and entertainment. Begun by Antonius Caracalla and inaugurated in 217 AD, the baths were used until the 6th century. From the 1930s to 1993 they were an atmospheric venue for opera performances in summer. These performances have now been banned to prevent further damage to the ruins. The baths are open in summer from 9 am to 6 pm and in winter until 3 pm. Entry is L8000.

Some Significant Churches Down Via Cavour from Stazione Termini is **Santa Maria Maggiore**, built in the 5th century. Its main baroque façade was added in the 18th century, preserving the 13th-century mosaics of the earlier façade. Its bell tower is Romanesque and the interior is baroque. There are 5th-century mosaics decorating the triumphal arch and nave. Follow Via Merulana to reach **San Giovanni in Laterano**, Rome's cathedral. The original church was built in the 4th century, the first Christian basilica in Rome. Largely destroyed over a long period of time, it was rebuilt in the 17th century. **San Pietro in Vincoli**, just off Via Cavour, is worth a visit because it houses Michelangelo's *Moses* and his unfinished statues of Leah and Rachel, as well as the chains worn by St Peter during his imprisonment before being crucified. **San Clemente**, in Via San Giovanni in Laterano, near the Colosseum, defines how history in Rome exists on many levels. The 12th-century church at street level was built over a 4th-century church which was, in turn, built over a 1st-century Roman house containing a temple dedicated to the pagan god of light, Mithras.

Santa Maria in Cosmedin, north-west of Circus Maximus, is regarded as one of the finest medieval churches in Rome. It has a seven-storey bell tower and its interior is heavily decorated with Cosmatesque inlaid marble, including the beautiful floor. The main attraction for the tourist hordes is, however, the **Bocca della Verità** (Mouth of Truth). Legend has it that if you put your right hand into the mouth, while telling a lie, it will snap shut. Located in Via Veneto, **Santa Maria della Concezione** is an austere 17th-century building; however, the Capuchin cemetery beneath the church (with access on the right of the church steps) features a bizarre display of monks' bones which were used to decorate the walls of a series of chapels.

Baths of Diocletian Started by Emperor Diocletian, these baths were completed in the 4th century. The complex of baths, libraries, concert halls and gardens covered about 13 hectares and could house up to 3000 people. After the aqueduct which fed the baths was destroyed by invaders in 536 AD, the complex fell into decay. Parts of the ruins are now incorporated into the church of Santa Maria degli Angeli and the Museo Nazionale Romano. The baths are open Tuesday to Saturday from 9 am to 2 pm and Sunday to 1 pm. Admission is L12,000.

Basilica di Santa Maria degli Angeli Designed by Michelangelo, this church incorporates what was the great central hall and tepidarium (lukewarm room) of the original baths. During the following centuries his work was drastically changed and little evidence of his design, apart from the great vaulted ceiling of the church, remains. An interesting feature of the church is a double meridian in the transept, one tracing the polar star and the other telling the precise time of the sun's zenith. The church is open from 7.30 am to 12.30 pm and from 4 to 6.30 pm. Through the sacristy is an entrance to a stairway leading to the upper terraces of the ruins. A plaque near the stairway records the traditional belief that the baths were built by thousands of Christian slaves.

Museo Nazionale Romano This museum houses an important collection of ancient art, including Greek and Roman sculpture. It also has a collection of frescos and mosaics from the Villa of Livia at Prima Porta. The museum is now largely located in the former Collegio Massimo, just across the road from the Baths of Diocletian, and is open from 9 am to 2 pm (1 pm on Sunday, closed Monday) and entry is L12,000.

Via Vittorio Veneto This was Rome's hot spot in the 1960s, where film stars could be spotted at the expensive outdoor cafés. These days you will find only tourists, and the atmosphere of Fellini's *Roma* is long dead.

Piazza di Spagna & Spanish Steps This piazza, church and famous staircase (Scalinata della Trinità dei Monti) have long provided a major gathering place for foreigners. Built with a legacy from the French in 1725, but named after the Spanish Embassy to the Holy See, the steps lead to the church of Trinità dei Monti, which was built by the French.

In the 18th century the most beautiful men and women of Italy gathered there, waiting to be chosen as artists' models. To the right as you face the steps is the house where Keats spent the last three months of his life, and where he died in 1821. In the piazza is the boat-shaped fountain of the **Barcaccia**, believed to be by Pietro Bernini, father of the famous Gian Lorenzo. One of Rome's most elegant shopping streets, **Via Condotti**, runs off the piazza towards Via del Corso.

Piazza del Popolo This vast piazza was laid out in the 16th century and redesigned in the early 19th century by Giuseppe Valadier. It is at the foot of the **Pincio Hill**, from where there is a panoramic view of the city.

Villa Borghese This beautiful park was once the estate of Cardinal Scipione Borghese. His 17th-century villa houses the **Museo e Galleria Borghese**, which has been undergoing renovations for more than a decade. It still houses a sculpture collection (entry L4000, open Tuesday to Saturday from 9 am to 1.30 pm and Sunday till 1 pm). Part of the gallery's collection of paintings is temporarily housed in the **Istituto San Michele a Ripa**, Via di San Michele a Ripa in Trastevere (open Tuesday to Saturday from 9 am to 7 pm, and Sunday 9 am to 1 pm). Entry is L4000. Just outside the park are the **Galleria Nazionale d'Arte Moderna**, Viale delle Belle Arti 131, and the important Etruscan museum, **Museo Nazionale di Villa Giulia**, along the same street in Piazzale di Villa Giulia. Both open Tuesday to Saturday from 9 am to 7 pm and Sunday to 1 pm. Entry at both is L8000.

Trevi Fountain The high-baroque Fontana di Trevi was designed by Nicola Salvi in 1732. Its water was supplied by one of Rome's earliest aqueducts. Work to clean the fountain and its water supply was completed in 1991. The famous custom is to throw a coin into the fountain (over your shoulder while facing away) to ensure your return to Rome. If you throw a second coin you can make a wish.

Pantheon This is the best-preserved building of ancient Rome. The original temple was built in 27 BC by Marcus Agrippa, son-in-law of Emperor Augustus, and dedicated to the planetary gods. Although the temple was rebuilt by Emperor Hadrian around 120 AD, Agrippa's name remains inscribed over the entrance.

Over the centuries the temple was consistently plundered and damaged. The gilded bronze roof tiles were removed by an emperor of the eastern empire, and Pope Urban VIII had the bronze ceiling of the portico melted down to make the canopy over the main altar of St Peter's and 80 cannons for Castel Sant'Angelo. The Pantheon's extraordinary dome is considered the most important achievement of ancient Roman architecture. In 608 AD the temple was consecrated to the Virgin and all martyrs.

The Italian kings Vittorio Emanuele II and Umberto I and the painter Raphael are buried there. The Pantheon is in Piazza della Rotonda and is open Monday to Saturday from 9 am to 4 pm (9 am to 2 pm in winter) and 9 am to 1 pm Sunday and public holidays year-round. Admission is free.

Piazza Navona This is a vast and beautiful square, lined with baroque palaces. It was laid out on the ruins of Domitian's stadium and features three fountains, including Bernini's masterpiece, the **Fontana dei Fiumi** (Fountain of the Rivers), in the centre. Take time to relax on one of the stone benches and watch the artists who gather in the piazza to work.

Campo de' Fiori This is a lively piazza where a flower and vegetable market is held every morning except Sunday. Now lined with bars and trattorias, the piazza was a place of execution during the Inquisition.

The **Palazzo Farnese** (Farnese Palace), in the piazza of the same name, is just off Campo de' Fiori. A magnificent Renaissance building, it was started in 1514 by Antonio da Sangello,

ITALY

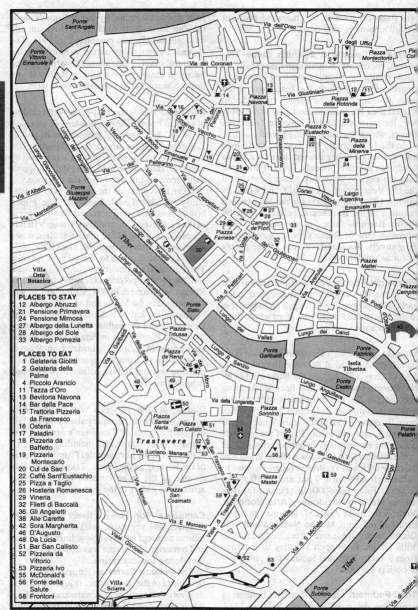

PLACES TO STAY
12 Albergo Abruzzi
21 Pensione Primavera
24 Pensione Mimosa
27 Albergo della Lunetta
28 Albergo del Sole
33 Albergo Pomezia

PLACES TO EAT
1 Gelateria Giolitti
2 Gelateria della
  Palme
4 Piccolo Arancio
11 Tazza d'Oro
13 Bevitoria Navona
14 Bar della Pace
15 Trattoria Pizzeria
   da Francesco
16 Osteria
17 Paladini
18 Pizzeria da
   Baffetto
19 Pizzeria
   Montecarlo
20 Cul de Sac 1
22 Caffé Sant'Eustachio
25 Pizza a Taglio
26 Hosteria Romanesca
29 Vineria
31 Filetti di Baccalà
36 Gli Angeletti
39 Alle Carette
42 Sora Margherita
46 D'Augusto
48 Da Lucia
51 Bar San Callisto
52 Pizzeria da
   Vittorio
53 Pizzeria Ivo
55 McDonald's
56 Fonte della
   Salute
58 Frontoni

ITALY

Pantheon & Trastevere Areas

0   200   400 m

OTHER

3	Fontana & Piazza di Trevi
5	Palazzo Quirinale
6	Chiesa di Sant'Andrea al Quirinale
7	Chiesa di San Carlo alle Quattro Fontane
8	Questura (Police Station)
9	Teatro dell'Opera
10	CTS Travel Agency
23	Pantheon
30	Palazzo Farnese & French Embassy
31	French Consulate
34	Palazzo Venezia
35	Monumento Vittorio Emanuele II
37	Basilica di San Pietro in Vincoli
39	Chiesa di Santa Maria d'Aracoeli
40	Palazzo del Museo Capitolino
41	Palazzo dei Conservatori
43	Teatro di Marcello
44	Arch of Constantine
45	Chiesa di San Clemente
47	Corner Bookshop
49	Pasquino Cinema
50	Basilica di Santa Maria in Trastevere
54	Hospital
57	Alcazar Cinema
59	Basilica di Santa Cecilia in Trastevere
60	Chiesa di Santa Maria in Cosmedin
61	Circus Maximus
62	Porta Portese Market Area
63	Porta Portese

work was carried on by Michelangelo and it was completed by Giacomo della Porta. Built for Cardinal Alessandro Farnese (later Pope Paul III), the palace is now the French Embassy. The piazza has two fountains, which were enormous granite baths taken from the Baths of Caracalla.

Via Giulia This street was designed by Bramante, who was commissioned by Pope Julius II to create a new approach to St Peter's. It is lined with Renaissance palaces, antique shops and art galleries.

Trastevere You can wander through the narrow medieval streets of this busy and Bohemian area. It is especially beautiful at night and is one of the more interesting areas for bar-hopping or a meal.

Of particular note here is the **Basilica di Santa Maria in Trastevere**, in the lovely piazza of the same name. It is believed to be the oldest church dedicated to the Virgin in Rome. Although the first church was built on the site in the 4th century, the present structure was built in the 12th century and features a Romanesque bell tower and façade, with a mosaic of the Virgin. Its interior was redecorated during the baroque period, but the vibrant mosaics in the apse and on the triumphal arch date from the 12th century. Also take a look at the **Basilica di Santa Cecilia in Trastevere**.

Gianicolo Go to the top of the Gianicolo (Janiculum), the hill between St Peter's and Trastevere, for a panoramic view of Rome.

Catacombs There are several catacombs in Rome, consisting of miles of tunnels carved out of volcanic rock, which were the meeting and burial places of early Christians in Rome. The largest are along the Via Appia Antica, just outside the city and accessible on bus No 218 (from Piazza di Porta San Giovanni – ask the driver when to get off). The **Catacombs of San Callisto** and **Catacombs of San Sebastiano** are almost next to each other on the Via Appia Antica. San Callisto is open from 8.30 am to noon and 2.30 to 5 pm (closed Wednesday). San Sebastiano is open from Friday to Wednesday, 9 am to noon and 2.30 to

5 pm. Admission to each costs L8000 and is with a guide only.

Vatican City After the unification of Italy, the Papal States of central Italy became part of the new Kingdom of Italy, causing a considerable rift between church and state. In 1929, Mussolini, under the Lateran Treaty, gave the pope full sovereignty over what is now the Vatican City.

The tourist office, in Piazza San Pietro to the left of the basilica, is open daily from 8.30 am to 7 pm. Guided tours of the Vatican City can be organised here. A few doors up is the Vatican Post Office, said to offer a much more reliable service than the normal Italian postal system. It is open Monday to Friday from 8.30 am to 7 pm and until 6 pm on Saturday (closed Sunday).

The city has its own postal service, currency newspaper, radio station, train station and army of Swiss Guards.

St Peter's Basilica & Square The most famous church in the Christian world, **San Pietro** stands on the site where St Peter was buried. The first church on the site was built during Constantine's reign in the 4th century and in 1506 work started on a new basilica designed by Bramante.

Although several architects were involved in its construction, it is generally held that St Peter's owes more to Michelangelo, who took over the project in 1547 at the age of 72 and was particularly responsible for the design of the dome. He died before the church was completed. The cavernous interior contains numerous treasures, including Michelangelo's superb *Pietà*, sculptured when he was only 25 years old and the only work to carry his signature (on the sash across the breast of the Madonna). It has been protected by bulletproof glass since an attack in 1972 by a hammer wielding Hungarian.

Bernini's huge, baroque *Baldacchino* (a heavily sculpted bronze canopy over the papal altar) stands 29 metres high and is an extraordinary work of art. Another point of note is the red porphyry disc near the central door, which marks the spot where Charlemagne and later emperors were crowned by the pope.

Entrance to Michelangelo's soaring dome is

to the right as you climb the stairs to the atrium of the basilica. Make the entire climb on foot for L5000, or pay L6000 and take the elevator for part of the way (recommended).

The basilica is open daily from 7 am to 7 pm (6 pm in winter) and dress rules are stringently enforced – no shorts, miniskirts or sleeveless tops. Prams and strollers must be left in a designated area outside the basilica.

Bernini's **Piazza San Pietro** (St Peter's Square) is considered a masterpiece. Laid out in the 17th century as a place for Christians of the world to gather, the immense piazza is bound by two semicircular colonnades, each of which is made up of four rows of Doric columns. In the centre of the piazza is an obelisk that was brought to Rome by Caligula from Heliopolis (in ancient Egypt). When you stand on the dark paving stones between the obelisk and either of the fountains, the colonnades look as though they have only one row of columns.

The pope usually gives a public audience at 10 or 11 am every Wednesday in the Papal Audience Hall. To attend, you must go to Prefettura della Casa Pontifica (☎ 69 88 30 17), through the bronze doors under the colonnade to the right as you face the basilica. The office is open from Monday to Saturday 9 am to 1 pm. Otherwise apply in writing to the Prefettura della Casa Pontifica, 00120 Città del Vaticano.

Vatican Museums From St Peter's follow the wall of the Vatican City (to the right as you face the basilica) to the museums, or catch the regular shuttle bus (L2000) from the piazza in front of the tourist office. The museums are open Monday to Saturday from 8.45 am to 1 pm. At Easter and during summer they are open to 4 pm. Admission is L15,000. The museums are closed on Sundays and public holidays, but open on the last Sunday of every month from 9 am to 1 pm (free admission, but queues are always very long). Guided visits to the Vatican gardens cost L18,000 and can be booked by calling ☎ 69 88 44 66.

The Vatican museums contain an incredible collection of art and treasures collected by the popes, and you will need several hours to see the most important areas and museums. The Sistine Chapel comes towards the end of a full visit, otherwise you can walk straight there and then work your way back through the museums.

The **Museo Pio-Clementino**, containing Greek and Roman antiquities, is on the ground floor near the entrance. Through the Tapestry and Map galleries are the **Stanze di Rafaello**, once the private apartment of Pope Julius II, decorated with frescos by Raphael. Of particular interest is the magnificent **Stanza della Segnatura**, which features Raphael's masterpieces *The School of Athens* and *Disputation on the Sacrament*.

From Raphael's Rooms, go down the stairs to the sumptuous **Appartamento Borgia**, decorated with frescos by Pinturicchio, then go down another flight of stairs to the **Sistine Chapel**, the private papal chapel built in 1473 for Pope Sixtus IV. Michelangelo's wonderful frescos of the *Creation* on the barrel-vaulted ceiling and *Last Judgment* on the end wall have both been recently restored. It took him four years, at the height of the Renaissance, to paint the ceiling. Twenty-four years later he painted the extraordinary *Last Judgment*. The other walls of the chapel were painted by artists including Botticelli, Ghirlandaio, Pinturicchio and Signorelli.

Organised Tours

Walk Through the Centuries (☎ 323 17 33), Via Silla 10, offers walking tours of the city's main sights for L25,000 per person. Bus No 110 leaves from Piazzo dei Cinquecento, in front of Stazione Termini, for a three-hour tour of the city. The cost is L15,000. Vastours (☎ 481 43 09), Via Piemonte 34, operates half-day coach tours of Rome from L43,000 and full-day coach tours of the city from L110,000, as well as tours to Tivoli, the Castelli Romani and other Italian cities. American Express (☎ 676 41) in Piazza di Spagna, and the CIT office in Piazza della Repubblica also offer guided tours of the city.

Special Events

Although Romans desert their city in summer, particularly in August, when the weather is relentlessly hot and humid, cultural and musical events liven up the place. The Comune di Roma coordinates a diverse series of concerts, performances and events throughout summer under the general title Estate Romana (Roman Summer). The series usually features major international performers. Information is published in Rome's daily newspapers. A jazz festival is held in July and August in the Villa Celimontana, a park on top of the Celian Hill (access from Piazza della Navicella). The Festa de' Noantri is held in Trastevere in the last two weeks of July in honour of Our Lady of Mt Carmel. Street stalls line Viale di Trastevere, but head for the back streets for live music and street theatre. The Festa di San Giovanni is held on 23 and 24 June in the San Giovanni district of Rome and features much dancing and eating in the streets. Part of the ritual is to eat stewed snails and suckling pig.

At Christmas the focus is on the many churches of Rome, each setting up its own Nativity scene. Among the most renowned is the 13th-century crib at Santa Maria Maggiore. During Holy Week, at Easter, the focus is again religious and events include the famous procession of the cross between the Colosseum and the Palatine on Good Friday, and the Pope's blessing of the city and the world in St Peter's Square on Easter Sunday.

The Spanish Steps become a sea of pink azaleas during the Spring Festival in April.

Places to Stay

Camping About 15 minutes from the centre by public transport is *Village Camping Flaminio* (☎ 333 26 04), at Via Flaminia 821. It costs L13,000 per person and L12,400 for a site. Tents and bungalows are available for rent. From Stazione Termini catch bus No 910 to Piazza Mancini, then bus No 200 to the camping ground. At night, catch bus No 24N from Piazzale Flaminio (just north of Piazza del Popolo).

Hostel The HI *Ostello Foro Italico* (☎ 323 62 67), Viale delle Olimpiadi 61, costs L23,000 a night, breakfast and showers included. Take Metro Linea A to Ottaviano, then bus No 32 to Foro Italico. The head office of the Italian Youth Hostels Association (☎ 487 11 52) is at Via Cavour 44, 00184 Rome. It will provide information about all the hostels in Italy. You can also join HI here.

Hotels & Pensioni There is a vast number of cheap hotels and pensioni in Rome, concentrated mainly to the north-east and south-west

of Stazione Termini. The private tourist office, Enjoy Rome (see the earlier Tourist Offices section), will book you a room, but if you want to go it alone, either phone ahead or check your bags in and walk the streets to the left and right of the station. The area south-west is crowded, noisy and swarms with thieves and pickpockets who prey on newly arrived tourists. It can be unpleasant and dangerous, particularly for women at night, so it is important always to remain extremely alert. The area north-east is quieter and somewhat safer.

North-East of Stazione Termini To reach the pensioni in this area, head to the right as you leave the train platforms onto Via Castro Pretorio. *Pensione Giamaica* (☎ 49 01 21), Via Magenta 13, has OK singles/doubles for L40,000/65,000 and triples at L25,000 per person. Nearby at Via Magenta 39 is the excellent *Fawlty Towers* (☎ 445 03 74), which offers hostel-style accommodation at L25,000 per person, or L27,000 with private shower. Run by the people at Enjoy Rome, it offers lots of information about Rome and added bonuses are the sunny terrace and satellite TV.

Nearby in Via Palestro there are several reasonably priced pensioni. *Pensione Restivo* (☎ 446 21 72), Via Palestro 55, has reasonable singles/doubles for L60,000/100,000, including the cost of showers. A triple is L27,000 per person. There is a midnight curfew. In the same building, *Albergo Mari* (☎ 446 21 37) has singles/doubles for L45,000/70,000. A good choice is *Hotel Positano* (☎ 49 03 60), Via Palestro 49, which has very pleasant rooms for L80,000/100,000 with bathroom. *Pensione Katty* (☎ 444 12 16), Via Palestro 35, has basic singles/doubles for up to L55,000/70,000. Around the corner at Viale Castro Pretorio 25 is *Pensione Ester* (☎ 495 71 23) with comfortable doubles for L70,000 and L90,000 for a triple.

At Via San Martino della Battaglia 11, are three good pensioni in the same building. The *Pensione Lachea* (☎ 495 72 56) has large newly renovated doubles/triples for L60,000/ 80,000. *Hotel Pensione Dolomiti* (☎ 49 10 58) has singles/doubles for L44,000/55,000; a triple is L25,000 per person. *Albergo Sandra* (☎ 44 26 12), Via Villafranca 10 (which runs between Via Vicenza and Via San Martino della

ITALY

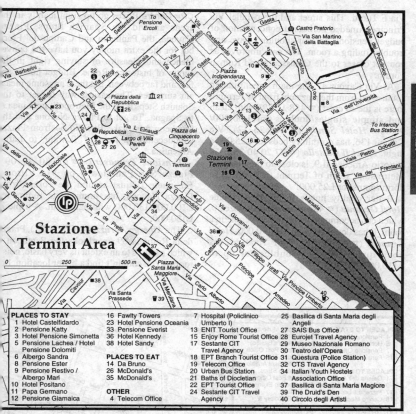

Stazione Termini Area

0   250   500 m

PLACES TO STAY
1 Hotel Castelfidardo
2 Pensione Katty
3 Hotel Pensione Simonetta
5 Pensione Lachea / Hotel Pensione Dolomiti
6 Albergo Sandra
8 Pensione Ester
9 Pensione Restivo / Albergo Mari
10 Hotel Positano
11 Papa Germano
12 Pensione Giamaica

16 Fawlty Towers
23 Hotel Pensione Oceania
33 Pensione Everist
36 Hotel Kennedy
38 Hotel Sandy

PLACES TO EAT
14 Da Bruno
26 McDonald's
35 McDonald's

OTHER
4 Telecom Office

7 Hospital (Policlinico Umberto I)
13 ENIT Tourist Office
15 Enjoy Rome Tourist Office
17 Sestante CIT Travel Agency
18 EPT Branch Tourist Office
19 Telecom Office
20 Urban Bus Station
21 Baths of Diocletian
22 EPT Tourist Office
24 Sestante CIT Travel Agency

25 Basilica di Santa Maria degli Angeli
27 SAIS Bus Office
28 Eurojet Travel Agency
29 Museo Nazionale Romano
31 Questura (Police Station)
32 CTS Travel Agency
34 Italian Youth Hostels Association Office
37 Basilica di Santa Maria Maggiore
39 The Druid's Den
40 Circolo degli Artisti

Battaglia), is clean, with dark but pleasant rooms. Singles/doubles cost L50,000/70,000, including the cost of a shower. *Hotel Pensione Simonetta* (☎ 444 13 02), across from Piazza dell'Indipendenza at Via Palestro 34, has decent rooms for L70,000/85,000.

Papa Germano (☎ 48 69 19), at Via Calatafimi 14a, is one of the more popular budget places in the area. It has singles/doubles for 40,000/65,000, or L50,000/80,000 with private bathroom.

Hotel Castelfidardo (☎ 446 46 38), Via Castelfidardo 31, off Piazza Indipendenza, is one of Rome's better one-star pensioni. It has singles/doubles for L50,000/65,000 and triples

for L28,000 per person, or L38,000 per person with private bathroom. *Pensione Stella* (☎ 444 10 78), Via Castelfidardo 51, is a friendly establishment, with decent rooms for L40,000/60,000. Across Via XX Settembre, at Via Collina 48 (a 10-minute walk from the station) is *Pensione Ercoli* (☎ 474 54 54) with singles/doubles for L43,000/60,000 and triples for L80,000.

West of Stazione Termini This area is decidedly seedier, but prices remain the same. As you exit to the left of the station, follow Via Gioberti to Via G Amendola, which becomes

Via F Turati. This street and the parallel Via Principe Amedeo harbour a concentration of budget pensioni, so you shouldn't have any trouble finding a room. The area improves as you get closer to the Colosseum and Roman Forum.

At Via Cavour 47, the main street running south-west from the piazza in front of Termini, there is the *Everest* (☎ 488 16 29), with clean and simple singles/doubles for L60,000/90,000. *Hotel Sandy* (☎ 445 26 12), Via Cavour 136, has dormitory beds for L25,000 a night. *Hotel Il Castello* (☎ 77 20 40 36), Via Vittorio Amedeo II 9, is close to the Manzoni Metro stop, south of Termini. It has beds in dorm rooms for L25,000.

Better quality hotels in the area include *Hotel Oceania* (☎ 482 46 96), Via Firenze 50, which can accommodate up to five people in a room. It has doubles for up to L170,000. *Hotel Kennedy* (☎ 446 53 73), Via F Turati 62, has good quality singles/doubles for up to L110,000/200,000.

City Centre Prices go up significantly in the areas around the Spanish Steps, Piazza Navona, the Pantheon and Campo de' Fiori but for the extra money you have the convenience and pleasure of staying right in the centre of historical Rome. Budget hotels are few and far between, but there are some pleasant surprises. The easiest way to get to the Spanish Steps is on the Metropolitana Linea A to Spagna. To get to Piazza Navona and the Pantheon area, take Bus No 64 from Piazza Cinquecento, in front of Termini, to Largo Argentina.

Pensione Primavera (☎ 68 80 31 09) Piazza San Pantaleo 3 on Via Vittorio Emanuele II, just around the corner from Piazza Navona, has immaculate rooms for L100,000/130,000 with bathroom. A triple is L150,000.

The *Albergo Abruzzi* (☎ 679 20 21), Piazza della Rotonda 69, overlooks the Pantheon – which excuses to an extent its very basic, noisy rooms. You couldn't find a better location, but

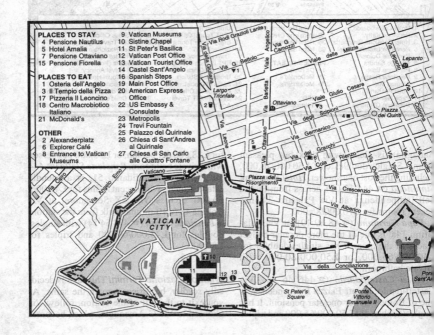

PLACES TO STAY
4 Pensione Nautilus
5 Hotel Amalia
7 Pensione Ottaviano
15 Pensione Fiorella

PLACES TO EAT
1 Osteria dell'Angelo
3 Il Tempio della Pizza
17 Pizzeria Il Leoncino
18 Centro Macrobiotico Italiano
21 McDonald's

OTHER
2 Alexanderplatz
6 Explorer Café
8 Entrance to Vatican Museums
9 Vatican Museums
10 Sistine Chapel
11 St Peter's Basilica
12 Vatican Post Office
13 Vatican Tourist Office
14 Castel Sant'Angelo
16 Spanish Steps
19 Main Post Office
20 American Express Office
22 US Embassy & Consulate
23 Metropolis
24 Trevi Fountain
25 Palazzo del Quirinale
26 Chiesa di Sant'Andrea al Quirinale
27 Chiesa di San Carlo alle Quattro Fontane

it is expensive at L83,000/110,000 for singles/ doubles. Triples are L150,000. Bookings are essential throughout the year at this popular hotel. *Pensione Mimosa* (☎ 68 80 17 53; fax 683 35 57), Via Santa Chiara 61 (off Piazza della Rotonda), has very pleasant singles/ doubles for L65,000/95,000. The owner imposes a strict no-smoking rule in the rooms.

The *Albergo del Sole* (☎ 654 08 73), Via del Biscione 76, off Campo de' Fiori, has expensive singles/doubles at L85,000/115,000 – but it's in a great location. Around the corner is *Albergo della Lunetta* (☎ 687 76 30; fax 689 20 28), Piazza del Paradiso 68, which charges L50,000/90,000 for singles/doubles, or L70,000/130,000 with private shower. Reservations are essential at both hotels.

The *Albergo Pomezia* (☎ & fax 686 13 71) at Via dei Chiavari 12 (which runs off Via dei Giubbonari from Campo de' Fiori) has doubles/triples for L100,000/130,000, breakfast included. Use of the communal shower is free.

Near the Spanish Steps is *Pensione Fiorella* (☎ 361 05 97), Via del Babuino 196; singles/ doubles cost L55,000/89,000, including breakfast.

Near St Peter's & the Vatican Bargains do not abound in this area, but it is comparatively quiet and still reasonably close to the main sights. Bookings are an absolute necessity because rooms are often filled with people attending conferences and so on at the Vatican. The simplest way to reach the area is on the Metropolitana Linea A to Ottaviano. Turn left into Via Ottaviano, and Via Germanico is a short walk away. Bus No 64 from Termini stops at St Peter's – walk away from the basilica along Via di Porta Angelica, which becomes Via Ottaviano after Piazza del Risorgimento, a five-minute walk.

The best bargain in the area is *Pensione Ottaviano* (☎ 39 73 72 53), Via Ottaviano 6, near Piazza Risorgimento. It has beds in dormitories for L25,000 per person. The owner

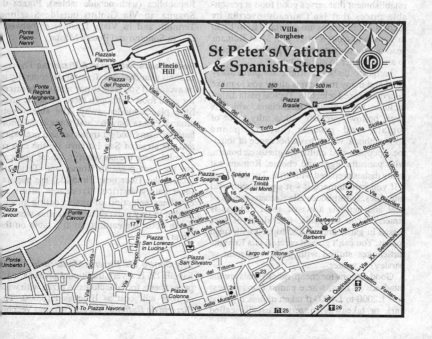

speaks good English. *Hotel Pensione Nautilus* (☎ 324 21 18), Via Germanico 198, offers basic doubles/triples for L90,000/L130,000 or L100,000/L140,000 with private bathroom (no singles). *Hotel Amalia* (☎ 39 72 33 56), Via Germanico 66 (near the corner of Via Ottaviano), has a beautiful courtyard entrance and clean, sunny rooms. Singles/doubles are L80,000/100,000 and include breakfast and use of the communal shower.

Rental Accommodation Apartments near the centre of Rome are expensive, so expect to pay around L2,000,000 a month. A good way to find a shared apartment is to buy *Wanted in Rome* or *Metropolitan*, two English-language fortnightly magazines which publish both classified advertisements and information about what's on in the city. Enjoy Rome (see Tourist Offices) can also help.

Places to Eat
Rome bursts at the seams with trattorias, pizzerias and restaurants – the trick is to locate an establishment that serves good food at reasonable prices that isn't already overrun by tourists. Eating times are generally from 12.30 to 3 pm and from 8 to 11 pm. Most Romans head out for dinner around 9 pm, so it's better to arrive earlier to claim a table.

Antipasto dishes in Rome are particularly good and many restaurants allow you to make your own mixed selection. Typical pasta dishes include: bucatini all'Amatriciana, which is large, hollow spaghetti with a salty sauce of tomato and *pancetta* (bacon); penne all'arrabbiata, which has a hot sauce of tomatoes, peppers and chilli; spaghetti carbonara, with pancetta, eggs and cheese. Romans eat many dishes prepared with offal. Try the paiata – if you can stomach it – it's pasta with veal intestines. Saltimbocca alla Romana (slices of veal and ham) is a classic meat dish, as is straccetti con la rucola, fine slices of beef tossed in garlic and oil and topped with fresh rocket. You can't go past carciofi alla Romana (artichokes stuffed with garlic and mint and parsley) in winter.

Good options for cheap, quick meals are the hundreds of bars, where panini (sandwiches) cost L2000 to L4000 if taken *al banco* (at the bar), or takeaway pizzerias, usually called *pizza a taglio*, where a slice of freshly cooked pizza, sold by weight, can cost as little as L2000. Bakeries are numerous and are another good choice for a cheap snack. Try a huge piece of pizza bianca, a flat bread resembling focaccia, costing from around L2000 a slice (sold by weight). Try *Paladini*, Via del Governo Vecchio 29, for sandwiches and *Pizza a Taglio*, Via Baullari, between Campo de' Fiori and Corso Vittorio Emanuele II, for takeaway pizza.

For groceries and supplies of cheese, prosciutto, salami and wine, shop at alimentari. For fresh fruit and vegetables there are numerous outdoor markets, notably the lively daily market in Campo de' Fiori. Other, cheaper food markets are held in Piazza Vittorio Emanuele, near the station, and in Via Andrea Doria, near Largo Trionfale, north of the Vatican. The huge wholesale food markets are in Via Ostiense, some distance from the centre, and are open to the public Monday to Saturday from 10 am to 1 or 2 pm.

But, if all you really want is a Big Mac you'll find McDonald's outlets in Piazza della Repubblica (with outside tables), Piazza di Spagna, in Via Giolitti outside Stazione Termini, and in Viale Trastevere (between Piazza Sonnino and Piazza Mastai).

Restaurants, Trattorias & Pizzerias The restaurants near Stazione Termini are generally to be avoided if you want to pay reasonable prices for good food – although there are some great little places hidden away. The side streets around Piazza Navona and Campo de' Fiori harbour many budget trattorias and pizzerias and the areas of San Lorenzo (to the east of Termini, near the university), where you can get the best pizza in Rome, and Testaccio (across the Tiber near Piramide) are popular local eating districts. Trastevere offers an excellent selection of rustic eating places hidden in tiny piazzas, and pizzerias where it doesn't cost the earth to sit at a table on the street.

City Centre The *Pizzeria Montecarlo*, Vicolo Savelli 12, is a very traditional pizzeria, with paper sheets for tablecloths. A pizza with wine or beer will cost as little as L15,000. The *Pizzeria da Baffetto*, Via del Governo Vecchio

1, on the corner of Via Sora, is a Roman institution. Expect to join a queue if you arrive after 9 pm and don't be surprised if you end up sharing a table. Funnily enough, for all this, the pizzas are nothing to write home about. Pizzas cost around L9000, a litre of wine costs L9000 and the coperto is only L1500. Further along the street at No 18 is a tiny, nameless *osteria* run by Antonio Bassetti, where you can eat an excellent, simple meal for around L20,000. There's no written menu, but don't be nervous - the owner/waiter will explain slowly (in Italian). Back along the street towards Piazza Navona, at Piazza Pasquino 73, is *Cul de Sac 1*, which has pleasant light meals at reasonable prices.

Trattoria Pizzeria da Francesco, Piazza del Fico 29, has good pasta dishes for around L12,000, as well as pizzas for L7000 to L14,000 and a good range of antipastos and vegetables. *Pizzeria Il Leoncino*, Via del Leoncino 28, going from Piazza Navona towards the Spanish Steps, has good pizzas at low prices. *Centro Macrobiotico Italiano*, Via della Vite 14, is a vegetarian restaurant. It charges an annual membership fee (which reduces as the year goes by), but tourists can usually eat there and pay only a small surcharge.

There are several small restaurants in the Campo de' Fiori. *Hostaria Romanesca* is tiny, so arrive early in winter. In summer there are numerous tables outside. A dish of pasta will cost around L10,000, a full meal around L25,000.

Along Via Giubbonari, off Campo de' Fiori, is *Filetti di Baccalà* in the tiny Largo dei Librari, which serves only deep-fried cod fillets for around L4000 and wine for L6000 a litre. Across Via Arenula, in the Jewish quarter, is *Sora Margherita*, Piazza delle Cinque Scole 30. It serves traditional Roman and Jewish food and a full meal will cost around L25,000.

Near the Trevi Fountain, in Vicolo Scanderbeg, you'll find *Piccolo Arancio*, which offers reasonable food at around L9000 for a first course and L9000 to L15,000 for a secondo. Most of the restaurants in this area are either high class and very expensive, or tourist traps.

West of the Tiber On the west bank of the Tiber, good-value restaurants are concentrated in Trastevere and the Testaccio district, past Piramide. Many of the establishments around St Peter's and the Vatican are geared for tourists and can be very expensive. There are, however, some good options. Try *Il Tempio della Pizza*, Viale Giulio Cesare 91, or *Osteria dell'Angelo*, Via G Bettolo 24, along Via Leone IV from the Vatican City, although this place can be difficult to get into.

In Trastevere's maze of tiny streets you will find any number of pizzerias and cheap trattorias. The area is beautiful at night and most establishments have outdoor tables. It is very popular, so arrive before 8.30 pm if you don't want to join a queue for a table.

Try *Frontoni*, on Viale di Trastevere, opposite Piazza Mastai, for fantastic panini made with pizza bianca. *D'Augusto*, Piazza dei Renzi, just around the corner from the Basilica Santa Maria in Trastevere (turn right as you face the church and walk to Via della Pelliccia), is one of the cheapest spots in town. The food might be average, but the atmosphere, especially in summer with tables outside in the piazza, is as traditionally Roman as you can get. A meal with wine will cost around L20,000. *Pizzeria Ivo*, Via di San Francesco a Ripa 158, has outdoor tables. It's popular with tourists, but the pizzas could be bigger for the price (from around L9000).

A much better pizza is to be had at *Pizzeria da Vittorio*, Via San Cosimato 14a. It is tiny and you have to wait if you arrive after 9 pm, but the atmosphere is great. A bruschetta, pizza and wine will cost around L15,000. *Da Lucia*, Vicolo del Mattinato 2, is more expensive at around L35,000 a full meal, but the food is good and the owners are delightful.

You won't find a cheaper, noisier, more chaotic pizzeria in Rome than *Pizzeria Remo*, Piazza Santa Maria Liberatrice 44, in Testaccio. *Il Canestro*, Via Maestro Giorgio, Testaccio, specialises in vegetarian food and is relatively expensive. *Augustarello*, Via G Branca 98, off the piazza, specialises in the very traditional Roman fare of offal dishes. The food is reasonable and a meal will cost around L20,000.

San Lorenzo District & between Termini & the Forum You will find typical local fare and good pizzas at prices students can afford at *Pizzeria l'Economica*, Via Tiburtina 44.

Another local favourite is *Formula 1*, Via degli Equi 13. Pizzas at both cost around L8000.

If you have no option but to eat near Stazione Termini, try to avoid the tourist traps offering overpriced full menus. *Trattoria da Bruno*, Via Varese 29, has great food at reasonable prices – around L8000 for pasta and up to L14,000 for a second course. They serve home-made gnocchi on Thursdays. A decent pizzeria is *Alle Carrette*, Vicolo delle Carrette 14, off Via Cavour near the Roman Forum. A pizza and wine will cost around L12,000. Just off Via Cavour in the tiny Via dell'Angeletto, is *Gli Angeletti*, an excellent little restaurant with prices at the higher end of the budget range. You'll pay around L12,000 for a pasta and around L15,000 for a second course.

Cafés & Bars Remember that prices skyrocket in bars as soon as you sit down, particularly near the Spanish Steps, in the Piazza della Rotonda and in Piazza Navona, where a cappuccino *a tavola* (at a table) can cost L5000 or more. The same cappuccino taken at the bar will cost around L1500 – but passing an hour or so watching the world go by over a cappuccino, beer or wine in any of the above locations can be hard to beat!

For the best coffee in Rome head for *Tazza d'Oro*, just off Piazza della Rotonda in Via degli Orfani, and *Caffè Sant'Eustachio*, Piazza Sant'Eustachio 82. Try the granita di caffè at either one. *Vineria* in Campo de' Fiori, also known as *Giorgio's*, has a wide selection of wine and beers. In summer it has tables outside, but prices are steep – better to stand at the bar. *Bar della Pace*, Via della Pace 3/7, is big with the young 'in' crowd, but 'cool' always has a price. *Bevitoria Navona*, Piazza Navona 72 has wine by the glass. *Bar San Callisto*, Piazza San Callisto, in Trastevere, has outside tables and you don't pay extra to sit down. The crowd is generally pretty scruffy. *The Druid's Den* is a popular Irish pub, which means you can get Guinness and Kilkenny on tap. It's at Via San Martino ai Monti 28, near Santa Maria Maggiore.

Gelati *Giolitti*, Via degli Uffici del Vicario 40, near the Pantheon and *Gelateria della Palma*, around the corner at Via della Maddalena 20, both have a huge selection of flavours. *Fonte della Salute*, Via Cardinale Marmaggi 2-6, in Trastevere, has arguably the best gelati in Rome.

Entertainment

Rome's primary entertainment guide is *Trovaroma*, a weekly supplement in the Thursday edition of the newspaper *La Repubblica*. Considered the bible for what is happening in the city, it provides a comprehensive listing but in Italian only. The newspaper also publishes a daily listing of cinema, theatre and concerts.

Metropolitan is a fortnightly magazine for Rome's English-speaking community (L1500). It has good entertainment listings and is available at outlets including the Economy Book & Video Center, Via Torino 136 and newsstands in the city centre, including at Largo Argentina. Another excellent guide is *Roma C'è*, available at newspaper stands.

For information on Internet cafés see the earlier Rome, Post & Communications section.

Exhibitions & Concerts From November to May, opera is performed at the *Teatro dell'Opera*, Piazza Beniamino Gigli (☎ 481 70 03). A season of concerts is held in October and November at the *Accademia di Santa Cecilia*, Via della Conciliazione 4, and the *Accademia Filarmonica*, Via Flaminia 118. A series of concerts is held from July to the end of September at the *Teatro Marcello*, Via Teatro di Marcello 44, near Piazza Venezia. For information call ☎ 482 74 03.

Rock concerts are held throughout the year and are advertised on posters plastered all over the city. For information and bookings, contact the ORBIS agency (☎ 475 14 03) in Piazza Esquilino near Stazione Termini.

Nightclubs Nightclubs and discotheques are popular during winter. Among the more interesting and popular Roman live music clubs is *Radio Londra*, Via di Monte Testaccio 67, in the Testaccio area. Although entry is free, you might find it hard to get in here because the bouncers tend to pick and choose, but give it a try anyway. In the same street are the more sedate music clubs *Caruso Caffè* at No 36 and *Caffè Latino* at No 96, both generally offering jazz or blues. More jazz and blues can be heard at *Alexanderplatz*, Via Ostia 9, and *Big Mama*, Via San Francesco a Ripa 18, in Trastevere.

Metropolis, Via Rasella 5, near Piazza Barberini, is a rock club which often stages live concerts by young overseas bands. Membership costs L10,000. *Circolo degli Artisti*, Via Lamarmora 28, near Piazza Vittorio Emanuele, is a lively club, popular among Rome's 'cool' set.

Roman discos are outrageously expensive. Expect to pay up to L30,000 to get in (although women are often allowed in free of charge), which may or may not include one drink. Perennials include: *Alien*, Via Velletri 13; *Piper '90*, Via Tagliamento 9; and *Gilda-Swing*, Via Mario de' Fiori 97. The best gay disco is *L'Alibi*, Via di Monte Testaccio 44.

Cinema The cinema *Pasquino* (☎ 580 36 22), Vicolo del Piede 19, in Trastevere, screens films in English. It is just off Piazza Santa Maria in Trastevere. *Alcazar* (☎ 588 00 99), Via Merry del Val 14, Trastevere, shows an English-language film every Monday.

Things to Buy

The first things that come to mind when thinking of shopping in Rome are clothing and shoes. But it can be difficult to find bargains here, except during the sales.

It is probably advisable to stick to window-shopping in the expensive Ludovisi district, the area around Via Veneto. The major fashion shops are in Via Sistina and Via Gregoriana, leading towards the Spanish Steps. Via Condotti and the parallel streets heading from Piazza di Spagna to Via del Corso are lined with moderately expensive clothing and footwear boutiques, as well as shops selling accessories.

It is cheaper, but not as interesting, to shop along Via del Tritone and Via Nazionale. There are some interesting second-hand clothes shops along Via del Governo Vecchio.

If clothes don't appeal, wander through the streets around Via Margutta, Via Ripetta, Piazza del Popolo and Via Frattina to look at the art galleries, artists' studios and antiquarian shops. Antique shops line Via Coronari, between Piazza Navona and Lungotevere di Tor di Nona.

Everyone flocks to the famous Porta Portese market every Sunday morning. Hundreds of stalls selling anything you can imagine line the streets of the Porta Portese area parallel to Viale di Trastevere, near Trastevere. Here you can pick up a genuine 1960s evening dress for L1000, an antique mirror for L10,000 or a leather jacket for L40,000. Take time to rummage through the piles of clothing and bric-a-brac and you will find some incredible bargains. Catch bus No 280 from Largo Argentina and ask the bus driver where to get off (it's a 10-minute ride).

The market in Via Sannio, near Porta San Giovanni, sells new and second-hand clothes and shoes at bargain prices.

Getting There & Away

Air The main airline offices are in the area around Via Veneto and Via Barberini, north of the station. Qantas, British Airways, Alitalia, Air New Zealand, Lufthansa and Singapore Airlines are all in Via Bissolati. The main airport is Leonardo Da Vinci, at Fiumicino (see the Getting Around section).

Bus The main terminal for intercity buses is in Piazzale Tiburtina, in front of the Stazione Tiburtina. Catch the Metropolitana Linea B from Termini to Tiburtina. Buses connect with cities throughout Italy. Numerous companies, some of which are listed below, operate these services. For information about which companies operate services to which destinations, go to the EPT office, or Enjoy Rome (see Tourist Offices). At Eurojet, Piazza della Repubblica 54, you can buy tickets for and get information about several bus services. Otherwise, there are ticket offices for all of the companies inside the Tiburtina station. COTRAL buses, which service Lazio, depart from numerous points throughout the city, depending on their destinations. Again, the EPT or Enjoy Rome should be able to help.

Some useful bus lines are:

COTRAL – services throughout Lazio – via Ostiense 131 (☎ 722 24 70)
Lazzi – services to other European cities (Eurolines) and the Alps – via Tagliamento 27r (☎ 884 08 40)
Marozzi – services to Bari and Brindisi, as well as to Pompeii, Sorrento and the Amalfi Coast – information at Eurojet

SAIS & Segesta – services to Sicily – Piazza della Repubblica 42 (☎ 481 96 76)
SENA – service to Siena – information at Eurojet
SULGA – services to Perugia and Assisi – information at Eurojet

Train Almost all trains arrive at and depart from Stazione Termini. There are regular connections to all major cities in Italy and throughout Europe. An idea of trip time and cost for intercity trains from Rome (which require the rapido supplement) is as follows: Florence (two hours, L31,500); Milan (five hours, L57,700) and Naples (two hours, L23,000). For train timetable information phone ☎ 4775 (from 7 am to 10.40 pm), or go to the information office at the station (English is spoken). Timetables can be bought at most newsstands in and around Termini and are particularly useful if you are travelling mostly by train. Services at Termini include luggage storage beside tracks 1 and 22 (L5000 per piece for 12 hours), telephones and money exchange (see the Information section). Some trains depart from the stations in Trastevere and at Tiburtina.

Car & Motorcycle The main road connecting Rome to the north and south is the Autostrada del Sole A1, which extends from Milan to Reggio di Calabria. On the outskirts of the city it connects with the Grande Raccordo Anulare (GRA), the ring road encircling Rome. If you are entering or leaving Rome, use the Grande Raccordo and the major feeder roads which connect it to the city; it might be longer, but it is simpler and faster. From the Grande Raccordo there are 33 exits into Rome. If you're approaching from the north, take the Via Salaria, Via Nomentana or Via Flaminia exits. From the south, Via Appia Nuova, Via Cristoforo Colombo and Via del Mare (which connects Rome to the Lido di Ostia) all provide reasonable direct routes into the city. The A12 connects the city to Civitavecchia and to Fiumicino airport.

To rent a car, you will need to be at least 21 years old and have a valid driver's licence. It is cheaper to organise a car from your own country if you want one for a long period. If you have a small child, you can organise to have a baby car seat. It will cost around L46,000 extra for the entire rental period.

Car rental companies in Rome include: Avis (☎ toll-free 1678-6 30 63), Piazza Esquilino 1 Hertz (☎ toll-free 1678-2 20 99), Viale Leonardo da Vinci 421; Europcar (☎ 1678-6 80 88), Via Lombardia 7; and Maggiore (☎ toll-free 1678-6 70 67), Via Po 8. All have offices at Stazione Termini and at both airports Happy Rent (☎ 481 81 85), Piazza Esquilino 8, rents cars, scooters and bicycles (with baby seats available), as well as videocameras Another option for scooters and bicycles is Bike Rome (☎ 322 52 40), Via Veneto 156.

Hitching It is illegal to hitchhike on the auto strade. To head north, wait for a lift on Via Salaria, near the autostrada exit. To go south to Naples, take the Metropolitana to Anagnin and wait in Via Tuscolana. Hitching is no recommended, particularly for women, eithe alone or in groups.

Boat Tirrenia and FS (state railway) ferrie leave from Civitavecchia, near Rome, fo various points in Sardinia (see Sardinia' Getting There & Away section). Bookings ca be made at Sestante CIT, or any travel agency displaying the Tirrenia or FS sign. You can als book directly with Tirrenia (☎ 474 20 41), Vi Bissolati 41, Rome, or at the *Stazione Marittim* (ferry terminal) at the port in Civitavecchia Bookings can be made at Stazione Termini fc FS ferries.

Getting Around
To/From the Airport The main airport i Leonardo da Vinci (☎ 65 95 1) at Fiumicino Access to the city is via the airport-Stazion Termini direct train (follow the signs to th station from the airport arrivals hall), whic costs L13,000. The train arrives at and leave from platform No 22 at Termini and there is ticket office on the platform. The trip takes 3 minutes. The first train leaves the airport fc Termini at 7 am and the last at 10.50 pn Another train makes stops along the way including at Trastevere and Ostiense, and ter minates at Stazione Tiburtina (L8000). A nigh bus runs from Stazione Tirburtina (accessibl by bus No 42N from Piazza Cinquecento i front of Termini) to the airport. The airport i connected to Rome by an autostrada, acces sible from the Grande Raccordo.

Taxis are prohibitively expensive from the airport (see Taxi in the main Getting Around section of this chapter).

The other airport is Ciampino, which is used for most domestic and international charter. Blue COTRAL buses (running from 5.45 am to 10.30 pm) connect with the Metropolitana Linea A at Anagnina), where you can catch the subway to Termini or the Vatican. But, if you arrive very late at night you could end up being forced to catch a taxi. A new metropolitan train line now under construction, which will be known as FM4, will connect the airport with Termini. The airport is connected to Rome by Via Appia Nuova.

Bus The city bus company is ATAC and most of the main buses terminate in Piazza Cinquecento in front of Stazione Termini. Details on which buses head where are available at the ATAC information booth in the centre of the piazza. Another central point for main bus routes in the centre is Largo Argentina, on Corso Vittorio Emanuele south of the Pantheon. Buses run from 6 am to midnight, with limited services throughout the night on some routes.

Travel on Rome's buses, subway and suburban railways has now been linked, and the same ticket is valid for all three. Tickets cost L1500 and are valid for 75 minutes. They must be purchased *before* you get on the bus and validated in the orange machine as you enter. The fine for travelling without a ticket is L50,000, to be paid on the spot, and there is no sympathy for 'dumb tourists'. Tickets can be purchased at any tobacconist, newsstand, or at the main bus terminals. Daily tickets cost L6000, weekly tickets cost L24,000 and monthly tickets are L50,000. ATAC was restructuring many routes in 1996. However, at the time of writing, useful bus numbers to remember were No 64 from Stazione Termini to St Peter's; No 27 from Termini to the Colosseum; No 218 from Piazza di Porta San Giovanni to the catacombs; and No 44 from Piazza Venezia to Trastevere.

Metropolitana The Metropolitana (Metro) has two lines, A and B. Both pass through Stazione Termini. Take Linea A for Piazza di Spagna, the Vatican (Ottaviano) and Villa Borghese (Flaminio), and Linea B for the Colosseum,

Circus Maximus and Piramide (for Testaccio and Stazione Ostiense). Tickets are the same as for city buses (see under Bus in this section). Trains run approximately every five minutes between 6 am and 11.30 pm.

Taxi Taxis are on radio call 24 hours a day in Rome. Cooperativa Radio Taxi Romana (☎ 3570) and La Capitale (☎ 4994) are two of the many operators. Major taxi ranks are at the airports and Stazione Termini and also at Largo Argentina in the historical centre. Remember that there are surcharges on Sunday and for luggage, night service, public holidays and travel to/from Fiumicino airport. The taxi flag fall is L6400 (for the first three km), then L1200 per km. There is a L3000 supplement from 10 pm to 7 am and L1000 from 7 am to 10 pm on Sunday and public holidays. There is a L15,000 supplement on travel to and from Fiumicino airport because it is outside the city limits. This means the fare will cost around L70,000.

Car & Motorcycle Negotiating Roman traffic by car is difficult enough, but be aware that you are taking your life in your hands if you ride a motorcycle in the city. The rule in Rome is to watch the vehicles in front and hope that the vehicles behind are watching you.

Most of the historic centre is closed to normal traffic, although tourists are permitted to drive to their hotels. *Vigili* (traffic police) control the entrances to the centre and will let you through once you mention the name of your hotel. Ask at the hotel for a parking permit for the centre, otherwise you might find a brace on your car wheel or, at worst, that the car has been towed away. If your car goes missing after being parked illegally, check with the traffic police (☎ 6 76 91). It will cost about L180,000 to get it back.

The major parking area close to the centre is at the Villa Borghese. Entrance is from Piazzale Brasile at the top of Via Veneto. There is a supervised car park at Stazione Termini. There are large car parks at Stazione Tiburtina and Piazza dei Partigiani at Stazione Ostiense (both accessible to the centre of Rome by the Metro). The EPT office has a list of cheap car parks on the outskirts of Rome; you can reach the centre by bus or Metro. (See the preceding

Getting There & Away section for information about car, scooter and bike rental.)

In Rome, be wary when crossing at traffic lights because most motorcyclists don't stop at red lights. Neither motorcyclists nor motorists are keen to stop at pedestrian crossings, so be extremely careful. The accepted mode of crossing a road is to step into the traffic and walk at a steady pace. If in doubt, follow a Roman.

Around Rome

Rome demands so much of your time and concentration that most tourists forget that the city is part of the region of Lazio. There are some interesting places within easy day-trip distance of the city. In summer, avoid the polluted beaches close to the city and head south to Sabaudia or Sperlonga, or take the train from Ostiense to Lago di Bracciano.

OSTIA ANTICA

The Romans founded this port city at the mouth of the Tiber in the 4th century BC and it became a strategically important centre of defence and trade. It was populated by merchants, sailors and slaves, and the ruins of the city provide a fascinating contrast to a place such as Pompeii. It was abandoned after barbarian invasions and the appearance of malaria, but Pope Gregory IV re-established the city in the 9th century.

The Rome EPT office or Enjoy Rome can provide information about the ancient city.

Things to See & Do

Of particular note in the excavated city are the **Terme di Nettuno**; a **Roman theatre** built by Augustus; the **forum** and **temple**, dedicated to Jupiter, Juno and Minerva; and the **Piazzale delle Corporazioni**, where you can see the offices of Roman merchants, distinguished by mosaics depicting their trades. The site is open from 9 am to about an hour before sunset and entry is L8000.

Getting There & Away

To get to Ostia Antica take the Metropolitana Linea B to Magliana and then the Ostia Lido train (getting off at Ostia Antica).

TIVOLI

Set on a hill by the Anio River, Tivoli was a resort town of the ancient Romans and became popular as a summer playground for the rich during the Renaissance. It is famous today for the terraced gardens and fountains of the Villa d'Este and the ruins of the spectacular Villa Adriana, built by the Roman emperor Hadrian.

The local AAST tourist office (☎ 0774-31 12 49) is in Largo Garibaldi near the COTRAL bus stop.

Things to See & Do

Hadrian built his summer villa, **Villa Adriana** in the 2nd century AD. Its construction was influenced by the architecture of the famous classical buildings of the day. It was successively plundered by barbarians and Romans for building materials and many of its original decorations were used to embellish the Villa d'Este. However, enough remains to give an idea of the incredible size and magnificence of the villa. You will need about four hours to wander through the vast ruins. Highlights include La Villa dell'Isola (the Villa of the Island), where Hadrian spent his pensive moments, the Imperial Palace and its Piazza d'Oro (Golden Square) and the floor mosaics of the Hospitalia. The villa is open from 9 am to about one hour before sunset, therefore to around 7 pm (last entry at 6 pm) in the warmer months and to around 5 pm in winter. Entry is L8000.

The Renaissance **Villa d'Este** was built in the 16th century for Cardinal Ippolito d'Este on the site of a Franciscan monastery. The villa's beautiful gardens are decorated with numerous fountains, which are its main attraction. Opening hours are the same as for Villa Adriana and entry is L8000. Villa d'Este is closed on Mondays.

Getting There & Away

Tivoli is about 40 km east of Rome and accessible by Cotral bus. Take Metro Linea B from Stazione Termini to Rebibbia; the bus leaves from outside the station every 15 minutes. The bus also stops near the Villa Adriana, about one km from Tivoli. Otherwise, catch local bus No 4 from Tivoli's Piazza Garibaldi to Villa Adriana.

ETRUSCAN SITES

Lazio has several important Etruscan archaeological sites, most within easy reach of Rome by car or public transport. These include Tarquinia (one of the most important cities of the Etruscan League), Cerveteri, Veio and Tuscania. The tombs and religious monuments discovered in the area have yielded the treasures which can now be seen in the large museums, including the Villa Giulia and the Vatican, although the small museums at Tarquinia and Cerveteri are worth visiting.

If you really want to lose yourself in a poetic journey, take along a copy of D H Lawrence's *Etruscan Places*.

Tarquinia

Believed to have been founded in the 12th century BC and to have been the home of the Tarquin kings who ruled Rome before the creation of the republic, Tarquinia was an important economic and political centre of the Etruscan League. The major attractions here are the painted tombs of its necropoli (burial grounds). The AAST tourist information office (☎ 0766-85 63 84) is at Piazza Cavour 1.

Things to See & Do The 15th-century Palazzo Vitelleschi houses the **Museo Nazionale de Tarquinia** and an excellent collection of Etruscan treasures, including frescos removed from the tombs. There are also numerous sarcophagi found in the tombs. The museum is open Tuesday to Sunday from 9 am to 7 pm (closed Monday). Admission costs L8000 and the same ticket admits you to the **necropolis**, a 15 to 20-minute walk away (same opening hours). Ask at the tourist office for directions. Only a small number of the thousands of tombs have been excavated and only a handful are open on any given day. You must wait until a group forms and a guide will then take you on a tour of four to six tombs. Beware of long waits in summer, when thousands of tourists visit the necropolis daily. The tombs are richly decorated with frescos, though many are seriously deteriorated. They are now maintained at constant temperatures to preserve the remaining decorations. This means that it is possible to see them only through glass partitions.

Take the time to wander through the streets of medieval Tarquinia and, if you have a car,

ask for directions to the remains of Etruscan Tarquinia, on the crest of the Civita Hill nearby. There is little evidence of the ancient city, apart from a few limestone blocks that once formed part of the city walls. However, a large temple, the **Ara della Regina**, was discovered on the hill and has been excavated this century.

Places to Stay & Eat There is a camping ground by the sea, *Tusca Tirrenia* (☎ 8 82 94), Viale Neriedi. There are no budget options if you want to stay overnight and it can be difficult to find a room if you don't book well in advance. Try the *Hotel all'Olivo* (☎ 85 73 18), Via Togliatti 15, in the newer part of town, about a 10-minute walk downhill from the medieval centre. Rooms with private bath cost L60,000/90,000 for singles/doubles.

For a good, cheap meal, try *Cucina Casareccia*, at Via G Mazzini 5, off Piazza Cavour, or *Trattoria Arcadia* opposite at No 6.

Getting There & Away Buses leave approximately every hour for Tarquinia from Via Lepanto in Rome, near the Metropolitana Linea A Lepanto stop, arriving at Tarquinia a few steps away from the tourist office. You can also catch a train from Ostiense, but Tarquinia's station is at Tarquinia Lido (beach), approximately three km from the centre. You will then need to catch one of the regular local buses.

Cerveteri

Ancient Caere was founded by the Etruscans in the 8th century BC and enjoyed a period of great prosperity as a maritime centre from the 7th to 5th centuries BC. The main attractions here are the tombs known as *tumoli*, great mounds with carved stone bases. Treasures taken from the tombs can be seen in the Vatican Museums, the Villa Giulia Museum and the Louvre. The Pro Loco tourist office is at Piazza Risorgimento 19.

The main necropolis area, **Banditaccia**, is open daily from 9 am to 4 pm in winter and 9 am to 7 pm in summer and entry is L8000. You can wander freely once inside the area, though it is best to follow the recommended routes in order to see the best preserved tombs. Signs detailing the history of the main tombs are in Italian only. Banditaccia is accessible by local bus in summer only from the main piazza in Cerveteri, but it is also a pleasant three-km walk west from the town.

There is also a small **museum** in Cerveteri that contains an interesting display of pottery and sarcophagi. It is in the Palazzo Ruspoli and is open from 9 am to 2 pm (closed Monday). Entry is free.

Cerveteri is accessible from Rome by COTRAL bus from Via Lepanto, outside the Lepanto stop on Metropolitana Linea A.

Northern Italy

Italy's northern regions are its wealthiest and offer many and varied attractions to travellers. A tour of the north could take you from the beaches of the Italian Riviera in Liguria, to Milan for a shopping spree, into Emilia-Romagna to sample its remarkable *cucina* (cuisine), through countless medieval and Renaissance towns and villages, and into the Alps to ski or trek in the Dolomites, before taking a boat trip down the Grand Canal of timeless Venice.

GENOA

Travellers who think of Genoa (Genova) as simply a dirty port town and bypass the city for the coastal resorts don't know what they're missing. This once powerful maritime republic, birthplace of Christopher Columbus (1451-1506) and now capital of the region of Liguria, can still carry the title La Superba (the proud). It is a fascinating city that is full of contrasts. Here you can meet crusty old seafarers in the markets and trattorias of the port area, where some of the tiny streets are so narrow it is difficult for two people to stand together. But go round a corner and you will find young Genoese in the latest Benetton gear strolling through streets lined with grand, black-and-white marble palaces.

Orientation

Most trains stop at both of the main stations in Genoa: Stazione Principe and Stazione Brignole. The area around Brignole is closer to the city centre and offers more pleasant accommodation than does Principe, which is close to the port. Women travelling alone should avoid staying in the port area.

From Brignole walk straight ahead along Via Fiume to get to Via XX Settembre and the historical centre. It is easier to walk around Genoa than to use the local ATM bus service, but most useful buses stop outside both stations.

Information

Tourist Offices There are APT tourist offices at Stazione Principe and at the airport (both open from 8 am to 8 pm Monday to Saturday and 9 am to midday on Sunday) and at Via del Porto Antico (☎ 2 4871) in the Palazzina Santa Maria, open 8.30 am to 6.30 pm seven days a week.

Post & Communications The main post office is in Via Dante, just off Piazza de Ferrari. There is a Telecom office at Stazione Brignole, open from 8 am to 10 pm.

Genoa's postcode is 16100 and its telephone code is ☎ 010.

Medical Services The Ospedale San Martino (☎ 55 51) is in Via Benedetto XV. For an ambulance call ☎ 570 59 51.

Emergency Call ☎ 113 for the police.

Things to See & Do

Start by wandering around the port area, the oldest part of Genoa, to see the huge, 12th-century, black-and-white marble **Cattedrale di San Lorenzo** and the nearby **Palazzo Ducale**, in Piazza Matteotti. In the beautiful, tiny **Piazza San Matteo** are the palaces of the Doria family, one of the most important families of the city in the 14th and 15th centuries. Take a walk along **Via Garibaldi**, which is lined with palaces. Some are open to the public and contain art galleries, including the 16th-century **Palazzo Bianco** and the 17th-century **Palazzo Rosso**, where the Flemish painter Van Dyck lived. Both are open from 9 am to 7 pm Tuesday to Saturday and on Sunday from 9 am to 12.30 pm. Entry to each is L4000.

Take the kids to the **aquarium** (Europe's biggest and well worth a visit) to see the sharks, dolphins, penguins and myriad other marine life. Located on Ponte Spinola, it opens from

9.30 am to 7 pm Tuesday, Wednesday and Friday and 9.30 am to 8.30 pm Thursday, Saturday and Sunday.

Places to Stay

The HI *Ostello Genova* (☎ 242 24 57), is at Via Costanzi 120, at Righi, just outside Genoa. Bed and breakfast costs L22,000 and a meal is L15,000. Catch bus No 40 from Stazione Brignole. The *Casa della Giovane* (☎ 20 66 32), Piazza Santa Sabina 4, has cheap beds for women only.

Turn right as you leave Stazione Brignole and walk up Via de Amicis to Piazza Brignole. Turn right into Via Gropallo where there are some good hotels in a lovely old palazzo at No 4. *Pensione Mirella* (☎ 839 37 22) has singles/doubles for L37,000/65,000. A shower costs L2000 extra. The *Carola* (☎ 839 13 40) has very pleasant rooms for L45,000/75,000. *Albergo Rita* (☎ 87 02 07), a few doors up at No 8, has recently renovated singles/doubles for L30,000/65,000. *Albergo Vittoria* (☎ 58 15 17), Largo Archimede 1 (turn left as you leave Stazione Brignole), has large rooms for L35,000/45,000.

Places to Eat

Don't leave town without trying pesto genovese (pasta with a sauce of basil, garlic and pine nuts), torta pasqualina (made with artichokes, cheese and eggs), pansoti (ravioli), farinata (a torte made with chickpea flour) and, of course, focaccia. The best deal in town is at *Da Maria*, Vico Testa d'Oro 14, where a full meal is a set L12,000, including wine. Students and old seafarers dine here. *Trattoria Walter*, Vico Colalanza 2r, concentrates on Genoese specialities. Pasta dishes cost from L7000.

Entertainment

The Genoa Theatre Company performs at the *Politeama Genovese* (☎ 89 35 89) and the *Teatro della Corte* (☎ 570 24 72). Its main season is January to May. *Teatro della Tosse in Sant'Agostino* (☎ 29 57 20), Piazza R Negri, has a season of diverse shows from October to May.

Getting There & Away

Air The Cristoforo Colombo international airport at Sestri Ponente, six km west of the city, has regular domestic and international connections. An airport bus service, the Volabus (☎ 59 94 14), leaves from Piazza Verdi, just outside Stazione Brignole and also stops at Stazione Principe.

Bus Buses leave from Piazza della Vittoria for Rome, Florence, Milan and Perugia. Eurolines buses leave from the same piazza for Barcelona, Madrid and Paris. You can make bookings at Geotravels (☎ 58 71 81) in the piazza.

Train Genoa is connected by train to Turin, Milan, Pisa and Rome. For train information call ☎ 28 40 81.

Boat The city's busy port is a major embarkation point for ferries to Sicily, Sardinia and Corsica. Major companies are: Corsica Ferries (for Corsica), Piazza Dante 1 (☎ 59 33 01); Moby Lines (for Corsica), Ponte Asserato (☎ 25 27 55); and Tirrenia (for Sicily and Sardinia), at the Stazione Marittima, Ponte Colombo (☎ 275 80 41). For more information, see the Getting There & Away sections under Sicily and Sardinia, and under Corsica in the France chapter.

RIVIERA DI LEVANTE

This coastal area of the region of Liguria from Genoa to La Spezia, on the border with Tuscany, has a spectacular beauty to rival that of the Amalfi Coast. It also has several resorts which, despite attracting thousands of summer tourists, manage to remain unspoiled. The region's climate means that both spring and autumn can bring suitable beach weather.

The telephone code is ☎ 0185.

There are tourist offices in most of the towns, including at Santa Margherita (☎ 78 74 85), Via XXV Aprile, between the station and the sea, and at Camogli (☎ 77 10 66), Via XX Settembre 33, just as you leave the station. They will advise on accommodation.

Things to See & Do

Santa Margherita Ligure, a pretty resort town noted for its orange blossoms, is a good base from which to explore the area.

From Santa Margherita, the resorts of **Portofino**, a haunt of the rich and famous, and **Camogli**, a fishing village turned major resort town (but which still manages to look like a fishing village), are a short bus ride away. The fascinating fishing village of **San Fruttuoso** and its medieval Benedictine monastery are also close by.

Easily accessible by train are the beautiful **Cinque Terre**, literally meaning Five Lands. These five coastal towns (Monterosso, Vernazza, Corniglia, Manarola and Riomaggiore) are linked by walking tracks along the coast. Make a point of walking from Monterosso to Riomaggiore (about five hours).

Places to Stay & Eat

There are some excellent options in Santa Margherita. The *Albergo Nuovo Riviera* (☎ 28 74 03), in an old villa at Via Belvedere 10, has singles/doubles for L45,000/60,000 or doubles with private shower for L70,000. It also offers half and full board, which is compulsory in the high season. Full board is L70,000 per person. The friendly owners impose a strict no-smoking rule in the hotel's public areas. *Albergo Annabella* (☎ 28 65 31), Via Costasecca 10, has large, bright rooms for L45,000/65,000. Triples are L90,000.

In Camogli try the *Albergo la Camogliese* (☎ 77 14 02), Via Garibaldi 55, on the seafront. Some rooms have balconies and views and prices are graded accordingly. The cheapest rooms cost L60,000/90,000 a single/double. Full board in the high season is L90,000.

In Santa Margherita, *Trattoria San Siso*, at Corso Matteotti 137 (about 10 minutes from the seafront), has great food at low prices, with a full meal costing around L20,000. Try the panzotti, which are small ravioli in a walnut sauce.

Getting There & Away

The entire coast is served by train and all points are accessible from Genoa. From Santa Margherita, Camogli and the Cinque Terre are both accessible by train. Buses leave from Santa Margherita's Piazza Martiri della Libertà for Portofino. You can walk to San Fruttuoso from either Portofino or Camogli.

Boats leave from near the bus stop in Santa Margherita for Portofino (L9000 return), San Fruttuoso (L23,000 return) and the Cinque Terre (L35,000 return).

TURIN

Turin (Torino) is the capital of the Piedmont region. The House of Savoy, which ruled this region for hundreds of years (and Italy until 1945), built for itself a gracious baroque city. Its grandeur is often compared to that of Paris. Italy's industrial expansion began here with companies like Fiat and Olivetti.

Orientation & Information

The Porta Nuova train station is the point of arrival for most travellers. To reach the city centre walk straight ahead over the main east-west route, Corso Vittorio Emanuele II, through the grand Piazza Carlo Felice and along Via Roma until you come to Piazza San Carlo. The APT tourist office (☎ 011-53 51 81) is at Via Roma 226. There is a smaller office at the main train station and both are open Monday to Saturday from 9 am to 7.30 pm.

Things to See & Do

In Piazza San Carlo, known as Turin's drawing room, are the baroque churches of **San Carlo** and **Santa Cristina**, the latter designed by Filippo Juvarra. **Piazza Castello**, the centre of historical Turin, features the sumptuous **Palazzo Madama**, once the residence of Victor Amadeo I's widow, Marie Cristina, and the **Museo Civico di Arte Antica**. Nearby is the **Palazzo Reale** (Royal Palace), an austere 17th-century building. The palace gardens were designed in 1697 by Louis le Nôtre, whose other works include the gardens at Versailles.

The **Cattedrale di San Giovanni**, west of the Palazzo Reale, off Via XX Settembre, houses the **Shroud of Turin**, the linen cloth which some believed was used to wrap the crucified Christ. Scientists have been able to categorically establish that the shroud is simply not that old – instead it dates back to somewhere around the 12th century. The actual shroud is in the **Cappella della Santa Sindone** (Chapel of the Holy Shroud), topped by Guarini's honeycomb-like, black marble dome, while a copy adorns the walls of a nearby chapel.

Places to Stay & Eat

Cheap rooms can be hard to find. Call the APT in advance for a suggestion, although the staff won't make a reservation.

Campeggio Villa Rey (☎ 819 01 17), Strada Val San Martino Superiore 27, is open from March to October. The *Ostello Torino* (☎ 660 29 39), Via Alby 1, on the corner of Via Gatti, is in the hills east of the Po River and can be reached by bus No 52 from the Porta Nuova station. Bed and breakfast is L18,000 and a meal is L14,000.

The *Canelli* (☎ 54 60 78), Via San Dalmazzo 5b, off Via Garibaldi, has singles/doubles for L25,000/35,000. The *Albergo Magenta* (☎ 54 26 49), Corso Vittorio Emanuele II 67, has singles/doubles for L45,000/50,000.

One of the better self-service restaurants is *La Grangia*, Via Garibaldi 21, where you can eat a full meal for around L14,000. At *Pizzeria alla Baita dei 7 Nani*, Via A Doria 5, you can have a pizza and a beer for around L10,000. For excellent gelati, head for *Caffè Fiorio*, Via Po 8, and try the gianduia.

Getting There & Away

Turin is serviced by Caselle international airport (☎ 567 63 61), with flights to European and national destinations. The SADEM bus company (☎ 30 16 16) runs a service to the airport every 30 minutes from the bus station at Corso Inghilterra 3. Intercity buses also terminate here. Buses serve the Aostan valley, most of the towns and ski resorts in Piedmont and major Italian cities. Regular trains connect with Milan, Aosta, Venice, Genoa and Rome.

Getting Around

The city is well serviced by a network of buses and trams. A map of public transport routes is available from the APT.

AROUND TURIN

The main attractions of the Piedmont region are the Alps, including the **Parco Nazionale del Gran Paradiso** and the beautiful natural reserve around **Monte Rosa** in the far north. Walkers can tackle sections of the Grande Traversata delle Alpi, a 200-km track through the Alps, running from the Ligurian border to Lago Maggiore on the border with Lombardy. Information is available at Turin's APT office. Wine-lovers can visit the vineyards around **Asti**, a pleasant town in the Monferrato hills, which gives its name to Italy's best known sparkling wine, Asti Spumante.

MILAN

The economic and fashion capital of Italy, Milan (Milano) has long been an elegant and cultural city. Its origins are believed to be Celtic, but it was conquered by the Romans in 222 BC, and later became an important trading and transport centre. From the 13th century the city flourished under the rule of two powerful families: the Visconti and later the Sforza.

Orientation

From Milan's central train station (Stazione Centrale), it is simple to reach the centre of town and other major points on the efficient Milan underground (known as the MM, or Metropolitana). The MM3 will take you from the station to the Duomo and the centre of town. The city of Milan is huge, but most sights are in the centre. Use the Duomo and the Castello Sforzesco, at the other end of Via Dante, as your points of reference. The main shopping areas and sights are around and between the two.

Note that Milan closes down almost completely in August, when most of the city's inhabitants take their annual holidays. You will find few restaurants and shops open at this time.

Information

Tourist Offices The main branch of the APT (☎ 80 96 62) is at Via Marconi 1, in Piazza del Duomo, where you can pick up the useful *Milan is Milano*, one of the most comprehensive city guides in Italy. It is open Monday to Saturday from 8 am to 7 pm and Sunday and public holidays from 9 am to 12.30 pm and 1.30 to 5 pm. There is a branch office (open the same hours) at the Stazione Centrale.

Milan City Council operates an information office in Galleria V Emanuele II, just off Piazza del Duomo, Monday to Saturday from 8 am to 8 pm.

Foreign Consulates You will find the consulates of the following countries in Milan: Australia (☎ 77 70 41), Via Borgogna 2; Canada (☎ 675 81), Via Vittorio Pisani 19; France (☎ 655 91 41), Via Mangili 1; the UK (☎ 72 30 01), Via San Paolo 7; and the USA (☎ 29 03 51), Via P Amadeo 2/10.

ITALY

ITALY

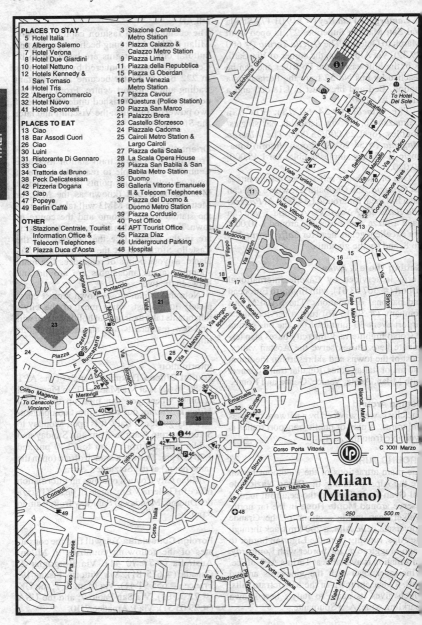

PLACES TO STAY
5 Hotel Italia
6 Albergo Salerno
7 Hotel Verona
8 Hotel Due Giardini
10 Hotel Nettuno
12 Hotels Kennedy & San Tomaso
14 Hotel Tris
22 Albergo Commercio
32 Hotel Nuovo
41 Hotel Speronari

PLACES TO EAT
13 Ciao
18 Bar Assodi Cuori
26 Ciao
30 Luini
31 Ristorante Di Gennaro
33 Ciao
34 Trattoria da Bruno
38 Peck Delicatessan
42 Pizzeria Dogana
43 Ciao
47 Popeye
49 Berlin Caffè

OTHER
1 Stazione Centrale, Tourist Information Office & Telecom Telephones
2 Piazza Duca d'Aosta
3 Stazione Centrale Metro Station
4 Piazza Caiazzo & Caiazzo Metro Station
9 Piazza Lima
11 Piazza della Repubblica
15 Piazza G Oberdan
16 Porta Venezia Metro Station
17 Piazza Cavour
19 Questura (Police Station)
20 Piazza San Marco
21 Palazzo Brera
23 Castello Sforzesco
24 Piazzale Cadorna
25 Cairoli Metro Station & Largo Cairoli
27 Piazza della Scala
28 La Scala Opera House
29 Piazza San Babila & San Babila Metro Station
35 Duomo
36 Galleria Vittorio Emanuele II & Telecom Telephones
37 Piazza del Duomo & Duomo Metro Station
39 Piazza Cordusio
40 Post Office
44 APT Tourist Office
45 Piazza Diaz
46 Underground Parking
48 Hospital

Milan
(Milano)

0   250   500 m

Money Banks in Milan are open Monday to Friday from 8.30 am to 1.30 pm and from 3 to 4 pm. Exchange offices open at weekends include Banca Ponti, Piazza del Duomo 19, from 8.30 am to 1 pm Saturday. There are also exchange offices open seven days a week at the Stazione Centrale. The American Express office (☎ 72 00 36 94) is at Via Brera 3 and opens Monday to Thursday from 9 am to 5.30 pm and Friday to 5 pm.

Post & Communications The main post office is at Via Cordusio 4, off Via Dante, near Piazza del Duomo. Fermo Posta is here, open Monday to Friday from 8.15 am to 7.40 pm and Saturday to 3.30 pm. There are also post offices at the station and at Linate airport.

There are Telecom telephone offices at the central station (open daily from 8 am to 9.30 pm – telephone directories are here for all of Italy, Europe and the Mediterranean) and in Galleria V Emanuele II, open daily from 8 am to 9.30 pm.

Telecom has been changing telephone numbers in Milan for some years. If you have problems call ☎ 12 (they speak Italian only).

Milan's postcode is 20100 and its telephone code is ☎ 02.

Bookshops The American Bookstore, Via Campiero 16, has a good selection of English-language books.

Medical Services For an ambulance call ☎ 77 33 and for emergency first-aid call the Italian Red Cross on ☎ 38 83. If you need a hospital, the Ospedale Maggiore Policlinico (☎ 551 35 18) is at Via Francesco Sforza 35, close to the centre. There is an all-night pharmacy in the Stazione Centrale (☎ 669 09 35).

Emergency In an emergency call the police on ☎ 113 or ☎ 112. The *questura centrale* (police headquarters) office for foreigners is at Via Montebello (☎ 62 26 34 00). They speak English. For lost property call the Milan City Council (☎ 551 61 41).

Dangers & Annoyances Milan's main shopping areas are popular haunts for local groups of thieves. They are as numerous here as in Rome and also lightning fast. They use the same technique of waving cardboard or newspaper in your face to distract your attention while they head for your pockets or purse. Be particularly careful in the piazza in front of the Stazione Centrale – it is a major haunt of thieves who prey on tourists.

Things to See & Do
Start with the extraordinary **Duomo**, commissioned by Gian Galeazzo Visconti in 1386. The first glimpse of this spiky, tumultuous structure, with its marble façade shaped into pinnacles, statues and pillars, is certainly memorable.

Walk through the graceful **Galleria Vittorio Emanuele II** to **La Scala**, Milan's famous opera house. The theatre's **museum** is open Monday to Saturday from 9 am to midday and 2 to 6 pm, and on Sunday from 9.30 am to 12.30 pm and 2.30 to 6 pm. Admission is L5000.

At the end of Via Dante is the huge **Castello Sforzesco**, which was originally a Visconti fortress but was entirely rebuilt by Francesco Sforza in the 15th century. Its museums contain an interesting collection of sculpture, including Michelangelo's *Pietà Rondanini*. It is open Tuesday to Sunday from 9.30 am to 5.30 pm. Admission is free.

Nearby in Via Brera is the 17th-century **Palazzo di Brera**, which houses the **Pinacoteca di Brera**. This gallery's vast collection of paintings includes Mantegna's masterpiece, the *Dead Christ*. The gallery is open Tuesday to Saturday from 9 am to 5.30 pm and Sunday from 9 am to 12.30 pm. Admission is L8000.

An absolute must is Leonardo da Vinci's *Last Supper*, in the Cenacolo Vinciano, next to the **Chiesa di Santa Maria delle Grazie**, noted for Bramante's tribune. The *Last Supper* was restored in 1995, but centuries of damage from floods, bombing and decay have left their mark. The building is open Tuesday to Saturday from 8 am to 1.45 pm. Admission is L12,000.

Special Events
St Ambrose's Day (7 December) is one of Milan's major festivals, and features a traditional street fair near the Basilica di Sant'Ambrogio, off Via Carducci.

Places to Stay
Hostels The HI *Ostello Piero Rotta* (☎ 39 26

70 95), Viale Salmoiraghi 2, is north-west of the city centre. Bed and breakfast is L23,000. Take the MM1 to the QT8 stop. The place is closed from 9 am to 5 pm and lights out is 12.30 am. *Protezione della Giovane* (☎ 29 00 01 64), Corso Garibaldi 123, is run by nuns for women aged 16 to 25 years. Beds cost from L26,000 a night.

Hotels Milan's hotels are among the most expensive and heavily booked in Italy, so it's strongly recommended that you book in advance. There are numerous budget hotels around Stazione Centrale, but quality varies. The tourist office will make bookings, which hotels will hold for one hour.

Stazione Centrale & Corso Buenos Aires
The *Nettuno* (☎ 29 40 44 81), Via Tadino 27 (turn right off Via D Scarlatti, which is to the left as you leave the station), is a 10-minute walk away. It has basic singles/doubles for L44,000/64,000. A triple with bathroom is L120,000.

In Via Vitruvio, to the left off Piazza Duca d'Aosta as you leave the station, there are two budget options. The *Albergo Salerno* (☎ 204 68 70) at No 18 has very clean singles/doubles for L40,000/60,000 – an extra L20,000 with bathroom. The *Italia* (☎ 669 38 26) at No 44 has less attractive rooms for L45,000/65,000. The *Due Giardini* (☎ 29 52 10 93), Via Lodovico Settala 46, has very comfortable singles/doubles for L60,000/80,000 and triples for L108,000, as well as a communal garden. The *Verona* (☎ 66 98 30 91), at Via Carlo Tenca 12, near Piazza della Repubblica, has rooms for L50,000/80,000 with TV and telephone.

At Viale Tunisia 6, just off Corso Buenos Aires, there are several hotels. The *Hotel Kennedy* (☎ 29 40 09 34) has reasonable singles/doubles for L60,000/80,000. A double with private bathroom is L120,000 and triples with bathroom are L40,000 per person. Bookings are accepted. The *Hotel San Tomaso* (☎ 29 51 47 47) has small, clean singles/doubles for L50,000/80,000 and triples for L35,000 per person.

Closer to the centre, off Piazza G Oberdan, is the quaint *Hotel Tris* (☎ 29 40 06 74), at Via

Sirtori 26. It has appealing doubles/triples with private shower for L80,000/105,000.

The Centre The *Albergo Commercio* (☎ 86 46 38 80), Via Mercato 1, has very basic singles/doubles with shower for L50,000 60,000. From Piazza Cordusio walk down Via Broletto, which becomes Via Mercato. The entrance to the hotel is around the corner in Via delle Erbe.

Very close to Piazza del Duomo is the *Hotel Speronari* (☎ 86 46 11 25), Via Speronari 4 which is eccentrically decorated but comfortable. Singles/doubles are L60,000/80,000. The *Hotel Nuovo* (☎ 86 46 05 42) at Piazza Beccaria 6, is in a great location just off Corso Vittorio Emanuele II and the Duomo. Singles doubles cost L50,000/65,000.

Places to Eat
Italians say that the cucina of Lombardy (Lombardia) is designed for people who don' have time to waste because they are always in a hurry to get to work. In Milan, traditiona restaurants are being replaced by fast-foo outlets and sandwich bars as the favoured eating places. Try the bar snacks laid in many bars around 5 pm.

Restaurants Avoid the area around the station and head for Corso Buenos Aires and the centre.

Around Stazione Centrale Ciao, Corso Buenos Aires 7, is part of a chain (there are others in Corso Europa, Piazza del Duomo and at Via Dante 5), but the food is first-rate and relatively cheap. Pasta dishes cost around L5000 and excellent salads go for around L3000. *Ristorante Primavera d'Oriente*, Via Palestrina 13, offers a standard Chinese mea from L16,000.

City Centre The first time the Milanese taste pizza it was cooked at *Ristorante Di Gennaro* Via S Radegonda 3, though today there is no much to set this place above others in the city The *Trattoria da Bruno*, Via Cavallotti 15, of Corso Europa, has a set-price lunch fo L17,000. *Pizzeria Dogana*, on the corner o Via Capellari and Via Dogana, also near th Duomo, has outside tables. Pasta and pizz each cost around L9000 and there's a good selection of contorni.

Popeye, Via San Tecla 8, near the Duomo, is reputed to have the best pizza in Milan. A pizza costs around L7000 to L10,000 and a full meal will come to around L25,000 or more.

Cafés & Sandwich Bars One of Milan's oldest fast-food outlets is *Luini*, Via S Radegonda 16, just off Piazza del Duomo. A popular haunt of teenagers and students, it sells panzerotti, similar to calzone (a savoury turn-over made with pizza dough) but stuffed with tomatoes, garlic and mozzarella. They cost L3000.

Berlin Caffè, Via G Mora 9 (to the left off Corso Porta Ticinese, near Largo Carrobbio), has a small menu at night (L12,000 for one dish). Otherwise it is a pleasant place for coffee or wine.

A good sandwich bar is *Bar Assodi Cuori*, Piazza Cavour (where you can sit down for no extra charge). Not far from Stazione Centrale is *Pattini & Marinoni*, at Corso Buenos Aires 53, which sells bread, and also pizza by the slice.

For gourmet takeaway head for *Peck*. Its rosticceria is at Via Cesare Cantù 11, where you can buy cooked meats and vegetables. Another outlet is at Via Spadari 9 (near the Duomo).

Entertainment

Music, theatre and cinema dominate Milan's entertainment calendar. The opera season at *La Scala* opens on 7 December. For tickets go to the box office (☎ 55 18 13 77), but don't expect a good seat unless you book well in advance. There is also a summer season, which features operas, concerts and ballet.

In March/April and October/November organ concerts are performed at the Church of San Maurizio in the Monastero Maggiore, at Corso Magenta 15, the continuation of Via Meravigli. In April/May there is a jazz festival, Città di Milano, and in summer the city stages Milano d'Estate, a series of concerts, theatre and dance performances.

The main season for theatre and concerts starts in October. Full details of all events are available from the tourist office in Piazza del Duomo. For details on cinema read the listings section in the daily newspaper *Corriere della Sera*.

Things to Buy

Every item of clothing you ever wanted to buy, but could never afford, is in Milan. The main streets for clothing, footwear and accessories are behind the Duomo around Corso Vittorio Emanuele II. You can window-shop for high-class fashions in Via Borgospesso and Via della Spiga.

The areas around Via Torino, Corso Buenos Aires and Corso XXII Marzo are less expensive. Markets are held in the areas around the canals (south-west of the centre), notably on Viale Papiniano on Tuesday and Saturday morning. A flea market is held in Viale Gabriele d'Annunzio each Saturday.

Getting There & Away

Air International flights use Malpensa airport, about 50 km north-west of Milan. Domestic and European flights use Linate airport, about seven km east.

Bus Bus stations are scattered throughout the city, although some major companies use Piazza Castello as a terminal. Check with the APT for assistance.

Train Regular trains go to Venice, Florence (and Bologna), Genoa, Turin and Rome, as well as major cities throughout Europe. For train timetable information go to the busy office in the station (they speak English), open 7 am to 11 pm or call ☎ 67 50 01.

Car & Motorcycle Milan is the major junction of Italy's motorways, including the Autostrada del Sole (A1) to Rome, the Milano-Torino (A5) and the Serenissima (A4) for Verona and Venice, and the A8 and A9 north to the lakes and the Swiss border.

All these roads meet with the Milan ring road, known as the Tangenziale Est and Tangenziale Ovest (the east and west bypasses). From here follow the signs which lead into the centre. The A4 in particular is an extremely busy road, where there are numerous accidents that can hold up traffic for hours. In winter all roads in the area become extremely hazardous because of rain, snow and fog.

ITALY

Getting Around

To/From the Airports STAM airport shuttle buses leave from Piazza Luigi di Savoia, on the east side of Stazione Centrale, for Malpensa airport (from 5.15 am to 10.15 pm, tickets L18,000) and for Linate airport (from 5.40 am to 9 pm, tickets L6000) every half-hour.

Bus & Metro Milan's public transport system is extremely efficient. The underground (MM) has three lines. The red MM1 provides the easiest access to the city centre. It is necessary to take the green MM2 from Stazione Centrale to Loreto metro station to connect with the MM1. The yellow MM3 also passes through Stazione Centrale and has a station in Piazza del Duomo. It's the easiest way to get around, but buses and trams are also useful. Tickets for the MM are L1500, valid for one underground ride and/or 75 minutes on buses and trams.

You can buy tickets in the MM stations, as well as at authorised tobacconists and newspaper stands.

Taxi Taxis won't stop if you hail them in the street – head for the taxi ranks, all of which have telephones. A few of the radio taxi companies serving the city are Radiotaxidata (☎ 53 53), Esperia (☎ 83 88) and Autoradiotaxi (☎ 85 85).

Car & Motorcycle Normal traffic is banned in the city centre from Monday to Friday 7.30 am to 6 pm, although tourists travelling to their hotels are allowed to enter. The city is dotted with expensive car parks (look for the blue sign with a white P). A cheaper alternative is to use one of the supervised car parks at the last stop on each MM line. Hertz, Avis, Maggiore and Europcar all have offices at Stazione Centrale.

MANTUA

Legend, perpetuated by Virgil and Dante, claims that Mantua (Mantova) was founded by the soothsayer Manto, daughter of Tiresias. Virgil was, in fact, born in a nearby village in 70 AD. From the 14th to the 18th century the city was ruled by the Gonzaga family, who embellished the town with their palaces and employed artists such as Andrea Mantegna and Pisanello to decorate them with their paintings

and frescos. You can easily see the city on a day trip from Milan, Verona or Bologna.

Information

The tourist office, Piazza Andrea Mantegna, is a 10-minute walk from the station along Corso Vittorio Emanuele, which becomes Corso Umberto 1. It is open from Monday to Saturday 9 am to noon and 3 to 6 pm.

Mantua's telephone code is ☎ 0376.

Things to See & Do

Start with the **Piazza Sordello**, which is surrounded by impressive buildings including the **cattedrale**, a strange building that combines a Romanesque tower, baroque façade and Renaissance interior. The piazza is dominated by the **Palazzo Ducale**, a huge complex of buildings, and seat of the Gonzaga family. There is much to see in the palace, in particular the Gonzaga **apartments** and art collection, and the famous **Camera degli Sposi** (Bridal Chamber), decorated with frescos by Andrea Mantegna in the 15th century. In the **Sala del Pisanello** (Pisanello's Room) are frescos by the Veronese painter (discovered in 1969 under two layers of plaster), depicting the cycle of chivalry and courtly love, which were. The palace is open Monday to Saturday from 9 am to 1 pm, 2.30 to 4.30 pm, and Sunday 9 am to 1 pm. Admission is L10,000.

Don't miss the **Palazzo Te**, the lavishly decorated summer palace of the Gonzaga. It is open Tuesday to Sunday from 9 am to 6 pm. Admission is L10,000. Take bus No 5 from the centre to the palace.

Places to Stay & Eat

The HI *Ostello per la Gioventù* (☎ 37 24 65) is just out of town at Lunetta San Giorgio. Take bus No 2M from the station. Bed and breakfast is L15,000. There is a *camping ground* next to the hostel which charges L4000 per person and L3500 for a tent space. Both are open from April to October.

At the *Albergo Roma Vecchia* (☎ 32 21 00) Via Corridoni 20, doubles cost L42,000. It is closed during August and part of December.

Self Service Nuvolari, Piazza Viterbi 11, is a self-service place with good food and cheap prices. *Caà Ramponi*, Piazza Broletto 7, offers pasta and pizza at reasonable prices. You could also buy fresh produce from the market in nearby Piazza Broletto and have a picnic in Piazza Virgiliana.

Getting There & Away

Mantua is accessible by train and bus from Verona (about 40 minutes), and by train from Milan and Bologna with a change at Modena.

VERONA

Forever associated with Romeo and Juliet, Verona has much more to offer than the relics of a tragic love story. Known as *la piccola Roma* (little Rome) for its importance as a Roman city, its golden era was during the 13th and 14th centuries, under the rule of the della Scala (also referred to as Scaliger) family. This was a period noted for the savage family feuding on which Shakespeare based his play.

Old Verona is small, but there is much to see and it is a popular base for exploring surrounding towns.

Orientation & Information

It's easy to find your way around Verona. Buses leave for the centre from outside the train station; otherwise walk to the right, past the bus station, cross the river and walk along Corso Porta Nuova to Piazza Brà. From there take Via Mazzini and turn left at Via Cappello to reach Piazza delle Erbe.

The main tourist office is at Via Leoncino 61 (☎ 59 28 28), on the corner of Piazza Brà facing the Roman Arena (open 8 am to 7 pm). There are branches at the train station (open 8 am to 6 pm) and at Piazza delle Erbe 42 (open only in summer from 8 am to 7 pm).

The main post office is at Piazza Viviani. The Ospedale Civile Maggiore (☎ 807 11 11) is at Piazza A Stefani.

Verona's telephone code is ☎ 045.

Things to See & Do

The pink-marble Roman amphitheatre, known as the **Arena**, in Piazza Brà, was built in the 1st century and is now Verona's opera house. Walk along Via Mazzini to Via Cappello and **Juliet's House** (Casa di Giulietta), its entrance smothered with lovers' graffiti. Further along the street to the right is **Porta Leoni**, one of the gates to the old Roman Verona; **Porta Borsari**, the other gate to the city, is north of the Arena at Corso Porta Borsari.

In the other direction is **Piazza delle Erbe**,

the former site of the Roman forum. Lined with the characteristic pink-marble palaces of Verona, the piazza today remains the lively centre of the city, but the permanent market stalls in its centre detract from its beauty. In the piazza is the **Fountain of Madonna Verona**. Just off the square is the elegant **Piazza dei Signori**, flanked by the Renaissance **Loggia del Consiglio**; the della Scala (Scaliger) residence now known as the **Governor's Palace** and partly decorated by Giotto; and the medieval town hall. Take a look at the **Duomo**, on Via Duomo, for its Romanesque main doors and Titian's *Assumption*.

Places to Stay & Eat

The HI *Ostello Villa Francescatti* (☎ 59 03 60), Salita Fontana del Ferro 15, should be your first choice. Bed and breakfast is L17,000 a night (including sheets) and a meal is L12,000. An HI or student card is necessary. Next door is a *camping ground*. To reserve a space, speak to the hostel management. Catch bus No 2 from the station to Piazza Isolo and then follow the signs.

The *Casa della Giovane* (☎ 59 68 80), Via Pigna 7, just off Via Garibaldi, is for women only and costs L25,000 or L30,000 a night for a bed in a small dormitory. Catch bus No 2 and ask the driver where to get off.

Albergo Castello (☎ 800 44 03), Corso Cavour 43, has singles/doubles for L30,000/48,000. *Albergo Ciopeta* (☎ 800 68 43), Vicolo Teatro Filarmonico 2, near Piazza Brà, has doubles for up to L100,000.

Known for its fresh produce, its crisp soave (a dry white wine) and its boiled meat, Verona offers delicious food at reasonable prices. In Piazza Brà, with a view of the Arena, is *Brek*, a good bet for cheap meals, with pasta dishes starting from around L6000. The *Pizzeria Liston*, Via dietro Liston 19, has good pizzas for around L8000. A full meal will cost around L24,000.

Entertainment

Throughout the year the city hosts musical and cultural events. These culminate in the season of opera and drama that runs from July to September at the *Arena* (tickets from around L40,000). There is a lyric-symphonic season in winter at the 18th-century *Teatro Filarmonico* (☎ 800 28 80), Via dei Mutilati 4, just off

ITALY

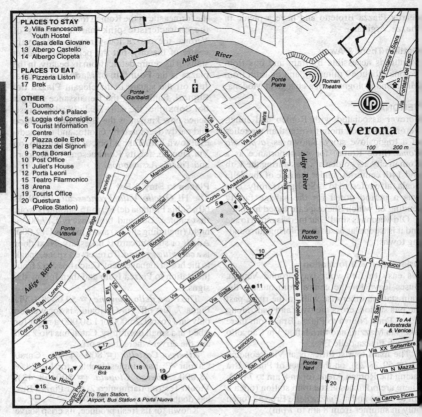

PLACES TO STAY
2 Villa Francescatti
   Youth Hostel
3 Casa della Giovane
13 Albergo Castello
14 Albergo Ciopeta

PLACES TO EAT
16 Pizzeria Liston
17 Brek

OTHER
1 Duomo
4 Governor's Palace
5 Loggia del Consiglio
6 Tourist Information
   Centre
7 Piazza delle Erbe
8 Piazza dei Signori
9 Porta Borsari
10 Post Office
11 Juliet's House
12 Porta Leoni
15 Teatro Filarmonico
18 Arena
19 Tourist Office
20 Questura
   (Police Station)

Verona

Piazza Brà, and Shakespeare is performed in the Roman Theatre in summer. Information and tickets for these events are available at the Ente Lirico Arena di Verona (☎ 800 51 51), Piazza Brà 28.

Getting There & Away

The Verona-Villafranca airport (☎ 51 30 39) is just outside the town and accessible by bus and train.

The main APT bus terminal is in the piazza in front of the station, an area known as Porta Nuova. Buses leave for surrounding areas, including Mantua, Ferrara and Brescia.

Verona is on the Brenner Pass railway line to Austria and Germany. It is directly linked by train to Milan, Venice, Florence and Rome.

The city is at the intersection of the Serenissima A4 (Milan-Venice) and the Brennero A22 autostrade.

Getting Around

There is an APT bus to the airport, which leaves from Porta Nuova and from Piazza Cittadella, off Corso Porta Nuova near Piazza Brà. Bus Nos 2 and 8 connect the station with Piazza Brà and No 32 with Piazza delle Erbe. A ticket costs L14000 and is valid for one hour. Otherwise it's a 15-minute walk along Corso Porta Nuova.

If you arrive by car, you should have no trouble reaching the centre. Simply follow the *centro* signs. There are also signs marking the directions to most hotels. There's a free car park in Via Città di Nimes (near the train station).

PADUA

Although famous as the city of St Anthony and for its university, which is one of the oldest in Europe, Padua (Padova) is often merely seen as a convenient and cheap place to stay while visiting Venice. The city, however, offers a rich collection of art treasures and its many piazzas and arcaded streets are a pleasure to explore.

Orientation & Information

From the train station it's a 10-minute walk to reach the centre of town, or you can take bus No 10 along Corso del Popolo, which becomes Corso Garibaldi, to the historical centre.

There is a tourist office at the station, open Monday to Saturday from 9.30 am to 5.30 pm and Sunday from 9 am to noon. There you can pick up a map, a list of hotels and other useful information.

The post office is at Corso Garibaldi 33 and there's a telephone office nearby at No 7, open 9 am to midday and 4 to 6 pm.

Padua's postcode is 35100 and its telephone code is ☎ 049.

Things to See & Do

Thousands of pilgrims arrive in Padua every year to visit the **Basilica del Santo** in the hope that St Anthony, patron saint of Padua and of lost things, will help them find whatever it is they are looking for. The saint's tomb is in the church along with important art works, including 14th-century frescos and bronze sculptures by Donatello which adorn the high altar. A bronze equestrian statue, known as the *Gattamelata* (Honeyed Cat), also by Donatello, is outside the basilica.

The **Cappella degli Scrovegni** is in the Giardini dell'Arena, off Piazza Eremitani. The interior walls of the chapel were completely covered in frescos by Giotto in the 14th century. Depicting the life of Christ and ending with the *Last Judgment*, the 38 panels are considered one of the greatest works of figurative art of all time. The chapel is open daily from 9 am to 7 pm. The **Palazzo della Ragione** (Law Courts) is remarkable for its sloping roof and loggias; inside is the enormous, entirely frescoed **salon**, containing a huge wooden horse built for a joust in 1466.

A special L15,000 ticket (L10,000 for students) allows entry to the city's main monuments and you can buy it at any of the main sights. Since entry to the Scrovegni Chapel alone is L10,000, it's worth the price.

Places to Stay & Eat

Padua has no shortage of budget hotels, but they fill up quickly in summer. The non-HI *Ostello della Città di Padova* (☎ 875 22 19) is at Via A Aleardi 30. Bed and breakfast is L19,000. Take bus No 3, 8 or 12 from the station to Prato della Valle (a piazza about five minutes away) and then ask for directions. The *Verdi* (☎ 875 57 44), Via Dondi dell'Orologio 7, has basic and clean singles/doubles for L39,000/52,000 and is located in the university district off Via Verdi. The *Pavia* (☎ 66 15 58) at Via dei Papafava 11 has slightly dingy singles/doubles for L35,000/45,000. Follow Corso del Popolo until it becomes Via Roma and then turn right into Via Marsala.

Daily markets are held in the piazzas around the Palazzo Ragione, with fresh produce sold in Piazza delle Erbe and Piazza della Frutta, and bread, cheese and salami sold in the shops *Trattoria Voglia Di*, Via Umberto, just before Prato della Valle, serves an excellent meal for around L20,000. It also has a bar where you can get a sandwich. A cheap but not very atmospheric place to eat a meal is the self-service restaurant, *Brek*, in Piazza Cavour. under the porticoes.

Getting There & Away

Padua is directly linked by train to Milan, Venice and Bologna and is easily accessible from most other major cities. Regular buses serve Venice, Milan, Trieste and surrounding towns. The terminal is in Piazzale Boschetti, off Via Trieste, near the station. There is a large public car park in Prato della Valle, a massive piazza near the Basilica del Santo.

VENICE

No other city in the world has inspired the superlatives heaped upon Venice (Venezia) by writers and travellers through the centuries. It

ITALY

was, and remains, a phenomenon – La Serenissima, the Most Serene Republic.

The secret to seeing and discovering the romance and beauty of Venice is to *walk*. Parts of Dorsoduro and Castello are devoid of tourists even in the high season (July to September). You could become lost for hours in the narrow winding streets between the Accademia and the station, where the signs pointing to San Marco and the Rialto never seem to make any sense – but what a way to pass the time!

After the fall of the Western Roman Empire, as waves of barbarians poured across the Alps, the people of the Veneto cities fled to the islands of the coastal lagoon. The waters that today threaten its existence once protected the city. Following years of Byzantine rule, Venice evolved into a republic ruled by a succession of doges (chief magistrates of the republic), a period of independence which lasted 1000 years. It was the point where East met West, and the city eventually grew in power to dominate the entire Mediterranean, the Adriatic and

the trade routes to the Levant. It was from here that Marco Polo set out on his voyage to China.

Today, most of Venice is under restoration and this, together with the annual winter floods (caused by high tides) and soaring property values, make it increasingly unattractive as a place of residence. Most of the 'locals' in fact live in industrial Mestre, which is linked to the city by the four-km-long bridge across the lagoon. A project to install massive floodgates at the main entrances to the lagoon has been approved by the Italian government, but work has been delayed by the country's seemingly endless political turmoil. The floodgates would be designed to protect the city from disaster-level floods. This and other projects to 'save' Venice are supported by local and international bodies.

Orientation

Venice is built on 117 small islands with some 150 canals and more than 400 bridges. Only three bridges cross the Grand Canal (Canale Grande): the Rialto, the Accademia

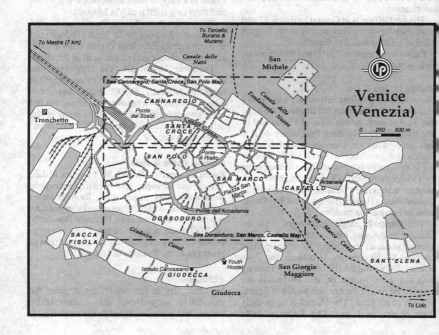

and the Scalzi at the train station. The city is divided into six *sestieri* (sections): Cannaregio, Castello, San Marco, Dorsoduro, San Polo and Santa Croce. The streets are called *calle*, *ruga* or *salizzada*; little side streets can be called *caletta* or *ramo*; a street beside a canal is a *fondamenta*; a canal is a *rio*; and a quay is a *riva*. The only square in Venice called a *piazza* is San Marco – all the others are called a *campo*. On maps, you will find the following abbreviations: Cpo for Campo, Sal for Salizzada, cl for Calle, Mto for Monumento and Fond for Fondamenta.

If all that isn't confusing enough, Venice also has its own style of street numbering. Instead of a system based on individual streets, there is instead a long series of numbers for each sestiere. There are no cars in the city and all public transport is via the canals, on *vaporetti*. To cross the Grand Canal between the bridges, use a *traghetto* (basically a public gondola) – a cheaper mode of transport than the tourist gondolas. Signs will direct you to the various traghetto points. The other mode of transportation is *a piedi* (on foot). To walk from the *ferrovia* (train station) to San Marco along the main thoroughfare, Lista di Spagna (whose name changes several times), will take a good half-hour – follow the signs to San Marco. From San Marco the routes to other main areas, such as the Rialto, the Accademia and the ferrovia, are well signposted but can be confusing, particularly in the Dorsoduro and San Polo areas.

The free map provided by the tourist office (see the following section) provides only a vague guide to the complicated network of streets. Pick up a cheap de Agostini map, simply titled *Venezia*, which lists all street names with map references.

Information

Tourist Offices There is an information office of the APT at the train station, open Monday to Saturday from 8 am to 7.30 pm. The main office (☎ 529 87 30) is in the Palazzetto Selva in the ex Giardini Reale. From Piazza San Marco, walk to the waterfront and turn right – the office is about 100 metres ahead. The staff will give you a map and list of hotels and will help you find a room.

Young people can buy a Rolling Venice card (L5000), which offers significant discounts on food, accommodation and entry to museums and galleries. It is available at the Assessorato all Gioventù, Corte Contarina 1529, just west of Piazza San Marco.

Foreign Consulates There is a British Consulate (☎ 522 72 07) at Palazzo Querini near the Accademia, Dorsoduro 1051. The French Consulate (☎ 522 23 92) is on the Fondamenta Zattere at Dorsoduro 1397.

Money Banks are always the most reliable places to change money and they offer the best rates. Most of the main banks have branches in the area around the Rialto and San Marco. After hours, the American Express office, Salizzada San Moisè (exit from the western end of Piazza San Marco onto Calle Seconda dell'Ascensione) will exchange money without charging commission. Normal opening hours are weekdays from 9 am to 5.30 pm and Saturday to 12.30 pm. For card-holders the office also has an ATM. Thomas Cook, in Piazza San Marco, is open Monday to Saturday from 9 am to 6 pm and Sunday from 9 am to 2 pm. There is also a bank at the train station, or you can change money at the train ticket office from 7 am to 8.30 pm daily.

Post & Communications The main post office is at Salizzada del Fontego dei Tedeschi, just near the Ponte di Rialto (Rialto Bridge) on the main thoroughfare to the station. You can buy stamps at window Nos 11 and 12 in the central courtyard. There is a branch post office just off the western end of Piazza San Marco.

A staffed Telecom office next to the main office is open Monday to Friday from 8 am to 12.30 pm and 4 to 7 pm.

Venice's postcode is 30100 and the telephone code is ☎ 041.

Bookshops There is a good selection of English-language guidebooks and general books on Venice at Studium, on the corner of Calle de la Canonica, on the way from San Marco to Castello. San Giorgio, Calle Larga XXII Marzo 2087, west of San Marco, has a good range of English-language books.

Medical Services If you need a hospital, the Ospedale Civili Riuniti di Venezia (☎ 520 56

22) is in Campo SS (Santissimi) Giovanni e Paolo. For an ambulance phone ☎ 523 00 00. Current information on all-night pharmacies is listed in *Un Ospite di Venezia*, available at the tourist offices.

Emergency For police emergencies call ☎ 113. The questura (☎ 520 32 22) is at Fondamenta di San Lorenzo in Castello.

Things to See & Do
Before you visit Venice's main monuments, churches and museums, catch the No 1 vaporetto along the Grand Canal and then go for a long walk around Venice. Start at **San Marco** and head for the **Accademia Bridge** to reach the narrow, tranquil streets and squares of **Dorsoduro** and **San Polo**. In these sestieri you will be able to appreciate just how beautiful and seductive Venice can be. Remember that most museums are closed on Monday.

Piazza & Basilica di San Marco One of the most famous squares in the world, San Marco was described by Napoleon as the finest drawing room in Europe. Enclosed by the basilica, the old Law Courts and the Libreria Vecchia (which houses the Archaeological Museum and the Marciana Library), the piazza hosts flocks of pigeons and tourists, both competing for space in the high season. Stand and wait for the famous bronze *mori* (Moors) to strike the bell of the Law Courts' 15th-century **clock tower**.

The **basilica**, with its elaborately decorated façade, was constructed to house the body of St Mark, which had been stolen from its burial place in Egypt by two Venetian merchants. The saint has been reburied several times in the basilica (at least twice the burial place was forgotten) and his body now lies under the high altar. The present basilica was built in the Byzantine style in the 11th century and richly decorated with magnificent mosaics and other embellishments over the next five centuries. The famous bronze horses which stood above the entrance have been replaced by replicas. The horses were part of Venice's booty from the famous Sack of Constantinople in 1204. The originals are now in the basilica's museum (entry is L3000).

Don't miss the stunning **Pala d'Oro**

(L3000), a gold altarpiece decorated with silver, enamel and precious stones. It is behind the basilica's altar.

In the piazza is the basilica's 99-metre-high freestanding **bell tower**. It was built in the 10th century, but suddenly collapsed on 14 July 1902 and was later rebuilt. It was closed to the public in 1996, but it normally costs L2000 to climb to the top.

Palazzo Ducale The official residence of the doges and the seat of the republic's government, this palace also housed many government officials and the prisons. The original palace was built in the 9th century, and later expanded and remodelled. Visit the **Sala del Maggior Consiglio** to see the paintings by Tintoretto and Veronese. The palace is open daily from 9 am to 7 pm. Admission is L10,000. The **Bridge of Sighs** (Ponte dei Sospiri) connects the palace to the old prisons. This bridge now evokes romantic images, probably because of its association with Casanova, a native of Venice who was incarcerated in the prisons. It was, however, the thoroughfare for prisoners being led to the dungeons.

Galleria dell'Accademia The Academy of Fine Arts contains an important collection of Venetian art, including works by Tintoretto, Titian and Veronese. It is open Wednesday to Monday from 9 am to 2 pm and Tuesday from 9 am to 7 pm, and admission is L12,000. For a change of pace visit the nearby **Collezione Peggy Guggenheim**, once the home of the American heiress. It contains her collection of modern art, including works by Jackson Pollock, Max Ernst, Salvador Dali and Marc Chagall, and is set in a sculpture garden where Miss Guggenheim and her many pet dogs are buried. It is open Wednesday to Sunday from 11 am to 6 pm (closed Tuesday). Admission is L10,000.

Churches On Giudecca Island, the **Chiesa del Redentore** (Church of the Redeemer) was built in the 16th century by the architect Palladio and is the scene of the annual Festa del Redentore (see the Special Events section). The **Chiesa di Santa Maria della Salute** was built at the entrance to the Grand Canal and dedicated to the Madonna after a plague in the

17th century. It contains works by Tintoretto and Titian. Be sure to visit the great Gothic churches **SS Giovanni e Paolo** and the **Frari**.

The Lido Easily accessible by vaporetto No 1, 2 or 82, this thin strip of land, east of the centre, separates Venice from the Adriatic. Once *the* most fashionable beach resort, it is still very popular and it is almost impossible to find a space on its long beach in summer.

Islands The island of **Murano** is the home of Venetian glass. Visit the Glassworks Museum to see the evolution of the famous glassware. **Burano**, despite the constant influx of tourists, is still a relatively sleepy fishing village, renowned for the lace-making of its women residents. Visit the tiny **Torcello** to see the Byzantine mosaics in its cathedral, notably the stunning mosaic of the Madonna in the apse. Excursion boats leave for the three islands from San Marco (L20,000 per hour). If you want to go it alone, vaporetto No 12 goes to all three and costs L4000 one way. It leaves from Fondamenta Nova.

Gondolas These might represent the quintessential romantic Venice, but at around L80,000 for a 50-minute ride they are very expensive. It is possible to squeeze up to five people into one gondola and still pay the same price. Prices are set for gondolas, so check with the tourist office if you have problems.

Organised Tours
Shop around the various travel agencies for the best deals, or try Ital-Travel (☎ 522 91 11), San Marco 72B, under the colonnade at Piazza San Marco's western end. It organises tours of the city on foot or by boat.

Special Events
The major event of the year is the famous Carnevale, held during the 10 days before Ash Wednesday, when Venetians don spectacular masks and costumes for what is literally a 10-day street party.

The Venice Biennale, a major exhibition of international visual arts, is held every odd-numbered year (for the time being), and the Venice International Film Festival is held every September at the Palazzo del Cinema, on the Lido.

The most important celebration on the Venetian calendar is the Festa del Redentore (Festival of the Redeemer), on the third weekend in July, which features a spectacular fireworks display. The regatta storica, a gondola race on the Grand Canal, is held on the first Sunday in September.

Places to Stay
Simply put, Venice is expensive. The average cost of singles/doubles without bath is now L40,000/60,000. The hostel and several religious institutions provide some respite for budget travellers. Hotel proprietors are inclined to inflate the bill by demanding extra for a compulsory breakfast, and, almost without exception, they increase their prices in the high season (usually July to October). It is advisable to make a booking before you arrive. As Venice does not have a traditional street numbering system, the best idea is to ring your hotel when you arrive and ask for specific directions. If you're travelling by car, you can save on car park costs by staying in Mestre.

Camping There are numerous camping grounds, many with bungalows, at Litorale del Cavallino, the coast along the Adriatic Sea, north-east of the city. The tourist office has a full list, but you could try the *Marina di Venezia* (☎ 96 61 46), Via Montello 6, at Punta Sabbioni, which is open from May to September.

Hostels The HI *Ostello Venezia* (☎ 523 82 11) is on the island of Giudecca, at Fondamenta delle Zitelle 86. It is open to members only, though you can buy a card there. Bed and breakfast is L23,000 and full meals are available for L14,000. Take vaporetto No 82 from the station (L4000 one way) and get off at Zitelle. The hostel is closed from 9 am to 2 pm and curfew is at 11.30 pm. *Istituto Canossiano* (☎ 522 21 57), nearby at Fondamenta del Piccolo 428, has dorm beds for women only at L18,000 per night. Take vaporetto No 82 and get off at Sant'Eufemia. The *Ostello Santa Fosca* (☎ 71 57 75), Cannaregio 2372, is about halfway between the station and San Marco. Walk along the Lista di Spagna for about 15 minutes and you will see signs directing you to the hostel. A bed in a dorm costs L23,000. It opens only in June, July and August. *Foresteria Valdese* (☎ 528 67 97), Castello 5150, has dorm beds for L25,000 a night. It also has beds in private rooms for L32,000 per night and two independent apartments at around L100,000 per day – great for families. Take Calle Lunga from Campo Santa Maria Formosa.

Hotels Most of the cheaper hotels are in Cannaregio; places around San Marco and in the Castello, Dorsoduro, San Polo and Santa Croce areas are more expensive.

Cannaregio This is the easiest area to find a bed because of the sheer number of pensioni, locande and alloggi. The *Locanda Antica Casa Carettoni* (☎ 71 62 31) at Lista di Spagna 130, has singles/doubles for L35,000/60,000. Just off the Lista di Spagna, at Calle della Misericordia 358, is *Hotel Santa Lucia* (☎ 71 51 80), in a newer building which has singles/doubles for up to L65,000/100,000. It also has small apartments for up to five people.

Hotel Villa Rosa (☎ 71 65 69), Calle della Misericordia 389, has singles/doubles for L60,000/90,000 and triples for L120,000, all with breakfast included. *Albergo Adua* (☎ 71 61 84) is at Lista di Spagna 233a, about 50 metres past Casa Carettoni on the right. It has slightly shabby but clean singles/doubles for L38,000/53,000 and triples for L80,000.

The *Hotel Rossi* (☎ 71 51 64) is also near the station in the tiny Calle de le Procuratie, off Lista di Spagna, and has singles/doubles for L60,000/90,000. Triples/quads with bathroom cost L120,000/180,000. At *Al Gobbo* (☎ 71 50 01), in Campo San Geremia, sparkling clean doubles are L90,000. In the same piazza at No 283 is the pleasant *Casa Gerotto*, with singles/doubles for L40,000/60,000 and triples for L75,000. Four-bed dorms cost L22,000 per person. In the same building is *Alloggi Calderan* (☎ 71 55 62), with singles/doubles for L40,000/60,000. *Alloggi Biasin* (☎ 72 06 42), Fondamenta di Cannaregio 1252, is just off the Lista di Spagna across the Ponte delle Guglie. Singles/doubles are L30,000/70,000

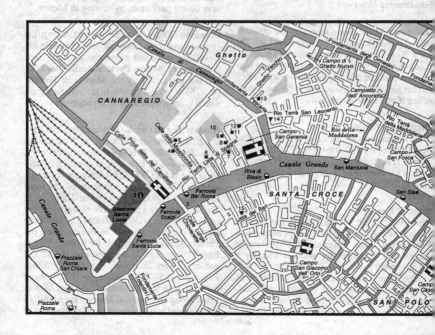

and rooms for three and four are around L30,000 a person. Rooms can be very small.

The **Hotel Minerva & Nettuno** (☎ 71 59 68), Lista di Spagna 230, has decent singles/doubles for L59,000/85,000.

San Marco Although this is the most touristy area of Venice, it has some surprisingly good-quality (relatively) budget pensioni. *Al Gambero* (☎ 522 43 84; fax 520 04 31), Calle dei Fabbri 4587, near Campo San Zulian, has small but pleasant singles/doubles for L61,000/100,000 and triples for L138,000, breakfast included. *Hotel Noemi* (☎ 523 81 44), at Calle dei Fabbri 909, is only a few steps from the piazza and has basic singles/doubles for L55,000/75,000. A triple is L94,000. Check the bed for comfort before accepting a room.

One of the nicest places in this area is *Locanda Casa Petrarca* (☎ & fax 520 04 30), San Marco 4386, which has singles/doubles for L60,000/90,000. Extra beds in a room are an additional 35%. Doubles with bath are L128,000. The friendly owner speaks English.

To get there, find Campo San Luca, go along Calle dei Fusari, then take the second street on the left and turn right into Calle Schiavone.

Castello This area is to the east of Piazza San Marco, and although close to the piazza, is less touristy. The easiest way to get there is to catch the No 1 vaporetto to Castello.

The *Locanda Piave* (☎ 528 51 74), is just off Campo Santa Maria Formosa at Ruga Giuffa 4838/40. Singles/doubles are L65,000/98,000, including breakfast. *Locanda Silva* (☎ 522 76 43), Fondamenta del Rimedio 4423, off Campo SM Formosa towards San Marco, has basic rooms for L50,000/85,000.

Dorsoduro, San Polo & Santa Croce The *Albergo Guerrato* (☎ 522 71 31) is just near the Rialto Bridge at Calle drio la Scimia 240a, to the right off Ruga de Speziale. Singles/doubles cost L95,000/125,000, but it's worth the extra expense. *Hotel Al Gallo* (☎ 523 67 61), Calle Amai 197, off Fondamenta Tolentini, has excellent doubles/triples for L80,000/130,000.

ITALY

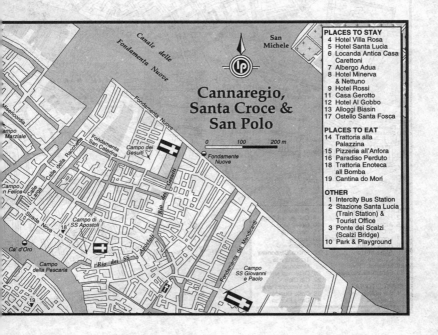

Cannaregio, Santa Croce & San Polo

0   100   200 m

PLACES TO STAY
4 Hotel Villa Rosa
5 Hotel Santa Lucia
6 Locanda Antica Casa Carettoni
7 Albergo Adua
8 Hotel Minerva & Nettuno
9 Hotel Rossi
11 Casa Gerotto
12 Hotel Al Gobbo
13 Alloggi Biasin
17 Ostello Santa Fosca

PLACES TO EAT
14 Trattoria alla Palazzina
15 Pizzeria all'Anfora
16 Paradiso Perduto
18 Trattoria Enoteca all Bomba
19 Cantina do Mori

OTHER
1 Intercity Bus Station
2 Stazione Santa Lucia (Train Station) & Tourist Office
3 Ponte dei Scalzi (Scalzi Bridge)
10 Park & Playground

The **Casa Peron** (☎ 71 00 21), Salizzada San Pantalon 84, has clean rooms with shower for L50,000/85,000, including breakfast. The same owners run **Casa Diana** next door, which has singles/doubles for young people for L35,000/65,000. To get there from the station, cross the bridge (Ponte Scalzi) and follow the signs to San Marco and the Rialto till you reach Rio delle Muneghette, then cross the wooden bridge.

Lido The **Pensione La Pergola** (☎ 526 07 84), Via Cipro 15, has pleasant singles/doubles for L53,000/80,000, including breakfast. It's open all year and has a shady terrace. To get there

turn left off the Gran Viale Santa Maria Elisabetta into Via Zara, then turn right into Via Cipro.

Mestre Only 15 minutes away on bus No 7, Mestre is an economical alternative to staying in Venice. There are a number of good hotels as well as plenty of cafés and places to eat around the pleasant main square. If you're travelling by car, the savings on car-parking charges are considerable. **Albergo Roberta** (☎ 92 93 55), Via Sernaglia 21, has good-sized, clean rooms for L50,000/70,000. **Albergo Giovannina** (☎ 92 63 96), Via Dante 113, has decent singles/doubles for L40,000/85,000.

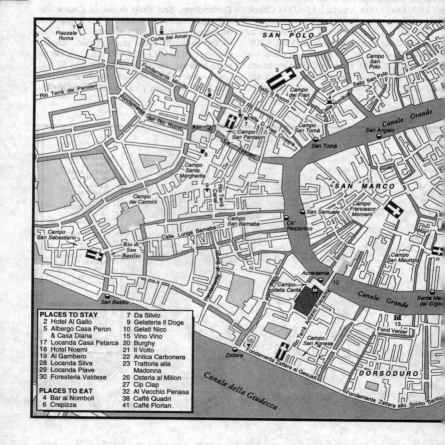

PLACES TO STAY
2 Hotel Al Gallo
5 Albergo Casa Peron & Casa Diana
17 Locanda Casa Petarca
18 Hotel Noemi
19 Al Gambero
28 Locanda Silva
29 Locanda Piave
30 Foresteria Valdese

PLACES TO EAT
4 Bar ai Nomboli
6 Crepizza
7 Da Silvio
9 Gelateria Il Doge
10 Gelati Nico
15 Vino Vino
20 Burghy
21 Il Volto
22 Antica Carbonera
23 Trattoria alla Madonna
26 Osteria al Milion
27 Cip Ciap
32 Al Vecchio Penasa
38 Caffè Quadri
41 Caffè Florian

Places to Eat

Eating in Venice can be an expensive pastime unless you choose very carefully. Many restaurants, particularly around San Marco, are tourist traps, where prices are high and the quality is poor.

Many bars serve a wide range of Venetian panini, with every imaginable filling. Tramezzini (three-pointed sandwiches) and huge bread rolls cost from L3000 to L5000 if you eat them while standing at the bar. Head for one of the many bacari or osterie, for wine by the glass and interesting snacks. The staples of the Veneto region's cucina are rice and beans. Try the risi e bisi (risotto with peas) and don't miss

a risotto or pasta dish with radicchio trevisano (red chicory). The rich mascarpone dessert, tiramisù, is a favourite here.

Self-Catering For fruit and vegetables, as well as delicatessans, head for the market in the streets on the San Polo side of the Rialto Bridge. There is a *Standa* supermarket on Strada Nova and a *Mega 1* supermarket in Campo Santa Margherita.

Cannaregio The *Trattoria alla Palazzina*, Canregio 1509, is just over the first bridge after Campo San Geremia. It has a garden at the rear and serves good pizzas for L6000 to L13,000.

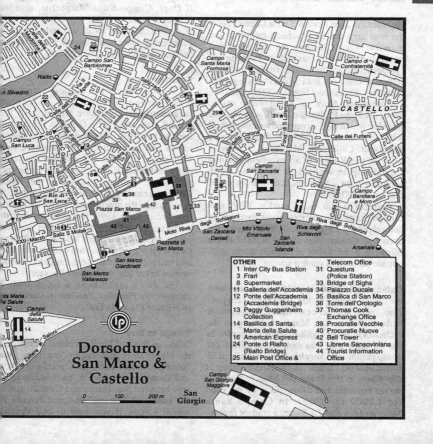

Dorsoduro, San Marco & Castello

0   100   200 m

OTHER	
1 Inter City Bus Station	31 Questura
3 Frari	(Police Station)
8 Supermarket	33 Bridge of Sighs
11 Galleria dell'Accademia	34 Palazzo Ducale
12 Ponte dell'Accademia	35 Basilica di San Marco
(Accademia Bridge)	36 Torre dell'Orologio
13 Peggy Guggenheim	37 Thomas Cook
Collection	Exchange Office
14 Basilica di Santa	39 Procuratie Vecchie
Maria della Salute	40 Procuratie Nuove
16 American Express	42 Bell Tower
24 Ponte di Rialto	43 Libreria Sansoviniana
(Rialto Bridge)	44 Tourist Information
25 Main Post Office &	Office

Telecom Office

A full meal will cost around L25,000. *Trattoria Enoteca all Bomba*, Calle de l'Oca, parallel to Strada Nova near Campo SS Apostoli, has a tourist menu for L20,000. *Paradiso Perduto*, Fondamenta della Misericordia, is a restaurant/bar with live music and outside tables in summer.

Around San Marco & Castello *Vino Vino*,
San Marco 2007, is a popular bar/osteria at Ponte Veste near Teatro La Fenice. The menu changes daily. A pasta or risotto costs L8000, a main dish around L13,000. Wine is sold by the glass. There's a *Burghy* outlet in Campo San Luca. At *Antica Carbonera*, in Calle Bembo, pasta costs around L8000.

Dorsoduro, San Polo & Santa Croce This is
the best area for small, cheap trattorias and pizzerias. Locals say that the best pizza and pasta in Venice is served at *Pizzeria al-l'Anfora*, across the Scalzi Bridge from the station at Lista dei Bari 1223. It has a garden at the rear. Pizzas cost from L6000 to L12,000.

Cantina do Mori, on Sottoportego dei do Mori, off Ruga Rialto, is a small, very popular wine bar which also serves sandwiches. A meal will cost around L25,000. *Trattoria alla Madonna*, Calle della Madonna, two streets west of the Rialto, is an excellent trattoria specialising in seafood. It might be worth splurging here – a full meal of seafood could cost up to L60,000.

Crepizza, Calle San Pantalon 3757, past Campo Santa Margherita, serves pasta, pizza and crêpes for L8000 to L10,000. Around the corner at Crosera San Pantalon 3817 is *Da Silvio*, a good value pizzeria/trattoria with outside tables in a garden setting.

Cafés, Snacks & Osterie If you can cope with
the idea of paying up to L10,000 for a cappuccino, spend an hour or so sitting at an outdoor table in Piazza San Marco, listening to the orchestra at either *Caffè Florian* or *Quadri*. In the Castello area you can get excellent but cheap panini at *Al Vecchio Penasa*, Calle delle Rasse. Just off Campo Santa Maria Formosa is *Cip Ciap*, at the Ponte del Mondo Novo. It serves fantastic and filling pizza by the slice for L2000 to L3000. In Campo Santa Margherita is *Bar La Sosta*, a student favour-

ite. Panini cost from L1500 to L4000 and yo[u] can sit outside at no extra charge. *Bar a[l] Nomboli*, between Campo San Polo and th[e] Frari on the corner of Calle dei Nomboli an[d] Rio Terrà di Nomboli, has a great selection o[f] gourmet sandwiches and tramezzini.

If you're looking for a good osteria, try *[Al] Volto*, Calle Cavalli, in the San Marco area, o[r] *Osteria Al Milion*, Corta Prima del Milior[e] behind the Chiesa di San Giovann[i] Crisostomo.

Gelati & Pastries The best ice cream in Venic[e]
is said to be at *Gelati Nico*, Fondament[a] Zattere 922. The locals take their evening stro[ll] along the fondamenta while eating their gelat[i]. *Il Doge*, Campo Santa Margherita, also ha[s] excellent gelati.

A popular place for cakes and pastries [is] *Pasticceria Marchini*, just off Campo Sant[o] Stefano, at Calle del Spezier 2769.

Entertainment
Exhibitions, theatre and musical events con[-] tinue throughout the year in Venice[.] Information is available (in English an[d] Italian) in the weekly *Un Ospite di Venezia* an[d] the tourist office also has brochures listin[g] events and performances for the entire yea[r]. Concerts of classical and chamber music a[re] often performed in churches and a contempo[-] rary music festival is staged at the *Teatr[o] Goldoni* annually in October. Venice lost i[ts] opera house, the magnificent Teatro La Fenic[e] to a fire in early 1996. It was hoped that th[e] building would be reconstructed quickl[y]. Major art exhibitions are held at the *Palazz[o] Grassi* (at the vaporetto stop of San Samuele[)] and you will find smaller exhibitions at variou[s] venues in the city throughout the year.

The city's nightlife is a bit dismal. [In] summer, try *Paradiso Perduto* in Cannaregi[o] (see under Places to Eat).

Things to Buy
Who can think of Venice without an image [of] its elaborately grotesque Venetian gla[ss] coming to mind? There are several worksho[ps] and showrooms in Venice, particularly in th[e] area between San Marco and Castello and o[n] the island of Murano, designed mainly f[or] tourist groups. If you want to buy Venetia[n]

glass, shop around carefully because quality and prices vary dramatically.

The famous Carnevale masks make a beautiful, though expensive, souvenir of Venice. A small workshop and showroom in a small street off Campo SS Filippo and Giacomo, towards Piazza San Marco, is worth a look. Venice is also famous for its *carta marmorizata* (marbled paper), sold at many outlets throughout the city.

The main shopping area for clothing, shoes, accessories and jewellery is in the narrow streets between San Marco and the Rialto, particularly the Merceria and the area around Campo San Luca. It is best to avoid shopping in the Piazza San Marco itself or at the Rialto bridge – prices are high for the tourists.

Getting There & Away

Air Marco Polo airport (☎ 260 92 60) is just east of Mestre and services domestic and European flights. It is accessible by regular *motoscafo* (motorboat) from San Marco and the Lido (L15,000). There are also ATVO buses from Piazzale Roma (L5000). A water taxi from San Marco will cost around L87,000.

Bus ACTV buses leave from Piazzale Roma or surrounding areas, including Mestre and Chioggia, a fishing port at the southernmost point of the lagoon. Buses also go to Padua and Treviso. Tickets and information are available at the office in the piazza.

Train The Stazione Santa Lucia, known in Venice as the *ferrovia*, is directly linked by train to Padua, Verona, Trieste, Milan and Bologna and thus is easily accessible from Florence and Rome. You can also leave from Venice for major points in Germany, Austria and the former Yugoslavia. The Venice Simplon Orient Express runs between Venice and London, via Verona, Zürich and Paris twice weekly. Ask at any travel agent.

Boat Kompas Italia (☎ 528 65 45), San Marco 1497, operates some ferry and hydrofoil services to Croatia. Kompas also operates day trips to towns on the Istrian peninsula.

Getting Around

As there are no cars in Venice, vaporetti are the city's mode of public transport.

Once you cross the bridge from Mestre, cars must be left at the car park on the island of Tronchetto or at Piazzale Roma (cars are allowed on the Lido – take car ferry No 17 from Tronchetto). The car parks are not cheap at around L22,000 a day. A cheaper alternative is to leave the car at Fusina, near Mestre, and catch the No 16 vaporetto to Zattere and then the No 82 either to Piazza San Marco or the train station. Ask for information at the tourist information office just before the bridge to Venice.

From Tronchetto or Piazzale Roma, vaporetto No 1 zigzags its way along the Grand Canal to San Marco and then to the Lido. There are faster and more expensive vaporetti if you are in a hurry. The No 12 vaporetto leaves from the Fondamenta Nuove for the islands of Murano, Burano and Torcello. A full timetable is available at the tourist office. Tickets cost L3000 for the No 1 and L4000 one way for all the other, faster vaporetti. A 24-hour ticket costs L15,000, a three-day ticket costs L30,000 and one week costs L55,000.

Water taxis are exorbitant, with a set charge of L27,000 for a maximum of seven minutes, then L500 every 15 seconds. It's an extra L8000 if you phone for a taxi, and various other surcharges add up to make a gondola ride seem cheap.

FERRARA

Ferrara was the seat of the Este dukes from the 13th century to the end of the 16th century. The city retains much of the austere splendour of its heyday – its streets are lined with graceful palaces and in its centre is the Castello Estense, surrounded by a moat.

Information

The tourist information office (☎ 20 93 70), Corso della Giovecca 21, opens Monday to Saturday from 9 am to 1 pm and from 2.30 to 5.30 pm. There's another office at Via Kennedy 2, open from April to October.

The Ferrara telephone code is ☎ 0532.

Things to See & Do

The historical centre is small, encompassing the medieval Ferrara to the south of the

Castello Estense, and the area to the north, built under the rule of Duke Ercole I during the Renaissance. The castello now houses government offices, but certain areas are open to the public. Visit the **medieval prisons**, where in 1425 Duke Nicolò d'Este had his young second wife, Parisina Malatesta, and his son Ugo beheaded after discovering they were lovers, thereby inspiring the poet Robert Browning to write *My Last Duchess*.

The beautiful Romanesque-Gothic **Duomo** has an unusual pink-and-white marble triple façade and houses some important works of art in its museum. The 14th-century **Palazzo Schifanoia**, at Via Scandiana 23, one of the Este palaces, houses the Civic Museum and features interesting frescos. It is open daily from 9 am to 7 pm; entry is L6000.

Places to Stay & Eat

Ferrara is a cheap alternative to Bologna, and it can even be used as a base for Padua and Venice. The *Tre Stelle* (☎ 20 97 48), Via Vegri 15, has very basic singles/doubles for L30,000/40,000. *Pensione Artisti* (☎ 76 10 38), Via Vittoria 66, has singles/doubles for L26,000/46,000. Better rooms are available at *Albergo Nazionale* (☎ 20 96 04), Corso Porta Reno 32, for L55,000/90,000 with private bathroom.

A popular budget restaurant is *Trattoria da Giacomino*, Via Garibaldi 135, where a full meal will cost around L24,000. *Royal Pizzeria*, Via Vignatagliata 11, has pizzas for around L9000.

Getting There & Away

Ferrara is on the Bologna-Venice train line, with regular trains to both cities. It is 40 minutes from Bologna and 1½ hours from Venice. Regular trains also run directly to Ravenna. Buses run from the train station to Modena (also in the Emilia-Romagna region).

BOLOGNA

Elegant, intellectual and wealthy, Bologna stands out among the many beautiful cities of Italy. The regional capital of Emilia-Romagna, Bologna is famous for its porticoes (arcaded streets), its harmonious architecture, its university (which is one of the oldest in Europe) and, above all, its gastronomic tradition. The Bolognese have given the world tortellini, lasagne, mortadella and the ubiquitous spa-

ghetti bolognese (known in Italy as *ragù*) hence one of the city's nicknames, Bologna la Grassa (Bologna the Fat).

Information

There is an Informazioni e Assistenza Turistica (IAT) office (☎ 23 96 60) in Piazza Maggiore inside the Centro d'Informazione Comunale. It is open Monday to Saturday from 9 am to 7 pm and Sunday from 9 am to 1 pm. There are branch offices at the train station and the airport. Pick up a map and the useful booklet *A Guest in Bologna*, published monthly in English.

The main post office is in Piazza Minghetti. Telecom telephone offices are at Piazza VIII Agosto 24, and the train station. In a medical emergency call ☎ 118, or Ospedale Maggiore on ☎ 634 81 11. For the police call ☎ 113 or 112.

Bologna's telephone code is ☎ 051.

Things to See

The **Piazza Maggiore**, the adjoining **Piazza del Nettuno** and **Fontana di Nettuno** (Neptune's Fountain), sculpted in bronze by a French artist who became known as Giambologna, and the **Piazza Porta Ravegnana** with its leaning towers to rival that of Pisa, form the beautiful centre of Bologna.

In Piazza Maggiore is the **Basilica di San Petronio**, dedicated to the city's patron saint. The red-and-white marble of its unfinished façade displays the colours of Bologna. It contains important works of art and it was here that Charles V was crowned emperor by the pope in 1530. The **Palazzo Comunale** (town hall) is a huge building, combining several architectural styles in remarkable harmony. It features a bronze statue of Pope Gregory XIII (a native of Bologna who created the Gregorian calendar), an impressive winding staircase and Bologna's collection of art treasures.

The **Chiesa di Santo Stefano** is in fact a group of four churches in the Romanesque style. In a small courtyard is a basin which legend says was used by Pontius Pilate to wash his hands after condemning Christ to death. In fact, it is an 8th century Lombard artefact.

Places to Stay & Eat

Budget hotels in Bologna are virtually nonexistent and it is almost impossible to find a single room. The city's busy trade-fair calen-

ITALY

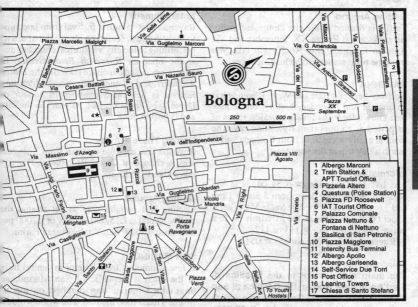

Bologna

0   250   500 m

1 Albergo Marconi
2 Train Station &
   APT Tourist Office
3 Pizzeria Altero
4 Questura (Police Station)
5 Piazza FD Roosevelt
6 IAT Tourist Office
7 Palazzo Comunale
8 Piazza Nettuno &
   Fontana di Nettuno
9 Basilica di San Petronio
10 Piazza Maggiore
11 Intercity Bus Terminal
12 Albergo Apollo
13 Albergo Garisenda
14 Self-Service Due Torri
15 Post Office
16 Leaning Towers
17 Chiesa di Santo Stefano

lar means that hotels are often heavily booked, so always book in advance. The best options are the two HI hostels: *Ostello San Sisto* (☎ 51 92 02), Via Viadagola 14, charges L18,000 with breakfast and *Ostello Due Torri* (☎ 50 18 10), in the same street at No 5, charges L20,000. Take bus No 93 or 20/b from Via merio, off Via Independenza near the station, and ask the bus driver where to get off, then follow the signs to the hostel.

Albergo Garisenda (☎ 22 43 69), Galleria del Leone 1, is under the two towers and has decent singles/doubles for L65,000/85,000. The *Apollo* (☎ 22 39 55), Via Drapperie 5, off Via Rizzoli, has singles/doubles for L49,000/81,000 and triples with bathroom for L140,000. The *Albergo Marconi* (☎ 26 28 32), at Via G Marconi 22, has pleasant singles/doubles/triples for L45,000/70,000/96,000.

Fortunately, it is cheaper to eat in Bologna, particularly in the university district north of Via Rizzoli. *Pizzeria Bella Napoli*, Via San Felice 40, serves good pizzas at reasonable prices. *Trattoria da Boni*, Via Saragozza 88, is

another good option. *Pizzeria Altero*, Via Ugo Bassi 10, has good, cheap pizzas. Try the self-service *Due Torri*, Via dei Giudei 4, under the towers. It opens only for lunch and the food is good value. You can buy panini in most cafès and eat them standing at the bar.

Shop at the *Mercato Ugo Bassi*, Via Ugo Bassi 27, a covered market offering all the local fare. There is also a market in the streets south-east of Piazza Maggiore.

Getting There & Away

Bologna is a major transport junction for northern Italy and trains from virtually all major cities stop here. The only hitch is that many are intercity trains, which means you have to pay the rapido supplement.

Buses to major cities depart from the terminal in Piazza XX Settembre, around the corner from the train station in Piazza delle Medaglie d'Oro.

The city is linked to Milan, Florence and Rome by the A1 (Autostrada del Sole). The A13 heads directly for Venice and Padua, and the A14 goes to Rimini and Ravenna.

Getting Around

Traffic is limited in the city centre and major car parks are at Piazza XX Settembre and Via Antonio Gramsci. Bus No 25 will take you from the train station to the historical centre.

RAVENNA

Halfway between East and West, Ravenna has an ancient and legendary history, but is now best known for its exquisite mosaics, relics of its period as an important Byzantine city. The town is easily accessible from Bologna and is worth a day trip at the very least.

Information

The IAT tourist office (☎ 3 54 04) is at Via Salara 8 and is open daily from 8 am to 1 pm and 3 to 6 pm. The Ospedale Santa Maria delle Croci (☎ 40 91 11) is at Via Missiroli 10. In a police emergency call ☎ 113 or 112.

Ravenna's telephone code is ☎ 0544.

Things to See

The main mosaics are in the **Basilica di Sant'Apollinare Nuovo**, the **Basilica di San Vitale**, the **Mausoleo di Galla Placidia**, which contains the oldest mosaics, and the **Battistero Neoniano**, also known as the Orthodox Baptistry. These are all in the town centre and an admission ticket to the four, as well as to the **Museo Arcivescovile**, costs L9000 – a bargain given that a ticket to only one monument costs L5000. The **Basilica di Sant'Apollinare Nuovo in Classe** is five km from Ravenna and accessible by bus No 4 from the station.

Places to Stay & Eat

The HI *Ostello Dante* (☎ 42 04 05) is at Via Aurelio Nicolodi 12. Take bus No 1 from Viale Pallavacini, to the left of the station. Bed and breakfast is L22,000 and family rooms are available. *Al Giaciglio* (☎ 3 94 03), at Via R Brancaleone 42, has singles/doubles for L35,000/50,000 and triples for L80,000. To find it, go straight ahead from the station along Viale Farini and turn right into Via Brancaleone from Piazza Mameli. The only other budget hotel, the Ravenna, at Via Maroncelli 12, was closed for renovation at the time of writing.

For a quick meal, try *Free Flow Bizantino*, Piazza Andrea Costa, next to the city's fresh-produce market.

Entertainment

Ravenna hosts a music festival from late June to early August, featuring international artists performing in the city's historical churches and at the open-air *Rocca di Brancaleone*. In winter, opera and dance are staged at the *Teatro Alighieri*, and an annual theatre and literature festival is held in September in honour of Dante, who spent his last 10 years in the city and is buried there.

Getting There & Away

Ravenna is accessible by train from Bologna, with a change at Castel Bolognese. The trip takes about 1½ hours.

Getting Around

Cycling is a popular way to get around the sights. Rental is L15,000 per day or L2000 per hour from COOP San Vitale, Piazza Farini.

SAN MARINO

A few kilometres from Rimini in central Italy is the ancient Republic of San Marino, an unashamed tourist trap perched on top of Monte Titano (600 metres). The world's oldest surviving republic, San Marino was formed in 300 AD by a stonemason said to have been escaping religious persecution. The tiny state (only 61 sq km) strikes its own coins, has its own postage stamps and its own army. Wander along the city walls and drop in at the two fortresses. The main attraction of a visit is the splendid view of the mountains and the coast. The Ufficio di Stato per il Turismo (☎ 0549-88 29 98), is in the Palazzo del Turismo, Contrada Omagnano 20.

The town is accessible from Rimini by ATR bus. There is no train to San Marino.

The Dolomites

This spectacular limestone mountain range in the Alps stretches across Trentino-Alto Adige into the Veneto. It is the Italians' favoured area for skiing and there are excellent hiking trails

Information

Information can be obtained at the APT de Trentino (Azienda per la Promozione Turistica del Trentino) in Trent (☎ 0461-90 00 00) at Corso III Novembre 134; in Rome (☎ 06-679 42 16) at Via Poli 47; or Milan (☎ 02-87 43 87) at Piazza Diaz 5. The provincial tourist office for Alto Adige (☎ 0472-99 38 08) is at Piazza Parocchia 11, Bolzano. The APT delle Dolomiti Bellunesii (☎ 0473-94 00 83) can provide information on trekking along the Sentiero della Pace (Path of Peace), which traces the Italian/German frontline of WWI.

Skiing

There are numerous excellent ski resorts, including the expensive and fashionable Cortina d'Ampezzo and the less pretentious, more family-oriented resorts, such as those in the Val Gardena in Trentino-Alto Adige. All have helpful tourist offices with loads of information on facilities, accommodation and transport (some are listed in this section).

The high season is generally from Christmas to early January and from early February to April, when prices go up considerably, but actual dates vary throughout the Alps. A good way to save money is to buy a *settimana bianca* (literally, 'white week' – a package-deal ski holiday) through Sestante CIT, CTS or other travel agencies throughout Italy. This covers accommodation, food and ski passes for seven days.

If you want to go it alone, but plan to do a lot of skiing, invest in a ski pass. Most resort areas offer their own passes for unlimited use of lifts at several resorts for a nominated period. The cost in the 1996/97 high season for a seven-day pass was around L245,000. However, the best value is the Superski Dolomiti pass, which allows access to 450 lifts and more than 1100 km of ski runs. In the 1996/97 high season, a superski pass for seven days cost L296,000. Ring Superski Dolomiti (☎ 0471-79 53 98) for information. The average cost of ski and boot hire in the Alps is from L17,000 to L25,000 a day for downhill and around L15,000 for cross-country.

Trekking

Without doubt, the Dolomites provide the most breathtaking opportunities for walking in the Italian Alps – from a half-day stroll with the kids, to walks/treks for as many days as you like, and demanding treks which combine walking with mountaineering skills. The walking season is roughly from July to late September. Alpine refuges usually close around September 20.

Buy a map of the hiking trails, which also shows the locations of Alpine refuges. The best maps are the Tabacco 1:25,000, which can be bought in newsagents and bookshops in the area where you plan to hike. They are also often available in major bookshops in larger cities. Lonely Planet's *Italy* guide has more detailed information about walking in the Dolomites, including suggested treks. A useful guide is *Walking in the Dolomites* by Gillian Price.

Hiking trails are generally very well marked with numbers on red-and-white painted bands (which you will find on trees and rocks along the trails), or by numbers inside different coloured triangles for the Alte Vie (the four High Routes through the Dolomites – ask for details at the tourist offices listed in this section). There are numerous organisations offering guided treks, climbs etc, as well as courses. One is the *Scuola Alpina Dolomiten* (☎ 0471-70 53 43; fax 0471-70 73 890), Via Vogelweider, Castelrotto, which has a summer programme including week-long treks, expeditions on horseback and mountain bike, and courses in rockclimbing. It also has a winter programme of ski expeditions and courses. Phone or fax for a programme.

Recommended areas to walk in the Dolomites include:

Brenta Group (Dolomiti di Brenta)
 accessible from either Molveno to the east or Madonna di Campiglio to the west
Sella Group
 accessible from either the Val Gardena to the west, or the Val Badia to the east
Pale di San Martino
 accessible from San Martino di Castrozza
Cortina area
 which straddles Trentino and Veneto and features the magnificent Parco Naturale di Fanes-Sennes-Braies, and, to the south, Mt Pelmo and Mt Civetta
Sesto Dolomites
 north of Cortina towards Austria.

Warning Remember that even in summer the weather is extremely changeable in the Alps and, though it might be sweltering when you set off, you should be prepared for very cold and wet weather on even the shortest of walks. Essentials include a pair of good-quality, worn-in walking boots, an anorak or pile/wind jacket, a lightweight backpack and water.

Getting There & Away

Trentino-Alto Adige has an excellent public transport network – the two main bus companies for the region are SAD in Alto Adige and Atesina in Trentino. The main towns and many of the ski resorts are also accessible from major cities throughout Italy, including Rome, Florence, Bologna, Milan and Genoa, by a network of long-distance buses operated by companies including Lazzi, SITA, Sena and STAT. Information about the services is available from tourist offices and *autostazioni* (bus stations) throughout Trentino-Alto Adige, or from the following offices: Lazzi Express (☎ 06-884 08 40), Via Tagliamento 27B, Rome, and in Florence at Piazza Adua 1 (055-21 51 55); SITA (☎ 055-21 47 21), Autostazione, Via Santa Caterina di Siena 17, Florence.

Getting Around

If you are planning to hike in the Alps during the warmer months, you will find that hitch-hiking is no problem, especially near the resort towns. The areas around the major resorts are well serviced by local buses, and tourist offices will be able to provide information on local bus services. During winter, most resorts have 'ski bus' shuttle services from the towns to the main ski facilities.

CORTINA D'AMPEZZO

The most famous, fashionable and expensive Italian ski resort, Cortina is also one of its best equipped and certainly the most picturesque. If you are on a tight budget, the prices for accommodation and food will be prohibitive, even in the low season. However, camping grounds and Alpine refuges (open only during summer) provide more reasonably priced alternatives.

Situated in the Ampezzo bowl, Cortina is surrounded by the stunning Dolomites, including the Cristallo and Marmarole groups and the Tofane. Facilities for both downhill and cross-country skiing are first class. The area is also very popular for trekking and climbing, with well-marked trails and numerous refuges. A memorable three-day walk starts at Passo Falzarego and incorporates sections of Alta Via No 1. It takes you through the beautiful Val di Fanes and ends at Passo Cimabanche. Buy a good 1:25,000 map and plan your route.

Information

The main tourist information office (APT ☎ 32 31) is at Piazzetta San Francesco 8, in the town centre. It has information on accommodation, ski passes and hiking trails. There is a small information office at Piazza Roma 1.

La Cortina's telephone code is 0436.

Places to Stay

The *International Camping Olympia* (☎ 50 57) is about five km north of Cortina at Fiame and is open all year. A local bus will take you there from Cortina. If you are trekking in the area, refuges are open from July to late September and charge roughly L20,000 per person. There are not many options for cheap accommodation in Cortina. You could try the *Albergo Cavallino* (☎ 26 14) or the *La Ginestrina* (☎ 86 02 55), both of which charge L70,000 or more per person, including breakfast, in the high season.

CANAZEI

Set in the Fassa Dolomites, the resort of Canazei has more than 100 km of trails and is linked to slopes in the Val Gardena and Val Badia by a network of runs known as the **Sella Ronda**, which enable skiers to make a day long skiing tour of the valleys surrounding the Sella Group. Canazei also offers cross-country skiing and summer skiing on the Marmolada glacier. (At 3342 metres, the Marmolada peak is the highest in the Dolomites.) The Marmolada *camping ground* (☎ 0462-6 16 60) is open all year, or you have a choice of hotels, furnished rooms and apartments. Contact the AAST tourist office (☎ 6 11 13) for full details. The resort is accessible by Atesina bus from Trent and SAD bus from Bolzano and the Val Gardena.

VAL GARDENA

This is one of the most popular skiing areas in the Alps, due to its reasonable prices and excellent facilities for downhill, cross-country and alpine skiing. There are excellent walking trails in the Sella group and the Alpi Siusi. The Vallunga, behind Selva, is great for family walks and cross-country skiing.

The valley's main towns are Ortisei, Santa

Cristina and Selva, all offering lots of accommodation and easy access to runs. The tourist offices at Santa Cristina (☎ 0471-79 30 46) and Selva (☎ 79 51 22) have extensive information on accommodation and facilities. Staff speak English and will send details on request.

The Val Gardena is accessible from Bolzano by SAD bus. It is connected to major Italian cities by coach services (Lazzi, SITA and STAT).

MADONNA DI CAMPIGLIO

One of the five major ski resorts in Italy and situated in the Brenta Dolomites, Madonna di Campiglio is one of the more beautiful and well-equipped places to ski, but also one of the more expensive. The Brenta group offers challenging trails for mountaineers and cross-country skiers, while the nearby, beautiful Val di Genova is perfect for family walks. The resort is accessible by Atesina bus from Trent, and from Rome, Florence and Bologna by Lazzi or SITA coach. More information is available from the helpful APT office (☎ 0465-4 20 00).

SAN MARTINO DI CASTROZZA

Located in a sheltered position beneath the Pale di San Martino, this resort is popular among Italians and offers good facilities and ski runs, as well as cross-country skiing and a toboggan run. The APT office (☎ 0439-76 88 7) will provide a full list of accommodation, or try the *Suisse* (☎ 6 80 87), Via Dolomiti 1. Its singles/doubles cost L50,000/85,000. Buses travel regularly from Trent and, during the high season, from Milan, Venice, Padua and Bologna.

Central Italy

The landscape in central Italy is a patchwork of textures bathed in a beautiful soft light – golden pink in Tuscany, and a greenish gold in Umbria and the Marches. The people remain close to the land, but in each of the regions here is also a strong artistic and cultural tradition – even the smallest medieval hill town can harbour extraordinary works of art.

FLORENCE

Cradle of the Renaissance, home of Dante, Machiavelli, Michelangelo and the Medici, Florence (Firenze) is overwhelming in its wealth of art, culture and history, and is one of the most enticing cities in Italy.

Florence was founded as a colony of the Etruscan city of Fiesole in about 200 BC and later became the strategic Roman garrison settlement of Florentia. In the Middle Ages the city developed a flourishing economy based on banking and commerce, which sparked a period of building and growth previously unequalled in Italy. It was a major focal point for the Guelph and Ghibelline struggle of the 13th century, which saw Dante banished from the city. But Florence truly flourished in the 15th century under the Medici, reaching the height of its cultural, artistic and political development as it gave birth to the Renaissance.

The Grand Duchy of the Medici was succeeded in the 18th century by the House of Lorraine (related to the Austrian Hapsburgs). As a result of the Risorgimento, the Kingdom of Italy was formally proclaimed in March 1861, and Florence was the capital of the new kingdom from 1865 to 1871. During WWII, parts of the city, including all of the bridges except the Ponte Vecchio, were destroyed by bombing, and in 1966 a devastating flood destroyed or severely damaged many important works of art. A worldwide effort helped Florence in its massive restoration works.

In 1993, a bomb seriously damaged one of the principal corridors of the Uffizi Gallery. Several important works of art were lost in the attack, which was executed by the Mafia.

Orientation

Whether you arrive by train, bus or car, the central train station, Santa Maria Novella, is a good reference point. Budget hotels and pensioni are concentrated around Via Nazionale, to the east of the station, and Piazza Santa Maria Novella, to the south. The main thoroughfare to the centre is Via de' Panzani and then Via de' Cerretani, about a 10-minute walk. You'll know you've arrived when you first glimpse the Duomo.

Once at Piazza del Duomo you will find Florence easy to negotiate, with most of the major sights within easy walking distance.

ITALY

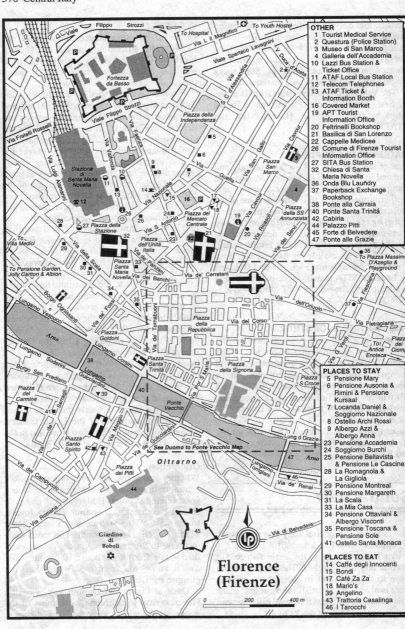

OTHER
1 Tourist Medical Service
2 Questura (Police Station)
3 Museo di San Marco
4 Galleria dell'Accademia
10 Lazzi Bus Station & Ticket Office
11 ATAF Local Bus Station
12 Telecom Telephones
13 ATAF Ticket & Information Booth
16 Covered Market
19 APT Tourist Information Office
20 Feltrinelli Bookshop
21 Basilica di San Lorenzo
22 Cappelle Medicee
26 Comune di Firenze Tourist Information Office
32 SITA Bus Station
33 Chiesa di Santa Maria Novella
36 Onda Blu Laundry
37 Paperback Exchange Bookshop
38 Ponte alla Carraia
40 Ponte Santa Trinità
42 Cabiria
44 Palazzo Pitti
45 Forte di Belvedere
47 Ponte alle Grazie

PLACES TO STAY
5 Pensione Mary
6 Pensione Ausonia & Rimini & Pensione Kursaal
7 Locanda Daniel & Soggiorno Nazionale
8 Ostello Archi Rossi
9 Albergo Azzi & Albergo Anna
23 Pensione Accademia
24 Soggiorno Burchi
25 Pensione Bellavista & Pensione Le Cascine
28 La Romagnola & La Gigliola
29 Pensione Montreal
30 Pensione Margareth
31 La Scala
33 La Mia Casa
34 Pensione Ottaviani & Albergo Visconti
35 Pensione Toscana & Pensione Sole
41 Ostello Santa Monaca

PLACES TO EAT
14 Caffé degli Innocenti
15 Bondi
17 Café Za Za
18 Mario's
39 Angelino
43 Trattoria Casalinga
46 I Tarocchi

Florence (Firenze)

0   200   400 m

Think carefully, though, about how you spend your time. Most important museums close by 2 pm (with the exception of the Uffizi Gallery) and virtually all are closed on Monday. You will need to start your day early, but be careful not to overload your itinerary. Florence is a living art museum and you won't waste your time by just wandering the streets. Take the city ATAF buses for longer distances such as to Piazzale Michelangelo or the nearby suburb of Fiesole, both of which offer panoramic views of the city (see the Getting Around section that follows).

Information

Tourist Offices The city council (Comune di Firenze) operates a tourist information office (☎ 21 22 45) just outside the main train station in the covered area where local buses stop. During high season it opens from Monday to Saturday 8 am to 7.30 pm. The main APT office (☎ 29 08 32) is just north of the Duomo at Via Cavour 1r and opens Monday to Saturday 8.15 am to 7.15 pm and Sunday from 8.15 am to 1.45 pm. At both offices you can pick up a map of the city, a list of hotels and other useful information. The Consorzio ITA (☎ 28 28 93), inside the station on the main concourse, can check availability of hotel rooms and book you a night for a small fee.

A good map of the city, on sale at newsstands, is the one with the white, red and black cover (*Firenze: Pianta della Città*), which costs L8000.

Foreign Consulates The US Consulate (☎ 239 82 76) is at Lungarno Vespucci 38, and the UK Consulate (☎ 21 25 94) is at Lungarno Corsini 2. The French Consulate (☎ 230 25 56) is at Piazza Ognissanti 2.

Money The main banks are concentrated around Piazza della Repubblica. You can use the service at the information office in the station, but it has bad exchange rates.

Post & Communications The main post office is in Via Pellicceria, off Piazza della Repubblica, open weekdays from 8.15 am to 7 pm and Saturday to midday. Poste restante mail can be addressed to 50100 Firenze. There is a Telecom office at Via Cavour 21, open daily from 8 am to 9.45 pm, and another at Stazione Santa Maria Novella, open Monday to Saturday from 8 am to 9.45 pm.

Florence's telephone code is ☎ 055.

Bookshops The Paperback Exchange, Via Fiesolana 31r (closed Sunday), has a vast selection of new and second-hand books. Internazionale Seeber, Via de' Tornabuoni 70r, and Feltrinelli, opposite the APT in Via Cavour, also have good selections of English-language books.

Laundry Onda Blu, Via degli Alfani 24bR, east of the Duomo, is self service and charges around L6000 for a 6.5 kilo load.

Medical Services The main public hospital is Ospedale Careggi (☎ 427 71 11), Viale Morgagni 85, north of the city centre. Tourist Medical Service (☎ 47 54 11), Via Lorenzo il Magnifico 59, is open 24 hours a day and the doctors speak English, French and German. An organisation of volunteer interpreters (English, French and German) called the Associazione Volontari Ospedalieri (☎ 234 45 67 or ☎ 40 31 26) will translate free of charge once you've found a doctor. Hospitals have a list of volunteers. All-night pharmacies include the Farmacia Comunale (☎ 28 94 35), inside the station, and Molteni (☎ 28 94 90), in the city centre at Via Calzaiuoli 7r.

Emergency For police emergency call ☎ 113. The questura (☎ 4 97 71) is at Via Zara 2. There is an office for foreigners where you can report thefts etc. Lost property (☎ 36 79 43) and towed-away cars can be collected from Via Circondaria 19 (south-west of the centre).

Dangers & Annoyances Crowds, heavy traffic and summer heat can combine to make Florence unpleasant. Air pollution can be a problem for small children, people with respiratory problems and the elderly, so check with your hotel or the tourist office. Pickpockets are active in crowds and on buses, and beware of the groups of dishevelled women and children carrying newspapers and cardboard. A few will distract you while the others rifle your bag and pockets.

ITALY

Things to See & Do

Duomo This beautiful cathedral, with its pink, white and green marble façade and Brunelleschi's famous dome dominating the Florence skyline, is one of Italy's most famous monuments. At first sight, no matter how many times you have visited the city, the Duomo will take your breath away. Named the Cattedrale di Santa Maria del Fiore, it was begun in 1296 by the Sienese architect Arnolfo di Cambio but took almost 150 years to complete. It is the fourth-largest cathedral in the world.

The Renaissance architect Brunelleschi won a public competition to design the enormous dome, the first of its kind since antiquity. Although now severely cracked and under restoration, it remains a remarkable achievement of design. The dome is decorated with frescos by Vasari and Zuccari and stained-glass windows by Donatello, Andrea del Castagno, Paolo Uccello and Lorenzo Ghiberti. Climb to the top of the dome for an unparalleled view of Florence (open from 9.30 am to 5.20 pm, entry L8000). The Duomo's marble façade was built in the 19th century to replace the original unfinished façade, which was pulled down in the 16th century.

Giotto designed and began building the **bell tower** next to the cathedral in 1334, but died before it was completed. This unusual and graceful structure is 82 metres high and you can climb its stairs from 9 am to 4.20 pm daily (L8000).

The Romanesque-style **baptistry**, believed to have been built between the 5th and 11th centuries on the site of a Roman temple, is the oldest building in Florence. Dante was baptised here. It is famous for its gilded bronze doors, particularly the celebrated east doors facing the duomo, the *Gates of Paradise*, by Lorenzo Ghiberti. The south door, by Andrea Pisano, dates from 1336 and is the oldest. The north door is also by Ghiberti, who won a public competition in 1401 to design it, but the *Gates of Paradise* remain his masterpiece. Most of the doors are copies – the original panels are being removed for restoration and are placed in the Museo dell'Opera del Duomo as work is completed. The baptistry is open Monday to Saturday from 1.30 to 6 pm and on Sunday from 9 am to 1.30 pm. An entry fee of around L3000 was to be introduced in 1996.

Uffizi Gallery The Palazzo degli Uffizi, built by Vasari in the 16th century, houses the most important art collection in Italy. The vast collection of paintings dating from the 13th to 18th centuries represents the great legacy of the Medici family.

You will need more than one visit to appreciate fully the extraordinary number of important works in the Uffizi, which include paintings by Giotto and Cimabue from the 14th century; 15th-century masterpieces including Botticelli's *Birth of Venus* and *Allegory of Spring*; and works by Filippo Lippi, Fra Angelico and Paolo Uccello. *The Annunciation* by Leonardo da Vinci is also here. There are 16th-century works by Raphael, Michelangelo's *Holy Family* and famous works by Titian, Andrea del Sarto, Tintoretto, Rembrandt, Caravaggio, Tiepolo, Rubens, Van Dyck and Goya. Most of the gallery's second corridor was damaged in the 1993 bomb attack. Restoration work on the art works and rooms was expected to be completed by the end of 1996. The gallery is open weekdays from 9 am to 7 pm and Sunday from 9 am to 2 pm (closed Monday). Entry is L12,000.

Piazza della Signoria & Palazzo Vecchio Built by Arnolfo di Cambio between 1299 and 1314, the Palazzo Vecchio is the traditional seat of the Florentine government. In the 16th century it became the ducal palace of the Medici before they moved to the Pitti Palace. Visit the beautiful Michelozzi courtyard just inside the entrance and the lavishly decorated apartments upstairs. It is open weekdays from 9 am to 7 pm and Sunday to 1 pm (closed Thursday). Admission is L10,000. The palace's turrets, battlements and 94-metre-high bell tower form an imposing and memorable backdrop to Piazza della Signoria scene of many important political events in the history of Florence, including the execution of the religious and political reformer Savonarola. A bronze plaque marks the spot where he was burned at the stake in 1498. The **Loggia della Signoria**, at a right angle to the Palazzo Vecchio, contains important sculptures including Cellini's *Perseus*.

Ponte Vecchio This famous 14th-century bridge, lined with gold and silversmiths' shops

ITALY

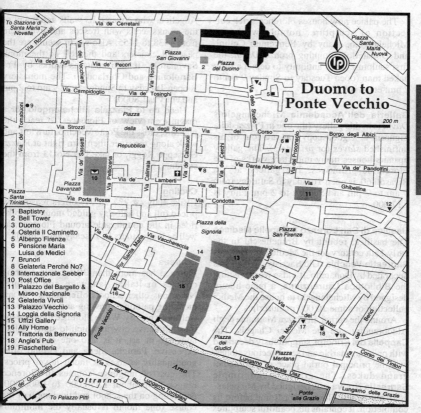

Duomo to Ponte Vecchio

1 Baptistry
2 Bell Tower
3 Duomo
4 Osteria Il Caminetto
5 Albergo Firenze
6 Pensione Maria
   Luisa de Medici
7 Brunori
8 Gelateria Perché No?
9 Internazionale Seeber
10 Post Office
11 Palazzo del Bargello &
   Museo Nazionale
12 Gelateria Vivoli
13 Palazzo Vecchio
14 Loggia della Signoria
15 Uffizi Gallery
16 Aily Home
17 Trattoria da Benvenuto
18 Angie's Pub
19 Fiaschetteria

was the only one to survive Nazi bombing in WWII. Originally, the shops housed butchers. A corridor along the 1st floor was built by the Medici to link the Pitti Palace and the Uffizi Gallery.

Palazzo Pitti The immense and imposing Palazzo Pitti, housing several museums, was originally designed by Brunelleschi. The **Galleria Palatina** (open Tuesday to Saturday from 9 am to 7 pm, Sunday 9 am to 2 pm; entry L12,000) has 16th and 17th-century works by Raphael, Filippo Lippi, Tintoretto, Veronese and Rubens, hung in lavishly decorated rooms. The royal apartments of the Medici, and later

of the Savoy, show the splendour in which these rulers lived.

The other museums are the Museo degli Argenti, the Galleria del Costume and the Galleria d'Arte Moderna. They open Tuesday to Sunday 9 am to 2 pm. After the Pitti Palace, visit the beautiful Renaissance **Giardino di Boboli** (entry L4000).

Palazzo Bargello & Museo Nazionale del Bargello A medieval palace, also known as the Palazzo del Podestà, the Bargello was the seat of the local ruler and, later, of the chief of police. People were tortured at the site of the well in the centre of the courtyard.

The palace now houses Florence's rich collection of sculpture, notably works by Michelangelo, many by Benvenuto Cellini, and Donatello's stunning bronze *David*, the first sculpture since antiquity to depict a fully naked man (open Tuesday to Sunday 9 am to 2 pm; entry is L8000).

Galleria dell'Accademia Michelangelo's *David* is in this gallery (the one in Piazza della Signoria is a good copy), as are four of his unfinished *slaves* (or *prisoners*). The gallery upstairs houses many important works of the Florentine primitives. The gallery, at Via Ricasoli 60, is open Tuesday to Saturday from 9 am to 7 pm and Sunday to 2 pm. Entry is L12,000.

Basilica di San Lorenzo & Capelle Medicee
The basilica, rebuilt by Brunelleschi in the early 15th century for the Medici, contains his **Sagrestia Vecchia** (Old Sacristy), which was decorated by Donatello. It's also worth visiting the **Biblioteca Laurenziana**, a huge library designed by Michelangelo to house the Medici collection of some 10,000 manuscripts.

Around the corner, in Piazza Madonna degli Aldobrandini, are the Medici Chapels. The **Cappella dei Principi**, sumptuously decorated with precious marble and semiprecious stones, was the principal burial place of the Medici grand dukes. The graceful and simple **Sagrestia Nuova** was designed by Michelangelo, but he left Florence for Rome before its completion. It contains his beautiful sculptures *Night & Day*, *Dawn & Dusk* and the *Madonna with Child*, which adorn the Medici tombs. The chapels are open Tuesday to Sunday from 9 am to 2 pm. Admission is L10,000.

Other Attractions The Dominican church of **Santa Maria Novella** was built during the 13th and 14th centuries, and its white-and-green marble façade was designed by Alberti in the 15th century. The church is decorated with frescos by Ghirlandaio (who was assisted by a very young Michelangelo) and Masaccio. The **Cappella di Filippo Strozzi** contains frescos by Filippo Lippi, and the beautiful **cloisters** feature frescos by Uccello and his students.

The **Convento di San Marco** (Monastery of St Mark) is a museum of the work of Fra

Angelico, who covered its walls and many of the monks' cells with frescos and lived here from 1438 to 1455. Also worth seeing are the peaceful cloisters and the cell of the monk Savonarola. It also contains works by Fra Bartolomeo and Ghirlandaio. The monastery is open Tuesday to Sunday from 9 am to 2 pm and entry is L8000.

Head up to **Piazzale Michelangelo** for a magnificent view of Florence. To reach the piazzale, cross the Ponte Vecchio, turn left and walk along the river, then turn right at Piazza Giuseppe Roggi, or take bus No 13 from the station.

Cycling
I Bike Italy (☎ 234 23 71) offers reasonably priced full and half-day guided mountain-bike rides in the countryside around Florence, as well as longer tours in Tuscany and Umbria.

Courses
Florence has more than 30 schools offering courses in Italian language and culture. Numerous other schools offer courses in art, including painting, drawing and sculpture, as well as art history. While Florence might be the most attractive city in which to study Italian language or art, it is also one of the more expensive. Perugia, Siena and Urbino offer good-quality courses at much lower prices. The cost of language courses in Florence ranges from about L450,000 to L900,000, depending on the school and the length of the course (one month is usually the minimum duration). Here are the addresses of some of the language courses available in Florence:

Centro Linguistico Italiano Dante Alighieri
    Via dei Bardi 12, 50125, Florence (☎ 234 29 86)
Istituto Europeo
    Piazzale delle Pallottole 1, 50122 Florence
    (☎ 238 10 71)
Istituto di Lingua e Cultura Italiana per Stranieri Michelangelo
    Via Ghibellina 88, 50122 Florence (☎ 24 09 75)

Art courses range from one-month summer workshops (costing from L500,000 to more than L1,000,000) to longer-term professional diploma courses. These can be expensive, some of them costing more than L6,500,000 a year. Schools will organise accommodation for students, upon request, either in private apartments or with Italian families.

Brochures detailing courses and prices are available at Italian cultural institutes throughout the world. You can write in English to request information and enrolment forms – letters should be addressed to the *segretaria*. Some art schools include:

Istituto d'Arte di Firenze Lorenzo de' Medici
  Via Faenza 43, 50122 Florence (☎ 28 71 43)
Istituto per l'Arte e il Restauro
  Palazzo Spinelli, Borgo Santa Croce 10, 50122 Florence (☎ 234 58 98)

Special Events

The major festivals include the Festa del Patrono (the Feast of St John the Baptist) on June 24; the Scoppio del Carro (Explosion of the Cart), held in front of the Duomo on Easter Sunday (see Facts for the Visitor at the start of this chapter); and the lively Calcio Storico (Historical Football), featuring football matches played in 16th-century costume, which is held in June.

Places to Stay

There are more than 150 budget hotels in Florence, so even in peak season when the city is packed with tourists, you should be able to find a room. However, it is always advisable to make a booking, and you should arrive by late morning to claim your room.

Always ask the full price of a room before putting your bags down. Hotels and pensioni in Florence are notorious for bill-padding, particularly in summer. Many require an extra L5000 for a compulsory breakfast and will charge L3000 and more for a shower. Prices listed here are for high season and, unless otherwise specified, are for rooms without private bathroom.

Camping The *Italiani e Stranieri* camping ground (☎ 681 19 77), Viale Michelangelo 80, is near Piazzale Michelangelo. Take bus No 13 from the train station. *Villa Camerata* (☎ 60 03 15), Viale Augusto Righi 2/4, is next to the HI hostel (see the next section), north-east of the centre (take bus 17B from the station, 30 minutes). There is another camping ground at Fiesole, *Campeggio Panoramico* (☎ 59 90 69)

at Via Peramonda 1, which also has bungalows. Take bus No 7 to Fiesole from the station.

Hostels The HI *Ostello Villa Camerata* (☎ 60 14 51), Viale Augusto Righi 2/4, charges L23,000 for B&B, dinner is L14,000 and there is also a bar. Take bus No 17B, which leaves from the right of the station as you leave the platforms. The trip takes 30 minutes. Daytime closing is 9 am to 2 pm. It is open to HI members only and reservations can be made by mail (essential in summer).

The private *Ostello Archi Rossi* (☎ 29 08 04), Via Faenza 94r, is another good option for a bed in a dorm room. *Ostello Santa Monaca* (☎ 26 83 38), Via Santa Monaca 6, is also private. It is a 15 to 20-minute walk from the station. Go through Piazza Santa Maria Novella, along Via de' Fossi, across the Ponte alla Carraia and directly ahead along Via de' Serragli. Via Santa Monaca is on the right. A bed costs L20,000 and meals are available.

Hotels – around the station The *Pensione Bellavista* (☎ 28 45 28), Largo Alinari 15 (at the start of Via Nazionale), is small, but a knockout bargain if you manage to book one of the two double rooms with balconies and a view of the Duomo and Palazzo Vecchio. Singles/doubles cost L55,000/70,000, but they will hit you for L3500 to use the bath. In the same building is the *Pensione Le Cascine* (☎ 21 10 66), a two-star hotel with beautifully furnished rooms, some with balconies. Singles/doubles are L65,000/95,000, including use of the communal bathroom. Prices double for rooms with private bathrooms.

Albergo Azzi (☎ 21 38 06), Via Faenza 56, has a helpful management and singles/doubles cost L45,000/70,000, breakfast included. The same management runs the *Albergo Anna* upstairs.

Across Via Nazionale at Via Faenza 7, is *Pensione Accademia* (☎ 29 34 51). It has pleasant rooms and incorporates an 18th-century palace, replete with magnificent stained-glass doors and carved wooden ceilings; singles cost L90,000 and a double with bathroom is L130,000, breakfast and TV included. *Soggiorno Burchi* (☎ 41 44 54), Via Faenza 20, has triples for L75,000 and there is free use of the kitchen.

The *Locanda Daniel* (☎ 21 12 93), Via Nazionale 22, has doubles for L60,000 and beds in a large room for L25,000 per person. One of the rooms has a panoramic view of the Duomo. The owner will not take bookings, so arrive very early. In the same building is *Soggiorno Nazionale* (☎ 238 22 03). Singles/doubles are L55,000/84,000 and triples are L114,000. Breakfast is included.

At No 24 is the *Pensione Ausonia & Rimini* (☎ 49 65 47), run by a young couple who go out of their way to help travellers. Singles/doubles are L65,000/84,000, and a triple is L108,000. The price includes breakfast and use of the communal bathroom. The same couple also operates the more expensive *Pensione Kursaal* downstairs.

Pensione Mary (☎ 49 63 10), Piazza della Indipendenza 5, has singles/doubles for L60,000/85,000.

Hotels – around Piazza Santa Maria Novella
In the piazza at No 25, *La Mia Casa* (☎ 21 30 61) is a rambling place filled with backpackers. Singles/doubles are L35,000/50,000 and triples/quads are L65,000/80,000.

Via della Scala, which runs north-west off the piazza, is lined with pensioni. *La Romagnola* (☎ 21 15 97) at No 40 has large, clean rooms for L39,000/64,000. A triple room is L90,000. The same family runs *La Gigliola* (☎ 28 79 81) upstairs. *La Scala* (☎ 21 26 29) at No 21 is small and has doubles/triples for L80,000/110,000. The *Pensione Margareth* (☎ 21 01 38) at No 25 is pleasantly furnished and has singles/doubles for L45,000/60,000. A triple is L90,000. Use of the communal shower is L2500. *Pensione Montreal* (☎ 238 23 31) at No 43 has singles for L40,000 and doubles/triples with bathroom for L80,000/120,000.

The *Sole* (☎ 239 60 94), Via del Sole 8, charges L45,000/65,000 for singles/doubles. A double with bathroom costs L85,000. Triples/quads cost L78,000/92,000. The curfew is 1 am. Ask for a quiet room. In the same building is the *Pensione Toscana* (☎ 21 31 56), with singles/doubles with bathroom for L70,000/110,000. The *Ottaviani* (☎ 239 62 23), at Piazza Ottaviani 1, just off Piazza Santa Maria Novella, has singles/doubles for L50,000/70,000, breakfast included. In the same building is the *Visconti* (☎ 21 38 77), with a pleasant

terrace garden where you can have breakfast. Singles/doubles are L55,000/84,000, and a triple is L115,000. Breakfast is included.

Hotels – from the Duomo to the Arno This area is a 15-minute walk from the station and is right in the heart of old Florence.

One of the best deals is the small *Aily Home* (☎ 329 65 05), overlooking the Ponte Vecchio at Piazza Santo Stefano 1. It has double rooms (three of which overlook the bridge) for L60,000 a night. *Albergo Firenze* (☎ 21 42 03; fax 21 23 70), Piazza dei Donati 4, just south of the Duomo, has singles/doubles for L55,000/82,000 including breakfast. The *Brunori* (☎ 28 96 48), Via del Proconsolo 5, has doubles for L66,000, or with private bathroom for L84,000. The *Maria Luisa de' Medici* (☎ 28 00 48), Via del Corso 1, is in a 17th-century palace. It has no singles, but its large rooms for up to five people cater for families. All prices include breakfast. A double is L93,000, a triple L129,000 and a quad L168,000.

Fiesole In the hills overlooking Florence is *Bencistà* (☎ 055-5 91 63), Via Benedetto da Maiano 4, about one km from Fiesole. It is an old villa and from its terrace there is a magnificent view of Florence. A double is L140,000, or L170,000 with bathroom, and half-pension is L105,000 per person. It might break the budget, but for one or two days it is well worth it.

Rental If you want an apartment in Florence, save your pennies and start searching well before you arrive. A one-room apartment with kitchenette, in the centre, will cost from L600,000 to L1,000,000 a month. Florence & Abroad (☎ 48 70 04), Via Zanobi 58, handles rental accommodation.

Places to Eat
Simplicity and quality best describe the food of Tuscany. Start your meal with fettunta (known elsewhere in Italy as bruschetta), a thick slice of toasted bread, rubbed with garlic and soaked with the rich, green Tuscan olive oil. Try the ribollita, a very filling soup of vegetables and white beans, reboiled with chunks of bread and garnished with olive oil. Another traditional dish is the deliciously simple fagiolini alla Fiorentina (green beans

and olive oil). Florence is renowned for its excellent bistecca Fiorentina (beefsteak Florentine) – thick, juicy and big enough for two people.

Eating at a good trattoria can be surprisingly economical, but many tourists fall into the trap of eating at the self-service restaurants which line the streets of the main shopping district between the Duomo and the Arno. Be adventurous and seek out the little eating places in the district of Oltrarno (the other side of the Arno from the centre) and near the Mercato Centrale (the covered market) in San Lorenzo. The market, open from Monday to Saturday 7 am to 2 pm (also Saturday from 4 to 8 pm), offers fresh produce, cheeses and meat at reasonable prices.

City Centre The *Trattoria da Benvenuto*, Via Mosca 16r, on the corner of Via dei Neri, is an excellent trattoria. A full meal will cost around L25,000 and a quick meal of pasta, bread and wine will cost around L12,000. *Angie's Pub*, Via dei Neri 35r, offers a vast array of sandwiches and focaccia (you can design your own) for L4500 to L6500, as well as hamburgers, served Italian-style with mozzarella and spinach, and hot dogs with cheese and mushrooms. There is a good range of beers and no extra charge if you sit down. At *Fiaschetteria*, Via dei Neri 17r, try the excellent ribollita for around L10,000. *Osteria Il Caminetto*, Via dello Studio 34, just south of Piazza del Duomo, has a small vine-covered terrace. A pasta dish costs around L9000, and a full meal around L30,000.

Around San Lorenzo Ask anyone in Florence where they go for lunch and they will answer *Mario's*. This small bar and trattoria at Via Rosina 2r, near the Mercato Centrale, is open only at lunchtime. It serves pasta dishes for around L4000 to L6000, and a secondo for L5000 to L9000. A few doors down, at Piazza del Mercato Centrale 20, is *Cafè Za Za*, another favourite with the locals. Prices are around the same as at Mario's. *Bondi*, Via dell'Ariento 85, specialises in focaccia and pizza from L2500.

In the Oltrarno A bustling place popular with the locals is *Trattoria Casalinga*, Via dei

Michelozzi 9r. The food is great and a filling meal of pasta, meat or contorni, and wine will cost you around L15,000 to L20,000. *I Tarocchi*, Via de' Renai 12-14r, serves excellent pizza, ranging from L6000 to L10,000, as well as dishes typical of the region, including a good range of pasta from L7000 to L8000, and plenty of salads and vegetable dishes from L5000 to L8000. The coperto is only L2000. *Angelino*, Via Santo Spirito 36, is an excellent trattoria where a full meal will cost around L35,000.

Cafés & Snack Bars Near the Mercato Centrale, Via Nazionale 57, *Caffè degli Innocenti* has a good selection of pre-prepared panini and cakes for around L2500 to L3500. The streets between the Duomo and the Arno harbour many pizzerias where you can buy pizza by the slice to take away for around L2000 to L4000, depending on the weight.

Gelati Among the best outlets for gelati are *Gelateria Vivoli*, Via dell'Isola delle Stinche, near Via Torta, and *Perché No?*, Via dei Tavolini 19r, off Via Calzaiuoli.

Entertainment
Several publications list the theatrical and musical events and festivals held in the city and surrounding areas. They include the bimonthly *Florence Today* and the monthly *Firenze Information* and *Firenze Avvenimenti*, all available at the tourist offices. *Firenze Spettacolo* is the city's definitive entertainment guide, available every 15 days for L2500 at newsstands.

Concerts, opera and dance are performed year-round at the *Teatro Comunale*, Corso Italia 16, with the main seasons running from September to December and from January to April. Contact the theatre's box office (☎ 277 92 36).

The *Astro Cinema* in Piazza San Simone, near Santa Croce, runs films in English every night except Monday. Nightclubs include *La Dolce Vita*, Piazza del Carmine, south of the Arno. *Cabiria*, in Piazza Santo Spirito, is a bar which is very popular among young people, especially in summer.

A more sedate pastime is the nightly passeggiata (stroll) in Piazzale Michelangelo, overlooking the city (take bus No 13 from the station or the Duomo).

Things to Buy

The main shopping area is between the Duomo and the Arno, with boutiques concentrated along Via Roma, Via dei Calzaiuoli and Via Por Santa Maria, leading to the goldsmiths lining the Ponte Vecchio. Window-shop along Via de' Tornabuoni, where the top designers, including Gucci, Yves Saint Laurent and Pucci, sell their wares.

The open-air market (open Monday to Saturday), located in the streets of San Lorenzo near the Mercato Centrale, offers leather goods, clothing and jewellery at low prices, but quality can vary greatly. Check the item carefully before you buy. You can bargain, but not if you want to use a credit card. The flea market at Piazza dei Ciompi, off Borgo Allegri near the Church of Santa Croce (Monday to Saturday), is not as extensive but there are great bargains. It opens roughly the same hours as retail shops and all day on the last Sunday of the month.

Florence is famous for its beautifully patterned paper, which is stocked in the many *cartolerie* (stationer's shops) throughout the city and at the markets.

Getting There & Away

Air The nearest international airport is Galileo Galilei at Pisa, just under an hour away from Florence. It has regular connections to major European and Italian cities. Amerigo Vespucci airport, a few km north-west of the city centre at Via del Termine, serves domestic flights only.

Bus The SITA bus terminal (☎ 21 47 21), Via Santa Caterina da Siena, is just to the west of the train station. Buses leave for Siena, the Colle Val d'Elsa, Poggibonsi (where there are connecting buses to San Gimignano and Volterra) and Arrezzo. Full details on other bus services are available at the APT.

Train Florence is on the main Rome-Milan line and most of the trains are the fast intercities, for which you have to pay a rapido supplement. Regular trains also go to/from Venice (three hours) and Trieste. For train information ring ☎ 28 87 85.

Car & Motorcycle Florence is connected by the Autostrada del Sole (A1) to Bologna and Milan in the north and Rome and Naples to the south. The motorway to the sea, Autostrada del Mare (A11), joins Florence to Prato, Lucca, Pisa and the Mediterranean coast, and a superstrada (dual carriageway) joins the city to Siena. Exits from the autostrade into Florence are well signed, and either one of the exits marked 'Firenze nord' or 'Firenze sud' will take you to the centre of town. There are tourist information offices on the A1 both to the north and south of the city.

Getting Around

To/From the Airports Regular trains leave from platform number 5 at Florence's Santa Maria Novella station for Pisa airport daily from 5.55 am to 8 pm. Check your bags in at the air terminal (☎ 21 60 73) near platform 5. ATAF bus No 62 leaves regularly from the train station for Amerigo Vespucci airport.

Bus ATAF buses service the city centre and Fiesole. The terminal for the most useful buses is in a small piazza to the left as you go out of the station onto Via Valfonda. Bus No 7 leaves from here for Fiesole and also stops at the Duomo. Tickets must be bought before you get on the bus and are sold at most tobacconists or from automatic vending machines at major bus stops (L1400 for one hour, L1900 for two hours, L5000 for 24 hours).

Car & Motorcycle If you're spending the day in Florence, park the car at the Fortezza da Basso. It costs L1500 an hour. More expensive car parks are in Piazza del Mercato Centrale.

To rent a car, try Hertz (☎ 28 22 60), Via M Finiguerra 17r, or Avis (☎ 21 36 29), Borgognissanti 128r. For motorcycles and bicycles try Alinari (☎ 28 05 00), Via Guelfa 85r.

Taxi You can find taxis outside the station, or call ☎ 4798 or ☎ 4390 to book one.

PISA

Once a maritime power to rival Genoa and Venice, Pisa now seems content to have one remaining claim to fame: its leaning tower. On the banks of the Arno River near the Ligurian Sea, Pisa was once a busy port, the site of an important university and the home of Galileo Galilei (1564-1642). Devastated by the Genoese in the 13th century, its history eventually merged with that of Florence. Today Pisa is a pleasant town, but there is not a lot to see after you have explored the main square, the Campo dei Miracoli, and taken a walk around the old centre.

Information

There are APT tourist information offices at the train station, the airport and at Piazza Arcivescovado, next to the Campo dei Miracoli. In summer the station and Campo offices open daily from 8 am to 8 pm but the station office is closed on Sunday. Take bus No 1 from the old town, to Piazza del Duomo.

Pisa's postcode is 56100 and the telephone code is ☎ 050.

Things to See & Do

The Pisans can justly claim that their **Campo dei Miracoli** (Field of Miracles) is one of the most beautiful squares in the world. Set in its sprawling lawns are the **cathedral**, the **baptistry** and the **leaning tower**. On any day the piazza is teeming with people – students studying, tourists wandering and Pisan workers eating their lunch.

The Romanesque cathedral, begun in 1064, has a beautiful façade of columns in four tiers and its huge interior is lined with 68 columns. The bronze doors of the transept, facing the leaning tower, are by Bonanno Pisano. The 16th-century bronze doors of the main entrance are by Giambologna and were made to replace the original doors which were destroyed in a fire. The marble baptistry, which was started in 1153 and took almost two centuries to complete, contains a beautiful pulpit by Nicola Pisano.

The famous leaning bell tower was in trouble from the start. Its architect, Bonanno Pisano, managed to complete three tiers before the tower started to lean. The problem is generally believed to have been caused by shifting soil, and the tower has continued to lean by an average one mm a year. Galileo climbed its 294 steps to experiment with gravity. Today it is no longer possible to follow in his footsteps. The tower has been closed for some years while the Italians have been trying to work out how to

stop its inexorable lean towards the ground. Finally, in early 1994, they found a solution – 600 tons of lead ingots which anchor the north foundation. The lean was stopped and the tower even began to straighten. However, in September 1995 the tower moved 2.5 mm in one night. While no-one has any intention of turning the leaning tower into a straight tower, many still believe that it will fall down eventually.

After seeing the Campo dei Miracoli, take a walk down Via Santa Maria, along the Arno and into the Borgo Stretto to explore the old city.

Places to Stay & Eat

Pisa has a reasonable number of budget hotels for a small town, but many double as residences for students during the school year, so it can be difficult to find a cheap room. The non-HI *Ostello per la Gioventù* (☎ 89 06 22), is at Via Pietrasantina 15 and is used by students. A bed is L20,000. The place is closed from 9 am to 6 pm. Take bus No 3 from the station. The *Albergo E Gronchi* (☎ 56 18 23), Piazza Arcivescovado 1, just near the Campo dei Miracoli, has modern singles/doubles for L32,000/50,000 and triples/quads for L68,000/84,000. *Albergo Giardino* (☎ 56 21 01), Piazza Manin 1, just west of Campo dei Miracoli, has singles/doubles for L40,000/60,000. The *Hotel di Stefano* (☎ 55 35 59), Via Sant'Apollonia 35, offers good-quality singles/doubles for L40,000/55,000.

Near the station is the *Albergo Milano* (☎ 23 162), Via Mascagni 14, with pleasant rooms and a friendly owner. Singles/doubles cost L45,000/60,000 and triples cost L80,000.

Being a university town, Pisa hosts a good range of cheap eating places. Head for the area around Borgo Stretto and the university. *Numeroundici*, Via Domenica Cavalca 11, has cheap snacks, as well as a full menu. *Pizzeria da Matteo*, Via Santa Maria 20, is another good choice. There is an open-air food market in Piazza delle Vettovaglie, off Borgo Stretto. Pick up supplies there and head for the Campo dei Miracoli for a picnic lunch.

Getting There & Away

The airport, with domestic and international (European) flights, is only a few minutes away by train, or by bus No 7 from the station. Lazzi (☎ 462 88) buses operate to Florence, Prato and Lucca. APT (☎ 233 84) runs buses to

Volterra and Livorno. The city is linked by direct train to Florence, Rome and Genoa. Local trains head for Lucca and Livorno.

SIENA

Italy's best preserved medieval town, Siena is built on three hills and is still surrounded by its historic ramparts. Its medieval centre is bristling with majestic Gothic buildings in various shades of the colour known as burnt sienna. According to legend, Siena was founded by the sons of Remus (one of the founders of Rome). In the Middle Ages the city became a free republic, but its success and power led to serious rivalry with Florence. In a famous incident in the 13th century, the Florentines hurled dead donkeys and excrement into Siena, hoping to start a plague.

Painters of the Sienese School produced important works of art and the city was home to St Catherine and St Benedict. Siena is divided into 17 *contrade* (districts) and each year 10 are chosen to compete in the Palio, an extraordinary horse race and pageant held in the shell-shaped Piazza del Campo on 2 July and 16 August.

Orientation

Siena is well geared for tourism. Signs direct you through the modern town to the medieval city, and within the walls there are easy-to-follow signs to all the major sights.

From the train station catch bus No 2, 3 or 10 to Piazza Matteotti and walk into the centre along Via dei Termini (it takes about five minutes to reach the Campo). From the bus terminal in Piazza San Domenico, it's a five-minute walk along Via della Sapienza and then left into Via delle Terme to the Campo. No cars, apart from those of residents, are allowed in the medieval centre.

Information

Tourist Office The APT office (☎ 28 05 51) is at Piazza del Campo 56 and during summer is open Monday to Saturday from 8.30 am to 7.30 pm. For the rest of the year it opens Monday to Friday from 9 am to 1 pm and 3.30 to 6.30 pm.

Post & Communications The main post office is at Piazza Matteotti 1. The Telecom office is at Via dei Termini 40.

Siena's telephone code is ☎ 0577.

Medical Services For an ambulance, call ☎ 28 00 28. The public hospital (☎ 29 08 07) is in Viale Bracci, just north of Siena at Le Scotte.

Emergency For a police emergency call ☎ 113. The questura is at Via del Castoro 23 (near the Duomo) and its Foreigners' Office is in Piazza Jacopo della Quercia.

Things to See & Do

The **Piazza del Campo**, known simply as the Campo, is a magnificent shell-shaped, slanting piazza, its paving divided into nine sectors. At the lowest point of the piazza is the imposing **Palazzo Pubblico** (also known as Palazzo Comunale or town hall), considered one of the most graceful Gothic buildings in Italy. Inside the town hall are numerous important Sienese works of art, including Simone Martini's *Maestà* and Ambrogio Lorenzetti's frescos, *Allegories of Good & Bad Government*. There is also a chapel with frescos by Taddeo di Bartolo. As with all museums and monuments in Siena, the opening hours for the palace vary depending on the time of year. In summer it opens Monday to Saturday from 9.30 am to 7.30 pm and Sunday from 9.30 am to 1.45 pm. Entry is L6000, or L3000 for students.

The spectacular **Duomo** is one of the most beautiful in Italy. Its black-and-white striped marble façade has a Romanesque lower section, with carvings by Giovanni Pisano. Its upper section is 14th-century Gothic and there are 19th-century mosaics at the top. The interior features an inlaid marble floor, with various works depicting biblical stories. The beautiful **pulpit** was carved in marble and porphyry by Nicola Pisano, the father of Giovanni Pisano. Other important art works include a bronze statue of St John the Baptist by Donatello and statues of St Jerome and Mary Magdalene by Bernini.

Through a door from the north aisle is the **Libreria Piccolomini**, which Pope Pius III (pope during 1503) built to house the magnificent, illustrated books of his uncle, the former pope Pius II. It features frescos by Pinturicchio and a Roman statue of the Three Graces. Entry is L2000.

ITALY

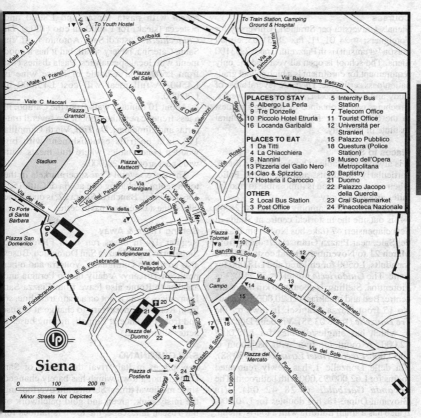

PLACES TO STAY
6 Albergo La Perla
9 Tre Donzelle
10 Piccolo Hotel Etruria
16 Locanda Garibaldi

PLACES TO EAT
1 Da Titti
4 La Chiacchiera
8 Nannini
13 Pizzeria del Gallo Nero
14 Ciao & Spizzico
17 Hostaria il Caroccio

OTHER
2 Local Bus Station
3 Post Office
5 Intercity Bus Station
7 Telecom Office
11 Tourist Office
12 Universitá per Stranieri
15 Palazzo Pubblico
18 Questura (Police Station)
19 Museo dell'Opera Metropolitana
20 Baptistry
21 Duomo
22 Palazzo Jacopo della Quercia
23 Crai Supermarket
24 Pinacoteca Nazionale

Siena

0   100   200 m

Minor Streets Not Depicted

The **Museo dell'Opera Metropolitana** (Duomo Museum) is in Piazza del Duomo. It houses many important works of art that formerly adorned the cathedral, including the famous *Maestà* by Duccio di Buoninsegna, formerly used as a screen for the cathedral's High Altar; and works by artists including Ambrogio Lorenzetti, Simone Martini and Taddeo di Bartolo. The collection also features tapestries and manuscripts. From mid-March to the end of September the museum is open daily from 9 am to 7.30 pm. In October it closes at 6 pm and during the rest of the year at 1.30 pm. Entry is L5000.

The **baptistry**, which is behind the cathedral, has a Gothic façade and is decorated with 15th-century frescos, a font by Jacopo della Quercia, and sculptures by artists such as Donatello and Ghiberti. Entry is L3000.

The 15th-century **Palazzo Buonsignori** houses the **Pinacoteca Nazionale** (National Picture Gallery), with innumerable masterpieces by Sienese artists, including the *Madonna dei Francescani* by Duccio di Buoninsegna, *Madonna col Bambino* by Simone Martini and a series of Madonnas by Ambrogio Lorenzetti. The gallery is open Tuesday to Saturday from 9 am to 7 pm and Sunday to 1 pm. Admission is L8000.

Courses

Siena's Università per Stranieri (University for Foreigners; ☎ 24 01 11; fax 28 31 63; e-mail unistra4@unisi.it) is in Piazzetta Grassi 2, 53100 Siena. The school is open all year and the only requirement for enrolment is a high school graduation/pass certificate. There are several areas of study and courses cost L725,000 for 10 weeks. Brochures can be obtained by making a request to the Secretary, or from the Italian Cultural Institute in your city.

Places to Stay

It is always advisable to book a hotel in Siena, particularly in August and during the Palio, when accommodation is impossible to find for miles around the city.

The **Colleverde** camping ground (☎ 28 00 44) is outside the historical centre at Strada di Scacciapensieri 47 (take bus No 8 from Piazza del Sale, near Piazza Gramsci). It opens from March 21 to November 10 and costs L13,000 for adults, L6500 for children and L18,000 for a site. The **Guidoriccio** hostel (☎ 52 212), Via Fiorentina, Stellino, is about two km out of the centre. Bed and breakfast is L20,000. Take bus No 15 from Piazza Gramsci. In town try the **Tre Donzelle** (☎ 28 03 58), Via delle Donzelle 5, which has singles/doubles for L38,000/62,000. A room for four with bathroom is L132,000. **Piccolo Hotel Etruria** (☎ 28 80 88), Via delle Donzelle 1, has newly renovated rooms for L62,000/95,000 with bathroom. The **Locanda Garibaldi** (☎ 28 42 04), Via Giovanni Dupré 18, has doubles for L70,000. It also has a small trattoria with a tourist menu.

The **Albergo La Perla** (☎ 47 144) is on the 2nd floor at Via delle Terme 25, a short walk from the Campo. Small but clean singles/doubles with shower are L60,000/90,000.

Agriturismo is well organised around Siena. The tourist office has a list of establishments, or contact Agriturismo in Rome (see Accommodation in the Facts for the Visitor section earlier in this chapter).

Places to Eat

Pizzeria del Gallo Nero, Via del Porrione 67, near the Campo, has good pizzas for around L8000 and there are no cover or service charges. In the Piazza del Campo is the cheap self-service **Ciao & Spizzico**. Off the Campo, at Via Casato di Sotto 32, is **Hostaria Il Car-**roccio with pasta for around L8000 and bistecca (steak) for L4000 an etto (100g). **La Chiacchiera**, Costa di Sant' Antonio 4, off Via Santa Caterina, is very small, but it has a good menu with local specialities. Pasta dishes cost from L5000 and a bottle of house wine is L4500. A full meal will cost L15,000 to L20,000.

About 10 minutes walk from the Campo, in a less frenetic neighbourhood, are several trattorias and alimentari. **Da Titti**, Via di Camollia 193, is a no-frills establishment with big wooden bench tables where full meals with wine cost around L20,000.

There are several **Crai** supermarkets in the town centre, including one at Via di Città 152-156. **Nannini**, Banchi di Sopra 22, is one of the city's finest cafés and pasticcerie.

Getting There & Away

Regular Tra-In buses run from Florence to Siena, arriving at Piazza San Domenico. Buses also go to San Gimignano, Volterra and other points in Tuscany. A daily bus to Perugia and another to Rome also leave from Piazza San Domenico. Siena is not on a main train line, so from Rome it is necessary to change at Chiusi and from Florence at Empoli, making buses a better alternative.

SAN GIMIGNANO

Few places in Italy rival the beauty of San Gimignano, a town which has barely changed since medieval times. Set on a hill overlooking the misty pink, green and gold patchwork of the Tuscan landscape, the town is famous for its towers (14 of the original 72 remain), built as a demonstration of power by its prominent families in the Middle Ages.

The town is packed with tourists at weekends, so try to visit during the week. The Pro Loco tourist information office (☎ 94 00 08) is in Piazza del Duomo in the town centre.

San Gimignano's telephone code is ☎ 0577.

Things to See

Climb San Gimignano's tallest tower, **Torre Grossa** (also known as the town hall tower), off Piazza del Duomo, for a memorable view of the Tuscan hills. The tower is reached from within the **Palazzo del Popolo**, which houses the **Museo Civico**, with paintings by Filippo Lippi and Pinturicchio. Also in the piazza is the

Duomo, with a Romanesque interior, frescos by Ghirlandaio in the **Cappella di Santa Fina** and a *Last Judgment* by Taddeo di Bartolo.

The **Piazza della Cisterna**, with a 13th-century well, is the most impressive piazza in San Gimignano. It is paved with bricks in a herringbone pattern and lined with towers and palaces.

Places to Stay & Eat

San Gimignano offers few options for budget travellers. The nearest camping ground is *Il Boschetto di Piemma* (☎ 94 03 52), about three km from San Gimignano at Santa Lucia. It costs L6000 a night for adults and L4000 for children, plus L8000 for a site. It is open from April until mid-October and there is a bus service to the site. The non-HI hostel (☎ 94 19 91) at Via delle Fonti opens from March 1 to October 31 and charges L21,000 for B&B. *Foresteria Convento di Sant'Agostino* (☎ 94 03 83), Piazza Sant'Agostino, has rooms for L25,000/35,000. Some rooms are very shabby, but the prices are hard to beat.

Hotels in town are expensive, but there are numerous rooms for rent in private homes. Agriturismo is well organised in this area. For information on both, contact the tourist office or the APT in Siena.

Pizzeria Pizzoteca, Via dei Fossi, outside the walls to the left of Porta San Matteo, has good pizzas, but forget about the pasta. *Trattoria Chiribiri*, Piazzetta della Madonna, off Via San Giovanni, has pasta at reasonable prices. Nearby is *Pizza a Taglio*, with pizza by the slice. There is a fresh produce market held on Thursday morning in Piazza del Duomo and there are several alimentari in Via San Matteo.

Getting There & Away

Regular buses connect San Gimignano with Florence and Siena, but for both you need to change at Poggibonsi. Buses arrive at Porta San Giovanni and timetables are posted outside the Pro Loco. Enter through the Porta and continue straight ahead to reach the Piazza del Duomo.

PERUGIA

One of Italy's best preserved medieval hill towns, Perugia, the capital of the Umbria Region, has a lively and bloody past. The city is noted for the internal feuding of its families, the Baglioni and the Oddi, and the violent wars against its neighbours during the Middle Ages. Perugia also has a strong artistic and cultural tradition. It was the home of the painter Perugino, and Raphael, his student, also worked here. Its University for Foreigners, established in 1925, offers courses in Italian language and attracts thousands of students from all over the world. A full calendar of musical and cultural events, including the noted Umbria Jazz in July, makes the city even more appealing.

Orientation & Information

The centre of all activity in Perugia is the Corso Vannucci. The APT tourist information office (☎ 572 33 27) is in Piazza IV Novembre, opposite the cathedral at one end of the Corso, and is open Monday to Saturday from 8.30 am to 1.30 pm and 4 to 7.30 pm and Sunday from 9 am to 1 pm. The main post office is in Piazza Matteotti. For all events and useful information, get a copy of the monthly *Perugia What, Where, When* (L1000 at newsstands).

Perugia's telephone code is ☎ 075.

Things to See & Do

The **Palazzo dei Priori**, on Corso Vannucci, is a rambling 13th-century palace housing the impressively frescoed **Sala dei Notari** and the **Galleria Nazionale dell'Umbria**, with works by Pinturicchio, Perugino and Fra Angelico. Opposite the palazzo is the **duomo**, with an unfinished façade in the characteristic Perugian red-and-white marble. Inside are frescos, decorations and furniture by well-known artists from the 15th to 18th centuries.

Between the two buildings, in Piazza IV Novembre, is the 13th-century **Fontana Maggiore**, designed by Fra Bevignate in 1278 and carved by Nicola and Giovanni Pisano. The bas-relief panels represent scenes of the history and trades of Perugia, the sciences and the seasons. At the other end of Corso Vannucci is the **Rocca Paolina** (Paolina Fortress), the ruins of a massive 16th-century fortress built upon the foundations of the palaces and homes of the powerful families of the day, notably the Baglioni. The homes were destroyed and the materials used to build the fortress, under the orders of Pope Paul III, as a means of suppressing the Baglioni. Destroyed by the Perugians after the declaration of the Kingdom of Italy in 1860, it remains a symbol of their defiance against oppression.

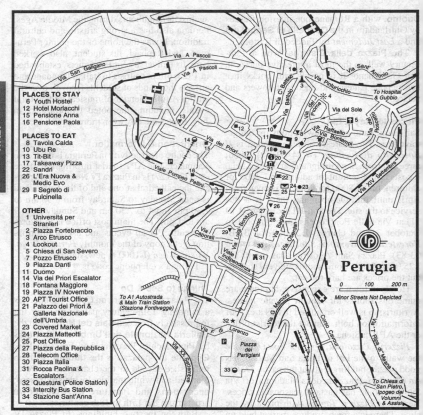

PLACES TO STAY
6 Youth Hostel
12 Hotel Morlacchi
15 Pensione Anna
16 Pensione Paola

PLACES TO EAT
8 Tavola Calda
10 Ubu Re
13 Tit-Bit
17 Takeaway Pizza
22 Sandri
26 L'Era Nuova &
   Medio Evo
29 Il Segreto di
   Pulcinella

OTHER
1 Universitá per
  Stranieri
2 Piazza Fortebraccio
3 Arco Etrusco
4 Lookout
5 Chiesa di San Severo
7 Pozzo Etrusco
9 Piazza Danti
11 Duomo
14 Via dei Priori Escalator
18 Fontana Maggiore
19 Piazza IV Novembre
20 APT Tourist Office
21 Palazzo dei Priori &
   Galleria Nazionale
   dell'Umbria
23 Covered Market
24 Piazza Matteotti
25 Post Office
27 Piazza della Repubblica
28 Telecom Office
30 Piazza Italia
31 Rocca Paolina &
   Escalators
32 Questura (Police Station)
33 Intercity Bus Station
34 Stazione Sant'Anna

Perugia

0   100   200 m

Minor Streets Not Depicted

In the **Chiesa di San Severo**, Piazza San Severo, is Raphael's magnificent fresco *Trinity with Saints*, one of the last works by the painter in Perugia and completed by Perugino after Raphael's death in 1520.

Etruscan remains in Perugia include the **Arco Etrusco** (Etruscan Arch), near the university, and the **Pozzo Etrusco** (Etruscan Well), off Piazza Piccinino, near the cathedral.

Courses

Perugia's University for Foreigners offers three and six-month courses in Italian language and culture for L720,000 for three months. The six-month courses are for advanced students.

Special one-month courses (L320,000) and intensive courses (L450,000 per month) are also offered. The quality of the courses is generally good, but there can be up to 70 students in a beginner's class during the summer months. You may need to apply for a study visa in your own country, and to obtain this you must have confirmation of enrolment in a course (see Visas & Embassies in the Facts for the Visitor section of this chapter). Since obtaining the necessary documentation from the university takes time, ensure that you send your enrolment form at least three to four months before your intended departure date.

The university will organise accommodation

on request. A room in an apartment (shared with other students), in a private room or with an Italian family will cost around L400,000 a month. Course details can be obtained from Italian cultural institutes in your country, or you can write to the secretary at the Università per Stranieri, Palazzo Gallenga, Piazza Fortebraccio 4, 06122 Perugia (☎ 574 62 11; fax 574 62 13).

Places to Stay

Perugia has a good selection of reasonably priced hotels, but if you arrive unannounced during Umbria Jazz in July, or during August, expect problems. The non-HI *Centro Internazionale per la Gioventù* (☎ 572 28 80), Via Bontempi 13, charges L14,000 a night. Sheets (for the entire stay) are an extra L1000. Its TV room has a frescoed ceiling and its terrace has one of the best views in Perugia (this floor was closed for renovation in 1996). Daylight closing is 9.30 am to 4 pm.

Pensione Anna (☎ 573 63 04), Via dei Priori 48, off Corso Vannucci, has singles/doubles for L36,000/55,000. The *Pensione Paola* (☎ 572 38 16), Via della Canapina 5, is five minutes from the centre, down the escalator from Via dei Priori. It has pleasant singles/doubles for L38,000/58,000. Just off Corso Vannucci, at Via Bonazzi 25, is the *Piccolo Hotel* (☎ 572 29 87), with small doubles for L60,000 (no singles). Showers cost an extra L3000.

The *Hotel Morlacchi* (☎ 572 03 19), Via Tiberi 2, north-west of Piazza IV Novembre, has singles/doubles for L45,000/70,000, or a triple with bathroom for L120,000.

The weekly *Cerco e Trovo* (L2500 at newsstands) lists rental accommodation.

Places to Eat

Being a student town, Perugia offers many budget eating options. Good places for pizza are *L'Era Nuova*, just behind the bar *Medio Evo* on Corso Vannucci, and *Tit-Bit*, Via dei Priori 105. Another option is the popular *Il Segreto di Pulcinella*, Via Larga 8. A pizza will cost from L5000 to L10,000 at each restaurant. There is a takeaway pizza place at Via dei Priori 3.

For a cheap meal try the *Tavola Calda* in Piazza Danti. For an excellent meal and lots of vegetables, try *Ubu Re*, Via Baldeschi 17. It's on the expensive side.

Sandri, in Corso Vannucci near the Palazzo dei Priori, is a great meeting place for a quiet coffee and cake, where you don't pay extra to sit down.

Getting There & Away

Perugia is not on the main Rome-Florence railway line. There are some direct trains from both cities, but most require a change, either at Foligno (from Rome) or Terontola (from Florence). Local trains (for towns such as Terni) leave from St Anna Station. Intercity buses leave from Piazza Partigiani, at the end of the Rocca Paolina escalators, for Rome (and Fiumicino airport), Florence, Siena and cities throughout Umbria including Assisi, Gubbio and nearby Lake Trasimeno. Full timetables for all trains and buses are available at the tourist office.

Getting Around

The main train station is a few km downhill from the historical centre. Catch any bus heading for Piazza Matteotti or Piazza Italia to get to this centre. Tickets cost L1000 and must be bought before you get on the bus.

If you arrive in Perugia by car, be prepared to be confused. Roads leading to the centre wind around a hill topped by the historical centre, and the normal driving time from the base of the hill to the centre is around 10 to 15 minutes. Signs to the centre are clearly marked 'centro' and by following these signs you should arrive at Piazza Italia, where you can leave the car and walk along Corso Vannucci to the tourist office.

Most of the centre is closed to normal traffic, but tourists are allowed to drive to their hotels. It is probably wiser not to do this, as driving in central Perugia is a nightmare because of the extremely narrow streets, most of which are one way. To accommodate other traffic, escalators from the historical centre take you to large car parks downhill. The Rocca Paolina escalator leads to Piazza Partigiani, where there is a supervised car park (L10,000 for one day, then L7500 per day), the intercity bus terminal, and escalators to Piazza Italia nearby. The Via dei Priori escalator leads to two major car parks.

ASSISI

Despite the millions of tourists and pilgrims it attracts every year, Assisi, home of St Francis, manages to remain a beautiful and tranquil refuge (as long as you keep away from the main tourist drags). From Roman times its inhabitants have been aware of the visual impact of the city, perched halfway up Mt Subasio. From the valley its pink-and-white marble buildings literally shimmer in the sunlight.

The APT tourist office (☎ 81 25 34), Piazza del Comune 12, has all the information you need on hotels, sights and events in Assisi.

The local telephone code is ☎ 075.

Things to See

Most people visit Assisi to see its religious monuments. **St Francis' Basilica** is composed of two churches, one built on top of the other. The lower church contains the crypt where St Francis is buried. The upper church was decorated by the great painters of the 13th and 14th centuries, including Giotto and Cimabue. Dress rules are applied rigidly – absolutely no shorts, miniskirts or low-cut dresses/tops are allowed.

The 13th-century **Basilica di Santa Chiara** has an impressive façade. Inside are interesting 14th-century frescos and the remains of St Clare, friend of St Francis and founder of the Order of Poor Clares. The **Cattedrale di San Rufino** is interesting for its impressive Romanesque façade. Its austere interior was altered in the 16th century, but retains the baptismal font where St Francis and St Clare were baptised. The **Piazza del Comune**, in the town centre, was the site of the Roman **Foro Romano**, parts of which have been excavated; access is from Via Portico (entry L3000). The piazza also contains the **Tempio di Minerva**. It is now a church, but retains its impressive pillared façade.

Assisi's 'crown' is the **Rocca Maggiore**, a remarkably well-preserved medieval castle. In the valley below Assisi is the **Basilica di Santa Maria degli Angeli**, a huge church built around the first Franciscan monastery, and the **Cappella del Transito**, where St Francis died in 1226.

Places to Stay & Eat

Assisi is well geared for tourists and there are numerous budget hotels and *affittacamere*

(rooms for rent). Peak periods, when you will need to book well in advance, are Easter, August and September, and the Feast of St Francis on 3 and 4 October. The tourist office has a full list of affittacamere and religious institutions.

The HI *Ostello della Pace* (☎ 81 67 67), Via Valecchi, is small and open all year. Bed and breakfast is L25,000. There is a non-HI *hostel* (L22,000 for B&B) and camping ground (☎ 81 36 36) just out of the town at Fontemaggio. From Piazza Matteotti, at the far end of town from St Francis' Basilica, walk uphill for about two km along Via Eremo delle Carceri till you reach the hostel. *Albergo La Rocca* (☎ 81 22 84), Via Porta Perlici 27, has singles/doubles for L31,000/48,000 and doubles with bath for L69,000. The *Albergo Italia* (☎ 81 26 25), Piazza del Comune, has singles/doubles for L35,000/47,000.

For a snack of pizza by the slice, head for *Pizza Vincenzo*, just off Piazza del Comune at Via San Rufina 1a. In the same complex as the camping ground at Fontemaggio is *La Stalla*, where you can eat a filling meal under an arbour for less than L20,000. In town try *Il Pozzo Romano*, Via Santa Agnese 10, off Piazza Santa Chiara. The pizzas cost around L7000. The restaurant at the *Albergo La Rocca* has home-made pasta for L5000 to L9000 and a three-course tourist menu for L19,000.

Getting There & Away

Buses connect Assisi with Perugia, Foligno and other local towns, leaving from Piazza Santa Chiara. Buses for Rome and Florence leave from Piazza San Pietro. Assisi's train station is in the valley, in the suburb of Santa Maria degli Angeli. It is on the same line as Perugia and there is a shuttle bus service between the town and the station.

SOUTH OF PERUGIA

Umbria is a mountainous region characterised by its many medieval hill towns. After Perugia and Assisi, visit **Orvieto**, **Spello** and **Spoleto** to appreciate the Romanesque and Gothic architecture, particularly Orvieto's cathedral, considered one of the most beautiful in Italy. Try to time your visit to take in the Festival of Two Worlds at Spoleto in late June and early July. These hill towns are accessible by bus or train from Perugia, and the tourist office there has information and timetables.

ANCONA

The main reason to visit Ancona is to catch a ferry to Croatia, Greece or Turkey. This industrial, unattractive port town in the region of the Marches does, however, have an interesting, though small and semi-abandoned, historical centre.

Orientation & Information

The easiest way to get from the train station to the port is by bus No 1. There are tourist information offices at the train station and the *stazione marittima* (seasonal). The main APT office (☎ 3 49 38) is out of the way at Via Thaon de Revel 4.

The main post office is at Piazza XXIV Maggio, open Monday to Saturday from 8.15 am to 7 pm. The Telecom office is opposite the train station.

The telephone code for Ancona is ☎ 071.

Things to See

Walk uphill to the old town and the **Piazzale del Duomo** for a view of the port and the Adriatic. The town's Romanesque **cathedral** was built on the site of a Roman temple and has Byzantine and Gothic features. The church of **San Francesco delle Scale** has a beautiful Venetian-Gothic doorway, and towards the port are the 15th-century **Loggia dei Mercanti** (Merchants' Loggia) and the Romanesque church of **Santa Maria della Piazza**, which has a remarkable, heavily adorned façade.

Places to Stay & Eat

Many people bunk down at the ferry terminal, although the city has many cheap hotels. *Albergo Fiore* (☎ 4 33 90), Piazza Rosselli 24, has singles/doubles for L40,000/65,000 and is just across from the train station. The *Pensione Centrale* (☎ 5 43 88), Via Marsala 10 (near Corso Stamira), has doubles for L50,000.

Trattoria da Dina, Vicolo ad Alto 17 in the old town, has full meals for around L10,000. *Osteria del Pozzo*, Via Bonda 2, just off Piazza del Plebiscito, has good, reasonably priced food. For atmosphere and good fare head for *Osteria Teatro Strabacco*, Via Oberdan 2, near Corso Stamira. The *Mercato Pubblico*, off

Corso Mazzini, has fresh fruit and vegetables and alimentari.

Getting There & Away

Bus Buses link Ancona with towns throughout the Marches region and also with major cities including Rome and Milan. Ancona is on the Bologna-Lecce train line and thus easily accessible from major towns throughout Italy. It is also directly linked to Rome via Foligno.

Car & Motorcycle Ancona is on the A14, which links Bologna and Bari. Tourists can park free at the port.

Boat All ferry operators have booths at the Stazione Marittima, off Piazza Kennedy. Here you can pick up timetables and price lists and make bookings. Remember that timetables are always subject to change and that prices fluctuate dramatically with the season. Most lines offer discounts on return fares. Prices listed are for one way, deck class in the 1996 high season.

Companies include the following: Minoan Lines (☎ 5 67 89) operates ferries to Igoumenitsa, Corfu, Kefallonia and Patras (Greece) for L123,000. Adriatica (☎ 207 43 34) ferries go to Durres in Albania (L155,000) and Split in Croatia (L70,000). Jadrolinija (☎ 20 28 05) goes to Patras (Greece) for L138,000. Marlines (☎ 20 25 66) goes to Patras (L110,000) and Kusadasi in Turkey (L270,000). Full information is available at the port.

URBINO

This town in the Marches can be difficult to reach, but it is worth the effort to see the birthplace of Raphael and Bramante, which has changed little since the Middle Ages and remains a centre of art, culture and learning.

The APT tourist information office (☎ 24 41) is at Piazza Duca Federico 35.

The telephone code for Urbino is ☎ 0722.

Things to See & Do

Urbino's main sight is the huge **Palazzo Ducale**, designed by Laurana and completed in 1482. The best view is from Corso Garibaldi to the west, from where you can appreciate the size of the building and see its towers and loggias. Enter the palace from Piazza Duca

Federico and visit the **Galleria Nazionale delle Marches**, featuring works by Raphael, Paolo Uccello and Verrocchio. The palace is open daily from 9 am to 2 pm and entry is L8000. Also visit the **Casa di Rafaello**, Vìa Raffaello 57, where the artist Raphael was born, and the **Oratorio di San Giovanni Battista**, with 15th-century frescos by the Salimbeni brothers.

Courses
Urbino's Università degli Studi offers an intensive course in Italian language and culture for foreigners in August. The one-month courses cost around L500,000.

Brochures and enrolment forms can be obtained from Italian cultural institutes in your country or by writing to the Secretary, Università degli Studi di Urbino, Via Saffi 2, 61029 Urbino (☎ 30 52 50). You can arrange accommodation through the university by writing to Ufficio Alloggi dell'ERSU, Via Saffi 46, 61029 Urbino (☎ 29 34). The cost of accommodation is around L350,000 per month.

Places to Stay & Eat
Urbino is a major university town and most cheap beds are taken by students during the school year. The tourist office has a full list of affittacamere. The *Pensione Fosca* (☎ 32 96 22), Via Raffaello 67, has doubles/triples for L55,000/68,000. *Albergo Italia* (☎ 27 01), Corso Garibaldi 32, is next to the Palazzo Ducale and has singles/doubles from L42,000/55,000.

There are numerous bars around Piazza della Repubblica in the town centre and near the Palazzo Ducale which sell good panini. Try *Il Cortigiano* in Piazza del Rinascimento or *Pizzeria Galli*, Via Vittorio Veneto 19, for takeaway pizza by the slice. *Ristorante Da Franco*, just off Piazza del Rinascimento, next to the university, has a self-service section where you can eat a full meal for around L20,000.

Getting There & Away
There is no train service to Urbino, but it is connected by SAPUM and Bucci buses on weekdays to cities including Ancona, Pesaro and Arezzo. There is a bus link to the train station at the town of Fossato di Vico, on the Rome-Ancona line. There are also buses to Rome twice a day. All buses arrive at Borgo Mercatale, down Via Mazzini from Piazza della Repubblica. The tourist office has timetables for all bus services.

Southern Italy

The land of the *mezzogiorno* (midday sun) will surprise even the most world-weary traveller. Rich in history and cultural traditions, the southern regions are poorer than those of the north, and certainly the wheels of bureaucracy grind increasingly more slowly as you travel closer to the tip of the boot. The attractions here are simpler and more stark, the people more vibrant and excitable, and myths and legends are inseparable from official history. Campania and Basilicata cry out to be explored and absolutely nothing can prepare you for Naples. Less well known among foreigners, Calabria has beautiful beaches and the striking scenery of the Sila Massif to offer visitors.

NAPLES
Crazy and confusing, but also seductive and fascinating, Naples (Napoli), capital of the Campania region, has an energy that is palpable. Beautifully positioned on the Bay of Naples and overshadowed by Mt Vesuvius, it is one of the most densely populated cities in Europe. You will leave Naples with a head full of its classic images – laundry strung across narrow streets, three people and a dog on one Vespa, cars speeding along alleys no wider than a driveway, and the same streets teeming with locals shopping at outdoor markets and drinking wine or caffè with friends.

Naples has its own secret society of criminals, the *Camorra*, which traditionally concentrated its activities on the import and sale of contraband cigarettes, but has now diversified into drugs, construction, finance and tourist developments.

Orientation
Both the Stazione Centrale (central train station) and the main bus terminal are in the vast Piazza Garibaldi. Naples is divided into *quartieri* (quarters). The main thoroughfare into the historical centre, Spaccanapoli, is

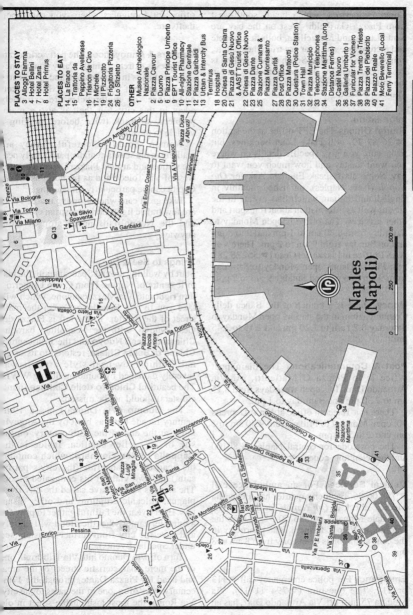

Naples (Napoli)

Corso Umberto I, which heads south-west from Piazza Garibaldi. West on the bay are Santa Lucia and Mergellina, both fashionable and picturesque and a far cry from the chaotic, noisy historical centre. South of Mergellina is Posillipo, where the ultra-wealthy live, and in the hills overlooking the bay is the residential Vomero district.

Information

Tourist Offices The EPT office at the station (☎ 26 87 79) will make hotel bookings, but make sure you give specific details on where you want to stay and how much you want to pay. Some staff speak English. Ask for *Qui Napoli* (Here Naples), published monthly in English and Italian, which lists events in the city, as well as information about transport and other services. The office is open Monday to Saturday from 8.30 am to 1 pm and 2 to 8 pm and on Sunday from 9 am to 2 pm. There's an AAST office in Piazza del Gesù (☎ 552 33 28), near Piazza Dante, open Monday to Saturday from 9 am to 6 pm and Sunday 9 am to 2 pm.

Money There is a branch of the Banca della Comunicazioni in the station, open Monday to Saturday 8.20 am to 1.20 pm and 2.45 to 3.45 pm.

Post & Communications The main post office is in Piazza G Matteotti, off Via Armando Diaz. It is open weekdays from 8.15 am to 7.30 pm and Saturday to 1 pm.

There is a Telecom office at Via A Depretis 40, open Monday to Friday from 9.30 am to 1 pm and 2 to 5.30 pm.

The postcode for central Naples is 80100 and the telephone code is ☎ 081.

Medical Services For an ambulance call ☎ 752 06 96. Each city quarter has a Guardia Medica, check in *Qui Napoli* for details. The Ospedale Monaldi (☎ 545 50 51) is near the Duomo, in Vico L Bianchi. The pharmacy in the central station is open daily from 8 am to 8 pm.

Emergency For police emergency call ☎ 113 or 112. The questura (☎ 794 11 11), Via Medina 75, just off Via Armando Diaz, has an office for foreigners where you can report thefts etc.

Dangers & Annoyances The petty crime rate in Naples is extremely high. Carry your money and documents in a money belt and never carry a bag or purse if you can help it. Pickpockets and thieves on motorcycles are extremely adept in this city. Car theft is also a major problem, so think twice before bringing a vehicle to the city.

Women should be careful if they are walking in the streets at night, particularly near the station and around Piazza Dante. The area west of Via Toledo and as far north as Piazza Capità can be particularly threatening.

Take great care when crossing roads. There are few traffic lights and pedestrian crossings, and the Neapolitans never stop at them anyway.

Things to See & Do

Start by walking around Spaccanapoli, the historic centre of Naples. From Corso Umberto I turn right into Via Mezzocannone, which will take you to Via Benedetto Croce, the main street of the quarter. To the left is Piazza del Gesù Nuovo, with the Neapolitan baroque **Chiesa di Gesù Nuovo** and the 14th-century **Chiesa di Santa Chiara**, restored to its original Gothic-Provençal style after it was severely damaged by bombing during WWII. The beautiful **Chiostro delle Clarisse** (nun's cloisters) should not be missed.

The **Duomo** (Via Duomo) has a 19th-century façade but was built by the Angevin kings at the end of the 13th century, on the site of an earlier basilica. Inside is the **Cappella di San Gennaro**, which contains the head of St Januarius (the city's patron saint) and two vials of his congealed blood. The saint is said to have saved the city from plague, volcanic eruptions and other disasters. Every year the faithful gather to pray for a miracle, namely that the blood will liquefy and save the city from further disaster (see under Special Events).

Turn off Via Duomo into **Via Tribunali**, one of the more characteristic streets of the area, and head for Piazza Dante, through the 17th-century **Port'Alba**, one of the gates to the city. Via Roma, the most fashionable street in old

Naples, heads to the left (becoming Via Toledo) and ends at Piazza Trento e Trieste and he **Piazza del Plebiscito**.

In the piazza is the **Palazzo Reale**, the former official residence of the Bourbon and Savoy kings, now a museum. It is open Monday to Saturday from 9 am to 2 pm and to pm Sunday and public holidays. Admission s L6000. Just off the piazza is the **Teatro San Carlo**, one of the most famous opera houses in he world thanks to its perfect acoustics and beautiful interior.

The 13th-century **Castel Nuovo** overlooks Naples' ferry port. The early Renaissance **triumphal arch** commemorates the entry of Alfonso I of Aragon into Naples in 1443. It is possible to enter the courtyard of the castle, but he building itself is not open to the public. South-west along the waterfront, at Porto Santa Lucia, is the **Castel dell'Ovo**, originally Norman castle, which is surrounded by a tiny fishing village, the **Borgo Marinaro**.

The **Museo Archeologico Nazionale** is in Piazza Museo, north of Piazza Dante. It contains one of the most important collections of Graeco-Roman artefacts in the world, mainly he rich collection of the Farnese family, and he art treasures that were discovered at Pompeii and Herculaneum. It is open Monday o Saturday from 9 am to 2 pm and Sunday to pm. Admission is L12,000.

From May to October, Naples' main museums are open until 7 pm.

To escape the noise and general chaos of historical Naples, catch the Funicolare Centrale in Via Toledo (funicular) to the suburb of Vomero and visit the **Certosa di San Martino**, a 14th-century Carthusian monastery, rebuilt n the 17th century in Neapolitan baroque style. t houses the **Museo Nazionale di San Martino**. The monastery's church is well worth a visit, as are its terraced gardens, which afford spectacular views of Naples and the bay. The monastery is open Tuesday to Sunday from 9 am to 2 pm. Entry is L8000.

Special Events

Religious festivals are lively occasions in Naples, especially the celebration of St Januarius, the patron saint of the city, held three times a year: on the first Sunday in May, 19 September and 16 December in the Duomo.

Places to Stay

Hostel The HI *Ostello Mergellina Napoli* (☎ 761 23 46), Salita della Grotta 23 in Mergellina, is modern, safe and the best budget option in the city. Bed and breakfast is L20,000, or L22,000 per person for a family room. Dinner is L14,000 and there is a bar. It is open all year and imposes a maximum three-night stay in summer. Take bus No 152 from the station, or the Metropolitana to Mergellina, and signs will direct you to the hostel from the waterfront.

Hotels Most of the cheap hotels are near the station and Piazza Garibaldi in a rather unsavoury area, and some of the cheaper hotels double as brothels. It is best to ask the tourist office at the station to recommend or book a room.

Station Area The following hotels are safe and offer a reasonable standard of accommodation. The *Hotel Zara* (☎ 28 71 25), Via Firenze 81, is clean with singles/doubles for L28,000/50,000. Doubles with private bath are L60,000. Via Firenze is off Corso Novara, to the right as you leave the train station. *Albergo Ginevra* (☎ 28 32 10), Via Genova 116, the second street to the right off Corso Novara, is another reliable and well-kept place with newly renovated singles/doubles for L36,000/60,000 and triples for L80,000. The *Casanova Hotel* (☎ 26 82 87), Corso Garibaldi 333, is quiet and safe. Singles/doubles are L28,000/51,000. Triples with shower are L78,000. *Hotel Primus* (☎ 554 73 54), Via Torino 26, has good standard, renovated rooms with bathroom for L50,000/90,000.

Piazza Dante Area The *Alloggi Fiamma* (☎ 45 91 87), Via Francesco del Giudice has basic singles/doubles with bathroom for L40,000/ 70,000. Another option is *Hotel Bellini* (☎ 45 69 96), Via San Paolo 44, with singles/doubles for L35,000/65,000.

Out of the Centre Just off Piazza Amedeo in Mergellina, at Via Martucci 72, is *Pensione Ruggiero* (☎ 761 24 60). It has clean, bright singles/doubles with bathroom for L90,000/120,000. In Santa Lucia *Pensione Astoria* (☎ 764 99 03), Via Santa Lucia 90, is a great

ITALY

bargain, with well-kept singles/doubles for L30,000/50,000. In the same building is *Albergo Teresita* (☎ 764 0105) with singles/doubles for L40,000/55,000. At Vomero, just near the funicular station, is *Pensione Margherita* (☎ 556 70 44), Via D Cimarosa 29. This hotel is more up-market and charges L46,000/82,000 for singles/doubles. Ask for a room with a bay view. Have a L50 coin on hand for the lift.

Places to Eat
Naples is the home of pasta and pizza. In fact, once you have eaten a good Neapolitan pizza, topped with fresh tomatoes, oregano, basil and garlic, no other pizza will taste the same. Try a calzone, a filled version of a pizza, or mozzarella in carozza, which is mozzarella deep-fried in bread, sold at tiny street stalls. Also sold at street stalls is the misto di frittura (deep-fried vegetables). Don't leave town without trying the sfogliatelle (light, flaky pastry filled with ricotta).

City Centre According to the locals the best pizza in Naples is served at *Trianon da Ciro*, Via Pietro Colletta 46, near Via Tribunali. There's a wide selection, costing from L5500 to L12,000. Across the street is *Michele*, another good pizzeria. Nearer the station is *Trattoria Avellinese*, Via Silvio Spaventa 31-35, just off Piazza Garibaldi, which specialises in cheap seafood. Just down the street at No 14 is *La Brace*, a no-nonsense cheap place to eat. *Il Pizzicotto*, Via Mezzocannone 129, has good pizzas and full meals cost around L15,000.

Mergellina & Vomero Neapolitans head for the area around Piazza Sannazzaro, south-west of the centre, for a good meal. It is also handy to the youth hostel. *Pizzeria da Pasqualino*, Piazza Sannazzaro 79, has outdoor tables and serves good pizzas and seafood. A meal will cost around L20,000 with wine. *Mario Daniele*, Via A Scarlatti 104, is a bar with a restaurant upstairs. *Cibo Cibo*, Via Cimarosa 150, is another good budget spot.

Food Stalls On the corner of Vico Basilico Puoti and Via Pignasecca is *Lo Sfizieto*. *Friggitoria Pizzeria* is at Piazza Montesanto. Both offer lots of cheap goodies.

Entertainment
The monthly *Qui Napoli* and the local newspapers are the only real guides to what's on. In July there is a series of free concerts called *Luglio Musicale a Capodimonte* outside the Capodimonte Palace. The *Teatro San Carlo* has year-round performances of opera, ballet and concerts. Tickets start at L20,000. Call ☎ 797 21 11 for bookings and information.

Things to Buy
The area around Naples is famous for its ceramic products and many small shops in the city and surrounding areas sell hand-painted ceramics at reasonable prices. Young people shop along Via Roma and Via Toledo. More exclusive shops are found in Santa Lucia, along Via Chiaia to Piazza dei Martiri and down towards the waterfront. Naples is renowned for the work of its goldsmiths and for its *presepi* (nativity scenes). Most artisans are in Spaccanapoli. The narrow streets of Naples are full of markets, notably in the area off Via Mancinio (off Piazza Garibaldi), near Piazza Carità (which separates Via Roma and Via Toledo) and around Piazza Montesanto.

Getting There & Away
Air The Capodichino airport (☎ 789 62 68), Viale Umberto Maddalena, is about five km north-east of the city centre. There are connections to most Italian and several European cities.

Bus Buses leave from Piazza Garibaldi, just outside the train station, for destinations including Salerno, Benevento, Caserta (every 20 minutes) and Bari, Lecce and Brindisi in Apulia.

Train Naples is a major rail transport centre for the south, and regular trains for most major Italian cities arrive and depart from the Stazione Centrale in Piazza Garibaldi. There are up to 30 trains a day for Rome.

Car & Motorcycle Driving in Naples is not recommended. The traffic is chaotic and car and motorcycle theft is rife. The city is easily accessible from Rome on the A1. The Naples-Pompeii-Salerno road connects with the coastal road to Sorrento and the Amalfi Coast

Boat Traghetti and *aliscafi* (hydrofoils) leave for Capri, Sorrento, Ischia and Procida from the Molo Beverello, in front of the Castel Nuovo. Some hydrofoils leave for the bay islands from Mergellina and ferries for Ischia and Procida also leave from Pozzuoli. All operators have offices at the various ports from which they leave. Tickets for the hydrofoils cost around double those for ferries, but the trip takes half the time.

Ferries to Palermo and Cagliari (Tirrenia ☎ 720 11 11) and to the Aeolian Islands (Siremar ☎ 761 36 88) leave from the Stazione Marittima on Molo Angioino, next to Molo Beverello (see the Getting There & Away sections under Sicily and Sardinia). SNAV (☎ 761 23 48) runs regular hydrofoils to the islands.

Getting Around

You can make your way around Naples by bus, tram, Metropolitana (underground) and funicular. City buses leave from Piazza Garibaldi in front of the central station bound for the centre of Naples, as well as Mergellina. Tickets, called *GiraNapoli*, cost L1200 for 90 minutes and are valid for buses, trams, the Metropolitana and funicular services. Day tickets cost L4000. Useful buses include: 14 to the airport; CD and CS to Piazza Dante; C4 Mergellina to the city centre; 127R from Piazza Garibaldi to Piazza Cavour and the archaeological museum. Tram No 1 leaves from east of Stazione Centrale for the city centre. To get to Molo Beverello and the Stazione Marittima, take Bus No R2, 152 or M1 from Stazione Centrale.

The Metropolitana station is downstairs at central station. Trains head west to Mergellina, topping at Piazza Amedeo and the funicular to Vomero, and Piazza Cavour, then head on to the Campi Flegrei and Pozzuoli. Another line, now under construction, will eventually connect Piazza Garibaldi and Piazza Medaglie d'Oro, with stops including the Duomo and the Museo Archeologico Nazionale.

The main funicular connecting the city centre with Vomero is the Funicolare Centrale, in Piazza Duca d'Aosta, next to Galleria Umberto I, on Via Toledo.

The Ferrovia Circumvesuviana operates trains for Pompeii, Herculaneum and Sorrento. The station is about 400 metres south-west of Stazione Centrale, in Corso Garibaldi (take the underpass from Stazione Centrale). The Ferrovia Cumana and the Circumflegrei, based at Stazione Cumana in Piazza Montesanto, operate services to Pozzuoli and Cumae every 20 minutes.

AROUND NAPLES

From Naples it is only a short distance to the **Campi Flegrei** (Phlegraean Fields) of volcanic lakes and mudbaths, which inspired both Homer and Virgil in their writings. Today part of suburban Naples, the area is dirty and over-developed, but still worth a day trip. The Greek colony of **Cumae** is certainly worth visiting, particularly to see the Cave of the Cumaean Sybil, home of one of the ancient world's greatest oracles. Also in the area is **Lake Avernus**, the mythical entrance to the underworld.

Reached by CPTC bus from Naples' Piazza Garibaldi or by train from the Stazione Centrale is the **Palazzo Reale** at Caserta, usually called the Reggia di Caserta. Built by the Bourbon king Charles III, this massive 1200-room palace is set in gardens modelled on Versailles.

Pompeii & Herculaneum

Buried under a layer of lapilli (burning fragments of pumice stone) during the devastating eruption of Mt Vesuvius in 79 AD, **Pompeii** provides a fascinating insight into how the ancient Romans lived. It was a resort town for wealthy Romans, and among the vast ruins are impressive temples, a forum, one of the largest known Roman amphitheatres, and streets lined with shops and luxurious houses. Many of the site's mosaics and frescos have been moved to Naples Museo Archeologico Nazionale. The exception is the Villa dei Misteri, where the frescos remain *in situ*.

Most of the houses and shops are locked, but there are numerous official attendants who are supposed to open them on request. Single women should avoid attendants who are a bit too willing to take you to the more secluded sights.

There are tourist offices (AAST) at Via Sacra 1 (☎ 850 72 55) in the new town, and just outside the excavations at Piazza Porta Marina Inferiore 12 (☎ 861 09 13). *How to Visit Pompeii* (talk them down to L8000), is a comprehensive guide to the ancient city. The ruins are open from 9 am to one hour before sunset and entry is L12,000.

Catch the Circumvesuviana train from Naples and get off at the Pompeii-Villa dei Misteri stop; the Porta Marina entrance is close by.

Herculaneum (Ercolano) is closer to Naples and is also a good point from which to visit Mt Vesuvius. Legend says the city was founded by Hercules. First Greek, then Roman, it was also destroyed by the 79 AD eruption, buried under mud and lava. Most inhabitants of Herculaneum had enough warning and managed to escape. The ruins here are smaller and the buildings, particularly the private houses, are remarkably well preserved. Here you can see better examples of the frescos, mosaics and furniture that used to decorate Roman houses.

Herculaneum is also accessible on the Circumvesuviana train from Naples. The ruins are open daily from 9 am to one hour before sunset. Entry is L12,000.

Catch the SITA bus from the piazza in front of the Ercolano train station to Mt Vesuvius (L4000 return). The first bus leaves the station at 8.15 am and the last returns at 5.45 pm. You'll then need to walk about 1.5 km to the summit, where you must pay L3000 to be accompanied by a guide to the crater.

SORRENTO

This major resort town is in a particularly beautiful area, but is heavily overcrowded in summer with package tourists and traffic. However, it is handy to the Amalfi Coast and Capri.

Orientation & Information

The centre of town is Piazza Tasso, a short walk from the train station along Corso Italia. The AAST tourist office (☎ 807 40 33), Via Luigi de Maio 35, is inside the Circolo dei Forestieri complex. The office is open from Monday to Saturday from 8.30 am to 2 pm and 4 to 7 pm. The postcode is 80067.

The post office is at Corso Italia 210 and the Telecom telephone office is at Piazza Tasso 37.

For medical assistance contact the Ospedale Civile (☎ 533 11 11). For the police call ☎ 113.

Sorrento's telephone code is ☎ 081.

Places to Stay

There are several camping grounds, includin *Nube d'Argento* (☎ 878 13 44), Via Capo 2 which costs L13,000 per person and up t L19,000 for a tent site.

The HI Ostello Surriento was closed at th time of writing.

Albergo City (☎ 877 22 10), Corso Italia 221, has singles/doubles with bathroom fo 60,000/85,000. *Pensione Linda* (☎ 878 2 16), Via degli Aranci 125, has singles/double for L40,000/70,000.

Places to Eat

You can get a cheap meal at *Self Servic Angelina Lauro*, Piazza Angelino Laur *Giardinello*, Via dell'Accademia 7, has pizza for around L7000 and pasta from L5000. In Vi San Cesareo, off Piazza Tasso, there are severa alimentari where you can buy food for picnics

Getting There & Away

Sorrento is easily accessible from Naples o the Circumvesuviana train line. SITA buse leave from outside the train station for th Amalfi Coast. Hydrofoils and ferries leav from the port, along Via de Maio and down th steps from the tourist office, for Capri an Ischia.

In summer, traffic is heavy along the coasta roads to Sorrento.

CAPRI

This beautiful island, an hour by ferry from Naples, retains the mythical appeal whicl attracted Roman emperors, including Augus tus and Tiberius, who built 12 villas here. Th town of Capri is packed with tourists i summer, but is more peaceful in the lov season. A short bus ride will take you t Anacapri, the town uphill from Capri – a goo alternative if rooms are full in Capri. The islan is famous for its grottoes, but is also a goo place for walking. There are tourist offices a Marina Grande (☎ 081-837 06 34), where al the ferries arrive, in Piazza Umberto I (☎ 83 06 86), in the centre of town, and at Piazz Vittoria 4 in Anacapri (☎ 837 15 24).

Things to See & Do

There are expensive boat tours of the grottoes including the famous Grotta Azzurra (Blu Grotto). Boats leave from the Marina Grand

and a round trip will cost about L23,000 (which includes the cost of a motorboat to the grotto, rowing boat into the grotto and entrance fee). It is cheaper to catch a bus from Anacapri although the rowboat and entrance fee still total around L15,000). It is possible to swim into the grotto before 9 am and after 5 pm, but do so only in company and when the sea is very calm. You can walk to most of the interesting points on the island (pick up a walking guide from the tourist office). Sights include the **Giardini d'Augusto**, in the town of Capri, and **Villa Jovis**, the ruins of one of Tiberius' villas, along the Via Longano and Via Tiberio. The latter is a one-hour walk uphill from Capri. Also visit the **Villa San Michele** at Anacapri.

Places to Stay & Eat
The *Stella Maris* (☎ 837 04 52), Via Roma 27, just off Piazza Umberto I, is right in the noisy heart of town. Singles/doubles are L60,000/90,000 and triples/quads are an additional 30%. Prices go down significantly in the off season. Bookings must be made well in advance for summer. *Villa Louisa* (☎ 837 01 28), Via D Birago 1, has rooms with great views for L80,000 a double.

In Anacapri, the *Loreley* (☎ 837 14 40), Via G Orlandi 16, near the town centre, is one of the better deals. Singles/doubles with bathroom are L50,000/90,000. The *Caesar Augustus* (☎ 837 14 21), Via G Orlandi 4, is a beautiful hotel which becomes a knockout bargain in the off season and when they have empty rooms. Prices can go as low as L40,000 per person, so it is worth checking out. Another option on the island is affittacamere. The tourist office has a full list.

In Capri, try *La Cisterna*, Via M Serafina 5, for a pizza. In Anacapri try the *Trattoria il Solitario*, in a garden setting at Via G Orlandi 54. Another good place is *Il Saraceno*, Via Trieste e Trento 18, where a full meal could cost up to L30,000. Try their lemon liqueur.

Getting There & Away
See the Getting There & Away section under Naples.

Getting Around
From Marina Grande, the funicular directly in front of the port takes you to the town of Capri (L1500), which is at the top of a steep hill some three km from the port up a winding road. Small local buses connect the port with Capri, Anacapri and other points around the island (L1500 for one trip).

AMALFI COAST
The Amalfi coast swarms with rich tourists in summer and prices are correspondingly high. However, it remains a place of rare and spectacular beauty and if you can manage to get there in spring or autumn, you will be surprised by the reasonably priced accommodation and peaceful atmosphere.

There are tourist information offices in the individual towns, including at Positano (☎ 87 50 67), Via Saracino 2, and Amalfi (☎ 87 11 07), on the waterfront at Marina Grande.

The telephone code for the area is ☎ 089.

Positano
This is the most beautiful town on the coast, but for exactly this reason it has also become the most fashionable. It is, however, still possible to stay here cheaply.

Villa Nettuno (☎ 87 54 01), Via Pasitea 208, has doubles for L90,000 in the high season, all with private bath, though prices vary according to the length of stay. Half of the rooms are new and have small balconies overlooking the sea. The older rooms are cheaper and open onto a large terrace. Book well in advance for summer.

Villa Maria Luisa (☎ 87 50 23), at Via Fornillo 40, has double rooms with terraces for L35,000 per person in the low season and L50,000 per person, breakfast included, in July. Half-pension (L85,000 per person) is obligatory during August. The *Villa delle Palme* (☎ 87 51 62), around the corner in Via Pasitea, is run by the same management and charges slightly higher prices. Next door is the pizzeria *Il Saraceno d'Oro*, Via Pasitea 254.

Around Positano
The hills behind Positano offer some great walks if you tire of lazing on the beach. The tourist office at Positano has a brochure listing four routes, ranging in length from two to four hours. Visit **Nocelle**, a tiny, isolated village above Positano, accessible by walking track from the end of the road from Positano. Have lunch at *Trattoria Santa Croce* (☎ 87 53 19), which has a terrace with panoramic views. It is

open for both lunch and dinner in summer, but at other times of the year it is best to telephone and check in advance. From Nocelle, a walking track leads directly up into the hills overlooking the Amalfi Coast. Nocelle is accessible by local bus from Positano, via Montepertuso; buses run roughly every half-hour in summer from 7.50 am to midnight.

On the way from Positano to Amalfi is the town of **Praiano**, which is not as scenic but has more budget options, including the only camping ground on the Amalfi Coast. *La Tranquillità* (☎ 87 40 84), has a pensione, bungalows and a small camping ground. It costs L14,000 per head to camp there if you have your own tent. For a double room or bungalow it is L80,000 (with breakfast) and in summer there is compulsory half-pension at L60,000 a head including room, private bathroom, breakfast and dinner. The SITA bus stops outside the pensione. The entire establishment closes down in winter, reopening at Easter. The *Pensione Aquila* (☎ 87 40 65) at Via degli Ulivi 15, charges L60,000 a double with breakfast, L70,000 with dinner and L90,000 in August. Signs from the coastal road make it easy to find.

Amalfi

One of the four powerful maritime republics of medieval Italy, Amalfi today is a major tourist resort. Despite this, it manages to retain a tranquil atmosphere. It has an impressive **Duomo**, and nearby is the **Grotta dello Smeraldo**, which rivals Capri's Blue Grotto.

In the hills behind Amalfi is **Ravello**, accessible by bus and worth a visit if only to see the magnificent 11th-century **Villa Rufolo**, once the home of popes and, later, of the German composer Wagner. The **Villa Cimbrone**, built this century, is set in beautiful gardens, which end at a terrace offering a spectacular view of the Gulf of Salerno. There are numerous walking paths in the hills between Amalfi and Ravello. Pick up the book *Walks from Amalfi – The Guide to a Web of Ancient Italian Pathways* (L10,000) in Amalfi.

Places to Stay & Eat The HI *Ostello Beato Solitudo* (☎ 081-802 50 48) is at Piazza G Avitabile, in Agerola, just west of Amalfi. It charges L13,000 for bed only. For a room in

Amalfi, try the *Albergo Proto* (☎ 87 10 03) Salita dei Curiali 4, which has singles/doubles from L50,000/80,000, breakfast included. The *Hotel Lidomare* (☎ 87 13 32) is at Via Piccolomini 9 (follow the signs from Piazza del Duomo and go left up a flight of stairs). A double costs more than L100,000 in high season, but rates are affordable at other times of the year.

Cheaper accommodation can be found at Atrani, just around the corner from Amalfi towards Salerno. *A Scalinetta* (☎ 87 14 92) just off Piazza Umberto, has beds in dorms for two, four and six people from L25,000 per person, breakfast included.

In Amalfi, *Trattoria Pizzeria al Teatro*, Via Mara Francesca Panza 19 (follow the signs to the left from Via Pietro Capuana, the main shopping street of Piazza del Duomo), offers good food in very pleasant surroundings. A pizza costs between L5000 and L10,000, pasta costs up to L7000 and fish up to L15,000 *Trattoria da Maria*, Via Genova 14, is good value with main courses around L10,000. *A Scalinetta* also has a trattoria.

Getting There & Away

Bus The coast is accessible by regular SITA buses, which run between Salerno (a 40-minute train trip from Naples) and Sorrento (accessible from Naples on the Circumvesuviana train line). Buses stop in Amalfi at Piazza Flavio Gioia, from where you can catch a bus to Ravello.

Car & Motorcycle The coastal road is narrow and in summer it is clogged with traffic, so be prepared for long delays. At other times of the year you should have no problems. Hire a motorcycle in Sorrento or Salerno.

Boat Hydrofoils and ferries also service the coast, leaving from Salerno and stopping at Amalfi and Positano. From Positano you can catch a boat to Capri.

PAESTUM

The evocative image of three Greek temples standing in fields of poppies is not easily forgotten and makes the trek to this archaeological site well worth the effort. The three temples, just south of Salerno, are among the world's best preserved monuments of the ancient Greek world. There is a tourist office (☎ 0828-81 10 16) and a museum at the site. The ruins are open Tuesday to Sunday from 9 am to one hour before sunset and entry is L10,000.

Paestum is accessible from Salerno by ATACS bus or by train.

MATERA

This ancient city in the region of Basilicata evokes powerful images of a peasant culture which existed until just over 30 years ago. Its famous *sassi* – the stone houses built in the two ravines which slice through the city – were home to more than half of Matera's population (about 20,000 people) until the 1950s, when the local government built a new residential area just out of Matera and relocated the entire population.

Information

The tourist office (☎ 33 19 83), Via Viti de Marco 9, off Via Roma (which runs off Piazza V Veneto) can organise a professional tour guide (about L25,000 for an hour).

Matera's telephone code is ☎ 0835.

Things to See

The two sassi wards, known as **Barisano** and **Caveoso**, had no electricity, running water or sewerage system until well into this century. The oldest sassi are at the top of the ravines, and the dwellings which appear to be the oldest were established in this century. As space ran out in the 1920s, the population started moving into hand-hewn or natural caves, an extraordinary example of civilisation in reverse.

The sassi zones are accessible from Piazza Vittorio Veneto and Piazza del Duomo, in the centre of Matera. Be sure to see the rock churches, **Santa Maria d'Idris** and **Santa Lucia alla Malve**, both with amazingly well-preserved Byzantine frescos. The 13th-century Apulian-Romanesque **cathedral**, overlooking Sasso Barisano, is also worth a visit. In Sasso Caveoso you will be approached by young children wanting to act as tour guides. They might be small, but they know their sassi, so pay them a few thousand lire and take up the offer, even if you can't speak Italian. Some sassi are now being restored and young people have begun to move back into the area.

Recent excavations in Piazza Vittorio Veneto have revealed the ruins of parts of Byzantine Matera, including a castle and a rock church decorated with frescos. Access is restricted, so enquire at the tourist office.

Places to Stay & Eat

There are not a lot of options for budget accommodation here and it is best to book in advance. Try the *Albergo Roma* (☎ 33 39 12), Via Roma 62. Singles/doubles are L38,000/55,000. The local fare is simple and the focus is on vegetables. *Da Aulo*, Via Anza di Lucana, is economical and serves typical dishes of Basilicata. There is a fruit and vegetable market near Piazza V Veneto, between Via Lucana and Via A Persio.

Getting There & Away

SITA buses connect Matera with Potenza, Taranto and Metaponto. The town is on the private Ferrovie Apulo-Lucane train line, which connects with Bari, Altamura and Potenza. There is also a twice-daily Marozzi bus from Rome to Matera (see the Rome Getting There & Away section). Buses arrive in Piazza Matteotti, a short walk down Via Roma to the town centre.

APULIA

For the dedicated traveller, the Apulia (Puglia) region offers many rich experiences. There are the many beautiful Romanesque churches, notably the cathedrals at Trani, Bari, Bitonto and Ruvo di Puglia. Or visit the beaches and forest of the Gargano Peninsula, stopping off at the famous sanctuary of St Michael the Archangel at Monte Sant'Angelo, and making a side trip to the unspoiled Tremiti Islands. Also visit Alberobello to see its *trulli*, which are whitewashed, conical-shaped buildings, both ancient and modern.

Lecce

Baroque can be grotesque, but never in Lecce. The style here is so refined and particular to the city that the Italians call it *barocco leccese* (Lecce baroque). Lecce's numerous bars and restaurants are a pleasant surprise in such a small city.

There is an EPT office (☎ 30 44 43) in Piazza Sant'Oronzo, the town's main piazza. Take bus No 4 from the station to the town centre.

Lecce's telephone code is ☎ 0832.

Things to See & Do The most famous example of Lecce baroque is the **Basilica di Santa Croce**. Artists worked for 150 years to decorate the building, creating an extraordinarily ornate façade. In the **Piazza del Duomo** are the 12th-century **cathedral** (which was completely restored in the baroque style by the architect Giuseppe Zimbalo of Lecce), and its 70-metre-high **bell tower**; the **Palazzo del Vescovo** (Bishop's Palace); and the **Seminario**, with its elegant façade and baroque well in the courtyard. In Piazza Sant'Oronzo are the remains of a **Roman amphitheatre**.

Places to Stay & Eat Cheap accommodation is not abundant in Lecce, but camping facilities abound in the province of Salento. Near Lecce is *Torre Rinalda* (☎ 65 21 61), near the sea at Torre Rinalda. You can get there by STP bus from the terminal in Via Adua. In town try *Hotel Cappello* (☎ 30 88 81) at Via Montegrappa 4, near the station. Singles/doubles are L40,000/60,000 with bathroom.

Eating in this city is both inexpensive and a pleasure. A good snack bar is *Guido e Figlio*, Via Trinchese 10. *Pizzeria Dolomiti*, Viale A Costa 5, has eat-in and takeaway pizzas.

Getting There & Away STP buses connect Lecce with towns throughout the Salentine Peninsula, leaving from Via Adua. Lecce is directly linked by train to Brindisi, Bari, Rome, Naples and Bologna. The Ferrovie del Sud Est runs trains to surrounding areas, including Otranto, Gallipoli and Taranto and major points in Apulia.

Otranto

Without a car it is difficult to tour the picturesque Adriatic coast of Salento, which extends to the tip of Italy's heel, at Capo Santa Maria di Leuca. However, Otranto is easy to reach by bus and on the Ferrovie del Sud Est train line.

The tourist office (☎ 80 14 36) is at Via Pantaleone Presbitero.

Otranto's telephone code is ☎ 0836.

Things to See This port town of whitewashed buildings is overrun by tourists in summer, but it is worth a visit if only to see the incredible **mosaic** that covers the floor of the Romanesque **cathedral**. The recently restored 12th-century mosaic, depicting the tree of life is a masterpiece unrivalled in southern Italy and is stunning in its simplicity.

The tiny Byzantine **Chiesa di San Pietro** contains some well-preserved Byzantine paintings.

Places to Stay Unfortunately, the town is not geared for budget tourism and has no one-star hotels. *Il Gabbiano* (☎ 80 12 51), Via Porto Craulo 5, has singles/doubles with bath for L35,000/80,000.

Getting There & Away A Marozzi bus runs daily from Rome to Brindisi, Lecce and Otranto (see Rome's Getting There & Away section). Ferries leave from here for Corfu and Igoumenitsa (Greece). For information and reservations for both ferries and the Marozzi bus, go to Ellade Viaggi (☎ 80 15 78) at the port.

Brindisi

Most travellers associate Brindisi with waiting. As the major embarkation point for ferries from Italy to Greece, the city swarms with travellers in transit. There is not much to do here, other than wait, so most backpackers gather at the train station or at the port in the Stazione Marittima. The two are connected by Corso Umberto I, which becomes Corso Garibaldi, and they are a 10-minute walk from each other; otherwise, you can take bus No 6, 9 or 12.

The EPT tourist information office (☎ 56 2 26) is at Lungomare Regina Margherita 12. Another information office is inside the Stazione Marittima.

Brindisi's telephone code is ☎ 0831.

Dangers & Annoyances Thieves are very active in the area between the station and the port. Carry valuables in a money belt, don't walk alone through the town at night and never leave luggage or valuables unattended in your car. It is inadvisable to sleep in any of the piazzas between the station and port (a homeless man was bashed to death by a group of youths in the piazza in front of the station a few years ago). If you arrive in Brindisi with a car during summer, allow extra time for the eternal traffic jam around the port.

Things to See & Do From ancient Roman times Brindisi has been Italy's gateway to the east. It was from here that the Crusaders set off for the Holy Land. Tradition has it that Virgil died in a Roman house near the columns marking the end of the **Appian Way** on his return from Greece. In Piazza del Duomo is the 14th-century **Palazzo Balsamo**, with a beautiful *loggetta* (a building open on one or more sides). The town's main monument is the **Chiesa di Santa Maria del Casale**, about four km from the centre. Built by Prince Philip of Taranto around 1300, it is a Romanesque church with Gothic and Byzantine touches.

Places to Stay & Eat The non-HI *Ostello per la Gioventù* (☎ 41 31 23) is about two km out of town at Via N Brandi 4, in Casale. B&B costs L17,000. Take bus No 3 or 4 from Via Cristoforo Colombo near the train station. *Hotel Venezia* (☎ 52 75 11), Via Pisanelli 4, has singles/doubles for L25,000/ 40,000. Turn left off Corso Umberto I onto Via S Lorenzo da Brindisi to get there.

There are numerous takeaway outlets along the main route between the train and boat stations, but if you want a meal, head for the side streets. The *Osteria Spaghetti House*, Via Mazzini 57, near the station, has good-value meals for around L20,000. There is a fruit and vegetable market in Via Battisti, off Corso Umberto I, open from 7 am to 1 pm daily except Sunday.

Getting There & Away Marozzi runs several buses a day to/from Rome (Stazione Tiburtina), leaving from Viale Regina Margherita in Brindisi (see the Rome Getting There & Away for information section). Appia Travel (☎ 52 16 84), Viale Regina Margherita 8-9, sells tickets (L52,000 or L58,000). Brindisi is directly connected by train to the major cities of northern Italy, as well as Rome, Ancona and Naples.

Boat Ferries leave Brindisi for Greek destinations including Corfu, Igoumenitsa, Patras and Cefalonia. The major companies operating ferries from Brindisi are: Adriatica (☎ 52 38 25), Corso Garibaldi 85-87 (open from 9 am to 1 pm, 4 to 7 pm) and on the 1st floor of the Stazione Marittima, where you must go to

check in; Hellenic Mediterranean Lines (☎ 52 85 31), Corso Garibaldi 8; and Med Link Lines (☎ 52 76 67), Corso Garibaldi 49.

Adriatica and Hellenic are the most expensive, but also the most reliable. They are the only lines which can officially accept Eurail and Inter-Rail passes, which means you pay only L5000 for deck class, L34,000 for a poltrona and L66,000 for a second-class cabin bed. If you want to use your Eurail or Inter-Rail pass, it is important to reserve some weeks in advance in summer. Even with a booking in summer, you must still go to the Adriatic or Hellenic embarkation office in the Stazione Marittima to have your ticket checked.

Discounts are available for travellers under 26 years of age and holders of some Italian rail passes. Note that fares increase by 40% in July and August. Ferry services are also increased during this period. Average prices in the 1996 high season for deck class were: Adriatica and Hellenic to Corfu, Igoumenitsa, Cefalonia or Patras – L90,000 (L76,000 for the return); Med Link to the same destinations – L75,000.

Prices go up by an average L15,000 for a poltrona, and for the cheapest cabin accommodation prices jump by L30,000 to L40,000. Bicycles can be taken aboard free, but the average fare for a motorcycle is L50,000 in the high season. Fares for cars are around L100,000 in the high season.

The port tax is L10,000, payable when you buy your ticket. It is essential to check in at least two hours prior to departure.

CALABRIA
Much of Calabria is still to be discovered by travellers, even though the region's beaches have become popular destinations. Tourist development has begun along the region's Ionian and Tyrrhenian coastlines, but in most areas it is minimal compared with Italy's more touristy regions. This is an area with many small villages in picturesque settings where the pace of life is slow and things have remained largely unchanged over the years. Market days are still an important local feature and this is when you will find most activity in the villages and towns.

Although the fierce feuding of the 'Ndrangheta, Calabria's version of the Sicilian Mafia, continues to cause havoc and atrocious deaths among Calabrians, tourists travelling in the region should not be concerned.

The Italian government's Southern Italy Development Fund, established in 1950 to invest money in the southern regions and in Sicily and Sardinia (for irrigation, road construction and industrial development), has basically succeeded in dragging the region into the 20th century, but many Calabrians, particularly those in more remote areas, still live in extreme poverty. Few locals speak English and you are more likely to be well received if you at least make an attempt to speak Italian.

Catanzaro & Cosenza

The old town of **Catanzaro**, the region's capital, is strikingly set, high on a hill top overlooking the Ionian Sea. Calabria's **riviera**, along the Ionian coast, is overdeveloped and pockmarked with heavy industry, but remains popular among Germans and Italians. **Tropea**, to the north of the region on the Tyrrhenian Sea, was an isolated paradise only a decade ago. Today it too has been affected by tourist development, but is certainly worth a visit, along with nearby **Pizzo** and **Scalea**, further north. For accommodation at Tropea try the *Vulcano* (☎ 0963-6 15 98), Via Campo Superiore. There are camping grounds at Scalea, including the *Camping La Pantera Rossa* (☎ 0985-2 15 46), Corso Mediterraneo.

If adventure appeals, Calabria's **Sila Massif** is the place to visit. This beautiful wilderness area remains on the verge of massive development and incorporates a major national park. The Sila is divided into three areas: the **La Greca**, **La Grande** and **La Piccola**. The best point from which to start exploring the Sila Massif is **Cosenza**, accessible by train from Paola, which is on the Rome-Reggio di Calabria railway line on the coast. From Cosenza catch a bus or train to **Camigliatello Silano**. (Cosenza has two train stations – the national FS Stazione Nuova, and the Ferrovie della Calabria serving the Sila Massif area. You can get from one to the other on local bus No 5.)

The Cosenza tourist office (☎ 0984-2 78 21) is at Corso Mazzini 92. For a room try the *Albergo Bruno* (☎ 0984-7 38 89), Corso Mazzini 27. Rooms are L30,000/ 50,000.

At Camigliatello Silano you can obtain trekking and tourist information from the Pro Loco (☎ 0984-57 80 91), Via Roma 5. Opening

hours are irregular. For accommodation try th *Miramonti* (☎ 0984-57 90 67), Via Forgitelle

Reggio di Calabria

The port city of Reggio di Calabria on the Strai of Messina is the capital of the province o Reggio di Calabria and was, until 1971, th capital of the region of Calabria. Founded i approximately 720 BC by Greek colonists, thi city was destroyed by an earthquake in 1908 which also razed Messina, and was totall rebuilt. There is a tourist information booth a the station (☎ 2 71 20) and the main office (☎ 89 20 12) is at Corso Garibaldi 329, wher you can pick up a map and a list of hotels.

Reggio's telephone code is ☎ 0965.

Things to See The **lungomare** (promenad along the port) overlooks Sicily and, in certai atmospheric conditions, such as at dawn, it i possible to see the fabled **mirage of Morgana** the reflection of Messina in the sea. Reggio' only really impressive sight is the **Museo Nazionale** (National Museum), which house a remarkable collection documenting Greel civilisation in Calabria. Of particular interes are the **Bronzi di Riace** (Bronze Warriors o Riace), two Greek statues found off the coas of Riace in the Ionian Sea in 1972.

Places to Stay & Eat Try *Albergo Noel* (☎ 89 09 65), Via Genoese Zerbi 13, north of th Stazione Lido, which has singles/doubles fo L55,000/65,000.

There are numerous alimentari along Cors Garibaldi, where you can buy cheese, brea and wine. *Ristorante La Pignata*, Via D Tripepi 122, off Corso Garibaldi, has reason ably priced food.

Getting There & Away Reggio is directly con nected by regular trains to Naples and Rome and also to Metaponto, Taranto and Bar (Apulia). Its two stations are the Lido, at th port, and Centrale, in the town centre at Piazz Garibaldi.

Up to 20 hyrofoils run by SNAV (☎ 2 95 68 leave the port just north of Stazione Lido ever day for Messina, some of them proceeding or to the Isole Eolie (Aeolian Islands). The FS runs several hydrofoils a day from the port to Messina.

It is easier, particularly if you arrive from the north by train, to depart from Villa San Giovanni, 15 minutes north of Reggio by train. Car ferries cross from here to Messina around the clock. All ferry companies have offices in Reggio or at the ferry terminal in Villa San Giovanni. If you arrive at Villa San Giovanni by train, you will most likely have already paid for the ferry passage across the strait. You can stay on your train (which is usually taken aboard the ferry), but the trip is short and it is more pleasant to sit on the boat deck.

Sicily

Think of Sicily (Sicilia) and two things immediately come to mind – beaches and the Mafia. While its beaches are beautiful and the Mafia still manages to assert a powerful influence on the Sicilian economy and way of life, Sicily is remarkably diverse.

The largest island in the Mediterranean, its strategic location made it a prize for successive waves of invaders and colonisers, so that it is now a place of Greek temples, Norman churches and castles, Arab and Byzantine domes and splendid baroque churches and palaces. Its landscape ranges from the fertile coast to the mountains of the north and the vast, dry plateau of its centre.

Sicily has a population of about five million. Long neglected by the Italian government after unification, it became a semiautonomous region in 1948, remaining under the control of the central Italian government, but with greater powers to legislate on regional matters. Although industry has developed on the island, its economy is still largely based on agriculture and its people remain strongly connected to the land.

Sicily's temperate climate means mild weather in winter, while summers are relentlessly hot and the beaches swarm with holidaying Italians and other Europeans. The best times to visit are in spring and autumn, when it is hot enough for the beach, but not too hot for sightseeing.

Sicilian food is hotter, spicier and sweeter than in other parts of Italy. The focus is on seafood, notably swordfish, and fresh produce.

Some say that fruit and vegetables taste better in Sicily. Their *dolci* (cakes and sweets) can be works of art but are very sweet. Try the cassata, both a ricotta cake (traditionally available only in winter) and a rich ice cream, and the *cannoli*, tubes of pastry filled with cream, ricotta or chocolate. Don't miss trying the *dolci di mandorle* (rich almond cakes and pastries) and the *granita*, a drink of crushed ice flavoured with lemon, strawberry or coffee, to name a few flavours.

As mentioned, the Mafia remains a powerful force in Sicily. Since the arrest of the Sicilian 'godfather', Salvatore 'Toto' Riina, in 1993, *Mafia pentiti* (grasses) have continued to blow the whistle on fellow felons, businesspeople and politicians, right up to former Prime Minister, Giulio Andreotti, who is on trial both in Palermo and Perugia. The Italian author Luigi Barzini wrote in his novel *The Italians*: 'The phenomenon has deep roots in history, in the character of the Sicilians, in local habits. Its origins disappear down the dim vistas of the centuries.' There is no need to fear you will be caught in the crossfire of a gang war while in Sicily. The 'men of honour' are little interested in the affairs of tourists.

Getting There & Away
Air There are flights from all major cities in Italy to Palermo and Catania. The two airports are also serviced by flights from major European cities. The easiest way to obtain information is from any Sestante CIT or Alitalia offices throughout Italy.

Bus & Train Direct bus services from Rome to Sicily are operated by two companies – SAIS and Segesta. In Rome the buses leave from Stazione Tiburtina. The SAIS bus runs to Agrigento, Catania and Syracuse, with connections to Palermo; it leaves daily from Rome at 8 pm. The Segesta bus runs directly to Palermo, leaving Rome at 7.45 am on Tuesday, Thursday and Saturday. One-way tickets for both cost L68,000.

One of the cheapest ways to reach Sicily is to catch a train to Messina. The cost of the ticket covers the ferry crossing from Villa San Giovanni (Calabria) to Messina. Direct trains run from Milan, Florence, Rome, Naples and Reggio di Calabria. (See the Getting There &

Away section under Reggio di Calabria for more details.)

Boat Sicily is accessible by ferry from Genoa, Livorno, Naples, Reggio di Calabria and Cagliari, and also from Malta and Tunisia. The main company servicing the Mediterranean is Tirrenia. Prices are determined by the season and jump considerably in the summer period (Tirrenia's high season varies according to your destination, but is usually from July to September). Timetables change completely each year and it is best to pick up the annual booklet listing all routes and prices at any Tirrenia office, or at a travel agency which takes ferry bookings. Be sure to book well in advance during summer, particularly if you have a car.

High-season prices in 1996 for a poltrona were: Genoa-Palermo – L109,700 (22 hours); Naples-Palermo – L69,000 (10½ hours); Palermo-Cagliari – L60,000 (14 hours); and Trapani-Tunisia – L92,000 (eight hours). A bed in a shared 2nd-class cabin costs an additional L10,000 to L20,000. Cars cost upwards of L100,000. Other main lines servicing the island are Grandi Traghetti for Livorno-Palermo and Gozo Channel for Sicily-Malta. For information on ferries going from the mainland directly to Lipari, see the Getting There & Away section under Aeolian Islands.

Getting Around

Bus is the best mode of public transport in Sicily. Numerous companies run services between Syracuse, Catania and Palermo as well as to Agrigento and towns in the interior. See the Getting Around section under each town for more details. The coastal train service between Messina and Palermo and Messina down to Syracuse is efficient and reliable.

Probably the best way to enjoy Sicily is by car. It is possible to hitchhike in Sicily, but don't expect a ride in a hurry. Women should not hitchhike alone under any circumstances.

PALERMO

An Arab emirate and later the seat of a Norman kingdom, Palermo was once regarded as the grandest and most beautiful city in Europe. Today it is in a remarkable state of decay – through neglect and heavy bombing during

WWII – yet enough evidence remains of its golden days to make Palermo one of the most fascinating cities in Italy.

Orientation

Palermo is a large but easily manageable city. The main streets of the historical centre are Via Roma and Via Maqueda, which extend from the central station to Piazza Castelnuovo, a vast square in the modern part of town.

Information

Tourist Offices The main APT tourist office (☎ 58 38 47) is at Piazza Castelnuovo 35. It opens Monday to Friday from 8 am to 8 pm and Saturday 8 am to 2 pm. The branch offices at the Stazione Centrale and at the port were closed indefinitely at the time of writing. There is a branch office at the airport.

Money There is an exchange office at the Stazione Centrale, open daily from 8 am to 8 pm.

Post & Communications The main post office is at Via Roma 322 and the main Telecom telephone office is opposite the station in Piazza G Cesare, open daily from 8.30 am to 9.30 pm.

The postcode for Palermo is 90100 and the telephone code is ☎ 091.

Medical Services For an ambulance call ☎ 30 66 44. There is a public hospital (☎ 666 11 11) at Via Carmelo Lazzaro. There is an all-night pharmacy, Lo Cascio, near the train station at Via Roma 1.

Emergency Call the police on ☎ 113. The police office for foreigners (☎ 21 01 11) is in Piazza della Vittoria, open 24 hours a day.

Dangers & Annoyances Petty crime is rife in Palermo and highly deft pickpockets and motorcycle bandits prey on tourists. Avoid wearing jewellery or carrying a bag and keep all your valuables in a money belt. It is unsafe for women to walk through the streets of the historical centre at night, even in Via Roma or Via Maqueda. At night, travellers should avoid the area north-east of the station, between Via Roma and the port.

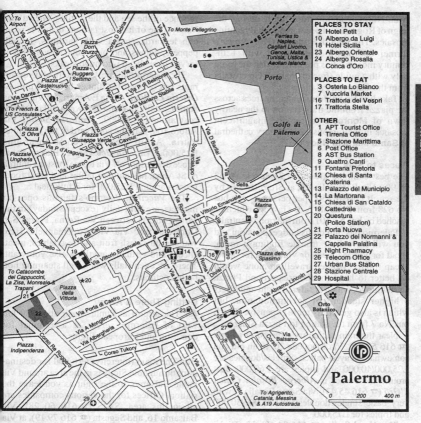

Map legend:

PLACES TO STAY
2 Hotel Petit
10 Albergo da Luigi
18 Hotel Sicilia
23 Albergo Orientale
24 Albergo Rosalia Conca d'Oro

PLACES TO EAT
3 Osteria Lo Bianco
7 Vuccria Market
16 Trattoria dei Vespri
17 Trattoria Stella

OTHER
1 APT Tourist Office
4 Tirrenia Office
5 Stazione Marittima
6 Post Office
8 AST Bus Station
9 Quattro Canti
11 Fontana Pretoria
12 Chiesa di Santa Caterina
13 Palazzo del Municipio
14 La Martorana
15 Chiesa di San Cataldo
19 Cattedrale
20 Questura (Police Station)
21 Porta Nuova
22 Palazzo dei Normanni & Cappella Palatina
25 Night Pharmacy
26 Telecom Office
27 Urban Bus Station
28 Stazione Centrale
29 Hospital

Palermo

0   200   400 m

Things to See

The intersection of Via Vittorio Emanuele and Via Maqueda marks the **Quattro Canti** (four corners of Palermo). The four 17th-century Spanish baroque façades are each decorated with a statue. Nearby is **Piazza Pretoria**, with a beautiful fountain (**Fontana Pretoria**), created by Florentine sculptors in the 16th century. Locals used to call it the Fountain of Shame because of its nude figures. Also in the piazza are the baroque **Chiesa di Santa Caterina** and the **Palazzo del Municipio** (town hall). Just off the piazza is Piazza Bellini and Palermo's most famous church, **La Martorana**, with a beautiful Arab-Norman bell

tower and its interior decorated with Byzantine mosaics. Next to it is the Norman **Chiesa di San Cataldo**, which also mixes Arab and Norman styles and is easily recognisable by its red domes.

The huge Norman **cattedrale** is along Via Vittorio Emanuele, on the corner of Via Bonello. Although modified many times over the centuries, it remains an impressive example of Norman architecture. Opposite Piazza della Vittoria and the gardens is the **Palazzo Reale**, also known as the Palazzo dei Normanni, now the seat of the government. Enter from Piazza Indipendenza to see the **Cappella Palatina**, a magnificent example of

Arab-Norman architecture, built during the reign of Roger II and decorated with Byzantine mosaics. The **Sala di Ruggero** (King Roger's former bedroom), is decorated with 12th-century mosaics. It is possible to visit the room only with a guide (free of charge). Go upstairs from the Cappella Palatina.

Take bus No 8/9 from under the trees across the piazza from the train station to the nearby town of **Monreale** to see the magnificent mosaics in the famous 12th-century cathedral of **Santa Maria la Nuova**.

Places to Stay

The best camping ground is *Trinacria* (☎ 53 05 90), Via Barcarello 25, at Sferracavallo by the sea. It costs L7500 per person. Catch bus No 628 from Piazzale A de Gasperi, which be reached by bus No 101 from Stazione Centrale.

Palermo has numerous budget pensioni and you will have little trouble finding a room. Head for Via Maqueda or Via Roma for basic, cheap rooms. Women travelling alone would do better to head for the area around Piazza Castelnuovo, which is safer at night and offers a higher standard of accommodation, but which is also generally more expensive. Catch bus No 7 from the station to Piazza Sturzo.

Near the train station try *Albergo Orientale* (☎ 616 57 25), Via Maqueda 26, in an old and somewhat decayed palace. Singles/doubles are L25,000/40,000 and triples are L60,000. Just around the corner is *Albergo Rosalia Conca d'Oro* (☎ 616 45 43), Via Santa Rosalia 7, with very basic singles/doubles for L35,000/50,000 and triples for L75,000.

The *Hotel Sicilia* (☎ 616 84 60), Via Divisi 99, on the corner of Via Maqueda, has rooms of a higher standard. Singles/doubles are L35,000/50,000, or L45,000/65,000 with private shower. *Albergo da Luigi* (☎ 58 50 85), Via Vittorio Emanuele 284, next to the Quattro Canti, has singles/doubles from L25,000/50,000, or L40,000/60,000 with bathroom. Ask for a room with a view of the fountain.

Near Piazza Castelnuovo is the *Hotel Petit* (☎ 32 36 16), Via Principe di Belmonte 84, with clean and comfortable singles/doubles for L50,000/65,000 with private shower. A single without shower is L35,000.

Places to Eat

Palermo's cucina takes advantage of the fresh produce of the sea and the fertile Conca d'Oro Valley. One of its most famous dishes is pasta con le sarde (pasta with sardines, fennel, peppers, capers and pine nuts). Swordfish is served here sliced into huge steaks.

The Palermitani are late eaters and restaurants rarely open for dinner before 8 pm. At *Osteria Lo Bianco*, Via E Amari, off Via Roma at the Castelnuovo end of town, a full meal will cost around L20,000. *Trattoria Stella*, Via Alloro 104, is in the courtyard of the old Hotel Patria. A full meal will come to around L25,000. *Trattoria dei Vespri*, Piazza Santa Croce dei Vespri, off Via Roma, past the church of St Anna, has outdoor tables and great food. It costs around L25,000 for a full meal.

The *Vucciria*, Palermo's famous open-air markets, are held daily (except Sunday) in the narrow streets between Via Roma, Piazza San Domenico and Via Vittorio Emanuele. Here you can buy fresh fruit and vegetables, meat, cheese and virtually anything else you want. There are even stalls which sell steaming hot, boiled octopus.

Getting There & Away

Air The airport at Punta Raisi, about 30 km west of Palermo, serves as a terminal for domestic and European flights.

Bus The main (intercity) terminal for destinations throughout Sicily is in the area around Via Paolo Balsamo, to the right as you leave the station. Offices for the various companies are all in this area. SAIS (☎ 616 60 28), Via Balsamo 16, and Segesta (☎ 616 79 19), at Via Balsamo 26, both run a daily bus to Rome.

Train Regular trains leave from the Stazione Centrale for Milazzo, Messina, Catania and Syracuse, as well as for nearby towns such as Cefalù. Direct trains go to Reggio di Calabria, Naples and Rome (L92,600 one way).

Boat Boats leave from the port (Molo Vittorio Veneto) for Sardinia and the mainland (see the Getting There & Away section under Sicily). The Tirrenia office (☎ 33 33 00) is at the port.

Getting Around

Taxis to the airport cost upwards of L60,000. The cheaper option is to catch one of the regular blue buses which leave every 40 minutes from outside the station from 5.25 am to 9.45 pm (L5000). Palermo's buses are efficient and most stop outside the train station. Useful numbers to remember are the No 7 along Via Roma from the train station to near Piazza Castelnuovo and the No 39 from the station to the port. You must buy tickets before you get on the bus; they cost L1500 for one hour.

AEOLIAN ISLANDS

Also known as the Lipari Islands, the seven islands of this archipelago just north of Milazzo are volcanic in origin. They range from the well-developed tourist resort of Lipari and the understated jet-set haunt of Panarea, to the rugged Vulcano, the spectacular scenery of Stromboli (and its fiercely active volcano), the fertile vineyards of Salina, and the solitude of Alicudi and Filicudi, which remain relatively undeveloped. The islands have been inhabited since the Neolithic era, when migrants sought the valuable volcanic glass, obsidian. The Isole Eolie (Aeolian Islands) are so named because the ancient Greeks believed they were the home of Aeolus, the god of wind. Homer wrote of the islands in the *Odyssey*.

Information

The main AAST tourist information office (☎ 988 00 95) for the islands is on Lipari at Corso Vittorio Emanuele 202. Offices open on Stromboli, Vulcano and Salina during summer.

The telephone code for the islands is ☎ 090.

Things to See & Do

On **Lipari** visit the **castello**, with its archaeological park and museum. You can also go on excellent walks on the island. Catch a local bus from the town of Lipari to the hill-top village of **Quattrocchi** for a great view of Vulcano. Boat trips will take you around the island – contact the tourist office for information.

Vulcano, a strange, desolate place, with the smell of sulphur always in the air, is a short boat trip from Lipari's port. The main volcano (**Vulcano Fossa**) is still active, though the last recorded period of eruption was from 1888 to 1890. Though you can do the one-hour hike to the crater, be extremely careful of sudden bursts of sulphurous gas and landslides.

Stromboli is the most spectacular of the islands. Its volcano is the most active in Europe – climb Stromboli at night to see the **Sciara del Fuoco** (Trail of Fire), lava streaming down the side of the volcano, and the volcanic explosions from the crater. Many people make the trip (four to five hours) without a guide during the day, but at night you should go with a guided group. The Club Alpino Italiano (☎ 98 62 63), off Piazza San Vincenzo, in San Vincenzo, organises guided tours which depart at around 4 pm and return at 11.30 pm. It is best to contact them in advance before making a booking, since they only depart if groups are large enough. Remember to take warm clothes, wear heavy shoes and carry a torch and plenty of water. The return trip from Lipari to Stromboli is L25,400 by ferry and L45,000 by hydrofoil.

Places to Stay & Eat

Lipari provides the best options for a comfortable stay. It has numerous budget hotels, affittacamere and apartments, and the other islands are easily accessible by regular hydrofoils. When you arrive on Lipari you are likely to be approached by someone offering accommodation. This is worth checking because the offers are usually genuine.

The island's camping ground, *Baia Unci* (☎ 981 19 09), is at Canneto, about two km out of the Lipari township. It costs L15,000 a night per person, plus L25,000 for a site. The HI *hostel* (☎ 981 15 40), Via Castello 17, is inside the walls of the castle. A bed costs L12,000 a night, plus L2000 for a hot shower, or L2500 for breakfast. A meal costs L15,000. *Cassarà Vittorio* (☎ 981 15 23), Vico Sparviero 15, costs L35,000 per person, or L40,000 with private bathroom. There are two terraces with views, and use of the kitchen is L5000. The owner can be found (unless he finds you first) at Via Garibaldi 78, on the way from the port to the centre.

You can eat surprisingly cheaply on Lipari. For a pizza try *Il Galeone*, Corso V Emanuele 222. For an excellent meal eat at *Trattoria d'Oro*, Corso Umberto I. There is a L20,000 tourist menu.

Panarea is a beautiful haunt of the jet set. If you want seclusion, head for Filicudi or Alicudi. However, the hotels aren't exactly cheap. The *Ericusa* (☎ 988 99 02) on Alicudi costs L90,000 a double and the *Locanda la Canna* (☎ 988 99 56) on Filicudi charges

L80,000 a double. On Stromboli try the *Locanda Stella* (☎ 98 60 20), Via Fabio Filzo 14, and on Vulcano, if you can cope with the sulphurous fumes, try *Pensione Agostino* (☎ 985 23 42), Via Favaloro 1 (close to the mud bath), which has doubles with bathroom for L85,000. Camping facilities are available on Salina and Vulcano. Most accommodation in summer is booked out well in advance on the smaller islands, particularly on Stromboli, and most hotels close during winter.

Getting There & Away

Ferries and hydrofoils leave for the islands from Milazzo (which is easy to reach by train from Palermo and Messina) and all ticket offices are along Via Rizzo at the port. SNAV runs hydrofoils (L18,100 one way). Siremar runs hydrofoils, as well as ferries for half the price. They both have offices at the port. SNAV runs hydrofoils from Palermo twice a day in summer and three times a week in the off season. If arriving at Milazzo by train, you will need to catch a bus to the port. If arriving by bus, simply make the five-minute walk back along Via Crispi to the port area.

You can travel directly to the islands from the mainland. Siremar runs regular ferries from Naples and SNAV runs hydrofoils from Naples (see the Naples Getting There & Away section), Messina and Reggio di Calabria. Note that the sea around the islands can be very rough.

Getting Around

Regular hydrofoil and ferry services operate between the islands. Both Siremar and Aliscafi SNAV have offices at the port on Lipari, where you can get full timetable information.

TAORMINA

Spectacularly located on a hill overlooking the sea and Mt Etna, Taormina has long ago discovered by the European jet set, which has made it one of the more expensive and touristy towns in Sicily. But its magnificent setting, its Greek Theatre and the nearby beaches remain as seductive now as they were for the likes of Goethe and D H Lawrence. The AAST tourist office (☎ 2 32 43) in Palazzo Corvaja, just off the main street, Corso Umberto, near Largo Santa Caterina, has extensive information on the town.

Taormina's telephone code is ☎ 0942.

Things to See

The **Greek Theatre** (entry L2000) was built in the 3rd century BC and later greatly expanded and remodelled by the Romans. Concerts and theatre are staged there in summer and it affords a wonderful view of Mt Etna. From the beautiful **villa comunale** (public gardens) there is a panoramic view of the sea. Along Corso Umberto is the **Duomo**, with a Gothic façade. The local beach is **Isola Bella**, a short bus ride from Via Pirandello. Trips to Mt Etna can be organised through CST (☎ 2 33 01), Corso Umberto 101.

Places to Stay & Eat

You can camp near the beach at *Campeggio San Leo* (☎ 2 46 58), Via Nazionale, at Capotaormina. The cost is L7500 per person per night, and L8000 for a tent site.

There are numerous affittacamere in Taormina and the tourist office has a full list. *Il Leone* (☎ 2 38 78), Via Bagnoli Croce 127, near the public gardens, has singles/doubles for L26,000/46,000, or L26,000 per person with private bathroom. *Pensione Ingeniere* (☎ 62 54 80), Via Timeo 8, charges L30,000 per person. At *Pensione Svizzera* (☎ 2 37 90), Via Pirandello 26, on the way from the bus stop to the town centre, very pleasant singles/doubles are L60,000/100,000, with private bathroom. Breakfast is included.

Eating is expensive here. For a light meal head for *Shelter Pub*, Via Fratelli Bandieri 10, off Corso Umberto, for sandwiches and salads from L4000 to L8000. *Ritrovo Trocadero*, Via Pirandello 1, has pizza and pasta at reasonable prices. At *Ristorante La Piazzetta*, Via Paladini 5, you can sit outside and an excellent full meal will cost around L30,000.

Getting There & Away

Bus is the easiest way to get to Taormina. SAIS buses leave from Messina and Catania. Taormina is on the main train line between Messina and Catania, but the station is on the coast and regular buses will take you to Via Pirandello, near the centre; bus services are heavily reduced on Sunday.

MT ETNA

Dominating the landscape in eastern Sicily between Taormina and Catania, Mt Etna (3350 metres) is Europe's largest live volcano and one of the world's most active. Eruptions occur frequently, both from the four live craters at the summit and on the volcano's slopes, which are littered with crevices and old craters. Its most recent eruption was in 1992, when a stream of lava threatened the town of Zafferana Etnea. The unpredictability of the volcano's activity means that people are no longer allowed to climb to the craters at the summit. Only a rope marks the point where it becomes unsafe to proceed, but it would be extremely foolish to ignore the warning signs and go further. To reach this point, you can either hike from the start of the cable car (a long, hard climb of about five hours return), or catch the cable car to 2500 metres (L25,000 return) and then one of the 4WD minibuses to 2920 metres (L27,000 return). Many people catch the minibuses uphill and then walk back to the cable car.

If you want to stay on the volcano, there is *Rifugio Sapienza* (☎ 095-91 10 62) near the cable car.

Mt Etna is best approached from Catania by AST bus (☎ 095-53 17 56), which leaves from Via L Sturzo in front of Catania's train station at 8.15 am and goes via Nicolosi to the cable car on Mt Etna. The bus returns to Catania at 4 pm. Another option is to circle Mt Etna on the private Circumetnea train line, which starts at Catania at Stazione Borgo, Via Caronda 352, accessible by bus No 29 or 36 from Catania's main train station. From Taormina, you can catch a train to Randazzo, where you can pick up the Circumetnea.

SYRACUSE

Once a powerful Greek city to rival Athens, Syracuse (Siracusa) is one of the highlights of a visit to Sicily. Founded in 743 BC by colonists from Corinth, it became a dominant sea power in the Mediterranean, prompting Athens to attack the city in 413 BC. In one of the great maritime battles in history, the Athenian fleet was destroyed. Syracuse was conquered by the Romans in 212 BC and, with the rest of Sicily, fell to a succession of invasions through the centuries. Syracuse was the birthplace of the Greek mathematician and physicist Archimedes, and Plato attended the court of the tyrant Dionysius, who ruled from 405 to 367 BC.

The main sights of Syracuse are in two areas: on the island of Ortygia and at the archaeological park two km across town. There are two tourist information offices. The AAT (☎ 46 42 55) is at Via Maestranza 33 on Ortygia. It opens Monday to Saturday from 8.30 am to 1.45 pm and 4.30 to 7.30 pm (closed afternoons in winter). The APT (☎ 677 10 10), Via San Sebastiano 43 (branch office at the archaeological zone), opens Monday to Saturday from 8 am to 7 pm and Sunday from 8 am to 1 pm.

The town's telephone code is ☎ 0931.

Things to See

The island of Ortygia is the spiritual and physical heart of the city. Its buildings are predominantly medieval, with some baroque palaces and churches. The 7th-century **Duomo** was built on top of the **Temple of Athena**, incorporating most of the original columns in its three-aisled structure. The **Piazza Duomo** is lined with baroque palaces. Walk down Via Picherali to the waterfront and the **Fonte Aretusa** (Fountain of Arethusa), a natural freshwater spring. According to Greek legend, the nymph Arethusa, pursued by the river god Alpheus, was turned into a fountain by the goddess Diana. Undeterred, Alpheus turned himself into the river which feeds the spring.

To get to the **Parco Archeologico**, catch bus No 1 from Riva della Posta on Ortygia. The main attraction here is the 5th-century BC **Greek theatre**, its seating area carved out of solid rock. Nearby is the **Orecchio di Dionisio**, an artificial grotto in the shape of an ear which the tyrant of Syracuse, Dionysius, used as a prison. Its extraordinary acoustics led the painter Caravaggio, during a visit in the 17th century, to give the grotto its current name. Caravaggio mused that the tyrant must have taken advantage of the acoustics to overhear the whispered conversations of his prisoners. The 2nd-century **Roman Amphitheatre** is impressively well preserved. The park is open daily from 9 am to one hour before sunset. Admission is L2000.

The **Museo Archeologico Paolo Orsi**, about 500 metres east of the archaeological zone, off Viale Teocrito, contains the best organised and most interesting archaeological collection in Sicily. The museum is open Tuesday to Saturday from 9 am to 1 pm and Wednesday also from 3.30 to 6.30 pm. Entry is L2000.

Special Events

Since 1914 Syracuse has hosted a festival of Greek classical drama in May and June of every even-numbered year. Performances are given at the Greek Theatre. Tickets are available at the APT, at the theatre ticket booth. For information call ☎ 6 53 73.

Places to Stay

Camping facilities are at *Agriturista Rinaura* (☎ 72 12 24), about four km out of the city near the sea. Catch bus No 21, 22 or 24 from Corso Umberto. It costs L6000 per person and L8500 for a site. The non-HI *Ostello della Gioventù* (☎ 71 11 18), Viale Epipoli 45, is eight km west of Syracuse. Catch bus No 11 or 25 from Piazza Marconi. Beds are L20,000. If you can afford it, stay at the *Gran Bretagna* (☎ 6 87 65), on Ortygia at Via Savoia 21, just off Largo XXV Luglio. It has very pleasant rooms for L46,000/76,000. *Hotel Centrale* (☎ 605 28), close to the train station at Corso Umberto 141, has singles/doubles for L25,000/40,000 and triples for L55,000.

Places to Eat

Spaghetteria do Schoggiu, Via Scina 11, serves all types of pasta from L6500 a plate. *Pizzeria La Dolce Vita*, Via Roma 112, has outside tables in a small courtyard.

There is an open-air, fresh produce market in the streets behind the Temple of Apollo, open daily (except Sunday) until 1 pm. You will find several alimentari and supermarkets along Corso Gelone.

Getting There & Away

SAIS buses leave from Riva della Posta on Ortygia, for Catania, Palermo, Enna and surrounding small towns. The SAIS service for Rome also leaves from the piazza, connecting with the Rome bus at Catania. AST buses also service Palermo from Piazza della Posta. Syracuse is easy to reach by train from Messina and Catania. Boat services from Syracuse to Malta are in a state of flux. Check with the tourist offices (see the Malta chapter's Getting There & Away section).

AGRIGENTO

Founded in approximately 582 BC as the Greek Akragas, it is today a pleasant medieval town, but the Greek temples in the valley below are the real reason to visit. The Italian novelist and dramatist Luigi Pirandello (1867-1936) was born here, as was the Greek philosopher and scientist Empedocles (circa 490-430 BC). The AAST tourist office (☎ 204 54), Via Cesare Battisti 15, opens Monday to Friday from 8.30 am to 1.45 pm and 4 to 7 pm, and in the morning only on Saturday.

Agrigento's telephone code is ☎ 0922.

Things to See & Do

Agrigento's **Valley of the Temples** is one of the major Greek archaeological sights in the world. Its five main Doric temples were constructed in the 5th century BC and are in various states of ruin because of earthquakes and vandalism by early Christians. The only temple to survive relatively intact is the **Tempio della Concordia**, which was transformed into a Christian church. The **Tempio di Giunone**, a five-minute walk uphill to the east, has an impressive sacrificial altar. The **Tempio di Ercole** is the oldest of the structures. Across the main road which divides the valley is the massive **Tempio di Giove**, one of the most imposing buildings of ancient Greece. Although now completely in ruins, it used to cover an area measuring 112 metres by 56 metres, with columns 18 metres high. **Telamoni**, colossal statues of men, were also used in the structure. The remains of one of them are in the **Museo Archeologico**, just north of the temples on Via dei Templi (a copy lies at the archaeological site). Close by is the **Tempio di Castore e Polluce**, which was partly reconstructed in the 19th century. The temples are lit up at night until 11.30 pm and are open until 9 pm. To get to the temples from the town, catch bus No 1, 2 or 3 from the train station.

Places to Stay & Eat

The *Bella Napoli* (☎ 2 04 35), Piazza Lena 6, off Via Bic Bac at the end of Via Atenea, has clean and comfortable singles/doubles for L30,000/55,000, or L40,000/75,000 with private bathroom. For a decent, cheap meal try the *Trattoria la Concordia*, Via Porcello 6.

Getting There & Away

Intercity buses leave from Piazza Rosselli, just off Piazza Vittorio Emanuele, for Palermo, Catania and surrounding small towns.

Sardinia

The second-largest island in the Mediterranean, Sardinia (Sardegna) was colonised and invaded by the Greeks, Phoenicians and Romans, followed by the Pisans, Genoese and finally the Spaniards. But it is often said that the Sardinians, known on the island as *Sardi*, were never really conquered – they simply retreated into the hills.

The Romans were prompted to call the island's eastern mountains *Barbagia* because of their views on the lifestyle of the locals. This area is still known as the Barbagia. Even today the Sardinians are a strangely insular people. In the island's interior, some women still wear the traditional costume and shepherds still live in almost complete isolation, building enclosures of stone or wood for their sheep and goats as the ancients did. If you venture into the interior, you will find the people incredibly gracious and hospitable, but easily offended if they sense any lack of respect.

The first inhabitants of the island were the Nuraghic people, thought to have arrived here around 2000 BC. Little is known about them, but the island is dotted with thousands of *nuraghi*, their conical-shaped stone houses and fortresses.

Sardinia became a semiautonomous region in 1948, and the Italian government's Sardinian Rebirth Plan of 1962 made some impact on the development of tourism, industry and agriculture.

The island's cuisine is as varied as its history. Along the coast most dishes feature seafood and there are many variations of *zuppa di pesce* (fish soup). Inland you will find *porcheddu* (roast suckling pig), kid goat with olives, and even lamb's trotters in garlic sauce. The Sardi eat *pecorino* (sheep's milk cheese) and you will rarely find *parmigiano* (Parmesan cheese) here. The preferred bread throughout the island is the paper-thin *carta musica* (literally, music paper), also called *pane carasau*, often sprinkled with oil and salt.

The landscape of the island ranges from the 'savage, dark-bushed, sky-exposed land' described by D H Lawrence, to the incredibly beautiful gorges and valleys near Dorgali, the rugged isolation of the Gennargentu mountain range and the unspoiled coastline between Bosa and Alghero. Although hunters have been traditionally active in Sardinia, some wildlife remains, notably the albino donkeys on the island of Asinara, colonies of griffon vultures on the west coast, and miniature horses in the inland area of Giara di Gesturi, in the southwest. The famous colony of Mediterranean monk seals at the Grotta del Bue Marino, near the beach of Cala Gonone, has not been sighted for some years.

Try to avoid the island in August, when the weather is very hot and the beaches are overcrowded. Warm weather generally continues from May to September.

Getting There & Away

Air Airports at Cagliari, Olbia and Alghero link Sardinia with major Italian and European cities. For information contact Alitalia or the Sestante CIT or CTS offices in all major towns.

Boat The island is accessible by ferry from Genoa, Livorno, Civitavecchia, Naples, Palermo, Trapani, Bonifacio (Corsica) and Tunis. The departure points in Sardinia are Olbia, Golfo Aranci and Porto Torres in the north, Arbatax on the east coast and Cagliari in the south.

The main company is Tirrenia, though the national railway, Ferrovie dello Stato, runs a slightly cheaper service between Olbia and Civitavecchia. Moby Lines (which also runs Navarma Lines and Sardegna Lines) and Sardinia Ferries (also known as Elba and Corsica Ferries) both operate services from the mainland to Sardinia, as well as to Corsica and Elba. They depart from Livorno, Civitavecchia and arrive at either Olbia or Golfo Aranci. Most travel agencies in Italy have brochures on the various companies' services.

Timetables change every year and prices fluctuate according to the season.

Prices for a poltrona on Tirrenia ferries in the 1996 high season were as follows: Genoa-Cagliari – L94,000 (19 hours); Genoa-Porto Torres or Olbia – L60,000 (12½ hours); Civitavecchia-Cagliari – L70,000 (13½ hours); Civitavecchia-Olbia – L33,900 (seven hours); Naples-Cagliari – L65,000 (15 hours); and Palermo-Cagliari – L60,000 (12½ hours). The cost of taking a small car ranged from

L138,000 to L241,000, and up to L50,000 for a motorcycle.

Getting Around

Bus The two main bus companies are ARST, which operates extensive services throughout the island, and PANI, which links the main towns.

Train The main FS train lines link Cagliari with Oristano, Sassari and Olbia. The private railways that link smaller towns throughout the island can be very slow. However, the *trenino* (little train), which runs from Cagliari to Arbatax through the Barbagia, is a relaxing way to see part of the interior (See the Getting There & Away section under Cagliari).

Car & Motorcycle The only way to explore Sardinia properly is by road. Rental agencies are listed under Cagliari and some other towns around the island.

Hitching You might find hitchhiking laborious once you get away from the main towns because of the light traffic. Women should not hitchhike in Sardinia under any circumstances.

CAGLIARI

This is a surprisingly attractive city which offers an interesting medieval section, a beautiful beach – Poetto – and a population of pink flamingos.

Orientation

If you arrive by bus, train or boat you will find yourself at the port area of Cagliari. The main street along the harbour is Via Roma, and the old city stretches up the hill behind it to the castle. Most of the budget hotels and restaurants are in the area near the port.

Information

Tourist Offices The AAST information booth (☎ 66 92 55) at Piazza Matteotti 1, is open daily from 8 am to 8 pm in the high season, and from 8 am to 2 pm in other months. There are also information offices at the airport and in the Stazione Marittima.

The ESIT (Ente Sardo Industrie Turistiche) office (☎ 6 02 31), Via Goffredo Mameli 97, is open daily from 8 am to 8 pm in high season.

Here you can pick up information on all of Sardinia.

Post & Communications The main post office is in Piazza del Carmine, up Via La Maddalena from Via Roma. The Telecom telephone office is at Via G M Angioj, north of Piazza Matteotti.

The postcode for Cagliari is 09100 and the telephone code is ☎ 070.

Medical Services For an ambulance ring ☎ 27 23 45, and for medical attention go to the Ospedale Civile (☎ 601 82 67), Via Ospedale.

Emergency Contact the police on ☎ 113, or go to the questura (☎ 4 44 44), Via Amat 9.

Things to See

The **Museo Archeologico Nazionale**, Piazza Arsenale, in the Citadella dei Musei, has a fascinating collection of Nuragic bronzes. It is open Monday to Saturday from 9 am to 2 pm, Sunday from 9 am to 1 pm and in the afternoon from 3.30 to 6.30 pm on Wednesday, Friday and Saturday. Entry is L4000.

It is enjoyable enough to wander through the medieval quarter. The Pisan-Romanesque **Duomo** was built in the 13th century, but later remodelled. It has an interesting Romanesque pulpit.

From the **Bastione di San Remy**, which is in the centre of town in Piazza Costituzione and once formed part of the fortifications of the old city, there is a good view of Cagliari and the sea.

The Pisan **Torre di San Pancrazio**, in Piazza Indipendenza, is also worth a look. The **Roman amphitheatre**, on Viale Buon Cammino, is considered the most important Roman monument in Sardinia. During summer, opera is performed here.

Spend a day on the **Spiaggia di Poetto** (east of the centre) and wander across to the salt lakes to see the flamingos.

Special Events

The Festival of Sant'Efisio, a colourful festival mixing the secular and the religious, is held annually for four days from 1 May.

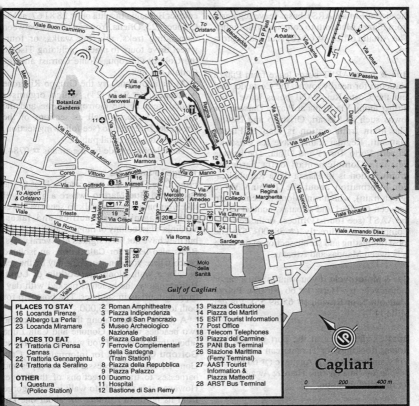

PLACES TO STAY
16 Locanda Firenze
20 Albergo La Perla
23 Locanda Miramare

PLACES TO EAT
21 Trattoria Ci Pensa Cannas
22 Trattoria Gennargentu
24 Trattoria da Serafino

OTHER
1 Questura (Police Station)

2 Roman Amphitheatre
3 Piazza Indipendenza
4 Torre di San Pancrazio
5 Museo Archeologico Nazionale
6 Piazza Garibaldi
7 Ferrovie Complementari della Sardegna (Train Station)
8 Piazza della Repubblica
9 Piazza Palazzo
10 Duomo
11 Hospital
12 Bastione di San Remy

13 Piazza Costituzione
14 Piazza dei Martiri
15 ESIT Tourist Information
17 Post Office
18 Telecom Telephones
19 Piazza del Carmine
25 PANI Bus Terminal
26 Stazione Marittima (Ferry Terminal)
27 AAST Tourist Information & Piazza Matteotti
28 ARST Bus Terminal

Cagliari

0   200   400 m

Places to Stay & Eat

There are numerous budget pensioni near the station. Try the *Locanda Firenze* (☎ 65 36 78), Corso Vittorio Emanuele 50, which has comfortable singles/doubles for L35,000/45,000. The *Locanda Miramare* (☎ 66 40 21), Via Roma 59, has singles/doubles for L55,000/60,000. Nearby is *Albergo La Perla* (☎ 66 94 46), Via Sardegna 18, with singles/doubles for L42,000/54,000.

Several reasonably priced trattorias can be found in the area behind Via Roma, particularly around Via Sardegna and Via Cavour. *Trattoria da Serafino*, Via Lepanto 6, on the corner of Via Sardegna, has excellent food at reasonable prices. *Trattoria Gennargentu*, Via Sardegna 60, has good pasta and seafood and a full meal costs around L20,000. *Trattoria Ci Pensa Cannas*, down the street at No 37, is another good choice, with meals for around L20,000. In Via Sardegna there are also grocery shops and bakeries.

Entertainment

During summer, opera is performed in the Roman amphitheatre.

Getting There & Away

Air The airport (☎ 24 00 47) is north-west of

the city at Elmas. ARST buses leave regularly from Piazza Matteotti to coincide with flights. The Alitalia office (☎ 60 10) is at Via Caprera 14.

Bus & Train ARST buses leave from Piazza Matteotti for nearby towns, the Costa del Sud and the Costa Rei. PANI buses leave from further along Via Roma at Piazza Darsena for towns such as Sassari, Oristano and Nuoro. The main train station is also in Piazza Matteotti. Regular trains leave for Oristano, Sassari, Porto Torres and Olbia. The private Ferrovie Complementari della Sardegna (train) station is in Piazza della Repubblica. For information about the Trenino Verde (green train), which runs along a scenic route between Cagliari and Arbatax, contact ESIT, the AAST (see Tourist Offices), or the Ferrovie Complementari directly (☎ 58 00 76). The most interesting and scenic section of the route is between Mandas and Arbatax.

Car & Motorcycle If you want to rent a car or motorcycle try Hertz (☎ 66 81 05), Piazza Matteotti 1, or Ruvioli (☎ 65 89 55), Via dei Mille 11.

Boat Ferries arrive at the port just off Via Roma. Bookings for Tirrenia can be made at Via Campidano 1, c/o Agenave (☎ 66 60 65). See the Sardinia Getting There & Away section for more information.

CALA GONONE
This fast-developing seaside resort is an excellent base from which to explore the coves along the coastline, as well as the Nuraghic sites and rugged terrain inland.

Major points are accessible by bus and boat, but you will need a car to explore.

Information
Tourist information is available at the boat ticket office at the port. There is a Pro Loco tourist office at nearby Dorgali (☎ 9 62 43) at Via Lamarmora 106, where you can pick up maps, a list of hotels and information to help you while visiting the area. The EPT office (☎ 3 00 83) in Nuoro, Piazza Italia 19, also has information on the area.

For information on trekking in the Barbagia,

contact Barbagia Insolita on ☎ 28 81 67, at Via Carducci 25, Oliena. You can choose between demanding treks, relaxing walks, or four-wheel drive tours to places including Tiscali, the Gola di Gorropu, Monte Corrasi and the Codula di Luna.

At Cala Gonone, try the Gruppo Ricerche Ambientali (☎ 9 34 24), which organises guided treks of the Gorropu Gorge and the Codula di Luna, as well as sections of the Grotta del Bue Marino (see following section) not open to the general public.

The telephone code for the area is ☎ 0784.

Things to See & Do
From Cala Gonone's port catch a boat to the **Grotta del Bue Marino**, where a guide will take you on a one-km walk to see vast caves with stalagmites, stalactites and lakes. Sardinia's last colony of monk seals lived here, but they have not been sighted in several years. Boats also leave for **Cala Luna**, an isolated beach where you can spend the day by the sea or take a walk along the **Codula di Luna**. Unfortunately, the beach is packed with day-tripping tourists in summer. The boat trip for both together costs L25,000.

A **walking track** along the coast links the two beaches of Cala Gonone and Cala Luna (about three hours). If you want to explore the **Gorropu Gorge**, ask for information at Cala Gonone, since it is necessary to use ropes and harnesses to traverse sections of the gorge. However, it is possible to walk into the gorge from its northern entrance for about one km before it becomes impossible to proceed.

Places to Stay
At Cala Gonone there is a *camping ground* (☎ 9 31 65) at Via Collodi. It is expensive in summer at up to L20,000 per person. Free camping is strictly forbidden throughout the area.

Hotels include the *Gabbiano* (☎ 9 31 30) at the port, with singles/doubles for L40,000/60,000.

Su Gologone (28 75 12), is a few km east of Oliena, near the entrance to the Lanaittu valley. It is on the expensive side at around L115,000 a double with bathroom, but it is in a lovely setting and organises guided tours and treks, as well as horse-riding expeditions. Its restaurant is renowned throughout the island.

Getting There & Away
Catch a PANI bus to Nuoro from Cagliari, Sassari or Oristano and then take an ARST bus to Dorgali and Cala Gonone. There is also a bus from Olbia's port to Dorgali, from where you can catch a bus (only every three hours) to Cala Gonone. If you are travelling by car, you will need a detailed road map of the area. One of the best is published by the Istituto Geografico de Agostini. The tourist office has maps which detail the locations of the main sights.

ALGHERO
One of the most popular tourist resorts in Sardinia, Alghero is on the island's west coast in the area known as the Coral Riviera.

The town is a good base from which to explore the magnificent coastline which links it to Bosa in the south and the famous Grotte di Nettuno (Neptune's Caves) on the Capocaccia, a cape just near Alghero, to the north.

Orientation & Information
The train station is in Via Don Minzoni, some distance from the centre, and is connected by a regular bus service to the centre of town.

The main tourist information office, AAST (☎ 97 90 54), is at Piazza Porta Terra 9, near the port and just across the gardens from the bus terminal. The old city and most hotels and restaurants are in the area west of the tourist office.

The main post office is at Via XX Settembre 108. There is a bank of public telephones on Via Vittorio Emanuele at the opposite end of the gardens from the tourist office.

The postcode for Alghero is 07041 and the telephone code is ☎ 079.

In an emergency ring the police on ☎ 113; for medical attention ring ☎ 93 05 33, or go to the Ospedale Civile (☎ 99 62 33), Via Don Minzoni.

Things to See & Do
It's worth wandering through the narrow streets of the old city and around the port. The most interesting church is the **Chiesa di San Francesco**, Via Carlo Alberto. The city's **cathedral** has been ruined by constant remodelling, but its bell tower remains a fine example of Gothic-Catalan architecture.

Near Alghero are the **Grotte di Nettuno**, accessible by hourly boats from the port (L15,000), or by the SFS bus from Via Catalogna. For some services you will need to change at Porto Conte (L2000 one way).

If you have your own means of transport, don't miss the beautiful **Capocaccia** and the **Nuraghe di Palmavera**, about 10 km out of Alghero on the road to Porto Conte.

The coastline between **Alghero** and **Bosa** is stunning. Rugged cliffs fall down to isolated beaches, and near Bosa is one of the last habitats of the griffon vulture. It is quite an experience if you are lucky enough to spot one of these huge birds. The only way to see the coast is by car or motorcycle, or by hitchhiking. If you want to rent a bicycle or motorcycle to explore the coast, try Cicloexpress (☎ 97 65 92), Via Lamarmora 39.

Places to Stay
It is virtually impossible to find a room in August unless you book months in advance. At other times of the year you should have little trouble.

Camping facilities include *Calik* (☎ 93 01 11) in Fertilia, about seven km out of town, at L15,000 per person.

The HI *Ostello dei Giuliani* (☎ 93 03 53) is at Via Zara 1, Fertilia. Take the hourly bus AF from Via Catalogna to Fertilia. Bed and breakfast costs L14,000, a shower is L1000 and a meal costs L14,000. The hostel is open all year.

In the old town is the *Hotel San Francesco* (☎ 97 92 58), Via Ambrogio Machin 2, with singles/doubles for L50,000/85,000. *Pensione Normandie* (☎ 97 53 02), Via Enrico Mattei 6, is out of the centre. To get there follow Via Cagliari, which becomes Viale Giovanni XXIII. It has slightly shabby but large singles/doubles for L35,000/65,000.

Places to Eat
A pleasant place to eat is *Trattoria il Vecchio Mulino*, Via Don Deroma 3. A full meal will cost around L25,000. A cheaper option is the *pizzeria* just off Via Roma at Vicolo Adami 17. Takeaway pizza by the slice costs about L2500. *Paninoteca al Duomo*, next to the cathedral in Piazza Civica, has good sandwiches.

ITALY

ITALY

Entertainment

In summer Alghero stages the Estate Musicale Algherese (Alghero's Summer Music Festival) in the cloisters of the church of San Francesco, Via Carlo Alberto.

A festival, complete with fireworks display, is held annually on 15 August for the Feast of the Assumption.

Getting There & Away

Alghero is accessible from Sassari by train. The main bus station is in Via Catalogna, next to the public park. ARST buses leave for Sassari and Porto Torres; SFS buses also service Sassari and there is a special service to Olbia to coincide with ferry departures. Buses also run between Alghero and Bosa.

Macedonia (Македонија)

Macedonia is at the south end of what was once the Yugoslav Federation. Its position in the centre of the Balkan Peninsula between Albania, Bulgaria, Serbia and Greece has often made it a political powder keg. The mix of Islamic and Orthodox influences tell of a long struggle which ended in 1913 when the Treaty of Bucharest divided Macedonia among its three neighbours. Serbia got the northern part while the southern half went to Greece. Bulgaria received a much smaller slice. Only in 1992 did ex-Yugoslav Macedonia become fully independent.

For travellers Macedonia is a land of contrasts, ranging from space-age Skopje with its modern shopping centre and timeworn Turkish bazar, to the many medieval monasteries of Ohrid. Macedonia's fascinating blend of Orthodox mystery and the exotic Orient combine with the world-class beauty of Ohrid Lake to make the country much more than just a transit route on the way to somewhere else.

Facts about the Country

HISTORY

Historical Macedonia (from whence Alexander the Great set out to conquer the ancient world in the 4th century BC) is today contained mostly in present Greece, a point Greeks are always quick to make when discussing contemporary Macedonia's use of that name. The Romans subjugated the Greeks of ancient Macedonia and the territory to the north in the mid-2nd century BC, and when the empire was divided in the 4th century AD this region became part of the Eastern Roman Empire ruled from Constantinople. Slav tribes settled here in the 7th century, changing the ethnic character of the area.

In the 9th century the region was conquered by the Bulgarian tsar Simeon (893-927) and later under Tsar Samuel (980-1014), Macedonia was the centre of a powerful Bulgarian state. Samuel's defeat by Byzantium in 1014

ushered in a long period when Macedonia passed back and forth between Byzantium, Bulgaria and Serbia. After the crushing defeat of Serbia by the Turks in 1389, the Balkans became part of the Ottoman Empire and the cultural character of the region again changed.

In 1878 Russia defeated Turkey, and Macedonia was ceded to Bulgaria by the Treaty of San Stefano. The Western powers, fearing the creation of a powerful Russian satellite in the heart of the Balkans, forced Bulgaria to give Macedonia back to Turkey.

In 1893 Macedonian nationalists formed the Internal Macedonian Revolutionary Organisation (IMRO) to fight for independence from Turkey, culminating in the Ilinden uprising of May 1903 which was brutally suppressed three months later. Although nationalist leader Goce Delčev died before the revolt he has become the symbol of Macedonian nationalism.

The First Balkan War in 1912 brought Greece, Serbia and Bulgaria together against Turkey. In the Second Balkan War in 1913 Greece and Serbia ousted the Bulgarians and

split Macedonia between themselves. Frustrated by this result IMRO continued the struggle against royalist Serbia; the interwar government in Belgrade responded by banning the Macedonian language and even the name Macedonia. Though some IMRO elements supported the Bulgarian occupation of Macedonia during WWII, many more joined Tito's partisans, and in 1943 it was agreed that postwar Macedonia would have full republic status in future Yugoslavia. The first Macedonian grammar was published in 1952 and an independent Macedonian Orthodox Church was allowed to form. By recognising Macedonians as an ethnic group distinct from both Serbs and Bulgarians, the Belgrade authorities hoped to weaken Bulgarian claims to Macedonia.

On 8 September 1991 a referendum on independence was held in Macedonia and 74% voted in favour, so in January 1992 the country declared its full independence from former Yugoslavia. For once Belgrade cooperated by ordering all federal troops present to withdraw and, because the split was peaceful, road and rail links were never broken. In mid-1993, however, about 1000 United Nations troops were sent to Macedonia to monitor the border with Yugoslavia, especially near the potentially volatile province of Kosovo.

Greece delayed diplomatic recognition of Macedonia by demanding that the country find another name, alleging that the term Macedonia implied territorial claims on northern Greece. The concern of Greece is that if the Macedonians use the term Macedonia they may aspire to greater de facto legitimacy to the ambit of ancient Macedonia, which included (and still includes) a large part of Greece. At the insistence of Greek officials, Macedonia was forced to use the absurd 'temporary' title FYROM (Former Yugoslav Republic of Macedonia) for the purpose of being admitted to the UN in April 1993. After vacillating for two years, six of the European Union (EU) countries established diplomatic relations with FYROM in December 1993 despite strong objections from Greece, and in February 1994 the USA also recognised FYROM. At this, Greece declared an economic embargo against Macedonia and closed the port of Thessaloniki to the country's trade. The embargo was lifted in November 1995 after Macedonia changed its flag and agreed to enter into discussions with Greece about the name of the country. Shortly after these decisions were made, president Kiro Gligorov was almost assassinated in a car-bombing. To date, no final resolution of this thorny issue has been arrived at. Macedonia is in the process of seeking possible accession to the EU in the future.

GEOGRAPHY

Much of 25,713-sq-km Macedonia is a plateau between 600 and 900 metres high. The Vardar River cuts across the middle of the country, passing the capital, Skopje, on its way to the Aegean Sea near Thessaloniki. Ohrid and Prespa lakes in the south-west drain into the Adriatic via Albania. These lakes are among the largest on the Balkan Peninsula, and Ohrid Lake is also the deepest (294 metres compared to Prespa Lake's 35 metres). In the north-west the Šar Planina marks Macedonia's border with Kosovo; Titov vrh (2748 metres) in this range is Macedonia's highest peak. The country's three national parks are Pelister (west of Bitola), Galičica (between Ohrid and Prespa lakes) and Mavrovo (between Ohrid and Tetovo).

ECONOMY

Macedonia is a rich agricultural area which feeds itself and exports tomatoes and cucumbers to Western Europe. Cereals, rice, cotton and tobacco are also grown and Macedonian mines yield chromium, manganese, tungsten, lead and zinc. The main north-south trade route from Western Europe to Greece via the valleys of the Danube, Morava and Vardar rivers passes through the country. Tourism is concentrated around Lake Ohrid. At present Macedonia is gradually recovering its economic equilibrium after the lifting of UN sanctions against Yugoslavia, which together with Greece, had provided the ports and land routes for Macedonia's trade. Economic relations with Greece, though not what they once were, are slowly improving.

With the changes in Eastern Europe and especially with the separation of Macedonia from Yugoslavia, a new east-west trading route is developing from Turkey to Italy via Bulgaria, Macedonia and Albania. Over the next decade US$2.5 billion is to be invested in a new railway and motorway corridor linking Sofia, Skopje and Tirana. At present this route is covered only by narrow secondary roads, a legacy of the political policies of former regimes.

Since the late 1960s, tens of thousands of Macedonians have emigrated, and remittances from the 100,000 Macedonians now resident in Germany and Switzerland are a major source of income.

POPULATION & PEOPLE

Of the republic's present population of over two million, 66% are Macedonian Slavs who bear no relation whatsoever to the Greek-speaking Macedonians of antiquity. The Macedonian language is much closer to Bulgarian than to Serbian and many ethnographers consider the Macedonians ethnic Bulgarians. The official position of the Bulgarian government is that Macedonians are Bulgarians, though only a minority of Macedonians support this view.

The largest minority groups are ethnic Albanians (22%), Turks (4%), Serbs (2%), Gypsies (2%) and others (4%). The birth rate of the mostly rural Albanians is three times the national average. Albanians are in a majority in the region between Tetovo and Debar in the north-west of the republic and there have been demonstrations in defence of the right to education in Albanian.

The 50,000 Macedonians living in northern Greece are subject to assimilatory pressures by the Greek government, which calls them 'Slavophone Greeks'. Education in Macedonian is denied and human rights groups such as Helsinki Watch have documented many cases of police harassment of Greek Macedonians who publicly protested against these policies.

ARTS
Music
In Macedonian folk music the drone of the *gajda* (bagpipes) and chords of the *tambura* (two-stringed lute) provide a background for the *kaval* (flute) and *tapan* (cylindrical drum).

Folk Dancing

The most famous and popular Macedonian folk dance is '*Teškoto*' (The Hard One). It is a male dance for which music is provided by the *tapan* (a huge Macedonian drum) and the *zurla* (large pipes). It starts very slowly and gets progressively faster. The finale is dynamic and beautiful to watch.

During the dance, many things take place simultaneously. The dance leader might climb on the tapan, for example. This dance symbolises the national awakening of the Macedonian people and is performed with dancers dressed in traditional Macedonian costumes.

There are many other very interesting folk dances, like the Komitsko, the Osogovka and the Tresenica, a women's dance from the Mariovo region.

CULTURE

Macedonians are a proud and hospitable people and welcome visitors. If invited out for a meal, it is assumed that your host will pay for you. Insist on contributing if you must, but don't overdo it. Show respect to your hosts by learning a few words of Macedonian. Be aware that churches and mosques are not built for tourists, but are working places of worship. Dress and behave accordingly. Tread carefully when talking politics, especially about Greeks and Albanians.

RELIGION

Most of the Albanians and Turks are Muslim, while the Slavs are Orthodox.

LANGUAGE

Macedonian is a South Slavic language divided into two large groups, the western and eastern Macedonian dialects. The Macedonian literary language is based on the central dialects of Veles, Prilep and Bitola. Macedonian shares all the characteristics which separate Bulgarian from the other Slavic languages, evidence that it's closely related to Bulgarian.

The Cyrillic alphabet is based on the alphabet developed by two Thessaloniki brothers, St Cyril and St Methodius, in the 9th century. It was taught by their disciples at a monastery in Ohrid, Macedonia, from whence it spread across the eastern Slavic world.

The Cyrillic alphabet is used predominantly in Macedonia. Street names are printed in Cyrillic script only, so it is imperative that you learn the Cyrillic alphabet if you don't want to get lost. Road signs use both Cyrillic and Latin scripts.

Lonely Planet's *Mediterranean Europe Phrasebook* contains a complete chapter on Macedonian with Cyrillic spellings provided. For a quick introduction to Macedonian, see the Language Guide at the end of the book.

Facts for the Visitor

PLANNING
Climate & When to Go

Macedonia's summers are hot and dry. In winter, warm Aegean winds blowing up the Vardar Valley moderate the continental conditions prevailing further north. However Macedonia receives a lot of snowfall, even if temperatures are warmer than those further north.

Books & Maps

A couple of good background books are *Who Are the Macedonians?* by Hugh Poulton, a political and cultural history of the region, and *Black Lamb and Grey Falcon* by Rebecca West, a between-the-wars Balkan travelogue.

Baedeker's Greece map also covers Macedonia. In Macedonia you should be able to get hold of the excellent *Republic of Macedonia* map, published by GiziMap of Hungary.

Online Services

A couple of useful World Wide Web sites are at http://www.duc.auburn.edu/mitrege/macedonia (*Macedonia Information Almanac*), and at http://www.isc.rit.edu/bvs4997/Macedonia (*Virtual Macedonia*). Both sites have useful background and practical information.

What to Bring

You can find most things in Macedonia, but do bring along a universal sink plug since hotels rarely have them.

SUGGESTED ITINERARIES

Depending on the length of your stay, you might want to see and do the following things in Macedonia:

Two days

Visit Skopje.

One week

Visit Skopje and Ohrid.

Two weeks

As above, plus some hiking in Pelister and Galičica national parks between Ohrid and Bitola.

HIGHLIGHTS

The Byzantine monasteries of Ohrid, particularly Sveti Sofija and Sveti Kliment, are worth a visit. Lake Ohrid itself is simply beautiful. The Čaršija (old Turkish bazar) in Skopje is very colourful.

TOURIST OFFICES

Makedonijaturist (☎ 115 051), based in the Hotel Turist in Skopje, is the state tourist organisation. Private agencies are also appearing on the scene.

VISAS & EMBASSIES
Visas

British and Yugoslav passport-holders require no visa. Canadians, Americans and Australians need a visa but it's issued free of charge at the border.

Foreign Embassies in Macedonia

The following embassies are in Skopje:

Albania

ulica Tome Arsovski (☎ 115 878; fax 226 459).

Bulgaria

ulica Zlatko Snajder 3 (☎ 229 444; fax 116 139); open weekdays from 9 am to noon.

UK

Veljko Vlahovic 26 (☎ 116 772); open weekdays from 10 am to 4 pm.

USA

Bulevar Ilinden(☎ 116 180; fax 117 103); open weekdays from 10 am to 4 pm.

Visa requirements and costs for travellers from all nearby countries change frequently, so check with the embassies in question.

CUSTOMS

Customs checks are generally cursory. They may be interested, however, if you are carrying a video camera – especially if you haven't declared it on entry.

MONEY

Macedonian denar (MKD) banknotes come in denominations of 10, 20, 50, 100 and 500 and there are coins of one, two and five denari. The denar is now a stable currency, but outside Macedonia the denar is worthless.

Travellers' cheques can be changed into Macedonian denari at most banks with no commission deducted. Small private exchange offices can be found throughout central Skopje and Ohrid and the rate they offer is generally good.

Conversion rates for major currencies in mid-1996 are listed below:

Exchange Rates

Australia	A$1	=	29MKD
Canada	C$1	=	32MKD
Germany	DM1	=	27MKD
United Kingdom	UK£1	=	61MKD
United States	US$1	=	39MKD

For up-to-date currency rates of the Macedonian denar, point your Web browser at: gopher://gopher.undp.org:70/00/uncurr/exch rates.

POST & COMMUNICATIONS
Post

Mail addressed c/o Poste Restante, 91000 Skopje 2, Macedonia, can be claimed at the post office next to Skopje train station, weekdays from 8 am to 1 pm.

Mail addressed c/o Poste Restante, 96000 Ohrid, Macedonia, can be picked up at Ohrid's main post office near the bus station.

Telephone

Long-distance phone calls cost less at main post offices, far more at hotels. To call Macedonia from abroad dial the international access code, ☎ 389 (the country code for Macedonia), the area code (without the initial zero) and the number. Area codes include ☎ 091 (Skopje), ☎ 096 (Ohrid) and ☎ 097 (Bitola). For outgoing calls the international access code in Macedonia is ☎ 99. Phonecard phones are now available in major centres. You can purchase phonecards, in 100 or 200-unit denominations, from post offices.

E-mail

Macedonia is connected to the Internet. You could e-mail the Open Society Foundation of Macedonia (vmilcin@soros.mk) for more

MACEDONIA

information. A number of private Internet service providers operate in Skopje, but there are no Internet cafés to date.

NEWSPAPERS & MAGAZINES

There are three local Macedonian-language papers, along with an Albanian and a Turkish daily. English-language papers can be bought at most central kiosks. There is also an English-language monthly called *Skopsko Metro* that you may be able to find at tourist locations.

RADIO & TV

You have a choice of two state TV stations and any number of private and satellite channels, including CNN, Eurosport and MTV. There are many local FM radio stations.

TIME

Macedonia goes on daylight-saving time at the end of March when clocks are turned one hour ahead. On the last Sunday of September they're turned back an hour. Bulgaria and Greece are always one hour ahead of Macedonia while Yugoslavia and Albania keep the same time as Skopje.

ELECTRICITY

Macedonia uses 220V AC, 50 Hz. A circular plug with two round pins is used.

WEIGHTS & MEASURES

Macedonia uses the metric system.

HEALTH

Basic health services are available free to travellers from state health centres. Health insurance to cover private health services is recommended.

WOMEN TRAVELLERS

Women travellers should feel no particular concern about travel in Macedonia. Other than possible cursory interest from men, travel is hassle-free and easy.

GAY & LESBIAN TRAVELLERS

Macedonia has a strange policy on homosexuality. Lesbians enjoy legal status but gay men do not. Prison terms of up to one year apply.

DISABLED TRAVELLERS

Few public buildings or streets have facilities for wheelchairs. Access could be problematic.

DANGERS & ANNOYANCES

Macedonia is a safe country in general. Travellers should be on the lookout for pickpockets in bus and train stations and exercise common sense in looking after belongings.

BUSINESS HOURS

Office and business hours are 8 am to 8 pm weekdays, 8 am to 2 pm on Saturday.

PUBLIC HOLIDAYS & SPECIAL EVENTS

Public holidays in Macedonia are New Year (1 and 2 January), Orthodox Christmas (7 January), Old New Year (13 January), Easter Monday and Tuesday (March/April), Labour Day (1 May), Ilinden or Day of the 1903 Rebellion (2 August), Republic Day (8 September and 1941 Partisan Day (11 October).

ACTIVITIES

Macedonia's top ski resort is Popova šapka (1845 metres) on the southern slopes of Šar Planina west of Tetovo. Hiking in any of the three national parks is a good way to get to know the countryside, but there do not seem to be organised outings for visitors.

ACCOMMODATION

Macedonia's hotels are very expensive but there are camping grounds and private-room agencies in Ohrid and Skopje. Skopje's convenient hostel is open throughout the year, and the Ohrid hostel opens in summer. Beds are available at student dormitories in Skopje in summer.

FOOD

Turkish-style grilled mincemeat is available almost everywhere and there are self-service cafeterias in most towns for the less adventurous. Balkan *burek* (cheese or meat pie) and yoghurt makes for a cheap breakfast. Watch for Macedonian *gravče na tavče* (beans in skillet) and Ohrid trout, which is priced according to weight.

Getting There & Away

AIR

With the demise of JAT Yugoslav Airlines a number of local carriers have emerged offering direct flights from Skopje to cities in Germany and Switzerland. Companies like Avioimpex and Palair cater mostly to Mace-donians resident in those countries. Some sample discount fares from Skopje are: Amsterdam 13,500 MKD; Düsseldorf 10,800 MKD (with Palair Macedonian); Ljubljana 5460 MKD; and Vienna 9750 MKD (with Avioimpex).

Any travel agent in Skopje or Ohrid can book these flights. Mata Travel (☎ 239 175), next to the international bus station, or Marco Polo Travel (☎ 222 340) at ulica Maksim Gorki are two agencies that you may like to approach.

LAND

Bus

The international bus station in Skopje is next to the City Museum. Mata Travel Agency (☎ 239 175; fax 230 269), at the international bus station, has buses to Sofia (twice daily, 216 km, 6½ hours, 450 MKD), Tirana (daily, 9½ hours, 840 MKD), İstanbul (four daily, 16 hours, 1150 MKD), Belgrade (daily, 5½ hours, 1050 MKD) and Munich (twice weekly, 27 hours, 4020 MKD).

To/from Croatia you must transit Belgrade and Hungary. Ask about overnight buses from Skopje to Belgrade and Podgorica. Buses between Skopje and Prizren in Kosovo, Yugoslavia (117 km), are fairly frequent. To/from Albania you can travel between Skopje and Tirana by bus or walk across the border at Sveti Naum (see the Ohrid section).

Train

Express trains run five times a day between Skopje and Belgrade (472 km, seven hours, 1125 MKD), via Niš. Sleepers are available on the overnight Skopje-Belgrade train. Trains run twice a day between Skopje and Thessaloniki.

Sample 2nd-class international train fares from Skopje are 500 MKD to Thessaloniki (285 km, five hours), 1310 MKD to Athens (795 km, 14 hours), 3050 MKD to Budapest (15 hours) and 4000 MKD to Vienna (20 hours).

Greece-bound, it's cheaper to buy a ticket only to Thessaloniki and get another on to Athens from there. There's no direct rail link between Macedonia and Bulgaria and the train is not recommended for travel between Sofia and Skopje as you must change trains in Yugoslavia and a visa will be required.

All the timetables and arrivals/departures boards at Skopje train station are in Cyrillic script only. For information in English go upstairs to Feroturist Travel Agency (open daily 7 am to 8.30 pm), which also sells international train tickets and books sleepers to Belgrade.

Car & Motorcycle

There are several main highway border crossings into Macedonia from neighbouring countries.

Yugoslavia You can cross at Blace (between Skopje and Uroševac) and Tabanovce (10 km north of Kumanovo).

Bulgaria The main crossings are Kriva Palanka (between Sofia and Skopje), Delčevo (26 km west of Blagoevgrad) and Novo Selo (between Kulata and Strumica).

Greece There are crossings at Gevgelija (between Skopje and Thessaloniki), Dojran (just east of Gevgelija) and Medžitlija (16 km south of Bitola).

Albania The crossings are Sveti Naum (29 km south of Ohrid), Ćafa San (12 km south-west of Struga) and Blato (five km north-west of Debar).

LEAVING MACEDONIA

The airport departure tax at Skopje and Ohrid is 470 MKD.

Getting Around

BUS

Bus travel is well developed in Macedonia with fairly frequent services from Skopje to

Ohrid and Bitola. Always book buses to/from Ohrid well in advance.

TRAIN

You won't find Macedonia's trains of much use, except perhaps for the overnight train from Skopje to Belgrade and trains to Greece. The local train from Skopje to Bitola takes four hours to cover 229 km. There is also a local service from Skopje to Kičevo.

CAR & MOTORCYCLE

Petrol coupons (the cheaper way of paying for petrol) can be purchased at the border crossings with Yugoslavia and Greece 24 hours a day (payment in cash Deutschmarks only). During business hours (weekdays from 7 am to 3 pm) coupons can also be purchased at Automoto Sojuz offices in Bitola, Gevgelija, Gostivar, Kavadarci, Kičevo, Kočani, Kumanovo, Prilep, Ohrid, Skopje, Štip, Strumica, Tetovo and Veles. The regulations surrounding petrol coupons change frequently, so check at the border.

Motorway tolls can be paid either in cash or with coupons purchased at the border.

Speed limits for cars and motorcycles are 120 km/h on motorways, 80 km/h on open roads and from 50 to 60 km/h in towns. Speeding fines are high (1400 MKD) and inflexibly enforced by radar-equipped highway police, so never speed! Parking tickets average 1600 MKD and wearing a seatbelt is compulsory.

The Macedonia-wide number for emergency highway assistance is ☎ 987.

Around the Country

SKOPJE (СКОПЈЕ)

Macedonia's capital, Skopje (population 600,000), is strategically set on the Vardar River at a crossroads of Balkan routes almost exactly midway between Tirana and Sofia, capitals of neighbouring Albania and Bulgaria. Thessaloniki, Greece, is 260 km south-east, near the point where the Vardar flows into the Aegean. The Romans recognised the location's importance long ago when they made Scupi the centre of-Dardania Province. Later conquerors included the Slavs, Byzantines, Bulgarians,

Normans and Serbs, until the Turks arrived in 1392 and managed to hold onto Uskup (Skopje) until 1912.

After a devastating earthquake in 1963 which killed 1066 people, aid poured in from the rest of Yugoslavia to create the modern urban landscape we see today. It's evident that the planners got carried away by the money being thrown their way, erecting oversized, irrelevant structures which are now crumbling due to lack of maintenance and function. The post office building and telecommunications complex next to it are particularly hideous examples of this architectural overkill. Fortunately, much of the old town survived, so you can still get a glimpse of the old Skopje.

Orientation

Most of central Skopje is a pedestrian zone, with the 15th-century Turkish stone bridge over the Vardar River linking the old and new towns. South of the bridge is Ploštad Makedonija (the former Ploštad Maršal Tito), which gives into ulica Maršal Tito leading south. The new railway station is a 15-minute walk south-east of the stone bridge. The old railway station, with its clock frozen at the moment the 1963 earthquake struck, is now the home of the City Museum and is at the south end of ulica Maršal Tito. The bus station is just over the stone bridge. Further north is Čaršija, the old Turkish bazar.

The left-luggage office at the bus station is open from 5 am to 10 pm. Each item left costs 40 MKD. Left luggage at the train station is open 24 hours.

Information

Tourist Offices The tourist information office is opposite the Daud Pasha Baths on the viaduct between the Turkish bridge and Čaršija. There is also a small tourist booth outside the railway station.

The office of the Automoto Sojuz or Automobile Club of Macedonia (☎ 116 011) is at Ivo Ribar Lola 51 just west of the downtown area. Petrol coupons are available here.

Money The Stopanska Banka facing the Turkish bridge opposite the bus station changes travellers' cheques on weekdays from 7 am to 7 pm, on Saturday from 7 am to 1 pm

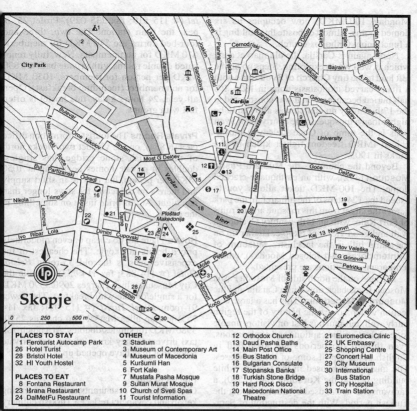

PLACES TO STAY
1 Feroturist Autocamp Park
26 Hotel Turist
28 Bristol Hotel
32 HI Youth Hostel

PLACES TO EAT
8 Fontana Restaurant
23 Išrana Restaurant
24 DalMetFu Restaurant

OTHER
2 Stadium
3 Museum of Contemporary Art
4 Museum of Macedonia
5 Kuršumli Han
6 Fort Kale
7 Mustafa Pasha Mosque
9 Sultan Murat Mosque
10 Church of Sveti Spas
11 Tourist Information

12 Orthodox Church
13 Daud Pasha Baths
14 Main Post Office
15 Bus Station
16 Bulgarian Consulate
17 Stopanska Banka
18 Turkish Stone Bridge
19 Hard Rock Disco
20 Macedonian National
   Theatre

21 Euromedica Clinic
22 UK Embassy
25 Shopping Centre
27 Concert Hall
29 City Museum
30 International
   Bus Station
31 City Hospital
33 Train Station

MACEDONIA

There are many private exchange offices scattered throughout the old and new towns where you can change your cash at a good rate.

Post & Communications Poste-restante mail is held at the train station post office, not the main post office. The telephone centre in the main post office near the city centre is open 24 hours. Skopje's telephone code is ☎ 091.

Travel Agencies Mata Travel Agency (☎ 239 175; fax 230 269) is at the international bus station next to the City Museum. Feroturist

Travel Agency (daily 7 am to 8.30 pm) is upstairs in the Skopje railway station.

Medical & Emergency Services The city hospital (☎ 221 133) is on the corner of ulica 11 Oktomvri and Moše Pijade. The Euromedica private clinic is just off ulica Veljno Vlahivič, near the British Embassy.

Things to See
As you walk north from the Turkish bridge you'll see the **Daud Pasha Baths** (1466) on the right, once the largest Turkish baths in the Balkans. The **City Art Gallery** (closed on

Monday, 100 MKD) now occupies its six domed rooms. Almost opposite this building is a functioning Orthodox church.

North again is Čaršija, the old market area, which is well worth exploring. Steps up on the left lead to the tiny **Church of Sveti Spas** with a finely carved iconostasis done in 1824. It's half buried because when it was constructed in the 17th century no church was allowed to be higher than a mosque. In the courtyard at Sveti Spas is the tomb of Goce Delčev, a mustachioed IMRO freedom fighter killed by the Turks in 1903.

Beyond the church is the **Mustafa Pasha Mosque** (1492), with an earthquake-cracked dome. The 100-MKD ticket allows you to ascend the 124 steps of the minaret. In the park across the street from this mosque are the ruins of **Fort Kale**, with an 11th-century Cyclopean wall and good views of Skopje. Higher up on the same hill is the lacklustre **Museum of Contemporary Art** (closed Monday), where temporary exhibitions are presented.

The lane on the north side of Mustafa Pasha Mosque leads back down into Čaršija and the **Museum of Macedonia**. This has a large collection which covers the history of the region fairly well, but much is lost on visitors unable to read the Cyrillic captions and explanations, even though the periods are identified in English at the top of some of the showcases. The museum is housed in the modern white building behind the **Kuršumli Han** (1550), a caravanserai or inn used by traders during the Turkish period. With the destruction of Sarajevo, Skopje's old Oriental bazaar district has become the largest and most colourful of its kind left in Europe.

Places to Stay

Camping From April to mid-October you can pitch a tent at *Feroturist Autocamp Park* (☎ 228 246) for 160 MKD per person and tent. Basic camping caravans are for hire year-round at 400 MKD per person. Late-night music from the restaurant can be a problem. This camping ground is between the river and the stadium, a 15-minute walk upstream from the Turkish stone bridge along the right (south) bank. It's always a good bet.

Hostels The HI *Dom Blagoj Šošolčev Hostel* (☎ 115 519; fax 235 029), Prolet 25, is near the train station. The two, three and four-bed dorms are 540 MKD for members, 610 MKD for nonmembers. New, fully renovated double rooms with private bath are 830 MKD per person for members, 1050 MKD for nonmembers (including breakfast). Open all year, 24 hours a day, this hostel is often full with groups.

Private Rooms The tourist information office (☎ 116 854), on the viaduct two blocks north of the Turkish stone bridge, has singles/doubles in private homes beginning at 1050 MKD per person, but they're in short supply and there's no reduction for stays longer than one night. At this price insist on something in the centre.

Hotels There are no cheap or even moderately priced hotels in Skopje. The cheapest of the expensive ones is the old 33-room *Bristol Hotel* (☎ 114 883; fax 114 753) opposite the City Museum which charges 2690/3590 MKD for a single/double with breakfast. The newer 91-room *Hotel Turist* (☎ 115 051; fax 114 753) just up ulica Maršal Tito charges 2570/3980 MKD for singles/doubles. At a pinch, ask taxi drivers if they know of any new private hotels that may have opened up.

Places to Eat

Colourful small restaurants in Čaršija serving kebab and čevapčiči reflect a Turkish culinary heritage still dear to the stomachs of many Macedonians. Try the *Fontana* restaurant. It is on a little square with a fountain in the Čaršija. The food is good and the atmosphere is great.

There are two easy-to-find restaurants in the modern city centre beyond Ploštad Makedonija on the south side of the Turkish stone bridge. The *DalMetFu Restaurant* is fairly obvious across the square at the beginning of ulica Maršal Tito, on the left as you come from the bridge. This place is good for pizza and pasta. *Išrana Self-Service* is half a block away down the next street over to the right. Look for the vertical sign reading 'Restaurant' in large blue letters.

There is also a nice restaurant in the basement of the youth hostel (see Places to Stay) which is open to the public.

Entertainment

Check the concert hall, ulica Maršal Tito 12, for performances. *Hard Rock*, facing the river behind the Academy of Sciences, is a large modern discotheque which opens nightly, except Monday, at 10 pm during the school year (closed July and August).

Club MNT, downstairs below the Macedonian National Theatre, also cranks up around 10 pm and is open in summer. The *Park Disco* at the stadium is another hot spot.

Getting There & Away

Bus There are buses to Ohrid, Bitola, Priština, Prizren, Peć, Podgorica and Belgrade. Book a seat on the bus of your choice the day before, especially if you're headed for Ohrid Lake. There are two bus routes from Skopje to Ohrid Lake: the one through Tetovo (167 km) is much faster and more direct than the bus that goes via Veles and Bitola (261 km). If you just want to get to the Adriatic from Skopje, catch the overnight bus to Podgorica in Montenegro (382 km).

If for some reason you can't take the direct bus to Sofia (see the Getting There & Away section earlier this chapter) there are 12 buses daily to Kriva Palanka (96 km), 13 km short of the Bulgarian border. Onward hitching should be possible.

Train All trains between central Europe and Greece pass through Skopje. There are two daily trains to/from Thessaloniki (285 km, five hours, 500 MKD) and Athens (795 km, 14 hours, 1310 MKD one way).

Several trains run to Belgrade (472 km, seven hours, 1125 MKD), and local trains run to Bitola (229 km, four hours) and, for what it's worth, Kičevo. Couchettes are available to Belgrade. Feroturist Travel Agency upstairs in the Skopje railway station sells international tickets and books couchettes and sleepers (700 MKD).

Getting Around

To/From the Airport There are 11 special airport buses daily which all pick up at the international bus station as well as major hotels. A ticket costs 100 MKD. Agree on a price if you take a taxi.

Bus City buses in Skopje use tokens (getone) which you must buy at kiosks at major stops.

OHRID (ОХРИД)

Ohrid Lake, a natural tectonic lake in the southwest corner of Macedonia, is the deepest lake in Europe (294 metres) and one of the oldest in the world. A third of its 450-sq-km surface area belongs to Albania. Nestled amid mountains at an altitude of 695 metres, the Macedonian section of the lake is the more beautiful, with striking vistas of the water from the beach and hills.

The town of Ohrid is *the* Macedonian tourist mecca and is popular with visitors from the Netherlands. Some 30 'cultural monuments' in the area keep visitors busy. Predictably, the oldest ruins readily seen today are Roman. Lihnidos (Ohrid) was on the Via Egnatia, which connected the Adriatic to the Aegean, and part of a Roman amphitheatre has been uncovered in the old town.

Under Byzantium Ohrid became the episcopal centre of Macedonia. The first Slavic university was founded here in 893 by Bishop Kliment of Ohrid, a disciple of St Cyril and St Methodius, and from the 10th century until 1767 the patriarchate of Ohrid held sway. The revival of the archbishopric of Ohrid in 1958 and its independence from the Serbian Orthodox Church in 1967 were important steps on the road to modern nationhood.

Many of the small Orthodox churches with intact medieval frescos have now been adapted to the needs of ticketed tourists. Nice little signs in Latin script direct you to the sights, but even these tourist touches don't spoil the flavour of enchanting Ohrid.

Orientation

Ohrid bus station is next to the post office in the centre of town. To the west is the old town and to the south is the lake.

The left-luggage office at the bus station is open from 5 am to 8.20 pm daily. Ask at the ticket windows.

Information

Tourist Offices Biljana tourist office is at Partizanska 3 in front of the bus station.

Automoto Sojuz (☎ 22 338) is on Galičica at Lazo Trpkoski, both backstreets behind the large 'Mini Market' on the corner of Jane

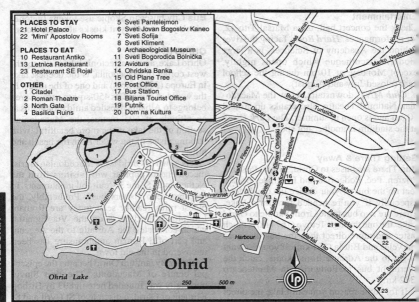

PLACES TO STAY
21 Hotel Palace
22 'Mimi' Apostolov Rooms

PLACES TO EAT
10 Restaurant Antiko
13 Letnica Restaurant
23 Restaurant SE Rojal

OTHER
1 Citadel
2 Roman Theatre
3 North Gate
4 Basilica Ruins

5 Sveti Pantelejmon
6 Sveti Jovan Bogoslov Kaneo
7 Sveti Sofija
8 Sveti Kliment
9 Archaeological Museum
11 Sveti Bogorodica Bolnička
12 Avioturs
14 Ohridska Banka
15 Old Plane Tree
16 Post Office
17 Bus Station
18 Biljana Tourist Office
19 Putnik
20 Dom na Kultura

Ohrid

Ohrid Lake

Sandanski and Bulevar Turistička, a major
intersection on the east side of town.

Money The Ohridska Banka agency, on Sveti
Kliment Ohridski mall (Monday to Saturday
from 8 am to 8 pm, Sunday 7 am to 1 pm),
changes travellers' cheques and cash without
commission. Travel agencies often exchange
cash as well.

Post & Communications The telephone
centre at the post office near the bus station is
open Monday to Saturday from 7 am to 9 pm,
and Sunday from 9 am to noon and 6 to 8 pm.
Phonecard phones are located outside the post
office. Ohrid's telephone code is ☎ 096.

Travel Agencies Putnik, Partizanska 2 opposite the bus station, sells train and plane tickets.

Things to See
The picturesque old town of Ohrid rises from
Sveti Kliment Ohridski, the main pedestrian

mall, up towards Sveti Kliment Church and the
citadel. A medieval town wall still isolates this
hill from the surrounding valley. Penetrate the
old town on Car Samoil as far as the **Archaeological Museum** in the four-storey dwelling of
the Robevu family (1827) at No 62. Admission
is 100 MKD. Further along Car Samuil is
11th-century **Sveti Sofija**, also worth the
100/50 MKD (full/student) admission price.
Aside from the frescos there's an unusual
Turkish *mimbar* (pulpit) remaining from the
days when this was a mosque, and an upstairs
portico with a photo display of the extensive
restoration work. An English-speaking guide
is on hand to fill you in.

From near here ulica Ilindenska climbs to
the North Gate, to the right of which is the
13th-century **Church of Sveti Kliment**, (100
MKD admission), almost covered inside with
vividly restored frescos of biblical scenes. An
icon gallery is opposite this church and there's
a fine view from the terrace. The walls of the
10th-century **citadel** to the west offer more
splendid views.

In the park below the citadel are the ruins of an Early Christian **basilica** with 5th-century mosaics covered by protective sand, and nearby is the shell of **Sveti Pantelejmon**, now a small museum. The tiny 13th-century **Church of Sveti Jovan Bogoslov Kaneo**, on a point overlooking the lake, occupies a very pleasant site. There's a beach at the foot of the cliffs and in summer young men perform death-defying leaps into the water from the clifftop above the lake. All churches and museums at Ohrid are open daily, except Monday, from 9 am to 3 pm with a morning break from 10.30 to 11 am.

The better part of a second day at Ohrid could be spent on a pilgrimage to the Albanian border to see the 17th-century **Church of Sveti Naum** on a hill above the lake, 29 km south of Ohrid by bus. From here you get a view of the Albanian town of Pogradec across the lake and inside the church is a finely carved iconostasis.

In summer you can also come by boat but it only leaves when a group is present; ask about times at the Putnik office opposite the bus station at the wharf the day before. The fare is 100 MKD each way). The mountains east of Ohrid Lake, between it and Prespa Lake, are included in Galičica National Park.

There's frequent bus service from Ohrid to **Struga**. This small Macedonian town at the northern end of the lake is divided by the Crni Drim River, which drains Ohrid Lake into the Adriatic near Shkodra, Albania. On Saturday there's a large market at Struga. Each year at the end of August, poets converge on Struga for an international festival of poetry.

Special Events

The Balkan Festival of Folk Dances & Songs, held at Ohrid in early July, draws folkloric groups from around the Balkans. The Ohrid Summer Festival, held from mid-July to mid-August, features classical concerts in the Church of Sveti Sofija as well as many other events.

Places to Stay

Camping The *Autocamp Gradište* (☎ 22 578), open from June to mid-September, is halfway to Sveti Naum. A secluded nudist beach is nearby. There's also *Autocamp Sveti Naum* (☎ 58 811) two km north of the monastery of the same name. Both camp sites are accessible on the Sveti Naum bus. Just between the Albanian border and Sveti Naum monastery is *Camp Vasko Karandžgleski* (open in July and August only). The caravans here are booked well ahead but you should be able to pitch a tent. The location is good, with a beach nearby and boat service to/from Ohrid in summer.

Private Rooms Private rooms are your best bet at Ohrid as the camping grounds and hostel are far from town and the hotels are pricey. Private rooms from the Biljana tourist office (☎ & fax 24 114), Partizanska 3, beside the bus station, cost 390 MKD per person (three nights or less) plus 39 MKD per person per day tax. Women who unofficially rent private rooms often wait just outside the Biljana office. Popular with the Tirana diplomatic community, *'Mimi' Apostolov Rooms* (☎ & fax 31 549) at ulica Strašo Pinđura 2 has several rooms with phone and TV for 590 MKD.

Other private rooms are available from Putnik (☎ 32 025) opposite the bus station; Avioturs (☎ & fax 32 110) on Kosta Abraš; or Palasturist (☎ 25 025) on Sveti Kliment Ohridski.

Hostels & Hotels The HI *Mladost Hostel* (☎ 21 626) is located on the lakeside a little over two km west of Ohrid, towards Struga. A bed in a dorm or a small four-berth caravan will cost around 230 MKD per person. Even if all the caravans are full they'll let you pitch a tent for 80 MKD per person, 120 MKD per tent (and 40 MKD per person tax).

The hostel is open from April to mid-October and YHA membership cards are not essential. In midsummer it will be full of children. Get there on the Struga bus (15 MKD) or, if you're walking, turn left after the fifth minaret, counting from the one opposite the old plane tree at the top of Sveti Kliment Ohridski.

Mladinski Centar-Hotel Magnus (☎ 21 671; fax 34 214), a modern hotel next to the hostel, charges 500 MKD per person in two or three-bed rooms, including three meals daily, provided you have a hostel card. Without the card the price will be 30% higher. In midsummer they're booked solid, but as they're open all year it's worth trying other months. Expect to pay 1521/2340 MKD per night, including breakfast, for a single/double room at the fairly central *Hotel Palace* (☎ 22 030; fax 35 460) on Partizanska.

Places to Eat

There are a number of fast-food and pizza joints in the old town area, but the easiest place to eat at is the *Letnica Self-Service Restaurant* on Bulevar Makedonski Prosvetiteli not far from the little harbour. The food is reasonably good and cheap.

A very pleasant mid-range restaurant is the *SE Rojal* at Jane Sandanski 2, about 200 metres south-east along the lakefront. Despite its smart décor, a meal is very affordable. The smartest and most atmospheric eating place is the *Restaurant Antiko*, Car Samoil 30, in an old house in the old town. It is expensive and ordering Ohrid Lake trout will break the budget. Ask before ordering how much it will cost.

Entertainment

Ohrid's movie theatre is *Dom Na Kultura* at Grigor Prličev, facing the lakeside park. Various cultural events are also held here.

Getting There & Away

Air Palair has flights from Ohrid to Zürich (10,240 MKD) on weekends (summer only), Amsterdam (13,500 MKD) on Monday, and Düsseldorf (12,150 MKD) on Sunday.

Bus No less than 10 buses a day run between Ohrid and Skopje (167 km, three hours, 235 MKD), via Kičevo. Another six go via Bitola. The former route is much shorter, faster and more scenic, so try to take it. It pays to book a seat the day before.

There are six buses a day to Bitola (80 km, 1¼ hours, 115 MKD). Buses to Struga (seven km) leave about every 15 minutes from stand No 1 at the bus station (enter through the back doors and pay the conductor).

Serbia An overnight bus from Ohrid to Belgrade (694 km, 1380 MKD), via Kičevo, leaves Ohrid at 5.45 pm, reaching Belgrade 14 hours later. Another two buses go to Belgrade via Bitola, leaving at 5 am and 3.30 pm.

Albania To go to Albania catch a bus or boat to Sveti Naum monastery, which is very near

the border crossing. In summer there are six buses a day from Ohrid to Sveti Naum (29 km, 65 MKD), in winter three daily. The bus continues on to the border post. From Albanian customs it's six km to Pogradec but hitching is easy (and it's an interesting walk, if necessary).

Greece To get to Greece you can take a bus from Ohrid to Bitola (80 km), then hitch or take a taxi 16 km to the Medžitlija highway border crossing. It's much easier, however, to go to Skopje and pick up a train to Thessaloniki (500 MKD) from there. Coming from Greece, try to get a cross-border taxi from Florina to Bitola directly. This will cost about 7000 dr.

BITOLA (БИТОЛА)

Bitola, the southernmost city of former Yugoslavia and second largest in Macedonia, sits on a 660-metre-high plateau between mountains 16 km north of the Greek border. The old bazaar area (Stara Čaršija) is colourful but the facilities at Bitola are poor.

Private rooms are unavailable and the hotels overpriced. No left-luggage office is provided at either the bus or train stations and the city is useless as a transit point to/from Greece as there's no bus or train to the border (Medžitlija). You must hitch the 16 km, or take a taxi. Bus services to Ohrid (80 km) and Skopje (18 km), on the other hand, are good.

The bus and train station are adjacent to each other, about one km south of the town centre. It's probably not worth dragging your luggage into town just to see Bitola's Turkish mosque and bazar but the **Heraclea ruins** beyond the old cemetery, one km south of the bus/train stations, are recommended (admission 100 MKD, photos 500 MKD and video an exorbitant 1000 MKD extra). Founded in the 4th century BC by Philip II of Macedonia, Heraclea was conquered by the Romans two centuries later and became an important stage on the Via Egnatia. From the 4th to 6th centuries AD it was an episcopal seat. Excavations continue but the Roman baths, portico and theatre can now be seen. More interesting are the two Early Christian basilicas and the episcopal palace, complete with splendid mosaics. There's also a small museum through the refreshment stand, and a nice terrace on which to have a Coke or beer.

Malta

Malta, Gozo and Comino don't take up much space on the map, but their strategic position in the eastern Mediterranean between Sicily and Tunisia has for centuries made them irresistible to both navigators and invaders. The British were merely the last of a long series of colonisers to leave, but, as a result, most Maltese, and most of the tourists who visit the country, speak English. Due to the islands' varied colonial history, the Maltese have developed and retained a unique language and culture in which it is possible to detect Italian, Arabic, English, Jewish, French and Spanish influences.

Malta has long been regarded as an economical and cheerful destination for a beach holiday. The weather is excellent, food and accommodation are good value and the water is clean. However, the coastline is mainly rocky and the few sandy beaches are often crowded. The real highlights are the magnificent 16th-century fortified city of Valletta with its glorious harbour; the bustling Mediterranean life of the city with its lively cafés and bars; the stone villages with their precious baroque churches and exuberant *festas*; the astonishing prehistoric temples and archaeological finds; the beautiful, medieval fortress town of Mdina; and, if you want to get away from it all, the quiet island of Gozo.

Maltese language (Malti) is Semitic in origin and is believed to be based on Phoenician. The colourful Maltese fishing boats – *luzzu* and *dghajsa* – which have watchful eyes painted on the prow, are scarcely changed from the Phoenician trading vessels that once plied the Mediterranean.

After the Punic Wars between Rome and Carthage and the defeat of the Carthaginian general Hannibal in 208 BC, Malta became part of the Roman Empire. In 60 AD, St Paul – a prisoner en route to Rome – was shipwrecked on the island. According to tradition, he converted the islanders to Christianity.

Arabs from North Africa arrived in 870, but tolerated the local Christian population. They introduced citrus fruits and cotton, and had a notable impact on Maltese customs and language. The Arabs were expelled in 1090 by the Norman King Roger of Sicily. For the next 400 years Malta's history was linked to Sicily, and its rulers were a succession of Normans, Angevins (French), Aragonese and Castilians (Spanish). The relatively small population of

Facts about the Country

HISTORY

Malta has a fascinating history, and the island is crowded with physical and cultural reminders of the past. The island's oldest legacy is the beautifully preserved megalithic temples built between 3800 and 2500 BC, which are the oldest surviving free-standing structures in the world.

From around 800 to 218 BC, Malta was colonised by the Phoenicians and, for the last 150 years of this period, by Phoenicia's principal North African colony, Carthage. The

MALTA

GOZO

COMINO

Marsalforn
Ramla Bay
Nadur
Zebbug
Gharb
Xaghra
Ġgantija
Xewkija
VICTORIA
Xlendi
Sannat
Azure Window
Inland Sea &
Qawra
Dwejra Point
Mġarr
North Comino Channel
Mġarr Harbour
Same Scale as Main Map

St Thomas
Bay
St George's
Bay
Marsaxlokk
Birzebbuga

Balluta Bay
Marsamxett Harbour
Grand Harbour
St Julian's
Sliema
Paceville
Gzira
Ta' Xbiex
VALLETTA
Vittoriosa
Senglea
Cospicua
White Rocks &
Splash & Fun Park
Msida
Tarxien
Paola
Ħamrun
Birkirkara
Zurrieq
Naxxar
Lija
Qormi
Mosta
Zebbug
Siggiewi
Malta
International
Airport
Qrendi
Ħaġar Qim
Mqabba
Bugibba
St Paul's
Bay
Imġiebaħ Bay
Rabat
Mdina
Dingli
Dingli
Cliffs

Victoria Lines
Victoria Lines

MEDITERRANEAN
SEA

Mellieħa
Mellieħa Bay

Golden Bay
Għajn Tuffieħa Bay

GOZO

COMINO

South Comino Channel

See Inset

Ċirkewwa (Marfa Point) -
Ramla tal-Bir Bay
Paradise
Bay

MALTA

GOZO

COMINO

MALTA

Malta

0   2.5   5 km

0   5   10 km

owntrodden islanders paid their taxes by trading, slaving and piracy, and were repaid in kind by marauding North Africans (Berbers and Arabs) and Turks.

In 1530, the islands were given to the Knights of the Order of St John of Jerusalem by Charles V, Emperor of Spain; their rent was two Maltese falcons a year, one to be sent to the emperor and the other to the Viceroy of Sicily. The 12,000 or so local inhabitants were given no say in the matter.

The Order of St John was founded during the crusades to protect Christian pilgrims travelling to and from the Holy Land, and to care for the sick. The knights were drawn from the younger male members of Europe's aristocratic families; in other words, those who were not the principal heirs. The order comprised eight nationalities or *langues* (languages). In order to preserve their identity, the langues built their own magnificent palaces, called *auberges*. The eight langues – Italy, Germany, France, Provence, Castile, Aragón, Auvergne and Bavaria – correspond to the eight points of the Maltese Cross. It was a religious order, with the knights taking vows of celibacy, poverty and obedience and handing over their patrimony. The Order of St John became extremely prestigious, wealthy and powerful as a military and maritime force, and as a charitable organisation which founded and operated several hospitals.

As soon as they arrived in Malta, the knights began to fortify the harbour and to skirmish with infidels. In May 1565, an enormous Ottoman fleet carrying more than 30,000 men laid siege to the island. The 700 knights and 8000 Maltese and mercenary troops were commanded by a 70-year-old grand master, Jean de la Vallette. The Great Siege lasted for more than three months, with continuous and unbelievably ferocious fighting; after enormous bloodshed on both sides, help finally arrived from Sicily and the Turks withdrew.

The knights were hailed as the saviours of Europe. Money and honours were heaped on them by grateful monarchs, and the construction of the new city of Valletta – named after the hero of the siege – and its enormous fortifications began. Malta was never again seriously threatened by the Turks.

Although the order continued to embellish Valletta, the knights sank into corrupt and ostentatious ways, largely supported by piracy. In 1798 Napoleon arrived, seeking to counter the British influence in the Mediterranean, and the knights, who were mostly French, surrendered to him without a fight.

The Maltese defeated the French in 1800 with the assistance of the British, and in 1814 Malta officially became part of the British Empire. The British decided to develop Malta into a major naval base. In WWII, Malta once again found itself under siege. Considered a linchpin in the battle for the Mediterranean, Malta was subjected to a blockade and, in 1942, to five months of day-and-night bombing raids, which left 40,000 homes destroyed and a population on the brink of starvation.

In 1947 the devastated island was given a measure of self-government. Malta's best known leaders in the postwar period have been the leader of the Nationalist Party and prime minister, Dr George Borg Olivier, who led the country to independence in 1964, and Mr Dominic Mintoff, who, as prime minister and leader of the Maltese Labour Party, established the republic in 1974. In 1979 links with Britain were reduced further when Mintoff expelled the British armed services and signed agreements with Libya, the Soviet Union and North Korea. Domestic policy focused on state enterprises.

In 1987 the Nationalist Party assumed power under the prime ministership of Dr Eddie Fenech Adami, and it was returned by a landslide victory in 1992. One of the party's main objectives was Malta's application to join the EU, a move opposed by the Labour Party. Negotiations to join the EU were under way in 1996.

During the past 10 years, the Maltese have achieved considerable prosperity, thanks largely to tourism, but increasingly because of trade and light industries.

GEOGRAPHY & ECOLOGY

The Maltese archipelago consists of three inhabited islands: Malta (246 sq km), Gozo (67 sq km) and Comino (2.7 sq km). They lie in the middle of the Mediterranean, 93 km south of Sicily and 350 km north of Libya.

The islands are formed of a soft limestone, which is the golden building material used in all Maltese buildings on the densely populated islands. There are some low ridges and out-crops, but no major hills. The Victoria Lines escarpment traverses the island of Malta from the coast near Paceville almost to Golden Bay. The soil is generally thin and rocky, although in some valleys it is terraced and farmed intensively. There are few trees and, for most of the year, little greenery to soften the stony, sun-bleached landscape. The only real exception is Buskett Gardens, a lush valley of trees and orange groves protected by the imposing southern Dingli Cliffs. There is virtually no surface water and there are no permanent creeks or rivers. The water table is the main source of fresh water, but it is supplemented by several large desalination plants.

The combined pressures of population, land use and development, as well as pollution, hunting and the lack of protection of natural areas, have had a significant environmental impact on the islands. In 1990 the Maltese government drew up a plan which designates development zones and identifies areas of ecological importance.

GOVERNMENT

Malta is an independent, neutral, democratic republic. The president has a ceremonial role and is elected by parliament. Executive power lies with the prime minister and the cabinet; the latter chosen from the majority party in the 65-member parliament.

There are two major parties: the Partit Tal-Haddiema, or Labour Party, and the Partit Nazzjonalista, or Nationalist Party.

ECONOMY

The Maltese enjoy a good standard of living, low inflation and low unemployment. The government's economic strategy is to concentrate on the development of the tourism industry, manufacturing, and financial services. The country's tourism industry, in particular, is rapidly growing in importance.

POPULATION & PEOPLE

Given its history, it's not surprising that Malta has been a melting pot of Mediterranean peoples. Malta's population is around 376,000, with most people living in Valletta and its satellite towns; Gozo has 29,000 inhabitants; Comino has a mere handful of farmers, six or seven in winter.

ARTS

Malta is noted for its fine crafts – particularly its handmade lace, hand-woven fabrics and silver filigree. Lace-making probably arrived with the knights in the 16th century. It was traditionally the role of village women – particularly on the island of Gozo – and, although the craft has developed into a healthy industry, it is still possible to find women sitting on their doorsteps making lace tablecloths.

The art of producing silver filigree was probably introduced to the island in the 17th century via Sicily, which was then under strong Spanish influence. Malta's silversmiths still produce beautiful filigree by traditional methods, but in large quantities to meet tourist demand.

Other handicrafts include weaving, knitting and glass-blowing; the latter is an especially healthy, small industry which produces glassware exported throughout the world.

CULTURE & RELIGION

In Malta, the Mediterranean culture is dominant, but there are quite a few signs of British influence. The Catholic Church is the custodian of national traditions, just as its enormous churches dominate the villages. Although its influence is waning, Catholicism is a real force in most people's daily lives. Divorce and abortion are illegal, although the voices of the islands' young people increasingly argue that abortion should be a personal choice.

LANGUAGE

Some linguists attribute the origins of the language to the Phoenician occupation of Malta and consider Maltese to be a Semitic offshoot of Phoenician. Others consider the Arabic period to be the more significant linguistic force. The Semitic base of Maltese grammar has persisted to this day despite the prominence of the Romance languages since the Europeanisation of Malta, which has led to the vocabulary becoming laced with Sicilian, Italian, Spanish, French and English words. The Maltese alphabet is a transliteration of Semitic sounds, written in Roman characters.

Nearly all Maltese in built-up areas speak English, and an increasing number speak Italian, helped by the fact that Malta receives Italian TV. French and German are also spoken.

See the Language Guide at the back of the book for pronunciation guidelines and useful words and phrases.

Facts for the Visitor

PLANNING
Climate & When to Go
Malta has an excellent climate, although it can get very warm (around 30°C) in midsummer and occasionally when the hot sirocco winds blow from Africa. The rainfall is low, at around 580 mm a year, and it falls mainly between November and February. However, there's still plenty of sun in winter, when temperatures average around 14°C.

The pleasant climate means you can visit Malta at any time. Outside the high season, which is between mid-June and late September, accommodation prices drop by up to 40%. The season of festas (or more correctly *festi*) begins in earnest at the beginning of June and lasts until the end of September.

Books & Maps
There are a number of useful guides; the best introduction and souvenir is Insight Guides' *Malta* (APA Publications), which has excellent photographs and articles. For detailed information on the historical sights, use the Blue Guide's *Malta* by Stuart Rossiter, but most people who are staying only a couple of days will find that Berlitz' *Malta* has sufficient detail.

The Kappillan of Malta by Nicholas Monsarrat is widely available and is a painless way of absorbing history. It tells the story of a priest's experiences during WWII, interwoven with other dramatic historical episodes. Monsarrat, also the author of *The Cruel Sea*, lived on Gozo for many years.

Malta has many fiction writers. Those writing in English include Francis Ebejer and Joseph Attard. A useful map is the *AA Macmillan Malta & Gozo Traveller's Map*, which shows street names in Maltese. This is important, because many street signs give the names in Maltese only, though in tourist areas there are increasing numbers of dual-language signs. The Maltese themselves rarely know the English names of streets other than the main thoroughfares. *Triq* means street in Maltese, but is used interchangeably with 'street'. The *Bartholomew Clyde Leisure Map Malta & Gozo* shows street names in English.

There are several good bookshops which stock guidebooks, maps and general books. Sapienza Bookshop (☎ 23 36 21), 26 Republic St, is recommended.

Online Services
The Malta National Tourism Organisation has a site at http://www.magnet.mt on the World Wide Web.

What to Bring
Summers can get very hot in Malta, so bring light, cool clothing and a hat (one which will not be blown off by the constant wind). Also bring along sunblock (it's always more expensive in tourist areas) and comfortable shoes if you plan to do some exploring on foot.

HIGHLIGHTS
The evocative Haga Qim prehistoric temples are without doubt the highlight of a visit to Malta. The hilltop medieval town, Mdina, is another must. On Gozo, visit the imposing megalithic temples of Ggantija and the fascinating Azure Window and nearby Inland Sea at Qawra.

TOURIST OFFICES
Local Tourist Offices
The Malta National Tourism Organisation information offices can provide a range of useful brochures, hotel listings and maps. There are offices at Malta international airport (☎ 24 96 00), open 24 hours a day; in Valletta (☎ 23 77 47) at 1 City Arcade; and on Gozo at Mgarr Harbour (☎ 55 33 43) and Victoria (☎ 55 81 06), 1 Palm St.

Maltese Tourist Offices Abroad
The Malta National Tourist Office has its main office in London (☎ 0171-292 4900) at Malta House, 36-38 Piccadilly, London, W1V OPP. Embassies and offices of Air Malta can provide information in other countries (see the following Visas & Embassies section).

VISAS & EMBASSIES
Entry visas are not required for holiday visits

of up to three months by Australians, Canadians, New Zealanders, North Americans or Britons.

Maltese Embassies Abroad

Malta has diplomatic missions in the following countries:

Australia
261 La Perouse St, Red Hill, Canberra, ACT 2603 (☎ 06-295 1586)

Canada
The Mutual Group Centre, 3300 Bloor St West, Suite 730, West Tower Etobicoke, Ontario (☎ 416-207 0922)

Italy
12 Lungotevere Marzio, 00186 Rome (☎ 06-687 99 47)

UK
36-38 Piccadilly, London, W1V OPQ (☎ 0171-292 4800)

USA
2017 Connecticut Ave, NW Washington, DC, 20008 (☎ 202-462 3611)

Foreign Embassies in Malta

The following countries have embassies in Malta:

Australia
Ta'Xbiex Terrace, Ta'Xbiex MSD 11 (☎ 33 82 01/05)

Canada
103 Archbishop St, Valletta (☎ 23 31 22)

Germany
Il-Piazzetta, Entrance B, 1st floor, Tower Rd, Sliema (☎ 33 65 31)

Italy
5 Vilhena St, Floriana (☎ 23 31 57/59)

Tunisia
Dar Carthage, Qormi Rd, Attard BZN 02 (☎ 43 51 75)

UK
7 St Anne St, Floriana (☎ 23 31 34/37)

USA
Development House, 3rd floor, St Anne St, Floriana (☎ 23 59 60/65)

CUSTOMS

Items for personal use are not subject to duty. One litre of spirits, one litre of wine and 200 cigarettes can be imported duty-free. Duty is charged on any gifts intended for local residents.

MONEY
Currency

The Maltese lira (Lm; a £ symbol is also sometimes used) is divided into 100 cents. There are

one, two, five, 10, 25, 50 cent and Lm1 coins and Lm2, Lm5, Lm10 and Lm20 notes.

Exchange Rates

Banks almost always offer significantly bette rates than hotels or restaurants. There is a 24 hour bureau at the airport available t passengers only. Travellers arriving by ferr should note that there are no exchange facili ties at the port.

Australia	A$1	=	Lm0.28
Canada	C$1	=	Lm0.26
France	1FF	=	Lm0.07
Germany	DM1	=	Lm0.24
Italy	L1000	=	Lm0.23
Japan	¥100	=	Lm0.33
New Zealand	NZ$1	=	Lm0.25
United Kingdom	UK£1	=	Lm0.55
United States	US$1	=	Lm0.36

Costs

By European standards, Malta is very goo value. If you can budget around Lm10 per day you'll get pleasant hostel accommodation, simple restaurant meal, a decent street-sid snack and enough cold drinks to keep yo going. If you cook your own meals and avoi Paceville (north-west of Valletta), your cost will be even lower.

Tipping & Bargaining

Restaurants and taxis expect a 10% tip. Bar gaining for handicrafts at stalls or markets i essential, but most shops have fixed prices Hotels will often be prepared to bargain in th off season between October and mid-June. Yo won't get far bargaining for taxis, but mak sure you establish the fare in advance.

Consumer Taxes

A 15% value-added tax (VAT) on all consume items has been introduced.

POST & COMMUNICATIONS
Post

Post office branches are found in most town and villages. There is a poste restante servic at the main post office, in the Auberge d'Itali Merchants St, Valletta; it's open from 8 am t 6 pm.

Local postage costs five cents; air mail t Europe costs 14 cents, to the USA 20 cents, an to Australia 25 cents. Postcards cost the same as letters, except those to Australia, which cost 30 cents.

Telephone & Fax

Public telephones tend to be a bit sparse (although their number is increasing) and they take only phonecards. You can buy Telecards (phonecards) at TeleMalta offices, post offices and stationery shops for Lm2, Lm3 or Lm5. There are rows of phones at the offices of TeleMalta (the country's phone company). The main office is at Mercury House, St George's Rd, St Julian's (open 24 hours). Other offices are at South St, Valletta (open from 8 am to 6.30 pm) and Bisazza St, Sliema (open 8 am to 11 pm).

For local telephone enquiries phone ☎ 190; for overseas enquiries phone ☎ 194. Local calls cost five cents. The international direct dialling code is ☎ 00. International calls are discounted by 25% between 9 pm and 8 am daily and all day Sunday. To call Malta from abroad, dial the international access code, ☎ 356 (the country code for Malta) and the number. There are no area codes in Malta.

Fax and telex services are available at TeleMalta offices.

NEWSPAPERS & MAGAZINES

The local English-language newspapers are the *Times* (15 cents) and the *Sunday Times* (18 cents). British, French, German and Italian newspapers are available on the evening of publication. A new local weekly, the *Malta Independent*, is available in English on Sunday (18 cents).

TV

Two local TV stations broadcast in Maltese. CNN can be picked up by satellite and cable TV is on the way. All of the Italian TV stations are received in Malta.

TIME

Malta is two hours ahead of GMT/UTC during summer (from the last Sunday in March to the last Sunday in September), and one hour ahead during winter.

ELECTRICITY

The electric current in Malta is 240V, 50 Hz and plugs have three flat pins. Malta has the same system as the UK, and therefore differs from most other Mediterranean European countries, which tend to run on 220V, 50 Hz.

WEIGHTS & MEASURES

The metric system is used in Malta.

TOILETS

Small blocks of public toilets are located throughout Malta.

HEALTH

The water is safe to drink but heavily chlorinated, so stick to the bottled variety. There are no unusual health risks and no inoculations are required. Citizens of Australia and the UK are entitled to free health care because there are reciprocal agreements for the Maltese in both countries. St Luke's Hospital (☎ 24 12 51) in Gwardamanga (on the rounded promontory at the north-western corner of the Valletta defences) is the main general hospital. Gozo General Hospital, also known as Craig Hospital (☎ 56 16 00), is the main hospital on Gozo. For health emergencies phone ☎ 196. Both hospitals have 24-hour emergency services.

WOMEN TRAVELLERS

Malta remains a conservative society by Western standards, and women are still expected to be wives and mothers; however an increasing number of women are now joining the workforce. Young males have adopted the Mediterranean macho style, but they are not usually aggressive. Normal caution should be observed, but problems are unlikely. If you are alone, Paceville – the nightclub zone at St Julian's – is hectic but not particularly unsafe. Walking alone at night in Gzira is not recommended because this is the centre for prostitution.

Dress conservatively, particularly if you intend to visit churches (shorts are out for both sexes in churches). Topless bathing is not acceptable.

DISABLED TRAVELLERS

The Association for the Physically Handicapped (☎ 69 38 63) is a good contact for disabled people wanting to travel to Malta. It is at the Rehabilitation Fund Rehabilitation Centre, Corradino Hill, Paola PLA 07. The National Tourism Organisation can provide details about hotels in Malta which have facilities for the disabled.

TRAVEL WITH CHILDREN

Pharmacies are well stocked with baby needs such as formula, bottles, pacifiers and nappies (diapers). It is always difficult to keep young kids amused, but you could try taking them to see the Malta Experience (see Things to See & Do in the Valletta section), or on a harbour tour (see Organised Tours in the Valletta section). In summer, you can hire snorkelling gear, boats etc at the NSTS Aquacentre beach club (see Activities in the Valletta section). There is a Splash & Fun Park, with water slides and a fairytale fun park (☎ 34 27 24), at Bahar Ic-Caghaq, White Rocks. Another option for older kids (who are not easily frightened) is a visit to the dungeons at Mdina, which are fitted out with spooky sound-and-light effects and life-size characters (see the Mdina section).

BUSINESS HOURS

Shops open at 9 am, close at 1 pm, and are open again between 3.30 or 4 and 7 pm. Between 1 October and 15 June, banks are open Monday to Friday from 8.30 am to 12.30 pm and on Saturday from 8.30 am to noon; they close half an hour earlier during summer.

Between 1 October and 30 June, offices are open Monday to Friday from 8 am to 1 pm and from 2.30 or 3 to 5.30 pm, and on Saturday from 8.30 am to 1 pm; from July to September they open Monday to Saturday from 7.30 am to 1.30 pm.

PUBLIC HOLIDAYS & SPECIAL EVENTS

Fourteen national public holidays are observed in Malta: New Year's Day (1 January); St Paul's Shipwreck (10 February); St Joseph's Day (19 March); Good Friday; Freedom Day (31 March); Labour Day (1 May); commemoration of 1919 independence riots (7 June); Feast of Sts Peter and Paul, and Harvest Festival (29 June); Feast of the Assumption (15 August); Feast of Our Lady of Victories (8 September); Independence Day (21 September); Feast of the Immaculate Conception (8 December); Republic Day (13 December); and Christmas (25 December).

Festi are important events in Maltese family and village life. During the past 200 years they have developed from simple village feast days into extravagant spectacles. Every village has a festa, usually to celebrate the feast day of its patron saint. Most of them are in summer, and for days in advance the island reverberates to the sound of explosions announcing the forth coming celebration.

The main fireworks display is usually on Saturday night, and is accompanied by one o more local brass bands. On Sunday evening the statue of the patron saint is paraded through the streets accompanied by brass bands, fireworks petards and church bells. Afterwards, people repair to the bars to drink and chat, or sample the *pastizzi* (savoury cheese pasties) and *qubbajt* (nougat) from elaborate, temporary stands.

If a festival is held while you are visiting you should definitely go. Tourist offices can provide details – check the time for the procession and the main fireworks display. At least one festa is held every weekend from the beginning of June to mid-September.

ACTIVITIES
Diving

Malta offers excellent conditions for diving and competitive rates on courses. Although there is not the colour or sea life you can expect in the Red Sea, there is fantastic clarity (visibility often exceeds 30 metres) and a dramatic underwater seascape, with caves and enormous drop-offs sometimes only metres from the shore. If you are a diver, at least one dive is a must. The water temperature drops to around 14°C in winter and reaches 25°C in summer. It is nearly always possible to find a protected site with easy access, so conditions are ideal for beginners.

Diving is strictly monitored by the Maltese government, and all divers must provide a medical certificate from either their own doctor or a local doctor (Lm4). The minimum age for diving is 14 years. People wanting to dive unaccompanied will also need a government permit (Lm2) – granted on presentation of the medical certificate, proof of qualification and two passport-sized photos. A PADI o NAUI open-water dive course will cost Lm125. A six-dive package including boat dives and equipment will cost around Lm3: (unaccompanied) or Lm45 (accompanied) i transfers are included. One escorted shore dive with equipment will cost about Lm7.50. Then are at least 10 licensed diving schools, so they can't all be listed here. Cresta (☎ 31 07 43), Villa Rosa Beach Club, Dragonara Rd, St George's Bay, Malta, and Calypso Diving (☎ 56 20 00), Calypso Hotel, Marsalforn, Gozo, have been recommended.

The National Tourism Organisation produces a useful brochure on diving, but there is also a book entitled *Diving the Maltese Islands*, available from SEA Publications, PO Box 247, Chester, East Cheshire, England.

Horse Riding

There are several registered riding schools – the National Tourism Organisation can provide a list. Try Darmanin's Riding School (☎ 23 56 49), Stables Lane, Marsa.

Walking

Distances on Malta are relatively small, so you can cover a lot of the island on foot. The *Bartholomew Clyde Leisure Map – Malta & Gozo* suggests some interesting routes. Unfortunately, the Maltese show little interest in the countryside, so a lot of it is unkempt, unattractive and littered with rubbish.

Sports Clubs

Sports clubs abound, and most of their facilities are available to visitors through temporary membership. One of the best is the Marsa Sports Club (☎ 23 28 42), four km south of Valletta, which offers golf, tennis, squash, cricket and swimming.

Beaches

The best sandy beaches on Malta are Gnejna Bay; Tuffieha (bus Nos 47 and 52); Golden Bay (bus Nos 47 and 47a); Cirkewwa and Paradise Bay (bus Nos 45 and 48); Ramla al-Bir Bay; Ramla tal-Qortin Bay; Armier Bay (bus No 50); Mellieha Bay (bus Nos 43 and 48); Imgiebah Bay; and St George's Bay (bus No 67).

The best sandy beaches on Gozo are Ramla Bay (bus No 42) and Xlendi Bay (bus No 87). On Comino, the best beaches are Santa Maria Bay and San Niklaw Bay. Where bus numbers are not shown, private transport is necessary.

WORK

It is difficult for foreigners to work legally in Malta. Those seriously seeking work should

contact the National Tourism Organisation for information about permits. Some casual (illegal) work waitering, washing dishes etc in bar and discos can be found.

ACCOMMODATION

The National Tourism Organisation produces a detailed listing of accommodation on Malta, Gozo and Comino. There's a full range of possibilities, from five-star hotels to small guesthouses.

One-star hotels have set B&B rates of Lm5 to Lm8 for one person in a single room. Fourth-class holiday complexes charge Lm4 to Lm6, for a bed only. Third-class guesthouses charge Lm3 to Lm5 for B&B, 2nd-class guesthouses charge Lm4 to Lm6, and 1st-class charge Lm5 to Lm7. Prices can be considerably lower in the off season. There are hostels on Malta and Gozo. Camping is not allowed.

Apart from hostels (see the Valletta, Sliema and St Julian's section), the cheapest option is boarding with families for around Lm3 a night. Try the National Student Travel Service (NSTS); see Air in the Getting There & Away section for details.

FOOD

You are unlikely to eat great cuisine in Malta, but food is both good and cheap. The most obvious influence is Sicilian, and most of the cheaper restaurants serve pasta and pizza. English standards (eg grilled chops, sausages and mash, and roast with three veg) are also commonly available, particularly in the tourist areas. Vegetarians are well catered for, with more than 40 restaurants offering vegetarian dishes as main courses.

It is definitely worth trying some of the Maltese specialties: pastizzi (savoury cheese pasties), which are available from small bakeries and bars; *timpana* (a macaroni, cheese and egg pie); and *bragioli* (spicy beef rolls). Two favourite, but relatively expensive, dishes are *fenech* (rabbit), which is fried or made as a casserole or pie, and *lampuka*, a fish (dorado), which is caught between September and November and usually served grilled, fried or made into a pie.

DRINKS

Local beers are good, with a range of lagers, stouts and pale ales: Hop Leaf (30 cents for a

MALTA

small bottle) is recommended. The local wines are fairly rough but quite acceptable. You get what you pay for (from 50 cents to Lm4 a bottle). Imported wines and beers are available at reasonable prices.

ENTERTAINMENT

Paceville is the centre of Malta's nightlife, with lots of bars, clubs and discos.

THINGS TO BUY

Hand-knitted clothing is produced in the villages and can be cheap. Traditional handicrafts include lace, silver filigree, blown glass and pottery. Shop around, though, before you make a purchase; the Malta Crafts Centre, St John's Square, Valletta, is a good place to start. The best bargains are found on Gozo.

Getting There & Away

AIR

Malta is well connected to Europe and North Africa. Scheduled prices aren't particularly cheap, but there are some excellent packages, and NSTS also has some bargains. It is the representative in Malta for most student travel organisations (including STA Travel, Campus Holidays, CTS and so on) and is an associate member of Hostelling International (HI). It has offices at 220 St Paul St, Valletta (☎ 24 66 28), and on Gozo (☎ 55 39 77) at 45 St Francis Square, Victoria.

Air Malta (☎ 66 22 11) has scheduled flights to/from Amsterdam, Athens, Berlin, Brussels, Cairo, Catania (Sicily), Damascus, Dubai, Dublin, Frankfurt, Geneva, Hamburg, London (Heathrow and Gatwick), Lyon, Madrid, Manchester, Munich, Palermo, Paris, Rome, Tunis, Vienna, Zürich and other destinations.

There are weekly direct Air Malta flights from Melbourne and Sydney. Air Malta's sales agents include:

Australia
World Aviation Systems, 403 George St, Sydney, NSW 2000 (☎ 02-9321 9111; fax 02-9290 3641)
Canada
British Airways offices throughout Canada
Egypt
Air Malta Office, 2 Tahir Square, Cairo (☎ 02-5782692)

UK
Air Malta House, 314-316 Upper Richmond R₀ Putney, London SW15 6TU (☎ 0181-785 3199)
USA
Air Malta Office, 630 Fifth Ave, Suite 2662, Nev York, NY 10111 (☎ 212-245 7768)

Other airlines servicing the country includ₀ Alitalia, KLM, Lufthansa, Swissair an₀ Tunisavia. Avoid buying tickets in Malta if yo₀ can, because prices are higher.

Charter flights, usually for trips of one o₀ two weeks from England or Scotland, offe₀ outstanding value, particularly in winter₀ Contact a travel agent specialising in budge₀ flights and packages.

SEA

Malta has regular sea links in summer wit₀ both Sicily (Palermo, Pozzallo, Syracuse an₀ Catania) and northern Italy (Genoa an₀ Livorno). Cars can be brought by ferry fro₀ Sicily and may be imported for up to thre₀ months. A Green Card (internationally rec₀ ognised proof of insurance) for Malta i₀ required. The main Italian ferry company ope₀ ating in the Mediterranean, Tirrenia, has cut it₀ service to Malta (Tirrenia ferries used to trave₀ regularly from Naples, Reggio di Calabri₀ Catania and Syracuse to Malta).

Since the Italy-Malta ferry link is in a stat₀ of flux and companies operating the service₀ can change, it is best to confirm the informa₀ tion given here with a travel agent. SM₀ Agency (☎ 23 22 11), 311 Republic St, Val₀ letta, will provide information about all of th₀ services on offer.

In 1996, Virtù Ferries ran a fast catamara₀ to Sicily (Pozzallo and Catania) up to fiv₀ times a week, depending on the season. Th₀ journey to Catania takes three hours and cos₀ Lm21 (one way, all seasons) and as little a₀ Lm14 for same-day return in winter, or Lm2₀ for same-day return in summer. Virtù Ferrie₀ has offices in Ta'Xbiex, near Valletta (3 Prin₀ cess Elizabeth Terrace; ☎ 31 88 54), an₀ Catania (Piazza Europa 1; ☎ 095-37 69 33).

Other Maltese companies operate regula₀ car-ferry services to Italian ports and t₀ Tunisia. The journey to Catania takes aroun₀ nine hours and a deck passenger is charge₀ from Lm17 to Lm21, depending on the seaso₀ Cars cost from Lm24 to Lm29 to transpor₀

Ferry companies include Grandi Traghetti (☎ 24 43 73) to Palermo, Genoa and Tunis, and EuroMalta (☎ 23 22 300), which runs car ferries and hydrofoils to Catania and Syracuse.

Ferries to Libya, which run irregularly, can be booked through Sea Malta (☎ 23 22 30/39). The one-way economy fare is Lm50.

It is important to note that ferries do not have exchange facilities and there are no exchange facilities at Malta's port. Neither is there public transport from the port up to the city of Valletta – you either catch a taxi or make the steep 15-minute walk.

LEAVING MALTA

All passengers departing by sea are required to pay a Lm4 departure tax, plus a 15% government levy. Both should be added by the travel agent when you buy your ticket.

Getting Around

HELICOPTER

There is a helicopter service between Malta and Gozo which might be worth the expense if you don't want to spend two hours catching buses and the ferry to reach your destination. Open return tickets cost Lm25 for adults and Lm12.50 for children. Same-day return costs Lm20 and Lm10. There are also helicopter tours of the islands. Contact any travel agency for information and bookings.

BUS

Malta and Gozo are served by a network of buses run by the Malta Public Transport Authority, many of them beautiful and uncomfortable relics of the 1950s. On Malta, fares range from 11 to 16 cents, depending on the number of fare 'stages' you pass through. Buses run until about 10 or 11 pm, depending on the route. Route numbers change frequently so check them locally. All buses on Malta originate from the main City Gate bus terminus, which is in a plaza area just outside Valletta's city gates (☎ 22 59 16 for information). The green, white and yellow *Malta Bus Map & Fares Guide* (20 cents) has useful information, including an official timetable. It's available from newsstands.

Bus Nos 45, 48 and 452 run regularly from Valletta to Cirkewwa to connect with the ferry to Gozo. Bus Nos 62 to 68 run from Valletta to Sliema and bus Nos 64, 65, 66 and 68 go on to St Julian's and Paceville.

On Gozo, the main bus terminus is on Main Gate St, just behind Republic St. A flat fare of nine cents will take you anywhere on the island. Note that few buses run after noon (for information phone ☎ 55 60 11). Bus No 25 runs from the ferry port of Mgarr to the main town of Victoria. In the villages, the bus stop is always in or near the church square.

TAXI

Taxis are expensive and should only be used as a last resort or with a group of people. A fare from the airport to Sliema is around Lm6; from Valletta to St Julian's, around Lm5. Make sure you establish a price in advance. White Taxi Service Amalgamated in Gzira (☎ 34 39 49) offers a 24-hour service.

CAR & MOTORCYCLE

Like the British, the Maltese drive on the left side of the road. Hiring a car in Malta is a good idea, partly because taxis are so expensive. One late-night fare between Paceville and Bugibba could easily cost Lm6, which is nearly the cost of a hire car for a day. Rates vary, so shop around. In 1996 Hertz was offering a daily rate of Lm8.60 for a small car (Lm6 a day for a week or more). Its head office (☎ 31 46 36) is at 66 Gzira Rd, Gzira. Local garages such as Merlin (☎ 22 31 31) charge slightly less. L'Aronde (☎ 33 40 79), Upper Gardens, St Julian's, hires out motorcycles from Lm3 per day (insurance and delivery included). One litre of petrol costs 26 cents. There is a speed limit of 64 km/h on highways and 40 km/h in urban areas. Call ☎ 24 22 22 for breakdown assistance and towing.

BICYCLE

Cycling can be an ideal way to get around Malta because of the small distances, but there are plenty of hills and it can be very hot. The Cycle Store (☎ 44 32 35), 135 Eucharistic Congress St, Mosta, has bikes for Lm1.50 a day. The Marsalforn Hotel (☎ 55 61 47) in Gozo has bikes for Lm2 a day, or less if rented for several days.

MALTA

HITCHING
Hitchhiking is very unusual on Malta and is frowned upon.

BOAT
Regular ferries link Malta and Gozo, and buses connect with all ferry services (see the Bus sections). Ferries depart from Cirkewwa in Malta and from Mgarr, Gozo. Services are more or less hourly from 6 am to 11 pm. The crossing takes 20 minutes and costs Lm1.50 return for passengers, and Lm3.50 return for cars. Even if you board at Cirkewwa, you still pay for your ticket at Gozo on the return leg; this means that car drivers arriving at Cirkewwa should head straight for the car queue.

Be warned that Maltese families flock to Gozo on Sunday, particularly in summer, which can cause long delays at ferry terminals despite the extra shuttle services which operate to accommodate the increased number of passengers. Traffic from Cirkewwa to the main towns is also very heavy on Sunday evening. All ferries are operated by the Gozo Channel Co (☎ 24 39 64, timetable recording ☎ 55 60 16). A ferry service also leaves from Sa Maison Creek in Marsamxett Harbour for Mgarr between 12.30 and 1.30 pm; it takes about 1¼ hours.

There is also a ferry service between Valletta's Marsamxett Harbour and Sliema's Tigne seafront (at the end of the Strand) approximately every half-hour from 8 am to 6 pm (☎ 33 56 89).

ORGANISED TOURS
A number of companies operate bus tours and they are highly competitive, so shop around the travel agencies. The tours will restrict you to the well-trampled tourist traps, but they can give you a good introduction to the islands nonetheless.

A typical full-day tour of Malta costs Lm2.50 to Lm5. If possible, choose tours without lunch, because these are generally half the price and you can buy lunch more cheaply yourself. There are also day tours to Gozo and Comino, and trips to see late-night festa fireworks. Tour guides expect tips.

There are day tours to Sicily (up to Lm30), available through the travel agencies. The journey takes 90 minutes by catamaran and the tour includes a visit to Mt Etna and Taormina.

Captain Morgan Cruises at Sliema Marina (☎ 34 33 73) has a great range of cruises sailing adventures and jeep safaris.

See the Valletta section for information on harbour tours.

Valletta, Sliema & St Julian's

Valletta, the city of the Knights of the Order of St John, is architecturally superb and seemingly unchanged since the 16th century. The city is the seat of Malta's government, and overlooks the magnificent Grand Harbour to the south-east and Marsamxett Harbour to the north-west.

On the south-eastern side of the Grand Harbour lie the fortified peninsulas of Vittoriosa and Senglea and the town of Cospicua (known collectively as the three cities, or the Cottonera). These are older and in some ways more interesting than Valletta itself. They are dominated by their docks, which date from the time of the Phoenicians and were the principal reason for their existence. They are definitely worth exploring.

On the northern side of Marsamxett Harbour lies Sliema, the most fashionable residential area. Restaurants and high-rise hotels line the shores. Further north-west are the tourist haunts of St Julian's and Paceville.

Orientation
The Maltese think of the suburbs that surround Valletta – Cospicua, Paola, Hamrun, Qormi, Birkirkara, Gzira, Sliema and St Julian's – as separate towns. This may well have been accurate in the relatively recent past, but they now run into one another and effectively create one large city with a population of around 250,000. The entire eastern half of the island is intensively developed, with large suburbs and towns, the airport and numerous industrial sites.

The ferries from Italy dock in the Grand Harbour below Valletta, and it's a steep 15-minute climb up the hill to the main City Gate bus terminus, outside the southern walls.

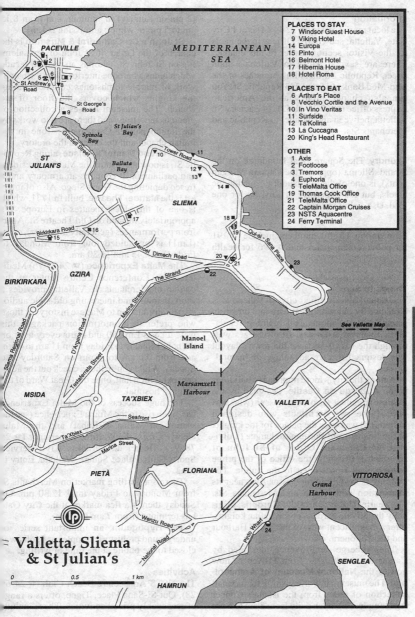

MEDITERRANEAN SEA

PACEVILLE

St Andrew's Road

St George's Road

Spinola Bay

Grenfell Street

St Julian's Bay

ST JULIAN'S

Balluta Bay

Tower Road

SLIEMA

Birkirkara Road

Manoel Dimech Road

Qui-si - Sana Place

GZIRA

The Strand

BIRKIRKARA

Sliema Regional Road

Marina Street

D'Argens Road

Testaferrata Street

MSIDA

TA'XBIEX

Ta'Xbiex

Seafront

Marina Street

PIETÀ

Manoel Island

Marsamxett Harbour

See Valletta Map

VALLETTA

FLORIANA

VITTORIOSA

Grand Harbour

Wenzu Road

National Road

Pinto Wharf

SENGLEA

HAMRUN

MALTA

PLACES TO STAY
7 Windsor Guest House
9 Viking Hotel
14 Europa
15 Pinto
16 Belmont Hotel
17 Hibernia House
18 Hotel Roma

PLACES TO EAT
6 Arthur's Place
8 Vecchio Cortile and the Avenue
10 In Vino Veritas
11 Surfside
12 Ta'Kolina
13 La Cuccagna
20 King's Head Restaurant

OTHER
1 Axis
2 Footloose
3 Tremors
4 Euphoria
5 TeleMalta Office
19 Thomas Cook Office
21 TeleMalta Office
22 Captain Morgan Cruises
23 NSTS Aquacentre
24 Ferry Terminal

Valletta, Sliema & St Julian's

0   0.5   1 km

Information

The local tourist office (☎ 22 44 44) is at 1 City Gate, Valletta; see Tourist Offices in the Facts for the Visitor section earlier in this chapter. There are several banks in Valletta's main street, Republic St, including branches of the Mid-Med Bank at 15 and 233 Republic St. You can also change money at the American Express office (☎ 23 21 41/42), 14 Zachary St, Valletta, between and parallel to Republic and Merchants Sts.

Laundry The Square Deal laundrette on the Strand, Sliema (opposite the Captain Morgan boats), is one of the few laundries outside the hotels, but it's expensive at Lm1.50 for one load. Use a sink instead.

Emergency Useful numbers include ☎ 191 for police emergencies and ☎ 196 for health emergencies.

Things to See

The remarkable fortified city of Valletta was built swiftly but with great care and attention paid to town planning and building regulations. Even on a hot day, fresh breezes waft through the streets because the town's layout was designed to take advantage of 'natural' air-con.

Among the city's more impressive buildings is the **Auberge de Castile**, designed by the Maltese architect Girolomo Cassar (who was one of the two architects who designed Valletta). It was once the palace for the knights of the Spanish and Portuguese langue (a division of the main Order of St John of Jerusalem). It is now the office of the prime minister and is not open to the public. The building is on Girolomo Cassar Ave, near its intersection with South and Merchants Sts. The nearby **Upper Barrakka Gardens**, originally the private gardens of the Italian knights, offer a magnificent view of the Grand Harbour and the Cottonera.

The Auberge de Provence, designed by Cassar for the knights from Provence, now houses the **National Museum of Archaeology**. The museum is worth visiting for its small collection of relics from the island's Copper Age temples. It's open daily from 8 am to 5 pm

(2 pm on Sunday) in summer, and from 8.15 am to 5 pm in winter; admission is Lm1.

St John's Co-Cathedral & Museum is the church of the Order of St John of Jerusalem. It's on St John St, and has an austere facade which hides a baroque interior. Note the patchwork of marble tombstones commemorating the knights which covers the floor of the church. The museum houses a collection of precious tapestries, and there are two works by the Italian painter Caravaggio – one in the Italian chapel and the other in the oratory.

The **Grand Master's Palace**, along Republic St, is now the seat of the Maltese president and parliament. It contains an armoury and a fresco depicting the Great Siege. Also of interest is the **Manoel Theatre**, built in 1731, which is one of the oldest theatres in Europe. It's appropriately located on Old Theatre St. Apart from performances (generally in winter), entry (Lm1) is by guided tour from Monday to Friday at 10.45 and 11.30 am.

The **Malta Experience** (☎ 24 37 76) Mediterranean Conference Centre (enter at the bottom of Merchants St, Valletta) provides a short, painless and interesting old-style audiovisual introduction to Maltese history for those who prefer their information packaged this way. It costs Lm2.50 and starts every hour on the hour Monday to Friday from 11 am to 4 pm and from 11 am to 1 pm on Saturday and Sunday. While you're there, check out the adjacent exhibition hall, once the Great Ward of the knights' hospital.

The huge success of the Malta Experience has given rise to the Mdina Experience (see the section on Mdina & Rabat) and the Malta George Cross: the Wartime Experience (☎ 24 78 91), Hostel de Verdelin, Civil Service Sports Club, Palace Square, Valletta. Entry is Lm2.

There's a bustling market on Merchants St from Monday to Friday until 12.30 pm. On Sunday there's a flea market at the City Gate bus terminus (from 7 am to 1 pm).

The **Hypogeum**, an important series of underground prehistoric temples at Paola, was closed to the public at the time of writing.

Activities

The NSTS Aquacentre Beach Club (☎ 24 66 28), Qui-Si-Sana Place, Tigne, offers a range of reasonably priced activities. These include

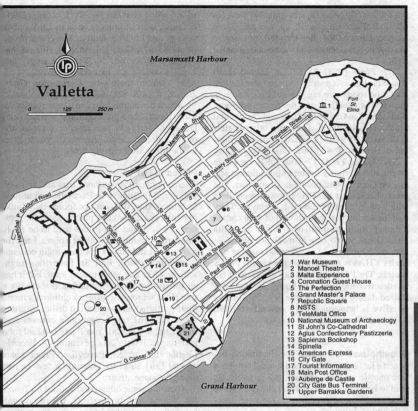

Valletta

Marsamxett Harbour

0   125   250 m

Grand Harbour

1 War Museum
2 Manoel Theatre
3 Malta Experience
4 Coronation Guest House
5 The Perfection
6 Grand Master's Palace
7 Republic Square
8 NSTS
9 TeleMalta Office
10 National Museum of Archaeology
11 St John's Co-Cathedral
12 Agius Confectionery Pastizzeria
13 Sapienza Bookshop
14 Spinella
15 American Express
16 City Gate
17 Tourist Information
18 Main Post Office
19 Auberge de Castile
20 City Gate Bus Terminal
21 Upper Barrakka Gardens

MALTA

the hire of flippers and masks for snorkelling (Lm1 per hour; 75 cents for students); paddle boats (Lm3.50/2.50 an hour); sailboards (Lm2.50/2 an hour; instruction available for Lm1); canoes (Lm1.20/1 an hour); water-skiing (Lm3/1.50 for five minutes, 6.50/5.50 for 15 minutes); sailing boats (Lm4/3 an hour); motorboats (Lm5/4 an hour); and scuba diving (Lm9/7.50 per dive, including equipment).

Organised Tours

Captain Morgan Cruises (☎ 34 33 73) operates short harbour cruises (Lm4.95) throughout the day, and a variety of half and full-day cruises around the islands, priced from Lm12 to Lm16,

including a buffet lunch. Boats leave from the Strand in Sliema and tickets can be purchased at any of the travel agencies on the waterfront. They also offer an underwater safari, with passengers seated in a glass observation keel, for Lm4.95.

Places to Stay

Hostels The NSTS is an associate member of Hostelling International (HI) and runs several hostels in Malta. The following prices are for high season. At *Hibernia House* (☎ 33 38 59) in Depiro St, Sliema, HI card-holders are charged Lm2.50 from 15 June to 31 October; nonmembers pay Lm3. Hibernia House also has reasonably priced apartments. Take bus No 62 to Balluta Bay, walk up the hill along Manoel Dimech Rd, then turn left into Depiro St – the hostel is about 100 metres along on the right.

The *Pinto* (☎ 31 98 52), in Sacred Heart Ave, St Julian's, is a steep walk up from Balluta Bay. The rooms are big, the ceilings are high, the view is excellent and the prices are right. Beds cost Lm4.50 per person and continental breakfast is included. There are other hostels at Rabat (☎ 45 94 45; Lm2.20 per night, groups only), and Lija (☎ 43 61 68; Lm4.95 per night).

The *Malta YHA*, 17 Triq Tal-Borg, Paola (☎ 69 39 57), runs a hostel at this address and one on Gozo at Ghajnsielem. In summer, you must check in at the Paola hostel, regardless which of the hostels you wish to stay in. They will then billet you in the hostel of your choice if there is room. You will need to join the Malta YHA (Lm2.50) to stay at these hostels. Note that the standard of accommodation at the Malta YHAs is much lower than at the NSTS hostels. The Paola hostel is not in a convenient or attractive location. The hostel is not always staffed during the day, so the best time to ring or arrive is between 5 and 7 pm; take bus No 8, 11 or 26 from City Gate bus station.

Guesthouses & Hotels The distinction between a large guesthouse and a small hotel is a fine one. In general, though, the guesthouses tend to be family operated and cheaper. Some good ones can be found in and around Paceville and St Julian's.

Right in the centre of Paceville (so it isn't quiet) is the *Windsor Guest House* (☎ 31 22 32 or 31 17 53), in Schreiber St, Paceville. Accommodation is simple but clean and prices are around Lm6 per person, depending on the season.

The *Viking Hotel* (☎ 31 67 02), Spinola Rd, St Julian's, has B&B doubles for Lm12 and singles for Lm8. In the top rooms you'll be charged extra for the view.

The *Belmont Hotel* (☎ 31 30 77), Mrabat St, Sliema, is a bit tacky, but it's clean, well located and cheap. Prices range up to Lm3.50 per person for a room with bathroom, plus breakfast.

The *Europa* (☎ 33 40 70), 138 Tower Rd, Sliema, is well located and has very pleasant rooms with bathroom and TV. It charges Lm11 a single, which drops to around Lm9 out of season, and Lm18 a double. The *Hotel Roma* (☎ 31 85 87), Ghar Il-Lembi St, Sliema, has rooms with shower for Lm17 a single and Lm25 a double, cheaper out of season.

In Valletta, there's the *Coronation Guest House* (☎ 23 76 52), 10E Miriel Anton Vassalli St, which has doubles for Lm10 and singles for Lm5. It could be a good option if you arrive by late-night ferry; if you reserve a room, the owner will make arrangements for you to enter the building after closing time.

Places to Eat

There are cheap restaurants, bars and cafés on the Strand in Sliema, in Paceville and around St Julian's Bay. But don't be fooled into thinking that cheap-looking places have the best deals. You'll find that prices tend to be fairly standard – around Lm1.60 for a pizza, Lm2 for pasta, and Lm2.50 to Lm4 for a main course.

Arthur's Place, Ball St, Paceville, might look just like any other tourist joint, but it has an interesting range of Maltese dishes. It's a fine place which also offers a children's menu (half-portions) and vegetarian dishes. Starters are in the Lm1 range, and main courses cost from Lm2 to Lm3.50. You'll pay Lm2.50 for a real Italian risotto alla pescatora at *Vecchio Cortile* in Gort St, Paceville. Pizza costs around Lm1.50 at the *Avenue*, a few metres along the same street.

There are some other good options on Tower Rd, Sliema. Try the *Surfside*, where you can eat pizza (around Lm1.60) on a terrace overlooking the sea. Opposite, at No 151, is *Ta'Kolina*, which offers good seafood and Maltese dishes for around Lm3.50 to Lm4.50. Around the corner is *La Cuccagna* at 47 Amery St; Italians would approve of its pasta and pizza, which cost around Lm1.60. For Maltese dishes at reasonable prices, go to the *King's Head Restaurant* in Triq Annunzjata, just off the Strand. This is where Maltese workers go for a feed. Soup costs 40 cents, pasta 60 cents, and a mixed grill is Lm2. The place is small, and don't expect luxury or gourmet food – the attraction is the prices.

Vegetarians (and others) could try *In Vino Veritas* at 59 Dingli St, on the corner of Tower Rd. The vegetarian lasagne (Lm1.65), vegetarian rice (Lm1.65) and home-made cakes are excellent. The atmosphere is lively and there are many regulars.

For lunch in Valletta, try the **Perfection** on Old Theatre St (down the hill from Republic Square, on the left just after Strait St). It has good coffee and inexpensive snacks. The cheapest lunch is a couple of delicious pastizzi from **Agius Confectionery Pastizzeria** at 273 St Paul's St – they're only 15 cents each. Also worth a visit is **Spinella**, 24 Republic St, which has pies, croissants and pastries for 25 to 45 cents, plus pasta and salads from Lm1.

The *Telecall Restaurant Guide Malta & Gozo* (Lm2.95) is widely available and lists restaurants by location and price. It also recommends restaurants that are suitable for vegetarians, those with nonsmoking areas and those with good wheelchair access.

Entertainment

Paceville is Malta's nightlife centre. It's quiet from Monday to Thursday but on Friday, Saturday and Sunday the place is jumping. Crowds spill out of the bars onto the street, policemen lounge around, elderly British tourists look bemused and cars crawl around trying to avoid pedestrian toes. Wander until you find the bar of your choice.

Tremors, a disco club for the young crowd, is in front of *Footloose*, a (loud) rock music pub, in St George's Rd. *Euphoria* and *Axis*, both in Paceville, are other places to dance and party till late. Discos cost around Lm2.50 to enter and drinks are expensive. Since bus services stop at around 10 pm, most Maltese group together and catch taxis home or walk.

Getting Around

To/From the Airport The short distance from Malta International Airport to the City Gate bus terminus is more problematical than it should be. The nearest bus stop is a 15-minute walk away and bus drivers generally refuse to carry suitcases. Most arrivals are transferred by courtesy car or coach to their hotels. Taxis operate on official rates; to Sliema or St Julian's it's Lm5.

Local Transport See the preceding Getting Around section in this chapter for more information on transport.

Around Malta

NORTH COAST

The north coast is fairly exposed and uninteresting until you get to St Paul's Bay. The sandy beach at Mellieha, east of St Paul's Bay, is the best on Malta, although it does get crowded. Catch bus No 43 or 48 from Valletta to reach the beach.

St Paul's Bay & Bugibba

Bugibba, the traditional name for the town on St Paul's Bay, is the main tourist centre – and it's ghastly. There is no reason to stay here unless you're on a very cheap package or have a liking for British food. However, the nightlife is apparently good in summer, and there are numerous cheap hotels and restaurants open throughout the year. Catch bus No 49 to get here from Valletta.

Cirkewwa

This is the port where the Gozo ferry docks. Paradise Bay, one of Malta's best sandy beaches, is a short walk to the south of the town. See the earlier Getting Around section for information on the ferry to Gozo.

WEST COAST

The west coast is a great place to get away from the crowds. The best access is by private boat. If you're looking for solitude, keep away from the big tourist development and crowded, sandy beach at Golden Bay.

MDINA & RABAT

Until the knights arrived and settled around the Grand Harbour, the political centre of Malta was Mdina. Set inland on an easily defendable rocky outcrop, it has been a fortified city for more than 3000 years. You could spend hours wandering through Mdina's narrow, cobbled streets.

The city is still home to the Maltese aristocracy and is sometimes called the Noble City, sometimes the Silent City. Much of it was rebuilt after an earthquake in 1693, but you can still see some original sections which survived the earthquake.

MALTA

Things to See & Do

The best preserved medieval building is the **Palazzo Falzon**, built in 1495, which has Norman architectural features and is generally known as the Norman House. Mdina has a beautiful main piazza, where you will find the Roman Catholic cathedral and the Mdina Cathedral Museum (open Monday to Saturday from 9 am to 1 pm and 1.30 to 4.30 pm).

The **Mdina Dungeons** (☎ 45 02 67), below the Vilhena Palace, St Publius Square, are medieval dungeons that have been restored to all their dubious glory and have tableaux depicting the victims. The dungeons are unlocked daily between 9.30 am and 5 pm and entry is Lm1.15.

The **Mdina Experience**, at 7 Mesquita Square, is the local version of Valletta's Malta Experience. It is shown from 11 am to 4 pm, Monday to Friday, and 11 am to 2 pm on Saturday. Entry is Lm1.10.

The adjacent township of Rabat is typically Maltese. **St Paul's Church** and **St Paul's Grotto** lie in the centre of the town, both of them classic examples of Maltese baroque. The grotto is believed to be the spot where St Paul lived.

Places to Stay & Eat

In Mdina, there is one budget hotel, the *Xara Palace* (☎ 45 05 60), St Paul's Square, which has double rooms for Lm13, and singles for Lm8, breakfast included. It has seen better days, but given the location, the price and the incredible views from some of its rooms, who's complaining? If you feel like a splurge, dine at the *Medina*, one of Malta's best restaurants, at 7 Holy Cross St, just off Mdina's main piazza. A really excellent meal with wine will come to around Lm12.

There are plenty of bars and a number of restaurants in Rabat. *Roman's Den Restaurant* (☎ 45 69 70) at 58 Main St is very good, though not especially cheap. At lunch, soup is 80 cents, lasagne is Lm1.20. Visit the *Baron* snack bar, 3 Republic St, not so much for the food as for the authentic local atmosphere.

Getting There & Away

Catch bus No 86 from Valletta or No 65 from Sliema to reach Mdina and Rabat.

SOUTH COAST

You can enjoy spectacular views from the 200-metre-high **Dingli Cliffs**. The most interesting and evocative prehistoric temples on Malta are **Hagar Qim** and **Mnajdra**, built between 3800 and 2500 BC near the village of Qrendi. The temples are open from 8 am to 2 pm in summer and to 5 pm in cooler weather; entry costs Lm1. These Copper Age megalithic temples are reminiscent of Stonehenge, and a visit is an absolute must.

EAST COAST

Marsaxlokk is an attractive fishing village with a couple of good fish restaurants and a touristy, harbourside market. Unfortunately, it is now overshadowed by the enormous, new power station. There are some pleasant swimming spots around **St Thomas Bay**, north-east of the village.

Gozo

Gozo is considerably smaller than Malta and has a distinctive character of its own; the countryside is more attractive, the pace is slower and there are far fewer tourists. It seems to have escaped the worst of the 20th century, so don't come for nightlife and bright lights. The capital is Victoria (also known as Rabat), but most people stay at the small resort town of Marsalforn. You can cram the sights into one day, but the real charm of Gozo can be appreciated only if you allow yourself to unravel it slowly.

VICTORIA

Victoria is an interesting, bustling town and the commercial centre of Gozo. It has a decent range of shops and banks, and there are tourist information and car-rental facilities. The *Three Hills Guest House* (☎ 55 18 95), on Xaghra Rd, has doubles for around Lm10.

There's a wonderful view over the island from the citadel which was constructed by the knights in the 17th century; it's worth visiting the cathedral and the archaeological and folklore museums.

The tourist office (☎ 55 81 06), on the corner of Palm and Republic Sts, has a useful brochure and map.

Victor Sultana (☎ 55 64 14), 50 Main Gate St (opposite the bus terminus), hires out bicycles (50 cents to Lm2.50 per day), motorcycles (minimum three days, Lm1 to Lm4 per day) and cars (minimum three days, Lm3 to Lm8 per day).

MARSALFORN

Marsalforn is the main resort town on the island and can become crowded on weekends. There's one large hotel, a scattering of smaller places to stay and a dozen restaurants, all built around an attractive bay.

You can change money at a branch of the Mid-Med Bank on the harbour front, which is open from 1 June to 31 October. Opening hours are from 9 am to 7 pm. The diving on Gozo is particularly good; visit the Calypso Diving Centre (see Activities in the Facts for the Visitor section for further information). The Marsalforn Hotel (☎ 55 61 47) hires out bicycles for Lm2 a day, or at reduced rates by the week.

Places to Stay

Outside the high season, the family-run *Atlantis Hotel* (☎ 55 46 85) in Qolla St should be considered. In winter, a poolside room and breakfast will cost Lm6.60 per person; this jumps to Lm15.50 per person in summer. Lower daily rates can be negotiated for stays of a week or more. They hire out cars and bicycles.

The *Marsalforn Hotel* (☎ 55 61 47), Rabat Rd, is a rather garish green and white hotel in the middle of town. B&B is between Lm3 and Lm5 per person, depending on the season. Self-catering flats are Lm5 to Lm12 per day. The *Electra Hotel* (☎ 55 33 23), 12 Valley Rd, is very simple, but clean. It charges Lm6.50/8.50 for a single/double.

Places to Eat

The restaurants are clustered around the harbour, and there's not really a great deal to distinguish between them. *Smiley's* is the cheapest, but it's pretty basic: burgers cost 40 cents, pizza costs 90 cents and fresh fish with salad and chips costs Lm2.

The *Il-Kartell*, on the west side of the bay, is a step up and has good fish, pasta and pizzas; spaghetti is Lm1.20 and main courses and fresh fish are from Lm3 to Lm5. The *Arzella Bar Restaurant Pizzeria*, on a terrace suspended over the east side of the bay, is similarly priced but also offers Maltese specialties such as timpana (Lm1.50) and bragioli (Lm3.20).

Getting There & Away

Marsalforn is a four-km walk from Victoria, or you can catch bus No 21 or 22 from the terminus in Main Gate St.

AROUND GOZO

Gozo measures only 14 km from east to west and six km from north to south, so a lot of the island can be covered on foot. The **Ggantija** temple complex near Xaghra village is the most spectacular in Malta – its walls are six metres high. There's a dramatic stretch of coastline around Dwejra Point, including the imposing Azure Window, a gigantic rock arch in the cliff, only few metres from the Inland Sea. This is the best area in Malta for walking along the scenic rocky coastline.

Xlendi

Xlendi is a small fishing village situated at the tip of a deep, rocky inlet on the south-west coast. It's a pretty spot, but it's fast becoming overdeveloped and has degenerated into something of a tourist trap (much loved by British day-trippers from Malta). The *Serena Apart-Hotel* (☎ 55 37 19), Upper St, is perched over the town and has great views. A superior suite with a sea view, plus breakfast, costs Lm11 per person, with reduced rates if you stay a week or more. Catch bus No 87 to get here from Victoria.

Morocco

Morocco is a fascinating mix of African, Islamic, Arab, Berber and even European influences and this, combined with its accessibility from Europe, makes it a popular and memorable place to visit. As well as the four imperial cities – Fès, Meknès, Marrakesh and Rabat – there are the natural attractions of the Atlantic beaches and the remote villages of the High Atlas and Rif mountains. The contrasts are stark: poverty and opulence, hospitality and aggression. You are unlikely to quickly forget a trip to Morocco.

Facts about the Country

HISTORY

Morocco is largely populated by descendants of the Berber settlers who came to the area thousands of years ago. Their independent spirit has outlived conquerors over the centuries and resulted in one of Africa's most colourful cultures.

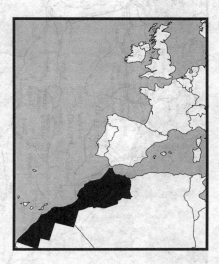

The first records of the Berbers recount their control of trans-Saharan trade. Later the Romans gained a tenuous hold in this part of North Africa, only to fade slowly away before the arrival of Islam in the 7th century. The Arab armies swept across Byzantine Egypt and eventually controlled the whole North African coast and much of Spain.

Basic tribal divisions soon reasserted themselves, however, and the Berbers, having adopted Islam, developed their own brand of Shi'ism, known as Kharijism. One of these Kharijite communities, the Idrissids, with their capital at Fès, would later form the core of a united Morocco.

By the 11th century the region had been plunged into chaos, when the Almoravids took control of Morocco and Muslim Spain (Al-Andalus) and founded Marrakesh. They were supplanted by the Almohads, who raised Fès, Marrakesh and Rabat to heights of splendour, before crumbling as Christian armies regained Spain. The Merenid dynasty revitalised the Moroccan heartland and established Fès el-Jdid (New Fès), but it too collapsed after Granada fell to the Christians in 1492 and Muslim refugees poured into Morocco.

The Merenids were followed by the Saadians but by the 1630s they had succumbed to the 'decadence' of urban living. The Alawites took over and constructed the Imperial City at Meknès during the rule of Sultan Moulay Ismail (1672-1727). It was a last gasp and Morocco increasingly became a neglected backwater as trans-Saharan trade disintegrated and Europe became industrialised.

Morocco managed to retain its independence as colonialism swept the rest of Africa until, by the 1912 Treaty of Fès, France took over much of the country, handing Spain a zone in the north. Under the enlightened French resident-general, Marshal Lyautey, the colonialists built the *villes nouvelles* (new cities) that are a feature of many larger Moroccan cities, thus preserving the more traditional medinas.

Rabat was made the capital and Casablanca

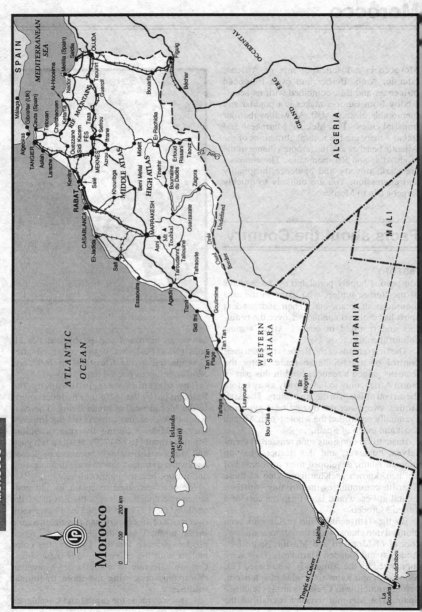

MOROCCO

developed as a major port. By 1934 the last opposition from Berber mountain tribes had been crushed, but Moroccan resistance moved into political channels in the Istiqlal (independence) party. After WWII, opposition again took a more violent turn and in 1953 the French exiled Sultan Mohammed V. This only succeeded in further stoking Moroccan discontent and he was allowed to return in 1955. Independence was granted the following year.

The Spanish withdrew from much of the country at about the same time but have retained the coastal enclaves of Ceuta and Melilla. Sultan Mohammed V became a king and, since his death, his son, King Hassan II, despite democratic noises and several coup attempts, has retained all effective power.

King Hassan's popularity soared with the 1975 'Green March', when 350,000 unarmed Moroccans marched into the Spanish colony of Western Sahara. Spanish troops left shortly after and the Polisario Front, which had been struggling for years against Spanish rule, turned to fight its new overlords. With Algerian support gone and a ceasefire in place since 1991, Morocco has a firm grip on the region.

Morocco today suffers from a batch of traditional Third World problems including breakneck population increase, high unemployment and a yawning gap between a wealthy elite and a huge section of the population living below the poverty line. Although economic reform has accelerated in the past 10 to 15 years, political change lags behind.

GEOGRAPHY & ECOLOGY

One of Africa's most geographically diverse areas, Morocco is spectacularly beautiful. It is traversed by four mountain ranges. From north to south, they are the Rif, the Middle Atlas, the High Atlas and the Anti-Atlas. Certain peaks of the High Atlas remain snowcapped all year and are among the highest in Africa.

Between the mountain ranges themselves, and between these ranges and the Atlantic Ocean, are plateaux and plains. Fed by melting snow, they are often, fertile and well watered. On many of the plains further south, agriculture is tenuous, except along certain river courses. In the extreme south, at the edge of the Anti-Atlas Mountains, the country is characterised by vast, eroded gorges which, like the rivers that flow at their bases, gradually peter

out in the endless sand and stone wastes of the Sahara Desert.

Deforestation and soil erosion are major problems in some areas. Between Ouezzane and Meknès, and Fès and Taza, for instance, vegetation is sparse after a dry winter. Nevertheless, springtime can see blazes of colourful wildflowers and there are still pine and cedar forests in the north and rolling wooded parkland towards the south. The fringes of the desert are graced with beautifully verdant palmeraies.

Wildlife includes little that is truly exotic, although wild boar inhabit the forested areas and a large wild sheep, the *mouflon*, is quite common in the Atlas, as is the Macaque monkey. The more arid regions are home to gazelles and fennec foxes but you will be very fortunate to spot either.

What you are almost certain to see are storks. They are common in country and town areas and almost every disused minaret and chimney stack supports a vast tangle of branches that the stork calls home. Egrets are also an everyday sight on cultivated land, and flights of iridescent bee-eaters can be seen swooping through the palm groves of the south.

GOVERNMENT & POLITICS

Morocco is officially a constitutional monarchy, but the power of the Crown has remained essentially absolute.

King Hassan II appoints all government ministers, who are directly answerable to him, and can dissolve parliament and rule by decree. While constitutional reforms enacted in 1992 pledged that future governments would 'reflect the balances of forces in parliament', the fact that only two-thirds of the 333-seat parliament is directly elected – the rest being chosen by local councils, chambers of commerce and salaried workers – means that the establishment effectively retains control.

Moves toward some form of bicameral parliamentary system are expected during 1996 and 1997, but just how this will be enacted (the next election is not due until 1999) and how it will affect the king's authority is unclear. The previous elections of 1993 saw opposition parties, including the Istiqlal Party, make big gains, but the present administration is largely made up of loyalist technocrats. For some, the most positive result of the polls was the first-ever election of women to parliament – only two, but a start.

The country is divided into provinces called *wilayat*, four of them making up the still-contested Western Sahara. Local government is in the hands of *pashas* and *qaids* (or *caids*).

ECONOMY

The mainstays of Morocco's economy are mining, agriculture, tourism, manufacturing, and remittances from Moroccans working abroad.

Morocco is the world's third-largest producer (and largest exporter) of phosphates but continues to suffer from low world-market prices. Tourism also took a battering during and after the Gulf War and is struggling to recover.

A decade of IMF-imposed austerity measures up to 1993, followed by continued public spending cuts and massive privatisation, has made the economy leaner and fitter, but with serious social costs, such as rising unemployment. External debt is still high, but Morocco hopes a mooted free trade zone pact with the EU will accelerate development. The payoff for Europe could be a tighter clamp on the flow of drugs from Morocco to Europe – a multibillion dollar trade that does neither side much good.

POPULATION & PEOPLE

The population stands at about 28 million, but, at present growth levels, is expected to double by early next century. Some 55% of the population is aged 20 or under. In 1990, more than half the male population and 70% of women were illiterate.

The largest city is Casablanca, with a population of around three million. It is followed by Rabat-Salé (1.23 million) and Fès (735,000).

ARTS

Two things that immediately strike the visitor to Morocco are the music and the architecture. The former is drawn from many traditions, from classics of the Arab-Andalusian heritage through to the more genuinely African rhythms of Berber music. Raï, a fusion of traditional, tribal and modern Western popular forms and instruments, began in Algeria and has become very popular in Morocco. Cheap cassettes are easily obtained throughout the country.

With the exception of what the Arabs left behind in Spain, nothing in Europe can prepare you for the visual feast of the great mosques and *medersas* (Qur'anic schools) that bejewel the major Moroccan cities. Lacking the extravagance of the Gothic or rococo, Moroccan monuments are virtuoso pieces of geometric design and harmony.

CULTURE

It is easy to be beguiled by appearances in Morocco. Despite the chic French women's fashions and many other signs of the impact of the West (and above all France), Morocco remains a largely conservative Muslim society.

Outsiders can save themselves some (but not all) hassle by dressing modestly (beach resorts like Agadir are an exception). Although not the problem it is in Algeria, Islamic fundamentalism is an issue in Morocco. Westerners' disregard for Muslim norms may well have contributed to its influence.

RELIGION

All but a tiny minority of the population is Sunni Muslim, but in Morocco, Islam is far from strictly orthodox. The main difference lies in the worship of local saints and holy people *(marabouts)* – a sort of resurgence of pre-Islamic traditions. The whitewashed *koubba* (tomb) of the marabout is a standard sight all over the Maghreb (north-west Africa).

Where these local saints have accumulated many followers, prosperous individuals have endowed the koubba with educational institutions known as *zawiyyas*, which offer an alternative to the orthodox medersas attached to mosques.

Until the establishment of Israel, Morocco was the home of many Jews. Traditionally, they lived in the *mellahs* of the main cities and were an important economic force. Few now remain, most having emigrated to Israel.

LANGUAGE

Arabic is the official language, but Berber and French are widely spoken. Spanish is spoken in former Spanish-held territory (particularly the north) and English in the main tourist centres. Arabic and French are taught in schools and French is important in university education and commerce – it is still the official language in banking.

Although many Moroccans speak many different languages passably, don't expect much beyond Moroccan Arabic and French outside the main cities and popular tourist spots.

Spoken Moroccan Arabic *(darija)* is considerably different from what you hear in the Middle East. Pick up a copy of Lonely Planet's *Moroccan Arabic Phrasebook*, by Dan Bacon, for more detailed coverage. Various Berber dialects are spoken in the countryside and particularly in the mountains.

See the Language Guide at the back of this book for pronunciation guidelines and useful words and phrases.

Facts for the Visitor

PLANNING

Climate & When to Go

In winter the coastal lowlands are pleasantly warm to hot during the day (average 18°C) and cool to cold at night (9°C). In summer, it's very hot during the day (30°C) and warm at night (18°C). A hot, dusty wind from the desert, the *chergui* can whip temperatures up above 40°C.

Winter in the higher regions demands clothing suitable for Arctic conditions; this is true anywhere in the vicinity of the High Atlas Mountains. In summer, it's hot during the day and cool at night.

Passes over the High Atlas can be blocked with snow during winter. Snowploughs usually clear them by the following day, but you may spend a bitterly cold night stuck in an unheated bus.

The main rainy season is between November and April but it usually brings only occasional light rain. Rain rarely falls on the eastern parts of the country, and humidity is generally low.

The most pleasant times to explore Morocco are during spring (April to May) and autumn (September to October). Midsummer can be very enjoyable on the coast but viciously hot in the interior. Likewise, winter can be idyllic in Marrakesh and further south during the day, but you can be chilled to the bone at night.

Books & Maps

See Lonely Planet's travel survival kits *Morocco* and (if you're planning on travelling

further) *North Africa* for more detailed information on the country.

The Moors: Islam in the West by Michael Brett & Werner Forman details Moorish civilisation at its height, with superb colour photographs. *The Conquest of Morocco* by Douglas Porch is recommended. Another good book, also by Porch, is *The Conquest of the Sahara*.

Doing Daily Battle by Fatima Mernissi, translated by Mary Jo Lakeland, is a collection of interviews with 11 Moroccan women giving a valuable insight into their lives and aspirations. A number of Western writers have connections with Morocco, including long-term Tangier resident, Paul Bowles.

The best map is the Michelin No 959 *Morocco* (scale 1:1,000,000).

Online Services

If you have access to the Web, there is good site about Morocco at http://maghreb.net/morocco/. A helpful location for further searches is http://bertie.la.utexas.edu/course-materials/government/mena/morocco.html.

What to Bring

Bring any special medication you need. Sun protection, including hat, glasses and suntan cream, is a good idea in much of the country for much of the year. You should also bring your own contraceptives. You can get hold of condoms and even the pill, but quality is dubious and availability uncertain.

SUGGESTED ITINERARIES

Depending on how much time you have, you might want to do the following things:

One to two weeks
Visit the imperial cities (Fès, Meknès, Marrakesh and Rabat).
Two to three weeks
Visit Marrakesh, the High Atlas (trekking from Imlil), the southern oases and gorges, and finish on the coast at Essaouira.
One month
At a pinch you could get in the imperial cities, some trekking, the southern oases and gorges, Essaouira and perhaps spend a little time in the Rif Mountains, preferably at Chefchaouen.
Two months
This should give you time to visit all of Morocco (or a good chunk of it).

MOROCCO

HIGHLIGHTS
Imperial Cities
The four great cities of Morocco's imperial past are Fès, Marrakesh, Meknès and Rabat. Here you will discover Morocco's greatest monuments – mosques and medersas surrounded by the chaos of the medina and *souqs* (markets).

Coastal Towns & Beaches
The Atlantic coast is dotted with tranquil towns bearing the marks of European occupation. Among the more interesting are Asilah and El-Jadida, which started life as Portuguese settlements, and Essaouira. There are plenty of beaches along the Atlantic coast, and a couple of decent ones on the Mediterranean too.

High Atlas & the South
In just a few days you can sample the breathtaking heights of the Atlas Mountains, sprinkled with Berber villages, and then head south for the oases and kasbahs (citadels) of the Drâa Valley and the Dadès and Todra gorges to the south-east of Marrakesh.

TOURIST OFFICES
Local Tourist Offices
The national tourist body, ONMT, has offices (usually called Délégation Régionale du Tourisme) in the main cities. They have brochures and simple maps of the major places. The head office is in Rabat, at Rue al-Abtal (☎ 681531). A few cities also have local offices known as *syndicats d'initiative*. The staff at these are more clued-up on local matters.

Moroccan Tourist Offices Abroad
The ONMT maintains offices in Australia (Sydney), Belgium (Brussels), Canada (Montreal), France (Paris), Germany (Düsseldorf), Italy (Milan), Japan (Tokyo), Portugal (Lisbon), Spain (Madrid), Sweden (Stockholm), Switzerland (Zürich), the UK (London) and the USA (New York and Orlando).

USEFUL ORGANISATIONS
The following organisations may prove helpful:

Club Alpin Français
  BP 6178, Casablanca 01 (☎ 270090; fax 297292). Useful if you want to book refuges in the High Atlas Mountains for trekking.

Division de la Cartographie
  This section of the Conservation & Topography Department, at 31 Ave Moulay Hassan in Rabat (☎ 705311; fax 705191), sells detailed survey maps of interest to people doing serious hiking or travelling well off the beaten track. Maps of the most popular areas of the High Atlas can be obtained on the spot (Dr 30 a sheet); for other areas you may need your passport and have to make an official request, which can take days.
Fédération Royale Marocaine des Auberges de Jeunes
  The head office of the Moroccan hostel organisation is on Blvd Oqba ben Nafii in Meknès (☎ 524698). There is another office in Casablanca on the Parc de la Ligue Arabe (☎ 970952 or 220551).
Fédération Royale Marocaine de Ski et Montagne
  Parc de la Ligue Arabe, BP 15899, Casablanca 01 (☎ 203798).

VISAS & EMBASSIES
Most visitors to Morocco need no visa and on entry are granted leave to remain in the country for 90 days. Visa requirements for nationals of South Africa have recently been waived and the process for Israelis is now simpler. They must apply through Moroccan consulates either within their home country or abroad. Cost varies according to length of stay and the number of entries requested.

Nationals of the following countries making organised tours to Morocco only need their national identity cards: Austria, Denmark, Finland, France, Germany, Iceland, Norway, Spain, Sweden and Switzerland.

Entry requirements for Ceuta and Melilla are the same as for Spain (see that chapter).

On entry, your passport is stamped and there are forms to fill in. If you're on the Algeciras-Tangier boat, this process begins on the boat, so look out for officials, or you may have long delays when you dock.

Visa Extensions
If the 90 days you are entitled to are insufficient, the simplest thing to do is leave (eg to the Spanish enclaves) and come back a few days later. Your chances improve if you re-enter by a different route.

People on visas may, however, prefer to try for an extension. Go to the Sûreté Nationale office in Rabat (off Ave Mohammed V) with your passport, a photo, a form (which you'll need to pick up beforehand at the same office) and a letter from your embassy requesting a visa extension on your behalf.

Should this fail, or if you want to get residency for any other reason, you will have to go to the Bureau des Etrangers at the police headquarters (Préfecture de Police) in the town you're in. You may well have to go to Rabat. The process is long and involves opening bank accounts, producing proof of your capacity to support yourself and reasons for staying – good luck.

Moroccan Embassies Abroad

Algeria
    8 Rue des Cèdres, Parc de la Reine, Algiers (☎ 02-607737, 607408)
Australia
    Suite 2, 11 West St, North Sydney, NSW 2060 (☎ 02-9957 6717, 9922 4999)
Canada
    38 Range Rd, Ottawa KIN 8J4 (☎ 416-236 7391/7392)
France
    5 Rue Le Tasse, Paris 75016 (☎ 01 45 20 69 35)
Germany
    Gotenstrasse, 7-9-5300, Bonn 2 (☎ 35 50 44)
Japan
    Silva Kingdom 3.16-3, Sendagaya, Shibuya-ku, Tokyo (☎ 03-3478 3271)
Netherlands
    Oranjestraat 9, 2514 JB, The Hague (☎ 70-346 6917)
Spain
    Calle Serrano 179, Madrid 2 (☎ 91-563 1090/1150)
Tunisia
    39 Rue du 1er Juin, Mutuelleville, Tunis (☎ 01-782775)
UK
    49 Queen's Gate Gardens, London SW7 5NE (☎ 0171-581 5001)
USA
    1601 21st St NW, Washington, DC, 20009 (☎ 202-462 7979)

Foreign Embassies in Morocco

Most embassies are in Rabat but there are also consulates in Tangier, Marrakesh and Casablanca. Embassies in Rabat (telephone code ☎ 07) include:

Algeria
    46 Ave Tariq ibn Zayid (☎ 765474)
Canada
    13bis Zankat Jaafar as-Sadiq, Agdal (☎ 672880)
France
    Embassy: 3 Rue Fahnoun, Agdal (☎ 777822; fax 777852)
    Consulate (Service de Visas): Rue Ibn al-Khattib (☎ 702404)
Germany
    7 Rue Madnine (☎ 709662)

Japan
    70 Ave Al Oumoum Al Mouttahida (☎ 674163)
Netherlands
    40 Rue de Tunis (☎ 733512)
Spain
    Embassy: 3-5 Rue Madnine (☎ 707600, 709481; fax 707964)
    Consulate: 57 Ave du Chellah (☎ 704147; fax 704694)
Tunisia
    6 Ave de Fès (☎ 730576, 730636; fax 727866)
UK
    17 Ave de la Tour Hassan (☎ 731403; fax 720906)
USA
    2 Ave de Marrakech (☎ 762265; fax 765661)

DOCUMENTS

Although officially required, an International Driving Permit is not generally necessary in Morocco, as most national licences are sufficient. Hostel membership cards are not obligatory for staying in most Moroccan hostels; they'll save a couple of dirham each night. An international student card, if you are under 31 years, can get you 50% reductions on internal flights.

CUSTOMS

You can import up to 200 cigarettes and a litre of spirits duty-free.

MONEY

The unit of currency is the dirham (Dr), which is equal to 100 centimes. The importation or exportation of local currency is prohibited and there's not much of a black market and little reason to use it. In the Spanish enclaves of Ceuta and Melilla the currency is the Spanish peseta (pta).

Exchange Rates

Australia	A$1	=	Dr 6.73
France	1FF	=	Dr 1.71
Germany	DM1	=	Dr 5.80
Japan	¥100	=	Dr 7.94
New Zealand	NZ$1	=	Dr 5.99
Spain	100 ptas	=	Dr 6.82
United Kingdom	UK£1	=	Dr 13.37
United States	US$1	=	Dr 8.58

Banking services are generally quick and efficient. Branches of BMCE (Banque Marocaine du Commerce Extérieur) are the most convenient and often have separate *bureau de change* sections. Avoid them for travellers' cheques, as

MOROCCO

they are one of the few banks to charge commission. Australian and New Zealand dollars are not quoted in banks and are generally not accepted.

Credit Cards
All major credit cards are widely accepted in the main cities and even in many small towns, although their use often attracts a 5% surcharge. American Express is represented by the travel agency Voyages Schwartz, which can be found in Casablanca, Marrakesh and Tangier.

Visa, MasterCard, Access and Carte Bleue are accepted by many banks, but usually only in head branches. The principal banks in all the main cities have automatic teller machines *(guichets automatiques)*, but only BMCE and sometimes BMCI ATMs accept foreign cards – if the machines are working and if they can be persuaded to recognise your PIN!

Costs
Moroccan prices are refreshingly reasonable. With a few small tips here and there plus entry charges to museums and the like, you could just about get by on US$15 to US$20 a day per person as long as you stay in cheap hotels, eat at cheap restaurants and are not in a hurry. If you'd prefer some of life's basic luxuries, such as hot showers, the occasional splurge at a good restaurant and the odd taxi, plan on US$25 to US$30 a day per person.

Tipping & Bargaining
Tipping is a way of life in Arab countries. Practically any service can warrant a tip, but don't be railroaded. The judicious distribution of a few dirham for a service willingly rendered can, however, make your life a lot easier. Between 5% and 10% of a restaurant bill is fine, but if you are waiting for Dr 1 change on a Dr 4 cup of coffee, don't bother!

Bargaining is also an integral part of Moroccan street life. Prices in hotels, on transport and in most 'normal' shops are generally fixed. In the souqs and when souvenir-hunting, meet the vendor's stated price with one as low as one-tenth, and bargain your way to the middle.

POST & COMMUNICATIONS
Post
The Moroccan post is fairly reliable, and you shouldn't have big problems receiving letters care of poste restante – although they are sometimes returned to sender a little hastily. Take your passport to claim mail. There's a small charge for collecting letters.

Outgoing parcels have to be inspected by customs (at the post office) before you seal them and pay for postage, so don't turn up with a sealed parcel. Some post offices offer a private packing service, but if you're not sure whether this is available, bring the requirements with you. Post offices are distinguished by the 'PTT' sign or the new 'La Poste' logo.

Telephone & Fax
The telephone system in Morocco is good. Most cities and towns have a phone office attached to the post office – the biggest are open 24 hours, seven days a week. For overseas calls you can either book a call at the office and pay at the counter, or dial direct. Private sector *téléboutiques* are widespread and much quicker than the official phone offices, though fractionally more expensive. The attendant sells phonecards *(télécartes)* and can provide as much change as you might need, which is a lot if you are ringing abroad. Calls are expensive; over US$2 a minute to Europe and about three times that to Australia. There is a 20% reduction between 10.30 pm and 6 am and 40% from 1 pm Saturday to 6 am Monday.

Reverse charges calls are possible from phone offices – ask to *téléphoner en PCV* (pronounced 'peh-seh-veh').

There is one standard phone book for all of Morocco in French – the *Annuaire des Abonnés au Téléphone*. Most phone offices have a copy lying around.

When calling overseas from Morocco, dial ☎ 00, your country code and then the city code and number.

When calling Morocco from overseas, the international direct telephone code is ☎ 212.

The police can be reached on ☎ 19 and the highway emergency service on ☎ 177.

Many *téléboutiques* have fax machines. Prices per page vary but you can expect to pay about Dr 40 to Europe and Dr 80 to North America and Australia. The better hotels also offer fax services.

MEDIA
Most French press is available in the big cities. You can also find *Time, Newsweek,* the *Inter-*

national Herald Tribune and the occasional English paper at selected newsstands – usually a couple of days late.

Local radio is in Arabic and French, and you can pick up Spanish broadcasts in most parts of the country. The BBC broadcasts into the area on shortwave frequencies MHz 15,070 and 12,095, from about 8 am to 11 pm.

PHOTOGRAPHY & VIDEO

Kodak and Fuji colour-negative and slide film, as well as video tapes, are readily available in all large Moroccan cities and towns.

Urban Moroccans are generally easy-going about being photographed but in the countryside you should ask permission beforehand. As a rule, women especially do *not* want to be photographed. Respect their right to privacy and don't take photos.

TIME

Moroccan time is GMT/UTC all year, so when it's summer in Europe, Morocco will be two hours behind Spanish time and one hour behind UK time.

ELECTRICITY

Morocco has 220 and sometimes 110V, depending on which area you are in, so check before plugging in any appliances. Plugs are of the European two-pin type.

WEIGHTS & MEASURES

Morocco uses the metric system. There is a standard conversion table at the back of this book.

LAUNDRY

You're better off doing it yourself. Some hotels will do it and charge – often you have to wait days to see your clothes again. There are plenty of dry-cleaners about, but few simple laundries.

TOILETS

Outside the major cities, public toilets are few, far between and usually require your own paper, a tip for the attendant, stout-soled shoes and a nose clip. They are mostly of the 'squatter' variety. If you get caught short, duck into the nearest hotel or café. No-one will refuse you.

HEALTH

The Moroccan health service is largely urban based; almost 50% of all public sector doctors are to be found in Casablanca and Rabat-Salé. Thus, if you're in serious trouble you need to get to one of the bigger towns. The number of rural health centres has, however, increased in recent years and they are quite adequate for dealing with minor complaints. There is also a growing private health sector but, in case of emergency, head for a public hospital outpatients department. Moroccan doctors are, on the whole, reasonably well trained and the top hospitals in the big cities are OK. Pharmacies are widespread and well stocked.

See also the Health section in the Facts for the Visitor chapter at the start of this book.

WOMEN TRAVELLERS

Although a certain level of sexual harassment is almost the norm, in some ways Morocco can be less problematic than more overtly macho countries such as Italy and Spain. Telling a Moroccan male to behave himself can sometimes have decisive results. Although it is wise to dress conservatively, you will see plenty of Moroccan women wearing miniskirts or shorts in the larger cities. See also the Women Travellers section in the Facts for the Visitor chapter at the start of this book.

DANGERS & ANNOYANCES

Morocco's era as a hippy paradise, riding the Marrakesh Express and all that, is long past. Plenty of fine dope may be grown in the Rif Mountains, but drug busts are common and Morocco is not a good place to investigate local prison conditions. Travellers have reported various drug-related rip-off rackets, including one where tourists are kidnapped and forced to smoke the stuff, photos are taken, and they are told they will be turned over to the police unless they cooperate. Morocco has its share of pickpockets and thieves but they're not a major problem.

Guides

What Morocco does have in abundance is touts, guides and a persistent background of 'hassles'. You can't totally ignore the frequent offers of paid assistance, and sometimes it's actually worth forking out a little money for expert local help. The big medinas, the one at

Fès in particular, really can be confusing at first, and once you have one guide you're not pestered to take another. Official guides carry badges and cost about Dr 50 for half a day. A tip will be expected. Negotiate carefully and, if you don't want to be dragged through shops, make sure they are quite clear about this. They make part of their living from commissions in shops, so it's hard to avoid ending up in some. You may occasionally be subjected to heavy pressure to buy items. If you don't want to, don't (but try to be polite about it).

BUSINESS HOURS

Banking hours are Monday to Thursday from 8.30 to 11.30 am and 2.30 to 4.30 pm; on Friday hours are from 8.30 to 11.15 am and 3 to 4.30 pm; and during Ramadan they're 9 am to 3 pm. These times can vary a little. In some of the main tourist cities, the BMCE head branch will have later opening times for currency exchange (often a small separate office). Post offices generally keep similar hours, but don't close until 6 pm or so. Phone offices in the bigger centres are open long hours and seven days a week.

Many museums and some monuments are closed on Tuesday.

PUBLIC HOLIDAYS & SPECIAL EVENTS

All banks, post offices and most shops are shut on the main public holidays: 1 January (New Year's Day); 3 March (Feast of the Throne); 1 May (Labour Day); 6 November (Anniversary of the Green March); 18 November (Independence Day).

In addition to secular holidays there are many Islamic holidays and festivals, all tied to the lunar calendar. Some are celebrated all over the country but others are less elaborate local events.

Probably the most important is the 'Eid al-Fitr, held at the end of the month-long Ramadan fast, which is fairly strictly observed by most Muslims.

Another important Muslim festival is 'Eid al-Adha, which marks the end of the Islamic year. It commemorates Abraham's submission to God through the offer of his son Isaac for sacrifice. The third main religious festival, known as Mawlid an-Nabi (or simply Mouloud), celebrates the Prophet Mohammed's birthday.

Local festivals, mostly in honour of marabouts (saints) and known as moussems or amouggars, are common among the Berbers and usually held in the summer months.

ACTIVITIES
Trekking & Hiking
It is worth doing some trekking in the High Atlas, a walking experience unlike anything you will find in Europe. Ascending Jebel Toubkal, the highest peak, takes just a matter of days, but you could easily spend weeks hiking across the mountains. See the High Atlas Trekking section.

Surfing & Windsurfing
There are plenty of beaches along the Atlantic coast to investigate, but it is the winds in the Essaouira region that have made it popular for windsurfing. There is no reason not to bring a surfboard, although often the waves are messy

Rock Climbing
The Dadès and Todra gorges in the south have some interesting and challenging climbs. Most of the hotels there have hand-drawn plans of various routes and can provide a certain amount of the necessary gear.

ACCOMMODATION
Camping
You can camp anywhere in Morocco if you have permission from the site's owner, but there are also many official camping grounds which vary in price depending on facilities.

Hostels
There are hostels (auberges de jeunesse) at Asni, Azrou, Casablanca, Chefchaouen, Fès, Marrakesh, Meknès, Rabat and Tangier. If you're travelling alone, they are among the cheapest places to stay. They usually cost Dr 20 to Dr 30 a night.

Hotels
Apart from unclassified hotels (usually the most basic), hotels in Morocco are classified under guidelines established by the Fèdèration Nationale de l'Industrie Hôtelière, and there's a fixed maximum price they can charge. You can choose from one to four-star hotels which are then subdivided as class A or B. A one-star B single with its own shower but shared toilet

is around Dr 80, and a two-star A single/double with shower and shared toilet is around Dr 150. A four-star A single with shower and toilet is around Dr 400. There are regional and seasonal variations.

Tourist tax is added to hotel prices, and ranges from Dr 3 per person in the lower classes to Dr 8 per person in the higher classes. Five-star luxury hotels are not regulated and have no ceiling on their prices.

The most basic unclassified hotels may have no shower facilities but there will always be a *hammam* (public bath) nearby, usually with separate times for male and female clientele.

FOOD

Morocco offers fewer gastronomic delights than you might expect. In average restaurants the food can be distinctly mundane, and it's worth the occasional splurge as an antidote to culinary boredom. Vegetarians may well be reduced to surviving on salads and fruit, though shops and markets are well stocked if you are self-catering.

In the larger towns many restaurants offer set meals – starter, main course, dessert – at reasonable prices. They typically cost Dr 40 to Dr 80 (US$5 to US$10), but you can spend up to Dr 350 (US$40) in the best places.

The French influence is still strong, and although traditionally baked bread is widely available, 'French sticks' are universal and every town has at least one *pâtisserie*, often attached to a café. Coffee and a croissant is a popular way to start the day.

Couscous, the staple of the region, consists of an enormous bowl of steamed semolina topped with a meat-and-vegetable sauce. It can vary enormously from the barely edible to the truly delicious. The other well-known Moroccan dish is *tajine*, a meat-and-vegetable stew cooked slowly in an earthenware pot.

Harira is the traditional Moroccan starter: it's a tasty and filling soup based on a meat stock thickened with macaroni, lentils and vegetables. With a chunk of bread it makes a cheap meal.

At the other extreme is *pastilla*, an incredibly rich pigeon pie made with layered *ouarka* pastry (like filo pastry), flavoured with nuts and spices, coated with sugar and baked. Fès is a major centre for pastilla.

All too often, however, you find yourself faced with chicken and chips. Kebab and *kefta* (meatballs) fast-food outlets and sandwich bars are popular and serve a filling meal for as little as Dr 10. Although they're generally quite healthy, it's wise to be cautious with salads until your stomach has had time to acclimatise. Mixed salad is known as *salade marocaine*. Seafood can be excellent along the coast.

Desserts and sweets are more often available from pâtisseries than in restaurants, but crème caramel, cakes and fruit are often served in the better restaurants.

DRINKS

Moroccan city streets are lined with cafés or tea rooms where sipping coffee or mint tea while the world passes by is a favourite occupation. Tea is served in glasses, very hot, very sweet and with a bush of mint leaves stuffed into the pot or glass. Coffee is served in the French style: short black or large white. Everything closes early though – except during Ramadan, the cities are dead by 10 pm.

Sidi Ali, Sidi Harazem and the fizzy Olmes are the most readily available bottled mineral waters. Popular international soft drinks are also widely available and cost about Dr 5. Beer is reasonably easy to find in the villes nouvelles, and even in some outdoor cafés. A bottle of Stork or Flag beer typically costs Dr 12 to Dr 15 in restaurants. Morocco produces some quite palatable wines for as little as Dr 35 in liquor stores. Freshly squeezed orange juice is cheap and delicious.

ENTERTAINMENT

Morocco is no nightlife paradise. The cities all have cinemas and a few discos, either dubious or rather exclusive – or both. You can see theatre in Rabat. Plenty of hotels and restaurants put on traditional dance and music shows, and you can usually find a bar (however dire).

THINGS TO BUY

Moroccan crafts are world-famous for their variety and quality. The souqs of Fès, Meknès and Marrakesh offer a full range.

Wooden boxes, marquetry and chessboards are best bought in Essaouira. Cedarwood screens are the things to buy in Fès or Meknès, while brightly painted chests and cradles are a speciality of Fès and Tetouan. Chased-copper and brass objects are good buys in Casablanca,

Fès, Marrakesh and Tetouan. Silverware is a speciality of Tiznit and Taroudannt.

The quality and softness of Morocco's leather work is legendary. For the best wallets, desk sets, slippers *(babouches)* and embossed poufs, go to Fès, Meknès, Marrakesh and Rabat. The carpet souqs of Fès, Meknès, Marrakesh and Rabat stock many styles and sizes – shop around for quality before buying.

Levis jeans at Dr 160 are a lot cheaper than in many European countries.

Getting There & Away

AIR
Although most travellers arrive by ferry from Spain or Gibraltar, Morocco is well served by air from Europe, the Middle East and West Africa. The main international airport is outside Casablanca, but there are smaller ones at Tangier, Agadir, Marrakesh and other centres. Airlines flying to Morocco include Air France, Alitalia, British Airways, GB Airways, Iberia, KLM, Lufthansa, Royal Air Maroc (RAM), Swissair and Tunis Air.

Europe
It is possible to find cheap charter-flight tickets to Morocco from northern European cities such as Amsterdam, London, Manchester or Paris. They're always return tickets and generally must be paid for in advance. Some agents will sell you a one-way ticket a few days before the flight or even on the day itself if they have a deal with the charter companies and there are spare seats going. The cheapest scheduled one-month return fares from London to, say, Casablanca, cost around UK£200. Scheduled tickets in the high season, or tickets valid for longer, are about UK£300.

It is generally cheaper to fly to Málaga in southern Spain, bus it to Algeciras and catch a ferry. The cheapest flights from London are often available in November and December – around UK£60 to UK£80 for a long-weekend return.

If you can find a cheap charter flight to Morocco (especially to Agadir or Marrakesh if you want to get straight to the south), it is often worth it even if you have to throw away the return half. Finding these tickets can involve a lot of work, and they get snapped up quickly. Trying to arrange them through provincial agents is usually a waste of time.

Regular fares from Morocco, which is all you're likely to find in the country, are becoming cheaper. A return ticket Casablanca-Paris can be found for around US$300.

North America
Royal Air Maroc has a direct Montreal-New York-Casablanca flight (Can$1650 return), but it would be more economical to take a cheap flight to London and continue from there.

Australasia
There are no direct flights between Australia or New Zealand and Morocco. The best bet is to get a flight to Europe and make your way to Morocco from there. Most people head for London or Amsterdam first.

LAND
Europe
Bus Eurolines and the Moroccan national bus line, CTM (Compagnie des Transports Marocains), operate buses between Morocco and many European cities. London-Marrakesh return costs UK£228. CTM buses to Paris and other French and Belgian cities run from most Moroccan cities and cost around Dr 1000 to Dr 1400 (US$118 to US$165) one way. These services usually run several times a week.

Train Buses are fine if you can handle them over long distances, but with a train you have the option of couchettes and can break the trip along the way (tickets are generally valid for two months, one way or return). The Moroccan rail system is part of Inter-Rail. The one-way fare from London to Tangier is UK£168 (30% less for those under 26).

Algeria
Car There are two crossing points from Morocco to Algeria when and if the border is open: between Oujda and Tlemcen in the north near the coast, and between Figuig and Beni Ounif, 300 km further south.

In the past, people bringing a vehicle *into* Morocco had to have a telex (as well as a Green Card) from their embassy in Rabat guaranteeing that they would take the vehicle out of the country. Check this well in advance, as getting such a telex can take up to a couple of weeks.

There are no direct buses between Morocco and Algeria.

Train The Al-Maghreb al-Arabi train used to link Morocco, Algeria and Tunisia daily, the trip taking about 44 hours. This service has been indefinitely suspended owing to the troubled situation in Algeria.

SEA
Spain
Car ferries are operated by Compañía Trasmediterranea, Islena de Navigación SA, Comarit, Limadet and Transtour. The most popular route is Algeciras-Tangier; others are Algeciras-Ceuta (Spanish Morocco), Almeria-Melilla (Spanish Morocco), Málaga-Melilla (Spanish Morocco) and Tarifa-Tangier. The vessels are mostly car ferries of the drive-on and drive-off type.

Algeciras-Tangier There are nine crossings a day in either direction (more in the high season). The crossing takes 2½ hours, and fares are 3065 ptas (pesetas) or Dr 210 (half-price for children under 12 years of age). A car up to six metres long costs 8500 ptas or Dr 618. Jetfoils do the crossing in an hour for the same price.

Algeciras-Ceuta There are up to 12 crossings a day (ferry and jetfoil) in either direction. The ferry trip takes 1½ hours and the fare is 1801 ptas. Cars cost from 8223 ptas. The jetfoil costs 2945 ptas and takes 30 minutes.

Almeria & Málaga-Melilla Compañía Trasmediterranea has six services a week from Almeria to Melilla and vice versa. The crossing takes 6½ to eight hours with fares from 3200 to 8500 ptas. Málaga-Melilla operates on a similar schedule and with similar fares but takes around eight hours.

Tarifa-Tangier The Transtour ferry operates once daily except Sunday in either direction. The crossing takes one hour and the fare is 3100 ptas or Dr 210. This is not a car ferry.

Gibraltar
The Gibraltar-Tangier service has had a rocky history but sometimes operates thrice-weekly in each direction. The two-hour crossing costs UK£19 (Dr 250) one way. There is an occasional catamaran service between Gibraltar and Restinga Smir, north of Tetouan. When it runs (mainly summer), it costs around UK£20 one way.

France
Sète-Tangier & Nador This car-ferry service is operated by the Compagnie Marocaine de Navigation and the crossing is usually made once every four to five days. The trip takes 38 hours, and the fare, depending on class, is between FF1250 and FF2100 (children half-price). Cars under four metres long cost FF1540. Departures, journey time and fares to Nador (summer only) are similar.

LEAVING MOROCCO
There are no departure taxes from Morocco. If you plan to buy a ferry ticket at the port in Tangier, keep enough dirham handy to do so.

Getting Around

AIR
If time is limited, it's worth considering the occasional internal flight with Royal Air Maroc (RAM). If you're under 22, or over 60, or under 31 years old with a valid international student card, you get 50% off all fares. The same reduction applies for families of three or more. There are various fares depending on days of the week but a cheap return flight from Casablanca to Fès (Dr 462) takes 50 minutes and can save a circuitous train trip.

Internal airports serviced by RAM are Agadir, Al-Hoceima, Casablanca, Dakhla, Fès, Laayoune, Marrakesh, Oujda, Ouarzazate, Rabat, Smara, Tangier and Tan Tan.

BUS
There is a good network of bus routes all over the country and departures are frequent. Most cities and towns have a central terminal (*gare routière*). Otherwise the various bus companies are usually clustered in the same area.

MOROCCO

CTM (Compagnie des Transports Marocains) is the only national company (privatised in 1994). On most main routes it runs two classes: *mumtaz* (deluxe) and 1st class. There are more of the former than the latter, so you'll often be paying the higher fare (about 25% more) unless you're very flexible about departure times. CTM runs only a handful of 2nd-class buses on less important routes. Generally booking is not necessary, but it's advisable (where they sell advance tickets) in smaller towns with few services. In some cities, CTM has its own terminal.

The biggest of the remaining companies is SATAS, which covers destinations south of Casablanca. It's just as good as CTM, slightly cheaper and has more services in the south. The other firms cover the whole range, right down to tiny local companies operating a couple of clapped-out buses. Sometimes you have a choice of 1st and 2nd class; often it's 2nd class only and the distinction is not always evident.

Bus transport is cheap; some examples of bus fares on CTM mumtaz class include:

Casablanca to:	Agadir (Dr 130), Fès (Dr 75), Marrakesh (Dr 60), Tangier (Dr 100)
Tangier to:	Fès (Dr 79), Tiznit (Dr 230)
Marrakesh to:	Fès (Dr 125), Ouarzazate (Dr 50)
Agadir to:	Laayoune (Dr 194.50), Tangier (Dr 230)

There is an official baggage charge on CTM buses – about Dr 5 for an average pack. On other lines you'll often be subject to demands for money from baggage handlers. It should rarely be more than Dr 2, but they often ask Dr 5 – and become quite irate about it. Theft is generally not a problem.

Only CTM mumtaz buses have heating, so have lots of warm clothes when crossing the Atlas – it's possible to be stuck for a night because of snowdrifts.

TRAIN
Morocco has one of the most modern rail systems in Africa and train is the preferred way to travel when you can. You have a choice of 1st and 2nd class in normal and *rapide* trains. The latter are in fact no faster, but have air-con and are more comfortable. The shuttle trains (TNR) between Rabat, Casablanca and Mohammed V international airport are in a class of their own. They are fast (Rabat to Casablanca in 55 minutes) and comfortable Fares in 2nd class are roughly comparable with bus fares, and there is no need to go 1st class

Couchettes are available on long-distance night trains (Casablanca-Oujda; Marrakesh Tangier) and sleepers on the Oujda run. There are refreshment trolleys and sometimes buffet cars on the longer journeys too.

Timetables are prominently displayed in train stations, and a free book of timetables *Indicateur Horaires,* is sometimes available at stations.

Supratours runs luxury buses in conjunction with trains to some destinations not on the rail network. Useful ones include Tetouan, Agadir and Essaouira. You can buy a bus-rail ticket to any place on the combined network.

CAR & MOTORCYCLE
You drive on the right in Morocco. Main roads are in decent condition, but many secondary roads are not so hot. Some mountain roads can be blocked by snow in winter, and desert roads are sometimes awash with sand drifts. There is only one motorway, between Casablanca Rabat and Kenitra. An extension to Larache and a Rabat-Fès link are expected to open in 1996. The speed limit on the motorway is 120 km/h. Elsewhere it is 100 km/h (60 or 40 km/h in built-up areas).

There are frequent police and customs road blocks, some set up with tyre-shredding traps Always stop; often you'll be waved through but have your licence and passport handy.

Most towns have paid parking areas. They give some peace of mind and cost a few dirham for a few hours or Dr 10 overnight.

Super (about Dr 7.50 a litre) and diesel are the most widely available types of fuel. They are much cheaper in the Spanish enclaves and the Western Sahara.

Rental
It is worth renting a car for at least a few days especially in the southern oases and kasba routes, for the freedom this gives you to explore.

All the major companies have reps in the main cities, and there are plenty of local companies. The cheapest car is a Renault 4, perfectly decent little vehicle. Rental for three days with unlimited mileage starts on paper at Dr 1962 but there seems no need to pay the price. On top comes a 19% tax, and it's worth taking out Collision Damage Waiver insurance (at least Dr 40 a day). You may be asked to leave a deposit of at least Dr 3000 if not paying by credit card, and need to be at least 21 years old. It's cheaper if you hire for a week and more so for a month or more (always shop around and always haggle for discounts). National licences are generally acceptable, although officially you need an International Driving Permit.

Agadir seems to be one of the few places where you can hire motorbikes or scooters.

BICYCLE

There's no better way to see some of the country, but you need to be fit to cycle in the mountains. Take plenty of water and a good repair kit when on the road. Many roads are narrow and dusty. You can transport bikes on the train and bus, although they could take a beating on the latter.

HITCHING

Hitching is OK, but can be tricky if you have to deal with hustlers – a problem in the north. Many drivers expect to be paid something for giving you a lift. Women should not hitch alone.

LOCAL TRANSPORT

The big cities all have reasonable local bus networks. A ride costs about Dr 2 and they can be useful for getting from the ville nouvelle to the medina in places like Marrakesh and Fès.

City taxis (petits taxis) are equally useful and cheap – you'll rarely pay more than Dr 10. Some are metered, in others you must haggle. Multiple hire is the rule, and fares rise by about 50% after 8 pm.

Shared taxis (grands taxis) work a little like buses. They take six passengers to a fixed destination for a standard fare and leave when full. They often leave more frequently than buses, are quicker and up to 50% more expensive. Over long distances they can be very cramped.

Grands taxis are a good idea where bus services are thin, or on scenic routes that buses might cover partially at night (grands taxis mostly stop running at dusk or cost 50% extra after this time). It is possible to hire these taxis privately (this is called corsa) – you must agree

on a price with the driver, and discuss beforehand if you will want to stop to take photos en route. They won't stop if you're travelling with other people on a standard run.

ORGANISED TOURS

Marrakesh and Agadir are the main centres for organised tours catering to package tourists. The trips work out much more expensive than going on your own. Otherwise, many hotels organise trips, particularly 4WD and camel desert excursions in the south.

The Mediterranean Coast & the Rif

TANGIER

All the peoples who have settled here at one time or another have left their mark on Tangier. The major port of entry for tourists, it has hordes of the world's best hustlers. Even if you know exactly which hotel you are heading for and require no help, they'll claim they found it for you. Every subterfuge in the book will be used to extract money. Welcome to Morocco!

Tangier has been coveted for millennia as a strategic site commanding the Strait of Gibraltar. The site has been occupied by the Romans, Vandals, Byzantines, Arabs, Berbers, Fatimids, Almoravids, Almohads, Merenids, Portuguese, Spanish, British and French.

In the late 19th and early 20th centuries, Tangier (Tanja to the locals) became the object of intense rivalry between the European powers. A final solution was only reached in 1923, when Tangier and the surrounding countryside were declared an 'international zone' controlled by the resident diplomatic agents of France, Spain, Britain, Portugal, Sweden, Holland, Belgium, Italy and the USA. Even the Moroccan sultan was represented by an agent, appointed by the French resident-general.

After independence in 1956, Tangier was reunited with the rest of the country. In the meantime it had become a fashionable Mediterranean resort and haven for freebooters, artists, writers, refugees, exiles and bankers; it was also renowned for its high-profile gay and paedophile scene.

MOROCCO

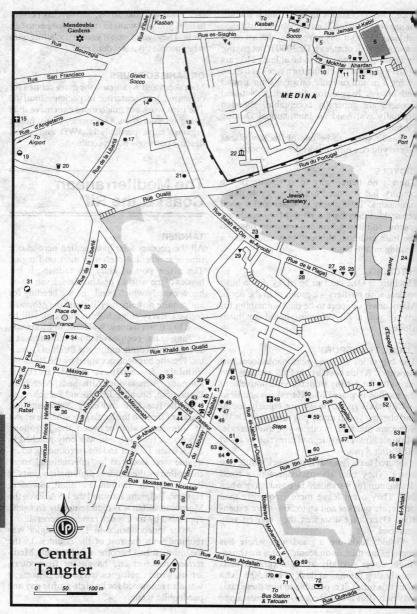

Central Tangier

0   50   100 m

PLACES TO STAY

1	Hôtel Mauritania
3	Pension Becerra
7	Pension Tan Tan
9	Hôtel Mamora
10	Pension Palace
12	Pension Karlton
13	Hôtel Olid
23	Pension Atou
28	Pension Miami
30	Hôtel El Minzah
44	Hôtel de Paris
50	Hôtel El Muniria & Tanger Inn
51	Hôtel Biarritz
52	Hôtel Cecil
53	Hôtel Marco Polo
54	Hôtel El Djenina
55	Hostel
56	Hôtel Bristol
57	Hôtel l'Amor
58	Hôtel Magellan
59	Hôtel Ibn Batouta
60	Hôtel Panoramic Massilia

PLACES TO EAT

2	Café Central
4	Restaurant Mamounia
5	Takeaway Snack Bar
8	Restaurant Moderne
11	Restaurant Ahlan
25	Restaurant/Bar La Paix
26	Restaurant Africa
27	Hassi Baida Restaurant
29	Restaurant Le Bon Goût
32	Café de Paris
33	Café de France
37	Big Mac
41	Restaurant Damascus
42	Morocco Palace Restaurant
47	Romero's Restaurant
62	Eric's Hamburger Shop

OTHER

6	Grand Mosque
14	Publi Bath
15	St Andrew's Church
16	Cinéma Rif
17	Glacier Liberté
18	Covered Market
19	Local Bus Terminal
20	Dean's Bar
21	Covered Market
22	American Legation Museum
24	Tanger-Gare Train Station
31	French Consulate
34	Royal Air Maroc
35	Cinéma Le Paris
36	Telephone & Fax Office
38	BMCE (Late Bank & ATMs)
39	Bar
40	Bar
43	Tourist Office
45	Telephone & Fax Office
46	Budget
48	Trasmediterranea/Limadet Office
49	Church
61	Iberia Airlines
63	Librairie des Colonnes
64	Avis
65	Voyages Schwartz (Amex)
66	Bar
67	Cinéma Roxy
68	Banque Populaire
69	Wafabank
70	Cady Rent-a-Car
71	Hertz
72	Post Office

Orientation

Tangier follows a pattern familiar to larger Moroccan towns. It's divided between the convoluted streets of the medina, redolent of Morocco prior to the French era, and the wide boulevards of the ville nouvelle, or new town. The modern shops, offices and services and most of the restaurants and better hotels are in the latter area. The medina has the markets, craft shops, cheaper hotels and smaller restaurants. The square known as the Petit Socco is in the heart of the medina. The larger Grand Socco lies between the medina and the ville nouvelle.

Information

Tourist Office The tourist office (☎ 948661) at 29 Blvd Pasteur has a limited range of maps and brochures.

Money There are plenty of banks along Blvd Pasteur and Blvd Mohammed V. The BMCE head office on Blvd Pasteur has ATMs and a change booth which should be open seven days a week from 10 am to 2 pm and 4 to 8 pm. The agent for American Express is Voyages Schwartz (☎ 330372), 54 Blvd Pasteur.

Post & Communications The main post office is on Blvd Mohammed V, a 20-minute walk from the Grand Socco. There is also a telephone office here.

Tangier's telephone code is ☎ 09.

Bookshops The Librairie des Colonnes (☎ 936955), on Blvd Pasteur, near the Voyages Schwartz office, is the best.

Things to See

In the heart of the medina the **Petit Socco**, with its cafés and restaurants, is the focus of activity. In the days of the international zone this was the sin and sleaze centre and it retains something of its seedy air.

MOROCCO

From the Petit Socco, the Rue des Almo-hades (ex-Rue des Chrétiens) takes you to the **kasbah**. Built on the highest point of the city, you enter from Bab el-Assa at the end of Rue Ben Raissouli in the medina. The gate opens onto a large open courtyard which leads to the 17th-century **Dar el-Makhzen**, the former sultan's palace and now a museum. The museum is open daily, except Tuesday, from 9 am to 3.30 pm in summer and 9 am to noon and 3 to 6 pm in winter; entry is Dr 10.

The **American Legation Museum** is a fas-cinating reminder that Morocco was the first country in the world to recognise US indepen-dence. It's in a fine old house in the medina. Opening hours are erratic, but entry is free. Knock to gain entrance.

Places to Stay

Camping Campers have a choice of two sites. The cheaper and more convenient is *Camping Miramonte*, about three km west of the centre. It's close to the beach and has a reasonable restaurant. To get there, take bus No 12 or 21 from near the Grand Socco.

Caravaning Tingis, about six km east of the centre of town, has a tennis court and swim-ming pool. To get there, take bus No 15 from the Grand Socco bus terminal.

Hostel The *hostel* (☎ 946127) is on Rue el-Antaki, just past the Hôtel El Djenina. Beds cost Dr 31. Dr 5 will get you a hot shower.

Hotels There are numerous small hotels in the medina around the Petit Socco and along Ave Mokhtar Ahardan (formerly Rue des Postes), which connects the Petit Socco and the port area. If you arrive by ferry, walk out of the port area until you pass through the main gates and then head right away from the train station and up the steps to Ave Mokhtar Ahardan.

If you prefer the more European-style hotels outside the medina, then, once out of the port gates, carry on past the train station and take the first street on your right (Rue de la Plage, also known as Rue Salah ed-Din el-Ayoubi), or the Rue Magellan 200 metres further on, where there's also a good choice of hotels. Prices rise by about Dr 30 in summer.

Medina Area There are plenty of cheap pen-sions here, most of them basic, although some offer hot water for a small extra charge. Singles cost Dr 30 to Dr 40 and doubles Dr 50 to Dr 80. They include the Hôtel *Mauritania* and the pensions *Becerra*, *Agadir*, *Karlton* and *Tan Tan* (see map).

Two of the best places are the *Pension Palace* (☎ 936128), at 2 Ave Moktar Ahardan, and the *Hôtel Olid* (☎ 931310), at No 12. They charge Dr 40/80 for singles/doubles. The Palace's rooms are small but otherwise OK, and many front on to a verdant courtyard. There are shared toilets and hot showers for Dr 10. The Olid has seen better days, but the rooms come with own shower, from which you can occasionally coax some hot water.

The two-star *Hôtel Mamora* (☎ 934105), 19 Ave Mokhtar Ahardan, offers spotlessly clean singles/doubles with shower for Dr 144/174 in the low season and Dr 194/224 in the high season.

The pick of the crop is the *Hôtel Continen-tal* perched above the port (☎ 931024; fax 931143). Used for some scenes in the film version of Paul Bowles' *The Sheltering Sky*, it is full of character. Singles/doubles cost Dr 150/200.

If you are staying in a place with no showers, there's a hammam at 80 Rue des Almohades and another by the Grand Socco.

Ville Nouvelle The unclassified hotels and pensions along Rue de la Plage are no better than the cheapies in the medina. Basic rooms with shared bath and toilet are similarly priced from Dr 30 to Dr 40 for a single and Dr 50 to Dr 80 for a double. The *Pension Miami* is popular and the *Pension Atou* is OK.

A much better selection of hotels can be found up the steep and winding Rue Magellan which starts between the hotels Biarritz and Cecil. The hotels *l'Amor* (☎ 931450) and *Magellan* (☎ 938726) have big, clean rooms for Dr 50/100. The latter has a hot trickle of water pretty much whenever you ask – it's difficult to describe it as a shower.

The *Hôtel Biarritz* (☎ 932473) has comfort-able, spacious old rooms overlooking the sea but is somewhat overpriced at Dr 70/133. Slightly better are the front rooms with balcony in the *Hôtel Cecil* (☎ 931087). Most of them are big and self-contained with phone. They charge Dr 100 per person, but this appears to be negotiable.

Further up Rue Magellan, you get to the *Hôtel El Muniria* (☎ 935337) and the *Hôtel Ibn Batouta* (☎ 937170), opposite one another just before you reach a flight of steps. They're both one-star hotels and offer immaculate singles/doubles with bath for Dr 100/120. William Burroughs wrote *The Naked Lunch* while staying at the Muniria.

Close by, with good front-room views over the harbour, is the one-star *Hôtel Panoramic Massilia* (☎ 935015), on the corner of Rue Ibn Jubair and Rue Targha. Rooms with shower, toilet and hot water cost Dr 80/130 including breakfast.

A good choice of mid-range hotels can be found in the streets off the Blvd Pasteur, close to the tourist office. One of the better ones is the two star *Hôtel de Paris* (☎ 931877), at 42 Blvd Pasteur. Good, comfortable rooms with own shower and breakfast cost Dr 167/220.

There's also a decent trio of places where Rue el-Antaki heads up from Ave d'Espagne on the waterfront. The German-run *Hôtel Marco Polo* (☎ 938213) has impeccable rooms and a restaurant and bar. Singles/doubles cost Dr 136/166. Next door is the two-star *Hôtel El Djenina* (☎ 942244), with decent rooms for Dr 148/186. A couple of floors up is the two-star *Hôtel Bristol* (☎ 942914). Doubles with shower, or shower and toilet, are Dr 150/180 which includes an obligatory breakfast.

Places to Eat
Medina Area There are plenty of small cafés and restaurants around the Petit Socco and the Grand Socco offering traditional fare for reasonable prices. Sipping a mint tea at the *Café Central* or one of the other places on the Petit Socco is a time-honoured pursuit. The Central was a favourite of Burroughs and other writers in the 1950s.

There's a good takeaway *snack bar* just where Rue Jemaa el-Kebir begins on the Petit Socco. Huge rolls filled with meat, salad and pickles cost about Dr 10. Just north of the Petit Socco, *Restaurant Andalus* and the *Grèce Restaurant* are two excellent little hole-in-the-wall places. For more substantial meals, try the popular *Restaurant Ahlan*, Ave Mokhtar Ahardan, which offers a filling meal of cous-

cous, salad and a drink for Dr 40. Also good value is the small and cheap *Restaurant Moderne*, across the road at No 21.

There are a couple of food stalls at the bottom of the steps at the end of Ave Mokhtar Ahardan, mainly serving fried fish.

A bit more expensive is the *Restaurant Mamounia* on Rue es-Siaghin, which offers full Moroccan feasts in more sumptuous surroundings than the other medina eateries.

Ville Nouvelle A good place for snacks is the *Restaurant Le Bon Goût* on Rue Salah ed-Din el-Ayoubi. Further down towards Ave d'Espagne are two reasonably priced sit-down restaurants, the *Africa* (No 83) and, next door, the *Hassi Baida*. Both offer set meals for around Dr 40 or main courses of fairly generous proportions for Dr 25 to Dr 35. The *Restaurant/Bar La Paix*, on the corner of Ave d'Espagne, is more a bar than a restaurant.

If you feel like Western-style fast food, you could do worse than *Big Mac*, on the corner of Blvd Pasteur and Rue Ahmed Chaouki. They do good hot dogs for Dr 15. *Eric's Hamburger Shop*, which claims to be open 24 hours, is in the arcade between Blvd Pasteur and Rue el-Moutanabi.

Somewhat more expensive meals can be had in the restaurants and cafés near Place de France (a coffee at the *Café de Paris* is a must). In Rue du Prince Moulay Abdallah, just around the corner from the tourist office, you can find everything from Moroccan/European takeaways to a full-on Moroccan banquet complete with belly dancers at the *Morocco Palace*. Try the *Damascus* for Moroccan food and *Romero's* for pricey, Spanish-style seafood.

On Rue de la Liberté, just up from the Grand Socco, *Glacier Liberté* does great ice cream. For a cold beer, try the *Tanger Inn*, below the Hôtel El Muniria, open from 9 pm to 1 am.

Getting There & Away
Bus Most CTM buses leave from an office near the port entrance. All others leave from the bus station on Place Jamia el-Arabia at the end of Ave van Beethoven. It's a long walk, so take a petit taxi.

Regular CTM departures include Casablanca (Dr 100), Rabat (Dr 75), Tetouan (Dr 13), and Fès (Dr 79).

Train There are two train stations: Tanger Gare and Tanger Port. The former is more convenient. Trains south from Tangier split at Sidi Kacem to Rabat (five hours), Casablanca (six hours) and Marrakesh (10 hours), or to Meknès (five hours) and Fès (six hours) and Oujda (12 hours).

Taxi Grands taxis leave from the bus station; there are frequent departures to Tetouan (Dr 20) and Asilah (Dr 19).

Car The following are among the car-rental agencies in Tangier:

Avis
 54 Blvd Pasteur (☎ & fax 933031)
Budget
 7 Rue du Prince Moulay Abdallah (☎ 937994)
Europcar
 87 Blvd Mohammed V (☎ 941938)
Goldcar
 Hôtel Solazur, Ave des FAR (☎ 940164, 946568)
Hertz
 36 Blvd Mohammed V (☎ 322210, 322165)

Boat If you're heading to Spain or Gibraltar by boat, you can buy tickets from virtually any travel agency or at the port itself. The Trasmediterranea office is on Rue du Prince Moulay Abdallah.

Getting Around
The local bus terminus is just up from the Grand Socco, on Rue d'Angleterre. Petits taxis are metered and cost under Dr 10 around town.

TETOUAN
With its busy whitewashed medina, dramatic setting and nearby beaches, Tetouan has an unmistakable Spanish-Moroccan flavour, as a result of its settlement by Arab-Berber and Jewish refugees from Muslim Andalucía in the 16th century and subsequent occupation by the Spanish during the protectorate years.

Information
The tourist office (☎ 961915; fax 961914) is at 30 Calle Mohammed V. Some of the staff speak English. There are plenty of banks along Calle Mohammed V. The most useful (with ATM) is the BMCE, below the Pension Iberia on Place Moulay el-Mehdi.

The post office is also on Place Moulay el-Mehdi, with the telephone office nearby

Spain has a consulate at Ave al-Massira (☎ 973941; fax 973946). It is open weekdays from 9 am to noon.

Tetouan's telephone code is ☎ 09.

Things to See
The **Place Hassan II**, the town's showpiece links the old and new parts of the city. The busiest entrance to the **medina** is Bab er-Rouah. In the area towards the eastern gate Bab el-Okla, are some fine houses built by the city's residents in the last century. Just inside Bab el-Okla, the excellent **Musée Marocain** is built in an old bastion in the town wall and has well-presented exhibits of everyday Moroccan and Andalusian life. It is open weekdays from 8.30 am to noon and 2.30 to 6 pm; admission is Dr 10.

Just outside Bab el-Okla is the **Artisanal School**, where you can see children learning traditional crafts such as leather work, wood work and the making of enamel *(zellij)* tiles The building itself is worth a visit. The school is open weekdays from 8.30 am to noon and 2.30 to 5.30 pm; entry is Dr 10.

Places to Stay
The nearest **camping ground** is on the beach at Martil, eight km away.

Tetouan has plenty of cheap, basic pensions some decidedly better than others in terms of facilities, views and character. The **Pension Iberia** (☎ 963679), on the 3rd floor above the BMCE bank on Place Moulay el-Mehdi, has great views over the square and rooms at Dr 70 with shared bath.

The **Hotel Bilbao** (☎ 964114), 7 Calle Mohammed V, has a lot of character. It costs Dr 52 for a room, regardless of whether one or two people occupy it, with shared bathroom and cold showers.

The one-star **Hotel Trebol** (☎ 962018) is close to the bus station and has singles/doubles without own shower for Dr 50/80, or Dr 70/102 with shower. There is hot water in the mornings.

More expensive is the **Hôtel Oumaime** (☎ 963473), Rue Achra Mai. It has rooms for Dr 166/198 in the low season and Dr 173/207 in summer. They turn on the central heating in winter – sometimes.

MOROCCO

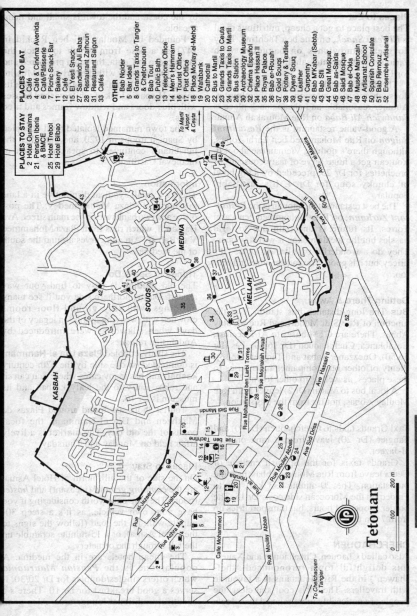

PLACES TO STAY
2 Hôtel Oumaima
21 Pension Iberia
& BMCE
25 Hôtel Trebol
29 Hôtel Bilbao

PLACES TO EAT
3 Café
4 Café & Cinéma Avenida
6 Café/Pâtisserie
11 Picnic Snack Bar
12 Bakery
12 Café
15 El Yesil Snack
27 Sandwich Ali Baba
28 Restaurant Zarhoun
31 Restaurant Saigon
33 Cafés

OTHER
1 Bab Noider
5 Bar Ideal
8 Grands Taxis to Tangier
   & Chefchaouen
9 Bab Tout
10 Public Bath
13 Telephone Office
14 Men's Hammam
16 Tourist Office
17 Post Office
18 Place Moulay el-Mehdi
19 Wafabank
20 Cathedral
22 Bus to Martil
23 Grands Taxis to Ceuta
24 Grands Taxis to Martil
26 Bus Station
30 Archaeology Museum
32 Cinéma Español
34 Place Hassan II
35 Royal Palace
36 Bab er-Rouah
37 Gold Souqs
38 Pottery & Textiles
39 Dyers' Souq
40 Leather
41 Carpentry
42 Bab M'Kabar (Sebta)
43 Bab Sfli
44 Great Mosque
45 Bab as-Saida
46 Saidi Mosque
47 Bab el-Okla
48 Musée Marocain
49 Artisanal School
50 Spanish Consulate
51 Bab Remouz
52 Ensemble Artisanal

MEDINA

SOUQS

KASBAH

MELLAH

To Martil
Airport
& Ceuta

To Chefchaouen
& Tangier

Tetouan

0   100   200 m

MOROCCO

Places to Eat

The best place to get a cheap, nutritious meal is *El Yesfi Snack*, on Rue ben Tachfine. They do great sandwiches on baguettes with various meats, potato salad, chips and salad for Dr 10.

The *Picnic* snack bar, on Rue Achra Mai, does an average version of a hamburger. Another reasonable and cheap snack place is *Sandwich Ali Baba* on Rue Mourakab Anual.

A good-value restaurant is the *Restaurant Saigon* on Rue Mohammed ben Larbi Torres, although there's nothing Vietnamese about it. You can get a huge serve of tasty couscous or brochettes for Dr 25, preceded by a big bowl of chunky soup for Dr 4. It's justifiably popular.

The best restaurant in Tetouan is the *Restaurant Zarhoun*, on Rue Mohammed ben Larbi Torres. Its future is uncertain due to legal hassles but the locals reckon it will stay open. They do a wonderful pastilla. At Dr 55, it's pricey, but it is good. You can get wine and beer too.

Getting There & Away

Bus The long-distance bus station is at the junction of Rue Sidi Mandri and Rue Moulay Abbas. There are CTM buses to Al-Hoceima, Casablanca, Chefchaouen (Dr 16.50), Fès (Dr 56.50), Ouezzane, Rabat and Tangier (Dr 13). Plenty of other bus companies have buses to these places, as well as to other towns.

A local bus to Martil (Dr 2) leaves from Rue Moulay Abbas, not far from the bus station.

Taxi Grands taxis to Chefchaouen (Dr 20) and Tangier (Dr 20) leave from a rank on Rue al-Jazeer.

Grands taxis for the Spanish enclave of Ceuta leave from Rue Moulay Abbas, near the bus station. The 20-minute (33 km) trip to Fnideq on the Moroccan side costs Dr 15. The border is open 24 hours, but transport dries up from 7 pm to 5 am.

CHEFCHAOUEN

Also called Chaouen, Chechaouen and Xauen, this delightful town (pronounced 'shefshawen') in the Rif Mountains is a favourite with travellers. The air is cool and clear, the people are noticeably more relaxed than down by the coast, and the town is small and manageable.

Founded by Moulay Ali ben Rachid in 1471 as a base from which to attack the Portuguese in Ceuta, the town prospered and grew considerably with the arrival of Muslim refugees from Spain. They gave the town its unique Hispanic look of whitewashed houses with blue doors and window frames and tiled roofs.

The town remained isolated until occupied by Spanish troops in 1920, and until then the inhabitants continued to speak a variant of medieval Castilian.

Information

There's a small syndicat d'initiative in a lane just north of Plaza Mohammed V. The post office and two banks are on the main street, Ave Hassan II, which runs from Plaza Mohammed V to Bab al-'Ain and curves around the south of the medina.

Things to See & Do

The old **medina** is easy to find your way around. On the northern side you'll see many buildings with tiny ground-floor rooms crowded with weaving looms – a legacy of the days when silkworms were introduced by Andalusian refugees.

The shady, cobbled **Plaza Uta el-Hammam** is dominated on one side by the 17th-century **kasbah** and has many cafés where you can sit and relax. Entry to the leafy kasbah and its museum is Dr 10.

Tourist shops are found around Plazas de Makhzen and Uta el-Hammam, the focal points of the old city. The **market** is a lively affair held on Monday and Thursday.

Places to Stay

On the side of the hill, north of Hôtel Asma, are the *camping ground* (pleasant) and *hostel* (poor). They are only worth considering if you have your own vehicle, as it's a steep 30-minute walk by the road (follow the signs to the Hôtel Asma), or a 15-minute scramble up the hill through the cemetery.

The cheap hotels are in the medina. A popular one is the *Pension Mauritania* which offers singles/doubles for Dr 20/30. It serves a good breakfast for Dr 10. There's a beautiful traditional lounge area. Also good

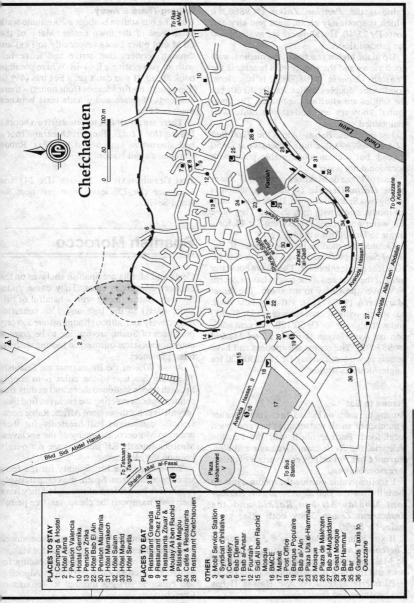

Chefchaouen

0   50   100 m

To Ras al-Ma'

To Ouezzane & Kalama

To Tetouan & Tanger

To Ouezzane

To Bus Station.

Oued Laou

Kasbeh

Blvd Sidi Abdel Hamid

Sharia Alal al-Fassi

Plaza Mohammed V

Avenida Hassan II

Avenida Allal ben Abdallah

Sharia Aksawr

Zankat al-Qadi

PLACES TO STAY
1   Camping & Hostel
2   Hôtel Asma
7   Pension Valencia
10 Hostal Gernika
13 Pension Znika
22 Hôtel Bab El Ain
30 Pension Mauritania
31 Hôtel Marrakech
32 Hôtel Salam
33 Hôtel Madrid
37 Hôtel Sevilla

PLACES TO EAT
8   Restaurant Granada
9   Restaurant Chez Fouad
14 Restaurants Zouar & Moulay Ali ben Rachid
20 Pâtisserie Magou
24 Cafés & Restaurants
28 Restaurant Chefchaouen

OTHER
3   Mobil Service Station
4   Syndicat d'Initiative
5   Cemetery
6   Bab Djenan
11 Bab al-Ansar
12 Fountain
15 Sidi Ali ben Rachid Mosque
16 Market
18 Post Office
19 Banque Populaire
21 Bab al-'Ain
23 Plaza Uta el-Hammam
26 Plaza de Makhzen
27 Bab al-Muqaddam
29 Great Mosque
34 Bab Hammar
35 Bar
36 Grands Taxis to Ouezzane

value is the **Pension Znika** (☎ 986624), which is spotlessly clean, light and airy and costs Dr 25/40. Hot showers are available on the ground floor.

Up in the higher reaches of the medina, with good views and the chance of a breeze, is the **Pension Valencia** (☎ 986088). It has clean, good-value doubles/triples for Dr 40/60, but the singles are glorified cupboards. The communal showers and toilets are quite well maintained.

Just inside the Bab al-'Ain is the **Hôtel Bab El Ain** (☎ 986935), a little expensive at Dr 50 a head, but a clean, comfortable place with occasional hot water.

East of Plaza de Makhzen near Bab al-Ansar is the **Hostal Gernika** (☎ 987434), which is run by two Spanish women. It has nine beautiful rooms, some with own shower. They have hot water and prices range from Dr 45 for a single to Dr 120 for a double.

Outside the medina on Ave Hassan II, the **Hôtel Salam** (☎ 986239) is a good deal at Dr 40/60 for singles/doubles. They have hot water most of the time and some rooms have a decent view over the valley to the south. The **Hôtel Marrakech** (☎ 987113), virtually next door, has rooms without own shower for Dr 50/100 and with shower for Dr 60/120. A recent addition on Ave Hassan II is the **Hotel Madrid** (☎ 987498). The rooms are spotless and have heaters in winter. You pay Dr 160/230/320 for singles/doubles/triples.

Places to Eat

Among the cafés on Plaza Uta el-Hammam are a number of small restaurants that serve good local food. Further north near the Pension Valencia, the **Restaurant Granada** and **Restaurant Chez Fouad** present a variety of dishes at reasonable cost.

Excellent value outside the medina, just up the hill from the Bab al-'Ain, are the **Restaurant Moulay Ali ben Rachid** and the **Restaurant Zouar**. They both offer good mains for Dr 20.

If you want to splurge, try the **Restaurant Chefchaouen** on the street leading up to Plaza de Makhzen. A full meal (soup, tajine/couscous and fruit) for lunch or dinner costs Dr 50.

Pâtisserie Magou on Ave Hassan II has good pastries and fresh bread.

Getting There & Away

Bus The bus station is about a 20-minute walk south-west of the town centre. Many of the CTM and other buses (especially to Fès) are through services that arrive and leave full without you getting a look-in. Where possible book ahead. If you can't get a Fès bus (4½ to five hours), try for Meknès (four hours) – there are loads of buses and grands taxis between there and Fès.

There are also buses to Tetouan (two hours), Fnideq (for Ceuta), Tangier, Ouezzane (not a bad alternative launch pad for Fès), Rabat, Casablanca and Nador.

Taxi Grands taxis to Tetouan (Dr 24) and Ouezzane (Dr 25) leave from just near the Hotel Sevilla.

Spanish Morocco

Ceuta and Melilla are Spanish enclaves on the northern Moroccan coast. They came under Spanish control (along with a handful of off-shore islets) in the 16th and 15th centuries respectively and, although administered as city provinces of Spain, are waiting to be granted autonomous status on an equal footing with the other provinces.

About 70% of the inhabitants are Spanish. The main function of the cities is to supply Spanish troops stationed there, and as duty free centres – goods entering the enclaves find their way all over north-western Africa. Rabat occasionally campaigns half-heartedly for their return to Morocco, but many of the enclaves' Muslims (mostly Rif Berbers) are not overly keen on the idea.

Travellers come here mainly for the ferry services to and from Spain, the comparatively hassle-free border formalities and (if they have their own transport) the cheap, tax-free petrol.

CEUTA

Known as Sebta in Arabic, Ceuta (pronounced 'thayuta') doesn't offer a great deal for visitors and it's not very cheap. If you're heading for Morocco, catch an early ferry from Algeciras and continue straight through to Tetouan or Chefchaouen.

Information

There's a tourist office near the local bus terminus (☎ 514092). It is open on weekdays from 8 am to 3 pm.

Plenty of banks (many with ATMs) line the main street, Paseo de Revellín, and its continuation, Calle Camoens. Outside business hours you can change money at the Hotel La Muralla, on Plaza de Africa. There's no need to buy dirham here, as you can do so at the border as long as you have cash.

The main post office (correos y telégrafos) is on Plaza de España, just off Calle Camoens.

The telephone code for Ceuta is ☎ 0956.

Things to See

The **Museo de la Legión** on Paseo de Colón holds a staggering array of military paraphernalia. It is open Monday to Saturday from 10 am to 2 pm, and on Saturday from 4 to 6 pm as well. Entry is free.

From the convent of the **Ermita de San Antonio**, there is an excellent view over the Mediterranean to Gibraltar. A large festival is held annually on 13 June at this 17th-century convent to mark St Anthony's Day.

Places to Stay

There is no shortage of fondas (inns) and casas de huéspedes (boarding houses), easily identifiable by the large blue-and-white F or CH on the entrance. Cheapest of these is the small **Pensión Charito** (☎ 513982), on the 1st floor at 5 Calle Arrabal, about 15 minutes walk along the waterfront from the ferry terminal. The only indication that it is a guesthouse is the 'Chambres' sign above the footpath, and the CH sign on the wall. Basic singles/doubles cost 800/1400 ptas. There are no hot showers.

If you can afford a little more, the two best deals in town are the **Casa de Huéspedes Tiuna** (☎ 517756), at 3 Plaza Teniente Ruiz, and the **Pensión Bohemia** (☎ 510615), 16 Paseo de Revellín. They both charge 2000/3000 ptas for good singles/doubles, but the Bohemia (look for the small sign in the shopping arcade) is definitely the better of the two. It has piping hot showers in spotless shared bathrooms.

Places to Eat

You won't find food as cheap here as in Morocco. There are plenty of cafés that serve snacks, such as bocadillos and pulgas, which are basically rolls with one or two fillings. Things get cheaper as you head east from the town centre along Calle Real.

Getting There & Away

Morocco Buses (No 7) run to the border every 15 minutes or so from Plaza de la Constitución for 65 ptas (20 minutes). If you arrive by ferry and want to head straight for the border, there is a stop for the No 7 just up from the port and off to the right opposite the ramparts.

The border crossing is straightforward and, once through, there are plenty of grands taxis to Tetouan (Dr 15 a seat). Unless the border is packed, the trip from Ceuta to Tetouan should take no more than two hours – often much less.

Mainland Spain The ferry terminal is west of the town centre, and there are frequent departures to Algeciras. You can take the bus marked Puerto-Centro from Plaza de la Constitución.

MELILLA

With a population of 70,000, Melilla retains a lingering fascination because of its medieval fortress. Until the end of the 19th century, almost all of Melilla was contained within these massive walls. This old part of town has a distinctly Castilian flavour with narrow, twisting streets, squares, gates and drawbridges.

The new part of town, west of the fortress, was begun at the end of the 19th century and still vaguely reflects the dictates of Spanish modernist architecture of the time.

Information

The well-stocked tourist office (☎ 684013) is at the junction of Calle de Querol and Avenida General Aizpuru (signposted from the port). Most of the banks are along the main street, Avenida de Juan Carlos I, and you can buy and sell dirham. Moneychangers hang around the cafés on the Plaza de España but they won't offer you better deals than those available in the banks.

The telephone code for Melilla is ☎ 0952.

Things to See

The fortress of **Melilla la Vieja**, also known as the Medina Sidonia, offers good views over the town and out to sea. Inside the walls, don't miss the **Iglesia de la Concepción** with its gilded reredos and shrine to Nuestra Señora la Virgen de la Victoria (the patron of the city), and the **Museo Municipal**.

The main entrance is through the massive **Puerta de la Marina**, or you can enter from the west side via the **Plaza de Armas** and the drawbridges of **Puerta de Santiago**.

Places to Stay

The cheapest option is the *Pension del Puerto*, a largely Moroccan establishment off Avenida General Macías. A bed should cost less than 1000 ptas.

Easily the best place for the tight budget is the *Hostal Rioja* (☎ 682709), at 6 Calle Ejército Español. It has decent singles/doubles for 2000/3000 ptas outside the high season, with communal hot showers.

Places to Eat

The best area to search for good cheap bocadillos and the like is along Calle Castelar (not far from the Mercado Municipal). The *Bodegas Madrid*, with its old wine casks for tables, is the most popular spot here for a beer and a bite.

In Melilla la Vieja, search out the *Casa El Manco/Meson de la Tortilla* or, for a splurge, the *Barbacoa de Muralla*, in the southern corner of the old town.

Getting There & Away

Morocco Local buses go from Plaza de España to the border from about 7.30 am until late in the evening. From where the buses stop, it's about 150 metres to Spanish customs and another 200 metres to Moroccan customs. On the other side of Moroccan customs there are frequent buses and grands taxis to Nador until about 8 pm.

Mainland Spain Trasmediterranea has an office on Plaza de España for ferries to the Spanish mainland. Otherwise, buy tickets at the ferry terminal itself (*estación marítima*). You can book Spanish rail tickets at the RENFE office. It's worth checking out flights to Málaga too.

The Middle Atlas

MEKNÈS

Although a town of considerable size even in the days of the 13th-century Merenids, Meknès didn't reach its peak until Moulay Ismail, the second Alawite sultan, made it his capital in 1672. Over the next 55 years an enormous palace complex encircled by some 25 km of walls was built, transforming Meknès out of all recognition.

Under Sultan Sidi Mohammed III, however, Morocco's capital was moved back to Marrakesh. The 1755 earthquake that severely damaged many Moroccan cities also took its toll on Meknès. No restoration was done and the city was allowed to decay until recently, when its tourism potential was recognised and major restoration begun. Oued Boufekrane divides the new town from the old.

Information

The tourist office (☎ 524426) and the main post office are next to each other on Place de France.

The banks are concentrated in the new city, mainly on Ave Hassan II, Ave Mohammed V and Blvd Allal ben Abdallah. The BMCE operates a bureau de change on Ave des FAR, opposite the Hôtel Volubilis, which is open daily from 10 am to 2 pm and 4 to 8 pm.

Meknès' telephone code is ☎ 05.

Things to See

The focus of the old city is the massive **Bab el-Mansour**, the main entrance to Moulay Ismail's 17th-century **Imperial City**. It is highly decorated and well preserved.

The gate faces Place el-Hedim. On the far north side of this square is the **Dar Jamai**, a late 19th-century palace that houses a good folk museum. It is open daily, except Tuesday, from 9 am to noon and 3 to 6 pm. Entry costs Dr 10.

The **medina** stretches north behind the Dar Jamai. The easiest access is through the arch left of the Dar Jamai. The covered main street leads to the **Grand Mosque** and the mid-14th century **Medersa Bou Inania**. Similar in design to the Fès medersas, it is open daily

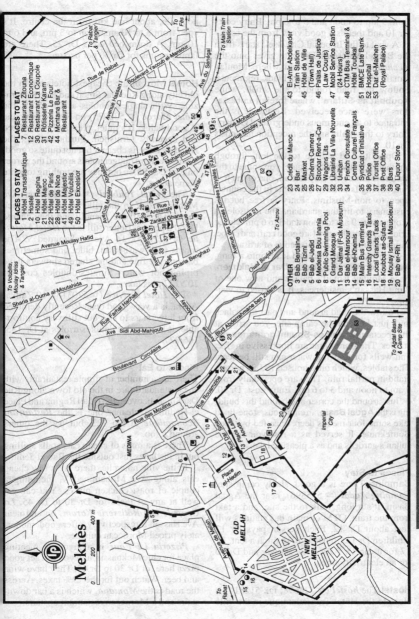

Meknès

PLACES TO STAY
1 Hôtel Transatlantique
2 Hostel
10 Hôtel Regina
21 Hôtel Maroc
22 Hôtel de Paris
28 Hôtel de Nice
41 Hôtel Majestic
49 Hôtel Volubilis
50 Hôtel Excelsior

PLACES TO EAT
7 Restaurant Zitouna
12 Restaurant Economique
30 Restaurant La Coupole
31 Rôtisserie Karam
42 Pizzeria Le Four
44 Montana Bar &
   Restaurant

OTHER
3 Bab Berdaine
4 Bab Tizimi
5 Bab el-Jedid
6 Medersa Bou Inania
8 Public Swimming Pool
9 Grand Mosque
11 Dar Jamaï (Folk Museum)
13 Bab el-Mansour
14 Bab el-Khemis
15 Main Bus Terminal
16 Intercity Grands Taxis
17 Local Grands Taxis
18 Koubbat as-Sufara'
19 Moulay Ismail Mausoleum
20 Bab er-Rih
23 Crédit du Maroc
24 Bar
25 Market
26 Cinéma Camera
27 Stopcar Rent-a-Car
29 Wagons Lits
32 Librairie La Ville Nouvelle
33 Uniban
34 French Consulate &
   Centre Culturel Français
35 Syndicat d'Initiative
36 Police
37 Tourist Office
38 Post Office
39 Bars
40 Liquor Store
43 El-Amir Abdelkader
   Train Station
45 Hôtel de Ville
   (Town Hall)
46 Palais de Justice
   (Law Courts)
47 Mobil Service Station
   (24 Hours)
48 CTM Bus Terminal &
   Hôtel Toubkal
51 BMCE Late Bank
52 Hospital
53 Dar el-Makhen
   (Royal Palace)

MOROCCO

from 9 am to noon and 3 to 6 pm. Entry costs Dr 10 and there's a good view from the roof.

A visit to the Imperial City itself starts from the Bab el-Mansour. The gate gives onto the *mechouar*, a parade ground where Moulay Ismail reviewed his famed black regiments. Follow the road round to the small, white **Koubbat as-Sufara'**, where foreign ambassadors were once received. Beside it is the entrance to an enormous underground granary. Entry to the vaults and the reception hall costs Dr 10.

Opposite and a little to the left, through another recently restored gate, you come to the **Mausoleum of Moulay Ismail**, one of the few functioning Islamic monuments in the country open to non-Muslims. Entry is free but it's customary to tip the guardian. The mausoleum is open from 9 am to noon and 3 to 6 pm (closed Friday). Across the road are good craft and carpet shops belonging to a cooperative of artisans.

From the tomb, the road leads into a long, walled corridor flanking the **Dar el-Makhzen**, once Moulay Ismail's palace and now one of King Hassan's residences. It is closed to visitors.

Follow the road around and past the palace and, just beyond the camp site, you arrive at the spectacular **Heri es-Souani granaries** and stables. The storerooms are impressive in size, and wells for drawing water can still be seen. The stables, which once housed 12,000 horses, stand in partial ruin. They are open daily from 9 am to noon and 3 to 6 pm. Entry costs Dr 10.

Just around the corner and behind this building is the **Agdal Basin**, an enormous, stone-lined lake some four metres deep, once fed by Oued Boufekrane. It served as a reservoir for the sultan's gardens and as a pleasure lake.

Places to Stay
Camping There is a good, shady camp site, *Camping Agdal* (☎ 555396), near the Agdal Basin. It's a long walk to the site, and a taxi from the train, CTM or main bus stations will cost about Dr 12. Each person pays Dr 17 (children Dr 12), plus Dr 10 to pitch a tent, Dr 17 for a car, Dr 7 for a hot shower and Dr 10 for an electricity line.

Hostel The *hostel* (☎ 524698; fax 512814) is close to the Hôtel Transatlantique in the ville

nouvelle, about one km from the centre. It's open from 8 to 10 am, noon to 3 pm, and 6 to 10 pm. A dorm bed costs Dr 25. There are family rooms for Dr 30 per person.

Hotels Most of the cheapest hotels are in the old city along Rue Dar Smen and Rue Rouamzine. With singles/doubles at Dr 45/85, the *Hôtel Maroc* (☎ 530075) on Rue Rouamzine is good value. It's quiet, pleasantly decorated and decently furnished. Further along, the *Hôtel de Paris* is cheaper but not quite so good. There are more budget hotels around the corner on Rue Dar Smen but they are nothing to write home about.

The *Hôtel Toubkal* (☎ 522218), on Ave Mohammed V in the ville nouvelle, is much better. The staff are friendly and they charge Dr 60 a person. Better still is the *Hôtel Majestic* (☎ 522035), 14 Ave Mohammed V. The rooms with washbasin, bidet and sometimes balcony are fine and the shared showers have piping hot water. Singles/doubles cost Dr 102/137 plus taxes.

The *Hôtel de Nice* (☎ 520318), 10 Zankat Accra, is a very good deal. Recently demoted from three-stars to two but still very comfortable, it has singles/doubles/triples at Dr 135/166/227.

Places to Eat
There are a number of simple restaurants with cheap standard fare in the old town along Rue Dar Smen, between the Hôtel Regina and Place el-Hedim. A cleaner one is the *Restaurant Économique* at No 123, but try the others around it too.

There is a mass of cheap eats stalls spilling out in the lanes just outside the Bab el-Jedid.

In the ville nouvelle, there are a few cheap eats along Ave Mohammed V, including a couple of roast chicken places. You can eat well at any of these for Dr 30 to Dr 45. *La Coupole* and *Rôtisserie Karam*, on and near Ave Hassan II respectively, offer good, moderately priced Moroccan cuisine.

Pizzeria Le Four is a favourite meeting place for chic Meknassis, and you can get good pizza here for Dr 30 to Dr 45. They have wine and beer. Watch out for the 19% taxes. Across the road is the *Montana*, which is a bar downstairs and a Moroccan restaurant upstairs.

To splash out in traditional Moroccan surroundings, look up the *Restaurant Zitouna* (☎ 532083), 44 Jamaa Zitouna, in the medina, though it is primarily designed for groups.

Getting There & Away

Bus The CTM bus terminal is on Ave Mohammed V near the junction with Ave des FAR. There are daily departures to Fès, Casablanca, Rabat, Tangier, Taza, Oujda, Marrakesh, Tetouan, Agadir, Ifrane, Azrou and Er-Rachidia.

The main bus terminal is outside Bab el-Khemis on the north side of the new mellah along Ave du Mellah. There are regular departures to most major destinations.

Train All trains stop at the centrally located Gare El-Amir Abdelkader, which is more convenient than the main station on Ave du Sénégal.

Taxi Grands taxis leave from a lot just outside the main bus station to Fès (Dr 15), Rabat (Dr 38) and Moulay Idriss (for Volubilis, Dr 7).

Getting Around

Local buses run between the medina and the new city, but they get crowded. Pale blue petits taxis are economical and easier to use.

AROUND MEKNÈS

About 33 km from Meknès are the best preserved Roman ruins in Morocco. **Volubilis** (Oualili in Arabic) dates largely from the 2nd and 3rd centuries AD, although the site was originally settled by Carthaginian traders in the 3rd century BC. It is noted for its superb mosaic floors, many of which have been left *in situ*.

The site is open daily from sunrise to sunset and entry is Dr 20. Buses (infrequent) and grands taxis leave from the main bus station in Meknès. Get them to drop you at the turn-off to Moulay Idriss, from where it's a half-hour walk. Going back, you can hitch or walk to Moulay Idriss and wait for a bus or taxi. If you have a group, you could negotiate to hire a grand taxi for a half-day trip (reckon on about Dr 150).

FÈS

Fès is the oldest of the imperial cities of Morocco, founded shortly after the Arabs swept across North Africa following the death of the Prophet Mohammed. It has been the capital of Morocco on several occasions and for long periods. The city's magnificent buildings reflect the brilliance of Arab-Berber imagination and artistry. Fassis, the people of Fès, justifiably look on their city as the cultural and spiritual capital of Morocco.

The medina of Fès el-Bali (Old Fès) is one of the largest in the world and the most interesting in Morocco. Its narrow, winding alleys and covered bazars are crammed with craft workshops, restaurants, mosques, medersas, food markets and extensive dye pits and tanneries. The exotic smells, the hammering of the metalworkers, the call of the muezzin, the crowded bazars and teams of uncooperative donkeys create an unforgettable experience.

Fès was founded in 789 AD by Idriss I on the right bank of the Oued Fès in what is now the Andalus Quarter. His son, Idriss II, extended the city onto the left bank in 809; these two parts of the city constitute Fès el-Bali.

The earliest settlers were mainly refugees from Córdoba (Spain) and Kairouan (Tunisia). Both groups were from well-established Islamic centres of brilliance and their skills laid the groundwork for one of the most important centres of Islamic intellectual and architectural development.

The city reached its heights under the Merenids, who took it from the Almohads in 1250 and erected a new quarter, Fès el-Jdid. Fès remained the capital throughout their rule. With the rise of the Saadians in the 16th century, Marrakesh once again gained the ascendancy and Fès slipped into relative obscurity, only to be revived under the Alawite ruler Moulay Abdallah in the 19th century. In 1916, the French began building the ville nouvelle on the plateau to the south-west of the two ancient cities.

Orientation

Fès consists of three distinct parts. The original walled city of Fès el-Bali lies to the east; to the south-west is the French-established ville nouvelle where most of the restaurants and hotels are located; between the two is the Merenid walled city of Fès el-Jdid.

MOROCCO

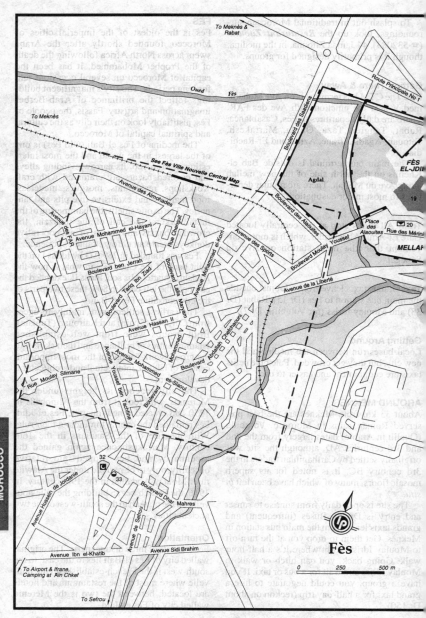

To Meknès &
Rabat

Route Principale No 1

Oued   Fès

To Meknès

See Fès Ville Nouvelle Central Map

Boulevard des Saâdiens

Boulevard des Alaouites

FÈS
EL-JDID

Agdal

19

Avenue des Almohades

Avenue des FAR

Avenue Mohammed el-Hayani

Rue Cherguit

Avenue des Sports

Place
des
Alaouites

Rue des Mérini

20

MELLAH

Boulevard ben Jerrah

Boulevard Tariq Ibn Ziad

Boulevard Lalla Maryam

Avenue Mohammed el-Korri

Boulevard Moulay Youssef

Avenue Hassan II

Avenue de la Liberté

Rue Moulay Slimane

Avenue Mohammed
Youssef ben
Tachfine

Boulevard
es-Siaoui

Mohammed
Boulevard Abdallah Chefchaouni

32

33

Boulevard Dhar
Mahres

Avenue Hussein de Jordanie

Fès

0   250   500 m

To Airport & Ifrane,
Camping at Aïn Chkef

Avenue Ibn el-Khatib

Avenue de Sefrou

Avenue Sidi Brahim

To Sefrou

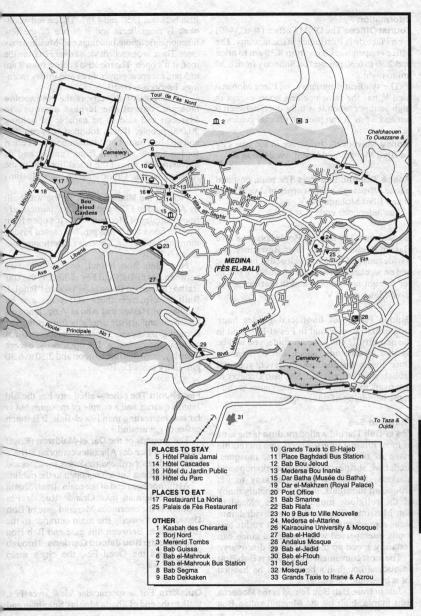

At-Talaa al-Kebir
At-Talaa as-Seghir

Tour de Fès Nord

Chefchaouen
To Ouezzane &

Bou Jeloud Gardens

Sharia Moulay Sulieman

Cemetery

Ave de la Liberté

Route Principale No 1

Blvd Mohammed el-Alaoui

MEDINA
(FÈS EL-BALI)

Oued Fès

Cemetery

To Taza &
Oujda

MOROCCO

PLACES TO STAY		OTHER	
5 Hôtel Palais Jamai		1 Kasbah des Cherarda	19 Dar el-Makhzen (Royal Palace)
14 Hôtel Cascades		2 Borj Nord	20 Post Office
16 Hôtel du Jardin Public		3 Merenid Tombs	21 Bab Smarine
18 Hôtel du Parc		4 Bab Guissa	22 Bab Riafa
		5 Bab el-Mahrouk	23 No 9 Bus to Ville Nouvelle
PLACES TO EAT		6 Bab el-Mahrouk Bus Station	24 Medersa el-Attarine
17 Restaurant La Noria		7 Bab Segma	25 Bab el-Hadid
25 Palais de Fès Restaurant		8 Bab Dekkaken	26 Kairaouine University & Mosque
		9 Grands Taxis to El-Hajeb	27 Bab el-Jedid
OTHER		10 Place Baghdadi Bus Station	28 Andalus Mosque
		11 Bab Bou Jeloud	29 Bab el-Ftouh
		12 Medersa Bou Inania	30 Borj Sud
		13 Dar Batha (Musée du Batha)	31 Mosque
		14 Dar el-Makhzen (Royal Palace)	32 Grands Taxis to Ifrane & Azrou

1 Kasbah des Cherarda	19 Dar el-Makhzen (Royal Palace)
2 Borj Nord	20 Post Office
3 Merenid Tombs	21 Bab Smarine
4 Bab Guissa	22 Bab Riafa
6 Bab el-Mahrouk	23 No 9 Bus to Ville Nouvelle
7 Bab el-Mahrouk Bus Station	24 Medersa el-Attarine
8 Bab Segma	26 Kairaouine University & Mosque
9 Bab Dekkaken	27 Bab el-Jedid
10 Grands Taxis to El-Hajeb	28 Andalus Mosque
11 Place Baghdadi Bus Station	29 Bab el-Ftouh
12 Bab Bou Jeloud	30 Borj Sud
13 Medersa Bou Inania	31 Mosque
15 Dar Batha (Musée du Batha)	32 Mosque
16 Hôtel du Jardin Public	33 Grands Taxis to Ifrane & Azrou

Information

Tourist Offices The ONMT office (☎ 623460) is on Place de la Résistance in the new city. The office is open weekdays from 8.30 am to noon and 2.30 to 6.30 pm, and on Saturday from 8.30 am to noon.

The syndicat d'initiative, on Place Mohammed V, has the same opening hours except in high summer when it is only open between 9 am and 3 pm. It can provide official guides.

Money Most of the banks are in the new city on Blvd Mohammed V and Ave Hassan II.

Post & Communications The main post and phone offices are on the corner of Ave Hassan II and Blvd Mohammed V.

Fès' telephone code is ☎ 05.

Bookshops The English Bookshop at 68 Ave Hassan II, close to Place de la Résistance, has a wide range of books. It's closed at lunchtime and on weekends. There are a number of places for foreign newspapers and magazines along Blvd Mohammed V.

Guides Plenty of unofficial guides hang around Bab Bou Jeloud in Fès el-Bali, and in the new city. If you have no guide, you will be hassled to take one, which can be wearing. Once inside the medina, however, you will probably not be pestered. See also Dangers & Annoyances in the Facts for the Visitor section at the beginning of this chapter.

Things to See

Fès el-Bali The old walled **medina** is the area of most interest to visitors. It's an incredible maze of twisting alleys, arches, mosques, medersas, shrines, fountains, workshops and markets. It takes a lot of walking to get around all the sights, but unfortunately many of the religious monuments are closed to non-Muslims. The medina is divided into areas representing different craft guilds and souqs interspersed with houses; a guide can certainly speed up the process of discovery.

The most convenient entry point is **Bab Bou Jeloud**, although it's here you'll be hassled most by would-be guides.

Just in from Bab Bou Jeloud is the **Medersa Bou Inania**, built by the Merenid sultan Bou Inan between 1350 and 1357. The carved woodwork is magnificent and it is one of the few functioning religious buildings non-Muslims may enter. There are excellent views over Fès from the roof, if it's open. The medersa is open from 8 am to 5 pm, except at prayer times and Friday mornings. Entry costs Dr 10.

In the guts of the city is the **Kairaouine Mosque**, one of the largest mosques in Morocco and said to be capable of holding 20,000 people. It was founded between 859 and 862 by Fatma bint Mohammed ben Feheri for her fellow refugees from Tunisia, and its university has one of the finest libraries in the Muslim world. Unfortunately, non-Muslims may not enter.

Nearby, the **Medersa el-Attarine** was built by Abu Said in 1325 and has some particularly fine examples of Merenid work. It's open from 9 am to noon and 2 to 6 pm, but closed Friday mornings and often Thursday afternoons too. Entry is Dr 10.

Near Bab Bou Jeloud, on the boundary between Fès el-Bali and Fès el-Jdid, is the **Dar Batha** (Musée du Batha) on Place de l'Istiqlal. Built as a palace about 100 years ago by Moulays al-Hassan and Abd al-Aziz, it houses historical and artistic artefacts from ruined or decaying medersas, Fassi embroidery, tribal carpets, and ceramics. It's open daily, except Tuesday, from 8.30 am to noon and 2.30 to 6.30 pm. Entry costs Dr 10.

Fès el-Jdid The other walled city has the old Jewish quarter and a couple of mosques but is far less interesting than Fès el-Bali. It is much easier to get around.

The grounds of the **Dar el-Makhzen** (Royal Palace) on Place des Alaouites comprise 80 hectares of palaces, pavilions, medersas, mosques and pleasure gardens but are not open to the public.

At the northern end of the main street, Sharia Moulay Suleiman (aka Grande Rue de Fès el-Jdid), is the enormous Merenid gate of **Bab Dekkaken**, formerly the main entrance to the royal palace. Between this gate and Bab Bou Jeloud are the **Bou Jeloud Gardens**. Through them flows the Oued Fès, the city's main source of water.

Outskirts For a spectacular view over Fès, walk to the end of Sharia Moulay Suleiman and through the Bab Dekkaken; continue straight on through the mechouar and Bab Segma, across the main road and around behind the Kasbah des Cherarda and cemetery to the Borj Nord fortress. The whole of Fès lies at your feet.

The **Borj Nord** was built in the late 16th century by the Saadian sultan Ahmed al-Mansour. It houses the **Arms Museum**. Opening hours are as for the Musée du Batha and entry is Dr 10.

Places to Stay
Camping The nearest site, *Camping Diamant Vert* (☎ 608367), is six km out of town off the Ifrane road. It sits in a valley through which a clean stream passes, and there's plenty of shade. Facilities include a swimming pool. Camping costs Dr 20 per person (children Dr 10) plus Dr 15 for a car and Dr 15 to pitch a tent. Public bus No 218 goes there from Fès.

Hostel The cheapest place in the ville nouvelle is the *hostel* (☎ 624085), 18 Rue Mohammed el-Hansali. It costs Dr 25 per person in dorms and the showers are cold. It's open from 8 to 9 am, noon to 3 pm and 6 to 10 pm.

Hotels Fès offers the usual trade-off between medina authenticity and ville nouvelle comfort, but in summer, when many of the smaller hotels fill up towards the end of the day, there's little point in heading for Fès el-Bali if it's late. Many medina cheapies hike up their prices in summer, so you pay what you would for better accommodation in the ville nouvelle.

Fès el-Bali The most colourful hotels are the cheapies around Bab Bou Jeloud. They're basic and most have cold showers or none at all. That's no problem, as there are hammams all over the medina. The best hotel is the *Hôtel du Jardin Public* down a side lane (signposted) just outside the Bab. It's clean, quiet, has cold showers and is good value at Dr 30/60 for a single/double (more in summer).

The most interesting place to stay in Fès is the *Hôtel Palais Jamai* (☎ 634331; fax 635096), once the pleasure dome of a late 19th-century grand vizier to the sultan. Set in

a lush Andalusian garden near Bab Guissa, its rooms start at Dr 900 and head for the sky.

Fès el-Jdid Staying in Fès el-Jdid doesn't offer the medina buzz but there are some basic places along Sharia Moulay Suleiman. Closest to Bab Dekkaken is the well-kept and keenly priced *Hôtel du Parc* (Dr 30 a head).

Ville Nouvelle The cheapest hotels here are the *Hôtel du Maghreb*, 25 Ave Mohammed es-Slaoui, the *Hôtel Regina*, 21 Rue Ghassan Kanfani, and the *Hôtel Renaissance*. They are basic but clean and cost Dr 40 to Dr 60 for a single, Dr 70 for a double and Dr 100 for a triple.

Slightly better are the *Hôtel Volubilis*, Blvd Abdallah Chefchaouni, and, just around the corner, the *Hôtel Savoy* (☎ 620608). Rooms cost about Dr 30/70/90 for singles/doubles/triples.

The ville nouvelle has a good selection of one and two-star hotels. Among the best is the *Hôtel Kairouan* (☎ 623596), 84 Rue du Soudan (a short walk from the train station). It has some spacious rooms with big clean beds for Dr 85/111. Rooms with private shower cost Dr 109/129. The nearby one-star *Hôtel Royal* (☎ 624656), 36 Rue du Soudan, charges Dr 109/129 for rooms with own shower.

The three-star *Grand Hôtel* (☎ 932026; fax 653847), on Blvd Abdallah Chefchaouni, still lives up to its name. It has rooms with all facilities for Dr 216/261.

Places to Eat
Fès el-Bali The best restaurants for a cheap meal in Fès el-Bali are around Bab Bou Jeloud. Just inside the Bab is the *Restaurant des Jeunes*, near the Hôtel Cascades, which offers harira for Dr 5 and mains for Dr 30. There are some wonderful snack stands where you can buy stuffed rolls for about Dr 10.

In the north-west corner of the Bou Jeloud Gardens, *La Noria* is a quiet place for a more expensive snack or cold drink in a pleasant garden with a large *noria*, or water wheel.

Fès is dotted with a good half dozen restaurants housed in old mansions and offering expensive Moroccan feasts. Possibly the pick of them is the *Palais de Fès* (☎ 634707), a gracious 14th-century building housing a restaurant and rooftop café. Coffee costs Dr 10 a

MOROCCO

shot, but is worth it for the views. Full meals, often with a performance of music and dance, come to around Dr 200 at these places. The tourist office can suggest others.

Ville Nouvelle There are a few cheap eats on or just off Blvd Mohammed V, especially around the central market. They are mixed in with pâtisseries, cafés and the like. A couple of these food places are on the same side street off Blvd Mohammed V as the Hôtel Olympic. Watch the prices.

The·*Restaurant Chamonix*, in a side street another block south, offers a limited range of good food, including a tasty set menu for Dr 47.50. Across the street is the *Oliverdi* (☎ 620231), a pizzeria that does home delivery.

If you want a drink with your meal, you could do worse than the *Restaurant du Centre*, not far from the Chamonix but directly on Blvd Mohammed V, which serves alcohol and a Dr 60 menu of simple French fare.

The restaurant *Golding Palm* (☎ 620019), on Blvd Mohammed V, just near the CTM station is an attractive, lively place with a bar attached. It offers good servings of Moroccan food for about Dr 50 a main course.

La Mamia on Place de Florence does eat-in and takeaway pizzas and hamburgers. The pizzas cost from Dr 30 to Dr 50 and are not bad.

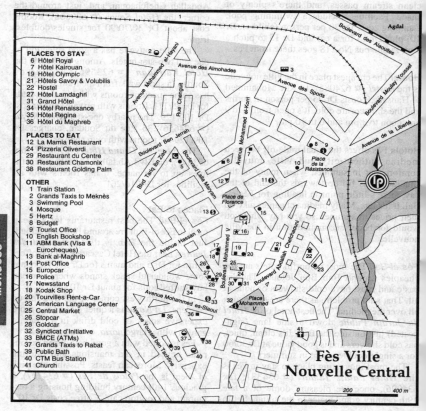

PLACES TO STAY
6 Hôtel Royal
7 Hôtel Kairouan
19 Hôtel Olympic
21 Hôtels Savoy & Volubilis
22 Hostel
27 Hôtel Lamdaghri
31 Grand Hôtel
34 Hôtel Renaissance
35 Hôtel Regina
36 Hôtel du Maghreb

PLACES TO EAT
12 La Mamia Restaurant
24 Pizzeria Oliverdi
29 Restaurant du Centre
30 Restaurant Chamonix
38 Restaurant Golding Palm

OTHER
1 Train Station
2 Grands Taxis to Meknès
3 Swimming Pool
4 Mosque
5 Hertz
8 Budget
9 Tourist Office
10 English Bookshop
11 ABM Bank (Visa & Eurocheques)
13 Bank al-Maghrib
14 Post Office
15 Europcar
16 Police
17 Newsstand
18 Kodak Shop
20 Tourvilles Rent-a-Car
23 American Language Center
25 Central Market
26 Stopcar
28 Goldcar
32 Syndicat d'Initiative
33 BMCE (ATMs)
37 Grands Taxis to Rabat
39 Public Bath
40 CTM Bus Station
41 Church

Fès Ville Nouvelle Central

0   200   400 m

Getting There & Away

Bus The CTM bus station is in the ville nouvelle on Blvd Mohammed V. Tickets can be bought up to five days in advance – a good idea as demand is high, especially on the Fès-Tangier and Fès-Marrakesh runs. There are daily departures to Casablanca, Marrakesh, Meknès, Oujda, Tangier and Tetouan.

Non-CTM buses use a brand new station just outside Bab el-Mahrouk, east of the kasbah. Buses depart from here for all destinations and reservations can be made for the most popular runs. CTM also has an office in the complex.

Train The train station is in the ville nouvelle, 10 minutes walk from the centre. Trains are the best bet to Oujda (five to six hours), Casablanca (five hours), Tangier (six hours) and Marrakesh (eight hours). Most trains from Fès to Marrakesh involve a change of trains at either Rabat or Casa-Voyageurs station in Casablanca. All trains between Fès and Casablanca or Marrakesh stop at Meknès and Rabat.

Taxi Grands taxis for Rabat (Dr 50) leave from the streets around the CTM station and those for Meknès (Dr 15) leave from in front of the train station. Grands taxis for all other destinations leave from the bus station at Bab el-Mahrouk.

Car The following are among the car-rental agencies located in Fès:

Avis
  50 Blvd Abdallah Chefchaouni (☎ 626746; fax 626746)
Budget
  Angle Ave Hassan II, Rue Bahrein (☎ 940092; fax 940091)
Europcar
  45 Ave Hassan II (☎ 626545)
Hertz
  Blvd Lalla Maryam (☎ 622812)

Getting Around

Bus Fès has a fairly good local bus service, although the buses are like sardine cans at certain times of the day. Useful routes include the following:

No 9 – Place de l'Atlas – Ave Hassan II – Dar Batha

No 10 – train station – Bab Guissa – Sidi Bou Jidda
No 11 – bus station – Ave Hassan II – Place de l'Atlas
No 12 – Bab Bou Jeloud – Bab Guissa – Bab el-Ftouh
No 16 – train station – airport
No 17 – Blvd Tariq ibn Ziad – 'Ain Chkef
No 18 – Bab el-Ftouh – Dar Batha
No 37 – train station – Bab Bou Jeloud

Taxi The red petits taxis are cheap and plentiful. The drivers use the meters without any fuss. Expect to pay about Dr 10 to Dr 15 from the CTM station to Bab Bou Jeloud and about Dr 10 from Bab el-Mahrouk to Blvd Mohammed V. Only grands taxis – from in front of the syndicat d'initiative – will go out to the airport and although it's only 15 km they're virtually impossible to beat down to less than Dr 70.

AROUND FÈS

Set against jagged mountain bluffs and rich farmland, the picturesque Berber town, **Sefrou**, makes a fine contrast to the intensity and size of Fès, just 28 km away. The town boasts a small but interesting walled **medina** and **mellah**. The best points of entry/exit are the Bab Taksebt, Bab Zemghila and the Bab Merba. There's a **waterfall** about 1.5 km from town.

Apart from a *camping ground*, you have no real accommodation options. Regular buses and taxis between Fès and Sefrou drop you off at Place Moulay Hassan in front of the Bab M'Kam and Bab Taksebt.

TAZA

Overlooking the Taza Gap – the only feasible pass from the east between the Rif Mountains and the Middle Atlas – Taza has been important throughout Morocco's history as a base from which to exert control over the country's eastern extremities.

If you have your own transport, the drive around **Mt Tazzeka**, with a visit to the incredible caverns of the **Gouffre du Friouato**, is superb. Said to be the deepest in North Africa, the caverns have only been partially explored. You can get down the first 100 metres easily, and there is plenty of natural light. To explore below this level you will need a torch (flashlight). Pay the guardian to get in (Dr 10 should suffice).

In the town itself, the old medina is relaxed and worth a wander, particularly around the ramparts to **Bab er-Rih** (Gate of the Wind), from where there are excellent views over the surrounding countryside. The **Grande Mosquée**, which was begun by the Almohads in 1135, is not open to non-Muslims.

Taza's telephone code is ☎ 05.

Places to Stay & Eat
The *Hôtel de la Gare* (☎ 672448), near the train station, has clean, simple singles/doubles without shower for Dr 48/64, and with shower for Dr 75/85.

In the centre of the new town, the *Hôtel Guillaume Tell* (☎ 672347) offers big rooms with double beds for Dr 41/62. Showers are cold. The nearby *Hôtel de la Poste* (☎ 672589) has small but comfortable rooms for Dr 48/64 but no shower.

The *Grand Hôtel du Dauphine* (☎ 673567) is an attractive colonial-style building and the best place to stay if you have the money. Rooms without bathroom cost Dr 70/87; with own shower Dr 96/120. There's hot water in the evenings. Downstairs is a lively bar and a sedate dining hall.

One of the best of the few eateries in town is the *Restaurant Majestic* on Ave Mohammed V, near the hotels. You can eat well for around Dr 30.

Getting There & Away
Buses and grands taxis leave for Fès, Oujda, Al-Hoceima and Nador several times a day from a lot on the Fès-Oujda road near the station. The CTM terminal is on Place de l'Indépendance, more convenient for the hotels.

There are daily trains to Oujda, Fès and Meknès. Some continue beyond Meknès to Tangier, others to Casablanca via Rabat.

OUJDA
This is the last town before the Algerian border, which is closed at this point so there's little reason to come here. The ville nouvelle is reminiscent of Casablanca and of little interest. The partially walled old medina is quite small.

Information
The tourist office (☎ 685631) is on Place du 16 Août at the junction with Blvd Mohammed V. The post office and banks are concentrated on Blvd Mohammed V.

Oudja's telephone code is ☎ 06.

The Algerian consulate (☎ 683740) is at 11 Blvd Bir Anzarane (aka Blvd de Taza). It is open Monday to Thursday from 8 am to 3 pm and Friday until noon. No visas were being issued at the time of writing.

Places to Stay
There are basic places in the medina, mostly near Bab el-Ouahab. Closer to the centre of town, along Rue de Marrakech, are more cheapies.

The best area to look, however, is in the pedestrian precinct behind the Bank al-Maghrib on Blvd Mohammed V. A cheap and showerless place here is the *Hôtel Majestic* (☎ 682948). The signs are that it doubles as a brothel.

The *Hôtel Isly* (☎ 683928), at 24 Rue Ramdane el-Gadhi, has reasonable budget singles/doubles/triples for Dr 45/70/90. The hot water in the showers is hit and miss but the management is friendly.

A little more money will get you a much better deal. The *Hôtel Simon* (☎ 686304) has singles/doubles with own shower and wrought iron balcony for Dr 70/93. Not far away, at 13 Blvd Zerktouni, the *Hôtel Royal* (☎ 682284) is another good bet. It charges Dr 64/94 for rooms without shower and Dr 109/125 with own hot shower and toilet.

Places to Eat
In the evenings, cheap food stalls are set up in the medina just inside Bab el-Ouahab.

Iris Sandwich is a good snack food place on Ave Idriss el-Akbar. You can get a baguette stuffed with meat, salad and chips for Dr 12 to Dr 16. Virtually next door is the *Restaurant Quick Food*, which offers a common Middle Eastern dish, shawarma. There are other cheap OK places in the pedestrian area off Blvd Mohammed V. The *Café Holiday*, for instance, does an unexciting tajine for Dr 30. There are a few nondescript places along Rue de Marrakech too.

Try the *Brasserie Restaurant de France*, on Blvd Mohammed V, for a Dr 100 splurge in air-conditioned comfort.

Getting There & Away
Bus CTM runs buses to Tangier, Rabat and Casablanca from an office behind the town hall. The bus station for all other buses is across Oued Nachef, about 15 minutes walk south

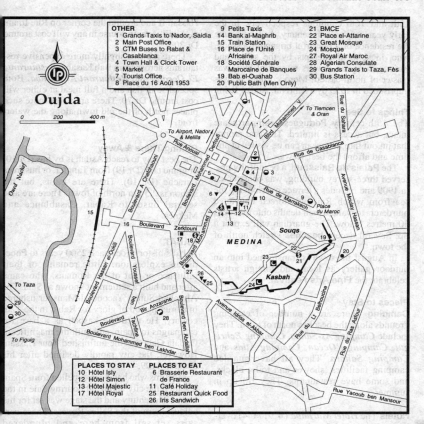

Oujda

0   200   400 m

from the train station. Advance booking is available on the major runs.

CTM has daily departures to Taza, Fès and Nador. Ligne du Sahara and Transports des Hauts Plateaux have departures to Figuig and Bouarfa. Ligne de Casablanca has buses to Fès and to Casablanca/Rabat.

Train The train station is close to the centre, at the end of Blvd Zerktouni. There are daily westbound departures, all stopping at Taza (four hours), Fès (6½ hours) and Meknès (7½ hours). Some trains continue to Tangier, others to Rabat and Casablanca. Sleepers and couchettes are available on the evening trains.

Taxi Grands taxis to Taza and Fès leave from near the bus station and to Nador and Saidia from Rue Foucauld just off Blvd Mohammed Derfoufi.

The Atlantic Coast

ASILAH
About 46 km south of Tangier, the small port of Asilah has enjoyed a tumultuous history disproportionate to its size. Settled first by the Carthaginians and then the Romans, it came under Portuguese and Spanish control in the

MOROCCO

15th and 16th centuries respectively. In the early years of the 20th century, Asilah became the residence of a powerful brigand, Raissouli, who, in spite of attempts by the sultan and various European powers to control him, was master of north-eastern Morocco until he was imprisoned in 1925 by a Rif rival, Abd el-Krim.

Things to See
The 15th-century Portuguese **ramparts** are intact, but access is limited. The two prongs that jut out into the ocean can be visited at any time and afford the best views.

The **Palais de Raissouli**, a beautifully preserved three-storey building, was constructed in 1909 and includes a terrace overlooking the sea from which Raissouli forced convicted murderers to walk to their deaths onto the rocks 30 metres below. The guardian will expect a tip. Several decent **beaches** stretch north of the town.

In August the town is transformed into an outdoor gallery as local and foreign artists celebrate the **Fine Arts Festival**.

Places to Stay
Camping There are a number of camping grounds along the beaches north of town. They include *Camping As-Saada*, *Camping Echrigui*, *Camping l'Océan*, *Camping Atlas* and *Camping Sahara*. They all have guarded camping facilities, shower and toilet blocks, and some have restaurants. They fill up in summer.

Hotels The *Hôtel Marhaba* (☎ 917144) overlooks Place Zelaka, in front of the main entrance (Bab Kasaba) to the old town, and is clean and pleasant. Singles/doubles cost Dr 60/80. Hot showers are Dr 5 extra. The *Hôtel Asilah* on Ave Hassan II has rooms for Dr 60/100 and free shower (hot water in the morning), and is a good alternative.

The *Hôtel Belle Vue* (☎ 917747), Rue al-Khansa, offers comfortable, clean rooms with shared shower and toilet and plenty of hot water. Rooms cost Dr 100/120, more in summer. It also has larger self-contained apartments with lounge, kitchen and fridge but no belle vue.

Places to Eat
There is a string of restaurants and cafés on Ave Hassan II and around the corner on Rue Imam al-Assili. A main course in any will cost around Dr 30.

There are two slightly more expensive restaurants across from Bab Kasaba, *Restaurante El Oceano* and *Restaurant Al Kasaba*. Both specialise in fish and a full meal at either will cost around Dr 70. There are a few more such places north of the old town along the waterfront.

Getting There & Away
The best way to reach Asilah is by bus (Dr 10) or grand taxi (Dr 19) from Tangier, or bus from Larache (Dr 10). There are trains, but the station is 2.5 km north of town. There are also several buses to Rabat, Casablanca and Meknès.

RABAT
Rabat's history goes back 2500 years to Phoenician exploration. Little remains of their influence or that of the Romans, who came after and built a settlement known as Sala. The Almohad Sultan Yacoub al-Mansour ushered in a brief period of glory for Rabat in the 12th century. He used the kasbah as a base for campaigns in Spain, and built the magnificent Oudaia Gate and the unfinished Tour Hassan. However, the city rapidly declined after his death in 1199.

Muslims who had been expelled from Spain resettled the city and neighbouring Salé in the early 17th century and the stage was set for the colourful era of the Sallee Rovers. These corsairs set sail from here and plundered thousands of merchant vessels returning to Europe from Asia, West Africa and the Americas throughout the 17th and 18th centuries

Rabat's role as Morocco's capital dates from the days of the French protectorate. Few of its people are involved in the tourist trade, which means you can walk through the souq without having to steel yourself against high-pressure sales tactics.

Orientation
Rabat lies on the west bank of the Oued Bou Regreg, and Salé lies on the east. The Roman ruins of Sala, later known as Chellah, are immediately south of the town centre, while the relatively small medina area is just north.

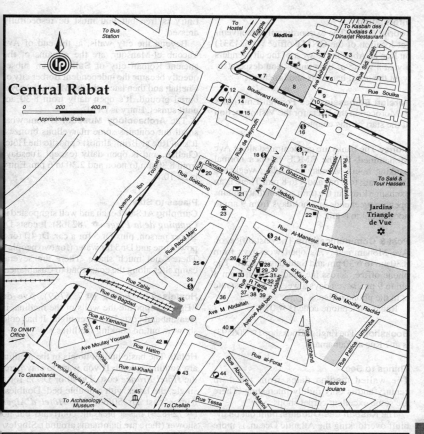

Central Rabat

0   200   400 m

Approximate Scale

To Bus Station
To Hostel
To Égypte
Medina
To Kasbah des Oudaias & Dinarjat Restaurant
Ave de Égypte
Ave Mohammed V
Rue Sidi Fatah
Rue Souika
Boulevard Hassan II
Rue de Beyrouth
Rue Damiate
Rue Halab
Rue Soékamo
Rue Mohammed V
R. Ghazzah
R. Jeddah
Rue de Monastir
Rue Yougoslavia
To Salé & Tour Hassan
Avenue Ibn Toumerte
Rue Raoul Marc
Rue Zahla
Rue Dimachk
Rue al-Mansour ad-Dahbi
Rue al-Kahira
Rue Moulay Rachid
Rue Patrice Lumumba
Rue Marchand
Rue al-Tanta
Ammane
Jardins Triangle de Vue
Rue de Bagdad
Rue al-Yamama
Rue Souta
Ave Moulay Youssef
Rue Hatim
Rue al-Khahil
Avenue Moulay Hassan
To ONMT Office
To Casablanca
Ave M Abdallah
Avenue Allal ben Abdallah
Rue al-Forat
Rue Abou Fars al-Marini
Place du Joulane
To Archaeology Museum
To Chellah
Rue Tessa

PLACES TO STAY
4 Hôtel France
5 Hôtel d'Alger
9 Hôtel Dorhmi
14 Hôtel Majestic
15 Hôtel Mamounia
19 Hôtel de la Paix
22 Hôtel Royal
27 Hôtel Central
33 Hôtel Balima
40 Hôtel Velleda
42 Hôtel Terminus

PLACES TO EAT
2 Restaurants de l'Union & de la Libération
3 Restaurant Taghazout
6 Café de la Jeunesse
7 Seafood Restaurants
10 Restaurant El Bahia
30 La Bidoche (Hamburgers)
31 Dolce Vita (Ice Cream)
32 Pizza La Mamma
37 Pizza Hot
38 Restaurant La Bamba
39 Restaurant Baghdad

OTHER
1 Public Bath
8 Municipal Market
11 Petit Taxi Stand
12 Public Bath
13 No 3 Bus (to Gare Routière) & No 17 to Temara via Zoo
16 Wafabank
17 BMCE (ATMs)
18 BMCE (ATM)
20 Immigration Office (Sûreté Nationale)
21 Post Office
23 Telephone Office
24 Bank al-Maghrib
25 House of Deputies
26 Air France
28 Bar Le Rêve
29 Bar de Tanger
34 BMCI (ATM)
35 Rabat Ville Train Station
36 Royal Air Maroc
41 English Bookshop
43 Hertz
44 French Consulate
45 Musée National des PTT

MOROCCO

Information

Tourist Office The extraordinarily inconvenient location of the ONMT office (☎ 681531) on Rue al-Abtal in the west of the city renders a visit a waste of time unless you desperately want the usual handouts and brochures.

Foreign Embassies See Foreign Embassies in Morocco in the Facts for the Visitor section at the start of this chapter.

Money The banks are concentrated along Ave Mohammed V. The BMCE is open normal banking hours Monday to Friday; weekends from 10 am to 2 pm and 4 to 8 pm. There is an exchange kiosk in the train station that remains open on weekends and holidays from 9 am to noon and 3 to 6 pm.

Post & Communications The post office, on Ave Mohammed V, is open weekdays from 8.30 am to 6.30 pm and Saturday to noon. The phone office, across the road, is open from 8 am to 9 pm, seven days a week. Poste restante is in the phone office.

Rabat's telephone code is ☎ 07.

Bookshops The English Bookshop (☎ 706593) is at 7 Rue al-Yamama.

Things to See

The walled **medina** dates from the 17th century and is only mildly interesting. There are some excellent carpet shops.

The **Kasbah des Oudaias**, built out on the bluff overlooking the Atlantic Ocean, is more interesting than the medina. The main entry is via the enormous **Almohad Bab Oudaia**, built in 1195. A 'guide' in here is quite unnecessary. The kasbah houses a palace built by Moulay Ismail that now contains a museum of traditional art. The palace is open every day from 9 am to noon and 3 to 5 pm (6 pm in summer). Entry to the museum is Dr 10. The pleasant **Andalusian Gardens** in the palace grounds were actually planted by the French.

Rabat's most famous landmark is the **Tour Hassan**, the incomplete minaret of the great mosque begun by Yacoub al-Mansour. The 1755 earthquake finished off the half-built mosque. On the same site is the **Mausoleum of Mohammed V**, the present king's father. Entry is free but you must be respectfully dressed.

Beyond the city walls, at the end of Ave Yacoub el-Mansour, are the remains of the ancient Roman city of **Sala**, which subsequently became the independent Berber city of Chellah and then later still the Merenids' royal burial ground. It's open daily from 8.30 am until sunset. Entry is Dr 10.

The **Archaeology Museum** is somewhat small but contains some marvellous bronzes. It's on Rue al-Brihi, almost opposite the Hôtel Chellah, and is open daily (except Tuesday) from 8.30 am to noon and 2.30 to 6 pm. Entry is Dr 10.

Places to Stay

Camping At Salé beach and well signposted is *Camping de la Plage* (☎ 782368). It costs Dr 10 per person, plus Dr 5 for a car, Dr 10 for a power line and Dr 5 for water (for two people). There's not much shade. There are several camp sites along the coast road to Casablanca.

Hostels The *hostel* (☎ 725769), Ave de l'Egypte, opposite the walls of the medina, is pleasant and costs Dr 31 per night. It has cold showers but no cooking facilities.

Hotels The basic budget hotels in the medina are nothing special. If you want to stay here, the *Hôtel France* costs Dr 30 or Dr 35 for a single, the latter with a double bed. Doubles/triples cost Dr 50/60. The *Hôtel d'Alger* (☎ 724829) has a pleasant courtyard but no shower (there are hammams around). Singles/doubles/triples/quadruples here cost Dr 35/60/90/110.

The best in the medina is the *Hôtel Dorhmi* (☎ 723898), at 313 Ave Mohammed V. It has been completely renovated and has singles/doubles for Dr 80/100. Hot showers are Dr 7 more.

A block south of Blvd Hassan II, the *Hôtel Mamounia* (☎ 724479), 10 Rue de la Mamounia, is a quiet place to stop. It has simple, clean rooms for Dr 60/80. Hot showers are Dr 5 extra.

One of the best budget deals is the *Hôtel Central* (☎ 707356), at 2 Zankat al-Basra. Spacious, furnished rooms with basin and bidet cost Dr 70/110. A hot shower costs Dr 9. A little more expensive for singles but a rival for value in doubles is the *Hôtel Velleda* (☎ 769531), 106 Ave Allal ben Abdallah. Generous rooms with own toilet cost Dr 83/99, or Dr 125/146 with shower as well.

The *Hôtel Royal* (☎ 721171), 1 Rue Jeddah Ammane, has comfortable rooms with telephone and bathroom. Singles with own shower are Dr 152, and Dr 185 with shower and toilet. Doubles are about Dr 40 more. There is hot water all day. Try for a room with views over the park. A bit cheaper but pretty much as good is the *Hôtel de la Paix* (☎ 722926) on Rue Ghazzah. Singles/doubles cost Dr 136/171.

Places to Eat
There are several good, cheap places to eat in the medina, including a group of restaurants under a common roofed area directly opposite the Hôtel Majestic on Blvd Hassan II. You can get meat dishes or sometimes freshly fried fish, salad and the like for as little as Dr 30.

At the popular *Café de la Jeunesse*, on Ave Mohammed V in the medina, you can get a full meal of kebabs and chips, salad and bread for Dr 25. On the ground floor it offers even cheaper takeaways. A little further along the same street there's similar food in a cleaner setting at the *Restaurant de l'Union* and the *Restaurant de la Libération*. Just round the corner on Rue Sebbahi is the *Restaurant Taghazout*.

The *Restaurant El Bahia*, on Blvd Hassan II close to the junction with Ave Mohammed V, is built into the walls of the medina. A meal will cost from Dr 30. You can eat outside or in a Moroccan-style salon.

The spot to splurge in the medina is *Dinarjat* (☎ 704239), 6 Rue Belgnaoui, off Blvd al-Alou. It's in an old mansion and is *the* place for a Moroccan feast experience.

There is quite a range of restaurants in the ville nouvelle. A block behind the Hôtel Balima is a cluster of them. *La Bamba* offers Moroccan food and fish dishes, including two set menus at Dr 65 and Dr 95. They promise paella too. Next door and across the road respectively are two pizza joints, *Pizza Hot* and *La Mamma*. The latter is the more expensive, but does a fine pizza with real ham, and it's licensed. The *Restaurant Baghdad* is primarily a bar but does shish kebabs, *La Bidoche* does hamburgers and *Dolce Vita* sells ice creams.

There are numerous popular cafés and pâtisseries along Ave Mohammed V.

Entertainment
There are several local bars in the ville nouvelle, including the *Bar de Tanger* and *Bar Le Rêve*, opposite the Hôtel Central on Rue Dimachk. There are a few expensive nightclubs scattered about Rabat. Entry is normally at least Dr 50 and subsequent drinks are also Dr 50.

Getting There & Away
Bus The bus station is inconveniently situated five km from the centre of town. There are local buses (No 30) and petits taxis (Dr 12) to the centre.

CTM has buses to Casablanca Er-Rachidia, Fès, Oujda, Tangier and Tiznit. Other companies cover most destinations of interest, including Marrakesh.

Train The Rabat Ville station is centrally located on Ave Mohammed V. Don't get off at Rabat Agdal station. There are 17 daily express trains to Casablanca from 6.20 am to 9.48 pm on weekdays (fewer on weekends and public holidays). They take 55 minutes and cost Dr 25 (2nd class) one way.

Other main daily departures are to Tangier (five hours), Meknès and Fès (four hours), Oujda (10 hours), Marrakesh (six hours) and El-Jadida (two hours).

Taxi Grands taxis for Casablanca (Dr 27) leave from outside the main bus station. Others leave from near the Hôtel Bou Regreg on Blvd Hassan II for Fès (Dr 50), Meknès (Dr 35) and Salé (Dr 2).

Car The following are among the car-rental agencies located in Rabat:

Avis
    7 Rue Abou Faris al-Marini (☎ 769759; fax 767503)
Budget
    train station, Ave Mohammed V (☎ 705789)
Europcar
    25bis Rue Patrice Lumumba (☎ 722328; fax 200241)
Hertz
    46 Ave Mohammed V (☎ 709227)

Getting Around
To/From the Airport Eleven express trains run

MOROCCO

daily between Rabat and Casablanca's Mohammed V international airport with a change at Casa-Port station. The fare is Dr 45 in 2nd class and the journey takes 90 minutes.

Local Transport Bus No 30 to the main bus station leaves from a stop just inside Bab al-Had. Others leave to Salé from the main local terminus on Blvd Hassan II. Most of Rabat's petits taxis are metered.

AROUND RABAT

The town of **Salé** is worlds away from Rabat. Largely left to itself since the demise of the corsairs who brought it prosperity, you can experience the sights, smells and sounds of the Morocco of yesteryear here without the tourist hordes.

In the 13th century the Merenid sultan built the walls and gates that stand today and a canal between the Oued Bou Regreg and the Bab Mrisa to allow safe access for shipping. Salé became the principal seaport through which the sultanate at Fès traded with the outside world until the end of the 16th century, when it was eclipsed by the rise of Rabat.

The **souqs** are worth wandering through, and the main sight inside the walls is the **medersa** built in 1333 next to the Grand Mosque. It is a classic example of Merenid artistry. Entry costs Dr 10.

Grands taxis to Rabat (Dr 2) leave from Bab Mrisa. Bus No 16 also links the two, or you could catch the rowboat across the river below Bab Bou Haja.

CASABLANCA

With a population already around three million and growing, Casablanca is Morocco's largest city and industrial centre.

Although it has a history going back many centuries and was colonised by the Portuguese in the 16th century (who stayed until 1755), it had declined into insignificance by the mid-1880s.

Its renaissance came when the resident-general of the French protectorate, Lyautey, decided to develop Casablanca as a commercial centre. It was largely his ideas that gave Casablanca its wide boulevards, public parks and fountains, and imposing Mauresque civic

buildings (a blend of French colonial and traditional Moroccan styles).

Look for the white, medium high-rise 1930s architecture, the many Art Deco touches and the pedestrian precincts thronged with speedy, fashion-conscious young people. Casablanca is cosmopolitan Morocco and an excellent barometer of liberal Islam.

Information

Tourist Offices The ONMT (☎ 271177) is at 55 Rue Omar Slaoui and the syndicat d'initiative (☎ 221524) at 98 Blvd Mohammed V. They have the usual brochures. The ONMT is open weekdays from 8.30 am to noon and 3 to 6.30 pm. The syndicat has the same hours Monday to Saturday and is open on Sunday from 9 am to noon.

Money There are BMCE branches with ATMs on Ave Lalla Yacout and Ave des FAR. The BMCI exchange office on Place des Nations Unies is open seven days a week.

American Express is represented by Voyages Schwartz (☎ 222947), 112 Rue Prince Moulay Abdallah. Thomas Cook is represented by KTI Voyages (☎ 398572/3/4; fax 398567), 4 Rue des Hirondelles.

Post & Communications The central post office is on Place Mohammed V. It's open weekdays from 8 am to 6.30 pm and Saturday until noon.

The poste-restante counter is in the same section as the international telephones, which is open from 9 am to 9 pm. The entrance is the third door along Blvd de Paris.

Casablanca's telephone code is ☎ 02.

Things to See

The **medina** is worth a look, although it has seen more dynamic days. Most of the surviving craft stalls are concentrated outside the walls along Blvd Houphouet Boigny. Prices are relatively high, but there are no hassles with guides.

The **Hassan II Mosque**, finished in 1993, overlooks the ocean just beyond the northern tip of the medina. It is one of the biggest mosques in the world and has the tallest minaret. Tours of the interior are guided and cost Dr 100 per person; Dr 50 for students.

The central **ville nouvelle** around Place des Nations Unies has some of the best examples of Mauresque architecture. They include the law courts, post office, French consulate and the Sacré Cœur cathedral.

Casablanca's **beaches** are to the west of town along the Blvd de la Corniche and beyond in the suburb of 'Ain Diab. It's a trendy area and very crowded in summer. The beaches are OK but nothing special. Bus No 9 goes to 'Ain Diab from the terminus at Place Oued al-Makhazine.

Places to Stay

Camping If you have a tent, head to *Camping de l'Oasis* (☎ 234257), Ave Mermoz (the main road to El-Jadida). It's a long way from the centre, so unless you have your own transport it's hardly worth it. Bus No 31 runs past it.

Hostel The *hostel* (☎ 220551; fax 227677), 6 Place de l'Amiral Philibert, faces a square in the medina, just off Blvd des Almohades. It's large, comfortable and clean, and costs Dr 40 per person, including breakfast. It's open daily from 8 to 10 am and noon to 11 pm.

Hotels The hotels in the medina are unclassified and seedy. None have hot showers, but there are several hammams around. They all cost around Dr 40 per person, but for a little more you can do better outside the medina. Check the map for the location of the medina hotels.

Outside the medina, the *Hôtel du Palais* (☎ 276191) is one of the best unclassified joints. Located at 68 Rue Farhat Hachad near the French consulate, it has clean and spacious singles/doubles for Dr 62/76. The showers are cold.

At No 38 Rue Chaoui is the pleasant *Hôtel Colbert* (☎ 314241). Singles/doubles/triples without shower or toilet start at Dr 63/78/114. Those with shower are Dr 84/100/136.

Two popular places are the *Hôtel du Périgord* (☎ 221085), 56 Rue Araibi Jilali (formerly Rue de Foucauld) and the *Hôtel de Foucauld* (☎ 222666) at No 52. The first has rooms for Dr 62/82/127. The singles are cramped. Cold showers only. The Foucauld has singles without own shower for Dr 70 and doubles with shower for Dr 110.

Hôtel du Louvre (☎ 273747), 36 Rue Nationale, is quite good, but some rooms are better than others. Prices start at Dr 70. Singles/doubles with own shower are Dr 94/120 including breakfast.

The *Hôtel du Centre* (☎ 312448), just off the Ave des FAR, is a good two-star place with clean, modern rooms (own bathroom and phone) for Dr 181/216. The *Hôtel de Lausanne* (☎ 268690), 24 Rue Tata (ex-Rue Poincaré), is similar in quality and price.

Places to Eat

There are a few cheap restaurants around the clock tower entrance to the medina. One good one is the *Restaurant Widad*, which serves generous helpings of Moroccan food. A big steaming bowl of soup costs Dr 3.50.

There are lots of Moroccan fast-food cafés along Ave Lalla Yacout such as *Kwiki Sandwich*. You can get a kefta sandwich with salad and chips here for Dr 10. A more up-market version is the *Snack Bohayra* at 62 Rue Nationale, where you can get filled sandwiches for about Dr 15 or filling sit-down meals of kefta, chips, salad and a soft drink for Dr 30 to Dr 35.

On Ave Hassan II is a particularly bright and popular snack bar, *Casablanca Lights*, where you can go downstairs for a game of pool. Another popular 'self-service' restaurant is *Welcome*, in from Place des Nations Unies.

The *Restaurant de l'Étoile Marocaine*, at 107 Rue Allal ben Abdallah, not far from the Hôtel Touring, is a friendly place where you can eat good Moroccan food in traditional surroundings. They have pastilla for Dr 45.

If you're hankering after South-East Asian food, you could head for the *Restaurant Le Tonkin* on the pedestrian mall, or *La Pagode*, close to the Hôtel du Palais. A meal at either will set you back around Dr 80. Or you could try the Korean restaurant, *Le Marignan*, on the corner of Blvd Mohammed V and Rue Mohammed Smiha. For seafood, go to the *Taverne du Dauphin* on Blvd Houphouet Boigny.

The *Centre 2000*, next to Casa-Port train station, houses several up-market restaurants.

Entertainment

Casablanca nightlife can be expensive, but you can join the throng promenading up and down

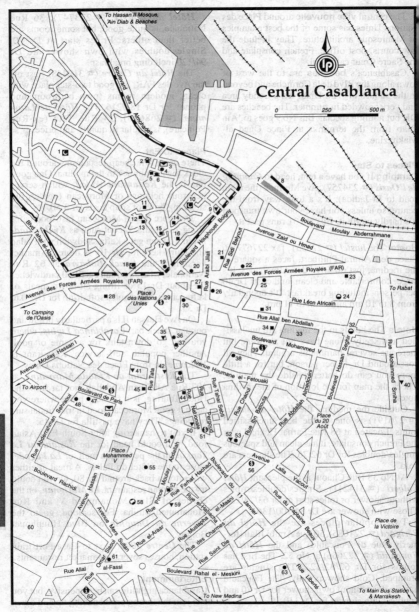

Central Casablanca

To Hassan II Mosque,
Ain Diab & Beaches

0   250   500 m

To Rabat

To Camping
de l'Oasis

To Airport

To Main Bus Station
& Marrakesh

To New Medina

Place
des Nations
Unies

Place
du 20
Août

Place
Mohammed
V

Place de
la Victoire

Boulevard des Almohades

Boulevard Moulay Abderrahmane

Avenue Zaid ou Hmad

Avenue des Forces Armées Royales (FAR)

Rue Léon Africain

Rue Allal ben Abdallah

Boulevard Mohammed V

Avenue Houmane el-Fetouaki

Avenue des Forces Armées Royales (FAR)

Bvd Tahar el-Alaoui

Avenue Moulay Hassan I

Boulevard de Paris

Boulevard Rachidi

Rue Abderrahman Senhadji

Rue Sidi Belyout

Rue Arabi Jilali

Boulevard Houphouet Boigny

Rue Tahar Sebti

Rue Tata

Rue Nationale

Rue Prince Moulay Abdallah

Rue Farhat Hachad

Rue Chaoui

Rue Ibn Batouta

Rue Abdallah Almejdouni

Boulevard Hassan Seghir

Rue Mohammed Smiha

Boulevard du 11 Janvier

Rue el-Habous el-Maani

Rue Mustapha el-Maani

Rue des Charmes

Rue Saint Die

Avenue Hassan II

Avenue Mers Sultan

Rue el-Nraar

Rue Allal

Rue Omar Slaoui

Sultan

al-Fassi

Boulevard Rahal el-Meskini

Rue Liberté

Rue Strasbourg

Lalla
Yacout

Rue du Capitaine Beaux

MOROCCO

PLACES TO STAY		40	Le Marignan	33	Central Market
2	Hostel		Restaurant	36	Trasmediterranea/
5	Hôtel Central	41	Casablanca Lights		Intercona
11	Hôtels des Amis, de	42	Restaurant Le Tonkin	37	Goethe Institut
	Medine & Gibraltar	50	Snack Bohayra	38	Cinéma Rialto
12	Hôtel Candide	52	Kwiki Sandwich	39	PTT & Syndicat
13	Hôtel Soussi	59	Restaurant La Pagode		d'Initiative
14	Hôtel Helvetia			43	Gelatino Ice Cream
15	Hôtel de Brésil	OTHER			Place
16	Hôtel Genève	1	Mosque	46	Citibank
21	Hôtel du Centre	3	Post Office	47	Parcel Post
23	Hôtel Safir	4	Hammam	48	Telex Office
27	Hôtels de Foucauld &	7	Centre 2000	49	Main Post Office
	Périgord	8	Casa-Port Train Station	51	BMCE (ATMs)
28	Hyatt Regency Hotel	10	Great Mosque	53	Cinéma Lux
31	Touring Hôtel	18	Mosque	54	Voyages Schwartz
34	Hôtel Colbert	19	Clock Tower		(Amex)
44	Hôtel du Louvre	20	Goldcar	55	Law Courts
45	Hôtel de Lausanne	22	Avis	56	BMCI (Exchange)
57	Hôtel du Palais	24	CTM Bus Terminal	58	French Consulate
		25	Budget & Europcar	60	Stadium
PLACES TO EAT		26	Hertz	61	Liquor Store
6	Café Central	29	BMC (ATMs) Weekend	62	ONMT Office
9	La Taverne du Dauphin		Banking	63	Cinéma Liberté
17	Restaurant Widad	30	British Centre		
35	Welcome Restaurant	32	Grands Taxis for Rabat		

the Rue Prince Moulay Abdallah pedestrian mall each evening. Or you can sit down at one of the cafés along it and watch life go by.

The best of the nightclubs are at the beaches but the clientele is ritzy and prices reflect this – entry is Dr 50 to Dr 100 and drinks cost Dr 50. There are plenty of largely men-only bars (some of the red-light variety) in the town centre.

Bogart fans could try the Hyatt Regency Hotel's *Casablanca Bar*, which has a happy hour from 6.30 to 7.30 pm (and still it's expensive). Posters aside, the place does little to evoke the Hollywood atmosphere.

Getting There & Away

Bus The CTM bus terminal is on Rue Léon Africain at the back of the Hôtel Safir. Most other lines use the chaotic main station just off Rue Strasbourg, two blocks south of Place de la Victoire – it's quite a hike, so a take a petit taxi or local bus No 4 or No 5.

There are CTM departures to Agadir (six daily), Essaouira, Fès and Meknès (nine daily), Marrakesh (five daily), Oujda, Rabat, Safi, Tangier (six daily), Taza and Tetouan.

CTM also operates international buses to France and Belgium from Casablanca.

If the CTM timetable doesn't suit, there are plenty of buses for most conceivable destinations from the main bus station.

Train Most train departures are from Casa-Voyageurs station, but where possible you should try to leave from the central Casa-Port station. Local bus No 30 runs to Casa-Voyageurs along Ave des FAR and Blvd Mohammed V. Otherwise it's an hour's walk or a Dr 15 petit taxi ride.

Trains to Tangier, Oujda and Fès leave from Casa-Port. Additional trains run to these destinations from Casa-Voyageurs as well as to Marrakesh and El-Jadida. All but those to Marrakesh and El-Jadida stop at Rabat. Oujda trains all stop at Fès and Meknès.

For Rabat, take one of the high-speed shuttles which take 55 minutes (Dr 25 in 2nd class). They leave from both Casablanca stations.

Taxi Grands taxis to Rabat leave from Blvd Hassan Seghir, near the CTM bus station. The fare is Dr 27.

Car The following are among the car-rental agencies in Casablanca, but check out some smaller agencies too.

MOROCCO

Avis
19 Ave des FAR (☎ 312424, 311135)
Mohammed V airport (☎ 339072)
Budget
Tour des Habous, Ave des FAR (☎ 313124)
Mohammed V airport (☎ 339157)
Europcar
Complexe des Habous, Ave des FAR (☎ 313737)
Mohammed V airport (☎ 339161; fax 339517)
Goldcar
5 Ave des FAR (☎ & fax 202510, 260109)
Hertz
25 Rue Araibi Jilali (☎ 484710)
Mohammed V airport (☎ 339181)

Getting Around

To/From the Airport Shuttle trains (TNR) run from Mohammed V airport to Casa-Voyageurs and Casa-Port train stations. They take 24 minutes and cost Dr 25 in 2nd class. A grand taxi to Mohammed V airport will cost you Dr 150 (Dr 200 after 8 pm).

Bus Local buses run from a terminus on Place Oued al-Makhazine to 'Ain Diab (No 9) and Place de la Victoire (No 5). Bus No 30 connects the Casa-Voyageurs train station to central Casablanca.

Taxi There's no shortage of metered petits taxis in Casablanca – just make sure the meter is on. Expect to pay Dr 10 for a ride in or around the city centre.

EL-JADIDA

The Portuguese founded El-Jadida (which they called Mazagan) in 1513 and held it until 1769, when it was besieged by Sultan Sidi Mohammed bin Abdallah. In the final evacuation, the Portuguese mined the ramparts and blew them to smithereens, taking with them a good part of the besieging army.

The fortress walls were rebuilt in 1820 by Sultan Moulay Abd ar-Rahman. The medina inside the walls was largely neglected until the mid-19th century, when it was recolonised by European merchants.

The massive bastioned fortress, with its enclosed medina, churches and enormous cistern, is still remarkably well preserved. These days, El-Jadida is also a popular beach resort.

Information

The tourist office (☎ 344788) is on Rue Ibn Khaldoun. There are several banks in the town centre.

El-Jadida's telephone code is ☎ 03.

Things to See

The old **Portuguese Fortress** (Cité Portugaise) is the focal centre of town. There are two entrance gates to the fortress; the southernmost one, which is more convenient, opens onto the main street through the medina, Rue Mohammed Ahchemi Bahbai. About halfway down this street is the **Citerne Portugaise** (Portuguese Cistern). The cistern, where Orson Welles filmed scenes for *Othello*, is open on weekdays from 8.30 am to noon and 2 to 6 pm. Entry is Dr 10.

Entry to the **ramparts**, which you can walk all the way around, is through the large door at the end of the tiny cul-de-sac on the right after entering the fortress. The man with the key to the door will expect a tip for letting you in.

Beaches stretch north and south but the northern ones are occasionally polluted by oil. They're pleasant enough but can get very crowded during July and August.

Places to Stay

Camping About a 15-minute walk south-east of the bus station, *Camping Caravaning International* (☎ 342755) is on Ave des Nations Unies. It's one of the better, treed Moroccan camping grounds and costs Dr 12 a person, Dr 6.50 per car, Dr 10 to pitch a tent, Dr 5 for a hot shower and Dr 11 for electricity.

Hotels Rooms can be hard to find in summer and prices tend to rise then too.

There are two hotels knocked into one just off Place Hansali. The *Hôtel du Maghreb* and *Hôtel de France* (☎ 342181) are owned by the same guy, and some of the big rooms look out to the sea. Singles/doubles cost Dr 41/57, and a hot shower costs Dr 4. The *Hôtel du Port* (☎ 342701), on Blvd de Suez, is less appealing and rooms cost Dr 31/47.

The *Hôtel Bruxelles* (☎ 342072), 40 Rue Ibn Khaldoun, offers clean if spartan rooms with own bathroom for Dr 70/110 plus taxes.

El-Jadida's only two-star hotel, the *Hôtel du Provence* (☎ 342347; fax 352115), 42 Ave Fkih Mohammed Errafil, is one of the most pleasant places in town. Singles/doubles,

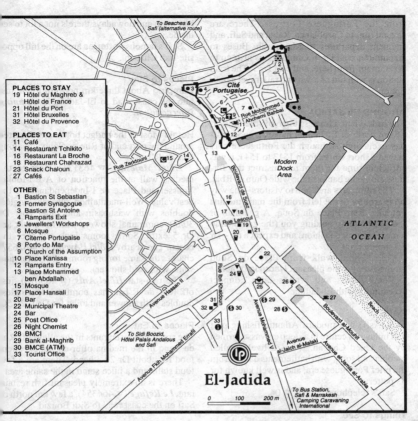

PLACES TO STAY
19 Hôtel du Maghreb &
   Hôtel de France
21 Hôtel du Port
31 Hôtel Bruxelles
32 Hôtel du Provence

PLACES TO EAT
11 Café
14 Restaurant Tchikito
16 Restaurant La Broche
18 Restaurant Chahrazad
23 Snack Chaloun
27 Cafés

OTHER
1 Bastion St Sebastian
2 Former Synagogue
3 Bastion St Antoine
4 Ramparts Exit
5 Jewellers' Workshops
6 Mosque
7 Citerne Portugaise
8 Porto do Mar
9 Church of the Assumption
10 Place Kanissa
12 Ramparts Entry
13 Place Mohammed
   ben Abdallah
15 Mosque
17 Place Hansali
20 Bar
22 Municipal Theatre
24 Bar
25 Post Office
26 Night Chemist
28 BMCI
29 Bank al-Maghrib
30 BMCE (ATM)
33 Tourist Office

El-Jadida

0   100   200 m

---

triples/quadruples with own shower and toilet
cost Dr 121/149/204/259.

The three-star *Hôtel Palais Andalous*
(☎ 343745), Blvd Docteur de la Lanouy, is a
converted pasha's residence and a luxurious
splurge. The rooms cost Dr 256/332/448 for
singles/doubles/triples plus tax.

Places to Eat

There's a string of pleasant little seafront cafés
on Blvd al-Mouhit that are great for breakfast.

Snack Chaloun is a popular place across
from the municipal theatre. A reasonable meal
of sausages, rice and chips and salad costs Dr
20. The *Restaurant Chahrazad*, on Place

Hansali, serves the old favourites for about Dr
30. The nearby family-run *Restaurant La
Broche* is a little more expensive and has a
cosier feel to it.

The *Restaurant Tchikito*, in a lane a short
walk north-west of Place Hansali, serves filling
meals of fresh fried fish for as little as Dr 25.

The *Hôtel du Provence* has a popular restaurant that offers a choice of good Moroccan,
French and seafood specialities. A three-course
meal with wine costs around Dr 120.

Getting There & Away

The bus terminal is south-east of town on Ave
Mohammed V. It's about a 20-minute walk

MOROCCO

from the Portuguese Fortress. There are several runs to Casablanca, Rabat and Safi, and frequent departures to Marrakesh. Buses to Azemmour cost Dr 3. Grands taxis also go to Azemmour from here, and cost Dr 5. The train station is well out of town and rail travel a poor option.

AROUND EL-JADIDA
The little-visited fortress town of **Azemmour**, 15 km north of El-Jadida, makes a good half-day excursion. Although the Portuguese only stayed a short while, from 1513 to 1541, it was sufficient time for them to construct this fortress along the banks of the wide Oum er-Rbia.

The **ramparts** are open to visitors – the way up is around to the left from the main medina entrance from Place du Souq. A guardian or kids will end up guiding you (the guardian in a more informed fashion) and expect a tip – Dr 10 should do it.

A half-hour walk from Place du Souq (signposted) is the pleasant **Haouzia beach**.

Local buses and grands taxis connect Azemmour with El-Jadida.

SAFI
Safi (Asfi) is a modern Atlantic fishing port and industrial centre in a steep crevasse formed by the Oued Chabah. It has a lively walled medina and souq, with battlements dating from the brief Portuguese era, and is well known for its pottery.

Safi's telephone code is ☎ 04.

Things to See
In the walled city the Portuguese built and to which the Moroccans later added, the **Qasr al-Bahr** (Castle on the Sea) is usually the first port of call. There are good views from the ramparts, as well as a number of 17th-century Spanish and Dutch cannons. It's open from 8.30 am to noon and 2.30 to 6 pm and entry costs Dr 10.

Across the street lies the **medina**, which is dominated by the **Kechla**, a massive defensive structure with ramps, gunnery platforms, living quarters, a ceramics museum and fine views out to the Qasr al-Bahr.

Inside the medina is the **Chapelle Portugaise**. It would have become the town cathedral had the Portuguese hung about long enough; instead it was converted into a

hammam and nowadays there's not a lot to see inside.

Safi's famous **potteries** are on the hill opposite Bab Chabah.

Places to Stay
Camping About three km north of town, just into the coast road to El-Jadida, is *Camping International*.

Hotels Most of the budget hotels are clustered around the port end of Rue du Souq and along Rue de R'bat.

Hôtel Majestic (☎ 463131), next to the medina wall at the junction of Ave Moulay Youssef and Place de l'Indépandance, is the best value. Well-maintained, pleasant singles/doubles with washbasin and bidet cost Dr 30/60; communal showers with hot water are Dr 5 extra. Some rooms look out over the ocean. The nearby *Hôtel l'Avenir* (☎ 462657) charges the same for big rooms with toilet (and some with cold shower).

The two-star *Hôtel Anis* (☎ 463078), just off Rue de R'bat, has comfortable singles/doubles with shower and toilet for Dr 122/150.

Places to Eat
The small fish restaurants in the alleys off Rue du Souq in the medina offer cheap, excellent food for about Dr 20 a head. There are a few food stalls and a juice stand in the same area.

There is an extremely pleasant fish restaurant, *Le Refuge* (☎ 464354), a few km north of Safi on the coast road to Sidi Bouzid.

Getting There & Away
CTM and other companies share a terminal south-east of the town centre. There are regular departures to Casablanca and several to Marrakesh, Essaouira and Agadir. A couple of buses head north to El-Jadida. Some are through services from elsewhere, but you shouldn't have too much trouble on main runs.

Two trains go daily from Safi to Casablanca (Casa-Voyageurs station) and both involve a change at Benguerir. From Benguerir you can also link up with a Marrakesh-bound train on the morning service (6 am from Safi).

ESSAOUIRA
Essaouira is one of the most popular coastal towns for independent travellers. Not only

does it have a long curve of magnificent beach (much appreciated by windsurfers), it also has a pleasantly hassle-free atmosphere.

Essaouira was founded in the 16th century by the Portuguese, but the present town dates largely from 1765, when Sultan Sidi Mohammed bin Abdallah hired a French architect to redesign the town for use as a trade centre with Europe.

The fortifications are thus an interesting mix of Portuguese, French and Berber military architecture, although the walls around the town date mainly from the 18th century. Their massiveness lends a powerful mystique to the town, yet inside the walls it's all light and charm. You'll find narrow, freshly white-washed streets, painted blinds, tranquil squares, artisans in tiny workshops beavering away at fragrant *thuya* wood, friendly cafés, and not a hustler in sight. In summer, unfortunately, it can get very crowded.

Information

Three banks are clustered around Place Prince Moulay Hassan. The post office is a 10-minute walk south of the city walls from the same square.

Essaouira's telephone code is ☎ 04.

Things to See

You can walk along most of the **ramparts** on the seaward part of town and visit the two main forts *(skalas)* during daylight hours. The **Skala de la Ville** (no entry fee) is impressive, with its collection of 18th and 19th-century brass cannons from various European countries. The **Skala du Port** is locked at lunchtime and on Sunday and there's a Dr 10 entry fee.

The **Museum of Traditional Art** on Darb Laalouj al-Attarine has displays of jewellery, costumes and weapons. It is open daily, except Tuesday, from 8.30 am to noon and 2.30 to 6.30 pm. Entry is Dr 10.

The **beach** stretches some 10 km down the coast to the sand dunes of Cap Sim. On the way you'll pass the ruins of an old fortress and pavilion partially covered in sand. There are a couple of stalls that hire out **windsurfing** gear on the beach near the town.

Just off the coast to the south-west is the **Île de Mogador**, on which there's another fortification. It's actually two islands and several tiny islets, the famed Iles Purpuraires of antiquity.

There is a disused prison on the biggest of the islands. These days the islands are a sanctuary for the rare Eleonora's falcon and other birds. Visits are normally prohibited.

Places to Stay

Camping The best *camping ground* is about three km past the village of Diabat, next to the Auberge Tangaro. Drive about six km south of Essaouira on the Agadir road and turn to the right just after the bridge. The camping ground in town, *Camping International*, is rather bare.

Hotels The popular *Hôtel Smara* (☎ 472655) on Rue de la Skala has sea views and is quiet and clean. Singles/doubles/triples cost Dr 50/70/100, showers are an extra Dr 2 and breakfast costs Dr 10. The well-kept *Hôtel Beau Rivage* (☎ 472925) overlooks Place Prince Moulay Hassan and is decent value. Rooms with two beds cost Dr 70, or Dr 120 with own shower. Hot water is available most of the time.

The *Hôtel du Tourisme*, Rue Mohammed ben Massaoud, has reasonable singles/doubles for Dr 36/47, and a few larger rooms sleeping up to four. The *Hôtel Tafraout* (☎ 472120), 7 Rue de Marrakech, off Rue Mohammed ben Abdallah, is excellent value and very well maintained. Rooms without shower cost Dr 59/77, or with shower Dr 75/90.

The two-star *Hôtel Sahara* (☎ 472292), Ave Oqba ben Nafii, has rooms with shower for Dr 125/150 plus taxes, and with shower and toilet for Dr 157/187 plus taxes. The rooms are a mixed bag, so try to have a look at a few before deciding.

The *Hôtel Villa Maroc* (☎ 473147; fax 472806), located just inside the city walls at 10 Rue Abdallah ben Yassin, consists of two stylishly renovated 18th-century houses. Booking ahead is advisable. Singles/doubles cost Dr 435/555 plus taxes.

Places to Eat

For breakfast you can't beat the cafés on Place Prince Moulay Hassan. The *Café/Pâtisserie l'Opéra* and the *Driss Pâtisserie* sell fine croissants and other pastries.

For simple snacks there are a few little places along Rue Mohammed ben Abdallah,

Essaouira

ATLANTIC
OCEAN

To Île de Mogador

Harbour

ATLANTIC
OCEAN

OLD
MELLAH

To Bus
Station

To Cap Sim,
Agadir &
Marrakesh

Place
Orson
Welles

Place Prince
Moulay Hassan

Place
Orson
Welles

PLACES TO STAY
6 Hôtel Smara
14 Hôtel Chakib
16 Hôtel Tafraout
17 Hôtel Mechouar
18 Hôtel Sahara
29 Hôtel Beau Rivage
34 Hôtel Villa Maroc
43 Hôtel du Tourisme
46 Hôtel des Îles
49 Camping International

PLACES TO EAT
1 Cheap Eats
8 Restaurant Riad
9 El Khaima Restaurant
15 Restaurant Dar Baba
19 Driss Pâtisserie
22 Restaurant Chez Toufik
26 Snack Stand
28 Café/Pâtisserie l'Opéra
32 Restaurant Essalam
35 Café
41 Grilled-Fish Stalls
42 Chez Sam Restaurant

OTHER
2 Bab Doukkala
3 Bab al-Bahr
4 Entry to Ramparts
5 Skala de la Ville
7 Museum of Traditional Art
10 Spice, Herb & Cures Shops
11 Souqs
12 Souqs
13 Mosque
20 BMCE
21 Carpet & Curio Shops
23 Carpet & Curio Shops
24 Mosque
25 Jack's Kiosk
27 Alfakai Art
30 Banque Populaire
31 Banque Commerciale
   du Maroc
33 Crédit du Maroc
36 Bab al-Minzah
37 Car Park
38 Customs & Fish Market
39 Skala du Port
40 Shipyards
44 Bab as-Sebaa
45 Bab Marrakech
47 Post Office
48 Church

Rue Zerktouni and in the old mellah just inside Bab Doukkala. On Place Prince Moulay Hassan you'll find two stands where you can get excellent baguettes stuffed with meat, salad and just about anything else you want. These cost from Dr 10 to Dr 15. There's a reasonable food stall next to the Hôtel Chakib too. Down by the port are a number of stalls selling fresh, grilled fish for about Dr 20.

At the popular **Restaurant Essalam** on Place Prince Moulay Hassan you can enjoy a decent meal for around Dr 35.

The **Restaurant Riad**, at the end of an alley off Rue Mohammed ben Abdallah can be a good place for seafood. The **Restaurant Dar Baba**, just near the Hôtel Tafraout, does a range of Italian dishes.

For something more indulgent, the **Restaurant Chez Toufik** offers a traditional Berber ambience, but the food is nothing amazing. The more formal **El Khaima Restaurant** has set menus for Dr 80.

Famous throughout Morocco is **Chez Sam** at the far end of the port area, past the boat builders. The restaurant is housed in a delightfully eccentric building and the seafood specialities are excellent. There are two set menus at Dr 60 to Dr 170 and it's licensed. You may have to book a table.

Entertainment
Apart from drinking in the licensed restaurants, there aren't very many night-time alternatives. Local drinkers gather in the bar under the Hôtel Mechouar. More up-market tipplers might be tempted by the Piano Bar in the *Hôtel des Îles* – which also has a nightclub.

Things to Buy
Essaouira is a centre for thuya carving, and the quality of the work is superb. Most of the carvers have workshops under the Skala de la Ville. Nearby are craft shops with an equally impressive range of goods. Try also Alfakai, on Place Prince Moulay Hassan.

Carpet, bric-a-brac, jewellery and brassware shops are in the narrow street and small square flanking Ave Oqba ben Nafii, between Place Prince Moulay Hassan and the ramparts.

Getting There & Away
The bus terminal is one km north-east of the town centre. There are regular departures to Safi, Marrakesh and Agadir. Grands taxis to Agadir (or neighbouring Inezgane) leave from a nearby lot.

AGADIR
Agadir was destroyed by an earthquake in 1960 and, although it has been rebuilt, it's hardly a typical Moroccan city any longer. Most of the activity centres on package tourists from Europe who flock in by the plane-load in search of sun, sand and a sanitised version of the mysteries of the Barbary Coast.

Agadir is one of the more expensive and least appealing cities in Morocco but it's a take-off point for visits east and further south, so you'll probably have to stay overnight at least.

Information
The ONMT tourist office (☎ 846377) is in the market area just off Ave Prince Sidi Mohammed; there's also a syndicat d'initiative (☎ 840307) on Blvd Mohammed V at the junction with Ave du Général Kettani.

Agadir's telephone code is ☎ 08.

Places to Stay
Camping Camper vans predominate at Agadir's camping ground (☎ 846683). There's a general store there.

Hotels Most of the budget hotels and a few of the mid-range ones are around the bus terminal area and along Rue Allal ben Abdallah. In the high seasons you must get into Agadir early to be sure of a room.

Cheapies such as the **Hôtel Canaria** (☎ 822299) and the **Hôtel Massa** are pretty dire. Better is the **Hôtel Select** (public bath next door), which has singles/doubles for Dr 63/81.

The **Hôtel Amenou** (☎ 823026), near the bus terminal on Rue Yacoub el-Mansour, and the **Hôtel La Tour Eiffel** (☎ 823712), around the corner, have doubles for Dr 70. The **Hôtel Aït Laayoune** (☎ 824375), also on Rue Yacoub el-Mansour, is slightly more expensive but for no obvious reason.

The two-star **Hôtel de Paris** (☎ 822694), Ave du Président Kennedy, is comfortable and has reliable hot water. It costs Dr 90/110 for singles/doubles without bathroom, or Dr 150/180 with shower and toilet.

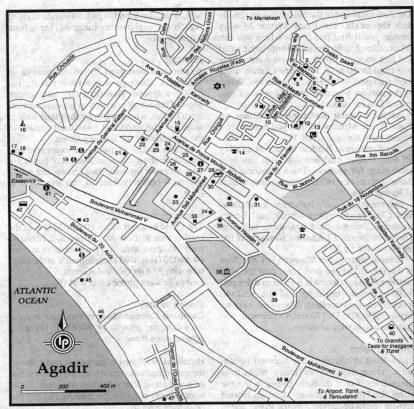

Agadir

ATLANTIC OCEAN

To Essaouira

To Marrakesh

To Grands Taxis for Inezgane & Tiznit

To Airport, Tiznit & Taroudannt

0   200   400 m

MOROCCO

The *Hôtel Aladin* (☎ 843228; fax 846071), Rue de la Jeunesse, has comfortable rooms and a pool. They charge Dr 236/290 in the low season, and Dr 245/302 in the high season.

Places to Eat
You'll find cheap restaurants and sandwich bars on the same street as the bus terminal. Also near here is a small plaza with the *Restaurant Chabab*, the *Restaurant Mille et Une Nuits*, the *Café Restaurant Coq d'Or* and the *Restaurant Ibtissam*, all next to each other. Typical offerings include couscous or tajine (about Dr 20), omelette (about Dr 10) and salads (up to Dr 10). They're good value.

The *Restaurant Select*, just by the hotel of the same name, does a solid range of old favourites and you can eat well for about Dr 20. Do *not* order the crêpes – they are awful.

For that international tourism feel, *La Dolce Vita* on Ave Hassan II has a varied menu. You can eat a good meal for around Dr 70 and it is licensed.

Set right on the beach near the Hôtel Tafouk is the *La Perla del Mare* (☎ 840065). It's not only classy, it's pricey.

Getting There & Away
Bus The buses leaving from Rue Yakoub el Mansour should be sufficient. CTM has daily

PLACES TO STAY		OTHER		30	Hôtel de Ville (Town
4	Hôtel Aït Laayoune	1	Jardin de Olhâo		Hall)
6	Hôtel Canaria	2	Bus Terminal	31	New Labcolor
7	Hôtel Amenou	3	Ensemble Artisanal		(Kodak)
9	Hôtel Select	8	Post Office	32	Liquor Store
11	Hôtel de Paris	13	Mohammed V Mosque	33	Place de l'Espérance
12	Hôtel La Tour Eiffel	14	Telephone Office	34	Car/Motorbike Hire
16	Camp Site	15	Bar Crystal	36	Travel Agents (Local
35	Hôtel Aladin	17	Budget		Excursions &
43	Sheraton	18	Hertz		Charter Flights)
45	Hôtel Tafoukt	19	BMCE (ATM & Bureau	37	Telephone Office
47	Hôtel Beach Club		de Change)	38	Musée Municipal
48	Hôtel Sahara	20	BMCI (ATM)	39	Stadium
		21	Tour Agents	40	Local Buses &
PLACES TO EAT		22	Supratours		Taghazout Grands
5	Restaurants	23	Tour Agents		Taxis
10	Café/Restaurant Select	24	Cinéma Rialto	41	Syndicat d'Initiative
26	Restaurant La Dolce	25	Central Market	42	Public Swimming Pool
	Vita	27	Tourist Office		& Café
46	Restaurant La Perla	28	Uniprix	44	Banque Populaire &
	del Mare	29	Post Office		Clinic

buses to Casablanca, Dakhla, El-Jadida, Essaouira/Safi, Marrakesh, Smara/Laayoune, Taroudannt and Tiznit.

SATAS has buses to Casablanca, Essaouira, Marrakesh, Tafraoute, Tan Tan, Taroudannt and Tiznit.

The region's main bus terminal is actually in Inezgane, 13 km south of Agadir, and you may arrive here.

Taxi Most of the grands taxis leave from Inezgane. They go to Essaouira, Taroudannt, Tiznit, Goulimime and Tan Tan.

Car The following are the main car-rental agencies in Agadir:

Avis
Ave Hassan II (☎ 841755)
airport (☎ 840345)

Budget
Bungalow Marhaba, Blvd Mohammed V (☎ 844600)
airport (☎ 839101)

Europcar
Bungalow Marhaba, Blvd Mohammed V (☎ 840203)
airport (☎ 839066)

Hertz
Bungalow Marhaba, Blvd Mohammed V (☎ 840939)

Motorcycle & Scooter A walk around the big hotels will soon reveal a series of booths that rent out motorbikes and scooters. Dr 100 a day or Dr 400 a week seems to be an average charge for a scooter but you should haggle.

Getting Around

There are local buses and grands taxis between Agadir and Inezgane. There are also local buses between Inezgane and the airport. A grand taxi from Agadir to the airport costs Dr 100.

AROUND AGADIR

For less crowded **beaches** and other independent travellers, head out of town. The quietest beaches are up around Aghrod, 27 km north of Agadir, and Cap Rhir. Closer to Agadir they tend to be crowded.

TAROUDANNT

Taroudannt, with its magnificent, extremely well preserved red-mud walls, has played an important part in the history of Morocco, and briefly became the capital under the Saadians in the 16th century. They built the old part of town and the kasbah.

The city narrowly escaped destruction in 1687 at the hands of Moulay Ismail, after it had become the centre of a rebellion opposing his rule. Instead, Moulay Ismail contented himself with massacring its inhabitants.

Taroudannt's telephone code is ☎ 08.

Things to See

You can explore the **ramparts** of Taroudannt on foot, but it is better to hire a bicycle or

MOROCCO

engage one of the horse-and-cart drivers. It's a long way around the walls!

You can find high-quality items in the small **souqs**, especially traditional Berber silver jewellery. Modest **tanneries** are located just beyond Bab Taghount, north-west of Place al-Alaouyine (ex-Assarag). Turn left outside the gate and follow the signs.

Places to Stay

There are many cheap hotels in the centre, around or close to Place al-Alaouyine. On the square, it's a toss-up between the *Hôtel de la Place* and the *Hôtel Roudani*. Prices hover around Dr 30/50 for singles/doubles. Closer to Place an-Nasr is the *Hôtel des Oliviers* (☎ 852021). It has clean rooms for Dr 40/60. The showers are cold. Another reasonable deal is the *Hôtel Mantaga*, which has clean rooms with big beds for Dr 35/70.

The best deal by far is the creaky old *Hôtel Taroudant* (☎ 852416). With rooms gathered around a tranquil, leafy courtyard, it's full of character. Singles/doubles/triples without bathroom cost Dr 50/68/105; with shower Dr 75/95/132; and with shower and toilet Dr 95/110/147. The water is boiling hot, the hotel has one of the few bars in town and the food in the restaurant is good and moderately priced.

Places to Eat

The small cafés that line the street between Place an-Nasr and Place al-Alaouyine serve traditional food such as soup, salads and tajine. Among these small cafés are several with seafood at rock-bottom prices.

Also good are the restaurants on the ground floors of the *Hôtel de la Place* and the slightly more expensive *Hôtel Roudani* (Dr 29 for generous serves of brochettes, chips and salad). The restaurant at the *Hôtel Taroudant* makes a good minor splurge with tasty French and Moroccan food.

Getting There & Away

CTM and SATAS have terminals on Place al-Alaouyine. Most of the others are on the nearby Place an-Nasr. SATAS buses run to Agadir and Marrakesh. CTM has a bus to Casablanca via Agadir and another to Ouarzazate. Only the 5 am bus of the Moulay Saïd Company goes over the Tizi n'Test pass to

Marrakesh. Grands taxis to Agadir (Inezgane) leave from Place an-Nasr.

TIZNIT

In an arid corner of the Souss Valley at the end of the Anti-Atlas range, is Tiznit. With its six km of encircling red-mud walls, it looks old but is actually a recent creation. It's a pleasant place to hang around and the silver jewellery is reputed to be some of the best in the south.

Places to Stay

The *camping ground* between Bab Oulad Jarrar and the main roundabout is nothing special.

The budget hotels are mostly on or near Place al-Machouar, the main square within the city walls, and are all pretty similar. One of the best is off the square on Impasse Idakchouch. The *Hôtel Belle-Vue* (☎ 862109) has clean singles/ doubles for Dr 40/70 and a hot shower costs Dr 5. The *Hôtel Atlas*, on the square itself, has rooms for Dr 35/60. Cold shower and toilets are communal. Similar are the *Hôtel des Amis* and *Hôtel de la Jeunesse*. Just off Impasse Idakchouch is a hammam, the Douche Atlas.

The *Hôtel Mauritania* (☎ 863632), on the road to Goulimime, has much better rooms for Dr 60/80.

Places to Eat

Several of the hotels on Place al-Machouar have restaurants, and there are a few cafés scattered around inside and outside the walls. The best is the *Restaurant Essaraha* (you can eat well for Dr 20), across Blvd Mohammed V from the main city gates. The market virtually next door is good for fresh food.

Getting There & Away

Buses (including CTM and SATAS) leave from Place al-Machouar to Agadir, Essaouira, Casablanca, Marrakesh, Tafraoute and Sidi Ifni. Grands taxis go to Agadir, Sidi Ifni and Goulimime.

TAFRAOUTE

Some 107 km east of Tiznit is the pretty Berber town of Tafraoute. The reason for visiting is the surrounding countryside. The nearby **Ameln Valley**, with its fields dotted with mud-brick villages, provides days of hiking possibilities. The journey up from Tiznit (or Agadir) into the heart of the Anti-Atlas to Tafraoute is itself well worth the effort.

Places to Stay & Eat

The cheapest places are the *Hôtel Tanger* (☎ 800033), which offers basic single/double rooms for Dr 35/45, and the *Hôtel Reddouane* (☎ 800066), where rooms cost Dr 40.

Much better altogether is the *Hôtel Tafraout* (☎ 800061 or 800121), where you can get clean modern rooms for Dr 60/100. There's steaming hot water in the communal showers. There is also a small *camping ground* attached to the hotel.

You can eat fairly well for about Dr 25 in either of the two cheap hotels. The *Restaurant l'Étoile du Sud*, opposite the post office, is a more luxurious splurge that will cost you Dr 70 for a tasty set menu.

Getting There & Away

Transport is thin. There are a few buses during the day to Tiznit, and possibly Agadir.

The High Atlas

MARRAKESH

Marrakesh is one of Morocco's most important artistic and cultural centres. It was founded in 1062 AD by the Almoravid sultan Youssef bin Tachfin but experienced its heyday under his son, Ali, who built the extensive underground irrigation canals *(khettara)* that still supply the city's gardens with water. Although Fès later gained in prominence as a result of the Almoravid conquest of Spain, Marrakesh remained the southern capital.

The city was largely razed by the Almohads in 1147, but they soon rebuilt what would remain the capital of the Almohad empire until its collapse in 1269. For the following 300 years the focus of Moroccan brilliance passed to Fès, but the Saadians made Marrakesh the capital again in the 16th century.

The mellah, Mouassine mosque and the mosque of Ali ben Youssef with its adjacent medersa were all built in Saadian times. In the 17th century, Moulay Ismail moved the capital to Meknès, and although Marrakesh remained an important base of central power, it only really came into its own again when the French built the ville nouvelle and revitalised the old town under the protectorate. Tourism has ensured its relative prosperity since then, producing some ugly side effects, as growing numbers of unemployed seek by any means possible to extract whatever they can from foreign visitors.

Orientation

As in other major Moroccan towns, the ville nouvelle and the medina are separate entities. The Djemaa el-Fna, Marrakesh's colourful and atmospheric main square, is the heart of the medina.

Information

Tourist Office On the Place Abdel Moumen ben Ali, in the ville nouvelle, the tourist office (☎ 448889) has the usual range of glossy leaflets and hotel lists. Official guides can be arranged here or in big hotels. If you don't take one, you may well be obliged to take an unofficial one. See also Dangers & Annoyances in the Facts for the Visitor section of this chapter.

Money Most banks are in the ville nouvelle but they can also be found near the Djemaa el-Fna. The BMCE opposite the tourist office and the one on Rue Moulay Ismail have ATMs and exchange facilities open daily, including weekends, from 9 am to 1 pm and 4 to 8 pm. On public holidays they open only in the afternoon.

American Express is represented by Voyages Schwartz (☎ 436600), Immeuble Moutaouakil, 1 Rue Mauritania, from 9 am to 1 pm (closed on Sunday).

Post & Communications The main post office is on Place du 16 Novembre in the ville nouvelle. There is a branch office on the Djemaa el-Fna.

Marrakesh's telephone code is ☎ 04.

Things to See

The focal point of Marrakesh is the **Djemaa el-Fna**, a huge square in the medina. Although lively at any time of day, it comes into its own in the late afternoon and evening. Then the

MOROCCO

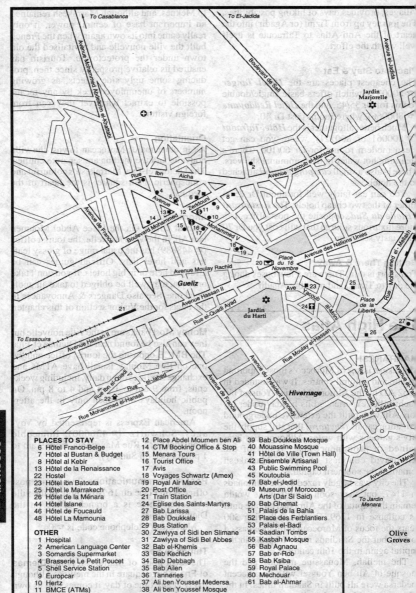

To Ouarzazate,
Meknès & Fès

Marrakesh

0   250   500 m

Route Principale No 24

Rue Assouel

Rue de Bab Khemis

Rue de Bab Tarroucout

Rue el Gza

Medina

Rue de Bab Doukkala

Rue Dar el-Glaoui

Rue Fatima Zahra

Rue Sidi el-Yamani

Rue Souq es-Smarine

Rue Mouassine

Rue el-Koutoubia

Rue Azbezt

Rue Issebbine

Rue de Bab Aïlen

Rue de Bab Debbagh

Remparts

Route des

Rue Dabach

Rue Graoui

Rue Riad Ba Ahmed

Place Djemaa
el-Fna

See Marrakesh
(Budget Hotel Area Map)

Avenue Mohammed V

Rue Abbes Sebti

Avenue
el-Mouahidine

Rue Riad Zitoun el-Jedid

Rue Riad Zitoun el-Qedim

To Ouarzazate

Ave Houmane el-Fetouaki

Rue Bab Agnaou

Ave Houmane
el-Fetouaki

Rue Sidi Mimoun

Mellah

Rue de la Kasbah

Kasbah

To Asni &
Taroudannt

Airport

Boulevard el-Yarmouk

MOROCCO

curtain goes up on a rather strange spectacle. Rows of open-air food stalls are set up and mouthwatering aromas quickly fill the air. Jugglers, storytellers, snake charmers, magicians, acrobats and benign lunatics take over the rest of the space. In between the groups weave hustlers, thieves, knick-knack sellers and bewildered tourists. It is a prime place for people-watching but if you stand still for too long someone will try to sell you something, dance for you, sing for you, or simply drape a large live serpent around your neck.

The **souqs** of Marrakesh are some of the best in Morocco, producing a wide variety of high-quality crafts, but they are also among the most commercialised. High-pressure sales tactics are the order of the day and you should never believe a word you are told about silver, gold or amber items. The gold and silver are always plated, and the amber is plastic (put a lighted match to it and smell it). Brass plates, leather work, woodwork and, up to a point, carpets can't be faked and there is some genuine jewellery, but it takes finding.

The **Ali ben Youssef Medersa**, next to the mosque of the same name, was built by the Saadians in 1565. It was once the largest theological college in the Maghreb – it is hard to imagine how, as is claimed, they crammed up to 900 students and teachers into these rooms. The mosque is closed to non-Muslims. Of its annexes, only the Koubba Ba'adiyn survives – one of the few relics of Almoravid Marrakesh. Entry is Dr 10.

The **Koutoubia**, across Place Foucauld from the Djemaa el-Fna, is the tallest and most famous landmark in Marrakesh. Built by the Almohads in the late 12th century, it is the oldest and best preserved of their three famous minarets, the other two being the Tour Hassan in Rabat and the Giralda in Seville (Spain).

Marrakesh's most famous palace was the **Palais el-Badi**, built by Ahmed al-Mansour between 1578 and 1602. Unfortunately, it was torn apart by Moulay Ismail in 1696 for materials to build his new capital at Meknès. All that remains are devastated mud walls enclosing a huge square with a sunken orange grove and some modern concrete pools. It's open daily, except on certain religious holidays, from 8.30 am to noon and 2.30 to 6 pm. Entry is Dr 10. The entrance to the palace is from the southern side of Place des Ferblantiers.

The **Palais de la Bahia** was built as the residence of the Grand Vizier of Sultan Moulay al-Hassan I, Si' Ahmed ben Musa (aka Bou Ahmed), towards the end of the 19th century. It's a rambling structure with fountains, living quarters, pleasure gardens and numerous secluded, shady courtyards. The palace is open daily from 8.30 am to 1 pm (11.45 am in winter) and 4 to 7 pm (2.30 to 6 pm in winter). Entry is free, but you must take and pay a guide.

Built about the same time and definitely worth a visit is the nearby **Dar Si Said**, now the Museum of Moroccan Arts. It served as a palace for Bou Ahmed's brother, Sidi Said, and houses a fine collection of Berber jewellery, carpets, Safi pottery and Marrakesh leather work. It's open from 9 am to noon and 4 to 7 pm (2.30 to 6 pm in winter); closed Tuesday. On Friday it's closed from 11.30 am to 3 pm. Entry costs Dr 10.

Next to the Kasbah Mosque are the **Saadian Tombs**, the necropolis begun by the Saadian sultan Ahmed al-Mansour. Sixty-six of the Saadians, including Al-Mansour, his successors and their closest family members, lie buried under the two main structures, and over 100 more outside them. The tombs are open every day, except Friday morning, from 8 am to noon and 2.30 to 7 pm (6 pm in winter). Entry costs Dr 10. To get there, follow Rue de Bab Agnaou to Bab Agnaou itself – the Kasbah Mosque is a prominent landmark.

Special Events

If you're in Marrakesh in June (the exact dates vary), don't miss the Festival of Folklore, which attracts some of the best troupes in Morocco. In July there's the famous Fantasia, featuring charging Berber horsemen outside the ramparts.

Places to Stay

Camping At the time of writing the *camping ground* was closed and there were no definite plans for it to be either reopened or replaced. Check with the tourist office.

Hostel The *hostel* (☎ 447713), close to the train station, costs Dr 20 a night and, although it's clean and pleasant, it's a long way from the action. You need your membership card.

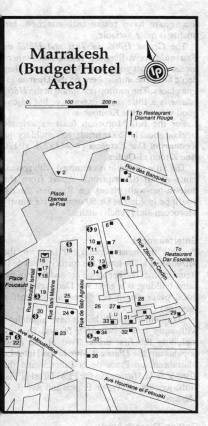

Marrakesh (Budget Hotel Area)

0   100   200 m

To Restaurant Diamant Rouge

Place Djemaa el-Fna

Rue des Banques

Place Foucauld

Rue Moulay Ismail

Rue Bani Marine

Rue de Bab Agnaou

Rue Zitoun el-Qedim

To Restaurant Dar Essalam

Ave el-Mouahidine

Ave Houmane el-Fetouaki

PLACES TO STAY
1	Hôtel Panorama
4	Hôtel/Café de France
5	Résidence de la Place
6	Hôtel CTM
7	Hôtel Cecil
8	Hôtel Menzah
10	Hôtel Hassan
17	Hôtel Ali
21	Hôtel de Foucauld
23	Hôtel La Gazelle
25	Hôtel Ichbilia
27	Hôtel Sahara
28	Hôtel Essaouira
29	Hôtel Chellah
30	Hôtel Arabia
31	Hôtel Gallia
32	Hôtel Souria
33	Hôtel El Atlal
36	Grand Hôtel du Tazi

PLACES TO EAT
2	Restaurant Argana
11	Restaurant Etoile
18	Restaurant Ali
26	Cafés

OTHER
3	Entrance to Hôtel/Café de France
9	Banque Populaire
12	Crédit du Maroc
13	Men's Hammam
14	Women's Hammam
15	Bank al-Maghrib
16	Post Office
19	Wafabank
20	BMCE (ATM)
22	BMCI (ATM)
24	Cinéma Mabrouka
34	Men's Hammam (Bain Polo)
35	Banque Populaire

Hotels Most of the city's cheap hotels are near the Djemaa el-Fna. The ville nouvelle has only a few good options.

Djemaa el-Fna There are many hotels in the area south of the Djemaa el-Fna. Most of the cheaper ones charge extra for hot showers, some even for cold showers. Singles/doubles typically cost about Dr 40/70, but price hikes in summertime can make them more expensive than much better rooms in a classified (price-controlled) hotel.

Better rock-bottom hotels in this area include the *Souria*, *El Atlal*, *Essaouira*, *Panorama* (☎ 445047) and *Chellah* (☎ 442977).

The *Hôtel/Café de France* (☎ 442319) on the Djemaa el-Fna is all right and the rooftop café is a good vantage point overlooking the square. The *Hôtel CTM* (☎ 442325), also on the square, is OK at Dr 78/103 for rooms with own shower and toilet.

Three decent one-star places just south of the Djemaa el-Fna are the *Hôtel Ichbilia* (☎ 390486), *Hôtel La Gazelle* (☎ 441112) and *Hôtel Ali* (☎ 444979). They all cost about Dr 70/110 for singles/doubles. At the latter you can sleep on the terrace for about Dr 30. It has a good restaurant and you can organise High Atlas treks from here too.

The two-star *Hôtel Gallia* (☎ 445913; fax

MOROCCO

444853), 30 Rue de la Recette, is a small hotel and top value. Singles/doubles with toilet cost Dr 99/126 and those with shower as well cost Dr 148/182. They have hot, steaming showers and central heating in winter. This place is often booked out, especially during holidays and on weekends. The *Grand Hôtel du Tazi* (☎ 442787; fax 442152) is considerably more expensive than the Gallia and not as nice (despite the small pool).

The *Hôtel Islane* (☎ 440081; fax 440085), at 279 Ave Mohammed V, has comfortable self-contained rooms for Dr 185/227. Some rooms have good views of the Koutoubia.

Ville Nouvelle The ville nouvelle has very few cheap hotels. The cheapest is the one-star *Hôtel Franco-Belge* (☎ 448472), 62 Blvd Mohammed Zerktouni. It has a pleasant courtyard and singles/doubles cost Dr 40/80 without shower and Dr 80/100 with shower and toilet.

Most of the mid-range and top-end hotels are in the ville nouvelle. Close to the medina, a fine choice is the *Hôtel de la Ménara* (☎ 436478; fax 436478), Ave des Remparts, overlooking Place de la Liberté. The large rooms are self-contained, have balconies and cost Dr 231/312 including breakfast. Other decent places in this class include the *Hôtel ibn Batouta* (☎ 438159; fax 434062), *Hôtel al Kebir* (☎ 439540) and the *Hôtel al Bustan* (☎ 446810).

Marrakesh has what is said to be the best hotel in Morocco: *La Mamounia* (☎ 448981; fax 444940). Be prepared to pay Dr 2500 a night (at least) to sample its delights.

Places to Eat

In the evening, the Djemaa el-Fna fills with all sorts of specialised food stalls. You can eat snacks for a few dirham, and a full meal won't cost you more than Dr 20. Otherwise there are several small restaurants along Rue Bani Marine and Rue de Bab Agnaou. The *Etoile*, for example, offers a filling set menu for Dr 40.

Excellent value is the self-service restaurant below the *Hôtel Ali* – all you can eat for Dr 60. Back on the Djemaa el-Fna itself, the *Restaurant Argana* has a decent set menu for Dr 65. The *Restaurant Diamant Rouge* isn't bad either. Most of the remaining rooftop cafés on

the square have restaurants attached, but quality is quite variable.

The *Grand Hôtel du Tazi* and *Hôtel de Foucauld* have licensed restaurants, where meals will cost you about Dr 80 a head. They don't have the atmosphere of the Djemaa el-Fna places. The rooftop restaurant at the *Hôtel Islane* is a little more expensive, but enjoys good views of the Koutoubia.

For the full Moroccan feast experience (reckon about Dr 200 a head), you could try the *Restaurant Dar Essalam* (☎ 443520), at 170 Rue Zitoun el-Qedim.

The ville nouvelle is crammed with restaurants of all descriptions. Apart from the hole-in-the-wall places on Rue Ibn Aicha, you'll be looking at Dr 60 or more for mostly Moroccan and French cuisine.

Entertainment

Possibly the most popular bar in town, the *Mirador*, is at the top of the former Hôtel de la Renaissance. The bar on the ground floor of the same building is a great Art Deco relic and a good place for a beer (inside) or coffee (outside).

Many ville nouvelle hotels have nightclubs with entry fees between Dr 50 and Dr 100, including the first drink. Two of the most popular are the *Diamant Noir* in the Hôtel Le Marrakech, on Place de la Liberté, and the *Temple de la Musique* in the PLM Hôtel N'Fis, at the junction of Ave de France and Ave de la Ménara.

Getting There & Away

Bus The bus station is just outside the city walls by Bab Doukkala. This is a 20-minute walk or a Dr 10 taxi ride from the Djemaa el-Fna.

Train The train station is on Ave Hassan II and a long way from the Djemaa el-Fna. Take a taxi or bus No 8 into the centre. Trains operate regularly from Marrakesh to Casablanca (four hours) and Rabat (five hours). From there they continue to either Tangier (10½ hours) or Meknès (seven hours) and Fès (eight hours). These trips sometimes involve changes.

Car The main rental agents in Marrakesh are:

Avis
    137 Ave Mohammed V (☎ 433727; fax 449485)
Budget
    68 Blvd Mohammed Zerktouni (☎ 431187; fax
    431180)
Europcar
    63 Blvd Mohammed Zerktouni (☎ 431228; fax
    432769)
Goldcar
    Hôtel Semiramis Méridien, Route de Casablanca
    (☎ 4431377)
Hertz
    154 Ave Mohammed V (☎ 431394; fax 439983)

Getting Around

A taxi to the airport should be no more than Dr
50. Occasionally bus No 11 runs between the
airport and the Djemaa el-Fna area.

A petit taxi between the train station and
Djemaa el-Fna should cost Dr 10 (with difficulty). Bus No 8 does the same run for Dr 2.

Horse carriages are an expensive way to get
around – the fares are posted in French and
Arabic in the cab.

AROUND MARRAKESH

The road between Marrakesh and Taroudannt
goes over the spectacular **Tizi n'Test pass**, one
of the highest passes in Morocco. It's a good,
if sometimes hairy, road and the views are
magnificent. From Taroudannt, the Moulay
Saïd Company bus leaves at 5 am and crosses
the pass in the early morning. On the way, a
worthwhile stop is the partly restored **Tin Mal
Mosque**, the launch pad for the Almohad campaign of conquest in the 12th century.

HIGH ATLAS TREKKING

If you have good shoes or boots, plenty of
warm clothes and a sleeping bag, the ascent of
Jebel Toubkal (4165 metres), Morocco's
highest mountain, is worth making. It's a beautiful area and, on clear days, there are
incredible views in all directions.

You don't need mountaineering skills, as
long as you go up the normal route from Imlil
and stay at the Toubkal (ex-Neltner) hut for the
night, although there are one or two semi-
dangerous patches of scree along the trail. You
can do this trek in two days – up to the Toubkal
hut the first day, and up to the summit and back
down again the second.

The usual starting point for the trek is the
village of Imlil, 17 km south of Asni on the Tizi
n'Test road from Marrakesh to Agadir. Other

possible starting points are the villages of Setti
Fatma and Oukaïmeden in the Ourika Valley,
but these involve longer treks.

Guides

You don't need a guide for the normal two-day
trek, but longer treks may require a guide and
mule. Arrange this in Imlil at the CAF Refuge
or Bureau des Guides. Official guides have
badges and the official prices for guides, mules
and muleteers are published annually in *La
Grande Traversée des Atlas Marocains
(GTAM)*, a useful tourist office brochure (generally *not* available in Imlil – get one in
Marrakesh).

If you start from the Ourika Valley, you
could ask for Lahcen Izahan at the Café
Azagya, about two km before the village of
Setti Fatma. He knows the region well.

Guidebooks

For information beyond the two-day trek,
consult *La Grande Traversée de l'Atlas Maro-
cain*. Volume I (Moussa Gorges to Ait ben
Wgemmez) covers the Toubkal massif.
Another excellent guide (in French) is *Le Haut
Atlas Central* by André Fougerolles (Guide
Alpin). Detailed maps are available in Rabat
(see Useful Organisations in the Facts for the
Visitor section).

Getting to Imlil & Asni

There are frequent buses (Dr 12.50) and grands
taxis (Dr 15) to Asni from Bab er-Rob in
Marrakesh. From Asni, trucks operate fairly
frequently to Imlil and will take passengers for
around Dr 15. You could also negotiate with
the odd taxi.

Imlil

Most trekkers stay in Imlil for the first night.
Stock up here for the trek, as there's nothing
available further up the mountain. The Imlil
shops have a wide range of food including
bread, canned and packaged goods, mineral
water, soft drinks and cigarettes, but no beer.

Places to Stay A good place to stay is the *CAF
(Club Alpin Français) Refuge* in the village
square. It offers dormitory-style accommodation for Dr 20 (CAF members), Dr 30 (YHA
members) and Dr 40 (nonmembers), plus
there's a common room with an open fireplace,

cooking facilities (Dr 5 for use of gas), cutlery and crockery. Bookings for *refuges* (huts) further up cannot be made from here, but instead must go through the Club Alpin Français (☎ 270090; fax 297292), 1 Rue 6ème Henri, BP 6178, Casablanca-Bourgoune, or through CAF, BP 888, Marrakesh.

The best deal in Imlil is probably the *Hôtel el Aine*, which charges Dr 25 per person in comfortable and bright rooms.

The 'luxury' place is the *Hôtel Étoile du Toubkal* (☎ 449767, 435663). You pay Dr 90/136/190/280 for clean singles/doubles/ triples/quadruples in the low season and Dr 20 more in the high season. There is occasionally hot water.

The Two-Day Trek

The first day takes you from Imlil to the Toubkal hut (3207 metres) via the villages of Aroumd and Sidi Chamharouch. This takes about five hours. Bottled drinks are usually available at both these villages. The Toubkal hut has beds for 29 people in two dorms, but you must provide your own bedding. There's a kitchen with a gas stove and cooking utensils. It costs Dr 52 per person for non-CAF members, plus an extra charge if you use the cooking facilities or hot water. There's a resident warden. You must bring all your own food, although the warden may, if given plenty of notice, prepare meals for you. Book in the high season or you may find it full.

The ascent from the hut to the summit should take you about four hours and the descent about two. It's best to take water in summer – any water from the streams on the mountainside should be boiled or there's a fair chance you'll pick up giardia. It can be bitterly cold at the top even in summer.

Other Treks

The five-hour trek from Imlil to Tacheddirt is a good, longer alternative. The walk takes you over a pass at 3000 metres, above the snow line, then down the other side and up again. There's a good CAF refuge here with panoramic views where you can stay for Dr 40, plus Dr 5 if you use the gas for cooking. Many other treks are possible from Tacheddirt, including a seven-hour trek at military pace back down to Asni.

The possibilities for even longer treks are

almost unlimited. You could do a week to 10-day circuit taking in Toubkal, Lake Sidi Ifni, Tacheddirt, Oukaïmeden and Tizi Oussem.

There's a CAF refuge at Tazarhart and the key for it can be found at Tizi Oussem village. All CAF refuges are open all year, but the one in Oukaïmeden is open to members only.

If you start out from the Ourika Valley, head first for Setti Fatma. Buses from Marrakesh go when full from Bab er-Rob and cost Dr 12. The best place to stay is the *Hôtel Tafoukt*, with singles/doubles for Dr 90/127. The *Hôtel Azrou* is an unpleasant, unclassified dump with rooms for about Dr 40/60.

Southern Morocco

OUARZAZATE

Ouarzazate (pronounced 'warzazat') was created by the French as a garrison and regional administrative centre in 1928 and now has about 30,000 inhabitants.

The best thing about Ouarzazate is the journey there from Marrakesh over the Tizi n'Tichka pass which offers superb views over the mountains and into the valleys. Ouarzazate's other drawing card is the **Kasbah of Aït Benhaddou**, 32 km north of Ouarzazate off the Marrakesh road – a popular location for film-makers.

Information

The helpful tourist office (☎ 882485) is in the centre of town, opposite the post office. The Banque Populaire on Blvd Mohammed V is sometimes open for exchange on weekends. For cash advances go to Crédit du Maroc. The Supermarché on Blvd Mohammed V carries a reasonable range of goods.

Ouarzazate's telephone code is ☎ 04.

Things to See

The only place worth visiting in Ouarzazate is the Glaoui **kasbah** at the eastern end of town. It is officially open from 9 am to noon and 3 to 6 pm and closed Sunday but you can often visit it all day and all week. Entry to the main building costs Dr 10; you can wander through the rest at liberty.

Places to Stay

Camping There's a *camping ground* (sign-posted) next to the so-called Tourist Complex off the main road out of town towards Tinerhir, about four km from the bus station. Charges are Dr 10 per person and Dr 7 to pitch a tent.

Hotels It can be difficult to find a cheap hotel in Ouarzazate if you arrive late in the day. The best cheap option is the *Hôtel Royal* (☎ 882258), which offers rooms ranging from Dr 31 for a small single to Dr 164 for a four-person suite. The nearby *Hôtel Atlas* (☎ 882307), 13 Rue du Marché, has singles/doubles/triples without own shower for Dr 36 per person. Doubles and triples with own shower are Dr 82/112.

The *Hôtel Amlal* (☎ 884030; fax 884600) is a decent one-star alternative, offering reasonable self-contained rooms for Dr 108/128/170/210.

Places to Eat

The *Restaurant Essalam* offers eight set menus for Dr 50. The restaurants at the hotels *Royal* and *Atlas* are also OK.

For a minor splurge, good French or Moroccan food and a great drink selection, you can't beat *Restaurant Chez Dimitri*, Blvd Mohammed V. It's very popular, but you won't get a lot of change from Dr 100.

Getting There & Away

CTM has a separate terminal on Blvd Mohammed V. SATAS and other lines depart from a new bus station at Douar Chems near the western entry to the town. It's a good 30-minute walk from the centre.

CTM buses go to Agadir, Casablanca, Er-Rachidia (via Boumalne du Dadès, seven hours), Marrakesh (five hours) and Zagora/M'Hamid (four hours to Zagora). The other companies have more and slightly cheaper services. Grands taxis leave from the main bus lot to Zagora (Dr 40), Boumalne (Dr 25) and Marrakesh (Dr 70).

Car Since the Drâa Valley makes such a spectacular journey, consider renting a car in Ouarzazate. Some of the main agencies are:

Avis
  Corner Blvd Mohammed V & Rue A Sehraoui (☎ 884870)
Budget
  Résidence Al-Warda, Blvd Mohammed V (☎ 882892)
Europcar
  Bureau 4, Place du 3 Mars (☎ 882035)
Hertz
  33 Blvd Mohammed V (☎ 882084)

THE DRÂA VALLEY & ZAGORA

The journey through the Drâa Valley, with its crumbling red-mud kasbahs and lush, green palmeraies hemmed in by craggy desert cliffs, is a thoroughly exotic experience.

Zagora, the valley's administrative centre, is fairly dull, but there are plenty of interesting places nearby. A freshly painted sign here proclaims, 'Timbuktoo 52 jours' – by camel.

Places to Stay

Camping A good camping ground is *Camping d'Amezrou*, about 200 metres past Hôtel La Fibule. *Camping Montagne* is signposted about two km away down a dirt track. Bring your own food. *Camping Sindbad* is in the town proper near the Hôtel Tinsouline.

Hotels Try to get a front room at the *Hôtel Vallée du Drâa* (☎ 847210; fax 847497) on Blvd Mohammed V. Singles/doubles cost Dr 46/65 with shared bathroom, Dr 69/85 with own shower and Dr 77/90 with full bathroom. Next door is the *Hôtel des Amis* (☎ 847924) with basic rooms for Dr 30 a head.

Most rooms at the two-star *Hôtel de la Palmeraie* (☎ 847008) on Blvd Mohammed V have balconies. They cost Dr 70/100 with own toilet and shared shower, and Dr 100/150 with own shower and toilet. An en suite, air-con double costs Dr 200. You can also sleep on the roof for Dr 15. The hotel has a bar and a restaurant. Camel treks can be arranged here, as in all the hotels.

One of Zagora's most relaxing places is the *Hôtel La Fibule* (☎ 847318; fax 847271), on the south side of the Oued Drâa, almost one km from the centre. Doubles cost Dr 160 with own shower but shared toilet (few of these) and Dr 360 with own shower, toilet and air-con. It has a restaurant, bar and swimming pool.

Places to Eat

All the hotels have restaurants, and they all try hard to produce tasty Moroccan dishes.

The *Hôtel Vallée du Drâa* and the *Hôtel de la Palmeraie* offer substantial servings and the latter is licensed. Even if you don't stay in *La Fibule*, try to have a meal there. The *Restaurant Timbouctou*, on Blvd Mohammed V, is popular with locals and offers full meals for around Dr 30.

Getting There & Away

There's a daily CTM bus for Dr 35 from Zagora to Ouarzazate (and on to Marrakesh) at 7 am; a 4 pm departure for M'Hamid; and an overnight bus to Casablanca at 7 pm. Other buses leave from a separate dirt lot by the market. Grands taxis cost Dr 40 per person to Ouarzazate. On market days you may be able to get a ride to Rissani. There are no car hire outlets in Zagora.

SOUTH OF ZAGORA

Across the Oued Drâa, about three km south of Zagora, the village of **Amezrou** has an interesting old Jewish mellah, which is still a centre for the casting of silver jewellery.

About 18 km south of Zagora, **Tamegroute** has a zawiyya (religious foundation) containing an old Qur'anic library – some of the texts are 700 years old. A donation is expected, and it's closed in the middle of the day.

Five km further south are some minor dunes and the *Auberge Repos du Sable*. Simple singles/doubles cost Dr 50/80. It's a rather dull desert hang-out. Camel treks can be organised.

The end of the road is at **M'Hamid**, about 95 km south of Zagora. M'Hamid is nothing special, but the journey through desert and oasis landscapes is well worth the trip. Watch out for the village of **Oulad Driss**, with its impressive mud-brick mosque and kasbah. There are a couple of basic hotels and camp sites in or near M'Hamid.

Getting There & Away

The CTM bus to Zagora leaves around 5 am from M'Hamid. Otherwise you'll have to hope for the rare grand taxi or a lift with tourists. You could hire a taxi, especially in Zagora – up to Dr 400 for the day, but this is negotiable.

BOUMALNE DU DADÈS & THE DADÈS GORGE

The Dadès, the first gorge on the road from Ouarzazate to Er-Rachidia, is peppered with magnificent ruined and lived-in *ksour* (fortified strongholds). The rock formations make this valley one of Morocco's most fantastic sites.

A bumpy tarmac road wiggles through this fantasia for about 27 km from the main Ouarzazate-Boumalne road, after which it reverts to a dirt track requiring a 4WD.

Places to Stay & Eat

In the Gorge There's a cluster of hotels right up where the bitumen road runs out. Just before, in Aït Oudinar, there's the *Auberge des Gorges du Dadès* (☎ 830762) on the river. You have a choice of camping for Dr 5 per person and Dr 5 for a vehicle, simple singles/doubles for Dr 40/60 (communal hot showers) or classier self-contained rooms for Dr 100/140.

Two km further on, there is a handful of places. The best deal is the *Hôtel La Gazelle du Dadès* where spotless rooms with two or three beds cost Dr 60. The *Hôtel La Kasbah de la Vallée* is bigger and fancier and has a few doubles at Dr 60 and lots more with *en suite* shower and toilet for anything from Dr 100 to Dr 180. At both you can pitch a tent by the river or sleep on the roof for Dr 10 to Dr 15. All these places have restaurants.

Boumalne du Dadès You can also stay in the town (though the gorge is the better option). The *Hôtel Adrar* (☎ 830355) is a popular cheapie with singles/doubles for Dr 40/60 if you claim to be a student and Dr 60/120 if you don't. Better and just as popular is the *Hôtel Restaurant Chems* (☎ 830041) further up the hill heading east. It has doubles with shower for Dr 130; slightly less for single occupancy. Both have their own restaurants.

Getting There & Away

A few buses pass through on their way to Ouarzazate and Er-Rachidia, but you're better off going for a grand taxi.

To get up the gorge, there's an occasional grand taxi to Aït Oudinar, but you'll probably have to hire one specially – Dr 50 will be the minimum to Aït Oudinar.

TINERHIR & THE TODRA GORGE

The Todra Gorge is 15 km from Tinerhir, at the end of a lush valley of palmeraies and mud-brick villages. Hemmed in by barren, craggy mountains, the gorge is 300 metres high but only 10 metres wide in places. A crystal-clear stream completes one of Morocco's most magnificent natural sights. You can explore the main gorge in half a day, or continue further up the gorge or walk through the palmeraies on the way to Tinerhir. The gorge is attracting more and more rock climbers and gear can now be rented through the hotels.

Those with more time could take a punt on the vagaries of local transport to villages further north into the High and Middle Atlas ranges.

Places to Stay & Eat

Camping There are three good camp sites six km short of the gorge entrance: *Auberge de l'Atlas*, *Camping Auberge* and *Camping Le Lac*. You'll pay about Dr 8 per person and up to Dr 15 to pitch a tent. There's a small grocery store here too. Two other sites, near Tinerhir, are not worth considering.

Hotels Just by the gorge entrance, the *Hôtel Le Mansour* (☎ 834213) offers rather ordinary singles/doubles for Dr 50/60 and the new *Etoile de la Gorge* has double rooms with shower and breakfast for Dr 100. Within the gorge, the *Hôtel Restaurant les Roches* (☎ 834814) offers dinner, bed and breakfast deals for Dr 100 per head or a place in a big tent for Dr 20. The *Hôtel Restaurant Yasmina* (☎ 833013) has rooms costing Dr 90/160 including breakfast (less in winter). In summer they'll let you sleep on the roof for about Dr 15 a head. It seems to be pretty much negotiable in all these hotels as to where and for how much you sleep.

In Tinerhir, the *Hôtel El Fath*, 56 Ave Hassan II, has acceptable rooms with single beds for Dr 35/60. Rooms with one single and a double bed cost Dr 75. They promise hot water in the shared shower. The *Hôtel Al-Qods*, at the end of the block, has bright, simple singles/doubles/triples for Dr 30/60/90.

Behind Ave Hassan II near the central market area is the Spanish-run *Hôtel de l'Avenir* (☎ 834599). It has a friendly atmosphere and the rooms are good at Dr 60/100/130. The restaurant serves paella. A good cheap eats area is the market just near the hotel.

Getting There & Away

CTM has a couple of buses east to Er-Rachidia and west to Ouarzazate and on to Marrakesh. Several other bus lines have services east and west, and there are grands taxis too. Some grands taxis head up to the Todra Gorge (stress you want a place in a shared taxi), and there are trucks to High Atlas villages beyond, especially on Monday after the market.

ER-RACHIDIA & THE ZIZ VALLEY

The road through the **Gorge du Ziz** north of Er-Rachidia (itself an uninteresting administrative town) is the main attraction of the place. Make sure you travel this route by day so you see the spectacular scenery.

The telephone code for this area is ☎ 05.

Places to Stay & Eat

Camping Source Bleue de Meski is 23 km south along the Erfoud road. It is a pleasant place with a great natural spring and pool.

The *Hôtel Restaurant Renaissance* (☎ 572633), Rue Moulay Youssef, is where most travellers stay. It costs Dr 80 for half-board, and there's hot water. The two-star *Hôtel Oasis* (☎ 572519), at Rue Sidi Bou Abdallah, offers good singles/doubles with attached facilities for Dr 121/140. There's a bar and restaurant.

The covered *market* on Ave Moulay Ali Cherif offers a wide variety of very reasonably priced food.

The *Restaurant Imilchil* has a leafy garden and does the usual grub for around Dr 30 for a main course. The *Restaurant Lipton* on the same side of the road has a similar menu but less attractive setting.

Getting There & Away

All buses operate out of the central bus station. CTM has daily departures to Rabat, Casablanca, Marrakesh, Meknès, Ouarzazate, Rissani (via Erfoud) and Tinerhir. Grands taxis go to Azrou, Erfoud, Fès and Meknès.

FIGUIG

The little villages of this vast oasis make up the last town before the Algerian border and as that

MOROCCO

was closed at the time of writing, it is even more laid-back than ever. A sea of palm trees is dotted by ksour and kasbahs. The best place to stay is the *Hôtel Diamant Vert*. You can camp here for Dr 10 a head, or take a room for Dr 30/40 single/double. They have cold showers and a pool.

Getting There & Away

There are daily buses north to Bouarfa and Oujda. It's a three-km walk to the border, should it be open, and another four km to Beni Ounif. Don't forget to visit the police for an exit stamp first, and be prepared for heavy searches on the Algerian side.

Portugal

Spirited yet unassuming, Portugal has a dusty patina of faded grandeur; the quiet remains of a far-flung colonialist realm. Even as it flows towards the economic mainstream of the European Union (EU), it still seems to gaze over its shoulder and out to sea.

For visitors, this far side of Europe offers more than beaches and port wine. Beyond the crowded Algarve, one finds wide appeal: a simple but hearty cuisine based on seafood and lingering conversation, an enticing architectural blend that wanders from the Moorish to Manueline to surrealist styles, and a changing landscape that occasionally lapses into impressionism. Like the *emigrantes*, economically inspired Portuguese vagabonds who eventually find their way back to their roots, *estrangeiros*, or foreigners, who have had a taste of the real Portugal can only be expected to return.

Facts about the Country

HISTORY

The early history of Portugal goes back to the Celts who settled the Iberian Peninsula around 700 BC. A subsequent pattern of invasion and reinvasion was established by the Phoenicians, Greeks, Romans and Visigoths in succession.

In the 8th century, the Moors crossed the Strait of Gibraltar and commenced a long occupation which introduced their culture, architecture and agricultural techniques to Portugal. Resistance to the Moors culminated in their ejection during the 12th century.

In the 15th century, Portugal entered a phase of conquest and discovery under the rule of Henry the Navigator. Famous explorers such as Vasco da Gama, Ferdinand Magellan and Bartolomeu Diaz set off to discover new trade routes and assisted in creating a huge empire that, at its peak, extended to India, the Far East, Brazil and Africa.

This period of immense power and wealth faded towards the end of the 16th century when Spain occupied Portugal. Although the Portuguese regained their country within a few decades, the momentum of the empire steadily declined over the following centuries.

At the close of the 18th century, Napoleon sent several expeditions to invade Portugal but he was eventually trounced by the troops of the Anglo-Portuguese alliance.

During the 19th century, Portugal's economy fell apart. There was a general muddle of civil war and political mayhem which culminated in the abolition of the monarchy in 1910 and the founding of a democratic republic.

The democratic phase was brief, lasting until a military coup in 1926 set the stage for a long period of dictatorship under Antonio de Oliveira Salazar, who clung tenaciously to power until 1968 when he died after falling off a chair! General dissatisfaction with the repressive regime and a pointless and ruinous colonial war in Africa led to the Revolution of the Carnations, a peaceful military coup on 25 April 1974.

During the 1970s and early 1980s, Portugal

To Tuy
Valença
Peneda-Gerês
National Park
To A Gudiña
Verín
MINHO
Rio Lima
Viana do Castelo
Ponte de Lima
Braga
Guimarães
Chaves
Bragança
TRÁS-OS-MONTES
Vila Real
To Zamora
Porto
DOURO LITORAL
Rio Douro
Pocinho
Peso da Régua
BEIRA ALTA
S P A I N
ATLANTIC OCEAN
Aveiro
Viseu
Guarda
Vilar Formoso
Luso & Buçaco Forest
Seia
Gouveia
To Salamanca
Manteigas
BEIRA LITORAL
Pampilhosa
Penhas da Saúde
Coimbra
Torre (1993 m)
Covilhã
Figueira da Foz
Serra da Estrela
Lousã
BEIRA BAIXA
Leiria
Castelo Branco
Nazaré
Batalha
Fátima
Tomar
Alcobaça
Entroncamento
Óbidos
ESTREMADURA
Santarém
Rio Tejo
To Cáceres
Castelo de Vide
Marvão
Portalegre
Mafra
Sintra
Queluz
Vila Franca de Xira
RIBATEJO
ALTO ALENTEJO
Estremoz
Badajoz
Cascais
Estoril
LISBON
Arraiolos
Vila Viçosa
To Mérida
Setúbal
Évora
Monsaraz
Sines
Beja
Serpa
To Seville
BAIXA ALENTEJO
Portugal
0   50   100 km
Monchique
Silves
Lagos
ALGARVE
To Seville
Vila Real de Santo António
Sagres
Faro
Tavira

went through some painful adjustments: the political scene was marked by extreme swings between right and left, and the economy suffered from strikes over government versus private ownership. The granting of independence to Portugal's African colonies in 1974-75 resulted in a flood of nearly a million refugees into the country. Entry into the EU in 1986 secured a measure of stability, buttressed by the acceptance of Portugal as a full member of the European Monetary System in 1992.

Although EU membership has given a tremendous boost to Portugal's development and modernisation, the 1990s have been troubled by recession, rising unemployment, and continuing backwardness in the agricultural and educational sectors. In the 1995 elections, the electorate showed its dissatisfaction with the scandal-tainted Social Democrat Party by switching back to socialism after 10 years of conservatism.

The next big dates on the country's calendar are the Lisbon Expo in 1998 which is expected to attract eight million visitors (and coincide with the opening of the new 12 km Vasco da Gama bridge across the Tejo), and the difficult goal of European monetary union in 1999.

GEOGRAPHY & ECOLOGY

Portugal is one of Europe's smaller countries – approximately twice the size of Switzerland. From north to south it's 560 km and from east to west, 220 km.

The northern and central regions are densely populated, particularly near the coast. The inland region is characterised by lush vegetation and mountains; the highest range is the Serra da Estrela, peaking at Torre (1993 metres). The south is less populated and, apart from the mountainous backdrop of the Algarve, much flatter and drier.

Portugal has one international-standard national park (70,290-hectare Peneda-Gerês), 10 *parques naturals* (natural parks) (of which the biggest and best known is 101,060-hectare Serra da Estrela), eight nature reserves and three other protected areas. The government's Instituto da Conservação da Natureza (ICN) manages all of them; its information office (☎ 01-352 3317) at Rua Ferreira Lapa 29-A, Lisbon, provides maps and information, though each park has its own information centre as well.

GOVERNMENT & POLITICS

Portugal has a Western-style democracy based on the Assembleia da República, a single-chamber parliament with 230 members and an elected president. The two main parties are the ruling Socialist Party (Partido Socialista or PS) and the opposition right-of-centre Social Democratic Party (Partido Social Democrata or PSD). There are several other parties, including the United Democratic Coalition (CDU), which links the Communist Party with the Greens (Partido Ecologista Os Verdes or PEV). The Greens are occasionally referred to as 'watermelons' – green on the outside and red on the inside!

The general election of October 1995 saw the ousting of the PSD after 10 years of rule and the return to power of the Socialist Party. The 46-year-old prime minister, António Guterres, has reassured many by expressing a strong commitment to budgetary discipline and to European monetary unification but it remains to be seen whether he can fulfil his promise to improve health care and education.

ECONOMY

After severe economic problems and rampant inflation in the 1980s, Portugal has tamed the inflation rate to around 4%. The tight grip of state ownership has been relaxed and privatisation continues to accelerate, even under the new socialist government. Agriculture plays a decreasing role in the economy as services (such as real estate, banking and tourism) and industry take over. In addition, Portugal looks set to benefit from its low labour costs, young population (nearly a quarter of the population is under 15 years old), and traditional trading links with South America and Africa. EU membership has led to dramatic changes: the EU provides vital funding (a stunning US$12.8 million a day for the rest of the century) which has already helped to improve the country's infrastructure. However, competition from within the single European market, and a massive budget deficit, are beginning to sour the EU honeymoon.

POPULATION & PEOPLE

Portugal's population of 10.6 million does not include an estimated three million Portuguese living abroad as migrant workers.

ARTS

Music

The best-known form of Portuguese music is the melancholy, nostalgic *fado*, songs popularly considered to have originated with the yearnings of 16th-century sailors. Much of what is offered in tourist shows in Lisbon is overpriced and far from authentic. Amália Rodrigues is *the* star of Portuguese fado; her recordings can be bought in most record shops in Portugal.

Literature

During the 16th century, Gil Vicente, who excelled at farces and religious dramas, set the stage for Portugal's dramatic tradition. Later in the same century, Luís de Camões wrote *Os Lusíadas*, an epic poem celebrating the age of discovery and exploration. He is now considered the national poet of Portugal. The romantic dramatist Almeida Garrett was one of Portugal's leading literary figures during the 19th century, while Fernando Pessoa is arguably the finest Portuguese poet and dramatist to emerge this century and one of the few contemporary Portuguese writers to be widely read abroad.

For a look at Portuguese literature in translation, try Camões' *The Lusiads* and works by Eça de Queiroz *(The Maias)*, Fernando Pessoa *(Selected Poems)*, Fernando Namora *(Mountain Doctor)* and Mario Braga. For a recent Portuguese 'whodunit' – close to the political bone – pick up *The Ballad of Dog's Beach* (Dent, 1986) by José Cardoso Pires.

Architecture

Of special interest is the development during the 16th century of Manueline architecture, named after King Manuel I (1495-1521). The style represents the zest for discovery during that era and is characterised by the use of boisterous twists and spirals as columns, and nautical themes for decoration.

Crafts

The most striking Portuguese craft is the making of decorative tiles known as *azulejos*, a technique learnt in the 15th century from the Moors. Today, superb examples of this craft are to be seen all over Portugal. Lisbon has its own azulejos museum.

CULTURE

Despite growing prosperity and influences from abroad, the Portuguese are keeping a firm grip on their culture. Traditional folk dancing is still the pride of villages throughout the land, and local festivals are celebrated with gusto. Soccer is one modern element now ingrained in male Portuguese life – watching matches on TV ensures the continuation of the traditional long lunch break.

The Portuguese are famous for their friendliness, but they're also fairly conservative: you'll endear yourself to them more quickly if you avoid looking too outlandish and if you greet and thank them in Portuguese. Skimpy beachwear is tolerated at beach resorts, but shorts (and hats) are considered very offensive inside churches.

RELIGION

The Portuguese population is 99% Roman Catholic. The Protestant community numbers less than 120,000 and there are approximately 5000 Jews.

LANGUAGE

Like French, Italian, Spanish and Romanian, Portuguese is a Romance language, closely derived from Latin. It is spoken by more than 10 million people in Portugal, 130 million in Brazil, and is also the official language of five African nations. In large cities such as Porto and Lisbon, it's easy to find Portuguese who speak English, but in remoter areas few locals speak foreign languages, unless they are returned emigrants. See the Language Guide at the back of the book for pronunciation guidelines and useful words and phrases.

Facts for the Visitor

PLANNING

Climate & When to Go

Portugal's climate is temperate; it's only searingly hot in midsummer in the Algarve and Alentejo. The tourist season in the Algarve lasts from late February to November. Peak season extends from June to September; prices for accommodation and museums outside peak season can be discounted by as much as 50%. Prices in this chapter are for peak season.

During winter, the north receives plenty of rain, and temperatures can be chilly. Snowfall is common in the mountains, particularly the Serra da Estrela, which has basic ski facilities. Tourist season in the north extends from approximately May to September.

You can take advantage of fewer crowds, seasonal discounts and spectacular foliage in spring (late March and April) and late summer (September and early October).

Books & Maps

They Went to Portugal and *They Went to Portugal Too* by Rose Macaulay follow the experiences of a wide variety of visitors from medieval times to the 19th century. For a general overview of Portugal and its place in the modern world try *The Portuguese: The Land and Its People* by Marion Kaplan.

The Michelin map of Portugal is accurate and extremely useful even if you are not using a car. The maps produced by the Automóvel Club de Portugal (ACP) provide slightly more up-to-date, but less detailed, coverage.

Walkers should pack the *Landscapes of Portugal* series (Sunflower Books, UK) by Brian & Aileen Anderson, with both car tours and walks in various regions, including the Algarve, Sintra/Estoril and the Costa Verde. More detailed is *Walking in Portugal* by Bethan Davies & Ben Cole.

Military and civilian topographic maps of Portugal are sold at the Porto Editora bookshop (☎ 02-200 7669), Rua da Fabrica 90, Porto. ICN (☎ 01-352 3317), Rua Ferreira Lapa 29-A, Lisbon, the state agency that administers national/natural parks, has a few maps. Better information is available at information offices in or near the parks, though little of it is in the kind of detail needed by trekkers.

SUGGESTED ITINERARIES

Depending on the length of your stay you might want to see the following places:

Two days
    Visit Lisbon.
One week
    Three days in Lisbon, two in Sintra, one in Óbidos and Nazaré.
Two weeks
    As above, plus the Algarve, including two days each in Tavira, Lagos and Sagres.

One month
    As above, plus three days each in Porto, Évora, Serra da Estrela Natural Park, Peneda-Gerês National Park, and two days in Castelo de Vide and Marvão.
Two months
    All of the above, but spending twice as long in each place.

HIGHLIGHTS

For scenery, you can't beat the wild mountain landscapes of the Serra da Estrela and Peneda-Gerês National Park. Architecture buffs should make a beeline for the monasteries at Belém and Batalha, and the palaces of Pena (in Sintra) and Buçaco. Combining the best of both worlds are Portugal's old walled towns such as Évora and Marvão, which are architectural gems surrounded by stunning scenery. Not to be missed in Lisbon is the Gulbenkian, a giant of a museum.

TOURIST OFFICES
Local Tourist Offices

Known as *postos de turismo* or *turismos*, local tourist offices are found throughout Portugal and will provide brochures and varying degrees of assistance.

Tourist Offices Abroad

Countries with Portuguese tourist offices operating under the administrative umbrella of ICEP (Investimentos, Comércio e Turismo de Portugal) include:

Canada
    Portuguese Trade & Tourism Office, 60 Bloor Street West, suite 1005, Toronto, Ont M4W 3B8 (☎ 416-921 7376)
Spain
    Oficina de Turismo de Portugal, Gran Via 27, 1st floor, 28013 Madrid (☎ 91-522 9354)
UK
    Portuguese Trade & Tourism Office, 22-25a Sackville St, London W1X 1DE (☎ 0171-494 1441)
USA
    Portuguese Trade & Tourism Office, 590 Fifth Ave, 4th floor, New York, NY 10036-4704 (☎ 212-354 4403)

There are ICEP offices in many other countries, including Austria, Belgium, France, Germany, Holland, Italy and Switzerland.

VISAS & EMBASSIES

Nationals of all EU countries, as well as those from Australia, Canada, Ireland, Israel, New

Zealand and the USA, can stay up to three months in any half-year without a visa. Some others, including nationals of South Africa and Singapore, need a visa and must produce evidence of financial responsibility, eg a fixed sum of money plus an additional amount per day of their stay (the amounts vary depending on nationality), unless they are the spouse or child of EU citizens.

Portugal is one of the signatories of the Schengen Convention on the abolition of mutual border controls (the others are Austria, Belgium, France, Germany, Greece, Italy, Luxembourg, Netherlands and Spain). You can apply for visas for more than one of these states on the same form, though a visa for one does not automatically grant you entry to the others.

Visa Extensions & Re-entry Visas

Outside Portugal, information is supplied by Portuguese consulates. Inside Portugal, contact the Foreigners' Registration Service (Serviço de Estrangeiros e Fronteiras), Avenida António Augusto de Aguiar 20, Lisbon (☎ 01-346 6141 or 01-352 3112), open 9 am to 3 pm on weekdays.

Portuguese Embassies Abroad

Australia
   23 Culgoa Circuit, O'Malley, ACT 2606 (☎ 06-290 1733)
Canada
   645 Island Park Drive, Ottawa, Ont K1Y OB8 (☎ 613-729 0883)
Ireland
   Knock Sinna House, Knock Sinna, Fox Rock, Dublin 18 (☎ 01-289 4416)
Spain
   Calle del Pinar 1, Madrid 6 (☎ 91-261 7808)
UK
   62 Brompton Road, London SW3 1BJ (☎ 0171-581 3598; premium-rate recorded message ☎ 0891-600202; fax 0171-581 3085)
USA
   2125 Kalorama Rd NW, Washington, DC, 20008 (☎ 202-328 8610)

Foreign Embassies in Portugal

Foreign embassies in Lisbon include:

Canada
   Edifício MCB, Avenida da Liberdade 144 (☎ 01-347 4892)
France
   Calçada Marquês de Abrantes (☎ 01-395 6056)
Germany
   Campo do Mártires da Pátria 38 (☎ 01-352 3961)
Ireland
   Rua da Imprensa à Estrela 1 (☎ 01-396 1569)
Spain
   Rua do Salitre 1 (☎ 01-347 2381)
UK
   Rua de São Domingos à Lapa 37 (☎ 01-396 1191)
USA
   Avenida das Forças Armadas (☎ 01-726 6600)

There are no embassies for Australia or New Zealand in Portugal, but both countries have honorary consuls in Lisbon. Australian citizens can call ☎ 01-353 0750 on weekdays between 1 and 2 pm (the nearest Australian embassy is in Paris); New Zealand citizens should call ☎ 01-357 4134 during business hours (the nearest New Zealand embassy is in Rome).

CUSTOMS

There is no limit on the importation of currency. But if you leave with more than 100,000$00 in escudos or 500,000$00 in foreign currency you will have to prove that you brought in at least this much. The duty-free allowance for travellers from non-EU countries is 200 cigarettes (or 250g of tobacco or 50 cigars or 100 cigarillos); one litre of alcoholic beverage over 22% alcohol by volume or two litres of wine or beer. EU travellers can arrive loaded up with 800 cigarettes, plus 10 litres of spirits, 20 litres of apéritifs or sparkling wine, or a mind-boggling 90 litres of still wine or 110 litres of beer! Everyone can bring in enough coffee, tea etc for personal use.

MONEY

Portuguese banks can change most foreign currencies and travellers' cheques but charge a nasty commission of at least 2000$00, plus 140$00 government tax. Eurocheques often have a 500$00 commission charge. The best deals for travellers' cheques are at private exchange bureaus in Lisbon, Porto and popular tourist resorts: these often charge no commission, but their exchange rates are fairly low.

Better value (and more convenient) are the 24-hour Multibanco credit-card machines found at nearly all banks. There's a handling fee of about 1.5% included in the transaction and exchange rates are reasonable. Automatic exchange machines are found only in a few major cities.

Major credit cards are widely accepted – especially Visa and MasterCard.

Currency

The unit of Portuguese currency is the escudo, further divided into 100 centavos. Prices are usually written with a $ sign between escudos and centavos; eg 25 escudos 50 centavos is written 25$50.

There are 200$00, 100$00, 50$00, 20$00, 10$00, 5$00, 2$50 and 1$00 coins. Notes currently in circulation are 10,000$00, 5000$00, 2000$00, 1000$00 and 500$00. The Portuguese frequently refer to 1000$00 as a *conto*.

Exchange Rates

Australia	A$1	=	119$25
Canada	C$1	=	110$90
France	1FF	=	30$35
Germany	DM1	=	102$85
Japan	¥100	=	140$70
New Zealand	NZ$1	=	106$15
Spain	100 ptas	=	120$90
United Kingdom	UK£1	=	237$00
United States	US$1	=	152$15

Costs

Although costs are beginning to rise noticeably, Portugal is still one of the cheapest places to travel in Europe. On a rock-bottom budget – using hostels or camping grounds, and mostly self-catering – you can squeeze by with about US$25 a day. With bottom-end accommodation and the occasional inexpensive restaurant meal, daily costs will hover around US$30. Travelling with a companion and timing your trip to take advantage of off-season discounts (see the Climate & When to Go section), you can eat and sleep in style for around US$70 per day for two. Outside major tourist areas, prices dip appreciably.

Tipping & Bargaining

A reasonable restaurant tip is 5% to 10%. For just a snack at a *cervejaria*, *pastelaria* (see the Food section that follows) or café, a bit of loose change is sufficient. Taxi drivers appreciate 5% to 10% of the fare, and petrol station attendants 30$00 to 60$00.

Good-humoured bargaining is acceptable in markets but you'll find the Portuguese tough opponents! Off season, you can sometimes bargain down the price of accommodation.

Consumer Taxes

A 17% sales tax, called IVA, is levied on hotel and other accommodation, restaurant meals, car rental and some other bills.

If they are resident outside the EU, foreign tourists can claim an IVA refund on goods from shops which are members of Europe Tax-Free Shopping Portugal. The minimum purchase eligible for a refund at the time of research was 11,700$00 in any one shop. The shop assistant fills in a cheque for the amount of the refund (minus an administration fee). When you leave Portugal present the goods, the cheque and your passport at the tax-refund counter at customs for a cash, postal-note or credit-card refund. This service is presently available at the airports in Lisbon, Porto and Faro, and at Lisbon harbour (customs section). If you are leaving overland, contact customs at the last EU border point. Further details are available from Europe Tax-Free Shopping Portugal (☎ 01-840 8813) in the international departures concourse of Lisbon airport.

POST & COMMUNICATIONS

Post

Postal Rates Postcards and letters up to 20g cost 140$00 to destinations outside Europe, 98$00 to non-EU European destinations and 78$00 to EU destinations. For delivery to the USA or Australia, allow eight to 10 days; delivery times for destinations within Europe average four to six days.

Sending Mail If you're sending a parcel, 'economy air' (or surface airlift – SAL) costs about a third less than air mail, but usually arrives a week or so later. Printed matter is cheapest (and simplest) to send in batches of under two kg. Postal regulations for large parcels can tie both you and the counter clerk in knots. The post office at Praça dos Restauradores in Lisbon and the main post office in Porto are open into the evening and on weekends.

Receiving Mail Most major towns have a post office with *posta restante* service, but it can take time to find out exactly which post office feels responsible. A charge of 60$00 is levied for each item of mail received, at least in Lisbon and Porto.

Addresses Addresses in Portugal are written with the street name first, followed by the building address and often a floor number with a ° symbol, eg 15-3°. An alphabetical tag on the address eg 2-A indicates an adjoining entrance or building. The tag R/C *(rés do chão)* means ground floor.

Telephone

The largest coin accepted by standard pay phones is 50$00, making these phones impractical for international calls. Local calls start at 20$00. Much more useful for both domestic and international calls are the increasingly common 'Credifones', which accept plastic cards available from news-agents, tobacconists and telephone offices. Credifone cards are currently in 875$00 or 2100$00 denominations. A separate TLP (Telefones de Lisboa e Porto) phonecard system is used in Lisbon and Porto as well.

Calls can be made from public telephones as well as booths in Portugal Telecom offices and post offices. International calls average 300$00 per minute to Europe; 450$00 per minute off-peak to Australia and the USA (600$00 per minute at peak times). Charges from private phones are about a third less than those from public phones. Calls from a hotel room are almost double the standard rate. It's generally cheapest to phone between 8 pm and 8 am and on weekends.

To call Portugal from abroad, dial the inter-national access code, ☎ 351 (the country code for Portugal), the area code and the number. Important area codes include ☎ 01 (Lisbon) and ☎ 02 (Porto). From Portugal, the interna-tional access code is ☎ 00.

Fax

Post offices now operate a domestic and inter-national fax service known as CORFAX, costing 1350$00 for the first page to Europe, North America or Australia.

E-mail

Telepac, Portugal's biggest Internet provider, has a public user's centre in Lisbon called Quiosque Internet (☎ 01-314 2527; e-mail email@telepac.pt), where you can plug into the net or send e-mail (but not receive it) for 125$00 per quarter-hour. It's open weekdays from 9 am to 5 pm in the Forum Picoas building beside Picoas metro station.

NEWSPAPERS & MAGAZINES

Major Portuguese-language newspapers include *Diário de Notícias*; the dailies *Público* and *Jornal de Notícias*; and the gossip tabloid *Correio da Manhã*, which may lack finesse but licks all the others for circulation. Weeklies include *O Independente* and *Expresso*. For entertainment listings, check the local dailies or the municipality's calendar of events (usually available at tourist offices).

English-language newspapers published in Portugal include *Portugal Post*, an English-language weekly which aims to serve all of Portugal; *The News*, 'Portugal's National English-Language Paper', which has various regional editions featuring relevant local news and classified pages; and the similar *APN* (Anglo-Portuguese News).

English-language newspapers and maga-zines from abroad are widely available in most major cities and tourist resorts.

RADIO & TV

Portuguese radio is represented by the state-owned stations *Antenna Um* and *Antenna Dois*, by *Rádio Renascença* and by a clutch of recently established local stations. *Rádio Difusão Portuguesa* transmits daily pro-grammes to visitors in English and other languages. Portuguese TV has expanded from two state-run channels (RTP-1 or Canal 1, and RTP-2 or TV2) to include two private channels (SIC and TVI). Soaps (known as *telenovelas*) take up the lion's share of broadcasting time.

BBC World Service broadcasts can be picked up on 15.070 MHz shortwave.

PHOTOGRAPHY & VIDEO

It's best to take film and camera equipment with you, especially if you hanker after Kodachrome, which is generally not available or very expensive. Other brands of E6 slide film, as well as print film and video cassettes, are widely available for reasonable prices at franchised photo shops in larger towns. Print film processing is as fast and inexpensive as anywhere in Europe.

TIME

Portugal is GMT/UTC in winter and GMT/UTC plus one hour in summer. Clocks are set forward by an hour on the last Sunday

ELECTRICITY

Electricity is 220V, 50 Hz. Plugs are normally of the two-round-pin variety.

WEIGHTS & MEASURES

Portugal uses the metric system; decimals are indicated with commas and thousands with points.

LAUNDRY

You'll find *lavandarias* providing laundry services at reasonable cost all over the place, though it make take a day or two. Genuine self-service is rare – though in Lisbon and Porto some can do your wash in a few hours, as cheaply as doing it yourself. Expect to pay around 1500$00 for a 10-kg load.

TOILETS

When available (which isn't often), public toilets in towns are of the sit-down variety, generally clean, and usually free. Most people, however, go to the nearest café for a drink or pastry and take advantage of the facilities there.

HEALTH

There is little to worry about in Portugal. Avoid swimming on beaches which are not marked as safe – Atlantic currents are notoriously dangerous. Take the usual precautions against sunburn and sunstroke. If you are an EU national, make sure you get an E111 or similar form a few weeks before your departure; this entitles you to free emergency medical treatment in Portugal. Considering the relatively small investment required, travel insurance is advisable as a backup.

For minor health problems you can pop into a local chemist (just ask directions to a *farmácia*). For more serious problems, ask your embassy or the local tourist office to refer you to the nearest hospital with an English-speaking doctor. The number to dial in any emergency is ☎ 112.

WOMEN TRAVELLERS

Women travelling around Portugal on their own or in small groups may be accorded attention by males who have the curious habit of hissing. The attention is wearisome, but generally unfocused and best ignored.

DISABLED TRAVELLERS

The Secretariado Nacional de Rehabilitação (☎ 01-793 6517; fax 01-796 5182), Avenida Conde de Valbom 63, Lisbon, publishes the Portuguese-language *Guia de Turismo* with sections on barrier-free accommodation, transport, shops, restaurants and sights in Portugal. It's only available at their offices.

A private agency called Turintegra, also called APTTO (Associação Portuguesa de Turismo Para Todos; ☎ & fax 01-859 5332), Praça Dr Fernando Amado, Lote 566-E, 1900 Lisbon, keeps a keener eye on developments and arranges holidays for disabled travellers. The public transport agencies of Lisbon, Coimbra and Porto offer dial-a-ride services at costs comparable to those of taxis.

DANGERS & ANNOYANCES

Crime against foreigners in Portugal usually involves pickpocketing, theft from cars or pilfering from camping grounds (though armed robberies are also on the increase), mostly in heavily touristed areas such as the Algarve, specific parts of Lisbon and a few other major cities. With the usual precautions (use a money belt or something similar and don't leave valuables in cars or tents) there is little cause for worry. For peace of mind take out travel insurance.

The national emergency number is ☎ 112, for police, fire and other emergencies anywhere in Portugal. For more routine police matters and direct access to the fire brigade there are also telephone numbers for each town or district.

BUSINESS HOURS

Most banks are open weekdays from 8.30 am to 3 pm. Most museums and other tourist attractions are open weekdays from 10 am to 5 pm but are often closed at lunchtime and all day Monday. Shopping hours generally extend from 9 am to 7 pm on weekdays, and from 9 am to 1 pm on Saturday. Lunch is given serious and lingering attention between noon and 3 pm.

PUBLIC HOLIDAYS & SPECIAL EVENTS

Public holidays in Portugal include New Year's Day, Carnival & Shrove Tuesday

(February/March), Good Friday, Anniversary of the Revolution (25 April), May Day, Corpus Christi (May), National Day (Camões Day; 10 June), Feast of the Assumption (15 August), Republic Day (5 October), All Saints' Day (1 November), Independence Day (1 December), Feast of the Immaculate Conception (8 December) and Christmas Day.

The most interesting cultural events in Portugal include:

Holy Week Festival
This is celebrated at Braga during Easter week and features a series of colourful processions of which the most famous is the Ecce Homo procession, featuring hundreds of barefoot penitents carrying torches.

Festas das Cruzes (Festival of the Crosses)
Held in Barcelos in May, this festival is noted for its processions, performances of folk music and dance, and exhibitions of regional handicrafts.

Feira Nacional da Agricultura (National Agricultural Fair)
In June, Santarém holds a grand country fair with bullfighting, folk singing and dancing.

Festa do Santo António (Festival of Saint Anthony)
This street festival is held in Lisbon (mainly in the Alfama district) on June 13.

Festas de São João (St John's Festival)
From 16 to 24 June, Porto parties – the night of the 23rd sees virtually all the townsfolk out on the streets amicably bashing each other over the head with leeks or plastic hammers.

Festas da Nossa Senhora da Agonia (Agonia Fair & Festival)
This is held in Viana do Castelo on the first Sunday after 15 August and is famed for its folk arts, parades, fireworks, and handicrafts fair.

Feira de São Martinho (National Horse Festival)
Equine enthusiasts will want to gallop off to Golegã between 3 and 11 November to see all manner of horses, riding contests and bullfights.

ACTIVITIES
Hiking & Pony Trekking
Despite some magnificent rambling country, walking ranks low among Portuguese passions: there are no national walking clubs or official cross-country trails, though some parks are establishing trails (see Serra da Estrela in the Central Portugal section and Peneda-Gerês in the North section). See Information under Lisbon, Évora and Serra da Estrela in the Central Portugal section, and Peneda-Gerês in the North section, for some local outfits specialising in walking and pony treks.

Water Sports
Water sports popular in Portugal include white-water rafting, water-skiing, surfing, windsurfing and motorised and unmotorised boating. For local specialists in these sports see Information under Lagos and Sagres in the Algarve section and Peneda-Gerês in the North section.

Canyoning & Hydrospeed
Canyoning is a relatively new adventure sport which involves tackling every possible outdoor challenge offered by a canyon: swimming, trekking, abseiling and rock climbing. Hydrospeed is a version of white-water boating, without the boat. A few agencies offer these high-adrenalin activities, including Trilhos (see Information under Porto).

Multi-Activity & Adventure Programmes
Movijovem, the country's central booking office for Hostelling International (see Lisbon), organises adventure holidays in Portugal for 16 to 26-year-olds, which include rafting, caving and horse riding. TurAventur (see Évora) offers walking, biking and jeep trips across the plains of the Alentejo. Montes d'Aventura and Trote-Gerês (see Peneda-Gerês) can organise trekking, horse riding, canoeing, cycling and combination trips in the Peneda-Gerês National Park.

For the full range of available sports, ask the National Tourist Office for its brochure.

ACCOMMODATION
Most local tourist offices have lists of accommodation to suit a wide range of budgets and they can help you locate and book it. Although the government uses one to five stars to grade some types of accommodation, the criteria seem erratic. For a room with a double bed, ask for a *quarto de casal*; for twin beds, ask for a *duplo*; and for a single room, ask for a *quarto individual*.

Camping
Camping is widespread and popular in Portugal, and easily the cheapest option. The *Roteiro Campista* (1500$00), published annually in March and sold in most large bookshops, is an excellent multilingual guide with details of camping grounds in Portugal and regulations for camping outside these sites. Depending on

the facilities and the season, prices per night run at about 500$00 to 600$00 for an adult (or child over 10 years old), plus 400$00 to 500$00 for a car and the same again for a small tent. Considerably lower prices apply in less touristed regions and in the low season.

Hostels

Portugal has a network of 20 youth hostels, called *pousadas de juventude*, part of the Hostelling International (HI) system. Low rates are offset by restrictions including a midnight curfew and exclusion from the hostel for part of the day at most (but not all) of them. Prices are higher for popular hostels, particularly Lisbon's, but for most others a dorm bed costs 1200$00 to 1400$00 in the low season and 1450$00 to 1600$00 in the high season. Some hostels also offer private doubles from 2200$00 to 3700$00 per room per night. Breakfast is included in the price; lunch or dinner costs 950$00 more.

Demand is high, so advance reservations (for which you are charged 1000$00) are essential. If you don't already have a card from your national hostel association, you can get an HI membership by paying an extra 400$00 each (and having a 'guest card' stamped) at the first six hostels you stay at. For more information, contact Movijovem (☎ 01-355 9081; fax 01-352 8621), Avenida Duque d'Ávila 137, 1000 Lisbon – Portugal's central HI reservations office, where you can book hostels anywhere in Portugal or abroad.

Cheap Rooms

Another cheap option is a *quarto particular* (private room), or *quarto*, usually just a room in a private house. Home-owners may approach you in the street or at the bus or train station; otherwise watch for 'quartos' signs. Tourist offices sometimes have relevant lists. The rooms are usually clean, cheap (around 3500$00 a double) and free from the restrictions of hostels, and the owners can be interesting characters. A more commercial variant is a *dormida* or rooming house, where doubles cost about 4000$00 in the high season. You may be able to bargain for less in the low season.

Guesthouses

The most common types of guesthouses, the Portuguese equivalent of B&Bs, are the *residencial* and the *pensão* (plural *pensões*). Both are graded from one to three stars, and the top-rated establishments are often cheaper and better-run than some hotels clinging to their last star(s). During the high season, rates for a double in the cheapest pensão start at around 4500$00; expect to pay slightly more for a residencial, where breakfast is normally included in the price. There are often cheaper rooms with communal bathrooms. During the low season, rates drop by at least a third.

Hotels

Hotels are graded from one to five stars. For a double in high season you'll pay between 15,000$00 and 30,000$00 at the top end and around 9000$00 to 12,000$00 at the low end. In the same category, but more like up-market inns, are the *estalagem* and *albergaria*. In the low season, prices drop spectacularly, with a double in a spiffy four-star hotel for as little as 8000$00. Breakfast is usually included.

Other Accommodation

There is a wide selection of other opulent accommodation. *Pousadas* are government-run former castles, monasteries or palaces, often in spectacular locations. Details are available from tourist offices.

Private counterparts of pousadas are mostly operated under a scheme called Turismo de Habitação ('Turihab') and smaller schemes called Turismo Rural and Agroturismo, which allow you to stay in anything from a farmhouse to a mansion as the guest of the owner. Some also have self-catering cottages. A hefty book, *Turismo no Espaço Rural*, describing most of the available places, is available for about 2800$00 from Turismo de Habitação, Praça da República 4990, Ponte de Lima (☎ 058-741 672; fax 058-741444), from the Lisbon tourist office or from Portuguese national tourist offices abroad.

Prices usually include breakfast and are graded by quality and season. For a double in high season you will pay a minimum of 14,500$00 in a pousada, and 11,500$00 in a manor house belonging to the Turihab scheme. In low season, prices drop by as much as 50% and you can literally stay in a palace for the price of an average B&B elsewhere in Europe.

FOOD

Eating and drinking get serious attention in Portugal, where hearty portions and excellent value for money are the norm. Portugal has solidly ignored the fast-food era in favour of leisurely dining and devotion to wholesome ingredients.

The line between snacks and full-scale meals is blurred. Bars and cafés often sell snacks or even offer a small menu. For full-scale meals try a *casa do pasto* (a simple and cheap eatery, most popular at lunchtimes), a *restaurante*, a *cervejaria* (a type of bar and restaurant), or a *marisqueira* (a restaurant with an emphasis on seafood). The *prato do dia* (dish of the day) is often an excellent deal at around 700$00. In more touristed regions, restaurants may advertise an *ementa turística* (tourist menu). In contrast to the prato do dia, these are not real bargains.

The titbits offered at the start of a meal, known as the *couvert*, often include bread rolls, cheese and butter; you will be charged additionally for this. A full portion, ample for two decent appetites, is a *dose*; or you can ask for a *meia dose* (half-portion) usually about a third cheaper. Lunchtime moves at a leisurely pace from noon to 3 pm; evening meals are taken between 7 and 10.30 pm.

Snacks

Typical snacks include *sandes* (sandwiches), *prego em pão* (a slab of meat with egg sandwiched in a roll), *pastéis de bacalhau* (cod fish cakes), and *tosta mista* (a toasted cheese and ham sandwich). Prices start at around 250$00. Soups are also cheap and filling.

Main Dishes

Seafood in Portugal offers exceptional value, especially fish dishes such as *linguado grelhado* (grilled sole), *bife de atúm* (tuna steak), and the omnipresent *bacalhau* (cod) cooked in dozens of different ways. Meat is hit-and-miss, but worth sampling are *presunto* (ham); lamb, usually roasted, and known as *borrego* by the gourmets of Alentejo; and *cabrito* (kid). Prices for main dishes start at around 900$00.

Desserts & Cheeses

In most cafés and *pastelarias* (pastry shops), you can gorge yourself on some of the sweetest desserts *(sobremesas)* and cakes *(bolos)* imaginable. Cheeses from Serra da Estrela, Serpa and the Azores are also worth sampling but relatively expensive at about 2300$00 a kg.

Self-Catering

The lively local markets offer excellent fresh seafood, vegetables and fruit. Go early to get the best choice.

DRINKS

Nonalcoholic Drinks

Surprisingly, fresh fruit juices are a rarity. Mineral water *(água mineral)* is excellent, either carbonated *(com gás)* or still *(sem gás)*.

Coffee is a hallowed institution with its own convoluted nomenclature. A small black espresso is usually called a *bica*. For coffee with lots of milk, ask for a *galão*. In the north, half coffee and half milk is a *meia de leite*; elsewhere, it's a *café com leite*. Tea *(chá)* comes with lemon *(com limão)* or with milk *(com leite)*.

Alcohol

Local brands of beer *(cerveja)* include Sagres, Super Bock and Tuborg (produced under licence). To order draught beer, ask for a *fino* or an Imperial.

Portuguese wine *(vinho)* offers excellent value in all its varieties: mature red *(tinto)*, white *(branco)* and semi-sparkling young *(vinho verde)*, which is usually white but occasionally red. Restaurants often have *vinho da casa* (house wine) for as little as 250$00 for a 350-ml bottle or jug, though for less than 800$00 you can buy a bottle to please the most discerning taste buds.

Port, synonymous with Portugal, is produced in the Douro Valley near Porto and drunk in three forms: ruby, tawny and white. Dry white port with sardines makes a memorable feast. Local brandy *(aguardente)* is also worth a try. For some rough stuff that tries hard to destroy your throat, ask for a *bagaço* (grape marc). Most bartenders in Portugal have the pleasant habit of serving large measures: a single brandy often contains the equivalent of a triple in the UK or the USA.

ENTERTAINMENT

Cinemas are inexpensive – around 700$00 a ticket – and prices are often reduced once a week in a bid to lure audiences from their home videos. Foreign films are normally shown in the original language with Portuguese subtitles.

For dance, music (rock, jazz and classical) and other cultural events, ask at the tourist offices or pick up a copy of the local newspaper for listings.

Discos abound in Lisbon, Porto and the Algarve (where the town of Albufeira has a reputation as Portugal's hot spot).

Perhaps the most original forms of entertainment are the local festivals (see the earlier Public Holidays & Special Events section).

SPECTATOR SPORT

Football (soccer) dominates the sporting scene – literally everything stops for a big match. The season lasts from August to May and almost every village and town finds enough players for a team. The three main teams are Benfica and Sporting in Lisbon, and FC Porto in Porto. Ask at the tourist office about forthcoming matches.

Bullfighting is still popular in Portugal, despite pressure from international animal-rights activists. If you want to see a *tourada*, the season runs from late April to October. The rules for the Portuguese version of bullfighting prohibit a public kill, though the hapless beast must often be dispatched in private afterwards. In Lisbon, bullfights are held at the Campo Pequeno on Thursday. Ribatejo is the region where most bulls are bred; major fights are staged in Vila Franca de Xira and Santarém.

THINGS TO BUY

Leather goods, especially shoes and bags, are good value, as are textiles such as lace and embroidered linen. Handicrafts range from inexpensive pottery and basketwork to substantial purchases like rugs from Arraiolos, filigree gold or silver jewellery, and sets of azulejos made to order.

Getting There & Away

AIR

British Airways and TAP (Air Portugal) have direct flights between London and Lisbon.

They also provide direct services to Porto and Faro. Fare categories are extremely complicated and seem to change every six months.

A discounted London-Lisbon return fare is about £130 in low season, or about £200 to £240 in high season. It's sometimes possible to get deals as low as £100 for charter or package return flights between London and Faro. For a general idea of prices from England, call TAP (☎ 0171-828 0262) or British Airways (☎ 0181-897 4000) direct. Both BA and TAP offer discounted youth and student fares. You could also try the travel agencies Abreu (☎ 0171-229 9905) or Latitude 40 (☎ 0171-229 3164), or ask the Portuguese National Tourist Office for its *Tour Operators' Guide: Portugal*. Campus Travel (☎ 0171-730 3402) is one of the UK's best youth-fare agencies.

For prices *to* England, try the youth travel agencies Tagus Travel (☎ 01-352 5509) and Jumbo Expresso (☎ 01-793 9264); other options are Top Tours (☎ 01-315 5885), TAP (☎ 01-841 6990) and British Airways (☎ 01-346 4353), all in Lisbon.

Since France, and Paris in particular, has a huge population of Portuguese immigrants, there are also frequent flights at reasonable prices between the two countries. For details, from France call Air France (☎ 01 44 08 24 24) or TAP (☎ 01 44 86 89 89). Both offer discounted prices to those under 26.

Madeira and the Azores are served by direct flights from Lisbon. There are also direct flights to Madeira from London, and to the Azores from New York and Montreal. The standard fare for a return flight with TAP from Lisbon is about UK£145 to Madeira or UK£210 to the Azores. Package deals offered by UK travel agencies may offer even better value.

LAND

Bus

Spain Intercentro, Portugal's main Eurolines agent, operates bus services three times a week between Lisbon and Madrid (11 hours) for 6860$00. Eurolines also has services between other Portuguese towns and Spain; for information and reservations, call ☎ 91-530 7600 (Madrid) or ☎ 01-357 7715 (Lisbon).

Internorte (☎ 02-600 4223 in Porto) runs coaches to/from northern Portuguese cities, including a service between Porto and Madrid

(5230$00) four times a week. In the Algarve, Intersul has express services between Lagos and Seville about four times weekly, via Vila Real de Santo António.

England & France Intercentro/Eurolines has regular services between central Portugal (Lisbon and other cities) and France, with a bus change in Paris for London, five times a week. Allow about 40 hours for the trip from London (Victoria coach station) to Lisbon; a standard ticket costs UK£112 one way. For more information call Eurolines in England on %y0990-143219 or in Portugal on %y01-357 7715.

Internorte (Porto ☎ 02-600 4223) has similar services to/from northern Portugal (Porto and other cities), with a change in Paris, as well as a once-weekly direct Porto-London coach. A one-way Porto-London ticket is about UK£95.

The private line IASA (☎ 01-793 6451 in Lisbon, ☎ 02-208 4338 in Porto) runs coaches five times a week between Lisbon and Paris (via Coimbra and other towns) and between Porto and Paris (via Braga and other towns). Both journeys take about 27 hours and cost about UK£65 one way.

Train

Spain The main rail route is Madrid-Lisbon via Valência de Alcântara; the journey (with an express departure daily) takes about 10 hours. Other popular routes include Vigo-Porto (expresses three times a day) and, in southern Spain, Seville-Ayamonte, across the river from the Portuguese town of Vila Real de Santo António in the Algarve. Also, the daily Lisbon-Paris train (see the following section) goes via Salamanca, Valladolid, Burgos, Vitória and San Sebastian.

England & France In general, it's only worth taking the train if you can take advantage of special under-26 rail passes such as Inter-Rail (see the Getting Around chapter at the beginning of this book for details).

Services from London to Lisbon and other destinations in Portugal run via Paris, where you change trains. There are two standard routes. The *Sud Express* runs from Paris via Irún (where you must change trains again) and across Spain to Pampilhosa in Portugal (con-

nections for Porto) before continuing to Lisbon. The other route runs from Paris to Madrid, where you can catch the *Lisboa Express* via Entroncamento (connections for Porto) to Lisbon. Allow at least 30 hours for the trip from London to Lisbon. A one-way 2nd class, under-26 ticket is UK£94.

Car & Motorcycle The quickest routes from the UK are by ferry via northern Spain – from Plymouth to Santander with Brittany Ferries (☎ 0990-360360) or from Portsmouth to Bilbao with P&O Ferries (☎ 0990-980111). Alternatively, take the ferry or Channel Tunnel to France, motor down the coast via Bordeaux through Spain via Burgos and Salamanca to Portugal. One option to reduce driving time on this route is to use Motorail for all or part of the trip from Paris to Lisbon; for information in England call French Railways (☎ 0171-803 3030).

All border posts are open around the clock.

LEAVING PORTUGAL

There is an airport departure tax of about 2000$00 for international departures and about 800$00 for domestic departures (the exact amount depends on your destination), but this is invariably included in the price of the ticket.

Getting Around

AIR

Flights inside Portugal are extremely expensive and hardly worth considering for the short distances involved – unless you have an under-26 card. Portugália operates daily flights between Lisbon, Porto and Faro (14,280$00 – about UK£65 – for the 50-minute Lisbon-Faro flight), with a handsome 50% discount for youth-card holders. For further information, phone Portugália in Lisbon (☎ 01-840 8999).

TAP also has some domestic connections, including Lisbon-Porto, and daily Lisbon-Faro flights that connect with all international TAP arrivals and departures at Lisbon.

BUS

The now defunct, state-run Rodoviária Nacional (RN) has spawned a host of private regional companies which together operate a dense network of bus services of two types: *expressos* which provide comfortable, fast and direct connections between major cities and towns, and *carreiras* which stop at every crossroad. Local weekend services, especially up north, can thin out to almost nothing, especially when school is out in summer. In the boondocks, timetables are a rare commodity: stock up on information at tourist offices or bus stations in major towns.

An express coach from Lisbon to Faro takes just under five hours and costs about 2000$00 (2500$00 for the luxury four-hour EVA express); Lisbon-Porto takes 3½ hours and costs about 1800$00.

TRAIN
Caminhos de Ferro Portugueses (CP), the state railway company, operates three main types of service: *rápido* or *intercidade* (marked IC on timetables); *interregional* (marked IR); and *regional* (marked R). Tickets for the first two types cost at least double the price of a regional service, and reservations are either mandatory or highly recommended. A special intercidade service called Alfa, with fewer stops than usual, operates between selected northern cities (eg Lisbon and Porto). Frequent train travellers may want to buy a copy of the *Guia Horário Oficial* (360$00), which lists all domestic and international timetables, from the ticket windows at all the major stations in Lisbon.

If you can match your itinerary and pace to a regional service, travel by rail is cheaper, if slower, than by bus. Children from four to 12 years old and adults over 65 travel at half-price. Holders of youth cards get 30% off regional and interregional services only. There are also family discounts. Tourist tickets (*bilhetes turísticos*) are available for seven (17,500$00), 14 (28,300$00) or 21 (40,000$00) days, but are only worthwhile if you plan to spend a great deal of time moving around. The same discounts apply as for regular tickets. With intercidade and Alfa services everyone – even rail-pass holders – must pay an additional booking charge.

CAR & MOTORCYCLE
ACP (Automóvel Club de Portugal) is Portugal's representative for various foreign car and touring clubs. It provides medical, legal and car breakdown assistance for its members, but anyone can get road information and maps from its head office (☎ 01-356 3931; fax 01-357 4732) at Rua Rosa Araújo 24, Lisbon.

Road Rules
There are indeed rules, but the two guiding principles for Portuguese drivers seem to be: find the fastest route between two points; and defy the law of mortality in doing so. Although city driving (and parking) is hectic, minor roads in the countryside have surprisingly little traffic. Recent EU subsidies have ensured that the road system has been upgraded and there are now several long stretches of motorway – some of which are toll roads.

Petrol is pricey – 156$00 and up for a litre of 95-octane unleaded fuel. Unleaded petrol (*sem chumbo*) is readily available in most parts of the country. Speed limits in Portugal are 60 km/h in cities and public centres, unless otherwise indicated; 90 km/h on normal roads; and 120 km/h on motorways. Driving is on the right, and front passengers are required by law to wear seat belts.

Car Rental
There are dozens of local car-rental firms in Portugal, but the best deals are often arranged from abroad, either as part of a package with the flight, or through an international car-rental firm. From the UK, for example, for a small car expect to pay about UK£130 for seven days in the high season or UK£65 in low season; in Portugal, figure on around UK£160 in the high season or UK£130 in the low season (including tax, insurance and unlimited mileage). You must be at least 23 years old and have held your licence for over a year.

BICYCLE
The Portuguese are still bemused by the idea of cycling for pleasure, though the rental of mountain bikes (nicknamed BTT, for *bicyclete tudo terrano*) is catching on in some touristed areas (for anywhere from 1500$00 to 3500$00 a day). Elsewhere, bike shops and rental outfits are rare; if you're bringing your own machine, pack plenty of spares.

You can take your bike on any regional or interregional train for 1200$00.

PORTUGAL

HITCHING

Thumbing a ride takes considerable time because drivers in remote regions tend to be going short distances. You get to meet some interesting characters, but you may only advance from one field to the next! You'll make more progress on major roads.

LOCAL TRANSPORT

Bus

Except in big cities like Lisbon there is little reason to take a municipal bus. Most areas have regional bus services of some kind, but timetables can be scarce and/or bewildering, with many new private companies operating similar routes – and services can simply disappear on summer weekends, especially in the north.

Metro

Lisbon's underground system, the metro, is handy for the city centre, and by the time of Expo '98 it will extend much further. See the Lisbon section for more details.

Taxi

Taxis offer good value over short distances – especially for two or more people – and are usually plentiful in towns. Flag fall is 250$00; a fare of 500$00 is often enough for a zip across town. Once a taxi leaves the town or city limits, you may pay a higher fare, and possibly the cost of a return trip – whether you take it or not.

Other Transport

Enthusiasts for stately progress should not miss the trams of Lisbon and Porto, an endangered species. Also worth trying are the funiculars and elevators (both called *elevadores*) in Lisbon, Bom Jesus (Braga), Nazaré and elsewhere.

Commuter ferries run back and forth across the Rio Tejo all day between Lisbon and Cacilhas (and other points).

ORGANISED TOURS

Gray Lines (☎ 01-352 2594; fax 01-353 3291), Avenida Praia da Vitória 12-B, Lisbon, organises three to seven-day bus tours to selected regions throughout Portugal, normally through local travel agents or upper-end tourist hotels. The AVIC coach company (☎ 058-829705), Avenida Combatentes 206, Viana do Castelo, entices travellers on short tours

of the lovely Douro and Lima valleys. Miltours (☎ 089-890 4600), Verissimo de Almeida 20, Faro, gives you a choice of day trips not only in the Algarve but all over Portugal; they also have offices in Lisbon (Rua Conde de Redondo 21, ☎ 01-352 4166) and Porto (Rua J Simão Bolivar 209, ☎ 02-941 4671).

Several unusual tours of Portugal are organised by UK travel agencies, eg art and music tours by Martin Randall Travel (☎ 0181-742 3355; fax 0181-742 1066) and wine tours in Alentejo and the Douro by Arblaster & Clarke Wine Tours (☎ 01730-893344). Further listings are available from the Portuguese National Tourist Office.

Two UK travel agencies that specialise in hiking holidays are Explore Worldwide (☎ 01252-319448) and Ramblers Holidays (☎ 01707-331133). Refer to Activities under Facts for the Visitor for information on adventure-travel specialists within Portugal.

Lisbon

Although it bustles with the crowds, noise and traffic of a capital city, Lisbon's low skyline and breezy position beside the Rio Tejo (River Tagus) lend it a small and manageable feel. Its unpretentious atmosphere and pleasant blend of architectural styles conspire with diverse attractions – and a few unique quirks – to make it a favourite with a wide range of visitors. Furthermore, Lisbon (Lisboa to the Portuguese) is one of Europe's most economical destinations. Lovers of Art Deco shouldn't wait: façades are fast disappearing in a frenzy of redevelopment.

Orientation

Apart from the puff required to negotiate the hills, orientation is straightforward. Activity centres on the lower part of the city, the Baixa district, focused on Praça Dom Pedro IV, which nearly everyone calls 'the Rossio'. Just north of the Rossio is Praça dos Restauradores, at the bottom of Avenida da Liberdade. West of the Rossio it's a steep climb to the Bairro Alto district where one section, the Chiado, is under renovation after a huge fire in 1988. East of the Rossio, it's another climb to the Castelo de São Jorge and the adjacent Alfama district, a maze of tiny streets. Several km to the west is Belém with its cluster of attractions.

Information

Tourist Offices The main tourist office (☎ 346 6307) in Palácio Foz, Praça dos Restauradores, near Restauradores metro station, offers brochures and can help with accommodation. Ask here about museum opening times, which delight in being fickle. The office is open from 9 am to 8 pm every day. There is also a tourist office at the airport (☎ 849 4323), open daily from 6 am to 2 am.

Money There are useful banks with 24-hour exchange machines (for foreign cash) at the airport; at Santa Apolónia train station; opposite Rossio station (at Rua 1 de Dezembro 118-A); and at Rua Augusta 24 near Praça do Comércio. A better deal is the private exchange bureau, Cota Câmbios, at Rua do Áurea 283, open from 9 am to 8 pm weekdays (to 6 pm Saturday). Banco Borges e Irmão (☎ 342 1068) at Avenida da Liberdade 9-A is open from 8.30 am to 7.30 pm on weekdays and on alternate Saturdays.

Post & Communications The central post office is on Praça do Comércio. Mail addressed to Posta Restante, Central Correios, Terreira do Paço, 1100 Lisboa, will go to counter 13 or 14 here. A fee of 60$00 is charged for each letter collected. A telephone office at Rossio 68 is open daily from 8 am to 11 pm. A more convenient post and telephone office (☎ 347 1122), on Praça dos Restauradores opposite the tourist office, is open weekdays from 8 am to 11 pm and weekends and holidays from 9 am to 6 pm.

The telephone code for Lisbon is ☎ 01.

Travel Agencies Top Tours (☎ 315 5885; fax 315 5873), Avenida Duque de Loulé 108, is Lisbon's American Express representative. It offers commission-free currency exchange, help with lost cards or travellers' cheques, and outbound ticketing, and will forward and hold mail and faxes. It's closed at weekends. Good youth travel agencies are Tagus Travel (☎ 352 5509 for air bookings, ☎ 352 5986 for youth cards and other services) at Rua Camilo Castelo Branco 20, and Jumbo Expresso

(☎ 793 9264), Avenida da República 97, near Entre Campos metro station.

Two agencies specialising in adventure travel are Rotas do Vento (☎ 364 9852; fax 364 9843) at Rua dos Lusíadas 5, which organises weekend guided walks to remote corners of Portugal; and Turnatur (☎ 207 6886; fax 207 7675), Rua Almirante Reis 60 in Barreiro, just across the Tejo, which organises nature walks, jeep safaris, canoeing and canyoning expeditions.

Bookshops The central Diário de Notícias at Rossio 11 has a modest range of guides and maps. The city's biggest bookseller is Livraria Bertrand, with at least half a dozen shops, the biggest at Rua Garrett 7. If you're into classy bookshops, seek out Livraria Buchholz at Rua Duque de Palmela 4 (by Rotunda metro station), with its extensive collection. For second-hand books, there are two or three shops along Calçada do Carmo, which climbs up behind Rossio station.

Cultural Centres The USA's Abraham Lincoln Center (☎ 357 0102), at Avenida Duque de Loulé 22-B, is open weekdays from 2 to 5.30 pm. The library has a massive stock of American books and magazines. The British Council (☎ 347 6141), at Rua de São Marçal 174, also has a good library. It's open Tuesday through Friday from noon to 6 pm. At Avenida Luís Bivar 91 is the Institut Franco-Portugais de Lisbonne (☎ 311 1400).

Maps Along with their microscopic city map the tourist office sometimes has a good 1:15,000 *Lisboa* map free of charge. The detailed, oblique-perspective *Lisbon City Map – Vista Aérea Geral*, available from kiosks and bookshops, is great for spotting landmarks.

Laundry Lavandaria Sous'ana (☎ 888 0820) on the 1st floor of the Centro Comércial da Mouraria on Largo Martim Moniz (metro: Socorro) is self-service, but they'll do your wash in a few hours for the same price; they're open 9.30 am to 8.30 pm except Sunday. The Texas Lavandaria at Rua da Alegria 7, with dry-cleaning, washing and ironing, is open weekdays.

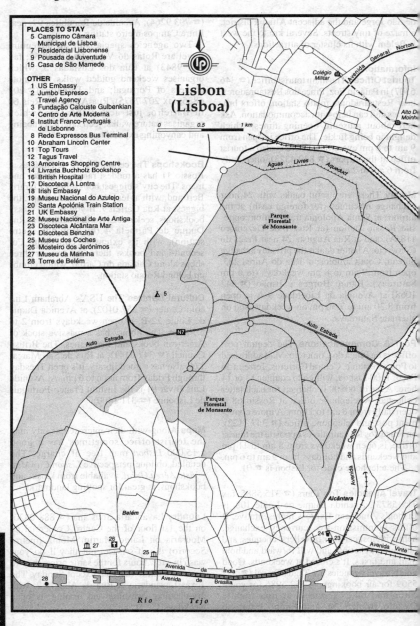

PLACES TO STAY
5 Campismo Câmara
   Municipal de Lisboa
7 Residencial Lisbonense
9 Pousada de Juventude
15 Casa de São Mamede

OTHER
1 US Embassy
2 Jumbo Expresso
   Travel Agency
3 Fundação Calouste Gulbenkian
4 Centro de Arte Moderna
6 Institut Franco-Português
   de Lisbonne
8 Rede Expressos Bus Terminal
10 Abraham Lincoln Center
11 Top Tours
12 Tagus Travel
13 Amoreiras Shopping Centre
14 Livraria Buchholz Bookshop
16 British Hospital
17 Discoteca A Lontra
18 Irish Embassy
19 Museu Nacional do Azulejo
20 Santa Apolónia Train Station
21 UK Embassy
22 Museu Nacional de Arte Antiga
23 Discoteca Alcântara Mar
24 Discoteca Benzina
25 Museu dos Coches
26 Mosteiro dos Jerónimos
27 Museu da Marinha
28 Torre de Belém

Lisbon
(Lisboa)

0   0.5   1 km

Aguas Livres Aqueduct

Parque Florestal de Monsanto

Parque Florestal de Monsanto

Colégio Militar

Avenida General Norton

Alto De Moinho

Auto Estrada

N7

N7

Auto Estrada

Avenida de Ceuta

Alcântara

Avenida Vinte e

Belém

Avenida da Índia

Avenida de Brasília

Rio Tejo

PORTUGAL

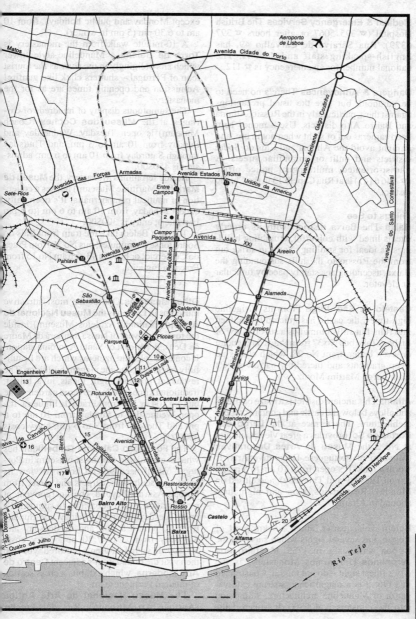

Medical & Emergency Services The British Hospital (☎ 395 5067 or after hours ☎ 397 6329), Rua Saraiva de Carvalho 49, has English-speaking staff and doctors. The national number for an emergency is ☎ 112.

Dangers & Annoyances There's no need to be paranoid, but take the usual precautions against theft, particularly in the Rossio, Alfama and Bairro Alto districts. Use a money belt, keep cameras out of sight when not in use, and at night avoid the Alfama and Cais do Sodré districts and unlit or unfamiliar streets. A tourist-oriented, multilingual police office (☎ 346 6141) is at Rua Capelo 13 in the Chiado district.

Things to See
Baixa The Baixa district, with its orderly streets lined with colourful, crumbling buildings, is ideal for strolling. You can strike out from the Rossio to the hills surrounding the Baixa, ascending at a stately pace by funicular or elevator.

Castelo de São Jorge From its Visigothic high times, the castle has gracefully declined into ruin, but still commands a superb view of Lisbon. Take bus No 37 from Praça da Figueira or, even better, tram No 28, which clanks up steep gradients and incredibly narrow streets from Largo Martim Moniz.

Alfama This ancient district is a maze of streets and alleys below the castle and contains superb architecture. The terrace at the **Largo das Portas do Sol** provides a great viewpoint, and at No 2 the **Museu de Artes Decorativas** (Museum of Portuguese Decorative Arts) is worth a look. It's open from 10 am to 5 pm (8 pm on Tuesday and Thursday), and closed on Monday. Restaurants, bars and nightclubs abound in Alfama.

Belém This quarter, about six km west of Rossio, has several sights which survived the Lisbon earthquake in 1755. **Mosteiro dos Jerónimos** (Jerónimos Monastery) is the city's finest sight – do not miss it. Constructed in 1496, it is a magnificent, soaring extravaganza of Manueline architecture. Admission into the cloisters is 400$00. It's open daily, except Monday and public holidays, from 10 am to 6.30 pm (5 pm in winter).

A 10-minute walk from the monastery is **Torre de Belém**, a Manueline-style tower which sits obligingly in the river as *the* tourist icon of Portugal – shutters click like gunfire! Admission and opening times are as for the monastery.

The sumptuous display of hundreds of carriages at the **Museu dos Coches** (Coach Museum) is open Tuesday, Wednesday and Sunday from 10 am to 3 pm, and Thursday through Saturday from 10 am to 6 pm; admission is 450$00.

Beside Jerónimos Monastery, the **Museu da Marinha** (Maritime Museum) houses a collection of nautical paraphernalia. It's open daily, except Monday, from 10 am to 6 pm (to 5 pm in winter); entry is 300$00.

To reach Belém take the train from Cais do Sodré for seven minutes; bus No 28 from Praça do Comércio; or bus No 43 or tram No 15 from Praça da Figueira.

Other Museums One of the most attractive museums in Lisbon is the **Museu Nacional do Azulejo** (National Azulejos Museum) inside the former convent of Nossa Senhora da Madre de Deus, north-east of Santa Apolónia station. It contains splendid azulejos which are beautifully integrated into the elegant buildings. The restaurant provides light meals in a bright, traditional kitchen or in a covered garden. Take bus No 104 or 105 from Praça da Figueira. It's open Wednesday to Sunday from 10 am to 6 pm and Tuesday from 2 to 6 pm; entry costs 350$00.

The **Fundação Calouste Gulbenkian** has what is considered the finest museum in Portugal. You'll need several hours to view its paintings, sculptures, carpets and more, from Europe, Asia and beyond. The most convenient metro station is São Sebastião. In summer it's open Tuesday, Thursday, Friday and Sunday from 10 am to 5 pm, and Wednesday and Saturday from 2 to 7.30 pm; entry costs 500$00. If your feet aren't too tired, you can then visit the Foundation's adjacent **Centro de Arte Moderna**, which exhibits a cross section of modern Portuguese art.

The **Museu Nacional de Arte Antiga** (Antique Art Museum), Rua das Janelas

Verdes, houses the national collection of works by Portuguese painters. Opening times are Wednesday to Sunday from 10 am to 6 pm and Tuesday from 2 to 6 pm. Admission costs 500$00. Take bus No 40 or 60 from Praça da Figueira.

Mercado da Ribeira This municipal market (also called Mercado Municipal 24 de Julho) is Lisbon's biggest market, diagonally opposite Cais do Sodré station. Get there early in the day to see vegetables, fruit, seafood and more, sold by feisty vendors.

Places to Stay
Camping The *Campismo Câmara Municipal de Lisboa* (☎ 760 2061/2063) in Parque Florestal de Monsanto is about six km northwest of Rossio. Take bus No 14 or 43 from Praća da Figueira.

Hostels Close to the centre is the *pousada de juventude* (☎ 353 2696) on Rua Andrade Corvo 46 (off Ave Fontes Pereira de Melo). It's open 24 hours a day. The closest metro station is Picoas, or take bus No 46 from Santa Apolónia station or Rossio and get off at Marquês de Pombal. It's very popular, so reservations are essential.

The *Pousada de Juventude de Catalazete* (☎ 443 0638) is at Estrada Marginal (next to Inatel) in Oeiras. This is a very pleasant beachside hostel, 12 km west of central Lisbon. Take the train from Cais do Sodré station to Oeiras, a trip of 20 to 25 minutes. The hostel is open 24 hours a day. Reservations are essential.

Hotels & Guesthouses The tourist office in Restauradores will make enquiries but not reservations for accommodation in Lisbon. During the high season advance bookings are imperative for accommodation near the centre.

Baixa & Chiado If you don't mind climbing four flights of stairs, the central *Pensão Galicia* (☎ 342 8430) at Rua do Crucifixo 50 and *Pensão Moderna* (☎ 346 0818) at Rua dos Correeiros 205 are good value, with doubles for 4500$00.

Pensão Estrela do Chiado (☎ 342 6110) at Rua Garrett 29, involves similar exercise and has doubles from 4000$00. Close to Rossio

station, *Residencial Estrela do Mondego* (☎ 346 7109) at Calçada do Carmo 25, has bigger rooms for the same price. Also up behind Rossio station at Calçada do Duque 53, *Pensão Duque* (☎ 346 3444) has plain, clean doubles with shared bathroom for about 3500$00.

Restauradores & Rato At Rua Jardim do Regedor 24, *Residencial Campos* (☎ 346 2864) is a friendly place surrounded by restaurants. Doubles start at 4000$00. At Rua da Glória 21, the *Pensão Monumental* (☎ 346 9807) has functional doubles from 6000$00, but street noise can be annoying. *Hotel Suiço-Atlântico* (☎ 346 1713), Rua da Glória 3, has well-maintained rooms and is close to the tourist office. Doubles start at around 9500$00.

Casa de São Mamede (☎ 396 3166), Rua Escola Politécnica 159, is a stylish hotel in an elegant old house with doubles from 10,000$00. With similar rates is the well-run *Hotel Jorge V* (☎ 356 2525), just off Avenida da Liberdade at Rua Mouzinho da Silveira 3.

Bairro Alto At Rua do Teixeira 37, close to the Elevador da Glória, the pleasant *Pensão Globo* (☎ 346 2279) has doubles without shower for as little as 3500$00. Nearby, the popular *Pensão Londres* (☎ 346 2203) at Rua Dom Pedro V 53 has several floors of spacious rooms, the upper ones with great city views. Doubles start at 5300$00.

Saldanha The bright and pleasant *Residencial Lisbonense* (☎ 354 4628), at Rua Pinheiro Chagas 1, has doubles from 7000$00.

Castelo de São Jorge Below the castle at Costa do Castelo 74, *Pensão Ninho das Aguias* (☎ 886 7008) offers amazing views after a steep climb. Reservations are essential. Doubles start at around 6500$00.

Places to Eat
Most of the city's good restaurants and cafés are in the Baixa and Bairro Alto districts. Eateries in the streets off Praça dos Restauradores tend to be poorer value or lower quality.

Baixa One of several similar bargain restaurants along Rua dos Coreeiros is *Lagosta*

PORTUGAL

Central Lisbon

0   200   400 m

RIO   TEJO

To Cacilhas

To Cacilhas,
Montijo & Seixal

To Barreiro
Train Station

Rua Alexandre Herculano

Rua Rosa Araújo

Rua Barata Salgueiro

Rua – do – Salitre

Jardim
Botânico
(Botanical
Gardens)

Rua da Escola Politécnica

Rua de
São Marçal

Rua Dom Pedro V

Rua do Século

Bairro
Alto

Calçada do Combro

Cais do Sodré

Rua de São Paulo

Avenida da Liberdade

Avenida da Liberdade

Rua Rodrigues Sampaio

Rua Gomes Freire

Avenida Almirante Reis

Rua Palmira

Intendente

Rua Andrade

Largo do
Intendente
Pina Manique

Campo dos
Mártires da
Pátria

Rua de São José

Rua das Portas de Santo Antão

Rua da Palma

Socorro

Largo
Martim
Moniz

Avenida

da – Alegria

Rua de Santa Marta

Rua da Glória

TV da Carra

Calçada
do Duque

Restauradores

Praça Dom
Pedro IV
(Rossio)

Rossio

Praça da
Figueira

Calçada do Carmo

Rua do Carmo

Rua Garrett

Chiado

Rua Capelo

Rua Nova do Almada

Rua do Alecrim

Rua do Loreto

Rua Diário de Notícias

Rua do Norte

Rua da Madalena

Rua Augusta

Rua da Prata

Rua dos Douradores

Rua dos Fanqueiros

Rua de São Mamede

Rua dos Correeiros

Rua Aurea

Rua da Vitória

Rua de Santa Justa

Rua da Conceição

Rua de São Nicolau

Rua do Crucifixo

Baixa

Rua São Julião

Rua do Comércio

Rua dos Bacalhoeiros

Rua da Alfândega

Castelo

Costa do Castelo

Alfama

Largo das
Portas do Sol

Rua de São Mamede

Rua das Remédios

R das Remédios

Av Vinte e Quatro de Julho

Av Vinte e Quatro de Julho

Rua do Arsenal

Avenida Ribeira das Naus

Praça do
Comércio

PORTUGAL

PLACES TO STAY					
1	Hotel Jorge V	40	Lagosta Vermelha	34	Diário de Notícias Bookshop
11	Pensão Monumental	44	A Brasileira	35	Cota Câmbios
12	Hotel Suíço-Atlântico	50	Martinho da Arcada	39	Elevador de Santa Justa
13	Pensão Londres	53	Pastelaria & Snack Bar Brasilia	41	Museu de Artes Decorativas
17	Residencial Campos	55	Restaurante Porto de Abrigo	43	Livraria Bertrand Bookshop
23	Pensão Globo			45	Elevador da Bica
26	Pensão Duque	**OTHER**		46	Fabrica Sant'Ana
28	Residencial Estrela do Mondego	2	Spanish Embassy	47	Tourist Police Office
31	Pensão Ninho das Aguias	3	Canadian Embassy	49	24-hour Exchange Machine
33	Pensão Moderna	4	Cerâmica Viúva Lamego	51	Resende, Caima and Frota Azul Bus Terminal
42	Pensão Estrela do Chiado	5	Hot Clube de Portugal		
48	Pensão Galicia	6	British Council	52	Central Post Office
		7	Texas Lavandaria	54	Ó Gilíns Irish Pub
PLACES TO EAT		8	Elevador de Lavra	56	Mercado da Ribeira
9	Restaurante O Brunhal	10	Banco Borges e Irmão	57	Cais do Sodré Train Station
16	Restaurante Pinóquio	14	Main Tourist Office	58	Cais do Sodré Ferry Terminal
22	Cafetaria Brasil	15	Post & Telephone Office	59	Cais de Alfândega Ferry Terminal
24	Restaurante O Tacão Pequeno	18	Lavandaria Sous'ana	60	Terréiro do Paço Ferry Terminal
27	Restaurante O Sol	19	24-hour Exchange Machine		
29	Nicola	20	Rossio Train Station		
36	Cervejaria da Trindade	21	Elevador da Glória		
37	Adega Machado (Casa de Fado)	25	Telephone Office		
38	Adega do Ribatejo (Casa de Fado)	30	Carris Kiosk		
		32	Castelo de São Jorge		

Vermelha (☎ 342 4832), a typically casual casa de pasto at No 155. *Restaurante Pinóquio* (☎ 346 5106), Praça dos Restauradores 79, is more expensive, though the seafood is good. *Restaurante O Sol* (☎ 347 1944), Calçada do Duque 23, is an inexpensive vegetarian option with set meals for under 1000$00.

For a coffee or a meal, *Nicola*, at Rossio 24, is the celebrated grande dame of Lisbon's turn-of-the-century cafés. It is closed on Sunday. *Martinho da Arcada* café (☎ 887 9259), Praça do Comércio 3, was once a haunt of the literary set, including Fernando Pessoa, but renovation has cost it some of that lustre. It closes at 9 pm; both the café and the adjacent, overpriced restaurant are closed on Sunday.

Bairro Alto The cavernous *Cervejaria da Trindade* (☎ 342 3506), Rua Nova da Trindade 20-C, is a converted convent decorated with azulejos. Main dishes start at around 1200$00. It stays open until 1 am.

Restaurante O Brunhal (☎ 347 8634), Rua

da Glória 27, close to the tourist office, is an unpretentious place with simple cheap food.

Restaurante Porto de Abrigo (☎ 346 0873) is at Rua dos Remolares 18, close to Cais do Sodré station. The seafood dishes are recommended: figure on 800$00 to 1700$00 a dish; it's closed on Sunday. One of several cheapies in the same area, the *Pastelaria & Snack Bar Brasilia* (☎ 346 6902) at Praça Duque da Terceira 10, has good-value daily specials.

Restaurante O Tacão Pequeno (☎ 347 2848) at Travessa da Carra 3-A, is a cosy dive with some unusual décor. Nearby, the bright, plain *Cafetaria Brasil* at Rua de São Pedro de Alcântara 51 has pratos do dia (dishes of the day) from 600$00.

A Brasileira (☎ 346 9547), Rua Garrett 120, is another venerable café with strong literary traditions.

Entertainment
For current listings, pick up a copy of the free monthly *Agenda Cultural* from the tourist office, or *Público* from a newsstand.

PORTUGAL

Music In its authentic form, fado is fascinating. However, the sad truth in Lisbon is that many casas de fado (which are also restaurants) produce pale tourist imitations, often at prices which may make you feel like groaning as much as the fado singer. Even the simplest places now have a minimum charge of 1800$00 to 3000$00. In the Bairro Alto you could try *Adega Machado* (☎ 342 8713), Rua do Norte 91, or the simpler *Adega do Ribatejo* (☎ 346 8343), at Rua Diário de Notícias 23. The tourist office can suggest others.

Hot Clube de Portugal (☎ 346 7369), Praça da Alegria 39, is at the centre of a thriving Lisbon jazz scene. You can listen to live music there three or four nights a week. It's open from 10 pm to 2 am, closed on Sunday and Monday.

Homesick Dubliners craving a draft Guinness should head down to *Ó Gilíns Irish Pub* (☎ 342 1899) at Rua dos Remolares 8-10, by Cais do Sodré station. It's open daily from 11 am to 2 am and has live Irish music most Saturday nights and jazz with brunch on Sunday.

Discos boom and bust at lightning speed. Try *Benzina* (☎ 363 3959), Travessa de Teixeira Júnior 6 in the Alcântara district, or *Alcântara Mar* (☎ 363 6432), just down the road at Rua da Cozinha Económica 11, both raving from midnight until 6 or 7 am.

The African music scene (predominantly Cape Verdean) bops in numerous bars in the area around Rua de São Bento; one of the best known is *Discoteca A Lontra* at No 155.

Cinemas There are plenty of cinemas around the city. The Amoreiras shopping centre has a multiscreen cinema (☎ 383 1275) showing almost a dozen different films every night. Tickets are 700$00 (500$00 on Monday).

Spectator Sport The local football teams are Benfica and Sporting. The tourist office can advise on match dates and tickets. If you must see one, bullfights are staged at Campo Pequeno between April and October.

Things to Buy
For azulejos, try Fabrica Sant'Ana at Rua do Alecrim 95, or Cerâmica Viúva Lamego (☎ 885 2402), Largo do Intendente Pina Manique 25 (metro: Intendente). The Museu Nacional do Azulejo also has a small shop. On Tuesday and Saturday mornings, visit the Feira da Ladra, a kind of flea market in the Alfama district. Or just wander the backstreets of Baixa and Bairro Alto.

Getting There & Away
For information on international and domestic connections, see the Getting There & Away and Getting Around sections at the beginning of this chapter.

Air Lisbon's airport is 20 minutes from the centre (but 45 minutes or more in rush hour). For arrival and departure information phone ☎ 840 4500.

Bus What's left of the state-run RN service (notably Rede Expressos), plus international coaches and a few private companies such as EVA (from the Algarve), uses the main bus terminal (☎ 354 5439) at Avenida Casal Ribeiro 18, not far from Picoas and Saldanha metro stations. The private Renex company (☎ 887 4871 or 888 2829), including Resende, Caima and Frota Azul services, operates from Rua dos Bacalhoeiros, a few blocks east of Praça do Comércio.

Train Santa Apolónia station (☎ 888 4025 for train information) is the terminus for trains from north and central Portugal, and for all international services. Cais do Sodré station is used by trains heading to Cascais and Estoril. Rossio station is centrally placed and serves Sintra and Estremadura. Barreiro station lies across the river and is the terminus for services from the south of Portugal and the Algarve; connecting ferries leave frequently from the pier at Terréiro do Paço, by Praça do Comércio.

Ferry Ferries of the Transtejo line run back and forth across the Rio Tejo from Praça do Comércio to Cacilhas (90$00) every 10 minutes all day, and to Montijo (270$00) and Seixal (200$00) every hour or so. There is also a car ferry to Cacilhas from Cais do Sodré.

Getting Around
To/From the Airport Bus No 91, called the Aero-Bus, is a special service running about every 20 minutes from 7 am to 9 pm and taking

20 to 45 minutes (depending on traffic) between the airport and the city centre, including a stop right outside the tourist office. It costs 430$00/1000$00 and includes a ticket useable for one/three days on all buses, trams and funiculars. Local bus Nos 8, 44, 45 and 83 also run near the tourist office but are a nightmare in rush hour if you have baggage. A taxi will cost about 1500$00, plus an extra 300$00 if your luggage needs to go in the boot.

Bus & Tram Individual bus and tram tickets cost 150$00 or half that if purchased beforehand. Prepaid tickets are sold at kiosks with the Carris logo, most conveniently at Praça da Figueira and the Santa Justa elevator. If you plan to spend a few days in Lisbon, tourist passes valid for all trams and buses and the metro are available for four days (1550$00) or one week (2190$00).

Buses and trams run from about 5 or 6 am to 1 am, with some night services. You can get a transport map *(Planta dos Transportes Públicas da Carris)* from the tourist office and sometimes from Carris kiosks, but thanks to the city's building frenzy, route changes are so frequent the map is not always reliable.

Wheelchair users can all Carris on ☎ 363 2044 for information on their dial-a-ride service. The clattering, antediluvian trams *(eléctricos)* are an endearing component of Lisbon. Don't leave without riding tram No 28 to the old quarter from Rua da Conceiçao.

Metro The metro isn't extensive (though plenty of expansion is underway), but it's useful for short hops across the centre of town. Individual tickets cost 70$00 or it's 500$00 for a *caderneta* of 10 tickets. A day ticket costs 200$00. The metro operates from 6.30 am to 1 am. Pickpockets can be a nuisance.

Taxi Compared with the rest of Europe, Lisbon's taxis are fast, cheap and plentiful. Either flag taxis down on the street or go to a rank. Some of the taxis that haunt the airport are a bit unscrupulous, so watch your map.

Car Car-rental companies in Lisbon include Avis (☎ 356 1176), Europcar (☎ 353 5115), Kenning (☎ 354 9182) and Solcar (☎ 356 0500).

Around Lisbon

SINTRA
If you make only one side trip from Lisbon, Sintra should receive top priority. Long favoured by Portuguese royalty and English nobility (Lord Byron was dotty about it), the thick forests and unusual architecture of Sintra provide a complete change from urban Lisbon. The very efficient tourist office (☎ 923 1157), on the ground floor of the Sintra Regional Museum on Praça da República (near the Palácio Nacional), has a good map and photos of accommodation options. During weekends and the annual music festival held in July expect droves of visitors. In high season it's wise to book ahead for more up-market accommodation.

The telephone code for Sintra is ☎ 01.

Things to See
The **Palácio Nacional de Sintra**, recently repainted a shocking bright white, dominates the town with its twin kitchen chimneys. From Moorish origins, the palace has been developed into a synthesis of Manueline and Gothic architecture. Highlights include the **Magpie Room** and the **Swan Room**. It's open daily, except Wednesday, from 10 am to 1 pm and 2 to 5 pm; entry is 400$00. Ticket sales finish 30 minutes before closing time.

A steep three-km climb from the centre leads to the **Palácio da Pena**, built in 1839 in exuberant Romantic style. The grounds are ideal for botanical forays. It's open daily, except Monday, from 10 am to 1 pm and from 2 to 5 pm; entry is 400$00. The nearby ruins of **Castelo dos Mouros**, which provide a magnificent view over the town and surroundings, are open daily from 10 am to 6 pm (5 pm in winter).

Rambling and romantic, the **Monserrate Gardens** are a four-km walk from the town, past the brazenly luxurious **Palácio de Seteais** hotel. The gardens are open from 10 am to 6 pm (5 pm in winter) and entry is 200$00.

More beguiling is the **Convento dos Capuchos**, a tiny 16th-century hermitage in the forest nine km from Sintra, with cells hewn from rock and lined with cork. Walkers can

PORTUGAL

approach it from Monserrate, though the path isn't always clear; guidance is provided in the *Landscapes of Portugal* walkers' guidebook for this area (see Books & Maps earlier in this chapter).

Places to Stay

The nearest decent camping ground is *Camping Praia Grande* (☎ 929 0581), on the coast 11 km from Sintra and linked by a frequent bus service.

The *pousada de juventude* (☎ 924 1210) is at Santa Eufémia, four km from the town centre. Along with dormitory beds, it has doubles for 3300$00. Advance reservations are essential.

Casa de Hospedes Adelaide (☎ 923 0873), Rua Guilherme Gomes Fernandes 11, a 10-minute walk from the station, has comfortable doubles without bath from around 3500$00. Closer to the station, at Largo Afonso d'Albuquerque 25, *Pensão Nova Sintra* (☎ 923 0220) is a cosy old house with doubles at 5000$00 (without private bath) and a pleasant outdoor patio. Across the railway, at Rua João de Deus 70, *Piela's* (☎ 924 1691) has immaculate doubles at 6500$00. For 24,000$00 you can have an exquisite double in the *Quinta da Capela* (☎ 929 0170), an 18th-century manor house in a wooded valley below Monserrate Gardens.

Places to Eat

Tulhas (☎ 923 2378), close to the tourist office at Rua Gil Vicente 4-6, is an excellent restaurant; it's closed on Wednesday. The simple *A Tasca do Manel* (☎ 923 0215) by the town hall at Largo Dr Vergilio Horta 5, serves all the usual favourite fare for around 800$00 a dish, while the nearby *Topico Bar & Restaurant* (☎ 923 4825) at Rua Dr Alfredo Costa 8, has live music on Wednesday, Friday and Saturday. For something special, try *Orixás* (☎ 924 1672), an expensive Brazilian restaurant-cum-art gallery at Avenida Adriano Júlio Coelho 7. *Fonte da Pipa* (☎ 923 4437), Rua Fonte da Pipa 11-13, is a cosy bar with snacks and inexpensive drinks.

Getting There & Away

The bus and train stations are together in the north of the town on Avenida Dr Miguel Bombarda, two km from the Palácio Nacional. Trains from Lisbon's Rossio station take about 50 minutes (180$00). Buses run from Sintra to Estoril, Cascais and Mafra.

Getting Around

Taxis are a convenient though expensive way to get around: a three-hour sightseeing trip is 6000$00 plus 20% at weekends and holidays (the tourist office has a full list of prices). Horse-drawn carriages are a romantic alternative: figure on 6000$00 to Monserrate and back. Horse riding is available at Centro Hipico Penha Longa Country Club (☎ 924 9033) for around 3500$00 an hour.

ESTORIL

Estoril is a beach resort with Europe's biggest casino and a genteel ambience favoured by the rich and famous. The tourist office (☎ 466 3813) is on Arcadas do Parque. Attractions are limited to the casino, and strolls in the public gardens. Estoril's telephone code is ☎ 01.

Accommodation and restaurants are both better value in Cascais, just a couple of km further west along the coastline, but if you feel like lingering to gamble your escudos away, the pick of the pensões is *Pensão Smart* on Rua José Viana 3 (☎ 468 2164). Doubles with breakfast start at 6500$00. Cheaper digs are at nearby *Casa de Hóspedes Paula Castro* (☎ 01-468 0699), Rua da Escola 4, which has basic doubles from 5000$00. From Cais do Sodré station in Lisbon it's a half-hour trundle by train to Estoril (180$00).

CASCAIS

Cascais is similar to Estoril, but has become the 'in' beach resort. Cascais tourist office (☎ 486 8204), Rua Visconde de Luz 14, has accommodation lists and bus timetables.

The telephone code for Cascais is ☎ 01.

Things to See & Do

Two km west of the town centre is the **Boca do Inferno** (literally, 'mouth of hell'), where the sea roars into the coast. **Cabo da Roca**, the westernmost point of Europe, is a spectacular and often very windy spot 16 km from Cascais and Sintra (served by buses from both towns) – pop into the tiny windswept post office for a commemorative certificate. Those who like their beaches long and wild will appreciate **Guincho**, three km from Cascais, the venue for the 1991 World Surfing Championships.

Bicycles and motorcycles can be rented from Gesrent at Centro Commercial Cisne (☎ 486 4566), Avenida Marginal Bloco 3 (near the post office).

Places to Stay
Camping Orbitur do Guincho (☎ 487 1014), seven km from Cascais near Guincho beach, is useful if you have your own transport.

Getting There & Away
From Cais do Sodré station in Lisbon it's a 25-minute train trip (180$00) to Cascais.

QUELUZ
The 17th-century **Palácio Nacional de Queluz**, with later additions inspired by Versailles, has sumptuous rooms and fine gardens. The throne room and the gargantuan kitchen (now a restaurant) are highlights. It's open Wednesday to Monday from 10 am to 1 pm and 2 to 5 pm; entry is 400$00.

Frequent trains from Rossio station make the 20-minute trip (150$00) to Queluz.

MAFRA
The only attraction here is the colossal **Palácio Nacional de Mafra**, which tops the league for size on the Iberian Peninsula. Its size (an estimated 4500 doors!) and austerity make the tour rather depressing. It's open from 10 am to 1 pm and from 2 to 5 pm, except Tuesday and public holidays; admission is 300$00 (free on Sunday mornings).

Buses from Lisbon take 1½ hours (530$00), or from Sintra it's a 45-minute bus ride (370$00).

The Algarve

Loud, boisterous and full of foreigners, the Algarve is about as far from quintessential Portugal as one can get. While sun and sand are the major drawcards, there are some other attractions. West of Lagos are wild and all-but-deserted beaches. The coast east of Faro is dotted with enticing, colourful fishing villages. And for those who've filled up on seascapes, there are the forested slopes of Monchique, the

fortified village of Silves and the past glory of Estói Palace tucked away in the mountains.

Orientation
The southernmost slice of Portugal, the Algarve divides neatly into five regions: the Costa Vicentina facing west into the teeth of Atlantic gales, the windward coast (Sotavento) from Sagres to Lagos, the central coast from Lagos to Faro, the leeward coast (Barlavento) from Faro to Vila Real de Santo António, and the interior.

The largest town, and district capital, is Faro. The easternmost town, Vila Real de Santo António, is a border crossing to Ayamonte, Spain – linked to it by a car ferry and a highway bridge across the mouth of Rio Guadiana. The beach, golf, disco and nightclub scenes are focused on the central Algarve, particularly Albufeira and Portimão. West of Lagos, the shore grows increasingly steep and rocky.

Information
Leaflets describing every Algarve community from tiny Alcoutim to booming Albufeira are available from the district tourist office in Faro. A host of English-language newspapers like the *Algarve News*, *APN* and *Algarve Resident*, which are aimed primarily at expatriates, provide entertainment listings and information on attractions and coming events. Walkers should pick up *Algarve: Guide to Walks* (250$00) from the Faro tourist office.

Dangers & Annoyances Take extra precautions against theft on the Algarve. Paranoia is unwarranted, but don't leave anything of value in your vehicle or unattended on the beach.

Swimmers should beware of dangerous currents, especially on the west coast. Beaches are marked by coloured flags: red means the beach is closed to bathing, yellow means swimming is prohibited but wading is fine, green means anything goes.

Things to Buy
Few souvenirs are actually made in the Algarve, but Moorish-influenced ceramics and local woollens (cardigans and fishing pullovers) are good value. You may want to try Algarviana, a local amaretto (bitter almond liqueur), or the salubrious bottled waters of Monchique, on sale everywhere.

To Sines, Odemira & Lisbon — To Ourique — To Castro Verde — To Mértola & Beja — SPAIN

ATLANTIC OCEAN

Algarve

0   10   20 km

Getting There & Away

The major airport at Faro serves both domestic and international flights. For details see the introductory Getting There & Away section of this chapter.

Several companies, including Rede Expressos and EVA, operate regular and express services to all the major towns on the Algarve. It's about 5½ hours from Lisbon to Faro. Services also run between Lagos and Seville (Spain) via major Algarve towns (5½ hours).

From Barreiro in Lisbon there are several trains daily to Lagos and Faro (four to five hours, half an hour less by intercidade train).

For motorists arriving from Ayamonte in Spain, a bridge completed in 1991 four km north of Vila Real de Santo António now bypasses the old ferry connection. The most direct route from Lisbon to Faro takes about five hours.

Getting Around

There's an efficient network of bus services between the major towns of the Algarve. Via Infante, the superhighway planned to run the length of the coast to Spain, is only partially completed. Bicycles, scooters and motorcycles can be rented all over; see individual town listings.

FARO

The capital of the Algarve, Faro is also the main transport hub and a thriving commercial centre, but is otherwise of little interest. The tourism office (☎ 803604), Rua da Misericórdia, can provide a wide range of tourist literature.

The telephone code for Faro is ☎ 089.

Things to See & Do

The waterfront around Praça de Dom Francisco Gomes has pleasant gardens and cafés. Faro's beach, **Praia de Faro**, is six km southwest of the city on Ilha de Faro. Take bus No 16 from in front of the tourist office; another option between May and September is a ferry from Arco da Porta Nova, close to Faro's port.

At Estói, 12 km north of Faro, the wonderful crumbling wreck of **Estói Palace** is a surreal garden of statues, balustrades and azulejos – highly recommended. The bus from Faro to São Brás de Alportel goes via Estói.

Places to Stay & Eat

There are some camping facilities at Faro beach. Conveniently close to the port and the train station is the *Residencial Avenida* (☎ 823347) at Avenida da República 150. A double costs 7000$00/5000$00 with/without bath. Singles/doubles at the nearby *Residencial Madalena* (☎ 805806), Rua Conselheiro Bivar 109, are about 5000$00/ 7000$00. Slightly cheaper is the good *Residencial Alameda* (☎ 801962), Rua José de Matos 31.

The *Restaurante Mariqueira Ramirez*, Rua Filipe Alistão 19, serves excellent seafood. *A Garrafeira do Vilaça* (☎ 802150) at Rua São Pedro 33 is popular with students; next door at No 31 is the pricier *Restaurante Queda d'Água*. Worth lingering at is *Café Aliança*, a turn-of-the-century gem on Rua Dom Francisco Gomes.

Getting There & Away

The airport is six km from the city centre. Bus No 18 runs there until around 8 pm. A taxi into town costs about 1100$00.

The bus station is in the centre, close to the harbour. There are at least 10 express buses to Lisbon (1900$00) daily, including four non-stops, and frequent buses to other coastal towns.

The train station is just a few minutes on foot west of the bus station. Around six trains go to Lisbon daily (1800$00), and a similar number go to Albufeira and Portimão.

TAVIRA

Tavira is one of the Algarve's oldest and most beautiful towns. Graceful bridges cross Rio Gilão which divides the town. The excellent tourist office (☎ 22511) is at Rua da Galeria 9. Bicycles and motorcycles can be rented from Loris rent, Rua Damiao Augusto de Brito, 4 (☎ 325203, mobile ☎ 0931-274766).

The telephone code for Tavira is ☎ 081.

Things to See & Do

In the old part of town is the **Igreja da Misericórdia**, with a striking Renaissance doorway. From there, it's a short climb to the **castle** dominating the town.

Two km from Tavira is **Ilha da Tavira**, an attractive island beach connected to the mainland by ferry. Walk two km beside the river to reach the ferry terminal at Quatro Águas or take the bus from the bus station.

For a look at the way the Algarve used to be, take a bus to **Cacela Velha**, an unspoilt hamlet eight km from Tavira. Another worthwhile day trip is to the church and colourful quay at **Olhão**, 22 km west of Tavira. Drop in for a delicious and fresh seafood lunch at *Papy's*, opposite the park.

Places to Stay & Eat

There's a *camping ground* on Ilha da Tavira, but the ferry stops running at 11 pm (usually 1 am from July to September). *Pensão Residencial Lagoas* (☎ 22252), at Rua Almirante Cândido dos Reis 24, has singles/doubles from 2500$00/4000$00 without bath. *Princesa do Gilão* (☎ 325171), Rua Borda d'Água de Aguiar 10, beside the river, charges 5000$00/ 6000$00 a single/double, but street-side rooms can be noisy. In the heart of town, *Pensão Residencial Castelo* (☎ 23942) at Rua da Liberdade 4, has rooms for 5000$00/5500$00 with bath.

Restaurante O Pátio (☎ 23008) at Rua António Cabreira 30 serves excellent Algarve specialties such as cataplana (shellfish cooked in a sealed wok).

Getting There & Away

Running between Faro and Tavora there are 15 trains a day (taking between 40 and 60 minutes) as well as seven buses a day (four at weekends), taking an hour.

LAGOS

Lagos is a major tourist resort with some of the finest beaches on the Algarve. The breathtakingly unhelpful tourist office (☎ 763031) is on Largo Marquês de Pombal in the centre of town.

The telephone code for Lagos is ☎ 082.

Things to See & Do

In the old part of town, the **municipal museum** houses an odd assortment of ecclesiastical treasures, handicrafts and preserved animal fetuses. The adjacent **Chapel of Santo António** contains some extraordinarily intricate baroque woodwork.

The beach scene includes **Meia Praia**, a vast strip of sand to the east; and to the west **Praia da Luz** and the more secluded **Praia do Pinhão**.

Espadarte do Sul (☎ 761820) operates **boat trips** from Docapesca harbour, including snorkelling and game fishing. Bom Dia (☎ 764670) has classier outings on a traditional schooner. Local fishermen trawl for customers along the seaside promenade and offer motorboat jaunts to the nearby grottoes.

Landlubbers can go **horse riding** at Tiffany's equestrian centre (☎ 69395), about 10 km west on the N125 road; they'll even come and get you in Lagos.

Places to Stay & Eat

Two nearby camping grounds are *Trindade* (☎ 763893), 200 metres south of the town walls, and *Imulagos* (☎ 760031), with a shuttle bus from the waterfront road. The *pousada de juventude* (☎ 761970) is at Rua Lançarote de Freitas 50. *Residencial Marazul* (☎ 769749), Rua 25 de Abril 13, has smart singles/doubles from 6500$00/8000$00. Private rooms are plentiful and usually cost around 5000$00 a double.

For standard food with fado accompaniment, try *Restaurante A Muralha* (☎ 763659), Rua da Atalaia 15. *O Cantinho Algarvio* (☎ 761289), at Rua Afonso d'Almeida 17, offers good Algarve specialities. The *Barroca Jazz Bar & Restaurant* (☎ 767162), at the south end of Rua da Barroca, is open from 7 pm to 2 am, with live jazz most nights in summer.

Getting There & Away

Both bus and train services depart up to six times daily to Lisbon.

Getting Around

You can rent bicycles and mopeds from Safari Moto (☎ 764314) at Rua Lucinda Santos 4 (near the main bus terminal), or from Motoride (☎ 761720) at Rua José Afonso 23. Figure on about 1300$00 a day for a mountain bike or 2000$00 for a moped.

MONCHIQUE

This quiet highland town in the forested Serra de Monchique offers an alternative to the discos and lazy beach life on the coast.

The telephone code for Monchique is ☎ 082.

Things to See & Do

In Monchique itself, the **Igreja Matriz** has an amazing Manueline portal – about the closest you'll get to seeing stone tied in knots! Follow the brown signs which lead pedestrians up above the bus station round the old town's narrow streets.

Six km south is the drowsy hot-spring community of **Caldas de Monchique**. Have a soak in the spa or try the bottled water.

The best excursion from Monchique is to drive or hike eight km through thick forest to the 'rooftop' of the Algarve at **Fóia**. If you can ignore the forests of radio masts, the views are terrific.

Places to Stay & Eat

The *Residencial Miradouro* (☎ 92163), Rua dos Combatentes do Ultramar, has singles/doubles for 3500$00/4500$00. *Restaurante A Charrete* (☎ 92142), Rua Samora Gil, is friendly and unpretentious. Winning rave reviews from travellers (who have scribbled recommendations on the walls) is the cosy *Restaurante Central*, Rua da Igreja 5. *Barle-fante* (☎ 92774), at Travessa da Guerreira, is a popular bar which stays open until 1 am.

Getting There & Away

Over a dozen daily buses run between Lagos and Portimão, where eight services daily run to Monchique.

SILVES

Silves was once the Moorish capital of the Algarve and rivalled Lisbon in its influence. Times are quieter now, but the town's huge castle is a reminder of past grandeur and well worth a visit.

The switched-on tourist office (☎ 442255), Rua 25 de Abril, can also help with accommodation.

The telephone code for Silves is ☎ 082.

Places to Stay & Eat

The *Residencial Sousa* (☎ 442502), Rua Samoura Barros 17, has singles/doubles for 3500$00/4000$00. The eye-catching *Residencial Ponte Romana* (☎ 443275) beside the old bridge has rooms for around 5000$00/6000$00.

Restaurante Rui (☎ 442682), Rua C Vitarinho 23, is the best (and most expensive) fish restaurant in town; it serves a memorable arroz de marisco (shellfish rice). For cheaper meals, head for the riverfront restaurants opposite the bus stop.

Getting There & Away

Silves train station is two km from town; buses meet Faro trains seven times daily (five times daily at weekends). Another bus service connects Silves with Portimão via Lagoa.

SAGRES

Sagres is a small fishing port perched on dramatic, windswept cliffs at the south-western extremity of Portugal.

The telephone code for Sagres is ☎ 082.

Things to See & Do

In the **fort**, on a wide windy promontory, Henry the Navigator established his school of navigation and primed the explorers who later founded the Portuguese empire.

There are several beaches close to Sagres. A particularly pleasant one is at the fishing village of **Salema**, 17 km east.

No visit to Sagres would be complete without a trip to precipitous **Cabo de São Vicente** (Cape St Vincent), six km from Sagres. A solitary lighthouse stands on this barren cape which proclaims itself the south-westernmost point of Europe.

Places to Stay & Eat

The well-maintained *Camping Sagres* (☎ 64351) is two km from town, off the Lisbon road. Scooters are available for hire here. Some locals in Sagres rent out rooms for around 3500$00 a double. Cheap, filling meals can be had at the *Restaurante A Sagres* (☎ 64171) at the roundabout as you enter the village, and the *Café Atlântico* (☎ 64236) on the main street near the turn-off to the elegant *Pousada do Infante* (☎ 64222).

Getting There & Away

There are about a dozen buses daily between Sagres and Lagos, fewer on Sundays and holidays; at least three connect Sagres to Faro.

Central Portugal

Central Portugal, good for weeks of desultory rambling, deserves more attention than it receives. From the beaches of the Costa de Prata to the lofty Serra da Estrela and the sprawling Alentejo plains dotted with curious megaliths, it is a landscape of extremes.

Some of Portugal's finest wines come from the Dão region, while further south, the hills and plains are studded with the country's equally famous cork oaks. To literally top it off, the centre is graced with scores of fortresses and walled cities where you can wander along ancient cobbled streets, breathe clean air, and contemplate the awe-inspiring expanses below.

ÉVORA

One of the architectural gems of Portugal, the walled town of Évora is the capital of Alentejo province – a vast district with surprisingly varied landscapes of olive groves, vineyards and wheat fields, and in spring brilliant wild flowers. Évora's charm lies in the narrow one-way streets (mind those wing mirrors!) of the remarkably well preserved inner town.

Orientation & Information

The focal point of Évora is Praça do Giraldo. From here you can wander through backstreets until you meet the city walls. Poor maps with some walking routes are available from the tourist office (☎ 22671), Praça do Giraldo 73, while the good *Planta de Évora* map, and a few books in English, can be found at Nazareth bookshop, Praça do Giraldo 46.

Outside the tourist office there's an automatic exchange machine which accepts a wide range of currencies. The post office is on Rua de Olivença. The hospital (☎ 22132) is on Rua do Valasco.

The telephone code for Évora is ☎ 066.

Things to See

On Largo do Marquês de Marialva is the **Sé**, Évora's cathedral. It has cloisters and a museum of ecclesiastical treasures, both closed Monday. Admission is 300$00.

Next door, the **Museu de Évora**, features Roman and Manueline sculptures, and also paintings by 16th-century Portuguese artists. Admission is 250$00. Opposite the museum is the Roman-era **Temple of Diana**, subject of Évora's top-selling postcard.

The **Igreja de São Francisco**, a few blocks south of Praça do Giraldo, includes the ghoulish Capela dos Ossos (Chapel of Bones),

Évora

To Estremoz
To Arraiolos
Circunvalação
University
To Lisbon
To Orbitur Camping
Jardim Público
Praça de Touros (Bullring)
To Train Station 700 m
To Beja
Praça da República
Quartel de Dragões

0   75   150 m

Rua Cândido dos Reis
Rua de Aviz
Rua de Caia
Rua da Mouraria
Rua do Menino Jesus
Rua João de Deus
R Nova
Rua 5 de Outubro
R Conde de Serra
Rua de Machede
Rua Mendo Estevens
Rua Serpa Pinto
Rua da Moeda
Rua dos Mercadores
Rua do Raimundo
Rua Miguel Bombarda
Rua da República
Rua do Valasco
Praça do Giraldo
Praça 1 de Maio

PLACES TO STAY
12 Pensão Policarpo
15 Residencial Riviera
17 Pensão Portalegre
19 Residencial Solar Monfalim

PLACES TO EAT
4 Restaurante-Bar
6 Restaurante Martinho Molhóbico
9 Restaurante O Garfo
14 Dom João Cafetaria
20 Gelataria Zoka
21 Café Restaurant O Cruz

OTHER
1 Club Dezasseis
2 Diplomata Pub
3 Pub O Trovador
5 Évora Rent-a-Bike
7 Post Office & Telecom
8 Temple of Diana
10 TurAventur
11 Museu de Évora
13 Sé (Cathedral)
16 Nazareth Bookshop
18 Tourist Office
22 Hospital
23 Igreja de São Francisco
24 Bus Terminal

constructed with the bones and skulls of several thousand people.

Places to Stay

Accommodation gets very tight in Évora, which is popular with Spanish tourists. The tourist office can help, but in summer you should definitely book ahead.

Camping *Orbitur* (☎ 25190) is about two km south of the town; take a bus towards Alcaçovas or a taxi.

Guesthouses The *Residencial Solar Monfalim* (☎ 22031), Largo da Misericórdia 1, is a mini-palace with fading singles/doubles from 10,000$00/12,000$00. Doubles at the *Pensão Policarpo* (☎ 22424), Rua da Freiria de Baixo 16, another historical charmer, are 8500$00/6500$00 with/without bath. In the backstreets at Travessa do Barão 18 is the run-down *Pensão Portalegre* (☎ 22326), with quiet rooms at 2000$00/3000$00. The *Residencial Riviera* (☎ 23304), Rua 5 de Outubro 49, is like a quality hotel and is good value with doubles for 9000$00.

Places to Eat

Restaurante O Garfo (☎ 29256), Rua de Santa Catarina 13, provides healthy servings of feijoada ha alentejana (lamb and bean stew) and other lamb dishes at reasonable prices in traditional surroundings. *Restaurante Martinho* (☎ 23057), Largo Luis de Camões 24-25, is one of many places specialising in borrego (lamb) dishes. The friendly *Café Restaurant O Cruz* (☎ 744779), at Praça 1 de Maio 20, dishes out good bacalhau and tasty carne com ameijoas (meat with clams). Another good-value place is the *Restaurante-Bar Molhóbico* (☎ 744343) at Rua de Aviz 91, offering meat dishes and half a dozen versions of bacalhau until 1.30 am. The town's most popular ice-cream parlour is *Gelataria Zoka* at Largo de São Vicente 14 (west end of Rua Miguel Bombarda).

Entertainment

Among popular student hang-outs are a cluster of bars north-west of the centre – *Club Dezasseis* (☎ 26559) at Rua do Escrivão da Cámara 16; the *Diplomata Pub* (☎ 25675), with frequent live music, at Rua do Apóstolo 4; and the *Pub O Trovador* (☎ 27370) at Rua da Mostardeira 4. Another student focal point that stays open late is *Dom João Cafetaria* (☎ 20493), Rua Vasco da Gama 10.

The Feira de São João is Évora's big bash, held from approximately 22 June to 2 July and renowned as one of Alentejo's biggest country fairs.

Getting There & Away

Bus There are at least five buses a day to Lisbon (3¾ hours) and to Estremoz, and at least three to Faro; all buses depart from the terminal (☎ 22121) on Rua da República.

Train There are several express trains to Lisbon (three hours) daily, plus slower services. There are also trains to the Algarve (tedious and indirect), Coimbra (changes required) and regional chug-a-lug services to Beja.

Getting Around

Évora Rent-a-Bike (☎ 761453), on Praça Joaquim António de Aguiar, has mountain bikes for about 1500$00 a day. TurAventur (☎ & fax 743134) at Rua João de Deus 21, can organise everything from walking and biking tours to drive-yourself jeep safaris.

MONSARAZ

Monsaraz, a magical walled town perched high above the plain, is well worth the effort spent getting there for its eerie medieval atmosphere, clear light and magnificent views. It's small and easily covered on foot in a couple of hours. Of architectural interest are the **Misericórdia** hospital and the **Museu de Arte Sacra**, probably a former tribunal which houses a rare 15th-century fresco of the allegory of justice. Clamber onto the castle's parapets for the best views.

Places to Stay & Eat

The tourist office (☎ 066-55136) on the main square can help with accommodation, including private rooms, Turihab places, and a couple of posh establishments just outside town. There are three fairly expensive restaurants and a tiny grocery store near the main gate. Eat before 8 pm, as the town goes to bed early.

Getting There & Away

With infrequent direct buses from Évora (only one or two a day), it's best to stay overnight in Monsaraz. There are also a few buses daily from Reguengos de Monsaraz (17 km west), which has more regular connections with Évora and several places to stay overnight.

ESTREMOZ

The Estremoz region is dominated by huge mounds of marble extracted from its quarries. The town's architectural appeal lies in its elegant, gently deteriorating buildings, which are liberally embellished with marble, of course.

Information

The welcoming tourist office (☎ 332071/2/3), in a kiosk on the south-western corner of the main square (known as the Rossio), has maps and accommodation lists.

The telephone code for Estremoz is ☎ 068.

Things to See & Do

The upper section of Estremoz is crowned by the **Torre de Menagem**. At the foot of the castle is a former palace, converted into a pousada. The focus of the lower section is the Rossio, and two interesting sights nearby are the **Igreja de São Francisco** and the **Misericórdia** hospital.

There's a small food and pottery **market** every Saturday in the Rossio. The clothes and shoes section is on the eastern outskirts of town. One of Portugal's most charming museums is the **Museu Rural** at Rossio 62 and full of handmade miniatures. It's open daily, except Monday, from 10 am to 1 pm and 3 to 5.30 pm; entry is 100$00.

Vila Viçosa, 17 km from Estremoz, is an easy bus trip. The major attraction is the **Palácio Ducal** – the ancestral home of the dukes of Bragança – with its horde of carpets, furniture and artworks. It's open daily, except Monday and public holidays, from 9.30 am to 1 pm and 2 to 6 pm (last tour at 5 pm). Admission (with a mandatory guided tour, usually in Portuguese only) costs 1000$00 which includes the fee for the armoury museum. The coach museum costs another 250$00.

Places to Stay & Eat
Spacious singles/doubles at the *Pensão-Restaurante Mateus* (☎ 22226), Rua Almeida 41, are good value at 2500$00/4500$00. Prices include breakfast in the restaurant which is also good for other meals.

Getting There & Away
About 12 buses daily (including three expressos) run from Estremoz to Évora, and six buses run to Portalegre daily, with less frequent connections to and from Lisbon.

CASTELO DE VIDE & MARVÃO
From Portalegre (near the Spanish border, north-east of Lisbon) it's a short hop to **Castelo de Vide**, noted for its mineral water and picturesque houses clustered around a castle. Highlights are the **Judiaria** (Old Jewish Quarter) in the well-preserved network of medieval backstreets, and the view from the castle.

Try to spend at least one night in **Marvão**, a magnificent medieval walled village tucked into a mountaintop 12 km from Castelo de Vide. The grand views from its castle encompass large chunks of Spain and Portugal.

Information
The tourist offices at Castelo de Vide (☎ 91361), Rua de Bartolomeu Álvares da Santa 81, and at Marvão (☎ 93104), Rua Dr Matos Magalhães, can both help with accommodation, including private rooms and Turihab places.

The telephone code for Marvão and Castelo de Vide is ☎ 045.

Getting There & Away
In summer, from Portalegre there are four or five buses daily to Castelo de Vide five times daily and one or two to Marvão. Two buses run daily from Lisbon to Castelo de Vide and Marvão. There are three direct connections daily between Castelo de Vide and Marvão. Outside the summer season you may find no buses at all on weekends and holidays.

NAZARÉ
The peaceful 17th-century fishing village of Nazaré was 'discovered' by tourism in the 1970s and dubbed Portugal's most picturesque fishing village. Today, the old fishing skills and distinctive local dress have gone overboard and in the high season the place is a tourist circus. But the beauty of the coastline and the superb seafood make it a worthwhile place to visit.

The tourist office (☎ 561194) is at the funicular end of Avenida da República. The telephone code for Nazaré is ☎ 062.

Things to See & Do
The lower part of Nazaré's beachfront has retained a core of narrow streets which now cater to the tourist trade. The upper section, O Sítio, on the cliffs overlooking the beach, is reached by a vintage funicular railway. The cliff-top view along the coast is superb.

The beaches attract huge summer crowds and pollution is an increasing problem. Beware of dangerous currents. The tourist office will tell you which beaches are safe for swimming.

Places to Stay & Eat
Many locals rent private rooms: you will probably be pounced on when you arrive at the bus station. Singles/doubles start around 3000$00/4500$00. *Camping Golfinho* (☎ 553680) is an inexpensive camping ground off the main Estrada Nacional 242 just north of town; two other sites, including an Orbitur one, are 2.5 km from Nazaré. There are dozens of pensões, but prices jump in high season.

One compelling reason to visit is the superb and abundant seafood, though the seafront restaurants are expensive. For cheaper fare in simple surroundings, try *Casa Marques* (☎ 551680) at Rua Gil Vicente 37, run by a troika of Nazarean women. The friendly *A Tasquinha* (☎ 551945) at Rua Adrião Batalha 54 does a superb carne de porco à Alentejana for under 1000$00. Another attractively priced place is *Casa O Pescador* (☎ 553326) at Rua António Carvalho Laranjo 18-A. The caldeirada (fish stew) is a tasty bargain at 900$00.

Getting There & Away

The nearest train station, six km away at Valado, is connected to Nazaré by frequent buses. There are numerous bus connections to Lisbon, Alcobaça, Óbidos and Coimbra.

ALCOBAÇA

Alcobaça's attraction is the immense **Mosteiro de Santa Maria de Alcobaça**, founded in 1178. The original Gothic style has undergone Manueline, Renaissance and baroque additions. Of interest are the tombs of Pedro I and Inês de Castro, the cloisters, the kings' room and the kitchens. It's open from 9 am to 7 pm (5 pm in winter); entry is 400$00.

The tourist office (☎ 062-42377) is opposite the monastery.

Getting There & Away

Alcobaça is an easy day trip from Nazaré. There are frequent buses to Nazaré, Batalha and Leiria. The closest train station is five km north-west at Valado dos Frades, from where there are buses to Alcobaça.

BATALHA

Batalha's single highlight is its monastery, the **Mosteiro de Santa Maria de Vitória**, a colossal Gothic masterpiece constructed between 1388 and 1533. Earthquakes and vandalism by French troops have taken their toll, but a full restoration was completed in 1965. Highlights include the Founder's Chapel (with the tomb of Henry the Navigator), the Royal Cloisters, Chapter House and the Unfinished Chapels. It's open from 9 am to 6 pm daily; entry is 400$00.

The tourist office (☎ 044-96180) is in a nearby shopping complex on Largo Paulo VI. The telephone code for Batalha is ☎ 044.

Getting There & Away

There are frequent bus connections to Alcobaça, Nazaré, Tomar and Leiria, and at least three direct buses to Lisbon daily.

ÓBIDOS

The impressive walled town of Óbidos has preserved its medieval streets and alleys almost too perfectly. It's easily seen in a day. The friendly tourist office (☎ 959231), Rua Direita, has information on Óbidos and the region.

The telephone code for Óbidos is ☎ 062.

Things to See

Climb onto the town walls and do a circuit for the views and your bearings. Then wander through the back alleys before popping into **Igreja de Santa Maria**, featuring fine azulejos, and the adjacent **museu municipal**.

Places to Stay & Eat

Accommodation in Óbidos isn't cheap but it's plentiful, with both residencials and a number of private rooms for around 4500$00 a double. Look for the signs around town. You might fancy dishing out for the romantic *Casa do Poço* (☎ 959358) in Travessa da Mouraria; its four double rooms around a courtyard are 11,500$00 each. A cheaper alternative is the *Residencial Martim de Freitas* (☎ 959185), just outside the walls on the Estrada Nacional 8, with doubles from 6000$00.

Restaurants are not cheap either. The supermarket inside the town gate would suit self-caterers. *Restaurante Alcaide* (☎ 959220) at Rua Direita has excellent main dishes from 1200$00 and you can eat on the terrace in warm weather. It's closed on Monday and during November.

Getting There & Away

There are excellent bus connections to Lisbon, Porto, Coimbra, Tomar and the surrounding region. From the train station, outside the walls at the foot of the hill, there are five services daily to Lisbon (most with a change at Cacém).

COIMBRA

Coimbra is famed for its university, dating back to the 13th century, and its traditional role as a centre of culture and art, complemented in recent times by industrial development.

The regional tourist office (☎ 23886) on Largo da Portagem has a good city map and information on cultural events. There are friendlier and more efficient municipal tourist offices (☎ 32591 or 33202) in Praça Dom Dinis by the university, and down below in Praça da República.

Coimbra's annual highlight is the Queima das Fitas (literally, 'burning of ribbons') when students celebrate the end of the academic year by burning their faculty ribbons. This boisterous week of fado and revelry begins the first Thursday in May.

The telephone code for Coimbra is ☎ 039.

Things to See

In lower Coimbra, the most interesting sight is **Mosteiro de Santa Cruz** with its ornate pulpit, medieval tombs and intricate sacristy.

In the upper town, the main attractions are the **old university** with its baroque library and Manueline chapel, and the **Machado de Castro Museum**, with a fine collection of sculpture and painting. The back alleys of the university quarter are filled with student hangouts and an exuberant atmosphere.

At **Conimbriga**, 16 km south of Coimbra, are the excavated remains of a Roman city (open from 9 am to 1 pm and 2 to 8 pm; to 6 pm in winter), including impressive mosaic floors, baths and fountains. The site museum (open from 10 am to 1 pm and 2 to 6 pm) has a variety of Roman artefacts and a good restaurant. Both are open daily except Monday. Entry costs 350$00. Buses run frequently to Condeixa, a km from the site, or you can take a direct bus (245$00) at 9.05 or 9.35 am (9.35 am only at weekends) from the AVIC terminal at Rua João de Ruão 18; it returns at 1 and 6 pm (6 pm only at weekends).

Activities

O Pioneiro do Mondego (☎ 478385) rents out kayaks at 2500$00 a day for paddling down the Rio Mondego (a free minibus whisks you upriver to Penacova at 10 am).

Horse riders can trot around Choupal Park by contacting the Coimbra Riding Centre (☎ 37695), Mata do Choupal.

Places to Stay & Eat

The *pousada de juventude* (☎ 22955), Rua Henriques Seco 12-14, is Coimbra's youth hostel; take bus No 5 from Largo de Portagem or No 5 from Coimbra A. *Residencial Antunes* (☎ 23048), Rua Castro Matoso 8, near the university, has singles/doubles from 3200$00/4800$00 (without bath) and deluxe doubles at 10,000$00. Overlooking the central Praça do Comércio, the quiet *Pensão Rivoli* (☎ 25550) has rooms for 2500$00/4500$00. One of the cheapest places in the town centre is the spartan *Hospedaria Simões* (☎ 34638), Rua Fernandes Tomás 69, where singles/doubles cost around 2000$00/3000$00.

There are numerous cheap eateries around the Praça do Comércio. *Diligência Bar* (☎ 27667), Rua Nova 30, is also a popular venue for amateur and professional fadistas. The vaulted *Café Santa Cruz*, in the Praça 8 de Maio, is an addictive place for coffee breaks. In a seedy backstreet at Beco do Forno 12, *Zé Manel* (☎ 23790) is a wacky little dive with crazy décor and huge servings. Go before 8 pm to beat the queues. The cosy *Restaurante Ticino* (☎ 35989), near the hostel at Rua Bernardo de Albuquerque 120, serves good Italian dishes from around 1200$00.

Getting There & Away

At least a dozen buses and an equal number of trains run daily to Lisbon and Porto and there are frequent express buses to Évora and Faro. Coimbra has three train stations: Coimbra Parque for Lousã; Coimbra A for Figueira da Foz; and the main Coimbra B for all other services (including international). Coimbra A and B are linked by a regular shuttle train service.

Getting Around

Mountain bikes can be rented from O Pioneiro do Mondego (☎ 478385) from 1 to 3 pm and 8 to 10 pm.

Car-rental agencies include Avis (☎ 34786), Hertz (☎ 37491) and Salitur (☎ 20594).

LUSO & BUÇACO FOREST

Walkers will appreciate the Buçaco Forest, which was chosen by monks as a retreat in the 6th century and has escaped serious harm since then. It's a few km from the spa resort of Luso, where the tourist office (☎ 939133) on Avenida Emídio Navarro has a general map of the forest and more detailed leaflets describing trails past wayside shrines and more than 700 species of trees and shrubs.

The telephone code for Luso is ☎ 031.

Places to Stay & Eat

The Luso tourist office has accommodation lists. *Pensão Central* (☎ 939254), Avenida Emídio Navarro, has bright singles/doubles from 2700$00/4500$00 and a good summer-time restaurant with patio seating.

For a touch of class, try the *Palace Hotel* (☎ 930101; fax 930509), a former royal hunting lodge in the forest and as zany and beautiful an expression of Manueline style as any in Portugal. Figure on spending at least 2500$00 per dish or 5000$00 for the restaurant's set menu. If you want to stay in this positively elegant five-star establishment, you'll pay around 25,000$00/30,000$00.

Getting There & Away

Five buses a day go to Luso and Buçaco from Coimbra and Viseu (only two on weekends). There are three trains daily from Coimbra to Luso.

SERRA DA ESTRELA

Serra da Estrela, Portugal's highest mountain range, stretches between Guarda and Castelo Branco. With steep valleys, forests and streams, it offers superb scope for hiking and is a designated parque natural. The highest peak, Torre (1993 metres), is snow-covered for much of the year.

Orientation & Information

The best sources of information are at the tourist offices in Covilhã (☎ 075-322170), Manteigas (☎ 075-981129) and Guarda (☎ 071-222251), and the park office in Manteigas (☎ 075-982382). Covilhã is an uninteresting industrial hub, but a good base for excursions; another is the hostel at Penhas da Saúde. The regional tourist administration publishes the walking guide *À Descoberta da Estrela*, with maps and narratives. It is available from the Covilhã, Manteigas and Seia tourist offices, and park offices in Gouveia, Seia and Manteigas, for 840$00 (English edition). A more detailed map for 1050$00 is also available.

Serious hikers might want to contact the Club Nacional de Montanhismo (☎ 075-323364; fax 075-313514) in Covilhã, which organises weekend walking, camping, skiing and other expeditions.

Places to Stay

The *pousada de juventude* (☎ 075-25375) at Penhas da Saúde, high in the mountains nine km from Covilhã, has full facilities for meals (theirs or do-it-yourself) and accommodation. There are buses from Covilhã on weekends in July and August only, and hitching is fairly safe and easy; the only other options are your feet or bike, or a taxi.

Getting There & Away

There are several buses a day from Coimbra to Seia, Covilhã and Guarda, as well as some from Porto and Lisbon to Covilhã and Guarda. Twice-daily intercidade trains link Coimbra to Guarda, and twice-daily interregional trains stop at Gouveia as well. Covilhã and Guarda are on the Lisbon-Paris line, with several fast trains a day and connections from Porto.

Getting Around

There are twice-daily buses (and some week-end express services) linking Guarda and Covilhã, but nothing across the park.

The North

Most visitors are surprised by Portugal's northern tier. With considerable tracts of forest, rich viticultural country, the peaks of Peneda-Gerês National Park, and a strand of undeveloped beaches, it is Portugal's new tourism horizon. The urban scene focuses on Porto with its magnificent vantage point on the Rio Douro. Within easy reach of Porto are a trio of stately historical cities: Braga, Portugal's religious centre; beautifully situated Viana do Castelo; and Guimarães, which proudly declares itself the country's birthplace.

PORTO

Porto is Portugal's second-largest city. Despite its reputation as a grimy industrial hub, it has considerable charm beyond the imbibing of port wine.

Orientation

The city is divided by the Rio Douro, which is spanned by four bridges. On the north bank is central Porto; on the south bank is Vila Nova de Gaia with its port-wine lodges.

The focus of central Porto is Avenida dos Aliados. Major shopping areas are eastward around Rua de Santa Catarina, and westward around Rua dos Clérigos. Praça da Liberdade marks the southern end of Avenida dos Aliados, close to São Bento station and its cavernous booking hall covered with superb azulejos. The picturesque Ribeira district lies below Ponte de Dom Luís I, several streets south of São Bento.

Information

Tourist Offices The municipal tourist office (☎ 312740) is at Rua Clube dos Fenianos 25, close to the town hall. It's open weekdays from 9 am to 5.30 pm (to 4 pm on Saturday). Between July and September it's open on weekdays until 7 pm and on Sunday from 10 am to 1 pm. A smaller national tourist office (☎ 317514) is found at Praça Dom João I, 43. It's open weekdays from 9 am to 7 pm and on weekends from 9 am to 3.30 pm.

Foreign Consulates There is no longer a US Consulate here. The UK Consulate (☎ 618 4789; fax 610 0438), Avenida da Boavista 3072, is open weekdays from 9.30 am to 12.30 pm and 3 to 5 pm.

Money Several banks line Avenida dos Aliados, with a currency exchange machine at No 138. Better deals are at Portocambios, Rua Rodrigues Sampaio 193, and at Intercontinental, Rua de Ramalho Ortigão 8.

Post & Communications The main post office (the place to collect poste-restante mail) is on Praça General Humberto Delgado, opposite the main tourist office; it's open weekdays from 8 am to 9 pm and weekends from 9 am to 6 pm. The main telephone office is at Praça da Liberdade 62; it's open weekdays from 8 am to midnight and on Sundays and holidays from 10 am to 1 pm and 2 pm to midnight. The telephone office in the main post office is open weekdays from 9 am to 6 pm.

The telephone code for Porto is ☎ 02.

Travel Agencies Top Tours (☎ 208 2785; fax 325367), Rua Alferes Malheiro 96, is the American Express representative. Youth travel specialist Jumbo Express Viagens (☎ 208 1561), Rua de Ceuta 47, can arrange youth and student travel, including car-rental discounts.

Laundry The Pinguim Lavandaria (☎ 609 5032), in the basement of the Brasília shopping centre, Praça Mouzinho de Albuquerque, Boavista, has laundry, dry-cleaning and self-service facilities. It's open from 10 am to 10.30 pm Monday to Saturday.

Medical Services The Santo António Hospital (☎ 200 5241 day; 200 7354 night) has some English-speaking staff.

Things to See & Do

The **Torre dos Clérigos** on Rua dos Clérigos is the highest tower in Portugal. Its 200-plus steps lead to the best panorama of the city. It's open daily, except Wednesday, from 10.30 am to noon and from 2.30 to 5 pm, for 100$00.

The formidable **Sé**, the cathedral dominating central Porto, is worth a visit for its mixture of architectural styles and ornate interior. It's open daily from 9 am to 12.30 pm and 2.30 to 6 pm. Admission to the cloisters and chapter house (closed Sunday) is 200$00.

The **Soares dos Reis National Museum**, on Rua Dom Manuel II, has finally reopened after renovation and is open daily except Monday, from 10 am to 12.30 pm and 2 to 5.30 pm. It displays masterpieces of Portuguese painting and sculpture from the 19th and 20th centuries. Admission is 350$00 (140$00 for students with youth cards) and is free on Sunday morning.

In Vila Nova de Gaia you can tour the cellars of some of the **port-wine lodges** and sample the goods. Large lodges include Porto Sandeman (☎ 370 2293), Largo Miguel Bombarda 3, and Ferreira (☎ 370 0010), Rua Carvalhosa 19.

In Porto the **Solar do Vinho do Porto** (☎ 694749) is at Rua de Entre Quintas 220. Select from a huge port list and sip it on a terrace offering excellent views across the city. It's open until 11.45 pm on weekdays and until 10.45 pm on Saturday (closed on Sunday and public holidays).

Bolhão is a fascinating market north-east of

PLACES TO STAY
9 Pensão Estoril
10 Pousada de Juventude
11 Pensão São Marino
13 Pensão Pão de Açucar
29 Pensão Mondariz
30 Pensão Aviz
37 Pensão Astória

PLACES TO EAT
16 Café Majestic
23 A Tasquinha
23 Restaurante Padeiro
24 Café Douro
40 Casa de Pasto Dura Sempre
41 Pesa Arroz

OTHER
1 Brasília Shopping Centre
 (Pinguim Lavandaria)
2 Top Tours
3 Trindade Train Station
4 Bolhão Market
5 Casa Januário
7 Main Post Office
7 Municipal Tourist Office
12 Intercontinental
12 Bus Station for REDM,
 AV Minho, João Terreira
 das Neves
14 Portocambios
15 Bus Station for Rodonorte
17 National Tourist Office
18 Jumbo Express Viagens
19 Solar do Vinho do Porto
20 Soares dos Reis National Museum
21 Santo António Hospital
25 Tram Stop No 18
26 Bus Station for Renex
27 Main Telephone Office
28 São Bento Train Station
31 Bus Station for Rede
 Expressos
32 Torre dos Clérigos
33 Casa Oriental
34 Bus Stop No 56
35 Museu dos Carros Eléctricos
 (Tram Museum)
36 Sé
38 Pinguim Café
39 Mercado Ferreira Borges
42 Aniki Bóbó
43 Capitólio Final Bar-Grill
44 Centre for Traditional
 Arts & Crafts

Porto

0   250   500 m

PORTUGAL

Avenida dos Aliados, where cheery strapping ladies offer everything from seafood to herbs and honey. It's open weekdays from 7 am to 5 pm and Saturday from 7 am to 1 pm.

Trilhos (☎ & fax 520740), Rua Dr Luis Pinto da Fonseca 137, can provide a weekend of canyoning or hydrospeed trips in the region. With advance notice, they can also organise everything from biking to potholing adventures.

Special Events

Porto is fond of festivals: the big one is the Festas de São João (St John's Festival) in June. Also worth catching is the unusual International Festival Intercéltico do Porto (Celtic Music Festival) in March and the Festival de Marionetas (Puppet Festival) in May.

Places to Stay

Camping *Camping da Prelada* (☎ 812616) is at Rua Monte dos Burgos, about five km northwest of the city centre. From Praça de Liberdade, take bus No 6. *Camping Marisol* (☎ 711 5942) is at Madalena, about 10 km south of Porto. Take bus No 57.

Hostels The central *pousada de juventude* (☎ 606 5535), Rua Rodrigues Lobo 98, has only 50 beds – reservations are essential. Take bus No 52, 20 or 3 from Praça da Liberdade.

Guesthouses *Pensão Mondariz* (☎ 200 5600), near São Bento train station in the rather seedy Rua Cimo de Vila at No 147, is cheap and cheerful; it has singles/doubles from 1500$00/3000$00. *Pensão Pão de Açucar* (☎ 200 2425; fax 310239), at Rua do Almada 262, has a pleasant terrace and singles/doubles with shower from 5500$00/7500$00. It's popular, so bookings are essential.

Rooms at the recently renovated *Pensão Aviz* (☎ 320722) at Avenida Rodrigues de Freitas 451, are 5000$00/6000$00. In the university neighbourhood, *Pensão Estoril* (☎ 200 2751; fax 208 2468) at Rua de Cedofeita 193 offers good-value doubles from 4000$00. The nearby *Pensão São Marino* (☎ 325499) at Praça Carlos Alberto 59 is prim and proper, with comfortable doubles for 6000$00.

Just outside the city walls, *Pensão Astória* (☎ 200 8175) is an unexpected gem where elegant old-fashioned rooms, many with stunning views over the Rio Douro, are 3000$00/5000$00.

Places to Eat

A Tasquinha (☎ 322145), Rua do Carmo 23 is a folksy place popular with students and families. It's closed on Sunday. Another student favourite is *Restaurant Padeiro* (☎ 200 7452), around the corner at Travessa do Carmo 28-A, with filling daily specials at 1200$00 and half-portions for around 800$00

The Ribeira district is crammed with restaurants, though most are over-priced and touristy Some of the cheapest eats are the daily special at the *Casa de Pasto Dura Sempre* (☎ 200 8488), on the backstreet Rua da Lada 106. *Pesa Arroz* (☎ 310291) on Cais da Ribeira, 41-42 is more up-market but has a congenial atmosphere.

Café Majestic at Rua de Santa Catarina 112 is an extravagantly decorated Art Nouveau relic with expensive coffees and afternoon teas. The liveliest student haunt in town, particularly at lunchtimes, is *Café Douro* at Praça de Parada Leitão 49.

Entertainment

The *Pinguim Café* (☎ 323100), Rua de Belomonte 67, is a cultural and musical meeting spot close to the Ribeira, paddling into life after 10 pm. Nearby are several lively pubs try *Aniki Bóbó* (☎ 324669) at Rua Fonte Taurina 36, or *Capitúlo Final Bar-Grill* (☎ 208 3640) at Rua Infante D'Henrique 35.

Puppet-fans will find the *Teatro de Marionetas do Porto* (☎ 208 3341) pulling strings at Rua de Belomonte 57.

Things to Buy

Port, of course, is a popular purchase. Casa Oriental, Rua dos Clérigos 111, has a good selection interspersed with dangling bacalhau (dried cod). Casa Januário, Rua do Bonjardim 352, is also a port specialist. Other good buys are shoes and gold-filigree jewellery. For handicrafts, there's the Centre for Traditional Arts & Crafts at Rua da Reboleira 37 in the Ribeira (closed Monday).

Getting There & Away

Air International and domestic flights use Porto's Pedras Rubras airport (☎ 941 3260), 20 km north-west of the city centre. Domestic connections include daily Portugália flights to/from Lisbon and Faro, and some TAP flights to/from Lisbon. Both TAP and British Airways link Porto with London.

Bus There are several places where you can catch long-distance buses. Renex (☎ 208 2398) at Rua Carmelitas 32 is the best choice for Lisbon and the Algarve, and also runs to Braga; the ticket office is open 24 hours a day. From Praça Filipa de Lencastre, REDM (☎ 200 3152) goes mainly to Braga; AV Minho (☎ 200 6121) to Viana do Castelo; and João Terreira das Neves (☎ 200 0881) to Guimarães. From a terminal at Rua Alexandre Herculano 370, Rede Expressos (☎ 200 6954) buses go all over Portugal. Rodonorte (☎ 200 5637) departs from Rua Ateneu Comércial do Porto 19 and goes mainly to Bragança and Vila Real.

Train Porto, a rail hub for northern Portugal, has three major stations. Most international connections, and all intercidade links throughout Portugal, start at Campanhã (☎ 564141), the main and largest station. Inter-regional and regional connections depart from either the very central São Bento station or from Campanhã (bus No 35 runs frequently between these two stations). Trindade station is for Póvoa de Varzim and Guimarães only.

Car & Motorcycle Driving in the city centre is a real pain, thanks to gridlocked traffic, one-way streets and scarce parking.

Getting Around

To/From the Airport Take bus No 56 from Jardim da Cordoaria or a taxi (2400$00 plus a possible baggage charge of 300$00). During peak times allow an hour from the city centre.

Bus An extensive bus system operates from Jardim da Cordoaria (also called Jardim de João Chagas) and Praça Dom João I. Individual tickets cost 160$00 or you can buy a caderneta (book of 20 tickets) for 1400$00, or a one-day (350$00), four-day (1700$00) or one-week (2200$00) Passe Turístico (Tourist Pass), from kiosks near the bus stops or opposite São Bento station.

Tram Porto's trams used to be one of the delights of the city but only one is left: the No 18, trundling from Carmo out to Foz and back to Boa Vista every quarter-hour all day (except Sunday when a No 18 bus does the route). Sentimental fans can stop en route at the **Museu dos Carros Eléctricos** (Tram Museum), Cais do Bicalho (look for the STCP building), which has dozens of restored old cars in a cavernous tram warehouse. It's open Tuesday to Saturday from 9 am to noon and 2 to 5 pm; entry is 100$00.

Taxi Taxis are good value. For a zip across town, figure on about 500$00. An additional charge is made if you cross the Ponte Dom Luís to Vila Nova de Gaia or leave the city limits.

Car Porto's car-rental agencies include Hertz (☎ 312387), Europcar (☎ 318398), Turiscar (☎ 600 8401), and AA Castanheira (☎ 606 5256).

ALONG THE DOURO

The Douro Valley is one of Portugal's scenic highlights, with some 200 km of bold, expansive panoramas from Porto to the Spanish border. In the upper reaches, port-wine vineyards wrap round every crew-cut hillside, interrupted only by the occasional bright-white port company manor house.

The river, tamed by eight dams and locks since the late 1980s, is now navigable all the way, making boat tours an ideal option. Vistadouro (☎ 938 7949) organises one or two-day cruises throughout the year. Highly recommended, too, is the train trip from Porto to Peso da Régua (about a dozen trains daily, 2½ hours). The last 50 km cling dramatically to the river bank. The further you go, the better it gets: four trains continue daily along the valley to Pocinho (4½ hours).

Bike and car travellers have an enticing choice of river-hugging roads along the south and north banks – but both are wriggly and crowded with Porto escapees at weekends. Grayline (☎ 316597), Rua Guedes de Azevedo, Edificio Silo-Auto, operates a day-long Douro Valley coach tour which includes some nearby attractions.

The detailed colour map *Rio Douro*

(1000$00), available from Porto bookshops, is a handy source of information.

VIANA DO CASTELO

This port, attractively set at the mouth of the Rio Lima, is renowned for its historic old town and its promotion of folk traditions.

The helpful tourist office (☎ 822620) on Praça da Erva has information on festivals and other tourist literature about the region. The telephone code for Viana do Castelo is ☎ 058.

During August, the town hosts the Festas de Nossa Senhora da Agonia. See the Facts for the Visitor section at the start of this chapter for more details.

Things to See & Do

The focal point of the town is the splendid Praça da República with its delicate fountain and elegant buildings, including the **Ingreja de Misericórdia**.

At the top of the steep Santa Luzia hill, four km above town, is **Ingreja de Santa Luzia**, with a grand panorama across the coast from its dome lookout. A funicular railway climbs the hill from 9 am to 7 pm (hourly in the morning, every 30 minutes in the afternoon) from behind the train station.

Places to Stay & Eat

The tourist office has extensive accommodation listings, and can book Turihab places from 6000$00 for a double. *Pensão Guerreiro* (☎ 822099), Rua Grande 14 (1st floor), has clean singles/doubles for 2000$00/4000$00 (without bath). The *Residencial Magalhães* (☎ 823293), Rua Manuel Espregueira 24, has comfortable doubles from 5000$00.

The family-run *Restaurante Minho* (☎ 823261), Rua Gago Coutinho 103-5, serves wholesome, inexpensive dishes until midnight. Folksy *Os Três Potes* (☎ 829928), Rua Beco dos Fornos 9, has seafood dishes from around 1300$00, and dancers skipping between the tables on Saturday nights in summer! For other seafood specials try *Neiva-Mar Marisqueira* (☎ 820669), Largo Infante D. Henrique 1 (at the corner of Largo de Santa Catarina), opposite the fish market.

Getting There & Away

During the week, over a dozen buses daily go to Porto including four express services (1½

hours). Ten buses daily go to Braga (one hour). Train services run north to Spain and south to Porto.

BRAGA

Crammed with churches, Braga is considered Portugal's religious capital. During Easter week huge crowds attend its Holy Week Festival.

The tourist office (☎ 22550), Avenida da Liberdade 1, can help with accommodation and maps. The telephone code for Braga is ☎ 053.

Things to See & Do

At Bom Jesus do Monte, a pilgrimage site on a hill seven km from the city, is an extraordinary stairway called **Escadaria do Bom Jesus**, with sculpted representations of the five senses, and a superb view. Buses run from Braga to the site, where you can either climb the steps or ride a funicular railway to the top

In the centre of Braga is the **Sé**, a bewildering cathedral complex. Admission to its rambling treasury museum and several tomb chapels is 300$00.

It's an easy day trip to **Guimarães**, considered the cradle of Portugal, of interest for its medieval town centre and the palace of the dukes of Bragança.

Places to Stay

The *pousada de juventude* (☎ 616163), Rua de Santa Margarida 6, is a friendly hostel near the city centre. The *Grande Residência Avenida* (☎ 22955), Avenida da Liberdade 738, is good value with doubles from around 4500$00. Cheap but not very cheerful is the *Casa Santa Zita* (☎ 618331), a hostel for pilgrims (and others) at Rua São João 20, with singles/doubles for 2750$00/5500$00. Rooms with stunning views at the *Hotel Sul-Americano* (☎ 481237) at Bom Jesus start at 5500$00/7500$00; it's very popular so reserve a place.

Places to Eat

Café Brasileira (☎ 22104) is a turn-of-the-century special at the corner of Rua de São Marcos and Rua do Souto, just off Praça da República; order a coffee and watch the world pass by. At *Retiro da Primavera* (☎ 72482) Rua Gabriel Pereira Castro 100, the prato do dia is probably the best-value meal in town More congenial is the rustic, family-run *Casa*

Grulha (☎ 22883) at Rua dos Biscainhos 95, with an excellent cabrito assado (roast kid, a local specialty). Two good-value places (pratos for under 1000$00) on Praça Velha are *Taberna Rexío da Praça* at No 17 (closed on Sunday) and the casa de pasto *Pregão* at No 18.

Getting There & Away

The completion of an expressway from Porto has put Braga within easy day-trip reach. Train services connect Braga north to Viana do Castelo and Spain and south to Porto and Coimbra. There are excellent bus services to Porto and Lisbon, and local bus lines to Guimarães and Bom Jesus.

PENEDA-GERÊS NATIONAL PARK

This fine wilderness park along the Spanish border has spectacular scenery and a wide variety of fauna and flora. The Portuguese day-trippers and holiday-makers tend to stick to the main camping areas, leaving the rest of the park to hikers.

The main centre for the park is **Caldas do Gerês** (also called just Gerês), a sleepy, hot-spring village.

Orientation & Information

You can obtain information from the tourist office (☎ 391133) in the colonnade at the upper end of Caldas do Gerês. The Peneda-Gerês National Park has a small information office nearby (☎ 391181), others at Arcos de Valdevez and Montalegre just outside the park, and a head office (☎ 600 3480) in Braga at Avenida António Macedo, Quinta das Parretas. All sell a useful park map (530$00), with some roads and tracks (but not trails), and a booklet (105$00) on the park's features; most other information is in Portuguese.

The telephone code for Braga and Caldas do Gerês is ☎ 053.

Activities

Hiking The lack of decent trail maps can be a problem on a long trip, though most tracks are pleasant enough for short walks. From Caldas do Gerês, avoid the popular **Miradouro do Gerês** route at weekends when it's packed with car-trippers. A good option which offers the possibility of a swim is an old Roman road from Albergaria (10 km up-valley from Caldas by taxi or hitching), past the **Vilarinho**

das Furnas reservoir to **Campo do Gerês**. Further afield, the walks to Ermida and Cabril are excellent and both have simple accommodation and cafés.

An official long-distance trail is slowly being established, with eight itineraries spanning the park, mostly following traditional routes. Five have been completed so far, and descriptive map-brochures (300$00, in Portuguese) are available for two of these; contact a park office for details.

Montes d'Aventura (mobile ☎ 0936-673739, or Porto ☎ 02-208 8175), with a base at the pousada de juventude in Campo do Gerês, and Trote-Gerês (☎ 053-659860) near Cabril, organise guided walks for under 1800$00 per person per day.

Horse Riding The national park operates horse-riding facilities (☎ 391181) from beside their Vidoeiro camping ground, near Caldas do Gerês, for around 1300$00 an hour. Two other equine outfits are Equi Campo (☎ 357022) at Campo do Gerês, and Trote-Gerês (☎ 659860) near Cabril.

Canoeing & Other Water Sports Rio Caldo, eight km south of Caldas do Gerês, is the base for water sports on the Caniçada reservoir. The English-run outfit Água Montanha Lazer (☎ 391740) rents out kayaks for 600$00 to 1000$00 per hour, four-person canoes for 1500$00, plus small outboard boats. For paddling the Salamonde reservoir, Trote-Gerês (☎ 659860) rents canoes at 1000$00 an hour from their camping ground at Cabril. There's a swimming pool in Caldas do Gerês' Parque das Termas; park admission is 130$00 and pool admission is 700$00 on weekdays or 1100$00 on weekends.

Organised Tours

For an organised spin through the major sights in the park, Agência no Gerês (☎ 391112), next to the Universal Hotel in Caldas do Gerês, operates two to five-hour trips for 1000$00 to 1250$00 per person.

Places to Stay

The *Pousada de Juventude de Vilarinho das Furnas* (☎ 351339) and the very good *Cerdeira Camping Ground*, both at Campo do Gerês, make good bases for hikes. One km north of Caldas do Gerês at Vidoeiro is a good park-run camping ground (☎ 391289). Other camping grounds are at Lamas de Mouro, Entre-Ambos-os-Rios and Cabril.

Caldas do Gerês has plenty of pensões, though these are often block-booked by spa patients in summer. Try *Pensão da Ponte* (☎ 391121) beside the gushing river, with doubles from 6000$00, or *Pensão Príncipe* (same owners, same rates) just up the hill. At the top of the hill, with the best views, is *Pensão Adelaide* (☎ 391188), with doubles from 5000$00/4000$00 with/without bath. For more rural accommodation, Trote-Gerês (☎ 659860) operates the cheerful, comfortable *Pousadinho* cottage in Paradela, with doubles from 4200$00.

Places to Eat
Most pensões at Caldas do Gerês provide hearty meals, usually available to non-guests,

too. Pensão Adelaide has a popular restaurant, or you can try the *Baltasar Pensão Restaurant* (☎ 391131), next to the park office, with huge servings from 900$00 a dish. There are several small stores in the main street for picnic provisions.

Getting There & Away
From Braga at least 10 buses a day run to Caldas do Gerês and at least two a day to Campo do Gerês (plus more on weekdays). Coming from Lisbon or Porto, change at Braga.

Getting Around
Unless you have your own transport, you must rely on infrequent bus connections to a limited number of places in or near the park or walk.

Mountain bikes are available from Trote-Gerês (☎ 659860) at its Cabril camping ground, and from Pensão Carvalho Araújo (☎ 391185) in Caldas do Gerês.

Slovenia

Little Slovenia (Slovenija) straddles Eastern and Western Europe. Many of its cities and towns bear the imprint of the Habsburg Empire and the Venetian Republic, while up in the Julian Alps you'd almost think you were in Bavaria. The two million Slovenes were economically the most well off among the peoples of what was once Yugoslavia, and the relative affluence of this nation on the 'sunny side of the Alps' is immediately apparent. Slovenia might be your gateway to the Balkans from Italy or Austria, but you'll feel you're still in central Europe.

Slovenia is one of Eastern Europe's most delightful surprises for travellers. Fairy-tale Bled Castle, breathtaking Lake Bohinj, scenic Postojna and Škocjan caves, the lush Soča Valley, Italianate Piran and Koper and thriving Ljubljana are ace attractions, all accessible at much less than the cost of similar places in Western Europe. The amazing variety of environments packed into one small area makes this country truly a 'Europe in miniature'. An added bonus is that Slovenia is a nation of polyglots, and communicating with these friendly, helpful people is never difficult.

The problems associated with the break-up of Yugoslavia touched Slovenia only briefly in mid-1991, and since then this independent republic has been a peaceful, safe place to visit. Slovenia escaped most war damage, but the ensuing publicity scared off many Europeans who used to holiday here; only now are they beginning to realise that things are back to normal. Meanwhile, you can enjoy Slovenia without the huge crowds of tourists found in Western Europe and without most of the hassles and discomforts sometimes encountered elsewhere in Eastern Europe.

Facts about the Country

HISTORY

The early Slovenes settled in the river valleys of the Danube Basin and the eastern Alps in the 6th century. In 748, Slovenia was brought under Germanic rule, first by the Frankish empire of the Carolingians, who converted the population to Christianity, and then as part of the Holy Roman Empire in the 9th century. The Austro-German monarchy took over in the early 14th century and continued to rule (as the Austrian Habsburg Empire from 1804) right up until 1918 – with only one brief interruption. Over these six centuries, the upper classes became totally Germanised, though the peasantry retained their Slavic (later Slovenian) identity. The Bible was translated into the vernacular during the Reformation in 1584, but Slovene did not come into common use as a written language until the early 19th century.

In 1809, in a bid to isolate the Habsburg Empire from the Adriatic, Napoleon established the so-called Illyrian Provinces (Slovenia, Dalmatia and part of Croatia), making Ljubljana the capital. Though the Habsburgs returned in 1814, French reforms in education, law and public administration endured. The democratic revolution that swept

Europe in 1848 also increased political and national consciousness among the Slovenes, and after WWI and the dissolution of the Austro-Hungarian Empire, Slovenia was included in the Kingdom of Serbs, Croats and Slovenes. During WWII much of Slovenia was annexed by Germany, with Italy and Hungary taking smaller shares. Slovenian partisans fought courageously against the invaders from mountain bases, and Slovenia joined the Socialist Federal Republic of Yugoslavia in 1945.

Moves by Serbia in the late 1980s to assert its leading role culturally and economically among the Yugoslav republics worried Slovenes. When Belgrade abruptly ended the autonomy of Kosovo (where 80% of the population is ethnically Albanian) in late 1988, Slovenes feared the same could happen to them. For some years, Slovenia's interests had been shifting to the capitalist west and north; the Yugoslav connection, on the other hand, had become not only an economic burden but a political threat.

In the spring of 1990, Slovenia became the first Yugoslav republic to hold free election and slough off 45 years of Communist rule; in December the electorate voted overwhelmingly in favour of independence. The Slovenian government began stockpiling weapons, and on 25 June 1991 it pulled its republic out of the Yugoslav Federation. To dramatise their bid for independence and to generate foreign sympathy, the Slovenian leaders deliberately provoked fighting with the federal army by attempting to take control of the border crossings, and a 10-day war ensued. But resistance from the Slovenian militia was determined and, as no territorial claims or minority issues were involved, the Yugoslav government agreed to a truce brokered by the European Community (EC). Slovenia got a new constitution in late December, and on 15 January 1992 the EC formally recognised the country. Slovenia was admitted to the United Nations in May 1992 and has applied for full membership of the European Union, expected by the year 2000.

GEOGRAPHY & ECOLOGY

Slovenia is wedged between Austria and Croatia and shares much shorter borders with Italy and Hungary. Measuring just 20,256 sq km, Slovenia is the smallest country in Eastern Europe, about the size of Wales or Israel. Much of the country is mountainous, culminating in the north-west with the Julian Alps and the nation's highest peak, Mt Triglav (2864 metres). From this jagged knot, the main Alpine chain continues east along the Austrian border, while the Dinaric range runs south-east along the coast into Croatia.

Below the limestone plateau of the Karst region between Ljubljana and Koper is Europe's most extensive network of karst caverns, which gave their name to other such caves around the world.

The coastal range forms a barrier isolating the Istrian Peninsula from Slovenia's corner of the Danube Basin. Much of the interior east of the Alps is drained by the rivers Sava (which rises near Lake Bohinj) and Drava (which passes through Maribor); both empty into the Danube. The Soča flows through western Slovenia into the Adriatic.

Slovenia is a very green country – just under half of its total area is covered in forest – and is home to 2900 plant species; Triglav National Park is especially rich in indigenous flowering plants. Common European animals (deer, boar, chamois) live here in abundance, and rare species include *Proteus anguinus*, the unique 'human fish' that inhabits karst caves.

ECONOMY

Although Slovenia had only 8% of former Yugoslavia's population, it accounted for up to 20% of the country's gross domestic product (GDP) and exported more than a quarter of its goods.

Separation from Yugoslavia meant the loss of markets accounting for some 30% of all exports, but the negative effects of that loss and the pain caused by reforms needed to modernise the economy are fading pretty rapidly.

Slovenia's per-capita GDP is more than double that of Hungary or the Czech Republic and is approaching the level of Greece. The growth rate was steady in mid-1996 at about 5%, inflation stood at just under 9% (down from more than 100% just after independence) and the unemployment rate was about 14% and

falling. Shipments to and from the former Yugoslavia have reduced drastically since independence, and Slovenia's furniture, textile and paper industries now export primarily to Germany, Italy, Austria and France.

Mass privatisation in Slovenia of unprofitable industries built up by the former regime came about much later than in some other Eastern European countries. A complicated 'transformation of ownership' scheme was put in place in 1994 but by 1996 less than a third of the 1400 eligible companies had actually been privatised. Thus a disproportionately high percentage of employees still work for the state.

There are major coal mines east of Ljubljana, steelworks at Jesenice and textile mills at Kranj. High-quality home appliances are produced by Gorenje, pharmaceuticals by Krka and electronic goods by Iskra.

Agriculture plays a remarkably minor role in the economy, considering how rural Slovenia appears at first. It comprises only 6% of GDP, as opposed to industry at 39% (manufacturing is 30% of that figure) and services at 55%. Despite this the country is virtually self-sufficient in food production.

POPULATION & PEOPLE

Slovenia was the most homogeneous of all the Yugoslav republics. About 88% of the two million inhabitants are Slovenes, 2.7% Croats and 2.5% Serbs, with smaller groups identified as Muslims, Hungarians, Italians and Gypsies. Roman Catholics account for about 82% of the total, followed by Eastern Orthodox Christians (2.4%), Muslims (1%) and Protestants (1%). The largest cities are Ljubljana (330,000), Maribor (108,000), Celje (42,000) and Kranj (37,000).

ARTS

Slovenia's most beloved writer is the Romantic poet France Prešeren (1800-49), whose lyric poems set new standards for Slovenian literature and helped to raise national consciousness. Disappointed in love, Prešeren wrote sensitive love poems but also satirical verse and epic poetry. A rather dashing portrait of the poet appears on the 1000 SIT banknote.

Many notable buildings and public squares in Ljubljana and elsewhere in Slovenia were designed by the extraordinary architect Jože

Plečnik (1872-1957), who studied under Otto Wagner in Vienna. Plečnik's likeness is on the 500 SIT note.

Postmodernist painting and sculpture has been dominated since the 1980s by the multimedia group Neue Slowenische Kunst (NSK) and the five-member artists' cooperative IRWIN. The latter, founded in 1983, spurns the sacred myth of the individual artist by exhibiting only as an anonymous group with jarring ideological or historical symbols juxtaposed in such a way as to bring out new meanings.

Avant-garde dance is best exemplified by Betontanc, an NSK dance company that combines live music and theatrical elements (called 'physical theatre' in Slovenia) with sharp political comment. In the rock ballet *Thieves of Wet Handkerchiefs*, members of the troupe murder one another and then are resurrected.

Since WWII, many Slovenian folk traditions have been lost, but compilations by the trio Trutamora Slovenica (available at music shops in Ljubljana) examine the roots of Slovenian folk music. Popular music runs the gamut from Slovenian *chanson* and jazz to Latin and house disco, but it was punk music in the late 1970s and early 1980s that put Slovenia on the world stage. The most celebrated groups, imitated throughout Eastern Europe, were Pankrti, Kuzle, Borghesia and Laibach (part of the NSK movement).

CULTURE

The Slovenes are an easy-going, industrious people, though in the former Yugoslavia they were considered the most strait-laced and formal of all the nationalities, perhaps reflecting those 600 years of Austro-German rule. There are few social taboos that the visitor runs the risk of transgressing, but try to remember that Slovenia is independent now for the first time in history. Slovenes are at once very proud of their new-found freedom and a bit unsure of finally 'owning' rather than 'renting'.

LANGUAGE

Slovene is a South Slavic language written in the Roman alphabet. It is closely related to Croatian and Serbian, but the languages are not mutually intelligible. Grammatically complex, with lots of cases, genders and tenses, Slovenian has something very rare in linguistics: the

dual number. It's one *miza* (table) and three or more *mize* (tables) but two *mizi*.

Virtually everyone in Slovenia speaks at least one other language: Croatian, Serbian, German, English and/or Italian (in that order). English is definitely the preferred language of the young. See the Language Guide at the end of the book for pronunciation guidelines and useful words and phrases. Lonely Planet's *Mediterranean Europe Phrasebook* contains a complete chapter on Slovene.

Facts for the Visitor

PLANNING

Climate & When to Go

Snow can linger in the mountains as late as June, but spring (April and May) is a good time to be in the lowlands and valleys of Slovenia when everything is fresh and in blossom (though April can be rainy). In July and August hotel rates are increased and there are lots more tourists, especially on the coast. September is an excellent month to visit Slovenia as the summer crowds have vanished, and it's the best time for hiking and climbing. December to March is for skiers.

Books & Maps

Books are very expensive in Slovenia so try to buy whatever you can on the country before you arrive. Lonely Planet's *Slovenia – a travel survival kit* is a complete guide to the country. *Discover Slovenia*, published by Cankarjev Založba, is a colourful and easy introduction.

Slovenia's main cartographer is the Geodesic Institute (Geodetski Zavod Slovenije; GZS) while the Alpine Association of Slovenia (Planinska Zveza Slovenije; PZS) produces hiking maps. Most of these are available from Kod & Kam, Trg Francoske Revolucije 7, in Ljubljana.

Online Services

Information on Slovenia can be found at the SloWWWenija web site (http://www.uvi.si/slo/).

What to Bring

You don't have to remember any particular

tems of clothing – a warm sweater (even in summer) for the mountains at night, perhaps, and an umbrella in the spring or autumn – unless you plan to do some serious hiking or other sport. One peculiarity here is that, while Slovenes drink lots of herbal teas, black tea is hard to find. Bring along a cup, coil water heater and tea bags and make your own.

SUGGESTED ITINERARIES

Depending on the length of your stay, you might want to see and do the following in Slovenia:

Two days
    Visit Ljubljana.
One week
    Visit Ljubljana, Bled, Bohinj, Škocjan Caves and Piran.
Two weeks
    Visit all the places covered in this chapter.

HIGHLIGHTS

Ljubljana, Piran and Koper have outstanding architecture; the hilltop castles at Bled and the capital are impressive. The Škocjan Caves are among the foremost underground wonders in the world. The Soča Valley is indescribably beautiful in spring. The frescoed Church of St John the Baptist is in itself worth the trip to Lake Bohinj.

TOURIST OFFICES

The best tourist office in Slovenia is the Tourist Information Centre (TIC) in Ljubljana. The staff know everything about the country. Bled, Bohinj (at Ribčev Laz), Kobarid and Portorož also have excellent tourist offices. Travel agencies in most other towns are much more willing to offer assistance to individual visitors than commercial ones in Western Europe. Companies to watch for are Kompas, Emona Globtour and Slovenijaturist.

Tourist Offices & Travel Agencies Abroad

Slovenia – sometimes in conjunction with the Kompas travel agency – maintains tourist offices in the following eight countries:

Austria
    Hilton Center, Landstrasser Hauptstrasse 2, A-1030 Vienna (☎ 0222-715 4010)
Germany
    Maximilliansplatz 12A, D-80333 Munich (☎ 089-228 3974)

Hungary
    Gellérthegy utca 28, 1013 Budapest (☎ 1-156 8223)
Italy
    Via Lazzaro Palazzi 2A, 20124 Milan (☎ 02-29 51 11 87)
Netherlands
    Goudent 10-13, NL-4330 GC Middelburg (☎ 0118-635 790)
Switzerland
    St Leodegarstrasse 2, CH-6006 Lucerne (☎ 041-410 8515)
UK
    2 Canfield Place, London NW6 3BT (☎ 0171-372 3767)
USA
    122 East 42nd St, Suite 3006, New York, NY 10168-0072 (☎ 212-682 5896)

In addition, Kompas offices in the following countries will be able to provide information on tourism in Slovenia.

Australia
    3/257 Boundary St, Spring Hill, Queensland 4000 (☎ 07-3831 4400)
Canada
    4060 Ste Catherine St West, Suite 535, Montreal, Que H3Z 2Z3 (☎ 514-938 4041)
France
    80 Rue Taitbout, Pavillion 7, 75009 Paris (☎ 01 44 63 57 83)
USA
    2826 East Commercial Blvd, Fort Lauderdale, FL 33308 (☎ 305-771 9200)

VISAS & EMBASSIES

Passport holders from Australia, Canada, the EU, Israel, Japan, New Zealand, Switzerland and the USA do not require visas for stays up to 90 days; those from any EU country as well as Switzerland can enter on just a valid personal identity document for up to 30 days. Citizens of other countries requiring visas (including South Africans) can get them at any Slovenian embassy or consulate for up to 90 days or at the border or Brnik airport for 30 days. They cost the equivalent of DM50.

Slovenian Embassies Abroad

In addition to the embassies listed here, Slovenia has honorary consuls in Sydney (☎ 02-9314 5116) and in Cleveland, Ohio (☎ 216-589 9220), and embassies or consulates in Budapest, Munich, Prague, Trieste and Zagreb.

SLOVENIA

Australia
Advance Bank Centre, Level 6, 60 Marcus Clark St,
Canberra, ACT 2608 (☎ 06-243 4830)
Austria
Niebelungengasse 13, A-1010 Vienna (☎ 0222-586
1307)
Canada
150 Metcalfe St, Suite 2101, Ottawa, Ont K2P 1P1
(☎ 613-565 5781)
UK
Suite 1, Cavendish Court, 11-15 Wigmore St, London
W1H 9LA (☎ 0171-495 7775)
USA
1525 New Hampshire Ave NW, Washington DC
20036 (☎ 202-667 5363)
600 Third Ave, 24th Floor, New York, NY 10016
(☎ 212-370 3006)

Foreign Embassies in Slovenia

Selected countries with representation in
Ljubljana appear below. Citizens of countries
not listed here (eg Australia, Canada, South
Africa) should contact their embassies in
Vienna or Budapest.

Croatia
Grubarjevo nabrežje 6 (☎ 061-125 7287)
Czech Republic
Riharjeva ulica 1 (☎ 061-125 2521)
France
Železna cesta 18/VI (☎ 061-173 4441)
Hungary
Ul Konrada Babnika 5 (☎ 061-152 1882)
UK
Trg Republike 3 (☎ 061-125 7191)
USA
Pražakova ulica 4 (☎ 061-301 485)

CUSTOMS

Travellers can bring in the usual personal
effects, a couple of cameras and electronic
goods for their own use, 200 cigarettes, a generous four litres of spirits and a litre of wine.

MONEY

Slovenia's currency, the tolar, is abbreviated
SIT. Prices in shops, at restaurants and train
and bus fares are always in tolars, but some
hotels, guesthouses and even camping grounds
still use Deutschmarks as the tolar is linked to
it. For that reason, some forms of accommodation listed in this chapter are quoted in DM
(though you are never required to pay in the
German currency). There are coins of 50 stotin
and one, two and five tolar and banknotes of
10, 20, 50, 100, 200, 500, 1000, 5000 and now
10,000 tolars.

It is very simple to change cash and
travellers' cheques at banks, post offices, trave
agencies and any *menjalnica*, the ubiquitou
private exchange offices. There's no blac
market, but exchange rates can vary some
what, so it pays to keep your eyes open. Bank
take a commission *(provizija)* of 1% or none a
all, but tourist offices, travel agencies
exchange bureaus and hotels have high fees ·
sometimes up to 5%.

Banks usually pay a higher rate fo
travellers' cheques than for cash, but som
private exchange offices (not travel agencies
do the opposite. Post offices are not the bes
places to change money as some may onl
want to accept cash and the rate is usually poo.

You can usually exchange excess tolar
back into US dollars or Deutschmarks (th
24-hour exchange office at Ljubljana's trai
station is a good place), but exchange receip
may be required. Slovenia is a good place t
trade your travellers' cheques for cash dollar
or Deutschmarks. Most Slovenian banks wil
carry out the transaction for a flat 3% commis
sion.

Exchange Rates

Australia	A$1	=	106 SIT
Canada	C$1	=	97 SIT
France	1FF	=	25 SIT
Germany	DM1	=	88 SIT
Japan	¥100	=	124 SIT
United Kingdom	UK£1	=	201 SIT
United States	US$1	=	133 SIT

Credit Cards

Visa, MasterCard and American Express card
are accepted at up-market restaurants, shop
and hotels; otherwise, it's cash. There are sti
no automatic teller machines (ATMs) open t
foreign-account holders in Slovenia, but Vis
card holders can get cash advances in tolar
from any A Banka branch nationwide
MasterCard and Eurocard holders from th
Nova Ljubljanska Banka (☎ 061-125 0155
Trg Republike 2, in Ljubljana and America
Express customers from Atlas (☎ 061-13
2028), Mestni trg 8.

Consumer Taxes

A 'circulation tax' called *prometni davek* an
not unlike value-added tax (VAT) covers th
purchase of most goods and services. Visitor

can claim refunds on total purchases of 12,500 SIT or more (not including tobacco products or spirits) through Kompas MTS, which has offices at Brnik airport and about 30 border crossings. Make sure you get the paperwork done at the time of purchase.

Most towns and cities in Slovenia levy a 'tourist tax' on overnight visitors of about 200 SIT (less for campers).

POST & COMMUNICATIONS

Post

Poste restante is sent to the main post office in a city or town (in the capital, it goes to the branch at Slovenska cesta 32, 1101 Ljubljana) where it is held for 30 days. American Express card holders can have their mail addressed c/o Atlas travel agency, Mestni trg 8, 1000 Ljubljana. Slovenia dropped the initial '6' from all its postal codes in 1996. They now have only four digits.

Telephone

The easiest place to make long-distance calls as well as send faxes and telegrams is from a post office or telephone centre; the one at Trg Osvobodilne Fronte near the train and bus stations in Ljubljana is open 24 hours a day. Public telephones on the street require a token (žeton) or a phone card; they never take coins.

Telephone tokens, available at post offices and some newsstands, come in three varieties. Token A (60 SIT) has five impulses and is used for brief local calls. Token B, with 25 impulses for 200 SIT, can be used for longer or domestic calls. Token C costs 400 SIT and has 50 impulses. Telekom Slovenije phone cards cost 750 SIT for 50 impulses, 1300 SIT for 100 and 3750 SIT for 400.

A local call absorbs about five impulses, and a three-minute call from Slovenia will cost about 360 SIT to neighbouring countries, 435 SIT to Western Europe (including the UK) and 750 SIT to the USA or Australia. Rates are 20% cheaper between 7 pm and 7 am.

The international access code in Slovenia is 00. The international operator can be reached on ☎ 901 and international directory enquiries on ☎ 989. To call Slovenia from abroad, dial the international access code, ☎386 (Slovenia's country code), the area code (without the initial zero) and the number.

E-mail

The only cybercafé open to the public in Slovenia at present is in the basement of the Student Organisation of the University of Ljubljana centre (ŠOU; ☎ 061-131 7010) at Kersnikova ulica 4 in Ljubljana.

MEDIA

There are no English-language newspapers, radio stations or TV channels in Slovenia though Radio Slovenija's Channel 1 broadcasts a news summary in English at 10.30 pm. In July and August, the same channel has a weather report in English at 6.35 am followed by news, traffic conditions and tourist information at 9.35 am. You can listen on FM frequencies 88.5, 90.0, 90.9, 91.8, 92.0, 92.9, 94.1 and 96.4 or kHz/AM frequency 3268.

PHOTOGRAPHY & VIDEO

Film and basic camera equipment are available throughout Slovenia, though the largest selection is in Ljubljana. Film prices vary but 24 exposures of 100 ASA Kodacolor II, Agfa or Fujifilm will cost from 700 to 900 SIT while Ektachrome 100 is 1300 SIT. Super 8 (P5-60) film costs about 1300 SIT while an EC45 video cassette is 1300 SIT. Developing print film costs about 2400 SIT for 36 prints (10 x 15 cm). For 36 framed transparencies, expect to pay around 1100 SIT.

TIME

Slovenia is one hour ahead of GMT/UTC. The country goes onto summer time (GMT/UTC +2) at the end of March when clocks are advanced by one hour. At the end of September they're turned back one hour.

ELECTRICITY

The electric voltage is 220V 50 Hz, AC. Plugs are the standard European two-pronged type.

WEIGHTS & MEASURES

Slovenia uses the metric system exclusively.

LAUNDRY

Commercial laundrettes are pretty much nonexistent in Slovenia. The best places to look for do-it-yourself washers and dryers are hostels, college dormitories and camp sites. In Ljubljana try the student dormitory Kam (Dom C) at Kardeljeva ploščad 14, north of the centre in Bežigrad, or Alba at Wolfova ulica 12.

HEALTH

Foreigners are entitled to emergency medical aid at the very least; for subsequent treatment entitlement varies. Some EU countries (including the UK) have contractual agreements with Slovenia allowing their citizens free medical care while travelling in the country. This may require carrying a special form so check with your Ministry of Health or equivalent before setting out.

GAY & LESBIAN TRAVELLERS

The best source of information for gays and lesbians is the Roza Klub branch of ŠOU (☎ 061-131 7010) at Kersnikova ulica 4 in Ljubljana. Among other things, it organises a disco every Sunday night at the Klub K4.

DISABLED TRAVELLERS

A group that looks after the interests and special needs of physically challenged people is the Zveza Paraplegikov Republike Slovenije (ZPRS; ☎ 061-123 7138) at Štihova ulica 19, Ljubljana. With advance notice, the TIC in Ljubljana can organise a guide for disabled people.

DANGERS & ANNOYANCES

Slovenia is hardly a violent or dangerous place. Police say that 90% of all crimes reported involve thefts so take the usual precautions. Be careful of your purse or wallet in bus and train stations and where you may consider leaving it unattended (on the beach, in a hut while hiking). Lock your car at all times, park in well-lit areas and do not leave valuables visible inside.

In the event of an emergency, the following numbers can be dialled nationwide:

☎ 92 – Police
☎ 93 – Fire
☎ 94 – First aid/ambulance
☎ 987 – Automobile assistance (AMZS)

BUSINESS HOURS

Shops, groceries and department stores are open from 7.30 or 8 am to 7 pm on weekdays and to 1 pm on Saturday. Bank hours are generally from 8 am to 4.30 or 5 pm on weekdays

(often with a lunchtime break) and till noon or Saturday. The main post office in any city or town is open from 7 am to 6 or 7 pm or weekdays and till 1 pm on Saturday. Most government offices close at 3 pm.

PUBLIC HOLIDAYS & SPECIAL EVENTS

Public holidays in Slovenia include a two-day New Year holiday (1 and 2 January), Prešeren Day (8 February), Easter Monday (March/April), Insurrection Day (27 April), two Labour Day holidays (1 and 2 May), National Day (25 June), Assumption Day (15 August) Reformation Day (31 October), All Saints' Day (1 November), Christmas (25 December) and Independence Day (26 December). If any of these falls on a Sunday, then the Monday becomes the holiday.

Though cultural events are scheduled year round, the highlights of Slovenia's summer season (July and August) are the International Summer Festival at Ljubljana and Bled, the Piran Musical evenings, the Primorska Summer Festival at Piran, Koper and Portorož, and summer in the Old Town in Ljubljana, with three or four cultural events a week taking place. The Cows' Ball (*kravji bal*) at Bohinj is a zany weekend of folk dance, music, eating and drinking in mid-September to mark the return of the cows to the valleys from their high pastures.

ACTIVITIES
Skiing

Skiing is by far the most popular sport in Slovenia, and every fourth Slovene is an active skier. The country has many well-equipped ski resorts in the Julian Alps, especially Vogel (skiing up to 1800 metres) above Bohinj, Kranjska Gora (1620 metres), Kanin (2200 metres) above Bovec, and Krvavec (1950 metres), east of Kranj. World Cup slalom and giant slalom events are held at Kranjska Gora in December, and the current world ski-jumping record (200 metres) was set at nearby Planica in 1994.

All these resorts have multiple chair lifts, cable cars, ski schools, equipment rentals and large resort hotels. December to March is the main ski season though it can stretch into May at Kanin.

Hiking

Hiking is almost as popular as skiing in Slovenia, and one of the nicest things about it is that it gives you a chance to meet local people in a relaxed, informal environment. This small country contains some 9000 km of marked hiking trails and 165 mountain huts. You'll experience the full grandeur of the Julian Alps in Triglav National Park at Bohinj, and for the veteran mountaineer there's the Slovenian Alpine Trail, which crosses all the highest peaks.

Kayaking, Canoeing & Rafting

These sports are practised anywhere there's running water, but the best white-water rafting is on the Soča, one of only half a dozen rivers in the European Alps whose upper waters are still unspoiled. The centre is at Bovec.

Cycling

Mountain bikes are for rent at Bled and Bohinj, and the uncrowded roads around these resorts are a joy to cycle on. You can also rent bikes on the coast.

ACCOMMODATION
Camping

In summer, camping is the cheapest way to go, and there are conveniently located camping grounds all over the country. You don't always need a tent as some camp sites have inexpensive bungalows, too. Two of the best camping grounds for those who want to experience the mountains or the sea are Zlatorog on Lake Bohinj and Jezero Fiesa near Piran, though they can be jammed in summer. It is forbidden to camp 'rough' in Slovenia.

Hostels & Colleges

Slovenia has only seven 'official' hostels including two in Ljubljana and one each in Bled (currently under renovation), Bohinj and Koper, but not all are open year round. Many college dormitories accept travellers in the summer months.

Private Rooms & Guesthouses

Private rooms arranged by tourist offices and travel agencies can be inexpensive, but a 30% surcharge is usually levied on stays of less than three nights. You can often bargain for rooms without the surcharge by going directly to any house with a sign reading 'sobe' (rooms). A small guesthouse (called *penzion* or *gostišče*) can also be good value, though in July and August you may be required to take at least one meal and the rates are higher then. These are also a good choice for solo travellers as rooms are usually priced per person.

Farmhouses

The agricultural cooperatives of Slovenia have organised a unique programme to accommodate visitors on working farms. It's like staying in a private room except that the 120 participating farms are in picturesque rural areas and may offer activities such as horse riding, kayaking, skiing and cycling. Prices range from DM21 per person for a 2nd-category room with shared bath and breakfast in the low season (from September to mid-December and mid-January to June) to around DM40 per person for a 1st-category room with private bath and all meals in the high season (July and August). Apartments for groups of up to 10 people are also available. There's a 30% surcharge on stays of less than three nights. Bookings should be made through the Vas travel agency (☎ 061-126 4252), Miklošičeva cesta 4, in Ljubljana. Their UK agent is Slovenija Pursuits (☎ 01763-852 646), 14 Hay St, Steeple Morden, Royston, Herts SG8 0PE.

Hotels

Hotels are more expensive than any of the other accommodation options and the rates vary according to season, with July and August being the peak season and May/June and September/October the shoulder seasons. In Ljubljana, prices are constant all year. Many resort hotels, particularly on the coast, are closed in winter. As hotels seldom levy a surcharge for stays of one or two nights they're worth considering if you're only passing through.

FOOD

Slovenian cuisine is heavily influenced by that of its neighbours. From Austria, it's *klobasa* (sausage), *zavitek* (strudel) and *Dunajski zrezek* (Wiener schnitzel). *Njoki* (potato dumplings), *rižota* (risotto) and the ravioli-like *žlikrofi* are obviously Italian, and Hungary has contributed *golaž* (goulash), *paprikaš* (chicken or beef 'stew') and *palačinke* (thin pancakes filled with jam or nuts and topped with chocolate). And then there's that old Balkan standby, *burek*, a greasy layered cheese, meat or even apple pie served at takeaway places everywhere.

There are many types of dumplings; cheese ones called *štruklji* are the most popular. Try also the baked delicacies, including *potica* (walnut roll) and *gibanica*, pastry filled with poppy seeds, walnuts, apple and/or sultanas and cheese and topped with cream.

No Slovenian meal is complete without soup, be it *goveja juha* (beef broth with little egg noodles), *gobova kremna juha* (creamed mushroom soup), *istrski brodet* (Istrian fish soup with polenta) or *jota* (sauerkraut and beans cooked with pork). Goulash is considered a main dish and not a soup. Traditional dishes are best tried at an inn *(gostilna* or *gostišče)*.

DRINKS

The wine-growing regions of Slovenia are Podravje in the east (noted for such white wines as Riesling and Traminec), Posavje in the south-east (try the distinctly Slovenian light-red Cviček) and Primorska near Koper, which produces hearty reds like Teran and Refošk. Slovenian wines are classed *vrhunsko* (premium), *kakovostno* (quality) and *namizno* (table wine) whether they be *suho* (dry), *polsuho* (semi-dry) or *sladko* (sweet).

An alcoholic drink as Slovenian as wine is *žganje*, a strong brandy or eau de vie distilled from a variety of fruits but most commonly plums. The finest is *pleterska hruška* made from pears by the monks at the Pleterje Monastery near Kostanjevica na Krki in south-east Slovenia.

Beer is very popular. Union, brewed in Ljubljana, is lighter-tasting and sweeter than Zlatorog, the excellent and ubiquitous beer made by Laško. Union also produces an alcohol-free beer called Uni and a decent stout.

Getting There & Away

AIR

Slovenia's national airline, Adria Airways (☎ 061-133 4336), has nonstop flights (some seasonal only) to Ljubljana's Brnik Airport from Amsterdam, Barcelona, Copenhagen, Frankfurt, Glasgow, London (Heathrow), Manchester, Moscow, Munich, Paris, Prague, Skopje, Split, Tel Aviv, Tirana, Vienna and Zürich.

LAND
Bus

Nova Gorica is the easiest exit/entry point between Slovenia and Italy as you can catch up to seven buses a day to/from the Italian city of Gorizia or simply walk across the border at Rožna Dolina. Koper also has good connections with Italy: some 17 buses a day go to/from Trieste, 21 km to the north-east.

To/from Hungary you can catch a bus from Ljubljana to Lenti twice a week (230 km, five hours, 2130 SIT). Otherwise take one of the six daily buses from Ljubljana to Lendava (21? km, four hours), then walk the four km through Lendava north to the Hungarian border. The first Hungarian railway station, Rédics, is only two km away with eight trains a day to Zalaegerszeg. From there three direct trains make their way to Budapest.

For information about getting to/from other neighbouring countries and ones farther afield, see Getting There & Away in the Ljubljana section.

Train

The main train routes into Slovenia from Austria are Vienna to Maribor and Salzburg to Jesenice. Tickets cost 4500 SIT from Ljubljana to Salzburg (300 km, 4½ hours), 6155 SIT to Vienna (460 km, six hours) and 28,975 SIT to Amsterdam (1429 km, 18 hours). For Austria it's cheaper to take a local train to Maribor (865 SIT) and buy your ticket on to Vienna from there. Similarly, from Austria only buy a ticket as far as Jesenice or Maribor as domestic fares are much lower than international ones.

There are two trains a day between Munich and Ljubljana (453 km, seven hours, 8117 SIT) via Salzburg (4500 SIT). The Eurocity *Mimara* travels by day, while the *Lisinski* express goes overnight (sleeping carriage available). An 800 SIT supplement is payable on the *Mimara*, and this includes a seat reservation if made the day before or earlier. Seat reservations (310 SIT) can be made on the *Lisinski* but are not required.

Four trains a day run from Trieste to Ljubljana (165 km, three hours, 1350 SIT) via Divača and Sežana. From Croatia it's Zagreb to Ljubljana (160 km, 2½ hours, 1012 SIT) via Zidani Most, or Rijeka to Ljubljana (155 km, 2½ hours) via Pivka. Most services between Slovenia and Croatia require a change of trains at some point but connections are immediate. The intercity *Drava* and *Venezia Express* trains link Ljubljana with Budapest (500 km, 7½ hours, 4925 SIT) via north-west Croatia and Zagreb respectively.

Car & Motorcycle

Slovenia maintains 14 international border crossings with Italy, 17 with Austria, 24 with Croatia and two with Hungary. Only rough secondary roads link Slovenia to Hungary, and there are often long lines of trucks waiting to cross on each side of the two international border crossings, especially at Dolga Vas.

SEA

Between April and mid-October, the 39-metre *Prince of Venice* catamaran sails between Venice and Portorož (2½ hours; DM63/90 one way/return) on Friday, Saturday and Sunday. The Russian-built catamaran *Kolhida* makes the same run on Wednesday and Saturday from mid-May to September for DM48/80.

LEAVING SLOVENIA

A departure tax of DM25/US$16 is levied on all passengers leaving Slovenia by air though this is usually included in the ticket price.

Getting Around

BUS

Except for long journeys, the bus is preferable to the train in Slovenia and departures are frequent. In some cases you don't have much of a choice; travelling by bus is the only practical way to get to Bled and Bohinj, the Julian Alps and much of the coast from Ljubljana.

In Ljubljana you can buy your ticket (with seat reservation, 100 SIT) the day before, but many people simply pay the conductor on the bus itself. The one time you really might need a reservation is Friday afternoon, when many students travel from Ljubljana to their homes or people leave the city for the weekend.

Footnotes you might see on Slovenian bus schedules include: *vozi vsak dan* (runs daily); *vozi ob delavnikih* (runs on working days – Monday to Friday); *vozi ob sobotah* (runs on Saturday); and *vozi ob nedeljah in praznikih* (runs on Sunday and holidays).

TRAIN

Slovenske Železnice (SŽ) operates on just over 1200 km of track. The country's most scenic rail route runs from Jesenice to Nova Gorica via Bled (Bled-Jezero station) and Bohinjska Bistrica. This 89-km route through the Julian Alps and Soča Valley opened for service in 1906. Either side will get you views of the blue-green Soča River. Between four and six local trains a day cover this route in each direction. The trip takes about two hours.

The 160-km train ride from Ljubljana to Zagreb is also worth taking as the line follows the Sava River along most of its route through a picturesque gorge. Sit on the right side eastbound, the left side westbound.

On posted timetables in Slovenia, *odhod* or *odhodi vlakov* means 'departures' and *prihod* (or *prihodi vlakov*) is 'arrivals'. If you don't have time to buy a ticket, seek out the conductor who will sell you one for an extra charge of 200 SIT.

CAR & MOTORCYCLE

Tolls are payable on the motorways from Ljubljana to Kranj (26 km), Ljubljana to Postojna (51 km) and Maribor to Celje (54 km) but they're not expensive; from Ljubljana to Postojna it's only 200 SIT for cars and motorcycles.

Speed limits for cars are 60 km/h in built-up areas, 80 km/h on secondary roads, 100 km/h on main highways and 120 km/h on motorways. In large towns illegally parked vehicles are routinely towed away, especially in Ljubljana. Petrol is relatively cheap in Slovenia: 69/74/82 SIT per litre for 91/95 (unleaded)/98 octane.

Slovenia's automobile club is the Avto Moto Zveza Slovenije (AMZS). For emergency road assistance, motorists can call them on ☎ 987.

Car Rental

Car rentals from Kompas Hertz, Globtour Budget, Europcar and Avis begin at around

US$27 a day plus US$0.27 a km, or US$450 a week with unlimited km for the cheapest car, usually a Renault 5 or Suzuki Swift. Optional collision insurance is about US$8 a day extra, theft insurance another US$8 a day and there's 15% tax.

Smaller agencies like ABC at Brnik airport and Avtoimpex in Ljubljana have much more competitive rates. Some agencies have minimum-age requirements or insist that those under 23 take out full insurance cover (always a good idea in any case).

HITCHING

Hitchhiking is legal everywhere except on motorways and some major highways and is generally easy; even young women do it. But hitching is never a totally safe way of getting around and, although we mention it as an option, we don't recommend it.

Ljubljana

With some 330,000 inhabitants, Ljubljana (Laibach in German) is by far Slovenia's largest and most populous city. But in many ways the city, whose name means 'Beloved' in Slovene, does not feel like an industrious municipality of national importance but a pleasant, self-contented little town. The most beautiful parts of the city are the Old Town below the castle and the embankments designed by Plečnik along the Ljubljanica River.

Ljubljana began as the Roman town of Emona, and legacies of the Roman presence can still be seen throughout the city. The Habsburgs took control of Ljubljana in the 15th century and later built many of the pale-coloured churches and mansions that earned the city the nickname 'White Ljubljana'. From 1809 to 1814, Ljubljana was the capital of the 'Illyrian Provinces', Napoleon's short-lived springboard to the eastern Adriatic.

Despite the patina of imperial Austria, contemporary Ljubljana has a vibrant Slavic air all its own. It's like a little Prague without the hordes of tourists but with all the facilities you'll need. Over 27,000 students attend Ljubljana University's 14 faculties and three

art academies so the city always feels young. Though you can easily see the best Ljubljana has to offer in a day or two, it's a lovely place to linger and recharge those batteries.

Orientation

The tiny bus station and renovated train station are adjacent on Trg Osvobodilne Fronte (Trg OF) at the northern end of the centre (called Center). The 24-hour left-luggage office (*garderoba*; 150 SIT per piece) is on the platform inside the train station. A smaller garderoba (open from 5.30 am to 8.30 pm) is inside the bus station.

The best source for hiking and other maps is Kod & Kam, Trg Francoske Revolucije 7, a travel bookshop opposite the Križanke concert hall.

Information

Tourist Offices The Tourist Information Centre (TIC; ☎ 224 222) has moved from Slovenska cesta 35 to the historical Kresija building south of Triple Bridge. It's open on weekdays from 8 am to 7 pm, and weekends from 8 am to noon and from 4 to 7 pm. The TIC is well worth visiting to pick up free maps and brochures especially the *Where? City Guide*, a goldmine of information. They also have a new office at the train station.

The Cultural Information Centre (☎214 025) next to Trg Francoske Revolucije 7 can answer questions about what's on in Ljubljana and has a free booklet listing all the city's museums and galleries.

The main office of the Alpine Association of Slovenia (☎ 312 553) is at Dvoržakova ulica 9, in a small house set back from the street.

Money The currency exchange office inside the train station is open 24 hours a day. They accept travellers' cheques, charge no commission and the rate is decent. The best rate anywhere in Slovenia, though, is at Nova Ljubljanska Banka, Trg Republike 2. There's an A Banka branch at Slovenska cesta 50.

The currency exchange machine outside the SKB Banka, in the very centre of the modern shopping mall at Trg Ajdovščina 4, changes the banknotes of 18 countries.

The Hida exchange bureau in the historical Seminary building near the open-air market in

Pogarčarjev trg is open on weekdays from 7 am to 7 pm and on Saturday to 2 pm.

Post & Communications Poste-restante mail is held for 30 days at the post office at Slovenska cesta 32. It is open weekdays from 7 am to 8 pm and to 1 pm Saturday.

To mail a parcel you must go to the special customs post office at Trg OF 5 opposite the bus station. Make sure you bring your package open for inspection; the maximum weight is about 15 kg, depending on the destination. You can make international telephone calls or send faxes from either post office or the main one at Pražakova ulica 3, but the Trg OF one is open round the clock.

The telephone code for Ljubljana is ☎ 061.

Travel Agencies Backpackers and students should head for the Erazem travel office (☎ 133 1076) at Trubarjeva cesta 7. They can provide information, make bookings and they have a message board. They also sell ISIC cards (550 SIT) and, for those under 26 but not studying, FIYTO cards (700 SIT). Mladi Turist (☎ 312 185), at Celovška cesta 49, is the office of the Slovenian Youth Hostel Association and sells hostel cards (600 to 1800 SIT, depending on your age).

Slovenijaturist (☎ 131 5206), Slovenska cesta 58, sells BIJ international train tickets (one third cheaper than regular fares) to persons aged under 26 years.

The American Express representative is Atlas (☎ 133 2028), Mestni trg 8. They will hold clients' mail but don't cash travellers' cheques.

Bookshops Ljubljana's largest bookshop is MK Knjigarna Konzorcij at Slovenska cesta 29. It also has a branch on Miklošičeva cesta 40, opposite the bus station. Another good chain with a shop at Slovenska cesta 37 is Cankarjeva Založba.

The best place for English and other foreign-language newspapers and magazines is the newsstand in the lobby of the Grand Hotel Union, Miklošičeva cesta 1.

Medical & Emergency Services You can see a doctor at the University Medical Centre (Klinični Center; ☎ 133 6236) at Zaloška cesta 2. Signposted 'urgenca', the emergency unit is open 24 hours a day.

Things to See
The most picturesque sights of old Ljubljana are along both banks of the Ljubljanica River, a tributary of the Sava that curves around the foot of Castle Hill.

Opposite the TIC in the Kresija building is the celebrated **Triple Bridge**. In 1931, Jože Plečnik added the side bridges to the original central span dating from 1842. On the northern side of the bridge is Prešernov trg with its inviting **Franciscan church** (1660), a statue (1905) of poet France Prešeren and some lovely Art Nouveau buildings. The lively pedestrian street Čopova ulica runs to the north-west.

On the south side of the bridge in Mestni trg, the baroque **Robba Fountain** stands before the **Town Hall** (1718). Italian sculptor Francesco Robba designed this fountain in 1751 and modelled it after one in Rome. Enter the Town Hall to see the double Gothic courtyard. To the south of Mestni trg is **Stari trg**, atmospheric by day or night. North-east are the twin towers of the **Cathedral of St Nicholas** (1708), which contains impressive frescos. Behind the cathedral is Ljubljana's colourful open-air **produce market** (closed Sunday) and a lovely **colonnade** along the riverside designed by Plečnik.

Študentovska ulica, opposite the Vodnik statue in the market square, leads up to **Ljubljana Castle** (closed Monday). The castle has been undergoing reconstruction for decades, but you can climb the 19th-century **Castle Tower** to the west and view the exhibits in a Gothic chapel and the **Pentagonal Tower**. The modern building to the south-east is used as a wedding hall. Reber ulica beside Stari trg 17 also leads up to the castle.

There's another interesting area worth exploring on the west side of the Ljubljanica River. The **Municipal Museum**, Gosposka ulica 15 (open Tuesday to Saturday from 9 am to 7 pm), is a good place to start. The museum has a well-presented collection of Roman artefacts, plus a scale model of Roman Emona (Ljubljana). Upstairs rooms contain period furniture and household objects.

At Gosposka ulica 14 near the Town Museum is the **National & University Library** (1941) designed by Plečnik, and north on

SLOVENIA

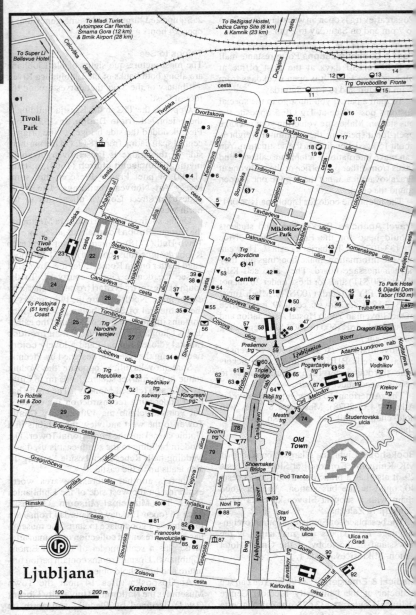

To Mladi Turist,
Avtoimpex Car Rental,
Šmarna Gora (12 km)
& Brnik Airport (28 km)

To Bežigrad Hostel,
Ježica Camp Site (6 km)
& Kamnik (23 km)

To Super Li
Bellevue Hotel

Trg Osvoboditne Fronte

Tivoli
Park

Tivoška

Dvoržakova   ulica

Prašakova

Čeligova

Gosposvetska

Kmetinova ulica

Voshakova ulica

Slovenska

Trdinova   ulica

Cigaletova

Tavčarjeva

Miklošičev
Park

Miklošičeva

Kolodvorska

Komenskega   ulica

Resljeva

To Park Hotel
& Dijaški Dom
Tabor (150 m)

Dalmatinova

Trg
Ajdovščina

Center

Puharjeva ulica

To Tivoli
Castle

Štefanova

Cankarjeva   cesta

Župančičeva

Prešernova

Beethovnova

Tomšičeva

Trg
Narodnih
Herojev

Nazorjeva   ulica

Čopova

Slovenska

Šubičeva   ulica

Prešernov
trg

Ljubljanica   River

Dragon Bridge

Trg
Republike

Plečnikov
trg
subway

Kongresni
trg

Wolfova ul

Triple
Bridge

Adamič-Lundrovo nab

Vodnikov
trg

To Rožnik
Hill & Zoo

Ribji trg

Ciril Metodov

Krekov
trg

Erjavčeva   cesta

Mestni
trg

Old
Town

Študentovska
ulcia

Gregorčičeva

Dvorni
trg

Cankarjevo

Shoemaker
Bridge

Pod Trančo

Ljubljanica River

Igriška

Rimska

Vegova

Turjaška ul

Novi trg

Stari
trg

Reber
ulica

Ulica na
Grad

Francoske
Revolucije

Gosposka

Breg

Gornji trg

Levstikov trg

Rožna ul

Slovenska

Zoisova   cesta

Ljubljanica

Karlovška   cesta

Ljubljana

Krakovo

0   100   200 m

PLACES TO STAY
42 Holiday Inn
43 Turist Hotel & Central Disco
51 Grand Hotel Union
55 Slon Hotel
81 Pri Mraku Guesthouse

PLACES TO EAT
5 Evropa Café
17 Mercator Delicatessen
32 Maximarket/Maxim Self-Service Restaurant
36 Dairy Queen
37 Daj-Dam
40 Super 5 Club Food Stand
46 Napoli Pizzeria
53 Šestica
57 McDonald's
64 Mercator Delicatessen
66 Ribca Seafood Bar
72 Kolovrat
77 Ljubljanski Dvor
89 Pizzeria Romeo
90 Sichuan

OTHER
1 Tivoli Recreation Centre
2 Ilirija Swimming Pool
3 Alpine Association of Slovenia
4 Adria Airways Office
6 Klub K4/University Student Centre
7 A Banka
8 City Bus Ticket Kiosks
9 Slovenijaturist Travel Agency
10 Main Post Office
11 Adria Airways Airport Buses

12 Post Office (Customs)
13 City Airport Buses
14 Train Station
15 Bus Station
16 Kompas Cinema
18 US Embassy
19 Kompas Hertz Car Rental
20 Kinoteka Cinema
21 Globtour Budget Car Rental
22 National Gallery
23 Serbian Orthodox Church
24 Museum of Modern Art
25 National Museum
26 Opera House
27 Parliament Building
28 UK Embassy
29 Cankarjev Dom (Cultural Centre)
30 Nova Ljubljanska Banka
31 Ursuline Church
33 Emona Globtour Travel Agency
34 MK Knjigarna Konzorcij Bookshop
35 Komuna Cinema
38 Cankarjeva Založba Bookshop
39 Skyscraper Building & Café
41 SKB Banka
44 TruBar
45 Irish Pub
47 Erazem Travel Agency
48 Urbanc Building/ Centromerkur Department Store
49 Vas Travel Agency
50 Art-Nouveau Bank Buildings

52 El Dorado Disco
54 Kompas Travel Agency
56 Post Office (Poste Restante)
58 Franciscan Church
59 Prešeren Monument
60 Horse's Tail Pub/Café
61 Cutty Sark Pub
62 Babilon Disco
63 Alba Laundry
65 Tourist Information Centre (TIC)
67 Bishop's Palace
68 Seminary/Hida Exchange Bureau
69 Cathedral of Saint Nicholas
70 Produce Market
71 Puppet Theatre
73 Robba Fountain
74 Town Hall
75 Castle
76 Atlas Travel Agency (American Express)
78 Filharmonija
79 Ljubljana University
80 Glej Theatre
82 Cultural Information Centre
83 National & University Library
84 Kod & Kam Bookshop
85 Križanke Ticket Office
86 Križanke/Summer Festival Theatre
87 Municipal Museum
88 Academy of Arts & Sciences
91 Church of St James
92 Church of St Florian

Gosposka ulica at Kongresni trg 12 is the main building of **Ljubljana University** (1902), formerly the regional parliament. The lovely **Filharmonija**, at No 10 on the south-east corner of the square, is home to the Slovenian Philharmonic Orchestra. The **Ursuline church** (1726) with an altar by Robba faces Kongresni trg to the west.

If you still have time, walk west on Šubičeva ulica where there are several museums. All are open Tuesday to Saturday from 10 am to 6 pm and Sunday to 1 pm, and each costs 300/200 SIT for adults/students and children. The **National Museum**, at Muzejska ulica 1, has prehistory, natural history and ethnography

collections. The highlight is a Celtic situla, a kind of pail or urn, from the 6th century BC sporting a fascinating relief. Most of the captions aren't in English, but the museum building, erected in 1885, is impressive.

The **National Gallery**, Cankarjeva ulica 20, offers portraits and landscapes from the 17th to 19th centuries, as well as copies of medieval frescos. Diagonally opposite, at Cankarjeva ulica 15, is the **Museum of Modern Art**, where the International Biennial of Graphic Arts is held every other summer in odd-numbered years. The Serbian Orthodox **Church of SS Cyril & Methodius** just opposite is worth entering to see the beautiful modern frescos (open Tuesday to Saturday from 3 to 6 pm). The subway from the Museum of Modern Art leads to the relaxing, if somewhat unkempt, **Tivoli Park**.

Activities
The **Tivoli Recreation Centre**, in the Tivoli Park at Celovška cesta 25, has bowling alleys, tennis courts, an indoor swimming pool, a fitness centre, a roller-skating rink and a popular sauna called **Zlati Klub** with several saunas, a steam room, warm and cold splash pools and a small outside pool surrounded by high walls so you can sunbathe in the nude (mixed sexes). Entry costs 1100 SIT. The outdoor **Ilirija pool** opposite the Tivoli Hotel at Celovška cesta 3 is open in summer from 10 am to 7 pm on weekdays, 9 am to 8 pm at the weekend.

Organised Tours
From June to September, a two-hour free guided tour of the city, in English, sponsored by the TIC departs daily at 5 pm from the Town Hall in Mestni trg. During the rest of the year there are tours at 11 am on Sunday only.

Places to Stay
Camping Six km north of Center on the Sava River at Dunajska cesta 270 (bus No 8 to the terminus) is *Camping Ježica* (☎ 371 382), with a large, shady camping area (860 SIT per person, 180 SIT per tent) and 38 cramped little bungalows costing 6500 SIT for two. The site is open all year.

Hostels Four student dormitories (*dijaški dom*) open their doors to foreign travellers in July and August. The most central by far is the *Dijaški Dom Tabor* (☎ 321 067), opposite the Hotel Park at Vidovdanska ulica 7 and affiliated with Hostelling International. They charge 1600 SIT for a single room and 1200 SIT per person for a bed in a double or triple. There is a discount of 10% if you pay three days in advance.

The *Dijaški Dom Bežigrad* (☎ 342 867), another HI member, is at Kardeljeva ploščad 28 in the Bežigrad district two km north of the train and bus stations. It has singles/ doubles/ triples with shower and toilet for 1800/3000/ 3600 SIT and triples with shared facilities for 1000 SIT per person. An HI card gets you 10%

off. The Bežigrad has 150 rooms available in July and August but only about 15 the rest of the year.

Private Rooms The TIC has about 40 rooms on their list but just a handful are in Center. Most of the others would require a bus trip up to Bežigrad.

Prices range from DM15 to DM20 for singles and DM25 to DM35, depending on the category. They also have eight apartments (again not central) for two or three people starting at about DM80 a day.

Hotels The 124-room *Hotel Park* (☎ 133 1306) at Tabor 9 is where most people usually end up as it's the city's only large budget hotel close to Center and the Old Town. It's pretty basic, but the price is right: DM49 for a single with breakfast and shower and DM75 for a double. Rooms without showers are 20% cheaper and students get a 20% discount (provided they have a student card). The staff are very helpful and friendly.

One of the best deals in Ljubljana is the 15-room *Super Li Bellevue Hotel* (☎ 133 4949) on the northern edge of Tivoli Park at Pod Gozdom 12. There are no rooms with private baths, but bright and airy singles/ doubles with wash basin are 3050/6000 SIT.

The closest thing to a guesthouse in Ljubljana is the 30-room *Pri Mraku* (☎ 223 412), west of Trg Francoske Revolucije at Rimska cesta 4. The rooms are quite small for what they charge: 4400 SIT for a single with shower and breakfast and 6900 SIT for a double.

The three-star Art Nouveau *Grand Hotel Union* (☎ 125 4133), Miklošičeva cesta 1, with 134 rooms, manages to preserve some of the elegance of its inaugural year (1905).

At DM150/220 for a single/double with bath and breakfast, rooms at the Grand Union are about 30% cheaper than those in the adjacent 133-room *Holiday Inn* (☎ 125 5051), but guests get to use the latter's swimming pool and gym.

Places to Eat
Restaurants The capital abounds in Italian restaurants and pizzerias. Among the best is the *Ljubljanski Dvor* at Dvorni trg 1 on the west bank of the Ljubljanica (pizzas from 600 SIT),

but there is also *Pizzeria Romeo* in the Old Town at Stari trg 6, *Napoli Pizzeria* off Trubarjeva cesta at Prečna ulica 7 and the studenty *Čerin* at the eastern end of Trubarjeva cesta on Znamenjska ulica.

The *Kolovrat* at Ciril Metodov trg 14 opposite the cathedral is an old gostilna with reasonably priced Slovenian meals, or you can try the 200-year-old standby *Šestica* with a pleasant courtyard at Slovenska cesta 38. Main courses start at about 750 SIT. If you've a yen for some Chinese food, the location of the *Sichuan* below St Florian's Church at Gornji trg 23 is wonderful.

Among the two cheapest places for lunch are the *Maxim* self-service restaurant in the basement of the Maximarket department store on Trg Republike, and *Daj-Dam* at Cankarjeva ulica 4. But don't expect cordon bleu food; it's real school cafeteria stuff.

For a quick and very tasty lunch, try the fried squid or whitebait (from 350 SIT) at *Ribca*, a basement seafood bar below the Plečnik colonnade in Pogarčarjev trg.

There are *burek stands* everywhere in Ljubljana, and one of the best is opposite the train station on Masarykova cesta. If you want something more substantial, head for the outdoor *Super 5 Club*, which faces Slovenska cesta from the shopping mall in Trg Ajdovščina. They serve cheap and cheerful Balkan grills like čevapčiči (550 SIT) and pleskavica (380 SIT) till very late.

Cafés For coffee and cakes head for the renovated *Evropa* café on the corner of Slovenska cesta and Gosposvetska cesta or the *Slon* café in the Slon Hotel, Slovenska cesta 34. Better still (at least for the views) is the *Nebotičnik Terasa* café on the top (12th) floor of the Art Deco skyscraper building at the corner of Slovenska cesta and Štefanova ulica.

Fast Food Ljubljana boasts a *Dairy Queen* and a *McDonald's* – at Cankarjeva cesta 2 and Čopova ulica 14 respectively.

Self-Catering The largest supermarket in the city is in the basement of the *Maximarket* department store in Trg Republike.

But the best places for picnic supplies are the *Mercator* delicatessen branches on Stritarjeva ulica, opposite the TIC, and the corner of Milošičeva cesta and Pražakova ulica.

Entertainment
Ljubljana enjoys a very rich cultural life so ask the TIC for its monthly programme of events called *Where to? in Ljubljana*.

Classical Music & Theatre The city's main venue – with up to 700 cultural events a year – is *Cankarjev Dom* on Trg Republike. It has two large auditoriums (the Great Hall has perfect acoustics) and a number of smaller ones. The ticket office, in the basement of the nearby Maximarket mall, is open on weekdays from 11 am to 1.30 pm and 4 to 8 pm, Saturday from 10 am to 1 pm and for an hour before performances. Also check for concerts at the beautiful *Filharmonija* in Kongresni trg. Tickets generally run between 600 and 1500 SIT.

The ticket office of the *Opera House*, where ballets are also performed, is at Župančičeva ulica 1 and opens Monday to Saturday from 11 am to 1 pm and an hour before each performance.

For tickets to the International Summer Festival and anything else staged at the *Križanke*, go to the booking office behind the Illirija Column at Trg Francoske Revolucije 1-2. It is open weekdays from 11 am to 6 or 7 pm and one hour before performances.

Ljubljana has six theatres and nine companies so there should be something for everyone. The *Glej Theatre*, Gregorčičeva ulica 3, is Ljubljana's foremost experimental theatre with three resident or affiliated companies, including the Betontanc dance troupe. They're often on tour and the theatre is closed in July and August; in other months your best chance to see a performance is on Thursday or Friday night.

The *Puppet Theatre* performs at the St James Theatre, south of Vodnikov trg at Krekov trg 2.

Cinemas For first-run films in Ljubljana, head for the *Kino Komuna* at Cankarjeva cesta 1 or *Kino Union* at Nazorjeva 2. *Kino Kompas* at Miklošičeva cesta 38 and the *Kinoteka* at No 28 both screen art and classic films. In general, tickets cost 400 to 550 SIT and discounts are offered on Monday.

Discos The most popular conventional discos are *El Dorado*, open daily to at least 2 am, behind Nazorjeva ulica 6, *Babilon* at Kongresni trg 2 (Tuesday to Saturday from 10 pm to 4 am) and *Central* next to the Hotel Turist at Dalmatinova ulica 15.

The student *Klub K4* at Keršnikova ulica 4 has a disco on some nights (Sunday is for gays and lesbians), but the most popular rave venue at present is *Dakota DC-3* in the BTC centre at far-flung Šmartinska cesta 152/g north-east of the train station (bus Nos 2, 7 and 12). It rages Thursday, Friday and Saturday from 10 pm to 4 pm.

Pubs Pleasant and congenial places for a pivo or glass of vino include the outdoor *Horse's Tail* (Konjski Rep) pub/café in Prešernov trg, the *TruBar* at Trubarjeva cesta 23, the *Irish Pub* at Prečna ulica 5 and the *Cutty Sark* on Wolfova ulica.

Things to Buy

Digitalia at Gregorčičeva ulica 9 and Muzikalje at Trg Francoske Revolucije 6 have CDs and cassettes of Slovenian folk music. Vinoteka Simon Bradeško at Dunajska cesta 18 has a huge selection of Slovenian wines, which you can taste first.

Getting There & Away

Bus You can reach virtually anywhere in the country by bus from the capital. If you're heading for Bled or Bohinj, take the bus not the train. The train from Ljubljana to the former will leave you at the Lesce-Bled station, four km south-east of the lake. The closest train station to Lake Bohinj is at Bohinjska Bistrica, six km to the east, and it's on the branch line linking Nova Gorica with Jesenice.

The timetable in the shed-like bus station lists all routings and times, but here are some sample frequencies and one-way fares: Bled (hourly, 590 SIT); Bohinj (hourly, 880 SIT); Jesenice (hourly, 660 SIT); Koper (13 a day, 1130 SIT); Maribor (half-hourly, 1230 SIT); Piran (10 a day, 1260 SIT); Postojna (half-hourly, 530 SIT).

Buses from Ljubljana serve a number of international destinations as well, including: Belgrade (one daily at 5.45 pm, 5500 SIT); Budapest (Thursday and Friday at 10 pm, 4050

SIT); Frankfurt (Wednesday and Sunday, 11,520 SIT); Lenti (Tuesday and Thursday at 5.30 am, 2130 SIT); Munich (Tuesday to Thursday and Sunday, 4950 SIT); Novigrad (one daily); Prague (Tuesday, Thursday and Saturday at 9 pm); Pula (one daily); Rijeka (two a day); Rovinj (daily at 1.45 pm); Split (daily at 7.40 pm); Trieste (daily at 6.25 am, 990 SIT); Varaždin (two a day); Villach (daily at 5.30 am, 1050 SIT); and Zagreb (eight a day).

Train All domestic and international trains arrive at and depart from the station at Trg OF 6. Local trains leave Ljubljana regularly for Bled (415 SIT), Jesenice (504 SIT) Koper (865 SIT) and Maribor (865 SIT). Return fares are usually 20% cheaper than double the price, and there's an 120 SIT surcharge on domestic inter-city train tickets.

For information on international trains to/from Ljubljana, see the introductory Getting There & Away section of this chapter.

Getting Around

To/From the Airport To get to Brnik airport (28 km north-west of Ljubljana) catch the city bus (hourly, 270 SIT) from platform 28 at the bus station. The Adria airport bus, a bit further west on Trg OF, leaves between six and nine times a day (400 SIT), depending on the flights. A taxi would cost about 3500 SIT.

Bus The local bus system, run by LPP, is excellent and very user-friendly. There are a total of 22 lines; five of them (Nos 1, 2, 3, 6 and 11) are considered main lines. These start at 3.15 am and run till midnight while the rest operate from 5 am to 10.30 pm. You can pay on board (80 SIT) or use a tiny yellow plastic token (60 SIT) available at newsstands, tobacco shops, post offices and the two kiosks on the pavement in front of Slovenska cesta 55. Bus passes good for a day (*enodnevna vozovnica*, 180 SIT) or a week (*tedenska vozovnica*, 840 SIT) are also available.

Car The international car-rental chains are Kompas Hertz (☎ 311 241), Miklošičeva ulica 11; Globtour Budget (☎ 126 3118), Štefanova ulica 13; Europcar (☎ 132 2238), Trdinova ulica 9; and Avis (☎ 168 7204), Dunajska 156. They all have counters at Brnik airport. Two excellent smaller agencies are ABC (☎ 261 684) at Brnik airport and Avtoimpex (☎ 133 6228), Celovška cesta 150.

Taxi You can call a taxi on one of seven numbers: ☎ 9700 to 9706.

Julian Alps

Slovenia shares the Julian Alps in the north-west corner of the country with Italy. Three-headed Mt Triglav (2864 metres), the

country's highest peak, is climbed regularly by hundreds of weekend warriors, but there are countless less-ambitious hikes on offer in the region. Lakes Bled and Bohinj make ideal starting points – Bled with its comfortable resort facilities, Bohinj right beneath the rocky crags themselves. Most of this spectacular area falls under Triglav National Park (founded in 1924).

BLED

Bled, a fashionable resort at 501 metres, is set on an idyllic, two-km-long, emerald-green lake that has a little island with a church in the

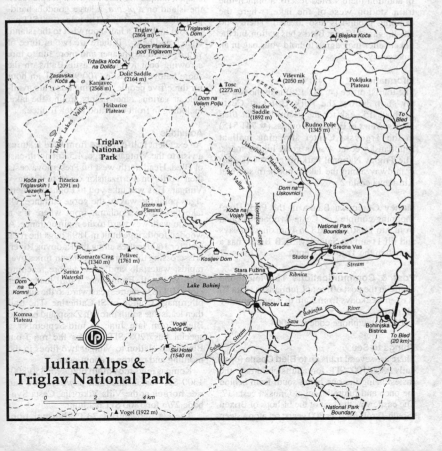

Julian Alps & Triglav National Park

middle and a castle towering overhead. Trout and carp proliferate in the clear lake water, which is surprisingly warm and a pleasure to swim in or go boating on. To the north-east, the highest peaks of the Karavanke Range form a natural boundary with Austria; the Julian Alps lie to the west. Bled has been a favourite destination for travellers for decades. All in all, it *is* beautiful but it can get very crowded – and pricey – in season.

Orientation

Bled village is at the east end of the lake below the castle. The bus station is also here, but the main Lesce-Bled train station is four km east. In addition there's Bled-Jezero, a branch-line train station west of the lake, where the camping ground is also located. There's no left-luggage office at Bled's bus station, but the ticket seller may agree to hold your bag in an emergency.

Information

The tourist office (☎ 741 122) is in the souvenir shop below the Park Hotel at Cesta Svobode 15. Ask for the useful booklet *Bled Tourist News* in English. Kompas (☎ 741 515) in the Trgovski Center shopping mall in Ljubljanska cesta 4 sells good hiking maps. The Triglav National Park office (☎ 741 188) is midway along the lake's northern shore at Kidričeva cesta 2.

Money Gorenjska Banka in the Park Hotel shopping complex on Cesta Svobode is open from 9 to 11.30 am and 1 to 4 pm on weekdays and till 11 am on Saturday. SKB Banka has a branch in the Trgovski Center.

Post & Communications The telephone centre in the post office at Ljubljanska cesta 10 is open weekdays from 7 am to 7 pm, Saturday till noon.

Bled's telephone code is ☎ 064.

Things to See

There are several trails up to **Bled Castle** (open daily, 300/100 SIT for adults/children), the easiest being the one going south from behind the once and future hostel at Grajska cesta 17. The castle was the seat of the bishops of Brixen (South Tyrol) for over 800 years; set atop a steep

cliff 100 metres above the lake, it offers magnificent views in clear weather. The castle's museum presents the history of the area and allows a peep into a small 16th-century chapel. You get free admission to the castle if you eat at the Blejski Grad restaurant there (a deposit against your meal must be paid at the gate).

Bled's other striking feature is tiny **Bled Island** at the west end of the lake. From the tall white belfry rising above the dense vegetation, the tolling 'bell of wishes' echoes across the lake. It's said that all who ring this bell will get what they ask for; naturally it chimes constantly. Beneath the present **baroque church** are the foundations of a pre-Romanesque chapel, unique in Slovenia. Most people reach the island on a *pletna*, a large gondola hand-propelled by a boatman. The price (900 SIT per person) includes a half-hour visit to the island, church and belfry. If there are two or three of you it would be cheaper and more fun to hire a rowing boat from the Castle Baths on the shore below the castle (700/900 SIT an hour for three/five people). Rowing boats are available at various other points around the lake, including in front of Grand Hotel Toplice.

Activities

An excellent half-day **hike** from Bled features a visit to the Vintgar Gorge, 4.5 km north-east of Bled. Head north-west on Prešernova cesta then north on Partizanska cesta to Cesta v Vintgar. This will take you to Podhom, where signs point the way to the gorge entrance. Or take the bus to Podhom, from where it's a 1.5-km walk westward to the main entrance. A wooden footbridge built in 1893 hugs the rock wall for 1600 metres along the Radovna River, crisscrossing the raging torrent four times over rapids, waterfalls and pools before reaching Šum Waterfall. From there a trail leads over Hom Hill (834 metres) eastward to the ancient pilgrimage Church of St Catherine. The trail then leads due south through Zasip and back to Bled. From late June to mid-September a special bus (200 SIT) makes the run from Bled's bus station to Vintgar two times in the morning and returns at about noon.

Kompas rents **mountain bikes** for 350/800/1300 SIT for an hour/half-day/day. You can ride **horses** at the Villa Viktorija, Cesta Svobode 27/a for 1800 SIT per hour.

There's a beautiful 23°C **thermal pool**

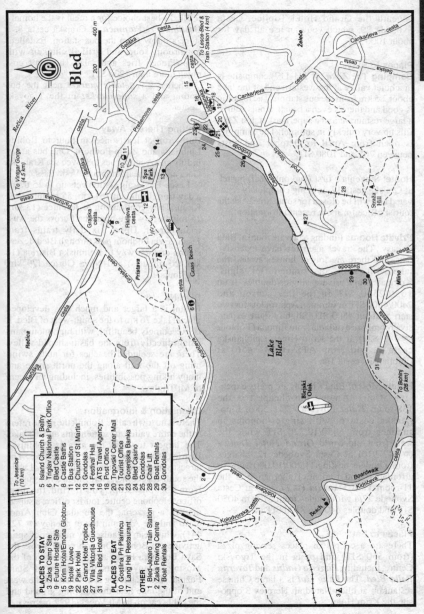

Bled

To Lesce-Bled &
Train Station (4 km)

To Vintgar Gorge
(4.5 km)

To Jesenice
(10 km)

To Bohinj
(26 km)

Lake
Bled

Blejski
Otok

Spa
Park

Grajska
cesta

Pristava

Mlino

Grass Beach

Boardwalk

Beach

Rečica River

Rečica

Stráza
Hill

PLACES TO STAY
3   Zaka Camp Site
6   Future Hostel Site
15 Krim Hotel/Emona Globtour
19 Hotel Lovec
22 Park Hotel
26 Grand Hotel Toplice
27 Villa Viktorija Guesthouse
31 Villa Bled Hotel

PLACES TO EAT
10 Gostilna Pri Planincu
17 Lang Hai Restaurant

OTHER
1   Bled-Jezero Train Station
2   Zaka Rowing Centre
4   Boat Rentals
5   Island Church & Belfry
6   Triglav National Park Office
7   Bled Castle
8   Castle Baths
11 Bus Station
12 Church of St Martin
13 Gondolas
14 Festival Hall
16 ATS Travel Agency
18 Post Office
20 Trgovski Center Mall
21 Tourist Office
23 Gorenjska Banka
24 Bled Casino
25 Gondolas
28 Chair Lift
29 Boat Rentals
30 Gondolas

beneath the Grand Hotel Toplice, Cesta Svobode 20, which you can use all day for about 1000 SIT.

Places to Stay

Camping The *Zaka* (☎ 741 117) camp site is in a quiet valley at the western end of the lake about 2.5 km from the bus station. The location is good and there's even a beach, tennis courts, a large restaurant and a supermarket, but Zaka fills up very quickly in summer. The camp site is open from April to October and costs between 765 and 1080 SIT.

Hostel Slovenia's first (and only real) hostel, at Grajska cesta 17, is being completely renovated and will be closed for some time. Ask the tourist office for more recent information.

Private Rooms Finding a private room at Bled is easy. The travel agencies have extensive lists, and there are lots of houses around the lake with 'sobe' or 'zimmer frei' signs. Kompas rents private singles/doubles from 1650/2340 SIT in the low season and 2400/4800 SIT in summer. Apartments for two start at about 4500 SIT. Slightly more expensive rooms are available from Emona Globtour (☎ 741 821) at the Krim Hotel, Ljubljanska cesta 7, and from ATS (☎ 741 456) at Ljubljanska cesta 1/a.

Hotels Most of Bled's hotels are pretty expensive affairs. Among the cheapest is the 138-room *Hotel Lovec* (☎ 741 500), Ljubljanska cesta 6, with singles/doubles in summer from 6450/10,320 SIT while the waterfront old-world *Grand Hotel Toplice* (☎ 647 910) at Cesta Svobode 12, charges from a budget-busting 11,200/19,000 SIT. An affordable (and romantic) alternative is the 11-room *Villa Viktorija* (☎ 77 344) at Cesta Svobode 27/a with singles from 2700 to 4050 SIT and doubles 5400 to 8100 SIT.

Places to Eat

There are a couple of places serving pizza (from 550 SIT) and pasta in the Trgovski Centre, including *Pizzeria Gallus* and *Taverna Bella Bled*. The *Lang Hai* is a large Chinese restaurant at ulica Narodnih Herojev 3 opposite the Krim Hotel.

Bled's best choice for a meal is the homely *Gostilna Pri Planincu* at Grajska cesta 8, a stone's throw from the bus station. Excellent mushroom soup and grilled chicken with chips/French fries and salad shouldn't cost much more than 1200 SIT.

There's a *vegetable market* near the bus station and a *supermarket* in the Trgovski Center.

Getting There & Away

Buses run at least once an hour to Bohinj, Ljubljana and Zasip-Podhom. One bus a day in July and August goes to Bovec via Kranjska Gora and the heart-stopping Vršič Pass.

Lesce-Bled train station gets up to 15 trains a day from Ljubljana (51 km, 55 minutes) via Kranj. They continue on to Jesenice (13 km; 15 minutes), where about half cross the Austrian border. Up to six daily trains from Jesenice via Podhom pass through Bled-Jezero station on their way to Bohinjska Bistrica (18 km; 20 minutes) and Nova Gorica (79 km, 1¾ hours).

BOHINJ

Bohinj is a larger and much less developed glacial lake 26 km to the south-west of Bled. It is exceedingly beautiful, with high mountains rising directly from the basin-shaped valley. There are secluded beaches for nude swimming off the trail along the north shore and many hiking possibilities, including an ascent of Mt Triglav.

Orientation & Information

There is no town called Bohinj; the name refers to the entire valley, its settlements and the lake. The largest town in the area is Bohinjska Bistrica, six km to the east of the lake. The largest settlement on the lake is Ribčev Laz in the south-east corner. Here, all in a row just up from the bus stop, you'll find the post office/telephone centre, tourist office, a supermarket, a pizzeria, the popular Club Amor disco and the Alpinum travel agency (☎ 723 441), which can organise any number of sport activities in Bohinj. One km north across the Sava Bohinjka River and at the mouth of the Mostnica Canyon sits the village of Stara Fužina. Hotel Zlatorog is at Ukanc at the west end of the lake near the camping ground and the cable car up to Mt Vogel (1922 metres).

Post & Communications The post office at Ribčev Laz 47 is open weekdays from 8 am to 6 pm (with a couple of half-hour breaks) and on Saturday till noon.

The telephone code for Bohinj is ☎ 064.

Things to See & Do

The **Church of St John the Baptist**, on the northern side of the Sava Bohinjka across the stone bridge from Ribčev Laz, has exquisite 15th-century frescos and can lay claim to being the most beautiful and evocative church in Slovenia. If the church is locked, ask the tourist office for the key.

The **Herders' Museum** at house No 181 in Stara Fužina, about 1.5 km north of Ribčev Laz, has a small but interesting collection related to Alpine dairy farming in the Bohinj Valley, once the most important such centre in Slovenia. If you have time, take a walk to the village of **Studor**, a couple of km to the east. It is renowned for its *kozolci* and *toplarji*; large single and double hayracks that are unique to Slovenia.

The Alpinum agency has an equipment rental kiosk at Ribčev Laz 53, to the right just before you cross the stone bridge over the Sava Bohinjka. **Bicycles** and mountain bikes are DM5/20 per hour/day while **canoes** and kayaks are DM6/25. They also organise guided mountain tours (from DM30), rafting trips on the Sava (DM30) and 'canyoning' through the rapids of the Mostnica Gorge safely stuffed into a neoprene suit, life jacket and helmet for DM80.

The **Vogel cable car**, above the camping ground at the western end of Lake Bohinj about five km from Ribčev Laz, will whisk you 1000 metres up into the mountains. It runs every half-hour year-round (except possibly in November) from 7.30 am to 6 pm (till 8 pm in July and August). Adults/children pay 900/600 SIT for a return ticket. From the Ski Hotel Vogel (1540 metres) at the upper station you can scale **Mt Vogel** (1922 metres) in a couple of hours for a sweeping view of the region. Be careful in the fog.

Places to Stay

Camping The large *Zlatorog* camp site (☎ 723 441) on the lake near the Zlatorog Hotel costs 720 to 900 SIT, depending on the season (May to September). It's one of the most beautifully situated camping grounds in Europe, close to a lake beach and a good base for hiking.

Hostel The *Apolon Hotel* (☎ 723 469), about two km west of Ribčev Laz on the lake's southern shore at Ribčev Laz 63, doubles as a hostel all year. A bed in a room for two or three (many with their own showers) costs about 2000 SIT.

Private Rooms & Pensions The tourist office can arrange private rooms in Ribčev Laz, Stara Fužina and neighbouring villages for as little as DM11 per person per night in the low season and up to DM20 in July and August (though there are 20% surcharges for stays of less than three nights and for guests on their own).

The *Stare Penzion* (☎ 723 403), with nine rooms on the Savica River north of the Zlatorog Hotel at Ukanc 128, has singles/doubles with shower and breakfast for 3500/5700 SIT.

Places to Eat

The *MK Pizzeria* next to the Alpinum travel agency at 50 Ribčev Laz is very popular all year round. If you've got wheels of any sort, head for *Gostilna Rupa* at house No 89 in the village of Srednja Vas, about five km north-east of Ribčev Laz. It has some of the best home-cooking in Slovenia. For something truly different at lunch, try *Planšar* opposite the Herders' Museum at Stara Fužina 179. It specialises in home-made dairy products, and you can taste a number of local specialities for about 500 SIT.

Getting There & Away

Buses to and from Ljubljana via Bled and Kranj are very frequent; count on up to a dozen departures a day. There are also three to five buses a day to Bohinjska Bistrica. All of these buses stop near the post office on Triglavska cesta in Bohinjska Bistrica and in Ribčev Laz before carrying on to the Zlatorog hotel in Ukanc. The closest train station is at Bohinjska Bistrica on the Jesenice-Nova Gorica line.

TREKKING MT TRIGLAV

The Julian Alps are one of the finest hiking areas in Eastern Europe. A mountain trip here is also an excellent way to meet Slovenes, so take advantage of this opportunity if you're in the country during the hiking season. A mountain hut (*planinska koča* or *planinski dom*) is normally less than five hours' walk away. The huts in the higher regions are open from July to September, and in the lower regions from June to October. You'll never be turned away if the weather looks bad, but some huts on Triglav get very crowded at weekends, especially in August and September. A bed for the night shouldn't be more than 1500 SIT per person. Meals are also available, so you don't need to carry a lot of gear. Leave most of your things below, but warm clothes, sturdy boots and good physical condition are indispensable.

The best months for hiking are August and September, though above 1500 metres you can encounter winter weather conditions at any time. Keep to the trails that are well-marked with red-and-white circles, rest frequently and never *ever* try to trek alone. Before you set out, pick up the 1:20,000 *Julijske Alpe – Triglav* and *Julijske Alpe – Bohinj* maps or something similar at a bookshop or tourist office.

The circular three-day route described here is not the shortest or the easiest way to climb Slovenia's highest mountain, but it is one of the most rewarding. Try to get hold of the brochure *An Alpine Guide*, which provides more detail than can be included here or the seminal *How to Climb Triglav* published by the Alpine Association.

The Route from Bohinj

An hour's hike west of the Zlatorog Hotel at Ukanc is the **Savica Waterfall**, the source of the Sava River, which gushes from a limestone cave and falls 60 metres into a narrow gorge.

From the waterfall a path zigzags up the steep Komarča crag. From the top of this cliff (1340 metres), there's an excellent view of Lake Bohinj. Further north, three to four hours from the falls, is the *Koča pri Triglavskih Jezerih* (1685 metres; mobile ☎ 0609-615 235), a 104-bed hut at the southern end of the fantastic Triglav Lakes Valley where you'll spend the night. If you want a good overview of the valley and its seven permanent lakes (the others fill up in spring only), you can climb to Mt Tičarica (2091 metres) to the north-east in about one hour. An alternative – though longer – route from the waterfall to the Triglav Lakes

Valley is via *Dom na Komni* and the Komna Plateau.

On the second day, you hike up the valley, past the largest glacial lakes then north-east to the desert-like Hribarice Plateau (2358 metres). You descend to the Dolič Saddle (2164 metres) where the *Tržaška Koča na Doliču* (2152 metres; mobile ☎ 0609-614 780) has 60 beds. You would have walked about four hours by this stage from the Koča pri Triglavskih Jezerih and could well carry on to *Dom Planika pod Triglavom* (2401 metres; mobile ☎ 0609-614 773), about 1½ hours to the north-east, but this 80-bed hut fills up quickly.

From Dom Planika it's just over an hour to the summit of Triglav (2864 metres), a well-trodden path indeed. Don't be surprised if you find yourself being turned over to have your bottom beaten with a birch switch. It's a long-established tradition for Triglav 'virgins'.

You could return the way you came, but it's far more interesting to go back to Bohinj southward via Stara Fužina. This way passes the 50-bed *Dom na Velem Polju* (1817 metres; mobile ☎ 0609-615 621) less than two hours from Dom Planika. There are two routes to choose from between Vodnikov Dom and Stara Fužina: down the Voje Valley or over Uskovnica, a highland pasture at about 1100 metres. The former takes about four hours; the route via Uskovnica is a little longer but affords better views.

If you decide to do the trip in reverse – starting from Stara Fužina and returning via the Savica Waterfall – count on walking about seven hours to Dom Planika through the Voje Valley and eight hours via Uskovnica.

Soča Valley

KOBARID & BOVEC

The Soča Valley, defined by the aquamarine Soča River, stretches from Triglav National Park to Nova Gorica and is one of the most beautiful and peaceful spots in Slovenia. Of course it wasn't always that way. During much of WWI, this was the site of the infamous Soča (or Isonzo) Front, which claimed the lives of an estimated one million people and was immortalised by the American writer Ernest Hemingway in his novel *A Farewell to Arms*. Today visitors flock to the town of **Kobarid** to relive these events at the award-winning **Kobarid Museum** (Gregorčičeva ulica 10; 400/250 SIT adults/students and children) or, more commonly, head for Bovec, 21 km north, to take part in some of the best white-water rafting in Europe. The season lasts from April to October.

The people to see for the latter are Soča Rafting (☎ 065-86 040) in the Alp Hotel at Trg Golobarskih Žrtev 18 or Bovec Rafting Team (☎ 065-86 128) further west on the same street opposite the Martinov Hram restaurant. Rafting trips on the Soča, taking 1½ hours with distances of up to 10 km, cost from 3050 to 5850 SIT (including neoprene long john, wind cheater, life jacket, helmet and paddle). A kayak/canoe for two is 3600/6000 SIT for the day. There are kayaking courses on offer in summer (eg a weekend for beginners costs 9000 SIT).

In Kobarid, the tourist office in the Kobarid Museum (☎ 065-85 055) and, in Bovec, the Avrigo travel agency (☎ 065-86 123) next to the Alp Hotel can organise *private rooms* for about 1800 SIT for a single and 3250 SIT for a double. There are *camp sites* in both towns.

Getting There & Away
Buses between Kobarid and Bovec and to Tolmin are frequent. Other destinations include: Bled (one a day); Ljubljana (up to six); and Nova Gorica (five). In summer one bus a day heads for Ljubljana via the Vršič Pass, Kranjska Gora, Bled and Kranj.

Karst Region

POSTOJNA
Vying with Bled as the top tourist spot in Slovenia, **Postojna Cave** continues to attract the hordes, but many travellers feel they've seen Disneyland after their visit – especially if they've first been to the more natural Škocjan Caves, 33 km to the south-west (see the following). Visitors get to see about 5.5 km of the cave's 27 km on a 1½-hour tour in their own language; about four km are covered by an electric train that will shuttle you through colourfully lit karst formations along the so-called Old Passage and the remaining 1700 metres is on foot. The tour ends with a viewing of a tank full of *Proteus anguinus*, the unique salamander-like beasties inhabiting Slovenia's karst caves.

There are at least two weekday visits (at 10 am and 2 pm) year round with two more (at noon and 4 pm) at the weekend. From March to October there are between four and 11 daily tours. Depending on the season, admission is 1440 or 1800 SIT for adults and 720 or 900 SIT for children. Dress warmly as the cave is a constant 8°C (with 95% humidity) all year.

If you have extra time, visit **Predjama Castle**, the awesome 16th-century fortress perched in the gaping mouth of a hill-top cavern nine km north-west of Postojna.

Orientation & Information
The cave is about two km north-west of Postojna's bus centre and bus station, which has a left-luggage office. The train station is a km east of the centre. Kompas (☎ 067-25 439) at Titov trg 1/a has private rooms from 1600 SIT per person.

Getting There & Away
Postojna can be a day trip from Ljubljana or a stopover on the way to/from the coast or Croatian Istria. There are direct trains to Postojna from Ljubljana (67 km), Koper (86 km) and Rijeka (79 km). The bus station in Postojna is much more conveniently located, and almost all buses between Ljubljana and the coast stop there.

ŠKOCJAN CAVES
The Škocjan Caves, in the village of Matavun five km south-east of Divača (between Postojna and Koper), have been heavily promoted since 1986 when they were entered on UNESCO's World Heritage List. There are between three and seven daily 1½-hour tours of the cave between April and October but at weekends only (at 10 am and 3.30 pm) the rest of the year. Admission is 1500/1000 SIT for adults/children. These caves are in more natural surroundings – some consider a visit the highlight of their stay in Slovenia – than Postojna Cave but tough to reach without your own transport. From the train station at Divača

(up to a dozen trains daily to/from Ljubljana), you can follow a three-km path leading south-east through the village of Dolnje Ležeče to Matavun. The driver of any bus heading along the highway to/from the coast will let you off at the access road (there are huge signs announcing the caves) if you ask in advance. From there you can walk the remaining 1.5 km to the caves' entrance.

LIPICA

This small village in the middle of the Karst some 10 km south-west of Divača is where the snow-white Lipizzaner horses of the imperial Spanish Riding School in Vienna were first bred in the 18th century. You can tour the 311-hectare **Lipica Stud Farm** all year round; there are between six and eight guided tours a day (from 9.30 am to 3 or 5 pm, depending on the season). Exhibition performances, where these intelligent creatures go through all their paces, take place on Tuesday and Friday (at 2.30 pm) and on Sunday (at 3.30 pm) from May to September. Admission costs 1000/700 SIT for adults/children (1800/1100 SIT including the performance as well). Riding costs 2160 SIT an hour. Two or three buses a day (week-days only) link Lipica with Divača and, to the north, Sežana.

The Coast

KOPER

Koper, only 21 km south of Trieste, is the first of several quaint old coastal towns along the north side of the Istrian Peninsula. The town's Italian name, Capodistria, recalls its former status as capital of Istria under the Venetian Republic in the 15th and 16th centuries. After WWII, Koper's port was developed to provide Slovenia with an alternative to Italian Trieste and Croatian Rijeka. Once an island but now firmly connected to the mainland by a cause-way, the Old Town's medieval flavour lingers despite the surrounding industry, container ports, high-rise buildings, superhighways and developments beyond its 'walls'. This admin-istrative centre and largest town on the Slovene coast makes a good base for exploring the region.

Orientation

The bus and train stations are adjacent, about a km south-east of the Old Town at the end of Kolodvorska cesta. There's a left-luggage office in the train station open daily from 5.30 am to 10 pm.

Information

There is no tourist office here, but Slovenija-turist (☎ 066-271 358), opposite the marina at Trg Antona Ukmarja 7, can help.

Money Splošna Banka Koper, at Kidričeva ulica 21 a few doors west of the regional museum, changes travellers' cheques without commission on weekdays from 8.30 am to noon and from 3 to 5 pm, and on Saturday morning. Compare their rates with those at the private Maki exchange office at Pristaniška ulica 13 next to Kompas and at Feniks in the east wing of the shopping mall and market across the street. Both of these are open weekdays from 7.30 am to 7 pm and on Saturday to 1 pm.

The Slovenijaturist counter inside the train station (open daily 6 am to 7.30 pm) changes travellers' cheques for a 3% commission.

Post & Communications The telephone centre in the post office branch at Muzejski trg 3 is open weekdays from 7 am to 7 pm, Satur-day to 1 pm. The main post office next to the train station is open on weekdays from 7 am to 8 pm, on Saturday to 7 pm, and on Sunday from 8 am to noon.

The telephone code for Koper is ☎ 066.

Things to See

From the stations you enter Prešernov trg through **Muda Gate** (1516). Follow the crowd past the bridge-shaped **Da Ponte Fountain** (1666) and into Čevljarska ulica (Shoemakers' Street), a narrow pedestrian way that opens onto Titov trg, the medieval central square. Most of the things to see in Koper are clustered here.

The 36-metre-high **City Tower** (1480), which you can climb, stands next to the mostly 18th-century **Cathedral of St Nazarius**. The lower portion of the cathedral's façade is Gothic, the upper part Renaissance. To the north is the sublime **Loggia** (1463), now a café, and to the south the **Praetorian Palace** (1452), both in the Venetian Gothic style. On the

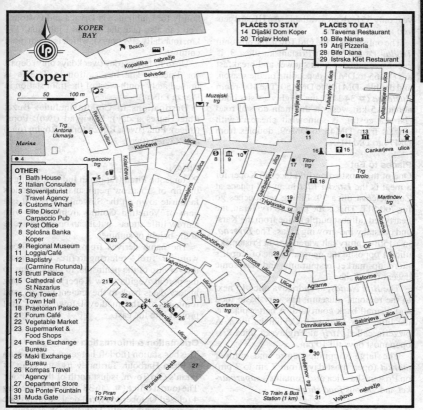

Koper

KOPER BAY

PLACES TO STAY
14 Dijaški Dom Koper
20 Triglav Hotel

PLACES TO EAT
5 Taverna Restaurant
10 Bife Nanas
19 Atrij Pizzeria
28 Bife Diana
29 Istrska Klet Restaurant

OTHER
1 Bath House
2 Italian Consulate
3 Slovenijaturist Travel Agency
4 Customs Wharf
6 Elite Disco/ Carpaccio Pub
7 Post Office
8 Splošna Banka Koper
9 Regional Museum
11 Loggia/Café
12 Baptistry (Carmine Rotunda)
13 Brutti Palace
15 Cathedral of St Nazarius
16 City Tower
17 Town Hall
18 Praetorian Palace
21 Forum Café
22 Vegetable Market
23 Supermarket & Food Shops
24 Feniks Exchange Bureau
25 Maki Exchange Bureau
26 Kompas Travel Agency
30 Department Store
30 Da Ponte Fountain
31 Muda Gate

To Piran (17 km)

To Train & Bus Station (1 km)

narrow lane beside the cathedral is a 14th-century Romanesque baptistry called the **Carmine Rotunda**. Trg Brolo to the east of the cathedral contains several more old Venetian buildings, including the **Brutti Palace** at No 1.

The **Koper Regional Museum** (supposedly open Tuesday to Sunday from 9 am to 1 pm and 6 to 8 pm) is in the Belgramoni-Tacco Palace at Kidričeva ulica 19. It contains old maps and photos of the port and coast, 16th to 18th century Italianate sculptures and paintings, and copies of medieval frescos.

Places to Stay
The closest *camp sites* are at Ankaran, about

10 km to the north by road, and at Izola, eight km to the west.

Slovenijaturist and Kompas (☎ 272 346), at Pristaniška ulica 17 opposite the vegetable market, have private rooms. Singles range from 1400 to 2400 SIT and doubles 2400 to 4800 SIT, depending on the season. Both levy a 30% surcharge if you stay less than three nights. Most of the rooms are in the new town beyond the train station.

Dijaški Dom Koper (☎ 391 154), an 'official' hostel at Cankarjeva ulica 5 in the Old Town east of Trg Brolo, rents out some 445 beds in three-bed rooms for 1650 SIT including breakfast in July and August; the rest of the year only 35 beds are available. An HI card gets you a small discount.

The only hotel in the Old Town, the 80-room *Triglav* (☎ 23 771) at Pristaniška ulica 3, is expensive: singles with shower and breakfast are DM65 to DM75, depending on the season, and doubles DM100 to DM150. The 100-room *Žusterna* (☎ 34 112), the Triglav's sister hotel about 1.5 km west on the main coastal road (Istrska cesta), is somewhat cheaper, with singles from DM48 to DM69, doubles from DM74 to DM103.

Places to Eat

One of the most colourful places in Koper for a meal is the *Istrska Klet* in an old palace at Župančičeva ulica 39. Filling set lunches go for 700 SIT. This is the place to try Teran, the hearty red (almost purple) wine from the Karst and coastal wine-growing areas. The *Taverna*, in a 15th-century salt warehouse at Pristaniška ulica 1 opposite the marina, is one of Koper's more up-market restaurants and has some decent fish dishes.

The *Bife Nanas*, at Kidričeva ulica 17 next to the regional museum, has very basic food and a small back courtyard. A better place is the little *Bife Diana* on Čevljarska ulica. A pizzeria called *Atrij* at Triglavska ulica 2 is open most days till 10 pm.

The large shopping centre and outdoor *market* (open most days from 7 am to 2 pm) on Pristaniška ulica also contains a *supermarket* and various *food shops*.

Entertainment

Koper often feels more Italian than Slovenian and at dusk, the *passeggiata* – a lot of strolling and strutting – begins. You can watch some of it from the lovely *Loggia Caffè* at Titov trg 1, but the *Forum* café/pub at the west wing of the market on Pristaniška ulica is where the action is.

The *Elite* is a high-class nightclub and disco at Carpacciov trg 6 (closed Sunday). The *Carpaccio Pub* next door is pleasant for a drink.

Getting There & Away

There are buses almost every 20 minutes on weekdays to Piran (17 km) and Portorož via Izola, and every 40 minutes at the weekend. The buses start at the train and bus stations and stop in front of the market on Pristaniška ulica before continuing on to Izola. Buses also leave hourly for Ljubljana via Divača and Postojna. You can also take the train to Ljubljana (175 km, four daily, 2½ hours), which is much more comfortable.

Up to 17 buses a day (weekdays only) depart for Trieste. The bus station in Trieste is immediately south-west of the train station in Piazza Libertà.

Destinations in Croatia include: Buzet (three buses a day); Novigrad (two); Poreč (three); Pula (two); Rijeka (one); Rovinj (one) and Zagreb (two).

PIRAN

Picturesque Piran (Pirano in Italian), sitting at the tip of a narrow peninsula, is everyone's favourite town on the Slovenian coast. It is a gem of Venetian Gothic architecture with narrow little streets, but it can be a mob scene at the height of summer.

The name derives from *pyr* – the Greek word for 'fire' – referring to fires lit at Punta, the very tip of the peninsula, to guide ships to the port at Aegida (now Koper). Piran's long history dates back to the ancient Greeks, and remnants of the medieval town walls still protect it to the east.

Orientation & information

The bus station (no left luggage) is just south of Piran Harbour. Tartinijev trg, the heart of Piran's Old Town, is just north of the harbour. The tourist office (☎ 746 3820) at Tartinijev trg 4 (closed October to April) deals with private accommodation only. Instead seek assistance from the helpful staff at the Maona travel agency (☎ 746 228), Cankarjevo nabrežje 7, who can arrange all sorts of activities, including excursions to the Brioni Islands off the Croatian Istrian coast on the *Marconi* and boat trips to Trieste.

Money The Splošna Banka Koper, Tartinijev trg 12, changes travellers' cheques from 8.30 am till noon and 3 to 5 pm on weekdays and on Saturday morning. At the entrance to the bank is a 24-hour exchange machine that accepts banknotes from 13 countries.

Post & Communications The post office and telephone centre in the town hall at Tartinijev

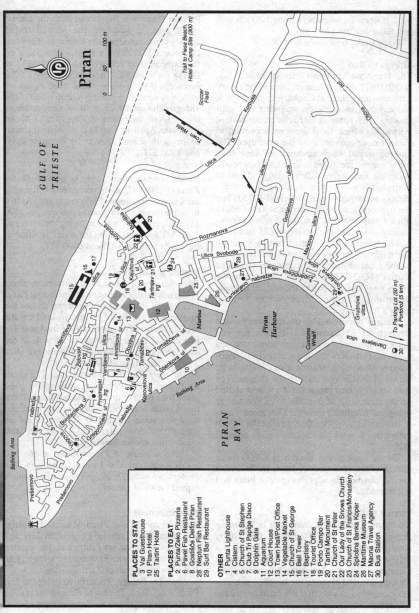

Piran

GULF OF TRIESTE

PIRAN BAY

Piran Harbour

Trail to Fiesa Beach, Hotel & Camp Site (300 m)

To Parking Lot (50 m) & Portorož (5 m)

Customs Wharf

Marina

Bathing Area

Bathing Area

Prešernovo

Prešernovo nabrežje

Soccer Field

Town Walls

Rozmanova

Ulica Svobode

Cankarjevo nabrežje

Gortanova ulica

Markova ulica

Adamičeva

Zidovski trg

Bonifacijeva ul

Gregorčičeva ul

Kosovelova ulica

Prvomajski trg

Obzidna ul

Levstikova ul

Tomažičev trg

Verdijeva ul

Tartinijev trg

Kajuhova ul

Korpusova ul

Bolniška ul

Čevljarska ulica

Župančičeva

Grudnova ulica

Danijeleva ulica

Tomažičeva ul

Stjenkova ul

PLACES TO STAY
3 Val Guesthouse
10 Piran Hotel
25 Tartini Hotel

PLACES TO EAT
2 Punta/Zeko Pizzeria
6 Pavel Fish Restaurant
8 Gostišče Delfin Piran
28 Neptun Fish Restaurant
29 Surf Bar Restaurant

OTHER
1 Punta Lighthouse
4 Cistern
5 Church of St Stephen
7 Club Tri Papige Disco
9 Dolphin Gate
11 Aquarium
12 Court House
13 Town Hall/Post Office
14 Vegetable Market
15 Church of St George
16 Bell Tower
17 Baptistry
18 Tourist Office
19 Porto Campo Bar
20 Tartini Monument
21 Church of St Peter
22 Church of the Snows Church
23 Church of St Francis/Monastery
24 Spločna Banka Koper
26 Maritime Museum
27 Maona Travel Agency
30 Bus Station

SLOVENIA

trg 2 is open on weekdays from 7.30 am to 8 pm, Saturday from to 1 pm.

Piran's telephone code is ☎ 066.

Things to See

The **Maritime Museum** (closed on Monday, 300/200 SIT adults/children), in a 17th century harbour-side palace at Cankarjevo nabrežje 3, has exhibits focusing on seafaring and salt-making (the latter at Sečovlje south-east of Portorož), which have been so important to Piran's development over the centuries. The antique model ships upstairs are very fine; other rooms are filled with old figureheads, weapons and votive folk paintings placed in church for protection against shipwreck. Piran's **aquarium** (open daily, 300/200 SIT) on the opposite side of the marina at Tomažičeva ulica 4 may be small, but there's a tremendous variety of sea life packed into its 25 tanks.

The **town hall** and **court house** stand on Tartinijev trg, in the centre of which is a statue of the local violinist and composer Giuseppe Tartini (1692-1770). A short distance to the north-west is Prvomajski trg and its baroque **cistern**, used in the 18th century to store the town's fresh water.

Piran is dominated by the tall tower of the **Church of St George**, a Renaissance and baroque structure on a ridge above the sea north of Tartinijev trg. It's wonderfully decorated with frescos, marble altars and a large statue of St George slaying the dragon. The free-standing **bell tower** (1609) was modelled on the campanile of San Marco in Venice; the octagonal **baptistry** from the 17th century next to it contains a wooden **Gothic crucifix** (1300) called the Tree of Life because of its unusual shape.

To the east of the church is a 200-metre stretch of the 15th-century **town walls**, which can be climbed for superb views of Piran and the Adriatic.

Places to Stay

Camping The closest camp site is *Camping Jezero Fiesa* (☎ 73 473) at Fiesa, four km by road from Piran (but less than a km if you follow the coastal trail east of the Church of St George). It's in a quiet valley by a small, protected pond and close to the beach, but it gets very crowded in summer. It's open from June to September.

Private Rooms & Pensions Both the tourist office and, in summer, the Maona travel agency can arrange *private rooms* for between DM18 and DM29 for a single, depending on the category and season, and from DM32 to DM48 for a double. They usually levy a 50% surcharge if you stay less then three nights.

A very central, relatively cheap place is the *Val* guesthouse (☎ 75 499) at Gregorčičeva ulica 38A on the corner of Vegova ulica. Open from late April to October, it has two dozen rooms with shared shower for between 2600 and 2900 SIT.

Hotels From October to May, your best bet is the *Fiesa* (☎ 746 897), a 21-room hotel overlooking the sea near the Jezero Fiesa camp site. At that time this pleasant four-storey hotel charges 3500 SIT per person for a room facing the hills and 3900 SIT for overlooking the water. In summer the prices jump to 5700 and 6100 SIT.

Places to Eat

Piran has a heap of seafood restaurants along Prešernovo nabrežje but most (including *Pavel* and less so *Portos* at the southern end of the promenade) are fairly pricey. Instead try the local favourites *Gostišče Delfin Piran* near Trg Prvomajski trg at Kosovelova ulica 4, or the more expensive *Neptun* at Župančičeva ulica 7 behind the Maona travel agency.

The *Surf Bar* at Grudnova ulica 1, a small street north-east of the bus station, is a good place for a meal or drink. It has a 'photo-album menu' with some 60 dishes – from ham and eggs and pizza (from 500 SIT) to Slovenian specialities (from 800 SIT) – and the staff speak most known languages.

Have a pizza at *Punta/Zeko*, about 150 metres east of the Punta lighthouse on Prešernovo nabrežje 26, and enjoy the uninterrupted views of the sea.

Entertainment

Many events of the Piran Musical Evenings and Primorska Summer Festival in July and August take place on Fridays in the vaulted cloister of the former Franciscan monastery on Bolniška ulica, east of Tartinijev trg.

Club Tri Papige, Prešernovo nabrežje 2, is Piran's top disco. The *Porto Campo* bar at ulica IX Korpusa 9 attracts a mixed and gay crowd.

Getting There & Away

Bus Local buses from Piran to Portorož, Izola and Koper are frequent. Other destinations that can be reached from Piran include Ljubljana via Divača and Postojna (10 a day), Nova Gorica (one) and Sečovlje via Seča (eight). Six buses head for Trieste on weekdays, and there's a daily departure at 4.25 am for Zagreb. One early-morning bus a day heads south for Croatian Istria, stopping at the coastal towns of Umag, Novigrad, Poreč and Rovinj.

Car & Motorcycle

Traffic is severely restricted in Piran. All cars must pay a parking fee if they intend to stay in the town for more than an hour and it's stiff – over six hours and you'll have to pay 4500 SIT! Leave your vehicle behind or in the lot south of the bus station, which charges only 50 SIT per hour.

PORTOROŽ

Every country with a sea coast has got to have a honky-tonk beach resort, and Portorož is Slovenia's very own Blackpool, Bondi or Atlantic City. The 'Port of Roses' is essentially a solid strip of high-rise hotels, restaurants, bars, travel agencies, shops, discos, beaches with turnstiles, parked cars and tourists, and it is not to everyone's taste. But its sandy beaches are the largest on the coast and relatively clean, there's a pleasant spa where you can take the waters; the list of other activities is endless. If you take it for what it is, Portorož can be a fun place to watch Slovenes, Italians, Austrians and others at play.

Orientation & Information

The bus station (no left-luggage facility) is opposite the main beach on Postajališka pot. The tourist office (☎ 747 015) is at No 6 of Obala, the main drag, a short distance to the west.

Money Splošna Banka Koper, next to the Sloveniya Hotel at Obala 33, is open from 8.30 am till noon and 5 to 7 pm on weekdays and on Saturday morning. It has an exchange machine outside that accepts the banknotes of 18 countries. Feniks, a private exchange bureau next to the tourist office, gives a good rate and does not charge commission. It is open daily from 9 am to midnight.

Post & Communications The post office/telephone centre is on K Stari cesta, opposite the once luxurious and now empty Palace Hotel (1891). It is open weekdays from 8 am to 7 pm, Saturday till 1 pm.

The telephone code for Portorož is ☎ 066.

Activities

The **beaches** at Portorož, including the main one accommodating some 6000 bodies, are 'managed' so you'll have to pay 250 SIT to use them. They are open from 7 am to 8 pm in season.

The **Palace Spa**, on K Stari cesta, is famous for its thalassotherapy (treatment using sea water and its by-products). The spa offers warm sea baths (850 SIT per half-hour), brine baths (2200 SIT), Sečovlje mud baths (2600 SIT) and a host of other therapies and beauty treatments from Monday to Saturday 7 am to 7 pm, Saturday to 2 pm. The palatial new indoor swimming pool there is open daily, except Monday, from 7 am to 7 pm.

The Atlas travel agency (☎ 73 264), at Obala 55, rents **boats** as well as **bicycles** (1800 SIT a day) and **motor scooters** (5400 SIT including insurance). Rosetour (☎ 76 364) opposite the Maritime Museum Collection on Obala has bicycles/motor scooters for 1600/4500 SIT a day.

Sightseeing by **ultra-light plane** is available at the Portorož airport (☎ 79 001), seven km to the south-east near Sečovlje on the Croatian border, from April to September. Flights over Portorož and Piran or the whole coast cost DM27 or DM45.

Places to Stay & Eat

The *Lucija* camp site (☎ 71 027) has two locations. The 2nd-category site is south-east of the marina at the end of Cesta Solinarjev less than two km from the bus station.

The 1st-category site, 600 metres to the west, is on the water. Both camps are open from May to September and get very crowded in summer. The charge per person ranges between DM12 and DM14, depending on the site and the month.

The tourist office and Atlas all have *private rooms* and *apartments*. You can also book them through Kompas (☎ 73 160), Obala 41, Emona Globtour (☎ 73 356) in the Slovenija Hotel at Obala 33 and at Top Line (☎ 747 161),

SLOVENIA

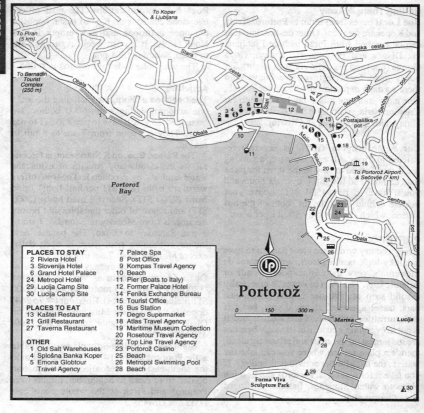

To Koper
& Ljubljana

To Piran
(5 km)

Stara

cesta

Koprska cesta

To Bernardin
Tourist
Complex
(250 m)

Obala

Obala

Senčna pot

2 3 4 5 6
8 9
K Štart c

12

Postajališka
pot

14 13
16
15

17

18

Main

Beach

Maritime Museum Collection

19

To Portorož Airport
& Sečovlje (7 km)

20

21

Senčna

23
24

Portorož
Bay

22

25

Obala

26

Portorož

0   150   300 m

Marina

Lucija

27

28

Forma Viva
Sculpture Park

29

30

PLACES TO STAY
2 Riviera Hotel
3 Slovenija Hotel
6 Grand Hotel Palace
24 Metropol Hotel
29 Lucija Camp Site
30 Lucija Camp Site

PLACES TO EAT
13 Kaštel Restaurant
21 Grill Restaurant
27 Taverna Restaurant

OTHER
1 Old Salt Warehouses
4 Splošna Banka Koper
5 Emona Globtour
   Travel Agency

7 Palace Spa
8 Post Office
9 Kompas Travel Agency
10 Beach
11 Pier (Boats to Italy)
12 Former Palace Hotel
14 Feniks Exchange Bureau
15 Tourist Office
16 Bus Station
17 Degro Supermarket
18 Atlas Travel Agency
19 Maritime Museum Collection
20 Rosetour Travel Agency
22 Top Line Travel Agency
23 Portorož Casino
25 Beach
26 Metropol Swimming Pool
28 Beach

Obala 22. Generally singles start at about 1800
SIT in the low season and rise to 3100 SIT in
summer; doubles are 3000 and 6200 SIT.
Apartments for two are a minimum of 4400
and 5900 SIT. Getting a room for less than
three nights or a single at any time can be
difficult.

Fast-food and pizza-pasta restaurants line
Obala. But if you want a proper sit-down meal,
the terrace at the *Taverna* in the sports field at
Obala 22 looks out over the marina and the bay.
The *Grill* restaurant, often with something
large being roasted on a spit near the entrance,
faces the main beach at Obala 20. The *Kaštel*
restaurant sits under an enormous marquee in

summer. The *Degro supermarket* is a few
steps away from the bus station.

Entertainment
The *Arcadia*, near the old church tower in the
centre of the Bernadin tourist complex north-
west of the centre, is a popular disco. For more
'mature' entertainment, there's also the *J&B
Club Venus* below the Riviera Hotel and the
Tivoli Club at the modern Grand Hotel Palace.

Getting There & Away
Buses to Piran, Izola and Koper run at least
every half-hour. Other destinations from
Portorož include Ljubljana via Divača and

Postojna (10 a day), Nova Gorica (one) and Sečovlje via Seča (eight).

International destinations include Poreč (three), Pula (two), Zagreb (two) and Trieste (eight a day on weekdays).

For information about the boat service to Venice from Portoro, see the introductory Getting There & Away section at the start of this chapter. Most of the travel agencies in Portorož can sell you a ticket.

Spain

Spaniards approach life with such exuberance that most visitors have to stop and stare. In almost every town in the country, the nightlife will outlast the foreigners. Then just when they think they are coming to terms with the pace, they are surrounded by the beating drums of a fiesta, with day and night turning into a blur of dancing, laughing, eating and drinking. Spain also holds its own in cultural terms with exciting museums like the Prado in Madrid, Cuenca's abstract art museum, the wacky Dalí museum in Figueres, and the Picasso and Miró museums in Barcelona.

Then, of course, you have the weather and the highly varied landscape. From April to October the sun shines with uncanny predictability on the Mediterranean coast and the Balearic Islands. Elsewhere you can enjoy good summer weather in the more secluded coves of Galicia, in the Pyrenees or the mountains of Andalucía, or on the surf beaches of western Andalucía or the País Vasco (Basque Country).

A wealth of history awaits the visitor to Spain: fascinating prehistoric displays at the archaeological museums in Teruel and Madrid; and from Roman times the aqueduct in Segovia, the seaside amphitheatre in Tarragona and the buried streets of Roman Barcelona made accessible via an underground walkway. After Roman times, the Moorish era left perhaps the most powerful cultural and artistic legacy – focused on Granada's Alhambra, Córdoba's mosque and Seville's *alcázar* – but Christian Spain also constructed hundreds of impressive castles, cathedrals, monasteries, palaces and mansions, which still stand throughout the length and breadth of the country.

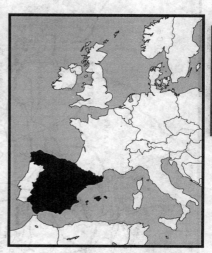

Facts about the Country

HISTORY
Ancient History
Located at the crossroads between Europe and Africa, the Iberian Peninsula has always been a target for invading peoples and civilisations. From around 8000 to 3000 BC, people from North Africa known as the Iberians crossed the Strait of Gibraltar and settled the peninsula. Around 1000 BC Celtic tribes entered northern Spain, while Phoenician merchants were establishing trading settlements along the Mediterranean coast. They were followed by Greeks and Carthaginians who arrived around 600 to 500 BC.

The Romans arrived in the 3rd century BC, but took two centuries to subdue the peninsula. Christianity came to Spain during the 1st century AD, but was initially opposed by the Romans, leading to persecution and martyrdoms. In 409 AD Roman Hispania was invaded by Germanic tribes and by 419 the Christian Visigoths, another Germanic people, had established a kingdom which lasted until 711, when the Moors – Muslim Berbers and Arabs from North Africa – crossed the Strait of Gibraltar and defeated Roderic, the last Visigoth king.

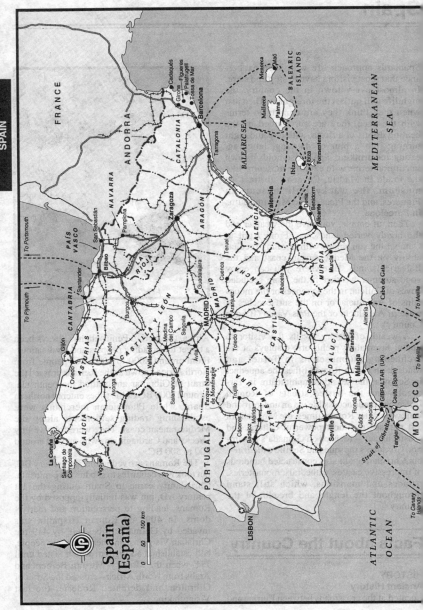

Spain
(España)

0   50   100 km

FRANCE

ANDORRA

Cadaqués
Girona – Figueres
Palafrugell
Tossa de Mar
Barcelona
CATALONIA

Tarragona

NAVARRA
Pamplona
San Sebastián
PAÍS VASCO
To Portsmouth
To Plymouth
Bilbao
Santander
CANTABRIA
LA RIOJA
Zaragoza
ARAGÓN
Teruel

MEDITERRANEAN SEA

BALEARIC ISLANDS
Menorca
Maó
Mallorca
Palma
BALEARIC SEA
Ibiza
Formentera

Valencia
Dénia
Benidorm
VALENCIA
Alicante
MURCIA
Murcia
Albacete
Cabo de Gata
Almería

Gijón
Oviedo
ASTURIAS
GALICIA
La Coruña
Santiago de Compostela
Vigo

León
Astorga
Burgos
CASTILLA Y LEÓN
Valladolid
Medina del Campo
Segovia
Ávila
Salamanca
Guadalajara
MADRID
MADRID
Aranjuez
Cuenca
CASTILLA-LA MANCHA
Toledo

Parque Natural de Montfragüe
Cáceres
Trujillo
Mérida
Badajoz
EXTREMADURA

PORTUGAL
LISBON

Córdoba
Seville
Cádiz
Algeciras
Ronda
ANDALUCÍA
Granada
Málaga

GIBRALTAR (UK)
Ceuta (Spain)
Strait of Gibraltar
Tangier
To Melilla
MOROCCO

ATLANTIC OCEAN

To Canary Islands

Moorish Spain & the Reconquista

By 714, the Muslim armies had occupied the entire peninsula, apart from some northern mountain regions. Moorish dominion was to last almost 800 years in parts of Spain. In the Moorish-held areas – known as al-Andalus – arts and sciences prospered, new crops and agricultural techniques were introduced, and palaces, mosques, schools, gardens and public baths were built.

In 722 a small army under the Visigothic leader Pelayo inflicted the first defeat on the Moors at Covadonga in northern Spain. This marked the beginning of the Reconquista, the very gradual and unsteady reconquest of Spain by the Christians. By the beginning of the 11th century the frontier between Christian and Muslim Spain stretched across the peninsula from Barcelona to the Atlantic.

In 1085 Toledo was taken by Alfonso VI, king of León and Castile, prompting the Moors to request military help from northern Africa which arrived in the form of the Almoravids, who recaptured much territory and ruled it until the 1140s. The Almoravids were followed by the Almohads, another north African people, who ruled until 1212. By the mid-13th century, the Christians had taken most of the peninsula except for the state of Granada.

In the process the kingdoms of Castile and Aragón emerged as Christian Spain's two main powers, and in 1469 they were united by the marriage of Isabel, princess of Castile, and Fernando, heir to the throne of Aragón. Known as the Catholic Monarchs, they united all of Spain and laid the foundations for the Spanish golden age. They also revived the notorious Inquisition, which expelled and executed thousands of Jews and other non-Christians. In 1492 the last Moorish ruler of Granada surrendered to them, marking the completion of the Reconquista.

The Golden Age

Also in 1492, while searching for an alternative passage to India, Columbus stumbled on the Bahamas and claimed the Americas for Spain. This sparked a period of exploration and exploitation which was to yield Spain enormous wealth while destroying the ancient American empires. For three centuries, gold and silver from the New World were used to finance the expansion of the Spanish empire.

In 1516 Fernando was succeeded by his grandson Carlos, of the Habsburg dynasty. Carlos was elected Holy Roman Emperor in 1519, and ruled over an empire that included Austria, southern Germany, the Netherlands, Spain and the American colonies. But he and his successors were to lead Spain into a series of expensive wars and, despite the influx of American gold and silver, the empire was soon bankrupt. In 1588 the mighty Spanish Armada was annihilated by Sir Francis Drake's English fleet. The Thirty Years' War (1618-48) saw Spain in conflict with the Netherlands, France and England. By the reign of the last Habsburg monarch, Carlos II (1655-1700), the Spanish empire was in debt and decline.

The 18th & 19th Centuries

Carlos II died without an heir. At the end of the subsequent War of the Spanish Succession (1702-13), Felipe V, grandson of French king Louis XIV, became the first of the Bourbon dynasty. The Bourbons unified Spain, overseeing a period of stability, enlightened reforms and economic growth, but this recovery was ended by events after the French Revolution of 1789.

When Louis XVI was guillotined in 1793, Spain initially declared war on the new French republic, but then turned to alliance with France and war against Britain, in which the Battle of Trafalgar (1805) ended Spanish sea power. In 1807-08 Napoleon's troops entered Spain, supposedly en route to invade Portugal, but Napoleon convinced Carlos IV, the Spanish king, to abdicate, and installed his own brother Joseph Bonaparte as king of Spain. The Spanish people united against the French and fought a five-year war of independence. In 1815 Napoleon was defeated by Wellington and a Bourbon, Fernando VII, was restored to the Spanish throne.

Fernando's reign was a disastrous advertisement for monarchy: the Inquisition was re-established, liberals and constitutionalists were persecuted, free speech was repressed, Spain entered a severe recession and the American colonies won their independence. After his death in 1833 came the First Carlist War (1834-39), fought between conservative forces led by Don Carlos, Fernando's brother, and liberals who supported the claim of Fernando's daughter Isabel (later Isabel II) to the throne.

SPAIN

In 1868 the monarchy was overthrown during the Septembrina Revolution and Isabel II was forced to flee the country. The First Republic was declared in 1873, but within 18 months the army had restored the monarchy, with Isabel's son Alfonso XII on the throne. Despite political turmoil, Spain's economy prospered in the second half of the 19th century, fuelled by industrialisation.

The disastrous Spanish-American War of 1898 marked the end of the Spanish empire. Spain was defeated by the USA in a series of naval battles, resulting in the loss of its last overseas possessions – Cuba won its independence and Puerto Rico, Guam and the Philippines passed to the USA.

The 20th Century

The early 20th century was characterised by military disasters in Morocco and growing political and social instability as radical forces struggled to overthrow the established order. In 1923, with Spain on the brink of civil war, Miguel Primo de Rivera made himself military dictator, and ruled until 1930. In 1931 Alfonso XIII fled the country, and the Second Republic was declared.

Like its predecessor, the Second Republic also fell victim to internal conflict. The 1936 elections told of a country split in two, with the Republican government (an uneasy alliance of leftist parties known as the Popular Front) and its supporters on one side, and the right-wing Nationalists (an alliance of the army, Church and the fascist-style Falange Party) on the other.

Nationalist plotters in the army rose against the government in July 1936. During the subsequent Spanish Civil War (1936-39), the Nationalists, led by General Francisco Franco, received almost unlimited military and financial support from Nazi Germany and fascist Italy, while the elected Republican government received support only from Russia and, to a lesser degree, from the International Brigades made up of foreign leftists.

By 1939 Franco had won and an estimated 350,000 Spaniards had died. After the war, thousands of Republicans were executed, jailed or forced into exile. Franco's 35-year dictatorship began with Spain isolated internationally and crippled by recession. It wasn't until the 1950s and 1960s, when the rise in

tourism and a treaty with the USA combined to provide much needed funds, that the country began to recover. By the 1970s Spain had the fastest-growing economy in Europe.

Franco died in 1975, having named Juan Carlos, grandson of Alfonso XIII, his successor. King Juan Carlos is widely credited with having overseen Spain's transition from dictatorship to democracy. The first elections were held in 1977, a new constitution was drafted in 1978, and a failed military coup in 1981 was seen as a futile attempt to turn back the clock. Spain joined the EU in 1986, and celebrated its return to the world stage in style in 1992, with Expo '92 in Seville and the Olympic Games in Barcelona.

GEOGRAPHY & ECOLOGY

Spain is probably Europe's most geographically diverse country, with landscapes ranging from the near-deserts of Almería to the green, Wales-like countryside and deep coastal inlets of Galicia, and from the sunbaked plains of Castilla-La Mancha to the rugged mountains of the Pyrenees.

The country covers around 80% of the Iberian Peninsula and spreads over nearly 505,000 sq km, more than half of which is high tableland – the *meseta*. This is supported and divided by several mountain chains. The main ones are the Pyrenees along the border with France; the Cordillera Cantábrica backing the north coast; the Sistema Ibérico from the central north towards the middle Mediterranean coast; the Cordillera Central from north of Madrid towards the Portuguese border; and three east-west chains across Andalucía, one of which includes the highest range of all, the Sierra Nevada.

The major rivers are the Ebro, Duero, Tajo (Tagus), Guadiana and Guadalquivir, each draining a different basin between the mountains and all flowing into the Atlantic Ocean, except for the Ebro which reaches the Mediterranean Sea.

Flora & Fauna

The brown bear, wolf, lynx and wild boar all survive in Spain, though only the boar exists in healthy numbers. Spain's high mountains harbour the goat-like chamois and Spanish ibex (the latter rare) and big birds of prey such as eagles, vultures and the lammergeier. The marshy Ebro delta and Guadalquivir estuary are very important for waterbirds, the spectacular greater flamingo among them. Many of Spain's 5500 seed-bearing plants occur nowhere else in Europe because of the barrier of the Pyrenees. Spring wildflowers are spectacular in many a country and hill areas.

The conservation picture has improved by leaps and bounds in the past 20 years and Spain now has 25,000 sq km of protected areas, including 10 national parks. But overgrazing, reservoir creation, tourism, housing developments, agricultural and industrial effluent, fires and hunting all still threaten plant and animal life.

GOVERNMENT & POLITICS

Spain is a constitutional monarchy. The 1978 constitution restored parliamentary government and grouped the country's 50 provinces into 17 autonomous communities, each with its own regional government. From 1982 to 1996 Spain was governed by the centre-left PSOE party led by Felipe González. In the 1996 election the PSOE, weakened by a series of scandals and long-term economic problems, was finally unseated by the right-of-centre Partido Popular, led by José María Aznar.

ECONOMY

Spain has experienced an amazing economic turnabout in the 20th century, raising its living standards from the lowest in Western Europe to a level comparable with the rest of the continent. But its booming economy came back to earth with a thud in the early 1990s, and has since recovered only slowly. The unemployment rate is by far the highest in Western Europe, at over 20%. Service industries employ over six million people and produce close to 60% of the country's GDP. The arrival of over 50 million tourists every year brings work to around 10% of the entire labour force. Industry accounts for about one-third of both workforce and GDP, but agriculture accounts for only 4% of GDP compared to 23% in 1960, although it employs one in 10 workers.

POPULATION & PEOPLE

Spain has a population of 39 million, descended from all the many peoples who have settled here over the millennia, among them Iberians, Celts, Romans, Jews, Visigoths and Moors. The biggest cities are Madrid (three million), Barcelona (1.7 million), Valencia (750,000) and Seville (715,000). Each region proudly preserves its own unique culture, and some – Catalonia and the País Vasco in particular – display a fiercely independent spirit.

ARTS
Cinema

Early Spanish cinema was hamstrung by a lack of funds and technology, and perhaps the greatest of all Spanish directors, Luis Buñuel, made his silent surrealist classics *Un Chien Andalou* (1928) and *L'Age d'Or* (1930) in France. Buñuel, however, returned to Spain to make *Tierra sin Pan* (Land without Bread, 1932), a film about rural poverty in the Las Hurdes area of Extremadura.

Under Franco there was strict censorship, but satirical and uneasy films like Juan Antonio Bardem's *Muerte de un Ciclista* (Death of a Cyclist, 1955) and Luis Berlanga's *Bienvenido Mr Marshall* (Welcome Mr Marshall, 1953) still managed to appear. Carlos Saura, with films like *Ana y los Lobos* (Anna & the Wolves, 1973), and Victor Erice, with *El Espiritu de la Colmena* (Spirit of the Beehive, 1973) and *El Sur* (The South, 1983), looked at the problems of young people scarred by the Spanish Civil War and its aftermath.

After Franco, Pedro Almodóvar broke away from this serious cinema dwelling on the past with his humorous films set amid the social and artistic revolution of the late 1970s and 80s – notably *Mujeres al Borde de un Ataque de Nervios* (Women on the Verge of a Nervous Breakdown, 1988). Almodóvar has brought Spanish films for the first time to a non-arthouse public outside Spain, and has made international stars of two of his actors, Antonio Banderas and Carmen Maura.

Painting

The golden age of Spanish art (1550-1650) was strongly influenced by Italy but the great Spanish artists developed their talents in unique ways. The giants were the Toledo-based El Greco (originally from Crete), and Diego Velázquez, perhaps Spain's most revered painter. Both excelled with insightful portraits, among other things. Francisco Zurbarán and Bartolomé Esteban Murillo were also prominent. The genius of the 18th and

19th centuries was Francisco Goya, whose versatility ranged from unflattering royal portraits and anguished war scenes to bullfight etchings.

Catalonia was the powerhouse of early 20th-century Spanish art, engendering the hugely prolific Pablo Picasso, the colourful symbolist Joan Miró, and Salvador Dalí, who was obsessed with the unconscious and weird. Works by these and other major Spanish artists can be found in galleries throughout the country.

Architecture

The earliest architectural relics are the prehistoric monuments on Menorca. Reminders of Roman times include the ruins of Mérida and Tarragona, and Segovia's amazing aqueduct. The Moors created some uniquely beautiful Islamic buildings such as Granada's Alhambra, Córdoba's mosque and Seville's alcázar (fortress) – the latter an example of Mudéjar architecture, the name given to Moorish work done in Christian-held territory.

The first main Christian architectural movement was Romanesque, in the north in the 11th and 12th centuries, which has left countless lovely country churches and several cathedrals, notably that of Santiago de Compostela. Later came the many great Gothic cathedrals (Toledo, Barcelona, León, Salamanca and Seville) of the 13th to 16th centuries, as well as Renaissance styles, such as the plateresque work so prominent in Salamanca and the austere work of Juan de Herrera, responsible for El Escorial. Spain then followed the usual path to baroque (17th and 18th centuries) and neoclassicism (19th century) before Catalonia produced its startling modernist movement around the turn of the 20th century, of which Antoni Gaudí's La Sagrada Família church is the most stunning example. More-recent architecture is only likely to excite specialists.

Literature

One of the earliest works of Spanish literature is the *Cantar de mío Cid*, an anonymous epic poem describing the life of El Cid, an 11th-century Christian knight. Miguel de Cervantes' novel *Don Quixote de la Mancha* is the masterpiece of the literary flowering of the 16th and 17th centuries, and one of the world's great works of fiction. The playwrights Lope de Vega and Pedro Calderón de la Barca were also leading lights of the age.

The next highpoint, in the early 20th century, grew out of the crisis of the Spanish-American War which spawned the intellectual 'Generation of '98'. Philosophical essayist Miguel de Unamuno was prominent, but the towering figure was poet and playwright Federico García Lorca, whose tragedies *Blood Wedding* and *Yerma* won international acclaim before he was murdered in the civil war for his Republican sympathies. Camilo José Cela, author of the civil war aftermath novel *The Family of Pascal Duarte*, won the 1989 Nobel Prize for literature. Juan Goytisolo is probably the major contemporary writer; his most approachable work is his autobiography *Forbidden Territory*. There has been a proliferation of women – particularly feminist – writers in the last 25 years, in which prominent figures include Adelaide Morales, Ana María Matute and Montserrat Roig.

CULTURE

Most Spaniards are economical with etiquette but this does not signify unfriendliness. They're gregarious people, on the whole very tolerant and easy-going towards foreigners. It's not easy to give offence. Disrespectful behaviour – including excessively casual dress – in churches won't go down well though.

Siesta

Contrary to popular belief, most Spaniards do not sleep in the afternoon. The siesta is generally devoted to a long leisurely lunch and lingering conversation. Then again, if you've stayed out until 5 am...

Flamenco

Getting to see real, deeply emotional, flamenco can be hard, as it tends to happen semi-spontaneously in little bars. Andalucía is its traditional home. You'll find plenty of clubs there and elsewhere offering flamenco shows: these are generally aimed at tourists and are expensive, but some are good. Your best chance of catching the real thing is probably at one of the flamenco festivals in the south, usually held in summer.

RELIGION

Only about 20% of Spaniards are regular churchgoers, but Catholicism is deeply ingrained in the culture. As the writer

Unamuno said, 'Here in Spain we are all Catholics, even the atheists'. Many Spaniards have a deep-seated scepticism of the Church: during the civil war, churches were burnt and clerics shot because they represented repression, corruption and the old order.

LANGUAGE

Spanish, or Castilian (*castellano*) as it is often and more precisely called, is spoken by just about all Spaniards, but there are also three widely spoken regional languages: Catalan (another Romance language, closely related to Spanish and French) is spoken by about two-thirds of people in Catalonia and the Balearic Islands and half the people in the Valencia region; Galician (another Romance language which sounds like a cross between Spanish and Portuguese) is spoken by many in the north-west; and Basque (of obscure, non-Latin origin) is spoken by a minority in the País Vasco and Navarra.

English isn't as widely spoken as many travellers seem to expect. In the main cities and tourist areas it's much easier to find people who speak at least some English, though generally you'll be better received if you at least try to communicate in Spanish.

See the Language Guide at the back of the book for pronunciation guidelines and useful words and phrases.

Facts for the Visitor

PLANNING

Climate & When to Go

For most purposes the ideal months to visit Spain are May, June and September (plus April and October in the south). At these times you can rely on good weather, yet avoid the sometimes extreme heat – and main crush of Spanish and foreign tourists – of July and August, when temperatures may climb to 45°C in parts of Andalucía and when Madrid is unbearably hot and almost deserted.

The summer overflows with festivals, including Sanfermines, with the running of the bulls in Pamplona, and Semana Grande all along the north coast (dates vary from place to place), but there are excellent festivals during the rest of the year too.

In winter the rains never seem to stop in the north, except when they turn to snow. Madrid regularly freezes in December, January and February. At these times Andalucía is the place to be, with temperatures reaching the mid-teens in most places and good skiing in the Sierra Nevada.

Books & Maps

The New Spaniards by John Hooper is a fascinating account of modern Spanish society and culture. For a readable and thorough, but not over-long, survey of Spanish history, *The Story of Spain* by Mark Williams is hard to beat.

Classic accounts of life and travel in Spain include Gerald Brenan's *South from Granada* (1920s), Laurie Lee's *As I Walked Out One Midsummer Morning* (1930s), George Orwell's *Homage to Catalonia* (the civil war), and *Iberia* by James Michener (1960s). Among the best of more recent books are *Homage to Barcelona* by Colm Tóibín, *Spanish Journeys* by Adam Hopkins and *Cities of Spain* by David Gilmour.

Of foreign literature set in Spain, Ernest Hemingway's civil war novel *For Whom the Bell Tolls* is a must.

If you're planning in-depth travels in Spain, get hold of Lonely Planet's *Spain – travel survival kit*.

Some of the best maps for travellers are published by Michelin, which produces a 1:1 million *Spain Portugal* map and six 1:400,000 regional maps. The country map doesn't show railways, but the regional maps do.

Online Services

An Internet search under 'Spain, Travel' will reveal dozens of sites including the national tourist office's useful *Discover Spain* (www.spaintour.com).

What to Bring

You can buy anything you need in Spain, but some articles, such as sun-screen lotion, are more expensive than elsewhere. Books in English tend to be expensive and are hard to find outside main cities.

A pair of strong shoes and a towel are essential. A money belt or shoulder wallet can be useful in big cities. Bring sunglasses if glare

SPAIN

SPAIN

gets to you. If you want to blend in, don't just pack T-shirts, shorts and runners – Spaniards are quite dressy and many tourists just look like casual slobs to them.

SUGGESTED ITINERARIES

If you want to whiz around as many places as possible in limited time, the following itineraries might suit you:

Two days
  Fly to Madrid, Barcelona or Seville, or nip into Barcelona or San Sebastián overland from France.
One week
  Spend two days each in Barcelona, Madrid and Seville, allowing one day for travel.
Two weeks
  As above, plus San Sebastián, Toledo, Salamanca and/or Cuenca, Córdoba and/or Granada, and maybe Cáceres and/or Trujillo.
One month
  As above, plus some of the following: side trips from the cities mentioned above; an exploration of the north, including Santiago de Compostela and the Picos de Europa; visits to Teruel, Mallorca, Formentera, Segovia, Ávila, or some smaller towns and more remote regions such as North-East Extremadura or Cabo de Gata.

HIGHLIGHTS
Beaches

Yes, it's still possible to have a beach to yourself in Spain. In summer it may be a little tricky, but spots where things are bound to be quiet are such gems as the beaches of Cabo Favàritx in Menorca, and some of the secluded coves on Cabo de Gata in Andalucía. There are also good, relatively uncrowded beaches on the Costa de la Luz, between Tarifa and Cádiz. On the Galician coast, between Noia and Pontevedra, are literally hundreds of beaches where even in mid-August you won't feel claustrophobic.

Museums & Galleries

Spain is home to some of the finest art galleries in the world. The Prado in Madrid has very few rivals, and there are outstanding art museums in Bilbao, Seville, Barcelona, Valencia and Córdoba. There are also fascinating smaller galleries, such as the Dalí museum in Figueres and the abstract art museum in Cuenca. Tarragona and Teruel have excellent archaeological museums.

Buildings

Try not to miss Andalucía's Moorish gems – the Alhambra in Granada, the alcázar in Seville and the mezquita in Córdoba – or Barcelona's extraordinary La Sagrada Família church. The fairy-tale alcázar in Segovia has to be seen to be believed. For even more exciting views, and loads of medieval ghosts, try to reach the ruined castle in Morella, Valencia province.

Scenery

There's outstanding mountain scenery – often coupled with highly picturesque villages – in the Pyrenees and Picos de Europa in the north and in parts of Andalucía such as the Alpujarras. On the coasts, the rugged inlets of Galicia and stark, hilly Cabo de Gata in Andalucía stand out.

TOURIST OFFICES

Most towns (and many villages) of any interest have a tourist office (oficina de turismo). These will supply you with a map and brochures with basic information on local sights, attractions, accommodation, history etc. Some can also provide info on other places too. Their staff are generally helpful and often speak some English.

Spanish Tourist Offices Abroad

Spain has tourist information centres in 20 countries including:

Canada
  102 Bloor St West, 14th floor, Toronto, Ontario M5S 1M8 (☎ 416-961 3131)
France
  43ter Ave Pierre 1er de Serbie, 75381 Paris (☎ 01 47 20 90 54)
Portugal
  Avenida Fontes Pereira de Melo 51, 4th floor, 1000 Lisbon (☎ 01-354 1992; fax 354 0332)
UK
  57-58 St James's St, London SW1A 1LD (☎ 0171-499 0901)
USA
  665 Fifth Ave, New York, NY 10022 (☎ 212-759 8822)

USEFUL ORGANISATIONS

The travel agency TIVE, with offices in major cities throughout Spain, specialises in discounted tickets and travel arrangements for students and young people. Its head office (☎ 91-347 7700) is at Calle José Ortega y Gasset 71, 28006 Madrid.

VISAS & EMBASSIES

Citizens of EU countries can enter Spain with their national identity card or passport. UK citizens must have a full passport – a British visitor passport won't do. Non-EU nationals must take their passport.

EU, Norway and Iceland citizens require no visa. Nationals of Canada, Israel, Japan, New Zealand, Switzerland and the USA need no visa for stays of up to 90 days but must have a passport valid for the whole visit.

Australians and South Africans are among nationalities who do need a visa for Spain. It's best to obtain the visa in your country of residence to avoid possible bureaucratic problems. Both 30-day single-entry and 90-day triple-entry visas are available, though if you apply in a country where you're not resident the 90-day option may not be available. Triple-entry visas will save you a lot of time and trouble if you plan to leave Spain – say to Gibraltar or Morocco – then re-enter it.

The Schengen 'System'

Spain is one of the seven Schengen countries – the others are Belgium, France, Germany, Luxembourg, the Netherlands and Portugal – which have theoretically done away with passport control on travel between them. (In fact some checks have still been known to occur at airports and on some Lisbon-Madrid trains.) But confusingly, the seven countries have not standardised their lists of nationalities that require visas. So Australians, for example, need a visa to visit France or Spain, but not for Portugal. Despite the removal of most passport controls between Schengen countries, it's still illegal for Australians to enter Spain without a visa, and can lead to deportation.

One good thing about the Schengen system is that a visa for one Schengen country is valid for other Schengen countries too – so, for instance, a French visa is good for Spain too, and vice-versa. Compare validity periods, prices and the number of permitted entries before you apply, as these can differ between countries.

Stays of Longer than 90 Days

EU, Norway and Iceland nationals planning to stay in Spain more than 90 days are supposed to apply during their first month in the country for a residence card. This is a lengthy, compli-

cated procedure: if you intend to subject yourself to it, consult a Spanish consulate before you go to Spain, as you'll need to take certain documents with you.

Other nationalities are not normally allowed more than one 90-day stay in any six-month period. Visa carriers may be able to get short visa extensions at their local Comisaría de Policía (National Police station), but don't count on it. Otherwise, for stays of longer than 90 days you're supposed to get a residence card. This is a nightmarish process, starting with a residence visa issued by a Spanish consulate in your country of residence: start the process light-years in advance.

Spanish Embassies Abroad

Spanish embassies include:

Australia
    15 Arkana St, Yarralumla, Canberra 2600, ACT (☎ 06-273 3555); consulates in Sydney and Melbourne
Canada
    350 Sparks St, suite 802, Ottawa K1R 7S8 (☎ 613-237 2193); consulates in Toronto and Montreal
France
    22 Ave Marceau, 75381 Paris (☎ 01 44 43 18 00); consulates in Marseille, Bayonne, Hendaye, Pau etc
New Zealand
    represented in Australia
Portugal
    Rua do Salitre 1, 1296 Lisbon (☎ 01-347 2381); consulates in Porto and Valença do Minho
UK
    39 Chesham Place, London SW1X 8SB (☎ 0171-235 5555); consulates in Edinburgh and Manchester
USA
    2375 Pennsylvania Ave NW, Washington, DC, 20037 (☎ 202-452 0100); consulates in New York, Los Angeles, San Francisco, Chicago Miami and other cities

Foreign Embassies in Spain

Some 70 countries have embassies in Madrid, including:

Australia
    Paseo de la Castellana 143 (☎ 579 04 28)
Canada
    Calle de Nuñez de Balboa 35 (☎ 431 43 00)
France
    Calle de Salustiano Olozoga 9 (☎ 435 55 60)
Germany
    Calle de Fortuny 8 (☎ 319 91 00)
Ireland
    Calle de Claudio Coello 73 (☎ 576 35 00)

Japan
Calle de Joaquín Costa 29 (☎ 562 55 46)
Morocco
Calle de Serrano 179 (☎ 562 42 84)
New Zealand
Plaza Lealtad 2 (☎ 523 02 26)
Portugal
Calle del Pinar 1 (☎ 561 78 00)
UK
Calle de Fernando el Santo 16 (☎ 319 02 00)
USA
Calle de Serrano 75 (☎ 577 40 00)

CUSTOMS

EU internal borders are customs-free. From outside the EU, you are allowed to bring in one litre of spirits, 50 grams of perfume and 200 cigarettes duty-free.

MONEY
Currency

Spain's unit of currency is the peseta (pta). The legal denominations are coins of one, five (known as a *duro*), 10, 25, 50, 100, 200 and 500 ptas. There are notes of 1000, 2000, 5000 and 10,000 ptas. In the past, several different forms of coin have circulated for each value, but from February 1997 only one type of coin for each value will be legal tender. Take care not to confuse the 500-pta coin with the 100-pta coin.

Exchange Rates

Banks – mostly open Monday to Friday from 8.30 am to 2 pm, Saturday from 8.30 am to 1 pm – generally give better exchange rates than currency-exchange offices, and travellers' cheques attract a slightly better rate than cash. ATMs accepting a wide variety of cards are common.

Australia	A$1	=	99 ptas
Canada	C$1	=	92 ptas
France	1FF	=	25 ptas
Germany	DM1	=	85 ptas
Japan	¥100	=	116 ptas
New Zealand	NZ$1	=	88 ptas
Portugal	100$00	=	83 ptas
United Kingdom	UK£1	=	196 ptas
United States	US$1	=	126 ptas

Costs

Spain is one of Western Europe's more affordable countries. If you are particularly frugal, it's possible to scrape by on US$20 to US$25 a day; this would involve staying in the cheapest possible accommodation, avoiding eating in restaurants or going to museums or bars, and not moving around too much. Places like Madrid, Barcelona, Seville and San Sebastián will place a greater strain on your money belt.

A more reasonable budget would be US$35 to US$40 a day. This would allow you 1500 to 2000 ptas for accommodation; 300 ptas for breakfast (coffee and a pastry); 800 to 1000 ptas for a set lunch; 250 ptas for public transport (two metro or bus rides); 500 ptas for a museum; and 600 ptas for a light dinner, with a bit over for a drink or two and intercity travel.

Tipping & Bargaining

In restaurants, menu prices include a service charge, and tipping is a matter of personal choice – most people leave some small change and 5% is plenty. It's common to leave small change in bars and cafés. The only places in Spain where you are likely to bargain are markets and, occasionally, cheap hotels – particularly if you're staying for a few days.

Consumer Taxes & Refunds

In Spain, VAT (value-added tax) is known as IVA (*impuesto sobre el valor añadido*). On accommodation and restaurant prices, there's a flat rate of 7% IVA which is usually – but not always – included in quoted prices. To check, ask if the price is 'con IVA' (with VAT) or 'sin IVA' (without VAT).

On retail goods, alcohol, electrical appliances etc, IVA is 16%. Visitors are entitled to a refund of IVA on any item costing more than 15,000 ptas that they are taking out of the EU. Ask the shop for a Europe Tax-Free Shopping Cheque when you buy, then present the goods and cheque to customs when you leave within three months. Customs stamps the cheque and you then cash it at a booth with the Tax-Free logo and Cash Refund sign. There are booths at all main Spanish airports, the border crossings at Algeciras, Gibraltar and Andorra, and similar refund points throughout the EU.

POST & COMMUNICATIONS
Post

Main post offices in towns are usually open Monday to Friday from about 8.30 am to 8.30 pm, and Saturday from about 9 am to 1.30 pm. Stamps are also sold at *estancos* (tobacconist shops with the 'Tabacos' sign in yellow letters on a maroon background). A standard air-mail letter or card costs 60 ptas to Europe, 87 ptas to the USA or Canada, and 108 ptas to Australia or New Zealand. Mail to/from Europe normally takes up to a week, and to North America, Australia or New Zealand around 10 days – but there may be some unaccountable long delays.

Poste-restante mail can be addressed to you at either poste restante or *lista de correos*, the Spanish name for it, in the city in question. It's a fairly reliable system, although you must be prepared for mail to arrive late. American Express card or travellers' cheque holders can use the free client mail service (see the Facts for the Visitor chapter at the beginning of this book).

Common abbreviations used in Spanish addresses are 1°, 2°, 3° etc, which mean 1st, 2nd, 3rd floor, and s/n *(sin número)*, which means the building has no number.

Telephone & Fax

When calling Spain from other countries, omit the initial 9 of the Spanish area code. Public pay phones are blue, common and easy to use. They accept coins, phonecards *(tarjetas telefónicas)* and, in some cases, credit cards. Phonecards come in 1000 and 2000-pta denominations and are available at main post offices and estancos. A three-minute call from a pay phone costs 15 ptas within a local area, 72 ptas to other places in the same province, or 184 ptas to other provinces. Calls are around 15% cheaper between 10 pm and 8 am and all day Sunday and holidays.

International reverse-charge (collect) calls are simple to make: from a pay phone or private phone dial ☎ 900 99 00 followed by ☎ 61 for Australia, ☎ 44 for the UK, ☎ 64 for New Zealand, ☎ 15 for Canada, and for the USA ☎ 11 (AT&T) or ☎ 14 (MCI).

Most main post offices have a fax service, but you'll often find cheaper rates at shops or offices with 'Fax Público' signs.

NEWSPAPERS & MAGAZINES

The major daily newspapers in Spain are the solid liberal *El País*, the conservative *ABC*, and *El Mundo*, which specialises in breaking political scandals. For a laugh, have a look at *¡Hola!*, a weekly magazine devoted to the lives

and loves of the rich and famous. There's also a welter of regional dailies, some of the best being in Barcelona, the País Vasco and Andalucía.

International press such as the *International Herald Tribune*, *Time* and *Newsweek*, and daily papers from Western European countries reach major cities and tourist areas on the day of publication; elsewhere they're harder to find and are a day or two late.

RADIO & TV

There are hundreds of radio stations, mainly on the FM band – you'll hear a substantial proportion of British and American music. The national pop/rock station, Radio 3, has admirably varied programming.

Spaniards are Europe's greatest TV-watchers after the British, but do a lot of their watching in bars and cafés which makes it more of a social activity. Most TVs receive six channels – two state-run (TVE1 and TVE2), three privately run (Antena 3, Tele 5 and Canal+), and one regional channel. Apart from news, TV seems to consist mostly of game and talk shows, sport, soap operas, sitcoms, and English-language films dubbed into Spanish.

PHOTOGRAPHY & VIDEO

Main brands of film are widely available and processing is fast and generally efficient. A roll of print film (36 exposures, 100 ASA) costs around 650 ptas and can be processed for around 1700 ptas – though there are often better deals if you have two or three rolls developed together. The equivalent in slide film is around 850 ptas plus the same for processing. Nearly all pre-recorded videos in Spain use the PAL image-registration system common to Western Europe and Australia. These won't work on many video players in France, North America and Japan.

TIME

Spain is one hour ahead of GMT/UTC during winter, and two hours ahead from the last Sunday in March to the last Sunday in September.

ELECTRICITY

Electric current in Spain is 220V, 50 Hz, but some places are still on 125 or 110V. In fact, the voltage sometimes differs in the same building. Plugs have two round pins.

WEIGHTS & MEASURES
The metric system is used. Like other Continental Europeans, the Spanish indicate decimals with commas and thousands with points.

LAUNDRY
Self-service laundrettes are rare. Laundries (lavanderías) are common but not particularly cheap. They will usually wash, dry and fold a load for 1000 to 1200 ptas.

HEALTH
Apart from the dangers of contracting STDs, the main thing you have to be wary of is the sun – in both cases, use protection. Tap water is safe to drink throughout most of the country – if in doubt ask ¿Es potable el agua? – although taste-wise it varies from great to blah. Bottled water is available everywhere, generally for 40 to 75 ptas for a 1.5-litre bottle.

Health care is available for free to EU citizens on provision of an E111 form (available free in your home country – contact your health service before you come to Spain to find out how to get it), but others will have to pay cash, so travel insurance is a must. In a health emergency, the local tourist office or police (☎ 091 or ☎ 092) can advise on where to go. Farmacias (chemists) can treat many ailments. Emergency dental treatment is available at most public hospitals.

WOMEN TRAVELLERS
The best way for women travellers to approach Spain is simply to be ready to ignore stares, cat calls and unnecessary comments. However, Spain has one of the lowest incidences of reported rape in the developed world, and even physical harassment is much less frequent than you might expect. The Asociación de Asistencia a Mujeres Violadas in Madrid (☎ 91-574 01 10, Monday to Friday from 10 am to 2 pm and 4 to 7 pm; recorded message in Spanish at other times) offers advice and help to rape victims, and can provide details of similar centres in other cities, though only limited English is spoken.

GAY & LESBIAN TRAVELLERS
Attitudes are pretty tolerant, especially in the cities. Madrid, Barcelona, Sitges, Ibiza and Cádiz all have active gay and lesbian scenes. Gay and lesbian travellers wanting information can call Gai-Inform in Madrid (☎ 91-523 00 70) daily from 5 to 9 pm.

DISABLED TRAVELLERS
Spanish tourist offices in other countries can provide a basic information sheet with some useful addresses, and give info on accessible accommodation in specific places. Mobility International (☎ 02-410 6274; fax 02-410 6297), Rue de Manchester 25, Brussels B1070, Belgium, has researched facilities for disabled tourists in Spain. INSERSO (☎ 91-347 88 88), Calle Ginzo de Limea 58, 28029 Madrid, is the government department for the disabled, with branches in all of Spain's 50 provinces.

You'll find some wheelchair-accessible accommodation in main centres, but it may not be in the budget category – although 25 Spanish youth hostels are classed as suitable for wheelchair users.

DANGERS & ANNOYANCES
It's a good idea to take your car radio and any other valuables with you any time you leave your car. In fact it's best to leave nothing at all – certainly nothing visible – in a parked car. In youth hostels, don't leave belongings unattended – there is a high incidence of theft. Beware of pickpockets in cities and tourist resorts (Barcelona and Seville have bad reputations). There is also a relatively high incidence of mugging in such places, so keep your wits about you. Emergency numbers for the police throughout Spain are ☎ 091 (national police) and ☎ 092 (local police).

Drugs
In 1992 Spain's liberal drug laws were severely tightened. No matter what anyone tells you, it is not legal to smoke dope in public bars. There is a reasonable degree of tolerance when it comes to people having a smoke in their own home, but not in hotel rooms or guesthouses.

BUSINESS HOURS
Generally, people work Monday to Friday from 9 am to 2 pm and then again from 4.30 or 5 pm for another three hours. Shops and travel

agencies are usually open these hours on Saturday too, though some may skip the evening session. Museums all have their own unique opening hours: major ones tend to open for something like normal business hours (with or without the afternoon break), but often have their weekly closing day on Monday, not Sunday.

PUBLIC HOLIDAYS

Spain has something like 15 official holidays a year – some observed nationwide, some very local – but you'll often find banks, post offices and shops winding down early before holidays or opening up late after them. When a holiday falls close to a weekend, Spaniards like to make a *puente* (bridge) – meaning they take the intervening day off too. The following holidays are observed just about everywhere: 1 January (New Year's Day), 6 January (Epiphany or Three Kings' Day, when children receive presents), Good Friday, 1 May (Labour Day), 15 August (Feast of the Assumption), 12 October (National Day), 1 November (All Saints' Day), 6 December (Constitution Day), 8 December (Feast of the Immaculate Conception) and 25 December (Christmas). The two main periods when Spaniards go on holiday are Semana Santa (the week leading up to Easter Sunday) and the month of August. At these times accommodation in resorts can be scarce and transport heavily booked, but other cities are often half-empty.

SPECIAL EVENTS

Spaniards indulge their love of colour, noise, crowds and partying at innumerable local fiestas and *ferias* (fairs): even small villages will have at least one, probably several, during the year. Many fiestas are religion-based but still highly festive. Local tourist offices can always supply detailed info.

Among festivals to look out for are La Tamborada in San Sebastián on 20 January, when the whole town dresses up and goes berserk; *carnaval*, a time of fancy-dress parades and merrymaking celebrated around the country about seven weeks before Easter (wildest in Cádiz and Sitges); Valencia's week-long mid-March party, Las Fallas, with all-night dancing and drinking, first-class fireworks, and processions; Semana Santa with its parades of holy images and huge crowds, notably in Seville; Seville's Feria de Abril, a week-long party in late April, a kind of counterbalance to the religious peak of Semana Santa; Sanfermines, with the running of the bulls, in Pamplona in July; Semana Grande, another week of heavy drinking and hangovers, all along the north coast during the first half of August; and Barcelona's week-long party, the Festes de la Mercè, around 24 September.

ACTIVITIES
Surfing & Windsurfing

The País Vasco has some good surf spots – San Sebastián, Zarauz and the legendary left at Mundaca, among others. Tarifa, Spain's southernmost point, is windsurfer's heaven, with constant strong breezes and long, empty beaches too.

Skiing

Skiing in Spain is cheap and the facilities and conditions are surprisingly good. The season runs from around December to May. The most accessible resorts are in the Sierra Nevada (very close to Granada), the Pyrenees (north of Barcelona) and in the ranges north of Madrid. The tourist offices in these cities have information on the various ski fields, and affordable day trips can be booked through travel agents.

Cycling

Bike touring isn't as common as in other parts of Europe because of deterrents like the often-mountainous terrain, crowded roads and summer heat. It's a more viable option on the Balearic Islands than on much of the mainland, though it's popular in autumn and spring in the south. Mountain biking is increasingly popular and areas like Andalucía and Catalonia have km upon km of good tracks for this. Finding bikes to rent is a hit-and-miss affair so if you're set on the idea it's best to bring your own.

Trekking & Walking

Spain is a trekker's paradise, so much so that Lonely Planet has published a guide to some of the best treks in the country, *Trekking in Spain*. See also the Mallorca and Picos de Europa sections of this chapter.

Walking country roads and paths, between villages, can also be highly enjoyable and a great way to meet the locals. Two organisations publish detailed maps of Spain.

The Instituto Geográfico Nacional (IGN) covers the country in over 4000 1:25,000 sheets, mostly fairly up-to-date. The IGN and the Army Cartographic Service (SCE) both publish 1:50,000 series – the SCE's tend to be more up to date, but the IGN's are more traveller/hiker oriented. Also very useful for hiking and exploring small areas are the *Guía Cartográfica* and *Guía Excursionista y Turística* booklets published in Spanish by Editorial Alpina. Covering most of the mountainous parts of the country (except the south), these include detailed maps at scales ranging from 1:25,000 to 1:50,000, and are well worth their price (around 500 ptas). You may well find IGE, SCE and Alpina publications in local bookshops but it's more reliable to get them in advance from specialist map or travel shops like La Tienda Verde in Madrid, and Altaïr and Quera in Barcelona, or you can obtain them from some overseas specialists. IGN (☎ 91-554 14 50), Calle General Ibañez de Íbero 3, 28003 Madrid, can supply you with a free catalogue.

If you fancy a really long walk, there's the Camino de Santiago. This route, which has been followed by Christian pilgrims for centuries, can be commenced at various places in France. It then crosses the Pyrenees and runs via Pamplona, Logroño and León all the way to the cathedral in Santiago de Compostela. There are numerous guidebooks explaining the route, and the best map is published by IGN.

COURSES
The best place to take a language course in Spain is generally at a university. Those with the best reputations include Salamanca, Santiago de Compostela and Santander. It can also be fun to combine study with a stay in one of Spain's most exciting cities such as Barcelona, Madrid or Seville. There are also dozens of private language colleges throughout the country; the Instituto Cervantes (☎ 0171-935 1518), at 22-23 Manchester Square, London W1M 5AP, can send you lists of these and of universities that run courses. Some Spanish embassies and consulates also have info.

Other courses available in Spain include art, cookery and photography. Spanish tourist offices can help with information.

WORK
EU, Norway and Iceland nationals are allowed to work in Spain without a visa, but if they plan to stay more than three months, they are supposed to apply within the first month for a residence card (see Visas & Embassies earlier in this chapter). Virtually everyone else is supposed to obtain, from a Spanish consulate in their country of residence, a work permit and, if they plan to stay more than 90 days, a residence visa. These procedures are even more difficult (see Visas & Embassies). That said, quite a few people do manage to work in Spain one way or another – though with Spain's unemployment rate running at over 20%, don't rely on it. Teaching English is an obvious option – a TEFL certificate will be a big help. Another possibility is summer work in a bar or restaurant in a tourist resort. Quite a lot of these are run by foreigners.

ACCOMMODATION
Camping
Spain has more than 800 camping grounds. Facilities and settings vary enormously, and grounds are officially rated from 1st class to 3rd class. You can expect to pay around 450 ptas per person, 450 ptas per car and 450 ptas per tent. Tourist offices can direct you to the nearest camping ground. Many sites are open all year, though quite a few close from around October to Easter. With certain exceptions (such as many beaches and environmentally protected areas), it is legal to camp outside camping grounds. You'll need permission to camp on private land.

Hostels
Spain's youth hostels *(albergues juveniles)* are often the cheapest place to stay for lone travellers, but two people can usually get a double room elsewhere for a similar price. With some notable exceptions, hostels are only moderate value. Many have curfews and/or are closed during the day, or lack cooking facilities (though if so they usually have a cafeteria). They can, too, be lacking in privacy, and are often heavily booked by school groups. Most are members of the country's Hostelling International (HI) organisation, Red Española de Albergues Juveniles (REAJ), whose head office (☎ 91-347 77 00) is at Calle José Ortega y Gasset 71, 28006 Madrid. Prices often

depend on the season or whether you're under 26: typically you pay 900 to 1500 ptas. Some hostels require HI membership, others don't but may charge more if you're not a member. You can buy HI cards for 1800 ptas at virtually all hostels.

Other Accommodation

Officially, all establishments are either *hoteles* (from one to five stars), *hostales* (one to three stars) or *pensiones*. In practice, there are all sorts of overlapping categories, especially at the budget end of the market. In broad terms, the cheapest are usually *fondas* and *casas de huéspedes*, followed by pensiones. All these normally have shared bathrooms, and singles/doubles for 1000/2000 to 1500/3000 ptas. Some hostales and *hostal-residencias* come in the same price range, but others have rooms with private bathroom costing anywhere up to 6000 ptas or so. Hoteles are usually beyond the budgets of shoestringers. The luxurious state-run *paradores*, often converted historic buildings, are prohibitively expensive.

Room rates in this chapter are high-season prices, which in most resorts and other heavily touristed places means July and August, Semana Santa and sometimes Christmas-New Year. At other times prices in many places go down by 5% to 25%.

FOOD

It's a good idea to reset your stomach's clock in Spain, unless you want to eat alone or only with other tourists. Most Spaniards start the day with a light breakfast *(desayuno)*, perhaps coffee with a *tostada* (toasted roll) or *pastel* (pastry). *Churros con chocolate* (long, deep-fried doughnuts with thick hot chocolate) are a delicious start to the day and unique to Spain. Lunch (*almuerzo* or *comida*) is usually the main meal of the day, eaten between about 1.30 and 4 pm. The evening meal *(cena)* is usually lighter and may be eaten as late as 10 or 11 pm. It's common (and a great idea!) to go to a bar or café for a snack around 11 am and again around 7 or 8 pm.

Spain has a huge variety of local cuisines. Seafood as well as meat is prominent almost everywhere. One of the most characteristic dishes, from the Valencia region, is paella – rice, seafood, the odd vegetable and often chicken or meat, all simmered up together,

with a yellow colour traditionally produced by saffron. Another dish, of Andalucian origin, is gazpacho, a soup made from tomatoes, breadcrumbs, cucumber and/or green peppers, eaten cold. *Tortillas* (omelettes) are an inexpensive standby and come in many varieties. *Jamón serrano* (cured ham) is a treat for meat-eaters but can be expensive.

Cafés & Bars

If you want to follow Spanish habits, you'll be spending plenty of time in cafés and bars. In almost all of them you'll find *tapas* available. These saucer-sized mini-snacks are part of the Spanish way of life and come in infinite varieties from calamari rings to potato salad to spinach with chickpeas to a small serving of tripe. A typical tapa costs 100 to 200 ptas, but check before you order because some are a lot dearer. A *ración* is a meal-sized serving of these snacks; a *media ración* is a half-ración.

The other popular snacks are *bocadillos*, long filled white bread rolls. Spaniards eat so many bocadillos that there are cafés that sell nothing else. Try not to leave Spain without sampling a *bocadillo de tortilla de patata* or *de jamón serrano*, a roll filled with potato omelette or cured ham.

You can often save 10% to 20% by ordering and eating food at the bar rather than at a table.

Restaurants

Throughout Spain, you'll find plenty of restaurants serving good, simple food at affordable prices, often featuring regional specialities. Many restaurants offer a *menú del día* – the budget traveller's best friend. For between 500 and 1200 ptas, you typically get a starter, a main course, dessert, bread and wine – often with a choice of two or three dishes for each course. The *plato combinado* is a near relative of the menú. It literally translates as 'combined plate' – maybe a steak and egg with chips and salad, or fried squid with potato salad. You'll pay more for your meals if you order à la carte, but the food will be better.

Vegetarian Food

Finding vegetarian fare can be a headache. It's not uncommon for 'meatless' food to be flavoured with meat stock. But in larger cities and important student centres there's a growing awareness of vegetarianism, so that if there isn't a vegetarian restaurant, there are often vegetarian items on menus. A good vegetarian snack at almost any place with bocadillos or sandwiches is a *bocadillo* (or *sandwich*) *vegetal*, which has a filling of salad and, often, fried egg (*sin huevo* means without egg).

Self-Catering

Every town of any substance has a *mercado* (food market). These are fun and great value. Even big eaters should be able to put together a filling meal of bread, chorizo (spiced sausage), cheese, fruit and a drink for 400 ptas or less. If you shop carefully you can eat three healthy meals a day for as little as 600 ptas.

DRINKS

Coffee in Spain is strong. Addicts should specify how they want their fix: *café con leche* is about 50% coffee, 50% hot milk; *café solo* is a short black; *café cortado* is a short black with a little milk.

The most common way to order a beer *(cerveza)* is to ask for a *caña* (pronounced 'can-ya'), which is a small draught beer. *Corto* and, in the País Vasco, *zurrito*, are other names for this. A larger beer (about 300 ml) is often called a *tubo*, or in Catalonia a *jarra*. All these words apply to draught beer *(cerveza de barril)* – if you just ask for a cerveza you're likely to get bottled beer, which is more expensive.

Wine *(vino)* comes white *(blanco)*, red *(tinto)* or rosé *(rosado)*. *Tinto de verano*, a kind of wine shandy, is good in summer. There are also many regional grape specialities such as *jerez* (sherry) in Jerez de la Frontera and *cava* (like champagne) in Catalonia. *Sangría*, a sweet punch made of red wine, fruit and spirits, is refreshing and very popular with tourists.

The cheapest drink of all is, of course, water. To specify tap water (which is safe to drink almost everywhere), just ask for *agua de grifo*.

ENTERTAINMENT

Spain has some of the best nightlife in Europe – wild and *very* late nights, especially on Friday and Saturday, are an integral part of the Spain experience. Many young Spaniards don't even think about going out till midnight or so. Bars, which come in all shapes, sizes and themes, are the main attractions until around 2 or 3 am. Some play great music which will get

you hopping before – if you can afford it – you move on to a disco till 5 or 6 am. Discos are generally expensive, but not to be missed if you can manage to splurge. Spain's contributions to modern dance music are *bakalao* and *makina*, kinds of frenzied (150 to 180 bpm) techno.

The live-music scene is less exciting. Spanish rock and pop tends to be imitative, though the bigger cities usually offer a reasonable choice of bands. See the earlier Culture section for info on flamenco.

Cinemas abound and are good value, though foreign films are usually dubbed into Spanish.

SPECTATOR SPORT

The national sport is *fútbol* (soccer). The best teams to see – for their crowd support as well as their play – are usually Real Madrid and Barcelona, though the atmosphere can be electric anywhere. The season runs from September to May.

Bullfighting is enjoying a resurgence despite continued pressure from international animal-rights activists. It's a complex activity that's regarded as much as an art form as a sport by aficionados. If you decide to see a *corrida de toros*, the season runs from March to October. Madrid, Seville and Pamplona are among the best places to see one.

THINGS TO BUY

Many of Spain's best handicrafts are fragile or bulky – inconvenient unless you're going straight home. Pottery comes in a great range of attractive regional varieties. Some lovely rugs and blankets are made in places like the Alpujarras and Níjar in Andalucía. There's some pleasing woodwork available too, such as Granada's marquetry boxes and chess sets. Leather jackets, bags and belts are quite good value in many places.

Getting There & Away

AIR

Spain has many international airports including Madrid, Barcelona, Bilbao, Santiago de Compostela, Seville, Málaga, Almería, Alicante, Valencia, Palma de Mallorca, Ibiza and Maó (Menorca). In general, the cheapest destinations are Málaga, the Balearic Islands, Barcelona and Madrid.

Australia

In general, the best thing to do is to fly to London, Paris, Frankfurt or Rome, and then make your way overland. Alternatively, some flight deals to these centres include a couple of short-haul flights within Europe, and Madrid or Barcelona are usually acceptable destinations for these. Some round-the-world (RTW) fares include stops in Spain. STA Travel should be able to help you out with a good price. Generally speaking, a return fare to Europe for under A$1700 is too good to pass up.

North America

Return fares to Madrid from Miami, New York, Atlanta or Chicago range from US$620 to US$680 on Iberia or Delta. On the west coast, agencies such as Pelican Travel in Concord, California, can put together return fares from around US$770.

London

Scheduled flights to Spain are generally expensive, but with the huge range of charter, discount and low-season fares, it's often cheaper to fly than to take a bus or train. Check the travel sections of *TNT* or *Time Out* magazines or the weekend newspapers. The following are examples of short-notice low-season return fares from London:

Destination	Fare	Agent	Phone
Barcelona	£109	Charter Flight Centre	☎ 0171-630 5757
Ibiza	£95	Flight Dealers	☎ 0171-630 9494
Madrid	£89	Comet Travel	☎ 0171-636 6060
Málaga	£79	Alpha Flights	☎ 0181-579 3508

From Spain

For northern Europe, check the ads in local English-language papers in tourist centres like the Costa del Sol, the Costa Blanca and the Balearic Islands. You may pick up a one-way fare to London for around 12,000 ptas. The youth and student travel agency TIVE, and the general travel agency Halcón Viajes, both with branches in most main cities, have some good fares: generally you're looking at around 13,000 to 15,500 ptas one way to London, Paris

or Amsterdam, and at least 30,000 ptas to the USA.

LAND

Bus

There are regular bus services to Spain from all major centres in Europe, including Lisbon, London and Paris. In London, Eurolines (☎ 0171-730 8235) has services at least twice a week to Barcelona (24 hours), Madrid (27 hours) and Málaga (34 hours). One-way fares are £70 to £90. Tickets are sold by major travel agencies, and people under 26 and senior citizens qualify for a 10% discount. In Spain, services to the major European cities are operated by Eurolines affiliates such as Linebús and Julià Via. There are also bus services to Morocco from some Spanish cities.

Train

Reaching Spain by train is more expensive than bus unless you have a rail pass, though fares for those under 26 come close to the bus price. Normal one-way fares from London to Madrid (via Paris) are around £115. For more details, contact British Rail International in London (☎ 0171-834 2345) or a travel agent. See the introductory Getting Around chapter for more on rail passes and train travel through Europe.

Car & Motorcycle

If you're driving or riding to Spain from England, you'll have to choose between going through France (check visa requirements) or taking a direct ferry from England to Spain (see the following section). The cheapest way is one of the shorter ferries from England to France, then a quick drive down through France.

SEA

Britain

There are two direct ferry services. Brittany Ferries (in England ☎ 0990-360360) runs Plymouth-Santander ferries twice weekly from about mid-March to mid-November (24 hours), and a Portsmouth-Santander service (30 hours), usually once a week, in other months. P&O European Ferries (in England ☎ 0990-980980) runs Portsmouth-Bilbao ferries twice weekly almost all year (35 hours). Prices on all services are similar: one-way passenger fares range from about £45 in winter to £75 in summer (cabins extra); a car and driver costs from £145 to £260, or you can take a vehicle and several passengers for £223 to £411.

Morocco

Ferry services between Spain and Morocco include Algeciras-Tangier, Algeciras-Ceuta, Gibraltar-Tangier, Málaga-Melilla and Almería-Melilla. Those to/from Algeciras are the fastest, cheapest and most frequent, with up to nine daily Ceuta sailings (1½ hours) and four Tangier sailings (2½ hours). One-way passenger/car/motorcycle fares are 1800/8250/1875 ptas (Ceuta) and 2960/9300/2650 ptas (Tangier). You can buy tickets at Algeciras harbour, but it's more convenient to go to one of the many agencies on the waterfront. The price doesn't vary from shop to shop, so just look for the place with the shortest queue. A word of advice – don't buy Moroccan currency until you reach Morocco, as you will get ripped off in Algeciras.

LEAVING SPAIN

There is no departure tax in Spain.

Getting Around

AIR

Spain now has four main domestic airlines – Iberia, Aviaco, Air Europa and Spanair – and competition produces some fares which can make flying worthwhile if you're in a hurry, especially for longer trips or return trips. Málaga or Seville to Barcelona with Air Europa, for example, is 13,900 ptas (20,900 ptas return), against 7000 to 9000 ptas each way by bus or train. You can fly from Barcelona to the Balearic Islands with Spanair for 7950 ptas, or there and back with Aviaco for 12,500 ptas, not very much more than the ferry fare.

Among travel agencies, TIVE and Halcón Viajes (see Air under Getting There & Away earlier) are always worth checking for fares. There are some useful deals if you're under 26 (or, in some cases, over 63).

BUS

Spain's bus network is operated by dozens of independent companies and is more extensive than its train system, serving remote towns and villages as well as the major routes. The choice between bus and train depends on the particular trip you're taking: for the best value, compare fares, journey times and frequencies each time you move. Buses to/from Madrid are often cheaper than cross-country routes: for instance Seville to Madrid costs 2680 ptas while the shorter Seville-Granada trip is 2710 ptas.

Many towns and cities have one main bus station where most buses arrive and depart, and these usually have an information desk giving info on all services. Tourist offices can also help with info but don't sell tickets.

TRAIN

The Spanish train system has improved beyond imagination in the last 15 years. Trains are mostly modern and comfortable, and late arrivals are now the exception rather than the rule. The main headache is deciding which compartment on which train gives you best value for money.

RENFE, the national railway company, runs numerous types of train, and travel times can vary a lot on the same route. So can fares, which may depend not just on the type of train but also the day of the week and time of day. Among long-distance *(largo recorrido)* trains the best, quickest and most expensive type is normally a Talgo. Next quickest is usually an Intercity, then a Diurno or Rápido and finally an Estrella. Some trains have both 1st and 2nd class, some have only one or the other. There's also a category of overnight train called Tren Hotel, usually 1st class only and quite quick. Best of all is the AVE high-speed service that links Madrid and Seville in just 2½ hours.

Regionales are RENFE trains which travel shorter distances, usually with a lot of stops and cheaper fares. *Cercanías* are suburban trains run by various local authorities, not RENFE.

There's also a bewildering range of accommodation types, especially on overnight trains. RENFE publishes a fare guide, but it's 500 pages long and to understand it fully you'd need a PhD in cryptography! For any one route, there are up to 24 different fares per class (fares quoted in this chapter are typical 2nd-class seat fares). Fortunately ticket clerks understand the problem and are usually happy to go through a few options with you. The cheapest sleeper option is usually a *litera*, a bunk in a six-berth 2nd-class compartment.

You can buy tickets and make reservations at stations, RENFE offices in many city centres, and travel agencies which display the RENFE logo. For long-distance trains a reservation is always needed and costs 500 ptas or more per ticket.

Train Passes
Rail passes are valid for all RENFE trains, but Inter-Rail users have to pay supplements on Talgo and Intercity services, and full fare on the high-speed AVE service between Madrid and Seville. All pass-holders, like everyone else, have to make reservations for long-distance trains and pay the reservation fee of 500 ptas or more.

RENFE's Tarjeta Turistica is a rail pass valid for four to 10-days travel in a two-month period: in 2nd class, four days costs 22,646 ptas, while 10 days is 48,374 ptas.

CAR & MOTORCYCLE
If you're driving or riding around Spain, consider investing 1900 ptas in the *Mapa Oficial de Carreteras*, which is published annually by the Ministry of Public Works, Transport & Environment. It's a handy atlas with detailed road maps as well as maps of all the main towns and cities.

Spain's roads vary enormously but are generally quite good. Fastest are the *autopistas*, multilane freeways between major cities. On some, mainly in the north, you have to pay hefty tolls (from the French border to Barcelona, for example, it's around 1750 ptas). Minor routes can often be slow going but are usually more scenic. Petrol is relatively expensive at around 110 ptas for a litre of unleaded.

The head office of the Spanish automobile club Real Automovil Club de España (RACE) is at Calle José Abascal 10, 28003 Madrid (☎ 91-447 32 00). For RACE's 24-hour, nationwide, on-road emergency service, call ☎ 91-593 3333.

Road Rules
A general disrespect for road rules has given Spain the dubious honour of having one of the highest road-death tolls in the developed world. Speed limits are 120 km/h on autopistas, 90 or 100 km/h on other country roads and 50 km/h in built-up areas. The maximum allowable blood-alcohol level is 0.08%. Seat belts must be worn, and motorcyclists must always wear a helmet.

Trying to find a parking spot can be a nightmare in larger towns and cities. Spanish drivers just park anywhere to save themselves the hassle of a half-hour search, but *grúas* (tow trucks) will tow your car away if given the chance. The cost of bailing out a car hovers around the 6000 ptas mark.

Rental
Rates vary widely from place to place. The best deals tend to be in major tourist areas, including at their airports. At Málaga airport you can rent a small car for under 20,000 ptas a week. More generally, you're looking at something like 2500 ptas for a day plus 25 ptas a km (taxes and insurance included), or around 40,000 ptas a week with unlimited km. Local companies often have better rates than the big firms.

BICYCLE
See the Activities section earlier.

HITCHING
It's still possible to thumb your way around parts of Spain, but large doses of patience and common sense are necessary. Women should avoid hitching alone. Hitching is illegal on autopistas and difficult on major highways. Your chances are better on minor roads, although the going can still be painfully slow.

BOAT
For information on ferries to, from and between the Balearic Islands, see that section of this chapter.

LOCAL TRANSPORT
In many Spanish towns you will not need to use public transport, as transport terminals and accommodation are centralised and within walking distance of most tourist attractions.

Most towns in Spain have an effective local bus system. In larger cities, these can be complicated, but tourist offices can advise on which buses you need. Barcelona and Madrid both have efficient underground systems which are cheaper, faster and easier to use than the bus systems.

Taxis are still pretty cheap. If you split a cross-town fare between three or four people, it can be a decidedly good deal. Rates vary slightly from city to city: in Barcelona, they cost 270 ptas, plus 92 to 107 ptas per km; in Madrid they're a bit cheaper. There are supplements for luggage and airport trips.

Madrid

Whatever apprehensions you may have about Madrid when you first arrive, Spain's capital is sure to grow on you. Madrid may lack the glamour or beauty of Barcelona and the historical richness of so many Spanish cities (it was insignificant until Felipe II made it his capital in 1561), but it more than makes up for this with a remarkable collection of museums and galleries, some lovely parks and gardens and a really wild nightlife.

Orientation

The area of most interest to visitors lies between Parque del Buen Retiro in the east and Campo del Moro in the west. These two parks are more or less connected by Calle de Alcalá and Calle Mayor, which meet in the middle at Puerta del Sol. Calle Mayor passes the main square, Plaza Mayor, on its way from Puerta del Sol to the Palacio Real in front of Campo del Moro.

The main north-south thoroughfare is Paseo de la Castellana, which runs (changing names to Paseo de Recoletos and finally Paseo del Prado) all the way from Chamartín train station in the north to Madrid's other big station, Atocha.

Information

Tourist Offices Madrid's main tourist office (☎ 541 23 25) is in the Torre de Madrid on Plaza de España. It's open weekdays from 9 am to 7 pm (to 1 pm on Saturday). There are other tourist offices at Calle Duque de Medinaceli 2 (☎ 429 49 51), open the same hours, and at Plaza Mayor 3 (☎ 366 54 77), open weekdays from 10 am to 8 pm (to 2 pm on Saturday). The offices in Chamartín train station and Barajas

airport are open weekdays from 8 am to 8 pm and Saturday from 9 am to 1 pm.

Money Large banks like the Caja de Madrid usually have the best rates, but check commissions first. Banking hours are weekdays from 9 am to 2 pm (Saturday to 1 pm). El Corte Inglés department stores (see Things to Buy earlier) and American Express (see Post & Communications following) also have reasonable exchange rates. If you're desperate there are plenty of *bureaux de change* around Puerta del Sol and Plaza Mayor, which offer appalling rates but are open until midnight. One exception on both counts is Cambios Uno, Calle de Alcalá 20 – open daily from 9 am to 9 pm (Sunday till 3 pm).

Post & Communications The main post office is in the gigantic Palacio de Comunicaciones on Plaza de la Cibeles. Poste restante (lista de correos) is at window 17 and is open weekdays from 8 am to 9.30 pm and on Saturday from 8.30 am to 2 pm. American Express (☎ 322 54 24) is not too far away for those using its client mail service, at Plaza de las Cortes 2. It's open weekdays from 9 am to 5.30 pm and Saturday from 9 am to noon.

There are plenty of public phones on the streets. The Telefónica *locutorios* (phone centres) at Gran Vía 30 and Paseo de Recoletos 41 (near Plaza Colón) have phone books for the whole country and cabins where you can make calls in relative peace. Both are open daily from 9.30 am to 11.30 pm. Madrid's telephone code is ☎ 91.

Travel Agencies For cheap travel tickets try Viajes Zeppelin (☎ 547 79 03), Plaza Santo Domingo 2; or TIVE, the student and youth travel organisation, at Calle Fernando el Católico 88 (☎ 543 02 08) or in the Instituto de la Juventud at Calle José Ortega y Gasset 71 (☎ 347 77 00), both open Monday to Friday from 9 am to 1 pm.

Bookshops Librería Turner, at Calle de Génova 3, has an excellent selection of English-language books – literature, fiction and guidebooks – as well as French and German books. Booksellers, at Calle José Abascal 48, is another good English bookshop.

Librería de Mujeres, Calle San Cristóbal 17, is a women's bookshop and a well-known feminist meeting place.

La Tienda Verde, Calle Maudes 38 (metro: Cuatro Caminos), has about the best selection of walking guides and maps for many parts of Spain, including many IGN and SCE 1:25,000, 1:50,000 and 1:100,000 maps.

Laundry Laundrettes include Lavandería España on Calle Infante, Lavomatique on Calle de Cervantes, and Lavandería Alba at Calle del Barco 26.

Medical & Emergency Services The most central police station is beside the ticket office in Puerta del Sol metro station. You can call the police on ☎ 091. For medical emergencies, there's a clinic and 24-hour first-aid station at the Centro de Salud (☎ 521 00 25), Calle Navas de Tolosa 10. You can also ring ☎ 061 in a medical emergency. For an ambulance ring the Cruz Roja (Red Cross) on ☎ 522 22 22. For English-speaking medical services, try the Anglo-American Medical Unit (☎ 435 18 23) at Calle Conde de Aranda 1 (metro: Retiro).

Things to See
Madrid will make a lot more sense if you spend some time just walking around before you start getting into the city's cultural delights. The following walking tour could take anywhere from a few hours to a few days – it's up to you. You'll find more detail on the major sights in following sections.

Walking Tour The most fitting place to start getting to know Madrid is **Puerta del Sol**. Sol, as it's known to locals, is not much more than a huge traffic-junction-cum-bus-stop, but it's as central as you can get – on the south side, a small plaque in the footpath marks **Km 0**, from which distances along Spain's highways are measured. The statue of a bear climbing a tree on the north side of Sol is one of Madrid's favourite meeting places.

Walk up Calle de Preciados and take the second street on the left, which will bring you to Plaza de las Descalzas. Note the **doorway** to the Caja de Ahorros in the Caja de Madrid building – it was built for King Felipe V in 1733. It faces the 16th-century **Convento de las Descalzas Reales**. Moving along, head south down Calle San Martín to the **Iglesia de San Ginés**. This is one of Madrid's oldest churches – there is evidence that it has been here in one form or another since the 14th century. It houses some fine paintings, including El Greco's *Cleansing of the Temple*, but is only open for services. Behind the church is the wonderful **Chocolatería de San Ginés**, which specialises in chocolate con churros; it's generally open from 7 to 10 pm and 1 to 7 am.

Continue down to and across Calle Mayor and into Madrid's most famous square. On a sunny day the cafés on the early 17th-century **Plaza Mayor** do a roaring trade, with some 500 tables on the square – definitely a place to be seen, as the prices indicate. In the middle is a **statue of Felipe III**, who was responsible for the building of the square. The colourful murals on the **Real Casa de la Panadería**, on the north side, were painted in the early 1990s.

From Plaza Mayor, head west along Calle Mayor to the historic **Plaza de la Villa**, with Madrid's 17th-century ayuntamiento (city hall). Also here are the 16th-century **Casa de Cisneros** and the Gothic-Mudéjar **Torre de los Lujanes**, one of the city's oldest buildings, dating from the Middle Ages.

Take the street down the left side of Casa de Cisneros, cross the road at the end, go down the stairs and follow cobbled Calle del Cordón out on to Calle Segovia. Almost directly in front of you is the Mudéjar tower of the **Iglesia de San Pedro**. Turn right when you come to Plaza de la Cruz Verde. A little way up the hill behind you is the domed **Iglesia de San Andrés** – the decoration inside the dome is rather unusual and worth a peek.

Walk up Calle de la Villa past the military church on to Calle Mayor, and turn left, passing the **Capitanía General**, the national military headquarters. Calle Mayor brings you out on to Calle Bailén.

As you walk northward, you will pass Madrid's cathedral, the **Iglesia de la Almudena**, a stark and cavernous building which was finally completed in mid-1992, after more than 110 years under construction. A little further along is the **Palacio Real**, opposite which is the lovely **Plaza de Oriente**, with its collection of statues, fountains and mazes. On the far side of the plaza is Madrid's **Teatro Real**.

SPAIN

SPAIN

To Museo
de América
(200 m)

To Universidad
Complutense
(1.25 km)

To Escuela Oficial
de Idiomas (400 m)

To La Tienda Verde
& Aviaco (750 m)

Calle de Isaac Peral

Calle de Hilarión Eslava

Paseo Moret

Moncloa

Calle de Gaztambide

Calle Fernández de los Ríos

Calle de Blasco de Garay

Calle de Fernando El Católico

Callede Menéndez Valdés

Calle de Bravo Murillo

Calle de Eloy Gonzalo

Paseo General Martínez Camp

Iglesia

Calle de Santa Engracia

Calle de Fernández de Hoz

Calle de Zurbano

Pas

Argüelles

Calle Martín de los Heros

Calle de la Princesa

Calle de Quintana

Serrano

Calle de Fuencarral

Quevedo

San
Bernardo

Jove

Calle de la Princesa

Calle Mártires de Alcalá

Calle Alberto Aguilera

Calle Carranza

Calle de Luchana

Calle de Sagasta

Bilbao

Alonso
Martínez

Calle de Génova

Ventura
Rodríguez

Calle San

Novicidado

Calle Divino Pastor

Calle Daoíz

Calle de
Vicente

Calle de
Ferrer

Malasaña
La Paima

Tribunal

Campoamor

Calle de Prim

Calle Almirante

See Central Madrid Map

Chueca

Plaza
de
España

Gran Vía

Bailén

San Vicente

Cuesta de

Gran Vía

Calle de la Montera

Calle de Augusto Figueroa

Plaza
de
la Cibeles

Príncipe
Pío Train
Station

Norte

To
Panteón
de Goya &
Casa Mingo
(500 m)

To Albergue
Richard
Schirmann
(Youth Hostel)

Campo
del Moro

Calle del Arenal

Calle de Alcalá

Puerta
del Sol

Plaza
de
Canalejas

Carrera de San Jerónimo

Plaza
Cánovas
del
Castillo

Calle Mayor

Plaza
Mayor

Calle de las Huertas

Calle de Segovia

Ronda

de

Segovia

Paseo

Imperial

Calle

de

Toledo

Puerta
Toledo

Latina

El Rastro
Market

Calle Ribera de Curtidores

Calle de Atocha

Calle de Santa Isabel

Lavapiés

Ronda

de

Toledo

Embajadores

Ronda Valencia

Ronda de Atocha

To Estadio Vicente
Calderón (700 m)

To Estación
Sur de Autobuses
(300 m)

Paseo del Prado

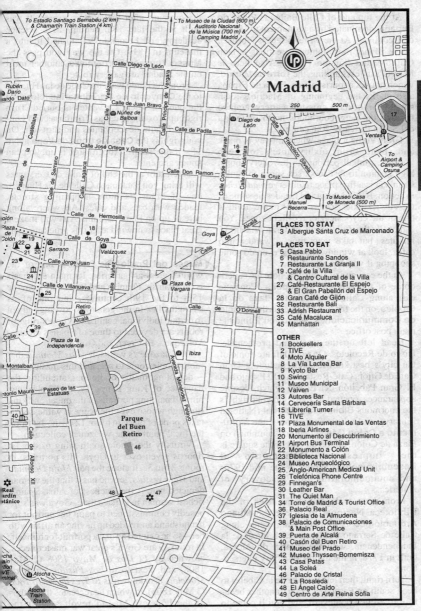

Madrid

0   250   500 m

To Estadio Santiago Bernabéu (2 km)
& Chamartín Train Station (4 km)

To Museo de la Ciudad (600 m),
Auditorio Nacional
de la Música (700 m) &
Camping Madrid

To Museo de la Ciudad

To Airport &
Camping
Osuna

To Museo Casa
de Moneda (500 m)

Parque
del Buen
Retiro

Atocha Train Station

PLACES TO STAY
3 Albergue Santa Cruz de Marcenado

PLACES TO EAT
5 Casa Pablo
6 Restaurante Sandos
7 Restaurante La Granja II
19 Café de la Villa
   & Centro Cultural de la Villa
27 Café-Restaurante El Espejo
   & El Gran Pabellón del Espejo
28 Gran Café de Gijón
32 Restaurante Bali
33 Adrish Restaurant
35 Café Macaluca
45 Manhattan

OTHER
1 Booksellers
2 TIVE
4 Moto Alquiler
8 La Vía Lactea Bar
9 Kyoto Bar
10 Swing
11 Museo Municipal
12 Vaivén
13 Autores Bar
14 Cervecería Santa Bárbara
15 Librería Turner
16 TIVE
17 Plaza Monumental de las Ventas
18 Iberia Airlines
20 Monumento al Descubrimiento
21 Airport Bus Terminal
22 Monumento a Colón
23 Biblioteca Nacional
24 Museo Arqueológico
25 Anglo-American Medical Unit
26 Telefónica Phone Centre
29 Finnegan's
30 Leather Bar
31 The Quiet Man
34 Torre de Madrid & Tourist Office
36 Palacio Real
37 Iglesia de la Almudena
38 Palacio de Comunicaciones
   & Main Post Office
39 Puerta de Alcalá
40 Casón del Buen Retiro
41 Museo del Prado
42 Museo Thyssen-Bornemisza
43 Casa Patas
44 La Soleá
46 Palacio de Cristal
47 La Rosaleda
48 El Ángel Caído
49 Centro de Arte Reina Sofía

At the top end of Calle Bailén is **Plaza de España**, dominated by a monument to Miguel de Cervantes. At the writer's feet is a bronze statue of his most famous creations – Don Quixote and Sancho Panza. Also here is Madrid's tallest building, the **Torre de Madrid**, which houses a tourist office. Plaza de España also marks the beginning of Madrid's main street – Gran Vía, a crosstown artery rammed through the neighbourhoods north of Puerta del Sol in the early 20th century.

Gran Vía is a place where money is made and spent. From luxury hotels to cheap hostales, pinball parlours to jewellery shops, high fashion to fast food, sex shops to banks, Gran Vía is a fine place to observe *madrileños* in action. Behind the grand façades lie some of the city's tackier scenes – just to the north is one of the city's sleazier red-light zones. You can walk the full length of Gran Vía in 15 minutes, but take your time – wander into cafés, look at window displays, even do some shopping if you can afford to.

At the east end of Gran Vía, note the superb dome of the **Edificio Metrópolis**. Continue east along Calle de Alcalá to **Plaza de la Cibeles**, on the far side of which is the **Palacio de Comunicaciones**, where you'll find the main post office.

Head left up the tree-lined promenade, Paseo de Recoletos. On your left are some of the city's best-known cafés, including Gran Café de Gijón, Café-Restaurante El Espejo and El Gran Pabellón del Espejo which, despite appearances, opened in 1990! On your right is the enormous **Biblioteca Nacional** (National Library), and a little further on is the **Monumento a Colón** (Monument to Columbus) on Plaza de Colón. At the far end of the square is the impressive **Monumento al Descubrimiento**, sculpted in the mid-1970s and commemorating the 'discovery' of America.

From here walk round the back of the Biblioteca Nacional to where the **Museo Arqueológico** is housed. Walk south along Calle de Serrano until you reach Plaza de la Independencia, with the **Puerta de Alcalá**, built in 1778, in the middle of a busy intersection.

Turn right, then left at Plaza de la Cibeles to head south on Paseo del Prado, another beautiful tree-lined boulevard, and you'll come to the museum after which it is named. It was built in the late 18th century as a science academy and Fernando VII turned it into a museum in 1819. On the way you pass the **Museo Thyssen-Bornemisza**, another must on the Madrid art-gallery route.

From the Prado walk up Calle de las Huertas to the **Convento de las Trinitarias** (closed to the public), where Cervantes is buried. Turn right up Costanilla de las Trinitarias and continue to Calle de Cervantes and turn left. On your right is the **Casa de Lope de Vega** at No 11 – if the 'abierto' (open) sign is up, you can knock and enter.

A left turn at the end of Calle de Cervantes will bring you back on to Calle de las Huertas, one of Madrid's more happening streets, loaded with bars and cafés. Anywhere along here or up on Plaza de Santa Ana will make a great place to unwind after this gruelling tour!

Museo del Prado The Prado is one of the world's great art galleries. Its main emphasis is on Spanish, Flemish and Italian art from the 15th to the 19th centuries, and one of its strengths lies in the generous coverage given to certain individual geniuses. Whole strings of rooms are devoted to three of Spain's greats – Velázquez, El Greco and Goya.

Of Velázquez's works, it's *Las Meninas* that most people come to see, and this masterpiece – depicting maids of honour attending the daughter of King Felipe IV, and Velázquez himself painting portraits of the queen and king (through whose eyes the scene is witnessed) – takes pride of place in room 12 on the 1st floor, the focal point of the Velázquez collection.

Virtually the whole south wing of the 1st floor is given over to Goya. His portraits, in rooms 34 to 38, include the pair *Maja Desnuda* and *Maja Vestida*: legend has it that the woman depicted here is the Duchess of Alba, Spain's richest woman in Goya's time. Goya was supposedly commissioned to paint her portrait for her husband and ended up having an affair with her – so he painted an extra portrait for himself. In room 39 are Goya's great war masterpieces, crowned by *El Dos de Mayo 1808* (2 May 1808) and, next to it, *Los Fusilamientos de Moncloa*, also known as *El Tres de Mayo 1808* (3 May 1808), in which he recreates the pathos of the hopeless Madrid revolt against the

Central Madrid

0   125   250 m

PLACES TO STAY
1 Hostal El Pinar
2 Hostal Besaya
6 Hostal Medieval
9 Hostal América
10 Hotel Laris
12 Hostal Flores
16 Hotel Regente
23 Pensión Luz
27 Hostal Eureka
35 Hostal Leonesa
36 Hostal Rifer
37 Hostal Riesco
40 Hostal Santa Cruz
43 Hostal Tineo & Hostal Gibert
46 Hostal La Rosa
51 Pensión Poza
52 Hostal Lucense & Hostal Prado
57 Hostal Mondragón & Hostal León
66 Hostal Vetusta

73 Hostal La Macarena
74 Hostal Los Gallegos
78 Hostal Castro & Hostal San Antonio
80 Hostal Casanova
83 Hostal López
85 Hostal Matute

PLACES TO EAT
11 Bar Restaurante Cuchifrito
15 Restaurante Integral Artemisa
19 Taberna del Alabardero
20 Restaurante La Paella Real
22 Café del Real
33 Chocolatería de San Ginés
38 Restaurante Pontejos
41 Museo de Jamón
44 La Casa del Abuelo
47 Las Bravas
48 La Trucha
53 La Trucha
56 Mesón La Caserola
58 Restaurante Integral Artemisa
64 Café Principal
67 Restaurante Madrid 1600
75 Restaurante Sobrino de Botín
79 Restaurante Pasadero
82 Restaurante La Biotika
84 Restaurante La Sanabresa

OTHER
3 Bali Hai Disco
4 Morocco Disco
5 Lavandería Alba (Laundrette)
7 Cruising Bar
8 Rimmel Bar
13 Telefónica Phone Centre

14 Cock Bar
17 Centro de Salud
18 Viajes Zeppelin
21 Teatro Real
24 Convento de las Descalzas Reales
25 El Corte Inglés Department Store
26 Police Station
28 Edificio Metropolis
29 RENFE Train Booking Office
30 Police Station
31 Teatro de la Zarzuela
32 Cambios Uno
34 Iglesia de San Ginés
39 Librería de Mujeres
42 La Cartuja Disco
45 Torero Disco
49 Suristán
50 Teatro de la Comedia
54 Viva Madrid
55 La Venencia Bar
59 Carbones Bar
60 American Express
61 Tourist Office
62 Casa de Lope de Vega
63 Lavomatique (Laundrette)
65 La Moderna Bar
68 Mercado de San Miguel
69 Capitanía General
70 Ayuntamiento (City Hall)
71 Casa de Cisneros
72 Torre de los Lujanes
76 Tourist Office
77 Lavandería España (Laundrette)
81 Convento de las Trinitarias
86 Iglesia de San Pedro
87 Iglesia de San Andrés

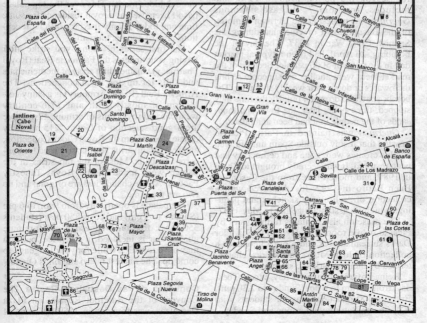

French. There's more Goya in rooms 66 and 67 on the ground floor.

Other well-represented artists include El Greco, the Flemish masters Hieronymus Bosch and Peter Paul Rubens, and the Italians Tintoretto, Titian and Raphael.

The Prado is open Tuesday to Saturday from 9 am to 7 pm, and on Sundays and holidays from 9 am to 2 pm. Entry is 400 ptas (200 ptas if you have a student card) and includes the Casón del Buen Retiro, a subsidiary a short walk east which contains the collection's 19th-century works. It's free for all on weekends from 2.30 to 7 pm, as well as on some national holidays. A 'Paseo del Arte' ticket for 1050 ptas gives a year's access to the Prado, Centro de Arte Reina Sofia and Museo Thyssen-Bornemisza.

Centro de Arte Reina Sofia At Calle de Santa Isabel 52, opposite Atocha station, the Reina Sofia museum houses a superb collection of predominantly Spanish art. The exhibition focuses on the period 1900 to 1940, and includes, in room 7, Picasso's famous *Guernica*, his protest at the German bombing of the Basque town of Guernica during the Spanish Civil War in 1937. The day of the bombing, 26 April, had been a typical market day in the town of 5000 people. Because of the market there were another 5000 people selling their wares or doing their weekly shopping. The bombs started to drop at 4 pm. By the time they stopped, three hours later, the town and thousands of the people in it had been annihilated.

Guernica was painted in Paris. Picasso insisted that it stay outside Spain until Franco and his cronies were gone and democracy had been restored. It was secretly brought to Spain in 1981, and moved here from the Casón del Buen Retiro in 1992. It's displayed with a collection of preliminary sketches and paintings which Picasso put together in May 1937.

The museum also contains further work by Picasso, while room 9 is devoted to Salvador Dalí's surrealist work and room 13 contains a collection of Joan Miró's late works, characterised by their remarkable simplicity.

Reina Sofia is open every day, except Tuesday, from 10 am to 9 pm (Sunday to 2.30 pm). Entry is 400 ptas (200 ptas for students with ID); free on Saturday afternoon and Sunday.

Museo Thyssen-Bornemisza Purchased by Spain in 1993 for something over US$300 million (a snip), this extraordinary collection of 800 paintings was formerly the private collection of the Dutch steel magnate Heinrich von Thyssen. Starting with medieval religious art, it moves on through Titian, El Greco and Rubens to Cézanne, Monet and Van Gogh, then from Miró, Picasso and Gris to Pollock, Dalí and Lichtenstein, thereby offering one of the best and most comprehensive art-history lessons you'll ever have. The museum is at Paseo del Prado 8, almost opposite the Prado, and opens Tuesday to Saturday from 10 am to 7 pm, and Sunday from 9 am to 2 pm. Entry is 600 ptas (350 ptas for students with ID); free from 2.30 pm on Saturday and Sunday.

Palacio Real Madrid's 18th-century Royal Palace is a lesson in what can happen if you give your interior decorators a free hand. You'll see some of the most elaborately decorated walls and ceilings imaginable, including the sublime Throne Room (and other rooms of more dubious merit). This over-the-top palace hasn't been used as a royal residence for some time and today is only used for official receptions and, of course, tourism.

The first series of rooms you strike after buying your ticket is the Farmacia Real (Royal Pharmacy), an unending array of medicine jars and stills for mixing royal concoctions. The Armería Real (Royal Armoury) is a shiny collection of mostly 16th and 17th-century weapons and royal suits of armour. Elsewhere are a good selection of Goyas, 215 absurdly ornate clocks from the Royal Clock Collection, and five Stradivarius violins, still used for concerts and balls. Most of the tapestries in the palace were made in the Royal Tapestry Factory. All the chandeliers are original and no two are the same.

The palace is open daily from 9 am to 6 pm (Sunday to 3 pm) and costs 850 ptas (students 350 ptas); free on Wednesday. A 50-minute guided tour is included in the price, but you may have to wait a while for your language to come up. The nearest metro station is Opera.

Convento de las Descalzas Reales The Convent of the Barefoot Royals, on Plaza Descalzas, was founded in 1559 by Juana of

Austria, daughter of the Spanish king Carlos I, and became one of Spain's richest religious houses thanks to gifts from noblewomen. Much of the wealth came in the form of art: on the obligatory guided tour you'll be confronted by a number of tapestries based on works by Rubens, and a wonderful painting entitled *The Voyage of the 11,000 Virgins*. Juana of Austria is buried here. Opening hours are Tuesday to Saturday from 10.30 am to 12.30 pm and (except Friday) from 4 to 5.30 pm. On Sunday it's open from 11 am to 1.30 pm. Entry is 650 ptas (students 250 ptas); free on Wednesday.

Panteón de Goya Also called the Ermita de San Antonio de la Florida, this little church contains not only Goya's tomb, directly in front of the altar, but also one of his greatest works – the entire ceiling and dome, beautifully painted with religious scenes (and recently restored). The scenes on the dome depict the miracle of St Anthony. The panteón is the first of two small churches 700 metres north-west along Paseo de la Florida from Norte metro station. It's open Tuesday to Friday from 10 am to 2 pm and 4 to 8 pm, and weekends from 10 am to 2 pm. Entry is 300 ptas (free on Wednesday and Sunday).

Museo Arqueológico This museum on Calle de Serrano traces the history of the peninsula from the earliest prehistoric cave paintings to the Iberian, Roman, Carthaginian, Greek, Visigothic, Moorish and Christian eras. Exhibits include mosaics, pottery, fossilised bones and a reconstructed prehistoric burial site. It's open Tuesday to Saturday from 9.30 am to 8.30 pm, and Sunday from 9 am to 2 pm. Entry is 400 ptas (students 200 ptas); free from 2 pm on Saturday and on Sunday.

Other Museums Madrid almost has more museums than the Costa del Sol has high-rise apartments. If you can digest any more, they include: the **Museo Municipal**, with assorted art including some Goyas, and some beautiful old maps, scale models, silver, porcelain and period furniture; the **Museo Casa de la Moneda**, which follows the history of coinage in great detail and contains a mind-boggling collection of coins and paper money; the **Museo de América** with stuff brought from the Americas from the 16th to 20th centuries; and even the **Museo de la Ciudad**, perfectly described by one traveller as 'a must for infrastructure buffs!', which rather drily traces the growth of Madrid. Check the tourist office's *Enjoy Madrid* brochure for more details.

Real Jardín Botánico The perfect answer to an overdose of art and history could be this beautiful botanic garden next door to the Prado. It's open daily from 10 am to 7 pm and entry costs 200 ptas (students 100 ptas).

Parque del Buen Retiro This is another great place to escape hustle and bustle. On a warm spring day walk between the flowerbeds and hedges or just sprawl out on one of the lawns.

Stroll along **Paseo de las Estatuas**, a path lined with statues originally from the Palacio Real. It ends at a lake overlooked by a **statue of Alfonso XII**. There are rowing boats for rent at the northern end when the weather is good.

Perhaps the most important, and certainly the most controversial, of the park's other monuments is *El Ángel Caído* (The Fallen Angel). First-prize winner at an international exhibition in Paris in 1878, this is said to be the first statue in the world dedicated to the devil.

You should also visit some of the park's gardens, such as the exquisite **La Rosaleda** (rose garden), and the **Chinese Garden** on a tiny island near the Fallen Angel. The all-glass **Palacio de Cristal** in the middle of the park occasionally stages modern-art exhibitions.

Campo del Moro This serene and stately garden is directly behind the Palacio Real, and the palace is visible through the trees from just about all points. This is one of the few places in the city where the roar of the traffic is reduced to a whisper and it's quite a haven for local birdlife. A couple of fountains and statues, a thatch-roofed pagoda and a carriage museum provide artificial diversions, but nature is the real attraction here.

El Rastro If you get up early on a Sunday morning you'll find the city almost deserted, until you get to El Rastro. The Rastro is one of the biggest flea markets you're ever likely to see, and if you're prepared to hunt around, you can find almost anything. The market spreads along and between Calle Ribera de Curtidores and Calle Embajadores (metro: Latina). It's said to be the place to go if you want to buy your car stereo back – watch your pockets and bags.

Language Courses

Madrid's Universidad Complutense offers a range of language and culture courses throughout the year, ranging from beginners to advanced. Contact the Secretaría de los Cursos para Extranjeros (☎ 394 53 25; fax 394 52 98), Facultad de Filosofía y Letras (Edificio A), Universidad Complutense, Ciudad Universitaria, 28040 Madrid. Another option is the rather overworked Escuela Oficial de Idiomas (☎ 533 58 05), Calle de Jesús Maestro s/n, which has Spanish-language courses at most levels from beginners up. There are many private language schools too.

Organised Tours

Madrid Vision tourist buses trace a circular route around the city, stopping at major sights, including the Prado and near Plaza Mayor, with taped commentaries in four languages including English. You can board at any of 13 clearly marked stops. One full round trip is 1500 ptas; a 2200-pta ticket gives you two full days. Either way, the metro is a quicker and cheaper way of getting around. The buses run five times daily except Sunday and holidays (when they go three times), and Monday when they don't run at all.

Special Events

Madrid's major fiesta celebrates its patron saint, San Isidro Labrador, throughout the third week of May. There are free music performances around the city and one of the country's top bullfight seasons at the Plaza Monumental de las Ventas. The Malasaña district, already busy enough (see Entertainment later), has its biggest party on 2 May, and the Fiesta de San Juan is held in the Parque del Buen Retiro for the seven days leading up to 24 June. The few locals who haven't left town in August will be celebrating the consecutive festivals of La Paloma, San Cayetano and San Lorenzo. The last week of September is Chamartín's Fiesta de Otoño (Autumn Festival) – about the only time you would go to Chamartín other than to catch a train.

Places to Stay

Finding a place to stay in Madrid is never really a problem.

Camping There are only two camping grounds relatively close to the city, but both are open all year, charging 525 ptas per person, 525 ptas per tent and 525 ptas per car. *Camping Osuna* (☎ 741 05 10), on Avenida de Logroño near the airport, is the better of the two (though smaller, with room for just 360): take the metro to Canillejas at the end of line 5, from where it's about 500 metres. *Camping Madrid* (☎ 302 28 35) is at Km 11 on the N-I road to Burgos. Take the Alcobendas bus from the stop outside Plaza de Castilla metro station to Los Dominicos, from where it's a 15-minute walk.

Hostels Madrid has two HI hostels within striking distance of the centre. Both are cheap (B&B at 900 ptas for those under 26, 1200 ptas for others), but they're also institutional, inconveniently located and almost always full with school groups. *Albergue Santa Cruz de Marcenado* (☎ 547 45 32), at Calle Santa Cruz de Marcenado 28, is a five-minute walk from Argüelles metro station, and has a 1.30 am curfew. *Albergue Richard Schirrmann* (☎ 463 56 99) is in Casa de Campo, a huge public park five km west of the centre. The hostel is a 15-minute walk from El Lago metro, but the park area is not safe to walk in at night. On the plus side, the hostel is open 24 hours a day and there's parking space.

Hostales & Pensiones These tend to cluster in three or four parts of the city and the price-to-quality ratio is fairly standard. In summer the city is drained of people, thanks to the horrific heat, so if you are mad enough to be here then, you may well be able to make a hot deal on the price. At other times it's only worth trying to bargain if you intend to stay a while.

Around Plaza de Santa Ana Santa Ana is well on the way to becoming one of Madrid's 'in' places. Close to Sol and within walking distance of the Prado and Atocha train station, it's also in one of Madrid's nightlife areas and has plenty of good budget restaurants.

North of the plaza, there's a choice of at least five hostales at Carrera de San Jerónimo 32.

Hostal Mondragón (☎ 429 68 16) (4th floor) is pretty good value at 1800/2700 ptas for biggish singles/doubles. *Hostal León* (☎ 429 67 78) in the same building is not bad and has heating in winter. It charges 2000/3500 ptas.

There are a number of very popular places on Calle Núñez de Arce. *Hostal Lucense* (☎ 522 48 88) at No 15 and *Pensión Poza* (☎ 232 20 65) at No 9 are owned by the same people (who used to live in Australia). Small, sometimes windowless, rooms start at 1000/2000 ptas, but there are better ones for 1500/2200 ptas. A hot shower is 200 ptas extra. In the same building as the Lucense, *Hostal Prado* (☎ 521 30 73) offers reasonable rooms from 1500/2800 ptas.

Hostal La Rosa (☎ 532 58 05), further up at Plaza de Santa Ana 15 (3rd floor), is good value with spacious rooms for 1800/3000 ptas.

Hostal Vetusta (☎ 429 64 04), Calle de las Huertas 3, has small but cute rooms with private shower for 2000/3500 ptas – try for one overlooking the street. On a quiet part of this street at No 54 (1st floor), *Hostal López* (☎ 429 43 49) is a good option. Rooms start at 2400/3800 ptas, or 3600/4800 ptas with private bath. The impressive *Hostal Matute* (☎ 429 55 85), Plaza de Matute 11, has spacious rooms for 2500/4300 ptas, or 3500/5500 ptas with private bath.

Hostal Casanova (☎ 429 56 91), Calle de Lope de Vega 8, has simple rooms at 1800/2600 ptas. Up around the corner at Calle de León 13, the attractive *Hostal Castro* (☎ 429 51 47) has good, clean rooms at 2000/3500 ptas with private bath. *Hostal San Antonio* (☎ 429 51 37), the next floor up, also has some nice rooms at similar prices.

Around Puerta del Sol You can't get more central than Plaza Puerta del Sol. Generally you'll pay for this privilege, but there are still some good deals in the surrounding streets.

Hostal Eureka (☎ 531 94 60), Calle de la Montera 7 (3rd floor), has bright, simple singles/doubles for 1500/2500 ptas. The pick of this area's bunch is *Hostal Riesco* (☎ 522 26 92) at Calle de Correo 2 (3rd floor), with comfortable rooms looking right on to the plaza. They cost 3200/4300 ptas with shower, or 3600/5000 ptas with full bathroom. *Hostal Rifer* (☎ 532 31 97) at Calle Mayor 5 (4th

floor) is not quite as good but still reasonable at 4000/5000 ptas.

Hostal Gibert (☎ 522 42 14), Calle Victoria 6 (2nd floor), has rooms for 2000/3500 ptas, or doubles with private bath for 4000 ptas. In the same building on the 1st floor, *Hostal Tineo* (☎ 521 49 43) is perfectly adequate with singles/doubles at 2000/3500 ptas.

Around Plaza Mayor Plaza Mayor, Madrid's true heart, is not a major accommodation area, but there are a few good options scattered among all the open-air cafés, tapas bars, ancient restaurants and souvenir shops.

Hostal Los Gallegos (☎ 366 58 84) at Calle de Toledo 4 has singles/doubles for 1400/3000 ptas and one of the best positions in the city. *Hostal Santa Cruz* (☎ 522 24 41) at Plaza de Santa Cruz 6 (2nd floor) is equally well positioned and has much better rooms for 2400/3600 ptas, or 2800/4400 ptas with bath. The more up-market *Hostal La Macarena* (☎ 365 92 21), Calle Cava San Miguel 8, is also perfectly located. All rooms have private bath and they cost 3500/5500 ptas.

Further north, *Hostal Leonesa* (☎ 559 43 60), Calle Costanilla de Santiago 2 (2nd floor), has bright rooms for 1800/2800 ptas. *Pensión Luz* (☎ 542 07 59), Calle de las Fuentes 10 (3rd floor), is a bargain at 2000/3500 ptas.

Around Gran Vía The hostales on and around Gran Vía tend to be a little more expensive. All the same, it's another popular area.

Hostal El Pinar (☎ 547 32 82), Calle Isabel la Católica 19, has singles/doubles at 2500/3800 ptas. The stylish *Hostal Besaya* (☎ 541 32 06), Calle San Bernardo 13, has good rooms from 3600/4800 ptas.

Hostal Flores (☎ 522 81 52) at Gran Vía 30 (entrance at Calle G Jiménez Quesada 2, 8th floor) offers good views and rooms for 2300/3500 ptas, or 3500/4500 ptas with private bath.

Hotel Laris (☎ 521 46 80), Calle del Barco 3, is a good mid-range hotel with rooms for 5000/7900 ptas, all with air-con and colour TV. Garage space is available (2000 ptas). *Hotel Regente* (☎ 521 29 41), Calle Mesoneros Romanos 9, has similar standards and prices.

There are loads of places on Calle Valverde. *Hostal América* (☎ 522 26 14) at No 9 (4th floor) is excellent value, with rooms at 1700/

3500 ptas. Calle de Fuencarral also has plenty of options. At No 45, **Hostal Medieval** (☎ 522 25 49) has spacious and bright rooms from 3000/4200 ptas.

Rental Many of the hostales mentioned above will do a deal on long stays. This may include a considerable price reduction, meals and laundry. It is simply a matter of asking. For longer stays, check the rental pages of *Segundamano* magazine or notice boards at universities, the Escuela Oficial de Idiomas and cultural institutes like the British Council or Alliance Française.

Places to Eat

Around Santa Ana If you are staying around Santa Ana, you needn't look far for good-value eats. *Restaurante La Sanabresa*, Calle Amor de Dios 12, has some of the brightest lights and best value food in the city – main meals start at about 500 ptas and desserts at 150 ptas. At No 3 in the same street, *Restaurante La Biotika* is an earthy and aromatic vegetarian restaurant, with a menú for 950 ptas and salads and mains from 700 ptas. *Restaurante Pasadero*, Calle Lope de Vega 9, is a popular local place with a solid set lunch for 975 ptas. *Restaurante Integral Artemisa* at Calle Ventura de la Vega 4 is an excellent vegetarian restaurant with a tasty set menú for 1200 ptas. They have another branch at Calle Tres Cruces 4 off Gran Vía. *Mesón La Caserola*, Calle de Echegaray 3, is an unassuming and popular place for seafood. Ask for a fritura, a mixed platter of deep-fried seafood.

The *Museo de Jamón*, Carrera de San Jerónimo 6, is one of several branches of this Madrid institution. Huge clumps of every conceivable type of ham dangle all over the place. Check prices as some are very expensive. There are cheap bocadillos and platos combinados too.

Excellent tapas joints in the Santa Ana area include *La Casa del Abuelo*, Calle Victoria 14, a classic old wine bar with superb grilled or garlic king prawns; *Las Bravas*, on Calle Álvarez Gato, with the best patatas bravas (spicy potatoes) you'll ever eat; and *La Trucha*, with two branches just off Plaza de Santa Ana on Calle Núñez de Arce and Calle Manuel Fernández y González.

Around Plaza Mayor You know you're getting close to Plaza Mayor when you see signs in English saying 'Typical Spanish Restaurant' and 'Hemingway Never Ate Here'. Nevertheless, when the sun's shining (or rising) there's not a finer or more popular place to be than at one of the outdoor cafés in the plaza.

Calle Cava San Miguel and Calle de Cuchilleros are packed with mesones that aren't bad for a little tapas hopping. Among them is *Restaurante Madrid 1600* at Cava San Miguel 7. A cut above the rest is *Restaurante Sobrino de Botín*, Calle de Cuchilleros 17, one of Europe's oldest restaurants (established in 1725), where the set menú costs about 3200 ptas – it's popular with those who can afford it.

The popular *Restaurante Pontejos*, Calle San Cristóbal 11, is a reliable place where you can often get a good paella. A full meal with wine will be about 2500 ptas.

Other Areas Just about anywhere you go in central Madrid, you can find cheap restaurants with good food.

Manhattan, half a km south of Plaza Mayor at Calle Encomienda 5, is a busy, no-frills establishment that fills up quickly for its 800-pta lunch menú. *Bar Restaurante Cuchifrito* at Calle Valverde 9 is a plain, simple eating house with a set menú for 900 ptas. *Casa Mingo* at Paseo de la Florida 2, near the Panteón de Goya, is a great old place for chicken and cider. A full roast bird, salad and bottle of cider – enough for two – comes to less than 2000 ptas.

If you're after paella at all costs, head for *Restaurante La Paella Real*, Calle de Arrieta 2 near Plaza de Oriente, which does a whole range of rice-based dishes from 1500 ptas. For a really first-class meal in a cosy atmosphere try *Taberna del Alabardero*, nearby at Calle Felipe V 6. Expect little change from 5000 ptas per person. If this is a bit steep, consider a couple of the mouthwatering tapas at the bar.

In the Malasaña area around Plaza Dos de Mayo, *Restaurante La Granja II* on Calle San Andrés has a vegetarian menú for 900 ptas. *Restaurante Sandos*, Plaza Dos de Mayo 8, can do you a cheap outdoor pizza and beer. A couple of blocks away, *Casa Pablo*, also known as La Glorieta, Calle de Manuela

Malasaña 37, is a rather polished place with good, modestly priced food – the 950-pta menú is excellent value.

The Plaza de España area is a good hunting ground for non-Spanish food, though you're looking at 2000 to 2500 ptas for a meal in the better places. *Restaurante Bali*, Calle San Bernardino 6, has authentic Indonesian fare. The *Adrish*, virtually across the street at No 1, is about Madrid's best Indian restaurant.

Cafés Madrid has so many fine places for a coffee and a light bite that you'll certainly find your own favourites. Ours include: *Café Principal*, Calle del Príncipe 33, an old-fashioned place near Plaza de Santa Ana; the historic, very elegant *Café-Restaurante El Espejo*, Paseo de Recoletos 31 (you could also sit at the turn-of-the-century-style *El Gran Pabellón del Espejo* outside); the equally graceful *Gran Café de Gijón* just down the road; the more down-to-earth *Café de la Villa* in the cultural centre of the same name on Plaza Colón, a cheery den for arty types and office workers; *Café del Real*, Plaza Isabel II, an atmospheric place with a touch of faded elegance, good for breakfast and busy at night too; and *Café Macaluca*, at Calle Juan Álvarez Mendizabal 4, just off Plaza de España, with fabulous crêpes and cheesecake.

Self-Catering The *Mercado de San Miguel*, just west of Plaza Mayor, is a good place to stock up on food for a cheap lunch.

Entertainment

A copy of the weekly *Guía del Ocio* (125 ptas at newsstands) will give you a good rundown of what's on in Madrid. Its comprehensive listings include music gigs, art exhibitions, cinema, TV and theatre. It's very handy even if you can't read Spanish.

Bars The epicentres of Madrid's nightlife are the Santa Ana-Calle de las Huertas area, and the Malasaña-Chueca zone north of Gran Vía. The latter has a decidedly lowlife element.

Any of the bars on Plaza de Santa Ana makes a pleasant stop, especially when you can sit outside in the warmer months. *La Moderna* attracts a mixed and buzzy crowd. Though it gets very crowded at weekends, you should look into *Viva Madrid*, Calle Manuel Fernández y González 7; its tiles and heavy wooden ceilings make a distinctive setting for the earlier stage of your evening. On the same street, *Carbones* is a busy place open till about 4 am with good mainstream music on the jukebox. *La Venencia*, Calle Echegaray 7, is an ill-lit, woody place that looks as if it hasn't been cleaned in years – perfect for sampling one of its six varieties of sherry.

In Malasaña, *Cervecería Santa Bárbara* at Plaza Santa Bárbara 8 is a classic Madrid drinking house and a good place to kick off a night out. Irish pubs are very popular in Madrid: two good ones are *The Quiet Man*, Calle Valverde 44, and *Finnegan's*, Plaza de las Salesas 9. *La Vía Lactea*, Calle Velarde 18, is a bright place with thumping mainstream music, a young crowd and a good drinking atmosphere. *Kyoto* bar on Calle Barceló is another popular hang-out. Calle de Pelayo Campoamor is lined with an assortment of bars, graduating from noisy rock bars at the north end to gay bars at the south end, where you've reached the Chueca area, the heart of Madrid's gay nightlife. *Autores*, No 6, can usually be relied on to be busy when other bars are thinning out in the wee hours. *Leather* at No 42 is just one of the many gay bars. *Rimmel*, Calle Luis de Góngora 4, and *Cruising*, Calle Pérez Galdós 5, are other popular gay haunts.

The quaintly named *Cock Bar*, Calle de la Reina 16, once served as a discreet salon for high-class prostitution. The ladies in question have gone but this popular bar retains plenty of atmosphere.

Live Music & Discos Latin rhythms have quite a hold in Madrid. A good place to indulge is *Vaiven*, Travesía de San Mateo 1 in Malasaña. Thursday is the big night, with the band La Única working magic. Entry is free and a beer is about 600 ptas. *Suristán*, Calle de la Cruz 7, near Plaza Santa Ana, pulls in a wide variety of bands, from Cuban to African, usually starting at 11.30 pm, sometimes with a cover charge up to 1000 ptas. *Swing*, Calle San Vicente Ferrer 23 in Malasaña, always has something on, including Caribbean music and, on Friday, pop and soul. Entry hovers around 1000 ptas. *Morocco*, at Calle Marqués de

Leganés 7 in Malasaña, is still a popular stop on the Madrid disco circuit, though some say it's past its prime. It gets going about 1 am. From 5 am a lively, noisy crowd makes for *Bali Hai*, nearby in Calle de la Flor Alta, where you can lose weight to the sound of bakalao.

Near Plaza de Santa Ana, Calle de la Cruz has a couple of good dance spaces: try to pick up fliers for them before you go – they may save you queueing. *Torero*, No 26, has Spanish music upstairs and international fare downstairs. *La Cartuja*, No 10, is also pretty popular and is open till 6 am.

La Soleá, Calle de la Cava Baja 27, is regarded by some as the last real flamenco bar in Madrid. *Casa Patas*, Calle Cañizares 10, hosts recognised masters of flamenco song, guitar and dance. Bigger flamenco names also play some of Madrid's theatres – check listings.

Concerts, Theatre & Opera There's plenty happening, except in summer. The city's grandest stage, the *Teatro Real*, is still undergoing an overhaul. The beautiful old *Teatro de la Comedia*, Calle del Príncipe 14, home to the Compañía Nacional de Teatro Clásico, often stages gems of classic Spanish and European theatre. The *Teatro de la Zarzuela*, Calle Jovellanos 4, fills the gap left by the Teatro Real as Madrid's top opera venue. The *Centro Cultural de la Villa*, under the waterfall at Plaza de Colón, stages everything from classical concerts to comic theatre, opera and even classy flamenco. Also important for classical music is the *Auditorio Nacional de Música*, Avenida Príncipe de Vergara 146 (metro: Cruz del Rayo), which often hosts the Orquesta Nacional de España.

Cinema Cinemas are very reasonably priced, with tickets around 700 ptas. Films in their original language (with Spanish subtitles) are usually marked VO (versión original) in listings. A good part of town for these is on and around Calle Martín de los Heros and Calle de la Princesa, near Plaza de España. The *Renoir*, *Alphaville*, *Lumière* and *Princesa* complexes here all screen VO movies.

Spectator Sport
Spending an afternoon or evening at a football (soccer) match provides quite an insight into Spanish culture. Tickets can be bought on the day of the match, starting from around 1000 ptas, although big games may be sold out. Real Madrid's home is the huge Estadio Santiago Bernabéu (metro: Lima). Atlético Madrid play at Estadio Vicente Calderón (metro: Pirámides).

Madrid is one of the best places in Spain to see a bullfight. These take place most Sundays between March and October – more often during the festival of San Isidro Labrador in May, and in summer. Madrid has Spain's largest bullring, Plaza Monumental de las Ventas (metro: Ventas), and a second bullring by metro Vista Alegre. Tickets are best bought in advance, from agencies or at the rings, and cost from about 2000 ptas.

Things to Buy
For general shopping needs, start at either the markets or the large department stores. The most famous market is El Rastro (see the section in Things to See, earlier). The largest department store chain is El Corte Inglés, with a central branch just north of Sol on Calle de Preciados.

The city's premier shopping street is Calle Serrano, a block east of Paseo de la Castellana. Calle del Almirante off Paseo de Recoletos has a wide range of engaging, less-mainstream shops. For guitars and other musical instruments, hunt around the area near the Palacio Real. For leather try the shops on Calle del Príncipe and Gran Vía, or Calle Fuencarral for shoes. For designer clothing, try the Chueca area.

Getting There & Away
Air Scheduled and charter flights from all over the world arrive at Madrid's Barajas airport, 13 km north-east of the city. With nowhere in Spain more than 12 hours away by bus or train, domestic flights are generally not very good value unless you're in a burning hurry. Nor is Madrid the budget international flight capital of Europe. That said, you *can* find bargains to popular destinations such as London, Paris and New York, and for domestic flights it's worth hunting around the airlines and a few travel agents. Some of the more interesting domestic fares from Madrid at the time of writing included:

Destination	Airline	Fare (one way/return)
Barcelona	Air Europa	6900/13,800 ptas (youth fare)
Canary Islands	Spanair	18,100/28,900 ptas
Palma de Mallorca	Spanair	9900/13,800 ptas
Málaga	Air Europa	9900/14,900 ptas
Santiago de Compostela	Spanair	9900/13,800 ptas

For more on fares and agents, see Travel Agencies under Information earlier in this Madrid section, and this chapter's introductory Getting There & Away and Getting Around sections.

Airline offices in Madrid include:

Air Europa
 Barajas airport (☎ 542 73 38, information ☎ 902-30 06 00)
American Airlines
 Calle de Pedro Teixeira 8 (☎ 597 20 68)
Aviaco
 Calle Maudes 51 (☎ 554 36 00)
British Airways
 Calle Serrano 60 (☎ 431 75 75)
Delta Airlines
 Calle de Goya 8 (☎ 577 06 50)
Iberia
 Calle de Goya 29 (☎ 587 87 87 or 587 81 09)
Spanair
 Barajas airport (☎ 393 67 35, information and reservations ☎ 902-13 14 15)

Bus There are eight bus stations dotted around Madrid. Tourist offices can tell you which you need for your destination. Most buses to the south, and some to other places (including a number of international services), use the Estación Sur de Autobuses (☎ 468 42 00 for information) at Calle de las Canarias 17 (metro: Palos de la Frontera). The choice between bus and train depends largely on where you're going – more detail on services to/from Madrid is given in other city sections in this chapter.

Train Atocha station, south of the centre, is used by most trains to/from southern Spain and many destinations around Madrid. Some trains from the north also terminate here, passing through Chamartín, the other main station (in the north of the city), on the way. Chamartín (metro: Chamartín) is smaller and generally serves destinations north of Madrid, though this rule is not cast-iron: some trains to the south use Chamartín and don't pass through

Atocha. A third station, Príncipe Pío (metro: Norte), is used by some trains to/from Galicia, Extremadura and Salamanca.

The main RENFE booking office (☎ 328 90 20) is at Calle Alcalá 44 and is open Monday to Friday from 9.30 am to 8 pm.

For information on fares, see the Getting There & Away section under the city you are going to.

Car & Motorcycle Madrid is surrounded by two ring-road systems, the older M-30 and the now almost completed M-40, considerably further out. Roads in and out of the city can get pretty clogged at peak hours (around 8 to 10 am, 2 pm, 4 to 5 pm and 8 to 9 pm), and on Sunday night.

Car-rental companies in Madrid include Atesa/Eurodollar (☎ 571 19 31), Avis (☎ 547 20 48), Budget (☎ 402 14 80), Europcar (☎ 541 88 92) and Hertz (☎ 900-10 01 11). All these have offices at the airport, in the city centre, and often at the main train stations. Recently there's been a spate of robberies on hire-cars leaving the airport, which makes it wiser to pick up your car elsewhere.

You can rent motorbikes from Moto Alquiler (☎ 542 06 57), Calle Conde Duque 13, but it's pricey, starting at 4000 ptas plus 16% tax a day for a 49-cc Vespino, with a 40,000-pta deposit. Something like a Yamaha 250 will cost you 10,000 ptas a day plus tax, with a 75,000-pta deposit.

Hitching & Car Pooling If you intend to hitch out of Madrid, you need to get well out of town first – choose a town along your route and start from there. For Andalucía, your chances of long rides improve dramatically south of Aranjuez.

A good alternative to hitching, and cheaper than buses and trains, is to prearrange a ride to your destination. You can do this through Auto Compartido (☎ 522 77 72), Calle de Santa Lucía 15. There's an annual membership fee of 1160 ptas, plus you pay 5 ptas per km.

Getting Around
To/From the Airport An airport bus service runs to/from an underground terminal in Plaza de Colón every 12 to 15 minutes. The trip takes 30 minutes in average traffic and costs 360

ptas. An alternative is to take bus No 1 (180 ptas) between the airport (where it uses the same stop as the airport bus) and Canillejas metro station. A taxi between the airport and city centre should cost around 2400 ptas.

Bus In general, the underground (metro) is faster and easier than city buses for getting around central Madrid. Bus route maps are available from tourist offices. A single ride costs 130 ptas. Night owls may find the 20 night bus lines, running from midnight to 6 am, useful. They run from Puerta del Sol and Plaza de la Cibeles.

Metro Madrid has a very efficient, safe and simple underground system. Trains run from 6.30 am to 1.30 am. Single rides cost 130 ptas and a ticket for 10 rides is 645 ptas.

Taxi Madrid's taxis are inexpensive by European standards. They're handy late at night, though in peak hours it's quicker to walk. From Chamartín station to Plaza de Colón costs about 1000 ptas.

Car & Motorcycle There's little point subjecting yourself to Madrid's traffic just to move from one part of the city to another, especially at peak hours. Most on-street parking space in central Madrid is designated for people with special permits, but almost everybody ignores this – also ignoring the 12,000 parking tickets slapped on vehicles every day. But you risk being towed if you park in a marked no-parking or loading zone, or if you double-park. There are plenty of car parks across the city, but they cost about 200 ptas an hour.

Around Madrid

EL ESCORIAL

The extraordinary 16th-century monastery-palace complex of San Lorenzo de El Escorial lies about one hour north-west of Madrid, just outside the town of the same name.

El Escorial was built by Felipe II, king of Spain, Naples, Sicily, Milan, the Netherlands and large parts of the Americas, to commemorate his victory over the French in the battle of

San Quintín (1557) and as a mausoleum for his father Carlos I, the first of Spain's Habsburg monarchs. Felipe began searching for a site in 1558, deciding on El Escorial in 1562. The last stone was placed in 1584, and the next 11 years were spent on decoration and other finishing touches. El Escorial's austere style, reflecting not only Felipe's wishes but also the watchful eye of architect Juan de Herrera, is loved by some, hated by others. Either way, it's a quintessential monument of Spain's golden age.

Almost all visitors to El Escorial make it a day trip from Madrid. It's open daily from 10 am to 6 pm (to 5 pm from October to March), and you should allow at least 2½ hours for a visit.

Information

You can get information on El Escorial from tourist offices in Madrid, or from the tourist office (☎ 91-890 15 54) close to the monastery at Calle Floridablanca 10. It's open weekdays from 10 am to 2 pm and 3 to 4.45 pm and on Saturday from 10 am to 1.45 pm.

You will have to pay for all but the most basic of the printed information at the monastery; guidebooks are on sale in the souvenir shop, starting from 700 ptas.

Things to See

Above the monastery's main gateway, on its west side, stands a **statue of San Lorenzo**, holding a symbolic gridiron, the instrument of his martyrdom (he was roasted alive on one). Inside, across the Patio de los Reyes, stands the restrained **basílica**, a cavernous church with a beautiful white-marble Crucifixion by Benvenuto Cellini, sculpted in 1576. At either side of the altar stand bronze statues of Carlos I and his family (to the left), and Felipe II with three of his four wives and his eldest son (on the right).

From the basílica, follow signs to the ticket office *(taquilla)*, where you must pay 850 ptas (students 350 ptas) to see the other open parts of El Escorial. The price includes an optional guided tour of the *panteones* and one or two other sections.

The route you have to follow leads first to the **Museo de Arquitectura**, detailing in Spanish how El Escorial was built, and the **Museo de Pintura**, with 16th and 17th-century Spanish, Italian and Flemish fine art

You then head upstairs to the richly decorated **Palacio de Felipe II**, in one room of which the monarch died in 1598; his bed was positioned so that he could watch proceedings at the basilica's high altar. Next you descend to the **Panteón de los Reyes**, where almost all Spain's monarchs since Carlos I, and their spouses, lie in gilded marble coffins. Three empty sarcophagi await future arrivals. Backtracking a little, you find yourself in the **Panteón de los Infantes**, a larger series of chambers and tunnels housing the tombs of princes, princesses and other lesser royalty.

Finally, the **Salas Capitulares** in the southeast of the monastery house a minor treasure trove of El Grecos, Titians, Tintorettos and other old masters.

When you emerge, it's worth heading back to the entrance, where you can gain access to the **biblioteca** (library), once one of Europe's finest and still a haven for some 40,000 books. You can't handle them, but many historic and valuable volumes are on display.

Getting There & Away

Herranz bus line runs up to 30 buses a day to El Escorial from Calle de la Princesa, near Moncloa metro station in Madrid. The bus (700 ptas return) takes around one hour and drops you off near the monastery. There are also frequent trains (costing about the same as the bus) from Madrid's Atocha station, and local buses will take you the two km from the train station up to the monastery. Some trains continue to Ávila from El Escorial.

Castilla y León

The one-time centre of the mighty Christian kingdom of Castile, Castilla y León is one of Spain's most historic regions. From Segovia's Roman aqueduct to the walled city of Ávila, and from León's magnificent cathedral to the beautifully preserved old centre of Salamanca, it is crowded with reminders of its prominent role in Spain's past.

SEGOVIA

Segovia is justly famous for its magnificent Roman aqueduct, but also has a splendid ridge-top old city which is worthy of more than a fleeting visit from Madrid. Originally a Celtic settlement, Segovia was conquered by the Romans around 80 BC. The Visigoths and Moors also left their mark before the city finally ended up in Castilian hands in the 11th century.

There are two tourist offices, one on Plaza Mayor (☎ 46 03 34) and another on Plaza del Azoguejo down beside the aqueduct.

The telephone code for Segovia is ☎ 921.

Things to See

You can't help but see the **aqueduct**, stretching away from the east end of the old city – it's over 800 metres long with 163 arches. The dates are a little hazy, but it was probably built in the 1st century AD.

At the heart of the old city is the 16th-century Gothic **catedral** on the very pretty Plaza Mayor. The first thing that catches your attention inside is its brightness. With a very high ceiling and no transepts, its sheer volume is quite overwhelming.

Perched on a craggy clifftop at the west end of the old city, Segovia's **alcázar**, with its turrets, towers and spires, is a fairy-tale 15th-century castle. It was virtually destroyed by fire in 1862, but has since been completely rebuilt and converted into a museum (open daily; entry 350 ptas).

Places to Stay

Two km along the road to La Granja is *Camping Acueducto* (☎ 42 50 00), open April to September.

Fonda Aragón (☎ 46 09 14) and *Fonda Cubo* (☎ 46 09 17), both at Plaza Mayor 4, are shabby but among the cheapest in town: 1200/2500 ptas for singles/doubles at the Aragón, a bit less at the Cubo. If you have no luck with these, *Hostal Juan Bravo* (☎ 43 55 21), Calle de Juan Bravo 12, will often have a room. Adequate rooms with private bath cost 4000/4200 ptas. There are a couple of dingy doubles without bath for 3300 ptas. More pleasant is *Hostal Plaza* (☎ 46 03 03), Calle Cronista Lecea 11, where rooms start at 3000/4000 ptas without private bath.

Further from the centre, but about the best deal in town, is the spick and span *Hostal Don Jaime* (☎ 44 47 87), near the aqueduct at Calle de Ochoa Ondategui 8. Rooms with TV cost 3000/5000 ptas.

If you can't find anywhere to stay in Segovia, it may be worth continuing to La Granja (see Around Segovia), which has a few cheap pensiones and considerably better nightlife.

Places to Eat
Bar Yiyo's, Calle de Doctor Sánchez 3, has hamburgers and the like and also one of the cheapest set lunches you're likely to find in Segovia – 875 ptas. At *Restaurante La Codorniz*, Calle Aniceto Marinas 3, you can expect to pay about 1500 ptas for a good main meal. Segovia's speciality is cochinillo asado (roast suckling pig); a set meal featuring this is 2100 ptas at one local favourite, *Mesón José María* at Calle del Cronista Lecea 11.

Getting There & Away
There are up to 16 buses a day to Madrid, and daily buses to Ávila and Salamanca. The bus station is 500 metres south of the aqueduct, just off Paseo Ezequiel González. There are also up to nine trains daily to Madrid (Chamartín or Atocha stations) but they are pretty slow. Trains also run north to Valladolid.

Getting Around
Bus No 3 runs between Plaza Mayor and the train station, passing the bus station on the way.

AROUND SEGOVIA
In the mountain village of San Ildefonso de la Granja, 11 km south-east, you can visit the royal palace and glorious gardens of **La Granja**, a Spanish version of Versailles built by Felipe V in 1720. Up to 10 buses daily run from Segovia to San Ildefonso.

About 50 km north-west of Segovia, the **Castillo de Coca** is also well worth a visit. One of the best known castles in Spain, this beautiful all-brick building dates from the 15th century. It is now a forestry school, but guided tours (☎ 911-58 63 59 or ☎ 911-58 66 47) are conducted by the students. Coca is on the Segovia-León railway, and up to three buses a day run from Segovia.

ÁVILA
Ávila deservedly lays claims to being one of the world's best preserved, and most impress-

ive, walled cities. The 11th and 12th-century walls surrounding the old town are 2.5 km long, up to 12 metres high and three metres thick, with 90 turrets. The city has nine gates, the most beautiful of which are those of San Vicente and the alcázar.

Ávila also is also distinguished by being the highest city in Spain (1127 metres); the birth-place of St Teresa de Ávila, the 16th-century mystical writer and reformer of the Carmelite order; and – less to be boasted about – the place where Tomás de Torquemada orchestrated the most brutal phase of the Spanish Inquisition, sending off 2000 people to be burnt at the stake in the late 15th century.

Ávila's tourist office (☎ 21 13 87) is at Plaza de la Catedral 4.

The telephone code for Ávila is ☎ 920.

Things to See & Do
Of the numerous convents, museums and mon-uments you can visit here, the most outstanding is the **catedral** (open daily), built into the eastern end of the walls. Construction started in the 12th century in Romanesque style, although other sections, such as the Gothic towers, date from the 14th and 15th centuries. Later renovations were carried out in the baroque style, and the facade is adorned with an intricate Renaissance frieze. Art works in the small museum include a portrait by El Greco.

A short distance outside the eastern walls is the 16th-century **Palacio de los Deanes**, on Plaza de Nalvillos, which houses Ávila's inter-esting provincial museum – mainly ethnological and archaeological exhibits (200 ptas). A couple of minutes walk further east, on Calle Duque de Alba, **Convento de San José** was the first convent founded by St Teresa. Its museum is full of memorabilia (open daily).

Los Cuatros Postes, a lookout point around 2.5 km from the city gates on the Salamanca road, has the best view of the city and its perfectly preserved walls.

If you are in the region in October, don't miss the Festival of Santa Teresa (8 to 15 October). Semana Santa in Ávila is also recom-mended.

Places to Stay & Eat
Hostal Las Cancelas (☎ 21 22 49), just south of the cathedral at Calle de la Cruz Vieja 6, has

simple singles/doubles from 2500/3500 ptas. *Hotel Jardín* (☎ 21 10 74), Calle de San Segundo 38, is a fairly scruffy place with rooms starting at 2500/3500 ptas. Better is the *Hostal Mesón El Rastro* (☎ 21 12 18), Plaza del Rastro 1, which is full of character and has a good restaurant. Rooms start at 3200/4000 ptas.

Restaurante Los Leales, Plaza de Italia 4, has a solid menú for 900 ptas. For a cheap, decent pizza, try *Telepizza* on the corner of Avenida de Portugal and Calle de San Segundo.

Getting There & Away
There are up to 17 trains a day between Ávila and Madrid. The two-hour trip costs 755 ptas. Trains to Salamanca cost the same. Buses also connect Ávila with Madrid, Segovia and Salamanca.

The bus and train stations are around 700 metres and 1.5 km east of the old town respectively. Bus No 1 links the train station with the old town.

SALAMANCA
Salamanca on a warm, sunny day is a great place to be. The cafés in the beautiful Plaza Mayor fill the square with tables and chairs, and the street artists and musicians come out of their winter hiding places. This is one of Spain's most inspiring cities, both in terms of history and modern life.

Information
The municipal tourist office (☎ 21 83 42) on Plaza Mayor, open daily, concentrates on information about the city. For more information, including details of language courses at Salamanca University, which is one of the best places in Spain to study Spanish, go to the oficina de turismo (☎ 26 85 71) in the Casa de las Conchas, open Monday to Friday from 10 am to 2 pm and 5 to 8 pm, and Saturday from 10 am to 2 pm.

The post office is at Gran Vía 25. There's no shortage of banks around the centre.

The telephone code for Salamanca is ☎ 923.

Things to See
As in many Spanish cities, one of the joys of Salamanca is to simply wander around the streets. Salamanca's beautiful **Plaza Mayor**

was designed in 1733 by the Spanish architect José Churriguera and built almost entirely in golden sandstone. The most outstanding building on the square, the **ayuntamiento** (town hall), was not completed until 1755.

The 15th-century **Casa de las Conchas** on the corner of Rua Mayor and Calle de la Compañía is a symbol of Salamanca. The original owner was a knight of St James *(caballero de Santiago)* and had the façades decorated with carved sandstone shells, the emblem of his order. The entrance to the **university**, on Calle Libreros, is another wonder. The best place to admire its intricacy from, the **Patio de las Escuelas**, is open from 9.30 am to 1.30 pm and 4 to 6.30 pm.

Next, brace yourself for the **Catedral Nueva** (New Cathedral) on Rua Mayor. This incredible Gothic structure, completed in 1733, took 220 years to build. As you try to take in the detailed relief around the entrance, you may wonder how they did it so fast. From inside the cathedral, you can enter the adjacent **Catedral Vieja** (Old Cathedral) for 300 ptas. A Romanesque construction begun in the early 11th century, this was consecrated in 1160, and has a particularly beautiful dome which helps to create a surprisingly spacious interior. Both cathedrals are open daily from 10 am to 1.30 pm and 4 to 7.30 pm.

At the southern end of Gran Vía is the magnificent **Convento de San Esteban**, where Columbus is said to have once stayed. Across the road, the smaller **Convento de las Dueñas** has a lovely courtyard with views of the cathedrals' domes and spires. Both convents are open daily.

Places to Stay
Salamanca is a very popular place to spend a few days, and accommodation can be hard to find. Persevere as it's worth the effort.

It is hard to beat a room in one of the little places right on Plaza Mayor. *Pensión Los Angeles* (☎ 21 81 66), No 10, has rather basic singles/doubles with washbasin for 1500/2500 ptas. Not far south of the plaza, *Hostal La Perla Salamantina* (☎ 21 76 56) at Calle de Sánchez Barbero 7 has rooms with bath for 2000/4000 ptas. *Hostal Tormes* (☎ 21 96 83) at Rua Mayor 20 has a range of rooms up to 2400/3300 ptas. The simple but decent *Pensión Estefanía* (☎ 21 73 72), Calle Jesús

SPAIN

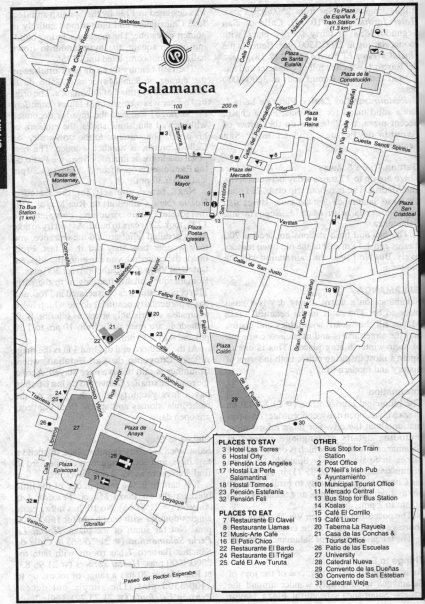

Salamanca

0   100   200 m

PLACES TO STAY
3 Hotel Las Torres
6 Hostal Orly
9 Pensión Los Angeles
17 Hostal La Perla
   Salamantina
18 Hostal Tormes
23 Pensión Estefanía
32 Pensión Feli

PLACES TO EAT
7 Restaurante El Clavel
8 Restaurante Llamas
12 Music-Arte Cafe
16 El Patio Chico
22 Restaurante El Bardo
24 Restaurante El Trigal
25 Café El Ave Turuta

OTHER
1 Bus Stop for Train
   Station
2 Post Office
4 O'Neill's Irish Pub
5 Ayuntamiento
10 Municipal Tourist Office
11 Mercado Central
13 Bus Stop for Bus Station
14 Koalas
15 Café El Corrillo
19 Café Luxor
20 Taberna La Rayuela
21 Casa de las Conchas &
   Tourist Office
26 Patio de las Escuelas
27 University
28 Catedral Nueva
29 Convento de las Dueñas
30 Convento de San Esteban
31 Catedral Vieja

SPAIN

3-5, has one single at 1750 ptas and doubles from 3000 ptas.

Further south, **Pensión Feli** (☎ 21 60 10), Calle de los Libreros 58, has a handy location near the university and cheerful rooms for 2000/2800 ptas.

If you're looking for a little extra comfort, **Hostal Orly** (☎ 21 61 25), at Calle del Pozo Amarillo 5-7, offers good, modern rooms with TV, phone and heating for 4280/5350 ptas. **Hotel Las Torres**, (☎ 21 21 00), Calle de Concejo 4, has comfortable rooms with all mod cons for 9630/12,840 ptas.

Places to Eat

The best place to look for cheap eats (for those on a really low budget) is the excellent *mercado central* (food market), right by Plaza Mayor. *Restaurante Llamas*, nearby at Calle del Clavel 9, has a tasty menú for 950 ptas. There are also dozens of eateries around Plaza Mayor. *Music-Arte Cafe*, Plaza del Corrillo 20, has tasty filled baguettes and croissants for 375 ptas and good pastries. *El Patio Chico* on Calle de Melendez is a lively place to sit around and drink beers; filling tapas are around 400 ptas a throw.

Restaurante El Bardo, inside the Casa de las Conchas, has a good menú at 900 ptas (vegetarian or carnivorous). Another vegetarian place with similar prices is *Restaurante El Trigal* at Calle Libreros 20. Along the street at No 24, there's a respectable 800-pta menú at *Café El Ave Turuta*.

For a splurge, try the *Restaurante El Clavel*, at Calle del Clavel 6. You're looking at about 4000 ptas for a full meal.

Entertainment

When the university is in session, the nightlife in Salamanca is bound to please. Most of the places to be seen are on or around Gran Vía. Make sure you see the amazing décor at *Cafe Luxor*, a little way east up Calle de San Justo from Gran Vía. *Koalas* at Gran Vía 63 is, of course, a must for homesick Aussies, and as the day grows old, this place can really start to move. A popular, pleasantly low-lit place for earlier in the evening is *Taberna La Rayuela*, Rúa Mayor 19. *O'Neill's Irish Pub*, Calle de Zamora 14, is one of the Irish-style pubs increasingly in vogue in Spain, and it's always busy. *Café El Corrillo* on Calle de Meléndez

is a great place to have a beer while catching some live jazz.

Getting There & Away

Bus Salamanca's bus station (☎ 23 67 17) is at Avenida Filiberto Villalobos 85, about a km north-west of Plaza Mayor. AutoRes has up to 16 express buses daily to Madrid, taking 2½ hours for 2210 ptas, plus stopping buses for 1770 ptas.

Among many other destinations served by regular buses are Santiago de Compostela, Cáceres, Ávila, Segovia, León and Valladolid.

Train The station is on Paseo de la Estación, 1.3 km north-east of the centre. At least five trains leave daily for Madrid (three hours, 1560 ptas) via Ávila (1¾ hours, 805 ptas). There are also direct trains daily to León, Valladolid and Barcelona. You can reach Santiago de Compostela via Medina del Campo, and Santander via Valladolid. A train for Lisbon leaves at 4.55 am.

Getting Around

From the train station, take bus No 1, which heads to the city centre along Calle Azafranal. Going the other way, it can be picked up on Gran Vía near the post office. From the bus station, bus No 4 runs round the old town perimeter to Gran Vía. Heading back, pick it up outside Plaza Mayor.

LEÓN

León is far too often left off travellers' itineraries. For those who get here, a fresh and pleasant city awaits. It's a city of long, wide boulevards, open squares and excellent nightlife, with one of Spain's greatest cathedrals. León was at its mightiest in the 10th to 13th centuries, as capital of the expanding Christian kingdom of the same name.

The tourist office (☎ 23 70 82), opposite the cathedral at Plaza de la Regla 3, is open Monday to Saturday from 10 am to 2 pm and 5 to 8 pm, and on Sunday from 11 am to 2 pm and 4.30 to 8.30 pm.

León's telephone code is ☎ 987.

Things to See

León's **catedral**, built primarily in the 13th century, is a wonder of Gothic architecture. Its

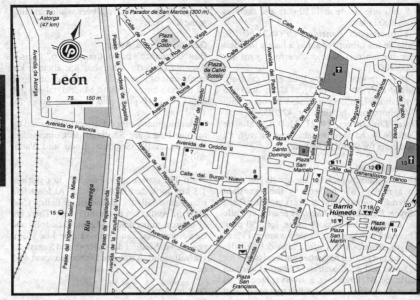

most outstanding feature is its breathtaking stained-glass windows. Of course, you'll have to go inside to appreciate their beauty. Opening hours are 9.30 am to 1 pm and 4 to 6.30 pm (closed Sunday afternoon). At the northern end of Calle del Cid is a great monument from the earlier Romanesque age: the **Real Basílica de San Isidoro** containing the **Panteón Real**, burial place of Leonese royalty with some wonderful 12th-century ceiling frescos. The panteón can be visited only by guided tour (300 ptas).

Plaza Mayor in the old town, a short distance south of the cathedral, is a little run down, but this is part of its romance. It is also the heart of León's buzzing nightlife. Also of interest is the **Casa de Botines** on Plaza San Marcelo, designed by the Catalan genius Antoni Gaudí, although it's rather conservative by his standards.

Places to Stay

There's plenty of budget accommodation, mostly on or near Avenida de Ordoño II,

Avenida de Roma and Plaza Mayor in the old town. *Pensión Berta* (☎ 25 70 39), Plaza Mayor 8, has basic singles/doubles for 1500/2200 ptas. The position is unbeatable.

Fonda Roma (☎ 22 46 63), Avenida de Roma 4, is in an attractive old building, with dirt-cheap rooms at 900/1500 ptas. More expensive is the *Hostal Central* (☎ 25 18 06), Avenida de Ordoño II 27, with reasonable rooms for 1800/2700 ptas. *Hostal Bayón* (☎ 23 14 46), Calle del Alcázar de Toledo 6, is run by a friendly woman who keeps clean rooms costing 2650/3500 ptas. *Hostal Orejas* (☎ 25 29 09), Calle de Villafranca 8, is a pretty good deal: rooms with bath and TV are 3200/5150 ptas.

Hotel Paris (☎ 23 86 00; fax 27 15 72), Calle de Generalísimo Franco 20, is a wonderful old hotel with moderate prices, at 4150/6250 ptas. If you're really an oil sheikh masquerading as a backpacker, you'll probably stay at the magnificent 15th-century *Parador de San Marcos* (☎ 23 73 00), Plaza de San Marcos 7. Doubles fit for royalty start from 17,500 ptas.

PLACES TO STAY
3 Fonda Roma
5 Hostal Bayón
6 Hostal Orejas
7 Hostal Central
11 Hotel Paris
19 Pensión Berta

PLACES TO EAT
10 Restaurante Bodega Regia
16 Restaurante El Tizón
17 Restaurante El Palomo
18 Restaurante & Sidrería Vivaldi
20 Restaurante Honoré

OTHER
1 Train Station
2 Pub La Morgue
4 Real Basílica de San Isidoro & Panteón Real
8 La Fundación
9 Casa de Botines
12 Tourist Office
13 Catedral
14 Mercado
15 Bus Station
21 Post Office

Places to Eat

There are lots of good places within a short walk of the cathedral or Plaza Mayor. *Restaurante Honoré*, Calle de los Serradores 4, has a good menú for 750 ptas. *Restaurante El Palomo*, on tiny Calle de la Escalerilla, is a quality establishment with a lunch menú for 1300 ptas. Next door is the popular *Restaurante & Sidrería Vivaldi*, where you can wash down your meal with a cider from Asturias.

Restaurante El Tizón, Plaza San Martín 1, is good for wine and meat dishes, and offers an abundant menú for 1600 ptas. There are a few decent pizzerías and bars on the same square. For a really good meal in a cosy atmosphere, you can't go past the award-winning *Restaurante Bodega Regia* at Calle General Mola 5. They have a menú for 1700 ptas, and you can eat really well à la carte from 2500 ptas or so.

Entertainment

León's nocturnal activity flows thickest in the aptly named Barrio Húmedo (Wet Quarter), the crowded tangle of lanes leading south off Calle del Generalísimo Franco. Plaza San Martín is a particularly pleasant spot for drinks. Calle de Cervantes and Calle de Fernando Regueral north of Calle del Generalísimo Franco, are also lined with bars to suit most tastes.

As the night grows older, the action slides west towards the river. Friday nights are the best for dancing till dawn at *Pub La Morgue*, a noisy place for the young bakalao scene on Avenida de Roma. A more mixed crowd and music can be had until 6 am at *La Fundación*, just off Calle del Burgo Nuevo. There are more places on and around Avenida de Lancia.

Getting There & Away

Bus The bus station is on Paseo del Ingeniero Saenz de Miera, on the west bank of the Río Bernesga. Empresa Fernández has as many as eight buses to Madrid a day. The trip takes $3\frac{1}{2}$ to $4\frac{1}{2}$ hours and costs 2600 to 4000 ptas. Other destinations include Bilbao, Zamora, Salamanca and Valladolid.

Train The train station too is across the river, on Avenida de Astorga. Up to 10 trains a day leave for Madrid. A regional train (the slowest) costs 2550 ptas. Plenty of trains head north to Oviedo and Gijón and south to Valladolid. There are three trains daily to Barcelona and up to five to La Coruña and other destinations in Galicia.

AROUND LEÓN

A more extravagant example of Gaudí's work is in the town of **Astorga**, 47 km south-west of León. His Palacio Episcopal (1889) is also home to the moderate Museo de los Caminos, with Roman artefacts and religious art. Next door, the cathedral is a hotchpotch of 15th to 18th-century styles. Both are open in summer from 10 am to 2 pm and 4 to 8 pm, and in winter from noon to 2 pm and 3.30 to 6.30 pm (250 ptas each or 400 ptas for both). Several buses a day go from León.

Castilla-La Mancha

Best known as the home of Don Quixote, Castilla-La Mancha conjures up images of endless empty plains and sweeping windmills.

This Spanish heartland is also home to two exceptionally scenic and fascinating cities, Toledo and Cuenca.

TOLEDO

Toledo is one of Spain's most magnificent historic cities. The narrow, winding streets of the old city, perched on a small hill above the Río Tajo, are crammed with fascinating museums, monuments, churches and castles. As the main city of Muslim central Spain, Toledo was the peninsula's leading centre of learning and the arts in the 11th century. Taken by the Christians in 1085, it soon became the headquarters of the Spanish Church and was one of the most important of Spain's numerous early capitals. Until 1492, Christians, Jews and Muslims coexisted peaceably here, for which Toledo still bears the label 'Ciudad de las Tres Culturas' (City of the Three Cultures). Its unique architectural combinations, with Arabic influences everywhere, are a strong reminder of Spain's mixed heritage. El Greco lived here from 1577 to 1614 and many of his works can still be seen in the city.

Toledo is quite expensive and packed with tourists and souvenir shops. Try to stay here at least overnight, since you can enjoy the street and café life after the tour buses have headed north in the evening.

Information

The main tourist office (☎ 22 08 43) is on Carretera de Madrid, just outside the Puerta Nueva de Bisagra gate at the northern entrance to the old city. There's also an information booth on Plaza de Zocodover, the main square of the old city. Both are open daily.

The telephone code for Toledo is ☎ 925.

Things to See

Most of Toledo's attractions open from about 10 am to 1.30 pm and about 4 to 6 pm (7 pm in summer). Many, including the alcázar, Sinagoga del Tránsito and Casa y Museo de El Greco – but not the cathedral – are closed Sunday afternoon and/or all day Monday.

The **catedral**, in the heart of the old city, is awesome. You could easily spend hours in here, admiring the glorious stone architecture, stained-glass windows, tombs of kings in the Capilla Mayor, and art by the likes of El Greco, Velázquez and Goya. Entry to the cathedral is free, but you have to buy a ticket (500 ptas) to enter four areas – the Coro, Sacristía, Capilla de la Torre and Sala Capitular – which contain some of the finest art and artisanry.

The **alcázar**, Toledo's number-one landmark, just south of Plaza de Zocodover, was fought over repeatedly from the Middle Ages to the civil war, when it was besieged by Republican troops. Today it's a military museum, created by the Nationalist victors of the civil war, with most of the displays – which are fascinating – relating to the 1936 siege. Entry is 125 ptas.

The **Museo de Santa Cruz** on Calle de Cervantes contains a large and sometimes surprising collection of furniture, fading tapestries, military and religious paraphernalia, and paintings. Upstairs is an impressive collection of El Grecos including the masterpiece *La Asunción* (Assumption of the Virgin). Note also *La Sagrada Familia*: during cleaning of the painting in the 1980s, San José appeared in the background to the surprise and delight of all concerned. Entry is 200 ptas (free on Saturday afternoon and Sunday).

In the south-west of the old city, the queues outside an unremarkable church, the **Iglesia de Santo Tomé** on Plaza del Conde, indicate there must be something special inside. That something is El Greco's masterpiece *El Entierro del Conde de Orgaz*. The painting depicts the burial of the Count of Orgaz in 1322 by San Esteban (St Stephen) and San Agustín (St Augustine), observed by a heavenly entourage, including Christ, the Virgin, John the Baptist and Noah. Entry is 150 ptas.

The so-called **Casa y Museo de El Greco** on Calle de Samuel Leví, in Toledo's former Jewish quarter, contains the artist's famous *Vista y Plano de Toledo*, plus about 20 of his minor works and other 17th-century Spanish artworks. The house was apparently not really El Greco's; it was simply decorated in the style of his era. Entry is 400 ptas (200 ptas for students).

Nearby, the **Sinagoga del Tránsito** on Calle de los Reyes Católicos is one of two synagogues left in Toledo. Built in 1355 and handed over to the Catholic church in 1492, when most of Spain's Jews were expelled from the country, it houses the interesting Museo Sefardí, examining Jewish culture in Spain before 1492. Entry is 400 ptas (free on Saturday afternoon and Sunday).

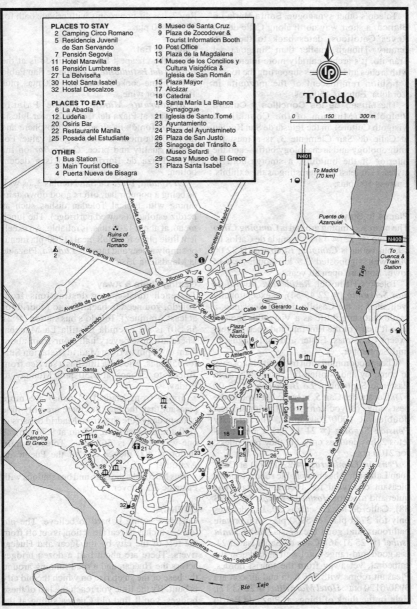

Toledo

0   150   300 m

To Madrid
(70 km)

N401

Puente de
Azarquiel

N400

To
Cuenca &
Train
Station

Río Tajo

PLACES TO STAY
2 Camping Circo Romano
5 Residencia Juvenil
   de San Servando
7 Pensión Segovia
11 Hotel Maravilla
16 Pensión Lumbreras
27 La Belviseña
30 Hotel Santa Isabel
32 Hostal Descalzos

PLACES TO EAT
6 La Abadía
12 Ludeña
20 Osiris Bar
22 Restaurante Manila
25 Posada del Estudiante

OTHER
1 Bus Station
3 Main Tourist Office
4 Puerta Nueva de Bisagra
8 Museo de Santa Cruz
9 Plaza de Zocodover &
   Tourist Information Booth
10 Post Office
13 Plaza de la Magdalena
14 Museo de los Concilios y
   Cultura Visigótica &
   Iglesia de San Román
15 Plaza Mayor
17 Alcázar
18 Catedral
19 Santa María La Blanca
   Synagogue
21 Iglesia de Santo Tomé
23 Ayuntamiento
24 Plaza del Ayuntamineto
26 Plaza de San Justo
28 Sinagoga del Tránsito &
   Museo Sefardi
29 Casa y Museo de El Greco
31 Plaza Santa Isabel

SPAIN

Toledo's other synagogue, **Santa María La Blanca**, a short way north along Calle de los Reyes Católicos, dates back to the 12th century. Though smaller than Sinagoga del Tránsito, it's architecturally more interesting, with arches and columns supporting the roof in a fashion reminiscent of the mezquita in Córdoba. Entry is 150 ptas.

The **Museo de los Concilios y Cultura Visigótica** (Museum of the Councils & Visigoth Culture), in the Iglesia de San Román at Calle de San Clemente 3, is a must for anthropology and archaeology buffs – and the interior of the building, a smorgasbord of styles, is at least as interesting as the exhibits. Entry is 100 ptas.

Places to Stay
The nearest camping ground is *Camping Circo Romano* (☎ 22 04 42) at Avenida de Carlos III 19, but better is *Camping El Greco* (☎ 22 00 90), well signposted 2.5 km south-west of town. Both are open all year.

Toledo's HI hostel, *Residencia Juvenil de San Servando* (☎ 22 45 54), is exceptionally well sited in the Castillo de San Servando, a castle that started life as a Visigothic monastery. It's east of the Río Tajo and open all year except Christmas, Easter and mid-August to mid-September.

Cheap accommodation in the city is not easy to come by and is often full, especially from Easter to September. *La Belviseña* (☎ 22 00 67), Cuesta del Can 5, is basic but among the best value (if you can get in), with singles/doubles at 1000/2000 ptas. The friendly *Pensión Segovia* (☎ 21 11 24), Calle Recoletos 2, has doubles only, but they're spotless, for 2100 ptas.

Pensión Lumbreras (☎ 22 15 71) at Calle Juan Labrador 9 has reasonable rooms round a pleasant courtyard for 1600/2500 ptas. The quiet and modern *Hostal Descalzos* (☎ 22 28 88), Calle de los Descalzos 30, has doubles only for 3745 ptas, or 5900 ptas with private bathroom, and good breakfasts. *Hotel Santa Isabel* (☎ 25 31 36), Calle de Santa Isabel 24, is a good mid-range hotel well placed near the cathedral, yet away from the tourist hordes. Pleasant rooms with TV, bath and air-con are 3930/6120 ptas. *Hotel Maravilla* (☎ 22 83 17), right in the thick of things at Plaza de Barrio

Rey 7, has air-con rooms with private bath for 3750/6000 ptas.

Places to Eat
About the cheapest lunch in Toledo is at the *Posada del Estudiante*, Callejón de San Pablo 2. The home-cooked menú costs 600 ptas, plus 100 ptas for wine.

Restaurante Manila, in the Palacio Fuensalida at Plaza del Conde 2 (near Iglesia de Santo Tomé), has loads of atmosphere and its 1100-ptas menú is usually good value. For similar quality and price, *Osiris Bar* on the shady Plaza de Barrio Nuevo is a decent option.

La Abadía, Plaza de San Nicolás 3, as well as being a popular bar, offers good downstairs dining with typical Toledan dishes such as perdiz estofada (stewed partridge). The lunch menú, at about 1200 ptas, is reliable. An excellent little place for a full meal (1200-pta menú) or simply a beer and tapas is *Ludeña*, Plaza de la Magdalena 13.

Getting There & Away
To reach most major destinations from Toledo, you need to backtrack to Madrid (or at least Aranjuez). Toledo's bus station (☎ 21 58 50) is on Avenida Castilla La Mancha. There are buses every half-hour from about 6 am to 10 pm to/from Madrid (Estación Sur) for 550 ptas. The Aisa line has a service from Toledo to Cuenca at 5.30 pm, Monday to Friday.

Trains from Madrid (Atocha) are more pleasant than the bus, but there are only nine of them daily (the first from Madrid departs at 7.20 am, the last from Toledo at 9.30 pm). A one-way ticket is 565 ptas. Toledo's train station is 400 metres east of the Puente de Azarquiel.

Bus No 5 links the train and bus stations with Plaza de Zocodover.

CUENCA
Cuenca's setting is hard to believe. The old town, which is its real attraction, is cut off from the rest of the city by the Júcar and Huécar rivers. There are about half a dozen bridges across the Huécar, and a road running around the base of the steep rise on which the old city is built. By the time you reach the last of these bridges, you'll find old Cuenca sitting at the

top of a deep gorge, with its most famous monuments teetering on the edge – a photographer's delight.

Don't follow the signs to the tourist office in the new town – there's a more useful one (☎ 23 21 19) up in the old town at Calle de San Pedro 6, just up the hill from Plaza Mayor.

The telephone code for Cuenca is ☎ 969.

Things to See & Do

Cuenca's **Casas Colgadas** (Hanging Houses) originally built in the 15th century, are precariously positioned on a clifftop, their balconies literally hanging over the gorge. A footbridge across the gorge provides access to spectacular views of these buildings (and the rest of the old town) from the other side. Inside the Casas Colgadas is the **Museo de Arte Abstracto Español**. This exciting collection is based around works by Spain's 'abstract generation', a group of artists who were particularly active in the 1950s. Opening hours are Tuesday to Friday from 11 am to 2 pm and 4 to 6 pm, Saturday from 11 am to 2 pm and 4 to 8 pm, and Sunday from 11 am to 2 pm. Entry is 300 ptas.

Nearby, on Calle del Obispo Valero, is the very different **Museo Diocesano**, with beautiful textiles, tapestries and religious art and artefacts dating as far back as the 13th century. Entry is 200 ptas; it's open Tuesday to Saturday from 11 am to 2 pm and 4 to 6 pm, Sunday from 11 am to 2 pm.

On Plaza Mayor you'll find Cuenca's strange **catedral**. The lines of the unfinished façade are Norman-Gothic and reminiscent of French cathedrals, and the stained-glass windows look like they'd be more at home in the abstract art museum.

As you wander the old town's beautiful streets, check the **Torre de Mangana**, the remains of a Moorish fortress in a square west of Calle de Alfonso VIII, overlooking the plain below.

Places to Stay & Eat

Pensión Real (☎ 22 99 77), in virtually the last house in the highest part of the old town at Calle Larga 99, is a typical family-run place with singles/doubles for 1700/4000 ptas. *Posada Huécar* (☎ 21 42 01), at Paseo del Huécar 3 at the foot of the old town, is quiet and comfortable with rooms from

2000/3800 to 3000/5000 ptas. *Posada de San José* (☎ 21 13 00), behind the tourist office at Ronda de Julián Romero 4, is a lovely 16th-century residence with doubles costing up to 4920 ptas, or up to 9500 ptas with private bathroom. Most of the restaurants and cafés around Plaza Mayor are better for a drink and people-watching than for good-value eating, but *Mesón Mangana* just down from the plaza has tasty tapas and a menú for 1500 ptas.

Down in the new town, there are several places on Calle Ramón y Cajal, which runs from near the train station towards the old town, including two no-frills pensiones at No 53: *Pensión Adela* (☎ 22 25 33) charging 1250 ptas per person plus 200 ptas for a shower, and *Pensión Marín* (☎ 22 19 78) upstairs, which is marginally better value at 1300/2400 ptas for singles/doubles. At No 49, *Hostal Cortés* (☎ 22 04 00) is more comfortable but characterless. Rooms with bath and TV are 3430/5350 ptas. *El Mesón*, Calle de Colón 56, is an atmospheric place to eat, with a good-value 1300-pta menú. It opens for lunch, and Friday and Saturday evenings only.

Getting There & Away

There are up to nine buses a day to Madrid (2½ hours, 1260 ptas), and daily buses to Barcelona, Teruel and Valencia. There are five trains a day direct to Madrid (Atocha), taking 2½ hours and costing 1215 ptas one way. There are also three trains a day to Valencia.

Bus No 1 or 2 from near the bus and train stations will take you up to Plaza Mayor in the old town.

AROUND CUENCA

A 35-km drive north of Cuenca is the bizarre **Ciudad Encantada** (Enchanted City). This 'city', open daily from 9.30 am to sunset (200 ptas), is a series of fantastically shaped rocks, many now given names that refer somewhat imaginatively to their shapes, such as Crocodile & Elephant Fighting, Mushrooms and Roller Coaster. If you have a car, it is worth the trip. The scenery on the way is great and the Ciudad Encantada itself makes a wonderful playground – a must if you are with kids. Take food and drink, as the café is expensive.

Catalonia

Catalonia (Catalunya in Catalan, Cataluña in Spanish) is one of the most fiercely independent regions in Spain and also the wealthiest. The Catalans speak a distinct language, Catalan, and many don't consider themselves Spanish. Catalonia's golden age was the 12th to 14th centuries, when it was the leading light in the medieval kingdom of Aragón, and Barcelona was capital of a big Mediterranean seafaring empire. The region has much to offer: Barcelona apart, there's the Costa Brava to its north, Tarragona with its fine Roman remains, Sitges with Spain's most forthright gay community and a vibrant carnaval, and Figueres with the bizarre Dalí museum. Away from the towns and cities, the Pyrenees offer good walking in many areas, especially the Parc Nacional d'Aigües Tortes i Sant Maurici, and skiing in winter.

BARCELONA

If you only visit one city in Spain, it probably should be Barcelona. After hosting the Olympic Games in 1992, it has finally taken its place on the list of the world's great cities. Catalonia's modernist architecture of the late 19th and early 20th centuries – a unique melting pot of Art Nouveau, Gothic, Moorish and other styles – climaxes here in the inspiring creations of Antoni Gaudí, among them La Sagrada Família church and Parc Güell. Barcelona also has world-class museums including two devoted to Picasso and Miró, a fine old quarter (the Barri Gòtic) and nightlife as good as anywhere in the country.

Orientation

Plaça de Catalunya is Barcelona's main square, and a good place to get your bearings when you arrive. The main tourist office is nearby at Gran via de les Corts Catalanes 658. Most travellers base themselves in Barcelona's old city (Ciutat Vella), the area bordered by the harbour Port Vell (south), Plaça de Catalunya (north), Ronda de Sant Pau (west) and Parc de la Ciutadella (east).

La Rambla, the city's best known boulevard, runs through the heart of the old city from Plaça de Catalunya down to the harbour. On the east side of La Rambla is the Gothic quarter (Barri Gòtic), and on the west the somewhat seedy Barri Xinès. North of the old city is the gracious suburb l'Eixample, where you'll find the most outstanding examples of Barcelona's modernist architecture.

Information

Tourist Offices Barcelona's main tourist office, the Catalunya Oficina de Turisme (☎ 301 74 43) at Gran Via de les Corts Catalanes 658, is open on weekdays from 9 am to 7 pm (Saturday to 2 pm). It can get very busy in summer but has a great deal of useful information and reasonable maps. There is another helpful office (☎ 412 91 71) at Estació Sants, the main train station, open on weekdays (and every day in summer) from 8 am to 8 pm, and on weekends from 8 am to 2 pm.

Money Banks usually have the best rates for both cash and travellers' cheques. Banking hours are usually weekdays from 8 am to 2 pm. The American Express office at Passeig de Gràcia 101 is open weekdays from 9.30 am to 6 pm and Saturday from 10 am to noon. You can also change money at El Corte Inglés department store on Plaça de Catalunya, open from 10.30 am to 9.30 pm except Sunday. Both these places have reasonable rates. For after-hours emergencies, there are currency exchanges along La Rambla.

Post & Communications The main post office is on Plaça d'Antoni López. For most services including poste restante (lista de correos), it's open weekdays from 8 am to 9 pm, and Saturday from 9 am to 2 pm.

Barcelona's telephone code is ☎ 93.

Travel Agencies Viva (☎ 483 83 78) at Carrer de Rocafort 116-122 (metro: Rocafort) offers youth and student fares. It's open weekdays from 10 am to 8 pm, and Saturday from 10 am to 1.30 pm, but expect long queues.

Bookshops In the Barri Gòtic, Quera at Carrer de Petritxol 2 specialises in maps and guides; Próleg at Carrer de la Dagueria 13 is a good women's bookshop.

In l'Eixample, Altaïr, Carrer de Balmes 71, is a superb travel bookshop; Librería Francesa at Passeig de Gràcia 91, Come In at Carrer de Provença 203 and BCN at Carrer d'Aragó 277 are good for novels and books on Spain, and dictionaries.

Laundry Lavandería Tigre at Carrer Rauric 20 in the Barri Gòtic will wash and dry five kg in a couple of hours for 1075 ptas. Doing it yourself saves 100 ptas.

Emergency There's a handy Guàrdia Urbana police station (☎ 301 90 60), with English spoken, at La Rambla 43 opposite Plaça Reial. The emergency police numbers are ☎ 091 or ☎ 092. For an ambulance or emergency medical help call ☎ 061.

Dangers & Annoyances Watch your pockets, bags and cameras on the train to/from the airport, on La Rambla, in the Barri Gòtic south of Plaça Reial and in the Barri Xinès – especially at night. These last two areas, once very seedy, have been somewhat cleaned up in recent years but there are still some pickpockets, bag-snatchers and intimidating beggars about.

Things to See
La Rambla The best way to introduce yourself to Barcelona is by a leisurely stroll from Plaça de Catalunya down **La Rambla**, the magnificent boulevard of a thousand faces. This long pedestrian strip, shaded by leafy trees, is an ever-changing blur of activity, lined with newsstands, bird and flower stalls, and cafés. It's populated by artists, buskers, human statues, shoe-shine merchants, beggars, and a constant stream of people promenading and just enjoying the sights.

About halfway down La Rambla is the wonderful **Mercat de la Boqueria**, which is worth going to just for the sights and sounds, but is also a good place to stock up on fresh fruit, vegetables, nuts, bread, pastries – everything you'll need for a park picnic. Just off La Rambla, further south, **Plaça Reial** was, until a few years ago, a seedy square of ill repute, but it's now quite pleasant, with numerous cafés, bars and a couple of music clubs. Just off the other side of La Rambla at Carrer Nou de la Rambla 3-5 is Gaudí's moody **Palau Güell**,

open daily, except Sunday, from 10 to 2 pm and 4 to 8 pm (300 ptas; students 150 ptas).

Down at the end of La Rambla stands the **Monument a Colom**, a statue of Columbus atop a tall pedestal. A small lift will take you to the top of the monument (225 ptas). Just west is the **Museu Marítim**, in the beautiful 14th-century Royal Shipyards, with an impressive array of boats, models, maps and more. If you like boats and the sea, you won't be disappointed – open daily, except Monday, from 10 am to 7 pm (800 ptas).

Barri Gòtic Barcelona's serene Gothic **cated-ral** is open daily from 8 am to 1.30 pm and 5 to 7.30 pm – be sure to visit the lovely cloister. Each Sunday at noon, crowds gather in front of the cathedral to dance the Catalan national dance, the *sardana*. Just east of the cathedral is the fascinating **Museu d'Història de la Ciutat** (City History Museum) composed of several buildings around **Plaça del Rei**, the palace courtyard of the medieval monarchs of Aragón. From the royal chapel, climb the multi-tiered Mirador del Rei Martí for good views. The museum also includes a remarkable subterranean walk through excavated portions of Roman and Visigothic Barcelona. It's all open Monday to Saturday from 10 am to 2 pm and 4 to 8 pm, and Sunday from 10 am to 2 pm. Entry is 500 ptas (250 ptas for students under 26 and pensioners).

A few minutes walk west of the cathedral, **Plaça de Sant Josep Oriol** is something of a hang-out for bohemian musicians and buskers. The plaza is surrounded by cafés and towards the end of the week becomes an outdoor art and craft market.

Waterfront For a look at the new face of Barcelona, take a stroll along the waterfront areas, once drab and seedy, but now attractively redeveloped with marinas, pedestrian promenades and more. From the bottom of La Rambla you can cross the Rambla de Mar footbridge to the **Moll d'Espanya**, a former wharf in the middle of the old harbour, Port Vell, where you'll find **L'Aquàrium**, one of Europe's best aquariums, open daily from 10 am to 9 pm, but not cheap at 1300 ptas. North-east of Port Vell, on the far side of the drab La Barceloneta area, begin the city **beaches**. Along the beachfront, after 1.25

SPAIN

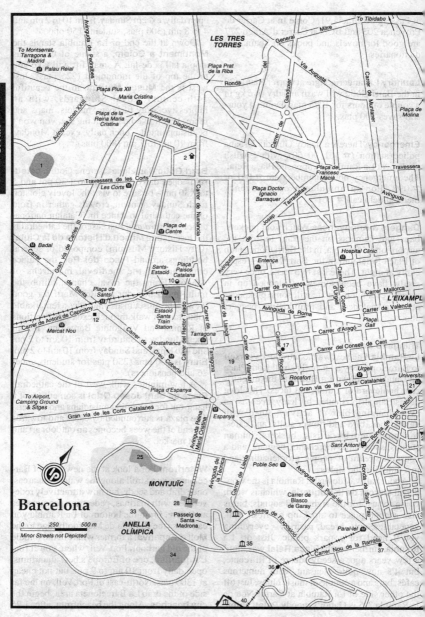

To Tibidabo

LES TRES
TORRES

Mitre

General

Via Augusta

Ronda

del

Plaça Prat
de la Riba

To Montserrat,
Tarragona &
Madrid

Palau Reial

Avinguda de Pedralbes

Plaça Pius XII

Maria Cristina

Plaça de la
Reina Maria
Cristina

Avinguda Joan XXIII

Avinguda Diagonal

Carrer de Ganduxer

Carrer de Muntaner

Plaça de
Molina

2

Travessera de les Corts

Les Corts

Carrer de Numància

Carrer de

Plaça Doctor
Ignacio
Barraquer

Plaça de
Francesc
Macià

Travessera

Avinguda

Plaça del
Centre

Badal

Carrer

Gran via de Carles III

de Sants

Josep

Tarradellas

Hospital Clínic

Entença

Carrer de Provença

Carrer del Comte d'Urgell

Carrer Mallorca

L'EIXAMPL

Carrer de València

Sants-
Estació

Plaça
Països
Catalans

10

Plaça de
Sants

Carrer d'Antoni de Capmany

12

Mercat Nou

Estació
Sants Train
Station

Hostafrancs

Carrer de la Creu Coberta

Carrer del Rector Triadó

Carrer de Llançà

11

Avinguda de Roma

Plaça
Gaíl

Carrer d'Aragó

Urgell

Carrer del Consell de Cent

Universitat

21

Tarragona

19

Carrer de Tarragona

Carrer de Vilamarí

Carrer de Rocafort

17

Rocafort

Gran via de les Corts Catalanes

To Airport,
Camping Ground
& Sitges

Plaça d'Espanya

Gran via de les Corts Catalanes

Espanya

Avinguda Reina
Maria Cristina

Sant Antoni

Ronda de Sant Antoni

Ronda de Sant Pau

25

Avinguda de la Tècnica

Carrer de Lleida

Poble Sec

Avinguda del Paral·lel

Barcelona

0   250   500 m

Minor Streets not Depicted

MONTJUÏC

33

ANELLA
OLÍMPICA

28

34

Passeig de
Santa
Madrona

29

Carrer de
Blasco
de Garay

Passeig de l'Exposició

35

Paral·lel

36

Carrer Nou de la Rambla

37

40

SPAIN

PLACES TO STAY
3 Alberg Pere Tarrés
11 Hostal Sofia
12 Hostal Sans
26 Hostal de Joves
31 Hostal Nuevo Colón

PLACES TO EAT
24 Restaurante Riera

OTHER
1 Otto Zutz
2 Camp Nou (FC Barcelona Stadium)
4 Martin's Disco
5 American Express
6 Come In Bookshop
7 Librería Francesa
8 La Pedrera
9 La Sagrada Família
10 Estació d'Autobuses de Sants
13 Altaïr Bookshop
14 BCN Bookshop
15 Els Encants Market
16 Casa Batlló & Casa Amatller
17 Viva Travel Agency
18 Iberia & Aviaco
19 Parc Joan Miró
20 Universitat de Barcelona
21 Metro Disco
22 Estació del Nord Bus Station
25 Poble Espanyol
27 Cascada
28 Palau Nacional & Museu Nacional d'Art de Catalunya
29 Museu d'Arqueologia
30 Bar Marsella
32 Museu Nacional d'Art Modern
33 Piscines Bernat Picornell
34 Estadi Olímpic
35 Fundació Joan Miró
36 Montjuïc Funicular Top Station & Chairlift Bottom Station
37 Club Apolo
38 Estació de França Train Station
39 Zoo
40 Castell de Montjuïc & Military Museum
41 Museu Marítim
42 Monument a Colom
43 L'Aquàrium

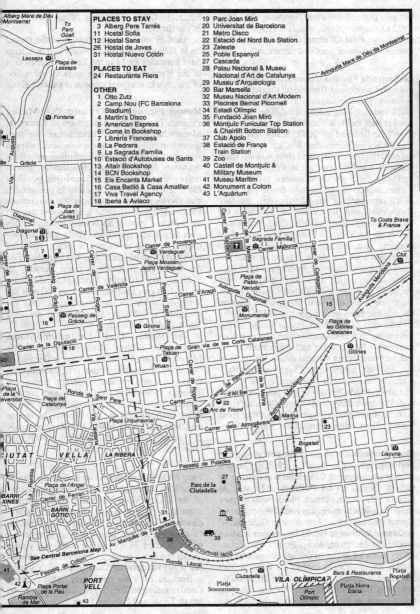

km you'll reach the **Vila Olímpica**, site of the 1992 Olympic village, which is fronted by the impressive **Port Olímpic**, a large marina with dozens of popular bars and restaurants.

La Sagrada Família Construction on Gaudí's principal work and Barcelona's most famous building (metro: Sagrada Família) began in 1882 and is taking a *long* time. The church is not yet half built: it's anyone's guess whether it will be finished by 2082. Many feel that it should not be completed but left as a monument to the master, whose career was cut short when he was hit by a tram in 1926.

Today there are eight towers, all over 100 metres high, with 10 more to come – the total of 18 representing the 12 Apostles, the four Evangelists and the mother of God, with the tallest tower (170 metres) standing for her son. Although La Sagrada Família is effectively a building site, the awesome dimensions and extravagant yet careful sculpting of what has been completed make it probably Barcelona's greatest highlight. The north-east Nativity Façade was done under Gaudí's own supervision, the very different north-west Passion Façade has been built since the 1950s.

You can climb high inside some of the towers by spiral staircases for a vertiginous overview of the interior and a panorama to the sea, or you can opt out and take a lift some of the way up. Entry to La Sagrada Família – which is on Carrer de Sardenya, on the corner of Carrer de Mallorca – is 750 ptas for everyone. It's open daily – May to September from 9 am to 9 pm, March, April and October from 9 am to 7 pm, other months from 9 am to 6 pm.

More Modernism Many of the best modernist buildings are in l'Eixample, including Gaudí's beautifully coloured **Casa Batlló** at Passeig de Gràcia 43 and his **La Pedrera** at Passeig de Gràcia 92, an apartment block with a grey stone façade which ripples round the corner of Carrer de Provença. Next door to Casa Batlló is **Casa Amatller** at No 41 by another leading modernist architect, Josep Puig i Cadafalch. Sadly none of these buildings is open to the public, except for the roof of La Pedrera with its giant chimney pots looking like multicoloured medieval knights. To see this you must book a free guided tour through the

Fundació Caixa Catalunya office (☎ 484 59 80) in the building.

Another modernist highpoint is the **Palau de la Música Catalana** concert hall at Carrer Sant Pere mes alt 11 in the La Ribera area east of the Barri Gòtic – a marvellous concoction of tile, brick, sculpted stone and stained glass.

Museu Picasso & Around The Museu Picasso, in a medieval mansion at Carrer de Montcada 15-19 in La Ribera, houses the most important collection of Picasso's work in Spain – more than 3000 pieces, including paintings, drawings, engravings and ceramics. It concentrates on Picasso's Barcelona periods (1895-1900 and 1901-04, early in his career), and shows fascinatingly how the precocious Picasso learned to handle a whole spectrum of subjects and treatments before developing his own forms of expression. There are also two rooms devoted to Picasso's 1950s series of interpretations of Velázquez's masterpiece *Las Meninas*. The museum is open Tuesday to Saturday from 10 am to 8 pm and Sunday from 10 am to 3 pm. Entry is 500 ptas (250 ptas for students under 26 and pensioners, and for everyone on Wednesday; free on the first Sunday of each month).

The **Museu Tèxtil i d'Indumentària** (Textile & Costume Museum), opposite the Museu Picasso, has a fascinating collection of tapestries, clothing and other textiles from centuries past and present. Opening hours are Tuesday to Saturday from 10 am to 5 pm and Sunday from 10 am to 2 pm (300 ptas). At the south end of Carrer de Montcada is the **Església de Santa Maria del Mar**, probably the most perfect of Barcelona's Gothic churches.

Parc de la Ciutadella As well as being a great place for a picnic or a stroll, this large park east of the Ciutat Vella has some more specific attractions. Top of the list are the monumental **cascada** (waterfall), a dramatic combination of statuary, rocks, greenery and thundering water created in the 1870s with the young Gaudí lending a hand; and the **Museu Nacional d'Art Modern de Catalunya**, with a good collection of 19th and early 20th-century Catalan art, open Tuesday to Saturday from 10 am to 7 pm, and Sunday from 10 am to 2 pm

(200 ptas). At the southern end of the park is Barcelona's **zoo**, open daily from 10 am to 5 pm (950 ptas) and famed for its albino gorilla.

Parc Güell This park, in the north of the city, is where Gaudí turned his hand to landscape gardening. It's a strange, enchanting place where Gaudí's passion for natural forms really took flight – to the point where the artificial almost seems more natural than the natural.

The main, lower gate, flanked by buildings which have the appearance of Hansel and Gretel's gingerbread house, sets the mood of the entire park, with its winding paths and carefully tended flower beds, skewed tunnels with rough stone columns resembling tree roots, and the famous dragon of broken glass and tiles. The house in which Gaudí lived most of his last 20 years has been converted into a museum, open Sunday to Friday from 10 am to 2 pm and 4 to 6 pm (250 ptas). The simplest way to Parc Güell is to take the metro to Lesseps then walk 10 to 15 minutes: follow the signs north-east along Travessera de Dalt then left up Carrer de Larrard. The park is open daily from 10 am – May to August to 9 pm, April and September to 8 pm, March and October to 7 pm, other months to 6 pm (free).

Montjuïc This hill overlooking the city centre from the south-west is home to some of Barcelona's best museums and attractions, some fine parks, and the main 1992 Olympics sites – well worth some of your time.

On the north side of the hill, the impressive **Palau Nacional** houses the **Museu Nacional d'Art de Catalunya**, with a wonderful collection of Romanesque frescos, woodcarvings and sculpture from medieval Catalonia. Opening hours are Tuesday to Saturday from 10 am to 7 pm, and Sundays and holidays from 10 am to 2.30 pm. Entry is 500 ptas.

Nearby is the **Poble Espanyol** (Spanish Village), by day a tour group's paradise with its craft workshops, souvenir shops and creditable copies of famous Spanish architecture; after dark it becomes a nightlife jungle, with bars and restaurants galore. It's open from 9 am daily (Monday to 8 pm; Tuesday to Thursday to 2 am; Friday and Saturday to 4 am; Sunday to midnight). Entry is 950 ptas (450 ptas with

a student card) but free after 9 pm except Friday and Saturday.

Downhill east of the Palau Nacional, the **Museu d'Arqueologia** (Archaeological Museum) has a good collection from Catalonia and the Balearic Islands. Opening hours are Tuesday to Saturday from 9.30 am to 1.30 pm and from 3.30 to 7 pm, and Sunday from 9.30 am to 2 pm. Entry is 200 ptas (free on Sunday).

Above the Palau Nacional is the **Anella Olímpica** (Olympic Ring), where you can swim in the Olympic pool, the **Piscines Bernat Picornell**, open daily from 7.30 am to 9 pm (2.30 pm on Sunday) for 1000 ptas, and wander into the main **Estadi Olímpic** (open daily from 10 am to 6 pm; admission free).

The **Fundació Joan Miró**, a short distance downhill east of the Estadi Olímpic, is one of the best modern art museums in Spain. Aside from many works by Miró, there are both permanent and changing exhibitions of other modern art. It's open Tuesday to Saturday from 11 am to 7 pm (Thursday to 9.30 pm), Sundays and holidays from 10.30 am to 2.30 pm. Entry is 600 ptas (300 ptas for students).

At the top of Montjuïc is the **Castell de Montjuïc**, with a military museum and great views.

To get to Montjuïc you can either walk or take a bus from Plaça d'Espanya (metro: Espanya). Bus No 61 from here links most of the main sights and ends at the foot of a chairlift (375 ptas) up to the castle. A funicular railway (185 ptas) from Paral-lel metro station also runs to the chairlift. From November to mid-June, the chairlift and funicular run only on weekends and holidays.

Tibidabo At 542 metres, this is the highest hill in the wooded range that forms the backdrop to Barcelona – a good place for a change of scene, some fresh air and, if the air's clear, 70-km views. At the top are the **Temple del Sagrat Cor**, a church topped by a giant Christ statue, and the **Parc d'Atraccions** funfair. A short distance along the ridge is the 288-metre **Torre de Collserola** telecommunications tower, with a hair-raising external glass lift – open daily from 11 am to 2.30 pm and 4 to 6 pm (500 ptas).

The fun way to Tibidabo is to take a suburban train from Plaça de Catalunya to Avinguda

SPAIN

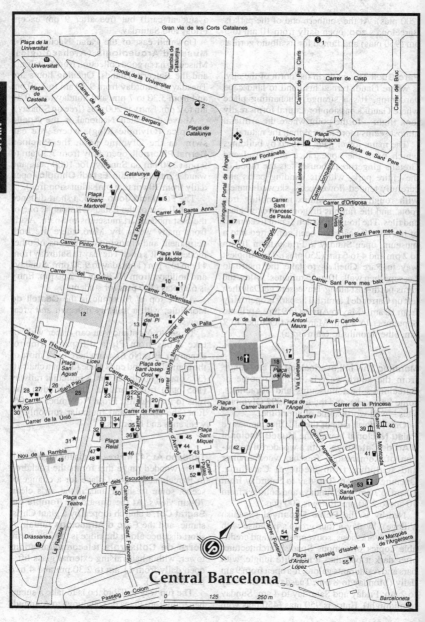

Gran via de les Corts Catalanes

Plaça de la
Universitat

Universitat

Plaça
de
Castella

Ronda de la Universitat

Carrer de Pelai

Carrer dels Tallers

Carrer de Palau

Carrer Bergara

Rambla de
Catalunya

Plaça de
Catalunya

Carrer de Pau Claris

Carrer de Casp

Carrer del Bruc

1

2

3

Urquinaona

Plaça
Urquinaona

Ronda de Sant Pere

Catalunya

La Rambla

Plaça
Vicenç Martorell

4

5

6

Carrer de Santa Anna

Avinguda Portal de l'Angel

Carrer Fontanella

Carrer
Sant
Francesc
de Paula

Via Laietana

Carrer Jonqueres

Carrer d'Ortigosa

9

Carrer Sant Pere mes alt

Carrer Pintor Fortuny

Carrer del Carme

Plaça Vila
de Madrid

7

8

Carrer Montsio

C. Amadors

Allada Vermell

Carrer Sant Pere mes baix

Carrer Portaferrissa

10   11

12

Plaça
del Pi

13

Carrer dels Nous

Carrer de la Palla

14

Av de la Catedral

Plaça
Antoni
Maura

Av F Cambó

Carrer de l'Hospital

Liceu

Carrer de Sant Pau

Carrer Boqueria

Plaça
San Agustí

Plaça de
Sant Josep
Oriol

15

19

Plaça
del Rei

Via Laietana

16

17

18

28 27

26

25

24

23

22

21

20

Raurió

Carrer de Ferran

Carrer de la Unió

30 29

31

32

33 34

35

36

37

38

Plaça
St Jaume

Plaça de
l'Angel

Carrer Jaume I

Carrer de la Princesa

Jaume I

Carrer Argenteria

Carrer de Montcada

39   40

41

Nou de la Rambla

47

48

49

Plaça
Reial

46

45

44

43

42

Plaça
Sant
Miquel

Carrer
Palau

51

52

Plaça
53
Santa
Maria

Carrer dels Escudellers

50

Carrer Nou de Sant Francesc

Plaça del
Teatre

Drassanes

La Rambla

54

Carrer Fusteria

Via Laietana

Plaça
d'Antoni
López

Passeig d'Isabel II

Av Marqués
de l'Argentera

55

Barceloneta

Central Barcelona

0   125   250 m

Passeig de Colom

PLACES TO STAY
5 Hotel Continental
7 Hostal Lausanne
10 Pensión-Hostal Fina
11 Hostal-Residencia Rembrandt
14 Hostal Galerias Maldà
15 Hotel Jardí
17 Hostal Layetana
20 Pensión Fernando
21 Pensión Bienestar
22 Pensión Europa
24 Hotel Internacional
27 Hotel Peninsular
45 Hostal Levante
46 Hotel Roma Reial
48 Youth Hostel Kabul
51 Casa Huéspedes Mari-Luz
52 Alberg Palau

PLACES TO EAT
6 Self-Naturista
8 Els Quatre Gats
12 Mercat de la Boqueria

19 Mesón Jesús
26 Bar-Restaurante Romescu
28 Restaurante Els Tres Bots
29 Restaurante Pollo Rico
30 Kashmir Restaurant Tandoori
34 Les Quinze Nits
43 Bar Restaurant Cervantes
44 El Gallo Kiriko
50 La Fonda Escudellers
55 Restaurante Set Portes

OTHER
1 Main Tourist Office
2 Catalunya Train Station
3 El Corte Inglés Department Store
4 L'Ovella Negra
9 Palau de la Música Catalana
13 Quera Bookshop
16 Catedral

18 Museu d'Història de la Ciutat
23 Cafè de l'Òpera
25 Gran Teatre del Liceu
31 Guàrdia Urbana (Police Station)
32 Barcelona Pipa Club
33 Glaciar Bar
35 Lavandería Tigre
36 Bar Malpaso
37 CIAJ (Youth Information Centre)
38 Próleg Bookshop
39 Museu Tèxtil i d'Indumentària
40 Museu Picasso
41 El Xampanyet Bar
42 Bar L'Ascensor
47 Jamboree & Sala Tarantos
49 Palau Güell
53 Església de Santa Maria del Mar
54 Main Post Office

de Tibidabo (10 minutes), then hop on the *tramvia blau* tram (175 ptas) across the road, which will take you up to the foot of the Tibidabo funicular railway. The funicular climbs to the church at top of the hill for 300 ptas. All these run every 10 or 15 minutes from at least 9 am to 9.30 pm.

Els Encants Market This good second-hand market by Plaça de les Glòries Catalanes, runs on Monday, Wednesday, Friday and Saturday between 8 am and 6 pm (8 pm in summer).

Courses
The Universitat de Barcelona runs good-value one-month Spanish courses (80 hours tuition, 40,000 ptas) about four times a year. Contact its Instituto de Estudios Hispánicos (☎ 318 42 66 ext 2084; fax 302 59 47) at Gran via de les Corts Catalanes 585. The main tourist office and the CIAJ youth information centre at Carrer de Ferran 32 in the Barri Gòtic have further information on courses. There are also notice boards with ads for classes at the above-mentioned university building and at Come In bookshop, Carrer de Provença 203. Also advertised at Come In are some jobs for English teachers.

Organised Tours
Bus No 100 (Bus Turístic), which starts at Plaça de Catalunya, is a special tourist bus that operates from mid-June to late October. It leaves every 20 minutes and does a city circuit linking virtually all the major sights. You can get on or off anywhere along the route. Tickets cost 1200 ptas for one day or 1700 ptas for two consecutive days, and include discounts to many attractions. This beats the other tours hands down on price.

Special Events
Barcelona's biggest festival is the Festes de la Mercè, several days of merrymaking around 24 September including *castellers* (human-castle builders), dances of giants and *correfocs* – a parade of firework-spitting dragons and devils. There are many others – tourist offices can clue you in.

Places to Stay
Camping *Camping Cala Gogo* (☎ 379 46 00), nine km south-west, is the closest camping ground to Barcelona and can be reached by bus No 65 from Plaça d'Espanya. Two to three km further out in Viladecans, on Carretera C-246, *El Toro Bravo* (☎ 637 34 62) and *La Ballena Alegre* (☎ 658 05 04) are much more pleasant,

and there are several more camping grounds within a few more km on Carretera C-246. To get to any of these, take bus No L95 from the corner of Ronda de la Universitat and Rambla de Catalunya.

Hostels A handful of places in Barcelona provide dormitory accommodation. For two people they're not great value, but they're certainly good places to meet other travellers. All require you to rent sheets, at 150 to 350 ptas for your stay, if you don't have them (or a sleeping bag). Ring before you go as the hostels can get booked up.

Youth Hostel Kabul (☎ 318 51 90), at Plaça Reial 17, is a rough-and-ready place but it has no curfew and is OK if you're looking for somewhere with a noisy party atmosphere; it has 150 places and charges 1300 ptas a night (no card needed). Security is slack but there are safes available for your valuables. Bookings are not taken.

Alberg Palau (☎ 412 50 80) at Carrer Palau 6 has just 40 places and is more pleasant. It charges 1200 ptas a night including breakfast and has a kitchen. It's open from 7 am to midnight. No card is needed.

Hostal de Joves (☎ 300 31 04), near metro Arc de Triomf at Passeig de Pujades 29, is quite clean and modern, with 68 beds and a kitchen, and charges 1300 ptas including breakfast; there's a 1 or 2 am curfew. A hostel card is only needed during the six peak summer weeks.

Alberg Mare de Déu de Montserrat (☎ 210 51 51) is the biggest and most comfortable hostel, but is four km north of the centre at Passeig Mare de Déu del Coll 41-51. It has 180 beds and charges 1500 ptas if you're under 26 or have an ISIC or IYTC card, 2075 ptas otherwise (breakfast included). A hostel card is needed. It's closed during the day and you can't get in after 3 am. It's a 10-minute walk from Vallcarca metro or a 20-minute ride from Plaça de Catalunya on bus No 28.

Alberg Pere Tarrés, (☎ 410 23 09) at Carrer de Numància 149 (about five minutes walk from Les Corts metro), has 90 beds at 1300 ptas for those under 26, 1550 ptas for others, plus 250 ptas for non-HI members (rates include breakfast). It has a kitchen, but is closed during the day and you can't get in after 2 am.

Pensiones & Hostales Most of the cheaper options are scattered through the old city, on either side of La Rambla. Generally, the areas closer to the port and on the west side of La Rambla are seedier and cheaper, and as you move north towards Plaça de Catalunya standards (and prices) rise.

Hostal Galerias Malda (☎ 317 30 02), upstairs in an arcade off Carrer del Pi 5, is about as cheap as you'll find. It's a rambling family-run establishment with basic but clean doubles at 2000 ptas and a couple of singles for 1000 ptas. The ever-popular *Casa Huéspedes Mari-Luz* (☎ 317 34 63), Carrer Palau 4, has doubles and dorms for 1300 ptas a person. The same people own the clean if somewhat spartan *Pensión Fernando* (☎ 301 79 93), Carrer de la Volta del Remei 4, with around 100 rooms, mostly doubles, for 1500 ptas a person. The nearby *Pensión Bienestar* (☎ 318 72 83), Carrer Quintana 3, has 30 clean, ordinary singles/doubles from 1500/2600 ptas. At Carrer Boqueria 18, *Pensión Europa* (☎ 318 76 20) has above-average security and 40 plain, reasonable-sized rooms for 1600/3200 ptas, or 2100/3400 ptas with shower.

Hostal Levante (☎ 317 95 65), Baixada de Sant Miquel 2, is a good family-run place with singles/doubles for 2500/4000 ptas and doubles with bath for 5000 ptas. Up near Plaça de Catalunya is the excellent *Hostal Lausanne* (☎ 302 11 39), Avinguda Portal de l'Angel 24 (1st floor), with good security and rooms from 2000/3200 ptas. Quiet Carrer Portaferrissa has a couple of good hostales: *Hostal-Residencia Rembrandt* (☎ 318 10 11) at No 23, and *Pensión-Hostal Fina* (☎ 317 97 87) at No 11. Both charge around 2500/3600 ptas for comfortable singles/doubles. *Hostal Layetana* (☎ 319 20 12) at Plaça de Berenguer Gran 2 is very well kept, with good-sized rooms at 2350/ 3650 ptas.

Opposite Estació de França, the impressive *Hostal Nuevo Colón* (☎ 319 50 77), Avinguda Marquès de l'Argentera 19, has rooms from 2000/3200 ptas.

Accommodation near Estació Sants is inconvenient for the centre, but if you arrive late at night, *Hostal Sofia* (☎ 419 50 40), at Avinguda de Roma 1-3, has very good rooms from 3500/4500 ptas. The modern *Hostal Sans* (☎ 331 37 00) at Carrer de Antoni de Capmany 82 charges 2100/3100 ptas, or 3100/4700 ptas with bath.

Hotels Higher up the scale, but good value, is the *Hotel Roma Reial* (☎ 302 03 66) at Plaça Reial 11. Modern singles/doubles with bath cost 3500/5800 ptas. The once-grand *Hotel Peninsular* (☎ 302 31 38), Carrer de Sant Pau 34, has singles/doubles from 3245/4815 ptas, although the rooms don't quite live up to the impressive foyer and central atrium.

Hotel Jardí (☎ 301 59 00), Plaça de Sant Josep Oriol 1, is well located, clean and plain, with rooms from 6500 to 8000 ptas single or double. On La Rambla itself, *Hotel Continental* (☎ 301 25 70) at No 138 and *Hotel Internacional* (☎ 302 25 66) at No 78-80 are among the best value. The Continental has pleasant, well-decorated rooms from 7450/9250 ptas including a good breakfast; the Internacional charges 6300/8100 ptas.

Places to Eat

For quick food, the *Bocatta* and *Pans & Company* chains, with numerous branches around the city, do good hot and cold baguettes with a range of fillings for 300 to 400 ptas.

The greatest concentration of cheaper restaurants is within walking distance of La Rambla. There are a few good-value ones on Carrer de Sant Pau, west off La Rambla. *Kashmir Restaurant Tandoori* at No 39 does tasty curries and biryanis from around 750 ptas. *Restaurante Pollo Rico*, No 31, has a somewhat seedy downstairs bar where you can have a quarter chicken or an omelette, with chips, bread and wine, for 300 to 400 ptas; the restaurant upstairs is more salubrious and only slightly more expensive. *Restaurante Els Tres Bots*, No 42, is grungy but cheap, with a menú for 750 ptas. Just off Carrer de Sant Pau on Carrer de l'Arc de Sant Agustí, tiny *Bar Restaurante Romescu* has good, home-style food at great prices, with most main courses around 400 or 500 ptas.

One of Barcelona's best value meals is the 695-pta, four-course menú (available evenings too) at the *Restaurante Riera*, Carrer de Joaquín Costa 30. Servings are generous and there's plenty to choose from (closed Friday night and Saturday).

There are lots more places in the Barri Gòtic. *Self-Naturista*, a self-service vegetarian restaurant at Carrer de Santa Anna 13, does a good lunch menú for 810 ptas. *Mesón Jesús*, at Carrer dels Cecs de la Boqueria 4, and *Bar-*

Restaurant Cervantes, Carrer de Cervantes 7, do good lunch menús for 900 to 1000 ptas. *El Gallo Kiriko* at Carrer d'Avinyó 19 is a friendly Pakistani restaurant busy with travellers. Tandoori chicken and salad, or couscous with beef or vegetables, is just 450 ptas.

For something a bit more up-market, *Les Quinze Nits* at Plaça Reial 6 and *La Fonda Escudellers* on Carrer dels Escudellers are two stylish bistro-like restaurants, under the same management, with a big range of good Catalan and Spanish dishes at reasonable prices – which can mean long queues in summer and at weekends. Three courses with wine and coffee will be about 2000 ptas. Carrer dels Escudellers also has a couple of good nighttime takeaway falafel joints – 200 to 300 ptas a serve. Or there's *Restaurante Set Portes* (☎ 319 30 33) at Passeig d'Isabel II 14, which dates from 1836 and specialises in paella (1200 to 2000 ptas). It's advisable to book. Another famous institution is *Els Quatre Gats*, Picasso's former hang-out at Carrer Montsió 3.

The *Mercat de la Boqueria* on La Rambla has a great selection of food.

Entertainment

Barcelona's entertainment bible is the weekly *Guía del Ocio* (125 ptas at newsstands). Its excellent listings (in Spanish) include films, theatre, music and art exhibitions.

Bars Barcelona's huge variety of bars are mostly at their busiest from about 11 pm to 1 am, especially on Friday and Saturday.

Cafè de l'Òpera at La Rambla 74, opposite the Liceu opera house, is the liveliest place on La Rambla. It gets packed with all and sundry at night. *Glaciar* on Plaça Reial gets very busy with a young crowd of foreigners and locals. Tiny *Bar Malpaso* at Carrer Rauric 20, just off Plaça Reial, packs in a young, casual crowd and plays great Latin and African music. Not far away, *Bar L'Ascensor*, Carrer de Bellafila 3, is a cosy little place with more good music and a young crowd.

El Xampanyet at Carrer de Montcada 22 near the Museu Picasso is another small place, specialising in cava (Catalan champagne, around 500 ptas a bottle), with good tapas too.

West of La Rambla, *L'Ovella Negra*, Carrer de les Sitges 5, is a noisy, barn-like tavern with a young crowd. **Bar Marsella**, Carrer de Sant Pau 65, specialises in absinthe (absenta in Catalan), a potent but mellow beverage with supposed narcotic qualities (500 ptas a shot).

Another great bar area is the Port Olímpic, with many bright and lively spots with open-air tables out front; some have good music inside too.

Live Music & Discos Many music places have dance space and some discos have bands on around midnight or so, to pull in some custom before the real action starts about 3 am. If you go for the band, you can normally stay for the disco at no extra cost and avoid bouncers' whims about what you're wearing etc. Women – and maybe male companions – may get in free at some discos if the bouncers like their looks. Count on 300 to 800 ptas for a beer in any of these places.

On Plaça Reial, **Barcelona Pipa Club**, No 3, has jazz Thursday to Saturday around midnight (ring the bell to get in); **Jamboree**, No 17, has jazz nightly and a lively disco later, from about 1.30 am; **Sala Tarantos**, next door, has classy flamenco some nights. **Club Apolo**, Carrer Nou de la Rambla 113, has live world music several nights a week, followed by live salsa or a varied disco.

Otto Zutz, Carrer de Lincoln 15, is, as its blurb says, 'where the beautiful people go...2000 ptas. Worth it'. The crowd's cool and the atmosphere's great – just don't wear running shoes and if in doubt, do wear black. **Zeleste**, Carrer dels Almogàvers 122, Poble Nou, is a cavernous warehouse-type club, regularly hosting visiting bands. **Mirablau** at the foot of the Tibidabo funicular is a bar with great views and a small disco floor; it's open till 4.30 am and entry is free.

The two top gay discos are **Metro**, Carrer de Sepúlveda 185, and **Martin's** at Passeig de Gràcia 130. Metro attracts some lesbians and heteros as well as gay men; Martin's is for gay men only.

Opera & Classical Music The Gran Teatre del Liceu opera house on La Rambla, gutted by fire in 1994, is due to reopen in 1998. Until then, opera and orchestral music are shared among other theatres, the lovely Palau de la Música

Catalana at Carrer de Sant Pere mes alt 11 being the chief venue.

Cinema For films in their original language (with Spanish subtitles), check listings for those marked VO *(versión original)*. A ticket is usually 600 to 700 ptas but many cinemas reduce prices on Monday.

Getting There & Away

Air Barcelona's airport, 14 km south-west of the city centre at El Prat de Llobregat, caters to international as well as domestic flights. For any flight it's well worth comparing the range of available fares, at any travel agent. One-way fares to Madrid range from 6900 ptas (Air Europa's youth fare) to 14,950 ptas on some Iberia flights. Other Air Europa fares include Seville or Santiago de Compostela for 13,900 ptas one way or 20,900 ptas return. Spanair flies to Palma de Mallorca from 9900 ptas return. One-way flights to London start from around 17,000 ptas, and to New York from 35,000 ptas (a bit less for students and those under 26).

Iberia and Aviaco (☎ 412 56 67) are at Passeig de Gràcia 30; Spanair (☎ 478 66 91) and Air Europa (☎ 412 77 33) are at the airport.

Bus The terminal for virtually all domestic and international buses is the Estació del Nord at Carrer d'Alí Bei 80 (metro: Arc de Triomf). Its information desk (☎ 265 65 08) is open daily from 7 am to 9 pm. A few international buses go from Estació d'Autobuses de Sants beside Estació Sants train station.

Several buses a day go to most main Spanish cities. Madrid is seven or eight hours away (2690 to 3450 ptas), San Sebastián 6½ hours (2375 ptas), Valencia 4½ hours (2650 ptas), Granada 13 to 15 hours (7540 ptas). Buses run several times a week to London (14,450 ptas), Paris (11,125 ptas) and other European cities.

Train Virtually all trains travelling to/from destinations within Spain stop at Estació Sants (metro: Sants-Estació); most international trains use Estació de França (metro: Barceloneta).

For some international destinations you have to change trains at Montpellier or the French border. A 2nd-class seat to Paris is

11,795 to 13,420 ptas, a sleeping berth 15,500 to 39,500 ptas.

Daily trains run to most major cities in Spain. To Madrid there are seven trains a day (6½ to 9½ hours, 4800 ptas); to San Sebastián two (eight to 10 hours, 4500 ptas); to Valencia 10 (four to 4½ hours, 3000 ptas), to Seville four (11 to 13½ hours, 6600 to 9200 ptas).

Tickets and information are available at the stations or from the RENFE office in Passeig de Gràcia metro/train station on Passeig de Gràcia, open daily from 7 am to 9 pm.

Car & Motorcycle Tolls on the A-7 autopista add up to over 1700 ptas from the French border to Barcelona, and over 6000 ptas from Barcelona to Alicante. The N-II from the French border and N-340 southbound are slower but toll-free. The fastest route to Madrid is via Zaragoza on the A-2 (1890 ptas), which heads west off the A-7 south of Barcelona, then the toll-free N-II from Zaragoza.

Getting Around

To/From the Airport Trains link the airport to Estació Sants and Catalunya station on Plaça de Catalunya every half-hour. They take 15 to 20 minutes and a ticket is 300 ptas (335 ptas at weekends). The A1 Aerobús does the 40-minute run between Plaça de Catalunya and the airport every 15 minutes, or every half-hour at weekends. The fare is 435 ptas. A taxi from the airport to Plaça de Catalunya is around 2000 ptas.

Bus, Metro & Train Barcelona's metro system spreads its tentacles around the city in such a way that most places of interest are within 10 minutes walk of a station. Buses and suburban trains are only needed for a few destinations – but note the Bus Turístic under Organised Tours earlier in this section.

A single metro, bus or suburban train ride costs 130 ptas, but a T-1 ticket, valid for 10 rides, costs only 700 ptas, while a T-DIA ticket (500 ptas) gives unlimited city travel in one day.

Car & Motorcycle While traffic flows smoothly thanks to an extensive one-way system, navigating can be extremely frustrating. Parking a car is also difficult and, if you

choose a parking garage, quite expensive. It's better to ditch your car and rely on public transport.

Taxi Barcelona's black-and-yellow taxis are plentiful, reasonably priced and especially handy for late-night transport. From Plaça de Catalunya, it costs around 600 ptas to Estació Sants.

MONESTIR DE MONTSERRAT

Unless you are on a pilgrimage, the prime attraction of Montserrat, 50 km north-west of Barcelona, is its setting. The Benedictine Monastery of Montserrat sits high on the side of an amazing 1236-metre mountain of truly weird rocky peaks, and is best reached by cable car. The monastery was founded in the 11th century to commemorate an apparition of the Virgin Mary on this site. Pilgrims still come from all over Christendom to pay homage to its Black Virgin (La Moreneta), a 12th-century wooden sculpture of Mary, regarded as Catalonia's patroness.

Information

Montserrat's information centre (☎ 835 02 51, ext 586), to the left along the road from the top cable-car station, is open daily from 9 am to 6 pm. It has a good free leaflet/map on the mountain and monastery, and an official guidebook for 475 ptas.

Montserrat's telephone code is ☎ 93.

Things to See & Do

If you are making a day trip to Montserrat, come early. Apart from the monastery, exploring the mountain is a treat.

The two-part **Museu de Montserrat**, on the plaza in front of the monastery's basilica (church), has an excellent collection ranging from an Egyptian mummy to art by El Greco, Monet and Picasso. It's open daily from 10.30 am to 2 pm and 3 to 6 pm (400 ptas, students 200 ptas).

Daily from 8 to 10.30 am, and noon to 6.30 pm, you can file past the image of the Black Virgin, high above the main altar of the 16th-century **basilica**, the only part of the monastery proper open to the public. The famous Montserrat Boys' Choir sings in the basilica every day at 1 and 7 pm, except in July.

SPAIN

The church fills up quickly, so try to arrive early.

You can explore the mountain above the monastery on a web of paths leading to small chapels and some of the peaks. The Funicular de Sant Joan (475/775 ptas one way/return) will lift you up the first 250 metres from the monastery.

Places to Stay & Eat

There are several accommodation options (all ☎ 835 02 51) at the monastery. A small camping ground 300 metres along the road past the lower Sant Joan funicular station is open from Semana Santa to October. The cheapest rooms are in the *Cel-les de Montserrat*, blocks of simple apartments, with showers, for up to 10 people. Two people pay 2360 ptas, or 2555 to 3155 ptas with kitchen. The *Hotel El Monestir*, open from Semana Santa to October, has singles/doubles from 2200/3800 ptas. *Hotel Abat Cisneros* charges from 4700/7900 ptas, but little more than half that in the off season.

The *Snack Bar* near the top cable-car station has platos combinados from 875 ptas and bocadillos from 325 ptas. *Cafeteria Self-Service* along the road has great views but is dearer – 1650 ptas for a three-course menú. *Hotel Abat Cisneros* has a menú for 2900 ptas.

Getting There & Away

Trains run from Plaça d'Espanya in Barcelona to Aeri de Montserrat daily, every two hours from 7.10 am to 9.10 pm – a 1½-hour ride. Return tickets for 1560 ptas include the exciting cable car up to the monastery from Aeri de Montserrat.

There's also a daily bus to the monastery from Estació d'Autobuses de Sants in Barcelona at 9 am (plus 8 am in July and August), for a return fare of 1090 ptas (1240 ptas at weekends).

COSTA BRAVA

The Costa Brava ranks with Spain's Costa Blanca and Costa del Sol among Europe's most popular holiday spots. It stands alone, however, in its spectacular scenery and proximity to northern Europe, both of which have sent prices skyrocketing in the most appealing places.

The main jumping-off points for the Costa Brava are the inland towns Girona (Gerona in Castilian) and Figueres (Figueras). Both places are on the A-7 autopista and the toll-free N-II highway which connect Barcelona with France. Along the coast the most appealing resorts are, from north to south, Cadaqués, L'Escala (La Escala), Tamariu, Llafranc and Calella de Palafrugell and Tossa de Mar.

Tourist offices along the coast are very helpful, with information on accommodation, transport and other things; they include Girona (☎ 22 65 75), Figueres (☎ 50 31 55), Palafrugell (☎ 30 02 28), and Cadaqués (☎ 25 83 15).

The telephone code for the Costa Brava is ☎ 972.

Coastal Resorts

The Costa Brava (Rugged Coast) is all about picturesque inlets and coves. Some of the longer beaches at places like L'Estartit and Empúries are worth visiting out of season, but there has been a tendency to build tall buildings wherever engineers think it can be done. Fortunately, in many places it just can't.

Cadaqués, about one hour's drive east of Figueres at the end of an agonising series of hairpin bends, is perhaps the most picturesque of all Spanish resorts, and haunted by the memory of the artist Salvador Dalí, who lived here. It's very short on beaches, so people tend to spend a lot of time sitting at waterfront cafés or wandering along the beautiful rocky coast. About 10 km north-east of Cadaqués is **Cap de Creus**, a rocky peninsula with a single restaurant at the top of a craggy cliff. This is paradise for anyone who likes to scramble around rocks risking life and limb with every step.

Further down the coast, past L'Escala and L'Estartit, you eventually come to Palafrugell, itself a few km inland with little to offer, but near three beach towns that have to be seen to be believed. The most northerly of these, and also the smallest, least crowded and most exclusive, is **Tamariu**. **Llafranc** is the biggest and busiest, and has the longest beach. **Calella de Palafrugell**, with its picture-postcard setting, is never overcrowded and always relaxed. If you're driving down this coast, it's worth making the effort to stop at some of these towns, particularly out of season.

Other Attractions

When you have had enough beach for a while, make sure you put the **Teatre-Museu Dalí**, on Plaça Gala i Salvador Dalí in Figueres, at the top of your list. This 19th-century theatre was converted by Dalí himself and houses a huge and fascinating collection of his strange creations. From July to September it's open from 9 am to 7.15 pm daily; in other months it's open from 10.30 am to 5.15 pm daily, except Mondays and 1 January and 25 December. Entry is 1000 ptas (students 700 ptas). Expect huge crowds and long queues in summer.

Historical interest is provided by **Girona**, with a lovely medieval quarter centred on a Gothic cathedral, and the ruins of the Greek and Roman town of **Empúries**, two km from L'Escala.

For a spectacular stretch of coastline, take a drive north from Tossa de Mar to San Feliu de Guíxols. There are 360 curves in this 20-km stretch of road, which, with brief stops to take in the scenery, can take a good two hours.

Among the most exciting attractions on the Costa Brava are the **Illes Medes**, off the coast from the package resort of L'Estartit. These seven islets and their surrounding coral reefs, with a total land area of only 21.5 hectares, have been declared a natural park to protect their extraordinarily diverse flora and fauna. Almost 1500 different life forms have been identified on and around the islands. A two-hour snorkelling or glass-bottom boat trip from L'Estartit costs around 1400 ptas; diving is easily arranged too.

Places to Stay

Most visitors to the Costa Brava rent apartments. If you are interested in renting an apartment for a week or so, contact local tourist offices in advance for information.

Figueres Figueres' HI hostel, the *Alberg Tramuntana* (☎ 50 12 13), is two blocks from the tourist office at Carrer Anicet Pagès 2. It charges 1500 ptas if you're under 26 or have an ISIC or IYTC card, 2075 ptas otherwise (breakfast included). Alternatively, *Hotel España* (☎ 50 08 69), a block east of the Dalí museum at Carrer de La Jonquera 26, has decent singles/doubles for 2000/4000 ptas. Don't sleep in Figueres' Parc Municipal – people have been attacked here at night.

Girona Girona's modern HI hostel, *Alberg Residencia Cerverí* (☎ 21 81 21), is perfectly situated in the middle of the old town at Carrer dels Ciutadans 9. The price is the same as at Figueres, if you can get a place – from October to June it's usually full with students. Otherwise, head down the road to *Pensión Viladomat* (☎ 20 31 76) at Carrer dels Ciutadans 5, which has comfortable singles/doubles for 1800/3600 ptas.

Cadaqués At the top of the town as you head towards Cabo de Creus is *Camping Cadaqués* (☎ 25 81 26). It charges 500 ptas a car, 650 ptas a tent and 525 ptas a person. At these prices, a single person is probably better off staying in town near the waterfront. *Hostal Marina* (☎ 25 81 99) at Carrer Riera 3 has singles/doubles from 2140/4280 ptas.

Near Palafrugell There are camping grounds at all three of Palafrugell's satellites. In Calella de Palafrugell try *Camping Moby Dick* (☎ 61 43 07); in Llafranc, *Kim's Camping* (☎ 30 11 56); and in Tamariu, *Camping Tamariu* (62 04 22).

Hotel and pensión rooms are relatively thin on the ground here, as many people come on package deals and stay in apartments. In Calella de Palafrugell, the friendly *Hostería del Plancton* (☎ 61 50 81) is one of the best deals on the Costa Brava, with rooms from 1500/3000 to 1800/3600 ptas, but it's only open from June to September. *Residencia Montaña* (☎ 30 04 04) at Carrer Cesárea 2 in Llafranc is well positioned near the beach and has singles/doubles for 2570/4815 ptas, or 2835/5450 ptas with shower, including breakfast. In Tamariu, the *Hotel Sol d'Or* (☎ 62 01 72), five minutes walk from the beach at Carrer Riera 18, has doubles with bathroom for 5620 ptas.

Getting There & Away

A few buses daily run from Barcelona to Tossa del Mar, L'Estartit and Cadaqués, but for the small resorts near Palafrugell you need to get to Girona first. Girona and Figueres are both on the railway connecting Barcelona to France. The dozen or so trains daily from Barcelona to Port Bou at the border all stop in Girona, and most in Figueres. The fare from Barcelona to Girona is 845 ptas, to Figueres 1195 ptas.

Getting Around

There are two or three buses a day from Figueres to Cadaqués and three or four to L'Escala. Figueres bus station (☎ 67 42 98) is across the road from the train station.

Several buses daily run to Palafrugell from Girona (where the bus station is behind the train station), and there are buses from Palafrugell to Calella de Palafrugell, Llafranc and Tamariu. Most other coastal towns (south of Cadaqués) can be reached by bus from Girona.

TARRAGONA

Tarragona makes a perfect contrast to the city life of Barcelona. Founded in 218 BC, it was for a long time the capital of much of Roman Spain, and Roman structures figure among its most important attractions. Other periods of history are also well represented, including the medieval cathedral and 17th-century British additions to the old city walls. The city's archaeological museum is one of the most interesting in Spain. Today, Tarragona is a modern city with a large student population and a lively beach scene – and Spain's answer to EuroDisney, Port Aventura, is just a few km south.

Orientation & Information

Tarragona's main street is Rambla Nova, which runs approximately north-west from a clifftop overlooking the Mediterranean. A couple of blocks to the east, parallel to Rambla Nova, is Rambla Vella, which marks the beginning of the old town. To the south-west, on the coast, is the train station.

Tarragona's main tourist office (☎ 24 50 64) is at Carrer Major 39. There is also a regional tourist office at Carrer Fortuny 4.

The telephone code for Tarragona is ☎ 977.

Things to See & Do

The **Museu d'Història de Tarragona** comprises four separate Roman sites. A single 400-pta ticket (free for students and pensioners) from any of them is good for all. The sites are open daily except Monday: from July to September, hours are 10 am to 8 pm; hours vary in other months. A good site to start with is the **Museu de la Romanitat** on Plaça del Rei,

which includes part of the vaults of the Roman circus, where chariot races were held. Nearby, close to the beach, is the very well preserved Roman **amphitheatre**, where gladiators battled each other, or wild animals, to the death. On Carrer Lleida, a few blocks west of Rambla Nova, are substantial remains of a **Roman forum**. The **Passeig Arqueològic** is a peaceful walkway along a stretch of the old city walls, which are a combination of Roman, Iberian and 17th-century British efforts.

Tarragona's **Museu Arqueològic**, on Plaça del Rei, gives further insight into the city's rich history. The carefully presented exhibits include frescos, mosaics, sculpture and pottery dating back to the 2nd century BC. The museum is open daily except Monday (100 ptas, free on Tuesday). Also worth seeing is the **Museu d'Art Modern** at Carrer Santa Anna 8.

The **catedral** sits grandly at the highest point of Tarragona, overlooking the old town. Some parts of the building date back to the 12th century AD. It's open for tourist visits Monday to Friday from 10 am to 2 pm (300 ptas). Entrance is through the beautiful cloister with the excellent Museu Diocesà.

If you're here in summer, Platja del Miracle is the main city beach. It is reasonably clean but can get terribly crowded. Several other beaches dot the coast north of town, but in summer you will never be alone.

Port Aventura

Port Aventura (☎ 902-20 22 20), which opened in 1995 near Salou, 10 km south-west of Tarragona, is Spain's newest, biggest and best funfair. It's divided into five theme areas – China, a Mediterranean fishing village, the Wild West, Polynesia and ancient Mexico. It has a hectic street life that includes wild-west shoot-outs and Polynesian dance troupes, theatres with Chinese acrobats, and of course hair-raising rides like the Dragon Khan, claimed to be Europe's biggest roller coaster. If you have 3900 ptas to spare, it makes a really fun day out with never a dull moment. Port Aventura is open daily, from Semana Santa to October, from 10 am to 8 pm. At peak periods it may stay open till midnight, with special night tickets, valid from 7 pm to midnight, costing 2300 ptas. Trains run to Port Aventura's own station several times a day from Tarragona and Barcelona.

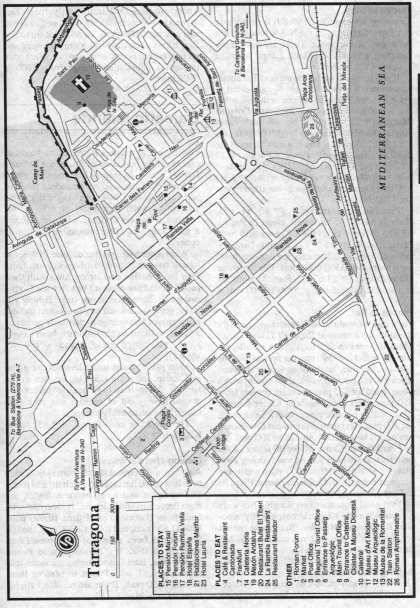

Tarragona

0   150   300 m

To Bus Station (275 m),
Barcelona & Valencia via A-7

To Port Aventura
& Valencia via N-340

To Camping Grounds
& Barcelona via N-340

MEDITERRANEAN SEA

SPAIN

PLACES TO STAY
15 Pensión Marsal
16 Pensión Forum
17 Pensión Rambla Vella
18 Hotel España
21 Habitaciones Mariflor
23 Hotel Lauria

PLACES TO EAT
4 Café & Restaurant
   Cantonada
7 Frankfurt
14 Cafetería Noria
19 Mesón Andaluz
20 Restaurant Bufet El Tiberi
24 La Rambla Restaurant
25 Restaurant Mirador

OTHER
1 Roman Forum
2 Market
3 Post Office
5 Regional Tourist Office
6 Entrance to Passeig
   Arqueológic
8 Main Tourist Office
9 Entrance to Catedral,
   Cloister & Museu Diocesà
10 Catedral
11 Museu d'Art Modern
12 Museu Arqueologic
13 Museu de la Romanitat
22 Train Station
26 Roman Amphitheatre

Places to Stay

Camping Tàrraco (☎ 23 99 89) is near Platja Arrabassada beach, off the N-340 road two km north-east of the centre. There are three more camping grounds on Platja Larga beach, a couple of km further on.

If you intend to spend the night in Tarragona in summer, it would be wise to call ahead to book a room. Plaça de la Font in the old town has a few good pensiones, including *Pensión Marsal* (☎ 22 40 69) at No 26, with clean singles/doubles with bath for 1500/3000 ptas (or 1300/2600 ptas if you can make it up to the 5th floor), and the better *Pensión Forum* (☎ 23 17 18) at No 37, charging 2140/3745 ptas, also with bath. *Habitaciones Mariflor* (☎ 23 82 31) at Carrer General Contreras 29 has clean rooms for 1400/2600 ptas.

Pensión Rambla Vella (☎ 23 81 15), Rambla Vella 31, has small, clean rooms for 1870/3750 ptas, or 2140/4280 ptas with bath. *Hotel España* (☎ 23 27 12), Rambla Nova 49, is a well-positioned, unexciting one-star hotel with rooms for 3300/6000 ptas. The three-star *Hotel Lauría* (☎ 23 67 12), Rambla Nova 20, is a worthwhile splurge at 5800/10,700 ptas.

Places to Eat

For a taste of traditional Catalan food, head for the stylish *Restaurant Bufet El Tiberi*, Carrer Martí d'Ardenya 5, which offers an all-you-can-eat buffet for 1390 ptas per person. Nearby *Mesón Andaluz*, upstairs at Carrer de Pons d'Icart 3, is a backstreet local favourite, with a good menú for 775 ptas and main courses from 350 ptas. *Café Cantonada* at Carrer Fortuny 23 is another popular place, with a lunch menú for 900 ptas; next door, *Restaurant Cantonada* has pizzas and pasta from 575 to 700 ptas.

Frankfurt at Carrer Major 30 is one of the better-value cafés in the old town, doing good platos combinados from 500 ptas and a big range of bocadillos. *Cafeteria Noria*, Plaça de la Font 53, has similar fare and prices.

Two good restaurants on Rambla Nova are *La Rambla* at No 10 and, almost directly opposite, *Restaurant Mirador*. Both have menús for about 1400 ptas and you can eat well à la carte for 2500 to 3000 ptas.

Getting There & Away

Over 20 regional trains a day run from Barcelona to Tarragona (one to 1½ hours, 650 ptas).

There are about 12 trains daily from Tarragona to Valencia, taking three to 3½ hours and costing 2500 ptas. To Madrid, there are four trains each day – two via Valencia and taking seven hours and two via Zaragoza taking six hours. Fares range from 3700 to 5600 ptas.

Balearic Islands

Floating out in the blue waters of the Mediterranean off the east coast of Spain, the Balearic Islands (Islas Baleares) are invaded every summer by a massive multinational force of hedonistic tourists. Not surprising really, when you consider the ingredients on offer – fine beaches, relentless sunshine, wild nightlife and a great range of accommodation and eating options.

What is surprising is that despite all this, the islands have managed, to a degree, to maintain their individuality and strong links with their past. Beyond the bars and beaches are Gothic cathedrals, Stone Age ruins, small fishing villages, some spectacular bushwalks and endless olive groves and orange orchards. It comes as a relief to discover that tourism hasn't *completely* consumed these islands – not yet anyway.

Most place names and addresses are given in Catalan, the main language spoken in the islands. Note that high-season prices are quoted here – out of season, you may find things are considerably cheaper.

The telephone code for all of the Balearic Islands is ☎ 971.

Getting There & Away

Air There are frequent flights from major cities to Palma de Mallorca, Maó (Mahón) and Ibiza. The cheapest and most frequent flights are from Barcelona and Valencia. Typical one-way fares from Barcelona are Palma 10,600 ptas, Maó 11,850 ptas, and Ibiza 12,700 ptas, though Spanair has fares as low as 7950 ptas. From Valencia to Ibiza it's 10,800 ptas, to Palma 12,100 ptas. Inter-island flights are quite reasonably priced, with Palma to Maó or Ibiza costing 6650 ptas. There are no direct flights from Ibiza to Maó.

Return fares are double the one-way fare, unless you can manage to meet the not-too-stringent advance-booking conditions for deals like Aviaco's *tarifa azul* (around 12,000 ptas return from Barcelona to Ibiza or Maó) or Spanair's *super reducida* Barcelona-Palma return fare of 9900 ptas.

Boat Trasmediterránea, with offices in (and services between) Barcelona (☎ 93-443 25 32), Valencia (☎ 96-367 65 12), Palma, Maó and Ibiza, is the major ferry company serving the islands.

It has a 'four seasons' timetable – the warmer it is, the more frequent the sailings. In summer, scheduled ferries are: Barcelona-Palma, nine a week; Barcelona-Ibiza, five a week; Barcelona-Maó, Valencia-Palma and Valencia-Ibiza, all six a week; and Valencia-Maó, one a week. There are also inter-island services, although it's not much more expensive to fly.

During summer, one-way fares from the mainland to any of the islands are 6300 ptas for a *butaca turista* (seat), except for Valencia-Ibiza which costs 5040 ptas. Alternatively, you can take a berth in a cabin, which ranges from around 10,500 ptas (four-share) to 15,750 ptas (twin-share) per person. To take a small car from the mainland costs around 18,000 ptas; a motorcycle is around 4500 ptas. Off-season fares are considerably lower.

Another company, Flebasa (☎ 96-578 40 11), has services from Denia on the mainland (between Valencia and Alicante) to both Ibiza and Formentera. See the Formentera section later for details on ferries there from Ibiza.

MALLORCA
Mallorca is the largest of the Balearic Islands. Most of the five million annual visitors to the island are here for the three *s* words: sun, sand and sea. There are, however, other reasons for coming to Mallorca. Palma, the main population centre, is in itself worth visiting, and the island offers a number of noncoastal attractions.

Orientation & Information
The capital, Palma de Mallorca, is on the southern side of the island, in a bay famous for its brilliant sunsets. The Serra de Tramuntana

mountain range, which runs parallel with the north-west coastline, is trekkers' heaven. Mallorca's best beaches are along the north-east and east coasts – so are most of the big tourist resorts.

All of the major resorts have at least one tourist office. Palma has four – on Plaça d'Espanya (☎ 71 15 27), at Carrer Sant Domingo 11 (☎ 72 40 90), on Plaça Major and at the airport. Palma's post office is on Carrer de la Constitució.

Things to See & Do
Palma is a pleasant town and worth spending a day or so exploring. The enormous **catedral** on Plaça Almoina is the first landmark you will see as you approach the island by ferry. It houses an excellent museum, and some of the cathedral's interior features were designed by Antoni Gaudí; entry costs 400 ptas.

In front of the cathedral is the **Palau de l'Almudaina**, the one-time residence of the Mallorcan monarchs. Inside is a collection of tapestries and artworks, although it's not really worth the 450 ptas entry. Instead, visit the rich and varied **Museu de Mallorca** (300 ptas).

Also near the cathedral are the interesting **Museu Diocesà** and the delicate **Banys Àrabs** (Arab baths), the only remaining monument to the Moorish domination of the island. Also worth visiting is the collection of the **Fundació Joan Miró**, housed in the artist's Palma studios at Carrer Joan de Saridakis 29, two km west of the centre.

Mallorca's north-west coast is a world away from the concrete jungles on the other side of the island. Dominated by the Serra de Tramuntana mountains, it's a beautiful region of olive groves, pine forests and small villages with stone buildings; it also has a rugged and rocky coastline. There are a couple of highlights for drivers: the hair-raising road down to the small port of **Sa Calobra** and the amazing trip along the peninsula leading to the island's northern tip, **Cap Formentor**.

If you don't have your own wheels, take the **Palma to Sóller train** (see Getting Around later). It's one of the most popular and spectacular excursions on the island. Sóller is also the best place to base yourself for trekking – the easy three-hour return walk from here to the beautiful village of Deiá is a fine introduction to trekking on Mallorca. The tourist office's

SPAIN

SPAIN

Palma de Mallorca

```
0        150        300 m
Some streets pedestrian-only
```

Parc de la Mar

PLACES TO STAY
7   Hotel Born
9   Pensión Costa Brava
11   Hostal Pons
13   Hostal Apuntadores
14   Hostal Ritzi

PLACES TO EAT
12   Vecchio Giovanni & Abaco
17   Casa Julio
20   Rincón del Artista
21   Restaurante Sa Impremta

23   Mario's Cafe

OTHER
1   Train Stations (to Sóller & Inca)
2   Bus Station & Airport Bus
3   Tourist Office
4   Hospital
5   Santa Magadalena Church
6   Mercat de l'Olivar (Market)
8   Teatro Principal

10   Tourist Office
15   Post Office
16   Main Tourist Office
18   Ayuntamiento (Town Hall)
19   Santa Eulalia Church
22   Basílica de Sant Francesc
24   Palau de l'Almudaina
25   Catedral
26   Museu Diocesà
27   Museu de Mallorca
28   Banys Árabs (Arab Baths)

Hiking Excursions brochure covers 20 of the island's better walks, or for more detailed information see Lonely Planet's *Trekking in Spain*.

Most of Mallorca's best beaches have been consumed by tourist developments, although there are exceptions. There are long stretches of sandy, undeveloped beach south of **Port d'Alcúdia** on the north-east coast. The lovely **Cala Mondragó** on the south-east coast is backed by a solitary hostal, and a little further south the attractive port town of **Cala Figuera** has escaped many of the ravages of mass tourism. There are also some good quiet beaches near the popular German resort of **Colonia San Jordi**, particularly Ses Arenes and Es Trenc, both a few km back up the coast towards Palma.

Places to Stay

Palma The *Pensión Costa Brava* (☎ 71 17 29), Carrer Martí Feliu 16, is a back-street cheapie with reasonable rooms from 1300/2300 ptas. The cluttered 19th-century charm of *Hostal Pons* (☎ 72 26 58), Carrer del Vi 8, overcomes its limitations (spongy beds, only one bathroom); it charges 2000 ptas per person. At Carrer Apuntadores 8, *Hostal Apuntadores* (☎ 71 34 91) has smartly renovated singles/doubles at 2000/3530 ptas and doubles with bathroom at 4100 ptas. Next door, *Hostal Ritzi* (☎ 71 46 10) has good security and comfortable rooms at 2300/3300 ptas, or doubles with shower/bath for 3800/4500 ptas.

The superb *Hotel Born* (☎ 71 29 42), in a restored 18th-century palace at Carrer de Sant Jaume 3, has B&B from 6000/8500 ptas.

Other Areas If you've got time (and sense), have a quick look around Palma and then head for the hills. In Deià, the charming *Pensión Villa Verde* (☎ 63 90 37) charges 2300 ptas per person for B&B, while *Hostal Miramar* (☎ 63 90 84), overlooking the town, has B&B at 3600/6000 ptas (during summer, it's half-board only, from 5100/9000 ptas). Beside the train station in Sóller, the popular *Hotel El Guía* (☎ 63 02 27) has rooms for 4815/6420 ptas, or nearby (go past El Guía and turn right) the cosy *Casa de Huéspedes Margarita Thás Vives* (☎ 63 42 14) has doubles/triples/quads at 2800/3600/5000 ptas.

If you want to stay on the south-east coast, the large *Hostal Playa Mondragó* (☎ 65 77 52) at Cala Mondragó has B&B for 3900/5800 ptas. At Cala Figuera, *Hostal Ca'n Jordi* (☎ 64 50 35) has rooms from 2500/4200 ptas.

If you're camping, *Camping Club Picafort* (☎ 53 78 63) on the north coast (nine km south of Port d'Alcúdia) has excellent facilities and good beaches opposite. There are also several youth hostels and a couple of quirky old monasteries around the island where you can sleep cheap – ask at the tourist offices for full details.

Places to Eat

For Palma's best range of eateries, wander through the maze of streets between Plaça de la Reina and the port. Carrer Apuntadors is lined with restaurants and should have something to suit everyone – seafood, Chinese, Italian – even a few Spanish restaurants! Around the corner at Carrer Sant Joan 1 is the deservedly popular *Vecchio Giovanni*, which has a good menú for 950 ptas. Right next door is the amazing *Abaco*, the bar of your wildest dreams (with the drinks bill of your darkest nightmares). At *Mario's Cafe*, on Carrer de la Mar, you can have pizza or pasta from 700 ptas.

There are a couple of good places over near Plaça de Santa Eulalia, both with menús for 800 ptas: the excellent *Casa Julio*, Calle Previsio 4, specialises in local rice dishes (open for lunch only, Monday to Saturday) and, nearby at Carrer d'En Morey 4, *Restaurante Sa Imprenta* is a friendly little bar-eatery.

Getting Around

Bus No 17 runs every half-hour between the airport and Plaça Espanya in central Palma (265 to 295 ptas). Alternatively, a taxi will cost around 1800 ptas.

Most parts of the island are accessible by bus from Palma. Buses generally depart from or near the bus station at Plaça Espanya – the tourist office's *Public Tourist Bus Routes* brochure lists all the gory details. Mallorca's two train lines also start from Plaça Espanya. One goes to the inland town of Inca (250 ptas one way) and the other goes to Sóller (420 ptas one way).

The best way to get around the island is by car – it's worth renting one just for the drive along the north-west coast. There are about 30 rental agencies in Palma. If you want to

SPAIN

compare prices many of them have harbour-side offices along Passeig Marítim. Rates vary substantially, depending on the season and hire period. If you're looking for a cheapish deal, places worth trying include Casa Mascaro (☎ 73 61 03), Iber-Auto (☎ 28 54 48) and Entercar (☎ 74 30 51).

IBIZA

Ibiza (Eivissa in Catalan) is the most extreme of the Balearic islands, both in terms of its landscape and the people it attracts. Hippies, gays, fashion victims, nudists, party animals – this is truly one of the world's most bizarre melting pots. The island receives over a million visitors each year. Apart from the weather and the desire to be 'seen', the main drawcards are the notorious nightlife and the many picturesque beaches.

Orientation & Information

The capital, Ibiza (Eivissa) city, is on the south-eastern side of the island. This is where most travellers arrive (the airport is to the south, and most ferries operate from the port here) and it's also the best base. The next-largest towns are Santa Eulária des Riu on the east coast and Sant Antoni de Portmany on the west coast. Other big resorts are scattered around the island.

In Ibiza city, the tourist office (☎ 30 19 00) is at Passeig Vara de Rey 13. There is a Telefónica phone centre on Avinguda Santa Eulària by the port, while the post office is at Carrer Madrid 23. You'll find a good laundrette, Lavandería Master Clean, at Carrer Felipe II 12.

Things to See & Do

Shopping seems to be a major pastime in Ibiza city – the port area of Sa Penya is crammed with funky and trashy clothes boutiques and hippy market stalls. From here you can wander up into the D'Alt Vila, the old walled town, with its up-market restaurants, galleries and the Museu d'Art Contemporani. There are fine views from the walls and from the catedral at the top, and the Museu Arqueològic nearby is worth a visit.

The heavily developed Platja de ses Figueretes beach is a 20-minute walk south of Sa Penya – you'd be better off taking the half-hour bus ride (105 ptas) south to the beaches at Ses Salines.

If you're prepared to explore, there are still numerous unspoiled and relatively undeveloped beaches around the island. On the north-east coast, Cala de Boix is the only black-sand beach in the islands, while further north are the lovely beaches of S'Aigua Blanca. On the north coast near Portinatx, Cala Xarraca is in a picturesque, semi-protected bay, and near Port de Sant Miquel is the attractive Cala Benirràs. On the south-west coast, Cala d'Hort has a spectacular setting overlooking two rugged rock-islets, Es Verda and Es Verdranell.

Places to Stay

Ibiza City There are quite a few hostales in the streets around the port, although in mid-summer cheap beds are as scarce as hen's teeth. The friendly Hostal Sol y Brisa (☎ 31 08 18), Avinguda Bartolomé Vincent Ramón 15, has excellent singles/doubles at 1800/3400 ptas. Nearby at Carrer Vincente Cuervo 14, Hostal Ripoll (☎ 31 42 75) has similar prices, as well as good studio apartments (2000 to 9000 ptas a night).

On the waterfront, Hostal-Restaurante La Marina (☎ 31 01 72), Andenes del Fuerto 4, has good doubles with sea views at 3200 ptas and sleepless singles with disco views at 1700 ptas. Casa de Huéspedes Navarro (☎ 31 08 25), Carrer de la Cruz 20 (3rd floor), also has some rooms with harbour views (and a sunny rooftop) for 1600/3200 ptas.

If you're after rooms with bath, Hostal-Residencia Parque (☎ 30 13 58) at Carrer Vincente Cuervo 3 has rooms for 3100/6200 ptas. Perfectly located at Passeig Vara del Rey 2, Hotel Montesol (☎ 31 01 61) has rooms with TV and phone for around 4900/7900 ptas.

Other Areas One of the best of Ibiza's half-dozen camping grounds is Camping Cala Nova (☎ 33 17 74), 500 metres north of the resort town of Cala Nova and close to a good beach.

If you want to get away from the resort developments the following places are all worth checking out. Near the Ses Salines beach (and bus stop), Casa de Huéspedes Escandel (☎ 39 65 83) is a simple six-room guesthouse with doubles from 3500 ptas; next door Hostal Mar y Sal (☎ 39 65 84) has doubles at 4600 ptas. On the south-west coast at Cala d'Hort, *Restaurante y Habitaciones Del Carmen* (☎ 14 26 61) has good rooms upstairs with bath and sea views from 4225/6500 ptas. Near the S'Aigua Blanca beaches, *Pensión Sa Plana* (☎ 33 5073) has a pool, rooms with bath from 4000/4500 ptas and a menú for 1000 ptas.

Places to Eat

Bland, overpriced eateries abound in the port area, but there are a few exceptions worth searching out. The no-frills *Comidas Bar San Juan*, Carrer Montgri 8, is outstanding value with main courses from 400 to 750 ptas. At Carrer de la Cruz 19, *Ca'n Costa* is another family-run eating house with a menú for 900 ptas. *Chi Chi's*, Carrer del Mar 16, isn't particularly cheap but its Tex-Mex tucker is particularly good. Pizzas and pastas are around 800 ptas at the *Pizzería Da Franco Er Romano* (below Hostal Sol y Brisa) – it also has a menú for 1250 ptas.

Entertainment

Ibiza's nightlife is renowned. The gay scene is wild and the dress code expensive. Dozens of bars keep Ibiza city's port area jumping until the early hours, and after they wind down you can continue on to one of the island's world-famous discos – if you can afford the 3000 to 5000 ptas entry, that is. The big-names are *Pacha*, on the north side of Ibiza city's port; *Privilege* and *Amnesia*, both six km out on the road to Sant Antoni; and *Kiss* and *Space*, both south of Ibiza city in Platja d'En Bossa.

Getting Around

Buses run between the airport and Ibiza city hourly (100 ptas); otherwise, a taxi costs around 1500 ptas. Buses to other parts of the island leave from the series of bus stops along Avenida Isidoro Macabich – pick up a copy of the handy bus timetable from the tourist office.

If you are intent on getting to some of the more secluded beaches you will need to rent wheels. Agencies in Ibiza city include Ribas (☎ 30 18 11), at Calle Vincente Cuervo 3, and Valentin (☎ 31 08 22), at Avinguda Bartolomé Vincent Ramón 19. Both have cars (4000 to 5000 ptas a day), scooters (2500 to 4000 ptas a day) and bicycles (700 to 1000 ptas a day).

FORMENTERA

A short boat ride south of Ibiza, Formentera is the smallest and least developed of the four main Balearic Islands. This idyllic island has fine beaches and some excellent short walking and cycling trails to explore. It's a popular day trip destination from Ibiza and can get pretty crowded in midsummer, but most of the time it is still possible to find yourself a strip of sand out of sight of tourist colonies and out of earshot of other tourists.

Orientation & Information

Formentera is about 20 km from east to west. Ferries arrive at La Savina on the north-west coast; the tourist office (☎ 32 20 57) is behind the rental agencies you'll see when you disembark. Three km south is the island's capital, Sant Francesc Xavier, where you'll find most of the banks. From here, the main road runs along the middle of the island before climbing to the highest point (192 metres). At the eastern end of the island is the Sa Mola lighthouse. Three km east of La Savina, Es Pujols is the main tourist resort (and the only place with any nightlife to speak of).

Things to See & Do

Some of the island's best and most popular beaches are the beautiful white strips of sand along the narrow promontory which stretches north towards Ibiza. A two-km walking trail leads from the La Savina-Es Pujols road to the far end of the promontory, from where you can wade across a narrow strait to **S'Espalmador**, a tiny islet with beautiful, quiet beaches. Along Formentera's south coast, **Platja de Migjorn** is made up of numerous coves and beaches – tracks lead down to these off the main road. On the west coast is the lovely **Cala Saona** beach.

The tourist office's *Green Tours* brochure outlines 19 excellent walking and cycling trails that take you through some of the island's most scenic areas.

Places to Stay

Camping is not allowed on Formentera. Sadly, the coastal accommodation places mainly cater to German and British package-tour agencies and are overpriced and/or booked out in summer. In Es Pujols you could try *Hostal Tahiti* (☎ 32 81 22), with B&B at 5200/8600 ptas. If you prefer peace and quiet you would be better off in Es Caló – **Fonda Rafalet** (☎ 32 70 16) has good rooms on the waterfront for 3000/5500 ptas, or across the road the tiny and simple **Casa de Huéspedes Miramar** (☎ 32 70 60) charges 2000/3000 ptas.

Perhaps the best budget bet is to base yourself in one of the small inland towns and bike it to the beaches. In Sant Ferran (1.6 km south of Es Pujols), the popular **Hostal Pepe** (☎ 32 80 33) has B&B with bath at 3110/4975 ptas. In Sant Francesc Xavier, **Restaurant Casa Rafal** (☎ 32 22 05) charges 2000/3500 ptas (3000/5000 ptas with bath). La Savina isn't the most thrilling place, but **Hostal La Savina** (☎ 32 22 79) has excellent rooms from 2750/4250 ptas.

Getting There & Away
There are 20 to 25 ferries daily between Ibiza city and Formentera. The trip takes about 25 minutes by jet ferry (3600 ptas return), or about an hour by car ferry (1500 to 2200 ptas return; 5000 ptas for a small car). Prices vary from company to company, so check around.

Getting Around
A string of rental agencies line the harbour in La Savina. Bikes are the best way to get around, and daily rates range from 500 ptas to 1000 ptas for a mountain bike. If you're in a tearing hurry (or lazy), there are also scooters (1500 to 4000 ptas) and cars (4000 to 7000 ptas). A regular bus service connects all the main towns.

MENORCA
Menorca is perhaps the least overrun and most low-key of the Balearic Islands. In 1993, the island was declared a Biosphere Reserve by UNESCO, with the aim of preserving its important environmental areas such as the Albufera d'es Grau wetlands and its unique collection of archaeological relics and monuments.

Orientation & Information
The capital, Maó (Mahón in Spanish), is at the eastern end of the island. Its busy port is the arrival point for most ferries, and Menorca's airport is seven km south-west. The main road runs down the middle of the island to Ciutadella, Menorca's second-largest town,

with secondary roads leading north and south to the major coastal resorts and beaches.

The main tourist office is in Maó (☎ 36 37 90) at Plaça de S'Esplanada 40. During summer there are offices at the airport and in Ciutadella on Plaça des Born. Maó's post office is on Carrer del Bon Aire.

Things to See & Do
Maó and Ciutadella are both harbour towns, and from either place you'll have to commute to the beaches. Maó absorbs most of the tourist traffic – while you're here you can take a boat cruise around its impressive harbour and sample the local gin at the **Xoriguer distillery**. Ciutadella, with its smaller harbour and historic buildings, has a more distinctively Spanish feel about it.

In the centre of the island, the 357-metre-high **Monte Toro** has great views of the whole island, and on a clear day you can see as far as Mallorca.

With your own transport and a bit of footwork you'll be able to discover some of Menorca's off-the-beaten-track beaches. North of Maó, a drive across a lunar landscape leads to the lighthouse at **Cap de Favàritx**. If you park just before the gate to the lighthouse and climb up the rocks behind you, you'll see a couple of the eight beaches that are just waiting for scramblers like yourself to grace their sands.

On the north coast, the picturesque town of **Fornells** is on a large bay that is popular with windsurfers. Further west at the beach of Binimella, you can continue (on foot) to the unspoilt Cala Pregonda.

North of Ciutadella is **La Vall**, another stretch of untouched beach backed by a private nature park (600 ptas entry per car). On the south coast, there are two good beaches either side of the resort of Santa Galdana – Cala Mitjana to the east, and Macarella to the west.

Menorca's beaches aren't its only attractions. The interior of the island is liberally sprinkled with reminders of its rich and ancient heritage. Pick up a copy of the tourist office's excellent *Archaeological Guide to Minorca*.

Places to Stay
The only **camping ground** is near the beach of Cala Galdana, 10 km south of Ferreries. It is only open in summer.

Maó and Ciutadella both have a handful of good budget options. In Maó at Carrer de la Infanta 19, *Hostal Orsi* (☎ 36 47 51) is owned by a young English couple who are a mine of information about the island. With singles/doubles/triples at 2200/3800/5400 ptas, it is highly recommended. *Hostal La Isla* (☎ 36 64 92), Carrer de Santa Catalina 4, has excellent rooms with bath at 2000/4000 ptas.

In Ciutadella at Carrer de Sant Isidre 33, *Hostal Oasis* (☎ 38 21 97) is set around a spacious courtyard and has its own Italian restaurant; rooms with bath are 2500/4300 ptas. *Hotel Geminis* (☎ 38 58 96), Carrer Josepa Rossinyol 4, is a friendly and stylish two-star with excellent rooms for 3500/6500 ptas.

In Fornells, *Hostal La Palma* (☎ 37 66 34), Plaça S'Algaret 3, has singles/doubles from 3000/5750 ptas.

Places to Eat
In Maó, the *American Bar* in Plaça Reial has a limited but tasty menú for 950 ptas. *La Dolce Vita*, an Italian bistro at Carrer de Sant Roc 25, has great home-made bread, pasta, fresh salads, pizza, and a menú for 1000 ptas. Maó's waterfront road, Andén de Levante, is lined with restaurants with outdoor terraces. The excellent *Roma*, at No 295, has pizzas and pastas from 700 ptas and a menú for 1100 ptas.

Ciutadella's port is also lined with restaurants, and you won't have any trouble finding somewhere to eat. After dinner, check out *Sa Clau*, a hip little jazz and blues bar set in the old city walls.

Getting Around
From the airport, a taxi into Maó costs around 1200 ptas – there are no buses.

TMSA (☎ 36 03 61) runs six buses a day between Maó and Ciutadella, with connections to the major resorts on the south coast. In summer there are also daily bus services to most of the coastal towns from both Maó and Ciutadella.

If you're planning to hire a car, rates vary seasonally (from around 3500 to 7000 ptas a day) – during summer, minimum hire periods apply. Places worth trying include Ibercars (☎ 36 42 08), GB International (☎ 36 24 32) and Autos Confort (☎ 36 94 70). In Maó, Hostal Orsi rents mountain bikes (800 ptas a day). Motos Rayda (☎ 35 47 86) also rents

bikes as well as a range of scooters (1500 to 2500 ptas a day).

Valencia & Murcia

Though perhaps best known for the package resorts of the Costa Blanca, this region also includes Spain's lively third city, Valencia, and a fairy-tale castle at Morella.

VALENCIA
Valencia comes as a pleasant surprise to many. Home to paella and, they claim, the Holy Grail, it is also blessed with great weather and Las Fallas (in March), one of the wildest parties in the country.

Orientation
Plaza del Ayuntamiento marks the centre of Valencia. Most points of interest lie to the north of the train station and are generally within easy walking distance. The Río Turia cuts the central region of the city from the northern and eastern suburbs. This once mighty river is now almost dry, and has been turned into a city-length park, the Jardines del Turia.

Many Valencian streets now have signs in Catalan as well as the Spanish used in this section. You'll often find Catalan and Spanish signs at opposite ends – or sides – of the street.

Information
Valencia's main tourist office (☎ 351 04 17) on Plaza del Ayuntamiento is open weekdays from 8.30 am to 2.15 pm and from 4.15 to 6.15 pm, and Saturday from 9.15 am to 12.45 pm. There's a regional tourist office (☎ 352 85 73) at the train station, open weekdays from 9 am to 6.30 pm.

The post office is on Plaza del Ayuntamiento, and there's a telephone centre at the train station. Valencia's telephone code is ☎ 96.

A good selection of English-language novels is available at the English Book Centre at Calle Pascual y Genis 16. There is a laundrette, Lavandería El Mercat, at Plaza del Mercado 12.

Things to See & Do

Valencia's **Museo de Bellas Artes**, north across the river on Calle San Pio V, ranks among the very best museums in the country. It contains a beautiful collection including works by El Greco, Goya, Velázquez and a number of Valencian impressionists. It opens Tuesday to Saturday between 9 am and 2 pm and 4 and 6 pm, and Sunday from 9 am to 2 pm; entry is free. Another museum with works by El Greco is the **Real Colegio del Patriarca** on Plaza del Patriarca (open daily 11 am to 1.30 pm; entry 100 ptas). The **Instituto Valenciano Arte Moderno (IVAM)**, north-west of the centre at Calle Guillem de Castro 118, houses an impressive collection of 20th-century Spanish art (open Tuesday to Sunday from 11 am to 6 pm; entry 350 ptas).

Valencia's **catedral** is also worth a visit. Climb to the top of the tower for a great view of the sprawling city. The cathedral's museum also claims to be home to the Holy Grail (Santo Cáliz), and contains works by Goya.

The baroque **Palacio de Marqués de dos Aguas**, on Calle Poeta Querol, is fronted by an extravagantly sculpted façade and houses the **Museo Nacional de Cerámica**. It was closed for renovations at the time of writing but should be open by the time you read this.

Valencia has OK city beaches east of the centre, but a better bet is to take a bus 10 km south to the **Playas del Saler**.

Special Events

Valencia's Las Fallas de San José is one of Spain's most unique festivals, an exuberant and anarchic blend of fireworks, music, festive bonfires *(fallas)* and all-night partying. If you're in Spain between 12 and 19 March, don't miss it.

Places to Stay

The nearest camping ground, *Camping del Saler* (☎ 183 00 23), is on the coast 10 km south of Valencia. There is an HI hostel, *Albergue La Paz* (☎ 369 01 52), three km east of the centre at Avenida del Puerto 69 (open July to mid-September).

Central Valencia's accommodation zones are distinctively different. A few dodgy hostales cluster around the train station but there are better options north of the mercado central, which puts you close to Valencia's best nightlife (and, unfortunately, the red-light district). *Hospedería del Pilar* (☎ 391 66 00), Plaza del Mercado 19, has clean and bright singles/doubles at 1300/2400 ptas (1900/3400 ptas with bath). At Calle de la Carda 11, the old *Hostal El Rincón* (☎ 391 79 98) has similar prices. *Hostal El Cid* (☎ 392 23 23), Calle Cerrajeros 13, charges 1400/2700 ptas, or 3000/3700 ptas for doubles with shower/bath.

The areas around and east of Plaza del Ayuntamiento are more up-market. At Calle Salva 12, *Pensión Paris* (☎ 352 67 66) has spotless singles/doubles/triples at 2000/3000/4500 ptas (doubles with shower 3600 ptas). The stylish *Hostal Comedias* (☎ 394 1692), Calle de las Comedias 19, has excellent rooms with bath at 2500/5000 ptas. *Hostal Moratín* (☎ 352 12 20), Calle Moratín 15, has spacious rooms for 2200/3750 ptas, while nearby at Calle Barcelonina 1, *Hotel Londres* (☎ 351 22 44) has well-worn but cosy rooms with TV, phone and bath for 4400/7600 ptas (3750/6500 ptas on weekends).

Places to Eat

The *mercado central* is on Plaza del Mercado. Across the road, *Café del Mercat* has tasty tapas, a lunchtime menú for 1200 ptas and a dinner menú for 1800 ptas. At Calle En Llop 2, *Bar Cafetería Olimpya* has an excellent menú for 950 ptas; they also do pretty good salads, breakfasts and tapas.

Restaurante El Generalife, just off Plaza de la Virgen at Calle Caballeros 5, has a menú for around 1000 ptas that often includes a Valencian paella. *Café de las Horas*, Conde de Almodóvar 1, is a wonderful Spanish-style tearoom serving up sandwiches, salads and cakes – very soothing. Across the road from here is the popular subterranean *Las Cuevas* restaurant. For a splurge, you can't go wrong at *Restaurante Nuevo Don Ramón*, Plaza Rodrigo Botet 4, with a weekday lunch menú for 1100 ptas and main courses in the 1000 to 2200 ptas range.

Entertainment

Valencia's 'what's on' guides, *Que y Donde* and *Turia*, are both available from newsstands. On Plaza Ayuntamiento, *Filmoteca* (☎ 351 23 36) screens classic and art-house films in their original language (200 ptas entry!).

Finnigan's, an Irish pub on Plaza de la

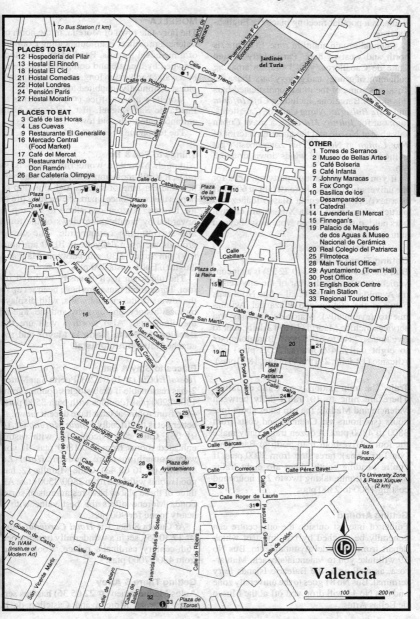

PLACES TO STAY
12 Hospedería del Pilar
13 Hostal El Rincón
18 Hostal El Cid
21 Hostal Comedias
22 Hotel Londres
24 Pensión Paris
27 Hostal Moratín

PLACES TO EAT
3 Café de las Horas
4 Las Cuevas
9 Restaurante El Generalife
16 Mercado Central (Food Market)
17 Café del Mercat
23 Restaurante Nuevo Don Ramón
26 Bar Cafetería Olimpya

OTHER
1 Torres de Serranos
2 Museo de Bellas Artes
5 Café Bolsería
6 Café Infanta
7 Johnny Maracas
8 Fox Congo
10 Basílica de los Desamparados
11 Catedral
14 Lavendería El Mercat
15 Finnegan's
19 Palacio de Marqués de dos Aguas & Museo Nacional de Cerámica
20 Real Colegio del Patriarca
25 Filmoteca
28 Main Tourist Office
29 Ayuntamiento (Town Hall)
30 Post Office
31 English Book Centre
32 Train Station
33 Regional Tourist Office

Valencia

0   100   200 m

Reina, is a popular meeting place for English-speakers.

Valencia's main nightlife zone, El Carme, is north and west of here. Particularly around Calle de Caballeros, you'll find an amazing collection of grungy and groovy bars. Plaza del Tosal has some of the most sophisticated bars this side of Barcelona, including *Café Infanta* and *Cafe Bolseria*. Along Calle de Caballeros, look out for *Johnny Maracas*, a suave Cuban salsa bar at No 39, and the amazing interior of *Fox Congo* at No 35. This zone doesn't get going until 11 pm, and winds down around 3 am.

If you want to continue partying, head for the university zone two km east (about 600 ptas in a taxi). Along Avenida Blasco Ibáñez and particularly around Plaza Xuquer are enough bars and discos to keep you busy beyond sunrise.

Getting There & Away
Bus The bus station (☎ 349 72 22) is an inconvenient two km north-west of the city centre on Avenida Menéndez Pidal – bus No 8 runs between the station and Plaza del Ayuntamiento (eventually). Major destinations and services include Madrid (10 to 12 daily, four to five hours, 2845 to 3145 ptas), Barcelona (six to eight daily, 4½ hours, 2650 ptas) and Alicante (12 daily, 2¼ to 4½ hours, 1890 ptas).

Train The train station is on Calle de Játiva. There are nine to 10 trains daily between Valencia and Madrid; the trip takes about four hours (six hours via Cuenca) and costs from 3800 to 4800 ptas. A dozen trains daily make the four to five-hour haul north to Barcelona (via Tarragona); fares start from 3000 ptas. If you're heading south, there are eight trains daily to Alicante, taking two to 2½ hours and costing 1800 to 2300 ptas.

Getting Around
Points of interest outside the city centre can generally be reached by bus, most of which depart from Plaza del Ayuntamiento. Bus No 19 will take you to Valencia's beach, Malvarrosa, as well as to the Balearic Islands ferry terminal. Bus No 81 goes to the university zone and bus No 11 will drop you off at the Museo de Bellas Artes.

MORELLA
The fairy-tale town of Morella, in the north of Valencia province, is an outstanding example of a medieval fortress. Perched on a hill top, crowned by a castle and completely enclosed by a wall over two km long, it is one of Spain's oldest continually inhabited towns.

Morella's tourist office (☎ 17 30 32) is at Puerta de San Miguel, just inside the main entrance gate to the old town.

The telephone code is ☎ 964.

Things to See & Do
Although Morella's wonderful castle is in ruins, it is still most imposing. You can almost hear the clashing of swords and clip-clop of horses that were once a part of everyday life in the fortress. A strenuous climb to the top is rewarded by breathtaking views of the town and surrounding countryside. The castle grounds are open daily from 10.30 am until 6.30 pm (until 7.30 pm between May and August). Entry costs 200 ptas.

The old town itself is easily explored on foot. Three small museums have been set up in the towers of the ancient walls, with displays on local history, photography and the 'age of the dinosaurs'. Also worth a visit are the **Basílica de Santa María la Mayor** and the attached **Museo Arciprestal**.

Places to Stay & Eat
Hostal El Cid (☎ 16 01 25), Puerta San Mateo 2, has reasonable if drab singles/doubles from 1300/2200 ptas (doubles with bath 3500 ptas) – the front rooms at least have decent views. A better bet is the friendly *Fonda Moreno* (☎ 16 01 05), Calle San Nicolás 12, with rustic, unheated rooms from 950/1800 ptas. If you want something more modern, *Hotel La Muralla* (☎ 16 02 43), Calle Muralla 12, has good rooms with bath from 2800/3500 ptas. All three of these places have restaurants of sorts; Fonda Moreno offers the best value with a hearty menú for 900 ptas.

At Cuesta Suñer 1 is *Hotel Cardenal Ram* (☎ 17 30 85), set in a wonderfully transformed 16th-century cardinal's palace. Rooms start from 4300/7000 ptas.

Getting There & Away
Autos Mediterraneo (☎ 22 05 36) has bus services between Morella and Castellón de la

Plana (daily, 1015 ptas) and Vinaròz (Monday to Saturday, 710 ptas), both on the coast north of Valencia, as well as to Alcañiz in Aragón (Monday, Wednesday and Thursday; 2000 ptas).

If you are driving to Morella in winter, check the weather forecast first, as the town is sometimes snowed in for days.

THE COSTA BLANCA

Alicante and the surrounding coastal area, the Costa Blanca, is one of Europe's most heavily touristed regions. Who hasn't heard of nightmares such as Benidorm and Torrevieja? If you want to find a secluded beach in midsummer, you should keep well away from here. If, however, you are looking for a lively social life, good beaches and a suntan...

The telephone code for the Costa Blanca is ☎ 96.

Alicante

Alicante is a surprisingly refreshing town with wide boulevards, long white sandy beaches and a number of other attractions.

The main tourist office (☎ 520 00 00) is at Explanada de España 2; there's another tourist office at the bus station on Calle Portugal.

Things to See & Do The most obvious of Alicante's attractions is the **Castillo de Santa Bárbara**, a 16th-century fortress overlooking the city. There is a lift shaft deep inside the mountain which will take you right to the castle (200 ptas return) – the lift entrance is opposite Playa del Postiguet. The castle opens daily from 10 am to 8 pm (9 am to 7 pm from October to March); entry is free.

The **Colección de Arte de Siglo XX** on Plaza Santa María houses an excellent collection of modern art including a handful of works by Dalí, Miró and Picasso. It opens daily from 10.30 am to 1.30 pm and 6 to 9 pm (but from October to April from 10 am to 1 pm and 5 to 8 pm) except for Monday, Sunday afternoon and public holidays. Entry is free.

Kontiki (☎ 521 63 96) runs boat trips most days to the popular **Isla de Tabarca** south of Alicante. The island has quiet beaches and good snorkelling, plus a small hotel. Return fares are 1500 ptas.

Playa del Postiguet is Alicante's city beach, but you are better off heading north to the cleaner and less-crowded beaches of San Juan or Campello.

Places to Stay At Calle Monges 2, the outstanding *Pensión Les Monges* (☎ 521 50 46) is more like a boutique hotel than a pensión. Its eight rooms range from 1800/3400 ptas to 2600/4200 ptas with bath – book ahead. At Calle Villavieja 8, *Pensión La Milagrosa* (☎ 521 69 18) has clean and bright rooms and a small guest kitchen; it charges 1200 to 1500 ptas per person. At Calle Mayor 5, *Hostal Mayor* (☎ 520 13 83) has singles/doubles/ triples with bath for 2200/4000/5700 ptas. Opposite the bus station at Calle Portugal 26, *Hostal Portugal* (☎ 592 92 44) charges 2000/3000 ptas, or 3000/3800 ptas with bath.

The three-star *Hotel Palas* (☎ 520 93 09), Plaza Puerta del Mar, is a rambling, semigrand hotel with a weird collection of art works, furniture and mirrors. Rooms with mod cons (and a few odd ones) cost 5240/8425 ptas.

Places to Eat The *Restaurante Ciudad Imperial*, Calle de Gravina 8, has tasty Chinese tucker, a budget menú at 500 ptas and banquet menús from 695 to 950 ptas. At Calle Maldonado 25, *Restaurante El Canario* is a no-frills local eatery with a hearty menú for 850 ptas. *Cafetería Capri*, Calle San Ildefonso 6, has 22 different platos combinados costing from 600 to 1400 ptas and a menú for 925 ptas. *Restaurante El Refugio*, at Calle Rafael Altamira 19, has menús from 1200 to 2400 ptas.

You can try local seafood specialties at the stylish *Boutique del Mar* at Calle San Fernando 16, where main courses range from 750 to 1500 ptas and the menú costs 1500 ptas.

Restaurante Mixto Vegetariano on Plaza Santa María is a basic little place doing reasonable vegetarian or carnivorous menús for 850 ptas

Entertainment Alicante's El Barrio nightlife zone clusters around the cathedral – look out for the heavenly (and very weird) *Celestial Copas*, *La Naya*, *Potato-Bar Cafe*, and *Jamboree Bar*. Down on Explanada de España, the very cool *Cool* has live salsa, jazz and blues bands.

SPAIN

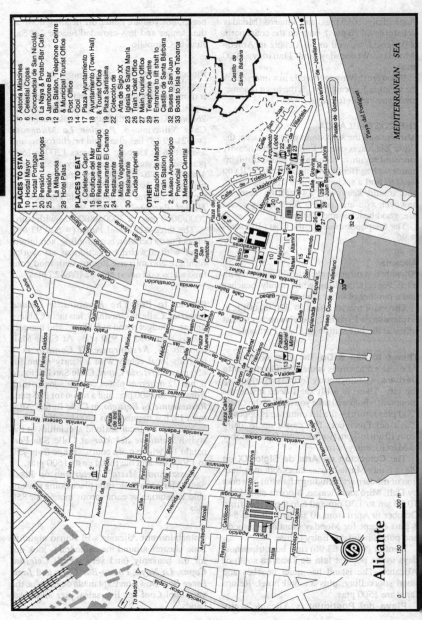

PLACES TO STAY
10 Hostal Mayor
11 Hostal Portugal
20 Pensión Les Monges
25 Pensión
      La Milagrosa
28 Hotel Palas

PLACES TO EAT
4   Cafetería Capri
15 Boutique del Mar
16 Restaurante El Refugio
21 Restaurante El Canario
24 Restaurante
      Mixto Vegetariano
30 Restaurante
      Ciudad Imperial

OTHER
1   Estación de Madrid
      (Train Station)
2   Museo Arqueológico
      Provincial
3   Mercado Central

5   Astoria Minicines
6   Celestial Copas
7   Concatedral de San Nicolás
8   La Naya & Potato-Bar Cafe
9   Jamboree Bar
12 Bus Station, Telephone Centre
      & Municipal Tourist Office
13 Post Office
14 Cool
17 Plaza Ayuntamiento
18 Ayuntamiento (Town Hall)
      & Tourist Office
19 Plaza Santísima
22 Colección de
      Arte de Siglo XX
23 Iglesia de Santa María
26 Train Ticket Office
27 Main Tourist Office
29 Telephone Centre
31 Entrance to lift shaft to
      Castillo de Santa Bárbara
32 Buses to San Juan
33 Boats to Isla de Tabarca

Alicante

Getting There & Away Alicante is the gateway to the Costa Blanca; the airport is 12 km west of the town centre.

There are daily services from the bus station (☎ 513 07 00) on Calle Portugal to Almería (2500 ptas), Granada (3090 ptas), Valencia (1890 ptas), Barcelona (4300 ptas), Madrid (2950 ptas) and the towns along the Costa Blanca.

The train station (☎ 521 02 02) is on Avenida Salamanca. Services include Madrid (10 daily, 3500 to 4500 ptas), Valencia (eight daily, 1800 to 2300 ptas) and Barcelona (three daily, 3500 to 5000 ptas).

Jávea

Jávea (Xábia), 10 km south-east of the port of Denia, is worth a visit early in the season, when the weather has started to improve but the masses haven't arrived yet. This laid-back place is in three parts: the old town (three km inland), the port and the beach zone of El Arenal, which is lined with pleasant bar-restaurants that stay open late during summer. If you have wheels, you might try to get to **Cabo La Nao**, known for its spectacular views, or **Granadella**, with its small, uncrowded beach – both are a few km to the south of Jávea.

Camping El Naranjal (☎ 579 29 89) is about 10 minutes walk from El Arenal. The port area is very pleasant and has some reasonably priced pensiones: *Fonda del Mar* (☎ 579 01 17) at Calle Cristo del Mar 12 has singles/doubles for 2000/4000 ptas, and a good restaurant with a menú for 1300 ptas. At Avenida de la Marina Española 8, *Hostal La Marina* (☎ 579 31 39) is run by an amiable Scottish family and has good rooms from 2000/3000 to 4500/5500 ptas with bath and sea views. In their restaurant you can try Valencian paella, or maybe the haggis?

Calpe

One of the Costa's more pleasant seaside towns, Calpe (22 km north-east of Benidorm) is dominated by the Gibraltaresque **Peñon de Ifach**, a towering monolith that juts out into the sea. The climb to the 332-metre-high summit is especially popular – while you're up there you can choose which of Calpe's two long sandy beaches to grace with your presence later in the day.

There are a couple of good places to bed down. *Pensión Centrica* (☎ 583 55 28) on Plaza de Ilfach has cosy, pretty rooms for 1600 ptas per person, while a stone's throw from the beachfront, *Hostal Crespo* (☎ 583 39 31) at Calle La Pinta 1 has doubles (some with sea views) ranging from 2500 to 4000 ptas.

Altea

Altea's beaches may be a blend of pebbles, rocks and sand, but it beats Benidorm hands down when it comes to character (which, admittedly, isn't saying much). With what's left of the old town perched on a hill top overlooking the sea, Altea (11 km north-east of Benidorm) is a good place to spend a few days relaxing away from the nearby hustle and bustle. The tourist office (☎ 584 41 14) is at Calle San Pedro 9.

Hotel San Miguel (☎ 584 04 00), on the waterfront at Calle La Mar 65, has pleasant rooms with bath for 3500/6000 ptas (plus IVA). The seafood restaurant downstairs has a good menú for 1650 ptas.

Benidorm

Infamous Benidorm supposedly represents all that is bad about tourism in Spain. If you're thinking about coming out of sheer curiosity – can it really be that bad? – allow us to save you the trip. It's worse – much, much worse than you could possibly imagine. Five km of white sandy beaches backed by a relentless jungle of concrete high-rise; streets overwhelmed with tourists toting tacky souvenirs and plastic beach toys; slabs of pasty-white flesh committing outrageous sins in the name of summer fashion...

Benidorm's tourist office (☎ 585 32 24) is near the waterfront in the old town at Calle Martínez Alejos 16. Almost everyone here is on some kind of package deal, but if you need to stay there are a few hostales in the old town. *Hostal Calpi* (☎ 585 78 48), Costera del Barco 6, has rooms with bath for 2000 to 3000 ptas per person. *Hostal La Santa Faz* (☎ 585 40 63), Calle Santa Faz 18, has dim rooms with bath for 3250/6000 ptas.

Santa Pola

Apart from being yet another beachfront concrete jungle, Santa Pola (20 km south of Alcante) is the jumping-off point for the Isla de Tabarca. The town's tourist office (☎ 669 22 76) is on Plaza de la Diputación.

Beaches in and around Santa Pola worth visiting include Gran Playa and Playa Lisa. Also try the beaches in Santa Pola del Este. In the centre of town on Plaza de la Glorieta, a well-preserved, 16th-century **fortress** stands besieged by 20th-century high-rise architecture. Inside there's a small **aquarium** and **archaeological museum** (100 ptas).

Camping Bahía (☎ 541 10 12) is about 15 minutes walk from the town centre at Calle Partida Rural de Valverde Bajo 9. The friendly *Hostal Chez Michel* (☎ 541 18 42), Calle Felipe 11, has refurbished rooms with bath at 2625/4000 ptas.

Torrevieja
A heavily developed but not completely unpleasant coastal resort, Torrevieja has good beaches and a lively nightlife, but be warned that you will probably not get to know many, if any, Spaniards here. The tourist office (☎ 571 59 36) is centrally located on Plaza Capdepont.

The best budget bet is *Hostal Fernández* (☎ 571 00 09), well located at Calle Ramón Gallud 16; rooms with bath are 3000/5000 ptas. Near the bus station at Calle Zoa 53, *Hotel Cano* (☎ 670 09 58) has modern rooms with bath at 3500/5000 ptas. At Avenida Dr Gregorio Marañón 22, *Hostal Reina* (☎ 670 19 04) has cheap rooms with marshmallow beds for 1800/3000 ptas.

MURCIA
The Murcian coast beyond Cartagena has some of the least developed beaches on the Mediterranean coast, and towns in the interior, such as Lorca, have a flavour unique to this part of the country.

The best known and most touristed beaches in the area are in the so-called Mar Menor, just south of the Valencia-Murcia border. You are better off passing them by and heading on to **Mazarrón** to the west of Cartagena, or even further south-west to the golden beaches at **Águilas**. Both Mazarrón and Águilas have camping grounds and it is possible to swim there (without dying of hypothermia) as early as the beginning of March.

Andalucía

The stronghold of the Moors for nearly eight centuries and the pride of the Christians for many more thereafter, Andalucía is perhaps Spain's most exotic and colourful region. The home of flamenco, bullfighting and some of the country's most brilliant fiestas, it's peppered with reminders of the Moorish past – from treasured monuments like the Alhambra in Granada and the mezquita in Córdoba to the white villages clinging to its hillsides. The regional capital, Seville, is one of Spain's most exciting cities.

Away from the main cities and resorts, Andalucía is surprisingly untouristed and makes for some great exploring. Its scenery ranges from semideserts to lush river valleys, from gorge-ridden mountains to the longest coastline of any Spanish region. The coast stretches from the quiet beaches of Cabo de Gata, past the mayhem of the Costa del Sol, to come within 14 km of Africa at the windsurfing centre Tarifa, before opening up to the Atlantic Ocean on the Costa de la Luz, where long beaches sweep by Cádiz and the famous wetlands of Doñana National Park to the Portuguese border.

SEVILLE
Seville (Sevilla) is one of the most exciting cities in Spain, with an atmosphere both relaxed and festive, a rich history, some great monuments, beautiful parks and gardens, and a large, lively student population. Located on the Río Guadalquivir, which is navigable to the Atlantic Ocean, Seville was once the leading Muslim city in Spain. It reached its height later, in the 16th and 17th centuries, when it held a monopoly on Spanish trade with the Americas. Expo '92, in 1992, once again plunged Seville into the international limelight.

Seville is an expensive place, so it's worth planning your visit carefully. In high summer, the city is stiflingly hot and not a fun place to be. It's best during its unforgettable spring festivals, though rooms then (if you can get one) are expensive.

Information
The main tourist office at Avenida de la Constitución 21 (☎ 422 14 04) is open week-

days from 9 am to 7 pm and Saturday from 10 am to 2 pm. It's often extremely busy, so you might try the other offices – at Paseo de las Delicias 9 (☎ 423 44 65), open Monday to Friday from 8.30 am to 6.30 pm, and on Calle Arjona (☎ 421 36 30), open weekdays from 9 am to 8.45 pm, and weekend mornings. There's also a tourist office (☎ 444 91 28) at the airport.

Seville's telephone code is ☎ 95.

Librería Beta, at Avenida de la Constitución 9 and 27, has guidebooks and novels in English. Tintorería Roma at Calle Castelar 4 will wash, dry and fold a load of washing for 1000 ptas.

Things to See & Do
Cathedral & Giralda Seville's immense cathedral – the biggest in the world, says the *Guinness Book of Records* – was built on the site of Moorish Seville's main mosque between 1401 and 1506. The structure is primarily Gothic, though most of the internal decoration is in later styles. The adjoining tower, La Giralda, was the mosque's minaret and dates from the 12th century. The climb up La Giralda affords great views and is quite easy as there's a ramp (not stairs) all the way up inside. One highlight of the cathedral's lavish interior is Christopher Columbus' supposed tomb inside the south door (no-one's 100% sure that his remains didn't get mislaid somewhere in the Caribbean). The four crowned sepulchre-bearers represent the four kingdoms of Spain at the time of Columbus' sailing. Entry to the cathedral and Giralda is 600 ptas (students and pensioners 200 ptas). Opening hours for both are Monday to Saturday from 11 am to 5 pm, and Sunday from 2 to 4 pm. The Giralda alone is open on Sunday from 10.30 am to 1.30 pm.

Alcázar Seville's alcázar, a residence of Muslim and Christian royalty for many centuries, was founded in the 10th century as a Moorish fortress. It has been adapted by Seville's rulers in almost every century since, which makes it a mish-mash of styles, but adds to its fascination. The highlights are the **Palacio de Don Pedro**, exquisitely decorated by Moorish artisans for the Castilian king Pedro the Cruel in the 1360s, and the large, immaculately tended **gardens** – the perfect place to ease your body and brain after some intensive sightseeing. The alcázar is open Tuesday to Saturday from 10.30 am to 5 pm, and Sundays and holidays from 10 am to 1 pm. Entry is 600 ptas (students free).

Walks & Parks If you're not staying in the **Barrio de Santa Cruz**, the old Jewish quarter immediately east of the cathedral and alcázar, make sure you take a stroll among its quaint streets and lovely plant-bedecked plazas. Another enjoyable walk is along the **riverbank**, where the 13th-century Torre del Oro contains a small, crowded maritime museum.

South of the centre, large **Parque de María Luisa** is a very pleasant place to get lost in, with its maze of paths, tall trees, flowers, fountains and shaded lawns.

Museums The **Archivo de Indias**, beside the cathedral, houses over 40 million documents dating from 1492 through to the decolonisation of the Americas. Most can only be consulted with special permission, but there are rotating displays of fascinating maps and documents. Entry is free, and it's open Monday to Friday from 10 am to 1 pm.

The **Museo de Bellas Artes**, on Calle Alfonso XII, has an outstanding, beautifully housed collection of Spanish art, focusing on Seville artists like Murillo and Zurbarán. It's open Tuesday to Sunday from 9 am to 3 pm (250 ptas, free for EU citizens).

Expo '92 Site The Expo '92 site is west of the Guadalquivir across the Puente del Cachorro. A **Parque de Atracciones** (adventure park) is due to reopen here in 1997. Two other areas are open to visitors. One is **Puerta de Triana**, with exhibits on sea exploration in the Pabellón de la Navegación (400 ptas). The other is the **Conjunto Monumental de La Cartuja**, a 15th-century monastery where Columbus used to stay, later converted into a china factory (300 ptas). Both sites are closed Monday. You can wander round the rest of the Expo grounds and admire the pavilions, but it's rather lifeless.

Special Events
The first of Seville's two great festivals is Semana Santa, held during the week leading up to Easter Sunday. Throughout the week,

SPAIN

SPAIN

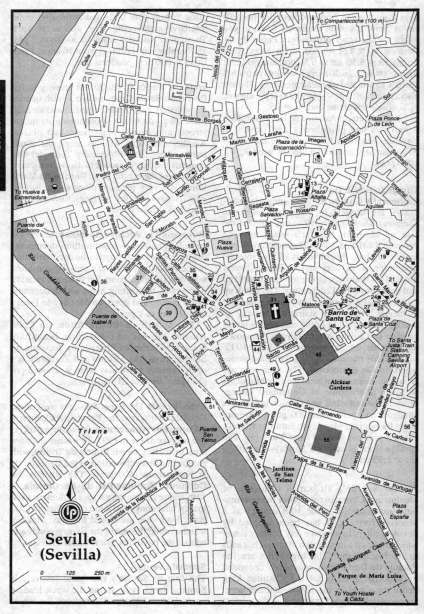

To Compartecoche (100 m)

Calle del Torno
Calle del Torno
Cisneros
Teniente Borges
Calle Alfonso XII
Monsalves
San Eloy
Murillo
O'Donnell
Pedro del Toro
Canalejas
San Pablo
Moratin
Reyes Católicos
Zaragoza
Santas Patronas
Calle Castelar
Calle de Adriano
Antonia Díaz
C. de Temprado
Dos de Mayo
Santander
Almirante Lobo
Calle Betis
Puente San Telmo

Jesús del Gran Poder
Martín Villa
Laraña
J Gestoso
Plaza de la Encarnación
Imagen
Apodaca
Velázquez
Cerrajería
Cuna
Sagasta
Plaza Salvador
Alvarez Quintero
Hernando Colón
Argote de Molina
Plaza Nueva
G Vinuesa
Avenida de la Constitución
Santo Tomás
Mateos
Gago
Santa María La Blanca
Levies
Virgenes
Aguilas
Sol
Plaza Ponce de León
Santiago
Imperial
Plaza de la Imagen
Plaza Alfalfa
Cta Rosario

Plaza Salvador

Barrio de Santa Cruz
Plaza de Santa Cruz

To Santa Justa Train Station, Camping Sevilla & Airport

Alcázar Gardens

Calle San Fernando
Av Sanjurjo
Avenida de Roma
Calle de Menéndez Pelayo
Avenida del Cid
Av Carlos V

Río Guadalquivir
Puente del Cachorro
Puente de Isabel II
Paseo de Cristóbal Colón

Triana

Avenida de la República Argentina
Asunción
Puente San Telmo

Jardines de San Telmo
Paseo de las Delicias

Río Guadalquivir

Palos de la Frontera
Avenida de Portugal
Plaza de España
Avenida de Isabel la Católica
Avenida María Luisa
Avenida del Perú

Parque de María Luisa

Avenida Rodríguez Caso

To Youth Hostel & Cádiz

To Huelva & Extremadura

Seville (Sevilla)

0   125   250 m

PLACES TO STAY		25	Restaurant El Cordobés	36	Tourist Office
2	Hostal Pino	28	Pizzeria San Marco	38	Arena
6	Hostal Alfonso XII	29	Bodega Santa Cruz	39	Plaza de Toros de la
7	Hostal Lis II	33	Bodega Paco Góngora		Maestranza (Bull-
10	Hostal Lis	37	Mercado del Arenal		ring)
17	Hostal Sierpes	46	El Rincon de Pepe	40	Habana
18	Hostal Sánchez	54	Pizzeria San Marco	41	A3
	Sabariego			42	Bar Populus
20	Huéspedes La	**OTHER**		44	Main Post Office
	Montoreña	1	Expo 92 Site	45	Archivo de Indias
21	Hostal Bienvenido	4	Museo de Bellas Artes	47	Los Gallos
23	Pensión Fabiola	5	Plaza de Armas Bus	48	Alcazar
24	Pensión San Pancracio		Station	49	Main Tourist Office
26	Pensión Cruces El	11	El Mundo	50	Librería Beta
	Patio	12	Sopa de Ganso	51	Torre del Oro & Museo
27	Hostal Toledo	13	Bare Nostrum		Marítimo
35	Hotel La Rábida	14	Lamentable	52	Alambique, Mui d'Aqui
43	Hotel Simón	16	Bestiario		& Big Ben
		16	American Express	53	SVQ
PLACES TO EAT		19	La Carbonería	55	University
3	Bodegón Alfonso XII	30	La Giralda	56	Prado de San
8	Patio San Eloy	31	Catedral		Sebastián Bus
9	Pizzeria San Marco	32	Librería Beta		Station
22	Cervecería Alta-Mira &	34	Tintorería Roma	57	Tourist Office
	Bar Casa Fernando		(Laundry)		

long processions of religious brotherhoods (*cofradías*), dressed in strange penitents' garb with tall pointed hoods, accompany sacred images through the city, watched by huge crowds. The Feria de Abril, a week in late April, is a kind of release after this solemnity: the festivities involve six days of music, dancing, horse riding and traditional dress on a site in the Los Remedios area west of the river, plus daily bullfights and a general city-wide party.

Places to Stay
The summer prices given here can come down substantially from October to March, but during Semana Santa and the Feria de Abril they can rise by anything up to 200%.

Seville's 200-place HI hostel *Albergue Juvenil Sevilla* (☎ 461 31 50) was closed for renovation but may be open by the time you get there. It's at Calle Isaac Peral 2, about 10 minutes by bus No 34 from opposite the main tourist office.

Barrio de Santa Cruz has a few fairly good-value places to stay. *Hostal Bienvenido* (☎ 441 36 55) at Calle Archeros 14 has singles for 1500 or 1700 ptas, and doubles for 3000 ptas. *Huéspedes La Montoreña* (☎ 441 24 07), Calle San Clemente 12, has clean, simple

singles/doubles at 1500/3000 ptas. *Pensión San Pancracio* (☎ 441 31 04), at Plaza de las Cruces 9, has small singles for 1800 ptas and bigger doubles for 3200 ptas, or 4000 ptas with bath. *Pensión Cruces El Patio* (☎ 422 96 33), Plaza de las Cruces 10, has a few dorm beds at 1200 ptas, singles at 2500 ptas, and doubles at 4000 and 5000 ptas. The friendly *Hostal Toledo* (☎ 421 53 35), Calle Santa Teresa 15, has good singles/doubles with bath for 2500/5000 ptas. *Pensión Fabiola* (☎ 421 83 46) at Calle Fabiola 16 has simple, well-kept rooms from 3000/5500 ptas.

The area north of Plaza Nueva, only 10 minutes walk from all the hustle and bustle, has some good value too. *Hostal Pino* (☎ 421 28 10), Calle Tarifa 6, is one of the cheapest, at 1600/2600 ptas, or 2000/3200 ptas with shower. *Hostal Lis II* (☎ 456 02 28), in a beautiful house at Calle Olavide 5, charges 1700 ptas for singles and 3500 ptas for doubles with toilet. The same family owns *Hostal Lis* (☎ 421 30 88) at Calle Escarpín 10, where singles/doubles with shower are 2000/3500 ptas. The friendly *Hostal Alfonso XII* (☎ 421 15 98) at Calle Monsalves 25 has singles for 2000 ptas and doubles with bath for 4000 ptas.

On Corral del Rey, east of Plaza Nueva, *Hostal Sánchez Sabariego* (☎ 421 44 70) at

No 23 has singles for 2000 ptas and doubles with bath for 4000 ptas. Almost opposite, at No 22, *Hostal Sierpes* (☎ 422 49 48) is a good larger place with a garage space. Singles with bath are 4300 ptas, doubles are 4300 to 6700 ptas. They'll pay your taxi fare from the train or bus station.

Hotel Simón (☎ 422 66 60), at Calle García de Vinuesa 19, in a typical 18th-century Seville house, has very pleasant singles/doubles with bath from 5350/7500 ptas. The impressive *Hotel La Rábida* (☎ 422 09 60), Calle Castelar 24, has rooms with bath at 5600/8825 ptas, and a restaurant.

Places to Eat

In central Seville, Barrio de Santa Cruz is the best area for decent-value eating. The excellent, very popular *Pizzeria San Marco*, in a stylishly refurbished building at Calle Mesón del Moro 6, has pizzas and pasta dishes for 700 to 800 ptas (there are two more branches at Calle de la Cuna 6 and Calle Betis 68). Calle Santa María La Blanca has several good places: at *Cervecería Alta-Mira*, No 6, a media-ración of tortilla Alta-Mira (made with potatoes and vegetables) is almost a full meal for 600 ptas; *Bar Casa Fernando* round the corner has a decent 800-pta lunch menú; *Restaurant El Cordobés* at No 20 is good for breakfasts such as eggs, bacon, bread and coffee for 350 ptas. *Bodega Santa Cruz* on Calle Mateos Gago is a popular bar with a big choice of good-sized tapas for 150 ptas. Near the alcázar, *El Rincón de Pepe* at Calle Gloria 6 has folksy décor and a menú of gazpacho or salad, paella and dessert for 1050 ptas.

West of Avenida de la Constitución, *Bodega Paco Góngora* at Calle Padre Marchena 1 has a huge range of good seafood at decent prices – media-raciones of fish a la plancha (grilled) are mostly 600 ptas. Further north, *Patio San Eloy* at Calle San Eloy 9 is a bright, busy place with lots of good tapas for 115 to 175 ptas. *Bodegón Alfonso XII* at Calle Alfonso XII 33 has deals like a breakfast of bacon, eggs and coffee for 350 ptas.

Mercado del Arenal, on Calle Pastor y Landero, is the only food market in the central area.

Entertainment

Seville's nightlife is among the liveliest in Spain. On fine nights throngs of people block the streets outside popular bars, while teenagers and students just bring their own bottles to mass gathering spots such as the Mercado del Arenal. Seville also has some great music bars, often with dance space. As everywhere in Spain, the real action is on Friday and Saturday nights.

Drinking & Dancing Until about midnight, Plaza Salvador is a popular spot for an open-air drink, with a student crowd and couple of little bars selling carry-out drinks. The east bank of the Guadalquivir is busy into the early hours – in summer it's dotted with temporary bars.

There are some hugely popular bars just north of the cathedral, but the crowds from about midnight around Calle de Adriano, west of Avenida de la Constitución, have to be seen to be believed. Busy music bars on Adriano itself include *A3*, *Habana*, *Bar Populus* and *Arena*. Nearby on Calle García de Vinuesa and Calle Dos de Mayo are some quieter bodegas (traditional wine bars), some with good tapas, that attract a more mature crowd.

Calle Pérez Galdós off Plaza Alfalfa has three lively music bars – *Lamentable*, *Bare Nostrum* and *Sopa de Ganso* which serves vegetarian tapas. It's fairly busy by midnight. Across the river, *Alambique*, *Mui d'Aqui* and *Big Ben*, side by side on Calle Betis two blocks north of the Puente de San Telmo, all play good music and attract an interesting mix of students and travellers.

For serious disco action, try the bakalao frenzy at *Bestiario* on Calle Zaragoza, or the funkier *SQV* at Calle Betis 67. SQV opens until around dawn from Thursday to Saturday and entry is free – though before about 2 am the crowd is *very* young.

Flamenco Seville is Spain's flamenco capital but even here it can be hard to find authentic flamenco unless you're present for the Feria de Abril, or the Bienal de Arte Flamenco festival, held in September and/or October in even-numbered years. Bars which put on fairly regular flamenco, of erratic quality, include *La Carbonería*, Calle Levies 18, and *El Mundo*, Calle Siete Revueltas 5 (usually Tuesday at midnight). There are several tourist-oriented venues with regular shows, and some of these, though hardly spontaneous, are good. The best is *Los Gallos* on Plaza Santa Cruz, with two shows nightly; entry is 3000 ptas.

Spectator Sport

Seville's bullfights are among the best in the country. The season runs from Easter to October, with fights most Sundays about 6 pm, and almost every day during the Feria de Abril and the week or two before it. The bullring is on Paseo de Cristóbal Colón. Tickets start around 2000 ptas.

Getting There & Away

Air Seville airport (☎ 451 06 77) has quite a range of domestic and international flights. Air Europa flies to Barcelona for 13,900 ptas (from 20,900 ptas return).

Bus Buses to Extremadura, Madrid, Portugal and Andalucía west of Seville leave from the Plaza de Armas bus station (☎ 490 80 40). Buses to other parts of Andalucía use the Prado de San Sebastián bus station (☎ 441 71 11).

Daily services include around 10 buses each to Córdoba (two hours, 1200 ptas), Granada (three hours, 2710 ptas), Málaga (three hours, 2245 ptas) and Madrid (six hours, 2680 ptas). To Lisbon there are three direct buses a week (eight hours, 4350 ptas), and daily buses with a transfer at the border (nine hours, 2540 ptas). For the Algarve you need to change buses at Huelva, or Ayamonte on the border.

Train Seville's Santa Justa train station (☎ 454 02 02) is about 1.5 km north-east of the city centre on Avenida Kansas City.

To/from Madrid, there are up to a dozen super-fast AVE trains each day, covering the 471 km in just 2½ hours and costing from 7600 to 9200 ptas in the cheapest class (turista); a couple of Talgos taking 3½ hours for 6700 to 7300 ptas in 2nd class; and the evening Tren Hotel, taking 3¾ hours for 5100 ptas in a seat. Inter-Rail cards are not valid on AVEs; Eurail pass-holders pay 1400 ptas.

Other daily trains include about 20 to Córdoba (43 minutes to 1¾ hours, 875 to 2500 ptas); four to Barcelona (11 to 14 hours, from 6600 ptas); and three each to Granada (4½ hours, 1950 ptas) and Málaga (three hours, 1790 ptas). For Lisbon (16 hours, 6500 ptas), there's one train a day with a change in Cáceres.

Car Pooling Compartecoche (☎ 490 78 52) at Calle González Cuadrado 49 is an intercity car-pooling service. Its service is free to drivers, while passengers pay an agreed transfer rate. Ring them for details.

Getting Around

The airport is about seven km from the centre, off the N-IV Córdoba road. Airport buses (750 ptas) run up to 12 times daily – tourist offices have details.

Bus Nos C1 and C2, across the road from the front of Santa Justa train station, follow a circular route via Avenida de Carlos V, close to Prado de San Sebastián bus station and the city centre, and Plaza de Armas bus station. Bus No C4, south on Calle de Arjona from Plaza de Armas bus station, goes straight to the centre.

GRANADA

From the 13th to 15th centuries, Granada was capital of the last Moorish kingdom in Spain, and the finest city on the peninsula. Today it's home to the greatest Moorish legacy in the country, and one of the most magnificent buildings on the continent – the Alhambra. South-east of the city, the Sierra Nevada mountain range (Spain's highest), and the Alpujarras valleys, with their picturesque, mysterious villages, are well worth exploring if you have time to spare.

Information

Granada's main tourist office (☎ 22 66 88), on Plaza de Mariana Pineda, opens on weekdays from 9.30 or 10.30 am to 1.30 or 2 pm (depending on the season) and from 4.30 to 6.30 or 7 pm, and on Saturday from 10 am to 1 pm. There's another office on Calle Mariana Pineda, open Monday to Friday from 9 am to 7 pm and Saturday from 10 am to 2 pm.

Granada's telephone code is ☎ 958.

Lavandería Duquesa, Calle de la Duquesa 26, will wash and dry a load of clothes for 900 ptas.

Things to See

La Alhambra One of the greatest accomplishments of Islamic art and architecture, the Alhambra is simply breathtaking. Much has

SPAIN

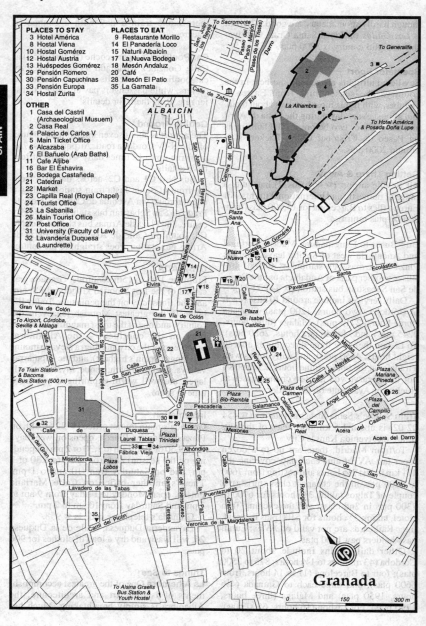

PLACES TO STAY
3 Hotel América
8 Hostal Viena
10 Hostal Gomérez
12 Hostal Austria
14 Huéspedes Gomérez
29 Pensión Romero
30 Pensión Capuchinas
33 Pensión Europa
34 Hostal Zurita

PLACES TO EAT
9 Restaurante Morillo
14 El Panadería Loco
15 Naturii Albaicín
17 La Nueva Bodega
18 Mesón Andaluz
20 Café
28 Mesón El Patio
35 La Garnata

OTHER
1 Casa del Castril (Archaeological Musuem)
2 Casa Real
4 Palacio de Carlos V
5 Main Ticket Office
6 Alcazaba
7 El Bañuelo (Arab Baths)
11 Cafe Aljibe
16 Bar El Eshavira
19 Bodega Castañeda
21 Catedral
22 Market
23 Capilla Real (Royal Chapel)
24 Tourist Office
25 La Sabanilla
26 Main Tourist Office
27 Post Office
31 University (Faculty of Law)
32 Lavandería Duquesa (Laundrette)

Granada

been written about its fortress, palace, patios and gardens, but nothing can really prepare you for what you will see.

The **Alcazaba** is the Alhambra's fortress, dating from the 11th to the 13th centuries. The views of the city from the tops of the towers are great. The **Casa Real** (Royal Palace), built for Granada's rulers in its 14th and 15th-century heyday, is the centrepiece of the Alhambra. The intricacy of the stonework, epitomised by the Patio de los Leones (Patio of the Lions) and Sala de las Dos Hermanas (Hall of the Two Sisters), is stunning. Finally, there is the **Generalife**, the summer palace of the sultans, set in soul-soothing gardens. This is a great spot to relax and contemplate the rest of the Alhambra from afar.

Cuesta de Gomérez leads up to the Alhambra from Plaza Nueva in the city. The complex opens at 9 am, closing at 7.45 pm in summer (5.45 pm on Sunday) and at 6 pm in winter. There are also night-time sessions. Admission is 675 ptas, but free on Sunday. You'll enjoy your visit much more if you can avoid the bus-tour crowds – go first thing in the morning or during siesta. On weekends and holidays and in high summer you'll have to queue a while for your ticket.

Other Attractions Simply wandering around the narrow streets of the **Albaicín** Moorish district, across the river from the Alhambra (not too late at night), or the area around **Plaza Bib-Rambla** is a real pleasure. On your way, stop by the **Casa del Castril** (archaeological museum) and **El Bañuelo** (Arab baths), both on Carrera del Darro in the Albaicín, and the **Capilla Real** (Royal Chapel) on Gran Vía de Colón in which Fernando and Isabel, the Christian conquerors of Granada in 1492, are buried along with their daughter and son-in-law. Next door to the chapel is Granada's **catedral**, which dates in part from the early 16th century. The Gypsy caves of **Sacromonte**, in the north of the city, are another popular attraction.

Places to Stay

Granada's youth hostel, *Albergue Juvenil Granada* (☎ 27 26 38), is near the bus station at Camino de Ronda 171. It charges 1100 ptas per person if you're under 26, 1400 ptas if you're older. An alternative budget option is

the *Posada Doña Lupe* (☎ 22 14 73), on Avenida del Generalife, just above the Alhambra car park, which has plentiful singles/doubles from 1000/1950 ptas including a light breakfast.

Most of Granada's budget accommodation clusters in two areas – on the east side of Plaza Nueva (well placed for the Albaicín and Alhambra) and around Plaza Trinidad. In the first area, *Hostal Gomérez* (☎ 22 44 37), Cuesta de Gomérez 10, is cheap and cheerful with rooms for 1400/2300 ptas. *Huéspedes Gomérez* (☎ 22 63 98), Cuesta de Gomérez 2, is also friendly and even cheaper at 1200/2000 ptas. *Hostal Viena* (☎ 22 18 59), in Calle Hospital de Santa Ana 2 (off Cuesta de Gomérez), has rooms from 1500/3000 ptas and doubles with bath for 3500 ptas. The same owners run *Hostal Austria* (☎ 22 70 75), Cuesta de Gomérez 4, where rooms with bath cost from 2500/3500 ptas.

Hotel América (☎ 22 74 71) is not a budget hotel, but it simply must be mentioned because of its magical position. Yes, you too can have a room within the walls of the Alhambra, if you can afford 6500/11,000 ptas.

Around Plaza de la Trinidad there's plenty of choice. *Pensión Romero* (☎ 26 60 79), Calle Sílleria 1, on the corner of Calle Mesones, has rooms from 1400/2600 ptas. The small *Pensión Capuchinas* (☎ 26 53 94), Calle Capuchinas 2 (2nd floor), has rooms from 1500/2500 ptas, but the proprietors can be picky about who they let in. *Pensión Europa* (☎ 27 87 44), Calle Fábrica Vieja 16, is run by a family and has rooms from 2000/3900 ptas; meals are available. *Hostal Zurita* (☎ 27 50 20), Plaza de la Trinidad 7, is friendly and good value with rooms from 1875/3750 ptas and off-street parking for 1000 ptas a day.

Places to Eat

There are some great deals on food in Granada, and bar flies will be delighted to hear that you often don't pay for tapas in Granada's bars. *La Nueva Bodega* in Calle Cetti Meriém has a menú for 850 ptas, and around the corner on Calle de Elvira, *Mesón Andaluz* has various menús from 950 ptas. There are a few cheapies on Cuesta de Gomérez, heading up to the Alhambra: *Restaurante Morillo* (summer only) at No 20 has 18 menús from 750 to 1400 ptas.

Don't miss the tasty Arabic food at the *Café* on Plaza Nueva – you can eat in or take away. The teterías (Arabic-style tea houses) on Calderería Nueva, a picturesque pedestrian street west of Plaza Nueva, are atmospheric but expensive. *Naturii Albaicín*, Calderería Nueva 10, is a good vegetarian restaurant. A few doors up the street is an excellent wholemeal bakery, *El Panadería Loco*.

Mesón El Patio, Calle Mesones 50, has an outdoor courtyard, cheap bocadillos, reasonably priced main dishes and excellent bread. For late-night snacks, but also open during the day, *La Garnata*, a modern cafeteria at Carril del Picón 22, is a great place for churros and chocolate and has delicious, affordable sandwiches including a very nice BLT.

Entertainment
The highest concentration of nightspots is on and around Calle Pedro Antonio de Alarcón: to get there, walk south on Calle Tablas from Plaza Trinidad. After 11 pm, you can't miss it. Another interesting street is Carrera del Darro and its continuation, known as Paseo de los Tristes, which leads from Plaza Nueva up into the Albaicín.

Bars in the streets west of Plaza Nueva get very lively on weekend nights. *Bodega Castañeda*, on Calle Almireceros, is one of the most famous bars in Granada and an institution among locals and tourists alike.

Granada's oldest bar, *La Sabanilla*, in Calle Tundidores, is showing its age but is worth a visit. Don't miss *Bar El Eshavira*, a basement jazz and flamenco club down a dark alley at Placeta de la Cuna. For great late-night music try *Cafe Aljibe*, above Plaza de Cuchilleros.

In the evening many travellers go to Sacromonte to see flamenco, but it's extremely touristy and a bit of a rip-off.

Getting There & Away
Most buses to other parts of Andalucía and further afield leave from the Alsina Graells bus station (☎ 25 13 58) on Camino de Ronda, 1.5 km south-west of the centre. Long-distance buses (to Madrid, Barcelona etc) are also run by Bacoma, on Avenida Andaluces opposite the train station, 1.5 km south-west of the centre.

Of the two trains daily to Madrid, one takes 9½ hours (3300 ptas), the other takes six hours (4000 ptas). To Seville, there are three trains a day (four hours, from 1950 ptas). For Málaga and Córdoba, you have to change trains in Bobadilla. There's one train daily to Valencia and Barcelona (6300 ptas).

CÓRDOBA
In Roman times Córdoba was the capital of Hispania Ulterior province and then, after a reorganisation, of Baetica province. With the building of the mezquita (mosque) in the 8th century it became the most important Moorish city in Spain and the most splendid city in Europe, a position it held for 200 or so years until the Córdoban Caliphate broke up after the death of its great ruler Al-Mansur in 1002. Thereafter Córdoba was overshadowed by Seville and in the 13th century both cities fell to the Christians in the Reconquista. The legacy of these great civilisations makes Córdoba one of the most interesting and important historical centres in Spain.

Orientation
Córdoba centres on and around the mezquita, which lies near the banks of the Río Guadalquivir. The mezquita is surrounded by the Judería (old Jewish quarter) to its west and the old Muslim quarter to its east, which make up the old town. The commercial centre of modern Córdoba is Plaza de las Tendillas, a few hundred metres north of the mezquita. Further north-west is the train station, on Avenida de América.

Information
There are two tourist offices: the municipal tourist office (☎ 47 20 00 ext 209) on Plaza de Judá Leví, and the provincial tourist office (☎ 47 12 35) on Calle Torrijos, near the entrance to the mezquita. The main post office is on Calle de José Cruz Conde. There are plenty of telephones on Plaza de las Tendillas.

Córdoba's telephone code is ☎ 957.

Things to See & Do
After Granada and Seville, Córdoba seems almost provincial. It is quite a laid-back town and a pleasant place to spend a couple of days just relaxing. Its most important attraction is the **mezquita**. Built by the Emir of Córdoba,

SPAIN

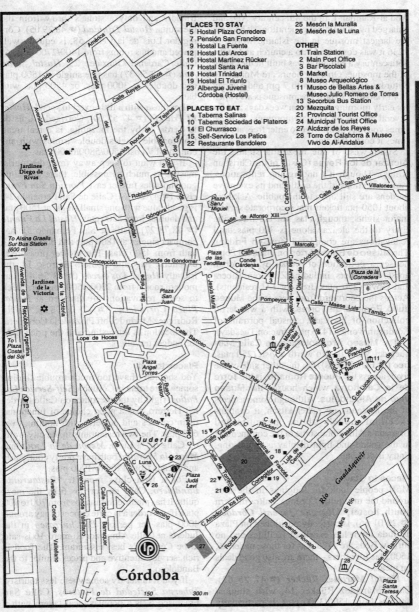

PLACES TO STAY
5 Hostal Plaza Corredera
7 Pensión San Francisco
9 Hostal La Fuente
12 Hostal Los Arcos
16 Hostal Martínez Rücker
17 Hostal Santa Ana
18 Hostal Trinidad
19 Hostal El Triunfo
23 Albergue Juvenil
   Córdoba (Hostel)

PLACES TO EAT
4 Taberna Salinas
10 Taberna Sociedad de Plateros
14 El Churrasco
15 Self-Service Los Patios
22 Restaurante Bandolero

25 Mesón la Muralla
26 Mesón de la Luna

OTHER
1 Train Station
2 Main Post Office
3 Bar Piscolabi
6 Market
8 Museo Arqueológico
11 Museo de Bellas Artes &
   Museo Julio Romero de Torres
13 Secorbus Bus Station
20 Mezquita
21 Provincial Tourist Office
24 Municipal Tourist Office
27 Alcázar de los Reyes
28 Torre de Calahorra & Museo
   Vivo de Al-Andalus

Córdoba

0   150   300 m

Abd al-Rahman I, in the 8th century AD, and enlarged by subsequent generations, it became the largest mosque in the Islamic world. In 1236 it was converted into a church and in the 16th century a cathedral was built in the centre of the mosque. Opening hours are Monday to Saturday from 10.30 am to 7 pm and Sunday from 1.30 to 7.30 pm. The mosque is also open for early morning masses on weekdays and for several masses on Sunday mornings. At these times you may be allowed to enter free; at other times it costs 750 ptas.

South-west of the mezquita stands the **Alcázar de los Reyes** (Castle of the Christian Kings). Though it's undergoing renovations, various sections of the castle and its extensive gardens are still open to the public. Ask here about 1050-pta tickets that incorporate several major sights, though alas not the mezquita. Entry to the alcázar alone is 300 ptas until renovations are completed (free on Friday). The **Museo de Bellas Artes** on Plaza del Potro houses a collection of works by Córdoban artists and others, including Zurbarán, Ribera and Goya (250 ptas, free for EU residents). Across the courtyard from here is the **Museo Julio Romero de Torres**, with a wonderful collection of his dark, sensual portraits of Córdoban women (425 ptas, free on Tuesday).

The **Museo Arqueológico** on Calle Marqués del Villar is also worth a visit (250 ptas, free for EU citizens). On the other side of the river, across the **Puente Romano**, is the **Torre de la Calahorra** which houses the **Museo Vivo de Al-Andalus**. Although some aspects of the museum are rather kitsch, it contains excellent models of the mezquita and Granada's Alhambra; some of the commentary in the sound-and-light display is interesting. Entry is 400 ptas.

Places to Stay

Most people look for lodgings in the area around the mezquita. Córdoba's ultra-modern youth hostel, *Albergue Juvenil Córdoba* (☎ 29 01 66), is perfectly positioned on Plaza de Judá Leví, has excellent facilities and no curfew. Beds are 1175 ptas for those under 26, 1500 ptas for others – there are also good deals on meals.

Hostal Martínez Rücker (☎ 47 25 62), Calle Mártinez Rücker 14, with singles/ doubles from 1500/3500 ptas, is particularly

friendly and only a stone's throw from the mezquita. *Hostal Trinidad* (☎ 48 79 05), Corregidor Luis de la Cerda 58, is equally well placed and has rooms from 1400/2700 ptas. At Calle Cardenal González 25, *Hostal Santa Ana* (☎ 48 58 37) has one single at 1500 ptas and doubles at 3000 ptas, or 4500 ptas with bath.

For those with a little extra to spend, *Hostal El Triunfo* (☎ 47 55 00), Corrigedor Luis de la Cerda 79 by the mezquita, is a real treat. Comfortable singles/doubles/triples with air-con and TV cost 3500/5800/6900 ptas.

If you want to keep away from the tourist masses as much as possible, there are some good hostales further east. *Pensión San Francisco* (☎ 47 27 16), Calle de San Fernando 24, is good value with one small single at 1500 ptas and doubles from 3500 ptas. *Hostal La Fuente* (☎ 48 78 27), Calle de San Fernando 51, has compact singles at 1800 ptas and doubles with bath from 4500 ptas. The shower pressure is excellent! At Calle Romero Barroso 14, the friendly *Hostal Los Arcos* (☎ 48 56 43) has modern rooms from 2000/3500 ptas. Or, check to see if renovations are finished at *Hostal Plaza Corredera* (☎ 47 05 81), Calle Rodriguez Marín 15, off Plaza de la Corredera. The location is interesting and the price right for budget travellers.

Places to Eat

You shouldn't have too much trouble finding somewhere to eat in Córdoba. *Self-Service Los Patios*, right by the mezquita on Calle Cardenal Herrero, has a good choice of functional main courses and desserts with nothing over 600 ptas. The two restaurants in the city walls on Calle de la Luna, *Mesón de la Luna* and *Mesón la Muralla*, both have pretty courtyards and menús from 1200 to 1900 ptas.

For a first-class meal try *Restaurante Bandolero*, Calle de Torrijos 6 by the mezquita. It has platos combinados from 700 to 900 ptas; if you order à la carte expect to pay around 4000 ptas per person. *El Churrasco* in the Judería at Calle Almanzor Romero 16 is said to be Córdoba's best restaurant. The food is rich, service attentive and prices similar to the Bandolero.

If you'd rather try somewhere less touristy, *Taberna Sociedad de Plateros*, Calle San Francisco 6, is a popular local tavern with a good range of tapas and raciones to choose from. Likewise *Taberna Salinas* at Calle Tundidores 3 offers good, cheap, local fare.

There is an excellent market in Plaza de la Corredera, another part of town beyond the tourist precinct. The market opens from Monday to Saturday and gets going at around 9.30 am – Saturday is the busiest day. There are lots of good bakeries with pastries, cakes and bocadillos in both the old and new parts of town; try Calle Concepción off the south end of the Avenida del Gran Capitán pedestrian mall.

Entertainment

As you might expect, Córdoba has pretty good nightlife. Most of the action is in the new town, in the area around Plaza de las Tendillas. In particular, try Plaza San Miguel and Calle del Caño. The pubs and bars around Plaza Costa del Sol in Ciudad Jardín, a km or so west of Plaza Tendillas, are also popular. If you're getting peckish in the early hours, head for *Bar Piscolabi* or one of its neighbours in Calle Conde de Cárdenas, for some of the cheapest bocadillos in Spain to go with your drink.

Getting There & Away

Buses to cities around Andalucía leave from the Alsina Graells Sur bus station (☎ 23 64 74) at Avenida Medina Azahara 29-31. Long-distance buses to Barcelona and other cities on the Mediterranean coast, operated by Bacoma (☎ 45 65 14), also leave from this bus station. Buses to Madrid are run by Secorbus (☎ 46 80 40), Camino de los Sastres, on the corner of Avenida República Argentina some 600 metres north-west of the mezquita and behind the big Hotel Melia.

There are plenty of trains daily from Córdoba to Seville. Options range from AVEs (45 minutes, from 2100 ptas) to stopping trains (1¾ hours, 875 ptas). From Córdoba to Madrid, AVEs take 1¾ to two hours (from 5500 ptas) and the night train takes 6½ hours (3400 ptas). There are around eight trains to Bobadilla daily (875 to 1400 ptas). Most of them continue to Málaga (1300 to 2400 ptas). For Granada, you usually need to change trains at Bobadilla but connections are good (3¾ to 5½ hours, from 1700 ptas).

COSTA DE ALMERÍA

The Costa de Almería in south-east Andalucía, running from the Golfo de Almería round Cabo de Gata to the border of Murcia, is perhaps the last section of Spain's Mediterranean coast where you can have a beach completely to yourself. In high summer forget it, but this is Spain's hottest region, so even in late March it can be warm enough to take in some rays and try out your new swimsuit.

Orientation & Information

The most useful tourist offices are in Almería (☎ 27 43 55), San José (☎ 38 02 99) and Mojácar (☎ 47 51 62). Change money before going to Cabo de Gata as there are no banks there.

The telephone code for the region is ☎ 950.

Things to See & Do

The **Alcazaba**, an enormous 10th-century Moorish fortress, is the highlight of Almería city. In its heyday the city it dominated was more important than Granada. In the desert 25 km inland on the N-340 is **Mini-Hollywood** (☎ 36 52 36), where *A Fistful of Dollars* and other classic Westerns were shot. It's fun to drop in: the Western town set is preserved and shoot-outs are staged daily (entry 925 ptas). From Almería you can get there on a Tabernas bus.

The best thing about the region is the wonderful 50-km coastline and semidesert scenery of **Cabo de Gata**. All along the coast from Cabo de Gata village to Agua Amarga, some of the most beautiful and empty beaches on the Mediterranean alternate with precipitous cliffs and scattered villages. At Las Salinas, three km south of Cabo de Gata village, is a famous **flamingo colony**. The main village is laidback **San José**, from where you can walk or drive to some of the best beaches such as **Playa Genoveses** and **Playa Monsul**. Some other beaches can only be reached on foot or by boat.

Mojácar, 30 km north of Agua Amarga, is a white town of Moorish origin, perched on a hill two km from the coast. Although a long resort strip, Mojácar Playa, has grown up below, Mojácar is still a very pretty place and it's not hard to spend some time here, especially if you fancy a livelier beach scene than Cabo de Gata offers.

Places to Stay & Eat

A good cheapie in Almería is *Hostal Universal* (☎ 23 55 57), in the centre at Puerta de Purchena 3, with singles/doubles for 1500/ 3000 ptas. *Restaurante Alfareros*, nearby at Calle Marcos 6, has a good three-course lunch and dinner menú for 900 ptas.

In high summer it's a good idea to ring ahead about accommodation on Cabo de Gata, as some places fill up. There are four camping grounds: *Camping Los Escullos* (☎ 38 98 11) and *Camping Las Negras* (☎ 52 52 37) are open year-round. San José's *albergue juvenil* (youth hostel; ☎ 38 03 53), on Calle Montemar, opens from late June to late September, plus holidays, and charges 1250 ptas. In San José village centre, *Fonda Costa Rica* has doubles with bath for 5000 ptas. *Hostal Bahía* (☎ 38 03 06) nearby on Calle Correo has lovely singles/doubles for 5000/7500 ptas. *Restaurante El Emigrante* across the road does good fish and meat dishes for 900 or 1000 ptas, and big salads and tortillas for 300 to 400 ptas. There's accommodation in other villages too.

In Mojácar, the cheaper places are mostly up in the town. *Pensión Casa Justa* (☎ 47 83 72), Calle Morote 7, is good value with rooms at 1500/3000 ptas, or 4000 ptas for doubles with bath. *Hostal La Esquinica* (☎ 47 50 09), nearby at Calle Cano 1, charges 1750/3500 ptas. *Pensión La Luna* (☎ 47 80 32), Calle Estación Nueva 15, is more comfortable with doubles at 5000 ptas and good meals available. *Restaurante El Viento del Desierto* on Plaza Frontón by the church is good value with main courses such as chicken kebabs or rabbit in mustard for 550 to 700 ptas. The only true budget place to stay down at the beach is *El Cantal* camping ground (☎ 47 82 04). *Antonella*, 1.5 km south, is popular for its pizzas and pasta for 600 to 1200 ptas.

Getting There & Away

Almería has an international and domestic airport and is accessible by bus and train from Madrid, Barcelona, Granada and Seville, and by bus from Málaga and Murcia. Buses run from Almería to Cabo de Gata village and (except on Sunday) to San José. Mojácar can be reached by bus from Almeriá, Murcia, Granada and Madrid.

MÁLAGA & THE COSTA DEL SOL

The Costa del Sol, a string of tightly packed high-rise resorts running south-west from Málaga towards Gibraltar, is geared for – and incredibly popular with – package-deal tourists from Britain and Germany and the time-share crowd. The main resorts are Torremolinos (which has acquired such a bad reputation that it has been dubbed 'Terrible Torre'), Fuengirola and Marbella. From Marbella onwards, you can see the Rif Mountains in Morocco on a clear day.

The telephone code for Málaga and the coast is ☎ 95.

Things to See & Do

The Costa del Sol pulls in the crowds because of its weather, beaches, warm Mediterranean water and cheap package deals. The resorts were once charming Spanish fishing villages, but that aspect has all but disappeared in most cases. If you're more interested in Spain than in foreign package tourists, **Málaga** itself is a better place to stop over. It has a bustling street life, a 16th-century cathedral and a Moorish palace/fortress, the Alcazaba, from which the walls of the Moorish castle, the Gibralfaro, climb to the top of the hill dominating the city.

Torremolinos and **Fuengirola** are a concrete continuum designed to squeeze as many paying customers as possible into the smallest possible area. You'll be surprised if you hear someone speak Spanish. **Marbella** is more inviting: its old town has managed to retain some of its original character and has a well-preserved 15th-century castle. **Puerto Banús**, four km west, is the only town on the Costa del Sol which could be called attractive. Consequently it's also exorbitant. Its harbour is often a port of call for yachts that moor in Monte Carlo at other times of the year. A lot of the money here is rumoured to be on the crooked side, but nobody asks any questions.

Probably the only reason to stay long on the Costa del Sol is to work. If you go about it the right way, you may get work on one of the yachts in Puerto Banús. Some young travellers make good money in Marbella, Fuengirola and Torremolinos, touting for time-share salespeople.

Places to Stay

In Málaga the friendly *Pensión Córdoba* (☎ 221 44 69), Calle Bolsa 9, has singles/

doubles at 1600/2800 ptas. The basic but clean *Hospedajes La Perla* (☎ 221 84 30), Calle Luis de Velázquez 5 (3rd floor), charges 1300/2600 ptas. Both are near the central Plaza de la Constitución.

Rooms down the coast are expensive in July, August and maybe September but prices usually come down sharply at other times from the levels given here. In Terrible Torre, *Hostal Prudencio* (☎ 238 14 52), Calle Carmen 43, at 2800/5600 ptas, is a stone's throw from the beach. *Hostal Guillot* (☎ 238 01 44), Calle Río Mundo 4, is nowhere near as pleasant, but has cheaper doubles at 3500 ptas.

At Fuengirola, the British-run *Pensión Coca* (☎ 247 41 89), Calle de la Cruz 3, has decent rooms at 2800/4800 ptas. *Pensión Andalucía* (☎ 246 33 30), Calle Troncón 59, has doubles only at 3300 ptas (4500 ptas in August). Both are just a short walk from the beach.

Marbella has an excellent modern HI *hostel* (☎ 277 14 91) at Calle Trapiche 2; rooms have just two or three beds and half have private bath. It's 1175 ptas for those under 26, and 1500 ptas for others. The British-run *Hostal del Pilar* (☎ 282 99 36), in the old town at Calle Mesoncillo 4, is popular with backpackers and charges 2000 ptas a person.

Places to Eat
Near the cathedral in Málaga, *Bar Restaurante Tormes*, Calle San Agustín 13 (closed Monday), and the slightly fancier *El Jardín* on Calle Cister both have good menús for 1100 ptas. For local flavour, sample fish dishes at outdoor tables at the reasonably priced marisquerías on Calle Comisario. In Torremolinos and Fuengirola, it's just a matter of going for a walk along the beachfront – you'll find plenty of places with menús for well under 1000 ptas.

In Marbella, *Bar El Gallo* at Calle Lobatos 44 in the old town does great-value burgers and fish and meat dishes for 325 to 475 ptas. *Restaurante Sol de Oro* on the seafront in front of the tourist office has a good menú for 925 ptas including wine.

Getting There & Away
Málaga is the main landing and launching pad for the Costa del Sol and its airport has a good range of domestic as well as international flights. Málaga is linked by train and bus to all

major Spanish centres, including Madrid, Barcelona, Seville, Granada and Algeciras. Málaga's bus and train stations are round the corner from each other, one km west of the centre.

Getting Around
Trains run every half-hour from Málaga airport to the city centre and west to Torremolinos and Fuengirola. There are even more frequent buses from Málaga to Torremolinos, Fuengirola and Marbella.

RONDA
One of the prettiest and most historic towns in Andalucía, Ronda is a world apart from the nearby Costa del Sol. Straddling the savagely deep and steep El Tajo gorge, the town stands at the heart of some lovely hill country dotted with white villages and ripe for exploring.

The main tourist office (☎ 287 12 72) is at Plaza de España 1.

Ronda's telephone code is ☎ 95.

Things to See & Do
Ronda is a pleasure to wander around, but during the day you'll have to contend with bus loads of day-trippers up from the coast.

The **Plaza de Toros** (1785) is considered the home of bullfighting and is something of a mecca for aficionados; inside is the small but fascinating **Museo Taurino**. Entry to both is 225 ptas.

To cross the gorge to the originally Moorish old town, you have a choice of three bridges. The 18th-century **Puente Nuevo** (New Bridge) is an amazing feat of engineering and the views from here are great. The old town itself is littered with ancient churches, monuments and palaces. The **Palacio de Mondragón** houses a rather inconsequential museum, but is almost worth the 200 ptas entry (students 100 ptas) for the views alone. You can walk down into the gorge from nearby Plaza María Auxiliadora. Also of interest are **Santa María la Mayor**, a medieval church whose tower was once the minaret of a mosque, and the **Baños Arabes** (Arab Baths), also dating from the 13th century.

Places to Stay & Eat
Camping El Sur (☎ 287 59 39) is in a pleasant

setting two km south-west of town and has a swimming pool and restaurant.

Fonda La Española (☎ 287 10 52), in the street behind the main tourist office at Calle José Aparicio 3, has clean, basic singles/doubles from 1200/2400 ptas. The friendly *Pensión La Purísima* (☎ 287 10 50), Calle Sevilla 10, is also good value with rooms for 1500/3000 ptas.

There are several good places to eat on and just off Plaza del Socorro, a block west of the bullring. *El Molino* here has pizzas, pasta and platos combinados from 500 to 700 ptas, and tables outside. A few metres up Calle Lorenzo Borrego, *Pizzería Michelangelo* is also good value; *Cervecería Patatín-Patatán* next door has great tapas.

Getting There & Away

There are several buses daily to Seville (2½ hours, 1235 ptas) and Málaga (two to three hours, 875 to 1100 ptas, some via the Costa del Sol), and one (except Sunday) to La Línea (Gibraltar) for 990 ptas. The bus station is on Plaza Concepción Garcia Redondo.

Daily trains go to Seville (three hours, 1650 ptas), Málaga (two to 2½ hours, 1080 ptas), Granada and Córdoba, mostly with a change at Bobadilla, and there are direct trains to Algeciras. The station is on Avenida de Andalucía.

Gibraltar

The British colony of Gibraltar occupies a huge lump of limestone, five km long and one km wide, at the mouth of the Mediterranean Sea. It's a curious and interesting port of call if you're in the region. Gibraltar has certainly had a rocky history; it was the bridgehead for the Moorish invasion of Spain in 711 AD and Castile didn't finally wrest it from the Moors until 1462. Then in 1704 an Anglo-Dutch fleet captured Gibraltar after a one-week siege. Spain gave up military attempts to regain it from Britain after the failure of the 3½-year Great Siege in 1779-83, but during the Franco period Gibraltar was an extremely sore point between Britain and Spain, and the border was closed for years.

Today Gibraltar is self-governing and depends on Britain only for defence. An overwhelming majority of Gibraltarians – many of whom are of Genoese or Jewish ancestry – want to remain with Britain.

Information

EU, US, Canada, Australia, New Zealand, Israel, South Africa and Singapore passport-holders are among those who do *not* need visas for Gibraltar, but anyone who needs a visa for Spain should have at least a double-entry Spanish visa if they intend to return to Spain from Gibraltar.

Gibraltar has helpful tourist offices at: the border; the Piazza, Main St (☎ 74982); and the Gibraltar Museum, 18-20 Bomb House Lane (☎ 74805). All are open Monday to Friday from 10 am to 6 pm, the last two are also open on Saturday from 10 am to 2 pm.

The currency is the Gibraltar pound or pound sterling. You can use pesetas but conversion rates aren't in your favour. Exchange rates for buying pesetas are, however, a bit better than in Spain. Change any unspent Gibraltar pounds before you leave.

To phone Gibraltar from Spain, the telephone code is ☎ 9567; from the UK dial ☎ 00, then ☎ 350 (the code for Gibraltar) and the local number.

Things to See & Do

Downtown Gibraltar is nothing very special – you could almost be in Bradford or Bletchley – but the **Gibraltar Museum**, 18-20 Bomb House Lane, has an interesting historical, architectural and military collection and includes a Moorish bathhouse. It's open the same hours as the tourist office. Entry is £2. Many graves in the **Trafalgar Cemetery** are of those who died at Gibraltar from wounds received in the Battle of Trafalgar (1805).

The large **Upper Rock Nature Reserve**, covering most of the upper rock, has spectacular views and several interesting spots to visit. It's open daily from 9.30 am to sunset. Entry, at £5 a person and £1.50 a vehicle, includes all the following sites, which are open to 6.15 pm. Cable-car tickets (see Getting Around later) include entry to the reserve, the Apes' Den and St Michael's Cave.

The rock's most famous inhabitants are its colony of **Barbary macaques**, the only wild

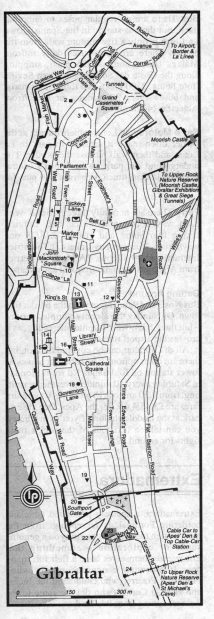

PLACES TO STAY
2 Emile Youth Hostel
5 Miss Seruya Guest House
11 Cannon Hotel
20 Toc H Hostel
22 Queen's Hotel

PLACES TO EAT
4 The Clipper
7 Viceroy of India
9 The Piazza
12 Three Roses Bar
16 Maxi Manger
19 Minister's Restaurant
23 Piccadilly Gardens

OTHER
1 Bus No 9
3 Tourafrica International
6 Post Office
8 St Bernard's Hospital
10 Tourist Office
13 Roman Catholic Cathedral
14 Gibraltar Museum & Tourist Office
15 Bus No 3
17 Anglican Cathedral
18 Gibraltar Bookshop
21 Trafalgar Cemetery
24 Bottom Cable-Car Station

SPAIN

Gibraltar

0   150   300 m

primates (apart from *Homo sapiens*) in Europe. Some of these hang around the **Apes' Den** near the middle cable-car station, others can often be seen at the top station or Great Siege Tunnels.

From the top cable-car station, there are views as far as Morocco in decent weather. **St Michael's Cave**, 20 minutes downhill walk south from here, is a big natural grotto renowned for its stalagmites and stalactites. Apart from attracting tourists in droves, it's used for concerts, plays and even fashion shows. The **Great Siege Tunnels**, 30 minutes walk north (downhill) from the top cable-car station, are a series of galleries in the rock hewn out by the British during the Great Siege to provide new gun emplacements. Worth a stop on the way down to the town from here are the **Gibraltar: a city under siege** exhibition and a **Moorish castle**.

Places to Stay

The *Emile Youth Hostel* (☎ 51106) at Montagu Bastion, Line Wall Rd, is a step up from Gibraltar's other budget options. It has 44 places in two to eight-person rooms for £10 including continental breakfast. The *Toc H Hostel* (☎ 73431), a ramshackle old place tucked into the city walls at the south end of Line Wall Road, has beds at £5 a night and cold showers. *Miss Seruya Guest House* (☎ 73220), 92/1A Irish Town (1st floor), has four very small and basic rooms and one shower. Singles/doubles cost from £8/12 to £16/18.

The *Queen's Hotel* (☎ 74000) at 1 Boyd St is in a different league, with a restaurant, bar, games room and singles/doubles at £16/24, or £20/36 with private bath or shower. Reduced rates of £14/20 and £16/24 are offered to students and young travellers. The *Cannon Hotel* (☎ 51711) at 9 Cannon Lane also has decent rooms, each sharing a bathroom with one other room, for £25 single or double.

There are some economical options in the Spanish border town La Línea. *Pensión La Perla* (☎ 95-76 95 13), Calle Clavel 10, has spacious pink-trimmed singles/doubles for 1700/3000 ptas.

Places to Eat

Most of the many pubs in town do pub meals with all sorts of British goodies on the menu. One of the best is *The Clipper* at 78B Irish Town, where a generous serve of fish and chips and a pint of beer will set you back £6. *Three Roses Bar* at 60 Governor's St does a huge all-day British breakfast for £2.80. At the popular *Piccadilly Gardens* pub on Rosia Rd you can sit in the garden and have a three-course lunch for £6. *Maxi Manger* on Main St is a good fast-food spot with burgers (including vegetarian) for £1.60 and calamari for £2.25.

If you fancy a restaurant meal, there's great Indian food at the *Viceroy of India*, 9-11 Horse Barrack Court, which has a three-course lunch special for £6.50. À la carte there are vegetarian dishes for £2 to £3 and main courses from £6 to £10. *The Piazza*, 156 Main St, does decent pizzas for £5 to £6, and fish and meat main courses from £5.50 to £8. *Minister's Restaurant*, 310 Main St, does good servings of fish and seafood for £3.50 to £4, or fish, meat or pasta with chips or salad from £5.

Getting There & Away

Air GB Airways (☎ 79300) flies daily to London for £99 one way. It also has flights to Morocco.

Bus There are no regular buses to Gibraltar itself, but the bus station in the Spanish town La Línea is only a five-minute walk from the border. There are four buses daily to/from Málaga (three hours, 1225 ptas), stopping along the Costa del Sol; three to/from Seville (four hours, 2500 ptas); two to/from Granada; and buses every 30 minutes or so to/from Algeciras (40 minutes).

Car & Motorcycle Long vehicle queues at the border often make it sensible to park in La Línea and then walk across the border. The underground car park on La Línea's central Plaza de la Constitución charges 810 ptas for 24 hours.

Ferry There are normally three ferries a week each way between Gibraltar and Tangier, taking two hours and costing £18/28 one way/return. You can buy tickets at Tourafrica International (☎ 77666), 2A Main St. Ferries from Algeciras are more frequent and cheaper.

Getting Around

Bus Nos 3 and 9 run direct from the border into town. On Sunday there's only a limited service – but the 1.5 km-walk is quite interesting, as it crosses the airport runway.

All of Gibraltar can be covered on foot, but there are other options. The cable car leaves its lower station on Red Sands Rd from Monday to Saturday every 10 minutes, weather permitting, from 9.30 am to 5.15 pm. One-way/return fares are £3.45/4.65. For the Apes' Den, disembark at the middle station. If you're in a hurry, you can take a taxi tour of the rock's main sights for around £25.

Extremadura

Extremadura, a sparsely populated tableland bordering Portugal, is far enough from the most beaten tourist trails to give you a genuine sense of exploration – something that *extremeños* themselves have a flair for: many epic 16th-century *conquistadores* including Francisco Pizarro (who conquered the Incas) and Hernán Cortés (who did the same to the Aztecs) sprang from this land.

Trujillo and Cáceres are the two not-to-be-missed old towns here, while a spot of hiking, or just relaxing, in the valleys of north-east Extremadura makes the perfect change from urban life. Elsewhere, Mérida has Spain's biggest collection of Roman ruins, and the Parque Natural de Monfragüe, famous for its birds of prey, is a great stop for drivers north of Trujillo. If you can, avoid June, July and August, when Extremadura is *very* hot.

The telephone code for all places in this section is ☎ 927.

TRUJILLO

With just 9000 people, Trujillo can't be much bigger now than in 1529, when its most famous son Francisco Pizarro set off with his three brothers and a few local buddies for an expedition that culminated in the bloody conquest of the Inca empire three years later. Trujillo is blessed with a broad and fine Plaza Mayor, from which rises its remarkably preserved old town, packed with aged buildings exuding history. If you approach from the Plasencia direction you might imagine that you've driven through a time warp into the 16th century. The tourist office (☎ 32 26 77) is on Plaza Mayor.

Things to See

A **statue of Pizarro**, done by an American, Charles Rumsey, in the 1920s, dominates the Plaza Mayor. On the plaza's south side, the **Palacio de la Conquista** (closed to visitors) sports the carved images of Francisco Pizarro and the Inca princess Inés Yupanqui. Their daughter Francisca lived in this house with her husband Hernando, the only Pizarro brother to return alive to Spain. Two noble mansions which you can visit are the 16th-century **Palacio de los Duques de San Carlos**, also on the Plaza Mayor, and the **Palacio de Orellana-Pizarro**, through the alley in the plaza's south-west corner.

Up the hill, the **Iglesia de Santa María la Mayor** is an interesting hotchpotch of 13th to 16th-century styles, with some fine paintings by Fernando Gallego of the Flemish school. Higher up, the **Casa-Museo de Pizarro** has informative displays (in Spanish) on the lives and adventures of the Pizarro family. At the top of the hill, Trujillo's **castillo** is an impressive though empty structure, primarily of Moorish origin.

Places to Stay & Eat

Cheap accommodation is in rather short supply. **Camas Boni** (☎ 32 16 04), about 100 metres east of Plaza Mayor at Calle Domingo Ramos 7, is good value with singles/doubles from 1500/3000 ptas and doubles with bath for 4000 ptas. **Casa Roque** (☎ 32 23 13), further along the street at No 30, is a second option, at 1500/3500 ptas. On Plaza Mayor at No 27, **Hostal Nuria** (☎ 32 09 07) has nice rooms with bath for 3000/5000 ptas. **Hostal La Cadena** (☎ 32 14 63) at No 8 is also good, with rooms for 4000/5000 ptas.

The menú at **Restaurante La Troya** on Plaza Mayor costs 1900 ptas, but if you're a meat-eater it will save you from eating much else for the next couple of days. Portions are gigantic and they also give you a large omelette and a salad for starters, and an extra main course later on! If you're not quite that hungry there are great tapas here too. Elsewhere on Plaza Mayor **Cafetería Nuria** has platos combinados for 750 to 900 ptas. **Café-Bar El Escudo** up the hill on Plaza Santiago is also moderately priced.

Getting There & Away

The bus station (☎ 32 12 02) is 500 metres south of Plaza Mayor, on Carretera de Badajoz. At least 12 buses daily run to Madrid (2000 ptas, 2½ to four hours), and seven or more run to Cáceres and Mérida. There's daily service to Salamanca, but only three buses a week to Parque Natural de Monfragüe and Plasencia.

CÁCERES

Cáceres is larger than Trujillo and has an even bigger old town, created in the 15th and 16th centuries and so perfectly preserved that it can seem lifeless at times – but if things seem a bit quiet, the student-led nightlife around Plaza Mayor, on the north-west side of the old town, more than makes up for that on weekends. The tourist office (☎ 24 63 47) is on Plaza Mayor.

Things to See

The old town is still surrounded by walls and towers raised by the Almohads in the 12th century. Entering it from Plaza Mayor, you'll see ahead the fine 15th-century **Iglesia de Santa María**, Cáceres' cathedral. Any time from February to September, Santa María's tower will be topped by the ungainly nests of the large storks which make their homes on every worthwhile vertical protuberance in the old city.

Many of the old city's churches and imposing medieval mansions can only be admired from outside, but you *can* enter the good **Museo de Cáceres** on Plaza Veletas, housed in a 16th-century mansion built over a 12th-century Moorish cistern *(aljibe)* which is the museum's prize exhibit. It's open daily, except Monday, from 9 am to 2.30 pm (200 ptas). Also worth a look is the **Casa-Museo Árabe Yussuf Al-Borch** at Cuesta del Marqués 4, a private house decked out with oriental and Islamic trappings to capture the feel of Moorish times. The **Arco del Cristo** at the bottom of this street is a Roman gate.

Places to Stay

The best area to stay is around Plaza Mayor, though it gets noisy at weekends. *Pensión Márquez* (☎ 24 49 60), just off the low end of the plaza at Calle Gabriel y Galán 2, is a friendly family-run place with clean singles/doubles at 1250/2500 ptas. *Hostal Castilla* (☎ 24 44 04), one block west at Calle Ríos Verdes 3, has adequate rooms for 2000/4000 ptas. *Hotel Iberia* (☎ 24 82 00), off the top end of the plaza at Calle Pintores 2, is a step up with characterful singles/doubles for 4000/5000 ptas including private bath, TV and air-con or heating.

Places to Eat

If you're hungry, Cáceres has another *Restaurante La Troya* on the same lines as the one in Trujillo, at Calle Juan XXIII 1, a 1.5-km walk south from Plaza Mayor.

On Plaza Mayor at No 9, the popular *Cafetería El Puchero* has a huge range of options from good bocadillos (around 300 ptas) and all sorts of raciones to sizeable platos combinados (675 to 900 ptas) and à la carte fare. *Cafetería El Pato*, a block down the arcade, has an upstairs restaurant with a good menú for 1285 ptas.

Cafetería Lux at Calle Pintores 32, off the high end of Plaza Mayor, does basic platos combinados from 375 to 650 ptas.

Getting There & Away

The bus and train stations are both a little over two km south-west of Plaza Mayor, more or less opposite each other. Bus No L-1 from the stop beside the petrol station by the big roundabout outside the train station will take you into town.

There are at least seven buses daily to Madrid (3½ to 4¼ hours, 2385 ptas) via Trujillo, and a handful each day to Mérida, Seville, Salamanca and points beyond.

Five trains a day go to Madrid (3½ to five hours, from 2200 ptas). If you're heading for Portugal, the daily train to Lisbon (six hours, from 4400 ptas) leaves in the middle of the night (3 am). One train a day, except Sunday, goes to Seville, and three a day go to Mérida and Plasencia.

NORTH-EAST EXTREMADURA

From Plasencia, the green, almost Eden-like valleys of La Vera, Valle del Jerte and Valle del Ambroz stretch north-east into the Sierra de Gredos and its western extensions. Watered by rushing mountain streams called *gargantas*, and dotted with medieval villages, these valleys offer some excellent walking routes and attract just enough visitors to provide a good network of places to stay.

Information

The Editorial Alpina booklet *Valle del Jerte, Valle del Ambroz, La Vera* (600 ptas) includes a 1:50,000 map of the area showing walking routes. Try to get it from a map or book shop before you come: if not, the tourist office in Cabezuela del Valle may have copies.

There are tourist offices at Plasencia (☎ 42 21 59), Jaraiz de la Vera (☎ 46 00 24), Jarandilla de la Vera (☎ 56 04 60) and Cabezuela del Valle (☎ 47 21 22). Most sizeable villages have banks.

Things to See & Do

La Vera About halfway up the valley, **Cuacos de Yuste** has its share of narrow village streets with half-timbered houses leaning at odd angles, their overhanging upper storeys supported by timber or stone pillars. Two km north-west up a side road is the **Monasterio de Yuste**, to which in 1555 Carlos I, once the world's most powerful man, retreated for his dying years. The simple royal chambers and the monastery church are open Monday to Saturday from 9.30 am to 12.30 pm and 3.30 to 6 pm and on Sundays and holidays from 9.30

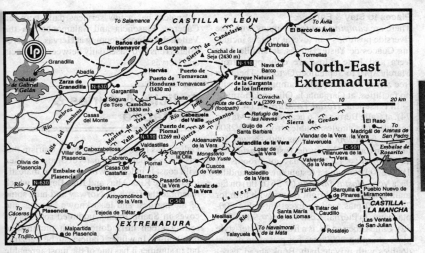

SPAIN

to 11.30 am, 1 to 1.30 pm and 3.30 to 6 pm.) Entry is 100 ptas.

The road continues past the monastery to **Garganta la Olla**, another typically picturesque village, from where you can head over the 1269-metre **Puerto del Piornal** pass into the Valle del Jerte.

Jarandilla de la Vera is a bigger village, with a 15th-century fortress-church on the main square (below the main road), and a parador occupying a castle-palace where Carlos I stayed while Yuste was being readied for him. The tourist office beside the church has a basic leaflet suggesting some good walks from Jarandilla. Of the longer hikes, the Ruta de Carlos V (see Valle del Jerte) is the most enticing. If you want to do it in reverse, ask for directions at Camping Jaranda.

Valle del Jerte This valley grows half of Spain's cherries and turns into a sea of white at blossom time in April. **Piornal**, high on the south flank, is a good base for walks along the Sierra de Tormantos. In the bottom of the valley, **Cabezuela del Valle** has a particularly medieval main street. A 35-km road crosses from just north of here over the 1430-metre

Puerto de Honduras pass to Hervás in the Valle del Ambroz. For hikers, the PR-10 trail climbs roughly parallel, to the south. From **Jerte** you can walk into the beautiful **Parque Natural de la Garganta de los Infiernos**.

Tornavacas, near the head of the valley, is the starting point of the **Ruta de Carlos V**, a 28-km marked trail following the route by which Carlos I (who was also Carlos V of the Holy Roman Empire) was carried over the mountains to Jarandilla on the way to Yuste. It can be walked in one long day – just as Carlos' bearers did it back then.

Valle del Ambroz Towards the head of the valley **Hervás**, a pleasant small town, has the best surviving 15th-century Barrio Judío (Jewish quarter) in Extremadura, where many Jews took refuge in hope of avoiding the Inquisition. About 22 km west by paved roads across the valley, **Granadilla** is a picturesque old fortified village that was abandoned after the Embalse de Gabriel y Galán reservoir almost surrounded it in the 1960s. Now it's restored as an educational centre and you can visit, free, from 10 am to 1 pm and 5 to 7 pm daily, except Saturday morning, Sunday afternoon and from 15 December to 30 January.

Places to Stay & Eat

There are *camping grounds* – many with fine riverside positions – in several villages including Cuacos de Yuste, Hervás, Jarandilla de la Vera and Jerte. Most are only open from March/April to September/October. There are free *zonas de acampada*, camping areas with no facilities, at Garganta la Olla and Piornal.

In Plasencia, *Hostal La Muralla* (☎ 41 38 74), at Calle Berrozana 6 near the Plaza Mayor, has adequate singles/doubles from 1500/2800 ptas, or from 2900/3000 ptas with shower. On the main road in Cuacos de Yuste, *Pensión Sol de Vettonia* (☎ 17 22 41) has good rooms for 1900/2700 ptas, and a restaurant. In Jarandilla de la Vera, *Hostal Jaranda* (☎ 56 02 06) on the main road has big, bright rooms with bath for 2675/5350 ptas, and an excellent-value 800-pta menú. In Piornal, *Casa Verde* (☎ 908-92 19 72), Calle Libertad 38, is a friendly hostel-style place charging 2000 ptas per person in decent doubles with private bath. Book ahead, especially in spring. *Pensión Los Piornos* (☎ 47 60 55) on Plaza de las Eras, has plain singles/doubles for 2000/2500 ptas.

In Cabezuela del Valle, the good *Hotel Aljama* (☎ 47 22 91), Calle Federico Bajo s/n, has nice modern rooms for 2500/4500 ptas. There are numerous places to eat and drink on nearby Calle El Hondón. *Hostal Puerto de Tornavacas* (☎ 47 01 01), a couple of km up the N-110 from Tornavacas, is a country inn-style place with rooms 2500/4600 ptas.

The only rooms in Hervás are at the dull *Hostal Sinagoga* (☎ 48 11 91), outside the town centre at Avenida de la Provincia 2, for 2500/5000 ptas with bath and TV.

Getting There & Away

Your own wheels are a big help but if you do use the buses, you can at least walk over the mountains without worrying about how to get back to your vehicle! The following bus services run Monday to Friday, with a much reduced service on weekends. Mirat (☎ 42 36 43) runs three or four Plasencia-Madrid buses daily along La Vera, and one from Cáceres to La Vera. Doaldi (☎ 17 03 59) and La Sepulvedana (☎ 91-530 48 00) also run Madrid-La Vera services.

León Álvarez runs four daily buses from Plasencia up the Valle del Jerte to Tornavacas, and one to Piornal.

Enatcar has a few services daily between Cáceres, Plasencia and Salamanca via the Valle del Ambroz, stopping at Hervás. Los Tres Pilares runs two buses daily between Plasencia and Hervás.

Galicia, Asturias & Cantabria

Galicia has been spared the mass tourism that has reached many other parts of Spain. Its often wild coast is indented with a series of majestic inlets – the Rías Altas and Rías Bajas – which resemble the fjords of Norway and hide some of the prettiest and least known beaches and coves in Spain. Inland, potholed roads cross rolling green hills dotted with picturesque farmhouses. In winter, Galicia can be freezing, but in summer it has one of the most agreeable climates in Europe – though you must expect a little rain.

Highlights of the Asturias and Cantabria regions, east of Galicia, are the wonderful cave paintings at Altamira and the Picos de Europa mountains.

SANTIAGO DE COMPOSTELA

This beautiful small city is the end of the Camino de Santiago, a collective name for several major medieval pilgrim routes from as far away as France, still followed by plenty of faithful today. Thanks to its university, Santiago is a lively city almost any time, but is at its most festive around 25 July, the Feast of Santiago (St James). Its tourist office (☎ 58 40 81) at Rúa do Vilar 43 is open from 10 am to 2 pm and 4 to 7 pm daily.

The city's telephone code is ☎ 981.

Things to See & Do

The goal of the Camino de Santiago is the **catedral** on magnificent **Praza do Obradoiro**. Under the main altar lies the supposed tomb of Santiago Apóstol (St James the Apostle). It's believed the saint's remains were buried here in the 1st century AD and rediscovered in 813, after which he grew into the patron saint of the Christian Reconquista, and his tomb attracted streams of pilgrims from all over western Europe. The cathedral is a superb

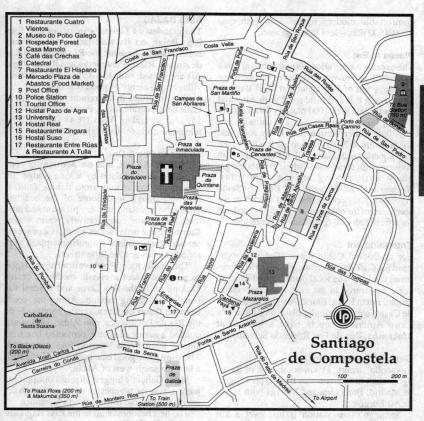

1 Restaurante Cuatro
   Vientos
2 Museo do Pobo Galego
3 Hospedaje Forest
4 Casa Manolo
5 Café das Crechas
6 Catedral
7 Restaurante El Hispano
8 Mercado Plaza de
   Abastos (Food Market)
9 Post Office
10 Police Station
11 Tourist Office
12 Hostal Pazo de Agra
13 University
14 Hostal Real
15 Restaurante Zingara
16 Hostal Suso
17 Restaurante Entre Rúas
   & Restaurante A Tulla

Santiago
de Compostela

SPAIN

Romanesque creation of the 11th to the 13th
century, with later decorative flourishes, and
its masterpiece is the Pórtico de la Gloria inside
the west façade.

Santiago's compact old town is a work of
art, and a walk around the cathedral will take
you through some of its most inviting squares.
It's also good to stroll in the beautifully land-
scaped **Carballeira de Santa Susana** park
south-west of the cathedral. Just north-east of
the old city, off Porta do Camino, an impressive
old convent houses the **Museo do Pobo
Galego**, covering Galician life from fishing
through music and crafts to traditional costume
(open Monday to Saturday, free).

Places to Stay

Santiago is jammed with cheap pensiones, but
many are full with students. A quiet and cheap
central option with decent rooms is *Hospedaje
Forest* (☎ 57 08 11), Callejón de Don Abril
Ares 7, where singles/doubles start at 1300/
2400 ptas. *Hostal Real* (☎ 56 66 56), Rúa da
Calderería 49, has good-sized rooms for 2000/
3000 ptas. The attractive *Hostal Pazo de Agra*
(☎ 58 90 45), at Rúa da Calderería 37, is a
spotless old house with rooms for 2000/3000
ptas, or 3000/4500 ptas with private bath.
Enquire at Restaurante Zingara, Rúa de Cardenal Payá. The popular little *Hostal Suso* (☎ 58
66 11), Rúa do Vilar 65, has amiable hosts;

comfortable modern rooms with bath cost 3200/4500 ptas – less in low season.

Places to Eat

The excellent and varied 600-pta menú at *Casa Manolo*, Rúa Travesa 27, ensures that the place is always full of foreigners and local students alike. For a full and solid meal with wine and dessert for less than 1000 ptas, try *Restaurante Cuatro Vientos*, Rúa de Santa Cristina 19.

A little dearer, *Restaurante Entre Rúas* and *Restaurante A Tulla*, next to each other in the tiny square on the lane called Entrerúas, both come up with some good dishes. You should get away with paying around 1500 ptas. *Restaurante El Hispano* on Rúa de Santo Agostiño, just opposite the food market in the south-east of the old town, is a good place to head for a fresh fish grill (parrillada de pescados).

Entertainment

For traditional Celtic music, Galician style, head for *Café das Crechas*, Via Sacra 3. Sometimes it's live. The local drinking and dancing scene is centred in the new town, especially around Praza Roxa. *Black*, Avenida de Rosalía de Castro s/n, is a popular disco. For more of a Latin American touch, have a look in at *Makumba*, Rúa de Frei Rodendo Salvado 16.

Getting There & Away

Lavacolla airport, 11 km south-east of Santiago, caters to international flights, plus flights to Madrid, Barcelona and Málaga with Iberia or Air Europa.

Santiago's bus station is just over a km north-east of the cathedral, on Rúa de Rodriguez Viguri. City bus No 10 runs to Praza de Galicia, on the south edge of the old town. Buses leave hourly to Vigo (900 ptas), via Pontevedra, and north to La Coruña (775 ptas), and there are regular buses to Salamanca, Madrid, Barcelona and Cáceres. Buses to Porto take five hours and cost 1800 ptas; there are two a week in winter, six a week in summer.

The train station is 600 metres south of the old town at the end of Rúa do Horreo. Bus Nos 6 and 9 from near the station go to Praza de Galicia. Up to four trains a day run to Madrid (eight to 11 hours, from 5000 ptas), and frequent trains head to La Coruña (1½ hours, 450 ptas), Pontevedra (one hour, 450 ptas) and Vigo.

RÍAS BAJAS

The grandest of Galicia's inlets are the four Rías Bajas, on its west-facing coast. From north to south these are the Ría de Muros, Ría de Arousa, Ría de Pontevedra and Ría de Vigo. All are dotted with low-key resorts, fishing villages and plenty of good beaches.

Tourist offices in the region include one at Calle del General Mola 3, Pontevedra (☎ 85 08 14) and several in Vigo (☎ 43 05 77). The telephone code for the region is ☎ 986.

Things to See & Do

On Ría de Arousa, **Isla de Arousa**, is connected to the mainland by a long bridge. Its inhabitants live mainly from fishing (and, it appears, smuggling). Some of the beaches facing the mainland are very pleasant and protected and have comparatively warm water. **Cambados**, a little further south, is a peaceful seaside town with a magnificent plaza surrounded by evocative little streets.

The small city of **Pontevedra** has managed to preserve intact a classic medieval centre backing on to the Río Lérez and is ideal for simply wandering around. Along the coast between **Cabo de Udra**, on the south side of the Ría de Pontevedra, and Aldán village are cradled a series of pretty, protected beaches, among them **Praia Vilariño** and **Areacova**. There are more good beaches around little **Hío**, a few km south-west of Aldán.

Vigo, Galicia's biggest city, is a disappointment given its wonderful setting, though its small, tangled old town is worth a wander.

The best beaches of all in the Rías Bajas are on the **Islas Cíes** off the end of the Ría de Vigo. Of the three islands, one is off limits for conservation reasons. The other two, Isla del Faro and Isla de Monte Agudo, are linked by a white sandy crescent – together forming a nine-km breakwater in the Atlantic. You can only visit the islands from mid-June to the end of September, and numbers are strictly limited. A return boat ticket from Vigo costs 1700 ptas: the frequency of services depends largely on the weather.

Places to Stay & Eat

A couple of *camping grounds* open in summer on Isla de Arousa. In Cambados, *Hostal Pazos Feijoo* (☎ 54 28 10), Calle de Curros Enriquez 1, near the waterfront in the newer part of town, has singles/doubles for 2500/4000 ptas. The *Café-Bar* on Rúa Caracol does reasonable seafood meals for about 1000 ptas.

In the old town in Pontevedra, *Hospedaje Penelas* (☎ 85 57 05) at Rúa Alta 17 has small but decent rooms for 2000/3000 ptas, and *Casa Alicia* (☎ 85 70 79), Avenida Santa María 5, has homely doubles for 2500 to 3000 ptas. You can eat cheaply on Calle de San Nicolás at *Casa Fidel O'Pulpeiro* at No 7, *Bar Barrantes* at No 6, or *O' Noso Bar* at No 5.

Hostal Stop (☎ 32 94 75) in Hío has rooms for as little as 1000/2000 ptas in winter, but more like 3000/5000 ptas in summer.

In Vigo, *Hostal Madrid* (☎ 22 55 23), Rúa de Alfonso XIII 63, near the train station, has doubles for 1800 ptas, or 2500 ptas with shower. Not too far away, *Hostal Krishna* (☎ 22 81 61), Rúa de Urzaiz 57, has modern singles/doubles for 2000/3000 ptas. Old Vigo is laced with tapas bars and eateries of all descriptions. *Patio Gallego* at Rúa dos Cesteiros 7, off Praza da Constitución, has a decent set lunch for 1000 ptas.

Camping is the only option if you want to stay on the Islas Cíes: you must book the camp site (520 ptas per person and per tent) at the office in the estación marítima in Vigo – places are limited. You can then organise a round-trip boat ticket for the days you require.

Getting There & Away
Pontevedra and Vigo are the area's transport hubs, with a reasonable network of local buses fanning out from them. Both are well served by buses and trains from Santiago de Compostela and La Coruña, and Vigo has services from more distant places like Madrid and Barcelona, as well as Aviaco flights from those cities. Three trains a day run from Vigo to Porto in Portugal (3½ hours).

LA CORUÑA
La Coruña (A Coruña in Galician), Galicia's capital, is an attractive port city with decent beaches and a wonderful seafront promenade, the Paseo Marítimo. The older part of town, the **Ciudad Vieja**, is huddled on the headland east of the port, while the most famous attraction, the **Torre de Hércules** lighthouse, originally built by the Romans (open daily from 10 am to 7 pm), caps the headland's northern end. The north side of the isthmus joining the headland

to the mainland is lined with sandy **beaches**, more of which stretch along the 30-km sweep of coast west of the city.

La Coruña's telephone code is ☎ 981.

Places to Stay & Eat
Calle de Riego de Agua, a block back from the waterfront Avenida de la Marina on the southern side of the isthmus, is a good spot to look for lodgings. *Hospedaje María Pita* (☎ 22 11 87) at No 38 (3rd floor), is good value with basic singles/doubles for 1200/1800 ptas. *Hostal Roma* (☎ 22 80 75), nearby at Rúa Nueva 3, offers basic doubles for 2100 ptas.

Calle de la Franja, the street behind Hospedaje María Pita, has several good places to eat. *Casa Jesusa* at No 8 offers a tasty seafood set lunch for 1000 ptas. You may have to queue for *O' Calexo* at No 34, but there's a good reason: the great fish grill (parrillada de pescado) for 2500 ptas for two.

Getting There & Away
There are daily trains and buses to Santiago de Compostela, Vigo, Santander, León, Madrid and Barcelona.

RÍAS ALTAS
North-east of La Coruña stretches the alternately pretty and awesome coast called the Rías Altas. This has some of the most dramatic scenery in Spain, and beaches that in good weather are every bit as inviting as those on the better known Rías Bajas. Spots to head for include the medieval towns **Betanzos, Pontedeume** and **Viveiro** (all of which have budget accommodation), the tremendous cliffs of **Cabo Ortegal** and the **beaches** between it and Viveiro. Buses from La Coruña and Santiago de Compostela will get you into the area – after that you'll need local buses and the occasional walk or lift.

PICOS DE EUROPA
This small mountainous region straddling Asturias, Cantabria and Castilla y León is some of the finest walking country in Spain. Spectacular scenery, combined with unique flora and fauna, ensures a continual flow of visitors from all over Europe and beyond.

The Picos are 25 km from the coast, and only around 40 km long and 40 km wide. They are comprised of three limestone massifs. In the south-east is the Andara Massif, with a summit of 2441 metres, and in the west is the Cornión Massif, with a summit of 2596 metres. In the centre is the best known and largest, the Uriello Massif, soaring to 2648 metres.

Books & Maps

Serious trekkers would be well advised to buy a copy of Lonely Planet's *Trekking in Spain*. If you want to buy detailed topographical maps of the area before coming to Spain, Edward Stanford, 12-14 Long Acre, London WC2E 9LP, can send you a list of those available. Try getting hold of the *Mapa Excursionista del Macizo Central de los Picos de Europa* by Miguel Andrade (1:25,000) and *Mapa del Macizo del Cornión* by José Ramón Lueje (1:25,000).

Things to See & Do

Serious trekkers should allow plenty of time for the Picos. If you're not quite that adventurous, perhaps the least strenuous way to get a feel for the area is to drive up to **Lago La Ercina** from Covadonga in the west of the Picos or to **Sotres** in the east. From either of these places you can set out on well-marked walking trails into the heart of the mountains.

Places to Stay & Eat

In a remote, beautiful setting off the road to Lago La Ercina, *Refugio de Enol* (☎ 98-584 85 76) is a simple stone building with bunk beds at 500 ptas (BYO sleeping bag) and good meals. In Sotres, *Pensión Los Picos* (☎ 98-594 50 24), also called Pensión Cipriano, is both the place to stay and the place to eat. Bunk beds cost 900 ptas, doubles range from 3000 to 4000 ptas and there is a menú for 1000 ptas. *Hostal Remoña* (☎ 942-73 66 05) in Espinama has singles/doubles from 2500/3500 ptas and a good menú for 950 ptas. The main access towns – Cangas de Onís, Arenas de Cabrales and Potes – all have a wide range of hostales.

Getting There & Away

The Picos are encircled by a ring road, from which three main routes lead into the heart of the mountains: from Cangas de Onís to Covadonga and Lago La Ercina; from Arenas de Cabrales to Sotres; and from Potes to Fuente Dé.

There are bus services from Santander, León, Oviedo and Gijón to the three main access towns, plus regular buses from Potes to Fuente Dé, and from Cangas de Onís to Covadonga and (in summer only) Lago La Ercina.

SANTANDER

Santander, capital of Cantabria, is a modern, cosmopolitan city with wide waterfront boulevards, leafy parks and crowded beaches. Semana Grande in August is a pretty wild party, but you won't find any accommodation here, or anywhere else on the north coast at that time, without booking well in advance.

The main tourist office (☎ 31 07 08) is in the estación marítima (ferry terminal); there's also a municipal tourist office (☎ 21 61 20) in the harbour-front Jardines de Pereda.

The telephone code for Santander is ☎ 942.

Things to See & Do

Santander's main attractions are the nightlife (see Entertainment later) and El Sardinero beach. As you come round to El Sardinero on bus No 1 or 2, you may notice an uncanny resemblance to Bondi Beach in Australia, with surfers out in force by mid-March, despite the cold. The streets back from the sea near El Sardinero are lined with beautiful houses. This is some of Spain's most expensive real estate.

Places to Stay

Camping Bellavista (☎ 27 48 43), on Cabo Mayor, is less than one km north of El Sardinero beach. From the centre, take bus No 9 (marked 'Cueto'), which stops 200 metres from the site – ask the driver when to get off.

Rooms are expensive in high summer, but the rates given here come down substantially from October to May. *Fonda Perla de Cuba* (☎ 21 00 41), Calle Hernán Cortés 8 (1st floor), is one of the better deals in town, with singles/doubles at 2000/4000 ptas. *Pensión La Corza* (☎ 21 29 50), down the same street at No 25 (3rd floor), has pleasant doubles for 5500 ptas. *Pensión Picos de Europa* (☎ 22 53 74), very near the bus station at Calle Calderón de la Barca 5 (3rd floor), is a cosy house with singles for around 2500 ptas and doubles with private shower for 4500 ptas.

If you have just arrived on the ferry from England, you might be looking for a little more luxury. *Hotel México* (☎ 21 24 50) at Calle

Calderón de la Barca 3 is a good bet. Featuring a collection of impressive paintings by the owners' son, it has singles/doubles with all mod cons for 5550/10,165 ptas.

Places to Eat

A good area for cheap eats is around Plaza Cañadio, three blocks back from the municipal tourist office. On the plaza itself the stylish *Restaurante Cañadio* serves first-class seafood and local specialities, with a lunch menú for 1550 ptas.

Just off the plaza, Calle Daoiz y Velarde has lots of options including *Mesón el Portón* at No 29 with a simple 850-pta lunch menú, and the *Bierhaus* at No 27 serving Spanish and German food. Also on this street are Tex-Mex and Chinese places and the old *Bodega Cigalaña* wine bar with good seafood.

Entertainment

Nightlife in Santander is centred around Calle Santa Lucía and is particularly good between Calle Santa Lucía and the waterfront. In summer, there is also quite a good scene in El Sardinero along the main drag.

Getting There & Away

Santander is one of the major entry points to Spain, thanks to its ferry link with Plymouth in England (see Getting There & Away at the start of this chapter).

The ferry terminal and train and bus stations are all in the centre of Santander, within 200 metres of each other. There are hourly buses to Bilbao (two hours, 875 ptas), five a day to San Sebastián (three hours, 1800 ptas), and two a day to La Coruña (10 hours, 5000 ptas) and Santiago de Compostela (11 hours, 5200 ptas).

Trains to Bilbao (one to three daily, 2½ hours, 855 ptas) and Oviedo are run by FEVE, a private line which does not accept rail passes. Trains to Madrid (via Ávila) and Galicia are run by RENFE, so rail passes are valid. To Madrid there are three trains daily (5½ to nine hours, from 3550 ptas). Trains to La Coruña and Santiago de Compostela follow a round-about route taking 13 hours or more, with changes at Palencia or Medina del Campo, and cost from 7100 ptas.

SANTILLANA DEL MAR

The beautiful village of Santillana del Mar, 30 km west of Santander, has a wonderful feeling of timelessness. Cobbled streets lined with well-preserved old houses give it a character all its own. When it rains, water pours off the overhanging roofs in a torrent, somehow adding to the unusual charm of the town.

The telephone code for Santillana is ☎ 942.

Things to See & Do

Santillana's fame lies as much in the **Cueva de Altamira**, two km west, as in the town itself. The 14,000-year-old animal paintings in the Altamira cave reduce many people to tears, and all those lucky enough to gain entry are deeply moved by what they see. A maximum of 20 people a day are allowed into the cave and if you want to be one of them, you must ask permission at least a year in advance, listing three or four preferred dates, by writing to: Centro de Investigación Altamira, 39330 Santillana del Mar, Cantabria, Spain. If you're one of the lucky ones, admission is 400 ptas. Some people turn up on the day in the hope that someone has cancelled and they can get lucky. There's a small museum, open to all, at the cave; its hours are Tuesday to Sunday from 9.30 am to 2.30 pm.

Places to Stay & Eat

The good *Camping Santillana* (☎ 81 82 50), about 500 metres west of town on the main highway, charges around 500 ptas per person, 500 ptas per tent and 500 ptas per car.

In the old town, the best place to stay is *Posada Octavio* (☎ 81 81 99) at Plaza Las Arenas 4, run by the friendly González family. In summer, singles cost 3000 to 3500 ptas and doubles are 4500 to 5000 ptas. Most of the other places in the old town are considerably dearer, but there are plenty of options along the highway to the east, among them *Hostal Montañes* (☎ 81 8177) at Calle Le Dorat 8, with singles/doubles at 3500/5000 ptas in summer. Restaurants here tend to be expensive. A couple of exceptions are *Casa Cossío*, Plaza Abad Francisco Navarro 12, which does good seafood and has a menú for 950 ptas, and *Restaurant Altamira*, at Calle del Cartón 1, with a reliable lunch menú for 1100 ptas.

Getting There & Away

There are four buses a day (six in summer) between Santander and Santillana del Mar.

País Vasco, Navarra & Aragón

The Basque people have lived for thousands of years in Spain's País Vasco (Basque Country, or Euskadi in the Basque language) and the adjoining Pays Basque across the border in France. They have their own ancient language (Euskara), a distinct physical appearance, a rich culture and a proud history. Along with this strong sense of identity has come, among a significant minority of Basques in Spain, a desire for independence. The Basque nationalist movement was born in the 19th century. During the Franco years the Basque people were brutally repressed and Euskadi ta Askatasuna (ETA), a radical separatist movement, began its terrorist activities. With Spain's changeover to democracy in the late 1970s, the País Vasco was granted a large degree of autonomy, but ETA has continued to pursue full independence with terrorist tactics.

While ETA terrorism is still a deterrent to tourism, the País Vasco remains one of the most beautiful regions of Spain. Although the Bilbao area is heavily industrialised, the region has a spectacular coastline, a green and mountainous interior and the elegance of San Sebastián. Another great reason to visit is to sample the delights of Basque cuisine, considered the best in Spain.

South-east of the País Vasco, the Navarra and Aragón regions reach down from the Pyrenees into drier, more southern lands. Navarra has a high Basque population and its capital is Pamplona, home of the Sanfermines festival with its world-famous running of the bulls. The Aragonese Pyrenees offer the best range of opportunities for walking and skiing on the Spanish side of this mountain range. Head for the Parque Nacional de Ordesa for the best walking (the park entrance is at Torla) but note – especially in the peak Spanish holiday period, mid-July to mid-August – that a maximum 1500 visitors are allowed into the park at any time. Weatherwise the best months up there are late June to mid-September. Aragón has half a dozen decent ski resorts – the regional tourist office in Zaragoza has plenty of information about them.

SAN SEBASTIÁN

San Sebastián (Donostia in Basque) is stunning. Famed as a ritzy resort for wealthy Spaniards who want to get away from the hordes in the south, it has also been a stronghold of Basque nationalist feeling since well before Franco. The surprisingly relaxed town, of 180,000 people, curves round the beautiful Bahía de la Concha. Those who live here consider themselves the luckiest people in Spain, and after spending a few days on the beaches in preparation for the wild evenings, you may well begin to understand why.

Information

The very helpful municipal tourist office (☎ 48 11 66) is on the corner of Paseo de la República Argentina and Calle Reina Regente. From June to September it's open daily from 8 am to 8 pm (Sunday from 10 am to 1 pm); otherwise it's open weekdays from 9 am to 2 pm and 3.30 to 7 pm, and Saturday from 9 am to 2 pm. There's also a Basque regional tourist office (☎ 42 62 82) at Paseo de los Fueros 1.

The main post office is on Calle Urdaneta, behind the cathedral. The telephone code for San Sebastián is ☎ 943.

Lavomatique, in the Parte Vieja (old town) at Calle de Iñigo 14, is a rarity in Spain – a good self-service laundrette.

Things to See

The **Playa de la Concha** and **Playa de Ondarreta** make up one of the most beautiful city beaches in Spain. You can get out to **Isla de Santa Clara**, in the middle of the bay, by boat from the port – but it's more exciting to swim. In summer, rafts are anchored about halfway from Ondarreta to the island to serve as rest stops.

If you intend to spend your evenings as the locals do, you won't be up to much more than sitting on the beach during the day. However, there is some worthwhile sightseeing to be done in and around San Sebastián.

The **Museo de San Telmo**, in a 16th-century monastery on Plaza de Zuloaga, has a bit of everything – ancient tombstones, agriculture and carpentry displays, a good art collection – and the squeakiest floors in Spain. It's open Tuesday to Saturday from 10.30 am to 1.30 pm and 4 to 7.30 pm and is free.

Overlooking Bahía de la Concha from the

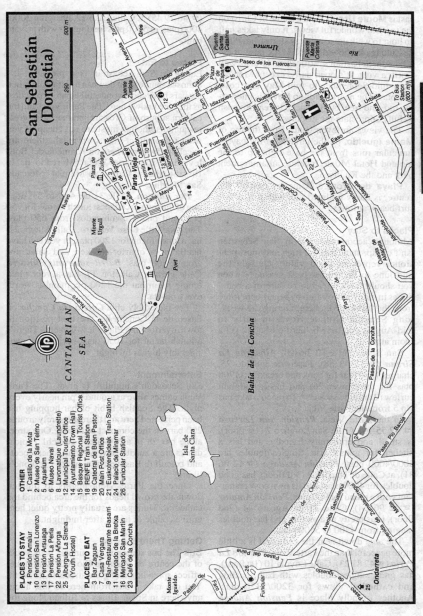

San Sebastián (Donostia)

CANTABRIAN SEA

Bahía de la Concha

Isla de Santa Clara

Monte Urgull

Parte Vieja

Port

Monte Igueldo

Ondarreta

PLACES TO STAY
4 Pensión Amaiur
10 Pensión San Lorenzo
13 Pensión Arsuaga
17 Pensión La Perla
22 Pensión Aforga
25 Albergue La Sirena (Youth Hostel)

PLACES TO EAT
3 Bar Zaguan
7 Casa Vergara
9 Bar-Restaurante Basarri
11 Mercado de la Bretxa
16 Mercado San Martín
23 Café de la Concha

OTHER
1 Castillo de la Mota
2 Museo de San Telmo
5 Aquarium
6 Museo Naval
8 Lavomatique (Laundrette)
12 Municipal Tourist Office
14 Ayuntamiento (Town Hall)
15 Basque Regional Tourist Office
18 RENFE Train Station
19 Catedral de Buen Pastor
20 Main Post Office
21 Euskotrenbideak Train Station
24 Palacio de Miramar
26 Funicular Station

SPAIN

east is **Monte Urgull**, with a statue of Christ on the top and wonderful views. It only takes half an hour to walk up: a stairway starts from Plaza de Zuloaga in the old town. At the base of the hill, San Sebastián's **aquarium** is also well worth a visit. It's open daily, except Monday from mid-September to mid-May and costs 450 ptas. The nearby **Museo Naval** is interesting too, and free, but you need to read Spanish to fully appreciate the displays.

The views are even better from the top of **Monte Igueldo**, on the far side of the bay. A funicular runs from the base right up to the top-end Hotel Monte Igueldo, an amusement park and the Ku disco.

Playa de Gros, 500 metres east of the centre, is badly polluted although it is a fine surf beach at times.

Places to Stay

Although accommodation in San Sebastián isn't cheap, standards are high and most pensiones represent good value. Outside the mid-June to September peak season – when you should book ahead to be sure of a bed – prices in many places drop by a quarter or more from the levels given here. During the week-long Semana Grande fiesta in early to mid-August you may be hard-pushed to get a room at all.

San Sebastián's HI hostel, *Albergue La Sirena* (☎ 31 02 68), Paseo de Igueldo 25, charges 1500 ptas for bunk and breakfast (1700 ptas for those over 26) and has a midnight curfew (2 am at weekends). To reach it take bus No 5 from the Parte Vieja.

In the Parte Vieja, *Pensión San Lorenzo* (☎ 42 55 16), Calle San Lorenzo 2 (1st floor), is small and eminently friendly, and has a kitchen for guests' use. Singles/doubles are 3000/4000 ptas. *Pensión Arsuaga* (☎ 42 06 81), at Calle de Narrika 3 (3rd floor), has good doubles for 4000 ptas, and its own cosy restaurant with a menú for 900 ptas. *Pensión Amaiur* (☎ 42 96 54), Calle 31 de Agosto 44 (2nd floor), is as pretty as a picture and has doubles ranging from 4300 to 5500 ptas.

The area down near the cathedral is a little more peaceful than the Parte Vieja. *Pensión La Perla* (☎ 42 81 23), Calle Loyola 10 (1st floor), has great singles/doubles with bath, heating and cathedral views for 3200/5350 ptas. Another friendly place is *Pensión Añorga*

(☎ 46 79 45) at Calle Easo 12, charging 3000/4000 ptas, or 5000 ptas for doubles with private bath.

Places to Eat

Eating in San Sebastián is a pleasure. It's almost a shame to sit down in a restaurant when the bars have such wonderful tapas, or pinchos, as they are known here. The Parte Vieja and the eastern suburb of Gros are jammed with great restaurants, though most are not cheap. If you want to construct your own meals, there are excellent *food markets* on Alameda del Boulevard in the Parte Vieja (Mercado de la Bretxa), and on Calle San Marcial (Mercado San Martín).

Bar Zaguan, Calle 31 de Agosto 31, does one of the town's cheapest lunch menús for 950 ptas, and platos combinados from 650 ptas. The good little *Casa Vergara*, Calle Mayor 21, has a lunch menú for 1200 ptas, or you can have paella or a quarter-chicken and salad for around 800 ptas. *Bar-Restaurante Basarri*, Calle Fermín Calbetón 17, has a very plain dining room but the 1200-pta menú is worth every peseta.

The incredibly chic *Café de la Concha* on Paseo de la Concha has the best position in town, overlooking Playa de la Concha. There's a lunch menú for 1050 ptas – prices are considerably higher by night.

Entertainment

San Sebastián's nightlife is great. The Parte Vieja comes alive at around 8 pm nearly every night. The Spanish habit of bar-hopping has been perfected here and there are surely around 200 bars in the compact old town. One street alone has 28 in a 300-metre stretch! Typical drinks are a zurrito (a very small, cheap beer) and txacolí (a Basque wine, not to everyone's liking).

Once the Parte Vieja begins to quieten down, the crowd heads for the area behind the cathedral. Things are usually pretty quiet here until a couple of hours after midnight.

Getting There & Away

Bus The bus station is 20 minutes walk south of the centre on Plaza de Pio XII, with ticket offices spreading along the streets to its north. You can take a bus from here to just about anywhere in Spain. Buses to Bilbao along the autopista go every half-hour, take a little over an hour and cost 1030 ptas. You can also go via Zarauz and the coast which takes about three hours. The bus to Pamplona takes over two hours and costs 750 ptas.

Train The RENFE train station is across the river on Paseo de Francia, on a line linking Paris with Madrid. There are six trains a day to Madrid (six to 8½ hours, from 4600 ptas), and two to Barcelona (nine to 10½ hours, from 4600 ptas) via Pamplona and Zaragoza. To Paris (six to eight hours, from 10,500 ptas), there's one direct train a day and several others with a change at Hendaye. Other destinations include Salamanca, La Coruña and Algeciras.

Trains to Bilbao, and some to Hendaye, are run by a private company, Euskotrenbideak, from a separate station on Calle de Easo.

COSTA VASCA
Spain's often ruggedly beautiful Costa Vasca (Basque Coast) is one of its least touristed coastal regions. A combination of cool weather, rough seas and terrorism tends to put some people off.

Things to See & Do
Between the French border and San Sebastián, **Fuenterrabia** (Hondarribia) is a picturesque fishing town with good beaches nearby, while **Pasajes de San Juan** (Pasaia Donibane) has a pretty old section and some good-value fish restaurants.

West of San Sebastián, the coast extends to Bilbao, passing through some of the finest **surfing** territory in Europe. Keep your wet suit handy though, as the water here can be pretty chilly. **Zarauz** (Zarautz), about 15 km west of San Sebastián, stages a round of the World Surfing Championship each September, when all the big names turn up for one of Europe's greatest surfing spectacles. Slightly west, the picturesque village of **Guetaria** (Getaria) has a small beach, but the main attraction is just in wandering around the narrow streets and the fishing harbour.

Mundaca (Mundaka), 12 km north of Guernica (Gernika), is a surfing town. For much of the year, surfers and beach bums hang around waiting for the almost legendary 'left-hander' to break. When it does, it's one of the

longest and best lefts you'll ever see! If you're interested in renting a surfboard or stocking up on Aussie surf gear, ask the locals to direct you to Craig's shop (Craig is an Australian who came here to surf some years ago and never managed to leave).

In Bilbao, the showpiece (when it opens in 1997) will be the **Museo Guggenheim de Arte Contemporáneo**, in a new waterfront building that looks for all the world like a huge scrap-metal yard seen through the eyes of someone on a strong dose of LSD. Inside will be art by Picasso, Dalí, Miró, Matisse, Pollock and other 20th-century greats. On a more old-fashioned note, the excellent **Museo de Bellas Artes** in Parque de Doña Casilda de Iturriza has works by El Greco, Velázquez and Goya, and an important collection of Basque art.

Places to Stay & Eat
San Sebastián and Bilbao are the most obvious bases for excursions along the Basque coast. In Bilbao you might try *Hostal Jofra* (☎ 94-421 29 49), at Calle Elcano 34, which has singles/doubles from 1700/3000 ptas.

In the smaller towns the easiest and cheapest option is generally camping. *Camping Talai-Mendi* (☎ 943-83 00 42) in Zarauz is 500 metres from the beach and signposted from the highway on the east side of town; it's open from July to mid-September only. Guetaria is well known for its excellent seafood and has a couple of harbourside restaurants where you can watch the fishing boats unload.

In Mundaca, *Camping Portuondo* (☎ 94-687 63 68) is on the riverfront about one km south of town, on the road to Guernica. For food, you will be pretty much limited to sand-wiches or do-it-yourself fare, as anything else is prohibitively expensive. There is an excellent *food market* in nearby Bermeo (west of Mundaca).

Getting Around
The coastal road is best explored by car. If you don't have your own transport, there are buses from San Sebastián to Zarauz and Guetaria, and from Bilbao to Guernica. From Guernica you can take a bus to Bermeo which will drop you in Mundaca. Hitching can be painfully slow.

PAMPLONA

The madcap festivities of Sanfermines in Pamplona (Iruñea in Basque) run from 6 to 14 July and are characterised by nonstop partying, out-of-control drunkenness and, of course, the bulls being set free in the streets of the old town. Every year there are injuries, and occasionally deaths, as the frenzied crowd runs through the streets in front of, behind and around the bulls. Inevitably, someone always gets a little too close, with predictably gory consequences.

The safest place to watch the running (*encierro*) is on TV. If this is too tame for you, see if you can sweet-talk your way on to a balcony in one of the streets where the bulls run. You might have to pay, but it is well worth the cost if you can afford it. The other places to watch from are Plaza Santo Domingo where the action begins, or near the entrance to the bullring. The bulls are let out at 8 am, but if you want to get a good vantage point you will have to be there around 6 am.

If you visit at any other time of year, you'll find a very pleasant and modern city, with lovely parks and gardens, a compact and partly walled old town, and a large proportion of students among the population of 185,000. The tourist office (☎ 22 07 41) is just south of the old town at Calle Duque de Ahumada 3.

Pamplona's telephone code is ☎ 948.

Places to Stay & Eat

The nearest camping ground is *Camping Ezcaba* (☎ 33 03 15), seven km north of the city. To get there, take an Arre or Oricain bus from Calle Teovaldos near the bullring. The camping ground fills up a couple of days before Sanfermines.

If you want to stay in a pensión or hostal during Sanfermines, you'll need to book well in advance (and pay a substantial premium). During the festival, beds are also available in private houses (casas particulares) – check with the tourist office or haggle with the locals at the bus and train stations. Otherwise, you'll have to do what everyone else does and sleep in one of the parks, plazas or shopping malls. You can leave your bags for 200 ptas in the consigna at the bus station. Alternatively, you could make day trips here from San Sebastián or other towns.

Fonda La Montañesa (☎ 22 43 80), Calle San Gregorio 2, has clean and basic singles/doubles for 1300/2600 ptas. *Pensión Casa García* (☎ 22 38 93), along the street at No 12, is a little better at 1400/2700 ptas.

The best way to eat cheaply in Pamplona is to fill up on tapas. There are some good places on Calle San Lorenzo; *Lanzale* at No 31 and *El Erburo* at No 19 have menús for 1000 and 1200 ptas respectively.

Getting There & Away

The bus station is on Avenida de Yanguas y Miranda, a five-minute walk south of the old town. There are up to 12 buses a day to San Sebastián (2½ hours, 700 ptas) and daily services to Madrid, Zaragoza and Bilbao.

The train station is about two km north-west of the old town. There are daily trains to San Sebastián (2½ hours, 1200 ptas), Zaragoza and Barcelona.

ZARAGOZA

Zaragoza, capital of Aragón and home to half its 1.2 million people, is often said to be the most Spanish city of all. Once an important Roman city, under the name Caesaraugusta, and later a Muslim centre for four centuries, it is today relatively untouched by tourism. The old town is full of lively bars and restaurants, and Aragonese cooking is good.

Information

The city tourist office (☎ 20 12 00) is in a surreal-looking glass cube on Plaza del Pilar. From Monday to Saturday, it's open from 9.30 am to 1.30 pm and from 4.30 to 7.30 pm; on Sunday it's open from 10 am to 2 pm. There's also a regional tourist office (☎ 39 35 37) in the Torreón de la Zuda, a Mudéjar tower on Plaza Cesar Augusto.

The post office is at Paseo de la Independencia 33. The telephone code for Zaragoza is ☎ 976.

Things to See

Zaragoza's focus is the vast 500-metre-long main square, **Plaza de Nuestra Señora del Pilar**. Dominating the north side is the **Basílica de Nuestra Señora del Pilar**, a 17th-century church of epic proportions. People flock to kiss a piece of marble pillar – believed to have been left by the Virgin Mary when she appeared to Santiago (St James) in a vision here in AD 40

SPAIN

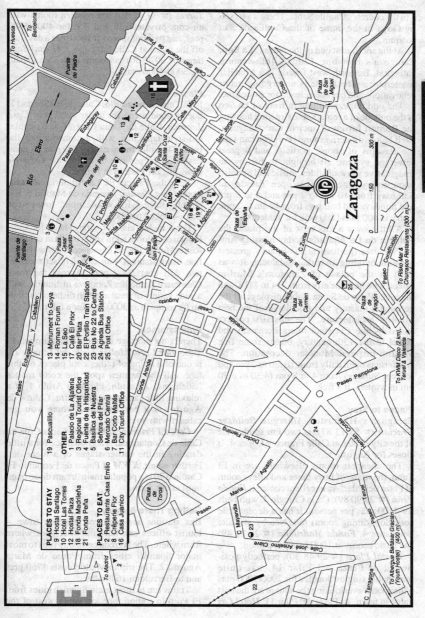

Zaragoza

300 m

0   150   300 m

To Huesca

To Barcelona

To Madrid

To KYM Disco (2 km),
Teruel & Valencia

To Risko Mar &
Churrasco Restaurants (300 m)

To Albergue Baldsar Gracián
(Youth Hostel) (400 m)

To Tarragona

PLACES TO STAY
9 Hostal Santiago
10 Hostal Las Torres
12 Hostal Plaza
18 Fonda Madrileña
21 Fonda Peña

PLACES TO EAT
2 Restaurante Casa Emilio
8 Crêperie Flor
16 Casa Juanico
19 Pascualillo

OTHER
1 Palacio de La Aljafería
3 Regional Tourist Office
4 Fuente de la Hispanidad
5 Basílica de Nuestra
   Señora del Pilar
6 Mercado Central
7 Bar Corto Maltés
11 City Tourist Office
13 Monument to Goya
14 Roman Forum
15 La Seo
17 Café El Prior
20 Bar Plata
22 El Portillo Train Station
23 Bus No 22 to Centre
24 Agreda Bus Station
25 Post Office

– in the church's Capilla Santa. There's a fresco by Goya in the dome of the Capilla de San Joaquín.

At the south-east end of the plaza is **La Seo**, Zaragoza's brooding 12th to 16th-century cathedral. Its north-west façade is a Mudéjar masterpiece. The inside is undergoing major renovations and has been closed for some time.

The odd trapezoid thing in front of La Seo is the outside of a remarkable structure housing the **Roman forum** of ancient Caesaraugusta. Well below modern ground level you can visit the remains of shops, porticos and a great sewerage system, all brought to life by an imaginative show of slides, music and Spanish commentary. The forum is open Tuesday to Saturday from 10 am to 2 pm and 5 to 8 pm and Sundays and holidays from 10 am to 2 pm. Entry is 400 ptas (200 ptas for students).

A little over a km west of the plaza, the **Palacio de La Aljafería**, today housing Aragón's *cortes* (parliament), is Spain's greatest Muslim building outside Andalucía. It was built as the palace of Zaragoza's Muslim rulers, who held the city from 714 to 1118, and the inner Patio de Santa Isabel displays all the geometric mastery and fine detail of the best Muslim architecture. The upstairs palace, added by the Christian rulers Fernando and Isabel in the 15th century, boasts some fine Muslim-inspired Mudéjar decoration. The Aljafería is open daily from 10 am to 2 pm and (except Sunday) from 4 to 8 pm (4.30 to 6.30 pm in winter). It's free.

Places to Stay

Zaragoza's HI hostel, *Albergue Baltásar Gracián* (☎ 55 13 87), is two km south-west of the city centre at Calle Franco y López 4. It closes for August.

The cheapest rooms elsewhere are in El Tubo, the maze of busy lanes and alleys south of Plaza del Pilar. An excellent choice is *Fonda Peña* (☎ 29 90 89), Calle Cinegio 3, with beds for 1100 ptas per person. It has a decent little comedor (dining room) too. Nearby at Calle Estébanes 4, *Fonda Madrileña* (☎ 29 81 49) has basic rooms at 1000 ptas per person.

Hostal Plaza (☎ 29 48 30), perfectly positioned at Plaza del Pilar 14, has quite reasonable singles/doubles for 2000/3000 ptas – the rooms overlooking the square are the best value in town. At Plaza del Pilar 11, *Hotel Las Torres* (☎ 39 42 50) has modern rooms with air-con, private bath and TV for 4000/6500 ptas, and parking spaces at 1000 ptas a day. Just off the plaza at Calle Santiago 3, *Hostal Santiago* (☎ 39 45 50) has rooms with TV and bath for 3000/4000 ptas.

Places to Eat

In El Tubo, *Pascualillo*, Calle de la Libertad 5, does a good menú for under 1000 ptas. *Casa Juanico*, Calle de Santa Cruz 21, is a popular old-style tapas bar with a comedor out the back. The solid menú costs 1100 ptas. A great dessert of crêpes can be had in the *Crêperie Flor*, just off Plaza San Felipe.

Near the Palacio de La Aljafería, *Restaurante Casa Emilio*, Avenida de Madrid 5, is a simple place with wholesome, low-priced home-cooked meals.

For a higher class of eating, head for Calle Francisco Vitoria, a km south of Plaza del Pilar. *Risko Mar*, Calle de Francisco Vitoria 16, is a fine fish restaurant – an excellent set meal for two will cost 5000 ptas. Across the road, *Churrasco* is another Zaragoza institution, with a wide variety of meat and fish dishes. You'll be up for as much as 3000 ptas for a full meal.

Entertainment

There's no shortage of bars in and around El Tubo. *Bar Corto Maltés*, Calle del Temple 23, is one of a string of rather cool places on this lane. All the barmen sport the corto maltés (sideburns). *Chastón*, Plaza de Ariño 4, is a relaxing little jazz club. *Bar Plata*, Calle 4 de Agosto, is a bar cantante, where you get cabaret with your drinks.

Café El Prior, near Plaza de Santa Cruz on Calle de Contamina, is a good place for a little dancing in the earlier stages of a night out. Further south, *KWM* at Paseo de Fernando El Católico 70 is a popular mainstream disco open until about 5 am.

Getting There & Away

Bus stations are scattered all over town – tourist offices can tell you what goes where from where. The Agreda company runs to most major Spanish cities from Paseo de María Agustín 7. The trip to Madrid costs 1750 ptas and to Barcelona 1640 ptas.

Trains run to most main Spanish cities from El Portillo station, one km south-west of the centre on Calle José Anselmo Clave, linked by bus No 22 to Plaza de España in the centre. Up to 14 trains daily run to both Madrid (three to 4½ hours, from 2600 ptas) and Barcelona (3½ to 4½ hours, from 3000 ptas). Some Barcelona trains go via Tarragona. There are two trains a day to Valencia (six hours, from 2200 ptas) via Teruel, and two to San Sebastián (four or 5½ hours, from 2400 ptas), with a stop in Pamplona.

TERUEL

Aragón's hilly deep south is culturally closer to Castilla-La Mancha or the backlands of Valencia than to some other regions of Aragón itself. A good stop on the way to the coast from Zaragoza, or from Cuenca in Castilla-La Mancha, is the town of Teruel, which has a flavour all its own thanks to four centuries of Muslim domination in the middle ages and some famous Mudéjar architecture dating from after its capture by the Christians in 1171.

The tourist office (☎ 60 22 79) is at Calle Tomás Nogués 1.

Teruel's telephone code is ☎ 978.

Things to See

Teruel has four magnificent Mudéjar towers, on the cathedral of **Santa María** (12th and 13th centuries) and the churches of **San Salvador** (13th century), **San Martín** and **San Pedro** (both 14th century). These, and the ceiling inside Santa María, are among Spain's best Mudéjar architecture. Note the complicated brickwork and colourful tiles on the towers, so typical of the style. A further example of Mudéjar work is **La Escalinata**, the flight of stairs leading down to the train station from Paseo del Óvalo, on the edge of the old town.

The **Museo Provincial de Teruel** on Plaza Padre Polanco is well worth a visit, mainly for its fascinating, well-presented archaeological collection going back to the days of *Homo erectus*. Entry is free; hours are Tuesday to Friday from 10 am to 2 pm and 4 to 7 pm, and weekends from 10 am to 2 pm.

Places to Stay & Eat

Fonda El Tozal (☎ 60 10 22) at Calle Rincón 5 is great value. It's an amazing rickety old house run by a wonderful, friendly family, and most of the rooms have cast-iron beds, enamelled chamber pots and exposed ceiling beams. Singles/doubles cost 1300/2500 ptas. In winter, you might prefer *Hostal Aragón* (☎ 60 13 87), Calle Santa María 4, which is also charming but has mod cons such as heating. Rooms are 1620/2750 ptas, or 2775/4450 ptas with private bath. Both these places are just a couple of minutes walk from the main square, Plaza Carlos Caste.

Teruel is famed for its jamón. If you can't fit a whole leg of ham in your backpack, at least sample a tostada con jamón, with tomato and olive oil. At *Bar Gregori*, Paseo del Óvalo 6, you can choose from a tasty range of tapas, or raciones from 400 to 900 ptas. *Bar El Torreón* at Ronda de Ambeles 28, in one of the turrets of what were the city walls, offers a filling lunch menú for 800 ptas.

Getting There & Away

The bus station (☎ 60 20 04) is on Ronda de Ambeles. There are daily buses to Barcelona (six hours, 3000 ptas), Cuenca (2¾ hours, 1050 ptas), Valencia (2½ hours, 1050 ptas) and Madrid (4½ hours, 2215 ptas).

By rail, Teruel is about midway between Valencia and Zaragoza, with three trains a day to both places, taking just under three hours and costing around 1100 ptas.

To get to the old town, walk out of the train station, take a deep breath, and start climbing the stairway in front of you.

Tunisia

Despite being the smallest country in North Africa, Tunisia boasts a rich cultural and social heritage – Phoenician, Roman, Byzantine, Arab, Ottoman and French empires have all come and gone in this part of the world.

Facts about the Country

HISTORY

The ancient city-state of Carthage, arch rival of Rome, was only a few km from the centre of the modern capital, Tunis. Carthage began life in 814 BC as one of a series of Phoenician staging posts. It remained relatively unimportant until Phoenicia (situated on what is now coastal Lebanon and Syria) was overrun by the Assyrians in the 7th century BC. As a result, Carthage rapidly grew into the metropolis of the Phoenician world, recording a population of about half a million at its peak.

By the 6th century BC, it had become the main power in the western Mediterranean – bringing it into inevitable conflict with the emerging Roman Empire. The two fought each other almost to a standstill in the course of the 128-year Punic Wars, which began in 264 BC. Carthage's legendary general Hannibal appeared to have brought the Romans to their knees after his invasion of Italy in 216 BC, but the wars ended in total victory for Rome. The Romans showed no mercy after the fall of Carthage in 146 BC. The city was razed and the population sold into slavery.

Carthage was rebuilt as a Roman city and it became the capital of the province of Africa, an area roughly corresponding to modern Tunisia. Africa's main attraction for the Romans was the grain-growing plains of the Medjerda Valley, west of Carthage, which became known as the bread basket of the empire. The remains of the cities they built on these plains, such as Dougga, are among Tunisia's best known attractions.

The Vandals captured Carthage in 439 AD and made it the capital of their North African

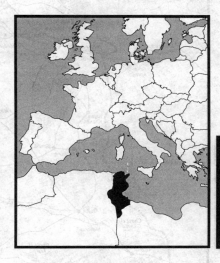

empire until they were ousted by the Byzantines in 533 AD. The Byzantines never managed more than a shaky foothold, and put up little resistance when the Arabs arrived from the east in 670 AD, ruling from the holy city of Kairouan, 150 km south of Carthage. They proved to be the most influential of conquerors, introducing both Islam and the social structure which remains the basis of Tunisian life today.

After the political fragmentation of the Arab empire, Tunisia became the eastern flank of a Moroccan empire belonging to the group of Islamic Berbers known as the Almohads. The Moroccans appointed the Hafsid family as governors and they ruled, eventually as an independent monarchy, from 1207 until 1574 – a period of stability and prosperity.

The Hafsids were defeated by the Ottoman Turks and Tunisia came to be ruled by a local elite of Turkish janissaries (the professional elite of the Ottoman armies). By the 18th century, this elite had merged with the local populace and produced its own national monarchy, the Huseinid beys.

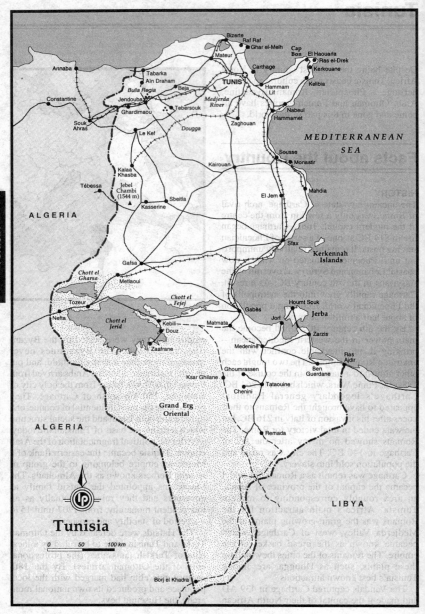

TUNISIA

Tunisia

0   50   100 km

In the 19th century, the beys were careful not to provoke the expansionist French. They managed to delay colonisation for some years by outlawing piracy, westernising the administration and, in 1857, adopting a constitution. However, serious financial mismanagement finally gave the French an excuse to invade from Algeria in 1881, and Tunisia became a French protectorate in 1883.

In the 1930s, the Néo-Destour movement for national liberation grew under the leadership of Habib Bourguiba, a Sorbonne-educated lawyer. The French banned the movement and jailed Bourguiba. The movement flourished briefly during the German occupation of Tunis in WWII when Bourguiba was released and the beys appointed ministers from the Néo-Destour movement. This came to an end with the Allied victory in North Africa, and Bourguiba went into exile. Bourguiba orchestrated two years of guerilla warfare against the French from Egypt, eventually forcing the French to grant autonomy in 1955. Bourguiba returned to head the new government, and Tunisia was granted independence a year later.

In 1957, the bey was deposed and Bourguiba became the first president of the new republic. In 1975, the national assembly made him president for life. Bourguiba consolidated his power in 1981 at the country's first multiparty elections.

However, as the 1980s progressed, Bourguiba began to loose touch with his people and became isolated from the rest of the Arab world. In November 1987, the interior minister, Zine el-Abidine ben Ali, orchestrated Bourguiba's downfall and was installed as president.

Tunisia remains one of the most stable and moderate Arab countries. It has developed close ties with both the USA and Germany, which supply the bulk of its foreign aid.

In recent years, the country has become one of the Mediterranean's major tourist attractions, drawing millions of northern Europeans to its shores each year.

GEOGRAPHY & ECOLOGY

Tunisia occupies an area of about 164,150 sq km, bordered by Algeria to the west, Libya to the south-east, and the Mediterranean to the east and north. The mountainous northern third of the country is dominated by the eastern extensions of the Atlas Mountains.

The north coast is Tunisia's green belt, with a fertile coastal plain backed by the densely forested Kroumirie Mountains. The forests are home to large numbers of wild boar, as well as jackals, mongooses and genets. The country's main mountain range is the rugged central Dorsale, further south. It runs from Kasserine in the west and peters out into Cap Bon in the east. It includes the country's highest peak, Jebel Chambi (1544 metres). Between these ranges lies the fertile Medjerda Valley, fed by the country's only permanent river. South of the Dorsale, a high plain falls away to a series of salt lakes (chotts) and then to a sandy desert on the edge of the Sahara known as the Grand Erg Oriental.

The east coast is remarkable for the vast areas under olive cultivation, particularly around Sfax.

GOVERNMENT & POLITICS

The republic of Tunisia is governed by a president and a chamber of deputies of 144 members. Political reforms since the ousting of Bourguiba in 1987 have legalised some opposition parties, although it hasn't done them much good: the ruling Rassemblement Constitutionnel Démocratique (RCD) won all 144 seats at elections held in March 1994, and President ben Ali got 99% of the presidential votes.

ECONOMY

Tunisia's oil is running out fast. Petroleum, which once contributed 25% of export income, now generates less than 10%. The economy relies heavily on tourism to bridge the gap. Leather and textiles are the biggest income earners, followed by phosphates, olive oil, fertilisers and chemicals. Food, raw materials and capital goods are the chief imports.

The main problem is unemployment, estimated to be as high as 30%. Living standards, however, are high compared to other developing countries. Education is free during primary and secondary school, but universities are now charging fees. Health care is no longer free for everyone.

POPULATION & PEOPLE

Tunisia has an estimated population of almost nine million, although no census has been taken since 1984. Most people are of Arab/ Berber stock. The original Berbers make up only 1% of the population and are confined mainly to the south of the country. Before the creation of Israel, Tunisia had a Jewish population of around 150,000. Only 2000 remain, mainly in Tunis and on Jerba. The major cities and their estimated populations are Tunis and suburbs (1.89 million), Sfax (380,000), Bizerte (135,000) and Sousse (110,000).

ARTS
Artistic activity is heavily focused on Tunis. Tunis has a large number of galleries – these are listed on the inside back page of the *Tunisia News*.

CULTURE
Tunisia is easy-going by Muslim standards, especially in Tunis and the major tourist areas. You'll find many Western trappings, such as fast food, pop music and women dressed in the latest European fashions. However, traditional life has changed little in rural areas, where the mosque, the hammam (bathhouse) and the café remain the focal points of life.

Avoiding Offence
The residents of Tunis and the resort towns have seen far too many Westerners to be offended easily, but the situation is different in rural areas. You can avoid any problems by dressing respectfully, which means long trousers for men and clothes that show off as little flesh as possible for women.

Women in Society
Thanks largely to the efforts of their secular, socialist, former president, Habib Bourguiba, conditions for women in Tunisia are better than just about anywhere in the Islamic world – to Western eyes, at least. His 1956 Personal Status Code banned polygamy and ended divorce by renunciation. He called the *hijab* (veil) an 'odious rag', and banned it from schools as part of a campaign to phase out a garment he regarded as demeaning. He didn't quite succeed, although it is very unusual to find a women under 30 wearing one. You will encounter some interesting mother-daughter combinations wandering around: mother wrapped in hijab, and daughter adorned in the latest Western fashions.

Women make up about 20% of the paid workforce.

RELIGION
Islam is the state religion and 99.75% of the population are Sunni Muslims. There are about 20,000 Roman Catholics and 2000 Jews.

Ramadan
Ramadan is the ninth month of the Muslim calendar, when all Muslims must abstain from eating, drinking, smoking and having sex between dawn and dusk. It commemorates the month when the Qur'an was revealed to Mohammed.

For the traveller it can be an interesting, though frustrating, time to travel. During the day it's often difficult to find a restaurant open, although the big tourist hotels usually function normally. Be discreet about where you drink and smoke – don't do it openly during the day. When the sun goes down, things get really busy, and restaurants and shops stay open late. It's a great contrast to the normal routine, when very little happens in towns after about 9 pm.

LANGUAGE
Tunisia is virtually bilingual. Arabic is the language of education and government, but almost everyone speaks some French. You are unlikely to come across many English, German or Italian-speakers outside the main tourist centres. You'll get a good reception if you try to speak Arabic rather than French. It's a good idea to learn the basic greetings. Tunisian Arabic is essentially the same as Moroccan Arabic (see the Language Guide at the back of the book for pronunciation guidelines and useful words and phrases).

Facts for the Visitor

PLANNING
Climate & When to Go
Northern Tunisia has a typical Mediterranean climate, with hot, dry summers and mild, wet winters. The further south you go, the hotter and drier it gets. Some Saharan areas go without rain for years.

Summer is the most popular time to visit, mainly because this is the European holiday season, but it is not the ideal time because it's so hot – hovering around 40°C for days on end. Transport during this period is also stretched to the limit and hotel rooms are hard to find after noon.

The best time to visit is in spring, when the north is still green, the south is pleasantly warm and the summer hordes have yet to arrive. Autumn is the next best time.

Books & Maps
Lonely Planet's *North Africa – travel survival kit* provides more-detailed information about the country, and Freytag & Berndt produce the best map. The tourist office in Tunis hands out a perfectly adequate road map.

What to Bring
Essential items for the summer visitor include a broad-brimmed hat, good sunglasses and a sunscreen. If you're planning on visiting the Sahara, a light sweater will come in handy even in summer because it gets surprisingly cold at night. In winter, you will need a warm sweater and – in the north – a raincoat. An alarm clock is important for catching early morning buses. Unless you're happy with a diet of expensive foreign papers, bring a supply of books.

SUGGESTED ITINERARIES
The following are three suggested one-week itineraries, based around arriving at one of the country's three major international airports:

Tunis and around
    Visit Tunis (medina and Bardo Museum), Carthage, Sidi Bou Said, Tabarka, Aïn Draham, Bulla Regia and Dougga.
Monastir and around
    Visit Sousse, Mahdia, Kairouan and El Jem.
Jerba and around
    Visit Houmt Souk (Jerba); the *ksour* near Tataouine; Douz; and Tozeur.

HIGHLIGHTS
Most of the highlights are in the south. The oasis towns of Tozeur and Nefta are full of surprises. The *palmeraie* (palm groves) are veritable gardens of Eden. Both towns are also famous for the intricate brickwork of their traditional quarters.

Other highlights include staying in the fine old *foundouks* (caravanserai) of Houmt Souk; early morning visits to the ksour around Tataouine; and camel trekking in the desert around Douz. Three Roman sites stand out among the crowd: El Jem, Dougga and Bulla Regia. The Bardo in Tunis and Dar Charait in Tozeur are easily the best of the museums.

TOURIST OFFICES
Local Tourist Offices
Don't hold your breath waiting for a tidal wave of information. There are offices of the government-run Office National du Tourisme Tunisien (ONTT) in all major towns and tourist centres, as well as local offices called *syndicats d'initiative* – a serious malapropism. There are a couple of exceptions, notably the Sousse ONTT office, but most have no more than a few glossy brochures and the odd map.

Tunisian Tourist Offices Abroad
There are Tunisian tourist offices in the following countries:

Belgium
    60 Galerie Ravenstein, 1000 Brussels (☎ 02-511 11 42)
Canada
    1253 McGill College, Montreal, Quebec (☎ 514-397 1182)
France
    32 Ave de l'Opéra, 75002 Paris (☎ 01 47 42 51 02)
Germany
    Am Hauptbahnhof 6, 60329 Frankfurt/Main (☎ 069-23 18 91/92)
Italy
    Via Baracchini 10, 20123 Milan (☎ 02-86 45 30 26)
Netherlands
    Muntplein 2, 1012 WR Amsterdam (☎ 020-622 49 71)
Sweden
    Stureplan 15, 11145 Stockholm (☎ 08-678 06 45)
Switzerland
    Bahnhofstrasse 69, 8001 Zürich (☎ 01-211 48 30)
UK
    77A Wigmore St, London W1H 9LJ (☎ 0171-224 5598)

VISAS & EMBASSIES
Nationals of most Western European countries can stay up to three months without a visa – you just roll up and collect a stamp in your passport. Americans, Canadians, Germans and Japanese can stay up to four months. The situation is a bit more complicated for other

nationalities. Most require no visa if arriving on an organised tour.

Australians and New Zealanders travelling independently can obtain a two-week visa at the airport for TD3, although some have reported being given a month. South Africans can stay a month. Those wanting to stay longer should get a three-month visa (TD6) before they arrive – available wherever Tunisia has diplomatic representation.

Israeli nationals are not allowed into the country.

Visa Extensions
It is unlikely that you will need to extend your visa because a month in Tunisia is ample for most people. Applications can be made only at the Interior Ministry on Ave Habib Bourguiba in Tunis. They cost TD3 (payable only in revenue stamps), take up to 10 days to issue, and require two photographs, bank receipts and a *facture* (receipt) from your hotel. It may sound simple, but the process is more hassle than it's worth.

Tunisian Embassies Abroad
Canada
  515 O'Connor St, Ottawa (☎ 613-237 0330)
France
  17 Rue de Lubeck, Paris (☎ 01 45 53 50 94)
  8 Blvd d'Athènes, 13001 Marseille (☎ 04 91 50 28 68)
Germany
  110 Esplanade 12, 1100 Berlin (☎ 030-472 20 64)
  Adimstrage 4, 8000 Munich 19 (☎ 089-55 45 51)
Italy
  Via Asmara 5, 00199 Rome (☎ 06-860 42 82)
  24 Piazza Ignazio Florio, 90100 Palermo (☎ 091-32 89 26)
Japan
  1-18-8 Wakaba Cho, Shinjuku-ku, 160 Tokyo (☎ 03-3353 41 11)
Morocco
  6 Ave de Fas, Rabat (☎ 07-73 06 36)
Spain
  Plaza Alonzo Martinez 3, 28004 Madrid (☎ 91-447 35 08)
UK
  29 Prince's Gate, London SW7 (☎ 0171-584 8117)
USA
  1515 Massachusetts Ave NW, Washington, DC, 20005 (☎ 202-862 1850)

Australia has an honorary Tunisian consulate in Sydney (☎ 02-9363 5588) which sends out visa application forms. The address is GPO Box 801, Double Bay, 2028.

Foreign Embassies in Tunisia
Countries with diplomatic representation in Tunis include:

Australia
  Australian affairs are handled by the Canadian Embassy in Tunis.
Canada
  3 Rue du Sénégal (☎ 796 577)
France
  Place de l'Indépendance, Ave Habib Bourguiba (☎ 347 838)
Germany
  1 Rue el Hamra (☎ 786 455)
Italy
  3 Rue de Russie (☎ 341 811)
Japan
  10 Rue el Matri (☎ 791 251)
Libya
  48 Rue du 1 Juin (☎ 780 866)
Morocco
  39 Rue du 1 Juin (☎ 782 775)
UK
  5 Place de la Victoire (☎ 341 444); consulate at 141 Ave de la Liberté (☎ 793 322)
USA
  144 Ave de la Liberté (☎ 782 566)

DOCUMENTS
People planning to hire a car or motorbike of more than 50 cc will need their national driving licence. It must be valid for a year.

Although there are no advertised discounts for students, it never hurts to ask, so bring your ID.

CUSTOMS
The duty-free allowance is 400 cigarettes, two litres of wine, a litre of spirits and 250 ml of perfume. It is advisable to declare valuable items (such as cameras) on arrival to ensure a smooth departure.

MONEY
The Tunisian dinar is a nonconvertible currency, and it's illegal to import or export it. All the major European currencies are readily exchangeable, as well as the US and Canadian dollars and the Japanese yen. Australian and NZ dollars and South African rand are not accepted. It is not necessary to declare your foreign currency on arrival. Foreign currency can be exchanged at banks, post offices and major hotels.

When leaving the country, you can re-exchange up to 30% of the amount you changed into dinar, up to a limit of TD100. You need to produce bank receipts to prove you changed the money in the first place.

Major credit cards such as Visa, American Express and MasterCard are widely accepted throughout the country at large shops, tourist hotels, car-rental agencies and banks. Cash advances are given in local currency only.

Currency

The unit of currency is the Tunisian dinar (TD), which is divided into 1000 millimes (mills). There are five, 10, 20, 50, 100 and 500-mill coins and one-dinar coins. There are five, 10 and 20-dinar notes. Changing the larger notes is not a problem.

Exchange Rates

Exchange rates are regulated, so the rate is the same everywhere. Banks charge a standard 351 mills commission per travellers' cheque, and the larger hotels take slightly more. Post offices will change cash only.

Australia	A$1	= TD0.75
Canada	C$1	= TD0.69
France	1FF	= TD0.19
Germany	DM1	= TD0.64
Italy	L1000	= TD0.62
Japan	¥100	= TD0.88
New Zealand	NZ$1	= TD0.66
United Kingdom	UK£1	= TD1.48
United States	US$1	= TD0.95

Costs

Tunisia is a cheap country to travel in, especially for Europeans. It's usually possible to find a clean room for about TD5 per person, main meals in local restaurants are seldom priced over TD3.500, and transport is cheap. If you're fighting to keep costs down, you can get by on TD20 a day. You'll have more fun with a budget of about TD30 per day and you can be quite lavish for TD50.

Tipping

Tipping is not a requirement. Cafés and local restaurants put out a saucer for customers to throw their small change into, but this is seldom more than 50 mills. Waiters in tourist restaurants are accustomed to tips – 10% is plenty. Taxi drivers do not expect tips from locals, but they often round up the fare for foreigners.

Bargaining

Handicrafts are about the only items you may have to bargain for in Tunisia. To be good at bargaining, you need to enjoy the banter. If you don't, you're better off buying your souvenirs from one of the government fixed-price ONAT craft shops (see Things to Buy). It's a good idea to go there anyway just to get an idea of prices.

POST & COMMUNICATIONS

Post

The Tunisian postal service is slow but reliable. Letters from Europe generally take about a week to arrive; letters from further afield take about two weeks. Delivery times are similar in the other direction, although it can take three weeks for a letter to reach Australia. Air-mail letters cost 550 mills to Europe, and 600 mills to Australia and the Americas; postcards cost 100 mills less. You can buy stamps at post offices, major hotels and some general stores and newsstands.

Post offices are open in summer (1 July until 30 September) from 7.30 am to 1.30 pm, Monday to Thursday, and 7.30 am to 12.30 pm on Friday. In winter, opening hours are 8 am to 6 pm, Monday to Saturday. During Ramadan, they open from 8 am to 3 pm, Monday to Saturday. The main post office in Tunis, on Rue Charles de Gaulle, is open seven days a week. Post office hours vary from town to town.

You can receive mail at any post office in the country. It should be addressed clearly, with your surname first.

Parcel Post Parcels should be taken along unwrapped for inspection. Parcels weighing less than two kg can be sent by ordinary mail. Larger parcels should be taken to the special parcel counter. In Tunis, this is at a separate post office on Ave de la République. Indicate clearly if you want to send something surface mail.

Telephone

The telephone system is modern and efficient. Public telephones, known as Taxiphones, are everywhere and it's rare to find one that doesn't work. Most places have Taxiphone offices, readily identified by the yellow sign, with about a dozen booths and attendants to give change. Local calls cost 100 mills. The number for directory information is ☎ 1818.

International Calls The same phones can also be used for international direct dialling, except that you will need to feed them one-dinar and half-dinar coins. International calls are not cheap: TD1.280 per minute to most European countries, and a prohibitive TD4 per minute to Australia and New Zealand. To dial out, phone the international access code ☎ 00, followed by the country code, then the local code and number.

If you're calling Tunisia from abroad, the country code is ☎ 216. Main area codes include: ☎ 01 (Tunis region), ☎ 02 (Bizerte), ☎ 03 (Sousse), ☎ 04 (Sfax), and ☎ 05 (Gabès and Jerba).

NEWSPAPERS & MAGAZINES

You will need to speak French or Arabic to make much sense of the Tunisian press. The weekly *Tunisian News* is the only local publication in English, but it's not much to get excited about. *La Presse* and *Le Temps* are the main French-language papers. They both have a couple of pages of international news as well as local service information such as train, bus and flight times. In the main centres you can buy two-day-old European newspapers.

RADIO & TV

There is a French-language radio station broadcasting on (or around) FM 98 MHz. It broadcasts in English from 2 to 3 pm, German from 3 to 4 pm and Italian from 4 to 5 pm. A much better source of English-language radio is the BBC World Service, which can be picked up on 15.07 MHz and 12.095 MHz.

The French-language TV station has half an hour of news at 8 pm every night, which includes foreign news and sport, but most programming consists of mindless game shows.

PHOTOGRAPHY & VIDEO

Kodak and Fuji film are widely available in Tunis and resort areas, but cost a good deal more – especially at resorts. All main towns have quick processing labs which can develop any type of print film.

Always ask before taking photographs of people. Although Tunisia is a relatively liberal country, photographing women is still a no-no in parts of the country. Photographing anything to do with the military or police is forbidden – and they mean it.

TIME

Tunisia is one hour ahead of GMT/UTC from October to April, and two hours ahead of GMT/UTC from May to September.

ELECTRICITY

The power supply is 220V and plugs have two round pins, as in Europe.

WEIGHTS & MEASURES

Tunisia uses the metric system. For readers more familiar with the imperial system, there's a conversion table at the back of this book.

LAUNDRY

Laundrettes don't exist in the Western sense, but there are a couple of places in Tunis filled with washing machines where you can pay for washing to be done by the kg. You just drop off the load and collect it later. Tourist areas and most larger towns have dry-cleaning shops. Typical prices are TD1.500 for a shirt, TD1.800 for jeans, and TD2 for a cloth jacket.

TOILETS

Public toilets are a rarity. About the only places you'll find them are at bus and railway stations. Otherwise, cafés are the best option – although you will be expected to buy a coffee or something for the privilege. Toilets are often of the Asian squat variety. Most are equipped with a hose for washing yourself; if you like to use paper, carry your own.

HEALTH

You will need to show a yellow-fever vaccination certificate if you have visited an infected area in the six days prior to arrival. The telephone number for an ambulance is ☎ 190.

WOMEN TRAVELLERS

Women should encounter few problems. It's advisable to dress more conservatively outside Tunis and the resort towns. A headscarf may come in handy in remote areas as proof of modesty. Cosmetics, tampons, etc are widely available.

GAY & LESBIAN TRAVELLERS

While the lifestyle is liberal by Islamic standards, society has yet to come to terms with homosexuality.

DANGERS & ANNOYANCES

Probably the worst hassles you will encounter are the carpet touts of Kairouan, but they don't hold a candle to their Moroccan counterparts. There have been isolated reports of beach thefts, but crimes such as mugging are very rare.

BUSINESS HOURS

Government offices and businesses are open Monday to Thursday from 8.30 am to 1 pm and 3 to 5.45 pm. They're also open on Friday and Saturday from 8.30 am to 1.30 pm. In summer, offices don't open in the afternoon.

Banks are open from 8 to 11 am and 2 to 4 pm Monday to Thursday, and 8 to 11 am and 1 to 3 pm Friday. Some banks in Tunis extend opening times beyond these hours. Banks are not open in the afternoons in summer.

Most shops are open Monday to Friday from 8 am to 12.30 pm and 2.30 to 6 pm, and from 8 am to noon on Saturday. Summer hours are usually 7.30 am to 1 pm.

PUBLIC HOLIDAYS

Public holidays and festivals are either religious celebrations or festivities marking the anniversary of historic events. The Islamic holidays fall 10 days earlier every Western calendar year because the Gregorian (Western) and Islamic calendars are of different lengths. Ramadan is the main one to watch out for, because opening hours and transport scheduled are disrupted for an entire month.

Other public holidays in Tunisia are: New Year's Day (1 January); Independence Day (20 March); Youth Day (21 March); Martyrs' Day (9 April); Labour Day (1 May); Republic Day (25 July); Public Holiday (3 August); Women's Day (13 August); Evacuation Day (15 October); Ben Ali's Presidential Anniversary (7 November).

Some of these holidays, such as Women's Day and Evacuation Day, pass without notice. On other holidays, everything except transport comes to a halt. Avoid travel before Eid al Fitr (celebrating the end of Ramadan) when everyone is trying to get home for the festivities.

SPECIAL EVENTS

The capital stages the annual Carthage Festival in July and August, with performances of classical theatre at Carthage's Roman theatre. It also hosts the biennial Carthage Film Festival (October, odd-numbered years).

Other cultural events of note are the El Jem Symphonic Music Festival, held every July in El Jem's spectacular floodlit colosseum, and the Dougga festival of classical theatre at the site's fine Roman theatre.

Almost every tourist town stages an annual festival, usually a week-long line-up of parades and fairly tacky folkloric events. The best of them is the Sahara Festival in Douz and Tozeur during December/February. The main festivals are:

Sahara Festival
    Held in December/January in Douz and Tozeur, this festival has everything from camel races and saluki dog trials to traditional marriages.
Nefta Festival
    Held in April, this festival features parades and folkloric events.
Monastir Festival
    This is held in May.
Siren Festival
    Held in July/August, this festival takes place on the Kerkennah Islands.
Hammamet Festival
    Held in July/August, this festival features music and cultural events.
Tabarka Festival
    This festival held in July/August features music, theatre, and a coral exhibition.
Ulysses Festival
    Held in July/August in Jerba, this festival is strictly for the tourists, right down to the Miss Ulysses competition.
Baba Aoussou Festival
    This is held in July/August in Sousse.

ACCOMMODATION

You'll find everything in Tunisia, from camp sites and basic hotels to five-star luxury resorts.

Camping

Most of the official camp sites have only basic facilities and charge about TD2.500 per person. It's technically possible to camp anywhere as long as you get the landowner's permission.

Sleeping on the beach is acceptable in the north (near Bizerte) at Raf Raf and Ghar el-Melh. The same applies to the remote beaches of the north coast, but in the resort areas of the Cap Bon peninsula and Sousse, this would definitely be frowned upon.

There are good camp sites – complete with electricity and hot water – at Aghir (Jerba), Douz, Gabès, Hammamet, Nabeul, Remel Plage (near Bizerte) and Tozeur.

Hostels

Hostels in Tunisia fall into two categories: the government-run *maisons des jeunes* and the *auberges de jeunesse*, affiliated to Hostelling International (HI) – and they couldn't be more different.

The auberges de jeunesse are thoroughly recommended; most have prime locations, such as a converted palace in the Tunis medina and a fascinating old foundouk at Houmt Souk, Jerba. They charge TD4.500 per night for bed and breakfast, with other meals available for TD3 each. You need an HI card to use the hostels. The address for HI in Tunisia is 25 Rue Saida Ajoula, Tunis medina (☎ 567 850).

Almost without exception, maisons des jeunes are characterless, concrete boxes with all the charm of army barracks. Almost every town has a maison des jeunes, normally stuck way out in the boondocks, and used primarily to house visiting sporting teams and for schoolchildren's holiday camps. The only reason to mention them is that sometimes they represent the only available budget accommodation. They all charge TD4 for a dormitory bed.

There are a couple of places where the maisons des jeunes concept has been expanded into a scheme called *centres des stages et vacances*. These are holiday camps which combine hostels and camp sites. There is one on the beach at Aghir (Jerba), and another in the oasis at Gabès. Camping charges are TD2 per person and 500 mills per tent. Electricity and hot showers are available.

Hotels

Tunisian hotels are generally clean, if a little shabby. All hotels must display the tariff by the reception desk, so you can always see what the top price should be. In most places, you can find a clean room with shared bathroom for TD5 to TD8 per person, and TD18 to TD25 will get you a comfortable double with bathroom. Prices for all but the most basic places

usually include breakfast, which means coffee, French bread, butter and jam.

FOOD

The national dish is couscous (semolina granules). There are apparently more than 300 ways of preparing the stuff – sweet as well as savoury. A bowl served with stew costs about TD3 in local restaurants. A curiosity in Tunisian cuisine is the *briq*, a crisp, very thin pastry envelope which comes with a range of fillings always including egg.

Other dishes include:

harissa
    fiery red chilli paste that comes as a side-serve
kammounia
    meat stew made with lots of cumin
lablabi
    spicy chickpea broth which is doled out on a bed of broken bread
mloukhia
    similar to kammounia, except that it's made with a blend of dried herbs; cuts of lamb or beef are simmered until they almost disappear into the rich, green sauce
salade mechouia
    very spicy mixture of mashed roast vegetables, often predominantly eggplant, which is served as an accompaniment to dishes such as roast chicken
salade tunisienne
    finely diced salad vegetables mixed with a dressing of lemon juice and olive oil
shakshuka
    thick vegetable soup based on onions and green peppers; unfortunately for vegetarians, it's normally made from a meat stock
tajine
    the Tunisian version is no relation to its Moroccan namesake; it's similar to quiche and is normally served cold with chips and salad

Restaurants

Restaurants can be divided into three broad categories.

You'll find most of the food mentioned above in *gargottes*. They vary from very basic to slightly up-market. Generally a main dish and salad won't cost much over TD3.500; many serve fish, lamb cutlets and kebabs.

Rotisseries are easy to spot because they normally have a rotating spit of roast chickens outside; that's about all they serve, usually with chips and salad. Prices start at TD1.600 for a quarter of a chicken.

Tourist restaurants serve what they like to call Franco-Tunisienne cuisine. If you can avoid lobster, most meals will cost under TD10. Tourist restaurants normally sell alcohol – unlike the others.

Fast Food
Almost every town has a shop selling *casse-croûtes*, half a French loaf stuffed with a choice of fillings – fried egg, chips and harissa is a favourite known as *khaftegi*. Western-style fast food is also becoming popular. Pizza parlours and hamburger joints can be found in most of the major towns.

DRINKS
Mineral water is cheap and available everywhere, as are soft drinks such as Coca-Cola. Alcohol is readily available. The Monoprix chain of supermarkets sells a good range of local wines. Supermarkets sell alcohol only from midday to 6.30 pm, and not on Friday.

The only local spirit is a fiery number called *boukha*, which is generally consumed with a mixer. If you're curious, a miniature bottle costs TD2.300.

Whisky drinkers are advised to bring a bottle as part of their duty-free allowance – a bottle costs at least TD60 locally.

Bars
Bars can be found in all the major towns. They are generally hard-drinking, smoke-filled, male preserves. Beer is the most popular drink and Celtia is the only beer. It sells for TD1.300 per bottle in Tunis and for as little as TD1 outside the capital. It is possible for accompanied foreign females to stop for a beer at these places, but don't be surprised by the attention levels. Most foreigners, particularly women, feel more comfortable drinking at the resort hotels.

ENTERTAINMENT
Nightlife is not promising outside Tunis and the resort areas. The favourite local entertainment is coffee and cards at the café, but that's strictly for the blokes. Almost every town has a cinema, but the posters don't look auspicious. If you like discos, stick to the resorts.

THINGS TO BUY
The most popular items to buy in Tunisia are rugs and carpets, jewellery, pottery, beaten copper and brass items, leather and straw

goods, and *chechias* (small, red, felt hats worn by Tunisian men).

Although they're not cheap, rugs and carpets are among the most readily available and beautiful souvenirs. The main carpet-selling centres are Tunis, Kairouan, Tozeur and Jerba. Look out for carpets which have been inspected by the Office National de l'Artisanat Tunisien (ONAT). It classifies the carpets by quality and affixes a label and seal on the back. Carpets not classified by ONAT are cheaper, but their quality may be suspect.

Jewellery, particularly gold, is very ornate. The Hand of Fatima (daughter of the Prophet) is a traditional Arabic design, usually made of silver.

Sand roses are sold all over the country. They are formed of gypsum, present in the desert sand, which crystallises into beautiful patterns.

ONAT has crafts shops in all the major towns and tourist destinations. The shop in Tunis, on Ave Mohamed V, has the best selection.

Markets
Town and village life revolves around the weekly markets. Market day is a good day to be in a town because it's far livelier than usual and the markets attract both itinerant merchants and people from outlying districts.

Getting There & Away

AIR
Tunisia has four international airports: Tunis, Jerba, Monastir and Tabarka. Tunis handles most of the scheduled flights, while Jerba and Monastir are the main charter airports.

Europe
British Airways flies to Tunis three times a week and does a 30-day return for UK£140, dropping as low as UK£85 at times. Most of the flights using Jerba and Monastir are charters. These can be incredibly cheap – as low as UK£69 return – if you don't mind minimum and maximum-stay restrictions; you get the biggest discounts at the last minute.

Overseas branches of the Tunisian National Tourist Office have lists of charter operators.

In the UK, Horizon Holidays (☎ 0181-200 8733) and Thomson Holidays (same number) are the two biggest operators.

North America
There are no direct flights between Tunisia and the USA or Canada. The cheapest way to travel between North America and Tunisia is to get a cheap fare to London and a charter flight or bucket-shop deal from there. The full one-way fare from New York is around US$850.

Australia
There are no direct flights to/from Australia either, so head for London and get a flight from there. You can fly Sydney-Tunis and return for under A$2000 if you shop around. Some airlines include Tunis on the list of free European side trips they offer if you're buying a ticket from Australia to Europe.

Morocco
Royal Air Maroc and Tunis Air fly regularly between the two countries. The standard economy fare is about US$500 return.

LAND
Algeria
It's years now since the last recorded crossing of this border by a tourist. The problems in Algeria have prompted the cancellation of bus and train services between Tunis and Annaba, leaving *louages* (shared taxis) as the only option. They operate from Place Sidi Bou Mendil in the Tunis medina to Annaba (TD25) and Constantine (TD30).

Libya
The border crossing between Tunisia and Libya on the coast at Ras Ajdir is open, but tourist visas are still as scarce as hen's teeth. There are regular buses (TD17.350) and louages (TD20) from Sfax to Tripoli, as well as a daily bus from Tunis to Tripoli for TD28.

SEA
Italy
There are ferries between Tunis and the Italian ports of Genoa, Naples and Trapani (Sicily). The shortest crossing is the weekly Tirrenia Lines service to Trapani (eight hours, TD53 one way). It leaves Trapani at 8 am on Monday morning and Tunis at 6 pm the same day.

Boats to Genoa and Naples are run by the Compagnie Tunisienne de Navigation (CTN). Services to Genoa vary between four a month in winter and 11 a month at the height of summer. The trip takes 24 hours and costs TD119 one way. There is a fortnightly boat to Naples (16 hours, TD87).

You can get tickets for all three services at 122 Rue de Yougoslavie.

France
CTN also operates regular ferries from Tunis to Marseille (24 hours, TD169 one way). There are at least seven ferries a month even in winter, and daily sailings in August. The service is packed in summer, so visitors taking cars will need to book ahead.

LEAVING TUNISIA
There is no departure tax to be paid when leaving the country. An TD8 airport tax is included in the price of an air ticket, and a similar TD2 port tax is included in the price of ferry tickets.

Getting Around

Tunisia has a well-developed transport network, and just about every town in the country has daily bus connections with Tunis. For most of the year public transport copes easily with demand, but things get pretty hectic during August and September and on public holidays. Book ahead if possible.

AIR
Tunisia's domestic air network is fairly limited because it's such a small country. The domestic airline, Tuninter, operates the following services: Tunis to Jerba (five flights per day); Tunis to Tozeur (every day except Tuesday and Wednesday); Tunis to Sfax (Monday to Friday); Monastir to Jerba (Tuesday and Saturday); and Tozeur to Jerba (Monday and Tuesday).

BUS
SNTRI, the national bus company, runs daily air-con buses to most towns in the country. These green-and-yellow buses are fast, comfortable,

not too expensive, and run pretty much to schedule. Many of the long-distance buses run at night to avoid the heat, which means you won't see much of the country you're travelling through. It's especially important to book in advance when leaving Tunis in summer.

There are also regional bus companies, which are reliable and cheap, but slow and without air-con. Booking in advance is both impossible and unnecessary. The only way to be sure of bus schedules is to go to the bus station and ask. Most stations do not have timetables displayed; those that do, have them in Arabic only – with the exception of Houmt Souk in Jerba. Departures tend to be early in the day. If you're seeking directions to the bus station, ask for the *gare routière*.

Some towns are served by two or three regional companies. These competing companies generally share stations, but in some cases, such as Tabarka, each company has its own station. Officials from one company never know about the schedules of another, so always ask if there is more than one company operating in town.

TRAIN
Tunisia's rail network is modern and efficient, but hardly comprehensive. There are passenger services from Tunis to Bizerte, El Jem, Gabès, Ghardimaou, Kalaa Khasba, Mahdia, Metlaoui, Monastir, Nabeul, Sfax and Sousse. The best service is on the main line south from Tunis to Sousse and Sfax.

Passenger trains offer three classes: second, first and *confort*. Second class costs about the same as a local bus, and is normally packed with people, produce and livestock. First-class carriages have reclining, upholstered seats, and cost about 40% more than 2nd class. Confort costs a bit more again, but doesn't offer much extra. Prices quoted in this chapter are for 2nd class.

LOUAGE
Louages are long-distance taxis offering a parallel service to the buses. Whereas buses leave to a timetable, louages leave when they're full. Most are station wagons with an extra bench seat in the back, designed to take five passengers. Drivers stand by their vehicles and call out their destinations. They seldom take long to fill up. Louages are the fastest way to get

around, and the fares are only slighter higher than the buses. Most louages are white with a red stripe.

In most towns, the louage 'station' is close to, or incorporated with, the bus station, enabling you to choose between the services.

CAR & MOTORCYCLE
Most of Tunisia's roads are excellent and tarsurfaced. The speed limit is 50 km/h in town and 100 km/h on the open road. The minor roads in the north are usually just single, narrow strips of bitumen. In the south there are more unsurfaced roads but they are usually easily negotiable. The worst road you are likely to encounter is the one from Matmata direct to Medenine; people will tell you it's for 4WD vehicles only, but it can be negotiated with caution in even the smallest cars rented by agencies.

Tunisian drivers generally drive safely and predictably. For someone used to driving in Europe, the greatest dangers are the thousands of suicidal moped riders who weave through the traffic, and the pedestrians who think that it is their inalienable right to walk on the road regardless of traffic conditions.

Although the short distances and good road conditions make motorcycling an ideal way to travel, you hardly see a bike bigger than 90 cc. If you're bringing your own motorbike, make sure you have basic spare parts; they're virtually impossible to find because of the scarcity of motorbikes.

Automobile Clubs
The Touring Club de Tunisie has reciprocal rights arrangements with many European automobile clubs, including Britain's Automobile Association (AA). If your car conks out, they can supply you with the name of the nearest affiliated breakdown service. The club's address in Tunis is 15 Rue d'Allemagne, Tunis 1000 (☎ 243 114).

Rental
Hiring a car can be a great way to see the country, but unless you have a fat wallet or are part of a small group, it's not a realistic option. All the major international operators have offices in the larger towns. Rental conditions are fairly straightforward. If you are paying by cash, you will be required to leave a deposit

roughly equivalent to the rental charge. Credit cards don't have the same restriction.

Typical rental charges for the smallest cars (Renault Esp or Citroën 15) are about TD22 per day plus 220 mills per km. It's cheaper to take an unlimited-km deal; these start at about TD380 per week. On top of these rates, you'll have to pay 17% tax, insurance at about TD10 per day, contract fees etc. By the time you've filled the petrol tank at 570 mills per litre, your wallet will be a lot lighter.

Unfortunately, there's only one motorcycle-rental agency in the country – *Holiday Bikes* (☎ 05-657 169) on Jerba, opposite the Penelope Club on the tourist strip. It has a range of bikes, from 50 cc mopeds for TD24 per day up to 600 cc Yamahas for an outrageous TD620 per week (plus TD400 deposit), fully inclusive.

When you hire a vehicle car, make sure there is an accident report form with the car's papers. If you have an accident, both parties involved must complete the form. If the form is not completed, you may be liable for the costs, whether you've paid for insurance or not.

Rental companies require that drivers be aged over 21 and hold a driver's licence valid for at least a year. No licence or insurance is required for a moped.

There are military checkpoints all over the country, and although officials are not too bothered about checking foreigners, make sure you have your passport handy.

BICYCLE

Cycling is an excellent way to see the country in spring or autumn. It's too hot to cycle in summer and a little bleak in winter, though it is possible to put a bike on the train if you get too exhausted or want to skip a long stretch.

A few places hire out bikes, normally for about TD7 per day. If there's no hire facility in town, it's worth asking at a local bike-repair shop to see if they'll rent a spare bike for a few hours. Make sure that the brakes work.

HITCHING

The following information is intended solely as an explanation of how hitching works in Tunisia, not as a recommendation. Although many people hitch in Tunisia, it is not an entirely safe method of transport, and you do so at your own risk. It is strongly recommended

that women do not attempt to hitch without a male companion.

Conditions for hitching vary throughout the country. The south is easiest because there is a great deal more tourist traffic – either people who hire cars in Jerba or overlanders heading for Tozeur and the Sahara. You shouldn't have to wait more than a couple of hours for a lift. In the north, people seem less inclined to pick up hitchers, particularly in the summer when there are so many tourists in the country.

Between small towns in the south, hitching is a standard way of getting around, although you will normally be expected to pay the equivalent of the bus fare. See the introductory Getting Around chapter for more information on hitching.

BOAT

There are two scheduled ferry services in the country. The first connects Sfax with the Kerkennah Islands. There are up to eight crossings a day in summer, dropping to four in winter. The trip takes 1½ hours and costs 570 mills. The second service runs from Jorf on the mainland to Ajim on Jerba. The crossing takes only a few minutes and the ferries run 24 hours.

LOCAL TRANSPORT

You'll find orange, metered taxis in almost every town. Flag fall is 280 mills, followed by 370 mills per km. In the south, *camionettes* (small trucks) operate between towns and outlying villages, such as between Douz and Zaafrane. They charge by the place, and leave when there are enough passengers to make it worthwhile.

Tunis

Tunis, the capital of Tunisia, is a major gateway to Africa and offers a range of attractions from lazing on the beach to exploring the medina and the ruins of Carthage.

Orientation

The medina, the original city of Tunis, was built on a narrow strip of land between Lake Tunis and the Sebkhet Sejoumi salt lake. When the French arrived, they built a new city, the *ville nouvelle*, on land reclaimed from Lake Tunis to the east of the medina. The main thoroughfare of the ville nouvelle is Ave Habib Bourguiba, which runs from Lake Tunis to the Bab Bhar, the medina's eastern gate – also known as the Porte de France.

Most of the budget hotels are in the area around the Bab Bhar and to the south of Ave Habib Bourguiba. A causeway at the eastern end of Ave Habib Bourguiba carries road and light-rail traffic across Lake Tunis to the port suburb of La Goulette, and north to the affluent beach suburbs of Carthage, Sidi Bou Said and La Marsa.

Information

Tourist Offices The tourist office (☎ 341 077) is on Ave Habib Bourguiba at Place de l'Afrique in the city centre. They have a free map of Tunis and good brochures on Carthage and the medina.

Money The major banks are on Ave Habib Bourguiba. A couple of them have 24-hour automatic exchange machines. American Express (☎ 254 304) is represented by Carthage Tours, 59 Ave Habib Bourguiba, and Thomas Cook (☎ 342 710) by the Compagnie Tunisienne de Tourisme, 45 Ave Habib Bourguiba.

1 UK Consulate
2 US Embassy
3 Northern Bus & Louage Station
4 Charles Nicolle Hospital
5 Auberge de Jeunesse
6 Restaurant Dar el Jeld
7 Souk des Chechias
8 Souk el Attarine
9 M'Rabet
10 Great Mosque
11 Hotel Majestic
12 ONAT
13 TGM Light-Rail Station
14 Tunis Marine Bus Station
15 Dar Ben Abdallah Museum
16 Southern Louage Station
17 Southern Bus Station

Tunis

TUNISIA

Post & Communications The main post office is on Rue Charles de Gaulle, and the telephone office is on the opposite side of the same building, entry is from Rue Jamel Abdelnasser. It was closed for repairs at the time of writing, but there are Taxiphone offices (see the Central Tunis map) on Rue de Hollande and Ave de Carthage.

The telephone code for Tunis is ☎ 01.

Laundry The laundry at 15 Rue d'Allemagne charges TD5.500 to wash and dry five kg.

Medical & Emergency Services The telephone number for the police and fire brigade is ☎ 197 (nationwide); the number for the ambulance service is ☎ 190. There is an anti-poison centre in Tunis (☎ 245 075).

Things to See

City Centre It's worth wandering around the medina for at least half a day. Don't miss the **Dar Ben Abdallah Museum**, a splendid old Turkish palace housing traditional costumes and local artefacts.

Two souks to check out are the **Souk el Attarine** (the perfume souk) and the **Souk des Chechias**, where Tunisia's traditional, red, felt caps are made – from Australian wool. They are worn only by older men these days.

The main street into the medina from the new city, Rue Jamaa Ez Zitouna, is virtually one continuous line of souvenir shops. This street has possibly the highest prices in the country, but it will give you a good idea of what is available.

One attraction not to be missed is the **Bardo Museum**, which has a magnificent collection of Roman mosaics and marble statues. The museum is housed in an old palace three km north-west of the city centre. It is open from 9 am to 5 pm in summer and 9.30 am to 4.30 pm in winter; closed on Monday. Entry costs TD3.100, plus TD1 to take photos. *Métro léger* (tram) line 4 has a stop (Le Bardo) almost right outside the museum, or you can catch bus No 3 from opposite the Hotel Africa on Ave Habib Bourguiba.

Carthage The Punic and Roman ruins of Carthage are scattered around Tunis and include Roman baths, houses, cisterns, basilicas and old streets. The best way to see Carthage is to take the TGM light rail from Ave Habib Bourguiba to Carthage Hannibal Station, and wander from there. If your time is limited, visit the **National Museum** (on top of the hill next to the deconsecrated cathedral) and the **Byrsa Quarter** (in the grounds of the museum). The Romans did such a good job of destroying Carthage that, apart from the ports, these are the only worthwhile Punic sites remaining; everything else is of Roman origin.

The enormous **Antonine Baths** on the water's edge are worth a quick look. Entry to all the sites at Carthage is by a multiple ticket (TD4.100), which can be bought only at the Antonine Baths, the Roman villas and the museum.

A few stops further along the TGM line is the beautiful, whitewashed, cliff-top village of **Sidi Bou Said**. It's really an outer suburb of Tunis, and is considered one of the city's most up-market residential areas. Although it's on every tour group's itinerary, it remains very relaxed, especially late in the afternoon after the tour buses have left. There are no specific attractions – it's just enjoyable to wander through the cobbled streets.

Places to Stay

Camping isn't really an option. The nearest camp site is 15 km south of the city near Hammam Lif.

Fortunately, Tunis has an excellent *auberge de jeunesse* (☎ 567 850). It occupies an old palace, the Dar Saida Ajoula, right in the heart of the medina on Rue Es Saida Ajoula. Rates range from TD4.500 for a dormitory bed and hot shower up to TD10.500 for full board. It even has a washing machine (500 mills). It has a three-day limit in the high season.

There are lots of cheap hotels in the medina charging TD3 for a bed in a shared room. They are not recommended for men, and are totally unsuitable for women. There are a couple of possibilities around Place de la Victoire. The *Hotel Medina* (☎ 255 056) is basic but clean enough with doubles for TD10. The *Hotel Marhaba* (☎ 343 118), on the opposite side of the square at 5 Rue de la Commission, has doubles for TD7.500.

Most travellers opt to stay outside the medina in the area south of Ave Habib Bourguiba. A popular choice is the *Hotel*

Bristol (☎ 244 836) on Rue Lt Mohamed Aziz Taj. It has the best budget rooms in town with singles for TD4.900 and doubles for TD7.800. The *Hotel Cirta* (☎ 241 583), at 42 Rue Charles de Gaulle, has long been a favourite with travellers. The place is shabby but clean, and charges TD6/10 for singles/doubles with shared bathroom. Showers, supposedly hot, cost TD1. The *Hotel de l'Agriculture* (☎ 246 394), opposite, was in the middle of a major facelift at the time of writing.

There are plenty of good mid-range hotels to choose from. They don't come any better than the *Hotel Maison Doree* (☎ 240 632), an old-style French hotel on Rue el Koufa, just north of Place de Barcelone, off Rue de Hollande. It is immaculately clean and well kept, the staff are friendly and efficient, and it even has a lift. Singles/doubles with shower cost TD21.650/23.900, including a breakfast which includes chocolate croissants. Two other good places nearby are the *Hotel Salammbô* (☎ 337 498), at 6 Rue de Grèce, and the *Hotel Transatlantique* (☎ 240 680), at 106 Rue de Yougoslavie.

The *Hotel Majestic* (☎ 242 848), at the northern end of Ave de Paris, is a splendid piece of fading grandeur with one of the finest

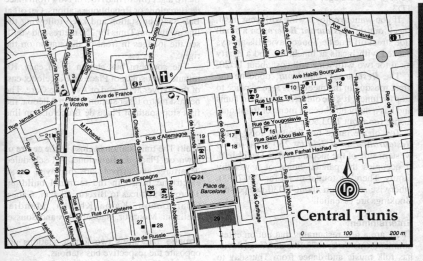

Central Tunis

0   100   200 m

TUNISIA

PLACES TO STAY		14	Restaurant Carcassonne & Le Palais	6	Cathedral
3	Hotel Medina			7	French Embassy
10	Hotel Africa	15	Restaurant Bolero	9	Taxiphone Office
13	Hotel Bristol	16	Restaurant Ezzeitonna	11	Tunis Air
17	Hotel Transatlantique			12	Interior Ministry
18	Hotel Salammbô	**OTHER**		20	Taxiphone Office
19	Hotel Maison Doree	1	Tourist Office	22	Louages to Algeria & Libya
21	Hotel Marhaba	2	Buses to Airport (No 35) & Bardo Museum (No 3)	23	Central Market
27	Hotel de l'Agriculture			24	Place de Barcelone Buses & Trams
28	Hotel Cirta	4	UK Embassy	25	Telephone Office
		5	American Express	26	Post Office
PLACES TO EAT				29	Train Station
8	Café de Paris				

French colonial façades in town. It has huge singles/doubles with bathroom and TV for TD30/40, including breakfast.

Places to Eat

There's a host of good places to choose from in the streets south of Ave Habib Bourguiba, particularly around Ave de Carthage and Rue Ibn Khaldoun. It's hard to beat the *Restaurant Carcassonne*, 8 Ave de Carthage, for value. It turns out a four-course menu for TD3.200, supplemented by as much bread as you can eat.

The *Restaurant Le Palais*, right next door, does a slightly better three-course menu for TD3.500, while the *Restaurant Ezzeitouna*, at 30 Ave de Carthage, offers three courses for TD3.

If you want to enjoy a wine with your meal, check out the *Restaurant Bolero*, on a small side street off Rue de Yougoslavie. It's always packed with locals at lunchtime and a hearty meal for two with wine will about TD20.

The *Restaurant Mahdaoui*, opposite the great mosque in the medina, is a good place to stop for lunch. It's the oldest restaurant in Tunis and has a daily blackboard menu of traditional dishes for about TD3.500.

Top of the range for Tunisian food is the *Restaurant Dar el Jeld* (☎ 260 916), on the western side of the medina in Rue Dar el Jeld. It occupies the palatial home of a wealthy family. There's a tourist menu for TD17.500, otherwise reckon on about TD30 per person. Bookings are essential.

Entertainment

There are a few restaurants that put on entertainment. *Gaston's*, at 73 Rue de Yougoslavie, has folk music and dance from Thursday to Saturday night for a TD5 surcharge. *M'Rabet* is an amazing old place in the heart of the medina, on Souk el-Trouk, which has dinner and belly dancing from 8 pm every night except Sunday. Reckon on spending about TD25.

Things to Buy

The ONAT store on Ave Mohamed V has the best selection of handicrafts in the country.

Getting There & Away

Air Domestic airline Tuninter flies at least five times daily to Jerba and less frequently to Tozeur and Sfax. Tickets can be bought from the Tunis Air office (☎ 330 100) on the corner of Ave Habib Bourguiba and Rue 18 Janvier 1952. Tuninter has a special reservations service (☎ 701 111).

Most of the international airline offices are along Ave Habib Bourguiba and Ave de Paris.

Bus Tunis has two bus stations; one for departures to the north (Gare Routière Nord de Bab Saadoun) and the other for buses heading south or to international destinations (Gare Routière Sud de Bab el Alleoua).

The north station is on the north-western side of Bab Saadoun. You can get there by métro léger (tram) line No 3 or No 4 from Place de Barcelone or République stations. Get off at Bab Saadoun station and keep following the line away from Tunis for 250 metres and you'll see the louages in front of the station on the right.

The southern bus station is an easy 10-minute walk south of Place de Barcelone; east of the flyover at the end of Ave de la Gare. The nearest métro léger station is Bab Alleoua, the first stop south of Place de Barcelone on line No 1.

Train The train station is close to the centre of town on Place de Barcelone. All scheduled departures and arrivals are displayed on an electronic board in the terminal building. There are services to Bizerte, El Jem, Gabès, Ghardimaou, Kalaa Khasba, Mahdia, Metlaoui, Monastir, Nabeul, Sfax and Sousse.

Louage The city's two louage stations are opposite the respective bus stations.

Car All the major car-rental companies have offices both at the airport and in town (most of them on Ave Habib Bourguiba).

Ferry Ferries from Europe arrive in Tunis at La Goulette, at the end of the causeway across Lake Tunis. The cheapest way to reach the city is by TGM light rail. From the port, walk straight out to the kasbah, turn left and walk about 500 metres until you come to a railway crossing; Vieille Goulette station is 100 metres to the right. A taxi from the port to Ave Habib Bourguiba shouldn't cost more than TD2.

The best place to buy boat tickets is the Tirrenia office (☎ 242 999) at 122 Rue de Yougoslavie.

Getting Around
To/From the Airport Tunis-Carthage Airport is eight km north-east of the city. Yellow city bus No 35 runs to the airport from the Tunis Marine bus station every 20 minutes from 6 am to 9 pm and costs 620 mills. The bus leaves the airport from just outside the terminal building, to the right of the exit. A taxi to the city centre from the airport costs about TD3.500.

Bus The yellow city buses operate to all parts of the city, but apart from getting to the airport, the Bardo Museum or the northern bus station, you should have little cause to use them. Fares are cheap – 330 mills to the Bardo, for example. Most conductors are happy to help by telling you where to disembark.

There are three main bus terminals: Tunis Marine, which is next to the TGM station at the causeway end of Ave Habib Bourguiba; Place de Barcelone; and Jardin Thameur, 500 metres north of Ave Habib Bourguiba, off Ave Habib Thameur.

Light Rail The TGM light-rail system connects central Tunis with the beachside suburbs of La Goulette, Carthage, Sidi Bou Said and La Marsa. Trains run from 4 am until midnight.

Tram The efficient new tram system (métro léger) has four routes. The most useful line is No 4, which has a new station right next to the Bardo Museum. Lines 3 and 4 stop at Bab Saadoun, close to the northern bus and louage stations, and Line 1 stops at Bab Alloua, close to the southern bus and louage stations.

Taxi Taxis are a cheap and easy way to get around. Flag fall is 280 mills and the meter then ticks over at about 380 mills per km. Sample fares from the city centre include TD3.500 to the airport and TD4 to the Bardo Museum. Taxis can be booked by phone, which is very handy if you're going to the airport with a mountain of baggage; ask at your hotel.

Cap Bon Peninsula

HAMMAMET
The fact that a third of all Tunisia's foreign visitors wind up here doesn't make it a great place to stay. The building of more than 80 huge resort hotels has transformed this part of Tunisia into a monument to the package-tourism industry. Don't even consider coming here in summer unless you want to rub shoulders with thousands of other foreigners.

NABEUL
These days Nabeul has virtually merged with its boomtown southern neighbour, Hammamet, although it's not quite as over the top. Nabeul is the major service town of the Cap Bon region, and it's economy is not entirely dependent on tourism.

Nabeul's telephone code is ☎ 02.

Places to Stay & Eat
Nabeul does at least have some decent budget accommodation (Hammamet doesn't). There's an *auberge de jeunesse* (☎ 286 689) right on the beach at the end of Ave Mongi Slim. Dormitory accommodation and breakfast costs TD3.500, half-board is TD6 and full board is TD8. The *Hotel Les Jasmins* (☎ 285 343), a couple of km towards Hammamet, has a good, shady camp site which is only a short walk from the beach.

In town, the *Pension Les Roses* is a friendly place offering spotless singles/doubles for TD6/10. It's right next to the main mosque in the middle of town.

Getting There & Away
There are frequent buses from Nabeul to Tunis (1½ hours, TD2.550), but louages do the trip in almost half the time for TD2.900. The bus and louage stations are about 400 metres from the town centre on Ave Habib Thameur. There's a train to Tunis every morning at the impossible time of 5.45 am. It leaves Tunis at a more respectable 2.20 pm. Louages to Kelibia and buses to other parts of Cap Bon leave from Ave Farhat Hached on the far side of the town centre.

TUNISIA

KELIBIA

Kelibia, 58 km north of Nabeul, remains relatively untouched by the ravages of mass tourism. There are a few big hotels at Mansourah Beach, just north of town, but it's still fairly low key. The nicest part of Kelibia is the old fishing port, two km from the town centre. The port is overlooked by a 16th-century Spanish fort. It's worth clambering up for the commanding views up and down the coast.

Kelibia's telephone code is ☎ 02.

Places to Stay

Camping (TD2.500 per person) is permitted in the grounds of the *maison des jeunes* hostel (☎ 296 105), for once conveniently located. It's between the fort and the port on the road to Mansourah Beach. The *Hotel Florida* (☎ 296 248), on the beach near the fort, charges TD14 per person with breakfast and turns out a good three-course dinner for TD5.500.

Getting There & Away

All forms of public transport leave from the main intersection in the middle of town. There are regular buses and louages (45 minutes, TD2.350) to Nabeul, and less frequent services to El Haouaria.

NORTH OF KELIBIA

The small town of **El Haouaria** sits under the mountainous northern tip of Cap Bon, 25 km from Kelibia. The **Roman caves** near the cape were cut when stone was quarried for the building of Roman Carthage. The three-km walk from town takes about 45 minutes. There is also a good beach at **Ras el-Drek**, on the southern side of the cape.

Halfway between Kelibia and El-Haouaria there's a signpost to **Kerkouane**, the country's best preserved Punic site. The site is about 1.5 km from the road, closed Monday.

Northern Tunisia

BIZERTE

Bizerte, 65 km north-west of Tunis, was the scene of a post-independence conflict between the French and Tunisian governments which resulted in the death of 1000 Tunisian soldiers in the early 1960s. The French fought to retain their naval base in the town after Tunisia was granted independence, and it was not until 1963 that the French finally withdrew.

Despite its interesting history, the town is dull and decrepit. The popular spots are the Corniche beaches north-west of town, and the beaches of Remel Plage and Ras Jebel to the east.

Orientation & Information

The centre of Bizerte is the ville nouvelle, built on the compact grid favoured by the French. It is flanked by a shipping canal connecting Lake Bizerte with the Mediterranean to the south-east and Ave Habib Bourguiba to the north-west. The old town – the kasbah and medina – is built around the edge of the old harbour at the end of Ave Habib Bourguiba.

The tourist office (☎ 432 897) is on the corner of Ave Taieb Mehiri and Quai Tarak ibn Ziad, close to the shipping canal. The post office is on Ave d'Algérie, and the telephone office is around the back. The banks are mostly grouped around the main square; one bank is rostered to be open on Saturday mornings (ask at the tourist office for details).

Bizerte's telephone code is ☎ 02.

Things to See

The **medina** and new city meet around the heavily polluted **old port**. Neither the medina nor the Spanish fort on the hill is of much interest.

The beach at **Remel Plage** is a few km south-east of the town on the road to Tunis. Buses going to Raf Raf or Ras Jebel can drop you off at the turn-off, one km from the beach. Tunisians consider **Raf Raf** to have the best beach in the country. It's a long streak of white sand which curves for a km or so and is backed by the pine-clad Cap Farina at its far end. It gets packed in summer. Regular buses travel from Bizerte and Ras Jebel to the beach.

Places to Stay & Eat

There is an *auberge de jeunesse* camp site (☎ 440 804) at the Remel Plage turn-off, open only during June, July and August. It's a laidback place just five minutes from the beach, charging TD4.500 for dorm bed and breakfast.

The hotels in Bizerte are a depressing bunch.

The **Hotel Continental** (☎ 431 327) is pretty decrepit, but the staff are friendly and the rates of TD6/10 are negotiable. At least there are several reasonable restaurants to choose from. The **Restaurant du Bonheur**, on Ave Thaalbi, specialises in traditional soups and stews and is worth seeking out. It also serves alcohol.

There is a cluster of up-market hotels along the Corniche, the best of which is the **Petite Mousse** (☎ 432 185), two km west of the city centre. It charges TD27/40 in summer for very comfortable singles/doubles with breakfast. The restaurant here is reputed to be one of the best in the country.

Getting There & Away
Most public transport leaves from the south-eastern edge of town near the shipping canal. The bus station is at the end of Ave d'Algérie. There are buses to Tunis every 30 minutes. SNTRI has a daily bus at 6 am to Tabarka (2½ hours, TD5.650) and Aïn Draham (3¼ hours, TD6.480). The train station is 300 metres from the bus station at the end of Rue de Russie. There are four trains a day to Tunis (1½ hours, TD2.550). Louages do the trip in 45 minutes for TD2.800, leaving from under the shipping bridge.

Getting Around
Local buses depart from the train station. Buses to the Corniche beaches can be caught at the corner of Ave Habib Bourguiba and Blvd Hassan en Nouri.

TABARKA
The densely forested Kroumirie Mountains provide a dramatic backdrop to the small coastal town of Tabarka, 170 km west of Tunis, near the border with Algeria. Tourism looks set to boom here following the building of an international airport (charter flights only to date).

Most of the tourist development is 10 km to the east of town, leaving the town itself relatively unspoiled. The small bay to the north is watched over by an impressive Genoese fort. There's not much to do except hang out, but the atmosphere is right for it.

Information
There is a tourist office (☎ 644 491) in the middle of town on Ave Habib Bourguiba,

although the opening hours are pretty erratic outside summer. The banks are nearby, and the post office is on Ave Hedi Chaker, diagonally opposite the Hotel de France. Tabarka's telephone code is ☎ 08.

Places to Stay & Eat
There are a couple of good places to stay, but neither is particularly cheap. **Pension Mamia** (☎ 644 058), on Rue de Tunis, has spotless rooms built around a central courtyard. It charges TD8.500 per person in winter, and twice that in summer – breakfast included. Next best is the **Hotel de la Plage** (☎ 644 039), on Rue des Pecheurs, which has rooms and breakfast for TD10/16 all year.

There are several small places around the town centre serving delicious freshly grilled rouget (small red mullet) for about TD2.500. You'll see the small **charcoal grills** out in the street around the junction of Rue du Peuple and Rue Farhat Hached. The restaurant at the **Hotel de France** does a good three-course meal for TD6.500.

Getting There & Away
The SNTRI bus office and louage station for Tunis are on Rue du Peuple. SNTRI has nine buses a day to Tunis (3¼ hours, TD7.120). SRN Jendouba office, east of the town centre on Ave Habib Bourguiba, has regular buses to Jendouba via Aïn Draham. Louages to these towns leave from the eastern end of Ave Habib Bourguiba.

AÏN DRAHAM
Aïn Draham is Tunisia's hill station, nestled among the cork forest of the Kroumirie Mountains at an altitude of about 900 metres. The climate is markedly cooler than on the coast in summer, and snow is quite common in winter. Other than walking, there's not much to do. The 25-km drive from Tabarka takes in some of the prettiest scenery in Tunisia. Aïn Draham's telephone code is ☎ 08.

Places to Stay & Eat
There is a **maison des jeunes** hostel at the top end of town on the road to Jendouba. The only hotel in town is the pleasant **Hotel Beauséjour** (☎ 647 005). Singles/doubles cost TD17.500/29 with breakfast. Full board is good value – two three-course meals for an extra TD6. The

TUNISIA

porcine trophies on the walls are evidence of the hotel's popularity as a hunting lodge in colonial times.

Getting There & Away
SNTRI has three buses a day to Tunis (four hours, TD7.350) from the bus station at the foot of the hill. SRN Jendouba has regular buses to Tabarka and Jendouba, and an 8.15 am service to Le Kef.

BULLA REGIA
Bulla Regia, 160 km west of Tunis near the town of Jendouba, is famous as the town where the Romans went underground to escape the summer heat in much the same way as the Berbers did around Matmata.

They built their villas with one level below ground, usually with a small courtyard open to the sky. They lived in some style, if the three underground homes on display are anything to go by. They are named after the mosaics that were found inside them: the Palace of Fishing; the House of Amphitrite (in Greek mythology, a sea goddess and wife of Poseidon); and the Palace of the Hunt. A few mosaics have been left *in situ*, but the best examples are now in the Bardo Museum in Tunis. The site is open from 8 am to 7 pm in summer, and 8.30 am to 5.30 pm in winter.

The telephone code for the nearest town, Jenjouba, is ☎ 08.

Places to Stay
There is nowhere to stay near the site. The closest accommodation is in the nearby town of Jendouba, a dull administrative centre that most people avoid. If you get stuck, the *Pension Saha en Noum*, near the main square on Blvd Khemais el Hajiri, has clean rooms at TD4 per person. The two-star *Hotel Atlas* (☎ 630 566) charges TD16/22 for singles/doubles with breakfast.

Getting There & Away
The turn-off to Bulla Regia is clearly signposted six km from Jendouba on the road to Aïn Draham. If you're coming by bus or louage from Aïn Draham, you can get off at the junction and walk the last three km. Much of the walk is along an avenue of eucalypts. Coming from Jendouba, the simplest solution is to catch a cab for about TD3. You can arrange

to be picked up later or take your chances; there's a fair amount of passing traffic.

Jendouba is a regional transport hub with a good range of options. Train is the most comfortable way to get to Tunis (2½ hours, TD5.050). The last of five daily services leaves at 5 pm. There are also frequent buses and louages to Tunis, as well as to Le Kef, Aïn Draham and Tabarka.

DOUGGA
Dougga is an excellent Roman ruin in a commanding position on the edge of the Tebersouk Mountains, 110 km south-west of Tunis. The site is home to the country's most photographed Roman monument, the imposing **Capitol of Dougga**. This huge monument is dedicated to the gods Jupiter, Juno and Minerva. Fragments of the enormous statue of Jupiter are now housed in the Bardo Museum in Tunis, along with the best mosaics from the site. Next to the capitol is the **Square of the Winds**. In the centre is an enormous circular inscription listing the names of the 12 winds. On the southern edge of the site is **Trifolium House**, once the town's brothel. Dougga's well-preserved **theatre** makes a spectacular setting for performances of classical drama during the Dougga Festival in July and August. The site is open from 8 am to 7 pm in summer, and from 8.30 am to 5.30 pm in winter.

Dougga's telephone code is ☎ 08.

Places to Stay
Tebersouk is the closest town to the site, and the only hotel is the *Hotel Thugga* (☎ 465 713). The place caters almost exclusively to tour groups and charges TD23/35 for singles/doubles with breakfast. It's easy to visit the site on a day trip from Tunis or Le Kef.

Getting There & Away
SNTRI's frequent buses between Tunis and Le Kef stop at Tebersouk, ensuring a steady flow of departures in both directions until about 6 pm. At the bus stop you'll find locals asking about TD5 per person to take you the remaining seven km to the site and pick you up at a time of your choice. You can also walk to the site from Nouvelle Dougga, a village on the Tunis-Le Kef road just west of Tebersouk. It's a solid three-km uphill hike to the site – too far in summer.

LE KEF
Le Kef is an agricultural town some 170 km
south-west of Tunis, near the Algerian border.
Although it has no specific attractions, its altitude and commanding position make it a
pleasant place to visit. Le Kef is generally a
welcome few degrees cooler than the surrounding plains. The city centre, Place de
l'Independance, is a 10-minute walk uphill
from the bus and louage station.

Le Kef's telephone code is ☎ 08.

Things to See
The regional **museum** occupies a beautifully
restored old *zaouia* (Sufic shrine) deep within
the old medina on Place ben Aissa – not far
from the presidential palace. It has put together
a good display on the lifestyle of the area's
nomads. The **kasbah** on top of the hill is very
rundown but offers some fine views of the
plains.

Places to Stay & Eat
The *Hotel Medina* (☎ 220 214), 18 Rue Farhat
Hached, is a safe choice with doubles for TD8,
but no singles. There are good views from the
rooms at the back, which are also much quieter.
Hot showers are 500 mills. The *Hotel de la
Source* (☎ 224 397) improves once you make
it past the yellow lobby. It has singles/doubles
for TD8/10. The best place in town is the
Residence Venus (☎ 224 695), nestled beneath
the walls of the old kasbah. It has excellent
singles/doubles for TD18/28 with breakfast.

There are a couple of popular restaurants
opposite the PTT on Ave Hedi Chaker serving
cheap traditional food.

Getting There & Away
SNTRI has regular buses to Tunis (2½ hours,
TD6.850) via Tebersouk. Louages do the
journey in two hours for TD7. There are local
buses to Jendouba and Kasserine.

Central Tunisia

SOUSSE
Sousse, 142 km south of Tunis, is the country's
third-largest city and a major port. The huge
medina and impressive fortifications are the
main pointers to the city's long history as a
commercial centre. It was an important Phoenician town, called Hadrumète, long before
Carthage was settled. In Roman times,
Hadrumetum was the capital of the province of
Byzacée; the Vandals renamed it Huneri-
copolis in honour of their chief's son.

The latest invaders are package tourists,
who rule from their custom-built tourist village
of Port el-Kantaoui, 14 km to the north. The
coastline here is one long line of giant hotel
complexes.

Orientation & Information
Everything of importance in Sousse happens
around the enormous Place Farhat Hached, the
town's main square. The medina is on its south-
western corner, the port lies to the south-east
and Ave Habib Bourguiba runs north to the
beaches. The Tunis-Sfax railway line runs
right through the centre of the square.

The efficient tourist office (☎ 225 157) is on
the corner of Place Farhat Hached and Ave
Habib Bourguiba. There's also a syndicat
d'initiative, dispensing smiles from a small,
white-domed building across the square, near
the medina. The post office and main train
station are close by.

Sousse's telephone code is ☎ 03.

Things to See
The main monuments of the medina are the
ribat, a sort of fortified monastery, and the
great mosque. Both are in the north-eastern
part of the medina, not far from Place Farhat
Hached, and were built in the 9th century.

The ribat was primarily a fort, but the men
could study the Qur'an in the small cells surrounding the courtyard when they weren't
fighting. The tower offers excellent views of
the medina and the courtyard of the great
mosque below.

The great mosque is open from 9 am to 1 pm
every day. The **kasbah museum** on top of the
hill, closed on Monday, has well-presented
mosaics from the area. There is no access to
the kasbah from the medina, so make sure
you're outside the medina wall before climbing the hill.

Places to Stay & Eat
The best budget place in town is the spotless
Hotel de Paris (☎ 220 564), just inside the

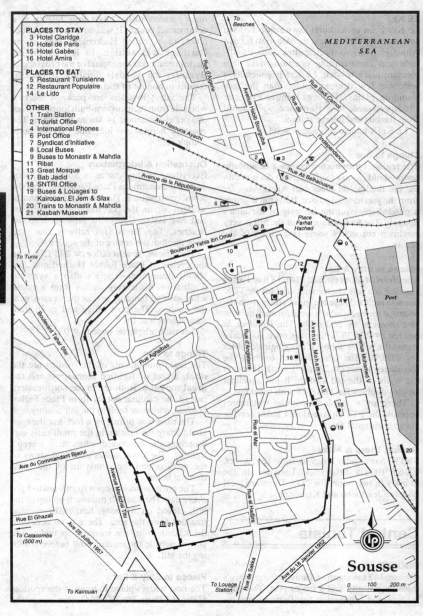

PLACES TO STAY
3 Hotel Claridge
10 Hotel de Paris
15 Hotel Gabès
16 Hotel Amira

PLACES TO EAT
5 Restaurant Tunisienne
12 Restaurant Populaire
14 Le Lido

OTHER
1 Train Station
2 Tourist Office
4 International Phones
6 Post Office
7 Syndicat d'Initiative
8 Local Buses
9 Buses to Monastir & Mahdia
11 Ribat
13 Great Mosque
17 Bab Jadid
18 SNTRI Office
19 Buses & Louages to
   Kairouan, El Jem & Sfax
20 Trains to Monastir & Mahdia
21 Kasbah Museum

MEDITERRANEAN
SEA

To Beaches

Rue d'Algerie

Rue Sadi Carnot

Avenue Habib Bourguiba

Rue de l'Independance

Ave Hasouna Ayachi

Rue Ali Belhaouane

1

2

3

5

Avenue de la République

6

7

Place
Farhat
Hached

Boulevard Yahia Ibn Omar

8

9

To Tunis

10

11

12

Port

13

14

Boulevard Tahar Sfar

Rue Aghalbas

15

16

Rue d'Angleterre

Avenue Mohamed Ali

Avenue Mohamed V

17

18

19

Ave du Commandant Bjaoul

Avenue Marechal Tito

Rue el Mar

Rue el Hadjira

20

Rue El Ghazali

Ave 25 Juillet 1967

21

To Catacombs
(500 m)

To Kairouan

To Louage
Station

Rue de Palais

Ave du 18 Janvier 1952

Sousse

0   100   200 m

TUNISIA

medina's north wall at 15 Rue du Rempart Nord. It has small singles for TD6, and larger singles/doubles for TD9/13 – rising to TD11/15 in summer, when you can also negotiate to sleep out on the roof. There are free hot showers and laundry facilities.

The *Hotel Gabès*, at 12 Rue de Paris, is the most presentable of the medina cheapies. It charges TD6 per person with free hot showers. If everywhere is full, you may still find a bed at the *Hotel Medina* (☎ 221 722), right next to the great mosque. It has good singles/doubles for TD13/18, including breakfast. The *Hotel Claridge* (☎ 224 759), on Ave Habib Bourguiba, is a fine older-style hotel charging TD27.500 for a large double with bathroom. Breakfast is served in the café next door.

The medina is the place to look for cheap local food. The *Restaurant Populaire*, at the entrance to the medina, is always packed. You pay for your meal before you sit down and hand the receipt to the waiter. There's keen competition for the tourist trade from the countless restaurants that line Ave Habib Bourguiba and Place Farhat Hached. You can get a good meal for TD10, plus wine. *Le Lido*, opposite the port on Ave Mohamed V, is well known for its seafood.

Getting There & Away
Train is the way to travel. There are eight trains a day to Tunis (2¼ hours, TD4.850), and four to Sfax (two hours, TD4.400) via El Jem. One train a day continues south to Gabès. Regular trains for Monastir and Mahdia leave from Bab Jedid station at the southern end of Ave Mohamed V. Buses leave from a variety of locations. Northbound SNTRI buses and regional buses to Monastir and Mahdia leave from the port side of Place Farhat Hached. Southbound SNTRI buses and regional buses to Kairouan (1½ hours, TD2.550) are to be found further south on Ave Mohamed Ali, near the medina's Bab Jedid gate. Catching a louage from Sousse has become a hassle since the louages were moved to a new station at the Souk el-Ahad, two km south of the city centre.

KAIROUAN
The old, walled city of Kairouan is historically the most important town in Tunisia. To Muslims, it ranks behind only Mecca, Medina and Jerusalem. The city, situated 150 km south of Tunis, is also famous for its carpets, its carpet salesmen and its orchards.

Orientation & Information
The medina is the focal point of Kairouan. Its busy main street, Ave Ali Belhouane, runs from Bab Tunis in the north to Bab ech Chouhada in the south. It's packed with carpet shops – and with bogus guides trying to get you into them. The tourist office (☎ 221 797) is inconveniently located right out on the northern edge of town, next to the Aghlabid Basins. Tickets for the main sites are sold here for TD2.100.

Kairouan's telephone code is ☎ 07.

Things to See
The city's main monument, the outwardly plain **great mosque**, is in the north-eastern corner of the medina. Much of the mosque dates from the 9th century, although the lowest level of the minaret is thought to have been built early in the 8th century, making it the oldest standing minaret in the world.

Other places of interest include the recently restored **Mosque of the Three Doors**, famous for the rare Arab inscriptions carved on its façade; the **Zaouia de Sidi Abid el Ghariani**; and the tourist trap known as **Bir Barouta**, which features a blindfolded camel drawing water from a well whose waters are said to be connected to Mecca.

Places to Stay & Eat
The best value is offered by the *Hotel Sabra* (☎ 220 260), just outside Bab ech Chouhada. It charges TD7.500/13 for clean rooms, breakfast and free hot showers. The *Hotel Marhala* (☎ 220 736), a converted madrese (Islamic college) in the medina, would be more enjoyable if the owner hadn't put a carpet shop in one of the rooms. It charges TD6.500 per person.

The *Restaurant de la Jeunesse*, on Ave Ali Belhouane, has excellent couscous. Stalls everywhere sell makhroud – a local speciality comprising honey-soaked pastry stuffed with dates.

Getting There & Away
The bus station is about 10 minutes walk southeast of town. There are regular buses to Sfax, Sousse and Tunis. Louages leave from a vacant lot north of the kasbah.

TUNISIA

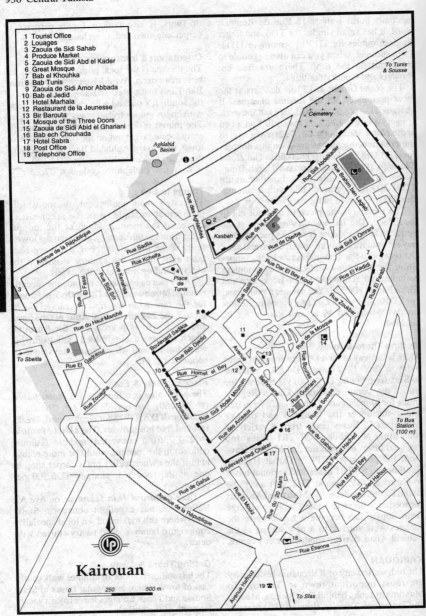

1 Tourist Office
2 Louages
3 Zaouia de Sidi Sahab
4 Produce Market
5 Zaouia de Sidi Abd el Kader
6 Great Mosque
7 Bab el Khouhka
8 Bab Tunis
9 Zaouia de Sidi Amor Abbada
10 Bab el Jedid
11 Hotel Marhala
12 Restaurant de la Jeunesse
13 Bir Barouta
14 Mosque of the Three Doors
15 Zaouia de Sidi Abid el Ghariani
16 Bab ech Chouhada
17 Hotel Sabra
18 Post Office
19 Telephone Office

To Tunis & Sousse

Cemetery

Aghlabid Basins

1

Rue Sidi Abdelkader

Rue Brahim ben Laghab

6

Rue des Aghlabites

2

Kasbah

Rue de la Kasbah

5

Rue de Djerba

Rue Sidi B Omrani

7

Rue El Kedidi

Rue El Farabi

Avenue de la République

Rue Sadlia

Rue Kchelfa

Rue Kenahsa

Rue Sidi Srif

Rue El Fassi

4

Place de Tunis

Rue Saili Soyssi

Rue Dar El Bey Koud

Rue Zouibar

Rue du Haut Marché

8

Boulevard Sadikia

Rue Bab Djedid

11

Avenue Ali Belhouane

Rue de la Mosque

14

To Sbeitla

9

Rue El Gadraoui

Rue El Zouacha

10

Rue Homet el Bey

12

13

Rue Bouras

Avenue Ali Zouaoui

Rue Sidi Abdel Moumen

Rue des Arceaux

15

16

Rue Guemiani

Rue de Soussa

To Bus Station (100 m)

Boulevard Hedi Chaker

17

Rue du Gafsa

Rue Farhat Hached

Rue Monced Bey

Rue Ouled Hafouz

Rue de Gafsa

Rue du 20 Mars

Rue El Mouiiz

To Sfax

Avenue de la République

18

Rue Étienne

19

Avenue Hafouz

Kairouan

0   250   500 m

MONASTIR

Monastir, 24 km south-east of Sousse, is another town that has surrendered lock, stock and barrel to the tourist trade. There's a nice sheltered **beach** – packed in summer, and scenes from Monty Python's *Life of Brian* were shot at the small, heavily restored **ribat**, but both can easily be visited on a day trip from Sousse.

MAHDIA

The eastern coastal town of Mahdia remains a relaxed place, despite the burgeoning tourist zone on the beaches to the north. The town was the capital of the early Fatimid rulers – a Muslim dynasty that ruled over North Africa from 909 to 1171. The site was chosen because its narrow promontory provided an ideal defensive position.

There is a small tourist office (☎ 681 098) just inside the medina.

Mahdia's telephone code is ☎ 03.

Things to See

The main gate to the old medina, **Skifa el Kahla**, is all that remains of the 10-metre-thick wall which once protected the city. The unadorned **great mosque** is a 20th-century replica of the mosque built by the Mahdi in the 10th century.

Places to Stay & Eat

The *Hotel el Jazira* (☎ 681 629) is the only medina hotel. It has a great location, with rooms overlooking the sea for TD8/13. Don't miss a meal at the *Restaurant El Moez*, on the edge of the medina near the market.

Getting There & Away

The bus, louage and train stations are about 500 metres from the town centre, past the fishing port. There are eight trains a day to Sousse (1½ hours, TD2).

EL JEM

This small town in the middle of Tunisia's olive-growing region is dominated by a very well-preserved **Roman amphitheatre** – arguably the most impressive Roman monument in North Africa. The amphitheatre suffered badly in the 17th century when one side was blown up to flush out rebels hiding inside. There is a good **museum** housing mosaics and local artefacts; it's about 500 metres south of the train station, on the road to Sfax. Both amphitheatre and museum are open daily from 7 am to 7 pm in summer and from 8 am to 5.30 pm in winter. Admission to the amphitheatre costs TD4.100.

Places to Stay

The *Hotel Julius* (☎ 690 044), right next to the train station, is the only hotel – and only bar – in town. It has singles/doubles around a pleasant, central courtyard for TD8.500/15.

Getting There & Away

All forms of transport leave from around the railway station, so just grab the first service that comes by – bus, louage or train.

SFAX

The unglamorous, eastern coastal town of Sfax is Tunisia's second-largest city. It has two big things going for it – its unspoiled old medina and the fact that there's hardly a package tourist in sight.

Orientation & Information

Sfax is a big, sprawling city. The only parts of interest to the visitor are the medina and the ville nouvelle, built on reclaimed land between the medina and the port.

There's a tourist office (☎ 224 606) in the small, green-roofed pavilion on Ave Habib Bourguiba. The post office occupies most of a block at the north-eastern end of Ave Habib Bourguiba, near the train station. There are plenty of banks, mostly along Ave Habib Bourguiba and Ave Hedi Chaker.

Sfax's telephone code is ☎ 04.

Things to See & Do

It's easy to spend hours wandering around the medina's maze of narrow streets. This is still a working medina, without the glitz and wall-to-wall tourist shops of the medinas in Tunis and Sousse. It's worth checking out the **Dar Jellouli Museum of Popular Traditions**, signposted off Rue de la Driba, a small street east off Rue Mongi Slim. It's open Tuesday to Saturday from 9.30 am to 4.30 pm.

Places to Stay & Eat

The cheap hotels are in the medina. Most charge about TD3.500 per person. The *Hotel Medina* (☎ 220 354), on Rue Mongi Slim, is the best of them with clean rooms for TD4 per person.

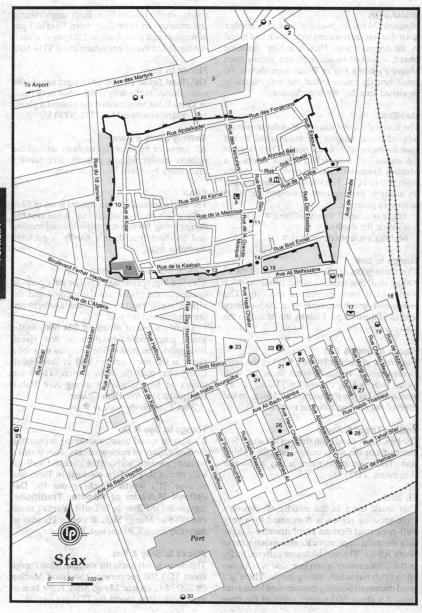

Ave des Martyrs

To Airport

Rue des Forgerons

Rue Abdelkader

Rue des Teinturiers

Rue Ahmed Bey

Rue Essour

Rue Sidi Kheilil

Rue Mong Slim

Rue de la Driba

Rue Sidi Ali Karral

Rue el Ksar

Rue de la Mercoue

Rue de la Grande Mosque

Rue Dar Essebai

Rue du 18 Janvier

Ave de l'Armée

Rue de la Kasbah

Rue Borj Ennar

Ave Ali Belhouane

Boulevard Farhat Hached

Ave Hedi Chaker

Ave de L'Algérie

Rue Dag Hammarskjold

Rue Halfouz

Rue de Tazarka

Rue Cheikh Megdiche

Rue Iribat

Rue al Arbi Zarrouk

Ave Taieb Mehin

Rue Imam Boukhari

Rue Alexandre Dumas

Rue Mong Bali

Ave Habib Bourguiba

Rue Salem Harzallah

Rue Habib Thameur

Rue de Kairouan

Ave Ali Bach Hamba

Rue Aboulkacem ech Chabi

Rue Tahar Star

Rue Patrice Lumumba

Rue Habib Maazoun

Ave Hedi Chaker

Rue Mohamed Ali

Ave Ali Bach Hamba

Ave Ali Bach Hamba

Rue de Remada

Ave Ali Bach Hamba

Port

Sfax

0   50   100 m

PLACES TO STAY		3	Market	18	Train Station
11	Hotel Medina	4	Local Buses	19	SNTRI Buses
20	Hotel Sfax Centre	5	Bab Jedid	21	Monoprix Supermarket
27	Hotels Alexander and	6	Bab Jabli	22	Tourist Office
	De la Paix	7	Bab el Chergui	23	International
29	Hotel Les Oliviers	8	Dar Jellouli Museum		Newspapers
		9	Great Mosque	24	Town Hall
PLACES TO EAT		10	Bab el Gharbi	25	Southern Bus Station
13	Café Diwan	12	Kasbah	26	Children's Playground
		14	Bab Diwan	28	ONAT
OTHER		15	Louages to Tripoli	30	Ferries to Kerkennah
1	Louages to Mahdia	16	Louage Station		
2	Northern Bus Station	17	Post Office		

There are a couple of good mid-range places on Rue Alexandre Dumas in the ville nouvelle. The *Hotel Alexander* (☎ 221 911) has large, comfortable rooms with bath for TD10.500/16, including breakfast. Give the place a miss on Saturday night when a folk band plays in the restaurant. The *Hotel de la Paix* (☎ 296 437), a few doors up from the Alexander, has singles/doubles for TD10/12. The *Hotel Les Oliviers* (☎ 225 188) is an elegant, older-style establishment on Ave Habib Thameur charging TD24/38 for singles/doubles with breakfast.

Getting There & Away

Sfax has direct flights to Tunis (45 minutes, TD37.600 one way) on weekdays only. The city is well served by the national bus line, SNTRI, which is conveniently located opposite the train station.

There are regular buses to Tunis (4½ hours, TD10.200) via Sousse (two hours, TD5.300); three a day to Jerba (four hours, TD9.300) via Gabès; and two a day to Tataouine (four hours, TD10.300). There's a daily train to Gabès at 11.25 am, and four trains a day to Tunis. Louages are spread out along Ave Ali Belhouane in front of the medina, but most leave from the shady square at the junction with Ave de l'Armée. The ferry port for the Kerkennah Islands is a 10-minute walk to the south of the city.

KERKENNAH ISLANDS

The Kerkennah Islands are a couple of depressing, flat, featureless islands 21 km from Sfax. The islands are linked by a causeway built in Roman times. Long used as a place of exile, the place has a general air of abandonment. Even the palm trees appear to be turning up

their toes. There was once a cluster of low-budget resort hotels at Sidi Fredj, but all bar two have closed down. The main town of Remla has a bank and a couple of restaurants, but the only hotel has closed.

There are between four and eight ferries a day to Sfax (1½ hours, 570 mills) depending on the season. All ferries are met by buses to Remla, at least one of which goes via Sidi Fredj. Bicycles are the best way of getting around; they can be rented at the resorts.

Southern Tunisia

GAFSA

Gafsa is the main service town for the phosphate-mining area of southern Tunisia. There's little of interest to the traveller apart from a couple of Roman pools, but they're not worth coming to Gafsa for. If you do get stuck, there are half a dozen cheap hotels around the bus station. The best of them is the *Hotel de la République* (☎ 221 807) on Rue Ali Belhouane. It charges a negotiable TD7/10 for singles/doubles with breakfast.

TOZEUR

Tozeur is a thriving town on the edge of the Chott el Jerid, the largest of Tunisia's salt lakes. The place has a relaxed atmosphere and is a popular destination for travellers.

The tourist office on Ave Abdulkacem Chebbi (☎ 450 088) and the syndicat d'initiative at Place ibn Châabat (☎ 450 034) have nothing to offer that you couldn't discover by asking the first person you meet on the street.

TUNISIA

There are several banks on Ave Habib Bourguiba. Ave Bourguiba is lined with souvenir shops selling the area's famous rugs. Bargain hard if you're buying.

Tozeur's telephone code is ☎ 06.

Things to See

The enormous **palmeraie** (palm grove) is best explored by bicycle, which can be hired on the road signposted to the **Zoo du Paradis** (home to a Coca-Cola-drinking camel). The impressive **Museum Dar Charait** is one km west of the tourist office at the western end of Ave Abdulkacem Chebbi. It's open every day from 8 am until midnight; admission is TD3.200. The **Ouled el Hadef**, the town's labyrinthine old quarter, is well worth exploring for its striking architecture and brickwork; enter by the road past the Hotel Splendid.

Places to Stay & Eat

Near the tourist office on Ave Abdulkacem Chebbi, **Camping Beaux Rêves** (☎ 451 242), is a good, shady site that backs onto the palmeraie. It charges TD3.500 per person, whether they sleep in their own tents or in one of the communal nomad-style tents. Hot showers are 900 mills.

The cheapest hotel in town is the grim **Hotel Essaada**, behind the carpet shops on Ave Habib Bourguiba. It charges TD3.500 per person. The nearby **Hotel Khalifa** isn't much better at TD6. Fortunately, there are a couple of good mid-range options. The **Residence Warda** (☎ 452 597) is an excellent place on Ave Abdulkacem Chebbi. It has singles/doubles with shared bathroom for TD10.300/15.600, and with bathroom for TD11.500/18. Prices include breakfast. If it's full, try the **Hotel Karim** (☎ 454 574) further along Ave Abdulkacem Chebbi at No 69. It's a new place offering a similar deal.

The inconspicuous **Restaurant du Sud**, north-east of the city centre on Ave Farhat Hached, gets the lion's share of local business. The Sfaxien food it advertises seems very similar to ordinary Tunisian food, but it's good and most meals cost under TD3. Other popular

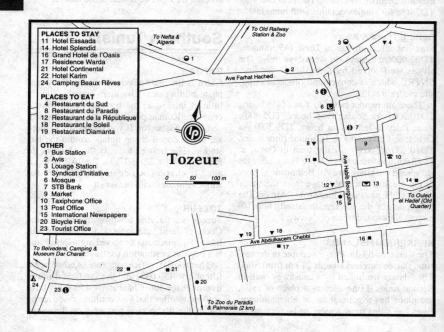

PLACES TO STAY
11 Hotel Essaada
14 Hotel Splendid
16 Grand Hotel de l'Oasis
17 Residence Warda
21 Hotel Continental
22 Hotel Karim
24 Camping Beaux Rêves

PLACES TO EAT
4 Restaurant du Sud
8 Restaurant du Paradis
12 Restaurant de la République
18 Restaurant le Soleil
19 Restaurant Diamanta

OTHER
1 Bus Station
2 Avis
3 Louage Station
5 Syndicat d'Initiative
6 Mosque
7 STB Bank
9 Market
10 Taxiphone Office
13 Post Office
15 International Newspapers
20 Bicycle Hire
23 Tourist Office

To Nefta & Algeria
To Old Railway Station & Zoo
Ave Farhat Hached

Tozeur

0   50   100 m

Ave Habib Bourguiba
Ave Abdulkacem Chebbi

To Ouled el Hadef (Old Quarter)

To Belvedere, Camping & Museum Dar Charait

To Zoo du Paradis & Palmeraie (2 km)

TUNISIA

places are the *Restaurant de la République*, just off Ave Bourguiba, and the *Restaurant le Soleil*, opposite the Residence Warda.

Getting There & Away

Tozeur has four flights a week to Tunis (70 minutes, TD43 one way), and three a week to Jerba (50 minutes, TD27 one way). The airport is four km from town off the road to Nefta. Tunis Air (☎ 450 038) has an office in town on Route de Nefta, about 200 metres beyond the new bus station.

SNTRI has five buses a day to Tunis (eight hours, TD16.500). The buses travelling inland via Gafsa and Kairouan are quicker than those going via Gabès and the coast. It also has one bus a day to Douz (two hours, TD5.350). There are local buses to Nefta (30 minutes, 950 mills). At the time of writing, louages were still leaving from a vacant lot off Ave Farhat Hached, but they were supposed to be moving out to the bus station.

NEFTA

Nefta is a sleepy oasis town close to the Algerian border. A daily bus goes to the border at 10 am. The palmeraie is worth exploring, and there are some beautiful examples of traditional brickwork in the old quarter. If you want to stay the night, there's an excellent place run by the Touring Club de Tunisie. The *Hotel Marhala* (☎ 05-457 027) occupies a converted brickworks and charges TD11/18 for singles/doubles with breakfast. To get there, follow the signs to the Zone Touristique and you'll find the Marhala on the way.

The bus station is on the main road into town. SNTRI has two buses a day to Tunis, and there are regular local buses and louages to Tozeur.

DOUZ

Situated right on the fringe of the Grand Erg Oriental (Great Eastern Desert), Douz promotes itself as the 'gateway to the Sahara'. The town centre is tiny, and everything of importance is within five minutes walk. You can change money at the bank on the Kebili road, and there's a post office on Ave des Martyrs.

Things to See & Do

Most people come to Douz to organise **camel trekking**. Trekking touts can now be found as far afield as the bus station in Gabès, and the offers are flying thick and fast by the time you reach Douz. Most of the time they are touting for a couple of big operators at Zaafrane – which is the place to go to get the best deals. There are regular camionettes and louages (both 500 mills) to Zaafrane from opposite the louage station in Douz. In Zaafrane you will be dropped at a huge vacant lot dotted with hundreds of camels. Among the camels are two small palm-thatch huts, bases for the rival organisations. Both offer trekking for as long as you care to nominate – from an hour (TD3.500) upwards. It's a good idea to sit on a camel for an hour before signing up for an adventure like an eight-day, oasis-hopping trek to Ksar Ghilane. You'll pay about TD30 a day for an experience like this, including all meals. Meals are cooked by campfire, and you'll sleep in basic nomad-style tents.

Douz is well known for its colourful Thursday **market**. Unfortunately, it's now on every tour group's itinerary. A more relaxing option is to wander through the extensive **palmeraie** to the **Great Dune** in the desert opposite the tour-group hotels.

Places to Stay & Eat

There's a good choice of budget accommodation, starting with the *Desert Club* camp site (☎ 05-495 595) in the palmeraie at the southern end of Ave 7 Novembre. The friendly *Hotel 20 Mars* (☎ 05-495 495), in the centre of town, has good rooms around a small courtyard for TD6 per person. At the time of writing, the smart new *Hotel de la Medina* was about to open up at the palmeraie end of Rue des Affections.

Getting There & Away

Buses leave from around the clock tower in the middle of town. SNTRI has buses to Tunis via Tozeur at 6 am and via the coast at 9 am. It also has a bus to Tozeur at 8 am. There are regular local buses to Kebili, and louages to Kebili and Gabès – but not Tozeur.

GABÈS

There is little reason to stay in this industrialised town on the Gulf of Gabès. Its only attraction is a mediocre palmeraie which tour groups get trotted through in *calèches* (horse carts). If you get stuck overnight, the *Hotel*

Ben Nejima is a spotless place charging TD7 per person. It's close to the bus station at the junction of Ave Farhat Hached and Rue Haj Djilani Lahbib. There's a restaurant downstairs.

The new bus and louage station is at the western end of Ave Farhat Hached. Three bus companies operate from here and can take you just about anywhere in Tunisia. SNTRI has regular departures to Tunis for TD12.100. There are two trains a day to Tunis.

MATMATA

It's easy to work out why the makers of *Star Wars* picked Matmata, 45 km south-west of Gabès, as the home planet of Luke Skywalker. Set amid a bizarre lunar landscape, the scattering of above-ground houses around the bus stop give little indication that you've arrived at a sizeable settlement. The Berbers of Matmata went underground centuries ago to escape the summer heat, and each of the many mounds that dot the landscape represents a home. They are all built along the same lines: a large central courtyard, usually circular, is dug out of the soft sandstone, and the rooms are then tunnelled into the perimeter.

Fascinating though Matmata might be, it's hard not to feel sorry for the long-suffering residents. The first tour buses roll up at 9 am every day, and they just keep on coming – day after day. The residents are sick of being stared at like goldfish. Many holes are surrounded by barbed wire to keep the tourists out.

Places to Stay

Three troglodyte homes have been transformed into interesting budget hotels. The *Sidi Driss* (☎ 05-230 005), setting for the bar scene in *Star Wars*, is the best of them – and the cheapest at TD6 per person for B&B.

MEDENINE

Medenine, 75 km south-east of Gabès, is the main town of the ksour (plural of *ksar*, a fortified Berber granary) area of the country's south. Medenine itself has a small ksar, which is something of a tourist trap, but the best examples are further south, near Tataouine, although the ksar which dominates the village of **Metameur**, six km north of Medenine, is impressive.

There's no reason to stay in Medenine, but the *Hotel Essaada* (☎ 05-640 300) on Ave Habib Bourguiba is OK if you get stuck. It asks TD4.500/7 for clean singles/doubles. The hotel is just a short walk from the bus and louage stations on Rue 18 Janvier. There are regular departures for Gabès, Jerba and Tataouine.

TATAOUINE

Tataouine is a fairly dull administrative centre 50 km south of Medenine, but it's a good base for visiting the surrounding Berber villages.

Things to See

The three-storey **Ksar Megabla** is a one-hour walk from the town centre, on the right side of the road to Remada. Locals still use the solid rooms to pen their sheep and goats.

Places to Stay & Eat

The *Hotel Medina* (☎ 05-860 999), on Rue Habib Mestaoui, charges TD5 per person and has the best budget restaurant in Tataouine. The *Hotel La Gazelle* is the up-market option, with singles/doubles for TD19/26 – often negotiable.

Getting There & Away

Buses and louages both leave from the city centre. There are frequent departures to Medenine, and occasional buses continuing to Jerba, Gabès and Tunis.

AROUND TATAOUINE
Chenini

This is a spectacular Berber village perched on the edge of an escarpment 18 km west of Tataouine. There are occasional camionettes to Chenini from the petrol station on the road to Remada. Otherwise you'll have to hitch or hire a taxi, which will cost about TD15 for the return journey. The journey is worth the effort, but get there early to avoid the tourist buses.

Ghoumrassen

This village is surrounded by rocky cliffs and has numerous cave dwellings that you can explore. It's the largest of the Berber villages and the only one serviced by public transport from Tataouine.

Jerba

Jerbans, especially those involved in the tourist industry, like to claim that their island is the legendary Land of the Lotus Eaters visited by Ulysses in the course of Homer's *Odyssey*. Whatever the story, there's something about the place that keeps drawing the tourists in ever increasing numbers – over a million in 1994.

The island now boasts a tourist strip covering more than 20 km of prime beachfront in the north-east. The island's main town and transport hub is Houmt Souk, in the middle of the north coast.

The island is linked to the mainland by a causeway, which was built in Roman times, and 24-hour car ferries between Ajim and Jorf.

Places to Stay

There are a couple of camp sites on the east coast near Aghir – at the *Auberge Centre Aghir* and attached to the *Hotel Sidi Slim*. The bus to Club Med from Houmt Souk goes right past both sites. If you want a hotel, the best place to look is Houmt Souk.

Getting There & Away

Air Tuninter flies to Tunis (one hour, TD45.300 one way) up to six times a day, depending on

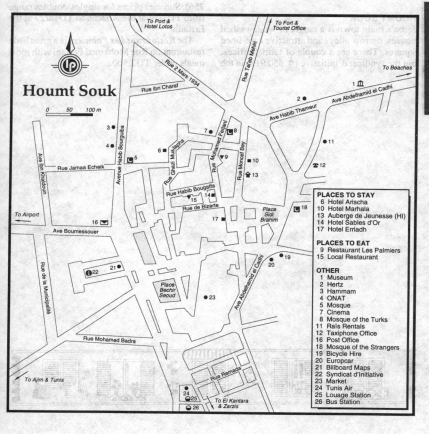

Houmt Souk

PLACES TO STAY
6 Hotel Arischa
10 Hotel Marhala
13 Auberge de Jeunesse (HI)
14 Hotel Sables d'Or
17 Hotel Erriadh

PLACES TO EAT
9 Restaurant Les Palmiers
15 Local Restaurant

OTHER
1 Museum
2 Hertz
3 Hammam
4 ONAT
5 Mosque
7 Cinema
8 Mosque of the Turks
11 Raïs Rentals
12 Taxiphone Office
18 Mosque of the Strangers
19 Bicycle Hire
20 Europcar
21 Billboard Maps
22 Syndicat d'Initiative
23 Market
24 Tunis Air
25 Louage Station
26 Bus Station

TUNISIA

the season. The airport is eight km from Houmt Souk – about TD3 by taxi.

Bus & Louage The bus and louages are side by side at the southern end of the Houmt Souk's main street. SNTRI has three buses a day to Tunis (eight hours, TD17.750), and there are also daily buses to Gabès and Tataouine. Gabès is the main louage destination.

Getting Around

Most of Jerba is flat, which makes it a good place to explore by bicycle or moped, both of which can be hired in Houmt Souk. The island's bus network is centred on Houmt Souk, where you'll find a timetable in English.

HOUMT SOUK

Jerba's main town is a tangle of whitewashed houses, narrow alleys and attractive café-lined squares. There are a couple of tourist offices, but the syndicat d'initiative (☎ 650 915) in the middle of town is the only one worth visiting. There are several banks, a post office and countless souvenir shops.

Houmt Souk's telephone code is ☎ 05.

Places to Stay & Eat

Houmt Souk has some of the most interesting places to stay in the country – old foundouks (caravanserai) that have been converted in a range of accommodation to suit every budget.

They start with the excellent *auberge de jeunesse* (☎ 650 619) on Rue Moncef Bey. It's great value at TD3.500. The other foundouk hotels are the *Arischa* (☎ 650 384), the *Marhala* (☎ 650 146), and the *Erriadh* (☎ 650 756). Summer prices for singles/doubles range from TD8/14 at the Arischa to TD18/27 at the Erriadh.

The *Restaurant Les Palmiers* is a great little restaurant on Rue Mohamed Ferjani with most meals under TD2.500.

Turkey

Turkey is usually considered Asia's foothold in Europe, the country that bridges two continents. There's no denying it's a Mediterranean country, with over 4000 km of warm-water coastline. A tourism boom in the 1980s put it on the travel map for everyone from package tourers to villa-renters. Holiday villages now share shore space with the hundreds of ruined Greek and Roman cities. The Turks are mostly quite friendly, especially when you escape the resorts and head into the heartland. The food can be marvellous, and prices are very low compared to Western Europe.

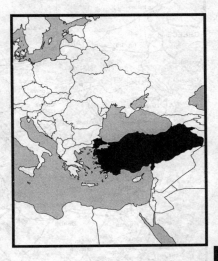

Facts about the Country

HISTORY

The Mediterranean region was inhabited as early as 7500 BC, and by 7000 BC a Neolithic city had grown up at Çatal Höyük, near Konya. The greatest of the early civilisations in Anatolia (Asian Turkey) was that of the Hittites. Long believed to be a purely mythical people, they were in fact a force to be reckoned with from 2000 to 1200 BC.

After the collapse of the Hittite empire, Anatolia broke up into a number of small states, and not until the Graeco-Roman period were parts of the country reunited. Later, Christianity spread through Anatolia, carried by the apostle Paul, a native of Tarsus (near Adana).

Byzantine Empire

In 330 AD the Roman emperor Constantine founded a new imperial city at Byzantium (modern İstanbul). Renamed Constantinople, this strategic city became the capital of the Eastern Roman Empire and was the centre of the Byzantine Empire for 1000 years. During the European Dark Ages, when the glories of Greece were just a memory and Rome had been overrun by barbarians, the Byzantine Empire kept alive the flame of Western culture. Through the centuries it was threatened by the powerful empires of the East (Persians, Arabs,

Turks) and West (the Christian powers of Europe).

The beginning of the Byzantine Empire's decline came with the arrival of the Seljuk Turks – they had previously conquered Persia and were beginning to encroach on Byzantine territory. The threat posed by the Seljuks precipitated the election of a new Byzantine emperor, Romanus IV Diogenes.

Romanus assembled an army to battle the Seljuks, but in August 1071 he was defeated at Manzikert, near Lake Van, and taken prisoner. The Seljuks took over most of Anatolia, and established a provincial capital at Nicaea/İznik. Their domains included today's Turkey, Iran and Iraq.

With significantly reduced territory, the Byzantines, under their new emperor, Alexius I Comnenus, endeavoured to protect Constantinople and reclaim Anatolia.

The Crusades

In 1095, Pope Urban II called for crusaders to fight in a holy war. To reach the Holy Land, it

945

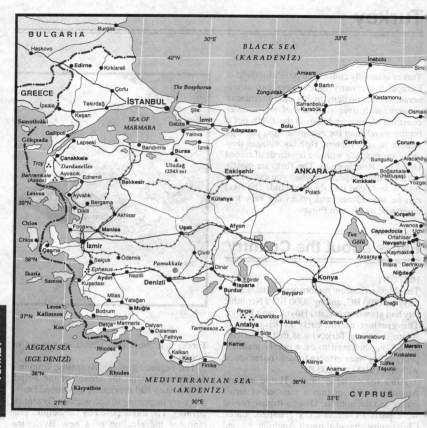

was necessary for the First Crusade to pass through Constantinople. In return for this right of passage, Alexius Comnenus struck a deal with the crusade leaders, demanding that any territories won from the Turks by the crusaders be returned to the Byzantines. Although the crusaders failed to cooperate totally with the terms of the pact, in 1097 the Byzantines were able to win back the city of Nicaea from the Seljuks and reoccupy western Anatolia, with the Seljuks maintaining their power in the rest of Anatolia. The Fourth Crusade (1202-04) proved less fruitful for the Byzantines, with a combined Venetian and crusade force taking and plundering the city of Constantinople. The

ravaged city was eventually regained by the Byzantines in 1261.

Ottoman Empire

A Mongol invasion of the late 1200s put an end to Seljuk power, but new small Turkish states were born soon after in western Anatolia. One of these, headed by Osman (1258-1326), grew into the Ottoman Empire, and in 1453 (just under 40 years before Columbus sailed for America), Constantinople fell to the Ottoman sultan Mehmet II (the Conqueror).

A century later, under Süleyman the Magnificent, the Ottoman Empire reached the peak of its cultural brilliance and power, spreading

deep into Europe, Asia and North Africa. The janissaries, members of the sultan's personal guard and the first modern standing army, gave the Turks an advantage, as the European nations had to raise armies anew for each war. The Turks also tolerated minority groups, including Christians and Jews.

Ottoman success was based on military expansion, not on industry or agriculture. When their march westwards was stalled at Vienna in 1683, the rot started. A succession of incompetent sultans hardly helped, especially when combined with discontent among the janissaries, who by now had become totally unreliable.

The great European powers began to covet the sultan's vast domains. Nationalist ideas swept through Europe after the French Revolution, and Turkey found itself with unruly subject populations in the Balkans. In 1829 the Greeks won their independence, followed by the Serbs, the Romanians and the Bulgarians in 1878. Italy took Tripolitania in North Africa from Turkey in 1911, and Albania and Macedonia escaped after the 1912-13 Balkan War.

Finally, the unfortunate Turks emerged from WWI stripped of their last non-Turkish provinces – Syria, Palestine, Mesopotamia (Iraq) and Arabia. Most of Turkey (Anatolia) itself was to be parcelled out to the victorious

Greeks, Italians, French and Russians, leaving the Turks virtually nothing.

Atatürk

At this low point in Turkish history, Mustafa Kemal, the father of modern Turkey, took over. Atatürk, as he was later called, had made his name by repelling the Anzacs in their heroic but futile attempt to capture Gallipoli. Rallying the tattered remnants of the army, he pushed the final, weak Ottoman rulers aside and outmanoeuvred the Allied forces in the War of Independence, a desperate affair.

Final victory for the Turks in the War of Independence came in 1923 at Smyrna – a city with a large Greek population on Turkey's Aegean coast, today known as İzmir – where invading Greek armies were literally pushed into the sea. This was followed by an exchange of populations similar to that which took place in India at the time of the India-Pakistan partition. Well over a million Greeks left Turkey and nearly half a million Turks moved in. Relations with Greece improved markedly in 1930, but were soured again after WWII by the conflict over Cyprus, particularly after the Greek-led anti-Makarios coup, and subsequent Turkish invasion of the island, in 1974.

With Turkey reduced to smaller but more secure boundaries, Atatürk embarked on a rapid modernisation programme centred on establishing a secular democracy, de-emphasising religion, introducing the Roman alphabet and European dress, and moving towards equal rights for women. In 1923 the country's capital was moved from 'decadent' İstanbul to Ankara, which was laid out anew to a modern plan. Naturally, such sweeping changes did not come easily, but Turkey is certainly more progressive in these areas than most of its neighbours.

Modern Turkey

The oil crisis of the 1970s, the Gulf War (1991) and continuing problems with separatist Kurds in the east have wreaked havoc on the Turkish economy, forcing the government to introduce unpopular austerity measures.

Still poor by Western standards, Turkey is developing rapidly. In 1995 it entered into a customs-union agreement with the EU, and hopes eventually for full membership.

Although resurgent Islam has recently gained some influence in the country, and the Islamic Welfare Party (Refah) won control of İstanbul and Ankara in 1994 local elections, Atatürk remains very much the symbol of modern Turkey, and secularism – not Islamic law – is the preference of the great majority of Turks. The collapse of the old Soviet Union has brought Turkey unparalleled opportunities for trade with Eastern Europe and the newly emerging Turkic republics of former Soviet Central Asia.

GEOGRAPHY

Turkey is divided into Asian and European parts by the Dardanelles, the Sea of Marmara and the Bosphorus. Thrace (European Turkey) comprises only 3% of the total 780,000-sq-km land area. The remaining 97% is Anatolia, a vast plateau rising eastward towards the Caucasus Mountains. Turkey's coastline is over 6000 km long and includes many popular resort areas.

GOVERNMENT & POLITICS

Turkey is a multiparty parliamentary democracy. Several times in the last 40 years, the army has stepped in to 'correct' what it saw as an undemocratic drift away from the principles set forth by Atatürk. During the 1970s, in shock from the oil crisis, the country became politically unstable and racked by left-right terrorism. To nobody's surprise (and to most people's relief), the army ousted the ineffectual civilian government in 1980, restored order and rewrote the constitution.

By 1983, its popularity waning, the military government held elections and, again to no-one's surprise, lost power to the new centre-right Anavatan (Motherland) party headed by economist Turgut Özal. Motherland held a parliamentary majority through the 1980s, with Özal first as prime minister (1983-89) and then as president for a seven-year term.

In 1993 Özal died and seven-times former prime minister Süleyman Demirel became president, with former economics minister Professor Tansu Çiller as Turkey's first female prime minister.

The elections of 24 December 1995 were a wake-up call against politics as usual: the pro-Islamic Welfare (Refah) Party won a relative majority of 23%, which was seen as a protest vote against the two big centre-right parties. After months of political wrangling, Welfare came to power as the senior member of a coalition with Çiller's True Path party, amidst bitter acrimony in the largely pro-secularist parliament.

ECONOMY

Turkey has a strong agricultural sector, being a net exporter of food. Wheat, cotton, sugar beet, sunflowers, hazelnuts, tobacco, fruit and vegetables are abundant. Sheep are the main livestock, and Turkey is the biggest wool producer in Europe. However, manufactured goods now dominate the economy. Turkey builds motor vehicles, appliances, consumer goods and large engineering projects, and exports them throughout the region. There is still a large Turkish workforce in the industrial sectors of Europe, particularly in Germany.

POPULATION & PEOPLE

Turkey's population of nearly 60 million is made up predominantly of Muslim Turks, with a significant minority (perhaps eight to 10 million) of Muslim Kurds and small groups of Jews, Greeks, Armenians, Laz (a Black Sea people) and Arabs. Its five biggest cities are İstanbul (12 million people), Ankara (3.2 million), İzmir (2.7 million), Adana (1.9 million) and Bursa (1.6 million).

ARTS

Islam discourages images of any being 'with a soul' (ie animal or human), so there was little sculpture or portraiture in Ottoman times (though there was Turkish miniature painting). Instead, Turkish artists pursued calligraphy, architecture, textile design (especially carpets and apparel), jewellery, faïence, glass-making and many crafts.

Ottoman literature and court music were mostly religious, and both sound pompous and lugubrious to Western ears. Folk music was (and is) sprightly; troubadours were highly skilled and very popular, although TV and cassettes have largely wiped them out.

As with all else, Atatürk changed Turkey's cultural picture overnight, encouraging painting, sculpture, Western music (he loved opera), dance and drama. In recent days, Ottoman arts

such as paper-marbling and the Karagöz shadow-puppet plays are enjoying a resurgence, and are seen as valuable traditions worthy of preservation. Carpet-weaving is, was, and always will be a Turkish passion.

CULTURE

Ottoman Turkey was ruled by the sharia (Islamic religious law), but republican Turkey – thanks to Atatürk – has largely adapted to a modern, westernised lifestyle. Although many Turks drink alcohol (and don't mind if others drink), they still revere the moral and spiritual teachings of their religion, and observe its customs, if sometimes loosely.

Liberal Western attitudes born of Atatürk's reforms are strongest in the urban centres of the west and along the coasts – among the middle and upper classes. You will feel quite comfortable among these Turks; they look to Western culture as the ideal, and accept the validity of other religious beliefs.

The working and farming classes, particularly in the east, are more conservative, traditional and religious. There is a small but growing segment of 'born-again' Muslims, fervent and strict in their religion but otherwise modern. Though always polite, these Turks may give you the feeling that East is East and West is West, and that the last echo of 'crusaders versus Saracens' has not yet died away.

RELIGION

Turkey is 99% Muslim, predominantly Sunni, with Shias in the east and south-east. When you visit mosques, dress conservatively (no 'revealing' clothing like shorts or sleeveless shirts), remove your shoes, don't take flash photographs and be respectful. Women should cover their head and shoulders.

LANGUAGE

Ottoman Turkish was written in Arabic script, but Atatürk decreed a change to Roman script in 1928. In big cities and tourist areas, many locals know at least some English and/or German. See the Language Guide at the back of the book for pronunciation guidelines and useful words and phrases.

TURKEY

Facts for the Visitor

PLANNING
Climate & When to Go

The Aegean and Mediterranean coasts have mild, rainy winters and hot, dry summers. In İstanbul, summer temperatures average around 28˚C to 30˚C; the winters are chilly but usually above freezing, with rain and perhaps a dusting of snow. The Anatolian plateau is cooler in summer and quite cold in winter. The Black Sea coast is mild and rainy in summer, and chilly and rainy in winter.

Mountainous eastern Turkey is very cold and snowy in winter, and only pleasantly warm in high summer. The south-east is dry and mild in winter and very hot in summer, with temperatures above 45˚C not unusual. In general, spring (April/May) and autumn (September/October) have the most pleasant weather.

Books & Maps

Lonely Planet also publishes the more detailed *Turkey – travel survival kit* and also the *Turkish phrasebook*.

For a short cut to an understanding of Turkey, read *Atatürk: The Rebirth of a Nation* by Lord Kinross (JPD Balfour). An absolutely gripping account of the decline of the Ottoman Empire from its peak under Süleyman the Magnificent is *Lords of the Golden Horn* by Noel Barber. Freya Stark's *Alexander's Path* retraces Alexander the Great's route across southern Turkey; it's good on the pre-tourist-boom south, if sometimes a little too learned. An easier read is Mary Lee Settle's *Turkish Reflections*, which casts a novelist's eye over the whole country.

The Bartholomew Euromap of Turkey, in two sheets at 1:800,000, is excellent. The forthcoming Lonely Planet *Turkey Travel Atlas* will cover the country in an easy-to-carry format. Inspect locally produced maps carefully to assess their probable usefulness before you buy.

What to Bring

You'll find the following items useful in Turkey: mosquito repellent (from April to September), sunblock cream (it's expensive in Turkey), a universal sink plug, a towel, and reading matter. Women should bring tampons or sanitary pads.

SUGGESTED ITINERARIES

İstanbul, the Aegean and Mediterranean coasts and Cappadocia are the areas most people come to see. The Black Sea coast can be travelled in a day or a week, as you wish. If your time is limited, you might like to consider the following itineraries:

Two days
　Explore İstanbul or Selçuk/Ephesus.
One week
　See İstanbul and the Aegean coast to Bodrum or Marmaris, with a quick trip to Pamukkale.
Two weeks
　Travel from İstanbul south and east along the coasts to Antalya or Alanya, then return to İstanbul via Cappadocia.
Three weeks or more
　Travel from İstanbul to İznik, Bursa, the Aegean coast and the Mediterranean coast to Silifke, then inland to Konya, Cappadocia and Ankara, and back to İstanbul.

HIGHLIGHTS

In İstanbul, don't miss Topkapı Palace, Aya Sofya (Hagia Sofia), the Blue Mosque or the Kariye Museum. The battlefields of Gallipoli, on the Dardanelles, are particularly moving. Many visitors find Troy disappointing, but not so Ephesus, the best-preserved classical city on the Mediterranean.

Seljuk Turkish architecture, earlier than Ottoman, is particularly fine. Alanya, Konya, Sivas and Erzurum have good Seljuk buildings.

Turkey's beaches are best at Pamucak (near Ephesus), Ölüdeniz, Bodrum, Patara, Antalya, Side and Alanya. The improbable 'lunar' landscapes of Cappadocia are perhaps the single most visually impressive feature in all Turkey. Further east, the great Commagenian heads on Nemrut Dağı certainly repay an early start to the day.

TOURIST OFFICES
Local Tourist Offices

Ministry of Tourism (Turizm Bakanlığı) offices exist in every tourist-oriented town. There may be provincial or local offices as well. The enthusiasm and helpfulness of the staff vary widely. Most offer regional brochures and local maps of minimal usefulness;

the big town maps, however, are excellent. Ask for the *Youth Travel Guide Book*, which has lots of advice for budget travellers.

Turkish Tourist Offices Abroad

Turkey has tourist offices in the following countries:

UK
170-173 Piccadilly, 1st floor, London WV1 9DD (☎ 0171-734 8681; fax 0171-491 0773)

USA
821 UN Plaza, New York, NY 10017 (☎ 212-687 2194; fax 212-599 7568)

VISAS & EMBASSIES

Have a passport valid for at least three months beyond your date of entry. Nationals of many Western European countries don't need visas for visits of up to three months. UK subjects pay UK£10, and US citizens US$20, for a visa on arrival. Embassies are in Ankara; many nations have consulates in İstanbul, and some have them in İzmir as well.

Turkish Embassies

Turkey has embassies in the following countries:

Australia
66 Ocean St, PO Box 222, Woollahra, NSW 2025 (☎ 02-9328 1155)

Bulgaria
Blvd Vasil Levski No 80, 1000 Sofia (☎ 02-872306)

Canada
197 Wurtemburg St, Ottawa, Ontario KlN 8LD (☎ 613-789 4044)

Greece
Vasilissis Georgiou B 8, 106 74 Athens (☎ 01-724 5915)

UK
43 Belgrave Square, London SW1X 8PA (☎ 0171-235 5252)

USA
1714 Massachusetts Ave NW, Washington, DC, 20036 (☎ 202-659 8200)

Foreign Embassies in Turkey

Countries with diplomatic representation in Turkey include:

Australia
consulate: Tepecik Yolu 58, 80630 Etiler, İstanbul (☎ 212-257 7050; fax 212-257 7054) open from 8.30 am to 12.30 pm weekdays

Canada
consulate: Büyükdere Caddesi 107/3, Bengün Han, 3rd floor, Gayrettepe, İstanbul (☎ 212-272 5174)

France
consulate: İstiklal Caddesi 8, Taksım, İstanbul (☎ 212-243 1852; fax 212-249 9168)

Germany
consulate: İnönü Caddesi, Selim Hatun Camii Sokak 46, Ayazpaşa, Taksim, İstanbul (☎ 212-251 5404; fax 249 9920)

Greece
consulate: Turnacıbaşı Sokak 32, Ağahamam, Beyoğlu, İstanbul (☎ 212-245 0596; fax 212-252 1365)

Japan
consulate: İnönü Caddesi 24, Ayazpaşa, Taksim, İstanbul (☎ 212-251 7605; fax 212-252 5864)

New Zealand
embassy: Kızkulesi Sokak 42/1, Gaziosmanpaşa, Ankara (☎ 312-446 0768, 446 0732; fax 312-445 0557)

UK
consulate: Meşrutiyet Caddesi 57, Tepebaşı, Beyoğlu, İstanbul (☎ 212-252 6436, 244 7540; fax 212-245 4989)

USA
consulate: Meşrutiyet Caddesi 104-108, Tepebaşı, Beyoğlu, İstanbul (☎ 212-251 3602; fax 212-252 7851)

CUSTOMS

You may import, duty-free, two cartons of cigarettes (that's 400), 50 cigars or 200 grams of smoking tobacco, and five litres of liquor. Duty-free items are on sale in both arrival and departure areas of Turkey's international airports.

Turkey is full of antiquities: ancient coins, figurines, pots and mosaics. *It is illegal to buy, sell or export antiquities!* Penalties are severe – if caught, *you may go to jail*. Customs officers spot-check the luggage of departing passengers. For information on bringing a motor vehicle into Turkey, see Car & Motorcycle in the Getting Around section of this chapter.

MONEY
Currency

The Turkish lira (TL) comes in coins of 1000, 2500, 5000, 10,000 liras, and notes (bills) of 10,000, 20,000, 50,000, 100,000, 250,000, 500,000 and one million liras, with higher denominations added regularly as inflation (close to 100% per annum) devalues the currency. Watch for three or more zeros to be dropped from the money in 1997, if not earlier. Prices in this chapter are quoted in more-stable US dollars.

Turkey has no black market; you can often spend US dollars or Deutschmarks in place of

TURKEY

liras. Exchanging cash of major currencies is fast and easy in most banks, exchange offices, post offices, shops and hotels. Cashing major travellers' cheques is less easy (some places resist) and the exchange rate is usually slightly lower. Many places charge a commission (*komisyon*); ask first.

Exchange Rates

Australia	A$1	=	65,448TL
Canada	C$1	=	60,848TL
France	1FF	=	16,642TL
Germany	DM1	=	56,426TL
Japan	¥100	=	77,216TL
New Zealand	NZ$1	=	58,244TL
United Kingdom	UK£1	=	130,038TL
United States	US$1	=	83,480TL

Costs

Turkey is Europe's budget destination, and you can travel on as little as US$10 to US$15 per person per day using buses, staying in pensions, and eating one restaurant meal daily. For US$15 to US$30 per day you can travel more comfortably by bus and train, staying in one and two-star hotels with private baths, and eating most meals in average restaurants. For US$30 to US$70 per person per day you can move up to three and four-star hotels, take the occasional airline flight and dine in restaurants all the time. Costs are highest in İstanbul and the big coastal resorts, and lowest in small eastern towns off the tourist track.

Tipping

Waiters appreciate a tip of 7 to 10% (15% in expensive places) of the bill; hotel porters, 50 cents to US$1; barbers, hairdressers and Turkish-bath attendants, 10 to 15%; and cinema ushers, a few coins or a small lira note. Porterage at airports and train and bus stations is set and should be posted. Except for special service, don't tip taxi drivers; rather, round up the fare. Minibus (*dolmuş*) drivers are not tipped.

Bargaining

In some shops prices are set, but in others, use your *pazarlık* (bargaining) skills. You *must* bargain for souvenirs. Even if the establishment has set prices, bargain if you are buying several items or are shopping in the off season. For hotel rooms, bargain if you visit any time between October and late May, or if you plan to stay more than a few days.

Consumer Taxes

A value-added tax (KDV, Katma Değer Vergisi) of 15 to 20% is included in the price of most items and services; this is known as KDV *dahil* (VAT included). A few hotels and shops give discounts if you agree not to request an official receipt; this way, they don't have to pay the tax, and you save. It's illegal but not unusual.

If you buy an expensive item (eg carpet, leather apparel) for export, ask the shopkeeper for a KDV *iade özel fatura* (special VAT refund receipt). Get the receipt stamped as you clear customs, then get your refund at a bank branch in the airport departure lounge; or you can mail the receipt and be sent a cheque.

POST & COMMUNICATIONS
Post

Turkish post offices are called PTT (*posta, telefon, telgraf*); look for the black-on-yellow signs. If you have mail addressed to you care of poste restante in a major city, the address should include Merkez Postane (central post office) or the name of the neighbourhood post office at which you wish to retrieve it.

Telephone & Fax

Turkey's public telephones, now separated from the PTT and operated by Türk Telekom, take either *jetonlar* (tokens) or a *telekart* (telephone card), both sold at telephone centres and some shops. Turkey's country code is ☎ 90.

To call from one city to another, dial ☎ 0 (zero), then the city code and number. To call abroad, dial ☎ 00, then the country and area codes and number.

It's easiest to send and receive faxes at your hotel for a fee (ask in advance). Türk Telekom telephone centres have faxes but require more paperwork.

E-mail

TURNET, Turkey's national Internet network, was established by Türk Telekom in 1996. IBM also has a Turkish network, but both require that you have an account. A better option is to have an account with CompuServe, the US company with offices and nodes in most countries. Turkish nodes (9600 bps) are in Ankara (modem 312-468 8042) and İstanbul (modem 212-234 5168). America Online's İstanbul node is at 212-234 5158 (28,800 bps).

NEWSPAPERS & MAGAZINES

The *Turkish Daily News* is the local English-language paper. In major tourist areas you'll find many day-old European and US newspapers and magazines.

RADIO & TV

Broadcasting is by the government-funded TRT (Turkish Radio & Television) and numerous independent stations. TRT offers short news broadcasts in English each morning and evening on radio and late each evening on TV.

PHOTOGRAPHY & VIDEO

Film costs about US$6, plus developing, for 24 Kodacolor exposures. Kodachrome is scarce, pricey and can't be developed in Turkey, though the simpler E-6 process films such as Ektachrome and Fujichrome are readily available and speedily processed in city photo shops.

Still cameras are subject to an extra fee in most museums; in some they are not allowed at all. For use of flash or tripod, you must normally obtain written permission from the staff (not easy). Video fees are usually even higher.

Don't photograph anything military. In areas off the tourist track, it's polite to ask 'Foto/video çekebilir miyim?' (May I take a photo/video?) before shooting close-ups of people.

TIME

Turkey is on Eastern European Time, two hours ahead of GMT/UTC. When it's noon in Turkey, it's 11 am in Paris and Frankfurt, 10 am in London, 5 am in New York and 2 am in Los Angeles. In summer/winter it's 5/7 pm in Perth and Hong Kong, 7/9 pm in Sydney and 9/11 pm in Auckland. From late March to late September, Turkey observes daylight-saving time and clocks are turned ahead one hour.

ELECTRICITY

The electric current in Turkey is 220V, 50 Hz. Cheap hotel rooms (up to two-star) usually have one power point/outlet. Most camp sites,

however, are very rudimentary, and power may not be easily available.

WEIGHTS & MEASURES

Turkey uses the metric system.

LAUNDRY

Attended laundrettes are beginning to appear in the larger cities, but most tourist laundry (*çamaşır*) is done in hotels. Talk to the staff. The cost may be negotiable. Dry cleaners (*kuru temizleme*) are readily found in the cities; ask at your hotel.

TOILETS

The word is *tuvalet*. All mosques have toilets, though most are at least a bit smelly. Major tourist sites have better ones. Almost all public toilets require payment of a small fee (10 to 30 cents).

Though most hotels and many public toilets have the familiar raised bowl commode, Turkey also has flat toilets, which are simply a hole in the floor with footrests on either side. You'll soon find squatting quite natural. Traditionally, one washes with water (from a spigot, jug or little pipe attached to the toilet), using the left hand. When not in your hotel, carry toilet paper with you.

HEALTH

Travellers in Turkey may experience 'traveller's diarrhoea', so take precautions. Drink bottled water; make sure fruit is washed in clean water or peeled with clean hands; avoid raw or undercooked seafood and meat; and don't eat food which has been standing unrefrigerated.

Pharmacists can advise you on minor problems and dispense on the spot many drugs for which you would need a prescription at home. Emergency medical and dental treatment is available at simple dispensaries, clinics and government hospitals. Look for signs with a red crescent or big 'H'. Payment is required, but is usually very low.

WOMEN TRAVELLERS

In traditional Turkish society, men and women have lives apart: the husband has his male friends, the wife has her female friends. Younger Turks are shedding these roles, and women now hold some positions of authority.

TURKEY

Still, foreign women are often hassled while travelling in Turkey. Men pinch, grab and make strange noises, which can become very tiresome; more serious assault is uncommon but possible. Travelling with a male improves matters, as does travelling with another female, or preferably two.

Turkish women completely ignore men who speak to them in the street. Wearing a headscarf, a skirt which comes below the knees, a wedding ring and sunglasses makes you less conspicuous. Away from beach resorts you should certainly avoid skimpy tops and brief shorts.

STUDENT TRAVELLERS
The International Student Identity Card (ISIC) gets you reductions at museums and archaeological sites (usually 50%), train travel (30%), on Turkish Maritime Lines ships (10%) and sometimes on private bus lines and Turkish Airlines.

GAY & LESBIAN TRAVELLERS
Homosexuality is illegal in Turkey, though it exists openly at a small number of gay bars and clubs in major cities and resorts. Be discreet.

DISABLED TRAVELLERS
Turkey is not well prepared for disabled travellers. Steps and obstacles are everywhere; ramps, wide doorways and properly equipped lodgings and toilets are rare. Crossing most streets is for the young and agile; all others are in peril. You must plan each hour of your trip carefully, and usually patronise luxury-level hotels, restaurants and transport.

SENIOR TRAVELLERS
Seniors (altın yaş, literally 'golden-agers') are welcomed and respected in Turkey, and sometimes receive discounts at hotels, museums and other touristic sites.

DANGERS & ANNOYANCES
Although Turkey is considered one of the safest countries in the region, you must still take precautions. Wear a money belt under your clothing. Be wary of pickpockets and purse-snatchers in buses, markets and other crowded places.

In İstanbul, single men have been victims of a thinly veiled form of extortion: after being lured to a bar or nightclub (often one of those along İstiklal Caddesi) by new Turkish 'friends', the man is then made to pay an outrageous bar bill whether he drank or not.

On intercity buses, there have been isolated incidents of theft by drugging: the person in the bus seat next to you buys you a beverage at a rest stop, slips a drug into it and, as you sleep, makes off with your luggage. More commonly, the hard-sell tactics of carpet sellers can drive you to distraction; be warned that 'free' lifts and suspiciously cheap accommodation often come attached to nearly compulsory visits to carpet showrooms.

BUSINESS HOURS
Banks and offices are open Monday to Friday, generally from 8.30 am to noon and from 1.30 to 5 pm; shops are open Monday to Saturday from 9.30 am to 6 or 7 pm, some taking a lunch break from 1 to 2 pm. Food shops open early (6 or 7 am) and close late (7 or 8 pm). One food shop in each neighbourhood opens on Sunday.

PUBLIC HOLIDAYS & SPECIAL EVENTS
Turkey celebrates the following holidays and events:

1 January
    New Year's Day
Mid-January
    camel-wrestling in Selçuk
23 April
    National Sovereignty Day – the first republican parliament was convened in Ankara on this day in 1920; and *Children's Day*
19 May
    Youth & Sports Day – the date of Atatürk's landing in Samsun to begin the War of Independence
Mid-May
    Ephesus festival of international dance and drama at Efes
June
    Oil-wrestling in Edirne (2nd week); *International İstanbul Music Festival* (late June to early July)
30 August
    Victory Day – victory over invading Greek armies at Dumlupınar in 1922
29 October
    Republic Day – proclamation of the republic in 1923
10 November
    Anniversary of Atatürk's death (1938) – although not a public holiday, special ceremonies are held
December
    Whirling dervishes in Konya

Religious Holidays
Muslim holidays follow the lunar calendar.

The holy month of Ramadan (Ramazan) is followed by the three-day Şeker Bayramı (Sweets Holiday). Ramadan runs from 10 January to 8 February 1997, 30 December 1997 to 28 January 1998, 19 December 1998 to 17 January 1999, and 8 December 1999 to 6 January 2000.

Kurban Bayramı, when millions of families sacrifice rams to celebrate Abraham's near sacrifice of Isaac, is a four-day holiday, the biggest of the year. It starts on 18 April 1997, 8 April 1998, 28 March 1999 and 16 March 2000. Plan ahead – almost everything closes.

ACTIVITIES

Archaeology

If you like archaeology, you've come to the right place. Turkey abounds with ancient sites. You may have some of the remote ones all to yourself.

Water Sports

The Aegean and Mediterranean coasts are the places to go; the Black Sea is too chilly, and most lakes are too salty or undeveloped. The big resort hotels have windsurfing, snorkelling, scuba-diving and rowing gear for hire.

Yacht Cruising

Turkey has lots of opportunities for yacht cruising, from day trips to two-week luxury charters. Kuşadası, Bodrum and Marmaris are the main centres, with more resorts developing yachting businesses all the time. You can hire crewless bareboats or flotilla boats, or take a cabin on a boat hired by an agency. Ask anywhere near the docks for information.

Hiking

Hiking and mountain trekking are becoming popular in Turkey, particularly in the northeast. For detailed information, see Lonely Planet's *Trekking in Turkey*.

Turkish Baths

The pleasures of the Turkish bath are famous: soaking in the steamy heat, getting kneaded and pummelled by a masseur, then being scrubbed squeaky clean and lathered all over by a bath attendant, before emerging swaddled in puffy Turkish towels for a bracing glass of tea.

Traditionally, men and women bathe separately, but in popular tourist areas baths often accept men and women at the same time for higher than usual prices. For safety's sake, women should know at least some of the men in the bath with them, and females might want to avoid male masseurs (a Turkish woman would only accept a masseuse). Not all baths accept women.

WORK

You must have residence and work permits to be legally employed; your employer can help you with these. Some people work illegally (as waiters, English teachers or journalists) and cross the border to Greece every three months to keep their visas current. If you're thinking of doing this, remember that after a while the immigration officer checking your passport is going to question all those exit and entry stamps. Job opportunities for English-speakers are listed in the classifieds of the *Turkish Daily News*.

ACCOMMODATION

You'll find camping facilities here and there throughout Turkey. Some hotels and pensions let you camp in their grounds and use their toilets and washrooms for a small fee. Well-equipped European-style camp sites are available in a few resort areas.

Turkey has plenty of cheap hotels, although the very cheapest are probably too basic for many tastes and not always suitable for women travelling alone. The cheaper places (up to US$20 a night) are usually subject to rating by municipalities. Above this level, ratings are by the national Ministry of Tourism.

The very cheap hotels are just dormitories where you're crammed into a room with whoever else fronts up. To avoid this, negotiate a price where you (and yours) have the whole room. Women travellers will get less unwanted attention in hotels by asking for *aile* (family/women's) accommodation.

There are a few very basic student hostels in the cities, available only in summer when they're not being used by Turkish students, and a couple of accredited Hostelling International (HI) youth hostels.

In tourist areas look for small *ev pansiyonu* (home pensions), which sometimes offer kitchen facilities too.

One and two-star hotels offer reasonable comfort and private bathrooms at excellent prices; three-star places can be quite luxurious.

TURKEY

FOOD

Turkish food, which is similar to Greek but more refined, has often with good reason been called the French cuisine of the East. Pop into the kitchen and see what's cooking. *Şiş kebap* (shish kebab), lamb grilled on a skewer, is a Turkish invention. You'll find the *kebapçı*, a cheap eatery specialising in roast lamb, everywhere. Try the ubiquitous *döner kebap* – lamb packed onto a vertical revolving spit and sliced off when done.

The best cheap and tasty meal is *pide*, Turkish pizza. Fish, though excellent, is often expensive – be sure to ask the price before you order. A proper meal consists of a long procession of dishes. First come the *meze* (hors d'oeuvres), such as:

beyaz peynir	– white sheep's-milk cheese
börek	– flaky pastry stuffed with white cheese and parsley
cacık	– yoghurt, cucumber and garlic
(kuru) fasulye	– (dried) beans
kabak dolması	– stuffed zucchini
patlıcan salatası	– puréed aubergine salad
patlıcan tava	– fried aubergine
pilaki	– beans vinaigrette
taramasalata	– fish-roe dip
yaprak dolması	– stuffed vine leaves

Dolma are vegetables (aubergine, zucchini, peppers, cabbage or vine leaves) stuffed with rice, currants and pine nuts, and served cold, or hot with lamb. The aubergine (eggplant) is the number one vegetable to the Turks. It can be stuffed as a dolma (*patlıcan dolması*), served puréed with lamb (*hünkar beğendi*), stuffed with minced meat (*karnıyarık*) or appear with exotic names like *imam bayıldı* – 'the priest fainted' – which means stuffed with ground lamb, tomatoes, onions and garlic. Well might he!

For dessert, try *fırın sütlaç* (baked rice pudding), *kazandibi* (caramelised pudding), *aşure* (fruit and nut pudding), baklava (flaky pastry stuffed with walnuts or pistachios, soaked in honey), or *tel kadayıf* or *burma kadayıf* (shredded wheat with nuts in honey).

Finally, Turkish fruit is terrific, particularly the melons.

DRINKS

Good bottled water is sold everywhere. Beers, such as Tuborg or Efes Pilsen, the sturdy Turkish pilsener, supplement the familiar soft drinks. There's also good Turkish wine – red or white – and fierce aniseed *rakı*, which is like Greek ouzo (the Turks usually cut it by half with water). Turkish coffee (*kahve*) is legendary. Turkish tea (*çay*), grown on the eastern Black Sea coast, is served in tiny glasses, sweet and without milk. A milder alternative is apple tea (*elma çay*).

ENTERTAINMENT

İstanbul, Ankara and İzmir have opera, symphony, ballet and theatre. Many smaller towns have folk-dance troupes. Every Turkish town has at least one cinema and one nightclub with live entertainment. In summer the seaside resorts throb to the sounds of innumerable clubs and discos.

THINGS TO BUY

Clothes, jewellery, handicrafts, leather apparel, carpets, brass and copperware and carved meerschaum are all good buys. Bargaining usually pays off.

Getting There & Away

There are plenty of ways to get in and out of Turkey – by air, sea, rail and bus, across the borders of seven countries.

AIR

International airports are at İstanbul, Ankara, İzmir, Dalaman, Antalya and Adana. Turkish Airlines has direct flights from İstanbul to two dozen European cities and New York, as well as the Middle East, North Africa, Bangkok, Karachi, Singapore and Tokyo.

Major European airlines such as Aeroflot, Air France, Alitalia, Austrian Airlines, British Airways, Finnair, KLM, Lufthansa, SAS and Swissair fly to İstanbul; British Airways, Lufthansa and the independent airline İstanbul Airlines have flights to Ankara, Antalya, İzmir and Dalaman as well. One-way full-fare tickets from London to İstanbul can cost as much as US$450, so it's usually advisable to buy an excursion ticket (US$250 to US$425) even if you don't plan to use the return portion.

The European airlines also fly one-stop services from many North American cities to İstanbul; Lufthansa flies to the most cities and has the best connections. Turkish Airlines flies the only nonstops from New York (Newark) to İstanbul. Delta flies as well. Return fares range from US$500 to US$1200.

There are no direct flights from Australia or New Zealand to Turkey, but you can fly Qantas or British Airways to London, or Olympic to Athens, and get a connecting flight from these cities. You can also fly Qantas or Singapore Airlines from most Australian cities, or Kuala Lumpur, to Singapore to connect with Turkish Airlines' thrice-weekly flights to İstanbul. Excursion fares start from around US$2200, which is almost as much as you would pay for a more versatile round-the-world (RTW) ticket.

LAND
Europe
The daily İstanbul Express train links Munich, Slovenia, Croatia, Yugoslavia and Bulgaria to İstanbul's Sirkeci train station. Travellers have reported passengers being knocked out with sleeping gas in their compartments and their gear stolen.

Several Turkish bus lines, including Ulusoy, Varan and Bosfor, offer a reliable, comfortable service between İstanbul and major European cities such as Frankfurt, Munich and Vienna. One-way tickets range from US$110 to US$175.

Greece There are daily train (Athens Express) and bus connections between Athens and İstanbul via Thessaloniki. The bus (US$45 to US$75) is much faster than the train.

SEA
Turkish Maritime Lines (TML) runs car ferries from Antalya, Marmaris and İzmir to Venice weekly from May to mid-October. The charge is US$236 to US$286 one way with reclining seat; mid-price cabins cost US$386 to US$493 per person. Greek and Italian lines also visit İzmir and İstanbul. There is a daily service to Turkish Cyprus from Taşucu (near Silifke).

Private ferries run between Turkey's Aegean coast and the Greek islands, which are in turn linked by air or boat to Athens. Services are frequent (usually daily) in summer, several times weekly in spring and autumn, and infre-

quent (perhaps once a week) in winter. The most reliable winter services are Chios-Çeşme, Rhodes-Marmaris and Samos-Kuşadası; warm-season services are Lesvos-Ayvalık, Lesvos-Dikili, Kos-Bodrum and Kastellorizo-Kaş.

LEAVING TURKEY
Don't carry any antiquities in your luggage. If you're caught smuggling them out, you'll probably go to jail. The departure tax is about US$12.

Getting Around

AIR
Turkish Airlines (Türk Hava Yolları, THY) links all the country's major cities, including the busy İstanbul-Ankara corridor (50 minutes, US$90), and flies to the Middle East, Europe, USA and the Far East. Domestic flights tend to fill up, so book in advance. İstanbul Airlines competes with Turkish Airlines on a few routes. Its fares are often lower, but its flights are less frequent. Smoking is prohibited on domestic flights.

BUS
Buses go everywhere in Turkey frequently and cheaply (around US$2.25 to US$2.75 per 100 km) and usually comfortably. Kamil Koç, Metro, Ulusoy and Varan are premium lines, and have better safety records than most. Traffic accidents take a huge number of lives on Turkish roads each year.

The bus station (otogar) is often on the outskirts of a city, but the bigger bus companies often have free şehiriçi servis (shuttle mini-buses) between the city-centre ticket office and the otogar. Many of the larger otogars have left-luggage rooms called emanet; there is a small charge. Don't leave valuables in unlocked luggage. If there's no emanet, leave luggage at your bus line's ticket office.

Everyone in Turkey – bus drivers included – seems to chain-smoke. Aside from getting a seat near a window vent, there doesn't seem to be a polite solution. Ask about sigarasız (no-smoking) buses when you buy a ticket.

TURKEY

TRAIN

Turkish State Railways (Türkiye Cumhuriyeti Devlet Demiryolları, TCDD or DDY) trains have a hard time competing with the best long-distance buses for speed and comfort. Only on the special express trains such as the *Fatih* and *Başkent* can you get somewhere faster than by bus.

Ekspres and *mototren* services sometimes have one class only. If they have 2nd class it costs 30% less. Student and return fares are discounted too. These trains are a little slower than buses, are comparable in price, and are often more pleasant (there are no-smoking cars, for one thing). On *yolcu* and *posta* trains you could grow old and die before you get to your destination. Trains east of Ankara are not as punctual or comfortable as those to the west.

Sleeping-car trains linking İstanbul, İzmir and Ankara are good value; the cheaper *örtülü kuşetli* carriages have four simple beds per compartment.

Major stations have emanet (left-luggage rooms).

CAR & MOTORCYCLE

An International Driving Permit may be handy if your licence is from a country likely to seem obscure to a Turkish police officer.

Türkiye Turing ve Otomobile Kurumu (TTOK), the Turkish Touring & Automobile Association (☎ 212-282 8140; fax 212-282 8042), Oto Sanayi Sitesi Yanı, Seyrantepe, 4 Levent, İstanbul, can help with questions and problems.

Carnets are not required if you're staying for less than three months, but details of your car are stamped in your passport to ensure it leaves the country with you.

Mechanical service is easy to find, reasonably competent and cheap. The most easily serviced cars are Fiat, Renault and Mercedes.

If you plan to spend time in a major city, park your car and use public transport: traffic is terrible and parking impossible. Your hotel will advise you on parking. Covered car parks are called *katotopark*.

BICYCLE

The countryside is varied and beautiful, and the road surfaces are acceptable (if a bit rough). Turkish drivers regard cyclists as a bit of a nuisance.

HITCHING

Because of the extensive, cheap bus system, hitching is not popular in Turkey. If you ask for a ride, the driver will expect you to offer the bus fare for the privilege. They may politely refuse to accept it, but if you don't offer, you will be considered a freeloader.

Women should not hitchhike alone; if you must hitch, do it with another woman or (preferably) a man, and don't accept a ride in a vehicle which has only men in it.

BOAT

Every Monday from June to early October, a comfortable Turkish Maritime Lines car ferry departs from İstanbul for Trabzon, calling at ports along the way. It leaves Trabzon on Wednesday for İstanbul, arriving on Friday. Fares from İstanbul to Trabzon (per person, no meals) range from US$15 for a reclining seat to US$50 for a bed in the best cabin. The fare for a car is US$20.

A similar car-ferry service departs from İstanbul on Friday (all year round) and arrives the next morning in İzmir. It departs in the afternoon for the return trip to İstanbul. Fares are US$16 (reclining seat) to US$50 (luxury cabin bed), and US$45 for a car.

A twice-daily ship/train service called the Marmara Ekspresi links İstanbul and İzmir via Bandırma, costing US$10 one way; no ships on Friday or Saturday though.

LOCAL TRANSPORT

The big towns all have local bus services, and also private *dolmuş* (shared taxi or minibus) services. İstanbul has a growing metro system of trains and trams. Ankara's metro is under construction.

In the big cities, taxis have digital meters and are required by law to run them. The greatest risk of taxi rip-offs (drivers refusing to run the meter, taking the long way etc) is in İstanbul. Service is usually fairly honest and efficient in the other big cities. In smaller places, where taxis have no meters, fares are set by the town, but you'll be at a loss to know what they are. Agree on a fare before you get in the car.

ORGANISED TOURS

Most independent travellers find tours in Turkey expensive. Almost all tours park you in a carpet shop for an hour (the guide gets a kickback). In general, it's faster and cheaper to make your own travel arrangements.

İstanbul

İstanbul, formerly Constantinople, is a treasure trove of places and things to see. After a day of wandering around tangled streets, mosques and ruins where empires have risen and fallen, you'll realise what is meant by the word 'Byzantine'. Nor should it be forgotten that it was here, five and a half centuries ago, that the final fragment of the Roman Empire crumbled, and that through Europe's Dark Ages this city carried European civilisation on from its Greek and Roman origins.

History
In the late 2nd century, Rome conquered the small city-state of Byzantium, and in 330 AD Emperor Constantine moved the capital of his empire there from Rome and renamed the city Constantinople.

The city walls kept out barbarians for centuries as the western part of the Roman Empire collapsed before Goths, Vandals and Huns. When Constantinople fell for the first time it was to the misguided Fourth Crusade in 1204. Bent on pillage, the crusaders abandoned their dreams of Jerusalem and ravaged Constantinople's churches, shipping out the art and melting down the silver and gold. When the Byzantines regained the city in 1261 it was only a shadow of its former glory.

The Ottoman Turks laid siege in 1314, but withdrew. Finally, in 1453, after a long and bitter siege, the walls were breached at Topkapı Gate on the west side of the city. Mehmet the Conqueror marched to Hagia Sofia (Aya Sofya) and converted the church to a mosque. The Byzantine Empire had ended.

As capital of the Ottoman Empire, the city entered a new golden age. During the glittering reign of Süleyman the Magnificent (1520-66), the city was graced with many new buildings of great beauty. Even during the empire's long and celebrated decline, the capital retained many of its charms. Occupied by Allied forces after WWI, it came to be thought of as the decadent capital of the sultans, just as Atatürk's armies were shaping a new republican state.

The Turkish Republic was proclaimed in 1923, with Ankara as its capital. But İstanbul, the much beloved metropolis, is still the centre of business, finance, journalism and the arts.

Orientation
The Bosphorus strait between the Black and Marmara seas divides Europe from Asia. On its western shore, European İstanbul is further divided by the Haliç (Golden Horn) into Old İstanbul in the south and the 'newer' quarter of Beyoğlu in the north.

İstanbul's bus terminal (otogar) is at Esenler, about 10 km west of the city on the metro tram line (Hızlı tramvay). Aksaray, halfway between the city walls and Sultanahmet, is a major traffic intersection and heart of a chaotic shopping district. East of Aksaray, the boulevard called Divan Yolu runs past İstanbul University, the Kapalı Çarşı (Grand Bazar) and other historic sites to Sultanahmet. Sultanahmet is the heart of Old İstanbul, with the ancient Hippodrome, the Sultan Ahmet Camii (Blue Mosque), Aya Sofya, Topkapı Palace and many cheap hotels and restaurants.

North of Sultanahmet, on the Golden Horn, is Sirkeci train station, the terminus for the European railway line. Ferries to Asian İstanbul and the Bosphorus run from Eminönü, just north-west of Sirkeci.

Beyoğlu, on the north side of the Golden Horn, is considered the 'new' or 'European' city, although there's been a city here since Byzantine times. Karaköy, formerly Galata, is where cruise ships dock at the yolcu salonu (maritime terminal). Ferries depart from Karaköy for Kadıköy and Haydarpaşa on the Asian shore, and hydrofoils head for more-distant Asian points.

A short underground railway (Tünel) runs up the hill from Karaköy to the southern end of Beyoğlu's main street, İstiklal Caddesi, now a pedestrian way. At its northern end is Taksim Meydanı (Taksim Square), heart of 'modern' İstanbul with its luxury hotels and airline offices.

On the Asian side, Haydarpaşa train station (served by ferry from Karaköy) is the terminus for Anatolian trains, and there's a major bus terminal at Harem, a 10-minute taxi ride north.

TURKEY

İstanbul

0   250   500 m

Minor Streets not Depicted

1	Kariye Müzesi (Chora Church)
2	Fatih Camii
3	Aqueduct of Valens
4	Süleymaniye Camii
5	Beyazıt Camii
6	Kapalı Çarşı (Covered Market/Grand Bazar)
7	Çemberlitaş Hamamı (Turkish Bath)
8	Topkapı Palace
9	Yeni Cami
10	Merkez Postane (Post Office)
11	Mısır Çarşısı (Egyptia Bazar)
12	Rüstem Paşa Camii
13	Galata Tower
14	US Consulate
15	Pera Palas Oteli
16	UK Consulate
17	French Consulate
18	Marmara Hotel
19	Turkish Airlines (THY) Office
20	German Consulate

Information

Ask at Sirkeci train station about trains. Budget travel agencies on Divan Yolu in Sultanahmet can get you bus, train and plane tickets. Bus companies have ticket offices near Aksaray and near Taksim Square on Mete Caddesi and İnönü Caddesi.

Tourist Offices The Ministry of Tourism has offices in the international arrivals hall at Atatürk airport (☎ 663 6363); in the yolcu salonu (maritime terminal; ☎ 249 5776) at Karaköy; in Sirkeci train station (☎ 511 5888); at the north-east end of the Hippodrome in Sultanahmet (☎ 518 1802); near the UK Consulate in Beyoğlu at Meşrutiyet Caddesi 57, Tepebaşı (☎ 243 2928); in Taksim Square (☎ 245 6876) on İstiklal Caddesi; and in the İstanbul Hilton arcade on Cumhuriyet Caddesi (☎ 233 0592), four long blocks north of Taksim Square.

Money Divan Yolu is lined with currency-exchange offices and travel agencies offering speedy, hassle-free exchange facilities at fairly high rates. Most are open from 9 am to 9 pm. Other good areas to look are Sirkeci, Taksim and along İstiklal Caddesi.

Post & Communications The main post office (*merkez postane*) is just south-west of Sirkeci station. Go here for poste-restante mail.

There are branch post offices in Aksaray and the Grand Bazar, and in Beyoğlu at Galatasaray and Taksim, as well as in the domestic and international departure areas at Atatürk airport.

İstanbul has two telephone codes: ☎ 212 for the European side and ☎ 216 for the Asian. Assume that phone numbers given here are ☎ 212 unless stated otherwise.

Travel Agencies Divan Yolu in Sultanahmet is lined with travel agencies, all of them selling cheap air and bus tickets; shop around for the best deals. Most also offer speedy foreign-exchange facilities and can arrange minibus transport to the airport. Ms Filiz Bingöl at the Overseas Travel Agency (☎ 513 4175; fax 513 41 77), Alemdar Caddesi 16, Sultanahmet, is a helpful Turkish-Australian woman. Backpackers Travel Agency (☎ 638 6343; fax 638 1483), Yeni Akbıyık Caddesi 22, is right among the hotels and pensions of Cankurtaran.

Bookshops Aypa (☎ 516 0100), Mimar Mehmet Ağa Caddesi 19, Sultanahmet, just down the hill from Aya Sofya and the Blue Mosque, has guides, maps and magazines in English, French and German.

The best stores are on İstiklal Caddesi near Tünel, including Robinson Crusoe (☎ 293 6968), İstiklal Caddesi 389; Dünya Aktüel (☎ 249 1006), İstiklal Caddesi 469; ABC Kitabevi (☎ 279 6610), İstiklal Caddesi 461; and Metro Kitabevi (☎ 249 5827), İstiklal Caddesi 513.

Laundry In the Sultanahmet area try the Hobby Laundry (☎ 513 6150), Caferiye Sokak 6/1, near the Yücelt Interyouth Hostel; Active Laundry, Dr Emin Paşa Sokak 14, off Divan Yolu beneath the Arsenal Youth Hostel; Sultan Laundry, İncili Çavuş Çıkmazı 21, opposite the Hotel Nomade.

Emergency Try the tourist police (☎ 527 4503), Yerebatan Caddesi 6, Sultanahmet, across the street from Yerebatan Saray (Sunken Palace Cistern). The ordinary police (☎ 155 in an emergency) are less experienced in dealing with foreigners.

As for hospitals, the Amerikan Bristol (☎ 231 4050), at Güzelbahçe Sokak, Nişantaşı

TURKEY

(two km north-west of Taksim Square), and the International (☎ 663 3000), Çınar Oteli Yanı, İstanbul Caddesi 82, in Yeşilköy near the airport, do good work.

Things to See & Do

Sultanahmet is the first place to go, with all the major sights arranged around the Hippodrome. There is a sound-and-light show on summer evenings – different nights, different languages. Ask at the Hippodrome tourist office.

Aya Sofya The Church of the Holy Wisdom (Hagia Sofia in Greek, Aya Sofya in Turkish) was begun under Emperor Justinian in 532 AD and was intended to be the grandest church in the world. For a thousand years it was the largest in Christendom. The interior reveals the building's magnificence; stunning even today, it must have been overwhelming centuries ago when it was covered in gilded mosaics.

Climb up to the gallery for a different view, and to see the splendid surviving mosaics. After the Turkish conquest the mosaics were covered over, as Islam prohibits images of beings. They were not revealed until the 1930s, when Atatürk declared Aya Sofya a museum. The minarets were added during the centuries when Aya Sofya was a mosque. The church is open from 9.30 am to 4.30 pm daily, till 7 pm in summer (closed on Monday); note that the gallery closes from 11.30 am to 1 pm. Admission is US$6.

Blue Mosque (Sultan Ahmet Camii) The Mosque of Sultan Ahmet I, just south-west of Aya Sofya, was built between 1609 and 1619. It's light and delicate compared with its squat, massive, ancient neighbour. The exterior is notable for its six slender minarets and cascade of domes and half-domes, but it's inside where you will find the blue, a luminous overall impression created by the tiled walls and painted dome. You're expected to make a small donation when visiting the mosque – and leave your shoes outside.

On the north side of the Blue Mosque, up the ramp, is a **carpet and textile museum** (open from 9.30 am to 4.30 pm, closed Sunday and Monday; entry US$1).

Rents from the **Arasta** (row of shops) on the street behind the Blue Mosque to the east provide support for the mosque's upkeep. In the Arasta is the entrance to the newly restored **mosaic museum**, with portions of ancient Byzantine pavements showing marvellous scenes from nature. The museum is open from 9.30 am to 4.30 pm (closed Monday) for US$1.

The Hippodrome (Atmeydanı) In front of the Blue Mosque is the Hippodrome, where chariot races and the Byzantine riots took place. Construction started in 203 AD and it was later enlarged by Constantine. Today, three ancient monuments remain. The **Obelisk of Theodosius** is an Egyptian column from the temple of Karnak, resting on a Byzantine base, with perfectly clear, 3500-year-old hieroglyphs.

The 10-metre-high **Obelisk of Constantine Porphyrogenitus** was once covered in bronze (the crusaders stole the bronze plates). The base rests at the former level of the Hippodrome, now several metres below the ground. Between these two monuments are the remains of a column of intertwined snakes. Erected at Delphi by the Greeks to celebrate their victory over the Persians, it was later transported to the Hippodrome and the snakes' heads disappeared. At the north-eastern end of the Hippodrome is a ceremonial fountain built to commemorate Kaiser Wilhelm's visit in 1901.

Turkish & Islamic Arts Museum On the west side of the Hippodrome, the Türk ve İslam Eserleri Müzesi (Turkish & Islamic Arts Museum) is housed in the former palace (built in 1524) of İbrahim Pasha, grand vizier and son-in-law of Süleyman the Magnificent. The exhibits run the gamut of Islamic history, from beautifully illuminated Qur'ans through to carpets and mosque furniture, crafts and Turkish miniature paintings. The museum is open daily from 10 am to 5 pm (closed on Monday); admission costs US$1.

Yerebatan Saray Across Divan Yolu from the north-eastern end of the Hippodrome is a small park; on the north side of the park is the entrance to Yerebatan Saray, the Sunken Palace Cistern. Built by Constantine and later enlarged by Justinian, this vast, columned cistern held water not only for summer use but also for times of siege. It's open daily from 9 am to 5.30 pm; admission costs US$1.

Topkapı Palace Just north-east of Aya Sofya is the fortified, sprawling Topkapı Sarayı, the palace of the sultans from 1462 until they moved to Dolmabahçe Palace, across the Golden Horn, last century. Topkapı is not just a palace but a collection of gardens, houses and libraries, and a 400-room harem. In the vast outer courtyard, where the crack troops known as janissaries once gathered, is the **Aya İrini** or Church of Divine Peace, dating from around 540 AD. Entrance is through the Ortakapı (middle gate).

Within the park-like Second Court are exhibits of priceless porcelain (in the former palace kitchens), silverware and crystal, arms and calligraphy. Right beside the Kubbealtı, or Imperial Council Chamber, is the entrance to the **harem**, a succession of sumptuously decorated rooms which served as the sultan's family quarters.

In the Third Court are the sultan's ceremonial robes and the fabulous **treasury**, which contains an incredible wealth of gold and gems. The **Shrine of the Holy Relics** holds a solid-gold casket containing the Prophet Mohammed's cloak and other Islamic relics. The beautiful little tiled kiosks have fine views of the city.

Topkapı is open daily from 9.30 am to 5 pm but is closed on Tuesday; admission costs US$6, with an extra US$2.50 payable to visit the harem, which is open from 10 am to noon and 1 to 4 pm.

Archaeological Museums Down the hill from the outer courtyard, to the west of Topkapı Palace, are the Arkeoloji Müzeleri, a complex of three museums. The **Archaeological Museum** has an outstanding collection of Greek and Roman statuary, and what is said to be Alexander the Great's sarcophagus (stone coffin). The **Museum of the Ancient Orient** (Eski Şark Eserleri Müzesi) is dedicated to the pre-Islamic and pre-Byzantine civilisations.

The **Çinili Köşk** (Tiled Pavilion), built by order of Sultan Mehmet the Conqueror in 1472, is among the oldest Turkish buildings in the city. It is now a museum of Turkish tile work.

The museums are open from 9.30 am to 5 pm (they're all closed on Monday; the Museum of the Ancient Orient only opens on Wednesday, Friday and Sunday, and the Tiled Pavilion opens on Tuesday, Thursday and Saturday); admission to all three costs US$3. Down the slope and west from the museums is **Gülhane Park**, the former palace park, now with a small zoo, restaurants and amusements. It's open from 7 am to 6 pm daily; entry is 30 cents.

Divan Yolu Walk westward up Divan Yolu from Sultanahmet. Near the top of the slope, on the right, is a complex of **tombs** of several 19th-century sultans, including Mahmut II (1808-39), Abdülaziz (1861-76) and Abdül-hamid II (1876-1909).

A bit further along, on the right, is the **Çemberlitaş** (Banded Stone), a monumental column erected by Constantine the Great some time during the 4th century. Within a century it had to be strengthened with iron bands. During a storm in 1105 Constantine's statue toppled off the top, killing several people sheltering below. In 1779 the column was badly damaged by a fire, and it was further strengthened with the iron hoops you see today.

Grand Bazaar (Kapalı Çarşı) This covered market is a labyrinthine medieval shopping mall. Most of the old stalls have been converted into modern, glassed-in stalls. Still, it's fun to wander among the 65 streets and 4400 shops, and a great place to get lost – which you certainly will.

The bazaar is divided into areas – carpets, jewellery, clothing, silverware and so on. West of the bazaar proper, across Çadırcılar Caddesi, beside the Beyazıt Camii mosque, is the **old book market** *(sahaflar çarşısı)* with many stalls selling second-hand books, most of them in Turkish. The bazaar is open Monday to Saturday from 8 am to 7 pm.

Beyazıt & Süleymaniye Beyazıt takes its name from the graceful mosque **Beyazıt Camii**, built in 1506 on the orders of Sultan Beyazıt II, son of Mehmet the Conqueror. In Byzantine times this plaza was the **Forum of Theodosius**, laid out in 393 AD. The great portal on the north side of the square is that of

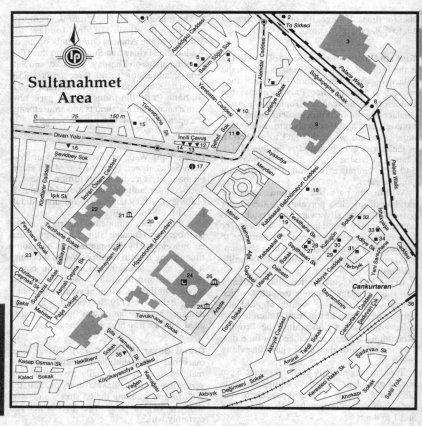

Sultanahmet Area

0   75   150 m

İstanbul University. The portal, enclosure and buildings behind it date mostly from Ottoman times, when this was the Ministry of War.

Behind the university to the north-west rises İstanbul's grandest mosque complex, the **Süleymaniye**. Construction was completed in 1557 on orders of Süleyman the Magnificent; he and his foreign-born wife Roxelana (Hürrem Sultan) are buried in a **mausoleum** behind the mosque to the south-east. Süleyman's great architect, Sinan, is entombed near the sultan. The buildings surrounding the mosque were originally a hospital, seminaries, soup kitchen, baths and hospice.

Theodosian Walls Stretching for seven km from the Golden Horn to the Sea of Marmara, the walls date back to about 420 AD, but many parts have been restored during the past decade.

At **Yedikule**, close to the Sea of Marmara, you can visit a Byzantine-Turkish fortress where obstreperous diplomats and 'inconvenient' princes were held in squalor and despair. The fortress is open daily from 9.30 am to 5 pm (closed on Monday); admission costs 75 cents. Get there on a *banliyö* (suburban) train from Sirkeci to Yedikule, or on İETT bus No 80 from Eminönü.

Near the **Edirnekapı** (Adrianople Gate) is the marvellous **Kariye Müzesi** (Chora Church), a Byzantine building with the best 14th-century mosaics east of Ravenna. Built in the 11th century, it was later restored, then converted to a mosque, and is now a museum. It's open daily from 9.30 am to 4.30 pm (closed on Tuesday), and admission costs US$3. To get there, take an Edirnekapı bus along Fevzipaşa Caddesi.

Turkish Baths İstanbul's most interesting historical baths are now very touristy. However attractive, the Cağaloğlu Hamamı, Yerebatan Caddesi 34, has priced itself out of most pockets. Instead, you could try **Çemberlitaş Hamamı**, off Divan Yolu at the Sultanahmet end, which was designed by the great Ottoman architect Sinan in 1584.

Both the men's and women's sections are open from 6 am to 12 pm daily. Prices here would be outrageous anywhere else in Turkey:

about US$10 for an assisted bath with massage, supposedly inclusive of tips.

Eminönü At Galata Bridge's southern end looms the large **Yeni Cami** (New Mosque), built between 1597 and 1663. Beside it is the **Mısır Çarşısı** (Egyptian Bazaar), full of spice and food vendors. To the west, in the fragrant market streets, is the **Rüstem Paşa Camii**, a small, richly tiled mosque also designed by Sinan.

Beyoğlu Cross the new Galata Bridge, completed only in 1992, and head uphill towards the **Galata Tower**. In its present form this tower dates from 1216, when Galata was a Genoese trading colony. Later it served as a prison, an observatory, then a fire lookout before it caught fire itself in 1835. In 1967 it was completely restored as a supper club. The observation deck, perfect for views and photos, is open daily from 9 am to 6 pm in winter and 7 pm in summer; admission costs US$1. Inside, a small sign announces that during the 17th century an intrepid local flier made the first intercontinental flight clear across to Asian İstanbul from the top of the Galata Tower.

At the top of the hill is **İstiklal Caddesi**, once called the Grand Rue de Péra, now a pedestrian way served by a restored tram. The famed Pera Palas Oteli (rooms for US$180 a double) is off to the west; huge consulates line the avenue. In Galatasaray are the colourful **Balık Pazar** (Fish Market) and **Çiçek Pasajı** (Flower Passage), and an assortment of fish restaurants. **Taksim Meydanı** (Taksim Square), with its huge hotels, park and Atatürk Cultural Centre, is the hub of modern İstanbul.

The Bosphorus North from İstanbul, towards the Black Sea, are some beautiful old Ottoman buildings, including the imposing **Dolmabahçe Palace** and several big mosques; **Rumeli Hisar**, the huge castle built by Mehmet the Conqueror on the European side to complete his stranglehold on Constantinople; and many small and surprisingly peaceful villages that are now the city's dormitory suburbs. Towns on the Asian side in particular have charm, open space and good food. A ferry ride up the Bosphorus is *de rigueur* for all visitors to İstanbul.

The Princes' Isles Once the site of monasteries and a haven for pirates, this string of nine spotless little islands is a popular weekend and summer getaway for İstanbul's middle class. With good beaches, lots of open woodland and transport by horse-drawn wagons, they make a pleasant escape from İstanbul's noise and hustle. Ferries (US$3.50) and hydrofoils *(deniz otobüsü,* US$5) depart the dock at Kabataş, just south of Dolmabahçe.

Organised Tours

The standard 1¾-hour tourist cruise from Eminönü (Boğaz dock No 3) to Sarıyer on a normal ferry costs US$4 one way (half-price on Sunday). Alternatively, you can take the shorter 'poor-person's sunset cruise' across the Bosphorus and back by boarding any boat for Üsküdar. A long-established, reputable travel agency and tour operator that has English-speaking staff is Orion-Tour (☎ 248 8437; fax 241 2808), Halaskargazi Caddesi 284/3, Marmara Apartımanı, Şişli, about two km north of Taksim. Orion (pronounced 'OR-yohn') sells tickets to just about anywhere and has tours all over Turkey.

Special Events

Celebration of the capture of Constantinople from the Byzantines (1453) are held on the anniversary, 29 May, near Edirnekapı in the city walls. The İstanbul International Music Festival is held each year from early June to early July, with top-name artists from around the world.

Places to Stay

Camping In this big city, camping is not particularly convenient and costs about as much as staying in a cheap hotel (US$8 to US$10 for a tent site). *Londra Camping* (☎ 560 4200) is a truck stop with a large camping area behind it; you'll find it on the south side of the Londra Asfaltı between Topkapı otogar and the airport (coming east from the airport, follow the *servis yolu* signs). *Ataköy Tatil Köyü* (☎ 559 6000), on the shore south-east of the airport, and *Florya Turistik Tesisleri* (☎ 663 1000) are holiday beach-hotel-bungalow complexes with camping facilities. To get to the Ataköy,

take bus No 81 from Eminönü; to get to the Florya, take the banliyö (suburban) train from Sirkeci train station.

Hostels & Hotels South-east of Sultanahmet is Cankurtaran, an area of quiet streets and good, cheap and moderate hotels. For four and five-star hotels, go to Taksim.

Sultanahmet The *Yücelt Interyouth Hostel* (☎ 513 6150), Caferiye Sokak 6/1, has dorm beds for US$6, beds in three or four-bed rooms for US$8 and doubles with toilet for US$18.

Arsenal Youth Hostel (☎ 513 6407), Dr Emin Paşa Sokak 12, off Divan Yolu by the Tarihi Park Hamamı, has dorm rooms with four beds each at US$6 per bed, and showers down the hall.

Yerebatan Caddesi runs west from Aya Sofya. A block past the Sunken Palace Cistern, turn right on Salkım Söğüt Sokak to find *Hotel Ema*, *Hotel Elit* (☎ 512 7566) and *Hotel Anadolu* (☎ 512 1035). The Anadolu and the Elit are the cheapest and quietest at US$12 and US$15 per person for rooms with sink; hot showers are free.

Cankurtaran Find the house-like Yeşil Ev hotel on the south-east side of the fountain park between Aya Sofya and the Blue Mosque, and walk down Tevkifhane Sokak on the hotel's left side. Downhill on the corner of Utangaç Sokak is the friendly *Hotel Park* (☎ 517 6596), Utangaç Sokak 26. Basic double rooms cost US$22, those with shower cost US$30, with breakfast included. The neighbouring *Hotel Side Pansiyon* (☎ 517 6590) costs a bit more. Slightly further downhill, at Kutlugün Sokak 27, is the friendly *Guesthouse Berk* (☎ 516 9671), where clean rooms with bath cost US$35/45 a single/double; it's a good place for single women.

Yusuf Guesthouse (☎ 516 5878), at Kutlugün Sokak 3, is friendly and quiet. Doubles cost US$14, with free, hot showers down the hall. Beds in four-bed dorms cost US$5; those on the roof cost US$3. *Star Hostel* (☎ 638 2302), Akbıyık Caddesi 18, has doubles with shower for US$20, and a public laundry as well. Walk down Adliye Sokak for the *Alp Guesthouse* (☎ 517 9570) at No 4; it's family-run and charges US$35 a double with shower and breakfast.

Around the corner at Akbıyık Caddesi 13 is the cheerful, friendly *Orient Youth Hostel* (☎ 517 9493); doubles cost US$12 with sink, US$3.50 for a dorm bed, and the top-floor café has marvellous Marmara views.

The best splurge in this area is *Hotel Empress Zoe* (☎ 518 2504; fax 518 5699; e-mail emzoe@ibm.net), Akbıyık Caddesi, Adliye Sokak 10, in a Byzantine cistern next to an old Ottoman hammam. The rooms are small but nice, with marble baths, at US$45/60 a single/double. The rooftop bar-lounge-terrace affords fine views of the sea and the Blue Mosque. Run by American expatriate Ann Nevens, it's a fine option for single women.

Places to Eat

Nowadays, the *Pudding Shop*, officially known as the Lale Restaurant and once a legend amongst travellers, is just one of a string of medium-priced lokanta (restaurants) along Divan Yolu opposite the Hippodrome – typical meals cost US$4 to US$6. Try the *Can Restaurant*, or the *Vitamin Restaurant*, a brightly lit, hyperactive and shifty place (the food's good, but check your bill). The *Sultanahmet Köftecisi* serves delicious grilled meatballs called köfte with salad, bread and a drink for US$4 or less. *Dedem Börekçisi*, Divan Yolu 21, is a streetside booth selling flaky pastry (börek) filled with sheep's-milk cheese for US$2, drink included.

At the far (south-western) end of the Hippodrome, walk up Peykhane Sokak one short block to the *Yeni Birlik Lokantası* (☎ 517 6465), at No 46, a large, light restaurant serving ready-made food and favoured by lawyers from the nearby law courts. Meals cost US$2.50 to US$4; no alcohol. *Doy Doy*, Sıfa Hamamı Sokak 13, downhill off the south-western end of the Hippodrome, is small, popular, cheap and good for stews, grills and pide.

The neighbourhood called Kumkapı, following the shoreline 800 metres south of Beyazıt along Tiyatro Caddesi, boasts dozens of good seafood restaurants. In fair weather the whole place is one big party. You can eat meat for US$8 or US$10, but are more likely to spend from US$12 to US$20 on fish and rakı. For a cheaper fish lunch, buy a filling fish sandwich from one of the boats near the Galata Bridge for just US$1.

Getting There & Away

Air İstanbul is Turkey's airline hub. Most foreign airlines have their offices near Taksim, or north of it, along Cumhuriyet Caddesi. You can buy Turkish Airlines tickets in Taksim (Cumhuriyet Caddesi 10), or at any travel agency. Most domestic flights cost under US$100. Call the airline's office (☎ 663 6363) for reservations.

İstanbul Airlines (☎ 509 2121; fax 593 6035) flies to Adana, Ankara, Antalya, Dalaman, İzmir and Trabzon, as well as many European cities. Most domestic flights cost US$55 to US$70.

Bus İstanbul's international bus terminal (Uluslararası İstanbul Otogarı, ☎ 658 0505) has 168 ticket offices and buses to all parts of Turkey and beyond. Get to it via metro train from Aksaray; get out at Otogar.

Buses depart for Ankara (seven hours, US$15 to US$24) roughly every 15 minutes, day and night, and to most other cities at least every hour. Heading east to Anatolia, you might want to board at the smaller otogar at Harem, north of Haydarpaşa on the Asian shore.

Train Sirkeci is the station for trains to Edirne, Greece and Europe. Haydarpaşa, on the Asian shore, is the terminus for trains to Anatolia. Ask at Sirkeci station (☎ 527 0050) or Haydarpaşa station (☎ 216-336 0475) for rail information. From Sirkeci there are four express trains daily to Edirne (6½ hours, US$4), but the bus is faster (3 hours, US$5.75). The nightly *İstanbul Express* goes to Munich.

From the Sarayburnu dock, just north of Topkapı Palace, ships depart each morning and evening (except Friday and Saturday) for Bandırma, from where you continue to İzmir on the *Marmara Ekspresi* (10½ to 12 hours, US$10).

From Haydarpaşa there are seven express trains daily to Ankara (7½ to 11 hours, US$11 to US$30); one of them is all sleeping cars.

Boat For information on car ferries to İzmir and along the Black Sea coast to Trabzon, see

TURKEY

the introductory Getting Around section in this chapter. Buy tickets at the Turkish Maritime Lines (Denizyolları) office (☎ 249 9222 for reservations, ☎ 244 0207 for information), Rıhtım Caddesi, Karaköy, just east of the Karaköy ferry dock.

Ferries and hydrofoils depart from İstanbul's Kabataş dock, south-east of Taksim and south of Dolmabahçe, for the Princes' Isles and Yalova on the south shore of the Sea of Marmara, half a dozen times daily in summer. From Yalova, buses run to İznik (ancient Nicaea) and Bursa.

Getting Around

To/From the Airport Havaş airport buses depart from the international terminal about every 30 minutes, stopping at the domestic terminal, Bakırköy and Aksaray (get out here for Sultanahmet) before terminating in Taksim Square. The trip takes 30 to 45 minutes and costs US$2.75. The metro is cheaper but less convenient; Dünya Ticaret Merkezi stop is closest to the airport. City buses from the airport to Sultanahmet are infrequent and slow.

An airport taxi costs about US$10 to US$12 for the 23 km to Old İstanbul, and US$12 to US$15 to Beyoğlu; it costs 50% more at night. Many of the Divan Yolu travel agencies and Sultanahmet hostels book minibus transport from your hotel to the airport for about US$3.50.

Bus City buses are crowded but useful. Destinations and intermediate stops are indicated at the front and side of the bus. You must have a ticket (50 cents) before boarding; some long routes require that you stuff two tickets into the box. You can buy tickets from the white booths near major stops or from nearby shops. Stock up in advance.

Train To get to Sirkeci train station, take the tramway (tram) from Aksaray or Sultanahmet, or any bus signed for Eminönü. Haydarpaşa train station is connected by ferry to Karaköy (at least every 30 minutes; 50 cents). Banliyö (suburban) trains (40 cents) run every 20 minutes along the southern walls of Old İstanbul and westward along the Marmara shore.

Underground The Tünel (İstanbul's underground train) mounts the hill from Karaköy to Tünel Square and İstiklal Caddesi (every 10 or 15 minutes; 35 cents). An underground line running north from Taksim may be operational in 1997. The Hızlı tramvay (50 cents), runs west from Aksaray via Adnan Menderes Bulvarı through the city walls to the otogar.

Tram The tramvay between Sirkeci and Aksaray via Divan Yolu and Sultanahmet is useful, and costs just 30 cents; buy a ticket before boarding from the booths near the stops. A different tram, the Hızlı tramvay, runs underground within the city walls and above ground in the western suburbs (see Underground, below). A third, restored tram trundles along İstiklal Caddesi to Taksim (30 cents).

Taxi İstanbul has 60,000 yellow taxis, all with digital meters; some are driven by lunatics who will really take you for a ride. From Sultanahmet to Taksim costs US$2.50 to US$3.50; to the otogar costs around US$10.

Around İstanbul

EDİRNE

European Turkey is known as Thrace (Trakya). If you pass through, stop in Edirne, a pleasant, undervisited town with decent cheap hotels and several striking mosques. Best is the **Selimiye Camii**, the finest work of Süleyman the Magnificent's master architect Sinan. The impressive **Beyazıt II Camii** is well worth a walk across the river. Both the **Üçşerefeli Cami** and the **Eski Cami** are currently undergoing restoration.

The tourist office (☎ 225 1518), Hürriyet Meydanı 17, is in the town centre. Edirne's telephone code is ☎ 284. Around the corner from the tourist office are the budget-priced *Anıl* (☎ 212 1482) and *Konak* (☎ 225 1348) hotels and the pricier but better *Park Hotel* (☎ 213 5276) which charges US$13/20 a single/ double, and the newer and slightly more expensive *Efe Hotel* (☎ 213 6166) nearby. Buses run very frequently to İstanbul (three hours, US$5.75) and five times daily south to Çanakkale.

BURSA

Sprawled at the base of Uludağ, Turkey's biggest winter sports centre, Bursa was the Ottoman capital prior to İstanbul's conquest. It retains several fine mosques and pretty neighbourhoods from early Ottoman times, but Bursa's big attraction, now and historically, is its thermal springs. Besides healthy hot water, Bursa produces lots of succulent fruit and most of the cars made in Turkey. It's also famous for its savoury kebabs.

Orientation & Information

The city centre, with its banks and shops, is along Atatürk Caddesi between the Ulu Cami (Grand Mosque) to the west and the main square, Cumhuriyet Alanı, commonly called Heykel (*heykel* means 'statue'), to the east. The post office is on the south side of Atatürk Caddesi across from the Ulu Cami. Bursa's Şehir Garajı (otogar) and some cheap hotels are 1.5 km down the mountain slope from the city centre. Çekirge, with its hot springs, is about six km west of Heykel.

You can get maps and brochures at the tourist office (☎ 251 1834) in the Orhangazi Altgeçidi subway, Ulu Cami Parkı, opposite the Koza Han (silk market).

Bursa's telephone code is ☎ 224.

Things to See & Do

The largest of Bursa's beautiful mosques is the 20-domed **Ulu Cami** (Grand Mosque), built in 1399; it's on Atatürk Caddesi in the city centre. About one km east of Heykel in a pretty pedestrian zone are the early Ottoman **Yeşil Cami** (Green Mosque, built in 1424), its beautifully tiled **Yeşil Türbe** (Green Tomb, open from 8 am to noon and 1 to 5 pm; entry free) and the **Turkish & Islamic Arts Museum**, or Türk İslam Eserleri Müzesi (open 8.30 am to noon and 1 to 5 pm; closed Monday; entry US$1.25).

A few hundred metres further east is the **Emir Sultan Camii** (1805). To get there, take a dolmuş or bus No 18 (marked Emir Sultan) from Heykel.

Uphill and west of the Grand Mosque, on the way to Çekirge, are the beautifully situated **Tombs of Osman & Orhan**, which house the remains of the first Ottoman sultans. A km beyond is the **Muradiye Mosque Complex**, with its decorated tombs dating from the 14th and 15th centuries. Nearby is the **17 YY**

Osmanlı Evi Müzesi (17th-century Ottoman House Museum).

On a clear day it's worth going up Uludağ. From Heykel you can get bus No 3 or a dolmuş east to the *teleferik*, or cable car, (US$5 one way) up the mountain, or take a dolmuş (US$6) from Orhangazi Caddesi for the entire 22 km to the top. The **mineral baths** are in the suburb of Çekirge.

Places to Stay

Camping is along the Yalova Highway at the **Kervansaray Kumluk Mocamp**, six km north, or the **Nur Mocamp**, eight km north.

Bursa's cheapest hotels are pretty seedy. **Hotel Mavi Ege** (☎ 254 8420), Fırın Sokak 17, down a side street opposite the otogar, has singles/doubles with sink for US$6/9; showers cost extra. Nearby, at Celal Bayar Caddesi 168 the **Hotel Belkis** (☎ 254 8322) costs the same. **Öz Uludağ Hotel**, a few doors to the left (west) of the Belkis, is not as comfortable. The **Otel Geçit** (☎ 254 1032), Celal Bayar Caddesi 175, charges US$15 a double with shower.

In Tahtakale, south of the Ulu Cami, the **Otel Çamlıbel** (☎ 221 2565), İnebey Caddesi 71, is past its prime; singles/doubles with a shower cost US$13/17. Better value with singles/ doubles at US$18/22 are the excellent, quiet **Hotel Çeşmeli** (☎ 224 1511), Gümüşçeken Caddesi 6, just north of Heykel, and the **Hotel Bilgiç** (☎ 220 3190), Başak Caddesi 30, south of Heykel.

Staying in Çekirge, you pay more but get free mineral baths. The **Yeşil Yayla Oteli** (☎ 236 8026), behind the Yıldız Hotel at the upper end of the village, charges US$14 a double for rooms with sink, and free use of the mineral baths. The **Hotel Eren** (☎ 236 8099), Birinci Murat Arkası 2, has a pleasant terrace, but charges US$22 for a double with shower.

For real luxury, try the **Termal Hotel Gönlü Ferah** (☎ 233 9210), Murat Caddesi 24, with its panoramic views and marble baths, charging US$50/70 for a single/double, including breakfast.

Places to Eat

Bursa is renowned for İskender kebap (döner kebap topped with savoury tomato sauce and browned butter). Competition for patrons is fierce among kebapçıs. **Kebapçı İskender**, Ünlü Caddesi 7 just east of Heykel, dates back to 1867 and has a posh, atmospheric dining

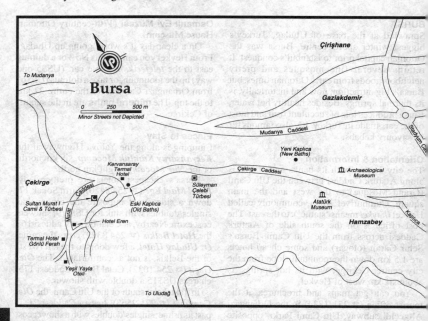

room but low prices – about US$6 with a soft drink. **Adanur Hacıbey**, opposite, charges the same but is less fancy.

Çiçek İzgara, Belediye Caddesi 15, just north of the half-timbered belediye (town hall) in the flower market, is bright and modern, good for women unaccompanied by men, and open every day from 11 am to 3.30 pm and from 5.30 to 9 pm.

For cheaper eats, head for the small eateries in the Tahtakale Çarşısı (the market across Atatürk Caddesi from the Ulu Cami). For a jolly evening of seafood and drinks, explore Sakarya Caddesi, off Altıparmak Caddesi.

Getting There & Away

The best way to İstanbul is by bus to Yalova (every half-hour, 70 minutes, US$3), then the fast (one hour) Yalova-İstanbul (Kabataş) *deniz otobüsü* (hydrofoil; five a day) for US$6.

Buses to İstanbul designated *feribot ile* use the Topçular-Eskihisar ferry, which is quicker (2½ hours) than the land route (*karayolu ile*) round the Marmara (four hours, US$9).

Getting Around

Dolmuş and buses to places all over Bursa leave from behind the otogar. Buy BOI city bus tickets (30 cents) at kiosks and shops. Bursa dolmuş with little 'D' plates on top charge 45 cents or more for a seat. Those marked 'SSK Hastanesi' go to Çekirge, those marked 'Dev(let) Hast(anesi)' go to the Orhan & Osman tombs, those marked 'Yeşil' go to the Yeşil Cami (Green Mosque) area, and those marked 'S Garaj' go to the bus station.

The Aegean Coast

Olive groves and a unique history distinguish this gorgeous coast. Gallipoli, Troy and Pergamum are only a few of the famous places to be visited.

ÇANAKKALE

Çanakkale, a laid-back town, is a hub for transport to Troy and across the Dardanelles to

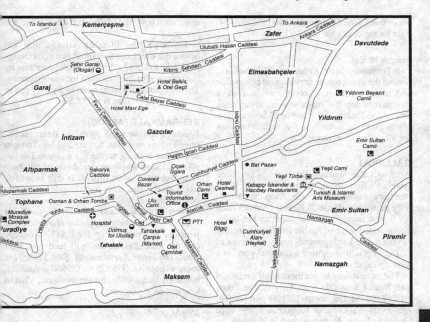

On the map:

To İstanbul — Kemerçeşme — To Ankara — Ankara Caddesi

Zafer — Davutdede

Uluabatlı Hasan Caddesi

Şehir Garajı (Otogar) — Kıbrıs Şehitleri Caddesi — Elmasbahçeler

Garaj — Hotel Belkis, & Otel Geçit — Celal Bayar Caddesi — Yıldırım Beyazıt Camii

Hotel Mavi Ege — Feyzi Çakmak Caddesi

İntizam — Gazcılar — Yıldırım

Emir Sultan Camii

Altıparmak — Sakarya Caddesi — Haşim İşcan Caddesi

Çiçek İzgara — Cumhuriyet Caddesi — Bat Pazarı — Yeşil Cami

Covered Bazar — Orhan Cami — Hotel Çeşmeli — Yeşil Türbe — Turkish & Islamic Arts Museum

Altıparmak Caddesi — Tourist Information Office — Kebapçı İskender & Hacıbey Restaurants

Tophane — Osman & Orhan Tombs — Ulu Cami — Atatürk Caddesi — Emir Sultan

Muradiye Mosque Complex — Hasta Yurdu Caddesi — Yiğitler Caddesi — Nadir Cad — PTT — Namazgah

Muradiye — Hospital — Cemal — Hotel Bilgiç — Namazgah Caddesi — Piremir

Dolmuş for Uludağ — Tahtakale Çarşısı (Market) — Otel Çamlibel — Cumhuriyet Alanı (Heykel)

Tahtakale — Maksem Caddesi — İpekçilik Caddesi — Namazgah

Maksem

Gallipoli. It was here that Leander swam across what was then called the Hellespont to his lover Hero, and here too that Lord Byron did his romantic bit and duplicated the feat. The defence of the straits during WWI led to a Turkish victory over Anzac forces on 18 March 1916, now a major local holiday.

The helpful tourist office (☎ 217 1187) and many cheap hotels and cafés are within a few blocks of the ferry pier, near the landmark clock tower.

The Ottoman **castle** built by Sultan Mehmet the Conqueror in 1452 is now the **Army & Navy Museum**. Just over two km south of the ferry pier, the **Archaeological Museum** holds artefacts found at Troy and Assos.

Çanakkale's telephone code is ☎ 286.

Places to Stay

Camping is at Güzelyalı Beach, 15 km south off the road to Troy. Most small hotels and pensions have identical city-regulated prices (singles/doubles for US$6/9, or US$7/10 with shower). All are heavily booked in summer and around Anzac Day, 25 April.

Hotel Efes (☎ 217 4687), behind the clock tower at Aralık Sokak 5, is modern, but the rooms have no running water. *Hotel Akgün* (☎ 217 3049), across the street, is similar, as are the *Hotel Erdem* (☎ 217 4986) and *Hotel Umut* (☎ 217 6473), nearer to the clock tower. The *Yellow Rose Pension* (☎ 217 3343) is quiet and tucked out of sight at Yeni Sokak 5. By the clock tower, the *Kervansaray* (☎ 217 8192), an attractive old house with a garden, is a good option, as is the more up-to-date *Konak* (☎ 217 1150).

Hotel Bakır (☎ 217 2908) is old, but has fine sea views and rooms with shower for US$24/30. *Otel Aşkın* (☎ & fax 217 4956), Hasan Mevsuf Sokak 53, less than a block north of the bus station, charges US$14 a double with shower and breakfast. The nearby *Aşkın Pansiyon* (same phone), has waterless doubles for US$8.

For two-star comfort, the *Otel Anzac* (☎ 217 7777), facing the clock tower, charges US$24/

TURKEY

30, or there's the *Otel Anafartalar* (☎ 217 4454) right by the docks for slightly more.

Places to Eat

The *Gaziantep Aile Kebap ve Pide Salonu*, behind the clock tower, serves good cheap pide and more substantial kebabs, while *Trakya Restaurant*, on the main square, always has lots of food ready and waiting 24 hours a day. If you eat at the waterfront fish restaurants, ask for all prices in advance.

GALLIPOLI

Although the Dardanelles had always been İstanbul's first line of defence, it was in WWI that they proved their worth. Atop the narrow, hilly peninsula, Mustafa Kemal (Atatürk) and his troops fought off a far superior but badly commanded force of Anzac and British troops. A visit to the battlegrounds and war graves of Gallipoli (Gelibolu), now a national park, is a moving experience.

The easiest way to get there is on a minibus tour from Çanakkale with Troy-Anzac Tours (☎ 217 5849) for about US$20 per person. However, it's cheaper to take a ferry from Çanakkale to Eceabat and a dolmuş to Kabatepe, and follow the trail around the sites described in a booklet sold at the visitor centre there.

Turkish Maritime Lines' car ferries cross the straits hourly from Lapseki to Gallipoli and from Çanakkale to Eceabat (50 cents per person). Small private 'dolmuş' ferries cross more frequently, more cheaply and more quickly (15 to 20 minutes) from Çanakkale (in front of the Hotel Bakır) to Kilitbahir. Buses also make the five-hour trip to Gallipoli from İstanbul's Esenler otogar.

TROY

There's not much of the historic 'Trojan Horse' Troy (Truva) to be seen, because it's estimated that nine successive cities have been built on this same site. Troy I goes right back to the Bronze Age. Legendary Troy is thought to be Troy VI. Most of the ruins you see are Roman ones from Troy IX. Still, it's nice to say you've been there.

Dolmuş run the 32 km from Çanakkale frequently for US$2. Walk straight inland from the ferry pier to Atatürk Caddesi, and turn right towards Troy; the dolmuş station is at the bridge.

Tevfikiye, the farming village one km before the site, has a few small pensions charging US$5 to US$7 a double. The restaurants by the entrance to the ruins are inevitably pricey. Troy is open daily from 8 am to 5 pm (7 pm in summer); admission is US$2.50.

BEHRAMKALE (ASSOS)

Nineteen km west of Ayvacık, Behramkale, once known as Assos, has the hill-top **Temple of Athena** looking across the water to Lesvos (Greece), and was considered one of the most beautiful cities of its time. It is still beautiful, particularly the tiny port *(iskele)* two km beyond the village.

Dost provides camping at the port for US$5.50. On the heights, *Halıcı Han* and other pensions can put you up for US$12 a double and the *Kale Restaurant* will feed you. Port hotels (*Behram*, *Kervansaray*, *Şen*, *Yıldız*) are more expensive (US$25 to US$60 a double), but also more comfy and atmospheric. Visit in low season if you can.

AYVALIK

Once inhabited by Ottoman Greeks, this popular beach resort is packed with Turkish vacationers in summer. The main street, İnönü Caddesi, links the otogar, 1.5 km north of the town centre, and the tourist office (☎ 312 2122), one km south, opposite the marina.

Offshore is **Alibey Island**, with open-air restaurants, linked by ferries and a causeway to the mainland (take the red 'Ayvalık Belediyesi' bus north). Six km south on a blue 'Sarımsaklı Belediyesi' bus is the 12-km-long **Sarımsaklı Plaj** (beach), also called Plajlar.

Turkish boats make the two-hour trip to Lesvos in the morning, Greek boats in the evening, for an outrageous US$50 one way and US$65 same-day return. Boats operate daily from late May to September.

Ayvalık's telephone code is ☎ 266.

Places to Stay & Eat

The best value in Ayvalık is the *Çiçek Pansiyon* (☎ 312 1201), 200 metres south of the town centre and one street in from the water (follow the signs), where clean, quiet singles/doubles with shower cost US$11/14; the *Biret* and *Melisa* round the corner take the overflow.

Taksiyarhis Pansiyon (☎ 312 1494), İsmetpaşa Mahallesi, Mareşal Çakmak Caddesi 71, is a renovated Ottoman house charging US$25 a double with shower.

Off İnönü Caddesi are several good, cheap restaurants such as the *Ayvalık* and the *Anadolu Döner ve Pide Salonu*. The ones in the market, east of the main road, are more atmospheric. The *Öz Canlı Balık Restaurant* on the waterfront is pricier but good for seafood.

BERGAMA

From the 3rd century BC to the 1st century AD, Bergama (Pergamum) was a powerful and cultured kingdom. A line of rulers beginning with a general under Alexander the Great ruled over this small but wealthy kingdom, whose **asclepion** (medical school, 3.5 km from the city centre, entry US$2.50) grew famous and whose library rivalled that of Alexandria in Egypt. The star attractions here are the city's ruins, especially the **acropolis** (a hill-top site six km from the city centre, entry US$2.50), and an excellent **archaeology & ethnography museum** (in the city centre, entry US$2.50).

The tourist office (☎ 633 1862) is at Cumhuriyet Meydanı in the town centre. Taxis wait here and charge US$5 to the acropolis, US$10 total if they wait and bring you back down. If you're a walker, follow the path down through the ruins instead. A tour of the acropolis, the asclepion and the museum costs US$21.

Bergama's telephone code is ☎ 232.

Places to Stay & Eat

There are camping grounds, including *Bergama Camping* (US$3 per person), between the town and the coast highway.

The spotless, family-run *Böblingen Pension* (☎ 633 2153), Asklepion Caddesi 2, is at the start of the road to the asclepion, with doubles for US$15. Near the çarşı hamamı (Turkish bath, for men only) on the main street, *Pergamon Pension* (☎ 633 2395), Bankalar Caddesi 3, has rooms of all sizes for US$8 to US$12. Across the street, *Acroteria Pension* (☎ 633 2469), set back from the road and thus quiet, charges just a bit more.

For luxury, there's the *Hotel Berksoy* (☎ 633 2595) east of the town, charging US$55 a double amid well-kept gardens with a pool.

About 150 metres south-west of the old red basilica on the main street is a square where you'll find the *Meydan Restaurant* charging about US$5 or US$6 for a three-course meal on vine-shaded terraces. The simpler *Sarmaşık Lokantası* has no outdoor seating, but is cheaper. Heading south-west towards the museum and pensions, the *Şen Kardeşler* and *Çiçek Sever Kebap Salonu* are good, cheap options.

Gözde Yemek ve Kebap Salonu, next to the çarşı hamamı, is also good.

Getting There & Away

Buses shuttle between Bergama and İzmir every half-hour in summer (1½ hours, US$4). Four buses connect Bergama's otogar and Ayvalık daily; or you can hitch out to the highway and catch a bus.

İZMİR

Turkey's third-largest city, once named Smyrna, is said to be the place where Homer was born in 700 BC. Today it's a transport hub, but otherwise a good place to skip. İzmir is spread out and baffling to find your way around, and its hotels are overpriced. If you stay, you can enjoy the good **bazar**, the 2nd-century Roman agora, the hill-top Kadifekale **fortress**, and the **archaeological and ethnographic museums**.

Turkish tourist literature 'regrets' that there is not much to see here because of the great fire of 1922. You can get to the Greek island of Chios from Çeşme, 90 km (two hours) west of İzmir.

Orientation

Central İzmir is a web of plazas linked by streets that aren't at right angles to each other. Instead of names, the back streets have numbers. Luckily, the tourist office hands out detailed maps.

Budget hotels are clustered near the Basmane train station. South-west, Anafartalar Caddesi twists and turns through the labyrinthine bazar to the waterfront at Konak, the commercial and government centre. Atatürk Caddesi, also called Birinci Kordon, runs north-east from Konak along the waterfront 1.4 km to Cumhuriyet Meydanı (and its equestrian statue of Atatürk), where you'll find the main post office, luxury hotels, and tourist and airline offices.

TURKEY

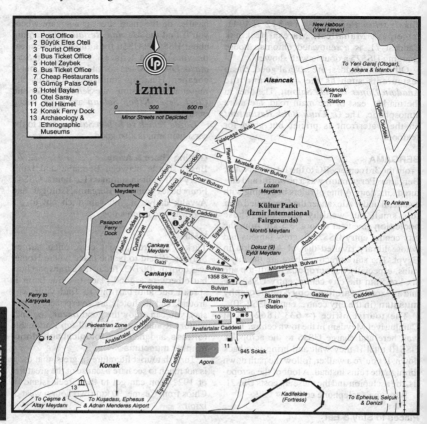

İzmir

1 Post Office
2 Büyük Efes Oteli
3 Tourist Office
4 Bus Ticket Office
5 Hotel Zeybek
6 Bus Ticket Office
7 Cheap Restaurants
8 Gümüş Palas Oteli
9 Hotel Baylan
10 Otel Saray
11 Otel Hikmet
12 Konak Ferry Dock
13 Archaeology &
   Ethnographic
   Museums

0   300   600 m
Minor Streets not Depicted

At Atatürk Caddesi's northern end is the harbour (Alsancak Yeni Limanı) and the smaller, mostly suburban Alsancak train station. İzmir's otogar is two km east of Alsancak train station.

Information

The tourist office (☎ 484 2147) is next to the Turkish Airlines office in the Büyük Efes Oteli at Gaziosmanpaşa Bulvarı 1/C, Cumhuriyet Meydanı, with another at Adnan Menderes airport. There's a good city information desk at the otogar.

İzmir's telephone code is ☎ 232.

Places to Stay

From Basmane train station, walk south along Anafartalar Caddesi. Turn right on 1296 Sokak, a quiet street lined with cheap hotels and restaurants. Hotels here include the *Yıldız Palas* at No 50 and the *Gümüş Palas* around the corner on 1299 Sokak. Both charge US$7 a double without running water, US$9 with a sink.

Anafartalar Caddesi winds into the bazar. Near the Hatuniye Camii (mosque) is the *Otel Saray* (☎ 483 6946), at Anafartalar Caddesi 635, which has been popular with backpackers for years. Get a room on the upper floor (it's quieter there) for US$14 a double with sink. Up 945 Sokak at No 26 is the cleaner, more comfortable *Otel Hikmet* (☎ 484 2672), which charges about the same prices.

For other hotels, walk straight down Fevzipaşa Bulvarı from Basmane station and turn right (north). 1368 Sokak and its westward continuation, 1369 Sokak, have half a dozen good, clean, quiet and cheap hotels such as the *Otel Özcan*, the *Akgün*, the *Ova* and the *Çiçek Palas*, with doubles for US$12 with sink, US$18 with shower. The *Hotel Zeybek* (☎ 489 6694), on 1368 Sokak, has two-star comforts in very small rooms for US$32/40, while the *Hotel Baylan* (☎ 483 1426), 1299 Sokak No 8, has good two-star rooms for US$35/53 with breakfast.

Places to Eat

Immediately opposite Basmane station, the *Ankara*, *Karaca Birtat*, *Ödemis Azim* and *Aydın-Denizli-Nazili* restaurants offer quick, cheap meals. Little eateries are also scattered along the budget-hotel streets.

On 1296 Sokak is the cheap *Güneydoğu Kebap Salonu*, where a kebab plate and a drink cost US$4 or less. But the restaurants on 1368 and 1369 sokaks, just across Fevzipaşa Bulvarı, are much more pleasant and some serve alcohol. The *Dört Mevsim Et Lokantası*, 1369 Sokak No 51/A, specialises in meats, serves drinks, and will fill you up for about US$5 or US$6.

The up-market restaurants are along Atatürk Caddesi, by the sea.

Getting There & Away

Air Turkish Airlines (☎ 484 1220), Gaziosmanpaşa Bulvarı 1/F, in the Büyük Efes Oteli at Cumhuriyet Meydanı, has flights to İstanbul (50 minutes, US$85) and Ankara, with connections to other places.

İstanbul Airlines (☎ 489 0541), Gaziosmanpaşa Bulvarı 2/E, has some flights to İstanbul, and numerous flights between İzmir and Europe.

Bus Many bus companies have ticket offices around Dokuz Eylül Meydanı, just north of Basmane, and west along Gazi Bulvarı. They may also provide a free (şehiriçi servis)

minibus shuttle service to İzmir's otogar (three km east of the city centre).

Train The evening *mavi tren* hauls sleeping and dining cars from Basmane station to Ankara (14 hours, US$13). The evening *İzmir Ekspresi* to Ankara (15 hours) has 1st/2nd-class carriages for US$10/7.

For İstanbul, take the Marmara Ekspresi (US$6) to Bandırma, then a ferry (no boats on Friday or Saturday); in total the journey costs US$10. Four pokey but cheap trains go from Basmane to Selçuk/Ephesus (2½ hours, US$1.50); three continue to Denizli (for Pamukkale, six hours, US$4).

Boat The Getting There & Away and Getting Around sections earlier in this chapter have information on ferries to the Greek Islands and Venice. Ferries to Chios depart from Çeşme, west of İzmir, daily in summer (US$25 one way). Catch a bus from Dokuz Eylül Meydanı to Altay Meydanı (Altay Square) in western İzmir. From there, buses go to Çeşme every 20 minutes.

Getting Around

To/From the Airport A Havaş bus (45 minutes, US$2) departs from the Turkish Airlines office at the Büyük Efes Oteli several times daily for the 25-km trip to Adnan Menderes airport. Trains (50 cents) run hourly from Alsancak train station to the airport, and *some* southbound trains from Basmane also stop at the airport. From Montrö Meydanı, 700 metres north of Basmane, southbound 'Adnan Menderes Belediyesi' buses go to the airport during the day for US$1. A taxi costs about US$12.

Local Transport City buses and dolmuş connect the bus and train stations for 70 cents; signs say 'Basmane' or 'Yeni Garaj'. The No 50 city bus (70 cents, buy your ticket before boarding) links the Yeni Garaj and Konak; Çankaya Meydanı is the closest stop to Basmane. A taxi from the city centre to the bus station costs about US$3.

SELÇUK & EPHESUS

Selçuk is an easy 1¼-hour (80 km) bus trip south of İzmir. Almost everybody comes here

TURKEY

to visit the splendid Roman ruins of Ephesus (Efes). In its Ionian heyday only Athens was more magnificent, and in Roman times this was Asia's capital.

Orientation & Information

Although Selçuk is touristy and has its share of irritatingly persistent carpet hawkers, it is modest compared with coastal resorts like Kuşadası. On the east side of the highway are the otogar, restaurants, some hotels and the train station; on the west side, behind the museum, are many pensions. There are a tourist office (☎ 232-892 6328) and a town map in the park on the west side of the main street, across from the otogar.

Selçuk's telephone code is ☎ 232.

Ephesus is a three-km, 35-minute walk west from Selçuk's otogar along a shady road – turn left (south) at the Tusan Motel. Or there are frequent minibuses from the otogar to the motel, leaving you just a one-km walk.

Things to See & Do

Ephesus flourished as the centre for worship of the Anatolian fertility goddess Cybele. The **Arcadian Way** through Ephesus was the main street to the port, which is long gone, having silted up. The immense **Great Theatre** holds 24,000 people. The **Temple of Hadrian**, the **Celsus Library**, the **Marble Way** (where the rich lived) and the **Fountain of Trajan** are still in amazingly good shape, or under painstaking restoration. The site, permanently swamped with coach groups, is open daily from 8 am to 5 pm. Entry fees are US$6, plus US$1 to park a car.

The excellent **Ephesus Museum** in Selçuk (open from 8.30 am to noon and 1 to 5.30 pm; closed Monday; entry $3.50) has a striking collection of artefacts from this period. The foundations of the **Temple of Artemis**, between Ephesus and Selçuk, are all that is left of one of the Seven Wonders of the World. Ephesus was later a centre of early Christianity. It was visited by St Paul, who wrote a famous letter to the Ephesians. Above Selçuk is the **Basilica of St John**, said to be built over his tomb. The Virgin Mary is said to have lived her last years at **Meryemana**, on a nearby mountain top.

Places to Stay

Garden Motel & Camping (☎ 892 1163) is west of Ayasoluk, the hill bearing the citadel and Basilica of St John; walk past the basilica, down the hill, then turn right at the İsabey Camii. Quiet tent and caravan sites amidst fruit orchards cost US$7. **Tusan Motel**, at the Ephesus turn-off, also has camp sites. Other sites are en route to, and at, Pamucak, seven km west of town.

There are many pensions up the hill behind the Selçuk Museum, charging about US$6 to US$8 per person. Good choices are the **Barım**, at Turgutreis Sokak 34, on the first street back from the museum, and the **Australia & New Zealand Pension** (☎ 892 6050) at Profesör Mitler Sokak 17, on the second street back. Also worth seeking out are the **Homeros** (☎ 892 3995), Asmali Sokak 17; **Abasız** (☎ 892 1367), Turgutreis Sokak 13, with nine rooms (some with views); and the eight-room **Akgüneş Pension** (☎ 892 3869), Turgutreis Sokak 14, with private showers.

For even cheaper rooms but without private showers, walk east from the otogar uphill to the section called 14 Mayıs Mahallesi and follow the signs to the **Yayla**, **Zümrüt** and **Panorama** pensions.

For luxury, the best place is the atmospheric, 50-room **Otel Kalehan** (☎ 892 6154), on the main road just north of the Shell station. Rooms with showers, mini-fridges and air-con cost US$30/50/70 a single/double/triple. There's a pool as well.

Cengiz Topel Caddesi, a pedestrian street between the Cybele fountain at the highway and the town square by the train station, has several decent hotels charging US$25 a double with private bath.

Places to Eat

Cengiz Topel Caddesi has many outdoor restaurants and cafés. For cheap pide, try the **Artemis Pide Salonu**, a half-block south of the tea garden at the eastern end of Cengiz Topel, where Turkish-style pizza goes for US$1.50 to US$2.50. **Okumuşlar Pide Salonu** on Namık Kemal Caddesi is similar. The **Kodalak Restaurant** at the otogar serves cheap stews, but ask for prices before you order.

Getting There & Away

Minibuses leave frequently for Kuşadası (20

km, 30 minutes, 80 cents) and Pamucak (seven km, 10 minutes, 70 cents), passing the Ephesus turn-off (five minutes, 50 cents). Taxis to Ephesus charge at least US$2.50; ask for the *güney kapısı* (southern gate) so you can walk downhill. A dolmuş to Pamucak leaves at 8 am daily from the otogar.

You can make a day trip to Pamukkale (195 km, three hours, US$8 one way) on direct buses leaving before 9 am and returning by 5 pm. Frequent buses and three cheap trains (US$3) daily go to Denizli, where you can get a dolmuş to Pamukkale. Hourly buses go to Bodrum and to Marmaris. Buses to İzmir leave regularly from 6.30 am to 7 pm (1¼ hours, US$2.25); the six daily trains are slower (2½ hours) but cheaper (US$2).

KUŞADASI

This is a cruise-ship port and a cheerfully shameless tourist trap. The main reason to visit is to catch a boat to the Greek island of Samos, although Kuşadası is a good base for visits to the ancient cities of **Priene**, **Miletus** and **Didyma** to the south. Tours are pricey at US$18 to US$25, so you might want to try a combination of local buses and hitching instead. There are also good beaches and a national park at **Güzelçamlı**, 25 minutes south by dolmuş.

The tourist office (☎ 614 1103) is right by the pier and the otogar 1.5 km south-east of the town centre on the highway. Boats to Samos (Sisam) sail daily in summer for US$30 one way, US$35 same-day return, or US$55 open return, including Turkish port tax; ticket offices are close to the tourist office.

Kuşadası's telephone code is ☎ 256.

Places to Stay

The *Önder* and *Tur-Yat Mocamp* camping grounds, north of town on the waterfront near the marina, charge US$8 for two people in a tent.

Decent cheap hotels and pensions (US$10 to US$12 per person with shower) are uphill behind the Akdeniz Apart-otel along Aslanlar Caddesi. *Su Pansiyon* (☎ 614 1453), at No 13, is an old reliable option; *Pension Golden Bed* (☎ 614 8708), just off Aslanlar Caddesi (follow the signs), is quiet and family-run, with a terrace café. Follow Aslanlar Caddesi to Bezirgan Sokak and turn right to find the *Pansiyon Dinç*

(☎ 614 4249), Mercan Sokak, which is small, simple and cheap at US$16 for a waterless double, breakfast included; the nearby *Enişte* and *Hasgül* are similar. *Stella* (☎ 614 1632) costs more (US$55 a double) but boasts stunning harbour views.

To stay in the historic *Hotel Kervansaray* (☎ 614 4115) in the centre of town costs US$50/65 for singles/doubles with breakfast; you're better off just enjoying a drink in the courtyard bar. For less money (US$22/36 a single/double) and more comfort, stay at a hotel (*Köken*, *Çidem* or *Akman*) on İstiklal Sokak one km north-east of the centre.

Places to Eat

Good seafood places along the waterfront close to the wharf charge US$8 to US$20 for a fish dinner, depending on the fish and the season. Cheaper meals (US$3 to US$6) are served on Sağlık Caddesi between Kahramanlar Caddesi and İnönü Bulvarı. Try the *Konyalı* at No 40.

The Kaleiçi district shelters several charming cafés, a million miles in atmosphere from the crass offerings of so-called Pub Lane.

PAMUKKALE

Three hours east of Selçuk by bus, this fascinating site has hot, calcium-rich waters that flow over a plateau edge and cool to form a series of pool-filled, brilliant white ledges, or travertines. Above and behind this natural wonder lie the extensive ruins of the Roman city of **Hierapolis**, an ancient spa.

There are tourist offices on the ridge at Pamukkale (☎ 272 2077) and in Denizli train station. You pay admission (US$4) to the ridge as you climb the hill. Soak your bones in one of the many **thermal baths**; one friend likened it to 'swimming in warm Perrier'. The most famous (and most expensive, at US$4.50 for two hours), complete with sunken Roman columns, is at the Pamukkale Motel on top of the ridge. Just south of it are the more mundane Belediye Turistik Tesisleri (municipal baths; open May to September only). Some pensions in the village at the bottom of the ridge have pools too.

Pamukkale's (and Denizli's) telephone code is ☎ 258.

A worthwhile but time-consuming detour on your way back to Selçuk or Kuşadası would

TURKEY

be to the beautiful ruined city of **Aphrodisias**, south of Nazilli near Karacasu. Many think it rivals Ephesus.

Places to Stay

The bargain pensions and hotels (over sixty of them) are in the village below – the further from the highway, the cheaper they are. For cheerful service and decent rooms, try the **Kervansaray Pension** (☎ 272 2209), where rooms cost US$12/18 a single/double, and the nearby **Aspawa** (☎ 272 2094). The friendly, tidy **Koray Otel** (☎ 272 2300), a few streets south, has a restaurant, bar and pool; doubles cost US$18, including breakfast.

The government has said that the ridge-top hotels must soon close. In the meantime the **Tusan Moteli** (☎ 272 2010) and the **Motel Koru** (☎ 272 2429) charge US$65/80 for a single/double, breakfast and dinner included.

Places to Eat

Taking meals in your pension or hotel is usually best here – but ask for prices in advance! Of the restaurants in the town, the **Gürsoy**, opposite the Yörük Motel in the village centre, has the nicest terrace, but the **Han**, around the corner facing the square, offers the best value for money. Meals at either cost US$4 to US$6.

BODRUM

Bodrum, formerly Halicarnassus, is the site of the **Mausoleum**, the monumental tomb of King Mausolus, which was another of the Seven Wonders of the World. Little now remains of the Mausoleum, which was probably partially destroyed by an earthquake and then demolished by the Knights of St John.

Placed between Bodrum's perfect twin bays is the medieval **Castle of St Peter**, built in 1402 and rebuilt in 1522 by the knights, using stones from the tomb. It's now a **museum of underwater archaeology** and contains finds from the oldest shipwreck ever discovered. The museum is open from 8 am to noon and from 1 to 5 pm; entry costs US$3, with another US$1.75 each to visit the ancient wreck and a model of a Carian princess' tomb.

Walk west past the marina and over the hill to **Gümbet**, which has a nicer beach than Bodrum proper, though it's a bit polluted. **Gümüşlük**, to the far west of the Bodrum

peninsula, is the best of the many smaller villages nearby. Dolmuş run there every hour.

The otogar is 500 metres inland along Cevat Şakir Caddesi from the Adliye Cami, a small mosque at the centre of the town. The post office and several banks are on Cevat Şakir Caddesi. The tourist office is at Barış Meydanı (☎ 316 1091), beside the castle.

Bodrum's telephone code is ☎ 252.

Places to Stay

Some of the smaller villages on the peninsula, such as Bitez Yalısı and Ortakent Yalısı, have camp sites. There are more on the peninsula's north shore.

Bodrum is full of pensions and hotels charging US$6 to US$10 per person; prices rise steeply as you approach the waterfront, but they drop in the off season.

Behind the belediye (town hall) on Türkkuyusu Sokak, try the **Sevin Pansiyon** (☎ 316 8361), which has doubles with shower for US$24; the cheaper **Titiz** (☎ 316 1534) at No 18; or **Melis** (☎ 316 1487) at No 50. Rooms in the nearby **Pansiyon Kaya** (☎ 316 5745) on Eski Hükümet Sokak also cost US$12 a double. The **Şenlik Pansiyon** (☎ 316 6382), at No 115, is right on the street and a bit pricey at US$28 a double, but behind it is the family-run **Sedan** (☎ 316 0355), Türkkuyusu 121. Newer double rooms with shower go for US$20; older, waterless doubles for US$15.

Best of all is the wonderful **Su Otel** (☎ 316 6906), Turgutreis Caddesi, 1201 Sokak (follow the signs), with a charming flower-filled courtyard, a swimming pool, and rooms decorated in local crafts; doubles with bath cost US$40 to US$55 in summer.

Places to Eat

For very cheap eats, buy a dönerli sandviç (sandwich with roast lamb) for less than US$2 at a streetside büfe. Look for the words in the window.

In July and August, the cheapest food is at simple local eateries well inland, without menus in English or German. Most serve no alcohol.

In the grid of small market streets just east of the Adliye Camii are several restaurants. **Babadan**, **Ziya'nin Yeri** and **Üsküdarlı** are patronised by locals as well as foreigners, and serve plates of döner for about US$2.75 and beer for US$1.30. For cheaper fare, continue eastward to a little plaza filled with open-air restaurants serving pide and kebab. The *Nazilli* is the favourite here, but the *Şahin* and the *Karadeniz* are almost as good. A pide topped with meat or cheese costs only US$3 or so.

In warm weather, inspect Meyhaneler Sokak, off İskele Caddesi. Wall-to-wall tavernas serve food and drink to happy crowds nightly for US$12 to US$18.

Of the up-market places, *Amphora* (☎ 316 2368), on the western bay, is the best, with meals for around US$15 a head. More expensive, but quite pleasant, is *Kocadon* (☎ 316 3705), back toward the centre a bit.

Getting There & Away

Bodrum has a fast and frequent bus service to all points in the region and some beyond, including Antalya (11 hours, US$22), Fethiye (4½ hours, US$14), İzmir (four hours, US$9), Kuşadası and Selçuk (three hours, US$9), Marmaris (three hours, US$8) and Pamukkale (five hours, US$13).

Hydrofoils and boats go to Kos (İstanköy) frequently in summer for US$22.50 one way and US$29 return (plus a US$13 Greek port tax at Kos). In summer there are also boats to Datça, Didyma, Knidos, Marmaris and Rhodes; check with the tourist office.

The Mediterranean Coast

Turkey's Mediterranean coastline winds eastward for more than 1200 km from Marmaris to Antakya on the Syrian border. East of Marmaris, the 'Turquoise Coast' is perfect for boat excursions, with many secluded coves and quiet bays all the way to Fethiye. The rugged coastline from Fethiye east to Antalya – immortalised by Homer as Lycia – and the Taurus Mountains east of Antalya are wild and beautiful. Further east you pass through fewer seaside resorts and more workaday cities. The entire coast is liberally sprinkled with impressive ruins, studded with beautiful beaches and washed by clear water ideal for sports.

MARMARİS

Even more than Kuşadası and Bodrum, Marmaris, sited on a beautiful bay at the edge of a hilly peninsula, has yielded to mass tourism. Nevertheless, the sculptured coastline and crystalline waters explain why it's become Turkey's premier yachting port. The Greek island of Rhodes (Rodos) is a short voyage south. Marmaris is not as pretty as Bodrum, although the swimming in the surrounding bays is probably safer.

Orientation & Information

Marmaris has a small castle overlooking the town centre. İskele Meydanı (the main square) and the tourist office (☎ 412 1035) are near the ferry pier just north-east of the castle. The centre is mostly a pedestrian precinct. New development stretches many km to the southeast around the bay.

The otogar is north of the yacht harbour. Hacı Mustafa Sokak, otherwise known as Bar Street, runs down from near the otogar to the bazar; action here keeps going until the early hours of the morning.

Marmaris' telephone code is ☎ 252.

Things to See & Do

The **castle** has a few unexciting exhibition rooms but offers fine views of Marmaris. It's open from 8 am to noon and 1 to 5 pm daily (closed on Monday); admission is US$1.

There are daily **boat trips** in summer to nearby Paradise Island (about US$15 a head) and further afield to **Dalyan** and **Caunus** (about US$30 a head). The beach at **İçmeler**, 10 km away by minibus, is marginally better than that at Marmaris.

Datça, a village two hours drive away, out on the peninsula, has now been 'discovered' but is still a great place to visit; less spoilt is **Bozburun**, not as far west. At the tip of the peninsula are the ruins of the ancient port of **Knidos**, accessible by road or excursion boat.

Places to Stay

Marmaris has hundreds of lodgings, but few are cheap. Ask at the tourism office about *ev pansiyonları* (home pensions), renting double rooms for US$8 to US$12. Some are inland from Abdi İpekçi Park on 97 Sokak, including the *Altun*, the *Taşkın*, the *Erdel*, the *Cihan* and the *Etem*.

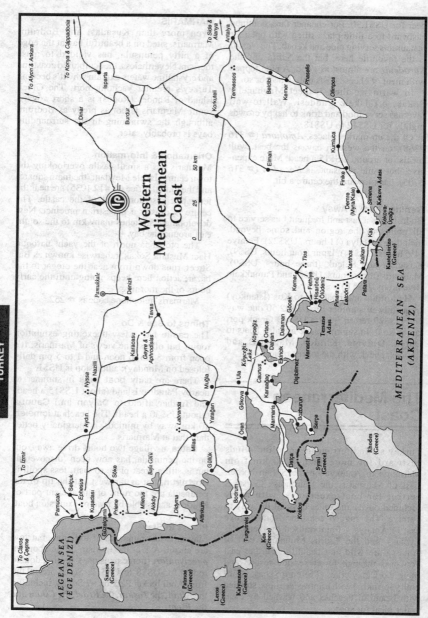

Western Mediterranean Coast

For lodgings and camping on the beach, take a 'Siteler-Turban' minibus along the waterfront road to the last stop at the Turban Marmaris Tatil Köyü holiday village, four km south-west of the main square. Besides *Berk Camping*, with tent sites for US$6 and cabins for US$18, there are several small pension-like hotels renting double rooms for around US$20: the *Birol*, *Yüzbaşı*, *Sembol*, *Panorama* and *Tümer*.

The original *Interyouth Hostel* (☎ 412 6432), at Kemeraltı Mahallesi, İyiliktaş Mevkii 14, has been joined by a second hostel deep in the bazar at Tepe Mahallesi, 42 Sokak No 45, which has cheekily co-opted the same *Interyouth Hostel* (☎ 412 3687) name. Neither is ideal – the original stranded in Marmaris' rear wastelands, its newer rival in the noisy bazar. Both charge US$6 for a dorm bed, US$8 per person in a double.

A few small old hotels remain just off the main square near the tourist office, including the *Otel İmbat* (☎ 412 1413) and the *Otel Karaaslan* (☎ 412 1867), which has no sign; both charge US$14 a double with private bath, but this area is now very noisy with disco-bars.

Pricier but charming is the *Hotel Begonya* (☎ 412 4095), Hacı Mustafa Sokak 101, northwest of the yacht harbour, one street inland. A stone house around a courtyard filled with flowers, it has singles/doubles with shower for US$35/45, including one of Turkey's best breakfasts. Noise from nearby bars, though, goes on until the early hours.

Places to Eat

The 'resort rule' applies: the further you go inland from the water, the higher the quality and the lower the price. Have some Marmaris honey while you're here – it's famous.

The *Ayyıldız Restaurant*, near the mosque in the bazar, is fairly dependable, with three-course meals for US$7.50 or so. Of the open-air restaurants along Fevzipaşa Caddesi (the street with the PTT), the *Marmaris Lokantası* is one of the best, offering İskender kebap for US$4. The *Yeni Liman* is also good and cheap, with full meals for US$8 to US$10, as is the *Öz 49*.

Hacı Mustafa Sokak harbours all sorts of possibilities for cheap eating, from filled baked potatoes through to pizzas. *Beyoğlu Café-Bar* has cheap fish meals for US$7.50. *Pizza Napoli* offers tasty, filling pizzas for around US$6.

Surprisingly, the pizza and steak meals at the posh *Pineapple International Restaurant* (☎ 412 4999) in the Netsel Marina (yacht harbour) cost only US$15 to US$20.

The best place for a sundowner is *Panorama Bar*; follow the signs from the castle end of the bazar.

Getting There & Away

Marmaris otogar, north of the yacht marina, has frequent direct buses and minibuses to all places in the region, including Antalya (eight hours, US$14), Bodrum (three hours, US$6.50), Dalyan (via Ortaca; two hours, US$4), Datça (1¾ hours, US$4), and Fethiye (three hours, US$6.50). Bozburun minibuses run once daily (1½ hours, US$2), more frequently in summer. Small car ferries run to Rhodes daily, except Sunday, in summer (less frequently in the off season) for US$41 one way or US$56 return (plus US$13 port tax at Rhodes and US$10 to re-enter Turkey).

KÖYCEĞİZ & DALYAN

Köyceğiz, 75 km east of Marmaris, stands at the edge of a great, placid lake. Although a pleasant, peaceful farming town with a few pensions and hotels, it's overshadowed by its smaller but more touristy neighbour, the town of Dalyan.

Set in lush river-delta farming country, Dalyan has it all: fertile soil, a river meandering by, excellent fishing and, to the south at İztuzu, beautiful **beaches** which are the natural nesting ground of the *Carretta carretta*, or ancient sea turtle.

As if that were not enough, Dalyan has ruins: dramatic rock-cut **Lycian tombs** in the cliff facing the town, and the ruined city of **Caunus** easily visited by boat excursion downriver. Upriver on the shores of Köyceğiz Lake are **hot springs** at Sultaniye Kaplıcaları.

Dozens of pensions and small but comfortable hotels are spread north and south of Dalyan's town centre. Cheapest are those nearest to the bus stop, but those further south along Maraş Caddesi, like the *Önder* and *Çinar Sahil* (☎ 252-284 2117) pansiyons, have better views.

The local boaters' cooperative sets rates for river excursions to points of interest. Daily

TURKEY

tours taking in the mud baths, the ruins at Caunus, and Turtle Beach cost about US$4.50 a head. Forty-minute runs just to the beach cost US$2.

For cheap eats try *Café Natural* in the main square where kebab and juice come to US$4.50. A small tourist office hides behind the boat cooperative on the quay.

DALAMAN & GÖCEK
Dalaman, 23 km south-east of Dalyan, is another farming community, but with an international airport *(hava limanı)*. A few scheduled flights supplement the holiday charters. The town has hotels and pensions in all price brackets, and you can camp in the Belediye Koru Parkı pine forest 300 metres north of the otogar. Buses run to all points along the coast and beyond.

Göcek, 23 km east of Dalaman through fragrant pine forests, is a small fishing town getting used to tourism. With an odd mix of cheap pensions and camping grounds for backpackers, and white-tablecloth restaurants for sailing enthusiasts, Göcek is pleasant and laidback, even though it lacks good beaches.

FETHİYE
Fethiye has superb beaches and cheap lodgings; it's crowded in summer but worth the diversion off the road. This is the site of ancient **Telmessos**, with giant Lycian stone **sarcophagi** from 400 BC littered about, and the rock-cut **Tomb of Amyntas** looming from a cliff above the town. There's a marked hiking trail over the hills to the Ottoman Greek ghost town of **Kayaköy**.

Four km north, the beach at **Çalış** is many km long, and backed by hotels and pensions. To the south, 12 km over the mountains, is the gorgeous lagoon of **Ölüdeniz** (Dead Sea), too beautiful for its own good and now one of the Mediterranean's most famous beach spots. Inland from the beach are moderately priced bungalows and camping areas, as well as some hotels. There are some even cheaper pensions several km inland on the Fethiye road at Ovacık and in Hisarönü village. Alternatively, you can sleep in Fethiye and come to Ölüdeniz for the day.

If you stay in Fethiye, be sure to take the '12 Island Tour' boat excursion. With its swimming, cruising and sightseeing, it may be your most pleasant day in Fethiye. Prices average around US$8 per person. Don't miss the Turkish bath in the bazar either. It's open from 7 am to midnight and the full treatment costs about US$10.

Orientation & Information
The otogar is two km east of the town centre. The tourist office (☎ 614 1527), next to the Dedeoğlu Otel, is near the yacht marina on the western side of the town.

Fethiye's telephone code is ☎ 252.

Places to Stay
There's a cluster of pensions near the stadium just west of the otogar. To find them walk straight down the road heading north from the minibus station.

Next to the stadium, *Göreme Pansiyon* (☎ 614 6944), Dolgu Sahası, Stadyum Yanı 25, has spotless singles/doubles for US$10/16, and a proprietor who lived in London. Across the road is the similar but cheaper *Moonlight Pension* (☎ 614 2178). Turn right and follow the signs for the *Olimpiyat Pansiyon* (☎ 614 3444), Yergüz Caddesi 48, with big, clean doubles for US$14, breakfast included.

Other pensions are uphill from the yacht marina along Fevzi Çakmak Caddesi. The *Yıldırım* (☎ 614 3913), the *Pınara* (☎ 614 2151), the *Derelioğlu* (☎ 614 5983), the *Polat* (☎ 614 2347) and the *İrem* (☎ 614 3985) all charge US$7 to US$9 per person; breakfast costs another US$1.

The *İdeal Pension* (☎ 614 1981), Zafer Caddesi 1, has superb views from its terrace, but is a bit more expensive. Even further uphill, the *İnci Pansiyon* (☎ 614 3325) has marvellous views and blissful quiet at similar prices. *Cesur Pansiyon* (☎ 614 3398), across the street, is similar.

Places to Eat
The market district is packed with open-air restaurants, where you should watch out for bill fiddling. The *Tahirağa Lokantası* (☎ 614 6308) on Çarşı Caddesi (the main market street) is not as fancy or pricey as many others, and alcohol is served.

Around the corner on Tütün Sokak is the *Refat Tuna Lokantası*, which is a bit quieter. Also nearby is *Nefis Pide Salonu*, which serves cheap pide, and soup, şiş kebap, bread and a soft drink only costs about US$3.

Pricier but with a wonderful choice of appetisers is **Restaurant Güneş** (☎ 614 2776) at Likya Caddesi 4 in the bazar. A good meal should cost between US$8 and US$12.

Getting There & Away

The coastal mountains force long-haul bus services to travel east and west – to Marmaris, Muğla and Antalya – before going anywhere else. If you're heading directly for Antalya, note that the *yayla* (inland) route is shorter and cheaper (US$8) than the *sahil* (coastal) route (US$12).

Buses from the otogar also serve Kalkan (US$2.75) and Kaş (US$3). Minibuses depart from their own terminal, one km west of the otogar toward the centre, on short hops to other points along the coast, like Patara (US$2.75), Kınık (for Xanthos, US$2) and Ölüdeniz (US$1).

RUINS NEAR FETHİYE

Lycia was heavily populated in ancient times, as shown by the large number of wonderful old cities, which can be reached by minibus from Fethiye. **Tlos** is 40 km up into the mountains near Kemer on the inland route to Antalya. **Pınara**, south of Fethiye, is an undervisited mountainous site.

Letoön, four km off the highway in a fertile valley filled with tomato greenhouses, has excellent mosaics, a good theatre and a pool sacred as the place of worship of the goddess Leto. **Xanthos**, a few km south-east of Letoön above the village of Kınık, is among the most impressive sites along this part of the coast, with its Roman theatre and Lycian pillar tombs.

At **Patara**, seven km further south (turn at Ovaköy), the attraction is not so much the ruins as the incredible 20-km-long beach. Lodgings in Patara village, 2½ km inland from the beach, range from camping through cheap pensions and hotels to the three-star *Otel Beyhan Patara* (☎ 242-843 5098).

KALKAN

Kalkan, everybody's idea of what a small Turkish fishing village should be, is 11 km east of the Patara turn-off. It tumbles down a steep hillside to a yacht marina (in ancient times, the port).

Kalkan's old stone and wood houses have been restored as lodgings – some expensive, some moderate, some still fairly cheap. The streets above the marina are chock-a-block with atmospheric open-air restaurants. There are no good beaches to speak of, but the inevitable excursion boat tours (or minibuses) can take you to Patara Beach and secluded coves along the coast.

Kalkan's telephone code is ☎ 242.

Places to Stay

If you decide to stay, look for cheap pensions (US$10/15 a single/double) at the top of the town.

On the main shopping street, **Özalp Pansiyon** (☎ 844 3486) charges US$9/13 for good, modern rooms with shower and balcony. Not far away, the **Çelik Pansiyon** (☎ 844 2126), Yalıboyu 9, is a standard simple pension charging US$9/16 for a single/double, breakfast included. Continue along the road to the end for the **Holiday Pension**, or go up the hill across the street for the **Gül Pansiyon** (☎ 844 3099); both are more primitive and slightly cheaper.

Further down towards the harbour, the **Akın Pansiyon** (☎ 844 3025) has some waterless rooms on the top floor priced at US$17 a double; rooms lower down with private showers cost US$22, breakfast included. The **Akgül** (☎ 844 3270) around the corner is similar.

Çetin Pansiyon (☎ 844 3094), in the southern part of town, is quieter and cheaper at US$16 a double. The nearby **Altan Pension** (☎ 844 1044) is similar.

Kalkan Han (☎ 844 3151) is charming but rather pricey, at US$38/55 for a single/double, including breakfast. Cheaper is the **Daphne Pansiyon** (☎ 844 3380), nicely decorated with kilims and carpets, with singles/doubles for US$16/32, including breakfast.

Places to Eat

Dominating the shopping centre is **Köşk** restaurant, where meals cost around US$5 to US$7. The **Smile Restaurant** and **Merkez Café** are cheaper. **Belgin's Kitchen**, which is downhill from the Kösk, serves a more limited range of moderately priced traditional dishes in an attractively Turkish setting.

KAŞ

Kaş, called Antiphellus in ancient times, has a picturesque quayside square, friendly people, a big Sunday **market**, Lycian stone **sarco-phagi** dotted about its streets and rock-cut tombs in the cliffs above the town – it's a fine, laid-back place.

The Greek island of Kastellorizo (Meis in Turkish) is visible just a short distance across the water and can be reached by daily boat.

Aside from enjoying the town's ambience and a few small pebble beaches, you can walk west a few hundred metres to the very well-preserved **theatre**, then take a boat excursion to Kalkan, Patara, the Blue Cave, Saklıkent Gorge, Üçağız (see the next section) or Demre.

The tourist office (☎ 836 1238) is on the main square.

Kaş's telephone code is ☎ 242.

Places to Stay

Kaş has everything from camp sites to cheap pensions and four-star hotels. *Kaş Camping*, in an olive grove a km west of town past the theatre, also has simple bungalows.

At the otogar you'll be accosted by pension-pushers. Yenicami Caddesi (or Recep Bilgin Caddesi), just south of the otogar, has lots of places, including the *Orion Hotel* (☎ 836 1938), with tidy rooms and sea views for US$13/22, breakfast included. Further along the street, or just off it, are the *Akkın Pansion* (☎ 836 1232), the *Anıl Motel* (☎ 836 1791), the *Hilal* (☎ 836 1207) and the *Melisa* (☎ 836 1068). At the southern end of the street by the mosque is the *Ay Pansiyon* (☎ 836 1562), where the front rooms have sea views.

Turn right at the Ay Pansiyon and follow the signs to the quieter *Çetin Pension* and the *Pansiyon Kale* (☎ 836 1094), right by the theatre ruins. Opposite the Çetin is the slightly pricier *Korsan Karakedi Motel* (☎ 836 1887) with a lovely roof terrace with bar. Singles/doubles here cost US$13/17.

On the other (eastern) side of town many more pensions offer similar accommodation. Try the *Koştur* (☎ 836 1264).

For more comforts and services, try the two-star *Hotel Kayahan* (☎ 836 1313) above Küçük Çakıl Plaj, where rooms with wonder-ful sea views cost US$28/30; or the three-star *Hotel Club Phellos* (☎ 836 1953), the fanciest place in town, with a swimming pool and comfortable rooms for US$40/65, including breakfast.

Places to Eat

Five popular restaurants fill a shady alley between the marketplace and the main square: the *Aslı Ocakbaşı*, *Derya*, *Orkinos*, *Evakent* and *Baba'nın Yeri*. All serve three-course meals for US$4 to US$8.

On the main square, the *Noel Baba* is a favourite café-restaurant for breakfast and light meals (US$1.50 to US$4). The *Corner Café*, at the PTT end of İbrahim Serin Caddesi, serves juices or a vegetable omelette for US$1, and yoghurt with fruit and honey for US$1.50. The *Café Merhaba* across the street is good for cakes.

The *Eriş*, behind the tourist office, is a favourite, as much for its setting as for its food. Also popular is *Smiley's Restaurant* nearby, where pizza or seafood meals cost around US$3 to US$6.

Round off the evening in the wonderfully decorated *Sun Café* (which sometimes has live music) at the western end of the quay behind the mosque.

KEKOVA & ÜÇAĞIZ

Up in the hills 14 km east of Kaş, a road goes south to Kekova and Ücağız, two villages amid partly sunken ancient ruins. Ücagız, 20 km from the highway, is a farming and fishing hamlet with a handful of very basic pensions and a few simple waterfront restaurants built on top of the ruins of ancient Teimiussa.

Boat owners will try to cajole you into taking a tour (US$10 to US$16 per person) of the bay, including a look at the picturesque little village of Kale (not to be confused with the other Kale, which is also known as Demre/Myra), and the sunken ruins (Batık Şehir) on **Kekova Adası** island. A swim near the ruins is included.

KAŞ TO ANTALYA

Hugging a coast backed by pine-clad mountains, the main road goes east from Kaş and then north to Antalya, passing a dozen ruined cities. From ancient times until the 1970s, virtually all transport to this region was by sea.

The modern towns built over or near the ancient ones are still deeply involved in maritime life.

Demre (Kale)

Demre (ancient Myra, also known as Kale), set in a rich alluvial plain covered in greenhouses, is interesting because of its generous 4th-century bishop, later canonised as St Nicholas, the original Father Christmas or Santa Claus.

For a lofty US$3 you can visit the restored 12th-century **Church of St Nicholas** (Noel Baba), which was built to hold his tomb; save your money, there's little to see inside. Two km inland from the church at Demre there is a rock face honeycombed with ancient **tombs**, right next to a large **Roman theatre**. Both are open from 7.30 am to 7 pm in summer; entry is cheap at US$1. Demre's telephone code is ☎ 242.

Most people don't stay overnight here, but if you do, head straight for the **Kekova Pansiyon** (☎ 871 2804), İlkokul Caddesi 38, 800 metres south of the main square past the otogar towards the beach. Clean and friendly, it costs only US$6/9 for singles/doubles with good bathroom facilities; excellent buffet meals are served as well. If it's full, try the neighbouring *Otel Topçu* (☎ 871 2200). The pricier *Hotel Simge* (☎ 871 3674), a block east of the main square near the PTT, charges US$20 for doubles with balconies, bathrooms and breakfast, but it needs updating.

As for meals, the *Şehir* and *Çinar* near the main square provide basic sustenance. In high season, better fare is offered five km west at **Çayağzı**, the ancient Andriake, Demre's harbour, where the beach, the views and the food are fine.

Finike

Known as Phoenicus in ancient times, Finike, 30 km east of Demre past wide beaches and along twisting mountain roads, is an attractive little town living on a mixture of farming, fishing and tourism. Small pensions and hotels provide for travellers, some of whom come to enjoy the vast 15-km-long pebble beach at **Sahilkent**, east of the town.

Olimpos & the Chimaera

After climbing into the mountains, you reach the turn-off for Olimpos. From here it's just over eight km down a winding, unpaved road

to the village, and a further 3.5 km along an ever-worsening road to the site of ancient Olimpos. Wild and abandoned, the Olimpos ruins peek out from forest copses, rock outcrops and riverbanks. A few small restaurants provide simple fare. Perfect for the rough camper, the beach is magnificent, although pebbly.

Çavuşköy/Adrasan, a cove to the east, has half a dozen hotels and pensions, ranging from very simple to quite comfortable.

According to legend, the Chimaera (Yanartaş), a natural eternal flame, was the hot breath of a subterranean monster. Easily sighted by mariners in ancient times, it's a mere glimmer of its former self today. Even so, it is a wonder, a flame which, when extinguished, always reignites.

Turn off the highway less than a km east of the eastern Olimpos turn-off; the road is marked for **Çıralı**, seven km towards the sea. To see the Chimaera, go three km east from Çıralı down a neighbouring valley. If you're driving, park at the end of the valley, then follow the signs for the half-hour climb.

Çıralı has lots of good cheap pensions and camping grounds, including the *Barış*, *Sahil* and *Bizim Cennet*, all charging US$4 or US$5 per person. Keep walking westwards for the small but friendly *Rüya Pansiyon* (☎ 242-825 7055), tucked away behind a school, and for the *Blue Blue Pansiyon* (☎ 242-825 7013). The *Florya Pension* trumpets its healthy food as a selling point.

Phaselis

Two km from the highway, Phaselis is a collection of ruins framing three small, perfect bays. It's a good place for a swim and a picnic. The ruins are open from 7.30 am to 7 pm in summer; entry costs US$1.

Kemer

Built to the specifications of resort planners and architects, Kemer was custom-made for the package-holiday traveller. Its white buildings and straight streets seem sterile, but there's a nice little beach by the marina and, above it, **Yörük Park** (Nomad Park), showing aspects of the region's traditional life. Kemer's telephone code is ☎ 242.

The place to stay here is the *King's Garden Pension* (☎ 814 1039), on the north side of

TURKEY

town, 400 metres north-east of the minibus station. From June to September double rooms with compulsory full board cost US$40 (US$20 for B&B at other times). You can camp in the grounds of the King's Garden for US$4 a tent. Too much? Then cross the canal and look for the *Portakal Pansiyon* (☎ 814 4701), opposite, which charges about US$15 for a double room with breakfast.

ANTALYA

The main town along the coast, Antalya has one of the most attractive harbour settings in the Mediterranean. It's fun to kick around in **Kaleiçi**, the old restored Ottoman town by the Roman harbour – now the yacht marina. The **bazar** is interesting and the archaeological museum outstanding. The best **beaches** are out of town, to the west (Konyaaltı Plajı, a pebble beach) and the east (Lara Plajı, a sand beach).

Orientation & Information

The main otogar is four km north of the centre on the D 650 highway to Burdur. The city centre is at Kalekapısı, a major intersection right next to Cumhuriyet Meydanı, with its dramatic equestrian statue of Atatürk. Kaleiçi, the old town, is south of Kalekapısı down the hill.

The Doğu Garaj (eastern otogar) is 600 metres east of Kalekapısı along Ali Çetinkaya Caddesi. Atatürk Caddesi, 100 metres east of Kalekapısı, goes south past Hadriyanüs Kapısı (Hadrian's Gate). A bit further along is the pleasant Karaalioğlu Park.

There are two tourist offices. One (☎ 247 6298) is in Kaleiçi on Mermerli Sokak across from the Hotel Aspen. The other (☎ 241 1747), at Cumhuriyet Caddesi 2, is 250 metres west of Kalekapısı (look for the sign 'Antalya Devlet Tiyatrosu' on the right-hand side; it's in this building). The Turkish Airlines office (☎ 241 0558) is in the same building. The central post office is around the corner on Anafartalar Caddesi.

Antalya's telephone code is ☎ 242.

Owl Bookshop, Akarçeşme Sokak 21 in Kaleiçi, offers a rare (for Turkey) chance to buy or exchange books in English.

Things to See & Do

Antalya's single most important sight is the **Antalya Museum**, west along Cumhuriyet Caddesi (catch a dolmuş from Kalekapısı). It houses the finds from Perge and some wonderful ethnographical exhibits; it's open daily from 9 am to 5 pm (closed Monday) and admission is US$2.

Ancient monuments are also scattered in and around Kaleiçi. **Hadriyanüs Kapısı** (Hadrian's Gate) was built for the Roman emperor's visit in 130 AD. Behind the clock tower is Antalya's graceful symbol, the **Yivli Minare** (Grooved Minaret), which rises above an old building, once a mosque and now a fine-arts gallery. In Kaleiçi, the **Kesik Minare** (Truncated Minaret) marks a ruined Roman temple.

From Antalya you can also visit Termessos, Perge, Aspendos and other sites in the region.

Places to Stay

The *Parlar Mocamp*, 14 km north on the Burdur highway (D 650), has unshaded tent and van sites. *Camping Bambus* (☎ 321 5263), on the road to Lara Plajı, has modern facilities on the beach.

Kaleiçi is full of pensions; find them by following the little signs. *Garden Pansiyon* (☎ 247 1930), Zafer Sokak 16 (or Hesapçı 44), has a few US$9 rooms, but most have showers and cost US$18, including breakfast. The *Bahar Aile Pansiyon* (☎ 248 2089), Akarçeşme Sokak 5, is unrestored and frankly unattractive, but its simple, basic, clean, waterless rooms are low in price at US$12 a double. The showers are clean. Other cheap places include *Adler* (☎ 241 7818) at Civelek Sokak 16, and the *Saltur Pansion* (☎ 247 6238), on the corner of Hesapçı and Hıdırlık sokaks, charging US$15 for a double with shower and breakfast. The *Bermuda* and *Senem* across the street are also good bets.

For a bit more money Kaleiçi has many other beautiful pensions and hotels, including the prettily decorated *Atelya Pension* (☎ 241 6416) at Civelek Sokak 21, where doubles cost US$26 including breakfast.

Pricier but worth it is the *Frankfurt Pansiyon* (☎ 247 6224), Hıdırlık Sokak 25, a spotless place charging US$28/38 for a single/double.

Places to Eat

Many pensions serve good meals at decent prices; ask at yours.

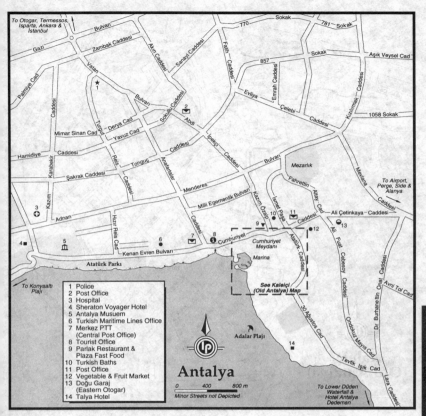

Antalya

Map legend:
1 Police
2 Post Office
3 Hospital
4 Sheraton Voyager Hotel
5 Antalya Musuem
6 Turkish Maritime Lines Office
7 Merkez PTT (Central Post Office)
8 Tourist Office
9 Parlak Restaurant & Plaza Fast Food
10 Turkish Baths
11 Post Office
12 Vegetable & Fruit Market
13 Doğu Garaj (Eastern Otogar)
14 Talya Hotel

0   400   800 m
Minor Streets not Depicted

See Kaleiçi (Old Antalya) Map

TURKEY

Eski Sebzeciler İçi Sokak, a short street just south-west of the junction of Cumhuriyet and Atatürk caddesis, is filled with open-air restaurants where a kebab, salad and drink can cost as little as US$4. The speciality is Antalya's own tandır kebap (mutton cooked in an earthenware pot), but döner kebap is also served.

Cheaper meals are to be had on a back street running from near Eski Sebzeciler İçi Sokak to Kalekapısı. Try the **Surkent Restaurant** for cheap lahmacun (pizza) and pide, the nearby **Sultanyar** for more substantial meals.

For grills, you can't beat the **Parlak Restaurant** (☎ 241 6553), a block up Kazım Özalp/Şarampol Caddesi on the left. Skewered chickens and lamb kebabs sizzle as patrons drink rakı and beer. A full meal of appetisers, grills and drinks costs from US$8 to US$12 a person. The neighbouring **Plaza Fast Food** is the sanitised version of the Parlak.

Getting There & Away

Turkish Airlines has flights daily from Antalya to Ankara and İstanbul, and flights weekly to Amman, Lefkoşa (Nicosia), London, Tel Aviv and Zürich. İstanbul Airlines also has frequent flights to İstanbul. The airport bus costs US$1, a taxi about $10, or take any eastbound minibus and walk the final two km.

Beach buses leave from the Doğu Garaj on

TURKEY

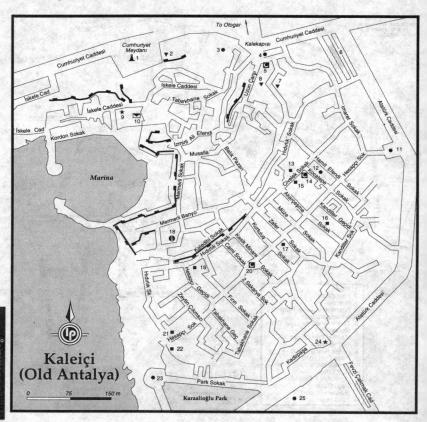

**Kaleiçi
(Old Antalya)**

0   75   150 m

Ali Çetinkaya Caddesi – the Konyaaltı minibus goes west, the Lara minibus east. You can get to the local ruins from here too: take an 'Aksu' dolmuş for Perge, or a 'Manavgat' for Side.

From the otogar, hourly buses go to Alanya (two hours, US$4), Konya (six hours, US$12), Nevşehir (for Cappadocia; nine hours, US$18), Side (1½ hours, US$3), and other towns.

AROUND ANTALYA

This stretch of coast has plenty more Greek and Roman ruins if you can take them. **Perge**, 15 km east of Antalya just north of Aksu, includes a 12,000-seat stadium and a theatre for 15,000.

Aspendos, 47 km east of Antalya, has Turkey's best preserved ancient theatre, dating from the 2nd century AD; it is still used for performances during the Antalya Festival in September. **Termessos**, high in the mountains off the Korkuteli road, has a spectacular setting and demands some vigorous walking and climbing if you want to see it all.

SİDE

Once an idyllic seaside village, Side (pronounced 'SEE-deh') has been overrun by tourists and by carpet and leather shops. Once the main slave market at this end of the Mediterranean and a base for pirates, it's now a

PLACES TO STAY		7	Sultanyar Restaurant	11	Hadriyanüs Kapısı
13	Adler Pension	8	Surkent Restaurant		(Hadrian's Gate)
15	Atelya Pension			12	Sefa Hamamí (Turkish
16	Bahar Aile Pansiyon	**OTHER**			Bath)
17	Garden Pansiyon	1	Atatürk Statue	14	Mosque
19	Frankfurt Pansiyon	3	Yivli Minare (Grooved	18	Tourist Office
21	Bermuda Pension		Minaret)	20	Kesik Minare & Korkut
22	Saltur Pension	4	Saat Kulesi (Clock		Camii
			Tower)	23	Hıdırlık Kulesi
PLACES TO EAT		5	Tepedelenli Ali Paşa		(Tower)
2	Hisar Restaurant		Camii	24	Police
6	Eski Sebzeciler İçi	9	Tourist Police	25	Belediye (Town
	Sokak (Meat	10	Post Office		Hall)
	Restaurants)				

tawdry, overcrowded caricature of its former self which you might prefer to visit as a day trip. Its impressive ancient structures include a **Roman bath** (now an excellent museum, open from 8 am to 5.15 pm daily; admission US$2), the old **city walls**, a huge **amphitheatre** (open from 8 am to 5.15 pm daily; US$2) and seaside marble **temples** to Apollo and Athena. Its excellent beaches are packed in summer.

The village is three km south of the highway from Manavgat; minibuses (70 cents) will run you between the two. Heading for Antalya or Alanya it's usually best to travel via Manavgat. The tourist office (☎ 242-753 1265) is on the road into town, 1.5 km from the village centre.

The village itself is packed willy-nilly with pensions and hotels which fill up quickly in summer. Most attractive are the ones near the sea behind the Apollo temple (there's camping in the grounds of the *Micro Pansiyon*), but there are cheaper offerings near the theatre and, less conveniently, on the road into town from Manavgat. The larger hotels and motels are east and west of the town along the beaches.

ALANYA

Dominated by the ruins of a magnificent Seljuk fortress perched high on a promontory, Alanya is second only to Antalya as a Turkish Mediterranean resort. Indeed, it was a resort in the 13th century, when the Seljuk sultans came down from Konya for sun and fun. Once a pretty, easy-going place, it has grown in recent years into a big, bustling and noisy city. The good beaches to the east and west are now lined with hotels.

The otogar is three km west of the centre; you can get to town in a dolmuş or a municipal bus – disembark at the roundabout by the little mosque. Downhill towards the big mosque is the old waterfront area with trendy shops, good food and a few cheap hotels. The tourist office (☎ 513 1240) is on Kalearkası Caddesi, on the western side of the promontory. Alanya's telephone code is ☎ 242.

Things to See & Do

If you stop here, visit the Seljuk Turkish **Kızıl Kule** (Red Tower, built in 1226), down by the harbour. It's open from 8 am to noon and from 1.30 to 5 pm (closed on Monday); entry is US$2. Also worth checking out is the *kale* (fortress, also built in 1226) atop the promontory. It's open from 8 am to 7 pm daily and entry is US$2. The hyper-touristy **Damlataş Mağarası** (Dripping Stones Cave), good for asthma sufferers, is on the western side of the promontory, near the tourist office and the **museum**. Hire a boat (US$17 to US$27) for an excursion to other caves beneath the promontory.

Places to Stay

Camping is available at the Forestry Department site of İncekum, 19 km west of town. Sad to say, cheap accommodation has virtually disappeared as pensions give way to self-catering flats for package holiday-makers.

There are a couple of places left on noise-ridden İskele Caddesi, above the harbour. *Baba Hotel* (☎ 513 1032), at No 6, has cheap doubles with/without bath for US$16/13. The adjacent *Alanya Palas* (☎ 513 1016) is similar. The *Hotel Emek* (☎ 512 1223) at İskele Caddesi 12, has rooms with bath and balcony for US$18. The *Çınar Otel* (☎ 512 0063),

TURKEY

Hürriyet Meydanı 6, on the plaza just north of the Hotel Baba, rents basic rooms for US$12/9 a double with/without shower.

Places to Eat

The best area for cheap food is between the first two waterfront streets, near the big mosque, where the alleys are filled with tables and chairs. Most places here will give you a big döner kebap, salad and beer for US$4.50. The *Yönet* and *Mahperi* along the waterfront promenade are worth visiting for evening meals (around US$8 to US$12).

THE EASTERN COAST

East of Alanya the coast sheds some of its touristic freight. Seven km east of **Anamur** there is a wonderful castle (Mamure Kalesi, built by the emirs of Karaman in 1230); there are pensions and camping grounds nearby. The ghostly ruins of Byzantine **Anamurium** are 8.5 km west of the town.

Silifke has a crusader castle and a ruined Roman temple, but is mostly a transport hub. At **Taşucu**, 11 km south-west of Silifke, boats and hydrofoils depart daily for Girne (Kyrenia) in Turkish Cyprus. **Kızkalesi** (Maiden's Castle) is a small holiday town with a striking crusader castle offshore. **Mersin** is a modern city of no great interest apart from being a port for car ferries to Famagusta (Magosa) in Turkish Cyprus. **Tarsus**, just east of Mersin, was the birthplace of St Paul and the place where Antony first ran into Cleopatra. Little is left to testify to these events, however. Smoky industry prevails.

Adana is the country's fourth-largest city, an important agricultural centre and a major bus interchange for eastern Turkey.

HATAY

South-east of Adana, a tongue of Turkish territory licks at the mountains of north-western Syria: the land is called Hatay. You'll pass several impressive castles on the way to the port city and pipeline terminus of **İskenderun** (formerly Alexandretta), where Alexander the Great defeated the Persians and Jonah is thought to have been coughed up by the whale.

Antakya

This is the biblical Antioch, where St Peter did a spell of converting. It was said to be the Roman Empire's most depraved city. You can see St Peter's church, the **Senpiyer Kilisesi**, three km outside the town, for free. **Antakya Museum** boasts some of the world's best Roman mosaics (open 8 am to noon and 1.30 to 5 pm, closed on Monday; entry costs US$2.50). Buses run from here to Aleppo and Damascus in Syria.

The provincial tourist office (☎ 216 0610) is one km north of the museum. Antakya's telephone code is ☎ 326.

Cheap hotels are south of the otogar. The *Jasmin Hotel* (☎ 212 7171), İstiklal Caddesi 14, has decent double rooms with shared baths for US$12. *Hotel Güney* (☎ 214 9713), İstiklal Sokak 28, is one narrow street east of İstiklal Caddesi. Big, bright and bare, it serves mostly Turkish families, who spend US$10 for a double without shower, or US$14 with one. The *Divan Oteli* (☎ 215 1518), İstiklal Caddesi 62, charges about the same, and the cross-ventilation is fairly good.

Hotel Orontes (☎ 214 5931), İstiklal Caddesi 58, is the best mid-range choice, with air-con singles/doubles at US$24/34, some with river views.

Central Anatolia

İstanbul may be exotic and intriguing, the coasts may be pretty and relaxing, but it's the Anatolian plateau which is Turkey's heartland, as Atatürk acknowledged when he moved the capital to Ankara. Don't think of this area as a great central nothingness; cruise across the undulating steppe to Cappadocia and you'll be amazed by a region that looks as if it belongs in another world.

ANKARA

The capital of Turkey since 1923, Ankara's site was a Hittite settlement nearly 4000 years ago. It's not an especially exciting city, but because of its central location there's a good chance you'll at least pass through here.

Orientation

Atatürk Bulvarı is the city's main north-south axis. Ankara's mammoth otogar is 6.5 km south-west of Ulus, the historic centre, and six

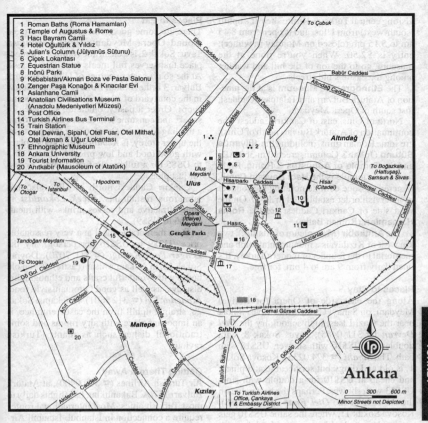

1 Roman Baths (Roma Hamamları)
2 Temple of Augustus & Rome
3 Hacı Bayram Camii
4 Hotel Oğultürk & Yıldız
5 Julian's Column (Jülyanüs Sütunu)
6 Çiçek Lokantası
7 Equestrian Statue
8 İnönü Parkı
9 Kebabistan/Akman Boza ve Pasta Salonu
10 Zenger Paşa Konağı & Kınacılar Evi
11 Aslanhane Camii
12 Anatolian Civilisations Museum
   (Anadolu Medeniyetleri Müzesi)
13 Post Office
14 Turkish Airlines Bus Terminal
15 Train Station
16 Otel Devran, Sipahi, Otel Fuar, Otel Mithat,
   Otel Akman & Uğur Lokantası
17 Ethnographic Museum
18 Ankara University
19 Tourist Information
20 Anıtkabir (Mausoleum of Atatürk)

km west of Kızılay, the modern centre. The Turkish Airlines city bus terminal is next to the train station *(gar)*, 1.4 km south-west of Ulus.

Opera Meydanı (Opera Square, also called İtfaiye Meydanı), just south of Ulus, has lots of cheap hotels.

The diplomatic area is Çankaya, five km south of Kızılay, and the adjoining districts of Gaziosmanpaşa and Kavaklıdere.

Information
The tourist office (☎ 229 2631) is on the square called Tandoğan Meydanı. The main post office is on Atatürk Bulvarı just south of Ulus,

although there's a handy branch beside the train station where you can also change cash and travellers' cheques. In an emergency, you could try the tourist police at Boncuk Sokak 10/2, but the tourist office is probably a better bet.

Ankara's telephone code is ☎ 312.

Things to See
The **Anatolian Civilisations Museum** (Anadolu Medeniyetleri Müzesi), on Hisarparkı Caddesi, is Ankara's most worthwhile attraction. With the world's richest collection of Hittite artefacts, it's an essential supplement to

visiting central Turkey's Hittite sites. It's uphill (south-west) from Ulus, and is open from 8.45 am to 5.15 pm (closed on Monday in winter); entry is $2.50. When you're done at the museum, go to the top of the hill and wander among the castle's old streets.

The **Ethnographic Museum** is at the junction of Atatürk Bulvarı and Talatpaşa Caddesi, just south of Opera Meydanı.

North of Ulus, east of Çankırı Caddesi (the continuation of Atatürk Bulvarı north of Ulus), are some Roman ruins, including the **Jülyanüs Sütunu** (Julian's Column, erected in 363 AD) and the **Temple of Augustus & Rome**. Right next to the temple is the **Hacı Bayram Camii**, a sacred mosque commemorating the founder of a dervish order established in 1400. On the west side of Çankırı Caddesi are the **Roma Hamamları** (Roman Baths).

The **Anıtkabir** (Mausoleum of Atatürk), two km west of Kızılay, is a monumental tomb and memorial to the founder of modern Turkey. It's open daily from 9 am to 4 pm, for free.

Places to Stay

Along the east side of Opera (or İtfaiye) Meydanı, on Sanayi Caddesi and Tavus Sokak near the Gazi Lisesi high school, try the *Otel Devran* (☎ 311 0485), Tavus Sokak 8, with doubles for US$16 with shower, US$18 with bath. The *Sipahi* (☎ 324 0235), Kosova Sokak 1, is old and dingy but serviceable at a pinch, and cheap at US$10 for a double with sink, US$13 with shower. Perhaps the best value on the street is at the *Otel Fuar* (☎ 312 3288), Kosova Sokak 11, where the same US$10 gets you a decent double room with sink, with showers down the hall.

For more comfort, the *Otel Mithat* (☎ 311 5410), Tavus Sokak 2, has shower-equipped doubles for US$18, and is a better choice than the adjoining *Otel Akman* (☎ 324 4140), Tavus Sokak 6, which charges more.

North of Ulus and one street west of Çankırı Caddesi, the three-star *Hotel Oğultürk* (☎ 309 2900), Rüzgarlı Eşdost Sokak 6, has singles/doubles with TV and minibar for US$26/40, breakfast included. The nearby *Yıldız* (☎ 312 7581) is similar.

In 'new' Ankara south of Kızılay, the one-star *Hotel Ergen* (☎ 417 5906), Karanfil Sokak 48, near Olgunlar Sokak, charges US$30/42 a single/double with bath.

Places to Eat

There are some good, cheap spots for a meal around Opera Meydanı. *Uğur Lokantası*, Tavus Sokak 2, is a clean aile (family-oriented) place that serves full meals for US$5 or less. At the south-eastern corner of Ulus at Atatürk Bulvarı 3 is the *Akman Boza ve Pasta Salonu*, in the courtyard of a huge block of offices and shops. Order a pastry, omelette, sandwich or snack, and consume it at terrace tables around a tinkling fountain. Overlooking this place, on the upper storey, is *Kebabistan*, a kebab place with good food and low prices – about US$3 to US$5 for a full meal of roast lamb, or less for just pide.

Çankırı Caddesi north of Ulus also has numerous restaurants. *Çiçek Lokantası* is quite attractive and serves drinks with meals (US$6 to US$9).

For a memorable meal at a very reasonable price (US$9 to US$16 per person), try the *Zenger Paşa Konağı* (☎ 311 7070), Doyran Sokak 13, in Ankara's hisar (castle). It's an old house with wonderful crafts and ethnographic displays, as well as good Ottoman-style food. *Kınacılar Evi* (☎ 312 5601), Kalekapısı Sokak 28, straight uphill from the castle entrance, is an imposing place with airy rooms and some traditional dishes such as mantı (Turkish ravioli).

Getting There & Away

Air Turkish Airlines (☎ 309 0400), at Atatürk Bulvarı 167/A, Bakanlıklar, has flights daily to most Turkish cities. Most international routes require a connection in İstanbul. İstanbul Airlines (☎ 432 2234), Atatürk Bulvarı 83, Kızılay, serves several Turkish cities, but more foreign ones.

Bus Ankara's huge otogar (AŞTİ) is the vehicular heart of the nation, with coaches to all places day and night. For İstanbul (six hours, US$9 to US$20) they go at least every 15 minutes. Other coaches go to Antalya (10 hours, US$17), Bodrum (13 hours, US$20), Erzurum (15 hours, US$23), İzmir (8½ hours, US$14.50 to US$20) and Ürgüp/Cappadocia (five hours, US$9).

Train Seven express trains, two of them with sleeping cars, connect Ankara and İstanbul

(7½ to 11 hours, US$12 to US$15). The Fatih and Başkent express trains are the fastest and most expensive.

The *İzmir Mavi Tren* (14 hours, US$13) hauls sleeping and dining cars. The evening *İzmir Ekspresi* (15 hours) has 1st and 2nd-class carriages (US$15 and US$13).

Trains heading east of Ankara are not as comfortable or as punctual as those travelling westward. The *Doğu Ekspresi*, hauling carriages and sleeping cars, departs each evening for Erzincan, Erzurum (25 hours; US$15, or US$32 for a bed) and Kars. On alternate mornings the *Güney Ekspresi* departs for Diyarbakır (26½ hours, US$15), and the *Vangölü Ekspresi* departs for Tatvan (31 hours, US$16); both haul sleeping cars (US$35).

Getting Around

To/From the Airport Ankara's Esenboğa airport is 33 km north of the city centre. Havaş buses (40 minutes in light traffic, US$3.50) depart from the Turkish Airlines city terminal at the train station 1½ hours before domestic and two hours before international Turkish Airlines flights. A taxi costs US$20 or more. Cheaper shared taxis run from the train station to the airport as well.

Local Transport Ankara's metro (underground transit system) is under construction. Many city buses run the length of Atatürk Bulvarı. Buy a *bilet* (ticket, 50 cents) from kiosks by bus stops, or from a shop with the sign 'EGO Bilet(i)'.

City bus No 198 departs from the otogar headed for the train station and Ulus; bus No 623 goes via Kızılay to Gazıler.

Taxis are multitudinous, suicidal and metered, charging about US$3 for an average ride, or US$4 to US$6 from one end of the city to the other.

BOĞAZKALE

The Hittites ruled central Anatolia from about 2000 to 1180 BC. To see where they lived, visit Boğazkale, 29 km off the Ankara-Samsun road. Called Hattuşaş in Hittite, this was the ancient capital of the Hittites until it was destroyed by the Phrygians.

Today there's little left apart from the walls and foundations of buildings. But what walls! Crumbling though they are, they stretch for over 10 km and have five entrances, including the **Kral Kapı** (King's Gate), the **Aslanlı Kapı** (Lion Gate) and an underground tunnel, **Yer Kapı**.

The massive, imposing foundations are also inspiring. Largest is the site of the **Büyük Mabed** (Great Temple of the Storm God), which has no fewer than 70 storerooms. The natural rock temple of **Yazılıkaya**, two km from the main site, has bas-reliefs of Hittite deities carved into the rock face.

Alacahöyük, 36 km from Boğazkale near the main road, is a pre-Hittite site, probably 6000 years old. The remains, however, including the **Sphinx Gate**, are Hittite.

To get to the sites, take a bus to Sungurlu, from where there should be minibuses to Boğazkale and Alacahöyük. Both villages have small **museums**.

Several small hotels with camping facilities open in Boğazkale in summer.

KONYA

Known as Iconium in Roman times, Konya is a humourless, conservative place, but it's one of the oldest continually occupied cities in the world, and a showplace for some striking Seljuk architecture. It was the capital of the Seljuk Turks, and it was here, in the 13th century, that the poet Celaleddin Rumi (Mevlana) founded the whirling dervishes, one of Islam's major mystical orders. Atatürk put a stop to the whirling except as 'folk dance'; you can see it here in May and during the **Mevlana Festival** every December.

Mevlana's **tomb** is topped by the brilliant green-tiled tower near the tourist office (☎ 332-351 1074) and hotel area; it's now the **Mevlana Müzesi**, open from 9 am to 5.30 pm daily (10 am to 5.30 pm Monday); 50 cents entry. Other fine Seljuk buildings include the **Karatay Müzesi**, once a Muslim theological seminary, now a ceramics museum, and the **İnce Minare Medresesi**, now a wood and stone-carving museum.

If you're staying, good budget places near the Mevlana Müzesi are the *Mavi Köşk* (☎ 332-350 1904) and *Derviş* (☎ 332-351 1688) hotels, side by side in Bostan Çelebi Sokak and both charging US$9/11 a single/double. Just doors away from them is *Öztemel Konya Fırın Kebap Salonu*, where you can

TURKEY

sample Konya's own fırın kebap (oven-roasted mutton) with a soft drink for US$4. The otogar is 3.5 km north of the city centre. Minibuses will ferry you to the town centre for 25 cents.

CAPPADOCIA

South-east of Ankara, almost in the centre of the country, the Cappadocia (Kapadokya in Turkish) region is famous for the fantastic natural **rock formations** of its valleys. Over the centuries people have carved rooms, houses, churches, fortresses and even complete underground cities into the soft, eerily eroded volcanic stone.

Attractions include the Göreme, Zelve and Soğanlı valleys with their scores of rock-cut chapels (early Christian monastics sought refuge throughout the region); the fortress towns of Uçhisar and Ortahisar; the huge underground cities at Kaymaklı and Derinkuyu (open from 8 am to 5 pm, to 6.30 pm in summer; US$2.50 entry); and rugged Ihlara Valley (south of Aksaray) dotted with ancient churches.

Nevşehir is the biggest town. Ürgüp has a good selection of hotels and pensions, but Göreme village is more attractive to budget travellers.

Transport is easy between Nevşehir and everywhere else, and buses run on the hour between Avanos and Ürgüp, stopping in Göreme.

Nevşehir

A loud, unattractive provincial capital, Nevşehir is good for information and for transport connections. Catch minibuses here for the astonishing underground cities of **Derinkuyu** and **Kaymaklı**, and for the rock-carved monasteries and churches, Hittite traces and interesting mosques much further south at **Niğde**.

Nevşehir's tourist office (☎ 384-213 3659) is sympathetic to budget travellers.

Göreme

The Göreme Valley is one of the most amazing sights in Turkey. Over the centuries a thick layer of volcanic tufa has eroded into fantastic shapes. Early Christians carved cross-shaped churches, stables and homes into the cliffs and cones. Painted **church murals** date from as

early as the 8th century, though the best are from the 10th to 13th centuries; unlit for many centuries, they've hardly faded at all, although vandals have left their indelible mark. The best are those in the **Göreme Open-Air Museum** (Göreme Açık Hava Müzesi), which is open from 8 am to 5.30 pm (4.30 pm in winter) daily; entry is US$5.

Altogether there are several dozen churches, a monastery and a nunnery in the valley. Less crowded is the **Zelve Valley**, east of the Göreme-Avanos road.

Three km south-west of Göreme village is picturesque **Uçhisar**, a town built around, and into, a prominent peak. A room-to-room scramble through its rock citadel leads to fine views from the summit. There's a similar complex south-east of Göreme at **Ortahisar**.

Göreme's telephone code is ☎ 384.

Good, reasonably priced tours of the region are offered by Turtle Tours (☎ 271 2388) across the road from Göreme otogar; and Hiro Tour (☎ 271 2542), in the otogar.

Places to Stay & Eat You can camp in the gardens of many pensions, or at the *Dilek* or *Berlin* camping grounds, side by side amid wonderful rock formations on the road leading from Göreme village to the open-air museum.

The many pensions in Göreme village charge identical rates of US$3.50 per bed in a dorm, US$4.50 in a waterless private room, or US$7 per bed with private facilities. One of the most popular is *Köse* (☎ 271 2294), on the right side of the flood channel, with a good café and a book-exchange scheme. Other favourites are the *Tan* (☎ 271 2445), *Rock Valley* (☎ 271 2153), *Paradise* (☎ 271 2248), *Ufuk* (☎ 271 2157), and the *Peri* (☎ 271 2136). The pretty *Cave Hotel Melek* (☎ 271 2463), high on the valley wall, has rock-cut waterless double rooms for US$10, or US$16 with private bath; breakfast is included. The aptly named *Ottoman House* (☎ 271 2616) offers luxury at affordable prices: US$9 a head.

Restaurants offering standard fare at slightly above average prices are clustered around the otogar. For a splurge, head uphill to the **Konak Türk Evi**, where a 19th-century paşa's house is now a fine restaurant. Expect to pay around US$8 to US$15 to dine in such opulence.

Avanos

On the north bank of the Kızılırmak (Red River), Avanos is known for its pottery, onyx and carved alabaster. Pensions here tend to be cheaper than in Göreme. Good value is *Kirkit Pansiyon* (☎ 511 3148), where beds cost US$6 in waterless doubles (US$8 with shower), breakfast included; from the tourist office (☎ 511 4360) at the northern end of the bridge, walk east and bear left at the first alley.

Other cheapies in the old town up behind the main square include the basic *Nomade* and the slightly cheerier *Panorama* and *Kervan*, all with doubles for US$6 to US$8. Moving up the price and comfort scale, the *Sofa Motel* (☎ 511 4489), across the bridge from the tourist office, has tastefully decorated rooms in a group of old houses for US$15/20 a single/double with private bath.

Avanos' telephone code is ☎ 384.

Ürgüp

In spite of heavy tourist traffic (Ürgüp seems to be the base for tour groups in Cappadocia), this low-rise town is still very appealing, with its old sandstone buildings, cobbled streets and a stone hill carved full of rooms and passages. You can go wine-tasting here; Cappadocia's best is bottled at wineries on Mustafapaşa Caddesi and at the top of the hill on the Nevşehir road.

The helpful tourist office (☎ 341 4059) is in the park, downhill from the main square. Ürgüp's telephone code is ☎ 384.

Places to Stay & Eat The *Belde* and *Yeni Hitit* hotels, with singles/doubles for US$10/16, are along Dumlupınar Caddesi, east of the otogar. The *Elvan*, west of the otogar past the Dutlu Cami, has doubles with shower for US$21. Follow Ahmet Refik Caddesi up the hill towards Nevşehir and you'll find *Born Hotel* (☎ 341 4756), an old paşa's house with singles/doubles for US$5/10.

Prettiest of all is the pristine *Esbelli Evi* (☎ 341 3395; fax 341 8848) behind the Turban Hotel, with singles/doubles at US$45/55, excellent breakfast included; reserve in advance.

Good food at reasonable prices can be had in *Sofa Restaurant*, a converted han (caravan-serai) on the main square, or in the newly expanded *Cappadocia Restaurant* beside the belediye (town hall) and just off Dumlupınar Caddesi.

Ihlara Valley

Ihlara is a remote canyon full of carved and painted Byzantine churches – a must for walkers.

The village of Ihlara Köyü is 85 km southwest of Nevşehir and 40 km south-east of Aksaray. *Star Pansiyon*, right in the village, has waterless rooms for US$6 a head. *Anatolia Pansiyon* (☎ 382-453 7128), on the road running along the top of the gorge between Ihlara village and the official entrance, has basic rooms without showers for about US$6 per person, or camping for US$2. There are more pensions and a camp site in the gorge itself at the village of Belisırma.

Ihlara Belediyesi buses run several times daily from Aksaray's otogar, charging 50 cents one way.

Kayseri & Sivas

Sitting in the shadow of snowy Mt Erciyes, Kayseri, known as Caesarea in Roman times, was the provincial capital of Cappadocia. Thankfully, its once notoriously persistent carpet merchants are learning the art of soft sell.

A religiously conservative town, it's full of mosques, tombs and old seminaries *(medrese)*. Near the tourist office (☎ 352-222 3903) is the beautiful **Hunat Hatun** mosque, tomb and seminary (now the Ethnographic Museum).

Opposite, behind the massive 6th-century city walls, are the **bazar** and the **Ulu Cami** (Great Mosque), begun by the Seljuks in 1136. Pride of place goes to the fine decorations on the **Döner Kümbet** (Revolving Tomb), one km south of the tourist office on Talas Caddesi.

Sivas, on the central route through Turkey, has many marvellous Seljuk buildings to prove its past importance as a crossroads on the caravan route to Persia and Baghdad. In 1919 it was the starting point for Atatürk's War of Independence.

The Black Sea Coast

This region is dramatically different from the rest of Turkey – steep and craggy, damp and lush, and isolated by the Pontic Mountains along most of its length. It's the country's dairy

TURKEY

belt, and the area's hazelnuts make Turkey the world's biggest exporter of them. The tea you drink in İstanbul probably comes from east of Trabzon; the cigarette smoke you endure probably comes from tobacco grown west of Samsun.

Legend has it that the coast was first settled by a tribe of Amazons. Its kingdoms have tended to be independent-minded; Trabzon was where the last Byzantines held out against the Ottomans. Even tourism hasn't penetrated far, though you'll find plenty of cheap hotels and camping grounds. Prices are lower than on the Mediterranean coast, and get even lower in the off season. With the exception of Samsun and Trabzon, less English is spoken than in other areas of Turkey.

Partly because of heavy industry around Zonguldak, the coast west from Sinop to the Bosphorus is almost unknown to tourists, though the fishing port of **Amasra**, with its Roman and Byzantine ruins, and **Safranbolu** and **Bartın**, with their traditional timber houses, are worth a look.

Good long-distance bus lines here are Ulusoy and Aydın, but there's plenty of much cheaper town-to-town dolmuş transport. On your way to the coast, stop at **Amasya**, an old Ottoman town in a dramatic mountain setting.

SİNOP

This fishing and boat-building town, three hours by bus west of Samsun, was the birthplace of Diogenes, the cynic philosopher. Thanks to the development of Samsun's harbour, Sinop is a fine little backwater now. There are miles of beaches on both sides of the peninsula.

SAMSUN

Under the Seljuks, Samsun was a major trading port and had its own Genoese colony. When the Ottomans looked set to capture it in the 15th century, the Genoese burned the city to the ground before fleeing. There's little of interest here now, but it's a good starting point for travel along the coast and a port of call for the ferry from İstanbul.

Atatürk landed here on 19 May 1919 to begin the Turkish War of Independence. The otogar is three km east of town by dolmuş.

SAMSUN TO TRABZON

There are excellent beaches (but chilly water) around the cheerful resort town of **Ünye**, on a wide bay 85 km east of Samsun.

Beaches are the only reason to stop in the glum town of **Ordu**, 80 km east of Ünye. There is a tourist office (☎ 452-223 1607) half a block east of the central Atatürk statue and mosque.

Europe's first cherry trees came from **Giresun** courtesy of Lucullus, the Roman general and famous epicure, and the town is still surrounded by cherry orchards.

Dramatic remains of a big Byzantine fortress are on a headland beside the friendly village of **Akçakale**, 22 km west of Trabzon.

TRABZON

Trabzon is certainly the most interesting place on the Turkish Black Sea coast, with mild weather, good-natured people, lots of Byzantine architecture, beaches and the amazing Sumela Monastery. Known as Trebizond in Byzantine times, this town was the last to fall to the Ottoman Turks, and earlier was a stronghold against the Seljuks and Mongols as well.

Orientation & Information

Modern Trabzon is centred on Atatürk Alanı (Atatürk Square), on a steep hill above the harbour. The helpful government tourist office (☎ 321 4659) is on the south side of the square (the Atatürk statue faces east), with a Turkish Maritime Lines (TML or Denizyollari; ☎ 321 7096) agency next door. Up behind it are Ulusoy and Metro bus ticket offices. Turkish Airlines is on the west side of the square. The long-distance otogar is three km east of the port.

Trabzon's telephone code is ☎ 462.

Things to See

A half-hour walk west from Atatürk Alanı the dark walls of the Byzantine city can be found. The **old town**, with its timber houses and stone bridges, still looks medieval.

Trabzon has many **Byzantine churches**. The best preserved, the 13th-century Aya Sofya, is now a museum (open from 8.30 am to 5 pm daily but closed on Monday in winter; entry US$1); take a minibus from Atatürk Alanı. Among its more beautiful Ottoman mosques are the **Gülbahar Hatun Camii** west

TURKEY

of the city walls and the **Çarşı Camii** (or Osmanpaşa Camii) in the bazar. For a look at a beautiful 19th-century villa, visit the **Atatürk Köşkü** high above the town.

Some travellers come to Trabzon just to visit the 14th-century **Sumela Monastery**, built into a cliff face like a swallow's nest. It was inhabited until 1923 and has many fine murals (much damaged by vandals, but being restored) and amazing views. In summer, Ulusoy runs an 11 am bus (returning at 2 and 3 pm) from the town-centre terminal just uphill from the tourist office. The 40-minute trip costs US$4.

Dolmuş depart from the tourist office and charge US$20 for a carload of five to the monastery and back. Entry to Sumela National Park and the monastery is US$2.50.

Places to Stay

Dalyan Camping is nine km west of Trabzon. Just before Dalyan, take the turn-off to Derecik; it's 1.5 km to the camping area at Sera Gölü Lake. On the road to Sumela there's camping two km beyond Maçka in the grounds of the *Coşandere Restaurant*.

Finding a decent cheap hotel is more problematic. Most of the places east of Atatürk Alanı on Güzelhisar Caddesi and adjacent streets are filled with traders and prostitutes from the former Soviet states.

The *Anıl* (☎ 321 9566), Güzelhisar Caddesi 10, has a flashy lobby and fairly clean rooms for US$11/18 a single/double. The *Gözde Aile Oteli* (☎ 321 9579), just off Güzelhisar Caddesi, offers reasonable rooms with sinks and showers, but no toilets, for about US$4 a head. This might be a good choice for lone women, though the *Sankta Maria Katolik Kilisesi Hostel* (☎ 321 2192), Sümer Sokak 26, is better. Built by French Capuchins in 1869 when Trabzon was a cosmopolitan trading port, the hostel offers clean, simple rooms and the use of hot showers in exchange for a donation. You needn't be Catholic to stay here.

Rooms at the family-run *Hotel Benli* (☎ 321 1022), behind the belediye at Cami Çıkmazı Sokak 5, smell a bit. The new *Nur* (☎ 321 2798), opposite, has spotless cell-like rooms with sinks for the same money. US$5/10 a single/double.

Hotel Toros (☎ 321 1212), Gençoğlu Sokak 3/A, has clean doubles with showers for US$14.

Probably the best bet, if you can afford it, is the *Otel Horon* (☎ 321 1199), Sıramağazalar 125, where spotless singles/doubles with shower cost US$30/40.

Places to Eat

Derya Restaurant, across from the belediye on the north-east corner of Atatürk Alanı, has a good selection of ready-made food and serves a tasty İskender kebap for US$3. Look also for the *Volkan 2* a few steps to the west. Close by is the *Tad Pizza ve Hamburger*, a US-style pizza parlour. Pizzas cost US$2.25 to US$3; burgers, half that.

At the nearby *Meydan Kebap Salonu*, have the çevirme piliç (rotisserie chicken). *Murat Balık Salonu*, facing Atatürk Alanı, does a good grilled uskumru (mackerel) for US$1.50 to US$3 per fish, or alabalık (trout) for more.

Across from the tourist office on the south side are the *İnan Kebap Salonu* and the *Çınar Lokantası*, both with a good selection of ready-made meals, best eaten fresh at lunchtime.

At the *Kıbrıs Restaurant* on the east side of the square you can get alcoholic drinks with your meal (US$6 or US$8), as you can at the *Şişman Restaurant*, on Maraş Caddesi just west of the square.

Getting There & Away

Air Turkish Airlines (☎ 321 1680), at the south-west corner of Atatürk Alanı, has flights daily to Ankara and İstanbul. An airport bus (US$1) leaves from outside the office 1½ hours before flights. İstanbul Airlines (☎ 322 3806), Kazazoğlu Sokak 9, Sanat İşhanı, on the north-west corner of Atatürk Alanı, flies four times weekly to İstanbul for a lower fare.

Bus Dolmuş taxis to the otogar leave from just up the hill from the tourist office.

From the otogar, minibuses go every half-hour to Rize (75 km, 1½ hours, US$2), Hopa (165 km, three hours, US$5) and Artvin (255 km, five hours, US$10). A dozen buses a day head for Erzurum (325 km, six hours, US$10), a beautiful but slow ride via Gümüşhane, or an equally beautiful and slow route via Artvin.

Boat See the Getting Around section at the

TURKEY

beginning of this chapter for information about car ferries to İstanbul.

KAÇKAR MOUNTAINS

The eastern end of the coastal mountain range is dominated by 3937-metre Kaçkar Dağı, inland from Rize. Around it are excellent opportunities for camping, wilderness treks, and even white-water rafting on the Çoruh River. There are many small villages with cheap accommodation.

At **Uzungöl**, 50 km east of Trabzon and 50 km inland, is an alpine lake, with camping, bungalows and a few small hotels. A good base for day hikes and trekking towards Kaçkar Dağı is **Ayder**, 40 km east of Rize and 40 km inland, with hot springs as a bonus. Necip in Trabzon tourist office can fill you in on camping, walking and white-water rafting possibilities in the area.

Eastern Turkey

Turkey's eastern region is the harshest, and the hardest, part of the country to travel in, but it rewards visitors with dramatic landscapes – like majestic views of the 5165-metre Mt Ararat (the legendary resting place of Noah's Ark) – and some unusual historical relics. In the winter, bitterly cold weather is imported direct from the Russian steppes, so unless you're well equipped and something of a masochist, avoid travelling here from October to April. For full coverage of this region see Lonely Planet's *Turkey – travel survival kit*.

Warning

In recent years, the Kurdistan People's Party (PKK) has carried out terrorist raids throughout Turkey, but particularly in the east, in pursuit of its goal of an independent Kurdistan. On isolated occasions the PKK have even kidnapped tourists to attract publicity.

At the time of writing, the region was still unstable, with incidents between the Turkish army and guerilla fighters. Check with your embassy or consulate before travelling east, especially to Diyarbakır, Mardin or any points east of them. If you do travel here, stick to the main roads and large towns, and travel only in daylight on recognised bus lines, trains and airlines.

ERZURUM

Eastern Turkey's main transport hub and a military centre, Erzurum is a fairly drab town famous for its harsh climate, although it has some striking Seljuk buildings that justify staying for a day or so.

Orientation & Information

The tourist office (☎ 218 5697) is on Cemal Gürsel Caddesi, the main street, just west of the Atatürk statue, although you may not find anyone there. The otogar is inconveniently located at the edge of town on the airport road, but the town centre itself is compact, with all the main sites within walking distance.

Erzurum's telephone code is ☎ 442.

Things to See & Do

From the well-preserved walls of a 5th-century **Byzantine fortress**, you get a good view of the town's layout and the bleak plains that surround it. The **Cifte Minareli Medrese** (built in 1253) is a seminary famous for its Seljuk architecture. It's beautifully symmetrical, with a classic carved portal flanked by twin minarets which frame a conical dome behind.

The oldest mosque, **Ulu Cami**, built in 1179, is next door. Further west along Cumhuriyet Caddesi, an open square marks the centre of town, with an Ottoman mosque and, at the western corner, another seminary, the **Yakutiye Medresesi**, built by the local Mongol emir in 1310. It's now the Turkish and Islamic Arts and Ethnography Museum, which is open from 8 am to noon and 12.30 to 5 pm (closed Monday); admission is 50 cents.

Take an excursion to **Yusufeli**, north of Erzurum, and neighbouring **Georgian Valleys** to see the ancient churches and to go white-water rafting on the Çoruh River.

Places to Stay

Erzurum has lots of cheapies, although showers and winter heating may cost extra, and some of the places are pretty dismal. The welcoming *Otel Polat* (☎ 218 1623), Kazım Karabekir Caddesi 3, has singles/doubles from US$7/10 and is well situated between the train station and the town centre.

Round the corner the *Hotel Sefer* (☎ 218

6714), İstasyon Caddesi, charges US$10/15/18 a single/double/triple including breakfast. The entrance is decrepit; the guest rooms are better.

Opposite the Yakutiye Medresesi, the *Kral Hotel* (☎ 218 7783) at Erzincankapı 18 has much nicer rooms than the lobby might suggest for US$9/14 a single/double with shower and TV.

The best rooms in town are at the three-star *Otel Oral* (☎ 218 9740), Terminal Caddesi 3, between the otogar and the centre, but they cost a hefty US$36/52, including breakfast, and can be noisy.

Places to Eat

There are a number of reasonable options along Cumhuriyet Caddesi near the Yakutiye Medresesi. *Güzelyurt Restorant*, although tarted up with tablecloths and uniformed waiters, is cheap and good (try the house speciality mantarlı güveç, a delicious lamb stew). Meals cost US$5 to US$8. The *Salon Çağın* and *Salon Asya* on Cumhuriyet are a bit cheaper.

Getting There & Away

Air Turkish Airlines (☎ 218 1904), on 100 Yıl Caddesi at the north-western end of Kazım Karabekir Caddesi, has two flights daily (US$45) to Ankara, with connections to İstanbul and İzmir. The airport bus (50 cents) departs 1½ hours before flight time from the Turkish Airlines office.

Bus Catch a No 2 bus into town from the otogar, which is three km north-east of the town centre.

There are plenty of bus company offices uphill from the train station.

Train The *Doğu Ekspresi* takes 25 hours to get to Ankara – if it's on time (which is rare). The bus is faster.

KARS

About 260 km north-east of Erzurum, this frontier town was much fought over and has a suitably massive fortress. The main reason to come here now is to see the ruins of ancient Ani and look across the border at Armenia. You'll need official permission to visit Ani; ask at the tourist office (☎ 474-223 2724), at Ordu Caddesi 241, but be wary of schemes to charge too much for transport to Ani.

There's not much to do in Kars, although there's a **museum** (closed on Monday), northeast of the train station on Cumhuriyet Caddesi, with exhibits dating from the Bronze Age.

Ani, 44 km east of Kars, was completely deserted in 1239 after a Mongol invasion, but before that it had been a major city and a capital of both the Urartian and Armenian kingdoms. Surrounded by huge walls, the ruins lie in fields overlooking the Arpaçay River, which forms the border with Armenia. The ghost city is extremely dramatic and there are several notable churches, including a cathedral built between 989 and 1010 that was the seat of the Armenian prelate.

DOĞUBEYAZIT

Known jocularly as 'dog biscuit', this drab town, dramatically sited at the far side of a sweeping grass plain that runs to the foot of Mt Ararat, is the departure point for people going to Iran. It doesn't take long to find your bearings, as everything is within a five-minute walk. Apart from spectacular views of Mt Ararat, there's an interesting palace-fort, the **İshak Paşa Sarayı** (open from 7 am to 5 pm; entry US$2), five km east of town. Perched romantically among rocky crags, it overlooks the town and the plains. The occasional dolmuş passes nearby, but unless you want to walk you'll probably have to negotiate for a taxi (about US$5 there and back).

Until recently Doğubeyazıt was also a base for climbing Mt Ararat, but because of the Kurdish revolt the area is now out of bounds to trekkers. Take excursions to the **meteor crater, Diyadin hot springs**, and the supposed resting-place of **Noah's Ark**.

If you decide to stay, the *Hotel İsfahan* (☎ 472-311 5159), Emniyet Caddesi 26, has extremely comfortable rooms (some with real bathtubs) for US$25/38 a single/double. Several smaller hotels nearby provide rooms for US$5 to US$7 a bed.

VAN

The town of Van, on the south-east shore of the vast salt lake of the same name, has a 3000-year-old **citadel** at Van Kalesi (Rock of Van) and a small **museum**. Tourists are beginning to return to Van after years of being scared off by the Kurdish revolt.

TURKEY

The helpful tourist office is at Cumhuriyet Caddesi 127 (☎ 216 2018). The otogar is several km north-west of the centre. Van's telephone code is ☎ 432.

There's a 10th-century church on **Akdamar Island** in the lake. The church is a fascinating piece of Armenian architecture in a beautiful setting, with frescos inside and reliefs outside depicting biblical scenes.

Dolmuş (US$2) from Beş Yol in Van take you to the dock for boats to Akdamar. Unless you can rustle up a group to share costs, expect to pay US$25 to US$35 for a boat.

Places to Stay

Cheap hotels in the bazar (çarşı) charge US$3.50 per person in rooms with sink and/or private shower. Among the better ones are the *İpek Otel* (☎ 216 3033) and the *Lüks Aslan Oteli* (☎ 216 2469), Eski Hal Civarı. The 63-room *Hotel Kent* (☎ 216 2404) charges a bit more for less.

For more comfort, try the places next to the government building (Van Valiliği): *Otel Sirhan* (☎ 214 3463) charges US$28 a double with bath, breakfast included. Avoid rooms right above the nightclub.

Best in town is the 75-room, three-star *Büyük Urartu Oteli* (☎ 212 0660), near the Devlet Hastanesi hospital, overpriced at US$42/60 a single/double.

SOUTH-EASTERN TURKEY

Turkey's south-east corner, along the border with Syria and Iraq, is the region once known as Upper Mesopotamia; it is drained by the historic Tigris (Dicle) and Euphrates (Fırat) rivers. It's the area with the largest Kurdish population and thus the area worst affected by PKK activity and government reprisals. If you do mean to travel here, it's vital to take heed of the warning given at the start of this section.

Nemrut Dağı

North of Şanlıurfa and south of Malatya, pretty much in the middle of nowhere, is Nemrut Dağı (Mt Nimrod), on whose summit is a 2000-year-old **memorial sanctuary** for an obscure Commagene king. It has huge statues of gods and kings, their heads toppled by earthquakes and scattered on the ground.

Malatya tourist office (☎ 422-323 3025), on the first floor of the Vilayet Binası in the main square, arranges minibus trips almost daily for around US$22 per person, including one night in a hotel near the summit. On the south side of the mountain in **Kahta**, the tourist office (☎ 416-725 5007) can help with minibus tours, though you should check around for better prices. All hotels in Kahta, including the *Kommagene* (☎ 715 1092) and *Mezopotamya* (☎ 725 5112), and *Zeus Camping* (☎ 725 5695) arrange tours.

Yugoslavia (Југославија)

The new Federal Republic of Yugoslavia (SRJ), made up of Serbia and Montenegro, occupies the heart of the Balkan Peninsula astride the main road, rail and river routes from Western Europe to Asia Minor.

Since the withdrawal of Croatia, Slovenia, Bosnia-Hercegovina and Macedonia in 1991, Yugoslavia (Jugoslavija) seems to have become a mere 'Greater Serbia', with oppressed Hungarian, Slavic Muslim and Albanian minorities.

This tragic outcome and the continuing ethnic strife have cast a pall over a country still rich in mountains, rivers, seascapes, cultures, customs, cuisines and peoples. Now shorn of most of its coastal tourist resorts, rump Yugoslavia seems destined to be forgotten by the world of mass tourism. However, awaiting those visitors who do stray beyond the transit corridors to Turkey and Greece are the glorious gorges and beaches of Montenegro, the mystical Orthodox monasteries of southern Serbia and Kosovo, the imposing fortresses along the Danube, and hundreds of other tangible traces of a tumultuous history stretching back thousands of years.

In this book we use the term Yugoslavia ('Land of the South Slavs') to refer to either pre-1991 Yugoslavia or present-day Yugoslavia (Serbia and Montenegro), depending on the context. By former or ex-Yugoslavia we mean the whole territory of pre-1991 Yugoslavia as it is today.

We make no judgment on whether present Yugoslavia is entitled to continue using the name Yugoslavia. If that's what they want to call their country, so be it. The same applies to Macedonia.

United Nations (UN) sanctions have come and gone and seem to have barely dented Yugoslavia's pride. Yugoslavia's tourist economy, though severely compromised as a result of internal upheavals and to a lesser degree by sanctions, is making a recovery and is seeking to attract visitors again. The country is a safe and relatively stable destination, and is beckoning.

Facts about the Country

HISTORY

The original inhabitants of this region were the Illyrians, followed by the Celts, who arrived in the 4th century BC. The Roman conquest of Moesia Superior (Serbia) began in the 3rd century BC and under Augustus the empire extended to Singidunum (Belgrade) on the Danube. In 395 AD Theodosius I divided the empire and what is now Serbia passed to the Byzantine Empire, while Croatia remained part of the Western Roman Empire.

In the middle of the 6th century, Slavic tribes (Serbs, Croats and Slovenes) crossed the Danube in the wake of the Great Migration of Nations and occupied much of the Balkan Peninsula. In 879 the Serbs were converted to the Orthodox Church by Sts Cyril and Methodius. In 969 Serbia broke free from Byzantium and established an independent state; however,

YUGOSLAVIA

Byzantium re-established its authority in the 11th century.

An independent Serbian kingdom reappeared in 1217 and during the reign of Stefan Dušan (1346-55) Serbia was a great power including much of present Albania and northern Greece within its boundaries. Numerous frescoed Orthodox monasteries were erected during this Serbian 'Golden Age'. After Stefan's death Serbia declined, and at the Battle of Kosovo on 28 June 1389 the Serbian army was defeated by the Ottoman Turks, ushering in 500 years of Islamic rule. The Serbs were pushed north as the Turks advanced into Bosnia in the 15th century and the city-state of Venice occupied the coast. By 1459 Serbia was a Turkish *pashalik* (province) and the inhabitants had become mere serfs. In 1526 the Turks defeated Hungary at the Battle of Mohács, expanding their realm north and west of the Danube.

The first centuries of Turkish rule brought stability to the Balkans but, as the power of the sultan declined, local Turkish officials and soldiers began to oppress the Slavs. After their defeat at Vienna in 1683, the Turks began a steady retreat.

By 1699 they had been driven out of Hungary and many Serbs moved north into Vojvodina, where they enjoyed Habsburg protection. Through diplomacy the sultan regained northern Serbia for another century, but a revolt in 1815 led to de facto Serbian independence in 1816.

Serbia's autonomy was recognised in 1829, the last Turkish troops departed in 1867, and in 1878, after Russia's defeat of Turkey in a war over Bulgaria, complete independence was achieved. Montenegro also declared itself independent of Turkey in 1878. Macedonia remained under Turkish rule into the 20th century.

The 20th Century

Tensions mounted after Austria's annexation of Bosnia-Hercegovina in 1908, with Russia backing Serbia. There was more overt trouble in Macedonia. In the First Balkan War (1912), Serbia, Greece and Bulgaria combined against Turkey for the liberation of Macedonia. The Second Balkan War (1913) saw Serbia and Greece join forces against Bulgaria, which had claimed all of Macedonia for itself. At about this time Serbia wrested control of Kosovo from Albania with the help of the Western powers.

WWI was an extension of these conflicts as Austria-Hungary used the assassination of Archduke Ferdinand by a Serb nationalist on 28 June 1914 as an excuse to invade Serbia. Russia and France came to Serbia's aid, while Germany backed Austria. Thus began 'the war to end all wars'. In the winter of 1915-16 a defeated Serbian army of 155,000 retreated across the mountains of Montenegro to the Adriatic from where it was evacuated to Corfu. In 1918 these troops fought their way back up into Serbia from Thessaloniki, Greece.

After WWI, Croatia, Slovenia and Vojvodina were united with Serbia, Montenegro and Macedonia to form the Kingdom of Serbs, Croats and Slovenes under the king of Serbia. In 1929 the name was changed to Yugoslavia. The Vidovdan constitution of 1921 created a centralised government dominated by Serbia. This was strongly opposed by the Croats and other minorities, forcing King Alexander to end the political turmoil by declaring a personal dictatorship in 1929. The 1934 assassination of the king by a Macedonian terrorist with links to Croat separatists brought to power a regent who continued the Serbian dictatorship. Corruption was rampant and the regent tilted towards friendship with Nazi Germany.

On 25 March 1941, Yugoslavia joined the Tripartite Alliance, a fascist military pact, after being promised Greek Macedonia and Thessaloniki by the Germans. This sparked mass protest demonstrations and a military coup that overthrew the profascist regency. Peter II was installed as king and Yugoslavia abruptly withdrew from the alliance. Livid, Hitler ordered an immediate invasion and the country was carved up between Germany, Italy, Hungary and Bulgaria. In Croatia a fascist puppet state was set up which massacred hundreds of thousands of ethnic Serbs and Jews.

Almost immediately the Communist Party, under Josip Broz Tito, declared an armed uprising. There was also a monarchist resistance group, the Četniks, but they proved far less effective than Tito's partisans, and after 1943 the British gave full backing to the communists. A 1943 meeting of the Antifascist

Council for the National Liberation of Yugo-slavia (AVNOJ) at Jajce, in Bosnia, laid the basis for a future communist-led Yugoslavia.

The partisans played a major role in WWII by tying down huge Italian and German armies, but Yugoslavia suffered terrible losses, especially in Croatia and Bosnia-Hercegovina, where most of the fighting took place. According to the Serbian author Bogoljub Kočović some 487,000 Serbs, 207,000 Croats, 86,000 Muslims, 60,000 Jews, 50,000 Montenegrins, 32,000 Slovenes, 7000 Macedonians and 6000 Albanians died in the war. The resistance did, however, guarantee Yugoslavia's postwar independence.

Postwar Communism

In 1945 the Communist Party (which had been officially banned since 1920) won control of the national assembly, which in November abolished the monarchy and declared Yugoslavia a federal republic. Serbia's size was greatly reduced when Bosnia-Hercegovina, Monte-negro and Macedonia were granted republic status within this 'second' Yugoslavia. The Albanians of Kosovo and Hungarians of Vojvodina were denied republics of their own, however, on the pretext that they were not nations because their national homelands were outside the boundaries of Yugoslavia. Under Tito's slogan *bratstva i jedinstva* (brotherhood and unity) nationalist tendencies were suppressed.

Tito broke with Stalin in 1948 and, as a reward, received US$2 billion in economic and military aid from the USA and UK between 1950 and 1960. For the West this was a cheap way of protecting NATO's southern flank, but for Yugoslavia the Western subsidies alleviated the need for reform, contributing to the eco-nomic problems of today.

After the break with the USSR, Yugoslavia followed its own 'road to socialism' based on a federal system, self-management, personal freedom and nonalignment. The decentralisa-tion begun in 1951 was to lead to the eventual 'withering away of the state' of classical Marxism. Yugoslavia never became a member of either the Warsaw Pact or NATO, and in 1956 the country played a key role in the formation of the nonaligned movement.

The 1960s witnessed an economic boom in the north-west accompanied by liberalisation throughout the country, and in July 1966 Tito

fired his hardline secret police chief Alexander Ranković. Growing regional inequalities led, however, to increased tension as Slovenia, Croatia and Kosovo demanded greater auton-omy within the federation. In 1971 Tito responded with a 'return to Leninism', which included a purge of party reformers and a threat to use military force against Croatia.

With the most talented members of the lead-ership gone, Yugoslavia stagnated through the 1970s while borrowing billions of recycled petrodollars from the West. A 1970 constitu-tional amendment declared that the federal government would have control of foreign policy, defence, trade, the national economy and human rights, and all residual powers were vested in the six republics (Croatia, Bosnia-Hercegovina, Macedonia, Montenegro, Serbia and Slovenia) and two autonomous provinces of Serbia (Kosovo and Vojvodina). The 1974 constitution strengthened the powers of the autonomous provinces.

After Tito

Tito died in 1980 and the presidency then became a collective post rotated annually among nine members who were elected every four years by the national assembly, the six republics and the two autonomous provinces. This cumbersome system proved unable to solve either Yugoslavia's deepening economic problems or its festering regional and ethnic antagonisms.

In 1986 a working group of the Serbian Academy of Sciences prepared a memoran-dum calling on Serbia to reassert its hegemony in Yugoslavia. A year later Slobodan Milošević took over as party leader in Serbia by portray-ing himself as the champion of an allegedly persecuted Serbian minority in Kosovo. Milošević hoped to restore the flagging popu-larity of the League of Communists by inciting the Serbs' latent anti-Albanian sentiments. When moves by Serbia to limit Kosovo's autonomy led to massive protest demonstra-tions in the province in late 1988 and early 1989, the Serbian government unilaterally scrapped Kosovo's autonomy. Thousands of troops were sent to intimidate Kosovo's 90% Albanian majority, and in direct confrontations with the security forces dozens of civilians were shot dead.

Milošević's vision of a 'Greater Serbia' horrified residents of Slovenia and Croatia, who elected non-communist republican governments in the spring of 1990. These called for the creation of a loose Yugoslav 'confederation' which would allow Slovenia and Croatia to retain most of their wealth for themselves, and both republics threatened to secede from Yugoslavia if such reforms were not forthcoming. In the Serbian elections of December 1990, however, Milošević's policies paid off when the communists won 194 of 260 seats (the Albanians boycotted the election). In the other republics communists held Montenegro but lost Bosnia-Hercegovina and Macedonia.

Meanwhile, the federal prime minister, Ante Marković (a Croat), tried to steer clear of the ethnic turmoil. In late 1989 Marković introduced major economic reforms to control inflation. Though Western governments verbally supported the Marković reforms, few came forward with material support in the form of new loans or investments. With the Soviet empire disintegrating, Yugoslavia was no longer of prime strategic importance.

In March 1991 Serbia's state-controlled media broadcast false reports of a massacre of ethnic Serbs in Croatia in an attempt to precipitate a crisis leading to a military takeover. This outraged prodemocratic Serbian students who, led by Serbian Renewal Movement leader Vuk Drašković, massed outside the TV studios in Belgrade demanding that those responsible be sacked.

Civil War

On 25 June 1991 Slovenia and Croatia declared themselves independent of Yugoslavia. This soon led to fighting as the federal army moved into Slovenia. Fearing a tidal wave of refugees, the European Community (EC), now known as the European Union (EU), rushed a delegation of foreign ministers to Yugoslavia to negotiate a truce, which soon broke down. In Belgrade, Milošević went on TV to reaffirm his support for Yugoslavia and the right of people to continue to live in it. He said the Yugoslav People's Army would intervene to defend Serbs wherever they lived.

On 7 July, federal and republican leaders met on Brijuni Island off Istria in the hope of

preventing a full-scale civil war, while the EC imposed a weapons embargo on Yugoslavia and froze US$1 billion in aid and credits. It soon became clear that the matter would be decided in Croatia; on 18 July the Yugoslav government announced that all federal troops would be withdrawn from Slovenia within three months.

Intervention by the federal army on the side of Serb separatists in Croatia led to months of heavy fighting, with widespread property damage and thousands of casualties. The EC sent unarmed cease-fire monitors to the trouble areas in September and organised a peace conference in the Netherlands but this failed, and in November the EC applied economic sanctions against Serbia and Montenegro. On 20 December 1991 the federal prime minister, Ante Marković, resigned after the army demanded 81% of the 1992 budget.

In December it was agreed that a UN peacekeeping force would be sent to Croatia and from 3 January 1992 a cease-fire generally held. On 15 January the EC recognised the independence of Croatia and Slovenia, whereupon Macedonia and Bosnia-Hercegovina demanded recognition of their own independence. Montenegro alone voted to remain in Yugoslavia. The secession of Bosnia-Hercegovina, with its large Serb population, sparked bitter fighting as Serb militants with army backing again used force to seize territory, as they had done in Croatia.

The Third Yugoslavia

On 27 April 1992 a 'third' Yugoslav federation was declared by Serbia and Montenegro in a rushed attempt to escape blame for the bloodshed in Bosnia-Hercegovina. The rump state disclaimed responsibility for the federal army in Bosnia-Hercegovina and announced that all soldiers hailing from Serbia and Montenegro would be withdrawn. In effect this manoeuvre didn't amount to much as 80% of the federal troops in the breakaway Serb Republic of Bosnia, which came into existence in late 1991, were Bosnian Serbs. Meanwhile, the federal army purged its ranks of officers who still supported the old concept of Yugoslavia and replaced them with Serb hardliners.

In May 1992, with Sarajevo under siege and the world losing patience with what was seen as Serbian aggression, the UN Security Council passed a sweeping package of economic and diplomatic sanctions against Yugoslavia. In mid-July US and Western European warships began patrolling the Adriatic off Montenegro to monitor the embargo. Yugoslavia was denied its old seat at the UN in September 1992 and in November a UN naval blockade was imposed. Sanctions against Yugoslavia were greatly strengthened in April 1993 after the Serb side rejected a peace plan for Bosnia-Hercegovina. Yet, despite severe economic hardship, the socialists won the December 1993 elections.

With the division of Bosnia into Serb and Croat-Muslim states in late 1995, the dream of a 'Greater Serbia' seemed close to reality, stained with the blood of tens of thousands of unfortunate people and soiled by the ashes of their burned homes. The new constitution of rump Yugoslavia makes no mention of 'autonomous provinces', and the Albanian majority in Kosovo continues to be brutally repressed by Serb officials, with an ever-present danger of uprising and Bosnia-style genocide (see the Kosovo section later in this chapter).

Meanwhile, five years of hostile relations with Croatia officially ended in August 1996, with the signing of a landmark treaty which recognised national borders and normalised relations between the two countries.

GEOGRAPHY

Mountains and plateaus account for the lower half of this 102,173-sq-km country (the size of the US state of Virginia), the remainder being the Pannonian Plain, which is drained by the Sava, Danube and Tisa rivers in the north-east. Yugoslavia's interior and southern mountains belong to the Balkan range, and the coastal range is an arm of the Alps. Most of the rivers flow north into the Danube, which runs through Yugoslavia for 588 km. In the south many smaller rivers have cut deep canyons in the plateau, which make for memorable train rides.

When the country split up in 1991, most of the Adriatic coast went to Slovenia and Croatia, though the scenically superb 150-km Montenegrin coast remains in Yugoslavia. The Bay of Kotor here is the only real fjord in southern Europe, and Montenegro's Durmitor National Park has ex-Yugoslavia's largest canyon. Between Ulcinj and Albania is one of the longest beaches on the eastern Adriatic.

ECONOMY

After WWII, Yugoslavia was a war-torn land of peasants. From 1948 to 1951 a concentrated attempt was made to form agricultural cooperatives. This failed, however, and most of the land continued to be worked privately by small farmers. In 1953 individual private holdings were reduced to a maximum of 10 hectares.

During the 1950s, state property was handed over to the workers in a reaction against Stalinist state socialism. The economy was thus reorganised on the basis of 'self-management', and elected workers' councils began running the factories and businesses, with coordination from producers' councils on a regional level. State control was limited to the broadest economic planning.

This system soon led to inefficiencies and an expensive duplication of services without the full benefits of open competition. Since collectively owned property had no clear owner, it was impossible to enforce economic efficiency or to guarantee profits. Initiative was stifled and employees often used self-management to improve their own financial standing without feeling any responsibility towards their property. Income was spent on higher wages and, with little or no capital left for development, companies turned to the banks. The cycle of inefficiency and dependency deepened as companies borrowed with little hope of ever paying off the loans.

The crisis of 2000% inflation in 1989 shattered the self-management ideal and led reformers to believe that a return to private property was inevitable. At the beginning of 1990 the government attempted to halt inflation by stopping the printing presses of the Belgrade mint and declaring a wage freeze. Prices still jumped by 75% but by mid-1990 inflation had levelled off to 13% a year. However, in 1992 hyperinflation returned as the government again turned to printing money to finance government operations and the war in Bosnia-Hercegovina. UN economic sanctions did the rest.

In 1993 incomes were a tenth of what they had been three years previously, industrial output had dropped 40% from that of a year before and 60% of factory workers were unemployed.

Over 80% of Yugoslav property is still collectively owned and if normal bankruptcy procedures were applied most firms would go broke. Instead, freshly printed banknotes keep them going and everyone pays the price in the form of inflation. People get by on remittances from relatives overseas or by subsisting on their gardens and livestock.

The end of the Cold War has greatly reduced the strategic importance of the entire Balkan region and Western countries are unlikely to rush in with 1950s-style aid or 1970s-style loans, even assuming that peace and stability do somehow return. Yugoslavia owes foreign governments and banks about US$16 billion, most of it dating back to the 1970s.

POPULATION & PEOPLE

The 11 million people of the 'third' Yugoslavia include Serbs (62.3%), Albanians (16.6%), Montenegrins (5%), Hungarians (3.3%) and Slavic Muslims (3.1%), plus a smattering of Croats, Gypsies, Slovaks, Macedonians, Romanians, Bulgarians, Turks and Ukrainians. The Montenegrins are officially considered ethnic Serbs. In 1991 an estimated 170,000 Gypsies lived in Yugoslavia, 100,000 of them in Kosovo. There are about 500,000 war refugees from Croatia and Bosnia-Hercegovina in Serbia and another 64,000 in Montenegro.

Nearly a quarter of the population of Vojvodina is Hungarian and 90% of Kosovars are Albanian. Around 200,000 Serbs also live in Kosovo and there are large Slavic Muslim and Albanian minorities in Montenegro. In total there are 1,800,000 ethnic Albanians in present-day Yugoslavia, a large number considering that the population of Albania itself is only 3,200,000. Some 250,000 Slavic Muslims live in the Sandžak region of Serbia and Montenegro between Novi Pazar and Berane (part of Bosnia until 1918). The human rights of all minorities are challenged by an increasingly nationalistic Serbia.

Yugoslavia's largest cities are Belgrade (population 1,500,000), Novi Sad (250,000), Niš (230,000), Priština (210,000) and Subotica (160,000).

ARTS

The artistic group FIA (☎ 011 347 355), Hilandarska 4, 11000 Belgrade, founded in 1989 by Stavislav Sharp and Nada Rajičić,

uses art to explore Serbia's tumultuous present through 'Phobjects', suggestive images juxtaposed against folk art, political symbols and provocative quotations.

At exhibitions, group members dress in black paramilitary uniforms and show videos of skits in which FIA 'conspiracies' are acted out. Their 1992 Belgrade exhibition was visited by over 50,000 people in two weeks before being suddenly closed by force.

Phobjects have been exhibited in the ruins of the railway station in Sarajevo and at the bombed-out zoo in Osijek (Croatia). Surrealist 'posters of conscience' bring the FIA message to the streets. Their works are often prophetic.

The award-winning film *Underground*, by Sarajevo-born director Emil Kusturica, is worth seeing. Told in a chaotic, colourful style, the film deals with the history of former Yugoslavia over the last 50 years.

Literature

Nobel Prize winner Ivo Andrić is Serbia's most respected and most translated writer. His novel *Na Drini Ćuprija* (Bridge over the Drina), which is about the gap between religions, accurately foresaw the disasters that befell the Balkans in the early 1990s. Respected writer Milorad Pavić's novel *Hazarski Rečnik* (Hazar Dictionary) is a historical narrative, interlaced with fact and fiction, which has also been translated into English.

Music

Serbia's vibrant dances are similar to those of neighbouring Bulgaria. Serbian folk musicians use the *caraba* (small bagpipes), *gajde* (larger bagpipes), *frula* (small flute), *duduk* (large flute) and the fiddle.

The gajde employed in much Balkan music probably dates back to 4th-century Celtic invasions; unlike Scottish sheepskin bagpipes, the gajde is made from goatskin. The music of the Albanians of Kosovo bears the deep imprint of five centuries of Turkish rule, with the high whine of an Arab *zorna* (flute) carrying the tune above the beat of a goatskin drum. The *kolo* (round dance) is often accompanied by Gypsy musicians.

Blehmuzika, or brass music, has become the national music of Serbia. Though documented as far back as 1335, blehmuzika evolved under the influence of Turkish and, later, Austrian military music. The heartland of blehmuzika is the area around Guča, a village south of the railway line between Kraljevo and Požega. Each year around the end of August more than 100,000 people attend the three-day Guča trumpet festival to hear 20 competing bands. A second centre for Serbian brass music is the Niš region, where Gypsy bands play wild Eastern-inspired dance music.

For popular modern music check out Momčilo Bajagić who often appears on CD together with his group Bajaga & Instruktori. His music fuses traditional elements with street poetry and jazz. He is very popular with the younger generation. Đorđe Balašević, equally if not more popular, appeals to a wider listening audience, combining once again traditional folkloric elements with modern musical motifs.

CULTURE
The Serbs are a proud and hospitable people, despite their newly-tarnished reputation. Visitors are a source of pride and are made to feel welcome. As in Macedonia, respect for all religious establishments and customs should be shown; these should not be treated as tourist entertainment. Dress appropriately at all times – look at what locals are wearing. Learning some basic Serbian, Hungarian or Albanian will open doors and create smiles.

RELIGION
The Serbs and Montenegrins are Orthodox, the Hungarians are Roman Catholic and the Albanians are predominantly Muslim.

LANGUAGE
Ordinary Yugoslavs are most likely to know German as a second language, though educated people in Kosovo and Serbia can often speak French. Serbian is the common language, and Albanian is spoken in Kosovo.

Serbian and Croatian are almost the same language, although Serbian is written in Cyrillic and Croatian is written in Latin characters (see the Croatian & Serbian language section at the end of the book). Before the break-up of the Yugoslav Federation, the language was referred to as Serbo-Croatian, but this term is now obsolete. Serbs in Yugoslavia call their language Serbian.

The Latin alphabet is used by the Albanians in Kosovo and the Hungarians in Vojvodina. In Montenegro you'll encounter a mixture of Latin and Cyrillic, but in Serbia most things are written only in Cyrillic. It's almost imperative to spend an hour or two studying the Cyrillic alphabet if you want to be able to read street and travel destination signs. (See the Macedonian language section at the end of the book for an explanation of the alphabet.)

Facts for the Visitor

PLANNING
Climate & When to Go
The interior has a more extreme continental climate than the Adriatic coast of Montenegro. Belgrade has average daily temperatures above 17°C from May to September, above 13°C in April and October and above 7°C in March and November. In winter a cold wind (koshava) often blows across Belgrade.

Books & Maps
Rebecca West's Black Lamb & Grey Falcon is a classic portrait of prewar Yugoslavia. Former partisan and leading dissident Milovan Djilas has written many fascinating books about history and politics in Yugoslavia, most of them published in English. Any good library will have a couple of them.

The disintegration of former Yugoslavia has produced a wealth of reading material. A highly recommended recent (updated to July 1991) book on the region's political upheaval is Remaking the Balkans by Christopher Cvilic (Pinter Publishers). The precise background information contained in this slim volume offers a clear explanation of events. The Destruction of Yugoslavia by Branka Magaš (Verso Publishers) offers many insights into the period from the death of Tito in 1980 to the end of 1992. Other titles dealing with the turbulence of the 1990s include The Fall of Yugoslavia by Misha Glenny and The Death of Yugoslavia by Laura Silber and Allan Little, based on the 1995 BBC documentary series of the same name.

Current Hallwag or Baedeker maps of Yugoslavia are hard to find or non-existent.

Older maps show the former borders. The *Savezna Republika Jugoslavija Autokarta* showing the new borders and a few regional town maps, and the detailed Belgrade city map *Plan Grada Beograd* are both available for 15 and 10 DIN respectively from the Tourist Organisation of Belgrade.

Online Services
A useful World Wide Web page to point your browser at for general information on Yugoslavia is http://www.umiacs.umd.edu/users/lpv/YU/HTML/yu.html (Yugoslavia). An excellent source of rare and out-of-print books on Serbia is Eastern Books (☎ 0181 871 0880), 125a Astonville St, Southfields, London SW18 5AQ. Point your WWW browser at their URL: http://ourworld.compuserve.com/home pages/EasternBooks/serbia htm, or e-mail them on 100753.1153@compuserve. com.

What to Bring
You should plan on bringing your own film and video requirements, to be on the safe side. Bring a universal bath plug, since hotels rarely supply them.

SUGGESTED ITINERARIES
Depending on the length of your stay, you might want to see and do the following things in Yugoslavia:

Two days
    Visit Novi Sad and Belgrade.
One week
    Visit Novi Sad, Belgrade, Ulcinj, Budva and Cetinje.
Two weeks
    Visit all areas covered in this chapter except Kosovo.
One month
    Visit all areas covered herein.

HIGHLIGHTS
Yugoslavia has a wealth of castles, such as Smederevo Castle on the Danube, which is Serbia's last medieval fortress. Petrovaradin Citadel at Novi Sad is one of Europe's great baroque fortresses and Belgrade's Kalemegdan Citadel must be mentioned for its historic importance. At Kotor the Venetian city walls creep right up the mountainside behind the town and the old Montenegrin capital of Cetinje will please romantics. Of the beach resorts, Budva is chic but Ulcinj has more atmosphere and is much cheaper.

TOURIST OFFICES
All overseas offices of the Yugoslav National Tourist Office closed in 1991 but should gradually be reopening. Municipal tourist offices still exist in Belgrade, Novi Sad and Podgorica. Commercial travel agencies such as Montenegroturist and Putnik will often provide general information on their area.

VISAS & EMBASSIES
Most visitors require visas and these are issued promptly at Yugoslav consulates, usually free of charge (Australians are charged A$5 as an administrative fee). Before the current troubles you could get a Yugoslav visa at the border but this is no longer possible; you *must* obtain your Yugoslav visa in advance at an embassy or consulate. Don't confuse Yugoslavia with Macedonia and Croatia, where visas *are* readily available at the border.

Don't count on obtaining a Yugoslav visa in Slovenia, Croatia or Macedonia. If you plan on entering Yugoslavia more than once, ask for a double or triple-entry visa, otherwise you'll have to apply for a visa again.

Yugoslav Embassies Abroad
In addition to those listed below, Yugoslav consulates or embassies are found in Bucharest, Budapest, Prague, Sofia, Timişoara, Tirana and Warsaw. Try to avoid the chaotic Tirana consulate.

Australia
    11 Nuyts St, Canberra, ACT 2603
    (☎ 06-295 1458; fax 06-239 6178)
Canada
    17 Blackburn Ave, Ottawa, Ontario, K1N 8A2
    (☎ 613-233 6289)
Netherlands
    Groot Hertoginnelaan 30, 2517 EG, The Hague
    (☎ 070-363 6800)
UK
    5-7 Lexham Gardens, London, W8 5JJ
    (☎ 0171-370 6105)
USA
    2410 California St NW, Washington DC, 20008
    (☎ 202-462 6566)

Foreign Embassies
Most consulates and embassies are on or near Belgrade's Kneza Miloša, a 10-minute walk south-east from the train station. Visas are payable in cash, hard currency only (prices below are given in Deutschmarks).

Albania
  Kneza Miloša 56 (☎ 646 864); open weekdays from 9 am to 1 pm.
Australia
  Čika Ljubina 13 (☎ 624 655).
Bulgaria (Consulate)
  Birčaninova 26 (open weekdays from 9 am to noon); visas cost DM50 for a same-day service or DM80 for on-the-spot express service.
Canada
  Kneza Miloša 75 (☎ 644 666).
Czech Republic (Consulate)
  Bulevar Revolucije 22 (open weekdays from 9 am to noon).
Hungary (Consulate)
  Ivana Milutinovića 74 (open weekdays 9 to 11 am); visas DM50.
Poland (Consulate)
  Kneza Miloša 38 (open weekdays from 8 am to noon); visas DM40 for same-day service or DM70 for a 25-minute express service).
Romania (Consulate)
  Kneza Miloša 70 (open weekdays from 9 am to 1 pm); visas DM25, issued on the spot.
Slovakia (Consulate)
  Bulevar Umetnosti 18 in Novi Beograd(☎ 222 2432).
UK
  Generala Ždanova 46 (☎ 645 034/645 055).
USA
  Kneza Miloša 50 (☎ 645 655).

You may encounter large queues seeking visas at the embassies of Western countries. This is an indication of the country's continuing economic plight.

MONEY
Currency
With the Belgrade mint working overtime printing money to finance an oversized military and a de facto Serb government in Bosnia-Hercegovina, the Yugoslav dinar has suffered repeated devaluations. In December 1993 Yugoslavia experienced the highest inflation in the history of Europe (higher even than the monthly 32,000% record set by Weimar Germany in 1923). To most of us, such a situation is inconceivable but the Yugoslavs are experienced at dealing with inflation.

In 1990 four zeros were knocked off the Yugoslav dinar, so 10,000 old dinars became one new dinar, and in mid-1993 another six zeros were dropped. When this currency in turn inflated into obsolescence, a 'super dinar' was issued in January 1994 with a value of one to 12 million old dinars. By mid-1996 a new currency, the 'novi dinar', was holding its own

against harder currencies. There are coins of five, 10 and 50 para and one novi dinar and notes of five, 10 and 20 dinars. This means that your wallet or pocket soon becomes over-stuffed with dinar notes if you change a largish amount of money into dinars.

Changing Money
All banks, travel agencies and hotels will change cash hard currency into Yugoslav dinars at the official rate; unlike in Western Europe, you won't be given a worse rate at the fancy hotels or on Sunday.

Bring cash, preferably Deutschmarks, as you can spend or change them almost anywhere. A few people in Yugoslavia still change money on the street and unlike Budapest, Bucharest and Prague, it's fairly straightforward to do so and you probably won't be ripped off (but still take care). It's technically illegal and you are better off using the private exchange offices to avoid flashing your cash out in the open.

Only change what you're sure you'll need, as it's difficult to change dinars back into hard currency. For the most recent exchange rates of the Yugoslav dinar, point your Web browser at: gopher://gopher.undp.org:70/00/uncurr/exchrates. Conversion rates for major currencies in late 1996 are listed below:

Exchange Rates
Australia	A$1	=	3.9DIN
Canada	C$1	=	3.6DIN
France	1FF	=	16.07DIN
Germany	DM1	=	3.3DIN
Japan	¥100	=	336.3DIN
United Kingdom	UK£1	=	7.5DIN
United States	US$1	=	5.05DIN

POST & COMMUNICATIONS
Post
To mail a parcel from Yugoslavia take it unwrapped to a main post office where the staff will wrap and seal it. You then fill out six or seven forms, stand in line for a while and with luck, it will be sent off. Not all post offices will do this, however. Allow plenty of time to complete the transaction.

Inflation is still at such a level in Yugoslavia that the post office has trouble printing stamps of higher and higher denominations fast enough to keep up. You're probably better off going to a post office to have your postcards meter-mailed rather than using stamps.

Receiving Mail You can receive mail addressed to poste restante in all towns for a small charge per letter.

Mail addressed c/o Poste Restante, 11101 Belgrade 1, Yugoslavia, will be held for one month at window No 2 in the main post office, Takovska 2.

Telephone

To place a long-distance phone call in Yugoslavia you usually go to the main post office. Avoid doing this on weekends as the office may be jammed with military personnel waiting to call home. International calls made from hotels are much more expensive. Calls from post offices go straight through and cost about 85 DIN a minute to the USA and Australia, with no minimum.

Magnetic telephone cards purchased at post offices or news kiosks are an inexpensive, easy way of making international calls, but only in Belgrade as card phones are hard to find elsewhere. Cards can be bought in units of 100 (17,70 DIN), 200 (28,90 DIN), 300 (42 DIN) and 400 (53 DIN). The international access code for outgoing calls is ☎ 99. To call another town within Yugoslavia dial the area code with the initial zero and the number.

To call Yugoslavia from Western Europe dial the international access code (which varies from country to country), ☎ 381 (the country code for Yugoslavia), the area code (without the initial zero) and the number.

E-mail & Fax

Yugoslavia is connected to the Internet, but access from within the country is fairly limited at present. Don't plan on doing any cybercafé e-mailing home just yet. Faxes can be sent from the main post office in Belgrade.

NEWSPAPERS & MAGAZINES

There is a wide selection of Serbian newspapers and magazines, as will be obvious by the displays at street kiosks. Not so useful if you do not read Serbian. *Politika* is the main daily for serious reading.

Until publication was suspended in 1993 as a consequence of UN sanctions, the English-

language *International Weekly* carried the best stories of the week from *Politika*. To date it has not made a reappearance.

Also before UN sanctions, many foreign-language publications were widely available in Yugoslavia. At the time of research, English-language publications were reappearing, but hadn't fully found their way back to the newsstands.

RADIO & TV

In Belgrade, there are some 11 local TV stations, including two from Novi Sad. Satellite TV stations such as CNN, Eurosport and MTV are also available if the receiver is suitably equipped. There are fewer stations in regional areas. Many FM and AM radio stations cater to all tastes.

PHOTOGRAPHY & VIDEO

Bring all your own film, as that sold locally is expensive and may be unreliable outside Belgrade. You're only allowed to bring five rolls per person, but because this isn't enforced, it's possible to distribute larger quantities through your luggage. Keep your camera stowed away while crossing the border and be careful about taking pictures of anything other than obvious tourist attractions, as you could arouse unwelcome curiosity. Taking photos from a train or bus is not advisable and photographing soldiers or military facilities will cause serious problems if you're caught. The funny little signs with a camera crossed out should be taken seriously.

Video paraphernalia – tapes and batteries – is available in Belgrade, but you are advised to bring your own since these things are generally more expensive in Yugoslavia.

TIME

Yugoslavia is one hour ahead of GMT/UTC. The country goes on summer time at the end of March when clocks are turned forward an hour. At the end of September they're turned back an hour.

ELECTRICITY

The electric current is 220 V, 50 Hz. Plugs are of the standard European two-pronged type.

WEIGHTS & MEASURES

Yugoslavia uses the metric system.

YUGOSLAVIA

TOILETS

Public toilets outside of Belgrade are probably better avoided. Make full use of the facilities at restaurants and hotels. A 1DIN charge is common for use of public toilets in Belgrade.

HEALTH

The cost of medical treatment in Yugoslavia is very low and if you're covered at home by a regular health insurance plan which includes treatment abroad, special travel medical insurance is unnecessary and a waste of money. Conditions, however, in state-run services may not be up to your expectations. Private clinics offer a more presentable level of service and will normally be covered by your travel insurance.

WOMEN TRAVELLERS

Women travellers should feel no particular concern about travel in Yugoslavia. Other than cursory interest shown by men towards solo women travellers, travel is hassle-free and easy. Dress more conservatively than usual in Albanian Muslim areas of Kosovo.

GAY & LESBIAN TRAVELLERS

Homosexuality has been legal in Yugoslavia since 1932. For more information, contact Arkadia, Brace Baruh 11, 11000 Belgrade (e-mail: Jelica.Todosijevic@zamir-bg.ztn.zer.de).

DISABLED TRAVELLERS

Few public buildings or streets have facilities for wheelchairs. Access could be problematic in Belgrade with its numerous inclines.

DANGERS & ANNOYANCES

Belgrade is a remarkably safe city, even late at night. The seediest area is around the train station but even there there's no particular danger. Throughout Yugoslavia theft is rare.

Many Yugoslavs are chain-smokers who can't imagine that anyone might be inconvenienced by their habit, so choose your seat in trains, restaurants, bars and other public places carefully. Buses are supposed to be smoke-free and there are no-smoking sections on trains but the interpretation of this prohibition is sometimes ignored by other passengers.

If the subject turns to politics, it's best to listen to what Yugoslavs say rather than to tell

them what you think, as nationalist passions can be unpredictable. It's striking the way Serbs who seem to be reasonable, nice people suddenly become tense and defensive as soon as the subject of Kosovo comes up.

Don't give the police the impression you are anything but a tourist, otherwise you may be in for a searching interrogation.

BUSINESS HOURS

Banks in Yugoslavia keep long hours, often from 7 am to 7 pm weekdays and 7 am to noon on Saturday. On weekdays many shops close for lunch from noon to 4 pm but stay open until 8 pm. Department stores, supermarkets and self-service restaurants generally stay open throughout the day. On Saturday most government offices are closed, though shops stay open until 2 pm; many other businesses close at 3 pm.

PUBLIC HOLIDAYS & SPECIAL EVENTS

Public holidays include New Year (1 and 2 January), Orthodox Christmas (6 and 7 January), Labour Days (1 and 2 May), Partisan Day (4 July) and Republic Days (29 and 30 November). In addition, 7 July (Uprising Day) is a holiday in Serbia and 13 July is a holiday in Montenegro. If any of these should fall on a Sunday, then the following Monday or Tuesday is a holiday.

Belgrade hosts a film festival in February, an international theatre festival in mid-September, a festival of classical music in October and a jazz festival in November. The Novi Sad Agricultural Fair is in mid-May. Budva has a summer festival in July and August.

ACTIVITIES

Skiing

Serbia's largest ski centre is Kopaonik (2017 metres), south of Kraljevo, with 26 different runs covering a total of 54 km. Get there from Belgrade by taking a bus to Brus (246 km, five hours), then a local bus to the resort at Brzeče (18 km). Otherwise take a bus from Belgrade to Kruševac (194 km) and another from there to Brus (52 km). Kopaonik has a 150-bed hostel (☎ 037-833 176) with three, four and five-bed rooms at 72 DIN per person, open year-round.

On the north side of the Šar Planina, which separates Kosovo from Macedonia, is

Brezovica (1750 metres), Kosovo's major ski resort. Montenegro's main ski resort is at Žabljak. The ski season is from about December to March.

White-Water Rafting & Hiking
White-water rafting is offered on the Tara River in Montenegro's Durmitor National Park. Turn to Travel Agencies in the Belgrade section for a contact address. For high-altitude lakes and one of the world's deepest canyons, Durmitor can't be beaten. This is also a popular hiking and skiing area.

LANGUAGE COURSES
Courses for linguists, or Slavists who wish to learn Serbian, are run in September each year by the International Slavic Centre (MSC) in Belgrade. For further details write to the MSC at Studenski trg 3, Belgrade.

ACCOMMODATION
You won't find many inexpensive hotels in Yugoslavia. Prices are often quoted in US dollars or Deutschmarks, although payment in dinars is OK. Foreigners pay up to three times as much as locals at state-owned hotels – a legacy of the old socialist days when foreigners were supposed to be able to afford higher rates. Food prices are the same for everyone, so at resort hotels compare the price of a room with all meals against the price of a room only, as it may only be a few dollars more.

In summer you can camp along the Montenegrin coast; organised camping grounds are few and many of those that do exist are closed due to the absence of tourists. There's a hostel in Belgrade but it's far from the centre, overcrowded and overpriced. Other HI hostels exist at Kopaonik and Ulcinj (summer only). At last report the Novi Sad hostel was still being used to house refugees. The hostel charges for foreigners are fixed in Deutschmarks and thus staying in hostels could be more expensive and often less convenient than taking a private room.

Private rooms are usually available along the coast but seldom inland. They are hard to find in Belgrade. There are steep surcharges if you stay less than three nights. If you plan to stay that long, Budva and Bar make good central bases from which to make side trips to Cetinje and Ulcinj.

An overnight bus or train can sometimes get you out of an accommodation jam. Book a sleeper or couchette on the train between Belgrade and Bar or buy a bus ticket with a seat reservation between Belgrade and Skopje/Ohrid as far ahead as possible. It will cost less than the cheapest hotel room and you'll reach your destination as well.

FOOD
The cheapest breakfast is Balkan *burek*, a greasy layered pie made with cheese (*sir*) or meat *(meso)*, and it's available everywhere. *Krompirusa* is potato burek. Food is cheaper in the interior than along the coast and meat dishes can be very cheap in Turkish-influenced areas.

Regional Dishes
Yugoslavia's regional cuisines range from spicy Hungarian goulash in Vojvodina to Turkish kebab in Serbia and Kosovo. A speciality of Vojvodina is *alaska čorba* (fiery riverfish stew). In Montenegro try the pastoral fare such as boiled lamb or *kajmak* (cream from boiled milk which is salted and turned into cheese).

Serbia is famous for grilled meats such as *čevapčići* (kebabs of spiced, minced meat, grilled), *pljeskavica* (a large spicy hamburger steak) and *ražnjići* (a pork or veal shish kebab with onions and peppers). If you want to try them all at once, order *mešano meso* (a mixed grill of pork cutlet, liver, sausage, and minced meat patties with onions). Serbian *duveč* is grilled pork cutlets with spiced stewed peppers, zucchini and tomatoes in rice cooked in an oven – delicious.

Other popular dishes are *musaka* (aubergine and potato baked in layers with minced meat), *sarma* (cabbage stuffed with minced meat and rice), *kapama* (stewed lamb, onions and spinach served with yoghurt), *punjena tikvica* (zucchini stuffed with minced meat and rice), and peppers stuffed with minced meat, rice and spices, cooked in tomato sauce.

Most traditional Yugoslav dishes are based on meat so vegetarians will have problems, though every restaurant menu will include a Serbian salad (*Srpska salata*) of raw peppers, onions and tomatoes, seasoned with oil, vinegar and chilli. Also ask for *gibanica* (a

YUGOSLAVIA

layered cheese pie) and *zeljanica* (cheese pie with spinach).

DRINKS

Beer (*pivo*) is always available. Nikšićko pivo brewed at Nikšić in Montenegro is terribly good when imbibed ice-cold at the beach on a hot summer day. Its taste has a smoky flavour in comparison with the Bip beer served around Belgrade, which tends to be on the flat side.

Yugoslav cognac (grape brandy) is called *vinjak*. Coffee is usually served Turkish-style, boiled in a small individual pot, 'black as hell, strong as death and sweet as love'. Hotel breakfast coffee is universally undrinkable.

Getting There & Away

AIR

Since the lifting of UN sanctions in November 1995, JAT has recommenced services and provides for a limited but growing number of domestic and international destinations. As at mid-1996, services to the US and Australia had not resumed but that may change.

LAND

In mid-1991, all rail and road links between Croatia and Serbia were cut, making it necessary to do a loop through Hungary to travel from Zagreb to Belgrade. Five years later the border was reopened. The main vehicle and rail crossing is at Batrovci, near the town of Šid, on the main Belgrade-Zagreb *autoput*. Other border crossings at Bačka Palanka, Bogojevo and Bezdan were still under the control of UNPROFOR in mid-1996. The southern border between Croatia and Montenegro had not reopened as of mid-1996.

Limited train and bus services use the main crossing instead of transiting Hungary but at the time of going to press there were no bus links between Yugoslavia and Croatia and few other details were available.

Bus

Buses travelling to/from Slovenia and Macedonia can use the main Yugoslavia-Croatia border crossing instead of going through Hungary.

In Belgrade, the travel agencies Basturist, Turist Biro Lasta and Putnik all sell tickets for international buses (see Travel Agencies in the Belgrade section for addresses and contact numbers). Sample fares from Belgrade, payable in Deutschmarks only, are:

Destination	Cost
Budapest	DM60
Lyon	DM180
Munich	DM155
Paris	DM230
Thessaloniki	DM50
Zürich	DM170

Train

Only buy a ticket as far as your first stop in Yugoslavia, as domestic fares are much cheaper than international fares. Consider breaking your journey in Subotica, Niš or Skopje for this purpose alone. A student card will get you a reduction on train fares from Yugoslavia to other Eastern European countries.

All the international 'name trains' mentioned here run daily all year unless otherwise stated.

Hungary & Beyond Since mid-1991, trains between Western Europe and Belgrade have run via Budapest, Subotica and Novi Sad. About six trains a day cover the 354 km between Budapest and Belgrade (six hours, 170 DIN). The *Avala* and *Beograd* express trains run between Belgrade and Vienna. Belgrade is 11 hours from Vienna (627 km, 302 DIN) and 17 hours from Munich. Reservations are usually required on these trains.

An unreserved local train runs three times a day between Subotica and Szeged in Hungary (45 km, 1½ hours, 15 DIN).

Croatia You can take a direct train from Zagreb to Budapest (140 DIN), then change to another train for Belgrade (170 DIN). Otherwise take the daily train from Zagreb to Pécs (Hungary), a bus from Pécs to Szeged and a train from Szeged across the border to Subotica in Vojvodina. You would have to spend at least one night somewhere along the way.

Romania From Romania the overnight *Bucureşti* express train runs between Bucharest and

Beograd-Dunav station (693 km, 13 hours, 156 DIN) via Timişoara. Reservations are required. Two daily unreserved local trains on this route connect Timişoara to Vršac (76 km).

Apart from this, there's an unreserved local train from Jimbolija (Romania) to Kikinda (Yugoslavia) twice a day (19 km). From Kikinda there are four local trains a day to Pančevo (161 km, 3½ hours), with hourly trains from there to Belgrade (23 km, 30 minutes). Four daily trains run between Jimbolija and Timişoara (39 km, one hour).

Bulgaria & Turkey The most reliable service to/from Bulgaria and Turkey is the *Balkan Express* train, which connects Budapest with Istanbul and runs through Belgrade. From Istanbul the train goes via Sofia, Niš, Belgrade and Novi Sad. If bound for Bulgaria you can board this overnight train in Novi Sad.

From Belgrade it's nine hours to Sofia (417 km, 98 DIN) and 26 hours to Istanbul (1051 km, 236 DIN). The *Balkan Express* departs Belgrade each evening at 10 pm and reservations are required.

Greece The southern main line between Belgrade and Athens (1267 km, 22 hours, 251 DIN) is through Skopje and Thessaloniki, with two trains a day. Reservations are recommended.

Car & Motorcycle
Following are the main highway entry/exit points around Yugoslavia (travelling clockwise), with the Yugoslav border post named.

Hungary There are crossings at Bački Breg (32 km south of Baja), Kelebija (11 km north-west of Subotica) and Horgoš (between Szeged and Subotica).

Romania You may cross at Sprska Crnja (45 km west of Timişoara), Vatin (between Timişoara and Belgrade), Kaluđerovo (120 km east of Belgrade) and Kladovo (10 km west of Turnu Severin).

Bulgaria You have a choice of Negotin (29 km north-west of Vidin), Zaječar (45 km south-west of Vidin), Gradina (at Dimitrovgrad

between Sofia and Niš) and Klisura (66 km west of Pernik).

Macedonia You can cross at Preševo (10 km north of Kumanovo) and Đeneral Janković (between Uroševac and Skopje).

Albania There are crossings at Vrbnica (18 km south-west of Prizren) and Božaj (24 km south-east of Podgorica).

SEA
A ferry service operates between Bari (Italy), and Bar in Montenegro. The Belgrade agent is Yugoagent at Kolarčeva 3. There are a couple of agents in Bar.

LEAVING YUGOSLAVIA
The airport departure tax on international flights is 70 DIN.

Getting Around

AIR
JAT domestic flights operate from Belgrade to Tivat (Montenegro) four to six times daily and to Podgorica (also in Montenegro) twice daily. Both fares cost about 300 DIN, plus 20 DIN domestic departure airport tax. These flights are heavily booked.

Only 15 kg of checked baggage is allowed on domestic flights. JAT runs inexpensive buses to the airports to and from city centres.

BUS
Though present-day Yugoslavia depends on railways far more than the other four countries of ex-Yugoslavia, there are also many buses. You'll depend on buses to travel along the Montenegrin coast from Bar to Budva and Ulcinj, to go from Montenegro to Kosovo and to get to Durmitor National Park and the monasteries of southern Serbia. On long hauls, overnight buses can be exhausting but they do save you time and money.

TRAIN
The Jugoslovenske Železnice (JŽ) provides adequate railway services along the main interior line from Subotica to Novi Sad, Belgrade,

Niš, Priština and Skopje and there's a highly scenic line from Belgrade down to the coast at Bar, especially between Kolašin and Bar. There are four classes of train: *ekspresni* (express), *poslovni* (rapid), *brzi* (fast) and *putnicki* (slow). Make sure you have the right sort of ticket for your train.

The train is cheaper than the bus and you don't have to pay for luggage. It is, however, slower and can get very crowded. The quality of the rolling stock varies enormously from OK to dilapidated and dirty. The international 'name' trains are usually of good quality. It's normally only possible to make seat reservations in the train's originating station, unless reservations are mandatory, in which case try to book the day before. Most trains have 'no smoking' compartments. Inter-Rail passes are valid in Yugoslavia, but Eurail passes are not.

All train stations (except in Kosovo) have left-luggage offices where you can dump your bag (passport required).

CAR & MOTORCYCLE

Yugoslavia's motorways *(autoput)* run southeast through Belgrade, Niš and Skopje towards Greece. Yugoslavs pay low tolls in dinars but foreign-registered vehicles pay much higher prices in Deutschmarks. Toll charges are posted at the motorway exit, not at the entrance. All other roads are free and, with a little time and planning, you can avoid the motorways.

Speed limits for private cars and motorcycles are 120 km/h on motorways, 100 km/h on 1st-class roads, 80 km/h on 2nd-class roads and 60 km/h in built-up areas.

Members of foreign automobile clubs get a reduced rate on towing services provided by the Automoto Savez Jugoslavije (AMSJ). It has branches in almost every town, with repair facilities available. Call ☎ 987 for AMSJ emergency assistance.

Petrol is available in regular (86 octane), super (98 octane) and unleaded or *bezolovni* (95 octane) varieties. There are no petrol coupons but queues may still form at government-owned Jugopetrol and Beopetrol stations. If you can find one, a private petrol station *(privatna benzinska pumpa)* may have slightly cheaper petrol. In mid-1996 the cost was about 3.4 DIN for a litre of super.

Driving around Yugoslavia should present no particular problems these days. The hoards of transiting tourists have backed off and the roads are relatively untravelled and in good repair. All borders are open, including the one with Croatia (although at the time of writing, train, bus and air routes had not been fully restored), and the large towns and the coast are quiet. The police are ever-vigilant and always on the lookout to fine unwary motorists on the spot for some minor infringement, so beware. Kosovo is probably better avoided because of ethnic tensions. Take reasonable security precautions when parking – an alarm or steering-wheel lock is a good idea.

LOCAL TRANSPORT

Public-transport strip tickets and tokens are available from newsstands in Belgrade. Punch your ticket as you board the vehicle.

ORGANISED TOURS

Day trips along the Danube and further afield are available. Check with the Tourist Organisation of Belgrade in the city centre for details. Ski Centar Durmitor organises one-week skiing packages and Putnik Tours in Belgrade have various tailored packages for visitors.

Belgrade (Београд)

The dominant role of Serbia (Srbija) in the former Yugoslav Federation was underlined by the inclusion within its boundaries of two formerly 'autonomous provinces', Vojvodina and Kosovo, and the national capital, Belgrade.

Belgrade (Beograd) is strategically situated on the southern edge of the Carpathian basin where the Sava River joins the Danube. Just east of the city is the Morava Valley, route of the famous 'Stamboul Road' from Turkey to Central Europe. At this major crossroads developed a city which has long been the flashpoint of the Balkans. It would be an interesting place to look around for a few days, if accommodation wasn't so absurdly expensive.

Until WWI Belgrade was right on the border of Serbia and Austria-Hungary, and its citadel has seen many battles. Destroyed and rebuilt 40 times in its 2300-year history, Belgrade has never quite managed to pick up all the pieces. It is nonetheless a lively, vibrant city with fine

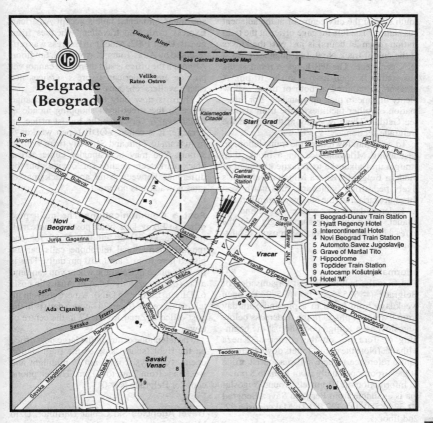

Belgrade (Beograd)

0   1   2 km

Danube River

Veliko Ratno Ostrvo

See Central Belgrade Map

To Airport

Leninov Bulevar

Druga Bulevar

Novi Beograd

Jurija Gagarina

Kalemegdan Citadel

Stari Grad

Central Railway Station

29 Novembra

Takovska

Partizanski Put

Mije Kovacevica

Sava River

Nemanjina

Gazela

Trg Slavija

Vracar

Bulevar Franše D'Eperea

Bulevar JNA

Bulevar Mira

1 Beograd-Dunav Train Station
2 Hyatt Regency Hotel
3 Intercontinental Hotel
4 Novi Beograd Train Station
5 Automoto Savez Jugoslavije
6 Grave of Maršal Tito
7 Hippodrome
8 Topčider Train Station
9 Autocamp Košutnjak
10 Hotel 'M'

Ada Ciganlija

Sapsko Jezero

Radnička

Bulevar Voj. Mišića

Bulevar Vojvode Mišića

Savski Venac

Stevana Provenčanceg

Teodora Drajzera

Bulevar JNA

Vojvode Stepe

Nemanjoda Junaka

Savska Magistrala

Požeška

---

restaurants and street cafés and a rhythm that reminds you of northern Europe rather than the Balkans.

History

The Celtic settlement of Singidunum was founded in the 3rd century BC on a bluff overlooking the confluence of the Sava and Danube rivers. The Romans arrived in the 1st century AD and stayed till the 5th century. The present Slavic name Beograd (White City) first appeared in a papal letter dated 16 April 878.

Belgrade became the capital of Serbia in 1403, when the Serbs were pushed north by the Turks. In 1456 the Hungarians, under János Hunyadi, succeeded in defeating a Turkish northward advance but in 1521 the Turks finally took Belgrade. In 1842 the city again became the capital of Serbia and in 1918, the capital of Yugoslavia. In April 1941, 17,000 lives were lost in a Nazi bombing raid on Belgrade. Soon after, on 4 July 1941, Tito and the Communist Party's central committee, meeting at Belgrade, decided to launch an armed uprising. Belgrade was liberated on 20 October 1944, and since then the population has grown six-fold to over 1.5 million.

Orientation

You'll probably arrive at the train station on the

south side of the city centre or at the adjacent bus station. The left-luggage office at the train station (open 24 hours) is just past the kiosks at the end of track No 9. Left luggage costs 4 DIN per piece. The left-luggage room at the bus station is open from 6 am to 10 pm. A passport is required at both of these. Allow plenty of time to pick up your bag. For information on other facilities at the train station, see Getting There & Away at the end of the Belgrade section.

To walk into town from the train station, go east along Milovanovića for a block, then straight up Balkanska to Terazije, the heart of modern Belgrade. Kneza Mihaila, Belgrade's lively pedestrian boulevard, runs north-west through Stari Grad (the old town) from Terazije to Kalemegdan Park, where you'll find the citadel. The crowds are surprisingly chic, the cafés well patronised and the atmosphere bustling and businesslike.

Information

The friendly, helpful Tourist Organisation of Belgrade (☎ 635 622; fax 635 343), open weekdays from 9 am to 8 pm and Saturday from 9 am to 4 pm, is in the underpass below Jugoslovenska Knjiga bookshop at the beginning of Terazije, on the corner of Kneza Mihaila. (Note the public toilets down there for future reference.) There's also a tourist office at the airport open daily from 8 am to 8 pm.

Information on HI hostels around Yugoslavia is available from Ferijalni Savez Beograd (☎ 324 8550; fax 322 0762), Makedonska 22, 2nd floor.

Motorists are assisted by the English-speaking staff at the special Informativni Centar around the corner from the Automoto Savez Jugoslavije (☎ 419 822), Ruzveltova 18, a little south-east of Tašmajdan Park.

Money The JIK Banka is across the park in front of the train station (open from 8 am to 8 pm weekdays and 8 am to 3 pm Saturday). The exchange window in the train station gives a less favourable rate.

In mid-1996 American Express travellers' cheques could only be changed at the Karić Banka on the corner of Maršala Birjuzova and Pop Lukina, or at the airport branch which is also open on weekends. Hyatt International

and InterContinental hotels accept American Express cards and travellers' cheques from guests. Until 1992, American Express was represented by Atlas Tours, Kosovska 8, 6th floor. Although the office is still there they cannot yet provide any American Express services nor cash travellers' cheques.

There is now only one private exchange office in the street-level shopping arcade at Kolarčeva 7, very near the tourist office on Terazije. It is called VODR (open weekdays from 9 am to 7 pm and Saturday from 9 am to 3 pm). You may occasionally come across black marketeers angling for 'devize', but the difference between bank and black market rates nowadays is not great.

Post & Communications The main post office, at Takovska 2, holds poste-restante mail (postcode 11101) at window No 2 for one month. International telephone calls can be placed here from 7 am to 10 pm daily. This is the only place in Belgrade where you can send a fax (one page to the USA or Australia costs 62 DIN, to Europe 45 DIN). A more convenient telephone centre (open 24 hours a day) is in the post office at Zmaj Jovina 17 in the centre of town.

The telephone centre in the large post office on the right (south) side of the train station opens weekdays from 7 am to midnight and weekends from 7 am to 10 pm. The telephone code for Belgrade is ☎ 011.

Travel Agencies Ski Centar Durmitor, Uzin Mirkova 7, has information on white-water rafting, skiing and hiking in Montenegro's Durmitor National Park.

Putnik Travel Agency (☎ 330 669; fax 334 505), Terazije 27, is the largest and oldest travel agency in Yugoslavia. It offers a wide range of services both domestically and internationally.

Basturist (the office with the JAT sign in the window between the bus and train station), Turist Biro Lasta (☎ 641 251; fax 642 473) and the adjacent Putnik office all sell tickets for international buses (see Getting There & Away for fare prices).

Beogradtours (☎ 641 258; fax 687 447), at Milovanovića 5, a block up the hill from the train station, will book couchettes and sleepers

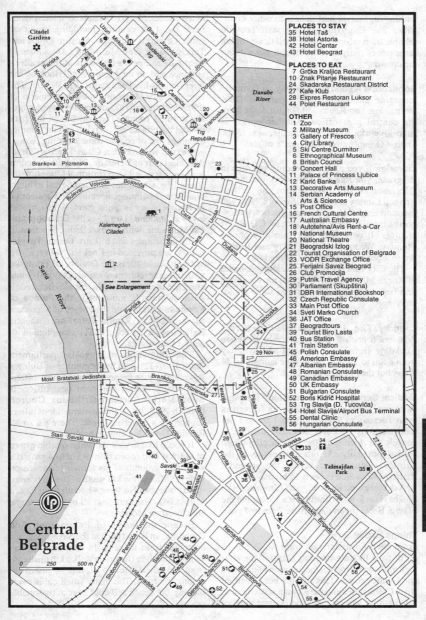

PLACES TO STAY
35 Hotel Taš
38 Hotel Astoria
42 Hotel Centar
43 Hotel Beograd

PLACES TO EAT
7 Grčka Kraljica Restaurant
10 Znak Pitanje Restaurant
24 Skadarska Restaurant District
27 Kafe Klub
28 Expres Restoran Luksor
44 Polet Restaurant

OTHER
1 Zoo
2 Military Museum
3 Gallery of Frescos
4 City Library
5 Ski Centre Durmitor
6 Ethnographical Museum
8 British Council
9 Concert Hall
11 Palace of Princess Ljubice
12 Karić Banka
13 Decorative Arts Museum
14 Serbian Academy of
   Arts & Sciences
15 Post Office
16 French Cultural Centre
17 Australian Embassy
18 Autotehna/Avis Rent-a-Car
19 National Museum
20 National Theatre
21 Beogradski Izlog
22 Tourist Organisation of Belgrade
23 VODR Exchange Office
25 Ferijalni Savez Beograd
26 Club Promocija
29 Putnik Travel Agency
30 Parliament (Skupština)
31 DBR International Bookshop
32 Czech Republic Consulate
33 Main Post Office
34 Sveti Marko Church
36 JAT Office
37 Beogradtours
39 Tourist Biro Lasta
40 Bus Station
41 Train Station
45 Polish Consulate
46 American Embassy
47 Albanian Embassy
48 Romanian Consulate
49 Canadian Embassy
50 UK Embassy
51 Bulgarian Consulate
52 Boris Kidrič Hospital
53 Trg Slavija (D. Tucovića)
54 Hotel Slavija/Airport Bus Terminal
55 Dental Clinic
56 Hungarian Consulate

Central Belgrade

0   250   500 m

within Yugoslavia and tickets to other countries. The English-speaking staff provide reliable train information and sell tickets at the same prices charged in the station, but without the crowds.

Bookshops A good place to get your favourite magazine and possibly newspaper is DBR International on Kneza Miloša just down from the central post office. Another option is Jugoslovenska Knjiga in Terazije, next to the Tourist Organisation of Belgrade office.

Libraries If you plan on spending any time in Belgrade, you might want to fork out the 50 DIN membership fee to join the British Council Library at Kneza Mihaila 48. Here you can read English-language magazines, borrow books and videos and access CD-ROM archives. It is open from 11 am to 4 pm on Monday, Wednesday and Friday and from 2 pm to 7 pm on Tuesday and Thursday.

The City Library is at the Kalemegdan end of Kneza Mihaila. Here you can have a coffee or a beer in the snack bar, or do some photocopying.

Laundry The dry cleaners at Generala Ždanova 6 just off Bulevar Revolucije (open weekdays from 7 am to 8 pm and Saturday from 8 am to 3 pm) can do your laundry in 24 hours but they charge per piece.

Medical Services The Boris Kidrič Hospital, Pasterova 1, has a special clinic for foreigners open Tuesday to Saturday from 7 am to 1 pm (consultations 20 DIN). It's also possible to consult the doctors in the regular clinic here until 7 pm daily. At other times go to the Klinički Centar just across the street at Pasterova 2, which is open 24 hours.

A dental clinic for foreigners (Stomatološka Služba) is at Ivana Milutinovića 15, behind the Slavija Hotel (open daily from 7 am to 7 pm).

Things to See

From the train station take tram No 1, 2 or 13 north-west to **Kalemegdan Citadel**, the strategic hill-top fortress at the junction of the Sava and Danube rivers. This area has been fortified since Celtic times and the Roman settlement of Singidunum was on the flood plain at the foot of the citadel. Much of what is seen today dates from the 17th century, including medieval gates, Orthodox churches, Muslim tombs and Turkish baths. Ivan Meštrović's *Monument of Gratitude to France* (1930) is at the citadel's entrance and on the ramparts overlooking the rivers stands his 1928 statue *The Winner*. The large **Military Museum** on the battlements of the citadel presents a complete history of Yugoslavia in 53 rooms. The benches in the park around the citadel are relaxing and on summer evenings lots of people come strolling past.

Next to Kalemegdan Citadel is Stari Grad, the oldest part of Belgrade. The best museums are here, especially the **National Museum**, trg Republike, which has archaeological exhibits downstairs, paintings upstairs. The collection of European art is quite good. A few blocks away at Studentski trg 13 is the **Ethnographical Museum**, with an excellent collection of Serbian costumes and folk art. Detailed explanations are provided in English. Not far away, at Cara Uroša 20, is the **Gallery of Frescos**, with full-size replicas of paintings from remote churches in Serbia and Macedonia. Belgrade's most memorable museum is the **Palace of Princess Ljubice**, on the corner of Svetozara Markovića and Kralija Petra, an authentic Balkan-style palace (1831) complete with period furnishings.

The **Skupština**, or Yugoslav parliament (built 1907-32), is at the beginning of Bulevar Revolucije, just before the main post office. East again, behind the main post office, is **Sveti Marko Serbian Orthodox Church** (built in 1932-39), with four tremendous pillars supporting a towering dome. There's a small Russian Orthodox church behind it.

If you'd like to visit the white marble **grave of Maršal Tito** (open from 9 am to 4 pm), it's within the grounds of his former residence on Bulevar Mira a few km south of the city centre (take trolleybus No 40 or 41 south from Kneza Miloša 64). The tomb and all of the museums are closed on Monday.

Escape the bustle of Belgrade on **Ada Ciganlija**, an island park in the Sava River just upstream from the city. In summer you can swim in the river (naturists walk a km upstream from the others), rent a bicycle or just stroll among the trees. The many small cafés overlooking the beach sell cold beer at reasonable prices.

Places to Stay

Accommodation in Belgrade is very expensive, compounded by the fact that foreigners can pay up to three times as much for accommodation as Yugoslavs. Budget places are hard to come by and private rooms almost impossible to find.

A valuable tip which will save a day's travelling time, a night's hotel bill and a lot of aggravation, is to book a sleeper or couchette out of Belgrade at the train station. This is easily done and costs from 18 to 36 DIN extra. Just try getting a room for that! There are overnight trains to Bar, Skopje and Peć. If you arrive in Belgrade in the morning, you'll have all day to look around before boarding the train late that evening (the main sights can be seen in a busy day). Don't forget that a train ticket is required in addition to the couchette ticket. If for some reason you can't get a couchette, consider an overnight bus with a seat reservation to your next destination. It's cheaper than the train and advance tickets are easily purchased at the bus station, but it's much more tiring.

Camping *Autocamp Košutnjak* (☎ 555 127), Kneza Višeslava 17, is about eight km southwest of the city centre. Camping is possible from May to September only, but there are expensive new bungalows open all year (120 DIN per person with private bath). The older, cheaper bungalows are permanently occupied by locals. It's a fairly pleasant wooded site with lots of shade, but pitch your tent far from the noisy restaurant. To get there take tram No 12 or 13 south from beside the train station to Kneza Višeslava, the next stop after you see the horse-racing track (hippodrome) on the left. From the tram stop it's a km up the hill.

Hostels Belgrade's HI hostel is the *Hotel M* (☎ 237 2560; fax 461 236), a modern three-storey building on Bulevar JNA at No 56a on the south side of the city. At 90 DIN for a bed in a six-bed dorm it's expensive but breakfast is included. A YHA card is not required. Individual single/doubles are 180/290 DIN. It's open all day (check in from noon) and there's no curfew or rules. From the railway station take tram No 2 or 3 up Nemanjina to trg Slavija (look out for McDonald's) and from here take

a No 47 Banjica bus for six stops. The hotel is 100 metres further on. For those arriving by train from Romania, bus No 47 departs from Beogad-Dunav station.

Private Rooms Private rooms have become more or less nonexistent in Belgrade. You will not be approached by anyone as you leave the bus or train station and finding one will be a challenge. Better opt for one of the cheap hotels (if there is a room available), or grit your teeth and fork out for a room at an inflated tourist price at a mid-range hotel in the centre.

Hotels Belgrade is full of state-owned B-category hotels charging 220/400 DIN and up for a single/double. One of the few privately owned hotels is the basic but clean *Hotel Taš* (☎ 343 507; fax 338 027), Beogradska 71, and here everyone pays the same: 84/108 DIN for a single/double. The Taš has only one single room and 18 doubles, and it's often full. Ask for a room away from the noisy street. Take tram No 12 from the train station to the end of the line, then walk across the park. Take the lift to the 3rd floor.

The next cheapest place is *Hotel Centar* (☎ 644 055; fax 657 838), Savski trg 7, opposite the train station. It's 135 DIN per person in a four-bed dorm or 140 DIN per person in a double room with bath. The only advantage of having to pay more than twice as much as a local is that they won't put a local in the room with you, which means you'll probably have it to yourself. This place is usually full.

If you are prepared to fork out more, the B-category *Hotel Beograd* (☎ 645 199; fax 643 746) at Nemanjina 6, directly opposite the main entrance to the train station, has singles/doubles for 160/240 DIN. The *Hotel Astoria* (☎ 645 422; fax 686 437), nearby at M.Milovanovića 1, has singles/doubles with breakfast for an even more inflated 210/330 DIN.

Places to Eat

For local colour and if the budget is up to it, try the expensive folkloric restaurants in the Bohemian quarter along ulica Skadarska. In the evening, open-air folkloric, musical and theatrical performances are often staged here.

The *Znak Pitanje* (Question Mark) restaurant, Kralja Petra 6 opposite the Orthodox church, is in an old Balkan inn serving traditional meat dishes, side salads and flat draught beer. You sit at low tables on low wooden stools. Look for the question-mark sign above the door. Prices are mid-range and the food is very good.

The *Grčka Kraljica*, at the Kalemegdan end of Kneza Mihaila, is a would-be Greek restaurant with vivid blue and white décor and Greek background muzak. The food is actually quite good, though heavy on the Serbian influence, and you can have Greek wine to accompany it. The location is particularly pleasant, situated as it is on a busy pedestrian mall. Prices are mid-range.

For inexpensive seafood try the *Polet Restaurant*, Njegoševa 1. The attractive maritime décor is designed to resemble the interior of a large ship. The menu is only in Serbian but all prices are clearly listed. On weekdays between 1 and 6 pm there's a special set menu of spicy fish soup (čorba), salad, bread and a main dish of fish and vegetables. The portions are large and the service is good.

Expres Restoran Luksor, at Balkanska 7, is the cheapest self-service place in town. Further up the street, the *Leskovac* takeaway window sells authentic Balkan-style hamburgers.

A great breakfast place near the train station is the burek counter at Nemanjina 5, just below Hotel Beograd (open weekdays from 5 am to 1 pm and Saturday from 5 to 11 am). Avoid the food kiosks right opposite the train station as they overcharge.

The *Kafe Klub*, at Terazije 4 near the tourist office, is perfect for a cappuccino with croissants.

Entertainment

During the winter season, opera is performed at the elegant *National Theatre* (1869) on trg Republike. Their box office opens Tuesday to Sunday from 10 am to 1 pm, and from 3 pm on performance days. The Yugoslavs aren't pretentious about theatre dress – jeans are OK even at the opera.

Concerts are held at the concert hall of *Kolarčev University*, Studentski trg 5 (box office open daily from 10 am to noon and 6 to 8 pm). In October a festival of classical music is held here. The *Belgrade Philharmonia* is hidden at the end of the passageway at Studentski trg 11, directly across the street from the Ethnographical Museum.

Concerts also take place in the hall of the *Serbian Academy of Arts & Sciences*, Kneza Mihaila 35. The *French Cultural Centre*, Kneza Mihaila 31 (closed weekends), often shows free films and videos. In the evening throngs of street musicians play along Kneza Mihaila.

The Bilet Servis, trg Republike 5, has tickets to many events and the friendly English-speaking staff will search happily through their listings for something musical for you. Ask them about the *Teatar T*, Bulevard Revolucije 77a, which stages musicals several times a week (but is closed Wednesday and Thursday).

Belgrade doesn't have a lot of discos. Most people do their socialising in the many fashionable cafés around trg Republike. One disco called *Club Promocija* is reached through a dark lane at Nušićeva 8 just off Terazije (open from 11 pm to 5 am daily except Sunday).

Things To Buy

There are thankfully – for the moment at least – few tacky tourist souvenirs on display to tempt you to part with your dollars or dinars. On trg Republike there is Beogradski Izlog (Belgrade Window), next to Bilet Servis, where you may find some tasteful local art and craftwork. Pottery features prominently, though you may also find souvenir sweaters and T-shirts emblazoned with 'Beograd' in Cyrillic.

Getting There & Away

Bus The bus station has computerised ticketing and there are overnight buses to many places around Yugoslavia. Buy your ticket as far ahead as you can to be assured of a good seat. Posted destinations are in Cyrillic only.

Train Belgrade is on the main railway lines from Istanbul and Athens to Western Europe. International trains on these routes are covered in the Getting There & Away section earlier in this chapter. Overnight domestic trains with couchettes or sleepers run from Belgrade to Bar (524 km, 7½ hours), Peć (490 km, 9½ hours) and Skopje (472 km, nine hours). Most of the above depart from the main station on

Savski trg. Trains to Romania depart from Beograd-Dunav Station, Đure Đakovića 39.

Sample fares from Belgrade to Bar are as follows: 88 DIN in 2nd class in a three-bed compartment, 79 DIN in a four-bed compartment, 70 DIN in a six-bed compartment; 1st-class sleepers are 129 DIN. These prices are all-inclusive. Regular train tickets for the Belgrade-Bar journey (524 km, 7½ hours) cost 52 DIN in 2nd class, or 75 DIN in 1st class.

Train Station At the main train station, the ticket counters are numbered 1 to 26. International tickets are sold at window Nos 3 and 4 and regular tickets at window Nos 7 to 20. Sleeper and couchette reservations are made in a separate office just off platform 1. Look for the blue and white 'bed' sign. Timetable and departure information is posted in Cyrillic only in the ticket hall. There is a currency-exchange window, a souvenir shop and an Avis car-rental office in the smaller building facing the end of the tracks. Toilets and left luggage are next to platform 9.

Getting Around
To/From the Airport The JAT bus (15 DIN) departs from the street next to Hotel Slavija, trg Slavija (D. Tucovića), roughly every hour. This bus also picks up from the forecourt of the main train station. Surčin airport is 18 km west of the city. If you're stuck at the airport waiting for a flight, visit the nearby Yugoslav Aviation Museum (closed Monday).

Public Transport Because Belgrade lacks a metro, the buses, trams and trolleybuses are tremendously overcrowded. Six-strip public transport tickets costing 7 DIN are sold at tobacco kiosks and you validate your own ticket by punching a strip once aboard. If you pay a city bus or tram driver directly it will be about double the fare. Fold the top of the strip over each time you use it. Local bus riders usually have monthly passes, so don't be surprised if they do not seem to use tickets.

Taxi A motley bunch of old and new vehicles all in different colours, Belgrade's taxis are in plentiful supply. Flag fall is 4 DIN. A trip around the centre should cost between 10 and 20 DIN. Check that the taxi meter is running. If not, point it out to the driver.

Car Rental Autotehna/Avis (☎ 620 362), Obilićev Venac 25, and Putnik Eurodollar (contact Putnik Travel) have cars beginning at an expensive 410 DIN per day. A cash bond equivalent to US$500 must be paid in advance. Their cars are only for use within Yugoslavia.

Vojvodina (Војводина)

Vojvodina (21,506 sq km) was an autonomous province until 1990 when Serbia scrapped this arrangement and annexed Vojvodina to the Republic of Serbia. Slavs settled here in the 6th century, followed by Hungarians in the 10th century. Following their defeat at the hands of the Turks in 1389, many Serbs fled north but they and the Hungarians were later swamped by the 16th-century Turkish conquest. When the Habsburgs drove the Turks back across the Danube in the late 17th century the Vojvodina region again became a refuge for the Serbs, who moved into this Hungarian-controlled area to escape unbroken Ottoman rule in the lands further south. The region remained a part of Hungary until 1918.

Today ethnic Serbs make up most of the population. Minorities include Hungarians (24%), Croats (8%), Slovaks (4%) and Romanians (3%). Some 170,000 ethnic Germans were expelled from Vojvodina after WWII and large numbers of Serbs immigrated here to occupy the areas the Germans formerly inhabited. As a result, the percentage of Serbs in the total population of Vojvodina increased from 37% in 1921 to 57.2% in 1991.

Until Serbian nationalists took control of the Vojvodina government in October 1988, the province's 345,000 Hungarians had fared better than Hungarian minorities in Romania and Slovakia, but since then they have come under increasing pressure. In July 1991 the Serbian parliament required all public signs to be written in Cyrillic, and teaching in Hungarian is being phased out in schools. Some 25,000 Hungarians fled to Hungary to escape war propaganda and forced mobilisation. As the Hungarians left, the Serbian government resettled some of the 140,000 Serbian refugees in Vojvodina into their homes. The 100,000 Croats of Bačka in northern Vojvodina are also suffering extreme repression as the Serbian government attempts to force them to leave.

This low-lying land of many rivers merges imperceptibly into the Great Hungarian Plain and Romania's Banat. The Tisa River cuts southward through the middle of the region, joining the Danube midway between Novi Sad and Belgrade. The Sava and Danube rivers mark Vojvodina's southern boundary with Serbia; the Danube also separates Vojvodina from Croatia in the west. Numerous canals crisscross this fertile plain which provides much of Yugoslavia's wheat and corn. Most of Yugoslavia's crude oil comes from wells here.

NOVI SAD (НОВИ САД)

Novi Sad (Hungarian: Újvidék), capital of Vojvodina, is a friendly, modern city situated at a strategic bend of the Danube. The city developed in the 18th century when a powerful fortress was built on a hill-top overlooking the river to hold the area for the Habsburgs. Novi Sad remained part of the Austro-Hungarian empire until 1918 and it still has a Hungarian air about it today. The main sights can be covered in a couple of hours or you can make a leisurely day of it.

Orientation & Information

The adjacent train and bus stations are at the end of Bulevar Oslobođenja, on the north-west side of the city centre. There is a tourist agency to the right as you come out of the train station.

It's a brisk 40-minute walk from the train station to the city centre, otherwise catch bus No 4 (pay the conductor 2 DIN) from the station to Bulevar Mihajla Pupina, then ask directions to the tourist office at Dunavska 27, in a quaint old part of town. This office has brochures on many parts of Yugoslavia besides Novi Sad.

The Automoto Klub Vojvodine is at Arse Teodorovića 15 off Pap Pavla.

Post & Communications

The telephone centre next to the main post office is open 24 hours. The telephone code for Novi Sad is ☎021 and the postcode is 21101.

Travel Agencies

Putnik (☎ 29 210), at Kraja Aleksandra 8 just off trg Slobode, sells train tickets.

Things to See

There are three **museums** on Dunavska near the tourist office: paintings at No 29 (closed Monday and Tuesday), archaeology at No 35 (closed Monday) and the history of the 1941-45 revolution at No 37. The latter museum is close to the Danube. Officially, the Museum of the Revolution is closed for 'rearrangement' but the old exhibits are still in place and the staff will let you see them if you say you're especially interested in Yugoslavia's WWII history.

Walk across the old bridge to majestic **Petrovaradin Citadel** (built 1699-1780), the 'Gibraltar of the Danube', designed by French architect Vauban. The stairs beside the large church in the lower town lead up to the fortress. Today the citadel contains an expensive hotel, a restaurant and two small museums (closed Monday), but the chief pleasure is simply to walk along the walls enjoying the splendid view of the city, river and surrounding countryside. There are up to 16 km of underground galleries and halls below the citadel, but these can only be visited by groups.

Other sights in Novi Sad include three substantial **art galleries** (closed Monday and Tuesday) side by side on Vase Stajića, not far from trg Slobode and the ultramodern **Serbian National Theatre** (1981).

Places to Stay

Camping There's a large *autocamp* (☎ 368 400) near the Danube at Ribarsko Ostrvo, with bungalows (120/140/160 DIN for a single/double/triple) available all year. Bus No 4 runs frequently from the train station to Liman via the city centre. From the end of the line walk towards the river. If you walk all the way from the centre of town, it will take about an hour.

Hostels The HI hostel across the river is still housing refugees and there is no other budget-friendly place to stay.

Hotels The nicest and oldest of Novi Sad's six hotels is *Hotel Vojvodina* (☎ 622 122; fax 615 445), right on trg Slobode. It has an attractive

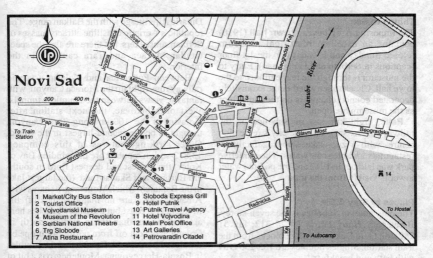

Novi Sad

0   200   400 m

To Train Station

To Hostel

To Autocamp

Danube River

Glavni Most

1 Market/City Bus Station	8 Sloboda Express Grill
2 Tourist Office	9 Hotel Putnik
3 Vojvodanski Museum	10 Putnik Travel Agency
4 Museum of the Revolution	11 Hotel Vojvodina
5 Serbian National Theatre	12 Main Post Office
6 Trg Slobode	13 Art Galleries
7 Atina Restaurant	14 Petrovaradin Citadel

pastel façade and is very conveniently located. The 62 rooms with private bath are a fairly pricey 200/300 DIN for a single/double, breakfast included.

The even more pricey *Hotel Putnik* (☎ 615 555; fax 622 561), round the corner from the Vojvodina, has singles/doubles for 300/400 DIN.

Places to Eat

The restaurant in the *Hotel Vojvodina* is reasonably priced, despite its elegant appearance. The food is good and the servings are large.

The *Atina Restaurant*, next to the large church on trg Slobode, has a self-service section for a quick lunch and a full-service restaurant at the back. It's nothing special but at least there's a menu with prices clearly listed.

The *Sloboda Express Grill*, on Modene in the centre, is cheap and unassuming. Take your pick and pay the cashier.

Getting There & Away

Novi Sad is on the main railway line between Belgrade, Budapest and Sofia. In the evening you can easily pick up the overnight *Balkan Express* train to Sofia (485 km, 12 hours). Trains to Subotica (99 km, two hours) and

Belgrade (80 km, 1½ hours) run every two hours.

SUBOTICA (СУБОТИЦА)

Subotica (Hungarian: Szabadka), is a large Hungarian-speaking city 10 km from the Hungarian border. Over half the 180,000 inhabitants are of Hungarian origin and another quarter are Croats. Subotica is a useful transit point to/from Szeged (Hungary) and the train station is just a short walk from the centre of town.

The left-luggage office at the train station is open 24 hours (passport required). You pay when you collect your luggage later. The cost is 4 DIN per item.

Information

Putnik (☎ 25 400), Borisa Kidriča 4, is helpful with information and sells train tickets. Subotica's telephone code is ☎ 024.

Money Vojvodanska Banka has a currency-exchange office in the old town hall (open weekdays from 7 am to 7.30 pm and Saturday from 7 am to 1.30 pm). Other exchange offices are at the train station and at the Hotel Patria.

Things to See

The imposing Art Nouveau **town hall** (1910) contains an excellent **historical museum** (closed Sunday and Monday) on the 1st floor (captions in Serbian and Hungarian). Entry to the museum is through the rear entrance to the town hall. Check to see whether the exquisitely decorated council chambers on the same floor as the museum are open.

Palić, eight km east of Subotica on the railway line to Szeged, is the city's recreation centre, with a zoo, lake, sporting facilities, restaurants and pleasant walks. The attractive park was laid out in 1912 and the pointed water tower is visible from the train.

Places to Stay & Eat

The only hotel in Subotica is the seven-storey, B-category *Hotel Patria* (☎ 26 312; fax 51 762), on Đure Đakovića, three blocks from the train station. Singles/doubles are 133/236 DIN with bath and breakfast.

Stara Pizzeria, Engelsova 7 off Borisa Kidriča, is a good choice for eating out.

There are three hotels at Palić. The best is the *Park* near the train station. The *Jezero* is also near the station, while the less expensive *Sport* is close to the camping ground, about 10 minutes walk away. In winter only the Park is open. The train to/from Szeged stops near these hotels. You can also get there on bus No 6 from the main bus station near Hotel Patria in Subotica.

Getting There & Away

There are four local trains a day to/from Szeged, Hungary (45 km, 1½ hours, 15 DIN). Several daily buses also shuttle between Szeged and Subotica (18 DIN), but the train is more convenient. A daily bus links Subotica to Budapest (216 km, 110 DIN).

Five express trains a day run north to Budapest (274 km, six hours, 102 DIN) and there are 12 trains a day to Novi Sad (99 km, two hours, 25 DIN).

Montenegro (Црна Гора)

The Republic of Montenegro (Crna Gora) occupies a corner of south-western Yugoslavia directly north of Albania, close to where the Dinaric Alps merge with the Balkan range. The republic's Adriatic coastline attracts masses of Serbian sunseekers, but there are also the spectacular Morača and Tara canyons in the interior.

Between Podgorica and Kolašin a scenic railway runs right up the Morača Canyon, with fantastic views between the countless tunnels. West of Mojkovac, the next station after Kolašin, is the 100-km-long Tara Canyon, thought to be the second-largest in the world. Other striking features of this compact, 13,812-sq-km republic are the winding Bay of Kotor (the longest and deepest fjord in southern Europe) and Skadar Lake (the largest lake in the Balkans), which Montenegro shares with Albania. There are no major islands off the Montenegrin coast but the sandy beaches here are far longer than those further north in Croatia. Now cut off from northern Europe by the closed border with Croatia and the troubles in Bosnia-Hercegovina, Montenegro is a bit of a backwater.

History

Only tiny Montenegro kept its head above the Turkish tide which engulfed the Balkans for over four centuries. Medieval Montenegro was part of Serbia, and after the Serbian defeat at Kosovo Polje in 1389 the inhabitants of this mountainous region continued to resist the Turks. In 1482 Ivan Crnojević established an independent principality at Cetinje ruled by *vladike* (bishops) who were popularly elected after 1516. Beginning in 1697 the succession was limited to the Petrović Njegoš family (each bishop being succeeded by his nephew), who forged an alliance with Russia in 1711.

Intermittent wars with the Turks and Albanians continued until 1878, when the European portion of the Ottoman Empire largely collapsed and Montenegrin independence was recognised by the Congress of Berlin. Nicola I Petrović, Montenegro's ruler from 1860, declared himself king in 1910. In 1916 the Austrians evicted the bishop-king and in 1918 Montenegro was incorporated into Serbia. During WWII Montenegrins fought valiantly in Tito's partisan army and after the war the region was rewarded with republic status within Yugoslavia. In 1946 the administration shifted from Cetinje to Podgorica (known until 1991 as Titograd), a modern city with little to interest the visitor.

The history of Montenegro is hard to follow unless you remember that, like the Albanians, the Montenegrins were divided into tribes or clans, such as the Njegoš clan west of Cetinje and the Paštrović clan around Budva. While blind obedience to the clan leader helped Montenegrins resist foreign invasions, it has not made the transition to democracy easy.

Getting There & Away

In the past, most visitors to Montenegro arrived from Dubrovnik by car or bus. The 1991 fighting closed this route and until the situation normalises the easiest way to get there is by train from Belgrade to Bar. You can also fly directly to Tivat or Podgorica airports from Belgrade.

BAR (БАР)

Backed by a barren coastal range, Bar (Italian: Antivari) is a modern city and the terminus of the railway from Belgrade. A daily ferry connects Bar with Bari, Italy. The development of Bar as an Adriatic port for landlocked Serbia was first proposed in 1879, yet it was not until 1976 that the dream became a reality, with the opening of the Belgrade-Bar train line.

As long as the border between Croatia and Yugoslavia remains closed, Bar will probably be your gateway to Montenegro. Bar is a convenient transport centre and if you find a cheap private room it makes a good base for day trips to Ulcinj, Podgorica, Cetinje, Kotor and Budva.

Orientation

The ferry terminal in Bar is only a few hundred metres from the centre of town, but the adjacent bus and train stations are about two km south-east of the centre. The beach is north of the port.

Information

The tourist office next to Putnik near the port has a few brochures and the adjacent Montenegro Express office can answer questions in English. Bar's telephone code is ☎ 085.

Money There are a number of banks in the port area and you can change money at the post office. You may encounter touts asking to change your money illegally.

Places to Stay & Eat

Autocamp Susanj, two km north of the ferry landing along the beach, is once again open for business during summer.

Putnik Turist Biro opposite the ferry terminal, open from 7 am to 9 or 10 pm in summer, arranges private rooms from 33 to 52 DIN per person, depending on facilities. Putnik is normally open to meet boat arrivals.

Hotel Topolica (☎ 11 244; fax 12 510), a modern five-storey hotel on the beach a few hundred metres north of the port, has single/doubles for 168/276 DIN with half-board, or 198/336 DIN with full board.

The *Grill Obala*, just up from the Putnik office, is handy if you are waiting for a ferry, and the *Grill Sidro*, between the bus and train stations, is convenient for a tasty hamburger if you are waiting for a bus or a train.

Getting There & Away

Four trains a day (two with couchettes) travel to/from Belgrade (524 km, eight hours, 52 DIN). The left-luggage office at the train station is open from 7 am to 9 pm. There are buses to all destinations along the coast. A daily ferry linking Bar to Bari (Italy) leaves Bar at either 9 or 10 pm. Fares on the *Sveti Stefan* may be paid for in dinars. Fares for the other two ferries, also Italy-bound, must be paid for in hard currencies. In midsummer all transport to/from Bar is very crowded as all of Serbia heads for the beach.

ULCINJ (УЛЦИНЬ)

A broad highway tunnels through hills between olive groves for 26 km from Bar to Ulcinj (Ulqin in Albanian, Dulcigno in Italian), near the Albanian border.

Founded by the Greeks, Ulcinj gained notoriety when it was used as a base by North African pirates from 1571 to 1878. There was even a slave market from which the few resident black families are descended.

The Turks held Bar and Ulcinj for over 300 years, and today there are many Muslim Albanians in Ulcinj. You'll notice the difference in people right away: the characteristic white headshawls of the women, the curious direct looks you get, the lively bazar atmosphere in the many small shops, and the sound of Albanian on the streets. Many older women in Ulcinj still wear traditional Islamic dress, especially on market day (Friday). It's a popular holiday resort for Serbs, who arrive en masse via the Belgrade-Bar train. In July and August it can get very crowded although accommodation is always available.

Orientation
Ulcinj's bus station is about two km south of Mala Plaža, the small beach below the old town. You will most likely be dropped off nearer the main drag, ulica 26 Novembar, rather than at the bus station proper. Walk uphill along ulica 26 Novembar to Mala Plaža and you'll pass several buildings with *sobe* and *zimmer* signs where you can rent a room.

Velika Plaža (Great Beach), Ulcinj's famous 12-km stretch of unbroken sand, begins about five km south-east of town (take the bus to Ada).

Information
Adriatours, at ulica 26 Novembar 18, is about 500 metres from the bus station on the way into town on the right.

Money There are several banks in town. Room proprietors and restaurant owners will often change hard cash for you.

Post & Communications The telephone centre in the main post office, at the foot of ulica 26 Novembar not far from the bus station, is open Monday to Saturday from 7 am to 9 pm and Sunday from 9 am to noon. The telephone code for Ulcinj is ☎ 085.

Things to See
The ancient **ramparts** of old Ulcinj overlook the sea, but most of the buildings inside were shattered by earthquakes in 1979 and later reconstructed. The **museum** (closed Monday) is by the upper gate. You can walk among the houses and along the wall for the view.

Places to Stay
Camping There are two camping grounds on Velika Plaža: *Milena* and *Neptun*. On Ada Island, just across the Bojana River from Albania, is *Camping Ada Bojana FKK*, a nudist camping ground accessible by bus (guests only).

Private Rooms Adriatours (☎ 52 057), at No 18 ulica 26 Novembar, is a private travel agency with helpful English-speaking staff who will find you a private room for about 33 DIN per person a night. They're open all year. If you arrive outside business hours knock on the door of the adjacent house with the *zimmer frei* signs (owned by the same family) and if they can't accommodate you they'll suggest someone else who can.

If you continue into town towards Mala Plaža, you'll pass Olcinium Travel Agency (more private rooms) nearly opposite Kino Basta (Basta Cinema). Facing Mala Plaža itself is Turist Biro 'Neptun' Montenegroturist, with another selection of private rooms (35 DIN per person).

Hotels The cheapest hotel is the 240-room *Mediteran* (☎ 81 411), a pleasant modern hotel which is a five-minute walk uphill from Mala Plaža. A single/double with private bath and breakfast will cost you 160/240 DIN and must have a balcony overlooking the sea. It's only open in the summer season.

Places to Eat
There are some chic eating places in the old town if your budget can stand a blowout. There are also numerous inexpensive restaurants around town offering cheap grilled meat or more expensive seafood. Try the *Dubrovnik Restaurant* next to the unfinished cultural centre on ulica 26 Novembar.

Getting There & Away
Buses to/from Bar (26 km, 8 DIN) run every couple of hours.

BUDVA (БУДВА)
Budva is Yugoslavia's top beach resort. A series of fine beaches punctuate the coastline all the way to Sveti Stefan, with the high coastal mountains forming a magnificent backdrop. Before the troubles, Budva used to cater mostly to people on package tours from northern Europe, but its main clientele these days is domestic. Although Budva is not cheap, you may find some good deals just outside the main tourist season of July and August. Though Bar is better positioned transport-wise as a base for making coastal day trips, Budva is far more beautiful and worth the extra effort and expense if you're not in a hurry.

Orientation & Information

The modern bus station is located in a new part of town about one km from the old town. Upon exiting the bus station turn left, walk for about 100 metres before heading right until you hit the main road. Turn right and follow this road to the traffic lights. Turn left here and follow the road round until you come to the main square, trg Republike. There's no left-luggage office at Budva bus station.

The people at Montenegro Express on trg Republike near the old town are good about answering questions.

The telephone code for Budva is ☎ 086.

Money There are two banks on trg Republike: Montenegro Bank and Jugobank. Hotels will normally exchange cash for you without any problem.

Things to See

Budva's big tourist-puller is its old **walled town.** This was levelled by two earthquakes in 1979, after which the residents were permanently evacuated. Since then it has been completely rebuilt as a tourist attraction and the main square with its three churches, museum and fortress (there's a great view from the ramparts) is so picturesque it seems almost contrived. It's possible to walk three-quarters of the way around the top of the town wall. Start from near the north gate.

Budva's main beach is pebbly and fairly average. A better beach is **Mogren Beach**, reached by following a coastal path northwards for 500 metres or so. The path starts in front of the Grand Hotel Avala.

Only a few km south-east of Budva is the former village of **Sveti Stefan**, an island now linked to the mainland. During the 1960s the entire village was converted into a luxury hotel but unlike Budva, which you may enter free, you will be charged to set foot on the hallowed soil of Sveti Stefan during the summer months. Settle for the long-range picture-postcard view and keep your money.

Places to Stay

Camping If you have a tent, try *Autocamp Avala* (☎ 51 205), behind Hotel Montenegro, two km south-east along the shore (through a small tunnel). It's crowded with caravans but at least it's near the beach. No bungalows are

available but the manager may help you find a private room nearby. Avala is open from June to September. Right next to Avala is *Autokamp Boreti*, which has less in the way of security (fences and gates especially).

Private Rooms *Maestral Tours* (☎ 52 250) at Mediteranska 23, just down from the post office, rents private rooms at 330 DIN per person in July and August only. *Emona Globe-tour* nearby may also have private rooms, and a third place to try is *Montenegro Express* (☎ 51 443) on trg Republike, closer to the old town. You may be able to find your own room by looking for signs, but from October to May finding a private room may take some searching.

Hotels The easiest and most convenient option is the modern *Hotel Mogren* (☎ 51 219; fax 52 041) just outside the north gate of the old town. Rates are a fairly pricey 200/330 DIN for singles/doubles but this place is open all year.

Maestral Tours runs the *Hotel Mediteran* (☎ 51 988), about two km south along the coast at Bečići. Prices here range from 120 to 140 DIN per person. Check with Maestral Tours for room availability first.

In the high season try asking for room-filler deals from the other resort hotels, though don't be too optimistic since room prices tend to be fixed by the government.

Places to Eat

Budva has no shortage of expensive bars and restaurants along the seafront and in the old town. Unfortunately these bars and restaurants don't often display their prices outside, so always ask to see a menu before ordering. Give the *Hong Kong* Chinese Restaurant a miss if you are hoping for real Chinese food.

Restoran Centar is upstairs beside the supermarket above the vegetable market, just inland from the post office. It's worth checking out for a meal without the frills. There is a reasonable *self-service restaurant* in the bus station.

Getting There & Away

There are 19 buses a day to Podgorica (74 km) via Cetinje (31 km) and 16 a day to Bar (38 km). There are also buses to Belgrade and other

YUGOSLAVIA

parts of Yugoslavia. The bus timetable at the Budva bus station is in Latin script.

If coming by train from Belgrade, get off at Podgorica and catch a bus from there to Budva. In the other direction it's probably best to take a bus from Budva to Bar and pick up the train to Belgrade there.

If you choose to fly to Tivat, a JAT bus (15 DIN) will take you to Budva and drop you off at trg Republike.

Getting Around

From May to September a small tourist train shuttles up and down the beach from Budva to Bečići for 10 DIN a ride. Ask around the harbour for tourist boats to the little island of Sveti Stefan just across the bay.

CETINJE (ЦЕТИЊЕ)

Cetinje, perched on top of a high plateau between the Bay of Kotor and Skadar Lake, is the old capital of Montenegro, subject of songs and epic poems. The open, easily defended slopes help to explain Montenegro's independence, and much remains of old Cetinje, from museums to palaces, mansions and monasteries. At the turn of the century all the large states of Europe had embassies here. Short hikes can be made in the hills behind Cetinje Monastery. It's well worth spending the night here if you can find an inexpensive place to stay.

Orientation & Information

The bus station is 500 metres from the main square, Balšića Pazar. From the station turn left and the first right and you will find it easily. There is a big wall map in the square to help you get oriented with the main sights and reference points.

Cetinje's telephone code is ☎ 086.

Things to See

The most imposing building in Cetinje is the **State Museum**, the former palace (1871) of Nicola I Petrović, the last king. Looted during WWII, only a portion of its original furnishings remain, but the many portraits and period weapons give a representative picture of the times.

Nearly opposite is the older 1832 residence of the prince-bishop Petar II Petrović Njegoš, who ruled from 1830 to 1851. This building,

now a museum, is also known as **Biljarda Hall** because of a billiard table installed in 1840.

Around the side of Biljarda Hall is a large glass-enclosed pavilion containing a fascinating relief map of Montenegro created by the Austrians in 1917 for tactical planning purposes. Ask one of the Biljarda Hall attendants to let you in.

Beyond the map is **Cetinje Monastery**, founded in 1484 but rebuilt in 1785. The monastery treasury contains a copy of the *Oktoih* or 'Octoechos' (Book of the Eight Voices) printed near here in 1494 – it's one of the oldest collections of liturgical songs in a Slavic language. Vladin Dom, the former Government House (1910) and now the National Gallery, is not far away.

Twenty km away at the summit of **Mt Lovćen** (1749 metres), the 'Black Mountain' which gave Montenegro its Italian name, is the mausoleum of Petar II Petrović Njegoš, a revered poet as well as ruler. The masterful statue of Njegoš inside is by Croatian sculptor Ivan Meštrović. There are no buses up Lovćen and taxis want 130 DIN return; the building is visible in the distance from Cetinje. From the parking lot you must climb 461 steps to the mausoleum and its sweeping view of the Bay of Kotor, mountains and coast. The whole of Mt Lovćen has been declared a national park.

Places to Stay & Eat

For a private room ask at *Intours* (☎ 21 157), the place marked 'Vincom Duty Free Shop' next to the post office. Chances are they'll send you to Petar Martinović, who lives a block away at Bajova Pivljanina 50, next to Belveder Mini Market.

If this fails you have a problem as the only hotel is the *Grand Hotel* (☎ 21 104), a modern so-called five-star hotel that would barely rate two stars anywhere else. Singles/doubles are 180/260 DIN with bath and breakfast. It's a five-minute walk from the centre.

There is not a glut of eating places in Cetinje. The *Restoran Cetinje* next to the post office and the *Mliječni Restoran* on the main square were closed out of season, but may be open in summer. Failing these two, you might opt for passable pasta or pizza at the *Spoleto* pizzeria further down from the post office.

Getting There & Away

There are 19 buses a day between Cetinje and Podgorica (45 km), and a similar number back to Budva (31 km).

You can easily make Cetinje a day trip from Bar by catching an early train to Podgorica, where you'll connect with a bus to Cetinje. An early afternoon bus down to Budva will give you some time at the beach and a chance to look around the reconstructed old town before taking a late afternoon bus back to Bar.

DURMITOR NATIONAL PARK

Montenegro's Durmitor National Park is a popular hiking and mountaineering area just west of Žabljak, a ski resort which is also the highest town in Yugoslavia (1450 metres). A chair lift from near Hotel Durmitor towards Mt Štuoc (1953 metres) operates in winter. Žabljak was a major partisan base during WWII, changing hands four times.

Some 18 mountain lakes dot the slopes of the Durmitor Range south-west of Žabljak. You can walk right around the largest lake, **Crno jezero** (Black Lake), three km from Žabljak, in an hour or two, and swim in its waters in summer. The rounded mass of Međed (2287 metres) rises directly behind the lake, surrounded by a backdrop of other peaks, including Savin kuk (2313 metres). You can climb Savin kuk in eight hours there and back. The national park office next to Hotel Durmitor sells good maps of the park.

Durmitor's claim to fame is the 1067-metre-deep **Tara Canyon**, which cuts dramatically into the mountain slopes and plateau for about 100 km. The edge of the Tara Canyon is about 12 km north of Žabljak, a three-hour walk along a road beginning near Hotel Planinka. Yugoslav tourist brochures maintain that this is the second-largest canyon in the world after the Grand Canyon in the USA, a claim other countries such as Mexico and Namibia also make for their canyons, but any way you look at it, it's a top sight.

White-Water Tours

Travel agencies sometimes offer rubber-raft trips on the clean green water, over countless foaming rapids, down the steep forested Tara Gorge. These begin at Splavište near the Đurđevića Tara bridge. Three-day raft expeditions go right down the Tara River to the junction with the Piva River at Šćepan Polje (88 km), near the border with Bosnia.

For advance information on white-water rafting on the Tara River contact Ski Centar Durmitor, (☎ 011-629 602; fax 011-634 944) Uzin Mirkova 7, Belgrade. At last report two-day, one-night raft trips departed from Žabljak every Monday from June to August; they cost about 450 DIN per person including transfers, meals and gear. There's a 10-person minimum to run a trip, so enquire well ahead. In winter the same Belgrade office will know all about ski facilities at Žabljak.

Places to Stay

The **tourist office** in the centre of Žabljak is not much help – it arranges expensive private rooms at 80 DIN a single and hands out brochures written in Serbian.

Žabljak has four hotels owned by Montenegroturist. The **Planinka** (☎ 083-88 344) and **Jezera** (☎ 083-88 226) are modern ski hotels charging 132 DIN per person with half-board in summer. The **Hotel Žabljak** (☎ 083-88 300) right in the centre of town also offers rooms with half-board for 132 DIN per person.

The cheapest of the bunch is the old four-storey wooden **Hotel Durmitor** (☎ 083-88 278), past Hotel Jezera at the entrance to the national park, a 15-minute walk from town. Singles/doubles with shared bath here are 76 DIN, with half-board. Although the Durmitor seems to have the reputation of being run-down and unfit for foreigners, some of the rooms are quite pleasant, with balconies facing the mountains. Just be aware that there's no hot water or showers in the building.

On a hill-top five minutes' walk beyond the national park office is **Autocamp Ivan-do** which is little more than a fenced-off field. People around here rent **private rooms** at rates far lower than those charged in town and you'll get an additional discount if you have a sleeping bag and don't require sheets. Set right in the middle of the forest, Ivan-do is a perfect base for hikers.

Places to Eat

The **Restoran Sezam** next to the small market just below the Turist Biro bakes its own bread and is one of the only places apart from the hotels that serves meals.

Getting There & Away

The easiest way to get to Žabljak is to take a bus from Belgrade to Pljevlja (334 km), then one of the two daily buses from Pljevlja to Žabljak (57 km). On the return journey, these buses leave Žabljak for Pljevlja at 5 am and 5 pm, connecting for Mojkovac and Podgorica at Đurđevića Tara, where there's a spectacular bridge over the canyon. If you have to change buses at Pljevlja, hurry as they don't wait long.

As soon as you arrive at Žabljak enquire about onward buses to Belgrade, Pljevlja, Mojkovac and Podgorica at the red kiosk marked 'Turist Biro' beside the bus stop. Seats should be booked the day before.

Another jumping-off point is Mojkovac on the Belgrade-Podgorica line. About four trains daily run from Bar to Mojkovac (157 km, two hours); catch the earliest one for the best connections. At Mojkovac you must walk two km from the train station to the bus station, where you can pick up buses running from Podgorica to Pljevlja. They'll usually drop you at Đurđevića Tara and from there you may have to hitch the remaining 22 km to Žabljak.

Coming from Bar, take a train to Podgorica and then take the afternoon bus from there direct to Žabljak.

Kosovo (Косово)

A visit to Kosovo (Kosova in Albanian) can be a traumatic experience. Probably nowhere in Europe are human rights as flagrantly and systematically violated as they are here. The people have an uninhibited friendliness and curiosity which sets them apart from other Yugoslavs and the direct looks you get are at first disconcerting. The region's poverty and backwardness are apparent, as is the watchful eye of the Serbian government. Police posts have taken the place of left-luggage facilities in the region's bus and train stations. Your presence won't go unnoticed.

Until recently an autonomous province, Kosovo is now an integral part of the Republic of Serbia. Just under two million people occupy Kosovo's 10,887 sq km, making it the most densely populated portion of Yugoslavia; it also has the highest birth rate. The Albanians

adopted Islam after the Turkish conquest and today the region has a definite Muslim air, from the inhabitants' food and dress to the ubiquitous mosques. The capital, Priština, is a depressing, redeveloped city with showplace banks and hotels juxtaposed against squalor, but in the west the Metohija Valley between Peć and Prizren offers a useful transit route from the Adriatic to Macedonia, or Belgrade to Albania, plus a chance to see another side of this troubled land.

History

Isolated medieval Serbian monasteries tell of an early period which ended in 1389 with the Serbs' crushing defeat at the hands of the Turks at Kosovo Polje, just outside Priština (Prishtinë in Albanian). After this disaster the Serbs moved north, abandoning the region to the Albanians, descendants of the ancient Illyrians, who had inhabited this land for thousands of years.

In the late 19th century the ethnic Albanians, who make up 90% of the population today, struggled to free themselves of Ottoman rule. Yet in 1913, when the Turkish government finally pulled out, Kosovo was handed over to Serbia. Over half a million ethnic Albanians emigrated to Turkey and elsewhere to escape Serbian rule and by 1940 at least 18,000 Serb families had been settled on the vacated lands. During WWII, Kosovo was incorporated into Italian-controlled Albania and in October 1944 it was liberated by Albanian communist partisans to whom Tito had promised an auto-nomous republic within Yugoslavia. The area came under Tito's forces in early 1945, not without force.

After the war Tito wanted Albania itself included in the Yugoslav Federation as a seventh republic, with Kosovo united to it. This never came to pass and thus began two decades of pernicious neglect. Between 1954 and 1957 another 195,000 Albanians were coerced into emigrating to Turkey. After serious rioting in 1968 (and with the Soviet invasion of Czechoslovakia pushing Yugoslavia and Albania closer together), an autonomous province was created in 1974 and economic aid increased. Due to these concessions Kosovo is one of the only parts of ex-Yugoslavia where Tito is still warmly remembered. You see his portrait in restaurants and cafés everywhere and the main street in Peć is still named after him.

Yet the changes brought only cosmetic improvements and the standard of living in Kosovo (which has some of the most fertile land in the Balkans) remained a quarter the Yugoslav average. Kosovo was treated as a colony, its mines providing raw materials for industry in Serbia. In 1981, demonstrations calling for full republic status were put down by military force at a cost of over 300 lives. The 7000 young Albanians subsequently arrested were given jail terms of six years and up. This brutal denial of equality within the Yugoslav Federation sowed the seeds which led to the violent break-up of the country a decade later.

State of Emergency Trouble began anew in November 1988 as Albanian demonstrators protested against the sacking by Belgrade of local officials, including the provincial president Azem Vllasi, who was later arrested. A Kosovo coal miners' strike in February 1989 was followed by new limits imposed by Serbia on Kosovo's autonomy, a curfew and a state of emergency. This resulted in serious rioting, and 24 unarmed Albanian civilians were shot dead by the Yugoslav security forces.

On 5 July 1990 the Serbian parliament cancelled Kosovo's political autonomy and dissolved its assembly and government. The only Albanian-language daily newspaper, *Rilindja*, was banned and TV and radio broadcasts in Albanian ceased. In a process termed 'differentiation' some 115,000 Albanians suspected of having nationalist sympathies were fired from their jobs and Serbs installed in their places. At Priština University, 800 Albanian lecturers were sacked, effectively ending teaching in Albanian and forcing all but 500 of the 23,000 Albanian students to terminate their studies. Albanian secondary-school teachers were forced to work without salaries, otherwise the schools would have closed. All Albanians working in state hospitals were sacked, creating a growth industry in private clinics where most Albanian women now give birth. (This happened after rumours that the survival rate for male Albanian babies born in hospitals had suddenly dropped.)

Large numbers of Albanians went abroad after losing their jobs and a third of adult male Kosovars now work in Western Europe. Ironically, with Yugoslavia now in an economic tailspin, the families of the émigrés are fairly well off thanks to the hard currency their men send home, while the Serbs who took their government jobs are paid in super-soft Yugoslav dinars. The 20% of ethnic Albanians who do have jobs in Kosovo work almost exclusively in private businesses.

In September 1991, Serbian police and militia mobilised to block a referendum on independence for Kosovo, turning voters away and arresting election officials. The vote went ahead anyway and, with a 90% turnout, 98% voted in favour of independence from Serbia. In further elections on 24 May 1992, also declared illegal by Serbia, the writer Ibrahim Rugova was elected president of Kosovo. The unrecognised parliament of the Republic of Kosovo, elected at the same time as Mr Rugova, is attempting to create a parallel administration that can offer passive resistance to Serbia and has requested UN peacekeeping troops for Kosovo.

The Spectre of War An Albanian national uprising would certainly unleash the bloodiest of ex-Yugoslavia's latest series of civil wars and the Kosovars are intensely aware of the way Western countries stood by and tolerated ethnic genocide in Bosnia, so to date they've resisted Serb aggression with non-violence. Yugoslavia has an estimated 40,000 troops and police in Kosovo and nobody doubts its readiness to use them. Serb nationalists are firmly convinced they have a historic right to Kosovo as part of a 'Greater Serbia' and a plan exists to colonise Kosovo with Serbs. In December 1992, Kosovo Serbs elected to parliament a thuggish militia leader named Arkan whose troops have been accused of murdering 3000 Muslims in northern Bosnia.

Given Albania's increasing ties with Islamic countries, a major disturbance in Kosovo would have serious repercussions. US presidents George Bush and Bill Clinton have warned Serbia that any repetition of the Bosnian scenario there could lead to US intervention. At the very least, a conflict would see tens of thousands of Kosovars fleeing towards Western Europe away from the notorious

YUGOSLAVIA

Serbian ethnic-cleansing machine, probably via Macedonia, where ethnic Albanians historically make up 20% of the population. This would quickly destabilise that small country and Greece has warned that it will take decisive action if its northern border is breached, possibly leading to military involvement by Bulgaria and Turkey. Considerations such as these have made even the rabble-rousers in Belgrade proceed with caution, at least until they've got what they want in Bosnia-Hercegovina.

Warning

Your luggage will probably be searched by Serbian police as you enter Kosovo. They're looking mostly for arms and printed matter published abroad about the conflict in ex-Yugoslavia. Anything printed in Albania or Albanian will raise a lot of questions and be confiscated. If the police suspect you're a journalist or human-rights activist you'll be taken to the station for questioning and your belongings, especially notebooks and other papers (put the names and addresses of any local contacts in code), will be carefully scrutinised again. If you are briefly detained look upon it as a unique experience. Once you convince them you're a harmless tourist you'll be released and have no further problems.

You may ask: why visit such a place? Although you should certainly not become involved in local politics, by observing conditions first-hand you'll gain a better understanding of the tragedy of ex-Yugoslavia. Although the Albanians of Kosovo are cheerful, they mention their 'situation' to foreigners whenever they get the chance and it's impossible not to feel the resentment. Listen, but beware of getting yourself and others into trouble. Individuals seen with you may later be questioned by the police. Be careful about taking photos.

Getting There & Away

Getting to Kosovo from Serbia and Macedonia is easy as there are direct trains from Belgrade to Peć (490 km, 9½ hours), and buses from Skopje to Prizren (117 km).

Getting from the Adriatic coast to Kosovo, on the other hand, takes a full night or day. From Budva or Cetinje catch a bus to Podgorica and look for a direct bus to Peć from

there. The buses usually go via Berane, though some may go via the 1849-metre Čakor pass. If you're leaving from Ulcinj, take an early bus to Bar, then a train to Podgorica.

Try to get as far as Peć or Prizren on the first day since accommodation between the coast and Kosovo is either non-existent or dire. If you do get stuck, *Autocamp Berane* (☎ 084-61 822) is less than one km from Berane bus station. If you are in a real bind, you could stop at Rožaje (32 km from Berane) and spend the night at the dreadful *Rožaje Hotel* (☎ 0871-54 335), which charges 100 DIN for a dingy single. An early bus will carry you the 37 km from Rožaje to Peć the next morning. There's nil to see or do in Rožaje. For the route to/from Albania, see the later Prizren section.

PEĆ

Peć (Peja in Albanian), below high mountains between Podgorica and Priština, is a friendly, untouristed town of picturesque dwellings with some modern development. Ethnic Albanian men with their white felt skullcaps and women in traditional dress crowd the streets, especially on Saturday (market day). The horse wagons carrying goods around Peć share the streets with lots of beggars.

Orientation

The bus and train stations are about 500 metres apart, both in the east part of Peć about a km from the centre. Neither station has a left-luggage room. Follow Rruga Maršal Tito west from the bus station into the centre of town.

Information

Try Kosmet Tours at Maršal Tito 102; Putnik, Maršal Tito 64; and Metohija Turist, Maršal Tito 20.

Post & Communications The main post office and telephone centre is opposite the Hotel Metohija.

The telephone code for Peć is ☎ 039.

Things to See

There are eight well-preserved, functioning mosques in Peć, the most imposing of which is the 15th-century **Bajrakli Mosque**. Its high dome rises out of the colourful **bazar** (čaršija), giving Peć an authentic Oriental air.

By the river two km west of Peć is the

Patrijaršija Monastery, seat of the Serbian Orthodox patriarchate in the 14th century, from 1557 to 1766 and again after 1920. The rebirth of the patriarchate in 1557 allowed the Serbs to maintain their identity during the darkest days of Ottoman domination, so this monastery is of deep significance to Serbs. Inside the high-walled compound are three mid-13th century churches, each of which has a high dome and glorious medieval frescos. There is a detailed explanation in English in the common narthex (admission 20 DIN). Two km west of the monastery along the main highway is the **Rugovo Gorge**, an excellent hiking area.

Peć's most impressive sight, however, is 15 km south and accessible by frequent local bus. The **Visoki Dečani Monastery** (1335), with its marvellous 14th-century frescos, is a two-km walk from the bus stop in Dečani (Deçan in Albanian) through beautiful wooded countryside. This royal monastery built under kings Dečanski and Dušan survived the long Turkish period intact. From Dečani you can catch an onward bus to Prizren.

Places to Stay

Camping Over the bridge and a km up the hill from the Metohija Hotel is the quiet and rather pleasant *Kamp Karagač* (☎ 22 358), with lots of shade. This camping ground has been privatised and its main business is now the restaurant. It doesn't really cater to campers any more, though this could change, so ask.

Hotels The A-category *Metohija Hotel* (☎ 22 611), Maršal Tito 60, is a budget-breaker at 180/280 DIN for a single/double with private bath and breakfast.

The B-category *Hotel Park* (☎ 21 864), just beyond Kamp Karagač, is your best bet. Prices here vary but it's not expensive. Also try *Motel Dardanija* which you can see from the train just before you arrive at Peć station.

None of the travel agencies in town offers private rooms.

Getting There & Away

Bus Services from Prizren (73 km) and Skopje (190 km) are good and there's a night bus to/from Belgrade (388 km). In July and August buses run direct to Peć from Ulcinj (279 km).

Train Express trains going between Belgrade and Peć stop at Kosovo Polje, a junction eight km west of Priština. From here, Peć is 91 km away (two hours) while a separate line runs to Prizren (125 km, three hours). There's an overnight train with couchettes to/from Belgrade.

PRIZREN

Prizren, the most Albanian-looking city in Yugoslavia, is midway between Peć and Skopje. The road from Shkodra reaches the Albanian border at Vrbnica, 18 km west of Prizren. A big military base is just outside Prizren on the way to Skopje.

Prizren was the medieval capital of 'Old Serbia' but much of what we see today is Turkish. Colourful houses climb up the hillside to the ruined citadel *(kalaja)*, from which the 15th-century Turkish bridge and 19 minarets are visible.

The Bistrica River emerges from a gorge behind the citadel and cuts Prizren in two on its way into Albania. East up this gorge is the Bistrica Pass (2640 metres), once the main route to Macedonia. Wednesday is market day, when the city really comes alive.

Orientation

The bus and train stations are adjacent on the west side of town, but there's no left-luggage facility in either. From the bus station follow Rruga Metohjska towards the mountains, then take Rruga Vidovdanska up the riverside into town.

Information

Try the Tourist Association of Prizren, Rruga Vidovdanska 51, or Putnik on trg Cara Dušana in the centre of town.

Post & Communications The main post office and telephone centre is adjacent to the Theranda Hotel.

Prizren's telephone code is ☎ 029.

Things to See

On your way into town from the bus station you'll see the huge white-marble Bankos Prizren building facing the river. On a back-street behind the bank is the **Church of Bogorodica Ljeviška** (1307), which has an open bell tower above and frescos inside. Nearby, a tall square tower rises above some

Turkish baths, now the **Archaeological Museum** (usually closed).

The **Sinan Pasha Mosque** (1561) beside the river in the centre is closed, as are the **Gazi Mehmed Pasha Baths** (1563) beyond the Theranda Hotel. A little back from these is the large dome of the beautifully appointed 16th-century **Bajrakli (Gazi Mehmed) Mosque**, which is still in use. Behind this mosque, on the side facing the river, is the **Museum of the Prizren League**, a popular movement which struggled for Albanian autonomy within the Ottoman Empire from 1878 to 1881. In 1881 Dervish Pasha suppressed the League, killing thousands of Albanians and exiling thousands more to Asia Minor.

The largest Orthodox church in Prizren is **Sveti Georgi** (1856) in the old town near the Sinan Pasha Mosque. Higher up on the way to the **citadel** is **Sveti Spas**, with the ruins of an Orthodox monastery.

Places to Stay & Eat

Unfortunately, no private rooms are available in Prizren. The B-category *Theranda Hotel* (☎ 22 292), by the river in the centre of town, charges 100/140 DIN for a single/double with private bath and breakfast.

Motel Putnik (☎ 43 107), near the river three blocks from the bus station (ask directions), charges similar prices for foreigners and locals, which makes it relatively cheap (prices vary). The camping ground behind the motel has been officially closed for years but they'll probably let you pitch a tent there at no cost.

Several good čevapčići places lie between Sveti Georgi and Sinan Pasha.

Getting There & Away

Bus service is good from Priština (75 km), Peć (73 km) and Skopje (117 km). Only slow local trains to Metohija junction (64 km, 1½ hours) and Kosovo Polje (125 km, three hours) leave from Prizren, so you're much better off coming and going by bus.

Buses to the Albanian border leave from the street beginning at Rruga Vidovdanska 77. Some buses run directly to the border post *(dogana)* at Vrbnica (18 km) but none cross into Albania. If you can't find a bus to Vrbnica take a local bus to Zhur, from where it's a six-km walk downhill to the border. It's only 200 metres between the Yugoslav and Albanian checkpoints, then you should be able to hitch a ride the 16 km to Kukës without difficulty.

Appendix I – International Country Abbreviations

The following is a list of official country abbreviations that you may encounter on motor vehicles in Europe. Other abbreviations are likely to be unofficial ones, often referring to a particular region, province or even city. A vehicle entering a foreign country must carry a sticker identifying its country of registration, though this rule is not always enforced.

A	–	Austria
AL	–	Albania
AND	–	Andorra
AUS	–	Australia
B	–	Belgium
BG	–	Bulgaria
BIH	–	Bosnia-Herzegovina
BY	–	Belarus
CC	–	Consular Corps
CD	–	Diplomatic Corps
CDN	–	Canada
CH	–	Switzerland
CY	–	Cyprus
CZ	–	Czech Republic
D	–	Germany
DK	–	Denmark
DZ	–	Algeria
E	–	Spain
EST	–	Estonia
ET	–	Egypt
F	–	France
FIN	–	Finland
FL	–	Liechtenstein
FR	–	Faroe Islands
GB	–	Great Britain
GBA	–	Alderney
GBG	–	Guernsey
GBJ	–	Jersey
GBM	–	Isle of Man
GBZ	–	Gibraltar
GE	–	Georgia
GR	–	Greece
H	–	Hungary
HKJ	–	Jordan
HR	–	Croatia
I	–	Italy
IL	–	Israel
IRL	–	Ireland
IS	–	Iceland
L	–	Luxembourg
LAR	–	Libya
LT	–	Lithuania
LV	–	Latvia
M	–	Malta
MA	–	Morocco
MC	–	Monaco
MD	–	Moldavia
MK	–	Macedonia
N	–	Norway
NL	–	Netherlands
NZ	–	New Zealand
P	–	Portugal
PL	–	Poland
RL	–	Lebanon
RO	–	Romania
RSM	–	San Marino
RUS	–	Russia
S	–	Sweden
SK	–	Slovakia
SLO	–	Slovenia
SYR	–	Syria
TN	–	Tunisia
TR	–	Turkey
UA	–	Ukraine
USA	–	United States of America
V	–	Vatican City
WAN	–	Nigeria
YU	–	Yugoslavia
ZA	–	South Africa

Appendix II – Alternative Place Names

The following abbreviations are used:

(A) Albanian	(Gr) Greek
(Ar) Arabic	(I) Italian
(B) Basque	(P) Portuguese
(C) Catalan	(S) Serbian
(Cr) Croatian	(Sle) Slovene
(E) English	(S) Spanish
(F) French	(T) Turkish
(G) German	

ALBANIA
Shgipëi
Durrës (A) – Durazzo
Korça (A) – Koritsa (Gr)
Lezha (A) – Allessio (I)
Saranda (E) – Sarandë (A)
Shkodra (E) – Shkodër (A), Scutari (I)
Tirana (E) – Tiranë (A)

CYPRUS
Kípros (Gr)
Kibris (T)
Gazimağusa (T) – Famagusta (Gr), Ammochostos (Gr)
Girne (T) – Kyrenia (Gr), Keryneia (Gr)
Lefkoşa (T) – Nicosia (Gr)
Limassol (Gr) – Lemessos (Gr)

CROATIA
Hrvatska
Brač (Cr) – Brazza (I)
Brijuni (Cr) – Brioni (I)
Cres (Cr) – Cherso (I)
Dalmatia (E) – Dalmacija (Cr)
Dubrovnik (Cr) – Ragusa (I)
Hvar (Cr) – Lesina (I)
Korčula – Curzola (I)
Krk (Cr) – Veglia (I)
Kvarner (Cr) – Quarnero (I)
Losinj (Cr) – Lussino (I)
Mljet Island (Cr) – Melita (I)
Poreč (Cr) – Parenzo (I)
Rab (Cr) – Arbe (G)
Rijeka (Cr) – Fiume (I)
Rovinj (Cr) – Rovigno (I)
Split (Cr) – Spalato (I)
Trogir (Cr) – Trau (I)
Zadar (Cr) – Zara (I)
Zagreb (Cr) – Agram (G)

FRANCE
Bayonne (F, E) – Baiona (B)
Basque Country (E) – Euskadi (B), Pays Basque (F)
Burgundy (E) – Bourgogne (F)
Brittany (E) – Bretagne (F)

Corsica (E) – Corse (F)
French Riviera (E) – Côte d'Azur (F)
Dunkirk (E) – Dunkerque (F)
Channel Islands (E) – Îles Anglo-Normandes (F)
English Channel (E) – La Manche (F)
Lake Geneva (E) – Lac Léman (F)
Lyons (E) – Lyon (F)
Marseilles (E) – Marseille (F)
Normandy (E) – Normandie (F)
Rheims (E) – Reims (F)
Rhine (River) (E) – Rhin (F), Rhein (G)
Saint Jean de Luz (F) – Donibane Lohizune (B)
Saint Jean Pied de Port (F) – Donibane Garazi (B)
Sark (Channel Islands; E) – Sercq (F)

GREECE
Hellas (or Ελλάς)
Athens (E) – Athina (Gr)
Corfu (E) – Kerkyra (Gr)
Crete (E) – Kriti (Gr)
Patras (E) – Patra (Gr)
Rhodes (E) – Rodos (Gr)
Salonica (E) – Thessaloniki (Gr)
Samothrace (E) – Samothraki (Gr)
Santorini (E, Gr, I) – Thira (Gr)

ITALY
Italia
Aeolian Islands (E) – Isole Eolie (I)
Apulia (E) – Puglia (I)
Florence (E) – Firenze (I)
Genoa (E) – Genova (I)
Herculaneum (E) – Ercolano (I)
Lombardy (E) – Lombardia (I)
Mantua (E) – Mantova (I)
Milan (E) – Milano (I)
Naples (E) – Napoli (I)
Padua (E) – Padova (I)
Rome (E) – Roma (I)
Sicily (E) – Sicilia (I)
Sardinia (E) – Sardegna (I)
Syracuse (E) – Siracusa (I)
Tiber (River) (E) – Tevere (I)
Venice (E) – Venezia (I)

MOROCCO
Ceuta (S) – Sebta (Ar)
Casablanca (F) – Dar al-Beida (Ar)
Marrakesh (E) – Marrakech (F)
Tangier (E) – Tanger (F), Tanja (Ar)

PORTUGAL
Cape St Vincent (E) – Cabo de São Vicente (P)
Lisbon (E) – Lisboa (P)
Oporto (E) – Porto (P)

SLOVENIA
Slovenija
Koper (Sle) – Capodistria (I)
Ljubljana (Sle) – Laibach (G)
Piran (Sle) – Pireos (Gk)
Postiojna Caves (Sle) – Adelsberger Grotten (G)
Vintgar Gorge (E) – Soteska Vintgar (Sle)

SPAIN
España
Andalusia (E) – Andalucía (S)
Balearic Islands (E) – Islas Baleares (S)
Basque Country (E) – Euskadi (B), País Vasco (S)
Catalonia (E) – Catalunya (C), Cataluña (S)
Cordova (E) – Córdoba (S)
Corunna (E) – La Coruña (S)
Majorca (E) – Mallorca (S)
Minorca (E) – Menorca (S)
Navarre (E) – Navarra (S)
San Sebastián (E, S) – Donostia (B)
Saragossa (E) – Zaragoza (S)
Seville (E) – Sevilla (S)

TURKEY
Türkiye
Cappadocia (E) – Kapadokya (T)
Ephesus (E) – Efes (T)
Euphrates River (E) – Firat (T)
Gallipoli (E) – Gelibolu (T)
İzmir (T) – Smyrna (G)
Mt Ararat (E) – Ağri Daği (T)
Mt Nimrod (E) – Nemrut Daği (T)
Thrace (E) – Trakya (T)
Tigris River (E) – Dicle (T)
Trebizond (E) – Trabzon (T)
Troy (E) – Truva (T)

YUGOSLAVIA
Jugoslavija
Bar (Se) – Antivari (I)
Belgrade (E) – Beograd (Se)
Deçan (A) – Dećani (Se)
Kotor (Se) – Cattaro (I)
Montenegro (E) – Crna Gora (Se)
Novi Sad (Se) – Neusatz (G)
Peć (Se) – Pejë (A)
Priština (Se) – Prishtinë
Serbia (E) – Serbija (Se)
Ulcinj (Se) – Ulqin (A), Dulcigno (I)

Appendix III – Telephones

Dial Direct

You can dial directly from public telephone boxes from almost anywhere in Europe to almost anywhere in the world. This is usually cheaper than going through the operator. In much of Europe, public telephones accepting phonecards are becoming the norm and in some countries coin-operated phones are increasingly difficult to find.

To call abroad you simply dial the international access code (IAC) for the country you are calling from (most commonly 00 in Europe but see the following table), the country code (CC) for the country you are calling, the local area code (usually dropping the leading zero if there is one) and then the number. If, for example, you are in Italy (international access code 00) and want to make a call to the USA (country code 1), San Francisco (area code 212), number ☎ 123 4567, then you dial ☎ 00-1-212-123 4567. To call from the UK (00) to Australia (61), Sydney (02), number ☎ 1234 5678, you dial ☎ 00-61-2-1234 5678.

Home Direct

If you would rather have somebody else pay for the call, you can, from many countries, dial directly to your home country operator and then reverse charges; you can also charge the call to a phone company credit card. To do this, simply dial the relevant 'home direct' number to be connected to your own operator. For the USA there's a choice of AT&T, MCI or Sprint Global One home direct services. Home direct numbers vary from country to country – check with your telephone company before you leave, or with the international operator in the country you're ringing from. Remember that from phone boxes in some countries you may need a coin or local phonecard to be connected with the relevant home direct operator.

In some places (particularly airports), you may find dedicated home direct phones where you simply press the button labelled USA, Australia, Hong Kong or whatever for direct connection to the operator. Note that the home direct service does not operate to and from all countries, and that the call could be charged at operator rates, which makes it quite expensive for the person who's paying. In general placing a call on your phone credit card is much more expensive than paying the local tariff.

Dialling Tones

In some countries (eg France, Hungary), after you've dialled the international access code, you have to wait for a second dial tone before proceeding with the code for your target country and the number. Often the same applies when you ring from one city to another within these countries: wait for a dialling tone after you've dialled the area code for your target city. If you're not sure what to do, simply wait three or four seconds after dialling a code – if nothing happens, you can probably keep dialling.

Phonecards

In major locations you may find phones which accept credit cards: simply swipe your card through the slot and the call is charged to the card, though rates can be very high. Phone company credit cards can be used to charge calls via your home country operator.

Stored-value phonecards are now almost standard all over Europe. You usually buy a card from a post office, telephone centre, newsstand or retail outlet and simply insert the card into the phone each time you make a call. The card solves the problem of finding the correct coins for calls (or lots of correct coins for international calls) and generally gives you a small discount.

Call Costs

Avoid ringing from a hotel room unless you really don't care what it's going to cost. The cost of making an international call varies widely from one country to another. A US$10 call from Britain could cost you US$30 from Spain. Choosing where you call from can make a big difference to your budget. The countries in the table are rated from * (cheap) to *** (expensive). Reduced rates are available at certain times (usually from mid-evening to early morning), though these vary from country to country and should make little difference to relative costs – check the local phone book or ask the operator.

Telephone Codes

	CC	cost (see text)	IAC	IO
Albania	355			
Andorra	376	***	00	821111
Austria	43	**	00	09
Belgium	32	***	00	1224 (private phone) 1223 (public phone)
Belarus	375		8(w)10	
Bulgaria	359	**	00	
Croatia	385	***	99	901
Cyprus	357	***	00	
Cyprus (Turkish)	905		00	
Czech Republic	42	***	00	0131
Denmark	45	**	00	141
Estonia	372	***	8(w)00	007
Finland	358	*	990	020222
France	33	**	00(w)	12
Germany	49	**	00	00118
Gibraltar	350	***	00	100
Greece	30	*	00	161
Hungary	36	*	00(w)	09
Iceland	354		90	09
Ireland	353	*	00	114
Italy	39	***	00	15
Latvia	371	***	00	115
Liechtenstein	41 75	***	00	114
Lithuania	370	***	8(w)10 8(w)	194/195
Luxembourg	352	**	00	0010
Macedonia	389		99	
Malta	356	**	00	194
Morocco	212	***	00(w)	12
Netherlands	31	***	00	060410
Norway	47	*	095	181
Poland	48	**	0(w)0	901
Portugal	351	**	00	099
Romania			40	071
Russia	7		8(w)10	
Slovakia	42	**	00	0131
Slovenia	386	**	00	901
Spain	34	***	07(w)	91389
Sweden	46	**	009(w)	0018
Switzerland	41	***	00	114
Tunisia	216	***	00	
Turkey	90	**	00	115
UK	44	*	00	155
Yugoslavia	381	**	99	901

CC – Country Code (to call *into* that country)
IAC – International Access Code (to call abroad *from* that country)
IO – International Operator (to make enquiries)
(w) – wait for dialling tone
Other country codes include: Australia 61, Canada 1, Hong Kong 852, India 91, Indonesia 62, Israel 972, Japan 81, Macau 853, Malaysia 60, New Zealand 64, Singapore 65, South Africa 27, Thailand 66, USA 1

Appendix IV – European Organisations

	Council of Europe	EU	EFTA	NATO	Nordic Council	OECD	WEU
Albania	✓	–	–	–	–	–	–
Andorra	✓	–	–	–	–	–	–
Austria	✓	✓	–	–	–	✓	–
Belgium	✓	✓	–	✓	–	✓	✓
Bulgaria	✓	–	–	–	–	–	–
Croatia	•	–	–	–	–	–	–
Cyprus	✓	–	–	–	–	–	–
Czech Republic	✓	–	–	–	–	✓	–
Denmark	✓	✓	–	✓	✓	✓	–
Estonia	✓	–	–	–	–	–	–
Finland	✓	✓	–	–	✓	✓	–
France	✓	✓	–	✓	–	✓	✓
Germany	✓	✓	–	✓	–	✓	✓
Greece	✓	✓	–	✓	–	✓	–
Hungary	✓	–	–	–	–	✓	–
Iceland	✓	–	✓	✓	✓	✓	–
Ireland	✓	✓	–	–	–	✓	–
Italy	✓	✓	–	✓	–	✓	✓
Latvia	✓	–	–	–	–	–	–
Lithuania	✓	–	–	–	–	–	–
Luxembourg	✓	✓	–	✓	–	✓	✓
Macedonia	✓	–	–	–	–	–	–
Malta	✓	–	–	–	–	–	–
Netherlands	✓	✓	–	✓	–	✓	✓
Norway	✓	–	✓	✓	✓	✓	–
Poland	✓	–	–	–	–	–	–
Portugal	✓	✓	–	✓	–	✓	✓
Romania	✓	–	–	–	–	–	–
Slovakia	✓	–	–	–	–	–	–
Slovenia	✓	–	–	–	–	–	–
Spain	✓	✓	–	✓	–	✓	✓
Sweden	✓	✓	–	–	✓	✓	–
Switerland	✓	–	✓	–	–	✓	–
Turkey	✓	–	–	✓	–	✓	–
UK	✓	✓	–	✓	–	✓	✓
Yugoslavia	–	–	–	–	–	✓	–

✓ – full member
• – special guest status

Council of Europe

Established in 1949, the Council of Europe is the oldest of Europe's political institutions. It aims to promote European unity, protect human rights, and assist in the cultural, social and economic development of its member states, but its powers are purely advisory. Founding states were Belgium, Denmark, France, Ireland, Italy, Luxembourg, the Netherlands, Norway, Sweden and the UK. Its headquarters are in Strasbourg.

European Union (EU)

Founded by the Treaty of Rome in 1957, the European Economic Community, or Common Market as it used to be known, broadened its scope far beyond economic measures as it developed into the European Community and finally the European Union. Its original aims were to develop and expand the economies of its member states by abolishing customs tariffs, coordinating transportation systems and general economic policies, establishing a common economic policy towards nonmember states, and promoting the free movement of labour and capital within its borders. Further measures included the abolishment of border controls and the linking of currency exchange rates. Since the Maastricht treaty of December 1991, the EU is committed to establishing a common foreign and security policy, close cooperation in home affairs and the judiciary, and a single European currency to be called the euro.

The EEC's founding states were Belgium, France, West Germany, Italy, Luxembourg and the Netherlands – the Treaty of Rome was an extension of the European Coal and Steel Community (ECSC) founded by these six states in 1952. Denmark, Ireland and the UK joined in 1973, Greece in 1981, Spain and Portugal in 1986 and Austria, Finland and Sweden in 1995. The main EU organisations are the European Parliament (elected by direct universal suffrage, with growing powers), the European Commission (the daily 'government'), the Council of Ministers (ministers of member states who make the important decisions) and the Court of Justice. The European Parliament meets in Strasbourg; Luxembourg is home to the Court of Justice. Other EU organisations are based in Brussels.

European Free Trade Association (EFTA)

Established in 1960 as a response to the creation of the European Economic Community, EFTA aims to eliminate trade tariffs on industrial products between member states, though each member retains the right to its own commercial policy towards nonmembers. Most members cooperate with the EU through the European Economic Area agreement. Denmark and the UK left EFTA to join the EU in 1973 and others have since followed suit, leaving EFTA's future in doubt. Its headquarters are in Geneva.

North Atlantic Treaty Organisation (NATO)

The document creating this defence alliance was signed in 1949 by the USA, Canada and 10 European countries to safeguard their common political, social and economic systems against external threats (read: against the powerful Soviet military presence in Europe after WWII). An attack against any member state would be considered an attack against them all. Greece and Turkey joined in 1952, West Germany in 1955, and Spain in 1982; France withdrew from NATO's integrated military command in 1966 and Greece did likewise in 1974, though both remain members. NATO's Soviet counterpart, the Warsaw Pact founded in 1955, collapsed with the democratic revolutions of 1989 and the subsequent disintegration of the Soviet Union; most of its former members are now NATO associates in the 'Partnership for Peace' programme. NATO's headquarters are in Brussels.

Nordic Council

Established in Copenhagen in 1953, the Nordic Council aims to promote economic, social and cultural cooperation among its member states (Denmark, Finland, Iceland, Norway and Sweden). Since 1971, the Council has acted as an advisory body to the Nordic Council of Ministers, a meeting of ministers from the member states responsible for the subject under discussion. Decisions taken by the Council of Ministers are usually binding, though member states retain full sovereignty. Environmental, tariff, labour and immigration policies are often coordinated.

Organisation for Economic Cooperation and Development (OECD)

The OECD was set up in 1961 to supersede the Organisation for European Economic Cooperation, which allocated US aid under the Marshall Plan and coordinated the reconstruction of postwar Europe. Sometimes seen as the club of the world's rich countries, the OECD aims to encourage economic growth and world trade. Its member states include most of Europe, as well as Australia, Canada, Japan, Mexico, New Zealand and the USA. Its headquarters are in Paris.

Western European Union (WEU)

Set up in 1955, the WEU was designed to coordinate the military defences between member states, to promote economic, social and cultural cooperation, and to encourage European integration. Social and cultural tasks were transferred to the Council of Europe in 1960, and these days the WEU is sometimes touted as a future, more 'European', alternative to NATO. Its headquarters are in Brussels.

Appendix V – Climate Charts

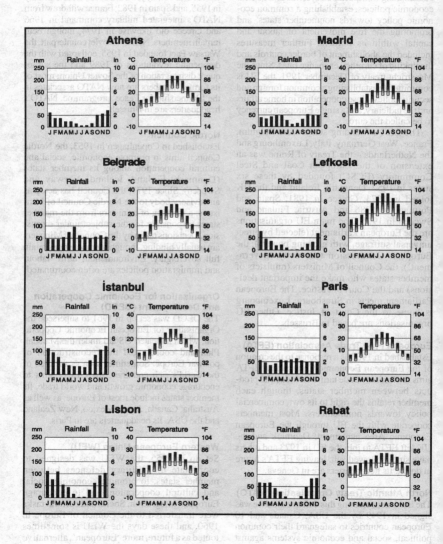

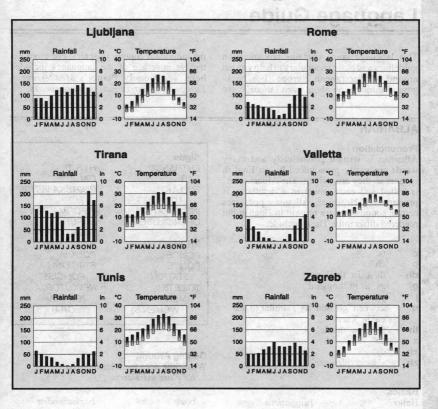

Language Guide

This language guide contains pronunciation guidelines and basic vocabulary to help you get around Mediterranean Europe. For background information about each language see the individual country chapters. For more extensive coverage of the languages included here, see Lonely Planet's *Mediterranean Europe* and *Western Europe phrasebooks*.

ALBANIAN

Pronunciation
Albanian is written phonetically and many words are easily pronounced by an English speaker as they are written. The Albanian 'rr' is trilled and each vowel in a diphthong is pronounced. However, Albanian possesses certain sounds that are present in English but rendered differently. These include:

c	'ts'
ç	'ch'
dh	'th' as in 'this'
gj	'gy' as in 'hogyard'
j	'y'
q	between 'ch' and 'ky', similar to the 'cu' in 'cure'
th	'th' as in 'thistle'
x	'dz'
xh	'dj'
zh	's' as in 'pleasure'

Basics

Hello	*Tungjatjeta*
Goodbye	*Lamtumirë*
	Mirupafshim (less formal)
Yes/No	*Po/Jo*
Please	*Ju lutem*
Thank you	*Ju falem nderit*
That's fine	*Eshtë e mirë*
You're welcome	*S'ka përse*
Excuse me	*Me falni*
Sorry (Excuse me, forgive me)	*Më vjen keq (Më falni, ju lutem)*
Do you speak English?	*A flisni anglisht?*
How much is it?	*Sa kushton?*
What is your name?	*Si quheni ju lutem?*
My name is ...	*Unë quhem .../Mua më quajnë*

Signs

ENTRANCE	*HYRJE*
EXIT	*DALJE*
FULL/NO VACANCIES	*PLOTŚKA VENDE TË*
INFORMATION	*INFORMACION*
OPEN/CLOSED	*HAPUR/ MBYLLUR*
PROHIBITED	*E NDALUAR*
POLICE	*POLICIA*
POLICE STATION	*STACIONI I POLICISË*
TOILETS (MEN'S/ WOMEN'S)	*NEVOJTORJA (BURRA/ GRA)*

Getting Around
What time does the... leave/arrive?
Në ç'orë niset/arrin...?

boat	*barka/lundra*
bus	*autobusi*
tram	*tramvaji*
train	*treni*
I would like...	*Dëshiroj...*
a one-way ticket	*një biletë vajtje*
a return ticket	*një biletë vajtje-ardhje*
1st class	*klas i parë*
2nd class	*klas i dytë*
timetable	*orar*
bus stop	*stacion autobusi*
Where is...?	*Ku është...?*
far/near	*larg/afër*
Go straight ahead.	*Shko drejt.*
Turn left.	*Kthehu majtas.*
Turn right.	*Kthehu djathtas.*

Around Town

a bank	një bankë
the...embassy	ambasadën
my hotel	hotelin tim
the post office	postën
the market	pazarin
chemist/pharmacy	farmaci
newsagency	agjensia e lajmeve
the telephone exchange	centrali telefonik
the tourist information office	zyra e informimeve turistike

What time does it open/close?
Në ç'ore hapet/mbyllet?

Accommodation

hotel	hotel
camping ground	vend kampimi

Do you have any rooms available?
A keni ndonjë dhomë të lirë?

a single room	një dhomë teke
a double room	një dhomë më dy krevatë

How much is it per night/per person?
Sa kushton një natë/për person?
Does it include breakfast?
A e përfshin edhe mëngjesin?

Time, Days & Numbers

What time is it?	Sa është ora?
today	sot
tomorrow	nesër
yesterday	dje
morning	mëngjes
afternoon	mbasdite
Monday	e hënë
Tuesday	e martë
Wednesday	e mërkurë
Thursday	e enjte
Friday	e premte
Saturday	e shtunë
Sunday	e diel

1	një
2	dy
3	tre
4	katër
5	pesë
6	gjashtë
7	shtatë
8	tetë
9	nëntë
10	dhjetë
100	njëqind
1000	njëmijë
one million	një milion

Emergencies

Help!	Ndihmë!
Call a doctor!	Thirrni doktorin!
Call the police!	Thirrni policinë!
Go away!	Zhduku!/Largohuni!
I'm lost.	Kam humbur rrugën.

CROATIAN & SERBIAN

Pronunciation

The spelling of both Croatian and Serbian is phonetically based: almost every word is written exactly as it is pronounced and every letter is pronounced. With regard to the position of stress, only one rule can be given: the last syllable of a word is never stressed. In most cases the accent falls on the first vowel in the word. Serbian uses the Cyrillic alphabet so it's worth familiarising yourself with it (see the Macedonian section later in this language guide).

There are 30 letters in the Croatian alphabet. Many letters are pronounced as in English – the following are some specific pronunciations.

c	'ts' as in 'cats'
ć	'kj' like the 'cu' in 'cure'
č	'tch' as in 'chop'
đ	'gj' like the 'gu' in 'legume'
dž	'j' as in 'just'
j	'y' as in 'young'
lj	'ly' like the 'lli' in 'million'
nj	'ny' as in 'canyon'
š	'sh' as in 'hush'
ž	'zh' like the 's' in 'treasure'

The principal difference between Serbian and Croatian is in the pronunciation of the vowel 'e' in certain words. A long 'e' in Serbian becomes 'ije' in Croatian (for example, *reka, rijeka*, 'river'), and a short 'e' in Serbian becomes 'je' in Croatian (for example, *pesma, pjesma*, 'song'). Sometimes, however, the vowel 'e' is the same in both languages, as in *selo*, 'village'. There are also a number of variations in vocabulary. These are indicated below with 'C' for Croatian and 'S' for Serbian.

Basics

hello	*zdravo*
	здраво
goodbye	*do viđenja*
	до виђења
yes	*da*
	да
no	*ne*
	не
please	*molim*
	молим
Thank you	*hvala*
	хвала

That's fine/You're welcome
  U redu je/Nema na čemu
  У реду је/Нема на чему
excuse me
  oprostite
  опростите
sorry (excuse me, forgive me)
  pardon (izvinite)
  пардон (опростите извините)
Do you speak English?
  Govorite li engleski?
  Говорите ли енглески?
How much is it ...?
  Koliko košta ...?
  Колико кошта ...?
What is your name?
  Kako se zovete?
  Како се зовете?
My name is ...
  Zovem se ...
  Зовем се ...

Getting Around

What time does ... leave/arrive?
  Kada ... dolazi (C)/polazi (S)?
  Када ... долази/полази?

boat	*brod*
	брод

Signs

ENTRANCE	
	ULAZ
	УЛАЗ
EXIT	
	IZLAZ
	ИЗЛАЗ
FULL/NO VACANCIES	
	SVE JE ZAUZETO/NEMA SLOBODNE SOBE
	СВЕ ЈЕ ЗАУЗЕТО/НЕМА СЛОБОДНЕ СОБЕ
INFORMATION	
	INFORMACIJE
	ИНФОРМАЦИЈЕ
OPEN/CLOSED	
	OTVORENO/ZATVORENO
	ОТВОРЕНО/ЗАТВОРЕНО
POLICE	
	MILICIJA (S)/POLICIJA (C)
	МИЛИЦИЈА
POLICE STATION	
	STANICA MILICIJE (S)/POLICIJA (C)
	СТАНИЦА МИЛИЦИЈЕ
PROHIBITED	
	ZABRANJENO
	ЗАБРАЊЕНО
ROOMS AVAILABLE	
	SLOBODNE SOBE
	СЛОБОДНЕ СОБЕ
TOILETS	
	TOALETI (S)/ZAHODI (C)
	ТОАЛЕТИ

bus (city)	*autobus (gradski)*
	аутобус (градски)
bus (intercity)	*autobus (međugradski)*
	аутобус (међуградски)
train	*voz* (S)/*vlak* (C)
	воз
tram	*tramvaj*
	трамвај

one-way ticket
  kartu u jednom pravcu
  карту у једном правцу
return ticket
  povratnu kartu
  повратну карту

1st class
prvu klasu
прву класу
2nd class
drugu klasu
другу класу

Where is the bus/tram stop?
Gde je autobuska/tramvajska stanica (S)/
postaja (C)?
Где је аутобуска/трамвајска станица?
Can you show me (on the map)?
Možete li mi pokazati (na karti)?
Можете ли ми показати (на карти)?

far/near
daleko/blizu
далеку/близу
Go straight ahead.
Idite pravo napred (S)/*naprijed* (C).
Идите право напред.
Turn left.
Skrenite lijevo. (C)
Skrenite levo. (S)
Скрените лево.
Turn right.
Skrenite desno.
Скрените десно.

Around Town

bank	*banka*
	банка
... embassy	*... ambasada*
	амбасада
my hotel	*moj hotel*
	мој хотел
post office	*pošta*
	пошта
market	*tržnica* (C)/*pijaca* (S)
	ријаца

telephone centre
telefonska centrala
телефонска централа
tourist information office
turistički informativni biro
туристички информативни ьиро

Accommodation

hotel
hotel
хотел
guesthouse
privatno prenoćište
приватно преноћиште

youth hostel
omladinsko prenoćište
омладинско преноћиште
camping ground
kamping
кампинг

Do you have any rooms available?
Imate li slobodne sobe?
Имате ли сльободне соье?

I would like ...
Želim ...
Желим ...
a single room
sobu sa jednim krevetom
собу са једним креветом
a double room
sobu sa duplim krevetom
собу са дуплим креветом

How much is it per night/per person?
Koliko košta za jednu noć/po osobi?
Колико кошта за једну ноћ/по особи?
Does it include breakfast?
Dali je u ceni (S)/*cijeni* (C) *uključen i
doručak?*
Дали је у цену укљчен и доручак?

Time, Days & Numbers

What time is it?	*Koliko je sati?*
	Колико је сати?
today	*danas*
	данас
tomorrow	*sutra*
	сутра
yesterday	*juče* (S)/*jučer* (C)
	јуче
in the morning	*ujutro*
	ујутро
in the afternoon	*popodne*
	поподне
Monday	*ponedeljak*
	понедељак
Tuesday	*utorak*
	уторак
Wednesday	*sreda* (S)/*srijeda* (C)
	среда
Thursday	*četvrtak*
	четвртак
Friday	*petak*
	петак

Saturday	*subota* субота		10	*deset* десет
Sunday	*nedelja* (S)/ *nedjelja* (C) недеља		100	*sto* сто
			1000	*hiljada* (S)/*tisuća* (C) хиљада
			one million	*jedan milion* (S)/ *jedan milijun* (C) један милион
1	*jedan* један			
2	*dva* два			
3	*tri* три			
4	*četiri* четири			
5	*pet* пет			
6	*šest* шест			
7	*sedam* седам			
8	*osam* осам			
9	*devet* девет			

Emergencies

Help! — Upomoć!
Упомоћ

Call a doctor!
Pozovite lekara (S)/*liječnika* (C)!
Позовите лекара!

Call the police!
Pozovite miliciju (S)/*policiju* (C)!
Позовите милицију!

Go away!
Idite!
Идите!

I'm lost.
Izgubio (m)/*Izgubina* (f) *sam se*.
Изгубљен /Изгубљена сам се.

FRENCH

Pronunciation

French has a number of sounds which are difficult for Anglophones to produce. These include:

- The distinction between the 'u' sound (as in *tu)* and 'oo' sound (as in *tout*). For both sounds, the lips are rounded and projected forward, but for the 'u' the tongue is towards the front of the mouth, its tip against the lower front teeth, whereas for the 'oo' the tongue is towards the back of the mouth, its tip behind the gums of the lower front teeth.

- The nasal vowels. During the production of nasal vowels the breath escapes partly through the nose and partly through the mouth. There are no nasal vowels in English; in French there are three, as in *bon vin blanc*, 'good white wine'. These

sounds occur where a syllable ends in a single 'n' or 'm'; the 'n' or 'm' is silent but indicates the nasalisation of the preceding vowel.

- The 'r'. The standard 'r' of Parisian French is produced by moving the bulk of the tongue backwards to constrict the air flow in the pharynx while the tip of the tongue rests behind the lower front teeth. It is similar to the noise made by some people before spitting, but with much less friction.

Basics

Hello	*Bonjour*
Goodbye	*Au revoir*
Yes/No	*Oui/Non*
Please	*S'il vous plaît*
Thank you	*Merci*
That's fine, you're welcome	*Je vous en prie*

Excuse me (attention)	*Excusez-moi*
Sorry (excuse me, forgive me)	*Pardon*
Do you speak English?	*Parlez-vous anglais?*
How much is it?	*C'est combien?*
What is your name?	*Comment vous appelez-vous?*
My name is ...	*Je m'appelle ...*

Getting Around

What time does the next ... leave/arrive?
À quelle heure part/arrive le prochain ...?

boat	*bateau*
bus (city)	*bus*
bus (intercity)	*car*
tram	*tramway*
train	*train*
I would like to hire a car/bicycle.	*Je voudrais louer une voiture/un vélo.*
I would like a one-way ticket.	*Je voudrais un billet aller simple.*
I would like a return ticket.	*Je voudrais un billet aller retour.*
1st/2nd class	*première/deuxième classe*
left luggage (office)	*consigne*

Signs

ENTRANCE	*ENTRÉE*
EXIT	*SORTIE*
FULL, NO VACANCIES	*COMPLET*
INFORMATION	*RENSEIGNE-MENTS*
OPEN/CLOSED	*OUVERT/FERMÉ*
PROHIBITED	*INTERDIT*
POLICE STATION	*(COMMIS-SARIAT DE) POLICE*
ROOMS AVAILABLE	*CHAMBRES LIBRES*
TOILETS (MEN'S/ WOMEN'S)	*TOILETTES, WC (HOMMES/ FEMMES)*

timetable	*horaire*
bus/tram stop	*arrêt d'autobus/de tramway*
train station/ferry terminal	*gare/gare maritime*
Where is ...?	*Où est ...?*
far/near	*loin/proche*
Go straight ahead.	*Continuez tout droit.*
Turn left/right.	*Tournez à gauche/à droite.*

Around Town

a bank	*une banque*
the ... embassy	*l'ambassade de ...*
my hotel	*mon hôtel*
post office	*le bureau de poste*
market	*le marché*
chemist/pharmacy	*la pharmacie*
newsagency/ stationer's	*l'agence de presse/ la papeterie*
a public telephone	*une cabine téléphonique*
the tourist information office	*l'office de tourisme/le syndicat d'initiative*

What time does it open/close?
Quelle est l'heure de l'ouverture?

Accommodation

the hotel	*l'hôtel*
the youth hostel	*l'auberge de jeunesse*
the camping ground	*le camping*

Do you have any rooms available?
Est-ce que vous avez des chambres libres?
for one/two people
pour une personne/deux personnes
How much is it per night/per person?
Quel est le prix par nuit/par personne?
Is breakfast included?
Est-ce que le petit déjeuner est compris?

Time, Days & Numbers

What time is it?	*Quelle heure est-il?*
today	*aujourd'hui*
tomorrow	*demain*
yesterday	*hier*
morning/afternoon	*matin/après-midi*

Monday	*lundi*	7	*sept*
Tuesday	*mardi*	8	*huit*
Wednesday	*mercredi*	9	*neuf*
Thursday	*jeudi*	10	*dix*
Friday	*vendredi*	100	*cent*
Saturday	*samedi*	1000	*mille*
Sunday	*dimanche*	one million	*un million*

1	*un*
2	*deux*
3	*trois*
4	*quatre*
5	*cinq*
6	*six*

Emergencies

Help!	*Au secours!*
Call a doctor!	*Appelez un médecin!*
Call the police!	*Appelez la police!*
Leave me alone!	*Fichez-moi la paix!*
I'm lost.	*Je me suis égaré/ée.*

GREEK

Pronunciation

Greek letters are shown by the closest English sound.

Α α	**a**	like the 'a' in 'father'
Β β	**v**	like the 'v' in 'vine'
Γ γ	**gh, y**	like a rough 'g', or like 'y' in 'yes'
Δ δ	**dh**	like the 'th' in 'there'
Ε ε	**e**	like the 'e' in 'egg'
Ζ ζ	**z**	like the 'z' in 'zoo'
Η η	**i**	like the 'ee' in 'feet'
Θ θ	**th**	like the 'th' in 'throw'
Ι ι	**i**	like the 'ee' in 'feet'
Κ κ	**k**	like the 'k' in 'kite'
Λ λ	**l**	like the 'l' in 'leg'
Μ μ	**m**	like the 'm' in 'man'
Ν ν	**n**	like the 'n' in 'net'
Ξ ξ	**x**	like the 'ks' in 'looks'
Ο ο	**o**	like the 'o' in 'hot'
Π π	**p**	like the 'p' in 'pup'
Ρ ρ	**r**	slightly trilled 'r'
Σ σ	**s**	like the 's' in 'sand' (ς at the end of a word)
Τ τ	**t**	like the 't' in 'tap'
Υ υ	**i**	like the 'ee' in 'feet'
Φ φ	**f**	like the 'f' in 'find'
Χ χ	**kh, h**	like the 'ch' in 'loch', or like a rough 'h'
Ψ ψ	**ps**	like the 'ps' in 'lapse'
Ω ω	**o**	like the 'o' in 'hot'

ει, οι		like the 'ee' in 'feet'
αι		like the 'e' in 'bet'
ου		like the 'oo' in 'mood'
μπ		like the 'b' in 'beer', or 'mb' as in 'amber', or 'mp' as in 'ample'
ντ		like the 'd' in 'dot', the 'nt' in 'sent', or the 'nd' in 'bend'
γκ, γγ		like the 'g' in 'god' or the 'ng' in 'angle'
γξ		like the 'ks' in 'minks'
τζ		like the 'ds' in 'hands'

Some pairs of vowels are pronounced separately if the first has an acute accent ( ), or the second has a dieresis ( ).

All Greek words of two or more syllables have an acute accent which indicates where the stress falls. The suffix of some Greek words depends on the gender of the speaker eg, *asthmatikos* (m) and *asthmatikya* (f), or *epileptikos* (m) and *epileptikya* (f).

Basics

Hello	*ya**su** (inf)/**yasas** (formal, plural)*
Goodbye	*andio*
Yes/No	*ne/okhi*
Please	*sas parakalo*
Thank you	*sas efkharisto*
That's fine/You're welcome.	*ine endak-si/parakalo*
Excuse me/Sorry	*signomi*
Do you speak English?	*milate anglika*
How much is it?	*poso kani*

Signs

ENTRANCE	ΕΙΣΟΔΟΣ
EXIT	ΕΞΟΔΟΣ
INFORMATION	ΠΛΗΡΟΦΟΡΙΕΣ
HOTEL	ΞΕΝΟΔΟΧΕΙΟ
ROOMS (DOMATIA)	ΔΩΜΑΤΙΑ
YOUTH HOSTEL	ΠΑΝΔΟΧΕΙΟ ΝΕΩΝ
CAMPING GROUND	ΚΑΤΑΣΚΗΝΩΣ
OPEN/CLOSED	ΑΝΟΙΚΤΟ/ ΚΛΕΙΣΤΟ
POLICE STATION	ΑΣΤΥΝΟΜΙΚΟΣ ΣΤΑΘΜΟΣ
PROHIBITED	ΑΠΑΓΟΡΕΥΕΤΑΙ
TOILETS	ΤΟΥΑΛΕΤΕΣ
(MEN'S/ WOMEN'S)	(ΑΝΔΡΩΝ/ ΓΥΝΑΙΚΩΝ)

What is your name? *pos sas lene/pos legeste*

My name is ... *me lene ...*

Getting Around

What time does ... leave/arrive?
ti ora fevyi/apohorito ...

boat	*to plio*
bus (city)	*to leoforio (ya tin boli)*
bus (intercity)	*to leoforio (ya ta proastia)*
tram	*to tram*
train	*to treno*

I would like a one-way ticket/a return ticket. *tha ithela isitirio horis epistrofi/ isitirio met epistrois*

1st class/2nd class *proti thesi/dhefteri thesi*

left luggage *horos aspokevon*
timetable *dhromologhio*
bus stop *i stasi tu leoforiu*
Go straight ahead. *pighenete efthia*
Turn left/right. *stripste aristera/dheksya.*

Around Town

a bank *mia trapeza*
the ... embassy *i ... presvia*

the hotel *to ksenodho khio*
the post office *to takhidhromio*
the market *i aghora*
pharmacy *farmakio*
newsagency *efimeridhon*
the telephone centre *to tilefoniko kentro*
the tourist information office *to ghrafio turistikon pliroforion*
What time does it open/close? *ti ora aniyi/klini*

Accommodation

a hotel *ena xenothohio*
a youth hostel *enas xenonas neoitos*
a camp site *ena kamping*

I'd like ... *thelo*
 a single room/ double room *ena dhomatio ya ena atomo/dhio atoma*
How much is it per night/per person? *poso kostizi ya ena vradhi/ya ena atomo*

Time, Days & Numbers

What time is it? *ti ora ine*
today *simera*
tomorrow *avrio*
yesterday *hthes*
in the morning/ afternoon *to proi/to apoyevma*

Monday	*dheftera*
Tuesday	*triti*
Wednesday	*tetarti*
Thursday	*pempti*
Friday	*paraskevi*
Saturday	*savato*
Sunday	*kiryaki*

1	*ena*	
2	*dhio*	
3	*tria*	
4	*tesera*	
5	*pende*	
6	*eksi*	
7	*epta*	
8	*okhto*	
9	*enea*	
10	*dheka*	

100	*ekato*
1000	*khilya*
one million	*ena ekatomirio*

Emergencies

| Help! | *voithia* |

Call a doctor!	*fona kste ena yatro*
Call the police!	*tilefoniste stin astinomia*
Go away!	*figheldhromo*
I'm lost.	*eho hathi*

ITALIAN

Pronunciation

Italian is not difficult to pronounce once you learn a few easy rules. Although some of the more clipped vowels and stress on double letters require careful practice for English speakers, it is easy enough to make yourself understood.

Vowels Vowels are generally more clipped than in English.

a	like the second 'a' in 'camera'
e	like the 'ay' in 'day', but without the 'i' sound
i	as in 'see'
o	as in 'dot'
u	as in 'too'

Consonants The pronunciation of many Italian consonants is similar to that of English. The following sounds depend on certain rules:

c	like 'k' before **a**, **o** and **u**; or like the 'ch' in 'choose' before **e** and **i**
ch	a hard 'k' sound
g	a hard 'g' as in 'get' before **a**, **o**
gh	a hard 'g' as in 'get'
gli	like the 'lli' in 'million'
gn	like the 'ny' in 'canyon'
h	always silent
r	a rolled 'rrr' sound
sc	like the 'sh' in 'sheep' before **e** and **i**; or a hard sound as in 'school' before **h**, **a**, **o** and **u**
z	like the 'ts' in 'lights' or as the 'ds' in 'beds'

Note that when 'ci', 'gi' and 'sci' are followed by **a**, **o** or **u**, unless the accent falls on the 'i', it's not pronounced. Thus the name 'Giovanni' is pronounced 'joh-VAHN-nee', with no 'i' sound after the 'G'.

Stress Double consonants are pronounced as a longer, often more forceful sound than a single consonant.

Stress often falls on the next to last syllable, as in 'spaghetti'. When a word has an accent, the stress is on that syllable, as in *città* (city).

Basics

Hello	*Buongiorno/Ciao*
Goodbye	*Arrivederci/Ciao*
Yes/No	*Sì/No*
Please	*Per favore/Per piacere*
Thank you	*Grazie*
That's fine/You're welcome	*Prego*
Excuse me	*Mi scusi*
Sorry (excuse me/ forgive me)	*Mi scusi/Mi perdoni*
Do you speak English?	*Parla (Parli) inglese?*
How much is it?	*Quanto costa?*
What is your name?	*Come si chiama?*
My name is ...	*Mi chiamo ...*

Getting Around

What time does the next ... leave/arrive?
A che ora parte/arriva ... ?

boat	*la barca*
ferry	*il traghetto*
bus	*l'autobus*
tram	*il tram*
train	*il treno*

| I'd like to hire a car/bicycle. | *Vorrei noleggiare una macchina/ bicicletta.* |

Signs

ENTRANCE	*INGRESSO/ ENTRATA*
EXIT	*USCITA*
FULL/NO VACANCIES	*COMPLETO*
INFORMATION	*INFORMAZIONE*
OPEN/CLOSED	*APERTO/ CHIUSO*
PROHIBITED	*PROIBITO/ VIETATO*
POLICE	*POLIZIA/ CARABINIERI*
POLICE STATION	*QUESTURA*
ROOMS AVAILABLE	*CAMERE LIBERE*
TOILETS (MEN'S/ WOMEN'S)	*GABINETTI/ BAGNI (UOMINI/ DONNE)*

I'd like a one-way/ return ticket.	*Vorrei un biglietto di solo andata/di andata e ritorno.*
1st class	*prima classe*
2nd class	*seconda classe*
left luggage	*deposito bagagli*
timetable	*orario*
bus stop	*fermata dell'autobus*
train station	*stazione*
ferry terminal	*stazione marittima*
Where is ...?	*Dov'è ...?*
far/near	*lontano/vicino*
Go straight ahead.	*Si va sempre diritto.*
Turn left/right.	*Gira a sinistra/ destra.*

Around Town

a bank	*una banca*
the ... embassy	*l'ambasciata di ...*
my hotel	*il mio albergo*
post office	*la posta*
market	*il mercato*
chemist/pharmacy	*la farmacia*
newsagency/ stationer's	*l'edicola/il cartolaio*
telephone centre	*il centro telefonico*
the tourist information office	*l'ufficio di turismo*

What time does it open/close?	*A che ora (si) apre/chiude?*

Accommodation

hotel	*albergo*
guesthouse	*pensione*
youth hostel	*ostello per la gioventù*
camping ground	*campeggio*

Do you have any rooms available?
Ha delle camere libere?/C'è una camera libera?
a single room
una camera singola
a double/twin room
una camera matrimoniale/doppia
for one/two nights
per una notte/due notti
How much is it per night/per person?
Quanto costa per la notte/ciascuno?
Is breakfast included?
È compresa la colazione?

Time, Days & Numbers

What time is it?	*Che ora è?/Che ore sono?*
today	*oggi*
tomorrow	*domani*
yesterday	*ieri*
morning/afternoon	*mattina/pomeriggio*
Monday	*lunedì*
Tuesday	*martedì*
Wednesday	*mercoledì*
Thursday	*giovedì*
Friday	*venerdì*
Saturday	*sabato*
Sunday	*domenica*

1	*uno*
2	*due*
3	*tre*
4	*quattro*
5	*cinque*
6	*sei*
7	*sette*
8	*otto*
9	*nove*
10	*dieci*
100	*cento*
1000	*mille*
one million	*un milione*

Emergencies

Help!	*Aiuto!*
Call a doctor!	*Chiama un dottore/un medico!*
Call the police!	*Chiama la polizia!*
Go away!	*Vai via!* (informal)
I'm lost.	*Mi sono perso/a.*

MACEDONIAN

Pronunciation

The spelling of Macedonian is basically phonetic: almost every word is written exactly as it is pronounced and every letter is pronounced. With regard to the position of the stress accent, only one rule can be given: the last syllable of a word is never stressed. There are 31 letters in the Cyrillic alphabet. The pronunciation of the Roman or Cyrillic letter is given to the nearest English equivalent.

Basics

hello	*zdravo*
	здраво
goodbye	*priatno*
	приатно
yes/no	*da/ne*
	да/не
please	*molam*
	молам
thank you	*blagodaram*
	благодарам

That's fine/You're welcome
Nema zošto/Milo mi e
Нема зошто/ мило ми е
Excuse me
Izvinete
извинете
sorry (excuse me, forgive me)
oprostete ve molam
опростете ве молам

Do you speak English?
Zboruvate li angliski?
Зборувате ли англиски?
How much is it?
Kolku čini toa?
Колку чини тоа?
What is your name?
Kako se vikate?
Како се викате?
My name is ...
Jas se vikam ...
Јас се викам ...

Getting Around

What time does the next ... leave/arrive?
Koga doagja/zaminuva idniot ...?
Кога доаѓа/заминува идниот ...?

boat	*brod*
	брод
bus (city)	*avtobus (gradski)*
	автобус (градски)

Roman	Cyrillic	English Pronunciation
a	Аа	'a' as in 'rather'
b	Бб	'b' as in 'brother'
v	Вв	'v' as in 'vodka'
g	Гг	'g' as in 'got'
gj	Ѓѓ	'gj' as in 'legume'
e	Ее	'e' as in 'bear'
zh	Жж	like the 's' in 'treasure'
z	Зз	'z' as in 'zero'
zj	Ѕѕ	like the 'ds' in suds
i	Ии	'i' as in 'machine'
j	Јј	'y' as in 'young'
k	Кк	'k' as in 'keg'
l	Лл	'l' as in 'lad'
lj	Љљ	like the 'lli' in 'million'
m	Мм	'm' as in 'map'
n	Нн	'n' as in 'no'
nj	Њњ	'ny' as in 'canyon'
o	Оо	like the 'aw' in 'shawl'
p	Пп	'p' as in 'pop'
r	Рр	'r' as in 'rock'
s	Сс	's' as in 'loss'
t	Тт	't' as in 'too'
ć	Ќќ	'kj' as in 'cure'
u	Уу	'oo' as in 'room'
f	Фф	'f' as in 'fat'
h	Хх	'h' as in 'hot'
c	Цц	'ts' as in 'cats'
č	Чч	'ch' as in 'chop'
dz	Џџ	'j' as in 'just'
š	Шш	'sh' as in 'hush'

Signs

ENTRANCE
VLEZ
ВЛЕЗ

EXIT
IZLEZ
ИЗЛЕЗ

FULL/NO VACANCIES
POLNO/NEMA MESTO
ПОЛНО/НЕМА МЕСТО

INFORMATION
INFORMACII
ИНФОРМАЦИИ

OPEN/CLOSED
OTVORENO/ZATVORENO
ОТВОРЕНО/ЗАТВОРЕНО

PROHIBITED
ZABRANETO
ЗАБРАНЕТО

POLICE
POLICIJA
ПОЛИЦИЈА

POLICE STATION
POLICISKA STANICA
ПОЛИЦИСКА СТАНИЦА

ROOMS AVAILABLE
SOBI ZA IZDAVANJE
СОБИ ЗА ИЗДАВАЊЕ

TOILETS (MEN'S/WOMEN'S)
KLOZETI, MAŠKI/ENSKI
КЛОЗЕТИ, МАШКИ/ЖЕНСКИ

---

bus (intercity)
avtobus (megjugradski)
автобус (меѓуградски)

train
voz
воз

tram
tramvaj
трамвај

I'd like to hire a car/bicycle.
Sakam da iznajmam kola/točak.
Сакам да изнајмам кола/точак.

I would like ...
Sakam ...
Сакам ...

a one-way ticket
bilet vo eden pravec
билет во еден правец

a return ticket
povraten bilet
повратен билет

1st class
prva klasa
прва класа

2nd class
vtora klasa
втора класа

timetable
vozen red
возен ред

bus stop
avtobuska stanica
автобуска станица

train station
elezniška stanica
железничка станица

Where is ...? *Kade je ...?*
Каде је ...?

far/near *daleku/blisku*
далеку/блиску

Go straight ahead. *Odete pravo napred.*
Одете право напред.

Turn left/right. *Svrtete levo/desno.*
Свртете лево/десно.

Around Town

bank *banka*
банка

the embassy *ambasadata*
амбасадата

my hotel *mojot hotel*
мојот хотел

the post office *poštata*
поштата

the market *pazarot*
пазарот

chemist/pharmacy *apteka*
аптека

newsagency/stationer's
kiosk za vesnici/knižarnica
киоск за весници/книжарница

the telephone centre
telefonskata centrala
телефонската централа

the tourist office
turističkoto biro
туристичкото биро

What time does it open/close?
Koga se otvora/zatvora?
Кога се отвора/затвора?

Accommodation
hotel
hotel
хотел
guesthouse
privatno smetuvanje
приватно сметување
youth hostel
mladinsko prenokevalište
младинско пренокевалиште
camping ground
kamping
кампинг

Do you have any rooms available?
Dali imate slobodni sobi?
Дали имате слободни соби?

a single room
soba so eden krevet
соба со еден кревет
a double room
soba so bračen krevet
соба со брачен кревет
for one/two nights
za edna/dva večeri
за една/два вечери

How much is it per night/per person?
Koja e cenata po noć/po osoba?
Која е цената по ноќ/по особа?
Does it include breakfast?
Dali e vključen pojadok?
Дали е вклучен ројадок?

Time, Days & Numbers
What time is it?   *Kolku e časot?*
                      Колку е часот?
today   *denes*
                      денес
tomorrow   *utre*
                      утре
yesterday   *včera*
                      вчера
morning   *utro*
                      утро
afternoon   *popladne*
                      попладне

Monday	*ponedelnik*	
	понеделник	
Tuesday	*vtornik*	
	вторник	
Wednesday	*sreda*	
	среда	
Thursday	*chetvrtok*	
	четврток	
Friday	*petok*	
	петок	
Saturday	*sabota*	
	сабота	
Sunday	*nedela*	
	недела	

1	*eden*	
	еден	
2	*dva*	
	два	
3	*tri*	
	три	
4	*četiri*	
	четири	
5	*pet*	
	пет	
6	*šest*	
	шест	
7	*sedum*	
	седум	
8	*osum*	
	осум	
9	*devet*	
	девет	
10	*deset*	
	десет	
100	*sto*	
	сто	
one million	*eden milion*	
	еден милион	

Emergencies
Help!   *Pomoš!*
                      Помош!
Call a doctor!   *Povikajte lekar!*
                      Повикајте лекар!
Call the police!   *Viknete policija!*
                      Викнете полиција!
Go away!   *Odete si!*
                      Одете си!
I'm lost.   *Jas zaginav.*
                      Јас загинав.

MALTESE

The following is a brief guide to Maltese pronunciation, and includes a few useful words and phrases.

Pronunciation

c like the 'ch' in child
g like the 'g' in good
g like the 'j' in job
gh takes the sound of the vowel following it
h silent, except when preceded by 'g'
h like the 'h' in hello
J like 'y'
aj like the 'igh' in high
ej like the 'ay' in say
q a very faint 'kh' sound
x like the 'sh' in shop
z like 'ts'
z a hard 'z'

Basics

Good morning/ Good day	Bongu
Goodbye	Sahha
Yes/No	Iva/Le
Please	Jekk joghgbok
Thank you	Grazzi
Excuse me	Skuzani

Do you speak English?	Titkellem bl-ingliz? (inf)
How much is it?	Kemm?
What is your name?	X'ismek?
My name is ...	Jisimni ...

Getting Around

When does the boat leave/arrive?
Meta jitlaq il-vapur?

When does the bus leave/arrive?
Meta titlaq il-karozza?
I'd like to hire a car/bicycle.
Nixtieq nikri karozza/rota.
I'd like a one-way/return ticket.
Nixtieq biljett 'one-way/return'.

1st/2nd class	Nixtieq biljett '1st/2nd class'.
left luggage	bagalji
bus/trolleybus stop	xarabank/coach

Where is a/the ...?	Fejn hi ...?
far/near	il-boghod/vicin
Go straight ahead.	Mur dritt.
Turn left/right.	Dur fuq il-lemin/ ix-xellug.

Around Town

the bank	il-bank
the ... embassy	l'ambaxxata ...
the hotel	il-hotel
the post office	il-posta
the market	is-suq
chemist/pharmacy	l-ispizerija
a public telephone	telefon pubbliku

What time does it open/close?
Fix'hin jiftah/jaghlaq?

Accommodation

Do you have a room available?
Ghandek kamra jekk joghgbok?
Do you have a room for one/two people
Ghandek kamra ghal wiehed/tnejn?
Do you have a room for one/two nights
Ghandek kamra ghal lejl/zewgt iljieli
Is breakfast included?
Il-breakfast inkluz?

Time, Days & Numbers

What time is it?	X'hin hu?
today	illum
tomorrow	ghada
yesterday	il-bierah
morning/afternoon	fil-ghodu/wara nofsiin-nhar

Monday	it-tnejn
Tuesday	it-tlieta
Wednesday	l-erbgha
Thursday	il-hamis

Friday	*il-gimgha*	9	*disgha*
Saturday	*is-sibt*	10	*ghaxra*
Sunday	*il-hadd*	100	*mija*
		1000	*elf*
1	*wiehed*	one million	*miljun*
2	*tnejn*		
3	*tlieta*		
4	*erbgha*	**Emergencies**	
5	*hamsa*	Help!	*Ajjut!*
6	*sitta*	Call a doctor.	*Qibghad ghat-tabib.*
7	*sebgha*	Police!	*Pulizija!*
8	*tmienja*	I'm lost.	*Ninsab mitluf.*

MOROCCAN ARABIC

Pronunciation

Arabic is a difficult language to learn, but even knowing a few words can win you a friendly smile from the locals.

Vowels There are at least five basic vowel sounds that can be distinguished:

a	like the 'a' in 'had' (sometimes very short)
e	like the 'e' in 'bet' (sometimes very short)
i	like the 'i' in 'hit'
o	like the 'o' in 'hot'
u	like the 'oo' in 'book'

The symbol over a vowel gives it a long sound. For example:

a	like the 'a' in 'father'
e	like the 'e' in 'ten', but lengthened
i	like the 'e' in 'ear', only softer, often written as 'ee'
o	like the 'o' in 'for'
u	like the 'oo' in 'food'

Combinations Certain combinations of vowels with vowels or consonants form other vowel sounds (diphthongs):

aw	like the 'ow' in 'how'
ai	like the 'i' in 'high'
ei and **ay**	like the 'a' in 'cake'

Consonants Many consonants are the same as in English, but there are some tricky ones:

j	more or less like the 'j' in 'John'
H	a strongly whispered 'h', almost like a sigh of relief
q	a strong guttural 'k' sound
kh	a slightly gurgling sound, like the 'ch' in Scottish 'loch'
r	a rolled 'r' sound
s	as in 'sit', never as in 'wisdom'
sh	like the 'sh' in 'shelf'
z	like the 's' in pleasure
gh	called 'ghayn', it is something like the French 'r', but more guttural

Glottal Stop (')

The glottal stop (') is the sound you hear between the vowels in the expression 'oh oh!', and can occur anywhere in the word at the beginning, middle or end. When the (') occurs before a vowel (eg 'ayn), the vowel is 'growled' from the back of the throat. If it is before a consonant or at the end of a word, it sounds like a glottal stop.

Basics

Hello	*as-salaam 'alaykum*
Goodbye	*ma' as-salaama*
Yes/No	*eeyeh/la*
Please	*'afak*
Thank you (very much)	*shukran (jazilan)*
You're welcome	*la shukran, 'ala wajib*
Excuse me	*smeH leeya*

Do you speak English?	*wash kayn shee Hedd henna lee kay'ref negleezeya*
How much (is it)?	*bish-hal*
What is your name?	*asmeetak*
My name is ...	*smeetee ...*

Getting Around

What time does the ... leave/arrive?
emta qiyam/wusuul ...

boat	*al-baboor*
bus (city)	*al-otobis*
bus (intercity)	*al-kar*
train	*al-masheena*

Where can I hire a car/bicycle?	*fein yimkin ana akra tomobeel/ beshkleeta*
1st/2nd class	*ddarazha lloola/ ttaneeya*
train station	*maHattat al-masheena/ al-qitar*
bus stop	*mawqif al-otobis*

Where is (the) ...?	*fein ...*
Go straight ahead.	*seer neeshan*
Turn right.	*dor 'al leemen*
Turn left.	*dor 'al leeser*

Around Town

the bank	*al-banka*
the embassy	*as-sifara*
the market	*as-suq*
the police station	*al-bolis*
the post office	*al-bosta, maktab al-barid*
a toilet	*bayt al-ma, mirHad*

Accommodation

hotel	*al-otel*

youth hostel	*dar shabbab*
camp site	*mukhaym*

Is there a room available?	*wash kayn shee beet xaweeya*
How much is this room per night?	*bshaHal al-bayt liyal*
Is breakfast included?	*wash lftor mHsoob m'a lbeet*

Time, Dates & Numbers

What time is it?	*shHal fessa'a*
today	*al-youm*
tomorrow	*ghaddan*
yesterday	*lbareH*
in the morning	*fis-sabaH*
in the evening	*fil-masa'*

Arabic numerals are simple enough to learn and, unlike the written language, run from left to right. In Morocco, European numerals often used anyway.

1	*waHid*
2	*jooj* or *itneen*
3	*talata*
4	*arba'a*
5	*khamsa*
6	*sitta*
7	*saba'a*
8	*tamanya*
9	*tissa'*
10	*'ashara*
100	*miyya*
1000	*alf*
one million	*melyoon*

Emergencies

Help!	*'teqnee*
Call a doctor!	*'eyyet at-tabeeb*
Call the police!	*'eyyet al-bolis*
Go away!	*seer fHalek*

PORTUGUESE

Pronunciation

Pronunciation of Portuguese is difficult; like English, vowels and consonants have more than one possible sound depending on position and stress. Moreover, there are nasal vowels and diphthongs in Portuguese with no equivalent in English.

Vowels Single vowels should present relatively few problems:

a	short, like the 'u' sound in 'cut', or long like the 'ur' sound in 'hurt'
e	short, as in 'bet', or longer as in French *été* and English 'laird'

é	short, as in 'bet'
ê	long, like the 'a' sound in 'gate'
e	silent final 'e', like the final 'e' in English 'these'; also silent in unstressed syllables
i	as in 'see', or short as in 'ring'
o	short, as in 'pot'; long as in 'note'; or like 'oo' as in 'good'
ô	long, as in 'note'
u	'oo', as in 'good'

Nasal Vowels Nasalisation is represented by an 'n' or an 'm' after the vowel, or by a tilde (~) over it. The nasal 'i' exists in English as the 'ing' in 'sing'. For other vowels, try to pronounce a long 'a', 'ah', or 'e', 'eh', holding your nose, as if you have a cold.

Diphthongs Double vowels are relatively straightforward:

au	as in 'now'
ai	as in 'pie'
ei	as in 'day'
eu	pronounced together
oi	similar to 'boy'

Nasal Diphthongs Try the same technique as for nasal vowels. To say *não*, pronounce 'now' through your nose.

ão	nasal 'now' (owng)
ãe	nasal 'day' (eing)
õe	nasal 'boy' (oing)
ui	similar to the 'uing' in 'ensuing'

Consonants The following consonants are specific to Portuguese:

c	hard, as in 'cat' before a, o or u
c	soft as in 'see' before e or i
ç	as in 'see'
g	hard, as in 'garden' before a, o or u
g	soft, as in 'treasure' before e or i
gu	hard, as in 'get' before e or i
h	never pronounced at the beginning of a word
nh	like the 'ni' sound in 'onion'
lh	like the 'lli' sound in 'million'
j	like the 's' in 'treasure'
m	in final position is not pronounced – it simply nasalises the previous vowel: *um* (oong), *bom* (bõ)

qu	like the 'k' in 'key' before e or i
qu	like the 'q' in 'quad' before a or o
r	at the beginning of a word, or rr in the middle of a word, is a harsh, guttural sound similar to the French *rue*, Scottish *loch*, or German *Bach*. In some areas of Portugal this r is not guttural, but strongly rolled.
r	in the middle or at the end of a word is a rolled sound stronger than the English 'r'
s	like the 's' in 'see' (at the beginning of a word)
ss	like the 's' in 'see' (in the middle of a word)
s	like the 'z' in 'zeal' (between vowels)
s	like the 'sh' in 'ship' (before another consonant, or at the end of a word)
x	like the 'sh' in 'ship'; the 'z' in 'zeal'; or the 'ks' sound in 'taxi'

Word stress is important in Portuguese, as it can change the meaning of the word. Many Portuguese words have a written accent and the stress must fall on that syllable when you pronounce the word.

Basics

Hello/Goodbye	*Olá/Adeus*
Yes/No	*Sim/Não*
Please	*Se faz favor*
Thank you	*Obrigado/a*
That's fine/You're welcome	*De nada*
Excuse me	*Desculpe/com licença*
Sorry (excuse me, forgive me)	*Desculpe*
Do you speak English?	*Fala Inglês?*
How much is it?	*Quanto custa?*
What is your name?	*Como se chama?*
My name is ...	*Chamo-me ...*

Getting Around

What time does the ... leave/arrive?
  A que horas parte/chega ...?

boat	*o barco*
bus (city)	*o autocarro*
bus (intercity)	*a camioneta*

the telephone centre	*da central de telefones*
the tourist information office	*do turismo/do serviço de informações para turistas*

What time does it open/close?
A que horas abre/fecha?

Accommodation

hotel	*hotel*
guesthouse	*pensão*
youth hostel	*albergue de juventude*
camping ground	*parque de campismo*

Do you have any rooms available?
Tem quartos livres?
a single room
um quarto individual
a double room
um quarto duplo/de casal
for one/two nights
para uma/duas noites
How much is it per night/per person?
Quanto é por noite/por pessoa?
Is breakfast included?
O pequeno almoço está incluído?

Time, Days & Numbers

What time is it?	*Que horas são?*
today	*hoje*
tomorrow	*amanhã*
yesterday	*ontem*
morning/afternoon	*manhã/tarde*
Monday	*segunda-feira*
Tuesday	*terça-feira*
Wednesday	*quarta-feira*
Thursday	*quinta-feira*
Friday	*sexta-feira*
Saturday	*sábado*
Sunday	*domingo*

Signs		
ENTRANCE	*ENTRADA*	
EXIT	*SAÍDA*	
FREE ADMISSION	*ENTRADA GRÁTIS*	
INFORMATION	*INFORMAÇÕES*	
OPEN/CLOSED	*ABERTO/ ENCERADO (OR FECHADO)*	
PROHIBITED	*PROIBIDO*	
POLICE STATION	*ESQUADRA DA POLÍCIA*	
ROOMS AVAILABLE	*QUARTOS LIVRES*	
TOILETS	*WC*	

tram	*o eléctrico*
train	*o comboio*
I'd like to hire a car/bicycle.	*Queria alugar um carro/uma bicicleta.*
I'd like a one-way ticket.	*Queria um bilhete simples/de ida.*
I'd like a return ticket.	*Queria um bilhete de ida e volta.*
1st class	*primeira classe*
2nd class	*segunda classe*
timetable	*horário*
bus stop	*paragem de autocarro*
train station	*estação ferroviária*
Where is ...?	*Onde é ...?*
far/near	*longe/perto*
Go straight ahead.	*Siga sempre a direito/sempre em frente.*
Turn left/right.	*Vire à esquerda/ direita.*

Around Town

a bank	*dum banco*
the ... embassy	*da embaixada de ...*
my hotel	*do meu hotel*
the post office	*dos correios*
the market	*do mercado/da praça*
chemist/pharmacy	*da farmácia*
newsagency/ stationer's	*papelaria/tabacaria*

1	*um/uma*
2	*dois/duas*
3	*três*
4	*quatro*
5	*cinco*
6	*seis*
7	*sete*
8	*oito*

9	*nove*
10	*dez*
100	*cem*
1000	*mil*
one million	*um milhão*

SLOVENE

Pronunciation

Slovene sounds are not difficult to learn. The alphabet consists of 25 letters, most of which are very similar to English. It does not have the letters q, w, x and y, but the following letters are added: č, š, ê, é, ó, ò and ž. Each letter has only one sound, with very few exceptions, and the sounds are pure and not diphthongal. The letters 'l' and 'v' at the end of syllables and before vowels are both pronounced like the English 'w'. Though words like *trn* (thorn) look unpronounceable, most Slovenes add a short vowel like an 'a' or the German 'ö' (depending on dialect) in front of the 'r' to give a Scot's pronunciation of 'tern' or 'tarn'. Here is a list of letters specific to Slovene.

c	'ts' as in 'pizza'
č	'ch' as in 'chocolate'
ê	'a' as in 'apple'
e	'er' as in 'opera' (when unstressed)
é	'ay' as in 'day'
j	'y' as in 'yellow'
ó	'o' as in 'more'
ò	'o' as in 'soft'
r	a rolled 'r' sound
š	'sh' as in 'ship'
u	'oo' as in 'good'
ž	'zh' like the 's' in 'treasure'

Basics

Hello	*Zdravo/*
	Živio (inf)
Goodbye	*Nasvidenje!*
Yes	*Ja*
No	*Ne*
Please	*Prosim*
Thank you (very much).	*Hvala (lepa).*
You're welcome.	*Prosim/Ni za kaj!*
Excuse me.	*Oprostite.*
Good day.	*Dober dan!*

My name is ...	*Moje ime je ...*
Where are you from?	*Od kod ste?*
I'm from ...	*Sem iz ...*

Getting Around

What time does ... leave/arrive?
Ob kateri uri ... odpelje/pripelge?

boat/ferry	*ladja/trajekt*
bus/tram	*avtobus/tramvaj*
train	*vlak*
one-way (ticket)	*enosmerna (vozovnica)*
return (ticket)	*povratna (vozovnica)*

Around Town

bank/exchange office	*banka/menjalnica*
embassy	*konzulat, ambasada*
post office	*pošta*
telephone centre	*telefonska centrala*
tourist information office	*turistični informacijski urad*

Accommodation

hotel	*hotel*
guesthouse	*gostišče*
camping ground	*kamping*

Do you have a ...?	*Ali imate prosto ...?*
bed	*posteljo.*
cheap room	*poceni sobo*
single/double room	*enoposteljno/*
	dvoposteljno sobo
for one night/two	*za eno noč/za dve*
nights	*noči*

How much is it per night/per person?
Koliko stane na noč/na osebo?

Time, Days & Numbers

today	*danes*
tonight	*danes zvečer*
tomorrow	*jutri*
in the morning	*zjutraj*
in the evening	*zvečer*

Monday	*ponedeljek*
Tuesday	*torek*
Wednesday	*sreda*
Thursday	*četrtek*

Friday	*petek*
Saturday	*sobota*
Sunday	*nedelja*

1	*ena*
2	*dve*
3	*tri*
4	*štiri*
5	*pet*
6	*šest*
7	*sedem*
8	*osem*
9	*devet*
10	*deset*
100	*sto*
1000	*tisoč*
one million	*milijon*

Emergencies

Help!	*Na pomoč!*
Call a doctor!	*Pokličite zdravnika!*
Call the police!	*Pokličite policijo!*
Go away!	*Pojdite stran!*

SPANISH

Pronunciation

Pronunciation of Spanish is not difficult, given that many Spanish sounds are similar to their English counterparts, and there is a clear and consistent relationship between pronunciation and spelling. If you stick to the following rules you should have very few problems in being understood.

Vowels Unlike English, each of the vowels in Spanish has a uniform pronunciation which does not vary. For example, the Spanish 'a' has one pronunciation rather than the numerous pronunciations we find in English, such as the 'a' in 'cake', 'art' and 'all'. Many Spanish words have a written accent. The acute accent (as in *días*) generally indicates a stressed syllable and it doesn't change the sound of the vowel. Vowels are pronounced clearly even if they are in unstressed positions or at the end of a word.

| a | like the 'u' in 'nut', or a shorter sound than the 'a' in 'art' |
| e | like the 'e' in 'met' |

i	somewhere between the 'i' sound in 'marine' and the 'i' in 'flip'
o	similar to the 'o' in 'hot'
u	like the 'oo' in 'hoof'

Consonants Some Spanish consonants are the same as their English counterparts. The pronunciation of other consonants varies according to which vowel follows and also according to which part of Spain you happen to be in. The Spanish alphabet also contains three consonants that are not found within the English alphabet: 'ch', 'll' and 'ñ'.

b	soft; also (less commonly) like the 'b' in 'book' when initial, or preceded by a nasal
c	a hard 'c' as in 'cat' when followed by **a**, **o**, **u** or a consonant; like the 'th' in 'thin' before **e** or **i**
ch	like the 'ch' in choose
d	like the 'd' in 'dog' when initial; elsewhere as the 'th' in 'then'
g	like the 'g' in 'gate' when initial and before **a**, **o** and **u**; elsewhere much

h	softer. Before **e** or **i** it's a harsh, breathy sound, similar to the 'h' in 'hit' silent
j	a harsh, guttural sound similar to the 'ch' in Scottish 'loch'
ll	like the 'lli' in 'million'; some people pronounce it rather like the 'y' in 'yellow'
ñ	a nasal sound like the 'ni' in 'onion'
q	like the 'k' in 'kick'; 'q' is always followed by a silent **u** and is combined only with the vowels **e** (as in *que*) and **i** as in *qui*
r	a rolled 'r' sound; longer and stronger when initial or doubled
s	like the 's' in 'send'
v	the same sound as **b**
x	like the 'ks' sound in 'taxi' when between two vowels; like the 's' in 'say' when it precedes a consonant
z	like the 'th' in 'thin'

Semiconsonant Spanish also has the semi-consonant 'y'. This is pronounced like the Spanish 'i' when it's at the end of a word or when it stands alone as a conjunction. As a consonant, its sound is somewhere between the 'y' in 'yonder' and the 'g' in 'beige', depending on the region.

Basics

Hello/Goodbye	*¡Hola!/¡Adiós!*
Yes/No	*Sí/No*
Please	*Por favor*

Signs	
ENTRANCE	*ENTRADA*
EXIT	*SALIDA*
FULL, NO VACANCIES	*OCUPADO, COMPLETO*
INFORMATION	*INFORMACIÓN*
OPEN/CLOSED	*ABIERTO/ CERRADO*
PROHIBITED	*PROHIBIDO*
POLICE STATION	*ESTACIÓN DE POLICÍA*
ROOMS AVAILABLE	*HABITACIONES LIBRES*
TOILETS (MEN'S/ WOMEN'S)	*SERVICIOS/ ASEOS (HOMBRES/ MUJERES*

Thank you	*Gracias*
That's fine/ You're welcome	*De nada*
Excuse me	*Permiso*
Sorry (excuse me, forgive me)	*Lo siento/ Discúlpeme*
Do you speak English?	*¿Habla inglés?*
How much is it?	*¿Cuánto cuesta?/ ¿Cuánto vale?*
What is your name?	*¿Cómo se llama?*
My name is ...	*Me llamo ...*

Getting Around

What time does the next ... leave/arrive?
¿A qué hora sale/llega el próximo ...?

boat	*barco*
bus (city)	*autobús, bus*
bus (intercity)	*autocar*
train	*tren*
tram	*tranvía*

I'd like to hire a car/bicycle.	*Quisiera alquilar un coche/una bicicleta.*
I'd like a one-way ticket.	*Quisiera un billete sencillo.*
I'd like a return ticket.	*Quisiera un billete de ida y vuelta.*
1st class	*primera clase*
2nd class	*segunda clase*
left luggage	*consigna*
timetable	*horario*
bus stop	*parada de autobus*
train station	*estación (de ferrocarril)*

Where is ...?	*¿Dónde está ...?*
far/near	*lejos/cerca*
Go straight ahead.	*Siga/Vaya todo derecho.*
Turn left.	*Doble a la izquierda.*
Turn right.	*Doble a la derecha.*

Around Town

a bank	*un banco*
the ... embassy	*la embajada ...*
my hotel	*mi hotel*
the post office	*los correos*
the market	*el mercado*
chemist/pharmacy	*la farmacia*

newsagency/ stationer's	papelería
the telephone centre	la central telefónica
the tourist office	la oficina de turismo

What time does it open/close
¿A qué hora abren/cierran?

Accommodation

hotel	hotel
guesthouse	pensión/casa de huespedes
youth hostel	albergue juvenile
camping ground	terreno de camping

Do you have any rooms available?
¿Tiene habitaciones libres?

a single room	una habitación individual
a double room	una habitación doble
for/one two nights	para una/dos noches

How much is it per night/per person?
¿Cuánto cuesta por noche/por persona?
Is breakfast included?
¿Incluye el desayuno?

Time, Days & Numbers

What time is it?	*¿Qué hora es?/* *¿Qué horas son?*
today	hoy
tomorrow	mañana

yesterday	ayer
morning/afternoon	mañana/tarde

Monday	lunes
Tuesday	martes
Wednesday	miércoles
Thursday	jueves
Friday	viernes
Saturday	sábado
Sunday	domingo

0	cero
1	uno, una
2	dos
3	tres
4	cuatro
5	cinco
6	seis
7	siete
8	ocho
9	nueve
10	diez
100	cien/ciento
1000	mil
one million	un millón

Emergencies

Help!	¡Socorro!/¡Auxilio!
Call a doctor!	¡Llame a un doctor!
Call the police!	¡Llame a la policía!
Go away!	¡Váyase!
I'm lost.	Estoy perdido/a.

TURKISH

Pronunciation

The new Turkish alphabet is phonetic and thus reasonably easy to pronounce, once you've learned a few important differences. Each Turkish letter is pronounced; there are no diphthongs, and the only silent letter is the 'ğ'.

Vowels Turkish vowels are pronounced as follows:

A, a	as 'ar', as in 'art' or 'bar'
E, e	as in 'fell'
İ, i	as 'ee'
I, ı	as 'uh'
O, o	as in 'hot'
U, u	like the 'oo' in 'moo'
Ö, ö	like the 'ur' in 'fur'
Ü, ü	like the 'ew' in 'few'

Note Both **ö** and **ü** are pronounced with pursed lips.

Consonants Most consonants are pronounced as in English, with a few exceptions:

Ç ç	like the 'ch' in 'church'
C c	just like the English 'j'
Ğ ğ	isn't pronounced but just draws out the preceding vowel a bit; don't pronounce it, ignore it!
G g	hard, as in 'gun'
H h	like the 'h' in 'half'
J j	like 's' in 'treasure'
S s	hard, as in 'stress'
Ş ş	like the 'sh' in 'shoe'
V v	like the 'w' in 'weather'

Basics

Hello	*Merhaba*
Goodbye	*Allahaısmarladık/ Güle güle*
Yes/No	*Evet/ Hayır*
Please	*Lütfen*
Thank you	*Teşekkür ederim*
That's fine/You're welcome	*Bir şey değil*
Excuse me	*Affedersiniz*
Sorry/Pardon	*Pardon*
Do you speak English?	*İngilizce biliyor musunuz?*
How much is it?	*Ne kadar?*
What is your name?	*Adınız ne?*
My name is ...	*Adim ...*

Signs

ENTRANCE	**GIRIS**
EXIT	**ÇIKIS**
FULL (NO VACANCIES)	**DOLU**
INFORMATION	**DANISMA**
OPEN/CLOSED	**AÇIK/KAPALI**
PROHIBITED	**YASAK(TIR)**
POLICE	**POLIS/EMNIYET**
POLICE STATION	**POLIS KARAKOLU/ EMNIYET MÜDÜRLÜĞÜ**
ROOMS AVAILABLE	**BOŞ ODA VAR**
TOILET	**TUVALET**

Getting Around

What time does the next ... leave/arrive?
Glecek ... ne zaman kalkar/gelir?

ferry/boat	*feribot/vapur*
bus (city)	*şehir otobüsü*
bus (intercity)	*otobüs*
tram	*tramvay*
train	*tren*
I would like ...	*... istiyorum*
a one-way ticket	*gidiş bileti*
a return ticket	*gidiş-dönüş bileti*
1st/2nd class	*birinci/ikinci mevkii*
left luggage	*emanetçi*
timetable	*tarife*
bus/tram stop	*otobüs/tramvay durağı*
train station	*gar/istasyon*
boat/ship dock	*iskele*

I'd like to hire a car/bicycle.
Araba/bisiklet kiralamak istiyorum.

Where is a/the ...?	*... nerede?*
far/near	*uzak/yakın*
Go straight ahead.	*Doğru gidin.*
Turn left.	*Sola dönün.*
Turn right.	*Sağa dönün.*

Around Town

a bank	*bir banka*
the ... embassy	*... büyükçiliğini*
my hotel	*otelimi*
the post office	*postane*
the market	*çarşıyı*
a chemist/pharmacy	*bir eczane*
the telephone centre	*telefon merkezi*
the tourist information office	*turizm danima bürosu*

What time does it open/close?
Ne zamam açılır/kapanır?

Accommodation

hotel	*otel(i)*
guesthouse	*pansiyon*
student hostel	*öğrenci yurdu*
camping ground	*kampink*

Do you have any rooms available?
Boş oda var mı?
a single room
tek kişilik oda
a double room
iki kişilik oda
How much is it per night/per person?
Bir gecelik/Kişibaşına kaç para?
Is breakfast included?
Kahvaltı dahil mi?

Time, Days & Numbers

What time is it?	*Saat kaç?*
today	*bugün*
tomorrow	*yarın*
yesterday	*dün*
morning	*sabah*
afternoon	*öğleden sonra*

Monday	*Pazartesi*	1	*bir*
Tuesday	*Salı*	2	*iki*
Wednesday	*Çarşamba*	3	*üç*
Thursday	*Perşembe*	4	*dört*
Friday	*Cuma*	5	*beş*
Saturday	*Cumartesi*	6	*altı*
Sunday	*Pazar*	7	*yedi*
		8	*sekiz*
January	*Ocak*	9	*dokuz*
February	*Şubat*	10	*on*
March	*Mart*	100	*yüz*
April	*Nisan*	1000	*bin*
May	*Mayıs*	one million	*bir milyon*
June	*Haziran*		
July	*Temmuz*	**Emergencies**	
August	*Ağustos*	Help!/Emergency!	*İmdat!*
September	*Eylül*	Call a doctor!	*Doktor çağırın!*
October	*Ekim*	Call the police!	*Polis çağırın!*
November	*Kasım*	Go away!	*Git!/Defol!*
December	*Aralık*	I'm lost.	*Kayboldum.*

Index

TEXT

Map references are in **bold** type.

LONELY PLANET JOURNEYS

FULL CIRCLE: A South American Journey by Luis Sepúlveda (translated by Chris Andrews)
Full Circle invites us to accompany Chilean writer Luis Sepúlveda on 'a journey without a fixed itinerary'. Extravagant characters and extraordinary situations are memorably evoked: gauchos organising a tournament of lies, a scheming heiress on the lookout for a husband, a pilot with a corpse on board his plane . . . Part autobiography, part travel memoir, *Full Circle* brings us the distinctive voice of one of South America's most compelling writers.

THE GATES OF DAMASCUS by Lieve Joris (translated by Sam Garrett)
This best-selling book is a beautifully drawn portrait of contemporary Syria. Through her intimate contact with local people, Lieve Joris explores women's lives and family relationships – the hidden world that lies behind the gates of Damascus.

IN RAJASTHAN by Royina Grewal
Indian travel writer Royina Grewal takes us behind the exotic facade of this fabled destination: here is an insider's perceptive account of India's most colourful state. *In Rajasthan* discusses folk music and architecture, feudal traditions and regional cuisine . . . Most of all, it focuses on people – from maharajahs to itinerant snake charmers – to convey the excitement and challenges of a region in transition.

ISLANDS IN THE CLOUDS: Travels in the Highlands of New Guinea by Isabella Tree
This is the fascinating account of a journey to the remote and beautiful Highlands of Papua New Guinea and Irian Jaya. The author travels with a PNG Highlander who introduces her to his intriguing and complex world. *Islands in the Clouds* is a thoughtful, moving book, full of insights into a region that is rarely noticed by the rest of the world.

KINGDOM OF THE FILM STARS: Journey into Jordan by Annie Caulfield
With honesty and humour, Annie Caulfield writes of travelling in Jordan and falling in love with a Bedouin. Her book offers fascinating insights into the country and unpicks some of the tight-woven Western myths about the Arab world within the intimate framework of a compelling love story.

LOST JAPAN by Alex Kerr
Lost Japan draws on the author's personal experiences of Japan over a period of 30 years. Alex Kerr takes his readers on a backstage tour: friendships with Kabuki actors, buying and selling art, studying calligraphy, exploring rarely visited temples and shrines . . . The Japanese edition of this book was awarded the 1994 Shincho Gakugei Literature Prize for the best work of non-fiction.

SEAN & DAVID'S LONG DRIVE by Sean Condon
Sean and David are young townies who have rarely strayed beyond city limits. One day, for no good reason, they set out to discover their homeland, and what follows is a wildly entertaining adventure that covers half of Australia. Sean Condon has written a hilarious, offbeat road book that mixes sharp insights with deadpan humour and outright lies.

SHOPPING FOR BUDDHAS by Jeff Greenwald
Shopping for Buddhas is Jeff Greenwald's story of his obsessive search for the perfect Buddha statue. In the backstreets of Kathmandu, he discovers more than he bargained for . . . and his souvenir-hunting turns into an ironic metaphor for the clash between spiritual riches and material greed. Politics, religion and serious shopping collide in this witty account of an enlightening visit to Nepal.

LONELY PLANET TRAVEL ATLASES

Lonely Planet has long been famous for the number and quality of its guidebook maps. Now we've gone one step further and in conjunction with Steinhart Katzir Publishers produced a handy companion series: Lonely Planet travel atlases – maps of a country produced in book form.

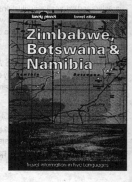

Unlike other maps, which look good but lead travellers astray, our travel atlases have been researched on the road by Lonely Planet's experienced team of writers. All details are carefully checked to ensure the atlas corresponds with the equivalent Lonely Planet guidebook.

The handy atlas format means no holes, wrinkles, torn sections or constant folding and unfolding. These atlases can survive long periods on the road, unlike cumbersome fold-out maps. The comprehensive index ensures easy reference.

- full-colour throughout
- maps researched and checked by Lonely Planet authors
- place names correspond with Lonely Planet guidebooks
  – no confusing spelling differences
- legend and travelling information in English, French, German, Japanese and Spanish
- size: 230 x 160 mm

Available now:
Chile & Easter Island; Egypt; India & Bangladesh; Israel & the Palestinian Territories; Jordan, Syria & Lebanon; Laos; Thailand; Vietnam; Zimbabwe, Botswana & Namibia

---

LONELY PLANET TV SERIES & VIDEOS

Lonely Planet travel guides have been brought to life on television screens around the world. Like our guides, the programmes are based on the joy of independent travel, and look honestly at some of the most exciting, picturesque and frustrating places in the world. Each show is presented by one of three travellers from Australia, England or the USA and combines an innovative mixture of video, Super-8 film, atmospheric soundscapes and original music.

Videos of each episode – containing additional footage not shown on television – are available from good book and video shops, but the availability of individual videos varies with regional screening schedules.

Video destinations include: Alaska; Australia (Southeast); Brazil; Ecuador & the Galápagos Islands; Indonesia; Israel & the Sinai Desert; Japan; La Ruta Maya (Yucatán, Guatemala & Belize); Morocco; North India (Varanasi to the Himalaya); Pacific Islands; Vietnam; Zimbabwe, Botswana & Namibia.

Coming soon: The Arctic (Norway & Finland); Baja California; Chile & Easter Island; China (Southeast); Costa Rica; East Africa (Tanzania & Zanzibar); Great Barrier Reef (Australia); Jamaica; Papua New Guinea; the Rockies (USA); Syria & Jordan; Turkey.

The Lonely Planet TV series is produced by:
Pilot Productions
Duke of Sussex Studios
44 Uxbridge St
London W8 7TG UK

Lonely Planet videos are distributed by:
IVN Communications Inc
2246 Camino Ramon
California 94583, USA

107 Power Road, Chiswick
London W4 5PL UK

Music from the TV series is available on CD & cassette.
For ordering information contact your nearest Lonely Planet office.

LONELY PLANET PRODUCTS

Lonely Planet is known worldwide for publishing practical, reliable and no-nonsense travel information in our guides and on our web site. The Lonely Planet list covers just about every accessible part of the world. Currently there are eight series: *travel guides, shoestring guides, walking guides, city guides, phrasebooks, audio packs, travel atlases* and *Journeys* – a unique collection of travellers' tales.

EUROPE

Austria • Baltic States & Kaliningrad • Baltic States phrasebook • Britain • Central Europe on a shoestring • Central Europe phrasebook • Czech & Slovak Republics • Denmark • Dublin city guide • Eastern Europe on a shoestring • Eastern Europe phrasebook • Finland • France • Greece • Greek phrasebook • Hungary • Iceland, Greenland & the Faroe Islands • Ireland • Italy • Mediterranean Europe on a shoestring • Mediterranean Europe phrasebook • Paris city guide • Poland • Prague city guide • Russia, Ukraine & Belarus • Russian phrasebook • Scandinavian & Baltic Europe on a shoestring • Scandinavian Europe phrasebook • Slovenia • St Petersburg city guide • Switzerland • Trekking in Greece • Trekking in Spain • Ukrainian phrasebook • Vienna city guide • Walking in Switzerland • Western Europe on a shoestring • Western Europe phrasebook

NORTH AMERICA

Alaska • Backpacking in Alaska • Baja California• California & Nevada • Canada • Florida • Hawaii • Honolulu city guide • Los Angeles city guide • Mexico • Miami city guide • New England • New Orleans city guide • Pacific Northwest USA • Rocky Mountain States • San Francisco city guide • Southwest USA • USA phrasebook

CENTRAL AMERICA & THE CARIBBEAN

Central America on a shoestring • Costa Rica • Cuba • Eastern Caribbean • Guatemala, Belize & Yucatán: La Ruta Maya • Jamaica

SOUTH AMERICA

Argentina, Uruguay & Paraguay • Bolivia • Brazil • Brazilian phrasebook • Buenos Aires city guide • Chile & Easter Island • Chile & Easter Island travel atlas • Colombia • Ecuador & the Galápagos Islands • Latin American Spanish phrasebook • Peru • Quechua phrasebook • Rio de Janeiro city guide • South America on a shoestring • Trekking in the Patagonian Andes • Venezuela

Travel Literature: Full Circle: A South American Journey

ANTARCTICA

Antarctica

ISLANDS OF THE INDIAN OCEAN

Madagascar & Comoros • Maldives & Islands of the East Indian Ocean • Mauritius, Réunion & Seychelles

AFRICA

Arabic (Moroccan) phrasebook • Africa on a shoestring • Cape Town city guide • Central Africa • East Africa • Egypt• Egypt travel atlas• Ethiopian (Amharic) phrasebook • Kenya • Morocco • North Africa • South Africa, Lesotho & Swaziland • Swahili phrasebook • Trekking in East Africa • West Africa • Zimbabwe, Botswana & Namibia • Zimbabwe, Botswana & Namibia travel atlas

ALSO AVAILABLE:

Travel with Children • Traveller's Tales

MAIL ORDER

Lonely Planet products are distributed worldwide. They are also available by mail order from Lonely Planet, so if you have difficulty finding a title please write to us. North American and South American residents should write to Embarcadero West, 155 Filbert St, Suite 251, Oakland CA 94607, USA; European and African residents should write to 10 Barley Mow Passage, Chiswick, London W4 4PH; and residents of other countries to PO Box 617, Hawthorn, Victoria 3122, Australia.

NORTH-EAST ASIA

Beijing city guide • Cantonese phrasebook • China • Hong Kong, Macau & Canton • Hong Kong city guide • Japan • Japanese phrasebook • Japanese audio pack • Korea • Korean phrasebook • Mandarin phrasebook • Mongolia • Mongolian phrasebook • North-East Asia on a shoestring • Seoul city guide • Taiwan • Tibet • Tibet phrasebook • Tokyo city guide

Travel Literature: Lost Japan

MIDDLE EAST & CENTRAL ASIA

Arab Gulf States • Arabic (Egyptian) phrasebook • Central Asia • Iran • Israel & the Palestinian Territories • Israel & the Palestinian Territories travel atlas • Jordan & Syria • Jordan, Syria & Lebanon travel atlas • Middle East • Turkey • Turkish phrasebook • Trekking in Turkey • Yemen

Travel Literature: The Gates of Damascus • Kingdom of the Film Stars: Journey into Jordan

INDIAN SUBCONTINENT

Bangladesh • Bengali phrasebook • Delhi city guide • Hindi/Urdu phrasebook • India • India & Bangladesh travel atlas • Indian Himalaya • Karakoram Highway • Nepal • Nepali phrasebook • Pakistan • Rajasthan • Sri Lanka • Sri Lanka phrasebook • Trekking in the Indian Himalaya • Trekking in the Karakoram & Hindukush • Trekking in the Nepal Himalaya

Travel Literature: In Rajasthan • Shopping for Buddhas

SOUTH-EAST ASIA

Bali & Lombok • Bangkok city guide • Burmese phrasebook • Cambodia • Ho Chi Minh city guide • Indonesia • Indonesian phrasebook • Indonesian audio pack • Jakarta city guide • Java • Laos • Lao phrasebook • Laos travel atlas • Malay phrasebook • Malaysia, Singapore & Brunei • Myanmar (Burma) • Philippines • Pilipino phrasebook • Singapore city guide • South-East Asia on a shoestring • Thailand • Thailand travel atlas • Thai phrasebook • Thai audio pack • Thai Hill Tribes phrasebook • Vietnam • Vietnamese phrasebook • Vietnam travel atlas

AUSTRALIA & THE PACIFIC

Australia • Australian phrasebook • Bushwalking in Australia • Bushwalking in Papua New Guinea • Fiji • Fijian phrasebook • Islands of Australia's Great Barrier Reef • Melbourne city guide • Micronesia • New Caledonia • New South Wales & the ACT • New Zealand • Northern Territory • Outback Australia • Papua New Guinea • Papua New Guinea phrasebook • Queensland • Rarotonga & the Cook Islands • Samoa • Solomon Islands • South Australia • Sydney city guide • Tahiti & French Polynesia • Tasmania • Tonga • Tramping in New Zealand • Vanuatu • Victoria • Western Australia

Travel Literature: Islands in the Clouds • Sean & David's Long Drive

THE LONELY PLANET STORY

Lonely Planet published its first book in 1973 in response to the numerous 'How did you do it?' questions Maureen and Tony Wheeler were asked after driving, bussing, hitching, sailing and railing their way from England to Australia.

Written at a kitchen table and hand collated, trimmed and stapled, *Across Asia on the Cheap* became an instant local bestseller, inspiring thoughts of another book.

Eighteen months in South-East Asia resulted in their second guide, *South-East Asia on a shoestring*, which they r. it together in a backstreet Chinese hotel in Singapore in 1975. The 'yellow bible', as it quickly became known to backpackers around the world, soon became *the* guide to the region. It has sold well over half a million copies and is now in its 8th edition, still retaining its familiar yellow cover.

Today there are over 180 titles, including travel guides, walking guides, language kits & phrasebooks, travel atlases and travel literature. The company is one of the largest travel publishers in the world. Although Lonely Planet initially specialised in guides to Asia, we now cover most regions of the world, including the Pacific, North America, South America, Africa, the Middle East and Europe.

The emphasis continues to be on travel for independent travellers. Tony and Maureen still travel for several months of each year and play an active part in the writing, updating and quality control of Lonely Planet's guides.

They have been joined by over 70 authors and 170 staff at our offices in Melbourne (Australia), Oakland (USA), London (UK) and Paris (France). Travellers themselves also make a valuable contribution to the guides through the feedback we receive in thousands of letters each year.

The people at Lonely Planet strongly believe that travellers can make a positive contribution to the countries they visit, both through their appreciation of the countries' culture, wildlife and natural features, and through the money they spend. In addition, the company makes a direct contribution to the countries and regions it covers. Since 1986 a percentage of the income from each book has been donated to ventures such as famine relief in Africa; aid projects in India; agricultural projects in Central America; Greenpeace's efforts to halt French nuclear testing in the Pacific; and Amnesty International.

'I hope we send the people out with the right attitude about travel. You realise when you travel that there are so many different perspectives about the world, so we hope these books will make people more interested in what they see. These are guidebooks, but you can't really guide people. All you can do is point them in the right direction.'

– Tony Wheeler

lonely planet

LONELY PLANET PUBLICATIONS

Australia
PO Box 617, Hawthorn 3122, Victoria
tel: (03) 9819 1877 fax: (03) 9819 6459
e-mail: talk2us@lonelyplanet.com.au

USA
Embarcadero West, 155 Filbert St, Suite 251,
Oakland, CA 94607
tel: (510) 893 8555 TOLL FREE: 800 275-8555
fax: (510) 893 8563
e-mail: info@lonelyplanet.com

UK
10 Barley Mow Passage, Chiswick,
London W4 4PH
tel: (0181) 742 3161 fax: (0181) 742 2772
e-mail: 100413.3551@compuserve.com

France:
71 bis rue du Cardinal Lemoine, 75005 Paris
tel: 1 44 32 06 20 fax: 1 46 34 72 55
e-mail: 100560.415@compuserve.com

World Wide Web: http://www.lonelyplanet.com